FACTITIOUS DISORDERS

Factitious Disorder
Factitious Disorder NOS

DISSOCIATIVE DISORDERS

Dissociative Amnesia
Dissociative Fugue
Dissociative Identity Disorder
Depersonalization Disorder
Dissociative Disorder NOS

SEXUAL DYSFUNCTIONS

Sexual Desire Disorders
- Hypoactive Sexual Desire Disorder
- Sexual Aversion Disorder

Sexual Arousal Disorders
- Female Sexual Arousal Disorder
- Male Erectile Disorder

Orgasmic Disorders
- Female Orgasmic Disorder
- Male Orgasmic Disorder
- Premature Ejaculation

Sexual Pain Disorders
- Dyspareunia (Not Due to a General Medical Condition)
- Vaginismus (Not Due to a General Medical Condition)

Sexual Dysfunction Due to a General Medical Condition [Specify Further]
Substance-Induced Sexual Dysfunction
Sexual Dysfunction NOS

PARAPHILIAS

Exhibitionism
Fetishism
Frotteurism
Pedophilia
Sexual Masochism
Sexual Sadism
Transvestic Fetishism
Voyeurism
Paraphilia NOS

GENDER IDENTITY DISORDERS

Gender Identity Disorder
Gender Identity Disorder NOS
Sexual Disorder NOS

EATING DISORDERS

Anorexia Nervosa
Bulimia Nervosa
Eating Disorder NOS

SLEEP DISORDERS

Primary Sleep Disorders
- Dyssomnias
  - Primary Insomnia
  - Primary Hypersomnia
  - Narcolepsy
  - Breathing-Related Sleep Disorder
  - Circadian Rhythm Sleep Disorder
  - Dyssomnia NOS
- Parasomnias
  - Nightmare Disorder
  - Sleep Terror Disorder
  - Sleepwalking Disorder
  - Parasomnia NOS

Sleep Disorders Related to Another Mental Disorder
- Insomnia Related to [Indicate Axis I or Axis II disorder]
- Hypersomnia Related to [Indicate Axis I or Axis II disorder]

Other Sleep Disorders
- Sleep Disorder Due to a General Medical Condition
- Substance-Induced Sleep Disorder

IMPULSE-CONTROL DISORDERS NOT ELSEWHERE CLASSIFIED

Intermittent Explosive Disorder
Kleptomania
Pyromania
Pathological Gambling
Trichotillomania
Impulse-Control Disorder NOS

ADJUSTMENT DISORDERS

Adjustment Disorder with Depressed Mood
Adjustment Disorder with Anxiety
Adjustment Disorder with Mixed Anxiety and Depressed Mood
Adjustment Disorder with Disturbance of Conduct
Adjustment Disorder with Mixed Disturbance of Emotions and Conduct

OTHER CONDITIONS THAT MAY BE A FOCUS OF CLINICAL ATTENTION

PSYCHOLOGICAL FACTORS AFFECTING MEDICAL CONDITION

MEDICALLY INDUCED MOVEMENT DISORDERS

OTHER MEDICALLY INDUCED DISORDERS

RELATIONAL PROBLEMS

Relational Problem Related to a Mental Disorder or General Medical Condition
Parent-Child Relational Problem
Partner Relational Problem
Sibling Relational Problem

PROBLEMS RELATED TO ABUSE OR NEGLECT

Physical Abuse of Child
Sexual Abuse of Child
Neglect of Child
Physical Abuse of Adult
Sexual Abuse of Adult

ADDITIONAL CONDITIONS THAT MAY BE A FOCUS OF CLINICAL ATTENTION

Noncompliance with Treatment
Malingering
Adult Antisocial Behavior
Child or Adolescent Antisocial Behavior
Borderline Intellectual Functioning
Age-Related Cognitive Decline
Bereavement
Academic Problem
Occupational Problem
Identity Problem
Religious or Spiritual Problem
Acculturation Problem
Phase of Life Problem

AXIS II

MENTAL RETARDATION

Mild Mental Retardation
Moderate Mental Retardation
Severe Mental Retardation
Profound Mental Retardation

PERSONALITY DISORDERS

Paranoid Personality Disorder
Schizoid Personality Disorder
Schizotypal Personality Disorder
Antisocial Personality Disorder
Borderline Personality Disorder
Histrionic Personality Disorder
Narcissistic Personality Disorder
Avoidant Personality Disorder
Dependent Personality Disorder
Obsessive-Compulsive Personality Disorder
Personality Disorder NOS

ABnormaL PSYCHOLOGY

ABNORMAL PSYCHOLOGY

THIRTEENTH EDITION

JAMES N. BUTCHER
University of Minnesota

SUSAN MINEKA
Northwestern University

JILL M. HOOLEY
Harvard University

PEARSON
A and B

Boston New York San Francisco
Mexico City Montreal Toronto London Madrid Munich Paris
Hong Kong Singapore Tokyo Cape Town Sydney

Editor in Chief:	Susan Hartman
Series Editorial Assistant:	Therese Felser
Development Editors:	Judith Hauck and Erin Liedel
Marketing Manager:	Karen Natale
Production Editor:	Susan Brown
Composition Buyer:	Linda Cox
Manufacturing Buyer:	Megan Cochran
Editorial-Production Service and Electronic Composition:	Elm Street Publishing Services, Inc.
Interior Design:	The Davis Group
Photo Researcher:	Sarah Evertson
Cover Administrator:	Kristina Mose-Libon

For related titles and support materials, visit our online catalog at www.ablongman.com.

Cataloging-in-Publication Data for this title is on file at the Library of Congress.

ISBN 0-205-45942-0

Printed in the United States of America

10 9 8 7 6 5 4 3 2 RRD-OH 10 09 08 07 06

Photo credits begin on page C-1, which constitutes a continuation of the copyright page.

Brief Contents

contents

CHAPTER 7 Mood Disorders and Suicide 225

CHAPTER 8 Somatoform and Dissociative Disorders 279

Features

Developments in Research

Developments in Thinking

Developments in Practice

The World Around Us

unresolved issues

DSM-IV-TR Boxes

Chapter 12: Addiction Disorders

Chapter 13: Sexual Variants, Abuse, and Dysfunctions

Chapter 14: Schizophrenia and Other Psychotic Disorders

Chapter 15: Cognitive Disorders

Chapter 16: Disorders of Childhood and Adolescence

Preface

Abnormal Psychology has a long and distinguished tradition as an undergraduate abnormal psychology text. Since 1948, when James Coleman wrote the first edition, this textbook has been considered the most comprehensive in its field. Through the years new authors have joined the writing team, offering fresh insights from their areas of expertise and continuing the unwavering commitment to thorough research coverage for which this book is known. In 1980, well-known psychologists Bob Carson and Jim Butcher developed the sixth edition of this classic text; in 1996 they were joined by esteemed researcher Susan Mineka to develop the tenth edition. In 2004 Bob Carson retired from the author team, but his contributions are immeasurable and his work will be well remembered. Jill Hooley of Harvard University provided a fresh perspective to the twelfth edition, and continues to offer exceptional insight, particularly in the field of schizophrenia research, for the thirteenth edition.

The abundance of research discoveries surfacing in the field today has broadened our understanding of psychopathology, improving upon theories and treatments practiced just a decade ago. The goal of this book is, and always has been, to present to students these exciting discoveries and to offer the most thoroughly researched and up-to-date explanation of psychopathology today. The Butcher-Mineka-Hooley team is unique. The depth and breadth of their research in the field of psychopathology provide students a learning experience that can provoke thought, increase awareness, and take them to new levels of understanding that other books do not offer. That this edition includes 63 pages of references speaks to its research base. The authors' work in the international arena provides a balance of multicultural studies and phenomena, which offer an integrative view of psychopathology.

What's New

The thirteenth edition of *Abnormal Psychology* features updated case studies and feature boxes; a new focus on research methodology, highlighted in the "Research Close-Up" key terms; the addition of DSM-IV-TR boxes; and a striking new design. *Abnormal Psychology* has been thoroughly updated—hundreds of new references throughout accurately reflect the ever-changing field of abnormal psychology. The thirteenth edition covers the most current and in-depth information about biological influences on the entire spectrum of behavioral abnormalities, while still maintaining its bio-psycho-social approach to abnormal behavior.

Features and Pedagogy

The extensive research base and accessible organization of this book are supported by high-interest features and helpful pedagogy to further engage students and support learning.

Features

- **FEATURE BOXES**

Special sections, called Developments in Research, Developments in Thinking, Developments in Practice, and The World Around Us, expand on topics of particular interest, focusing on applications of research to everyday life, current events, and the latest research methodologies, technologies, and findings.

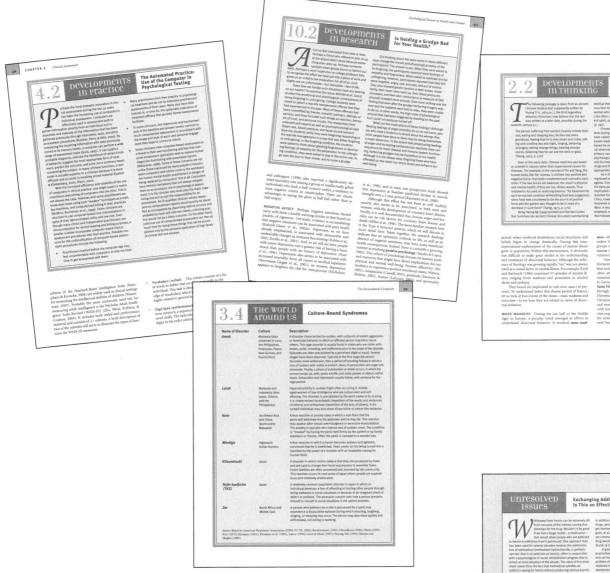

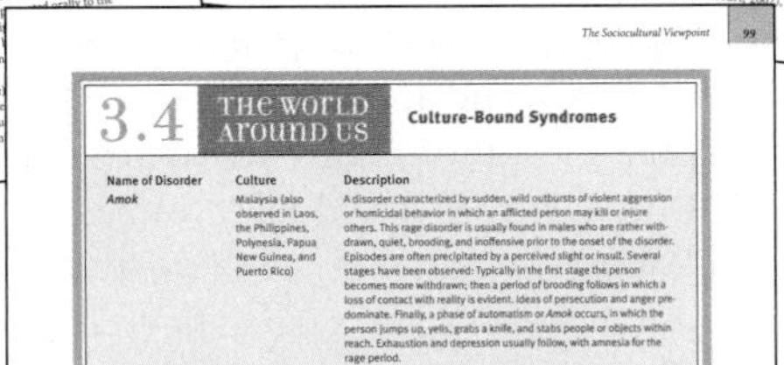

- **UNRESOLVED ISSUES**

Selected chapters include end-of-chapter sections that demonstrate how far we have come and how far we have yet to go in our understanding of psychological disorders. The topics covered here provide insight into the future of the field.

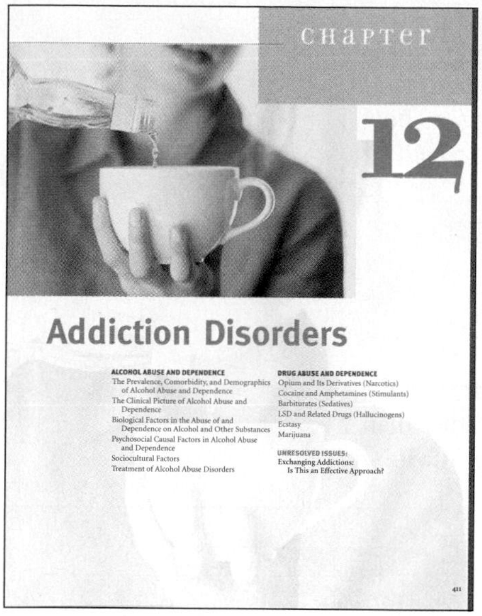
Chapter 12

Addiction Disorders

Pedagogy

- **CHAPTER OUTLINE**

Each chapter begins with a detailed outline that introduces the content and provides an overview of what is to come. This and the extensive chapter summary found at the end of each chapter are excellent tools for study and review.

CHAPTER 1 Abnormal Psychology: An Overview

How Does Culture Affect What Is Considered Abnormal?

case study A Native American Elder

- **CASE STUDIES**

Extensive case studies of individuals with various disorders appear throughout the book. Some are brief excerpts; others are detailed analyses. These cases bring disorders to life, while reminding students of the human factor that is so intimately a part of the subject matter of this text.

CHAPTER 6 Panic, Anxiety, and Their Disorders

Overview of the Anxiety Disorders and Their Commonalities

In Review

- **IN REVIEW QUESTIONS**

Questions appear at the end of each major section within the chapter, providing regular opportunities for self-assessment as students read and further reinforce their learning.

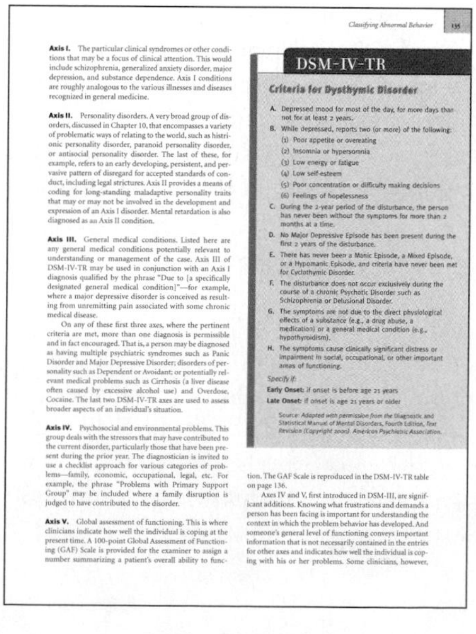
DSM-IV-TR

Criteria for Dysthymic Disorder

- **NEW! DSM-IV-TR BOXES**

These boxes summarize the essential criteria from the *Diagnostic and Statistical Manual of Mental Disorders* for the disorders discussed. A helpful study tool that reflects current diagnostic practice and helps students understand disorders in a real-world context.

Psychosocial Causal Factors 95

to 60 percent of children born in the 1990s will live at some point in single-parent families (Hetherington, Bridges, & Insabella, 1998).

Effects of Divorce on Parents Unhappy marriages are difficult, but ending a marital relationship can also be enormously stressful for the adults, both mentally and physically. The negative effects are temporary, with most people being able to adapt constructively within 2 to 3 years, but some adults never fully recover (Amato, 2000; Hetherington, 2003a). Divorced and separated persons are overrepresented among psychiatric patients, although the ***direction of the causal relationship*** is not always clear. In their comprehensive reviews of the effects of divorce on adults, Amato and Keith (1991b) concluded that it is a major source of psychopathology, as well as of physical illness, death, suicide, and homicide. It should also be recognized, however, that divorce actually benefits some individuals (Amato, 2000)—with some evidence that women are more likely to benefit than men (Hetherington, 2003a). Overall, good adjustment after divorce is positively associated with higher income, dating someone steadily, remarriage, having had relatively favorable attitudes toward divorce before it happened, and being the partner who initiated the divorce (Amato, 2000).

research close-up

direction of the causal relationship

Recall that, in a correlational or observational study, an association between two variables does not allow us to make inferences about causal direction. For example, divorce could precipitate psychological problems. Alternatively, people with psychological disorders might be more likely to have problematic marriages and end up divorced.

Effects of Divorce on Children Divorce can have traumatic effects on children, too. Feelings of insecurity and rejection may be aggravated by conflicting loyalties and, sometimes, by the spoiling the children may receive while staying with one of the parents. Not surprisingly, some children do develop serious maladaptive responses. Temperamentally difficult children are likely to have a more difficult time adjusting than are temperamentally easy children (Hetherington, Stanley-Hagan, & Anderson, 1989). Somewhat ironically, difficult children may be the ones whose parents are more likely to divorce, perhaps because having difficult children is likely to exacerbate marital problems (Block, Block, & Gjerde, 1986; Hetherington, 1999).

Delinquency and a wide range of other psychological problems are much more frequent among children and adolescents from divorced families than among those from intact families, although it is likely that a contributing factor here is prior or continuing parental strife (Chase-Lansdale, Cherlin, & Kiernan, 1995; Rutter, 1979). In addition, a number of studies have demonstrated that the adverse effects of divorce on adaptive functioning may persist into adulthood. On average, compared to young adults from families without divorce, young adults from divorced families have somewhat lower educational attainment, lower incomes, lower life satisfaction, and an increased probability of being on welfare and having children out of wedlock (Chase-Lansdale et al., 1995; Hetherington et al., 1998). Children from divorced families are also more likely to have their own marriages end in divorce (Amato & DeBoer, 2001; Hetherington, 2003b). One particularly interesting new study found that these long-lasting effects even occurred in a subsequent third generation. Specifically, in a study of nearly 700 grandparents and their grandchildren, Amato and Cheadle (2005) found that divorce in the grandparents was associated with lower education, more marital discord, and weaker parental ties in the grandchildren.

Nevertheless, many children adjust quite well to the divorce of their parents. Indeed, a quantitative review of 92 studies on parental divorce and the well-being of children, conducted on 13,000 children since the 1950s, concluded that the average negative effects of divorce on children are actually quite modest (Amato & Keith, 1991a; see also Emery, 1999; Hetherington, 2003b), as are the negative effects persisting into adulthood (Amato & Keith, 1991b). Amato and Keith (1991a, 1991b) also found that the negative effects of divorce seemed to decrease from the 1950s through the 1980s (particularly since 1970), perhaps because the stigma of divorce was decreasing. However, a follow-up review of 67 such studies published in the 1990s showed no further decreases in these negative effects since 1990 (Amato, 2001).

The effects of divorce on children are often more favorable than the effects of remaining in a home torn by marital conflict and dissension (Amato & Keith, 1991a; Emery & Kitzmann, 1995; Hetherington et al., 1998). At one time it was thought that the detrimental effects of divorce might be minimized if a successful remarriage provided an adequate environment for childrearing. Unfortunately, however, the Amato and Keith (1991a) review revealed that children living with a stepparent were often no better off than children living with a single parent, although this was more true for girls than for boys. Other studies have shown that children—especially very young children—living with a stepparent are at increased risk for physical abuse (injury and even death) by the stepparent, relative to children living with two biological parents (Daly & Wilson, 1988, 1996).

Maladaptive Peer Relationships

Important peer relationships usually begin in the preschool years. Children at this stage are hardly masters of the fine points of human relationships or diplomacy.

- **NEW! RESEARCH CLOSE-UP TERMS**

Appearing throughout each chapter, these terms illuminate research methodologies and give students a clear understanding of how research works in the ever-changing field of Abnormal Psychology.

- **CHAPTER SUMMARY**

Each chapter ends with a summary of what the chapter discussed, in bulleted lists rather than in paragraph form. This makes the information more accessible for students and easier to scan.

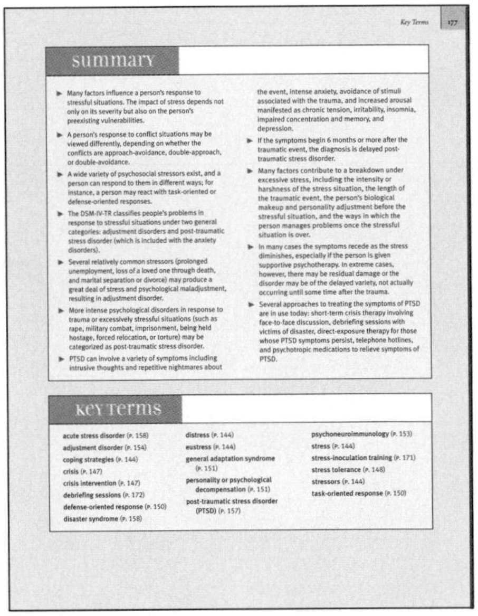
Key Terms 177

summary

- Many factors influence a person's response to stressful situations. The impact of stress depends not only on its severity but also on the person's preexisting vulnerabilities.
- A person's response to conflict situations may be viewed differently, depending on whether the conflicts are approach-avoidance, double-approach, or double-avoidance.
- A wide variety of psychosocial stressors exist, and a person can respond to them in different ways; for instance, a person may react with task-oriented or defense-oriented responses.
- The DSM-IV-TR classifies people's problems in response to stressful situations under two general categories: adjustment disorders and post-traumatic stress disorder (which is included with the anxiety disorders).
- Several relatively common stressors (prolonged unemployment, loss of a loved one through death, and marital separation or divorce) may produce a great deal of stress and psychological maladjustment, resulting in adjustment disorder.
- More intense psychological disorders in response to trauma or excessively stressful situations (such as rape, military combat, imprisonment, being held hostage, forced relocation, or torture) may be categorized as post-traumatic stress disorder.
- PTSD can involve a variety of symptoms including intrusive thoughts and repetitive nightmares about the event, intense anxiety, avoidance of stimuli associated with the trauma, and increased arousal manifested as chronic tension, irritability, insomnia, impaired concentration and memory, and depression.
- If the symptoms begin 6 months or more after the traumatic event, the diagnosis is delayed post-traumatic stress disorder.
- Many factors contribute to a breakdown under excessive stress, including the intensity or harshness of the stress situation, the length of the traumatic event, the person's biological makeup and personality adjustment before the stressful situation, and the ways in which the person manages problems once the stressful situation is over.
- In many cases the symptoms recede as the stress diminishes, especially if the person is given supportive psychotherapy. In extreme cases, however, there may be residual damage or the disorder may be of the delayed variety, not actually occurring until some time after the trauma.
- Several approaches to treating the symptoms of PTSD are in use today: short-term crisis therapy involving face-to-face discussion, debriefing sessions with victims of disaster, direct-exposure therapy for those whose PTSD symptoms persist, telephone hotlines, and psychotropic medications to relieve symptoms of PTSD.

key terms

acute stress disorder (p. 158)
adjustment disorder (p. 154)
coping strategies (p. 144)
crisis (p. 147)
crisis intervention (p. 147)
debriefing sessions (p. 172)
defense-oriented response (p. 150)
disaster syndrome (p. 158)
distress (p. 144)
eustress (p. 144)
general adaptation syndrome (p. 151)
personality or psychological decompensation (p. 151)
post-traumatic stress disorder (PTSD) (p. 157)
psychoneuroimmunology (p. 153)
stress (p. 144)
stress-inoculation training (p. 171)
stress tolerance (p. 148)
stressors (p. 144)
task-oriented response (p. 150)

- **KEY TERMS**

Key terms appear at the end of every chapter with the page numbers referencing where they are found in the body of the text. Key terms are also defined in the Glossary at the end of the book.

SUPPLEMENTS PACKAGE

For the Instructor

These supplements are available for qualified instructors only. Please contact your local Allyn & Bacon representative for more information.

Instructor's Manual

Robin K. Morgan, *Indiana University—Southeast*

A wonderful tool for classroom preparation and management. Each chapter includes an At-A-Glance Grid, with detailed pedagogical information linking to other available supplements; a detailed chapter outline; teaching objectives covering major concepts within the chapter; a list of Key Terms with page references; lecture material, including launchers, outlines, and suggested discussion questions; demonstrations and activities; an updated list of video, media, and Web resources; and an updated list of suggested readings.

In addition, this Instructor's Manual contains a preface with introductory letter from the author, a sample syllabus, and an appendix with a comprehensive list of student handouts.

Test Bank

Judith S. Rauenzahn, *Kutztown University*

Thoroughly revised by Judith Rauenzahn for the thirteenth edition, the Test Bank is composed of approximately 2,000 fully referenced multiple-choice, true/false, short-answer, and essay questions. Each question is accompanied by a page reference, difficulty level, type designation, topic, and an answer justification.

This product is also available in TestGen computerized version, for use in creating tests in the classroom.

Powerpoint™ Presentation
David Lundberg-Kenrick

An exciting interactive tool for use in the classroom. Each chapter includes key points covered in the textbook, images from the textbook, and a link to the companion website for corresponding activities.

Allyn and Bacon Digital Media Archive for Abnormal Psychology
A comprehensive source for images, including charts, graphs, and figures, with PowerPoint lectures for classroom presentation. Video clips include patient footage and news reels.

Abnormal Psychology Video: ABC News and Client Interviews
A wonderful classroom tool, including over 10 video clips from ABC News and some patient footage. Critical thinking questions accompany each clip. In addition, the video guide provides further critical thinking questions and Internet resources for more information.

MyPsychLab for Abnormal Psychology
This interactive and instructive multimedia resource can be used to supplement a traditional lecture course or to administer a course entirely online. It is an all-inclusive tool, a text-specific e-book plus multimedia tutorials, audio, video, simulations, animations, and controlled assessments to engage completely students and reinforce learning. Fully customizable and easy to use, MyPsychLab for Abnormal Psychology meets the individual teaching and learning needs of every instructor and every student. Visit the site at www.mypsychlab.com.

NEW! Interactive Lecture Questions for Clickers
To jumpstart exciting classroom discussions.

APPI Video Library
The APPI Video Library contains two video series which may be used individually or together to enrich classroom learning. The DSM-IV: New Diagnostic Issues Video Series is a series of clinical programs revealing additions and changes from DSM-III-R to DSM-IV for mood, psychotic, and anxiety disorders. Each videotape contains enactments of actual patient interviews, beginning with an introductory discussion between the clinician and the moderator, and continuing with diagnostic interviews and analysis of the major issues. The Treatment of Psychiatric Disorders Video Series features videos in which multiple clinicians present up-to-date information on treatments for psychiatric disorders, based on material discussed and presented at American Psychiatric Association meetings.

Transparencies for Abnormal Psychology
Approximately 125 full-color acetates to enhance classroom lecture and discussion. Includes images from Allyn and Bacon's major Abnormal Psychology texts.

For the Student

Companion Website (http://www.ablongman.com/butcher13e)
A unique resource for connecting the textbook to the Internet. Each chapter includes learning objectives, updated and annotated Web links for additional sources of information, Flash Card glossary terms, and online practice tests with page references.

Grade Aid Study Guide
Mary McNaughton-Cassill, *University of Texas at San Antonio*

This robust study guide, written by Mary McNaughton-Cassill of University of Texas at San Antonio, is filled with guided activities and in-depth exercises to promote student learning. Each chapter includes "Before You Read," presenting a brief chapter summary and learning objectives; "As You Read," offering a collection of demonstrations, activities, and exercises; "After You Read," containing three short practice quizzes and one comprehensive chapter exam; "When You Have Finished," presenting Web links for further information and a crossword puzzle using key terms from the text. An appendix includes answers to all practice tests and crossword puzzles.

Study Card for Abnormal Psychology
Colorful, affordable, and packed with useful information, Allyn & Bacon/Longman's Study Cards make studying easier, more efficient, and more enjoyable. Course information is distilled down to the basics, helping students quickly master the fundamentals, review a subject for understanding, or prepare for an exam.

Research Navigator™
www.ablongman.com/researchnavigator
The easiest way for students to start a research assignment or research paper. Research Navigator™ helps students quickly and efficiently make the most of their research time and write better papers. The program provides extensive help with the research process and includes three exclusive databases of credible and reliable source material: EBSCO's ContentSelect Academic Journal Database, The New York Times Search by Subject Archive, and our own "Best of the Web" Link Library.

Tutor Center One-on-One Tutoring
www.ablongman.com/tutorcenter/psych
A support service that's available when a tutor is not! *Abnormal Psychology* can be packaged with access to the Tutor Center, providing free, high-quality, one-on-one tutoring to students. Qualified tutors will answer questions students have about material in the text. The Tutor Center is open during peak study hours—in the late afternoon and evenings, 5–12 PM (EST), Sunday–Thursday during the academic calendar.

Acknowledgments

We want to single out for special praise and appreciation our development editors, Judy Hauck and Erin Liedel, who provided substantial editorial expertise and insightful and timely recommendations. Thank you to Susan Hartman, executive editor, for her guidance and support during the writing process. Another special thank you goes to Susan Brown and Eric Arima for managing the production of this book. And thank you to Jennifer Trebby for her work in coordinating the supplements package.

We are greatly indebted to the experts and researchers who gave us their comments on individual chapters. Their knowledge and expertise help give this text its currency.

Paul Arbisi, University of Minnesota, Chapter 10; David Baker, University of Akron, Chapter 2; Dianne Chambless, University of Pennsylvania, Chapters 6 and 17; Emily Durbin, Northwestern University, Chapter 3; John P. Forsyth, The State University of New York at Albany, Chapter 6; David Gleaves, Texas A& M University-College Station, Chapter 8; Michael Green, University of California at Los Angeles, Chapter 14; Chris Hayward, Stanford University Medical School, Chapter 6; Kathi Heffner, Ohio University, Chapter 10; William G. Iacono, University of Minnesota, Chapter 7; Kelly Klump,

Michigan State University, Chapter 9; Gerald Koocher, Simmons College, Chapter 16; David Kosson, Chicago Medical School, Chapter 11; Brett Litz, Boston University, Chapter 5; Edwin Megargee, Florida State University, Chapter 18; William Milberg, Harvard Medical School, Chapter 15; Matthew Nock, Harvard University, Chapters 1, 16, and 17; Shige Oishi, University of Virginia, Chapter 3; Walter Penk, Memorial Veterans Hospital, Bedford, MA, Chapter 5; Diego Pizzagalli, Harvard University, Chapter 7; Rick Seime, Mayo Clinic, Chapter 4; Eric Stice, University of Texas at Austin, Chapter 9; Nathan Weed, Central Michigan University, Chapter 12; and Ken Zucker, Clarke Institute of Psychiatry, Toronto, Chapter 13.

Book projects of this magnitude typically require a great deal of author preoccupation that tends to usurp "quality" time from deserving family members. James Butcher would like to thank his wife, Carolyn L. Williams, and his children, Holly Butcher, Sherry Butcher, and Jay Butcher, for their patience and support during this time. Susan Mineka wishes to thank her graduate students and friends for their patience and support for the duration of this project. Jill Hooley wishes to thank Kip Schur for his love, support, and endless patience. She is also grateful to her graduate students, especially Jason Angel and Sarah St. Germain, for their suggestions and comments.

We would also like to thank the many reviewers who have contributed helpful comments on this and previous editions of *Abnormal Psychology*.

Angela Bragg, Mount Hood Community College; Greg Carey, University of Colorado; Louis Castonguay, Pennsylvania State University; Lee Anna Clark, The University of Iowa; Barbara Cornblatt; William Paul Deal, University of Mississippi; Raymond L. Eastman, Stephen F. Austin State University; John F. Edens, Sam Houston State University; Colleen Ehrnstrom, University of Colorado at Boulder; William Fals-Stewart, The State University of New York at Buffalo; Louis R. Franzini, San Diego State University; David H. Gleaves, Texas A & M University; Michael Green, University of California at Los Angeles; Steven Haynes, University of Hawaii at Manoa; Daniel Holland, University of Arkansas at Little Rock; Steven Hollon, Vanderbilt University; Joanne Hoven Stohs, California State University Fullerton; Robert Howland, University of Pittsburgh, School of Medicine; Jean W. Hunt, Cumberland College; Alexandrea Hye-Young Park, Virginia Tech; Erick Janssen, Indiana University; Sheri Johnson, University of Miami; Alan Kazdin, Yale University; Carolin Keutzer, University of Oregon; John F. Kihlstrom, University of California at Berkeley; Brendan Maher, Harvard University; Richard McNally, Harvard University; William Miller, University of New Mexico; Robin Morgan, Indiana University Southeast; Chris Patrick, University of Minnesota; Harvey Richman, Columbus State University; Lizabeth Roemer, University of Massachusetts at Boston; Fran Sessa, Pennsylvania State University, Abington; Brad Schmidt, Ohio State University; Kandy Stahl, Stephen F. Austin State University; Stephanie Stein, Central Washington University; Marcus Tye, Dowling College; Michael E. Walker, Stephen F. Austin State University; and Kenneth J. Zucker, Centre for Addiction and Mental Health, Ontario, Canada.

JAMES N. BUTCHER
University of Minnesota

James N. Butcher was born in West Virginia. He enlisted in the Army when he was 17 years old and served in the airborne infantry for 3 years, including a 1-year tour in Korea during the Korean War. After military service, he attended Guilford College, graduating in 1960 with a BA in psychology. He received an MA in experimental psychology in 1962 and a PhD in clinical psychology from the University of North Carolina at Chapel Hill. He was awarded Doctor Honoris Causa from the Free University of Brussels, Belgium, in 1990. He is currently professor of psychology in the Department of Psychology at the University of Minnesota and was associate director and director of the clinical psychology program at the university for 19 years. He was a member of the University of Minnesota Press's MMPI Consultative Committee, which under-took the revision of the MMPI in 1989. He was formerly the editor of *Psychological Assessment*, a journal of the American Psychological Association, and serves as consulting editor or reviewer for numerous other journals in psychology and psychiatry. Dr. Butcher has been actively involved in developing and organizing disaster response programs for dealing with human problems following airline disasters. He organized a model crisis intervention disaster response for the Minneapolis-St. Paul Airport and organized and supervised the psychological services offered following two major airline disasters: Northwest Flight 255 in Detroit, Michigan, and Aloha Airlines on Maui. He is a fellow of the American Psychological Association and the Society for Personality Assessment. He has published 40 books and more than 175 articles in the fields of abnormal psychology, cross-cultural psychology, and personality assessment.

SUSAN MINEKA
Northwestern University

Susan Mineka, born and raised in Ithaca, New York, received her undergraduate degree magna cum laude in psychology at Cornell University. She received a PhD in experimental psychology from the University of Pennsylvania, and later completed a formal clinical retraining program from 1981–1984. She taught at the University of Wisconsin-Madison and at the University of Texas at Austin before moving to Northwestern University in 1987. Since 1987 she has been Professor of Psychology at Northwestern and since 1998 she has served as Director of Clinical Training there. She has taught a wide range of undergraduate and graduate courses, including introductory psychology, learning, motivation, abnormal psychology, and cognitive-behavior therapy. Her current research interests include cognitive and behavioral approaches to understanding the etiology, maintenance, and treatment of anxiety and mood disorders. She is currently a Fellow of the American Psychological Association, the American Psychological Society, and the Academy of Cognitive Therapy. She has served as Editor of the *Journal of Abnormal Psychology* (1990–1994). She is currently serving as an Associate Editor for *Emotion*, and is on the editorial boards of several of the leading journals in the field. She was also President of the Society for the Science of Clinical Psychology (1994–1995) and was President of the Midwestern Psychological Association (1997). She also served on the American Psychological Association's Board of Scientific Affairs (1992–1994, Chair 1994), on the Executive Board of the Society for Research in Psychopathology (1992–1994, 2000–2003), and on the Board of Directors of the American Psychological Society (2001–2004). During 1997–1998 she was a fellow at the Center for Advanced Study in the Behavioral Sciences at Stanford.

JILL M. HOOLEY
Harvard University

Jill M. Hooley is a professor of psychology at Harvard University. She is also head of the experimental psychopathology and clinical psychology program at Harvard. Dr. Hooley was born in England and received a B.Sc. in Psychology from the University of Liverpool. This was followed by research work at Cambridge University. She then attended Magdalen College, Oxford, where she completed her D.Phil. After a move to the United States and additional training in clinical psychology at SUNY Stony Brook, Dr. Hooley took a position at Harvard, where she has been a faculty member since 1985.

Dr. Hooley has a long-standing interest in psychosocial predictors of psychiatric relapse in patients with severe psychopathology such as schizophrenia and depression. She is currently conducting neuroimaging studies of emotion in depression. She is the author of many scholarly publications and has served on the editorial boards of several prestigious journals. She has also reviewed applications for research grants both in the United States and internationally. At Harvard, she has taught graduate and undergraduate classes in introductory psychology, abnormal psychology, schizophrenia, mood disorders, psychiatric diagnosis, and psychological treatment. When she is not teaching, conducting research, or treating clinical patients, Dr. Hooley is most likely to be found riding her horse.

ABNORMAL PSYCHOLOGY

CHAPTER

1

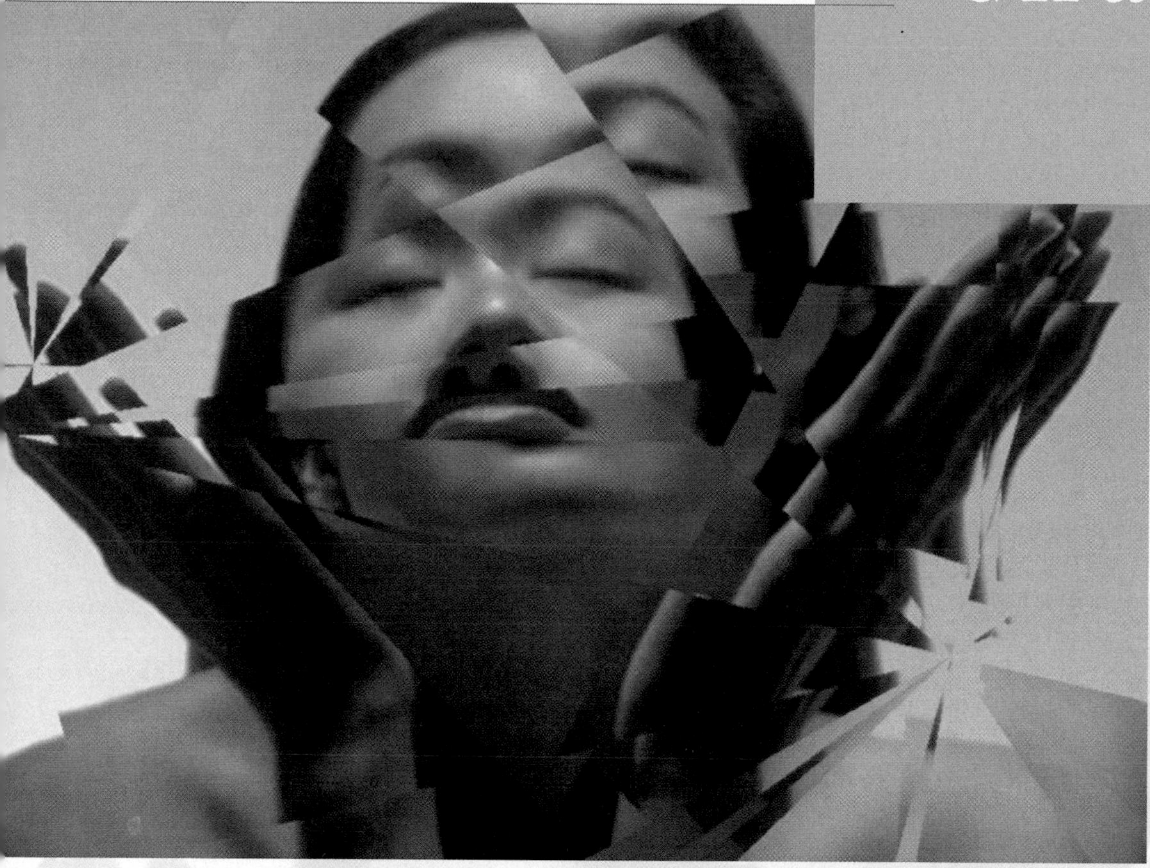

Abnormal Psychology: An Overview

The topics and problems central to abnormal psychology surround us every day. You have only to pick up a newspaper, read a magazine, watch TV, or go to a movie to be exposed to some of the issues that clinicians and researchers deal with on a day-to-day basis. Almost weekly, it seems, some celebrity is in the news because of a drug or alcohol problem, an eating disorder, or some other psychological difficulty. Bookstore shelves are lined with personal accounts of struggles with schizophrenia, depression, phobias, and panic attacks. Films such as *A Beautiful Mind* portray aspects of psychopathology with varying degrees of accuracy. And then there are the tragic news stories of mothers who kill their children, where problems with depression, schizophrenia, or postpartum difficulties seem to be implicated.

Abnormal psychology also exists much closer to home. Walk around any college campus, and you will see notices about peer support groups for people with eating disorders, depression, and a variety of other problems. You may even know someone who has experienced a clinical problem. It may be a cousin with a cocaine habit, a roommate with bulimia, or a grandparent who is developing Alzheimer's disease. It may be a co-worker of your mother's who is hospitalized for depression, a neighbor who is afraid to leave the house, or someone at your gym who works out intensely while looking worrisomely thin. It may even be the disheveled man in the aluminum foil hat who shouts, "Leave me alone!" to voices only he can hear.

The issues of abnormal psychology capture our interest, demand our attention, and trigger our concern. They also compel us to ask questions. To illustrate further, let's consider two clinical cases.

case STUDY Monique

Monique is a 24-year-old law school student. She is attractive, neatly dressed, and clearly very bright. If you were to meet her, you would think that she had few problems in her life. But Monique has been drinking alcohol since she was 14, and she smokes marijuana every day. Although she describes herself as "just a social drinker," she drinks four or five glasses of wine when she goes out with friends and also drinks a couple of glasses of wine a night when she is alone in her apartment watching TV in the evening. She frequently misses early morning classes because she feels too hungover to get out of bed, and on several occasions her drinking has caused her to black out. Although she denies having any problems with alcohol, Monique admits that her friends and family have started to get very concerned about her and have suggested that she seek help. Monique, however, says, "I don't think I am an alcoholic because I never drink in the mornings." The previous week she decided to stop smoking marijuana entirely because she was concerned that she might have a drug problem. However, she found it impossible to stop and is now smoking regularly again.

case STUDY Donald

Donald is 33 years old. Although Donald is of relatively high intelligence, he has never been employed for more than a few days at a time, and he currently lives in a sheltered community setting. Donald has brief but frequent periods when he needs to be hospitalized. His hospitalizations are triggered by episodes of great agitation during which Donald hears voices. These voices heap insulting and abusive comments on him. In most social situations, Donald appears awkward and painfully unsure of himself, as well as rather socially inappropriate.

In his mid-teens Donald began to withdraw socially from his friends and family. When he was 17, he suddenly, and without any obvious trigger, began to hear voices. At that time he was stubbornly insistent that the voices were coming, with malicious intent, from within a neighbor's house and were being transmitted electronically to the speakers of the family television. More recently he has begun to consider the possibility that he somehow produces them within himself. During periods of deterioration, Donald can be heard arguing vehemently with the voices. The rest of the time he appears to be reasonably able to ignore them, although his voices are never entirely absent for sustained periods.

Prior to his breakdown, Donald lived a relatively normal middle-class life. He was reasonably popular among peers and showed considerable athletic prowess. He earned passing grades in school, although his parents and teachers often complained that he seemed inattentive and preoccupied. There was no evidence of his ever having abused drugs.

Perhaps you found yourself asking questions as you read about Monique and Donald. For example, because Monique doesn't drink in the mornings, you might have wondered whether she could really have a serious alcohol problem. She does. This is a question that concerns the criteria that someone has to meet before getting a particular diagnosis. Or perhaps you wondered whether other people in Monique's family also have drinking problems. They do. This is a question about what we call **family aggregation,** or whether a disorder runs in families. No doubt you were also curious about what is wrong with Donald and why he is hearing voices. Donald suffers from schizophrenia. Also, as Donald's case illustrates, it is not unusual for someone who develops schizophrenia to be apparently perfectly normal before suddenly becoming ill.

These cases give some indication of how profoundly lives can be derailed because of mental disorders. Although the names of the people have been changed to protect their identities, these cases describe real people with real problems. It is hard to read about difficulties such as these without feeling compassion for the people who are struggling. But in addition to compassion, clinicians and researchers who want to help people like Monique and Donald must have other skills. If we are to understand mental disorders, we must learn to ask the kinds of questions that will enable us to help the patients and the families who suffer from mental disorders. These questions are at the very heart of a research-based approach that looks to use scientific inquiry and careful observation to understand abnormal psychology.

Just under 50 percent of people will suffer from a mental disorder at some point in their lives, with anxiety disorders being especially common.

Asking questions is an important aspect of being a psychologist. Psychology is a fascinating field, and (although we are undoubtedly biased) abnormal psychology is one of the most interesting areas of psychology. Psychologists are trained to ask questions and to conduct research. Though not all people who are trained in abnormal psychology (sometimes called "psychopathology") conduct research, they still rely heavily on their scientific skills and ability both to ask questions and to put information together in coherent and logical ways. For example, when a clinician first sees a new client or patient, he or she asks a lot of questions to try and understand the issues or problems related to that person. The clinician will also rely on current research to choose the most effective treatment. The "best treatments" of 20, 10, or even 5 years ago are not invariably the best treatments of today. Knowledge progresses, and advances are made. And research is the engine that drives all of these developments.

In this chapter, we will outline the field of abnormal psychology and the varied training and activities of the people who work in it. First we describe the ways in which abnormal behavior is defined and classified so that researchers and mental health professionals can communicate with each other about the people they see. Some of the issues here are probably more complex and controversial than you might expect. We also outline basic information about the extent of behavioral abnormalities in the population at large.

You will notice that a large section of this chapter is devoted to research. We make every effort to convey how abnormal behavior is studied. Research is at the heart of progress and knowledge in abnormal psychology. The more you know and understand about how research is conducted, the more educated and aware you will be about what research findings mean and what they do not mean. For example, read Developments in Research 1.1 before you buy a magnet to help you with a repetitive-stress injury caused by typing too many term papers!

What Do We Mean By Abnormal Behavior?

It may come as a surprise to you that there is still no universal agreement about what we mean by *abnormality* or *disorder.* This is not to say we do not have definitions; we

1.1 Developments in Research

Do Magnets Help with Repetitive-Stress Injury?

There is a growing trend for people to use alternative medical therapies when they experience problems (Eisenberg et al., 1998). One form of "energy healing" therapy that is growing in popularity is the use of magnets. Many companies now sell therapeutic magnets, and there are many testimonials that can be found on the Internet that extol their healing powers.

Magnets are often marketed to people who have chronic hand or wrist pain. This type of problem is known as repetitive-stress injury (RSI). A common source of such problems is extensive computer use. But do magnets really relieve the chronic pain that is associated with repetitive-stress injury? Testimonials notwithstanding, the only way to answer this question is by controlled research. To investigate this issue, Pope and McNally (2002) randomly assigned college students with RSI to one of three groups. One group was asked to wear wristbands containing magnets for a 30-minute period (magnet group). A second group was also given apparently identical bracelets to wear. In this case, however, and unknown both to the participants and to the assistant running the study, the magnets had been removed from the wristbands (sham group). A third group of subjects did not receive any magnets (no-treatment group).

You should note here that this study is an example of what we call a **double-blind study.** In other words, neither the subjects nor the experimenter who was working with the subjects knew who got the genuine magnets. The use of the wristbands with the magnets removed is called a *placebo treatment* condition (the word **placebo** comes from the Latin meaning "I shall please"). Placebo treatment conditions enable experimenters to control for the possibility that simply believing one is getting an effective type of treatment produces a therapeutic benefit. Finally, the no-treatment control group enables the experimenters to see what happens when they don't provide any treatment (or expectation of treatment) at all.

At the start of the study, all of the student participants completed a 4-minute typing test. This provided a measure of how many words they could type in this time. Then, 30 minutes after wearing the magnets or fake wristbands (or, for the no-treatment subjects, after waiting 30 minutes), all participants completed another 4-minute typing test. In addition, those who had been assigned to either the genuine or the placebo magnet group were asked to rate their degree of pain relief (from no improvement to complete relief) using an 8-point scale.

What were the results? As might be expected, those people who had been assigned to the no-treatment group did not report that their level of pain changed in any appreciable way. This is hardly surprising, because nothing had been done to them at all. They typed an average of about four more words on the second test (the post-test) than on the first (the pretest).

Did the people who wore the magnets do better than this? The answer is yes. Those who wore the genuine magnets reported that their pain was diminished. They also typed an average of 19 more words on the second typing test than they did on the first! In other words, with respect to both their self-report data (their pain improvement ratings) and their behavioral data (how rapidly they could type), they clearly did better than the no-treatment group.

Before you rush out to buy magnetic bracelets, however, let us look at the performance of the people who received the fake bracelets. Like the subjects who wore the genuine magnets, these participants also reported that their pain had improved. And, in fact, on the behavioral typing test, subjects in the placebo treatment group typed even more words on the second test (an average of 26 words more) than subjects who wore the real magnets did! With respect to their self-reports and their behavioral data, therefore, the group who wore the fake bracelets improved just as much as the group who wore the real magnets! Judging on the basis of this study, then, we must conclude that magnet therapy works via the placebo effect, not because there is any genuine clinical benefit that comes from the magnets themselves. If you believe that the magnet will help your RSI, you don't actually need a magnet to bring about any clinical improvement. And this, in a nutshell, is why we need controlled research trials.

do. However, every definition provided so far has proved problematic (Maddux, Gosselin, & Winstead, 2005). What is perhaps more remarkable is that even though we lack consensus on a definition, there is still a lot of agreement about which conditions are disorders and which are not (Spitzer, 1999). How do we manage this? In part, the answer lies in the fact that there are some clear elements of abnormality (Lilienfeld & Marino, 1999; Seligman et al., 2001). No one element of abnormality is sufficient in and of itself to define or determine abnormality, but the greater the similarity between a given person's behavior and the elements of abnormality described in The World Around Us 1.2, the more likely it is that the person is abnormal or mentally disordered in some way. In other words, we adopt a "prototype" kind of model of abnormality and assess the degree to which a given person

1.2 THE WORLD AROUND US

The Elements of Abnormality

There is no one behavior that makes someone abnormal. This has made the definition of mental disorders problematic. However, there are certainly elements of abnormality. The more that someone has difficulties in the following areas, the more likely it is that he or she has some form of mental disorder.

1. Suffering: If people suffer psychologically, we are inclined to consider this as indicative of abnormality. Depressed people clearly suffer, as do people with anxiety disorders. But what about the patient who is manic? He or she may not be suffering (indeed, many such patients dislike taking medications because they don't want to lose their manic "highs"). You may have a test tomorrow and be suffering because of that. But we would hardly label your suffering abnormal. Although suffering is an element of abnormality in many cases, it is neither a sufficient condition (all that is needed) nor even a necessary condition (that all cases of abnormality must show) for us to consider something as abnormal.
2. Maladaptiveness: Maladaptive behavior is often an indicator of abnormality. The person with anorexia may restrict her intake of food to the point where she becomes so emaciated that she needs to be hospitalized. The person with depression may withdraw from friends and family and may be unable to work for weeks or months. Maladaptive behavior interferes with our well-being and with our ability to enjoy our work and our relationships. But not all disorders involve maladaptive behavior. Consider the con artist and the contract killer, both of whom have antisocial personality disorder (see Chapter 11). One may be able glibly to talk people out of their life savings, the other to take someone's life in return for payment. Is this behavior maladaptive? Not for them, because it is the way they make their respective livings. We consider them abnormal, however, because their behavior is maladaptive for society.
3. Deviancy: The word *abnormal* literally means "away from the normal." But simply considering statistically rare behavior to be abnormal does not provide us with a solution to our problem of defining abnormality. Genius is statistically rare, as is perfect pitch. However, we do not consider people with such uncommon talents to be abnormal in any way. On the other hand, mental retardation (which is also statistically rare and represents a deviation from normal) is considered to reflect abnormality. This tells us that in defining abnormality, we make value judgments. If something is statistically rare and undesirable (as is mental retardation), we are more likely to consider it abnormal than something that is statistically rare and highly desirable (such as genius) or something that is undesirable but statistically common (such as rudeness).
4. Violation of the Standards of Society: All cultures have rules. Some of these are formalized as laws. Others form the norms and moral standards that we are taught to follow. Although many social rules are arbitrary to some extent, when people fail to follow the conventional social and moral rules, we may consider their behavior abnormal. Of course, much depends on the magnitude of the violation and on how commonly it is violated by others. For example, most of us have parked illegally at some time or other. This failure to follow the rules is so statistically common that we tend not to think of it as abnormal. On the other hand, when a mother drowns her children, there is instant recognition that this is abnormal behavior.
5. Social Discomfort: When someone violates a social rule, those around him or her may experience a sense of discomfort or unease. For example, imagine you are traveling home on the bus, and there is no one else on the bus except the driver. Then the bus stops and someone else gets on. Even though there are rows and rows of empty seats, this person sits down next to you. How do you feel? In a related vein, how do you feel when someone you met only 4 minutes before starts to tell you of her suicide attempt? Unless you are a therapist working in a crisis intervention center, you would probably consider this an example of abnormal behavior.
6. Irrationality and Unpredictability: As we have already noted, we expect people to behave in certain ways. Although a little unconventionality may add some spice to life, there is a point at which we are likely to consider a given unorthodox behavior abnormal. For example, if the person next to you suddenly started to scream and yell obscenities at nothing, you would probably regard that behavior as abnormal. It would be unpredictable, and it would make no sense to you. The disordered speech and the disorganized behavior of patients with schizophrenia (see Chapter 14) are often irrational. Such behaviors are also a hallmark of the manic phases of bipolar disorder. Perhaps the most important factor, however, is our evaluation of whether the person can control his or her behavior.

(continued)

Few of us would consider a roommate who began to recite speeches from *King Lear* to be abnormal if we knew that he was playing Lear in the next campus Shakespeare production—or even if he was a dramatic person given to extravagant outbursts. On the other hand, if we discovered our roommate lying on the floor, flailing wildly, and reciting Shakespeare, we might consider calling for assistance if this was entirely out of character and we knew of no reason why it should be happening.

As with most accomplished athletes, Venus and Serena Williams' physical ability is "abnormal" in a literal and statistical sense. Yet their behavior would not be labeled as being "abnormal" by psychologists. Why not?

Twenty years ago, pierced noses, lips, and navels were regarded as highly deviant. Now, such adornments are considered fashionable by many, and attract little attention.

resembles it. Using the elements of abnormality described in The World Around Us 1.2, consider the case in The World Around Us 1.3 on the following page.

Finally, we should note the additional problem of changing values and expectations in society at large. Because society is constantly evolving and becoming more or less tolerant of certain behaviors, what is considered abnormal or deviant in one decade may not be considered deviant or abnormal a decade or two later. For example, at one time, homosexuality was classified as a mental disorder. It is no longer viewed as such today (see Chapter 13). And 20 years ago, pierced noses, lips, and navels were regarded as highly deviant and prompted questions about a person's mental health. Now, however, such adornments are quite commonplace, are considered fashionable by many, and generally attract little attention. What other behaviors can you think of that are considered normal by today's standards but were regarded as deviant in the past?

Why Do We Need to Classify Mental Disorders?

If defining abnormality is so difficult, why do we do it? One simple reason is that most sciences rely on classification (e.g., the periodic table in chemistry and the classification of living organisms into kingdoms, phyla, classes, and so on in biology). At the most fundamental level, classification systems provide us with a **nomenclature** (a naming system) and enable us to *structure information* in a more helpful manner. Organizing information within a classification system also allows us to study the different disorders that we classify and therefore to learn more, not only about what causes them but also how they might best be treated. For example, thinking back to the cases you read about, Monique has alcohol and drug dependence, and Donald suffers from schizophrenia. Knowing what disorder each of them has is clearly very helpful, as Donald's treatment would likely not work for Monique.

A final effect of classification system usage is somewhat more mundane. As others have pointed out, the classification of mental disorders has social and political implications (see Blashfield & Livesley, 1999; Kirk & Kutchins, 1992). Simply put, defining the domain of what is considered to be pathological establishes the range of problems that the mental health profession can address.

1.3 The World Around Us

Extreme Generosity or Pathological Behavior?

Zell Kravinsky grew up in a working-class neighborhood in Philadelphia. A brilliant student, he won prizes at school and began investing in the stock market when he was 12. Despite his abilities, his Russian immigrant parents were, in the words of a family friend, "steadfast in denying him any praise." Kravinsky went to Dartmouth, where he majored in Asian studies, and, after graduation, he took a job at an insurance company. Later he became a teacher, working with children who had social and emotional problems. Eventually he returned to school himself, completing two Ph.D.s—the first in education, the second in literature. Throughout this time, he also indulged his growing interest in real estate. By the time he was 45, he was married with children, and his assets amounted to almost $45 million.

Although Kravinsky had a talent for making money, he found it difficult to spend it. He drove an old car, did not give his children pocket money, and lived with his family in a modest home. As his fortune grew, however, he began to talk to his friends about his plans to give all of his assets to charity. His philanthropy began in earnest when he and his wife gave two gifts, totalling $6.2 million, to the Centers for Disease Control Foundation. They also donated an apartment building to a school for the disabled in Philadelphia. The following year the Kravinskys gave gifts of real estate that were worth around $30 million to Ohio State University.

Kravinsky's motivation for his giving was to help others. According to one of his friends, "He gave away the money because he had it and there were people who needed it. But it changed his way of looking at himself. He decided the purpose of his life was to give away things." After he had put some money aside in trust for his wife and his children, Kravinsky's personal assets were reduced to a house (on which he had a substantial mortgage), two minivans, and around $80,000 in stocks and cash. He had essentially given away his entire fortune.

Kravinsky's giving did not end when his financial assets were gone. He began to be preoccupied with the idea of nondirected organ donations, in which an altruistic person gives an organ to a total stranger. When he learned that he could live quite normally with only one kidney, Kravinsky decided that the personal costs of giving away one of his kidneys were minimal compared to the benefits that someone with kidney disease would receive from being given a matching kidney. His wife, however, did not share his view. Although she had consented to giving away large sums of money to good causes, when it came to her husband giving away his kidney, she could not agree.

For Kravinsky, however, the burden of not being able to do something that would help alleviate the suffering of someone in need was almost unbearable. He called the Albert Einstein Medical Center and spoke to a transplant coordinator. He met with a surgeon, and then with a psychiatrist. Kravinsky told the psychiatrist that he suffered from depression and that his wife did not support his desire to donate one of his kidneys. When the psychiatrist told him that he was doing something that he did not have to do, Kravinsky's response was, "I do have to do it. You're missing the whole point. It's as much a necessity as food, water, and air."

Three months later, Kravinsky left his home in the early hours of the morning and drove to the hospital. In an operation that took 3 hours, he gave his right kidney to Donnell Reid, a 29-year-old single black woman who was studying social work and who had been on dialysis for the previous 8 years. The day after the operation, he called his wife to tell her what he had done.

In spite of the turmoil that his kidney donation created within his family, Kravinsky's mind turned back to philanthropy almost immediately. "I lay there in the hospital, and I thought about all my other good organs. When I do something good, I feel that I can do more. I burn to do more. It's a heady feeling." By the time he was discharged, he was wondering about giving away his one remaining kidney.

In the months after the operation, Kravinsky experienced a loss of his sense of direction. He had come to view his life as a continuing donation. But now that his financial assets and his kidney were gone, what could be next? His current dilemma is how he can continue to give in the way that matters most to him, and how he can continue to live if

(continued)

he carries out the organ donations he envisions. Sometimes he imagines offering his entire body for donation. "My organs could save several people if I gave my whole body away." He also acknowledges that he feels unable to do that to his family. At the present time, Kravinsky is involved in a real estate partnership with the goal of giving his shares in the business endeavor to charity.

Peter Singer, a Princeton philosopher, has called Kravinsky "a remarkable person who has taken very seriously questions about the nature of our moral obligations to assist people." Others who hear Kravinsky's story may think that he is quite mad. What do you think? Is Kravinsky's behavior abnormal? Or is this a man of profound moral commitment who possesses a degree of courage that allows him to act on his personal convictions? (Taken from Parker, 2004)

And on a purely pragmatic level, it also delineates which types of problems warrant insurance reimbursement, and how much reimbursement.

What Are the Disadvantages of Classification?

Of course, there are also some drawbacks to having a classification system. Classification, by its very nature, provides information in a shorthand form. However, using any form of shorthand inevitably leads to a *loss of information.* For example, learning about a person who has a particular type of disorder (e.g., by reading a case summary) tells you much more than just being told that the person is suffering from "schizophrenia." In other words, as we simplify through classification, we inevitably lose an array of personal details about the actual person who has the disorder.

Moreover, although things are changing, there can also still be some **stigma** (or disgrace) attached to receiving a psychiatric diagnosis. People who would readily disclose that they have an illness such as diabetes are much more likely to be silent if the diagnosis involves a mental disorder. In part, this is because of a fear (real or imagined) that talking candidly about having psychological problems will have unwanted social or occupational consequences. James McNulty, who has suffered from bipolar disorder for many years, provides the following example.

case STUDY — The Stigma of Mental Illness

I have lived with bipolar disorder for more than 35 years—all of my adult life. The first 15 years were relatively conventional, at least on the surface. I graduated from an Ivy League university, started my own business, and began a career in local politics. I was married, the father of two sons. I experienced mood swings during these years, and as I got older the swings worsened. Eventually, I became so ill that I was unable to work, my marriage ended, I lost my business, and I became homeless.

At this point I had my most powerful experience with stigma. I was 38 years old. I had recently been discharged after a psychiatric hospitalization for a suicide attempt, I had no place to live, my savings were exhausted, and my only possession was a 4-year-old car. I contacted the mental health authorities in the state where I then lived and asked for assistance in dealing with my mental illness. I was told that to qualify for assistance I would need to sell my car and spend down the proceeds. I asked how I was supposed to get to work when I recovered enough to find a job. I was told, "Don't worry about going back to work. People like you don't go back to work" (McNulty, 2004).

The experiences of James McNulty also illustrate another component of stigma, which is the problem of **stereotyping.** Stereotypes are automatic beliefs that people have about other people based on knowing one (often trivial) thing about them (e.g., people who wear glasses are more intelligent; New Yorkers are rude; everyone in the South has a gun). Because we may have heard about certain behaviors that can accompany mental disorders, we may automatically and incorrectly infer that this will also be true for any person we meet who has a psychiatric diagnosis. This is reflected in the comment, "People like you don't go back to work." Take a moment to consider honestly your own stereotypes about people with mental disorders. What assumptions do you tend to make? Do you view people with mental illness as less competent, more irresponsible, more dangerous, and more unpredictable? Research has shown that such attitudes are not uncommon (see Watson et al., 2004).

Finally, stigma can be perpetuated by the problem of **labeling.** A person's self-concept may be directly affected by being given a diagnosis of schizophrenia, depression, or some other form of mental illness. How might you react if you were told something like this? Also, once a group of symptoms (see Table 1.1) is given a name and identified by

TABLE 1.1 Symptoms and Syndromes

Symptom: A symptom is a single indicator of a problem. It can involve affect (e.g., sad mood, anxiousness), behavior (problems sleeping, lethargy), or cognition (excessive worry, suicidal thoughts).

Syndrome: A syndrome is a group or cluster of symptoms that all occur together. For example, sad or depressed mood, problems sleeping, concentration problems, weight loss, and suicidal thinking are all symptoms that reflect the syndrome of depression. Note that in the case of depression, depression can be a symptom (when it refers to depressed mood). It is also the name of the syndrome (when it refers to the cluster of symptoms).

TABLE 1.2 DSM-IV Definition of Mental Disorders

- A clinically significant behavioral or psychological syndrome or pattern
- Associated with distress or disability (i.e., impairment in one or more important areas of functioning)
- Not simply a predictable and culturally sanctioned response to a particular event (e.g., the death of a loved one)
- Considered to reflect behavioral, psychological, or biological dysfunction in the individual (adapted from American Psychiatric Association, DSM-IV, 2000, p. xxi)

means of a diagnosis, this "diagnostic label" can be hard to shake, even if the person later makes a full recovery.

It is important to keep in mind, however, that diagnostic classification systems do not classify people. Rather, they classify *the disorders that people have.* In other words, it is essential to note that a person has an illness, but is not defined by that illness. Language is therefore very important. At one time it was quite common for mental health professionals to describe a given patient as "a schizophrenic" or "a manic-depressive." Now, however, it is widely acknowledged that it is more accurate (not to mention more respectful) to say, "a person with schizophrenia" or "a person who suffers from manic depression." Simply put, the person is not the diagnosis.

The DSM-IV Definition of Mental Disorder

In the United States, the gold standard for defining various types of mental disorders is the American Psychiatric Association's *Diagnostic and Statistical Manual of Mental Disorders,* commonly known as "the DSM." The DSM is currently in its fourth edition (hence, DSM-IV). DSM-IV was first published in 1994 and then was revised slightly in 2000. This most recent edition of the DSM is known as "DSM-IV-TR" (the TR stands for *text revision*). Table 1.2 summarizes the current DSM-IV definition of a mental disorder.

This DSM definition does not refer to the causes of mental disorder. In other words, the DSM attempts to be "atheoretical." It also carefully rules out, among other things, behaviors that are culturally sanctioned, such as (depressive) grief following the death of a significant other. The text of the DSM is also careful to assert that mental disorders are always the product of "dysfunctions," dysfunctions that in turn always reside in individuals, not in groups.

Though widely accepted, the DSM definition of mental disorder still has problems. For example, what exactly is meant by the term "clinically significant" and how should this be measured? Also, how much distress or disability should someone experience before he or she can be considered to be suffering from a mental disorder? Who determines what is "culturally sanctioned"? And what exactly constitutes a "behavioral, psychological, or biological dysfunction"? Obviously, the problematic behavior cannot itself be the "dysfunction," for that would be like saying mental disorders are due to mental disorders. If a dysfunction is caused by a dysfunction, we have a definition that is based on circular reasoning.

Identifying this flaw in the DSM definition, Jerome Wakefield (1992a, 1992b, 1997) has proposed the idea of mental disorder as "harmful dysfunction." In his own definition (see Table 1.3), Wakefield classifies "harm" in

TABLE 1.3 Wakefield's Definition of a Mental Disorder

A mental disorder is a mental condition that

- causes significant distress or disability,
- is not merely an expectable response to a particular event, and
- is a manifestation of a mental dysfunction. (Wakefield, 1992b, p. 235)

terms of social values (e.g., suffering, being unable to work, etc.), and "dysfunction" refers to some underlying mechanism that fails to perform according to its (presumably evolutionary) "design" (see Clark, 1999).

One merit of Wakefield's approach is that he acknowledges the role played by social values in the definition of a mental disorder. He also tries to use scientific theory (the theory of evolution) in his conception of mental disorder. Nonetheless, there are still various logical and philosophical problems with this proposed solution (e.g., Lilienfeld & Marino, 1999; Maddux et al., 2005). How are we to know if a problematic behavior is caused by a dysfunction? Evolutionary theory does not provide us with a convenient list of what is functional and what is not. Rather, we are left to base these evaluations on social norms, not on scientific observations. Moreover, to imagine that we might someday be able to pinpoint a distinct underlying and presumably biological dysfunction for each of the nearly 300 DSM diagnoses seems rather an impossible task. As you can see, the term *mental disorder* defies simple, straightforward definition.

Despite the frustrations in trying to pin down such notions as distress and dysfunction, and in developing a consensus definition of mental disorder, clinical research and patient care must continue. We cannot wait until the experts have worked out all the details before we explore the nature, origins, and best forms of treatment for a wide range of disorders. Therefore, the "prototype" model of abnormality discussed earlier is the best attempt we have to identify and help those suffering from mental disorders. Any definition of abnormality or mental disorder must be somewhat arbitrary, and the DSM-IV definition is no exception. The DSM is a work in progress. Much thought is now being given to issues that will need to be dealt with as we begin to move toward DSM-V (e.g., Widiger & Clark, 2000). As our understanding of different disorders changes and as our thinking evolves, so too will the DSM and its definition of mental disorder.

How Does Culture Affect What Is Considered Abnormal?

It is difficult to consider the concepts of normal and abnormal without reference to culture. Within a given culture, there are many shared beliefs and behaviors that are widely accepted and that form part of customary practice. For example, many people in Christian countries believe that the number 13 is unlucky. The origins of this may be linked to the Last Supper, when 13 people were present. Many of us try to be especially careful on Friday the 13th. Some hotels and apartment buildings do not have a thirteenth floor, and there is often no bed number 13 in hospitals. The Japanese, in contrast, do not care about the number 13 but try to avoid the number 4 if they can. This is because in Japanese, the sound of the word for "four" is similar to the sound of the word for "death" (see Tseng, 2001, pp. 105–6).

There is also considerable variation in the way different cultures describe psychological distress. For example, there is no word for "depressed" in the languages of certain Native Americans, Alaska Natives, and some Southeast Asian groups (Manson, 1995). Of course, this does not mean that people from such cultural groups do not experience clinically significant depression. As the accompanying case illustrates, however, the way some disorders present themselves may depend on culturally sanctioned ways of describing distress.

case study: A Native American Elder

JGH is a 71-year-old member of a southwestern tribe who has been brought to a local Indian Health Service hospital by one of his granddaughters and is seen in the general medical outpatient clinic for multiple complaints. Most of Mr. GH's complaints involve nonlocalized pain. When asked to point to where he hurts, Mr. GH indicates his chest, then his abdomen, his knees, and finally moves his hands "all over." Barely whispering, he mentions a phrase in his native language that translates as "whole body sickness." His granddaughter notes that he "has not been himself" recently. Specifically, Mr. GH, during the past 3–4 months, has stopped attending or participating in many events previously important to him and central to his role in a large extended family and clan. He is reluctant to discuss this change in behavior as well as his feelings. When questioned more directly, Mr. GH acknowledges that he has had difficulty falling asleep, sleeps intermittently through the night, and almost always awakens at dawn's first light. He admits that he has not felt like eating in recent months, but denies weight loss, although his clothes hang loosely in many folds. Trouble concentrating and remembering are eventually disclosed as well. Asked why he has not participated in family and clan events in the last several months, Mr. GH describes himself as "too tired and full of pain" and "afraid of disappointing people." Further pressing by the clinician is met with silence. Suddenly the patient states, "You know, my sheep haven't been doing well lately. Their coats are ragged; they're thinner. They just wander aimlessly; even the ewes don't seem to care about the little ones." Physical examination and laboratory tests are normal. Mr. GH continues to take two tablets of acetaminophen daily for mild arthritic pain. Although he describes himself as a "recovering alcoholic," Mr. GH reports not having consumed alcohol during the last 23 years. He denies any prior episodes of depression or other psychiatric problems (Manson, 1995, p. 488).

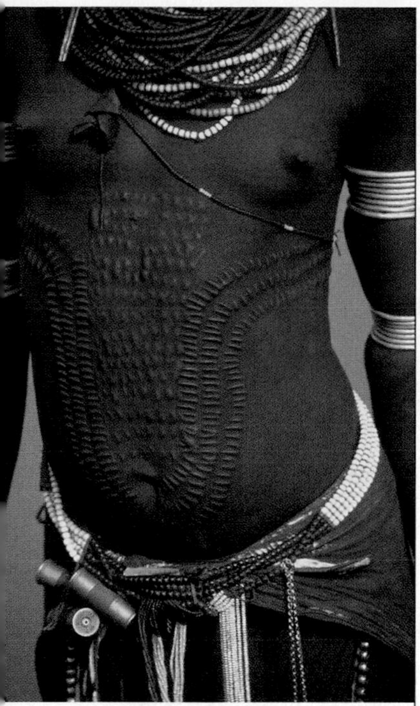

Some African tribe members inflict painful and permanent scars (a process called scarification*) on their faces and torsos in an effort to beautify themselves. Such a practice might be viewed as "abnormal" by Western European cultures but it is quite common among African tribes.*

As is apparent in the case of JGH, culture can shape the clinical presentation of disorders like depression, which are found all over the world (see Draguns & Tanaka-Matsumi, 2003). In China, for example, people who are suffering from depression most typically focus on physical concerns (fatigue, dizziness, headaches) rather than saying that they feel sad or down (Kleinman, 1986; Parker et al., 2001). This focus on physical pain rather than emotional pain is also noteworthy in Mr. GH's case.

Although things are slowly improving, we still know relatively little about the cultural aspects of abnormal psychology (Arrindell, 2003). The vast majority of the psychiatric literature originates from Euro-American countries (Western Europe, North America, and Australia/New Zealand). Astonishingly, of the papers submitted to and published in the six leading psychiatric journals between 1996 and 1998, only 6 percent came from areas of the world where 90 percent of the world's population actually lives (Patel & Sumathipala, 2001)! Moreover, when research is published in languages other than English, it tends to get disregarded (Draguns, 2001).

There is no word for "depressed" in the languages of certain Native American tribes. People from this culture tend to describe their symptoms of depression in physical rather than emotional terms.

Culture-Specific Disorders

Certain forms of psychopathology seem to be highly culture-specific. In other words, they are found only in certain areas of the world and appear to be highly linked to culturally bound concerns. One example is *taijin kyofusho.* This syndrome, which is a form of anxiety disorder (see Chapter 6), is quite prevalent in Japan. It involves a marked fear that one's body, body parts, or body functions may offend or embarrass others or make them feel uncomfortable. Often, people with this disorder are afraid of blushing or fear upsetting others by their gaze, facial expression, or body odor (Levine & Gaw, 1995).

Another culturally based way of showing distress that is found in Latinos, especially those from the Caribbean, is *ataque de nervios* (Lopez & Guarnaccia, 2005). The symptoms of an *ataque de nervios,* which is often triggered by a stressful event like divorce or loss of a loved one, include crying, trembling, uncontrollable screaming, and a general feeling of being out of control. Sometimes the person may become aggressive physically or verbally. In other cases, the person may faint or experience something that looks like a seizure. Once the *ataque* is over, the person may quickly return to normal and have no memory of what happened.

As we can see from these examples, **abnormal behavior** is behavior that deviates from the norms of the society in which it is enacted (e.g., see Gorenstein, 1992; Scheff, 1984). Experiences such as hearing the voice of a dead relative might be regarded as normative in one culture (e.g., in many Native American tribes) but as abnormal in another. Nonetheless, certain unconventional actions and behaviors are almost universally considered to be the product of mental disorder. For example, many years ago the anthropologist Jane Murphy (1976) studied what was regarded as abnormal behavior by the Yoruba of Africa and also by Yupik-speaking Eskimos living on an island in the Bering Sea. Both societies had words that were used to denote abnormality or "craziness." In addition, the clusters of behaviors that were considered to reflect abnormality in these cultures were behaviors that most of us would also

Some disorders are highly culture-specific. For example, taijin kyofusho *is a disorder that is prevalent in Japan and is characterized by a fear that one may upset others by one's gaze, facial expression, or body odor.*

regard as abnormal, such as hearing voices, laughing at nothing, defecating in public, drinking urine, and believing things that no one else believes. Why do you think these behaviors are universally considered to be abnormal?

In Review

- Why is abnormality so difficult to define? What characteristics help us recognize abnormality?
- Explain the differences between a symptom and a syndrome. Is depression a symptom or a syndrome?
- In what ways can culture shape the clinical presentation of mental disorders?

How Common are Mental Disorders?

How many and what kind of people actually have diagnosable psychological disorders today? This is an important question for a number of reasons. First, this kind of information is essential for planning mental health services. Mental health planners need to have a clear picture of the nature and extent of psychological problems within a given area, state, or country so that they can determine how resources, such as funding of research projects or services provided by community mental health centers, can be most effectively allocated. For example, it would obviously be foolish to have a treatment center filled with many experts able to treat anorexia nervosa (a very severe but rare clinical problem) while at the same time providing few treatment resources for people suffering from anxiety or depression, which are much more common.

Estimates of the frequency of mental disorders in different groups of people may provide valuable clues about their causes. For example, it is generally found that women with depression outnumber men with depression by a ratio of about 2:1 (Culbertson, 1997). This suggests that gender is an important factor to consider in any efforts to understand depression. What is also very interesting, however, is that among Jews, the genders are affected about equally (Levav et al., 1997). This is not true for other religious groups. Looking more closely at this ratio, it becomes apparent that Jewish males have a higher risk for depression than do men of non-Jewish descent. Why should this be? Although we do not yet know for sure, there are some interesting leads that we will discuss later in this chapter.

Prevalence and Incidence

Before we can discuss the extent of mental disorders in society, we must clarify how psychological problems are counted. **Epidemiology** is the study of the distribution of diseases, disorders, or health-related behaviors in a given population. Mental health epidemiology is the study of the distribution of mental disorders. A key component of an epidemiological survey is determining the frequencies of mental disorders. There are several ways of doing this. The term **prevalence** refers to the number of active cases in a population during any given period of time. Prevalence figures are typically expressed as percentages (i.e., the percentage of the population that has the disorder). There are several different types of prevalence estimates that can be made.

Point prevalence refers to the estimated proportion of actual, active cases of the disorder in a given population at any instant in time. For example, if we were to conduct a study and count the number of people who are suffering from major depression (see Chapter 7) on January 1 of next year, this would provide us with a point prevalence estimate of active cases of depression. Anyone who was suffering from depression during November and December but who managed to recover by January 1 would not be included in our point prevalence figure. The same is true of someone whose depression didn't begin until January 2. If, on the other hand, we wanted to get a **1-year prevalence** figure, we would count everyone who suffered from depression at any time during the whole year. As you might imagine, this prevalence figure would be higher than the point prevalence figure, because it would cover a much longer time. It would also include people who had recovered before the point prevalence assessment and people whose disorders did not begin until after the point prevalence estimate was made. Finally, we might also wish to get an estimate of how many people had suffered from a particular disorder at any time in their lives (even if they are now recovered). This would provide us with a **lifetime prevalence** estimate. Because they cover full life spans and include both currently ill people and recovered people who have had the disorder, lifetime prevalence estimates tend to be higher than other kinds of prevalence estimates.

The other important term you should be familiar with is **incidence.** This refers to the number of new cases that occur over a given period of time (typically 1 year). Incidence figures are typically lower than prevalence figures because they exclude already existing cases. In other words, if we were assessing the 1-year incidence of schizophrenia, we would not count people whose schizophrenia began before our January 1 starting date (even if they were still ill), because theirs would not be "new" cases of schizophrenia. On the other hand, someone who was quite well previously but who then developed schizophrenia during our 1-year window would be included in our incidence estimate.

Prevalence Estimates for Mental Disorders

Now that you understand some basic terms, let's look at the 1-year prevalence rates for several important disorders. Three major national mental health epidemiology studies, with direct and formal diagnostic assessment of participants, have been carried out in the United States in recent years. One, the Epidemiologic Catchment Area (ECA) study, concentrated on sampling the citizens of five communities: Baltimore, New Haven, St. Louis, Durham (NC), and Los Angeles (Myers et al., 1984; Regier et al., 1988; Regier et al., 1993). Another, the National Comorbidity Survey (NCS), was more extensive. It sampled the entire U.S. population and had a number of sophisticated methodological improvements as well (Kessler et al., 1994). A replication of the NCS (the NCS-R) has recently been completed (Kessler et al., 2004; Kessler, Berglund, et al., 2005; Kessler & Merikangas, 2004). The most current 1-year and lifetime prevalence estimates (based on NCS-R survey data) of different types of DSM-IV mental disorders are shown in Table 1.4.

The lifetime prevalence of having any DSM-IV disorder is 46.4 percent. This means that almost half of the Americans who were questioned had been affected by mental illness at some point in their lives (Kessler, Berglund, et al., 2005). Although this figure may seem very high, it may well be an underestimate because the NCS studies did not assess for eating disorders (see Chapter 9), schizophrenia, (see Chapter 14), or autism (see Chapter 16) or include measures of most personality disorders (see Chapter 11). As you can see from Table 1.4, the most prevalent kind of psychological disorders are anxiety disorders. The most common individual disorders are major depression, alcohol abuse, and specific phobias (e.g., fear of small animals, insects, flying, heights, etc.). Social phobias (e.g., fear of public speaking) are also very common (see Table 1.5).

Although lifetime rates of mental disorders appear to be quite high, it is important to remember that, in some cases, the duration of the disorder may be relatively brief (e.g., depression that lasts for a few weeks after the

TABLE 1.4 Prevalence of DSM-IV Disorders in Adults

	One-Year (%)	Lifetime (%)
Any mood disorder	9.5	20.8
Any anxiety disorder	18.1	28.8
Any substance-abuse disorder	3.8	14.6
Any disorder	26.2	46.4

Source: Kessler, Berglund, et al. (2005); Kessler, Chiu, et al. (2005).

TABLE 1.5 Most Common Individual DSM-IV Disorders

Disorder	One-Year Prevalence (%)	Lifetime Prevalence (%)
Major depressive disorder	6.7	16.6
Alcohol abuse	3.1	13.2
Specific phobia	8.7	12.5
Social phobia	6.8	12.1
Conduct disorder	1.0	9.5

Source: Kessler, Berglund, et al. (2005); Kessler, Chiu, et al. (2005).

Disorders do not always occur in isolation. A person who abuses alcohol may also be depressed or have an anxiety disorder.

breakup of a romantic relationship). Also, many people who meet criteria for a given disorder will not be seriously affected by it. For example, in the NCS-R study, almost half (48 percent) of the people diagnosed with a specific phobia had disorders that were rated as mild in severity, and only 22 percent of phobias were regarded as severe (Kessler, Chiu, et al., 2005). Meeting diagnostic criteria for a particular disorder and being seriously impaired by it are not always the same thing.

A final finding from the NCS-R study was the widespread occurrence of **comorbidity** among diagnosed disorders (Kessler, Chiu, et al., 2005). *Comorbidity* is the term used to describe the presence of two or more disorders in the same person. Comorbidity seems to be especially high in people who have severe forms of mental disorders. In the NCS-R study, half of the people with a disorder that was rated as serious on a scale of severity (mild, moderate, serious) also had two or more additional disorders (for example, a person who drinks excessively may also be depressed and have an anxiety disorder). In contrast, only 7 percent of the people who had a mild form of a disorder also had two or more other diagnosable conditions. What this tells us is that comorbidity is much more likely to occur in people who have the most serious forms of mental disorders. When the condition is mild, comorbidity is the exception and not the rule.

Treatment

Not all people with psychological disorders receive treatment. In some cases, people deny or minimize their problems. Others try to cope on their own with their problems and may manage to recover without ever seeing a mental health professional. Even when they recognize that they have a problem, it is typical for people to wait a long time before they decide to seek help. Half of the people who suffer from depression delay seeking treatment for more than 6–8 years. For anxiety disorders, the delay ranges from 9 to 23 years (Wang, Berglund, et al., 2005)!

When people with mental disorders do seek help, they are often treated by their family physician rather than a mental health specialist (Wang, Lane, et al., 2005). It is also the case that the vast majority of mental health treatment is now done on an outpatient (as opposed to an inpatient) basis (Narrow et al., 1993; O'Donnell et al., 2000). Outpatient treatment requires that patients visit a mental health facility or mental health practitioner, but the patient does not have to be admitted to the hospital or stay there overnight. Patients may attend a community mental health center, see a private therapist, or receive treatment through the outpatient department of a hospital.

Hospitalization and inpatient care are the preferred options for people who need more intensive treatment than can be provided on an outpatient basis. Various surveys indicate that admission to mental hospitals has decreased substantially over the past 45 years. The development of medications that control the symptoms of the most severe disorders is one reason for this change. Budget cuts have also forced many large state or county facilities to close. Patients who need inpatient care are now typically admitted to the psychiatric units of general hospitals (Narrow et al., 1993) or to private psychiatric hospitals that specialize in mental disorders (Kiesler & Simpkins, 1993). Because of their high cost, stays in private inpatient facilities now tend to be much shorter than they were in the past, with patients receiving additional treatment on an outpatient basis. This trend away from the use of traditional hospitalization, a trend often referred to as "deinstitutionalization," will be discussed more extensively in Chapters 2 and 18.

The Mental Health "Team"

In many clinical settings, diagnosis and assessment may involve a number of participants who play differing roles in the process and who gather data germane to a comprehensive evaluation of the patient's (or client's) situation. These professionals gather information from several perspectives and sources. The latter may include family members, friends, school officials (if the client is a child or adolescent), and any mental health professionals and social agencies with which the patient may have had contact. All these contributors then meet to process and integrate all the available information, arrive at a consensus diagnosis, and plan the initial phase of treatment. The World Around Us 1.4 briefly summarizes the training and professional identities of the mental health personnel likely to be found on such treatment teams.

In Review

- What is epidemiology?
- What is the difference between prevalence and incidence?
- What are the most common mental disorders?
- How is illness severity associated with comorbidity?

1.4 The World Around Us — Personnel in Mental Health

Professional

CLINICAL PSYCHOLOGIST Ph.D. in psychology, with both research and clinical skill specialization. One-year internship in a psychiatric hospital or mental health center. Or, Psy.D. in psychology (a professional degree with more clinical than research specialization) plus 1-year internship in a psychiatric hospital or mental health center. In some states, clinical psychologists with additional training are permitted, like psychiatrists, to prescribe medications to patients.

COUNSELING PSYCHOLOGIST Ph.D. in psychology plus internship in a marital- or student-counseling setting; normally, a counseling psychologist deals with adjustment problems not involving severe mental disorder.

SCHOOL PSYCHOLOGIST Ideally, a person having doctoral training in child-clinical psychology, with additional training and experience in academic and learning problems. At present, many school systems lack the resources to maintain an adequate school psychology program.

PSYCHIATRIST M.D. with residency training (usually 3 years) in a psychiatric hospital or mental health facility.

PSYCHOANALYST M.D. or Ph.D. plus intensive training in the theory and practice of psychoanalysis.

CLINICAL SOCIAL WORKER M.S.W. or Ph.D. with specialized clinical training in mental health settings.

PSYCHIATRIC NURSE R.N. certification plus specialized training in the care and treatment of psychiatric clients. Nurses can attain M.A. and Ph.D. in psychiatric nursing.

OCCUPATIONAL THERAPIST B.S. in occupational therapy plus internship training with physically or psychologically handicapped individuals, helping them make the most of their resources.

PASTORAL COUNSELOR Ministerial background plus training in psychology. Internship in mental health facility as a chaplain.

Paraprofessional

COMMUNITY MENTAL HEALTH WORKER Person with limited professional training who works under professional direction; usually involved in crisis intervention.

ALCOHOL- OR DRUG-ABUSE COUNSELOR Limited professional training but trained in the evaluation and management of alcohol- and drug-abuse problems.

In both mental health clinics and hospitals, personnel from several fields may function as an interdisciplinary team—for example, a psychiatrist, a clinical psychologist, a psychiatric social worker, a psychiatric nurse, and an occupational therapist may work together.

Research Approaches in Abnormal Psychology

As is apparent from the NCS-R study, the lives of large numbers of people are affected by mental disorders. To learn all that we can about these conditions, we need research. Through research we can study the nature of disorders—what their symptoms are, how **acute** (short in duration) or **chronic** (more long-lasting) they are, what kinds of deficits they are associated with, and so forth. Research also helps us understand the etiology (or causes) of disorders. Finally, we need research so that we can provide the best care for the patients who come to us for help. All of the authors of this book are practicing clinicians. As such, we turn to the research literature to help us provide the most effective and up-to-date care for the patients we see.

Students new to the field of abnormal psychology often assume that all the answers we need can come solely from studying individual cases. But when we study individual cases and make inferences from them, we are likely to have errors in our thinking. One such error is that we often attend only to data that confirm our view of how things are. For example, Dr. Smart might believe that drinking milk causes schizophrenia. When we ask Dr. Smart why he holds this view, he might say it is because every patient he has ever treated who has schizophrenia has drunk milk at some time in his or her life. Given that Dr. Smart has treated a lot of patients with schizophrenia and clearly has a great deal of experience with the disorder, we might be persuaded that he is right. Then along comes Dr. Notsofast. Dr. Notsofast decides to conduct a research study. He studies two groups of people. One group has schizophrenia. The other group does not have schizophrenia. Dr. Notsofast asks all of them about their milk-drinking habits. He finds that everyone has drunk milk at some point in his or her life and that there are no differences between the two groups. As this simple example illustrates, research prevents us from being misled by natural errors in thinking. In short, research protects investigators from their own biases in perception and inference (Raulin & Lilienfeld, 1999).

Not all research is done in a laboratory. Abnormal psychology research can be conducted in clinics, hospitals, schools, prisons, and even highly unstructured situations such as with the homeless on the streets. It is not the setting that determines whether research can be done. As Kazdin aptly points out (1998c, p. x), "methodology is not merely a compilation of practices and procedures. Rather it is an approach toward problem solving, thinking, and acquiring knowledge." As such, research methodology is constantly evolving. As new techniques become available (for example, brain-imaging techniques and new statistical procedures), methodology evolves. In the sections that follow, we introduce some fundamental research concepts so that you can start to think like a clinical scientist. To further help you, we sometimes use a Research Close-Up highlight to draw your attention to some key terms that are important to know and understand.

Sources of Information

As humans, we typically pay a lot of attention to the people around us. If you were asked to describe your best friend, your father, or even the professor teaching your abnormal psychology class, you would undoubtedly have plenty to say. As in virtually all other sciences, the foundation of psychological knowledge comes from observation. Indeed, much early knowledge about a wide range of psychopathological disorders came from case studies in which specific individuals were described in great detail. Astute clinicians such as the German psychiatrist Emil Kraepelin (1856–1926) and the Swiss psychiatrist Eugen Bleuler (1857–1939) provided us with detailed accounts of patients whom a modern-day reader would easily recognize as suffering from disorders such as schizophrenia and manic depression. Alois Alzheimer (1864–1915) described a patient with an unusual clinical picture that subsequently became known as Alzheimer's disease (see Chapter 15). Sigmund Freud (1856–1939), the founder of psychoanalysis, published many interesting clinical cases describing what we now recognize as phobia (the case of "Little Hans") and obsessive-compulsive disorder ("the Rat Man"). Such cases make for interesting reading, even today.

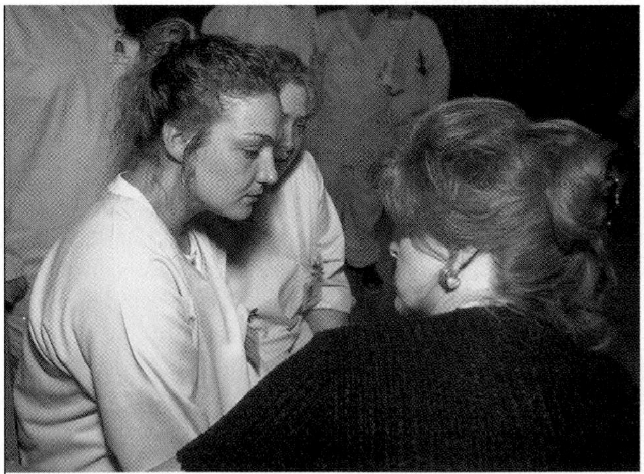

Abnormal psychology research can be conducted in a variety of settings outside the research laboratory, including clinics, hospitals, schools, or, as shown in this photo, prisons.

Much can be learned when skilled clinicians use the **case study** method, and case studies are a wonderful source of research ideas. But the information acquired is often relevant only to the individual being described and may be flawed, especially if we seek to apply it to other cases involving an apparently similar abnormality. When there is only one observer and one subject, and when the observations are made in a relatively uncontrolled context and are anecdotal and impressionistic in nature, the conclusions we can draw are very narrow and may be mistaken.

If we wish to study behavior in a more rigorous manner, how do we go about doing it? Much depends on what we want to know. For example, if we are studying aggressive children, we might wish to have trained observers count how many times children who are classified as being aggressive hit, bite, push, punch, or kick other children they play with. This would involve **direct observation** of the children's behavior. But there are also other behaviors we can study. For example, we might collect information about biological variables (such as heart rate) in our sample of aggressive children. Alternatively, we could collect information about stress hormones, such as cortisol, by asking them to spit into a plastic container (saliva contains cortisol) and then sending the saliva sample to the lab for analysis. This too is a form of observational data; it tells us something that we want to know using a variable that is relevant to our interests.

In addition to observing people's behavior directly, researchers can also collect **self-report data** from the research participants themselves. We could, for example, collect information from the children by asking them to fill out age-appropriate questionnaires. Or we could interview them and ask them how many friends they have. In other words, we can ask our research participants to report on their subjective experiences. Although this might seem like a good way to get information, it is not without its limitations. Self-report data can sometimes be misleading. One child might say that he has 20 "best friends" and yet, when we observe him, he may always be playing alone. Another child might say she has only one best friend and yet is always surrounded by peers who are soliciting her attention. Because people sometimes deliberately lie, misinterpret the question, or want to present themselves in a particularly favorable (or unfavorable) light, self-report data, although valuable and widely used in abnormal psychology research, cannot always be

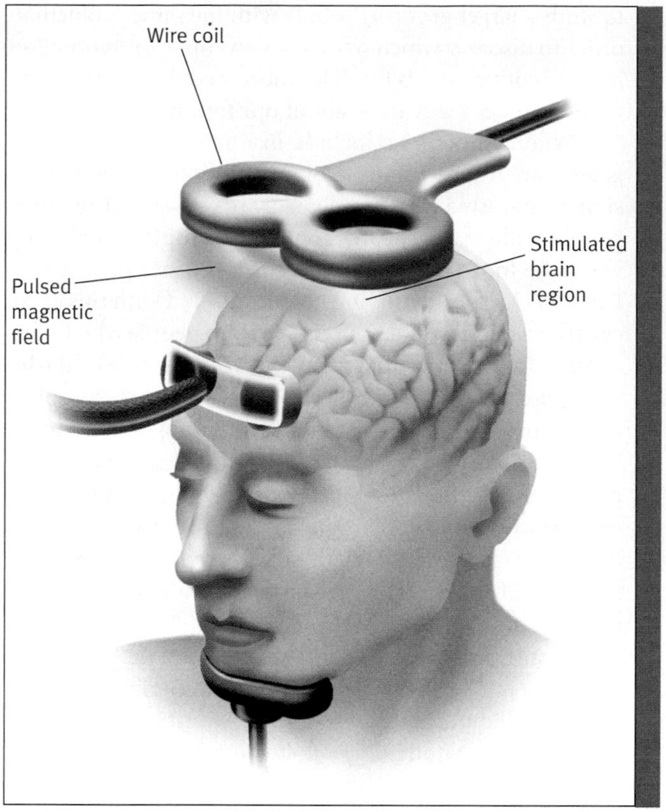

FIGURE 1.1

Researchers use technology, such as transcranial magnetic stimulation (TMS), to study how the brain works. This TMS technique generates a magnetic field on the surface of the head, through which underlying brain tissue is stimulated. Researchers can evaluate and measure behavioral consequences of this non-invasive and painless brain stimulation.

regarded as highly accurate and truthful. This is something that anyone who has ever answered a personal ad knows only too well!

Technology has advanced, and we are now developing ways to study behaviors, moods, and cognitions that have long been considered inaccessible. For example, as illustrated in Figure 1.1, we can now use brain-imaging techniques to study people's brains at work. We can study blood flow to various parts of the brain during memory tasks. We can look at which brain areas influence imagination. With techniques such as transcranial magnetic stimulation (TMS), which generates a magnetic field on the surface of the head, we can stimulate underlying brain tissue (for an overview, see Fitzgerald et al., 2002). This can be done painlessly and noninvasively while the person receiving the TMS sits in an armchair. Using TMS, we can even take a particular area of the brain "off-line" for a few seconds and measure the behavioral consequences. In short, we can collect behavioral data that would have been impossible to obtain even a few years ago.

Essentially, when we talk about observing behavior, we mean much more than simply watching people. Observing behavior really means studying what people (e.g., healthy people, depressed people, anxious people, people with schizophrenia) do and what they do not do. We may study social behavior in a sample of depressed patients by getting trained observers to rate how often they smile or make eye contact, or we may ask the patients themselves to fill out self-report questionnaires that assess social skills. If we think that sociability in depressed patients might be related to (or correlated with) how depressed they are, we might also ask patients to complete self-report measures designed to assess the severity of depression, and we might even measure levels of certain substances in patients' blood, urine, or cerebrospinal fluid (the clear fluid that bathes the brain and that can be obtained by performing a lumbar puncture; see Chapter 14). We could possibly even study our depressed patients' brains directly via brain-imaging approaches. All of these sources of information provide us with potentially valuable data that are the basis of scientific inquiry.

Forming Hypotheses about Behavior

To make sense of behavior, researchers generate hypotheses. Hypotheses are efforts to explain, predict, or explore something—in this case, behavior. What distinguishes scientific hypotheses from the speculation we all experience in response to the question "Why?"? The difference is that scientists attempt to test their hypotheses. In other words, they try to design research studies that will help them get closer to a full understanding of how and why things happen.

Anecdotal accounts such as case studies can be very valuable in helping us develop hypotheses, although case studies are not well suited for testing them. Other sources of hypotheses are unusual or unexpected research findings. For example, earlier you learned that although men generally have lower rates of depression than women, this is not the case for Jewish men. This is clearly an observation in search of an explanation. Why should Jewish men be more at risk for depression than non-Jewish men? One hypothesis is that there may be an interesting (and inverse) relationship between depression and alcohol use (Levav et al., 1997). Jewish men have lower rates of alcohol abuse and alcohol dependence than do non-Jewish men. Consistent with this idea, a study of members of Orthodox synagogues in London found no alcoholism and similar rates of depression in females and males (i.e., a 1:1 gender ratio instead of the typical 2:1 ratio; Loewenthal et al., 1995). Although much more remains to be learned, the hypothesis that the higher rates of depression in Jewish men may have something to do with their lower rates of alcohol abuse appears to have some value for further study (see Loewenthal et al., 2003).

Hypotheses are also important because they frequently determine the therapeutic approaches used to treat a particular clinical problem. For example, suppose we are confronted with someone who washes his or her hands 60 to 100 times a day, causing serious injury to the

Although men generally have lower rates of depression than women, the rate of depression for Jewish men and women is equal. Why would this be so? A correlation between higher rates of depression and lower rates of alcohol abuse in Jewish men provides interesting ground for further study.

skin and underlying tissues (this is an example of obsessive-compulsive disorder). If we believe that this behavior is a result of subtle problems in certain neural circuits, we might try to identify which circuits are dysfunctional in the hope of eventually finding a way to correct them (probably by medication). On the other hand, if we view the excessive hand washing as reflecting a symbolic cleansing of sinful and unacceptable thoughts, we might try to unearth and address the sources of the person's excessive concern with morals and scruples. Finally, if we regard the hand washing as merely the product of unfortunate conditioning or learning, we might devise a means to extinguish the problematic behavior. In other words, our working hypotheses about the causes of different disorders very much shape what kinds of approaches we adopt both when we study disorders and when we try to treat them.

Sampling and Generalization

As we have already noted, single-case studies can be very valuable because they help us to generate ideas and working hypotheses. But although we can occasionally get important leads from the intensive observation of a single case, such a strategy rarely yields enough information to allow us to reach firm conclusions. Research in abnormal psychology is concerned with gaining enhanced understanding and, where possible, control of abnormal behavior (that is, the ability to alter it in predictable ways). Ed may accost women in supermarkets and try to lick their feet because his mother always gave him attention when, as a child, he tried on her shoes. But George may engage in the same behavior for an entirely different reason. We need to study a larger group of people with the same problem in order to discover which of our observations or hypotheses have scientific credibility. The more people we study, the more confident we can be about our findings.

Whom should we include in our research study? In general we want to study groups of individuals who have similar abnormalities of behavior. If we wanted to study people with major depression, for example, a first step would be to determine criteria such as those provided in DSM-IV-TR for identifying people affected with this clinical disorder. We would then need to find people who fit our criteria. Ideally, we would study everyone in the world who met our criteria, because these people constitute our population of interest. This, of course, is impossible to do, so instead we would try to get a representative sample of people who are drawn from this underlying population. To do this, we would use a technique called **sampling.** What this means is that we would try to select people who are representative of the much larger group of individuals having major depressive disorders.

Ideally, we would like our smaller sample (our study group) to mirror the larger group (the underlying population) in all important ways (e.g., in severity and duration of disorder and in demographics such as age, gender, and marital status). If we could do everything perfectly, our research sample would be randomly selected from the larger population of people with depression, which is tantamount to ensuring that every person in that population would have an equal chance of being included in our study. Such a procedure would automatically adjust for potential biases in sample selection. In practice, however, this does not happen, and researchers must simply do the best they can given real-world constraints (which include the fact that some people just don't want to be in a research study!).

From a research perspective, the more representative our sample is, the better able we are to generalize, to the larger group, the findings derived from our work with the sample. A sample that involves depressed men and women of all ages, income groups, and education levels is more representative of the underlying population of depressed people than is a sample of depressed kindergarten teachers who are all female, unmarried, and aged 23–25. In addition, when we study a group of people who have something important in common (e.g., depression), we can then infer that anything else they turn out to have in common, such as a family history of depression or low levels of certain neurotransmitters, may be related to the behavioral disorder itself. Of course, this assumes that the characteristic in question is not widely shared by people who do not have the abnormality.

Criterion and Comparison Groups

To explain the idea of criterion and comparison groups let's go back to our example about schizophrenia and milk. Dr. Smart's hypothesis was that milk drinking causes schizophrenia. However, when a group of patients with schizophrenia (the criterion group, or group of interest) was compared with a group of patients who did not have schizophrenia (the comparison group), it was clear that there were no differences in milk drinking between the two groups.

To test their hypotheses, researchers use a **comparison group** (sometimes called a **control group**). This is a group of people who do not exhibit the disorder being studied but who are comparable in all other major respects to the **criterion group** (i.e., people with the disorder). By "comparable" we might mean that the two groups are similar in age, number of males and females in each group, education level, and similar demographic kinds of variables. Typically, the comparison group is psychologically healthy, or "normal," according to certain specified criteria. We can then compare the two groups on the variables we are interested in.

Using the controlled research approaches we have just described, researchers have discovered many things about large numbers of psychological disorders. We can also use extensions of this kind of approach not only to compare one group of patients with healthy controls, but also to compare groups of patients who have different disorders. For example, Cutting and Murphy (1990) studied how well (1) patients with schizophrenia, (2) patients with depression or mania, and (3) healthy controls did on a test of social knowledge. This involved a series of multiple-choice questions that presented a social problem (e.g., "How would you tell a friend politely that he had stayed too long?"). Answer choices included responses such as, "There's no more coffee left" and "You'd better go. I'm fed up with you staying too long." (In case you are wondering, both of these are incorrect choices; the preferred answer for this example was, "Excuse me. I've got an appointment with a friend.") Consistent with the literature showing social deficits associated with schizophrenia, the patients with schizophrenia did worse on this test than the healthy controls and the depressed/manic patients. The finding that the patients with schizophrenia did worse than the depressed/manic patients also allowed the researchers to rule out the possibility that simply being a psychiatric patient is linked to poor social knowledge.

Studying the World as It Is: Observational Research Designs

A major goal of researchers in abnormal psychology is to learn about the causes of different disorders. But for obvious ethical and practical reasons, we often cannot do this directly. Perhaps we want to know what causes depression. We may hypothesize that factors such as stress or losing a parent early in life might contribute to the development of depression. Most certainly, however, we cannot create such situations and then see what happens! Instead, the researcher uses what is known as an observational or correlational research design. Unlike a true experimental design (described below), **observational research** does not involve any manipulation of variables. Instead, the researcher selects groups of interest (people who have recently been exposed to a great deal of stress or people who lost a parent when they were growing up) and then compares the groups on a variety of different characteristics (including, in this example, measures of depression). Any time we study differences between people who have a particular disorder and people who do not (i.e., whenever we have a comparison group of some kind), we are using this kind of observational or correlational research design. Essentially, we are capitalizing on the fact that the world works in ways to create natural groupings of people (people with specific disorders, people who have had traumatic experiences, people who win lotteries, etc.) whom we can then study. Using these kinds of research designs, we can then identify factors that seem to go along with being depressed, having alcohol problems, binge eating, and the like (for a more comprehensive description of this kind of research approach, see Kazdin, 1998c).

But mere correlation, or association, between two or more variables can never by itself be taken as evidence of causation—that is, a relationship in which one of the associated variables (e.g., stress) causes the other (e.g., depression). This is an important caveat to bear in mind. Many studies in abnormal psychology show that two (or more) things regularly occur together, such as poverty and retarded intellectual development, or depression and reported prior stressors. For example, even as late as the 1940s, it was thought that masturbation caused insanity. As we discuss in Chapter 13, this hypothesis no doubt arose from the fact that historically, patients in mental asylums could often be seen masturbating in full view of others. Of course, we now know that masturbation and insanity were correlated not because masturbation caused insanity but because sane people are much more likely to masturbate in private than in public. In other words, the key factor was one of social awareness.

Even though correlational studies may not be able to pin down causal relationships, they can be a powerful and rich source of inference. They often suggest causal hypotheses and occasionally provide crucial data that confirm or refute these hypotheses. Much of what we know about mental disorders comes from correlational studies. The fact that we cannot manipulate many of the variables we study does not mean that we cannot find out a great deal.

Retrospective versus Prospective Strategies

Observational research designs can be used to study different groups of patients as they are now (that is, concurrently). For example, if we used brain imaging to look at the size of certain brain structures in patients with schizophrenia and in healthy controls, we would be using this type of approach. But if we wanted to try to learn what our patients were like before they developed a specific mental disorder like schizophrenia, we might adopt a retrospective research approach. In other words, we would try to collect information about how the patients behaved early in their lives in the hope of identifying factors that might have been associated with what went wrong later. In some cases, our source material might be limited to patients' recollections or the recollections of family members, or material from diaries or other records. A challenge with this kind of research design is that memories can be both faulty and selective. There are certain difficulties in attempting to reconstruct the pasts of people already experiencing a disorder. Apart from the fact that a person who is currently suffering from a mental disorder may not be the most accurate or objective source of information, such a strategy invites investigators to discover what they already expect to discover about the background factors theoretically linked to a disorder.

For example, reports of a link between early sexual abuse and various forms of psychopathology (e.g., see Chapters 8 and 11) started to emerge in the 1980s. After this, many therapists began to suggest to their patients who had these conditions that perhaps they too had been abused. For some overzealous therapists, the fact that many patients had no memories of any abuse was taken as evidence that the painful memories had simply been "repressed." In other cases, simply having such common problems as difficulty sleeping or being easily startled was taken as evidence of past abuse. Over time, many patients became as convinced as their therapists that they must have been abused and that this accounted for all their current difficulties and problems. But for many patients, it simply wasn't true that they had been abused. There are pitfalls in trying to reinterpret a person's past (or past behavior) in light of his or her present problems. Adherence to good scientific principles is as important in the clinical domain as it is in the research laboratory.

Another approach is to use **prospective** (as opposed to **retrospective**) **strategies.** Here the idea is to identify individuals who have a higher-than-average likelihood of becoming psychologically disordered and to focus on them before the disorder develops. We can have much more confidence in our hypotheses about the causes of a disorder if we have been tracking various influences and measuring them ahead of time. When our hypotheses correctly predict the behavior that a group of individuals will develop, we are much closer to establishing a causal relationship. In a typical instance, children who share a risk factor known to be associated with relatively high rates of subsequent breakdown (such as having been born to a mother with schizophrenia) are studied over the course of many years. Those who do break down are compared with those who do not in the hope that important differentiating factors will be discovered.

Manipulating Variables: The Experimental Method in Abnormal Psychology

Correlational research takes things as they are and determines covariations among observed phenomena. Do things vary together in a direct, corresponding manner (known as a **positive correlation**—see Figure 1.2) such as in the case of female gender and increased risk of depression? Or is there an inverse correlation, or **negative correlation,** between our variables of interest (such as high socioeconomic status and generally less risk of mental disorder)? Or are the variables in question entirely independent of one another, or *uncorrelated,* such that a given state or level of one variable fails to predict reliably anything about that of another, as in our earlier example of milk and schizophrenia?

Even when we find strong positive or negative associations between variables, however, correlational research does not allow us to conclude anything about directionality (i.e., does variable A cause B, or does B cause A?). However, correlational studies often provide crucial information that cannot be obtained in any other way and that might suggest certain causal influences.

Scientific research is most rigorous, however, and its findings most compelling and reliable, when it employs the full power of the experimental method. In such cases, scientists control all factors except one—one that could have an effect on a variable or outcome of interest; then they actively manipulate that one factor. This factor is referred to as the **independent variable.** If the outcome of interest, called the **dependent variable,** is observed to change as the manipulated factor is changed, that variable can be regarded as a cause of the outcome (see Figure 1.3 on p. 22). For example, if a proposed treatment is provided to a given group of patients but withheld from an otherwise completely comparable one (giving or not giving the treatment is the experimental manipulation), and if the former group experiences positive changes significantly in excess of those experienced by the latter group, then a causal inference can be made regarding the treatment's efficacy.

Studying the Efficacy of Therapy

Used in the context of treatment research, the experimental method has proved indispensable. It is a relatively simple and straightforward matter to set up a study in which a proposed treatment is given to a designated group of patients and withheld from a similar group of patients. Should the treated group show significantly more improvement than the untreated group, we can have confidence in the treatment's efficacy. We may not, however, know why the treatment works, although investigators are becoming increasingly sophisticated in fine-tuning their experiments to tease out the mechanisms through which

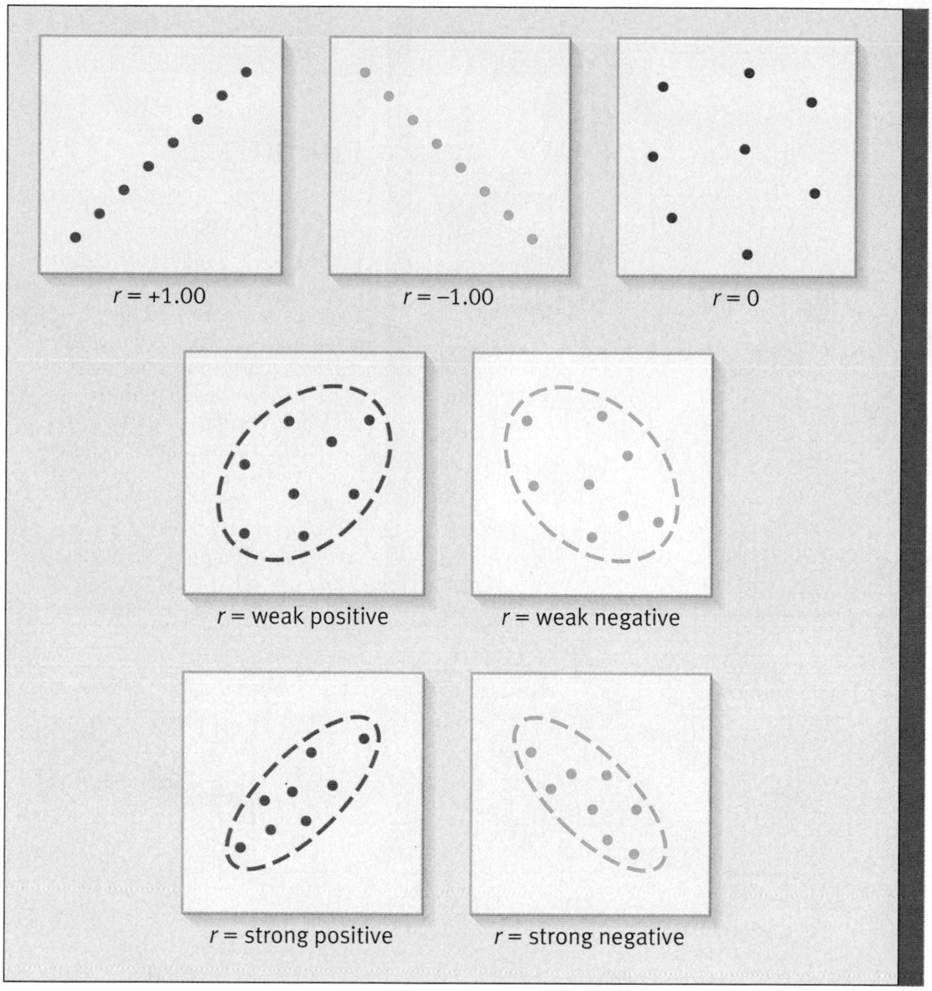

FIGURE 1.2

Scatterplots of data illustrating positive, negative, and no correlation between variables.

therapeutic change is induced (e.g., Jacobson et al., 1996; Hollon, DeRubeis, & Evans, 1987; Kazdin & Nock, 2003).

In treatment research it is important that the two groups (treated and untreated) be as comparable as possible except for the presence or absence of the proposed active treatment. To facilitate this, patients are typically randomly assigned to the treatment condition or the no-treatment condition. Once a treatment has been established as effective, it can then be provided for members of the original control (untreated) group, leading to improved functioning for everyone.

Sometimes, however, this "waiting list" control group strategy is deemed inadvisable for ethical or other reasons. For example, withholding a treatment that has already been established as beneficial just to evaluate some new type of treatment may deprive control subjects of valuable clinical help for longer than would be considered ethical. For this reason, there need to be stringent safeguards regarding the potential costs versus benefits of conducting the particular research project. In some cases, an alternative research design may be called for, in which two (or more) treatments are compared in different equivalent groups. This type of study is called a standard treatment comparison study. Typically, the efficacy of the treatment that is used as the control condition has already been established, so patients who are assigned to this condition are not disadvantaged. The issue then is whether patients who get the new treatment do even better than those getting the control (established) treatment. Such comparative-outcome research has much to recommend it and is being increasingly employed (Barlow & Kazdin, 1998; Kendall et al., 2004).

Single-Case Experimental Designs

Does **experimental research** always involve testing hypotheses by manipulating variables across groups? The simple answer is no. We have already noted the importance of case studies as a source of ideas and hypotheses. In addition, case studies can be used to develop and test therapy techniques within a scientific framework. Such approaches are called **single-case research designs** (Hayes, 1998; Kazdin, 1998b, 1998c). A central feature of these designs is that the same subject is

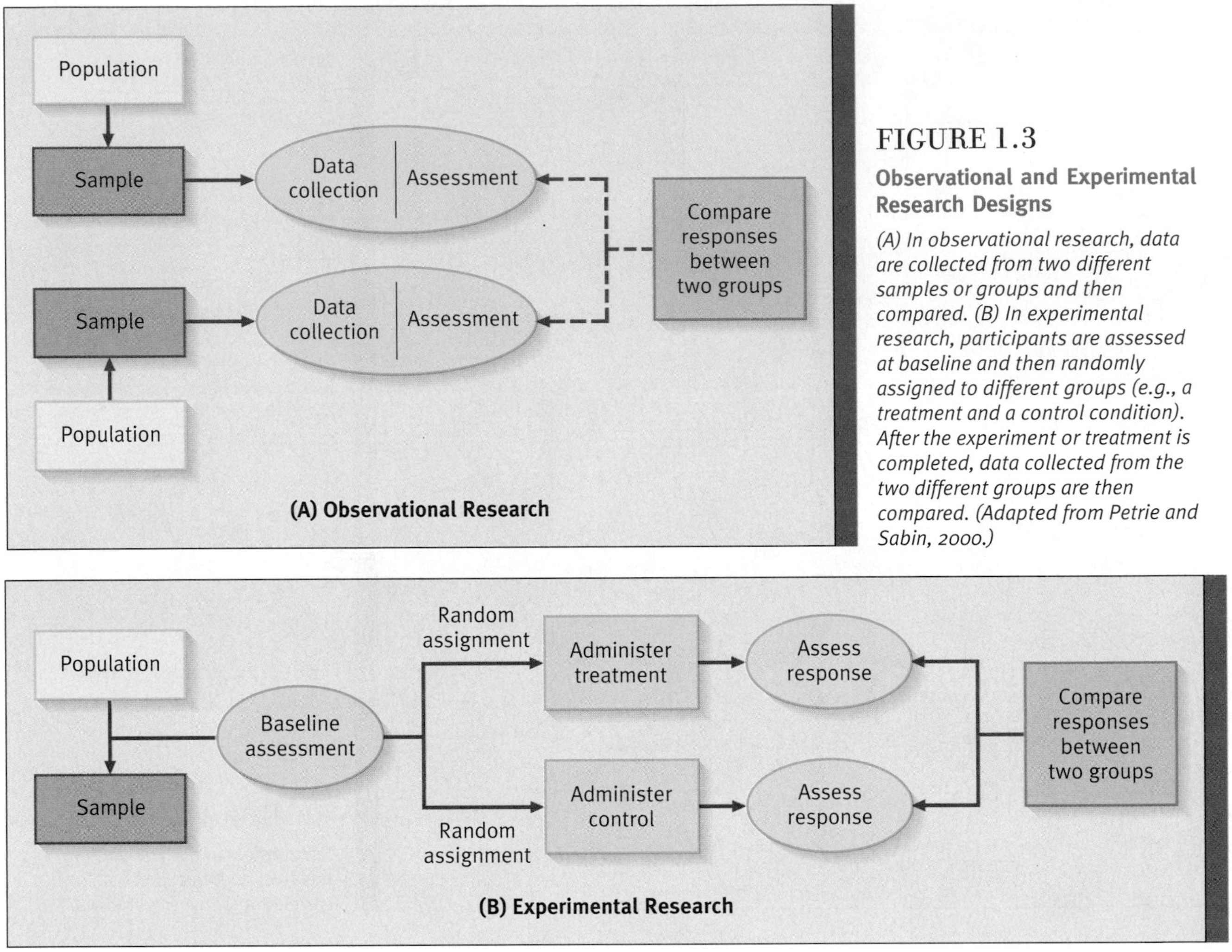

FIGURE 1.3

Observational and Experimental Research Designs

(A) In observational research, data are collected from two different samples or groups and then compared. (B) In experimental research, participants are assessed at baseline and then randomly assigned to different groups (e.g., a treatment and a control condition). After the experiment or treatment is completed, data collected from the two different groups are then compared. (Adapted from Petrie and Sabin, 2000.)

studied over time. Behavior or performance at one point in time can then be compared to behavior or performance at a later time, after a specific intervention or treatment has been introduced.

One of the most basic experimental designs in single-case research is called the **ABAB design.** The different letters refer to different phases of the intervention. The first A phase serves as a baseline condition. Here we simply collect data on or from the subject. Then, in the first B phase, we introduce our treatment. Perhaps the subject's behavior changes in some way. But even if there is a change, we are not justified in concluding that it was the introduction of our treatment that caused the change in the subject's behavior. Something else could have happened that coincided with our introducing the treatment, so any association between the treatment and the behavior change might be spurious. The way we can establish whether it really was what we did in the first B phase that was important is to withdraw the treatment and see what happens. This is the reasoning behind the second A phase (i.e., at the ABA point). Then, to demonstrate that we can again get the behavior to change back to how it was in the first B phase, we reintroduce our treatment and observe what happens. To illustrate this, let's consider the case of Kris (see Rapp et al., 2000).

case STUDY Kris

Kris was a 19-year-old female who was severely retarded. Since the age of 3 she had pulled her hair out. This disorder is called trichotillomania (pronounced tricko-tillomania). Kris's hair pulling was so severe that she had a bald area on her scalp that was about 2.5 in. in diameter.

The researchers used an ABAB experimental design (see Figure 1.4) to test a treatment for reducing Kris's hair pulling. In each phase, they used a video camera to observe Kris while she was alone in her room watching TV. During the baseline phase (phase A), observers mea-

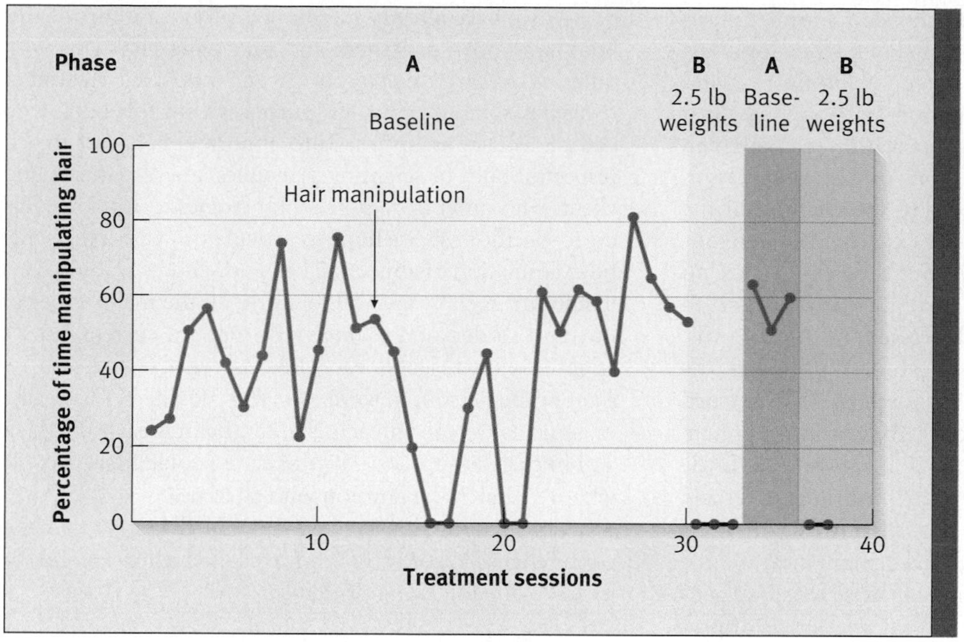

FIGURE 1.4

An ABAB Experimental Design: Kris's Treatment

In the A phase baseline data are collected. In the B phase a treatment is introduced. This treatment is then withdrawn (second A phase) and then reinstated (second B phase). In this example, hair manipulation declines with use of wrist weights, goes back to pretreatment (baseline) levels when they are withdrawn, and declines again when they are reintroduced.

(Data adapted from Rapp et al., 2000.)

sured the percentage of time that Kris either touched or manipulated her hair (42.5 percent of the time) and how much hair pulling she did (7.6 percent of the time). In the treatment phase (B), a 2.5-lb weight was put around Kris's wrist when she settled down to watch TV. When she was wearing the wrist weight, Kris's hair manipulation and hair pulling went down to zero. This, of course, suggested that Kris's behavior had changed because she was wearing a weight on her wrist. To verify this, the wrist weight was withdrawn in the second A phase (i.e., ABA). Kris immediately started to touch and manipulate her hair again (55.9 percent). She also showed an increase in hair pulling (4 percent of the time). When the wrist weight was reintroduced in the second B phase (ABAB), Kris's hair manipulation and hair pulling once again decreased, at least for a while. Although additional treatments were necessary (see Rapp et al., 2000), Kris's hair pulling was eventually totally eliminated. Most important for our purposes, the ABAB design allowed the researchers to explore systematically the treatment approaches that might be beneficial for patients with trichotillomania, using experimental techniques and methods.

Animal Research

Yet another way in which we can use the experimental method is to conduct research with animals. Although ethical considerations are still important in animal research, we can perform studies using animal subjects (e.g., giving them experimental drugs, implanting electrodes to record brain activity, etc.) that it would not be possible to do with humans. Of course, one major assumption is that the findings from animal studies will apply (that is, can be generalized) to humans. Experiments of this kind are generally known as **analogue studies** (in which we study not the real thing but some approximation to it). Analogue studies can also involve humans (for example, when we try to study depression by studying normal individuals whom we have made mildly and transiently sad using one technique or another).

One current model of depression, called "hopelessness depression" (see Chapter 7), has its roots in some early research that was done with animals (Seligman, 1975). Laboratory experiments with dogs had demonstrated that,

Animal research allows behavioral scientists to manipulate and study behavior under controlled conditions that would not be possible to replicate using humans as subjects. However, results of this research may not hold up when extended to humans outside the laboratory in a "real-world" setting.

when subjected to repeated experiences of painful, unpredictable, and inescapable electric shock, the dogs lost their ability to learn a simple escape response to avoid further shock in a different situation later on. They just sat and endured the pain. This observation led Seligman and his colleagues to argue that human depression (which he believed was analogous to the reaction of the helpless dogs) is a reaction to the experience of uncontrollable stressful events where one's behavior has no effect on one's environment, leading him or her to become helpless, passive, and depressed. In other words, the findings from these animal studies provided the impetus for what first became known as "the learned helplessness theory of depression" (Abramson, Seligman, & Teasdale, 1978; Seligman, 1975) and is now called "the hopelessness theory of depression" (Abramson et al., 1989). These theories of depression are not without their own problems, but it is important to remain aware of the broader issue: Although problems can arise when we generalize too readily from animal to human models of psychopathology, the learned helplessness analogy has generated much research and has helped us refine and develop our ideas about depression.

In Review

- How is experimental research different from observational (correlational) research?
- Explain what an ABAB design is. Why are such designs helpful to clinicians and researchers?
- If two variables are correlated, does this mean that one variable causes the other? If so, why? If not, why not?

The Focus of This Book

To provide consistency, when we discuss disorders we will try to focus on three significant aspects: (1) the clinical picture, in which we will describe what is going on with the disorder; (2) the possible causal factors; and (3) treatments. In each case, we will examine the evidence for biological, psychosocial (i.e., psychological and interpersonal), and sociocultural (the broader social environment of culture and subculture) influences. In short, we will strive to give you a sophisticated appreciation of the total context in which abnormalities of behavior occur.

As we have already mentioned, all the authors of this book are both researchers and practicing clinicians with differing research backgrounds and preferred treatment strategies. One of our main purposes with this book is to educate you in an approach to abnormal behavior that is respectful both of scientific principles and of patients and clients who suffer from psychopathological conditions. At a more specific level, we hope to provide you with a thoughtful examination of abnormal behavior and its place in contemporary society. We will focus on all the major types of mental disorders and acquaint you with the current state of scientific knowledge for each. Because we wish never to lose sight of the person, however, we also provide as much case material as we can in each chapter. Behind each disorder, and in each scientific study, there are people first—people who have much in common with all of us.

Throughout this text we assume that a sound and comprehensive study of abnormal behavior should be based on the following principles:

1. A SCIENTIFIC APPROACH TO ABNORMAL BEHAVIOR. Any comprehensive view of human behavior must draw on concepts and research findings from a variety of scientific fields. Of particular relevance are genetics, neuroanatomy, neurochemistry, sociology, anthropology, and, of course, psychology. Because we believe an understanding of the scientific approach to acquiring knowledge in abnormal psychology rests on an understanding of research principles, we hope this book will help you develop your ability to think like a research scientist. It is our belief that the benefits of acquiring such skills will persist long after your course in abnormal psychology has ended and will make it possible for you to understand and have a sophisticated appreciation of the research the field generates in the future.

2. OPENNESS TO NEW IDEAS. Science is progressive and cumulative. Knowledge builds upon knowledge. But science is also creative. And as scientists, we owe it to ourselves and to the field to be willing to consider new ideas—even if they contradict our favorite theories. This does not mean that we should ever blindly accept something just because it is different and new. But we believe that if something that is different and new is supported by credible scientific data, all of us should be willing to consider developing a fresh perspective. Scientists who are closed-minded and dogmatic are not true scientists at all.

3. RESPECT FOR THE DIGNITY, INTEGRITY, AND GROWTH POTENTIAL OF ALL PERSONS. In attempting to provide a broad perspective on abnormal behavior, we will focus not only on how maladaptive patterns are perceived by clinical psychologists and other mental health personnel, but also on how such disorders are perceived by those experiencing them, as well as by their families and friends. Historically, many of the disorders described in this book were conceptualized in extremely pessimistic terms. This is not an attitude we share. As our understanding of abnormal psychology grows, we become better able to help patients previously considered to be hopeless cases. New developments will only provide us with more of what we need to help our patients. In short, we are optimistic about the current state of the field and about what the future holds.

In Review

- Why do we need a research-based approach in order to learn about psychopathology?

Unresolved Issues

Are We All Becoming Mentally Ill? The Expanding Horizons of Mental Disorder

Because the concept of mental disorder, as we have seen, lacks a truly objective means of settling on its limits, and because it is in the economic and other interests of mental health professionals to designate larger and larger segments of human behavior as within the purview of "mentally disordered," there is constant pressure to include in the DSM more and more kinds of socially undesirable behavior. For example, one proposal was to include "road rage" (anger at other drivers) as a newly discovered mental disorder in the DSM-IV (Sharkey, 1997). However, anger at other drivers is so common that almost all of us would be at risk of being diagnosed with this new disorder if it had been added to the DSM. There is considerable informal evidence that the steering committee responsible for the production of DSM-IV worked hard to fend off a large number of such frivolous proposals, and in fact they largely succeeded in avoiding additional diagnoses beyond those that appeared in the previous edition (DSM-III-R) by adopting stringent criteria for inclusion. Nevertheless, this promises to be an uphill battle. Mental health professionals, like the members of other professions, tend to view the world through a lens that enhances the importance of phenomena related to their own expertise. And, of course, inclusion of a disorder in the DSM is a prerequisite for health insurers' reimbursement of services rendered.

It is thus in the interests of the public at large to keep a wary eye on proposed expansions of the "mentally disordered" domain. It is conceivable that failure to do so might eventually lead to a situation where almost anything but the most bland, conformist, and conventional behavior could be declared a manifestation of mental disorder. By that point, the concept would have become so indiscriminate as to lose most of its scientifically productive meaning.

Summary

- Encountering instances of abnormal behavior is a common experience for all of us. This is not surprising, given the high prevalence of many forms of mental disorder.
- A precise definition of "abnormality" is still elusive. Elements that can be helpful in considering whether something is abnormal include suffering, maladaptiveness, deviancy, violations of society's standards, causing discomfort in others, irrationality, and unpredictability.
- Wakefield's notion of "harmful dysfunction" is a helpful step forward but still fails to provide a fully adequate definition of mental disorder. It is nonetheless a good working definition.
- Culture shapes the presentation of clinical disorders in some cases. There are also certain disorders that appear to be highly culture-specific.
- The DSM employs a category type of classification system similar to that used in medicine. Disorders are regarded as discrete clinical entities, though not all clinical disorders may be best considered in this way.
- Even though it is not without problems, the DSM provides us with working criteria that help clinicians and researchers to identify and study specific and important problems that affect people's lives. It is far from a "finished product." However, familiarity with the DSM is essential to serious study in the field.

- To avoid misconception and error, we must adopt a scientific approach to the study of abnormal behavior. This requires a focus on research and research methods, including an appreciation of the distinction between what is observable and what is hypothetical or inferred.
- To produce valid results, research must be done on people who are truly representative of the diagnostic groups to which they purportedly belong.
- Research in abnormal psychology may be observational or experimental. Observational research studies things as they are. Experimental research involves manipulating one variable (the independent variable) and seeing what effect this has on another variable (the dependent variable).
- Mere correlation between variables does not enable us to conclude that there is a causal relationship between them. Simply put, correlation does not equal causation.
- Although most experiments involve studies of groups, single-case experimental designs (e.g., ABAB designs) can also be used to make causal inferences in individual cases.
- Analogue studies (e.g., animal research) are studies that provide an approximation to the human disorders of interest. Although generalizability can be a problem, animal research in particular has been very informative.

Key Terms

ABAB design (P. 22)
abnormal behavior (P. 11)
acute (P. 15)
analogue studies (P. 23)
case study (P. 16)
chronic (P. 15)
comorbidity (P. 14)
comparison or control group (P. 19)
criterion group (P. 19)
dependent variable (P. 20)
direct observation (P. 16)
double-blind study (P. 4)
epidemiology (P. 12)
experimental research (P. 21)
family aggregation (P. 3)
incidence (P. 13)
independent variable (P. 20)
labeling (P. 8)
lifetime prevalence (P. 13)
negative correlation (P. 20)
nomenclature (P. 6)
observational research (P. 19)
1-year prevalence (P. 12)
placebo (P. 4)
point prevalence (P. 12)
positive correlation (P. 20)
prevalence (P. 12)
prospective strategy (P. 20)
retrospective strategy (P. 20)
sampling (P. 18)
self-report data (P. 16)
single-case research design (P. 21)
stereotyping (P. 8)
stigma (P. 8)
symptom (P. 9)
syndrome (P. 9)

CHAPTER

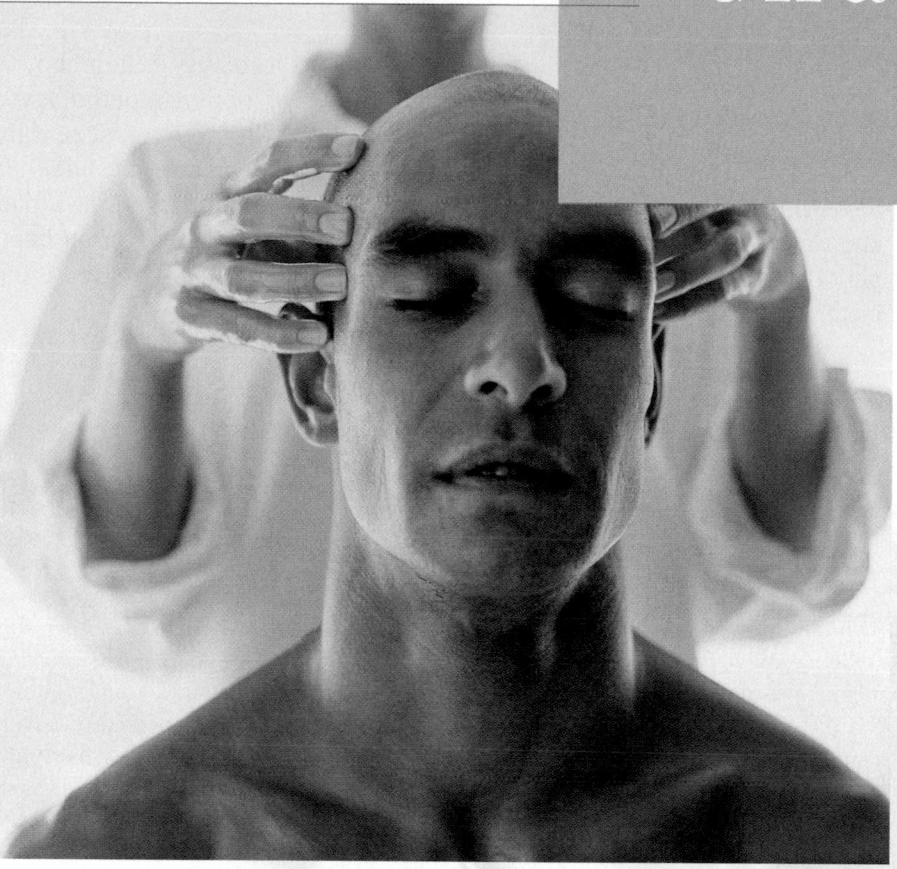

2

Historical and Contemporary Views of Abnormal Behavior

Our historical efforts to understand abnormal psychology include both humor and tragedy. In this chapter, we will highlight some views of psychopathology, and some of the treatments administered, from ancient times to the twenty-first century. In a broad sense, we will see a progression of beliefs from what we now consider superstition to those based on scientific awareness—from a focus on supernatural explanations to a knowledge of natural causes. The course of this evolution has often been marked by periods of advancement or unique individual contributions, followed by long years of inactivity or unproductive backward steps.

Historical Views of Abnormal Behavior

The earliest treatment of mental disorders was that practiced by Stone Age cave dwellers some half a million years ago. For certain forms of mental disorders (probably those in which the individual complained of severe headaches and developed convulsive attacks), the early shaman, or medicine man, treated the disorder by means of an operation now called "trephining." This operation was performed with crude stone instruments and consisted of chipping away one area of the skull in the form of a circle until the skull was cut through. This opening, called a "trephine," presumably permitted the evil spirit that was thought to be causing all the trouble to escape—and may incidentally have relieved a certain amount of pressure on the brain. In some cases, trephined skulls of primitive people show healing around the opening, indicating that the patient survived the operation and lived for many years afterward (Arnott, Finger, & Smith, 2003; Selling, 1943).

Although human life appeared on earth some 3 million or more years ago, written records extend back only a few thousand years. Thus our knowledge of our early ancestors is limited. Two Egyptian papyri dating from the sixteenth century B.C. provide some clues to the earliest treatments of diseases and behavior disorders (Okasha & Okasha, 2000). The Edwin Smith papyrus (named after its nineteenth-century discoverer) contains detailed descriptions of the treatment of wounds and other surgical operations. In it, the brain is described—possibly for the first time in history—and the writing clearly shows that the brain was recognized as the site of mental functions. The Ebers papyrus offers another perspective on treatment. It covers internal medicine and the circulatory system but relies more on incantations and magic for explaining and curing diseases that had unknown causes. Although surgical techniques may have been used, they were probably coupled with prayers and the like that reflected the prevailing view of the origin of behavior disorders.

Demonology, Gods, and Magic

References to abnormal behavior in early writings show that the Chinese, Egyptians, Hebrews, and Greeks often attributed such behavior to a demon or god who had taken possession of a person. Whether the "possession" was assumed to involve good spirits or evil spirits usually depended on the affected individual's symptoms. If a person's speech or behavior appeared to have a religious or mystical significance, it was usually thought that he or she was possessed by a good spirit or god. Such people were often treated with considerable awe and respect, for people believed they had supernatural powers.

Most possessions, however, were considered to be the work of an angry god or an evil spirit, particularly when a person became excited or overactive and engaged in behavior contrary to religious teachings. Among the ancient Hebrews, for example, such possessions were thought to represent the wrath and punishment of God. Moses is quoted in the Bible as saying, "The Lord shall smite thee with madness." Apparently this punishment was thought to involve the withdrawal of God's protection and the abandonment of the person to the forces of evil. In such cases, every effort was made to rid the person of the evil spirit. Jesus reportedly cured a man with an "unclean spirit" by transferring the devils that plagued him to a herd of swine, which, in turn, became possessed and "ran violently down a steep place into the sea" (Mark 5:1–13).

The primary type of treatment for demonic possession was exorcism, which included various techniques for casting an evil spirit out of an afflicted person. These techniques varied but typically included magic, prayer, incantation, noisemaking, and the use of horrible-tasting concoctions made from sheep's dung and wine.

Hippocrates' Early Medical Concepts

The Greek temples of healing ushered in the Golden Age of Greece under the Athenian leader Pericles (461–429 B.C.). This period saw considerable progress in the understanding and treatment of mental disorders, in spite of the fact

Hippocrates' (460–377 B.C.) belief that mental disease was the result of natural causes and brain pathology was revolutionary for its time.

that Greeks of the time considered the human body sacred, so little could be learned of human anatomy or physiology. During this period the Greek physician Hippocrates (460–377 B.C.), often referred to as the father of modern medicine, received his training and made substantial contributions to the field.

Hippocrates denied that deities and demons intervened in the development of illnesses and insisted that mental disorders, like other diseases, had natural causes and appropriate treatments. He believed that the brain was the central organ of intellectual activity and that mental disorders were due to brain pathology. He also emphasized the importance of heredity and predisposition and pointed out that injuries to the head could cause sensory and motor disorders.

Hippocrates classified all mental disorders into three general categories—mania, melancholia, and phrenitis (brain fever)—and gave detailed clinical descriptions of the specific disorders included in each category. He relied heavily on clinical observation, and his descriptions, which were based on daily clinical records of his patients, were surprisingly thorough.

Maher and Maher (1994) pointed out that the best known of the earlier paradigms for explaining personality or temperament is the doctrine of the four humors, associated with the name of Hippocrates and later with the Roman physician Galen. The four elements of the material world were thought to be earth, air, fire, and water, which had attributes of heat, cold, moistness, and dryness. These elements combined to form the four essential fluids of the body—blood (sanguis), phlegm, bile (choler), and black bile (melancholer). The fluids combined in different proportions within different individuals, and a person's temperament was determined by which of the humors was dominant. From this view came one of the earliest and longest-lasting typologies of human behavior: the sanguine, the phlegmatic, the choleric, and the melancholic. Each of these "types" brought with it a set of personality attributes. For example, the person of sanguine temperament was optimistic, cheerful, and unafraid.

Hippocrates considered dreams to be important in understanding a patient's personality. On this point, he was a harbinger of a basic concept of modern psychodynamic psychotherapy. The treatments advocated by Hippocrates were far in advance of the exorcistic practices then prevalent. For the treatment of melancholia (see Developments in Thinking 2.1 on p. 30), for example, he prescribed a regular and tranquil life, sobriety and abstinence from all excesses, a vegetable diet, celibacy, exercise short of fatigue, and bleeding if indicated. He also recognized the importance of the environment and often removed his patients from their families.

Hippocrates' emphasis on the natural causes of diseases, on clinical observation, and on brain pathology as the root of mental disorders was truly revolutionary. Like his contemporaries, however, Hippocrates had little knowledge of physiology. He believed that hysteria (the appearance of physical illness in the absence of organic pathology) was restricted to women and was caused by the uterus wandering to various parts of the body, pining for children. For this "disease," Hippocrates recommended marriage as the best remedy.

Early Philosophical Conceptions of Consciousness and Mental Discovery

The Greek philosopher Plato (429–347 B.C.) studied mentally disturbed individuals who had committed criminal acts and how to deal with them. He wrote that such persons were, in some "obvious" sense, not responsible for their acts and should not receive punishment in the same way as normal persons: "[S]omeone may commit an act when mad or afflicted with disease.... [If so,] let him pay simply for the damage; and let him be exempt from other punishment" (Plato, n.d.). Plato also made provision for mental cases to be cared for in the community.

Plato viewed psychological phenomena as responses of the whole organism, reflecting its internal state and natural appetites. In *The Republic,* Plato emphasized the importance of individual differences in intellectual and other abilities, and took into account sociocultural influences in shaping thinking and behavior. His ideas regarding

2.1 Developments in Thinking: Hysteria and Melancholia through the Ages

Although the modern mental health sciences have made great strides in defining, describing, classifying, determining the causes of, and treating psychological disorders, we should not ignore or minimize the contributions to understanding these conditions that were made by many individuals in antiquity. Actually, some mental health problems that are receiving a great deal of research and clinical attention today have been recognized and well described for millennia. One recent study of surviving letters from patients who were hospitalized in Edinborough Asylum between 1873 and 1906 concluded that mental health problems in the nineteenth century were very similar to those in our day (Beveridge, 1997). Two such disorders are hysteria and depression.

Hysteria

The disorder formerly known as "hysteria" is referred to as "conversion disorder" in DSM-IV-TR and has a long history going back to ancient Greek and Egyptian medicine (Adair, 1997; Mersky, 1995; Mersky & Potter, 1989). The term *hysteria* derives from the Greek word for "uterus" (*hystera*), which comes from an earlier Sanskrit term for "belly or stomach" (Micale, 1995). The ancient Greek philosopher Plato wrote in the *Timaeus* (see *Great Books of the Western World,* edited by Hutchins, 1952) about the uterus as follows: "When it remains barren for a long time after puberty it finds it difficult to bear, it feels wrath, it goes about the whole body, closing the tissues for air, stopping the respiration, putting the body into extreme dangers, and occasioning various diseases." Awareness of psychological problems identified as hysteria can be dated even earlier, to 1900 B.C. in ancient Egypt. Okasha and Okasha (2000) dated the understanding of this condition to the Kahun Papyrus. Although the papyrus has been partially destroyed over time, the fragments nevertheless describe a series of morbid states that are attributed to the uterus. "Most of these diseases are defined clearly enough to be recognizable today as hysterical disorders: a woman 'who loves bed, she does not rise and does not shake it'; 'who is ill in seeing, who has pain in her mouth'; 'pained in her teeth and jaws, she does not know how to open her mouth'; aching in all her limbs with pain in the sockets of her eyes, she can not hear what is spoken'; these and similar disturbances were believed to be caused by the 'starvation' of the uterus, by its upward displacement with a consequent crowding of other organs" (Okasha & Okasha, 2000, p. 418). Physicians held the view that hysteria was caused by "wandering of the uterus," until the seventeenth century when Willis (1621–1675) theorized that this disorder resulted from a disorder of the brain (Ng, 1999).

Melancholia

Perhaps no other mental disorder received so much attention from earlier scholars as depression, or (as it has been referred to in the past) melancholia. Efforts to understand melancholia have been undertaken by physicians, philosophers, writers, painters, and religious leaders in Western civilization for over 2,000 years. Moreover, conditions similar to depression were described in surviving writings from ancient Egypt (Okasha & Okasha, 2000) These disorders might have been viewed variously as medical conditions or religious states or human frailties; however, the symptom structure and behavior described were unmistakable.

Radden (2000) published an interesting compendium of important writings on melancholia that spanned 24 cen-

treatment included a provision for "hospital" care for individuals who developed beliefs that ran counter to those of the broader social order. There they would be engaged periodically in conversations comparable to psychotherapy to promote the health of their souls (Milns, 1986). Despite these modern ideas, however, Plato shared the belief that mental disorders were in part divinely caused.

The celebrated Greek philosopher Aristotle (384–322 B.C.), who was a pupil of Plato, wrote extensively on mental disorders. Among his most lasting contributions to psychology are his descriptions of consciousness. He held the view that "thinking" as directed would eliminate pain and help to attain pleasure. On the question of whether mental disorders could be caused by psychological factors such as frustration and conflict, Aristotle discussed the possibility and rejected it; his lead on this issue was widely followed. Aristotle generally subscribed to the Hippocratic theory of disturbances in the bile. For example, he thought that very hot bile generated amorous desires, verbal fluency, and suicidal impulses.

Later Greek and Roman Thought

Hippocrates' work was continued by some of the later Greek and Roman physicians. Particularly in Alexandria, Egypt (which became a center of Greek culture after its founding in 332 B.C. by Alexander the Great), medical practices developed to a higher level, and the temples dedicated to Saturn were first-rate sanatoria. Pleasant surroundings were considered of great therapeutic value for mental patients, who were provided with constant activities including parties, dances, walks in the temple gardens,

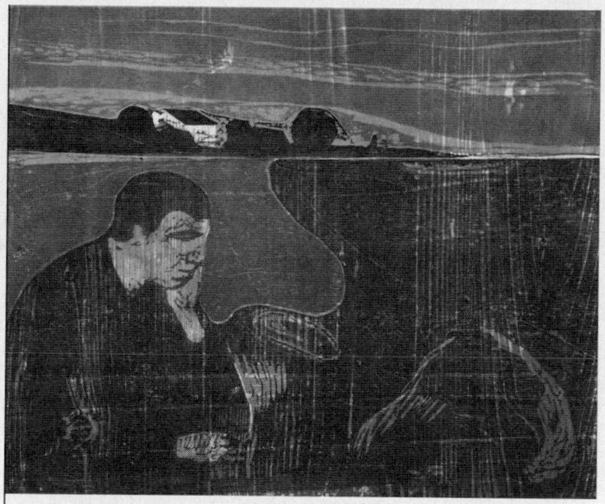

Evening (Melancholy), *1896. Edvard Munch. Efforts to understand melancholia have been undertaken by physicians, philosophers, writers, painters, and religious leaders in Western civilization for over 2,000 years.*

turies, some highlights of which are provided here. The understanding of depression, beginning with Aristotle and Galen during the Greek and Roman eras, provides lucid descriptions of the disorder melancholy. Even in the Middle Ages, when scholarship and inquiry were hindered by religious persecution, there were scholars interested in mental states such as melancholia. Hildegard (1098–1179), a nun whose intellectual brilliance was rewarded by the Pope even though she had little formal education, made significant contributions to understanding this mental disorder. Hildegard, known as the "first published woman physician," wrote a treatise on causes and cures in which she carried the Greek views of melancholia further by noting, among other things, that melancholia took different forms in men and women.

Even during the late medieval period when the Spanish Inquisition took a heavy toll on intellectual understanding, several writers contributed further to our comprehension of melancholia. Johann Weyer (1515–1588) provided astute descriptions of melancholia and examined characteristics of persons who might be so affected, even though these observations were often couched in terms of demonic possession—perhaps as a concession to leaders of the Inquisition in order to avoid persecution. Similarly, Teresa of Avila (1515–1582), even though she espoused the demonic view of melancholia, nevertheless promoted humane treatment of those afflicted.

The premodern view of melancholia as a disorder (without the taint of demonic possession or ancient Greek humors) was introduced by Philippe Pinel (1745–1826). A French physician widely recognized for his contributions to the humane treatment of people with mental disorders, Pinel also advanced our scholarly understanding of mental disorders such as melancholia by improving a classification schema and examining the causes of the disorder.

Two early modern contributors to our understanding of depression were Griesinger (1817–1868) and Kraepelin (1856–1926). Griesinger's views on the underlying biological basis for disorders such as melancholia focused the field of psychiatry on the need to seek biological determinants for disorders. Kraepelin is credited with preparing the way for the modern view of psychiatry. His classification schema is still cited today in contemporary writings as seminal in the evolution of diagnostic classification systems. Among other contributions to our understanding of melancholia, he identified manic depression as a major category of depression.

Even though much of our understanding of depression and our development of effective treatment methods has emerged over the past three decades, our debt to the ancients who struggled with describing and understanding this disorder needs to be recognized.

rowing along the Nile, and musical concerts. Physicians of this time also used a wide range of therapeutic measures including dieting, massage, hydrotherapy, gymnastics, and education, as well as some less desirable practices such as bleeding, purging, and mechanical restraints.

One of the most influential Greek physicians was Galen (A.D. 130–200), who practiced in Rome. Although he elaborated on the Hippocratic tradition, he did not contribute much that was new to the treatment or clinical descriptions of mental disorders. Rather, he made a number of original contributions concerning the anatomy of the nervous system. (These findings were based on dissections of animals; human autopsies were still not allowed.) Galen also took a scientific approach to the field, dividing the causes of psychological disorders into physical and mental categories. Among the causes he named were injuries to the head, excessive use of alcohol, shock, fear, adolescence, menstrual changes, economic reversals, and disappointment in love.

Roman medicine reflected the characteristic pragmatism of the Roman people. Roman physicians wanted to make their patients comfortable and thus used pleasant physical therapies such as warm baths and massage. They also followed the principle of *contrariis contrarius* (opposite by opposite)—for example, having their patients drink chilled wine while they were in a warm tub.

Abnormality during the Middle Ages

During the Middle Ages, the more scientific aspects of Greek medicine survived in the Islamic countries of the Middle East. The first mental hospital was established in

Galen (A.D. 130–200) believed that psychological disorders could have either physical causes, such as injuries to the head, or mental causes, such as disappointment in love.

Baghdad in A.D. 792; it was soon followed by others in Damascus and Aleppo (Polvan, 1969). In these hospitals, mentally disturbed individuals received humane treatment. The outstanding figure in Islamic medicine was Avicenna from Arabia (c. 980–1037), called the "prince of physicians" (Campbell, 1926), and the author of *The Canon of Medicine,* perhaps the most widely studied medical work ever written. In his writings, Avicenna frequently referred to hysteria, epilepsy, manic reactions, and melancholia. The following case study illustrates Avicenna's unique approach to the treatment of a young prince suffering from mental disorder.

case STUDY — An Early Treatment Case

A certain prince was afflicted with melancholia and suffered from the delusion that he was a cow.... He would low like a cow, causing annoyance to everyone,... crying, "Kill me so that a good stew may be made of my flesh." Finally...he would eat nothing.... Avicenna was persuaded to take the case.... First of all he sent a message to the patient bidding him be of good cheer because the butcher was coming to slaughter him, whereat... the sick man rejoiced. Some time afterward Avicenna, holding a knife in his hand, entered the sickroom saying, "Where is this cow that I may kill it?" The patient lowed like a cow to indicate where he was. By Avicenna's orders he was laid on the ground bound hand and foot. Avicenna then felt him all over and said, "He is too lean, and not ready to be killed; he must be fattened." Then they offered him suitable food of which he now partook eagerly, and gradually he gained strength, got rid of his delusion, and was completely cured. (Browne, 1921, pp. 88–89)

During the Middle Ages in Europe (c. 500–1500), scientific inquiry into abnormal behavior was limited, and the treatment of psychologically disturbed individuals was characterized more often by ritual or superstition than by attempts to understand an individual's condition. In contrast to Avicenna's era in the Islamic countries of the Middle East or to the period of enlightenment during the seventeenth and eighteenth centuries, the Middle Ages in Europe were largely devoid of scientific thinking and humane treatment for the mentally disturbed. A similar sequence of events occurred in other parts of the world, as can be seen in Developments in Thinking 2.2.

Mental disorders were quite prevalent throughout the Middle Ages in Europe, especially toward the end of the

Islamic physician Avicenna (c. 980–1037) approached the treatment of mental disorders with humane practices unknown to Western medical practitioners of the time.

2.2 Developments in Thinking

Early Views of Mental Disorders in China

The following passage is taken from an ancient Chinese medical text supposedly written by Huang Ti (c. 2674 B.C.), the third legendary emperor. Historians now believe that the text was written at a later date, possibly during the seventh century B.C.:

> The person suffering from excited insanity initially feels sad, eating and sleeping less; he then becomes grandiose, feeling that he is very smart and noble, talking and scolding day and night, singing, behaving strangely, seeing strange things, hearing strange voices, believing that he can see the devil or gods. (Tseng, 1973, p. 570)

Even at this early date, Chinese medicine was based on a belief in natural rather than supernatural causes for illnesses. For example, in the concept of Yin and Yang, the human body, like the cosmos, is divided into positive and negative forces that both complement and contradict each other. If the two forces are balanced, the result is physical and mental health; if they are not, illness results. Thus treatments focused on restoring balance: "As treatment for such an excited condition withholding food was suggested, since food was considered to be the source of positive force and the patient was thought to be in need of a decrease in such force" (Tseng, 1973, p. 570).

Beng-Yeong Ng (1999) pointed out that the Golden Box Summary (an ancient Chinese document summarizing medical theory and treatment) presented *zang-zao,* an illness that resembled a symptom pattern of hysteria: "A woman who suffers from *zang-zao* is easily saddened and cries often, is emotionally unstable as if influenced by an evil spirit, yawns, and stretches her limbs frequently" (p. 291).

Chinese medicine reached a relatively sophisticated level during the second century, and Chung Ching, who has been called the Hippocrates of China, wrote two well-known medical works around A.D. 200. Like Hippocrates, he based his views of physical and mental disorders on clinical observations, and he implicated organ pathologies as primary causes. However, he also believed that stressful psychological conditions could cause organ pathologies, and his treatments, like those of Hippocrates, utilized both drugs and the regaining of emotional balance through appropriate activities.

As in the West, Chinese views of mental disorders regressed to a belief in supernatural forces as causal agents. From the later part of the second century through the early part of the ninth century, ghosts and devils were implicated in "ghost-evil" insanity, which presumably resulted from possession by evil spirits. The "Dark Ages" in China, however, were neither so severe (in terms of the treatment of mental patients) nor so long-lasting as in the West. A return to biological, somatic (bodily) views and an emphasis on psychosocial factors occurred in the centuries that followed.

period, when medieval institutions, social structures, and beliefs began to change drastically. During this time, supernatural explanations of the causes of mental illness grew in popularity. Within this environment, it obviously was difficult to make great strides in the understanding and treatment of abnormal behavior. Although the influence of theology was growing rapidly, "sin" was not always cited as a causal factor in mental illness. For example, Kroll and Bachrach (1984) examined 57 episodes of mental illness ranging from madness and possession to alcohol abuse and epilepsy.

They found sin implicated in only nine cases (16 percent). To understand better this elusive period of history, let us look at two events of the times—mass madness and exorcism—to see how they are related to views of abnormal behavior.

MASS MADNESS During the last half of the Middle Ages in Europe, a peculiar trend emerged in efforts to understand abnormal behavior. It involved **mass madness**—the widespread occurrence of group behavior disorders that were apparently cases of hysteria. Whole groups of people were affected simultaneously. Dancing manias (epidemics of raving, jumping, dancing, and convulsions) were reported as early as the tenth century.

One such episode that occurred in Italy early in the thirteenth century was known as **tarantism**—a disorder that included an uncontrollable impulse to dance that was often attributed to the bite of the southern European tarantula or wolf spider. This dancing mania later spread to Germany and the rest of Europe, where it was known as **Saint Vitus's dance.** Similar to the ancient orgiastic rites through which people had worshiped the Greek god Dionysus, these rites had been banned with the advent of Christianity, but they were deeply embedded in the culture and were apparently kept alive in secret gatherings. Then, with time, the meaning of the dances changed. The old rites reappeared, but they were attributed to symptoms of the tarantula's bite. The participants were no longer "sinners" but the unwilling victims of the tarantula's spirit. The dancing became the "cure" and is the source of the dance we know today as the tarantella.

Isolated rural areas were also afflicted with outbreaks of **lycanthropy**—a condition in which people believed themselves to be possessed by wolves and imitated their behavior. In 1541 a case was reported in which a person suffering from lycanthropy told his captors, in confidence, that he was really a wolf but that his skin was smooth on the surface because all the hairs were on the inside (Stone, 1937). To cure him of his delusions, his extremities were amputated, following which he died, still uncured.

Mass madness occurred periodically all the way into the seventeenth century but reached its peak during the fourteenth and fifteenth centuries—a period noted for social oppression, famine, and epidemic diseases. During this time, Europe was ravaged by a plague known as the Black Death, which killed millions (according to some estimates, 50 percent of the population of Europe died) and severely disrupted social organization. Undoubtedly, many of the peculiar cases of mass madness were related to the depression, fear, and wild mysticism engendered by the terrible events of this period. People simply could not believe that frightening catastrophes such as the Black Death could have natural causes and thus could be within their power to control, prevent, or even create.

Today, so-called "mass hysteria" occurs occasionally; the affliction usually mimics some type of physical disorder such as fainting spells or convulsive movements. A case of apparent mass hysteria occurred among hundreds of West Bank Palestinian girls in April 1983. This episode threatened to have serious political repercussions, because some Arab and Israeli leaders initially thought that the girls had been poisoned by Israelis. Health officials later concluded that psychological factors had played a key role in most of the cases (Hefez, 1985).

Ilechukwu (1992) described an epidemic of mass hysteria that occurred in Nigeria in 1990 in which many men feared that their genitals had simply vanished. This fear of genital retraction accompanied by a fear of death is referred to as "Koro" (see Chapter 3) and has been widely documented in Southeast Asia. The afflicted persons believe this genital disappearance was caused by a supernatural occurrence in which they were robbed of their genitalia in order to benefit other people magically. Ilechukwu attributed some of this panic to male resentment of women's success during a period of social strain and the symbolic equation between masculine sexuality and economic, social, and creative prowess.

EXORCISM AND WITCHCRAFT In the Middle Ages in Europe, management of the mentally disturbed was left largely to the clergy. Monasteries served as refuges and places of confinement. During the early part of the medieval period, the mentally disturbed were, for the most part, treated with considerable kindness. "Treatment" consisted of prayer, holy water, sanctified ointments, the breath or spittle of the priests, the touching of relics, visits to holy places, and mild forms of exorcism. In some monasteries and shrines, **exorcisms** (which are symbolic acts that are performed to drive out the devil from persons believed to be possessed) were performed by the gentle "laying on of hands." Such methods were often joined with vaguely understood medical treatments derived mainly from Galen, which gave rise to prescriptions such as the following: "For a fiend-sick man: When a devil possesses a man, or controls him from within with disease, a spewdrink of lupin, bishopswort, henbane, garlic. Pound these together, add ale and holy water" (Cockayne, 1864–1866).

Interestingly, there has been a recent resurgence of superstition. For example, one can find those who believe that supernatural forces cause psychological problems and that "cures" should involve exorcism to rid people of unwanted characteristics or "spells." Unfortunately, exorcism is still practiced as two recent examples attest. Fries (2001) reported on a woman tragically drowning her 4-year-old daughter in an exorcism ritual attempting to rid her of demons that she believed possessed her. In a more recent example, *CBS News* reported an incident in which an autistic boy was killed in an exorcism at a church in Milwaukee (*CBS News*, 2003).

It had long been thought that during the Middle Ages, many mentally disturbed people were accused of being witches and thus were punished and often killed (e.g., Zilboorg & Henry, 1941). But several more recent interpretations have questioned the extent to which this was so (Maher & Maher, 1985; Phillips, 2002; Schoeneman, 1984). For example, in a review of the literature, Schoeneman notes that "the typical accused witch was not a mentally ill person but an impoverished woman with a sharp tongue and a bad temper" (p. 301). He goes on to say that "witchcraft was, in fact, never considered a variety of possession either by witch hunters, the general populace, or modern historians" (p. 306). To say "never" may be overstating the case; clearly, some mentally ill people were punished as witches. Otherwise, as we will see in the next section, why did some physicians and thinkers go to great lengths to expose the fallacies of the connection? In the case of witchcraft and mental illness, the confusion may be due, in part, to confusion about demonic possession. Even Robert Burton (1576–1640), an enlightened scholar, in his classic work *The Anatomy of Melancholia* (1621) considered demonic possession a potential cause of the disorder. There were two types of demonically possessed people: Those physically possessed were considered mad, whereas those spiritually possessed were likely to be considered witches. Over time, the distinctions between these two categories may have blurred in the eyes of historians, resulting in the perception that witchcraft and mental illness were connected more frequently in the medieval mind than was the case.

The changing view of the relationship between witchcraft and mental illness points to an even broader issue—the difficulties of interpreting historical events accurately. We will discuss this concept in more depth in the Unresolved Issues section at the end of this chapter.

In Review

- What aspects of Hippocrates' alternative approach to mental disorders were truly revolutionary?
- What is mass madness? Give some examples of this phenomenon.
- Describe the historical development of humanitarian reform, and give some of the reasons why it occurred.
- What was the role of supernatural beliefs in efforts to understand mental disorders during the Middle Ages?
- What were the historical views of the disorder of melancholia (known as "depression" today)?

Toward Humanitarian Approaches

During the latter part of the Middle Ages and the early Renaissance, scientific questioning reemerged and a movement emphasizing the importance of specifically human interests and concerns began—a movement (still with us today) that can be loosely referred to as "humanism." Consequently, the superstitious beliefs that had hindered the understanding and therapeutic treatment of mental disorders began to be challenged.

The Resurgence of Scientific Questioning in Europe

Paracelsus (1490–1541), a Swiss physician, was an early critic of superstitious beliefs about possession. He insisted that the dancing mania was not a possession, but a form of disease, and that it should be treated as such. He also postulated a conflict between the instinctual and spiritual natures of human beings, formulated the idea of psychic causes for mental illness, and advocated treatment by "bodily magnetism," later called *hypnosis* (Mora, 1967). Although Paracelsus rejected demonology, his view of abnormal behavior was colored by his belief in astral influences (*lunatic* is derived from the Latin word *luna*, or "moon"). He was convinced that the moon exerted a supernatural influence over the brain—an idea, incidentally, that persists among some people today.

Johann Weyer (1515–1588), a German physician and writer who wrote under the Latin name of "Joannus Wierus," was so deeply disturbed by the imprisonment, torture, and burning of people accused of witchcraft that he made a careful study of the entire problem. About 1563 he published a book, *The Deception of Demons,* that contains a step-by-step rebuttal of the *Malleus Maleficarum,* a witch-hunting handbook published in 1486 for use in recognizing and dealing with those suspected of being witches. In his book, Weyer argued that a considerable number, if not all, of those imprisoned, tortured, and burned for witchcraft were really sick in mind or body and that, consequently, great wrongs were being committed against innocent people. Weyer's work enjoyed the approval of a few outstanding physicians and theologians of his time. Mostly, however, it met with vehement protest and condemnation.

Johann Weyer, a sixteenth-century German physician, became so concerned over the torture and imprisonment of people accused of being witches that he wrote a book rebutting the church's witch hunting handbook the Malleus Maleficarum.

Weyer was one of the first physicians to specialize in mental disorders, and his wide experience and progressive views justify his reputation as the founder of modern psychopathology. Unfortunately, however, he was too far ahead of his time. He was scorned by his peers, many of whom called him "Weirus Hereticus" and "Weirus Insanus." His works were banned by the Church and remained so until the twentieth century.

The clergy, however, were beginning to question the practices of the time. For example, St. Vincent de Paul (1576–1660), at the risk of his life, declared, "Mental disease is no different to bodily disease and Christianity demands of the humane and powerful to protect, and the skillful to relieve the one as well as the other" (Castiglioni, 1924).

In the face of such persistent advocates of science, who continued their testimonies throughout the next two centuries, demonology and superstition gave ground. These advocates gradually paved the way for the return of observation and reason, which culminated in the development of modern experimental and clinical approaches.

The Establishment of Early Asylums and Shrines

From the sixteenth century on, special institutions called **asylums,** sanctuaries or places of refuge meant solely for the care of the mentally ill, grew in number. The early asylums were begun as a way of removing from society troublesome individuals who could not care for themselves. Although scientific inquiry into abnormal behavior was on the increase, most early asylums, often referred to as "madhouses," were not pleasant places or "hospitals" but primarily residences or storage places for the insane. The unfortunate residents lived and died amid conditions of incredible filth and cruelty.

The first hospital established in Europe was probably in Spain in 1409—the Valencia mental hospital founded by Father Juan Pilberto Jofre (Villasante, 2003)—although this point has been the subject of considerable discussion (Polo, 1997; Trope, 1997). Little is known about the treatment of patients in this asylum. In 1547 the monastery of St. Mary of Bethlehem in London (initially founded as a monastery in 1247; see O'Donoghue, 1914) was officially made into an asylum by Henry VIII. Its name soon was contracted to "Bedlam," and it became widely known for its deplorable conditions and practices. The more violent patients were exhibited to the public for one penny a look, and the more harmless inmates were forced to seek charity on the streets of London in the manner described by Shakespeare: "Bedlam beggars, who, with roaring voices . . . Sometime with lunatic bans, sometime with prayers, enforce their charity" (*King Lear,* II, iii). Tuke (1882) describes Ned Ward's account, in the *History of the Insane in the British Isles,* of a visit to Bedlam:

> Accordingly we were admitted in thro' an iron gate, within which sat a brawny Cerberus, of an Idico-colour, leaning upon a money-box; we turned in through another Iron-Barricado, where we heard such a rattling of chains, drumming of doors, ranting, hollowing, singing, and running, that I could think of nothing but Don Quevedo's Vision where the lost souls broke loose and put Hell in an uproar. The first whimsey-headed wretch of this lunatic family that we observed, was a merry fellow in a straw cap, who was talking to himself, "that he had an army of Eagles at his command," then clapping his hand upon his head, swore by his crown of moonshine, he would battle all the Stars in the Skies, but he would have some claret. . . . We then moved on till we found another remarkable figure worth our observing, who was peeping through his wicket, eating of bread and cheese, talking all the while like a carrier at his supper, chewing his words with his victuals, all that he spoke being in praise of bread and cheese: "bread was good with cheese, and cheese was good with bread, and bread and cheese was good together"; and abundance of such stuff; to which my friend and I, with others stood listening; at last he counterfeits a sneeze, and shot such a

The monastery of St. Mary of Bethlehem in London became an asylum for the mentally ill in the reign of King Henry the VIII during the sixteenth century. The hospital, known as "Bedlam," became infamous for its deplorable conditions and practices.

mouthful of bread and cheese amongst us, that every spectator had some share of his kindness, which made us retreat. (pp. 76–77)

Such asylums for the mentally ill were gradually established in other countries. The San Hipolito, established in Mexico in 1566 by philanthropist Bernardino Alvares, was the first asylum established in the Americas. The first such hospital in France, La Maison de Charenton, was founded in 1641 in a suburb of Paris. An asylum was established in Moscow in 1764, and the notorious Lunatics' Tower in Vienna was constructed in 1784. This structure was a showplace in Old Vienna, an ornately decorated round tower within which were square rooms. The doctors and "keepers" lived in the square rooms, while the patients were confined in the spaces between the walls of the rooms and the outside of the tower, where they were put on exhibit to the public for a small fee.

These early asylums were primarily modifications of penal institutions, and the inmates were treated more like beasts than like human beings. The following case study describes the treatment of the chronically insane in La Bicêtre, a hospital in Paris. This treatment was typical of the asylums of the period and continued through most of the eighteenth century.

This painting depicts Philippe Pinel supervising the unchaining of inmates at La Bicêtre hospital. Pinel's experiment represented both a great reform and a major step in devising humanitarian methods of treating mental disorders.

CASE STUDY — Treatment in Early Hospitals

The patients were ordinarily shackled to the walls of their dark, unlighted cells by iron collars that held them flat against the wall and permitted little movement. Oftentimes there were also iron hoops around the waists of the patients and both their hands and feet were chained. Although these chains usually permitted enough movement that the patients could feed themselves out of bowls, they often kept them from being able to lie down at night. Since little was known about nutrition, and the patients were presumed to be animals anyway, little attention was paid to whether they were adequately fed or to whether the food was good or bad. The cells were furnished only with straw and were never swept or cleaned; the patient remained in the midst of all the accumulated odor. No one visited the cells except at feeding time, no provision was made for warmth, and even the most elementary gestures of humanity were lacking. (Adapted from Selling, 1943, pp. 54–55)

In the United States, the Pennsylvania Hospital in Philadelphia, completed under the guidance of Benjamin Franklin in 1756, provided some cells or wards for mental patients. The Public Hospital in Williamsburg, Virginia, constructed in 1773, was the first hospital in the United States devoted exclusively to mental patients. The treatment of mental patients in the United States was no better than that offered by European institutions. Zwelling's 1985 review of the Public Hospital's treatment methods shows that, initially, the philosophy of treatment involved the belief that the patients needed to choose rationality over **insanity.** Thus the treatment techniques were aggressive, aimed at restoring a "physical balance in the body and brain." These techniques, though based on the scientific views of the day, were designed to intimidate patients. They included powerful drugs, water treatments, bleeding and blistering, electric shocks, and physical restraints. For example, a violent patient might be plunged into ice water or a listless patient into hot water; frenzied patients might be administered drugs to exhaust them; or patients might be bled in order to drain their system of "harmful" fluids.

Humanitarian Reform

Clearly, by the late eighteenth century, most mental hospitals in Europe and America were in great need of reform. The humanitarian treatment of patients received great impetus from the work of Philippe Pinel (1745–1826) in France.

Viewed from a contemporary perspective, the scene depicted in this nineteenth-century drawing appears inhumane and degrading. However, hydrotherapy treatment, as shown here at St. Anne's Hospital in Paris in 1868, was considered a standard treatment method.

PINEL'S EXPERIMENT In 1792, shortly after the first phase of the French Revolution, Pinel was placed in charge of La Bicêtre in Paris. In this capacity, he received the grudging permission of the Revolutionary Commune to remove the chains from some of the inmates as an experiment to test his views that mental patients should be treated with kindness and consideration—as sick people, not as vicious beasts or criminals. Had his experiment proved a failure, Pinel might have lost his head, but fortunately it was a great success. Chains were removed; sunny rooms were provided; patients were permitted to exercise on the hospital grounds; and kindness was extended to these poor beings, some of whom had been chained in dungeons for 30 or more years. The effect was almost miraculous. The previous noise, filth, and abuse were replaced by order and peace. As Pinel said, "The whole discipline was marked with regularity and kindness which had the most favorable effect on the insane themselves, rendering even the most furious more tractable" (Selling, 1943, p. 65). Interestingly, a historical document, subsequently found in the French Archives, raises some question about the date at which humanitarian reforms were begun in France. The document, provided by Jean-Baptiste Pussin (Pinel's predecessor at La Bicêtre), indicated that he had been the head of the hospital beginning in 1784 and had removed some of the chains from patients and employed slightly more humane straitjackets instead. He also pointed out in the document that he had issued orders forbidding the staff from beating patients (Weiner, 1979).

TUKE'S WORK IN ENGLAND At about the same time that Pinel was reforming La Bicêtre, an English Quaker named William Tuke (1732–1822) established the York Retreat, a pleasant country house where mental patients lived, worked, and rested in a kindly, religious atmosphere (Narby, 1982). This retreat represented the culmination of a noble battle against the brutality, ignorance, and indifference of Tuke's time.

The Quakers believed in treating all people, even the insane, with kindness and acceptance. Their view that kind acceptance would help mentally ill people recover sparked the growth of more humane psychiatric treatment during a period when mental patients were ignored and mistreated (Glover, 1984).

The Quaker retreat at York has continued to provide humane mental health treatment for over 200 years (Borthwick, Holman, et al., 2001) even though the mental hospital movement spawned by its example evolved into large mental hospitals that became crowded and often offered less-than-humane treatment in the late nineteenth and early twentieth centuries. (See the picture of the York Retreat today.)

As word of Pinel's amazing results spread to England, Tuke's small force of Quakers gradually gained the support of English medical practitioners such as John Connolly and Samuel Hitch. In 1841 Hitch introduced trained nurses into the wards at the Gloucester Asylum and put trained supervisors at the head of the nursing staffs. These innovations, quite revolutionary at the time, not only improved the care of mental patients but also changed public attitudes toward the mentally disturbed.

The historic mental health facility, the York Retreat, continues to provide services in York, England, over 200 years since it was founded by William Tuke in 1796. This mental health facility is sponsored by the Quakers and provides a broad range of services in both inpatient and outpatient care.

RUSH AND MORAL MANAGEMENT IN AMERICA The success of Pinel's and Tuke's humanitarian experiments revolutionized the treatment of mental patients throughout the Western world. In the United States, this revolution was reflected in the work of Benjamin Rush (1745–1813), the founder of American psychiatry, who was also one of the signers of the Declaration of Independence. While he was associated with the Pennsylvania Hospital in 1783, Rush encouraged more humane treatment of the mentally ill; wrote the first systematic treatise on psychiatry in America, *Medical Inquiries and Observations of the Diseases of the Mind* (1812); and was the first American to organize a course in psychiatry. But even he did not escape entirely from established beliefs of his time. His medical theory was tainted with astrology, and his principal remedies were bloodletting and purgatives. In addition, he invented and used a device called "the tranquilizing chair," which was probably more torturous than tranquil for patients. The chair was thought to lessen the force of the blood on the head while the muscles were relaxed. Despite these limitations, we can consider Rush an important transitional figure between the old era and the new.

During the early part of this period of humanitarian reform, the use of **moral management**—a wide-ranging method of treatment that focused on a patient's social, individual, and occupational needs—became relatively widespread. This approach, which stemmed largely from the work of Pinel and Tuke, began in Europe during the late eighteenth century and in America during the early nineteenth century.

Moral management in asylums emphasized the patients' moral and spiritual development and the rehabilitation of their "character" rather than their physical or mental disorders, in part because very little effective treatment was available for these conditions at the time. The treatment or rehabilitation of the physical or mental disorders was usually through manual labor and spiritual discussion, along with humane treatment.

Moral management achieved a high degree of effectiveness—which is all the more amazing because it was done without the benefit of the antipsychotic drugs used today and because many of the patients were probably suffering from syphilis, a then-incurable disease of the central nervous system. In the 20-year period between 1833 and 1853, Worcester State Hospital's discharge rate for patients who had been ill less than a year before admission was 71 percent. Even for patients with a longer preadmission disorder, the discharge rate was 59 percent (Bockhoven, 1972).

Despite its reported effectiveness in many cases, moral management was nearly abandoned by the latter part of the nineteenth century. The reasons were many and varied. Among the more obvious ones were ethnic prejudice against the rising immigrant population, leading to tension between staff and patients; the failure of the movement's leaders to train their own replacements; and the overextension of hospital facilities, which reflected the misguided belief that bigger hospitals would differ from smaller ones only in size.

Two other reasons for the demise of moral management are, in retrospect, truly ironic. One was the rise of the **mental hygiene movement,** which advocated a method of treatment that focused almost exclusively on the physical well-being of hospitalized mental patients. Although the patients' comfort levels improved under the mental hygienists, the patients received no help for their mental problems and thus were subtly condemned to helplessness and dependency.

Advances in biomedical science also contributed to the demise of moral management and the rise of the mental hygiene movement. These advances fostered the notion that all mental disorders would eventually yield to biological explanations and biologically based treatments (Luchins, 1989). Thus the psychological and social environment of a patient was considered largely irrelevant; the best one could do was keep the patient comfortable until a biological cure was discovered. Needless to say, the anticipated biological cure-all did not arrive, and by the late 1940s and early 1950s, discharge rates were down to about 30 percent. Its negative effects on the use of moral management notwithstanding, the mental hygiene movement has accounted for many humanitarian accomplishments.

DIX AND THE MENTAL HYGIENE MOVEMENT Dorothea Dix (1802–1887) was an energetic New Englander who became a champion of poor and "forgotten" people in prisons and mental institutions for decades during the nineteenth century. Dix, herself a child of very difficult and impoverished circumstances (Viney, 1996), later became an important driving force in humane treatment for psychiatric patients. She worked as a schoolteacher as a young adult but was later forced into early retirement because of recurring attacks of tuberculosis. In 1841 she began to teach in a women's prison. Through this contact she became acquainted with the deplorable conditions in jails, almshouses, and asylums. In a "Memorial" submitted to the U.S. Congress in 1848, she stated that she had seen "more than 9000 idiots, epileptics and insane in the United States, destitute of appropriate care and protection... bound with galling chains, bowed beneath fetters and heavy iron bails attached to drag-chains, lacerated with ropes, scourged with rods and terrified beneath storms of execration and cruel blows; now subject to jibes and scorn and torturing tricks; now abandoned to the most outrageous violations." (Zilboorg & Henry, 1941, pp. 583–584)

As a result of what she had seen, Dix carried on a zealous campaign between 1841 and 1881 that aroused people and legislatures to do something about the inhuman treatment accorded the mentally ill. Through her efforts, the mental hygiene movement grew in America: Millions of dollars were raised to build suitable hospitals, and 20 states

Dorothea Dix (1802–1887) was a tireless reformer who made great strides in changing public attitudes toward the mentally ill.

responded directly to her appeals. Not only was she instrumental in improving conditions in American hospitals, but she also directed the opening of two large institutions in Canada and completely reformed the asylum system in Scotland and several other countries. She is credited with establishing 32 mental hospitals, an astonishing record given the ignorance and superstition that still prevailed in the field of mental health. Dix rounded out her career by organizing the nursing forces of the northern armies during the Civil War. A resolution presented by the U.S. Congress in 1901 characterized her as "among the noblest examples of humanity in all history" (Karnesh, with Zucker, 1945, p. 18).

Later critics have claimed that establishing hospitals for the mentally ill and increasing the number of people in them spawned overcrowded facilities and custodial care (Bockhoven, 1972; Dain, 1964). These critics have further claimed that housing patients in institutions away from society interfered with the treatment of the day (moral therapy) and deferred the search for more appropriate and effective treatments for mental disorders (Bockhoven, 1972). These criticisms, however, do not consider the context in which Dix's contributions were made (see the Unresolved Issues at the end of this chapter). Her advocacy of the humane treatment of the mentally ill stood in stark contrast to the cruel treatment common at the time (Viney & Bartsch, 1984).

THE MILITARY AND THE MENTALLY ILL Mental health treatment was also advanced by military medicine. The first mental health facility for treating mentally disordered war casualties was opened by the Confederate Army in the American Civil War (Deutsch, 1944; Gabriel, 1987). An even more extensive and influential program of military psychiatry evolved in Germany during the late 1800s. Lengweiler (2003) reviewed the evolution of military psychiatry in Germany between the Franco-Prussian War in 1870 and World War I in 1914. During this period, psychiatrists, a number of whom made great contributions to the field of abnormal psychology (e.g., Emil Kraepelin and Richard Kraft-Ebbing), worked with the military administration, conducting research and training doctors to detect mental health problems that could interfere with performance of duty. One early research program illustrates the interplay between medicine and military administration. Kraepelin, who viewed alcohol as a key cause of psychological problems among soldiers, conducted a research project evaluating the extent to which alcohol consumption adversely affected the soldiers' ability to fire their rifles effectively.

Nineteenth-Century Views of the Causes and Treatment of Mental Disorders

In the early part of the nineteenth century, mental hospitals were controlled essentially by laypersons because of the prominence of moral management in the treatment of "lunatics." Medical professionals—or "alienists," as psychiatrists were called at this time in reference to their treating the "alienated," or insane—had a relatively inconsequential role in the care of the insane and the management of the asylums of the day. Moreover, effective treatments for mental disorders were unavailable, the only measures being such procedures as drugging, bleeding, and purging, which produced few objective results. However, during the latter part of the century, alienists gained control of the insane asylums and incorporated the traditional moral management therapy into their other rudimentary physical-medical procedures.

Over time, the alienists acquired more status and influence in society and became influential as purveyors of morality, touting the benefits of Victorian morality as important to good mental health. Mental disorders were only vaguely understood, and conditions such as depression were considered to be the result of nervous exhaustion. That is, psychiatrists of the time thought that emotional problems were caused by the expenditure of energy or by the depletion of bodily energies as a result of excesses in living. The mental deterioration or "shattered nerves" that supposedly resulted from a person's using up precious nerve force came to be referred to as "neurasthenia," a condition that involved pervasive feelings of low mood, lack of energy, and physical symptoms that were thought to be related to "lifestyle" problems brought on by the demands of civilization. These vague symptoms, viewed by the alienists/psychiatrists as a definable medical condition, were then considered treatable by medical men of the times.

Changing Attitudes toward Mental Health in the Early Twentieth Century

It is difficult to partition modern views of abnormal behavior into discrete, uniform attitudes or to trace their historical precedents without appearing arbitrary and overly simplistic. However, a brief, selective overview here will bring us into the contemporary era and set the scene for our discussion of the major viewpoints and causal considerations discussed in Chapter 3. By the end of the nineteenth century, the mental hospital or asylum—"the big house on the hill"—with its fortress-like appearance, had become a familiar landmark in America. In it, mental patients lived under relatively harsh conditions, despite the inroads made by moral management. To the general public, however, the asylum was an eerie place, and its occupants a strange and frightening lot. Little was done by the resident psychiatrists to educate the public or reduce the general fear and horror of insanity. A principal reason for this silence, of course, was that early psychiatrists had little actual information to impart.

Gradually, however, important strides were made toward changing the general public's attitude toward mental patients. In America, the pioneering work of Dix was followed by that of Clifford Beers (1876–1943), whose book *A Mind That Found Itself* was first published in 1908. Beers, a Yale graduate, described his own mental collapse and told of the bad treatment he received in three typical institutions of the day. Although chains and other torture devices had long since been given up, the straitjacket was still widely used as a means of "quieting" excited patients. Beers experienced this treatment and supplied a vivid description of what such painful immobilization of the arms means to an overwrought mental patient:

> No one incident of my whole life has ever impressed itself more indelibly on my memory. Within one hour's time I was suffering pain as intense as any I ever endured, and before the night had passed that pain had become almost unbearable. My right hand was so held that the tip of one of my fingers was all but cut by the nail of another, and soon knife-like pains began to shoot through my right arm as far as the shoulder. If there be any so curious as to wish to get a slight idea of my agony, let him bite a finger tip as hard as he can without drawing blood. Let him continue the operation for two or three minutes. Then let him multiply that effect, if he can, by two or three hundred. In my case, after four or five hours the excess of pain rendered me partially insensible to it. But for nine hundred minutes—fifteen consecutive hours—I remained in that strait-jacket; and not until the twelfth hour, about breakfast time the next morning, did an attendant so much as loosen a cord. (Beers, 1970, pp. 127–128)

After Beers recovered in the home of a kind attendant, he launched a campaign to make people realize that such treatment was no way to handle the sick. He soon won the interest and support of many public-spirited individuals, including the eminent psychologist William James and the "dean of American psychiatry," Adolf Meyer.

Mental Hospital Care in the Twentieth Century

The twentieth century began with a continued period of growth in asylums for the mentally ill; however, the fate of mental patients during that century was neither uniform nor entirely positive (see The World Around Us 2.3, Chaining Mental Health Patients). At the beginning of the twentieth century, with the influence of enlightened people such as Clifford Beers, mental hospitals grew substantially in number—predominantly to house persons with severe mental disorders such as schizophrenia, depression, organic mental disorders, tertiary syphilis and paresis, and severe alcoholism. By 1940 the public mental hospitals housed over 400,000 patients, or roughly 90 percent of mentally ill persons residing in large state-funded hospitals, the remainder of patients in private hospitals (Grob, 1994). During this period, hospital stays were typically quite lengthy, and many mentally ill individuals were destined to be hospitalized for many years. For the first half of the twentieth century, hospital care was accompanied by little in the way of effective treatment, and the care was often harsh, punitive, and inhumane. The year 1946, however, marked the beginning of an important period of change. In that year, Mary Jane Ward published a very influential book, *The Snake Pit,* which was popularized in a movie of the same name. This work called attention to the plight of mental patients and helped to create concern over the need to provide more humane mental

In the first half of the twentieth century, hospital care for the mentally ill afforded very little in the way of effective treatment. In many cases, the care was considered to be harsh, punitive, and inhumane.

2.3 The World Around Us

Chaining Mental Health Patients

Because of limited mental health treatment resources in some countries, it is not uncommon for mentally ill people to be chained. Westermeyer and Kroll (1978) conducted an epidemiologic study on the use of restraints for mentally ill people in 27 villages in Laos. They reported that mentally ill people who were aggressive toward others or who were considered to be a danger to themselves were sometimes restrained by being chained to posts. The woman in the picture shown here suffered from a psychotic disorder and reportedly felt compelled to sweep her platform for 6 or 7 hours a day. She was restrained at a Buddhist temple in Laos in order to keep her from wandering into the jungle (Westermeyer, 2001).

Many temples even provide homes for psychologically disturbed individuals, although the care is typically inadequate. For example, Erwady, India, near Madras, has 15 privately run homes, many of which are without electricity, tap water, toilet facilities, and beds. In 2000, six people died from waterborne disease at one of the Erwady asylums, prompting the government to direct an inquiry into the conditions of the mental health asylums. The investigation has not yet been completed. Recently, fire swept through a palm-thatched shed that housed mentally ill people at the Erwady Moslem shrine near Madras, killing 25 patients and injuring 5 others, many of whom were chained to heavy stones or pillars (Associated Press, 2001). At the time of the fire, the asylum housed 46 residents; only 16 of the patients escaped uninjured.

health care in the community in place of the overcrowded mental hospitals. Also in 1946, the National Institutes of Mental Health was organized, and provided active support for research and training through psychiatric residencies and (later) clinical psychology training programs. Moreover, the Hill-Burton Act, a program that funded community mental health hospitals, was passed during this period. This legislation, along with the Community Health Services Act of 1963, helped to create a far-reaching set of programs to develop outpatient psychiatric clinics, inpatient facilities in general hospitals, and community consultation and rehabilitation programs.

The need for reform in psychiatric hospitals was a prominent concern of many professionals and laypersons alike during the 1950s and 1960s. A great deal of professional attention was given to the need to improve conditions in mental hospitals following the publication of another influential book, *Asylums,* by the sociologist Erving Goffman (1961). This book further exposed the inhumane treatment of mental patients, and provided a detailed account of neglect and maltreatment in mental hospitals. The movement to change the mental hospital environment was enhanced significantly by scientific advances in the last half of the twentieth century, particularly the development of effective medications for many disorders—for example, the use of lithium in the treatment of manic depressive disorders (Cade, 1949) and the introduction of phenothiazines for the treatment of schizophrenia. (See Developments in Research 2.4 and Chapter 17 for further discussion.)

During the latter decades of the twentieth century, our society had seemingly come full circle with respect to the means of providing humane care for the mentally ill in the hospital environment. Vigorous efforts were made to close down mental hospitals and return psychiatrically disturbed people to the community, ostensibly as a means of providing more integrated and humane treatment than was available in the "isolated" environment of the psychiatric hospital. Large numbers of psychiatric hospitals were closed, and there was a significant reduction in state and county mental hospital populations, from over half a million in 1950 (Lerman, 1981) to about 100,000 by the early 1990s (Narrow et al., 1993). These reductions are all the more impressive given that the U.S. population increased substantially over those years. This movement, referred to as **deinstitutionalization,** although motivated by benevolent goals, created great difficulties for many psychologically disturbed persons and for many communities as well (see Chapter 18).

As a phenomenon, deinstitutionalization is an international movement. For example, there has been a shift in the locus of care of patients with chronic psychiatric illnesses from psychiatric hospitals to community-based residential services in Hong Kong (Chan, 2001), in the

2.4 Developments in Research: The Search for Medications to Cure Mental Disorders

Although there are records of early efforts to use drugs to treat mental disorders, the effective use of medications has a very recent history. For centuries physicians have sought a medicinal cure for mental disorder. One of the earliest known treatises on the use of drugs to treat mental disorders is the work of the Roman physician Galen (A.D. 130–200). Galen coined the term *apotherapy* for the use of medications to treat human disorders, and his writing details both the concoction of various medications and the clinical use of drug therapy with patients experiencing mental disorders. Most of his medications were laxatives and emetics (purgatives) that were used to cleanse the body of nonhuman materials believed to be causing the person's ills. During the Middle Ages, another notable but highly controversial physician–chemist named Paracelsus (1490–1541) experimented with various chemicals as medications to treat human disorders. He even used a substance referred to as "mummy powder" (ground up particles of mummies) and various other, seemingly more potent substances such as mercury.

A more recent phase in the development of psychotropic medicine began in the 1950s. The root *Rauwolfia serpentina* had been used for centuries as an herbal folk medicine in India, where it had been prescribed for a wide array of afflictions, including serpent bites, epilepsy, cataracts, and insanity. The Indian name for the root, *pagla-ka-dawa,* means "insanity herb." In the early 1950s the active ingredient in *Rauwolfia,* reserpine, was isolated by Ciba, a Swiss drug company, and in 1953, the psychiatrist R. A. Hakim wrote a prize-winning paper in India on using *Rauwolfia* to treat psychosis (as cited in Gupta, Deb, & Kahali, 1943). Today reserpine has been surpassed as a treatment for psychoses because of the development of other drugs and because of its side effects, which include tremors, referred to as "Parkinsonian symptoms." Today reserpine is mostly used in the treatment of hypertension.

The second psychoactive drug to emerge in the 1950s as a treatment for severe mental disorder was chlorpromazine. A German chemist named Bernthesen, searching for compounds that would operate as dyes, first developed the drug in the latter part of the nineteenth century. He synthesized a compound that is referred to as "the phenothiazines." Paul Erlich, a medical researcher and father of the field of chemotherapy, thought that this compound might be effective in treating human diseases by killing nonhuman cells while preserving human tissue. The drug was first tried as a means of treating malaria, and by the 1930s it was being employed as an anesthetic because of its sedating qualities. In 1951, the French surgeon Henri Labroit employed the drug as an "artificial hibernator" to prevent shock among surgical patients. It was not until 1952 that two French psychiatrists, Jean Delay and Pierre Deniker, finding that the drug reduced psychotic symptoms, began to use chlorpromazine to treat psychiatric patients.

The almost magical impact of antipsychotic medication was immediately felt in the psychiatric community in the United States. By 1956, the first year of widespread use of reserpine and chlorpromazine, the impact on psychiatric hospitalization had begun to show a remarkable effect. The previously increasing admission rate to psychiatric hospitals leveled off at 560,000 psychiatric inpatients in the United States. This number dropped to 490,000 by 1964 and to 300,000 by 1971!

The effectiveness of drugs in reducing psychotic symptoms has also led researchers to develop more specific causal hypotheses for mental disorders such as schizophrenia. Researchers have noted that antipsychotic drugs such as the phenothiazines modify the levels of dopamine, a neurotransmitter associated with schizophrenia. These observations have led theoreticians to the "dopamine hypothesis"—that the metabolism of dopamine is associated with the cause of schizophrenia. This development will be discussed further in Chapter 14.

Sources: Frankenburg, 1994; Green, 1951; Moriarty, Alagna, & Lake, 1984; Pachter, 1951.

Netherlands (Pijl & Pijl, 2001), and in Finland (Korkeila, Lehtinen, et al., 1998). Some countries have experienced extensive deinstitutionalization over the past 20 years. For example, in England and Wales during the last decades of the nineteenth century, only 14 of 130 psychiatric institutions remained open; and Australia showed a 90 percent reduction in hospital beds over the same period (Goldney, 2003). In a follow-up study of patients from 22 hospitals in Italy, D'Avanzo, Barbato, et al. (2003) reported that all were closed and 39 percent of the patients in these hospitals had been discharged to nursing homes, 29 percent to residential facilities, and 29 percent to other psychiatric hospitals; only 2 percent were returned to their families.

The original impetus behind the deinstitutionalization policy was that it was considered more humane (and cost-effective) to treat disturbed people outside of large mental hospitals, because doing so would prevent people from acquiring negative adaptations to hospital confinement. Many professionals were concerned that the mental

Freed from the confines of institutionalized care, or abandoned by society? Many homeless people suffer from one or more mental disorders. Deinstitutionalization, though motivated by benevolent goals, has created great difficulties for many psychologically disturbed individuals who have been released to a cruel and harsh existence.

hospitals were becoming permanent refuges for disturbed people who were "escaping" from the demands of everyday living and were settling into a chronic sick role with a permanent excuse for letting other people take care of them. There was great hope that new medications would promote a healthy readjustment and enable former patients to live more productive lives outside the hospital. Many former patients have not fared well in community living, however, and authorities now frequently speak of the "abandonment" of chronic patients to a cruel and harsh existence. Evidence of this failure to treat psychiatric patients successfully in the community can be readily seen in our cities: Many of the people living on the streets in large cities today are homeless mentally ill. The problems caused by deinstitutionalization appear to be due, in no small part, to the failure of society to develop ways to fill the gaps in mental health services in the community (Grob, 1994).

The mental institution, once thought to be the most humane way to manage the problems of the severely mentally ill, came to be seen as obsolete or as an evil alternative, more of a problem than a solution to mental health problems. By the end of the twentieth century, inpatient mental hospitals had been substantially replaced by community-based care, day treatment hospitals, and outreach programs (King, 1999).

The twentieth century closed on a note of uncertainty with respect to the best ways to manage the needs of severely disturbed psychiatric patients. It is clear that closing mental hospitals and providing treatment for severely disturbed people in the community has not proved to be the panacea it was touted to be only a few years ago. As we will discuss further in Chapter 18, deinstitutionalization has created problems for both patients and society as a whole. The role of the psychiatric hospital in helping those with severe psychiatric problems is likely to undergo further evolution as society again finds itself unable to deal effectively with the problems that severe mental illness can create if ignored or left unattended (see Grob, 1994).

In Review

- Describe the changing views toward mental illness that evolved as scientific thinking came to have greater influence in Europe in the sixteenth and seventeenth centuries.
- Discuss the development of the psychiatric hospital.
- Describe the changes in social attitudes that brought about major changes in the way persons with mental disorders have been treated.

Contemporary Views of Abnormal Behavior

While the mental hygiene movement was gaining ground in the United States during the latter years of the nineteenth century, great technological discoveries occurred both at home and abroad. These advances helped usher in what we know today as the scientific, or experimentally oriented, view of abnormal behavior and the application of scientific knowledge to the treatment of disturbed individuals. We will describe four major themes in abnormal psychology that spanned the nineteenth and twentieth centuries and generated powerful influences on our contemporary perspectives in abnormal behavior: (1) biological discoveries, (2) the development of a classification system for mental disorders, (3) the emergence of psychological causation views, and (4) experimental psychological research developments.

Biological Discoveries: Establishing the Link between the Brain and Mental Disorder

Advances in the study of biological and anatomical factors as underlying both physical and mental disorders developed in this period. A major biomedical breakthrough, for example, came with the discovery of the organic factors underlying general paresis—syphilis of the brain. One of the most serious mental illnesses of the day, general paresis produced paralysis and insanity and typically caused death within 2–5 years. This scientific discovery, however, did not occur overnight; it required the combined efforts of many scientists and researchers for nearly a century.

GENERAL PARESIS AND SYPHILIS The discovery of a cure for general paresis began in 1825, when the French physician A. L. J. Bayle differentiated general paresis as a specific type of mental disorder. Bayle gave a complete and accurate description of the symptom pattern of paresis and convincingly presented his reasons for believing paresis to be a distinct disorder. Many years later, in 1897, the Viennese psychiatrist Richard von Krafft-Ebbing conducted experiments involving the inoculation of paretic patients with matter from syphilitic sores. None of the patients developed secondary symptoms of syphilis, which led to the conclusion that they must previously have been infected. This crucial experiment established the relationship between general paresis and syphilis. It was almost a decade later, in 1906, when August von Wassermann devised a blood test for syphilis. This development made it possible to check for the presence of the deadly bacteria in the bloodstream of an individual before the more serious consequences of infection appeared.

Finally, in 1917, Julius von Wagner-Jauregg, chief of the psychiatric clinic of the University of Vienna, introduced the malarial fever treatment of syphilis and paresis because he knew that the high fever associated with malaria killed off the bacteria. He infected nine paretic patients with the blood of a malaria-infected soldier and found marked improvement in paretic symptoms in three patients and apparent recovery in three others. By 1925 several hospitals in the United States were incorporating the new malarial treatment for paresis into their hospital treatments. One of the earliest controlled studies of malarial treatment for paresis was conducted by Bahr and Brutsch in Indiana in 1928. They found that out of the 100 patients studied, 37 percent of paresis patients showed significant recovery, 25 percent had been discharged, and 21 percent of those had returned to their previous or similar occupations. This treatment, though clearly effective in many paresis patients, was short-lived because of the introduction of effective medicines. Today, of course, we have penicillin as an effective, simpler treatment of syphilis, but the early malarial treatment represented the first clear-cut conquest of a mental disorder by medical science. The field of abnormal psychology had come a long way—from superstitious beliefs to scientific proof of how brain pathology can cause a specific disorder. This breakthrough raised great hopes in the medical community that organic bases would be found for many other mental disorders—perhaps for all of them.

BRAIN PATHOLOGY AS A CAUSAL FACTOR With the emergence of modern experimental science in the early part of the eighteenth century, knowledge of anatomy, physiology, neurology, chemistry, and general medicine increased rapidly. Scientists began to focus on diseased body organs as the cause of physical ailments. It was the next logical step for these researchers to assume that mental disorder was an illness based on the pathology of an organ—in this case, the brain. In 1757 Albrecht von Haller (1708–1777), in his *Elements of Physiology,* emphasized the importance of the brain in psychic functions and advocated postmortem dissection to study the brains of the insane. The first systematic presentation of this viewpoint, however, was made by the German psychiatrist Wilhelm Griesinger (1817–1868). In his textbook *The Pathology and Therapy of Psychic Disorders,* published in 1845, Griesinger insisted that all mental disorders could be explained in terms of brain pathology. Following the discovery that brain pathology resulted in general paresis, other successes followed. Alois Alzheimer and other investigators established the brain pathology in cerebral arteriosclerosis and in the senile mental disorders. Eventually, in the twentieth century, the organic pathologies underlying the toxic mental disorders (disorders caused by toxic substances such as lead), certain types of mental retardation, and other mental illnesses were discovered.

It is important to note here that although the discovery of the organic bases of mental disorders addressed the "how" behind causation, it did not, in most cases, address the "why." This is sometimes true even today. For example, although we know what causes certain "presenile" mental disorders—brain pathology—we do not yet know why some individuals are afflicted and others are not. Nonetheless, we can predict quite accurately the courses of these disorders. This ability is due not only to a greater understanding of the organic factors involved but also, in large part, to the work of a follower of Griesinger, Emil Kraepelin.

The Development of a Classification System

Emil Kraepelin (1856–1926) played a dominant role in the early development of the biological viewpoint. His textbook *Lehrbuch der Psychiatrie,* published in 1883, not only emphasized the importance of brain pathology in mental disorders but also made several related contributions that helped establish this viewpoint. The most important of these contributions was his system of classification of mental disorders, which became the forerunner of today's DSM-IV-TR (introduced in Chapter 1). Kraepelin noted that certain symptom patterns occurred together regularly enough to be regarded as specific types of mental disease. He then proceeded to describe and clarify these types of mental disorders, working out a scheme of classification that is the basis of our present system. Integrating all of the clinical material underlying this classification was a herculean task and represented a major contribution to the field of psychopathology.

Kraepelin saw each type of mental disorder as distinct from the others and thought that the course of each was as predetermined and predictable as the course of measles. Thus the outcome of a given type of disorder could presumably be predicted, even if it could not yet be controlled. Such claims led to widespread interest in the accurate description and classification of mental disorders.

Emil Kraepelin (1856–1926) was a German psychiatrist who developed an early synthesis and classification system of the hundreds of mental disorders by grouping diseases together based on common patterns of symptoms. Kraepelin also demonstrated that mental disorders showed specific patterns in the genetics, course, and outcome of disorders.

Causation Views: Establishing the Psychological Basis of Mental Disorder

Despite the emphasis on biological research, understanding of the psychological factors in mental disorders was progressing, too. The first major steps were taken by Sigmund Freud (1856–1939), the most frequently cited psychological theorist of the twentieth century (Street, 1994). During five decades of observation, treatment, and writing, Freud developed a comprehensive theory of psychopathology that emphasized the inner dynamics of unconscious motives (often referred to as *psychodynamics*) that are at the heart of the **psychoanalytic perspective.** The methods he used to study and treat patients came to be called **psychoanalysis.** We can trace the ancestral roots of psychoanalysis to a somewhat unexpected place—the study of hypnosis, especially in its relation to hysteria. Hypnosis, an induced state of relaxation in which a person is highly open to suggestion, first came into widespread use in late-eighteenth- and early-nineteenth-century France.

MESMERISM Our efforts to understand psychological causation of mental disorder start with Franz Anton Mesmer (1734–1815), an Austrian physician who further developed the ideas of Paracelsus (the influential sixteenth-century physician and scholar) about the influence of the planets on the human body. Mesmer believed that the planets affected a universal magnetic fluid in the body, the distribution of which determined health or disease. In attempting to find cures for mental disorders, Mesmer concluded that all people possessed magnetic forces that could be used to influence the distribution of the magnetic fluid in other people, thus effecting cures.

Mesmer attempted to put his views into practice in Vienna and various other cities, but it was in Paris in 1778 that he gained a broad following. There he opened a clinic in which he treated all kinds of diseases by using "animal magnetism." In a dark room, patients were seated around a tub containing various chemicals, and iron rods protruding from the tub were applied to the affected areas of the patients' bodies. Accompanied by music, Mesmer appeared in a lilac robe, passing from one patient to another and touching each one with his hands or his wand. By this means, Mesmer was reportedly able to remove hysterical anesthesias and paralyses. He also demonstrated most of the phenomena later connected with the use of hypnosis.

Eventually branded a charlatan by his medical colleagues and an appointed body of noted scholars that included the American scientist Benjamin Franklin (Van

Mesmer believed that the distribution of magnetic fluid in the body was responsible for determining health or disease. He further thought that all people possessed magnetic forces that could be used to influence the distribution of fluid in others, thus effecting cures. In this painting of his therapy, Mesmer stands on the far right, holding a wand. He was eventually branded a fraud by his colleagues. His theories did, however, demonstrate most of the phenomena later connected with the use of hypnosis.

Doren, 1938), Mesmer was forced to leave Paris and quickly faded into obscurity. His methods and results, however, were at the center of scientific controversy for many years—in fact, **mesmerism,** as his technique came to be known, was as much a source of heated discussion in the early nineteenth century as psychoanalysis became in the early twentieth century. This discussion led to renewed interest in hypnosis itself as an explanation of the "cures" that took place.

THE NANCY SCHOOL Ambrose August Liébeault (1823–1904), a French physician who practiced in the town of Nancy, used hypnosis successfully in his practice. Also in Nancy at the time was a professor of medicine, Hippolyte Bernheim (1840–1919), who became interested in the relationship between hysteria and hypnosis. His interest was piqued by Liébeault's success in using hypnosis to cure a patient whom Bernheim had been treating unsuccessfully by more conventional methods for 4 years (Selling, 1943). Bernheim and Liébeault worked together to develop the hypothesis that hypnotism and hysteria were related and that both were due to suggestion (Brown & Menninger, 1940). Their hypothesis was based on two lines of evidence: (1) The phenomena observed in hysteria—such as paralysis of an arm, inability to hear, and anesthetic areas in which an individual could be stuck with a pin without feeling pain (all of which occurred when there was apparently nothing organically wrong)—could be produced in normal subjects by means of hypnosis. (2) The same symptoms also could be removed by means of hypnosis. Thus it seemed likely that hysteria was a sort of self-hypnosis. The physicians who accepted this view ultimately came to be known as the **Nancy School.**

Meanwhile, Jean Charcot (1825–1893), who was head of the Salpêtrière Hospital in Paris and the leading neurologist of his time, had been experimenting with some of the phenomena described by the mesmerists. As a result of his research, Charcot disagreed with the findings of the Nancy School and insisted that degenerative brain changes led to hysteria. In this, Charcot was eventually proved wrong, but work on the problem by so outstanding a scientist did a great deal to awaken medical and scientific interest in hysteria.

The dispute between Charcot and the Nancy School was one of the major debates of medical history, and many harsh words were spoken on both sides. The adherents to the Nancy School finally triumphed. This first recognition of a psychologically caused mental disorder spurred more research on the behavior underlying hysteria and other disorders. Soon it was suggested that psychological factors were also involved in anxiety states, phobias, and other psychopathologies. Eventually, Charcot himself was won over to the new point of view and did much to promote the study of psychological factors in various mental disorders.

The debate over whether mental disorders are caused by biological or psychological factors continues to this day. The Nancy School/Charcot debate represented a major step forward for psychology, however. Toward the end of the nineteenth century, it became clear that mental disorders could have psychological bases, biological bases, or both. But a major question remained to be answered: How do the psychologically based mental disorders actually develop?

THE BEGINNINGS OF PSYCHOANALYSIS The first systematic attempt to answer this question was made by Sigmund Freud (1856–1939). Freud was a brilliant young Viennese neurologist who received an appointment as lecturer on nervous diseases at the University of Vienna. In 1885 he went to study under Charcot and later became acquainted with the work of Liébeault and Bernheim at Nancy. He was impressed by their use of hypnosis with hysterical patients and came away convinced that powerful mental processes could remain hidden from consciousness.

On his return to Vienna, Freud worked in collaboration with another physician, Josef Breuer (1842–1925), who had incorporated an interesting innovation into the use of hypnosis with his patients. Unlike hypnotists before them, Freud and Breuer directed patients to talk freely about their problems while under hypnosis. The patients usually displayed considerable emotion and, on awakening from their hypnotic states, felt a significant emotional release, which was called a **catharsis.** This simple innovation in the use of hypnosis proved to be of great significance: It not only helped patients discharge their emotional tensions by discussing their problems but also revealed to the therapist the nature of the difficulties that had brought about certain symptoms. The patients, on awakening, saw no relationship between their problems and their hysterical symptoms.

It was this approach that thus led to the discovery of the **unconscious**—the portion of the mind that contains experiences of which a person is unaware—and with it the belief that processes outside of a person's awareness can play an important role in determining behavior. In 1893 Freud and Breuer published their joint paper *On the Psychical Mechanisms of Hysterical Phenomena,* which was one of the great milestones in the study of the dynamics of the conscious and unconscious. Freud soon discovered, moreover, that he could dispense with hypnosis entirely. By encouraging patients to say whatever came into their minds without regard to logic or propriety, Freud found that patients would eventually overcome inner obstacles to remembering and would discuss their problems freely.

Two related methods enabled him to understand patients' conscious and unconscious thought processes. One method, **free association,** involved having patients talk freely about themselves, thereby providing information about their feelings, motives, and so forth. A second method, **dream analysis,** involved having patients record and describe their dreams. These techniques helped analysts and patients gain insights and achieve a better understanding of the patients' emotional problems. Freud devoted the rest of his long and energetic life to the development and elaboration of psychoanalytic principles. His views were formally introduced to American scientists in 1909, when he was invited to deliver a series of lectures at Clark University by the eminent psychologist G. Stanley Hall, who was then president of the university. These lectures created a great deal of controversy and helped popularize psychoanalytic concepts with scientists as well as with the general public.

We will discuss the psychoanalytic viewpoint further in Chapter 3. Freud's lively and seminal views attracted a substantial following over his long career, and interest in his ideas persists today, more than 100 years after he began writing. Numerous other clinician-theorists—such as Carl Jung, Alfred Adler, and Harry Stack Sullivan—launched

Psychoanalysis was introduced to North America at a famous meeting at Clark University in Worcester, Massachusetts, in 1909. Among those present were (back row) A. A. Brill, Ernest Jones, and Sandor Ferenczi; (front row) Sigmund Freud, G. Stanley Hall, and Carl Jung.

"spin-off" theories that have elaborated on the psychoanalytic viewpoint. More will also be said of these views in Chapter 3. Here we will examine the early development of psychological research and explore the evolution of the behavioral perspective on abnormal behavior.

The Evolution of the Psychological Research Tradition: Experimental Psychology

The origins of much of the scientific thinking in contemporary psychology lie in early rigorous efforts to study psychological processes objectively, as demonstrated by Wilhelm Wundt (1832–1920) and William James (1842–1910). Although the early work of these experimental psychologists did not bear directly on clinical practice or on our understanding of abnormal behavior, this tradition was clearly influential a few decades later in molding the thinking of the psychologists who brought these rigorous attitudes into the clinic. (For a discussion of the history of clinical psychology, see Benjamin, 2005.)

THE EARLY PSYCHOLOGY LABORATORIES In 1879 Wilhelm Wundt established the first experimental psychology laboratory at the University of Leipzig. While studying the psychological factors involved in memory and sensation, Wundt and his colleagues devised many basic experimental methods and strategies. Wundt directly influenced early contributors to the empirical study of abnormal behavior; they followed his experimental methodology and also applied some of his research strategies to study clinical problems. For example, a student of Wundt's, J. McKeen Cattell (1860–1944), brought Wundt's experimental methods to the United States and used them to assess individual differences in mental processing. He and other students of Wundt's work established research laboratories throughout the United States.

It was not until 1896, however, that another of Wundt's students, Lightner Witmer (1867–1956), combined research with application and established the first American psychological clinic at the University of Pennsylvania. Witmer's clinic focused on the problems of mentally deficient children in terms of both research and therapy. Witmer, considered to be the founder of clinical psychology (McReynolds, 1996, 1997), was influential in encouraging others to become involved in this new profession. Other clinics were soon established. One clinic of great importance was the Chicago Juvenile Psychopathic Institute (later called the "Institute of Juvenile Research"), established in 1909 by William Healy (1869–1963). Healy was the first to view juvenile delinquency as a symptom of urbanization, not as a result of inner psychological problems. In so doing, he was among the first to recognize a new area of causation—environmental, or sociocultural, factors.

By the first decade of the twentieth century, psychological laboratories and clinics were burgeoning, and a great deal of research was being generated (Reisman, 1991). The rapid and objective communication of scientific findings was perhaps as important in the development of modern psychology as the collection and interpretation of research findings. This period saw the origin of many scientific journals for the propagation of research and theoretical discoveries. Two notable publications in the field of abnormal psychology were the *Journal of Abnormal Psychology,* founded by Morton Prince in 1906, and *The Psychological Clinic,* founded by Lightner Witmer in 1907. As the years have passed, the number of journals has grown. The American Psychological Association now publishes 38 scientific journals, many of which focus on research into abnormal behavior and personality functioning.

THE BEHAVIORAL PERSPECTIVE Although psychoanalysis dominated thought about abnormal behavior at the end of the nineteenth century and in the early twentieth century, another school—behaviorism—emerged out of experimental psychology to challenge its supremacy. Behavioral psychologists believed that the study of subjective experience—through the techniques of free association and dream analysis—did not provide acceptable scientific data, because such observations were not open to verification by other investigators. In their view, only the study of directly observable behavior—and the stimuli and reinforcing conditions that "control" it—could serve as a basis for formulating scientific principles of human behavior.

The **behavioral perspective** is organized around a central theme: the role of learning in human behavior. Although this perspective was initially developed through research in the laboratory rather than through clinical practice with disturbed individuals, its implications for explaining and treating maladaptive behavior soon became evident.

Classical Conditioning The origins of the behavioral view of abnormal behavior and its treatment are tied to experimental work on the type of learning known as **classical conditioning**—a form of learning in which a neutral stimulus is paired repeatedly with an unconditioned stimulus that naturally elicits an unconditioned behavior. After repeated pairings, the neutral stimulus becomes a conditioned stimulus that elicits a conditioned response. This work began with the discovery of the conditioned reflex by Russian physiologist Ivan Pavlov (1849–1936). Around the turn of the twentieth century, Pavlov demonstrated that dogs would gradually begin to salivate in response to a nonfood stimulus such as a bell after the stimulus had been regularly accompanied by food.

Pavlov's discoveries in classical conditioning excited a young American psychologist, John B. Watson (1878–1958), who was searching for objective ways to study human behavior. Watson reasoned that if psychology was to become a true science, it would have to abandon the subjectivity of inner sensations and other "mental" events and

Ivan Pavlov (1849–1936), a pioneer in demonstrating the part conditioning plays in behavior, is shown here with the staff and some of the apparatus used to condition reflexes in dogs.

limit itself to what could be objectively observed. What better way to do this than to observe systematic changes in behavior brought about simply by rearranging stimulus conditions? Watson thus changed the focus of psychology to the study of overt behavior rather than the study of theoretical mentalistic constructs, an approach he called **behaviorism.**

Watson, a man of impressive energy and demeanor, saw great possibilities in behaviorism, and he was quick to point them out to his fellow scientists and a curious public. He boasted that through conditioning, he could train any healthy child to become whatever sort of adult one wished. He also challenged the psychoanalysts and the more biologically oriented psychologists of his day by suggesting that abnormal behavior was the product of unfortunate, inadvertent earlier conditioning and could be modified through reconditioning.

By the 1930s Watson had had an enormous impact on American psychology. Watson's approach placed heavy emphasis on the role of the social environment in conditioning personality development and behavior, both normal and abnormal. Today's behaviorally oriented psychologists still accept many of the basic tenets of Watson's doctrine, although they are more cautious in their claims. Why do you think this is?

Operant Conditioning While Pavlov and Watson were studying antecedent stimulus conditions and their relation to behavioral responses, E. L. Thorndike (1874–1949) and subsequently B. F. Skinner (1904–1990) were exploring a different kind of conditioning, one in which the consequences of behavior influence behavior. Behavior that operates on the environment may be instrumental in producing certain outcomes, and those outcomes, in turn,

B. F. Skinner (1904–1990) formulated the concept of operant conditioning, in which reinforcers could be used to make a response more or less probable and frequent.

determine the likelihood that the behavior will be repeated on similar occasions. For example, Thorndike studied how cats could learn a particular response, such as pulling a chain, if that response was followed by food reinforcement. This type of learning came to be called "instrumental conditioning" and was later renamed **operant conditioning** by Skinner. Both terms are still used today. In Skinner's view, behavior is "shaped" when something reinforces a particular activity of an organism—which makes it possible "to shape an animal's behavior almost as a sculptor shapes a lump of clay" (Skinner, 1951, pp. 26–27).

In this chapter we have touched on several important trends in the evolution of the field of abnormal psychology and have recounted the contributions of numerous individuals from history who have shaped our current views. The vast amount of information available can cause confusion and controversy when efforts are made to obtain an integrated view of behavior and causation. We may have left supernatural beliefs behind, but we have moved into something far more complex in trying to determine the role of natural factors—be they biological, psychological, or sociocultural—in abnormal behavior. For a recap of some of the key contributors to the field of abnormal psychology, see Table 2.1.

In Review

- Compare the views of the Nancy School with those of Charcot. How did this debate influence modern psychology?
- Evaluate the impact of the work of Freud and that of Watson on psychology today.
- How did early experimental science help to establish brain pathology as a causal factor in mental disorders?

TABLE 2.1 Major Figures in the Early History of Abnormal Psychology

The Ancient World

Hippocrates

Hippocrates (460–377 B.C.) A Greek physician who believed that mental disease was the result of natural causes and brain pathology rather than demonology.

Plato (429–347 B.C.) A Greek philosopher who believed that mental patients should be treated humanely and should not be held responsible for their actions.

Aristotle (384–322 B.C.) A Greek philosopher and a pupil of Plato who believed in the Hippocratic theory that various agents, or humors, within the body, when imbalanced, were responsible for mental disorders. Aristotle rejected the notion of psychological factors as causes of mental disorders.

Galen (A.D. 130–200) A Greek physician and advocate of the Hippocratic tradition who contributed much to our understanding of the nervous system. Galen divided the causes of mental disorders into physical and mental categories.

Galen

The Middle Ages

Avicenna

Avicenna (980–1037) An Islamic Arabian-born physician who adopted principles of humane treatment for the mentally disturbed at a time when Western approaches to mental illness were inhumane.

Martin Luther (1483–1546) A German theologian and leader of the Reformation who held the belief, common in his time, that the mentally disturbed were possessed by the devil.

Paracelsus (1490–1541) A Swiss physician who rejected demonology as a cause of abnormal behavior. Paracelsus believed in psychic causes of mental illness.

The Sixteenth through the Eighteenth Centuries

Teresa of Avila (1515–1582) A Spanish nun, since canonized, who argued that mental disorder was an illness of the mind.

(continued)

TABLE 2.1 (continued)

Johann Weyer (1515–1588) A German physician who argued against demonology and was ostracized by his peers and the Church for his progressive views.

Reginald Scot (1538–1599) An Englishman who refuted the notion of demons as the cause of mental disorders and was castigated by King James I.

Robert Burton (1576–1640) An Oxford scholar who wrote a classic, influential treatise on depression, *The Anatomy of Melancholia,* in 1621.

William Tuke (1732–1822) An English Quaker who established the York Retreat, where mental patients lived in humane surroundings.

Philippe Pinel (1745–1826) A French physician who pioneered the use of moral management in La Bicêtre and La Salpêtrière hospitals in France, where mental patients were treated in a humane way.

Benjamin Rush (1745–1813) An American physician and the founder of American psychiatry who used moral management, based on Pinel's humanitarian methods, to treat the mentally disturbed.

Benjamin Rush

The Nineteenth and Early Twentieth Centuries

Dorothea Dix

Dorothea Dix (1802–1887) An American teacher who founded the mental hygiene movement in the United States, which focused on the physical well-being of mental patients in hospitals.

Clifford Beers (1876–1943) An American who campaigned to change public attitudes toward mental patients after his own experiences in mental institutions.

Franz Anton Mesmer (1734–1815) An Austrian physician who conducted early investigations into hypnosis as a medical treatment.

Emil Kraepelin (1856–1926) A German psychiatrist who developed the first diagnostic system.

Sigmund Freud (1856–1939) The founder of the school of psychological therapy known as "psychoanalysis."

Sigmund Freud

Wilhelm Wundt (1832–1920) A German scientist who established the first experimental psychology laboratory in 1879 and subsequently influenced the empirical study of abnormal behavior.

J. McKeen Cattell (1860–1944) An American psychologist who adopted Wundt's methods and studied individual differences in mental processing.

Lightner Witmer (1867–1956) An American psychologist who established the first psychological clinic in the United States, focusing on problems of mentally deficient children. He also founded the journal *The Psychological Clinic* in 1896.

Ivan Pavlov (1849–1936) A Russian physiologist who published classical studies in the psychology of learning.

William Healy (1869–1963) An American psychologist who established the Chicago Juvenile Psychopathic Institute and advanced the idea that mental illness was due to environmental, or sociocultural, factors.

John B. Watson (1878–1958) An American psychologist who conducted early research into learning principles and came to be known as the father of behaviorism.

John B. Watson

UNRESOLVED ISSUES

Interpreting Historical Events

Understanding current events and phenomena depends to a substantial degree on having an accurate understanding of the historical development of knowledge. Many psychologists hold the view that psychological theorizing can be advanced by greater use of historical data (McGuire, 1994). This chapter has attempted to provide a historical perspective on some of the concepts you will encounter in the chapters that follow. You might think that looking back in history to get a picture of events that occurred long ago would not be a difficult task—that it would be a simple matter of reviewing some history books and some publications from the time in question. Those who try to understand the historical context of particular phenomena or ideas are sometimes confronted with what Burton (2001) referred to as the tenacity of historical misinformation. He pointed out that there is one discouraging theme in the history of science—the widespread acceptance of false accounts. He noted that it is not uncommon for psychological findings and theories to be exaggerated or distorted and that the exaggerations frequently spread much further through public sources than do the authentic facts. For example, he noted the widespread acceptance, and inclusion in many textbooks, of inaccurate restatements of the widely cited study of Little Albert's fear of furry objects:

Little Albert

> Little Albert was the famous toddler who, originally unafraid of rats, exhibited such a fear when J. B. Watson and Rayner (1920) paired the presence of a rat with a loud noise. Harris (1979), Samelson (1980), and Gilovich (1991) are among the critics who have noted how frequently and consistently this case is misrepresented and exaggerated, in particular in terms of the permanence of Little Albert's fear (which is actually unknown, because the child was withdrawn from the study), the reversal of his fear (which was never attempted), and the generalization of Albert's fear of rats to other objects. J. B. Watson and Rayner described pairing the loud noise with the rat and later testing Albert's reaction to a rat and a rabbit, as well as to blocks, a seal coat, cotton wool, the hair of Watson and some assistants, and a Santa Claus mask. Albert never reacted to the blocks or the assistants' hair, always reacted to the rat, and reacted to the other objects with various degrees of agitation that were sometimes vividly described but sometimes merely (and vaguely) termed "negative reaction." According to Harris (1979, p. 153), secondary sources have erroneously reported the testing of "a fur pelt, . . . a man's beard, . . . a cat, a pup, a fur muff, . . . a white furry glove, . . . Albert's aunt, who supposedly wore fur, . . . either the fur coat or the fur neckpiece of Albert's mother, . . . and even a teddy bear." (pp. 228–29)

Another factor that can affect the quality of historical information is that our views of history and our understanding of events are sometimes open to reinterpretation. As Schudson (1995) pointed out, "Collective memory, more than individual memory, at least in liberal pluralistic societies, is provisional. It is always open to contestation" (p. 16). Any number of obstacles can stand in the way of our gaining an accurate picture of the attitudes and behaviors of people who lived hundreds of years ago. This has certainly been the case with our views of the Middle Ages (Kroll & Bachrach, 1984).

The foremost problem in retrospective psychological analysis is that we cannot rely on direct observation, a hallmark of psychological research. Instead, we must turn to written documents or historical surveys of the times. Although these sources are often full of fascinating information, they may not reveal directly the information we seek; we must therefore extrapolate "facts" from the information we have, which is not always an easy task. We are restricted in our conclusions by the documents or sources available to us. Attempting to learn about people's attitudes and subtle social perceptions hundreds of years ago by examining surviving church documents or biographical accounts is less than ideal. First, we inevitably view these documents out of the context in which they were written. Second, we do not know whether the authors had ulterior motives or what the real purposes of the documents were. For example, some historians have concluded erroneously that people of the Middle Ages considered sin to be a major causal factor in mental illness. This misconception may have been due in part to zealous authors invoking "God's punishment" against the victims of mental illnesses who happened to be their enemies. Apparently, if the victims happened to be friends, sin was typically not mentioned as a causal factor (Kroll & Bachrach, 1984). Such writings, of course, are biased, but we may have no way of knowing this. The fewer the sources surveyed, the more likely that any existing bias will go undetected.

In other cases, concepts important to historical interpretation may have quite a different meaning to us today than they had in the past. Or the meaning may simply be unclear. Kroll and Bachrach (1984) pointed out that the concept of "possession," so critical to our views of the Middle Ages, is a very vague and complex concept for which we have no helpful natural models. Our language fails us, except for colorful analogies and metaphors. Just as the term *nervous breakdown* means different things to different people, so too *possession* means and meant many different things and undoubtedly had a different range of meanings to medieval persons from what it has to us. This kind of

(continued)

uncertainty can make definitive assessments of things that happened during the Middle Ages difficult, if not impossible (Phillips, 2002).

Bias can come into play during interpretation also. Our interpretations of historical events or previously held beliefs can be colored by our own views of what is normal and what is abnormal. In fact, it is difficult to conduct a retrospective analysis without taking current perspectives and values as a starting point. For example, our modern beliefs about the Middle Ages have led, says Schoeneman (1984), to our contemporary misinterpretation that during the fifteenth and sixteenth centuries, the mentally ill were typically accused of being witches. For most of us, this mistaken interpretation makes sense simply because we do not understand the medieval perspective on witchcraft.

Although reevaluations of the Middle Ages have discredited the view that demonology, sin, and witchcraft played key roles in the medieval understanding of mental illness, it is also clear that in some cases, these concepts were associated with mental illness. Where does the truth lie? It appears that the last word has not been written on the Middle Ages, nor on any period of our history, for that matter. At best, historical views—and, therefore, retrospective psychological studies—must be regarded as working hypotheses that are open to change as new perspectives are applied to history and as "new" historical documents are discovered.

summary

- Understanding of abnormal behavior has not evolved smoothly or uniformly over the centuries; the steps have been uneven with great gaps between, and unusual—even bizarre—views or beliefs have often sidetracked researchers and theorists.
- The dominant social, economic, and religious views of the times have had a profound influence over how people view abnormal behavior.
- In the ancient world, superstitious explanations for mental disorders were followed by the emergence of medical concepts in many places such as Egypt and Greece; many of these concepts were developed and refined by Roman physicians.
- After the fall of Rome near the end of the fifth century A.D., superstitious views dominated popular thinking about mental disorders for over 1,000 years. In the fifteenth and sixteenth centuries, it was still widely believed, even by scholars, that some mentally disturbed people were possessed by a devil.
- Great strides have been made in our understanding of abnormal behavior. For example, during the latter part of the Middle Ages and the early Renaissance, a spirit of scientific questioning reappeared in Europe, and several noted physicians spoke out against inhumane treatments. There was a general movement away from superstitions and "magic" toward reasoned, scientific studies.
- With recognition of a need for the special treatment of disturbed people came the founding of various "asylums" toward the end of the sixteenth century. However, institutionalization brought the isolation and maltreatment of mental patients. Slowly this situation was recognized, and in the eighteenth century, further efforts were made to help afflicted individuals by providing them with better living conditions and humane treatment, although these improvements were the exception rather than the rule.
- The reform of mental hospitals continued into the twentieth century, but over the last four decades of the century there was a strong movement to close mental hospitals and release people into the community. This movement remains controversial here in the early part of the twenty-first century.
- The nineteenth and early twentieth centuries witnessed a number of scientific and humanitarian advances. The work of Philippe Pinel in France, of William Tuke in England, and of Benjamin Rush and Dorothea Dix in the United States prepared the way for several important developments in contemporary abnormal psychology. Among these were the gradual acceptance of mental patients as afflicted individuals who need and deserve professional attention; the successful application of biomedical methods to disorders; and the growth of scientific research into the biological, psychological, and sociocultural roots of abnormal behavior.
- In the nineteenth century, great technological discoveries and scientific advancements that were made in the biological sciences enhanced the understanding and treatment of disturbed individuals. A major biomedical breakthrough, for example, came with the discovery of the organic factors underlying general paresis—syphilis of the brain—one of the most serious mental illnesses of the day.
- In the early part of the eighteenth century, knowledge of anatomy, physiology, neurology, chemistry, and general medicine increased rapidly. These advances

led to the identification of the biological, or organic, pathology underlying many physical ailments.

- The development of a psychiatric classification system by Kraepelin played a dominant role in the early development of the biological viewpoint. Kraepelin's work (a forerunner to the DSM system) helped to establish the importance of brain pathology in mental disorders and made several related contributions that helped establish this viewpoint.
- The first major steps toward understanding psychological factors in mental disorders were taken by Sigmund Freud. During five decades of observation, treatment, and writing, he developed a theory of psychopathology, known as "psychoanalysis," that emphasized the inner dynamics of unconscious motives. Over the last half-century, other clinicians have modified and revised Freud's theory, which has thus evolved into new psychodynamic perspectives.
- Scientific investigation into psychological factors and human behavior began to make progress in the latter part of the nineteenth century. The end of the nineteenth century and the early twentieth century saw experimental psychology evolve into clinical psychology with the development of clinics to study, as well as intervene in, abnormal behavior.
- Two major schools of learning paralleled this development, and behaviorism emerged as an explanatory model in abnormal psychology. The behavioral perspective is organized around a central theme—that learning plays an important role in human behavior. Although this perspective was initially developed through research in the laboratory (unlike psychoanalysis, which emerged out of clinical practice with disturbed individuals), it has been shown to have important implications for explaining and treating maladaptive behavior.
- Understanding the history of psychopathology, its forward steps and missteps alike, helps us understand the emergence of modern concepts of abnormal behavior.

Key Terms

chapter

3

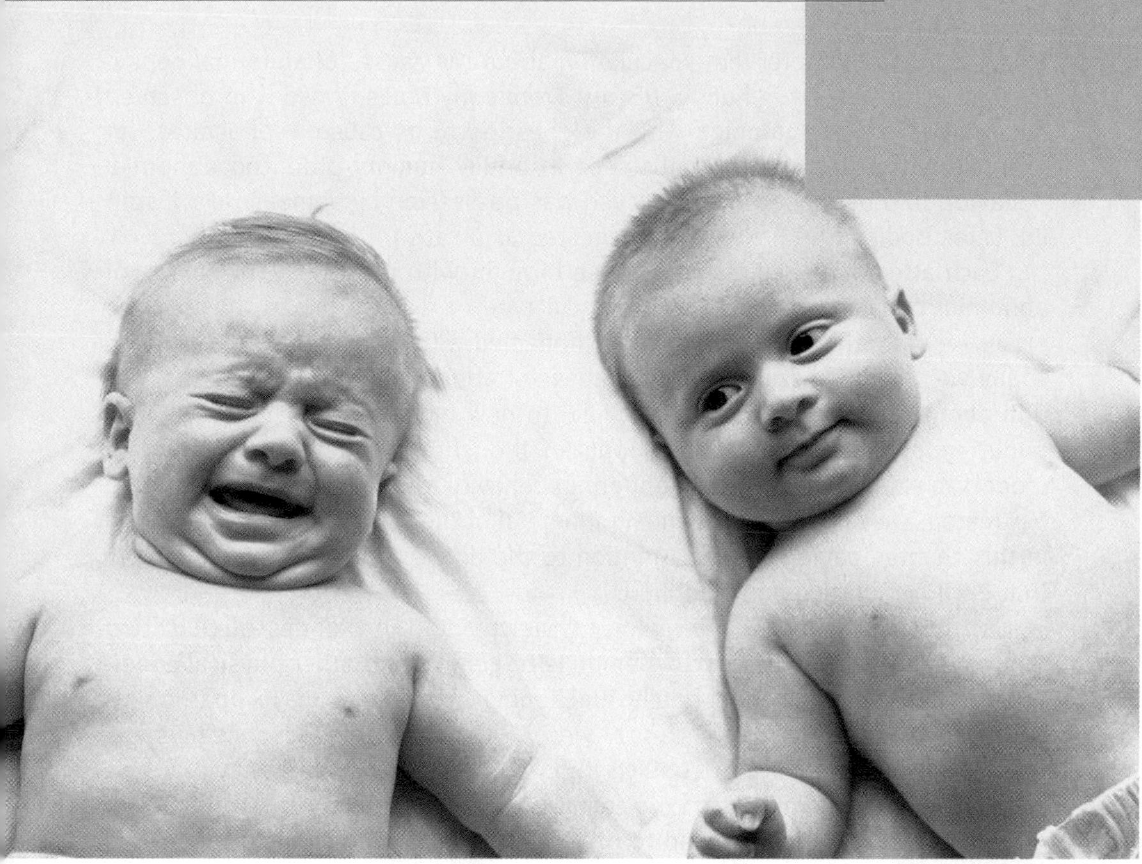

Causal Factors and Viewpoints

We saw in the last chapter that speculation about the causes of abnormal behavior goes back very far in human history. From early times, those who observed disordered behavior grappled with the question of its cause. Hippocrates, for example, suggested that an imbalance in bodily humors produced abnormal behavior. To other observers, the cause was possession by demons or evil spirits. Later, bodily dysfunction was suggested as a cause.

Each attempt at identifying a cause brought with it a theory, or model, of abnormal behavior. Hippocrates' theory, a type of disease model, posited the existence of four bodily humors, each connected with certain kinds of behavior. Today we are still puzzling over the causes of abnormal behavior, and speculation about causes continues to give rise to new models of abnormality. Since about 1900, several important schools of thought have developed elaborate models to explain the origins of abnormal behavior and to suggest how it might be treated. We will discuss the most influential of these theoretical perspectives in this chapter, paying special attention to the different types of causal factors that each perspective has identified.

We will first consider the biological viewpoint. The theories of causation that emerge from this perspective emphasize genetic and other physical conditions that impair brain and bodily functioning and lead to psychopathology. Next we will move on to psychosocial viewpoints: The psychodynamic perspective focuses on intrapsychic conflicts that lead to anxiety, the behavioral perspective on faulty learning, and the cognitive-behavioral perspective on types of information processing that lead to distorted thinking. We will look, too, at the sociocultural viewpoint, which focuses on pathological social conditions and on the importance of differing cultural backgrounds in shaping both vulnerability to psychopathology and the form that psychopathology may take. First, however, we need to address the very nature of the concept of causation as it is applied to abnormal behavior.

Causes and Risk Factors for Abnormal Behavior

Central to the field of abnormal psychology are questions about what causes people to behave maladaptively. If we knew the causes for given disorders, we might be able to prevent conditions that lead to them and perhaps reverse those that maintain them. We could also classify and diagnose disorders better if we clearly understood their causes rather than relying on clusters of symptoms, as we usually do now.

Although understanding the causes of abnormal behavior is clearly a desirable goal, it is enormously difficult to achieve because human behavior is so complex. Even the simplest human behavior, such as speaking or writing a single word, is the product of thousands of prior events—the connections among which are not always clear. Attempting to understand a person's life, even an "adaptive" life, in causal terms is a task of enormous magnitude; when the life is a maladaptive one, it is even more difficult. As a result, many investigators now prefer to speak of risk factors (variables correlated with an abnormal outcome) rather than of causes. Nevertheless, understanding causes remains the ultimate goal.

Necessary, Sufficient, and Contributory Causes

Regardless of one's theoretical perspective, several terms can be used to specify the role a factor plays in the **etiology,** or causal pattern, of abnormal behavior. A **necessary cause** (e.g., cause X) is a condition that must exist for a disorder (e.g., disorder Y) to occur. For example, general paresis (Y)—a degenerative brain disorder—cannot develop unless a person has previously contracted syphilis (X). Or more generally, if Y occurs, then X must have preceded it. Another example is post-traumatic stress disorder (PTSD)—one of the anxiety disorders—which cannot develop unless someone has experienced a severe trau-

Necessary Cause	If Disorder Y occurs, then Cause X must have preceded it.
Sufficient Cause	If Cause X occurs, then Disorder Y will also occur.
Contributory Cause	If X occurs, then the probability of Disorder Y increases.

FIGURE 3.1
Abnormal Behavior: Types of Causes

matic event. A necessary cause, however, is not always sufficient by itself to cause a disorder; other factors may also be required such as in PTSD, where several psychological and social variables determine which individuals undergoing such an event develop the disorder. Many mental disorders do not seem to have necessary causes, although there continues to be a search for such causes.

A **sufficient cause** (e.g., cause X) of a disorder is a condition that guarantees the occurrence of a disorder (e.g., disorder Y). For example, one current theory hypothesizes that hopelessness (X) is a sufficient cause of depression (Y); (Abramson, Alloy, & Metalsky, 1995; Abramson, Metalsky, & Alloy, 1989). Or, more generally, if X occurs, then Y will also occur. According to this theory, if you are hopeless enough about your future, then you will become depressed. However, a sufficient cause may not be a necessary cause. Continuing with the depression example, Abramson and colleagues (1989) acknowledge that hopelessness is not a necessary cause of depression; there are other causes of depression as well.

Finally, what we study most often in psychopathology research are **contributory causes.** A contributory cause (e.g., cause X) is one that increases the probability of a disorder (e.g., disorder Y) developing but is neither necessary nor sufficient for the disorder to occur. Or, more generally, if X occurs, then the probability of Y increases. For example, parental rejection could increase the probability that a child will later have difficulty in handling close personal relationships or could increase the probability that being rejected in a relationship in adulthood will precipitate depression. We say here that parental rejection is a contributory cause for the person's later difficulties, but it is neither necessary nor sufficient (Abramson et al., 1989; Abramson et al., 1995).

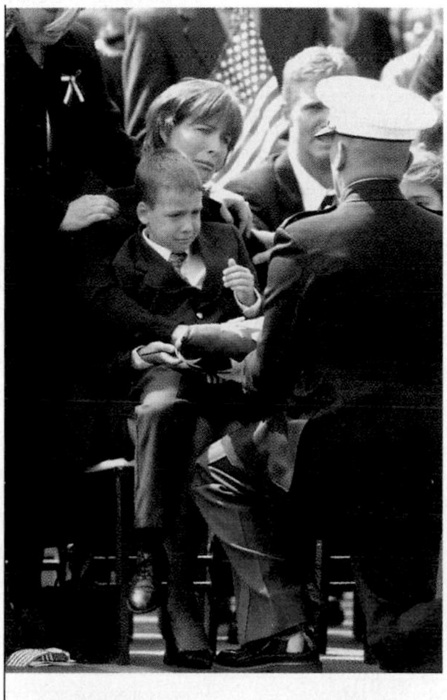

The loss of a parent at an early age may be a contributory cause for a child to develop depression in adulthood. Factors that may not show their effects for many years are called distal causal factors.

In addition to distinguishing among necessary, sufficient, and contributory causes of abnormal behavior, we must also consider the time frame under which the different causes operate. Some causal factors occurring relatively early in life may not show their effects for many years; these would be considered *distal causal factors* that may contribute to a predisposition to develop a disorder. For example, loss of a parent early in life, or having abusive or neglectful parents as a child, may serve as a distal contributory cause predisposing the person to depression or antisocial behaviors in adulthood. By contrast, other causal factors operate shortly before the occurrence of the symptoms of a disorder; these would be considered *proximal causal factors*. Sometimes a proximal causal factor may be a condition that proves too much for a person and triggers the onset of a disorder. A crushing disappointment at work or school, or severe marital difficulties are examples of more proximal causal factors that could lead to depression. In other cases, proximal factors might involve biological changes such as damage to certain parts of the left hemisphere of the brain, which can lead to depression.

A *reinforcing* contributory cause is a condition that tends to maintain maladaptive behavior that is already occurring. An example is the extra attention, sympathy, and relief from unwanted responsibility that may come when a person is ill; these pleasant experiences may unintentionally discourage recovery. Another example occurs when a depressed person's behavior alienates friends and family, leading to a greater sense of rejection that reinforces the existing depression (Joiner, 2002; Joiner & Metalsky, 1995).

For many forms of psychopathology, we do not yet have a clear understanding of whether there are necessary or sufficient causes, although answering this question remains the goal of much current research. However, we do have a good understanding of many of the contributory causes for most forms of psychopathology. Some of the distal contributory causes, to be discussed later in this chapter, set up vulnerability during childhood to some disorder later in life. Other more proximal contributory causes appear to bring on a disorder directly, and still others may contribute to maintenance of a disorder. This complex causal picture is further complicated by the fact that what may be a proximal cause for a problem at one stage in life may also serve as a distal contributory cause that sets up a predisposition for another disorder later in life. For example, the death of a parent can be a proximal cause of a child's subsequent grief reaction that might last a few months or a year; however, the parent's death may also serve as a distal contributory factor that increases the probability that when the child grows up, he or she will become depressed in response to certain stressors.

Feedback and Circularity in Abnormal Behavior

Traditionally in the sciences, the task of determining cause-and-effect relationships has focused on isolating the condition X (cause) that can be demonstrated to lead to condition Y (effect). For example, when the alcohol content of the blood reaches a certain level, alcoholic intoxication occurs. Where more than one causal factor is involved, the term *causal pattern* has been used. Here, conditions A, B, C, etc., lead to condition Y. In either case, this concept of cause follows a simple linear model in which a given variable or set of variables leads to a result either immediately or later. In the behavioral sciences, not only do we usually deal with a multitude of interacting causes, but we also often have difficulty distinguishing between what is cause and what is effect. In other words, the effects of feedback and the existence of mutual, two-way influences must be taken into account.

Consider the following example, which illustrates that our concepts of causal relationships must take into account the complex factors of feedback, patterns of interaction, and circularity.

case STUDY — Perceived Hostility

A boy with a history of disturbed interactions with his parents routinely misinterprets the intentions of his peers as being hostile. He develops defensive strategies to counteract the supposed hostility of those around him such as rejecting the efforts of others to be friendly, which he misinterprets as patronizing. Confronted by the boy's prickly behavior, those around him become defensive, hostile, and rejecting, thus confirming and strengthening the boy's distorted expectations. In this manner, each opportunity for new experience and new learning is in fact subverted and becomes yet another encounter with a social environment that seems perversely and persistently hostile—exactly in line with the boy's expectations.

Diathesis-Stress Models

One feature that many of the viewpoints or models of abnormal behavior that we will be discussing in this chapter share is that they can be considered diathesis-stress models. A predisposition toward developing a disorder is termed a *diathesis*. It can derive from biological, psychosocial, and/or sociocultural causal factors, and the different viewpoints that we will be discussing tend to emphasize the importance of different kinds of diatheses. Many mental disorders are believed to develop as the result of some kind of stressor operating on a person who has a diathesis or vulnerability for that disorder. Hence we will discuss what are commonly known as **diathesis-stress models** of abnormal behavior (e.g., Meehl, 1962; Monroe & Simons, 1991; see Ingram & Luxton, 2004, for a recent review). To translate these terms into the types of causal factors described earlier, the diathesis is a relatively distal necessary or contributory cause, but it is generally not sufficient to cause the disorder. Instead, there must be a more proximal undesirable event or situation (the stressor), which may also be contributory or necessary but is generally not sufficient by itself to cause the disorder except in someone with the diathesis.

Stress, the response of an individual to demands that he or she perceives as taxing or exceeding his or her personal resources (Folkman & Moskovitz, 2004; Lazarus, 1993), will be the focus of Chapter 5. It usually occurs when an individual experiences chronic or episodic events that are undesirable. The presence of a diathesis or vulnerability is often inferred only after stressful circumstances have led to maladaptive behavior. To complicate matters further, factors contributing to the development of a diathesis are themselves sometimes highly potent stressors, as when a child experiences the death of a parent, and may thereby acquire a predisposition or diathesis for becoming depressed later in life.

There are several different ways that researchers have proposed that a diathesis and stress may combine to produce a disorder (Ingram & Luxton, 2004; Monroe & Simons, 1991). In what is called the *additive model,* individuals who have a high level of a diathesis may need only a small amount of stress before a disorder develops, but those who have a very low level of a diathesis may need to experience a large amount of stress for a disorder to develop. In other words, the diathesis and the stress sum together and when one is high the other can be low, and vice versa; thus, a person with no diathesis or a very low level of diathesis could still develop a disorder when faced with truly severe stress. In what is called an *interactive model,* some amount of diathesis must be present before stress will have any effect. Thus, in the interactive model, someone with no diathesis will never develop the disorder, no matter how much stress he or she experiences, whereas someone with the diathesis will show increasing likelihood of developing the disorder with increasing levels of stress. More complex models are also possible because diatheses often exist on a continuum, ranging from zero to high levels. Each of these possibilities is illustrated in Figure 3.2.

Since the late 1980s, attention has been focused on the concept of **protective factors,** which are influences that

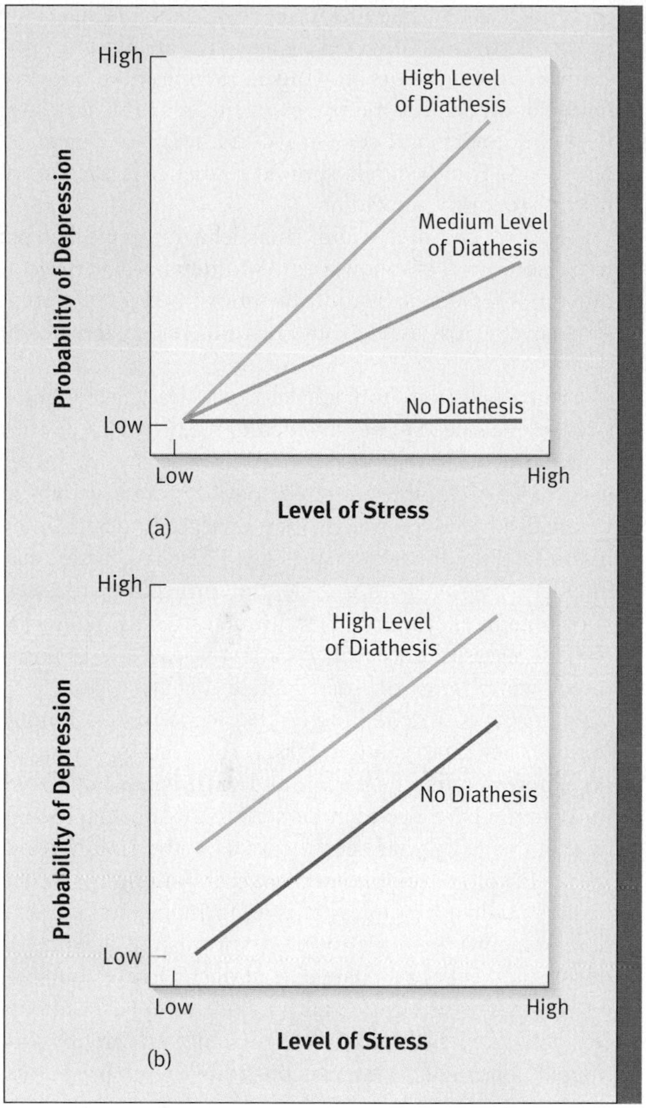

FIGURE 3.2

Diathesis-Stress Model

(a) Interactive model of diathesis-stress interaction. (b) Additive model of diathesis-stress interaction.

Source: *Adapted from S. M. Monroe & A. D. Simons (1991). Diathesis-stress theories in the context of life stress research: Implications for the depressive disorders.* Psychological Bulletin, 110, *406–414.*

modify a person's response to environmental stressors, making it less likely that the person will experience the adverse consequences of the stressors (Cicchetti & Garmezy, 1993; Masten, 2001; Masten et al., 2004; Rutter, 1985). One important protective factor in childhood is having a family environment in which at least one parent is warm and supportive, allowing the development of a good attachment relationship between the child and parent (Masten & Coatsworth, 1998). However, protective factors are not necessarily positive experiences. Indeed, sometimes exposure to stressful experiences that are dealt with successfully can promote a sense of self-confidence or self-esteem and thereby serve as a protective factor; thus some stressors paradoxically promote coping. This "steeling" or "inoculation" effect is more likely to occur with moderate stressors than with mild or extreme stressors (Barlow, 2002a; Hetherington, 1991; Rutter, 1987). And some protective factors have nothing to do with experiences at all but are simply some quality or attribute of a person. For example, for reasons that are not yet well understood, girls are less vulnerable than boys to many psychosocial stressors such as parental conflict and to physical hazards (Rutter, 1982). Other protective attributes include an easygoing temperament, high self-esteem, high intelligence, and school achievement (Masten, 2001; Masten & Coatsworth, 1998; Rutter, 1987).

Protective factors most often, but not always, lead to **resilience**—the ability to adapt successfully to even very difficult circumstances. An example is the child who perseveres and does well in school despite his parent's drug addiction or physical abuse (Garmezy, 1993; Luthar, 2003; Masten, 2001). The term *resilience* has been used to describe three distinct phenomena: "(1) good outcomes despite high-risk status, (2) sustained competence under threat, and (3) recovery from trauma" (Masten, Best, & Garmezy, 1990, p. 426). A more everyday way of thinking of resilience is in terms of "overcoming the odds" against you. There is increasing evidence that if a child's fundamental systems of adaptation (such as intelligence and cognitive development, ability to self-regulate, motivation to achieve mastery, and effective parenting) are operating normally, then most threatening circumstances will have minimal impact on him or her (Masten, 2001). Problems tend to arise when one or more of these systems of adaptation are weak to begin with (e.g., low intelligence), or when a serious stressor damages one or more of these systems (e.g., when a parent dies), or when the level of challenge far exceeds human capacity to adapt (e.g., exposure to chronic trauma as in war or to chronic maltreatment as in abusive families; Cicchetti, 2004; Cicchetti & Toth, 2005; Masten & Coatsworth, 1998). We should also note, however, that resilience should not be thought of as an all-or-none capacity, and some research has shown that resilient children (that is, those who show high social competence despite high

A child growing up under conditions of adversity may be protected from problems later in life if he or she has a warm and supportive relationship with some adult—such as a grandmother. Encouraging children to ask questions, taking the time to listen to their problems and concerns, and trying to understand the conflicts and pressures they face are the important elements of such a supportive and protective relationship.

stress) may nonetheless also experience considerable self-reported emotional distress. Moreover, children who show resilience in one domain may show significant difficulties in other domains (Luthar, Doernberger, & Zigler, 1993).

In sum, we can distinguish between causes of abnormal behavior that lie within and are part of the biological makeup or prior experience of a person—diatheses, vulnerabilities, or predispositions—and causes that pertain to current challenges in a person's life—stressors. Typically, neither the diathesis nor the stress is by itself sufficient to cause the disorder, but in combination they can sometimes lead the individual to behave abnormally. In addition, we can also examine protective factors, which may derive either from particular types of experiences or from certain qualities of the person, that can promote resilience in the face of vulnerability and stress. The following hypothetical but highly plausible scenario nicely illustrates these concepts.

case STUDY Nature and Nurture

Melinda and Tracy were identical twins whose parents were killed in a car accident when they were 1 year old. Their mother and grandmother both had histories of recurrent major depressive episodes. The twins were adopted into two loving middle-class families without a history of depression. Melinda's adoptive family provided a loving and supportive environment and supported her through school and college. Tracy's adoptive parents, by contrast, soon divorced and she was raised by her adoptive mother, who developed a serious alcohol dependence disorder and who could not hold a job. Her mother's living circumstances deteriorated and Tracy was forced to change schools four times. Because of her adoptive mother's alcohol and other mental problems, she was unable to provide Tracy with a consistently loving and supportive environment, and she frequently punished Tracy for no good reason when she was drunk. Tracy somehow managed to graduate from high school and supported herself through a state college. Both Tracy and Melinda married after they graduated from college but by age 27, both marriages resulted in divorce. Although Melinda developed some depressive symptoms for the first 6 weeks following the divorce, the depression was not severe and she quickly recovered. Tracy, by contrast, developed a major depressive episode that lasted for over a year.

In this example, both Tracy and Melinda have identical genetic makeup and therefore the same genetic diathesis for depression. Both had experienced the same distal stressor (death of parents at an early age), and the same proximal stressor (divorce) at age 27. But Melinda had many protective factors growing up (loving and supportive family and adequate resources) that Tracy did not have (lack of a loving and supportive mother and inadequate resources). Thus Melinda showed resilience in the face of her divorce but Tracy did not.

Different models of abnormal behavior, as we shall see in the sections that follow, identify different diatheses and different stressors as the route to abnormality and different protective factors as the route to resilience in the face of adversity.

This discussion should make it very clear that diathesis-stress models need to be considered in a broad framework of *multicausal developmental models*. Specifically, in the course of development a child may acquire a variety of cumulative risk factors that may interact in determining his or her risk for psychopathology. These risk factors also interact, however, with a variety of protective processes, and sometimes with stressors, to determine whether the child develops in a normal and adaptive way—as opposed to showing signs of maladaptive behavior and psychopathology—in childhood, adolescence, or adulthood (e.g., Masten, 2001; Rutter, 2001). It is also important to note, however, that to understand what is abnormal, one must always have a good understanding of normal human development. This has been the focus of the rapidly growing field of **developmental psychopathology,** which focuses on determining what is abnormal at any point in development by comparing and contrasting it with the normal and expected changes that occur in the course of development (e.g., Rutter, 2001). For example, an intense fear of the dark in a 3-to-5-year-old child may not be considered abnormal, given that most children have at least one specific fear that they bring into early adolescence (Antony et al., 1997; Barlow, 2002a). However, an intense fear of the dark that causes considerable distress and avoidance behavior in a high school or college-age student would be considered a phobia.

in Review

- What is a necessary cause? a sufficient cause? a contributory cause?
- What is a diathesis-stress model of abnormal behavior?
- Define the terms *protective factors* and *resilience*. Give examples of each.
- Explain why diathesis-stress models are essentially multicausal developmental models.

Viewpoints for Understanding the Causes of Abnormal Behavior

Students are often perplexed by the fact that in the behavioral sciences there often are several competing explanations for the same thing. In general, the more complex the phenomenon being investigated, the greater the number of viewpoints that develop in an attempt to explain it, although inevitably they are not all equally valid. In each case, a particular viewpoint helps professionals organize the observations they have made, provides a system of thought in which to place the observed data, and suggests areas of focus for research and treatment. In a fundamental way they also help determine the kinds of potential causes that are even examined in the first place. It is important to remember, however, that each of these viewpoints is a theoretical construction devised to orient psychologists in the study of abnormal behavior. One potential problem is that when adherents of a particular viewpoint are overly confident about the validity of that viewpoint, they may become blind to alternative interpretations.

As we saw in Chapter 2, Sigmund Freud helped shift the focus of abnormal psychology from biological illness or moral infirmity to unconscious mental processes within the person. In recent years, three other shifts in focus seem to have been occurring in parallel in the study of abnormal behavior. First, a newer, slightly different biological viewpoint is having a significant impact; it is the dominant force in psychiatry and has become very influential in clinical science more generally. Second, the behavioral and cognitive-behavioral viewpoints have become very influential paradigms among many empirically oriented clinical psychologists and some psychiatrists. Third, a sociocultural viewpoint has also become influential among psychologists and psychiatrists interested in the effects of sociocultural factors on abnormal behavior. In the long run, however, we also know from biological, psychosocial, and sociocultural research that only an integrated approach is likely to provide anything close to a full understanding of the origins of various forms of psychopathology, or of a long-lasting cure for many serious forms of psychopathology. Thus, in recent years, many theorists have come to recognize the need for a more integrative **biopsychosocial viewpoint** that acknowledges that biological, psychosocial, and sociocultural factors all interact and play a role in psychopathology and treatment.

With this in mind, we now turn to the major different viewpoints themselves. We will present the key ideas of each perspective, along with information about attempts to evaluate its validity. We will also describe the kinds of causal factors that each model tends to emphasize.

In Review

- What are the three traditional viewpoints that have dominated the study of abnormal behavior in recent years?
- What is the central idea of the more current, biopsychosocial viewpoint?

The Biological Viewpoint and Biological Causal Factors

As we saw in Chapter 2 in the discussion of general paresis and its link to syphilis, the traditional biological viewpoint focuses on mental disorders as diseases, many of the primary symptoms of which are cognitive, emotional, or behavioral. Mental disorders are thus viewed as disorders of the central nervous system, the autonomic nervous system, and/or the endocrine system that are either inherited or caused by some pathological process. At one time, people who adopted this viewpoint hoped to find simple biological explanations. Today, however, most clinical psychologists and psychiatrists recognize that such explanations are rarely simple, and many also acknowledge that psychosocial and sociocultural causal factors play a role as well.

The disorders first recognized as having biological or organic components were those associated with gross destruction of brain tissue. These disorders are neurological diseases—that is, they result from the disruption of brain functioning by physical or biochemical means and often involve psychological or behavioral aberrations. For example, damage to certain areas in the brain can cause memory loss, and damage to the left hemisphere that occurs during a stroke can cause depression.

Nevertheless, most mental disorders are not caused by neurological damage per se. For example, biochemical imbalances in the brain can lead to mental disorders without causing damage to the brain. Moreover, the bizarre content of delusions and other abnormal mental states like hallucinations can never be caused simply and directly by brain damage. Consider the example of a person with schizophrenia or general paresis who claims to be Napoleon. The content of such delusions must be the by-product of some sort of functional integration of different neural structures, some of which have been "programmed" by personality and learning based on past experience (e.g., having learned who Napoleon was).

People's behavior during alcohol intoxication is one good example of how a temporary biological condition can dramatically affect functioning—in this case engaging in behavior that normally would be inhibited.

We will focus here on four categories of biological factors that seem particularly relevant to the development of maladaptive behavior: (1) neurotransmitter and hormonal imbalances in the brain, (2) genetic vulnerabilities, (3) temperament, and (4) brain dysfunction and neural plasticity. Each of these categories encompasses a number of conditions that influence the quality and functioning of our bodies and our behavior. They are often not independent of each other, and they often occur in varying combinations in different people.

- ► Neurotransmitter and hormonal imbalances in the brain
- ► Genetic vulnerabilities
- ► Temperament
- ► Brain dysfunction and neural plasticity

FIGURE 3.3
Biological Causal Factors

Neurotransmitter and Hormonal Imbalances

In order for the brain to function adequately neurons, or nerve cells, need to be able to communicate effectively with one another. The site of communication between the axon of one neuron and the dendrites or cell body of another neuron is the **synapse**—a tiny filled space between neurons. These interneuronal transmissions are accomplished by **neurotransmitters**—chemical substances that are released into the synapse by the presynaptic neuron when a nerve impulse occurs (for details, see Developments in Research 3.1). There are many different kinds of neurotransmitters; some increase the likelihood that the postsynaptic neuron will "fire" (produce an impulse), and others inhibit the impulse. Whether the neural message is successfully transmitted to the postsynaptic neuron depends, among other things, on the concentration of certain neurotransmitters within the synapse.

IMBALANCES OF NEUROTRANSMITTERS The belief that *neurotransmitter imbalances* in the brain can result in abnormal behavior is one of the basic tenets of the biological perspective today, although today most researchers agree that this is only part of the causal pattern involved in the etiology of most disorders. Sometimes psychological stress can bring on neurotransmitter imbalances. These imbalances can be created in a variety of ways (see the figure in Developments in Research 3.1):

- There may be excessive production and release of the neurotransmitter substance into the synapses, causing a functional excess in levels of that neurotransmitter.
- There may be dysfunctions in the normal processes by which neurotransmitters, once released into the synapse, are deactivated. Ordinarily this deactivation occurs either through a process of reuptake of the released neurotransmitter from the synapse into the axon ending, or through a process of degradation by certain enzymes that may be present in the synapse and in the presynaptic axon ending.
- Finally, there may be problems with the receptors in the postsynaptic neuron, which may be either abnormally sensitive or abnormally insensitive.

Neurons that are sensitive to a particular neurotransmitter tend to cluster together, forming neural paths between different parts of the brain known as *chemical circuits.* As we will see, different disorders are thought to stem from different patterns of neurotransmitter imbalances in various brain areas (e.g., Lambert & Kinsley, 2005; Thompson, 2000). And different medications used to treat various disorders are often believed to operate by correcting these imbalances. For example, the widely prescribed antidepressant Prozac appears to slow the reuptake of the neurotransmitter serotonin, thereby prolonging how long serotonin remains in the synapse (see Chapters 7 and 17).

Although over a hundred neurotransmitters have been discovered to date, four different kinds of neurotransmitters have been most extensively studied in relationship to psychopathology: (1) norepinephrine, (2) dopamine, (3) serotonin, and (4) gamma aminobutyric acid (known as "GABA"; Lambert & Kinsley, 2005; Thompson, 2000). The first three belong to a class of neurotransmitters called *monoamines* because each is synthesized from a single amino acid (*monoamine* means "one amine"). Norepinephrine has been implicated as playing an important role in the emergency reactions our bodies show when we are exposed to an acutely stressful or dangerous situation

3.1 Developments in Research

Neurotransmission and Abnormal Behavior

A nerve impulse, which is electrical in nature, travels from the cell body of a neuron (nerve cell) down the axon. Although there is only one axon for each neuron, axons have branches at their end called axonal endings or terminal buttons. These are the sites where neurotransmitter substances are released into a synapse—a tiny, fluid-filled gap between the axon endings of one neuron (the presynaptic neuron) and the dendrites or cell body of another neuron (the postsynaptic neuron). The synapse is the site of neural transmission—that is, of communication between neurons. The neurotransmitter substances are contained within synaptic vesicles near the axon endings. When a nerve impulse reaches the axon endings, the synaptic vesicles travel to the presynaptic membrane of the axon and release the neurotransmitter substance into the synapse. The neurotransmitter substances released into the synapse then act on the postsynaptic membrane of the dendrite of the receiving neuron, which has specialized receptor sites where the neurotransmitter substances pass on their message. The receptor sites then initiate the receiving cell's response. The neurotransmitters can either stimulate that postsynaptic neuron to initiate an impulse, or to inhibit impulse transmission. Both kinds of messages are important. Once the neurotransmitter substance is released into the synapse, it does not stay around indefinitely (otherwise, the second neuron would continue firing in the absence of a real impulse). Sometimes the neurotransmitters are quickly destroyed by an enzyme such as monoamine oxidase, and sometimes they are returned to storage vesicles in the axonal button by a "reuptake" mechanism—a process of reabsorption by which the neurotransmitters are reabsorbed or effectively sucked back up into the axon ending. The enzyme monoamine oxidase is also present in the presynaptic terminal and can destroy excess neurotransmitter there too.

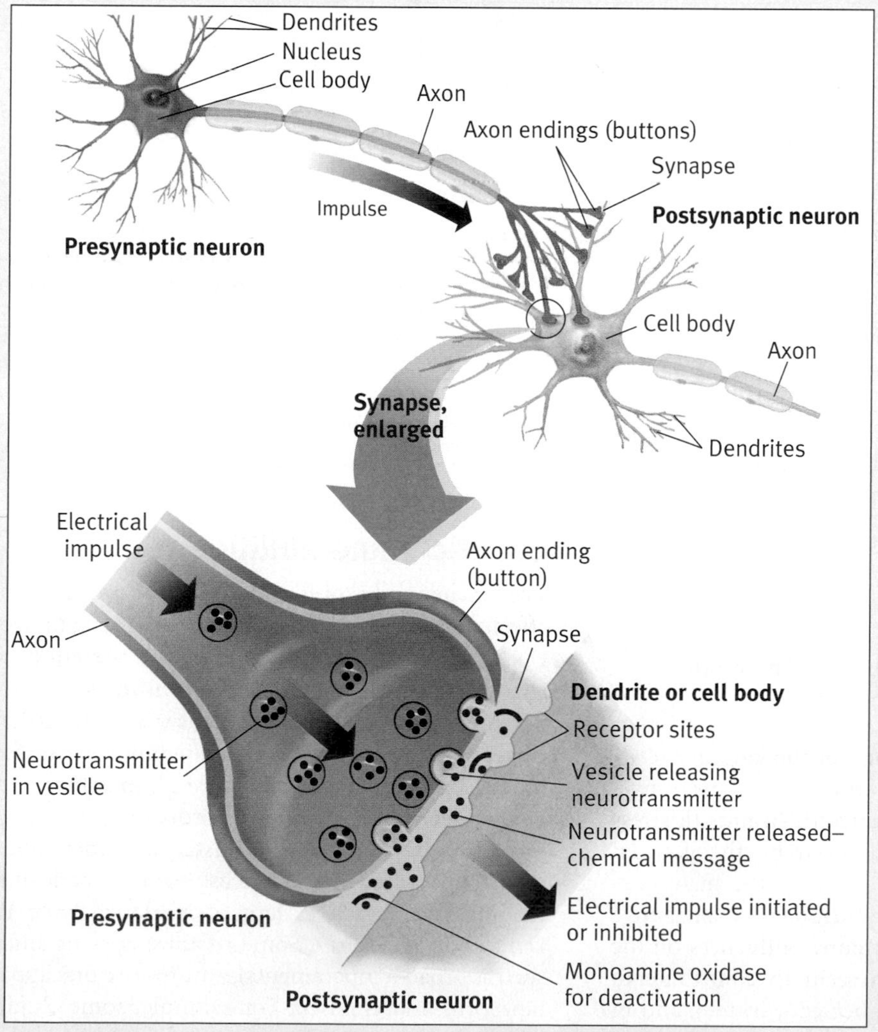

Given that many forms of psychopathology have been associated with various imbalances in neurotransmitter substances and with altered sensitivities of receptor sites, it is not surprising that many of the medications used to treat various disorders have the synapse as their site of action. For example, certain medications act to increase or decrease the concentrations of pertinent neurotransmitters in the synaptic gap. They may do so by blocking the reuptake process, by altering the sensitivity of the receptor sites, or by affecting the actions of the enzymes that ordinarily break down the neurotransmitter substances.

(see Chapters 5 and 6). Dopamine has been implicated in schizophrenia (see Chapter 14) as well as in addictive disorders (see Chapter 12). Serotonin has been found to have important effects on the way we think and process information from our environment (e.g., Meneses, 1999, 2001) as well as on behaviors and moods. Not surprisingly, then, it seems to play an important role in emotional disorders such as anxiety and depression as well as in suicide, as we will see in Chapters 6 and 7. Finally, in Chapter 6, we discuss the neurotransmitter GABA, which is strongly implicated in reducing anxiety as well as other emotional states characterized by high levels of arousal.

HORMONAL IMBALANCES Some forms of psychopathology have also been linked to *hormonal imbalances.* **Hormones** are chemical messengers secreted by a set of endocrine glands in our bodies. Each of the endocrine glands produces and releases its own set of hormones, which travel through our bloodstream and affect various parts of our brain and body. Our central nervous system is linked to the endocrine system (in what is known as the *neuroendocrine system*) by the effects of the hypothalamus on the **pituitary gland** (see Figure 3.4), which is the master gland of the body, producing a variety of hormones that regulate or control the other endocrine glands.

One particularly important set of interactions occurs in the **hypothalamic-pituitary-adrenal-cortical axis.** Activation of this axis involves:

1. Messages in the form of corticotrophin-releasing hormone (CRH) travel from the hypothalamus to the pituitary.
2. In response to CRH, the pituitary releases adrenocorticotrophic hormone (ACTH), which stimulates the cortical part of the adrenal gland (located on top of the kidney) to produce epinephrine (adrenaline) and the stress hormone **cortisol.** Cortisol mobilizes the body to deal with stress.
3. Cortisol in turn provides negative feedback to the hypothalamus and pituitary to decrease their release of CRH and ACTH, which in turn reduces the release of adrenaline and cortisol. This negative feedback system operates much as a thermostat does to regulate temperature.

As we will see, malfunctioning of this negative feedback system has been implicated in various forms of psychopathology such as depression and post-traumatic stress disorder. Sex hormones are produced by the gonadal glands, and imbalance in these (such as the male hormones, the *androgens*) can also contribute to maladaptive behavior. Moreover, gonadal hormonal influences on the developing nervous system also seem to contribute to some of the differences between behavior in men and in women (e.g., Collaer & Hines, 1995; Hayward, 2003; Money & Ehrhardt, 1972).

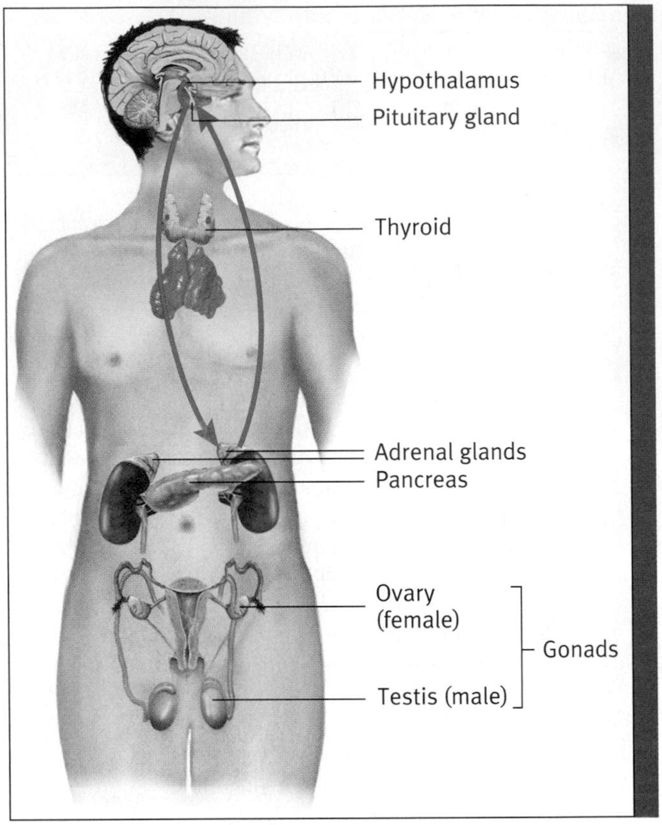

FIGURE 3.4

Major Glands of the Endocrine System

This figure illustrates some of the major glands of the endocrine system, which produce and release hormones into the bloodstream. The hypothalamic-pituitary-adrenal-cortical axis is also shown (blue arrows). The hypothalamus and pituitary are closely connected, and the hypothalamus periodically sends hormone signals to the pituitary (the master gland), which in turn sends another hormone to the cortical part of the adrenal glands (above the kidneys) to release epinephrine and the stress hormone cortisol.

Genetic Vulnerabilities

The biochemical processes described above are themselves affected by **genes,** which consist of very long molecules of DNA (deoxyribonucleic acid) and are present at various locations on chromosomes. **Chromosomes** are the chain-like structures within a cell nucleus that contain the genes. Genes are the carriers of genetic information that we inherit from our parents and other ancestors. Although neither behavior nor mental disorders are ever determined exclusively by genes, there is substantial evidence that most mental disorders show at least some genetic influence ranging from small to large (e.g., Jang, 2005; Plomin, DeFries, et al., 2001). Some of these genetic influences, such as broad temperamental features, are first apparent in newborns and children. For example, some children are just naturally more shy or anxious, whereas others are more outgoing (e.g., Carey & DiLalla, 1994; Kagan, Snidman, McManis, & Woodward, 2001). However, some genetic sources of vulnerability do not manifest themselves until adolescence or adulthood when most mental disorders appear for the first time.

Normal human cells have 46 *chromosomes* containing genetic materials that encode the hereditary plan that provides the potentialities for development and behavior throughout a lifetime (see Figure 3.5). The normal inheritance consists of 23 pairs of chromosomes, one of each pair from the mother and one from the father. Twenty-two of these chromosome pairs determine, by their biochemical action, the individual's general anatomical and other physiological characteristics. The remaining pair, the *sex chromosomes*, determine the individual's sex. In a female, both of these sex chromosomes—one from each parent—are designated as X chromosomes. In a male, the sex chromosome from the mother is an X, but that from the father is a Y chromosome.

Research in developmental genetics has shown that abnormalities in the structure or number of the chromosomes are associated with major defects or disorders. For example, Down syndrome is a type of mental retardation (also associated with recognizable facial features such as a flat face and slanted eyes) in which there is a trisomy (a set of three chromosomes instead of two) in chromosome 21 (see Chapter 16). Here the extra chromosome is the primary cause of the disorder. Anomalies may also occur in the *sex chromosomes,* producing a variety of complications, such as ambiguous sexual characteristics, that may predispose a person to develop abnormal behavior. Fortunately, advances in research have enabled us to detect chromosomal abnormalities even before birth, thus making it possible to study their effects on future development and behavior.

More typically, however, personality traits and mental disorders are not affected by chromosomal abnormalities per se, but rather by abnormalities in some of the genes on the chromosomes. Although you will often hear about discoveries that "the gene" for a particular disorder has been discovered, vulnerabilities to mental disorders are almost always *polygenic*, which means they are influenced by multiple genes. In other words, a genetically vulnerable person has usually inherited a large number of genes that collectively represent faulty heredity and that operate together in some sort of additive or interactive fashion (e.g., Plomin, 1990; Plomin et al., 2001). These faulty genes may, for example, lead to structural abnormalities in the central nervous system, to errors in the regulation of brain chemistry and hormonal balance, or to excesses or deficiencies in the reactivity of the autonomic nervous system, which is involved in mediating many of our emotional responses.

In the field of abnormal psychology, genetic influences rarely express themselves in a simple and straightforward manner. This is because behavior, unlike some physical characteristics such as eye color, is not determined exclusively by genetic endowment: It is a product of the organism's interaction with the environment. In other words, genes can affect behavior only indirectly. Gene "expression" is normally not a simple outcome of the information encoded in DNA but is, rather, the end product of an intricate process that may be influenced by the internal (e.g., intrauterine) and external environment. Indeed, genes can actually be "turned on" and "turned off" in response to environmental influences such as stress (e.g., Dent, Smith, & Levine, 2001; Jang, 2005; Sanchez, Ladd, & Plotsky, 2001).

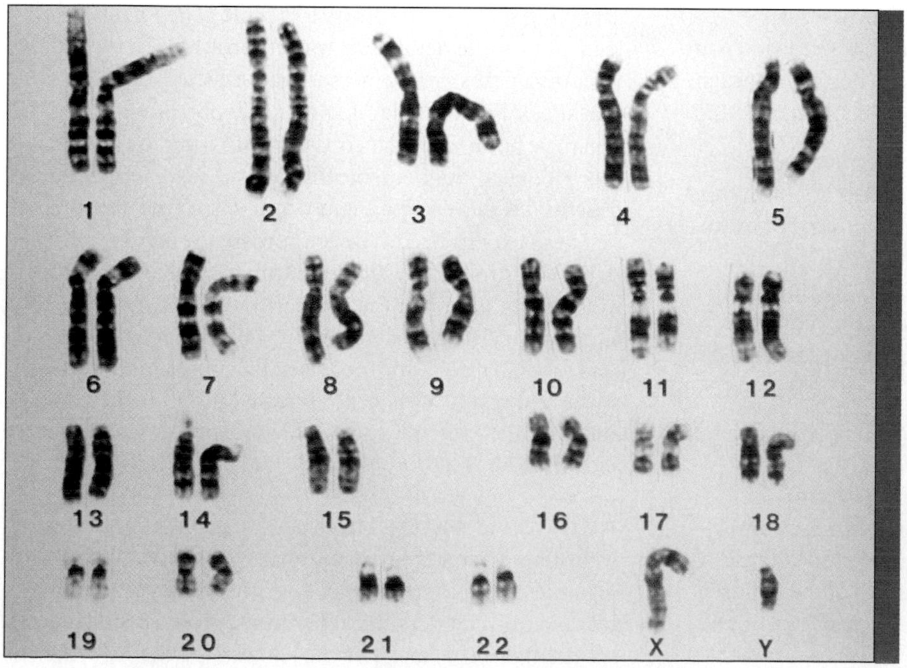

FIGURE 3.5

Human Chromosome Pairs

A normal human male has 22 pairs of autosomes, an X chromosome, and a Y chromosome.

The specific features of genetic endowment vary widely. Except for identical twins, no two humans ever begin life with the same endowment. Thus heredity not only provides the potentialities for development and behavior typical of the species but is also an important source of individual differences. Heredity determines not the specifics of human behavior but the ranges within which characteristic behavior can be modified by environmental or experiential influences. For example, a child born with an introverted disposition may become more or less introverted, depending on various experiences growing up, but it is unlikely that he or she will ever be truly extraverted.

THE RELATIONSHIP OF GENOTYPES TO PHENOTYPES

A person's total genetic endowment is referred to as her or his **genotype.** The observed structural and functional characteristics that result from an interaction of the genotype and the environment are referred to as a person's **phenotype.** In some cases, the genotypic vulnerability present at birth does not exert its effect on the phenotype until much later in life. In many other cases, the genotype may shape the environmental experiences a child has, thus affecting the phenotype in yet another very important way. For example, a child who is genetically predisposed to aggressive behavior may be rejected by his or her peers in early grades because of the aggressive behavior. Such rejection may lead the child to go on to associate with similarly aggressive and delinquent peers in later grades, leading to an increased likelihood of developing a full-blown pattern of delinquency in adolescence. When the genotype shapes the environmental experiences a child has in this way, we refer to this phenomenon as a **genotype-environment correlation.**

GENOTYPE-ENVIRONMENT CORRELATIONS

Researchers have found three important ways in which an individual's genotype may shape his or her environment (Jang, 2005; Plomin et al., 2001; Scarr & McCartney, 1983).

- The genotype may have what has been termed a *passive effect* on the environment resulting from the genetic similarity of parents and children. For example, highly intelligent parents may provide a highly stimulating environment for their child, thus creating an environment that will interact in a positive way with the child's genetic endowment for high intelligence.
- The child's genotype may evoke particular kinds of reactions from the social and physical environment—a so-called *evocative effect.* For example, active, happy babies evoke more positive responses from others than do passive, unresponsive infants (Lytton, 1980). Similarly, musically talented children may be picked out at school and given special opportunities (Plomin et al., 2001).
- The child's genotype may play a more active role in shaping the environment—a so-called *active effect.* In this case the child seeks out or builds an environment that is congenial—a phenomenon known as "niche building." Extraverted children may seek the company of others, for example, thereby enhancing their own tendencies to be sociable (Baumrind, 1991; Plomin et al., 2001).

GENOTYPE-ENVIRONMENT INTERACTIONS With the type of genotype-environment correlations just discussed, we see the effects that genes have on a child's exposure to the environment. But an additional, fascinating complication is that people with different genotypes may be differentially sensitive or susceptible to their environments; this is known as a **genotype-environment interaction.** One important example is illustrated by a disorder known as "PKU-induced mental retardation" (see Chapter 16). Children with the genetic vulnerability to PKU react very differently to many common foods with phenylalanine than do normal children because they cannot metabolize the phenylalanine, and as its metabolic products build up, they damage the brain (Jang, 2005; Plomin et al., 2001). Fortunately, this mental retardation syndrome can be prevented if the young child's diet changes (until about age 5 or 6) so as to eliminate foods with phenylalanine.

Another example occurs in people who are at genetic risk for depression who have been shown to be more likely to respond to stressful life events by becoming depressed than are people without the genetic risk factors who experience the same stressful life events (Kendler, Kessler, et al., 1995; Moffitt, Caspi, & Rutter, 2005; Silberg, Rutter, Neale, & Eaves, 2001). In one landmark study of nearly 850 individuals who had been followed since age 3, investigators found evidence for a genotpe-environment interaction involving several variants on a specific gene involved in the transport of the neurotransmitter serotonin. Which of two variants of this gene a person had affected the likelihood that she or he would develop major depression in her or his twenties, but only when considered in interaction with life stress (Caspi, Sugden, Moffitt, et al., 2003). Specifically, individuals with one variant of the gene (the short allele) who also experienced four or more major life stressors had twice the probability of developing major depression as individuals with another variant of the gene (the long allele) who also experienced four or more major life stressors (see Chapter 7 for more details). Since then, this basic pattern of results has been replicated in four other studies, and has failed to replicate in only one published study (see Moffitt et al., 2005).

METHODS FOR STUDYING GENETIC INFLUENCES

Although advances are beginning to be made in identifying faulty genetic endowment, for the most part we are not yet able to isolate, on the genes themselves, specific defects for mental disorders. Therefore, most of the information we have on the role of genetic factors in mental disorders is based not on studies of genes but on studies of people who are related to each other. Three primary methods have traditionally been used in **behavior genetics,** the field that focuses on studying the heritability of mental disorders (as well as other aspects of psychological functioning): (1) the family history (or pedigree) method, (2) the twin method, and (3) the adoption method. More recently, two additional methods, linkage studies and association studies, have also been developed.

The **family history** (or *pedigree*) **method** requires that an investigator observe samples of relatives of each *proband* or *index case* (the subject, or carrier, of the trait or disorder in question) to see whether the incidence increases in proportion to the degree of hereditary relationship. In addition, the incidence of the trait in a normal population is compared (as a control) with its incidence among the relatives of the index cases. The main limitation of this method is that people who are more closely related genetically also tend to share more similar environments, which makes it difficult to disentangle genetic and environmental effects.

The **twin method** is the second approach used to study genetic influences on abnormal behavior. *Identical* (*monozygotic*) twins share the same genetic endowment because they develop from a single zygote, or fertilized egg. Thus if a given disorder or trait were completely heritable, one would expect the **concordance rate**—the percentage of twins sharing the disorder or trait—to be 100 percent. That is, if one identical twin had a particular disorder, the other twin would as well. However, there are no forms of psychopathology in DSM-IV-TR where the concordance rates for identical twins are this high, so we can safely conclude that no mental disorders are completely heritable. However, as we will see, there are relatively high concordance rates for identical twins in some common and severe forms of psychopathology. These concordance rates are particularly meaningful when they differ from those found for nonidentical twins. *Nonidentical* (*dizygotic*) twins do not share any more genes than do siblings from the same parents because they develop from two different fertilized eggs. One would therefore expect concordance rates for a disorder to be much lower for dizygotic (DZ) than for monozygotic (MZ) twins if the disorder had a strong genetic component. Thus evidence for genetic transmission of a trait or a disorder can be obtained by comparing the concordance rates between identical and nonidentical twins. For most of the disorders we will discuss, concordance rates are much lower for nonidentical twins than for identical twins.

Some researchers have argued that finding higher concordance rates for a disorder in monozygotic twins than in dizygotic twins is not conclusive evidence of a genetic contribution, because it is always possible that identical twins are treated more similarly by their parents than are nonidentical twins (Bouchard & Propping, 1993; Torgersen, 1993). However, research has provided reasonably strong evidence that the genetic similarity is more important than

This set of identical twins from Bouchard's University of Minnesota Study of Twins Reared Apart pose here with Dr. Nancy Segal, Co-director of the project. Mark Newman (left) and Gerry Levey (right) were separated at birth and raised by different parents. Both were dedicated firefighters in different New Jersey towns and met after someone mistook one of them at a firemen's convention for his twin. Both had highly similar patterns of baldness, and were 6'4" tall. They both loved Budweiser beer (which they both held by placing their pinky finger under the beer can), as well as Chinese and Italian food. Both had been smokers until recently when one had quit. They both also liked hunting and fishing, and always carried knives. These eerie similarities between identical twins reared apart have been observed in many other such twins as well (Segal, 2005).

the similarity of the parents' behavior (e.g., Hettema, Neale, & Kendler, 1995; Jang, 2005; Plomin et al., 2001). Nevertheless, the ideal study of genetic factors in psychopathology involves identical twins who have been reared apart in significantly different environments. Unfortunately, finding such twins is extremely difficult (there are probably only a few hundred pairs in the United States), and so only a few such small studies have been done.

The third method used to study genetic influences is the **adoption method.** In one variation on this method, the biological parents of individuals who have a given disorder (and who were adopted away shortly after birth) are compared with the biological parents of individuals without the disorder (who also were adopted away shortly after birth) to determine their rates of disorder. If there is a genetic influence, one expects to find higher rates of the disorder in the biological relatives of those with the disorder than in those without the disorder. In another variation, researchers compare the rates of disorder in the adopted-away offspring of biological parents who have a disorder with those seen in the adopted-away offspring of normal biological parents. If there is a genetic influence, then there should be higher rates of disorder in the adopted-away offspring of the biological parents who have the disorder.

Although pitfalls can arise in interpreting each of these methods, if the results from studies using all three

3.2 Developments in Thinking

"Nature, Nurture, and Psychopathology: A New Look at an Old Topic"

People have abundant misconceptions and stereotypes about studies of genetic influences on behavior, traits, and psychopathology. Several of the more important ones are presented here (Plomin et al., 2001; Rutter, 1991; Rutter et al., 1993).

1. *Misconception*: Strong genetic effects mean that environmental influences must be unimportant. *Fact*: Even if we are discussing a trait or disorder that has a strong genetic influence, environmental factors can have a major impact on the level of that trait. Height, for example, is strongly genetically determined, and yet nutritional factors have a very large effect on the actual height a person attains. Between 1900 and 1960 the average height of boys reared in London increased about 10 cm thanks only to improvements in diet (Tizard, 1975).
2. *Misconception*: Genes provide a limit to potential. *Fact*: One's potential can change if one's environment changes, as the height example above illustrates. Another example comes from children born to socially disadvantaged parents but who are adopted and reared with socially advantaged parents. These children have a mean IQ about 12 points higher than those reared in the socially disadvantaged environment (Capron & Duyme, 1989; Plomin et al., 2001).
3. *Misconception*: Genetic strategies are of no value for studying environmental influences. *Fact*: The opposite is true because genetic research strategies provide critical tests of environmental influences on personality and psychopathology. For example, because monozygotic twins have identical genes, concordance rates of less than 100 percent clearly illustrate the importance of environmental influences, particularly those of the nonshared environment (Bouchard & Loehlin, 2001; Jang, 2005; Plomin et al., 2001).
4. *Misconception*: Nature and nurture are separate. *Fact*: Genetic effects "operate mainly through their effect on susceptibility to environmental influences" (Rutter, 1991, p. 129). For example, babies born with the genetic defect causing phenylketonuria (PKU), a metabolic disease, develop the disease only if they are environmentally exposed to diets with phenylalanine. In addition, genes affect the kinds of experiences people have, as is immediately evident if one thinks about the effects that gender, IQ, and temperament have on one's life experiences (Jang, 2005; Plomin et al., 2001).
5. *Misconception*: Genetic effects diminish with age. *Fact*: Although many people assume that genetic effects should be maximal at birth, with environmental influences getting stronger with increasing age, it is now evident that this is not always true (Carey, 2003; Plomin, 1986). For height, weight, and IQ, dizygotic twins are almost as alike as monozygotic twins in early infancy, but over time dizygotic twins show greater differences than monozygotic twins. For whatever reasons, many genetic effects on psychological characteristics increase with age up to at least middle childhood or even young adulthood. Moreover, other genetic effects do not appear until much later in life, as in cases like Huntington's disease, to be discussed in Chapter 15.
6. *Misconception*: Disorders that run in families must be genetic, and those that do not run in families must not be genetic. *Fact*: Many examples contradict these misconceptions. For example, teenage-onset juvenile delinquency tends to run in families, and yet this seems to be due primarily to environmental rather than genetic influences (Plomin et al., 2001). Conversely, autism is such a rare disorder that it doesn't appear to run in families (only about 3 percent of siblings have the disorder), and yet there seems to be a very powerful genetic effect (Plomin et al., 2001; Rutter et al., 1993).

strategies converge, one can draw reasonably strong conclusions about the genetic influence on a disorder (Plomin et al., 2001; Rutter, 1991). Developments in Thinking 3.2 considers various misconceptions about studies of genetics and psychopathology.

SEPARATING GENETIC AND ENVIRONMENTAL INFLUENCES Because each of the three types of heritability studies separate heredity from environment to some extent, they also allow for testing the influence of environmental factors and even for differentiating "shared" and "nonshared" environmental influences (Jang, 2005; Plomin & Daniels, 1987; Plomin et al., 2001). *Shared environmental influences* are those that would affect all children in a family similarly, such as overcrowding, poverty, and sometimes family discord. *Nonshared environmental influences* are those in which different children in a family differ. These would include unique experiences at school and also some unique features of upbringing in the home such as a parent treating one child in a qualitatively different way from another. An example of the latter occurs when parents who are quarreling and showing hostility to one another draw some children into the conflict while others are able to remain outside it (Plomin et al., 2001; Rutter et al., 1993). For many important psychological characteristics and forms of psychopathology, nonshared influences appear to be more important—that is, experiences that are specific to a child may do more to influence his or her behavior and adjustment than experiences shared by all children in the family (Jang, 2005; Plomin et al., 2001; Rutter, 1991).

LINKAGE ANALYSIS AND ASSOCIATION STUDIES

More recent molecular genetic methods used to study genetic influences on mental disorders include *linkage analysis* and *association studies*. Whereas the methods previously described attempt to obtain quantitative estimates of the degree of genetic influence for different disorders, linkage analysis and association studies attempt to determine the actual location of genes responsible for mental disorders. Considerable excitement surrounds such work, because identifying the location of genes for certain disorders could provide promising leads for new forms of treatment and even prevention of those disorders.

Linkage analysis studies of mental disorders capitalize on several currently known locations on chromosomes of genes for other inherited physical characteristics or biological processes (such as eye color, blood group, etc.). For example, researchers might conduct a large family pedigree study on schizophrenia, looking at all known relatives of a person with schizophrenia going back several generations. At the same time, however, they might keep track of something like the eye color of each individual (as well as their diagnostic status). Eye color might be chosen because it has a known genetic marker located on a particular chromosome. If the researchers found that the familial patterns for schizophrenia in one family pedigree were closely linked to the familial patterns for eye color in the same pedigree, they could infer that a gene affecting schizophrenia must be located very nearby on the chromosome that contains the known genetic marker for eye color. In other words, in this case one would expect all members of a particular family pedigree with schizophrenia to have the same eye color (e.g., blue), even though all members of a different family pedigree with schizophrenia might have brown eyes.

Although a number of published studies over the past 20 years using linkage analysis have provided evidence supporting, for example, the location of a gene for bipolar disorder on chromosome 11 (e.g., Egeland et al., 1987) and of genes for schizophrenia on particular parts of chromosomes 22, 6, 8, and 1 (e.g., Heinrichs, 2001), numerous other studies have failed to replicate these results. Therefore, most results are considered inconclusive at the present time (see Carey, 2003; Jang, 2005). Part of the problem in coming up with replicable results in such studies is that most of these disorders are influenced by many different genes spread over multiple chromosomes. To date, these linkage analysis techniques have been most successful in locating the genes for single-gene brain disorders such as Huntington's disease (Carey, 2003; Plomin et al., 2001).

Association studies start with a large group of individuals both with and without a given disorder. Researchers then compare the frequencies, in the people with and those without the disorder, of certain genetic markers that are known to be located on particular chromosomes (such as eye color, blood group, etc.). If one or more of the known genetic markers occur with much higher frequency in the individuals with the disorder than in the people without the disorder, the researchers infer that one or more genes associated with the disorder are located on the same chromosome. Ideally, the search for gene candidates for a given disorder starts with known genes for some biological process that is disrupted in the disorder (see Moffitt et al., 2005). For example, one study found that the genetic markers for certain aspects of dopamine functioning occurred significantly more frequently in the children with hyperactivity than in the children without hyperactivity. This led researchers to infer that some of the genes involved with hyperactivity are located near the known genetic markers for dopamine functioning (Thapar, Holmes, Poulton, & Harrington, 1999; see Plomin et al., 2001). For most mental disorders that are known to be influenced polygenically, association studies are more promising than linkage studies for identifying small effects of any particular gene.

In summary, these molecular genetic studies using linkage and association methodologies may hold tremendous promise for identifying new prevention or treatment approaches. However, at present that promise has not been fulfilled because of difficulties in producing replicable results.

Temperament

Temperament refers to a child's reactivity and characteristic ways of self-regulation. When we say that babies differ in temperament, we mean that they show differences in their characteristic emotional and arousal responses to various stimuli, and in their tendency to approach, withdraw, or attend to various situations (Rothbart, Derryberry, & Hershey, 2000). Some babies are startled by slight sounds or cry when sunlight hits their faces; others are seemingly insensitive to such stimulation. These behaviors are strongly influenced by genetic factors but prenatal and postnatal environmental factors also play a role in their development (Goldsmith, 2003; Rothbart et al., 2000).

Our early temperament is thought to be the basis from which our personality develops. Starting at about 2 to 3 months of age, approximately five dimensions of temperament can be identified: fearfulness, irritability and frustration, positive affect, activity level, and attentional persistence, although some of these emerge later than others. These seem to be related to the three important

A child with a fearful and anxious temperament can become very distressed with changes in the environment, such as the mother leaving for work.

dimensions of adult personality: (1) neuroticism or negative emotionality, (2) extraversion or positive emotionality, and (3) constraint (conscientiousness and agreeableness; Rothbart & Ahadi, 1994; Watson, Clark, & Harkness, 1994). The infant dimensions of fearfulness and irritability correspond to the adult dimension of neuroticism—the disposition to experience negative affect. The infant dimensions of positive affect and possibly activity level seem related to the adult dimension of extraversion, and the infant dimension of attentional persistence seems related to the adult dimension of constraint or control. At least some aspects of temperament show a moderate degree of stability from late in the first year of life through at least middle childhood, although temperament can also change (e.g., Fox et al., 2005; Kagan, 2003; Rothbart et al., 2000).

Just as we saw in the discussion of gene-environment correlations, the temperament of an infant or young child has profound effects on a variety of important developmental processes (Rothbart & Ahadi, 1994; Rothbart et al., 2000). For example, a child with a fearful temperament has many opportunities for the classical conditioning of fear to situations in which fear is provoked; later the child may learn to avoid entering those feared situations, and recent evidence suggests that he or she may be especially likely to learn to fear social situations (Kagan, 2003; Schwartz, Snidman, & Kagan, 1999). A child with a low threshold for distress may also learn to regulate distress by keeping the level of stimulation low, whereas a child with a high need for stimulation may do things to increase excitement (Rothbart et al., 2000).

Not surprisingly, temperament may also set the stage for the development of various forms of psychopathology later in life. For example, children who are fearful in many situations have been labeled *behaviorally inhibited* by Kagan and his colleagues. This trait has a significant heritable component (Kagan, 2003), and when it is stable, it is a risk factor for the development of anxiety disorders later in childhood and probably in adulthood (e.g., Fox et al., 2005; Kagan, 2003). Conversely, 2-year-old children who are highly *uninhibited*, showing little fear of anything, may have difficulty learning moral standards for their behavior from parents or society (Frick et al., 2003; Rothbart, Ahadi, & Evans, 2000), and they have been shown at age 13 to exhibit more aggressive and delinquent behavior (Schwartz, Snidman, & Kagan, 1996). If these personality ingredients were combined with high levels of hostility, the stage also could be set for the development of conduct disorder and antisocial personality disorder (Harpur, Hart, & Hare, 1993).

Brain Dysfunction and Neural Plasticity

As noted earlier, specific brain lesions with observable defects in brain tissue are rarely a primary cause of psychiatric disorders. However, advances in understanding how more subtle deficiencies of brain structure or function are implicated in many mental disorders have been increasing at a rapid pace in the past few decades. Some of these advances come from the increased availability of sophisticated new neuroimaging techniques to study the function and structure of the brain (see Chapter 4 for more details). These and other kinds of techniques have shown that genetic programs for brain development are not so rigid and deterministic as was once believed (e.g., Gottesman & Hanson, 2005; Nelson & Bloom, 1997; Thompson & Nelson, 2001). Instead, there is considerable *neural plasticity*—i.e., flexibility of the brain in making changes in organization and/or function in response to pre- and postnatal experiences, stress, diet, disease, drugs, maturation, etc. Existing neural circuits can be modified, or new neural circuits can be generated (e.g., Kolb, Gibb, & Robinson, 2003). The effects can either be beneficial or detrimental to the animal or person, depending on the circumstances.

One example of the positive effects of prenatal experiences comes from an experiment in which pregnant rats housed in complex enriched environments had offspring that responded less to brain injury that occurred early in development (Kolb et al., 2003). One example of negative effects of prenatal experiences comes from another experiment in which pregnant monkeys that were exposed to unpredictable loud sounds had infants that were jittery and showed neurochemical abnormalities (specifically, elevated levels of circulating catecholamines; Schneider, 1992). Many environmental events that occur postnatally also affect the brain development of the infant and child (Nelson &

Bloom, 1997; Thompson & Nelson, 2001). For example, the formation of new neural connections (or synapses) after birth is dramatically affected by the experience a young organism has (e.g., Greenough & Black, 1992; Rosenzweig et al., 2002). Rats reared in enriched environments (as opposed to in isolation) show heavier and thicker cell development in certain portions of the cortex (as well as more synapses per neuron). Similar but less extensive changes can occur in older animals exposed to enriched environments; hence neural plasticity continues to some extent throughout the life span (see Lambert & Kinsley, 2005).

The early implications of this kind of work were taken to suggest that human infants should be exposed to highly enriched environments. However, subsequent work has shown that normal rearing conditions with caring parents are perfectly adequate. What the more recent work really suggests is that unstimulating, deprived environments can cause retarded development (Thompson, 2000; Thompson & Nelson, 2001).

This research on neural and behavioral plasticity, in combination with the work described earlier on genotype-environment correlations, makes it clear why developmental psychopathologists have been devoting increasing attention to a **developmental systems approach.** This approach acknowledges not only that genetic activity influences neural activity, which in turn influences behavior, which in turn influences the environment, but also that these influences are bidirectional. As illustrated in Figure 3.6, various aspects of our environment (physical, social, and cultural) also influence our behavior, which in turn affects our neural activity, and this in turn can even influence genetic activity (Gottlieb, 1992, 2002; see also Gottesman & Hanson, 2005).

The Impact of the Biological Viewpoint

Biological discoveries have profoundly affected the way we think about human behavior. We now recognize the important role of biochemical factors and innate characteristics, many of which are genetically determined, in both normal and abnormal behavior. In addition, since the 1950s we have witnessed many new developments in the use of drugs that can dramatically alter the severity and course of certain mental disorders—particularly the more severe ones such as schizophrenia. The host of new drugs has attracted a great deal of attention to the biological viewpoint, not only in scientific circles but also in the popular media. Biological treatments seem to have more immediate results than other available therapies, and the hope is that they may in most cases lead to a "cure-all"—immediate results with seemingly little effort.

However, as Gorenstein (1992) argued, there are several common errors in the way many people interpret the meaning of recent biological advances. Gorenstein points out that it is illusory to think—as some prominent biological researchers have—that establishing biological differences between, for example, individuals with schizophrenia and those without schizophrenia in and of itself substantiates that schizophrenia is an illness (e.g., Andreasen, 1984; Kety, 1974). All behavioral traits (introversion and extraversion, for example, or high and low sensation seeking) are characterized by distinctive biological characteristics, yet we do not label these traits as illnesses. Thus the decision about what constitutes a mental illness or disorder ultimately still rests on clinical judgment regarding the functional effects of the disordered behavior—specifically whether it leads to clinically significant distress or impairment in functioning. Establishing the biological substrate does not bear on this issue because all behavior—normal and abnormal—has a biological substrate.

The second important misconception discussed by Gorenstein (1992) concerns the idea that most, if not all, mental disorders are biological conditions with biological causes (Andreasen, 1984; Kety, 1974). Given that all of our behavior and cognitions are ultimately reducible to a set of biological events occurring in the brain, it is a mistake to distinguish between biological and psychological causes in this way. As Gorenstein argued, psychological causes can be distinguished from biological causes "only prior to their entry into the central nervous system" (1992, p. 123). This is because once a psychological cause has had its effect on a

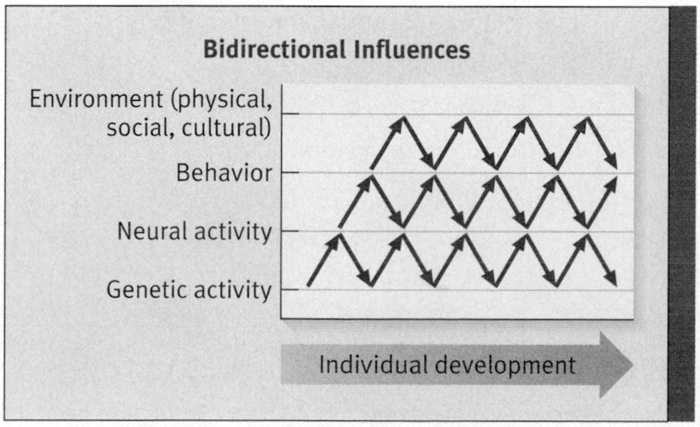

FIGURE 3.6

Bidirectional Influences

A systems view of psychobiological development.

Source: *Gilbert Gottlieb, from* Individual Development and Evolution: The Genesis of Novel Behavior. *New York: Oxford University Press, 1992. Reprinted by permission of Lawrence Erlbaum Associates.*

person, the effect of that psychological event is also ***mediated*** through the activities of the central nervous system. In actuality, then, if we find some dysfunction of the nervous system, this dysfunction could as well have arisen from psychosocial as from biological causes. In addition, psychosocial treatments are often as effective as drugs in producing changes in brain structure and function (e.g., Baxter et al., 2000; Schwartz, Stoessel, et al., 1996).

At a more general level, we must remind ourselves again that few, if any, mental disorders are independent of people's personalities or of the problems they face in trying to live their lives. We will examine viewpoints that emphasize these psychosocial and sociocultural considerations in the pages that follow, keeping in mind that the ultimate challenge will be to integrate these varying perspectives into a theoretically consistent biopsychosocial perspective on psychopathology.

research close•up

mediate

A mediator (or mediating variable) lies between two other variables and helps explain the relationship between them. You can think of it as being like an intermediate variable, hence the name.

in review

- ► Describe the sequence of events involved in the transmission of nerve impulses, and explain how imbalances of neurotransmitters might produce abnormal behavior.
- ► What is the relationship between genotypes and phenotypes, and how can genotypes shape and interact with the environment?
- ► What is temperament, and why is it important for the origins of abnormal behavior?
- ► What do we mean by "neural plasticity"?

THE PSYCHOSOCIAL VIEWPOINTS

There are many more psychosocial than biological interpretations of abnormal behavior, reflecting a wider range of opinions on how best to understand humans as people with motives, desires, perceptions, thoughts, and so on, rather than just as biological organisms. We will examine in some depth three perspectives on human nature and behavior that have been particularly influential: psychodynamic, behavioral, and cognitive-behavioral. Developments in Thinking 3.3 presents a few of the major themes of two additional perspectives: the humanistic and existential perspectives.

The three viewpoints we will discuss here represent distinct and sometimes conflicting orientations, but they are in many ways complementary. All of them emphasize the importance of early experience and an awareness of social influences and psychological processes within an individual—hence the term *psychosocial.*

The Psychodynamic Perspectives

As we noted in Chapter 2, Sigmund Freud founded the psychoanalytic school, which emphasized the role of unconscious motives and thoughts, and their dynamic interrelationships in the determination of both normal and abnormal behavior. A key concept here is the *unconscious.* According to Freud, the conscious part of the mind represents a relatively small area, whereas the unconscious part, like the submerged part of an iceberg, is the much larger portion. In the depths of the unconscious are the hurtful memories, forbidden desires, and other experiences that have been repressed—that is, pushed out of consciousness. However, unconscious material continues to seek expression and emerges in fantasies, dreams, slips of the tongue, and so forth, as well as when the individual is under hypnosis. Until such unconscious material is brought to awareness and integrated into the conscious part of the mind—for example, through psychoanalysis (a form of psychotherapy Freud developed—see Chapter 17)—it may lead to irrational and maladaptive behavior. For our purposes, a general overview of the principles of classical psychoanalytic theory will suffice (see Alexander, 1948; Arlow, 2000; or any of Freud's original work for more

- ► The psychosocial perspectives attempt to understand humans not just as biological organisms but also as people with motives, desires, and perceptions.
- ► There are three major psychosocial perspectives on human nature and behavior:
  1. Psychodynamic
  2. Behavioral
  3. Cognitive-behavioral
- ► Also includes two other perspectives:
  1. The humanistic perspective
  2. The existential perspective

FIGURE 3.7
Psychosocial Perspectives

3.3 Developments in Thinking: The Humanistic and Existential Perspectives

The Humanistic Perspective

The *humanistic perspective* views human nature as basically "good." Paying less attention to unconscious processes and past causes, it emphasizes present conscious processes and places strong emphasis on people's inherent capacity for responsible self-direction. Humanistic psychologists think that much of the empirical research designed to investigate causal factors is too simplistic to uncover the complexities of human behavior. Instead, this perspective is concerned with processes such as love, hope, creativity, values, meaning, personal growth, and self-fulfillment. Although these abstract processes are not readily subject to empirical investigation, certain underlying themes and principles of humanistic psychology can be identified, including the self as a unifying theme and a focus on values and personal growth.

In using the concept of self as a unifying theme, humanistic psychologists emphasize the importance of individuality. Among humanistic psychologists, Carl Rogers (1902–1987) developed the most systematic formulation of the *self-concept*, based largely on his pioneering research into the nature of the psychotherapeutic process. Rogers (1951, 1959) stated his views in a series of propositions that may be summarized as follows:

- Each individual exists in a private world of experience of which the *I, me,* or *myself* is the center.
- The most basic striving of an individual is toward the maintenance, enhancement, and actualization of the self, and his or her inner tendencies are toward health and wholeness under normal conditions.
- A perceived threat to the self is followed by a defense, including a tightening of perception and behavior and the introduction of self-defense mechanisms.

Humanistic psychologists emphasize that values and the process of choice are key in guiding our behavior and achieving meaningful and fulfilling lives. Each of us must develop values and a sense of our own identity based on our own experiences, rather than blindly accepting the values of others; otherwise, we deny our own experiences and lose touch with our own feelings. Only in this way can we become *self-actualizing,* meaning that we are achieving our full potential. According to this view, psychopathology is essentially the blocking or distortion of personal growth and the natural tendency toward physical and mental health. Chapter 17 presents the humanistic approach to psychotherapy.

The Existential Perspective

The *existential perspective* resembles the humanistic view in its emphasis on the uniqueness of each individual, the quest for values and meaning, and the existence of freedom for self-direction and self-fulfillment. However, it takes a less optimistic view of human beings and places more emphasis on their irrational tendencies and the difficulties inherent in self-fulfillment—particularly in a modern, bureaucratic, and dehumanizing mass society. In short, living is much more of a "confrontation" for the existentialists than for the humanists. Existential thinkers are especially concerned with the inner experiences of an individual in his or her attempts to understand and deal with the deepest human problems. There are several basic themes of existentialism:

- **Existence and essence.** Our existence is a given, but what we make of it—our essence—is up to us. Our essence is created by our choices, because our choices reflect the values on which we base and order our lives.
- **Meaning and value.** The will-to-meaning is a basic human tendency to find satisfying values and guide one's life by them.
- **Existential anxiety and the encounter with nothingness.** Nonbeing, or nothingness, which in its final form is death, is the inescapable fate of all human beings. The awareness of our inevitable death and its implications for our living can lead to existential anxiety, a deep concern over whether we are living meaningful and fulfilling lives.

Thus existential psychologists focus on the importance of establishing values and acquiring a level of spiritual maturity worthy of the freedom and dignity bestowed by one's humanness. Avoiding such central issues creates corrupted, meaningless, and wasted lives. Much abnormal behavior, therefore, is seen as the product of a failure to deal constructively with existential despair and frustration.

information). Then we will discuss newer *psychodynamic perspectives,* which were the second generation of theories that stemmed in some important way out of Freud's original psychoanalytic theory and yet also departed from it in significant ways.

FUNDAMENTALS OF FREUD'S PSYCHOANALYTIC THEORY

The Structure of Personality: Id, Ego, and Superego

Freud theorized that a person's behavior results from the interaction of three key components of the personality or psyche: the id, ego, and superego (e.g., see Arlow, 2000; Engler, 2006). The **id** is the source of instinctual drives and is the first structure to appear in infancy. These drives are inherited and are considered to be of two opposing types: (1) *life instincts,* which are constructive drives primarily of a sexual nature and which constitute the **libido,** the basic emotional and psychic energy of life; and (2) *death instincts,* which are destructive drives that tend toward aggression, destruction, and eventual death. Freud used the term *sexual* in a broad sense to refer to almost anything pleasurable, from eating to painting. The id operates on the **pleasure principle,** engaging in completely selfish and pleasure-oriented behavior, concerned only with the immediate gratification of instinctual needs without reference to reality or moral considerations. Although the id can generate mental images and wish-fulfilling fantasies, referred to as **primary process thinking,** it cannot undertake the realistic actions needed to meet instinctual demands.

Consequently, after the first few months of life, a second part of the personality, as viewed by Freud, develops—the ego. The **ego** mediates between the demands of the id and the realities of the external world. For example, during toilet training the child learns to control a bodily function to meet parental-societal expectations, and it is the developing ego that assumes the role of mediating between the physical needs of the body/id and the need to find an appropriate place and time. One of the basic functions of the ego is to meet id demands, but in such a way as to ensure the well-being and survival of the individual. This role requires the use of reason and other intellectual resources in dealing with the external world, as well as the exercise of control over id demands. The ego's adaptive measures are referred to as **secondary process thinking,** and the ego operates on the **reality principle.**

Freud viewed id demands, especially sexual and aggressive strivings, as inherently in conflict with the rules and prohibitions imposed by society. He postulated that as a child grows and gradually learns the rules of parents and society regarding right and wrong, a third part of the personality gradually emerges from the ego—the **superego.** The superego is the outgrowth of internalizing the taboos and moral values of society concerning what is right and wrong. It is essentially what we refer to as the *conscience.* As the superego develops, it becomes an inner control system that deals with the uninhibited desires of the id. Because the ego mediates among the desires of the id, the demands of reality, and the moral constraints of the superego, it is often called the *executive branch of the personality.*

Freud believed that the interplay of id, ego, and superego is of crucial significance in determining behavior. Often inner mental conflicts arise because the three subsystems are striving for different goals. If unresolved, these **intrapsychic conflicts** lead to mental disorder.

Anxiety is almost universally experienced at some point. This woman shows her anxiety while awaiting news about the outcome of surgery on her sick child.

Anxiety, Defense Mechanisms, and the Unconscious The concept of *anxiety*—generalized feelings of fear and apprehension—is prominent in the psychoanalytic viewpoint because it is an almost universal symptom of neurotic disorders. Indeed, Freud believed that anxiety played a key causal role in most of the forms of psychopathology that will be discussed in this book. Sometimes the anxiety is overtly experienced, and sometimes it is repressed and then transformed into and manifested in other overt symptoms.

Anxiety is a warning of impending real or imagined dangers as well as a painful experience, and it forces an individual to take corrective action. Often, the ego can cope with objective anxiety through rational measures. However, neurotic and moral anxiety, because they are unconscious, usually cannot be dealt with through rational measures. In these cases the ego resorts to irrational protective measures that are referred to as **ego-defense mechanisms,** some of which are described in Table 3.1. These defense mechanisms discharge or soothe anxiety, but they do so by helping a person push painful ideas out of consciousness (such as when we "forget" a dental appointment) rather than by dealing directly with the problem. These mechanisms result in a distorted view of reality, although some are clearly more adaptive than others.

Psychosexual Stages of Development In addition to his concept of the structure of personality, Freud also conceptualized five **psychosexual stages of development** that we all pass through from infancy through puberty. Each stage is characterized by a dominant mode of achieving libidinal (sexual) pleasure:

Oral stage: During the first 2 years of life, the mouth is the principal erogenous zone: An infant's

TABLE 3.1 Ego-Defense Mechanisms

Mechanism	Example
Displacement. Discharging pent-up feelings, often of hostility, on objects less dangerous than those arousing the feelings.	A woman harassed by her boss at work initiates an argument with her husband.
Fixation. Attaching oneself in an unreasonable or exaggerated way to some person, or arresting emotional development on a childhood or adolescent level.	An unmarried, middle-aged man still depends on his mother to provide his basic needs.
Projection. Attributing one's unacceptable motives or characteristics to others.	An expansionist-minded dictator of a totalitarian state is convinced that neighboring countries are planning to invade.
Rationalization. Using contrived "explanations" to conceal or disguise unworthy motives for one's behavior.	A fanatical racist uses ambiguous passages from the Scriptures to justify his hostile actions toward minorities.
Reaction formation. Preventing the awareness or expression of unacceptable desires by an exaggerated adoption of seemingly opposite behavior.	A man troubled by homosexual urges initiates a zealous community campaign to stamp out gay bars.
Regression. Retreating to an earlier developmental level involving less mature behavior and responsibility.	A man with shattered self-esteem reverts to childlike "showing off" and exhibits his genitals to young girls.
Repression. Preventing painful or dangerous thoughts from entering consciousness.	A mother's occasional murderous impulses toward her hyperactive 2-year-old are denied access to awareness.
Sublimation. Channeling frustrated sexual energy into substitutive activities.	A sexually frustrated artist paints wildly erotic pictures.

Source: Based on A. Freud (1946) and DSM-IV (1994).

greatest source of gratification is sucking, a process that is necessary for feeding.

Anal stage: From ages 2 to 3, the anus provides the major source of pleasurable stimulation during the time when toilet training is often going on and there are urges both for retention and for elimination.

Phallic stage: From ages 3 to 5 or 6, self-manipulation of the genitals provides the major source of pleasurable sensation.

Latency period: From ages 6 to 12, sexual motivations recede in importance as a child becomes preoccupied with developing skills and other activities.

Genital stage: After puberty, the deepest feelings of pleasure come from sexual relations.

Freud believed that appropriate gratification during each stage is important if a person is not to be stuck, or fixated, at that level. For example, he maintained that an infant who does not receive adequate oral gratification may, in adult life, be prone to excessive eating or other forms of oral stimulation, such as biting fingernails or drinking.

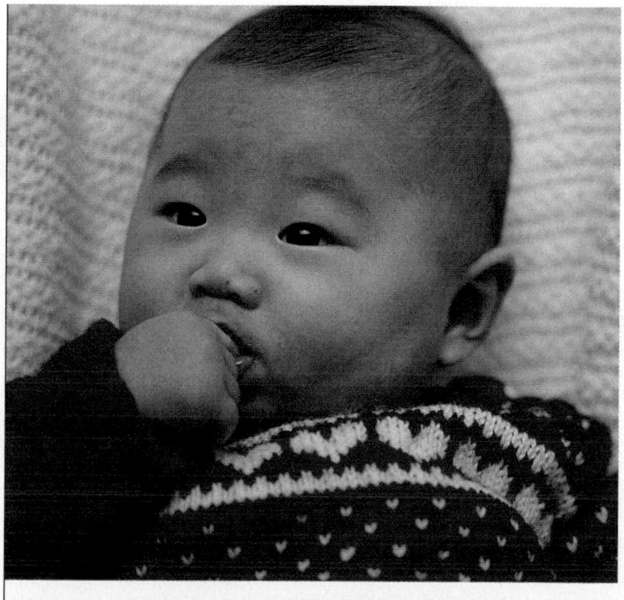

The demands of the id are evident in early childhood. According to Freud, babies pass through an oral stage, in which sucking is a dominant pleasure.

The Oedipus Complex and the Electra Complex In general, each psychosexual stage of development places demands on a child and arouses conflicts that Freud believed must be resolved. One of the most important conflicts occurs during the phallic stage, when the pleasures of self-stimulation and accompanying fantasies pave the way for the **Oedipus complex.** According to Greek mythology, Oedipus unknowingly killed his father and married his mother. Each young boy, Freud thought, symbolically relives the Oedipus drama. He longs for his mother sexually and views his father as a hated rival; however, each young boy also fears that his father will punish his son's lust by cutting off his penis. This **castration anxiety** forces the boy to repress his sexual desire for his mother and his hostility toward his father. Eventually, if all goes well, the boy identifies with his father and comes to have only harmless affection for his mother, channeling his sexual impulses toward another woman.

The **Electra complex** is the female counterpart of the Oedipus complex and is also drawn from a Greek tragedy. It is based on the view that each girl desires to possess her father and to replace her mother. Freud also believed that each girl at this stage experiences penis envy, wishing she could be more like her father and brothers. She emerges from the complex when she comes to identify with her mother and settles for a promissory note: One day she will have a man of her own who can give her a baby—which unconsciously serves as a type of penis substitute.

Resolution of this conflict is considered essential if a young adult of either sex is to develop satisfactory heterosexual relationships. The psychoanalytic perspective holds that the best we can hope for is to effect a compromise among our warring inclinations—and to realize as much instinctual gratification as possible with minimal punishment and guilt. This perspective thus presents a deterministic view of human behavior that minimizes rationality and freedom of self-determination. On a group level, it interprets violence, war, and related phenomena as the inevitable products of the aggressive and destructive instincts present in human nature.

NEWER PSYCHODYNAMIC PERSPECTIVES In seeking to understand his patients and develop his theories, Freud was chiefly concerned with the workings of the id, its nature as a source of energy, and the manner in which this id energy could be channeled or transformed. He also focused on the superego but paid relatively little attention to the importance of the ego. Later theorists developed some of Freud's basic ideas in three somewhat different directions. One new direction was that taken by his daughter Anna Freud (1895–1982), who was much more concerned with how the *ego* performed its central functions as the "executive" of personality. She and some of the other influential second generation of psychodynamic theorists refined and elaborated on the ego-defense reactions and put the ego in the foreground, giving it an important organizing role in personality development (e.g., A. Freud, 1946). According to this view, psychopathology develops when the ego does not function adequately to control or delay impulse gratification or does not make adequate use of defense mechanisms when faced with internal conflicts. This school became known as **ego psychology.** Embarking in a second new direction, other theorists focused the role of an infant's very early relationships (especially the *mother-infant relationship*) on the development of his or her personality and self-concept. The third group of influential second-generation psychodynamic theorists focused on social determinants of behavior and on the importance of people's *interpersonal relationships.* All three of these new directions omit the traditional (Freudian) psychoanalytic theory's emphasis on the primacy of libidinal energies and intrapsychic conflicts.

Object-Relations Theory Object-relations theory was developed by a number of prominent theorists including Melanie Klein, Margaret Mahler, W. R. D. Fairburn, and D. W. Winnicott, starting in the 1930s and 1940s. Although there are many variations on **object-relations theory,** they share a focus on individuals' interactions with real and imagined other people (external and internal objects) and on the relationships that people experience between their external and internal objects (Engler, 2006; Greenberg & Mitchell, 1983). *Object* in this context refers to the symbolic representation of another person in the infant's or child's environment, most often a parent. Through a

Anna Freud (1895–1982) elaborated the theory of ego-defense mechanisms and pioneered the psychoanalytic treatment of children.

Margaret Mahler (1897–1985) elaborated the object-relations approach, which many see as the main focus of contemporary psychoanalysis.

process of *introjection*, a child symbolically incorporates into his or her personality (through images and memories) important people in his or her life. For example, a child might internalize images of a punishing father; that image then becomes a harsh self-critic, influencing how the child behaves. The general notion is that internalized objects could have various conflicting properties—such as exciting or attractive versus hostile, frustrating, or rejecting—and also that these objects could split off from the central ego and maintain independent existences, thus giving rise to inner conflicts. An individual experiencing such splitting among internalized objects is, so to speak, "the servant of many masters" and cannot therefore lead an integrated, orderly life.

Erich Fromm (1900–1980) focused on the orientations that people adopt in their interactions with others. He believed that these basic orientations to the social environment were the bases of much psychopathology.

Erik Erikson (1902–1994) elaborated and broadened Freud's psychosexual stages into more socially oriented concepts. Erikson described conflicts that occurred at eight stages, each of which could be resolved in a healthy or unhealthy way.

In the past few decades, several other influential American analysts have become advocates of the object-relations point of view. Among them is Otto Kernberg, noted especially for his studies of both borderline and narcissistic personalities (Kernberg, 1985, 1996; see Chapter 11). Kernberg's view is that people with a borderline personality, whose chief characteristic is instability (especially in personal relationships), are individuals who are unable to achieve a full and stable personal identity (self) because of an inability to integrate and reconcile pathological internalized objects. Because of their inability to structure their internal world in such a way that the people they know (including themselves) can have a mixture of both good and bad traits, they also perceive the external world in abrupt extremes. For example, a person may be "all good" one moment and "all bad" the next (Koenigsberg, Kernberg, et al., 2000).

The Interpersonal Perspective We are social beings, and much of what we are is a product of our relationships with others. It is logical to expect that much of psychopathology reflects this fact—that psychopathology is rooted in the unfortunate tendencies we have developed while dealing with our interpersonal environments. This is the focus of the **interpersonal perspective,** which began with the defection in 1911 of Alfred Adler (1870–1937) from the psychoanalytic viewpoint of his teacher, Freud, and instead emphasizes social and cultural forces rather than inner instincts as determinants of behavior. In Adler's view, people are inherently social beings motivated primarily by the desire to belong to and participate in a group (see Engler, 2006; Mosak, 2000, for recent reviews).

Over time, a number of other psychodynamic theorists also took issue with psychoanalytic theory for its neglect of crucial social factors. Among the best known of these theorists were Erich Fromm (1900–1980) and Karen Horney (1885–1952). Fromm focused on the orientations, or dispositions (exploitive, for example), that people adopted in their interactions with others. He believed that when these orientations to the social environment were maladaptive, they served as the bases of much psychopathology. Horney independently developed a similar view and, in particular, vigorously rejected Freud's demeaning psychoanalytic view of women (for instance, the idea that women experience penis envy).

Erik Erikson (1902–1994) also extended the interpersonal aspects of psychoanalytic theory. He elaborated and broadened Freud's psychosexual stages into more socially oriented concepts, describing crises or conflicts that occurred at eight stages, each of which could be resolved in a healthy or unhealthy way. For example, Erikson believed that during what Freud called the "oral stage," when a child is preoccupied with oral gratification, a child's real development centers on learning either "basic trust" or "basic mistrust" of her or his social world. Learning a certain amount of trust, for instance, is necessary for later competence in many areas of life.

Attachment Theory Finally, John Bowlby's **attachment theory,** which can in many ways be seen as having its roots in the interpersonal and object-relations perspectives, has become an enormously influential theory in child psychology and child psychiatry, as well as in adult psychopathology. Drawing on Freud and others from these perspectives, Bowlby's theory (1969, 1973, 1980) emphasizes the importance of early experience, especially early experience with attachment relationships, as laying the foundation for later functioning throughout childhood, adolescence, and adulthood. He stressed the importance of the quality of parental care to the development of secure attachments, but he also saw the infants as playing a more active role in shaping the course of their own development than had most of the earlier theorists (Carlson & Sroufe, 1995; Sroufe, Carlson, Levy, & Egeland, 2003).

IMPACT OF THE PSYCHODYNAMIC PERSPECTIVES

Freud's psychoanalytic theory can be seen as the first systematic approach to showing how human psychological processes can result in mental disorders. Much as the biological perspective had replaced superstition with organic pathology as the suspected cause of mental disorders for many psychiatrists and psychologists, the psychoanalytic perspective replaced brain pathology with intrapsychic conflict and exaggerated ego defenses as the suspected cause of at least some mental disorders.

Freud greatly advanced our understanding of both normal and abnormal behavior. Many of his original concepts have become fundamental to our thinking about human nature and behavior, and have even had an important influence on the intellectual history of Western civilization. Two of Freud's contributions stand out as particularly noteworthy:

1. He developed therapeutic techniques such as free association and dream analysis for becoming acquainted with both the conscious and the unconscious aspects of mental life (see Chapter 17). The results obtained led Freud to emphasize several points that have been incorporated (in modified forms) into current thinking: (a) the extent to which unconscious motives and defense mechanisms affect behavior, meaning that the causes of human behavior are generally not obvious or available to conscious awareness; (b) the importance of early childhood experiences in the development of both normal and abnormal personality; and (c) the importance of sexual factors in human behavior and mental disorders. Although, as we have said, Freud used the term *sexual* in a much broader sense than usual, the idea struck a common chord, and the role of sexual factors in human behavior was finally brought out into the open as an appropriate topic for scientific investigation (see Chapter 13).
2. He demonstrated that certain abnormal mental phenomena occur in the attempt to cope with difficult problems and are simply exaggerations of normal ego-defense mechanisms. This realization that the same psychological principles apply to both normal and abnormal behavior dissipated much of the mystery and fear surrounding mental disorders.

The psychoanalytic perspective has come under attack, however, from many directions. Two important criticisms of traditional psychoanalytic theory center on its failure as a scientific theory to explain abnormal behavior. First, many believe that it fails to recognize sufficiently the scientific limits of personal reports of experience as the primary mode of obtaining information. Second, there is a lack of scientific evidence to support many of its explanatory assumptions or the effectiveness of traditional psychoanalysis (Erdelyi, 1992; but see also Westen, 1998). In addition, Freudian theory in particular has been criticized for an overemphasis on the sex drive, for its demeaning view of women, for pessimism about basic human nature, for exaggerating the role of unconscious processes, and for failing to consider motives toward personal growth and fulfillment.

IMPACT OF NEWER PSYCHODYNAMIC PERSPECTIVES

The second generation of psychodynamic theorists has done much to improve scientific efforts to measure concepts such as a person's core (but unconscious) conflictual relationships (e.g., Henry et al., 1994; Horowitz et al., 1991). Some progress has also been made in understanding how psychodynamic therapy works and in documenting its effectiveness for certain problems (e.g., Crits-Christoph & Barber, 2000; Crits-Christoph et al., 2004). In addition, Bowlby's attachment theory has generated an enormous amount of research supporting many of its basic tenets about normal and abnormal child development and adult psychopathology (e.g., Carlson & Sroufe, 1995; Rholes & Simpson, 2004).

The interpersonal perspective has also done a good deal to establish its scientific validity. In the area of diagnosis, many supporters of the interpersonal perspective believe that the reliability and validity of psychological diagnoses could be improved if a new system based on interpersonal functioning were developed, and some progress has been made toward developing such a system (e.g., Benjamin, 1993, 2005; Benjamin & Pugh, 2001). The focus of interpersonal therapy is on alleviating problem-causing relationships and on helping people achieve more satisfactory relationships. In recent years, major progress has been made in documenting that interpersonal psychotherapy for certain disorders such as depression, bulimia, and some personality disorders can be as effective, or nearly as effective, as cognitive-behavioral treatment—considered by many to be the treatment of choice for these disorders (Agras et al., 2000; Benjamin, 2004; Benjamin & Pugh, 2001; Hollon, Thase, & Markowitz, 2002b).

The Behavioral Perspective

The behavioral perspective arose in the early twentieth century in part as a reaction against the unscientific methods of psychoanalysis. Behavioral psychologists believed that the study of subjective experience (e.g., free association and dream analysis) did not provide acceptable scientific data because such observations were not open to verification by other investigators. In their view, only the study of directly observable behavior and of the stimuli and reinforcing conditions that control it could serve as a basis for understanding human behavior, normal and abnormal.

Although this perspective was initially developed through laboratory research rather than clinical practice with disturbed patients, its implications for explaining and treating maladaptive behavior soon became evident. As we noted in Chapter 2, the roots of the behavioral perspective are in Pavlov's study of classical conditioning and in Thorndike's study of instrumental conditioning (later renamed operant conditioning by Skinner; today both terms are used). In the United States, Watson did much to promote the behavioral approach to psychology with his book *Behaviorism* (1924).

Learning—the modification of behavior as a consequence of experience—is the central theme of the behavioral approach. Because most human behavior is learned, the behaviorists addressed the question of how learning occurs. Behaviorists focused on the effects of environmental conditions (stimuli) on the acquisition, modification, and possible elimination of various types of response patterns, both adaptive and maladaptive.

CLASSICAL CONDITIONING A specific stimulus may come to elicit a specific response through the process of **classical conditioning.** For example, although food naturally elicits salivation, a stimulus that reliably precedes and signals the presentation of food will also come to elicit salivation (Pavlov, 1927). In this case, food is the *unconditioned stimulus* (UCS) and salivation the *unconditioned response* (UCR). A stimulus that signals food delivery and eventually elicits salivation is called a *conditioned stimulus* (CS). Conditioning has occurred when presentation of the conditioned stimulus alone elicits salivation—the *conditioned response* (CR). The same general process occurs when a neutral CS is paired with a painful or frightening stimulus such as a mild electric shock or loud noise, as illustrated in Figure 3.8, although in this case fear is conditioned rather than salivation.

The hallmark of classical conditioning is that a formerly neutral stimulus—the CS—acquires the capacity to elicit biologically adaptive responses through repeated pairings with the UCS (e.g., Domjan, 2005). However, we also now know that this process of classical conditioning is not as blind or automatic as was once thought. Rather, it seems that animals (and people) actively acquire information about what CSs allow them to predict, expect, or prepare for an upcoming biologically significant event (the UCS). That is, they learn what is called a *stimulus-stimulus expectancy*. Indeed, only CSs that provide reliable and nonredundant information about the occurrence of a UCS acquire the capacity to elicit CRs (Hall, 1994; Rescorla, 1988). For example, if UCSs occur as often without being preceded by a CS as they do with the CS, conditioning will not occur because the CS in this case does not provide reliable information about the occurrence of the UCS.

Classically conditioned responses are well maintained over time; that is, they are not simply forgotten (even over many years). However, if a CS is repeatedly presented without the UCS, the conditioned response gradually extinguishes. This gradual process, known as **extinction,** should not be confused with the idea of unlearning, because we know that the response may return at some future point in time (a phenomenon Pavlov called **spontaneous recovery**). Moreover, a somewhat weaker CR may also still be elicited in different environmental contexts than in the one where the extinction process took place (Bouton, 1994, 2002, in press). Thus any extinction of fear that has taken place in a therapist's office may not necessarily generalize completely and automatically to other contexts outside the therapist's office (see Craske & Mystkowski, in press; Mystkowski & Mineka, in press). As we shall see later, these principles of extinction and spontaneous recovery have important implications for many forms of behavioral treatment.

Classical Conditioning

Prior to conditioning:
Conditioned stimulus (neutral) (CS) (Light) .... Orientation response to light
Unconditioned stimulus (UCS) (Painful stimulus) .... Unconditioned response (UCR) (Pain and fear)

During conditioning:
Conditioned stimulus (light) (CS) + Unconditioned stimulus (UCS) (painful stimulus) .... Conditioned response (fear) (CR)

Following conditioning:
Conditioned stimulus (alone) (CS) .... Conditioned response (fear) (CR)

FIGURE 3.8

Classical Conditioning

Before conditioning, the CS has no capacity to elicit fear, but after being repeatedly followed by a painful or frightening UCS that elicits pain or distress, the CS gradually acquires the capacity to elicit a fear CR. If there are also interspersed trials in which the UCS occurs not preceded by the CS, conditioning does not occur because in this case the CS is not a reliable predictor of the occurrence of the UCS.

Classical conditioning is important in abnormal psychology because many physiological and emotional responses can be conditioned, including those related to fear, anxiety, or sexual arousal and those stimulated by drugs of abuse. Thus, for example, one can learn a fear of the dark if fear-producing stimuli (such as frightening dreams or fantasies) occur regularly in the dark, or one can acquire a fear of snakes if bitten by a snake (e.g., Mineka & Sutton, in press; Mineka & Zinbarg, 2006). In addition, fears and other responses can be conditioned to internal bodily cues (known as *interoceptive cues*), as, for example, when a person's heart palpitations that occurred early during an acute panic attack acquire the capacity to elicit panic when they occur at other times (Bouton, Mineka, & Barlow, 2001).

INSTRUMENTAL CONDITIONING In **instrumental** (or **operant**) **conditioning,** an individual learns how to achieve a desired goal. The goal in question may be to obtain something that is rewarding or to escape from something that is unpleasant. Essential here is the concept of **reinforcement,** which refers either to the delivery of a reward or pleasant stimulus, or to the escape from an aversive stimulus. New responses are learned and tend to recur if they are reinforced. Although it was originally thought that instrumental conditioning consisted of simple strengthening of a stimulus-response connection every time that reinforcement occurred, it is now believed that the animal or person learns a *response-outcome expectancy* (e.g., Domjan, 2005)—that is, learns that a response will lead to a reward outcome. If sufficiently motivated for that outcome (e.g., being hungry), the person will make the response that he has learned produces the outcome (e.g., opening the refrigerator).

Initially a high rate of reinforcement may be necessary to establish an instrumental response, but lesser rates are usually sufficient to maintain it. In fact, an instrumental response appears to be especially persistent when reinforcement is intermittent—when the reinforcing stimulus does not invariably follow the response—as demonstrated in gambling when occasional wins seem to maintain high rates of responding. However, when reinforcement is consistently withheld over time, the conditioned response—whether classical or instrumental—gradually extinguishes. In short, the subject eventually stops making the response.

A special problem arises in extinguishing a response in situations in which a subject has been conditioned to anticipate an aversive event and to make an instrumental response to avoid it. For example, a boy who has nearly drowned in a swimming pool may develop a fear of water and a *conditioned avoidance response* in which he consistently avoids all large bodies of water. When he sees a pond, lake, or swimming pool, he feels anxious; running away and avoiding contact lessens his anxiety and thus is reinforcing. As a result, his avoidance response is highly resistant to extinction. It also prevents him from having experiences with water that could bring about extinction of his fear. In later discussions, we will see that conditioned avoidance responses play a role in many patterns of abnormal behavior.

Continuing to play blackjack after an occasional unpredictable win is an example of intermittent reinforcement. Behavior that is reinforced in this unpredictable manner occurs at high rates and is highly resistant to extinction.

As we grow up, instrumental learning becomes an important mechanism for discriminating between what will prove rewarding and what will prove unrewarding—and thus for acquiring the behaviors essential for coping with our world. Unfortunately, what we learn is not always useful in the long run. We may learn to value things (such as cigarettes or alcohol) that seem attractive in the short run but that can actually hurt us in the long run, or we may learn coping patterns (such as helplessness, bullying, or other irresponsible behaviors) that are maladaptive rather than adaptive in the long run.

GENERALIZATION AND DISCRIMINATION In both classical and instrumental conditioning, when a response is conditioned to one stimulus or set of stimuli, it can be evoked by other, similar stimuli; this process is called **generalization.** A person who fears bees, for example, may generalize that fear to all flying insects. A process complementary to generalization is **discrimination,** which occurs when a person learns to distinguish between similar stimuli and to respond differently to them based on which ones are followed by reinforcement. For example, because red strawberries taste good and green ones do not, a conditioned discrimination will occur if a person has experience with both.

The concepts of generalization and discrimination have many implications for the development of maladaptive behavior. Although generalization enables us to use past experiences in sizing up new situations, the possibility of making inappropriate generalizations always exists, as when a troubled adolescent fails to discriminate between friendly and hostile teasing from peers. In some instances, an important discrimination seems to be beyond an individual's capability (as when a bigoted person deals with others on the basis of stereotypes rather than as individuals) and may lead to inappropriate and maladaptive behavior.

OBSERVATIONAL LEARNING Human and nonhuman primates are also capable of **observational learning**—that is, learning through observation alone, without directly experiencing an unconditioned stimulus (for classical conditioning) or a reinforcement (for instrumental conditioning). For instance, children can acquire fears simply observing a parent or peer behaving fearfully with some object or situation that the child was not initially afraid of. In this case, they experience the fear of the parent or peer vicariously, and that fear becomes attached to the formerly neutral object (Mineka & Ben Hamida, 1998; Mineka & Cook, 1993). For observational instrumental learning, Bandura did a classic series of experiments in the 1960s on how children observationally learned various novel aggressive responses toward a large Bobo doll after they had observed models being reinforced for these responses (cf. Bandura, 1969). Although the children themselves were never directly reinforced for showing these novel aggressive responses, they nonetheless showed them when given the opportunity to interact with the Bobo doll themselves. The possibilities for observational conditioning of both classical and instrumental responses greatly expand our opportunities for learning both adaptive and maladaptive behavior.

IMPACT OF THE BEHAVIORAL PERSPECTIVE In the classic book *Personality and Psychotherapy*, Dollard and Miller (1950) reinterpreted psychoanalytic theory in the terminology of learning principles. They asserted that the ungoverned pleasure-seeking impulses of Freud's id were merely an aspect of the principle of reinforcement (the behavior of organisms being generally determined by the maximization of pleasure and the minimization of pain); that Freud's concept of anxiety was merely a conditioned fear response; that repression was merely conditioned thought stoppage reinforced by anxiety reduction; and so on. Dollard and Miller's ideas laid the groundwork for a behavioral assault on the prevailing psychodynamic doctrines of the time (e.g., Salter, 1949; Wolpe, 1958). However, behavior therapy did not become well established as a powerful way of viewing and treating abnormal behavior for another 15 to 20 years because there was so much resistance by well-entrenched supporters of psychoanalysis.

By means of relatively few basic concepts, the behavioral perspective attempts to explain the acquisition, modification, and extinction of nearly all types of behavior. Maladaptive behavior is viewed as essentially the result of (1) a failure to learn necessary adaptive behaviors or competencies, such as how to establish satisfying personal relationships, and/or (2) the learning of ineffective or maladaptive responses. Maladaptive behavior is thus the result of learning that has gone awry and is defined in terms of specific, observable, undesirable responses.

For the behavior therapist, the focus of therapy is on changing specific behaviors and emotional responses—eliminating undesirable reactions and learning desirable ones. For example, fears and phobias can be successfully treated by prolonged exposure to feared objects or situations—a kind of extinction procedure derived from principles of extinction of classically conditioned responses. Classic work using the principles of instrumental conditioning also showed that chronically mentally ill people can be retaught basic living skills such as clothing and feeding themselves through the use of tokens that are earned for appropriate behavior and that can be turned in for desirable rewards (candy, time watching television, passes to go outside, etc.).

The behavioral approach is well known for its precision and objectivity, for its wealth of research, and for its demonstrated effectiveness in changing specific behaviors. A behavior therapist specifies what behavior is to be changed and how it is to be changed. Later, the effectiveness of the therapy can be evaluated objectively by the degree to which the stated goals have been achieved. On the other hand, the behavioral perspective has been criticized for being concerned only with symptoms. However, this criticism is considered unfair by many contemporary behavior therapists, given that successful symptom-focused treatment often has very positive effects on other aspects of a person's life (e.g., Borkovec, Abel, & Newman, 1995; Lenz & Demal, 2000; Telch et al., 1995). Still others have argued that the behavioral approach oversimplifies human behavior and is unable to explain all of its complexities. This latter criticism stems at least in part from misunderstandings about current developments in behavioral approaches (e.g., Bouton et al., 2001; Mineka & Zinbarg, 1996, 2006). Whatever its limitations, the behavioral perspective has had a tremendous impact on contemporary views of human nature, behavior, and psychopathology.

The Cognitive-Behavioral Perspective

Since the 1950s many psychologists, including some learning theorists, have focused on cognitive processes and their impact on behavior. Cognitive psychology involves the study of basic information-processing mechanisms such as attention and memory, as well as higher mental processes such as thinking, planning, and decision making. The current emphasis within psychology as a whole on understanding all of these facets of normal human cognition originally began as a reaction against the relatively mechanistic nature of the traditional radical behavioral viewpoint (espoused by Watson and Skinner), including its failure to attend to the importance of mental processes—both in their own right and for their influence on emotions and behavior.

Albert Bandura (b. 1925) stressed that people learn more by internal than external reinforcement. They can visualize the consequences of their actions rather than rely exclusively on environmental reinforcements.

Albert Bandura (b. 1925), a learning theorist who developed a cognitive-behavioral perspective, placed considerable emphasis on the cognitive aspects of learning. Bandura stressed that human beings regulate behavior by internal symbolic processes—thoughts. That is, we learn by *internal reinforcement*. According to Bandura, we prepare ourselves for difficult tasks, for example, by visualizing what the consequences would be if we did not perform them. Thus we take our automobiles to the garage in the fall and have the antifreeze checked because we can "see" ourselves stranded on a road in winter. We do not always require external reinforcement to alter our behavior patterns; our cognitive abilities allow us to solve many problems internally. Bandura (1974) went so far as to say that human beings have "a capacity for self-direction" (p. 861). Bandura later developed a theory of *self-efficacy*, the belief that one can achieve desired goals (1986, 1997). He posited that cognitive-behavioral treatments work in large part by improving self-efficacy.

SCHEMAS AND COGNITIVE DISTORTIONS Other cognitive-behavioral theorists abandoned the learning theory framework more vigorously than did Bandura and focused almost exclusively on cognitive processes and their impact on behavior. Today the **cognitive** or **cognitive-behavioral perspective** on abnormal behavior focuses on how thoughts and information processing can become distorted and lead to maladaptive emotions and behavior. One central construct for this perspective is the concept of a schema that was adapted from cognitive psychology by Aaron Beck (b. 1921), another pioneering cognitive theorist (e.g., Beck, 1967; Neisser, 1967, 1982). A **schema** is an underlying representation of knowledge that guides the current processing of information and often leads to distortions in attention, memory, and comprehension. People develop different schemas based on their temperament, abilities, and experiences.

Our schemas about the world around us and about ourselves (self-schemas) are our guides, one might say, through the complexities of living in the world as we understand it. For example, we all have schemas about other people (for example, expectations that they are lazy or very career oriented). We also have schemas about social roles (for example, expectations about what the appropriate behaviors for a widow are) and about events (for example, what sequences of events are appropriate for a particular situation such as someone coping with a loss; Clark, Beck, & Alford, 1999; Fiske & Taylor, 1991). Our **self-schemas** include our views on who we are, what we might become, and what is important to us. Other aspects of our self-schemas concern our notions of the various roles we occupy or might occupy in our social environment such as woman, man, student, parent, physician, American, and so on. Most people have clear ideas about at least some of their own personal attributes and less clear ideas about other attributes (Fiske & Taylor, 1991; Kunda, 1999).

Schemas about the world and self-schemas are vital to our ability to engage in effective and organized behavior because they enable us to focus on what are the most relevant and important bits of information among the amazingly complex array of information that is available to our senses. However, schemas are also sources of psychological vulnerabilities, because some of our schemas or certain aspects of our self-schemas may be distorted and inaccurate. In addition, we often hold some schemas—even distorted ones—with conviction, making them resistant to change. This is in part because we are usually not completely conscious of our schemas. In other words, although our daily decisions and behavior are largely shaped by these frames of reference, we may be unaware of the assumptions

Our self-schemas—our frames of reference for what we are, what we might become, and what is important to us—influence our choice of goals and our confidence in attaining them. A probable element of this older woman's self-schema was that she could accomplish her lifelong goal of obtaining a college education once her children were grown in spite of the fact she was nearly 40 years older than the average college student.

Aaron Beck (b. 1921) pioneered the development of cognitive theories of depression, anxiety, and personality disorders. He also developed highly effective cognitive-behavioral treatments for these disorders.

on which they are based—or even of having made assumptions at all. We think that we are simply seeing things the way they are and often do not consider the fact that other views of the "real" world might be possible or that other rules for what is "right" might exist.

We tend to work new experiences into our existing cognitive frameworks, even if the new information has to be reinterpreted or distorted to make it fit—a process known as *assimilation.* In other words, we are likely to cling to existing assumptions and to reject or distort new information that contradicts them. *Accommodation*—changing our existing frameworks to make it possible to incorporate new information that doesn't fit—is more difficult and threatening, especially when important assumptions are challenged. Accommodation is, of course, a basic goal of psychosocial therapies—explicitly in the case of the cognitive and cognitive-behavioral therapies, but deeply embedded in virtually all other approaches as well.

According to Beck (1967; Beck, Freeman, & Davis, 2004; Beck & Weishaar, 2000), different forms of psychopathology are characterized by different maladaptive schemas that have developed as a function of adverse early learning experiences. These maladaptive schemas lead to the distortions in thinking that are characteristic of certain disorders such as anxiety, depression, and personality disorders. In addition to studying the nature of dysfunctional schemas associated with different forms of psychopathology, researchers have also studied several different patterns of distorted information processing exhibited by people with various forms of psychopathology. This research has illuminated the cognitive mechanisms that may be involved in causing or maintaining certain disorders. For example, depressed individuals show memory biases favoring negative information over positive or neutral information. Such biases are likely to help reinforce or maintain one's current depressed state (e.g., Mathews & MacLeod, 1994, 2005; Mineka, Rafaeli, & Yovel, 2003).

Another important feature of information processing is that a great deal of information is processed *nonconsciously*, or outside of our awareness. Note that the term *nonconscious* does not refer to Freud's concept of the unconscious in which primitive emotional conflicts are thought to simmer. Instead, the term *nonconscious mental activity* as studied by cognitive psychologists is simply a descriptive term for mental processes that are occurring without our being aware of them. One example relevant to psychopathology is that anxious people seem to have their attention drawn to threatening information even when that information is presented subliminally (that is, without the person's awareness); (e.g., Mathews & MacLeod, 1994, 2005). Another relevant example occurs in the well-known phenomenon of *implicit memory*, which is demonstrated when a person's behavior reveals that she or he remembers a previously learned word or activity even though she or he cannot consciously remember it. For example, if someone asks you for your old home phone number from about 10 years ago, you may not be able to recall it (no explicit memory for it), but if you picked up a phone you might dial it correctly (intact implicit memory for it).

ATTRIBUTIONS, ATTRIBUTIONAL STYLE, AND PSYCHOPATHOLOGY *Attribution theory* has also contributed significantly to the cognitive-behavioral approach (Anderson, Krull, & Weiner, 1996; Fiske & Taylor, 1991; Gotlib & Abramson, 1999). **Attribution** is simply the process of assigning causes to things that happen. We may attribute behavior to external events such as rewards or punishments ("He did it for the money"), or we may assume that the causes are internal and derive from traits within ourselves or others ("He did it because he is so generous"). Causal attributions help us explain our own or other people's behaviors and make it possible to predict what we or others are likely to do in the future. A student who fails a test may attribute the failure to a lack of intelligence (a personal trait) or to ambiguous test questions or unclear directions (environmental causes).

Attribution theorists have been interested in whether different forms of psychopathology are associated with distinctive and dysfunctional attributional styles. *Attributional style* is a characteristic way in which an individual tends to assign causes to bad events or good events. For example, depressed people tend to attribute bad events to internal, stable, and global causes ("I failed the test because I'm stupid" as opposed to "I failed the test because the teacher was in a bad mood and graded it unfairly"). However inaccurate our attributions may be, they become important parts of our view of the world and can have significant effects on our emotional well-being (Abramson, Seligman, & Teasdale, 1978; Buchanan & Seligman, 1995; Mineka et al., 2003). Interestingly, nondepressed people tend to have what is called a *self-serving bias* in which they are more likely to make internal, stable, and global attributions for positive rather than negative events (e.g., Mezulis, Abramson, Hyde, & Hankin, 2004).

COGNITIVE THERAPY Beck, who is generally considered the founder of cognitive therapy, has been enormously influential in the development of cognitive-behavioral treatment approaches to various forms of psychopathology. Following Beck's lead, cognitive-behavioral theorists and clinicians have simply shifted their focus from overt behavior itself to the underlying cognitions assumed to be producing the maladaptive emotions and behavior. Fundamental to Beck's perspective is the idea that the way we interpret events and experiences determines our emotional reactions to them. Suppose, for example, that you are sitting in your living room and hear a crash in the adjacent dining room. You remember that you left the window open in the dining room and conclude that a gust of wind must have knocked over your favorite new vase that was sitting on the table. What would your emotional reaction be? Probably you would be annoyed or angry with yourself either for having left the window open or for having left the vase out (or both!). By contrast, suppose you conclude that a burglar must have climbed in the open window. What would your emotional reaction be then? In all likelihood, you would feel frightened. Thus your interpretation of the crash you heard in the next room fundamentally determines your emotional reaction to it. Moreover, certain individuals with prominent danger schemas may be especially prone to making the burglar assumption in this example, leaving them at risk for anxiety and worry.

One central issue for cognitive therapy, then, is how best to alter distorted and maladaptive cognitions, including the underlying maladaptive schemas that lead to different disorders and their associated emotions. For example, cognitive-behavioral clinicians are concerned with their clients' self-statements—that is, with what their clients say to themselves by way of interpreting their experiences. People who interpret what happens in their lives as a negative reflection of their self-worth are likely to feel depressed; people who interpret the sensation that their heart is racing as meaning that they may have a heart attack and die are likely to have a panic attack. Cognitive-behavioral clinicians use a variety of techniques designed to alter whatever negative cognitive biases the client harbors (e.g., see Beck, 2005; Beck et al., 2004; Hollon & Beck, 1994, in press). This is in contrast to, for example, psychodynamic practice, which assumes that diverse problems are due to a limited array of intrapsychic conflicts (such as an unresolved Oedipus complex) and tends not to focus treatment directly on a person's particular problems or complaints. The most widely used cognitive-behavioral therapies will be described in greater detail in Chapters 6, 7, 11, and 17.

Some interpret terrifying scenes in a horror movie and the sensations of their heart pounding as a sign of excitement and having a good time; others interpret the same scenes and sensations as if something dangerous and scary is really *happening. Cognitive-behavioral psychologists emphasize that the way we interpret an event can dramatically color our emotional reactions to it.*

THE IMPACT OF THE COGNITIVE-BEHAVIORAL PERSPECTIVE The cognitive-behavioral viewpoint has had a powerful impact on contemporary clinical psychology. Many researchers and clinicians have found support for the principle of altering human behavior through changing the way people think about themselves and others. Many traditional behaviorists, however, have remained skeptical of the cognitive-behavioral viewpoint. B. F. Skinner (1990), in his last major address, remained true to behaviorism. He questioned the move away from principles of operant conditioning. He reminded his audience that cognitions are not observable phenomena and, as such, cannot be relied on as solid empirical data. Although Skinner is gone, this debate will surely continue in some form. Indeed, Wolpe (1988, 1993), who was another founder of behavior therapy, also remained highly critical of the cognitive perspective until his death in 1997. However, these criticisms have seemed to be decreasing over the past 10 to 15 years as more and more evidence accumulates for the efficacy of cognitive-behavioral treatments for various disorders ranging from schizophrenia to anxiety, depression, and personality disorders. This approach has also been greatly advanced by the accumulation of sophisticated information-processing studies of the effects of emotion on cognition and behavior (e.g., Mathews & MacLeod, 2005). This is because such studies do not rely on the self-report techniques that were originally central to this approach, which are especially open to the kinds of criticisms raised by Skinner and Wolpe.

What the Adoption of a Perspective Does and Does Not Do

Each of the psychosocial perspectives on human behavior—psychodynamic, behavioral, and cognitive-behavioral—contributes to our understanding of psychopathology, but none alone can account for the complex variety of human maladaptive behaviors. Because different causal perspectives influence which components of maladaptive behavior the observer focuses on, each perspective depends on generalizations from limited observations and research. For example, in attempting to explain a complex disorder such as alcohol dependence, the more traditional psychodynamic viewpoint focuses on intrapsychic conflict and anxiety that the person attempts to reduce through the intake of alcohol; the more recent interpersonal variant on the psychodynamic perspective focuses on difficulties in a person's past and present relationships that contribute to drinking; the behavioral viewpoint focuses on faulty learning of habits to reduce stress (drinking alcohol) and environmental conditions that may be exacerbating or maintaining the condition; and the cognitive-behavioral viewpoint focuses on maladaptive thinking including deficits in problem solving and information processing, such as irrational beliefs about the need for alcohol to reduce stress.

Thus which perspective we adopt has important consequences: It influences our *perception* of maladaptive behavior, the *types of evidence we look for,* and *the way in which we are likely to interpret data.* A range of psychosocial causal factors have been implicated in the origins of maladaptive behavior, and some of these different viewpoints provide contrasting (or sometimes complementary) explanations for how the causal factors exert their effects.

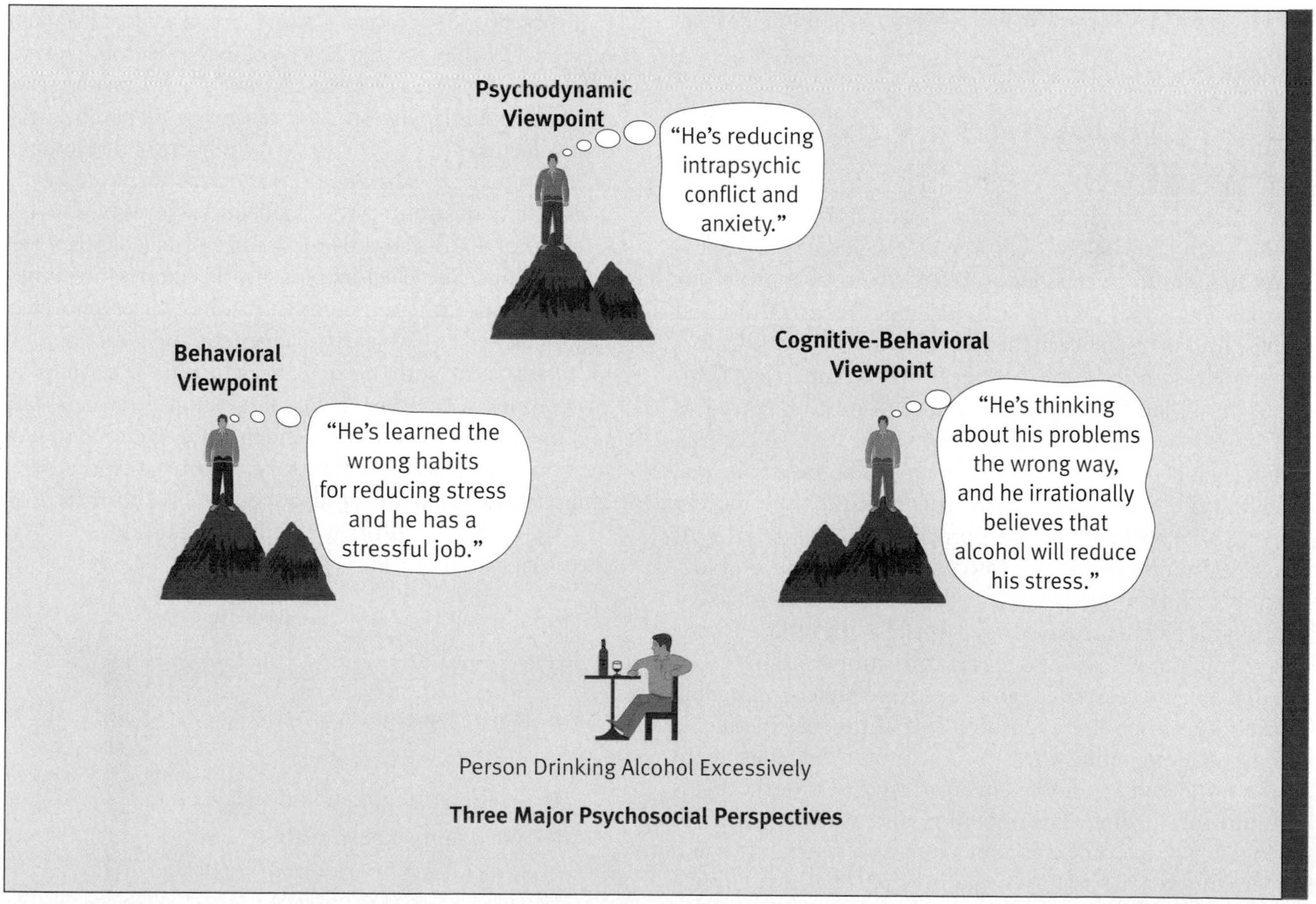

FIGURE 3.9
Three Major Psychosocial Perspectives on Alcohol Dependence

In Review

- Contrast the newer psychodynamic perspectives—ego psychology, object-relations theory, and the interpersonal perspective—with the earlier, Freudian perspective.
- What is the central theme of the behavioral perspective, and what has been its impact?
- How do classical and instrumental conditioning, generalization, discrimination, and observational learning contribute to the origins of abnormal behavior?
- What is the focus of the cognitive-behavioral perspective, and what has been its impact?
- Why are schemas and self-schemas so important for understanding abnormal behavior and its treatment?
- What role do cognitive distortions and attributions have in psychopathology according to the cognitive-behavioral perspective?

Psychosocial Causal Factors

We begin life with few built-in patterns and a great capacity to learn from experience. What we do learn from our experiences may help us face challenges resourcefully and may lead to resilience in the face of future stressors. Unfortunately, some of our experiences may be much less helpful in our later lives, and we may be deeply influenced by factors in early childhood over which we have no control. One good example of ways in which the events in one child's life may be vastly different from those in another child's life is whether they are *predictable* or *controllable*. At one extreme are children who grow up in stable and lovingly indulgent environments, buffered to a large extent from the harsher realities of the world; at the other extreme are children whose experiences consist of constant exposure to unpredictable and uncontrollable frightening events or unspeakable cruelties. Such different experiences have corresponding effects on the adults' schemas about the world and about the self: Some suggest a world that is uniformly loving, unthreatening, and benign, which of course it is not; others suggest a jungle in which safety and perhaps even life itself is constantly in the balance. Given a preference in terms of likely outcomes, most of us would opt for the former of these sets of experiences. However, these actually may not be the best blueprint for engaging the real world, because it may be important to encounter some stressors and learn ways to deal with them in order to gain a sense of control (e.g., Barlow, 2002a; Seligman, 1975) or self-efficacy (Bandura, 1986, 1997).

Exposure to multiple uncontrollable and unpredictable frightening events is likely to leave a person vulnerable to anxiety and negative affect, a central problem in a number of mental disorders such as anxiety and depression. For example, Barlow's (1988, 2002) and Mineka's (1985a; Mineka & Zinbarg, 1996, 2006) models emphasize the important role that experience with unpredictable and uncontrollable negative outcomes has in creating stress, anxiety, and depression (see also Abramson et al., 1978; Chorpita, 2001; Chorpita & Barlow, 1998; Seligman, 1975). It is important to note that a person exposed to the same frequency and intensity of negative outcomes that are predictable and/or controllable will experience less stress and be less likely to develop anxiety or depression.

In this section we will examine the types of psychosocial factors that make people vulnerable to disorder or that may precipitate disorder. Psychosocial factors are those developmental influences—often unpredictable and uncontrollable negative events—that may handicap a person psychologically, making him or her less resourceful in coping with events. (However, it is important to remember that psychosocial causal factors are always ultimately mediated by changes that take place in our nervous systems when emotions are activated and when new learning takes place.) We will focus on four categories of psychosocial causal factors that can each have important detrimental effects on a child's socioemotional development: (1) early deprivation or trauma, (2) inadequate parenting styles, (3) marital discord and divorce, and (4) maladaptive peer relationships. Such factors typically do not operate alone. They interact with each other and with other psychosocial factors, as well as with particular genetic and temperamental factors and with particular sociocultural settings or environments. In other words, although psychosocial factors are often studied independent of genetic, temperamental, and sociocultural factors, a more comprehensive biopsychosocial understanding should be the ultimate goal.

We now turn to the four different categories of psychosocial causal factors.

- Early deprivation or trauma
- Inadequate parenting styles
- Marital discord and divorce
- Maladaptive peer relationships

FIGURE 3.10
Examples of Psychosocial Causal Factors

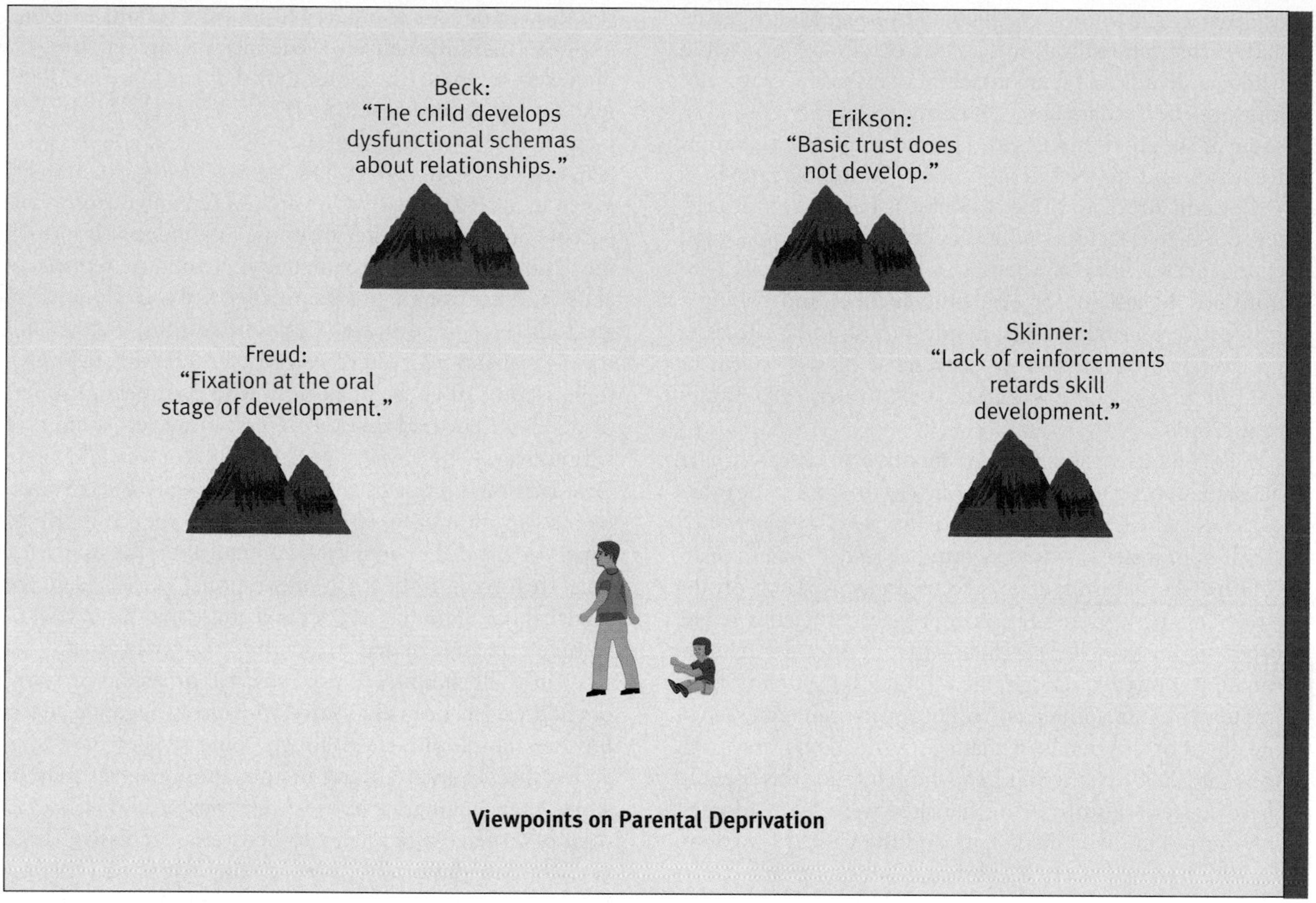

FIGURE 3.11
Viewpoints on Parental Deprivation

Early Deprivation or Trauma

Children who do not have the resources that are normally supplied by parents or parental surrogates may be left with deep and sometimes irreversible psychological scars. The needed resources range from food and shelter to love and attention. Deprivation of such resources can occur in several forms. The most severe manifestations of deprivation are usually seen among abandoned or orphaned children, who may be either institutionalized or placed in a succession of unwholesome and inadequate foster homes. However, it can also occur in intact families where, for one reason or another, parents are unable (for instance, because of mental disorder) or unwilling to provide close and frequent human attention and nurturing.

We can interpret the consequences of parental deprivation from several psychosocial viewpoints. Such deprivation might result in fixation at the oral stage of psychosexual development (Freud); it might interfere with the development of basic trust (Erikson); it might retard the attainment of needed skills because of a lack of available reinforcements (Skinner); or it might result in the child's acquiring dysfunctional schemas and self-schemas in which relationships are represented as unstable, untrustworthy, and without affection (Beck). Any of these viewpoints might be the best way of conceptualizing the problems that arise in a particular case, or some combination of them might be superior to any single one because, as we have noted, the causal pathways are usually multidimensional.

INSTITUTIONALIZATION In some cases children are raised in an institution where, compared with an ordinary home, there is likely to be less warmth and physical contact; less intellectual, emotional, and social stimulation; and a lack of encouragement and help in positive learning. Research done when institutionalization was more common in the United States and the United Kingdom makes it clear that the long-range prognosis for most children who suffer early and prolonged environmental and social deprivation through institutionalization is unfavorable (Rutter, 1990; Rutter & Quinton, 1984a; Sigal, Rossignol, & Perry, 1999). Many children institutionalized in infancy and early childhood show severe emotional, behavioral, and learning problems and are at risk for disturbed attachment relationships and psychopathology (e.g., Ellis, Fisher,

& Zaharie, 2004; Johnson, 2000; O'Conner, Maurn, et al., 2003). Institutionalization later in childhood of a child who has already had good attachment experiences was not found to be so damaging (Rutter, 1987). However, even some of the children institutionalized at an early age show resilience and do well in adulthood (Rutter, Kreppner, & O'Connor, 2001). In some cases this is because of influential protective factors, which include having some good experiences at school, whether in the form of social relationships or athletic or academic success, and having a supportive marital partner in adulthood; these successes probably contributed to a better sense of self-esteem or self-efficacy (Quinton & Rutter, 1988; Rutter, 1985; Rutter et al., 2001).

Fortunately, the results of this line of research have had a major impact on public policy in this and some other societies, which have recognized the need to place such children in foster or adoptive families rather than in institutions (see Johnson, 2000). Accordingly, research on the effects of institutionalization in Western societies is less urgent today—and less feasible—than it once was. Unfortunately, however, enlightened policies have not been implemented in some Eastern European countries, where the plight of children in orphanages is still deplorable (e.g., Johnson, 2000). Many children whose infancy was spent in these Eastern European orphanages were later adopted into homes in the United States and the United Kingdom. For children who spent a significant period of time in one of these deplorable institutions in their first year or two of life, there were very significant intellectual, language, and growth deficits, and more time in the institution was related to more severe deficits. Serious physiological, behavioral, psychological, and social problems also arose (e.g., Beckett et al., 2002; Gunnar et al., 2001; Rutter et al., 2001). When retested several years after being placed in good adoptive homes, most such children showed significant improvement in most of these areas, although they still showed deficits compared to adoptive infants who had not been institutionalized. Generally, the earlier the children were adopted, the better they did (see Johnson, 2000, for a review; Rutter et al., 1999).

NEGLECT AND ABUSE IN THE HOME Most infants subjected to parental deprivation are not separated from their parents but, rather, suffer from maltreatment at home. In the United States, approximately 2.6 million reports of abuse and neglect are made annually, and about one-third are found to be accurate (Cicchetti & Toth, 2005). This means that about 12 out of every 1,000 children are known to be victims of abuse or neglect, with countless numbers of other unreported cases. Parents can neglect a child in various ways—by physical neglect, denial of love and affection, lack of interest in the child's activities and achievements, or failure to spend time with the child or to supervise his or her activities. Parental abuse cases involve cruel treatment in the form of emotional, physical, and/or sexual abuse. Parental neglect and abuse may be partial or complete, passive or active, or subtly or overtly cruel.

Outright parental abuse (physical or sexual or both) of children has been associated with many negative effects on their development, although some studies have suggested that, at least among infants, gross neglect may be worse than having an abusive relationship. Abused children often have a tendency to be overly aggressive (both verbally and physically), even to the extent of bullying. Some even respond with anger and aggression to friendly overtures from peers (e.g., Cicchetti & Toth, 2005; Emery & Laumann-Billings, 1998). Researchers have also found that maltreated children have difficulties in linguistic development and significant problems in behavioral, emotional, and social functioning, including conduct disorder, depression and anxiety, and impaired relationships with

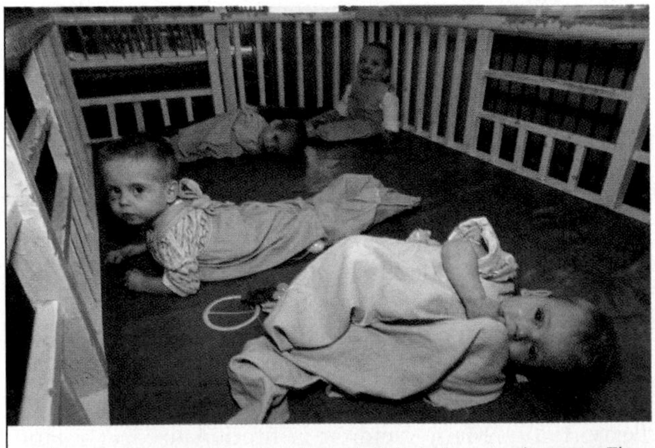

These Russian orphans spend most of their days in playpens. The lack of physical contact and social stimulation and support cause many children institutionalized in infancy and early childhood to show severe emotional, behavioral, and learning problems. They are also at elevated risk for psychopathology.

In February 1994 during a drug raid, Chicago police discovered 19 children in this freezing, squalid, cockroach-infested apartment. The stove in the kitchen did not work, and children were found sharing food with dogs off the floor. The six adults in the apartment were charged with child neglect, and child abuse charges were also considered. Growing up in such a setting may predispose children to later psychological problems.

peers, who tend to avoid or reject them (Cicchetti & Toth, 1995a, 1995b; Shonk & Cicchetti, 2001).

Abused and maltreated infants and toddlers are also quite likely to develop atypical patterns of attachment—most often a *disorganized* and *disoriented* style of attachment (Barnett, Ganiban, & Cicchetti, 1999; Crittenden & Ainsworth, 1989), characterized by insecure, disorganized, and inconsistent behavior with the caregiver. For example, such a child might at one point act dazed and show frozen behavior when reunited with his or her caregiver. However, at another point he or she might actually approach the mother but then immediately reject and avoid her. A significant portion of these children continue to show these "confused" patterns of relating to their mother up to at least age 13. A review of research in this area concluded that "Internal representational models of these insecure and often atypical attachments, with their complementary models of self and others, may generalize to new relationships, leading to negative expectations of how others will behave and how successful the self will be in relation to others" (Cicchetti & Toth, 1995a, p. 549; Shields et al., 2001).

Even children who have been maltreated can improve their damaged self-schemas if one or more protective factors—for example, a positive experience at school—is present.

The detrimental effects of such early traumas may never be completely overcome, partly because experiences that would provide the necessary relearning may be selectively avoided. According to the cognitive viewpoint, for example, a child whose schemas do not include the possibility that others can be trusted may not venture out toward others far enough to learn that some people in the world are in fact trustworthy, which is consistent with findings that they tend to be aggressive and/or socially withdrawn from peers (Cicchetti & Toth, 1995a, 2005; Shields, Ryan, & Cicchetti, 2001). This idea is also supported by the work of Dodge and colleagues (1990, 1995), who found that abused children are hypervigilant for hostile cues from peers (which they've learned to expect from their parents). If they believe others are behaving in a hostile manner toward them (as they are prone to do), this increases the chance that they will behave aggressively, and they may learn that aggressive responses can lead to positive consequences such as getting their own way or feeling good about their anger.

These effects of early abuse may endure into adolescence and adulthood. For example, several reviews concluded that childhood physical abuse predicts both familial and nonfamilial violence in adolescence and adulthood, especially in abused men (Cicchetti & Toth, 1995a; Emery & Laumann-Billings, 1998). Thus, a significant proportion of parents who reject or abuse their children have themselves been the victims of parental rejection. Their early history of rejection or abuse would clearly have had damaging effects on their schemas and self-schemas, and they were probably unable to internalize good models of parenting (e.g., Shields et al., 2001). Kaufman and Zigler (1989) estimated that there is about a 30 percent chance of this pattern of intergenerational transmission of abuse (see also Cicchetti & Toth, 1995a).

Nevertheless, maltreated children—whether the maltreatment comes from abuse or from deprivation—can improve to at least some extent when the caregiving environment improves (Cicchetti & Toth, 1995a; Emery & Laumann-Billings, 1998). Moreover, there are always a range of effects, and those who were least likely to show these negative outcomes tended to have one or more protective factors such as a good relationship with some adult during childhood, a higher IQ, positive school experiences, or physical attractiveness.

SEPARATION Bowlby (1960, 1973) summarized the traumatic effects, for children from 2 to 5 years old, of being separated from their parents during prolonged periods of hospitalization. First, there are the short-term or acute effects of the separation, which can include significant despair during the separation as well as detachment from the parents upon reunion; Bowlby considered this to be a normal response to prolonged separation, even in securely attached infants. Children who undergo such separations may develop an insecure attachment. In addition, there can be longer-term effects of early separation from one or both parents. For example, such separations can cause an increased vulnerability to stressors in adulthood, making it more likely that the person will become depressed (Bowlby, 1980) or show other psychiatric symptoms (Canetti, Bachar, et al., 2000; Carlson, Sampson, & Sroufe, 2003). As with other early traumatic experiences, the long-term effects of separation depend heavily on whether support and reassurance are given a child by parents or other significant people, which is most likely if the child has a secure relationship with at least one parent (Canetti et al., 2000; Carlson & Sroufe, 1995). Interestingly, many children who experience even a parent's death do not exhibit discernible long-term effects (Brown, Harris, & Bifulco, 1985; Canetti et al., 2000).

Inadequate Parenting Styles

Even in the absence of severe deprivation, neglect, or trauma, many kinds of deviations in parenting can have profound effects on a child's subsequent ability to cope with life's challenges and thus can create a child's vulnerability to various forms of psychopathology. Therefore,

Inadequate parenting styles can have profound effects on a child's subsequent ability to cope with life's challenges, and thus create vulnerability to various forms of psychopathology.

although their explanations vary considerably, the psychosocial viewpoints on causes of psychopathology all focus on the behavioral tendencies a child acquires in the course of early social interaction with others—chiefly parents or parental surrogates (e.g., Sroufe et al., 2000).

You should keep in mind that a parent-child relationship is always bidirectional: As in any continuing relationship, the behavior of each person affects the behavior of the other. Some children are easier to love than others; some parents are more sensitive than others to an infant's needs (e.g., Parke, 2005). For example, parents who have babies with difficult temperaments (who are very prone to negative moods) find it difficult and stressful to deal with their babies (e.g., Putnam, Sanson, & Rothbart, 2002). In an early study, Rutter and Quinton (1984b) found that parents tended to react with irritability, hostility, and criticism to children who were high in negative mood and low on adaptability (see also Crouter & Booth, 2003). This in turn may set such children at risk for psychopathology because they become "a focus for discord" in the family (Rutter, 1990, p. 191).

PARENTAL PSYCHOPATHOLOGY In general, it has been found that parents who have various forms of psychopathology (including schizophrenia, depression, antisocial personality disorder, and alcohol abuse or dependence) tend to have children who are at heightened risk for a wide range of developmental difficulties. The focus of most research in this area has been on mothers, but there is good evidence that disordered fathers also make significant contributions to child and adolescent psychopathology, especially to problems such as depression, conduct disorder, delinquency, and attention-deficit disorder (e.g., McMahon & Giannini, 2003; Phares, Duhig, & Watkins, 2002). Although some of these effects undoubtedly have a genetic component, many researchers believe that genetic influences cannot account for all of the adverse effects that parental psychopathology has on children (e.g., Goodman & Gotlib, 2002; Hammen, 2002; Sher, Grekin, & Williams, 2005).

For example, although many children of alcoholics do not have difficulties, others have elevated rates of truancy, substance abuse, and a greater likelihood of dropping out of school, as well as higher levels of anxiety and depression and lower levels of self-esteem (Chassin, Rogosch, & Barrera, 1991; Grekin, Brennan, & Hammen, 2005; Sher et al., 2005). In addition, the children of seriously depressed parents are at enhanced risk for depression and other disorders themselves (Burt et al., 2005; Cicchetti & Toth, 1998; Hammen, 2002), at least partly because depression makes for unskillful parenting—notably including inattentiveness to children's many needs (Gelfand & Teti, 1990), excessive criticism, and ineffectiveness in managing and disciplining the children (Cicchetti & Toth, 1998; Rogosch, Cicchetti, & Toth, 2004). Not surprisingly, children of depressed mothers are also more likely than children of nondepressed mothers to have insecure attachment relationships (Cicchetti & Toth, 1995b) and to live in environments with high levels of stress (e.g., Hammen, 2002).

Again, it is important to note that many children raised in such families do just fine, sometimes because of a variety of protective factors that may be present in the child or in the child's environment. For example, a child who lives with a parent with a serious disorder, but who also has a warm and nurturing relationship with that parent or the other parent or with another adult outside the family, has a significant protective factor (e.g., Brennan, Le Brocque, & Hammen, 2003). Other important protective factors that promote resilience include having good intellectual skills, having social and academic competence, and being appealing to adults (Masten & Coatsworth, 1995, 1998).

PARENTING STYLES: WARMTH AND CONTROL Less extreme differences in parenting styles than those that may occur with various forms of parental psychopathology can also have a significant impact on children's development and increase their risk for psychopathology. In the past, discipline was conceived of as a method for both punishing undesirable behavior and preventing or deterring such behavior in the future. Discipline is now thought of more positively as providing needed structure and guidance for promoting a child's healthy growth. Such guidance provides a child with schemas similar to outcomes actually meted out by the world, which are contingent on a person's behavior. This allows the child a sense of control over these outcomes and his or her freedom to make deliberate choices. When punishment is deemed necessary, it is important that a parent make clear exactly what behavior is inappropriate and what behavior is expected, and that positive and consistent methods of discipline be worked out for dealing with infractions.

Researchers have been interested in how parenting styles—including their disciplinary styles—affect chil-

Healthy parenting styles are those that reflect warmth and clear limits and restrictions regarding certain kinds of behaviors, while allowing considerable freedom within certain boundaries. The children raised in these environments tend to be energetic and friendly, and show general competencies for dealing with others.

dren's behavior over the course of development. Four types of parenting styles have been identified that seem to be related to different developmental outcomes for the children: (1) authoritative, (2) authoritarian, (3) permissive/indulgent, and (4) neglectful/uninvolved. These styles vary in the degree of *parental warmth* (amount of support, encouragement, and affection versus shame, rejection, and hostility) and in the degree of *parental control* (extent of discipline and monitoring versus leaving the children largely unsupervised; Emery & Kitzmann, 1995; Maccoby & Martin, 1983; Morris, 2001).

Authoritative Parenting The *authoritative style* is one in which the parents are both very warm and very careful to set clear standards and limits on certain kinds of behaviors, while allowing considerable freedom within these limits. They tend to be attentive and sensitive to their child's needs while still enforcing their limits. This style of parenting is associated with the most positive early social development; the children tend to be energetic and friendly and to show development of general competencies for dealing with others and with their environments (Baumrind, 1993; Emery & Kitzmann, 1995; Siegler, DeLoache, & Eiserberg, 2003). They also usually have secure attachment relationships (Karavasilis, Doyle, & Markiewicz, 2003) and show high levels of overall well-being, as well as good school performance in late adolescence (Berk, 2003; Slicker & Thornberry, 2002). When followed into adolescence in a longitudinal study, children of authoritative parents continued to show positive outcomes.

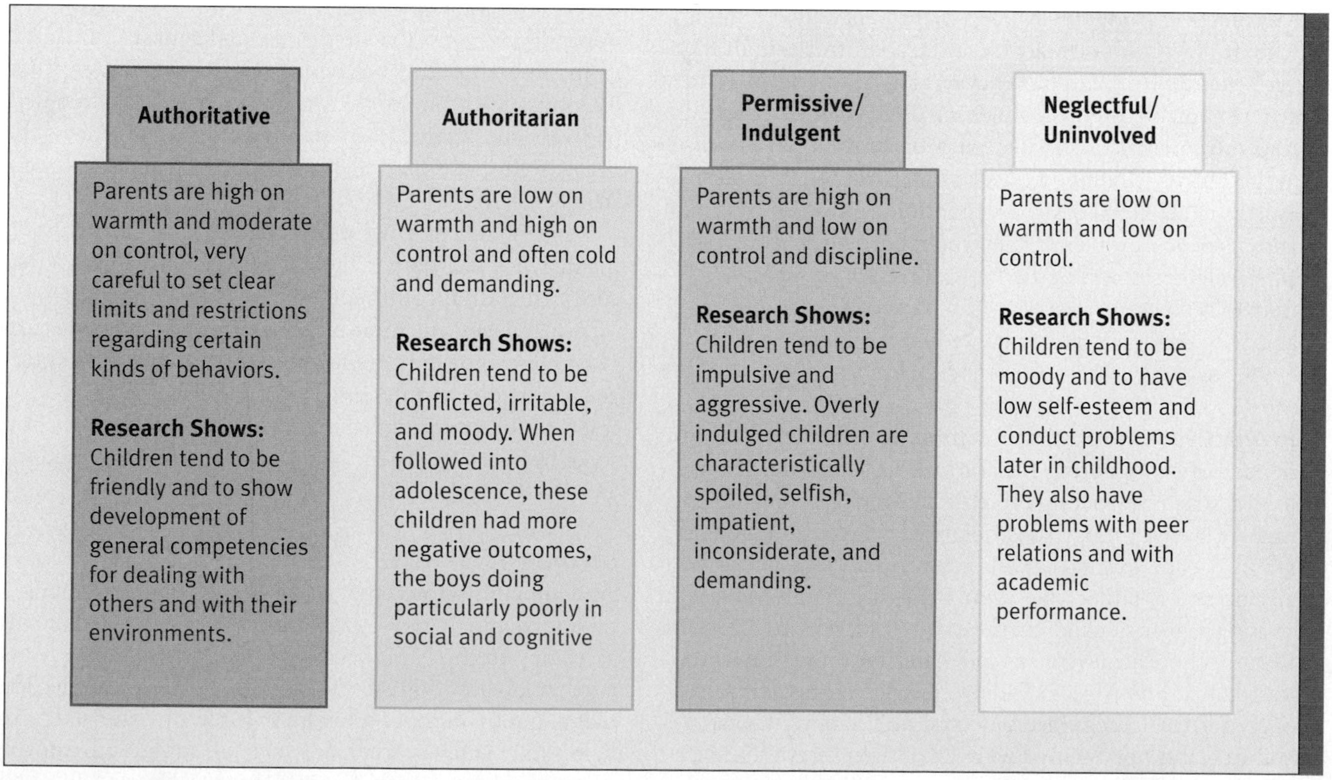
Authoritative
Parents are high on warmth and moderate on control, very careful to set clear limits and restrictions regarding certain kinds of behaviors.
Research Shows:
Children tend to be friendly and to show development of general competencies for dealing with others and with their environments.
Authoritarian
Parents are low on warmth and high on control and often cold and demanding.
Research Shows:
Children tend to be conflicted, irritable, and moody. When followed into adolescence, these children had more negative outcomes, the boys doing particularly poorly in social and cognitive
Permissive/ Indulgent
Parents are high on warmth and low on control and discipline.
Research Shows:
Children tend to be impulsive and aggressive. Overly indulged children are characteristically spoiled, selfish, impatient, inconsiderate, and demanding.
Neglectful/ Uninvolved
Parents are low on warmth and low on control.
Research Shows:
Children tend to be moody and to have low self-esteem and conduct problems later in childhood. They also have problems with peer relations and with academic performance.

FIGURE 3.12
Parenting Styles

Authoritarian Parenting Parents with an *authoritarian style* are high on control but low on warmth. They often appear quite cold and demanding, favoring punitive methods if their children disobey. Their children tend to be conflicted, irritable, and moody (Baumrind, 1975, 1993; Berk, 2003; Siegler et al., 2003). When followed into adolescence, these children tend to be lower in social and academic competence than children of authoritative parents, with boys doing particularly poorly in social and cognitive skills. If such authoritarian parents also use overly severe discipline in the form of physical punishment—as opposed to the withdrawal of approval and privileges—the result tends to be increased aggressive behavior on the part of the child (Emery & Kitzmann, 1995; Eron et al., 1974; Patterson, 1979).

Permissive/Indulgent Parenting *Permissive/indulgent* parents are high on warmth but low on discipline and control. This lenient style of parenting is associated with impulsive and aggressive behavior in childhood and adolescence (Baumrind, 1967; Hetherington & Parke, 1993; Siegler et al., 2003). Overly indulged children are characteristically spoiled, selfish, impatient, inconsiderate, and demanding (Baumrind, 1971, 1975). In adolescence, they tend to do less well academically and to show more antisocial behaviors. Confusion and difficulties in adjustment may occur when "reality" forces them to reassess their assumptions about themselves and the world.

Neglectful/Uninvolved Parenting Finally, parents who are low both on warmth and on control exhibit the *neglectful/uninvolved style.* They tend to be disengaged and not supportive of their children. This style of parental uninvolvement is associated with disruptions in attachment during childhood (Egeland & Sroufe, 1981; Karavasilis et al., 2003) and with moodiness, low self-esteem, and conduct problems later in childhood (Baumrind, 1991; Hetherington & Parke, 1993). These children of uninvolved parents also have problems with peer relations and with academic performance (Hetherington & Parke, 1993; see also Berk, 2003).

Restrictiveness Research examining only the effects of *restrictiveness* (ignoring the warmth variable) has shown that restrictiveness can protect children growing up in high-risk environments, as defined by a combination of family occupation and education level, minority status, and absence of a father (Baldwin, Baldwin, & Cole, 1990). Among high-risk children, those who did well in terms of IQ and school achievement tended to have more restrictive, less democratic parents. Indeed, restrictiveness was positively related to cognitive outcome only among high-risk children and not among low-risk children. Restrictiveness was also particularly helpful for families living in areas with high crime rates.

Marital Discord and Divorce

Disturbed parent-child patterns such as parental rejection are rarely found in severe form unless the total familial context is also abnormal. Thus disturbed family structure is an overarching risk factor that increases an individual's vulnerability to particular stressors. We will distinguish between intact families where there is significant marital discord and families that have been disrupted by divorce or separation.

MARITAL DISCORD Whatever the reasons for marital discord, when it is long-standing, it is likely to be frustrating, hurtful, and generally damaging in its effects on both adults and their children (e.g., Amato & Booth, 2001; Parke, 2005). More severe cases of marital discord may expose children to one or more of the stressors we have already discussed: child abuse or neglect, the effects of living with a parent with a serious mental disorder, authoritarian or neglectful/uninvolved parenting, and spouse abuse. But even less severe cases of marital discord also have negative effects on many children. For example, one recent study showed that children of parents with high levels of overt conflict showed a greater disposition to behave aggressively toward both their peers and their parents than children from less conflictual marriages (Cummings, Goeke-Morey, & Papp, 2004; Du Rocher et al., 2004). Interestingly, one study found that children could be buffered against many of the damaging effects of marital conflict if one or both parents had the following characteristics: warmth, proneness to giving praise and approval, and ability to inhibit rejecting behavior toward their children (Katz & Gottman, 1997). Another study found that children who had very supportive peers were also buffered against the negative effects of marital discord in their parents (Wasserstein & La Greca, 1996).

Several recent longitudinal studies have clearly documented that the damaging effects of serious marital discord on children continue into adulthood: The offspring's own marriages are more likely to be marked by discord (whether or not the parents divorced). Some of this intergenerational transmission of marital discord may be the result of the offspring having learned negative interaction styles by observing their own parents' marital interactions (Amato & Booth, 2001).

DIVORCED FAMILIES Partly as a consequence of a growing cultural acceptance of divorce, approximately a million divorces now occur yearly in the United States according to the National Center for Health Statistics (as cited in Divorce Statistics Collection, 2005). Estimates are that about 20 percent of children under the age of 18 are living in a single-parent household—some with unwed parents and some with divorced parents. Nearly half of all marriages end in divorce, and it has been estimated that 50 to 60 percent of children born in the 1990s will live at some point in single-parent families (Hetherington, Bridges, & Insabella, 1998).

Effects of Divorce on Parents Unhappy marriages are difficult, but ending a marital relationship can also be enormously stressful for the adults, both mentally and physically. The negative effects are temporary, with most people being able to adapt constructively within 2 to 3 years, but some adults never fully recover (Amato, 2000; Hetherington, 2003a). Divorced and separated persons are overrepresented among psychiatric patients, although the ***direction of the causal relationship*** is not always clear. In their comprehensive reviews of the effects of divorce on adults, Amato and Keith (1991b) concluded that it is a major source of psychopathology, as well as of physical illness, death, suicide, and homicide. It should also be recognized, however, that divorce actually benefits some individuals (Amato, 2000)—with some evidence that women are more likely to benefit than men (Hetherington, 2003a). Overall, good adjustment after divorce is positively associated with higher income, dating someone steadily, remarriage, having had relatively favorable attitudes toward divorce before it happened, and being the partner who initiated the divorce (Amato, 2000).

> research close•up
>
> ***direction of the causal relationship***
>
> *Recall that, in a correlational or observational study, an association between two variables does not allow us to make inferences about causal direction. For example, divorce could precipitate psychological problems. Alternatively, people with psychological disorders might be more likely to have problematic marriages and end up divorced.*

Effects of Divorce on Children Divorce can have traumatic effects on children, too. Feelings of insecurity and rejection may be aggravated by conflicting loyalties and, sometimes, by the spoiling the children may receive while staying with one of the parents. Not surprisingly, some children do develop serious maladaptive responses. Temperamentally difficult children are likely to have a more difficult time adjusting than are temperamentally easy children (Hetherington, Stanley-Hagan, & Anderson, 1989). Somewhat ironically, difficult children may be the ones whose parents are more likely to divorce, perhaps because having difficult children is likely to exacerbate marital problems (Block, Block, & Gjerde, 1986; Hetherington, 1999).

Delinquency and a wide range of other psychological problems are much more frequent among children and adolescents from divorced families than among those from intact families, although it is likely that a contributing factor here is prior or continuing parental strife (Chase-Lansdale, Cherlin, & Kiernan, 1995; Rutter, 1979). In addition, a number of studies have demonstrated that the adverse effects of divorce on adaptive functioning may persist into adulthood. On average, compared to young adults from families without divorce, young adults from divorced families have somewhat lower educational attainment, lower incomes, lower life satisfaction, and an increased probability of being on welfare and having children out of wedlock (Chase-Lansdale et al., 1995; Hetherington et al., 1998). Children from divorced families are also more likely to have their own marriages end in divorce (Amato & DeBoer, 2001; Hetherington, 2003b). One particularly interesting new study found that these long-lasting effects even occurred in a subsequent third generation. Specifically, in a study of nearly 700 grandparents and their grandchildren, Amato and Cheadle (2005) found that divorce in the grandparents was associated with lower education, more marital discord, and weaker parental ties in the grandchildren.

Nevertheless, many children adjust quite well to the divorce of their parents. Indeed, a quantitative review of 92 studies on parental divorce and the well-being of children, conducted on 13,000 children since the 1950s, concluded that the average negative effects of divorce on children are actually quite modest (Amato & Keith, 1991a; see also Emery, 1999; Hetherington, 2003b), as are the negative effects persisting into adulthood (Amato & Keith, 1991b). Amato and Keith (1991a, 1991b) also found that the negative effects of divorce seemed to decrease from the 1950s through the 1980s (particularly since 1970), perhaps because the stigma of divorce was decreasing. However, a follow-up review of 67 such studies published in the 1990s showed no further decreases in these negative effects since 1990 (Amato, 2001).

The effects of divorce on children are often more favorable than the effects of remaining in a home torn by marital conflict and dissension (Amato & Keith, 1991a; Emery & Kitzmann, 1995; Hetherington et al., 1998). At one time it was thought that the detrimental effects of divorce might be minimized if a successful remarriage provided an adequate environment for childrearing. Unfortunately, however, the Amato and Keith (1991a) review revealed that children living with a stepparent were often no better off than children living with a single parent, although this was more true for girls than for boys. Other studies have shown that children—especially very young children—living with a stepparent are at increased risk for physical abuse (injury and even death) by the stepparent, relative to children living with two biological parents (Daly & Wilson, 1988, 1996).

Maladaptive Peer Relationships

Important peer relationships usually begin in the preschool years. Children at this stage are hardly masters of the fine points of human relationships or diplomacy.

Empathy—the appreciation of another's situation, perspective, and feelings—is at best only primitively developed. We can see this in a child who turns on and rejects a current playmate when a more favored playmate arrives. The child's own immediate satisfaction tends to be the primary goal of any interaction, and there is only an uncertain recognition that cooperation and collaboration may bring even greater benefits. A substantial minority of children seem somehow ill-equipped for the rigors and competition of the school years, often because of temperamental factors in the child and/or psychosocial deficits in their family. A significant number of them withdraw from their peers and become schoolyard loners. A significant number of others (especially males) adopt physically intimidating and aggressive lifestyles, often becoming neighborhood bullies. Being either a loner or a bully does not bode well for good mental health outcomes (e.g., Coie et al., 1992; Dodge et al., 1997).

Several studies have found bullies to show high levels of both proactive aggression (where they initiate the aggressive behavior) and reactive aggression (where they overreact when confronted; e.g., Salmivalli & Nieminen, 2002). Although some bullies probably behave this way because of deficits in social skills, others (often the ringleader in a group of bullies) have a more sophisticated understanding of social behavior, which enables them to manipulate and organize their peers so that they can avoid being caught while making others suffer (Sutton, Smith, & Swettenham, 1999). Although most children profess attitudes against bullying, when bullying actually occurs, most students do nothing to intervene or support the victim (and as many as 20 to 30 percent actually encourage the bully; Salmivalli & Voeten, 2004). A small percentage (approximately 20 percent), however, do take the side of the victim and may even help defend him or her.

Fortunately, there is another side to this coin. Peer relations can be difficult, but they can also be sources of key learning experiences that stand an individual in good stead for years, perhaps for a lifetime. For a resourceful child, the winning and losing and the successes and failures of the school years provide excellent training in coming to grips with the real world and with her or his developing self—its capabilities and limitations, its attractive and unattractive qualities. The experience of intimacy with a friend has its beginning in this period of intense social involvement. If all goes well, a child emerges into adolescence with a considerable repertoire of social knowledge and skills that add up to *social competence*. Such resources can be strong protective factors against frustration, demoralization, despair, and mental disorder (Masten & Coatsworth, 1998).

Juvenile socializing is a risky business in which a child's hard-won prestige in a group is probably perceived as being constantly in jeopardy. Actually, reputation and status in a group tend to be stable, and a child who has been rejected by peers is likely to continue to have problems in peer relationships.

SOURCES OF POPULARITY VERSUS REJECTION What determines which children will be popular and which will be rejected? There seem to be two types of popular children—the prosocial and the antisocial types. Prosocial popular children communicate with their peers in friendly and assertive yet cooperative ways. They tend to be good students relative to their less popular peers (Zettergreen, 2003). Antisocial popular children—usually boys—tend to be "tough boys" who may be athletically skilled but who do poorly academically. They tend to be highly aggressive and defiant of authority (see Berk, 2003).

Far more attention has been devoted to determining why some children are persistently rejected by their peers and what the consequences are of such rejection. There also appear to be two types of rejected children—those who are too aggressive and those who are very withdrawn. The first category of rejected children takes an excessively demanding or aggressive approach when interacting with their peers. They often take offense too readily and attribute hostile intent to the teasing of their peers, thus escalating confrontations to unintended levels. They also tend to take a more punitive and less forgiving attitude toward such situations (Coie et al., 1991; Crick & Dodge, 1994). This may be especially likely in children who have been maltreated by their parents and have therefore developed maladaptive mental representations of caregivers and expect maltreatment. Expecting maltreatment, they may approach social situations with hyperarousal, anxiety, and angry reactivity, which may be consistent with what they have experienced at home but is out of synch with the context they share with peers (Cicchetti & Toth, 2005; Shields, Ryan, & Cicchetti, 2001). In addition, having a poor ability to understand a peer's emotions (such as fear and sadness) in kindergarten also predicts aggressive behavior toward peers in the third grade (Dodge, Laird, Lochman, & Zelli, 2002).

Being rejected and being aggressive at one point in childhood greatly increases the probability of aggressive and delinquent behavior later on, especially in boys (Coie, 2004). For example, one study followed 585 children from kindergarten through the eighth grade. Results showed that those who had hostile knowledge structures (schemas) early in childhood were more likely to develop consistent aggressive behaviors over an 8-year follow-up period (Burks, Laird, et al., 1999; see also Laird, Jordan, et al., 2001).

The second subset of children who may become chronic victims of rejection are not aggressive but, rather, are highly unassertive and quite submissive toward their peers, often because of social anxiety and fear of being scorned or attacked (Schwartz, Dodge, & Coie, 1993). Such isolation is likely to have serious consequences, because it deprives a child of further opportunities to learn the rules of social behavior and interchange, rules that become more sophisticated and subtle with increasing age (Coie, 1990). Repeated social failure and/or becoming the victim of bullies is the usual result, which has further damaging effects on self-confidence and self-esteem and sometimes leads to loneliness and depression (Berk, 2003; Burks, Dodge, & Price, 1995).

In summary, both logic and research findings suggest the same conclusion: A child who fails to establish satisfactory relationships with peers during the developmental years is deprived of a crucial set of background experiences and is at higher-than-average risk for a variety of negative outcomes in adolescence and adulthood including depression, school dropout, and delinquency (Burks et al., 1995; Coie, 2004; Kupersmidt et al., 1990). However, one should also remember that the peer social problems may also be early markers of disorders that have a heritable component but do not become full-blown until later in adolescence or adulthood. What is often going on is that the peer social problems indeed reflect some heritable diathesis, but they also serve as stressors that make it more likely that the underlying vulnerability will lead to full-blown disorder later (Parker et al., 1995; see also Coie, 2004).

In Review

- What are the most important effects of a child's being exposed to early deprivation and/or abuse?
- What kinds of effects do parental psychopathology have on children?
- What kinds of influences do parenting styles tend to have on children's development? (Consider especially the variables of parental warmth and parental control.)
- What is the typical range of effects that divorce and marital discord can have on children?

The Sociocultural Viewpoint

By the beginning of the twentieth century, sociology and anthropology had emerged as independent scientific disciplines and were making rapid strides toward understanding the role of sociocultural factors in human development and behavior. Early sociocultural theorists included such notables as Ruth Benedict, Abram Kardiner, Margaret Mead, and Franz Boas. Their investigations and writings showed that individual personality development reflected the larger society—its institutions, norms, values, and ideas—as well as the immediate family and other groups. Studies also made clear the relationship between various sociocultural conditions and mental disorders (for example, the relationship between the particular stressors in a given society and the types of mental disorders that typically occur in it). Further studies showed that the patterns of both physical and mental disorders within a given society could change over time as sociocultural conditions changed. These discoveries have added important new dimensions to modern perspectives on abnormal behavior (Fabrega, 2001; Tsai, Butcher, Munoz, & Vitousek, 2001; Westermeyer & Janca, 1997).

Uncovering Sociocultural Factors through Cross-Cultural Studies

The sociocultural viewpoint is concerned with the impact of culture and other features of the social environment on mental disorders. The relationships are complex. It is one thing to observe that a person with a psychological disorder has come from a harsh environment. It is quite another to show empirically that these circumstances were contributory causes of the disorder as opposed to being mere correlates of the disorder. Yet people raised in different societies and exposed to very different environments have provided natural "laboratories" of sorts, and cross-cultural research can enhance our knowledge about the range of variation that is possible in human behavioral and emotional development. It can also generate ideas about what causes normal and abnormal behavior—ideas that can later be tested more rigorously in the laboratory (e.g., Rothbaum, Weisz, et al., 2000, 2001; Weisz et al., 1997).

UNIVERSAL AND CULTURE-SPECIFIC DISORDERS AND SYMPTOMS Research supports the view that many psychological disturbances—in both adults and children—are universal, appearing in most cultures studied (Butcher, 1996a; Kleinman, 1988; Verhulst & Achenbach, 1995). Studying such issues is, of course, never easy because of the need to adapt psychological tests across barriers of language and culture and to validate their use in other cultures. One example of such research has shown that when some tests are translated into the language of different cultures, they need to be adapted so that they are appropriate for the new cultural context. In addition, care must be taken not to miss what may be culture-specific elements of various disorders such as anxiety and depression (e.g., Sue & Chang, 2003).

The Minnesota Multiphasic Personality Inventory (MMPI-2; see Chapter 4) is the best validated and most widely used test that has been adapted for use in many cultures (e.g., Butcher, Cheung, & Kim, 2003; Butcher, Derksen, Sloore, & Sirigatti, 2003). For example, the basic pattern of disturbed thoughts and behaviors that we call "schizophrenia" (Chapter 14) can be found among nearly all peoples, although the prevalence and symptoms vary to some degree (Kulhara & Chakrabarti, 2001). Moreover, certain psychological symptoms, as measured, are consistently found among similarly diagnosed clinical groups in many other countries. For example, Butcher (1996a) found that psychiatric patients from Italy, Switzerland, Chile, India, Greece, and the United States who were all diagnosed with paranoid schizophrenia produced similar general personality and symptom patterns on the MMPI.

Sociocultural factors influence the form and course of certain disorders. For example, in Western societies people suffering from stress frequently will become depressed. In China, stress is not manifested as depression but in physical problems such as fatigue and weakness.

Nevertheless, although some universal symptoms and patterns of symptoms appear, sociocultural factors often influence which disorders develop, the forms that they take, how prevalent they are, and their courses. For example, the prevalence of major depressive disorder varies widely across the cultures of the world. In a recent study conducted in ten countries around the world, the prevalence ranged from 3 percent in Japan to nearly 17 percent in the United States (Andrade et al., 2004). Differences can also emerge in the prognosis or outcomes of several severe mental disorders in different countries. Several international studies have found a more favorable course of schizophrenia in developing countries than in developed countries (Kulhara & Chakrabarti, 2001).

In another example, Kleinman (1986, 1988) compared the ways in which Chinese people (in Taiwan and the People's Republic of China) and Westerners deal with stress. He found that in Western societies, depression was a frequent reaction to individual stress. In China, on the other hand, he noted a relatively low rate of reported depression (Kleinman, 2004; see also Kirmayer & Groleau, 2001). Instead, the effects of stress were more typically manifested in physical problems such as fatigue, weakness, and other complaints. Moreover, Kleinman and Good (1985) surveyed the experience of depression across cultures. Their data show that important elements of depression in Western societies—for example, the acute sense of guilt typically experienced—do not appear in many other cultures. They also point out that the symptoms of depression such as sadness, hopelessness, unhappiness, and a lack of pleasure in the things of the world and in social relationships have dramatically different meanings in different societies. For Buddhists, seeking pleasure from things of the world and social relationships is the basis of all suffering; a willful disengagement is thus the first step toward achieving enlightenment. For Shi'ite Muslims in Iran, grief is a religious experience associated with recognition of the tragic consequences of living justly in an unjust world; the ability to experience grief fully is thus a marker of depth of personality and understanding. Several examples of abnormal behavior that appear only in certain cultures are given in The World Around Us 3.4 on culture-bound syndromes.

CULTURE AND OVER- AND UNDERCONTROLLED BEHAVIOR Studies of the prevalence of different kinds of childhood psychopathology in different cultures raise some fascinating issues. In cultures such as that of Thailand, adults are highly intolerant of *undercontrolled behavior* such as aggression, disobedience, and disrespectful acts in their children (e.g., Weisz, Weiss, Suwanlert, & Chaiyasit, 2003). Children are explicitly taught to be polite and deferential and to inhibit any expression of anger. This raises interesting questions about whether childhood problems stemming from undercontrolled behavior are lower in Thailand than in the United States, where such behavior seems to be tolerated to a greater extent. It also raises the question of whether problems related to *overcontrolled behavior* such as shyness, anxiety, and depression would be overrepresented in Thailand relative to the United States.

Two cross-national studies (Weisz, Suwanlert, et al., 1987, 1993) confirmed that Thai children and adolescents do indeed have a greater prevalence of overcontrolled problems than do American children. Although there were no differences in the rate of undercontrolled behavior problems between the two countries, there were differences in the kinds of undercontrolled behavior problems reported. For example, Thai adolescents had higher scores than American adolescents on indirect and subtle forms of undercontrol not involving interpersonal

3.4 THE WORLD AROUND US

Culture-Bound Syndromes

Name of Disorder	Culture	Description
Amok	Malaysia (also observed in Laos, the Philippines, Polynesia, Papua New Guinea, and Puerto Rico)	A disorder characterized by sudden, wild outbursts of violent aggression or homicidal behavior in which an afflicted person may kill or injure others. This rage disorder is usually found in males who are rather withdrawn, quiet, brooding, and inoffensive prior to the onset of the disorder. Episodes are often precipitated by a perceived slight or insult. Several stages have been observed: Typically in the first stage the person becomes more withdrawn; then a period of brooding follows in which a loss of contact with reality is evident. Ideas of persecution and anger predominate. Finally, a phase of automatism or *Amok* occurs, in which the person jumps up, yells, grabs a knife, and stabs people or objects within reach. Exhaustion and depression usually follow, with amnesia for the rage period.
Latah	Malaysia and Indonesia (also Japan, Siberia, and the Philippines)	Hypersensitivity to sudden fright often occurring in middle-aged women of low intelligence who are subservient and self-effacing. The disorder is precipitated by the word *snake* or by tickling. It is characterized by *echolalia* (repetition of the words and sentences of others) and *echopraxia* (repetition of the acts of others). A disturbed individual may also show dissociative or trance-like behavior.
Koro	Southeast Asia and China (particularly Malaysia)	A fear reaction or anxiety state in which a man fears that his penis will withdraw into his abdomen and he may die. This reaction may appear after sexual overindulgence or excessive masturbation. The anxiety is typically very intense and of sudden onset. The condition is "treated" by having the penis held firmly by the patient or by family members or friends. Often the penis is clamped to a wooden box.
Windigo	Algonquin Indian hunters	A fear reaction in which a hunter becomes anxious and agitated, convinced that he is bewitched. Fears center on his being turned into a cannibal by the power of a monster with an insatiable craving for human flesh.
Kitsunetsuki	Japan	A disorder in which victims believe that they are possessed by foxes and are said to change their facial expressions to resemble foxes. Entire families are often possessed and shunned by the community. This reaction occurs in rural areas of Japan where people are superstitious and relatively uneducated.
Taijin kyofusho (TKS)	Japan	A relatively common psychiatric disorder in Japan in which an individual develops a fear of offending or hurting other people through being awkward in social situations or because of an imagined physical defect or problem. The excessive concern over how a person presents himself or herself in social situations is the salient problem.
Zar	North Africa and Middle East	A person who believes he or she is possessed by a spirit may experience a dissociative episode during which shouting, laughing, singing, or weeping may occur. The person may also show apathy and withdrawal, not eating or working.

Source: Based on American Psychiatric Association (DSM-IV-TR, 2000); Bartholomew (1997); Chowdhury (1996); Hatta (1996); Kiev (1972); Kirmayer (1991); Kirmayer et al. (1995); Lebra (1976); Lewis & Ednie (1997); Sheung-Tak (1996); Simons and Hughes (1985).

In Thailand, children tend to exhibit overcontrolled behavior *and are explicitly taught by their parents to be polite and deferential and to inhibit any expression of anger. This is in contrast to American children, whose parents tend to tolerate* undercontrolled behavior *to a greater extent. We all receive a sociocultural inheritance that is the end product of thousands of years of social evolution, and this inheritance influences and defines the types of problems we tend to have within a given society.*

aggression such as having difficulty concentrating or being cruel to animals; American adolescents, on the other hand, had higher scores than Thai adolescents on behaviors like fighting, bullying, and disobeying at school (Weisz et al., 1993). In addition, these investigators found that Thai and American parents differ a good deal in which problems they will bring for treatment. In general, Thai parents seem less likely than American parents to refer their children for psychological treatment (Weisz & Weiss, 1991; Weisz et al., 1997). This may be in part because of their Buddhist belief in the transience of problems and their optimism that their child's behavior will improve. Alternatively, Thai parents may not refer their children with undercontrolled problems for treatment simply because these problems are so unacceptable that the parents are embarrassed to go public with them (Weisz et al., 1997).

Cultural differences in psychopathology may also result from differences in what cultures consider to be the ideal kinds of parent-child attachment relationships. The World Around Us 3.5 discusses recent research on cultural differences in what Japanese and Western cultures believe to be the nature of ideal versus disordered attachment relationships.

3.5 The World Around Us — Culture and Attachment Relationships

Recently research has shown that there are significant cross-cultural differences in views of the nature of ideal parent-child attachment relationships. Accordingly, there are different views of what constitutes disordered attachment relationships that can increase risk for psychopathology. Views on the function of good attachment relationships (and the nature of disordered attachment) in Western cultures have been found to differ rather dramatically from those seen in Japan (Rothbaum, Weisz, et al., 2000, 2001, 2002). In Western societies, secure attachment relationships are thought to occur when a mother responds in a sensitive fashion to a child's signals (e.g., signs of hunger or discomfort), yet gradually allows the child to explore the environment and develop some autonomy. Securely attached children (relative to insecurely attached children) are thought to be less anxious and depressed, better able to cope with negative emotional states, and better able to form close relationships with peers. However, in Japan, parents' goals are to anticipate all the child's needs and thereby avoid any exposure to stress such as hunger or discomfort and to foster dependency (Rothbaum, Weisz, et al., 2000, 2002). Indeed, children who are considered securely attached in Japan are very dependent on their mothers, and independent children are thought to have disturbed attachments. Moreover, because the Japanese value social harmony, children who are dependent and emotionally restrained and who express their feelings only indirectly are the ones viewed as competent; they also tend to be self-critical and self-effacing. This is very different from Western cultures, where children who show exploration and autonomy and are willing to express strong feelings and even disagreement openly are considered to be socially competent. Such children in Western cultures also tend to have positive self-views (Rothbaum, Weisz, et al., 2000).

Given such differences, it is not surprising that different clinical interventions are appropriate for children with behavior problems in these two cultures! For example, American therapists often help their clients to develop their own separate identities and assume that expression of negative feelings toward others (including parents) may be necessary. By contrast, Japanese therapists are more likely to encourage clients to be grateful to others (especially parents) and encourage devotion (see Rothbaum, Weisz, et al., 2000, 2001, 2002).

In Review

- Give some examples of universal and culture-specific disorders.
- What cultural factors help account for differences in problems involving overcontrolled and undercontrolled behavior in Thai versus American children?

Sociocultural Causal Factors

The Sociocultural Environment

We all receive a sociocultural inheritance that is the end product of thousands of years of social evolution just as we receive a genetic inheritance that is the end product of millions of years of biological evolution. Because each sociocultural group fosters its own cultural patterns by systematically teaching its offspring, all its members tend to be somewhat alike. Children reared among headhunters tend to become headhunters; children reared in societies that do not sanction violence usually learn to settle their differences in nonviolent ways. The more uniform and thorough the education of the younger members of a group, the more alike they will become. Thus, in a society characterized by a limited and consistent point of view, there are not the wide individual differences that are typical in a society like ours, where children have contact with diverse, often conflicting beliefs. Even in our society, however, there are certain core values that most of us consider essential.

Subgroups of a general sociocultural environment—such as family, sex, age, class, occupational, ethnic, and religious groups—foster beliefs and norms of their own, largely by means of social roles that their members learn to adopt. Expected role behaviors exist for a student, a teacher, an army officer, a priest, a nurse, and so on. Because most people are members of various subgroups, they are subject to various role demands, which also change over time. When social roles are conflicting, unclear, or difficult to achieve, healthy personality development may be impaired.

Pathogenic Societal Influences

There are many sources of pathogenic social influences. Some of these stem from socioeconomic factors. Others stem from sociocultural factors regarding role expectations and from the destructive forces of prejudice and discrimination. We will briefly look at some of the more important ones here.

LOW SOCIOECONOMIC STATUS AND UNEMPLOYMENT In our society the lower the socioeconomic class, the higher the incidence of mental disorder (e.g., Caracci & Mezzich, 2001; Kessler et al., 1994). The strength of this inverse correlation seems to vary with different types of mental disorder, however. For example, antisocial personality disorder is strongly related to socioeconomic status (SES), occurring about three times as often in the lowest income category as in the highest income category, whereas depressive disorders occur only about 1.5 times as often in the lowest income category (Kessler et al., 1994; see also Eaton & Muntaner, 1999; Kessler & Zhao, 1999).

There are many reasons for this general inverse relationship. There is evidence that some people with mental disorders slide down to the lower rungs of the economic ladder and remain there, sometimes because they do not have the economic or personal resources to climb back up (e.g., Gottesman, 1991) and sometimes because of prejudice and stigma against those with mental illness (e.g., Caracci & Mezzich, 2001). At the same time, more affluent people are better able to get prompt help or to conceal their problems. However, it is also true that, on average, people who live in poverty encounter more, and more severe, stressors in their lives, including lower self-esteem, than do more affluent people, and they usually have fewer resources for dealing with them (e.g., Twenge & Campbell, 2002). Thus lower socioeconomic groups may show increased prevalence of mental disorders due at least partly to increased stress on the people at risk (Eaton & Muntaner, 1999; Gottesman, 1991; Hobfoll et al., 1995).

Children from lower-SES families also tend to have more problems. A number of studies have documented a strong relationship between the parents' poverty and lower IQs in their children at least up to age 5. Persistent poverty has the most adverse effects (Duncan, Brooks-Gunn, & Klebanov, 1994; McLoyd, 1998), including greater mental distress, as well as greater risk-taking and affiliating with

- Low socioeconomic status and unemployment
- Prejudice and discrimination in race, gender, and ethnicity
- Social change and uncertainty
- Urban stressors: Violence and homelessness

FIGURE 3.13
Pathogenic Societal Influences

deviant peers (Sampson, Morenoff, & Gannon-Rowley, 2002). Children from low-SES families who were assessed when they were in preschool showed more acting-out and aggressive behaviors over the next 4 years (Dodge, Pettit, & Bates, 1994). Nevertheless, many inner-city children from high-risk socioeconomic backgrounds do very well, especially those with higher IQs and those with adequate relationships at home, in school, and with peers (Felsman & Valliant, 1987; Long & Valliant, 1984; Masten & Coatsworth, 1995).

Other studies have examined the effects of unemployment per se on adults and children. Since the 1970s, there have been a number of severe economic recessions experienced worldwide, and significant rates of unemployment have accompanied each. Studies have repeatedly found unemployment—with its financial hardships, self-devaluation, and emotional distress—to be associated with enhanced vulnerability and elevated rates of psychopathology (e.g., Dooley & Catalano, 1980; Dooley, Prause, & Ham-Rowbottom, 2000; Grzywacz & Dooley, 2003).

In particular, rates of depression, marital problems, and somatic complaints increase during periods of unemployment but usually normalize when employment rates recover (Dew et al., 1991; Jones, 1992; Murphy & Athanasou, 1999). It is not simply that people who are mentally unstable tend to lose their jobs. These effects occur even when mental health status before unemployment is taken into account. Not surprisingly, the wives of unemployed men are also adversely affected, exhibiting higher levels of anxiety, depression, and hostility, which seem to be at least partially caused by the distress of the unemployed husband (Dew, Bromet, & Schulberg, 1987). Children too can be seriously affected. In the worst cases, unemployed fathers are much more likely to engage in child abuse (Cicchetti & Lynch, 1995; Dew et al., 1991).

Finally, economic crises since 1990 have centered not only on unemployment but also on the effects that corporate restructuring and downsizing have had on upper-middle-class people, many of whom find themselves having to look for jobs requiring lower skills and paying much lower incomes than they earned in the past. In other cases people are forced to work only part time and often do not make enough to live on. In such cases of underemployment (or inadequate employment), several large studies of people who were underemployed found that rates of depression were comparable or nearly comparable to those seen in unemployed individuals (Dooley et al., 2000; Grzywacz & Dooley, 2003).

PREJUDICE AND DISCRIMINATION IN RACE, GENDER, AND ETHNICITY Vast numbers of people in our society have been subjected to demoralizing stereotypes, as well as both overt and covert discrimination in areas such as employment, education, and housing. We have made progress in race relations since the 1960s, but the lingering effects of mistrust and discomfort among various ethnic and racial groups can be clearly observed in many places (e.g., Eagly, 2004). For example, on most college campuses, many students socialize informally only with members of their own subcultures, despite the attempts of many well-meaning college administrators to break down the barriers. These tendencies needlessly limit students' educational experiences and probably contribute to continued misinformation about, and prejudice toward, others. Perceived discrimination seems to predict lower levels of well-being for women on dimensions relating to a sense of growth, autonomy, and self-acceptance (Ryff, Keyes, & Hughes, 2003). Prejudice against minority groups may also explain why these groups sometimes show increased prevalence of certain mental disorders such as depression (Cohler et al., 1995; Kessler et al., 1994). One possible reason for this is that perceived discrimination may serve as a stressor that threatens self-esteem, which in turn increases psychological distress (e.g., Cassidy, O'Connor, Howe, & Warden, 2004).

We have made progress in recognizing the demeaning and often disabling social roles our society has historically assigned to women. Again, though, much remains to be done. Many more women than men suffer from various emotional disorders, most notably depression and anxiety disorders, which are two of the three most common categories of disorders. This may be at least partly a consequence of the vulnerabilities (such as passivity and dependence) intrinsic to the traditional roles assigned to women and of the sexual discrimination that still occurs. There are two primary types of discrimination that occur: *access discrimination*, wherein women are not hired because they are women, and *treatment discrimination*, wherein women who have a job are paid less and receive fewer opportunities for promotion (Eagly & Karau, 2002; Helgeson, 2002). Sexual harassment in the workplace is another type of stress that women may experience. In addition, the special stressors with which many modern women must cope (being full-time mothers, full-time homemakers, and full-time employees) as their traditional roles rapidly change have also been implicated in higher rates of depression, anxiety, and marital dissatisfaction in women than in the past. This is especially true if a woman works long hours (over 40 hours a week), has a higher income than her husband, and has more children at home. However, it should also be noted that under at least some circumstances, working outside the home has also been shown to be a protective factor against depression and marital dissatisfaction (e.g., Brown & Harris, 1978; Helgeson, 2002).

SOCIAL CHANGE AND UNCERTAINTY The rate and pervasiveness of change today are different from anything our ancestors ever experienced. All aspects of our lives are affected—our education, our jobs, our families, our leisure pursuits, our finances, and our beliefs and values. Constantly trying to keep up with the numerous adjustments demanded by these changes is a source of considerable stress. Simultaneously, we confront inevitable crises as the earth's consumable natural resources dwindle and as our environment becomes increasingly noxious with pollutants. No longer are Americans confident that the future will be better than the past or that technology will solve all our problems. On the contrary, our attempts to cope with existing problems seem increasingly to create new problems that are as bad or worse. The resulting despair, demoralization, and sense of helplessness are well-established predisposing conditions for abnormal reactions to stressful events (Dohrenwend et al., 1980; Seligman 1990, 1998). This sense of helplessness was also exacerbated for Americans by the September 11, 2001, terrorist attacks on the World Trade Center in New York and the Pentagon, with many people now living under increased worry and uncertainty over the possibility of terrorist attacks. Yet in other parts of the world such as Israel and Palestine, people have lived with this uncertainty and worry over terrorist attacks for decades.

URBAN STRESSORS: VIOLENCE AND HOMELESSNESS Every year, all over the world, vast numbers of people in big cities of both developed and developing countries are direct or secondhand victims of *urban violence* (Caracci & Mezzich, 2001). It has been estimated that at least 3.5 million people worldwide lose their lives to violence each year (World Health Organization, 1999). Domestic violence against women and children is especially widespread (e.g., Caracci, 2003). Such violence takes its toll on the victims not only in the areas of medical care and lost productivity but also in increased rates of anxiety, post-traumatic stress disorder, depression, and suicidality (e.g., Caracci & Mezzich, 2001).

Another severe stress in urban areas worldwide is *homelessness*, which has been rapidly growing for the past few decades. Estimates are that approximately one-third of homeless people are affected by severe mental illness, but many people who are not mentally ill also become homeless because they are victims of violence or poverty (e.g., Caracci & Mezzich, 2001). Needless to say, the major stressors experienced by being homeless create mental distress including anxiety, depression, suicidality, and physical illness, even in those who started out healthy.

Today many major metropolitan areas in the United States have problems with gangs and urban violence.

Impact of the Sociocultural Viewpoint

With our increased understanding of sociocultural influences on mental health, what was previously an almost exclusive concern with individuals has broadened to include a concern with societal, communal, familial, and other group settings as factors in mental disorders. Sociocultural research has led to programs designed to improve the social conditions that foster maladaptive behavior and mental disorder, and to community facilities for the early detection, treatment, and long-range prevention of mental disorder. In Chapter 18 we will examine some clinical facilities and other programs—both governmental and private—that have been established as a result of community efforts.

There is strong evidence of cultural influences on abnormal behavior, and this area of research may yet answer many questions about the origins and courses of behavior problems, as well as their treatment (Cohler et al., 1995; Fabrega, 2001; Miranda, Bernal, et al., 2005; Sue, 1999). Nevertheless, in spite of increasing research showing that patients may do better when treated by therapists from their own ethnic group (or at least by someone familiar with the patient's culture), many professionals may fail to adopt an appropriate cultural perspective when dealing with mental illness. Instead, many simply assume that treatments that have been shown to be useful with one culture will fare as well with other cultures, when in fact this is always an empirical question (e.g., Lam & Sue, 2001; Miranda et al., 2005; Sue, 1998). In a world of instant communication with people from any country, it is crucial for our sciences and professions to take a worldview. In fact, Kleinman and Good (1985) consider cultural factors so important to our understanding of depressive disorders that they have urged the psychiatric community to incorporate another axis in the DSM diagnostic system to reflect cultural factors in psychopathology.

Although this has not yet happened, advocates are keeping up the pressure to do so (e.g., Mezzich, Kirmayer, et al., 1999), and authors of DSM-IV (APA, 1994) and DSM-IV-TR (APA, 2000) did take two big steps toward acknowledging the importance of cultural factors in diagnosing patients. First, they included an Appendix in which they suggested ways in which cultural factors should be considered when making psychiatric diagnoses and encouraged clinicians to include cultural considerations when evaluating patients. They recommended that the clinician attend to an individual's cultural identity, to possible cultural explanations for an individual's disorder, and to cultural factors that might affect that clinician's relationship with the individual. They also provided a glossary of culture-bound syndromes that usually occur only in specific societies or cultural areas and are described as "localized, folk, diagnostic categories" (APA, 1994, p. 844). Some of these are described in The World Around Us 3.4 on page 99.

In Review

- What kinds of effects do low SES and unemployment have on adults and children?
- Describe how prejudice and discrimination, social change and uncertainty, and urban stress can have adverse effects on the development of abnormal behavior.
- In what ways did DSM-IV and DSM-IV-TR begin to acknowledge the importance of sociocultural factors in mental disorders?

Unresolved Issues

Theoretical Viewpoints and the Causes of Abnormal Behavior

The viewpoints described in this chapter are theoretical constructions devised to orient psychologists in the study of abnormal behavior. As a set of hypothetical guidelines, each viewpoint emphasizes the importance and integrity of its own position to the exclusion of other explanations. Most psychodynamically oriented clinicians, for example, value those traditional writings and beliefs consistent with Freudian or later psychodynamic theories, and they minimize or ignore the teachings of opposing viewpoints. They usually adhere to prescribed practices of psychodynamic therapy and do not use other methods such as exposure therapy.

Advantages of Having a Theoretical Viewpoint

Theoretical integrity and adherence to a systematic viewpoint have a key advantage: They ensure a consistent approach to one's practice or research efforts. Once mastered, the methodology can guide a practitioner or researcher through the complex web of human problems. But such adherence to a theory has its disadvantages. By excluding other possible explanations, it can blind researchers to other factors that may be equally important. The fact is that none of the theories devised to date addresses the whole spectrum of abnormality—each is limited in its focus.

Two general trends have occurred as a result. First, the original model or theory may be revised by expanding or modifying some elements of the system. The many examples of such corrective interpretations include Adler's and Erikson's modifications of Freudian theory and the more recent cognitive-behavioral approach's modification of behavior therapy. But many of the early Freudian theorists did not accept the neo-Freudian additions, and some classical behavior therapists today do not accept the revisions proposed by cognitive behaviorists. Therefore, theoretical viewpoints tend to multiply and coexist—each with its own proponents—rather than being assimilated into previous views.

The Eclectic Approach

Alternatively, aspects of two or more diverse approaches may be combined in a more general eclectic approach. In practice, many psychologists have responded to the existence of many perspectives by adopting an eclectic stance; that is, they accept working ideas from several viewpoints and incorporate whichever they find useful. For example, a psychologist using an eclectic approach might accept causal explanations from psychodynamic theory while applying techniques of anxiety reduction from behavior therapy. Another psychologist might combine techniques from the cognitive-behavioral approach with those from the interpersonal approach. Purists in the field—those who advocate a single viewpoint—are skeptical about eclecticism, claiming that the eclectic approach tends to lack integrity and produces a "crazy quilt" of inconsistent practice with little rationale. This criticism may be true, but the approach certainly seems to work for many psychotherapists.

Typically, those who use an eclectic approach make no attempt to synthesize the theoretical perspectives. Although the approach can work in practical settings, it is not successful at a theoretical level, because the underlying principles of many of the theoretical perspectives are incompatible as they now stand. Thus the eclectic approach still falls short of the final goal, which is to tackle the theoretical clutter and develop a single, comprehensive, internally consistent viewpoint that accurately reflects what we know empirically about abnormal behavior.

The Biopsychosocial Unified Approach

At present, the only attempt at such a unified perspective that has been developing is called the *biopsychosocial viewpoint*. The name reflects the conviction that most disorders, especially those occurring beyond childhood, are the result of many causal factors—biological, psychosocial, and sociocultural—interacting with one another. Moreover, for any given person, the particular combination of causal factors may be unique, or at least not widely shared by large numbers of people with the same disorder. For example, some children may become delinquents because of having a heavy genetic loading for antisocial behavior, whereas others may become delinquent because of environmental influences such as living in an area with a large number of gangs. Therefore, we can still hope to achieve a scientific understanding of many of the causes of abnormal behavior, even if we cannot predict such behavior with exact certainty in each individual case and are often left with some "unexplained" influences.

summary

- Usually the occurrence of abnormal or maladaptive behavior is considered to be the joint product of a person's vulnerability (diathesis) to disorder and of certain stressors that challenge his or her coping resources.
- In considering the causes of abnormal behavior, it is important to distinguish among necessary, sufficient, and contributory causal factors, as well as between relatively distal causal factors and those that are more proximal.
  - The concept of protective factors is important for understanding why some people with both a diathesis and a stressor may remain resilient and not develop a disorder.
  - Both the distal (long ago) and proximal (immediate) causes of mental disorder may involve biological, psychosocial, and sociocultural factors. These three classes of factors can interact with each other in complicated ways.
- This chapter discussed biological, psychosocial, and sociocultural viewpoints, each of which tends to emphasize the importance of causal factors of a characteristic type.
- In examining biologically based vulnerabilities, we must consider genetic endowment, biochemical and hormonal imbalances, temperament, and brain dysfunction and neural plasticity.
- Investigations in this area show much promise for advancing our knowledge of how the mind and the body interact to produce maladaptive behavior.
- The oldest psychosocial viewpoint on abnormal behavior is Freudian psychoanalytic theory. For many years this view was preoccupied with questions about libidinal energies and their containment.
  - More recently, psychodynamic theories have shown a distinctly social or interpersonal thrust under the influence, in part, of object-relations theory, which emphasizes the importance of the quality of very early (pre-Oedipal) mother-infant relationships for normal development.
  - The originators of the interpersonal perspective were defectors from the psychoanalytic ranks who took exception to the Freudian emphasis on the internal determinants of motivation and behavior and instead emphasized that important aspects of human personality have social or interpersonal origins.
  - Psychoanalysis and closely related therapeutic approaches are termed psychodynamic in recognition of their attention to inner, often unconscious forces.
  - The behavioral perspective focuses on the role of learning in human behavior and attributes maladaptive behavior either to a failure to learn appropriate behaviors or to the learning of maladaptive behaviors.
  - Adherents of the behavioral viewpoint attempt to alter maladaptive behavior by extinguishing it and/or providing training in new, more adaptive behaviors.
- The cognitive-behavioral viewpoint attempts to incorporate the complexities of human cognition, and how it can become distorted, into an understanding of the causes of psychopathology.
  - Adherents to the cognitive-behavioral viewpoint attempt to alter maladaptive thinking and improve a person's abilities to solve problems and to plan.

- People's schemas and self-schemas play a central role in the way they process information, in how they attribute outcomes to causes, and in their values. The efficiency, accuracy, and coherence of a person's schemas and self-schemas appear to provide an important protection against breakdown.
- Sources of psychosocially determined vulnerability include early social deprivation or severe emotional trauma, inadequate parenting styles, marital discord and divorce, and maladaptive peer relationships.
- The sociocultural viewpoint is concerned with the contribution of sociocultural variables to mental disorder.
  - Although many serious mental disorders are fairly universal, the form that some disorders take and their prevalence vary widely among different cultures.
  - Low socioeconomic status, unemployment, and being subjected to prejudice and discrimination are associated with greater risk for various disorders.
- To obtain a more comprehensive understanding of mental disorder, we must draw on a variety of sources including the findings of genetics, biochemistry, psychology, and sociology.
- The biopsychosocial approach is promising, but in many ways it is merely a descriptive acknowledgment of these complex interactions rather than a clearly articulated theory of how they interact. It is up to future generations of theorists to devise a general theory of psychopathology, if indeed one is possible.

Key Terms

adoption method (p. 69)
association studies (p. 71)
attachment theory (p. 79)
attributions (p. 85)
behavior genetics (p. 69)
biopsychosocial viewpoint (p. 63)
castration anxiety (p. 78)
chromosomes (p. 66)
classical conditioning (p. 81)
cognitive-behavioral perspective (p. 84)
concordance rate (p. 69)
contributory cause (p. 59)
cortisol (p. 66)
developmental psychopathology (p. 62)
developmental systems approach (p. 73)
diathesis-stress models (p. 60)
discrimination (p. 82)
ego (p. 76)
ego psychology (p. 78)
ego-defense mechanisms (p. 76)
Electra complex (p. 78)
etiology (p. 58)
extinction (p. 81)
family history (or pedigree) method (p. 69)
generalization (p. 82)
genes (p. 66)
genotype (p. 68)
genotype-environment correlation (p. 68)
genotype-environment interaction (p. 68)
hormones (p. 66)
hypothalamic-pituitary-adrenal-cortical axis (p. 66)
id (p. 76)
instrumental (or operant) conditioning (p. 82)
interpersonal perspective (p. 79)
intrapsychic conflicts (p. 76)
libido (p. 76)
linkage analysis (p. 71)
necessary cause (p. 58)
neurotransmitters (p. 64)
object-relations theory (p. 78)
observational learning (p. 83)
Oedipus complex (p. 78)
phenotype (p. 68)
pituitary gland (p. 66)
pleasure principle (p. 76)
primary process thinking (p. 76)
protective factors (p. 60)
psychosexual stages of development (p. 76)
reality principle (p. 76)
reinforcement (p. 82)
resilience (p. 61)
schema (p. 84)
secondary process thinking (p. 76)
self-schema (p. 84)
spontaneous recovery (p. 81)
sufficient cause (p. 59)
superego (p. 76)
synapse (p. 64)
temperament (p. 71)
twin method (p. 69)

chapter

4

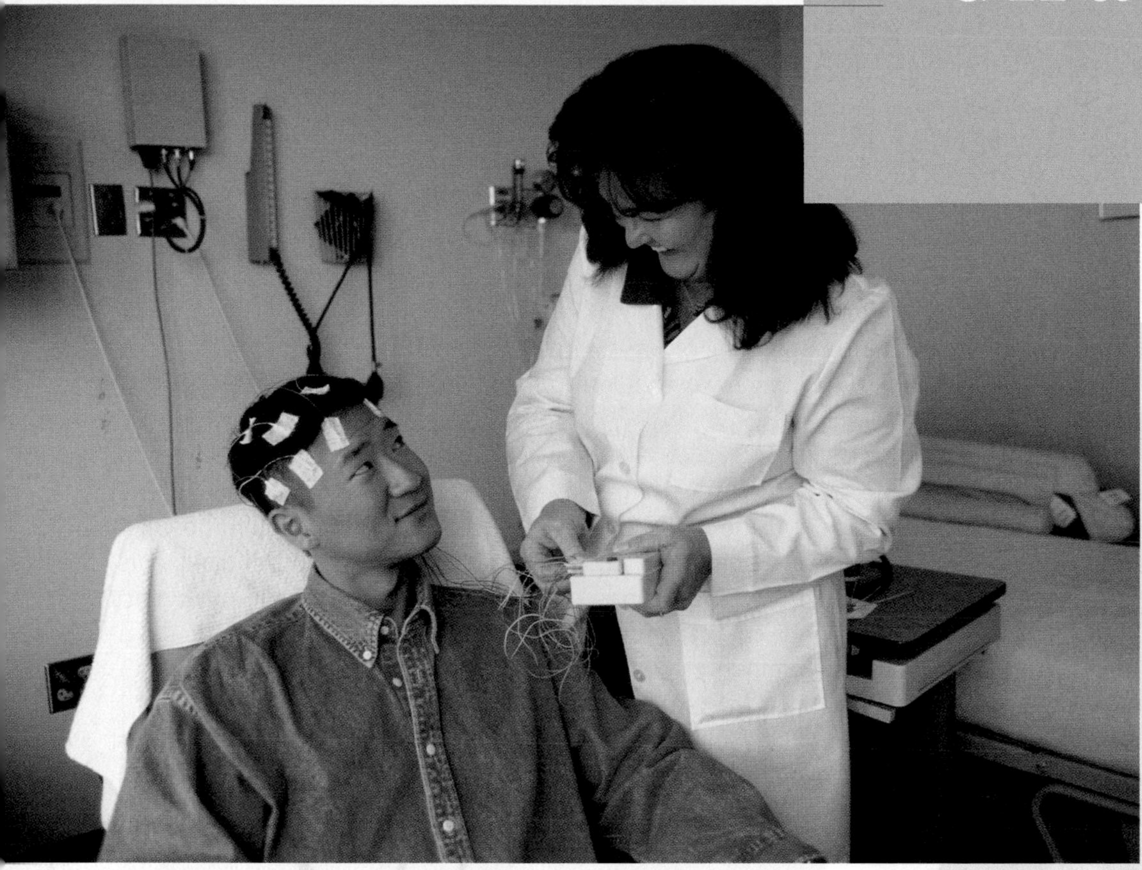

Clinical Assessment

We will focus in this chapter on the initial clinical assessment and on arriving at a clinical diagnosis according to DSM-IV-TR. Psychological assessment refers to a procedure by which clinicians, using psychological tests, observation, and interviews, develop a summary of the client's symptoms and problems. Clinical diagnosis is the process through which a clinician arrives at a general "summary classification" of the patient's symptoms by following a clearly defined system such as DSM-IV-TR or ICD-10 (International Classification of Diseases) published by the World Health Organization.

Assessment is an ongoing process and may be important at other points during treatment—for example, to evaluate outcome. In the initial clinical assessment, an attempt is made to identify the main dimensions of a client's problem and to predict the probable course of events under various conditions. It is at this initial stage that crucial decisions have to be made—such as what (if any) treatment approach is to be offered, whether the problem will require hospitalization, to what extent family members will need to be included as co-clients, and so on. Sometimes these decisions must be made quickly, as in emergency conditions, and without critical information. As will be seen, various psychological measurement instruments are employed to maximize assessment efficiency in this type of pretreatment examination process (Beutler & Harwood, 2002).

A less obvious but equally important function of pretreatment assessment is establishing baselines for various psychological functions so that the effects of treatment can be measured. Criteria based on these measurements may be established as part of the treatment plan such that the therapy is considered successful and is terminated only when the client's behavior meets these predetermined criteria. Also, as we will see in later chapters, comparison of posttreatment with pretreatment assessment results is an essential feature of many research projects designed to evaluate the effectiveness of various therapies.

In this chapter, we will review some of the more commonly used assessment procedures and show how the data obtained can be integrated into a coherent clinical picture for making decisions about referral and treatment. Our survey will include a discussion of neurological and neuropsychological assessment, the clinical interview, behavioral observation, and personality assessment through the use of projective and objective psychological tests. Later in this chapter we will examine the process of arriving at a clinical diagnosis using DSM-IV-TR.

Let us look first at what, exactly, a clinician is trying to learn during the psychological assessment of a client.

THE BASIC ELEMENTS IN ASSESSMENT

What does a clinician need to know? First, of course, the **presenting problem,** or major symptoms and behavior, must be identified. Is it a situational problem precipitated by some environmental stressor such as divorce or unemployment, a manifestation of a more pervasive and long-term disorder, or some combination of the two? Is there any evidence of recent deterioration in cognitive functioning? What is the duration of the current complaint and how is the person dealing with the problem? What, if any, prior help has been sought? Are there indications of self-defeating behavior and personality deterioration, or is the individual using available personal and environmental resources in a good effort to cope? How pervasively has the problem affected the person's performance of important social roles? Does the individual's symptomatic behavior fit any of the diagnostic patterns in the DSM-IV-TR?

The Relationship between Assessment and Diagnosis

It is important to have an adequate classification of the presenting problem for a number of reasons. In many cases, a formal diagnosis is necessary before insurance claims can be filed. Clinically, knowledge of a person's type of disorder can help in planning and managing the appropriate treatment. Administratively, it is essential to know the range of diagnostic problems that are represented among the patient or client population and for which treatment facilities need to be available. If most patients at a facility have been diagnosed as having personality disorders, for example, then the staffing, physical environment, and treatment facilities should be arranged accordingly. Thus the nature of the difficulty needs to be understood as clearly as possible, including a diagnostic categorization if appropriate (see the section "Classifying Abnormal Behavior" at the end of this chapter).

Taking a Social or Behavioral History

For most clinical purposes, assigning a formal diagnostic classification per se is much less important than having a clear understanding of the individual's behavioral history, intellectual functioning, personality characteristics, and environmental pressures and resources. That is, an adequate assessment includes much more than the diagnostic label. For example, it should include an objective description of the person's behavior. How does the person characteristically respond to other people? Are there excesses in behavior present, such as eating or drinking too much? Are there notable deficits, for example, in social skills? How appropriate is the person's behavior? Is the person manifesting behavior that is plainly unresponsive or uncooperative? Excesses, deficits, and appropriateness are key dimensions to be noted if the clinician is to understand the particular disorder that has brought the individual to the clinic or hospital.

PERSONALITY FACTORS Assessment should include a description of any relevant long-term personality characteristics. Has the person typically responded in deviant ways to particular kinds of situations—for example, those requiring submission to legitimate authority? Are there personality traits or behavior patterns that predispose the individual to behave in maladaptive ways? Does the person tend to become enmeshed with others to the point of losing his or her identity, or is he or she so self-absorbed that intimate relationships are not possible? Is the person able to accept help from others? Is the person capable of genuine affection and of accepting appropriate responsibility for the welfare of others? Such questions are at the heart of many assessment efforts.

THE SOCIAL CONTEXT It is also important to assess the social context in which the individual operates. What kinds of environmental demands are typically placed on the person, and what supports or special stressors exist in his or her life situation? For example, being the primary caretaker for a spouse suffering from Alzheimer's disease is so challenging that relatively few people can manage the task without significant psychological impairment, especially where outside supports are lacking.

The diverse and often conflicting bits of information about the individual's personality traits, behavior patterns, environmental demands, and so on, must then be integrated into a consistent and meaningful picture. Some clinicians refer to this picture as a "dynamic formulation," because it not only describes the current situation but also includes hypotheses about what is driving the person to behave in maladaptive ways. At this point in the assessment, the clinician should have a plausible explanation for why a normally passive and mild-mannered man suddenly flew into a rage and started breaking up furniture, for example. The formulation should allow the clinician to develop hypotheses about the client's future behavior as well. What is the likelihood of improvement or deterioration if the person's problems are left untreated? Which behaviors should be the initial focus of change, and what treatment methods are likely to be most efficient in producing this change? How much change might be expected from a particular type of treatment?

Where feasible, decisions about treatment are made collaboratively with the consent and approval of the individual. In cases of severe disorder, however, they may have to be made without the patient's participation or, in rare instances, even without consulting responsible family members. As has already been indicated, knowledge of the patient's strengths and resources is important; in short, what qualities does the patient bring to treatment that can enhance the chances of improvement?

Because a wide range of factors can play important roles in causing and maintaining maladaptive behavior, assessment may involve the coordinated use of physical, psychological, and environmental assessment procedures. As we have indicated, however, the nature and comprehensiveness of clinical assessments vary with the problem and the treatment agency's facilities. Assessment by phone in a suicide prevention center (Stolberg & Bongar, 2002), for

Some patients with cognitive deterioration are difficult to evaluate and to provide health care, often requiring special facilities.

example, is quite different from assessment aimed at developing a treatment plan for a person who has come to a clinic for help (Perry, Miller, & Klump, 2006).

The Influence of Professional Orientation

How clinicians go about the assessment process often depends on their basic treatment orientations. For example, a biologically oriented clinician—typically a psychiatrist or other medical practitioner—is likely to focus on biological assessment methods aimed at determining any underlying organic malfunctioning that may be causing the maladaptive behavior. A psychodynamic or psychoanalytically oriented clinician may choose unstructured personality assessment techniques, such as the Rorschach inkblots or the Thematic Apperception Test (TAT), to identify intrapsychic conflicts or may simply proceed with therapy, expecting these conflicts to emerge naturally as part of the treatment process. A behaviorally oriented clinician, in an effort to determine the functional relationships between environmental events or reinforcements and the abnormal behavior, will rely on such techniques as behavioral observation and self-monitoring to identify learned maladaptive patterns; for a cognitively oriented behaviorist, the focus would shift to the dysfunctional thoughts supposedly mediating those patterns. A humanistically oriented clinician might use interview techniques to uncover blocked or distorted personal growth, and an interpersonally oriented clinician might use such techniques as personal confrontations and behavioral observations to pinpoint difficulties in interpersonal relationships.

The preceding examples represent general trends and are in no way meant to imply that clinicians of a particular orientation limit themselves to a particular assessment method or that each assessment technique is limited to a particular theoretical orientation. Such trends are instead a matter of emphasis and point to the fact that certain types of assessments are more conducive than others to uncovering particular causal factors, or for eliciting information about symptomatic behavior central to understanding and treating a disorder within a given conceptual framework.

As you will see in what follows, both physical and psychosocial data can be extremely important to understanding the patient. In the sections below we will examine in some detail an actual psychological study that has drawn on a variety of assessment data.

Trust and Rapport between the Clinician and the Client

In order for psychological assessment to proceed effectively and to provide a clear understanding of behavior and symptoms, the client being evaluated must feel comfortable with the clinician. In a clinical assessment situation, this means that a client must feel that the testing will help the practitioner gain a clear understanding of her or his problems and must understand how the tests will be used and how the psychologist will incorporate them into the clinical evaluation. The clinician should explain what will happen during assessment and how the information gathered will help provide a clearer picture of the problems the client is facing.

Clients need to be assured that the feelings, beliefs, attitudes, and personal history that they are disclosing will be used appropriately, will be kept in strict confidence, and will be made available only to therapists or others involved in the case. An important aspect of confidentiality is that the test results are released to a third party only if the client signs an appropriate release form. In cases in which the person is being tested for a third party such as the court system, the client in effect is the referring source—the judge ordering the evaluation—not the individual being tested. In these cases the testing relationship is likely to be strained, and rapport is likely to be difficult. Of course, in a court-ordered evaluation, the person's test-taking behavior is likely to be very different from what it would be otherwise, and interpretation of the test needs to reflect this different motivational set created by the client's possible unwillingness to cooperate.

Clients being tested in a clinical situation are usually highly motivated to be evaluated and like to know the results of the testing. They generally are eager for some definition of their discomfort. Moreover, providing test feedback in a clinical setting can be an important element in the treatment process (Beutler & Harwood, 2002). Interestingly, when patients are given appropriate feedback on test results, they tend to improve—just from gaining a perspective on their problems from the testing. The test feedback process itself can be a powerful clinical intervention (Finn & Kamphuis, 2006; Finn & Tonsager, 1997). When persons who were not provided psychological test feedback were compared with those who were provided with feedback, the latter group showed a significant decline in reported symptoms and an increase in measured self-esteem as a result of having a clearer understanding of their own resources.

In Review

- What is the difference between diagnosis and clinical assessment? What components must be integrated into a dynamic formulation?
- Describe the important elements in a social history.
- What is the impact of professional orientation on the structure and form of a psychological evaluation?

Assessment of the Physical Organism

In some situations and with certain psychological problems, a medical evaluation is necessary to rule out the possibility that physical abnormalities may be causing or contributing to the problem. The medical evaluation may include both a general physical examination and special examinations aimed at assessing the structural (anatomical) and functional (physiological) integrity of the brain as a behaviorally significant physical system (Rozensky, Sweet, & Tovian, 1997).

The General Physical Examination

In cases in which physical symptoms are part of the presenting clinical picture, a referral for a medical evaluation is recommended. A physical examination consists of the kinds of procedures most of us have experienced in getting a "medical checkup." Typically, a medical history is obtained, and the major systems of the body are checked (LeBlond, DeGowin, & Brown, 2004). This part of the assessment procedure is of obvious importance for disorders that entail physical problems, such as somatoform, addictive, and organic brain syndromes. In addition, a variety of organic conditions, including various hormonal irregularities, can produce behavioral symptoms that closely mimic those of mental disorders usually considered to have predominantly psychosocial origins. Although some long-lasting pain can be related to actual organic conditions, other such pain can result from strictly emotional factors. A case in point is chronic back pain, in which psychological factors may sometimes play an important part (Arbisi & Butcher, 2004). A diagnostic error in this type of situation could result in costly and ineffective surgery; hence, in equivocal cases, most clinicians insist on a medical clearance before initiating psychosocially based interventions.

The Neurological Examination

Because brain pathology is sometimes involved in some mental disorders (e.g., unusual memory deficits or motor impairments), a specialized neurological examination can be administered in addition to the general medical examination. This may involve the client's getting an **electroencephalogram (EEG)** to assess brain wave patterns in awake and sleeping states. An EEG is a graphical record of the brain's electrical activity. It is obtained by placing electrodes on the scalp and amplifying the minute brain wave impulses from various brain areas; these amplified impulses drive oscillating pens whose deviations are traced on a strip of paper moving at a constant speed. Much is known about the normal pattern of brain impulses in waking and sleeping states and under various conditions of sensory stimulation. Significant divergences from the normal pattern can thus reflect abnormalities of brain function such as might be caused by a brain tumor or other lesion. When an EEG reveals a **dysrhythmia** (irregular pattern) in the brain's electrical activity (for example, that adult males with ADHD or adult hyperactivity disorder show abnormal brain activity; see Hermens, Williams, Lazzaro, et al., 2004), other specialized techniques may be used in an attempt to arrive at a more precise diagnosis of the problem.

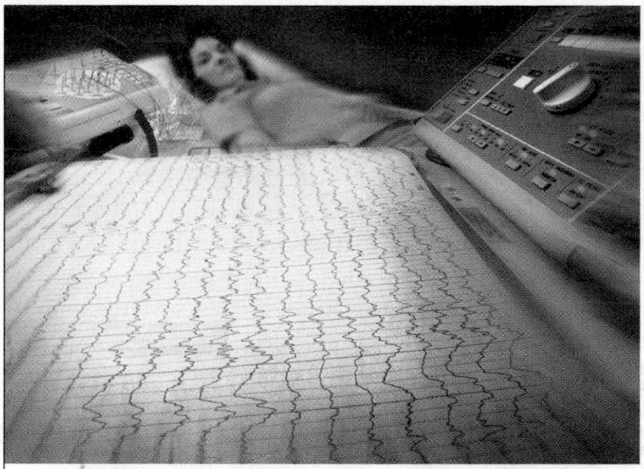

An EEG is a graphical record of the brain's electrical activity. Electrodes are placed on the scalp and brain wave impulses are amplified. The amplified impulses drive oscillating pens whose deviations are traced on a strip of paper moving at a constant speed. Significant differences from the normal pattern can reflect abnormalities of brain function.

ANATOMICAL BRAIN SCANS Radiological technology, such as **computerized axial tomography,** known in brief as the **CAT scan,** is one of these specialized techniques. Through the use of X rays, a CAT scan reveals images of parts of the brain that might be diseased. This procedure has aided neurological study in recent years by providing rapid access, without surgery, to accurate information about the localization and extent of anomalies in the brain's structural characteristics. The procedure involves the use of computer analysis applied to X-ray beams across sections of a patient's brain to produce images that a neurologist can then interpret.

CAT scans have been increasingly replaced by **magnetic resonance imaging (MRI).** The images of the interior of the brain are frequently sharper with MRI because of its superior ability to differentiate subtle variations in soft tissue. In addition, the MRI procedure is normally far less complicated to administer, and it does not subject the patient to ionizing radiation.

Essentially, MRI involves the precise measurement of variations in magnetic fields that are caused by the varying amounts of water content of various organs and parts of organs. In this manner the anatomical structure of a cross section at any given plane through an organ such as the brain can be computed and graphically depicted with astonishing structural differentiation and clarity. MRI thus makes possible, by noninvasive means, visualization of all but the most minute abnormalities of brain structure. It has been particularly useful in confirming degenerative brain processes as shown, for example, in enlarged areas of the brain. Therefore, MRI studies have considerable potential to illuminate the contribution of brain anomalies to "nonorganic" psychoses such as schizophrenia, and some progress in this area has already been made (Mathalondolf, Sullivan, Lim, & Pfefferbaum, 2001). The major problem encountered with MRI is that some patients have a claustrophobic reaction to being placed into the narrow cylinder of the MRI machine that is necessary to contain the magnetic field and block out external radio signals.

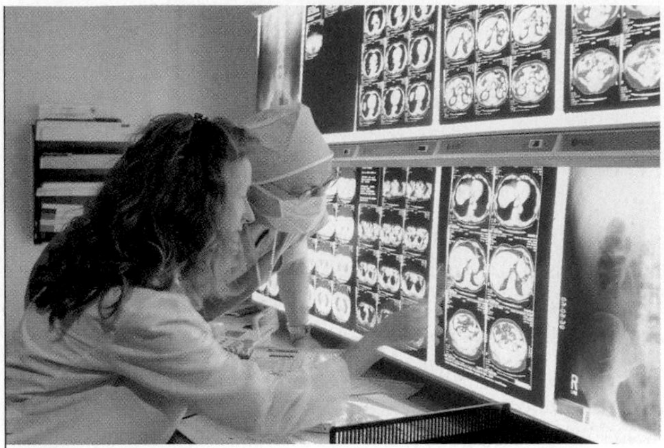

The functional MRI (fMRI), like the MRI, allows clinicians to "map" brain structure. However, the exciting breakthrough in fMRI technology gives clinicians the ability to measure brain activity such as sensations, images, and thoughts, revealing the specific areas of the brain that appear to be involved in their neurophysiological mediation.

PET SCANS: A METABOLIC PORTRAIT Another scanning technique is **positron emission tomography,** the **PET scan.** Although a CAT scan is limited to distinguishing anatomical features such as the shape of a particular internal structure, a PET scan allows for an appraisal of how an organ is functioning (Mazziotta, 1996). The PET scan provides metabolic portraits by tracking natural compounds, such as glucose, as they are metabolized by the brain or other organs. By revealing areas of differential metabolic activity, the PET scan enables a medical specialist to obtain more clear-cut diagnoses of brain pathology by, for example, pinpointing sites responsible for epileptic seizures, trauma from head injury or stroke, and brain tumors. Thus the PET scan may be able to reveal problems that are not immediately apparent anatomically. Moreover, the use of PET scans in research on brain pathology that occurs in abnormal conditions such as schizophrenia, depression, and alcoholism may lead to important discoveries about the organic processes underlying these disorders, thus providing clues to more effective treatment (Zametkin & Liotta, 1997). Unfortunately, PET scans have been of limited value thus far because of the low-fidelity pictures obtained (Fletcher, 2004; Videbech, Ravnkilde, Kristensen, et al., 2003).

THE FUNCTIONAL MRI The technique known as **functional MRI (fMRI)** has been used in the study of psychopathology for more than a decade. As originally developed and employed, the MRI could reveal brain structure but not brain activity. For the latter, clinicians and investigators remained dependent upon positron emission tomography (PET) scans, whose principal shortcoming is the need for a very expensive cyclotron nearby to produce the short-lived radioactive atoms required for the procedure. Simply put, in its most common form, fMRI measures changes in local oxygenation (i.e., blood flow) of specific areas of brain tissue that in turn depend on neuronal activity in those specific regions (Morihisa, 2001). Ongoing psychological activity, such as sensations, images, and thoughts, can thus be "mapped," at least in principle, revealing the specific areas of the brain that appear to be involved in their neurophysiological mediation. Because the measurement of change in this context is critically time-dependent, the emergence of fMRI required the development of high-speed devices for enhancing the recording process, as well as the computerized analysis of incoming data. These improvements are now widely available and will likely lead to a marked increase in studies of disordered persons using functional imaging.

Optimism about the ultimate value of fMRI in mapping cognitive processes in mental disorders is still strong. The fMRI is thought by some to hold more promise for depicting brain abnormalities than currently used procedures such as the neuropsychological examination (MacDonald & Carter, 2002). A number of published studies have provided support for this optimism. Research using fMRI has explored the cortical functioning that underlies various psychological processes; for example, one recent study showed that psychological factors or environmental events can affect brain processes as measured by fMRI. Eisenberger, Lieberman, and Williams (2003) found that participants who were excluded from social participation showed a similar pattern of brain activation (in the right ventral prefrontal cortex) as participants experiencing physical pain. (See photo on p. 113.)

Other studies have addressed problems in abnormal behavior. One study showed that impaired time estimation found in schizophrenics might result from dysfunction in specific areas of the brain, thalamus, and prefrontal cortex (Suzuki, Zhou, et al., 2004; Volz, Nenadic, et al., 2001); cortical functioning in auditory hallucinations in schizophrenia (Shergill, Brammer, et al., 2000); effects of neuroleptic medication with schizophrenics (Braus, Ende, et al., 1999); and the neuroanatomy of depression (Brody, Saxena, et al., 2001). Finally, Whalley et al. (2004) recently reported that fMRI technique has the potential of adding to our understanding of the early development of psychological disorder.

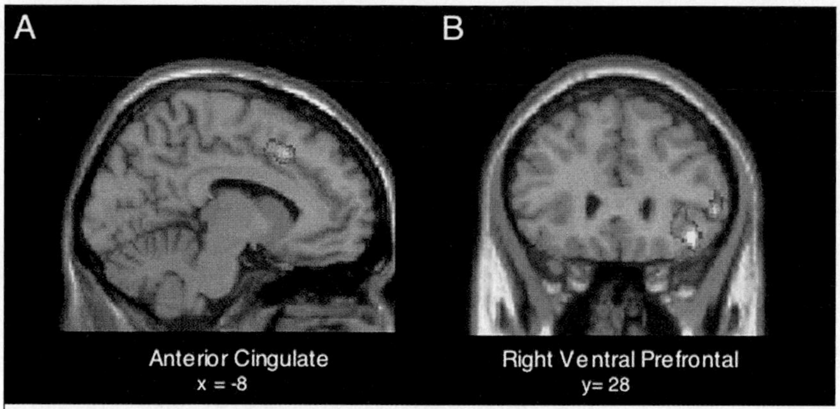

A pattern of increased activity in the anterior cingulated cortex (ACC) and the right ventral prefrontal cortex (RVPFC) shown here in persons who were excluded from participating in a game are similar to cortical activity of persons experiencing physical pain.

There are some clear methodological limitations that can influence fMRI results. For example, both MRI and fMRI are quite sensitive to artifacts as a result of slight movements of the person being evaluated (Davidson, Thomas, & Casey, 2003). Additionally, the results of fMRI studies are often difficult to interpret. Even though group differences emerge between a cognitively impaired group and a control sample, the results usually do not provide much specific information about the processes studied. Fletcher (2004) provided a somewhat sobering analysis of the current status of fMRI in contemporary psychiatry, noting that many professionals who had hoped for intricate and unambiguous results might be disappointed with the overall lack of effective, pragmatic methodology in fMRI assessment of cognitive processes.

At this point the fMRI is not considered to be a valid or useful diagnostic tool for mental disorders. The primary value of this procedure continues to be research into cortical activity and cognitive processes.

The Neuropsychological Examination

The techniques described so far have shown success in identifying brain abnormalities that are very often accompanied by gross impairments in behavior and varied psychological deficits. However, behavioral and psychological impairments due to organic brain abnormalities may become manifest before any organic brain lesion is detectable by scanning or other means. In these instances, reliable techniques are needed to measure any alteration in behavioral or psychological functioning that has occurred because of the organic brain pathology. This need is met by a growing cadre of psychologists specializing in **neuropsychological assessment,** which involves the use of various testing devices to measure a person's cognitive, perceptual, and motor performance as clues to the extent and location of brain damage (Franzen, 2001; Rohling, Meyers, & Millis, 2003).

In many instances of known or suspected organic brain involvement, a clinical neuropsychologist administers a test battery to a patient. The person's performance on standardized tasks, particularly perceptual-motor tasks, can give valuable clues about any cognitive and intellectual impairment following brain damage (La Rue & Swanda, 1997; Lezak, 1995; Reitan & Wolfson, 1985). Such testing can even provide clues to the probable location of the brain damage, although PET scans, MRIs, and other physical tests may be more effective in determining the exact location of the injury.

Many neuropsychologists prefer to administer a highly individualized array of tests, depending on a patient's case history and other available information. Others administer a standard set of tests that have been preselected to sample, in a systematic and comprehensive manner, a broad range of psychological competencies known to be adversely affected by various types of brain injury. The use of a constant set of tests has many research and clinical advantages, although it may compromise flexibility. The components of one such standard procedure, the Halstead-Reitan battery, are described in Developments in Practice 4.1.

In summary, the medical and neuropsychological sciences are developing many new procedures to assess brain functioning and behavioral manifestations of organic disorder (Snyder & Nussbaum, 1998). Medical procedures to assess organic brain damage include EEGs and CAT, PET, and MRI scans. The new technology holds great promise for detecting and evaluating organic brain dysfunction and increasing our understanding of brain function. Neuropsychological testing provides a clinician with important behavioral information on how organic brain damage is affecting a person's present functioning. However, in cases where the psychological difficulty is thought to result from nonorganic causes, psychosocial assessment is used.

in review

- Compare and contrast five important neurological procedures. What makes each one particularly valuable?
- Describe the use of neuropsychological tests in evaluating the behavioral effects of organic brain disorders.
- What is the difference between a PET scan and an fMRI?

4.1 Developments in Practice: Neuropsychological Examinations: Determining Brain-Behavior Relationships

The Halstead-Reitan battery is a neuropsychological examination composed of several tests and variables from which an "index of impairment" can be computed (Reitan & Wolfson, 1985). In addition, it provides specific information about a subject's functioning in several skill areas. Although it typically takes 4 to 6 hours to complete and requires substantial administrative time, it is being used increasingly in neurological evaluations because it yields a great deal of useful information about an individual's cognitive and motor processes (La Rue & Swanda, 1997; Reitan & Wolfson, 2000). The Halstead-Reitan battery for adults is made up of the following tests:

1. Halstead Category Test: Measures a subject's ability to learn and remember material and can provide clues as to his or her judgment and impulsivity. The subject is presented with a stimulus (on a screen) that suggests a number between 1 and 4. The subject presses a button indicating the number she or he believes was suggested. A correct choice is followed by the sound of a pleasant doorbell, an incorrect choice by a loud buzzer. The person is required to determine from the pattern of buzzers and bells what the underlying principle of the correct choice is.
2. Tactual Performance Test: Measures a subject's motor speed, response to the unfamiliar, and ability to learn and use tactile and kinesthetic cues. The test surface is a board that has spaces for ten blocks of varied shapes. The subject is blindfolded (never actually seeing the board) and asked to place the blocks into the correct grooves in the board. Later, the subject is asked to draw the blocks and the board from tactile memory.
3. Rhythm Test: Measures attention and sustained concentration through an auditory perception task. It is a subtest of Seashore's Test of musical talent and includes 30 pairs of rhythmic beats that are presented on a tape recorder. The subject is asked whether the pairs are the same or different.
4. Speech Sounds Perception Test: Determines whether an individual can identify spoken words. Nonsense words are presented on a tape recorder, and the subject is asked to identify the presented word from a list of four printed words. This task measures the subject's concentration, attention, and comprehension.
5. Finger Oscillation Task: Measures the speed at which an individual can depress a lever with the index finger. Several trials are given with each hand.

In addition to the Halstead-Reitan battery, other tests, referred to as "allied procedures," may be used in a neuropsychology laboratory. For example, Boll (1980) recommends use of the modified Halstead-Wepman Aphasia Screening Test for obtaining information about a subject's language ability and about her or his abilities to identify numbers and body parts, to follow directions, to spell, and to pantomime simple actions.

Psychosocial Assessment

Psychosocial assessment attempts to provide a realistic picture of an individual in interaction with his or her social environment. This picture includes relevant information about the individual's personality makeup and present level of functioning, as well as information about the stressors and resources in her or his life situation. For example, early in the process, clinicians may act as puzzle solvers, absorbing as much information about the client as possible—present feelings, attitudes, memories, demographic facts—and trying to fit the pieces together into a meaningful pattern. Clinicians typically formulate hypotheses and discard or confirm them as they proceed. Starting with a global technique such as a clinical interview, clinicians may later select more specific assessment tasks or tests. The following are some of the psychosocial procedures that may be used.

Assessment Interviews

An assessment interview, often considered the central element of the assessment process, usually involves a face-to-face interaction in which a clinician obtains information about various aspects of a patient's situation, behavior, and personality (Barbour & Davison, 2004; Craig, 2004). The interview may vary from a simple set of questions or prompts to a more extended and detailed format (Kici & Westhoff, 2004). It may be relatively open in character, with an interviewer making moment-to-moment decisions about his or her next question on the basis of responses to previous ones, or it may be more tightly controlled and structured so as to ensure that a particular set of questions is covered. In the latter case, the interviewer may choose from a number of highly structured, standardized interview formats whose ***reliability*** has been established in prior research.

research close-up

reliability

As used here, reliability *means simply that two or more interviewers assessing the same client will generate highly similar conclusions about the client, a type of consensus that research shows can by no means be taken for granted.*

STRUCTURED AND UNSTRUCTURED INTERVIEWS Although many clinicians prefer the freedom to explore as they feel responses merit, the research data show that the more controlled and structured type of assessment interviews yields far more reliable results than the flexible format. There appears to be widespread overconfidence among clinicians in the accuracy of their own methods and judgments (Taylor & Meux, 1997). Every rule has exceptions, but in most instances, an assessor is wise to conduct an interview that is carefully structured in terms of goals, comprehensive symptom review, other content to be explored, and the type of relationship the interviewer attempts to establish with the person. See Figure 4.1 for a description of the differences between structured and unstructured interviews.

The reliability of the assessment interview may also be enhanced by the use of rating scales that help focus inquiry and quantify the interview data. For example, the person may be rated on a 3-, 5-, or 7-point scale with respect to self-esteem, anxiety, and various other characteristics. Such a structured and preselected format is particularly effective in giving a comprehensive impression, or "profile," of the subject and his or her life situation and in revealing specific problems or crises—such as marital difficulties, drug dependence, or suicidal fantasies—that may require immediate therapeutic intervention.

Clinical interviews can be subject to error because they rely on human judgment to choose the questions and process the information. Evidence of this unreliability includes the fact that different clinicians have often arrived at different formal diagnoses on the basis of the interview data they elicited from a particular patient. It is chiefly for this reason that recent versions of the DSM (that is, III, III-R, IV, and IV-TR) have emphasized an "operational" assessment approach, one

Unstructured Interviews

Unstructured assessment interviews are typically subjective and do not follow a predetermined set of questions. The beginning statements in the interview are usually general, and follow-up questions are tailored for each client. The content of the interview questions is influenced by the habits or theoretical views of the interviewer. The interviewer does not ask the same questions of all clients; rather, he or she subjectively decides what to ask based on the client's response to previous questions. Because the questions are asked in an unplanned way, important criteria needed for a DSM-IV diagnosis might be skipped. Interview responses based on unstructured procedures are difficult to quantify or compare with responses of clients from other interviews. Thus, uses of unstructured interviews in mental health research are limited.

On the positive side, unstructured interviews can be viewed by clients as being more sensitive to their needs or problems than more structured procedures. Moreover, the spontaneous follow-up questions that emerge in an interview can, at times, provide valuable information that would not emerge in a structured interview.

Structured Interviews

Structured interviews follow a predetermined set of questions throughout the interview. The beginning statements or introduction to the interview follow set procedures. The themes and questions are predetermined to obtain particular responses for all items. The interviewer cannot deviate from the question lists and procedures. All questions are asked of each client in a preset way. Each question is structured in a manner so as to allow responses to be quantified or clearly determined.

On the negative side, structured interviews typically take longer to administer than unstructured interviews and may include some seemingly tangential questions. Patients can sometimes be frustrated by the overly detailed questions in areas that are of no concern to them.

FIGURE 4.1

Differences between Unstructured and Structured Interviews

During an assessment interview, a clinician obtains information about various aspects of a patient's situation, behavior, and personality makeup. The interview is usually conducted face-to-face and may have a relatively open structure or be more tightly controlled depending on the goals and style of the clinician.

that specifies observable criteria for diagnosis and provides specific guidelines for making diagnostic judgments. "Winging it" has limited use in this type of assessment process. The operational approach leads to more reliable psychiatric diagnoses, perhaps at some cost in reduced interviewer flexibility. For further discussion and illustration of the differences between structured and unstructured diagnostic interviewing see Figure 4.1 on page 115 .

The Clinical Observation of Behavior

One of the traditional and most useful assessment tools that a clinician has available is direct observation of a patient's characteristic behavior (Hartmann, Barrios, & Wood, 2004). The main purpose of direct observation is to learn more about the person's psychological functioning through the objective description of appearance and behavior in various contexts. Clinical observation is the clinician's objective description of the person's appearance and behavior—his or her personal hygiene and emotional responses and any depression, anxiety, aggression, hallucinations, or delusions he or she may manifest. Ideally, clinical observation takes place in a natural environment (such as observing a child's behavior in a classroom or at home), but it is more likely to take place upon admission to a clinic or hospital (Leichtman, 2002). For example, a brief description is usually made of a subject's behavior upon hospital admission, and more detailed observations are made periodically on the ward.

Some practitioners and researchers use a more controlled, rather than a naturalistic, behavioral setting for conducting observations in contrived situations. These *analogue situations*, which are designed to yield information about the person's adaptive strategies, might involve such tasks as staged **role-playing,** event reenactment, family interaction assignments, or think-aloud procedures (Haynes, 2001).

In addition to making their own observations, many clinicians enlist their patients' help by providing them instruction in **self-monitoring:** self-observation and objective reporting of behavior, thoughts, and feelings as they occur in various natural settings. This method can be a valuable aid in determining the kinds of situations in which maladaptive behavior is likely to be evoked, and numerous studies also show it to have therapeutic benefits in its own right. Alternatively, a patient may be asked to fill out a more or less formal self-report or a checklist concerning problematic reactions experienced in various situations. Many instruments have been published in the professional literature and are commercially available to clinicians. These approaches recognize that people are excellent sources of information about themselves. Assuming that the right questions are asked and that people are willing to disclose information about themselves, the results can have a crucial bearing on treatment planning.

The procedures described above focus on a subject's overt behavior, omitting the often equally important consideration of concurrent mental events—that is, the individual's ongoing thoughts. In an attempt to sample naturally occurring thoughts, psychologists are experimenting with having individuals carry small electronic beepers that produce a signal, such as a soft tone, at unexpected intervals. At each signal, the person is to write down or electronically record whatever thoughts the signal interrupted. These "thought reports" can then be analyzed in various ways, and they can be used for some kinds of personality assessment and diagnosis as well as for monitoring progress in psychological therapy (Klinger & Kroll-Mensing, 1995).

RATING SCALES As in the case of interviews, the use of **rating scales** in clinical observation and in self-reports helps both to organize information and to encourage reliability and objectivity (Aiken, 1996). That is, the formal structure of a scale is likely to keep observer inferences to a minimum. The most useful rating scales are those that enable a rater to indicate not only the presence or absence of a trait or behavior but also its prominence or degree. The following item is an example from such a rating scale; the observer would check the most appropriate description.

Sexual Behavior

______ **1.** Sexually assaultive: aggressively approaches males or females with sexual intent.

______ **2.** Sexually soliciting: exposes genitals with sexual intent, makes overt sexual advances to other patients or staff, masturbates openly.

______ **3.** No overt sexual behavior: not preoccupied with discussion of sexual matters.

______ **4.** Avoids sex topics: made uneasy by discussion of sex, becomes disturbed if approached sexually by others.

______ **5.** Excessive prudishness about sex: considers sex filthy, condemns sexual behavior in others, becomes panic-stricken if approached sexually.

Ratings like these may be made not only as part of an initial evaluation but also to check on the course or outcome of treatment.

One of the rating scales most widely used for recording observations in clinical practice and in psychiatric research is the Brief Psychiatric Rating Scale (BPRS) (Overall & Hollister, 1982; Serper, Goldberg, & Salzinger, 2004). The BPRS provides a structured and quantifiable format for rating clinical symptoms such as somatic concern, anxiety, emotional withdrawal, guilt feelings, hostility, suspiciousness, and unusual thought patterns. It contains 18 scales that are scored from ratings made by a clinician following an interview with a patient. The distinct patterns of behavior reflected in the BPRS ratings enable clinicians to make a standardized comparison of their patients' symptoms with the behavior of other psychiatric patients. The BPRS has been found to be an extremely useful instrument in clinical research (for example, see Davidson, Shahar, Stayner, et al., 2004; Lachar, Bailley, et al., 2001), especially for the purpose of assigning patients to treatment groups on the basis of similarity in symptoms. However, it is not widely used for making treatment or diagnostic decisions in clinical practice. The Hamilton Rating Scale for Depression (HRSD), a similar but more specifically targeted instrument, is one of the most widely used procedures for selecting clinically depressed research subjects and also for assessing the response of such subjects to various treatments (see Beevers & Miller, 2004; Santor & Coyne, 2001).

Psychological Tests

Interviews and behavioral observation are relatively direct attempts to determine a person's beliefs, attitudes, and problems. Psychological tests are a more indirect means of assessing psychological characteristics. Scientifically developed psychological tests (as opposed to the recreational ones sometimes appearing in magazines or on the Internet) are standardized sets of procedures or tasks for obtaining samples of behavior. A subject's responses to the standardized stimuli are compared with those of other people who have comparable demographic characteristics, usually through established test norms or test score distributions. From these comparisons, a clinician can then draw inferences about how much the person's psychological qualities differ from those of a reference group, typically a psychologically normal one. Among the characteristics that these tests can measure are coping patterns, motive patterns, personality characteristics, role behaviors, values, levels of depression or anxiety, and intellectual functioning. Impressive advances in the technology of test development have made it possible to create instruments of acceptable reliability and validity to measure almost any conceivable psychological characteristic on which people may vary. Moreover, many procedures are available in a computer-administered and computer-interpreted format (see Developments in Practice 4.2, p. 118).

Although psychological tests are more precise and often more reliable than interviews or some observational techniques, they are far from perfect tools. Their value often depends on the competence of the clinician who interprets them. In general, they are useful diagnostic tools for psychologists in much the same way that blood tests, X-ray films, and MRI scans are useful to physicians. In all these cases, pathology may be revealed in people who appear to be normal, or a general impression of "something wrong" can be checked against more precise information.

Two general categories of psychological tests for use in clinical practice are intelligence tests and personality tests (projective and objective).

INTELLIGENCE TESTS A clinician can choose from a wide range of intelligence tests. The Wechsler Intelligence Scale for Children-Revised (WISC-III) and the current

There are a wide variety of psychological tests that measure the intellectual abilities of children. The researcher in this photo is measuring this child's cognitive development by evaluating how she classifies and sorts the candy.

4.2 Developments in Practice

The Automated Practice: Use of the Computer in Psychological Testing

Perhaps the most dramatic innovation in clinical assessment during the last 40 years has been the increasing use of computers in individual assessment. Computers are effectively used in assessment both to gather information directly from an individual and to assemble and evaluate all the information that has been gathered previously through interviews, tests, and other assessment procedures (Butcher, Perry, & Atlis, 2000). By comparing the incoming information with data previously stored in its memory banks, a computer can perform a wide range of assessment tasks (Garb, 1995). It can supply a probable diagnosis, indicate the likelihood of certain kinds of behavior, suggest the most appropriate form of treatment, predict the outcome, and print out a summary report concerning the subject. In many of these functions, a computer is actually superior to a clinician because it is more efficient and accurate in recalling stored material (Epstein & Klinkenberg, 2001; Olson, 2001).

With the increased efficiency and reliability of the use of computers in clinical practice, one might expect a nearly unanimous welcoming of computers into the clinic. This is not always the case, however, and some practitioners we know even resist using such "modern" techniques as e-mail, fax machines, and computerized billing in their practices (McMinn, Buchanan, et al., 1999). Some clinicians are reluctant to use computer-based test interpretations in spite of their demonstrated utility and low cost. Even though many clinics and independent practitioners use microcomputers for record keeping and billing purposes, a smaller number incorporate computer-based clinical assessment procedures into their practice. Possible reasons for the underutilization of computer-based assessment procedures include the following:

- Practitioners trained before the computer age may feel uncomfortable with computers or may not have time to get acquainted with them.
- Many practitioners limit their practice to psychological treatment and do not do extensive pretreatment assessments of their cases. Many also have little interest in, or time for, the systematic evaluation of treatment efficacy that periodic formal assessments facilitate.
- To some clinicians, the impersonal and mechanized look of the booklets and answer sheets common to much computerized assessment is inconsistent with the image and style of warm and personal engagement they hope to convey to clients.
- Some clinicians view computer-based assessment as a threat to their own functioning and fear that computer-assessment specialists seek to replace human diagnostic functioning with automated reports (Matarazzo, 1986). Some of these concerns are not unlike those expressed by many people in industry when computers and robots come to the workplace. Are human mental health practitioners in danger of being replaced by computers? Not at all. Computers have intrinsic limitations that will always relegate them to an accessory role in psychological assessment. It is the clinician who must play the major organizing role and accept the responsibility for an assessment. An ill-qualified clinician wholly dependent on computerized reports would quickly be identified as incompetent by discerning referral sources and probably by most self-referred clients; a thriving practice would not be a likely outcome. On the other hand, judicious use of computerized assessment can free up much time for doing those things that can be accomplished only by the personal application of high levels of clinical skill and wisdom.

edition of the Stanford-Binet Intelligence Scale (Kamphaus & Kroncke, 2004) are widely used in clinical settings for measuring the intellectual abilities of children (Wasserman, 2003). Probably the most commonly used test for measuring adult intelligence is the Wechsler Adult Intelligence Scale-Revised (WAIS-III) (Zhu, Weiss, Prifitera, & Coalson, 2004). It includes both verbal and performance material and consists of 11 subtests. A brief description of two of the subtests will serve to illustrate the types of functions the WAIS-III measures.

- **Vocabulary (verbal):** This subtest consists of a list of words to define that are presented orally to the individual. This task is designed to evaluate knowledge of vocabulary, which has been shown to be highly related to general intelligence.
- **Digit Span (performance):** In this test of short-term memory, a sequence of numbers is administered orally. The individual is asked to repeat the digits in the order administered. Another task in this

David Wechsler (1896–1981) served in the military testing army recruits during World War I. He came to believe that the ways in which psychologists viewed and measured "intelligence" was inadequate. In 1934 he began construction of the most widely used adult intelligence test battery, the Wechsler Adult Intelligence Scale (WAIS) that has set the standard for practical measurement of intelligence.

subtest involves the individual's remembering the numbers, holding them in memory, and reversing the order sequence—that is, the individual is instructed to say them backward (Psychological Corporation, 1997, WAIS-III).

Individually administered intelligence tests—such as the WISC-III, the WAIS-III, and the Stanford-Binet—typically require 2 to 3 hours to administer, score, and interpret. In many clinical situations, there is not enough time or funding to use these tests. In cases where intellectual impairment or organic brain damage is thought to be central to a patient's problem, intelligence testing may be the most crucial diagnostic procedure in the test battery. Moreover, information about cognitive functioning can provide valuable clues to a person's intellectual resources in dealing with problems (Kihlstrom, 2002). Yet in many clinical settings and for many clinical cases, gaining a thorough understanding of a client's problems and initiating a treatment program do not require knowing the kind of detailed information about intellectual functioning that these instruments provide. In these cases, intelligence testing is not recommended.

PROJECTIVE PERSONALITY TESTS There are a great many tests designed to measure personal characteristics other than intellectual facility. It is customary to group these personality tests into projective and objective measures. **Projective tests** are unstructured in that they rely on various ambiguous stimuli such as inkblots or vague pictures, rather than on explicit verbal questions, and in that the person's responses are not limited to the "true," "false," or "cannot say" variety. Through their interpretations of these ambiguous materials, people reveal a good deal about their personal preoccupations, conflicts, motives, coping techniques, and other personality characteristics. An assumption underlying the use of projective techniques is that in trying to make sense out of vague, unstructured stimuli, individuals "project" their own problems, motives, and wishes into the situation. Such responses are akin to the childhood pastime of seeing objects or scenes in cloud formations, with the important exception that the stimuli are in this case fixed and largely the same for all subjects. It is the latter circumstance that permits determination of the normative range of responses to the test materials, which in turn can be used to identify objectively deviant responding. Thus projective tests are aimed at discovering the ways in which an individual's past learning and personality structure may lead him or her to organize and perceive ambiguous information from the environment. Prominent among the several projective tests in common use are the Rorschach Inkblot Test, the Thematic Apperception Test, and sentence completion tests.

The Rorschach The **Rorschach Test** is named after the Swiss psychiatrist Hermann Rorschach, who initiated the experimental use of inkblots in personality assessment in 1911. The test uses ten inkblot pictures to which a subject responds in succession after being instructed as follows (Exner, 1993):

> People may see many different things in these inkblot pictures; now tell me what you see, what it makes you think of, what it means to you.

The following excerpts are taken from a subject's responses to one of the actual blots:

> This looks like two men with genital organs exposed. They have had a terrible fight and blood has splashed up against the wall. They have knives or sharp instruments in their hands and have just cut up a body. They have already taken out the lungs and other organs. The body is dismembered . . . nothing remains but a shell . . . the pelvic region. They were fighting as to who will complete the final dismemberment. . . like two vultures swooping down. . . .

The extremely violent content of this response was not common for this particular blot or for any other blot in the series. Although no responsible examiner would base conclusions on a single instance, such content was consistent with other data from this subject, who was diagnosed as an antisocial personality with strong hostility.

Use of the Rorschach in clinical assessment is complicated and requires considerable training (Exner & Erdberg, 2002; Weiner, 1998). Methods of administering the test vary; some approaches can take several hours and hence must compete for time with other essential clinical services. Furthermore, the results of the Rorschach can be unreliable because of the subjective nature of test interpretations. For example, interpreters might disagree on the symbolic significance of the response "a house in flames." One person might interpret this particular response as suggesting great feelings of anxiety, whereas another interpreter might see it as suggesting a desire on the part of the patient to set fires. One reason for the diminished use of the Rorschach in projective testing today comes from the fact that many clinical treatments used in today's mental health facilities generally require specific behavioral descriptions rather than descriptions of deep-seated personality dynamics, such as those that typically result from interpretation of the Rorschach Test.

In the hands of a skilled interpreter, however, the Rorschach can be useful in uncovering certain psychodynamic issues, such as the impact of unconscious motivations on current perceptions of others. Furthermore, there have been attempts to objectify Rorschach interpretations by clearly specifying test variables and empirically exploring their relationship to external criteria such as clinical diagnoses (Exner, 1995). The Rorschach, although generally considered an open-ended, subjective instrument, has been adapted for computer interpretation. Exner (1987) has developed a computer-based interpretation system that, after scored Rorschach responses are input, provides scoring summaries and a list of likely personality descriptions and references about a person's adjustment. The Exner Comprehensive Rorschach System may, to some extent, answer the criticism that Rorschach interpretation is unreliable, because the use of standard norms (that is, an established distribution of scores based on a sample of normal individuals) can result in more reliable and invariant scoring of descriptors for any given set of Rorschach responses. In a recent study to assess the reliability of conclusions drawn from the Rorschach using the Exner Sys-

The Rorschach Test, which uses inkblots similar to those illustrated here, is a well-known projective test. What do you see in these inkblots?

Hermann Rorschach (1884–1922), a Swiss psychiatrist, received his M.D. in 1912. He worked in Russia before returning to Zurich to work in mental hospitals. His interest in inkblots developed when he was a young child and enjoyed an activity called "Klecksography," the making of pictures by using inkblots. In his work with psychiatric patients he began to use their responses to inkblots as a way of understanding their personality and motivation. In 1921 he published his major work, "Psychodiagnostics," which described his experience with using inkblots to understand personality.

tem, Meyer, Mihura, and Smith (2005) found that clinicians tended to draw the same conclusions from Rorschach responses.

Some researchers, however, have raised questions about the norms on which the Comprehensive System is based (Shaffer, Erdberg, & Haroian, 1999; Wood, Nezworski, Garb, & Lilienfeld, 2001). The Rorschach was shown to "overpathologize" persons taking the test—that is, the test appears to show psychopathology even when the person is a "normal" person randomly drawn from the community. The extent to which the Rorschach provides valid information beyond what is available from other, more economical instruments has not been demonstrated. Although some researchers have rallied support for the Comprehensive System (Hibbard, 2003), the Rorschach test has also been widely criticized as an instrument with low or negligible validity (Garb, Florio, & Grove, 1998; Hunsley & Bailey, 1999). The use of the test in clinical assessment has diminished (Piotrowski, Belter, & Keller, 1998), in part because insurance companies do not pay for the considerable amount of time needed to administer, score, and interpret the test.

The Thematic Apperception Test The **Thematic Apperception Test (TAT)** was introduced in 1935 by its authors, C. D. Morgan and Henry Murray of the Harvard Psychological Clinic. It still is widely used in clinical practice (Rossini & Moretti, 1997) and personality research (Cramer, 2003; Paul, Schieffer, & Brown, 2004). The TAT uses a series of simple pictures, some highly representational and others quite abstract, about which a subject is instructed to make up stories. The content of the pictures, much of it depicting people in various contexts, is highly ambiguous as to actions and motives, so subjects tend to project their own conflicts and worries onto it (see Morgan, 2002, for a historical description of the test stimuli).

Several scoring and interpretation systems have been developed to focus on different aspects of a subject's stories such as expressions of needs (Atkinson, 1992), the person's perception of reality (Arnold, 1962), and the person's fantasies (Klinger, 1979). It is time-consuming to apply these systems, and there is little evidence that they make a clinically significant contribution. Hence, most often a clinician simply makes a qualitative and subjective determination of how the story content reflects the person's underlying traits, motives, and preoccupations. Such interpretations often depend as much on "art" as on "science," and there is much room for error in such an informal procedure.

An example of the way a subject's problems may be reflected in TAT stories is shown in the following case, which is based on Card 1 (a picture of a boy staring at a violin on a table in front of him). The client, David, was a 15-year-old boy who had been referred to the clinic by his parents because of their concern about his withdrawal and poor work at school.

case STUDY David's TAT Response

David was generally cooperative during the testing, although he remained rather unemotional and unenthusiastic throughout. When he was given Card 1 of the TAT, he paused for over a minute, carefully scrutinizing the card.

"I think this is a . . . uh . . . machine gun . . . yeah, it's a machine gun. The guy is staring at it. Maybe he got it for his birthday or stole it or something." [Pause. The examiner reminded him that he was to make up a story about the picture.]

"OK. This boy, I'll call him Karl, found this machine gun . . . a Browning automatic rifle . . . in his garage. He kept it in his room for protection. One day he decided to take it to school to quiet down the jocks that lord it over everyone. When he walked into the locker hall, he cut loose on the top jock, Amos, and wasted him. Nobody bothered him after that because they knew he kept the BAR in his locker."

It was inferred from this story that David was experiencing a high level of frustration and anger in his life. The extent of this anger was reflected in his perception of the violin in the picture as a machine gun—an instrument of violence. The clinician concluded that David was feeling threatened not only by people at school but even in his own home, where he needed "protection."

This example shows how stories based on TAT cards may provide a clinician with information about a person's conflicts and worries as well as clues as to how the person is handling these problems.

The TAT has been criticized on several grounds in recent years. There is a "dated" quality to the test stimuli: The pictures, developed in the 1930s, appear quaint to many contemporary subjects, who have difficulty identifying with the characters in the pictures. Subjects often preface their stories with, "This is something from a movie I saw on the Late Show." Additionally, the TAT can require a great deal of time to administer and interpret. Interpretation of responses to the TAT is generally subjective, which limits the reliability and validity of the test.

A recent review (Rossini & Moretti, 1997) pointed out an interesting paradox: Even though the TAT remains popular among practicing clinicians, clinical training programs have reduced the amount of time devoted to teaching graduate students about the TAT, and relatively few contemporary training resources (such as books and manuals) exist. Again, we must note that some examiners, notably those who have long experience in the instrument's use, are capable of making astonishingly accurate interpretations with TAT stories. Typically, however, they have difficulty teaching these skills to others. On reflection, such an observation should not be unduly surprising, but it does point to the essentially "artistic" element involved at this skill level.

Sentence Completion Test Another projective procedure that has proved useful in personality assessment is the **sentence completion test.** A number of such tests have been designed for children, adolescents, and adults (for example, see Novy, Blumentritt, et al., 1997). Such tests consist of the beginnings of sentences that a person is asked to complete, as in these examples:

1. I wish ____________________
2. My mother ____________________
3. Sex ____________________
4. I hate ____________________
5. People ____________________

Sentence completion tests, which are related to the free-association method, are somewhat more structured than the Rorschach and most other projective tests. They help examiners pinpoint important clues to an individual's problems, attitudes, and symptoms through the content of his or her responses. Interpretation of the item responses, however, is generally subjective and unreliable. Despite the fact that the test stimuli (the sentence stems) are standard, interpretation is usually done in an ad hoc manner and without benefit of normative comparisons.

In sum, projective tests have an important place in many clinical settings, particularly those that attempt to obtain a comprehensive picture of a person's psychodynamic functioning and those that have the necessary trained staff to conduct extensive individual psychological evaluations. The great strengths of projective techniques—their unstructured nature and their focus on the unique aspects of personality—are at the same time their weaknesses because they make interpretation subjective, unreliable, and difficult to validate. Moreover, projective tests typically require a great deal of time to administer and advanced skill to interpret—both scarce quantities in many clinical settings.

OBJECTIVE PERSONALITY TESTS **Objective tests** are structured—that is, they typically use questionnaires, self-report inventories, or rating scales in which questions or items are carefully phrased and alternative responses are specified as choices. They therefore involve a far more controlled format than projective devices and thus are more amenable to objectively based quantification. One virtue of such quantification is its precision, which in turn enhances the reliability of test outcomes.

The MMPI One of the major structured inventories for personality assessment is the **Minnesota Multiphasic Personality Inventory (MMPI),** now called the "MMPI-2" after a revision in 1989. We focus on it here because in many ways it is the prototype and the standard of this class of instruments.

Several years in development, the MMPI was introduced for general use in 1943 by Starke Hathaway and J. C. McKinley; it is today the most widely used personality test for both clinical assessment and psychopathology research in the United States (Lally, 2003; Piotrowski & Keller, 1992). It is also the assessment instrument most frequently taught in graduate clinical psychology programs (Piotrowski & Zalewski, 1993). Over 14,000 books and articles on the MMPI instruments have been published since the test was introduced (Butcher, Atlis, & Hahn, 2003). Moreover, translated versions of the inventory are widely used internationally (the original MMPI was translated over 150 times and used in over 46 countries; Butcher, 2004). International use of the revised inventory is increasing rapidly; over 32 translations have been made since it was published in 1989 (Arbisi & Butcher, 2004). The original MMPI, a self-report questionnaire, consisted

Starke R. Hathaway (1903–1984), clinical psychologist, was a pioneer in physiological psychology and personality assessment. In 1940, he and J. C. McKinley published the Minnesota Multiphasic Personality Inventory (MMPI) for evaluating symptoms and behavior of psychiatric and medical patients. The MMPI became the most widely used personality assessment instrument in use and its revised version (MMPI-2) is the most frequently used personality measure today.

J. C. McKinley (1891–1950), a neuropsychiatrist at the University of Minnesota Hospital, co-authored the MMPI with Starke Hathaway and conducted research on the MMPI with both medical and psychiatric populations.

of 550 items covering topics ranging from physical condition and psychological states to moral and social attitudes. Normally, subjects are encouraged to answer all of the items either "true" or "false."

The Clinical Scales of the MMPI The pool of items for the MMPI was originally administered to a large group of normal individuals (affectionately called the "Minnesota normals") and several quite homogeneous groups of patients with particular psychiatric diagnoses. Answers to all the items were then item-analyzed to see which ones differentiated the various groups. On the basis of the findings, ten clinical scales were constructed, each consisting of the items that were answered by one of the patient groups in the direction opposite to the predominant response of the normal group. This rather ingenious method of selecting scorable items, known as "empirical keying," originated with the MMPI and doubtless accounts for much of the instrument's power. Note that it involves no subjective prejudgment about the "meaning" of a true or false answer to any item; that meaning resides entirely in whether the answer is the same as the answer deviantly given by patients of varying diagnoses. Should an examinee's pattern of true and false responses closely approximate that of a particular pathological group, it is a reasonable inference that he or she shares other psychiatrically significant characteristics with that group—and may in fact "psychologically" be a member of that group. (See the MMPI-2 profile of Esteban in Developments in Practice 4.3 on p. 124.)

Each of these ten "clinical" scales thus measures tendencies to respond in psychologically deviant ways. Raw scores on these scales are compared with the corresponding scores of the normal population, many of whom did (and do) answer a few items in the critical direction, and the results are plotted on the standard MMPI profile form. By drawing a line connecting the scores for the different scales, a clinician can construct a profile that shows how far from normal a patient's performance is on each of the scales. The Schizophrenia scale, for example (and to reiterate the basic strategy), is made up of the items that schizophrenic patients consistently answered in a way that differentiated them from normal individuals. People who score high (relative to norms) on this scale, though not necessarily schizophrenic, often show characteristics typical of the schizophrenic population. For instance, high scorers on this scale may be socially inept, may be withdrawn, and may have peculiar thought processes; they may have diminished contact with reality and, in severe cases, may have delusions and hallucinations.

The MMPI also includes a number of validity scales to detect whether a patient has answered the questions in a straightforward, honest manner. For example, there is one scale that detects lying or claiming extreme virtue and several scales that detect faking or malingering. Extreme endorsement of the items on any of these scales may invalidate the test, whereas lesser endorsements frequently contribute important interpretive insights. In addition to the validity scales and the ten clinical scales, a number of "special problem" scales have been devised—for example, to detect substance abuse, marital distress, and post-traumatic stress disorder.

Clinically, the MMPI is used in several ways to evaluate a patient's personality characteristics and clinical problems. Perhaps the most typical use of the MMPI is as a diagnostic standard. As we have seen, the individual's profile pattern is compared with profiles of known patient groups. If the profile matches a group, information about patients in this group can suggest a broad descriptive diagnosis for the patient under study.

Criticisms of the MMPI The original MMPI, in spite of being the most widely used personality measure, has not been without its critics. Some psychodynamically oriented clinicians felt that the MMPI (like other structured, objective tests) was superficial and did not adequately reflect the complexities of an individual taking the test. Some behaviorally oriented critics, on the other hand, criticized the

4.3 Developments in Practice

Esteban's MMPI-2 Profile and Computer-Based Report

Esteban was first tested with the original MMPI. His responses from that testing were converted to the MMPI-2 format by J. N. Butcher (1993). The computer-based report for the MMPI-2 norms is provided. The validity scales are shown in the figure in the left column in which MALE appears. The clinical scales are to the right. The special scales are not included in this version of the profile. (Table 4.1 on p. 126 describes each of these scales.) On the basis of the scores originally obtained and those you see displayed in the chart, a computer produced the narrative descriptions given here.

Computer-Based Report: The MMPI-2 Profile Validity

This MMPI-2 profile should be interpreted with caution. There is some possibility that the clinical report is an exaggerated picture of Esteban's present situation. He presented an unusual number of psychological problems and symptoms. His test-taking attitudes should be evaluated to determine whether his response pattern is a valid approach to the testing. This extreme response set could result from poor reading ability, confusion, disorientation, stress, or a need to seek attention for his problems. Clinical patients with this profile are often confused and distractible, and they show memory problems. Evidence of delusions and thought disorder may be present.

Symptomatic Pattern

Esteban's MMPI-2 profile reflects a high degree of psychological distress at this time. The client exhibits a mixed pattern of psychological symptoms. He appears to be tense, apathetic, and withdrawn and is experiencing some personality deterioration. He seems to be quite confused and disorganized, and he probably secretly broods about unusual beliefs and suspicions. Autistic behavior and inappropriate affect are characteristic features of individuals with this profile. Some evidence of an active psychotic process exists. He may have delusions and occult preoccupations and may feel that others are against him because of his beliefs. In interviews, he is likely to be vague, circumstantial, and tangential and may be quite preoccupied with abstract ideas.

He is having problems concentrating, feels agitated, and is functioning at a very low level of psychological efficiency. He feels apathetic and indifferent and believes he is a passive participant in life. He also feels that he has little energy left over from mere survival to expend on any pleasure in life. He may be showing signs of serious psychopathology, such as delusions, problems in thinking, and inappropriate affect. His long-standing lack of achievement and his work behavior have caused him many problems.

Many individuals with this profile consider committing suicide, and Esteban may actually have serious plans for self-destruction.

He experiences some conflicts concerning his sex-role identity, appearing somewhat passive and effeminate in his orientation toward life. He may appear somewhat insecure in the masculine role and may be uncomfortable in his relationships with women.

Esteban's response content indicates that he is preoccupied with feeling guilty and unworthy and feels that he deserves to be punished for wrongs he has committed. He feels regretful and unhappy about life, complains about having no zest for life, and seems plagued by anxiety and worry about the future. According to his response content, there is a strong possibility that he has contemplated suicide. A careful evaluation of this possibility is suggested. He views his physical health as failing and reports numerous somatic complaints. He feels that life is no longer worthwhile and that he is losing control of his thought processes. He reports in his response content that he feels things more, or more intensely, than others do.

Interpersonal Relations

Disturbed interpersonal relationships are characteristic of individuals with this profile. Esteban feels vulnerable to interpersonal hurt, lacks trust, and may never form close, satisfying interpersonal ties. He feels very insecure in relationships and may be preoccupied with guilt and self-defeating behavior. Many individuals with this profile are so self-preoccupied and unskilled in sex-role behavior that they never develop rewarding heterosexual relationships. Some never marry.

MMPI (and in fact the entire genre of personality tests) as being too oriented toward measuring unobservable "mentalistic" constructs such as traits.

A more specific criticism was leveled at the datedness of the MMPI. In response to these criticisms, the publisher of the MMPI sponsored a revision of the instrument. The scales listed on the standard original MMPI-2 profile form are described in Table 4.1 on page 126. This revised MMPI, designated "MMPI-2" for adults, became available for general professional use in mid-1989 (Butcher, Graham, et al., 2001), and the MMPI-A, for adolescents (Butcher et al., 1992), was published in 1992. However, the MMPI-2 has now effectively replaced the original instrument, which is no longer available from the publisher. The revised ver-

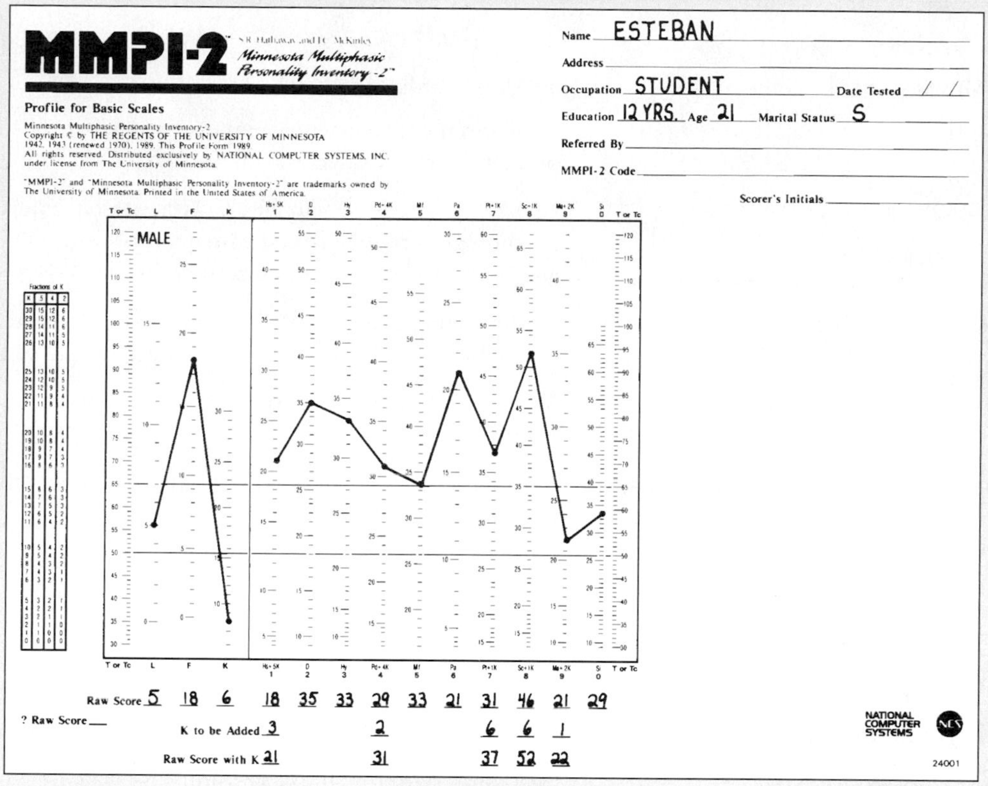

Behavioral Stability

Individuals with this profile type often lead chronically stormy, chaotic lives.

Diagnostic Considerations

The most likely diagnosis for individuals with this MMPI-2 profile type is Schizophrenia, possibly Paranoid type, or Paranoid Disorder. Similar clients tend also to have features of an affective disorder. In addition, there seems to be a long-standing pattern of maladjustment that is characteristic of people with severe personality disorders.

Because this behavioral pattern may also be associated with Organic Brain Syndrome or Substance-Induced Organic Mental Disorder, these possibilities should be evaluated.

Treatment Considerations

Individuals with this profile may be experiencing considerable personality deterioration, which may require hospitalization if they are considered dangerous to themselves or others. Psychotropic medication may reduce their thinking disturbance and mood disorder. Outpatient treatment may be complicated by their regressed or disorganized behavior. Multiple-problem life situations and difficulties forming interpersonal relationships make patients with this profile poor candidates for relationship-based psychotherapy. Day treatment programs or other such structured settings may be helpful in providing a stabilizing treatment environment. Long-term adjustment is a problem. Frequent, brief "management" therapy contacts may be helpful in structuring his activities. Insight-oriented or relationship therapies tend not to be helpful for individuals with these severe problems and may actually exacerbate the symptoms. Esteban probably would have difficulty establishing a trusting working relationship with a therapist.

sions of the MMPI have been validated in several clinical studies (Butcher, Rouse, & Perry, 2000; Graham, Ben-Porath, & McNulty, 1999).

Recent research (Arbisi, Ben-Porath, & McNulty, 2002; Greene, Robin, Albaugh, et al., 2003) has provided strong support for the revised versions of the MMPI. The clinical scales, which, apart from minimal item deletion or rewording, have been retained in their original form, seem to measure the same properties of personality organization and functioning as they always have. A comparable stability of meaning is observed for the standard validity scales (also essentially unchanged), which have been reinforced with three additional scales to detect tendencies to respond untruthfully to some items.

TABLE 4.1 The Scales of the MMPI-2

Validity Scales	
Cannot say score (?)	Measures the total number of unanswered items
Lie scale (L)	Measures the tendency to claim excessive virtue or to try to present an overall favorable image
Infrequency scale (F)	Measures the tendency to falsely claim or exaggerate psychological problems in the first part of the booklet; alternatively, detects random responding
Infrequency scale (FB)	Measures the tendency to falsely claim or exaggerate psychological problems on items toward the end of the booklet
Defensiveness scale (K)	Measures the tendency to see oneself in an unrealistically positive way
Response Inconsistency scale (VRIN)	Measures the tendency to endorse items in an inconsistent or random manner
Response Inconsistency scale (TRIN)	Measures the tendency to endorse items in an inconsistent true or false manner

Clinical Scales		
Scale 1	Hypochondriasis (Hs)	Measures excessive somatic concern and physical complaints
Scale 2	Depression (D)	Measures symptomatic depression
Scale 3	Hysteria (Hy)	Measures hysteroid personality features such as a "rose-colored glasses" view of the world and the tendency to develop physical problems under stress
Scale 4	Psychopathic deviate (Pd)	Measures antisocial tendencies
Scale 5	Masculinity–femininity (Mf)	Measures gender-role reversal
Scale 6	Paranoia (Pa)	Measures suspicious, paranoid ideation
Scale 7	Psychasthenia (Pt)	Measures anxiety and obsessive, worrying behavior
Scale 8	Schizophrenia (Sc)	Measures peculiarities in thinking, feeling, and social behavior
Scale 9	Hypomania (Ma)	Measures unrealistically elated mood state and tendencies to yield to impulses
Scale 0	Social introversion (Si)	Measures social anxiety, withdrawal, and overcontrol
Special Scales		
Scale APS	Addiction Proneness Scale	Assesses the extent to which the person matches personality features of people in substance use treatment
Scale AAS	Addiction Acknowledgment Scale	Assesses the extent to which the person has acknowledged substance abuse problems
Scale MAC-R	Mac Andrew Addiction Scale	An empirical scale measuring proneness to become addicted to various substances
MDS	Marital Distress Scale	Assesses perceived marital relationship problems

Advantages and Limitations of Objective Personality Tests

Self-report inventories, such as the MMPI, have a number of advantages over other types of personality tests. They are cost-effective, highly reliable, and objective; they also can be scored and interpreted (and, if desired, even administered) by computer. A number of general criticisms, however, have been leveled against the use of self-report inventories. As we have seen, some clinicians consider them too mechanistic to portray the complexity of human beings and their problems accurately. Also, because these tests require the subject to read, comprehend, and answer verbal material, patients who are illiterate or confused cannot take the test. Furthermore, the individual's cooperation is required in self-report inventories, and it is possible that the person might distort his or her answers to create a particular impression. The validity scales of the MMPI-2 are a direct attempt to deal with this last criticism.

Because of their scoring formats and emphasis on test validation, scientifically constructed objective personality inventories lend themselves particularly well to automated interpretation. The earliest practical applications of computer technology to test scoring and interpretation involved the MMPI. Over 40 years ago, psychologists at the Mayo Clinic programmed a computer to score and interpret clinical profiles. Computerized personality assessment has evolved substantially over the past few years and other highly sophisticated MMPI and MMPI-2 interpretation systems have been developed (Butcher, Perry, & Hahn, 2004). Computer-based MMPI interpretation systems typically employ powerful **actuarial procedures** (Grove, Zald, Lebow, et al., 2000). In such systems, descriptions of the actual behavior or other established characteristics of many subjects with particular patterns of test scores have been stored in the computer. Whenever a person turns up with one of these test score patterns, the appropriate description is printed out in the computer's evaluation. Such descriptions have been written and stored for a number of different test score patterns, most of them based on MMPI-2 scores.

The accumulation of precise actuarial data for an instrument like the MMPI-2 is difficult, time-consuming, and expensive. This is in part because of the complexity of the instrument itself; the potential number of significantly different MMPI-2 profile patterns is legion. The profiles of many subjects therefore do not "fit" the profile types for which actuarial data are available. Problems of actuarial data acquisition also arise at the other end: the behaviors or problems that are to be detected or predicted by the instrument. Many conditions that are of vital clinical importance are relatively rare (for example, suicide) or are psychologically complex (for example, possible psychogenic components in a patient's physical illness). Thus it is difficult to accumulate enough cases to serve as an adequate actuarial database. In these situations, the interpretive program writer is forced to fall back on general clinical lore and wisdom to formulate clinical descriptions appropriate to the types of profiles actually obtained.

Examples of computer-generated descriptions for the accompanying case of Esteban appear in the evaluations reprinted in Developments in Practice 4.3. Sometimes the different paragraphs generated by the computer have inconsistencies resulting from the fact that different parts of a subject's test pattern call up different paragraphs from the computer. The computer simply prints out blindly what has been found to be typical for people making similar scores on the various clinical scales and cannot integrate the descriptions it picks up. At this point the human element comes in: In the clinical use of computers, it is always essential that a trained professional further interpret and monitor the assessment data (Atlis, Hahn, & Butcher, 2006).

Computerized personality assessment is no longer a novelty but an important, dependable adjunct to clinical assessment. Computerized psychological evaluations are a quick and efficient means of providing a clinician with needed information early in the decision-making process.

A Psychological Case Study: Esteban

In this section, we will illustrate psychological assessment through a diagnostic case study of a young man who presented a complicated clinical picture that was substantially clarified through psychological and neuropsychological assessment. This is an unusual case in several respects: The young man's problems were quite severe and involved both psychological and organic elements; the case involved cross-cultural considerations—the young man was from South America and assessment was done in both English and Spanish (the latter only as necessary); and a number of psychological specialists participated in the assessment study, including a neuropsychologist, a behaviorally oriented clinical psychologist, a Hispanic clinical psychologist, and a psychiatrist.

SOCIAL HISTORY Esteban, a 21-year-old student from Colombia, had been enrolled in an English-language program at a small college in the United States. He had become disruptive in school, evidencing loud, obnoxious behavior in class and quarreling with his roommates (whom he accused of stealing his wallet). After a period of time during which his behavior did not improve, he was expelled from the program. The director of the program indicated that he felt Esteban needed psychological help for his problems, which included not only the behavioral problems but also, reportedly, severe headaches and confused thinking. The director added that Esteban would be considered for readmission only if he showed significant improvement in therapy.

On hearing of his expulsion, Esteban's parents, who were wealthy international banking entrepreneurs, flew in from Colombia and arranged for a complete physical examination for him at a well-known medical center in New York. After an extensive medical and neurological examination to determine the source of his headaches and confusion, Esteban was diagnosed as having some "diffuse" brain impairment, but he was found to be otherwise in good health. His parents then sought a further, more definitive neurological examination. The neurologist at the second hospital recommended a psychological and neuropsychological examination because he suspected that Esteban's mild neurological condition would not account for his extreme psychological and behavioral symptoms. He referred the family to a psychologist for assessment and treatment. Esteban was experiencing a number of pressing situational problems—for example, his behavior problems continued, he appeared eager to find a new English program, and, as we will see, he had some hard issues to face about his career aspirations to become a physician. Therefore, the psychologist decided to begin with therapy immediately, concurrent with the additional assessment evaluation.

INTERVIEWS AND BEHAVIOR OBSERVATIONS Esteban was seen in the initial session with his parents. The interview was conducted in English with some translation into Spanish (mostly by Esteban) because the parents knew little English. Throughout the session, Esteban was disorganized and distractible. He had difficulty staying on the topic being discussed and periodically interrupted his own conversation with seemingly random impulses to show the interviewer papers, books, pamphlets, and the like from his knapsack. He talked incessantly, often loudly. He was not at all defensive about his problems and talked freely about his symptoms and attitudes. His behavior resembled that of a hyperactive child—he was excitable, impulsive, and immature. He did not appear to be psychotic; he reported no hallucinations or delusions and was in touch with reality. He related well with the interviewer, seemed to enjoy the session, and expressed an interest in having additional sessions.

During subsequent interviews, Esteban expressed frequent physical complaints such as headaches, tension, and sleeping problems. He reported that he had a great deal of difficulty concentrating on his studies. He could not study because he always found other things to do—particularly talking about religion. He was seemingly outgoing and sociable and had no difficulty initiating conversations with other people. He tended, however, to say socially inappropriate things and to become frustrated and lose his temper easily. For example, during one family interview, he became enraged and kicked his mother.

FAMILY HISTORY Esteban's father was a Spanish-Colombian banker in his mid-sixties. He was well dressed and somewhat passive, though visibly quite warm toward his son. He had had his share of difficulties in recent years; severe business problems, coupled with two heart attacks, had brought on a depressive episode that had left him ineffective in dealing with his business. His wife and her brother, an attorney from Madrid, had had to straighten out the business problems. She reported that her husband had had several depressive episodes in the past and that Esteban's moods resembled her husband's in his earlier years.

Esteban's mother was a tense, worried, and somewhat hypochondriacal woman who appeared to be rather domineering. Before the first and second interviews, she handed the therapist, in secret, written "explanations" of her son's problems. Her own history revealed that she was unhappy in her marriage and that she lived only for her children, on whom she doted.

Esteban's brother, Juan, was an engineering student at an American university and apparently was doing well academically and socially. He was a year older than Esteban.

Esteban's childhood had been marked with problems. His mother reported that although he had been a good baby and had been pretty happy as a small child, he had changed after age 2½. At about that time, he had fallen on his head and was unconscious for a while; he was not hospitalized. Beginning in the preschool years, he exhibited behavioral problems including temper tantrums, negativism, and an inability to get along with peers. These problems continued when he began school. He frequently refused to go to school, had periods of aggressive behavior, and appeared in general to be "hyperactive." It seemed that he was probably overprotected and "infantilized" by his mother.

Esteban was quite close to his brother, Juan, with whom he reported having had extensive homosexual relations when they were growing up. The "darkest day" in Esteban's life was reportedly when Juan broke off the homosexual relationship with him at age 16 and told him to "go and find men." Although he later carried on a platonic relationship with a woman in Colombia, it was never a serious one. Esteban had strong homosexual urges of which he was consciously aware and which he attempted to control through a growing preoccupation with religion.

Esteban had been in psychotherapy on several occasions since he was 11 years old. After he graduated from high school, he attended law school in Colombia for a quarter but dropped out because he "wanted to become a doctor instead." (In Colombia, professional schools are combined with college.) He left school, according to his parents' report, because he could not adapt. He worked for a time in the family business but had difficulty getting along with other employees and was encouraged to try other work. When that failed, his parents sent him to the United States to study English, rationalizing that Colombia was not as good an environment for him as the United States.

INTELLIGENCE TESTING Esteban underwent psychological testing to evaluate further the possibility of neurological deficits and to determine whether he had the intellectual capabilities to proceed with a demanding academic career. He scored in the "borderline to average" range of intelligence on the WAIS-R (English version) and on the WAIS (Spanish version). He was particularly deficient in tasks involving practical judgment, common sense, concentration, visual-motor coordination, and concept formation. In addition, on memory tests he showed a below-average memory ability, such as a poor immediate recall of ideas from paragraphs read aloud (in both English and Spanish). Under most circumstances, people with similar deficits are able to live comfortable, fulfilling lives in careers whose formal intellectual demands are relatively modest. It was clear from the test data and Esteban's behavior during testing that his stated career aspirations—seemingly nurtured by his parents—exceeded his abilities and might well be a factor in much of his frustration.

PERSONALITY TESTING Esteban was given both the Rorschach Test and the MMPI. Both tests have been used extensively with Hispanic subjects. The Rorschach is believed by some to be particularly well suited for cases like Esteban's, because the test stimuli are relatively unstructured and not culture-bound. Esteban's Rorschach protocol was computer-analyzed using the Exner Comprehensive Rorschach System.

The computer-based interpretation of Esteban's Rorschach protocol provided the following hypotheses about his psychological adjustment: The Rorschach record appears to be valid and interpretively useful. The interpretation focused more on personality factors and interpersonal behavior than on severe psychopathology. For example, the report noted that the patient tends to internalize feelings and this often results in substantial tension and anxiety. There is a strong possibility that the patient avoids initiating behaviors and, instead, tends toward a more passive role in problem solving and interpersonal relationships. This patient's basic coping style tends to be maladaptive when new situations and/or stresses occur. He is likely to experience frequent social difficulties. There is evidence indicating the presence of considerable subjectively felt distress.

Serious personality problems were noted. For example, Esteban tends to use fantasy to cope rather than confront problems directly. This is a serious problem because his basic coping style is being used more to flee than to adapt to the external world. Emotional control problems were noted in the interpretation. The client does not modulate emotional displays as much as most adults. He is a person who is very emotional. This may pose a significant problem in adaptation because of problems in control.

Esteban's interpersonal distance was cited in the report. For example, the interpretation noted that he is an individual who does not experience a need for closeness in ways most people do. As a result, he is typically less comfortable in interpersonal situations, has difficulties in creating and sustaining deep relationships, is more concerned with issues of personal space, and may appear much more guarded and/or distant to others. He is prone to interpret new situations in a unique and overpersonalized manner. People such as this often view their world with their own special set of biases and are less concerned with being conventional and/or acceptable to others. The computerized interpretation also noted that Esteban appears to have an unusual body preoccupation and a marked sexual preoccupation.

His Rorschach responses were considered to be less sophisticated or less mature than expected. This may be a function of a developmental lag, disorganization, or simply a reluctance to commit resources to a task. These individuals often come to decisions prematurely and erroneously simply because they have not processed all available information adequately. This should not be confused with impulsiveness although some decisions and behaviors that result may have that feature. It should also be noted for this subject that the composite emotional controls is one important factor that leads to impulsive-like behaviors.

People with his approach to the test are often very resistive during early phases of intervention as this tendency toward denial causes them to avoid any affective confronting. The computer-based Rorschach interpretation did not address Esteban's severe emotional problems and lack of contact with reality that intrudes into his adjustment.

In summary, Esteban's performance on the Rorschach revealed tension, anxiety, and a preoccupation with morbid topics. He appeared to be overly concerned about his health, prone to depression, indecisive, and yet at other times impulsive and careless. His responses were often immature, and he showed a strong and persistent ambivalence toward females. In some responses, he viewed females in highly aggressive ways; often a fusion of sexual and aggressive images was evident. In general, he demonstrated aloofness and an inability to relate well to other people. Although his Rorschach responses suggested that he could view the world in conventional ways and was probably not psychotic, at times he had difficulty controlling his impulses.

Esteban took the original version of the MMPI in both English and Spanish. His MMPI profile was virtually identical in both languages. It has been converted to MMPI-2 format and is reproduced in Developments in Practice 4.3, along with the MMPI-2-based computer interpretation of his test scores.

SUMMARY OF THE PSYCHOLOGICAL ASSESSMENT OF ESTEBAN Esteban showed mild neurological deficits on neuropsychological testing and borderline intellectual ability. He clearly did not have the academic ability to pursue a medical career. Demanding intellectual tasks placed a great deal of stress on him and resulted in frustration. Furthermore, his poor memory made learning complex material very difficult.

The MMPI-2 interpretation indicated that Esteban's disorganized behavior and symptomatic patterns reflected a serious psychological disorder. Although he was not currently psychotic, both his past behavior and his test performance suggested that he was functioning marginally and that he showed the potential for personality deterioration in some situations.

Esteban's most salient psychological problems concerned his tendency to become frustrated and his ready loss of impulse control. He was volatile and became upset easily. It also appeared that Esteban's relative isolation during his early years (due in part to his overprotective mother) did not prepare him to function adequately in many social situations. Another important problem area for Esteban was in psychosexual adjustment. The psychological test results and his personal history clearly indicated gender-identity confusion.

Within the parameters of DSM-IV-TR, Esteban would receive an Axis I diagnosis of organic personality syndrome and an Axis II diagnosis of borderline personality disorder. Furthermore, it was recommended that he undertake social-skills training and that—rather than a career in medicine—he be encouraged to pursue occupational goals more in keeping with his abilities. Psychotropic medication (lithium and Mellaril) were prescribed for his problems with emotional control.

A FOLLOW-UP NOTE Esteban was seen in psychological therapy twice a week and remained on medication. He was also seen in a social-skills training program for ten sessions. Through the help of his therapist, he was admitted to a less demanding English program, which seemed more in keeping with his abilities.

For the first 6 months, Esteban made considerable progress, especially after his behavior became somewhat stabilized, largely, it appeared, as a result of the medications. He became less impulsive and more in control of his anger. He successfully completed the English classes in which he was enrolled. During this period, he lived with his mother, who had taken up a temporary residence near the college. She then returned to Colombia, and Esteban moved into an apartment with a roommate, with whom, however, he had increasing difficulty.

Several weeks after his mother had left, Esteban stopped going to therapy and stopped taking his medication. He began to frequent local gay bars, at first out of curiosity but later to seek male lovers. At the same time, his preoccupation with religion increased, and he moved into a house near campus that was operated by a fundamentalist religious cult. His parents, quite concerned by his openly homosexual behavior (which he described in detail over the phone, adding the suggestion that they visit the gay bar with him), returned to the United States. Realizing that they could not stay permanently to supervise Esteban, they then sought a residential treatment program that would provide him with a more structured living arrangement. All assessment and therapy records were forwarded to those in charge of the residential program.

In Review

- What are the assumptions behind the use of projective tests? How do they differ from objective tests?
- What advantages do objective personality tests offer over less structured tests?
- What is the Minnesota Multiphasic Personality Inventory (MMPI-2)? Describe how the scales work.

The Integration of Assessment Data

As assessment data are collected, their significance must be interpreted so that they can be integrated into a coherent working model for use in planning or changing treatment. Clinicians in individual private practice normally assume this often arduous task on their own. In a clinic or hospital setting, assessment data are often evaluated in a staff conference attended by members of an interdisciplinary team (perhaps a clinical psychologist, a psychiatrist, a social worker, and other mental health personnel) who are concerned with the decisions to be made regarding treatment. By putting together all the information they have gathered, they can see whether the findings complement each other and form a definitive clinical picture or whether gaps or discrepancies exist that necessitate further investigation.

This integration of all the data gathered at the time of an original assessment may lead to agreement on a tentative diagnostic classification for a patient. In any case, the findings of each member of the team, as well as the recommendations for treatment, are entered into the case record so that it will always be possible to check back and see why a certain course of therapy was undertaken, how accurate the clinical assessment was, and how valid the treatment decision turned out to be.

New assessment data collected during the course of therapy provide feedback on its effectiveness and serve as a basis for making needed modifications in an ongoing treatment program. As we have noted, clinical assessment data are also commonly used in evaluating the final outcome of therapy and in comparing the effectiveness of different therapeutic and preventive approaches.

Ethical Issues in Assessment

The decisions made on the basis of assessment data may have far-reaching implications for the people involved. A staff decision may determine whether a severely depressed person will be hospitalized or remain with her or his family or whether an accused person will be declared competent to stand trial. Thus a valid decision, based on accurate assessment data, is of far more than theoretical importance. Because of the impact that assessment can have on the lives of others, it is important that those involved keep several factors in mind in evaluating test results:

In a clinic or hospital setting, assessment data are usually evaluated in a staff conference attended by members of an interdisciplinary team—including, for example, a clinical psychologist, a psychiatrist, a social worker, and a psychiatric nurse. A staff decision may determine whether a severely depressed person will be hospitalized or remain with his or her family, or whether an accused person will be declared competent to stand trial. Because these decisions can have such great impact on the lives of the clients/patients, it is critical that clinicians be well aware of the limitations of assessment.

1. POTENTIAL CULTURAL BIAS OF THE INSTRUMENT OR THE CLINICIAN: There is the possibility that some psychological tests may not elicit valid information for a patient from a minority group (Gray-Little, 2002). A clinician from one sociocultural background may have trouble assessing objectively the behavior of someone from another background, such as a Southeast Asian refugee. It is important to ensure—as Greene, Robin, Albaugh, Caldwell, and Goldman (2003) and Hall, Bansal, and Lopez (1999) have shown with the MMPI-2—that the instrument can be confidently used with persons from minority groups.

2. THEORETICAL ORIENTATION OF THE CLINICIAN: Assessment is inevitably influenced by a clinician's assumptions, perceptions, and theoretical orientation. For example, a psychoanalyst and a behaviorist might assess the same behaviors quite differently. The psychoanalytically oriented professional is likely to view behaviors as reflecting underlying motives, whereas the behavioral clinician is likely to view the behaviors in the context of the immediate or preceding stimulus situations. Different treatment recommendations are likely to result.

3. UNDEREMPHASIS ON THE EXTERNAL SITUATION: Many clinicians overemphasize personality traits as the cause of patients' problems without paying enough attention to the possible role of stressors and other circumstances in the patients' life situations. An undue focus on a patient's personality, which some assessment techniques encourage, can divert attention from potentially critical environmental factors.

4. INSUFFICIENT VALIDATION: Some psychological assessment procedures in use today have not been sufficiently validated. For example, unlike many of the personality scales, widely used procedures for behavioral observation and behavioral self-report and the projective techniques have not been subjected to strict psychometric validation.

5. INACCURATE DATA OR PREMATURE EVALUATION: There is always the possibility that some assessment data—and any diagnostic label or treatment based on them—may be inaccurate or that the team leader (usually a psychiatrist) might choose to ignore test data in favor of other information. Some risk is always involved in making predictions for an individual on the basis of group data or averages. Inaccurate data or premature conclusions not only may lead to a misunderstanding of a patient's problem but also may close off attempts to get further information, with possibly grave consequences for the patient.

In Review

- What are some ethical issues that clinicians should be aware of when evaluating a patient's test results?
- How are computer-based psychological test interpretations incorporated into a test interpretation?
- What is test validity?

Classifying Abnormal Behavior

Classification is important in any science, whether we are studying chemical elements, plants, planets, or people. With an agreed-upon classification system, we can be confident that we are communicating clearly. If someone says to you, "I saw a dog running down the street," you can probably produce a mental image broadly approximating the appearance of that dog—not from seeing it but rather from your knowledge of animal classifications. There are of course many breeds of dogs, which vary widely in size, color, muzzle length, and so on, and yet we have little difficulty in recognizing the essential features of "dogness." "Dogness" is an example of what psychologists refer to as a "cognitive prototype" or "pattern."

In abnormal psychology, classification involves the attempt to delineate meaningful subvarieties of maladaptive behavior. Like defining abnormal behavior, classification of some kind is a necessary first step toward introducing order into our discussion of the nature, causes, and treatment of such behavior. Classification makes it possible to communicate about particular clusters of abnormal behavior in agreed-upon and relatively precise ways. For example, we cannot conduct research on what might cause eating disorders unless we begin with a more or less clear definition of the behavior under examination; otherwise, we would be unable to select, for intensive study, persons whose behavior displays the aberrant eating patterns we hope to understand. There are other reasons for diagnostic classifications, too, such as gathering statistics on how common the various types of disorders are and meeting the needs of medical insurance companies (which insist on having formal diagnoses before they will authorize payment of claims).

Keep in mind that, just as with the process of defining abnormality itself, all classification is the product of human invention—it is, in essence, a matter of making generalizations based on what has been observed. Even when observations are precise and carefully made, the generalizations we arrive at go beyond those observations and enable us to make inferences about underlying similarities and differences. For example, it is common for people experiencing episodes of panic to feel they are about to die. When "panic" is carefully delineated, we find that it is not in fact associated with any enhanced risk of death but, rather, that the people experiencing such episodes tend to share certain other characteristics, such as recent exposure to highly stressful events.

It is not unusual for a classification system to be an ongoing work in progress as new knowledge demonstrates an earlier generalization to be incomplete or flawed. It is important to bear in mind, too, that formal classification is successfully accomplished only through precise techniques of psychological, or clinical, assessment—techniques that have been increasingly refined over the years.

In this carnival game, the man is trying to hit the mark and ring the bell as a measure of his strength. How reliable do you think this measure is? If the man hit the mark in the same place each time and with the same amount of force but achieved different results, the measure would not be considered reliable. Is the measure valid? If the man misses the mark, and, consequently, the bell, does that mean he is not strong?

Reliability and Validity

A classification system's usefulness depends largely on its reliability and validity. Reliability is the degree to which a measuring device produces the same result each time it is used to measure the same thing. If your scale showed a significantly different weight each time you stepped on it over some brief period, you would consider it a fairly unreliable measure of your body mass. In the context of classification, **reliability** is an index of the extent to which different observers can agree that a person's behavior fits a given diagnostic class. If observers cannot agree, it may mean that the classification criteria are not precise enough to determine whether the suspected disorder is present.

The classification system must also be valid. **Validity** is the extent to which a measuring instrument actually measures what it is supposed to measure. In the context of classification, validity is the degree to which a diagnosis accurately conveys to us something clinically important about the person whose behavior fits the category, such as helping to predict the future course of the disorder. If, for example, a person is diagnosed as having schizophrenia, we should be able to infer the presence of some fairly precise characteristics that differentiate the person from individuals who are considered normal, or from those suffering from other types of mental disorder. The diagnosis of schizophrenia, for example, implies a disorder of unusually stubborn persistence, with recurrent episodes being common.

Normally, validity presupposes reliability. If clinicians can't agree on the class to which a disordered person's behavior belongs, then the question of the validity of the diagnostic classifications under consideration becomes irrelevant. To put it another way, if we can't confidently pin down what the diagnosis is, then whatever useful information a given diagnosis might convey about the person being evaluated is lost. On the other hand, good reliability does not in itself guarantee validity. For example, handedness (left, right, ambidextrous) can be assessed with a high degree of reliability, but handedness accurately predicts neither mental health status nor countless other behavioral qualities on which people vary; that is, it is not a valid index of these qualities (although it may be a valid index for success in certain situations involving the game of baseball, for example). In like manner, reliable assignment of a person's behavior to a given class of mental disorder will prove useful only to the extent that the validity of that class has been established through research.

Differing Models of Classification

There are currently three basic approaches to classifying abnormal behavior: the categorical, the dimensional, and the prototypal (Widiger & Frances, 1985). The categorical approach, like the diagnostic system of general medical diseases, assumes that (1) all human behavior can be divided into the categories of "healthy" and "disordered," and that (2) within the latter there exist discrete, nonoverlapping classes or types of disorder that have a high degree of within-class homogeneity in both "symptoms" displayed and the underlying organization of the disorder identified.

THE DIMENSIONAL APPROACH The dimensional and prototypal approaches differ fundamentally in the assumptions they make, particularly with respect to the requirement of discrete and internally homogeneous classes of behavior. In the dimensional approach, it is assumed that a person's typical behavior is the product of differing strengths or intensities of behavior along several definable dimensions such as mood, emotional stability, aggressiveness, gender identity, anxiousness, interpersonal trust, clarity of thinking and communication, social introversion, and so on. The important dimensions, once established, are the same for everyone. People are assumed to differ from one another in their configuration or profile of these dimensional traits (each ranging from very low to very high), not in terms of behavioral indications of a corresponding "dysfunctional" entity presumed to underlie and give rise to the disordered pattern of behavior (Miller, Reynolds, & Pilkonis, 2004; Widiger, Trull, Clarkin, Sanderson, & Costa, 2002). "Normal" is discriminated from "abnormal," then, in terms of precise statistical criteria derived from dimensional intensities among unselected people in general, most of whom may be presumed to be close to average, or mentally "normal." We could decide, for example, that anything above the ninety-seventh normative percentile on aggressiveness and anything below the third normative percentile on sociability would be considered "abnormal" findings.

Dimensionally based diagnosis has the incidental benefit of directly addressing treatment options. Because the patient's profile of psychological characteristics will normally consist of deviantly high and low points, therapies can be designed to moderate those of excessive intensity (e.g., anxiety) and to enhance those that constitute deficit status (e.g., inhibited self-assertiveness).

Of course, in taking a dimensional approach, it would be possible (perhaps even probable) to discover that such profiles tend to cluster together in types—and even that some of these types are correlated, though imperfectly, with recognizable sorts of gross behavioral malfunctions such as anxiety disorders or depression. It is highly unlikely, however, that any individual's profile will exactly fit a narrowly defined type or that the types identified will not have some overlapping features. This brings us to the prototypal approach.

THE PROTOTYPAL APPROACH A prototype (as the term is used here) is a conceptual entity depicting an idealized combination of characteristics that more or less regularly occur together in a less-than-perfect or standard way at the level of actual observation. Recall our earlier example of the "dogness" prototype. Prototypes are actually an aspect of our everyday thinking and experience. We can all readily generate in our mind's eye an image of a dog, while recognizing that we have never seen, nor will we ever see, two identical dogs. Thus no member of a prototypally defined group may actually have *all* of the characteristics of the defined prototype, even though it will have at least some of the more central of them. Also, some characteristics may be shared among differing prototypes—for example, many animals other than dogs have tails.

As we shall see, the official diagnostic criteria defining the various recognized classes of mental disorder, although explicitly intended to create categorical entities, more often than not result in prototypal ones. The central features of the various identified disorders are often somewhat vague, as are the boundaries purporting to separate one disorder from another. Much evidence suggests that a strict categorical approach to identifying differences among types of human behavior, whether normal or abnormal, may well be an unattainable goal. Bearing this in mind as we proceed may help you avoid some confusion. For example, we commonly find that two or more identified disorders regularly occur together in the same psychologically disordered individuals—a situation known as **comorbidity.** Does this really mean that such a person has two or more entirely separate and distinct disorders? In the typical instance, probably not.

Formal Diagnostic Classification of Mental Disorders

Today, there are two major psychiatric classification systems in use: the *International Classification of Disease System* (ICD-10), published by the World Health Organization, and the *Diagnostic and Statistical Manual of Mental Disorders* (DSM), published by the American Psychiatric Association. The ICD-10 system is widely used in Europe and many other countries, whereas the DSM system is the standard guide for the United States. Both systems are similar in many respects, such as in using symptoms as the focus of classification and in defining problems into different facets (the multiaxial system to be described below).

Certain differences in the way symptoms are grouped in these two systems can sometimes result in a different classification on the DSM-IV than on the ICD-10. We will focus on the DSM system in our discussion of what is to be considered a mental disorder. This manual specifies what subtypes of mental disorders are currently officially recognized and provides, for each, a set of defining criteria in the United States and some other countries. As already noted, the system purports to be a categorical one with sharp boundaries separating the various disorders from one another, but it is in fact a prototypal one with much fuzziness of boundaries and considerable interpenetration, or overlap, of the various "categories" of disorder it identifies.

The criteria that define the recognized categories of disorder consist for the most part of symptoms and signs. The term **symptoms** generally refers to the patient's subjective description, the complaints she or he presents about what is wrong. **Signs,** on the other hand, are objective observations that the diagnostician may make either directly (such as the patient's inability to look another person in the eye) or indirectly (such as the results of pertinent tests administered by a psychological examiner). To make any given diagnosis, the diagnostician must observe the particular criteria—the symptoms and signs that the DSM-IV indicates must be met.

THE EVOLUTION OF THE DSM The DSM is currently in its fourth edition (DSM-IV), with some recent modifications, referred to as "DSM-IV-TR," having been made in 2000. The classes of mental disorder recognized in the DSM-IV are reproduced on the endpapers of this book. This system is the product of a five-decade evolution involving increasing refinement and precision in the identification and description of mental disorders. The first edition of the manual (DSM-I) appeared in 1952 and was largely an outgrowth of attempts to standardize diagnostic practices in use among military personnel in World War II. The 1968 DSM-II reflected the additional insights gleaned from a markedly expanded postwar research effort in mental health sponsored by the federal government. Over time, practitioners recognized a defect in both these early efforts: The various types of disorders identified were described in narrative and jargon-laden terms that proved too vague for mental health professionals to agree on their meaning. The result was a serious limitation of diagnostic reliability; that is, two professionals examining the same patient might very well come up with completely different impressions of what disorder(s) the patient had.

To address this clinical and scientific impasse, the DSM-III of 1980 introduced a radically different approach, one intended to remove, as far as possible, the element of subjective judgment from the diagnostic process. It did so by adopting an "operational" method of defining the various disorders that would officially be recognized. This innovation meant that the DSM system would now specify the exact observations that must be made for a given diagnostic label to be applied. In a typical case, a specific number of signs or symptoms from a designated list must be present before a diagnosis can properly be assigned. The new approach, continued in the DSM-III's revised version of 1987 (DSM-III-R) and in the 1994 DSM-IV, clearly enhanced diagnostic reliability. As an example of the operational approach to diagnosis, the DSM-IV diagnostic criteria for Dysthymic Disorder are reproduced in the table on page 135.

The number of recognized mental disorders has increased enormously from DSM-I to DSM-IV, due both to the addition of new diagnoses and to the elaborate subdivision of older ones. Because it is unlikely that the nature of the American psyche has changed much in the interim period, it seems more reasonable to assume that mental health professionals view their field in a different light than they did 50 years ago. The DSM system is now both more comprehensive and more finely differentiated into subsets of disorders.

THE LIMITATIONS OF DSM CLASSIFICATION As already noted, there are limits on the extent to which a conceptually strict categorical system can adequately represent the abnormalities of behavior to which human beings are subject (Beutler & Malik, 2002). The real problems of real patients often do not fit into the precise lists of signs and symptoms that are at the heart of the modern DSM effort. How should we deal, for example, with the patient who meets three of the criteria for a particular diagnosis, if four is the minimum threshold for rendering the diagnosis? The clinical reality is that the disorders people actually suffer are often not so finely differentiated as the DSM grid on which they must be mapped. Increasingly fine differentiation also produces more and more recognized types of disorder. Too often, we believe, the unintended effect is to sacrifice validity in an effort to maximize interdiagnostician agreement—reliability. This makes little sense. For example, blends of anxiety and depression are extremely common in a clinical population, and they typically show much overlap (correlation) in quantitative scientific investigations as well. Nevertheless, the DSM treats the two as generically distinct forms of disorder, and as a consequence, a person who is clinically both anxious and depressed may receive two diagnoses, one for each of the supposedly separate conditions.

THE FIVE AXES OF DSM-IV-TR DSM-IV-TR evaluates an individual according to five foci, or "axes." The first three axes assess an individual's present clinical status or condition:

Axis I. The particular clinical syndromes or other conditions that may be a focus of clinical attention. This would include schizophrenia, generalized anxiety disorder, major depression, and substance dependence. Axis I conditions are roughly analogous to the various illnesses and diseases recognized in general medicine.

Axis II. Personality disorders. A very broad group of disorders, discussed in Chapter 10, that encompasses a variety of problematic ways of relating to the world, such as histrionic personality disorder, paranoid personality disorder, or antisocial personality disorder. The last of these, for example, refers to an early developing, persistent, and pervasive pattern of disregard for accepted standards of conduct, including legal strictures. Axis II provides a means of coding for long-standing maladaptive personality traits that may or may not be involved in the development and expression of an Axis I disorder. Mental retardation is also diagnosed as an Axis II condition.

Axis III. General medical conditions. Listed here are any general medical conditions potentially relevant to understanding or management of the case. Axis III of DSM-IV-TR may be used in conjunction with an Axis I diagnosis qualified by the phrase "Due to [a specifically designated general medical condition]"—for example, where a major depressive disorder is conceived as resulting from unremitting pain associated with some chronic medical disease.

On any of these first three axes, where the pertinent criteria are met, more than one diagnosis is permissible and in fact encouraged. That is, a person may be diagnosed as having multiple psychiatric syndromes such as Panic Disorder and Major Depressive Disorder; disorders of personality such as Dependent or Avoidant; or potentially relevant medical problems such as Cirrhosis (a liver disease often caused by excessive alcohol use) and Overdose, Cocaine. The last two DSM-IV-TR axes are used to assess broader aspects of an individual's situation.

Axis IV. Psychosocial and environmental problems. This group deals with the stressors that may have contributed to the current disorder, particularly those that have been present during the prior year. The diagnostician is invited to use a checklist approach for various categories of problems—family, economic, occupational, legal, etc. For example, the phrase "Problems with Primary Support Group" may be included where a family disruption is judged to have contributed to the disorder.

Axis V. Global assessment of functioning. This is where clinicians indicate how well the individual is coping at the present time. A 100-point Global Assessment of Functioning (GAF) Scale is provided for the examiner to assign a number summarizing a patient's overall ability to function. The GAF Scale is reproduced in the DSM-IV-TR table on page 136.

Axes IV and V, first introduced in DSM-III, are significant additions. Knowing what frustrations and demands a person has been facing is important for understanding the context in which the problem behavior has developed. And someone's general level of functioning conveys important information that is not necessarily contained in the entries for other axes and indicates how well the individual is coping with his or her problems. Some clinicians, however,

DSM-IV-TR

Criteria for Dysthymic Disorder

A. Depressed mood for most of the day, for more days than not for at least 2 years.

B. While depressed, reports two (or more) of the following:

(1) Poor appetite or overeating
(2) Insomnia or hypersomnia
(3) Low energy or fatigue
(4) Low self-esteem
(5) Poor concentration or difficulty making decisions
(6) Feelings of hopelessness

C. During the 2-year period of the disturbance, the person has never been without the symptoms for more than 2 months at a time.

D. No Major Depressive Episode has been present during the first 2 years of the disturbance.

E. There has never been a Manic Episode, a Mixed Episode, or a Hypomanic Episode, and criteria have never been met for Cyclothymic Disorder.

F. The disturbance does not occur exclusively during the course of a chronic Psychotic Disorder such as Schizophrenia or Delusional Disorder.

G. The symptoms are not due to the direct physiological effects of a substance (e.g., a drug abuse, a medication) or a general medical condition (e.g., hypothyroidism).

H. The symptoms cause clinically significant distress or impairment in social, occupational, or other important areas of functioning.

Specify if:

Early Onset: if onset is before age 21 years

Late Onset: if onset is age 21 years or older

DSM-IV-TR

The Global Assessment of Functioning (GAF) Scale

Consider psychological, social, and occupational functioning on a hypothetical continuum of mental health/illness. Do not include impairment in functioning due to physical (or environmental) limitations. (*Note:* Use intermediate codes when appropriate, e.g., 45, 68, 72.)

Code	
100–91	Superior functioning in a wide range of activities, life's problems never seem to get out of hand, is sought out by others because of his or her many positive qualities. No symptoms.
90–81	Absent or minimal symptoms (e.g., mild anxiety before an exam), good functioning in all areas, interested and involved in a wide range of activities, socially effective, generally satisfied with life, no more than everyday problems or concerns (e.g., an occasional argument with family members).
80–71	If symptoms are present, they are transient and expectable reactions to psychosocial stressors (e.g., difficulty concentrating after family argument); no more than slight impairment in social, occupational, or school functioning (e.g., temporarily falling behind in school work).
70–61	Some mild symptoms (e.g., depressed mood and mild insomnia) OR some difficulty in social, occupational, or school functioning (e.g., occasional truancy or theft within the household), but generally functioning pretty well, has some meaningful interpersonal relationships.
60–51	Moderate symptoms (e.g., flat affect and circumstantial speech, occasional panic attacks) OR moderate difficulty in social, occupational, or school functioning (e.g., few friends, conflicts with peers or coworkers).
50–41	Serious symptoms (e.g., suicidal ideation, severe obsessional rituals, frequent shoplifting) OR any serious impairment in social, occupational, or school functioning (e.g., no friends, unable to keep a job).
40–31	Some impairment in reality testing or communication (e.g., speech is at times illogical, obscure, or irrelevant) OR major impairment in several areas, such as work or school, family relations, judgment, thinking or mood (e.g., depressed man avoids friends, neglects family, and is unable to work; child frequently beats up younger children, is defiant at home, and is failing at school).
30–21	Behavior is considerably influenced by delusions or hallucinations OR serious impairment in communication or judgment (e.g., sometimes incoherent, acts grossly inappropriately, suicidal preoccupation) OR inability to function in almost all areas (e.g., stays in bed all day; no job, home, or friends).
20–11	Some danger of hurting self or others (e.g., suicide attempts without clear expectation of death; frequently violent; manic excitement) OR occasionally fails to maintain minimal personal hygiene (e.g., smears feces) OR gross impairment in communication (e.g., largely incoherent or mute).
10–1	Persistent danger of severely hurting self or others (e.g., recurrent violence) OR persistent inability to maintain minimal personal hygiene OR serious suicidal act with expectation of death.
0	Inadequate information.

Source: *Reprinted with permission from the* Diagnostic and Statistical Manual of Mental Disorders, Fourth Edition, *Text Revision (Copyright 2000). American Psychiatric Association.*

object to the routine use of these axes for insurance forms and the like, on the grounds that such use unnecessarily compromises a patient's right to privacy by revealing, for example, a recent divorce (Axis IV) or a suicide attempt (Axis V). Because of such concerns, Axes IV and V are now considered optional for diagnosis and in fact are rarely used in most clinical settings.

MAIN CATEGORIES OF AXIS I AND AXIS II DISORDERS

The different Axis I and II disorders are identified in the list of DSM-IV mental disorder diagnoses that appears on the endpapers of this book. They also serve as the means by which the clinical material in this book is organized. These diagnoses may be regarded as fitting into several broad etiological (major causal) groupings, each containing several subgroupings:

- Disorders secondary to gross destruction or malfunctioning of brain tissue, as in Alzheimer's dementia and a wide range of other conditions based on permanent or irreversible organic brain pathology. These disorders are described in Chapter 15.
- Substance-use disorders, involving problems such as habitual drug or alcohol abuse. These are discussed in Chapter 12.
- Disorders of psychological or sociocultural origin having no known brain pathology as a primary causal factor. This very large group includes a majority of the mental disorders discussed in this book, among them anxiety disorders (Chapter 6), somatoform and dissociative disorders (Chapter 8), psychosexual disorders (Chapter 13), and the Axis II personality disorders (Chapter 11). Traditionally, this group also includes severe mental disorders for which a specific organic brain pathology has not been demonstrated—such as major mood disorders (Chapter 7) and schizophrenia (Chapter 14)—although it appears increasingly likely that they may be caused at least in part by certain types of aberrant brain functioning.
- Disorders usually arising during childhood or adolescence, including a broad group of disorders featuring cognitive impairments such as mental retardation and specific learning disabilities (Chapter 16), and a large variety of behavioral problems, such as attention-deficit/hyperactivity disorder, that constitute deviations from the expected or normal path of development (Chapter 16).

In referring to mental disorders, several qualifying terms are commonly used. **Acute** is used to describe disorders of relatively short duration, usually under 6 months, such as transitory adjustment disorders (Chapter 5). In some contexts, it also connotes behavioral symptoms of high intensity. **Chronic** refers to long-standing and often permanent disorders such as Alzheimer's dementia and some forms of schizophrenia. The term can also be applied generally to low-intensity disorders, because long-term difficulties are often of this sort. **Mild, moderate,** and **severe** are terms that reflect different points on a dimension of severity or seriousness. **Episodic** and **recurrent** are used to describe unstable disorder patterns that tend to come and go, as with some mood and schizophrenic conditions.

THE PROBLEM OF LABELING The psychiatric diagnoses of the sort typified by the DSM-IV system are not uniformly revered among mental health professionals (e.g., Sarbin, 1997). Not even all psychiatrists (e.g., Tucker, 1998) are content with them. One important criticism is that a psychiatric diagnosis is little more than a label applied to a defined category of socially disapproved or otherwise problematic behavior.

The diagnostic label describes neither a person nor any underlying pathological condition ("dysfunction") the person necessarily harbors but, rather, some behavioral pattern associated with that person's current level of functioning. Yet once a label has been assigned, it may close off further inquiry. It is all too easy—even for professionals—to accept a label as an accurate and complete description of an individual rather than of that person's current behavior. When a person is labeled "depressed" or "schizophrenic," others are more likely to make certain assumptions about that person that may or may not be accurate. In fact, a diagnostic label can make it hard to look at the person's behavior objectively, without preconceptions about how he or she will act. These expectations can influence even clinically important interactions and treatment choices. For example, arrival at the diagnosis Major Depressive Disorder may cut off any further inquiry about the patient's life situation and lead abruptly to a prescription for antidepressant medication (Tucker, 1998), or the application of a label such as "borderline personality" might cause the mental health treatment staff to be less optimistic about the patient's prognosis (Markham, 2003).

Once an individual is labeled, he or she may accept a redefined identity and play out the expectations of that role. ("I'm nothing but a substance abuser. I might as well do drugs—everyone expects me to anyway. Furthermore, this is a condition deemed out of my control, so it is pointless for me to be an active participant in my treatment.") This acquisition of a new social identity can be harmful for a variety of reasons. The pejorative and stigmatizing implications of many psychiatric labels can mark people as second-class citizens with severe limitations that are often presumed to be permanent (Link, 2001; Slovenko, 2001). They can also have devastating effects on a person's morale, self-esteem, and relationships with others. The person so labeled may decide that he or she "is" the diagnosis and may thus adopt it as a life "career."

Clearly, it is in the disordered person's best interests for mental health professionals to be circumspect in the diagnostic process, in their use of labels, and in ensuring confidentiality with respect to both. A related change has developed over the past 50 years: For years the traditional term for a person who goes to see a mental health professional was *patient,* a term that is closely associated with medical sickness and a passive stance, waiting (patiently) for the doctor's cure. Today many mental health professionals, especially those trained in nonmedical settings, prefer the term *client* because it implies greater participation on the part of an individual and more responsibility for bringing about his or her own recovery. We shall be using these terms interchangeably in this text.

LIMITED USEFULNESS OF DIAGNOSIS It should be kept in mind that a DSM diagnosis per se may be of limited usefulness. The DSM-IV acknowledges this in its Introduction: "Making a DSM-IV diagnosis is only the first step in a comprehensive evaluation. To formulate an adequate treatment plan, the clinician will invariably require considerable additional information about the person being evaluated beyond that required to make a DSM-IV-TR diagnosis" (American Psychiatric Association, 2000, *DSM-IV-TR,* pp. xxxiv–xxxv). Arriving at a diagnosis is usually required, at least in the form of a "diagnostic impression," before the commencement of clinical services. This is necessitated, perhaps unwisely, by medical insurance requirements and long-standing clinical administrative tradition. The additional information required for adequate clinical assessment may be extensive and extremely difficult to unearth. For the most part, in keeping with psychiatric tradition, that process is interview-based. That is, the examiner engages the patient (or perhaps a family member of the patient) in a conversation designed to elicit the information necessary to place the patient in one or more DSM diagnostic categories. The interviewer introduces various questions and probes, typically becoming increasingly specific as he or she develops diagnostic hypotheses and checks these out with additional probes related to the criteria for particular DSM diagnoses. Physicians in general medical practice do something similar in the course of an examination.

Gladys Burr (shown here with her attorney) is a tragic example of the dangers of labeling. Involuntarily committed by her mother (apparently because of some personality problems) in 1936 at the age of 29, Ms. Burr was diagnosed as psychotic and was later declared to be mentally retarded. Though a number of IQ tests administered from 1946 to 1961 showed her to be of normal intelligence, and though a number of doctors stated that she was of normal intelligence and should be released, she was confined in a residential center for the mentally retarded or in a state boarding home until 1978. Though a court did give her a financial reward in compensation, surely nothing can compensate for 42 years of unnecessary and involuntary commitment.

UNSTRUCTURED DIAGNOSTIC INTERVIEWS Like assessment interviews described earlier, diagnostic interviews are of two general types, unstructured and structured. In the unstructured interview, the examiner follows no preexisting plan with respect to content and sequence of the probes introduced. Unstructured interviews, as their name implies, are somewhat freewheeling. The therapist/clinician asks questions as they occur to him or her, in part on the basis of the responses to previous questions. For example, if the patient/client mentioned a father who traveled a lot when he or she was a child, the clinician is free to ask, "Did you miss your father?" or (pursuing a different tack), "How did your mother handle that?" rather than being required to ask the next question in a predetermined list. Many clinical examiners prefer this unfettered approach because it enables them to follow perhaps idiosyncratic "leads." In the above example, the clinician might have chosen to ask about the mother's reaction on the basis of a developing suspicion that the mother may have been depressed during the client's childhood years. There is one serious drawback to the freewheeling style, however: The information that an interview yields is limited to the content of that interview. Should another clinician conduct another unstructured interview of the same patient, he or she might come up with a different clinical picture.

STRUCTURED DIAGNOSTIC INTERVIEWS The structured interview probes the client in a manner that is highly controlled. Guided by a sort of master plan (sometimes to the extent of specifying the examiner's exact wording), the clinician using a structured interview typically seeks to discover whether the person's symptoms and signs "fit" diagnostic criteria that are more precise and "operational" than in the past. The use of more precise criteria and of highly structured diagnostic interviewing has substantially improved diagnostic reliability, but the structured interview format is still used only sporadically in routine clinical work. Nevertheless, the precision of clinical research, including epidemiological research to be discussed later, has profited enormously with these developments.

There are a number of structured diagnostic interviews that may be used in various contexts. In clinical and

4.4 Developments in Practice

Schedules for Clinical Assessment in Neuropsychiatry (SCAN)

The SCAN (Schedules for Clinical Assessment in Neuropsychiatry) is a formal system of interview questions developed by the World Health Organization (WHO) for assessing and classifying psychopathology (1994). The SCAN (formerly known as the "Present State Exam") is the latest version of a long-term project undertaken by WHO to provide a systematic diagnostic schedule for classifying mental health problems. The SCAN is widely used around the world and has been translated into more than 35 languages.

The SCAN is a structured diagnostic interview in which the clinician records the patient's responses on a computer and rates the severity of the problem behavior during an interview. Although the SCAN was developed for use by trained clinicians, some research suggests that experienced laypersons can be trained to administer the SCAN with effective results (Brugha et al., 1999). The clinician follows a clearly defined set of structured questions covering a broad range of information such as demographic data and physical and mental health symptoms. The patient's responses are elicited for both the present state (e.g., the last month) and any period over the lifetime in order to obtain an evaluation of present and prior psychiatric conditions. For example, the clinician would ask:

- "Some people have phobias. They feel anxious or panicky or scared in certain situations, like being afraid of heights, or open spaces, or certain animals or insects, or in some social situations. They try to avoid them or even think about them. Would that be your experience?"

The interviewer then records the appropriate rating:

1 Phobias absent

0 Phobias may be present

Here is another example:

- "You have mentioned that in the last month you have had difficulty sleeping. Overall, how much interference has there been with your everyday activities because of this problem?"

Rate interference due to sleep problems:

0 No symptoms present to a significant degree

1 Symptoms present but of little interference

2 Moderate or intermittent symptoms

3 Severe to incapacitating symptoms

Upon completion of the interview, the clinician can readily obtain clinical diagnoses by instructing the computer program to run a diagnostic algorithm. The practitioner has the option of selecting DSM-IV or ICD-10 or both. In addition, the practitioner can select whether the diagnosis covers the present symptoms (e.g., the past 28 days) or symptoms that have occurred at any time in the person's lifetime. Only Axis I diagnoses are provided.

The SCAN procedure has been the subject of a number of comparative research studies—for example, in Taiwan (Cheng et al., 2001), Spain (Roca-Bennasar et al., 2001), Holland (Rijnders et al., 2000), and the United States (Hesselbrock et al., 1999). Investigators have found satisfactory concordance between the SCAN procedure and clinical diagnosis. The computer administration version of the SCAN provides more reliable diagnoses than diagnostic interviews conducted by clinicians without benefit of structured computer processing.

research situations, a popular instrument has been the Structured Clinical Interview for DSM Diagnosis (SCID), which yields, almost automatically, diagnoses carefully attuned to the DSM diagnostic criteria. Another structured diagnostic instrument, the Schedules for Clinical Assessment in Neuropsychiatry (SCAN), published by the World Health Organization (World Health Organization, 1994), enables the diagnostician to arrive at either an ICD-10 or a DSM-IV diagnosis (see Developments in Practice 4.4).

In Review

- Why is a classification system needed in abnormal psychology?
- What is the meaning of reliability and validity in the context of such a classification system?
- What are the three basic approaches to classifying abnormal behavior?

summary

- Clinical assessment is one of the most important and complex responsibilities of mental health professionals. The extent to which a person's problems are understood and appropriately treated depends largely on the adequacy of the psychological assessment.
- The goals of psychological assessment include identifying and describing the individual's symptoms; determining the chronicity and severity of the problems; evaluating the potential causal factors in the person's background; and exploring the individual's personal resources that might be an asset in his or her treatment program.
- Because many psychological problems have physical components, either as underlying causal factors or as symptom patterns, it is often important to include a medical examination in the psychological assessment.
- In cases where organic brain damage is suspected, it is important to have neurological tests—such as an EEG or a CAT, PET, or MRI scan—to help determine the site and extent of organic brain disorder.
- It is often important for someone with suspected organic brain damage to take a battery of neuropsychological tests to determine whether or in what manner the underlying brain disorder is affecting his or her mental and behavioral capabilities.
- Psychosocial assessment methods are techniques for gathering psychological information relevant to clinical decisions about patients.
- The most widely used and most flexible psychosocial assessment methods are the clinical interview and behavior observation. These methods provide a wealth of clinical information.
- Psychological tests include standardized stimuli for collecting behavior samples that can be compared with other individuals' behavior via test norms.
- Two different personality-testing approaches have been developed: (1) projective tests, such as the Rorschach, in which unstructured stimuli are presented to a subject, who then "projects" meaning or structure onto the stimulus, thereby revealing "hidden" motives, feelings, and so on; and (2) objective tests, or personality inventories, in which a subject is required to read and respond to itemized statements or questions.
- Objectively scored personality tests, such as the MMPI-2 and MMPI-A, provide a cost-effective means of collecting a great deal of personality information rapidly.
- Possibly the most dramatic recent innovation in clinical assessment involves the widespread use of computers in the administration, scoring, and interpretation of psychological tests. It is now possible to obtain immediate interpretation of psychological test results, either through a direct computer interactive approach or through a modem to a computer network that interprets tests.
- The formal definition of mental disorder, as offered in the fourth edition of the *Diagnostic and Statistical Manual of Mental Disorders* (DSM-IV-TR), has certain problems that limit its clarity (i.e., what exactly are "dysfunctions"?).
- There are problems with the category type of classification system adopted in DSM-IV-TR. Notably, the categories do not always result in within-class homogeneity or between-class discrimination. This can lead to high levels of comorbidity among disorders. Several possible solutions to this problem include dimensionalizing the phenomena of mental disorder and adopting a prototypal approach.
- For all of its problems, however, knowledge of the DSM-IV-TR is essential to serious study in the field of abnormal behavior.

Key Terms

actuarial procedures (P. 127)
acute (P. 137)
chronic (P. 137)
comorbidity (P. 133)
computerized axial tomography (CAT scan) (P. 111)
dysrhythmia (P. 111)
electroencephalogram (EEG) (P. 111)
episodic (P. 137)
functional MRI (fMRI) (P. 112)
magnetic resonance imaging (MRI) (P. 111)
mild (P. 137)
Minnesota Multiphasic Personality Inventory (MMPI) (P. 122)
moderate (P. 137)
neuropsychological assessment (P. 113)
objective tests (P. 122)
positron emission tomography (PET scan) (P. 112)
presenting problem (P. 108)
projective tests (P. 119)
rating scales (P. 116)
recurrent (P. 137)
reliability (P. 132)
role-playing (P. 116)
Rorschach Test (P. 119)
self-monitoring (P. 116)
sentence completion test (P. 122)
severe (P. 137)
signs (P. 134)
symptoms (P. 134)
Thematic Apperception Test (TAT) (P. 121)
validity (P. 132)

CHAPTER

5

Stress and Adjustment Disorders

Life can be stressful. Everyone faces a different mix of demands and adjustments in life, and any one of us may break down if the going gets tough enough. Under conditions of overwhelming stress, even a previously stable person may develop temporary (transient) psychological problems and lose the capacity to gain pleasure from life (Berenbaum & Connelly, 1993). This breakdown may be sudden, as in the case of a person who has gone through a severe accident or fire, or it may be gradual, as in the case of a person who, in a deteriorating marriage or other intimate relationship, has been subjected to prolonged periods of tension and challenges to his or her self-esteem. Most often the individual recovers once the stressful situation is over, although in some cases there may be long-lasting damage to self-concept and an increased vulnerability to certain types of stressors (Resick, 2001). Today's stress can be tomorrow's vulnerability. In the case of a person who is quite vulnerable to begin with, of course, a stressful situation may precipitate more serious and lasting psychopathology.

What Is Stress?

Life would be simple indeed if all of our needs were automatically satisfied. In reality, however, many obstacles, both personal and environmental, prevent this ideal situation. We may be too short for professional basketball or have less money than we need. Such obstacles place adjustive demands on us and can lead to stress. The term *stress* has typically been used to refer both to the adjustive demands placed on an organism and to the organism's internal biological and psychological responses to such demands. To avoid confusion, we will refer to adjustive demands as **stressors,** to the effects they create within an organism as stress, and to efforts to deal with stress as **coping strategies. Stress** is a by-product of poor or inadequate coping.

All situations, positive and negative, that require adjustment can be stressful. Thus, according to Canadian physiologist Hans Selye (1956, 1976a), the notion of stress can be broken down further into **eustress** (positive stress) and **distress** (negative stress). (In most cases, the stress experienced during a wedding would be eustress; during a funeral, distress.) Both types of stress tax a person's resources and coping skills, although distress typically has the potential to do more damage.

Stress can result from both negative and positive events—distress (negative stress) from tragic circumstances found in events such as funerals and eustress (positive stress) found in events like weddings. Both types of stress can tax a person's resources and coping skills, although distress typically has the potential to do more damage.

Research findings and clinical observations on the relationship between stress and psychopathology are so substantial that the role of stressors in symptom development is now formally emphasized in diagnostic formulations. In DSM-IV-TR (American Psychiatric Association, 2000), for example, a diagnostician can specify on Axis IV the specific psychosocial stressors facing a person. The Axis IV scale is particularly useful in relation to three Axis I categories: adjustment disorder, acute stress disorder, and post-traumatic stress disorder (acute, chronic, or delayed). These disorders involve patterns of psychological and behavioral disturbances that occur in response to identifiable stressors. The key differences among them lie not only in the severity of the disturbances but also in the nature of the stressors and the time frame during which the disorders occur (Cardeña, Butler, & Spiegel, 2003). In these disorders, the stressors supposedly can be identified as causal factors and specified on Axis IV.

Categories of Stressors

Adjustive demands, or stressors, stem from sources that fall into three basic categories: (1) frustrations, (2) conflicts, and (3) pressures. Although we will consider these categories separately, they are closely related.

FRUSTRATIONS A wide range of obstacles, both external and internal, can lead to frustration (see Penk, Drebing, & Schutt, 2002, for a discussion of PTSD in the workplace). Prejudice and discrimination, unfulfillment in a job, and the death of a loved one are common frustrations stemming from the environment; physical handicaps, limited ability to perform certain tasks, loneliness, guilt, and inadequate self-control are sources of frustration based on personal limitations. Frustrations can be particularly difficult for a person to cope with because they often lead to self-devaluation, making the person feel that she or he has failed in some way or is incompetent.

CONFLICTS In many instances, stress results from the simultaneous occurrence of two or more incompatible needs or motives: The requirements of one preclude satisfaction of the others. For example, if a woman is committed to a career but must decide whether to uproot her family for a promotion or decline it and leave her family undisturbed, she will experience conflict while trying to make the choice. Conflicts with which everyone has to cope may be classified as approach-avoidance, double-approach, and double-avoidance types (see Table 5.1). Classifying conflicts in this manner is somewhat arbitrary, and various combinations among the different types are perhaps the rule rather than the exception. Thus a double-approach conflict between alternative careers may also have approach-avoidance aspects because of the responsibilities that either career will impose. Regardless of how we categorize conflicts, they represent a major source of stress that can often become overwhelmingly intense.

PRESSURES Stress may stem not only from frustrations and conflicts but also from pressures to achieve specific goals or to behave in particular ways. Pressures force us to speed up, redouble our effort, or change the direction of goal-oriented behavior, which can seriously tax our coping resources or even lead to maladaptive behavior.

TABLE 5.1 Classification of Conflict Situations

1. *Approach-avoidance conflicts* involve strong tendencies to approach and to avoid the same goal. Mary has been offered an appealing new job in another department of the company in which she is employed. The job is one that she has had her eye on for several years and includes a substantial pay raise and better benefits. Unfortunately, her ex-husband, with whom she has been having great difficulty, also works in that department. She becomes very upset when she has to deal with him and is concerned that the work atmosphere would be unbearable.

2. *Double-approach conflicts* involve choosing between two or more desirable goals. Although the experience may cause more eustress than distress, the stress is still real and the choice difficult. In either case, the person gives up something. Charles G. is faced with a decision that many would envy but that is giving him a lot of sleepless nights. He has been admitted into two graduate programs that have almost equal appeal. One is a program at a highly prestigious university whose graduates tend to get the best positions. The other school is also highly respected (though not as much as the first school) and has exactly the type of specialization he has wanted, with an outstanding faculty. Choosing one, of course, means turning down the other. He has been vacillating between the choices, sometimes changing his decision every 5 minutes.

3. *Double-avoidance conflicts* are those in which the choices are between undesirable alternatives. Neither choice will bring satisfaction, so the task is to decide which course of action will be least disagreeable—that is, the least stressful. Jenny's mother sent her an airline ticket to enable her to attend an "important" family outing the likes of which Jenny has grown to despise. She is considering a course of action that she finds very distasteful—lying to her mother about being so busy that she cannot attend. She knows that her mother will be very punitive if she fails to go, but the family gatherings have become very stressful.

Pressures can originate from both external and internal sources. For example, students may feel under severe pressure to make good grades because their parents demand it (external pressure) and because they want to get into graduate school (internal pressure). The long hours of study, the tension of examinations, and the sustained concentration of effort over many years result in considerable stress for many students. Many students preparing for important, career-determining examinations such as the Graduate Record Exam (GRE) or the Medical College Admissions Test (MCAT) experience considerable anxiety as the examination date approaches. Fifty premedical students reported their anxiety levels for 17 days before and 17 days after the MCAT. The experience of anxiety was greater in the days preceding the examination, with peak anxiety occurring as the examination day approached (Bolger, 1990). People who were prone to dealing with stress by overusing defense mechanisms such as wishful thinking or self-blame tended to show increased maladaptive behavior and increased anxiety under high stress. Performance on the examination, however, did not appear to be related to the use of various coping strategies to deal with the stress; that is, those students who used maladaptive behaviors did not appear to do worse on the exam.

Occupational demands can also be highly stressful, and many jobs make severe demands in terms of responsibility, time, and performance (Roberts & Levinson, 2001; Tennant, 2001). Although we have arbitrarily separated stress into three categories, a given situation may involve elements of all three categories. The following case illustrates this point:

case STUDY Dejected Premed Student

A premed student whose lifelong ambition was to become a doctor received rejection letters from all the medical schools to which he had applied. This unexpected blow left him feeling depressed and empty. He felt extreme frustration over his failure and great conflict over what his next steps should be. He was experiencing pressure from his family and peers to try again, but he was also overwhelmed by a sense of failure. He felt so bitter that he wanted to drop everything and become a beach bum or a blackjack dealer in Las Vegas. The loss of self-esteem he was experiencing left him with no realistic backup plans and little interest in pursuing alternative careers.

Although a particular stressor may predominate in any situation, we rarely deal with an isolated demand. Instead, we usually confront a continuously changing pattern of interrelated and sometimes contradictory demands.

Living in extreme poverty with insufficient life resources can be a powerful stressor in a person's life at any age, but especially for children.

Factors Predisposing a Person to Stress

The severity of stress is gauged by the degree to which it disrupts functioning. The actual degree of disruption that occurs or is threatened to occur depends partly on a stressor's characteristics; partly on a person's resources, both personal and situational, for meeting the demands resulting from the stress; and partly on the relationship between the two. Everyone faces a unique pattern of adjustive demands. This is because people perceive and interpret similar situations differently and also because, objectively, no two people are faced with exactly the same pattern of stressors. Some individuals are more highly resistant to developing long-term problems under stress than others; that is, some individuals are more resilient as a result of personality characteristics and background experiences. (For an informative discussion of resiliency among Holocaust survivors, see the recent article by de Vries and Suedfeld, 2005.)

THE NATURE OF THE STRESSOR Although most minor stressors, such as misplacing one's keys, may be dealt with as a matter of course, stressors that involve important aspects of a person's life—such as the death of a loved one, a divorce, a job loss, or a serious illness—tend to be highly stressful for most people. Furthermore, the longer a stressor operates, the more severe its effects. Prolonged exhaustion, for example, imposes a more intense stress than temporary fatigue. Also, stressors often appear to have a cumulative effect. A married couple may maintain amicable relations through a long series of minor irritations or frustrations, only to dissolve the relationship in the face of "one last straw" of a precipitating stressor. Sometimes key stressors in a person's life center on a continuing, difficult life situation (Tein, Sandler, & Zautra, 2000). These stressors are considered chronic, or long-lasting. A person may be frustrated in a boring and unrewarding job from which there is seemingly no escape, suffer for years in an unhappy and conflict-filled marriage, or be severely frustrated by a physical handicap or a long-term health problem.

Encountering a number of stressors at the same time also makes a difference. If a man has a heart attack, loses his job, and receives news that his son has been arrested for selling drugs, all at the same time, the resulting stress will be more severe than if these events occurred separately.

Finally, the symptoms of stress intensify when a person is more closely involved in an immediately traumatic situation. Pynoos and colleagues (1987) conducted an extensive investigation of children's symptoms and behavior 1 month after a shooting incident in a schoolyard (1 child was killed and several others wounded when a sniper randomly fired into the playground). A total of 159 children from the school were interviewed. Depending on where they were at the time of the shooting—on the playground, in the school, in the neighborhood, on the way home, absent from school, or out of the vicinity—the children experienced different stress levels. Children on the playground, closest to the shooting, had the most severe symptoms, whereas children who were not at school during the shooting experienced no symptoms.

THE EXPERIENCE OF CRISIS From time to time, most of us experience periods of especially acute (sudden and intense) stress. The term **crisis** is used to refer to times when a stressful situation approaches or exceeds the adaptive capacities of a person or group. Crises are often especially stressful because the stressors are so potent that the coping techniques we typically use do not work. Stress can be distinguished from crisis in this way: A traumatic situation or crisis overwhelms a person's ability to cope, whereas stress does not necessarily overwhelm the person.

A crisis or trauma may occur as a result of an acrimonious divorce, a natural disaster such as a flood (Waelde, Koopman, et al., 2001), or the aftermath of an injury or disease that forces difficult readjustments in a person's self-concept and way of life. The outcome of such crises has a profound influence on a person's subsequent adjustment. If a crisis leads a person to develop an effective new method of coping—perhaps joining a support group or accepting help from friends—then he or she may emerge from the crisis even better adjusted than before. But if the crisis impairs the person's ability to cope with similar stressors in the future because of an expectation of failure, then his or her overall adjustment will suffer. For this reason, **crisis intervention** (to be discussed below)—providing psychological help in times of severe and special stress—has become an important element in contemporary treatment and prevention approaches (Arehart-Treichler, 2004).

The trauma of sudden and powerful disasters can produce intense stress. These people are reacting to the collapse of the World Trade Towers.

LIFE CHANGES It is important to remember that life changes, even some positive ones such as winning a desired promotion or getting married, place new demands on us and thus may be stressful. Our psychosocial environments (including such things as our friendship networks, work relationships, and social resources) can play a significant role in causing disorders or precipitating their onset, even in biological disorders such as bipolar disorder (see Chapter 7; Johnson & Miller, 1997). The faster the changes, the greater the stress. Early research efforts on life changes focused on developing scales that could measure the relationship between stress and possible physical and mental disorders. In one early attempt, Holmes and Rahe (1967), for example, developed the Social Readjustment Rating Scale, an objective method for measuring the cumulative stress to which a person has been exposed over a period of time (see also Bühler & Pagels, 2003). This scale measures life stress in terms of life change units (LCU): The more stressful the event, the more LCUs assigned to it. At the high end of the scale, "death of a spouse" rates 100 LCUs and "divorce" rates 73 LCUs; at the low end of the scale, "vacation" rates 13 LCUs and "minor violations of the law" rates 11 LCUs. Holmes and his colleagues found that people with LCU scores of 300 or more for recent months were at significant risk for getting a major illness within the next 2 years. In another effort, Horowitz and his colleagues (1979) developed the Impact of Events Scale (see also Shevlin, Hunt, & Robbins, 2000). This scale measures a person's reaction to a stressful situation by first identifying the stressor and then posing a series of questions to determine how he or she is coping.

Although the use of life event scales in the assessment of stress has shown promise (Gray, Litz, et al., 2004), this approach has been criticized for numerous methodological problems. For example, a number of criticisms have targeted the items selected for different scales, the subjectivity of the scoring, the failure to take into account the relevance of items for the populations studied, and the reliance on subjects' memory of events (Monroe & Simons, 1991). Other limitations of life event scales is that they tend to measure chronic problems rather than reactions to specific environmental events (Depue & Monroe, 1986; Monroe, Roberts, Kupfer, & Frank, 1996), and, depending on what mood the person is in, the scales' rating of how stressful something is can vary. Perhaps the most problematic aspect of life event scales is that they serve only as a general indicator of distress and do not provide useful information about specific types of disorders. Despite the limitations of scales devised to measure life stressors, however, the evidence supports the stressfulness of life changes (Maddi, Bartone, & Puccetti, 1987).

Another approach to the assessment of significant life events that has received attention among researchers is the Life Event and Difficulty Schedule by Brown and Harris (1989) and Brown and Moran (1997). This approach involves a semistructured interview that places the life event rating variables in a clearly defined context in order to increase interrater reliability. This approach makes it possible to assess the meaning of the event to the individual more directly. Although this approach is more labor-intensive and costly to administer, the resulting ratings are considered more reliable than those of other life event approaches.

A PERSON'S PERCEPTION OF THE STRESSOR Most of us are well aware that in some cases, one person's stressor is another person's thrill. Some look forward to a chance to be on stage; others dread it. The different reactions that people have to environmental events are due in part to the way they perceive the situation—the same event will be interpreted differently by different people. A study by Clark, Salkovskis, Öst, et al. (1997) found that persons who are prone to having panic attacks tend to interpret body sensations in a more catastrophic way than patients who do not experience panic attacks. A person who feels overwhelmed and is concerned that he or she will be unable to deal with a stressor is more likely to experience panic in the situation than a person who feels able to manage it. For example, a mother who is overwhelmed by the feeling that her three unruly children are unmanageable and leaves them unattended is more likely to experience negative consequences than a similarly stressed mother who stays with them.

Often, new adjustive demands that have not been anticipated (and for which no ready-made coping strategies are available) will place a person under severe stress. A devastating house fire and the damage it brings are not occurrences anyone has learned to cope with. Likewise, recovery from the stress created by major surgery can be markedly facilitated when a patient is given realistic expectations beforehand; knowing what to expect adds predictability to the situation, which reduces stress and anxiety (Leventhal, Patrick-Muller, & Leventhal, 1998; MacDonald & Kuiper, 1983). Understanding the nature of a stressful situation, preparing for it, and knowing how long it will last all lessen the severity of the stress when it does come.

Perceiving some benefit from a disaster, such as growing closer to your family because of a tragedy, can moderate the effects of a trauma somewhat and make adjustment to the circumstances easier. In fact some theorists (e.g., Christopher, 2004) have pointed out that trauma always leaves the person transformed in some way and that one natural outcome of the stress process is adaptation and growth. Of course, some stressors are more difficult to adapt to or accommodate than others. A study by McMillan, Smith, and Fisher (1997) found that an individual's ability to perceive some benefit in adapting to the consequences of a disaster depended in part on the nature of the disaster itself. For example, it was much more difficult for victims to perceive some "silver lining" from a tragic airplane crash in which many people died than it was for them to adapt to the damage from a tornado. In the case of an airplane crash, no "benefit" can be found, whereas the tornado offers more opportunity: "It could have been worse, the school might have been hit" or "Thank goodness so many were off at work!"

THE INDIVIDUAL'S STRESS TOLERANCE People who do not handle changing life circumstances well may be particularly vulnerable to the slightest frustration or pressure. Children are particularly vulnerable to severe stressors such as war and terrorism (Petrovic, 2004; Shaw, 2003). People who are generally unsure of their adequacy and worth are much more likely to experience threat than those who feel generally confident and secure. The term **stress tolerance** refers to a person's ability to withstand stress without becoming seriously impaired. People vary greatly in overall vulnerability to stressors. Blanchard, Hickling, Taylor, and Loos (1995) found that an individual's prior history of major depression is a ***risk factor*** for the development of severe psychological symptoms related to stress after a

> **research close-up**
>
> ***risk factor***
>
> *A* risk factor *is any variable that increases the likelihood of a specific (and usually negative) outcome occurring at a later point in time. For example, obesity is a risk factor for heart disease; perfectionism is a personality trait that is a risk factor for eating disorders.*

People who have a closer network of friends tend to have reduced vulnerability to depression when they experience extreme stress.

motor vehicle accident (see Chapter 7). Some individuals appear to be constitutionally more "frail" than others and tend to have more difficulty handling even relatively minor change. They do not have much physical stamina and may become fatigued or sick in the face of stressful situations. In addition, different people are vulnerable to different stressors. They may have failed to learn effective adaptive strategies for certain kinds of stressors. An individual's learning history plays a crucial part in this general capacity to deal with stress. Early traumatic experiences can leave a person especially vulnerable to—or especially well equipped to handle—certain stressors (see Chapter 3 for diathesis-stress models). Having a poor "track record" at handling difficult circumstances leaves one vulnerable to new challenges. For example, a person who has been subjected to uncontrollable stressors (such as being sexually abused at an early age) tends to become vulnerable or highly sensitized to later assault or abuse. For these and other reasons, emergencies and disappointments that one person can take in stride may prove incapacitating to another.

A LACK OF EXTERNAL RESOURCES AND SOCIAL SUPPORTS Considerable evidence suggests that positive social and family relationships can moderate the effects of stress on a person (Ozer, Best, et al., 2004). Conversely, the lack of external supports, either personal or material, can make a given stressor more potent and weaken a person's capacity to cope with it. A nationwide survey of stressful life events in mainland China found that problems with interpersonal relationships were the most commonly reported stressors in daily life (Zheng & Lin, 1994). A divorce or the death of a mate evokes more stress if people are left feeling alone and unloved than if they are surrounded by people they care about and feel close to. Siegel and Kuykendall (1990), for example, found that widowed men who attended church or temple experienced less depression than those who did not. This study also found that men who had lost a spouse were more often depressed than women who had done so. The reasons for this finding remain unclear, although others have found similar results (e.g., Stroebe & Stroebe, 1983). It could be that the women had a closer network of friends from the outset, which may have reduced their vulnerability to depression (Kershner, Cohen, & Coyne, 1998).

In other situations, a person may be adversely affected by family members who are experiencing problems. The level of tension for all family members can be increased if one member experiences extreme difficulty such as a chronic or life-threatening illness or a psychiatric disability. A person whose spouse is experiencing psychological disturbance is likely to experience more stress than one whose spouse is psychologically better adjusted (Yager, Grant, & Bolus, 1984). The stress of the illness is compounded by the loss of support.

Often a culture offers specific rituals or courses of action that support people as they attempt to deal with certain types of stress. For example, most religions provide rituals that help the bereaved, and in some faiths, confession and atonement help people deal with stresses related to guilt and self-recrimination.

Coping with Stress

Sometimes inner factors such as a person's frame of reference, motives, competencies, or stress tolerance play the dominant role in determining his or her coping strategies. For example, a person who has successfully handled adversity in the past may be better equipped to deal with similar problems in the future (Masten & Coatsworth, 1998). (See the discussion on resilience in Bonanno, 2004; see also

Chapter 3.) At other times environmental conditions, such as extreme social pressures, are of primary importance. Any stress reaction, of course, reflects the interplay of inner strategies and outer conditions—some more influential than others but all working together to make the person react in a certain way. Ironically, some people create stress for themselves rather than coping. Recent studies have shown that stressful situations may be related to or intensified by a person's cognitions (Nixon & Bryant, 2005). For example, if you're feeling depressed or anxious already, you may perceive a friend's canceling a movie date as an indication that she doesn't want to be with you rather than that perhaps a demand in her own life has kept her from making your date (Simons et al., 1993).

In reviewing certain general principles of coping with stress, it is helpful to conceptualize three interactional levels: (1) on a biological level, there are immunological defenses and damage-repair mechanisms; (2) on a psychological and interpersonal level, there are learned coping patterns, self-defenses, and support from family and friends; and (3) on a sociocultural level, there are group resources such as labor unions, religious organizations, and law enforcement agencies.

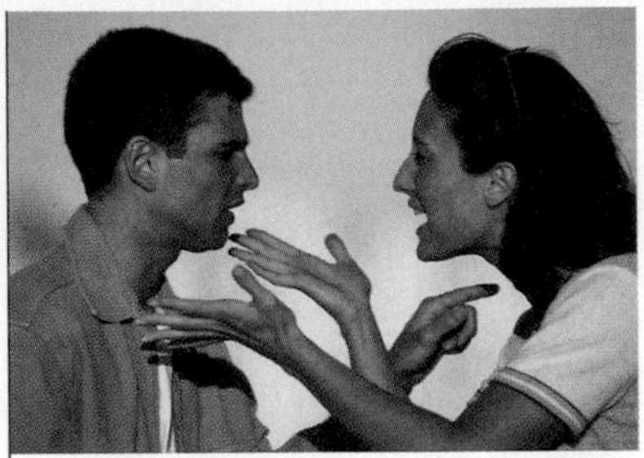

In defense-oriented coping, behavior is directed at protecting the self from hurt and disorganization, rather than solving the problem. So, for example, this couple is engaged in an argument, projecting blame on each other, instead of working together toward a task-oriented solution.

The failure of coping efforts on any of these levels may seriously increase a person's vulnerability on other levels. For example, a breakdown of immunological defenses may impair not only bodily functioning but psychological functioning as well; chronically poor psychological coping patterns may lead to other diseases. The impact of stress on bodily functioning and physical disorder will be discussed more fully in Chapter 10. In coping with stress, a person is confronted with two challenges: (1) meeting the requirements of the stressor, and (2) protecting himself or herself from psychological or physical damage and disorganization. These challenges can be met in two general ways:

TASK-ORIENTED COPING A **task-oriented response** may involve making changes in one's self, one's surroundings, or both, depending on the situation. The action may be overt, as in showing one's spouse more affection, or it may be covert, as in lowering one's level of aspiration. The action may involve retreating from the problem, attacking it directly, or trying to find a workable compromise. Each of these actions is appropriate under certain circumstances. For instance, if one is faced with a situation of overwhelming physical danger such as a forest fire, the logical task-oriented response might well be to run.

DEFENSE-ORIENTED COPING When a person's feelings of adequacy are seriously threatened by a stressor, a **defense-oriented response** tends to prevail—that is, behavior is directed primarily at protecting the self from hurt and disorganization, rather than at resolving the situation. Typically, the person using defense-oriented responses has forsaken more productive task-oriented action in favor of an overriding concern for maintaining the integrity of the self, however ill-advised and self-defeating the effort may prove to be.

There are two common types of defense-oriented responses. The first consists of responses such as crying, repetitive talking, and mourning that seem to function as psychological damage-repair mechanisms. The second type consists of the ego-defense or self-defense mechanisms discussed in Chapter 3. These mechanisms, including such responses as denial and repression, relieve tension and anxiety and protect the self from hurt and devaluation. For example, the person who fears that her or his difficulties with intimacy and warmth may have caused a relationship to end might cope defensively by projecting blame on the other person. Ego-defense mechanisms such as these protect a person from external threats such as failures in work or relationships, and from internal threats such as guilt-arousing desires or actions. They appear to protect the self in one or more of the following ways: (1) by denying, distorting, or restricting a person's experience; (2) by reducing emotional or self-involvement; and/or (3) by counteracting threat or damage.

These defense mechanisms are ordinarily used in combination rather than singly, and often they are combined with task-oriented behavior. Ego-defense mechanisms are considered maladaptive when they become the predominant means of coping with stressors and are applied in excess (Erickson, Feldman, Shirley, & Steiner, 1996). A recent theoretical examination of coping has attempted to refine and clarify the adaptation process through an interdisciplinary approach. Greve and Strobl (2004) view adaptation to stressors in terms of three modes of adaptation: defensive, proactive, and accommodative reactions. As noted earlier, defensive-responding efforts attempt to reject the problem or threat. The proactive approach, like the task-oriented responding noted above, involves the individual's attempting to cope with the stress by modifying the situation. The third strategy outlined is the accommodative effort. This approach involves the person's reevaluating the situation and adapting to changed circumstances by modifying goals and searching for more positive ways of responding to the crisis. In the view of Greve and Strobl, the only successful coping reaction is the one that stabilizes or increases well-being.

In Review

- Distinguish among stressors, stress, and coping strategies.
- How can the nature of the stressor, the individual's perception of it, his or her stress tolerance, and his or her external resources and supports modify the effects of stress?
- What are the differences between task-oriented and defense-oriented responses to stress?

The Effects of Severe Stress

When stressors are sustained or severe—for example, when a child is repeatedly abused—a person may not be able to adapt and may experience lowered capability to deal with future events and may eventually break down under stress. This lowering of adaptive functioning is referred to as **personality or psychological decompensation.**

Our reactions to stress can give us competencies that we need but would not develop unless we were challenged to do so. Stress can be damaging, however, if certain demands are too severe for our coping resources or if we believe they are and act as though they are. Severe stress can exact a high cost in terms of lowered efficiency, depletion of adaptive resources, wear and tear on the biological system, and, in extreme cases, severe personality and physical deterioration—even death.

In using its resources to meet one severe stressor, an organism may suffer a lowering of tolerance for other stressors. Selye (1976b) demonstrated that successions of noxious stimuli can have lethal effects on animals. It appears that an organism's coping resources are limited. In attempting to understand how stress affects the organism, Selye incorporated the concept of *homeostasis,* or the "balanced" state in which an organism finds itself when basic biological needs are being met. When the organism is stressed, it is thrown out of homeostatic balance. Another phenomenon involved in the effects of stress on an organism is *allostasis,* the process of adaptation or achieving stability through change. For example, in order to meet the demands of a stressor, the organism mobilizes bodily resources via the action of adrenaline. Under prolonged stress, these bodily systems are activated on a continuing basis—that is, they fail to shut down when no longer needed. The frequent mobilization of these systems under stress is referred to as an allostatic load (McEwen & Stellar, 1993), and it results in wear and tear on the body. If the organism's resources are already mobilized against one stressor, they are less available to react to others. This finding helps explain how sustained psychological stress can lower biological resistance to disease (see Chapter 10). Interestingly, prolonged stress may lead either to pathological overresponsiveness to stressors, as illustrated by the "last straw" response, or to pathological insensitivity to stressors, as shown by the loss of hope or extreme apathy in some "stressed out" people. In general, severe and sustained stress on any level leads to a serious reduction in an organism's overall adaptive capacity.

Biological Effects of Stress

Persistent or severe stress (trauma) can markedly alter a person's physical health, as will be further detailed in Chapter 10. It is difficult to specify the exact biological processes underlying a person's response to traumatic situations. Fullerton and Ursano (1997) pointed out that there are substantial gaps in psychiatry's current understanding of responses to trauma. However, one model that helps explain the course of biological decompensation under excessive stress is the **general adaptation syndrome** introduced by Selye (1956, 1976b). This explanatory view has been supported by research in the field (Cooper & Dewe, 2004). Selye found that the body's reaction to sustained and excessive stress typically occurs in three major phases: (1) an alarm reaction, in which the body's defensive forces are "called to arms" by activation of the autonomic nervous system; (2) a stage of resistance, in which biological adaptation is at the maximal level in terms of bodily resources used; and (3) exhaustion, in which bodily resources are depleted and the organism loses its ability to resist—and at this point, further exposure to stress can lead to illness and death. A diagram of Selye's general adaptation syndrome is shown in Figure 5.1 on page 152.

Stress and the Sympathetic Nervous System

Ever since the pioneering work of Cannon (1915), we have been aware of the important role the sympathetic nervous system (SNS) plays in response to stressful or dangerous situations. When an organism is faced with danger, the sympathetic nervous system discharges adrenaline to prepare the organism for "flight or fight" as follows: (1) The heart rate is increased, and blood flow (and blood pressure) are increased to the large muscles to provide the organism with the capability of reacting to physical threats. (2) The pupils are dilated so that more light enters the eye. (3) The skin constricts to limit blood loss in the event of injury. (4) Blood sugar is increased to provide more ready energy. Through this biological reaction, the organism is made ready for "emergency" physical effort, although most people today are seldom in situations that require the kind of activation provided by our ancestor's biological makeup. Our biochemistry and physiology, which are similar to those of our Stone Age

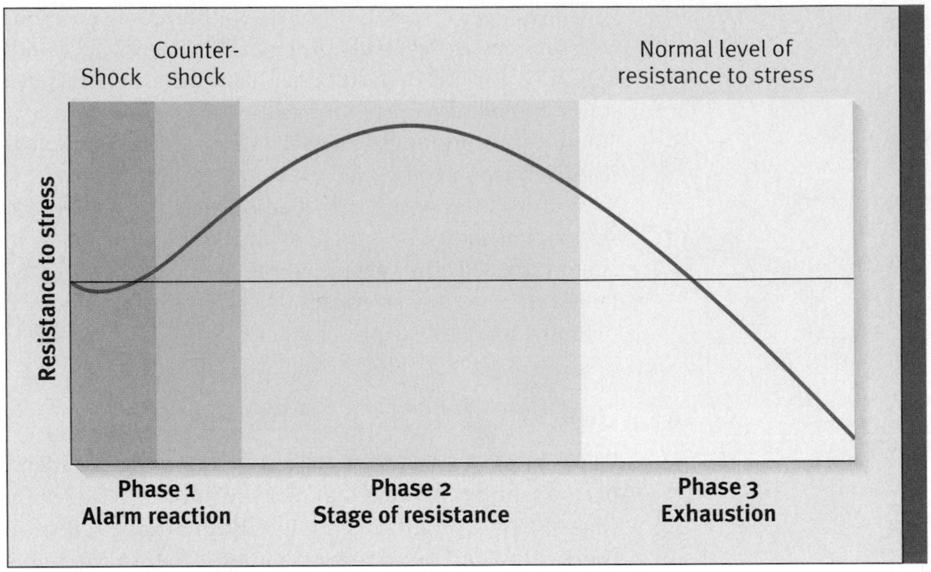

FIGURE 5.1

Selye's General Adaptation Syndrome (GAS)

Selye found that a typical person's general response to stress occurs in three phases. In the first phase (alarm reaction), the person shows an initial lowered resistance to stress or shock. If the stress persists, the person shows a defensive reaction or resistance (resistance phase) in an attempt to adapt to stress. Following extensive exposure to stress, the energy necessary for adaptation may be exhausted, resulting in the final stage of the GAS—collapse of adaptation (exhaustion phase).

ancestors, have in several important respects failed to adapt to our present circumstances (Carruthers, 1980). Our biology is perhaps more geared to such physical challenges as escaping from wild animals than to modern-day activities. Moreover, once the stress response has been activated over long periods or in an extreme manner, it becomes more difficult to return to homeostasis—that is, it is hard to shut off the organism's natural stress response.

In his informative book on the biological consequences of stress *Why Zebras Don't Get Ulcers* (1994), Robert Sapolsky has pointed out that "it might seem . . . that chronic or repeated stressors make you sick. It is actually more accurate to say that chronic or repeated stressors can potentially make you sick or can increase your risk of being sick" (p. 17).

After we have had our sympathetic nervous systems activated and are biologically ready for physical combat, what happens after the physical threat vanishes? Most of us probably believe that even after a very stressful experience, rest can completely restore us. However, any employment of the stress response inflicts a degree of wear and tear on the system. In his pioneering studies of stress, Selye found this evidence:

> Experiments on animals have clearly shown that each exposure leaves an indelible scar, in that it uses up reserves of adaptability, which cannot be replaced. It is true that immediately after some harassing experience, rest can restore us almost to the original level of fitness by eliminating acute fatigue. But the emphasis is on the word *almost*. Since we constantly go through periods of stress and rest during life, even a minute deficit of adaptation energy every day adds up—it adds up to what we call aging. (1976a, p. 429)

Considerable research has been devoted to exploring the impact of sympathetic nervous system overactivation in traumatized populations (Shalev, 2000). Many studies have examined the neurotransmitters that are involved when the SNS is activated: norepinephrine, epinephrine, and dopamine. For example, studies have compared the levels of these substances in patients undergoing severe stress and in control samples (Yehuda, 2002; Yehuda et al., 1992). Several studies have shown marked elevations in different physiological parameters such as heart rate and blood pressure. Davidson and Baum (1986) studied the effects of stress over a 5-year period following the March 1979 nuclear accident at Three Mile Island. They found that even 5 years after the incident, people who had been exposed to the incident showed elevated blood pressure and the presence of urinary noradrenaline (often associated with a persistent arousal state). These people also reported more intense psychological symptoms of stress such as intrusive thoughts than residents in the control community did.

Another way to evaluate the effects of stress on biological systems under controlled conditions involves what is referred to as a "challenge" study. In this approach, the research subject, a trauma victim perhaps, is later exposed to external stimuli resembling the original trauma—such as an audio recording of an event that is similar to the traumatic situation—while the researcher records the individual's biological response. One study found increased subjective distress, blood pressure, heart rate, and epinephrine levels in combat veterans with PTSD when they listened to tapes of war sounds (McFall, Murburg, Ko, & Veith, 1990).

Research on the role of the sympathetic nervous system in stressful situations has demonstrated that the stress response can have a significant impact on an individual's cardiovascular system (see Figure 5.2). Severe trauma and persistent stress can increase an individual's blood pressure so much that arteriosclerotic damage can occur in the

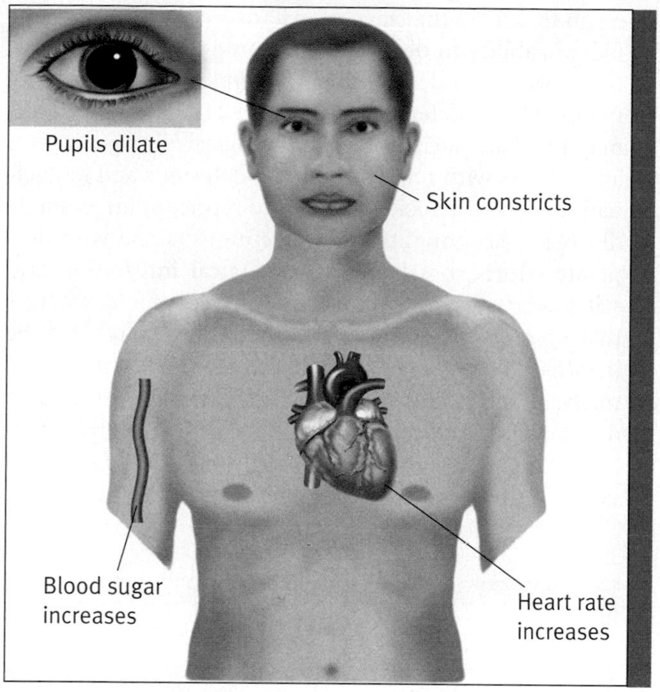

FIGURE 5.2

"Flight or Fight" Response

This drawing illustrates the situation when an organism is faced with danger and the sympathetic nervous system discharges adrenaline to prepare the organism for "flight or fight." Several processes are involved: (1) The heart rate increases, and blood flow (and blood pressure) increase to the large muscles, providing the organism with the capability of reacting to physical threats. (2) The pupils dilate so that more light enters the eye. (3) The skin constricts to limit blood loss in the event of injury. (4) Blood sugar increases to provide more ready energy.

heart and blood vessels, placing the individual at risk for hypertension, heart attack, and stroke (see Chapter 10).

STRESS AND THE IMMUNE SYSTEM Stress can also act through the hypothalamic-pituitary-adrenal glands to produce a serious endocrine imbalance that takes a major toll on a person's immune system (see Figure 5.3). The hypothalamus releases hormones that stimulate the pituitary to release other hormones that regulate many bodily functions such as tissue and bone growth and reproduction. Stress, operating through the hypothalamic-pituitary-adrenal system, can result in a suppression of the immune system (Shigenobu, 2001; Yehuda, 2002), making people vulnerable to diseases to which they would normally be immune (Maier, 2001). Although no one really knows why the immune system is suppressed during periods of stress, this emergency response process probably served a protective function in the evolution of our species. For example, it may have prevented an organism from acquiring autoimmune diseases by developing resistance (Sapolsky, 1994). However, it is clear that suppression of the immune system under chronic stress can have dire long-range health consequences. The relatively new field of **psychoneuroimmunology** focuses on the effects of stressors on the immune system. Having a lowered immune system response can mean that an individual is vulnerable to communicable diseases as well as to major mental health problems such as depression (O'Shea, 2001).

Numerous studies have shown a link between stress and the experience of extreme emotional states such as grief (Irwin et al., 1987), marital conflict (Loving, Heffner,

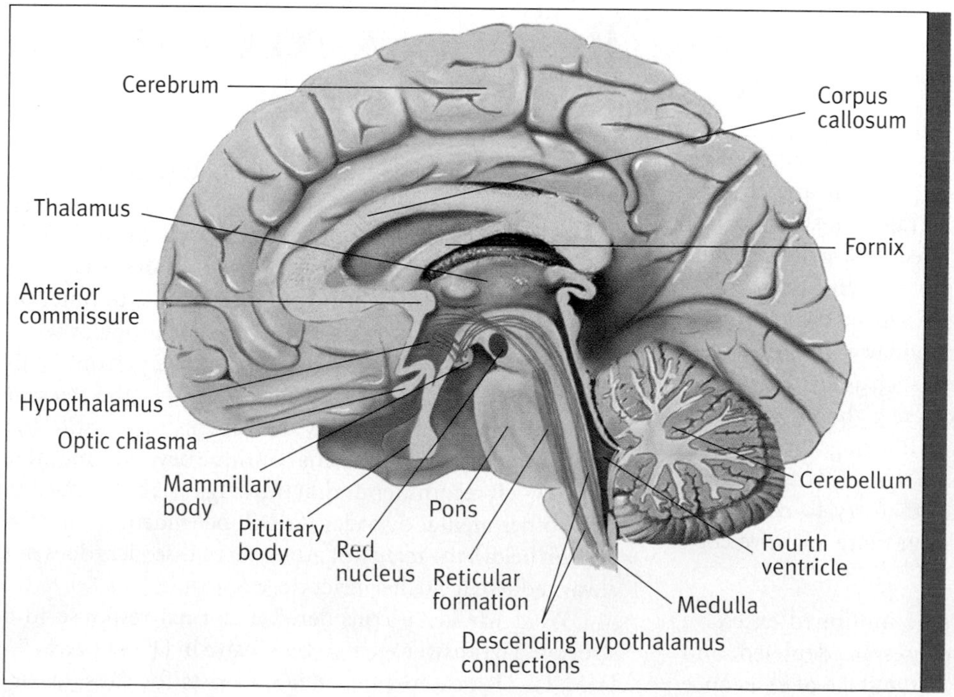

FIGURE 5.3

This diagram shows a cross section of brain structures such as the hypothalamus that are involved in human stress responses.

et al., 2004), separation and divorce (Kiecolt-Glaser & Glaser, 1988), recovery from surgery (Kiecolt-Glaser et al., 1998), and examination stress (Workman & La Via, 1987). In their evaluation of research on how changes in the immune system could affect health, Zakowski, Hall, and Baum (1992) noted the extreme importance of the immune system in response to stress. The organs and cells associated with the immune system provide the body's major defense against foreign organisms and other potential dangers. The skin prevents the intrusion of a vast onslaught of microbes and molecules in the air and water around us; and the rest of the immune system provides a strong defense against diseases such as cancer and human immunodeficiency virus (HIV) disease. They concluded that the immune system protects us against autoimmune diseases and maintains a balance of cells that maximizes our survival.

Psychological Effects of Long-Term Stress

Personality decompensation in the face of trauma is somewhat easier to specify. It appears to follow a course resembling that of biological decompensation and may in fact involve specific biological responses:

1. ALARM AND MOBILIZATION. First, a person's resources for coping with a trauma are alerted and mobilized. Typically involved at this stage are emotional arousal, increased tension, heightened sensitivity, greater alertness (vigilance), and determined efforts at self-control. At the same time, in attempts to meet the emergency, the person undertakes various coping measures that may be task-oriented, defense-oriented, or a combination of the two. During this stage, symptoms of maladjustment may appear, such as continuous anxiety and tension, gastrointestinal upset or other bodily diseases, and lowered efficiency, signs that the mobilization of adaptive resources is inadequate.

2. RESISTANCE. If trauma continues, a person is often able to find some means of dealing with it and thus to maintain some adjustment to life. Trauma resistance may be achieved temporarily by concerted, task-oriented coping measures; the use of ego-defense mechanisms may also be intensified during this period. Even in the resistance stage, however, indications of strain may exist. For example, psychophysiological symptoms such as acute stomach distress and mild reality distortions (e.g., hypersensitivity to sounds during the late phases of this stage) may occur. In addition, the person may become rigid and cling to previously developed defenses rather than try to reevaluate the traumatic situation and work out more adaptive coping patterns.

3. EXHAUSTION. In the face of continued excessive trauma, a person's adaptive resources are depleted, and the coping patterns called forth in the stage of resistance begin to fail. As the stage of exhaustion begins, the individual's ability to deal with continuing stress is substantially lowered, and she or he may employ exaggerated and inappropriate defensive measures. The latter reactions may be characterized by psychological disorganization and a break with reality involving delusions and hallucinations. These delusions appear to represent increasingly disorganized thoughts and perceptions, along with desperate efforts to salvage psychological integration and self-integrity by restructuring reality. Metabolic changes that impair normal brain functioning may also be involved in delusional and hallucinatory behavior. Eventually, if the excessive stress continues, the process of decompensation proceeds to a stage of severe psychological disorganization involving continuous, uncontrolled violence, apathy, stupor, and perhaps even death.

In Review

- Describe the three phases of Selye's general adaptation syndrome. Compare them with the three stages of personality decompensation.
- What is the effect of stress on the sympathetic nervous system?
- What is the effect of stress on the immune system?

Adjustment Disorder: Reactions to Common Life Stressors

A person whose response to a common stressor such as marriage, divorce, childbirth, or losing a job is maladaptive and occurs within 3 months of the stressor can be said to have an **adjustment disorder.** The person's reaction is considered maladaptive if he or she is unable to function as usual or if the person's reaction to the particular stressor is excessive. In adjustment disorder, the person's maladjustment lessens or disappears when (1) the stressor has subsided or (2) the individual learns to adapt to the stressor. Should the symptoms continue beyond 6 months, DSM-IV-TR recommends that the diagnosis be changed to some other mental disorder. As will be evident in the discussion below, the reality of adjustment disorders does not always adhere to such a strict time schedule.

What would be considered a normal response to a stressor? The answer seems a bit elusive in DSM criteria. In DSM-IV-TR no separate category exists for stress disorders; rather, acute stress disorder and post-traumatic stress disorder are categorized under the anxiety disorders.

Clearly, not all reactions to stressors are adjustment disorders. What seems to push a normal reaction into this category of post-traumatic stress disorder is the inability to function as usual, and yet this criterion applies to many other disorders (such as anxiety disorder) as well. We will not resolve this uncertainty any time soon; it is perhaps more important to recognize that adjustment disorder is probably the least stigmatizing and mildest diagnosis a therapist can assign to a client.

Managing the stress associated with unemployment requires great coping strength. Some people can deal with setbacks and can adapt without suffering long-range adjustment difficulties once the initial stressful situation has ended. The impact of chronic unemployment, however, can be shattering and can have serious long-term effects.

Adjustment Disorder Caused by Unemployment

Work-related problems can produce great stress in employees (Williams, Barefoot, et al., 1997). One extremely stressful situation that occurs all too frequently in today's business climate is loss of gainful employment. Managing the stress associated with unemployment requires great coping strength, especially for people who have previously earned an adequate living. The misfortune of losing one's job and being unable to find suitable employment has been common in the United States since the Great Depression of the 1930s. The frequent restructuring of businesses has resulted in the laying off of many people, transforming many thriving communities into depressed areas and many industrious employees into unemployed or underemployed people. In almost every community, one can find workers who have been laid off from jobs they had held for many years and who are facing the end of their unemployment compensation.

Unemployment is an especially acute problem in some population subgroups. For example, many young minority males live in a permanent economic depression that is more pervasive and just as debilitating as the Great Depression was for the white majority (Department of Labor, 1999). Indeed, for young black men, rates of unemployment are over twice those for whites. The long-range psychological consequences of unemployment can be devastating. Some people can deal with the setback of sudden job loss and can adapt without long-range adjustment difficulties once the initial stressful situation has ended. For others, however, unemployment can have serious long-term effects. The impact of chronic unemployment on a person's self-concept, sense of worth, and feeling of belongingness is shattering, especially in an affluent society.

Adjustment Disorder Caused by Bereavement

The sudden, unexpected death of a loved one accounts for about one-third of all post-traumatic stress disorder, or PTSD, cases seen in a community (Breslau, Kessler, Chilcoat, et al., 1998). When someone close to us dies, we are psychologically stunned. Often the first reaction is disbelief. Then, as we begin to realize the significance of the death, our feelings of sadness, grief, and despair (even, perhaps, anger at the departed person) frequently overwhelm us.

Grief over the loss of a loved one is a natural process that allows the survivors to mourn their loss and then free themselves for life without the departed person. Some people do not go through the typical process of grieving, perhaps because of their personality makeup (defensive coping styles) or as a consequence of their particular situations. A person may, for instance, be expected to be stoical about his or her feelings or may have to manage the family's affairs. Another person may develop exaggerated or prolonged depression after the grieving process should have ended. A normal grieving process typically lasts up to about a year and may involve negative health effects such as high blood pressure, changes in eating habits, and even thoughts of suicide (Prigerson, Bierhals, Kasl, Reynolds, et al., 1997).

Complicated or prolonged bereavement is often found in situations where there has been an untimely or unexpected death (Kim & Jacobs, 1995). Pathological reactions to death are also more likely to occur in people who have a history of emotional problems or who harbor a great deal of resentment and hostility toward the deceased and thus experience intense guilt. They are usually profoundly depressed and may, in some instances, be suffering from major depression (see Chapter 7). The following case illustrates an extreme pattern of withdrawal or pathological grief reaction (and, in this instance, a positive outcome) following a tragic death.

Some people express extreme reactions to death of a loved one. When Marine casualty officers told Carlos Arredondo of his son's death in Iraq, Arredondo became distraught. He smashed the windows of the Marine Corps van, climbed inside, and then lit the van on fire. Arredondo was saved by the marine officers, though he suffered severe burns.

case STUDY — Nadine's Grief

Nadine, a 66-year-old former high school teacher, lived with Charles, age 67, her husband of 40 years (also a retired teacher). The couple had been nearly inseparable from the time they first met—they even taught at the same schools during most of their teaching careers. They lived in a semirural community where they had worked and raised their three children, all of whom had married and moved to a large metropolitan area about 100 miles away. For years they had planned their retirement and had hoped to travel around the country visiting friends. A week before their fortieth anniversary, Charles had a heart attack and, after 5 days in the intensive care unit, had a second heart attack and died.

Nadine took Charles' death quite hard. Even though she had much emotional support from her many friends and her children, she had great difficulty adjusting. Elaine, one of her daughters, went and stayed a few days and encouraged her to come to the city for a while. Nadine declined the persistent invitation even though she had little to do at home. Friends called on her frequently, but she seemed almost to resent their presence. In the months following the funeral, Nadine's reclusive behavior persisted. Several well-wishers told Elaine that her mother was not leaving the house even to go shopping. They reported that Nadine sat alone in the darkened house, not answering the phone and showing reluctance to come to the door. She had also lost interest in activities she had once enjoyed.

Greatly worried about her mother's welfare, Elaine organized a campaign to get her mother out of the house. Each of Nadine's children and their families took turns visiting and taking her places until she finally began to show interest in living again. In time, Nadine agreed to go to each of their homes for visits. This proved a therapeutic step—Nadine had always been fond of children and took pleasure in the time spent with her eight grandchildren—and she actually extended the visits longer than she had planned.

Adjustment Disorder Caused by Divorce or Separation

The deterioration or ending of an intimate relationship is a potent stressor that is frequently cited as the reason why people seek psychological treatment. Divorce, though more generally accepted today, is still a tragic and usually stressful outcome to a once close and trusting relationship. We noted in Chapter 3 that marital disruption is a major source of vulnerability to psychopathology: People who are recently divorced or separated are markedly overrepresented among people with psychological problems.

Many factors make a divorce or separation unpleasant and stressful for everyone concerned: the acknowledgment of failure in a relationship important both personally and culturally; the necessity of explaining the failure to family and friends; the loss of valuable friendships that often accompanies the rupture; the economic uncertainties and hardships that both partners frequently experience; and, when children are involved, the problem of custody, including court battles, living and visitation arrangements, and so on.

After the divorce or separation, new problems typically emerge. Adjustment to a single life, perhaps after many years of marriage, can be a difficult experience. Because in many cases it seems that friends as well as assets have to be divided, new friendships need to be made. New romantic relationships may require a great deal of personal change. Even when the separation was relatively amicable, new strength to adapt and cope is needed. Thus it is not surprising that divorce may motivate the task-oriented coping response of seeking counseling.

In Review

- What is an adjustment disorder according to DSM-IV-TR?
- What "level of stressor" is required for a diagnosis of Adjustment Disorder?

Post-Traumatic Stress Disorder: Reactions to Catastrophic Events

Severe psychological and physical symptoms can result from sudden, unexpected environmental crises. These severe symptoms, often referred to as **post-traumatic stress disorder (PTSD),** can include some or many of the following:

- The traumatic event is persistently reexperienced by the person through intrusive, recurring thoughts or nightmares.
- The person avoids stimuli associated with the trauma (such as cars if the person was in a car crash).
- The person may experience chronic tension or irritability, often accompanied by insomnia and the inability to tolerate noise.
- The person may have impaired concentration and memory.
- Feelings of depression may take over, and the individual may avoid social situations or environments where he or she would be exposed to excitable stimuli.

Clearly, PTSD includes elements of anxiety—generalized feelings of fear and apprehension—but because it bears such a close relationship to the experience of major stress, we discuss it here and follow in Chapter 6 with coverage of the other anxiety disorders.

Prevalence of PTSD in the General Population

Until quite recently, no estimates of the prevalence of the disorder in the general population had been available. Many potential sources of crisis or trauma exist in contemporary society, and post-traumatic stress disorder symptoms are by no means rare in the general population. One recent study reported that nearly half of adults living in the United States will experience a traumatic event in their lives, but only 10 percent of women and 5 percent of men develop post-traumatic stress disorder (Ozer & Weiss, 2004). One example of a traumatizing event that resulted in adaptation challenges is a recent earthquake in Turkey. Başoğlu, Kiliç, et al., 2004 reported that the rates of PTSD and depression that was comorbid with PTSD were, respectively, 23 and 16 percent at the epicenter of the quake and 14 and 8 percent in Istanbul, about 100 kilometers distance from the center of the quake. More common traumatic events such as accidents and violence can result in long-term adjustment problems for victims (Falsetti et al., 1995; Norris & Kaniasty, 1994). The formal diagnosis of PTSD was not defined until 1980, and the known cases of the disorder were largely limited to war veterans and disaster victims (Breslau, 2001). Estimates of the prevalence of PTSD in the general population have been variable, but the disorder appears to occur in about 1 in 12 adults at some time in their lives (Breslau, 2001). The U.S. National Comorbidity study (Kessler et al., 1995) estimated the rate to be at about 7.8 percent of the population (5 percent for men and 10.4 percent for women). The reported rates are lower in national populations with fewer natural disasters and lower crime. In a review of the published research on the prevalence of PTSD, Resick (2001) recently estimated that 5 to 6 percent of men and 10 to 12 percent of women in the United States have experienced PTSD at some time in their lives. Breslau (2001) concluded that PTSD is about twice as prevalent in females as in males, largely because of the more common occurrence of assaultive violence—for example, beatings and sexual assault—against women.

PTSD, of course, can also occur along with other disorders (Ouimette & Brown, 2004). Brown, Stout, & Mueller (1999) found that 54 percent of their substance abusers also had diagnosable PTSD. Kessler et al. (1995) noted that approximately 16 percent of people with PTSD had one other disorder and that 54 percent of people with PTSD had three or more other diagnoses.

Many, if not most, people who are exposed to plane crashes, automobile accidents, explosions, fires, earthquakes, tornadoes, sexual assaults, or other terrifying experiences show psychological shock reactions such as confusion and disorganization. The symptoms may vary greatly, depending on the nature and severity of the terrifying experience, the degree of surprise, and the personality of the individual. For example, 6 flight attendants who survived a plane crash in which 47 passengers died were evaluated 8 months after the crash—all 6 met criteria for PTSD. Eighteen months after the crash they showed no depression but continued to experience a high level of stress (Marks, Yule, & De Silva, 1999).

Distinguishing between Acute Stress Disorder and Post-Traumatic Stress

The DSM-IV-TR provides two major classifications for post-traumatic stress disorder: Acute Stress Disorder and Post-Traumatic Stress Disorder. For both of these disorders, the stressor is unusually severe, such as the destruction of one's home, seeing another person hurt or killed, or being the victim of physical violence. Where the disorders

DSM-IV-TR

Criteria for Acute Stress Disorder

A. The person has been exposed to a traumatic event in which both of the following were present:
   (1) the person experienced, witnessed, or was confronted with an event or events that involved actual or threatened death or serious injury, or a threat to the physical integrity of self or others
   (2) the person's response involved intense fear, helplessness, or horror.

B. Either while experiencing or after experiencing the distressing event, the individual has three (or more) of the following dissociative symptoms:
   (1) a subjective sense of numbing, detachment, or absence of emotional responsiveness
   (2) a reduction in awareness of his or her surroundings (e.g., "being in a daze")
   (3) de-realization
   (4) depersonalization
   (5) dissociative amnesia (i.e., inability to recall an important aspect of the trauma)

C. The traumatic event is persistently re-experienced in a least one of the following ways: recurrent images, thoughts, dreams, illusions, flashback episodes, or a sense of reliving the experience; or distress on exposure to reminders of the traumatic event.

D. Marked avoidance of stimuli that arouse recollections of the trauma (e.g., thoughts, feelings, conversations, activities, places, people).

E. Marked symptoms of anxiety or increased arousal (e.g., difficulty sleeping, irritability, poor concentration, hypervigilance, exaggerated startle response, motor restlessness).

F. The disturbance causes clinically significant distress or impairment in social, occupational, or other important areas of functioning or impairs the individual's ability to pursue some necessary task, such as obtaining necessary assistance or mobilizing personal resources by telling family members about the traumatic experience.

G. The disturbance lasts for a minimum of 2 days and a maximum of 4 weeks and occurs within 4 weeks of the traumatic event.

H. The disturbance is not due to the direct physiological effects of a substance (e.g., a drug of abuse, a medication) or a general medical condition, is not better accounted for by the Brief Psychotic Disorder, and is not merely an exacerbation of a preexisting Axis I or Axis II disorder.

Source: *American Psychiatric Association, 2000.*

differ is in timing and duration of symptoms. **Acute stress disorder** occurs within 4 weeks of the traumatic event and lasts for a minimum of 2 days and a maximum of 4 weeks. If the symptoms last longer, the appropriate diagnosis is post-traumatic stress disorder. The latter diagnosis, which is not given unless the symptoms last for at least 1 month, can be further specified in terms of when the PTSD symptoms begin. If the symptoms begin within 6 months of the traumatic event, then the reaction is considered to be acute. If symptoms begin more than 6 months after the traumatic situation, the reaction is considered to be delayed (see the study by Gray, Bolen, & Litz, 2004, on Somalia peacekeepers). The delayed version of PTSD is less well defined and more difficult to diagnose than disorders that emerge shortly after the precipitating incident. Some authorities have questioned whether a delayed reaction should be diagnosed as PTSD at all; instead, some would categorize such a reaction as some other anxiety-based disorder. It is important to keep in mind that the criteria for post-traumatic stress disorders specify that the reactions last for at least 1 month.

A **disaster syndrome** appears to characterize the reactions of many victims of major catastrophes in which great loss or public suffering has been identified (see The World Around Us 5.1 on p. 160). This syndrome may be described in terms of the reactions during the traumatic experience, the initial reactions after it (the acute post-traumatic stress), and the long-lasting or late-arising complications (the chronic or delayed post-traumatic stress).

A victim's initial responses following a disaster typically involve three stages: (1) the shock stage, in which the victim is stunned, dazed, and apathetic; (2) the suggestible stage, in which the victim tends to be passive, suggestible, and willing to take directions from rescue workers or others; and (3) the recovery stage, in which the victim may be tense and apprehensive and show generalized anxiety but gradually regains psychological equilibrium, often showing a need to tell repeatedly about the catastrophic event. It is in the third stage that post-traumatic stress disorder may develop. Recurrent nightmares and the typical need to tell the same story about the disaster again and again appear to be mechanisms for reducing anxiety and desensitizing the self to the traumatic experience. Tension, apprehensiveness, and hypersensitivity appear to be residual effects of the shock reaction and to reflect the person's realization that the world can become overwhelmingly dangerous and threatening.

In some cases, the clinical picture may be complicated by intense grief and depression. When a person feels that his or her own personal inadequacy contributed to the loss of loved ones in a disaster, the picture may be further complicated by strong feelings of guilt, and the post-traumatic stress may last for months.

In some instances the guilt of the survivors seems to center on the belief that they deserved to survive no more,

DSM-IV-TR

Criteria for Post-Traumatic Stress Disorder

A. The person has been exposed to a traumatic event in which: They experienced, witnessed, or were confronted with an event or events that *involved* actual or threatened death or serious injury, or a threat to the physical integrity of self or others; and the person's response involved intense fear, helplessness, or horror.

B. The traumatic event is persistently re-experienced in one (or more) of the following:

(1) recurrent and intrusive distressing recollections of the event

(2) recurrent distressing dreams of the event; acting or feeling as if the traumatic event were recurring

(3) intense psychological distress at exposure to internal or external cues that symbolize or resemble an aspect of the traumatic event

(4) psychological reactivity on exposure to internal or external cues that symbolize or resemble an aspect of the traumatic event

C. Persistent avoidance of stimuli associated with the trauma and numbing of general responsiveness (not present before the trauma), as indicated by three (or more) of the following:

(1) efforts to avoid thoughts, feelings, or conversations associated with the trauma

(2) efforts to avoid activities, places, or people that arouse recollections of the trauma

(3) inability to recall an important aspect of the trauma

(4) markedly diminished interest or participation in significant activities

(5) feelings of detachment or estrangement from others

(6) restricted range of affect (e.g., unable to have loving feelings)

(7) sense of a foreshortened future (e.g., does not expect to have a career, marriage, children, or a normal life span)

D. Persistent symptoms of increased arousal that were not present before the trauma), as indicated by two (or more) of the following:

(1) difficulty falling or staying asleep

(2) irritability or outburst of anger

(3) difficulty concentrating

(4) exaggerated startle response

E. The duration of the disturbance is more than 1 month.

F. The disturbance causes clinically significant distress or impairment in social, occupational, or other important areas of functioning.

Specify if:

Acute: if duration of symptoms is less than 3 months;

Chronic: if duration of symptoms is 3 months or more

Specify if:

With delayed Onset: if onset of symptoms is at least 6 months after the stressor.

Source: *American Psychiatric Association, 2000.*

or perhaps even less, than those who died. As one flight attendant explained after the crash of a Miami-bound jet in the Florida Everglades that took many lives, "I kept thinking, I'm alive. Thank God. But I wondered why I was spared. I felt, It's not fair" (*Time*, 1973, p. 53).

Extreme post-traumatic symptoms are not uncommon following serious accidents. Blanchard, Hickling, Barton, and Taylor (1995) followed up with a group of motor vehicle accident victims who had sought medical attention as a result of their accidents. They found that one-third of those who initially met PTSD diagnostic criteria had not experienced a reduction in symptoms at a 12-month follow-up. In another incident, 1 month after a mass-murder spree by a gunman in Texas, psychologists interviewed 136 terrorized survivors and diagnosed 20 percent of the men and 36 percent of the women as having PTSD. In a review and comparison of all published disaster research in which estimates of postdisaster psychopathology were included,

5.1 THE WORLD AROUND US

A Trauma of Incredible Proportions

Tragedy can occur suddenly, unexpectedly, and on an unimaginable scale, leaving survivors in a state of shock. On September 11, 2001, anti-American terrorists struck the World Trade Center in New York with devastating effect. Flying two passenger jets into both towers of the World Trade Center, a third airliner into the Pentagon Building in Washington, DC, and a fourth into the ground in rural Pennsylvania, groups of terrorists left the world in a state of stunned disbelief. These acts killed over 3,000 people from 80 nations, including hundreds of emergency personnel attempting to rescue victims from the fire-ravaged buildings as they collapsed, leaving tens of thousands of people to face the incredible aftermath of loss.

The events of September 11 produced an intense period of grief, not only for the families and friends of the victims, but for the entire nation and many people around the world. Thousands of tragic stories unfolded over the days following the attack.

Even those who did make it out of the buildings alive were scarred by the experience. For example, Dwyer (2001) recounted the experiences of a window washer, Jan D., who was riding up the elevators of the World Trade Center with several other people to the sixty-ninth floor to work. Suddenly they felt a muted thud. Next the elevator swung from side to side like a pendulum and then fell until someone pushed the emergency button. The elevator finally came to a stop, and they found themselves trapped between floors. Shortly afterward they heard an announcement that there had been an explosion. Smoke began to seep into the elevator. After a few moments, they forced open the elevator door:

> They faced a wall, stenciled with the number "50." That particular elevator bank did not serve the 50th floor, so there was no need for an opening. To escape they would have to make one themselves. Mr. D. felt the wall. Sheetrock. Having worked in construction in his early days, he knew that it could be cut with a sharp knife. No one had a knife. From his bucket, Mr. D. drew his squeegee. He slid its metal edge against the wall, back and forth, over and over. He was relieved by other men. Against the smoke, they breathed through handkerchiefs dampened in a con-

This Indian child shows distress as he looks over the damage done to his home by the December 26, 2004, Asian Tsunami. Many people, including children, will suffer post-traumatic stress after extreme events such as the tsunami.

on average 17 percent of victims showed psychological adjustment problems in the aftermath of the disaster (Rubonis & Bickman, 1991). This is similar to the findings of La Greca, Silverman, Vernberg, and Prinstein (1996) that 18 percent of the children studied after Hurricane Andrew had symptoms of PTSD.

A person's traumatic reaction state may be more complicated in cases of severe loss. For example, an individual who becomes paralyzed in an automobile accident in which his wife is killed not only has to deal with the grief over the loss of a close relationship but also must do so during a long period of rehabilitation and a severely changed life. The psychological effects of applying for disability compensation may also complicate recovery from a disaster. Personal damage lawsuits tend to prolong post-traumatic symptoms because of the emotional hardships of litigation (Egendorf, 1986).

The Trauma of Rape

Rape is the act of forcing someone to engage in sexual intercourse against his or her will—a situation that can inflict severe trauma on a victim. In our society, rape occurs with alarming frequency. An extensive

tainer of milk that Mr. P. (another occupant of the elevator) had just bought.

Sheetrock comes in panels about one inch thick, Mr. D. recalled. They cut an inch, then two inches. Mr. D.'s hand ached. As he carved into the third panel, his hand shook, he fumbled the squeegee and it dropped down the shaft.

He had one tool left: a short metal squeegee handle. They carried on with fists, feet, and handle, cutting an irregular rectangle about 12 by 18 inches. Finally, they hit a layer of white tiles. A bathroom. They broke the tiles. One by one, the men squirmed through the opening, headfirst, sideways, popping into the floor near a sink. . . .

By then, about 9:30, the 50th floor was already deserted, except for firefighters astonished to see the six men emerge. . . . On the excruciating single-file descent through the smoke, someone teased Mr. D. about bringing his bucket. "The company might not order me another one," he replied. At the 15th floor, Mr. L. said, "We heard a thunderous, metallic roar. I thought our lives had surely ended then." The south tower was collapsing. It was 9:59. Mr. D. dropped his bucket. The firefighters shouted to hurry. At 23 minutes past 10, they burst onto the street, ran for phones, sipped oxygen, and, five minutes later, fled as the north tower collapsed. Their escape had taken 95 of the 100 minutes. "It took up to one and a half minutes to clear each floor, longer at the lower levels," said Mr. M., an engineer with the Port Authority. "If the elevator had stopped at the 60th floor, instead of the 50th, we would have been five minutes too late."

"And that man with the squeegee was like our guardian angel."

Since that day, Mr. D. has stayed home with his wife and children. He has pieced together the faces of the missing with the men and women he knew in the stations of his old life: The security guard at the Japanese bank on the 93rd floor who used to let him in at 6:30; the people at Carr Futures on 92; the head of the Port Authority. Their faces keep him awake at night.

His hands, the one that held the squeegee and the other that carried the bucket, shake with absence. (Dwyer, 2001)

Following the tragedy, thousands of family members and survivors sought crisis intervention assistance in their efforts to deal with the incredible losses. Many organizations and individuals joined in the effort to help the survivors deal with the devastating trauma by providing emotional support and counseling for victims (McCaslin, Jacobs, et al. 2005).

survey of college health behavior reported that 20 percent of female students acknowledged having been forced to have sexual intercourse (Brener, McMahon, et al., 1999). Although men and boys can and do experience rape, in most cases the victim is a woman. Rape is the most frequent cause of PTSD in women (Cloitre, 2004). In Chapter 13 we consider the pathology of rapists; our concern in this chapter is with a victim's response to rape. In stranger rape—a rape in which the victim does not know the offender—the victim is likely to experience strong fear of physical harm and death. In acquaintance rape, the reaction is apt to be slightly different (Frazier & Burnett, 1994). In such a situation the victim may feel not only fear but also betrayal by someone she had trusted. She may feel more responsible for what happened and experience greater guilt. She may also be more hesitant to seek help or report the rape to the police out of fear that she will be held partially responsible for it.

The age and life circumstances of a victim may also influence her reaction (Ullman & Filipas, 2001). For a young child who knows nothing about sexual behavior, rape can lead to sexual scars and confusion, particularly if the child is encouraged to forget about the experience without thoroughly talking it over first (Browne & Finkelhor, 1986). For young adult women, rape can increase the conflicts over independence and separation that are normal in this age group. In an effort to be helpful, parents of these victims may encourage various forms of regression, such as moving back to the family home, which may interfere with mastery of this developmental phase. Married rape victims with children face the task of explaining their experience to their children. Sometimes the sense of vulnerability that results from rape leaves a woman feeling temporarily unable to care for her children.

Husbands and boyfriends, if unsympathetic to what a woman is undergoing after being raped, can negatively influence a rape victim's adjustment. Rejection, blaming, uncontrolled anger at the offender, or insistence on a quick resumption of sexual activity can serve to increase a victim's negative feelings.

McCann, Sakheim, and Abrahamson (1988) found that the experience of rape affected women in five areas of functioning. First, physical disturbances, including hyperarousal or anxiousness (typical symptoms of PTSD), were common. One recent study found that women who had a history of sexual assault tended to see themselves as in poorer health (Golding, Cooper, & George, 1997). Second, women who had been sexually assaulted tended to experience emotional problems such as anxiety, depressed mood, and low self-esteem. Fierman and colleagues (1993) found that prior trauma, particularly sexual abuse, physical abuse, and rape, were prominent in the life histories of patients seeking treatment at an anxiety clinic. Falsetti and colleagues (1995) reported that 94 percent of their sample of women with panic disorders had histories of criminal victimization. Third, following rape, women tended to report cognitive dysfunction, including disturbed concentration and the experience of intrusive thoughts (Valentiner, Foa, Riggs, & Gershuny, 1996), and some reported negative beliefs about other people and concerns for their own safety even a year later (Frazier, Conlon, & Glaser, 2001). Fourth, many women reported engaging in atypical behavioral acts such as aggressive, antisocial actions and substance abuse after being raped. Finally, many women who experience rape tend to report having interference in their social relationships, including sexual problems, intimacy problems, and further victimization. All these symptoms reflect those of PTSD. See Figure 5.4 for a summary of the psychological processes rape victims go through as they cope with their experiences.

LONG-TERM EFFECTS Whether a rape victim will experience serious psychological problems depends to a large extent on her past coping skills, resiliency in dealing with problems, and level of psychological functioning. A resilient and previously well-adjusted woman usually will regain her prior equilibrium, but rape can precipitate severe pathology in a woman with psychological difficulties (Meyer & Taylor, 1986). Victims' perceptions of whether they can control future circumstances influence the recovery process. Women who tended to blame themselves or thought more about why the rape occurred were slower to recover from the trauma than those who believed that future assaults were less likely (Frazier & Schauben, 1994). When problems do continue, or when they become manifest later in a delayed post-traumatic stress disorder, they are likely to involve anxiety, depression, withdrawal, and difficulties in heterosexual relationships (Gold, 1986; Koss, 1983).

COUNSELING RAPE VICTIMS Although many survivors of sexual assault postpone seeking help with their emotional recovery (Symes, 2000), some research has suggested that women who participate in disclosure about the rape tend to have more positive and fewer negative outcomes (Wasco, Campbell, et al., 2004). The women's movement has played a crucial role in establishing specialized rape counseling services such as hotlines and rape crisis centers staffed by trained paraprofessionals who provide general support for victims, both individually and in groups. In some situations, specific trauma intervention programs have proved effective in treating rape victims (Petrak & Hedge, 2002). Many crisis centers also have victim advocacy services in which a trained volunteer accompanies a woman to a hospital or police station, helps her understand the procedures, and assists her with the red tape. The advocate may also accompany the person to meetings with legal representatives and to the trial—experiences that tend to temporarily reactivate the trauma of the rape.

The Trauma of Military Combat

Many people who have been involved in the turmoil of war experience devastating psychological problems for months or even years afterward (Garakani, Hirschowitz, & Katz, 2004). During World War I, traumatic reactions to combat conditions were called "shell shock," a term coined by a British pathologist, Col. Frederick Mott (1919), who regarded these reactions as organic conditions produced by minute brain hemorrhages. It was gradually realized, however, that only a small percentage of such cases represented physical injury. Most victims were suffering instead from the general combat situation, with its physical fatigue, ever-present threat of death or mutilation, and severe psychological shocks. During World War II, traumatic reactions to combat were known as *operational fatigue* and *war neuroses,* before finally being termed *combat fatigue* or *combat exhaustion* in the Korean and Vietnam Wars. Even the latter terms were none too aptly chosen, because they implied that physical exhaustion played a more important role than was usually the case. They did, however, serve to distinguish such disorders from other psychological disorders, such as drug use, that happened to occur under war conditions but might well have occurred in civilian life.

It has been estimated that in World War II, 10 percent of Americans in combat developed combat exhaustion. However, the actual incidence is not known, because many soldiers received supportive therapy at their battalion aid stations and were returned to combat within a few hours. In fact, combat exhaustion caused the single greatest loss of personnel during that war (Bloch, 1969). During the Korean War the incidence of combat exhaustion dropped from an initial high of over 6 percent to 3.7 percent; 27 percent of medical discharges were for psychiatric reasons (Bell, 1958). In the Vietnam War the figure dropped to less than 1.5 percent for combat exhaustion, with a negligible number of discharges for psychiatric disorders (Allerton, 1979; Bourne, 1970). The prevalence of PTSD symptoms among Gulf War veterans was reported to be 12.1 percent compared with non–Gulf War veterans (4.3 percent) (Kang, Natelson, et al., 2003). A recent survey of military personnel serving in Afghanistan and Iraq reported significant percentages of soldiers who met the criteria for depression, PTSD, and generalized anxiety disorder. Hoge, Castro, et al. (2004) found that between 15.6 percent and 17.1 percent of participants reported these symptoms after duty in Iraq compared with 11.2 percent

Anticipatory Phase

This period occurs before an actual rape, when an offender "sets up" a victim and the victim begins to perceive that a dangerous situation exists. In the early minutes of this phase, the victim often uses defense mechanisms such as denial to preserve an illusion of invulnerability. Common thoughts are, "This isn't really happening to me" or "He doesn't really mean that."

↓

Impact Phase

This phase begins with a victim's recognition that she is actually going to be raped and ends when the rape is over. The victim's first reaction is usually intense fear for her life, a fear much stronger than her fear of the sexual act itself. Symonds (1976) has described the paralytic effect of intense fear on victims of crime, showing that this fear usually leads to varying degrees of disintegration in the victim's functioning and possibly to a complete inability to act. Barlow (Anxiety, 2002) indicated that there is evidence that people experiencing intense anxiety go into a state of immobility. Roth and Lebowitz (1988) found that the sexual trauma confronts the individual with emotions and images that are difficult to manage and may have long-term adjustment consequences. When the victim later recalls her behavior during the assault, she may feel guilty about not reacting more efficiently, and she needs to be reassured that her actions were normal.

↓

Post-Traumatic Recoil Phase

Following rape, many women experience symptoms of hyperarousal and numbing along with continuing intrusive symptoms and avoidance behavior (Feuer, Nishith, & Resick, 2005). This phase begins immediately after a rape. Burgess and Holmstrom (1974, 1976) observed two emotional styles among the rape victims they interviewed in hospital emergency rooms: (1) an expressed style, in which feelings of fear and anxiety were shown through crying, sobbing, and restlessness, and (2) a controlled style, in which feelings appeared to be masked by a calm, controlled, subdued facade. Regardless of style, most victims felt guilty about the way they had reacted to the offender and wished that they had reacted faster or fought harder. (Excessive self-blame has been associated with poor long-term adjustment; see Meyer & Taylor, 1986.) Feelings of dependency were increased, and victims often had to be encouraged and helped to call friends or parents and to make other arrangements.

↓

Reconstitution Phase

This phase begins as a victim starts to make plans for leaving the emergency room or crisis center. It ends, often many months later, when the stress of the rape has been assimilated, the experience shared with significant others, and the victim's self-concept restored. Certain behaviors and symptoms are typical during this phase:

1. Self-protective activities, such as changing one's telephone number and moving to a new residence, are common. The victim's fear is often well justified at this point, because even in the unlikely event that the offender has been arrested and charged with rape, he is often out on bail.
2. Frightening nightmares in which the rape is relived are common. As the victim moves closer to assimilating the experience, the content of the dreams may gradually shift until the victim successfully fights off the assailant.
3. Phobias often develop immediately following rape, including fear of the indoors or outdoors (depending on where the rape took place), fear of being alone, fear of crowds, fear of being followed, and sexual fears.

FIGURE 5.4

Coping with Rape

Research with rape victims soon after the trauma has provided clear insights into the emotional turmoil and psychological processes they go through in coping with their experiences (Frazier & Burnett, 1994; Koss & Figueredo, 2004). Coping actually begins before the rape occurs and ends many months after the attack. The categories outlined in this figure summarize these findings and integrate the feelings and problems that women experience at different points of their traumas.

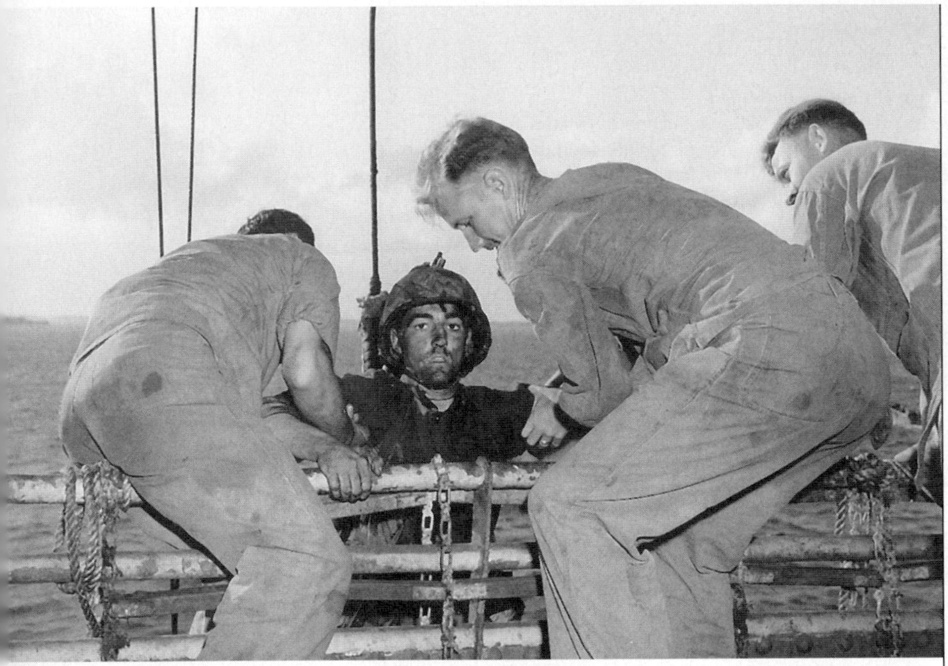

It has been estimated that in World War II, 10 percent of Americans in combat developed combat exhaustion. The stress of combat clearly took its toll on this Marine, who had just finished 2 days of heavy fighting in the Pacific.

in Afghanistan or 9.3 percent compared to reported symptoms before going to Iraq. The rates of disorder increased with the reported extent of combat and with being wounded in combat.

CLINICAL PICTURE IN COMBAT-RELATED STRESS

The specific symptoms of combat-related stress vary considerably, depending on the type of duty, the severity and nature of the traumatic experience, and the personality of the individual. Just being in a war zone, with the ever-present possibility that a shell can explode and kill or injure anyone in the area, is a frightening experience (Zeidner, 1993). In fact, civilians living in war zones are also at risk for PTSD. Studies of 492 Israeli elementary school children who were exposed to SCUD missile attacks during the first war with Iraq found that higher stress responses occurred in areas that were hit by missiles (Schwarzwald et al., 1993). In another study, the anxiety levels of the civilians exposed to the threat of attack were significantly higher during the war than when they were retested after the war was over (Weizman et al., 1994). Moreover, anxiety was higher during the evenings (when the SCUD attacks usually occurred) than during the day.

Many studies have documented the importance of war-zone stressors and the development of PTSD symptoms (Dohrenwend, Neria, et al., 2004; Ford, 1999; Prigerson, Maciejewski, & Rosenheck, 2002). One study evaluated the self-reports of 251 Vietnam veterans, grouping them according to three levels of experienced stress: (1) exposed to combat; (2) exposed to abusive violence in combat; and (3) participated in abusive violence in combat (Laufer, Brett, & Gallops, 1985). They found that post-traumatic symptoms including intrusive imagery, hyperarousal, numbing, and cognitive disruption were associated with exposure to combat violence. Participation in abusive violence was most highly associated with more severe pathologies marked by cognitive disruptions such as depression. The authors concluded that the clinical picture of post-traumatic stress disorder varies according to the stressors experienced. Combat involvement is also not the only stressor in a war zone. Soldiers involved in graves registration duties (i.e., handling corpses) had high rates of PTSD symptoms such as anger, anxiety, and somatic complaints compared with soldiers not assigned to such duties (McCarroll, Ursano, & Fullerton, 1995). Moreover, some people entering the military are more vulnerable to developing stress-related symptoms than others.

Despite these variations, the general clinical picture was surprisingly uniform for soldiers who developed combat stress in different wars. The first symptoms were increasing irritability and sensitivity, sleep disturbances, and often recurrent nightmares. One empirical study of the emotional components of PTSD in combat veterans found anger and anger control problems to be strong components in post-traumatic stress among combat veterans (Chemtob et al., 1994).

Interestingly, most physically wounded soldiers have shown less anxiety or less combat exhaustion symptoms than soldiers not physically wounded, except in cases of permanent mutilation. Apparently a wound, in providing an acceptable escape from a stressful combat situation, removes the source of anxiety. A similar finding was reported among Israeli soldiers hospitalized during the 5-to 6-week Yom Kippur War in 1973 when Egyptian and Syrian forces attacked Israel (Merbaum & Hefez, 1976). In fact, it is not unusual for soldiers to admit that they have prayed to be hit or to have something honorable happen to them to remove them from battle. When approaching full recovery and the necessity of returning to combat, injured soldiers sometimes show prolonged symptoms or delayed traumatic reactions of nervousness, insomnia, and other symptoms that they did not exhibit when they were first hospitalized.

PRISONERS OF WAR AND HOLOCAUST SURVIVORS

Among the most stressful and persistently troubling wartime experiences is that of being a prisoner of war (Beal, 1995; Page, Engdahl, & Eberly, 1997). Although some people have been able to adjust to the stress (especially as part of a supportive group), the toll on most pris-

5.2 Developments in Research

Unpredictable and Uncontrollable Stressors

For the past 30 years, extensive research in animals has shown that two of the most important determinants of how an organism responds to stress are whether the stressors are unpredictable and whether they are uncontrollable. An unpredictable stressor occurs without warning, and its nature may be unforeseen. With an uncontrollable stressor, there is no way to reduce its impact, such as by escape or avoidance. In general, both people and animals are more stressed by unpredictable and uncontrollable stressors than by stressors that are of equal physical magnitude but are either predictable or controllable or both (e.g., Evans & Stecker, 2004; Maier & Watkins, 1998).

There are many parallels between the symptoms of PTSD and the behavioral and physiological consequences of unpredictable and uncontrollable stressors in animals (e.g., Başoğlu & Mineka, 1992; Foa, Zinbarg, & Rothbaum, 1992; Friedman & Yehuda, 1995). It is known, for example, that uncontrollable stressors stimulate some brain systems and increase the levels of central and peripheral norepinephrine (Friedman & Yehuda, 1995; Southwick, Yehuda, & Morgan, 1995). This led PTSD researchers to hypothesize that administering a drug called yohimbine to persons with PTSD might increase their symptoms, because yohimbine (a naturally occurring substance) is known to activate noradrenergic neurons. In a result consistent with this hypothesis, Southwick and colleagues (1995) found that 40 percent of a group of 20 Vietnam veterans with PTSD given yohimbine experienced flashbacks. In addition, the veterans with PTSD showed increases in other symptoms, such as intrusive traumatic thoughts, emotional numbing, and grief.

Uncontrollable stressors in animals are also known to cause stress-induced analgesia (SIA), or diminished sensitivity to pain. Formerly neutral conditioned stimuli that are paired with uncontrollable stressors can also come to elicit this analgesia. SIA is known to work through the production of endogenous, or internally produced, opiate-like substances in the brain (Southwick et al., 1995; van der Kolk & Saporta, 1993). PTSD researchers now believe that many of the symptoms of emotional numbing seen in people with PTSD may be caused by this same kind of SIA, rather than a psychological defensive reaction against remembering the trauma.

If unpredictable and uncontrollable stressors are most likely to produce PTSD, what factors determine which of the people who experience those stressors will be most likely to develop PTSD? Again, researchers have turned to the animal literature for answers (e.g., Mineka & Zinbarg, 1995). For example, it is known that prior experience with uncontrollable stressors can sensitize the organism—that is, make it more susceptible to the negative consequences of later experiences with uncontrollable trauma. Several studies of PTSD have confirmed that this is indeed the case; for example, victims of childhood abuse are more susceptible than others to PTSD if they experience sexual or nonsexual assault in adulthood (see Foa, Zinbarg, & Rothbaum, 1992; Mineka & Zinbarg, 1995). In addition, soldiers who had been physically abused in childhood were more likely than others to develop PTSD during the Vietnam War (Post, Weiss, & Smith, 1995). There is some evidence that individual characteristics such as neuroticism might be more important than the uncontrollability of stressors in understanding subjective arousal to aversive stimuli (Vogeltanz & Hecker, 1999).

Considerable research now supports the hypotheses that perceptions of uncontrollability and unpredictability play an important role in the development and maintenance of PTSD symptoms (Anisman & Merali, 1999), although the associations between these perceptions and the symptoms that emerge are often complex (Zakowski, Hall, et al., 2001).

oners is great. About 40 percent of the American prisoners in Japanese POW camps during World War II died during their imprisonment; an even higher proportion of prisoners of Nazi concentration camps died. Many survivors of Nazi concentration camps sustained residual organic and psychological damage, along with a lowered tolerance to stress of any kind. Symptoms were often extensive and commonly included anxiety, insomnia, headaches, irritability, depression, nightmares, impaired sexual potency, and functional diarrhea (which may accompany even relatively mild stress). Such symptoms were attributed not only to the psychological stressors but also to biological stressors such as head injuries, prolonged malnutrition, and serious infectious diseases (Sigal et al., 1973; Warnes, 1973).

Among returning POWs, the effects of the psychological trauma they had suffered were often masked by the feelings of relief and jubilation that accompanied release from confinement. Even when there was little evidence of residual physical pathology, however, survivors of prisoner-of-war camps commonly showed impaired resistance to physical illness, low frustration tolerance, frequent dependence on alcohol and drugs, irritability, and other indications of emotional instability (Chambers, 1952; Goldsmith & Cretekos, 1969; Hunter, 1978; Strange

& Brown, 1970; Wilbur, 1973). Many veterans experience, at times, overwhelming anger over minor events that for some is difficult to control. Such maladaptive behaviors may require intervention even years after the stress of military combat has faded (Chemtob, Novaco, Hamada, & Gross, 1997). There is also evidence that combat exposure can result in severe adjustment problems including antisocial behavior (Barrett, Resnick, Foy, & Dansky, 1996).

In a retrospective study of psychological maladjustment symptoms following repatriation, Engdahl and colleagues (1993) interviewed a large sample of former POWs and found that half of them reported symptoms that met standard criteria for PTSD in the year following their releases from captivity; nearly a third met PTSD criteria 40 to 50 years after their wartime experiences.

Another measure of the toll taken by the prolonged stress of being in a POW or concentration camp is the higher death rate after return to civilian life. Among returning World War II POWs from the Pacific area, Wolff (1960) found that within the first six years, nine times as many died from tuberculosis as would have been expected in civilian life; four times as many from gastrointestinal disorders; over twice as many from cancer, heart disease, and suicide; and three times as many from accidents. Many problems of adjustment and post-traumatic symptoms can be found in POWs years after their release (Sutker & Allain, 1995). Bullman and Kang (1997) found an increased risk of death due to external causes (for example, from overdose and accidents) associated with PTSD in Vietnam veterans.

Some of the lingering problems experienced by former POWs might be a direct result of harsh treatment and starvation during captivity. Sutker and colleagues (1992) conducted a study of memory and cognitive performance of POW survivors and found that those who experienced the greatest trauma-induced weight loss, defined as greater than 35 percent of their weight before captivity, performed significantly worse on memory tasks than POWs who experienced less malnutrition.

Severe Threats to Personal Safety and Security

Some of the most traumatic and psychologically disabling circumstances a person can experience involve those in which he or she faces drastic threats to personal security. Even living in a modern, civilized world is no guarantee of uninterrupted peaceful pursuit of our dreams and ambitions. All too often in the modern world, we hear about tragic sociopolitical circumstances that require large populations to leave their homeland and join a scattered trail of refugees to some unknown place where they are subject to lawless and inhumane treatment (Miller & Rasco, 2004).

THE TRAUMA OF FORCED MIGRATION In 1999 more than 14.1 million refugees and asylum seekers fled their countries, and another 21 million were displaced within their own countries (U.S. Committee for Refugees, 2001).

In the United States, recent refugees have come from many countries—Ethiopia, the former Soviet Union, Iran, Cuba, Haiti, Laos, Vietnam, Cambodia, and Somalia. The Southeast Asians who began arriving in America after 1975 perhaps had the most difficult adjustment. Although many of these people were functioning well in their homeland and in time became successful and happy American citizens, others have had difficulty adjusting (Carlson & Rosser-Hogan, 1993; Westermeyer, Williams, & Nguyen, 1991). Not surprisingly, refugees with low self-esteem tend to have the most difficulty adjusting to new cultures (Nesdale, Rooney, & Smith, 1997). A 10-year longitudinal study of Hmong refugees from Laos found that many refugees had made considerable progress in their acculturation (Westermeyer, Neider, & Callies, 1989). Many had improved economically—about 55 percent were employed, with incomes approaching those of the general population. The percentage of people living on welfare had dropped from 53 percent initially to 29 percent after 10 years. Psychological adjustment had also improved, with symptoms of phobia, somatization, and low self-esteem showing the most positive changes. Considerable problems remained, however. Many refugees still had not learned English, some seemingly had settled permanently onto the welfare rolls, and some still showed symptoms such as anxiety, hostility, and paranoia that had changed little over the period studied. Although many refugees had adapted to their new culture, many were still experiencing considerable adjustment problems even after 10 years in the United States (Hinton, Tiet, et al., 1997; Westermeyer, 1989) or in other refugee countries such as Norway (Hauff & Vaglum, 1994).

Many adults who emigrate—especially those forced to leave their homes—experience a high degree of stress and problems in psychological adjustment. However, even greater degrees of stress can occur in their children (Rousseau, Drapeau, & Corin, 1996). In a study of Chinese migrants to Canada, Short and Johnston (1997) found that the degree of stress in children was often buffered by greater adjustment in the parents. Their study highlighted the importance of measuring stress levels of adults and implementing strategies to alleviate their settlement concerns in order to lower the level of stress for children. In many cases, however, young refugees do not live with their parents but with distant relatives or friends, a situation that can result in added adaptation stress (Halcón, Robertson, et al., 2004).

THE TRAUMA OF BEING HELD HOSTAGE Being held as a hostage can produce disabling psychological symptoms in victims (Allodi, 1994). The following case (adapted from Sonnenberg, 1988) describes a man who experienced a horrifying ordeal that left him with intense symptoms of anxiety and distress for months following the incident.

case study **Mr. A.'s Two-Year Terror**

Mr. A. was a married accountant, the father of two, in his early thirties. One night, while out performing an errand, he was attacked by a group of youths. These youngsters made him get into their car and took him to a deserted country road.

There they pulled him from the car and began beating and kicking him. They took his wallet, began taunting him about its contents (they had learned his name, his occupation, and the names of his wife and children), and threatened to go to his home and harm these family members. Finally, after brutalizing him for several hours, they tied him to a tree, one youth held a gun to his head, and after Mr. A. begged and pleaded for his life, the armed assailant pulled the trigger. The gun was empty, but at the moment the trigger was pulled, the victim defecated and urinated in his pants. Then the youths untied him and left him on the road.

This man slowly made his way to a gas station he had seen during his abduction and called the police. [One of the authors] was called to examine him and did so at intervals for the next 2 years. The diagnosis was PTSD. He had clearly experienced an event outside the range of normal human experience and was at first reexperiencing the event in various ways: intrusive recollections, nightmares, flashbacks, and extreme fear upon seeing groups of unsavory-looking youths. He was initially remarkably numb in other respects: He withdrew from the members of his family and lost interest in his job. He felt generally estranged and detached. He expected to die in the near future. There were also symptoms of increased psychophysiological arousal: poor sleeping, difficulty concentrating, and exaggerated startle response. When [the authors] first spoke about his abduction in detail, he actually soiled himself at the moment he described doing so during the original traumatic experience.

This man received treatment from another psychiatrist during the next 2 years, consisting of twice-weekly intensive individual psychotherapy sessions and the concurrent administration of a tricyclic antidepressant. The individual psychotherapy consisted of discussions that focused on the sense of shame and guilt this man felt over his behavior during his abduction. He wished he had been more stoic and had not pleaded for his life. With the help of his psychotherapist, he came to see that he could accept responsibility for his behavior during his captivity; that his murderous rage at his abductors was understandable, as was his desire for revenge; and that his response to his experience was not remarkable compared with what others might have felt and done.

Eventually he began to discuss his experience with his wife and friends, and by the end of the 2 years over which [the author] followed him, he was essentially without symptoms, although he still became somewhat anxious when he saw groups of tough-looking youths. Most important, his relationship with his wife and children was warm and close, and he was again interested in his work.

PSYCHOLOGICAL TRAUMA AMONG VICTIMS OF TORTURE Among the most highly stressful experiences human beings have reported are those inhuman acts perpetrated upon them by other human beings in the form of systematic torture. From the beginning of human history to the present, some people have subjected others to pain, humiliation, and degradation for political or inexplicable personal reasons (Jaranson & Popkin, 1998). History and literature are full of personal accounts of intense suffering and lifelong dread resulting from maltreatment by ruthless captors. In addition, several empirical studies have reported on the prevalence of torture in the modern world: Allden and colleagues (1996) reported that 38 percent of Burmese political dissidents who escaped to Thailand had been tortured before their escape. Shrestha, Sharma, and colleagues (1998) compared Bhutanese survivors of torture in a Nepalese refugee camp with matched controls and found that torture survivors had more PTSD, anxiety, and depressive symptoms than the controls. Van Ommeren, de Jong, et al. (2001) compared tortured and nontortured Bhutanese refugees and reported that those acknowledging being tortured had had more PTSD, somatoform pain, and dissociative disorders over the past year, as well as having had more lifetime mood affective and generalized anxiety disorders. Silove, Steel, et al. (2002) also found higher PTSD scores in a sample of Tamil torture victims living in Australia when compared with refugees who had not been tortured.

These studies are somewhat limited in terms of their generalizability in that they typically have used small or nonrepresentative samples of torture survivors. One recent study conducted with a substantial and representative sample of African refugees from Somalia and Ethiopia living in the United States provided a reliable estimate of the prevalence rates for torture for a large sample of 1,134 refugees. The sample contained approximately 600 refugees of each nationality, with equal numbers of men and women. Of the participants in the study, only about 56 percent met the criteria for no torture, while the remainder reported a history of having been tortured. These rates of torture were substantially higher than other studies have reported. The experience of torture varied by gender and ethnicity: 45 percent men (n = 272) and 43 percent women (n = 228) had approximately equal exposure to torture. More of the Ethiopians were exposed to torture (n = 286, 55 percent) than Somalis (n = 224, 36 percent) (Jaranson, Butcher, et al., 2004).

Psychological symptoms experienced after torture have been well documented and involve a range of problems including physical symptoms (such as pain, nervousness, insomnia, tremors, weakness, fainting, sweating, and diarrhea); psychological symptoms (such as night terrors and nightmares, depression, suspiciousness, social withdrawal and alienation, irritability, and aggressiveness); cognitive impairments (such as trouble concentrating, disorientation, confusion, and memory deficits); and unacceptable behaviors (such as aggressiveness, impulsivity, and suicidal attempts; see Başoğlu & Mineka, 1992; Burnett & Peel, 2001).

The following case is illustrative of the post-torture experience:

case STUDY Muhammad B.'s Captivity

Muhammad B., a 21-year-old Ethiopian refugee, lives with his mother, father, two younger brothers, and two younger sisters in a small center-city apartment building in a large Midwestern city. He works part time as a parking lot attendant and attends night school, majoring in business. Muhammed has been in the United States for 5 years after a very tumultuous period in his home country. He was held for interrogation, along with several other youths from his village, in a government prison compound for several months when he was 15 years old. The treatment received by the captives was severe, including starvation and frequent physical punishment. During a 7-month period of confinement, he was interrogated, usually after a severe beating or after being shown the bodies of other prisoners, in an effort by his captors to obtain information about the whereabouts of antigovernment guerilla fighters. On one occasion he was questioned while one of the guards held a rifle barrel in his mouth, and on another occasion he was subjected to a "staged execution" in order to get him to talk. After the captors determined that he had no relevant information, he was released. His family was able to escape the country shortly afterward.

Since his release from imprisonment, Muhammed has experienced severe PTSD symptoms including night terrors, sleeping disturbances, attacks of intense anxiety, and depression. He reports almost constant headaches and pains in the hand that was broken by his captors.

Although Muhammad has been able to complete high school successfully in the United States and has accumulated a year of college credit going to school part time, his day-to-day functioning is characterized by disabling, intrusive thoughts, anxiety, nightmares, and recurring depression.

Most of what we know about the psychological consequences of torture comes from anecdotal reports by victims. The experiences of torture victims have also been empirically evaluated in well-controlled studies of victims. In the study of Somali and Ethiopian torture victims noted above (Jaranson, Butcher, et al., 2004), torture survivors reported substantially higher numbers of physical and psychological problems and also scored higher on a PTSD checklist (the PCL-C) than refugees who had not been tortured.

In another study, Başoğlu and his colleagues (1994) studied the long-term consequences of torture, and possible rehabilitation strategies. They reported the results of a unique empirical study in which 55 former Turkish prisoners who were political activists were compared with 55 political activists who were not tortured. The torture victims and control subjects were located through articles and ads in newspapers and political journals. The investigators were able to match the victims and controls closely on a number of variables including age, gender, education level, ethnic status, and occupation. To obtain an objective picture of each person's adjustment and psychological symptoms, they used a number of standard assessment techniques: a psychiatric interview and a number of standardized psychological tests including the Turkish language MMPI, the Beck Depression Scale, and the State–Trait Anxiety Inventory.

Although the victims of torture were for the most part not found to be extremely psychiatrically disturbed compared with the controls, the victims of imprisonment and torture were found to experience significant symptoms of post-traumatic stress disorder related to being uprooted, being a refugee, living in a repressive political environment, and living through related traumatic events. Moreover, Başoğlu and his colleagues found evidence that torture induces psychological effects independent of other stressors (1994). Interestingly, the authors found that traumatic experience from torture had a differential impact depending on the manner in which the torture was applied—that is, whether the torture was perceived by the victim as uncontrollable and unpredictable (Başoğlu & Mineka, 1992). Victims who were able to assert some element of cognitive control over the circumstances (for example, those who were able to predict and ready themselves for the pain they were about to experience) tended to be less affected over the long term (see Developments in Research 5.2). These investigators concluded that prior knowledge of and preparedness for torture, strong commitment to a cause, immunization against traumatic stress as a result of repeated exposure, and strong social supports have protective value against PTSD in survivors of torture.

In a further follow-up study of torture victims, Başoğlu, Mineka, and colleagues (1997) found additional support for the idea that psychological preparedness for trauma is an extremely important protective factor for lessening the psychological effects of torture.

Causal Factors in Post-Traumatic Stress

Most people function relatively well in catastrophes, and many behave with heroism (Rachman, 1990). Whether or not someone develops post-traumatic stress disorder depends on a number of factors. Some research suggests that personality plays a role in reducing vulnerability to stress when the stressors are severe (Clark, Watson, & Mineka, 1994). At high levels of traumatic exposure, the nature of the traumatic stressor can account for much of the differences in stress response (e.g., Lifton, 2005). In other words, everyone has a breaking point, and at sufficiently high levels of stress, the average person can be expected to develop some psychological difficulties (which may be either short-lived or long term) following a traumatic event. Epstein, Fullerton, and Ursano (1998) found that workers who provide support to bereaved families of disaster victims are themselves at risk for increased illness, psychiatric symptoms, and negative psychological well-being for up to 18 months following the disaster. They also reported that individuals with lower levels of education, those who had exposure to grotesque burns, and those who had strong feelings of numbness following exposure were more likely to experience later psychological symptoms after an air disaster.

Even a seasoned police officer can experience a disabling level of stress, as shown in the following case.

case STUDY — The Police Officer and the Plane Crash

Don had been a model police officer during his 14 years on the force. He was evaluated highly by his superiors, had an M.A. in social work, and had attained the rank of sergeant. While patrolling in a squad car, he heard that there had been an aircraft accident, and he quickly drove to the scene to give aid to any survivors. After he arrived, he wandered around in a daze looking for someone to help, but there was only destruction. He later remembered the next few days as a bad dream.

For several days after the cleanup he was quite depressed, had no appetite, couldn't sleep, and was impotent. Images and recollections of the accident would come to him out of nowhere. He reported having a recurring dream in which he came upon an airplane crash while driving a car or flying a plane. In his dream, he would rush to the wreckage and help some passengers to safety.

Don decided that he needed help and sought counseling. Because of his deteriorating mood and physical condition, he was placed on medical leave from the police force. Eight months after the accident he was still in therapy and had not returned to work. During therapy it became apparent that Don had been experiencing a great deal of personal dissatisfaction and anger prior to the crash. His prolonged psychological disorder was not only a result of his anguish over the air crash but also a vehicle for expressing other problems. (Based on Davidson, 1979a, 1979b; O'Brien, 1979.) See Davis and Stewart (1999) for a discussion of the aftermath of this accident 20 years later.

In all cases of post-traumatic stress, conditioned fear—the fear associated with the traumatic experience—appears to be a key causal factor. Thus prompt psychotherapy following a traumatic experience is considered important in preventing conditioned fear from establishing itself and becoming resistant to change.

CAUSAL FACTORS IN COMBAT STRESS PROBLEMS

In a combat situation, with the continual threat of injury or death and repeated narrow escapes, a person's ordinary coping methods are relatively useless. The adequacy and security the person has known in the relatively safe and dependable civilian world are completely undermined. In a study of psychiatric war casualties from data going back to the Boer War at the beginning of the twentieth century, Jones and Wessely (2002) pointed out that there is a constant relationship between the incidence of total killed and wounded and the number of psychiatric casualties in war. At the same time, we must not overlook the fact that most soldiers subjected to combat have not become psychiatric casualties, although most of them have evidenced severe fear reactions and other symptoms of personality disorganization that were not serious enough to be incapacitating. In addition, many soldiers have tolerated almost unbelievable stress before they have broken down, whereas others have become casualties under conditions of relatively little combat stress or even as noncombatants—for example, during basic training.

In order to understand traumatic reactions to combat, we need to look at factors such as constitutional predisposition, personal maturity, loyalty to one's unit, and confidence in one's officers, as well as at the actual stress experienced.

Temperament Do constitutional differences in sensitivity, vigor, and temperament affect a soldier's resistance to combat stress? They probably do, but little actual evidence supports this assumption. We have more information about the conditions of battle that tax a soldier's emotional and physical stamina. Add other factors that often occur in combat situations (such as severe climatic conditions, malnutrition, and disease) to the strain of continual emotional mobilization, and the result is a general lowering of a person's physical and psychological resistance to all stressors.

Psychosocial Factors A number of psychological and interpersonal factors may contribute to the overall stress experienced by soldiers and predispose them to break down under combat. Such factors include reductions in personal freedom, frustrations of all sorts, and separation from home and loved ones. Central, of course, are the many stresses arising from combat including constant fear, unpredictable and largely uncontrollable circumstances, the necessity of killing, and prolonged harsh conditions. Personality (which is shaped by temperamental differences beginning in infancy) is an important determinant of adjustment to military experiences. Personality characteristics that lower a person's resistance to stress or to particular stressors may be important in determining his or her reactions to combat. Personal immaturity, sometimes stemming from parental overprotection, is commonly cited as making a soldier more vulnerable to combat stress.

Worthington (1978) found that American soldiers who had trouble readjusting after they returned home from the Vietnam War also tended to have had greater difficulties before and during their military service than soldiers who adjusted readily. In their study of the personality characteristics of Israeli soldiers who had broken down in combat during the Yom Kippur War, Merbaum and Hefez (1976) found that over 25 percent reported having had psychological treatment prior to the war. Another 12 percent had experienced difficulties previously in the 6-day Israeli–Arab War of 1967. Thus about 37 percent of these soldiers had clear histories of some personality instability that may have predisposed them to break down under combat stress. On the other hand, of the other soldiers who broke down, over 60 percent had not shown earlier difficulties and would not have been considered to be at risk for such breakdown.

A background of personal maladjustment does not always make a person a poor risk for withstanding combat stress. Some people are so accustomed to anxiety that they cope with it more or less automatically, whereas soldiers who are feeling severe anxiety for the first time may be terrified by the experience, lose their self-confidence, and panic.

Sociocultural Factors Several sociocultural factors play an important part in determining a person's adjustment to combat. These general factors include clarity and acceptability of war goals, identification with the combat unit, esprit de corps, and quality of leadership.

An important consideration is how clear and acceptable the war's goals are to the individual. If the goals can be concretely integrated into the soldier's values in terms of his or her "stake" in the war and the worth and importance of what he or she is doing, this will help support the soldier psychologically. Another important factor is a person's identification with the combat unit. In fact, the stronger the sense of group identification, the less the chance that a soldier will break down in combat. Feelings of esprit de corps influence a person's morale and adjustment to extreme circumstances. Finally, if a soldier respects his or her leaders, has confidence in their judgment and ability, and can accept them as relatively strong parental or sibling figures, the soldier's morale and resistance to stress are bolstered. On the other hand, lack of confidence or dislike of leaders is detrimental to morale and to tolerance of combat stress.

Many factors may contribute to traumatic reactions to combat—constitutional predisposition, personal immaturity, compromised loyalty to one's unit, diminished confidence in one's officers, as well as the actual stress experienced. Thus, although combat situations completely undermine a person's ordinary coping methods, some soldiers can tolerate great stress without becoming psychiatric casualties, while others may break down under only slight combat stress.

It also appears that returning to an unaccepting social environment can increase a soldier's vulnerability to post-traumatic stress. For example, in a 1-year follow-up of Israeli men who had been psychiatric war casualties during the Yom Kippur War, Merbaum (1977) found not only that they continued to show extreme anxiety, depression, and extensive physical complaints, but also that in many instances they appeared to have become more disturbed over time. Merbaum hypothesized that their psychological deterioration had probably been due to the unaccepting attitudes of the community; in a country so reliant on the strength of its army for survival, considerable stigma is attached to psychological breakdown in combat. Because of this stigma, many of the men were experiencing not only isolation within their communities, but also self-recrimination about what they perceived as failure on their own parts. These feelings exacerbated the soldiers' already stressful situations.

The stressful events that veterans experience can also have a negative impact on their families when they return home. A recent study of the families of Dutch peacekeeping soldiers returning home from stressful assignments reported that partners and parents of former peacekeepers showed signs of secondary traumatic stress responses (Dirkzwager, Bramsen, et al., 2005).

Long-Term Effects of Post-Traumatic Stress

In some cases, soldiers who have experienced combat exhaustion may show symptoms of post-traumatic stress for sustained periods of time (Penk, Rierdan, et al., in press). In cases of delayed post-traumatic stress, some soldiers who stood up exceptionally well under intensive combat have experienced post-traumatic stress upon their return home, often in response to relatively minor stresses that they had handled easily before. Evidently, these soldiers have suffered long-term damage to their adaptive capabilities, in some cases complicated by memories of killing enemy soldiers or civilians as well as by feelings tinged with guilt and anxiety (Horowitz & Solomon, 1978).

The nature and extent of delayed post-traumatic stress disorder are somewhat controversial (Burstein, 1985). Reported cases of delayed stress syndrome among Vietnam combat veterans are often difficult to relate explicitly to combat stress, because these people may also have other significant adjustment problems. People with adjustment difficulties may erroneously attribute their present problems to specific incidents from their past, such as experiences in combat. The wide publicity given to delayed post-traumatic stress disorder has made it easy for clinicians to find a precipitating cause in their patients' backgrounds. Indeed, the frequency with which this disorder has recently been diagnosed in some settings suggests that its increased use is as much a result of its plausibility and popularity as of its true incidence.

In Review

- What are the main differences between acute stress disorder and post-traumatic stress disorder?
- What are the three stages of disaster syndrome? At which stage might PTSD develop?
- What is controversial about the frequency of diagnosis of delayed PTSD?

Prevention and Treatment of Stress Disorders

Prevention of Stress Disorders

If we know that extreme or prolonged stress can produce maladaptive psychological reactions that have predictable courses, is it possible to prevent maladaptive responses to stress by preparing a person in advance to deal with the stress? When a predictable and unusually stressful situation is about to occur, is it possible to "inoculate" a person by providing information ahead of time about probable stressors and suggesting ways of coping with them? If preparation for battle stressors can help soldiers avoid breakdowns, why not prepare other people to meet anticipated stressors effectively?

This approach to stress management has been shown to be effective in cases where the person is facing a known traumatic event such as major surgery or the breakup of a relationship. In these cases a professional attempts to prepare the person in advance to cope better with the stressful event by teaching the person to develop more realistic and adaptive attitudes toward the problem. The use of cognitive-behavioral techniques to help people manage potentially stressful situations or difficult events has been widely explored (Brewin & Holmes, 2003). This preventive strategy, often referred to as **stress-inoculation training,** prepares people to tolerate an anticipated threat by changing the things they say to themselves before the crisis. A three-stage process is employed. In the first stage, information is provided about the stressful situation and about ways people can deal with such dangers. In the second stage, self-statements that promote effective adaptation—for example, "Don't worry, this little pain is just part of the treatment"—are rehearsed. In the third stage, the person practices making such self-statements while being exposed to a variety of ego-threatening or pain-threatening stressors such as unpredictable electric shocks, stress-inducing films, or sudden cold. This last phase allows the person to apply the new coping skills learned earlier. We shall discuss stress-inoculation training and the use of self-statements in greater detail in Chapter 17. Unfortunately, one cannot be prepared psychologically for most disasters or traumatic situations, which by their nature are often unpredictable and uncontrollable.

Treatment for Stress Disorders

Although a significant proportion of people in distress are reluctant to seek help for their symptoms, many people in crisis are in a state of acute turmoil and feel overwhelmed and incapable of dealing with the stress by themselves. They do not have time to wait for the customary initial therapy appointment, nor are they usually in a position to continue therapy over a sustained period of time. They need immediate assistance (Brown, Shiang, & Bongar, 2003; Schnyder, 2005). Crisis intervention has emerged in response to a widespread need for immediate help for individuals and families confronted with especially stressful situations—be they disasters or family situations that have become intolerable (Butcher & Dunn, 1989; McNally, Bryant, & Ehlers, 2003; Ritchie & Owens, 2004). But there are several approaches to treating the symptoms of PTSD: (1) short-term crisis therapy involving face-to-face discussion, (2) postdisaster debriefing sessions, (3) direct-exposure therapy for those whose PTSD symptoms persist, (4) telephone hotlines, and (5) psychotropic medications.

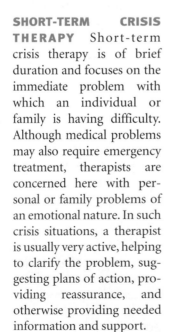

Short-term crisis therapy is geared to help the individual or family gain clarity, form a plan of action, obtain support and reassurance, and move forward through the immediate problem. Over the course of no more than six sessions, the therapist tries to provide as much help as the individual or family needs and will accept. In the wake of the September 11, 2001, terrorist attacks, many people found themselves in a crisis situation and sought psychological assistance to cope with the disaster.

SHORT-TERM CRISIS THERAPY Short-term crisis therapy is of brief duration and focuses on the immediate problem with which an individual or family is having difficulty. Although medical problems may also require emergency treatment, therapists are concerned here with personal or family problems of an emotional nature. In such crisis situations, a therapist is usually very active, helping to clarify the problem, suggesting plans of action, providing reassurance, and otherwise providing needed information and support.

If the problem involves psychological disturbance in one of the family members, emphasis is usually placed on mobilizing the support of other family members. Often this enables the person to avoid hospitalization and a disruption of family life. Crisis intervention may also involve bringing other mental health or medical personnel into the treatment picture. Most individuals and families who come for short-term crisis therapy do not continue in treatment for more than one to six sessions.

A central assumption in crisis-oriented therapy is that the individual was well functioning psychologically before the trauma. Thus therapy is focused only on helping the person through the immediate crisis, not on "remaking" her or his personality. As a central strategy, traumatized victims are provided emotional support and are encouraged to talk about their experiences during the crisis (Cigrang, Pace, & Yasuhara, 1995).

POSTDISASTER DEBRIEFING SESSIONS Those who appear to function well at a disaster site may experience difficulties after the immediate crisis has subsided and they have returned to their families and their normal duties. Even experienced disaster workers who are well trained and effective at the site can be affected later by the pressures and problems experienced during the disaster (Flannery, 2004). One approach to helping people who have been involved in a disaster is to arrange **debriefing sessions** to allow them to discuss their experiences with others, usually shortly after the trauma has subsided. To "unwind" in a psychologically safe environment and to share one's experience of the disaster are universal needs of people following a traumatic situation (Raphael & Wooding, 2004).

A widespread movement has evolved over the past 20 years to provide (even to mandate) debriefing sessions for those who have experienced a disaster (Zeev, Iancu, & Bodner, 2001). Such sessions are not always provided by mental health professionals. In fact, a small industry has sprung up to provide debriefing services, and disaster scenes are often swarmed by service providers—most well meaning but many with little or no mental health training. Further confusing the aftermath of a disaster are non–mental health "intruders," such as attorneys who are seeking to enlist potential litigants for lawsuits. For example, at the airport in Detroit, following the Northwest Airlines crash in 1987, a man dressed in the attire of a priest was providing counseling services to family members and airline personnel for several days following the accident. Employees became suspicious when he told one of the counselees that he had been at the airport for several days and needed to take some time off to go see his wife. It turned out that he was not a priest at all but a front man for a law firm. He had been passing out business cards for the law firm to every person he counseled.

DIRECT-EXPOSURE THERAPY One behaviorally oriented treatment strategy that has been used effectively for PTSD clients, particularly those with delayed-onset or

5.3 Developments in Practice

Crisis Intervention and Airline Disasters

There are many situations in which crisis intervention is necessary, but one crisis in particular requires additional effort in counseling—airline crashes. The immediate consequences of an air crash are devastating. Survivors typically have traumatic responses to the accident that impair their immediate functioning and place great demands on their psychological adjustment for weeks after the disaster. Family members of victims often experience great psychological trauma as well; they may need to make extensive changes during their loved one's lengthy recovery period, or they may need to make major life changes to adjust to their loved one's death. Even rescue personnel caught up in dealing with the aftermath of an airline disaster may suffer from post-traumatic stress disorder (Davis & Stewart, 1999).

Like natural disasters, airplane crashes are sudden and unexpected, and they are usually quite chaotic. There is little of the sense of community, however, that characterizes the response to many natural disasters. In fact, air crashes usually involve considerable blame and anger toward airline companies, which can aggravate or intensify the emotional reactions of survivors even months after the crash.

Most airports are required to have a disaster plan that includes rescue and evacuation procedures to deal with an airplane crash. Some airport disaster plans have also incorporated a psychological support program to provide emergency mental health services to survivors, the family members of crash victims, and rescue workers (Butcher & Dunn, 1989; Carlier, Lamberts, & Gersons, 1997).

How Crisis Counselors Help During Air Disasters

Crisis intervention supplied in the immediate aftermath of a disaster can reduce the emotional distress experienced and can result in a more effective future psychological adjustment (Butcher & Hatcher, 1988). A crisis counselor offers objective emotional support and tries to provide a long-term perspective—to allow victims to see that there is hope of surviving psychologically. Disasters are always followed by periods of confusion and misinformation. One important role of the mental health professional in disaster response efforts is to obtain, decipher, and clearly communicate to victims the most accurate picture of the situation obtainable at the moment. Finally, a crisis counselor provides practical suggestions to promote adaptation. In an extreme crisis, people often lose perspective and "forget" that they are usually quite effective in dealing with life problems.

Air Disasters and Telephone Hotline Counseling

After an air disaster, considerable psychological turmoil prevails among passengers and crew members. This state of tension can result in demoralization and negative behavior such as absenteeism from work, excessive drinking, and morale problems. An effective way to deal with this psychological uncertainty and reduce the negative atmosphere following an air disaster is to provide telephone counseling services for all those who feel the need to discuss their concerns, be they airline employees or the families of passengers.

Debriefing Sessions

Debriefing sessions are typically conducted in groups after the intensity of the immediate crisis has subsided. Debriefing sessions allow the participants in the disaster (such as aid workers) to express their feelings and emotions and to learn what people in similar situations have experienced. These sessions are effective in reducing the negative impact of people's emotional reactions to traumatic events.

chronic PTSD, is direct-therapeutic exposure (Taylor, 2003). In this approach, the client is exposed or reintroduced to stimuli that have come to be feared or to be associated with the traumatic event (McIvor & Turner, 1995). This procedure involves repeated or extended exposure, either *in vivo* or in the imagination, to objectively harmless but feared stimuli for the purpose of reducing anxiety (Foa & Rauch, 2004; Foa, Zoellner, et al., 2002). Exposure to stimuli that have come to be associated with fear-producing situations might also be supplemented by other behavioral techniques in an effort to reduce the symptoms of PTSD. For example, the use of traditional behavioral therapy methods such as relaxation training and assertiveness training might also be found to be effective in helping a client deal with anxiety following a traumatic event.

TELEPHONE HOTLINES Today, most major cities in the United States and many smaller ones have developed some form of telephone hotline to help people undergoing periods of severe stress. In addition, there are specific hotlines in many communities for rape victims and for runaways who need help.

As with other crisis intervention approaches, a person handling hotline calls must rapidly assess what is wrong and how bad it is. Even if an accurate assessment is possible and the hotline worker does everything within his or her power to help the caller, a distraught person may hang up without leaving any name, telephone number, or address. This can be a disturbing experience for the hotline counselor. Even in less severe cases, of course, the hotline worker may never learn whether the caller's problem has been solved. In other instances, however, the caller may be persuaded to come in for counseling, making more personal contact possible.

PSYCHOTROPIC MEDICATIONS As we have seen, persons experiencing traumatic situations usually report intense feelings of anxiety or depression; numbing, intrusive thoughts; and sleep disturbance. Several medications can be used to provide relief for intense PTSD symptoms (see the Unresolved Issues section of this chapter). Antidepressants, for example, are sometimes helpful in alleviating PTSD symptoms of depression, intrusion, and avoidance (Marshall & Klein, 1995; Shalev, Bonne, & Eth, 1996). However, because the symptoms can fluctuate over a brief period of time, careful monitoring of medications and dosage is required. The use of medication tends to focus on specific symptoms—for example, intrusive, distressing symptoms or nightmares; images of horrible events; startle reaction; and so forth (see Chapter 17).

Challenges in Studying Crisis Victims

In order to be effective and valid, psychological research conducted under field conditions must be carefully planned and organized. Research on the victims of a disaster is extremely difficult to implement for a number of reasons. It is virtually impossible to have an ideal, well-controlled, and well-funded experiment set up "awaiting a disaster." One cannot predict natural disasters such as a sudden tornado or fire, so it is difficult to have qualified staff ready to conduct research. Sound psychological research requires careful definition of the variables and meticulous management of the details in order to ensure that appropriate and effective measures are implemented. The variables we are interested in studying, such as the victims' grief response, are typically difficult to assess, and the extraneous conditions are difficult if not impossible to control. Often in disaster situations (for example, airplane crashes), therapy sessions are conducted in noisy, makeshift quarters such as crew lounges, hallways, and gate areas. Moreover, federal disaster funds that might be made available are typically for immediate intervention and cannot be used for long-term care or evaluation research (Pfefferbaum, Call, & Sconzo, 1999).

The events of September 11, 2001, produced an intense period of grief for families and friends of the victims, rescue workers, and people around the world who witnessed the attacks on television. Following the attacks, many people felt the need to tell the same story about the disaster again and again as a way to reduce anxiety and to desensitize themselves to the traumatic experience.

What We Are Learning about Crisis Intervention

Research on the efficacy of crisis intervention is usually designed and implemented after the fact. In some cases, it gets under way months after the disaster occurred and is constructed with available resources in a post-hoc fashion. Even so, a number of studies have provided valuable information. For example, Brom, Kleber, and Defares (1989) conducted a controlled study of the effectiveness of brief therapy with people experiencing PTSD and found that treatment immediately following the traumatic event significantly reduced their PTSD symptoms. Sixty percent of the treated persons showed improvement, whereas only 26 percent of the untreated group improved. Treatment did not benefit everyone, however, and some people maintained their PTSD symptoms even after therapy was terminated.

The disaster response strategy that has received the most attention over the past few years and is presently embroiled in controversy is postdisaster debriefing. Some believe that postdisaster counseling (much of which is conducted by people who are not mental health professionals) should be mandated for disaster victims in order to provide a quick fix (Conlon & Fahy, 2001). However, single debriefing sessions have not been demonstrated to reduce psychological distress or to prevent the development of stress-related disorders. In fact, some evidence suggests that the disaster victims who underwent debriefing fared worse than controls (Mayou, Ehlers, & Hobbs, 2000).

On the other hand, some investigators have reported that debriefing sessions following a disaster are effective. Chemtob, Tomas, Law, and Cremniter (1997), for example, explored the use of debriefing sessions and found this approach to be effective in reducing the emotional reactions to traumatic events. In another study, firefighters in Australia who participated in crisis debriefing after their ordeal perceived the intervention as beneficial in reducing their stress (Regehr & Hill, 2000). Everly, Boyle, and Lating (1999), after surveying the existing outcome literature on debriefing and conducting a meta-analysis of ten published studies, concluded that debriefings are effective in alleviating the effects of stress.

Hurricane Katrina left tens of thousands of people in dangerous and stressful circumstances. Here several hurricane victims attempt to attract the attention of rescuers.

In a thoughtful review, Deahl (2000) concluded that demonstrating the efficacy of debriefing presents a major challenge to investigators and that the controversy is not likely to be resolved soon.

In Review

- What strategies are useful for preventing or reducing maladaptive responses to stress?
- Describe crisis intervention therapy. How is this treatment approach different from psychotherapy for other mental health conditions?
- In what way are medications used in treating individuals in crisis?
- Describe the current controversy surrounding the use of "debriefing interventions."

Unresolved Issues

Psychotropic Medication in the Treatment of PTSD

Most authorities accept the view that PTSD results as a human response to extremely stressful events—even though the criteria for diagnosis differ somewhat between the two major diagnostic systems, DSM-IV and ICD-10 (Shalev, 2001). In both systems, however, exposure to an extreme stressor is one of the criteria for diagnosis. The treatment for PTSD has characteristically involved social or behavioral intervention—that is, primarily the use of interventions to alter the stressful situation or the individual's response to the stressor and to promote future adaptation (Hammer, Robert, & Frueh, 2004). Over the past few years, psychotropic medications have been used increasingly to relieve the symptoms of PTSD. For example, two recent studies have found that risperidone is effective at reducing the symptoms of chronic post-traumatic stress disorder (Bartzokis, Lu, et al., 2005; David, De Faria, et al., 2004).

The symptoms of PTSD, whatever their cause, can be extremely disabling and may leave a person unable to deal effectively with everyday demands. In some cases, the symptoms may be so intense and disabling that medication is prescribed to enable the patient to deal with the situation. Several medications are used to provide relief for intense PTSD symptoms. For example, antidepressants are sometimes considered helpful in improving symptoms of depression, intrusion, and avoidance (Pearlstein, 2000; Shalev, Bonne, & Eth, 1996).

Berlant (2001) recently reported on a novel use of the drug topiramate, an anti-epileptic or seizure medication, to reduce a patient's intrusive memories and nightmares, allowing her to deal more effectively with troubling events:

> Ms. A., a 35-year-old woman, presented with occasional "post-traumatic dreams" related to the death of

(continued)

her child 15 years previously, in addition to irritability, depressed mood, impulsivity, and marijuana abuse. Fluoxetine (an antidepressant), which had provided some relief for 5 years, had stopped helping. She had been unable to give up cannabis use for 15 years, finding that it helped suppress her nightmares. Preceding the loss of her child, Ms. A. had grown up in a household where she remembered feeling terrified and hiding when her parents argued and threatened to kill each other. At the age of 12 years, she was molested by her aunt's husband. When she sought her aunt's intervention, Ms. A. was not believed. At 13 years, her father died, leaving her in the care of a "hateful mother," who abandoned her and her sister to live on the street and later with relatives. As she grew older, she found that sex, alcohol, and marijuana provided her with some happiness.

At 20 years, Ms. A. became pregnant, only to lose the child to neonatal herpes at the age of 1 week. She described in vivid detail the experience of watching the baby's skin erupt with lesions and then watching as the baby went into cardiac arrest while being attended in an emergency room. She refused to be ushered from the resuscitation room, thereby subjecting herself to viewing the doctor's interventions, which included the futile insertion of a "7-inch needle into the baby's heart." Thereafter, she found herself besieged by nightmares of the death and by intrusive memories of the nightmares. She used alcohol and marijuana to suppress these symptoms for 15 years but finally decided that she wanted to stop using addictive drugs and come to terms with her problems.

Within 10 days of her stopping drugs and alcohol, and despite the introduction of sertraline, nightmares reemerged every few days, accompanied by almost daily intrusive reexperiencing of the nightmares. Especially troubling were the dreams of seeing her baby's corpse rotting in the ground and calling for her. Accompanying these symptoms were severe startle responses, social avoidance, and very low social functioning. (pp. 60–61)

Berlant (2001) noted that after topiramate was prescribed, Ms. A. reported that her nightmares had become less intense and that her dreams were difficult to remember and were not "grossly bloody," as they had been before. She also felt that her emotional reaction to the dreams had lessened. There were no longer any daytime intrusions, and the startle reaction had not recurred. She was maintained on topiramate for 30 days, after which the dosage was decreased. The nightmares recurred with the lower dosage level. The higher dosage level was reinstated, and there were no additional nightmares or intrusive memories.

Other antidepressant medications have been used in treating PTSD symptoms. Examples include trazodone (Warner, Dorn, & Peabody, 2001); nefazodone (Davis et al., 2000); fluoxetine (Davidson, Payne, et al., 2005); and sertraline (Comer & Figgitt, 2000). These drugs are targeted at reducing specific symptoms such as intrusive, distressing thoughts or nightmares; images of horrible events; startle reaction; and so forth. Vargas and Davidson (1993) concluded that psychotherapy administered along with medications was more effective in improving PTSD symptoms than medications taken alone. In general, most authorities agree that medications do not provide a quick fix to treatment of traumatized patients.

The idea that an environmentally or socially induced disorder can be treated biologically by altering a person's mental state through medications may seem incongruous. Also, the use of medications could have some unwelcome consequences. Medications might, for example, suppress the natural "warning signs" (the anxiety symptoms accompanying distress) and lull the person into a false sense of having escaped the effects of the traumatic experience. That misconception could lower her or his ultimate adaptive capabilities. Interestingly, medications actually may reinforce one of the main symptoms of PTSD—avoidance—by allowing the person respite from the intense symptoms. As Ehlers (2000) pointed out, "Avoidance is one of the main symptoms of PTSD, and it can thus take years for the person to seek help for this condition. It is important for clinicians to bear in mind [that] even those who seek help may find it hard to talk about the traumatic experience, and may show signs of avoidance such as irregular attendance or failure to disclose the worst moments of the trauma initially . . . " (p. 768).

Finally, the use of tranquilizing medications can promote an overreliance (psychological if not physiological) on medication.

The practitioner cannot simply prescribe medications and monitor their effect in brief follow-up visits. Rather, in the case of severe PTSD symptoms, the practitioner needs to integrate any medications carefully into the psychological and environmental treatment efforts. Recovery from severe PTSD often requires a drastic life reorientation. Overmedicated, tranquilized victims might feel less stressed but may not recognize the urgency of establishing new life circumstances.

In summary, a variety of psychotropic medications are increasingly being used in the treatment of traumatized patients. It is important to keep in mind that we do not yet know to what extent medications are effective in the treatment of PTSD symptoms (Ehlers, 2000; Jaranson, Kinzie, et al., 2001).

summary

- Many factors influence a person's response to stressful situations. The impact of stress depends not only on its severity but also on the person's preexisting vulnerabilities.
- A person's response to conflict situations may be viewed differently, depending on whether the conflicts are approach-avoidance, double-approach, or double-avoidance.
- A wide variety of psychosocial stressors exist, and a person can respond to them in different ways; for instance, a person may react with task-oriented or defense-oriented responses.
- The DSM-IV-TR classifies people's problems in response to stressful situations under two general categories: adjustment disorders and post-traumatic stress disorder (which is included with the anxiety disorders).
- Several relatively common stressors (prolonged unemployment, loss of a loved one through death, and marital separation or divorce) may produce a great deal of stress and psychological maladjustment, resulting in adjustment disorder.
- More intense psychological disorders in response to trauma or excessively stressful situations (such as rape, military combat, imprisonment, being held hostage, forced relocation, or torture) may be categorized as post-traumatic stress disorder.
- PTSD can involve a variety of symptoms including intrusive thoughts and repetitive nightmares about the event, intense anxiety, avoidance of stimuli associated with the trauma, and increased arousal manifested as chronic tension, irritability, insomnia, impaired concentration and memory, and depression.
- If the symptoms begin 6 months or more after the traumatic event, the diagnosis is delayed post-traumatic stress disorder.
- Many factors contribute to a breakdown under excessive stress, including the intensity or harshness of the stress situation, the length of the traumatic event, the person's biological makeup and personality adjustment before the stressful situation, and the ways in which the person manages problems once the stressful situation is over.
- In many cases the symptoms recede as the stress diminishes, especially if the person is given supportive psychotherapy. In extreme cases, however, there may be residual damage or the disorder may be of the delayed variety, not actually occurring until some time after the trauma.
- Several approaches to treating the symptoms of PTSD are in use today: short-term crisis therapy involving face-to-face discussion, debriefing sessions with victims of disaster, direct-exposure therapy for those whose PTSD symptoms persist, telephone hotlines, and psychotropic medications to relieve symptoms of PTSD.

key terms

acute stress disorder (p. 158)
adjustment disorder (p. 154)
coping strategies (p. 144)
crisis (p. 147)
crisis intervention (p. 147)
debriefing sessions (p. 172)
defense-oriented response (p. 150)
disaster syndrome (p. 158)
distress (p. 144)
eustress (p. 144)
general adaptation syndrome (p. 151)
personality or psychological decompensation (p. 151)
post-traumatic stress disorder (PTSD) (p. 157)
psychoneuroimmunology (p. 153)
stress (p. 144)
stress-inoculation training (p. 171)
stress tolerance (p. 148)
stressors (p. 144)
task-oriented response (p. 150)

CHAPTER

6

Panic, Anxiety, and Their Disorders

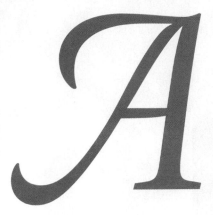

As we noted in Chapter 5, even stable, well-adjusted people may break down if forced to face extensive combat stress, torture, or devastating natural disaster. But for some people, simply performing everyday activities can be stressful. Faced with the normal demands of life—socializing with friends, waiting in line for a bus, being on an airplane, touching a doorknob—they become seriously fearful or anxious. In the most severe cases, people with anxiety problems may be unable even to leave their homes for fear of having a panic attack, or may spend much of their time in maladaptive behavior such as constant hand washing.

Anxiety—a general feeling of apprehension about possible danger—was, in Freud's formulation, a sign of an inner battle or conflict between some primitive desire (from the id) and prohibitions against its expression (from the ego and superego). Today the DSM has identified a group of disorders that share obvious symptoms and features of fear and anxiety. These **anxiety disorders,** as they are known, affect approximately 25 to 29 percent of the U.S. population at some point in their lives (over 23 million Americans) and are the most common category of disorders for women and the second most common for men (Kessler et al., 1994; Kessler, Berglund, et al., 2005b). In any 12-month period, about 23 percent of women and 12 percent of men suffer from at least one anxiety disorder (Kessler et al., 1994). Anxiety disorders create enormous personal, economic, and health care problems for those affected. For example, in 1990 anxiety disorders cost the United States $42.3 billion in direct and indirect costs, with 90 percent of these being direct costs (about 30 percent of the nation's total mental health bill of $148 billion in 1990; Greenberg et al., 1999).

Consider the following case of an anxious electrician:

case STUDY Edgy Electrician

A 27-year-old married electrician complains of dizziness, sweating palms, heart palpitations, and ringing of the ears of more than 18 months' duration. He has also experienced dry mouth and throat, periods of extreme muscle tension, and a constant "edgy" and watchful feeling that has often interfered with his ability to concentrate. These feelings have been present most of the time during the previous 2 years... Because of these symptoms the patient has seen a family practitioner, a neurologist, a neurosurgeon, a chiropractor, and an ear-nose-throat specialist.... He also has many worries. He constantly worries about the health of his parents... He also worries about whether he is a "good father," whether his wife will ever leave him (there is no indication that she is dissatisfied with the marriage), and whether he is liked by co-workers on the job. Although he recognizes that his worries are often unfounded, he can't stop worrying. For the past 2 years the patient has had few social contacts because of his nervous symptoms... he sometimes has to leave work when the symptoms become intolerable. (Adapted from Spitzer et al., 2002.)

Source: Adapted with permission from the *DSM-IV-TR Casebook* (Copyright 2000.) American Psychiatric Publishing, Inc.)

The physicians this man consulted could not determine the cause of his physical symptoms, and one of them finally referred him for treatment at a mental health clinic, where he was diagnosed as having *generalized anxiety disorder*—one of seven primary anxiety disorders.

Historically, cases like this and other cases of anxiety disorders were considered to be classic examples of **neurotic behavior.** Although neurotic behavior is maladaptive and self-defeating, a neurotic person is not out of touch with reality, incoherent, or dangerous. To Freud, **neuroses** were psychological disorders that resulted when intrapsychic conflict produced significant anxiety. Sometimes this anxiety was overtly expressed (as in those disorders known today as the anxiety disorders). In certain other neurotic disorders, however, he believed that the anxiety might *not* be obvious, either to the person involved or to others, if psychological defense mechanisms were able to deflect or mask it. In 1980 the DSM-III dropped the term *neurosis* and reclassified most of these disorders that did not involve obvious anxiety symptoms as either dissociative or somatoform disorders (see Chapter 8). DSM-III made this change in order to group together smaller sets of disorders that share more obvious symptoms and features.

We begin by discussing the nature of fear and anxiety as emotional states, both of which have an extremely important adaptive value but to which humans at times seem all too vulnerable. We will then move to a discussion of the anxiety disorders.

The Fear and Anxiety Response Patterns

It is difficult to define *fear* and *anxiety,* and there has never been complete agreement about how distinct the two emotions are from each other. Historically, the most common way of distinguishing between fear and anxiety has been whether there is a clear and obvious source of danger that would be regarded as real by most people. When the source of danger is obvious, the experienced emotion has been called *fear* (e.g., "I'm afraid of snakes"). With *anxiety,* however, we frequently cannot specify clearly what the danger is (e.g., "I'm anxious about my parents' health"). Intuitively, anxiety seems to be experienced as an unpleasant inner state in which we are anticipating something dreadful happening that is not entirely predictable from our actual circumstances (e.g., Barlow, 2002a).

Fear or panic is a basic emotion that is shared by many animals, including humans, and may activate the "fight-or-flight" response of the sympathetic nervous system. This allows us to respond rapidly when faced with a dangerous situation, such as being threatened by a predator. In humans who are having a panic attack, there is no external threat; panic occurs because of some misfiring of this response system.

FEAR In recent years, many prominent researchers have proposed a more fundamental distinction between fear and anxiety (e.g., Barlow, 1988, 2002a; Gray & McNaughton, 1996). According to these theorists, **fear** or **panic** is a basic emotion (shared by many animals) that involves activation of the "fight-or-flight" response of the sympathetic nervous system. This is an almost instantaneous reaction to any imminent threat such as a dangerous predator or someone pointing a loaded gun. Its adaptive value is that it allows us to escape from imminent danger. When the fear/panic response occurs in the absence of any obvious external danger, we say the person has had a spontaneous or uncued *panic attack.* The symptoms of a panic attack are nearly identical to those experienced during a state of fear except that panic attacks are often accompanied by a subjective sense of impending doom, including fears of dying, going crazy, or losing control. These latter cognitive symptoms do not generally occur during fear states. Thus fear and panic have three components:

1. cognitive/subjective components ("I feel afraid/terrified"; "I'm going to die");
2. physiological components (such as increased heart rate and heavy breathing);
3. behavioral components (a strong urge to escape or flee; Lang, 1968, 1971).

These components are only "loosely coupled" (Lang, 1985), which means that someone might show, for example, physiological and behavioral indications of fear without much of the subjective component, or vice versa. As a primitive alarm response to danger, the fear response must be activated with great speed to serve its adaptive purpose: enabling us to escape or avoid danger. Indeed, we often seem to go from a normal state to a state of intense fear almost instantaneously.

ANXIETY In contrast to fear and panic, **anxiety** is a complex blend of unpleasant emotions and cognitions that is both more oriented to the future and much more diffuse than fear (Barlow, 1988, 2002a). But like fear, it has not only cognitive/subjective components but also physiological and behavioral components. At the cognitive/subjective level, anxiety involves negative mood, worry about possible future threat or danger, self-preoccupation, and a sense of being unable to predict the future threat or to control it if it occurs. At a physiological level, anxiety often creates a state of tension and chronic overarousal, which may reflect readiness for dealing with danger should it occur ("Something awful may happen and I had better be ready for it if it does"). Although there is no activation of the fight-or-flight response as in fear, anxiety does prepare or prime a person for the fight-or-flight response should the anticipated danger occur. At a behavioral level, anxiety may create a strong tendency to avoid situations where danger might be encountered, but there is not the immediate urge to flee with anxiety as there is with fear (Barlow, 1988, 2002a). Support for the idea that anxiety is descriptively and functionally distinct from panic comes both from complex statistical analyses of subjective reports of panic and anxiety, and from a great deal of neurobiological evidence (e.g., Bouton, Mineka, & Barlow, 2001; Gorman et al., 2000).

The adaptive value of anxiety may be that it helps us plan and prepare for possible threat. In mild to moderate degrees, anxiety actually enhances learning and performance. For example, a mild amount of anxiety about how you are going to do on your next exam, or in your next tennis match, can actually be helpful. But although anxiety is often adaptive in mild or moderate degrees, it is maladaptive when it becomes chronic and severe, as we see in people diagnosed with anxiety disorders.

Although there are many threatening situations that provoke fear or anxiety unconditionally, many of our sources of fear and anxiety are learned. Years of human and nonhuman animal experimentation have established that the basic fear and anxiety response patterns are highly conditionable. That is, previously neutral and novel stimuli that are repeatedly paired with, and reliably predict, frightening or unpleasant events such as various kinds of physical or psychological trauma can acquire the capacity to elicit fear or anxiety themselves. Such conditioning is a completely normal and adaptive process that allows all of us to learn to anticipate upcoming frightening events if they are reliably preceded by a signal. Yet this normal and adaptive process can also lead in some cases to the development of clinically significant fears and anxieties, as we will see.

For example, a girl named Angela sometimes saw and heard her father physically abuse her mother in the evening. After this happened four or five times, Angela started to became anxious as soon as she heard her father's car arrive in the driveway at the end of the day. In such situations a wide variety of initially neutral stimuli may accidentally come to serve as cues that something threatening and unpleasant is about to happen—and thereby come to elicit fear or anxiety themselves. Our thoughts and images can also serve as conditioned stimuli capable of eliciting the fear or anxiety response pattern. For example, Angela came to feel anxious even when thinking about her father.

In Review

- Compare and contrast fear or panic with anxiety, making sure to note that both emotions involve three response systems.
- Explain the significance of the fact that both fear and anxiety can be classically conditioned.

Overview of the Anxiety Disorders and Their Commonalities

Anxiety disorders all have unrealistic, irrational fears or anxieties of disabling intensity as their principal and most obvious manifestation. DSM-IV-TR recognizes seven primary types of anxiety disorders:

- phobic disorders of the "specific" or of the "social" type;
- panic disorder with or without agoraphobia;
- generalized anxiety disorder;
- obsessive-compulsive disorder;
- post-traumatic stress disorder (discussed in Chapter 5).

People with these varied disorders differ from one another both in terms of the relative preponderance of fear/panic versus anxiety symptoms that they experience, and in the kinds of objects or situations that they are most concerned about. For example, people with specific or social phobias exhibit many anxiety symptoms about the possibility of encountering their phobic situation, but they may also experience a fear/panic response when they actually encounter the situation. People with panic disorder experience both frequent panic attacks and intense anxiety focused on the possibility of having another one. By contrast, people with generalized anxiety disorder mostly experience a general sense of diffuse anxiety and worry about many potentially bad things that may happen; some may also experience an occasional panic attack, but it is not a focus of their anxiety. Finally, people with obsessive-compulsive disorder experience intense anxiety or distress in response to intrusive thoughts or images and feel compelled to engage in compulsive, ritualistic activities that temporarily help to reduce the anxiety. It is also important to note that many people with one anxiety disorder will experience at least one more anxiety disorder and/or depression either concurrently or at a different point in their lives (e.g., Brown & Barlow, 2002; Kessler, Berglund, et al., 2005c; see also Developments in Thinking 7.2).

Given these commonalities across the anxiety disorders, it should come as no surprise that there are some important similarities in the basic causes of these disorders (as well as many differences). Among biological causes, we will see that there are modest genetic contributions to each of these disorders, and that at least part of the genetic vulnerability may be nonspecific, or common across the disorders (e.g., Barlow, 2002a). The common genetic vulnerability is manifested at a psychological level by the personality trait called *neuroticism*—a proneness to experience negative mood states. The brain structures most centrally involved are generally in the limbic system (often known as the emotional brain), and the neurotransmitter substances that are most centrally involved are GABA, norepinephrine, and serotonin (see Chapter 3).

Among common psychological causes, we will see that classical conditioning of fear/panic and/or anxiety to a range of stimuli plays a prominent role in most of these disorders (Mineka & Zinbarg, 1996, 2006). In addition, people who have perceptions of a lack of control over their environments and/or their own emotions seem more vulnerable to developing anxiety disorders. The development of such perceptions of uncontrollability depends heavily on the social environment people are raised in (Chorpita & Barlow, 1998; Mineka & Zinbarg, 1996). Finally, the sociocultural environment that people are raised in also has prominent effects on the kinds of things people become afraid of, or anxious about. Moreover, parenting styles can significantly influence the likelihood that children will develop phobic fears and other anxiety disorders (e.g., Craske & Waters, 2005; Rapee, 2002). Ultimately what we must strive for is a good biopsychosocial understanding of how all these different kinds of causes interact with one another in the development of these disorders. Now we will turn to a more detailed discussion of each disorder to highlight both their common and distinct features, as well as what is known about their causes.

Finally, there are many commonalities across the effective treatments for these different anxiety disorders, as we will see (e.g., Barlow, 2002a, 2004). For each disorder, graduated exposure to feared cues, objects, and situations—until fear/anxiety begins to habituate—constitutes the single most powerful therapeutic ingredient. Further, for certain disorders the addition of cognitive-restructuring techniques can provide added benefit, although for other disorders the addition of these techniques does not seem to be especially beneficial. What these cognitive-restructuring techniques for different disorders have in common is that they help the individual understand his or her distorted patterns of thinking about anxiety-related situations and how these patterns can be changed. Medications can also be useful for all disorders except specific phobias, and nearly all tend to fall into two primary medication categories: benzodiazepines (known as anti-anxiety drugs) and antidepressants. The advantages of behavioral and cognitive-behavioral treatments over medications are that they produce much lower relapse rates than medications once they are discontinued, and they do not have unpleasant side effects that medications often have.

We start with the *phobic disorders,* which are are the most common anxiety disorders. A **phobia** is a persistent and disproportionate fear of some specific object or situation that presents little or no actual danger and yet leads to a great deal of avoidance of these feared situations. As we will see in DSM-IV-TR, there are three main categories of phobias: (1) specific phobia, (2) social phobia, and (3) agoraphobia.

In Review

- What is the central feature of all anxiety disorders? That is, what do they have in common?
- What differentiates the anxiety disorders from one another?
- What are some common kinds of biological and psychosocial causes of the different anxiety disorders?
- What is the most important commonality across effective psychosocial treatments for the anxiety disorders?

Specific Phobias

A person is diagnosed as having a **specific phobia** if she or he shows strong and persistent fear that is excessive or unreasonable and is triggered by the presence of a specific object or situation (see DSM table on page 184). When individuals with specific phobias encounter a phobic stimulus, they often show an immediate fear response that often resembles a panic attack except for the existence of a clear external trigger (APA, *DSM-IV-TR,* 2000). Not surprisingly, such individuals go to great lengths to avoid encounters with their phobic stimulus and sometimes even avoid seemingly innocent representations of it such as photographs or television images. For example, claustrophobic persons may go to great lengths to avoid entering a closet or an elevator, even if this means climbing many flights of stairs or turning down jobs that might require them to take an elevator. This avoidance is a cardinal characteristic of phobias; it occurs both because the phobic

People with claustrophobia may find elevators so frightening that they go to great lengths to avoid them. If for some reason they have to take an elevator, they will be very frightened and may have thoughts about the elevator falling, the doors never opening, or there not being enough air to breathe.

response itself is so unpleasant and because of the phobic person's irrational appraisal of the likelihood that something terrible will happen. Table 6.1 lists the five subtypes of specific phobias in DSM-IV-TR, along with some examples.

The following case is typical of specific phobia:

case STUDY — A Pilot's Wife's Fear

Mary, a married mother of three, was 47 at the time she first sought treatment for both claustrophobia and acrophobia. She reported having been intensely afraid of enclosed spaces and of heights since her teens. She remembered having been locked in closets by her older siblings when she was a child; the siblings also confined her under blankets to scare her and added to her fright by showing her pictures of spiders after releasing her from under the blankets. She traced the onset of her claustrophobia to those traumatic incidents, but she had no idea why she was afraid of heights. While her children had been growing up, she had been a housewife and had managed to live a fairly normal life in spite of her two specific phobias. However, her children were now grown, and she wanted to find a job outside her home. This was proving to be very difficult, however, because she could not take elevators and was not comfortable being on anything other than the first floor of an office building. Moreover, her husband had for some years been working for an airline, which entitled him to free airline tickets. The fact that Mary could not fly (due to her phobias) had become a sore point in her marriage because they both wanted to be able to take advantage of these free tickets to see distant places. Thus, although she had had these phobias for many years, they had become truly disabling only in recent years as her life circumstances had changed and she could no longer easily avoid heights or enclosed spaces.

DSM-IV-TR

Criteria for Specific Phobia

A. Marked or persistent fear that is excessive or unreasonable, cued by the presence or anticipation of a specific object or situation.

B. Exposure to phobic stimulus almost invariably provokes an immediate anxiety response or panic attack.

C. Person recognizes that the fear is excessive or unreasonable.

D. Phobic situation avoided or endured with intense anxiety or distress.

E. Symptoms interfere significantly with normal functioning, or there is marked distress about the phobia.

F. Duration of at least 6 months.

Source: *Adapted with permission from the* Diagnostic and Statistical Manual of Mental Disorders, Fourth Edition, Text Revision *(Copyright 2000). American Psychiatric Association.*

Although people who suffer from phobias usually know that their fears are somewhat irrational, they say that they cannot help themselves. If they attempt to approach the phobic situation, they are overcome with fear or anxiety, which may vary from mild feelings of apprehension and distress (usually while still at some distance) to full-fledged activation of the fight-or-flight response. Regardless of how it begins, phobic behavior tends to be reinforced because every time the person with a phobia avoids a feared situation, his or her anxiety decreases. In addition, the benefits derived from being disabled, such as increased attention, sympathy, and some control over the behavior of others, may also sometimes reinforce a phobia.

TABLE 6.1 Subtypes of Specific Phobias in DSM-IV-TR

Phobia Type	Examples
Animal	Snakes, spiders, dogs, insects, birds
Natural Environment	Storms, heights, water
Blood-Injection-Injury	Seeing blood or an injury, receiving an injection, seeing a person in a wheelchair
Situational	Public transportation, tunnels, bridges, elevators, flying, driving, enclosed spaces
Other	Choking, vomiting, "space phobia" (fear of falling down if away from walls or other support)

Source: Reprinted with permission from the *Diagnostic and Statistical Manual of Mental Disorders, Fourth Edition, Text Revision* (Copyright 2000). American Psychiatric Association.

This boy suffers from height phobia and can only barely peer over the end of the diving board after watching his friends all dive successfully.

Blood-Injection-Injury Phobia

One category of specific phobias that probably occurs in about 3 to 4 percent of the population has a number of interesting and unique characteristics (Öst & Hellström, 1997; Page, 1994). In **blood-injection-injury phobia,** afflicted people typically experience at least as much (if not more) disgust as fear (Woody & Teachman, 2000). They also show a unique physiological response when confronted with the sight of blood or injury. Rather than showing the simple increase in heart rate and blood pressure seen when most people with phobias encounter their phobic object, these people show an initial acceleration, followed by a dramatic drop in both heart rate and blood pressure. This is very frequently accompanied by nausea, dizziness, and/or fainting, which do not occur with other specific phobias (Öst & Hellström, 1997).

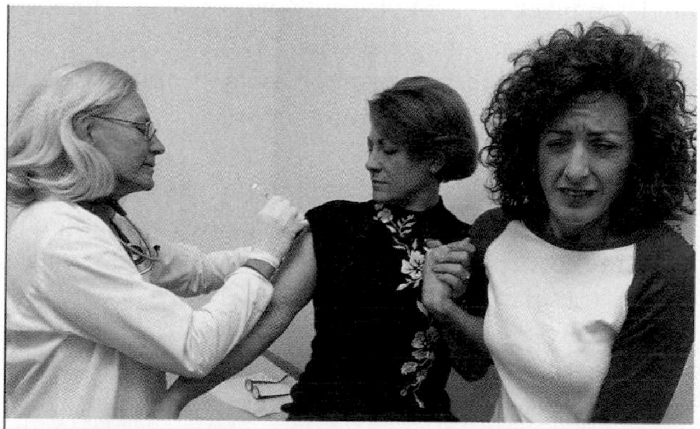

In blood-injection-injury phobia, the afflicted person experiences disgust and fear at the sight of someone receiving an injection. When confronted with the sight of blood or injury, people with this phobic disorder often experience nausea, dizziness, and fainting.

Interestingly, people with this phobia show this unique physiological response pattern only in the presence of blood and injury stimuli; they exhibit the more typical physiological response pattern characteristic of the fight-or-flight response to other feared objects (see Dahlloef & Öst, 1998; Öst & Hugdahl, 1985). From an evolutionary and functional standpoint, this unique physiological response pattern may have evolved for a specific purpose: By fainting, the person being attacked might inhibit further attack, and if an attack did occur, the drop in blood pressure would minimize blood loss (Craske, 1999; Marks & Nesse, 1991).

Age of Onset and Gender Differences in Specific Phobias

Specific phobias are quite common, especially in women. Results of the National Comorbidity Survey-Replication revealed a lifetime prevalence rate of about 12 percent (Kessler, Chiu, et al., 2005c). Among people with one specific phobia, over 75 percent have at least one other specific fear that is excessive (Curtis, Magee, et al., 1998). The relative gender ratios vary considerably according to the type of specific phobia, but phobias are always considerably more common in women than in men. For example, about 90 to 95 percent of people with animal phobias are women, but the gender ratio is less than 2:1 for blood-injury phobia. The average age of onset for different types of specific phobias also varies widely. Animal phobias usually begin in childhood, as do blood-injury phobias and dental phobias. However, other phobias such as claustrophobia and driving phobia tend to begin in adolescence or early adulthood (Barlow, 2002a; Öst, 1987).

Psychosocial Causal Factors

A variety of psychosocial causal factors has been implicated in the origins of specific phobias, ranging from deep-seated psychodynamic conflicts to relatively straightforward traumatic conditioning of fear. According to the psychodynamic view, phobias represent a defense against anxiety that stems from repressed impulses from the id. Because it is too dangerous to "know" the repressed id impulse, the anxiety is displaced onto some external object or situation that has some symbolic relationship to the real object of the anxiety. For example, in his classic case of Little Hans, Freud (1909) postulated that 5-year-old Hans had developed a phobia for horses as a result of anxiety stemming from a repressed Oedipal conflict in which Hans unconsciously desired his mother and wanted to kill his father so that he could have his mother all to himself. This led him unconsciously to fear that his father would want to "kill" or castrate him. The intense internal conflict created by all these unconscious feelings was not acceptable to Hans's conscious mind, so the anxiety was displaced onto horses, which supposedly bore some symbolic relationship to his father.

This prototypical psychodynamic account of how phobias are acquired has long been criticized as being far too speculative, and an alternative, simpler account of the origins of Hans's phobia for horses derives from learning theory (e.g., Wolpe & Rachman, 1960). When Hans was 4 years old, he had witnessed a horse being badly hurt in an accident; Hans had become very upset witnessing this incident (an example of traumatic classical conditioning) and later began to avoid leaving the house so as not to encounter horses in the street.

PHOBIAS AS LEARNED BEHAVIOR Building on these observations of Wolpe and Rachman (1960), numerous theorists in the 1960s proposed that the principles of classical conditioning appeared to account for the acquisition of irrational fears and phobias. The fear response can readily be conditioned to previously neutral stimuli when these stimuli are paired with traumatic or painful events. We would also expect that, once acquired, phobic fears would generalize to other, similar objects or situations. Recall, for example, that Mary's claustrophobia had probably been caused by multiple incidents as a child when her siblings locked her in closets and confined her under blankets to scare her. But as an adult Mary feared elevators and caves as well as other enclosed places. The powerful role of classical conditioning in the development of phobias was supported in a survey by Öst and Hugdahl (1981), who administered questionnaires to 106 adult phobic clients that concerned, among other things, the purported origins of their fears (see Mineka & Sutton, in press, for a review). Fifty-eight percent cited traumatic conditioning experiences as the sources of their phobias. Some of these traumatic conditioning events were simply uncued panic attacks, which are now known to effectively condition fear (e.g., Forsyth & Eiffert, 1998). Direct traumatic conditioning may be especially common in the onset of dental phobia (Kent, 1997), claustrophobia (Rachman, 1997), and accident phobia (Kuch, 1997).

Vicarious Conditioning of Phobic Fears Direct traumatic conditioning is not the only way people can learn irrational, phobic fears. Simply watching a phobic person behaving fearfully with his or her phobic object can be distressing to the observer and can result in fear being transmitted from one person to another through vicarious or observational classical conditioning. For example, one man, as a boy, had witnessed his grandfather vomit while dying. Shortly after this traumatic event, the boy had developed a strong and persistent vomiting phobia. Indeed, when this man was in middle age he even contemplated suicide one time when he was nauseated and feared vomiting (Mineka & Zinbarg, 2006).

Monkeys who watch a model monkey (such as the one illustrated here) behaving fearfully with a live boa constrictor will rapidly acquire an intense fear of snakes themselves. Fears can thus be learned vicariously, without any direct traumatic experience.

Animal research using rhesus monkeys has increased our confidence that vicarious conditioning of intense fears can indeed occur. In these experiments, Mineka and Cook and their colleagues (e.g., Mineka, Davidson, Cook, & Keir, 1984; Mineka & Cook, 1993; Cook & Mineka, 1991) showed that laboratory-reared monkeys who were not initially afraid of snakes rapidly developed a phobic-like fear of snakes simply through observing a wild-reared monkey behaving fearfully with snakes. Significant fear was acquired after only 4 to 8 minutes of exposure to the wild-reared monkey with snakes, and there were no signs that the fear had diminished 3 months later. The monkeys could also learn the fear simply through watching a videotape of the wild-reared model monkey behaving fearfully with snakes. This suggests that the mass media also play a role in the vicarious conditioning of fears and phobias in people (Cook & Mineka, 1990; Mineka & Sutton, in press).

Sources of Individual Differences in the Learning of Phobias Does the direct and vicarious conditioning model really explain the origins of most phobias? Given all the traumas that people undergo, why don't more people develop phobias (Mineka & Sutton, in press; Mineka & Zinbarg, 1996, 2006, Rachman, 1990)? The answer seems to be that differences in life experiences among individuals strongly affect whether or not conditioned fears or phobias actually develop. For example, years of positive experiences with friendly dogs before being bitten by one will probably keep the bite victim from developing a dog phobia. Thus, to understand individual differences in the development and maintenance of phobias, we need to understand the role of the different life experiences of people who undergo the same trauma. Some of these life experiences may make certain people more vulnerable to phobias than others, and other experiences may serve as protective factors for the development of phobias (Mineka & Sutton, in press).

Children who have had more previous nontraumatic experiences with a dentist are less likely to develop dental anxiety after a bad and painful experience than are children with fewer previous nontraumatic experiences (de Jongh et al., 1995; Kent, 1997). This shows the importance of the individual's prior familiarity with an object or situation in determining whether a phobia develops following a fear-conditioning experience. Moreover, Mineka and Cook (1986) showed that monkeys who first simply watched nonfearful monkeys behaving nonfearfully with snakes were immunized against acquiring a fear of snakes when they later saw fearful monkeys behaving fearfully with snakes. By analogy, if a child has extensive exposure to a nonfearful parent behaving nonfearfully with the phobic object (e.g., spiders) or situation (e.g., heights) of the other parent, this may immunize the child against the effects of later seeing the phobic parent behaving fearfully with the phobic object (Mineka & Sutton, in press).

A person who has had good experiences with a potentially phobic stimulus, such as the young woman romping here with her dog, is likely to be immunized from later acquiring a fear of dogs even if she has a traumatic encounter with one.

Events that occur *during* a conditioning experience, as well as before it, are also important in determining the level of fear that is conditioned. For example, experiencing an inescapable and uncontrollable event, such as being attacked by a dog that one cannot escape from after being bitten, is expected to condition fear much more powerfully than experiencing the same intensity of trauma that is escapable or to some extent controllable (e.g., by running away after the attack; Mineka, 1985a; Mineka & Zinbarg, 1996, 2006). In addition, the experiences that a person has *after* a conditioning experience may affect the strength and maintenance of the conditioned fear (Rescorla, 1974; White & Davey, 1989). For example, the *inflation effect* suggests that a person who acquired, for example, a mild fear of driving following a minor crash might be expected to develop a full-blown phobia if he or she later were physically assaulted, even though no automobile was present during the assault (Dadds, Davey, & Field, 2001; Mineka, 1985a; Mineka & Zinbarg, 1996, 2006). Even verbal information that later alters one's interpretation of the dangerousness of a previous trauma can inflate the level of fear (e.g., being told, "You're lucky to be alive because the man who crashed into your car last week had lost his license due to a record of drunk driving leading to fatal car crashes"; Dadds et al., 2001). These examples show that the factors involved in the origins and maintenance of fears and phobias are more complex than suggested by the traditional, simplistic conditioning view, although they are nevertheless consistent with contemporary views of conditioning.

Recently it has been shown that our cognitions, or thoughts, can help maintain our phobias once they have been acquired. For example, people with phobias are constantly on the alert for their phobic objects or situations and for other stimuli relevant to their phobia. Nonphobic persons tend to direct their attention away from threatening stimuli (see Mineka, Rafaeli, & Yovel, 2003). In addition, phobics also markedly overestimate the probability that feared objects have been, or will be, followed by frightening events. This cognitive bias may help maintain or strengthen phobic fears with the passage of time (Öhman & Mineka, 2001; Tomarken, Mineka, & Cook, 1989).

Evolutionary Preparedness for the Development of Fears and Phobias Consider the observation that people are much more likely to have phobias of snakes, water, heights, and enclosed spaces than of motorcycles and guns, even though the latter objects may be at least as likely to be associated with trauma. This is because our evolutionary history has affected which stimuli we are most likely to come to fear. Primates and humans seem to be evolutionarily prepared to rapidly associate certain objects—such as snakes, spiders, water, and enclosed spaces—with frightening or unpleasant events (e.g., Mineka & Öhman, 2002; Öhman, 1996; Seligman, 1971). This *preparedness* occurs because, over the course of evolution, those primates and humans who rapidly acquired fears of certain objects or situations that posed real threats to our early ancestors may have enjoyed a selective advantage. Thus "prepared" fears are not inborn or innate but, rather, are easily acquired or especially resistant to extinction. Guns and motorcycles, by contrast, were not present in our early evolutionary history and so did not convey any such selective advantage.

There is now a large amount of experimental evidence supporting the preparedness theory of phobias. In one important series of experiments using human subjects, Öhman and his colleagues (see Öhman, 1996; Öhman & Mineka, 2001, for reviews) found that fear is conditioned more effectively to fear-relevant stimuli (slides of snakes and spiders) than to fear-irrelevant stimuli (slides of flowers and mushrooms). These researchers also found that once the individuals acquired the conditioned responses to fear-relevant stimuli, these responses (including activation of the relevant brain area, the amygdala) could be elicited even when the fear-relevant stimuli (but not the fear-irrelevant stimuli) were presented subliminally (that is, presentation was so brief that the stimuli were not consciously perceived; e.g., Carlsson et al., 2004). This subliminal activation of responses to phobic stimuli may help to account for certain aspects of the irrationality of phobias. That is, people with phobias may not be able to control their fear because the fear may arise from cognitive structures that are not under conscious control (Öhman & Mineka, 2001; Öhman & Soares, 1993).

Another series of experiments showed that lab-reared monkeys in a vicarious conditioning paradigm can easily acquire fears of fear-relevant stimuli such as toy snakes and toy crocodiles, but not of fear-irrelevant stimuli such as flowers and a toy rabbit (Cook & Mineka, 1989, 1990). Thus both monkeys and humans seem selectively to associate certain fear-relevant stimuli with threat or danger. Moreover, these lab-reared monkeys had had no prior exposure to any of the stimuli (e.g., snakes or flowers) before participating in these experiments. Thus the monkey results support the evolutionarily based preparedness hypothesis even more strongly than the human experiments. For example, human subjects (unlike the lab-reared monkeys) might show superior conditioning to snakes or spiders because of preexisting negative associations to snakes or spiders, rather than because of evolutionary factors (Mineka & Öhman, 2002).

Genetic and Temperamental Causal Factors

Genetic and temperamental variables affect the speed and strength of conditioning of fear (e.g., Gray, 1987; Zinbarg & Mohlman, 1998). That is, depending on their temperament or personality, people are more or less likely to acquire phobias. Indeed, Kagan and his colleagues (2001) have found that behaviorally inhibited toddlers (who are excessively timid, shy, easily distressed, etc.) at 21 months of age were at higher risk of developing multiple specific phobias at 7 to 8 years of age than were uninhibited children (32 versus 5 percent). The average number of reported fears in the inhibited group was three to four per child (Biederman et al., 1990).

Several studies also suggest a modest genetic contribution to the development of specific phobias. For example, a large female twin study found that monozygotic (identical) twins were more likely to share animal phobias, blood-injury phobias, and situational phobias (such as of heights or water) than were dizygotic (nonidentical) twins (Kendler, Karkowski, & Prescott, 1999b; Kendler et al., 1992b). However, the same study also found evidence that nonshared environmental factors (i.e., individual specific experiences not shared by twins) also played a very substantial role in the origins of specific phobias, a result that supports the idea that phobias are learned behaviors.

Treating Specific Phobias

Exposure therapy—the best treatment for specific phobias—involves controlled *exposure* to the stimuli or situations that elicit phobic fear (Antony & Barlow, 2002; Craske & Mystkowski, in press). Clients are gradually placed—symbolically or increasingly under "real-life" conditions—in those situations they find most frightening. In treatment, clients are encouraged to expose themselves (either alone, or with the aid of a therapist or friend) to their feared situations for long enough periods of time that their fear begins to subside. One variant on this procedure, known as *participant modeling,* is often more effective than exposure alone. Here the therapist calmly models ways of interacting with the phobic stimulus or situation (Bandura, 1977a, 1997b). These techniques enable clients to learn that these situations are not as frightening as they had thought and that their anxiety, while unpleasant, is not harmful and will gradually dissipate (Craske & Mystkowski, in press; Craske & Rowe, 1997). For certain phobias such as small-animal phobias, flying phobia, claustrophobia, and blood-injury phobia, exposure therapy is often highly effective when administered in a single long session (up to 3 hours; Öst, 1997; Öst, Alm, Brandberg, & Breitholtz, 2001). This can be an advantage, because some people are more likely to seek treatment if they have to go only once.

One variation on exposure therapy is called participant modeling. *Here the therapist models how to touch and pick up a live tarantula and encourages the spider-phobic client to imitate her behavior. This treatment is graduated, with the client's first task being simply to touch the tarantula from the outside of the cage, then to touch the tarantula with a stick, then with a gloved hand, then with a bare hand, and finally to let the tarantula crawl over his hand. This is a highly effective treatment, with the most spider-phobic clients being able to reach the top of the hierarchy within 60–90 minutes.*

An example of the use of exposure therapy comes from the treatment of Mary, the housewife whose acrophobia and claustrophobia we described earlier.

case STUDY — Mary's Treatment

Treatment consisted of 13 sessions of graduated exposure exercises in which the therapist accompanied Mary first into mildly fear-provoking situations and then gradually into more and more fear-provoking situations. Mary also engaged in homework, doing these exposure exercises by herself. The prolonged *in vivo* ("real-life") exposure sessions lasted as long as necessary for her anxiety to subside. Initial sessions focused on Mary's claustrophobia and on getting her to be able to ride for a few floors in an elevator, first with the therapist and then alone. Later she took longer elevator rides in taller buildings. Exposure for the acrophobia consisted of walking around the periphery of the inner atrium on the top floor of a tall hotel and, later, spending time at a mountain vista overlook spot. The top of the claustrophobia hierarchy consisted of taking a tour of an underground cave. After 13 sessions, Mary successfully took a flight with her husband to Europe and climbed to the top of many tall tourist attractions there.

Recently, some therapists have begun to use *virtual reality environments* to simulate certain kinds of phobic situations, such as heights and airplanes, as places to conduct exposure treatment. If such techniques were highly effective and widely available, there would be no need to conduct treatment in real situations (such as real airplanes). A few controlled studies have yielded promising results, but it is too soon to draw any strong conclusions about the relative efficacy of virtual reality versus live exposure (Craske & Mystkowski, in press; Rothbaum, Hodges, et al., 2002).

Some researchers have also tried combining cognitive techniques or medications with exposure-based techniques to see if this can produce additional gains. In general, studies using cognitive techniques alone have not produced results as good as those using exposure-based techniques, and the addition of cognitive techniques has generally not added much (Antony & Barlow, 2002; Craske & Mystkowski, in press). Similarly, medication treatments are ineffective by themselves, and there is even some evidence that anti-anxiety medications may interfere with the beneficial effects of exposure therapy (Antony & Barlow, 2002). Very recently, however, preliminary evidence has shown that a drug known as d-cycloserine, which is known to facilitate extinction of conditioned fear in animals (e.g., Walker, Ressler, Lu, & Davis, 2002), may also enhance the effectiveness of small amounts of exposure therapy for fear of heights in a virtual reality environment (Ressler, Rothbaum, et al., 2004). These results are very promising, but much more work is necessary before it will be known how useful this drug will be in enhancing the effects of exposure therapy for many different kinds of phobias.

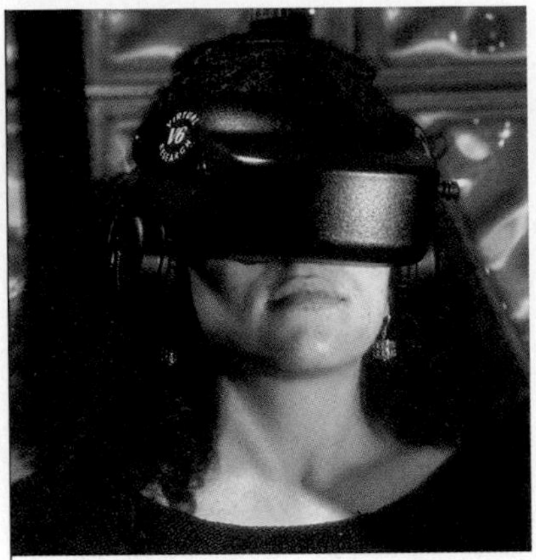

New treatments using virtual reality environments allow therapists to simulate certain kinds of phobic situations, such as standing at heights or sitting in airplanes, in a contrived setting. Unfortunately, the equipment is currently quite costly, which makes access to this treatment somewhat limited.

In Review

- What are the five subtypes of specific phobias listed in the DSM-IV-TR?
- Describe the original classical-conditioning explanation for the origins of specific phobias, and identify the primary criticisms of this hypothesis.
- Explain how recent behavioral and evolutionary explanations have improved and expanded the basic conditioning hypothesis of phobia acquisition.
- Describe the most effective treatment for specific phobias.

Social Phobias

Social phobia (or social anxiety disorder), as the DSM-IV-TR describes it, is characterized by disabling fears of one or more specific social situations (such as public speaking, urinating in a public bathroom, or eating or writing in public; see the DSM-IV-TR Table). In these situations, a person fears that she or he may be exposed to the scrutiny and potential negative evaluation of others and/or that she or he may act in an embarrassing or humiliating manner. Because of their fears, people with social phobias either avoid these situations or endure them with great distress. Intense fear of public speaking is the single most common type of social phobia. DSM-IV-TR also identifies one subtype of social phobia known as *generalized social phobia.* People with generalized social phobia have significant fears of most social situations (rather than simply a few) and often also have a diagnosis of avoidant personality disorder (see Chapter 11; e.g., Hofmann & Barlow, 2002; Skodol et al., 1995).

The diagnosis of social phobia is very common and occurs even in famous performers such as Barbra Streisand and Carly Simon. The National Comorbidity Survey-Replication estimated that about 12 percent of the population will qualify for a diagnosis of social phobia at some point in their lives (Kessler, Berglund, et al., 2005b; see also Tillfors, 2004); this disorder is somewhat more common among women than men (about 60 percent are women).

DSM-IV-TR

Criteria for Social Phobia

A. Marked or persistent fear of one or more social or performance situations in which the person is exposed to unfamiliar people or possible scrutiny of others.

B. Exposure to feared social situation almost invariably provokes anxiety or panic.

C. Person recognizes that the fear is excessive or unreasonable.

D. Feared social or performance situation avoided or endure with great distress or anxiety.

E. Symptoms interfere significantly with person's normal routine, or occupational or social functioning.

Source: *Adapted with permission from the* Diagnostic and Statistical Manual of Mental Disorders, Fourth Edition, Text Revisio *(Copyright 2000). American Psychiatric Association.*

Unlike specific phobias, which most often originate in childhood, social phobias typically begin somewhat later, during adolescence or early adulthood (Tillfors, 2004; Wells & Clark, 1997). More than half of people with social phobia suffer from one or more additional anxiety disorders at some point in their lives, and about 50 percent also suffer from a depressive disorder at the same time (Kessler, Chiu, et al., 2005c). Approximately one-third abuse alcohol to reduce their anxiety and help them face the situations they fear (for example, drinking *before* going to a party; Magee et al., 1996).

The case of Paul is typical of social phobia (except that not all people with social phobia have full-blown panic attacks, as Paul did, in their social phobic situations).

case STUDY **A Surgeon's Social Phobia**

Paul was a single white male in his mid-thirties when he first presented for treatment. He was a surgeon who reported a 13-year history of social phobia. He had very few social outlets because of his persistent concerns that people would notice how nervous he was in social situations, and he had not dated in many years. Convinced that people would perceive him as foolish or crazy, he particularly worried that people would notice how his jaw tensed up when around other people. Paul frequently chewed gum in public situations, believing that this kept his face from looking distorted. Notably, he had no particular problems talking with people in professional situations. For example, he was quite calm talking with patients before and after surgery. During surgery, when his face was covered with a mask, he also had no trouble carrying out surgical tasks or interacting with the other surgeons and nurses in the room. The trouble began when he left the operating room and had to make small talk—and eye contact—with the other doctors and nurses or with the patient's family. He frequently had panic attacks in these social situations. During the panic attacks he experienced heart palpitations, fears of "going crazy," and a sense of his mind "shutting down." Because the panic attacks occurred only in social situations, he was diagnosed as having social phobia rather than panic disorder.

Paul's social phobia and panic had begun about 13 years earlier when he was under a great deal of stress. His family's business had failed, his parents had divorced, and his mother had had a heart attack. It was in this context of multiple stressors that a personally traumatic incident probably triggered the onset of his social phobia. One day he had come home from medical school to find his best friend in bed with his fiancée. About a month later he had his first panic attack and started avoiding social situations.

Interaction of Psychosocial and Biological Causal Factors

Social phobias generally involve learned behaviors that have been shaped by evolutionary factors. Such learning is most likely to occur in people who are genetically or temperamentally at risk.

SOCIAL PHOBIAS AS LEARNED BEHAVIOR Like specific phobias, social phobias often seem to originate from simple instances of *direct* or *vicarious classical conditioning* such as experiencing or witnessing a perceived social defeat or humiliation, or being or witnessing the target of anger or criticism (Mineka & Zinbarg, 1995, 2006; Tillfors, 2004). In two studies, 56 to 58 percent of people with social phobia recalled and identified direct traumatic experiences as having been involved in the origin of their social phobias (Öst & Hugdahl, 1981; Townsley et al., 1995). Another study reported that 92 percent of an adult sample of people with social phobia reported a history of severe teasing in childhood, compared to only 35 percent in a group of people with obsessive-compulsive disorder (McCabe, Antony, et al., 2003). Öst and Hugdahl (1981) also reported that another 13 percent of their subjects recalled vicarious conditioning experiences of some sort. Another recent study interviewed a group of people with social phobia about their images of themselves in social phobic situations and asked where those images originated (Hackmann, Clark, & McManus, 2000). Ninety-six percent of these people remembered some socially traumatic experience that was linked to their own current image of themselves in socially phobic situations. The themes of these memories included having been "criticized for having an anxiety symptom" (e.g., being red or blushing), and having felt "self-conscious and uncomfortable in public as a consequence of past criticism" such as "having previously been bullied and called a 'nothing'" (Hackmann et al., 2000, p. 606).

Intense fear of public speaking is the single most common social phobia.

People with generalized social phobia also may be especially likely to have grown up with parents who were socially isolated and avoidant and who devalued sociability, thus providing ample opportunity for vicarious learning of social fears (Morris, 2001; Rapee & Melville, 1997). More generally, parents with anxiety disorders are more likely than nonanxious parents to tell their children about the potential dangers of a novel situation such as a playground, and thereby strengthen anxious children's avoidant tendencies (Morris, 2001). However, as with specific phobias, it is important to recognize that not everyone who experiences direct or vicarious conditioning in social situations, or who grows up with socially avoidant parents, develops social phobia. This is because individual differences in experiences play an important role in who develops social phobia, as is the case with specific phobias.

SOCIAL FEARS AND PHOBIAS IN AN EVOLUTIONARY CONTEXT Social fears and phobias by definition involve fears of members of one's own species. By contrast, animal fears and phobias usually involve fear of potential predators. Although animal fears probably evolved to trigger activation of the fight-or-flight response to potential predators, Öhman and colleagues proposed that social fears and phobias evolved as a by-product of dominance hierarchies that are a common social arrangement among animals such as primates (Dimberg & Öhman, 1996; Öhman et al., 1985). Dominance hierarchies are established through aggressive encounters between members of a social group, and a defeated individual typically displays fear and submissive behavior but only rarely attempts to escape the situation completely. Thus, these investigators argued, it is not surprising that people with social phobia endure being in their feared situations rather than running away and escaping them, as people with animal phobias often do.

If social phobias evolved as a by-product of dominance hierarchies, it is not surprising that humans have an *evolutionarily based predisposition* to acquire fears of social stimuli that signal dominance and aggression from other humans. These social stimuli include facial expressions of anger or contempt, which on average all humans seem to process more quickly and readily than happy or neutral facial expressions (Öhman et al., 2001; Schupp, Öhman, Junghöfer, et al., 2004). In a series of experiments that paralleled ones for specific phobias, Öhman, Dimberg, and their colleagues demonstrated that subjects develop stronger conditioned responses when slides of angry faces are paired with mild electric shocks than when happy or neutral faces are paired with the same shocks (Dimberg & Öhman, 1996). Indeed, even very brief subliminal (not consciously perceived) presentations of the angry face were sufficient to activate the conditioned responses (e.g., Parra, Esteves, Flykt, & Öhman, 1997). Such results may help explain the seemingly irrational quality of social phobia, in that the angry faces are processed very quickly and an emotional reaction can be activated without a person's awareness of any threat.

GENETIC AND TEMPERAMENTAL FACTORS As with specific phobias, not everyone who undergoes or witnesses traumatic social humiliation or defeat goes on to develop full-blown social phobia. Results from one large study of female twins and another study of male twins suggested that there is a modest genetic contribution to social phobia; estimates were that the proportion of variance due to genetic factors was about 30 percent (Kendler, Myers, Prescott, & Neale, 2001; Kendler et al., 1992b). Nevertheless, both studies suggest that an even larger proportion of variance in who develops social phobia is due to nonshared environmental factors, which is consistent with a strong role for learning.

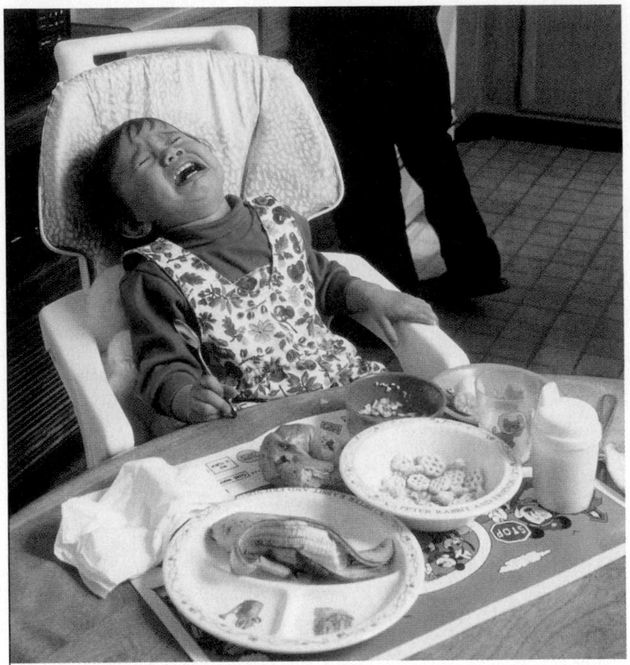

Infants and young children who are fearful and easily distressed by novel people or situations are sometimes high on the temperamental variable called behavioral inhibition. *Such infants show an increased risk of developing social phobia in adolescence.*

The most important temperamental variable is behavioral inhibition. Behaviorally inhibited infants who are easily distressed by unfamiliar stimuli and who are shy and avoidant are more likely to become fearful during childhood and, by adolescence, show increased risk of developing social phobia (Hayward et al., 1998; Kagan, 1997). For example, children classified as behaviorally inhibited when they are toddlers had higher rates of social anxiety by age 13 than children who were not behaviorally inhibited as toddlers (Schwartz et al., 1999). Another longitudinal study found that children who reported that they had been behaviorally inhibited as children were four times more likely to develop social phobia in adolescence than were adolescents who were not behaviorally inhibited as children (Hayward et al., 1998).

PERCEPTIONS OF UNCONTROLLABILITY AND UNPREDICTABILITY Being exposed to uncontrollable and unpredictable stressful events (such as Paul finding his fiancée in bed with his best friend) may play an important role in the development of social phobia (Barlow, 2002a; Mathew, Coplan, & Gorman, 2001; Mineka & Zinbarg, 1995, 2006). Perceptions of uncontrollability and unpredictability often lead to submissive and unassertive behavior, which is characteristic of socially anxious or phobic people. This kind of behavior is especially likely if the perceptions of uncontrollability stem from an actual social defeat, which is known in animals to lead to both increased submissive behavior and increased fear (Mineka & Zinbarg, 1995, 2006). Consistent with this, people with social phobia have a diminished sense of personal control over events in their lives (Leung & Heimberg, 1996). This diminished sense of personal control may develop, at least in part, as a function of having been raised in families with somewhat overprotective (and sometimes rejecting) parents (Lieb et al., 2000).

COGNITIVE VARIABLES Cognitive factors also play a role in the onset and maintenance of social phobia. Beck and Emery (1985) suggested that people with social phobia tend to expect that other people will reject or negatively evaluate them. This leads to a sense of vulnerability when they are around people who might pose a threat. Clark and Wells (1995; Wells & Clark, 1997) also argued that these danger schemas of socially anxious people lead them to expect that they will behave in an awkward and unacceptable fashion, resulting in rejection and loss of status. Such expectations lead to their being preoccupied with bodily responses and with negative self-images in social situations, and to overestimating how easily others will detect their anxiety (Hirsch, Meynen, & Clark, 2004). Such intense self-preoccupation during social situations, even to the point of attending to their own heart rate, interferes with their ability to interact skillfully (Hirsch, Clark, Mathews, & Williams, 2003; Pineles & Mineka, 2005). A vicious cycle may evolve: Social phobics' inward attention and somewhat awkward behavior may lead others to react to them in a less friendly fashion, confirming their expectations (Clark, 1997; Clark & McManus, 2002).

People with social phobia interpret ambiguous social events (such as a dinner companion's brief distraction) to be negative, and mildly negative social events (such as a dinner companion's apparent disinterest) as catastrophic.

Treating Social Phobias

There are very effective forms of behavior therapy, and of cognitive-behavioral therapy, for social phobia. As for specific phobias, behavioral treatments were developed first and generally involve prolonged and graduated exposure to social situations that evoke fear. More recently, as research has revealed the underlying distorted cognitions that characterize social phobia, cognitive techniques have been added to the behavioral techniques, generating a form of cognitive-behavioral therapy. The therapist attempts to help clients with social phobia identify their underlying negative automatic thoughts ("I've got nothing interesting to say" or "No one is interested in me"). After helping clients understand that these automatic thoughts often involve cognitive distortions, the therapist helps the clients change these inner thoughts and beliefs through logical reanalysis. The process of logical reanalysis might involve asking oneself questions to challenge the automatic thoughts: "Do I know for certain that I won't have anything to say?" "Does being nervous have to lead to or equal looking stupid?" In addition, in one highly effective version of such treatments, the client may receive videotaped feedback to help modify her or his distorted self-images. Such techniques have now been very successfully applied to the treatment of social phobia (Clark, Ehlers, et al., 2003; Heimberg, 2002).

An example of successful combined treatment can be seen in the case of Paul, the surgeon described earlier who had social phobia.

case study **Paul's Treatment**

Since the onset of his social phobia 13 years earlier, Paul had taken a tricyclic antidepressant at one point. The drug had helped stop his panic attacks, although he continued to fear them intensely and still avoided social situations. Thus there was little effect on his social phobia. He had also been in supportive psychotherapy, which helped his depression at the time but not his social phobia or his panic. When he went for treatment at an anxiety clinic, he was not on any medication or in any other form of treatment. Treatment consisted of 14 weeks of cognitive-behavioral therapy. By the end of treatment, Paul was not panicking at all and was quite comfortable in most social situations that he had previously avoided. He was seeing old friends whom he had avoided for years because of his anxiety, and he was beginning to date. Indeed, he even asked his female therapist for a date during the last treatment session! Although such a request was clearly inappropriate, it did indicate how much progress he had made.

Unlike specific phobias, social phobias can also sometimes be treated with medications. The most effective and widely used medications are several categories of antidepressants (including the monoamine oxidase inhibitors and the selective serotonin reuptake inhibitors discussed in Chapters 7 and 17; Blanco et al., 2002; Roy-Byrne & Cowley, 2002). In some studies the effects of these medications have been comparable to those seen with cognitive-behavioral treatments. However, in one recent study a new version of cognitive-behavior therapy produced much more substantial improvement than did medication (Clark, Ehlers, et al., 2003). Moreover, the medications must be taken over a long period of time to help ensure that relapse does not occur (Blanco et al., 2002; Hayward & Wardle, 1997). A distinct advantage of behavioral and cognitive therapies over medications, then, is that they generally produce much more long-lasting improvement, with very low relapse rates; indeed, clients often continue to improve after treatment is over.

In Review

- What are the primary diagnostic criteria for social phobia and for the subtype of generalized social phobia?
- Identify the psychosocial and biological causal factors of social phobia, and explain how they interact.
- Describe the major treatment approaches used for social phobias.

Panic Disorder with and without Agoraphobia

Panic Disorder

Diagnostically, **panic disorder** is defined and characterized by the occurrence of "unexpected" panic attacks that often seem to come "out of the blue." According to the DSM-IV-TR definition (see the DSM tables), the person must have experienced recurrent unexpected attacks and must have been persistently concerned about having another attack or worried about the consequences of having an attack (e.g., of "losing control" or "going crazy") for at least a month. For such an event to qualify as a full-blown panic attack, there must be abrupt onset of at least 4 of 13 symptoms, most of which are physical although three are cognitive: (1) depersonalization (a feeling of being detached from one's body) or derealization (a feeling that the external world is strange or unreal), (2) fear of dying, or (3) fear of "going crazy" or "losing control." Panic attacks are brief and intense, with symptoms developing abruptly and usually reaching peak intensity within 10 minutes; the attacks usually subside in 20 to 30 minutes and rarely last more than an hour. Periods of anxiety, by contrast, do not usually have such an abrupt onset and are more long-lasting.

Panic attacks are often "unexpected" or "uncued" in the sense that they do not appear to be provoked by identifiable aspects of the immediate situation. Indeed, they sometimes occur in situations in which they might be least

DSM-IV-TR

Criteria for Panic Attack

A discrete period of intense fear in which four or more of the following symptoms develop abruptly and reach a peak within 10 minutes:

1. Palpitations or pounding heart.
2. Sweating.
3. Trembling or shaking.
4. Sensations of shortness of breath or being smothered.
5. Feeling of choking.
6. Chest pain or discomfort.
7. Nausea or abdominal distress.
8. Feeling dizzy, lightheaded, or faint.
9. Derealization (feelings of unreality) or depersonalization (being detached from oneself).
10. Fear of losing control or going crazy.
11. Fear of dying.
12. Paresthesias (numbness or tingling sensations).
13. Chills or hot flushes.

Source: *Adapted with permission from the* Diagnostic and Statistical Manual of Mental Disorders, Fourth Edition, Text Revision *(Copyright 2000). American Psychiatric Association.*

DSM-IV-TR

Criteria for Panic Disorder without Agoraphobia

A. Both (1) and (2):
   (1) Recurrent, unexpected panic attacks.
   (2) At least one of the attacks followed by 1 month or more of
      (a) Concern about having another one.
      (b) Worry about consequences of an attack ("heart attack").
B. Absence of agoraphobia.
C. Panic attack not due to physiological effects of a substance or medical condition.
D. Panic attacks not better explained by another mental disorder such as social or specific phobia.

Source: *Adapted with permission from the* Diagnostic and Statistical Manual of Mental Disorders, Fourth Edition, Text Revision *(Copyright 2000). American Psychiatric Association.*

expected, such as during relaxation or during sleep (known as *nocturnal panic*). In other cases, however, the panic attacks are said to be "situationally predisposed," occurring only sometimes while the person is in a particular situation such as while driving a car or being in a crowd.

Because the majority of the 13 symptoms of a panic attack are physical, is not surprising that as many as 85 percent of people having a panic attack may show up repeatedly at emergency rooms or physicians' offices for what they are convinced is a medical problem—usually cardiac, respiratory, or neurological (White & Barlow, 2002). Unfortunately, a correct diagnosis is often not made for years, in spite of normal results on numerous costly medical tests. Prompt diagnosis and treatment is also important because panic disorder causes approximately as much impairment in social and occupational functioning as that caused by major depression (Hirschfeld, 1996) and because panic disorder can contribute to the development or worsening of a variety of medical problems (White & Barlow, 2002).

The case of Mindy Markowitz is typical of someone who has panic disorder without agoraphobia.

case study: Art Director's Panic Attacks

Mindy Markowitz is an attractive . . . 25-year-old art director . . . who comes to an anxiety clinic . . . seeking treatment for "panic attacks" that have occurred with increasing frequency over the past year, often two or three times a day. These attacks begin with a sudden, intense wave of "horrible fear" that seems to come out of nowhere, sometimes during the day, sometimes waking her from sleep. She begins to tremble, is nauseated, sweats profusely, feels as though she is choking, and fears that she will lose control and do something crazy, like run screaming into the street.

Mindy remembers first having attacks like this when she was in high school. She was dating a boy her parents disapproved of, and had to do a lot of "sneaking around" to avoid confrontations . . . she was under a lot of pressure as the principal designer of her high school yearbook, and [she] was applying to Ivy League colleges. She remembers that her first panic attack occurred just after the yearbook went to press and she was accepted by Harvard, Yale, and Brown. The attacks lasted only a few minutes, and she would just "sit through them." She was worried enough to mention them to her mother; but . . . she did not seek treatment.

Mindy has had panic attacks intermittently over the 8 years since her first attack, sometimes not for many months, but sometimes, as now, several times a day. There have been extreme variations in the intensity of the attacks, some being so severe and debilitating that she has had to take a day off from work.

Mindy has always functioned extremely well in school, at work, and in her social life, apart from her panic attacks. . . . She is a lively, friendly person who is respected by her friends and colleagues. . . . Mindy has never limited her activities, even during the times that she was having frequent, severe attacks, although she might stay home from work for a day because she was exhausted from multiple attacks. She has never associated the attacks with particular places. She says . . . she is as likely to have an attack at home in her own bed as on the subway, so there is no point in avoiding the subway. Whether she has an attack on the subway, in a supermarket, or at home by herself, she says, "I just tough it out." (Spitzer et al., 2002, pp. 201–2.)

Source: Reprinted with permission from the *DSM-IV-TR Casebook* (Copyright 2000.) American Psychiatric Publishing, Inc.

Agoraphobia

Historically, *agoraphobia* was thought to involve a fear of the "agora"—the Greek word for public places of assembly (Marks, 1987). In **agoraphobia** the most commonly feared and avoided situations include streets and crowded places such as shopping malls, movie theaters, and stores. Standing in line can be particularly difficult. See Table 6.2 for a description of situations commonly avoided by agoraphobics. What is the common theme that underlies this seemingly diverse cluster of fears? Today we think that agoraphobia usually develops as a complication of having panic attacks in one or more such situations. Concerned that they may have a panic attack or get sick, people with agoraphobia are anxious about

TABLE 6.2 Situations Frequently Avoided by People with Agoraphobia

Crowds	Standing in line
Theaters	Restaurants
Shopping malls	Sports arenas
Cars and buses	Trains and airplanes
Bridges	Tunnels
Escalators	Elevators
Being home alone	Being far away from home
Aerobic exercise	Sauna baths
Getting angry	Sexual activity
Watching exciting or scary movies	

being in places or situations from which escape would be physically difficult or psychologically embarrassing, or in which immediate help would be unavailable if something bad happened (see DSM table). Typically people with agoraphobia are also frightened by their own bodily sensations, so they also avoid activities that will create arousal such as exercising, watching scary movies, drinking caffeine, and even engaging in sexual activity.

As agoraphobia first develops, people tend to avoid situations in which attacks have occurred, but usually the avoidance gradually spreads to other situations where attacks might occur. In moderately severe cases, people with agoraphobia may even be anxious when venturing outside their homes alone. In very severe cases, agoraphobia is an utterly disabling disorder in which a person cannot go beyond the narrow confines of home—or even particular parts of the home.

The case of John D. is typical of panic disorder with agoraphobia.

DSM-IV-TR

Criteria for Agoraphobia

A. Anxiety about being in places from which escape might be difficult/embarrassing, or in which help may not be available in the event of a panic attack.

B. Situations are avoided or endured with marked distress or anxiety about having a panic attack.

C. Anxiety or avoidance not better accounted for by another anxiety disorder.

Source: *Adapted with permission from the* Diagnostic and Statistical Manual of Mental Disorders, Fourth Edition, Text Revision *(Copyright 2000). American Psychiatric Association.*

DSM-IV-TR

Criteria for Panic Disorder with Agoraphobia

A. Both (1) and (2):

(1) Recurrent, unexpected panic attacks.

(2) At least one of the attacks followed by 1 month or more of

(a) Concern about having another one.

(b) Worry about consequences of an attack ("heart attack").

B. Presence of agoraphobia.

C. Panic attack not due to physiological effects of a substance or medical condition.

D. Panic attacks not better explained by another mental disorder such as social or specific phobia.

Source: *Adapted with permission from the* Diagnostic and Statistical Manual of Mental Disorders, Fourth Edition, Text Revision *(Copyright 2000). American Psychiatric Association.*

case STUDY **John D.**

John D. was a 45-year-old married Caucasian man with three sons. Although well-educated and successful... John had been experiencing difficulties with panic attacks for 15 years... experiencing two to five panic attacks per month. The previous week John had had a panic attack while driving with his family to a computer store. He recollected that before the panic attack, he might have been "keyed up" over the kids making a lot of noise in the back seat; the attack began right after he had quickly turned around to tell the kids to "settle down." Immediately after he turned back to look at the road, John felt dizzy. As soon as he noticed this, John experienced a rapid and intense surge of other sensations including sweating, accelerated heart rate, hot flushes, and trembling. Fearing that he was going to crash the car, John quickly pulled to the side of the road. He jumped out and walked around to the passenger's side. He lowered himself into a squatting position and tried to gain control over his breathing.

John was having only a few panic attacks per month, but he was experiencing a high level of anxiety every day, focused on the possibility that he might have another panic attack at any time. Indeed, John had developed extensive apprehension or avoidance of driving, air travel, elevators, wide-open spaces, taking long walks alone, movie theaters, and being out of town.

[His] first panic attack had occurred 15 years ago. John had fallen asleep on the living room sofa at around 1:00 A.M., after returning from a night of drinking with some of his friends. Just after awakening at 4:30, John felt stomach pains and a pulsating sensation in the back of his neck. All of a sudden, John noticed that his heart was racing, too.... Although he did not know what he was suffering from, John was certain that he was dying.

John remembered having a second panic attack about a month later. From then on, the panic attacks began to occur more regularly. When the panic attacks became recurrent, John started to avoid situations in which the panic attacks had occurred, as well as situations in which he feared a panic attack was likely to occur. On three occasions during the first few years of his panic attacks, John went to the emergency room of his local hospital because he was sure that his symptoms were a sign of a heart attack. (Adapted from Brown & Barlow, 2001, pp. 19–22.)

AGORAPHOBIA WITHOUT PANIC Although agoraphobia is a frequent complication of panic disorder, it can also occur without prior full-blown panic attacks. When this happens, there is usually a gradually spreading fearfulness in which more and more aspects of the environment outside the home become threatening. Cases of agoraphobia without panic are extremely rare in clinical settings, and over half the time when they *are* seen, there is a history of what are called "limited symptom attacks" (with fewer than four symptoms), or of some other unpredictable physical ailment such as epilepsy or colitis that makes the person afraid of being suddenly incapacitated (McNally, 1994; White & Barlow, 2002). The most recent estimate of the lifetime prevalence of agoraphobia without panic from the National Comorbidity Survey-Replication is 1.4 percent (e.g., Kessler, Berglund, et al., 2005b).

People with severe agoraphobia are often fearful of venturing out of their homes into public places, in part because of their fear of having a panic attack in a place in which escape might prove physically difficult or psychologically embarrassing. They may even become housebound unless accompanied by a spouse or trusted companion.

Prevalence, Gender, and Age of Onset of Panic Disorder with and without Agoraphobia

Many people suffer from panic disorder with and without agoraphobia. The National Comorbidity Survey-Replication found that approximately 4.7 percent of the adult population has had panic disorder with or without agoraphobia at some time in their lives (Kessler, Berglund, et al., 2005b). Another study found that the prevalence of panic disorder (and of social phobia) seems to be increasing in younger generations (Magee et al., 1996), which is consistent with an increase in lifetime prevalence estimates from 1994 to 2005 of 3.5 to 4.7 percent (Kessler et al., 1994; Kessler, Berglund, et al., 2005b).

The usual age of onset for panic disorder with or without agoraphobia is between 15 and 24, especially for men, but it can also begin when people, especially women, are in their thirties and forties (Eaton et al., 1994; Hirschfeld, 1996). The median age of onset has been estimated at 24 years. Once panic disorder develops, it tends to have a chronic and disabling course, although the intensity of symptoms often waxes and wanes over time (Keller et al., 1994; White & Barlow, 2002). Panic disorder is about twice as prevalent in women as in men (Eaton et al., 1994; White & Barlow, 2002). Agoraphobia also occurs much more frequently in women than in men, and the percentage of women increases as the extent of agoraphobic avoidance increases. Among people with severe agoraphobia, approximately 80 to 90 percent are female (Bekker, 1996; White & Barlow, 2002). Table 6.3 on page 198 outlines gender differences in the prevalence of anxiety disorders.

The most common explanation of the pronounced gender difference in agoraphobia is a sociocultural one. In our culture (and many others as well), it is more acceptable for women who experience panic to avoid the situations they fear and to need a trusted companion to accompany them when they enter feared situations. Men who experience panic are more prone to "tough it out" because of societal expectations and their more assertive instrumental approach to life (Bekker, 1996). Although there is very little research on this topic, one study consistent with this idea was conducted by Chambless and Mason (1986), who administered a sex-role scale to both male and female agoraphobics and found that the less "masculine" one scored on the scale, the more extensive the agoraphobic avoidance, for both males and females. In addition, some evidence indicates that men with panic disorder may be more likely to self-medicate with nicotine or alcohol as a way of coping with and enduring panic attacks, rather than developing agoraphobic avoidance (White & Barlow, 2002).

Comorbidity with Other Disorders

More than 50 percent of people with panic disorder with or without agoraphobia have one or more additional diagnoses. These include generalized anxiety, social phobia, specific phobia, PTSD, depression, and substance-use disorders (Kessler, Chiu, et al., 2005c; Magee et al., 1996). It is estimated that 30 to 50 percent of people with panic disorder will experience a serious depression at some point in their lives (Gorman & Coplan, 1996). They may also meet criteria for dependent or avoidant personality disorder (see Chapter 11; White & Barlow, 2002). The issue of whether people with panic disorder show an increased risk

TABLE 6.3 **Gender Differences in the Anxiety Disorders: Lifetime Prevalence Estimates**

Disorder	Prevalence in Men (%)	Prevalence in Women (%)	Ratio
Specific phobias	6.7	15.7	2.34
Social phobia	11.1	15.5	1.4
Panic disorder	2.0	5.0	2.5
Generalized anxiety disorder	3.6	6.6	1.8
Obsessive-compulsive disorder	2.0	2.9	1.45
Post-traumatic stress disorder	5	10.4	2.08

Note: Because these figures are from different studies and may not be strictly comparable, they should be taken as approximations of current estimates of gender differences.

Sources: Barlow, 2002a; Eaton et al., 1994; Karno et al., 1988; Kessler et al., 1994, 1995; Magee et al., 1996.

of suicidal ideation and suicide attempts has been controversial. Several reviews have concluded, however, that there is little evidence that panic disorder, by itself, increases the risk for suicide; however, it may do so indirectly by increasing people's risk for depression and substance use, both of which are risk factors for suicide (Vickers & McNally, 2004; White & Barlow, 2002).

The Timing of a First Panic Attack

Although panic attacks themselves appear to come "out of the blue," the first one frequently occurs following feelings of distress or some highly stressful life circumstance such as loss of a loved one, loss of an important relationship, loss of a job, or criminal victimization (see Barlow, 2002a; Falsetti et al., 1995, for reviews). Indeed, approximately 80 to 90 percent of clients report that their first panic attack occurred after one or more negative life events.

Nevertheless, not all people who have a panic attack following a stressful event go on to develop full-blown panic disorder. Current estimates are that 7 to 30 percent of adults have experienced at least one panic attack in their lifetimes, but most have not gone on to develop full-blown panic disorder. People who have other anxiety disorders and/or major depression often experience occasional panic attacks (Barlow, 2002a; Brown, 1996). Given that panic attacks are much more frequent than panic disorder, this leads us to an important question: What causes full-blown panic disorder to develop in only a subset of these people? Several very different prominent theories about the causes of panic disorder have addressed this question.

Biological Causal Factors

GENETIC FACTORS According to family and twin studies, panic disorder has a moderate heritable component (e.g., Kendler et al., 1992b, 1992d, 2001; Mackinnon & Foley, 1996). In a large twin study, Kendler and colleagues (2001) estimated that 33 to 43 percent of the variance in liability to panic disorder was due to genetic factors. Some studies have suggested that this heritability is at least partly specific for panic disorder (rather than all anxiety disorders; e.g., see Barlow, 2002a, for a review), but a large female twin study suggests that there is overlap in the genetic vulnerability factors for panic disorder and phobias (Kendler, Walters, et al., 1995).

BIOCHEMICAL ABNORMALITIES Several decades ago, Klein (1981) and others (Sheehan, 1982, 1983) argued that panic attacks are alarm reactions caused by biochemical dysfunctions. This hypothesis initially appeared to be supported by numerous studies over the past 40 years, showing that people with panic disorder are much more likely to experience panic attacks when they are exposed to various *biological challenge procedures* than are normal people or people with other psychiatric disorders. For example, infusions of sodium lactate, a substance resembling the lactate our bodies produce during exercise (e.g., Gorman et al., 1989), or inhaling carbon dioxide (e.g., Woods et al., 1987), or ingesting caffeine (e.g., Uhde, 1990) produce panic attacks in panic disorder clients at a much higher rate than in normal subjects (see Barlow, 2002a, for review). There is a broad range of these so-called **panic provocation agents,** and some of them are associated with quite different and even mutually exclusive neurobiological processes. Thus no single neurobiological mechanism could possibly be implicated (Barlow, 2002a). This observation originally led biologically oriented theorists to speculate that there are multiple different biological causes of panic (Krystal, Deutsch, & Charney, 1996). Alternatively, others believe there are simpler biological and psychological explanations for this pattern of results. These alternative explanations stem from the observation that what all these biological challenge procedures have in common is that they put stress on certain neurobiological systems, which in turn produce intense physical symptoms (such as increased heart rate, respiration, and blood pressure).

At present, two primary neurotransmitter systems are most implicated in panic attacks—the noradrenergic and the serotonergic systems. Noradrenergic activity in certain brain areas can stimulate cardiovascular symptoms associated with panic (Gorman et al., 2000). Increased serotonergic activity also decreases noradrenergic activity. This fits with results showing that the medications most widely used to treat panic disorder today (the SSRIs—selective serotonin reuptake inhibitors) seem to increase serotonergic activity in the brain but also decrease noradrenergic activity. By decreasing noradrenergic activity, these medications decrease many of the cardiovascular symptoms associated with panic that are ordinarily stimulated by noradrenergic activity (Gorman et al., 2000). Recently the inhibitory neurotransmitter GABA has also been implicated in the anticipatory anxiety that many people with panic disorder have about experiencing another attack. GABA is known to inhibit anxiety and has been shown to be abnormally low in certain parts of the cortex in people with panic disorder (Goddard, Mason, et al., 2001, 2004).

PANIC AND THE BRAIN One relatively early prominent theory about the neurobiology of panic attacks implicated the *locus coeruleus* in the brain stem (see Figure 6.1) and a particular neurotransmitter—norepinephrine—that is centrally involved in brain activity in this area. For example, Redmond (1985) showed that electrical stimulation of the locus coeruleus in monkeys leads to a constellation of responses that strongly resembles a panic attack; moreover, destruction of this area left the monkeys seemingly unable to experience fear even in the presence of real danger. Such research led to the idea that abnormal norepinephrine activity in the locus coeruleus may play a crucial causal role in panic attacks (e.g., Goddard et al., 1996). However, today it is recognized that it is increased activity in the *amygdala* that plays a more central role in panic attacks than does activity in the locus coeruleus. (See Figure 6.1.) The **amygdala** is a collection of nuclei in front of the hippocampus in the limbic system of the brain that is critically involved in the emotion of fear. Stimulation of the central nucleus of the amygdala is known to stimulate the locus coeruleus, as well as the other autonomic, neuroendocrine, and behavioral responses that occur during panic attacks (e.g., Gorman et al., 2000; LeDoux, 2000).

Recently, some research has suggested that the amygdala is the central area involved in what has been called a "fear network," with connections not only to lower areas in the brain like the locus coeruleus but also to higher brain areas like the prefrontal cortex (e.g., Gorman et al., 2000). According to this view, panic attacks occur when the fear network is activated, either by cortical inputs or by inputs from lower brain areas. So according to this theory, panic disorder is likely to develop in people who have abnormally sensitive fear networks that get activated too readily to be adaptive. Abnormally sensitive fear networks may have a partially heritable basis but may also develop as a result of repeated stressful life experiences, particularly early in life (e.g., Gorman et al., 2000; Ladd et al., 2000).

But panic attacks are only one component of panic disorder. People with panic disorder also become anxious

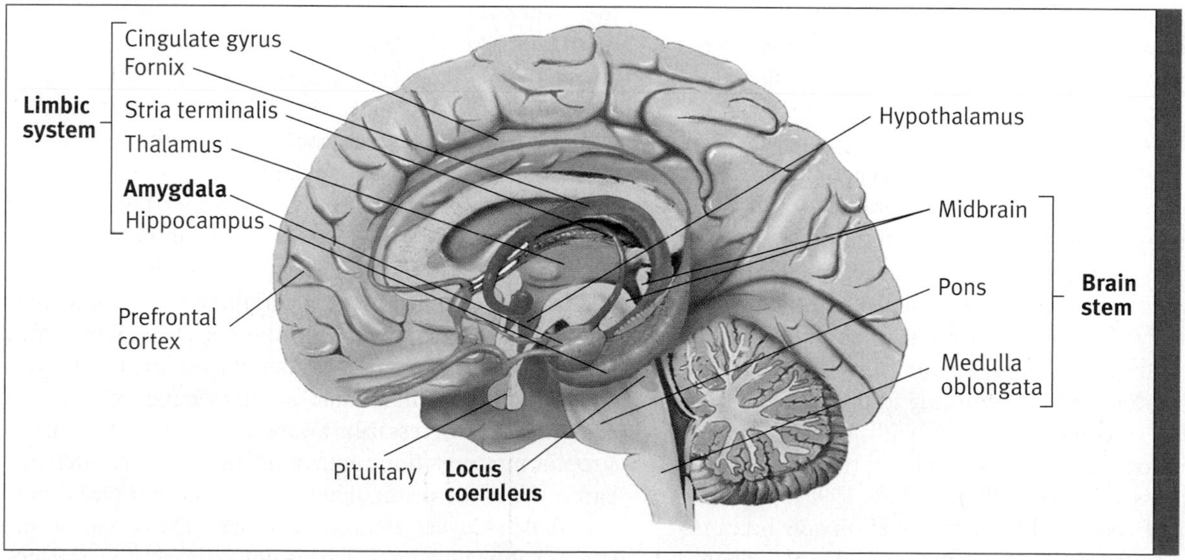

FIGURE 6.1

A Biological Theory of Panic, Anxiety, and Agoraphobia

According to one theory, panic attacks may arise from abnormal activity in the amygdala, a collection of nuclei in front of the hippocampus in the limbic system. The anticipatory anxiety that people develop about having another panic attack is thought to arise from activity in the hippocampus of the limbic system, which is known to be involved in the learning of emotional responses. Phobic avoidance, also a learned response, may also involve activity of the hippocampus (Gorman et al., 2000).

about the possibility of another attack, and those with agoraphobia also engage in phobic avoidance behavior (e.g., Gorman et al., 1989, 2000). Different brain areas are probably involved in these different aspects of panic disorder. The panic attacks themselves arise from activity in the amygdala, either by cortical inputs (e.g., evaluating a stimulus as highly threatening) or by activity coming from more downstream areas like the locus coeruleus. For people who have one or more panic attacks and who go on to develop significant conditioned anxiety about having another one in particular contexts, the *hippocampus* (a part of the limbic system, below the cortex, that is very involved in the learning of emotional responses) generates this conditioned anxiety (e.g., Charney, Grillon, & Bremner, 1998; Gray & McNaughton, 1996), and is probably also involved in the learned avoidance associated with agoraphobia (Gorman et al., 2000). Finally, the cognitive symptoms that occur during panic attacks (fears of dying or of losing control) and overreactions to the danger posed by possibly threatening bodily sensations are likely to be mediated by higher cortical centers (see Gorman et al., 2000).

Behavioral and Cognitive Causal Factors

COMPREHENSIVE LEARNING THEORY OF PANIC DISORDER One early psychological hypothesis about the origins of agoraphobia was the "fear of fear" hypothesis. The idea was that through a process of *interoceptive conditioning,* initial internal bodily sensations of anxiety or arousal effectively become conditioned stimuli (CSs) associated with higher levels of anxiety or arousal (Goldstein & Chambless, 1978). For example, heart palpitations may occur at the beginning of a full-blown attack, and because they become predictors of the rest of the attack, they may themselves acquire the capacity to provoke panic attacks.

Since 1978 researchers have made many advances in understanding the relationship between agoraphobia and panic disorder, and the differences between anxiety and panic as distinct emotional states. Building on these, as well as on advances in the study of classical conditioning, investigators have recently proposed a comprehensive learning theory of panic disorder that accounts for most of the known findings about panic disorder (Bouton, Mineka, & Barlow, 2001). According to this theory, initial panic attacks become associated with initially neutral internal (interoceptive) and external cues through a conditioning process (e.g., Forsyth & Eiffert, 1998). One primary effect of this conditioning is that *anxiety* becomes conditioned to these CSs, and the more intense the panic attack, the more robust the conditioning that will occur (Forsyth, Daleiden, & Chorpita, 2000). This conditioning of anxiety to the internal or external cues associated with panic thus sets the stage for the development of two of the three components of panic disorder: anticipatory anxiety, and agoraphobic fears. Specifically, when people experience their initial panic attacks (which are terrifying emotional events replete with strong internal bodily sensations), conditioning can occur to multiple different kinds of cues, ranging from heart palpitations and dizziness to shopping malls. Because anxiety becomes conditioned to these CSs, anxious apprehension about having another attack, particularly in certain contexts, may develop, as may agoraphobic avoidance of contexts in which panic attacks might occur.

However, another important effect is that panic attacks themselves (the third component of panic disorder) are also likely to be conditioned to certain internal cues. This leads to the occurrence of panic attacks that seemingly come out of the blue when people unconsciously experience certain internal bodily sensations (CSs). For example, one young man with panic disorder who was particularly frightened of signs that his heart was racing experienced a surprising and unexpected panic attack after hearing that his favorite presidential candidate had won. The panic attack thus occurred when he was happy and excited (which is what made it so surprising for him). However, from the standpoint of this theory, the attack was actually not surprising. Because the man was excited, his heart was racing, which probably served as an internal CS that triggered the panic (Mineka & Zinbarg, 2006). This theory also underscores why not everyone who experiences an occasional panic attack goes on to develop panic disorder. Instead, people with certain genetic, temperamental, or cognitive-behavioral vulnerabilities will show stronger conditioning of both anxiety and panic (Bouton et al., 2001).

THE COGNITIVE THEORY OF PANIC An earlier cognitive theory of panic proposed that panic clients are hypersensitive to their bodily sensations and are very prone to giving them the direst possible interpretation (Beck & Emery, 1985; D. M. Clark, 1986, 1997). Clark referred to this as a tendency to catastrophize about the meaning of their bodily sensations. For example, a person who develops panic disorder might notice that his heart is racing and conclude that he is having a heart attack, or that he is dizzy, which may lead to fainting or to the thought that he may have a brain tumor. These very frightening thoughts may cause many more physical symptoms of anxiety, which further fuel the catastrophic thoughts, leading to a vicious circle culminating in a panic attack (see Figure 6.2). The person is not necessarily aware of making these catastrophic interpretations; rather, the thoughts are often just barely out of the realm of awareness (Rapee, 1996). These *automatic thoughts,* as Beck calls them, are in a sense the triggers of panic. Although it is not yet clear how the tendency to catastrophize develops, the cognitive model proposes that only people with this tendency to catastrophize go on to develop panic disorder (e.g., D. M. Clark, 1997).

Several lines of evidence are consistent with the cognitive theory of panic. For example, people with panic disorder are much more likely to interpret their bodily sensations in a catastrophic manner (e.g., see D. M. Clark,

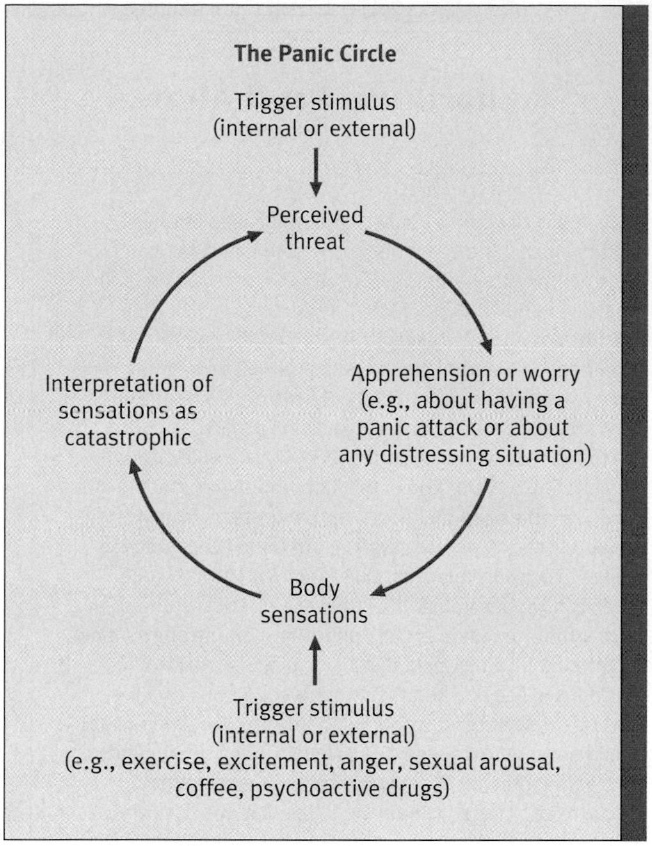

FIGURE 6.2

The Panic Circle

Any kind of perceived threat may lead to apprehension or worry, which is accompanied by various bodily sensations. According to the cognitive model of panic, if a person then catastrophizes about the meaning of his or her bodily sensations, this will raise the level of perceived threat, thus creating more apprehension and worry, as well as more physical symptoms, which fuel further catastrophic thoughts. This vicious circle can culminate in a panic attack. The initial physical sensations need not arise from the perceived threat (as shown at the top of the circle), but may come from other sources (exercise, anger, psychoactive drugs, etc., as shown at the bottom of the circle). (Adapted from Clark, 1986, 1997.)

1997, for a review). The model also predicts that changing their cognitions about their bodily symptoms should reduce or prevent panic. Evidence that cognitive therapy for panic works is consistent with this prediction (D. M. Clark et al., 1994, 1999; see below). In addition, a brief explanation of what to expect in a panic provocation study can apparently prevent panic (D. M. Clark, 1997). People with panic disorder either were given a brief but detailed explanation of what physical symptoms to expect from an infusion of sodium lactate, and why they should not worry about these symptoms, or were given a minimal explanation. The people with the cognitive rationale about what to expect were significantly less likely to say that they had had the subjective experience of a panic attack in response to the lactate (30 percent) than were control individuals (90 percent).

PSYCHOLOGICAL EXPLANATIONS OF RESULTS FROM PANIC PROVOCATION STUDIES Earlier we noted that there are simpler psychological explanations that provide a common mechanism for understanding how so many varied panic provocation agents can all provoke panic at high rates in people with panic disorder. Because these agents produce arousal, they mimic the physiological cues that normally precede a panic attack or may be taken as a sign of some other impending catastrophe (Barlow, 2002a; Bouton et al., 2001; Margraf, Ehlers, & Roth, 1986a, 1986b). People with panic disorder already start at a higher level of arousal than others and are very familiar with these early warning cues. Thus, according to the cognitive theory, people with panic attacks frequently misinterpret these symptoms as the beginning of a panic attack or a heart attack, which in turn induces the vicious circle of panic described above; this would not happen in controls who do not have the same tendency to catastrophize. Alternatively, according to the learning theory of panic, it would be only those with panic disorder for whom these cues might serve as interoceptive CSs that can trigger anxiety and panic because of their prior associations with panic.

The key difference between these two theories in explaining the results of panic provocation studies lies in the great importance that the cognitive model places on the *meaning* that people attach to their bodily sensations; they will experience panic only if they make catastrophic interpretations of certain bodily sensations. Such catastrophic cognitions are not necessary with the interoceptive conditioning model, because anxiety and panic attacks can be triggered by unconscious interoceptive (or exteroceptive) cues (Bouton et al., 2001). Thus the learning theory model is better able to explain the occurrence of the panic attacks that often occur without any preceding negative (catastrophic) automatic thoughts, as well as the occurrence of *nocturnal panic attacks* that occur during sleep; the occurrence of both of these kinds of attacks are difficult for the cognitive model to explain (see Developments in Research 6.1 on p. 202).

ANXIETY SENSITIVITY AND PERCEIVED CONTROL Other cognitive and behavioral explanations of panic and agoraphobia have looked at a number of different factors that can generally be explained within either the conditioning or the cognitive perspective. For example, several researchers have shown that people who have high levels of *anxiety sensitivity* are more prone to developing panic attacks and perhaps panic disorder (Cox, 1996; McNally, 2002). **Anxiety sensitivity** is a trait-like belief that certain bodily symptoms may have harmful consequences. Such a person would endorse statements such as, "When I notice that my heart is beating rapidly, I worry that I might have a heart attack." In one important study, Schmidt, Lerew, and Jackson (1997) followed over 1,400 young adults undergoing basic military training for 5 weeks. Schmidt and colleagues found that high levels of anxiety sensitivity predicted the development of spontaneous panic attacks

6.1 Developments in Research: Nocturnal Panic Attacks

Although the majority of panic attacks experienced by people with panic disorder occur during waking hours, approximately 50 to 60 percent of people report that they have experienced a panic attack during sleep at least once (Barlow, 2002a; O'Mahoney & Ward, 2003). Nocturnal panic refers to waking from sleep in a state of panic. It seems to occur with some regularity in about 20 to 40 percent of people with panic disorder (Craske, Lang, et al., 2002). Although one might think that such panic attacks occur in response to nightmares, considerable research shows that this is not the case. Sleep has five stages that occur in a fairly invariant sequence multiple times throughout the night: one stage called REM sleep (rapid eye movement sleep) when vivid dreaming occurs, and four stages of non-REM sleep (Stages 1–4) when vivid dreams do not occur. If nocturnal panic attacks occurred in response to dreams, we would expect them to occur during REM sleep, but in fact they occur during Stage 2 and early Stage 3 sleep, usually a few hours after falling asleep.

It is important to note that nocturnal panic attacks are different from "sleep terrors" or *"night terrors,"* which usually occur during Stage 4 sleep. Night terrors are usually experienced by children who often scream and then fear that someone or something is chasing them around the room; however, they do not wake up (Barlow, 2002a). Nocturnal panic attacks also differ from *isolated sleep paralysis,* which can sometimes occur during the transition from sleep to waking. It involves a stark sense of terror (resembling that during a panic attack) *and an inability to move,* which seems to occur because the individuals are waking from REM (dream) sleep, when there is suppression of muscle activity below the neck. Isolated sleep paralysis occurs much more commonly among African-Americans than among other ethnic groups, for reasons that are still unclear (Barlow, 2002a; McNally, 1994).

Although early research suggested that people who experience nocturnal panic attacks as well as daytime attacks may show overall higher levels of psychopathology, recent research has been showing otherwise, with few differences being reported (e.g., Craske et al., 2002; O'Mahoney & Ward, 2003). Similarly, biological models have hypothesized that nocturnal panic stems from dysregulation of the respiratory system, but there is no good evidence to support this idea. One reason nocturnal panic attacks have been of interest from a theoretical standpoint is that they appear to be very difficult for any strong version of the cognitive theory of panic to explain, in part because it is hard to see how the catastrophic cognitions that are posited to be necessary for the occurrence of a panic attack could occur during Stage 2 or 3 sleep. On the other hand, the learning theory of panic disorder can explain their occurrence because internal bodily sensations occurring during sleep that have been previously conditioned to elicit panic can do so without the person being consciously aware of them (Bouton et al., 2001). Consistent with this, one recent study has shown that panic attacks are less strongly related to catastrophic cognitions in people who sometimes experience nocturnal panic than in people who experience only daytime panic. Moreover, individuals who sometimes experience nocturnal panic show higher levels of anxiety sensitivity than do individuals without nocturnal panic (O'Mahoney & Ward, 2003). Because anxiety sensitivity involves fears of bodily sensations, this finding is more consistent with the learning theory of panic disorder.

during this highly stressful period. For example, of the trainees scoring in the top 10 percent on a scale measuring anxiety sensitivity, 20 percent experienced at least one panic attack during the 5 weeks of basic training; only 6 percent of the remaining study participants had a panic attack in the same time period. Several other studies examining the same issues have obtained very similar results, thus boosting confidence in the reliability of anxiety sensitivity as a predictor of panic attacks (e.g., Hayward et al., 2000; Li & Zinbarg, submitted).

In addition, several important studies have shown that simply having a sense of *perceived control*—for instance, over the amount of carbon-dioxide-altered air that is inhaled (a panic provocation procedure known frequently to bring on anxiety and panic)—reduces anxiety and even blocks panic (e.g., Sanderson, Rapee, & Barlow, 1989; Zvolensky et al., 1998, 1999). In addition, if a person with panic disorder has a "safe" person with her or him when s/he undergoes a panic provocation procedure, s/he is likely to show reduced distress, lowered physiological arousal, and reduced likelihood of panic, relative to someone who came alone (without a "safe" person; Carter et al., 1995). Moreover, people high in anxiety sensitivity may be protected against having panic attacks during stressful periods if they have a sense of perceived control and predictability over their life situation (Schmidt & Lerew, 2002).

SAFETY BEHAVIORS AND THE PERSISTENCE OF PANIC

Why do people who have developed panic disorder continue to have panic attacks in spite of the fact that their direst predictions rarely, if ever, come true? Some people with panic disorder may, for example, have three or four panic attacks a week for 20 years; each time they may believe they are having a heart attack, and yet they never do. After experiencing hundreds or thousands of panic attacks without having a heart attack, one would think, from the cognitive perspective, that this catastrophic thought would have been proven wrong so many times that it would finally go away. However, evidence suggests that such disconfirmation does not occur because people with panic disorder frequently engage in "safety behaviors" (such as breathing slowly) before or during an attack. They then mistakenly tend to attribute the lack of catastrophe to their having engaged in this safety behavior rather than to the idea that panic attacks actually do not lead to heart attacks. Similarly, people who think they may faint will tend to lean against solid objects (Clark, 1997; Salkovskis et al., 1996). Research suggests that it is important during treatment to identify these safety behaviors so that the person can learn to give them up and finally see that their feared catastrophe still does not occur.

Many people experiencing a panic attack mistake their symptoms (for example, chest pain and shortness of breath) for another medical problem—most often, a heart attack.

COGNITIVE BIASES AND THE MAINTENANCE OF PANIC Finally, many studies have shown that people with panic disorder are biased in the way they process threatening information. Such people not only interpret ambiguous bodily sensations as threatening (Clark, 1997) but also interpret other ambiguous situations as more threatening than do controls. People with panic disorder also seem to have their attention automatically drawn to threatening information in their environment such as words that represent things they fear, such as *palpitations, numbness,* or *faint* (see Mathews & MacLeod, 2005; Mineka et al., 2003, for reviews). A recent study using fMRI techniques demonstrated that people with panic disorder showed greater activation to threat words than did normals in brains areas involved in memory processing of threatening material (Maddock, Buonocore, Kile, & Garrett, 2003). Whether these information-processing biases are present before the disorder begins and help to cause it is as yet unclear, but these biases are certainly likely to help maintain the disorder once it has begun. For example, having one's attention automatically drawn to threatening cues in the environment is likely to provoke more attacks.

In summary, research into both biological and psychological factors involved in panic disorder has provided important insights into this disorder since it was first identified as a distinct disorder in 1980. It seems unlikely that research from either tradition alone will ever provide a complete account of this disorder, and we eagerly await more attempts at synthesizing these findings into a biopsychosocial theory of this disorder.

Treating Panic Disorder and Agoraphobia

MEDICATIONS Many people with panic disorder (with or without agoraphobia) are prescribed minor tranquilizers from the benzodiazepine category such as alprazolam (Xanax) or clonazepam. These people frequently show some symptom relief with these minor tranquilizers (also known as anxiolytics, or anti-anxiety medications), and many can function more effectively. One major advantage of these drugs is that they act very quickly (in ½ to 1 hour) and so can be useful in acute situations of intense panic or anxiety. However, these anxiolytic medications can also have quite undesirable side effects such as drowsiness and sedation, which can lead to impaired cognitive and motor performance. Moreover, they are potentially quite addictive, which means that with prolonged use, most people using moderate to high doses develop physiological dependence on the drug, which results in withdrawal symptoms when the drug is discontinued (e.g., nervousness, sleep disturbance, and dizziness). Withdrawal from these drugs can be very slow and difficult, and it precipitates relapse in a very high percentage of cases (Ballenger, 1996; Roy-Byrne & Cowley, 2002).

The other categories of medication that are useful in the treatment of panic disorder and agoraphobia are the antidepressants (including primarily the tricyclics and the SSRIs—selective serotonin reuptake inhibitors). These medications have both advantages and disadvantages compared with anxiolytics. One major advantage is that they are not addictive. However, it takes about 4 weeks before they have any beneficial effects, so they are not useful in an acute situation where a person is having a panic attack. Troublesome side effects (such as dry mouth, constipation, and blurred vision with the tricyclics, and interference with sexual arousal with the SSRIs) mean that large numbers of people refuse to take the medications or discontinue their use (White & Barlow, 2002). Moreover, relapse rates when the drugs are discontinued are quite high (although not as high as with the benzodiazepines).

Today the SSRIs are more widely prescribed than the tricyclics because the SSRIs are generally better tolerated by most patients. In addition, some (but not all) comparative studies have shown that the SSRIs may be even slightly more effective than the tricyclic antidepressants (Roy-Byrne & Cowley, 2002).

6.2 Developments in Practice: Cognitive-Behavioral Therapy for Panic Disorder

The cognitive and conditioning models of panic disorder have contributed to the formulation of new treatments that have been shown to be highly effective in dozens of different studies in many countries around the world (see Ruhmland & Margraf, 2001; White & Barlow, 2002). Although the treatments vary somewhat, each is a form of behavioral or cognitive-behavioral therapy. In one widely used version of the "Panic Control Treatment" developed by Barlow and colleagues, several different cognitive and behavioral techniques are combined in a program that typically lasts for 12 to 15 sessions (Barlow & Craske, 2000; Craske, Barlow, & Meadows, 2000).

There are three aspects to Panic Control Treatment. First, clients are taught about the nature of anxiety and panic and how the capacity to experience both is adaptive. By learning about the nature of the fight-or-flight response experienced during panic, clients come to understand that the sensations they experience during panic are normal and harmless. Clients are also taught to self-monitor their experiences with anxiety and panic through daily diaries.

The second part of treatment involves teaching people with panic disorder to control their breathing. First they are asked to hyperventilate, or overbreathe. Hyperventilation is known to create a variety of unpleasant physical sensations (such as lightheadedness, dizziness, and tightness of the chest) that often occur during panic attacks. (You can see this for yourself by breathing very fast and deeply for 1 to 2 minutes.) By then learning how to control their breathing, they master a new coping tool that will reduce the likelihood that they themselves will create some of the symptoms they are so frightened of.

BEHAVIORAL AND COGNITIVE-BEHAVIORAL TREATMENTS The original behavioral treatment for agoraphobia from the early 1970s involved prolonged exposure to feared situations, often with the help of a therapist or family member. The idea was to make people gradually face the situations they feared and learn that there was nothing to fear. Such exposure-based treatments were quite effective, and helped about 60 to 75 percent of people with agoraphobia show clinically significant improvement. These effects were generally well maintained at 2- to 4-year follow-up. But this left approximately 25 to 40 percent not improved to a ***clinically significant*** degree (Barlow, Raffa, & Cohen, 2002; McNally, 1994).

One limitation of these original treatments was that they did not specifically target panic attacks. In the mid-1980s, two new techniques were developed as clinical researchers increasingly recognized the importance of panic attacks to most people with agoraphobia. One new technique involves a variant on exposure known as *interoceptive exposure,* which means deliberate exposure to feared internal sensations. As we have noted, people with panic disorder have prominent fears of their bodily sensations, and panic attacks may be conditioned responses to interoceptive conditioned stimuli. The idea is that fear of these internal sensations should be treated in the same way that fear of external agoraphobic situations is treated—namely, through prolonged exposure to those internal sensations so that the fear may extinguish. Thus people with panic disorder in treatment are asked to do a variety of exercises (such as hyperventilating, running in place, holding their breath, ingesting caffeine, etc.) that bring on the physical sensations they may fear. Whichever exercises bring on the symptoms that most resemble those they experience during panic are then targeted for practice to promote extinction of the anxiety for these physical sensations.

> **research close•up**
>
> ***clinically significant***
>
> *Not all statistically significant changes are of sufficient magnitude to be clinically significant. Clinical significance reflects how large the effects of a particular treatment or intervention are with respect to how much meaningful change they provide in a person's level of functioning or well-being.*

The second set of techniques that were developed are cognitive techniques, in recognition that catastrophic automatic thoughts may help maintain panic attacks. Developments in Practice 6.2 illustrates one kind of integrative cognitive-behavioral treatment for panic disorder. This approach targets both agoraphobic avoidance and panic attacks. Generally, this integrative treatment produces better results than the original exposure-based techniques that focused exclusively on exposure to external situations (Clark, 1997; White & Barlow, 2002). However, results of a quantitative review of 51 studies showed that intensive exposure-based treatment that involves both intensive interoceptive and exteroceptive exposure may be just as effective as the integrative treatment (Ruhmland & Margraf, 2001). Indeed, in many of the studies conducted using one of the variants on these treatments, 75 to 95 percent of people with panic disorder were panic-free at the end of 8 to 14 weeks of treatment, and gains were well

Third, clients are taught to identify the automatic thoughts they have during panic attacks, as well as during anxiety-provoking situations. They are then taught about the logical errors that people who have panic are prone to making and learn to subject their own automatic thoughts to a logical reanalysis. For example, a person who fears having a heart attack at the first sign of heart palpitations is asked to examine the evidence that this might be true. (When did the doctor last tell him or her that his or her heart was perfectly healthy? What is the likelihood of having a heart attack at age 30?) In later sessions the cognitive part of the treatment is focused on teaching people how to decatastrophize—that is, to learn how to think through what the worst possible outcome might be if they did have a panic attack (e.g., if they had a panic attack while driving, they might have to pull their car over to the side of the road until the attack subsided). The entire experience of panic usually becomes less terrifying once they learn to decatastrophize.

Finally, another part of the treatment involves exposure to feared situations and feared bodily sensations. Because of the importance of **interoceptive fears** (fears of bodily sensations), clients are asked to do a variety of exercises with the therapist that bring on different bodily sensations. These include hyperventilating, breathing through a straw, shaking one's head from side to side, jogging in place, holding one's breath for a minute, and the like. After each exercise, clients describe the sensations produced, discuss how similar these sensations are to those that they experience during panic, and evaluate how scary those sensations are. Whichever exercises produce the symptoms most similar to their own during panic attacks are targeted for practice. The idea is that if clients practice inducing these sensations, their anxiety about the sensations will gradually extinguish. Later, clients who also have extensive agoraphobic avoidance begin to expose themselves to their feared situations for long enough that their anxiety diminishes. This part of the treatment is delayed until clients have learned a variety of coping skills (cognitive techniques as well as breathing skills).

maintained at 1- to 2-year follow-up (D. M. Clark, 1996; White & Barlow, 2002). Overall, the magnitude of improvement is greater with these cognitive and behavioral treatments than with medications (Barlow et al., 2002a).

What about the combination of medication and cognitive-behavioral therapy? In the short term, such combined treatment may sometimes produce a slightly superior result, compared to either type of treatment alone. However, in the long term after medication has been tapered, clients who have been on medication (with or without cognitive or behavioral treatment) seem to show a greater likelihood of relapse (Barlow et al., 2002a; Marks et al., 1993). Perhaps this is because they have attributed their gains to the medication rather than to their personal efforts (Başoğlu et al., 1994).

In Review

- Describe the major diagnostic features of both panic disorder and agoraphobia, and explain how they are thought to be related.
- What biological causal factors have been implicated in panic disorder?
- Compare and contrast the learning theory and cognitive models of panic disorder.
- Describe the major treatment approaches for panic disorder and their relative advantages and disadvantages.

Generalized Anxiety Disorder

Most of us worry and get anxious occasionally, and anxiety is an adaptive emotion that helps us plan for and prepare for possible threat. But for some people, anxiety and worry about many different aspects of life (including minor events) becomes chronic, excessive, and unreasonable. In these cases, **generalized anxiety disorder (GAD)** may be diagnosed (formerly known as *free-floating anxiety*). DSM-IV-TR criteria specify that the worry must occur more days than not for at least 6 months and that it must be experienced as difficult to control (see DSM table). The worry must be about a number of different events or activities, and its content cannot be exclusively related to the worry associated with another concurrent Axis I disorder such as the possibility of having a panic attack. The subjective experience of excessive worry must also be accompanied by at least three of six other symptoms listed in the table. Frequently people with GAD also show marked vigilance for possible signs of threat in the environment and engage in certain subtle avoidance activities such as procrastination, checking, or calling a loved one frequently to see if he or she is safe.

General Characteristics

The general picture of people suffering from generalized anxiety disorder is that they live in a relatively constant future-oriented mood state of anxious apprehension,

DSM-IV-TR

Criteria for Generalized Anxiety Disorder

A. Excessive anxiety and worry occurring more days than not for at least 6 months about a number of events or activities
B. Person finds it difficult to control the worry
C. Anxiety and worry associated with 3 or more of following 6 symptoms for more days than not:
(1) restlessness or feeling keyed up
(2) being easily fatigued
(3) difficulty concentrating
(4) irritability
(5) muscle tension
(6) sleep disturbance
D. Anxiety and worry not confined to features of another Axis I disorder
E. Symptoms cause clinically significant distress or impairment in functioning

Muscle tension, chronic overarousal, restlessness, and difficulty concentrating are all symptoms that people with generalized anxiety disorder may have. Such individuals also worry excessively and are hypervigilant for possible signs of threat in their environment.

chronic tension, worry, and diffuse uneasiness. They attempt to be constantly ready to deal with upcoming negative events and have a strong sense of lacking control over the worry process (Barlow, 2002a; Barlow et al., 1996). Such *anxious apprehension* is also part of other anxiety disorders (for example, the person with agoraphobia is anxious about future panic attacks and about dying, and the person with social phobia is anxious about possible negative social evaluation). But this apprehension is the essence of GAD, leading Barlow and others to refer to GAD as the "basic" anxiety disorder (Roemer, Orsillo, & Barlow, 2002; Wells & Butler, 1997).

The nearly constant worries of people with generalized anxiety disorder leave them continually upset, uneasy, and discouraged. In one study, their most common spheres of worry were found to be family, work, finances, and personal illness (Roemer, Molina, & Borkovec, 1997). Not only do they have difficulty making decisions, but after they have managed to make a decision, they worry endlessly, even after going to bed, over possible errors and unforeseen circumstances that may prove the decision wrong and lead to disaster. They have no appreciation of the logic by which most of us conclude that it is pointless to torment ourselves about possible outcomes over which we have no control.

The following case is fairly typical of generalized anxiety disorder.

case study — A Graduate Student with GAD

John was a 26-year-old single graduate student in the social sciences at a prestigious university. Although he reported that he had had problems with anxiety nearly all his life, even as a child, the past 7 to 8 years since he had left home and gone to an Ivy League college had been worse. During the past year his anxiety had seriously interfered with his functioning, and he worried about several different spheres of his life. He was very concerned about his own health and that of his parents. During one incident a few months earlier, he had thought that his heart was beating more slowly than usual and he had experienced some tingling sensations; this led him to worry that he might die. In another incident he had heard his name spoken over a loudspeaker in an airport and had worried that someone at home must be dying. He was also very worried about his future, because his anxiety had kept him from completing his master's thesis on time. John also worried excessively about getting a bad grade, even though he had never had one either in college or in graduate school. In classes he worried excessively about what the professor and other students thought of him, and he tended not to talk unless the class was small and he was quite confident about the topic. Although he had a number of friends, he had never had a girlfriend because of his shyness about dating. He had no problem talking or socializing with women as long as it was not defined as a dating situation. He worried that he should date a woman only if he was quite sure, from the outset, that it could be a serious relationship. He also worried excessively that if a woman did not want to date him, it meant that he was boring.

In addition to his worries, John reported muscle tension and easily becoming fatigued. He also reported great difficulty concentrating and a considerable amount of restlessness and pacing. When he couldn't work, he spent a great deal of time daydreaming, which worried him because he didn't seem able to control it. At times he had difficulty falling asleep if he was particularly anxious, but at other times he slept excessively, in part to escape from his worries. He frequently experienced dizziness and palpitations, and in the past he had had full-blown panic attacks. Overall, he reported frequently feeling paralyzed and unable to do things.

Both of John's parents were professionals; his mother was also quite anxious and had been treated for panic disorder. John was obviously extremely bright and had managed to do very well in school in spite of his lifelong problems with anxiety. But as the pressures of finishing graduate school and starting his career loomed before him, and as he got older and still had never dated, the anxiety became so severe that he sought treatment.

Prevalence and Age of Onset

Generalized anxiety disorder is a relatively common condition; current estimates from the National Comorbidity Survey-Replication are that approximately 3 percent of the population suffers from it in any 1-year period and 5.7 percent at some point in their lives (Kessler et al., 1994; Kessler, Chiu et al., 2005c, Kessler, Berglund, et al., 2005b). GAD is approximately twice as common in women as in men (a somewhat less dramatic difference than is seen with many specific phobias or severe agoraphobia; see Table 6.3 on p. 198 for summaries of gender differences in the different anxiety disorders). Although GAD is quite common, most people with this disorder manage to function in spite of their high levels of worry and low perceived well-being (Stein, Heimberg, & Stein, 2004). They are less likely to go to clinics for psychological treatment than are people with panic disorder or major depression, which are frequently more debilitating conditions. However, people with GAD do frequently show up in physicians' offices with medical complaints (such as muscle tension or fatigue) and are known to be overusers of health care resources (similar to people with panic disorder; Greenberg et al., 1999; Roy-Byrne & Katon, 2002).

Age of onset is often difficult to determine because 60 to 80 percent of people with GAD remember having been anxious nearly all their lives, and many others report a slow and insidious onset (Roemer et al., 2002; Wells & Butler, 1997). However, recent research has also documented that GAD often occurs in older adults where it is the most common anxiety disorder (e.g., Roemer et al., 2002; Stein, 2004).

Comorbidity with Other Disorders

Generalized anxiety disorder often co-occurs with other Axis I disorders, especially other anxiety and mood disorders such as panic disorder, social phobia, specific phobia, and PTSD (Brown, Campbell, et al., 2001; Kessler, Chiu, et al., 2005c). In addition, many people with GAD (like John) experience occasional panic attacks without qualifying for a diagnosis of panic disorder (Barlow, 1988, 2002a). Many of these people are mildly to moderately depressed as well as chronically anxious, which is not surprising given their generally gloomy outlook on the world (Roemer et al., 2002; Stein et al., 2004). Nor is it surprising that excessive use of tranquilizing drugs, sleeping pills, and alcohol often complicates the clinical picture in generalized anxiety disorder.

Psychosocial Causal Factors

THE PSYCHOANALYTIC VIEWPOINT According to this viewpoint, generalized or free-floating anxiety results from an unconscious conflict between ego and id impulses that is not adequately dealt with because the person's defense mechanisms have either broken down or have never developed. Freud believed that it was primarily sexual and aggressive impulses that had been either blocked from expression, or punished upon expression, that led to free-floating anxiety. Defense mechanisms may become overwhelmed when a person experiences frequent and extreme levels of anxiety, as might happen if expression of id impulses were frequently blocked from expression (e.g., under periods of prolonged sexual deprivation). According to this view, the primary difference between specific phobias and free-floating anxiety is that in phobias, the defense mechanisms of repression and displacement actually work, whereas in free-floating anxiety these defense mechanisms do not work, leaving the person anxious nearly all the time. Unfortunately this viewpoint is not testable and has therefore been largely abandoned among clinical researchers.

THE ROLE OF UNPREDICTABLE AND UNCONTROLLABLE EVENTS Uncontrollable and unpredictable aversive events are much more stressful than controllable and predictable aversive events, so it is perhaps not surprising that the former create more fear and anxiety (Barlow, 2002a; Craske & Waters, 2005; Mineka, 1985a; Mineka & Zinbarg, 1996). Conversely, experience with controlling aspects of one's life may immunize one against developing general anxiety (Chorpita, 2001; Mineka & Kelly, 1989).

This has led researchers to hypothesize that people with GAD may have a history of experiencing many important events in their lives as unpredictable and/or uncontrollable. For example, having a boss or spouse who has unpredictable bad moods or outbursts of temper for seemingly trivial reasons might keep a person in a chronic state of anxiety. Although the unpredictable and uncontrollable events involved in GAD are generally not as severe and traumatic as those involved in the origins of PTSD, there is some evidence that people with GAD may be more likely to have had a history of trauma in childhood than individuals with several other anxiety disorders (Borkovec et al., 2004). Moreover, people with GAD clearly have far less tolerance for uncertainty than nonanxious controls (Dugas, Buhr, & Ladoucer, 2004), which suggests that they are especially disturbed by not being able to predict the future (as none of us can; Roemer et al., 2002).

In addition, perhaps some of these people's intolerance for uncertainty, as well as their tension and hypervigilance (the sense of always looking for signs of threat), stems from their lacking safety signals in their environment. If a person mostly experiences predictable stressors (e.g., on Mondays the boss is always in a bad mood and is likely to be highly critical), he or she can predict when something bad is likely to happen by paying attention to this signal (e.g., Mondays at work). Such a person then feels safe when that signal is missing (*a safety signal*) (e.g., Tuesdays through Fridays at work). But if another person has experienced many unpredictable or unsignaled stressors (e.g., the boss or one's parent is in a bad mood and highly critical on random days of the week), she or he will not have developed safety signals for when it is appropriate to relax and feel safe, and this uncertainty may lead to chronic anxiety (Mineka, 1985a; Mineka & Zinbarg, 1996; Seligman & Binik, 1977). Thus a relative lack of safety signals may help explain why people with GAD feel constantly tense and vigilant for possible threats (Rapee, 2001).

It is possible that some of the chronic tension and hypervigilance that individuals with generalized anxiety disorder experience stem from their lacking safety signals in their environment. Without such safety signals, such as knowing when their boss or spouse will or will not be angry with them, they may never be able to relax and feel safe.

A SENSE OF MASTERY: THE POSSIBILITY OF IMMUNIZING AGAINST ANXIETY Although we cannot study whether controlling different aspects of our lives may immunize us from developing generalized anxiety by directly manipulating the controllability and predictability of our life experiences over prolonged periods of time, we can learn a lot from laboratory analogue studies in animals. One longitudinal experiment with infant rhesus monkeys supports the hypothesized role of experiences with control in immunizing individuals against fear and anxiety (Mineka, Gunnar, & Champoux, 1986). In this experiment, two groups of infant monkeys called "Master" monkeys were reared in peer groups (without their mothers) in which they gained extensive experience with control and mastery by pressing bars and pulling chains to obtain reinforcers like food, water, and treats. Two other groups of monkeys called "Yoked" monkeys were reared in identical environments but had no control over their reinforcers; instead, they received reinforcers when a member of the Master group exerted control. The Master and Yoked groups had equal exposure to reinforcers; they differed only in whether they controlled access to the reinforcers.

Between 7 and 11 months of age, all monkeys were tested for their responses to several fear- and anxiety-provoking situations. Master monkeys habituated more rapidly to frightening and stressful experiences than did Yoked monkeys, and the Master monkeys were also bolder and more willing to enter and explore a novel, somewhat frightening playroom situation. Finally, Master monkeys also coped better when they were separated from their peers and placed as an intruder in the Yoked group than Yoked monkeys did when placed in the Master group. Thus it appears that early experiences with control and mastery can immunize the individual to some extent against the harmful effects of exposure to stressful situations—and, by analogy, perhaps against the development of generalized anxiety (see also Chorpita, 2001; Craske, 2003; Mineka & Zinbarg, 1996, in press). In human children, experiences with control and mastery often also occur in the context of the parent-child relationship and so parents' responsiveness to their children's needs directly influences their children's developing sense of mastery (e.g., Craske, 2003; Mineka et al., 1986).

THE CENTRAL ROLE OF WORRY AND ITS POSITIVE FUNCTIONS The worry process is now considered the central feature of GAD and has been the focus of much research in recent years. Here we will first consider the nature and functions of worry. Next, we will consider why worry comes to be such a self-sustaining process in some people and why it may be perceived to be uncontrollable.

Borkovec (1994) and colleagues (2004) investigated both what people with GAD think the benefits of worrying are and what actual functions worry serves. The five benefits that people with GAD most commonly think derive from worrying are:

1. Superstitious avoidance of catastrophe ("Worrying makes it less likely that the feared event will occur").
2. Actual avoidance of catastrophe ("Worrying helps to generate ways of avoiding or preventing catastrophe").
3. Avoidance of deeper emotional topics ("Worrying about most of the things I worry about is a way to distract myself from worrying about even more emotional things, things that I don't want to think about").

4. Coping and preparation ("Worrying about a predicted negative event helps me to prepare for its occurrence").
5. Motivating device ("Worrying helps to motivate me to accomplish the work that needs to be done"; Borkovec, 1994, pp. 16–17; Borkovec et al., 2004).

In addition, exciting new discoveries about the functions that worry actually serves help reveal why the worry process is so self-sustaining. When people with GAD worry, their emotional and physiological responses to aversive imagery are actually suppressed. This suppression of emotional and aversive physiological responding may serve to reinforce the process of worry (that is, to increase its probability; Borkovec et al., 2004). Because worry suppresses physiological responding, it also insulates the person from fully experiencing or processing the topic that is being worried about, and it is known that such full processing is necessary if extinction of that anxiety is to occur. Thus the threatening meaning of the topic being worried about is maintained (Borkovec, 1994; Borkovec et al., 2004). Finally, Borkovec also believes that the worry process is further reinforced superstitiously, because most things that people worry about never happen.

THE NEGATIVE CONSEQUENCES OF WORRY In spite of these positive functions that worry serves, some of its effects are negative (Mineka, 2004; Mineka, Yovel, & Pineles, 2002). For example, worry itself is certainly not an enjoyable activity and can actually lead to a greater sense of danger and anxiety because of all the possible catastrophic outcomes that the worrier envisions. In addition, people who worry about something tend subsequently to have more negative intrusive thoughts than people who do not worry. For example, Wells and Papageorgiou (1995) had people watch a gruesome film. Following the film, some were told to relax and settle down, some were told to imagine the events in the film, and some were told to worry in verbal form about the film. Over the next several days, people in the worry condition showed the most intrusive images from the film. Wells and Butler (1997, p. 167) concluded, "Individuals who are prone to worry . . . are likely to engage in an activity that pollutes the stream of consciousness with an increasing frequency of intrusive thoughts."

Finally, there is now considerable evidence that attempts to control thoughts and worry may paradoxically lead to increased experience of intrusive thoughts and enhanced perception of being unable to control them (Abramowitz et al., 2001; Wells, 1999; Wells & Butler, 1997). Somewhat paradoxically, these intrusive thoughts can then serve as further trigger topics for more worry, and a sense of uncontrollability over worry may develop in people caught in this cycle that occurs in GAD. As we have noted, perceptions of uncontrollability are also known to be associated with increased anxiety, so a vicious circle of anxiety, worry, and intrusive thoughts may develop (Mineka, 2004; Mineka et al., 2002).

COGNITIVE BIASES FOR THREATENING INFORMATION Not only do people with GAD have frequent frightening thoughts, they also process threatening information in a biased way. Many studies have shown that generally anxious people tend to preferentially allocate their attention toward threatening cues when both threat and nonthreat cues are present in the environment. Nonanxious people show, if anything, the opposite bias (see Mathews & MacLeod, 1994, 2005; J. M. Williams et al., 1997, for reviews). Moreover, this attentional vigilance for threat cues occurs at a very early stage of information processing, even before the information has entered the person's conscious awareness. If a person is already anxious, having her or his attention automatically focused on threat cues in the environment would seem only to maintain the anxiety or even make it worse. Moreover, recent evidence also strongly supports the idea that such attentional biases play a causal role in anxiety as well (e.g., Mathews & MacLeod, 2002; MacLeod et al., 2004). Generally anxious people are also more likely than nonanxious people to think that bad things are likely to happen in the future (A. K. MacLeod, 1999), and they have a much stronger tendency to interpret ambiguous information in a threatening way. For example, when clinically anxious subjects read a series of ambiguous sentences (e.g., "The doctor examined little Emma's growth" or "They discussed the priest's convictions"), they are more likely than nonanxious controls to remember the threatening interpretation of the sentences (Eysenck et al., 1991; see also MacLeod et al., 2004; Richards, 2004).

In summary, several psychosocial variables seem to promote the onset of generalized anxiety as well as its maintenance. Experience with unpredictable and/or uncontrollable life events may create a vulnerability to anxiety and promote current anxiety. People also believe that worry serves a number of important functions, and it may actually be reinforced because it dampens physiological arousal. But worry also has some negative consequence, including the fact that worry begets further worry and creates a sense of perceived uncontrollability over the worry process, which further enhances anxiety. Finally, anxiety is associated with an automatic attentional and interpretive bias toward threatening information.

Biological Causal Factors

GENETIC FACTORS Although evidence for genetic factors in GAD is mixed, it does seem likely that there is a modest heritability, although perhaps smaller than for most other anxiety disorders (Hettema, Prescott, & Kendler, 2001; Kendler et al., 1992a; Plomin et al., 2001). Part of the problem for research in this area has been the evolving nature of our understanding of GAD and what its diagnostic criteria are. Several large twin studies reveal exactly how heritability estimates vary as a function of one's definition of GAD (Hettema et al., 2001; Kendler et al., 1992a). The largest and most recent of these twin studies estimates the heritability of GAD at about 15 to 20 percent.

The evidence is increasingly strong that GAD and major depressive disorder (to be discussed in Chapter 7) have a common underlying genetic predisposition (Kendler, 1996; Kendler et al., 1992d). What determines whether individuals with a genetic risk for GAD and/or major depression develop one or the other disorder seems to depend entirely on the specific environmental experiences they have (nonshared environment). This common genetic predisposition for GAD and major depression is best conceptualized as the basic personality trait commonly known as *neuroticism,* a proneness to experience negative mood states (e.g., L. A. Clark et al., 1994; Hettema, Prescott, & Kendler, 2004; Mineka, Watson, & Clark, 1998).

A FUNCTIONAL DEFICIENCY OF GABA In the 1950s certain drugs called the benzodiazepines were found to reduce anxiety. This discovery was followed in the 1970s by the finding that the drugs probably exert their effects by stimulating the action of gamma aminobutyric acid (GABA), a neurotransmitter now strongly implicated in generalized anxiety (Barlow, 2002a; Davis, 2002; LeDoux, 2002). It appears that highly anxious people have a kind of functional deficiency in GABA, which ordinarily plays an important role in the way our brain inhibits anxiety in stressful situations. The benzodiazepine drugs appear to reduce anxiety by increasing GABA activity in certain parts of the brain implicated in anxiety, such as the limbic system, and by suppressing the stress hormone cortisol. Whether the functional deficiency in GABA in anxious people causes their anxiety, or occurs as a consequence of it, is not yet known, but it does appear that this functional deficiency promotes the maintenance of anxiety.

More recently, researchers have discovered that another neurotransmitter—serotonin—is also involved in modulating generalized anxiety (Glitz & Balon, 1996; Goodman, 2004). At present, it seems that GABA, serotonin, and perhaps norepinephrine all play a role in anxiety, but the ways in which they interact remain largely unknown (LeDoux, 2002).

THE CORTICOTROPHIN-RELEASING HORMONE SYSTEM AND ANXIETY An anxiety-producing hormone called *corticotrophin-releasing hormone (CRH)* has also been strongly implicated as playing an important role in generalized anxiety (and depression). When activated by stress or perceived threat, CRH stimulates the release of ACTH (adrenocorticotrophic hormone) from the pituitary gland, which in turn causes release of the stress hormone cortisol from the adrenal gland (Thompson, 2000); cortisol helps the body deal with stress. The CRH hormone may play an important role in generalized anxiety through its effects on the *bed nucleus of the stria terminalis* (an extension of the amygdala; see Figure 6.1 on p. 199), which is now believed to be an important brain area mediating generalized anxiety (e.g., Lang, Davis, & Öhman, 2000).

NEUROBIOLOGICAL DIFFERENCES BETWEEN ANXIETY AND PANIC As we noted at the beginning of this chapter, contemporary theorists are drawing several fundamental distinctions between fear, or panic, and anxiety, including their neurobiological bases. Fear and panic involve activation of the fight-or-flight response, and the brain areas and neurotransmitters that seem most strongly implicated in these emotional responses are the amygdala (and locus coeruleus) and the neurotransmitters norepinephrine and serotonin. Generalized anxiety or anxious apprehension is a more diffuse emotional state involving arousal and a preparation for possible impending threat, and the brain area, neurotransmitters, and hormones that seem most strongly implicated are the limbic system (especially the bed nucleus of the stria terminalis, an extension of the amygdala), GABA, and CRH (Lang et al., 2000). Although serotonin may play a role in both anxiety and panic, it probably does so in somewhat different ways.

Treating Generalized Anxiety Disorder

Many clients with generalized anxiety disorder consult family physicians, seeking relief from their "nerves" or anxieties and/or their various functional (psychogenic) physical problems. Most often in such cases, medications from the benzodiazepine (anxiolytic) category such as Valium are used—and misused—for tension relief, reduction of other somatic symptoms, and relaxation. Their effects on worry and other psychological symptoms are not as great. Moreover, they can be quite habit forming and difficult to taper. A newer medication called buspirone (from a different medication category) also seems effective, and it is neither sedating nor addictive. However, it may take several weeks to show results (Glitz & Balon, 1996; Roy-Byrne & Cowley, 2002). Several categories of antidepressant medications are also useful in the treatment of GAD, and they seem to have a greater effect on the psychological symptoms than do the benzodiazepines (Goodman, 2004; Roy-Byrne & Cowley, 2002).

Cognitive-behavioral therapy (CBT) for generalized anxiety disorder has also become increasingly effective as clinical researchers have refined the techniques used. It usually involves a combination of behavioral techniques such as training in applied muscle relaxation, and cognitive-restructuring techniques aimed at reducing distorted cognitions and information-processing biases associated with GAD, as well as reducing catastrophizing about minor events (Borkovec, Newman, et al., 2002; Roemer et al., 2002). GAD initially appeared to be among the most difficult of the anxiety disorders to treat, and to some extent this is still true. However, advances have been made, and a quantitative review of 13 controlled studies showed that CBT approaches resulted in large changes on most symptoms measured (Borkovec & Ruscio, 2001).

case study — CBT for John's GAD

The case of John, the graduate student with GAD discussed earlier, serves as an example of the success of cognitive-behavioral therapy with this condition. Before receiving cognitive-behavioral therapy, John had seen someone at a student counseling center for several months, but he hadn't found the "talk therapy" very useful. He had heard that cognitive-behavioral therapy might be useful and had sought such treatment. He was in treatment for about 6 months, during which time he found training in deep muscle relaxation helpful in reducing his overall level of tension. Cognitive restructuring helped reduce his worry levels about all spheres of his life. He still had problems with procrastinating when he had deadlines, but this too was improving. He also began socializing more frequently and had tentatively begun dating, when treatment ended for financial reasons. He could now see that if a woman didn't want to go out with him again, this did not mean that he was boring but simply that they might not be a good match.

in review

- What are the key characteristics of GAD, and what is its typical age of onset?
- Describe the various cognitive factors that may be involved in GAD, and indicate what functions worry may serve for those with GAD.
- What are the major biological causal factors in GAD?
- Compare and contrast the biological and cognitive-behavioral treatments for GAD.

Obsessive-Compulsive Disorder

Diagnostically, **obsessive-compulsive disorder (OCD)** is defined by the occurrence of unwanted and intrusive obsessive thoughts or distressing images; these are usually accompanied by compulsive behaviors performed to neutralize the obsessive thoughts or images or to prevent some dreaded event or situation (see DSM table). More specifically, according to DSM-IV-TR, **obsessions** involve persistent and recurrent intrusive thoughts, images, or impulses that are experienced as disturbing and inappropriate. People who have such obsessions try to resist or suppress them, or to neutralize them with some other thought or action. **Compulsions** can involve either overt repetitive behaviors (such as hand washing, checking, or ordering) or more covert mental acts (such as counting, praying, or saying certain words silently). A

DSM-IV-TR

Criteria for Obsessive-Compulsive Disorder

A. Either obsessions or compulsions

Obsessions as defined by (all 4 required)

(1) recurrent and persistent thoughts, impulses or images that are experienced at some time as intrusive and cause marked anxiety

(2) thoughts, impulses, or images are not simply excessive worries about real life problems

(3) person attempts to ignore or suppress or neutralize them with some other thought or action

(4) person recognizes they are a product of his or her own mind

Compulsions as defined by (1 and 2)

(1) repetitive behaviors (hand washing, ordering, checking) or mental acts (praying, counting, etc.) the person feels driven to perform in response to an obsession, or according to rigid rules

(2) behaviors or mental acts aimed at preventing or reducing distress or preventing some dreaded event or situation

B. At least at some point person recognizes the obsessions or compulsions are excessive or unreasonable

C. Obsessions or compulsions cause marked distress, are time-consuming (more than 1 hour a day) or interfere significantly with normal functioning

person with OCD usually feels driven to perform this compulsive ritualistic behavior in response to an obsession, and there are often very rigid rules regarding how the compulsive behavior should be performed. The compulsive behaviors are performed with the goal of preventing or reducing distress or preventing some dreaded event or situation.

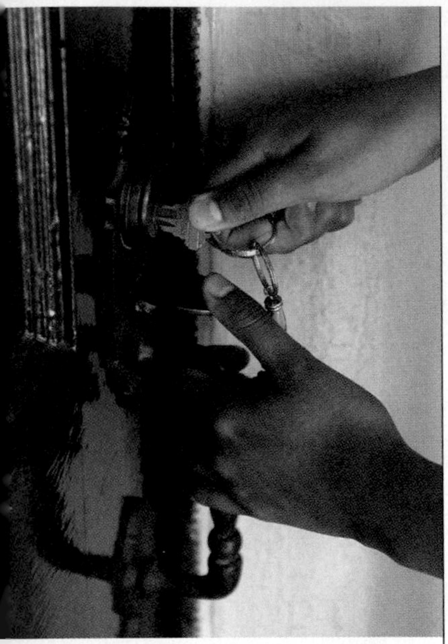

People who suffer from OCD often exhibit repetitive behaviors that are structured around rigid rules for performance. For example, this person turns the key in the lock a set number of times every time she leaves the house.

In addition, the person must recognize that the obsession is the product of his or her own mind rather than being imposed from without (as might occur in schizophrenia). However, there is a continuum of "insight" among obsessive-compulsives about exactly how senseless and excessive their obsessions and compulsions are (Foa & Kozak, 1995; Steketee & Barlow, 2002). In a minority of cases, this insight is absent most of the time.

The following is a fairly typical case of severe obsessive-compulsive disorder.

case STUDY — Obsessions about Confessing and Compulsive Checking

Mark was a 28-year-old single male who, at the time he entered treatment, suffered from severe obsessive thoughts and images about causing harm to others such as running over pedestrians while he was driving. He also had severe obsessions that he would commit a crime such as robbing a store of a large amount of money or poisoning family members or friends. These obsessions were accompanied by lengthy and excessive checking rituals. For example, one day when he drove, he began obsessing that he had caused an accident and hit a pedestrian at an intersection, and he felt compelled to spend several hours driving and walking around all parts of that intersection to find evidence of the accident.

At the time Mark went to an anxiety disorder clinic, he was no longer able to live by himself, after having lived alone for several years since college. He was a very bright young man with considerable artistic talent. He had finished college at a prestigious school for the arts and had launched a successful career as a young artist when the obsessions began in his early twenties. At first they were focused on the possibility that he would be implicated in some crime that he had not committed; later they evolved to the point where he was afraid that he might actually commit a crime and confess to it. The checking rituals and avoidance of all places where such confessions might occur eventually led to his having to give up his career and his own apartment and move back in with his family.

At the time he presented for treatment, Mark's obsessions about harming others and confessing to crimes (whether or not he had committed them) were so severe that he had virtually confined himself to his room at his parent's house. Indeed, he could leave his room only if he had a tape recorder with him so that he would have a record of any crimes he confessed to out loud, because he did not trust his memory. The clinic was several hours' drive from his home; his mother usually had to drive because of his obsessions about causing accidents with pedestrians or moving vehicles, and because the associated checking rituals could punctuate any trip with several very long stops. He also could not speak at all on the phone for fear of confessing some crime that he had (or had not) committed, and he could not mail a letter for the same reason. He also could not go into a store alone or into public bathrooms, where he feared he might write a confession on the wall and be caught and punished.

Prevalence, Age of Onset, and Comorbidity

Obsessive-compulsive disorder is much more prevalent than it was once thought to be (see Antony, Downie, & Swinson, 1998). Specifically, the average 1-year prevalence rate of OCD in the National Comorbidity Survey-Replication was 1 percent, and the average lifetime prevalence was 1.6 percent (Kessler, Berglund, et al., 2005b, 2005c), although estimates from the earlier Epidemiological Catchment Area study were slightly higher (1.6 one year, and 2.5 lifetime; Robins & Regier, 1991). These latter figures appear to be similar in other cultures that have been studied (Steketee & Barlow, 2002). Over 90 percent of those people with OCD who come for treatment experience both obsessions and compulsions (Foa & Kozak, 1995). When mental rituals and compulsions such as counting are included as compulsive behaviors, this figure jumps to 98 percent.

Divorced (or separated) and unemployed people are usually somewhat overrepresented among people with OCD (Karno et al., 1988), which is not surprising given the difficulties this disorder creates for interpersonal and occupational functioning. The results of the ECA study showed little or no gender difference in adults, which makes OCD quite different from most of the rest of the anxiety disorders. Although the disorder generally begins in late adolescence or early adulthood, it is not uncommon

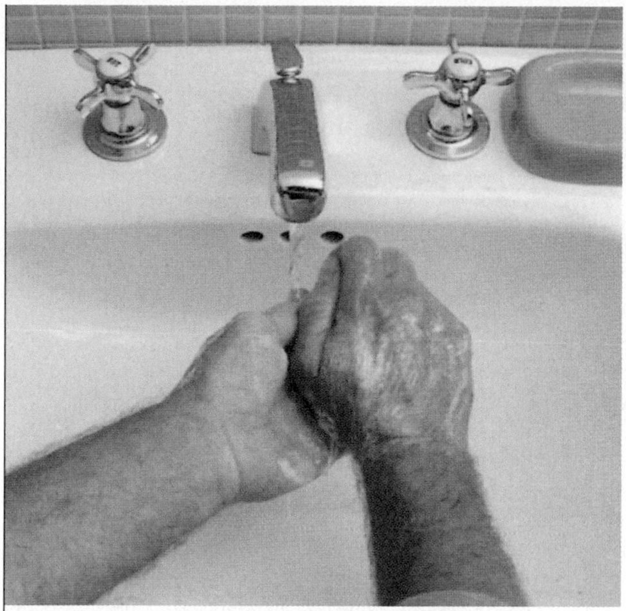

Many of us show some compulsive behavior, but people with obsessive-compulsive disorder feel compelled to perform repeatedly some action in response to an obsession, in order to reduce the anxiety or discomfort created by the obsession. Although the person may realize that the behavior is excessive or unreasonable, he or she does not feel able to control the urge. Obsessive-compulsive hand washers may spend hours a day washing, and may even use abrasive cleansers to the point that their hands bleed.

in children, where its symptoms are strikingly similar to those of adults (March & Leonard, 1998; Steketee & Barlow, 2002). Childhood or early adolescent onset is more common in boys than in girls and is often associated with greater severity. In most cases the disorder has a gradual onset, but once it becomes a serious condition, it tends to be chronic, although the severity of symptoms usually waxes and wanes over time (e.g., Mataix-Cols, Rauch, et al., 2002; Stewart, Geller, et al., 2004).

Like all the anxiety disorders, obsessive-compulsive disorder frequently co-occurs with other mood and anxiety disorders. Depression is especially common, and estimates are that at least one-third of people with OCD may experience major depression at some time in their lives, and as many as 80 percent may experience significant depressive symptoms (Steketee & Barlow, 2002). Given the chronic and debilitating nature of this disorder, it may not be surprising that many develop depression at least partly in response to having OCD. The anxiety disorders with which OCD most often co-occurs include social phobia, panic disorder, GAD, and PTSD (Kessler, Berglund, et al., 2005c). The personality disorders (see Chapter 11) most commonly found in people with OCD are dependent and avoidant.

Another related disorder that has been studied extensively only in the past 15 years—*body dysmorphic disorder (BDD)*—also co-occurs rather commonly with OCD. In one large study, 12 percent of patients with OCD also had body dysmorphic disorder, which many researchers believe to be a closely related disorder (e.g., Phillips, 2000, 2005; Simeon et al., 1995; see Chapter 8 for a discussion of body dysmorphic disorder).

Characteristics of OCD

Most of us have experienced minor obsessive thoughts, such as whether we remembered to lock the door or turn the stove off. In addition, most of us occasionally engage in repetitive or stereotyped behavior, such as checking the stove or the lock on the door or stepping over cracks on a sidewalk. With OCD, however, the thoughts are excessive and much more persistent and distressing, and the associated compulsive acts interfere considerably with everyday activities. Nevertheless, research indicates that normal and abnormal obsessions and compulsive behaviors exist on a continuum, differing primarily in the frequency and intensity of the obsessions and in the degrees to which the obsessions and compulsions are resisted and are troubling (Salkovskis & Kirk, 1997; Steketee & Barlow, 2002).

TYPES OF OBSESSIVE THOUGHTS Obsessive thoughts consist most often of contamination fears, fears of harming oneself or others, and pathological doubt. Other fairly common themes are concerns about or need for symmetry, sexual obsessions, and obsessions concerning religion or aggression. These themes are quite consistent cross-culturally and across the life span (Gibbs, 1996; Steketee & Barlow, 2002).

Obsessive thoughts involving themes of violence or aggression might include a wife being obsessed with the idea that she might poison her husband or child, or a daughter constantly imagining pushing her mother down a flight of stairs. Even though such obsessive thoughts are only very rarely carried out in action, they remain a source of often excruciating torment to a person plagued with them. This pattern is particularly well illustrated in a classic case described by Kraines (1948) of a woman who

> complained of having "terrible thoughts." When she thought of her boyfriend she wished he were dead; when her mother went down the stairs, she "wished she'd fall and break her neck"; when her sister spoke of going to the beach with her infant daughter, the patient "hoped that they would both drown." These thoughts "make me hysterical. I love them; why should I wish such terrible things to happen? It drives me wild, makes me feel I'm crazy and don't belong to society; maybe it's best for me to end it all than to go on thinking such terrible things about those I love." (p. 183)

TYPES OF COMPULSIONS People with OCD feel compelled to perform acts repeatedly that often seem pointless and absurd even to them and that they in some

6.3 Developments in Research

Compulsive Hoarding: Is It a Subtype of OCD?

Compulsive hoarding is a fascinating condition that has received less attention than other forms of OCD. Shirley, a 24-year-old woman, described her classic hoarding symptoms as follows:

> For the past 7 years, I have saved virtually everything that has come into my ownership with the exception of used Kleenexes, gum wrappers, torn movie tickets . . . I save receipts, even ones for low-cost items, paper bags, boxes, newspapers, magazines, notes and lists to myself . . . advertisements, empty . . . bottles . . . and jars, old TV guides, catalogs . . . clothing I don't wear anymore and know I never will . . . The worst is my mail. For the past 7 years, I have kept 99 percent of all the mail I've received. Most of it I . . . don't even open, because you can see that it is junk mail . . . Even after I read my personal mail, I save it. I save it all! . . . because . . . I feel compelled to save everything. . . . My bedroom at home is a monumental junk heap of all my collections. Strewn and piled and boxed everywhere in the most disorderly fashion are all the items I mentioned. There is a narrow path from my bedroom door to my bed and even there I walk on mail and newspapers. Aside from this path, there is no other place for me to walk. . . . And there are piles of my stuff in other parts of the apartment too, growing larger and larger every day. (Rapoport, 1989, pp. 190–91.)

Compulsive hoarding is a symptom seen in approximately 10 to 30 percent of people diagnosed with OCD (Steketee & Frost, 2004). Many have other OCD rituals as well, although some show only compulsive hoarding. Such individuals both acquire and fail to discard many possessions that seem useless or of very limited value. In addition, their living spaces are very cluttered and disorganized to the point of interfering with normal activities that would otherwise occur in those spaces, such as cleaning, cooking, and walking through the house. On average they are more disabled than people with OCD without compulsive hoarding (Frost, Steketee, Williams, & Warren, 2000), and they may be at risk for fire, falling, poor sanitation, and health risks (Frost, Steketee, & Williams, 2000).

Compulsive hoarding has only recently been the subject of significant research, in part because of increasing recognition that these individuals have a much poorer prognosis for treatment than do people without hoarding symptoms (Steketee & Frost, 2004). Medications usually used to treat OCD are usually not effective in treating people with compulsive hoarding symptoms. Traditional behavioral therapy using exposure and response prevention is also less effective than in other forms of OCD, although there are some promising new behavioral treatments that may be more effective.

Other recent neuroimaging research has found that people diagnosed with OCD who have compulsive hoarding symptoms also show patterns of brain activation in certain areas when their symptoms are provoked different from those of people diagnosed with OCD who do not have hoarding symptoms (Mataix-Cols, Wooderson, et al., 2004; Saxena, Brody, et al., 2004). This has led some to suggest that people with compulsive hoarding may be a neurologically distinct subgroup or variant of OCD (Saxena et al., 2004). This conclusion would also be consistent with findings of lack of responsiveness to the same medications that are often successful in reducing the severity of other forms of OCD.

But another possibility is that at least some people with compulsive hoarding actually have a form of psychopathology distinct from OCD (Steketee & Frost, 2004). This would be consistent with findings that a substantial number of people with hoarding symptoms do not show other obsessive-compulsive symptoms. This possibility would also be consistent with another marked difference between people with compulsive hoarding and with other forms of OCD: Compulsive hoarding symptoms are generally not experienced as repugnant and are not resisted in the same way that other obsessive-compulsive symptoms are (Steketee & Frost, 2004). Only further research will be able to help resolve this debate in the literature about the relationship of compulsive hoarding to other forms of OCD.

sense do not want to perform. There are of five primary types of compulsive acts: cleaning, checking, repeating, ordering/arranging, and counting (Antony et al., 1998), and many people show multiple kinds of rituals. For a smaller number of people, the compulsions are to perform various everyday acts (such as eating or dressing) extremely slowly (primary obsessional slowness), and for others the compulsions are to have things exactly symmetrical or "evened up" (Rasmussen & Eisen, 1991; Steketee & Barlow, 2002). Hoarding is another form of compulsive behavior that is only recently receiving research attention (see Developments in Research 6.3).

Washing rituals vary from relatively mild ritual-like behavior such as spending 15 to 20 minutes washing one's hands after going to the bathroom, to more extreme behavior such as washing one's hands with disinfectants for hours every day to the point where the hands bleed. Checking rituals also vary from relatively mild such as checking all the lights, appliances, and locks two or three times before leaving the house, to very extreme such as going back to an intersection where one thinks one may have run over a pedestrian and spending hours checking for any sign of the imagined accident, much as Mark did. Both cleaning and checking rituals are often performed a specific number of times and thus also involve counting. The performance of the compulsive act or the ritualized series of acts usually brings a feeling of reduced tension and satisfaction, as well as a sense of control, although this anxiety relief is typically fleeting, which is why the same rituals need to be repeated over and over (Rachman & Hodgson, 1980; Steketee & Barlow, 2002).

Howard Stern, as with other people who have suffered from OCD, found relief in a compulsive act or ritualized series of acts to bring about a feeling of reduced tension as well as a sense of control. In his book Miss America, *Stern describes behaviors such as turning pages in magazines only with his pinky finger, walking through doors with the right side of his body leading, and flipping through television stations in a particular order before turning the set off. Obsessive-compulsive disorder is more prevalent than it was once thought to be and its prevalence rate shows little or no difference across cultures and between men and women.*

CONSISTENT CHARACTERISTICS Given its many variations, OCD is in some ways more homogeneous than one might expect (Rasmussen & Eisen, 1991). Certain characteristics seem consistent across nearly all the different clinical presentations: (1) Anxiety is the affective symptom (except with primary obsessional slowness). (2) Compulsions usually reduce the anxiety to some degree, at least in the short term. (3) Nearly all people afflicted with OCD fear that something terrible will happen to themselves or others for which they will be responsible.

This latter consistent characteristic has led some to describe OCD as a "what if" illness (Rasmussen & Eisen, 1991). Most people with obsessive-compulsive disorder are continually worried about the possibility that something terrible will happen—e.g., "The very fact that it is within the realm of possibility, however unlikely, that I will stab my baby, or poison my child, is enough to terrify me so that I can think of nothing else no matter how hard I try" (Rasmussen & Eisen, 1991, p. 37). This tendency to judge risks unrealistically seems to be a very important feature of OCD.

Psychosocial Causal Factors

THE BEHAVIORAL VIEWPOINT The dominant behavioral view of obsessive-compulsive disorder derived from O. H. Mowrer's two-process theory of avoidance learning (1947). According to this theory, neutral stimuli become associated with frightening thoughts or experiences through classical conditioning and come to elicit anxiety. For example, touching a doorknob or shaking hands might become associated with the "scary" idea of contamination. Once having made this association, the person may discover that the anxiety produced by shaking hands or touching a doorknob can be reduced by hand washing. Washing his or her hands extensively reduces the anxiety, and so the washing response is reinforced, which makes it more likely to occur again in the future when other situations evoke anxiety about contamination (Rachman & Shafran, 1998). Once learned, such avoidance responses are extremely resistant to extinction (Mineka, 2004; Mineka & Zinbarg, 1996; Salkovskis & Kirk, 1997). Moreover, any stressors that raise anxiety levels can lead to a heightened frequency of avoidance responses in animals or compulsive rituals in humans.

Several classic experiments conducted by Rachman and Hodgson (1980) supported this theory. They found that for most people with OCD, exposure to a situation that provoked their obsession (e.g., a doorknob or toilet seat for someone with obsessions about contamination) did indeed produce distress, which would continue for a moderate amount of time and then gradually dissipate. If the person was allowed to engage in the compulsive ritual immediately after the provocation, however, her or his anxiety would generally decrease rapidly (although only temporarily) and therefore reinforce the compulsive ritual. This model predicts, then, that exposure to feared objects or situations should be useful in treating OCD if the exposure is followed by prevention of the ritual, enabling the person to see that the anxiety will subside naturally in time without the ritual (see also Rachman & Shafran, 1998).

This is indeed the core of the most effective form of behavior therapy for OCD (see Developments in Practice 6.4 on p. 219). Thus the early behavioral model has been very useful in helping us understand what factors maintain obsessive-compulsive behavior, and it has also generated an effective form of treatment. However, it has not been so helpful in explaining why people with OCD develop obsessions in the first place and why they have such abnormal assessments of risk.

OCD AND PREPAREDNESS Just as the preparedness concept has us consider specific and social phobias in the evolutionary context of fears that may have been adaptive for our early ancestors, we have also enlarged our understanding of obsessive-compulsive disorder by looking at it in an evolutionary context (e.g., De Silva, Rachman, & Seligman, 1977; Rapoport, 1989). For example, thoughts about dirt and contamination associated with compulsive washing are so common as to make their occurrence seem nonrandom. The overall consensus seems to be that humans' obsessions with dirt and contamination and certain other potentially dangerous situations did not arise out of a vacuum but rather have deep evolutionary roots (Mineka & Zinbarg, 1996, 2006).

In addition, some theorists have argued that the displacement activities that many species of animals engage in under situations of conflict or high arousal resemble the compulsive rituals seen in obsessive-compulsive disorder (Craske, 1999; Mineka & Zinbarg, 1996; Rapoport, 1989; Winslow & Insel, 1991). Displacement activities often involve grooming (such as a bird preening his feathers) or nesting under conditions of high conflict or frustration. They may therefore be related to the distress-induced grooming (such as washing) or tidying rituals seen in people with OCD, which are often provoked by obsessive thoughts that provoke anxiety.

THE EFFECTS OF ATTEMPTING TO SUPPRESS OBSESSIVE THOUGHTS When normal people attempt to suppress unwanted thoughts (for example, "Don't think about white bears"), they may experience a paradoxical increase in those thoughts later (Abramowitz et al., 2001; Wegner, 1994). In addition, two studies showed that if thought suppression occurs during a negative mood, a connection is produced between the thought and the negative mood. When the negative mood occurred again later, the thought was more easily experienced, or when the thought was later experienced, the mood returned (Wenzlaff, Wegner, & Klein, 1991).

As already noted, people with normal and abnormal obsessions differ primarily in the degree to which they resist their own thoughts and find them unacceptable. Thus a major factor contributing to the frequency of obsessive thoughts and negative moods may be these attempts to suppress them (similar to what was discussed earlier about the effects of attempts to control worry in people with generalized anxiety disorder). For example, when people with OCD were asked to record intrusive thoughts in a diary, both on days when they were told to try to suppress those thoughts and on days without instructions to suppress, the people with OCD reported approximately twice as many intrusive thoughts on the days when they were attempting to suppress them (Salkovskis & Kirk, 1997). In addition, some other research suggests that thought suppression leads to a more general increase in obsessive-compulsive symptoms beyond just the frequency of obsessions (Purdon, 2004).

APPRAISALS OF RESPONSIBILITY FOR INTRUSIVE THOUGHTS Salkovskis (e.g., 1989), Rachman (1997), and others have distinguished between obsessive or intrusive thoughts per se and the negative automatic thoughts and catastrophic appraisals that people have about them. For example, people with OCD often seem to have an inflated sense of responsibility, possibly encouraged during childhood if parents instill extremely high standards or show excessive criticism. In turn, this inflated sense of responsibility can in some vulnerable people be associated with beliefs that having a thought about doing something (e.g., hitting a pedestrian) is equivalent to actually having done it (e.g., having hit the pedestrian), or that thinking about committing a sin is as bad as doing so (Steketee & Barlow, 2002). This is known as *thought-action fusion* (see Shafran & Rachman, 2004, for a review). This inflated sense of responsibility for the harm they may cause adds to the "perceived awfulness of any harmful consequences" (Salkovskis et al., 2000, p. 348), and also motivates compulsive behaviors such as compulsive washing and checking to try to reduce the likelihood of anything harmful happening. Part of what differentiates normal people who have obsessions and can ordinarily dismiss them (without a perception of responsibility) from people with OCD is this sense of responsibility that makes the thought so "awful."

COGNITIVE BIASES AND DISTORTIONS Cognitive factors have also been implicated in obsessive-compulsive disorder. Research on people with OCD has shown that their attention is drawn to disturbing material relevant to their obsessive concerns, much as occurs in the other anxiety disorders (see McNally, 2000, for a review). People with OCD seem to have difficulty blocking out negative irrelevant input or distracting information, so they may attempt to suppress negative thoughts stimulated by this information (Enright & Beech, 1993a, 1993b; McNally, 2000). As we have noted, trying to suppress negative thoughts may paradoxically increase their frequency. These people also have low confidence in their memory ability, which may contribute to their repeating their ritualistic behaviors over and over again (Dar et al., 2000; McNally, 2000).

Biological Causal Factors

In the past 25 years there has been an explosion of research investigating the possible biological basis for obsessive-compulsive disorder, ranging from studies about its genetic basis, to studies about brain and neurotransmitter abnormalities. The evidence accumulating from all three kinds of studies suggests that biological causal factors are

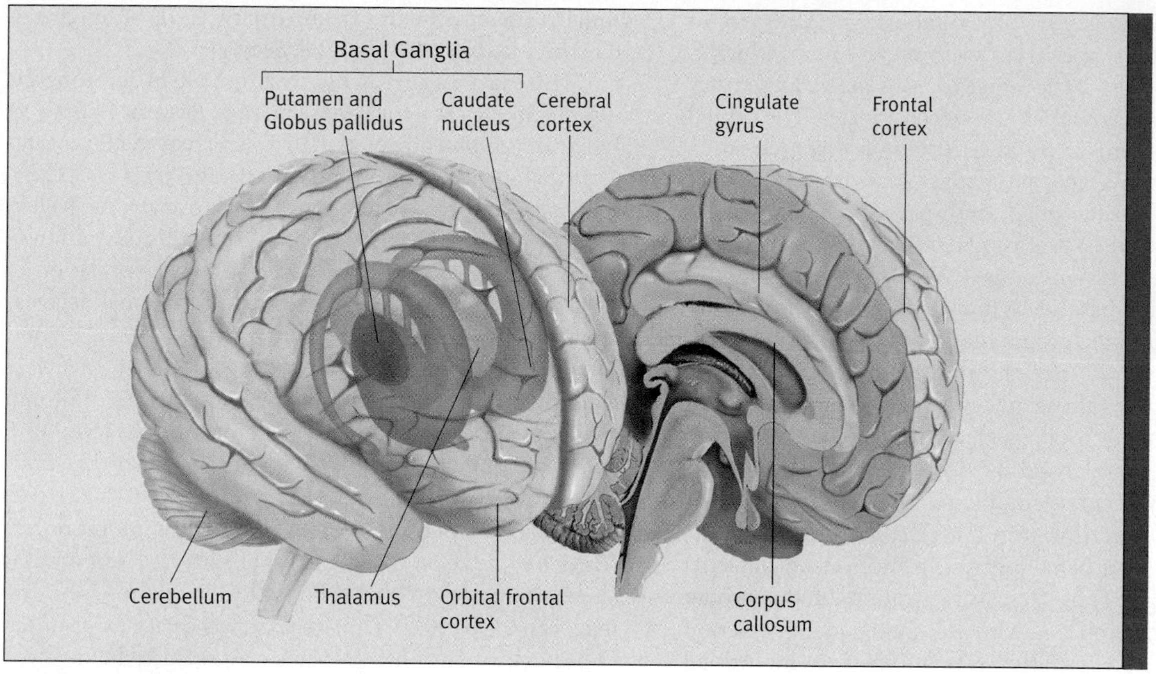

FIGURE 6.3

Neurophysiological Mechanisms for Obsessive-Compulsive Disorder

The orbital frontal cortex and the basal ganglia (especially the caudate nucleus) are the brain structures most often implicated in OCD. Increased metabolic activity has been found in both the orbital frontal cortex and the caudate nucleus in people with OCD.

perhaps more strongly implicated in the causes of OCD than in any of the other anxiety disorders.

GENETIC INFLUENCES Genetic studies have included both twin studies and family studies. Evidence from twin studies reveals a moderately high concordance rate for monozygotic twins and a lower rate for dizygotic twins. One review of 14 published studies included 80 monozygotic pairs of twins, of whom 54 were concordant for the diagnosis of OCD, and 29 pairs of dizygotic twins, of whom 9 were concordant. This is consistent with a moderate genetic heritability (Billett, Richter, & Kennedy, 1998). Most family studies have also found substantially higher rates of OCD in first-degree relatives of OCD clients than would be expected from current estimates of the prevalence of OCD (Hettema et al., 2001; Pauls et al., 1995).

Finally, the most compelling evidence of a genetic contribution to some forms of OCD is for a form of OCD that often starts in childhood and is characterized by chronic motor tics (Lochner & Stein, 2003). This form of tic-related OCD is linked to *Tourette's syndrome,* a disorder characterized by severe chronic motor and vocal tics that is suspected to have a substantial genetic basis (see Chapter 16). For example, one study found that 23 percent of first-degree relatives of people with Tourette's syndrome had diagnosable OCD (Pauls et al., 1986, 1991, 1995). Overall, it seems that there is probably a moderate genetic contribution to OCD, although it may be a rather nonspecific "neurotic" predisposition (Hanna, 2000; MacKinnon & Foley, 1996).

ABNORMALITIES IN BRAIN FUNCTION The search for abnormalities in the brains of people with OCD has been intense in the past 20 years as advances have been made in brain-imaging techniques. Findings from at least half a dozen studies using PET scans have shown that people with OCD have abnormally active metabolic levels in the caudate nucleus, the orbital frontal cortex, and the cingulate cortex. The caudate nucleus is part of the basal ganglia, which are a set of large nuclei lying just below the cerebral cortex; they in turn surround the thalamus (see Figure 6.3). Moreover, activity in some of these areas is further increased when symptoms are provoked by relevant phobic stimuli (see Evans, Lewis, & Iobst, 2004; Rauch & Savage, 2000, for reviews). Some of these studies have also shown partial normalization of at least some of these abnormalities with successful treatment through either medication or behavior therapy (Baxter et al., 2000; Saxena, Brody, et al., 2002).

Exactly how these areas are implicated is still unclear, although several different theories are currently being tested. For example, Baxter and colleagues (1991, 2000) have speculated that part of the primary dysfunction in OCD may be in an area of the brain called the corpus striatum (which includes the caudate nucleus). The corpus striatum/caudate nucleus (part of a set of structures called the basal ganglia) is part of an important neural circuit linking the orbital frontal cortex to the thalamus, which is an important relay station that receives nearly all sensory input and passes it back to the cerebral cortex. The orbital frontal cortex seems to be where primitive urges regarding sex, aggression, hygiene, and danger come from (the "stuff of obsessions"; Baxter et al., 1991, p. 116). These urges are ordinarily filtered by the caudate nucleus, allowing only the strongest to pass on to the thalamus.

This cortico-basal-ganglionic-thalamic circuit is normally involved in the preparation of complex sets of interrelated behavioral responses used only in specific situations such as those involved in territorial or social concerns. Baxter et al. cite evidence that when this circuit is not functioning properly, inappropriate behavioral responses may occur, including repeated sets of behaviors stemming from territorial and social concerns (e.g., checking and aggressive behavior) and from hygiene concerns (e.g., cleaning). Thus the overactivation of the orbital frontal cortex, combined with a dysfunctional interaction among the corpus striatum/caudate nucleus, the orbital frontal cortex, and the thalamus (which is downstream from the corpus striatum) may be the central component of the brain dysfunction in OCD. This in turn prevents people with OCD from showing the normal inhibition of sensations, thoughts, and behaviors that would occur if the circuit were functioning properly. In this case, impulses toward aggression, sex, hygiene, and danger that most people keep under control with relative ease "leak through" as obsessions and distract people with OCD from ordinary goal-directed behavior.

In summary, in people with OCD there seems to be overactivation of the orbital frontal cortex, which delivers the "stuff of obsessions" (Baxter et al., 1991, p. 116). Moreover, there is also a dysfunction of the cortico-basal-ganglionic-thalamic circuit, which leads to inappropriate behavioral responses that are not inhibited as they ordinarily would be. Considering these problems, we can begin to understand how the prolonged and repeated bouts of obsessive-compulsive behavior in people with OCD may occur (Baxter et al., 1991, 1992, 2000).

THE ROLE OF SEROTONIN Pharmacological studies of causal factors in obsessive-compulsive disorder intensified with the discovery in the 1970s that a drug called Anafranil (clomipramine) is often effective in the treatment of OCD. Clomipramine is closely related to other tricyclic antidepressants (see Chapter 7) but is more effective in the treatment of OCD (Pigott & Seay, 2000). Research shows that this is because it has greater effects on the neurotransmitter serotonin, which is now strongly implicated in OCD (Pogarell, Hamann, Popperl, et al., 2003). Moreover, several other antidepressant drugs from the SSRI category that also have relatively selective effects on serotonin, such as fluoxetine (Prozac), have also been shown to be about equally effective in the treatment of OCD (Dougherty, Rauch, & Jenike, 2002; Pigott & Seay, 2000).

The exact nature of the dysfunction in serotonergic systems in OCD is unclear (see Gross, Sasson, Chopra, & Zohar, 1998; Murphy et al., 1996). Current evidence suggests that increased serotonin activity and increased sensitivity of some brain structures to serotonin are involved in OCD symptoms. In this view, long-term administration of clomipramine or fluoxetine causes a down-regulation of certain serotonin receptors, causing a functional decrease in availability of serotonin (Dolberg et al., 1996a, 1996b). That is, although the immediate short-term effects of clomipramine or fluoxetine may be to increase serotonin levels (and exacerbate OCD symptoms too), the long-term effects are quite different. This is consistent with the finding that these drugs must be taken for at least 6 to 12 weeks before significant improvement in OCD symptoms occurs (Baxter et al., 2000; Dougherty et al., 2002). However, it is also becoming clear that dysfunction in serotonergic systems cannot by itself fully explain this complex disorder. Other neurotransmitter systems also seem to be involved although their role is not yet well understood (Baxter et al., 2000; Hollander et al., 1992).

In summary, there is now a substantial body of evidence implicating biological causal factors in OCD. This evidence comes from genetic studies, from studies of brain structure and functioning, and from psychopharmacological studies. Although the exact nature of these factors and how they are interrelated is not yet understood, major research efforts that are currently under way are sure to enhance our understanding of this very serious and disabling disorder.

Treating Obsessive-Compulsive Disorder

A behavioral treatment that combines exposure and response prevention may be the most effective approach to obsessive-compulsive disorders (e.g., Franklin & Foa, 1998, 2002; Steketee & Barlow, 2002). This treatment involves having the OCD clients repeatedly expose themselves to stimuli that will provoke their obsession (such as, for someone with compulsive washing, touching the bottom of their shoe or a toilet seat in a public bathroom) and then preventing them from engaging in their compulsive rituals, which they ordinarily would engage in to reduce the anxiety/distress provoked by their obsession. Preventing the rituals is essential so that they can see that the anxiety created by the obsession will dissipate naturally if they allow enough time to pass. This treatment is examined in more detail in Developments in Practice 6.4.

This treatment tends to help clients who stick with the treatment, most of whom show a 50 to 70 percent reduction in symptoms (Steketee, 1993). About 50 percent are much improved or very much improved, and another 25

6.4 Developments in Practice

Exposure and Response Prevention as Treatments for Obsessive-Compulsive Disorder

Foa and Franklin (2001, pp. 241–48; see also Steketee & Foa, 1985) presented the following case as an illustration of their recommended approach to the behavioral treatment of obsessive-compulsive disorders. The patient, June, was a 26-year-old, recently married nursing graduate who complained of washing and cleaning problems so severe that she was unable to seek work in her profession. On initial evaluation she was agitated and distressed, feeling helpless to control her need to take at least two 45-minute showers daily (each with a lot of counting and ordering rituals) and to wash her hands some 20 times a day for 5 minutes or more. She also spent a great deal of time wiping various objects with alcohol. Inquiry soon determined that she was terrified of becoming "contaminated," particularly by "dog dirt" and bathroom germs mostly coming from human feces, and she took great pains to avoid anything that could have had contact with either dog dirt or bathroom germs. She also had problems with garbage and with dead animals on the road. Previous treatments had been ineffective. Her relationship with her husband was very stressed because of her husband's frustration with her excessive cleanliness.

Exposure Treatment

The therapist and patient worked together to create a hierarchy of upsetting stimuli, rating them on a scale of 1 through 100 according to their capacity to evoke disgust and the impulse to wash. For example, the patient gave ratings of 100 to touching "dog dirt" (if unable to wash immediately), 90 to automobile tires (which might have contacted a dead animal), 90 to garbage cans outdoors (but only 50 to garbage in her own sink), and 40 to the outside doorknob of a public bathroom (the inside doorknob rated 80 and a public toilet seat 95). Subsequently, in treatment sessions five times weekly, June was instructed to expose herself deliberately to these stimuli either in guided fantasy or directly, beginning with those rated relatively low in the hierarchy and moving gradually to the more severely threatening ones. Systematic exposure continued until the patient appeared at ease with a particular confrontation and her discomfort rating of it dropped to the range of 40 to 50.

In addition to the exposures conducted during therapy sessions, "homework" was liberally assigned. Subjective ratings of discomfort were carefully monitored during these encounters. On one occasion well into treatment, the therapist drove with the patient to a place where she had observed a dead cat on the roadside and insisted that the patient approach the "smelly" corpse, touch it with the sole of her shoe, and then touch her shoe. A pebble lying close by and a stick with which she had touched the cat were presented to the patient with the instruction that she keep them in her pocket and touch them frequently throughout the day. The patient was also told to drive her car past the spot on subsequent days.

Response Prevention

After obtaining June's commitment to the full treatment procedure, the therapist instituted a no-washing rule after the first exposure session. Specifically, the patient was to remain completely unwashed for a period of 3 days, after which she could take a 10-minute shower to be followed by another wash-free 3 days. As anticipated, June was notably upset by this proposed regimen and strongly doubted that she could carry it off. The therapist was encouraging but insistent, promising support through the hard times, and the patient was indeed successful. The transition to "normal washing and cleaning behavior" was instituted shortly before the end of the planned 15 therapy sessions of several hours each. This plan consisted of one 10-minute shower per day and 30-second hand washings not to exceed five per day at mealtimes, after bathroom use, and after touching clearly soiled or greasy objects.

In an evaluation 9 months following the initiation of treatment, June described herself as "definitely a lot better . . . maybe about 80 percent better." She acknowledged that she still had obsessions "once every week or two" (most often still about dog feces), but she was now employed and her relationship with her husband was much improved. She felt she was living a "normal life."

As Foa and Franklin (2001) and Steketee and Foa (1985) have pointed out, obsessive-compulsive disorders rarely remit completely; even a successfully treated patient usually has some residual obsessive problems or rituals, as in June's case. The behavioral treatment undertaken here was of course rigorous and demanding, but it appears to have been the treatment of choice.

percent are moderately improved. These results are considered superior to those obtained with medication (Franklin & Foa, 2002; Steketee & Barlow, 2002).

The successful use of this treatment in the case of Mark, the young artist with severe OCD, is described here briefly.

case STUDY **Mark's Treatment**

Mark was initially treated with medication and with exposure and response prevention. He found the side effects of the medication (clomipramine) intolerable and gave it up within a few weeks. For the behavioral treatment, he was directed to get rid of the tape recorder and was given a series of exercises in which he exposed himself to feared situations where he might confess to a crime or cause harm to others, including making phone calls, mailing letters, and entering stores and public bathrooms (all things he had been unable to do). Checking rituals (including the tape recorder) were prevented. Although the initial round of treatment was not especially helpful, in part because of difficulty in getting to treatment, he did eventually make a commitment to more intensive treatment by moving to a small apartment closer to the clinic. Thereafter, he did quite well.

To date, medications that affect the neurotransmitter serotonin seem to be the primary class of medication that has reasonably good effects in the treatment of persons with OCD. The other anxiety and mood disorders respond to a wider range of drugs (Dougherty, Rauch, & Jenike, 2002; Pigott & Seay, 2000). These medications that alter functioning of the serotonin system, such as clomipramine (Anafranil) and fluoxetine (Prozac), appear to reduce the intensity of the symptoms of this disorder; approximately 50 to 70 percent of OCD clients show at least a 25 percent reduction in symptoms (relative to 4 to 5 percent on placebo; Iancu et al., 2000; Pigott & Seay, 2000). Some clients may show greater improvement than this, but about 30 to 50 percent do not show any clinically significant improvement.

A major disadvantage of medication treatment for OCD, as for other anxiety disorders, is that when the medication is discontinued, relapse rates are generally very high (as high as 90 percent) following discontinuation of the medication (Dolberg et al., 1996a, 1996b; Franklin & Foa, 2002). Thus many people who do not seek alternative forms of behavior therapy that have more long-lasting benefits may have to stay on these medications indefinitely. Studies in adults have generally not found combining medication with exposure and response prevention to be much more effective than behavior therapy alone (Franklin & Foa, 2002; Foa, Liebowitz, & Kozak, 2005), although one recent study showed that a combination treatment was superior in the treatment of children and adolescents with OCD (Pediatric OCD Treatment Study, 2004).

Finally, because OCD in its most severe form is such a crippling and disabling disorder, in recent years psychiatrists have begun to reexamine the usefulness of certain neurosurgical techniques for the treatment of severe intractable OCD (which may afflict as many as 10 percent of people diagnosed with OCD; Mindus, Rasmussen, & Lindquist, 1994). Before such surgery is even contemplated, the person must have had severe OCD for at least 5 years and must not have responded to any of the known treatments discussed so far (medication or behavior therapy). Several studies have shown that approximately one-third of these intractable cases respond quite well to neurosurgery designed to destroy brain tissue in one of the areas implicated in this condition (Dougherty et al., 2002; Jenike, 2000). The results of these techniques will be discussed in greater detail in Chapter 17.

IN REVIEW

- Summarize the major symptoms of obsessive-compulsive disorder.
- How have conditioning and cognitive factors been implicated in OCD?
- What are the major biological causal factors for OCD?
- Describe the major treatment approaches for OCD and their relative advantages and disadvantages.

SOCIOCULTURAL CAUSAL FACTORS FOR ALL ANXIETY DISORDERS

Cross-cultural research suggests that although anxiety is a universal emotion, and anxiety disorders probably exist in all human societies, there are some differences in prevalence and in the form in which the different disorders are expressed in different cultures (Barlow, 2002a; Good & Kleinman, 1985; Kirmayer, Young, & Hayton, 1995). Within the United States, however, prevalence rates of the different anxiety disorders are quite similar across different racial groups, including whites, African-Americans, and Hispanic Americans, although phobic disorders are somewhat more common among African-Americans and Hispanic Americans.

However, Latin Americans from the Caribbean, and other people from the Caribbean, do show higher rates of a variant of panic disorder called *ataque de nervios* (Barlow, 2002a; Liebowitz et al., 1994) than do other groups. Most of the symptoms of *ataque de nervios* are the same as in a panic attack but may also include bursting into tears and uncontrollable shouting. Other symptoms can include trembling, verbal or physical aggression, dissociative experiences, and seizure-like or fainting episodes. Such attacks are often associated with a stressful event relating to the family (e.g., news of a death) and the person may have amnesia for the episode (APA, *DSM-IV-TR,* 2000).

Looking at anxiety disorders from a cross-national perspective, one recent study of over 60,000 people across 14 countries (8 developed and 6 less developed) by the World Health Organization (WHO World Mental Health Survey Consortium, 2004) showed that anxiety disorders were the most common category of disorder reported in all but one country (Ukraine), but that reported prevalence rates for all the anxiety disorders combined varied from 2.4 percent (Shanghai, China) to 18.2 percent (United States). Other countries with moderately high rates of reported anxiety disorders were Colombia, France, and Lebanon, and other countries with moderately low rates were China, Japan, Nigeria, and Spain. We now turn to several examples of cultural variants on anxiety disorders that illustrate the range of expressions of anxiety that are exhibited worldwide.

Cultural Differences in Sources of Worry

In the Yoruba culture of Nigeria, there are three primary clusters of symptoms associated with generalized anxiety: worry, dreams, and bodily complaints. However, the sources of worry are very different than in Western society; they focus on creating and maintaining a large family and on fertility. Dreams are a major source of anxiety because they are thought to indicate that one may be bewitched. The common somatic complaints are also unusual from a Western standpoint: "I have the feeling of something like water in my brain," "Things like ants keep on creeping in various parts of my brain," and "I am convinced some types of worms are in my head" (Ebigbo, 1982; Good & Kleinman, 1985). Nigerians with this syndrome often have paranoid fears of malevolent attack by witchcraft (Kirmayer et al., 1995). In India also there are many more worries about being possessed by spirits and about sexual inadequacy than are seen in generalized anxiety in Western cultures (Carstairs & Kapur, 1976; Good & Kleinman, 1985).

Another culture-related syndrome that occurs in places like China is *Koro,* which for men involves intense, acute fear that the penis is shrinking into the body and that when this process is complete, the sufferer will die. Koro occurs less frequently in women, for whom the fear is that their nipples are retracting and their breasts shrinking. Koro tends to occur in epidemics—especially in cultural minority groups when their survival is threatened. It occurs in a cultural context where there are serious concerns about male sexual potency (Barlow, 2002a; Kirmayer et al., 1995).

Taijin Kyofusho

There is also some evidence that the form that certain anxiety disorders take has actually evolved to fit certain cultural patterns. A good example is the Japanese disorder *taijin kyofusho (TKS),* which is related to the Western diagnosis of social phobia. Like social phobia, it is a fear of interpersonal relations or of social situations (Kirmayer, 1991; Kleinknecht et al., 1997; Tseng et al., 1992). However, Westerners with social phobia are afraid of social situations where they may be the object of scrutiny or criticism. By contrast, most people with TKS are concerned about doing something that will embarrass or offend others (Barlow, 2002a). For example, they may fear offending others by blushing, emitting an offensive odor, or staring inappropriately into the eyes of another person, or through their perceived physical defects or imagined deformities. This fear of bringing shame on others or offending them is what leads to social avoidance (Kleinknecht et al., 1997). Two of the most common symptoms (phobias about eye contact and blushing) are not mentioned in the DSM-IV-TR description of social phobia (Kirmayer, 1991). Body dysmorphic disorder—the fear that some part of the body is defective or malformed (see Chapter 8)—also commonly occurs in TKS sufferers.

Kirmayer (1991) and colleagues (1995) have argued that the pattern of symptoms that occurs in taijin kyofusho has clearly been shaped by cultural factors. Japanese children are raised to be highly dependent on their mothers and to have a fear of the outside world, especially strangers. As babies and young children, they are praised for being obedient and docile. There is also a great deal of emphasis on implicit communication—being able to guess another's thoughts and feelings and being sensitive to them. People who make too much eye contact are likely to be considered aggressive and insensitive, and children are taught to look at the throat of people with whom they are conversing rather than into their eyes. The society is also very hierarchical and structured, and many subtleties in language and facial communication are used to communicate one's response to social status.

At a more general level, cross-cultural researchers have noted that recognition of the cognitive component of most anxiety disorders leads one to expect many cross-cultural variations in the form that different anxiety disorders take. Anxiety disorders can be considered, at least in part, disorders of the interpretive process. Because cultures influence the categories and schemas that we use to interpret our symptoms of distress, there are bound to be significant differences in the form that anxiety disorders take in different cultures (e.g., Barlow, 2002a; Good & Kleinman, 1985; Kirmayer et al., 1995).

In Review

- What are some examples of cultural differences in sources of worry?
- How is taijin kyofusho related to social phobia, and what kinds of cultural forces seem to have shaped it?

summary

- The anxiety disorders have anxiety or panic or both at their core. They were initially considered a subset of the neuroses, but recent versions of the DSM-III and DSM-IV-TR have largely abandoned this term.
- Fear or panic is a basic emotion that involves activation of the fight-or-flight response of the autonomic nervous system.
- Anxiety is a more diffuse blend of emotions that includes high levels of negative affect, worry about possible threat or danger, and the sense of being unable to predict threat or to control it if it occurs.
- Anxiety and panic are each associated with a number of distinct anxiety disorder syndromes.
- With **specific phobias,** there is an intense and irrational fear of specific objects or situations; when confronted with a feared object, the phobic person often shows activation of the fight-or-flight response, which is also associated with panic.
  - Many sources of fear and anxiety are believed to be acquired through conditioning or other learning mechanisms. However, some people (because of either temperamental or experiential factors) are more vulnerable than others to acquiring such responses.
  - We seem to have a biologically based preparedness to acquire readily fears of objects or situations that posed a threat to our early ancestors.
- In **social phobia,** a person has disabling fears of one or more social situations usually because of fears of negative evaluation by others or of acting in an embarrassing or humiliating manner; in some cases a person with social phobia may actually experience panic attacks in social situations.
  - We seem to have an evolutionarily based predisposition to acquire fears of social stimuli signaling dominance and aggression from other humans.
  - People with social phobia are also preoccupied with negative self-evaluative thoughts that tend to interfere with their ability to interact in a socially skillful fashion.
- In **panic disorder,** a person experiences unexpected panic attacks that often create a sense of stark terror, which usually subsides in a matter of minutes.
  - Many people who experience panic attacks develop anxious apprehension about experiencing another attack; this apprehension is required for a diagnosis of panic disorder.
  - Many people with panic disorder also develop agoraphobic avoidance of situations in which they fear that they might have an attack.
  - The conditioning theory of panic disorder proposes that panic attacks cause the conditioning of anxiety primarily to external cues associated with the attacks, and conditioning of panic itself primarily to interoceptive cues associated with the early stages of the attacks.
  - The cognitive theory of panic disorder holds that this condition may develop in people who are prone to making catastrophic misinterpretations of their bodily sensations, a tendency that may be related to preexisting high levels of anxiety sensitivity.

- Other biological theories of panic disorder emphasize that the disorder may result from biochemical abnormalities in the brain as well as abnormal activity of the neurotransmitters norepinephrine and serotonin.
- Panic attacks may arise primarily from the brain area called the amygdala, although many other areas are also involved.

- In **generalized anxiety disorder,** a person has chronic and excessively high levels of worry about a number of events or activities and responds to stress with high levels of psychic and muscle tension.
  - Generalized anxiety disorder may occur in people who have had extensive experience with unpredictable and/or uncontrollable life events.
  - People with generalized anxiety seem to have schemas about their inability to cope with strange and dangerous situations that promote worries focused on possible threats.
  - The neurobiological factor most implicated in generalized anxiety is a functional deficiency in the neurotransmitter GABA, which is involved in inhibiting anxiety in stressful situations; the limbic system is the brain area most involved.
- Thus different neurotransmitters and brain areas are involved in panic attacks and generalized anxiety.
- In **obsessive-compulsive disorder,** a person experiences unwanted and intrusive distressing thoughts or images that are usually accompanied by compulsive behaviors performed to neutralize those thoughts or images. Checking and cleaning rituals are most common.
  - Biological causal factors also seem to be involved in obsessive-compulsive disorder, with evidence coming from genetic studies, studies of brain functioning, and psychopharmacological studies.
  - Once this disorder begins, the anxiety-reducing qualities of the compulsive behaviors may help to maintain the disorder.
- Once a person has an anxiety disorder, mood-congruent information processing, such as attentional and interpretive biases, seems to help maintain it.
- Many people with anxiety disorders are treated by physicians, often with medications designed to allay anxiety or with antidepressant medications that also have anti-anxiety effects.
  - Such treatment focuses on suppressing the symptoms, and some medications have addictive potential.
  - Once the medications are discontinued, relapse rates tend to be high.
- Behavioral and cognitive therapies have a very good track record with regard to treatment of the anxiety disorders.
  - Behavior therapies focus on prolonged exposure to feared situations; with obsessive-compulsive disorder, the rituals also must be prevented following exposure to the feared situations.
  - Cognitive therapies focus on helping clients understand their underlying automatic thoughts, which often involve cognitive distortions such as unrealistic predictions of catastrophes that in reality are very unlikely to occur. Then they learn to change these inner thoughts and beliefs through a process of logical reanalysis known as cognitive restructuring.

Key Terms

agoraphobia (P. 195)
amygdala (P. 199)
anxiety (P. 181)
anxiety disorders (P. 180)
anxiety sensitivity (P. 201)
blood-injection-injury phobia (P. 185)
compulsions (P. 211)
fear (P. 181)
generalized anxiety disorder (GAD) (P. 205)
interoceptive fears (P. 205)
neuroses (P. 180)
neurotic behavior (P. 180)
obsessions (P. 211)
obsessive-compulsive disorder (OCD) (P. 211)
panic (P. 181)
panic disorder (P. 194)
panic provocation agent (P. 198)
phobia (P. 183)
social phobia (P. 190)
specific phobia (P. 183)

CHAPTER 7

Mood Disorders and Suicide

Most of us get depressed from time to time. Failing an exam, not getting into one's first choice of college or graduate school, and breaking up with a romantic partner are all examples of events that can precipitate a depressed mood in many people. However, **mood disorders** involve much more severe alterations in mood and for much longer periods of time. In such cases the disturbances of mood are intense and persistent enough to be clearly maladaptive, and often lead to serious problems in relationships and work performance. In fact, it has been estimated that in 2000, depression ranked among the top-five health conditions in terms of years lost to disability in all parts of the world except Africa, and it was the number-one such health condition in the United States, ranking above heart disease and stroke (Üstün et al., 2004). Overall the "disease-burden" of depression to society—that is, the total direct costs (such as for treatment) and indirect costs (such as days missed from work, disability, and premature deaths)—totalled $83.1 billion in the United States alone, with over 60 percent of the reported costs resulting from problems in the workplace (Greenberg, Kessler, et al., 2003). Consider the following case.

case STUDY **A Successful "Total Failure"**

Margaret, a prominent businesswoman in her late-forties, noted for her energy and productivity, was unexpectedly deserted by her husband for a younger woman. Following her initial shock and rage, she began to have uncontrollable weeping spells and doubts about her business acumen. Decision making became an ordeal. Her spirits rapidly sank, and she began to spend more and more time in bed, refusing to deal with anyone. Her alcohol consumption increased to the point where she was seldom entirely sober. Within a period of weeks, she had suffered serious financial losses owing to her inability, or refusal, to keep her affairs in order. She felt she was a "total failure," even when reminded of her considerable personal and professional achievements; indeed, her self-criticism gradually spread to all aspects of her life and her personal history. Finally, alarmed members of her family essentially forced her to accept an appointment with a clinical psychologist.

Was something "wrong" with Margaret, or was she merely experiencing normal human emotions because of her husband's deserting her? The psychologist concluded that she was suffering from a serious mood disorder and initiated treatment. The diagnosis, based on the severity of the symptoms and the degree of impairment, was major depressive disorder. Secondarily, she had also developed a serious drinking problem—a condition that frequently co-occurs with major depressive disorder.

Mood disorders are diverse in nature, as is illustrated by the many types of depression recognized in the DSM-IV-TR that we will discuss. Nevertheless, in all mood disorders (formerly called *affective disorders*), extremes of emotion or *affect*—soaring elation or deep depression—dominate the clinical picture. Other symptoms are also present, but the abnormal mood is the defining feature.

What Are Mood Disorders?

The two key moods involved in mood disorders are **mania,** often characterized by intense and unrealistic feelings of excitement and euphoria, and **depression,** which usually involves feelings of extraordinary sadness and dejection. Some people experience both of these kinds of moods at one time or another, but other people experience only the depression. These mood states are often conceived to be at opposite ends of a mood continuum, with normal mood in the middle. Although this concept is accurate to a degree, sometimes a patient may have symptoms of mania and depression during the same time period. In these *mixed episode* cases, the person experiences rapidly alternating moods such as sadness, euphoria, and irritability, all within the same episode of illness.

We will first discuss the **unipolar disorders,** in which the person experiences only depressive episodes, and then we will discuss the bipolar disorders, in which the person experiences both manic and depressive episodes. This distinction is prominent in DSM-IV-TR, and although the unipolar and bipolar forms of mood disorder may not be wholly separate and distinct, there are notable differences in symptoms, causal factors, and treatments. As we will see, it is also customary to differentiate among the mood disorders in terms of (1) *severity*—the number of dysfunctions experienced and the relative degree of impairment evidenced in those areas; and (2) *duration*—whether the disorder is acute, chronic, or intermittent (with periods of relatively normal functioning between the episodes of disorder).

As just noted, diagnosing unipolar or bipolar disorder first requires diagnosing what kind of mood episode the person presents with. The most common form of mood episode that people present with is a **major depressive episode.** As detailed in the DSM-IV-TR table, Criteria for Major Depressive Episode, to receive this diagnosis, the person must be markedly depressed (or show a marked loss of interest in pleasurable activities) for most of every day and for most days for at least 2 weeks. In addition, he or she must show at least three or four other symptoms (for a total of five) that range from cognitive symptoms (such as feelings of worthlessness or guilt, and thoughts of suicide), to behavioral symptoms (such as fatigue or physical agitation), to physical symptoms (such as changes in appetite and sleep patterns).

The other primary kind of mood episode is a **manic episode,** in which the person shows markedly elevated, euphoric, or expansive mood, often interrupted by occasional outbursts of intense irritability or even violence—particularly when others refuse to go along with the manic person's wishes and schemes. These extreme moods must persist for at least a week for this diagnosis to be made. In addition, three or more additional symptoms must occur in the same time period, ranging from behavioral symptoms (such as a notable increase in goal-directed activity, often involving loosening of personal and cultural inhibitions as in multiple sexual, political, or religious activities), to mental symptoms where self-esteem becomes grossly inflated and mental activity may speed up (such as a "flight of ideas" or "racing thoughts"), to physical symptoms (such as a decreased need for sleep, psychomotor agitation). (See the DSM-IV-TR table, Criteria for a Manic Episode on p. 228.)

Research suggests that mild mood disturbances are on the same continuum as the more severe disorders. That is, the differences seem to be chiefly of degree, not of kind, a conclusion supported in several large studies examining the issue (e.g., Kendler & Gardner, 1998; Ruscio & Ruscio, 2000). However, there is also considerable heterogeneity in the ways in which the mood disorders manifest themselves. Thus there are multiple different subtypes of both unipolar and bipolar disorders, and somewhat different causal pathways and treatments are important for different subtypes.

It is also important to remember that suicide is a distressingly frequent outcome (and always a potential outcome) of significant depressions, both unipolar and bipolar. In fact, as discussed in the latter part of this chapter, depressive episodes are clearly the most common of the predisposing causes leading to suicide.

DSM-IV-TR

Criteria for Major Depressive Episode

A. Five (or more) of the following symptoms have been present during the same 2-week period and represent a change from previous functioning; at least one of the symptoms is either 1) depressed mood or 2) loss of interest or pleasure.

   (1) Depressed most of the day, nearly every day, as indicated by either subjective reports or observation made by others.

   (2) Markedly diminished interest or pleasure in all, or almost all, activities most of the day, nearly every day.

   (3) Significant weight loss (when not dieting) or weight gain.

   (4) Insomnia or hypersomnia nearly every day.

   (5) Psychomotor agitation or retardation nearly every day.

   (6) Fatigue or loss of energy nearly every day.

   (7) Feelings of worthlessness or excessive or inappropriate guilt nearly every day.

   (8) Diminished ability to think or concentrate, or indecisiveness, nearly every day.

   (9) Recurrent thoughts of death or suicide, or recurrent suicidal ideation without a plan, or a suicide attempt or plan.

B. The symptoms do not meet criteria for a Mixed Episode.

C. The symptoms cause clinically significant distress or impairment.

The Prevalence of Mood Disorders

Major mood disorders occur with alarming frequency—at least 15 to 20 times more frequently than schizophrenia, for example, and at almost the same rate as all the anxiety disorders taken together. Of the two types of serious mood disorders, *unipolar major depression* is much more common, and its occurrence has apparently increased in recent decades (Kaelber, Moul, & Farmer, 1995; Kessler, Berglund, et al., 2003). The most recent epidemiological results from the National Comorbidity Survey-Replication study found lifetime prevalence rates of unipolar major depression at nearly 17 percent (12-month prevalence rates were nearly 7 percent) (Kessler, Chiu, et al., 2005). Moreover, rates for unipolar depression are always much higher for women than for men (usually about 2:1), similar to the sex differences for most anxiety disorders (see Chapter 6). The issue of sex differences in unipolar depression will be discussed

DSM-IV-TR

Criteria for a Manic Episode

A. A distinct period of abnormally and persistently elevated, expansive, or irritable mood, lasting at least 1 week.

B. During the period of mood disturbance, three or more of the following symptoms have persisted and have been present to a significant degree.

(1) Inflated self-esteem or grandiosity.

(2) Decreased need for sleep (e.g., feels rested after only 3 hours of sleep).

(3) More talkative than usual or pressure to keep talking.

(4) Flight of ideas or subjective experience that thoughts are racing.

(5) Distractibility.

(6) Increase in goal-directed activity (either socially, at work, or sexually), or psychomotor agitation.

(7) Excessive involvement in pleasurable activities that have a high potential for painful consequences (e.g., unrestrained buying sprees, sexual indiscretions, or foolish business investments).

C. The symptoms do not meet criteria for a Mixed Episode.

D. The mood disturbance is sufficiently severe to cause marked impairment in occupational functioning or in usual social activities, or to necessitate hospitalization to prevent harm to self or others, or there are psychotic features.

in detail later in the chapter (see Developments in Research 7.1 on p. 248). The other type of mood disorder, *bipolar disorder* (in which both manic and depressive episodes occur), is much less common. DSM-IV-TR estimates that the lifetime risk of developing this disorder ranges from 0.4 to 1.6 percent, and there is no discernible difference in the prevalence rates between the sexes.

In Review

- What is the major difference between unipolar disorders and bipolar disorders, and how prevalent are the two types of mood disorders?
- How do the prevalence rates of unipolar and bipolar disorders differ between the sexes?

Unipolar Mood Disorders

Sadness, discouragement, pessimism, and hopelessness about matters improving are familiar feelings to most people. Depression is unpleasant when we are experiencing it, but it usually does not last long, dissipating on its own after a period of days or weeks or after it has reached a certain intensity level. Indeed, mild and brief depression may actually be "normal" and adaptive in the long run because much of the "work" of depression seems to involve facing images, thoughts, and feelings that one would normally avoid, and, at the same time, it is usually self-limiting. By slowing us down, mild depression sometimes saves us from wasting a lot of energy in the futile pursuit of unobtainable goals (Keller & Nesse, 2005; Nesse, 2000). Usually, normal depressions would be expected to occur in people undergoing painful but common life events such as significant personal, interpersonal, or economic losses.

Depressions That Are Not Mood Disorders

Normal depressions are nearly always the result of recent stress. We will consider two fairly common causes of depressive symptoms that are generally not considered mood disorders except when they are unusually severe and/or prolonged.

LOSS AND THE GRIEVING PROCESS We usually think of grief as the psychological process one goes through following the death of a loved one—a process that appears to be more difficult for men than for women (Bonanno & Kaltman, 1999). Grief often has certain characteristic qualities. Indeed, Bowlby's (1980) classic observations revealed that there are usually four phases of *normal response* to the loss of a spouse or close family member:

1. Numbing and disbelief that may last from a few hours to a week and may be interrupted by outbursts of intense distress, panic, or anger.
2. Yearning and searching for the dead person (more similar to anxiety than depression), which may last for weeks or months. Typical symptoms include restlessness, insomnia, and preoccupation (or anger) with the dead person.
3. Disorganization and despair that set in after yearning and searching diminish. This is when the person finally accepts the loss as permanent and tries to establish a new identity (e.g., as a widow or widower). Criteria for major depressive disorder may be met during this phase.

4. Some level of reorganization when people gradually begin to rebuild their lives, sadness abates, and zest for life returns.

This has generally been considered the normal pattern. Some people, however, become stuck somewhere in the middle of the normal response sequence. The normal nature of exhibiting a certain number of grief symptoms has led DSM-IV-TR to suggest that major depressive disorders usually not be diagnosed for the first 2 months following the loss, even if all the symptom criteria are met.

Ignoring for the moment the people who are eventually diagnosed as having major depressive disorder, it is easy to see uncomplicated grief as having an adaptive function (Bowlby, 1980). Traditionally, failing to exhibit grief under conditions in which it seems warranted has been a cause of concern because it was thought to suggest that the person was not fully processing the loss, at least at a psychological level. However, recent studies of bereaved individuals following the loss of a spouse, life partner, or parent have found that about 50 percent exhibit genuine resilience in the face of loss, with minimal, very short-lived symptoms of depression or bereavement. And contrary to what was previously thought, these resilient individuals are not emotionally maladjusted or unattached to their spouses (e.g., Bonanno, Moskowitz, Papa, & Folkman, 2005; Bonanno, Wortman, & Nesse, 2004).

We usually think of grief as the psychological process a person goes through following the death of a loved one. We see here a young woman grieving at her father's grave. Grief may accompany other types of loss as well, including separation or divorce, or loss of a pet.

POSTPARTUM "BLUES" Even though the birth of a child would usually seem to be a happy event, postpartum depression sometimes occurs in new mothers (and occasionally fathers) following the birth of a child. In the past it was believed that postpartum major depression was relatively common, but more recent evidence suggests that only "postpartum blues" are very common. The symptoms of postpartum blues typically include emotional lability, crying easily, and irritability, often liberally intermixed with happy feelings (Miller, 2002; O'Hara et al., 1990, 1991). Such symptoms occur in as many as 50 to 70 percent of women within 10 days of the birth of their child and usually subside on their own (APA, DSM-IV-TR, 2000; Miller, 2002).

It appears that major depression occurs no more frequently in the postpartum period than would be expected in women of the same age and socioeconomic status who had not given birth (Hobfoll et al., 1995; O'Hara et al., 1990, 1991). Especially rare are instances where the major depression is accompanied by psychotic features. Thus the once firmly held notion that women are at especially high risk for major depression in the postpartum period has not been upheld. There is, however, a greater likelihood of developing major depression if the postpartum blues are severe (Henshaw, Foreman, & Cox, 2004).

Hormonal readjustments may play a role in postpartum blues and depression, although the evidence on this issue is mixed (Miller, 2002; O'Hara et al., 1991). It is obvious that a psychological component is present as well. Postpartum blues or depression may be especially likely to occur if the new mother has a lack of social support and/or has difficulty adjusting to her new identity and responsibilities and/or if the woman has a personal or family history of depression that leads to heightened sensitivity to

This new mother is experiencing post-partum blues; her mood is very labile and she cries easily.

the stress of childbirth (Collins et al., 2004; Miller, 2002; O'Hara & Gorman, 2004).

Dysthymic Disorder

The point at which mood disturbance becomes a diagnosable mood disorder is a matter of clinical judgment and usually concerns the degree of impairment in functioning that the individual experiences. Dysthymic disorder is considered to be of mild to moderate intensity, but its primary hallmark is its chronicity. To qualify for a diagnosis of **dysthymic disorder** (or dysthymia), a person must have a persistently depressed mood most of the day, for more days than not, for at least 2 years (1 year for children and adolescents). In addition, individuals with dysthymic disorder must have at least two of six additional symptoms when depressed (see the DSM-IV-TR table, Criteria for Dysthymic Disorder). Periods of normal mood may occur briefly, but they usually last for only a few days to a few weeks (and for a maximum of 2 months). These intermittently normal moods are one of the most important characteristics distinguishing dysthymic disorder from major depressive disorder.

Dysthymia is also quite common, with a lifetime prevalence estimated between 2.5 and 6 percent (Kessler et al., 1994; Kessler, Berglund, et al., 2005). The average duration of dysthymia is 5 years, but it can persist for 20 years or more (Keller et al., 1997). Chronic stress has been shown to increase the severity of symptoms over a 7.5-year follow-up period (Dougherty, Klein, & Davila, 2004). Even among those who seem to recover from dysthymia within 5 years, nearly half may relapse within an average of about 2 years (Klein, Schwartz, Rose, & Leader, 2000). Dysthymia often begins during the teenage years, and over 50 percent have an onset before age 21.

The following case is typical of this disorder.

DSM-IV-TR

Criteria for Dysthymic Disorder

A. Depressed mood for most of the day, for more days than not, for at least 2 years (1 year for children or adolescents).

B. Presence, while depressed, of two (or more) of the following:

(1) Poor appetite or overeating.

(2) Insomnia or hypersomnia.

(3) Low energy or fatigue.

(4) Low self-esteem.

(5) Poor concentration or difficulty making decisions.

(6) Feelings of hopelessness.

C. During the 2-year period of the disturbance, the person has never been without symptoms in Criteria A or B for 2 months at a time.

D. No Major Depressive Disorder has been present during the first 2 years of the disturbance.

E. There has never been a Manic Episode, a Mixed Episode, or a Hypomanic Episode, and criteria have never been met for Cyclothymic Disorder.

F. The symptoms cause clinically significant distress or impairment in functioning.

case STUDY — A Dysthymic Executive

A 28-year-old junior executive. . . . complained of being "depressed" about everything: her job, her husband, and her prospects for the future. . . . Her complaints were of persistent feelings of depressed mood, inferiority, and pessimism, which she claims to have had since she was 16 or 17 years old. Although she did reasonably well in college, she constantly ruminated about those students who were "genuinely intelligent." She dated during college and graduate school but claimed that she would never go after a guy she thought was "special," always feeling inferior and intimidated. . . .

Just after graduation, she had married the man she was going out with at the time. She thought of him as reasonably desirable, though not "special," and married him primarily because she felt she "needed a husband" for companionship. Shortly after their marriage, the couple started to bicker. She was very critical of his clothes, his job, and his parents; and he, in turn, found her rejecting, controlling, and moody. She began to feel that she had made a mistake in marrying him.

Recently she has also been having difficulties at work. She is assigned the most menial tasks at the firm and is never given an assignment of importance or responsibility. She admits that she frequently does a "slipshod" job of what is given her, never does more than is required, and never demonstrates any assertiveness or initiative. . . . She feels that she will never go very far in her profession because she does not have the right "connections" and neither does her husband, yet she dreams of money, status, and power. Her social life with her husband involves several other couples. The man in these couples is usually a friend of her husband. She is sure that the women find her uninteresting and unimpressive and that the people who seem to like her are probably no better off than she.

Under the burden of her dissatisfaction with her marriage, her job, and her social life, feeling tired and uninterested in "life," she now enters treatment for the third time. (Spitzer et al., 2002, pp. 110–11)

A person with major depressive disorder may experience a loss of energy, too much or too little sleep, decreased appetite and weight loss, an increase or slowdown in mental and physical activity, difficulty concentrating, irrational guilt, and recurrent thoughts of death or suicide.

Major Depressive Disorder

The diagnostic criteria for **major depressive disorder** require that the person exhibit more symptoms than are required for dysthymia and that the symptoms be more persistent (not interwoven with periods of normal mood). To receive a diagnosis of major depressive disorder, a person must be in a *major depressive episode* (initial or *single*, or *recurrent*). An affected person must experience either markedly depressed moods or marked loss of interest in pleasurable activities most of every day, nearly every day, for at least 2 consecutive weeks. In addition to showing one or both of these symptoms, the person must experience at least three or four additional symptoms during the same period (for a total of at least five symptoms), as detailed in the DSM-IV-TR table, Criteria for Major Depressive Episode. These symptoms include cognitive symptoms (such as feelings of worthlessness or guilt, and thoughts of suicide), behavioral symptoms (such as fatigue, or physical agitation), and physical symptoms (such as changes in appetite and sleep patterns).

It should be noted that few if any depressions—including milder ones—occur in the absence of significant anxiety (e.g., Akiskal, 1997; Merikangus et al., 2003; Mineka et al., 1998). Indeed, there is a high degree of overlap between measures of depressive and anxious symptoms in self-reports and in clinician ratings. At the diagnostic level, there are very high levels of comorbidity between mood and anxiety disorders. As discussed later in this chapter (see Developments in Thinking 7.2 on p. 250), the issues surrounding the co-occurrence of depression and anxiety, which have received a great deal of attention in recent years, are very complex.

The following account illustrates a moderately severe case of major depressive disorder.

DSM-IV-TR

Criteria for Major Depressive Disorder, Single Episode

A. Presence of a single (initial) Major Depressive Episode
B. The Major Depressive Episode is not better accounted for by another disorder.
C. There has never been a Manic Episode or a Mixed Episode, or a Hypomanic Episode.

case STUDY Connie

Connie, a 33-year-old homemaker and mother of a 4-year-old son, Robert, is referred . . . to a psychiatric outpatient program because . . . she has been depressed and unable to concentrate ever since she separated from her husband 3 months previously. Connie left her husband, Donald, after a 5-year marriage. Violent arguments between them, during which Connie was beaten by her husband, had occurred for the last 4 years of their marriage, beginning when she became pregnant with Robert. There were daily arguments during which Donald hit her hard enough to leave bruises on her face and arms. . . .

Before her marriage . . . she was close to her parents [and] had many friends whom she also saw regularly. . . . In high school she had been a popular cheerleader and a good student. . . . She had no personal history of depression and there was no family history of . . . mental illness.

During the first year of marriage, Donald became increasingly irritable and critical of Connie. He began to request that Connie stop calling and seeing her friends after work, and refused to allow them or his in-laws to visit their apartment. . . . Despite her misgivings about Donald's behavior toward her, Connie decided to become pregnant. During the seventh month of the pregnancy . . . Donald began complaining [and] began hitting her with his fists. She left him and went to live with her parents for a week. He expressed remorse . . . and . . . Connie returned to her apartment. No further violence occurred until after Robert's birth. At that time, Donald began using cocaine every weekend and often became violent when he was high.

In the 3 months since she left Donald, Connie has become increasingly depressed. Her appetite has been poor and she has lost 10 pounds. She cries a lot and often wakes up at 5:00 A.M. and is unable to get back to

(continued)

sleep. . . . Connie is pale and thin. . . . She speaks slowly, describing her depressed mood and lack of energy. She says that her only pleasure is in being with her son. She is able to take care of him physically, but feels guilty because her preoccupation with her own bad feelings prevents her from being able to play with him. She now has no contacts other than with her parents and her son. She feels worthless and blames herself for her marital problems, saying that if she had been a better wife, maybe Donald would have been able to give up the cocaine. . . . (Adapted from Spitzer et al., 2002, pp. 411–13)

Note that Connie's case nicely illustrates that a person with major depressive disorder shows not only mood symptoms of sadness but also a variety of symptoms that are more severe than in milder forms of depression. Connie shows various cognitive distortions, including feeling worthless and guilty. She complains of a lack of energy and inability to play with her child. Her biological symptoms include loss of appetite and early morning awakening. The loss of contact with friends also occurs commonly with depression, in part because the person is unmotivated to seek contact. Connie's case also nicely illustrates the multiple complex, interacting factors that may be involved in the etiology of depression. Although Connie did not have a personal or a family history of depression, the experiences from 5 years of a very difficult marriage with a violent and abusive husband were sufficient to finally precipitate her major depression.

DEPRESSION THROUGHOUT THE LIFE CYCLE Although the onset of unipolar mood disorder most often occurs during late adolescence up to middle adulthood, such reactions may begin at any time from early childhood to old age. Depression was once thought not to occur in childhood, but more recent research has found major depressions in preadolescent children, and it is estimated that about 2 to 3 percent of school-age children meet the criteria for some form of unipolar disorder, with perhaps another 2 percent exhibiting chronic mild depression (see Garber & Horowitz, 2002). Even infants may experience a form of depression (commonly known as *anaclitic depression* or despair) if they are separated for a prolonged period from their attachment figure (usually their mother; Bowlby, 1973, 1980; Speier et al., 1995).

The incidence of depression rises sharply during adolescence—a period of great turmoil for many people. Indeed, one review estimated that approximately 15 to 20 percent of adolescents experience major depressive disorder at some point during their adolescent years (Lewinsohn & Essau, 2002), and the average age of onset for adolescent depression has been decreasing over the past few decades (Lewinsohn et al., 1993; Speier et al., 1995). It is during this time period that sex differences in rates of depression first emerge (Hankin & Abramson, 2001; Nolen-Hoeksema, 2002; Nolen-Hoeksema & Girgus, 1994). (See Developments in Research 7.1 on p. 248.) The long-term effects of major depressive disorder in adolescence can last at least through young adulthood when such individuals show small but significant psychosocial impairments in many domains, including their occupational life, their interpersonal relationships, and their general quality of life (e.g., Lewinsohn, Rohde, et al., 2003). (See also Chapter 16.)

The occurrence of major depression continues into later life. Although the 1-year prevalence of major depression is significantly lower in people over age 60 than in younger adults (Kessler et al., 2003), major depression and dysthymia in older adults are still considered a major public health problem today (Beekman, Deeg, et al., 2004). Moreover, research suggests that rates of depression among physically ill residents of nursing homes or residential care facilities are substantially higher than among older adults living at home (see Powers et al., 2002). Unfortunately, depression in later life can be difficult to diagnose because many of the symptoms overlap with those of several medical illnesses and dementia (Alexopoulos et al., 2002). Yet it is very important to try and diagnose it reliably because depression in later life has many adverse consequences for a person's health, including doubling the risk of death in people who have had a heart attack or stroke (e.g., Schultz et al., 2002) (see Chapter 10).

SPECIFIERS FOR MAJOR DEPRESSION Some individuals who meet the basic criteria for diagnosis of major depression also have additional patterns of symptoms or features that are important to note when making a diagnosis because they have implications for understanding more about the course of the disorder and/or its most effective treatment. These different patterns of symptoms or features are called **specifiers** in DSM-IV-TR. One such specifier is **major depressive episode with melancholic features.** This designation is applied when, in addition to meeting the criteria for major depression, a patient either has lost interest or pleasure in almost all activities or does not react to usually pleasurable stimuli or desired events. In addition, the patient must experience at least three of the following: (1) early morning awakenings, (2) depression being worse in the morning, (3) marked psychomotor retardation or agitation, (4) significant loss of appetite and weight, (5) inappropriate or excessive guilt, and (6) depressed mood that is qualitatively different from the sadness experienced during a nonmelancholic depression. This severe subtype of depression is associated with a higher genetic loading than other forms of depression (Kendler, 1997).

Psychotic symptoms, characterized by loss of contact with reality and delusions (false beliefs) or hallucinations (false sensory perceptions), may sometimes accompany other symptoms of major depression. In such cases the specifier to the diagnosis that is noted is **severe major depressive episode with psychotic features.** Ordinarily, any delusions or hallucinations present are **mood-congruent**—that is, they seem in some sense "appropriate" to serious depression because the content is negative in tone, such as themes of personal inadequacy, guilt, deserved punishment, death, and disease. For example, the delusional idea that one's internal organs have totally deteriorated—an idea sometimes held by severely depressed people—ties in with the mood of a despondent person. Feelings of worthlessness and guilt are also commonly part of the clinical picture (Ohayon & Shatzberg, 2002). Psychotically depressed individuals are likely to have a poorer long-term prognosis than nonpsychotic depressives (Coryell, 1997), and any recurrent episodes are also likely to be characterized by psychotic symptoms (Fleming et al., 2004). Treatment generally involves an antipsychotic medication as well as an antidepressant. In very rare cases, psychotic depression occurs in the context of postpartum depression (Miller, 2002), where mothers may kill their babies because of the hallucinations or delusions they have.

A third important specifier is used when the individual shows "atypical features." **Major depressive episode with atypical features** includes a pattern of symptoms characterized by mood reactivity; that is, the person's mood brightens in response to potential positive events. In addition, the person must show two or more of the following four symptoms: (1) significant weight gain or increase in appetite, (2) hypersomnia (sleeping too much), (3) leaden paralysis (heavy feelings in arms or legs), and (4) a long-standing pattern of being acutely sensitive to interpersonal rejection. A disproportionate number of individuals who have atypical features are females, who have an earlier-than-average age of onset and who are more likely to show suicidal thoughts (Matza, Revicki, Davidson, & Stewart, 2003). This is also an important specifier because there are indications that individuals with atypical features may preferentially respond to a different class of antidepressants—the monoamine oxidase inhibitors—than do most other depressed individuals. See Table 7.1 for a summary of the major specifiers.

Although not recognized as an official specifier, it is not uncommon that major depression may coexist with dysthymia in some people, a condition given the designation **double depression** (Boland & Keller, 2002; Keller, Hirschfeld, & Hanks, 1997). People with double depression are moderately depressed on a chronic basis (meeting symptom criteria for dysthymia) but undergo increased problems from time to time, during which they also meet criteria for a major depressive episode. Among clinical samples of people with dysthymia, the experience of double depression appears to be common, although it may be much less common in people with dysthymic disorder who never seek treatment (Akiskal, 1997). For example, one clinical sample of nearly 100 individuals with early onset dysthymia (onset before age 21) were followed for 5 years, during which time 77 percent experienced at least one major depressive episode (see also Keller et al., 1997; Klein et al., 2000). Although nearly all individuals with double depression appear to recover from their major depressive episodes (at least for a while), recurrence is common (Boland & Keller, 2002; Klein et al., 2000).

DEPRESSION AS A RECURRENT DISORDER When a diagnosis of major depressive disorder is made, it is usually also specified whether this is a first and therefore *single*

TABLE 7.1 **Specifiers of Major Depressive Episodes**

Specifier	Characteristic Symptoms
With Melancholic Features	Three of the following: Early morning awakening, depression worse in the morning, marked psychomotor agitation or retardation, loss of appetite or weight, excessive guilt, qualitatively different depressed mood.
With Psychotic Features	Delusions or hallucinations (usually mood-congruent); feelings of guilt and worthlessness common.
With Atypical Features	Mood reactivity—brightens to positive events; two of the four following symptoms: weight gain or increase in appetite, hypersomnia, leaden paralysis, being acutely sensitive to interpersonal rejection.
With Seasonal Pattern	At least two or more episodes in past 2 years that have occurred at the same time (usually fall or winter), and full remission at the same time (usually spring). No other nonseasonal episodes in same 2-year period.

(initial) episode or a *recurrent* episode (preceded by one or more previous episodes). This reflects the fact that depressive episodes are usually time-limited; according to DSM-IV-TR, the average duration of an untreated episode is about 6 months. In a large untreated sample of depressed women, certain predictors pointed to a longer time to spontaneous remission of symptoms: having financial difficulties, severe stressful life events, and high genetic risk (Kendler, Walters, & Kessler, 1997). In some cases major depression does not remit for over 2 years, in which case **chronic major depressive disorder** is diagnosed.

Although most depressive episodes remit (which is not said to occur until symptoms have remitted for at least 2 months), depressive episodes usually recur at some future point. In recent years, **recurrence** has been distinguished from **relapse,** where the latter term refers to the return of symptoms within a fairly short period of time and probably reflects the fact that the underlying episode of depression has not yet run its course (Boland & Keller, 2002; Frank et al., 1991). Relapse may commonly occur, for example, when pharmacotherapy is terminated prematurely after symptoms have remitted but before the underlying episode is really over (Hollon et al., 2002a, 2002b; 2005).

The proportion of patients who will exhibit a recurrence of major depression is very high (about 80 percent, according to Judd, 1997), although the time period before a recurrence occurs is highly variable. In one very large national study of over 400 patients across 5 sites followed for more than a decade, 25 to 40 percent had a recurrence within 2 years, 60 percent within 5 years, 75 percent within 10 years, and 87 percent within 15 years (Boland & Keller, 2002; Keller & Boland, 1998). There is also evidence that the probability of recurrence increases with the number of prior episodes.

The traditional view was that between episodes, a person suffering from a recurrent major mood disorder is essentially normal. However, as more research data on the course of depression became available (e.g., Coryell & Winokur, 1992; Judd et al., 1998), it became clear this is frequently not the case. For example, in a large 5-site study with over 400 patients, Judd et al. (1998) found that even patients experiencing their first episode at the time the study began showed no symptoms at all during only 54 percent of weeks during a 12-year follow-up period, relative to only 37 percent showing no symptoms among those experiencing a second or later episode at the start of the study. Moreover, people with some residual symptoms, and/or with significant psychosocial impairment, following an episode are even more likely to have recurrences than those whose symptoms remit completely (Judd, Paulus, Zeller, et al., 1999; Solomon et al., 2004).

People who live in higher latitudes (northern climates for those in the northern hemisphere) are more likely to exhibit seasonal affective disorder in which depression occurs primarily in the fall and winter months and tends to remit in the spring or summer months.

SEASONAL AFFECTIVE DISORDER Some people who experience recurrent depressive episodes show a seasonal pattern commonly known as **seasonal affective disorder.** To meet DSM-IV-TR criteria for *recurrent major depression with a seasonal pattern,* the person must have had at least two episodes of depression in the past 2 years occurring at the same time of the year (most commonly, fall or winter), and full remission must also have occurred at the same time of the year (most commonly, the spring). In addition, the person cannot have had other, nonseasonal depressive episodes in the same 2-year period, and most of the person's lifetime depressive episodes must have been of the seasonal variety. Prevalence rates suggest that winter seasonal affective disorder is more common in people living at higher latitudes (northern climates) and in younger people.

In Review

- What are the major features that differentiate dysthymic disorder and major depressive disorder?
- What are three common specifiers of major depressive disorder?
- Distinguish between "recurrence" and "relapse."

Causal Factors in Unipolar Mood Disorders

In considering the development of unipolar mood disorders, researchers have focused on the possible roles of biological, psychosocial, and sociocultural factors. Although each set of factors has usually been studied separately, ultimately the goal should be to understand how these different kinds of causal factors are interrelated, in order to develop a biopsychosocial model.

Biological Causal Factors

It has long been known that a variety of diseases and drugs can affect mood, leading sometimes to depression and sometimes to elation or even hypomania. Indeed, this idea goes back to Hippocrates, who hypothesized that depression was caused by an excess of "black bile" in the system (c. 400 B.C.). As we will discuss, in the past half-century investigators attempting to establish a biological basis for unipolar disorders have considered a wide range of factors.

GENETIC INFLUENCES *Family studies* have shown that the prevalence of mood disorders is approximately three times higher among blood relatives of persons with clinically diagnosed unipolar depression than in the population at large (e.g., Sullivan, Neale, & Kendler, 2000; Wallace, Schneider, & McGuffin, 2002). More importantly, however, *twin studies,* which can provide much more conclusive evidence of genetic influences on a disorder, also suggest a moderate genetic contribution to unipolar depression. Sullivan et al. (2000) did a quantitative review of numerous twin studies (the total number of twins studied was over 21,000) and found that monozygotic co-twins of a twin with unipolar major depression are about twice as likely to develop major depression as are dizygotic co-twins. Averaging across the results of these studies, this review suggested that about 31 to 42 percent of the variance in liability to major depression was due to genetic influences. The estimate was even higher for more severe, recurrent depressions. Notably, however, the same review concluded that even more variance in the liability to major depression is due to nonshared environmental influences (i.e., experiences that family members do not share) than to genetic factors.

research close-up

adoption method

A research method that suggests if a predisposition to develop a given disorder is heritable, it should show up more often among biological relatives of the affected adoptees than among biological relatives of control adoptees.

A number of years ago, the ***adoption method*** of genetic research (see Chapter 3) was applied to the study of mood disorders. Of the three adoption studies on mood disorders published thus far, the most adequate one (Wender et al., 1986) found that unipolar depression occurred about seven times more often in the biological relatives of the severely depressed adoptees than in the biological relatives of control adoptees (Wallace et al., 2002; Wender et al., 1986).

Taken together, the results from family, twin, and adoption studies make a strong case for a moderate genetic contribution to the causal patterns of unipolar major depression, although not as large a genetic contribution as for bipolar disorder (Farmer, Eley, & McGuffin, 2005; Wallace et al., 2002). However, the evidence for a genetic contribution is much less consistent for milder but chronic forms of unipolar depression such as dysthymia, with some studies finding no evidence of genetic contributions (Roth & Mountjoy, 1997; Wallace et al., 2002). Finally, attempts to identify specific genes that may be responsible for these genetic influences have not yet been successful, although there are some promising leads (Plomin et al., 2001; Wallace et al., 2002).

One promising candidate for a specific gene that might be implicated is the *serotonin-transporter gene*—a gene involved in the transmission and reuptake of serotonin, which is one of the key neurotransmitters involved in depression. There are two different kinds of versions or alleles involved—the short allele (*s*) and the long allele (*l*), and people have two short alleles (*ss*), two long alleles (*ll*), or one of each (*sl*). Prior work with animals had suggested that having *ss* alleles might predispose to depression relative to having *ll* alleles, but human work on this issue had provided mixed results. In 2003, Caspi, Sugden, Moffitt, and colleagues published a landmark study in which they tested for the possibility of a *gene-environment interaction* involving this serotonin-transporter gene (see Chapter 3). They used 847 people in New Zealand who had been followed from birth until 26 years of age, at which time the researchers assessed diagnoses of major depression in the past year, and the occurrence of stressful life events in the previous 5 years. Their results were very striking: Individuals who possessed the *ss* alleles were twice as likely to develop depression following four or more stressful life events in the past 5 years as those who possessed the *ll* alleles and had four or more stressful events (those with the *sl* alleles were intermediate). See Figure 7.1. Moreover, they also found that those who had the *ss* alleles and had had severe maltreatment as children were also twice as likely to develop depression as those with the *ll* alleles who had had severe maltreatment, and as those with the *ss* alleles who had not been maltreated as children. These exciting findings have since led to several other studies that have found similar (although not identical) results

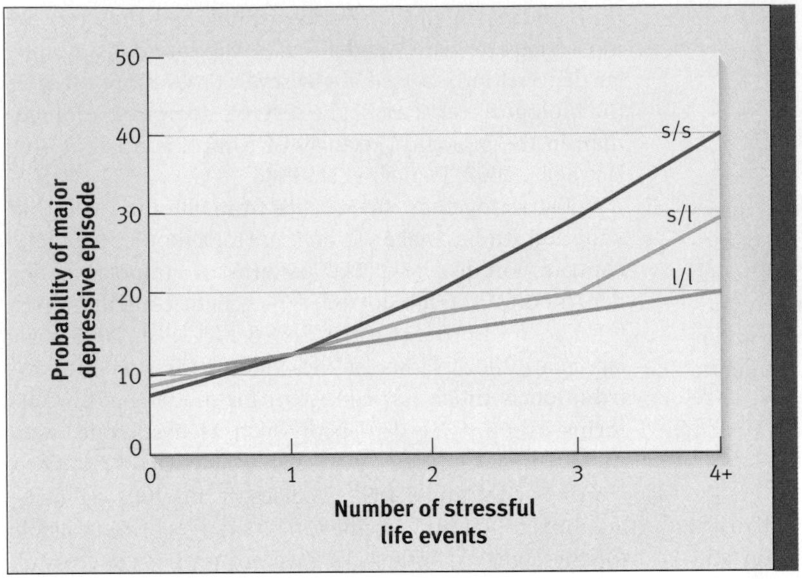

FIGURE 7.1

Number of Stressful Life Events vs. Probability of Major Depressive Episode

Results demonstrating the association between number of stressful life events (between ages 21 and 26 years) and probability of a major depression episode at age 26 as a function of 5-HTT genotype. Life events predicted a diagnosis of major depression among carriers of the s allele (ss or sl), but not among carriers of two l alleles (ll).

Source: *Caspi, A. Sugden, K., Moffitt, T. E., Taylor, A., Craig, I. W., et al. (2003) Influence of life stress on depression: Moderation by a polymorphism in the 5-HTT gene.* Science, 301, *386–389. Reprinted with permission from* Science, *18 July 2003, Vol. 301. Copyright © 2003 AAAS.*

(e.g., Kendler, Kuhn, et al., 2005). Such results suggest that the search for candidate genes that are likely to be involved in the etiology of major depression is likely to be much more fruitful if researchers also test for gene-environment interactions (see Moffitt, Caspi, et al., 2005).

NEUROCHEMICAL FACTORS Ever since the 1960s, the view that depression may arise from disruptions in the delicate balance of neurotransmitter substances that regulate and mediate the activity of the brain's nerve cells has received a great deal of attention. A large body of evidence suggested that various biological therapies (discussed later in this chapter) that are often used to treat severe mood disorders—such as electroconvulsive therapy and antidepressant medications—affect the concentrations or the activity of neurotransmitters at the synapse. Such early findings encouraged the development of neurochemical theories of the etiology of major depression.

Early attention in the 1960s and 1970s focused primarily on three neurotransmitter substances of the monoamine class—norepinephrine, dopamine, and serotonin—because researchers observed that antidepressant medications seemed to have the effect of increasing their availability at synaptic junctions. This observation led to the influential *monoamine hypothesis*—that depression was at least sometimes due to an absolute or relative depletion of one or all of these neurotransmitters at important receptor sites in the brain (Schildkraut, 1965). This depletion could come about through impaired synthesis of these neurotransmitters in the presynaptic neuron, through increased degradation of the neurotransmitters once they had been released into the synapse, or through altered functioning of postsynaptic receptors (Thase & Howland, 1995; Thase, Jindal, & Howland, 2002). Collectively, these neurotransmitters are now known to be involved in the regulation of behavioral activity, emotional expression, and vegetative functions—all of which are disturbed in mood disorders (Garlow & Nemeroff, 2003; Southwick, Vythilingam, & Charney, 2005).

However, by the 1980s it was clear that no such straightforward mechanisms could possibly be responsible for causing depression (e.g., Southwick et al., 2005; Thase et al., 2002). For example, some studies have found exactly the opposite of what is predicted by the monoamine hypothesis—that is, net increases in norepinephrine activity in depressed patients—especially in those with severe or melancholic depression (see Thase et al., 2002). Moreover, only a minority of depressed patients have lowered serotonin activity, and these tend to be patients with high levels of suicidal ideation and behavior. Finally, even though the immediate short-term effects of antidepressant drugs are to increase the availability of norepinephrine and serotonin, the long-term clinical effects of these drugs do not emerge until 2 to 4 weeks later, when neurotransmitter levels may have normalized.

Unfortunately, the early monoamine theory has not been replaced by a compelling alternative. Altered neurotransmitter activity in several systems is clearly associated with major depression, but research for the past 20 to 25 years has focused on complex interactions of neurotransmitters and how they affect cellular functioning. A number of integrative theories have been proposed that include a role for neurotransmitters, not alone but rather as they interact with other disturbed hormonal and neurophysiological patterns and biological rhythms (e.g., Garlow & Nemeroff, 2003). An interesting new focus of some of this research is on understanding how interactions among these different neurobiological systems can promote resilience in the face of major stress (a very common precipitant for depression), which in turn may help explain why only a subset of people undergoing major stressors develop depression (Southwick et al., 2005).

ABNORMALITIES OF HORMONAL REGULATORY SYSTEMS There has also been a good deal of research on possible hormonal causes or correlates of some forms of mood disorder (Checkley, 1992; Southwick et al., 2005; Thase et al., 2002). The majority of attention has been focused on the *hypothalamic-pituitary-adrenal (HPA) axis,* and in particular on the hormone *cortisol,* which is excreted by the outermost portion of the adrenal glands and is regulated through a complex feedback loop (see Figure 3.1 in Chapter 3; e.g., Howland & Thase, 1999). As we noted in Chapters 3, 5, and 6, the human stress response is associated with elevated activity of the HPA axis, which is partly controlled by norepinephrine and serotonin. The perception of stress or threat can lead to norepinephrine activity in the hypothalamus, causing the release of corticotrophin-releasing hormone (CRF) from the hypothalamus, which in turn triggers release of adrenocorticotrophic hormone (ACTH) from the pituitary. The ACTH then typically travels through the blood to the adrenal cortex of the adrenal glands, where cortisol is released. Blood plasma levels of cortisol are known to be elevated in some 20 to 40 percent of depressed outpatients and in about 60 to 80 percent of severely depressed hospitalized patients (Thase et al., 2002). Sustained elevations in cortisol can result from increased CRH activation (for example, during sustained stress or threat), increased secretion of ACTH, or the failure of feedback mechanisms. See Figure 7.2.

One line of evidence that implicates the failure of feedback mechanisms in some depressed patients comes from robust findings that in about 45 percent of seriously depressed patients, a potent suppressor of plasma cortisol in normal individuals, *dexamethasone,* either fails entirely to suppress cortisol or fails to sustain its suppression (Thase et al., 2002). This means that the HPA axis is not operating properly in these "dexamethasone nonsuppressors." It was initially thought that DST nonsuppressor patients constituted a distinct subgroup of people with severe or melancholic depression (Holsboer, 1992). However, subsequent research showed that several other groups of psychiatric patients, such as those with panic disorder, also exhibit high rates of nonsuppression. This suggests that nonsuppression may merely be a nonspecific indicator of generalized mental distress.

Recent findings have revealed that depressed patients with elevated cortisol also tend to show memory impairments and problems with abstract thinking and complex problem solving (Belanoff et al., 2001). Some of these cognitive problems may be related to other findings showing that prolonged elevations in cortisol such as seen in moderate to severe depression result in cell death in the

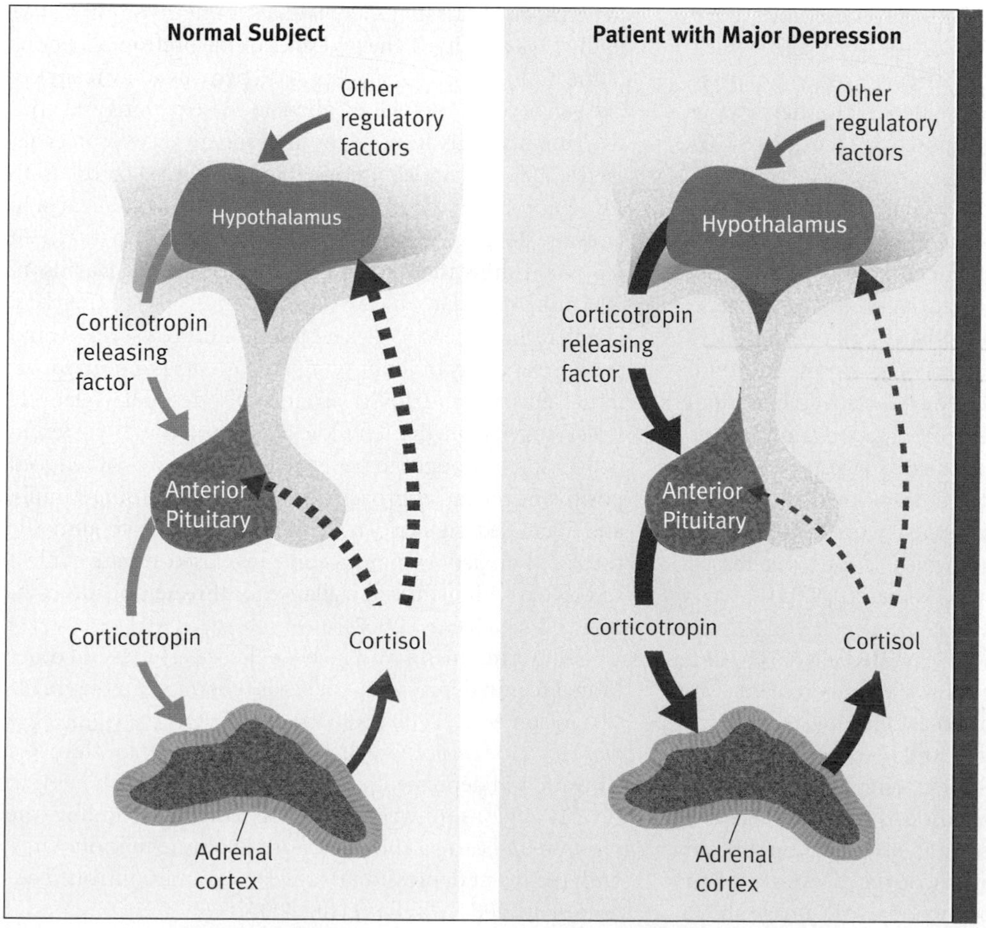

FIGURE 7.2

Response to Stress in a Normal Subject and a Patient with Major Depressive Disorder

In normal subjects and in patients with major depression, periods of stress are typically associated with increased levels of both cortisol and corticotropin-releasing factor. Corticotropin-releasing factor stimulates the production of corticotropin, which in turn stimulates the production of cortisol. Cortisol inhibits the release of corticotropin from the pituitary and the release of corticotropin releasing factor from the hypothalamus. In patients with major depression the sensitivity of this negative-feedback system is often decreased, leading to elevated levels of cortisol.

Source: *From "Post-Traumatic Stress Disorder" by Rachel Yehuda, Ph.D.* New England Journal of Medicine, *Vol. 346, No. 2, January 10, 2002, p. 111. Reprinted with permission from Massachusetts Medical Society. Copyright © 2002 Massachusetts Medical Society. All rights reserved.*

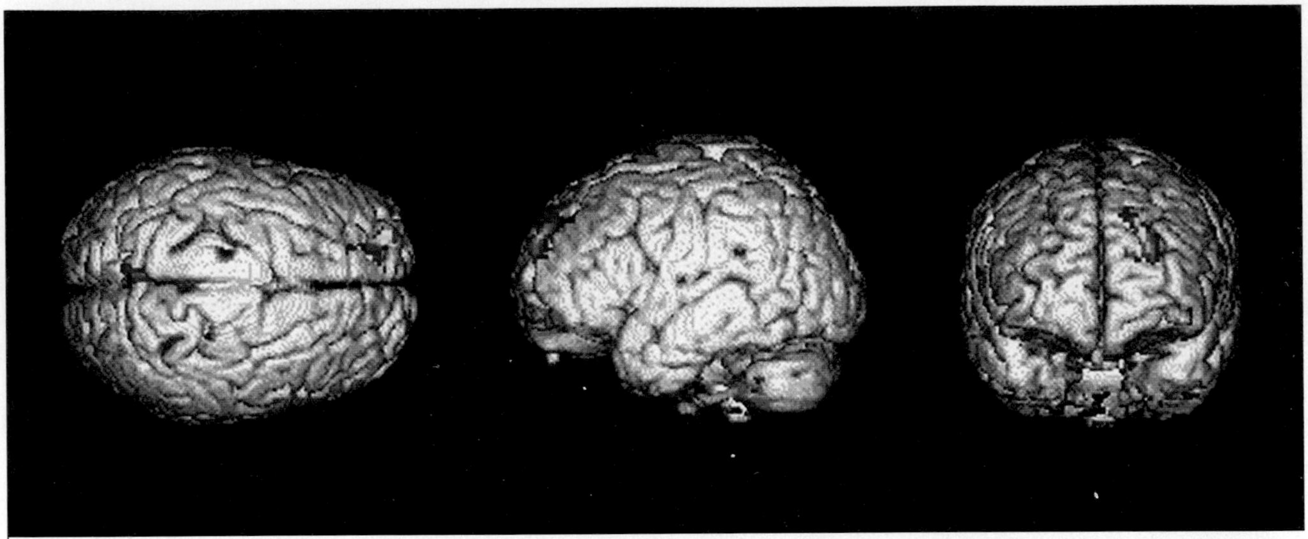

Functional MRI changes (see Chapter 4) in depressed patients in response to affective stimuli from pre- to post-treatment. These red and yellow images illustrate (in three different views) the increase in left prefrontal activation that occurred in a group of depressed patients following treatment compared to their activation pattern during an acute depressive episode. Thus, the red and yellow images depict the increase in cerebral blood in the left prefrontal area in response to affective stimuli from before to after successful antidepressant treatment. The second scan was obtained 8 weeks following the first scan. Patients were treated with an antidepressant medication during those 8 weeks. (This image courtesy of Richard Davidson.)

hippocampus—a part of the limbic system heavily involved in memory functioning (e.g., Southwick et al., 2005). Other interesting research has shown that stress in infancy and early childhood can promote long-term changes increasing the reactivity of the HPA axis, which may in turn help explain why children reared in environments with early adversity are at higher risk for developing depression later in life when exposed to acute stressors (e.g., Southwick et al., 2005).

The other endocrine system that has relevance to depression is the *hypothalamic-pituitary-thyroid axis.* Disturbances to this axis are also linked to mood disorders (Garlow & Nemeroff, 2003; Marangell et al., 1997; Thase et al., 2002). For example, people with low thyroid levels (*hypothyroidism*) often become depressed. In addition, about 20 to 30 percent of depressed patients who have normal thyroid levels nevertheless show dysregulation of this axis. Moreover, preliminary findings suggest that some patients who have not responded to traditional antidepressant treatments may show improvement when administered thyrotropin-releasing hormone, which leads to increased thyroid hormone levels (Garlow & Nemeroff, 2003).

NEUROPHYSIOLOGICAL AND NEUROANATOMICAL INFLUENCES Exciting neurophysiological research in recent years has followed up on earlier neurological findings that damage (for example, from a stroke) to the left, but not the right, anterior or prefrontal cortex often leads to depression (e.g., Davidson, 2000; Robinson & Downhill, 1995). This led to the idea that depression in people without brain damage may nonetheless be linked to lowered levels of brain activity in this same region (see functional MRI image above and Figure 7.3). A number of studies have supported this idea. When one measures the electroencephalographic (EEG) activity of both cerebral hemispheres in depressed patients, one finds that there is an asymmetry or imbalance in the EEG activity of the two sides of the prefrontal regions of the brain. In particular, depressed persons show relatively low activity in the left hemisphere in these regions and relatively high activity in the right hemisphere (Davidson et al., 2002a, 2002b). Similar findings have been reported using PET neuroimaging techniques (see Davidson et al., 2002b; Drevets, 2000; Phillips et al., 2003). Notably, patients in remission show the same pattern (Henriques & Davidson, 1990), as do children at risk for depression (Tomarken, Siemien, & Garber, 1994). These latter findings seem to hold promise as a way of identifying persons at risk, both for an initial episode and for recurrent episodes. The relatively lower activity on the left side of the prefrontal cortex in depression is thought to be related to symptoms of reduced positive affect and approach behaviors to rewarding stimuli, and increased right-sided activity is thought to underlie increased anxiety symptoms and increased negative affect associated with increased vigilance for threatening information (Pizzagalli et al., 2002).

Abnormalities have also been detected in several other brain areas in depressed patients as illustrated in Figure 7.3 (Davidson et al., 2002a, 2002b). One such area is *the anterior cingulate cortex,* which shows abnormally low levels of activation in depressed patients. Other research shows that several regions of the prefrontal cortex, including the *orbitofrontal cortex,* show decreased volume in individuals with recurrent depression relative to normal controls (Lacerda et al., 2004; Phillips et al., 2003).

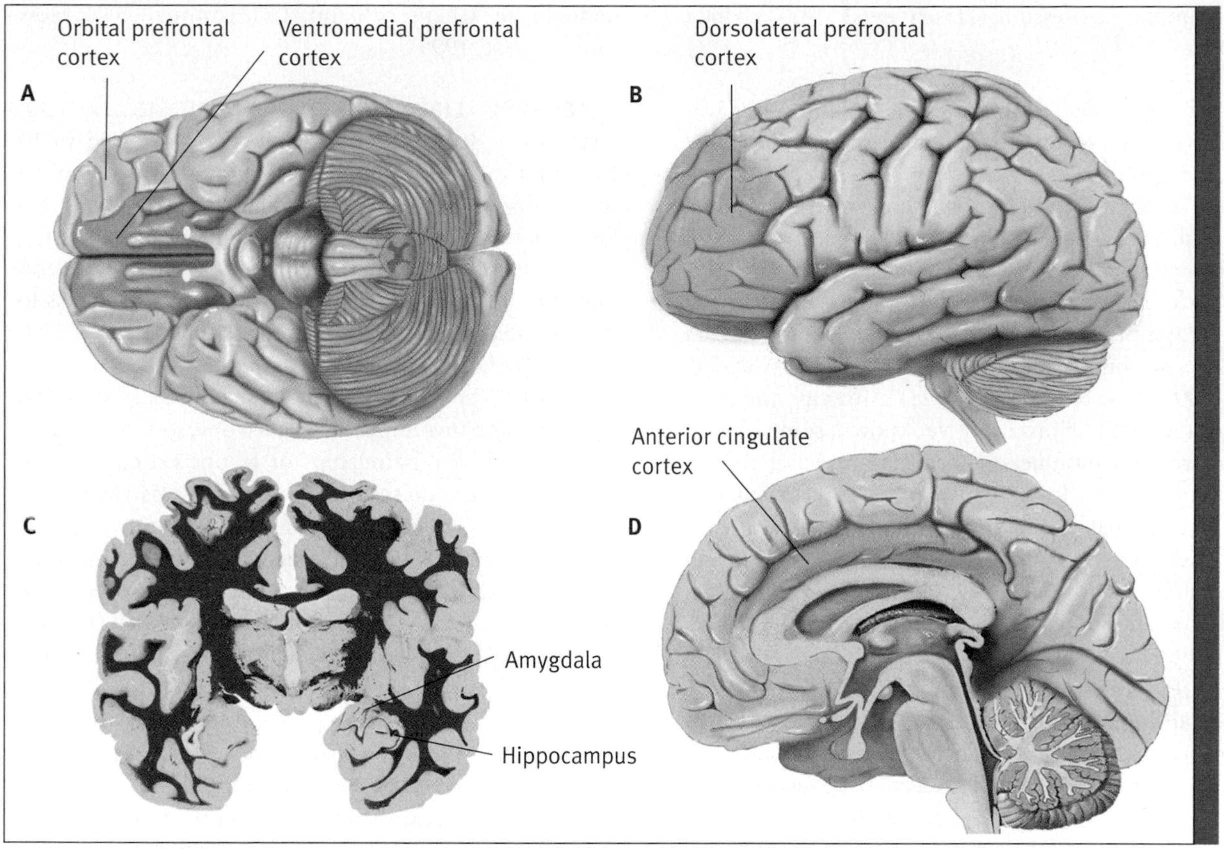

FIGURE 7.3

The key brain regions involved in affect and mood disorders are (A) orbital prefrontal cortex and ventromedial prefrontal cortex, (B) dorsolateral prefrontal cortex, (C) hippocampus and amygdala, and (D) anterior cingulate cortex.

Source: *From R. J. Davidson, Diego Pizzagalli, and Jack Nitschke (2002). "The Representation and Regulation of Emotion in Depression." In I. H. Gotlib and C. L. Hammen (Eds.),* Handbook of Depression *(pp. 219–244). New York: Guilford.*

Another area involved is the *hippocampus;* as already noted, prolonged depression often leads to decreased hippocampal volume (similar to what is seen in chronic PTSD), which could be due to cell atrophy or cell death (e.g., Southwick et al., 2005). Finally, the *amygdala* tends to show increased activation in individuals with depression, which may be related to their biased attention to negative emotional information (Phillips et al., 2003).

SLEEP AND OTHER BIOLOGICAL RHYTHMS Although findings of sleep disturbances in depressed patients have existed as long as depression has been studied, only recently have some of these findings been linked to more general disturbances in biological rhythms.

Sleep Sleep is characterized by five stages that occur in a relatively invariant sequence throughout the night (Stages 1 to 4 of non-REM sleep and REM sleep). REM sleep (rapid eye movement sleep) is characterized by rapid eye movements and dreaming, as well as other bodily changes; the first REM period does not usually begin until near the end of the first sleep cycle, about 75 to 80 minutes into sleep. Depressed patients, especially those with melancholic features, show a variety of sleep problems, ranging from early morning awakening, periodic awakening during the night (poor sleep maintenance), and, for some, difficulty falling asleep. Such changes occur in about 80 percent of hospitalized depressed patients and in about 50 percent of depressed outpatients.

Moreover, research using EEG recordings has found that many depressed patients enter the first period of REM sleep after only 60 minutes or less of sleep (i.e., 15 to 20 minutes sooner than nondepressed patients do), and also show greater amounts of REM sleep early in the night than are seen in nondepressed persons. The intensity and frequency of their rapid eye movements are also greater than in nondepressed patients (Thase et al., 2002). Because this is the period of the night when most deep sleep (Stages 3 and 4) usually occurs, the depressed person also gets a lower-than-normal amount of deep sleep. Both the reduced latency to REM sleep and the decreased amount of deep sleep often precede the onset of depression and persist following recovery, which suggests that they may be vulnerability markers for certain forms of major depression (Hasler et al., 2004; Thase et al., 2002).

Circadian Rhythms Humans have many circadian (24-hour, or daily) cycles other than sleep, including body temperature, propensity to REM sleep, and secretion of cortisol, thyroid-stimulating hormone, and growth hormone (Thase et al., 2002). These circadian rhythms are controlled by two related central "oscillators," which act as internal biological clocks. Research has found some abnormalities in all of these rhythms in depressed patients, though not all patients show abnormalities in all rhythms (Howland & Thase, 1999; Thase & Howland, 1995). Although the exact nature of the dysfunctions is not yet known, some kind of circadian rhythm dysfunction may play a causal role in many of the clinical features of depression. Two current theories are (1) that the size or magnitude of the circadian rhythms is blunted, and (2) that the various circadian rhythms that are normally well synchronized with each other become desynchronized or uncoupled (Howland & Thase, 1999; Thase et al., 2002).

Sunlight and Seasons Another, rather different kind of rhythm abnormality or disturbance is seen in *seasonal affective disorder,* in which most patients seem to be responsive to the total quantity of available light in the environment (Oren & Rosenthal, 1992). A majority (but not all) become depressed in the fall and winter and normalize in the spring and summer (Howland & Thase, 1999; Whybrow, 1997). Research in animals has also documented that many seasonal variations in basic functions such as sleep, activity, and appetite are related to the amount of light in a day (which, except near the equator, is much greater in summer than in winter). Depressed patients who fit the seasonal pattern usually show increased appetite and hypersomnia rather than decreased appetite and insomnia (Howland & Thase, 1999). They also have clear disturbances in their circadian cycles, showing weaker 24-hour patterns than nondepressed individuals (Howland & Thase, 1999; Teicher et al., 1997). A good deal of research on patients with seasonal affective disorder supports the therapeutic use of controlled exposure to light, even artificial light, which may work by reestablishing normal biological rhythms (Fava & Rosenbaum, 1995; Oren & Rosenthal, 1992).

Psychosocial Causal Factors

The evidence for important psychological causal factors in most unipolar mood disorders is at least as strong as evidence for biological factors. However, it is likely that the effects of at least some psychological factors such as stressful life events are mediated by a cascade of underlying biological changes that they initiate. One way in which stressors may act is through their effects on biochemical and hormonal balances and on biological rhythms (see Chapters 5 and 10) (Hammen, 2005; Howland & Thase, 1999).

STRESSFUL LIFE EVENTS AS CAUSAL FACTORS

Psychosocial stressors are known to be involved in the onset of a variety of disorders, ranging from some of the anxiety disorders to schizophrenia, but nowhere has their role been more carefully studied than in the case of unipolar depression. Many studies have shown that severely stressful life events often serve as precipitating factors for unipolar depression (e.g., Hammen, 2005; Kessler, 1997; Monroe & Harkness, 2005).

Most of the stressful life events involved in precipitating depression involve loss of a loved one, serious threats to important close relationships or to one's occupation, or severe economic or serious health problems (Monroe & Hadjiyannakis, 2002). For example, separations through death or divorce are strongly associated with depression, although such losses tend to precede other disorders such as panic disorder and generalized anxiety as well (Kendler, Hettema, et al., 2003; Kessler, 1997). Losses that involve an element of humiliation can be especially potent. The stress of caregiving to a spouse with a debilitating disease such as Alzheimer's is also known to be associated with the onset of both major depression and generalized anxiety disorder for the caregiver (e.g., Russo et al., 1995).

An important distinction has been made between stressful life events that are independent of the person's behavior and personality (*independent life events,* such as losing a job because one's company is shutting down or having one's house hit by a hurricane), and events that may have been at least partly generated by the depressed person's behavior or personality (*dependent life events*). For example, depressed people sometimes generate stressful life events because of their poor interpersonal problem solving (such as being unable to resolve conflicts with a spouse), which is often associated with depression. The poor problem solving in turn leads to higher levels of interpersonal stress, which in turn leads to further symptoms of depression. Another example of a dependent life event is failing to keep up with routine tasks such as paying bills, which may lead to a variety of troubles. Recent evidence suggests that dependent life events play an even stronger role in the onset of major depression than do independent life events (Hammen, 2005; Kendler et al., 1999a).

Research on stress and the onset of depression is complicated by the fact that depressed people have a distinctly negative view of themselves and the world around them (Beck, 1967; Clark, Beck, & Alford, 1999). Thus, their own perceptions of stress may result at least to some extent from the cognitive symptoms of their disorder, rather than causing their disorder (Hammen, 2005; Monroe & Hadjiyannakis, 2002). That is, their pessimistic outlook may lead them to evaluate events as stressful that an independent evaluator (or a nondepressed friend) would not.

Therefore, researchers have developed more sophisticated measures of life stress that do not rely on the depressed person's self-report of how stressful an event is and that take into account the biographical context of a person's life. For example, a divorcing woman who has already begun to establish a new relationship will probably not be as stressed by the divorce as one whose husband left her for a younger woman (e.g., Dohrenwend et al., 1995; Monroe & Hadjiyannakis, 2002). There is widespread agreement that conclusions derived from studies using these more sophisticated techniques are the most reliable.

Several recent reviews of studies that employed these sophisticated measurements of life stress show that severely stressful life events play a causal role (most often within a month or so after the event) in about 20 to 50 percent of cases (e.g., Hammen, 2005; Kendler, Karkowski, & Prescott, 1998; Monroe & Harkness, 2005). Moreover, depressed people who have experienced a stressful life event tend to show more severe depressive symptoms than those who have not experienced a stressful life event (Monroe and Hadjiyannakis, 2002). This relationship between severely stressful life events and depression is much stronger in people who are having their first onset than in those undergoing recurrent episodes (e.g., Kendler, Thorton, & Gardner, 2000; Monroe & Harkness, 2005). Indeed, Monroe and Harkness (2005) have estimated that about 70 percent of people with a first onset of depression have had a recent major stressful life event, whereas only about 40 percent of people with a recurrent episode have had a recent major life event.

Mildly Stressful Events and Chronic Stress Whether mildly stressful events are also associated with the onset of depression is much more controversial, with conflicting findings in the literature. However, studies applying the more sophisticated and complex strategies for assessing life stress have not found minor stressful events to be associated with the onset of clinical depression (e.g., Dohrenwend et al., 1995; Stueve, Dohrenwend, & Skodol, 1998). An interesting hypothesis has recently been raised that minor events may play more of a role in the onset of recurrent episodes than the initial episode, although new research strategies will be needed to confirm this hypothesis (Monroe & Harkness, 2005).

Although the relationship of chronic stress to the onset of depression has not been as thoroughly studied as has the relationship with episodic life events, in a number of good studies chronic stress has been associated with increased risk for the onset and maintenance of major depression (Hammen, 2005). Different studies have used the term *chronic strain* or *stress* in different ways, although it usually refers to one or more forms of stress ongoing for at least several months (e.g., poverty, lasting marital discord, medical disabilities, having a disabled child). One well-validated chronic stress interview assesses chronic stress in eight to ten different domains (e.g., intimate relationships, close friends, family relationships, health of self and family members, etc.; Hammen, 2005).

If a woman living in poverty is already genetically at risk for depression, the stresses associated with living in poverty may be especially likely to precipitate a major depression.

Individual Differences in Responses to Stressors: Vulnerability and Invulnerability Factors Women (and perhaps men) at genetic risk for depression not only experience more stressful life events (especially dependent life events) (Kendler & Karkowski-Shuman, 1997; Kendler, Karkowski, & Prescott, 1999a), but also are more sensitive to them (Kendler et al., 1995a). In one large study, women at genetic risk were three times more likely than those not at genetic risk to respond to severely stressful life events with depression (a good example of a genotype-environment interaction as discussed in Chapter 3). Conversely, those at low genetic risk for depression are more invulnerable to the effects of major stressors (Kendler et al., 1995a). Moreover, the findings discussed earlier by Caspi et al. (2003) have also now shown that at least part of this gene-environment interaction is mediated by the presence of the two short alleles of the serotonin-transporter gene rather than two long alleles. Specifically, individuals with two short alleles were twice as likely to develop depression following major stressful life events than were those with two long alleles.

In addition to genetic variables, there are a host of other variables that may make some people more vulnerable to developing depression after experiencing one or more stressful life events. Brown and Harris (1978) found some interesting examples in their classic study of relatively poor women living in inner London. Among the women who experienced a severe event, four factors were associated with not becoming depressed: (1) having an intimate relationship with a spouse or lover, (2) having no more than three children still at home, (3) having a job outside the home, and (4) having a serious religious commitment. Conversely, not having a close relationship with a spouse or lover, having three children under age 5 at home, not having a job, and having lost a parent by death before the age of 11 were strongly associated with the onset of depression following a major negative life event. Such research on vulnerability and invulnerability factors, building on Brown and Harris' example, has been integrated into more comprehensive diathesis—stress theories of depression, which will be reviewed more extensively below.

DIFFERENT TYPES OF VULNERABILITIES FOR UNIPOLAR DEPRESSION Before considering several influential **diathesis-stress theories,** we will first consider work on psychological diatheses—that is, vulnerability factors that may increase the risk for depression (whether or not they interact with stress).

Personality and Cognitive Diatheses Researchers have concluded that neuroticism is the primary personality variable that serves as a vulnerability factor for depression (and anxiety disorders as well) (for reviews, see Clark, Watson, & Mineka, 1994; Klein et al., 2002; see also Hayward et al., 2000; Kendler, Kuhn, & Prescott, 2004; Watson, Gamez, & Simms, 2005). Recall that *neuroticism,* or *negative affectivity,* refers to a stable and heritable personality trait that involves a temperamental sensitivity to negative stimuli. Thus, people who have high levels of this trait are prone to experiencing a broad range of negative moods, including not only sadness but also anxiety, guilt, and hostility. Moreover, several studies have also shown that neuroticism predicts the occurrence of more stressful life events (e.g., Kendler, Gardner, & Prescott, 2003). In addition to serving as a vulnerability factor, neuroticism is associated with a worse prognosis for complete recovery from depression.

There is some more limited evidence that high levels of introversion (or low positive affectivity) may also serve as vulnerability factors for depression, either alone or when combined with neuroticism (e.g., Gershuny & Sher, 1998; Watson et al., 2005). Positive affectivity involves a disposition to feel joyful, energetic, bold, proud, enthusiastic, and confident; people low on this disposition tend to feel unenthusiastic, unenergetic, dull, flat, and bored. It is therefore not surprising that this might make them more prone to developing clinical depression.

Children who have lost a parent through death or permanent separation may become vulnerable to depression if they receive poor subsequent care from another parent or guardian and if the child's environment and routine are disrupted.

The cognitive diatheses that have been studied for depression generally focus on particular negative patterns of thinking that make people who are prone to depression more likely to become depressed when faced with one or more stressful life events. For example, people who attribute negative events to internal, stable, and global causes may be more prone to becoming depressed than people who attribute the same events to external, unstable, and specific causes (e.g., Abramson et al., 1978, 1989, 2002). A pessimistic or depressive attribution for receiving a low grade on an exam might be, "I'm stupid," whereas a more optimistic attribution for the same event might be, "The teacher wrote the test in a bad mood and made it especially difficult."

Early Adversity and Parental Loss as a Diathesis Decades ago, evidence suggested that early parental loss through death or permanent separation seemed to create a vulnerability to depression in adulthood. For example, in their classic study of women in inner London, Brown and Harris (1978) found that the incidence of depression was three times higher in women who had lost their mothers before the age of 11 (see also Bowlby, 1980). Subsequently, however, a number of studies found no evidence that early parental loss produces a vulnerability to depression. Further research indicated that what determines a child's response to the loss has a lot to do with what happens following the loss. In cases where the child continues to receive good parental care, and there are not too many disruptions to the child's environment, a vulnerability to depression is usually not created (e.g., Goodman, 2002). However, if parental loss is followed by poor parental care, a vulnerability to adult depression is likely to be created (Bifulco, Brown, & Harris, 1987; Harris, Brown, & Bifulco, 1986).

Subsequent research has revealed that a range of other adversities in the early environment (such as family turmoil, parental psychopathology, physical or sexual abuse, and other forms of intrusive, harsh, and coercive parenting) can also create a long-term vulnerability to depression. Such factors operate, at least in part, by increasing an individual's sensitivity to stressful life events in adulthood (see also

Hammen, 2005, for a review). The long-term effects of such early environmental adversities may be mediated by biological variables (such as alterations in the regulation of the hypothalamic-pituitary stress response system) and psychological variables (such as lower self-esteem, insecure attachment relationships, difficulty relating to peers, and pessimistic attributions) (e.g., Goodman, 2002). However, it is also important to realize that certain individuals who have undergone early adversity remain resilient, and if the exposure to early adversity is moderate rather than severe, a form of stress inoculation may occur that makes the individual less susceptible to the effects of later stress (e.g., Parker et al., 2004). These stress inoculation effects seem to be mediated by strengthening socioemotional and neuroendocrine resistance to subsequent stressors.

Summary of Different Types of Vulnerabilities Several different types of diatheses for unipolar depression have been studied. Some propose a genetic diathesis that, often in conjunction with stressful life events, can lead to depression. Other models suggest that personality variables (such as neuroticism) or cognitive variables (such as pessimism or dysfunctional beliefs) provide a diathesis that, perhaps in interaction with negative life events, can produce depression. Finally, models proposing the importance of early parental loss or dysfunctional parenting or other forms of early adversity have also received a good deal of attention.

These models are not mutually exclusive, and some may simply be describing the same diathesis in different terms or at different levels of analysis. For example, there is a genetic basis for neuroticism, and neuroticism is correlated with pessimism (L. A. Clark et al., 1994; Luten, Ralph, & Mineka, 1997), so these three proposed diatheses may be somewhat interrelated. Moreover, dysfunctional early parenting, emotional abuse, and parental loss have been strongly implicated in the formation of some of the other cognitive diatheses (Alloy, Abramson, et al., 2004; Beck, 1967; Bowlby, 1980). Thus, these two proposed diatheses may simply differ in whether they operate distally (poor early parenting) or proximally (negative thinking patterns) in contributing to vulnerability for depression.

We now turn to five major psychological theories of depression that have received much attention over the years.

PSYCHODYNAMIC THEORIES In his classic paper "Mourning and Melancholia" (1917; 1957), Freud noted the important similarity between the symptoms of clinical depression and the symptoms seen in people mourning the loss of a loved one. Freud and a colleague, Karl Abraham (1924, 1927), both hypothesized that when a loved one dies, the mourner regresses to the oral stage of development (when the infant cannot distinguish self from others) and introjects or incorporates the lost person, feeling all the same feelings toward the self as toward the lost person. These feelings were thought to include anger and hostility because Freud believed that we unconsciously hold negative feelings toward those we love, in part because of their power over us. This is what led to the psychodynamic idea that depression is anger turned inward. Freud hypothesized that depression could also occur in response to imagined or symbolic losses. For example, a student who fails in school or who fails at a romantic relationship may experience this symbolically as a loss of his or her parents' love.

Freud also hypothesized that someone who has either experienced the loss of a mother or whose parents did not fulfill the infant's needs for nurturance and love develops a vulnerability to depression. In either case, the infant will grow up feeling unworthy of love, will have low self-esteem, and will be prone to depression when faced with real or symbolic losses (Bemporad, 1995).

Later psychodynamic theorists such as Klein (1934) and Jacobson (1971) emphasized even more than Freud the importance of the quality of the early mother-infant relationship in establishing a vulnerability to depression, and also emphasized a decrease in or threat to self-esteem as a critical issue (Bibring, 1953). Bowlby (1973, 1980), who started as a psychoanalyst before developing attachment theory (see Chapter 3), also extensively documented a child's need for a secure attachment to parental figures in order to be resistant to depression (and anxiety) in later life. As we saw earlier, much research supports this position.

Perhaps the most important contribution of the psychodynamic approaches to depression has been their noting the importance of loss (both real and symbolic or imagined) to the onset of depression and noting the striking similarities between the symptoms of mourning and the symptoms of depression (Bowlby, 1980). Even theorists who disagree with many of the specific details of these theories recognize that their own theories must account for these basic observations.

BEHAVIORAL THEORIES In the 1970s and 1980s, several theorists in the behavioral tradition developed behavioral theories of depression proposing that people become depressed either when their responses no longer produce positive reinforcement or when their rate of negative reinforcements increases (such as experiencing stressful life events; e.g., Ferster, 1974; Lewinsohn, 1974; Lewinsohn et al., 1985; Lewinsohn & Gotlib, 1995). Such theories are consistent with research showing that depressed persons do indeed receive fewer positive verbal and social reinforcements from their families and friends than do nondepressed persons, as well as experience more negative events. Moreover, they have lower activity levels, and their moods seem to vary with both their positive and their negative reinforcement rates (see Lewinsohn & Gotlib, 1995; Rehm & Tyndall, 1993). Nevertheless, although such findings are consistent with behavioral theories, they do not show that depression is caused by these factors. Instead, it may be that some of the primary symptoms of depression, such as pessimism and low levels of energy, cause the depressed person to experience these lower rates of reinforcement. For this and other reasons, behavioral theories of the origins of depression are no longer very influential.

BECK'S COGNITIVE THEORY Since 1967 one of the most influential theories of depression has been that of Aaron Beck—a psychiatrist who became disenchanted with psychodynamic theories of depression early in his career and developed his own cognitive theory of depression (e.g., Beck, 1967; Clark, Beck, & Alford, 1999). Whereas the most prominent symptoms of depression have generally been considered to be the affective or mood symptoms, Beck hypothesized that the cognitive symptoms of depression often precede and cause the affective or mood symptoms, rather than vice versa (see Figure 7.4). For example, if you think that you're a failure or that you're ugly, it would not be surprising if those thoughts led to a depressed mood.

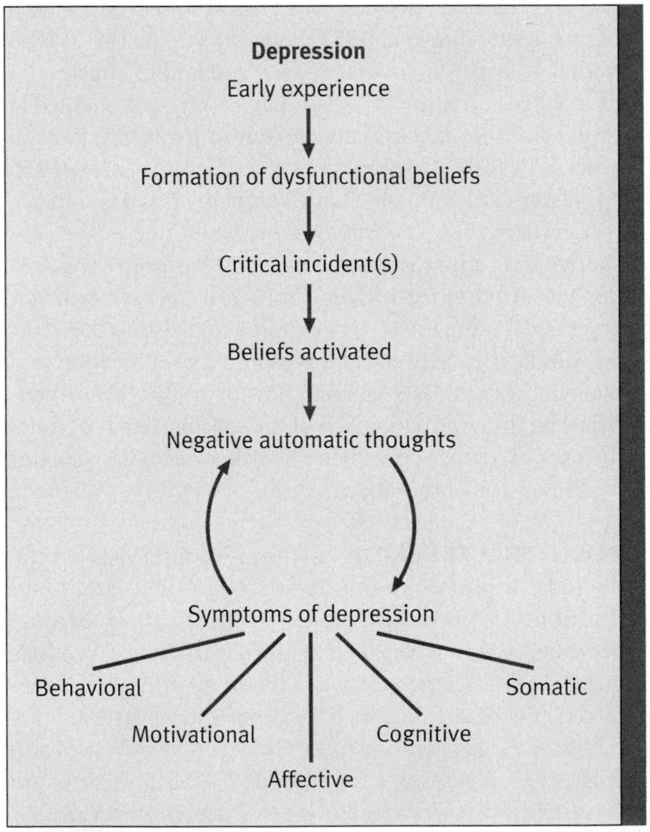

FIGURE 7.4

Beck's Cognitive Model of Depression

According to Beck's cognitive model of depression, certain kinds of early experiences can lead to the formation of dysfunctional assumptions that leave a person vulnerable to depression later in life if certain critical incidents (stressors) activate those assumptions. Once activated, these dysfunctional assumptions trigger automatic thoughts that in turn produce depressive symptoms, which further fuel the depressive automatic thoughts. (Adapted from Fennell, 1989.)

Beck's theory—in which negative cognitions are central—has become somewhat more elaborate over the years, while still retaining its primary tenets (e.g., Beck, 1967, 1983; Clark, Beck, & Alford, 1999). First, there are the underlying **depressogenic schemas** or **dysfunctional beliefs,** which are rigid, extreme, and counterproductive. An example of a dysfunctional belief (that a person is usually not consciously aware of) is, "If everyone doesn't love me, then my life is worthless." According to cognitive theory, such a belief would predispose the person holding it to develop depression if he or she perceived social rejection. Alternatively, a person with the dysfunctional belief, "If I'm not perfectly successful, then I'm a nobody" would be vulnerable to developing negative thoughts and depressed affect if she or he felt like a failure.

These depression-producing beliefs or schemas are thought to develop during childhood and adolescence as a function of one's negative experiences with one's parents and significant others, and they are thought to serve as the underlying diathesis, or vulnerability, to develop depression (Beck, 1967; Scher, Ingram, & Segal, 2005). Although they may lie dormant for years in the absence of significant stressors, when dysfunctional beliefs are activated by current stressors or depressed mood, they tend to fuel the current thinking pattern, creating a pattern of **negative automatic thoughts**—thoughts that often occur just below the surface of awareness and involve unpleasant pessimistic predictions. These pessimistic predictions tend to center on the three themes of what Beck calls the **negative cognitive triad:** (1) negative thoughts about the self ("I'm ugly"; "I'm worthless"; "I'm a failure"); (2) negative thoughts about one's experiences and the surrounding world ("No one loves me"; "People treat me badly"); and (3) negative thoughts about one's future ("It's hopeless because things will always be this way"; Clark & Beck, 1999; see Figure 7.5).

Beck also postulates that the negative cognitive triad tends to be maintained by a variety of negative cognitive biases or errors (see also Scher et al., 2005). Each of these involves biased processing of negative self-relevant information. Examples include:

- *Dichotomous or all-or-none reasoning,* which involves a tendency to think in extremes. For example, someone might discount a less-than-perfect performance by saying, "If I can't get it 100 percent right, there's no point in doing it at all."
- *Selective abstraction,* which involves a tendency to focus on one negative detail of a situation while ignoring other elements of the situation. Someone might say, "I didn't have a moment of pleasure or fun today" not because this is true but because he or she selectively remembered only the negative things that happened.
- *Arbitrary inference,* which involves jumping to a conclusion based on minimal or no evidence. A

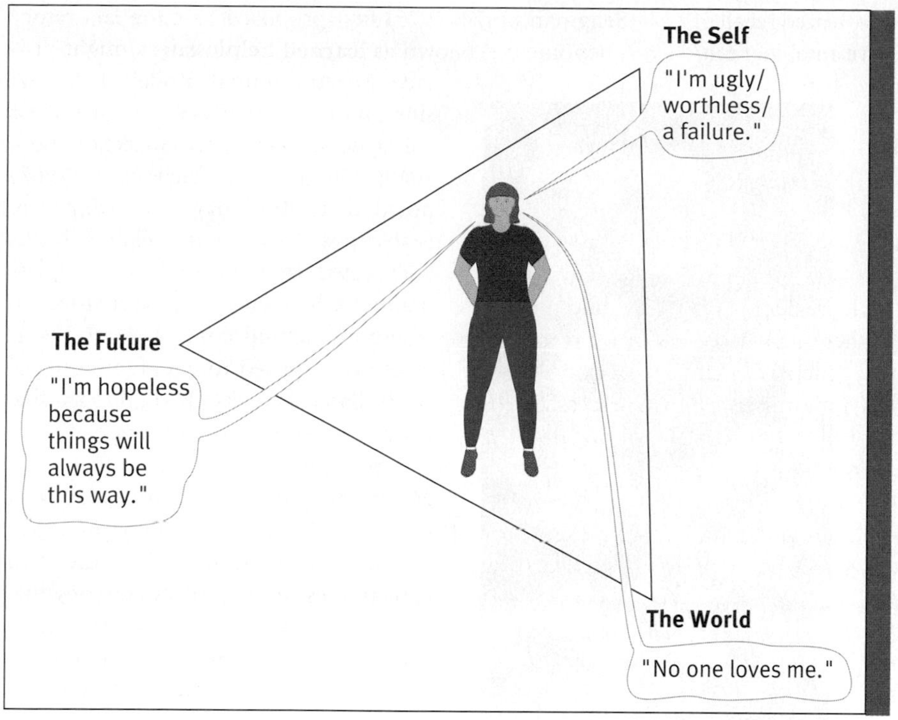

FIGURE 7.5
Negative Cognitive Triad
Beck's cognitive model of depression describes a pattern of negative automatic thoughts. These pessimistic predictions center on three themes: the self, the world, and the future.

depressed person might say, after an initial homework assignment from a cognitive therapist did not work, "This therapy will never work for me." (Examples from Fennell, 1989, p. 193)

It is easy to see how each of these cognitive distortions tends to maintain the negative cognitive triad. That is, if the content of your thoughts regarding your views of your self, your world, and your future is already negative, and you tend to minimize the good things that happen to you or draw negative conclusions based on minimal evidence, those negative thoughts are not likely to disappear. In addition, just as the underlying dysfunctional beliefs (such as, "If everybody doesn't love me, then my life is worthless") elicit the negative cognitive triad when activated, so too does the negative thinking produced by the negative triad serve to reinforce those underlying beliefs. Thus each of these components of cognitive theory serves to reinforce the others, as shown in Figure 7.4. Moreover, these negative thoughts can produce some of the other symptoms of depression such as sadness, dejection, and lack of motivation.

Evaluating Beck's Theory as a Descriptive Theory Over the past 35 years, an enormous amount of research has been conducted to test various aspects of Beck's theory. As we will see, it has generated a very effective form of treatment for depression known as cognitive therapy. In addition, it has been well supported as a descriptive theory that explains many prominent characteristics of depression (e.g., Clark & Beck, 1999; Haaga, Dyck, & Ernst, 1991). Depressed patients of all the subtypes are considerably more negative in their thinking, especially about themselves or issues highly relevant to the self, than are nondepressed persons, and more negative than they usually are when they are not depressed. Moreover, depressed persons do think more negatively about themselves and the world around them (especially their own personal world) than do nondepressed persons and are quite negative about the future (especially their own future) (the negative cognitive triad). By contrast, nondepressed people show a large positivity bias in attributions that may serve as a protective factor against depression. A positivity bias is a tendency to process emotional information in an overly optimistic, self-enhancing manner (Mezulis, Abramson, Hyde, & Hankin, 2004).

Beck's theory originally proposed that stressors are necessary to activate depressogenic schemas or dysfunctional attitudes that lie dormant between episodes, but more recent research has shown that stressors are not necessary to activate the latent depressive schemas between episodes. Indeed, simply inducing a depressed mood (e.g., through listening to sad music or recalling sad memories) in a previously depressed (that is, at-risk) individual is generally sufficient to activate latent depressogenic schemas (e.g., Scher et al., 2005).

In addition to evidence for dysfunctional attitudes and negative automatic thoughts, there is also considerable evidence for certain cognitive biases for negative self-relevant information in depression. For example, depressed people show better or biased recall of negative information and negative autobiographical memories, whereas nondepressed people tend to show biased recall of positive emotional information and positive autobiographical memories (Mathews & MacLeod, 1994, 2005; Mineka et al., 2003). In addition, depressed people are more likely than nondepressed people to draw negative conclusions that go beyond the information presented in a scenario and to underestimate the positive feedback they have received (Clark & Beck, 1999). It is easy to see how, if one is already depressed, remembering primarily the bad things that have happened is likely to maintain or exacerbate the depression. Teasdale (1988, 1996) aptly called this the "vicious cycle of depression."

If a celebrity comes to depend on the love and adoration of his fans to feed his feelings of self-worth, the celebrity is at great risk for developing depression when that positive attention subsides.

Evaluating the Causal Aspects of Beck's Theory Although research supports most of the descriptive aspects of Beck's theory, research directed toward confirming the causal hypotheses of Beck's theory has been more mixed. The causal hypotheses are usually tested with some kind of prospective study design. People who are not depressed are tested for their cognitive vulnerability (usually dysfunctional attitudes) at Time 1 and then are followed for 1 or more months or years, after which measurements of life stress are administered. Only some studies have found that dysfunctional beliefs or attitudes at Time 1, in interaction with stressful life events, predict depression at Time 2. However, some of the studies that yielded negative results may have used inadequate study designs. Several very large recent studies using more adequate designs have found results quite supportive of the causal aspects of Beck's theory (e.g., Hankin, Abramson, Miller, & Haeffel, 2004; Lewinsohn, Joiner, & Rohde, 2001). For example, Lewinsohn et al. (2001) assessed about 1,500 adolescents for their dysfunctional attitudes and then followed them for 1 year, at which point stressful life events during that year were assessed. Results indicated that those who started with high levels of dysfunctional attitudes and who experienced high stress were more likely to develop major depression than those with low stress, or than those with low dysfunctional attitudes and high stress.

THE HELPLESSNESS AND HOPELESSNESS THEORIES OF DEPRESSION Whereas Beck's theory grew out of his clinical observations and research on the pervasive patterns of negative thinking seen in depressed patients, the learned helplessness theory of depression originated out of observations in an animal research laboratory. Martin Seligman (1974, 1975) first proposed that the laboratory phenomenon known as **learned helplessness** might provide a useful animal model of depression. In the late 1960s, Seligman and his colleagues (Maier, Seligman, & Solomon, 1969; Overmier & Seligman, 1967) noted that laboratory dogs who were first exposed to uncontrollable shocks later acted in a passive and helpless manner when they were in a situation where they could control shocks. Animals first exposed to equal amounts of controllable shocks had no trouble learning to control the shocks.

Seligman and his colleagues (e.g., Maier, Seligman, & Solomon, 1969; Overmier & Seligman, 1967) developed the learned helplessness hypothesis to explain these effects. It stated that when animals or humans find that they have no control over aversive events (such as shock), they may learn that they are helpless, which makes them unmotivated to try to respond in the future; instead they exhibit passivity and even depressive symptoms. They are also slow to learn that any response they do make is effective, which may parallel the negative cognitive set in human depression. His observations that the animals looked depressed captured Seligman's attention and ultimately led to his proposing a learned helplessness model of depression (Seligman, 1974, 1975). Subsequent research demonstrated that helpless animals also show other depressive symptoms such as lower levels of aggression, loss of appetite and weight, and changes in monoamine neurotransmitter levels. After demonstrating that learned helplessness also occurs in humans (e.g., Hiroto & Seligman, 1975), he went on to propose that learned helplessness may underlie some types of human depression. That is, people undergoing stressful life events over which they have little or no control may develop a syndrome like the helplessness syndrome seen in animals.

The Reformulated Helplessness Theory Some of the research on helplessness with humans led to a major reformulation of the helplessness theory, addressing some of the complexities of what humans do when faced with uncontrollable events (Abramson, Seligman, & Teasdale, 1978). In particular, Abramson et al. proposed that when people (probably unlike animals) are exposed to uncontrollable negative events, they ask themselves why, and the kinds of **attributions** that people make are, in turn, central to whether they become depressed. These investigators proposed three critical dimensions on which attributions are made: (1) internal/external, (2) global/specific, and (3) stable/unstable. They proposed that a depressogenic or pessimistic attribution for a negative event is an internal, stable, and global one. For example, if your boyfriend treats you badly and you conclude that "It's because I'm ugly and boring," you are much more likely to become depressed than if you conclude that "It's because he's in a bad mood today after failing his exam and he is taking it out on me."

Abramson et al. (1978) proposed that people who have a relatively stable and consistent **pessimistic attributional style** have a vulnerability or diathesis for depression when faced with uncontrollable negative life events. This kind of cognitive style seems to develop, at least in part, through social learning (Abramson & Alloy, in press). For example, children may learn this cognitive style by observing and modeling inferences made by their parents. Alternatively or additionally, the parents may communicate their own inferences about negative events happening to their children, or by engaging in generally negative parenting practices.

This *reformulated helplessness theory* led to a great deal of research. Many studies demonstrated that depressed people do indeed have this kind of pessimistic attributional style, but of course this does not mean that pessimistic attributional style plays a causal role (e.g., Abramson et al., 1995; Buchanan & Seligman, 1995). Using designs similar to those used to test the causal aspects of cognitive theory, many studies have examined the ability of a pessimistic attributional style to predict the onset of depression in interaction with negative life events (Abramson et al., 1989; Peterson, Maier, & Seligman, 1993). Some results have supported the theory and some have not. Developments in Research 7.1 (p. 248) discusses the helplessness approach, as well as other approaches to understanding sex differences in depression.

The Hopelessness Theory of Depression A further revision of this theory, known as the *hopelessness theory,* was later presented (Abramson et al., 1989). Abramson et al. (1989) proposed that having a pessimistic attributional style in conjunction with one or more negative life events was not sufficient to produce depression unless one first experienced a state of hopelessness. A *hopelessness expectancy* was defined by the perception that one had no control over what was going to happen and by absolute certainty that an important bad outcome was going to occur or that a highly desired good outcome was not going to occur. They also proposed that the internal/external dimension of attributions was not important to depression. Instead, they proposed two other dimensions of pessimistic attributional style as being important components of this cognitive diathesis. Specifically, they proposed that depression-prone individuals not only tend to make global and stable attributions for negative events, but they also make negative inferences about other likely negative consequences of the event (e.g., that this means more bad things will also happen), and negative inferences about the implications of the event for the self-concept (e.g., that one is unworthy or deficient; Abramson, Alloy, et al., 2002).

Research is currently testing this theory. A major longitudinal prospective study of several hundred college students who were hypothesized to be at high risk for unipolar depression (because they have a pessimistic attributional style and have dysfunctional beliefs) is beginning to yield evidence quite supportive of some of the major tenets of the hopelessness theory (e.g., Abramson et al., 2002; Alloy, Abramson, et al., in press). For example, students in the high-risk group were about four times more likely than those in the low-risk group to develop a first or a recurrent episode of major depression (or comorbid depression and anxiety) in a 2.5-year follow-up period. Moreover, the high-risk students in this study who also had a tendency to ruminate about their negative thoughts and moods were even more likely to become depressed than the high-risk nonruminators.

These results are still somewhat preliminary with regard to hopelessness theory itself in that Abramson, Alloy, and colleagues (2002) have not yet presented findings on whether stress interacts with negative cognitive styles in the way postulated by the theory, or whether hopelessness mediates these effects. However, two smaller studies with similar designs have recently appeared that have shown evidence for the predicted interaction of cognitive vulnerability with life stress in predicting depressive symptoms and onset of diagnosable depression (Hankin et al., 2004). Thus, future research on the hopelessness theory is likely to continue to provide important insights into psychosocial causes of depression.

Developments in Thinking 7.2 on page 250 discusses how the helplessness and hopelessness theories help explain why anxiety and depression are so often comorbid.

INTERPERSONAL EFFECTS OF MOOD DISORDERS

Although there is no interpersonal theory of depression that is as clearly articulated as the cognitive theories, there has been a considerable amount of research on interpersonal factors in depression. Interpersonal problems and social-skills deficits may well play a causal role in at least some cases of depression. In addition, depression creates many interpersonal difficulties—with strangers and friends as well as with family members (Hammen, 1995, 2004; Joiner, 2002).

Lack of Social Support and Social-Skills Deficits Brown and Harris (1978), in their classic study of community women in a poor area of inner London, reported that women without a close, confiding relationship were more likely than those with at least one close confidant to become depressed if they experienced a severely stressful

7.1 Developments in Research

Sex Differences in Unipolar Depression

It has long been observed that women are about twice as likely as men to develop unipolar depression (either dysthymia or major depression). These differences occur in most countries around the world; the few exceptions are developing and rural countries such as Nigeria and Iran. In the United States, this sex difference starts in adolescence and continues until about age 65, when it seems to disappear. Yet among schoolchildren, boys are equally likely or slightly more likely to be diagnosed with depression (Nolen-Hoeksema, 1990, 2002).

Questions have been raised about whether these differences stem from some kind of artifact, such as young women in adolescence becoming more willing to report their feelings, but the data do not support this idea (Kessler, 2003; Nolen-Hoeksema, 1990). Moreover, this higher prevalence of depression in women than men applies only to first onsets and not to recurrences, and it would be hard to explain such results from the artifact hypothesis. What kinds of theories have been proposed that could explain these interesting observations?

An unemployed woman living in poverty may experience a sense of lack of control over her environment, and these feelings of helplessness may greatly enhance her vulnerability to depression.

One set of theories is biological. For example, it has been suggested that hormonal factors such as normal fluctuations in ovarian hormones account for the differences. Studies examining this hypothesis have yielded inconsistent results but overall are not very supportive (Brems, 1995; Nolen-Hoeksema, 1990, 2002). It seems that for the majority of women, hormonal changes occurring at various points (e.g., at the onset of puberty, before menstruation, in the postpartum period, and at menopause) do not play a significant role in causing depression. However, it remains possible that there is a causal association that has not yet been discovered because of real methodological difficulties in conducting conclusive research on this topic (Sanborn & Hayward, 2003). Moreover, for a small minority of women who are already at high risk (for example, by being at high genetic risk), hormonal fluctuations may trigger depressive episodes, possibly by causing changes in the normal processes that regulate neurotransmitter systems. Some studies have suggested that women have a greater genetic vulnerability to depression than men, but many other studies have not supported this idea (e.g., Nolen-Hoeksema, 2002; Wallace et al., 2002).

Given that biological theories have received mixed support at best, many researchers have focused on social and psychological factors that may be responsible for these sex differences in depression (e.g., Helgeson, 2002; Nolen-Hoeksema, 1990, 2002). One relevant theory is that sex differences in depression occur because of sex differences in neuroticism, which as discussed earlier is a very strong risk factor for depression (e.g., Goodwin & Gotlib, 2004; Kendler, Gardner, & Prescott, 2002). Another psychological theory proposes that by virtue of their roles in society, women are more prone to experiencing a sense of lack of control over negative life events. These feelings of helplessness might stem from poverty, discrimination in the workplace leading to unemployment or underemployment, the relative imbalance of power in many heterosexual relationships, high rates of sexual and physical abuse against women (either currently or in childhood), role overload (e.g., being a working wife and mother), and less perceived control over traits that men value when choosing a long-term mate, such as beauty, thinness, and youth (e.g., Ben Hamida, Mineka, & Bailey, 1998; Heim et al., 2000; Nolen-Hoeksema, 2002). There is at least some evidence that each of these conditions is associated with higher-than-expected rates of depression, although whether the effects involve a

event. Many more studies have since supported the idea that people who are socially isolated or lack social support are more vulnerable to becoming depressed (e.g., Joiner, 1997; Southwick et al., 2005) and that depressed individuals have smaller and less supportive social networks, which tend to precede the onset of depression (e.g., Gotlib & Hammen, 1992). In addition, some depressives have social-skills deficits. For example, they seem to speak more

sense of helplessness has not yet been established (Brems, 1995; Nolen-Hoeksema, Larson, & Grayson, 1999; Whiffen & Clark, 1997). Combining the neuroticism theory with the helplessness theory, it is important to note that a recent very large study has confirmed that people who are high on neuroticism are more sensitive to the effects of adversity, relative to those low on neuroticism (a gene-environment interaction) (Kendler, Kuhn, and Prescott, 2004). So given that women have higher levels of neuroticism and experience more uncontrollable stress, the increased prevalence of depression in women becomes less surprising.

Another intriguing hypothesis is that women have different responses to being in a depressed mood than men. In particular, it seems that women are more likely to ruminate when they become depressed. Rumination includes responses such as trying to figure out why you are depressed, crying to relieve tension, or talking to friends about your depression. It is known that rumination is likely to maintain or exacerbate depression, in part by interfering with instrumental behavior (i.e., taking action) and with effective interpersonal problem solving (Nolen-Hoeksema & Corte, 2004; Nolen-Hoeksema, Morrow, & Fredrickson, 1993). Moreover, self-focused rumination leads to increased recall of more negative autobiographical memories, thereby feeding a vicious circle of depression (Lyubomirsky, Caldwell, & Nolen-Hoeksema, 1998; Nolen-Hoeksema, 2002; Teasdale, 1988).

Men, by contrast, are more likely to engage in a distracting activity (or consume alcohol) when they get in a depressed mood, and distraction seems to reduce depression (Nolen-Hoeksema, 1990; Nolen-Hoeksema & Corte, 2004). Distraction might include going to a movie, playing a sport, or avoiding thinking about why they are depressed. The origin of these sex differences in response to depression is unclear, but if further research supports this hypothesis, it would certainly suggest that effective prevention efforts might include teaching girls to seek distraction rather than to ruminate as a response to depression.

Finally, we must consider why the sex difference starts in adolescence (Hankin & Abramson, 2001; Nolen-Hoeksema & Girgus, 1994), beginning to emerge between ages 12 and 13 and reaching its most dramatic peak between ages 14 and 16, although it is actually more tied to pubertal status than to age per se (Sanborn & Hayward, 2003; Twenge & Nolen-Hoeksema, 2002). This is a time of rapid physiological, environmental, and psychological changes known to create turmoil for many adolescents, but why are adolescent females more likely to become depressed? Hankin and Abramson (2001) proposed an intriguing cognitive vulnerability-stress model of the development of gender differences during adolescence. Building on ideas from the reformulated helplessness and hopelessness models of depression for adults, they summarize research indicating that children and adolescents, like adults, are prone to experiencing increases in depressive symptoms if they have a pessimistic attributional style and experience stressful life events (e.g., Hankin & Abramson, 2001; Hilsman & Garber, 1995). Moreover, during early adolescence, gender differences in attributional style, in rumination, and in stressful life events emerge, such that girls tend to have a more pessimistic attributional style, to show more rumination, and to experience more negative life events (especially interpersonal events). Thus one can see how, with all three of these risk factors showing gender differences in adolescence, a synergistic effect might lead to the dramatic rise in depression in adolescent girls. Moreover, Hankin and Abramson (2001) review evidence that the experience of negative life events may contribute to greater cognitive vulnerability, which in turn further increases susceptibility to depressive symptoms. Furthermore, depressive symptoms in adolescent girls, as in adults, are likely to result in more dependent life stress being generated, which in turn may exacerbate depression. Finally, girls not only experience more negative life events than boys but also encode them in greater detail and show better memory for emotional events (though not for nonemotional events).

Hankin and Abramson (2001) also emphasize the role of negative cognitions about attractiveness and body image in the emergence of sex differences in depression during adolescence. There is evidence that the development of secondary sexual characteristics is harder psychologically for girls than for boys. Body dissatisfaction goes up for females at this time, and down for males; moreover, body dissatisfaction is more closely related to self-esteem for girls than for boys. Much of girls' dissatisfaction with their bodies comes from their realization of the discrepancy between our society's ideal of a thin, prepubescent body shape for females and the fact that they are gaining fat as they mature sexually. Hankin and Abramson (2001) summarize evidence that girls are more likely than boys to make pessimistic attributions and other negative inferences about negative events that may occur (such as negative remarks) related to the domain of physical attractiveness. Given that physical attractiveness may be more motivationally significant for girls than for boys, it becomes plausible that this may be one important factor that makes depression especially likely in adolescent girls.

slowly and monotonously and to maintain less eye contact; they are also poorer than nondepressed people at solving interpersonal problems (e.g., Ingram, Scott, & Siegle, 1999; Joiner, 2002).

The Effects of Depression on Others Not only do depressed people have interpersonal problems, but unfortunately, their own behavior also seems to make these problems worse. For example, the behavior of a depressed

7.2 Developments in Thinking

Comorbidity of Anxiety and Mood Disorders

The issue of whether depression and anxiety can be differentiated in a reliable and valid way has received a good deal of attention over the years. Only recently, however, have researchers begun to make significant advances in understanding the real scope of the problem. The overlap between measures of depression and anxiety occurs at all levels of analysis: patient self-report, clinician ratings, diagnosis, and family/genetic factors (Barlow, 2002; Clark & Watson, 1991a, 1991b; Mineka et al., 1998). That is, persons who rate themselves high on symptoms of anxiety also tend to rate themselves high on symptoms of depression, and clinicians rating these same individuals do the same thing. The overlap also occurs at the diagnostic level. One review of the literature estimated that just over half of the patients who receive a diagnosis of a mood disorder also receive a diagnosis of an anxiety disorder at some point in their lives, and vice versa (e.g., Mineka et al., 1998). Although the vast majority of research on this topic has concerned comorbidity of anxiety and unipolar depressive disorders (which is the focus of this highlight), recent evidence has shown that comorbid anxiety disorders are equally common in bipolar disorder as well (e.g., Simon, Otto, et al., 2004). The importance of these high levels of comorbidity stems from research showing that the prognosis for people with comorbid depression and anxiety is generally worse than for people with either one alone.

Finally, there is considerable evidence from genetic and family studies of the close relationship between anxiety and unipolar depressive disorders (Kendler, 1996; Kendler et al., 1995; Mineka et al., 1998). Several very large twin studies and a recent review have shown that liability for unipolar depression and liability for generalized anxiety disorder come from the same genetic factors, and which disorder develops is a result of what environmental experiences occur (Barlow, 2002a; Kendler, 1996; Kendler et al., 1992d, 1995a). The genetic relationships between panic disorder and depression and between the other anxiety disorders and depression are more modest (Kendler et al., 1995b; Mineka et al., 1998). The shared genetically based factor among these disorders seems to be neuroticism personality traits—a major risk factor for all of these disorders (Middeldorp, Cath, & Boomsma, 2005).

At present the dominant theoretical approach to the overlap between depressive and anxiety symptoms is to assume that most of the measures used to assess both sets of symptoms tap the broad mood and personality dimension of *negative affect,* which includes affective states such as distress, anger, fear, guilt, and worry (Clark et al., 1994; Watson et al., 1995a, 1995b; Watson, Gamez, & Simms, 2005). Depressed and anxious individuals cannot be differentiated on the basis of their high level of negative affect. But these researchers have also shown that anxiety and depression can be distinguished from one another on the basis of a second dimension of mood and personality known as positive affect, which includes affective states such as excitement, delight, interest, and pride. Depressed persons tend to be characterized by low levels of positive affect, but anxious individuals usually are not (with the exception of people with social phobia; Watson et al., 2005). That is, only depressed individuals show the signs of fatigue and lack of energy and enthusiasm characteristic of low positive affect. A number of investigators have also shown that some anxious people (especially panic patients), but not depressed people, tend to be characterized by high levels of yet another mood dimension known as *anxious hyperarousal,* symptoms of which include racing heart, trembling, dizziness, and shortness of breath. This tripartite model of anxiety and depression thus explains what features anxiety and depression share (high negative affect) and what features they differ on (low positive affect for depression and anxious hyperarousal for panic; Mineka et al., 1998). Each of the other anxiety disorders has its own separate and relatively unique component as well (Barlow, 2002a; Brown et al., 1998; Mineka et al., 1998).

Beck and D. A. Clark have presented evidence that anxiety and depression also differ somewhat in the kinds of cognitions the patients show (e.g., D. A. Clark, Beck, & Alford, 1999; D. A. Clark, Steer, & Beck, 1994; Steer et al., 1995). For example, cognitions about loss, failure, and hopelessness are more common in major depression and dysthymia than in panic disorder and generalized anxiety disorder (although they are elevated in all of these disorders). Threat-related cognitions were significantly elevated in panic disorder (but not generalized anxiety disorder) relative to major depression and dysthymia.

Several aspects of the comorbidity between anxiety and mood disorders at the diagnostic level raise interesting questions about what common and what distinct causal factors may exist. For example, there is usually a sequential relationship between the symptoms of anxiety and depression, both within an episode and between episodes. For example, Bowlby (1973, 1980) described a biphasic response to separation and loss in which agitation and anxiety are followed by despair and depression. And across a lifetime, individuals are more likely to experience an anxiety disorder first and a depressive disorder later (T. Brown et al., 2001; Merikangus et al., 2003; Mineka et al., 1998). There is also differential comorbidity between depression and the different anxiety disorders: Panic disorder, posttraumatic stress disorder, and obsessive-compulsive disorder are more likely to be accompanied by depression than, for example, is simple or social phobia (Brown et al., 2001; Kessler et al., 1996; Mineka et al., 1998).

Alloy, Mineka, and colleagues (1990; see also Mineka et al., 1998) proposed an expansion of the hopelessness model of depression to account for these and other features of comorbidity. In their helplessness/hopelessness model they proposed that anxiety and anxiety disorders are characterized by prominent feelings of helplessness. People with these disorders expect that they may be helpless in controlling important outcomes, but they also believe that future control might be possible and so are likely to experience increased arousal and anxiety and an intense scanning of the environment in efforts to gain control. If the person becomes convinced of his or her helplessness to control important outcomes but is still uncertain about whether the bad outcome will actually occur, a mixed anxiety/depression syndrome is likely to emerge. And finally, if the person is convinced not only that he or she is helpless but also that bad outcomes will occur, helplessness becomes hopelessness, and depression sets in. Alloy, Mineka, and colleagues (1990) show how this perspective can explain certain features of comorbidity between anxiety and depressive disorders. For example, the sequential relationship is explained by the fact that one is likely to feel helpless for some time before coming to feel totally hopeless. And some anxiety disorders may be more closely associated with depression precisely because the symptoms of the disorders themselves (for example, obsessive thoughts and compulsions, panic attacks and related agoraphobic avoidance, flashbacks, and nightmares, etc.) are so distressing and seemingly uncontrollable. These symptoms may firmly convince the individual of her or his helplessness, leading to the mixed anxiety/depressive diagnostic picture.

People without social support networks are more prone to depression when faced with major stressors. Depressed people also have smaller and less supportive social support networks while they are depressed and to some extent even after their depression has remitted.

individual often places others in the position of providing sympathy, support, and care. However, such positive reinforcement does not necessarily follow. Depressive behavior can, and over time frequently does, elicit negative feelings (sometimes including hostility) and rejection in other people, including strangers, roommates, and spouses (Coyne, 1976; Ingram et al., 1999; Joiner, 2002). Although these negative feelings may initially make the nondepressed person feel guilty, which leads to sympathy and support in the short term, ultimately a downwardly spiraling relationship usually results, making the depressed person feel worse (e.g., Joiner, 2002; Joiner & Metalsky, 1995). Social rejection may be especially likely if the depressed person engages in excessive reassurance seeking.

Marriage and Family Life Interpersonal aspects of depression have also been carefully studied in the context of marital and family relationships. A significant proportion of couples experiencing marital distress have at least one partner with clinical depression, and there is a high correlation between marital dissatisfaction and depression for both women and men (e.g., Beach & Jones, 2002; Whisman, Uebelacker, & Weinstock, 2004). In addition, marital distress spells a poor prognosis for a depressed spouse whose symptoms have remitted. That is, a person whose depression clears up is likely to relapse if he or she has an unsatisfying marriage (Butzlaff & Hooley, 1998; Hooley & Teasdale, 1989).

Marital distress and depression may co-occur because the depressed partner's behavior triggers negative affect in the spouse. Depressed individuals may also be so preoccupied with themselves that they are not very sensitive or responsive to the needs of their spouses. A recent review by Beach and Jones (2002) adapted Hammen's (1991) stress-generation model of depression to help explain the two-way relationship between marital discord and depression (that is, marital distress can lead to depression, and depression can lead to marital distress). As noted earlier, a significant amount of the stress that depressed individuals experience is somehow at least partially generated by their own behaviors, but this stress in turn also serves to exacerbate depressive symptoms. Developments in Research 7.3 on page 252 also discusses how depression all too often sets

7.3 Developments in Research

Depression and Marital Violence

A strong concordance exists between distressed adult relationships and the presence of a mood disorder in one or both partners (Beach & Jones, 2002; Fruzzetti, 1996). These forms of relationship distress may include the occurrence of violent abuse. It has long been known that mood-disordered persons have an enhanced risk for engaging in violence, including family violence. Until recently, however, virtually all of that enhanced risk was thought to be related to the lack of control and disinhibition associated with manic or hypomanic episodes. Continuing research developments, begun in the 1980s (e.g., Maiuro et al., 1988), increasingly called that view into question and implicated depressive disorders in the occurrence of much violence, specifically domestic violence.

Men who attack their partners violently—some women also attack men, but usually less violently (Jacobson et al., 1994; O'Leary, 2000)—commonly do so as a means of attempting, by inspiring fear in the partner, to control and change a situation they perceive as threatening to their "proprietary" assumptions about the partnership (e.g., Berns, Jacobson, & Gottman, 1999; Maiuro et al., 1988; Wilson & Daly, 1996). Despite appearances to the contrary, many of these men tend to be highly emotionally dependent on their partners, and they tolerate poorly any signs of a partner's autonomy. Their underlying sense of inadequacy fuels their desperate attempts to maintain control over the partnership and change their wives' behavior. Too often, the result is a violent attack (Murphy, Meyer, & O'Leary, 1994).

Many partnered men who experience marital distress and become depressed tend to be "unsuccessful," either chronically or in response to recent reversals of fortune. Self-perceived "failure," in terms of conventional male values such as providing for the economic needs of the family, is thus often a complicating factor (e.g., Pan, Neidig, & O'Leary, 1994; Vinokur, Price, & Caplan, 1996). Although these men frequently exhibit high levels of "rejection sensitivity," their behavior in fact invites rejection, which increases the likelihood of heightened relationship friction (Downey & Feldman, 1996) and thus the further development of depressive symptoms (Fruzzetti, 1996). In this process of escalating dysphoria, many men turn to alcohol or other disinhibiting drugs as a type of "self-medication" to reduce stress and relieve depression, thus making it even more likely that they will impulsively attempt a violent solution to end their acute despair (Leonard & Senchak, 1996; Pan, Neidig, & O'Leary, 1994). Like other dysfunctional reactions to a deteriorating relationship, this one, too, nearly always makes matters worse.

It is also important to recognize, however, that not all men who violently attack their partners are depressed. Indeed, a subset of these men show more general antisocial and violent behavior in other parts of their lives as well (e.g., Holtzworth-Munroe & Meehan, 2004). In addition, more general risk factors besides depression for partner abuse include traditional sex-role ideology, alcohol abuse, and illicit drug use (Stith et al., 2004).

The causal relationships among depression, marital distress, and familial violence thus appear to be mutually reinforcing and multidirectional in nature. In fact, the victims of physical abuse are themselves likely to become clinically depressed (Cascardi, O'Leary, & Schlee, 1999; Stith et al., 2004; Street et al., 2003), thus diminishing their ability to take effective action. Once these behaviors are established as a pattern, it becomes extremely difficult, even with professional help, to disentangle cause from effect and to restore mutual understanding, respect, trust, and effective nonviolent functioning. Unfortunately, DSM-IV-TR, which recognizes disorders as exclusively "within" individuals, provides no adequate diagnostic recognition of this common scenario.

Despite the difficulties of establishing primacy within the entangled causal pattern in abusive relationships, contemporary research suggests that there is often evidence of problematic early attachment relationships among the people involved. Deriving from the work of Bowlby (1980) in England, psychologists have in recent years developed apparently reliable and valid means of measuring adults' propensities for attachment, usually differentiating among three "levels" that have significant implications for adult relationships. A person with a secure attachment pattern comfortably "connects with" and engages others at optimal levels of intimacy and mutual autonomy. Insecure attachment patterns include the anxious-ambivalent pattern, which involves high intimacy needs mixed with anxiety and conflictual, unstable attachments, and the avoidant pattern, which involves an active distancing of the self from others. The general hypothesis advanced here is that partners with insecure attachment patterns, particularly the anxious-ambivalent variety, are at significantly increased risk for marital distress, depression, and domestic violence.

In support of this hypothesis, Woike, Osier, and Candela (1996) demonstrated a significantly high level of violent relationship imagery (male perpetrators, female victims) among anxiously attached male college students. Anxiously attached women in this study also had more violent imagery, specifically involving female victims, than did secure women or women who exhibited avoidant attachment. The import of such findings, however, may go beyond mere violent imagery. For example, one recent study found an overrepresentation of insecure attachment patterns in a sample of maritally distressed violent men (Babcock, Jacobson, et al., 2000).

the scene for marital violence—particularly of husbands against wives.

The effects of depression in one family member extend to children of all ages as well. Parental depression puts children at high risk for many problems, but especially for depression (Goodman & Gotlib, 1999; Murray et al., 1996). A skeptic might argue that such studies merely prove that these disorders are genetically transmitted. However, the evidence for genetic influences on childhood depression is much more mixed than the evidence for genetic influences on adult depression (Goodman & Gotlib, 1999). Moreover, many studies have documented the damaging effects of negative interactional patterns between depressed mothers and their children. For example, depressed mothers show more friction and have less playful, mutually rewarding interactions with their children (see Goodman & Gotlib, 1999; Murray & Cooper, 1997). They are also less sensitively attuned to their infants and less affirming of their infants' experiences (Murray et al., 1996). Furthermore, their young children are given multiple opportunities for observational learning of negative cognitions, depressive behavior, and depressed affect. Thus, although genetically determined vulnerability may be involved, psychosocial influences probably play a more decisive role (Goodman & Gotlib, 1999; Murray & Cooper, 1997).

In Review

- Summarize the major biological causal factors for unipolar depression, including hereditary, biochemical, neuroendocrinological, and neurophysiological factors.
- What is the role of stressful life events in unipolar depression, and what kinds of diatheses have been proposed to interact with them?
- Describe the following theories of depression: Beck's cognitive theory, the helplessness and hopelessness theories, and interpersonal theories.

Bipolar Disorders

Bipolar disorders are distinguished from unipolar disorders by the presence of manic or hypomanic symptoms. A person who experiences a manic episode has a markedly elevated, euphoric, and expansive mood, often interrupted by occasional outbursts of intense irritability or even violence—particularly when others refuse to go along with the manic person's wishes and schemes. These extreme moods must persist for at least a week for this diagnosis to be made. In addition, three or more additional symptoms must occur in the same time period. There must also be significant impairment of occupational and social functioning, and hospitalization is often necessary during manic episodes.

In milder forms, similar kinds of symptoms can lead to a diagnosis of **hypomanic episode,** in which a person experiences abnormally elevated, expansive, or irritable mood for at least 4 days. In addition, the person must have at least three other symptoms similar to those involved in mania but to a lesser degree (e.g., inflated self-esteem, decreased need for sleep, flights of ideas, pressured speech, etc.). Although the symptoms listed are the same for manic and hypomanic episodes, there is much less impairment in social and occupational functioning in hypomania, and hospitalization is not required.

Cyclothymic Disorder

It has long been recognized that some people are subject to cyclical mood changes less severe than the mood swings seen in bipolar disorder. These are the symptoms of the disorder known as **cyclothymic disorder.** In DSM-IV-TR, cyclothymia is defined as a less serious version of major bipolar disorder, minus certain extreme symptoms and psychotic features, such as delusions, and minus the marked impairment caused by full-blown manic or major depressive episodes.

In the depressed phase of cyclothymic disorder, a person's mood is dejected, and he or she experiences a distinct loss of interest or pleasure in customary activities and pastimes. In addition, the person may show other symptoms such as low energy, feelings of inadequacy, social withdrawal, and a pessimistic, brooding attitude. Essentially, the symptoms are similar to those in someone with dysthymia except without the duration criterion.

Symptoms of the hypomanic phase of cyclothymia are essentially the opposite of the symptoms of dysthymia. In this phase of the disorder, the person may become especially creative and productive because of increased physical and mental energy. There may be significant periods between episodes in which the person with cyclothymia functions in a relatively adaptive manner. For a diagnosis of cyclothymia, there must be at least a 2-year span during which there are numerous periods with hypomanic and depressed symptoms (1 year for adolescents and children), and the symptoms must cause clinically significant distress or impairment in functioning (although not as severe as in bipolar disorder). (See the DSM-IV-TR table, Criteria for Cyclothymic Disorder.) Because individuals with cyclothymia are at increased risk of later developing full-blown bipolar disorder (e.g., Akiskal & Pinto, 1999), DSM-IV-TR recommends that they be treated.

The following case illustrates cyclothymia.

DSM-IV-TR

Criteria for Cyclothymic Disorder

A. For at least 2 years, the presence of numerous periods with hypomanic symptoms and numerous periods with depressive symptoms that do not meet criteria for a Major Depressive Episode.

B. During the 2-year period, the person has not been without the symptoms of Criterion A for more than 2 months at a time.

C. No Major Depressive Episode, Manic Episode, or Mixed Episode has been present during the first 2 years of the disturbance.

D. The symptoms in Criterion A are not better accounted for by another disorder.

E. The symptoms cause clinically significant distress or impairment in functioning.

case STUDY

A Cyclothymic Car Salesman

A 29-year-old car salesman was referred by his current girlfriend, a psychiatric nurse, who suspected he had a mood disorder even though the patient was reluctant to admit that he might be a "moody" person. According to him, since the age of 14 he has experienced repeated alternating cycles that he terms "good times and bad times." During a "bad" period, usually lasting 4 to 7 days, he sleeps 10 to 14 hours daily [and] lacks energy, confidence, and motivation—"just vegetating," as he puts it. Often he abruptly shifts, characteristically upon waking up in the morning, to a 3- to-4-day stretch of overconfidence, heightened social awareness, promiscuity, and sharpened thinking—"things would flash in my mind." At such times he indulges in alcohol to enhance the experience, but also to help him sleep. Occasionally the "good" periods last 7 to 10 days but culminate in irritable and hostile outbursts, which often herald the transition back to another period of "bad" days....

In school, A's and B's alternated with C's and D's, with the result that the patient was considered a bright student whose performance was mediocre overall because of "unstable motivation." As a car salesman his performance has also been uneven, with "good days" canceling out the "bad days"; yet even during his "good days" he is sometimes perilously argumentative with customers and loses sales that appeared sure. Although considered a charming man in many social circles, he alienates friends when he is hostile and irritable.... (Spitzer et al., 2002, pp. 155–56)

Bipolar Disorders (I and II)

Although recurrent cycles of mania and melancholia were recognized as early as the sixth century, it remained for Kraepelin, in 1899, to introduce the term *manic-depressive insanity* and to clarify the clinical picture. Kraepelin described the disorder as a series of attacks of elation and depression, with periods of relative normality in between, and a generally favorable prognosis. Today DSM-IV-TR calls this illness bipolar disorder, although the term *manic-depressive illness* is still commonly used as well.

Bipolar I disorder is distinguished from major depressive disorder by at least one episode of *mania* or a **mixed episode.** A mixed episode is characterized by symptoms of both full-blown manic and major depressive episodes for at least 1 week, whether the symptoms are intermixed or alternate rapidly every few days. Such cases were once thought to be relatively rare but are increasingly being recognized as relatively common (e.g., Cassidy et al., 1998). Moreover, many patients in a manic episode have some symptoms of depressed mood, anxiety, guilt, and suicidal thoughts, even if these are not severe enough to qualify as a mixed episode. See the DSM-IV-TR table, Criteria for Bipolar I Disorder.

Even though a patient may be exhibiting only manic symptoms, it is assumed that a bipolar disorder exists and that a depressive episode will eventually occur. Thus there are no officially recognized "unipolar" manic or hypomanic counterparts to dysthymia or major depression. Although some researchers have noted the probable existence of a unipolar type of manic disorder (e.g., Kessler et al., 1997; Solomon, Leon, et al., 2003), critics of this diagnosis argue that such patients usually have bipolar relatives and may well have had mild depressions that went unrecognized (Winokur & Tsuang, 1996).

DSM-IV-TR

Criteria for Bipolar I Disorder

A. Presence (or history) of one or more Manic or Mixed Episodes (necessary for the diagnosis).

B. Presence (or history) of one or more Major Depressive Episodes (not necessary for the diagnosis).

C. The mood symptoms in Criteria A or B are not better accounted for by another disorder.

D. The symptoms cause clinically significant distress or impairment in functioning.

E. Specify if current or most recent episode is:
   (1) Hypomanic
   (2) Manic
   (3) Mixed
   (4) Depressive

The following case illustrates both phases of Bipolar I disorder:

case STUDY **Roller Coaster**

When Ernest Eaton's desperate wife finally got him to agree to a comprehensive inpatient evaluation, he was 37, unemployed, and had been essentially nonfunctional for several years. After a week during which he was partying all night and shopping all day, Mrs. Eaton said she would leave him if he did not check into a psychiatric hospital. The admitting psychiatrist found him to be a fast-talking, jovial, seductive man with no evidence of delusions or hallucinations.

Mr. Eaton's troubles began 7 years before when he . . . had a few months of mild, intermittent depressive symptoms, anxiety, fatigue, insomnia, and loss of appetite [but] within a few months he was back to his usual self. A few years later . . . after removal of [an asymptomatic] mass . . . Mr. Eaton noted dramatic mood changes. Twenty-five days of remarkable energy, hyperactivity, and euphoria were followed by 5 days of depression during which he slept a lot and felt that he could hardly move. This pattern of alternating periods of elation and depression, apparently with few "normal" days, repeated itself continuously over the following years.

During his energetic periods, Mr. Eaton was optimistic and self-confident, but short tempered and easily irritated. His judgment at work was erratic. He spent large sums of money on unnecessary and, for him, uncharacteristic purchases, such as a high-priced stereo system and several Doberman pinschers. He also had several impulsive sexual flings. During his depressed periods, he often stayed in bed all day because of fatigue, lack of motivation, and depressed mood. He felt guilty about the irresponsibilities and excesses of the previous several weeks. He stopped eating, bathing, and shaving. After several days of this withdrawal, Mr. Eaton would rise from bed one morning feeling better and, within 2 days, he would be back at work, often working feverishly, though ineffectively, to catch up on work he had let slide during his depressed periods. (Adapted from Spitzer et al., 2002, pp. 23–24.)

DSM-IV-TR also identifies a distinct form of bipolar disorder called **Bipolar II Disorder,** in which the person does not experience full-blown manic episodes but has experienced clear-cut hypomanic episodes, as well as major depressive episodes as in Bipolar I disorder (Akiskal & Benazzi, 2005). Bipolar II disorder is somewhat more common than Bipolar 1 disorder, and, when combined, estimates are that about 3 percent of the U.S. population will suffer from one or the other disorder (e.g., Kupfer, 2005). Bipolar II disorder evolves into Bipolar I disorder in only about 5 to 15 percent of cases, suggesting that they are distinct forms of the disorder (APA, 2000; Coryell, Endicott, et al., 1995).

Bipolar disorder, which occurs equally in males and females and usually starts in adolescence and young adulthood, is typically a recurrent disorder, with people experiencing single episodes extremely rarely (Winokur & Tsuang, 1996). In about two-thirds of cases, the manic episodes either immediately precede or immediately follow a depressive episode; in other cases, the manic and depressive episodes are separated by intervals of relatively normal functioning. Figure 7.6 illustrates the different patterns of manic, hypomanic, and depressive episodes that can be seen in bipolar disorders. Most patients with bipolar disorder experience periods of remission during which they are relatively symptom-free, but as many as 20 to 30 percent continue to experience significant impairment (occupational and/or interpersonal) and mood lability, and as many as 60 percent have chronic occupational or interpersonal problems between episodes. As with unipolar major depression, the recurrences can be seasonal in nature, in which case **bipolar disorder with a seasonal pattern** is diagnosed.

FEATURES OF BIPOLAR DISORDER The symptoms of the depressive episodes of bipolar disorder are usually clinically indistinguishable from those of unipolar major depressive disorder (Cuellar, Johnson, & Winters, 2005; Perris, 1992), although some studies report higher rates of psychomotor retardation, and atypical depressive symptoms such as oversleeping and/or overeating in the depressed phase of bipolar disorder (e.g., Ghaemi et al., 2004; Mitchell et al., 2001; Whybrow, 1997). Suicidal attempts are at least as common as in unipolar depression and probably higher.

Because a person who is depressed cannot be diagnosed as bipolar unless he or she has exhibited at least one manic episode in the past, many people with bipolar disorder whose initial episode or episodes are depressive are misdiagnosed at first, and possibly throughout their lives (for instance, if no manic episodes are observed or reported, or if they die before a manic episode is experienced). Averaging across studies, one review estimated that about 10 to 13 percent of people who have an initial major depressive episode will later have a manic or hypomanic episode and will be diagnosed at that time as having Bipolar I or II disorder (Akiskal et al., 1995; see also Coryell et al., 1995). One recent study has shown that people presenting initially with a major depressive disorder who have a history of creative achievements, professional instability, multiple marriages, and flamboyant behavior may be especially likely to be diagnosed later with Bipolar II disorder (Akiskal, 2005).

Misdiagnoses are unfortunate because there are somewhat different treatments of choice for unipolar and bipolar depression. Moreover, there is evidence that some

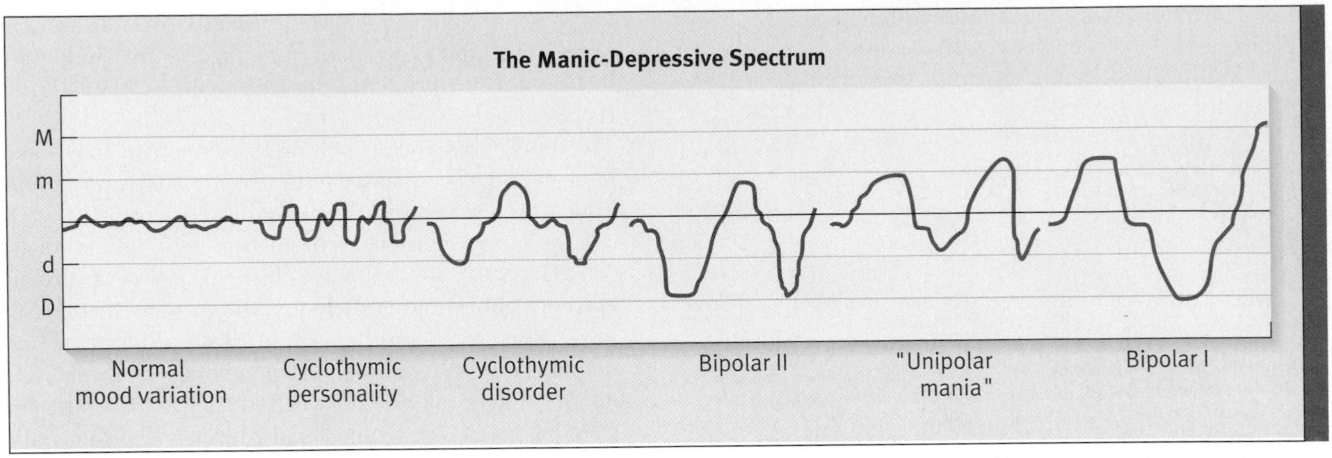

FIGURE 7.6

The Manic-Depressive Spectrum

There is a spectrum of bipolarity in moods. All of us have our ups and downs, which are indicated here as normal mood variation. People with a cyclothymic personality have more marked and regular mood swings, and people with cyclothymic disorder go through periods when they meet the criteria for dysthymia (except for the 2-year duration), and other periods when they meet the criteria for hypomania. People with Bipolar II disorder have periods of major depression and periods of hypomania. Unipolar mania is an extremely rare condition. Finally, people with Bipolar I disorder have periods of major depression and periods of mania. (Adapted from Goodwin & Jamison, 1990.)

Source: *From Frederick K. Goodwin and Kay R. Jamison,* Manic Depressive Illness. *Copyright © 1990 Oxford University Press, Inc. Used by permission of Oxford University Press, Inc.*

antidepressant drugs used to treat what is thought to be unipolar depression may actually precipitate manic episodes in patients who actually have as-yet-undetected bipolar disorder, thus worsening the course of the illness (Ghaemi, Hsu, Soldani, & Goodwin, 2003; Whybrow, 1997).

Many highly creative people are believed to have had bipolar disorder, going through periods of intense creative productivity during manic phases, and often through unproductive periods when clinically depressed. Two such individuals are the German composer Robert Schumann (1810–1856) and the British novelist Virginia Woolf (1882–1941). Schumann was committed to a mental asylum in 1854 and died there two years later. Woolf committed suicide by drowning herself.

On average, people with bipolar disorder suffer from more episodes during their lifetimes than do persons with unipolar disorder (although these episodes tend to be somewhat shorter, averaging 3 to 4 months; Angst & Sellaro, 2000). As many as 5 to 10 percent of persons with bipolar disorder experience at least four episodes (either manic or depressive) every year, a pattern known as **rapid cycling.** In fact, those who go through periods of rapid cycling usually experience many more than four episodes a year. Our case example of Robert Eaton (Roller Coaster) was diagnosed with Bipolar I disorder with rapid cycling. People who develop rapid cycling are more likely to be women, have an earlier average age of onset, and make more suicide attempts (Coryell, Solomon, et al., 2003). Rapid cycling is sometimes precipitated by taking certain kinds of antidepressants (Kilzieh & Akiskal, 1999; Whybrow, 1997). Fortunately, for many, rapid cycling is a temporary phenomenon and gradually disappears within about 2 years (Coryell et al., 1995; Coryell, Solomon, et al., 2003).

Overall, the probabilities of "full recovery" from bipolar disorder are discouraging even with the widespread use of mood-stabilizing medications such as lithium. One 10-year prospective study of over 200 patients found that 24 percent had relapsed within 6 months of recovery; 77 percent had had at least one new episode within 4 years of recovery; and 82 percent had relapsed within 7 years (Coryell et al., 1995). Another prospective study of 146 bipolar patients found that they experienced some symptoms (mostly subsyndromal) on an average of 47 percent of the weeks during the 13-year follow-up period. During the follow-up period, depressive symptoms were three times more common than manic or hypomanic symptoms (Judd et al., 2002; see also Judd, Shettler, et al., 2003). The long-term course of bipolar disorder is even more severe for patients who have comorbid substance abuse or dependence disorders (which is even more common than with unipolar disorders) (e.g., Levin & Hennessey, 2004).

In Review

- Describe the symptoms and clinical features of cyclothymia and bipolar disorder.
- Describe the typical course of Bipolar I and Bipolar II disorders.

Causal Factors in Bipolar Disorder

As for unipolar disorder, a host of causal factors for bipolar disorder have been posited over the past century. However, biological causal factors are clearly dominant, and the role of psychosocial causal factors has received significantly less attention.

Biological Causal Factors

GENETIC INFLUENCES There is a greater genetic contribution to bipolar disorder than to unipolar disorder. A summary of studies using refined diagnostic procedures suggests that about 8 to 9 percent of the first-degree relatives of a person with bipolar illness can be expected to have bipolar disorder relative to 1 percent in the general population (Katz & McGuffin, 1993; Plomin et al., 2001). The first-degree relatives of a person with bipolar disorder are also at elevated risk for unipolar major depression (especially atypical depression), although the reverse is not true (Akiskal & Benazzi, 2005).

Although family studies cannot by themselves establish a genetic basis for the disorder, results from early twin studies dating back to the 1950s also point to a genetic basis because the concordance rates for these disorders are much higher for identical than for fraternal twins. For example, one review of numerous twin studies found that the average concordance rate was about 60 percent for monozygotic twins and about 12 percent for dizygotic twins (Kelsoe, 1997). The best study to date (McGuffin et al., 2003) found that 67 percent of monozygotic twins with bipolar disorder had a co-twin who shared the diagnosis of bipolar or unipolar disorder (60 percent of these concordant co-twins had bipolar disorder, and 40 percent had unipolar disorder). The concordance rate in dizygotic twins was 19 percent. This and other studies suggest that genes account for about 80 to 90 percent of the variance in the tendency to develop (that is, the liability for) bipolar depression (Katz & McGuffin, 1993; McGuffin et al., 2003). This is higher than heritability estimates for unipolar disorder or any of the other major adult psychiatric disorders, including schizophrenia (Torrey et al., 1994).

The finding of elevated rates of both bipolar and unipolar forms of the disorder in the relatives of bipolars may be explained in several ways. One possibility is related to the idea that bipolar disorder may be a more severe form of the same underlying disorder as unipolar disorder. If this were the case, then the increased rate of unipolar disorder in relatives of patients with bipolar disorder would occur because bipolar is the more severe disorder—not all relatives have as severe a form of the disorder as the identified patient (Plomin et al., 2001). At least one good study, however, found no support for this hypothesis (McGuffin et al., 2003). Instead, their results suggested that about 70 percent of the genetic liability for mania is distinct from the genetic liability for depression. In other words, their results suggest that people with bipolar disorder are genetically susceptible to both depression and to mania, and that these susceptibilities are largely independent.

Efforts to locate the chromosomal site(s) of the implicated gene or genes in this genetic transmission of bipolar disorder suggest that they are polygenic. Although a great deal of research has been directed at identifying candidate genes through linkage analysis and association studies, no consistent support yet exists for any specific mode of genetic transmission of bipolar disorder, according to several recent comprehensive reviews (Potash & DePaulo, 2000; Tsuang, Taylor, & Faraone, 2004).

NEUROCHEMICAL FACTORS The early monoamine hypothesis for unipolar disorder was extended to bipolar disorder, the hypothesis being that if depression is caused by deficiencies of norepinephrine and/or serotonin, then perhaps mania is caused by excesses of these neurotransmitters. There is some evidence for increased norepinephrine activity during manic episodes and for lowered norepinephrine activity during depressive episodes (Manji & Lenox, 2000). However, serotonin activity appears to be low in both depressive and manic phases.

As noted earlier, norepinephrine, serotonin, and dopamine are all involved in regulating our mood states (Howland & Thase, 1999; Southwick et al., 2005). Evidence for the role of dopamine stems in part from research showing that increased dopaminergic activity in several brain areas may be related to manic symptoms of hyperactivity, grandiosity, and euphoria (Howland & Thase, 1999). High doses of drugs such as cocaine, which are known to stimulate dopamine, also produce manic-like behavior; in depression there appear to be decreases in both norepinephrine and dopamine functioning (Manji & Lenox, 2000). Thus disturbances in the balance of these neurotransmitters seem to be one of the keys to understanding this debilitating illness, which can send its victims on an emotional roller coaster.

One of the thorniest issues that must be addressed by any theory is how lithium, the most effective and widely prescribed drug used in the treatment of bipolar disorder, can stabilize individuals from both depressive and manic episodes. We know that lithium is closely related chemically to sodium and that sodium plays a key role in the passage of the neural impulse down an axon. Therefore, questions have been raised about whether bipolar patients have abnormalities in the way ions (such as sodium) are transported across the neural membranes. Research suggests that there is indeed some such abnormality in bipolar disorder (Goodwin & Jamison, 1990; Whybrow, 1997). One possibility is that lithium may substitute for sodium ions.

OTHER BIOLOGICAL CAUSAL FACTORS Some neurohormonal research on bipolar depression has focused on the hypothalamic-pituitary-adrenal axis. Cortisol levels are elevated in bipolar depression (as in unipolar depression), and they are also elevated during manic episodes. Similarly, bipolar depressed patients show evidence of abnormalities on the dexamethasone suppression test (DST), described earlier, at about the same rate as do unipolar depressed patients, and these abnormalities persist even when the patients have been fully remitted and asymptomatic for at least 4 weeks (e.g., Watson, Gallagher, et al., 2004). During a manic episode, however, their rate of DST abnormalities has generally (but not always) been found to be much lower (Manji & Lenox, 2000). Research has also focused on abnormalities of the hypothalamic-pituitary-thyroid axis because abnormalities of thyroid function are frequently accompanied by changes in mood. Many bipolar patients have subtle but significant abnormalities in the functioning of this axis, and administration of thyroid hormone often makes antidepressant drugs work better (Altshuler et al., 2001; Goodwin & Jamison, 1990). Moreover, thyroid hormone can also precipitate manic episodes in bipolar patients (Wehr & Goodwin, 1987).

With positron emission tomography (PET) scans, it has even proved possible to visualize variations in brain glucose metabolic rates in depressed and manic states. Several summaries of the evidence from studies using PET and other neuroimaging techniques show that, whereas blood flow to the left prefrontal cortex is reduced during depression, during mania it is reduced in the right frontal and temporal regions (Howland & Thase, 1999; Whybrow, 1997). During normal mood, blood flow across the two brain hemispheres is approximately equal. Thus there are shifting patterns of brain activity during mania and during depressed and normal moods.

Other neurophysiological findings from patients with bipolar disorder have shown both similarities and differences from patients with unipolar disorder and normal controls. For example, several recent reviews have summarized evidence that there are deficits in activity in the dorsolateral prefrontal cortex in bipolar disorder, which seem related to neuropsychological deficits that people with bipolar disorder have in problem solving, planning, working memory, shifting of attentional sets, and sustained attention on cognitive tasks (e.g., Haldane & Frangou, 2004; Malhi, Ivanovski, et al., 2004a). This is similar to what is seen in unipolar depression, as are deficits in the anterior cingulate cortex. However, structural imaging studies suggest that certain subcortical structures, including the basal ganglia and amygdala, are enlarged in bipolar disorder but reduced in size in unipolar depression. In other words, there appear to be more changes in subcortical structures in bipolar than in unipolar disorders (Malhi, Ivanovski, et al., 2004a). Studies using fMRI also find increased activation in bipolar patients in subcortical brain regions involved in emotional processing, such as the thalamus and amygdala, relative to unipolar patients and normals (Malhi, Lagopoulos, et al., 2004b).

There is considerable evidence regarding disturbances in biological rhythms such as circadian rhythms in bipolar disorder, even when symptoms have mostly remitted (e.g., Jones, Hare, & Evershed, 2005). During manic episodes, bipolar patients tend to sleep very little (seemingly by choice, not because of insomnia), and this is the most common symptom to occur prior to the onset of a manic episode (e.g., Jackson, Cavanagh, & Scott, 2003). During depressive episodes, they tend toward hypersomnia (too much sleep). Even between episodes people with bipolar disorder show substantial sleep difficulties, including high rates of insomnia (e.g., Harvey et al., 2005; Millar, Espie, & Scott, 2004). Bipolar disorder also sometimes shows a seasonal pattern the way unipolar disorder does, suggesting disturbances of seasonal biological rhythms, although these may be the result of circadian abnormalities in which the onset of the sleep-wake cycle is set ahead of the onset of other circadian rhythms. Given the cyclic nature of bipolar disorder itself, this focus on disturbances in biological rhythms holds promise for future integrative theories of the biological underpinnings of bipolar disorder. This is particularly true because bipolar patients seem especially sensitive to, and easily disturbed by, any changes in their daily cycles that require a resetting of their biological clocks (Jones et al., 2005; Whybrow, 1997).

Psychosocial Causal Factors

STRESSFUL LIFE EVENTS Stressful life events appear to be as important in precipitating bipolar depression as unipolar depression, and there is good evidence that stressful life events are often involved in precipitating manic episodes as well. One study also found that patients who experienced severe negative events took an average of three times longer to recover from manic, depressive, or mixed episodes than those without a severe negative event (395 versus 112 days; Johnson & Miller,

1997). Even minor negative events were found to increase time to recovery.

It has long been argued that as the illness unfolds, the manic and depressive episodes become more autonomous and do not usually seem to be precipitated by stressful events (e.g., Post, 1992). Some of these conclusions may be premature, however, given that most studies addressing this issue have relied on patients' memories of events before episodes, which may be unreliable (Johnson & Roberts, 1995). In several good prospective studies using more sophisticated stress measurement techniques, Ellicott, Hammen, and colleagues (1990; see also Hammen, 1995) did not find that stress played a less important role in precipitating episodes for people who had had more episodes of illness (Hammen, 1995; Swendsen et al., 1995). Indeed, one study even found that patients with more prior episodes were more likely to have episodes following major stressors than patients with fewer prior episodes (Hammen & Gitlin, 1997).

How might stressful life events operate to increase the chance of relapse? One hypothesized mechanism is through the destabilizing effects that stressful life events may have on critical biological rhythms. Although evidence in support of this idea is still preliminary, it appears to be a promising hypothesis, especially for manic episodes (e.g., Malkoff-Schwartz, Frank, et al., 1998).

OTHER PSYCHOLOGICAL FACTORS IN BIPOLAR DISORDER There is also some evidence that other social environmental variables may affect the course of bipolar disorder. For example, one recent study found that people with bipolar disorder who reported low social support showed more depressive recurrences over a 1-year follow-up, independent of the effects of stressful life events, which also predicted more recurrences (Cohen, Hammen, Henry, & Daley, 2004). There is also some evidence that personality and cognitive variables may interact with stressful life events in determining the likelihood of relapse. For example, two studies found that the personality variable neuroticism predicts increases in depressive symptoms in people with bipolar disorder, just as in unipolar disorder. Moreover, two personality variables associated with high levels of achievement striving and increased sensitivity to rewards in the environment predicted increases in manic symptoms (Lozano & Johnson, 2001; Meyer et al., 2001). Another study found that students with a pessimistic attributional style who also had negative life events showed an increase in depressive symptoms whether they were bipolar or unipolar depressives. Interestingly, however, the bipolar students who had a pessimistic attributional style and experienced negative life events also showed increases in manic symptoms at other points in time (Reilly-Harrington et al., 1999).

PSYCHODYNAMIC PERSPECTIVE According to psychodynamic theorists, manic reactions are an extreme defense against or reaction to depression. A contemporary reformulation of the early psychodynamic hypotheses was presented by Neale (1988), who argued that individuals with unstable self-esteem, along with unrealistic standards for what constitutes success, are at risk for bipolar disorder. Neale argued that the grandiose ideas that often occur during manic states may serve the purpose of defending against distressing thoughts (fueled by low self-esteem) by distracting the individual from them.

Several studies have provided some support for this view. For example, one study examined the reactions of actively manic patients, actively depressed (bipolar) patients, and normal controls on several self-esteem and cognitive tasks (Lyon, Startup, & Bentall, 1999). On overt self-report measures of self-esteem and attributional style, bipolar manic and bipolar depressed patients showed what might be expected from their overt mental and behavioral states: Manic patients, like the normal controls, seemed to show high self-esteem and an optimistic attributional style, whereas depressed patients showed low self-esteem and a pessimistic attributional style. However, when the manic patients were tested on indirect measures of attention, memory, and attributional style (where one would expect their psychological defenses not to be operating as they can with self-report measures), the manic patients showed patterns of responses just like the depressed patients and different from normal controls. For example, on an indirect test of attributional style, the manic patients showed evidence of a pessimistic rather than an optimistic attributional bias. These results, along with those of Winters and Neale (1985), provide some support for the idea that manic reactions may in part be a defense against underlying low self-esteem and depressive cognition.

Although the view of manic and depressive reactions as exaggerated defenses may seem plausible up to a point, it is difficult to account satisfactorily for the more extreme versions of these states without acknowledging biological causal factors. The effectiveness of biological treatment in alleviating severe manic and depressive episodes testifies to the importance of biological causal factors, although the importance of psychological treatments as adjuncts to medication has been increasingly recognized in recent years.

In Review

- Summarize the major biological causal factors for bipolar disorder, including hereditary, biochemical, and other biological factors.
- What role do psychological factors, including stressful life events, seem to play in bipolar disorder?

Sociocultural Factors Affecting Unipolar and Bipolar Disorders

In some cultures the concept of depression as we know it simply does not exist. For example, Australian aborigines who are "depressed" show none of the guilt and self-abnegation commonly seen in more "developed" countries. They also do not show suicidal tendencies, but instead are more likely to vent their hostilities onto others rather than onto themselves.

Research on the association of sociocultural factors with bipolar and unipolar mood disorders is discussed together because much of the research conducted in this area has not made clear-cut diagnostic distinctions between the two types of disorders. The prevalence of mood disorders seems to vary considerably among different societies: In some, mania is more frequent, whereas in others, depression is more common. However, it has been difficult to provide conclusive evidence for this because of various methodological problems, including widely differing diagnostic practices in different cultures, and because the symptoms of depression appear to vary considerably across cultures (Kaelber et al., 1995; Tsai & Chentsova-Dutton, 2002).

Cross-Cultural Differences in Depressive Symptoms

Although depression occurs in all cultures that have been studied, the form that it takes differs widely, as does its prevalence (e.g., Marsella, 1980; Tsai & Chentsova-Dutton, 2002). For example, in some non-Western cultures such as China and Japan where rates of depression are relatively low, many of the psychological symptoms of depression are often not present. Instead people tend to exhibit so-called somatic and vegetative manifestations such as sleep disturbance, loss of appetite, weight loss, and loss of sexual interest (Kleinman, 1986, 2004; Tsai & Chentsova-Dutton, 2002). The psychological components of depression that often seem to be missing (from a Western standpoint) are the feelings of guilt and self-recrimination that are so commonly seen in the "developed" countries (Kidson & Jones, 1968; Tsai & Chentsova-Dutton, 2002).

Several possible reasons for these symptom differences stem from Asian beliefs in the unity of the mind and body, a lack of expressiveness about emotions more generally, and the stigma attached to mental illness in these cultures (e.g., Kleinman, 2005; Tsai & Chentsova-Dutton, 2002). Another reason why guilt and negative thoughts about the self may be common in Western but not in Asian cultures is that Western cultures view the individual as independent and autonomous, so when failures occur, internal attributions are made. However, as countries like China have incorporated some Western values over the course of becoming increasingly industrialized and urbanized, the rates of depression have risen a good deal relative to several decades ago (e.g., Dennis, 2004; Zhou et al., 2000). Indeed, one recent study of adolescents from Hong Kong and the United States found levels of depressive symptoms and hopelessness to be higher in the adolescents from Hong Kong (Stewart, Kennard, et al., 2004).

Another example of symptom differences comes from several groups of Australian aborigines, among whom Kidson and Jones (1968) found not only an absence of guilt and self-recrimination in depressive reactions but also no attempted or actual suicide. In connection with the latter finding, they stated, "The absence of suicide can perhaps be explained as a consequence of strong fears of death and also because of the tendency to act out and project hostile impulses" (p. 415). That is, these groups of aborigines are more likely to vent their hostility onto others than onto themselves through suicide.

Another society relatively untouched by Western culture, where it is still very difficult to detect any sign of depression, is the Kaluli—a primitive tribe in New Guinea studied by Schieffelin (1985). Indeed, in his 3 years working with this tribe, Schieffelin identified only one case of depression, and it involved primarily physical complaints. A summary of Schieffelin's work by Seligman (1990) provides interesting suggestions on why this might be the case:

> Briefly, the Kaluli do not seem to have despair, hopelessness, depression, or suicide in the way we know it. What they do have is quite interesting. If you lose something valuable, such as your pig, you have a right to recompense. There are rituals (such as dancing and screaming at the neighbor who you think killed the pig) that are recognized by the society. When you demand recompense for loss, either the neighbor or the whole tribe takes note of your condition and usually recompenses you one way or another. The point I want to make here

is that reciprocity between the culture and the individual when loss occurs provides strong buffers against loss becoming helplessness and hopelessness. I want to suggest that a society that prevents loss from becoming hopelessness, and that prevents sadness from becoming despair, breaks up the process of depression. Societies that promote, as ours does, the transition from loss to helplessness to hopelessness, promote depression. (Seligman, 1990, pp. 4–5)

Cross-Cultural Differences in Prevalence

Prevalence rates for depression (whether expressed primarily through somatic or psychological symptoms) vary a great deal across countries, as revealed by many epidemiological studies. (See Figure 7.7.) For example, in Taiwan the lifetime prevalence has been estimated at 1.5 percent, whereas in the United States and Lebanon it has been estimated at 17 to 19 percent (Tsai & Chentsova-Dutton, 2002). The reasons for such wide variation are undoubtedly very complex, and much work remains to be done before we fully understand them. The ideas that are being explored include different levels of important psychosocial risk variables in different cultures and different levels of stress. For example, there appear to be cross-cultural differences in hypothesized risk variables such as pessimistic attributional style, although how these differences might translate into different rates of depression is unclear because we do not yet know whether the same risk variables are operative in different cultures.

Demographic Differences in the United States

In our own society, the role of sociocultural factors in mood disorders is also evident. The three large epidemiological studies conducted in the United States since the early 1980s did not find any large racial differences. However, in each study the prevalence was slightly lower among African-Americans than among European White Americans. The rates for Hispanics fell in between the other two in the first two studies (e.g., Regier et al., 1993), but in the more recent National Comorbidity Survey-Replication study (Kessler et al., 2005b) the prevalence rates among European White Americans and Hispanics were comparable.

Other research indicates that rates of unipolar depression are inversely related to socioeconomic status; that is, higher rates occur in lower socioeconomic groups (e.g., Kessler et al., 2005). This may well be because low SES leads to adversity and life stress (Dohrenwend, 2000; Monroe & Hadjiyannakis, 2002). However, for bipolar disorder the findings are the opposite: A number of studies show that bipolar disorder is more common in the higher socioeconomic classes (see Goodwin & Jamison, 1990). Moreover, some studies show that individuals with bipolar disorder tend to have more education and that they come, on average, from families with higher socioeconomic status than those with unipolar depression (e.g., Coryell et al., 1989). Some have suggested that this association of bipolar disorder with higher socioeconomic status might come about because some of the personality and behavioral correlates

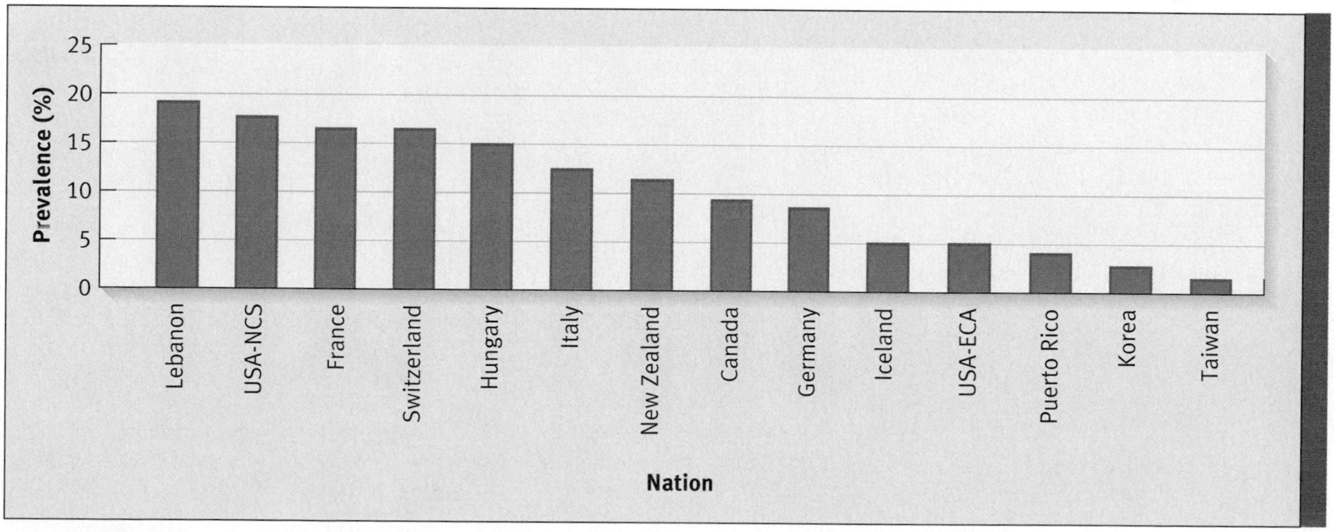

FIGURE 7.7

Prevalence Rates for Depression Across Several Nations

USA-NCS, United States according to the National Comorbidity Study; USA-ECA, United States according to Epidemiological Catchment Area Study.

Source: *Tsai, J. L., and Chentsova, Dalton, Y. "Understanding depression across cultures." In I. H. Gotlib and C. L. Hammen (Eds.),* Handbook of Depression, *p. 471. The Guilford Press © 2002. Reprinted with permission.*

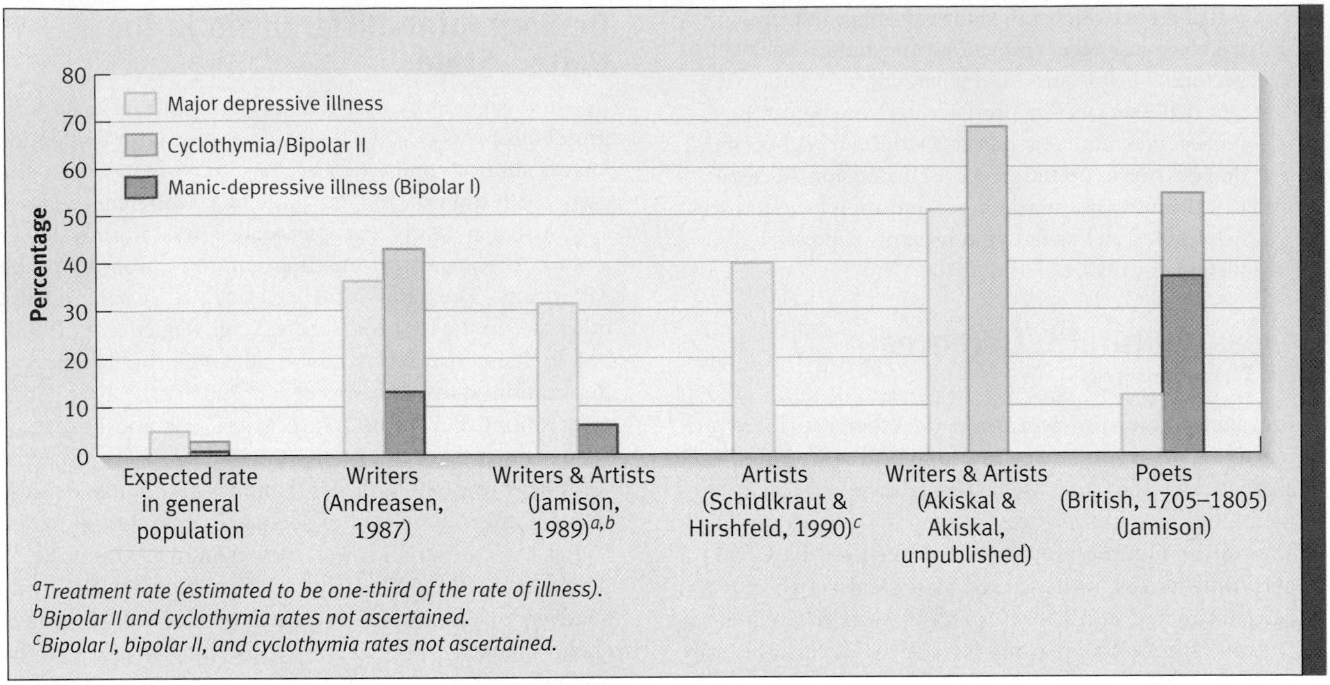

FIGURE 7.8

Rates of Mood Disorders in Writers and Artists

Although it is difficult to determine a reliable diagnosis of influential writers, poets, and artists (many of whom are long ago deceased), a number of psychological historians have compiled figures such as these, which clearly indicate that such individuals are far more likely than the general population to have had a unipolar or bipolar mood disorder. (Adapted from Jamison, 1993.)

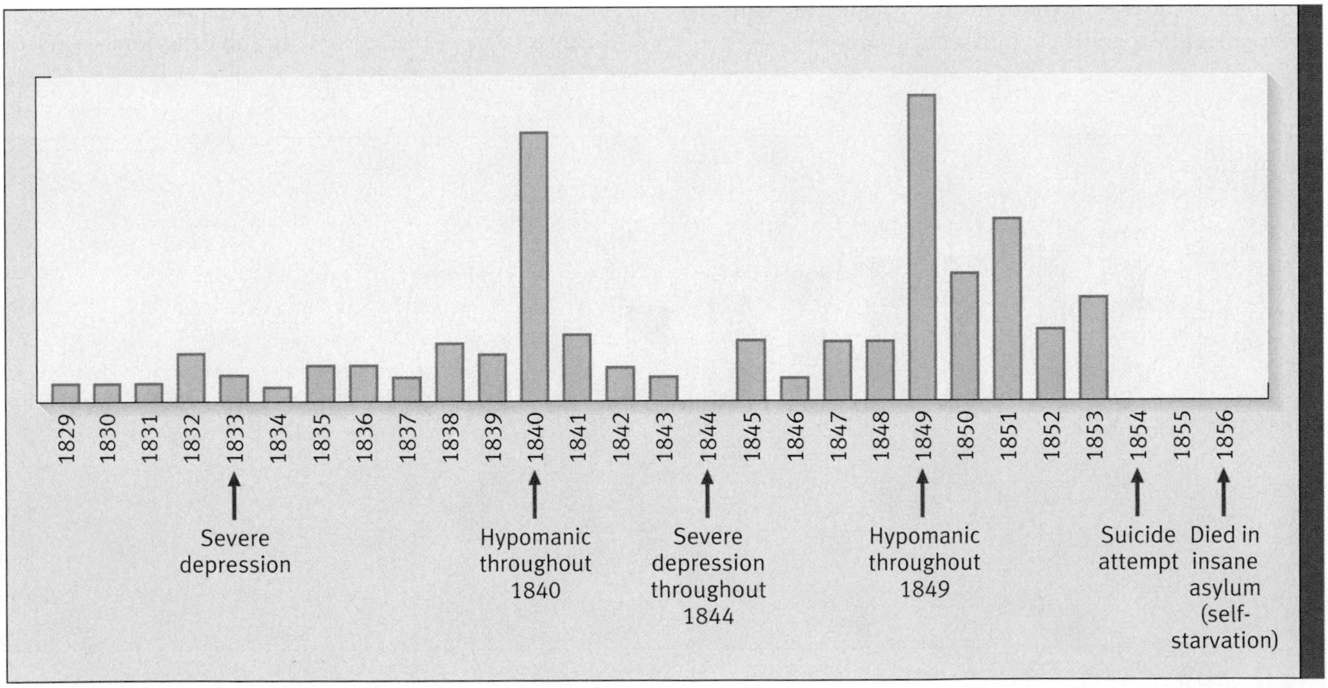

FIGURE 7.9

Robert Schumann's Work: Number of Compositions by Year

Number of Robert Schumann's compositions by year as they covaried with manic and depressive phases of his bipolar disorder. (Adapted from Jamison, 1993.)

Source: *Adapted from E. Slater and A. Meyer, "Contributions to a Pathography of the Musicians: Robert Schumann." In* Confinia Psychiatrica, *2 (1959), pp. 65–94. Reprinted by permission of S. Karger AG, Basel, Switzerland.*

of bipolar illness, at least in hypomanic phases (such as outgoingness, increased energy, and increased productivity), may lead to increased achievement and accomplishment (Goodwin & Jamison, 1990; Jamison, 1993; Whybrow, 1997).

These ideas about personality and behavioral correlates of mood disorders leading to increased accomplishments in the arts are consistent with a good deal of evidence (see Figure 7.8) that both unipolar and bipolar disorder, but especially bipolar disorder, occur with alarming frequency in poets, writers, composers, and artists (Jamison, 1993). Jamison has also documented for a number of such famous creative individuals how their periods of productivity covary with the manic, or hypomanic, and depressive phases of their illnesses (see Figure 7.9). One possible hypothesis to explain this relationship is that mania or hypomania actually facilitates the creative process, and/or that the intense negative emotional experiences of depression provide material for creative activity. A recent study of the eminent nineteenth-century American poet Emily Dickinson provides support for the latter part of this hypothesis—that is, evidence supports the idea that Dickinson's painful experiences with panic disorder and depression provided ideas for her especially high-quality work during those times. However, a detailed analysis of her hypomanic periods suggests that her hypomanic symptoms increased her motivation and output, but not her creativity per se (Ramey & Weisberg, 2004).

In Review

- What kinds of cross-cultural differences are there in depressive symptoms and what kinds of cross-cultural factors influence the prevalence of unipolar depression?
- What are some of the basic demographic differences in the United States influencing rates of unipolar and bipolar disorders?

Treatments and Outcomes

Many patients who suffer from mood disorders (especially unipolar disorder) never seek treatment, and without formal treatment, the great majority of manic and depressed patients will recover (often only temporarily) within less than a year. However, given the wide variety of treatments that are available today, and given the enormous amount of personal suffering and lost productivity that depressed and manic individuals endure, more and more people who experience these disorders are seeking treatment. This is happening in an era where there is greatly increased public awareness of the availability of effective treatments and during a time where significantly less stigma is associated with experiencing a mood disorder. Nevertheless, results from the recently completed National Comorbidity Survey-Replication study showed that only about 40 percent of people with mood disorders receive minimally adequate treatment, with the other 60 percent receiving no treatment or inadequate care (Wang, Lane, et al., 2005).

Pharmacotherapy

Antidepressant, mood-stabilizing, and antipsychotic drugs are all used in the treatment of unipolar and bipolar disorders (see Chapter 17 for a description of how these drugs work). The first category of antidepressant medications was developed in the 1950s; these medications are known as *monoamine oxidase inhibitors (MAOIs)* because they inhibit the action of monoamine oxidase—the enzyme responsible for the breakdown of norepinephrine and serotonin once released. The MAOIs can be quite effective in treating depression—especially atypical depression—but they can have potentially dangerous, even sometimes fatal, side effects if certain foods rich in the amino acid tyramine are consumed (e.g., red wine, beer, aged cheese, salami) and so are not used very often today unless other classes of medication have failed.

For most moderately to seriously depressed patients, including those with dysthymia (Kocsis et al., 1997), the drug treatment of choice since the early 1960s until about 1990 was one of the standard antidepressants (called *tricyclic antidepressants* because of their chemical structure), such as imipramine, which are known to increase neurotransmission of the monoamines (primarily norepinephrine and serotonin) (Hollon, Thase, Markowitz, 2002b; Nemeroff & Schatzberg, 2002). The efficacy of the tricyclics in significantly reducing depressive symptoms has been demonstrated in hundreds of studies where the response of depressed patients given these drugs has been compared with the response of patients given a placebo. Unfortunately, however, only about 50 percent show what is considered clinically significant improvement, and many of these patients still have significant residual depressive symptoms. Fortunately, about 50 percent of those who do not respond to an initial trial of medication will show a clinically significant response when switched to a different antidepressant or to a combination of medications (Hollon et al., 2002b).

Unfortunately, the tricyclics have unpleasant side effects for some people (dry mouth, constipation, sexual dysfunction, and weight gain may occur), and many patients do not continue long enough with the drug for it to have its antidepressant effect. In addition, because these drugs are highly toxic when taken in large doses, there is some risk in prescribing them for suicidal patients, who might use them for an overdose. (See also Chapter 17.)

Primarily because of the side effects and toxicity of tricyclics, physicians have increasingly chosen to prescribe one of the antidepressants from the *selective serotonin reuptake inhibitors (SSRIs).* These SSRI medications are generally no more effective than the tricyclics; indeed some findings suggest that the tricyclics are more effective than SSRIs for severe depression. However, the SSRIs tend to have many fewer side effects and are better tolerated by patients, as well as being less toxic in large doses. The primary negative side effects of the SSRIs are problems with orgasm and lowered interest in sexual activity, although insomnia, increased physical agitation, and gastrointestinal distress also occur in some patients.

Three of these medications—fluoxetine, sertraline, and paroxetine (Prozac, Zoloft, and Paxil, respectively)—are now extremely popular among physicians in various specialties and were 3 of the 11 most prescribed drugs of any type in 2000 (Gitlin, 2002). SSRIs are used not only to treat significant depression but also for people with mild depressive symptoms (Gitlin, 2002). Many mental health professionals believe that prescriptions for SSRIs are being written for these milder cases at an excessive rate. Prescribing drugs to essentially healthy people merely because the drugs make them feel more energetic, outgoing, and productive raises many ethical questions. These issues are considered further in The World Around Us 17.1 (Chapter 17).

In the past decade, several new atypical antidepressants (neither tricyclics nor SSRIs) have also become increasingly popular, and each has its own advantages. For example, bupropion (Wellbutrin) does not have as many side effects (especially sexual side effects) as the SSRIs and, because of its activating effects, is particularly good for depressions with significant weight gain, loss of energy, and oversleeping. In addition, venlafaxine (Effexor) seems superior to the SSRIs in the treatment of severe or chronic depression, although the profile of side effects is similar to that for the SSRIs. Nefazadone (Serzone) and mirtazapine (Remeron) are two other atypical antidepressants that have also been shown to be effective (see Chapter 17). (See Gitlin, 2002, for discussion of other newer medications.)

THE COURSE OF TREATMENT WITH ANTIDEPRESSANT DRUGS Unfortunately, antidepressant drugs usually require at least 3 to 5 weeks to take effect. Generally, if there are no signs of improvement after about 6 weeks, physicians should try a new medication, because about 50 percent of those who do not respond to the first drug prescribed do respond to a second one (Hollon et al., 2002b). Also, discontinuing the drugs when symptoms have remitted may result in relapse. Recall that the natural course of an untreated depressive episode is typically 6 to 9 months. Thus, when depressed patients take drugs for 3 to 4 months and then stop because they are feeling better, they are likely to relapse because the underlying depressive episode is actually still present, and only its symptomatic expression has been suppressed (Gitlin, 2002; Hollon et al., 2002b, 2006). Because depression tends to be a recurrent disorder, physicians have increasingly recommended that patients continue for very long periods of time on the drugs (ideally at the same dose) in order to prevent recurrence. Thus, these medications can often be effective in prevention, as well as treatment, for patients subject to recurrent episodes (Gitlin, 2002; Hollon et al., 2002b; see also Chapter 17). Nevertheless one recent study found that 25 percent of patients receiving medication during the maintenance phase of treatment showed recurrence of major depression even while on drugs (e.g., Solomon, Leon, et al., 2005). Other studies have indicated that patients showing even a few residual symptoms are most likely to relapse, indicating the importance of trying to treat the patient to full remission of symptoms (e.g., Keller, 2004).

LITHIUM AND OTHER MOOD-STABILIZING DRUGS Lithium therapy has now become widely used as a mood stabilizer in the treatment of both depressive and manic episodes of bipolar disorder. The term *mood stabilizer* is often used to describe lithium and related drugs because they have both antimanic and antidepressant effects—that is, they exert mood-stabilizing effects in either direction. Lithium has been more widely studied as a treatment of manic episodes than of depressive episodes, and estimates are that about three-quarters of manic patients show at least partial improvement. In the treatment of bipolar depression, lithium may be no more effective than traditional antidepressants (study results are inconsistent), and about three-quarters show at least partial improvement (Keck & McElroy, 2002b). However, treatment with antidepressants is associated with some risk of precipitating manic episodes or rapid cycling (e.g., Gitlin, 2002).

Lithium is also often effective in preventing cycling between manic and depressive episodes (although not necessarily for patients with rapid cycling), and bipolar patients are frequently maintained on lithium therapy over long time periods, even when not manic or depressed, simply to prevent new episodes. Although early studies indicated that lithium was quite effective in preventing repeated bipolar attacks, more recently several large studies have found that only slightly more than one-third of patients maintained on lithium remained free of an episode over a 5-year follow-up period. Nevertheless, maintenance on lithium does clearly lead to having fewer episodes than are experienced by patients who discontinue their medication. In a quantitative study of patients discontinuing medication, the risk of having a new episode was 28 times higher per month when not on medication than when on medication (Keck & McElroy, 2002b; Nemeroff & Schatzberg, 1998).

Lithium therapy has some unpleasant side effects such as lethargy, decreased motor coordination, and gastrointestinal difficulties in some patients. Long-term use of lithium is sometimes associated with kidney malfunction and sometimes permanent kidney damage (Gitlin, 1996;

Goodwin & Jamison, 1990). Not surprisingly, these side effects, combined with the fact that many bipolar patients seem to miss the highs and the abundance of energy associated with their hypomanic and manic episodes, sometimes create problems with compliance in taking the drug (see Chapter 17).

In the past several decades, evidence has emerged for the usefulness of another category of drugs known as the *anticonvulsants* (such as carbamazepine, divalproex, and valproate) in the treatment of bipolar disorder (Keck & McElroy, 2002a). These drugs are often effective in patients who do not respond well to lithium or who develop unacceptable side effects from it (Nemeroff & Schatzberg, 1998). However, a number of studies have indicated that risk for attempted and completed suicide was nearly two to three times higher for patients on anticonvulsant medications than for those on lithium (Goodwin et al., 2003), suggesting one major advantage of giving lithium to patients who can tolerate its side effects. Both bipolar and unipolar patients who show signs of psychosis (hallucinations and delusions) may also receive treatments with antipsychotic medications (see Chapters 14 and 17) in conjunction with their antidepressant or mood-stabilizing drugs (Keck & McElroy, 2002b; Rothschild et al., 2004).

Alternative Biological Treatments

ELECTROCONVULSIVE THERAPY Because antidepressants often take 3 to 4 weeks to produce significant improvement, electroconvulsive therapy (ECT) is often used with severely depressed patients (especially among the elderly) who may present an immediate and serious suicidal risk, including those with psychotic or melancholic features (Gitlin, 2002; Hollon et al., 2002b). It is also used in patients who cannot take antidepressant medications or who are otherwise resistant to medications (e.g., Mathew, Amiel, & Sackeim, 2005; Niederehe & Schneider, 1998). When selection criteria for this form of treatment are carefully observed, a complete remission of symptoms occurs for many after about 6 to 12 treatments (with treatments administered about every other day). This means that a majority of severely depressed patients can be vastly better in 2 to 4 weeks (Hollon et al., 2002b; Mathew et al., 2005). The treatments, which induce seizures, are delivered under general anesthesia and with muscle relaxants. The most common immediate side effect is confusion, although varying levels of transient amnesia in some cases may last for several months. Maintenance dosages of an antidepressant and a mood-stabilizing drug such as lithium are then ordinarily used to maintain the treatment gains achieved, until the depression has run its course (Mathew et al., 2005; Sackeim et al., 2001). ECT is also very useful in the treatment of manic episodes; reviews of the evidence suggest that it is associated with remission or marked improvement in 80 percent of manic patients (Gitlin, 1996; Mukherjee, Sackeim, & Schnur, 1994). Maintenance on mood-stabilizing drugs following ECT is usually required to prevent relapse (see also Chapter 17).

TRANSCRANIAL MAGNETIC STIMULATION (TMS) Although transcranial magnetic stimulation has been available as an alternative biological treatment for some time now, it has only recently begun to receive a good deal of attention. TMS is a noninvasive technique allowing focal stimulation of the brain in patients who are awake. Brief but intense pulsating magnetic fields that induce electrical activity in certain parts of the cortex are delivered (Janicak et al., 2005). The procedure is painless, and thousands of stimulations are delivered in each treatment session. Treatment usually occurs 5 days a week for 2 to 6 weeks. Although not all studies have found TMS to be effective in treating depression (see Couturier, 2005, for one review), many studies have shown it to be quite effective—indeed quite comparable to unilateral ECT and antidepressant medications in some studies (Janicak et al., 2005; Schulze-Rauschenbach et al., 2005). Moreover, TMS has advantages over ECT in that cognitive performance and memory problems are not affected adversely and sometimes even improve, relative to ECT where memory-recall deficits are common (Schulze-Rauschenbach et al., 2005).

BRIGHT LIGHT THERAPY In the past decade an alternative nonpharmacological biological method has received increasing attention—bright light therapy. This was originally used in the treatment of seasonal affective disorder, but it has now been shown to be effective in nonseasonal depressions as well (see Golden et al., 2005, for a quantitative review).

Psychotherapy

There are several forms of specialized psychotherapy, developed since the 1970s, that have proved effective in the treatment of unipolar depression, and the magnitude of improvement of the best of these is approximately equivalent to that observed with medications. Considerable evidence also suggests that these same forms of psychotherapy for depression, alone or in combination with drugs, significantly decrease the likelihood of relapse within a 2-year follow-up period (Hollon et al., 2002b; Hollon et al., 2005). Other specialized treatments have been developed to address the problems of people (and their families) with bipolar disorder.

COGNITIVE-BEHAVIORAL AND BEHAVIORAL ACTIVATION THERAPY One of the two best-known psychotherapies for unipolar depression with documented effectiveness is cognitive-behavioral therapy (CBT), developed by Beck and colleagues (Beck et al., 1979; Clark, Beck, & Alford, 1999). It is a relatively brief form of treatment (usually 10 to 20 sessions) that focuses on here-and-now problems rather than on the more remote causal issues that psychodynamic psychotherapy often addresses. For example, cognitive-behavioral therapy consists of highly structured, systematic attempts to teach people with unipolar depression to evaluate their beliefs and negative automatic thoughts systematically. They are also taught to identify and correct their biases or distortions in information processing and to uncover and challenge their underlying depressogenic assumptions. Cognitive therapy relies heavily on an empirical approach in that patients are taught to treat their beliefs as hypotheses that can be tested through the use of behavioral experiments.

One example of challenging a negative automatic thought through a behavioral experiment can be seen in the following interchange between a cognitive therapist and a depressed patient.

case STUDY **Therapy Session**

"My Husband Doesn't Love Me Any More"

PATIENT: My husband doesn't love me any more.

THERAPIST: That must be a very distressing thought. What makes you think that he doesn't love you?

PATIENT: Well, when he comes in in the evening, he never wants to talk to me. He just wants to sit and watch TV. Then he goes straight off to bed.

THERAPIST: OK. Now, is there any evidence, anything he does, that goes against the idea that he doesn't love you?

PATIENT: I can't think of any. Well, no, wait a minute. Actually it was my birthday a couple of weeks ago, and he gave me a watch which is really lovely. I'd seen them advertised and mentioned I liked it, and he took notice and went and got me one.

THERAPIST: Right. Now how does that fit with the idea that he doesn't love you?

PATIENT: Well, I suppose it doesn't really, does it? But then why is he like that in the evening?

THERAPIST: I suppose him not loving you any more is one possible reason. Are there any other possible reasons?

PATIENT: Well, he has been working very hard lately. I mean, he's late home most nights, and he had to go in to the office at the weekend. So I suppose it could be that.

THERAPIST: It could, couldn't it? How could you find out if that's it?

PATIENT: Well, I could say I've noticed how tired he looks and ask him how he's feeling and how the work's going. I haven't done that. I've just been getting annoyed because he doesn't pay any attention to me.

THERAPIST: That sounds like an excellent idea. How would you like to make that a homework task for this week? (From Fennell, 1989)

The usefulness of cognitive therapy has been amply documented in dozens of studies, including several studies on unipolar depressed inpatients and on patients diagnosed with depression with melancholic features (Hollon et al., 2002a, 2002b, 2006). When compared with pharmacotherapy, it is at least as effective when delivered by well-trained cognitive therapists. It also seems to have a special advantage in preventing relapse, similar to that obtained by staying on medication. Moreover, evidence is beginning to accumulate that it can prevent recurrence several years following the episode when the treatment occurred. When compared with pharmacotherapy, it seems to be at least as effective (DeRubeis, 1997; Hollon et al., 2002a, 2002b). However, some recent interesting brain-imaging studies have shown that the biological changes in certain brain areas that occur following effective treatment with cognitive therapy versus medications are somewhat different, suggesting that the mechanisms through which they work are also different (e.g., Goldapple et al., 2004).

Whether cognitive therapy is as effective as medication in the treatment of severe unipolar depression has been the more controversial question. However, recent evidence suggests that CBT and medications are also equally effective in the treatment of severe depression (DeRubeis et al., 1999; Hollon et al., 2002a, 2002b). For example, a recent two-site study of moderate to severe depression found that 58 percent responded to either cognitive therapy or to medication (DeRubeis, Hollon, et al., 2005). However, by the end of the 2-year follow-up when all cognitive therapy and medications had been discontinued for 1 year, only 25 percent of patients treated with cognitive therapy had had a relapse versus 50 percent in the medication group (a highly significant difference) (Hollon, DeRubeis, et al., 2005). (See Figure 7.10.)

A relatively new and promising treatment for unipolar depression is called *behavioral activation treatment.* This treatment approach focuses intensively on getting patients to become more active and engaged with their environment and with their interpersonal relationships. These techniques include scheduling daily activities and rating pleasure and mastery while engaging in them, exploring alternative behaviors to reach goals, and role-playing to address specific deficits. Traditional cognitive therapy attends to these same issues, but to a lesser extent. Behavioral activation treatment, by contrast, does not

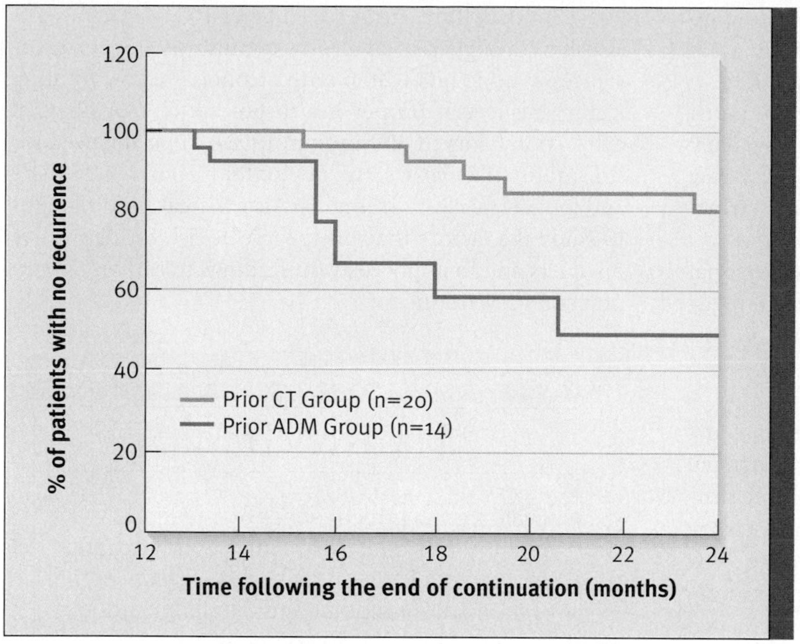

FIGURE 7.10

ADM indicates antidepressant medication; CT, cognitive therapy.

Source: *From "Prevention of Relapse Following Cognitive Therapy vs. Medications in Moderate to Severe Depression," by Hollon, S. D., DeRubeis, R. J., Shelton, R. C., et al.,* Arch Gen Psychiatry/*Vol. 62, no. 4, April 2005, pp. 417–426. © 2005 American Medical Association. Reprinted with permission.*

focus on implementing cognitive changes. Early results have been very promising, suggesting it may be as effective as more traditional cognitive therapies (Jacobson, Martell, & Dimidjian, 2001). Indeed, one very recent study found that moderately to severely depressed patients who received behavioral activation treatment did as well as those on medication and even slightly better than those who received cognitive therapy (Dimidjian, Hollon, et al., submitted). Moreover, the effects of behavioral activation treatment seem to be as enduring as those of cognitive therapy (and more than medications) (Hollon, Stewart, & Strunk, 2006). Because it is easier to train therapists to administer behavioral activation treatment than cognitive therapy, it seems likely that there will be increased attention paid to this relatively new treatment in the coming years.

Although the vast majority of research on CBT has focused on unipolar depression, recently there have been indications that a modified form of CBT may be very useful, in combination with medication, in the treatment of bipolar disorder as well (Craighead, Miklowitz, Frank, & Vajk, 2002; Lam et al., 2003, 2005).

Another variant on cognitive therapy, called *mindfulness-based cognitive therapy,* has been developed in recent years to be used in people with highly recurrent depression who have been treated with medication in order to help prevent further recurrences (e.g., Segal, Williams, & Teasdale, 2002; Teasdale, 2004). The logic of this treatment is based on findings that people with recurrent depression are likely to have negative thinking patterns activated when they are simply in a depressed mood. Perhaps rather than trying to alter the content of their negative thinking as in traditional cognitive therapy, it might be more useful to change the way in which people relate to their thoughts, feelings, and bodily sensations. This group treatment involves training in mindfulness meditation techniques aimed at developing patients' awareness of their unwanted thoughts and feelings and sensations so that they no longer automatically try to avoid them, but rather learn to accept them for what they are—simply thoughts occurring in the moment rather than a reflection of reality. For people who have had three or more recurrences of depression and have been treated with antidepressant medications, this form of treatment has been shown in at least two major studies to be very effective in reducing further recurrences (e.g., Ma & Teasdale, 2004; Teasdale, Segal, et al., 2000).

INTERPERSONAL THERAPY The *interpersonal therapy (IPT)* approach has not yet been subjected to as extensive an evaluation as cognitive-behavioral therapy, nor is it as widely available. However, the studies that have been completed strongly support its effectiveness for treating unipolar depression (see de Mello, Feijo, et al., 2005, for a quantitative review). Indeed, interpersonal therapy seems to be about as effective as medications or cognitive-behavioral treatment (Hollon et al., 2002b; Weissman & Markowitz, 2002). This IPT approach focuses on current relationship issues, trying to help the person understand and change maladaptive interaction patterns (Gillies, 2001). Interpersonal therapy can also be useful in long-term follow-up for individuals with severe recurrent unipolar depression (Frank et al., 1990; Weissman & Markowitz, 2002). Patients who received continued treatment with IPT once a month or who received continued medication were much less likely to have a recurrence than those maintained on a placebo over a 3-year follow-up period (although those maintained on medication were even less likely to relapse than those with monthly IPT).

In addition, IPT has been adapted for treatment of bipolar disorder by adding a focus on stabilizing daily social rhythms that, if they become destabilized, may play a role in precipitating bipolar episodes. In this new treatment, called *interpersonal and social rhythm therapy,* patients are taught to recognize the effect of interpersonal events on their social and circadian rhythms and to regularize these rhythms. As an adjunct to medication, this treatment seems promising (Craighead et al., 2002).

FAMILY AND MARITAL THERAPY Of course, in any treatment program, it is important to deal with unusual stressors in a patient's life, because an unfavorable life situation may lead to a recurrence of the depression and may necessitate longer treatment. This point has been well established in studies indicating that relapse in unipolar and bipolar disorders, as in schizophrenia, is correlated with certain noxious elements in family life (Butzlaff & Hooley, 1998; Hooley & Hiller, 2001). Behavior by a spouse that can be interpreted by a former patient as criticism seems especially likely to produce depression relapse. For example, for bipolar disorder, some types of family interventions directed at reducing the level of expressed emotion or hostility, and at increasing the information available to the family about how to cope with the disorder, have been found to be very useful in preventing relapse in these situations (e.g., Craighead et al., 2002; Miklowitz, 2002; Miklowitz et al., 2003). For married people who have unipolar depression and marital discord, marital therapy (focusing on the marital discord rather than on the depressed spouse alone) is as effective as cognitive therapy in reducing unipolar depression for the depressed spouse. Marital therapy has the further advantage of producing greater increases in marital satisfaction than cognitive therapy (Beach & Jones, 2002).

CONCLUSIONS Even without formal therapy, as we have noted, the great majority of manic and depressed patients recover from a given episode in less than a year. With the modern methods of treatment discussed here, the general outlook for a given episode has become increasingly favorable for many, but by no means all, afflicted individuals. Although relapses and recurrences often occur, these can now often be prevented or at least reduced in frequency by maintenance therapy—through continuation of medication and/or through follow-up therapy sessions at regular intervals.

At the same time, the mortality rate for depressed patients is significantly higher than that for the general population, partly because of the higher incidence of suicide, but there is also an excess of deaths due to natural causes (see Coryell & Winokur, 1992; Futterman et al., 1995), including coronary heart disease (e.g., Glassman, 2005; Smith & Ruiz, 2002; see Chapter 10). Manic patients also have a high risk of death, because of such circumstances as accidents (often with alcohol as a contributing factor), neglect of proper health precautions, or physical exhaustion (Coryell & Winokur, 1992). Thus, the need for still-more effective treatment methods, both immediate and long term, clearly remains. Also, a great need remains to study the factors that put people at risk for depressive disorders and to apply relevant findings to early intervention and prevention.

In Review

- Evaluate the effectiveness of antidepressant medications, electroconvulsive therapy, and mood-stabilizing drugs such as lithium in the treatment of unipolar and bipolar disorders.
- Describe the three major forms of psychotherapy that have been shown to be effective for treating depression.

SUICIDE

The risk of **suicide**—taking one's own life—is a significant factor in all types of depression. Although it is obvious that people also commit suicide for reasons other than depression, estimates are that about 40 to 60 percent of those who complete the act do so during a depressive episode or in the recovery phase (Isacsson & Rich, 1997; Stolberg, Clark, & Bongar, 2002). Paradoxically, the act often occurs at a point when a person appears to be emerging from the deepest phase of the depressive attack. The risk of suicide is about 1 percent during the year in which a depressive episode occurs, but the lifetime risk for someone who has recurrent depressive episodes is about 15 percent (D. C. Clark, 1995; Stolberg et al., 2002). To put it in a different way, depressed people are 50 times more likely to commit suicide than nondepressed people (Beutler, Clarkin, & Bongar, 2000). Moreover, even when suicide is not associated with depression, it is still generally associated with some other mental disorder; estimates are that approximately 90 percent of people who either attempted or successfully committed suicide had some psychiatric disorder at the time (Kessler, Berglund, et al., 2005; Stolberg et al., 2002).

Suicide now ranks among the ten leading causes of death in most Western countries (Kessler, Berglund, et al., 2005). In the United States, it is the eighth or ninth leading cause of death, with current estimates of about 31,000 suicides each year (National Vital Statistics Report, 2003). Moreover, most experts agree that the number of actual suicides is at least two to four times higher than the number officially reported because many self-inflicted deaths are attributed in official records to other, more "respectable" causes (e.g., O'Donnell & Farmer, 1995; M. M. Silverman, 1997). In addition to completed suicides, estimates are that approximately half a million people attempt suicide each year and that nearly 3 percent of Americans have made a suicide attempt at some time in their lives (Jamison, 1999).

Statistics, however accurate, cannot begin to convey the tragedy of suicide in human terms. Most people who commit suicide are ambivalent about taking their own lives and make this irreversible choice when they are alone and in a state of severe psychological distress and anguish, unable to see their problems objectively or to evaluate alternative courses of action. Thus one tragedy is that many do not really want to die. A second tragic concern arises from the long-lasting distress among those left behind. Studies of survivors show that the loss of a loved one through suicide "is one of the greatest burdens individuals and families may endure" (Dunne, 1992, p. 222).

In the discussion that follows, we will focus on various aspects of the incidence and clinical picture of suicide, on factors that appear to be of causal significance, on degrees of intent and ways of communicating it, and on issues of treatment and prevention.

The Clinical Picture and the Causal Pattern

Who commits suicide? What are the motives for taking one's own life? What general sociocultural variables appear to be relevant to an understanding of suicide? These are the questions we will consider.

WHO ATTEMPTS AND WHO COMMITS SUICIDE? Until recently, *suicide attempts* were most common in people between 25 and 44 years old (Stolberg et al., 2002), but it is now people between 18 and 24 years old who have the highest rates (Kessler, Berglund, et al., 2005). In the United States, women are about three times as likely to attempt suicide as men (National Vital Statistics Report, 2003). Rates of suicide attempts are also about three or four times higher in people who are separated or divorced than for those with any other marital status. Most attempts occur in the context of interpersonal discord or other severe life stress. The story is different, however, for *completed suicides;* about four times more men than women die by suicide each year in the United States (National Vital Statistics Report, 2003). The highest rate of completed suicides is in the elderly (aged 65 and over). Although these rates had been coming down since 1930, especially for elderly men (Stolberg et al., 2002), the 1980s and 1990s saw a trend back upward. Among elderly victims, a high proportion are divorced or widowed, or suffer from a chronic physical illness that can lead to increased risk for suicide, usually because the person is depressed (Conwell, Duberstein, & Canne, 2002; National Vital Statistics Report, 2003). For women, the method most commonly used is drug ingestion; men tend to use methods more likely to be lethal, particularly gunshot, which may be a good part of the reason why completed suicides are higher among men.

Kurt Cobain, lead vocalist with the rock band Nirvana, died from a self-inflicted gunshot wound on April 8, 1994. He left behind his wife, Courtney Love, and their daughter Frances, to deal with the emotional burden of his suicide. Forty to sixty percent of those who successfully commit suicide are depressed.

Besides the elderly, persons with mood disorders, and separated or divorced persons, there are a number of other high-risk groups among adults. For example, although people with mood disorders have the highest risk of suicide at some point in their lives (about a 15 percent risk), those with schizophrenia have about a 10 percent risk, and those hospitalized for alcohol dependence have about a 3 to 4 percent risk, relative to the average risk of 1.4 percent in the general population (e.g., Haas, 1997; Stolberg et al., 2002). The depressed mood and hopelessness that often occur in these other disorders are often implicated. People living alone and people from socially disorganized areas are also at heightened risk. Finally, certain highly creative or successful scientists, health professionals (e.g., physicians and psychologists), businessmen, composers, writers, and artists are at higher-than-average risk (Jamison, 1999).

SUICIDE IN CHILDREN Another disturbing trend is that rates of completed suicide among children, while still very low, have been increasing (King, 1997; Stolberg et al., 2002). For children between the ages of 5 and 14, suicide is rare in absolute terms (0.7 per 100,000), but suicide is nevertheless the seventh leading cause of death in the United States for this age group and has increased by 70 percent since 1981 (National Youth Violence Prevention Statistics, 2003). Further, the trend is by no means limited to youngsters from deprived or troubled backgrounds. Children are at increased risk for suicide if they have lost a parent or have been abused (Jamison, 1999). Several forms of psychopathology—depression, antisocial behavior, and high impulsivity—are also known to be risk factors for suicide in children (Sokol & Pfeffer, 1992).

SUICIDE IN ADOLESCENTS AND YOUNG ADULTS For persons between the ages of 15 and 24, the rate of successful suicides essentially tripled between the mid-1950s and the mid-1980s. From 1981–2000, the suicide rate in this age group declined slightly but remained unacceptably high. Suicide ranks as the third-most-common (National Vital Statistics Report, 2003) cause of death in the United States for 15-to-24-year-olds (after accidents and homicide), occurring in about 13 per 100,000 in this age group (King, 1997). The increases in suicide rates for adolescents are not unique to this country but, rather, have been observed in most of the many countries studied (Jamison, 1999).

As for suicide attempts, several recent surveys of high school students have estimated the rates of self-reported suicide attempts to be an alarming 10 percent, with about twice that many reporting that they have seriously considered it (Jamison, 1999). In recent years, these have been the highest rates of suicide attempts at any point in the human life span. Most of these attempts have very low lethality and do not require medical attention, but they do need to be taken seriously. Indeed, one study found that among male adolescents who had attempted suicide, nearly 9 percent completed suicide within 5 years; the comparable rates for girls were 1 to 4 percent (King, 1997). Suicide rates in college students are also high, and it is the second leading cause of death in this group. One large survey found that about 10 percent of college students had seriously contemplated suicide in the past year and that most of these had some sort of plan (Jamison, 1999).

Known Risk Factors for Adolescent Suicide Studies have found that mood disorder, conduct disorder, and substance abuse (especially alcohol) are relatively more common in both completers and nonfatal attempters. Among those with two or more of these disorders, risk for completion increases. Unfortunately, recent evidence suggests that treatment of adolescent mood disorders with antidepressant medication also seems to produce a very slightly increased risk for suicidal ideation and behavior in children and adolescents, and so now pharmaceutical companies must put warnings to this effect on these medications (e.g., Whittington, Kendall, & Pilling, 2005).

Why has there been such a surge in suicide attempts and completed suicides in adolescence? One obvious reason is that this is a period during which depression, anxiety, alcohol and drug use, and conduct disorder problems also show increasing prevalence, and these are all associated with increased risk for suicide (e.g., Evans, Hawton, & Rodham, 2004). Exposure to suicides (especially those of celebrities) through the media, where they are often portrayed in dramatic terms, has probably also contributed to these aggregate increases in adolescent suicide, perhaps because adolescents are highly susceptible to suggestion and imitative behavior (Hawton & Williams, 2002; Jamison, 1999). The fact that the media rarely discuss the mental disorders suffered by the suicide victims may further increase the likelihood of imitation. One review estimated that between 1 and 13 percent of adolescent suicides occur as a result of contagion factors (Velting & Gould, 1997).

Many college students also seem very vulnerable to the development of suicidal motivations. The combined stressors of academic demands, social interaction problems, and career choices—perhaps interacting with challenges to their basic values—evidently make it impossible for some students to continue making the adjustments their life situations demand. For an overview of warning signs for student suicide, see The World Around Us 7.4.

OTHER PSYCHOSOCIAL FACTORS ASSOCIATED WITH SUICIDE The specific factors that lead a person to suicide may take many forms. For example, one middle-aged man developed profound feelings of guilt after being promoted to the presidency of the bank for which he worked; shortly after his promotion, he fatally slit his throat. Such "success suicides" are undoubtedly related to those occasional depressive episodes that seem to be precipitated by positive life events. Much more often, suicide is associated with negative events such as severe financial reversals, imprisonment, and interpersonal crises of various sorts. Some believe the common denominator may be either that these events lead to the loss of a sense of meaning in life and/or to hopelessness about the future (e.g., Beck et al., 1993), which can both produce a mental state that looks to suicide as a possible way out. However, hopelessness about the future may be a better long-term predictor of suicide (say, 1 or 2 years later) than it is for the short term (for instance, weeks or months; Coryell & Young, 2005; Stolberg et al., 2002). Other symptoms that seem to predict suicide more reliably in the short term in patients with major depression include severe psychic anxiety, panic attacks, severe anhedonia, global insomnia, delusions, and alcohol abuse (Busch, Fawcett, & Jacobs, 2003; Fawcett et al., 1990). Indeed, in one study of 76 people who had committed suicide while being hospitalized, the hospital records revealed that 79 percent of these people had been severely anxious and agitated in the week prior to committing suicide (Busch et al., 2003).

Shneidman, a leading suicidologist for over 30 years, has written extensively about "the suicidal mind." For example, he wrote,

> In almost every case suicide is caused by . . . psychological pain, or "psychache". . . . Suicidal death, in other words, is an escape from pain. . . . Pain is nature's great signal. Pain warns us; pain both mobilizes us and saps our strength; pain, by its very nature, makes us want to stop it or escape from it. . . . Psychache is the hurt, anguish, or ache that takes hold in the mind . . . the pain of excessively felt shame, guilt, fear, anxiety, loneliness, angst, and dread of growing old or of dying badly. . . . [I]ts introspective reality is undeniable. Suicide happens when the psychache is deemed unbearable and death is actively sought to stop the unceasing flow of painful consciousness. (Shneidman, 1997, pp. 23, 24, 29)

7.4 THE WORLD AROUND US

Warning Signs for Student Suicide

A marked change in a student's mood and behavior may be a significant warning of possible suicide. Characteristically, the student becomes depressed and withdrawn, undergoes a marked decline in self-esteem, and shows deterioration in personal hygiene. He or she may also show uncharacteristically impulsive or reckless behavior, including self-mutilating behavior. The student may also write about death or suicide. These signs are accompanied by a profound loss of interest in studies. Often he or she stops attending classes and stays at home most of the day. The student's distress is usually communicated to at least one other person, often in the form of a veiled suicide warning.

When college students attempt suicide, one of the first explanations to occur to those around them is that they may have been doing poorly in school. As a group, however, they are superior students, and although they tend to expect a great deal of themselves in terms of academic achievement, their grades and academic competition are not regarded as significant precipitating stressors. Also, although many lose interest in their studies before becoming suicidal and thus receive worse grades, this loss of interest appears to be associated with depression and withdrawal caused by other problems. Moreover, in that minority of cases where academic failure does appear to trigger suicidal behavior, the underlying cause of the behavior seems to be loss of self-esteem and failure to live up to parental expectations, rather than academic failure itself.

For most suicidal students, both male and female, the major precipitating stressor appears to be either the failure to establish, or the loss of, a close interpersonal relationship. Often the breakup of a romance is the key precipitating factor. It has also been noted that significantly more suicide attempts and suicides are made by students from families that have experienced separation, divorce, or the death of a parent.

Although most colleges and universities have mental health facilities to assist distressed students, few suicidal students seek professional help. Thus it is of vital importance for those around a suicidal student to notice any warning signs and try to obtain assistance.

But what psychological factors lead one to this state? Research indicates that suicide is the end product of a long sequence of events that begins in childhood. People who become suicidal often come from backgrounds in which there was some combination of a good deal of family psychopathology, child maltreatment, and/or family instability (e.g., Molnar, Berkman, & Buka, 2001). These early experiences are in turn associated with the child (and later the adult) having low self-esteem, hopelessness, and poor problem-solving skills. Such experiences may affect the person's cognitive functioning in a very negative way, and these cognitive deficits may in turn mediate the link with suicidal behavior (e.g., Yang & Clum, 1996).

Ernest Hemingway (left) committed suicide on July 2, 1961. Thirty-five years later to the day, his granddaughter Margaux (right) took her own life as well. The Hemingway family has endured five suicides over four generations—Ernest's father Clarence, Ernest and his siblings Ursula and Leicester, and granddaughter Margaux.

BIOLOGICAL CAUSAL FACTORS There is strong evidence that suicide sometimes runs in families (see Figure 7.11 on p. 272) and that genetic factors may play a role in the risk for suicide (Baldessarini & Hennen, 2004; Mann, Brent, & Arango, 2001; Roy et al., 1999). For example, the concordance rate for suicide in identical twins is about 19 times higher than that in fraternal twins (Roy et al., 1999). Moreover, this genetic vulnerability seems to be at least partly independent of the genetic vulnerability for major depression.

There is also increasing evidence that this genetic vulnerability may be linked to the neurochemical correlates of suicide that have now been found in numerous studies. Specifically, suicide victims often have alterations

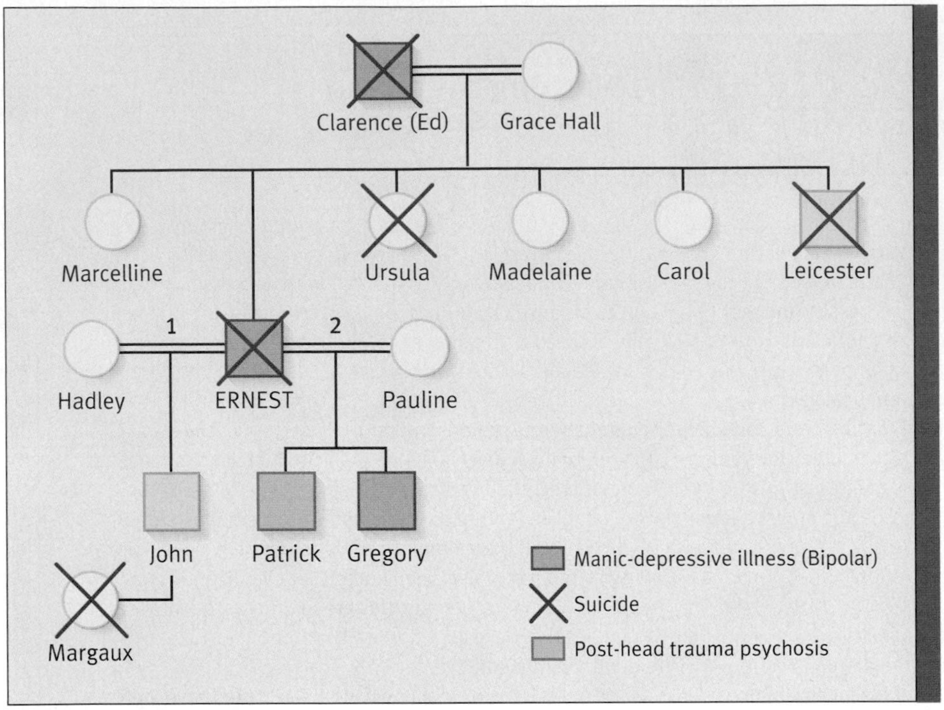

FIGURE 7.11

Psychiatric and suicidal family history of the writer Ernest Hemingway. Squares indicate males and circles indicate females.

Source: *Adapted with the permission of The Free Press, a division of Simon & Schuster Adult Publishing Group from* Touched with Fire: Manic Depressive Illness and the Artistic Temperament *by Kay Redfield Jamison. Copyright © 1993 by Kay Redfield Jamison.*

in serotonin functioning, with reduced serotonergic activity being associated with increased suicide risk—especially for violent suicide. Such studies have been conducted not only in postmortem studies of suicide victims but also in people who have made suicide attempts and survived. This association appears to be independent of psychiatric diagnosis, including suicide victims with depression, schizophrenia, and personality disorders (Mann et al., 2001). People hospitalized for a suicide attempt who have low serotonin levels are also ten times more likely to kill themselves in the next year than are those without low serotonin levels. Even in nonsuicidal individuals, low serotonin levels are associated with a tendency toward impulsive aggression (Oquendo & Mann, 2000). Recently several studies have tried to document an association between suicide and the serotonin-transporter gene (which controls the uptake of serotonin from the synapse) previously discussed as being implicated in the vulnerability to depression. Unfortunately, results of several studies to date have been inconsistent and inconclusive (Correa et al., 2004).

SOCIOCULTURAL FACTORS Substantial differences in suicide rates occur among different ethnic/racial groups in the United States. For example, Whites have much higher rates of suicide than African-Americans, except among young males, where rates are similar between White and African-American men (see Figure 7.12). Only young Native American men show a suicide rate similar to that of White American males.

Suicide rates also appear to vary considerably from one society to another. Hungary, with an annual incidence of more than 40 per 100,000, has the world's highest rate (about four times that of the United States). Other Western countries with high suicide rates—20 per 100,000 or higher—are Switzerland, Finland, Austria, Sweden, Denmark, and Germany. Rates in Japan and China are also high; indeed, in China the estimated suicide rate is three times the global average (Hesketh, Ding, & Jenkins, 2002). The United States has a rate of approximately 11 or 12 per 100,000. Countries with low rates (less than 9 per 100,000) include Greece, Italy, Spain, and the United Kingdom (Maris et al., 2000). Some have estimated the global mortality from suicide at 16 per 100,000 (WHO, International Suicide Statistics Resource Page, 2005). These estimates should, however, be considered in light of the fact that there are wide differences across countries in the criteria used for determining whether a death was due to suicide, and such differences may well contribute to the apparent differences in suicide rates.

Religious taboos concerning suicide and the attitudes of a society toward death are also apparently important determinants of suicide rates. Both Catholicism and Islam strongly condemn suicide, and suicide rates in Catholic and Islamic countries are correspondingly low. In fact, most societies have developed strong sanctions against suicide, and many still regard it as a crime as well as a sin.

Japan is one of the few societies in which suicide has been socially approved under certain circumstances—such as conditions that bring disgrace to an individual or group. During World War II, many Japanese villagers and Japanese military personnel were reported to have committed mass suicide when faced with defeat and imminent capture by Allied forces. There were also reports of group sui-

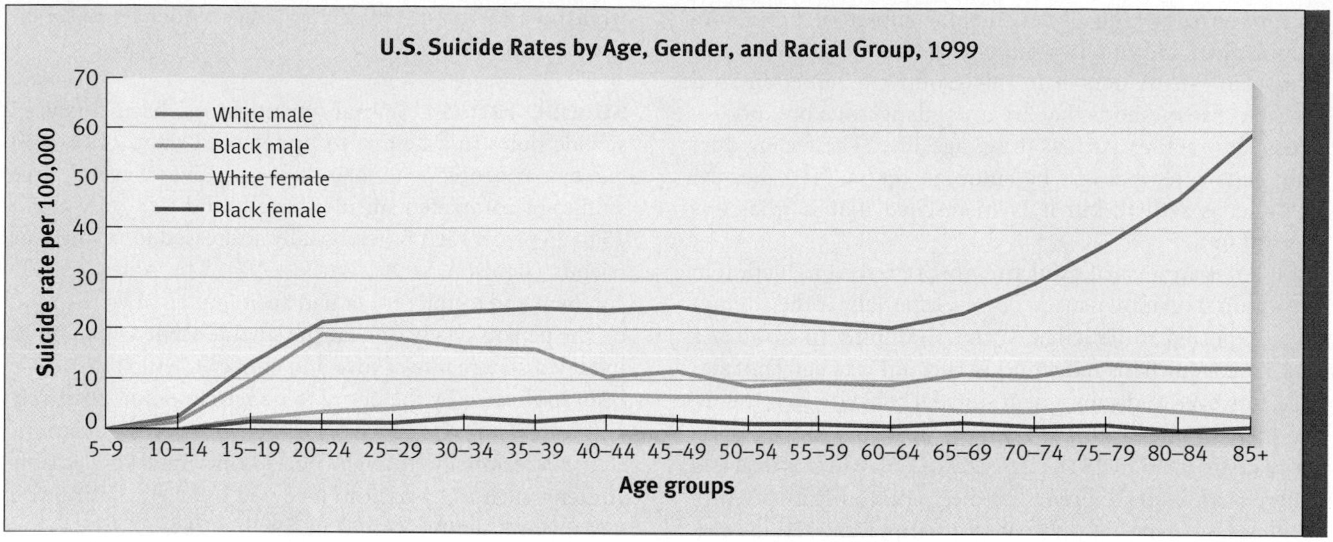

FIGURE 7.12

U.S. Suicide Rates by Age, Gender, and Racial Group

Suicide rates are higher in males than in females and higher in Whites than African-Americans.

Source: *National Institute of Mental Health, October 20, 2002. Data: Center for Disease Control and Prevention, National Center for Health Statistics.*

cide by Japanese military personnel under threat of defeat. In the case of the kamikaze, approximately 1,000 young Japanese pilots deliberately crashed their explosives-laden planes into American warships during the war's final stages as a way of demonstrating complete personal commitment to the national purpose. Comparable acts of self-destruction still occur today in the Middle East, where Muslim extremists and terrorists all too often commit suicide in order to ensure that a bomb explodes in a designated target area. In the case of the al Qaeda attacks on September 11, 2001, terrorists took over commercial jets and then flew them into the World Trade Center and the Pentagon, killing themselves and over 3,000 innocent people. More recently in Iraq, after the fall of Saddam Hussein, suicide bombers have formed a major part of the insurgency in Iraq against U.S. and other foreign soldiers, as well as against members of Iraq's newly formed government forces.

There are also interesting cross-cultural gender differences in whether men or women are more likely to attempt and complete suicide. Although women are more likely to attempt and men to complete suicide in the United States, in India, Poland, and Finland, men are more likely than women to engage in nonfatal suicide attempts. In China, India, and Papua New Guinea, women are more likely to complete suicide than men (Canetto, 1997; Jamison, 1999).

In a pioneering study of sociocultural factors in suicide, the French sociologist Emile Durkheim (1897/1951) attempted to relate differences in suicide rates to differences in group cohesiveness. Analyzing records of suicides in different countries and during different historical periods, Durkheim concluded that the greatest deterrent to committing suicide in times of personal stress is a sense of involvement and identity with other people. More contemporary studies tend to confirm this idea, showing, for example, that being married and having children tends to protect one from suicide (Maris, 1997; Stolberg et al., 2002).

Durkheim's views also seem relevant to understanding the higher incidence of suicide among individuals subjected to conditions of uncertainty and social disorganization in the absence of strong group ties. For example, there is a well-known association between unemployment and suicide (especially for men), which may well be related to the effects that unemployment has on mental health (Jamison, 1999; Maris, Berman, & Silverman, 2000). Similarly, suicide rates have been found to be higher among groups subject to severe social pressures. For example, in 1932, at the height of the Great Depression in the United States, the suicide rate increased from less than 10 to 17.4 per 100,000.

Suicidal Ambivalence

Ambivalence often accompanies thoughts of suicide. Some people (most often women) do not really wish to die but instead want to communicate a dramatic message to others concerning their distress. Their suicide attempts tend to involve nonlethal methods such as minimal drug ingestion or minor wrist slashing. They usually arrange matters so that intervention by others is almost inevitable. In stark contrast, a small minority of suicidal people are seemingly intent on dying. They give little or no warning of their intent, and they generally rely on the more violent and certain means of suicide such as shooting themselves or jumping from high places. A third subset of people are ambivalent about dying and tend to leave the question of death to fate. A person in this group may entertain and tend to use methods that are often dangerous but moderately slow acting, such as drug ingestion. The feeling during such attempts can be summed up as, "If I die, the conflict is settled, but if I am rescued that is what was meant to be."

After an unsuccessful attempt, a marked reduction in emotional turmoil usually occurs, especially if the attempt was expected to be lethal, such as jumping in front of a moving train. This reduction in turmoil is usually not stable, however, and subsequent suicidal behavior may follow. In the year after a suicide attempt, repetition of the behavior occurs in 15 to 25 percent (Zahl & Hawton, 2004), and there is an increased risk that the second or third attempt will be fatal, especially if the first attempt was a serious one. Long-term follow-ups of those who have made a suicide attempt show that about 7 to 10 percent will eventually die by suicide, a risk about five times greater than the average risk of 1.4 percent (Stolberg et al., 2002). Of people who do kill themselves, about 20 to 40 percent have a history of one or more previous attempts; however, more than half of those who commit suicide have no previous attempts (Zahl & Hawton, 2004; Stolberg et al., 2002).

COMMUNICATION OF SUICIDAL INTENT Research has clearly disproved the tragic belief that those who threaten to take their lives seldom do so. One review of many studies conducted around the world that involved interviewing friends and relatives of people who had committed suicide revealed that more than 40 percent had communicated their suicidal intent in very clear and specific terms and that another 30 percent had talked about death or dying in the months preceding their suicide. These communications were usually made to several people and occurred a few weeks or months before the suicide (D. C. Clark, 1995). Nevertheless, most of those interviewed said the suicide came as a surprise. It is also interesting that most of these communications of intent were to friends and family members and not to mental health professionals. Indeed, nearly 50 percent of people who die by suicide have never seen a mental health professional in their lifetime, and less than a third are under the care of one at the time of their death (Stolberg et al., 2002).

On the other hand, if a clinician knows that someone has been suicidal (for example, he or she is being hospitalized for a suicide attempt), he or she should also not take the patient's denial of suicidal intent as necessarily being valid. One fascinating study of clinical correlates of inpatients who had committed suicide revealed some sobering statistics: Among patients who were being hospitalized for having had either suicidal ideation or intent, nearly 80 percent denied suicidal ideation the last time they spoke with a clinician before actually committing suicide; moreover, over 50 percent of those who committed suicide did so while on a 15-minute suicide watch or under 1:1 observation (Busch et al., 2003).

SUICIDE NOTES Several investigators have analyzed suicide notes in an effort to understand the motives and feelings of people who take their own lives. Several large studies of completed suicides have found that only about 15 to 25 percent left notes, usually addressed to relatives or friends (Jamison, 1999; Maris, 1997). The notes, usually coherent and legible, either had been mailed or were found on the person's body or near the suicide scene. Some notes included statements of love and concern, which may have been motivated by the desire to be remembered positively and to reassure the survivor of the worth of the relationship. Occasionally, though, notes contained very hostile content, such as, "I used to love you but I die hating you and my brother too" (Jamison, 1999, p. 78).

Although one might think that such notes would express deep and tragic emotions, this is typically not the case. Many notes are often quite short and straightforward: "I am tired of living" or "I could not bear it any longer" or "No one is to blame for this. It's just that I could never be reconciled with life itself. God have mercy on my soul" (Jamison, 1999, pp. 77–78).

Suicide Prevention and Intervention

Preventing suicide is extremely difficult. Most people who are depressed and contemplating suicide do not realize that their thinking is restricted and irrational and that they are in need of assistance. Rather than seeking psychological help, more are likely to visit a doctor's office with multiple vague complaints of physical symptoms that the doctor often does not detect as symptoms of depression or alcoholism. Others are brought to the attention of mental health personnel by family members or friends who are concerned because the person appears depressed or has made suicide threats. The vast majority, however, do not receive the help they desperately need, which is unfortunate because if a person's cry for help can be heard in time, it is often possible to intervene successfully.

Currently, there are three main thrusts of preventive efforts: treatment of the person's current mental disorder(s) as noted above, crisis intervention, and working with high-risk groups.

CRISIS INTERVENTION The primary objective of crisis intervention is to help a person cope with an immediate life crisis. If a serious suicide attempt has been made, the first step involves emergency medical treatment, followed by referral to inpatient or outpatient mental health facilities in order to reduce the risk for future attempts (e.g., Stolberg et al., 2002).

When people contemplating suicide are willing to discuss their problems with someone at a suicide prevention center, it is often possible to avert an actual suicide

In recent years, the availability of competent assistance at time of suicidal crisis has been expanded through the establishment of suicide prevention centers. These centers are geared toward crisis intervention—usually via 24-hour telephone hotlines.

attempt. Here the primary objective is to help these people regain their ability to cope with their immediate problems as quickly as possible. Emphasis is usually placed on (1) maintaining supportive and often highly directive contact with the person over a short period of time—usually one to six contacts; (2) helping the person to realize that acute distress is impairing his or her ability to assess the situation accurately and to see that there are better ways of dealing with the problem; and (3) helping the person to see that the present distress and emotional turmoil will not be endless.

Since the 1960s, the availability of competent assistance at times of suicidal crisis has been expanded through the establishment of suicide hotlines for suicide prevention centers. There are now more than several thousand such hotlines in the United States, but only a relatively small proportion are members of the American Association of Suicidology, so questions have been raised about the quality of care offered by the majority (e.g., Seeley, 1997). These centers are geared primarily toward crisis intervention, usually via the 24-hour-a-day availability of telephone contact. Suicide hotlines are usually staffed primarily by nonprofessionals who are supervised by psychologists and psychiatrists. The worker attempts to establish the seriousness of the caller's intent and simultaneously tries to show empathy and to convince the person not to attempt suicide. Efforts are also made to mobilize support from family or friends. Unfortunately, good information on the assessment of the effects of these hotlines and suicide prevention centers has not revealed much impact on suicide rates.

FOCUS ON HIGH-RISK GROUPS AND OTHER MEASURES Many investigators have emphasized the need for broad-based prevention programs aimed at alleviating the life problems of people who are in groups at high risk for suicide (Institute of Medicine, 2002; Maris et al., 2000). Few such programs have actually been initiated, but one approach has been to involve older men—a high-risk group—in social and interpersonal activities that help others. Playing such roles may lessen these men's sense of isolation and meaninglessness, which often stems from forced retirement, financial problems, the deaths of loved ones, impaired physical health, and feeling unwanted. For adults who have already made at least one attempt, a recent study found that ten sessions of cognitive therapy focused on suicide prevention was beneficial in reducing further attempts (Brown, Have, et al., 2005). In the 18 months subsequent to receiving treatment, patients in the cognitive therapy group were 50 percent less likely to reattempt suicide than participants in the usual care group, and their depressive and hopelessness symptoms were also lower than in the usual care group. Other programs have been targeted at young adolescents who are at higher risk because of previous suicidal ideation and behavior, and/or mood or substance-use disorders (Zahl & Hawton, 2004).

In Review

- Which groups of people are most likely to attempt suicide and which groups are most likely to complete suicide, and what are some of the major precipitants of suicide?
- Summarize the psychosocial, biological, and sociocultural causal factors associated with suicide.
- What is meant by suicidal ambivalence, and how may it be related to communication of suicidal intent?
- What are the goals of suicide intervention programs, and how successful do they seem to be?

UNRESOLVED ISSUES

Is There a Right to Die?

Most of us respect the preservation of human life as a worthwhile value. Thus, in our society, suicide is generally considered not only tragic but also "wrong." Efforts to prevent suicide, however, involve ethical problems. If people wish to take their own lives, what obligation—or right—do others have to interfere? Not all societies have taken the position that others should interfere when someone wishes to commit suicide. For example, the classical Greeks believed in dignity in death, and people who were extremely ill could get permission from the state to commit suicide. Officials of the state gave out hemlock (a poison) to those who received such permission (Humphry & Wickett, 1986). Today, in certain Western European countries such as the Netherlands, the law allows terminally ill people to be given access to drugs that they can use to commit suicide (Maris et al., 2000). In 1997 the State of Oregon passed the Oregon Death with Dignity Act (ODDA), allowing physician-assisted suicide for terminally ill patients who request a prescription for lethal medications that they will ingest to end their own lives (e.g., Sears & Stanton, 2001).

Passage of the ODDA was (and is) highly controversial in the United States, and was challenged several times by U.S. Attorney General John Ashcroft in federal courts. So far the law remains in effect but was reviewed by the Supreme Court in the fall of 2005. Indeed, there is very heated debate all over the country about the right of people who are terminally ill or who suffer chronic and debilitating pain to shorten their agony. One group, the Hemlock Society, supports the rights of terminally ill people to get help in ending their own lives when they wish (this is often called physician-assisted suicide); the society also provides support groups for people making this decision.

Several other groups press related issues at a legislative level. One physician in Michigan, Dr. Jack Kevorkian, helped over 130 gravely ill people commit suicide and, in so doing, tried to get Michigan to pass laws permitting such acts. For years the state tried to block Kevorkian from assisting in any further suicides, and at several points he was even imprisoned, and his medical license revoked, because he refused to obey injunctions not to assist with any more suicides. In 1998 Kevorkian invited further attention—and prosecution—when he released a videotape to the CBS program *60 Minutes,* and millions watched him assisting in a suicide. He was later charged, and convicted in April 1999, of second-degree murder and is serving a 10-to-25-year term in prison. In spite of Kevorkian's failure to prompt the passage of laws supporting assisted suicide for such gravely ill individuals (indeed, Michigan passed a law prohibiting assisted suicide!), substantial numbers of people have come to sympathize with this position (Maris et al., 2000; see also Szasz's 1999 book *Fatal Freedom: The Ethics and Politics of Suicide*).

Arguments against this position have included fears that the right to suicide might be abused. For example, people who are terminally ill and severely incapacitated might feel pressured to end their own lives rather than burden their families with their care or with the cost of their care in a medical facility or hospice. However, neither the Netherlands nor Oregon, where assisted suicide is legal, has seen this happen. Indeed, physicians in Oregon seem to have become more aware of and sensitive to the needs of terminally ill patients in terms of recommending hospice care and learning more about prescribing the high doses of pain medication needed to relieve suffering (Ganzini et al., 2001).

But what about the rights of suicidal people who are not terminally ill and who have dependent children, parents, a spouse, or other loved ones who will be adversely affected, perhaps permanently (Lukas & Seiden, 1990; Maris et al., 2000), by their death? Here a person's "right to suicide" is not immediately obvious, and physicians are very unlikely to provide assistance in such cases (Rurup, Muller et al., 2005). The right to suicide is even less clear when we consider that, through intervention, many suicidal people regain their perspective and see alternative ways of dealing with their distress.

Rather than focusing on suicide "prevention," some have suggested suicide "intervention" as both a more appropriate term and as descriptive of a more ethically defensible professional approach to suicidal behavior. According to this perspective, suicide intervention embodies a more neutral moral stance than suicide prevention—it means interceding without the implication of preventing the act—and, in certain circumstances, such as when people are terminally ill, it may even encompass the possibility of facilitating the suicidal person's objective (e.g., M. M. Silverman, 1997).

The dilemma about the prevention concept becomes even more intense when prevention requires that a person be hospitalized involuntarily, when personal items (such as belts and sharp objects) are taken away, and when calming medication is more or less forcibly administered. Sometimes considerable restriction is needed to calm the individual. Not uncommonly, particularly in these litigious times, the responsible clinician feels trapped between threats of legal action on both sides of the issue. Undue restriction of the patient might lead to a civil rights suit, whereas failure to employ all available safeguards could, in the case of the patient's injury or death, lead to a potentially ruinous malpractice claim initiated by the patient's family (Maris et al., 2000). Currently, most practitioners resolve this dilemma by taking the most cautious and conservative course. Thus many patients are hospitalized with insufficient clinical justification. Even when the decision to hospitalize is made on good grounds, however, preventive efforts may be fruitless; truly determined persons may find a way to commit suicide even on a "suicide watch." Indeed, about 5 percent of all completed suicides are committed by psychiatric patients while they are hospitalized in inpatient psychiatric units that are supposed to help prevent suicide (Stolberg et al., 2002).

Thus the vexing ethical problems of whether and to what extent one should intervene in cases of threatened suicide have now been complicated by no-less-vexing legal problems. As in other areas of professional practice, clinical judgment is no longer the only consideration in intervention decisions. This is a societal problem, and the solutions—if any—will have to be societal ones.

summary

- Mood disorders are those in which extreme variations in mood—either low or high—are the predominant feature. Although some variations in mood are normal, for some people the extremity of moods in either direction becomes seriously maladaptive, even to the extent of suicide.
- Most people with mood disorders have some form of unipolar depression—dysthymia or major depression. Such individuals experience a range of affective, cognitive, motivational, and biological symptoms including persistent sadness, negative thoughts about the self and the future, lack of energy or initiative, too much or too little sleep, and gaining or losing weight.
    - Among biological causal factors for unipolar disorder, there is evidence of a moderate genetic contribution to the vulnerability for major depression, but probably not for dysthymia. Moreover, major depressions are clearly associated with multiple interacting disturbances in neurochemical, neuroendocrine, and neurophysiological systems. Disruptions in circadian and seasonal rhythms are also prominent features of depression.
    - Among psychosocial theories of the causes of unipolar depression are Beck's cognitive theory and the reformulated helplessness and hopelessness theories, which are formulated as diathesis-stress models. The diathesis is cognitive in nature (e.g., dysfunctional beliefs and pessimistic attributional style, respectively), and stressful life events are often important in determining when those diatheses actually lead to depression.
    - Personality variables such as neuroticism may also serve as diatheses for depression.
    - Psychodynamic and interpersonal theories of unipolar depression emphasize the importance of early experiences (especially early losses and the quality of the parent-child relationship) as setting up a predisposition for depression.
- In the bipolar disorders (cyclothymia and Bipolar I and II disorders), the person experiences episodes of both depression and hypomania or mania. During manic or hypomanic episodes, the symptoms are essentially the opposite of those experienced during a depressive episode.
    - Biological causal factors probably play an even more prominent role for bipolar disorders than for unipolar disorders. The genetic contribution to bipolar disorder is among the strongest of such contributions to the major psychiatric disorders. Neurochemical imbalances, abnormalities of the hypothalamic-pituitary-adrenal axis, and disturbances in biological rhythms all play a role in bipolar disorder.
    - Stressful life events may be involved in precipitating manic or depressive episodes, but it is unlikely that they cause the disorder.
- Biologically based treatments such as medications or electroconvulsive therapy are often used in the treatment of the more severe major disorders. Increasingly, however, psychosocial treatments are also being used to good effect in many cases of these more severe disorders, as well as in the milder forms of mood disorder. Considerable evidence suggests that recurrent depression is best treated by specialized forms of psychotherapy or by maintenance for prolonged periods on medications.
- Suicide is a constant danger with depressive syndromes of any type or severity. Accordingly, an assessment of suicide risk is essential in the proper management of depressive disorders.
    - A small minority of suicides appear unavoidable—chiefly those where the person really wants to die and uses a highly lethal method. However, a substantial amount of suicidal behavior is performed as a means of indirect interpersonal communication.
    - Somewhere between these extremes is a large group of people who are ambivalent about killing themselves and who initiate dangerous actions

(continued)

that they may or may not carry to completion, depending on momentary events and impulses.

- Suicide prevention (or intervention) programs generally consist of crisis intervention in the form of suicide hotlines. Although these programs undoubtedly avert fatal suicide attempts in some cases, the long-term efficacy of treatment aimed at preventing suicide in those at high risk is much less clear at the present time.

Key Terms

attributions (p. 246)
Bipolar I disorder (p. 254)
bipolar disorder with a seasonal pattern (p. 255)
Bipolar II disorder (p. 255)
chronic major depressive disorder (p. 234)
cyclothymic disorder (p. 253)
depression (p. 226)
depressogenic schemas (p. 244)
diathesis-stress theories (p. 242)
double depression (p. 233)
dysfunctional beliefs (p. 244)
dysthymic disorder (p. 230)
hypomanic episode (p. 253)
learned helplessness (p. 246)
major depressive disorder (p. 231)
major depressive episode (p. 227)
major depressive episode with atypical features (p. 233)
major depressive episode with melancholic features (p. 232)
mania (p. 226)
manic episode (p. 227)
mixed episode (p. 254)
mood disorders (p. 226)
mood-congruent delusions (p. 233)
negative automatic thoughts (p. 244)
negative cognitive triad (p. 244)
pessimistic attributional style (p. 247)
rapid cycling (p. 256)
recurrence (p. 234)
relapse (p. 234)
seasonal affective disorder (p. 234)
severe major depressive episode with psychotic features (p. 233)
specifiers (p. 232)
suicide (p. 268)
unipolar disorder (p. 226)

CHAPTER

8

Somatoform and Dissociative Disorders

SOMATOFORM DISORDERS
Hypochondriasis
Somatization Disorder
Pain Disorder
Conversion Disorder
Body Dysmorphic Disorder

DISSOCIATIVE DISORDERS
Depersonalization Disorder
Dissociative Amnesia and Fugue
Dissociative Identity Disorder (DID)
General Sociocultural Causal Factors in Dissociative Disorders
Treatment and Outcomes in Dissociative Disorders

UNRESOLVED ISSUES:
DID and the Reality of "Recovered Memories"

Have you ever had the experience, particularly during a time of serious stress, when you felt like you were walking around in a daze or like you just weren't all there? Or have you known people who constantly complained about being sure they had a serious illness even though several medical tests their doctor had performed failed to show anything wrong? Both of these are examples of mild dissociative and somatoform symptoms experienced at least occasionally by many people. However, when these symptoms become frequent and severe and lead to significant distress or impairment, a somatoform or dissociative disorder may be diagnosed. *Somatoform* and *dissociative disorders* appear to involve more complex and puzzling patterns of symptoms than those we have so far encountered. As a result, they confront the field of psychopathology with some of its most fascinating and difficult challenges, although unfortunately we do not know much about them—in part because many of them are quite rare.

The **somatoform disorders** are a group of conditions that involve physical symptoms and complaints suggesting the presence of a medical condition but without any evidence of physical pathology to account for them (APA, 2000). Despite the range of clinical manifestations—from blindness or paralysis to hypochondriacal complaints about stomach pains thought to be a sign of cancer—in each case the person is preoccupied with some aspect of her or his health or appearance to the extent that she or he shows significant impairments in functioning. These individuals therefore frequently show up in the practices of primary-care physicians, who then have the difficult task of deciding how to manage their complaints, which have no known physical basis.

The **dissociative disorders,** on the other hand, are a group of conditions involving disruptions in a person's normally integrated functions of consciousness, memory, identity, or perception (APA, 2000). Included here are some of the more dramatic phenomena in the entire domain of psychopathology: people who cannot recall who they are or where they may have come from, and people who have two or more distinct identities or personality states that alternately take control of the individual's behavior. The term **dissociation** refers to the human mind's capacity to engage in complex mental activity in channels split off from, or independent of, conscious awareness.

As we have seen (Chapter 6), both somatoform and dissociative disorders were once included with the anxiety disorders under the general rubric *neuroses*, where anxiety was thought to be the underlying cause of all neuroses whether or not the anxiety was experienced overtly. But in 1980, when DSM-III abandoned attempts to link disorders together on the basis of hypothesized underlying causes and instead focused on grouping disorders together on the basis of overt symptomatology, the somatoform and dissociative disorders became separate categories from the anxiety disorders.

Somatoform Disorders

Soma means "body," and somatoform disorders involve patterns in which individuals complain of bodily symptoms or defects that suggest the presence of medical problems, but for which no organic basis can be found that satisfactorily explains the symptoms such as paralysis or pain. Such individuals are typically preoccupied with their state of health and with various presumed disorders or diseases of bodily organs. Equally key to these disorders is the fact that the affected patients have no control over their symptoms. They are also not intentionally faking symptoms or attempting to deceive others. For the most part, they genuinely and sometimes passionately believe something is terribly wrong with their bodies. The prevalence of somatoform disorders appears to vary considerably among differing cultures (e.g., Isaac et al., 1995; Janca et al., 1995).

In our discussion, we will focus on five more or less distinct somatoform patterns that have been identified: (1) hypochondriasis, (2) somatization disorder, (3) pain disorder, (4) conversion disorder, and (5) body dysmorphic disorder.

Hypochondriasis

According to DSM-IV-TR, people with **hypochondriasis** are preoccupied either with fears of contracting a serious disease or with the idea that they actually have such a disease even though they do not. Their preoccupations are all based on a misinterpretation of one or more bodily signs or symptoms (e.g., being convinced that their slight cough is a sign of lung cancer). Of course the decision that a hypochondriacal complaint is based on a misinterpretation of bodily signs or symptoms can be made only after a thorough medical evaluation does not find a medical condition that could account for the signs or symptoms. Another defining criterion for hypochondriasis is that the person is not reassured by the results of a medical evaluation; that is, the fear or idea of having a disease persists despite medical reassurance. Indeed, these individuals are sometimes disappointed when no physical problem is found. Finally, the condition must persist for at least 6 months for the diagnosis to be made, so as to not diagnose relatively transient health concerns.

Not surprisingly, people with hypochondriasis usually first go to a medical doctor with their physical complaints. Because they are never reassured for long, and are inclined to suspect that their doctor has missed something, they sometimes shop for additional doctors, hoping one might discover what their problem really is. Because they repeatedly seek medical advice (e.g., Fink et al., 2004), it is not surprising that their yearly medical costs are much higher than those of most of the rest of the population (e.g., Hiller, Kroymann, et al., 2004; Salkovskis & Bass, 1997). These individuals generally resist the idea that their problem is a psychological one that might best be treated by a psychologist or psychiatrist.

Hypochondriasis may be the most commonly seen somatoform disorder, with a prevalence in general medical practice officially estimated at between 2 and 7 percent (APA, 2000). It occurs about equally often in men and women and can start at almost any age, although early adulthood is the most common age of onset. Once hypochondriasis develops, it tends to be a chronic disorder if left untreated, although the severity may wax and wane over time. Individuals with hypochondriasis often also suffer from mood disorders, panic disorder, and/or other somatoform disorders (especially somatization disorder; Creed & Barsky, 2004).

MAJOR CHARACTERISTICS Individuals with hypochondriasis are often anxious and highly preoccupied with bodily functions (e.g., heart beats or bowel movements) or with minor physical abnormalities (e.g., a small sore or an occasional cough) or with vague and ambiguous physical sensations (such as a "tired heart" or "aching veins"; APA, 2000). They attribute these symptoms to a suspected disease, and often have intrusive thoughts about it. The diagnoses they make for themselves range from tuberculosis to cancer, exotic infections, AIDS, and numerous other diseases.

Although people with hypochondriasis are usually in good physical condition, they are sincere in their conviction that the symptoms they detect represent real illness. They are not *malingering*—consciously faking symptoms to achieve specific goals such as winning a personal injury lawsuit. Not surprisingly, given their tendency to doubt the soundness of their doctor's conclusions (i.e., that they have no medical problem) and recommendations, the doctor-patient relationships are often marked by conflict and hostility.

The following case captures a typical clinical picture in hypochondriasis and incidentally demonstrates that a high level of medical sophistication does not necessarily rule out a person's developing this disorder.

DSM-IV-TR

Criteria for Hypochondriasis

A. Preoccupation with fears of contracting, or the idea that one has, a serious disease, based on misinterpretation of bodily symptoms.

B. Preoccupation persists despite appropriate medical evaluation and reassurance.

C. Preoccupation causes clinically significant distress or impairment.

D. Duration of at least 6 months.

Source: *Adapted with permission from the* Diagnostic and Statistical Manual of Mental Disorders, Fourth Edition, Text Revision *(Copyright 2000). American Psychiatric Association.*

case study: An "Abdominal Mass"

This 38-year-old physician/radiologist initiated his first psychiatric consultation after his 9-year-old son accidentally discovered his father palpating (examining by touch) his own abdomen and said, "What do you think it is this time, Dad?" The radiologist describes the incident and his

(continued)

accompanying anger and shame with tears in his eyes. He also describes his recent return from a 10-day stay at a famous out-of-state medical diagnostic center to which he had been referred by an exasperated gastroenterologist colleague who had reportedly "reached the end of the line" with his radiologist patient. The extensive physical and laboratory examinations performed at the center had revealed no significant physical disease, a conclusion the patient reports with resentment and disappointment rather than relief.

The patient's history reveals a long-standing pattern of overconcern about personal health matters, beginning at age 13 and exacerbated by his medical school experience. Until fairly recently, however, he had maintained reasonable control over these concerns, in part because he was embarrassed to reveal them to other physicians. He is conscientious and successful in his profession and active in community life. His wife, like his son, has become increasingly impatient with his morbid preoccupation about life-threatening but undetectable diseases.

In describing his current symptoms, the patient refers to his becoming increasingly aware, over the past several months, of various sounds and sensations emanating from his abdomen and of his sometimes being able to feel a "firm mass" in its left lower quadrant. His tentative diagnosis is carcinoma (cancer) of the colon. He tests his stool for blood weekly and palpates his abdomen for 15 to 20 minutes every 2 to 3 days. He has performed several X-ray studies of himself in secrecy after hours at his office. (Adapted from Spitzer et al., 2002, pp. 88–90.)

Source: Adapted with permission from the *DSM-IV-TR Casebook* (Copyright 2000). American Psychiatric Publishing, Inc.

Hypochondriacal individuals are preoccupied with health matters and unrealistic fears of disease. They are convinced that they have symptoms of physical illness, but their complaints typically do not conform to any coherent symptom pattern, and they usually have trouble giving a precise description of their symptoms.

THEORETICAL PERSPECTIVES ON CAUSAL FACTORS Knowledge of causal factors in somatoform disorders, including hypochondriasis, is quite minimal compared to many other Axis I disorders such as the mood and anxiety disorders discussed in the previous few chapters. Today many people think hypochondriasis is closely related to the anxiety disorders. Indeed, many researchers today prefer the term *health anxiety* to *hypochondriasis* (e.g., Taylor & Asmundson, 2004). Today, cognitive-behavioral views of hypochondriasis are perhaps most widely accepted and have as a central tenet that it is a disorder of cognition and perception. Misinterpretations of bodily sensations are currently a defining feature of the syndrome, but in the cognitive-behavioral view, these misinterpretations also play a causal role. It is believed that an individual's past experiences with illnesses (in both themselves and others, and as observed in the mass media) lead to the development of a set of dysfunctional assumptions about symptoms and diseases that may predispose a person to developing hypochondriasis (Bouman, Eifert, & Lejuez, 1999; Salkovskis & Bass, 1997; Salkovskis & Warwick, 2001). These dysfunctional assumptions might include notions such as, "Bodily changes are usually a sign of serious disease, because every symptom has to have an identifiable physical cause" or "If you don't go to the doctor as soon as you notice anything unusual, then it will be too late" (Salkovskis & Bass, 1997, p. 318).

Because of these dysfunctional assumptions, individuals with hypochondriasis seem to focus excessive attention on symptoms, with recent experimental evidence showing that these individuals do in fact have an attentional bias for illness-related information (Owens, Asmundson, et al., 2004). They also perceive their symptoms as more dangerous than they really are, and judge a particular disease to be more likely or dangerous than it really is. Once they have misinterpreted a symptom, they tend to look for confirming evidence and to discount evidence that they are in good health; in fact, they seem to believe that being healthy means being completely symptom-free (Rief, Hiller, & Margraf, 1998a). They also perceive their probability of being able to cope with the illness as extremely low

(Salkovskis & Bass, 1997) and see themselves as weak and unable to tolerate physical effort or exercise (Rief et al., 1998a). All this tends to create a vicious cycle in which their anxiety about illness and symptoms results in physiological symptoms of anxiety, which then provide further fuel for their convictions that they are ill.

If we consider the secondary reinforcements that individuals with hypochondriasis obtain, we can better understand how such patterns of thought and behavior are maintained in spite of the misery these individuals often experience. Most of us learn as children that when we are sick, special comforts and attention are provided and, furthermore, that we may be excused from a number of responsibilities. Barsky and colleagues (1994) found that their hypochondriacal patients reported much childhood sickness and missing of school. They also tend to have an excessive amount of illness in their families while growing up, which may lead to strong memories of being sick or in pain (Pauli & Alpers, 2002), and perhaps also of having observed some of the secondary benefits that sick people sometimes reap (Cote et al., 1996; Kellner, 1985).

Interestingly, one study retested hypochondriacal patients again 4 to 5 years later and found that those who had remitted at follow-up had acquired significantly more (real) major medical problems than their nonremitting counterparts (Barsky et al., 1998). In other words, it appears that hypochondriacal tendencies were reduced by the occurrence of serious medical conditions. The authors suggested that having a serious medical illness "served to legitimize the patients' complaints, sanction their assumption of the sick role, and lessen the skepticism with which they had previously been regarded.... As one noted, "'Now that I know Dr. X is paying attention to me, I can believe him if he says nothing serious is wrong"' (p. 744).

TREATMENT OF HYPOCHONDRIASIS At least a half dozen studies on cognitive-behavioral treatment of hypochondriasis have found that it can be a very effective treatment for hypochondriasis (e.g., Barsky & Ahern, 2004; Looper & Kirmayer, 2002; Wattar et al., 2005). The cognitive components of this treatment approach focus on assessing the patient's beliefs about illness and modifying misinterpretations of bodily sensations. The behavioral techniques include having patients induce innocuous symptoms by intentionally focusing on parts of their body so that they can learn that selective perception of bodily sensations plays a major role in their symptoms. Sometimes they are also directed to engage in response prevention by not checking their body as they usually do and by stopping their constant seeking of reassurance. The treatment, which is relatively brief (6–16 sessions), produced large changes in hypochondriacal symptoms and beliefs, as well as in levels of anxiety and depression. There is also some preliminary evidence that certain antidepressant medications (especially SSRIs) may be effective in treating hypochondriasis as well (e.g., Fallon, 2004).

Somatization Disorder

Somatization disorder is characterized by many different complaints of physical ailments, over at least several years beginning before age 30, that are not adequately explained by independent findings of physical illness or injury and that lead to medical treatment or to significant life impairment. Not surprisingly, therefore, somatization disorder is seen most often among patients in primary medical care settings in cultures all over the world (Guerje et al., 1997; Iezzi et al., 2001). Indeed, patients with somatization disorder are enormously costly to health care systems because they often have multiple unnecessary hospitalizations and surgeries (Hiller, Fichter, & Rief, 2003).

In addition to the requirement of multiple physical complaints, DSM-IV-TR (APA, 2000) lists four other symptom criteria that must be met at some time during the course of the disorder before a diagnosis of somatization disorder can be made. A diagnostician need not be convinced that these claimed illnesses actually existed in a patient's background history; the mere reporting of them is sufficient. The four other criteria that must be met are:

1. **Four pain symptoms.** The patient must report a history of pain experienced with respect to at least four different sites or functions—for example, head, abdomen, back, joints, or rectum, or during sexual intercourse or urination.
2. **Two gastrointestinal symptoms.** The patient must report a history of at least two symptoms, other than pain, pertaining to the gastrointestinal system—such as nausea, bloating, diarrhea, or vomiting when not pregnant.
3. **One sexual symptom.** The patient must report at least one reproductive system symptom other than pain—for example, sexual indifference or dysfunction, menstrual irregularity, or vomiting throughout pregnancy.
4. **One pseudoneurological symptom.** The patient must report a history of at least one symptom, not limited to pain, suggestive of a neurological condition—for example, various symptoms that mimic sensory or motor impairments such as loss of sensation or involuntary muscle contraction in a hand.

If the symptoms of somatization disorder seem similar to you in some ways to those of hypochondriasis, that is because there are indeed significant similarities between the two conditions (and they sometimes co-occur; Mai, 2004), but there are also enough distinguishing features that they are considered two separate disorders in DSM-IV-TR. For example, although both disorders are characterized by preoccupation with physical symptoms, only people with hypochondriasis tend to be convinced that they have an organic disease. Moreover, with hypochondriasis the

DSM-IV-TR

Criteria for Somatization Disorder

A. History of many physical complaints starting before age 30 that occur over several years and result in treatment being sought, or significant impairment in functioning.

B. Each of the following criteria must have been met at some time during the disturbance:

(1) Four pain symptoms in different sites.

(2) Two gastrointestinal symptoms other than pain.

(3) One sexual symptom.

(4) One pseudoneurological symptom.

C. Either (1) or (2):

(1) After appropriate investigation, each of the symptoms under Criterion B cannot be fully explained by a medical condition.

(2) When there is a related general medical condition, the physical complaints are in excess of what would be expected.

D. Symptoms not intentionally produced or feigned.

Source: *Adapted with permission from the* Diagnostic and Statistical Manual of Mental Disorders, Fourth Edition, Text Revision *(Copyright 2000). American Psychiatric Association.*

person usually has only one or a few primary symptoms, but in somatization disorder, by definition, there are multiple symptoms.

The main features of somatization disorder are illustrated in the following case summary, which also involves a secondary diagnosis of depression.

case STUDY — Not-Yet-Discovered Illness

This 38-year-old married woman, the mother of five children, reports to a mental health clinic with the chief complaint of depression, meeting diagnostic criteria for major depressive disorder. . . . Her marriage has been a chronically unhappy one; her husband is described as an alcoholic with an unstable work history, and there have been frequent arguments revolving around finances, her sexual indifference, and her complaints of pain during intercourse.

The history reveals that the patient . . . describes herself as nervous since childhood and as having been continuously sickly beginning in her youth. She experiences chest pain and reportedly has been told by doctors that she has a "nervous heart." She sees physicians frequently for abdominal pain, having been diagnosed on one occasion as having a "spastic colon." In addition to M.D. physicians, she has consulted chiropractors and osteopaths for backaches, pains in her extremities, and a feeling of anesthesia in her fingertips. She was recently admitted to a hospital following complaints of abdominal and chest pain and of vomiting, during which admission she received a hysterectomy. Following the surgery she has been troubled by spells of anxiety, fainting, vomiting, food intolerance, and weakness and fatigue. Physical examinations reveal completely negative findings. (Adapted from Spitzer et al., 2002, pp. 404–5.)

Source: Adapted with permission from the *DSM-IV-TR Casebook* (Copyright 2000). American Psychiatric Publishing, Inc.

DEMOGRAPHICS, COMORBIDITY, AND COURSE OF ILLNESS Somatization disorder (formerly called *Briquet's syndrome* after the French physician who first described it) has not been as extensively researched as several other somatoform disorders. It usually begins in adolescence and is believed by many to be about three to ten times more common among women than among men. It also tends to occur more in lower socioeconomic classes. The lifetime prevalence has been estimated to be between 0.2 and 2.0 percent in women and less than 0.2 percent in men (APA, 2000). Somatization disorder very commonly co-occurs with several other disorders including major depression, panic disorder, phobic disorders, and generalized anxiety disorder. Although it has generally been considered to be a relatively chronic condition with a poor prognosis, some recent studies have begun to challenge this view with some evidence that a significant number of patients remit spontaneously (e.g., Creed & Barsky, 2004).

CAUSAL FACTORS IN SOMATIZATION DISORDER Despite its significant prevalence in medical settings, we remain quite uncertain about the developmental course and specific etiology of somatization disorder. There is evidence that it runs in families and that there is a familial linkage between antisocial personality disorder in men (see Chapter 11) and somatization disorder in women. That is, one possibility is that some common, underlying predisposition, probably with an at least partly genetic basis, leads to antisocial behavior in men and to somatization disorder in women (Cale & Lilienfeld, 2002; Guze et al., 1986; Lilienfeld, 1992). Moreover, somatic symptoms and antisocial symptoms in women tend to co-occur (Cale & Lilienfeld, 2002). However, we do not yet have a clear understanding of this relationship. One possibility is that the two disorders may be linked through a common trait of impulsivity, but the nature of this relationship is not yet understood.

In addition to a possible genetic predisposition to developing somatization disorder, other contributory causal factors probably include an interaction of personality, cognitive, and learning variables. People high on neuroticism who come from certain kinds of family backgrounds may develop a tendency to misinterpret their bodily sensations as threatening or even disabling. This might be especially likely in families where a child is frequently exposed to models complaining of pain and vicariously learns that complaining about physical symptoms can lead to the garnering of sympathy and attention (social reinforcement) and even to avoidance of responsibilities (a secondary gain; Iezzi et al., 2001). This may be especially common in rather disorganized and uncohesive families with inconsistent parental care—more often from lower socioeconomic classes.

It has also become clear that people with somatization disorder selectively attend to bodily sensations and tend to see bodily *sensations* as somatic *symptoms*. Like patients with hypochondriasis, they tend to catastrophize about minor bodily complaints and to think of themselves as physically weak and unable to tolerate stress or physical activity (Rief et al., 1998a). One possible scenario suggested by Rief et al. (1998a) is that a vicious cycle may develop. If one thinks of oneself as being weak, has low tolerance for pain and stress, and selectively attends to bodily sensations (while assuming that being healthy equals being without bodily sensations), one will avoid many daily activities that require much exertion, including physical activity. Ironically, however, lowered physical activity can lead to being physically unfit, which can in turn increase bodily sensations about which to catastrophize. Moreover, selectively attending to bodily sensations may actually increase the intensity of the sensations, further exacerbating the vicious cycle. Finally, Rief, Shaw, and Fichter (1998b) also found that patients with somatization disorder had elevated levels of cortisol (a stress hormone) and did not show normal habituation to psychological stressors. Thus the physiological arousal caused by psychological stressors remains elevated and may further contribute to the bodily sensations that individuals suffering from this condition worry about.

TREATMENT OF SOMATIZATION DISORDER

Somatization disorder has long been considered to be extremely difficult to treat, but some recent treatment research has begun to suggest that a certain type of medical management and cognitive-behavioral treatments may be quite helpful. One moderately effective treatment involves identifying one physician who will integrate the patient's care by seeing the patient at regular visits (i.e., trying to anticipate the appearance of new problems) and by providing physical exams focused on new complaints (i.e., accepting her or his symptoms as valid). At the same time, however, the physician avoids unnecessary diagnostic testing and makes minimal use of medications or other therapies (Looper & Kirmayer, 2002; Mai, 2004). Several studies have found that patients show substantial decreases in health care expenditures over subsequent months and sometimes an improvement in physical functioning (although not in psychological distress; Rost, Kashner, & Smith, 1994; Smith, Monson, & Ray, 1986). This type of medical management can be even more effective when combined with cognitive-behavioral therapy that focuses on promoting appropriate behavior such as better coping and personal adjustment, and discouraging inappropriate behavior such as illness behavior and preoccupation with physical symptoms (e.g., Mai, 2004). As with hypochondriasis, the focus is on changing the way the patient thinks about bodily sensations and reducing any secondary gain the patients may receive from physicians and family members. There are also some promising but still preliminary results that antidepressants can sometimes be useful in treating somatization disorder.

When one physician can integrate a patient's care by providing regular office visits but minimum treatment, the physical functioning of patients with somatization disorder may improve.

Pain Disorder

The symptoms of pain disorder resemble the pain symptoms seen in somatization disorder, but with pain disorder, the other kinds of symptoms of somatization disorder are not present. Thus **pain disorder** is characterized by the experience of persistent and severe pain in one or more areas of the body. Although a medical condition may contribute to the pain, psychological factors must be judged to play an important role. In approaching the phenomenon of pain disorder, it is very important to remember that the pain that is experienced is very real and can hurt as much as pain with purely medical causes. It is also important to note that pain is always, in part, a subjective experience that is private and cannot be objectively identified by others.

DSM-IV-TR specifies two coded subtypes: (1) pain disorder associated with psychological factors, and (2) pain disorder associated with both psychological factors and a general medical condition. The first subtype applies where psychological factors are judged to play a major role in the onset or maintenance of the pain—that is, where any

DSM-IV-TR

Criteria for Pain Disorder

A. Pain in one or more sites as primary focus of clinical presentation.
B. Pain causes significant distress or impairment in functioning.
C. Psychological factors judged to have an important role in the pain.
D. Symptom or deficit is not intentionally produced or feigned.

Source: *Adapted with permission from the* Diagnostic and Statistical Manual of Mental Disorders, Fourth Edition, Text Revision *(Copyright 2000). American Psychiatric Association.*

The experience of pain is always subjective and private, making pain impossible to assess with pinpoint accuracy. Pain does not always exist in perfect correlation with observable tissue damage or irritation.

coexisting general medical condition is considered to be of minimal causal significance in the pain complaint. The second subtype applies where the experienced pain is considered to result from both psychological factors and some medical condition that could cause pain. In either case, the pain disorder may be *acute* (duration of less than 6 months) or *chronic* (duration of over 6 months).

The prevalence of pain disorder in the general population is unknown. It is definitely quite common among patients at pain clinics. It is diagnosed more frequently in women than in men and is very frequently comorbid with anxiety and/or mood disorders, which may occur first or may arise later as a consequence of the pain disorder (APA, 2000). People with pain disorder are often unable to work (they sometimes go on disability) or to perform some other usual daily activities. Their resulting inactivity (including an avoidance of physical activity) and social isolation may lead to depression and to a loss of physical strength and endurance. This fatigue and loss of strength can then exacerbate the pain in a kind of vicious cycle (Bouman, Eifert, & Lejuez, 1999; Flor, Birbaumer, & Turk, 1990). In addition, the behavioral component of pain is quite malleable in the sense that it can increase when it is reinforced by attention, sympathy, or avoidance of unwanted activities (Bouman et al., 1999). Such individuals may also repeatedly seek out new doctors in the hope of getting medical confirmation of their pain or to obtain medications to relieve their suffering.

TREATMENT OF SOMATOFORM PAIN DISORDER

Perhaps because it is a less complex and multifaceted disorder than somatization disorder, pain disorder is usually also easier to treat. Indeed, cognitive-behavioral techniques have been widely used in the treatment of both physical and "psychogenic" pain syndromes. Treatment programs using these techniques generally include relaxation training, support and validation that the pain is real, scheduling of daily activities, cognitive restructuring, and reinforcement of "no-pain" behaviors (Simon, 2002). Patients receiving such treatments tend to show substantial reductions in disability and distress although changes in the intensity of their pain tend to be smaller in magnitude. In addition, antidepressant medications (especially the tricyclic antidepressants) have been shown to reduce pain intensity in a manner independent of the effects the medications may have on mood (Simon, 2002).

Conversion Disorder

Conversion disorder involves a pattern in which symptoms or deficits affecting sensory or voluntary motor functions lead one to think a patient has a medical or neurological condition. However, upon medical examination, it becomes apparent that the pattern of symptoms or deficits cannot be fully explained by any known medical condition. A few typical examples include partial paralysis, blindness, deafness, and pseudoseizures. In addition, psychological factors must be judged to play an important role in the symptoms or deficits, because the symptoms usually either start or are exacerbated by preceding emotional or interpersonal conflicts or stressors. Finally, the person must not be intentionally producing or faking the symptoms, as will be discussed later (APA, 2000).

Early observations dating back to Freud suggested that most people with conversion disorder showed very little of the anxiety and fear that would be expected in a person with a paralyzed arm or loss of sight. This seeming lack of concern (known as *la belle indifférence*—French for "the beautiful indifference") in the way the patient describes what is wrong was thought for a long time to be an important diagnostic criterion for conversion disorder. However, more careful research later showed that *la belle indifférence* actually occurs in only about 30 to 50 percent of patients with conversion disorder, so it has been dropped as a criterion from recent editions of DSM. In fact, it is now thought that most patients with conversion disorder are actually quite anxious and concerned about their symptoms (Iezzi et al., 2001).

Conversion disorder is one of the most intriguing and baffling patterns in psychopathology, and we still have much to learn about it. Unfortunately, contemporary research on this disorder has been very sparse. The term *conversion disorder* is relatively recent, and historically this disorder was one of several disorders that were grouped together under the term **hysteria** (the others being somatization disorder and hysterical personality; see Chapter 2).

Freud used the term *conversion hysteria* for these disorders (which were fairly common in his practice), because he believed that the symptoms were an expression of repressed sexual energy—that is, the unconscious conflict that a person felt about his or her sexual desires was repressed. However, in Freud's view, the anxiety threatens to become conscious, so it is unconsciously *converted* into a bodily disturbance, thereby allowing the person to avoid having to deal with the conflict. For example, a person's guilty feelings about the desire to masturbate might be solved by developing a paralyzed hand. This is not done consciously, of course, and the person is not aware of the origin or meaning of the physical symptom. Freud also thought that the reduction in anxiety and intrapsychic conflict was the primary gain that maintained the condition, but he noted that patients often had many sources of secondary gain as well, such as receiving sympathy and attention from loved ones.

PRECIPITATING CIRCUMSTANCES, ESCAPE, AND SECONDARY GAINS Although Freud's theory that conversion symptoms are caused by the conversion of sexual conflicts or other psychological problems into physical symptoms is no longer accepted outside psychodynamic circles, many of Freud's astute clinical observations about primary and secondary gain are still incorporated into contemporary views of conversion disorder. Although the condition is still called a conversion disorder, the physical symptoms are usually seen as serving the rather obvious function of providing a plausible excuse, enabling an individual to escape or avoid an intolerably stressful situation without having to take responsibility for doing so. Typically, it is thought that the person first experiences a traumatic event that motivates the desire to escape the unpleasant situation, but literal escape may not be feasible or socially acceptable. Moreover, although becoming sick or disabled is more socially acceptable, this is true only if the person's motivation to do so is unconscious.

Thus, in contemporary terms, the **primary gain** for conversion symptoms is continued escape or avoidance of a stressful situation. Because this is all unconscious (that is, the person sees no relation between the symptoms and the stressful situation), the symptoms go away only if the stressful situation has been removed or resolved. Relatedly, the term **secondary gain,** which originally referred to advantages that the symptom(s) bestow beyond the "primary gain" of neutralizing intrapsychic conflict, has also been retained. Generally, it is used to refer to any "external" circumstance, such as attention from loved ones or financial compensation, that would tend to reinforce the maintenance of disability.

DSM-IV-TR

Criteria for Conversion Disorder

A. One or more symptoms affecting voluntary motor or sensory function that suggest a neurological or other medical condition.

B. Psychological factors judged to be associated with the symptoms because they were preceded by conflicts or other stressors.

C. Symptom or deficit cannot be fully explained by a general medical condition.

D. Symptom or deficit causes distress or impairment in functioning.

Source: *Adapted with permission from the* Diagnostic and Statistical Manual of Mental Disorders, Fourth Edition, Text Revision *(Copyright 2000). American Psychiatric Association.*

DECREASING PREVALENCE AND DEMOGRAPHIC CHARACTERISTICS Conversion disorders were once relatively common in civilian and (especially) military life. In World War I, conversion disorder was the most frequently diagnosed psychiatric syndrome among soldiers; it was also relatively common during World War II. Conversion disorder typically occurred under highly stressful combat conditions and involved men who would ordinarily be considered stable. Here, conversion symptoms—such as paralysis of the legs—enabled a soldier to avoid an anxiety-arousing combat situation without being labeled a coward or being subject to court-martial.

Today, however, conversion disorders constitute only some 1 to 3 percent of all disorders referred for mental health treatment. The prevalence in the general population is unknown, but even the highest estimates have been

Conversion disorders were fairly common during World War I and World War II. The disorder typically occurred in otherwise "normal" men during stressful combat conditions. The symptoms of conversion disorder (e.g., paralysis of the legs) enabled a soldier to avoid high-anxiety combat situations without being labeled a coward or being court-martialed.

around 0.005 percent (APA, 2000). Interestingly enough, the decreasing prevalence of conversion disorder seems to be closely related to our growing sophistication about medical and psychological disorders: A conversion disorder apparently loses its defensive function if it can be readily shown to lack an organic basis. When it does occur today, it is most likely to occur in rural people from lower socioeconomic circles who are medically unsophisticated. For example, a highly unusual recent "outbreak" of cases of severe conversion disorder involving serious motor weakness and wasting symptoms were reported in five 9- to 13-year-old girls living in a poor rural Amish community (all within a 21-month period and all within a close distance of one another). Each of these girls had experienced substantial psychosocial stressors including behavioral problems and dysfunctional family dynamics. There had also been a serious crisis in the local church, leading to a great deal of community stress (see Cassady, Kirschke, et al., 2005). Fortunately, after the caregivers of these girls were educated regarding the psychological nature of the symptoms and given advice to stick with one doctor, minimize stress, and avoid reinforcement of the "sick role," four of the five girls showed significant improvement over the next 3 months. In the fifth case the family refused to acknowledge the psychological component of the illness, holding to the belief that the symptoms were caused by parasites.

Conversion disorder occurs two to ten times more often in women than in men. It can develop at any age but most commonly occurs between early adolescence and early adulthood (Maldonado & Spiegel, 2001). It generally has a rapid onset after a significant stressor and often resolves within 2 weeks if the stressor is removed, although it commonly recurs. In many other cases, however, it has a more chronic course. Like most other somatoform disorders, conversion disorder frequently occurs along with other disorders, especially major depression, anxiety disorders, and somatization and dissociative disorders.

RANGE OF CONVERSION DISORDER SYMPTOMS

The range of symptoms for conversion disorder is practically as diverse as for physically based ailments. In describing the clinical picture in conversion disorder, it is useful to think in terms of four categories of symptoms: (1) sensory, (2) motor, (3) seizures, and (4) mixed presentation from the first three categories (APA, 2000).

Sensory Symptoms or Deficits Conversion disorder can involve almost any sensory modality, and it can often be diagnosed as a conversion disorder because symptoms in the affected area are inconsistent with how known anatomical sensory pathways operate. Today the sensory symptoms or deficits are most often in the visual system (especially blindness and tunnel vision), in the auditory system (especially deafness), or in the sensitivity to feeling (especially the anaesthesias). In the anaesthesias, the person loses her or his sense of feeling in a part of the body. One of the most common is *glove anaesthesia,* in which the person cannot feel anything on the hand in the area where gloves are worn, although the loss of sensation usually makes no anatomical sense.

With conversion blindness, the person reports that he or she cannot see and yet can often navigate about a room without bumping into furniture or other objects. With conversion deafness, the person reports not being able to hear and yet orients appropriately upon "hearing" his or her own name. Such observations lead to obvious questions: In conversion blindness (and deafness), can affected persons actually not see or hear, or is the sensory information received but screened from consciousness? In general, the evidence supports the idea that the sensory input is registered but that it is somehow screened from explicit conscious recognition. This *implicit perception* will be discussed later in Developments in Thinking 8.2 on page 299.

Motor Symptoms or Deficits Motor conversion reactions also cover a wide range of symptoms (e.g., Maldonado & Spiegel, 2001). For example, conversion paralysis is usually confined to a single limb such as an arm or a leg, and the loss of function is usually selective for certain functions. For example, a person may not be able to write but may be able to use the same muscles for scratching, or a person may not be able to walk most of the time but may be able to walk in an emergency such as a fire where escape is important. The most common speech-related conversion disturbance is *aphonia,* in which a person is able to talk only in a whisper, although he or she can usually cough in a normal manner. (In true, organic laryngeal paralysis, both the cough and the voice are affected.) Another common motor symptom is difficulty swallowing or the sensation of a lump in the throat (Finkenbine & Miele, 2004).

Seizures Conversion seizures, another relatively common form of conversion symptom, involve pseudoseizures, which resemble epileptic seizures in some ways but can usually be fairly well differentiated via modern medical technology (Bowman & Markand, 2005). For example, patients with pseudoseizures do not show any EEG abnormalities and do not show confusion and loss of memory afterward, as patients with true epileptic seizures do. Moreover, patients with conversion seizures often show excessive thrashing about and writhing not seen with true seizures, and they rarely injure themselves in falls or lose control over their bowels or bladder, as patients with true seizures frequently do.

The following case of conversion disorder clearly shows how "functional" a conversion disorder may be in the overall life circumstances of a patient, despite its exacting a certain cost in illness or disability.

case STUDY **A Wife with "Fits"**

Mrs. Chatterjee, a 26-year-old patient, attends a clinic in New Delhi, India, with complaints of "fits" for the last 4 years. The "fits" are always sudden in onset and usually last 30 to 60 minutes. A few minutes before a fit begins, she knows that it is imminent, and she usually goes to bed. During the fits she becomes unresponsive and rigid throughout her body, with bizarre and thrashing movements of the extremities. Her eyes close and her jaw is clenched, and she froths at the mouth. She frequently cries and sometimes shouts abuses. She is never incontinent of urine or feces, nor does she bite her tongue. After a "fit" she claims to have no memory of it. These episodes recur about once or twice a month. She functions well between the episodes.

Both the patient and her family believe that her "fits" are evidence of a physical illness and are not under her control. However, they recognize that the fits often occur following some stressor such as arguments with family members or friends.... She is described by her family as being somewhat immature but "quite social" and good company. She is self-centered, she craves attention from others, and she often reacts with irritability and anger if her wishes are not immediately fulfilled. On physical examination, Mrs. Chatterjee was found to have mild anemia but was otherwise healthy. A mental status examination did not reveal any abnormality... and her memory was normal. An electroencephalogram showed no seizure activity. (Adapted from Spitzer et al., 2002, pp. 469–70.)

Source: Adapted with permission from the *DSM-IV-TR Casebook* (Copyright 2000). American Psychiatric Publishing, Inc.

IMPORTANT ISSUES IN DIAGNOSING CONVERSION DISORDER Because the symptoms in conversion disorder can simulate a variety of medical conditions, accurate diagnosis can be extremely difficult. It is crucial that a person with suspected conversion symptoms receive a thorough medical and neurological examination. Unfortunately, however, misdiagnoses can still occur. Nevertheless, as medical tests have become increasingly sophisticated, the rate of misdiagnoses has declined substantially from in the past, with estimates of misdiagnoses in the 1990s ranging from about 5 to 10 percent (e.g., Stone, Zeidler & Sharpe, 2002).

Several other criteria are also commonly used for distinguishing between conversion disorders and true organic disturbances:

- The frequent failure of the dysfunction to conform clearly to the symptoms of the particular disease or disorder simulated. For example, little or no wasting away or atrophy of a "paralyzed" limb occurs in conversion paralyses, except in rare and long-standing cases.
- The selective nature of the dysfunction. As already noted, in conversion blindness the affected individual does not usually bump into people or objects, and "paralyzed" muscles can be used for some activities but not others.

Virtually all the symptoms of conversion disorder can be temporarily reduced or reproduced by hypnotic suggestion.

- Under hypnosis or narcosis (a sleeplike state induced by drugs) the symptoms can usually be removed, shifted, or reinduced at the suggestion of the therapist. Similarly, a person abruptly awakened from a sound sleep may suddenly be able to use a "paralyzed" limb.

DISTINGUISHING CONVERSION FROM MALINGERING AND FROM FACTITIOUS DISORDER Sometimes, of course, people do deliberately and consciously feign disability or illness. For these instances, the DSM distinguishes between *malingering* and *factitious disorder* on the basis of the feigning person's apparent goals. The **malingering** person is intentionally producing or grossly exaggerating physical symptoms and is motivated by external incentives such as avoiding work or military service, obtaining financial compensation, or evading criminal prosecution (APA, 2000; Maldonado & Spiegel, 2001). In **factitious disorder** also, the person intentionally produces psychological or physical symptoms (or both), but there are no external incentives. Instead, the person's goal is simply to obtain and maintain the personal benefits that playing the "sick role" (even undergoing repeated hospitalizations) may provide, including the attention and concern of family and medical personnel. Frequently these patients surreptitiously alter their own physiology—for example, by taking drugs—in order to simulate various real illnesses. Indeed, they may be at risk for serious injury or death and may even need to be committed to an institution for their own protection. (See The World Around Us 8.1 for a particularly pathological variation on this.) In the past, severe and chronic forms of factitious disorder with physical symptoms were called "Munchausen's syndrome," where the general idea was that the person had some kind of "hospital addiction" or a "professional patient" syndrome.

It is sometimes possible to distinguish between a conversion (or other somatoform) disorder and malingering, or factitiously "sick" role-playing, with a fair degree of confidence, but in other cases it is more difficult to make the correct diagnosis. Persons engaged in malingering and those who have factitious disorder are consciously perpetrating frauds by faking the symptoms of diseases or disabilities, and this fact is often reflected in their demeanor. Individuals with conversion disorders are not consciously producing their symptoms, feel themselves to be the "victims of their symptoms," and are very willing to discuss them, often in excruciating detail (Maldonado & Spiegel, 2001, p. 109). When inconsistencies in their behaviors are pointed out, they are usually unperturbed. Any secondary gains they experience are by-products of the conversion symptoms themselves and are not involved in motivating the symptoms. By contrast, persons who are feigning symptoms are inclined to be defensive, evasive, and suspicious when asked about them; they are usually reluctant to be examined and slow to talk about their symptoms, lest the pretense be discovered. Should inconsistencies in their behaviors be pointed out, deliberate deceivers as a rule immediately become more defensive. Thus conversion disorder and deliberate faking of illness are considered distinct patterns.

TREATMENT OF CONVERSION DISORDER Our knowledge of how best to treat conversion disorder is extremely limited, because no well-controlled studies have yet been conducted (e.g., Bowman & Markand, 2005; Looper & Kirmayer, 2002). Some hospitalized patients with motor conversion symptoms have been successfully treated with a behavioral approach in which specific exercises are prescribed in order to increase movement or walking, and then reinforcements are provided when patients show improvements (e.g., praise and gaining privileges). Any reinforcements of abnormal motor behaviors are removed in order to eliminate any sources of secondary gain. In one small study using this kind of treatment for ten patients, all had regained their ability to move or walk in an average of 12 days, and for seven of the nine available at approximately 2-year follow-up, the improvements had been maintained (Speed, 1996). Some studies have used hypnosis combined with other problem-solving therapies, and there are some suggestions that hypnosis, or adding hypnosis to other therapeutic techniques, can be useful (Looper & Kirmayer, 2002; Moene et al., 2003).

DSM-IV-TR

Criteria for Factitious Disorder

A. Intentional production or feigning of physical or psychological signs of symptoms.
B. Motivation for the behavior is to assume the sick role.
C. There are no external incentives for the behavior (e.g., economic gain or avoiding legal responsibilities, as seen in Malingering).

Source: *Adapted with permission from the* Diagnostic and Statistical Manual of Mental Disorders, Fourth Edition, Text Revision *(Copyright 2000). American Psychiatric Association.*

Body Dysmorphic Disorder

Body dysmorphic disorder (BDD) is officially classified in DSM-IV-TR (APA, 2000) as a somatoform disorder because it involves preoccupation with certain aspects of the body. People with BDD are obsessed with some *perceived* or *imagined flaw* or flaws in their appearance. This preoccupation is so intense that it causes clinically significant distress and/or impairment in social or occupational functioning. Although it is not considered necessary for the diagnosis, most people with BDD have compulsive checking behaviors (such as checking their appearance in the mirror excessively or hiding or repairing a perceived flaw). Another very common symptom is avoidance of usual activities because of fear that other people will see the imaginary defect and be repulsed. In severe cases they may become so isolated that they lock themselves up in

8.1 THE WORLD AROUND US

Factitious Disorder by Proxy (Munchausen's Syndrome by Proxy)

In a somewhat bizarre variant of factitious disorder, called **factitious disorder by proxy** (or *Munchausen's syndrome by proxy*), the person seeking medical help or consulting a mental health professional falsely reports, or even induces, medical or psychological symptoms in another person who is under his or her care (usually a child). In a typical instance, a mother presents her own child for treatment of a medical condition she has deliberately caused, disclaiming any knowledge of its origin. The majority of such cases involve the gastrointestinal, genitourinary, or central nervous systems, apparently because diseases or dysfunctions in these systems are most readily simulated by excessive administration of widely available drugs (emetics, laxatives, diuretics, CNS stimulants or depressants) or other illness-inducing chemicals (such as cleaning products). Of course, the health of such victims is often seriously endangered by this repeated abuse, and the intervention of social service agencies or law enforcement is sometimes necessary. In as many as 10 percent of cases, this form of child abuse may lead to a child's death (Hall, Eubanks, et al., 2000).

This disorder may be indicated when the victim's clinical presentation is atypical, when lab results are inconsistent with each other or with recognized diseases, or when there are unduly frequent returns or increasingly urgent visits to the same hospital or clinic. The perpetrators (who often have extensive medical knowledge) tend to be highly resistant to admitting the truth (McCann, 1999), and it has been estimated that the average length of time to confirm the diagnosis is 14 months (Rogers, 2004). If they sense that the medical staff is suspicious, they may abruptly terminate contact with that facility, only to show up at another one to begin the entire process anew. Compounding the problem of detection is the fact that health care professionals who realize they have been duped may be reluctant to acknowledge their fallibility for fear of legal action. Misdiagnosing the disorder when the parent is in fact innocent can also lead to legal difficulties for the health care professionals (McNicholas, Slonims, & Cass, 2000). One technique that has been used with considerable success is covert video surveillance of the mother and child during hospitalizations. In one study, 23 of 41 suspected cases were finally determined to have factitious disorder by proxy, and in 56 percent of those cases, video surveillance was essential to the diagnosis (Hall et al., 2000).

Over a period of 20 months, Jennifer, 8, shown here with her mother, Kathy Bush, had been taken to the hospital more than 130 times, underwent 40 surgeries, and amassed over $3 million in medical expenses. Doctors and nurses testified that Jennifer's condition always worsened after her mother visited her daughter at the hospital behind closed doors. In addition, Jennifer's health had significantly improved since being removed from her mother's care. The jury was convinced that Kathy Bush was responsible for causing Jennifer's illnesses. Bush was arrested and diagnosed with Munchausen's syndrome by proxy.

their house and never go out even to work, with the average employment rate estimated at only about 50 percent (Neziroglu et al., 2004).

People with BDD may focus on almost any body part: Their skin has blemishes, their breasts are too small, their face is too thin (or too fat) or disfigured by visible blood vessels that others find repulsive, and so on. One large study found that some of the more common locations for perceived defects included skin (73 percent), hair (56 percent), nose (37 percent), eyes (20 percent), legs (18 percent), chin (11 percent), breasts/chest/nipples (21 percent), stomach (22 percent), lips (12 percent), body build (16 percent), and face size/shape (12 percent; Phillips, 2005); many sufferers have perceived defects in more than one body part. It is very important to remember that these are not the ordinary concerns that most of us have about our appearance; they are far more extreme, leading in many cases to complete preoccupation and significant emotional pain. Some researchers estimate that about half the people with BDD have concerns about their appearance that are of delusional intensity (e.g., Allen & Hollander, 2004). Yet it is important to remember that

TABLE 8.1 Interference in Functioning

Problem	% of People with BDD Who Experienced the Problem or Average Number of Days
Interference with social functioning (e.g., with friends, family, or intimate relationships) due to BDD	99%
Periods of avoidance of nearly all social interactions because of BDD	95%
Interference with work or academic functioning because of BDD	90%
Periods of complete avoidance of work, school, or one's role (e.g., maintaining a household) because of BDD	80%
Days of work missed because of BDD*	52 days
Days of school missed because of BDD*	49 days
Completely housebound for at least 1 week because of BDD	29%
Ever felt depressed because of BDD	94%
Psychiatrically hospitalized at least once because of BDD	26%
Ever thought about suicide because of BDD*	63%
Ever attempted suicide	25%
Ever attempted suicide because of BDD	14%

*Since BDD began

Source: Adapted from *The Broken Mirror: Understanding and Treating Dysmorphic Disorder* by Katherine A. Phillips. © 2005 Oxford University Press. Reprinted by permission.

DSM-IV-TR

Criteria for Body Dysmorphic Disorder

A. Preoccupation with an imagined defect in appearance. If slight physical anomaly is present, person's concern is markedly excessive.

B. Preoccupation causes significant distress or impairment.

Source: *Adapted with permission from the* Diagnostic and Statistical Manual of Mental Disorders, Fourth Edition, Text Revision *(Copyright 2000). American Psychiatric Association.*

People with body dysmorphic disorder often seek plastic surgery for what they perceive to be serious flaws in their appearance. Here the actress Goldie Hawn (as she naturally looks on the left, and as a character in First Wives Club *on the right). Hawn's character is unhappy with her lips, wishing them to be fuller in shape. She has plastic surgery to make them fuller, and yet is still quite unhappy with the outcome, as is typical of individuals with body dysmorphic disorder who undergo such surgery.*

others do not even see the defects that the person with BDD has, or if they do, they see only a very minor defect within the normal range.

Another common feature of BDD is that people with this condition frequently seek reassurance from friends and family about their defects, but the reassurances almost never provide more than very temporary relief. They also frequently seek reassurance for themselves by checking their appearance in the mirror countless times in a day (although some avoid mirrors completely). They are usually driven by the hope that they will look different, and sometimes they may think their perceived defect does not look as bad as it has at other times. However, much more commonly they feel worse after mirror gazing (Veale & Riley, 2001). They frequently engage in excessive grooming behavior, often trying to camouflage their perceived defect through their hairstyle, clothing, or makeup (Sarwer, Gibbons, & Crerand, 2004).

The following case illustrates the primary features of this disorder.

case STUDY — The Elephant Man

Chris is a shy, anxious-looking, 31-year-old carpenter who has been hospitalized after making a suicide attempt.... He asks to meet with the psychiatrist in a darkened room. He is wearing a baseball cap pulled down over his forehead. Looking down at the floor, Chris says he has no friends, has just been fired from his job, and was recently rejected by his girlfriend. "It's my nose... these huge pockmarks on my nose. They're grotesque! I look like a monster. I'm as ugly as the Elephant Man! These marks on my nose are all that I can think about. I've thought about them every day for the past 15 years, and I think that everyone can see them and that they laugh at me because of them. That's why I wear this hat all the time. And that's why I couldn't talk to you in a bright room... you'd see how ugly I am."

The psychiatrist couldn't see the huge pockmarks that Chris was referring to, even in a brightly lit room. Chris is, in fact, a handsome man with normal-appearing facial pores. [Later Chris says,] "I've pretty much kept this preoccupation a secret because it's so embarrassing. I'm afraid people will think I'm vain. But I've told a few people about it, and they've tried to convince me that the pores really aren't visible.... This problem has ruined my life. All I can think about is my face. I spend hours a day looking at the marks in the mirror.... I started missing more and more work, and I stopped going out with my friends and my girlfriend... staying in the house most of the time...."

Chris... had seen a dermatologist to request dermabrasion, but was refused the procedure because "there was nothing there." He finally convinced another dermatologist to do the procedure but thought it did not help. Eventually he felt so desperate that he made two suicide attempts. His most recent attempt occurred after he looked in the mirror and was horrified by what he saw... "I saw how awful I looked, and I thought, I'm not sure it's worth it to go on living if I have to look like this and think about this all the time." (Adapted from Spitzer et al., 2002, pp. 7–9.)

Source: Adapted with permission from the *DSM-IV-TR Casebook* (Copyright 2000). American Psychiatric Publishing, Inc.

PREVALENCE, GENDER, AND AGE OF ONSET There are no official estimates of the prevalence of BDD, and they might actually be difficult to obtain because of the great secrecy that usually surrounds this disorder. Some leading researchers estimate that it is not a rare disorder, affecting perhaps 1 to 2 percent of the general population, up to 8 percent of people with depression (e.g., Allen & Hollander, 2004; Phillips, 2005). The prevalence seems to be approximately equal in men and women (Phillips, 2005; Phillips & Diaz, 1997). The age of onset is usually in adolescence, when many people start to become preoccupied with their appearance. People with BDD very commonly also have a depressive diagnosis (with most estimates being over 50 percent; Allen & Hollander, 2004), and, as in Chris's case, it often leads to suicide attempts or completed suicide (Neziroglu et al., 2004; Phillips, 2001). Rates of comorbid social phobia and obsessive-compulsive disorder are also quite substantial, although not as high as for depression (Allen & Hollander, 2004).

Sufferers of BDD like Chris commonly make their way into the office of a dermatologist or plastic surgeon, one recent estimate being that over 75 percent seek nonpsychiatric treatment (Phillips, Grant, Siniscalchi, & Albertini, 2001). One recent study found that 8 percent of those seeking cosmetic medical treatments met criteria for BDD (Crerand, Sarwer, et al., 2004), although other studies have estimated this to be 20 percent (Phillips, 2005). An astute doctor will not do the requested procedures and may instead make a referral to a psychologist or psychiatrist. All too often, though, the patient, like Chris, does get what he or she requests—and unfortunately is almost never satisfied with the outcome.

RELATIONSHIP TO OCD AND EATING DISORDERS Many researchers believe that BDD is closely related to obsessive-compulsive disorder and have proposed it as one of the obsessive-compulsive spectrum disorders (e.g., Allen & Hollander, 2004). At this point, the similarities to OCD should be fairly obvious. Like people with OCD, those with BDD have prominent obsessions, and they engage in a variety of ritualistic-like behaviors such as reassurance seeking, mirror checking, comparing themselves to others, and camouflage. Moreover, they are even more convinced that their obsessive beliefs are accurate than are people with OCD (Eisen, Phillips, Coles, & Rasmussen, 2003). But in addition to these similarities in symptoms, research is also increasingly suggesting an overlap in causes. For example, the same sets of brain structures are implicated in the two disorders (Rauch et al., 2003; Rivera & Borda, 2001), and, as we will discuss later, the same kinds of treatments that work for OCD are also the treatments of choice for BDD (Phillips, 2005).

Other researchers have also noted significant overlapping features between BDD and eating disorders (especially anorexia nervosa), the most striking similarity being the body image distortion in both kinds of conditions. Specifically, excessive concerns and preoccupation about physical appearance, dissatisfaction with one's body, and a distorted image of certain features of one's body are central to the diagnostic criteria for each (Allen & Hollander, 2004; Cororve & Gleaves, 2001). (See Chapter 9.)

WHY NOW? BDD has clearly existed for centuries, if not for all time. Why, then, did its examination in the literature begin only recently? One possible reason is that its prevalence may actually have increased in recent years as contemporary Western culture has become increasingly focused on "looks as everything," with billions of dollars spent each year on enhancing appearance through makeup, clothes, plastic surgery, etc. (Fawcett, 2004). A second reason BDD has been understudied is that most people with this condition never seek psychological or psychiatric treatment. Rather, they suffer silently or go to dermatologists or plastic surgeons (Crerand, Sarwer, et al., 2004; Phillips, 1996, 2001). Reasons for this secrecy and shame include worries that others will think they are superficial, silly, or vain and that if they mention their perceived defect, others will notice it and focus more on it. Part of the reason why more people are now seeking treatment is that the disorder has received a good deal of media attention in the past decade. It has even been discussed on some daily talk shows, where it is sometimes called "imaginary defect disorder." As increasing attention is focused on this disorder, the secrecy and shame often surrounding it should decrease, and more people will seek treatment. A leading researcher in this area is Katharine Phillips (1996, 2005), who carefully described the condition in *The Broken Mirror: Understanding and Treating Body Dysmorphic Disorder,* a book that was written (and later revised) for people who suffer from this disorder as well as for their families and clinicians.

A BIOPSYCHOSOCIAL APPROACH TO BDD Our understanding of what causes BDD is still in a preliminary stage, but recent research seems to suggest that a biopsychosocial approach offers some reasonable hypotheses. First, it seems likely that there is a partially genetically based personality predisposition that people with BDD may share in common with people who have OCD and perhaps other anxiety disorders (such as neuroticism), although evidence for this currently is minimal. Second, BDD seems to be occurring, at least today, in a sociocultural context that places great value on attractiveness and beauty, and people who develop BDD often hold attractiveness as their primary value, meaning that their self-schemas are heavily focused around such ideas as, "If my appearance is defective, then I am worthless" (endorsed by 60 percent in one study; Buhlmann & Wilhelm, 2004, p. 924). One possibility why this occurs is that in many cases they were reinforced as children for their overall appearance more than for their behavior (Neziroglu et al., 2004). Another possibility is that they later were teased or criticized for their appearance, which caused conditioning of disgust, shame, or anxiety to their own image of some part of their body. In addition, substantial empirical evidence now demonstrates that people with BDD show biased attention and interpretation of information relating to attractiveness (e.g., Buhlmann & Wilhelm, 2004). They selectively attend to positive or negative words such as *ugly* or *beautiful* more than to other emotional words not related to appearance, and they tend to interpret ambiguous facial expressions as contemptuous or angry more than do controls. Whether or not these attentional and interpretive biases play a causal role is not yet known, but certainly having such biases in processing information relating to attractiveness would, at a minimum, serve to perpetuate the disorder once it has developed.

TREATMENT OF BODY DYSMORPHIC DISORDER As we have already noted, the treatments that are effective for BDD are closely related to those used in the effective treatment of obsessive-compulsive disorder (see Chapter 6). There is some evidence that antidepressant medications from the selective serotonin reuptake inhibitor category often produce moderate improvement in patients with BDD, but many are not helped or show only a modest improvement (Phillips, 2004, 2005). In addition, a form of cognitive-behavioral treatment emphasizing exposure and response prevention has been shown to produce marked improvement in 50 to 80 percent of treated patients (Sarwer et al., 2004; Simon, 2002). These treatment approaches focus on getting the patient to identify and change distorted perceptions of his or her body during exposure to anxiety-provoking situations (e.g., wearing something that highlights rather than disguises the "defect"), and on prevention of checking responses (e.g., mirror checking, reassurance seeking, and repeated examining of the imaginary defect). The treatment gains are generally well maintained at follow-up (Looper & Kirmayer, 2002; Sarwer et al., 2004).

In Review

- What are the primary characteristics of hypochondriasis and how does the cognitive-behavioral viewpoint explain their occurrence?
- What are the symptoms of somatization disorder and of pain disorder?
- What are sources of primary and secondary gains involved in conversion disorders and how is conversion disorder distinguished from malingering and from factitious disorder?
- What are the primary symptoms of body dysmorphic disorder and how are they related to obsessive-compulsive disorder?

Dissociative Disorders

The concept of dissociation, which is over a century old, refers to the human mind's capacity to mediate complex mental activity in channels split off from, or independent of, conscious awareness (Kihlstrom, 1994, 2001, 2005). We all dissociate to a degree some of the time. Mild dissociative symptoms occur when we daydream or lose track of what is going on around us, when we drive miles beyond our destination without realizing how we got there, or when we miss part of a conversation we are engaged in. As these everyday examples of acts performed without conscious awareness suggest, there is nothing inherently pathological about dissociation itself.

More specifically, much of a normal individual's mental life involves nonconscious processes that are to a large extent autonomous with respect to deliberate, self-aware monitoring and direction. Such unaware processing extends to the areas of memory and perception, where it can be demonstrated that normal persons routinely show indirect evidence of remembering things they cannot consciously recall (*implicit memory*), and respond to sights or sounds as if they had perceived them (as in conversion blindness or deafness), even though they cannot report that they have seen or heard them (*implicit perception*; Kihlstrom, 2001, 2005; Kihlstrom, Tataryn, & Hoyt, 1993). As we have seen, the general idea of unconscious mental processes has been embraced by psychodynamically oriented clinicians for many years. But only in the past quarter-century has it also become a major research area in the field of cognitive psychology (though without any of the psychodynamic implications for why so much of our mental activity is unconscious).

In the dissociative disorders, however, this normally integrated and well-coordinated multichannel quality of human cognition becomes much less coordinated and integrated. When this happens, the affected person may be unable to access information that is normally in the forefront of consciousness, such as his or her own personal identity or details of an important period of time in the recent past. That is, the normally useful capacity to maintain ongoing mental activity outside of awareness appears to be subverted, sometimes for the purpose of managing severe psychological threat. When that happens, we observe the pathological dissociative symptoms that are the cardinal characteristic of dissociative disorders. As we will see, it is likely that some people have certain personality traits that make them more susceptible than others to developing dissociative symptoms and disorders.

Like somatoform disorders, dissociative disorders appear mainly to be ways of avoiding anxiety and stress and of managing life problems that threaten to overwhelm the person's usual coping resources. Both types of disorders also enable the individual to deny personal responsibility for his or her "unacceptable" wishes or behavior. In the case of DSM-defined dissociative disorders, the person avoids the stress by pathologically dissociating—in essence by escaping from his or her own autobiographical memory, or personal identity. The DSM-IV-TR recognizes several types of pathological dissociation.

DSM-IV-TR

Criteria for Depersonalization Disorder

A. Persistent or recurrent experiences of feeling detached from one's mental processes or body.

B. During this experience, reality testing remains intact.

C. Causes significant distress or impairment in functioning.

Source: *Adapted with permission from the* Diagnostic and Statistical Manual of Mental Disorders, Fourth Edition, Text Revision *(Copyright 2000). American Psychiatric Association.*

Depersonalization Disorder

Two of the more common kinds of dissociative symptoms are derealization and depersonalization, which we mentioned in Chapters 5 and 6 because they sometimes occur during stress disorders and panic attacks. In **derealization** one's sense of the reality of the outside world is temporarily lost, and in **depersonalization** one's sense of one's own self and one's own reality is temporarily lost. As many as half of us have such experiences in mild form at least once in our lives, usually during or after periods of severe stress, sleep deprivation, or sensory deprivation (e.g., Khazaal, Zimmerman, & Zullino, 2005). But when episodes of depersonalization (and derealization) become persistent and recurrent and interfere with normal functioning, **depersonalization disorder** may be diagnosed.

People with derealization symptoms experience the world as hazy and indistinct.

In this disorder, people have persistent or recurrent experiences of feeling detached from (and like an outside observer of) their own bodies and mental processes. They may even feel they are, for a time, floating above their physical bodies, which may suddenly feel very different—as if drastically changed or unreal. During periods of depersonalization, unlike during psychotic states, reality testing remains intact. The related experience of derealization, in which the external world is perceived as strange and new in various ways, may also occur. As one leader in the field described it, in both states "the feeling puzzles the experiencers: the changed condition is perceived as unreal, and as discontinuous with his or her previous ego-states. The object of the experience, self (in depersonalization) or world (in derealization), is commonly described as isolated, lifeless, strange, and unfamiliar; oneself and others are perceived as 'automatons,' behaving mechanically, without initiative or self-control" (Kihlstrom, 2001, p. 267). Often sufferers also report feeling as though they are living in a dream or movie (Maldonado, Butler, & Spiegel, 2002). In keeping with such reports, recent research has shown that emotional experiences are attenuated during depersonalization—both at the subjective level and at the level of neural and autonomic activity that normally accompanies emotional responses (Phillips & Sierra, 2003).

The following case is fairly typical.

case STUDY A Foggy Student

A 20-year-old male college student sought psychiatric consultation because he was worried that he might be going insane. For the past 2 years he had experienced increasingly frequent episodes of feeling "outside" himself. These episodes were accompanied by a sense of deadness in his body. In addition, during these periods he was uncertain of his balance and frequently stumbled into furniture; this was more apt to occur in public, especially if he was somewhat anxious. During these episodes he felt a lack of easy, natural control of his body, and his thoughts seemed "foggy" as well. . . .

The patient's subjective sense of lack of control was especially troublesome, and he would fight it by shaking his head and saying "stop" to himself. This would momentarily clear his mind and restore his sense of autonomy, but only temporarily, as the feelings of deadness and of being outside himself would return. Gradually, over a period of several hours, the unpleasant experiences would fade . . . At the time the patient came for treatment, he was experiencing these symptoms about twice a week, and each incident lasted from 3 to 4 hours. On several occasions the episodes had occurred while he was driving his car and was alone; worried that he might have an accident, he had stopped driving unless someone accompanied him. (Adapted from Spitzer et al., 2002, pp. 270–71.)

Source: Adapted with permission from the *DSM-IV-TR Casebook* (Copyright 2000). American Psychiatric Publishing, Inc.

In a study of 30 cases of depersonalization disorder, Simeon et al. (1997) noted elevated levels of comorbid anxiety and mood disorders, as well as avoidant, borderline, and obsessive-compulsive personality disorders (see also Hunter, Phillips, et al., 2003). Another study of over 200 cases found that the disorder had an average age of onset of 23. Moreover, in nearly 80 percent of cases the disorder has a fairly chronic course (with little or no fluctuation in intensity; Baker, Hunter, et al., 2003). Another study by Simeon et al. (2001) also revealed more self-reported emotional abuse among those with depersonalization disorder than in a nondissociative control group.

The lifetime prevalence of depersonalization disorder is unknown, but occasional depersonalization symptoms are not uncommon in a variety of other disorders such as schizophrenia, borderline personality disorder, panic disorder, acute stress disorder, and PTSD (Hunter, Phillips, et al., 2003). Although severe depersonalization symptoms can be quite frightening and may make the victim fear imminent mental collapse, such fears are usually unfounded. Sometimes, however, feelings of depersonalization are early manifestations of impending decompensation and the development of psychotic states (Chapter 14). In either case, professional assistance in dealing with the precipitating stressors and in reducing anxiety may be helpful.

Dissociative Amnesia and Fugue

Retrograde amnesia is the partial or total inability to recall or identify previously acquired information or past experiences; by contrast, *anterograde amnesia* is the partial or total inability to retain new information (Kapur, 1999; McNally, 2003). Persistent amnesia may occur in several Axis I disorders such as dissociative amnesia and dissociative fugue, and in organic brain pathology including traumatic brain injury and diseases of the central nervous system. If the amnesia is caused by *brain pathology* (diagnosed as "Amnestic Disorder Due to a General Medical Condition"; see Chapter 15), it most often involves failure to retain new information and experiences (anterograde amnesia). That is, the information contained in experience is not registered and does not enter memory storage (Kapur, 1999).

In the movie Memento, *the lead character has anterograde amnesia, which makes him unable to form any short-term memories. He has to write notes to himself and refer to them constantly in order to function on a daily basis.*

On the other hand, **dissociative amnesia** (or *psychogenic amnesia*) is usually limited to a failure to recall previously stored personal information, when that failure cannot be accounted for by ordinary forgetting (retrograde amnesia). The gaps in memory most often occur following intolerably stressful circumstances—wartime combat conditions, for example, or catastrophic events such as serious car accidents, suicide attempts, or violent outbursts. In this disorder, apparently forgotten personal information is still there beneath the level of consciousness, as sometimes becomes apparent in interviews conducted under hypnosis or narcosis (induced by sodium amytal, or so-called "truth serum") and in cases where the amnesia spontaneously clears up. Four primary types of psychogenic amnesia are recognized by DSM-IV-TR: *localized* (a person remembers nothing that happened during a specific period, most commonly the first few hours or days following some highly traumatic event); *selective* (a person forgets some but not all of what happened during a given period); *generalized* (a person forgets his or her life history including his or her identity); and *continuous* (a person remembers nothing beyond a certain point in the past until the present). The latter two types occur rarely.

Usually amnesic episodes last between a few days and a few years, and although some people experience only one such episode, many people have multiple episodes in their lifetimes (Maldonado et al., 2002). In typical dissociative amnesic reactions, individuals cannot remember certain aspects of their personal life history or important facts about their identity. Yet their basic habit patterns—such as their abilities to read, talk, perform skilled work, and so on—remain intact, and they seem normal aside from the memory deficit (Kihlstrom, 2005; Kihlstrom & Schacter, 2000). Thus only a particular type of memory is affected, the type of memory psychologists refer to as *episodic* (pertaining to events experienced) or *autobiographical* memory. The other recognized forms of memory—semantic (pertaining to language and concepts), procedural (how to do things), and short-term storage—seem usually to remain intact, although there is very little research on this topic (Kihlstrom, 2005; Kihlstrom & Schacter, 2000).

In very rare cases, a person may retreat still further from real-life problems by going into an amnesic state called a **dissociative fugue,** which, as the term implies (the French word *fugue* means "flight"), is a defense by actual flight—a person not only is amnesic for some or all aspects of his or her past but also departs from home surroundings. This is accompanied by confusion about personal identity or even the assumption of a new identity (although the identities do not alternate as in dissociative identity disorder). During the fugue, such individuals are unaware of memory loss for prior stages of their life, but their memory for what happens during the fugue state itself is intact (Kihlstrom, 2005; Kihlstrom & Schacter, 2000). Their behavior during the fugue state is usually quite normal and unlikely to arouse suspicion that something is wrong. However, behavior during the fugue state often reflects a rather different lifestyle from the previous one (the rejection of which is sometimes fairly obvious). Days, weeks, or sometimes even years later, such people may suddenly emerge from the fugue state and find themselves in a strange place working in a new occupation, with no idea how they got there. In other cases, recovery from the fugue state occurs only after repeated questioning and reminders of who they are. In either case, as the fugue state remits, their initial amnesia remits—but a new, apparently complete amnesia for their fugue period occurs.

The pattern in dissociative amnesia and fugue is essentially similar to that in conversion symptoms, except that instead of avoiding some unpleasant situation by becoming physically dysfunctional, a person unconsciously avoids thoughts about the situation or, in the extreme, leaves the scene (Maldonado et al., 2002). Thus people experiencing dissociative amnesia and fugue are typically faced with extremely unpleasant situations from which they see no acceptable way to escape. Eventually the stress becomes so

DSM-IV-TR

Criteria for Dissociative Amnesia

A. Primary disturbance is one or more episodes of inability to recall important personal information too extensive to be explained by ordinary forgetfulness.

B. Symptoms cause distress or impairment in functioning.

DSM-IV-TR

Criteria for Dissociative Fugue

A. Primary disturbance is sudden, unexpected travel away from home or work with inability to recall one's past.

B. Confusion about personal identity or assumption of a new identity.

C. Symptoms cause distress or impairment in functioning.

intolerable that large segments of their personalities and all memory of the stressful situations are suppressed.

Several of these aspects of dissociative fugue are illustrated in the following case.

case STUDY **A Middle Manager Transformed into a Short-Order Cook**

Burt Tate, a 42-year-old short-order cook in a small-town diner, was brought to the attention of local police following a heated altercation with another man at the diner. He gave his name as Burt Tate and indicated that he had arrived in town several weeks earlier. However, he could produce no official identification and could not tell the officers where he had previously lived and worked. Burt was asked to accompany the officers to the emergency room of a local hospital so that he might be examined....

Burt's physical examination was negative for evidence of recent head trauma or any other medical abnormality.... He was oriented as to current time and place, but manifested no recall of his personal history prior to his arrival in town. He did not seem especially concerned about his total lack of a remembered past....

Meanwhile, the police...discovered that Burt matched the description of one Gene Saunders, a resident of a city some 200 miles away who had disappeared a month earlier. The wife of Mr. Saunders...confirmed the real identity of Burt, who...stated that he did not recognize Mrs. Saunders.

Prior to his disappearance, Gene Saunders, a middle-level manager in a large manufacturing firm, had been experiencing considerable difficulties at work and at home. A number of stressful work problems, including failure to get an expected promotion, the loss of some of his key staff, failure of his section to meet production goals, and increased criticism from his superior—all occurring within a brief time frame—had upset his normal equanimity. He had become morose and withdrawn at home, and had been critical of his wife and children. Two days before he had left, he had had a violent argument with his 18-year-old son, who'd declared his father a failure and had stormed out of the house to go live with friends. (Adapted from Spitzer et al., 2002, pp. 215–16.)

Source: Adapted with permission from the *DSM-IV-TR Casebook* (Copyright 2000). American Psychiatric Publishing, Inc.

MEMORY AND INTELLECTUAL DEFICITS IN DISSOCIATIVE AMNESIA AND FUGUE Unfortunately, very little systematic research has been conducted on individuals with dissociative amnesia and fugue. What is known comes largely from intensive studies of the memory and intellectual functioning of isolated cases with these disorders, so any conclusions should be considered tentative pending further study of larger samples with appropriate control groups. What can be gathered from a handful of such case studies is that these individuals' semantic knowledge (assessed via the vocabulary subtest of an IQ test) seems to be generally intact. The primary deficit these individuals exhibit is their compromised episodic or autobiographical memory (Kihlstrom, 2005; Kihlstrom & Schacter, 2000). Indeed, several studies using brain-imaging techniques have confirmed that when people with dissociative amnesia are presented with autobiographical memory tasks, they show reduced activation in their right frontal and temporal brain areas relative to normals doing the same kinds of tasks (Kihlstrom, 2005; Markowitsch, 1999).

However, several cases (some nearly a century old) have suggested that implicit memory is generally intact. For example, Jones (1909, as cited in Kihlstrom & Schacter, 2000) studied a patient with dense amnesia and found that although he could not remember his wife's or daughter's names, when asked to guess what names might fit them, he produced their names correctly. In a more recent case (Lyon, 1985, as cited in Kihlstrom & Schacter, 2000), a patient who could not retrieve any autobiographical information was asked to dial numbers on a phone randomly. Without realizing what he was doing, he dialed his mother's phone number, which then led to her identifying him. In one particularly fascinating recent case of dissociative fugue, Glisky and colleagues (2004) described a German man who had come to work in the United States several months before he experienced a traumatic incident in which he was robbed and shot, at which point he wandered along unfamiliar streets for an unknown period of time. Finally, he stopped at a motel and asked if the police could be called because he did not know who he was (and had no ID because he'd been robbed) and could not recall any personal details of his life. He spoke in English (with a German accent) but could not speak German and did not respond to German instructions (which he denied that he spoke). In spite of his extensive loss of autobiographical memory (and the German language), when given a variety of memory tasks, he showed intact implicit memory. Especially striking was his ability to learn German-English word pairs, which he learned much faster than did normal controls, suggesting implicit knowledge of German even though he had no conscious knowledge of it.

Some of these memory deficits in dissociative amnesia and fugue have been compared to related deficits in explicit perception that occur in conversion disorders. This has convinced a good number of current theorists that conversion disorder should be classified with dissociative disorders rather than with somatoform disorders, as discussed in Developments in Thinking 8.2.

Dissociative Identity Disorder (DID)

According to DSM-IV-TR, **dissociative identity disorder (DID),** formerly called *multiple personality disorder* (MPD), is a dramatic dissociative disorder in which a

8.2 Developments in Thinking

Should Conversion Disorder Be Classified as a Dissociative Disorder?

Starting with Freud and Janet, and for a large portion of the twentieth century prior to the publication of DSM-III in 1980, conversion disorders were classified together with dissociative disorders as subtypes of hysteria (e.g., Hysterical Neurosis, Dissociative Type rather than the Hysterical Neurosis, Conversion Type listed in DSM-II). When it was determined that DSM-III would rely heavily on overt behavioral symptoms rather than on presumed underlying etiology (namely repressed anxiety) for classifying disorders, the decision was made to include conversion disorder with the other somatoform disorders, because the symptoms always appeared to be physical ones with no demonstrable organic basis. However, as Kihlstrom (1994, 2001, 2005) and others have pointed out, this way of linking conversion disorders together with all the other somatoform disorders, by focusing on their all having baseless physical complaints, ignores several important differences between conversion disorders and other somatoform disorders. The most important overall difference is that conversion symptoms (but not those of the other somatoform disorders) are nearly always pseudoneurological in nature (blindness, paralysis, anaesthesias, deafness, seizures, etc.), mimicking some true neurological syndromes, just as most of the dissociative disorders do.

The disorders we currently classify as dissociative disorders (such as dissociative amnesia and fugue and dissociative identity disorder) involve disruptions in explicit memory for events that have occurred, or who or what one's identity is, or both. However, it is clear that events occurring during a period of amnesia or in the presence of one identity are indeed registered in the nervous system, because they influence behavior indirectly even when the person cannot consciously recollect them (i.e., *implicit memory* remains at least partially intact in dissociative disorders). Similarly, Kihlstrom and others have argued that the conversion disorders involve disruptions in *explicit perception* and *action*. That is, people with conversion disorders have no conscious recognition that they can see or hear or feel, or no conscious knowledge that they can walk or talk. However, patients with conversion disorder can see, hear, feel, or move when tricked into doing so or when indirect physiological or behavioral measures are used (see Janet, 1901, 1907; Kihlstrom, 1994, 2001, 2005). Thus Kihlstrom (1994, 2001, 2005) makes a compelling argument that when the next edition of DSM appears, the term *conversion disorder* should be dropped and the sensory and motor types of the syndrome should be reclassified as forms of dissociative disorders. This way, the central feature of all dissociative disorders would be a disruption of the normally integrated functions of consciousness (memory, perception, and action). Such a proposal is also consistent with observations that dissociative symptoms and disorders are quite common in patients with conversion disorder (e.g., Sar et al., 2004).

patient manifests two or more distinct identities that alternate in some way in taking control of behavior. There is also an inability to recall important personal information that cannot be explained by ordinary forgetting. Each identity may appear to have a different personal history, self-image, and name, although there are some identities that are only partially distinct and independent from other identities. In most cases the one identity that is most frequently encountered and carries the person's real name is the **host identity.** In most cases the host is not the original identity, and it may or may not be the best-adjusted identity. The **alter identities** may differ in striking ways involving gender, age, handedness, handwriting, sexual orientation, prescription for eyeglasses, predominant affect, foreign languages spoken, and general knowledge. For example, one alter may be carefree, fun-loving, and sexually provocative, and another alter quiet, studious, serious, and prudish. Needs and behaviors inhibited in the primary or host identity are usually liberally displayed by one or more alter identities. Certain roles such as a child and someone of the opposite sex are extremely common.

DSM-IV-TR

Criteria for Dissociative Identity Disorder

A. Presence of two or more distinct identities, each with its own relatively enduring pattern of perceiving, relating to, and thinking about the environment and the self.

B. At least two of the identities recurrently take control of the person's behavior.

C. Inability to recall important personal information that is too extensive to be explained by ordinary forgetfulness.

Source: *Adapted with permission from the* Diagnostic and Statistical Manual of Mental Disorders, Fourth Edition, Text Revision *(Copyright 2000). American Psychiatric Association.*

Much of the reason for abandoning the older diagnostic term *multiple personality disorder* in favor of DID was the growing recognition that it conveyed misleading information, suggesting multiple occupancy of space, time, and victims' bodies by differing, but fully organized and coherent, "personalities." In fact, alters are not in any meaningful sense personalities but rather reflect a failure to integrate various aspects of a person's identity, consciousness, and memory (APA, 2000). The term *DID* betters captures these changes in consciousness and identity than does *MPD*.

Alter identities take control at different points in time and the switches typically occur very quickly (in a matter of seconds), although more gradual switches can also occur (APA, 2000). When switches occur in people with DID, it is often easy to observe the gaps in memories for things that have happened—often for things that have happened to other identities. But this amnesia is not always symmetrical; that is, some identities may know more about certain alters than do other identities. Sometimes one submerged identity gains control by producing hallucinations (such as a voice inside the head giving instructions). In sum, DID is a condition in which normally integrated aspects of memory, identity, and consciousness are no longer integrated.

The presence of more than one identity and significant amnesia for what alter identities have experienced are not the only symptoms of DID. Other symptoms include depression, self-mutilation, and frequent suicidal ideation and attempts. People with DID often show moodiness and erratic behavior, headaches, hallucinations, substance abuse, post-traumatic symptoms, and other amnesic and fugue symptoms (APA, 2000; Maldonado et al., 2002).

The disorder usually starts in childhood, although most patients are in their twenties or thirties at the time of diagnosis (Ross, 1997). Approximately three to nine times more females than males are diagnosed as having the disorder, and females tend to have a larger number of alters than do males (APA, 2000). Some believe that this pronounced gender discrepancy is due to the much greater proportion of *childhood sexual abuse* among females than among males (see Chapter 13), but this is a highly controversial point, as discussed later.

Many of these features are illustrated in the case of Mary Kendall.

case study — Mary and Marian

Mary, a 35-year-old divorced social worker, had . . . in her right forearm and hand . . . chronic pain. Medical management of this pain had proved problematic, and it was decided to teach her self-hypnosis as a means whereby she might control it. She proved an excellent hypnotic subject and quickly learned effective pain control techniques.

Her hypnotist/trainer, a psychiatrist, describes Mary's life in rather unappealing terms. She is said to be competent professionally but has an "arid" personal and social life. Although her brief marriage ended some 10 years ago, she evidences little interest in men and doesn't seem to have any close friends. She spends most of her free time doing volunteer work in a hospice . . .

In the course of the hypnotic training, Mary's psychiatrist discovered that she seemed to have substantial gaps in her memory. One phenomenon in particular was very puzzling: She reported that she could not account for what seemed an extraordinary depletion of the gasoline in her car's tank. She would arrive home from work with a nearly full tank, and by the following morning as she began her trip to work would notice that the tank was now only half-full. When it was advised that she keep track of her odometer readings, she discovered that on many nights on which she insisted she'd remained at home, the odometer showed significant accumulations of up to 100 miles. The psychiatrist, by now strongly suspecting that Mary had a dissociative disorder, also established that there were large gaps in her memories of childhood. He shifted his focus to exploring the apparently widespread dissociative difficulties.

In the course of one of the continuing hypnotic sessions, the psychiatrist again asked about "lost time," and was greeted with a response in a wholly different voice tone that said, "It's about time you knew about me." Marian, an apparently well-established alter identity, went on to describe the trips she was fond of taking at night . . . Marian was an extraordinarily abrupt and hostile "person," the epitome in these respects of everything the compliant and self-sacrificing Mary was not. Marian regarded Mary with unmitigated contempt, and asserted that "worrying about anyone but yourself is a waste of time."

In due course some six other alter identities emerged . . . There was notable competition among the alters for time spent "out," and Marian was often so provocative as to frighten some of the more timid others, which included a six-year-old child. . . .

Mary's history, as gradually pieced together, included memories of physical and sexual abuse by her father as well as others during her childhood. . . . Her mother was described . . . as having abdicated to a large extent the maternal role, forcing Mary from a young age to assume these duties in the family.

Four years of subsequent psychotherapy resulted in only modest success in achieving a true "integration" of these diverse trends in Mary Kendall's selfhood. (Adapted from Spitzer et al., 2002, pp.56–57.)

Source: Adapted with permission from the *DSM-IV-TR Casebook* (Copyright 2000). American Psychiatric Publishing, Inc.

Chris Sizemore was the inspiration for the book and movie Three Faces of Eve, *which explore her multiple personality disorder (now known as DID). Sizemore recovered in 1975 and then worked as an advocate for the mentally ill.*

The number of alter identities in DID varies tremendously and has increased over time. One review of 76 classic cases published in 1944 reported that two-thirds of these cases had only two personalities and most of the rest had three (Taylor & Martin, 1944). Yet more recent estimates in DSM-IV-TR are that about 50 percent now show over ten identities (APA, 2000), with some respondents claiming as many as a hundred. This historical trend of increasing multiplicity suggests the operation of social factors, perhaps through the encouragement of therapists, as we discuss below (e.g., Lilienfeld et al., 1999; Piper & Merskey, 2004a, 2004b; Spanos, 1996). Another recent trend is that many of the reported cases of DID now include more unusual and even bizarre identities than in the past (such as being an animal) and more highly implausible backgrounds (for example, ritualized satanic abuse in childhood).

PREVALENCE—WHY HAS DID BEEN INCREASING? Owing to their dramatic nature, cases of DID have received a great deal of attention and publicity in fiction, television, and motion pictures. But in fact, until relatively recently, DID was extremely rare—or at least rarely diagnosed—in clinical practice. Prior to 1979, only about 200 cases could be found in the entire psychological and psychiatric literature worldwide. By 1999, however, over 30,000 cases had been reported in North America alone (Ross, 1999), although as we will discuss later, many researchers in this area believe that this is a gross overestimate of true cases (e.g., Piper & Merskey, 2004b). Although their diagnosed occurrence in clinical settings has increased enormously in recent years, prevalence estimates in the general population vary tremendously, and it is possible that no such estimates are valid, given how hard it is to make this diagnosis reliably. (For example, recall that Mary's DID was uncovered only in the course of hypnotic sessions for pain management.)

Many factors probably have contributed to the drastic increase in the reported prevalence of DID (although in an absolute sense it is still very rare, and most practicing psychotherapists never see a person with DID in their entire careers). For example, the number of cases began to rise in the 1970s after the publication of Flora Rhea Schreiber's *Sybil* (1973), which increased public awareness of the condition (although ironically the case was later thoroughly discredited; see Borch-Jacobsen, 1997; Rieber, 1999). At about the same time, the diagnostic criteria for DID (then MPD) were clearly specified for the first time in 1980 with the publication of DSM-III. This seems to have led to increased acceptance of the diagnosis by clinicians, which may have encouraged reporting in the literature. Clinicians were traditionally (and often still are today) somewhat skeptical of the astonishing behavior these patients often display—such as undergoing sudden and dramatic shifts in personal identity before the clinicians' eyes.

Another reason why the diagnosis may be made more frequently since 1980 is that the diagnostic criteria for schizophrenia were tightened in DSM-III (1980). A good number of people who had been inappropriately diagnosed with schizophrenia before that time probably began to receive the appropriate diagnosis of MPD (now DID). (See The World Around Us 8.3 on p. 302.) Beginning in about 1980, prior scattered reports of instances of childhood abuse in the histories of adult DID patients began building into what would become a crescendo. As we will see later, many controversies have arisen regarding how to interpret such findings, but it is definitely true that these reports of abuse in patients with DID drew a great deal of attention to this disorder, which in turn may have increased the rate at which it was being diagnosed.

Finally, it is almost certain that some of the increase in the prevalence of DID is *artifactual* and has occurred because some therapists looking for evidence of DID in certain patients may suggest the existence of alter identities (especially when the person is under hypnosis and very suggestible); (e.g., Kihlstrom, 2005; Piper & Merskey, 2004b). The therapist may also subtly reinforce the emergence of new identities by showing great interest in these new identities. The way in which this might occur will be discussed in more detail later.

EXPERIMENTAL STUDIES OF DID The vast majority of what is known about DID comes from patients' self-reports and clinical observations by therapists or researchers. Indeed, only a small number of experimental studies of people with DID have been conducted to corroborate clinical observations that go back a hundred years. Moreover, most of these studies have been conducted on only one or a few cases, although very recently a few larger studies have been done that include appropriate control groups (e.g., Dorahy, Middleton, & Irwin, 2005; Huntjens et al., 2003). In spite of such shortcomings, most

8.3 THE WORLD AROUND US

Schizophrenia, Split Personality, and DID: Clearing Up the Confusion

The general public has long been confused by the distinction between DID and schizophrenia. It is not uncommon for people diagnosed with schizophrenia to be referred to as having a "split personality." We have even heard people say such things as, "I'm a bit schizophrenic on this issue" to mean that they have more than one opinion about it!

This misuse of the term *split personality* reflects the public's general misunderstanding of schizophrenia, which does not involve a "split" or "Jekyll and Hyde" personality at all. The original confusion may have stemmed from the term *schizophrenia,* which was first coined by a Swiss psychiatrist named Bleuler. *Schizien* is German for "split," and *phren* is the Greek root for "mind." The notion that schizophrenia is characterized by a split mind or personality may have arisen this way.

However, this is not at all what Bleuler intended the word *schizophrenia* to mean. Rather, Bleuler was referring to the splitting of the normally integrated *associative threads* of the mind—links between words, thoughts, emotions, and behavior. Splits of this kind result in thinking that is not goal-directed or efficient, which in turn leads to the host of other difficulties known to be associated with schizophrenia.

It is very important to remember that people diagnosed with schizophrenia do *not* have multiple distinct identities that alternately take control over their mind and behavior. They may have a delusion and believe they are someone else, but they do not show the changes in identity accompanied by changes in tone of voice, vocabulary, and physical appearance that are often seen when identities "switch" in DID. Furthermore, people with DID (who are probably closer to the general public's notion of "split personality") do not exhibit such characteristics of schizophrenia as disorganized behavior, hallucinations coming from outside the head, and delusions.

of the findings from these studies are generally consistent with one another and reveal some very interesting features of DID.

The primary focus of these studies has been to determine the nature of the amnesia that exists between different identities. As we have already noted, most people with DID have at least some identities that seem completely unaware of the existence and experiences of certain alter identities, although other identities may be only partially amnesic of some alters (e.g., Elzinga et al., 2003; Huntjens et al., 2003). This feature of DID has been corroborated by studies showing that when one identity (Identity 1) is asked to learn a list of word pairs, and an alter identity (Identity 2) is later asked to recall the second word in each pair, using the first word as a cue, there seems to be no transfer of what was learned by Identity 1 to Identity 2. This interpersonality amnesia with regard to conscious recall of the activities and experiences of at least some other identities has generally been considered a fundamental characteristic of DID (Kihlstrom, 2001, 2005; Kihlstrom & Schacter, 2000). Nevertheless, one interesting recent study of 21 DID patients has challenged the idea that this interpersonality amnesia is complete. As expected, the DID patients all reported complete subjective amnesia of a list of words (List A) learned by Identity 1 when Identity 2 was "out" and was asked if s/he had any recall of having learned List A. However, when Identity 2 was given a recognition test of his or her knowledge of List A, s/he actually recognized about 50 percent of the words (Huntjens et al., 2003), suggesting partial transfer of explicit memory across identities in this task.

As noted earlier, there are kinds of memory other than simply what can be brought to awareness (*explicit memory*). As with dissociative amnesia and fugue, there is evidence that Identity 2 has some *implicit memory* of things that Identity 1 learned. That is, although Identity 2 may not be able to recall consciously the things learned by Identity 1, these apparently forgotten events may influence Identity 2's experiences, thoughts, and behaviors unconsciously (Kihlstrom, 2001, 2005). This might be reflected in a test asking Identity 2 to learn the list of words previously learned by Identity 1. Even though Identity 2 could not consciously recall the list of words, Identity 2 would learn that list more rapidly than a brand-new list of words, an outcome that suggests the operation of implicit memory (e.g., Eich et al., 1997; Elzinga et al., 2003; see Kihlstrom, 2001, 2005, for reviews).

Related studies on implicit transfer of memories have shown that emotional reactions learned by one identity often transfer across identities, too. Thus, even though Identity 2 may not be able to recall an emotional event that happened to Identity 1, a visual or auditory reminder of the event (a conditioned stimulus) administered to Identity 2 may elicit an emotional reaction even though Identity 2 has no knowledge of why it did so (e.g., Ludwig et al., 1972; Prince, 1910; see Kihlstrom & Schacter, 2000, for a review). Moreover, a very recent study by Huntjens et al. (2005) had 22 DID patients in Identity 1 learn to reevaluate a neutral word in a positive or negative manner through a simple evaluative conditioning procedure in which neutral words are simply paired with positive or negative words; the neutral words then come to take on positive or negative connotations. When Identity 2 was later asked to emerge, s/he also categorized the formerly neutral word in the same positive or negative manner as learned by Identity 1, showing implicit memory for the reevaluation of the word learned by Identity 1 (although complete subjective amnesia was reported by Identity 2). Nevertheless, other sophisticated studies have made it clear that implicit memory transfer across personalities does not always occur, particularly with certain kinds of implicit memory tasks where memory performance may be strongly influenced by the identity currently being tested (e.g., Dorahy, 2001; Eich et al., 1997; Nissen et al., 1988). But whatever the reasons why only some implicit memory tests show evidence of transfer across identities, the results that do show implicit memory transfer are very important. This is because they demonstrate that explicit amnesia across identities cannot occur simply because one identity is trying actively to suppress any evidence of memory transfer; if this were possible, there would be no leakage of implicit memories across identities (Dorahy, 2001; Eich et al., 1997).

An even smaller number of experimental studies have examined differences in brain activity when individuals with DID are tested with different identities at the forefront of consciousness. For example, in an early classic study, Putnam (1984) investigated EEG activity in 11 DID patients during different identities, and ten control subjects who were simulating different personality states, in order to determine whether there were different patterns of brain wave activity during different identities (real or simulated), as would be found if separate individuals were assessed. The study found that there were indeed differences in brain wave activity when the patients with DID were in different personality states and that these differences were greater than those found in the simulating subjects (see Kihlstrom et al., 1993; Putnam, 1997). Tsai and colleagues (1999) used fMRI brain-imaging techniques to study different identities of a woman with DID while the switch from one identity to another was occurring. They found that changes in hippocampal and medial temporal lobe activity occurred during the switches. These brain areas are involved in memory, so finding activity there during switches of identity (which involve changes in patterns of memory) might be expected.

CAUSAL FACTORS AND CONTROVERSIES ABOUT DID

There are at least four serious interrelated controversies surrounding DID and how it develops. First, some have been concerned with whether DID is a real disorder or is faked, and whether, even if it is real, it can be faked. The second major controversy is about how DID develops. Specifically, is DID caused by early childhood trauma, or does the development of DID involve some kind of social enactment of multiple different roles that have been inadvertently encouraged by careless clinicians? Third, those who maintain that DID is caused by childhood trauma cite mounting evidence that the vast majority of individuals diagnosed with DID report memories of an early history of abuse. But are these memories of early abuse real or false? Finally, if abuse has occurred in most individuals with DID, did the abuse play a *causal role*, or was something else correlated with abuse actually the cause?

Is DID Real or Is It Faked? The issue of possible factitious or malingering origins of DID has dogged the diagnosis of DID for at least a century. One obvious situation in which this issue becomes critical is when it has been used by defendants and their attorneys to try to escape punishment for crimes ("My other personality did it"). For example, this defense was used, ultimately unsuccessfully, in the famous case of the Hillside Strangler, Kenneth Bianchi (Orne, Dinges, & Orne, 1984), but it has probably been used successfully in other cases that we are unaware of (almost by definition because the person is not sent to prison but rather to a mental hospital in most cases). Bianchi was accused of brutally raping and murdering ten young women in the Los Angeles area. Although there was a great deal of evidence that he had committed these crimes, he steadfastly denied it, and some lawyers thought perhaps he had DID. He was subsequently interviewed by a clinical psychologist, and under hypnosis a second personality, "Steve," emerged who confessed to the crimes, thereby creating the basis for a plea of "not guilty by reason of insanity" (see Chapter 18). However, Bianchi was examined even more closely by a renowned psychologist and psychiatrist specializing in this area, the late Martin Orne. Upon closer examination, Orne determined that Bianchi was faking the condition. Orne drew this conclusion in part because when he suggested to Bianchi that most people with DID have more than two identities, Bianchi suddenly produced a third (Orne et al., 1984). Moreover, there was no evidence of multiple identities existing prior to the trial. When Bianchi's faking the disorder was discovered, he was convicted of the murders. In other words, some cases of DID may involve complete fabrication orchestrated by criminal or other

Kenneth Bianchi, know as the "Hillside Strangler," brutally raped and murdered 10 women in the Los Angeles area. Hoping to create a plea of "not guilty by reason of insanity," Bianchi fabricated a second personality—"Steve"—who "emerged" while Kenneth was under hypnosis. A psychologist and psychiatrist specializing in DID determined he was faking the diagnosis and Bianchi was subsequently convicted of the murders.

unscrupulous persons seeking unfair advantages, and not all prosecutors have as clever and knowledgeable an expert witness as Martin Orne to help detect this. But most researchers think that factitious and malingering cases of DID (such as the Bianchi case or cases in which the person has a need to be a patient) are relatively rare.

If DID Is Not Faked, How Does It Develop: Post-Traumatic Theory or Sociocognitive Theory? Many professionals acknowledge that in most cases, DID is a real syndrome (not consciously faked), but there is marked disagreement about how it develops and how it is maintained. In the contemporary literature, the original major theory of how DID develops is *post-traumatic theory* (Gleaves, 1996; Ross, 1997, 1999). The vast majority of patients with DID (over 95 percent by some estimates) report memories of severe and horrific abuse as children (see Figure 8.1). According to this view, DID starts from the child's attempt to cope with an overwhelming sense of hopelessness and powerlessness in the face of repeated traumatic abuse. Lacking other resources or routes of escape, the child may dissociate and escape into a fantasy, becoming someone else. This escape may occur through a process like self-hypnosis (Butler et al., 1996), and if it helps to alleviate some of the pain caused by the abuse, it will be reinforced and occur again in the future. Sometimes the child simply imagines the abuse is happening to someone else. If the child is fantasy-prone, and this continues, the child may unknowingly create different selves at different points in time, possibly laying the foundation for multiple dissociated identities.

But only a subset of children who undergo traumatic experiences are prone to fantasy or self-hypnosis, which leads to the idea that a diathesis-stress model may be appropriate here. That is, children who are prone to fantasy and/or those who are easily hypnotizable may have a diathesis for developing DID (or other dissociative disorders) when severe abuse occurs (e.g., Butler et al., 1996; Kihlstrom, Glisky, & Angiulo, 1994). Moreover, it should also be emphasized that there is nothing inherently pathological about being prone to fantasy or readily hypnotizable (Kihlstrom et al., 1994).

Increasingly, those who view childhood abuse as playing a critical role in the development of DID are beginning to see DID as perhaps a complex and chronic variant of post-traumatic stress disorder, which by definition is caused by exposure to some kind of highly traumatic event(s), including abuse (e.g., Brown, 1994; Maldonado et al., 2002; Zelikovsky & Lynn, 1994). Anxiety symptoms are more prominent in PTSD than in DID, and dissociative symptoms are more prominent in DID than in PTSD. Nevertheless, both kinds of symptoms are present in both disorders (Putnam, 1997).

At the other extreme from post-traumatic theory is *sociocognitive theory*, which claims that DID develops when a highly suggestible person learns to adopt and enact the roles of multiple identities, mostly because clinicians have inadvertently suggested, legitimized, and reinforced them, and because these different identities are geared to the individual's own personal goals (Lilienfeld et al., 1999; Lilienfeld & Lynn, 2003; Spanos, 1994, 1996). It is important to realize that at the present time, the sociocognitive perspective maintains that this is not done intentionally or consciously by the afflicted individual but, rather, occurs spontaneously with little or no awareness (Lilienfeld et al., 1999). The suspicion is that overzealous clinicians, through fascination with the clinical phenomenon of DID and unwise use of such techniques as hypnosis, are them-

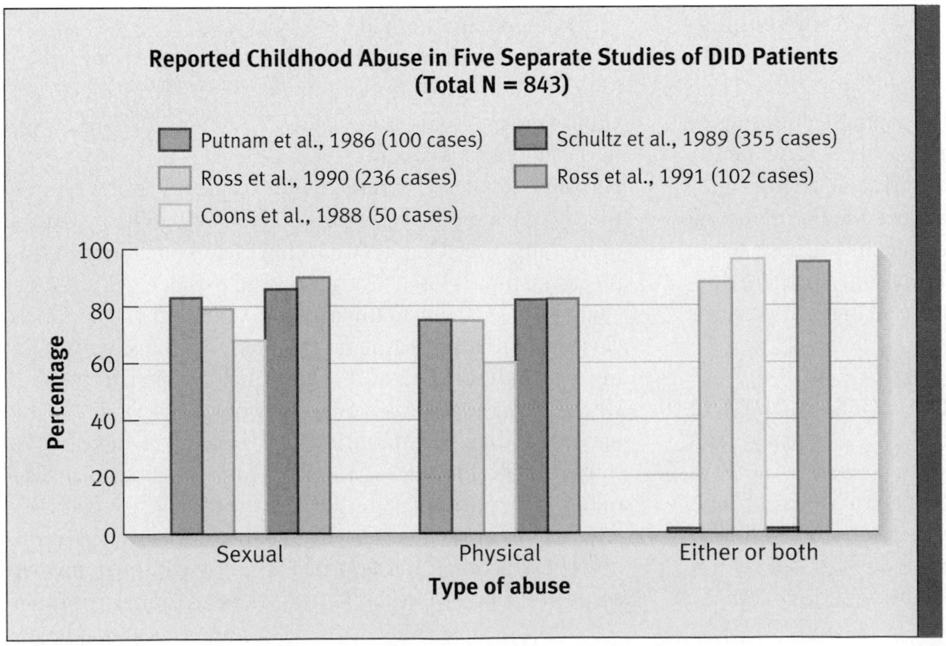

FIGURE 8.1

Reported childhood abuse in five separate studies of DID patients (Total N = 843).

selves largely responsible for eliciting this disorder in highly suggestible, fantasy-prone patients (e.g., Piper & Merskey, 2004a, 2004b; Spanos, 1996). Consistent with this hypothesis, Spanos, Weekes, and Bertrand (1985) demonstrated that normal college students can be induced by suggestion under hypnosis to exhibit some of the phenomena seen in DID, including the adoption of a second identity with a different name that shows a different profile on a personality inventory. Thus people can enact a second identity when situational forces encourage it. Related situational forces that may affect the individual outside the therapist's office include memories of one's past behavior (e.g., as a child), observations of other people's behavior (e.g., others being assertive and independent, or sexy and flirtatious), and media portrayals of DID (Lilienfeld et al., 1999; Piper & Merskey, 2004b; Spanos, 1994).

Sociocognitive theory is also consistent with evidence that most DID patients did not show unambiguous signs of the disorder before they entered therapy and with evidence that the number of alter identities often increases (sometimes dramatically) with time in therapy (Piper & Merskey, 2004b). It is also consistent with the increased prevalence of DID since the 1970s, when the first popular accounts of DID reached the general public, and since 1980, when therapist awareness of the condition increased as well (Lilienfeld et al., 1999; Piper & Merskey, 2004a).

However, there are also many criticisms of sociocognitive theory. For example, Spanos' demonstration of role-playing in hypnotized college students is interesting, but it does not show that this is the way DID is actually caused in real life. For example, someone might be able to give a convincing portrayal of a person with a broken leg, but this would not establish how legs are usually broken. Moreover, the hypnotized participants in this and other experiments showed only a few of the most obvious symptoms of DID (such as more than one identity) and showed them only under short-lived, contrived laboratory conditions. No such studies have shown that other symptoms such as depersonalization, memory lapses for prolonged periods, or auditory hallucinations can occur under such laboratory conditions. Thus, although some of the *symptoms* of DID could be created by social enactment, there is no evidence that the *disorder* can be created this way (e.g., Gleaves, 2. 1996).

Are Recovered Memories of Abuse in DID Real or False? Case reports of the cruelty and torture that some DID patients suffered as children are gut-wrenching to read or hear. However, the accuracy and trustworthiness of these reports of widespread sexual and other forms of childhood abuse in DID (as well as in other disorders—see Chapters 11 and 13) have become a matter of major controversy in recent years. Critics argue that many of these reports of DID patients, which generally come up in the course of therapy, may be the result of false memories, which are in turn a product of highly leading questions and suggestive techniques applied by well-meaning but inadequately skilled and careless psychotherapists (Kihlstrom, 2005; Lilienfeld et al., 1999; Yapko, 1994). It seems quite clear to many investigators that this sort of thing has happened, often with tragic consequences. Innocent family members have been falsely accused by DID patients, convicted, and imprisoned. But it is also true that brutal abuse of children occurs far too often and that it can have very adverse effects on development, perhaps encouraging pathological dissociation (e.g., Maldonado et al., 2002; Nash et al., 1993). In such cases, prosecution of the perpetrators of the abuse is indeed appropriate. Of course, the real difficulty here is in determining when the recovered memories of abuse are real and when they are false (or some combination of the two). This bitter controversy about the issue of false memory is more extensively considered in the Unresolved Issues section at the end of this chapter.

One way to document that particular recovered memories are real might be if some reliable physiological test could be developed to distinguish between them. Thus, some researchers are currently trying to determine whether there are different neural correlates of real and false memories that could be used to make this determination reliably. Another somewhat easier way to document whether a particular recovered memory is real would be to have independent verification that the abuse had actually occurred, such as through physician, hospital, and police records. A number of studies have indeed reported that they have confirmed the reported cases of abuse, but critics have shown that the criteria used for corroborating evidence are almost invariably very loose and suspect as to their validity. For example, Chu and colleagues (1999) simply asked their subjects, "Have you had anyone confirm these events?" (p. 751) but did not specify what constituted confirmation and had no way of determining if subjects were exaggerating or distorting the information they provided as confirming evidence (Piper & Merskey, 2004a). In another example of a flawed study, Lewis and colleagues (1997) studied 12 convicted murderers and then confirmed through medical, social service, and prison records that all 12 had been severely abused as children. Unfortunately, this study did not include a control group of otherwise comparable murderers who did not exhibit DID symptoms. Hence we cannot be certain that the childhood abuse of these subjects is not as much (or more) associated with violence or conviction for murder as with the development of DID specifically. Moreover, Lewis and colleagues should have carefully assessed for the possibility that some of the murderers might have been malingering (faking DID; Lilienfeld et al., 1999). Thus, although this study may have been one of the most impressive attempts yet to document abuse independently in people with DID, it was significantly flawed, and therefore highly inconclusive.

If Abuse Has Occurred, Does It Play a Causal Role in DID? Let us put the last controversy about the reality of recovered memories of abuse aside for a moment and assume that severe abuse has occurred in the early childhood backgrounds of many people with DID. How can we determine whether this abuse has played a critical *causal role* in the development of DID (e.g., Piper & Merskey, 2004a)? Unfortunately, many difficulties arise in answering this question. For example, child abuse usually happens in family environments plagued by many other sources of adversity and trauma (for example, various forms of psychopathology and extreme neglect and poverty). One or more of these other, correlated sources of adversity could actually be playing the causal role (e.g., Lilienfeld et al., 1999; Nash et al., 1993; Tillman, Nash, & Lerner, 1994). Another difficulty for determining the role of abuse is that people who have experienced child abuse as well as symptoms of DID may be more likely to seek treatment than people with symptoms of DID who did not experience abuse. Thus the individuals in most studies about the prevalence of child abuse in DID may not be representative of the population of all people who suffer from DID. Finally, childhood abuse has been claimed by some to lead to many different forms of psychopathology including depression, PTSD, eating disorders, somatoform disorders, and borderline personality disorder, to name just a few. Perhaps the most we will ever be able to say is that childhood abuse may play a *nonspecific causal role* for many disorders, with other, more specific factors determining which disorder develops (see Chapters 11 and 13).

Comments on a Few of These Controversies about DID

As we have seen, numerous studies indicate that the separate identities harbored by DID patients are somewhat physiologically and cognitively distinct. For example, EEG activity of various alters may be quite different. Because such differences cannot in any obvious way be simulated (e.g., Eich et al., 1997), it seems that DID must, in at least some cases, involve more than simply the social enactment of roles. Moreover, this should not be too surprising, given the widespread evidence of separate (dissociated) memory subsystems and nonconscious active mental processing, which indicates that much highly organized mental activity is normally carried on in the background, outside of awareness (e.g., Kihlstrom, 2005). Moreover, some people seem to be especially prone to pathological variants of these dissociative processes (Waller, Putnam, & Carlson, 1996; Waller & Ross, 1997).

We should also note that each of these controversies has usually been stated in a dichotomous way: Is DID real or faked? What causes DID—spontaneous social enactment of roles or repeated childhood trauma? Are recovered memories of abuse real or false? If abuse occurs, does it play a primary causal role? Unfortunately, however, such dichotomously stated questions encourage oversimplified answers. The human mind does not seem to operate in these dichotomous ways, and we need to address the complex and multifaceted nature of the dissociated mental processes that these often miserable and severely stressed patients are experiencing. Fortunately, theorists on both sides of these controversies have begun to soften their positions just a bit and acknowledge that multiple different causal pathways are likely to be involved. For example, Ross (1997, 1999), a long-time advocate for a strong version of post-traumatic theory, has more recently acknowledged that some cases are faked and that some may be inadvertently caused by unskilled therapists in the course of treatment. In addition, other advocates of post-traumatic theory have recently acknowledged that both real and false memories do occur in these patients, noting that it is critical that a method for determining which is which be developed (e.g., Gleaves, Smith, Butler, & Spiegel, 2004). From the other side, Lilienfeld and colleagues (1999), who have been vocal advocates for Spanos' sociocognitive theory since his death in 1994, have acknowledged that some people with DID may have undergone real abuse, although they believe it occurs far less often, and is less likely to play a real causal role, than the trauma theorists maintain (see also Kihlstrom, 2005).

General Sociocultural Causal Factors in Dissociative Disorders

There seems little doubt that the prevalence of dissociative disorders, especially their more dramatic forms such as DID, is influenced by the degree to which such phenomena are accepted or tolerated either as normal or as legitimate mental disorders by the surrounding cultural context. Indeed, in our own society, the acceptance and tolerance of DID as a legitimate disorder has varied tremendously over time. Nevertheless, although its prevalence varies, DID has now been identified in all racial groups, socioeconomic classes, and cultures where it has been studied. For example, outside North America it has been found in countries ranging from Nigeria and Ethiopia to Turkey, India, Australia, and the Caribbean, to name a few (Maldonado et al., 2002).

Many seemingly related phenomena, such as spirit possession and dissociative trances, occur very frequently in many different parts of the world where the local culture sanctions them (Krippner, 1994). When entered into voluntarily, trance and possession states are not considered pathological and should not be construed as mental disorders. But DSM-IV-TR has noted that some people who enter into these states voluntarily because of cultural norms develop distress and impairment; in such cases, they might be diagnosed with *dissociative trance disorder* (a provisional diagnostic category in DSM-IV-TR). People receiving this provisional diagnosis must either experience trances or possession trances. A *trance* is said to occur when someone experiences a temporary marked alteration in state of consciousness or identity (but with no replacement by an alternative identity). It is usually associated with either a narrowing of awareness of the immediate surroundings, or stereotyped behaviors or movements that are experienced as beyond one's control. A *possession trance* is similar except that the alteration of consciousness or identity is replaced by a new identity that is attributed to the influence of a spirit, deity, or other power. One study of 58 individuals from Singapore with this diagnosis, as well as 58 individuals with a diagnosis of major depression, found that conflicts over religious or cultural issues, prior exposure to trance states, and being a spiritual healer or healer's helper were most predictive of who had dissociative trance disorder relative to major depression (Ng & Chan, 2004).

There are also cross-cultural variants on dissociative disorders, such as *Amok*, which is often thought of as a rage disorder (see The World Around Us 3.4 in Chapter 3). Amok occurs when a dissociative episode leads to violent, aggressive, or homicidal behavior directed at other people and objects. It occurs mostly in men and is often precipitated by a perceived slight or insult. The person often has ideas of persecution, anger, and amnesia, often followed by a period of exhaustion and depression. Amok is found in Malaysia, Laos, the Philippines, Papua New Guinea, and Puerto Rico and among Navajo Indians (APA, 2000).

Treatment and Outcomes in Dissociative Disorders

Unfortunately, virtually no systematic controlled research has been conducted on treatment of dissociative amnesia, fugues, and depersonalization disorder and so very little is known about how to treat them successfully. Numerous case histories, sometimes presented in small sets of cases, are available, but without control groups who are assessed at the same time or who receive nonspecific treatments, it is impossible to know the effectiveness of the varied treatments that have been attempted (Kihlstrom, 2005). Depersonalization disorder is generally thought to be resistant to treatment (e.g., Simeon et al., 1997), although treatment may be useful for associated psychopathology such as anxiety and depressive disorders. Some think that hypnosis, including training in self-hypnosis techniques, may be useful, because patients with depersonalization disorder can learn to dissociate and then "reassociate," thereby gaining some sense of control over their depersonalization and derealization experiences (Maldonado et al., 2002). Single case studies have also supported the idea that antidepressant medications from the serotonin reuptake inhibitor category may have positive effects, but a recent randomized controlled study showed no difference between treatment with Prozac versus with placebo (Simeon et al., 2004).

In dissociative amnesia and fugue, it is important for the person to be in a safe environment, and simply removing her or him from what s/he perceives as a threatening situation sometimes allows for spontaneous recovery of memory. Hypnosis, as well as drugs such as benzodiazepines, barbiturates, sodium pentobarbital, and sodium amobarbital, are often used to facilitate recall of repressed and dissociated memories (Maldonado et al., 2002). After memories are recalled, it is important for the patient to work through the memories with the therapist so that the experiences can be reframed in new ways. However, unless the memories can be independently corroborated, they should not be taken at their face value (Kihlstrom, 2005).

For DID patients, most current therapeutic approaches are based on the assumption of post-traumatic theory that the disorder was caused by abuse (Kihlstrom, 2005). Most therapists set integration of the previously separate alters, together with their collective merging into the host personality, as the ultimate goal of treatment. When successful integration occurs, the patient eventually develops a unified personality, although it is not uncommon for only partial integration to be achieved. But it is also very important to assess whether improvement in other symptoms of DID and associated disorders has occurred. Indeed, it seems that treatment is more likely to produce symptom improvement, as well as associated improvements in functioning, than to achieve full and stable integration of the different alter identities (Maldonado et al., 2002).

Typically the treatment is psychodynamic and insight-oriented, focused on uncovering and working through the trauma and other conflicts that are thought to have led to the disorder (Kihlstrom, 2005). One of the primary techniques used in most treatments of DID is hypnosis (e.g., Kluft, 1993; Maldonado et al., 2002). Most DID patients are hypnotizable, and hypnotized DID patients are often able to recover past unconscious and frequently traumatic memories, often from childhood. Then these memories can be processed, and the patient can become aware that the dangers once present are no longer there. (There is another danger here, however. People are more suggestible under hypnosis, and much of what is recalled may not be accurate. See Kihlstrom, 2005, and the Unresolved Issues section.) Through the use of hypnosis, therapists are often able to make contact with different identities and reestablish connections between distinct, seemingly separate identity states. An important goal is to integrate the personalities into one identity that is better able to cope with current stressors. Clearly, successful negotiation of this critical phase of treatment requires therapeutic skills of the highest order; that is, the therapist must be strongly committed as well as professionally competent. Regrettably, not all therapists are.

Most reports in the literature are treatment summaries of single cases, and reports of successful cases should always be considered with caution, especially given the large bias in favor of publishing positive rather than negative results. Treatment outcome data for large groups of DID patients have been reported in only four studies we are aware of, and none of these included a control group, although it is quite clear that DID does not spontaneously remit simply with the passage of time, nor if a therapist chooses to ignore DID-related issues (Kluft, 1999; Maldonado et al., 2002). For example, Ellason and Ross (1997) reported on a 2-year postdischarge follow-up of DID patients originally treated in a specialized inpatient unit. Of the original 135 such patients, 54 were located and systematically assessed. All these patients, and especially those who had achieved full integration, generally showed marked improvements in various aspects of their lives. However, only 12 of 54 had achieved full integration of their identities. Such results are promising, but we must wonder about the clinical status of the 81 "lost" patients who may well have done less well. Another 10-year follow-up study reported similar results in a smaller sample of 25 treated DID patients. Only 12 were located 10 years later; of these, six had achieved full integration, but two of those had partially relapsed (Coons & Bowman, 2001). In general it has been found that (1) for treatment to be successful, it must be prolonged, often lasting many years, and (2) the more severe the case, the longer that treatment is needed (Maldonado et al., 2002).

In Review

- Describe the symptoms known as depersonalization and derealization, and indicate which disorder is primarily characterized by their appearance.
- Describe dissociative amnesia and dissociative fugue, and indicate what aspects of memory are affected.
- What are the primary symptoms of dissociative identity disorder (DID) and why is its prevalence thought to have been increasing?
- Review the four major controversies surrounding DID that were discussed in this chapter.

Unresolved Issues

DID and the Reality of "Recovered Memories"

As we have seen in this chapter, many controversies surround the nature and origins of DID. None have been more bitter than those related to the truth value of "recovered" memories of childhood abuse, particularly sexual abuse, which post-trauma theorists assert is the major causal factor in the development of DID. Indeed, a virtual chasm has developed between the "believers" (mostly but not exclusively private practitioners who treat people with DID) and the "disbelievers" (mostly but not exclusively the more academic and science-oriented mental health professionals). The disbelievers are sympathetic to people suffering DID symptoms, but they have tended to doubt that the disorder is usually caused by childhood abuse and have challenged the validity or accuracy of recovered memories of abuse.

For nearly 20 years, these controversies have moved beyond professional debate and have become major public issues, leading to countless legal proceedings. DID patients who recover memories of abuse (often in therapy) have often sued their parents for having inflicted abuse. But ironically, therapists and institutions have also been sued for implanting memories of abuse that they later came to believe had not actually occurred. Some parents, asserting they had been falsely accused, formed an international support organization—the False Memory Syndrome Foundation—and have sometimes sued therapists for damages, alleging that the therapists induced false memories of parental abuse in their child. Many families have been torn apart in the fallout from this remarkable climate of suspicion, accusation, litigation, and unrelenting hostility.

Whether DID originates in childhood abuse and whether recovered memories of abuse are accurate are basically separate issues, but they have tended to become fused in the course of the debate. Hence those who doubt the validity of memories of abuse are also likely to regard the phenomenon of DID as stemming from the social enactment of roles encouraged or induced—like the memories of abuse themselves—by misguided therapy (e.g., see Bjorklund, 2000; Lilienfeld et al., 1999; Lynn et al., 2004; Piper & Merskey, 2004a, 2004b). Believers, on the other hand, usually take both DID and the idea that abuse is its cause to be established beyond doubt (e.g., see Gleaves, 1996; Gleaves et al., 2001; Ross, 1997, 1999).

Much of the controversy about the validity of recovered memories is rooted in disagreements about the nature, reliability, and malleability of human autobiographical memory. With some exceptions, evidence for childhood abuse as a cause of DID is restricted to the "recovered memories" (memories not originally accessible) of adults being treated for dissociative experiences. Believers argue that before treatment, such memories had been "repressed" because of their traumatic nature or had been available only to certain alter identities that the host identity was generally not aware of. Treatment, according to this view of believers, dismantles the repressive defense and thus makes available to awareness an essentially accurate memory recording of the past abuse.

Disbelievers counter with several scientifically well-supported arguments. For example, scientific evidence in support of the repression concept is quite weak (e.g., Kihlstrom, 2005; Lilienfeld & Loftus, 1998; Piper, 1998). In many alleged cases of repression, the event may have been lost to memory in the course of ordinary forgetting rather than repression, or it may have occurred in the first 3 to 4 years of life, before memories can be recorded for retrieval in adulthood. In many other cases, evidence for repression has been claimed in studies where people may simply have failed to report a remembered event, often because they were never asked or were reluctant to disclose such very personal information (Kihlstrom, 2005; Lilienfeld & Loftus, 1999; Pope et al., 1998).

In addition, even if memories can be repressed, there are very serious questions about the accuracy of recovered memories. Human memory of past events does not operate in a computer-like manner, retrieving with perfect accuracy an unadulterated record of information previously stored and then repressed. Rather, human memory is malleable, constructive, and very much subject to modification on the basis of events happening after any original memory trace is established (Loftus & Bernstein, 2005; Schacter, Norman, & Koutstaal, 2000; Tsai, Loftus, & Polage, 2000). Directly addressing the abuse issue, Kirsch, Lynn, and Rhue (1993) put it this way:

> A traumatic history . . . consists not only of past childhood events but also of the person's interpretations, embellishments, and distortions of those events from the perspective of recent events, accomplishments, behaviors, and relationships that constitute life in the present. . . . In short, memory is not immutable or preserved like a fly in amber, nor is the mind like a vast storehouse of indelible impressions, facts, and information. (p. 18)

Indeed, there is now good evidence that people are sometimes very prone to the development of false memories. For example, a number of studies have now shown that when normal adult subjects are asked to imagine repeatedly events that they are quite sure had not happened to them before age 10, they later increase their estimate of the likelihood that these events actually had happened to them (Tsai et al., 2000). Moreover, even in a relatively short time frame, adult subjects sometimes come to believe they have performed somewhat bizarre acts (e.g., kissing a magnifying glass), as well as common acts (e.g., flipping a coin), after simply having imagined they had engaged in these acts several times 2 weeks earlier (Thomas & Loftus, 2002). These and other studies clearly show that repeated imagining of certain events (even somewhat bizarre events) can lead people to have false memories of events that never happened (Loftus & Bernstein, 2005). In addition, a recent experimental study by McNally and colleagues (2005) looked at individuals who reported either repressed or recovered memories of childhood sexual abuse and found some evidence that they had greater difficulty on at least some measures than normal controls in distinguishing between words that they had seen versus words that they had only imagined. This suggests that people with repressed or recovered memories of abuse may have greater difficulty distinguishing between what has actually happened to them and what they have imagined happened to them.

By the early 1990s, however, many poorly trained therapists, uninformed about how the human memory system works, bought into the notion that a suitably vigorous therapeutic approach could uncover a true and accurate record of the traumatic childhood experiences of their clients. In addition, many were convinced that certain rather common adult symptoms and complaints (e.g., headaches, poor self-esteem, unexplained anxiety) were indicative of a history of childhood trauma (e.g., see Bass & Davis, 1988; Blume, 1990) and justified relentless demands that the client remember the traumatic abuse. Persuaded by the therapist's certainty and persistence, which were accompanied by liberal use of techniques such as hypnosis and age regression, techniques known to enhance suggestibility, many clients did eventually "remember" such incidents, confirming the therapist's "expert" opinion.

Attempting to mediate the conflict and to provide both its members and the public with guidance on the issues involved, in the mid-1990s the American Psychological Association (APA) convened a bipartisan panel of experts on both sides called the Working Group on the Investigation of Memories of Childhood Abuse (Alpert et al., 1996). As one further measure of the amount of dissent and controversy raging in this field, the Working Group agreed on almost nothing, and each side wrote an independent report rather than contributed to an integrated one as originally hoped for. Unfortunately, no significant progress toward consensus has been made since the publication of that report in 1996. Thus the public and many professionals who are not directly involved remain divided and confused about what to believe about dissociative phenomena and their connection (if any) with actual childhood abuse.

summary

- Somatoform disorders are those in which psychological problems are manifested in physical disorders (or complaints of physical disorders) that often mimic medical conditions but for which no evidence of corresponding organic pathology can be found.
  - In hypochondriasis, an anxious preoccupation with having a disease is based on a misinterpretation of bodily signs or symptoms. Medical reassurance does not help.
  - Somatization disorder is characterized by many different complaints of physical ailments, in four symptom categories, over at least several years. The symptoms need not actually have existed as long as they were complained about.
  - Pain disorder is characterized by pain severe enough to disrupt life but in the absence of enough medical pathology to explain its presence.
  - Conversion disorder involves patterns of symptoms or deficits affecting sensory or voluntary motor functions, leading one to think there is a medical or neurological condition, even though medical examination reveals no physical basis for the symptoms.
  - Body dysmorphic disorder involves obsessive preoccupation with some perceived flaw or flaws in one's appearance. Compulsive checking behaviors (such as mirror checking) and avoidance of social activities because of fear of being rejected are also common.
- Dissociative disorders occur when the processes that normally regulate awareness and the multi-channel capacities of the mind apparently become disorganized, leading to various anomalies of consciousness and personal identity.
  - Depersonalization disorder occurs in people who experience persistent and recurrent episodes of derealization (losing one's sense of reality of the outside world) and depersonalization (losing one's sense of oneself and one's own reality).
  - Dissociative amnesia involves an inability to recall previously stored information that cannot be accounted for by ordinary forgetting and seems to be a common initial reaction to highly stressful circumstances. The memory loss is primarily for episodic or autobiographical memory.
  - In dissociative fugue, a person not only goes into an amnesic state but also leaves his or her home surroundings and becomes confused about his or her identity, sometimes assuming a new one.
  - In dissociative identity disorder, the person manifests at least two or more distinct identities that alternate in some way in taking control of behavior. Alter identities may differ in many ways from the host identity. There are many controversies about DID, including whether it is real or faked; how it develops; whether memories of childhood abuse are real; and, if the memories are real, whether the abuse played a causal role.

Key Terms

alter identities (P. 299)
body dysmorphic disorder (BDD) (P. 290)
conversion disorder (P. 286)
depersonalization (P. 295)
depersonalization disorder (P. 295)
derealization (P. 295)
dissociation (P. 280)
dissociative amnesia (P. 297)
dissociative disorders (P. 280)
dissociative fugue (P. 297)
dissociative identity disorder (DID) (P. 298)
factitious disorder (P. 290)
factitious disorder by proxy (P. 291)
host identity (P. 299)
hypochondriasis (P. 281)
hysteria (P. 287)
malingering (P. 290)
pain disorder (P. 285)
primary gain (P. 287)
secondary gain (P. 287)
soma (P. 280)
somatization disorder (P. 283)
somatoform disorders (P. 280)

CHAPTER 9

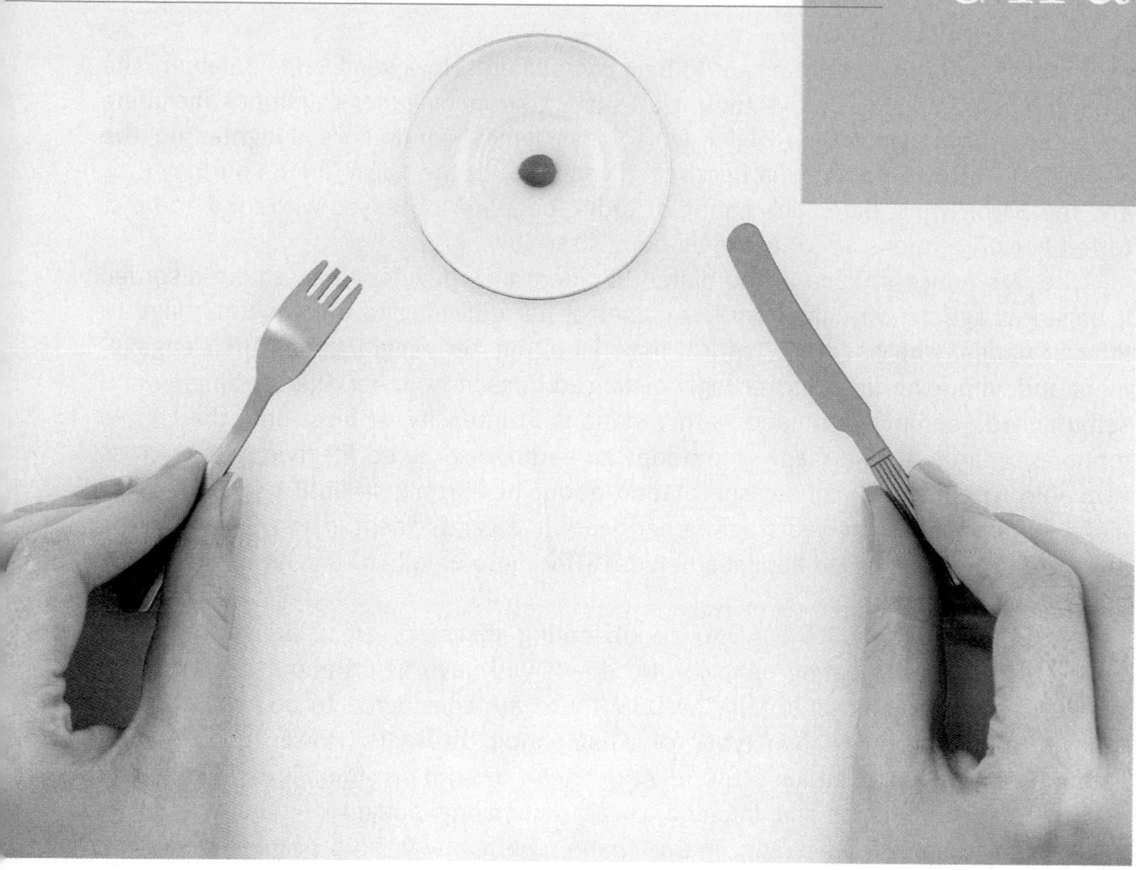

Eating Disorders and Obesity

"You look anorexic." It was not meant to be a compliment. However, Justine Bateman, the former *Family Ties* star, always took it as such. Like many other celebrities including Mary-Kate Olsen, Jamie-Lynn Sigler (who plays James Gandolfini's daughter on the *Sopranos*), Tracey Gold, Victoria Beckham (Posh Spice of the Spice Girls), Courtney Cox, and the Barbi Twins, Bateman's eating disorder made her obsessed with food and distorted her perceptions about her ideal body size.

The late Princess Diana of the United Kingdom also developed an eating disorder. It began at age 20, virtually from the outset of her difficult and unhappy marriage to Prince Charles, who had made critical remarks about her weight during their engagement and who, over time, increasingly distanced himself from her. Diana's binging and self-induced vomiting continued, with variations in intensity, at least until the couple formally separated. Like many who adopt an eating-disordered lifestyle, the princess was able to contain or ignore speculation about her problems until she decided to make them public, some years before her death in a car accident in 1997. Diana's type of eating disorder is called "bulimia nervosa" (for more details of this case, see Meyer, 2003, Chapter 10).

According to the DSM-IV (APA, 2000), **eating disorders** are characterized by a severe disturbance in eating behavior. No doubt you have heard about anorexia nervosa and bulimia nervosa. Within the DSM these are considered to be separate syndromes, and they reflect two types of adult eating disorders. However, disordered eating is not their most striking feature. At the heart of both disorders is an intense fear of becoming overweight and fat, and an accompanying pursuit of thinness that is relentless and sometimes deadly. In this chapter we focus on both of these disorders. We also examine obesity. Obesity is not considered an eating disorder or a psychopathological condition in the DSM; however, its prevalence is rising at an alarming rate. Obesity also accounts for more morbidity and mortality than all other eating disorders combined. Because obesity clearly involves disordered eating patterns, we include it in this chapter.

Like many other celebrities, Mary-Kate Olsen (shown here with her twin sister Ashley) has struggled with anorexia nervosa.

The late Princess Diana's courage in discussing her own struggles with bulimia nervosa helped many others with the same problem to seek help in treating their disorder.

Clinical Aspects of Eating Disorders

Anorexia Nervosa

The term *anorexia nervosa* literally means "lack of appetite induced by nervousness." However, this definition is something of a misnomer, because lack of appetite is not the real problem. At the heart of anorexia nervosa is an intense *fear of gaining weight* or becoming fat, combined with a *refusal to maintain even a minimally low body weight.* The DSM-IV criteria for anorexia nervosa are shown in the DSM criteria box.

Descriptions of extreme fasting or ascetic food refusal that were probably signs of **anorexia nervosa** can be found in the early religious literature (Vandereycken, 2002). The first known medical account of anorexia nervosa, however, was published in 1689 by Richard Morton (see Silverman, 1997, for a good general historical overview). Morton described two patients, an 18-year-old girl and a 16-year-old boy who suffered from a "nervous consumption" that caused wasting of body tissue. The female patient eventually died because she refused treatment. The disorder did not receive its current name, however, until 1873, when Charles Lasègue in Paris and Sir William Gull in London independently described the clinical syndrome. In his last publication on the condition, Gull (1888) described a 14-year-old girl who began "without apparent cause, to evince a repugnance to food; and soon afterwards declined to take any whatever, except half a cup of tea or coffee." After being prescribed to eat light food every few hours, the patient made a good recovery. Gull's illustrations of the patient before and after treatment appear in Figure 9.1.

Although the DSM-IV criteria for anorexia nervosa require that postmenarcheal females stop menstruating in order to be diagnosed with the disorder, some have questioned the value of this diagnostic criterion. Studies have suggested that women who continue to menstruate but meet all the other diagnostic criteria for anorexia nervosa are just as ill as those who have amenorrhea (Cachelin &

DSM-IV-TR

Criteria for Anorexia Nervosa

- Refusal to maintain a body weight that is normal for the person's age and height (i.e., a reduction of body weight to about 85 percent of what would normally be expected).
- Intense fear of gaining weight or becoming fat, even though underweight.
- Distorted perception of body shape and size.
- Absence of at least three consecutive menstrual periods.

Source: *Adapted with permission from the* Diagnostic and Statistical Manual of Mental Disorders, Fourth Edition, Text Revision *(Copyright 2000). American Psychiatric Association.*

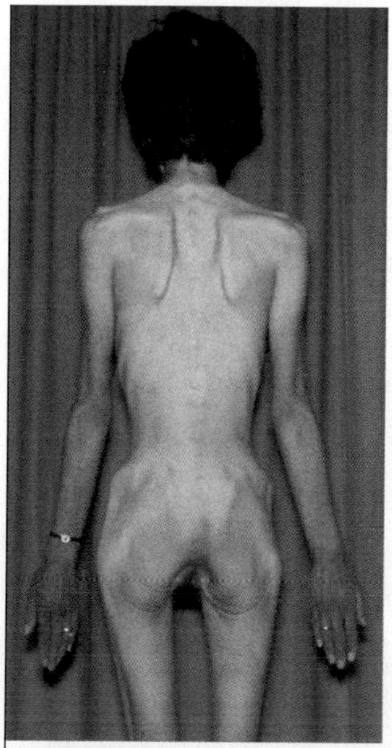

Patients with anorexia nervosa may be emaciated yet deny having any problems with their weight. They will go to great lengths to conceal their thinness by wearing baggy clothes or drinking massive amounts of water prior to being weighed (for example, in a hospital setting).

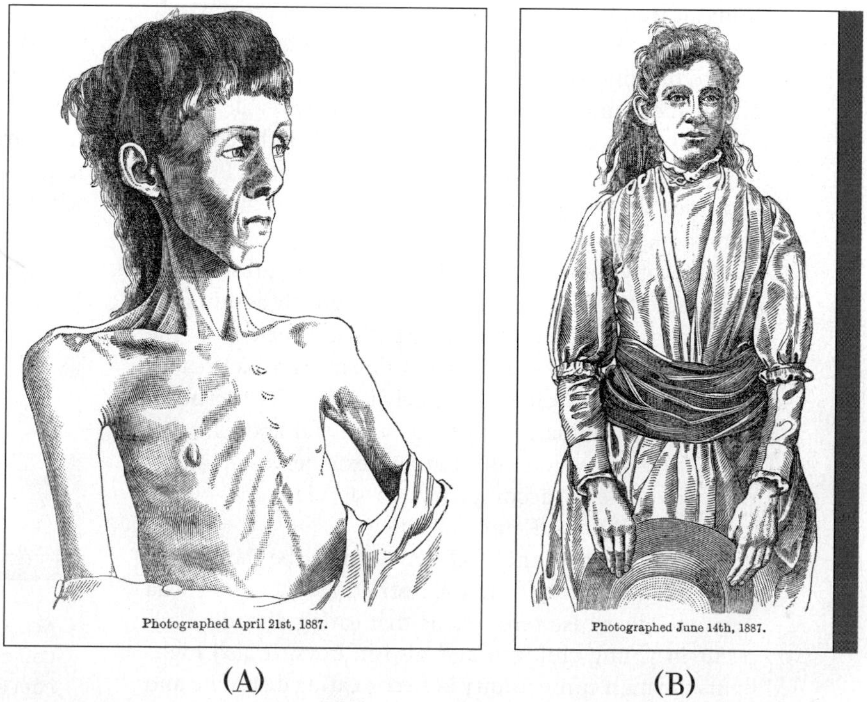

FIGURE 9.1

Gull's anorexic patient. (A) Before treatment. (B) After treatment.
Source: *Gull (1888).*

Maher, 1998; Garfinkel, 2002). For men, the equivalent of the menstruation criterion is diminished sexual appetite and lowered testosterone levels (Beaumont, 2002).

Even though they may look painfully thin or even emaciated, many patients with anorexia nervosa deny having any problems. Indeed, they may be quietly proud of their weight loss. Despite this, efforts may be made to conceal their thinness by wearing baggy clothes or sometimes even carrying hidden bulky objects to make themselves look heavier than they are. If they are being weighed (for example, in a hospital setting), patients with anorexia nervosa may drink large amounts of water to increase their weight temporarily.

There are two types of anorexia nervosa: the restricting type and the binge-eating/purging type. The central difference between these two types concerns how patients maintain their very low weight. In the *restricting type,* every effort is made to limit how much food is eaten, and caloric intake is tightly controlled. Patients often try to avoid eating in the presence of other people. When they are at the table, they may eat excessively slowly, cut their food into very small pieces, and dispose of food secretly (Beaumont, 2002). The relentless restriction of food intake is not possible for all patients with anorexia nervosa. Patients with the *binge-eating/purging type* of anorexia nervosa differ from patients with restricting anorexia nervosa because they either binge, purge, or binge *and* purge. A binge involves the out-of-control eating of amounts of food that are far greater than what most people would eat in the same amount of time and under the same circumstances. These binges may be followed by efforts to **purge,** or to remove from their bodies the food they have eaten. Approximately 30 to 50 percent of patients transition from the restricting type to the binge-eating/purging type of anorexia nervosa during the course of their disorder (see Löwe et al., 2001). Methods of purging commonly include self-induced vomiting or misuse of laxatives, diuretics, and enemas. Purging strategies do not prevent the absorption of all calories from food, however.

Indicative of the distorted values of eating-disordered patients, restricting anorexics are often greatly admired by others with eating disorders. One patient reported that she had not been "successful" in her anorexia nervosa because of her failure to reach an extremely low weight. Her belief was that the hallmark of a truly successful anorexic was death from starvation and that anorexia nervosa patients who were able to accomplish this should somehow be revered (see Bulik & Kendler, 2000).

In the example that follows, we describe the case of Tim, who is suffering from the restricting type of anorexia nervosa. Tim's case reminds us that eating disorders can occur in young children and also in boys. It also highlights the high comorbidity between eating disorders and obsessive-compulsive symptoms and personality traits that we will discuss later. In fact, Tim warrants an additional diagnosis of Obsessive-Compulsive Disorder (see Chapter 6).

case STUDY — Tim: Obsessed with His Weight

Eight-year-old Tim was referred by a pediatrician who asked for an emergency evaluation because of a serious weight loss during the past year for which the pediatrician could find no medical cause. Tim is extremely concerned about his weight and weighs himself daily. He complains that he is too fat, and if he does not lose weight, he cuts back on food. He has lost 10 pounds in the past year and still feels that he is too fat, though it is clear that he is underweight. In desperation, his parents have removed the scales from the house; as a result, Tim is keeping a record of the calories that he eats daily. He spends a lot of time on this, checking and rechecking that he has done it just right.

In addition, Tim is described as being obsessed with cleanliness and neatness. Currently he has no friends because he refuses to visit them, feeling that their houses are "dirty"; he gets upset when another child touches him. He is always checking whether he is doing things the way they "should" be done. He becomes very agitated and anxious about this. He has to get up at least two hours before leaving for school each day in order to give himself time to get ready. Recently, he woke up at 1:30 A.M. to prepare for school. (From Spitzer et al., 1994.)

Source: Reprinted with permission from the *DSM-IV-TR Casebook* (Copyright 2000). American Psychiatric Publishing, Inc.

Because the artistic standards of their profession emphasize a slender physique, ballet dancers are at especially high risk for eating disorders. Gelsey Kirkland, who developed an eating disorder while she was a premier ballerina with the New York City Ballet, described the existence of a "concentration camp aesthetic" within the company. This was no doubt fostered by the famous choreographer George Balanchine, who, as described by Kirkland in her autobiography, tapped her on the ribs and sternum after one event and exhorted "must see the bones" (Kirkland, 1986, pp. 55–56).

case STUDY — Ms. R.: Going to Extremes

Ms. R. is a very thin 19-year-old single ballet student who comes in at the insistence of her parents for a consultation concerning her eating behavior. The patient and her family report that Ms. R. has had a lifelong interest in ballet. She began to attend classes at age 5, was recognized by her teachers as having impressive talent by age 8, and since

Ballet dancers are at very high risk for developing eating disorders. According to Gelsey Kirkland, once the premier ballerina at the New York City Ballet, the value placed on being thin can create a "concentration camp aesthetic" supported and encouraged by the dance company.

age 14 has been a member of a national ballet company. The patient has had clear difficulties with eating since age 15 when, for reasons she is unable to explain, she began to induce vomiting after what she felt was overeating. The vomiting was preceded by many years of persistent dieting, which began with the encouragement of her ballet teacher. Over the past 3 years, Ms. R.'s binges have occurred once a day in the evening and have been routinely followed by self-induced vomiting. The binges consist of dozens of rice cakes or, more rarely, half a gallon of ice cream. Ms. R. consumes this food late at night after her parents have gone to bed. For some time, Ms. R.'s parents have been concerned that their daughter has a problem with her eating, but she consistently denied difficulties until about a month before this consultation.

Ms. R. reached her full height of 5 feet 8 inches at age 15. Her greatest weight was 120 pounds at age 16, which she describes as being fat. For the past 3 years, her weight has been reasonably stable at between 100 and 104 pounds. She exercises regularly as part of her profession, and she denies using laxatives, diuretics, or diet pills as a means of weight control. Except when she is binge eating she avoids the consumption of high-fat foods and sweets. Since age 15, she has been a strict vegetarian and consumes no meat or eggs and little cheese. For the past 3 or 4 years, Ms. R. has been uncomfortable eating in front of other people and goes to great lengths to avoid such situations. This places great limitations on her social life. Ms. R. had two spontaneous menstrual periods at age 16 when her weight was about 120 pounds, but she has not menstruated since. (Adapted from Frances & Ross, 1996, pp. 240–41.)

As we see in the case of Ms. R., anorexia nervosa is often a stubbornly persistent and potentially life-threatening disorder. The mortality rate for females with anorexia nervosa is more than 12 times higher than the mortality rate for females aged 15 to 24 in the general population (Sullivan et al., 1995). When death occurs, it is usually the result of either the physiological consequences of starvation or, more intentionally, suicidal behavior. This is one of the few very sharp contrasts to bulimia nervosa, where death as a direct outcome of the disorder is rare (Keel & Mitchell, 1997; Mitchell, Pomeroy, & Adson, 1997). There is growing evidence that the severe anorexic, even if she does survive, may suffer from irreversible brain atrophy (Garner, 1997; Lambe et al., 1997).

Bulimia Nervosa

Bulimia nervosa is characterized by binge eating and by efforts to prevent weight gain using such inappropriate behaviors as self-induced vomiting and excessive exercise. Bulimia nervosa was recognized as a psychiatric syndrome relatively recently. The British psychiatrist G. F. M. Russell (1997) proposed the term in 1979, and it was adopted into the DSM in 1987. The word *bulimia* comes from the Greek *bous* (which means "ox"), and *limos* ("hunger") and is meant to denote a hunger of such proportions that the person "could eat an ox." The DSM-IV-TR (APA, 2000) criteria for bulimia nervosa are shown in the DSM criteria box.

DSM-IV-TR

Criteria for Bulimia Nervosa

- Recurrent episodes of binge eating. Binges involve eating, in a fixed period of time, amounts of food that are far greater than anyone might eat under normal circumstances. For example, a person might eat a gallon of ice cream, a family-sized package of Oreo cookies, and a whole chocolate cake during a single short binge. While the binge is occurring, there is also a complete lack of control over eating and the person is unable to stop.
- Recurrent and inappropriate efforts to compensate for the effects of binge eating. Typical strategies include self-induced vomiting, use of laxatives, or excessive exercise. Some patients even take thyroid medication to enhance their metabolic rate.
- Self-evaluation is excessively influenced by weight and body shape.

Source: *Adapted with permission from the* Diagnostic and Statistical Manual of Mental Disorders, Fourth Edition, Text Revision *(Copyright 2000). American Psychiatric Association.*

TABLE 9.1 Differential Diagnostic Criteria in Anorexia Nervosa, Bulimia Nervosa, and Binge-Eating Disorder

Criterion	Anorexia		Bulimia		Binge Eating
	Restricting	*Binge/Purge*	*Purging*	*Nonpurging*	
Maintaining of extremely low weight	yes	yes	no	no	no
Fear of weight gain, becoming fat	yes	yes	yes	yes	no
Denial of seriously low weight	?	?	no	no	no
Body image distortion	?	?	no	no	no
Amenorrhea	yes	yes	no	no	no
Frequent binge eating	no	?	yes	yes	yes
Frequent purging	no	?	yes	no	no
Frequent use of nonpurging methods to avoid weight gain	yes	?	yes	yes	no
Sensed lack of control over eating	no	?	yes	yes	yes
Self-evaluation unduly influenced by shape/weight	?	?	yes	yes	no

Notes: Based on criteria sets provided in the DSM-IV-TR (APA, 2000), "?" indicates that the feature may or may not be present, as in the form of an either-or criterion alternative.

The clinical picture of the binge-eating/purging type of anorexia has much in common with bulimia nervosa. Indeed, some researchers have argued that the bulimic type of anorexia nervosa should really be considered another form of bulimia.The difference between a person with bulimia nervosa and a person with the binge-eating/purging type of anorexia nervosa is weight. By definition, the person with anorexia nervosa is severely underweight. This is not true of the person with bulimia nervosa (see Table 9.1). Consequently, if the person who binges or purges also meets criteria for anorexia nervosa, the diagnosis is anorexia nervosa (binge-eating/purging type) and not bulimia nervosa. In other words, the anorexia nervosa diagnosis "trumps" the bulimia nervosa diagnosis. This is because there is much greater mortality associated with anorexia nervosa than with bulimia nervosa. Recognizing this, the DSM requires that the most severe form of eating pathology take precedence diagnostically.

It is important to understand that people with anorexia nervosa and bulimia nervosa share a common and overwhelming fear of being or becoming "fat." However, unlike patients with anorexia nervosa, bulimic patients are typically of normal weight. Sometimes they may even be slightly overweight. The fear of becoming fat helps explain the development of bulimia nervosa. Bulimia typically begins with restricted eating motivated by the desire to be slender. During these early stages, the person diets and eats low-calorie foods. Over time, however, the early resolve to restrict gradually erodes and the person starts to eat "forbidden foods." These typically include snack and dessert food such as potato chips, pizza, cake, ice cream, and chocolate. However, some patients binge on whatever food they have available, including such things as raw cookie dough. During an average binge, someone with bulimia nervosa may consume as many as 4,800 calories (Johnson et al., 1982)! After the binge, in an effort to manage the breakdown of self-control, the person begins to vomit, fast, exercise excessively, or abuse laxatives. This pattern then persists because, even though bulimic individuals are disgusted by their behavior, the purging serves to alleviate the extreme fear of gaining weight that comes from eating.

Bulimia is a costly disorder for many patients. High food bills can create financial difficulties, and patients sometimes resort to stealing food from housemates. The DSM-IV-TR distinguishes between *purging* and *nonpurging types* of bulimia nervosa on the basis of whether, in the current episode, the person has employed purgative methods of preventing weight gain (e.g., vomiting, use of laxatives). The purging type is by far the most common and accounts for about 80 percent of cases. In the nonpurging type, the person may fast or exercise but does not vomit or use laxatives or diuretics to counteract the effects of binging.

The typical patient with anorexia nervosa often denies the seriousness of her disorder and may remain seemingly unaware of the shock and concern with which others view her emaciated condition. In contrast, the mind-set of the average bulimia nervosa patient is anything but complacent. Preoccupied with shame, guilt, self-deprecation, and efforts at concealment, she struggles painfully and often unsuccessfully to master the frequent impulse to binge. The case described below depicts a typical pattern.

case STUDY **Nicole: Too Full to Eat**

Nicole awakens in her cold, dark room and already wishes it were time to go back to bed. She dreads the thought of going through this day, which will be like so many others in her recent past. She asks herself the same question every morning: "Will I be able to make it through the day without being totally obsessed by thoughts of food, or will I blow it again and spend the day binging?" She tells herself that today she will begin a new life, today she will start to live like a normal human being. However, she is not at all convinced that the choice is hers.

She feels fat and wants to lose weight, so she decides to start a new diet: "This time it'll be for real! I know I'll feel good about myself if I'm thinner. I want to start my exercises again because I want to make my body more attractive." Nicole plans her breakfast but decides not to eat until she has worked out for a half-hour or so. She tries not to think about food because she is not really hungry. She feels anxiety about the day ahead of her. "It's this tension," she rationalizes. That is what is making her want to eat.

Nicole showers and dresses and plans her schedule for the day—classes, studying, and meals. She plans this schedule in great detail, listing where she will be at every minute and what she will eat at every meal. She does not want to leave blocks of time when she might feel tempted to binge. "It's time to exercise, but I don't really want to; I feel lazy. Why do I always feel so lazy? What happened to the will power I used to have?" Gradually, Nicole feels the binging signal coming on. Halfheartedly she tries to fight it, remembering the promises she made to herself about changing. She also knows how she is going to feel at the end of the day if she spends it binging. Ultimately, Nicole decides to give in to her urges because, for the moment, she would rather eat.

Nicole is not going to exercise, because she wants to eat, so she decides that she might as well eat some "good" food. She makes a poached egg and toast and brews a cup of coffee, all of which goes down in about 30 seconds. She knows this is the beginning of several hours of craziness!

After rummaging through the cupboards, Nicole realizes that she does not have any binge food. It is cold and snowy outside and she has to be at school fairly soon, but she bundles up and runs down the street. First she stops at the bakery for a bagful of sweets—cookies and doughnuts. While munching on these, she stops and buys a few bagels. Then a quick run to the grocery store for granola and milk. At the last minute, Nicole adds several candy bars. By the time she is finished, she has spent over $15.

Nicole can hardly believe that she is going to put all of this food, this junk, into her body. Even so, her adrenaline is flowing and all she wants to do is eat, think about eating, and anticipate getting it over with. She winces at the thought of how many pounds all of this food represents but knows she will throw it all up afterward. There is no need to worry.

At home Nicole makes herself a few bowls of cereal and milk, which she gobbles down with some of the bagels smothered with butter, cream cheese, and jelly (not to mention the goodies from the bakery and the candy bars, which she is still working on). She drowns all of this with huge cups of coffee and milk, which help speed up the process even more. All this has taken no longer than 45 minutes, and Nicole feels as though she has been moving at 90 miles an hour.

Nicole dreads reaching this stage, where she is so full that she absolutely has to stop eating. She will throw up, which she feels she has to do but which repels her. At this point, she has to acknowledge that she's been binging. She wishes she were dreaming but knows all too well that this is real. The thought of actually digesting all of those calories, all of that junk, terrifies her.

In her bathroom, Nicole ties her hair back, turns on the shower (so none of the neighbors can hear her), drinks a big glass of water, and proceeds to force herself to vomit. She feels sick, ashamed, and incredulous that she is really doing this. Yet she feels trapped—she does not know how to break out of this pattern. As her stomach empties, she steps on and off the scale to make sure she has not gained any weight.

Nicole knows she needs help, but she wants someone else to make it all go away. As she crashes on her bed to recuperate, her head is spinning. "I'll never do this again," she vows. "Starting tomorrow, I'm going to change. I'll go on a fast for a week and then I'll feel better." Unfortunately, deep inside, Nicole does not believe any of this. She knows this will not be the last time. Reluctantly, she leaves for school, late and unwilling to face the work and responsibilities that lie ahead. She almost feels as though she could eat again to avoid going to school. She wonders how many hours it will be until she starts her next binge, and she wishes she had never gotten out of bed this morning. (Adapted from Boskind-White & White, 1983, pp. 29–32.)

Age of Onset and Gender Differences

Anorexia nervosa and bulimia nervosa are often considered "modern" disorders, yet pathological patterns of eating date back several centuries (Silverman, 1997). St. Catherine of Sienna began to starve herself when she was around 16 years of age. She died in 1830 (at the age of 32 or 33) because she refused to consume either food or water (Keel & Klump, 2003). And, as far back as the second century, the Greek physician Galen referred to a syndrome characterized by overeating, vomiting, and fainting, which he termed *bulimos* (see Ziolko, 1996). It was not until the 1970s and 1980s, however, that eating disorders began to attract a great deal of attention. Clinicians began seeing more and more patients with pathological eating patterns, and it soon became apparent that this was a problem of considerable magnitude.

Anorexia nervosa and bulimia nervosa do not occur in appreciable numbers before adolescence. Children as young as 7, though, have been known to develop eating disorders, especially anorexia nervosa (Bryant-Waugh & Lask, 2002). Anorexia nervosa is most likely to develop in 15- to 19-year-olds; for bulimia nervosa, the age group at highest risk are young women aged 20–24 (Hoek & van Hoecken, 2003). We need to keep in mind, however, that there are always exceptions to statistical trends. For example, there is a case report of a woman who developed an eating disorder for the first time when she was 92 (Mer-

9.1 THE WORLD AROUND US — Eating Disorders in Men

From a clinical perspective, men with eating disorders look very similar to women with eating disorders (Carlat et al., 1997). However, doctors are not especially likely to think of anorexia nervosa when they see male patients. A growing awareness that anorexia nervosa is not just a "young women's disorder" is slowly leading to better detection of cases of anorexia nervosa in men and is resulting in a slight increase in the prevalence of anorexia nervosa in men. Male cases of bulimia, however, are quite uncommon (Andersen, 2002). Although very little is currently known about binge-eating disorder, it may well turn out to be the most prevalent form of eating disorder in males.

One established risk factor for eating disorders in men is homosexuality (Carlat et al., 1997), perhaps because thinness is highly valued in the gay community as a hallmark of attractiveness. Another important risk factor is premorbid obesity and being teased as a child. Other specific subgroups of men who may also be at higher risk of eating disorders are wrestlers and jockeys, who need to "make weight" in order to compete or work.

To the extent that eating disorders begin with dieting and a desire to lose weight, men (as we have already seen) are at much lower risk than women of developing eating disorders. Men tend to diet when their weight is 15 percent higher (considering height and weight norms) than the weight at which women begin to diet. In general, there are four major reasons why men diet: to avoid being teased again about childhood weight problems, to improve their performance in a sport, to avoid a weight-related medical illness that they have seen their fathers suffer from, and to improve a gay relationship (Andersen, 1999).

Men are now experiencing sociocultural pressures to have toned and muscular bodies. As levels of body dissatisfaction rise, eating disorders in men may become more prevalent.

Although most typical eating disorders occur less frequently in men, one disorder that is found almost exclusively in men is "reverse anorexia" or "muscle dysmorphia" (Pope et al., 1997). This condition is characterized by a fear of being thin, despite being highly muscular. Males with this disorder often go to extreme efforts to "bulk up" and resort to the use of anabolic steroids to achieve their desired appearance. The growing prevalence of this phenomenon may be associated with changing cultural norms about the most desired body type for men. Leit et al. (2001) estimated the body fat content and level of muscularity of male centerfolds in *Playgirl* from 1973 to 1997. The results showed that over time, the bodies of the centerfold men had become more "dense." In other words, the level of muscularity went up and the level of body fat went down. As more and more men begin to experience sociocultural pressures to have a toned body and "six-pack" abs, we can anticipate that their levels of body dissatisfaction may begin to rise. To the extent that this happens, we can expect eating problems and eating disorders in men to become increasingly prevalent.

melstein & Basu, 2001)! Eating disorders in the elderly are easily missed or attributed to other problems, because clinicians mistakenly assume that eating disorders are always disorders of the young.

Although eating disorders occur in males (see The World Around Us 9.1), they are far more common in women. Estimates indicate that there are ten females for every male with an eating disorder (Hoek & van Hoecken, 2003). This striking imbalance suggests that variables associated with gender may be centrally involved in the nature and genesis of these disorders.

Medical Complications of Anorexia Nervosa and Bulimia Nervosa

Anorexia nervosa is one of the most lethal psychiatric disorders. Not surprisingly, many patients with this disorder look extremely unwell. The hair on the scalp thins and becomes brittle, as do the nails. The skin becomes very dry, and downy hair (called "lanugo") starts to grow on the face, neck, arms, back, and legs. Many patients also develop a yellowish tinge to their skin, especially on the palms of their hands. Because they are so undernourished, people with this disorder have a difficult time dealing with cold. Their hands and feet are often cold to the touch and have a purplish-blue tinge due to problems with temperature regulation and lack of oxygen to the extremities. As a consequence of chronically low blood pressure, patients often feel tired, weak, dizzy, and faint (de Zwaan & Mitchell, 1999). Thiamin (vitamin B1) deficiency may also be present; this could account for some of the depression and cognitive changes found in low-weight anorexics (Winston et al., 2000).

People with anorexia nervosa can die from heart arrhythmias (irregular heartbeats). Sometimes this is caused by major imbalances in key electrolytes such as potassium. Chronically low levels of potassium can also result in kidney damage and renal failure severe enough to require dialysis.

Although bulimia nervosa is much less lethal than anorexia nervosa, it also causes a number of medical problems. Purging can cause electrolyte imbalances and low potassium (hypokalemia), which, as we have already mentioned, puts the patient at risk for heart abnormalities. Another complication is damage to the heart muscle, which can be caused by using ipecac to induce vomiting (Pomeroy & Mitchell, 2002). More typically, however, patients develop calluses on their hands from sticking their fingers down their throat to make themselves sick. In extreme cases, where objects such as a toothbrush are used to induce vomiting, tears to the throat can occur.

Because the contents of the stomach are acidic, patients damage their teeth when they throw up repeatedly. Brushing the teeth immediately after vomiting damages the teeth even more. Mouth ulcers and dental cavities are a common consequence of repeated purging, as are small red dots around the eyes that are caused by the pressure of throwing up. Finally, patients with bulimia very often have swollen parotid (salivary) glands caused by repeatedly vomiting. These are known as "puffy cheeks" or "chipmunk cheeks" by many bulimics. Although such swellings are not painful, they are often quite noticeable to others.

Other Forms of Eating Disorders

In addition to anorexia nervosa and bulimia nervosa, the DSM-IV-TR includes the diagnosis of **eating disorder not otherwise specified (EDNOS).** This diagnostic category is used for patterns of disordered eating that do not exactly fit the criteria for any of the more specific diagnoses. For example, a woman who meets all criteria for anorexia nervosa except disrupted menstrual periods would be diagnosed as having EDNOS. A diagnosis of EDNOS is given to approximately one-third of all patients who seek treatment for an eating disorder. Still another group of people with eating disorders is diagnosed as having **binge-eating disorder (BED;** see DSM criteria).

Although it is not yet formally in the DSM, binge-eating disorder has been proposed as a separate disorder distinct from bulimia nervosa, nonpurging type. The difference is that the individual with BED binges at a level comparable to a patient with bulimia nervosa but does not regularly engage in any form of inappropriate "compensatory" behavior (such as purging, using laxatives, or even exercise) to limit weight gain (see Table 9.1 on p. 316). There is also much less dietary restraint in BED than is

DSM-IV-TR

Criteria for Binge-Eating Disorder

- Eating, in a limited amount of time, an amount of food that is considerably larger than most people would eat under similar circumstances.
- A sense of lack of control over eating.
- Three or more of the following:
  - (a) Eating much more rapidly than normal.
  - (b) Eating to the point of feeling uncomfortably full.
  - (c) Eating large amounts of food when not hungry.
  - (d) Eating alone due to embarrassment about how much one is eating.
  - (e) Feelings of disgust, guilt, or depression after overeating.
- Marked distress about binge eating.
- Binge eating occurs at least twice a week for 6 months.

Source: *Adapted with permission from the* Diagnostic and Statistical Manual of Mental Disorders, Fourth Edition, Text Revision *(Copyright 2000). American Psychiatric Association.*

typical of either bulimia nervosa or anorexia nervosa (Wilfley, Friedman, et al., 2000). Most patients with binge-eating disorder are older than those with anorexia nervosa or bulimia nervosa (they are generally between 30 and 50 years of age). It is also worth noting that binge-eating disorder is not uncommon in men; only 1.5 females are affected for each male with this disorder (Grilo, 2002). Not surprisingly, most people with BED are overweight or even obese (Pike et al., 2001). Regardless, being overweight is not a factor that is used diagnostically to distinguish people with BED from nonpurging bulimia nervosa patients (Walsh & Garner, 1997). As evidence grows to support the idea that BED is a distinct clinical syndrome (e.g., Williamson et al., 2002), we expect that it will eventually move out of the DSM Appendix and become a formal diagnosis.

case STUDY

Ms. A.: Feeling Out of Control

Ms. A. was a 38-year-old African-American woman who was single, lived alone, and was employed as a personnel manager at a hotel in New York. Her height was 6 feet 0 inches, and she weighed 292 pounds (body mass index = 39.7; see Table 9.3 on p. 334) when she was initially seen at the eating disorders research clinic of a university hospital for the treatment of binge-eating disorder and obesity. Her chief reason for going to the clinic was that she felt her eating was out of control and, as a result, she had gained approximately 80 pounds over the previous year.

Ms. A. reported a lifetime history of obesity and a history of binge eating beginning at approximately age 11. At her intake session, she described her eating. She felt out of control and ate large amounts of food nearly every day, typically in the evenings when she was on her way home from work or alone at home. She tended to feel out of control throughout the day, which contributed to her snacking on three or four regular candy bars or three or four medium cookies and one ice cream bar during the day. Ms. A. then felt that a binge episode was inevitable.

A typical binge episode consisted of the ingestion of two pieces of chicken, one small bowl of salad, two servings of mashed potatoes, one hamburger, one large serving of french fries, one fast-food serving of apple pie, one large chocolate shake, one large bag of potato chips, and 15 to 20 small cookies—all within a 2-hour period. During her binge episodes, Ms. A. ate much more rapidly than usual until she felt uncomfortably full, ate large amounts of food when she didn't feel physically hungry, ate alone because she was embarrassed by how much she was eating, and felt disgusted with herself and very guilty after eating. She was also extremely distressed about her weight and acknowledged that her weight and shape were the most important factors that affected how she felt about herself. (Adapted from Goldfein et al., 2000.)

Distinguishing among Diagnoses

The diagnosis of an eating disorder is not always clear-cut. The distinction between normal and disordered eating, particularly in a time when very large numbers of young women perceive themselves as overweight and therefore indulge in one or another form of "dieting," is at best a fuzzy one. And, as indicated by the well-populated EDNOS category, failure to meet diagnostic criteria for either anorexia nervosa or bulimia nervosa does not imply that the individual is free of disorder. Furthermore, the distinction between anorexia nervosa and bulimia nervosa is often less than clear, and whether the two disorders should be separated at all has been seriously debated. In fact, many persons who presently meet the criteria for bulimia nervosa have been diagnosed with anorexia nervosa in the past and, less commonly, vice versa (Garner & Garfinkel, 1997). One 21-year follow-up of patients with anorexia nervosa suggests that patients tend not to maintain a restricting form of the disorder and instead progress to binging and purging over time (Löwe et al., 2001). It has been suggested that some cases of EDNOS may reflect a long-term end state of anorexia nervosa (Bulik, 2002). In short, as Figure 9.2 highlights, the diagnosis given at one time may not be the diagnosis given at a later date. The clinical features of eating disorders seem to evolve, and one common pattern is anorexia nervosa "morphing" into bulimia nervosa.

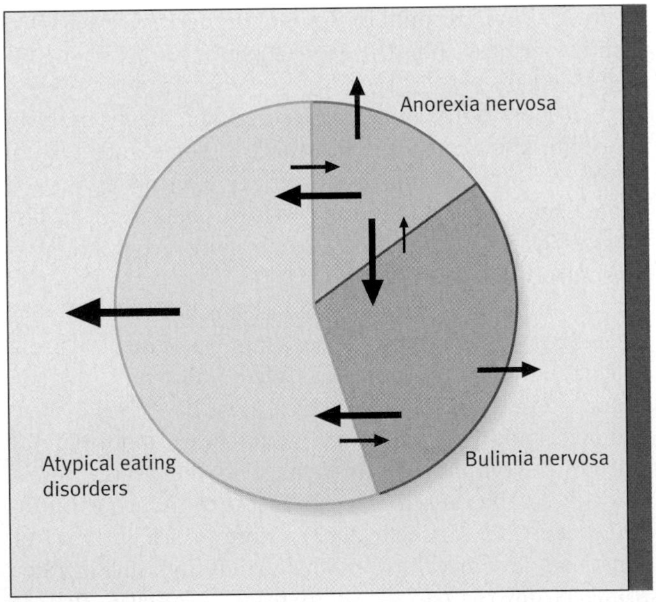

FIGURE 9.2

Temporal Movement between the Eating Disorders

The size of the arrow indicates likelihood of movement in shown direction. The larger the arrow, the more likely the movement from one eating disorder to another. Arrows that point outside of the circle indicate recovery.

Source: *Reprinted from* The Lancet, *V361:409, Fairburn et al., © 2003, with permission from Elsevier.*

Association of Eating Disorders with Other Forms of Psychopathology

Eating disorder diagnoses are commonly associated with other diagnosable psychiatric conditions. In other words, there is a great deal of comorbidity. For example, around 68 percent of patients with anorexia nervosa and 63 percent of patients with bulimia nervosa are also diagnosed with depression (Brewerton et al., 1995; Halmi et al., 1991; O' Brien & Vincent, 2003). Obsessive-compulsive disorder is also often found in patients with anorexia nervosa and bulimia nervosa (Kaye et al., 2004; Milos et al., 2002; O'Brien & Vincent, 2003). In addition, there is frequent co-occurrence of substance-abuse disorders in the binge-eating/purging subtype of anorexia nervosa as well as in bulimia nervosa. The restrictive type of anorexia nervosa, however, tends not to be associated with higher rates of substance abuse (Steiger & Seguin, 1999).

Comorbid personality (Axis II) disorders are also frequently diagnosed in people with eating disorders (Rø et al., 2005). Those with the restrictive type of anorexia nervosa are inclined toward personality disorders in the avoidant cluster (i.e., Cluster C; see Chapter 11; Skodol et al., 1993). In contrast, eating disorders that involve binge/purge syndromes (both anorexia nervosa and bulimia nervosa) are more likely to be associated with dramatic, emotional, or erratic (Cluster B) problems, especially borderline personality disorder (O'Brien & Vincent, 2003). Consistent with this, more than a third of patients with eating disorders have engaged in the kind of self-harming behaviors (cutting or burning themselves, for example) that are symptomatic of borderline personality disorder (Paul et al., 2002). Personality disorders are also found in patients with BED, although no clear pattern has emerged (Wilfley, Friedman, et al., 2000). Some evidence (Wilson, 1993) suggests that alcohol abuse is less common in this group than in binge-eating/purging anorexia nervosa or in bulimia nervosa and that there is also less comorbidity with other psychiatric disorders (Telch & Stice, 1998).

One problem with simple examinations of personality disorders in patients with eating disorders is that some of the disturbances found in these patients could reflect the consequences of malnourishment. Starvation is known to increase both irritability and obsessionality (Keys et al., 1950). We must therefore be cautious in our conclusions. Current thinking, however, is that even though the physiological consequences of eating disorders may exacerbate personality disturbances, they may be only enhancing traits that were there in the first place. Research suggests that some personality traits in eating-disordered patients might both predate the onset of the disorder and remain even when the eating disorder remits and the patient has recovered (Kaye et al., 2004; Klump et al., 2004). Consistent with this, around two-thirds of a sample of patients with anorexia nervosa reported that they were rigid and perfectionistic, even as children (Anderluh et al., 2003).

Prevalence of Eating Disorders

If we were to look only at the number of reports in the popular media about eating disorders, it would be easy to get the impression that there is an epidemic. However, this is not exactly true. When strict diagnostic criteria are applied, the prevalence of anorexia nervosa at any one time is around 0.3 percent (Hoek & van Hoecken, 2003) with a lifetime prevalence of 0.5 percent (APA, 2000). For bulimia, the point prevalence is around 1 percent (Hoek & van Hoecken, 2003), and the lifetime prevalence 1 to 3 percent (APA, 2000). In other words, the prevalence of these disorders is actually quite low.

Very little is currently known about binge-eating disorder because it is a newly proposed diagnosis. However, it may be relatively common. Community-based estimates indicate a prevalence of 2 to 3 percent in the general population and a much higher prevalence (around 8 percent) in obese people (Grilo, 2002).

We should keep in mind here that we are talking about clinically diagnosable eating disorders. Many people, particularly young women in their teens and twenties, have disordered eating patterns. For example, questionnaire studies suggest that up to 19 percent of students report some bulimic symptoms (Hoek, 2002). For some, this is a temporary condition, according to a published 10-year follow-up of people who were in college at initial assessment (Heatherton et al., 1997). At follow-up, the women in this study had experienced significant declines in disordered eating and increased satisfaction with their bodies, despite a continuing preoccupation with losing weight. In contrast, many men in the study reported increased concern about their eating habits.

There was a slight increase in the number of new cases (i.e., the incidence) of anorexia nervosa over the twentieth century (Keel & Klump, 2003). This increase is not fully explained by increased awareness of the disorder and better detection by clinicians. The number of new cases of bulimia nervosa has also increased significantly over the period 1970–1993, with the rise in the number of cases being much more dramatic than is found for anorxia nervosa. The reasons for the increase in these disorders are not fully understood. However, it is likely that changing norms regarding the "ideal" size and shape of women is an important factor. The type of body that used to be regarded as glamorous and attractive (e.g., Marilyn Monroe) is no longer considered desirable, especially by women.

Eating Disorders across Cultures

Although the majority of research on eating disorders is conducted in the United States and Europe, eating disorders are not confined to these areas. Le Grange, Telch, and Tibbs (1998) have reported widespread eating disorder difficulties among both Caucasian and non-Caucasian South African college students. Anorexia nervosa and (more recently) bulimia nervosa have also become clinical problems in Japan, Hong Kong, Taiwan, Singapore, and Korea (Lee & Katzman, 2002). Cases of eating disorders have been reported in India and Africa, and the prevalence of eating disorders in Iran is comparable to that in the United States (Nobakht & Dezhkam, 2000). Recently, the first published account of five males in central China who were diagnosed with eating disorders has appeared (Tong et al., 2005). Far from being confined to industrialized Western countries, eating disorders are becoming a problem worldwide.

Being white, however, does appear to be associated with having the kinds of subclinical problems that may put people at high risk for developing eating disorders. Examples of such problems include body dissatisfaction, dietary restraint, and a drive for thinness. A ***meta-analysis*** involving a total of 17,781 participants has shown that such attitudes and behaviors are significantly more prevalent in whites than in nonwhites (Wildes et al., 2001). Although Asian women exhibit levels of pathological eating similar to those of white women (Wildes et al., 2001), African-Americans in particular seem to be much less susceptible to subclinical types of eating problems and body image concerns than either whites or other minorities. This may help explain why eating disorders are less commonly found in black women than they are in white women. In a sample of 1,061 black women, for example, no case of anorexia nervosa was found. In contrast, out of a sample of 985 white women, 15 (1.5 percent) met clinical criteria for this disorder. More white than black women also had bulimia nervosa (2.3 percent versus 0.4 percent; see Striegel-Moore et al., 2003).

An important factor is how assimilated into white culture minority women are. In contrast to young white girls, black adolescent girls seem less inclined to use weight and appearance to fuel their sense of identity and self-worth (Polivy et al., 2005). However, young minority-group women are at increased risk of developing eating disorders if they are heavy and if they identify more strongly with white middle-class values (Cachelin et al., 2000). When the symptoms of eating disorders do occur in ethnic minorities, they appear to be linked to the same risk factors that have been found for whites, which we will describe in later sections (Polivy et al., 2005).

Some of the clinical features of *diagnosed* forms of eating disorders may also vary according to culture. For example, about 58 percent of anorexia nervosa patients in Hong Kong are not excessively concerned about fat. The reason they give for refusing food is fear of stomach bloating (Lee et al., 1993). Anorexia nervosa patients who were living in Britain but who had South Asian (Indian, Pakistani, Bangladeshi) ethnic origins also were less likely than patients with English ethnic origins to show evidence of fat phobia (Tareen et al., 2005). In yet another study, young women in Ghana who had anorexia nervosa were also not especially concerned about their weight or shape. Rather, they emphasized religious ideas of self-control and denial of hunger as the motivation for their self-starvation (Bennett et al., 2004). In a final example, Japanese women with eating disorders reported significantly lower levels of perfectionism and less of a drive for thinness than did American women with eating disorders (Pike & Mizushima, 2005). Findings such as these highlight the likely role culture plays in the clinical presentation of eating disorders.

Cases of anorexia nervosa have been reported throughout history. They have also been shown to occur all over the world. In light of this, Keel and Klump (2003) have concluded that anorexia nervosa is not a culture-bound syndrome. Of course, as we have just noted, culture may influence how the disorder manifests itself clinically. The more important point, however, is that anorexia nervosa is not a disorder that occurs simply because of exposure to Western ideals and the modern emphasis on thinness. In contrast, bulimia nervosa seems to occur only in people who have had some exposure to Western culture and ideals. Based on this, we conclude that bulimia nervosa is a culture-bound syndrome but that anorexia nervosa is not.

> **research close•up**
>
> ***meta-analysis***
>
> *A meta-analysis is a statistical method used to combine the results of a number of similar research studies. The data from each separate study are transformed into a common metric called the "effect size." Doing this allows data from the various studies to be combined and then analyzed. You can think of a meta-analysis as being just like research that you are already familiar with, except that the "participants" are individual research studies, not individual people!*

Course and Outcome

Eating disorders are notoriously difficult to treat, and relapse rates are high. However, over the very long term, recovery is a possibility. Löwe and colleagues (2001) looked at the clinical outcomes of patients with anorexia nervosa 21 years after they had first sought treatment. Reflecting the high morbidity associated with anorexia nervosa, 16 percent of the patients (all of whom were women) were no longer alive, having died primarily from complications of starvation or from suicide. Another 10 percent were still suffering from anorexia nervosa, and a further 21 percent had partially recovered. However, 51 percent of the sample were fully recovered at the time of the follow-up. These findings tell us that even after a series of treatment failures, it is still possible for women with anorexia nervosa to get well again. They also serve to highlight the dangers of this disorder. People with anorexia nervosa are at higher risk of suicide than people in the general population (Pompili et al., 2004), and those with both anorexia nervosa and substance abuse are at especially high risk of early death (Herzog et al., 2000; Keel et al., 2003).

With regard to bulimia nervosa, the long-term mortality rate is much lower, at around 0.5 percent. In a long-term outcome study in which the mean length of follow-up was around 11 years, Keel et al. (1999) found that about 70 percent of initially bulimic women were in remission and no longer met diagnostic criteria for any eating disorder. The remaining 30 percent continued to have problems with their eating. Because 20 percent of the women could not be contacted or refused to be interviewed, this figure could be an underestimate (women with severe problems may be especially inclined to refuse an interview). Again, substance-abuse problems (as well as a longer duration of illness prior to entry into the study) predicted patients doing worse over time.

Finally, it is worth noting that even when they are well, many people who recover from anorexia nervosa and bulimia nervosa still have some residual food issues. They may be excessively concerned about shape and weight, restrict their dietary intakes, and overeat and purge in response to negative mood states (Sullivan, 2002). In other words, the idea of recovery is relative. Someone who no longer meets all of the diagnostic criteria for an eating disorder may still have issues with food and body image.

In Review

- How do the prevalence rates for eating disorders vary according to socioeconomic status, gender, sexual orientation, and ethnicity?
- What are the major clinical differences between patients with anorexia nervosa and patients with bulimia nervosa? What clinical features do these two forms of eating disorder have in common?
- What kinds of medical problems do patients with eating disorders suffer from?

Risk and Causal Factors in Eating Disorders

There is no single cause of eating disorders. In all probability, anorexia nervosa and bulimia nervosa result from the complex interaction of biological, sociocultural, family, and individual variables.

Biological Factors

GENETICS The tendency to develop an eating disorder runs in families (Bulik & Tozzi, 2004). The biological relatives of people with anorexia nervosa or bulimia nervosa have elevated rates of anorexia nervosa and bulimia nervosa themselves. In one large family study of eating disorders, the risk of anorexia nervosa for the relatives of people with anorexia nervosa was 11.4 times greater than for the relatives of the healthy controls; for the relatives of people with bulimia nervosa, the risk of bulimia nervosa was 3.7 times higher than it was for the relatives of the healthy controls (Strober et al., 2000). However, eating disorders are not densely clustered in certain pedigrees the way mood disorders and schizophrenia sometimes are. It is also interesting that the relatives of patients with eating disorders are more likely to suffer from other problems, especially mood disorders (Lilenfield et al., 1998; Mangweth et al., 2003).

As you know, family studies do not allow us to untangle the different contributions of genetic and environmental influences. These kinds of questions are best resolved by twin studies and adoption studies. Presently, we have none of the latter, but a small number of twin studies do exist. Considered together, these studies suggest that both anorexia nervosa and bulimia nervosa are heritable disorders (Bulik & Tozzi, 2004; Fairburn & Harrison, 2003). There is also provocative evidence for a gene (or genes) on chromosome 1 that might be linked to susceptibility to the restrictive type of anorexia nervosa (Grice et al., 2002). Recent evidence has suggested that susceptibility to bulimia nervosa, particularly self-induced vomiting, may be linked to chromosome 10 (Bulik et al., 2003). Of course, until these findings are widely replicated, they should be treated as preliminary.

Eating disorders have also been linked to genes that are involved in the regulation of the neurotransmitter serotonin (Bulik & Tozzi, 2004). This makes sense, given the role that serotonin is known to play in the regulation of eating behavior. Furthermore, serotonin, as you have learned from Chapter 7, is also involved in mood. With this in mind, it is interesting to note that mood disorders and eating disorders often cluster together in families (Mangweth et al., 2003).

At present, researchers are still some distance away from understanding the role genes play in the development of eating disorders. Given the high degree of overlap between anorexia nervosa and bulimia nervosa (many women with AN later develop BN and many women with BN report histories of AN), it is possible that they may have some genetic factors in common. Moreover, in light of the continuum between more mild (subthreshold) eating disorders and disorders that are severe enough to warrant a clinical diagnosis, researchers are now considering the possibility that there may be an even broader eating disorder phenotype that has shared genetic predispositions at its core. As you will soon learn, being exposed to cultural attitudes that emphasize thinness is important for the development of eating disorders. However, only a small number of people who are exposed to such attitudes go on to develop eating disorders. In the future, we may be able to use genetic knowledge to help us understand why some people are more sensitive than others to these and other environmental risk factors.

SET POINTS There is a well-established tendency for our bodies to "resist" marked variation from some sort of biologically determined "set point" or weight that our individual bodies try to "defend" (Garner, 1997). Anyone intent on achieving and maintaining a significant decrease in body mass below his or her individual set point may be trying to do this in the face of internal physiologic opposition, which is aimed at trying to get the body back close to its original set-point weight.

One important kind of "physiologic opposition" designed to prevent us from moving far from our set point is hunger. As we lose more and more weight, hunger may rise to extreme levels, encouraging eating, weight gain, and a return to a state of equilibrium. Far from having little or no appetite, patients with anorexia nervosa think about food constantly and make intense efforts to suppress their increasing hunger. Accordingly, chronic dieting may well enhance the likelihood that a person will encounter periods of seemingly irresistible impulses to gorge on large amounts of high-calorie food. For patients with bulimia nervosa, these hunger-driven impulses may lead to "uncontrollable" binge eating.

SEROTONIN **Serotonin** is a neurotransmitter that has been implicated in obsessionality, mood disorders, and impulsivity. It also modulates appetite and feeding behavior. Because many patients with eating disorders respond well to treatment with antidepressants (which target serotonin), some researchers have concluded that eating disorders involve a disruption in the serotonin system (Kaye, 2002).

Evidence of disturbances in this neurotransmitter system can certainly be found. People with anorexia nervosa who are underweight have low levels of 5-HIAA, which is a major metabolite of serotonin. The same is true of people with bulimia nervosa. Moreover, upon recovery, both of these groups appear to have higher levels of 5-HIAA than control women (Kaye et al., 1991, 1998, 2001). Both of these findings suggest a problem in the serotonergic system.

Now researchers are studying brain serotonin receptors in women who have recovered from anorexia to try to learn more about how altered serotonergic function may play a role in this disorder. The early findings suggest that altered serotonergic function can be found, even after recovery. However, increased activity of the serotonin receptors seems to be more characteristic of the bulimia type of AN rather than the restricting type of AN (see Bailer et al., 2005), although why this should be is not yet clear.

Interpreting the data on serotonin is difficult because we cannot be sure if any disturbances in neurochemistry that we find are a primary cause of the problem (in this case, eating disorders) or whether such disturbances simply reflect the fact that patients are malnourished, restricting, purging, or whatever (that is, they are a consequence of the disorder itself). Studies of recovered patients certainly help in this regard. However, we cannot assume that any dysfunctions or dysregulations that remain after recovery must have *predated* the onset of the illness itself. It is equally possible that these dysregulations are a residual neurochemical "scar" that results from years of eating (or not eating) in a pathological manner. There is also another problem. As you already know, the comorbidity between eating disorders and depression is very high and the serotonin system is implicated in depression. This makes it difficult to be sure that dysregulation in the serotonergic system is related to eating disorders and is not simply a reflection of this susceptibility to depression.

Sociocultural Factors

PEER AND MEDIA INFLUENCES What is the ideal body shape for women in Western culture? Next time you glance at a glossy fashion magazine, take a moment to consider the messages you are getting concerning what is attractive. The overall body size of the models who appear on the

The fashion industry promotes an ideal of unnaturally thin women. Supermodel Carre Otis, who is 5 feet 9 inches, weighed 118 pounds at one point in her career, and took drugs to assist in keeping the weight off. Her unhealthy dietary habits eventually led to a heart condition, for which she had to have surgery. Today, Carre eats a healthy, balanced diet, exercises regularly, and sustains a strong support system with her friends. "I no longer let my size dictate who I am or how I feel," says Otis. "I let my achievements, goals, and compassion be the ruling force in my self-esteem."

covers of such magazines as *Vogue, Mademoiselle,* and *Cosmopolitan* has become increasingly thinner over the years (Sypeck, Gray, & Ahrens, 2004). Young adolescent women are avid consumers of such magazines and they are regularly bombarded with images of unrealistically thin models. These magazines are also widely available all over the world. For example, *British Vogue* is published in 40 or more countries and can be found in India, Argentina, and Kenya, among other widely diverse places (see Gordon, 2000). Moreover, social pressures toward thinness may be particularly powerful in higher-SES backgrounds, from where a majority of girls and women with anorexia nervosa appear to come (McClelland & Crisp, 2001).

It is likely that thinness became deeply rooted as a cultural ideal in the 1960s, although prior to this time, women had certainly been concerned with their weight and appearance. One landmark event was the arrival of Twiggy on the fashion scene. Twiggy was the first superthin supermodel. Although her appearance was initially regarded as shocking, it did not take long for the fashion industry to embrace the look she exemplified. The names of the models have changed over time, but little else has. The "waif-look" models of the early 1990s, as epitomized by Kate Moss, are a good example. Although from time to time there are proclamations of a shift in body standards toward a more "athletic" ideal, how many successful Hollywood actresses can you name who have this kind of build?

A provocative illustration of the importance of the media in creating pressures to be thin comes from a fascinating study that was done by Anne Becker and her colleagues (2002). In the early 1990s, when Becker was conducting research in Fiji, she became aware of the considerable percentage of Fijians who were overweight with respect to their Western counterparts. This was especially true of women. Within Fijian culture, being fat was associated with being strong, being able to work, and being kind and generous (these latter qualities are highly valued in Fiji). Being thin, in contrast, was regarded in a highly negative manner and was thought to reflect being sickly, being incompetent, or having somehow received poor treatment.

Through the early 1990s, being fat was considered the ideal in Fiji, where carrying extra weight was associated with strength, work aptitude, and being kind and generous. After television programs showing Western ideals of female figures started being broadcast in Fiji in the late 1990s, women started expressing dissatisfaction with their bodies and started dieting.

In other words, fatness was preferred over thinness, and dieting was viewed as offensive. What was also striking was the total absence of anything that could be considered an eating disorder.

After television came to Fiji, things changed, however. Not only were Fijians able to see programs such as *Beverly Hills 90210* and *Melrose Place,* but many young women also began to express concerns about their weight and dislike of their bodies. Moreover, for the first time, women in Fiji started to diet in earnest. As indicated in Table 9.2, the comments of the young Fijian women studied by Becker suggested that their body dissatisfaction and wish to lose weight were motivated by a desire to emulate the characters they had seen on television.

This "natural experiment" provides us with some anecdotal information on how Western values about thinness might begin to insin uate themselves into different cultural environments. Although Becker did not collect information about eating disorders themselves (she

TABLE 9.2 The Impact of Television on Fijian Adolescent Girls' Attitudes about Their Bodies

"I just want to be slim because [the television characters] are slim. Like it's influencing me so much that I have to be slim."

"... the actresses and all those girls, especially those European girls, I just like, I just admire them and I want to be like them. I want their body, I want their size."

"I want to be like [Cindy Crawford] ... I want to be like that, very tall, [I] want to be taller and thinner. [TV] always affects me like that."

Source: Becker et al., 2002.

measured attitudes toward eating), and although this was far from a controlled research study, the findings from the Fiji study are both provocative and alarming.

Family Influences

Clinicians have long been aware that certain problems seem regularly to characterize the families of patients with anorexia nervosa, prompting many clinicians to advocate a family therapy approach to treatment intervention (Lock et al., 2001). Echoing this sentiment, more than one-third of patients with anorexia nervosa reported that family dysfunction was a factor that contributed to the development of their eating disorder (Tozzi et al., 2003). However, there is no "typical" family profile. Rather, the types of family behaviors that tend to be noted are such things as rigidity, parental overprotectiveness, excessive control, and marital discord between parents (see Strober, 1997).

In addition, many of the parents of patients with eating disorders have long-standing preoccupations regarding the desirability of thinness, dieting, and good physical appearance (Garner & Garfinkel, 1997). And, like their children, they have perfectionistic tendencies (Woodside et al., 2002). However, in attempting to depict family characteristics associated with eating disorders, we must remember that having a patient with an eating disorder in the family is likely to affect family functioning in a negative way. That is, the causal connection, if any, might be in the other direction.

Family factors also seem to play a role in bulimia nervosa. Fairburn and colleagues (1997) noted that bulimic women were statistically differentiated from the general psychiatric control group and from the normal control group on such risk factors as high parental expectations, other family members' dieting, and degree of critical comments from other family members about shape, weight, or eating. In a large sample of college-age women, the strongest predictor of bulimic symptoms was the extent to which family members made disparaging comments about the woman's appearance and focused on her need to diet (Crowther et al., 2002). There is also some reason to believe that certain individual vulnerability factors may increase the impact of negative aspects of the family environment. For example, research has shown that an excessive focus on appearance is most predictive of a preoccupation with weight for young women who are generally more prone to anxiety (Davis et al., 2004). This highlights the importance of individual risk factors, which we now consider.

Individual Risk Factors

Not everyone who lives in a society that places excessive emphasis on being thin goes on to develop an eating disorder. If that were the case, eating disorders would be much more prevalent than they are. There must be other factors that increase a given person's susceptibility to developing problems. As we noted earlier, some of these differences may be biological. Others may be more psychological in nature.

INTERNALIZING THE THIN IDEAL The Duchess of Windsor once said that you could never be too rich or too thin. Clearly she had internalized the thin ideal, buying

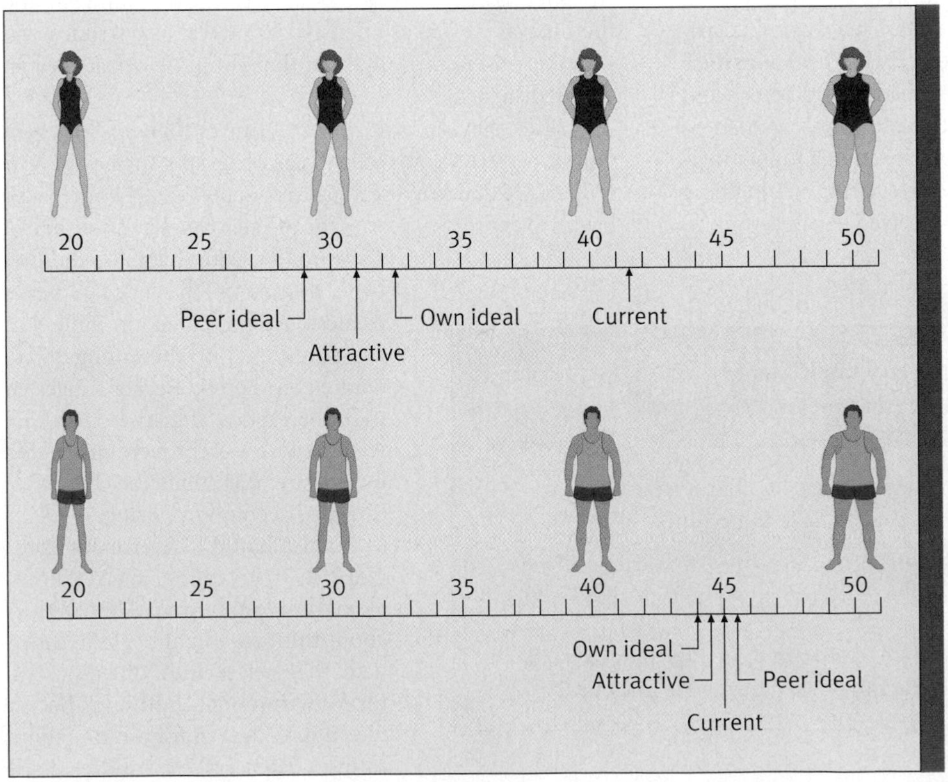

FIGURE 9.3

Mean body figure ratings of women (top) and men (bottom). Total scale values range from 10 to 90. Ratings reflect participants' responses to four questions: (a) "Which drawing looks most like your figure?" (current), (b) "Which figure do you most want to look like?" (own ideal), (c) "Which figure do you think most members of the opposite sex find most attractive?" (attractive), and (d) "Which figure do you think members of your own sex find most attractive?" (peer ideal). (Adapted from Cohn & Adler, 1992.)

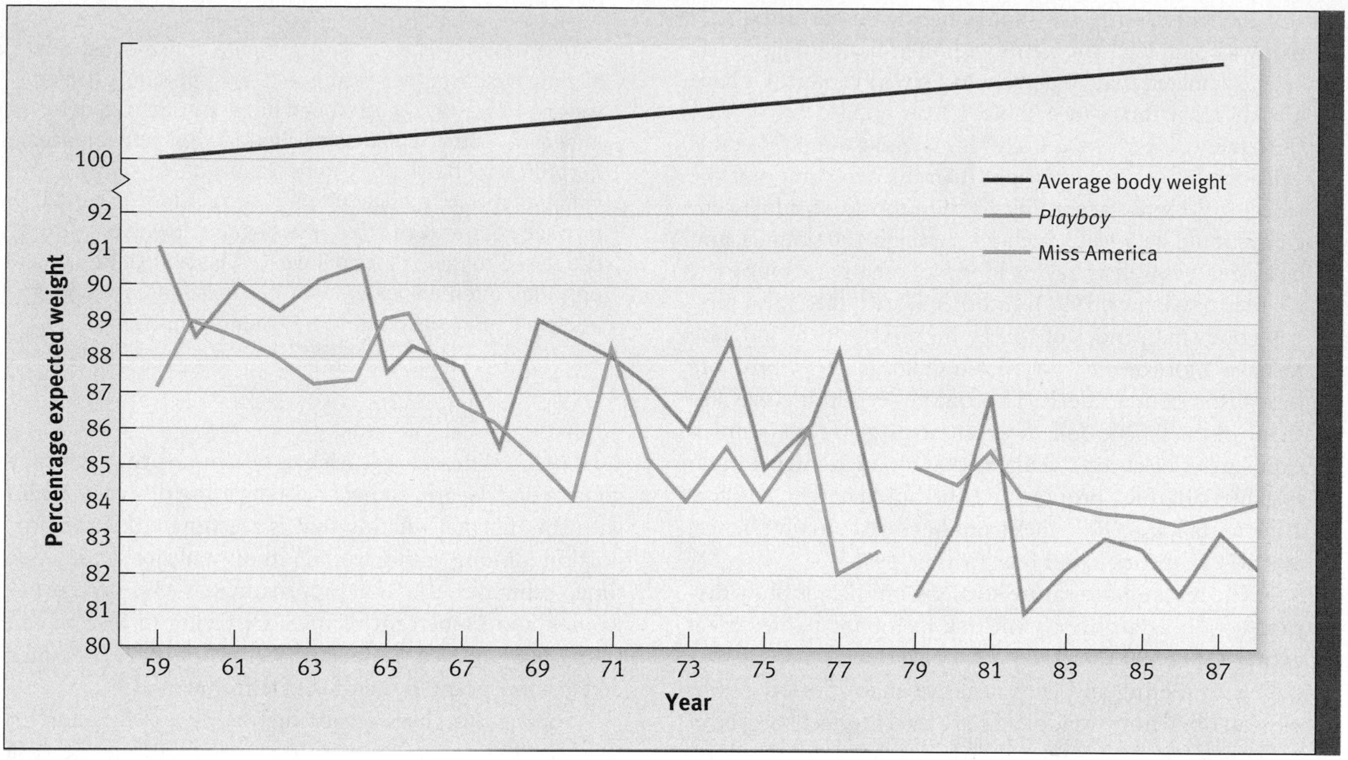

FIGURE 9.4

Prorated Trend of Women's Actual Body Weights Compared with the Trend for *Playboy* Centerfolds and Miss America Contestants

Changes in the average percentage of expected weight of Playboy *centerfolds and Miss America contestants, 1959–1978 (data from Garner, Garfinkel, Schwartz, & Thompson, 1980) and 1979–1988 (data from Wiseman, Gray, Mosimann, & Ahrens, 1992). The function above the broken verticals represents prorated changes in the average weights for women over the first 20-year period, based on the 1959 and revised 1979 Society of Actuaries norms. According to later population studies, this trend has continued. Adapted from Garner (1997), page 148.*

into the notion that being thin is highly desirable. Think for a moment about the extent to which you subscribe to this way of thinking. Do you regard thin people as unhealthy and weak? Or do you associate being thin with feeling attractive, being popular, and being happy? The extent to which people internalize the thin ideal is associated with a range of problems that are thought to be risk factors for eating disorders. These include body dissatisfaction, dieting, and negative affect (Stice, 2002). In fact, there is some empirical evidence that internalizing the thin ideal may be an early component of the causal chain that culminates in disordered eating (McKnight Investigators, 2003; Stice, 2001).

BODY DISSATISFACTION One consequence of sociocultural pressure to be thin is that some young girls and women develop highly intrusive and pervasive perceptual biases regarding how "fat" they are (e.g., Fallon & Rozin, 1985; Rodin, 1993; Wiseman et al., 1992; Zellner et al., 1989). In sharp contrast, young Amish people (who live radically separated from the modern world) do not show such body image distortions (Platte et al., 2000). This supports the idea that sociocultural influences are implicated in development of the discrepancy between the way many young girls and women perceive their own bodies and the "ideal" female form as represented in the media. Such perceptual biases lead girls and women to believe that men prefer more slender shapes than they in fact do. Many women also feel evaluated by other women, believing that their female peers have even more stringent standards about weight and shape than they themselves do (see Figure 9.3).

It would be one thing if women had a reasonable chance of attaining their "ideal" bodies simply by not exceeding an average caloric intake or by maintaining a healthy weight. But this is not possible for most people. In fact, as pointed out by Garner (1997), the average body weight of American young women has been increasing over at least the past four decades, probably as a consequence of general improvements in nutrition, pediatric health care, and other factors as well (e.g., the widespread availability of high-calorie foods). Yet, as women's average weight has been increasing since the late 1950s, the weight of such cultural icons of attractiveness as *Playboy* centerfolds and Miss America contestants has decreased at a roughly comparable rate. Figure 9.4 depicts these trends.

In light of this, we should hardly be surprised that many women have problems with their body image. It has been calculated that 70 percent of *Playboy* centerfolds have a body mass index (see Table 9.3 on p. 334) below 18.5 (Katzmarzyk & Davis, 2001). This is underweight, but it is considerably less underweight than the description of the "ideal girl," who, according to the reports of adolescent girls, should be 5 feet 7 inches tall, weigh 100 pounds, and be a size 5 (as well as having long blond hair and blue eyes; Nichter & Nichter, 1991). In other words, the "ideal girl" has a body mass index of 15.61 (this means she would have to have anorexia nervosa). Even children's toys promote unrealistic slender ideals. This can be seen in the size and shape of the Barbie doll, to which many girls receive much exposure. It has been calculated that for an average woman to achieve Barbie's proportions, she would have to be 7 feet 2 inches tall, lose 10 inches from her waist circumference, and add 12 inches to her bust (Moser, 1989).

The research literature strongly implicates body dissatisfaction as an important risk factor for pathological eating (Stice, 2002). Body dissatisfaction is also associated with dieting and with negative affect. Simply put, if we don't like how we look, we are likely to feel bad about ourselves. We may also try to lose weight in order to look better. Rebecca's eating disorder was triggered by the dissatisfaction she felt about her body after her boyfriend criticized her and pressured her to lose weight.

case study — Disgusted by Her Body

Rebecca, a 25-year-old Hispanic female, referred herself for treatment of eating difficulties and depressed mood. At intake she was 6 feet tall and weighed 150 pounds (body mass index = 20.3). She reported binging and inducing vomiting approximately once per week, and dated the onset of this behavior at 3 months before coming to therapy. She recalled that she had never had any concerns about her physical appearance until the time of her first romantic relationship at age 21. Apparently, her first boyfriend criticized her 175-pound (BMI = 23.7) physique and pressured her to lose weight, substantially affecting the way she viewed her body. At the end of this relationship, Rebecca felt disgusted with her appearance and decided that the only way to ensure success in future relationships was to lose weight. An additional precipitating factor for her eating disturbance appeared to be graduation from college at age 22. Feeling that she had little control over the direction of her life, Rebecca restricted her eating behavior in an attempt to "have control over something" (Hendricks & Thompson, 2005, p. 172) in her life. At one point, her body weight dropped to 135 pounds (BMI = 18.3). Alarmed at her behavior, Rebecca moved to her hometown to be closer to family and friends. She slightly increased her food intake and gradually gained weight. However, she remained unhappy and was determined to restrict her diet and modify her appearance. According to her report, Rebecca began to binge and vomit as a way to cope with her depression. To further manage her negative affect, she began drinking to intoxication two to three times per week. These binge-drinking episodes often coincided with her episodes of binging and purging. (From Hendricks & Thompson, 2005.)

DIETING When people wish to be thinner, they typically go on a diet. Nearly all instances of eating disorders begin with the "normal" dieting that is reaching epidemic proportions among young women in our culture. At any one time, estimates are that approximately 39 percent of women and 21 percent of men are trying to lose weight (Hill, 2002). Indeed, the majority of people have been on a diet at some point in their lives (Jeffrey et al., 1991).

Some researchers regard dieting as a risk factor for the development of anorexia nervosa and bulimia nervosa in young women (Polivy & Herman, 1985; Wilson, 2002). However, there is currently some debate about whether this is so. For example, even though a large-scale longitudinal study showed that the majority of adolescent girls who went on to develop anorexia nervosa had been dieters (Patton et al., 1990), it is obvious to all of us that not everyone who diets develops anorexia nervosa. Other factors, (e.g., personality factors like perfectionism—discussed below) must clearly be in operation. It has also been suggested that dietary restraint is a cause of binge eating. However, when overweight women were randomly assigned to either a low-calorie diet or to a waiting list control group (that did not involve a diet), those who received the diet lost weight and showed a *decrease* in bulimic symptoms (Presnell & Stice, 2003).

So why has dieting been linked to eating disorders? One possibility is that the people who self-report that they often diet or try to restrain their eating may be people who are dissatisfied with their bodies. It may be this dissatisfaction that is the important variable (Johnson & Wardle, 2005). Another factor to keep in mind is that there is a difference between going on a supervised diet that is monitored by therapists (which was the experience of the subjects in the Presnell and Stice study) and going on a self-started diet that might be characterized by periods of fasting and overeating. Moreover, as Stice (2002) notes in his comprehensive review of this topic, when our efforts to diet fall short, it is almost inevitable that we will feel bad about ourselves (see also Ackard et al., 2002). Dieting itself may therefore not be the real problem (which is good news for people who are obese and who need to lose weight). Rather, it may be the case that people who often report that they are trying to lose weight are the people who are most unhappy with their bodies and who are most inclined to feel bad about themselves when they don't stick with their diet plans.

NEGATIVE AFFECT **Negative affect** (feeling bad) is a causal risk factor for body dissatisfaction (Stice, 2002). When we feel bad, we tend to become very self-critical. We may focus on our limitations and shortcomings and magnify our flaws and defects. This seems to be especially true of people who have eating disorders. People with eating disorders, like those with depression, tend to exhibit *distorted ways of thinking* and of processing information received from the environment (e.g., Butow et al., 1993; Garner et al., 1997). In many cases, there is widespread negative self-evaluation (e.g., Fairburn et al., 1997). These cognitive distortions (I'm fat; I'm a failure; I'm useless) have the potential to make people feel even worse about themselves.

Longitudinal studies involving young people have confirmed that depression and general negative affect are predictive of high risk for later eating disorders (Johnson et al., 2002a; Leon et al., 1997). Moreover, evidence suggests that negative affect may work to maintain binge eating (see Stice, 2002). Patients often report that they engage in binges when they feel stressed, down, or bad about themselves. They also say that in the very short term, eating offers them some comfort. These reports are highly consistent with affect-regulation models (e.g., McCarthy, 1990) that view binge eating as a distraction from negative feelings. Of course, a major problem is that after binges, patients feel disappointed or even disgusted with themselves. In short, a bad situation leads to behavior that makes things even worse.

PERFECTIONISM **Perfectionism** (needing to have things exactly right) has long been regarded as an important risk factor for eating disorders (Bruch, 1973). This is because people who are perfectionistic may be much more likely to subscribe to the thin ideal and relentlessly pursue the "perfect body." It has also been suggested that perfectionism helps maintain bulimic pathology through the rigid adherence to dieting that then drives the binge/purge cycle (Fairburn et al., 1997).

In general, research supports the association of perfectionism and eating disorders. Halmi and her colleagues (2000) studied 322 women with anorexia nervosa and found that they scored higher on a measure of perfectionism than did a sample of controls without an eating disorder. The women with anorexia nervosa scored higher on perfectionism regardless of whether they had the restricting subtype of anorexia nervosa or subtypes that involved either purging or binge eating and purging. A large proportion of bulimia nervosa patients also show a longstanding pattern of excessive perfectionism (Anderluh et al., 2003; Garner & Garfinkel, 1997).

Large Seated Bather, *Pierre-Auguste Renoir. This painting by the eighteenth-century French painter Renoir depicts an idealized view of the female body. Note how ideas about feminine beauty in the 1800s differ from what is considered attractive today.*

As we have already noted, any personality characteristics found in eating-disordered patients could be the result of the eating disorders themselves, rather than contributory in a causal sense. However, even when they have recovered from their anorexia nervosa, former patients still score higher on perfectionism than do controls to whom they are compared (Bastiani et al., 1995; Srinivasagam et al., 1995). This suggests that perfectionism may be an enduring personality trait of people who are susceptible to developing eating pathology (see also Fairburn, Cooper, et al., 1999; Stice, 2002). Interestingly, men with eating disorders are less perfectionistic than are women with eating disorders (Woodside et al., 2004). If men are generally less perfectionistic than women, this might help them avoid some of the weight and shape concerns that seem to be a stepping stone to the development of eating disorders.

CHILDHOOD SEXUAL ABUSE Childhood sexual abuse has been implicated in the development of eating disorders (Connors, 2001; Fairburn et al., 1997; Fallon & Wonderlich, 1997). However, there is some debate about whether sexual abuse is truly a risk factor for eating disorders (see Stice, 2002). In the only prospective study to date that has examined this issue, Vogeltanz-Holm and colleagues (2000) failed to find that early sexual abuse predicted the later onset of binge eating. On the other hand, a meta-analysis of

53 studies did reveal a weak but positive association between childhood sexual abuse and eating pathology (Smolak & Murnen, 2002). This suggests that the two variables are linked in some way, although the precise nature of the link is not yet clear. One possibility is that being sexually abused increases the risk of developing other known risk factors for eating disorders such as having a negative body image or high levels of negative affect. In other words, the causal pathway from early abuse to later eating disorder may be an indirect one (rather than a direct one) that involves an array of other intervening variables.

In Review

- What individual characteristics are associated with increased risk for eating disorders? How might these risk factors work together to result in pathological eating?
- What role do sociocultural factors play in the development of eating disorders?

Treating Eating Disorders

The clinical management of eating disorders presents a serious challenge. Patients with eating disorders are often very conflicted about getting well, and around 17 percent of patients with severe eating disorders have to be committed to a hospital for treatment against their will (Watson et al., 2000). Suicide attempts are also often made and clinicians need to be mindful of this risk, even when patients have received a great deal of treatment (Franko et al., 2004).

Some of this ambivalence is apparent in the behavior of patients admitted to inpatient units. When one of the authors of this book was working on an inpatient unit that had a large number of patients with eating disorders, it was not uncommon for staff to find food vomited into small cups and hidden in patients' rooms. The World Around Us 9.2 describes how patients with eating disorders are now using the Internet to communicate with each other—again in ways that are very countertherapeutic.

Treating Anorexia Nervosa

Individuals with anorexia nervosa view the disorder as a chronic condition and are generally pessimistic about their potential for recovery (Holliday et al., 2005). They have a high dropout rate from therapy, and patients with the binge-eating/purging subtype of anorexia nervosa are especially likely to terminate inpatient treatment prematurely (Steinhausen, 2002; Woodside et al., 2004). Making the situation even worse, there have been surprisingly few controlled studies on which to base an informed judgment about what treatment will work best (le Grange & Lock, 2005). This is probably due to the fact that the disorder is rare. Moreover, patients who suffer from it are often very reluctant to seek treatment. These factors combine to make treatment research very difficult.

The most immediate concern with patients who have anorexia nervosa is to restore their weight to a level that is no longer life-threatening. In severe cases, this requires hospitalization and such extreme measures as tube feeding. This is followed by rigorous control of the patient's eating and progress toward a targeted range of weight gain (Andersen et al., 1997). Normally, this short-term effort is successful. However, without treatment designed to address the psychological issues that fuel the anorexic behavior, any weight gain will be temporary and the patient will soon need medical attention again. Also, in some cases, aggressive treatment efforts can backfire. What mistakes do you think are made in the clinical management of the following case?

case study — Hospitalized against Her Will

M., a 29-year-old woman, had been chronically ill since age 13. She had been hospitalized numerous times throughout the country and treated by exceptionally skilled therapists. Coming close to death on several occasions, she still managed to pursue a doctoral degree in mathematics and volunteered at a local community center for senior citizens, despite having a BMI of 12.2. A female aide at the center eventually struck up a friendship with M., but M. declined her repeated requests to socialize after work. This aide, increasingly worried that M.'s emaciation and ongoing resistance to eating might be a form of suicidal depression, took her concern to the center's director, who intervened by persuading M. to seek medical evaluation at a local hospital. Concerned about the gravity of her condition, the evaluating physician had M. detained involuntarily for psychiatric treatment. M. was soon judged by the psychiatric staff to be incompetent to make medical decisions despite her acknowledgment that she had anorexia nervosa, that the illness was resistant to usual care, and that she was aware of the detrimental effects of the disease. M. implored staff not to attempt any weight gain, explaining why this would only aggravate her psychological state. She proposed instead that she be allowed the alternative of supportive outpatient care. M.'s request to be released was summarily rejected. Over the next month, there were various clumsy, at times coercive, attempts to increase her weight. M. then sought legal counsel and was ordered released into her own custody. Fearing any further contact with health professionals, her weight dropped precipitously and she died 3 months later of cardiac arrest. (From Strober, 2004.)

MEDICATIONS There is no strong evidence that medications are particularly helpful in the treatment of patients with anorexia nervosa (Fairburn & Harrison, 2003). However, antidepressants as well as antipsychotic medications (to help with the disturbed thinking) are sometimes used (Ferguson & Pigott, 2000; Walsh, 2002).

FAMILY THERAPY For adolescents with anorexia nervosa, family therapy is now considered to be the treatment of choice (le Grange & Lock, 2005). In family therapy, the therapist works with the parents to help them help their anorexic child (typically a daughter) to begin to eat again. Family meals are observed by the therapist, and efforts are made to get the parents functioning as a team where their daughter's eating is concerned. After the patient starts to gain weight, other family issues and problems begin to be addressed. Later, in the final phase of treatment, the therapist works with both the patient and her parents to help the patient develop more independent and healthy relationships with her father and mother (see Lock et al., 2001).

research close•up

randomized controlled trials

A randomized controlled trial involves a specific treatment group (which is the group the researchers are most interested in) as well as a control treatment group (against which the treatment group will be compared). Participants have an equal chance of being placed in either group because which group they go into is determined randomly.

Randomized controlled trials have shown that patients treated with family therapy for 1 year do better than patients who are assigned to a control treatment (where they receive supportive counseling on an individual basis). Five years after treatment, 75 to 90 percent of patients show full recovery (le Grange & Lock, 2005). However, it is clear that family treatment works better for some patients than for others. In particular, patients who developed anorexia nervosa

9.2 THE WORLD AROUND US

Eating Disorders and the Internet

For most of us, the Internet is a valuable source of information, help, and advice. Many people use it to connect with like-minded others. For the person with anorexia nervosa, however, connecting with others via the Internet may have problematic consequences. A growing number of Web sites now provide help and support to anorexia nervosa sufferers. But these are not sites that encourage anorexics to seek treatment. On the contrary, these *pro-ana* (short for "pro-anorexia") Web sites provide information and inspiration to those who want to keep starving themselves.

Rather than regarding anorexia nervosa as a disorder, many young women view it as a lifestyle choice. For some, it is almost like a religion. One Web site contains the "Ana Prayer," which begins, "Strict is my diet. I must not want." The same site also lists the "Thin Commandments" ("If you aren't thin, you aren't attractive" and "Being thin is more important than being healthy"). The "Ana Creed" contains even more statements that express the thinking of severe anorexics with chilling clarity ("I believe in bathroom scales as an indicator of my daily successes and failures" and "I believe in Control, the only force mighty enough to bring order to the chaos that is my world").

The typical person with anorexia nervosa is silent and secretive about her disorder. In the past, the only way for patients with eating disorders to meet and to exchange ideas was during inpatient treatment. Now, the anonymity of the Internet provides for instant bonding with others who share similar, if distorted, values. A major problem is that this contact provides anorexia nervosa sufferers with a sense of validation. It also gives them ideas and information that supports their potentially deadly pursuit of thinness (how to cope with starvation headaches; how to diet so your body doesn't go into starvation mode and make it difficult to continue to lose weight). In response to pressure from the treatment community and others who run sites designed to provide genuine help for people with eating disorders, many large Web servers have recently made efforts to shut down pro-ana sites. However, the Internet is difficult to patrol, and many pro-ana (or pro-ED) sites have simply "gone underground," becoming more difficult to find and to access. Without question, the girls and young women who continue to visit these sites need help. But the people least able to offer the help they really need are other young girls and women with online names such as "PurfectLeighThin" and "Neverthinenuf."

before age 19 and had been ill for less than 3 years did much better than patients who had been ill for longer or who had bulimia nervosa (Dare & Eisler, 2002). These results suggest that family therapy may be most effective when it is used to treat adolescents (as opposed to adults) whose anorexia nervosa is of fairly recent onset.

COGNITIVE-BEHAVIORAL THERAPY **Cognitive-behavioral therapy (CBT),** which involves changing behavior and maladaptive styles of thinking, has proved to be very effective in bulimia. Because anorexia nervosa shares many features with bulimia, CBT is often used with anorexia nervosa patients too (Vitousek, 2002). The recommended length of treatment is 1 to 2 years. A major focus of the treatment involves modifying distorted beliefs about weight and food, as well as distorted beliefs about the self that may have contributed to the disorder (e.g., "People will reject me unless I am thin").

Pike and her colleagues (2003) treated a sample of 33 women who had anorexia after they had been discharged from the hospital. Over the course of a year, the women received either 50 sessions of CBT or nutritional counseling. Despite this, only 17 percent of patients who received CBT showed full recovery, and none of the women who received nutritional counseling was fully well (i.e., normal weight, no binge eating or purging, and with eating attitudes and concerns about weight within normal limits) at the end of treatment. These results highlight the current limitations of CBT for this group of patients and also the pressing need for new treatment developments, particularly for older patients with more long-standing problems.

Treating Bulimia Nervosa

MEDICATIONS It is quite common for patients with bulimia nervosa to be treated with antidepressant medications. Researchers became interested in using these medications to treat bulimic patients after it became clear that many patients with bulimia also suffer from mood disorders. Generally speaking, patients taking antidepressants do better than patients who are given inert, placebo medications. Perhaps surprisingly, antidepressants seem to decrease the frequency of binges, as well as improving patients' mood and their preoccupation with shape and weight (Fairburn & Harrison, 2003; Walsh, 2002).

COGNITIVE-BEHAVIORAL THERAPY The treatment of choice for bulimia is cognitive-behavioral therapy (CBT). Most of the current treatment approaches are based on the work of Fairburn and his colleagues in Oxford, England. Multiple controlled studies that include post-treatment and long-term follow-up outcomes attest to the clinical benefits of CBT for bulimia (e.g., Agras et al., 1992; Fairburn, Marcus, & Wilson, 1993, 1995; Fichter et al., 1991; Leitenberg et al., 1994; Walsh et al., 1997; Wilson & Fairburn, 1993, 1998). Such studies have included comparisons with medication therapy (chiefly antidepressants; see Wilson & Fairburn, 1998) and with interpersonal psychotherapy (IPT; see Agras et al., 2000), and they generally show CBT to be superior. In fact, combining CBT and medications produces only a modest increment in effectiveness over that achievable with CBT alone.

The "behavioral" component of CBT for bulimia focuses on normalizing eating patterns. This includes meal planning, nutritional education, and ending binging and purging cycles by teaching the person to eat small amounts of food more regularly. The "cognitive" element of the treatment is aimed at changing the cognitions and behaviors that initiate or perpetuate a binge cycle. This is done by challenging the dysfunctional thought patterns usually present in bulimia such as the "all-or-nothing" thinking described earlier. For example, CBT disputes the tendency to divide all foods into "good" and "bad" categories by providing factual information and by arranging for the patient to demonstrate to herself that ingesting "bad" food does not inevitably lead to a total loss of control over eating. Figure 9.5 shows a cognitive worksheet that was completed by a patient. It provides a good example of the kind of "hot thought" that can facilitate a binge.

Treatment with CBT clearly helps to reduce the severity of symptoms in patients with bulimia nervosa (Fairburn & Harrison, 2003). However, patients with the disorder are rarely completely well at the end of treatment (Lundgren et al., 2004). Most change occurs in such behaviors as binging and dietary restraint. Even after treatment, however, weight and shape concerns are likely to remain.

Treating Binge-Eating Disorder

As of now, we know little of a systematic nature about effective treatment for binge-eating disorder (BED). Significant depression is a common condition for binge eaters; some 60 percent have a lifetime diagnosis of mood disorder (Wilfley, Schwartz, et al., 2000). For this reason, antidepressant medications are sometimes used (Carter et al., 2003). Other categories of medications such as appetite suppressants and anticonvulsant medications are also being explored (Carter et al., 2003).

Clinicians have tried to apply aspects of the treatments of other eating disorders to BED patients. For example, Marcus (1997) has suggested adapting CBT techniques already established in the treatment of anorexia nervosa and bulimia nervosa to BED. BED patients are typically overweight and subject to chaotic eating patterns. They also typically have a variety of illogical and contradictory "rules" about food ingestion—for example, they share the bulimic's rigid distinction between "good" and "bad" foods. They may also have stereotypic attitudes about the character flaws of overweight people and so lack the self-esteem

Emma's completed worksheet:
Identifying permissive thoughts

Situation	Feelings and sensations	Permissive thoughts
Friday, at college, alone, had a free period, thinking about my assignment (how difficult it was going to be). Ate a bar of chocolate, knew I was going to binge. Got on the bus to town, went to Burger King—had a burger, two portions of fries, a milkshake, one big bar of chocolate, another smaller bar of chocolate.	Anxious Heavy Blank	I might as well keep eating now I've started. I can make myself sick afterwards—so it doesn't matter—I can have what I want and I won't gain weight. (circled) I might as well carry on until my money has run out. I've got to eat more and more.
• When was it? • Where were you? • Who were you with? • What were you doing? • What were you thinking about?	• What feelings did you have? • What body sensations did you notice?	• What were you saying to yourself that made it easier to keep eating? • Identify and circle the hot thought. This is the thought that makes it most likely that you will binge.

FIGURE 9.5
Cognitive Worksheet

Source: *Reproduced from M. Cooper, G. Todd, & A. Wells,* Bulimia Nervosa: A Cognitive Therapy Programme for Clients *with permission from Jessica Kingsley Publishers. Copyright © 2000 Myra Cooper, Gillian Todd, and Adrian Wells.*

that might motivate them to stop their binging. Somewhat curiously, most binge-eating disorder patients do not appear to overvalue thinness, although they do disparage their own bodies (Marcus, 1997). In general, a well-planned program of CBT, together with corrective and factual information on nutrition and weight loss, is often helpful (see Goldfein et al., 2000; Wilfley et al., 2002). Fairburn and Carter (1997) also suggest incorporating selected self-help reading materials into such a therapeutic program.

In Review

- Compare the treatment approaches that are used for anorexia nervosa and bulimia nervosa. Why do you think cognitive-behavioral therapy is so beneficial for patients with eating disorders?
- What factors make eating disorders (especially anorexia nervosa) so difficult to treat?

Obesity

There is now a worldwide epidemic of obesity, and prevalence rates are rising rapidly. To get an idea of how extensive the problem of obesity is, just look around. In the United States, almost two-thirds of the adult population is overweight. Of those, 31 percent are considered to be obese, up from 23 percent in 1994. And by 2008, it is predicted that 39 percent of the adults in America will be classified as obese (Hill et al., 2003).

Waistlines have not been increasing just in the United States. In China, the number of overweight women doubled between 1989 and 1997, and the number of overweight men tripled during this same period. Worldwide, there are more than 1 billion overweight adults and 300 million adults who are obese (Hill et al., 2003). It is no surprise that the World Health Organization has now recognized obesity as one of the top-ten global health problems.

Obesity is defined on the basis of a statistic called the **body mass index (BMI).** You can calculate your BMI by following the instructions in Table 9.3. Generally speaking, people with a BMI below 18.5 are considered underweight, 18.5 to 24.9 is considered normal, 25.0 to 29.9 is overweight, and obesity is defined as having a BMI above 30.

TABLE 9.3 Calculating Body Mass Index

$$\frac{\text{weight (lb)}}{\text{height (in.)}^2} \times 703 = \text{BMI}$$

	BMI
Healthy	18.5–24.9
Overweight	25–29.9
Obese	30–39.9
Morbidly obese	40+

Within our own society, obesity seems to be related to social class, occurring six times as often in lower-SES adults, and nine times as often in lower-SES children (Ernst & Harlan, 1991). Other demographic and behavioral factors that are linked to obesity are shown in Table 9.4. In addition, Lissau and Sorenson (1994) have found that children who were seriously neglected had a greater risk of obesity in young adulthood than well-cared-for children. Low parental education also seems to be an important risk factor (Johnson, Cohen, Kasen, et al., 2002).

Obesity can be a life-threatening disorder. It results in such conditions as diabetes, joint disease, high blood pressure, coronary artery disease, sleep apnea (breathing problems), and, in all likelihood, certain forms of cancer (e.g., Kenchaiah et al., 2002; Pi-Sunyer, 2003). In the United States, more than 300,000 people die each year from the consequences of obesity. The heavier the person, the greater the health risks.

From a diagnostic perspective, obesity is not an eating disorder. Many clinicians, however, regard the central problem as the habit of overeating. Although some cases of obesity result from metabolic or hormonal disorders, this is extremely uncommon. Put simply, obese persons just take in more calories than they burn.

In Review

- What demographic factors seem to place people at higher risk for becoming obese?
- Explain the importance of the body mass index in the definition of obesity.

Risk and Causal Factors in Obesity

The Role of Genes

Are you the kind of person who can eat high-calorie foods without significant weight gain? Or does it seem that you need only to look at a piece of chocolate cake to gain a few pounds? Genetic inheritance contributes substantially to the tendency for some people to become obese or, alternatively, to remain thin.

Thinness seems to run in families (Bulik & Allison, 2002). Genes associated with thinness and leanness have been found in certain animals, and a special type of rat has now been bred that does not become obese even when fed a high-fat diet. Twin studies further suggest that genes play a role both in the development of obesity and in the tendency to binge (Bulik, Sullivan, & Kendler, 2003; Friedman, 2003). Indeed, a genetic mutation has recently been discovered that is specifically associated with binge eating (Branson et al., 2003). Although this mutation was found only in a minority (5 percent) of the obese people in the study, all of the obese people with the gene reported problems with binge eating. In contrast, only 14 percent of obese people who did not have the genetic mutation had a pattern of binge eating.

TABLE 9.4 Demographic and Behavioral Factors Related to Obesity

Factor	Prevalence of obesity is increased if subjects are . . .
Age	Older
Sex	Female
Race or ethnicity	Of racial and ethnic minorities
Socioeconomic status	Of low SES
Family history	Children of obese parents
Marital status	Married
Children	If the person has more children
Smoking	Ex-smokers

From Valdez & Williamson (2002), p. 419.

Hormones Involved in Appetite and Weight Regulation

Over a 10-year period, the average person will consume approximately 10 million calories while keeping a reasonably stable overall weight. How do we accomplish this? The answers lie in the ability of our bodies to regulate how much we eat on a daily basis and in our body's ability to balance food intake and energy output over the longer term. One key element of this homeostatic system is a hormone called **leptin.** Leptin is a hormone that acts to reduce our intake of food and is produced by fat cells. Increased body fat leads to increased levels of leptin, which leads to decreased food intake. When body fat levels decrease, leptin production decreases and food intake is stimulated. Rare genetic mutations that result in an inability to produce leptin are associated with morbid obesity. One 9-year-old girl in England weighed 200 pounds and could hardly walk because her legs were so fat. When it was discovered that she was lacking leptin, she was treated with injections of the hormone and her weight returned to normal (Farooqi et al., 2002; Montague et al., 1997).

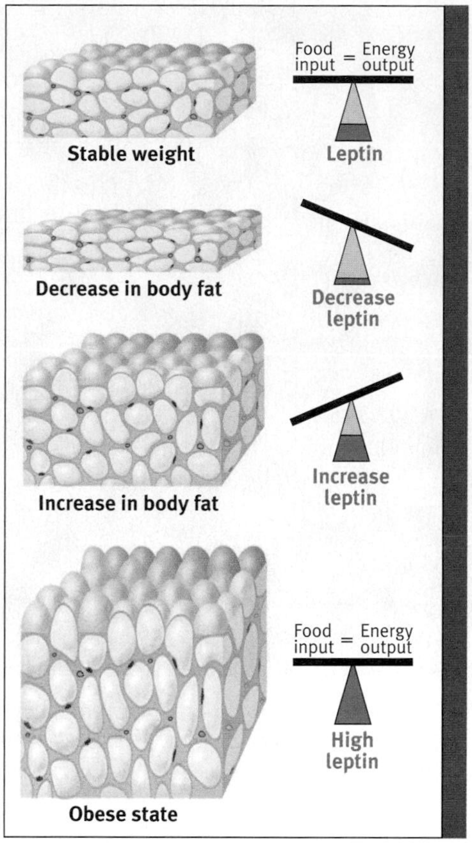

FIGURE 9.6
Leptin's Effect on Fat Cells

Leptin levels help the body regulate weight.

Source: *Reprinted with permission from Marx, SCIENCE 299:846–849 (2003). Illustration: Katherine Sutliff. Copyright 2003 AAAS.*

Unfortunately, when leptin is given to overweight people, in the majority of cases it has little effect. People who are overweight generally have high levels of leptin in their bloodstream (see Figure 9.6). The problem is that they are resistant to its effects (Friedman, 2003). Despite this, the leptin system is still a major focus of interest in the search for anti-obesity drugs.

Why do we get hungry at regular times during the day even if we don't even see or smell food? The reason may be another hormone of interest to researchers called **grehlin.** Grehlin is a recently discovered hormone that is produced by the stomach. Grehlin is a powerful appetite stimulator. Under normal circumstances, grehlin levels rise before a meal and go down after we have eaten. When grehlin is injected into human volunteers, it makes them very hungry. This suggests that grehlin is a key part of the appetite control system. People with a rare condition called Prader-Willi syndrome have chromosomal abnormalities that create many problems, one of which is very high levels of grehlin. Sufferers are extremely obese and often die before age 30 from obesity-related causes. Although this genetic disorder is very unusual, findings such as this highlight the role of genetics in the regulation of eating behavior and weight.

Sociocultural Influences

Although genes are important for understanding why people differ in their weight and eating patterns, rates of obesity are rising far more rapidly than genetics alone could explain. This implicates environmental factors in the development of extreme problems with weight. Particularly problematic for all of us is a culture that encourages consumption and discourages exercise. In the last week, how often have you had a "supersized" portion of food? How often have you worked out?

But why is the obesity epidemic happening now? A major culprit is probably time pressure. Because we are so chronically short of time, we drive rather than walk or we take the elevator rather than climb the stairs. Also, as the pace of life gets faster, we have less time to prepare food. This means that we eat out more or buy more prepackaged or fast food (Reich, 2003).

As Brownell (2003) has observed, the food industry is highly skilled at getting us to maximize our food intake. Restaurants in the United States serve large portions. One comparison of the same fast-food chains and eateries in Philadelphia and Paris found that the average portion sizes in Paris were 25 percent smaller (Rozin et al., 2003)! The culture of supersizing also tempts us to buy more than we really want because it costs only a small amount more (Brownell, 2003).

Family Influences

In many cases the key determinants of excessive eating and obesity appear to be family-behavior patterns. In some families, a high-fat, high-calorie diet or an overemphasis on food may produce obesity in many or all family members,

In many families, a pattern of high-fat, high-calorie diets or an overemphasis on food may be the key determining factor for producing obesity in many or all family members, including the family pet.

including the family pet! In such families, a fat baby may be seen as a healthy baby, and great pressure may be exerted on infants and children to eat more than they want. In other families, eating (or overeating) becomes a habitual means of alleviating emotional distress (Musante et al., 1998).

Family attitudes to food are important because their consequences are likely to remain with us for a long time. Obesity is related to the number and size of fat (adipose) cells in the body (Heymsfield et al., 1995). People who are obese have markedly more adipose cells than people of normal weight (Peeke & Chrousos, 1995). When obese people lose weight, the size of the cells is reduced, but not their number. Some evidence suggests that the total number of adipose cells stays the same from childhood on (Crisp et al., 1970). It is possible that overfeeding infants and young children causes them to develop more adipose cells and may thus predispose them to weight problems in adulthood. Consistent with this, DiPietro, Mossberg, and Stunkard (1994) found that, in a 40-year follow-up study, the majority of a sample of 504 overweight children became overweight adults.

We are all conditioned to eat in a number of situations including when watching TV or going to movies or to parties. However, obese people are conditioned to many more cues that may lead to overeating—for example, anger, anxiety, and boredom. The taste of food is pleasurable, lessens anxiety, and, as a result, encourages more eating.

Stress and "Comfort Food"

When you are stressed or unhappy, what kind of food do you want to eat? Do you crave a carrot or a piece of chocolate? Foods that are high in fat or carbohydrates are the foods that console us when we are feeling bad (Canetti, Bachar, & Berry, 2002). Workers who say that they are under a lot of stress report that they eat less healthy foods and foods that are higher in fat than their less stressed counterparts (Ng & Jeffery, 2003). Eating for comfort is found in rats too. When rats were placed under chronic stress (being subjected to cold), they selected diets that were higher in fat and sugar (Dallman et al., 2003). What was also interesting in this study was that the rats who ate the comfort food gained weight in their bellies and became calmer in the face of new acute stress, prompting the researchers to speculate that the sugary and fatty foods helped to reduce activation in the stress response system.

Might overeating function as a means of reducing feelings of distress or depression? Certainly many people with obesity experience psychological problems such as depression. One study reported that 26 percent of patients seeking help with weight loss were diagnosed as having a mood disorder and that 55 percent had at least one diagnosis of mood disorder in their lifetimes (Goldsmith et al., 1992). Other research has found that a striking percentage of subjects with an eating disorder binge eat in response to aversive emotional states such as feeling depressed or anxious (Kenardy et al., 1996).

In light of Dallman's data from the stressed rats, it is easy to see how weight gain or a tendency to maintain excessive weight might be explained quite simply in terms of learning principles (Fairburn et al., 1998). We are all conditioned to eat in response to a wide range of environmental stimuli (at parties, during movies, while watching TV). Obese people have also been shown to be conditioned to more cues—both internal and external—than are people of normal weight. Anxiety, anger, boredom, and depression may lead to overeating. Eating in response to such cues is then reinforced because the taste of good food is pleasurable and because the individual's emotional tension is reduced.

Food portions have increased significantly over the past several decades. In 1957 a fast-food hamburger weighed 1 ounce and contained around 210 calories. Today a typical hamburger weighs 6 ounces and contains 618 calories.

Pathways to Obesity

In a prospective study of 231 adolescent girls, Stice, Presnell, and Spangler (2002) established that binge eating is a predictor of later obesity. The idea that overeating is implicated in the development of obesity is hardly surprising. However, the association between binge eating and obesity suggests that we should pay close attention to the causes of binge eating.

Research suggests that one pathway to binge eating may be via social pressure to conform to the thin ideal (Stice et al., 2002). Being heavy often leads to dieting, which may lead to binge eating when willpower wanes (see Figure 9.7). Another pathway to binge eating may operate through depression and low self-esteem. In Stice and colleagues' prospective study, low levels of support from peers, as well as depression, made girls more at risk for binging. We also know that when children are fat, they are more likely to be rejected by their peers (Latner & Stunkard, 2003; Strauss & Pollack, 2003), thus increasing their negative affect. As Figure 9.7 shows, a pattern of binge eating in response to negative emotions may make a bad situation worse, increasing weight, depression, and fostering alienation from peers in a vicious cycle.

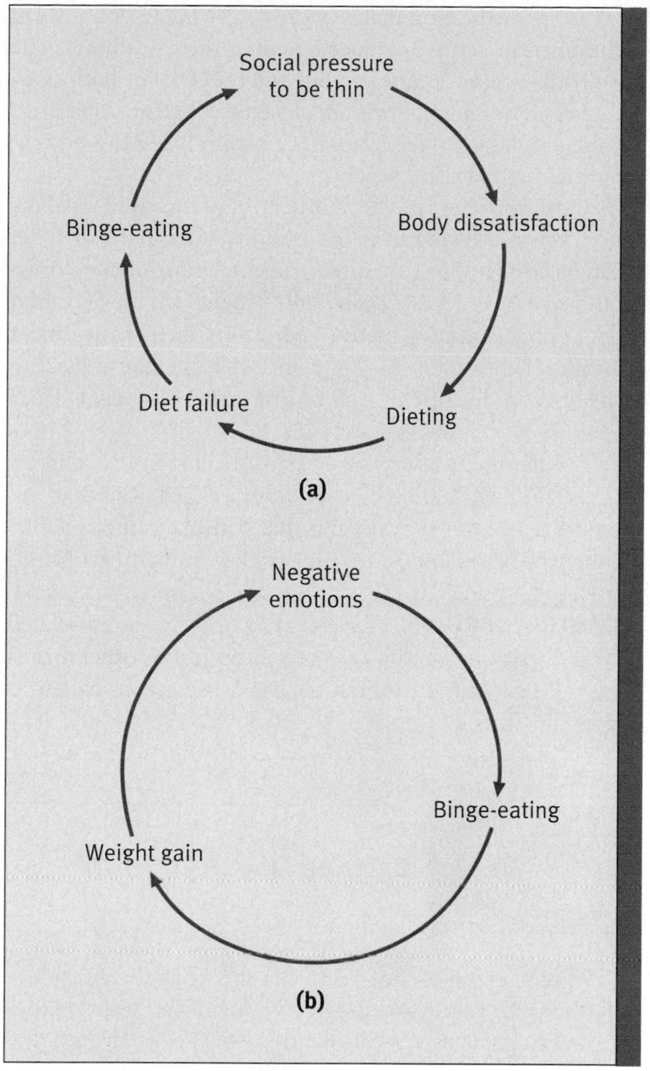

FIGURE 9.7

Pathways to Obesity

One pathway to obesity is via social pressure to be thin. Another pathway may operate via depression and low self-esteem.

Treatment of Obesity

Losing weight is a preoccupation of many Americans. New diet books, Internet-based interventions, dietary aids, and weight-loss programs are big business. Unfortunately, the success rates of most of these devices and programs are quite low (Tsai & Wadden, 2005). For those who are obese, losing weight and maintaining the weight loss presents a formidable challenge (Yanovski & Yanovski, 2002).

WEIGHT-LOSS GROUPS A number of weight-loss group programs are conducted by organizations such as Overeaters Anonymous and Weight Watchers. These programs provide education, encourage record keeping in the form of food diaries, and also provide support and encouragement. However, Weight Watchers is the only commercial weight-loss program with demonstrated efficacy in a randomized controlled trial. Over the course of 6 months, overweight and obese people who attended Weight Watchers lost more weight (10.5 versus 3 pounds) than did people who received self-help materials and two brief sessions with a nutritionist (Heshka et al., 2000).

MEDICATIONS Drugs that are used to promote weight loss fall into two main categories. One group of medications reduces eating by suppressing appetite, typically by increasing the availability of neurotransmitters. A second group of medications works by preventing some of the nutrients in food from being absorbed.

One medication that is approved by the FDA for use in conjunction with a reduced-calorie diet is sibutramine (Meridia). Sibutramine inhibits the reuptake of both serotonin and norepinephrine and, to a lesser extent, dopamine. Patients who use it for 6 months typically lose 5 to 8 percent of their pretreatment weight.

Orlistat (Xenical) is another FDA-approved medication. It works by reducing the amount of fat in the diet that can be absorbed once it enters the gut. Unfortunately, orlistat does not work especially well. Patients who take orlistat for 1 year lose approximately 9 percent of their pretreatment weight. The weight loss for controls who take a placebo medication during this time is just under 6 percent (Heck et al., 2000; Yanovski & Yanovski, 2002).

Other medications for obesity are currently in clinical trials (Vastag, 2003). One of these, called Rimonabant, blocks a receptor for cannabis that stimulates the appetite. It may be better known to some as the "munchie receptor."

GASTRIC SURGERY Given major health risks associated with obesity, those who cannot lose weight by other means may use extreme treatment measures. One such patient is Vincent Caselli.

case study — Battling Obesity

Vincent Caselli's battle with obesity began in his late twenties. "I always had some weight on me," he said. He was 200 pounds when he married his wife, and a decade later he reached 300. He would diet and lose 75 pounds, only to put 100 back on. By 1985 he weighed 400 pounds. On one diet, he got down to 190, but he gained it all back. "I must have gained and lost a thousand pounds," he said. He developed high blood pressure, high cholesterol, and diabetes. His knees and his back ached all the time, and he had limited mobility. He used to get season tickets to the local hockey games and go out regularly to the track every summer to see auto racing. Years ago, he drove in races himself. Now he could barely walk to his pickup truck. He hadn't been on an airplane since 1983, and it had been 2 years since he had visited the second floor of his own house, because he couldn't negotiate the stairs. He had to move out of the bedroom upstairs into a small room off the kitchen. Unable to lie down, he had slept in a recliner ever since. Even so, he could doze only in snatches, because of sleep apnea (a breathing problem), which is common among the obese and is thought to be related to excessive fat in the tongue and soft tissues of the upper airway. Every 30 minutes his breathing would stop, and he'd wake up asphyxiating. He was perpetually exhausted. (Adapted from Gawande, 2001.)

One increasingly popular method for treating obesity like Vincent Caselli's involves bariatric or gastric bypass surgery (Benotti & Forse, 1995; Santry et al., 2005). This current surgery of choice for the morbidly obese involves placing lines of staples in the intestines to develop a holding pouch for food that is ingested. Before the operation, the stomach might be able to hold about a quart of food and liquid. After the procedure, the stomach might be able to hold only the contents of a shot glass. Binge eating becomes virtually impossible. The operation takes a couple of hours, but because it is performed on an obese patient, recovery can be difficult.

Weight loss is quite dramatic after bariatric surgery. Vincent Caselli, the patient described above, weighed 250 pounds a year and a half after his surgery and was still losing weight. His case fits well with some of the empirical research findings. Pories and MacDonald (1993) reported that 2 years after the surgery, 89 percent of patients could no longer be considered morbidly obese. In another study, patients lost, on average, about 60 percent of their excess weight and retained most of this weight loss even 8 or 9 years after surgery (Sugerman et al., 1992). Nonetheless, some patients manage to find ways to continue to binge eat after surgery (Kalarchian et al., 1998) and tend to regain their weight over an 18-month period (Hsu et al., 1998).

PSYCHOLOGICAL TREATMENTS The most effective psychological treatment procedures for extremely obese patients are behavioral-management methods. A number

In March of 2002, Al Roker, the NBC weatherman on the Today *show, had gastric bypass surgery, one form of bariatric surgery. He weighed 320 pounds at the time of his surgery. By the end of the year, Roker had shed 100 pounds.*

of methods using positive reinforcement, self-monitoring, and self-reward can produce moderate weight loss over time (Agras, Telch, et al., 1997). Considerable support for treatment of binge eating using cognitive-behavioral methods has been found (Carter & Fairburn, 1998; Wilson & Fairburn, 1993). Research also suggests that highly motivated people can lose weight and keep it off (Klem et al., 1997; Tinker & Tucker, 1997). In these studies, clients identified strong reasons for losing weight such as medical problems aggravated by obesity (for example, varicose veins) or concerns over their appearance. These individuals were able to reduce their weight through diet and exercise in a long-term weight-loss program.

However, not every obese person has the strong motivation it takes to lose weight under a behavior-management regimen. Obese people may feel a great sense of shame and failure because they have tried many diets but either have failed to lose weight or have regained the lost weight soon afterward. Brownell and Wadden (1992) found that their patients had undertaken an average of five major diets on which they lost (and eventually regained) a total of 56 kilograms, or 123.2 pounds. People who go on very low-calorie diets that produce dramatic weight loss are especially likely to regain the weight they lost and may weigh more at follow-up than people who go on a more gradual (balanced-diet) weight-loss program (Wadden et al., 1994).

An active lifestyle combined with reduced food intake promotes health and prevents obesity.

The Importance of Prevention

Our bodies have evolved to survive in times of frequent famine. Losing weight is difficult because it is a battle against biological mechanisms that are designed to keep us at the weight we already are. Gaining weight, as we all know, is much more easy. Interestingly, populations who were most susceptible to starvation throughout history (e.g., Pima Indians, Pacific Islanders) are those who are most inclined to become obese when they have a sedentary lifestyle and a Western diet (see Friedman, 2003).

All of this speaks to the importance of not gaining weight in the first place. But what can we do? Some simple but important suggestions that are valuable for all of us are provided in Developments in Practice 9.3. In addition, given the powerful environmental forces at work,

9.3 Developments in Practice — Avoiding Age-Related Weight Gain

Over an 8-year period, the average adult (in the 20–40 age range) will gain about 14 to 16 pounds (Hill et al., 2003). How can we avoid this? Hill et al. (2003) estimate that most of the weight gain that people frequently regard as inevitable could be prevented through a combination of increased energy expenditure and reduced food intake. What is most encouraging is that this may be easier to do than we might imagine. Hill and colleagues (2003) have calculated that all that we need to do is cut back on our intake of calories by a mere 100 calories per day or walk an extra mile each day. A mile of walking is only 2,000 to 2,500 extra steps, and we can add these in small increments during the day. Here are some simple things to do:

1. Eat three fewer bites of food when you eat a meal. Three bites of hamburger, for example, equals 100 calories.
2. Take the stairs, combine a meeting with a walk, or park a little farther from your destination.

By making these habits part of your daily routine, you will be able to prevent weight gain as you age and improve your overall health.

Brownell (2002) makes several specific public policy recommendations. These include (1) improving opportunities for physical activity, (2) regulating food advertising aimed at children, (3) prohibiting the sale of fast food and soft drinks in schools, and (4) subsidizing the sale of healthful foods. Although some of these measures may seem extreme, the more we can focus on prevention, the better our chance to stop the nationwide problem of obesity from escalating even further out of control.

In Review

- What biological factors are implicated in obesity?
- In what ways might negative emotional states contribute to the development of obesity?
- What treatment approaches are currently being used to help obese patients?

summary

- DSM-IV-TR recognizes three different eating disorders: anorexia nervosa, bulimia nervosa, and eating disorder NOS (not otherwise specified). A fourth type of eating disorder, binge-eating disorder, is listed in the Appendix and is not yet part of the formal DSM.
- Both anorexia nervosa and bulimia nervosa are characterized by an intense fear of becoming fat and a drive for thinness. Patients with anorexia nervosa are seriously underweight. This is not true of patients with bulimia nervosa.
- Eating disorders are more common in women than in men. They can develop at any age, although they typically begin in adolescence.
- Anorexia nervosa has a lifetime prevalence of around 0.5 percent. Bulimia nervosa is more common, with a lifetime prevalence of 1 to 3 percent. Many more people suffer from less severe forms of disturbed eating patterns.
- Genetic factors play a role in eating disorders, although exactly how important genes are in the development of pathological eating patterns is still unclear.
- The neurotransmitter serotonin has been implicated in eating disorders. This neurotransmitter is also involved in mood disorders, which are highly comorbid with eating disorders.
- Sociocultural influences are important in the development of eating disorders. Our society places great value on being thin. Western values about thinness may be spreading, which may help explain why eating disorders are now found throughout the world.
- Individual risk factors such as internalizing the thin ideal, body dissatisfaction, dieting, negative affect, and perfectionism have been implicated in the development of eating disorders.
- Anorexia nervosa is very difficult to treat. Treatment is long term, and many patients resist getting well. Current treatment approaches include tube feeding (in severe cases), family therapy, and CBT. Medications are also used.
- The treatment of choice for bulimia nervosa is CBT. CBT is also helpful for binge-eating disorder.
- Obesity is defined as having a body mass index of 30 or above. Being obese is associated with many medical problems and with increased risk of death from heart attack. Obesity is not viewed as an eating disorder or as a psychiatric condition.
- A tendency to being thin or heavy may be inherited. However, unhealthful lifestyles are the most important cause of obesity.
- People are more likely to be obese if they are older, are female, or are of low socioeconomic status. Being a member of an ethnic minority group is also a risk factor for obesity.
- Obesity is a chronic problem. Medications help patients to lose small amounts of weight; drastic weight loss usually requires bariatric surgery.
- Because obesity tends to be a lifelong problem, and treating obesity is so difficult, there is now a focus on trying to prevent people from becoming obese in the first place. Implementing many approaches that have been recommended will require major changes in social policy.

Key Terms

anorexia nervosa (p. 313)
binge-eating disorder (BED) (p. 319)
body mass index (BMI) (p. 333)
bulimia nervosa (p. 315)
cognitive-behavioral therapy (CBT) (p. 332)
eating disorder (p. 312)
eating disorder not otherwise specified (EDNOS) (p. 319)
grehlin (p. 335)
leptin (p. 335)
negative affect (p. 329)
obesity (p. 333)
perfectionism (p. 329)
purge (p. 314)
serotonin (p. 324)

CHAPTER

10

Health Problems and Behavior

Are you under a lot of stress? Do you feel socially isolated? Do you tend often to be rather hostile and angry? There is now a growing recognition that what we are like as people and the way we live our lives have important implications for our overall health and physical well-being.

You may have noticed that when you are tired or have a cold, you seem to have a much lower tolerance for psychological stress. You may also have observed that when you are emotionally upset or are feeling pressured in some way, your body seems to have a lower resistance to physical disease. The medical profession has traditionally concentrated on understanding and treating anatomical and physiological factors in disease. In psychopathology, on the other hand, the main focus of interest has been to identify and remedy psychological factors associated with mental disorders. Now we are coming to understand that, although a disorder may be primarily physical or primarily psychological, it is always a disorder of the whole person—not just of the body or of the psyche. In other words, there is now a growing appreciation for how the mind and the body work in concert.

A person's overall life situation influences when a disorder first develops and the nature, duration, and prognosis of that disorder. Recovery is likely to be more rapid for a patient who is eager to get back to work and to family than for the person who will be returning to a frustrating job or an unpleasant home life. In addition, sociocultural influences affect the types and incidence of disorders found in members of different cultures and different gender and age groups. For example, men die an average of 7 years earlier than women; mortality from stroke in the United States is 10 percent higher than average in 11 southern states that make up the "Stroke Belt" (e.g., Alabama, Arkansas, and Georgia); African-Americans have more coronary heart disease than Caucasians; Latinos are less likely to smoke daily than are Caucasians; and Asian-Americans and Pacific Islanders are among the healthiest groups in the United States (see Whitfield et al., 2002). The ailments to which people are most vulnerable—whether physical, psychological, or both—are determined in no small part by who we are, where we live, and how we live (see Figure 10.1).

Behavioral medicine is an interdisciplinary field that focuses on the role that psychological factors play in the occurrence, maintenance, and prevention of medical problems. The field of behavioral medicine naturally involves professionals from many disciplines (such as medicine, psychology, and sociology) who take into account biological, psychological, and sociocultural influences when considering a person's health and well-being.

People who are hostile are more likely to develop cardiovascular disease.

Health psychology is a psychological subspecialty within behavioral medicine. It deals with psychology's contributions to the diagnosis, treatment, and prevention of psychological components of medical problems. Over the last 30 years, the field has developed rapidly and has had a notable impact on almost the entire range of clinical medicine (Belar, 1997; Smith, Kendall & Keefe, 2002; Smith et al., 2005).

A behavioral medicine approach to physical illness is concerned with the following types of issues (adapted from Gentry, 1984).

- The psychological factors that may predispose an individual to physical illness. Such psychological factors include critical life events, particular types of behavior, and personality.
- The ways in which the negative effects of stress can be reduced or buffered by personal resources. Examples of such resources include coping styles, social supports, and certain personality traits.
- The biological mechanisms by which human physiology is altered by stressors, particularly those arising

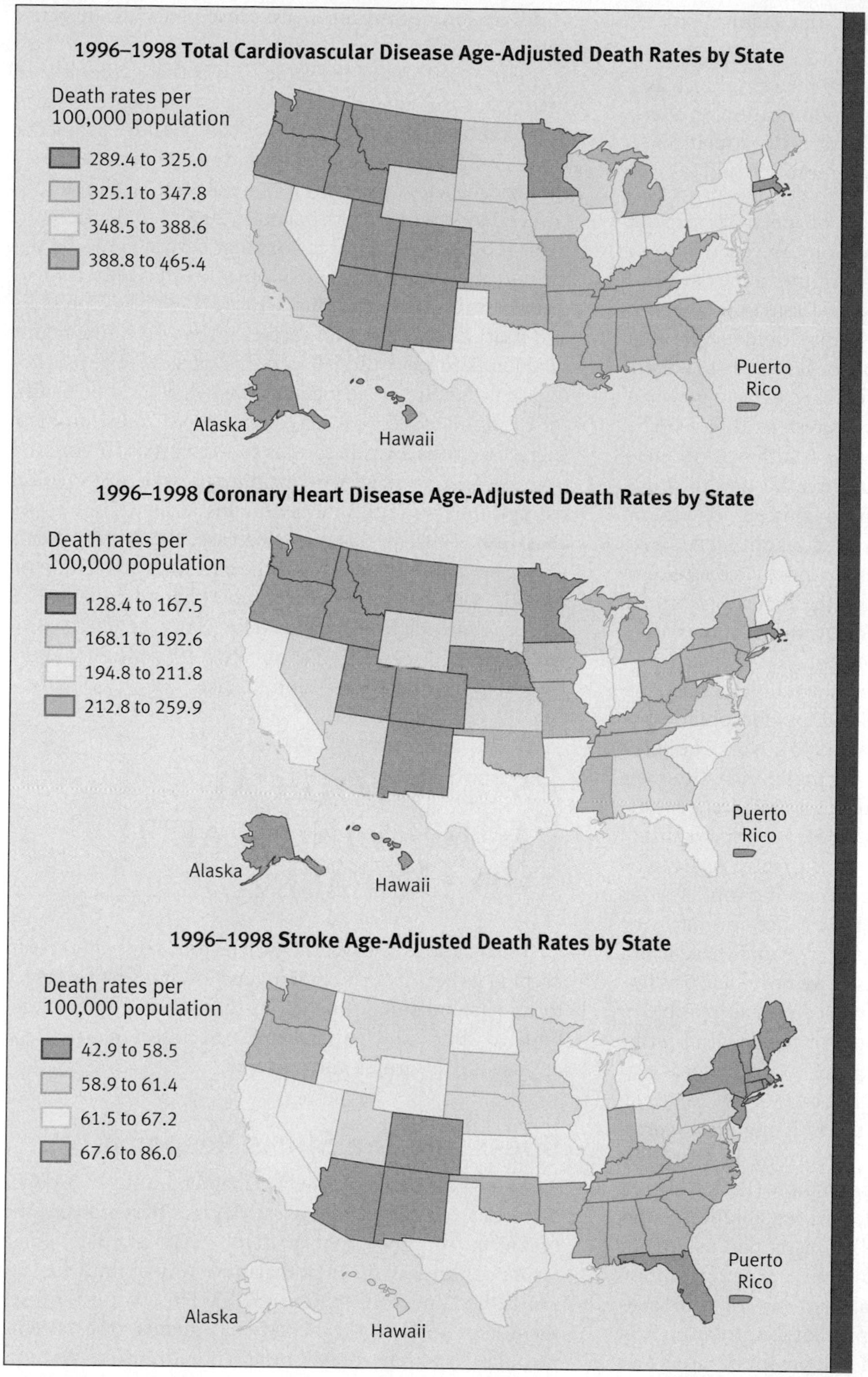

FIGURE 10.1

Age-Adjusted Death Rates by State

Source: *American Heart Association (2002).*

from maladaptive behavior, and the effects of stress on the immune, endocrine, gastrointestinal, and cardiovascular systems, among others.

- The psychological processes involved in the health choices individuals make with respect to such matters as hazardous lifestyles, health care decisions, and adherence to preventive regimens.
- The factors that determine compliance with sound medical advice. These include the nature of the relationship between the medical practitioner and the

patient, cultural factors, and personal factors (e.g., denial of illness).

- The effectiveness of psychological measures, such as health education and behavior modification, in altering unhealthful lifestyles and in directly reducing illness at both individual and community levels.

Consider, for example, the case of Joe, a 52-year-old man who is suffering from depression. As you will soon learn, Joe's depression may also contribute to the advancement of his cardiovascular disease (Glassman & Shapiro, 1998; Smith & Ruiz, 2002). And it may hinder efforts to treat his heart problems by making Joe less likely to adhere to a prescribed exercise regimen (it's hard to exercise when you are depressed and have no interest in things). The behavioral medicine perspective gives health practitioners extra tools for conceptualizing and treating health problems like Joe's. It encourages them to consider job and/or family circumstances that, if addressed, might make treatment of the primary medical problem more successful. Far from being merely supplementary, the behavioral medicine viewpoint may be critical in determining clinical outcomes, including survival versus death.

Years ago, the disorders in which psychological factors were thought to play a role were called "psychosomatic disorders" (Alexander, 1950; Dunbar, 1943). Now, the term **psychophysiological disorders** is preferred. Although some people may think that the word *psychosomatic* means that a disorder is "all in your head," these are not imaginary disorders but medical conditions that involve real symptoms. In addition, whereas the focus in earlier times was on a limited set of disorders thought to be caused primarily by psychological factors (e.g., ulcers, chronic headaches, asthma, and cardiovascular disease), we now view psychological factors as important for almost any health problem. We have also discovered that some of the medical problems that were thought to have purely psychological origins can also have nonpsychological causes. For example, one important cause of gastric ulcers is the *Helicobacter pylori* bacterium. However, only about one in every five people who has *H. pylori* develops an ulcer (Peek & Blaser, 1997), and ulcers can also develop in the absence of this bacterium (Ciociola et al., 1999). This is because major stressors (earthquakes, economic disasters) and common lifestyle factors (skipping breakfast, use of stomach-irritating medications such as aspirin or ibuprofen, lack of sleep) are also important in the development of ulcers (see Levenstein, 2002).

To recognize that psychological problems can be directly related to medical problems, Axis I of DSM-IV-TR provides a major category called "Mental Disorders Due to a General Medical Condition" (American Psychiatric Association, 2000, p. 181). This diagnosis is to be used when a general medical condition has played a direct role in the development of a psychological disorder. Some cases of depression, for example, are caused by an underactive thyroid.

The other side of the same coin is that psychological factors can also play a role in the development, aggravation, or maintenance of physical health problems. DSM-IV-TR acknowledges this with its reference to "Psychological Factors Affecting a General Medical Condition" (American Psychiatric Association, 2000, p. 731). Here the focus is on psychological factors that have a "clinically significant effect on the course or outcome of a general medical condition." An individual who has high blood pressure and heart disease but who refuses to give up eating highly salted junk food would fall into this category. The psychological factor (here, the maladaptive behavior of unhealthful eating) is coded on Axis I, and the medical problem (here, cardiovascular disease) is coded on Axis III. Another example is a man with schizophrenia who hears voices telling him to refuse dialysis for his kidney disease (see Morrison, 1995, p. 534). In this case, the schizophrenia would be coded on Axis I and the chronic renal failure on Axis III. Other psychological factors that could be coded on Axis I include hostile personality traits (linked to coronary artery disease, CAD, on Axis III), alcohol abuse (linked to liver problems), and the like.

Psychological Factors in Health and Disease

To understand how psychological factors may play a role in keeping us healthy or in making us sick, it is first necessary to understand something about the way our bodies react both to stress and to challenges by infectious or toxic agents such as viruses and bacteria.

Stress and the Stress Response

As we have already discussed in Chapter 5, a stress response involves a cascade of biological changes that prepares the organism for the fight-or-flight reaction. The stress response begins in the hypothalamus, which stimulates the sympathetic nervous system (SNS). This, in turn, causes the inner portion of the adrenal glands (the adrenal medulla) to secrete adrenaline and noradrenaline. As these circulate through the blood, they cause an increase in heart rate (familiar to all of us). They also get the body to metabolize glucose more rapidly.

In addition to stimulating the SNS, the hypothalamus releases a hormone called "corticotropin-releasing hormone" (or CRH). Traveling in the blood, this hormone stimulates the pituitary gland. The pituitary then secretes adrenocorticotrophic hormone (ACTH), which induces

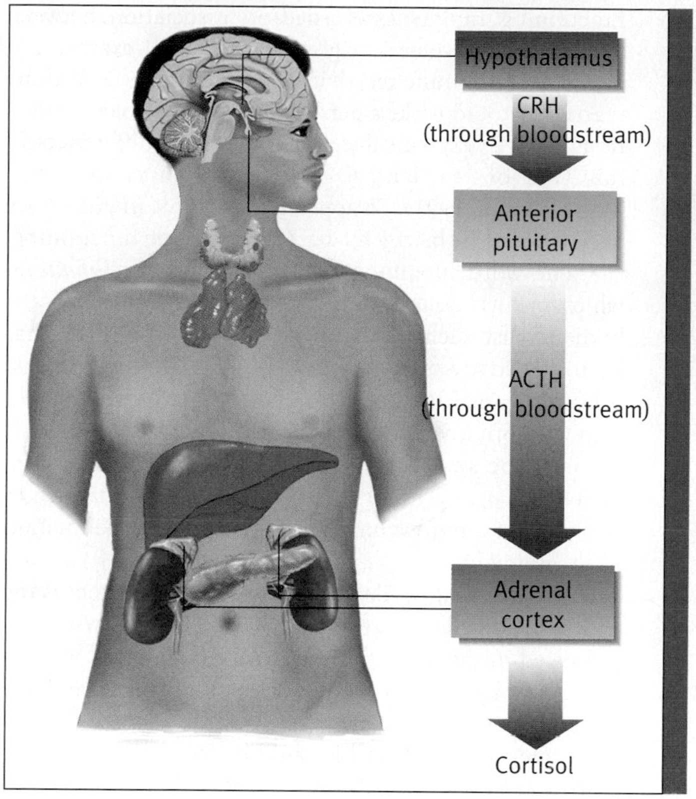

FIGURE 10.2

The Hypothalamic-Pituitary-Adrenal (HPA) Axis

Prolonged stress leads to secretion of the adrenal hormone cortisol, which elevates blood sugar and increases metabolism. These changes help the body sustain prolonged activity but at the expense of decreased immune system activity.

Source: *J. W. Kalat.* Biological Psychology, *7th ed. Belmont, CA: Wadsworth, 2001.*

the adrenal cortex (the outer portion of the adrenal gland) to produce the stress hormones called "glucocorticoids." In humans, the stress glucocorticoid that is produced is called **cortisol.** Figure 10.2 illustrates this sequence of events.

Cortisol is a good hormone to have around in an emergency. It prepares the body for fight or flight. It also inhibits the innate immune response. This means that if an injury does occur, the body's inflammatory response to it is delayed. In other words, escape has priority over healing, and tissue repair is secondary to staying alive. This obviously has survival value if you need to run away from a lion that has just mauled you. It also explains why cortisone injections are sometimes used to reduce inflammation in damaged joints.

But there is also a downside to cortisol. If the cortisol response is not shut off, cortisol can damage brain cells, especially in the hippocampus (see Sapolsky, 2000). At a very fundamental level, stress is bad for your brain. It may even stunt growth (babies who are stressed don't gain weight in the normal way and "fail to thrive"). Accordingly, the brain has receptors to detect cortisol. When these are activated, they send a feedback message that is designed to dampen the activity of the glands involved in the stress response. These are the ones described in Figure 10.2, which illustrates the **HPA axis** (the hypothalamic-pituitary-adrenal axis). But if the stressor remains, the HPA axis stays active and cortisol release continues. Although short-term cortisol production is highly adaptive, a chronically overactive HPA axis, with high levels of circulating cortisol, may be more problematic.

Biological Costs of Stress

The biological cost of adapting to stress is called the **allostatic load** (McEwan, 1998). When we are relaxed and not experiencing stress, our allostatic load is low. When we are stressed and feeling pressured, our allostatic load will be higher. Although efforts to relate specific stressors to specific medical problems have not generally been successful, stress is becoming a key underlying theme in our understanding of the development and course of virtually all physical illness. Moreover, the focus is now not just on major stressors such as job loss or the death of a loved one, but also on daily stressors such as commuting, unexpected work deadlines, or even computer problems (Almeida, 2005). These ideas are in keeping with the diathesis-stress model we discussed in Chapter 3. For example, a person with allergies may find his or her resistance further lowered by emotional tension; similarly, as we will see, when a virus has already entered a person's body—as is thought to be the case in multiple sclerosis, for example—emotional stress may interfere with the body's normal defensive forces or immune system. In like manner, any stress may tend to aggravate and maintain certain disorders, such as migraine headaches (Levor et al., 1986) and rheumatoid arthritis (Affleck et al., 1994; Keefe et al., 2002).

When we are relaxed and calm, our allostatic load is low.

When our allostatic load is high, we experience the biological signs of stress including high heart rate and increased levels of cortisol.

Stress and the Immune System

The link between stress and physical illness involves diseases (like colds) that are not directly related to nervous system activity. This suggests that stress may cause an overall vulnerability to disease by compromising immune functioning. We turn now to this issue.

We have already seen how glucocorticoids can cause stress-induced immunosuppression. In the short term, this can be adaptive (escape first, heal later). However, it is easy to see how longer-term stress might compromise the body's ability to heal and to fight infections. Early studies that examined the association between stress and immune functioning rapidly established an association between stressful circumstances (e.g., medical school exams) and diminished immune reactivity. Such diminished immune reactivity would make a person more susceptible to infections. There may be substantial individual differences in this type of reactivity to stress (Kosslyn et al., 2002; Manuck et al., 1991). To appreciate why this might be, we need to describe briefly the basics of immune functioning.

The word *immune* comes from the Latin *immunis*, which means "exempt." The immune system protects the body against such things as viruses and bacteria. It has been likened to a police force (Kalat, 1998). If it is too weak, it cannot function effectively, and the body succumbs to damage from invading viruses and bacteria. Conversely, if the immune system is too strong and unselective, it can turn on its own normal cells. This is what may happen in the case of autoimmune diseases such as rheumatoid arthritis and lupus.

The front line of defense in the immune system is the white blood cells. These leukocytes (or lymphocytes) are produced in the bone marrow and then stored in various places throughout the body, such as the spleen and the lymph nodes. There are two important types of leukocytes. One type, called a **B-cell** because it matures in the bone marrow, produces specific antibodies that are designed to respond to specific antigens. **Antigens** (the word is a contraction of *antibody generator*) are foreign bodies such as viruses and bacteria, as well as internal invaders such as tumors and cancer cells. The second important type of leucocyte is the **T-cell** (so named because it matures in the thymus, which is an important endocrine gland). When the immune system is stimulated, B-cells and T-cells become activated and multiply rapidly, mounting various forms of counterattack (see Figure 10.3).

T-cells circulate through the blood and lymph systems in an inactive form. Each T-cell has receptors on its surface that recognize one specific type of antigen. However, the T-cells are unable to recognize antigens by themselves. They become activated when immune cells called "macrophages" (the word means "big eater") detect antigens and start to engulf and digest them. To activate the T-cells, the macrophages release a chemical known as interleukin-1. Interleukins are a class of chemicals called **cytokines.** Cytokines are chemical messengers that appear to be of crucial importance for health (see Developments in Research 10.1). With the help of the macrophages, the T-cells become activated and are able to begin to destroy antigens (Maier et al., 1994).

B-cells are different in structure from T-cells. When a B-cell recognizes an antigen, it begins to divide and to produce antibodies that circulate in the blood. This process is facilitated by cytokines that are released by the T-cells. Production of antibodies takes 5 days or more (Maier et al., 1994). However, the response of the immune system will be much more rapid if the antigen ever appears in the future, because the immune system has a "memory" of the invader.

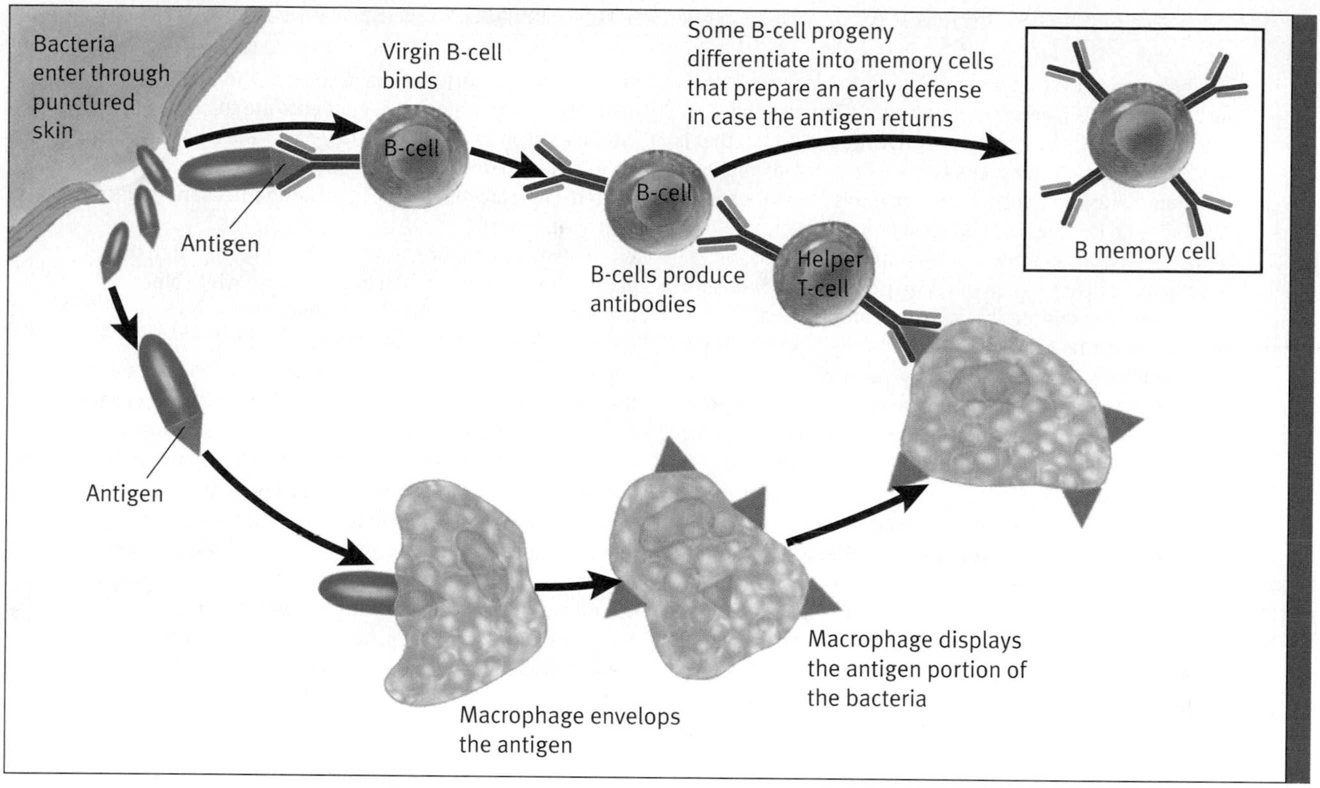

FIGURE 10.3

Immune System Responses to a Bacterial Infection

Source: *J. W. Kalat.* Biological Psychology, *7th ed. Belmont, CA: Wadsworth, 2001.*

10.1 Developments in Research

Cytokines: The Link between the Brain and the Immune System

Cytokines are chemical messengers that allow immune cells to communicate with each other. Cytokines are small protein molecules—you can think of them as being like hormones of the immune system. Currently there are about 18 known cytokines, although more may have been identified by the time you read this. A cytokine that you may already have heard about is interferon, which is given to patients with cancer, multiple sclerosis, and hepatitis C.

Cytokines play an important role in mediating the inflammatory and immune response (see Kronfol & Remick, 2000, for a review). They can be divided into two main categories: pro-inflammatory cytokines and anti-inflammatory cytokines. Pro-inflammatory cytokines such as interleukin-1 (IL-1), IL-6, or tumor necrosis factor help us deal with challenges to our immune system by augmenting the immune response. In contrast, anti-inflammatory cytokines such as IL-4, IL-10, and IL-13 decrease or dampen the response that the immune system makes. Sometimes they accomplish this by blocking the synthesis of other cytokines.

What makes cytokines so interesting is that in addition to communicating with the immune system, they also signal to the brain. Because the brain and the immune system can communicate via the cytokines, we can regard the immune system almost as another sensory organ. Far from being a self-contained system, the immune system can monitor our internal state and send the brain information about infection and injury. The brain can then respond. What this means is that *the brain is capable of influencing immune processes.* With this in mind, some of the findings discussed in this chapter (the link between depression and heart disease, for example, and the health benefits of optimism and social support) make much more sense. In a very tangible way, what is going on at the level of the brain can affect what is going on with the body, and vice versa.

(continued)

We also know that IL-1 and other cytokines can stimulate the HPA axis (see again Figure 10.2). The resulting increase in cortisol sets off a negative feedback loop that is designed to prevent an excessive or exaggerated immune or inflammatory response. However, if this feedback system fails and is either too sensitive or not sensitive enough, serious disorders such as cancer, infection, or autoimmune diseases can develop. Because the brain is also involved in this feedback loop, emotional factors and psychosocial stresses may tilt the balance in the feedback loop in either a helpful or a detrimental way.

One implication of developments in cytokine research is that disorders of the brain could potentially have "downstream" effects on the immune system. In the opposite direction, problems with the immune system may also lead to some behavioral changes or even to psychiatric problems. For example, when you are ill you sleep more, have a diminished appetite, and have little sexual interest. This is classic sickness behavior. It may also result, at least in part, from the effects of specific cytokines on the brain. When cytokines such as IL-1 or interferon are injected, subjects become lethargic, lose their appetites, and have trouble concentrating, among other problems (Reichenberg et al., 2001). In short, they have some of the symptoms of depression. And when cancer patients are treated with cytokines such as interferon, they experience both flu-like symptoms and depression, the latter of which is typically treated with paroxetine (Paxil), an antidepressant (Musselman et al., 2001).

A century ago, Bruce and Peebles (1904) noted that patients in a mental asylum in Britain had white blood cells that were abnormal in type and number. As knowledge of cytokine biology progresses, we may finally begin to understand why this would be. It is plausible to suggest that mental disorders will be found to have immune consequences (psychotic patients have already been found to have elevated levels of IL-6; see Smith & Maes, 1995). We should also not be too surprised if future research reveals that perturbations of the immune system also result in psychological changes. Although this idea is highly speculative at present, it may eventually explain why depression is so closely linked to chronic fatigue syndrome (see The World Around Us 10.7 on p. 367). In short, cytokines may have great potential for helping us understand the links between physical and mental well-being that are at the heart of behavioral medicine.

The protective activity of the B- and T-cells is supported and reinforced by other specialized components of the system, most notably natural killer cells, macrophages (which we have already mentioned), and granulocytes. The immune system's response to antigen invasion is intricately orchestrated, requiring the intact functioning of numerous components. And, as Developments in Research 10.1 illustrates, it is certain that the brain is centrally involved in this control of immune system events.

PSYCHOLOGICAL FACTORS AND IMMUNE FUNCTIONING AIDS is a disease of the immune system. After exposure to the virus that causes AIDS, the person becomes HIV (human immunodeficiency virus) positive. Leserman and her colleagues (2000) followed 82 men who were HIV positive, interviewing them every 6 months for over 7 years. Specifically, the researchers wanted to learn which psychological, behavioral, and biological factors were associated with faster progression from HIV to full-blown AIDS. Illustrating the interrelationship between stress and the immune response, greater overall levels of stressful life events were associated with more rapid transition from HIV-positive status to AIDS. Higher levels of circulating stress hormones (serum cortisol), use of denial as a means of coping, and greater dissatisfaction with available social support were also predictive of faster development of AIDS.

As the study described above highlights, the early cross-sectional investigations that showed a relationship between stress and illness have now been fortified by studies that support a stronger causal inference concerning the role of stress in reducing immunocompetence (see Kiecolt-Glaser et al., 2002a, 2002b; Schneiderman et al., 2005). For example, after the death of a spouse, there is a period of **immunosuppression** that can last 1 to 3 years (Hafen et al., 1996, p. 25). Immunosuppression can also be caused by short-term threats to our sense of well-being. Strauman, Lemieux, and Coe (1993) designed an experiment that (temporarily) manipulated the self-evaluations of their subjects. They found that natural killer cell cytotoxicity (i.e., its power to eradicate an antigen) was significantly diminished with induced negative self-evaluations, an effect that was especially strong for persons who were anxious and/or dysphoric in mood before the experiment.

Finally, there is evidence from animal studies that being exposed to a single stressful experience can enhance responsiveness to stressful events that occur later (Johnson, O'Connor, et al., 2002). Rats that were exposed to stressful tail shocks produced more of the stress hormone cortisol when they were later exposed to another stressful experience (being placed on a platform). Levels of ACTH (see again Figure 10.2) were also higher in these rats. These results suggest that prior stressful experiences may sensitize the HPA axis to later stressful experiences.

Psychoneuroimmunology

Psychoneuroimmunology is the study of the interaction between the nervous system and the immune system (Kiecolt-Glaser et al., 2002a, 2002b; Maier & Watkins,

1998; Maier et al., 1994). It is a developing field that is yielding exciting new findings. Although it was once thought that the immune system was essentially "closed" and responsive only to challenges from foreign substances (i.e., antigens), we now realize that this is not the case. The nervous system and the immune system communicate in ways that we are only just beginning to understand. Evidence continues to grow that the brain influences the immune system and that the immune system influences the brain. Maier and colleagues (Maier & Watkins, 1998; Maier et al., 1994) present strong evidence that a person's behavior and psychological states do indeed affect immune functioning, but the status of immunologic defenses also feeds back to influence current mental states and behavioral dispositions by affecting the blood levels of circulating neurochemicals, which in turn modify brain states.

STRESS, DEPRESSION, AND SUPPRESSION OF THE IMMUNE SYSTEM Research over the past 30 years has demonstrated a link between chronic stress and suppression of the immune system (Segerstrom & Miller, 2004), with the most enduring stressors (e.g., unemployment) being associated with the most global immunosuppression. Reviews (see Kiecolt-Glaser et al., 2002a; Weisse, 1992) also indicate a strong association between dysphoric mood and compromised immune function, which is, at least partially, independent of specific situations or events that may have provoked depressed feelings. (In other words, the state of being depressed adds something beyond any negative effects of the stressors precipitating this depressed mood.) Another review of the relevant research found that depressed affect was reliably associated with lowered numbers of white cells following challenge by a foreign protein, with lowered natural killer cell activity, and with lowered quantities of several varieties of circulating white cells (Herbert & Cohen, 1993).

The list of conditions that have been demonstrated to be associated with diminished immune function is a long one. Besides psychological depression, it includes sleep deprivation, marathon running, spaceflight, being the caregiver for a patient with dementia, and death of a spouse (Cacioppo, et al., 1998; Schleifer, Keller, & Stein, 1985; Schleifer et al., 1989; Vasiljeva et al., 1989). Immune responsiveness has also been shown to vary with even normal, diurnal variations in mood (Stone et al., 1987). Relevant to many readers of this book, a group of researchers has repeatedly demonstrated the compromise of white blood cell proliferation, including diminished natural killer cell activity, among students undergoing the stress of academic examinations (Glaser et al., 1985, 1987). Natural killer cells are believed to play a key role in tumor surveillance and in the control of viral infections. Stress has even been shown to slow the healing of wounds by as much as 24 to 40 percent (Kiecolt-Glaser et al., 1998). For anyone about to have surgery, this is clearly a very important finding.

STRESS, DEPRESSION, AND INCREASED IMMUNE RESPONSIVENESS There is a great deal of evidence linking stress to suppression of the immune system. However, a shift in thinking is now taking place. Researchers are beginning to pay attention to the possibility that chronic stress and depression may actually *enhance* certain immune system responses, although not in a good way (Robles et al., 2005). Chronic stress and depression may trigger the production of pro-inflammatory cytokines such as interleukin-6 (IL-6). One study showed that women who were caring for a family member with Alzheimer's disease had higher levels of IL-6 than women who were either anticipating the stress of relocation or who were experiencing neither of these stressors (Lutgendorf et al., 1999). This difference was found even though the women who were caregivers were 6 to 9 years younger than the women in the other two groups and even though IL-6 levels are known to increase with age. Major depression has also been linked to enhanced production of pro-inflammatory cytokines, including IL-6, and treatment with antidepressant medications can reduce this elevation (Kenis & Maes, 2002).

These findings are especially interesting in light of research showing a relationship between IL-6 and aging, as well as to chronic diseases including certain cancers and cardiovascular disease (Papanicolaou et al., 1998). Also, higher levels of IL-6 are associated with being overweight, smoking, and having a sedentary lifestyle (Ferrucci et al., 1999).

One group of investigators has reported that older adults (average age 71 years) who regularly attended church had lower levels of IL-6 and were less likely to die during the course of a 12-year follow-up than those who did not (Lutgendorf et al., 2004). These findings also held when other potential confounding variables such as age, social support, being overweight, having medical problems, or being depressed were also considered. Given all of these findings, it is not hard to see why researchers are becoming excited about the possibility that pro-inflammatory cytokines like IL-6 could be key mediators in the link between psychosocial factors and disease. Overall, what the research findings suggest is that chronic stress and depression can result in the immune system *going out of balance* in ways that may compromise health (see Robles et al., 2005). In short, the potential for psychological factors to influence our health and for our health to affect our psychological well-being is becoming ever more apparent.

Lifestyle Factors in Health and Illness

A great deal of attention is being paid today to the role of lifestyle in the development and/or maintenance of many health problems. Do you smoke? How often do you exercise? Numerous aspects of the way we live have been implicated in the development of some severe medical problems. Death from heart disease is linked to lack of physical exercise (Dubbert, 2002). Tobacco use contributes

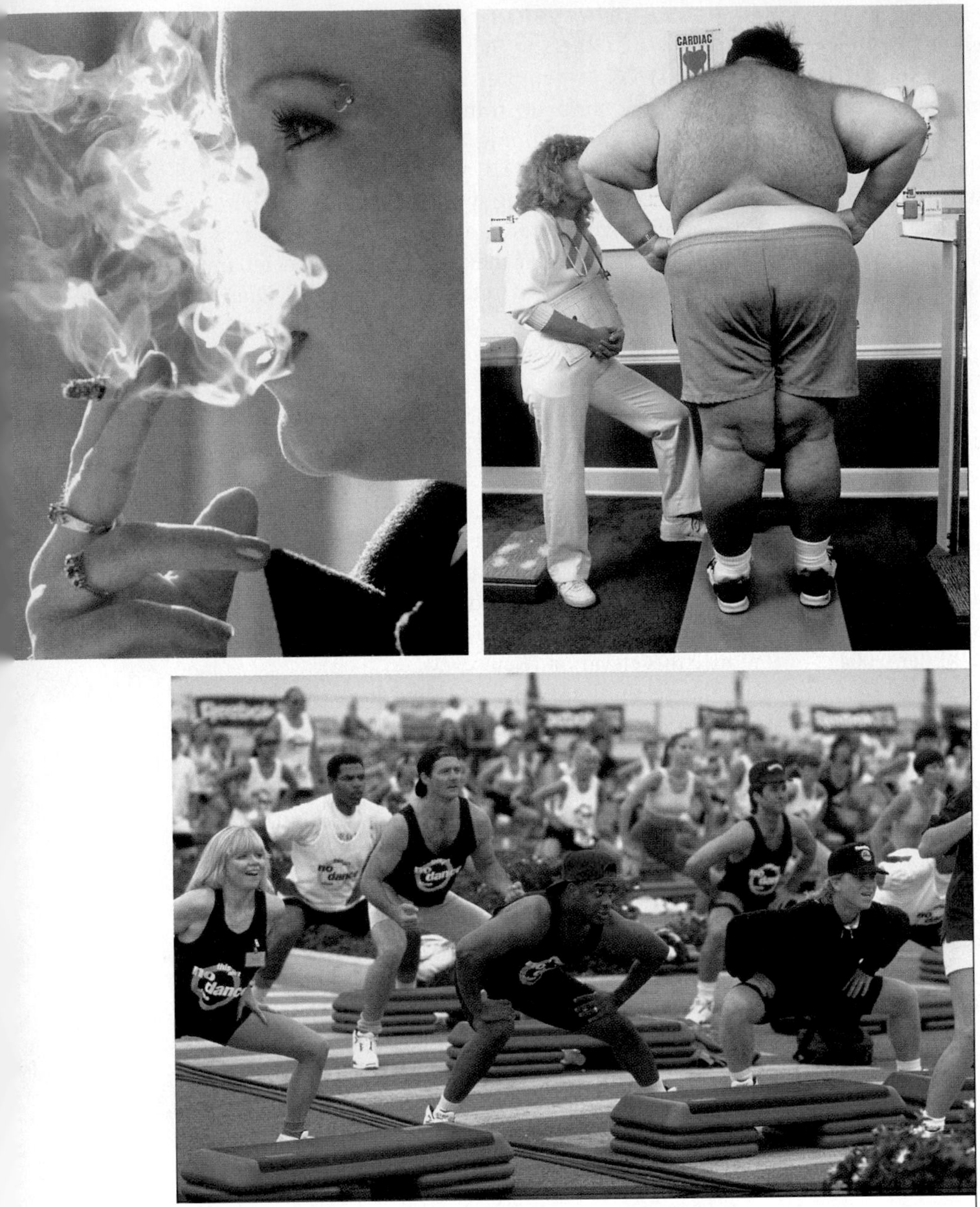

Lifestyle factors play a major role in determining health and risk for disease.

to 450,000 deaths each year (Niaura & Abrams, 2002). Some 61 percent of adult Americans are either overweight or obese (Wadden et al., 2002). Particularly relevant for college students, even partial sleep loss for as little as one night is associated with elevated levels of cortisol the following evening (Leproult et al., 1997).

Lifestyle factors—habits or behavior patterns presumably under our own control—play a major role in three of the leading causes of death in this country: coronary heart disease, automobile accidents, and alcohol-related deaths. Even when they know they are doing things that can cause irreparable physical harm, it is difficult for many people to change their lifestyles to reduce their risk of disease. Even after having two heart attacks and surgery to remove a cancerous lung, one man continued to smoke 2½ packs of cigarettes a day. He frequently said, "I know these things are killing me a little at a time . . . , but they have become so much a part of my life I can't live without them!" Most of us know someone who behaves in a similar way.

Health, Attitudes, and Coping Resources

Because the brain influences the immune system, a variety of psychological factors may be of great importance to our health and well-being. You have already learned how important depression is with regard to the immune system. How you view problems, cope with challenges, and even your temperament may directly affect your underlying physical health.

OPTIMISM Hopeless and helpless attitudes can have devastating effects on organic functioning. For example, a sense of hopelessness accelerates progression of atherosclerosis, the underlying process leading to heart attacks and strokes (Everson et al., 1997). Optimists, who expect that good things will happen, may fare much better (Carver & Scheier, 2002). Today, many surgeons will delay a major operation until they are convinced that the patient is reasonably optimistic about the outcome. Optimism in a more global, everyday sense seems to serve as a buffer against disease (Scheier & Carver, 1987, 1992). Although it is possible that being too optimistic about their health could cause people not to seek help for potentially dangerous health problems (e.g., Davidson & Prkachin, 1997; Fisher & Fisher, 1992; Friedman et al., 1994; Kalichman et al., 1993; Tennen & Affleck, 1987), most of the data suggest that the benefits of being optimistic outweigh the possible disadvantages (Carver & Scheier, 2002).

People with too little optimism experience a psychological sense of helplessness. As we saw in Chapter 5, this can be associated with poor health outcomes. In an interesting study of Hall of Fame baseball players, Peterson and Seligman (1987) found that in this group of athletes, negative attitudes were significantly associated with health problems following their active playing years. Peterson

10.2 Developments in Research

Is Holding a Grudge Bad for Your Health?

All of us feel mistreated from time to time. Perhaps a friend who offered to pick us up at the airport didn't show because something else came up. Perhaps someone spreads mean gossip about us behind our back. Perhaps a work supervisor or college professor fails to recognize the effort we have put into a piece of work and gives us an unfairly low evaluation. For all of us, such slights are an unfortunate—but inevitable—fact of life.

Does how we handle such situations have any bearing on our health? To examine this issue, Witvliet et al. (2001) studied the emotional and physiological consequences of being forgiving or unforgiving. College students were asked to select a real-life interpersonal offense that they had experienced in the past. Most of these offenses had been committed by friends, romantic partners, siblings, or parents, and they included such things as rejection, betrayals of trust, and personal insults. The researchers then collected self-reports as well as psychophysiological data (heart rate, blood pressure, and facial muscle tension) from the students while they were imagining responding to the real-life transgression in a way that was either forgiving or unforgiving. In the forgiving condition, the students were asked to think about granting forgiveness or developing feelings of empathy for the perpetrator. In the unforgiving condition, they were asked to stay in the victim role, to go over the hurt in their minds, and to nurse a grudge.

Did thinking about the same event in these different ways change the moods and physiological states of the participants? The answer is yes. When they were asked to be forgiving, the participants reported more feelings of empathy and forgiveness. When asked to ruminate and be unforgiving, however, participants reported that they felt more negative, angry, sad, aroused, and out of control. They also showed greater tension in their brows. Importantly, their heart rates went up, their blood pressures increased, and their skin conductance (a measure of SNS arousal) revealed more arousal. Even more striking was the finding that even after the grudge-harboring imagery was over and the subjects were told to relax, they were unable to do so. In other words, the high state of physiological arousal that had been triggered by dwelling on the past hurt could not easily be turned off.

What are the implications of these findings? Although fleeting feelings of anger probably do us no real harm, people who have a tendency to brood about the wrongs that other people have done to them may be doing themselves a major disservice. To the extent that perpetuating feelings of anger and increasing cardiovascular reactivity have consequences for heart disease and immune system functioning, harboring grudges may be hazardous to our health. Although it is not always easy, forgiving those who have offended us may lower our stress levels and enhance our well-being.

and colleagues (1998) also reported a significantly elevated mortality rate among a group of intellectually gifted individuals who had, a half-century earlier, a tendency to treat negative events as catastrophes. There are clearly advantages to seeing the glass as half full rather than as half empty.

NEGATIVE AFFECT Perhaps negative emotions should carry with them a health warning similar to that found on packets of cigarettes. Certainly, evidence is accumulating that negative emotions can be associated with poor health (Kielcolt-Glaser et al., 2002a). *Depression,* as we have already emphasized, is associated with measurable and undesirable changes in immune functioning (Robles et al., 2005; Zorillo et al., 2001). And, as we will see later, people with major depression run a greater risk of having a heart attack than people with no history of depression (Pratt et al., 1996). Depression also seems to be associated with increased mortality from all causes in medical inpatients (Herrmann-Lingen et al., 2001). In women, depression appears to heighten the risk for osteoporosis (Michelson et al., 1996), and in men, one prospective study showed that depression at baseline predicted decline in muscle strength over a 3-year period (Rantanen et al., 2000).

Although this effect has not been as well studied, *anxiety* also seems to be associated, in both men and women, with the development of coronary heart disease. Finally, it is well documented that chronic *anger and hostility* can be risk factors for coronary heart disease and death (Miller et al., 1996). The most familiar example here is the Type A behavior pattern, which we will discuss in more detail later. Taken together, the research findings indicate that an optimistic outlook on life, as well as an absence of negative emotions, may have some beneficial health consequences. Indeed, there is currently a growing interest in studying **positive psychology** (Snyder & Lopez, 2002). This school of psychology focuses on human traits and resources that might have direct implications for our physical and mental well-being. Positive affectivity (the tendency to experience positive emotional states; Watson, 2002), compassion (Cassell, 2002), gratitude (Emmons & Shelton, 2002), humor (Lefcourt, 2002), and spirituality

(Pargament & Mahoney, 2002) are valuable human gifts. Although research into these and other aspects of "accentuating the positive" is still in its infancy, there are already hints of their potential health benefits. For example, there is evidence that laughter is associated with enhanced immune functioning (Berk et al., 1988; Lefcourt, 2002). There are also physiological benefits associated with forgiving people who have wronged us (see Developments in Research 10.2).

Ironically, some of the positive characteristics of humans may also complicate efforts to determine the true effectiveness of new treatment techniques, such as new drugs. A patient who believes a treatment is going to be effective has a much better chance of showing improvement than one who is neutral or pessimistic—even when the treatment is subsequently shown to have no direct or relevant physiological effects. This **placebo effect** accounts in part for the controversies that arise periodically between the scientific community and the general public about the efficacy of certain drugs or other treatments. As you may recall from Chapter 1, the placebo effect appears to explain why people experience clinical benefit from magnet therapy.

It has even been suggested that without the placebo effect, the medical profession as we know it would not have survived to the twentieth century. Until the early 1900s, medical practitioners had little else to offer disease sufferers; indeed, many widely employed specific treatments (such as bleeding) were plainly harmful (bleeding killed George Washington, for example). The profession's survival and prosperity from ancient times is to a large extent a demonstration of the power of faith in healing (Shapiro & Morris, 1978). Thus the fundamental intimacy of the mind and body is perhaps nowhere better documented than in the history of the medical profession itself.

In Review

- How does a person's attitude and outlook on life affect health maintenance and deterioration?
- How can optimism or negative attitudes either enhance or compromise a person's ability to cope with illness?
- What physiological mechanisms are involved in autonomic nervous system arousal?
- Describe the relationship between stress and the immune system.

Cardiovascular Disease

Because cardiovascular disease is the leading cause of death in the United States (American Heart Association, 2001), we will use this disease to illustrate the many links between psychological factors and physical disease. Some of these are highlighted in the following case.

Case Study: The Angry Physician

Dr. M was a 44-year-old physician. The middle son of parents who had emigrated from Italy, he was ambitious and determined to make a successful life for himself and his family. He worked long hours helping patients with cancer, and he was caring and compassionate. His patients loved him. But his job was also very stressful. Added to the many demands of maintaining a busy medical practice was the great sadness that he felt when (inevitably) many of his terminally ill patients died.

At home Dr. M was a loyal husband and devoted father to his three children. But he was not an easy person to live with. He found it hard to relax, and he had a very volatile disposition. He was frequently angry and would shout at everyone whenever he had a bad day. Often his moods were caused by his feeling that he was not fully appreciated by the other doctors with whom he worked. Although his wife realized that he "just needed to vent," his moods took a toll on the family. His children distanced themselves from him much of the time, and his wife became less and less happy in the marriage.

One day at work, Dr. M started to feel unwell. He began to sweat and experienced a heavy pressure in his chest. It was difficult for him to breathe. Dr. M recognized the severity of his problem and called out for medical help. He had a sudden and severe heart attack and survived only because he was working in a hospital at the time of the attack. If he had not received prompt medical attention, he almost certainly would have died.

After his heart attack Dr. M became very depressed. It was almost as though he could not accept that he, a physician, had a severe medical problem. Although he lived in fear of having another heart attack, his efforts to lose weight (which his doctor had told him to do) were sabotaged by his unwillingness to follow any diet. He would try and then give up, coming back from the Italian bakery with bags of pastries. Making the problem worse was the fact that because he was a doctor, his own doctors were somewhat reticent about telling him what he had to do to manage his illness. He went back to work and

10.3 The World Around Us

Cardiovascular Disease in a 33-Year-Old Athlete

Darryl Kile was a Major League baseball all-star pitcher who died suddenly of a heart attack in his hotel room at the age of 33. His death emphasizes the importance of health knowledge and intervention in the prevention of cardiovascular disease, especially in young people.

Many young people mistakenly assume that cardiovascular disease is not something they should be concerned about. Research suggests otherwise. Iribarren and colleagues (2000) examined 374 Caucasian and African-American men and women between the ages of 18 and 30, looking for signs of calcification in the subjects' coronary arteries (a warning sign of the hardening of arteries, or atherosclerosis). Even when controlling for demographics, lifestyle, and physiological variables, the researchers found that those subjects who had scored higher on an initial measure of hostility that had been completed 10 years earlier were more than twice as likely to have coronary calcification as those subjects who had scored low in hostility. These findings not only challenge the common belief that cardiovascular disease is of little concern to young people but also accentuate the importance of starting as early as possible to engage in preventive measures (e.g., minimizing hostile attitudes, getting treated for depression, avoiding weight gain, and not smoking).

Prevention of cardiovascular disease begins with health education, which includes knowing your medical history. Kile's father, for example, had died from a stroke after suffering a heart attack at the age of 44. It is also important to be able to recognize the symptoms of a heart attack. Kile had mentioned to his brother, the night before his death, that he was tired and was experiencing soreness in his shoulder (Gorman, 2002). But because of his age, and because he was a pitcher, he may not have attributed these symptoms to an impending heart problem. The following warnings of heart attack are often (but not always) present: (1) a pain that spreads along the shoulders, arm, neck, or jaw; (2) sudden sweating; (3) a heavy pressure and pain in the center of the chest; and (4) nausea, vomiting, and shortness of breath. The symptoms may come and go. Denial of symptoms and stubbornness are common reasons why people who are having myocardial infarctions delay getting medical help (O'Carroll et al., 2001). Awareness of these findings is extremely important for young adults, who often think they are impervious to physical problems. In 1998 more than 3,000 people in America between the ages of 15 and 34 died suddenly of heart disease (Gorman, 2002). Although we may all want to assume that it could never happen to us, it is wise for all of us to know our family histories and be able to recognize the early signs of potential problems.

The second major study of Type A behavior and CHD was the Framingham Heart Study. This began in 1948 and has involved the long-term follow-up of a large sample of men and women from Framingham, Massachusetts (see Kannel et al., 1987). Approximately 1,700 CHD-free subjects were typed as A or B in the mid-1960s. Analysis of the data for CHD occurrence during an 8-year follow-up period not only confirmed the major findings of the earlier Western Collaborative Group Study but extended them to women as well.

Not all studies reported positive associations between Type A behavior and risk of coronary artery disease, however (Case et al., 1985; Shekelle et al., 1985). Moreover, as research with the construct has continued, it has become clear that it is the hostility component of the Type A construct (including anger, contempt, scorn, cynicism, and mistrust) that is most closely correlated with coronary artery deterioration (see Rozanski et al., 1999, for a summary of studies).

A recent development is the identification of the "distressed" or **Type D personality** type (Denollet et al., 2000). As shown in Figure 10.5 on page 358, people with Type D personality have a tendency to experience negative emotions and also to feel insecure and anxious. Although research exploring Type D personality is just beginning, men with CHD who scored high on measures of chronic emotional distress were more likely have fatal and nonfatal heart attacks over the 5-year follow-up period than were men who did not have these Type D personality traits (Denollet et al., 2000). The Type D personality construct also provides a way to tie in some of the other findings linking negative emotions and CHD, which we discuss below.

DEPRESSION Depression is commonly found in people who already have heart disease. People with heart disease are approximately three times more likely than healthy people to be depressed (Chesney, 1996; Shapiro, 1996). Furthermore, if heart attack patients are depressed at the time of their heart attack or shortly afterward, they show a greatly increased risk for future coronary events and cardiac death (Chesney, 1996; Shapiro, 1996). In one study of 222 patients who had experienced a heart attack, those who were clinically depressed were five times more likely than their nondepressed counterparts to die in the next

TEST: ARE YOU A TYPE D?

The social and emotional problems associated with Type D personality can increase your chances of developing heart disease. Read each statement and circle the appropriate number to indicate your answer. There are no right or wrong answers: your own impression is the only thing that matters.

1 TAKE THE TEST
Circle your answers:

	False	Less false	Neutral	Less true	True
1. I make contact easily when I meet people	4	3	2	1	0
2. I often make a fuss about unimportant things	0	1	2	3	4
3. I often talk to strangers	4	3	2	1	0
4. I often feel unhappy	0	1	2	3	4
5. I am often irritated	4	3	2	1	0
6. I often feel inhibited in social interactions	0	1	2	3	4
7. I take a gloomy view of things	4	3	2	1	0
8. I find it hard to start a conversation	0	1	2	3	4
9. I am often in a bad mood	4	3	2	1	0
10. I am a closed kind of person	0	1	2	3	4
11. I would rather keep people at a distance	4	3	2	1	0
12. I often find myself worrying about something	0	1	2	3	4
13. I am often down in the dumps	4	3	2	1	0
14. When socializing, I don't find the right things to talk about	0	1	2	3	4

2 ADD YOUR ANSWERS
Negative Affectivity:
Add scores for questions 2, 4, 5, 7, 9 12 and 13

Social Inhibition:
Add scores for questions 1, 3, 6, 8, 10, 11, and 14

3 SCORE THE RESULTS
You qualify as a Type D personality if your Negative Affectivity is 10 or higher and your Social Inhibition is 10 or higher.

FIGURE 10.5
Characteristics of the Type D Personality

Source: *Adapted from "DS14: Standard Assessment of Negative Affectivity, Social Inhibition, and Type D Personality" by Johan Denollet, PhD.* Psychosomatic Medicine, *2005. January–February;67(1);89–97. Used with permission by Lippincott/Williams & Wilkins.*

6 months (Frasure-Smith et al., 1993). Moreover, depression was as good a predictor of death from heart disease as were medical variables such as prior heart attacks and poor heart functioning. After adjustment for these other variables, it was estimated that the relative risk of death associated with depression was still four times greater. Risk of death is also increased even if the symptoms of depression are not especially severe (Bush et al., 2001).

Depression also appears to be a risk factor for the development of CHD. Pratt and her colleagues (1996) followed over 1,500 men and women with *no prior history of heart disease* for 14 years. They found that 8 percent of those who had suffered major depression at one time and 6 percent of those who had suffered mild depression at some point had a heart attack during the 14-year follow-up interval. By contrast, only 3 percent of those without a history of depression suffered heart attacks. When medical history and other variables were taken into account, those who had suffered major depression were found to be four times more likely to have had a heart attack. Similar findings have also been reported in other studies (Ferketich et al., 2000; Ford et al., 1998).

Evidence further points to the importance of *hopelessness* (an important element of depression) in increasing risk for CHD. For example, Anda and colleagues (1993) found that people who answered yes to the question, "In the past month, have you felt so sad, discouraged, hopeless, or had so many problems that you wondered if anything was worthwhile?" had twice the risk for CHD than did people who answered no to this question. Experiencing what is referred to as *vital exhaustion* (fatigue, irritability, and demoralization) also predicts future CHD and cardiac events, even in people who are currently quite healthy (Appels & Mulder, 1988).

Why should depression and CHD be linked? Two mechanisms have been proposed to explain the association. The first possibility is that depressed people may engage in more behaviors known to put them at risk for CHD. For example, depressed people are less likely to eat well or exercise, are more likely to smoke, and may not take their medications appropriately (e.g., Carney, Freedland, et al., 1995). Depressed people are also known to lack social support, another factor linked to CHD (Eriksen, 1994).

Second, it is likely that depression is linked to CHD through various biochemical mechanisms (Krantz & McCeney, 2002; Lesperance et al., 2004; Markovitz et al., 2000; Miller et al., 2002; Musselman et al, 2000). As we noted in Chapter 7, many depressed people have elevated levels of the stress hormone cortisol as well as elevated levels of interleukin-6 (Robles et al., 2005). They also have elevated levels of norepinephrine in their blood, which can increase blood pressure. Thus, although depressed people may appear lethargic, their elevated stress hormones may damage their hearts. Furthermore, depressed individuals show less variability in heart rate in response to behavioral changes (for example, the heart rate when walking should be different from the heart rate when sitting down). High heart rate levels and low heart rate variability are also known to be associated with changes in sympathetic-parasympathetic balance, which may increase the cardiac arrhythmias that often precede sudden death (Carney, Saunders, et al., 1995; Frasure-Smith et al., 1993).

ANXIETY Given the strong links between anxiety and mood disorders discussed in Chapter 6, it is not surprising

Depression increases the risk of developing heart disease and of dying from a heart attack.

that a similar link may exist between anxiety and CHD. Research has demonstrated a relationship between phobic anxiety and increased risk for sudden cardiac death. Kawachi, Colditz, and colleagues (1994) followed for 2 years nearly 34,000 male professionals who had been assessed for panic disorder, agoraphobia, and generalized anxiety. Men with the highest levels of phobic anxiety were three times more likely to have a fatal heart attack than men with the lowest levels of phobic anxiety. Sudden cardiac death was six times higher in the men with the highest levels of anxiety. However, *no* association was found between anxiety and *nonfatal* attacks. The findings were replicated in a second study of nearly 2,300 men who were participating in a normative aging study (Kawachi, Sparrow, et al., 1994, 1995).

SOCIAL ISOLATION AND LACK OF SOCIAL SUPPORT Studies point to the strong link between social factors and the development of CHD. For example, monkeys housed alone have four times more atherosclerosis (fatty deposits in blood vessels that eventually create a blockage) than monkeys housed in social groups (Shively et al., 1989). Similarly, people who have a relatively small social network or who consider themselves to have little emotional support are more likely to develop CHD over time (see Rozanski et al., 1999, for a review).

For people who already have CHD, there is a similar association. In one study among people who had already suffered a heart attack, those who reported that they had low levels of emotional support were almost three times more likely to experience another cardiac event (Berkman et al., 1992). And in another study, death in CHD patients was three times more likely over the next 5 years if they were unmarried or had no one that they could confide in (Williams et al., 1992). Echoing these findings, Coyne and his colleagues (2001) have shown that the quality of the marital relationship predicts 4-year survival rates in patients with congestive heart failure.

CHRONIC AND ACUTE STRESS Stress can come in a variety of forms. In some respects, all of the factors we have just described can be considered forms of stress. Certainly, having little or no social support can be stressful. Anger, depression, and anxiety can also be viewed as forms of internal stress.

What is perceived as stressful is often highly subjective. One person may sit in terror on a roller-coaster ride while the person in the next seat is exhilarated by the experience. Going to a party may be stressful for the shy person but not for the extrovert. What we experience as stressful is very much linked to who we are. This makes the measurement of stressful experiences very problematic.

Although some forms of stress may have a large subjective element, there are other forms of stress that we universally recognize as severe, objective, and external. An obvious example is earthquakes. Several researchers have now reported that deaths from CHD rise in the days and weeks following a severe earthquake (see Pickering, 2001). After the Northridge earthquake in Los Angeles in 1995, the number of sudden deaths due to CHD rose from an average of 4.6 (in the days preceding the earthquake) to 24 on the day of the earthquake (Kloner et al., 1997). There was also an increase in sudden death from cardiac events after the Hanshin-Awaji earthquake in Japan (Kario & Ohashi, 1997).

Everyday forms of stress can also elevate risk for CHD and death (Matthews & Gump, 2002; Smith & Ruiz, 2002). A good example is work-related stress (see The World Around Us 10.4). Here the key factors appear to be having a highly demanding job and having little control over decision making. Both of these types of job stress increase risk for future CHD. Moreover, this association still holds when other negative health behaviors (such as smoking) are controlled (see Peter & Siegrist, 2000).

Finally, simply being asked to give a 5-minute speech about an assigned topic to a small (but evaluative) audience was enough to produce detectable changes in cardiac function in about 20 percent of patients with existing coronary artery disease (see Sheps et al., 2002). Moreover, the patients who were most reactive to this form of mental stress were almost three times as likely as the less reactive patients to die in the next 5 to 6 years. Mental stress is known to raise systolic blood pressure and also to cause an elevation in epinephrine. Mental stress may also reduce the oxygen supply to the heart muscle (Yeung et al., 1991). What the results of the Sheps study illustrate, however, is that stress does not have to be extreme or severe to be associated with lethal consequences "down the road."

10.4 The World Around Us

Is Your Job Bad for Your Health?

Americans are working more and taking fewer vacations. The pace of life is fast and work is no exception. Deadlines loom, bosses threaten, and expectations are high. For many people, work is a major source of stress in their daily lives.

Does stress in the workplace affect our health? Research indicates that people who report facing a sudden short-term increase in work pressure or a great deal of competition at work have a sixfold greater risk of having a heart attack during the next 24 hours (Möller et al., 2005).

Work stress also seems to increase our risk for developing depression. Wang (2005) recently reported the results of a study of 6,633 workers in Canada. The employed participants were interviewed about their lives, their health, their jobs, and about how much work stress they experienced (see Figure accompanying this feature). Two years later, they were interviewed again. The results showed that workers who reported the highest levels of work stress (i.e., highest quartile) were 2.3 times more likely to have developed an episode of major depression in the time between the two interviews. This is an interesting finding, especially because people with a past history of depression were excluded from the analysis. Moreover, the association between work stress and the development of depression was not explained by other variables such as education level, chronic medical problems, trauma, or other negative life events that the workers experienced. Overall, the results of this study indicate that work stress may be a risk factor for the development of depression. The findings also highlight the potential importance of modifying work conditions to help employees stay healthy and productive (e.g., Theorell et al., 2001).

Key Elements of Work-Related Stress

- Not being required to learn new things
- Not having a job that requires a high level of skill
- Having to do the same things over and over
- Not having freedom to decide how to do your job
- Not having a say in what happens in your job
- Having a hectic job
- Having others make conflicting demands on you
- Having little job security
- Having a job that requires a lot of physical effort
- Being exposed to conflict and hostility at work
- Having an unhelpful supervisor
- Not having helpful co-workers

(From Wang, 2005.)

In Review

- What is essential hypertension, and what are some of the factors that contribute to its development?
- What are the clinical manifestations of, and potential risk factors for, coronary heart disease (CHD)?
- What is a Type A personality? What is the most important element of the Type A pattern? What evidence links this behavior pattern to coronary heart disease?

General Causal Factors in Physical Illness and Disease

What factors determine who gets one disorder and who gets another? Why does Michael suffer from migraines and why does Sam develop hypertension? Genetic differences may be part of the answer.

Genetic Factors

Our understanding of genetic contributions to disease, including diseases with a psychological component, is still quite limited. Genetic contributions may include:

- an underlying physical vulnerability to the disease in question, such as excessive cardiovascular reactivity in hypertension;
- the psychological makeup of the individual and his or her stress tolerance, such as an aggressive or inhibited temperament; and
- the nature of any interaction between factors (1) and (2).

If biological and psychological contributions to enhanced risk are both partly inherited, then disentangling their separate influences is bound to be difficult—all the more so if the expression of one influence is somehow modified by the presence of the other (that is, if they "interact").

Despite these difficulties of interpretation, nearly all diseases of genetic/psychological origin can be shown to run in families to at least some extent. We must keep in mind that social learning (for example, children modeling the inadequate coping skills of their parents) could be a factor in such family resemblances. As in other areas of psychopathology, whenever we assess the psychological aspects of physical illness, we struggle with the problem of differentiating the effects of shared genes from those of shared environments.

We will undoubtedly discover more as the Human Genome Project progresses and identifies all of the genes in the human organism (see Plomin & McGuffin, 2003). Genes that are associated with increased risk of hypertension in Caucasians and African-Americans (Kumar et al., 2005) have already been identified. A genetic polymorphism (variant form of a specific gene) of the serotonin-transporter gene has also been linked to increased risk of depression, but only when carriers of the gene are under stress (Caspi et al., 2003). As this study nicely illustrates, life circumstances (e.g., stress) may interact with inherited genetic vulnerabilities to determine who develops a specific problem or disease. The likelihood that genetic risk can be modified by psychosocial factors is a major reason why all of us should pay close attention to lifestyle factors in our efforts to stay well.

INDIVIDUAL DIFFERENCES IN STRESS RESPONSES

Even very young infants reveal marked differences in their sensitivities to upsetting stimuli. Some infants react to such stressors by developing digestive upsets, others by developing sleep disturbances. These differences in reactivity continue into adult life and may be linked to individual differences in susceptibility to disease and in the types of diseases a given person is most likely to develop (see Blanchard & Scharff, 2002; Schneiderman et al., 2005).

Genetic inheritance undoubtedly plays a role in determining how we respond to stress. However, early experiences are also crucially important. Studies show that rats that were repeatedly exposed to 3-hour separations from their mothers were hyperactive when they were placed in a novel environment and had more extreme responses to stress compared to rats that were separated from their mothers for only 15 minutes each time (Brake et al., 2004). Also, rats that are raised by highly nurturing and attentive mothers develop into low-anxious adults compared to rats that are raised by mothers who have a less caring maternal style (see Fish et al., 2004). Moreover, when rat pups that were born to less attentive biological mothers were cross-fostered so that they were raised by more attentive adoptive mothers, they developed into less stress-sensitive adults compared with their original littermates who remained with their biological mothers. Conversely, when rats pups were removed from their attentive, nurturing biological mothers and raised by adoptive mothers who were less attentive and less nurturing, the rat pups developed into more reactive and stress-sensitive adults compared with their biological siblings who stayed with their biological mothers (see Fish et al., 2004). Overall, the animal data suggest that differences in maternal care are causally related to individual differences in stress sensitivity later in life.

Characteristics of the early family environment are also associated with physiological vulnerability to stress in humans (see Luecken & Lemery, 2004). For example, children raised in high-conflict families show greater cardiovascular reactivity when they hear audiotapes of arguments compared to children who come from families where there is less conflict and marital friction (El-Sheikh & Harger, 2001).

Finally, research illustrating the interaction of genes and environment shows that children who have fearful or negative temperaments may be especially vulnerable to the negative effects of stress. These children showed much more extreme physiological reactivity in the face of stress than did their more laid-back peers (Gunnar et al., 1996). This highlights the importance of the interaction between

Children who are exposed to a lot of marital conflict in the home are more reactive physiologically when they are stressed.

genetic predispositions and environmental factors in our understanding of how people respond to negative situations in their lives.

Psychosocial Factors

PERSONALITY CHARACTERISTICS If we could clearly describe a "disease-prone" or "hypertensive" personality linked to particular diseases, it would be of great value in understanding and treating illnesses and perhaps even in preventing them. Just as useful would be a clear picture of the so-called "disease-resistant personality"—one possessing a high degree of "hardiness"—or the ability to withstand stress and bounce back from it (e.g., see Hafen et al., 1996). Research has shown that negative attitudes are associated with higher levels of physical and mental illness (especially depression). Developmental research, such as that described above, also indicates that children with fearful or negative temperaments tend to be especially reactive when they experience stress. However, as of now, no clear associations between specific personality characteristics and particular diseases have been identified.

SOCIAL SUPPORT In our previous discussions, we have repeatedly noted the destructive effects that stressful interpersonal patterns—including marital unhappiness and divorce—may have on personality adjustment. Such patterns may also influence physiological functioning (Graham et al., in press). In fact, death rates from various causes, including physical disease, are markedly higher in people who have recently experienced marital problems or divorce than in the general population (Burman & Margolin, 1992; Johnson et al., 2000). Loss of a spouse through death also puts the survivor at elevated risk, but men are more adversely affected by the death of their wives than are women by the death of their husbands (Helsing et al., 1981; Stroebe & Stroebe, 1983).

Findings such as these suggest that being "connected" with others in mutually supportive ways—such as in well-functioning families—is a significant protective factor in maintaining physical health. Available research strongly supports that conclusion and extends it beyond the confines of the family. Having a good social support system is a significant predictor of good health maintenance (see Graham et al., in press; Uchino et al., 1996). As Developments in Practice 10.5 also shows, high-quality support may even prolong life in terminally ill patients. More specifically, people with higher levels of social support have lower blood pressure than people with lower levels of social support. Social support is important for the immune system too. College freshman who reported low numbers of social ties showed a poorer immune system response when they were vaccinated for influenza than did freshmen with more extensive social networks (Pressman et al., 2005). In other words, the same vaccination provided less protection for the more isolated students than it did for the students who were more socially integrated. Natural killer cell activity (those are the cells that kill tumors) is also

10.5 Developments in Practice — Visiting the Terminally Ill

Do regular visits from volunteers who have been trained to provide emotional and practical support extend the lives of people who are terminally ill? In an effort to address this question, one group of researchers studied hospice patients who were not expected to live more than 6 months (Herbst-Damm & Kulik, 2005). These patients were, on average, about 73 years old and were living in their own homes. Because their conditions were considered hopeless, they were not receiving any curative medical treatments. The researchers then looked to see if those patients who had requested and received visits from hospice volunteers survived longer than those who either did not request any visits or those who requested visits but did not receive any (usually because of scheduling reasons). Hospice volunteers are people who visit terminally ill patients in their homes and are trained to listen, provide conversation, read to them, or help with basic grooming tasks.

The majority of patients (58 percent) did not request any visits from the volunteers. However, patients who requested and received visits lived an average of 80 days longer than patients who did not receive any visits. Importantly, patients who had requested visits but who had not received them for various reasons had survival times that were just like those of the patients did not want to be visited. This suggests that what was important to survival time was actually being visited by the hospice volunteer.

The data from this study provide no clues as to why the patients who received the social support lived longer. Information about the quality of the patients' lives during this time was also not available. However, the finding that patients who received support visits from volunteers lived almost 3 months longer than those who did not is an interesting and potentially very important finding. Brief, regular visits from caring people who are good listeners may be a relatively simple way of helping dying patients live slightly longer and better-quality lives.

10.6 The World Around Us

Who Catches a Cold?

It is a situation that we are all familiar with. We are rushed, busy, and under pressure. There is a deadline to meet, or an exam is imminent. Or perhaps we have had a major argument with a parent, a friend, or a romantic partner. And then, just when it seems like life is against us and it couldn't get much worse, it does. We get a cold.

As we have repeatedly pointed out in this chapter, stress causes our immune systems to function less efficiently. Evidence from our everyday lives confirms this, as does scientific evidence from the laboratory. Sheldon Cohen and his colleagues at Carnegie Mellon University have studied people's susceptibility to the common cold for many years. By deliberately exposing healthy college students to the common cold virus by means of nasal drops, they have been able to record exactly who gets a cold in the days afterward and who doesn't.

In one study Cohen and his colleagues exposed quarantined, healthy volunteer subjects to the cold virus and assessed the outcome in terms of actual contraction of an upper respiratory infection (URI). Stressful life events, self-perceived stress, and negative emotion, all assessed before exposure, each significantly predicted which subjects would come down with colds (Cohen, Tyrrell, & Smith, 1993).

In another study they showed that people who had more extensive social support networks (friends in a variety of domains such as work, home, and church) were less likely to develop a cold than people who had less diverse social networks (Cohen, Doyle, et al., 1997). This highlights the protective effects of social support on the immune system. Most recently, Cohen and his colleagues have used a prospective research design to explore how stress and social support variables interact (Hamrick et al., 2002). Healthy students came to the laboratory and completed measures of life events, measures of social network diversity, and some other scales. Then, for the next 12 weeks, they kept a diary about any cold or flu symptoms they noticed. If they felt unwell, they were asked to go to the clinic so that the researchers could confirm that the students had an upper respiratory infection.

Who developed colds in this **observational study?** Interestingly, the students who developed colds were the ones who had experienced higher levels of negative life events *and* who also had highly diverse social networks. These findings suggest that although it is generally beneficial to the immune system to have a broad network of friends, this is not the case when we are under stress and our resistance to infection is compromised. Under these circumstances, having more friends in different places means that we are exposed to a greater range of infectious agents than would otherwise be the case. In short, when we are not stressed, being popular is a good thing. When we are stressed, however, the fewer people we come into contact with, the better.

Stress causes our immune system to function less efficiently.

higher in people who have more social support than in people who have less. Such findings may help explain why being alone and lonely predicts vulnerability to illness and death from multiple causes (Graham et al., in press; Taylor et al., 2005).

To what extent do such factors as social support predict even minor health problems such as colds? As The World Around Us 10.6 illustrates, social support is important here too, although there is also a downside to being popular.

THE LEARNING OF ILLNESSES Although Pavlov and many subsequent investigators have demonstrated that autonomic responses can be conditioned—as in the case of salivation—it was long assumed that people could not learn to control such responses "voluntarily." We now know that this assumption was wrong. Not only can autonomic reactivity be conditioned involuntarily via the classic Pavlovian model, but operant conditioning of the autonomic nervous system can also take place.

What this means is that certain physical disorders may arise through accidental reinforcement of symptom-and-behavior patterns. In short, it appears that some physical disorders may be acquired and/or maintained in much the same way as other behavior patterns. As Lang (1970, p. 86) noted long ago, "A child who is repeatedly allowed to stay home from school when he has an upset stomach may be learning the visceral responses of chronic indigestion." Some of these factors are apparent in the case of Annette.

research close•up

observational research

In contrast to experimental research (which involves manipulating variables in some way and seeing what happens), in observational research the researcher observes or assesses the characteristics of different groups, learning much about them without manipulating the conditions to which they are exposed. Observational research is sometimes called "correlational research," although the former term is the preferred term.

case study **Annette**

Annette was 27 years old when she was referred to a therapist by her doctor. She had graduated from college and worked for a large insurance company. Although she was good at her job, her life was miserable. She was plagued by stomach problems and was always fearful that she would have a stomach upset at work. Her biggest fear was that she would become sick and throw up.

A review of Annette's history revealed that she had always been a nervous child. She was very attached to her mother and hated to leave her. Going to school was a big worry for her, and she often developed stomach pains or felt sick shortly before the school bus arrived. When this happened, Annette's mother would allow her to stay home, and Annette would soon feel better.

Annette's problems with anxiety and stomach upsets continued into her adult life. When she was at home, and on weekends, she usually felt fine and would eat full meals without any problem. Weekdays, however, were a different matter. She became highly attentive to how she was feeling, and she avoided eating before she went to work. On days when she knew she would have to make a presentation at work, she often felt particularly bad. Sometimes when she got to work and was busy, she would feel better. But whenever she felt bored or stressed, she usually noticed that she felt a little nauseated. If this did not resolve after eating a cracker, she would start to worry that she was going to be sick. At least once a week, things got so bad that she left work early.

Sociocultural Factors

As we have seen, the incidence of specific disorders, both physical and mental, varies in different societies, in different strata of the same society, and over time. In general, what Cannon (1915) called diseases of civilization do not occur among nonindustrialized societies such as the aborigines of the Australian Western Desert (Kidson & Jones, 1968), the Navajo Indians of Arizona, and certain isolated groups in South America (Stein, 1970). As these societies are exposed to social change, however, gastrointestinal, cardiovascular, and other diseases begin to appear. There is also evidence of change in the nature and incidence of such disorders in Japan, paralleling the tremendous social changes that have taken place there since World War II (Ikemi et al., 1974). For example, hypertension and coronary heart disease have increased markedly with the postwar westernization of Japanese culture. In general, it appears that any sociocultural conditions that boost life stress tend to play havoc with the biological human organism and lead to an increase in disease as well as in other physical and mental problems.

In Review

- What biological factors are important in determining what disorders people are susceptible to?
- What personality and psychosocial factors appear to be associated with resistance to disease?
- Explain how learning may be involved in the development of certain illnesses.

Treatments and Outcomes

Even though a particular environmental stressor may have been closely linked to the development of a physical illness, removal of this stressor, even when combined with learning more effective coping techniques, may not be enough to bring about recovery if organic changes have already taken place. Such changes may have become chronic and irreversible. This further emphasizes the importance of prevention.

Biological Interventions

Aside from immediate and long-range medical measures, such as emergency care for a hypertensive crisis or bypass surgery for coronary heart disease, good clinical practice requires that patients receive appropriate biological treatments for their problems. For patients with CHD, such treatments might include lipid-lowering medications, as well as aspirin or other drugs that can act as anticoagulants. Anxiolytic (anxiety-reducing) medications of the benzodiazepine family, such as clonazepam (Klonopin) or alprazolam (Xanax), might also be used to reduce emotional tension. Such drugs do not address the stressful situation or the coping reactions involved; but by alleviating emotional tension and distress they may give the person an opportunity to regroup his or her resources and develop more effective means of coping with life's problems. Of course, clinicians must guard against too readily prescribing tranquilizers to insulate patients against everyday stress that they might be better off facing and resolving in some manner. Some patients may also come to rely too much on their prescriptions for easy cures, and fail to address aspects of their lifestyles that are unhealthy and destructive. The development of dependence on anxiolytic medications is also a very real problem.

In light of the strong associations between depression and risk for CHD, treating depression is of the utmost importance. Unfortunately, most people with clinical depression go untreated, giving them unnecessary added risk for CHD. Moreover, even though there is no medical risk factor that is more important in predicting mortality for patients who have already had a heart attack (Welin et al., 2000), physicians often fail to treat depression in their cardiac patients. Instead, they dismiss it as an understandable consequence of having had a life-threatening medical scare (Glassman, 2005). Of those with major depression at the time of a heart attack, approximately one-half of those who have gone without treatment remain depressed or else have relapsed again 1 year later (Hance et al., 1996).

New research data are highlighting the thousands of lives that can be saved each year by giving antidepressant medications to patients who have suffered a myocardial infarction and who are depressed. In the most thorough investigation of this issue to date, Taylor et al. (2005) reported that patients treated with selective serotonin reuptake inhibitors (SSRIs) were much less likely to die or have another heart attack than patients who were not taking antidepressant medications. Perhaps surprisingly, in this study treatment with cognitive behavior therapy (CBT) was not associated with reduced mortality in the patients, although CBT treatment did help alleviate depression (see Berkman et al., 2003; Glassman, 2005).

Psychological Interventions

TRADITIONAL PSYCHOTHERAPY Even though psychoanalytic theory has long emphasized associations between emotions and physical illness, psychotherapy has been largely ineffective in treating psychophysiological disorders (Agras, 1982). One-on-one, nonspecifically directed, verbally oriented psychotherapies—aimed at helping patients understand their personality problems—just don't seem to help alleviate psychophysiological illnesses. On the other hand, "opening up" and writing expressively about life problems in a systematic way does seem to be an effective therapy for many persons with illnesses (Pennebaker, 1997; Smyth, 1998).

In the first study of emotional disclosure in people with rheumatoid arthritis, Kelley, Lumley, and Leisen (1997) found that people who had written about their emotions had significantly less physical dysfunction than those assigned to a control condition. In another study, people with either rheumatoid arthritis or asthma were asked either to write about their most traumatically stressful life experience or (in the case of the control group) to write about their plans for the day. Subjects wrote for 20 minutes for 3 consecutive days. When they were assessed 4 months later, the participants with rheumatoid arthritis who were assigned to the emotional disclosure condition were doing significantly better than the participants with rheumatoid arthritis who were assigned to the control group.

In studies that involve emotional disclosure, patients often experience initial increases in emotional distress during the writing phase but then show improvement in their medical status over follow-up. Why emotional disclosure provides clinical benefits for patients is still not clear, however. One reason could be that patients are given an opportunity for emotional catharsis, or "blowing off steam." Another possibility is that writing gives people an opportunity to rethink their problems. Given what we know about the link between emotional and physical well-being, it is not unreasonable to speculate that both of these processes could help improve immune function or perhaps decrease levels of circulating stress hormones.

There is also some evidence that psychological interventions can help post–heart attack patients who are depressed. In a review of the literature, Linden and colleagues (1996) reported that psychosocial interventions can decrease depression, systolic blood pressure, heart rate, and cholesterol levels in CHD patients. Moreover, patients who did not receive psychosocial treatment were 1.7 times more likely to die from their CHD—and 1.8 times more likely to have another heart attack in a 2-year follow-up period—than patients who were treated for their depression and anxiety. Another study has shown that the cardiac rehabilitation and exercise programs that are frequently suggested to patients who have had a heart attack to improve their physical condition also significantly improve their depression (Milani et al., 1996).

BIOFEEDBACK Somewhat ironically in light of its focus on altering physiological states, **biofeedback** treatment has generally failed to live up to the enthusiasm it generated when it was first introduced. However, biofeedback does seem to be helpful in treating some conditions, such as headaches, for example (E. B. Blanchard, 1992, 1994; Blanchard, Appelbaum, Radnitz, Morrill, et al., 1990). Flor and Birbaumer (1993) have also reported impressive effectiveness, especially in long-term follow-up, for electromyographic (muscle tonus) biofeedback in the control of musculoskeletal pain. In general, however, the effects of biofeedback tend to be small and they rarely exceed those that could be obtained in simpler (and less expensive) ways, such as by providing systematic relaxation training without biofeedback equipment (Carlson & Hoyle, 1993; Reed, Katkin, & Goldband, 1986).

BEHAVIOR THERAPY Behavioral approaches play a major role in helping people alter dangerous lifestyle choices such as smoking and excessive alcohol use (see Chapter 12). These obviously have major implications for physical health. Giving up smoking, for example, leads to a 40 percent reduction in mortality in patients with CHD (Wilson, Gibson, et al., 2000).

Researchers have also examined the effects of various behavioral relaxation techniques on selected stress-related illnesses. The results have been variable, though generally encouraging. For example, simple tension headaches have proved quite amenable to general relaxation treatment procedures (E. B. Blanchard, 1992; Blanchard, Appelbaum, Radnitz, Michultka, et al., 1990; see also Holroyd, 2002). In addition, there is evidence that relaxation techniques can help patients with essential hypertension (see Blumenthal et al., 2002).

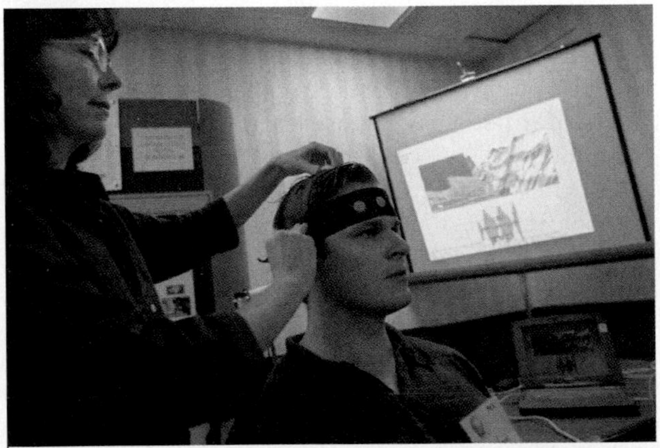

Though biofeedback may be nothing more than an elaborate means to teach patients how to relax, it has been used effectively to control musculoskeletal pain and reduce headache pain.

A growing topic of interest is meditation. Schneider and colleagues (2005) have recently shown that the daily practice of Transcendental Meditation may be helpful in reducing blood pressure. In this study, 194 African-American patients with chronic hypertension were randomly assigned to receive training in either Transcendental Meditation or progressive muscle relaxation (which involves tensing and relaxing various muscle groups in a systematic way), or else to receive general information about lifestyle changes that would be helpful to them. Patients who practiced Transcendental Meditation for 20 minutes twice a day reduced their diastolic blood pressure significantly more than did patients who practiced muscle relaxation or who received sound health care advice.

COGNITIVE-BEHAVIOR THERAPY CBT has been shown to be an effective intervention for headache (E. B. Blanchard, 1992; Blanchard et al., 1990a, 1990b; Holroyd, 2002) as well as for other types of pain (Keefe et al., 1992). CBT-oriented family therapy was markedly more successful than routine pediatric care in alleviating children's complaints of recurrent abdominal pain (Sanders et al., 1994). Deale and colleagues (1997) have also demonstrated that CBT is an effective treatment for chronic fatigue syndrome (see The World Around Us 10.7), the clinical status of which continues to be a matter of controversy (e.g., Jason et al., 1997). Some CBT techniques have also been used for stress management (Hafen et al., 1996).

Sociocultural Approaches

Sociocultural treatment measures are aimed more at prevention and are typically applied to selected populations or subcultural groups thought to be at risk for developing disorders, as we will discuss more in Chapter 18. Within these groups, people attempt to alter certain lifestyle behaviors to reduce their overall level of susceptibility to a disorder. For example, cigarette smoking is associated with increased risk for lung cancer and heart disease; to reduce the general risk of these illnesses, persistent efforts have been made to reduce or prevent smoking. Similarly, some association exists between high-cholesterol diets and coronary heart disease, and efforts are made to convince people to alter their diets to reduce the rate of coronary heart disease in the total population. Obviously, such intervention efforts involve substantial amounts of persuasion—often employing the media and, in the case of smoking, changes in federal and local laws restricting airline, restaurant, and workplace smoking. If you smoke and need yet another reason to quit, you might also con-

10.7 THE WORLD AROUND US

Chronic Fatigue Syndrome

We have all had days when we feel so tired that even small tasks seem to require too much effort. For most of us, this situation is usually temporary and is alleviated by rest. Imagine what life would be like, however, if you felt physically exhausted for months or years on end. This is what chronic fatigue syndrome is like.

Chronic fatigue syndrome (CFS) is distinguished by debilitating fatigue that cannot be explained by a known medical condition, substance use, or mental disorder. To meet the criteria for this diagnosis, the fatigue has to last 6 months or more. For many sufferers, however, CFS can last for years. Many patients also report diminished appetite, low-grade fever, balance problems, nausea, and night sweats. Although it was initially thought that CFS might be a form of "atypical depression," evidence is growing that this is not the case (e.g., Moss-Morris & Petrie, 2001). Some of the symptoms of CFS (such as sore throat, joint pain, and swollen lymph nodes) are not characteristic of depression. In addition, many of the symptoms that are typical of depression, such as guilt and lack of motivation, are virtually absent in CFS (Komaroff & Buchwald, 1998).

The typical patient with CFS is a white, middle-class female in her thirties. However, CFS is found in both children and adults and in people of all races, ethnicities, and social classes. The prevalence of the disorder in adults is around 0.1 percent. Although the causes of CFS are still unclear, viral infection and immunological and neuroendocrine abnormalities seem to be involved. Very often CFS begins with a sudden flu-like illness or another kind of medical problem. However, when the medical condition subsides, the physical problems and the social and occupational impairments continue (Komaroff & Buchwald, 1998). Keith Jarrett, the jazz pianist, suffers from CFS. So does Laura Hillenbrand, author of the best-selling book about the racehorse called "Seabiscuit." She describes the onset of her CFS in the following way:

> "In the spring of 1987 I was a sophomore at Kenyon College, majoring in English and history. I was nineteen, healthy and fit, playing tennis and cycling several times a week. On the night of March 20th, while traveling back to Kenyon from spring break, I developed apparent food poisoning and became sick enough that my roommates called paramedics. For three weeks, I couldn't seem to shake the stomach upset. Then one morning, I awoke so weak that I was unable to sit up. It took me two hours to work up the strength to stand. I expected the exhaustion to pass, but it didn't. For weeks, I couldn't even make the short walk to the dining hall. . . . I had to drop out of school. I spent the next eight months bedridden. I was under siege from constant infections, unremitting fever, chills, soaking sweats, acute light sensitivity, and balance and cognitive problems. In the first month alone I lost twenty pounds, weight I couldn't afford to lose; I finally leveled off at one hundred pounds. I was diagnosed with Chronic Fatigue Syndrome by the head of infectious diseases at Johns Hopkins.
>
> Though my health has fluctuated since then, and at times I have enjoyed improvement, I've never recovered."

CFS is still poorly understood. There is controversy over the direction of the correlation between fatigue and distress: whether psychological disorder is a cause of CFS, whether psychological problems maintain CFS, or whether psychological problems are a secondary reaction to CFS. Some of the confusion may stem from diagnostic problems. People who are depressed or overworked but who present to their doctors with extreme fatigue may be misdiagnosed as having CFS. Certainly there is evidence that the immune system is activated in CFS sufferers. Given what we know about cytokines (see Developments in Research 10.1), it is quite possible that CFS reflects the body's inability to return to a state of equilibrium after being challenged by an infectious agent. Moreover, in view of the links between the brain and the immune system, it is not surprising that the treatments of choice for CFS do not involve antiviral agents or medications of any sort. Rather, patients appear to do best when they are involved in a graded exercise program or else receive cognitive-behavioral therapy (Whiting et al., 2001), although these treatments are not curative.

sider the following: One study has shown that 41 percent of all current smokers have some form of current mental disorder (Lasser et al., 2000). The fact that someone smokes is therefore a cue that she or he might be more likely to have mental problems than someone who does not smoke.

As we learn more about the role of biological, psychosocial, and sociocultural factors in the etiology of disease, it becomes increasingly possible to identify high-risk persons and groups, such as heart-attack-prone personalities with chronic negative affect, young singles who engage in unsafe sex, and groups living in precarious and rapidly changing life situations. This ability to identify those at risk enables treatment efforts to focus on early intervention and prevention. In this context, programs aimed at fostering changes in maladaptive lifestyles and at remedying pathological social conditions seem highly worthwhile.

In Review

- What psychosocial approaches are helpful for people with diseases that have a psychological component?
- What are the major objectives of sociocultural measures taken to treat diseases that have a psychological component?
- Why is it important that patients with heart disease be screened for depression and treated if depression exists?

Unresolved Issues

Does Clinical Practice Ignore the Doctor–Patient Relationship?

As we've already mentioned in this chapter, for most of its history the medical profession survived and prospered not so much because it had available, effective remedies for illnesses but, rather, because physicians were able unwittingly to rely on the power of the placebo response in their patients. As medicine moved into the modern era, treatment of illness became increasingly an application of rapidly advancing and technologically sophisticated biological science. Enormous progress has been made in the control and actual conquering of many diseases that were once scourges of humankind. Virtually all of this progress has been due to medicine's adoption of a relentlessly scientific approach.

There are increasing signs, however, that something valuable may have been lost in this enthusiastic embrace of science and the "objectivity" it both bestows on and demands of its practitioners. The inherent temptation is for the physician to become a mere technician who administers the marvels of modern medical science to objectified patients (or, in a worse scenario, to objectified parts of patients). That temptation is strengthened by economic trends and the related development of "managed care" medicine, wherein physicians have fewer options and patients are often "processed" in assembly-line fashion. There is obvious and growing public restlessness about this model of "service delivery." The need for something more satisfying to patients shows up in the increasing interest in "alternative" varieties of medicine, the proliferation of medical self-help publications, and a heightened interest among members of the U.S. Congress in the details of medical practice.

Given what we now know about the intricate connections among mind, body, and society in disease processes, the ongoing reorganization of the medical care delivery system seems thus far to have ignored what behavioral medicine has taught us: It is important to treat not only the disease but also the *person* with the disease.

summary

- Emotional factors influence the development of many physical disorders and play an important role in the course of disease. DSM-IV-TR recognizes this with the category called "Psychological Factors Affecting a General Medical Condition."
- To recognize that psychological problems can also result from medical problems, DSM-IV-TR also has a category called "Mental Disorders Due to a General Medical Condition."
- The field of behavioral medicine grew out of the general recognition that physical and emotional well-being are intimately interrelated. It seeks to extend our conception of disease beyond the traditional medical focus on physical breakdown of organs and organ systems.
- When we are stressed, the autonomic nervous system responds in a variety of ways. One consequence of stress is increased production of cortisol. High levels of this stress hormone may be beneficial in the short term but problematic over the longer term.
- In the immune system, specialized white blood cells called B-cells and T-cells respond to antigens such as viruses and bacteria. They are assisted by natural killer cells, granulocytes, and macrophages.
- Psychoneuroimmunology is an exciting and developing field. It is concerned with the interactions between the nervous system and the immune system.
- Cytokines are chemical messengers that allow the brain and the immune system to communicate with each other. Some cytokines respond to a challenge to the immune system by causing an inflammatory response. Other cytokines, called "anti-inflammatory cytokines," dampen the response that the immune system makes when it is challenged.
- Negative emotional states, such as being under a lot of stress or having low social support, can impair the functioning of the immune system and the cardiovascular system, leaving a person more vulnerable to disease and infection. Damaging habits and lifestyles such as smoking and obesity also enhance risk for physical disease.
- Many physical illnesses seem to be linked to chronic negative emotions such as anger, anxiety, and depression. Hostility is well established as an independent risk factor for CHD. The same is true of depression.
- Positive psychology is an emerging field that is concerned with human traits and resources associated with health and well-being. One factor that is associated with greater well-being is having an optimistic outlook on life.
- Factors such as genetic vulnerabilities, excessive autonomic reactivity, and possible organ weaknesses remain important in our understanding of the causes of physical diseases. They must be a part of treatment considerations whenever physical disease occurs, regardless of strong evidence of psychological contributions to its development.
- A common factor in much psychosocially mediated physical disease is inadequacy in an individual's coping resources for managing stressful life circumstances. Cognitive-behavioral therapy, in particular, shows much promise in alleviating this type of health-endangering problem.

Key Terms

allostatic load (P. 347)
antigens (P. 348)
B-cell (P. 348)
behavioral medicine (P. 344)
biofeedback (P. 366)
chronic fatigue syndrome (CFS) (P. 367)
cortisol (P. 347)
cytokines (P. 348)
essential hypertension (P. 355)
health psychology (P. 344)
HPA axis (P. 347)
hypertension (P. 355)
immunosuppression (P. 350)
observational study (P. 363)
placebo effect (P. 354)
positive psychology (P. 353)
psychoneuroimmunology (P. 350)
psychophysiological disorders (P. 346)
T-cell (P. 348)
Type A behavior pattern (P. 356)
Type D personality (P. 357)

CHAPTER

11

Personality Disorders

Bob, age 21, comes to the psychiatrist's office accompanied by his parents . . . he begins the interview by announcing he has no problems . . . The psychiatrist was able to obtain the following story from Bob and his parents. Bob had apparently spread malicious and false rumors about several of the teachers who had given him poor grades, implying that they were having homosexual affairs with students. This, as well as increasingly erratic attendance at his classes over the past term, following the loss of a girlfriend, prompted the school counselor to suggest to Bob and his parents that help was urgently needed. Bob claimed that his academic problems were exaggerated, his success in theatrical productions was being overlooked, and he was in full control of the situation. He did not deny that he spread the false rumors, but showed no remorse or apprehension about possible repercussions for himself.

Bob is a tall, stylishly dressed young man. His manner is distant, but charming. . . . However, he assumes a condescending, cynical, and bemused manner toward the psychiatrist and the evaluation process. He conveys a sense of superiority and control over the evaluation. . . . His mother . . . described Bob as having been a beautiful, joyful baby, who was gifted and brilliant. The father . . . noted that Bob had become progressively more resentful with the births of his two siblings. The father laughingly commented that Bob "would have liked to have been the only child." . . . In his early school years, Bob seemed to play and interact less with other children than most others do. In fifth grade, after a change in teachers, he become arrogant and withdrawn and refused to participate in class. Nevertheless, he maintained excellent grades. . . . It became clear that Bob had never been "one of the boys". . . . When asked, he professed to take pride in "being different" from his peers. . . . Though he was well known to classmates, the relationships he had with them were generally under circumstances in which he was looked up to for his intellectual or dramatic talents. Bob conceded that others viewed him as cold or insensitive . . . but he dismissed this as unimportant. This represented strength to him. He went on to note that when others complained about these qualities in him, it was largely because of their own weakness. In his view, they envied him and longed to have him care about them. He believed they sought to gain by having an association with him. (Spitzer et al., 2002, pp. 239–41.)

Source: Adapted with permission from *DSM-TR-Casebook: A Learning Companion to the Diagnostic and Statistical Manual of Mental Disorders,* Fourth Edition, Text Revision (Copyright 2002). American Psychiatric Publishing, Inc.

A person's broadly characteristic traits, coping styles, and ways of interacting in the social environment emerge during childhood and normally crystallize into established patterns by the end of adolescence or early adulthood. These patterns constitute the individual's *personality*—the set of unique traits and behaviors that characterize the individual. Today there is reasonably broad agreement among personality researchers that about five basic personality trait dimensions can be used to characterize normal personality. This five-factor model of personality traits includes the following five trait dimensions: neuroticism, extraversion/introversion, openness to experience, agreeableness/antagonism, conscientiousness (e.g., Costa & McCrae, 1992; Widiger, 2005; Widiger & Costa, 2002).

Clinical Features of Personality Disorders

For most of us, our adult personality is attuned to the demands of society. In other words, we readily comply with most societal expectations. In contrast, there are certain people like Bob who, although they do not necessarily display obvious symptoms of an Axis I disorder, nevertheless have certain traits that are so inflexible and maladaptive that they are unable to perform adequately at least some of the varied roles expected of them by their society, in which case we may say that they have a **personality disorder.** Personality disorders were formerly known by psychodynamic theorists as *character disorders.* Bob was diagnosed with *narcissistic personality disorder.* Two of the general features that characterize most personality disorders are chronic interpersonal difficulties and problems with one's identity or sense of self (Livesley, 2001).

research close•up

epidemiological study

Epidemiological studies are designed to establish the prevalence (number of cases) of a particular disorder in a very large sample (usually many thousands) of people living in the community.

According to general DSM-IV-TR criteria for diagnosing a personality disorder, the person's enduring pattern of behavior must be *pervasive* and *inflexible,* as well as *stable* and of *long duration.* It must also cause either *clinically significant distress* or *impairment in functioning* and be manifested in at least two of the following areas: cognition, affectivity, interpersonal functioning, or impulse control. From a clinical standpoint, people with personality disorders often cause at least as much difficulty in the lives of others as in their own lives. Other people tend to find the behavior of individuals with personality disorders confusing, exasperating, unpredictable, and, to varying degrees, unacceptable. Whatever the particular trait patterns affected individuals have developed (obstinacy, covert hostility, suspiciousness, or fear of rejection, for example), these patterns color their reactions to each new situation and lead to a repetition of the same maladaptive behaviors, since they do not learn from previous mistakes or troubles. For example, a dependent person may wear out a relationship with someone such as a spouse by incessant and extraordinary demands such as never being left alone. After that partner leaves, the person may go immediately into another dependent relationship without choosing the new partner carefully.

The category of personality disorders is broad, encompassing behavioral problems that differ greatly in form and severity. In the milder cases we find people who generally function adequately but who would be described by their relatives, friends, or associates as troublesome, eccentric, or hard to get to know. Like Bob, they may have difficulties developing close relationships with others or getting along with those with whom they do have close relationships. One especially severe personality disorder results in extreme and often unethical "acting out" against society. Many such individuals are incarcerated in prisons, although some are able to manipulate others and keep from getting caught.

Personality disorders typically do not stem from debilitating reactions to stress in the recent past, as in post-traumatic stress disorder or many cases of major depression. Rather, these disorders stem largely from the gradual development of inflexible and distorted personality and behavioral patterns that result in persistently maladaptive ways of perceiving, thinking about, and relating to the world. In many cases, major stressful life events early in life also help set the stage for the development of these inflexible and distorted personality patterns.

There is not as much evidence for the prevalence of personality disorders as there is for most of the other disorders discussed in this book, in part because there has never been a really large ***epidemiological study*** examining all the personality disorders the way the two National Comorbidity Surveys examined the Axis I disorders (Kessler et al., 1994; Kessler, Berglund, et al., 2005). However, one review averaging across six relatively small epidemiological studies estimated that about 13 percent of the population meets criteria for at least one personality disorder at some point in their lives (Mattia & Zimmerman, 2001; see also Weissman, 1993). Several studies from Sweden yielded very similar estimates (Ekselius et al., 2001; Torgersen et al., 2001).

In DSM-IV-TR, as in DSM-III and DSM-III-R, the personality disorders are coded on a separate axis, Axis II (along with mental retardation; see Chapter 16), because they are regarded as different enough from the standard psychiatric syndromes (which are coded on Axis I) to warrant separate classification. Although a person might be diagnosed on Axis II only, Axis I disorders are frequently also present in people with personality disorders (leading to diagnoses on both Axes I and II). For example, personality disorders are often associated with anxiety disorders (Chapters 5 and 6), mood disorders (Chapter 7), substance abuse and dependence (Chapter 12), and sexual deviations (Chapter 13; e.g., Grant et al., 2004a, 2004b; Mattia & Zimmerman, 2001). A summary of evidence estimated that about three-quarters of people diagnosed with a personality disorder also have an Axis I disorder (Dolan-Sewell, Krueger, & Shea, 2001).

In Review

- What is the definition of a personality disorder?
- What are the general DSM criteria for diagnosing personality disorders?

Difficulties Doing Research on Personality Disorders

Before we consider what is known about the clinical features and causes of personality disorders, we should note that several important aspects of doing research in this area have hindered progress relative to what is known about many Axis I disorders. Two major categories of difficulties are briefly described.

Difficulties in Diagnosing Personality Disorders

A special caution is in order regarding the diagnosis of personality disorders because more misdiagnoses probably occur here than in any other category of disorder. There are a number of reasons for this. One problem is that diagnostic criteria for personality disorders are not as sharply defined as for most Axis I diagnostic categories, so they are often not very precise or easy to follow in practice. For example, it may be difficult to diagnose reliably whether someone meets a given criterion for dependent personality disorder such as "goes to excessive lengths to obtain nurturance and support from others" or "has difficulty making everyday decisions without an excessive amount of advice and reassurance from others." Because the criteria for personality disorders are defined by inferred traits or consistent patterns of behavior rather than by more objective behavioral standards (such as having a panic attack or a prolonged and persistent depressed mood), the clinician must exercise more judgment in making the diagnosis than is the case for many Axis I disorders.

One of the problems with the diagnostic categories of personality disorders is that the exact same observable behaviors may be associated with different personality disorders and yet have different meanings with each disorder. For example, this woman's behavior and expression looking out this closed window could suggest the suspiciousness and avoidance of blame seen in paranoid personality disorder, or it could indicate social withdrawal and absence of friends that characterize schizoid personality disorder, or it could indicate social anxiety about interacting with others because of fear of being rejected or negatively evaluated as seen in avoidant personality disorder.

With the development of semistructured interviews and self-report inventories for the diagnosis of personality disorders, certain aspects of diagnostic reliability have increased substantially. However, because the agreement between the diagnoses made on the basis of different structured interviews or self-report inventories is often rather low, there are still substantial problems with the reliability and validity of these diagnoses (Clark & Harrison, 2001; Livesley, 2001; Trull & Durrett, 2005). This means, for example, that three different researchers using three different assessment instruments may identify groups of individuals with substantially different characteristics as having a particular diagnosis such as borderline or narcissistic personality disorder. Of course, this virtually ensures that few research results obtained will be replicated by other researchers even though the groups studied by the different researchers have the same diagnostic label (e.g., Clark & Harrison, 2001).

A second problem is that the diagnostic categories are not mutually exclusive: People often show characteristics of more than one personality disorder (e.g., Grant et al., 2005; Livesley, 2003; Widiger & Sanderson, 1995). For example, someone might show the suspiciousness, mistrust, avoidance of blame, and guardedness of paranoid personality disorder, along with the withdrawal, absence of friends, and aloofness that characterize schizoid personality disorder. It should be noted, however, that this problem also occurs with Axis I disorders, where many individuals have symptoms of multiple disorders.

These problems often lead to unreliability of diagnoses (Clark & Harrison, 2001; Livesley, 2001; Trull & Durrett, 2005). Someday a more accurate way of diagnosing the personality disorders may be devised. In the meantime, however, the categorical system of symptoms and traits will continue to be used, tempered by the recognition that it is more dependent on the observer's judgment than one might wish. Several theorists have attempted to deal with the problems inherent in categorizing personality disorders by developing dimensional systems of assessment for symptoms and traits involved in personality disorders (e.g., Clark & Harrison, 2001; Livesley, 2001; Widiger, 2001, 2005). However, no one theoretical view on the dimensional classification of personality disorders has yet emerged as superior, and some researchers are trying to develop an approach that will integrate the many different existing approaches (Markon, Krueger, & Watson, 2005; Widiger & Simonsen, 2005).

The model that has perhaps been most influential is the five-factor model, which builds on the five-factor model of normal personality mentioned earlier to help understand the commonalities and distinctions between the different personality disorders by assessing how these individuals score on the five basic personality traits (e.g., Costa & Widiger, 2002; Widiger, Trull, et al., 2002). In order to fully account for the myriad ways in which people with personality disorders differ, it is necessary also to measure the six different facets or components of each of the five basic personality traits. For example, the trait of neuroticism is comprised of the following six facets: anxiety, angry-hostility, depression, self-consciousness, impulsiveness, and vulnerability. And the trait of extraversion is composed of the following six facets: warmth, gregariousness, assertiveness, activity, excitement seeking, and positive emotions. (All the facets of each of the five basic trait dimensions and how they differ across people with different personality disorders are explained later in Table 11.2.) By assessing whether a person scores low, high, or somewhere in between on each of these 30 facets, it is easy to see how this system can account for an enormous range of different personality patterns—far more than the mere ten personality disorders currently classified in DSM-IV-TR.

With these cautions and caveats in mind, we will look at the elusive and often exasperating clinical features of the personality disorders. It is important to bear in mind, however, that what we are describing is merely the prototype for each personality disorder. In reality, as would be expected from the standpoint of the five-factor model of personality disorders, it is rare for any individual to fit these "ideal" descriptions.

Difficulties in Studying the Causes of Personality Disorders

Little is yet known about the causal factors in most personality disorders, partly because such disorders have received consistent attention by researchers only since DSM-III was published in 1980 and partly because they are less amenable to thorough study. One major problem in studying the causes of personality disorders stems from the high level of comorbidity among them. For example, in an early review of four studies, Widiger and colleagues found that 85 percent of patients who qualified for one personality disorder diagnosis also qualified for at least one more, and many qualified for several more (Widiger & Rogers, 1989; Widiger et al., 1991). Even in a nonpatient sample, Zimmerman and Coryell (1989) found that of those with one personality disorder, almost 25 percent had at least one more (see also Mattia & Zimmerman, 2001). This substantial comorbidity adds to the difficulty of untangling which causal factors are associated with which personality disorder.

Another problem in drawing conclusions about causes occurs because researchers have more confidence in prospective studies, in which groups of people are observed before a disorder appears and are followed over a period of time to see which individuals develop problems and what causal factors have been present. Very little prospective research has yet been conducted with the personality disorders. Instead, the vast majority of research is conducted on people who already have the disorders; some of it relies on retrospective recall of prior events, and some of it relies on observing current biological, cognitive, emotional, and interpersonal functioning. Thus, any conclusions about causes that are suggested must be considered very tentative.

Of possible biological factors, it has been suggested that infants' temperament (an inborn disposition to react affectively to environmental stimuli; see Chapter 3) may predispose them to the development of particular personality traits and disorders (Mervielde et al., 2005). Several of the most important dimensions of temperament that have been studied are negative emotionality, sociability versus social inhibition or shyness, and activity level. One way of thinking about temperament is that it lays the early foundation for the development of the adult personality, but it is not the sole determinant of adult personality. Given that most temperamental and personality traits have been found to be moderately heritable (e.g., Bouchard & Loehlin, 2001; Livesley, 2005), it is not surprising that there is increasing evidence for genetic contributions to certain personality disorders (e.g., Livesley, 2005; Livesley et al., 1998; Torgersen et al., 2000). However, the genetic contribution to personality disorders appears to be mediated by the genetic contributions to the primary trait dimensions most implicated in each disorder rather than to the disorders themselves (Livesley, 2005). In addition, some progress is being made in understanding the psychobiological substrate of at least some of the traits prominently involved in the personality disorders (e.g., Coccaro, 2001; Depue & Lenzenweger, 2001; Paris, 2005).

Genetic propensities and temperament may be important predisposing factors for the development of particular personality traits and disorders. Parental influences, including emotional, physical, and sexual abuse, may also play a big role in the development of personality disorders.

Among psychological factors, psychodynamic theorists originally attributed great importance in the development of character disorders to an infant's getting excessive versus insufficient gratification of his or her impulses in the first few years of life. More recently, learning-based habit patterns and maladaptive cognitive styles have received more attention as possible causal factors (e.g., Beck, Freeman, & Associates, 1990; Beck, Freeman, & Davis, 2003; Millon & Davis, 1999). Many of these maladaptive habits and cognitive styles that have been hypothesized to play important roles for certain disorders may originate in disturbed parent–child attachment relationships, rather than derive simply from differences in temperament (e.g., Bartholomew, Kwong, & Hart, 2001). Parental psychopathology and ineffective parenting practices have also been implicated (Paris, 2001). Many studies have also suggested that early emotional, physical, and sexual abuse may be important factors in a subset of cases for several different personality disorders.

Various kinds of social stressors, societal changes, and cultural values have also been implicated as sociocultural causal factors (Paris, 2001). Ultimately, of course, the goal is to achieve a biopsychosocial perspective on the origins of each personality disorder, but today we are far from reaching that goal.

In Review

- What are three reasons for the high frequency of misdiagnoses of personality disorders?
- What are two reasons why it is difficult to conduct research on personality disorders?

Categories of Personality Disorders

The DSM-IV-TR personality disorders are grouped into three clusters on the basis of similarities of features among the disorders.

- **Cluster A:** ***Includes paranoid, schizoid, and schizotypal personality disorders.*** People with these disorders often seem odd or eccentric, with unusual behavior ranging from distrust and suspiciousness to social detachment.
- **Cluster B** **:** ***Includes histrionic, narcissistic, antisocial, and borderline personality disorders.*** Individuals with these disorders share a tendency to be dramatic, emotional, and erratic.
- **Cluster C:** ***Includes avoidant, dependent, and obsessive-compulsive personality disorders.*** In contrast to the other two clusters, anxiety and fearfulness are often part of these disorders.

Two additional personality disorders—depressive and passive-aggressive personality disorders—are listed in DSM-IV-TR in a provisional category in the appendix.

Paranoid Personality Disorder

Individuals with **paranoid personality disorder** have a pervasive suspiciousness and distrust of others, leading to numerous interpersonal difficulties. They tend to see themselves as blameless, instead blaming others for their own mistakes and failures—even to the point of ascribing evil motives to others. Such people are chronically "on guard," constantly expecting trickery and looking for clues to validate their expectations, while disregarding all evidence to the contrary. They are often preoccupied with doubts about the loyalty of friends and hence are reluctant to confide in others. They commonly bear grudges, refuse to forgive perceived insults and slights, and are quick to react with anger (Bernstein, Useda, & Siever, 1995; Miller et al., 2001).

DSM-IV-TR

Criteria for Paranoid Personality Disorder

A. Evidence of pervasive distrust or suspiciousness of others present in at least four of the following ways:

(1) Pervasive suspiciousness of being deceived, harmed, or exploited.

(2) Unjustified doubts about loyalty or trustworthiness of friends or associates.

(3) Reluctance to confide in others because of doubts of loyalty or trustworthiness.

(4) Hidden demeaning or threatening meanings read into benign remarks or events.

(5) Bears grudges; does not forgive insults, injuries, or slights.

(6) Angry reactions to perceived attacks on his or her character or reputation.

(7) Recurrent suspicions regarding fidelity of spouse or sexual partner.

B. Does not occur exclusively during course of Schizophrenia Mood Disorder with Psychotic Features, or other psychotic disorder.

Source: *Adapted with permission from the* Diagnostic and Statistical Manual of Mental Disorders, Fourth Edition, Text Revision *(Copyright 2000). American Psychiatric Association.*

It is important to keep in mind that paranoid personalities are not usually psychotic; that is, most of the time they are in clear contact with reality, although they may experience transient psychotic symptoms during periods of stress (Miller et al., 2001). People with paranoid schizophrenia (see Chapter 14) share some symptoms found in paranoid personality, but they have many additional problems including more persistent loss of contact with reality, delusions, and hallucinations.

case STUDY Paranoid Construction Worker

A 40-year-old construction worker believes that his co-workers do not like him and fears that someone might let his scaffolding slip in order to cause him injury on the job. This concern followed a recent disagreement on the lunch line when the patient felt that a co-worker was sneaking ahead and complained to him. He began noticing his new "enemy" laughing with the other men and often wondered if he were the butt of their mockery....

The patient offers little spontaneous information, sits tensely in the chair, is wide-eyed, and carefully tracks all movements in the room. He reads between the lines of the interviewer's questions, feels criticized, and imagines that the interviewer is siding with his co-workers....

He was a loner as a boy and felt that other children would form cliques and be mean to him. He did poorly in school, but blamed his teachers—he claimed that they preferred girls or boys who were "sissies." He dropped out of school and has since been a hard and effective worker; but he feels he never gets the breaks. He believes that he has been discriminated against because of his Catholicism, but can offer little convincing evidence. He gets on poorly with bosses and co-workers, is unable to appreciate joking around, and does best in situations where he can work and have lunch alone. He has switched jobs many times because he felt he was being mistreated.

The patient is distant and demanding with his family. His children call him "Sir" and know that it is wise to be "seen but not heard" when he is around.... He prefers not to have people visit his house and becomes restless when his wife is away visiting others. (Adapted from Spitzer et al., 1981, p. 37.)

Source: Reprinted with permission from the *DSM-TR-Casebook: A Learning Companion to the Diagnostic and Statistical Manual of Mental Disorders*, Fourth Edition, Text Revision (Copyright 2002). American Psychiatric Publishing, Inc.

CAUSAL FACTORS Little is known about important causal factors for paranoid personality disorder at this point. Some have argued for partial genetic transmission that may link the disorder to schizophrenia, but results examining this issue are inconsistent (Miller et al., 2001). Genetic transmission might occur through the heritability of high levels of antagonism (low agreeableness) and neuroticism (angry-hostility) that are among the primary traits in paranoid personality disorder (Widiger, Trull, et al., 2002). (See Table 11.2 on p. 383.) Psychosocial causal factors that are suspected to play a role include parental neglect or abuse and exposure to violent adults, although any links between early adverse experiences and adult paranoid personality disorder are clearly not specific to this one personality disorder but may play a role for other disorders as well.

Schizoid Personality Disorder

Individuals with **schizoid personality disorder** are usually unable to form social relationships and lack interest in doing so. Consequently, they typically do not have good friends, with the possible exception of a close relative. Such people are unable to express their feelings and are seen by others as cold and distant. They often lack social skills and can be classified as loners or introverts, with solitary interests and occupations, although not all loners or introverts have schizoid personality disorder (Miller et al., 2001). They tend not to take pleasure in

DSM-IV-TR

Criteria for Schizoid Personality Disorder

A. Evidence of a pervasive pattern of detachment from social relationships and a restricted range of expression of emotions in interpersonal settings shown in at least four of the following ways:

(1) Neither desires nor enjoys close relationships.
(2) Almost always chooses solitary activities.
(3) Has little if any interest in sexual experiences with another person.
(4) Takes pleasure in few if any activities.
(5) Lacks close friends or confidants.
(6) Appears indifferent to the praise or criticism of others.
(7) Shows emotional coldness, detachment, or flat affect.

B. Does not occur exclusively during course of Schizophrenia, Mood Disorder with Psychotic Features, or other psychotic disorder, or a Pervasive Developmental Disorder.

Source: *Adapted with permission from the* Diagnostic and Statistical Manual of Mental Disorders, Fourth Edition, Text Revision *(Copyright 2000). American Psychiatric Association.*

TABLE 11.1 Summary of Personality Disorders

Personality Disorder	Characteristics	Prevalence	Gender Ratio Estimate
Cluster A			
Paranoid	Suspiciousness and mistrust of others; tendency to see self as blameless; on guard for perceived attacks by others	0.5–2.5%	males > females
Schizoid	Impaired social relationships; inability and lack of desire to form attachments to others	<1%	males > females
Schizotypal	Peculiar thought patterns; oddities of perception and speech that interfere with communication and social interaction	3%	males > females
Cluster B			
Histrionic	Self-dramatization; over concern with attractiveness; tendency to irritability and temper outbursts if attention seeking is frustrated	2–3%	males = females
Narcissistic	Grandiosity; preoccupation with receiving attention; self-promoting; lack of empathy	<1%	males > females
Antisocial	Lack of moral or ethical development; inability to follow approved models of behavior; deceitfulness; shameless manipulation of others; history of conduct problems as a child	1% females 3% males	males > females
Borderline	Impulsiveness; inappropriate anger; drastic mood shifts; chronic feelings of boredom; attempts at self-mutilation or suicide	2%	females > males (by 3:1)
Cluster C			
Avoidant	Hypersensitivity to rejection or social derogation; shyness; insecurity in social interaction and initiating relationships	0.5–1%	males = females
Dependent	Difficulty in separating in relationships; discomfort at being alone; subordination of needs in order to keep others involved in a relationship; indecisiveness	2%	males = females
Obsessive-compulsive	Excessive concern with order, rules, and trivial details; perfectionistic; lack of expressiveness and warmth; difficulty in relaxing and having fun	1%	males > females (by 2:1)

Source: APA, DSM-IV-TR 1994; Weissman, 1993; Zimmerman & Coryell, 1990.

many activities, including sexual activity, and rarely marry. More generally, they are not very emotionally reactive, rarely experiencing strong positive or negative emotions, but rather show a generally apathetic mood. These deficits contribute to their appearing cold and aloof (Miller et al., 2001; Rasmussen, 2005). In terms of the five-factor model, they show high levels of introversion (especially low on warmth, gregariousness, and positive emotions). They are also low on openness to feelings (one facet of openness to experience; Widiger, Trull, et al., 2002).

case STUDY The Introverted Computer Analyst

Bill, a highly intelligent but quite introverted and withdrawn 33-year-old computer analyst, was referred for psychological evaluation by his physician, who was concerned that Bill might be depressed and unhappy. Bill had virtually no contact with other people. He lived alone in his apartment, worked in a small office by himself, and usually saw no one at work except his supervisor, who occasionally visited to give him new work and pick up completed projects. He ate lunch by himself, and about once a week, on nice days, went to the zoo for his lunch break.

Bill was a lifelong loner; as a child he had had few friends and had always preferred solitary activities over family outings (he was the oldest of five children). In high school he had never dated and in college had gone out with a woman only once—and that was with a group of students after a game. He had been active in sports, however, and had played varsity football in both high school and college. In college he had spent a lot of time with one relatively close friend—mostly drinking. However, this friend now lived in another city.

Bill reported rather matter-of-factly that he had a hard time making friends; he never knew what to say in a conversation. On a number of occasions he had thought of becoming friends with other people but simply couldn't think of the right words, so "the conversation just died." He reported that he had given some thought lately to changing his life in an attempt to be more "positive," but it had never seemed worth the trouble. It was easier for him not to make the effort because he became embarrassed when someone tried to talk with him. He was happiest when he was alone.

CAUSAL FACTORS We know very little about the causes of schizoid personality disorder. Early theorists considered a schizoid personality to be a likely precursor to the development of schizophrenia, but this viewpoint has been challenged (Kalus, Bernstein, & Siever, 1995; Miller et al., 2001). Research on the possible genetic transmission of schizoid personality has failed to establish either a link between the two disorders or any hereditary basis for schizoid personality disorder.

People with schizoid personality disorder are often loners interested in solitary pursuits, such as assembling odd collections of objects.

Cognitive theorists propose that individuals with schizoid personality disorder exhibit cool and aloof behavior because of maladaptive underlying schemas that lead them to view themselves as self-sufficient loners and to view others as intrusive. Their core dysfunctional belief might be, "I am basically alone" (Beck, Freeman, & Associates, 1990, p. 51) or "Relationships are messy [and] undesirable" (Pretzer & Beck, 1996, p. 60; see also Beck et al., 2003). Unfortunately, we do not know how some people might develop such dysfunctional beliefs.

Schizotypal Personality Disorder

Individuals with **schizotypal personality disorder** are also excessively introverted and have pervasive social and interpersonal deficits (like those that occur in schizoid disorder), but in addition they have cognitive and perceptual distortions and eccentricities in their communication and behavior (Miller et al., 2001; Widiger, Trull, et al.,

DSM-IV-TR

Criteria for Schizotypal Personality Disorder

A. A pervasive pattern of social and interpersonal deficits marked by acute discomfort with, and reduced capacity for, close relationships as well as by cognitive or perceptual distortions and behavioral eccentricities as indicated by at least five of the following:

(1) Ideas of reference.
(2) Odd beliefs or magical thinking.
(3) Unusual perceptual experiences.
(4) Odd thinking and speech.
(5) Suspiciousness or paranoid ideation.
(6) Inappropriate or constricted affect.
(7) Behavior or appearance that is odd, eccentric, or peculiar.
(8) Lack of close friends or confidants.
(9) Excessive social anxiety that does not diminish with familiarity.

B. Does not occur exclusively during the course of Schizophrenia, Mood Disorder with Psychotic Features, or other psychotic disorder, or a Pervasive Developmental Disorder.

2002). Although contact with reality is usually maintained, highly personalized and superstitious thinking is characteristic of people with schizotypal personality, and under extreme stress they may experience transient psychotic symptoms (APA, 2000; Widiger & Frances, 1994). Indeed, they often believe that they have magical powers and may engage in magical rituals. Other cognitive-perceptual problems include ideas of reference (the belief that conversations or gestures of others have special meaning or personal significance), odd speech, and paranoid beliefs. Their oddities in thinking, talking, and other behaviors are the most stable characteristics of this disorder (McGlashan et al., 2005) and are similar to those often seen in schizophrenic patients. In fact, they are sometimes first diagnosed as exhibiting simple or latent schizophrenia.

case STUDY **The "Spacey" Lady**

The patient is a 32-year-old unmarried, unemployed woman on welfare who complains that she feels "spacey." Her feelings of detachment have gradually become stronger and more uncomfortable. For many hours each day, she feels as if she were watching herself move through life, and the world around her seems unreal. She feels especially strange when she looks into a mirror. For many years she has felt able to read people's minds by a "kind of clairvoyance I don't understand." According to her, several people in her family apparently also have this ability. She is preoccupied by the thought that she has some special mission in life, but is not sure what it is; she is not particularly religious. She is very self-conscious in public, often feels that people are paying special attention to her, and sometimes thinks that strangers cross the street to avoid her. She has no friends, feels lonely and isolated, and spends much of each day lost in fantasies or watching TV soap operas.

The patient speaks in a vague, abstract, digressive manner, generally just missing the point, but she is never incoherent. She seems shy, suspicious, and afraid she will be criticized. She has no gross loss of reality testing such as hallucinations or delusions. She has never had treatment for emotional problems. She has had occasional jobs, but drifts away from them because of lack of interest. (From Spitzer et al., 1989, pp. 173–74.)

Source: Reprinted with permission from the *DSM-TR-Casebook: A Learning Companion to the Diagnostic and Statistical Manual of Mental Disorders,* Fourth Edition, Text Revision (Copyright 2002). American Psychiatric Publishing, Inc.

CAUSAL FACTORS According to DSM-IV-TR, the prevalence of this disorder in the general population is about 3 percent, but other estimates are considerably lower (e.g., Mattia & Zimmerman, 2001). Unlike schizoid personality disorder, schizotypal personality disorder is moderately heritable (Linney et al., 2003), and a genetic and biological association with schizophrenia has been clearly documented (Jang, Woodward, et al., 2005; Meehl, 1990a; Siever & Davis, 2004). For example, a number of studies on patients, as well as on college students, with schizotypal personality disorder (e.g., Lencz et al., 1993; Siever et al., 1995) have shown the same deficit in their ability to track a moving target visually that is common in schizophrenia (Coccaro, 2001; see also Chapter 14). They also show numerous other mild impairments in cognitive functioning (Voglmaier et al., 2005), including deficits in their ability to sustain attention (Coccaro, 2001; Lees-Roitman et al., 1997) and deficits in working memory (e.g., being able to remember a span of digits), both common in schizophrenia (Farmer et al., 2000; Squires-Wheeler et al., 1997). In addition, individuals with schizotypal personality disorder, like patients with schizophrenia, show deficits in their ability to inhibit attention to a second stimulus that rapidly follows presentation of a first stimulus. For example, normal individuals presented with a weak auditory stimulus about 0.1 second before a loud sound that elicits a startle response show a smaller startle response than those not presented the weak auditory stimulus first (Cadenhead et al., 2000a, 2000b). This normal inhibitory effect is reduced in people with schizotypal personality disorder and with schizophrenia, a phenomenon that may be related to their high levels of distractibility and difficulty staying focused (see also Hazlett et al., 2003).

A genetic relationship to schizophrenia has long been suspected. In fact, this disorder appears to be part of a spectrum of schizophrenia that often occurs in some of the first-degree relatives of people with schizophrenia (Kendler & Gardner, 1997; Nicolson et al., 2003; Tienari et al., 2003). Moreover, teenagers who have schizotypal personality disorder have been shown to be at increased risk for developing schizophrenia and schizophrenia-spectrum disorders in adulthood (Siever et al., 1995; Tykra, Cannon, et al., 1995).

Histrionic Personality Disorder

Excessive attention-seeking behavior and emotionality are the key characteristics of individuals with **histrionic personality disorder.** According to DSM-IV-TR (APA, 2000), these individuals tend to feel unappreciated if they are not the center of attention, and their lively, dramatic, and excessively extraverted styles often ensure that they can charm others into attending to them. But these qualities do not lead to stable and satisfying relationships because others tire of providing this level of attention. In seeking attention, their appearance and behavior are often quite theatrical and emotional as well as sexually provocative and seductive. They may attempt to control their partner through seductive behavior and emotional manipulation, but they also show a good deal of dependence (e.g., Rasmussen, 2005). Usually they are considered self-centered, vain, and excessively concerned about the approval of others, who see them as overly reactive, shallow, and insincere.

The prevalence of this disorder in the general population is estimated at 2 to 3 percent, and some (but not all) studies suggest that this disorder occurs more often in women than in men (APA, 2000; Widiger & Bornstein, 2001). Although reasons for the possible sex difference have been very controversial, one review of these controversies has suggested that this sex difference is not surprising given the number of traits, which occur more often in females that are involved in the diagnostic criteria. For example, many of the criteria for histrionic personality disorder (as well as for several other personality disorders such as dependent) involve maladaptive variants of female-related traits (e.g., Widiger & Bornstein, 2001). For histrionic personality disorder, these include overdramatization, vanity, seductiveness, and overconcern with physical appearance. This automatically increases the chances that women will be diagnosed as having the disorder.

case STUDY A Histrionic Housewife

Lulu, a 24-year-old housewife, was seen in an inpatient unit several days after she had been picked up for "vagrancy" after her husband had left her at the bus station to return her to her own family because he was tired of her behavior and of taking care of her. Lulu showed up for the interview all made-up and in a very feminine robe, with her hair done in a very special way. Throughout the interview with a male psychiatrist, she showed flirtatious and somewhat childlike seductive gestures and talked in a rather vague way about her problems and her life. Her chief complaints were that her husband had deserted her and that she couldn't return to her family because two of her brothers had abused her. Moreover, she had no friends to turn to and wasn't sure how she was going to get along. Indeed, she complained that she had never had female friends, whom she felt just didn't like her, although she wasn't quite sure why, assuring the interviewer that she was a very nice and kind person.

Recently she and her husband had been out driving with a couple who were friends of her husband's. The wife had accused Lulu of being overly seductive toward the wife's husband, and Lulu had been hurt, thinking her behavior was perfectly innocent and not at all out-of-line. This incident led to a big argument with her own husband, one in a long series over the past 6 months in which he complained about her inappropriate behavior around other men and about how vain and needing of attention she was. These arguments and her failure to change her behavior had ultimately led her husband to desert her.

DSM-IV-TR

Criteria for Histrionic Personality Disorder

A pervasive pattern of excessive emotionality and attention seeking, as indicated by at least five of the following:

1. Discomfort in situations in which s/he is not the center of attention.
2. Inappropriate sexually seductive or provocative behavior.
3. Displays rapidly shifting and shallow expression of emotions.
4. Consistently uses physical appearance to draw attention to self.
5. Has an excessively impressionistic style of speech.
6. Shows self-dramatization and exaggerated expressions of emotion.
7. Is overly suggestible.
8. Considers relationships to be more intimate than they actually are.

Source: *Adapted with permission from the* Diagnostic and Statistical Manual of Mental Disorders, Fourth Edition, Text Revision *(Copyright 2000). American Psychiatric Association.*

CAUSAL FACTORS Very little systematic research has been conducted on individuals with histrionic personality disorder. There is some evidence for a genetic link with antisocial personality disorder, the idea being that there may be some common underlying predisposition that is more likely to be manifested in women as histrionic personality disorder and in men as antisocial personality disorder (e.g., Cale & Lilienfeld, 2002). The suggestion of some genetic propensity is also supported by findings that histrionic personality disorder may be characterized as involving extreme versions of two common normal personality traits, neuroticism and extraversion—two normal personality traits known to have a partial genetic basis (Widiger & Bornstein, 2001). In terms of the five-factor model (see Table 11.2), their very high levels of extraversion include high levels of gregariousness, excitement seeking, and positive emotions. Their high levels of neuroticism particularly involve the depression and self-consciousness facets; they are also high on openness to fantasies (Widiger, Trull, et al., 2002).

Cognitive theorists emphasize the importance of maladaptive schemas revolving around the need for attention to validate self-worth. Core dysfunctional beliefs might include, "Unless I captivate people, I am nothing" and "If I can't entertain people, they will abandon me" (Beck, Freeman, & Associates, 1990, p. 50; Beck et al., 2003). No systematic research has yet explored how these dysfunctional beliefs might develop.

This woman could be just "clowning around" one night in a bar with friends. But if she frequently seeks opportunities to engage in seductive and attention-seeking behavior, she could have histrionic personality disorder.

DSM-IV-TR

Criteria for Narcissistic Personality Disorder

A pervasive pattern of grandiosity (in fantasy and behavior), need for admiration, and lack of empathy, as indicated by at least five of the following:

1. Grandiose sense of self-importance.
2. Preoccupation with fantasies of unlimited success, power, brilliance, beauty.
3. Belief that s/he is "special" and unique.
4. Excessive need for admiration.
5. Sense of entitlement.
6. Tendency to be interpersonally exploitative.
7. Lacks empathy.
8. Is often envious of others or believes that others are envious of him or her.
9. Shows arrogant, haughty behaviors or attitudes.

Source: *Adapted with permission from the* Diagnostic and Statistical Manual of Mental Disorders, Fourth Edition, Text Revision *(Copyright 2000). American Psychiatric Association.*

Narcissistic Personality Disorder

Individuals with **narcissistic personality disorder** show an exaggerated sense of self-importance, a preoccupation with being admired, and a lack of empathy for the feelings of others (Ronningstan, 1999; Widiger & Bornstein, 2001). It appears that grandiosity is the most important and widely used diagnostic criterion for diagnosing narcissistic patients. The grandiosity is manifested by a strong tendency to overestimate their abilities and accomplishments, while underestimating the abilities and accomplishments of others. Their sense of entitlement is frequently a source of astonishment to others, although they themselves seem to regard their lavish expectations as merely what they deserve. They behave in stereotypical ways (for example, with constant self-references and bragging) to gain the acclaim and recognition they crave. Because they believe they are so special, they often think they can be understood only by other high-status people or should associate only with such people as was the case with Bob presented at the beginning of the chapter. Finally, their sense of entitlement is also associated with an unwillingness to forgive others for perceived slights, and they easily take offense (Exline, Baumeister, et al., 2004).

Most researchers and clinicians believe that people with narcissistic personality disorder have a very fragile and unstable sense of self-esteem underneath all their grandiosity (Widiger & Bornstein, 2001). This may be why they are often preoccupied with what others think and why they are so preoccupied with fantasies of outstanding achievement. Their great need for admiration may help regulate and protect their fragile sense of self-esteem.

Narcissistic personalities share another central trait other than grandiosity—they are unwilling or unable to take the perspective of others, to see things other than "through their own eyes." Moreover, if they do not receive the validation or assistance they desire, they are inclined to be hypercritical and retaliatory (Rasmussen, 2005). Indeed, one study of male students with high levels of narcissistic traits showed that they had greater tendencies toward sexual coercion when they were rejected by the target of their sexual desires than did men with lower levels of narcissistic traits. They also rated filmed depictions of rape less unfavorably and more enjoyable and sexually arousing than did the men with low levels of narcissistic traits (Bushman et al., 2003).

TABLE 11.2	DSM-IV Personality Disorders and the Five-Factor Model									
NEO-PI-R domains and facets	**PAR**	**SZD**	**SZT**	**ATS**	**BDL**	**HST**	**NAR**	**AVD**	**DEP**	**OBC**
Neuroticism										
Anxiety			H		H			H	H	
Angry-hostility	H			H	H		H			
Depression					H	H		H		
Self-consciousness			H			H	H	H	H	
Impulsiveness					H					
Vulnerability					H			H	H	
Extraversion										
Warmth		L	L			H			H	
Gregariousness		L	L			H		L		
Assertiveness								L	L	H
Activity										
Excitement seeking				H		H		L		
Positive emotions		L	L			H				
Openness to Experience										
Fantasy			H			H	H			
Aesthetics										
Feelings		L				H				
Actions			H							
Ideas			H							
Values										L
Agreeableness										
Trust	L		L		L	H			H	
Straightforwardness	L			L						
Altruism				L			L		H	
Compliance	L			L	L				H	L
Modesty							L		H	
Tender mindedness				L			L			
Conscientiousness										
Competence					L					H
Order										H
Dutifulness				L						H
Achievement striving							H			H
Self-discipline				L						
Deliberation				L						

Note: NEO-PI-R = Revised NEO Personality Inventory. H, L = high, low, respectively, based on the fourth edition of the *Diagnostic and Statistical Manual of Mental Disorders* (*DSM-IV;* American Psychiatric Association, 1994) diagnostic criteria. Personality disorders: PAR = paranoid; SZD = schizoid; SZT = schizotypal; ATS = antisocial; BDL = borderline; HST = histrionic; NAR = narcissistic; AVD = avoidant; DEP = dependent; OBC = obsessive-compulsive.

Source: Adapted from Widiger, T. A., Trull, T. J., Clarkin, J. F., Sanderson, C., & Costa, P. T. (2002). A description of the DSM-IV personality disorders with the five-factor model of personality. (P. 90.) In P. T. Costa & T. A. Widiger (Eds.), *Personality Disorders and the Five-Factor Model of Personality,* Second Edition. Washington D. C.: APA Books.

case STUDY A Narcissistic Student

A 25-year-old single graduate student complains to his psychoanalyst of difficulty completing his Ph.D. in English literature and expresses concerns about his relationships with women. He believes that his thesis topic may profoundly increase the level of understanding in his discipline and make him famous, but so far he has not been able to get past the third chapter. His mentor does not seem sufficiently impressed with his ideas, and the patient is furious at him, but also self-doubting and ashamed. He blames his mentor for his lack of progress, and thinks that he deserves more help with his grand idea, that his mentor should help with some of the research. The patient brags about his creativity and complains that other people are "jealous" of his insight. He is very envious of students who are moving along faster than he and regards them as "dull drones and ass-kissers." He prides himself on the brilliance of his class participation and imagines someday becoming a great professor.

He becomes rapidly infatuated with women and has powerful and persistent fantasies about each new woman he meets, but after several experiences of sexual intercourse feels disappointed and finds them dumb, clinging, and physically repugnant. He has many "friends," but they turn over quickly, and no one relationship lasts very long. People get tired of his continual self-promotion and lack of consideration of them. For example, he was lonely at Christmas and insisted that his best friend stay in town rather than visit his family. The friend refused, criticizing the patient's self-centeredness; and the patient, enraged, decided never to see this friend again. (Adapted from Spitzer et al., 1981, pp. 52–53.)

Source: Reprinted with permission from the *DSM-TR-Casebook: A Learning Companion to the Diagnostic and Statistical Manual of Mental Disorders,* Fourth Edition, Text Revision (Copyright 2002). American Psychiatric Publishing, Inc.

From the perspective of the five-factor model, individuals with narcissistic personality disorder are characterized by low agreeableness/high antagonism (which includes traits of low modesty, arrogance, grandiosity, and superiority), low altruism (expecting favorable treatment and exploiting others), and tough-mindness (lack of empathy). (See Table 11.2 on p. 383.) They also show high levels of fantasy-proneness (openness to experience) and high levels of angry-hostility and self-consciousness (facets of high neuroticism; Widiger, Trull, et al., 2002). Given the features that histrionic and narcissistic personality disorders share, Widiger and Trull (1993) attempted to summarize the major differences in this way: "The histrionic tends to be more emotional and dramatic than the narcissistic, and whereas both may be promiscuous, the narcissistic is more dispassionately exploitative, while the histrionic is more overtly needy. Both will be exhibitionistic, but the histrionic seeks attention, whereas the narcissistic seeks admiration" (p. 388).

According to DSM-IV-TR, narcissistic personality disorder may be more frequently observed in men than in women (APA, 2000; Golomb et al., 1995), although not all studies show this (Ronningstam, 1999). Compared with some of the other personality disorders, it is thought to be relatively rare and is estimated to occur in about 1 percent of the population.

CAUSAL FACTORS Very different theories about the causal factors involved in the development of narcissistic personality disorder have been proposed, and each has strong advocates. On the one hand, influential psychodynamic theorists like Heinz Kohut argued that all children go through a phase of primitive grandiosity during which they think that all events and needs revolve around them. For normal development beyond this phase to occur, according to this view, parents must do some mirroring of the child's grandiosity. This helps children develop normal levels of self-confidence and a sense of self-worth to sustain them later in life, when the realities of life expose them to blows to their grandiosity (Kohut & Wolff, 1978; Ronningstam, 1999; Widiger & Trull, 1993). Kohut and Kernberg (1978) further proposed that narcissistic personality disorder is likely to develop if parents are neglectful, devaluing, or unempathetic to the child; this individual will be perpetually searching for affirmation of an idealized and grandiose sense of self (see also Kernberg, 1998; Widiger & Bornstein, 2001). Although this theory has been very influential among psychodynamic clinicians, it unfortunately has little empirical support.

From a very different theoretical stance, Theodore Millon—a personality disorder researcher from the social-learning tradition of Bandura—has argued quite the opposite. He believes that narcissistic personality disorder comes from unrealistic parental overvaluation (Millon & Davis, 1995; Widiger & Bornstein, 2001). For example, he has proposed that "these parents pamper and indulge their youngsters in ways that teach them that their every wish is a command, that they can receive without giving in return, and that they deserve prominence without even minimal effort" (Millon, 1981, p. 175; from Widiger & Trull, 1993). That theorists from these two quite different traditions (psychoanalytic and social learning) can come to such opposite conclusions illustrates the current paucity of empirical knowledge regarding particular antecedents for these disorders.

Antisocial Personality Disorder

Individuals with **antisocial personality disorder (ASPD)** continually violate and show disregard for the rights of others through deceitful, aggressive, or antisocial behavior, typically without remorse or loyalty to anyone. They tend to be impulsive, irritable, and aggressive and to show a pattern of generally irresponsible behavior. This pattern of behavior must have been occurring since the age of 15, and before age 15 the person must have had symptoms of conduct disorder, a similar disorder occurring in children and young adolescents who show persistent patterns of aggression toward people or animals, destruction of property, deceitfulness or theft, and serious violation of rules at home or in school (see Chapter 16). Because this personality disorder and its causes have been studied far more extensively than the others, and because of its enormous costs to society, it will be examined in some detail later (see also Table 11.2 on p. 383).

case STUDY — A Thief with Antisocial Personality Disorder

Mark, a 22-year-old, was awaiting trial for car theft and armed robbery. His case records included a long history of arrests beginning at age 9, when he had been picked up for vandalism. He had been expelled from high school for truancy and disruptive behavior. On a number of occasions he had run away from home for days or weeks at a time—always returning in a disheveled and "rundown" condition. To date he had not held a job for more than a few days at a time, even though his generally charming manner enabled him to obtain work readily. He was described as a loner with few friends. Although initially charming, Mark usually soon antagonized those he met with his aggressive, self-oriented behavior. Shortly after his first therapy session, he skipped bail and presumably left town to avoid his trial.

Otto Kernberg (b. 1928) is an influential contemporary psychoanalytic theorist who has written a great deal about borderline and narcissistic personality disorders.

Heinz Kohut (1913–1981), another contemporary psychoanalytic thinker, theorized that poor parenting can cause narcissistic personality disorder by failing to build a child's normal self-confidence.

Borderline Personality Disorder

According to DSM-IV-TR (APA, 2000), individuals with **borderline personality disorder (BPD)** show a pattern of behavior characterized by impulsivity and instability in interpersonal relationships, self-image, and moods. However, the term *borderline personality* has a long and rather confusing history (Paris, 1999). Originally it was most often used to refer to a condition that was thought to occupy the "border" between neurotic and psychotic disorders (as in the term *borderline schizophrenia*) (Skodol, Gunderson, et al., 2002a). Later, however, this sense of the term *borderline* became identified with schizotypal personality disorder, which (as we noted earlier) is biologically related to schizophrenia. The current diagnosis of borderline personality disorder is no longer considered to be biologically related to schizophrenia.

People with borderline personalities have a highly unstable self-image or sense of self, as well as highly unstable interpersonal relationships. They commonly have a history of intense but stormy relationships, typically involving overidealizations of friends or lovers that later end in bitter disillusionment and disappointment (Gunderson, Zanarini, & Kisiel, 1995; Lieb et al., 2004). Nevertheless, they may make desperate efforts to avoid real or imagined abandonment, perhaps because their fears of abandonment are so intense (Lieb et al., 2004). Their mood or affect is also highly unstable and characterized by drastic mood shifts. Symptoms of affective instability and intense anger are the two most stable features of borderline personality disorder (McGlashan et al., 2005).

Their extreme affective instability combined with their high levels of impulsivity often lead to erratic self-destructive behaviors such as gambling sprees or reckless driving. Suicide attempts, often flagrantly manipulative, are frequently part of the clinical picture (Paris, 1999). However, such attempts are not always simply manipulative; prospective studies suggest that approximately 8 to 10 percent may ultimately complete suicide (Adams et al., 2001; Skodol, Gunderson, et al., 2002a). *Self-mutilation* (such as repetitive cutting behavior) is another characteristic feature of borderline personality. In some cases the self-injurious behavior is associated with relief from anxiety or dysphoria. Research has also documented that borderline personality is associated with analgesia in as many as 70 to 80 percent of women with BPD (analgesia is the absence of the experience of pain in the presence of a theoretically painful stimulus; Figueroa & Silk, 1997; Schmahl

DSM-IV-TR

Criteria for Borderline Personality Disorder

A pervasive pattern of instability of interpersonal relationships, self-image, and affects, and marked impulsivity as indicated by at least five of the following:

1. Frantic efforts to avoid real or imagined abandonment.
2. A pattern of unstable and intense interpersonal relationships.
3. Identity disturbance characterized by a persistently unstable self-image or sense of self.
4. Impulsivity in at least two potentially self-damaging areas (e.g., spending, sex, substance abuse, reckless driving).
5. Recurrent suicidal behavior, gestures, or self-mutilating behavior.
6. Affective instability due to a marked reactivity of mood.
7. Chronic feelings of emptiness.
8. Inappropriate, intense anger.
9. Transient, stress-related paranoid ideation or severe dissociative symptoms.

Source: *Adapted with permission from the* Diagnostic and Statistical Manual of Mental Disorders, Fourth Edition, Text Revision *(Copyright 2000). American Psychiatric Association.*

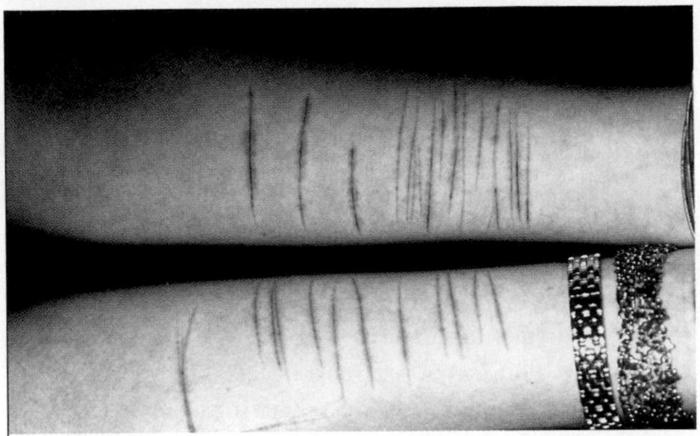

People with borderline personalities often engage in self-destructive behaviors including repetitive cutting behavior and other forms of self-mutilation. Suicide attempts among those with borderline personality disorder are common, with some studies suggesting that 8 percent may ultimately complete suicide.

et al., 2004). The following prototypic case illustrates the frequent risk of suicide and self-mutilation among borderline personalities.

case STUDY Self-Mutilation in Borderline Personality Disorder

A 26-year-old unemployed woman was referred for admission to a hospital by her therapist because of intense suicidal preoccupation and urges to mutilate herself with a razor. The patient was apparently well until her junior year in high school, when she became preoccupied with religion and philosophy, avoided friends, and was filled with doubt about who she was. Academically she did well, but later, during college, her performance declined. In college she began to use a variety of drugs, abandoned the religion of her family, and seemed to be searching for a charismatic religious figure with whom to identify. At times, massive anxiety swept over her and she found it would suddenly vanish if she cut her forearm with a razor blade.

Three years ago she began psychotherapy, and initially rapidly idealized her therapist as being incredibly intuitive and empathic. Later she became hostile and demanding of him, requiring more and more sessions, sometimes two in one day. Her life centered on her therapist, by this time to the exclusion of everyone else. Although her hostility toward her therapist was obvious, she could neither see it nor control it. Her difficulties with her therapist culminated in many episodes of her forearm cutting and suicidal threats, which led to the referral for admission. (From Spitzer et al., 2002, p. 233.)

Source: Reprinted with permission from the *DSM-TR-Casebook: A Learning Companion to the Diagnostic and Statistical Manual of Mental Disorders,* Fourth Edition, Text Revision (Copyright 2002). American Psychiatric Publishing, Inc.

In addition to affective and impulsive behavioral symptoms, as many as 75 percent of people with borderline personality disorder have cognitive symptoms that include relatively short or transient episodes in which they appear to be out of contact with reality and experience delusions or other psychotic-like symptoms such as hallucinations, paranoid ideas, or severe dissociative symptoms (Lieb et al., 2004; Skodol, Gunderson, et al., 2002a).

Estimates are that only about 1 to 2 percent of the population may qualify for the diagnosis of BPD, but they represent about 10 percent of patients in outpatient and 20 percent of patients in inpatient clinical settings (Lieb et al., 2004; Torgersen et al., 2001). Approximately 75 percent of individuals receiving this diagnosis are women.

COMORBIDITY WITH OTHER AXIS I AND AXIS II DISORDERS Given the many and varied symptoms of BPD, it is not surprising that this personality disorder produces significant impairment in social, academic, and occupational functioning (Bagge et al., 2004). BPD commonly co-occurs with a variety of Axis I disorders ranging from mood and anxiety disorders (especially panic and PTSD) to substance use and eating disorders (Adams et al., 2001; Skodol, Gunderson, et al., 2002a). In the past, many clinical researchers hypothesized that BPD had a special relationship with mood disorders, because about 50 percent of those with BPD also qualified for a mood disorder diagnosis at some point (Adams et al., 2001; Widiger & Trull, 1993). However, other Axis II disorders (such as dependent, avoidant, and obsessive-compulsive personality disorders) are actually more commonly associated with depression than is borderline personality disorder.

There is also substantial co-occurrence of BPD with other personality disorders—especially histrionic, dependent, antisocial, and schizotypal personality disorders. Nevertheless, Widiger and Trull (1993) noted the following differences in prototypic cases of these personality disorders: "The prototypic borderline's exploitative use of others is usually an angry and impulsive response to disappointment, whereas the antisocial's is a guiltless and calculated effort for personal gain. Sexuality may play a more central role in the relationships of histrionics than in [those of] borderlines, evident in the histrionic's tendency to eroticize situations... and to be inappropriately seductive. The prototypic schizotypal lacks the emotionality of the borderline, and tends to be more isolated, odd and peculiar" (p. 377). These differences can also be seen using the five-factor model of personality disorders (see Table 11.2).

CAUSAL FACTORS Research suggests that genetic factors play a significant role in the development of BPD (Paris, 1999; Skodol, Siever, et al., 2002b). This heritability may be partly a function of the fact that personality traits of impulsivity and affective instability, which are very prominent in borderline personality disorder, are themselves partially heritable.

There has also been a search for the biological substrate of BPD. For example, people with BPD often appear to be characterized by lowered functioning of the neurotransmitter serotonin, which is involved in inhibiting behavioral responses. This may be why they show impulsive-aggressive behavior, as in acts of self-mutilation; that is, their serotonergic activity is too low to put "the brakes on" impulsive behavior (e.g., Figueroa & Silk, 1997; Skodol et al., 2002b). Patients with BPD may also show disturbances in the regulation of noradrenergic neurotransmitters that are similar to those seen in chronic stress conditions such as PTSD (see Chapter 5). In particular, their hyperresponsive noradrenergic system may be related to their hypersensitivity to environmental changes (Figueroa & Silk, 1997; Skodol et al., 2002b). Moreover, certain brain areas that ordinarily serve to inhibit aggressive behavior when activated by serotonin (such as the orbital prefrontal and medial prefrontal cortex) seem to show decreased activation in BPD (Skodol et al., 2002b; see also Lieb et al., 2004).

Much theoretical and research attention has also been directed to the role of psychosocial causal factors in borderline personality disorder. Unfortunately, most of this research is retrospective in nature, relying on people's memories of their past to discover the antecedents of the disorder. Many such studies have found that people with this disorder usually report a large number of negative—even traumatic—events in childhood. These experiences include abuse and neglect, and separation and loss. For example, in one large study on abuse and neglect, Zanarini and colleagues (1997) reported on the results of detailed interviews of over 350 patients with BPD and over 100 patients with other personality disorders. Patients with BPD reported significantly higher rates of abuse than patients with other personality disorders: emotional abuse (73 versus 51 percent), physical abuse (59 versus 34 percent), and sexual abuse (61 versus 32 percent). Overall, about 90 percent of patients with borderline personality disorder reported some type of childhood abuse or neglect (emotional, physical or sexual). (See also Battle, Shea, et al., 2004.) Although these rates of abuse and neglect seem alarming, remember that the majority of children who experience early abuse and neglect do not end up with any serious personality disorders or Axis I psychopathology. (See Paris, 1999; Rutter & Maughan, 1997; Chapter 13.)

Although this and many other related studies (see Dolan-Sewell et al., 2001; Paris, 1999) suggest that BPD (and perhaps other personality disorders as well) is often associated with early childhood trauma, such studies have

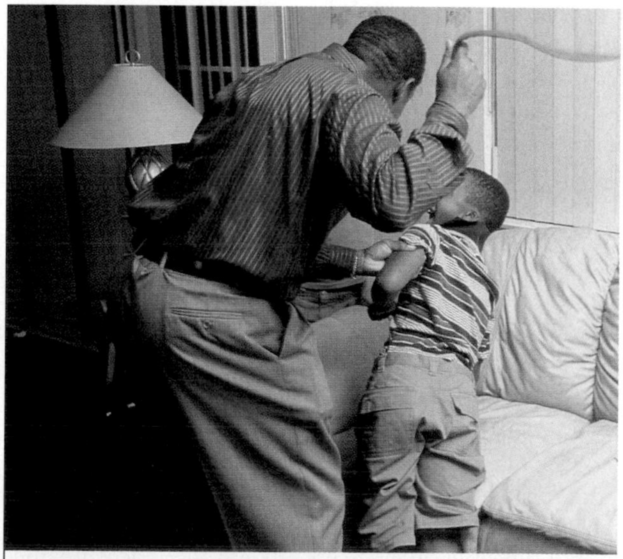

Many studies have shown that people with borderline personality disorder report a large number of negative, even traumatic events in childhood. These include abuse and neglect, separation and loss. When these psychological risk factors occur in individuals with high levels of impulsivity and affective instability, there is heightened risk for developing BPD.

many shortcomings and cannot tell us that such early childhood trauma plays a causal role. First, they rely on retrospective self-reports of individuals who are known for their exaggerated and distorted views of other people (Paris, 1999; Rutter & Maughan, 1997). Second, childhood abuse is certainly not a specific risk factor for borderline pathology, because it is also reported at relatively high rates with other personality disorders as well as with disorders such as dissociative identity disorder (see Chapter 8). Third, childhood abuse nearly always occurs in families with various other pathological dynamics, such as marital discord and family violence, that actually may be more important than the abuse per se in the development of BPD (Paris, 1999).

Paris (1999) has offered an interesting multidimensional theory of BPD. He proposes that people who have high levels of two normal personality traits—impulsivity and affective instability—may have a diathesis to develop borderline personality disorder, but only in the presence of certain psychological risk factors such as trauma, loss, and parental failure (see Figure 11.1). When such nonspecific psychological risk factors occur in someone who is affectively unstable, he or she may become dysphoric and labile and, if he or she is also impulsive, may engage in impulsive acting out to cope with the dysphoria. Thus the dysphoria and impulsive acts fuel each other. In addition, Paris proposes that children who are impulsive and unstable tend to be "difficult" or troublesome children and therefore may be at increased risk for being rejected and/or abused. If the parents are personality-disordered themselves, they may be especially insensitive to their difficult children, leading to a vicious cycle in which the child's problems are exacerbated by inadequate parenting, which in turn leads to increased dysphoria, and so on. Paris further suggests that borderline personality disorder may be more prevalent in our society than in many other cultures, and more prevalent today than in the past, because of the weakening of the family structure in our society.

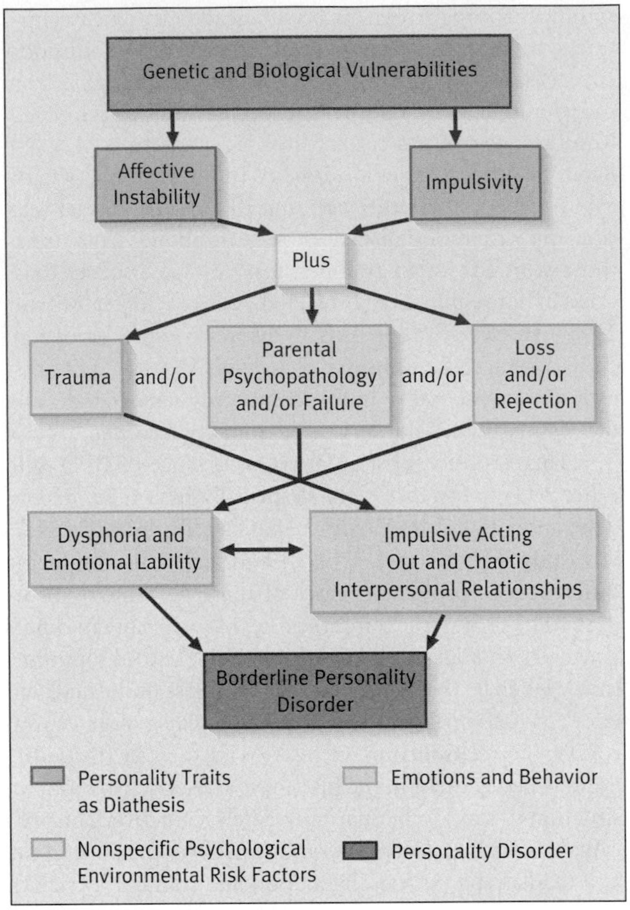

FIGURE 11.1

Multidimensional Diathesis-Stress Theory of Borderline Personality Disorder

Source: *Paris, 1999.*

Avoidant Personality Disorder

Individuals with **avoidant personality disorder** show extreme social inhibition and introversion, leading to lifelong patterns of limited social relationships and reluctance to enter into social interactions. Because of their hypersensitivity to, and their fear of, criticism and rebuff, they do not seek out other people; yet they desire affection and are often lonely and bored. Unlike schizoid personalities, people with avoidant personality disorder do not enjoy their aloneness; their inability to relate comfortably to other people causes acute anxiety and is accompanied by low self-esteem and excessive self-consciousness, which in turn are often associated with depression (Grant, Hasin, et al., 2005). Feeling inept and socially inadequate are the two most prevalent and stable features of avoidant personality disorder (McGlashan et al., 2005). In addition, researchers have recently documented that individuals with this disorder also show more generalized timidity and avoidance of many novel situations and emotions (including positive emotions), and show deficits in their ability to experience pleasure as well (Taylor, LaPosa, & Alden, 2004).

case STUDY — The Avoidant Librarian

Sally, a 35-year-old librarian, lived a relatively isolated life and had few acquaintances and no close personal friends. From childhood on, she had been very shy and had withdrawn from close ties with others to keep from being hurt or criticized. Two years before she entered therapy, she had had a date to go to a party with an acquaintance she had met at the library. The moment they had arrived at the party, Sally had felt extremely uncomfortable because she had not been "dressed properly." She left in a hurry and refused to see her acquaintance again.

In the early treatment sessions, she sat silently much of the time, finding it too difficult to talk about herself. After several sessions, she grew to trust the therapist, and she related numerous incidents in her early years in which she had been "devastated" by her alcoholic father's obnoxious behavior in public. Although she had tried to keep her school friends from knowing about her family problems, when this had become impossible, she instead had limited her friendships, thus protecting herself from possible embarrassment or criticism.

When Sally first began therapy, she avoided meeting people unless she could be assured that they would "like her." With therapy that focused on enhancing her assertiveness and social skills, she made some progress in her ability to approach people and talk with them.

DSM-IV-TR

Criteria for Avoidant Personality Disorder

A pervasive pattern of social inhibition, feelings of inadequacy, and hypersensitivity to negative evaluation, as indicated by at least four of the following:

1. Avoids occupational activities that involve significant interpersonal contact.
2. Unwillingness to get involved with people unless certain of being liked.
3. Restraint within intimate relationships because of the fear of being shamed or ridiculed.
4. Preoccupation with being criticized or rejected.
5. Is inhibited in new interpersonal situations because of feelings of inadequacy.
6. Views self as socially inept or inferior to others.
7. Extreme reluctance to take personal risks or engage in any new activities for fear of embarrassment.

Source: *Adapted with permission from the* Diagnostic and Statistical Manual of Mental Disorders, Fourth Edition, Text Revision *(Copyright 2000). American Psychiatric Association.*

The key difference between the loner with schizoid personality disorder and the loner who is avoidant is that the one with an avoidant personality is shy, insecure, and hypersensitive to criticism, whereas the one with a schizoid personality is aloof, cold, and relatively indifferent to criticism (Millon & Martinez, 1995). The avoidant personality also desires interpersonal contact but avoids it for fear of rejection, whereas the schizoid lacks the desire or ability to form social relationships. A less clear distinction is that between avoidant personality disorder and generalized social phobia (Chapter 6). Numerous studies found substantial overlap between these two disorders, leading some investigators to conclude that avoidant personality disorder may simply be a somewhat more severe manifestation of generalized social phobia (Alpert et al., 1997; Dolan-Sewell et al., 2001; Tillfors et al., 2004). This is consistent with the finding that there are cases of generalized social phobia without avoidant personality disorder, but very few cases of avoidant personality disorder without generalized social phobia. Somewhat higher levels of dysfunction and distress were also found in the individuals with avoidant personality disorder, including more consistent feelings of low self-esteem (Millon & Martinez, 1995; Tillfors et al., 2004).

The key difference between the loner with schizoid personality disorder and the loner who is avoidant is that the avoidant personality is shy, insecure, and hypersensitive to criticism. The schizoid personality is cold, aloof, and indifferent to criticism.

CAUSAL FACTORS Some research suggests that avoidant personality may have its origins in an innate "inhibited" temperament that leaves the infant and child shy and inhibited in novel and ambiguous situations. Moreover, there is now evidence that the fear of being negatively evaluated, which is prominent in avoidant personality disorder, is moderately heritable (Stein, Jang, & Livesley, 2002); introversion and neuroticism are both elevated (see Table 11.2) and are also moderately heritable. This genetically and biologically based inhibited temperament may often serve as the diathesis that leads to avoidant personality disorder in some children who experience emotional abuse, rejection, or humiliation from parents who are not particularly affectionate (Alden et al., 2002; Bernstein & Travaglini, 1999; Kagan, 1997). Such abuse and rejection would be especially likely to lead to anxious and fearful attachment patterns in temperamentally inhibited children (Bartholomew et al., 2001).

Dependent Personality Disorder

Individuals with **dependent personality disorder** show an extreme need to be taken care of, which leads to clinging and submissive behavior. They also show acute fear at the possibility of separation or sometimes of simply having to be alone, because they see themselves as inept (Widiger & Bornstein, 2001). These individuals usually build their lives around other people and subordinate their own needs and views to keep these people involved with them. Accordingly, they may be indiscriminate in selection of mates. They often fail to get appropriately angry with others because of a fear of losing their support, which means that dependent personalities may remain in psychologically or physically abusive relationships. They have great difficulty making even simple everyday decisions without a great deal of advice and reassurance, because they lack self-confidence and feel helpless even when they have actually developed good work skills or other competencies. They may function well as long as they are not required to be on their own.

DSM-IV-TR

Criteria for Dependent Personality Disorder

A pervasive and excessive need to be taken care of that leads to submissive and clinging behavior and fears of separation, as indicated by at least five of the following:

1. Difficulties making everyday decisions without excessive advice and reassurance from others.
2. Needs others to take responsibility for most major areas of life.
3. Difficulty expressing disagreement with others because of fear of loss of support or approval.
4. Difficulty initiating projects or doing things on his or her own.
5. Goes to excessive lengths to obtain nurturance and support from others.
6. Feels uncomfortable or helpless when alone because of fears of being unable to care for self.
7. Urgently seeks another relationship for care and support when a close relationship ends.
8. Unrealistic preoccupation with fears of being left to take care of himself or herself.

Source: *Adapted with permission from the* Diagnostic and Statistical Manual of Mental Disorders, Fourth Edition, Text Revision *(Copyright 2000). American Psychiatric Association.*

case study — The Dependent Wife

Sarah, a 32-year-old mother of two and a part-time tax accountant, came to a crisis center late one evening after Michael, her husband of a year and a half, abused her physically and then left home. Although he never physically harmed the children, he frequently threatened to do so when he was drunk. Sarah appeared acutely anxious and worried about the future and "needed to be told what to do." She wanted her husband to come back and seemed rather unconcerned about his regular pattern of physical abuse. At the time, Michael was an unemployed resident in a day treatment program at a halfway house for paroled drug abusers. He was almost always in a surly mood and "ready to explode."

Although Sarah had a well-paying job, she voiced great concern about being able to make it on her own. She realized that it was foolish to be "dependent" on her husband, whom she referred to as a "real loser." (She had had a similar relationship with her first husband, who had left her and her oldest child when she was 18.) Several times in the past few months, Sarah had made up her mind to get out of the marriage but couldn't bring herself to break away. She would threaten to leave, but when the time came to do so, she would "freeze in the door" with a numbness in her body and a sinking feeling in her stomach at the thought of "not being with Michael."

Estimates are that dependent personality disorder occurs in 2 to 4 percent of the population and is more common in women than in men. It is quite common for people with dependent personality disorder to have a comorbid diagnosis of mood and anxiety disorders (Bornstein, 1999; Grant, Hasin, et al., 2005).

Some features of dependent personality disorder overlap with those of borderline, histrionic, and avoidant personality disorders, but there are differences as well (see also Table 11.2). For example, both borderline personalities and dependent personalities fear abandonment. However, the borderline personality, who usually has intense and stormy relationships, reacts with feelings of emptiness or rage if abandonment occurs, whereas the dependent personality reacts initially with submissiveness and appeasement and then finally with an urgent seeking of a new relationship. Histrionic and dependent personalities both have strong needs for reassurance and approval, but the histrionic personality is much more gregarious, flamboyant, and actively demanding of attention, whereas the dependent personality is more docile and self-effacing. It can also be hard to distinguish between dependent and avoidant personalities. As noted, dependent personalities have great difficulty separating in relationships because they feel incompetent on their own and have a need to be taken care of, whereas avoidant personalities have trouble initiating relationships because they fear criticism or rejection, which will be humiliating (APA, *DSM-IV-TR,* 2000; Millon & Martinez, 1995). Even so, we should remember that avoidant personality occurs with dependent personality disorder rather frequently (Alden et al., 2002; Bernstein & Travaglini, 1999). This fits with the observation that people with avoidant personality disorder do not avoid absolutely everyone and that their dependent personality disorder characteristics are focused on the one or few individuals whom they do not avoid (Alden et al., 2002).

CAUSAL FACTORS Some evidence indicates that there may be a small genetic influence on dependent personality traits. Moreover, several other personality traits such as neuroticism and agreeableness that are also prominent in dependent personality disorder also have a genetic component (Widiger & Bornstein, 2001). It is possible that people with these partially genetically based predispositions to dependence and anxiousness may be especially prone to the adverse effects of parents who are authoritarian and overprotective (not promoting autonomy and individuation in their child but instead reinforcing dependent behavior). This might lead children to believe that they are reliant on others for their own well-being and are incompetent on their own (Widiger & Bornstein, 2001). Cognitive theorists describe the underlying maladaptive schemas for these individuals as involving core beliefs about weakness and competence and needing others to survive (Rasmussen, 2005), such as, "I am completely helpless" and "I can function only if I have access to somebody competent" (Beck, Freeman, & Associates, 1990, p. 60; Beck et al., 2003).

Obsessive-Compulsive Personality Disorder

Perfectionism and an excessive concern with maintaining order and control characterize individuals with **obsessive-compulsive personality disorder (OCPD).** Their preoccupation with maintaining mental and interpersonal control occurs in part through careful attention to rules, order, and schedules. They are very careful in what they do so as not to make mistakes, but because the details they are preoccupied with are often trivial, they use their time poorly and have a difficult time seeing the larger picture (Yovel, Revelle, & Mineka, 2005). This perfectionism is also often quite dysfunctional in that it can result in their never finishing projects. They also tend to be devoted to work to the exclusion of leisure activities and may have difficulty relaxing or doing anything just for fun (Widiger & Frances, 1994). At an interpersonal level, they have difficulty delegating tasks to others and are quite rigid, stubborn, and cold, which is how others tend to view them. Research indicates that rigidity and stubbornness, as well as reluctance to delegate, are the most prevalent and stable features of OCPD (Grilo et al., 2004; McGlashan et al., 2005).

DSM-IV-TR

Criteria for Obsessive-Compulsive Personality Disorder

A pervasive pattern of preoccupation with orderliness, perfectionism, and mental and interpersonal control, as indicated by at least four of the following:

1. Preoccupation with details, rules, order, or schedules to the extent that the major point of an activity is lost.
2. Extreme perfectionism that interferes with task completion.
3. Excessive devotion to work to the exclusion of leisure and friendships.
4. Overly inflexible and overconscientious about matters of morality, ethics, or values.
5. Inability to discard worn-out or worthless objects.
6. Reluctance to delegate tasks or work with others unless others do exactly the same things.
7. Miserliness in spending style toward both self and others.
8. Shows rigidity and stubbornness.

Source: *Adapted with permission from the* Diagnostic and Statistical Manual of Mental Disorders, Fourth Edition, Text Revision *(Copyright 2000). American Psychiatric Association.*

It is important to note that people with OCPD do not have true obsessions or compulsive rituals that are the source of extreme anxiety or distress in people with Axis I obsessive-compulsive disorder (see Chapter 6). Instead,

Individuals with obsessive-compulsive personality disorder are highly perfectionistic, leading to serious problems finishing various projects. They are also excessively devoted to work, inflexible about moral and ethical issues, and have difficulty delegating tasks to others. They are also inclined to be ungenerous with themselves and others.

people with OCPD have lifestyles characterized by overconscientiousness, inflexibility, and perfectionism, but without the presence of true obsessions or compulsive rituals (e.g., Barlow, 2002a). Indeed only about 20 percent of patients with obsessive-compulsive disorder have a comorbid diagnosis of OCPD (not significantly different from the rate of OCPD in patients with panic disorder; Albert et al., 2004).

case STUDY **The Perfectionist Train Dispatcher**

Alan appeared to be well suited to his work as a train dispatcher. He was conscientious, perfectionistic, and attended to minute details. However, he was not close to his co-workers, and they reportedly thought him "off." He would get quite upset if even minor variations to his daily routine occurred. For example, he would become tense and irritable if co-workers did not follow exactly his elaborately constructed schedules and plans.

In short, Alan got little pleasure out of life and worried constantly about minor problems. His rigid routines were impossible to maintain, and he often developed tension headaches or stomachaches when he couldn't keep his complicated plans in order. His physician, noting the frequency of his physical complaints and his generally perfectionistic approach to life, referred him for a psychological evaluation. Psychotherapy was recommended, but he did not follow up on the treatment recommendations because he felt that he could not afford the time away from work.

Some features of obsessive-compulsive personality disorder overlap with some features of narcissistic, antisocial, and schizoid personality disorder, although there are also distinguishing features. For example, individuals with narcissistic and antisocial personality disorders may share the lack of generosity toward others that characterizes OCPD, but the former tend to indulge themselves, whereas those with OCPD are equally unwilling to be generous with themselves. In addition, both the schizoid and the obsessive-compulsive personalities may have a certain amount of formality and social detachment, but only the schizoid personality lacks the capacity for close relationships. The person with OCPD has difficulty in interpersonal relationships because of excessive devotion to work and great difficulty expressing emotions.

CAUSAL FACTORS Theorists who take a five-factor dimensional approach to understanding obsessive-compulsive personality disorder note that these individuals have excessively high levels of conscientiousness (Widiger et al., 2002), which leads to extreme devotion to work, perfectionism, and excessive controlling behavior (McCann, 1999). They are also high on assertiveness (a facet of extraversion) and low on compliance (a facet of agreeableness). (See Table 11.2.) Another influential biological dimensional approach—that of Cloninger (1987)—posits three primary dimensions of personality: novelty seeking, reward dependence, and harm avoidance. Individuals with obsessive-compulsive personalities have low levels of novelty seeking (i.e., they avoid change) and reward dependence (i.e., they work excessively at the expense of pleasurable pursuits) but high levels of harm avoidance (i.e., they respond strongly to aversive stimuli and try to avoid them). At present little is known about what kinds of genetic and environmental factors contribute to the development of these traits proposed to be central to OCPD.

Provisional Categories of Personality Disorder in DSM-IV-TR

PASSIVE-AGGRESSIVE PERSONALITY DISORDER

The provisional diagnosis of **passive-aggressive personality disorder** (also known as *negativistic personality disorder,* listed in the Appendix of DSM-IV-TR) is controversial because empirical support for the reliability and validity of the diagnosis is limited (McCann, 1999; Millon & Radovanov, 1995). Nevertheless, as currently characterized, people with passive-aggressive personality disorder show a pervasive pattern of passive resistance to demands in social or work situations, sometimes being highly critical or scornful of authority. They also show a strong pattern of negativistic attitudes unrelated to any concurrent depression. Their passive resistance to demands is shown in many ways ranging from simple resistance to fulfilling routine tasks, to being sullen or argumentative, or to alternating between defiance and submission. They commonly complain about their personal misfortunes or of being misunderstood and unappreciated.

DEPRESSIVE PERSONALITY DISORDER A second provisional category in the DSM-IV-TR Appendix is **depressive personality disorder.** People with this disorder show a pattern of depressive cognitions and behaviors that is pervasive in nature. Their usual mood state is one of unhappiness, gloom, or dejection (although not necessarily sadness), and they tend to feel inadequate, worthless, remorseful, or guilty. They also tend to be pessimistic and prone to worry. Although the focus of this diagnosis is more on distorted cognitions and interpersonal traits than is true for dysthymic disorder (see Chapter 7), some questions remain about the validity of the distinction between these two diagnoses because it may be difficult to distinguish early onset dysthymia from depressive personality disorder (Klein, 1999; Ryder & Bagby, 1999). Nevertheless, Klein and colleagues (Klein & Shih, 1998; Klein & Vocisano, 1999) provided preliminary evidence that the depressive personality diagnosis is somewhat distinct and that most patients who receive the diagnosis do not meet the criteria for dysthymia, which is a disorder of mood regulation (see also Markowitz et al., 2005; McDermut, Zimmerman, & Chelminski, 2003); indeed, sadness or depressed mood and vegetative symptoms do not appear among the diagnostic criteria.

General Sociocultural Causal Factors for Personality Disorders

The sociocultural factors that contribute to personality disorders are not well understood. As with other forms of psychopathology, the incidence and particular features of personality disorders vary somewhat with time and place, although not as much as one might guess (Allik, 2005). Indeed there is less variance across cultures than within cultures. This may be related to findings that all cultures (both Western and non-Western, including Africa and Asia) share the same five basic personality traits discussed earlier, and their patterns of covariation also seem universal (see Allik, 2005, for a review).

Some researchers believe that certain personality disorders have increased in American society in recent years (e.g., Paris, 2001). If this claim is true, we can expect to find the increase related to changes in our culture's general priorities and activities. Is our emphasis on impulse gratification, instant solutions, and pain-free benefits leading more people to develop the self-centered lifestyles that we see in more extreme forms in the personality disorders? For example, there is some evidence that narcissistic personality disorder is more common in Western cultures where personal ambition and success are encouraged and reinforced (e.g., Widiger & Bornstein, 2001). There is also some evidence that histrionic personality might be expected to be (and is) less common in Asian cultures where sexual seductiveness and drawing attention to oneself are frowned on; by contrast, it may be higher in Hispanic cultures where such tendencies are common and well tolerated (e.g., Bornstein, 1999). Within the United States, rates of borderline personality disorder are higher in Hispanic Americans than in African-Americans and Caucasians, but rates of schizotypal personality disorder are higher in African-Americans than in Caucasians (Chavira, Grilo, et al., 2005).

It has also been suggested that known increases over the 60 years since World War II in emotional dysregulation (e.g., depression, parasuicide, and suicide) and impulsive behaviors (substance abuse and criminal behavior) may be related to increases in borderline and antisocial personality disorders over the same time period. This could stem from increased breakdown of the family and other traditional social structures (Paris, 2001).

In Review

- What are the general characteristics of the three clusters of personality disorders?
- Describe and differentiate among the following Cluster A personality disorders: paranoid, schizoid, and schizotypal.
- Describe and differentiate among the following Cluster B personality disorders: histrionic, narcissistic, antisocial, and borderline.
- Describe and differentiate among the following Cluster C personality disorders: avoidant, dependent, and obsessive-compulsive.

Treatments and Outcomes

Personality disorders are generally very difficult to treat, in part because they are, by definition, relatively enduring, pervasive, and inflexible patterns of behavior and inner experience. Moreover, many different goals of treatment can be formulated, and some are more difficult to achieve than others. Goals might include reducing subjective distress, changing specific dysfunctional behaviors, and changing whole patterns of behavior or the entire structure of the personality.

In many cases people with personality disorders enter treatment only at someone else's insistence, and they often do not believe that they need to change. Moreover, those from the odd/eccentric Cluster A and the erratic/dramatic Cluster B have general difficulties in forming and maintaining good relationships, including with a therapist. For those from the erratic/dramatic Cluster B, the pattern of acting out, typical in their other relationships, is carried into the therapy situation, and instead of dealing with their problems at the verbal level, they may become angry at their therapist and loudly disrupt the sessions.

In addition, people who have both an Axis I and an Axis II disorder do not, on average, do as well in treatment for their Axis I disorders as patients without comorbid personality disorders (Crits-Cristoph & Barber, 2002; Pilkonis, 2001). This is partly because people with personality disorders have rigid ingrained personality traits that often lead to poor therapeutic relationships and additionally make them resist doing the things that would help improve their Axis I condition.

Adapting Therapeutic Techniques to Specific Personality Disorders

Therapeutic techniques must often be modified. For example, recognizing that traditional individual psychotherapy tends to encourage dependence in people who are already too dependent (as in dependent, histrionic, and borderline personality disorders), it is often useful to develop treatment strategies specifically aimed at altering these traits. Patients from the anxious/fearful Cluster C, such as dependent and avoidant personalities, may also be hypersensitive to any criticism they may perceive from the therapist, so therapists need to be extremely careful to make sure that this does not happen.

For people with severe personality disorders, therapy may be more effective in situations where acting-out behavior can be constrained. For example, many patients with borderline personality disorder are hospitalized at times, for safety reasons, because of their frequent suicidal behavior. However, partial-hospitalization programs are increasingly being used as an intermediate and less expensive alternative to inpatient treatment (Azim, 2001). In these programs, patients live at home and receive extensive group treatment and rehabilitation only during the weekdays.

Specific therapeutic techniques are a central part of the relatively new cognitive approach to personality disorders that assumes that the dysfunctional feelings and behavior associated with the personality disorders are largely the result of schemas that tend to produce consistently biased judgments, as well as tendencies to make cognitive errors (e.g., Beck, Freeman, & Associates 1990; Beck et al., 2003; Cottraux & Blackburn, 2001). Changing these underlying dysfunctional schemas is difficult but is at the heart of cognitive therapy for personality disorders, which uses standard cognitive techniques of monitoring automatic thoughts, challenging faulty logic, and assigning behavioral tasks in an effort to challenge the patient's dysfunctional beliefs.

Treating Borderline Personality Disorder

Of all the personality disorders, the most clinical and research attention has probably been paid to the treatment of borderline personality disorder, partly because the treatment prognosis (probable outcome) is typically considered guarded because of these patients' long-standing problems and extreme instability. Treatment often involves a judicious use of both psychological and biological treatment methods, the drugs being used as an adjunct to psychological treatment, which is considered essential.

BIOLOGICAL TREATMENTS The use of medications is controversial with this disorder because it is so frequently associated with suicidal behavior. Today, antidepressant medications from the SSRI category are considered most safe and useful for treating rapid mood shifts, anger, and anxiety (Lieb et al., 2004), with more mixed evidence of their usefulness for impulsivity symptoms including impulsive aggression such as self-mutilation (Koenigsberg et al., 2002; Markovitz, 2001, 2004). In addition, low doses of antipsychotic medication (see Chapters 14 and 17) have modest but significant effects that are broad-based; that is, patients show some improvement in depression, anxiety, suicidality, rejection sensitivity, and especially transient psychotic symptoms (APA, 2001; Markovitz, 2001, 2004). Finally, mood-stabilizing medications such as carbazemine may be useful in reducing irritability, suicidality, and impulsive aggressive behavior (Lieb et al., 2004).

PSYCHOSOCIAL TREATMENTS Traditional psychosocial treatments for BPD involve variants of psychodynamic psychotherapy adapted for the particular problems of persons with this disorder. For example, Kernberg and colleagues (1985, 1996; Koenigsberg, Kernberg, et al., 2000) developed a form of psychodynamic psychotherapy that is much more directive than is typical of psychodynamic treatment. The primary goal is seen as strengthening the weak egos of these individuals, with a particular focus on their primary primitive defense mechanism of *splitting*, which leads them to black-and-white, all-or-none thinking, as well as to rapid shifts in their reactions to themselves and to other people (including the therapist) as "all good" or "all bad." One major goal is to help them see the shades of gray between these extremes and integrate positive and negative views of the self and others into more nuanced views. Although this treatment can be effective in some cases, it is expensive and time-consuming (often lasting a good number of years) and is only beginning to be subjected to controlled research (APA, 2001; Clarkin et al., 2004; Crits-Cristoph & Barber, 2002).

Linehan's (1993; Robins, Ivanoff, & Linehan, 2001) very promising *dialectical behavior therapy*—a unique kind of cognitive and behavioral therapy specifically adapted for this disorder—is now being widely used. Linehan believes that patients' inability to tolerate strong states of negative affect is central to this disorder, and one of the primary goals of treatment is to encourage patients to accept this negative affect without engaging in self-destructive or other maladaptive behaviors. Accordingly, she has developed a problem-focused treatment based on a clear hierarchy of goals: (1) decreasing suicidal and other self-harming behavior; (2) decreasing behaviors that interfere with therapy such as missing sessions, lying, and getting hospitalized; (3) decreasing escapist behaviors that interfere with a stable lifestyle, such as substance abuse; (4) increasing behavioral skills in order to regulate emotions, to increase interpersonal skills, and to increase tolerance for distress; and (5) other goals the patient chooses.

Dialectical behavior therapy combines individual and group components, with the group setting focusing more on training in interpersonal skills, emotion regulation, and stress tolerance. This all occurs in the presence of a therapist who is taught to accept the patient for who he or she is, in spite of behaviors on the part of the patient that make it difficult to do so (such as bursts of rage, suicidal behaviors, missing appointments, etc.). Linehan makes a clear distinction between accepting the patient for who he or she is and approving of the patient's behavior. For example, a therapist cannot *approve* of self-mutilation, but he or she should indicate *acceptance* of that as part of a patient's problem.

Initial results from one important controlled study using this form of treatment were very encouraging (Linehan, Heard, & Armstrong, 1993; Linehan et al., 1991; Linehan et al., 1994). Borderline patients who received dialectical behavior therapy were compared with patients who received treatment as usual in the community over a 1-year treatment and 1-year follow-up period. Patients who received dialectical behavior therapy showed greater reduction in self-destructive and suicidal behaviors, as well as in levels of anger, than those in the treatment-as-usual group. They were also more likely to stay in treatment and to require fewer days of hospitalization. At follow-up they were doing better occupationally and were rated as better adjusted in terms of interpersonal and emotional regulation skills than the control group. Although modest in some ways, these results are considered extraordinary by most therapists who work with this population, and many psychodynamic therapists are incorporating important components of this treatment into their own treatment. More recently, several other good controlled studies on dialectical behavior therapy have been published, and they have achieved similarly impressive results (APA, 2001; Bohus et al., 2004; Robins & Chapman, 2004).

Treating Other Personality Disorders

TREATING OTHER CLUSTER A AND B DISORDERS Treatment of schizotypal personality disorder is not, so far, as promising as some of the recent advances that have been made in the treatment of borderline personality disorder. Low doses of antipsychotic drugs (including the newer atypical antipsychotics; e.g., Keshavan et al., 2004) may result in modest improvements, and antidepressants from the SSRI category may also be useful. However, no treatment has yet produced anything approaching a cure for most people with this disorder (Koenigsberg et al., 2002, 2003; Markovitz, 2001, 2004). Other than uncontrolled studies or single cases, no systematic studies of treating people with either medication or psychotherapy yet exist for paranoid, schizoid, narcissistic, or histrionic disorder (Crits-Cristoph & Barber, 2002; Pretzer & Beck, 1996).

TREATING CLUSTER C DISORDERS Treatment of some of the personality disorders from Cluster C such as dependent and avoidant personality disorders has not been extensively studied but appears somewhat more promising. For example, Winston and colleagues (1994) found significant improvement in patients with Cluster C disorders using a form of short-term psychotherapy that is active and confrontational (see also Pretzer & Beck, 1996). Several studies using cognitive-behavioral treatment with avoidant personality disorder have also reported significant gains. Moreover, antidepressants from the MAO inhibitor and SSRI categories may sometimes help in the treatment of avoidant personality disorder, just as in closely related social phobia (Koenigsberg et al., 2002; Markovitz, 2001).

In Review

- Why are personality disorders especially resistant to therapy?
- Under what circumstances do individuals with personality disorders generally get involved in psychotherapy?
- What is known about the effectiveness of treatments for borderline personality disorder?

Antisocial Personality Disorder and Psychopathy

The outstanding characteristic of people with **antisocial personality disorder (ASPD)** is their tendency to persistently disregard and violate the rights of others. They do this through a combination of deceitful, aggressive, and antisocial behaviors. These people have a lifelong pattern of unsocialized and irresponsible behavior, with little regard for safety—either their own or that of others. These characteristics bring them into repeated conflict with society, and a high proportion become incarcerated. Only individuals 18 or over are diagnosed with antisocial personality disorder. According to DSM-IV-TR, this diagnosis is made if, after age 15, the person repeatedly performs acts that are grounds for arrest; shows repeated deceitfulness, impulsivity, irritability, and aggressiveness; shows disregard for safety; and shows consistent irresponsibility in work or financial matters. Moreover, the person must also have shown symptoms of conduct disorder before age 15 (see Chapter 16).

Psychopathy and ASPD

The use of the term *antisocial personality disorder* dates back only to DSM-III in 1980, but many of the central features of this disorder have long been labeled **psychopathy**

DSM-IV-TR

Criteria for Antisocial Personality Disorder

A. A pervasive pattern of disregard for and violation of the rights of others occurring since age 15, as indicated by at least three of the following:

(1) Failure to conform to social norms and repeated lawbreaking.

(2) Deceitfulness.

(3) Impulsivity or failure to plan ahead.

(4) Irritability and aggressiveness.

(5) Reckless disregard for safety of self or others.

(6) Consistent irresponsibility.

(7) Lack of remorse.

B. The individual is at least 18 years of age.

C. There is evidence of Conduct Disorder with onset before age 15.

Source: *Adapted with permission from the* Diagnostic and Statistical Manual of Mental Disorders, Fourth Edition, Text Revision *(Copyright 2000). American Psychiatric Association.*

or *sociopathy.* Although several investigators identified the syndrome in the nineteenth century under such labels as "moral insanity" (Prichard, 1835), the most comprehensive, systematic early description of psychopathy was made by Cleckley (1941, 1982) in the 1940s. In addition to the defining features of antisocial personality in DSM-III and DSM-IV-TR, psychopathy also includes such affective and interpersonal traits as lack of empathy, inflated and arrogant self-appraisal, and glib and superficial charm (see Patrick, 2005b, for a recent analysis of Cleckley's work in light of contemporary research). In their strong emphasis on behavioral criteria that can be measured reasonably objectively, DSM-III and DSM-IV-TR broke with the tradition of psychopathy researchers in an attempt to increase the reliability of the diagnosis (the level of agreement of clinicians on the diagnosis). However, much less attention has been paid to the validity of the diagnosis—that is, whether it measures a meaningful construct and whether that construct is the same as psychopathy.

According to DSM-IV-TR, the prevalence of ASPD in the general population is about 3 percent for males and about 1 percent for females; these estimates are based on several large epidemiological studies. There are no epidemiological studies estimating the prevalence of psychopathy, but Hare, Cooke, and Hart (1999) believe it is likely to be about 1 percent in North America.

TWO DIMENSIONS OF PSYCHOPATHY Research since 1980 by Robert Hare and his colleagues suggests that ASPD and psychopathy are related but differ in significant ways. Hare (1980, 1991; Hare et al., 2003) developed a 20-item Psychopathy Checklist-Revised (PCL-R) as a way for clinicians and researchers to diagnose psychopathy on the basis of the Cleckley criteria following an extensive interview and careful checking of past school, police, and prison records. Extensive research with this checklist has shown that there are two related but separable dimensions of psychopathy, each predicting different types of behavior:

- The first dimension involves the affective and interpersonal core of the disorder and reflects traits such as lack of remorse or guilt, callousness/lack of empathy, glibness/superficial charm, grandiose sense of self-worth, and pathological lying.
- The second dimension reflects behavior—the aspects of psychopathy that involve an antisocial, impulsive, and socially deviant lifestyle such as the need for stimulation, poor behavior controls, irresponsibility, and parasitic lifestyle.

The second dimension is much more closely related than the first to the DSM-III and DSM-IV-TR diagnosis of antisocial personality disorder (Clark & Harrison, 2001; Hare, Cooke, & Hart et al., 1999). Not surprisingly, therefore, when comparisons have been made in prison settings to determine what percentage of prison inmates qualify for a diagnosis of psychopathy versus antisocial personality disorder, it is typically found that about 70 to 80 percent qualify for a diagnosis of ASPD, but only about 25 to 30 percent meet the criteria for psychopathy (Patrick, 2005a). That is, a significant number of the inmates show the antisocial and aggressive behaviors necessary for a diagnosis of antisocial personality disorder, but not enough selfish, callous, and exploitative behaviors to qualify for a diagnosis of psychopathy (Hare et al., 1999).

The issues surrounding these diagnoses remain highly controversial. Although there was considerable discussion about expanding the DSM-IV criteria for antisocial personality disorder to include more of the traditional affective and interpersonal features of psychopathy, a conservative approach was taken and such changes were not made (Sutker & Allain, 2001; Widiger & Corbitt, 1995). However, many researchers continue using the Cleckley/Hare psychopathy diagnosis rather than the DSM-IV-TR ASPD diagnosis both because of the long and rich research tradition on psychopathy and because the psychopathy diagnosis has been shown to be a better predictor of a variety of important facets of criminal behavior than the ASPD diagnosis. Overall, a diagnosis of psychopathy appears to be the single best predictor we have of violence and recidivism (offending again after imprisonment; Gretton et al., 2004; Hart, 1998; Hare et al., 1999). For example, one review estimated that people with psychopathy are three

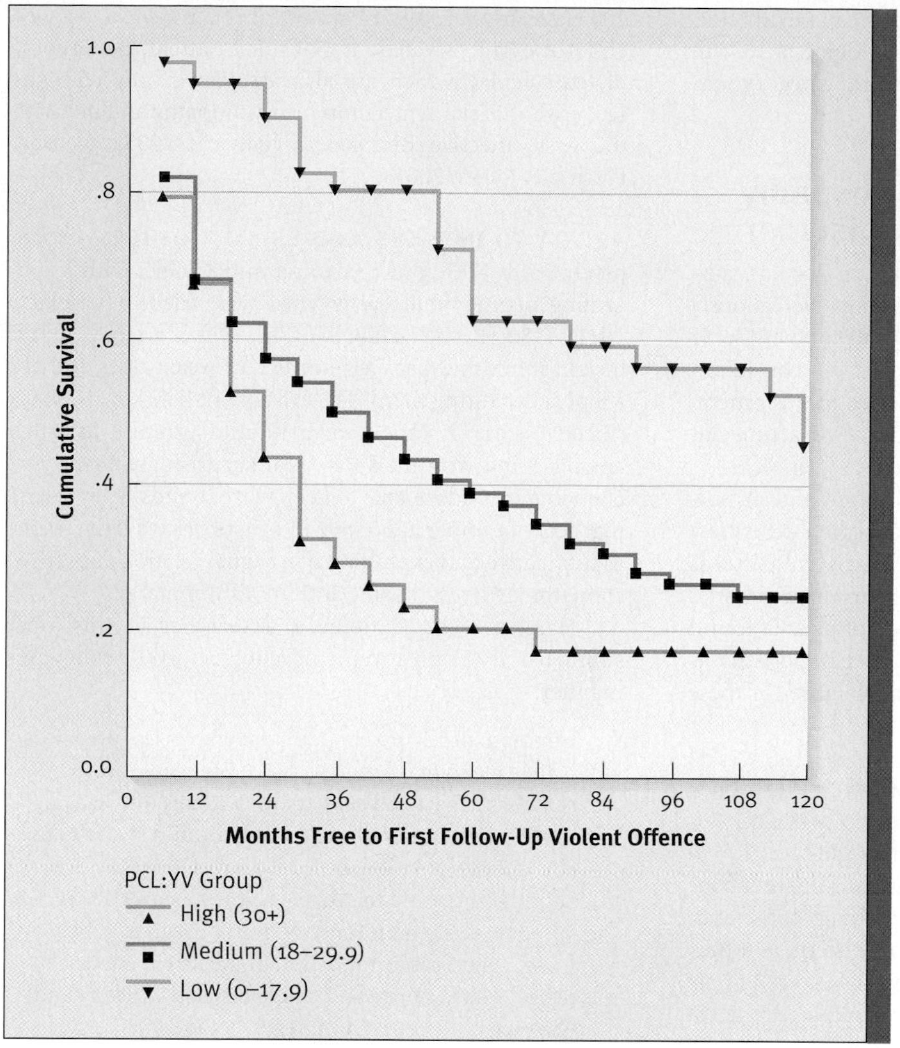

FIGURE 11.2

Survival curve of months free in the community until first violent reoffence by Hare Psychopathy Checklist: Youth Version (PCL:YV) group. The survival curve illustrates the percentage of individuals in each group who have not shown a violent reoffense at 12-month intervals. Those in the High-PCL-YV group were more likely to have violent reoffenses than the other two groups (lower probability of survival) and were more likely to have them sooner after release (indicated by a steeper slope).

Source: *From Gretton, H., Hare, R. D., & Catchpole, R. (2004). Psychopathy and offending from adolescence to adulthood: A Ten-year Follow-up.* Journal of Consulting and Clinical Psychology, *72, 636–645. Copyright © 2004 by the American Psychological Association. Reproduced with permission.*

times more likely to reoffend and four times more likely to reoffend *violently* following prison terms than are people without a psychopathy diagnosis (Hemphill et al., 1998). Moreover, adolescents diagnosed with psychopathy are not only more likely to show violent reoffending, but also more likely to reoffend more quickly (Gretton et al., 2004). (See Figure 11.2.)

An additional concern about the current conceptualization of ASPD is that it does not include what may be a substantial segment of society who shows many of the features of the first, affective and interpersonal dimension of psychopathy but not as many features of the second, antisocial dimension, or at least few enough that these individuals do not generally get into trouble with the law. Cleckley clearly did not believe that aggressive behavior was central to the concept of psychopathy (Patrick, 2005b). This group might include, for example, some unprincipled and predatory business professionals, high-pressure evangelists, and crooked politicians (Hare et al., 1999). Unfortunately, little research has been conducted on such psychopathic persons who manage to stay out of correctional institutions, because they are very difficult to find to study. One researcher (Widom, 1977) who wanted to study these individuals ran an ingenious ad in local newspapers:

> Are you adventurous? Psychologist studying adventurous, carefree people who've led exciting, impulsive lives. If you're the kind of person who'd do almost anything for a dare and want to participate in a paid experiment, send name, address, phone, and short biography proving how interesting you are to . . . (p. 675)

When those who responded were given a battery of tests, they turned out to be similar in personality makeup to institutionalized psychopaths. Several further studies on people with noncriminal psychopathy confirmed this finding (Hare et al., 1999). However, some experimental research to be discussed later suggests that these two groups may also differ biologically in some significant ways (Ishikawa, Raine, et al., 2001).

These controversies over the use of a diagnosis of psychopathy versus ASPD are not likely to be resolved soon. Different researchers in this area make different choices, so interpreting the research on causal factors can be difficult. Because the causal factors may well not be identical, we will attempt to make it clear which diagnostic category was used in different studies.

The Clinical Picture in Psychopathy and Antisocial Personality Disorder

Often charming, spontaneous, and likable on first acquaintance, psychopaths are deceitful and manipulative, callously using others to achieve their own ends. Many of them seem to live in a series of present moments, without consideration for the past or future. But also included in this general category are hostile people who are prone to acting out impulses in remorseless and often senseless violence.

We will summarize the major characteristics of psychopaths and antisocial personalities and then describe a case that illustrates the wide range of behavioral patterns that may be involved. Although all the characteristics examined in the following sections are not usually found in a particular case, they are typical of psychopaths as described by Cleckley (1941, 1982), and a subset of these characteristics occur in ASPD as well.

INADEQUATE CONSCIENCE DEVELOPMENT Psychopaths appear unable to understand and accept ethical values except on a verbal level. They may glibly claim to adhere to high moral standards that have no apparent connection with their behavior. In short, their conscience development is severely retarded or nonexistent, and they behave as though social regulations and laws do not apply to them. These characteristics of psychopathy are most strongly related to the interpersonal and affective core of psychopathy (Fowles & Dindo, 2005). In spite of their retarded conscience development, their intellectual development is typically normal. Nevertheless, intelligence is one trait that has different relationships with the two dimensions of psychopathy. The first, affective and interpersonal dimension is positively related to verbal intelligence (Salekin et al., 2004), but the second, antisocial dimension is negatively related to intelligence (Frick, 1998; Hare et al., 1999).

IRRESPONSIBLE AND IMPULSIVE BEHAVIOR Psychopaths have learned to take rather than earn what they want. Prone to thrill seeking and deviant and unconventional behavior, they often break the law impulsively and without regard for the consequences. They seldom forgo immediate pleasure for future gains and long-range goals. These aspects of psychopathy are most closely related to the second, antisocial dimension of psychopathy (Patrick, 2005a).

Many studies have shown that antisocial personalities and some psychopaths have high rates of alcohol abuse and dependence and other substance-abuse/dependence disorders (e.g., Cloninger, Bayon, & Przybeck, 1997; Waldman & Slutske, 2000). Alcohol abuse is related only to the antisocial or deviant dimension of the PCL-R (Patrick, 2005a; Reardon, Lang, & Patrick, 2002). Antisocial personalities also have elevated rates of suicide attempts and completed suicides, which are also associated only with the second, antisocial dimension of psychopathy and not with the first, affective dimension (Patrick, 2005a; Verona, Patrick, & Joiner, 2001).

ABILITY TO IMPRESS AND EXPLOIT OTHERS Some psychopaths are often charming and likable, with a disarming manner that easily wins new friends (Cleckley, 1941, 1982; Patrick, 2005b). They seem to have good insight into other people's needs and weaknesses and are adept at exploiting them. These frequent liars usually seem sincerely sorry if caught in a lie and promise to make amends—but will not do so. Not surprisingly, then, psychopaths are seldom able to keep close friends. They seemingly cannot understand love in others or give it in return. Manipulative and exploitative in sexual relationships, psychopaths are irresponsible and unfaithful mates.

Hare, a highly influential researcher in this area, summarized the prototypic psychopath in the following manner:

> Conceptualizing psychopaths as remorseless predators helped me to make sense of what often appears to be senseless behavior. These are individuals who, lacking in conscience and feelings for others, find it easy to use charm, manipulation, intimidation, and violence to control others and to satisfy their own social needs.... without the slightest sense of guilt or regret.... they form a significant proportion of persistent criminals, drug dealers, spouse and child abusers, swindlers and con men.... They are well represented in the business and corporate world, particularly during chaotic restructuring, where the rules and their enforcement are lax.... Many psychopaths emerge as "patriots" and "saviors" in societies experiencing social, economic, and political upheaval (e.g., Rwanda, the former Yugoslavia, and the former Soviet Union).... by callously exploiting ethnic, cultural, or racial tensions and grievances. (1998b, pp. 128–129)

Psychopathy is well illustrated in the following classic case study published by Hare (1970).

case study — A Psychopath in Action

Donald, 30 years old, has just completed a 3-year prison term for fraud, bigamy, false pretenses, and escaping lawful custody. The circumstances leading up to these offenses are interesting and consistent with his past behavior. With less than a month left to serve on an earlier 18-month term for fraud, he faked illness and escaped from the prison hospital. During the 10 months of freedom that followed, he engaged in a variety of illegal enterprises; the activity that resulted in his recapture was typical of his method of operation. By passing himself off as the "field executive" of an international philanthropic foundation, he was able to enlist the aid of several religious organizations in a fund-raising campaign. The campaign moved slowly at first, and in an attempt to speed things up, he arranged an interview with the local TV station. His performance during the interview was so impressive that funds started to pour in. However, unfortunately for Donald, the interview was also carried on a national news network. He was recognized and quickly arrested. During the ensuing trial it became evident that he experienced no sense of wrongdoing for his activities.... At the same time, he stated that most donations to charity are made by those who feel guilty about something and who therefore deserve to be bilked.

While in prison he was used as a subject in some of the author's research. On his release he applied for admission to a university and, by way of reference, told the registrar that he had been one of the author's research colleagues! Several months later the author received a letter from him requesting a letter of recommendation on behalf of Donald's application for a job.

Background. Donald was the youngest of three boys born to middle-class parents. Both of his brothers led normal, productive lives. His father spent a great deal of time with his business; when he was home he tended to be moody and to drink heavily when things were not going right. Donald's mother was a gentle, timid woman who tried to please her husband and to maintain a semblance of family harmony.... However,... on some occasions [the father] would fly into a rage and beat the children and on others he would administer a verbal reprimand, sometimes mild and sometimes severe.

By all accounts Donald was considered a willful and difficult child. When his desire for candy or toys was frustrated he would begin with a show of affection, and if this failed he would throw a temper tantrum; the latter was seldom necessary because his angelic appearance and artful ways usually got him what he wanted.... Although he was obviously very intelligent, his school years were academically undistinguished. He was restless, easily bored, and frequently truant... when he was on his own he generally got himself or others into trouble. Although he was often suspected of being the culprit, he was adept at talking his way out of difficulty.

Donald's misbehavior as a child took many forms including lying, cheating, petty theft, and the bullying of smaller children. As he grew older he became more and more interested in sex, gambling, and alcohol. When he was 14 he made crude sexual advances toward a younger girl, and when she threatened to tell her parents he locked her in a shed. It was about 16 hours before she was found. Donald at first denied knowledge of the incident, later stating that she had seduced him and that the door must have locked itself.... His parents were able to prevent charges being brought against him....

When he was 17, Donald... forged his father's name to a large check and spent about a year traveling around the world. He apparently lived well, using a combination of charm, physical attractiveness, and false pretenses to finance his way. During subsequent years he held a succession of jobs, never... for more than a few months. Throughout this period he was charged with a variety of crimes, including theft, drunkenness in a public place, assault, and many traffic violations. In most cases he was either fined or given a light sentence.

A Ladies' Man. His sexual experiences were frequent, casual, and callous. When he was 22, he married a 41-year-old woman whom he had met in a bar. Several other marriages followed, all bigamous.... The pattern was the same: He would marry someone on impulse, let her support him for several months, and then leave. One marriage was particularly interesting. After being charged with fraud Donald was sent to a psychiatric institution for a period of observation. While there he came to the attention of a female member of the professional staff. His charm, physical attractiveness, and convincing promises to reform led her to intervene on his behalf. He was given a suspended sentence and they were married a week later. At first things went reasonably well, but when she refused to pay some of his gambling debts he forged her name to a check and left. He was soon caught and given an 18-month prison term.... He escaped with less than a month left to serve.

It is interesting to note that Donald sees nothing particularly wrong with his behavior, nor does he express remorse or guilt for using others and causing them grief. Although his behavior is self-defeating in the long run, he considers it to be practical and possessed of good sense. Periodic punishments do nothing to decrease his egotism and confidence in his own abilities.... His behavior is entirely egocentric, and his needs are satisfied without any concern for the feelings and welfare of others. (Reprinted with permission of Robert P. Hare, University of British Columbia, rhare@interchange.ubc.ca)

The repetitive behavior pattern shown by Donald is common among people diagnosed as psychopathic. Some of the multitude of etiological factors that are involved in the development of this very serious personality disorder are considered next.

Causal Factors in Psychopathy and Antisocial Personality

Contemporary research has variously stressed the causal roles of genetic factors, temperamental characteristics, deficiencies in fear and anxiety, more general emotional

Serial killer Ted Bundy exhibited antisocial behavior at its most extreme and dangerous. From January of 1974 through February of 1977, Bundy used his clean-cut image to get close to his victims—mainly young university women—whom he sexually assaulted and then savagely murdered. From all outward appearances, Bundy was a fine, upstanding citizen: He campaigned for the Republican party and for the Crime Commission in Washington State. He was also a rape counselor at a Seattle crisis center after being screened for "maturity and balance." Bundy's charm was so strong that he even received marriage proposals while sitting on death row. Bundy was executed in Florida in 1989 after confessing, without showing any remorse, to the murder of 28 women (some authorities estimate the number was probably closer to 40).

deficits, the early learning of antisocial behavior as a coping style, and the influence of particular family and environmental patterns. Because an antisocial person's impulsiveness, acting out, and intolerance of discipline and a psychopathic person's callous interpersonal traits tend to appear early in life, many investigators have focused on the role of early biological and environmental factors as causative agents in antisocial and psychopathic behaviors.

GENETIC INFLUENCES Most behavior genetic research has focused on genetic influences on criminality rather than on psychopathy per se. There have been many studies comparing concordance rates between monozygotic and dizygotic twins, as well as a number of studies using the adoption method, wherein rates of criminal behavior in the adopted-away children of criminals are compared with the rates of criminal behavior in the adopted-away children of normals. The results of both kinds of studies show a moderate heritability for antisocial or criminal behavior (Carey & Goldman, 1997; Sutker & Allain, 2001), and at least one study reached similar conclusions for psychopathy (Schulsinger, 1972). Moreover, twin studies of some of the personality traits that are elevated in psychopathy (e.g., callousness, conduct problems, and narcissism) show moderate heritabilities as well (Hare et al., 1999; Livesley et al., 1998). For example, a recent twin study of 3,687 twin pairs at age 7 found that the early signs of callous/unemotional traits in these children were highly heritable (Viding et al., 2005; see also Blonigen et al., 2005).

However, researchers also note that strong environmental influences (to be discussed later) interact with genetic predispositions (a *genotype-environment interaction*) to determine which individuals become criminals or antisocial personalities (Carey & Goldman, 1997; Moffitt, 2005b). Indeed, this must be the case given the dramatic increases in crime that have occurred in the United States and the United Kingdom since 1960, as well as the tenfold higher murder rate in the United States than in the United Kingdom (Rutter, 1996); such findings cannot be accounted for by genetic factors alone but must involve psychosocial or sociocultural causal factors.

One excellent study of Cadoret and colleagues (1995; see also Riggins-Caspers et al., 2003) found that adopted-away children of biological parents with ASPD were more likely to develop antisocial personalities if their adoptive parents exposed them to an adverse environment than if their adoptive parents exposed them to a more normal environment. Adverse environments were characterized by some of the following: marital conflict or divorce, legal problems, and parental psychopathology. Similar findings of a gene-environment interaction were also found in twins at high or low risk for conduct disorder (typically a childhood precursor of ASPD); in this study the environmental risk factor was physical maltreatment (Jaffee, Caspi, et al., 2005).

The most exciting recent study on gene-environment interactions and ASPD identified a candidate gene that seems to be very involved (Caspi, McClay, et al., 2002). The gene is known as the *monoamine oxidase-A gene (MAO-A gene)*, and it is involved in the breakdown of neurotransmitters like norepinephrine, dopamine, and serotonin—all neurotransmitters affected by maltreatment stress that can lead to aggressive behavior. In this study over a thousand children from New Zealand were followed from birth to age 26. Researchers found that individuals with low MAO-A activity were far more likely to develop ASPD if they had experienced early maltreatment than were individuals with high MAO-A activity and early maltreatment, and than individuals with low levels of MAO-A activity without early maltreatment. (See also Moffitt, 2005b.) Similar findings have been reported for conduct disorder (Foley et al., 2004).

The relationship between antisocial behavior and substance abuse is sufficiently strong that some have ques-

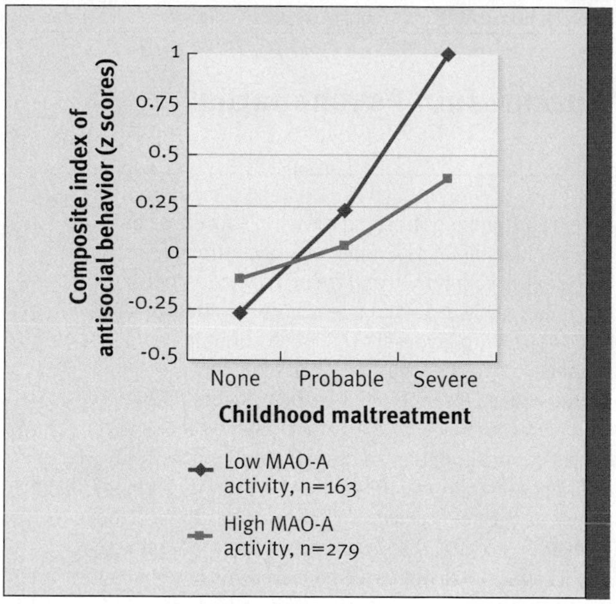

FIGURE 11.3

Means on the composite index of antisocial behavior as a function of high or low MAO-A gene activity and a childhood history of maltreatment.

Source: *Reprinted with permission from Caspi et al.,* Science *297:851–54 (2 Aug 2002). Copyright © 2002 AAAS.*

tioned whether there may be a common factor leading to both alcoholism and antisocial personality. Early studies of genetic factors involved in the predisposition to antisocial personality and to alcoholism were inconsistent (Carey & Goldman, 1997), but most recent research suggests that there is significant genetic involvement in their high level of comorbidity (e.g., Krueger et al., 2002; Slutske et al., 1998). Moreover, one recent study found that ASPD and other externalizing disorders (like alcohol and drug dependence and conduct disorder) all shared a strong common genetic vulnerability; environmental factors were more important in determining which disorder a particular person developed (Hicks, Krueger, et al., 2004).

THE LOW-FEAR HYPOTHESIS AND CONDITIONING Research evidence indicates that psychopaths who are high on the egocentric, callous, and exploitative dimension have low trait anxiety and show poor conditioning of fear (Lykken, 1995; Patrick, 2005a; Patrick & Lang, 1999). In an early classic study, for example, Lykken (1957) found that psychopaths showed deficient conditioning of skin conductance responses (reflecting activation of the sympathetic nervous system) when anticipating an unpleasant or painful event and that they were slow at learning to stop responding in order to avoid punishment. As a result, psychopaths presumably fail to acquire many of the conditioned reactions essential to normal passive avoidance of punishment, to conscience development, and to socialization (Trasler, 1978; see also Fowles & Dindo, 2005; Fowles & Kochanska, 2000). Hare aptly summarized work on this issue: "It is the emotionally charged thought, images, and internal dialogue that give the 'bite' to conscience, account for its powerful control over behavior, and generate guilt and remorse for transgressions. This is something that psychopaths cannot understand. For them conscience is little more than an intellectual awareness of rules others make up—empty words" (1998b, p. 112).

An impressive array of studies since the early work of Lykken has confirmed that psychopaths are deficient in the conditioning of at least subjective and certain physiological components of fear (e.g., Birbaumer et al., 2005; Flor et al., 2002; Fowles, 2001; Lykken, 1995), although they do learn that the CS predicts the US at a purely cognitive level (Birbaumer et al., 2005). Because such conditioning may underlie successful avoidance of punishment, this may also explain why their impulsive behavior goes unchecked. According to Fowles, the deficient conditioning of fear seems to stem from psychopaths' having a deficient *behavioral inhibition system* (Fowles, 1993, 2001; Fowles & Dindo, 2005; Hare et al., 1999). The behavioral inhibition system has been proposed by Gray (1987; Gray & McNaughton, 1996, 2000) to be the neural system underlying anxiety (Fowles, in press). It is also the neural system responsible for learning to inhibit responses to cues that signal punishment. In this *passive avoidance learning,* one learns to avoid punishment by not making a response (for example, by not committing robbery, one avoids punishment). Thus deficiencies in this neural system (currently identified as involving the septohippocampal system and the amygdala) are associated both with deficits in conditioning of anticipatory anxiety and, in turn, with deficits in learning to avoid punishment. Recent research suggests that "successful" psychopaths do not show these same deficits. This may be why they are successful at not getting caught, as discussed in The World Around Us 11.1 on page 402.

Other support for the low-fear hypothesis comes from work by Patrick and colleagues on the human startle response. Both humans and animals show a larger startle response if a startle probe stimulus (such as a loud noise) is presented when the subject is already in an anxious state (e.g., Patrick, Bradley, & Lang, 1993); this is known as *fear-potentiated startle.* Comparing psychopathic and nonpsychopathic prisoners, Patrick and colleagues found that the psychopaths did not show this effect, although the nonpsychopathic prisoners did. Indeed, the psychopaths showed smaller rather than larger startle responses when viewing unpleasant and pleasant slides than when watching neutral slides (see also Patrick, 1994; Sutton, Vitale, & Newman, 2002, for related results). These deficits in fear-potentiated startle responding are related only to the first, affective dimension of psychopathy (not to the second, antisocial dimension) (Patrick, 2005a).

The second important neural system in Gray's model is the *behavioral activation system.* This system activates

11.1 THE WORLD AROUND US

"Successful" Psychopaths

As already noted, most research on antisocial and psychopathic personalities has been conducted on institutionalized individuals, leaving us quite ignorant about the large number who stop short of criminal activity or who never get caught. Several early studies found the personality makeup of such individuals (as solicited from ads such as Widom's) to be very similar to that of institutionalized individuals. However, Widom (1978) also speculated that the "everyday," noncriminal psychopaths she had studied might well not show the same autonomic nervous system deficits that are typically seen in criminal psychopaths. Specifically, as noted earlier, criminal psychopaths typically show smaller skin conductance (sweaty palm) responses in anticipation of punishment than criminal nonpsychopaths, and several other studies showed that criminal psychopaths also showed lower cardiovascular (heart rate) reactivity during fear imagery or anticipation of punishment (e.g., Patrick et al., 1994; Arnett et al., 1993).

Several later studies provided tentative support for Widom's hypothesis that successful psychopaths would not show these deficits. One study, for example, showed that 15-year-old antisocial boys who later managed to avoid criminal convictions through age 29 showed increased autonomic arousal (heart rate and skin conductance) relative to 15-year-old antisocial boys who were later convicted of crimes (Raine, Venables, & Williams, 1995; see also Brennan et al., 1997). Recently, more direct support for Widom's hypothesis was provided by a study examining autonomic stress reactivity in successful and unsuccessful criminal psychopaths and control subjects, all living in the community and trying to find temporary employment (Ishiwaka, Raine, Lencz, et al., 2001). Each subject was told to give a short speech about his personal faults and weaknesses, during which time he was observed and videotaped. While subjects were preparing for and giving the speech, their heart rate was monitored. The results indicated that successful psychopaths (who had committed approximately the same number and type of crimes as the unsuccessful psychopaths, although they had never been caught) showed greater heart rate reactivity to this stressful task than did the controls or the unsuccessful psychopaths. Thus, just as Widom had predicted, the successful psychopaths did not show the reduced cardiovascular responsivity that the unsuccessful psychopaths exhibited when anticipating and experiencing a stressor. This is consistent with the idea that the increased cardiac reactivity of the successful psychopaths may serve them well in processing what is going on in risky situations and in making decisions that may prevent their being caught. Additional neuropsychological tests revealed that the successful psychopaths also showed superior "executive functioning" (higher-order cognitive processes such as planning, abstraction, cognitive flexibility, and decision making), which also probably enhances their ability to elude punishment. Clearly, more research is needed on this important group of successful psychopaths, who commit a great deal of crime but somehow manage to avoid being caught.

behavior in response to cues for reward (positive reinforcement), as well as to cues for *active avoidance* of threatened punishment (such as in lying or running away to avoid punishment that one has been threatened with). According to Fowles's theory, the behavioral activation system is thought to be normal or possibly overactive in psychopaths, which may explain why they are quite focused on obtaining reward. Moreover, if they are caught in a misdeed, they are very focused on actively avoiding threatened punishment (e.g., through deceit and lies, or running away). This hypothesis of Fowles that psychopaths have a deficient behavioral inhibition system and a normal or possibly overactive behavioral activation system seems to be able to account for three features of psychopathy: (1) psychopaths' deficient conditioning of anxiety to signals for punishment, (2) their difficulty learning to inhibit responses that may result in punishment (such as illegal and antisocial acts), and (3) their normal or hypernormal active avoidance of punishment (by deceit, lies, and escape behavior) when actively threatened with punishment (Fowles, 1993, p. 9; see also Hare, 1998b).

Newman and colleagues (e.g., Newman & Lorenz, 2003) have also conducted research suggesting that people with psychopathy have a dominant response set for reward. Their excessive focus on reward is thought to interfere with their ability to use punishment or other contextual cues or information to modulate (or modify) their responding when rewards are no longer forthcoming at the same rate that they once were. Moreover, Newman and colleagues believe that this response modulation deficit is more central to psychopathy than is a fear deficit (or even a general emotional deficit). A number of interesting studies they have conducted are consistent with their theory. However, there is still significant controversy over whether this response modulation deficit hypothesis can account for the wide array of findings in support of the low-fear (and other emotional deficit) hypothesis. Only future research will be able to resolve these controversies.

MORE GENERAL EMOTIONAL DEFICITS Researchers have also been interested in whether there are more general emotional deficits in psychopaths than simply deficits in the conditioning of anxiety (Fowles & Dindo, 2005; Hare et al., 1999; Patrick, 2005a). Psychopaths showed less significant physiological reactivity to distress cues (slides of people crying who are obviously quite distressed) than nonpsychopaths, a result consistent with the idea that they are low on empathy (Blair et al., 1997), in addition to being low on fear. However, they were not underresponsive to unconditioned threat cues such as slides of sharks, pointed guns, or angry faces. Consistent with this, Patrick and colleagues showed that this effect of smaller (rather than larger) startle responses when viewing unpleasant slides is especially pronounced with slides depicting scenes of victims who have been mutilated or assaulted, but not with slides representing threats to the self (aimed weapons or looming attackers; Levenston, Patrick, Bradley, & Lang, 2000). This specific failure to show larger startle responses with victim scenes might be related to the lack of empathy common in psychopathy (e.g., Blair et al., 1997).

Hare has hypothesized that the kinds of emotional deficits discussed so far are only a subset of more general difficulties that psychopaths have with processing and understanding the meaning of affective stimuli including positive and negative words and sounds (e.g., Lorenz & Newman, 2002; Verona et al., 2004; Williamson et al., 1991). Hare summarized work in this area as follows: "Psychopaths . . . seem to have difficulty in fully understanding and using words that for normal people refer to ordinary emotional events and feelings. . . . It is as if emotion is a second language for psychopaths, a language that requires a considerable amount of . . . cognitive effort on their part" (1998b, p. 115). One study using fMRI brain-imaging techniques showed that these emotional deficits may be related to reduced brain activity in the limbic area of the brain, which is prominently involved in affect-related processing (Kiehl, Smith, Hare, et al., 2001).

EARLY PARENTAL LOSS, PARENTAL REJECTION, AND INCONSISTENCY In addition to genetic factors and emotional deficits, slow conscience development and aggression are influenced by the damaging effects of parental rejection, abuse, and neglect, accompanied by inconsistent discipline (e.g., Luntz & Widom, 1994). However, studies of gene-environment interactions reviewed earlier clearly indicate that these kinds of disturbances are not sufficient explanations for the origins of psychopathy or antisocial personality. Moreover, these same conditions have been implicated in a wide range of later maladaptive behaviors. In the following section, we present an integrated developmental perspective using a biopsychosocial approach with multiple interacting causal pathways.

A Developmental Perspective on Psychopathy and Antisocial Personality

It has long been known that these disorders generally begin early in childhood, especially for boys, and that the number of antisocial behaviors exhibited in childhood is the single best predictor of who develops an adult diagnosis of ASPD, and the younger they start, the higher the risk (Robins, 1978, 1991). These early antisocial symptoms are today associated with a diagnosis of conduct disorder (see Chapter 16) and include theft, truancy, running away from home, and associating with delinquent peers. But what causes these early antisocial symptoms in some children?

Prospective studies have shown that it is children with an early history of *oppositional defiant disorder*—characterized by a pattern of hostile and defiant behavior toward authority figures that usually begins by the age of 6 years, followed by early onset conduct disorder around age 9—who are most likely to develop ASPD as adults (e.g., Lahey et al., 2005). For these children, the types of antisocial

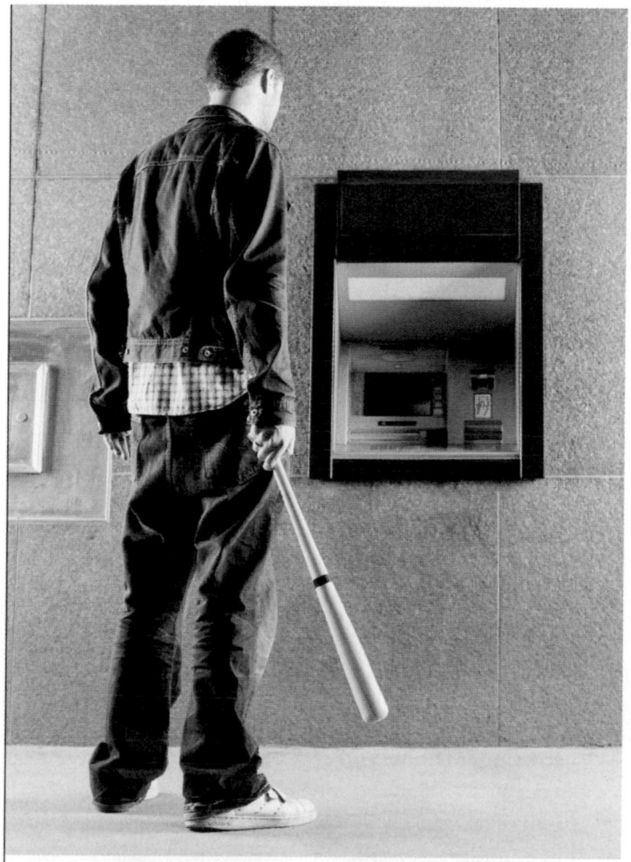

Children and adolescents who show persistent patterns of aggression toward people or animals, destruction of property, deceitfulness or theft, and serious violation of rules at home or in school may be at risk for developing conduct disorder and antisocial personality disorder.

behaviors exhibited across the first 25 years of life change a great deal with development but are persistent in nature (Hinshaw, 1994). By contrast, children without the pathological background who develop conduct disorder in adolescence do not usually become lifelong antisocial personalities but instead have problems largely limited to the adolescent years (Moffitt, 1993a; Moffitt & Caspi, 2001; Patterson & Yoerger, 2002).

The second early diagnosis that is often a precursor to adult psychopathy or ASPD is *attention-deficit/hyperactivity disorder* (ADHD). ADHD is characterized by restless, inattentive, and impulsive behavior, a short attention span, and high distractibility (see Chapter 16). When ADHD occurs with conduct disorder (which happens in at least 30 to 50 percent of cases), this leads to a high likelihood that the person will develop ASPD, and possibly psychopathy (Abramowitz, Kosson, & Seidenberg, 2004; Lahey et al., 2005; Lynam, 1996; Patterson et al., 2000). Indeed, Lynam (1996, 1997, 2002) has referred to children with ADHD and conduct disorder as "fledgling psychopaths," and several ways of assessing psychopathy in youth have been developed, with the Psychopathy Checklist—Youth Version (Forth, Kosson, & Hare, 2003) being perhaps the best validated (Salekin et al., 2004).

There is increasing evidence that genetic propensities to mild neuropsychological problems such as those leading to hyperactivity or attentional difficulties, along with a difficult temperament, may be important predisposing factors for early onset conduct disorder, which often leads to life-course persistent adult ASPD. The behavioral problems that these predisposing factors create have a cascade of pervasive effects over time. For example, on the basis of extensive longitudinal prospective research, Moffitt, Caspi, and colleagues (2002) have suggested that

> "Life-course-persistent" antisocial behavior originates early in life, when the difficult behavior of a high-risk young child is exacerbated by a high-risk social environment. According to the theory, the child's risk emerges from inherited or acquired neuropsychological variation, initially manifested as subtle cognitive deficits, difficult temperament, or hyperactivity. The environment's risk comprises factors such as inadequate parenting, disrupted family bonds, and poverty. The environmental risk domain expands beyond the family as the child ages, to include poor relations with people such as peers and teachers, then later with partners and employers. Over the first 2 decades of development, transactions between individual and environment gradually construct a disordered personality with hallmark features of physical aggression, and antisocial behavior persisting to midlife. (p. 180)

Many other psychosocial and sociocultural contextual variables contribute to the probability that a child with the genetic or constitutional liabilities discussed above will develop conduct disorder and later ASPD. As summarized by Patterson and colleagues (Dishion & Patterson, 1997; Reid, Patterson, & Snyder, 2002) and by Dodge and Petit (2003), these include: parents' own antisocial behaviors, divorce and other parental transitions, poverty and crowded inner-city neighborhoods, and parental stress. All of these contribute to poor and ineffective parenting skills—especially ineffective discipline, monitoring, and supervision. Moreover, antisocial behavior involving coercive interchanges trains children in these behaviors. This in turn all too often leads to association with deviant and aggressive peers and to the opportunity for further learning of antisocial behavior (Capaldi et al , 2002; Dodge & Petit, 2003). A general mediational model for how all this occurs is shown in Figure 11.4.

Until fairly recently it was not apparent how this integrated model applied to the development of the traits and behaviors representing the affective-interpersonal core of psychopathy. In the past decade, Frick and colleagues have developed a way of assessing children's callous and unemotional traits that seem to represent early manifestations of this first dimension of psychopathy observed (e.g., Frick & Morris, 2004; Frick et al., 2003). They have noted that there are at least two different dimensions of children's difficult temperament that seem to lead to different developmental outcomes. Some children have great difficulty learning to regulate their emotions and show high levels of emotional reactivity including aggressive and antisocial behaviors when responding to stressful demands and negative emotions like frustration and anger. Such children are at increased risk for developing ASPD and high scores on the antisocial dimension of psychopathy. But other children may have few problems regulating negative emotions, instead showing fearlessness and low anxiety, as well as callous/unemotional traits. These are the children most likely to show poor development of conscience, and their aggressive behaviors are more instrumental and premeditated rather than reactive as seen with those with emotional regulation difficulties. These latter children are likely to develop high scores on the first interpersonal affective core of psychopathy, leading to the cold, remorseless psychopaths described earlier by Hare (1998b), who show low fear and lack of empathy (Fowles & Dindo, 2005).

SOCIOCULTURAL CAUSAL FACTORS AND PSYCHOPATHY Cross-cultural research by Murphy on psychopathy reveals that it occurs in a wide range of cultures including nonindustrialized ones as diverse as the Inuit of northwest Alaska and the Yorubas of Nigeria. The Yorubas' concept of a psychopath is "a person who always goes his own way regardless of others, who is uncooperative, full of malice, and bullheaded," and the Inuit's concept is of someone whose "mind knows what to do but he does not do it.... This is an abstract term for the breaking of the many rules when awareness of the rules is not in question" (Murphy, 1976, p. 1026, cited in Cooke, 1996, p. 23). Nevertheless, the exact manifestations of the disorder are influenced by

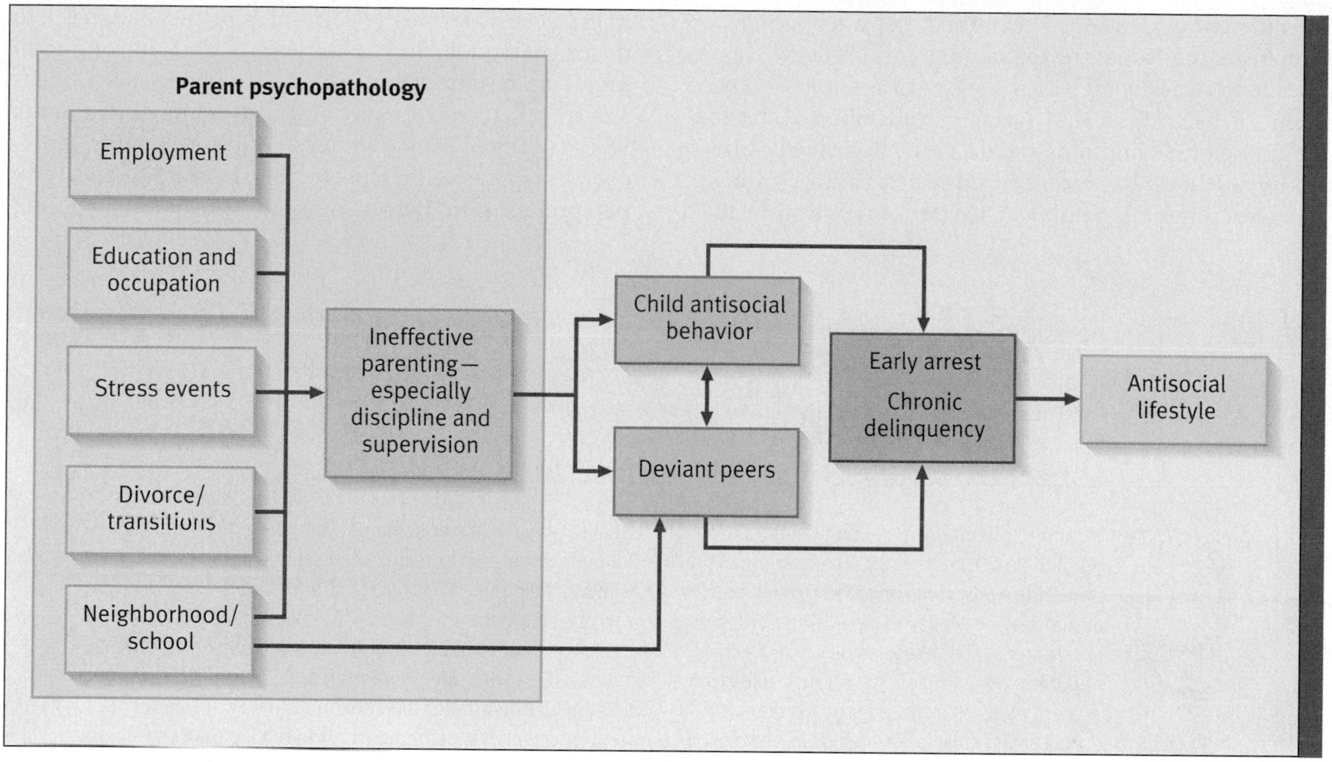

FIGURE 11.4

A model for the association of family context and antisocial behavior. Each of the contextual variables in this model has been shown to be related to antisocial behavior in boys, which in turn is related to antisocial behavior in adults. Antisocial behavior in girls is far less common and has also been found to be less stable over time, making it more difficult to predict (Capaldi & Patterson, 1994).

cultural factors. Moreover, the prevalence of the disorder also seems to vary with sociocultural influences that encourage or discourage its development (Cooke & Michie, 1999; Cooke et al., 2005; Hare et al., 1999).

Regarding different cross-cultural manifestations of the disorder, one of the primary symptoms where cultural variations occur is the frequency of aggressive and violent behavior. Socialization forces have an enormous impact on the expression of aggressive impulses. Thus it is not surprising that in some cultures, such as China, psychopaths may be much less likely to engage in aggressive, especially violent behavior than they are in most Western cultures (Cooke, 1996).

Moreover, cultures can be classified along a dimension distinguishing between individualistic and collectivist societies. Competitiveness, self-confidence, and independence from others are emphasized in relatively individualistic societies, whereas contributions and subservience to the social group, acceptance of authority, and stability of relationships are encouraged in relatively collectivist societies (Cooke, 1996; Cooke & Michie, 1999). Thus we would expect individualistic societies (such as in the United States) to be more likely to promote some of the behavioral characteristics that, carried to the extreme, result in psychopathy. These characteristics include "grandiosity, glibness and superficiality, promiscuity... as well as a lack of responsibility for others.... The competitiveness... not only produces higher rates of criminal behavior but also leads to an increased use of... deceptive, manipulative, and parasitic behavior" (Cooke & Michie, 1999, p. 65). Although the evidence bearing on this is minimal, it is interesting to note that estimates of the prevalence of ASPD are much lower in Taiwan, a relatively collectivist society, than in the United States (approximately 0.1 to 0.2 percent versus 1.5 to 5 percent).

Treatments and Outcomes in Psychopathic and Antisocial Personality

Most people with psychopathic and antisocial personalities do not suffer from much personal distress and do not believe they need treatment. Those who run afoul of the law may participate in rehabilitation programs in penal institutions, but they are rarely changed by them. Even when more and better therapeutic facilities are available, effective treatment will still be a challenging task, and many clinical researchers working with these populations have concluded that these disorders are extraordinarily difficult, if not impossible, to treat at this time (e.g., Hare et al., 1999). However, one review by Salekin and colleagues (2002) of several dozen treatment studies came to a different conclusion. They found that a few studies of intensive individual treatment programs (as many as four sessions a week for at least a year) led to as many as 60 percent of individuals showing significant improvement in psychopathic symptoms and decreases in recidivism (relative to about 20 percent in untreated control groups). However, there is reason to temper any optimism that might stem from this review; most of these studies had major methodological shortcomings and no long-term follow-up results were reported. In addition, such intensive treatment is not really practical to implement in the vast majority of people with ASPD or psychopathy. Moreover, less intensive therapeutic communities often run by paraprofessionals (which are more widely available) did

11.2 Developments in Practice

Prevention of Psychopathy and Antisocial Personality Disorder

Given the difficulties in treating conduct disorder and ASPD, there is an increasing focus on prevention programs oriented toward both minimizing some of the developmental and environmental risk factors described earlier and breaking some of the vicious cycles that at-risk children seem to get into. Intelligence is one naturally occurring protective factor for some adolescents who are at risk for psychopathy or antisocial personality in adulthood (Hawkins, Arthur, & Olson, 1997). For example, several studies found that many adolescents with conduct disorder never get involved in criminal behavior because they are positively influenced by schooling and focus their energies on more socially accepted behaviors (e.g., White, Moffitt, & Silva, 1989). Of course, not all at-risk adolescents have high intelligence, and these children may benefit from more structured prevention programs. The early results of such prevention efforts seem promising, but it will be many years before we understand their true potential for preventing adult psychopathy and antisocial personality disorder.

Given the life-course developmental model for the etiology of ASPD, devising prevention strategies becomes very complex, because many different stages present targets for preventive interventions (e.g., Dodge & Petit, 2003). Some interventions that have been shown to help are aimed at mothers estimated to be at high risk (poor, first-time, and single mothers) for producing children who could be at risk and include prenatal care aimed at improving maternal nutrition, decreasing smoking and other substance use, and improving parenting skills (Olds et al., 1986, 1994; Reid & Eddy, 1997).

For young children, Patterson, Dishion, Reid, and colleagues have developed programs that target the family environment and teach effective parental discipline and supervision (e.g., Dishion & Kavanaugh, 2002; Reid, Patterson, & Snyder 2002). At-risk children whose families receive such interventions do better academically, are less likely to associate with delinquent peers, and are less likely to get involved in drug use. Such family or parent training can even be effective at reducing or preventing further antisocial behavior in children and adolescents already engaged in antisocial behavior, although conducting the intervention with pre-elementary school children was more effective and less labor-intensive (see Reid & Eddy, 1997, for a review). In general, the earlier the prevention and intervention efforts are started, the greater the likelihood that they might succeed. However, it is also important to realize that any single intervention is unlikely to be successful because there are so many different kinds of forces that influence at-risk children throughout their development (Dodge & Pettit, 2003).

Some significant advances have also been made in prevention programs targeting the school environment or the school and family environments concurrently. One especially promising ongoing multisite intervention study of this sort is called the FAST Track (Families and Schools Together) intervention. Kindergarten students starting in 1990 who attended schools associated with high risk (generally those that serve inner-city and poor neighborhoods) and who already showed poor peer relations and high levels of disruptive behavior were recruited for this intensive program, which included parent training and school interventions. There was a focus on interpersonal problem-solving skills, emotional awareness, and self-control. Teachers and parents were taught how to manage disruptive behavior, and parents were informed of what their children were being taught. Early results through the third grade were quite promising in terms of reducing later conduct problems (Conduct Problems Prevention Research Group, 1999, 2002; see also Lochman et al., 2003). Parenting behavior and children's social cognitive skills also showed significant improvement. Children in FAST Track were also less likely to be nominated by peers as aggressive, and they tended to be better liked and to show better reading skills (Coie, 1996; Reid & Eddy, 1997). Although such interventions are expensive, if they can prevent (or at least dramatically reduce) the extremely costly effects on society of these children developing full-blown adult ASPD or psychopathy, the long-term benefits will outweigh the initial costs.

not show significantly more improvement than untreated control groups (Salekin et al., 2002).

Biological treatment approaches for antisocial and psychopathic personalities—including electroconvulsive therapy and drugs—have not been widely studied in a systematic way, partly because the few results that have been reported suggest modest changes at best. Drugs such as lithium and carbazemine used to treat bipolar disorder have had some success in treating the aggressive/impulsive behavior of violent aggressive criminals, but evidence on this is scanty (Lösel, 1998; Markovitz, 2001). There have also been some tentative but promising results using antidepressants from the SSRI category, which can sometimes reduce aggressive/impulsive behavior and increase interpersonal skills (Lösel, 1998). However, none of these biological treatments has any substantial impact on the disorder as a whole. Moreover, even if effective pharmacological treatments were found, the problem of these individuals generally having little motivation to take their medications would remain (Markowitz, 2001).

COGNITIVE-BEHAVIORAL TREATMENTS Cognitive-behavioral treatments are often thought to offer the greatest promise of more effective treatment (Lösel, 1998; Piper & Joyce, 2001; Rice & Harris, 1997). Common targets of cognitive-behavioral interventions include the following: (1) increasing self-control, self-critical thinking, and social perspective-taking; (2) increasing victim awareness; (3) teaching anger management; (4) changing antisocial attitudes; (5) curing drug addiction. Such interventions require a controlled situation in which the therapist can administer or withhold reinforcement and the individual cannot leave treatment (such as an inpatient or prison setting), because when treating antisocial behavior, we are dealing with a total lifestyle rather than with a few specific maladaptive behaviors (e.g., Piper & Joyce, 2001). For reasons discussed earlier, punishment by itself is ineffective for changing antisocial behavior.

Beck and Freeman's (1990; see also Beck et al., 2003) cognitive treatment for personality disorders also offers an interesting approach that can be incorporated into the treatment of antisocial personality disorder. It focuses on improving social and moral behavior by examining self-serving dysfunctional beliefs that psychopaths tend to have. These beliefs include, "Wanting something or wanting to avoid something justifies my actions" or "The views of others are irrelevant to my decisions, unless they directly control my immediate consequences" (Beck & Freeman, 1990, p. 154; Beck et al., 2003). In cognitive therapy, the therapist, using principles based on theories of moral and cognitive development, tries to guide the patient toward higher and more abstract kinds of thinking. This is done through guided discussions, structured cognitive exercises, and behavioral experiments.

Even the best of these multifaceted cognitive-behaviorally oriented treatment programs generally produce only modest changes, although they are somewhat more effective in treating young offenders (teenagers) than older offenders, who are often hard-core, lifelong psychopaths. In addition, some evidence suggests that psychopathy is more difficult to treat than antisocial personality disorder (Lösel, 1998; Rice & Harris, 1997). Clearly, research on developing effective treatments for these disorders is still in its very early stages.

Fortunately, the criminal activities of many psychopathic and antisocial personalities decline after the age of 40 even without treatment, possibly because of weaker biological drives, better insight into self-defeating behaviors, and the cumulative effects of social conditioning. Such individuals are often referred to as "burned-out psychopaths." For example, one important study that followed a group of male psychopaths over many years found a clear and dramatic reduction in levels of criminal behavior after age 40. However, over 50 percent of these people continued to be arrested after age 40 (Hare, McPherson, & Forth, 1988). Moreover, it is only the antisocial behavioral dimension of psychopathy that diminishes with age; the egocentric, callous, and exploitative affective and interpersonal dimension persists (Cloninger et al., 1997; Hare et al., 1999).

In view of the distress and unhappiness that psychopaths inflict on others and the social damage they cause, it seems desirable—and more economical in the long run—to put increased effort into the development of effective prevention programs. Longitudinal prevention research on children at risk for conduct disorder is discussed in Developments in Practice 11.2.

In Review

- List the three DSM criteria that must be met before an individual is diagnosed with antisocial personality disorder, and cite the additional personality traits that define psychopathy.
- What are several reasons why many researchers believe psychopathy is a more valid construct than antisocial personality disorder?
- What biological factors contribute to these disorders?
- What are the primary features of today's developmental perspective on these disorders?

Unresolved Issues

Axis II of DSM-IV-TR

While reading this chapter and focusing primarily on the categorical diagnostic system of DSM-IV-TR, you may have had some difficulty in capturing a clear, distinctive picture of each of the personality disorders. It is quite likely that as you studied the descriptions of the different disorders, the characteristics and attributes of some of them, say, the schizoid personality disorder, seemed to blend with other conditions, such as the schizotypal or the avoidant personality disorders. Although we attempted to highlight the apparent differences between prototypic cases of the different personality disorders with the greatest potential for overlap, patients usually do not fit these prototypes neatly and instead qualify for a diagnosis of more than one personality disorder (e.g., Grant et al., 2005; Widiger et al., 1991). Indeed, some studies have found that patients were given an average of four or more personality disorder diagnoses (Shea, 1995; Skodol et al., 1991). In addition, one of the most common diagnoses is the grab-bag category of "Personality disorder not otherwise specified" (e.g., Livesley, 2001; Verheul & Widiger, 2004); this category is reserved for persons who exhibit features from several different categories but do not cleanly fit within any of them.

A second major difficulty with the unreliability of Axis II diagnoses stems from the assumption in DSM-IV-TR that we can make a clear distinction between the presence and the absence of a personality disorder (Livesley, 1995, 2001; Widiger, 2005). As noted earlier, the personality processes classified on Axis II are dimensional in nature. For example, everyone is suspicious at times, but the degree to which this trait exists in someone with paranoid personality disorder is extreme. Suspiciousness can be viewed as a personality dimension on which essentially all people can be rated or given scores. On a hypothetical "scale of suspiciousness," the scores might range as follows:

Extremely Low		Low		Average		High		Extremely High		
0	10	20	30	40	50	60	70	80	90	100

Many studies have been conducted in an effort to find discrete breaks in such personality dimensions—that is, points at which normal behavior becomes clearly distinct from pathological behavior—and none have been found (Livesley, 2001; Widiger & Sanderson, 1995). Indeed, Livesley summarized the issue by stating that "the features of personality disorder whether described using diagnostic criteria or traits in patient or nonpatient samples are continuous, and . . . it is not possible to identify a discontinuity in the distributions of the kind that would support categorical diagnoses" (2001, pp. 18–19). Moreover, changes in the cut-points, or thresholds for diagnosis of a personality disorder, can have drastic effects on the apparent prevalence rates of a particular personality disorder diagnosis. For example, changes made when DSM-III was revised to DSM-III-R resulted in "an 800 percent increase in the rate of schizoid personality disorder and a 350 percent increase in narcissistic personality disorder" (Morey, 1988, p. 575).

A third problem inherent in Axis II classifications is that there are enormous differences in the kinds of symptoms that people can have who nevertheless are assigned the same diagnosis (e.g., Clark, 1992; Widiger & Sanderson, 1995). For example, to obtain a DSM-IV-TR diagnosis of borderline personality disorder, a person has to meet five out of nine possible symptom criteria. This means that there are 126 different ways (through different combinations of symptoms) to meet the DSM-IV-TR criteria for borderline personality disorder (Trull & Durrett, 2005; see also Widiger & Sanderson, 1995). Moreover, two people with the same diagnosis might share only one symptom. For example, one person might meet criteria 1–5, and a second person might meet criteria 5–9. By contrast, a third individual who met only criteria 1–4 would obtain no borderline personality diagnosis at all, yet surely that individual would be more similar to the first person than the first two people would be to each other.

In spite of all these problems with Axis II classification, researchers and clinicians usually agree that the developers of DSM-III made a crucial theoretical leap when they recognized the importance of weighing premorbid personality factors in the clinical picture and thus developed the second axis (Widiger, 2001). Use of the Axis II concepts can lead to a better understanding of a case, particularly with regard to treatment outcomes. Strong, ingrained personality characteristics can work against treatment interventions. The use of Axis II can help a clinician to attend to these long-standing and difficult-to-change personality factors in planning treatment.

What can be done to address the difficulties with Axis II? As noted earlier, many researchers feel that the psychiatric community should give up on the categorical approach to classification in favor of a dimensional approach and rating methods that would take into account the relative "amounts" of the primary traits shown by patients (e.g., Clark & Harrison, 2001; Livesley, 2001, 2005; Widiger, 2001, 2005). Some of the resistance to the dimensional approach to classification stems from the fact that medically oriented practitioners have a pronounced preference for categorical diagnosis. Moreover, there are fears that the dimensional approach to personality measurement might not be accepted because sound quantitative ratings might demand far too much time for most busy clinicians both to learn and to apply. Nevertheless, reviews of the evidence show that many clinicians are unhappy with the current categorical system, which is cumbersome when used properly because of the need to assess nearly 80 diagnostic criteria for DSM-IV-TR personality disorders (Widiger & Sanderson, 1995). Indeed, Widiger has argued persuasively that the use of a dimensional model may require less time because it would reduce the redundancy and overlap that currently exists across the categories. As one example, the five-factor model briefly described earlier in the chapter describes most of the many varied features of personality disorders using the five primary dimensions of personality traits, along with each of their six facets. Moreover, a dimensional model clearly helps make sense out of the patterns of comorbidity we have noted that stem from overlapping personality traits and facets (see Table 11.2).

In sum, the ultimate status of Axis II in future editions of the DSM is uncertain. Many problems inherent in using diagnostic categories for essentially dimensional behavior (traits) have yet to be resolved, although they are now almost universally recognized. One of the primary reasons why dimensional models have not yet replaced categorical models is that 18 different dimensional systems have been proposed, and there is still no clear evidence as to which one is best (e.g., Clark & Harrison, 2001; Livesley, 2001, 2005; Widiger, 2001). Fortunately, efforts are underway to try to integrate many of these different systems into one comprehensive framework (e.g., Markon, Krueger, & Watson, 2005; Widiger & Simonsen, 2005).

summary

- Personality disorders appear to be inflexible and distorted behavioral patterns and traits that result in maladaptive ways of perceiving, thinking about, and relating to other people and the environment.
- Even with structured interviews, the reliability of diagnosing personality disorders typically is less than ideal. Most researchers agree that a dimensional approach for assessing personality disorders would be preferable.
- It is difficult to determine the causes of personality disorders because most people with one personality disorder also have at least one more and because most studies to date are retrospective.

Three general clusters of personality disorders have been described in DSM:

- Cluster A includes paranoid, schizoid, and schizotypal personality disorders; individuals with these disorders seem odd or eccentric. Little is known about the causes of paranoid and schizoid disorders, but genetic and other biological factors are implicated in schizotypal personality disorder.
- Cluster B includes histrionic, narcissistic, antisocial, and borderline personality disorders; individuals with these disorders share a tendency to be dramatic, emotional, and erratic. Little is known about the causes of histrionic and narcissistic disorders. Certain biological and psychosocial causal factors have been identified as increasing the likelihood of developing borderline personality disorder in those at risk because of high levels of impulsivity and affective instability.
- Cluster C includes avoidant, dependent, and obsessive-compulsive personality disorders; individuals with these disorders show fearfulness or tension, as in anxiety-based disorders. Children with an inhibited temperament may be at heightened risk for avoidant personality disorder, and individuals high on neuroticism and agreeableness, with authoritarian and overprotective parents, may be at heightened risk for dependent personality disorder.
- There is relatively little research on treatments for most personality disorders.
  - Treatment of the Cluster C disorders seems most promising, and treatment of Cluster A disorders is most difficult.
  - A new form of behavior therapy (dialectical behavior therapy) shows considerable promise for treating borderline personality disorder, which is in Cluster B.
- A person with psychopathy is callous and unethical, without loyalty or close relationships, but often with superficial charm and intelligence. Individuals with a diagnosis of ASPD (and often psychopathy) engage in an antisocial, impulsive, and socially deviant lifestyle.
  - Genetic and temperamental, learning, and adverse environmental factors seem to be important in causing psychopathy and ASPD.
  - Psychopaths also show deficiencies in fear and anxiety as well as more general emotional deficits.
  - Treatment of individuals with psychopathy is difficult, partly because they rarely see any need to change and tend to blame other people for their problems.

Key Terms

antisocial personality disorder (ASPD) (p. 384)

avoidant personality disorder (p. 388)

borderline personality disorder (BPD) (p. 385)

dependent personality disorder (p. 390)

depressive personality disorder (p. 392)

histrionic personality disorder (p. 380)

narcissistic personality disorder (p. 382)

obsessive-compulsive personality disorder (OCPD) (p. 391)

paranoid personality disorder (p. 376)

passive-aggressive personality disorder (p. 392)

personality disorder (p. 373)

psychopathy (p. 395)

schizoid personality disorder (p. 377)

schizotypal personality disorder (p. 379)

chapter

12

Addiction Disorders

The increasing problem of substance abuse and dependence in our society has drawn both public and scientific attention. Although our present knowledge is far from complete, investigating these problems as maladaptive patterns of adjustment to life's demands, with no social stigma involved, has led to clear progress in understanding and treatment. Such an approach, of course, does not mean that an individual bears no personal responsibility in the development of a problem. Individual lifestyles and personality features are thought by many to play important roles in the development of addictive disorders and are central themes in some types of treatment.

Addictive behavior—behavior based on the pathological need for a substance or activity—may involve the abuse of substances such as nicotine, alcohol, or cocaine. Addictive behavior is one of the most pervasive and intransigent mental health problems facing our society today. Addictive disorders can be seen all around us: in extremely high rates of alcohol abuse and dependence, in tragic exposés of cocaine abuse among star athletes and entertainers, and in reports of pathological gambling, which has increased with the widening opportunity for legalized gambling today.

The most commonly used problem substances are those drugs that affect mental functioning, or **psychoactive drugs:** alcohol, nicotine, barbiturates, tranquilizers, amphetamines, heroin, ecstasy, and marijuana. Some of these drugs, such as alcohol and nicotine, can be purchased legally by adults; others, such as the barbiturates or pain killers, can be used legally under medical supervision; still others, such as heroin, ecstasy, and methamphetamine, are illegal.

For diagnostic purposes, addictive or substance-related disorders are divided into two major categories. The first category includes those conditions that involve organic impairment resulting from the prolonged and excessive ingestion of psychoactive substances—for example, an alcohol-abuse dementia disorder involving amnesia, formerly known as "Korsakoff's syndrome." The other category comprises substance-induced organic mental disorders and syndromes (the latter of which are included within the organic mental disorders). These conditions stem from **toxicity,** the poisonous nature of the substance (leading to, for example, amphetamine delusional disorder, alcoholic intoxication, or cannabis delirium), or physiological changes in the brain due to vitamin deficiency.

The majority of addictive disorders fall into the second category, which focuses on the maladaptive behaviors resulting from regular and consistent use of a substance and includes substance-abuse disorders and substance-dependence disorders. The system of classification for substance-abuse disorders that is followed by both DSM-IV-TR and ICD-10 (International Classification of Disease System, published by the World Health Organization) provides two major categories: substance-dependence disorders and substance-abuse disorders. Although some researchers and clinicians disagree with the dichotomous grouping, others consider this classification approach to have both research and clinical utility (Epstein, 2001).

Substance abuse generally involves a pathological use of a substance resulting in (1) potentially hazardous behavior such as driving while intoxicated, or (2) continued use despite a persistent social, psychological, occupational, or health problem. **Substance dependence** includes more severe forms of substance-use disorders and usually involves a marked physiological need for increasing amounts of a substance to achieve the desired effects. Dependence in these disorders means that an individual will show a tolerance for a drug and/or experience withdrawal symptoms when the drug is unavailable. **Tolerance**—the need for increased amounts of a substance to achieve the desired effects—results from biochemical changes in the body that affect the rate of metabolism and elimination of the substance from the body. **Withdrawal symptoms** are physical symptoms such as sweating, tremors, and tension that accompany abstinence from the drug.

Alcohol Abuse and Dependence

The terms alcoholic and **alcoholism** have been subject to some controversy and have been used differently by various groups in the past. The World Health Organization no longer recommends the term *alcoholism* but prefers the term *alcohol dependence syndrome*—"a state, psychic and usually also physical, resulting from taking alcohol, characterized by behavioral and other responses that always include a compulsion to take alcohol on a continuous or periodic basis in order to experience its psychic effects, and sometimes to avoid the discomfort of its absence; tolerance may or may not be present" (1992, p. 4). However, because the terms "alcoholic" and "alcoholism" are still widely used in practice, in scientific journals, and in government agencies and publications, we will sometimes use them in this book.

People of many ancient cultures, including the Egyptian, Greek, and Roman, made extensive and often excessive use of alcohol. Beer was first made in Egypt around 3000 B.C. The oldest surviving wine-making formulas were recorded by Marcus Cato in Italy almost a century and a half before the birth of Christ. About A.D. 800, the process of distillation was developed by an Arabian alchemist, thus making possible an increase in both the range and the potency of alcoholic beverages. Problems with excessive use of alcohol were observed almost as early as its use began. Cambyses, King of Persia in the sixth century B.C., has the dubious distinction of being one of the first alcoholic abusers on record.

The Prevalence, Comorbidity, and Demographics of Alcohol Abuse and Dependence

Alcohol abuse and dependence are major problems in the United States and are among the most destructive of the psychiatric disorders (Volpicelli, 2001). In 2003, 22.6 percent of Americans 12 or older reported binge drinking, and 6.8 percent were found to be heavy drinkers (Substance Abuse and Mental Health Services Administration, 2004). In the recent National Comorbidity Survey-Replication study, the lifetime prevalence for alcohol abuse in the United States is 13.4 percent (Kessler, Chiu, et al., 2005).

The potentially detrimental effects of excessive alcohol use—for an individual, his or her loved ones, and society—are legion. Heavy drinking is associated with vulnerability to injury (Shepherd & Brickley, 1996) and becoming involved in intimate partner violence (O'Leary & Schumacher, 2003). The life span of the average person with alcohol dependence is about 12 years shorter than that of the average person without this disorder. Alcohol significantly lowers performance on cognitive tasks such as problem solving—and the more complex the task, the more the impairment (Pickworth, Rohrer, & Fant, 1997). Organic impairment, including brain shrinkage, occurs in a high proportion of people with alcohol dependence (Gazdzinski, Durazzo, & Meyerhoff, 2005; Harper, Dixon, et al., 2003), especially among binge drinkers—people who abuse alcohol following periods of sobriety (Hunt, 1993).

Over 37 percent of alcohol abusers suffer from at least one coexisting mental disorder (Lapham, Smith, et al., 2001). Not surprisingly, given that alcohol is a depressant, depression ranks high among the mental disorders often comorbid with alcoholism. It is no surprise that many alcoholics commit suicide (Hufford, 2001; McCloud, Barnaby, et al., 2004). In addition to the serious problems that excessive drinkers create for themselves, they also pose serious difficulties for others (Gortner et al., 1997). Alcohol abuse also co-occurs with high frequency with personality disorder. Grant, Stinson, et al. (2004) reported that among individuals with a current alcohol-use disorder, 28.6 percent had at least one personality disorder.

Alcohol abuse is associated with over half the deaths and major injuries suffered in automobile accidents each year (Brewer, Morris, et al., 1994) and with about 40 to 50 percent of all murders (Bennett & Lehman, 1996), 40 percent of all assaults, and over 50 percent of all rapes (Abbey, Zawacki, et al., 2001). About one of every three arrests in the United States is related to alcohol abuse, and over 43 percent of violent encounters with the police involve alcohol (McClelland & Teplin, 2001). In a study of substance abuse and violent crime, Dawkins (1997) found that alcohol is more frequently associated with both violent and nonviolent crime than other drugs such as marijuana and that people with violence-related injuries are more likely to have a positive Breathalyzer test (Cherpitel, 1997). An estimated 13.6 percent of people 12 or older drove under the influence of alcohol in the past year (Substance Abuse and Mental Health Services Administration, 2004).

Alcohol abuse and dependence in the United States cuts across all age, educational, occupational, and socioeconomic boundaries. One recent study reported that in 2001, there were an estimated 244,331 alcohol-related visits to an emergency room among people ages 13 to 25. Of these, an estimated 119,503 involved people below the legal drinking age of 21 (Elder, Shults, et al., 2004). However, alcohol abuse is considered a serious problem in industry, in the professions, and in the military as well; alcohol abuse is found among such seemingly unlikely candidates as priests, politicians, surgeons, law enforcement officers, and teenagers. The image of the alcohol-dependent person as an unkempt resident of skid row is clearly inaccurate. Further myths about alcoholism are noted in Table 12.1 on page 415.

Alcohol is associated with over half of the deaths and serious injuries suffered in automobile accidents in the United States each year.

The Clinical Picture of Alcohol Abuse and Dependence

Exactly how alcohol works on the brain is only beginning to be understood, but several physiological effects are common. The first is a tendency toward decreased sexual inhibition but, simultaneously, lowered sexual performance. An appreciable number of alcohol abusers also experience blackouts—lapses of memory. At first these occur at high blood alcohol levels, and a drinker may carry on a rational conversation or engage in other relatively complex activities but have no trace of recall the next day. For heavy drinkers, even moderate drinking can elicit memory lapses. Another phenomenon associated with alcoholic intoxication is the hangover, which many drinkers experience at one time or another. As yet, no one has come up with a satisfactory explanation of or remedy for the symptoms of headache, nausea, and fatigue that are characteristic of the hangover.

Most problem drinkers—people experiencing life problems as a result of alcohol abuse—are men; men become problem drinkers at about five times the frequency of women (Helzer et al., 1990). This ratio, however, may change in time, because women's drinking patterns appear to be changing (Zilberman, Tavares, & el-Guebaly, 2003). There do not seem to be important differences in rates of alcohol abuse between black and white Americans. It appears that problem drinking may develop during any life period from early childhood through old age. (See Chapter 18 for further discussion on this topic.) Marriage, higher levels of education, and being older are associated with a lower incidence of alcoholism (Helzer et al., 1990). About 10 percent of men over age 65 were found to be heavy drinkers (Breslow, Faden, & Smothers, 2003). Surveys of alcoholism rates across different cultural groups around the world have found varying rates of the disorder across diverse cultural samples (Caetano et al., 1998; Hibell, Anderson, et al., 2000).

The course of alcohol-related problems can be both erratic and fluctuating. A recent survey found that some alcohol-dependent persons go through long periods of abstinence only to start drinking again later. Of 600 respondents in the study (most of whom were alcohol-dependent), over half (56 percent) had periods of abstinence lasting 3 months, and 16 percent reported a period of 5 years of abstinence (Schuckit, Tipp, Smith, & Buckholz, 1997). It is therefore important to keep in mind that the course of alcohol abuse and dependence can vary and may even include periods of remission.

ALCOHOL'S EFFECTS ON THE BRAIN Alcohol has complex and seemingly contradictory effects on the brain. At lower levels, alcohol stimulates certain brain cells and activates the brain's "pleasure areas," which release opium-like endogenous opioids that are stored in the body (Braun, 1996; Van Ree, 1996). At higher levels, alcohol depresses brain functioning, inhibiting one of the brain's excitatory neurotransmitters, glutamate, which in turn slows down activity in parts of the brain (Koob, Mason, et al., 2002). Inhibition of glutamate in the brain impairs the organism's ability to learn and affects the higher brain centers, impairing judgment and other rational processes and lowering self-control. As behavioral restraints decline, a drinker may indulge in the satisfaction of impulses ordinarily held in check. Some degree of motor uncoordination soon becomes apparent, and the drinker's discrimination and perception of cold, pain, and other discomforts are dulled. Typically the drinker experiences a sense of warmth, expansiveness, and well-being. In such a mood, unpleasant realities are screened out and the drinker's feelings of self-esteem and adequacy rise. Casual acquaintances become the best and most understanding of friends, and the drinker enters a generally pleasant world of unreality in which worries are temporarily left behind.

In most states, when the alcohol content of the bloodstream reaches 0.08 percent, the individual is considered intoxicated, at least with respect to driving a vehicle. Muscular coordination, speech, and vision are impaired, and thought processes are confused (NIAAA, 2001). Even before this level of intoxication is reached, however, judg-

TABLE 12.1 Some Common Misconceptions about Alcohol and Alcoholism

Fiction	Fact
Alcohol is a stimulant.	Alcohol is actually both a nervous system stimulant and a depressant.
You can always detect alcohol on the breath of a person who has been drinking.	It is not always possible to detect the presence of alcohol. Some individuals successfully cover up their alcohol use for years.
One ounce of 86-proof liquor contains more alcohol than two 12-ounce cans of beer.	Two 12-ounce cans of beer contain more than an ounce of alcohol.
Alcohol can help a person sleep more soundly.	Alcohol may interfere with sound sleep.
Impaired judgment does not occur before there are obvious signs of intoxication.	Impaired judgment can occur long before motor signs of intoxication are apparent.
An individual will get more intoxicated by mixing liquors than by taking comparable amounts of one kind—e.g., bourbon, Scotch, or vodka.	It is the actual amount of alcohol in the bloodstream rather than the mix that determines intoxication.
Drinking several cups of coffee can counteract the effects of alcohol and enable a drinker to "sober up."	Drinking coffee does not affect the level of intoxication.
Exercise or a cold shower helps speed up the metabolism of alcohol.	Exercise and cold showers are futile attempts to increase alcohol metabolism.
People with "strong wills" need not be concerned about becoming alcoholics.	Alcohol is seductive and can lower the resistance of even the "strongest will."
Alcohol cannot produce a true addiction in the same sense that heroin can.	Alcohol has strong addictive properties.
One cannot become an alcoholic by drinking just beer.	One can consume a considerable amount of alcohol by drinking beer. It is, of course, the amount of alcohol that determines whether one becomes an alcoholic.
Alcohol is far less dangerous than marijuana.	There are considerably more individuals in treatment programs for alcohol problems than for marijuana abuse.
In a heavy drinker, damage to the liver shows up long before brain damage appears.	Heavy alcohol use can be manifested in organic brain damage before liver damage is detected.
The physiological withdrawal reaction from heroin is considered more dangerous than is withdrawal from alcohol.	The physiological symptoms accompanying withdrawal from heroin are no more frightening or traumatic to an individual than alcohol withdrawal. Actually, alcohol withdrawal is potentially more lethal than opiate withdrawal.
Everybody drinks.	Actually, 28 percent of men and 50 percent of women in the United States are abstainers.

ment becomes impaired to such an extent that the person misjudges his or her condition. For example, drinkers tend to express confidence in their ability to drive safely long after such actions are in fact quite unsafe. When the blood alcohol level reaches approximately 0.5 percent (the level differs somewhat among individuals), the entire neural balance is upset and the individual passes out. Unconsciousness apparently acts as a safety device, because concentrations above 0.55 percent are usually lethal.

In general, it is the amount of alcohol actually concentrated in the bodily fluids, not the amount consumed, that determines intoxication. The effects of alcohol, however, vary for different drinkers, depending on their physical condition, the amount of food in their stomach, and the duration of their drinking. In addition, alcohol users may gradually build up a tolerance for the drug so that ever-increasing amounts may be needed to produce the desired effects. Women metabolize alcohol less effectively than

DSM-IV-TR

Criteria for Substance-Dependence and Substance-Abuse Disorders

Substance-Dependence Disorder

A maladaptive pattern of substance use leading to clinically significant distress or impairment, as manifested by at least three of the following occurring at any time in the same 12-month period:

A. Tolerance as defined by either a need for increased amounts of the substance to achieve intoxication or desired effect, or diminished effect with continued use of the same amount of substance.

B. Withdrawal as manifested by either the characteristic withdrawal syndrome for the substance, or same or closely related substance is taken to relieve or avoid withdrawal symptoms.

C. Substance is often taken in larger amounts or over a longer period than was intended.

D. Persistent desire or unsuccessful effort to cut down or control substance use.

E. The person spends a great deal of time engaging in activities necessary to obtain the substance, use the substance, or recover from its effects.

F. The person has given up or reduced the amount of important social, occupational, or recreational activities because of substance use.

G. Continued substance use despite persistent or recurrent physical or psychological problem caused or exacerbated by the substance.

Substance-Abuse Disorder

A. A maladaptive pattern of substance use leading to clinically significant impairment or distress, as manifested by at least one of the following occurring within a 12-month period:

(1) Recurrent substance use that results in a failure to fulfill some major role obligations at work, school, or home.

(2) Recurrent substance use in situations in which it is physically hazardous (e.g., driving).

(3) Recurrent substance-related legal problems (e.g., arrest for disorderly conduct).

(4) Continued substance use despite persistent or recurrent social or interpersonal problems caused or exacerbated by the effects of the substance.

B. Person has never had symptoms or problems that have met the criteria for Substance Dependence for this class of substance.

Source: *Adapted from* American Psychiatric Association, DSM-IV-TR *(2000)*.

Excessive use of alcohol can produce unexpected and often dramatic changes in behavior. The men shown here illustrate the behavioral disinhibition that can occur following alcohol abuse.

men and thus become intoxicated on lesser amounts of alcohol (Gordis et al., 1995).

DEVELOPMENT OF ALCOHOL DEPENDENCE Excessive drinking can be viewed as progressing insidiously from early- to middle- to late-stage alcohol-abuse disorder, although some abusers do not follow this pattern. Many investigators have maintained that alcohol is a dangerous systemic poison even in small amounts, but others believe that in moderate amounts it is not harmful to most people. For pregnant women, however, even moderate amounts are believed to be dangerous; in fact, no safe level has been established, as is discussed in Developments in Research 12.1. The photo on page 417 shows the differences between the brain of a normal teenager and those born with fetal alcohol syndrome (FAS), a condition that is caused by excessive alcohol consumption during pregnancy and results in birth defects such as mental retardation.

THE PHYSICAL EFFECTS OF CHRONIC ALCOHOL USE For individuals who drink to excess, the clinical picture is highly unfavorable (White, Altmann, & Nanchahal, 2002). Alcohol that is taken in must be assimilated by the body, except for about 5 to 10 percent that is eliminated through breath, urine, and perspiration. The work of assimilation is done by the liver, but when large amounts of alcohol are ingested, the liver may be seriously overworked and eventually suffer irreversible damage (Martin, Singleton, & Hiller-Sturmhöfel, 2003; Ramstedt, 2003). In fact, from 15 to 30 percent of heavy drinkers develop cirrhosis of the liver, a disorder that involves extensive stiffening of the blood vessels. About 40 to 90 percent of the 26,000 annual cirrhosis deaths every year are alcohol-related (DuFour, Stinson, & Cases, 1993).

12.1 Developments in Research

Fetal Alcohol Syndrome: How Much Drinking Is Too Much?

Research indicates that heavy drinking by expectant mothers can affect the health of unborn babies, particularly binge drinking and heavy drinking during the early days of pregnancy (Maler & West, 2001). Newborn infants whose mothers drank heavily during pregnancy have been found to have frequent physical and behavioral abnormalities (Alison, 1994), including aggressiveness and destructiveness (Gardner, 2000), and may experience symptoms of withdrawal (Thomas & Riley, 1998). For example, such infants have shown growth deficiencies, facial and limb irregularities, damage to the central nervous system (Goodlett & Horn, 2001; Mattson & Riley, 1998), and impairment in cognitive functioning (Kodituwakku, Kalberg, & May, 2001). As noted in *The Third Report on Alcohol and Health* (HEW 1978), alcohol abuse in pregnant women is the third-leading cause of birth defects (the first two being Down syndrome and spina bifida, the incomplete formation and fusion of the spinal canal). Fetal alcohol syndrome is also associated with the development of mental disorder in adults (Famy, Streissguth & Unis, 1998). Although data on fetal alcohol syndrome are often difficult to obtain the prevalence has been estimated at between 0.5 and 2 cases per 1,000 births (May & Gossage, 2001).

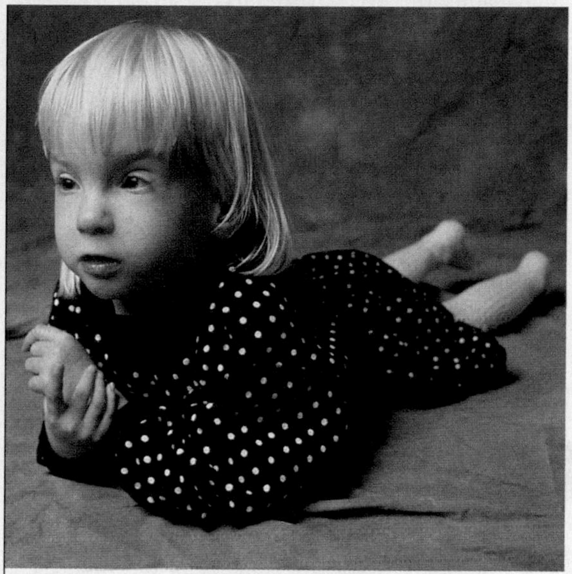

The effects of fetal alcohol syndrome can be both dramatic and long-lasting. This child shows some of the permanent physical abnormalities characteristic of the syndrome: widely spaced eyes, short broad nose, underdeveloped upper lip, and receding chin.

Research in laboratory animals has confirmed the devastating neurological effects of alcohol exposure *in utero* (Hannigan, 1996). Interestingly, research shows fetal alcohol syndrome has largely been reported in the United States and not in other countries, some of which have higher rates of alcohol use than the United States. The phenomenon of fetal alcohol syndrome has been referred to as an "American Paradox" (Abel, 1998) by researchers noting that fetal alcohol syndrome is strongly related to lower SES.

How much drinking endangers a newborn health? The HEW report warns against drinking more than 1 ounce of alcohol per day (one 12-ounce can of beer or one 5-ounce glass of wine, for example). The actual amount of alcohol that can safely be ingested during pregnancy is not known, but existing evidence for fetal alcohol syndrome is strongest when applied to binge drinkers or heavy alcohol users rather than to light or moderate users (Kolata, 1981). Nonetheless the surgeon general and many medical experts have concurred that pregnant women should abstain from using alcohol as the "safest course" until safe amount of alcohol consumption can be determined (Raskin, 1993).

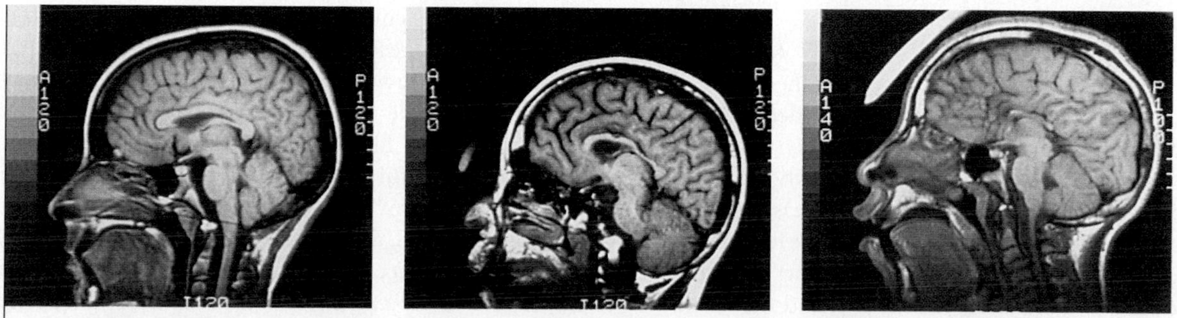

MRIs of three children: (left) Normal control, 13-year-old female; (center) FAS, 13-year-old male with focal thinning of the corpus callosum; (right) FAS, 14-year-old male with complete agenesis (nondevelopment) of the corpus callosum.

Alcohol is also a high-calorie drug. A pint of whiskey—enough to make about eight to ten ordinary cocktails—provides about 1,200 calories, which is approximately half the ordinary caloric requirement for a day (Flier, Underhill, & Lieber, 1995). Thus consumption of alcohol reduces a drinker's appetite for other food. Because alcohol has no nutritional value, the excessive drinker can suffer from malnutrition (Derr & Gutmann, 1994). Furthermore, heavy drinking impairs the body's ability to utilize nutrients, so the nutritional deficiency cannot be made up by popping vitamins. Many alcohol abusers also experience increased gastrointestinal symptoms such as stomach pains (Fields et al., 1994).

PSYCHOSOCIAL EFFECTS OF ALCOHOL ABUSE AND DEPENDENCE In addition to various physical problems, an excessive drinker usually suffers from chronic fatigue, oversensitivity, and depression. Initially, alcohol may seem to provide a useful crutch for dealing with the stresses of life, especially during periods of acute stress, by helping screen out intolerable realities and enhancing the drinker's feelings of adequacy and worth. The excessive use of alcohol eventually becomes counterproductive and can result in impaired reasoning, poor judgment, and gradual personality deterioration. Behavior typically becomes coarse and inappropriate, and the drinker assumes increasingly less responsibility, loses pride in personal appearance, neglects spouse and family, and becomes generally touchy, irritable, and unwilling to discuss the problem.

As judgment becomes impaired, an excessive drinker may be unable to hold a job and generally becomes unqualified to cope with new demands that arise (Frone, 2003). General personality disorganization and deterioration may be reflected in loss of employment and marital breakup. By this time, the drinker's general health is likely to have deteriorated, and brain and liver damage may have occurred. For example, there is some evidence that an alcoholic's brain is accumulating diffuse organic damage even when no extreme organic symptoms are present (Sullivan, Deshmukh, et al., 2000), and even mild to moderate drinking can adversely affect memory and problem solving (Gordis, 2001). Other researchers have found extensive alcohol consumption to be associated with an increased amount of organic damage in later life (Lyvers, 2000).

PSYCHOSES ASSOCIATED WITH SEVERE ALCOHOL ABUSE Several acute psychotic reactions fit the diagnostic classification of substance-induced disorders. These reactions may develop in people who have been drinking excessively over long periods of time or who have a reduced tolerance for alcohol for other reasons—for example, because of brain lesions from excessive long-term use. Such acute reactions usually last only a short time and generally consist of confusion, excitement, and delirium. There is some evidence that delirium may be associated with lower levels of thiamine in alcoholics (Holzbeck, 1996). These disorders are often called "alcoholic psychoses" because they are marked by a temporary loss of contact with reality.

Among those who drink excessively for a long time, a reaction called "alcohol withdrawal delirium" (formerly known as "delirium tremens") may occur (Palmstierno, 2001). This reaction usually happens following a prolonged drinking spree when the person is in a state of withdrawal. Slight noises or suddenly moving objects may cause considerable excitement and agitation. The full-blown symptoms include (1) disorientation for time and place in which, for example, a person may mistake the hospital for a church or jail, no longer recognize friends, or identify hospital attendants as old acquaintances; (2) vivid hallucinations, particularly of small, fast-moving animals like snakes, rats, and roaches; (3) acute fear, in which these animals may change in form, size, or color in terrifying ways; (4) extreme suggestibility, in which a person can be made to see almost any animal if its presence is merely suggested; (5) marked tremors of the hands, tongue, and lips; and (6) other symptoms including perspiration, fever, a rapid and weak heartbeat, a coated tongue, and foul breath.

The delirium typically lasts from 3 to 6 days and is generally followed by a deep sleep. When a person awakens, few symptoms—aside from possible slight remorse—remain, but frequently the individual is badly scared and may not resume drinking for several weeks or months. Usually, however, drinking is eventually resumed, followed by a return to the hospital with a new attack. The death rate from withdrawal delirium as a result of convulsions, heart failure, and other complications once approximated 10 percent (Tavel, 1962). With drugs such as chlordiazepoxide, however, the current death rate during withdrawal delirium and acute alcoholic withdrawal has been markedly reduced.

A second alcohol-related psychosis is the disorder referred to as "alcohol amnestic disorder" (formerly known as "Korsakoff's syndrome"). This condition was first described by the Russian psychiatrist Korsakoff in 1887 and is one of the most severe alcohol-related disorders (Oscar-Berman, Shagrin, Evert, & Epstein, 1997). The outstanding symptom is a memory defect (particularly with regard to recent events), which is sometimes accompanied by falsification of events (confabulation). Persons with this disorder may not recognize pictures, faces, rooms, and other objects that they have just seen, although they may feel that these people or objects are familiar. Such people increasingly tend to fill in their memory gaps with reminiscences and fanciful tales that lead to unconnected and distorted associations. These individuals may appear to be delirious, delusional, and disoriented for time and place, but ordinarily their confusion and disordered actions are closely related to their attempts to fill in memory gaps. The memory disturbance itself seems related to an inability to form new associations in a manner that renders them readily retrievable. Such a reaction usually occurs in older alcoholics, after many years of excessive drinking. These patients have also been observed to show other cognitive impairments such as planning deficits (Brokate, Hildebrandt, et al., 2003), intellectual decline, and emotional deficits (Snitz, Hellinger, & Daum, 2002) and judgment (Brand, Fujiwara, et al., 2003). Research with sophisticated brain-imaging techniques has found that patients with alcohol amnestic disorders show cortical lesions (Estruch, Bono, et al., 1998).

The symptoms of alcohol amnestic disorder are now thought to be due to vitamin B (thiamine) deficiency and other dietary inadequacies. Although it had been believed that a diet rich in vitamins and minerals generally restores such a patient to more normal physical and mental health, some research evidence suggests otherwise. Lishman (1990) reported that alcohol amnestic disorder did not respond well to thiamine replacement. Some memory functioning appears to be restored with prolonged abstinence. However, some personality deterioration usually remains in the form of memory impairment, blunted intellectual capacity, and lowered moral and ethical standards.

case STUDY **Alcohol Amnestic Disorder**

Averill B. was brought into the detoxification unit of a local county hospital by the police after an incident at a crowded city park. He was arrested because of his assaultive behavior toward others (he was walking through the crowded groups of sunbathers muttering to himself, kicking at people). At admission to the hospital, Averill was disoriented (did not know where he was), incoherent, and confused. When asked his name, he paused a moment, scratched his head, and said, "George Washington." When asked about what he was doing at the park he indicated that he was "marching in a parade in his honor."

Biological Factors in the Abuse of and Dependence on Alcohol and Other Substances

In trying to identify the causes of problem drinking, some researchers have stressed the role of genetic and biochemical factors; others have pointed to psychosocial factors, viewing problem drinking as a maladaptive pattern of adjustment to the stress of life; and still others have emphasized sociocultural factors such as the availability of alcohol and social approval of excessive drinking. As we will see, some combination of all of these factors seems to influence risk for developing alcohol abuse or alcohol dependence. As with most other forms of maladaptive behavior, there may be several types of alcohol dependence, each with somewhat different patterns of biological, psychosocial, and sociocultural causal factors.

How do substances such as alcohol, cocaine, and opium (discussed below) come to have such powerful effects—an overpowering hold that occurs in some people after only a few uses of the drug? Although the exact mechanisms are not fully agreed on by experts in the field, two important factors are apparently involved. The first is the ability of most, if not all, addictive drugs to activate areas of the brain that produce intrinsic pleasure and sometimes immediate, powerful reward. The second factor involves the person's biological makeup, or constitution, including his or her genetic inheritance and the environmental influences (learning factors) that enter into the need to seek mind-altering substances to an increasing degree as use continues. The development of an alcohol addiction is a complex process involving many elements—constitutional vulnerability and environmental encouragement, as well as the unique biochemical properties of certain psychoactive substances. Let's examine each of these elements in more detail.

THE NEUROBIOLOGY OF ADDICTION Let's first examine the role that drugs like alcohol play in the process of addiction. Drugs differ in their biochemical properties as well as in how rapidly they enter the brain. There are several routes of administration—oral, nasal, and intravenous. Alcohol is usually drunk, the slowest route, whereas cocaine is often self-administered by injection or taken nasally. Central to the neurochemical process underlying addiction is the role the drug plays in activating the "pleasure pathway." The **mesocorticolimbic dopamine pathway (MCLP)** is the center of psychoactive drug activation in the brain. The MCLP is made up of axons or neuronal cells in the middle portion of the brain known as the "ventral tegmental area" (see Figure 12.1) and connects to other brain centers such as the nucleus accumbens and then to the frontal cortex. This neuronal system is involved in such functions as control of emotions, memory, and gratification. Alcohol produces euphoria by stimulating this area in the brain. Research has shown that direct electrical stimulation of the MCLP produces great pleasure and has strong reinforcing properties (Liebman & Cooper, 1989; Littrell, 2001). Other psychoactive drugs also operate to change the brain's normal functioning and to activate the pleasure pathway. Drug ingestion or behaviors that lead to activation of the brain reward system are reinforced, so further use is promoted. The exposure of the brain to an addictive drug alters its neurochemical structure and results in a number of behavioral effects. With continued use of the drug, neuroadaptation or tolerance and dependence to the substance develop.

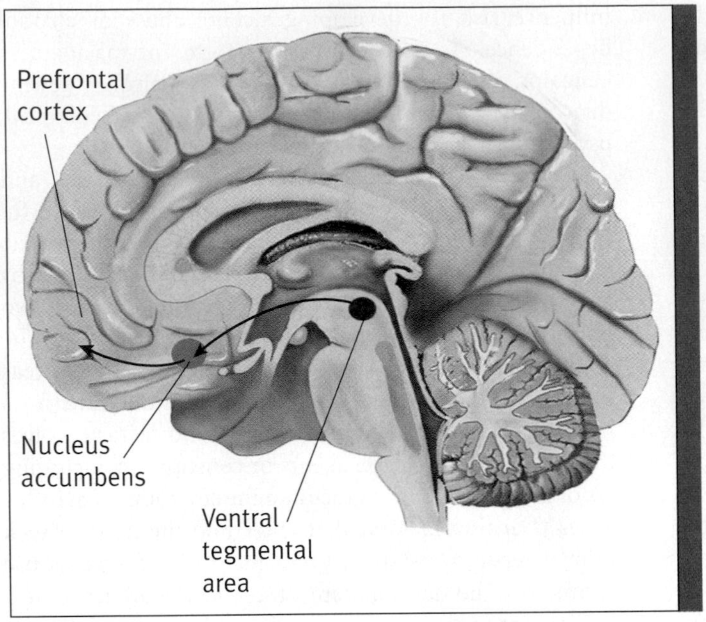

FIGURE 12.1

The Mesocorticolimbic Pathway

The mesocorticolimbic pathway (MCLP), running from the ventral tegmental area to the nucleus accumbens to the frontal cortex, is central to the release of the neurotransmitter dopamine and in mediating the rewarding properties of drugs.

Source: *Office of Technology Assessment, 1993.*

GENETIC VULNERABILITY The possibility of a genetic predisposition to developing alcohol-abuse problems has been widely researched. Many experts today agree that genetics probably plays an important role in developing sensitivity to the addictive power of drugs like alcohol (Mustanski, Viken, et al., 2003; Plomin & DeFries, 2003). Several lines of research point to the importance of genetic factors in substance-abuse disorders.

A review of 39 studies of the families of 6,251 alcoholics and of 4,083 nonalcoholics who had been followed over 40 years reported that almost one-third of alcoholics had at least one parent with an alcohol problem (Cotton, 1979). Likewise, a study of children of alcoholics by Cloninger and colleagues (1986) reported strong evidence for the inheritance of alcoholism. They found that for males, having one alcoholic parent increased the rate of alcoholism from 12.4 percent to 29.5 percent, and having two alcoholic parents increased the rate to 41.2 percent. For females with no alcoholic parents, the rate was 5.0 percent; for those with one alcoholic parent, the rate was 9.5 percent; and for those with two alcoholic parents, it was 25.0 percent.

Alcoholism clearly tends to run in families (Wall, Shea, et al., 2001). Research has shown that some people, such as the sons of alcoholics, have a high risk for developing problems with alcohol because of an inherent motivation to drink or sensitivity to the drug (Conrod, Pihl, & Vassileva, 1998). Research on the children of alcoholics who were adopted by other (nonalcoholic) families has also provided useful information. Studies have been conducted of alcoholics' children who were placed for adoption early in life and so did not come under the environmental influences of their biological parents. For example, Goodwin and colleagues (1973) found that children of alcoholic parents who had been adopted by nonalcoholic foster parents were nearly twice as likely to have alcohol problems by their late-twenties as a control group of adopted children whose real parents were not alcoholics. In another study, Goodwin and colleagues (1974) compared alcoholic parents' sons who were adopted in infancy by nonalcoholic parents with sons raised by their alcoholic parents. Both adopted and nonadopted sons later evidenced high rates of alcoholism—25 percent and 17 percent, respectively. These investigators concluded that being born to an alcoholic parent, rather than being raised by one, increases the risk of a son's becoming an alcoholic.

Another approach to understanding the precursors to alcohol-abuse disorders is to study prealcoholic personalities—individuals who are at high risk for substance abuse but who are not yet affected by alcohol. The heritability of personality characteristics has been widely explored (Bouchard & Loehlin, 2001). An alcohol-risk personality has been described as an individual (usually an alcoholic's child) who has an inherited predisposition toward alcohol abuse and who is impulsive, prefers taking high risks, and is emotionally unstable.

Research has shown that prealcoholic men (those who are genetically predisposed to developing drug or alcohol problems but who have not acquired the problem) show different physiological patterns than nonalcoholic men in several respects. Prealcoholic men tend to experience a greater lessening of feelings of stress with alcohol ingestion than do nonalcoholic men (Finn, Sharkansky, et al., 1997). They also show different alpha wave patterns on EEGs (Stewart, Finn, & Pihl, 1990). Prealcoholic men were found to show larger conditioned physiological responses to alcohol cues than individuals who were considered at a low risk for alcoholism, according to Earleywine and Finn (1990). These results suggest that prealcoholic men may be more prone to develop tolerance for alcohol than low-risk men.

Some research has suggested that certain ethnic groups, particularly Asians and Native Americans, have abnormal physiological reactions to alcohol—a phenomenon referred to as "alcohol flush reaction." Fenna and colleagues (1971) and Wolff (1972) found that Asian and Eskimo subjects showed a hypersensitive reaction including flushing of the skin, a drop in blood pressure, heart palpitations, and nausea following the ingestion of alcohol (see also Gill, Eagle,, et al., 1999). This physiological reaction is found in roughly half of all Asians (Chen & Yeh, 1997) and results from a mutant enzyme that fails to break down alcohol molecules in the liver during the metabolic process (Takeshita et al., 1993). Although cultural factors may also play a role, the relatively lower rates of alcoholism among Asian groups might be related to the extreme discomfort associated with the alcohol flush reaction (Higuci, Matsushita, et al., 1994).

GENETICS—THE WHOLE STORY? As with the other disorders described in this book, genetics alone is not the whole story, and the exact role it plays in the development of alcoholism remains unclear. This issue continues to be debated, and some experts are not convinced of the primary role of genetics in alcoholism. The genetic mechanism or model for the generally agreed-upon observation that alcoholism is familial is insufficient to explain the behavior fully. That is, genetic transmission in the case of alcoholism does not follow the hereditary pattern found in strictly genetic disorders. Some investigators have employed the evidence that genetics appears to play a stronger role in men than in women (Merikangus & Swendsen, 1997) to question the relative power of genetics as an explanatory factor in substance abuse. Searles (1991) points to the ambiguous evidence for the genetics of alcoholism and cautions against interpreting genetics as a causal factor in its development. Negative results have been found in both twin and adoptive studies and in studies designed to follow up the behavior of high-risk individuals. The great majority of children who have alcoholic parents do not themselves become alcoholics—whether or not they are raised by their real parents. The children of alcoholics who make successful life adjustments have not been sufficiently studied. In one study of high-risk children of alcoholics, a group of young men 19 to 20 years of age who were presumably at high risk for developing alcoholism were carefully studied for symptoms of psychopathology. Schulsinger and colleagues (1986) found that they did not differ in psychopathology or in alcohol-abuse behavior from a control sample similar to the general population. In another study of high-risk individuals, Alterman, Searles, and Hall (1989) failed to find differences in drinking behavior or alcohol-related symptoms between a group of high-risk subjects (those who had alcoholic fathers) and a group of non-high-risk subjects.

Although much evidence implicates genetic factors in the etiology of alcoholism, we do not know what precise role they play. At present, it appears that the genetic interpretation of alcoholism remains an attractive hypothesis; however, additional research is needed for us to hold this view with confidence. It is not likely that genetics alone will account for the full range of alcohol and drug problems. Social circumstances are still considered powerful forces in providing both the availability and the motivation to use alcohol and other drugs. McGue (1998) has noted that the mechanisms of genetic influence should be viewed as compatible, rather than competitive, with psychological and social determinants of this disorder.

GENETIC INFLUENCES AND LEARNING When we talk about familial or constitutional differences, we are not strictly limiting our explanation to genetic inheritance. Rather, learning factors appear to play an important part in the development of constitutional reaction tendencies. Having a genetic predisposition or biological vulnerability to alcohol abuse, of course, is not a sufficient cause of the disorder. The person must be exposed to the substance to a sufficient degree for the addictive behavior to appear. In the case of alcohol, almost everyone in America is exposed to the drug to some extent—in most cases through peer pressure, parental example, and advertising. The development of alcohol-related problems involves living in an environment that promotes initial as well as continuing use of the substance. People become conditioned to stimuli and tend to respond in particular ways as a result of learning. Learning appears to play an important part in the development of substance abuse and antisocial personality disorders (see Chapter 11). There clearly are numerous reinforcements for using alcohol in our social environments and everyday lives. However, research has also shown that psychoactive drugs such as alcohol contain intrinsic rewarding properties—apart from the social context or the drug's operation to diminish worry or frustration. As we saw earlier, the drug stimulates pleasure centers in the brain and develops a reward system of its own.

Psychosocial Causal Factors in Alcohol Abuse and Dependence

Not only do alcoholics become physiologically dependent on alcohol, they develop a powerful psychological dependence as well—they become socially dependent on the drug to help them enjoy social situations. Because excessive drinking is ultimately so destructive to a person's total life adjustment, the question of how psychological dependence is learned arises (Gordis, 2000). A number of psychosocial factors have been advanced as possible answers.

FAILURES IN PARENTAL GUIDANCE Stable family relationships and parental guidance are extremely important molding influences for children (Ramirez, Crano, et al.,

2004), and this stability is often lacking in families of substance abusers. Children who have parents who are extensive alcohol or drug abusers are vulnerable to developing substance-abuse and related problems themselves (Erblich, Earleywine, & Erblich, 2001). The experiences and lessons we learn from important figures in our early years have a significant impact on us as adults. Parent substance use is associated with early adolescent substance use (Brown, Tate, et al., 1999). Children who are exposed to negative role models and family dysfunction early in their lives or experience other negative circumstances because the adults around them provide limited guidance often falter on the difficult steps they must take in life (Fischer, Pidcock, et al., 2005). These formative experiences can have a direct influence on whether a youngster becomes involved in maladaptive behavior such as alcohol or drug abuse. And negative parental models can have longer-range negative consequences once children leave the family situation. For example, in a study of the health behavior of college students, college freshmen from families with alcohol-abusing parents viewed their families as less healthy and had more problematic family relationships than those with non-alcohol-abusing parents (Deming, Chase, & Karesh, 1996).

In one sophisticated program of research aimed at evaluating the possibility that negative socialization factors influence alcohol use, Chassin and colleagues (1993; Trim & Chassin, 2004) replicated findings that alcohol abuse in parents was associated with substance use in adolescents. They then evaluated several possible mediating factors that can affect whether adolescents start using alcohol. They found that parenting skills or parental behavior was associated with substance use in adolescents. Specifically, alcohol-abusing parents are less likely to keep track of what their children are doing, and this lack of monitoring often leads to the adolescents' affiliation with drug-using peers. In addition, Chassin and colleagues (1993) found that stress and negative affect (more prevalent in families with an alcoholic parent) were associated with alcohol use in adolescents. They reported that "parental alcoholism was associated with increases in negative uncontrollable life events which, in turn, were linked to negative affect, to associations with drug-using peers, and to substance use" (p. 16). In a follow-up study, Chassin et al. (1996) reported that the direct effect of fathers' alcohol abuse was strong, even after controlling for stress and negative affect. Extremely stressful childhood experiences such as child sexual abuse might make a person vulnerable to later problems. Women who have a history of child sexual abuse are at risk for developing a wide range of psychological problems including substance abuse (Kendler, Bulik, et al., 2000).

Parent substance use is associated with early adolescent substance use, and negative parental models can have longer-range negative consequences once children leave home.

PSYCHOLOGICAL VULNERABILITY Is there an "alcoholic personality"—a type of character organization that predisposes a person to use alcohol rather than adopt some other defensive pattern of coping with stress? Do some individuals self-medicate or reduce their discomfort by excessive use of alcohol? In efforts to answer this question, investigators have found that many potential alcohol abusers tend to be emotionally immature, expect a great deal of the world, require an inordinate amount of praise and appreciation, react to failure with marked feelings of hurt and inferiority, have low frustration tolerance, and feel inadequate and unsure of their abilities to fulfill expected male or female roles. Persons at high risk for developing alcohol-related problems are significantly more impulsive and aggressive than those at low risk for abusing alcohol (Morey, Skinner, & Blashfield, 1984).

In recent years, substantial research has focused on the link between alcohol-abuse disorders and such other disorders as antisocial personality, depression, and schizophrenia. About half of the persons with schizophrenia have either alcohol or drug abuse or dependence as well (Kosten, 1997). By far, most of the research on comorbidity has related antisocial personality (discussed in Chapter 11) and addictive disorders, where about 75 to 80 percent of the studies have shown a strong association (Alterman, 1988), and conduct disorder (Slutsky, Heath, et al., 1998). Interestingly, antisocial personality disorder, alcohol, and aggression are strongly associated (Moeller & Dougherty, 2001). High rates of substance abuse are found among antisocial personalities (Clark, Watson, & Reynolds, 1995), and in a survey of eight alcohol treatment programs, Morganstern, Langenbucher, and colleagues (1997) found that 57.9 percent had a personality disorder, with 22.7 percent meeting criteria for antisocial personality disorder.

Considerable research has suggested that there is a relationship between depressive disorders and alcohol abuse, and there may be gender differences in the association between these disorders (Kranzler et al., 1997). One group of researchers (Moscato, Russell, et al., 1997) found the degree of association between depression and alcohol-abuse problems stronger among women. For whatever reason they co-occur, the presence of other mental disorders in alcohol- or drug-abusing patients is a very important consideration when it comes to treatment, as will be discussed later in this chapter (Petrakis, Gonzalez, et al., 2002; Samet, Liu, & Hasin, 2004). In order to ensure more effective treatment with these complicated problems, Brems and Johnson (1997) recommended that treatment of co-occurring mental health problems involve more cross-disciplinary collaboration, greater integration of substance-abuse and mental health treatments, and modification of training of caregivers to sensitize them to the difficulties of treating patients with comorbid disorders.

STRESS, TENSION REDUCTION, AND REINFORCEMENT A number of investigators have pointed out that the typical alcohol abuser is discontented with his or her life and is unable or unwilling to tolerate tension and stress (Rutledge & Sher, 2001). For example, Hussong, Hicks, et al. (2001) and Kushner, Thuras, et al. (2000) reported a high degree of association between alcohol consumption and negative affectivity such as anxiety and somatic complaints. In other words, alcoholics drank to relax. In this view, anyone who finds alcohol tension-reducing is in danger of becoming an alcoholic, even without an especially stressful life situation. However, the tension reduction causal model is difficult to accept as a sole explanatory hypothesis. If this process were a main cause, we would expect alcoholism to be far more common than it is, because alcohol tends to reduce tension for most people who use it. In addition, this model does not explain why some excessive drinkers are able to maintain control over their drinking and continue to function in society, whereas others are not.

Cox and Klinger (1988) and Cooper (1994) describe a motivational model of alcohol use that places a great deal of responsibility on the individual. According to this view, the final common pathway of alcohol use is motivation; that is, a person decides, consciously or unconsciously, whether to consume a particular drink of alcohol. Alcohol is consumed to bring about affective changes, such as the mood-altering effects, and even indirect effects, such as peer approval. In short, alcohol is consumed because it is reinforcing.

> **research close•up**
>
> ***moderating***
>
> *A moderating variable is a variable that influences the association between two other variables. For example, depression is common after bereavement. However, men who have lost a spouse tend to be more likely to be depressed than women who have lost a spouse. In this case, gender is a key moderating variable for the bereavement–depression relationship.*

EXPECTATIONS OF SOCIAL SUCCESS A number of investigators have been exploring the idea that cognitive expectation may play an important role both in the initiation of drinking and in the maintenance of drinking behavior once the person has begun to use alcohol (Marlatt, Baer, et al., 1998). Many people, especially young adolescents, expect that alcohol use will lower tension and anxiety and increase sexual desire and pleasure in life (Seto & Barbaree, 1995). According to the reciprocal influence model, adolescents begin drinking as a result of expectations that using alcohol will increase their popularity and acceptance by their peers. Research has shown that expectancies of social benefit can influence adolescents' decisions to start drinking and predict their consumption of alcohol (Christiansen et al., 1989).

This view gives professionals an important and potentially powerful means of deterring drinking among young people, or at least of delaying its onset. From this perspective, alcohol use in teenagers can be countered by providing young people with more effective social tools and with ways of altering these expectancies before drinking begins. Smith and colleagues (1995) have suggested that prevention efforts should be targeted at children before they begin to drink so that the positive feedback cycle of reciprocal reinforcement between expectancy and drinking will never be established (see the discussion on prevention of alcohol use in Chapter 18).

Time and experience do have ***moderating*** influences on these alcohol expectancies. In a longitudinal study of college drinking, Sher, Wood, and colleagues (1996) found that there was a significant decrease in outcome expectancy over time. Older students showed less expectation of the benefits of alcohol than beginning students (see The World Around Us 12.2 on p. 424).

MARITAL AND OTHER INTIMATE RELATIONSHIPS Adults with less intimate and supportive relationships tend to show greater drinking following sadness or hostility than those with close peers and with more positive relationships (Hussong et al., 2001). Excessive drinking often begins during crisis periods in marital or other intimate personal relationships, particularly crises that lead to hurt and self-devaluation. The marital relationship may actually serve to maintain the pattern of excessive drinking. (See Case Study on p. 425.) Marital partners may behave toward each other in ways that promote or enable a spouse's excessive drinking. For example, a husband who lives with an alcoholic wife is often unaware of the fact that, gradually and inevitably, many of the decisions he makes every day are based on the expectation that his wife will be drinking. These expectations, in turn, may make the drinking behavior more likely. Eventually an entire marriage may center on the drinking of an alcoholic spouse. In some instances, the husband or wife may also begin to drink excessively. Thus one important concern in many treatment programs today involves identifying the personality or lifestyle factors in a

12.2 THE WORLD AROUND US

Binge Drinking in College

Two alcohol-related student deaths shocked the Colorado college community in the fall of 2004. Lynn B., an entering freshman at the University of Colorado, drank so much whiskey and wine during a fraternity initiation that he became unconscious and died as a result of alcohol poisoning. This tragic incident occurred just 2 weeks after a 19-year-old sophomore, Samantha S. at Colorado State University, died of alcohol poisoning after a party in which she consumed an estimated 40 drinks (Sink, 2004).

How extensive is college binge drinking? In spite of the fact that alcohol use is illegal for most undergraduates, binge drinking on campus is widespread (Rabow & Duncan-Schill, 1995). According to a survey by Wechsler, Davenport, et al. (1994), 44 percent of college students in the United States are binge drinkers, and Goodwin (1992) reports that 98 percent of fraternity and sorority members drink some amount every week. Some research has suggested, however, that the pattern of drinking can vary widely with binge drinking being more of an occasional rather than a regular event (Del Boca, Darkes, et al., 2004). Wechsler and colleagues (1994) conducted a nationwide survey of 140 college campuses in 40 states and obtained survey information pertaining to the drinking behavior and health consequences of drinking on 17,592 students (with approximately a 69 percent response rate). Students completed a 20-page survey of their drinking practices, including such information as recency of last drink, how many times they had five drinks or more in a row, and how many times they had four drinks in a row. They were also asked to provide information as to whether they experienced any of the following consequences after drinking: had a hangover, missed a class, got behind in schoolwork, did something they later regretted, forgot where they were or what they did, argued with friends, engaged in unplanned sexual activities, failed to use protection when having sex, damaged property, got into trouble with the campus police, got hurt, or required medical treatment for an alcohol overdose.

The colleges surveyed in the study varied widely in the extent of binge drinking among the student body. As one might expect—some colleges earn reputations as being "party schools"—some institutions had a large number of students (70 percent) heavily involved in alcohol and binge drinking, but the problem occurred to some degree across most college campuses. What are the reasons for the widespread problem of binge drinking in college? Many factors can be cited such as students' expressing independence from parental influence (Turrisi, Wiersma, & Hughes, 2000); peer group and situational influences (Read, Wood, et al., 2003); developing and asserting gender role, particularly for men adopting a "macho" role (Capraro, 2000); and holding beliefs that alcohol can help make positive transformations (e.g., "having a few drinks to celebrate special occasions"; Turrisi, 1999). The consequences of college binge drinking can be far-reaching. In their survey, Wechsler and colleagues (1994) reported a strong association between the frequency of binge drinking and alcohol-related health and life problems. In fact, binge drinkers were nearly ten times more likely than those who did not indulge in binge drinking to engage in unplanned sexual activity, not to use protection when having sex, to get into trouble with campus police, to damage property, and to get hurt after drinking. Men and women tended to report similar problems, except that men engaged in more property damage than women. Over 16 percent of the men and 9 percent of the women reported having gotten in trouble with the campus police. About 47 percent of the frequent binge drinkers, compared with 14 percent of the nonbinge drinkers, indicated that they had experienced five or more of the problems surveyed. In a recent follow-up survey of college drinking in 1997, Wechsler and colleagues (1998) reported strikingly similar results.

The results of studies bearing on the long-range consequences of college drinking have been somewhat equivocal (Granfield, 2005). One recent study suggested that extensive drinking in college, even among the heaviest drinkers from sororities and fraternities, might be determined to a great extent by situational factors. In a follow-up study of drinking behavior a year after graduation, Sher, Bartholow, and Nanda (2001) reported that being a member of a fraternity or sorority did not predict postcollege drinking. Interestingly, a long-term follow-up of over 11 years has shown that the heavy drinking during college did not relate to heavy drinking during later years (Bartholow, Sher, & Krull, 2003). These investigators found that heavy drinking that is associated with Greek society involvement does not generally lead to sustained heavy drinking in later life.

relationship that tend to foster the drinking in the alcohol-abusing person. Of course, such relationships are not restricted to marital partners but may also occur in those involved in love affairs or close friendships.

Excessive use of alcohol is one of the most frequent causes of divorce in the United States (Perreira & Sloan, 2001) and is often a hidden factor in the two most common causes—financial and sexual problems. The deterioration in alcoholics' interpersonal relationships, of course, further augments the stress and disorganization in their lives. The breakdown of marital relationships can be a highly stressful situation for many people. The stress of divorce and the often erratic adjustment period that follows can lead to increased substance abuse.

Family relationship problems have also been found to be central to the development of alcoholism. In a classic longitudinal study of possible etiologic factors in alcohol abuse, Vaillant, Gale, and Milofsky (1982) described six family relationship factors that were significantly associated with the development of alcoholism in the individuals they studied. The most important family variables that were considered to predispose the individual to substance-use problems were the presence of an alcoholic father, acute marital conflict, lax maternal supervision and inconsistent discipline, many moves during the family's early years, lack of "attachment" to the father, and lack of family cohesiveness.

The cultural influences on alcoholism are clear when one looks at the extremely low incidence of alcoholism among Muslims, Mormons, and orthodox Jews, whose religious values prohibit social drinking.

case STUDY The Drunken Wife and Mother

Evelyn C., a 36-year-old homemaker and mother of two school-age children (from a previous marriage), began to drink to excess especially following intense disagreements with her husband, John, a manager of a retail business. Over the past several months, she began drinking during the day when her children were at school and on two occasions was inebriated when they came home. On one recent occasion, Evelyn failed to pick up her older daughter after an after-school event. Her daughter called John's cell phone (he was out of town on a business trip), and he had an assistant pick her up. When they arrived home, Evelyn (apparently unaware of the problem she had caused) created a scene and was verbally abusive toward the assistant. Her out-of-control drinking increased when her husband of 3 years began staying out all night. These emotionally charged encounters resulted in John's physically abusing her one morning when he came back home after a night away. John moved out of the house and filed for divorce.

Sociocultural Factors

Alcohol use is a pervasive component in the social life in Western civilization. Social events often revolve around alcohol use, and alcohol use before and during meals is commonplace. Alcohol is often seen as a "social lubricant" or tension reducer that enhances social events. Thus investigators have pointed to the role of sociocultural as well as physiological and psychological factors in the high rate of alcohol abuse and dependence among Americans (Vega et al., 1993).

The effect of cultural attitudes toward drinking is well illustrated by Muslims and Mormons, whose religious values prohibit the use of alcohol, and by orthodox Jews, who have traditionally limited its use largely to religious rituals. The incidence of alcoholism among these groups is minimal. In comparison, the incidence of alcoholism is high among Europeans. For example, one survey showed the highest alcohol-use rates among young people to be in Denmark and Malta, where one in five students reported having drunk alcohol ten times within the past 30 days (ESPAD, 2000). Interestingly, Europe and six countries that have been influenced by European culture—Argentina, Canada, Chile, Japan, the United States, and New Zealand—make up less than 20 percent of the world's population yet consume 80 percent of the alcohol (Barry, 1982). Alcohol abuse continues to be a problem in Europe, and these problems greatly enhance accidents (Lehto, 1995), crime (Rittson, 1995), liver disease (Medical Council on Alcoholism, 1997), and the extent to which young people are becoming involved in substance-use problems (Anderson & Lehto, 1995). The French appear to have the highest rate of alcoholism in the world, approximately 15 percent of the population. France has both the highest per capita alcohol consumption and the highest death rate from cirrhosis of the liver (Noble, 1979). In addition, France shows the highest prevalence rates: In a broad survey of hospital patients, 18 percent (25 percent for men and 7 percent for women) were reported to have alcohol-use disorders, although only 6 percent of admissions were for alcohol problems (Reynaud, Leleu, et al., 1997). In Sweden, another country with high rates of alcoholism, 13.2 percent of men's hospital admissions, and 1.1 percent of women's, were attributed to alcohol (Andreasson & Brandt, 1997). Thus it appears that religious sanctions and social customs can influence whether alcohol is one of the coping methods commonly used in a given group or society.

The behavior that is manifested under the influence of alcohol seems to be influenced by cultural factors. Lindman and Lang (1994), in a study of alcohol-related behavior in eight countries, found that most people expressed the view that aggressive behavior frequently followed their drinking "many" drinks. However, the expectation that alcohol leads to aggression is related to cultural traditions and early exposure to violent or aggressive behavior.

In sum, we can identify many reasons why people drink—as well as many conditions that can predispose them to do so and reinforce drinking behavior—but the exact combination of factors that result in a person's becoming an alcoholic are still unknown.

Treatment of Alcohol Abuse Disorders

Alcohol abuse and dependence are difficult to treat because many alcoholics refuse to admit that they have a problem or to seek assistance before they "hit bottom," and many that do go into treatment leave before therapy is completed. DiClemente (1993) refers to the addictions as "diseases of denial." However, in a review of several large alcohol-treatment studies, Miller, Walters, and Bennett (2001) reported that two-thirds of studies show large and significant decreases in drinking and related problems. In this section, we will examine both biological and psychosocial treatment strategies. As we will see, some treatment approaches appear to reduce drinking-related problems more effectively than others (Miller & Wilbourne, 2002; Zweben, 2001). In general, a multidisciplinary approach to the treatment of drinking problems appears to be most effective, because the problems are often complex, requiring flexibility and individualization of treatment procedures (Margolis & Zweben, 1998). Also, a substance abuser's needs change as treatment progresses. Treatment objectives usually include detoxification, physical rehabilitation, control over alcohol-abuse behavior, and the individual's realizing that he or she can cope with the problems of living and lead a much more rewarding life without alcohol. Traditional treatment programs usually have as their goal abstinence from alcohol (Ambrogne, 2002). However, some programs attempt to promote controlled drinking as a treatment goal for problem drinkers. No matter what the treatment method, relapse is common, and many in the field see relapse as a factor that must be addressed in the treatment and recovery process (Tims, Leukefeld, & Platt, 2001).

USE OF MEDICATIONS IN TREATING ALCOHOL ABUSERS Biological approaches include a variety of treatment measures such as medications to reduce cravings, to ease the detoxification process, and to treat co-occurring health (National Institutes of Health, 2001) and mental health problems that may underlie the drinking behavior (Romach & Sellers, 1998).

MEDICATIONS TO BLOCK THE DESIRE TO DRINK Disulfiram (Antabuse), a drug that causes violent vomiting when followed by ingestion of alcohol, may be administered to prevent an immediate return to drinking (Niederhofer & Staffen, 2003). However, such deterrent therapy is seldom advocated as the sole approach, because pharmacological methods alone have not proved effective in treating alcoholism (Gorlick, 1993). For example, because the drug is usually self-administered, an alcohol-dependent person may simply discontinue the use of Antabuse when he or she is released from a hospital or clinic and begins to drink again. In fact, the primary value of drugs of this type seems to be their ability to interrupt the alcohol-abuse cycle for a period of time, during which therapy may be undertaken. Uncomfortable side effects may accompany the use of Antabuse; for example, alcohol-based aftershave lotion can be absorbed through the skin, resulting in illness. Moreover, the cost of Antabuse treatment, which requires careful medical maintenance, is higher than for many other, more effective treatments (Holder et al., 1991).

Another type of medication that has been used in a promising line of research (Kranzler, Armeli, et al., 2004; O'Malley, Krishnan-Sarin, et al., 2002) is naltrexone, an opiate antagonist that helps reduce the "craving" for alcohol by blocking the pleasure-producing effects of alcohol (NIAAA, 2004). O'Malley, Jaffe, Rode, and Rounsaville (1996) have shown that naltrexone reduced the alcohol intake and lowered the incentive to drink for alcohol abusers, compared with a control sample given a placebo. Some research has suggested that naltrexone is particularly effective with individuals who have a high level of craving (Monterosso, Flannery, et al., 2001). Some research, however, has failed to find naltrexone effective at reducing craving (Krystal, Cramer, et al., 2001), so confidence in its use for this purpose must await further research.

MEDICATIONS TO REDUCE THE SIDE EFFECTS OF ACUTE WITHDRAWAL In acute intoxication, the initial focus is on detoxification (the elimination of alcoholic substances from an individual's body), on treatment of the withdrawal symptoms described earlier, and on a medical regimen for physical rehabilitation. One of the primary goals in treatment of withdrawal symptoms is to reduce the physical symptoms characteristic of the syndrome such as insomnia, headache, gastrointestinal distress, and tremulousness. Central to the medical treatment approaches are the prevention of heart arrhythmias, seizures, delirium, and death (Bohn, 1993). These steps can usually best be handled in a hospital or clinic, where drugs such as Valium have largely revolutionized the treatment of withdrawal symptoms. Such drugs overcome motor excitement, nausea, and vomiting; prevent withdrawal delirium and convulsions; and help alleviate the tension and anxiety associated with withdrawal. Pharmacological treatments with long-lasting benzodiazepines such as diezepam to reduce the severity of withdrawal symptoms have been shown to be effective (Malcolm, 2003).

Concern is growing, however, that the use of tranquilizers at this stage does not promote long-term recovery and may foster addiction to another substance. Accordingly, some detoxification clinics are exploring alternative approaches including a gradual weaning from alcohol instead of a sudden cutoff. Maintenance doses of mild tranquilizers are sometimes given to patients withdrawing from alcohol to reduce anxiety and help them sleep. Such use of tranquilizers may be less effective than no treatment at all, however. Usually patients must learn to abstain from tranquilizers as well as from alcohol, because they tend to misuse both. Further, under the influence of tranquilizers, patients may even return to alcohol use.

PSYCHOLOGICAL TREATMENT APPROACHES Detoxification is optimally followed by psychological treatment, including family counseling and the use of community resources related to employment and to other aspects of a person's social readjustment. Although individual psychotherapy is sometimes effective, the focus of psychosocial measures in the treatment for alcohol-related problems often involves group therapy, environmental intervention, behavior therapy, and the approach used by Alcoholics Anonymous and family groups such as Al-Anon and Alateen.

Group Therapy Group therapy has been shown to be effective for many clinical problems (Pines & Schlapobersky, 2000), especially substance-abuse disorders (Velasquez, Maurer, et al., 2001). In the confrontational give-and-take of group therapy (see Chapter 17), alcohol abusers are often forced (perhaps for the first time) to face their problems and their tendencies to deny or minimize them. These group situations can be extremely difficult for those who have been engrossed in denial of their own responsibilities, but such treatment also helps them see new possibilities for coping with circumstances that have led to their difficulties. Often, though not always, this paves the way to learning more effective ways of coping and other positive steps toward dealing with their drinking problem.

In some instances, the spouses of alcohol abusers and even their children may be invited to join in group therapy meetings. In other situations, family treatment is itself the central focus of therapeutic efforts. In that case, the alcohol abuser is seen as a member of a disturbed family in which all the members have a responsibility for cooperating in treatment. Because family members are frequently the people most victimized by the alcohol abuser's addiction, they often tend to be judgmental and punitive, and the person in treatment, who has already passed harsh judgment on himself or herself, may tolerate this further source of devaluation poorly. In other instances, family members may unwittingly encourage an alcohol abuser to remain addicted—for example, a man with a need to dominate his wife may find that a continually drunken and remorseful spouse best meets his needs.

ENVIRONMENTAL INTERVENTION As with other serious maladaptive behaviors, a total treatment program for alcohol abuse usually requires measures to alleviate a patient's aversive life situation. Environmental support has been shown to be an important ingredient of an alcohol abuser's recovery (Booth et al., 1992a, 1992b). People often become estranged from family and friends because of their drinking and either lose or jeopardize their jobs. As a result, they are often lonely and live in impoverished neighborhoods. Typically, the reaction of those around them is not as understanding or as supportive as it would be if the alcohol abuser had a physical illness of comparable magnitude. Simply helping people with alcohol-abuse problems learn more effective coping techniques may not be enough if their social environment remains hostile and threatening. For those who have been hospitalized, halfway houses—designed to assist them in their return to family and community—are often important adjuncts to their total treatment program.

BEHAVIORAL AND COGNITIVE-BEHAVIORAL THERAPY One interesting and often effective form of treatment for alcohol-abuse disorders is behavioral therapy, of which several types exist (see Chapter 17). One is aversive conditioning, which involves the presentation of a wide range of noxious stimuli with alcohol consumption in order to suppress drinking behavior. For example, the ingestion of alcohol might be paired with an electric shock or a drug that produces nausea. A variety of pharmacological and other deterrent measures can be used in behavioral therapy after detoxification. One approach involves an intramuscular injection of emetine hydrochloride, an emetic. Before experiencing the nausea that results from the injection, a patient is given alcohol, so that the sight, smell, and taste of the beverage become associated with severe retching and vomiting. That is, a conditioned aversion to the taste and smell of alcohol develops. With repetition, this classical conditioning procedure acts as a strong deterrent to further drinking—probably in part because it adds an immediate and unpleasant physiological consequence to the more general socially aversive consequences of excessive drinking.

One of the most effective contemporary procedures for treating alcohol abusers has been the cognitive-behavioral approach recommended by Alan Marlatt (1985) and Witkiewitz and Marlatt (2004). This approach combines cognitive-behavioral strategies of intervention with social-learning theory and modeling of behavior. The approach, often referred to as a "skills training procedure," is usually aimed at younger problem drinkers who are considered to be at risk for developing more severe drinking problems because of an alcohol-abuse history in their family or their heavy current consumption. This approach relies on such techniques as imparting specific knowledge about alcohol, developing coping skills in situations associated with increased risk of alcohol use, modifying cognitions and expectancies, acquiring stress-management skills, and providing training in life skills (Connors & Walitzer, 2001). Cognitive-behavioral treatments have been shown to be effective; for example, O'Farrell, Murphy, et al. (2004) reported that partner violence was significantly reduced following cognitive-behavioral treatment.

Self-control training techniques (Miller, Brown, et al., 1995), in which the goal of therapy is to get alcoholics to reduce alcohol intake without necessarily abstaining altogether, have a great deal of appeal for some drinkers. There is now even a computer-based self-control training program available that has been shown to reduce problem drinking in a controlled study (Hester & Delaney, 1997; Neighbors, Larimer, & Lewis, 2004). It is difficult, of course, for individuals who are extremely dependent on the effects of alcohol to abstain totally from drinking. Thus many alcoholics fail to complete traditional treatment programs.

CONTROLLED DRINKING VERSUS ABSTINENCE Other psychological techniques have also received attention in recent years, partly because they are based on the hypothesis that some problem drinkers need not give up drinking altogether but, rather, can learn to drink moderately (Miller, Walters, & Bennett, 2001; Sobell & Sobell, 1995). Several approaches to learning controlled drinking have been attempted (McMurran & Hollin, 1993), and research has suggested that some alcoholics can learn to control their alcohol intake (Senft, Polen, et al., 1997). Miller and colleagues (1986) evaluated the results of four long-term follow-up studies of controlled-drinking treatment programs. Although they found a clear trend of increased numbers of abstainers and relapsed cases at long-term follow-up, they also found that a consistent percentage (15 percent) of subjects across the four studies controlled their drinking. The researchers concluded that controlled drinking was more likely to be successful in persons with less severe alcohol problems. The finding that some individuals are able to maintain some control over their drinking after treatment (without remaining totally abstinent) was also reported in a classic study by Polich, Armor, and Braiker (1981). These researchers found that 18 percent of the alcoholics they studied had reportedly been able to drink socially without problems during the 6-month follow-up of treatment.

However, many people in the field have rejected the idea that alcohol abusers can learn to control their drinking, and these theorists insist on a total abstinence approach. The debate over whether problem drinkers can learn moderate drinking continues after 25 years. Some researchers (Heather, 1995; Kahler, 1995; Sobell & Sobell, 1995) maintain the efficacy of controlled drinking. Others such as Glatt (1995) point to difficulties that alcohol abusers have in maintaining control. And some groups, such as Alcoholics Anonymous, are adamant in their opposition to programs aimed at controlled drinking for alcohol-dependent individuals.

ALCOHOLICS ANONYMOUS A practical approach to alcoholism that has reportedly met with considerable success is that of Alcoholics Anonymous (AA). This organization was started in 1935 by two men, Dr. Bob and Bill W., in Akron, Ohio. Bill W. recovered from alcoholism through a "fundamental spiritual change" and immediately sought out Dr. Bob, who, with Bill's assistance, achieved recovery. They in turn began to help other alcoholics. Since that time, AA has grown to over 51,000 groups in the United States and Canada, with an annual growth rate of about 6 to 7 percent (Alcoholics Anonymous, 2002). In addition, there are over 5,000 AA groups in Canada and over 41,000 groups in many other countries.

Alcoholics Anonymous operates primarily as a self-help counseling program in which both person-to-person and group relationships are emphasized. AA accepts both teenagers and adults with drinking problems, has no dues or fees, does not keep records or case histories, does not participate in political causes, and is not affiliated with any religious sect, although spiritual development is a key aspect of its treatment approach. To ensure anonymity, only first names are used. Meetings are devoted partly to social activities, but they consist mainly of discussions of the participants' problems with alcohol, often with testimonials from those who have stopped drinking. Such members usually contrast their lives before they broke their alcohol dependence with the lives they now live without alcohol. We should point out here that the term *alcoholic* is used by AA and its affiliates to refer either to persons who currently are drinking excessively or to people who have stopped drinking but must, according to AA philosophy, continue to abstain from alcohol consumption in the future. That is, in the AA view, one is an alcoholic for life, whether or not one is drinking; one is never "cured" of alcoholism but is instead "in recovery."

An important aspect of AA's rehabilitation program is that it appears to lift the burden of personal responsibility by helping alcoholics accept that alcoholism, like many other problems, is bigger than they are. Henceforth, they can see themselves not as weak-willed or lacking in moral strength, but rather simply as having an affliction—they cannot drink—just as other people may not be able to tolerate certain types of medication. Through mutual help and reassurance from group members who have had similar experiences, many alcoholics acquire insight into their problems, a new sense of purpose, greater ego strength, and more effective coping techniques. Continued participation in the group, of course, can help prevent the crisis of a relapse.

These people are participating in an Alcoholics Anonymous (AA) meeting. AA accepts both teenagers and adults, has no dues or fees, does not keep records or case histories, does not participate in political causes, and is not affiliated with any religious sect, although spiritual development is a key aspect of its treatment approach. To ensure anonymity, only first names are used at meetings. AA is one of the most popular alcohol treatment programs, promoting total abstinence rather than controlled drinking.

Affiliated movements such as Al-Anon family groups and Alateen (which has over 35,000 groups in the United States and Canada) are designed to bring family members together to share experiences and problems, to gain understanding of the nature of alcoholism, and to learn techniques for dealing with their own problems living in a family with one or more affected individuals. The reported success of Alcoholics Anonymous is based primarily on anecdotal information rather than on objective study of treatment outcomes, because AA does not directly participate in external comparative research efforts. However, several studies have found "AA" conditions effective in helping people avoid drinking (Gossop, Harris, et al., 2003; McCrady, Epstein, & Kahler, 2004). In a classic study, Brandsma, Maultsby, and Welsh (1980) included an AA program in their extensive comparative study of alcoholism treatments. The success of this treatment method with severe alcoholics was quite limited. One important finding was that the AA method had high dropout rates compared with other therapies. About half of the people who go to AA drop out of the program within 3 months. Chappel (1993) attributes the very high dropout rate to alcoholics' denial that they have problems, resistance to external pressure, and resistance to AA itself. Apparently many alcoholics are unable to accept the quasi-religious quality of the sessions and the group-testimonial format that is so much a part of the AA program. In the Brandsma study, the participants who were assigned to the AA group subsequently encountered more life difficulties and drank more than people in other treatment groups. On the positive side, however, a study by Morganstern, Labouvie, and colleagues (1997) reported that affiliation with AA after alcohol treatment was associated with better outcomes than no such involvement, and a study by Tonigan, Toscova, and Miller (1995) found that AA involvement was strongly associated with success in outpatient samples.

OUTCOME STUDIES AND ISSUES IN TREATMENT

The outcome of alcoholism treatment varies considerably, depending on the population studied and on the treatment facilities and procedures employed. Results range from low rates of success for hard-core substance abusers to recovery rates of 70 to 90 percent where modern treatment and aftercare procedures are used. Substance abusers who are also diagnosed as having a personality disorder or affective disorder tended to have poorer outcomes in alcohol treatment than those for whom the diagnosis was simply alcohol-abuse problems (Woelwer, Burtscheidt, et al., 2001). Treatment is most likely to be effective when an individual realizes that he or she needs help, when adequate treatment facilities are available, and when the individual attends treatment regularly. Having a positive relationship with the therapist was associated with better treatment outcome (Connors et al., 1997). One important new treatment strategy is aimed at reinforcing treatment motivation and abstinence early in the treatment process by providing "check-up" follow-ups on drinking behavior. Miller, Benefield, and Tonigan (1993) reported that "Drinking Check-Up" sessions during the early stages of therapy resulted in a reduction of drinking in the first 6 weeks of therapy, compared with clients who did not have check-up sessions.

Some researchers have maintained that treatment for alcohol-use and -abuse disorders would be more effective if important patient characteristics were taken into account (Mattson, Allen, Longabaugh, et al., 1994). That is, patients with certain personality characteristics or with differing degrees of severity might do better in one specific therapeutic approach rather than in another. This view was evaluated in a study of patient-treatment matching (referred to as "Project MATCH") that was sponsored by the National Institute on Alcohol Abuse and Alcoholism (NIAAA, 1997). This extensive study, initiated in 1989, involved 1,726 patients who were treated in 26 alcohol-treatment programs in the United States by 80 different therapists representing three treatment approaches. The research design included both an inpatient and an outpatient treatment component.

Project MATCH compared the treatment effectiveness of three different approaches to alcohol treatment: (1) a 12-step program along the lines of Alcoholics Anonymous (but not sponsored by AA) and referred to as "Twelve-Step Facilitation Therapy" (TSF); (2) a cognitive-behavioral therapy program (CBT); and (3) a treatment technique referred to as "Motivational Enhancement Therapy" (MET), which attempts to get clients to assume responsibility for helping themselves. These approaches were chosen because they were considered effective in treating alcoholics and had been reported to have potential for clear matching (Gordis, 1997). The researchers in Project MATCH evaluated patients on ten characteristics that had been shown in the literature to be related to treatment outcome (Babor, 1996; Project MATCH Group, 1997): diagnosis as alcoholics, cognitive impairment, conceptual ability level, gender, desire to seek meaning in life, motivation, psychiatric severity, severity of alcohol involvement, social support for drinking versus abstinence, and presence of sociopathy (personality disorder).

The results of this study were unexpected: Matching the patients to particular treatments did not appear to be important to having an effective outcome. The treatments studied all had equal outcomes. Gordis (1997) concluded that patients from competently run alcoholism treatment programs will do as well in any of the three treatments studied.

RELAPSE PREVENTION One of the greatest problems in the treatment of addictive disorders is maintaining abstinence or self-control once the behavioral excesses have been checked (Tims, Leukefeld, & Platt, 2001). Most alcohol-treatment programs show high success rates in "curing" the addictive problems, but many programs show lessening rates of abstinence or controlled drinking at various periods of follow-up. Many treatment programs do not pay enough attention to maintaining effective behavior and preventing relapse into previous maladaptive patterns (Miller & Rollnick, 2003).

Given that alcohol-dependent people are highly vulnerable to relapse, some researchers have focused on the need to help them remain abstinent. In one cognitive-behavioral approach, relapse behavior is a key factor in alcohol treatment (Marlatt & Vandenbos, 1997; Witkiewitz & Marlatt, 2004). The behaviors underlying relapse are seen as "indulgent behaviors" that are based on an individual's learning history. When an individual is abstinent or has an addiction under control, he or she gains a sense of personal control over the indulgent behavior. The longer the person is able to maintain this control, the greater the sense of achievement—the self-efficacy or confidence—and the greater the chance that he or she

Appealing advertisements and displays that encourage drinking can make abstinence particularly difficult and can contribute, at the very least on a subconscious level, to a relapse.

will be able to cope with the addiction and maintain control. However, a person may violate this rule of abstinence through a gradual, perhaps unconscious, process rather than through the sudden "falling off the wagon" that constitutes the traditional view of craving and relapse. In the cognitive-behavioral view, a person may, even while maintaining abstinence, inadvertently make a series of mini-decisions that begin a chain of behaviors that render relapse inevitable. For example, an abstinent alcohol abuser who buys a quart of bourbon just in case his friends drop by is unconsciously preparing the way for relapse.

Another type of relapse behavior involves the "abstinence violation effect," in which even minor transgressions are seen by the abstainer as having drastic significance. The effect works this way: An abstinent person may hold that he or she should not, under any circumstance, transgress or give in to the old habit. Abstinence-oriented treatment programs are particularly guided by this prohibitive rule. What happens, then, when an abstinent man becomes somewhat self-indulgent and takes a drink offered by an old friend or joins in a wedding toast? He may lose some of the sense of self-efficacy—the confidence—needed to control his drinking. Feeling guilty about having technically violated the vow of abstinence, he may rationalize that he "has blown it and become a drunk again, so why not go all the way?"

In relapse prevention treatment, clients are taught to recognize the apparently irrelevant decisions that serve as early warning signals of the possibility of relapse. High-risk situations such as parties or sports events are targeted, and the individuals learn to assess their own vulnerability to relapse. Clients are also trained not to become so discouraged, if they do relapse, that they lose their confidence. Some cognitive-behavioral therapists have even incorporated a "planned relapse" phase into the treatment. Research with relapse prevention strategies has shown them to be effective in providing continuing improvement over time (Rawson et al., 2002). In other words, when patients are taught to expect a relapse, they are better able to handle it.

In Review

- What is the difference between alcohol abuse and alcohol dependence?
- What are the three major physiological effects of alcohol?
- Identify the physical, interpersonal, and social/occupational problems that can result from chronic alcohol abuse.
- What are five major psychosocial factors that may contribute to alcohol dependence?
- Describe four psychosocial interventions used to treat alcohol dependence.

Drug Abuse and Dependence

Aside from alcohol, the psychoactive drugs most commonly associated with abuse and dependence in our society appear to be (1) narcotics such as opium and its derivatives, which include heroin; (2) sedatives such as barbiturates; (3) stimulants such as cocaine and amphetamines; (4) anti-anxiety drugs such as benzodiazepines; (5) pain killers such as OxyContin; and (6) hallucinogens such as LSD and PCP. (The effects of these and other drugs are summarized in Table 12.2 on p. 434.)

Caffeine and **nicotine** are also drugs of dependence, and disorders associated with tobacco withdrawal and caffeine intoxication are included in the DSM-IV-TR diagnostic classification system. The World Around Us 12.3 discusses these drugs further.

12.3 The World Around Us

Caffeine and Nicotine

The DSM-IV-TR includes addictions to two legally available and widely used substances: caffeine and nicotine. Although these substances do not represent the extensive and self-destructive problems found in drug and alcohol disorders, they create important physical and mental health problems in our society for several reasons:

- These drugs are easy to abuse. It is easy to become addicted to them because they are widely used and most people are exposed to them early in life.
- These drugs are readily available to anyone who wants to use them; in fact, because of peer pressure, it is usually difficult to avoid using them in our society.
- Both caffeine and nicotine have clearly addictive properties; use of them promotes further use, until one craves a regular "fix" in one's daily life.
- It is difficult to quit using these drugs both because of their addictive properties and because they are so embedded in the social context. (Nicotine use, however, is falling out of favor in many settings.)
- The extreme difficulty most people have in dealing with the withdrawal symptoms when trying to "break the habit" often produces considerable frustration.
- The health problems and side effects of these drugs, particularly nicotine, have been widely noted (USDHHS, 1994). One in seven deaths in the United States is associated with cigarette consumption.

Because of their tenacity as habits and their contributions to many major health problems, we will examine each of these addictions in more detail.

Caffeine

The chemical compound caffeine is found in many commonly available drinks and foods. Although the consumption of caffeine is widely practiced and socially promoted in contemporary society, problems can result from excessive caffeine intake. The negative effects of caffeine involve intoxication rather than withdrawal. Unlike addiction to drugs such as alcohol or nicotine, withdrawal from caffeine does not produce severe symptoms, except for headache, which is usually mild.

As described in DSM-IV-TR, caffeine-induced organic mental disorder (also referred to as "caffeinism") involves symptoms of restlessness, nervousness, excitement, insomnia, muscle twitching, and gastrointestinal complaints. It follows the ingestion of caffeine-containing substances, such as coffee, tea, cola, and chocolate. The amount of caffeine that results in intoxication differs among individuals.

(continued)

Nicotine

Because they are socially acceptable and readily available, caffeine and nicotine can be insidiously addictive substances. Though they do not represent the same kind of extensive, self-destructive problems as alcohol and drug disorders, caffeine and nicotine addiction can cause a myrlad of health problems, and are now included in the DSM-IV-TR.

The poisonous alkaloid nicotine is the chief active ingredient in tobacco; it is found in such items as cigarettes, chewing tobacco, and cigars, and it is even used as an insecticide.

Strong evidence exists for a nicotine-dependence syndrome (Malin, 2001; Watkins, Koob, & Markou, 2000), which nearly always begins during the adolescent years and may continue into adult life as a difficult-to-break and health-endangering habit. The surgeon general's report (USDHHS, 1994) estimates that there are 3.1 million adolescents and 25 percent of 17- to 18-year-olds who are current smokers. The "nicotine withdrawal disorder," as it is called in DSM-IV-TR, results from ceasing or reducing the intake of nicotine-containing substances after an individual has developed physical dependence on them. The diagnostic criteria for nicotine withdrawal include (1) the daily use of nicotine for at least several weeks, and (2) the following symptoms after nicotine ingestion is stopped or reduced: craving for nicotine; irritability, frustration, or anger; anxiety; difficulty concentrating; restlessness; decreased heart rate; and increased appetite or weight gain. Several other physical concomitants are associated with withdrawal from nicotine including decreased metabolic rate, headaches, insomnia, tremors, increased coughing, and impairment of performance on tasks requiring attention.

These withdrawal symptoms usually continue for several days to several weeks, depending on the extent of the nicotine habit. Some individuals report a desire for nicotine continuing for several months after they have quit smoking. In general, nicotine withdrawal symptoms operate in a manner similar to other addictions—they are "time limited and abate with drug replacement or gradual reduction" (Hughes, Higgins, & Hatsukami, 1990, p. 381).

Treatment of Nicotine Withdrawal

Over the past three decades, since the surgeon general's report that detailed the health hazards of smoking cigarettes, numerous treatment programs have been developed to help smokers quit (Curry, 1993; McEwen, Preston, & West, 2002; Smith, Reilly, et al., 2002). Such programs use many different methods including social support groups; various pharmacologic agents that replace cigarette consumption with safer forms of nicotine such as candy or gum; self-directed change which involves giving individuals guidance in changing their own behaviors; and professional treatment using psychological procedures such as behavioral or cognitive-behavioral interventions. One recent study provided smokers with ultrasound photographs of their carotid and femoral arteries along with quit-smoking counseling. This group showed higher quit rates than controls (Bovet, Perret, et al., 2002).

In general, tobacco dependence can be successfully treated, and most of the quit-smoking programs enjoy some success. They average only about a 20 to 25 percent success rate, however, although rates have been reported to be higher with treatment (Hays et al., 2001). This same level of success appears to result from the use of nicotine replacement therapy (NRT). Killen, Fortmann, and colleagues (1997) found that a controlled study of nicotine replacement treatment that employed a nicotine patch as well as video and printed materials for self-study produced a significant abstinence rate at 2 months (36 percent compared with 20 percent for the placebo condition). However, this abstinence rate dropped to only 22 percent at 6 months and was equal to that of the placebo or control sample. Recently, encouraging results have been reported on the use of the drug bupropion (Zyban) in preventing relapse for smokers trying to quit smoking. The drug reduced relapse as long as the person was taking it, but relapse rates were similar to those of other treatments once the drug was discontinued (Barringer & Weaver, 2002). The highest self-reported quit rates for smokers were reportedly among patients who were hospitalized for cancer (63 percent), cardiovascular disease (57 percent), or pulmonary disease (46 percent; Smith, Reilly, et al., 2002).

An estimated 28 million people worldwide incur significant health risks by using various psychoactive substances other than alcohol, tobacco, and volatile solvents such as glue (World Health Organization, 1997). The extent of drug abuse in the population is likely to be underestimated because many abusers do not seek help. In fact, one recent study (Newcomb, Galaif, & Locke, 2001) noted that one-third of abusers remitted without treatment. Although they may occur at any age, drug abuse and dependence are most common during adolescence and young adulthood (NIAAA, 2002; Smith, 1989) and vary according to metropolitan area, race and ethnicity, labor force status, and other demographic characteristics (Hughes, 1992). Substance-abuse problems are relatively more prominent in economically depressed minority communities (Akins, Mosher, et al., 2003; Beauvais, 1998). The reasons for this will be discussed later in this section.

The extent to which drug abuse has become a problem for society is reflected in a study of drug involvement among applicants for employment at a large teaching hospital in Maryland (Lange et al., 1994). Beginning in 1989, and for a 2-year period, all applicants for employment were screened through a preemployment drug-screening program (individuals were not identified in the initial study). Of 593 applicants, 10.8 percent were found to have detectable amounts of illicit drugs in their systems. The most frequently detected drug was marijuana (55 percent of those who tested positively), followed by cocaine (36 percent) and opiates (28 percent). The impact of drug use among employed people has also been reported to be significant. In a study of job satisfaction in a community sample of 470 adults, Galaif, Newcomb, and Carmona (2001) found that polydrug use (that is, use of multiple drugs) predicted impaired work functioning and job dissatisfaction 4 years later.

In one study, applicants for employment at a large teaching hospital were put through a pre-employment drug-screening program. Nearly 11 percent of the applicants were found to have detectable amounts of illicit drugs in their systems, including marijuana, cocaine, and opiates.

Among those who abuse drugs, behavior patterns vary markedly, depending on the type, amount, and duration of drug use; on the physiological and psychological makeup of the individual; and, in some instances, on the social setting in which the drug experience occurs. Thus it appears most useful to deal separately with some of the drugs that are more commonly associated with abuse and dependence in contemporary society.

Opium and Its Derivatives (Narcotics)

People have used opium and its derivatives for over 5,000 years. Galen (A.D. 130–201) considered theriaca, whose principal ingredient was opium, to be a panacea:

> It resists poison and venomous bites, cures inveterate headache, vertigo, deafness, epilepsy, apoplexy, dimness of sight, loss of voice, asthma, coughs of all kinds, spitting of blood, tightness of breath, colic, the iliac poisons, jaundice, hardness of the spleen, stone, urinary complaints, fevers, dropsies, leprosies, the trouble to which women are subject, melancholy and all pestilences. (See Brock, 1979 for a discussion of Galen)

Even today, opium derivatives are still used for some of the conditions Galen mentioned.

Opium is a mixture of about 18 chemical substances known as "alkaloids." In 1805 the alkaloid present in the largest amount (10 to 15 percent) was found to be a bitter-tasting powder that could serve as a powerful sedative and pain reliever; it was named **morphine** after Morpheus, god of sleep in Greek mythology. The hypodermic needle was introduced in America around 1856, allowing morphine to be widely administered to soldiers during the Civil War—not only to those wounded in battle but also to those suffering from dysentery. As a consequence, many Civil War veterans returned to civilian life addicted to the drug, a condition euphemistically referred to as "soldier's illness."

Scientists concerned with the addictive properties of morphine hypothesized that one part of the morphine molecule might be responsible for its analgesic properties (that is, its ability to eliminate pain without inducing unconsciousness) and another for its addictiveness. At about the turn of the century, it was discovered that if morphine was treated with an inexpensive and readily available chemical called "acetic anhydride," it would be converted into another powerful analgesic called **heroin.** Heroin was hailed enthusiastically by its discoverer, Heinrich Dreser (Boehm, 1968). Leading scientists of his time agreed on the merits of heroin, and the drug came to be widely prescribed in place of morphine for pain relief and related medicinal purposes. However, heroin was a cruel disappointment, for it proved to be an even more dangerous drug than morphine, acting more rapidly and more intensely and being equally if not more addictive. Eventually, heroin was removed from use in medical practice.

As it became apparent that opium and its derivatives—including codeine, which is used in some cough syrups—were perilously addictive, the U.S. Congress enacted the Harrison Act in 1914. Under this and later legislation, the unauthorized sale and distribution of certain drugs became a federal offense; physicians and pharmacists were held accountable for each dose they dispensed. Thus, overnight, the role of a chronic narcotic user changed from that of addict—whose addition was considered a vice, but was tolerated—to that of criminal. Unable to obtain drugs through legal sources, many turned to illegal channels, and eventually to other criminal acts, as a means of maintaining their suddenly expensive drug supply.

In one survey, about 2.4 million Americans acknowledged having tried heroin, and almost a quarter of a million

TABLE 12.2 Psychoactive Drugs Commonly Involved in Drug Abuse

Classification	Drug	Effect
Sedatives	Alcohol (ethanol)	Reduce tension Facilitate social interaction "Blot out" feelings or events
	Barbiturates Nembutal (pentobarbital) Seconal (secobarbital) Veronal (barbital) Tuinal (secobarbital and amobarbital)	Reduce tension
Stimulants	Amphetamines Benzedrine (amphetamine) Dexedrine (dextroamphetamine) Methedrine (methamphetamine) Cocaine (coca)	Increase feelings of alertness and confidence Decrease feelings of fatigue Stay awake for long periods Increase endurance Stimulate sex drive
Narcotics	Opium and its derivatives Opium Morphine Codeine Heroin	Alleviate physical pain Induce relaxation and pleasant reverie Alleviate anxiety and tension
	Methadone (synthetic narcotic)	Treatment of heroin dependence
Psychedelics and hallucinogens	Cannabis Marijuana Hashish	Induce changes in mood, thought, and behavior
	Mescaline (peyote) Psilocybin (psychotogenic mushrooms) LSD (lysergic acid diethylamide-25) PCP (phencyclidine)	"Expand" one's mind Induce stupor
Antianxiety drugs (minor tranquilizers)	Librium (chlordiazepoxide) Miltown (meprobamate) Valium (diazepam) Xanax	Alleviate tension and anxiety Induce relaxation and sleep

Note: This list is by no means complete; for example, it does not include newer drugs, such as Ritalin, which are designed to produce multiple effects; it does not include the less commonly used volatile hydrocarbons, such as glue, paint thinner, gasoline, cleaning fluid, and nail polish remover, which are highly dangerous when sniffed for their psychoactive effects; and it does not include the antipsychotic and antidepressant drugs, which are abused, but relatively rarely. We shall deal with these and the antianxiety drugs in our discussion of drug therapy in Chapter 17.

people admitted to using it within the past 12 months (U.S. Department of Health and Human Services, 1997). In 2000, heroin overdose accounted for 16 percent of all drug-related emergency room admissions (DAWN Report, 2001).

BIOLOGICAL EFFECTS OF MORPHINE AND HEROIN Morphine and heroin are commonly introduced into the body by smoking, snorting (inhaling the powder), eating, "skin popping," or "mainlining," the last two being methods of introducing the drug via hypodermic injection. Skin popping is injecting the liquefied drug just beneath the skin, and mainlining is injecting the drug directly into the bloodstream. In the United States, a young addict usually moves from snorting to mainlining.

Among the immediate effects of mainlined or snorted heroin is a euphoric spasm (the rush) lasting 60 seconds or so, which many addicts compare to a sexual orgasm. However, vomiting and nausea have also been known to be part of the immediate effects of heroin and morphine use. This rush is followed by a high, during which an addict typically is in a lethargic, withdrawn state in which bodily needs, including needs for food and sex, are markedly diminished; pleasant feelings of relaxation, euphoria, and reverie tend to dominate. These effects last from 4 to 6 hours and are followed—in addicts—by a negative phase that produces a desire for more of the drug.

The use of opium derivatives over a period of time generally results in a physiological craving for the drug. The time required to establish the drug habit varies, but it has been estimated that continual use over a period of 30 days is typically sufficient. Users then find that they have become physiologically dependent on the drug in the sense that they feel physically ill when they do not take it. In addition, users of opium derivatives gradually build up a tolerance to the drug, so increasingly larger amounts are needed to achieve the desired effects.

When people addicted to opiates do not get a dose of the drug within approximately 8 hours, they start to experience withdrawal symptoms. The character and severity of these reactions depend on many factors including the amount of the narcotic habitually used, the intervals between doses, the duration of the addiction, and especially the addict's health and personality.

Withdrawal from heroin is not always dangerous or even very painful. Many addicted people withdraw without assistance. Withdrawal can, however, be an agonizing experience for some people, with symptoms including runny nose, tearing eyes, perspiration, restlessness, increased respiration rate, and an intensified desire for the drug. As time passes, the symptoms may become more severe. Typically, a feeling of chilliness alternates with flushing and excessive sweating, vomiting, diarrhea, abdominal cramps, pains in the back and extremities, severe headache, marked tremors, and varying degrees of insomnia. Beset by these discomforts, an individual refuses food and water, and this, coupled with the vomiting, sweating, and diarrhea, results in dehydration and weight loss. Occasionally, symptoms include delirium, hallucinations, and manic activity. Cardiovascular collapse may also occur and can result in death. If morphine is administered, the subjective distress experienced by an addict temporarily ends, and physiological balance is quickly restored.

Withdrawal symptoms are usually on the decline by the third or fourth day and by the seventh or eighth day have disappeared. As the symptoms subside, the person resumes normal eating and drinking and rapidly regains lost weight. After withdrawal symptoms have ceased, the individual's former tolerance for the drug is reduced; as a result, there is a risk that taking the former large dosage might result in overdose.

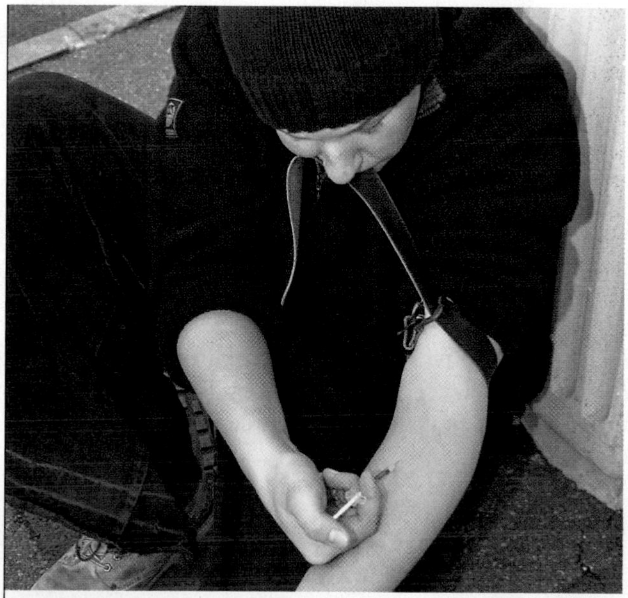

The adolescent shown here is injecting the drug heroin—a dangerous and highly addictive substance that is widely available to adolescents today.

SOCIAL EFFECTS OF MORPHINE AND HEROIN

Typically, the life of a narcotics addict becomes increasingly centered on obtaining and using drugs, so the addiction usually leads to socially maladaptive behavior as the individual is eventually forced to lie, steal, and associate with undesirable contacts to maintain a supply of drugs. Many addicts resort to petty theft to support their habits, and some addicts turn to prostitution as a means of financing their addictions.

Along with the lowering of ethical and moral restraints, addiction has adverse physical effects on an individual's well-being—for example, disruption of the immune system (Theodorou & Haber, 2005). Lifestyle factors can lead to further problems; an inadequate diet, for example, may lead to ill health and increased susceptibility to a variety of physical ailments. The use of unsterile equipment may also lead to various problems including liver damage from hepatitis and transmission of the AIDS virus. In addition, the use of such a potent drug without medical supervision and government controls to ensure its strength and purity can result in fatal overdose. Injection of too much heroin can cause coma and death. In fact, heroin-related deaths have shown an increase in cities where data are collected (National Institute for Drug Abuse, 1998). The most common drug-related deaths in the United States involve combinations of heroin, cocaine, and alcohol (DAWN, 2002). Women who use heroin during pregnancy subject their unborn children to the risk of dire consequences. One tragic outcome is premature babies who are themselves addicted to heroin and vulnerable to a number of diseases (Anand & Arnold, 1994).

Addiction to opiates usually leads to a gradual deterioration of well-being (Brown & Lo, 2000). The ill health and general personality deterioration often found in opium addiction do not result directly from the pharmacological effects of the drug but, rather, are usually products of the sacrifices of money, proper diet, social position, and self-respect as an addict becomes more desperate to procure the required daily dosage.

CAUSAL FACTORS IN OPIATE ABUSE AND DEPENDENCE No single causal pattern fits all addictions to narcotic drugs. A study by Fulmer and Lapidus (1980) concluded that the three most frequently cited reasons for beginning to use heroin were pleasure, curiosity, and peer pressure. Pleasure was the single most widespread reason—given by 81 percent of addicts. Heavy opiate use may in some part be influenced by genetic inheritance (Kendler, Karkowski, et al., 2000), perhaps through inheritance of personality characteristics (Bouchard & Loehlin, 2001). Other reasons such as a desire to escape life stress, personal maladjustment, and sociocultural conditions also play a part (Bry, McKeon, & Pandina, 1982).

NEURAL BASES FOR PHYSIOLOGICAL ADDICTION Research teams have isolated and studied receptor sites for narcotic drugs in the brain (Goldstein et al., 1974; Office of Technology Assessment, 1993; Pert & Snyder, 1973). Such receptor sites are specific nerve cells into which given psychoactive drugs fit like keys into the proper locks. This interaction of drug and brain cells apparently results in a drug's action and, in the case of narcotic drugs, may lead to addiction. The repeated use of opiates results in changes in neurotransmitter systems that regulate incentive/motivation and the ability to manage stress (DeVries & Shippenberg, 2002).

The human body produces its own opium-like substances, called **endorphins,** in the brain and pituitary gland. These substances are produced in response to stimulation and are believed to play a role in an organism's reaction to pain (Bolles & Fanselow, 1982). Some investigators have suspected that endorphins play a role in drug addiction, speculating that chronic underproduction of endorphins leads to a craving for narcotic drugs. Research on the role of endorphins in drug addiction has generally been inconclusive, and no effective treatment has resulted from this line of research.

ADDICTION ASSOCIATED WITH PSYCHOPATHOLOGY A high incidence of antisocial personality has been found among heroin addicts (Alterman, McDermott, et al., 1998). In a comparison between a group of 45 young institutionalized male addicts and a control group of nonaddicts, Gilbert and Lombardi (1967) found that the distinguishing features were "the addict's antisocial traits, his depression, tension, insecurity, and feelings of inadequacy, and his difficulty in forming warm and lasting interpersonal relationships" (p. 536). Meyer and Mirin (1979) found that opiate addicts were highly impulsive and unable to delay gratification. Kosten and Rounsaville (1986) reported that about 68 percent of heroin abusers were also diagnosed as having a personality disorder. As in the case of alcoholism, however, it is essential to exercise caution in distinguishing between personality traits before and after addiction; the high incidence of psychopathology among narcotics addicts may in part result from, rather than precede, the long-term effects of addiction.

ADDICTION ASSOCIATED WITH SOCIOCULTURAL FACTORS In our society, a so-called "narcotics subculture" exists in which addicts can obtain drugs and protect themselves against society's sanctions. The decision to join this culture has important future implications, for from that point on, addicts' activities will revolve around their drug-user role. In short, addiction becomes a way of life. In a survey of three large cities in Texas, Maddux and colleagues (1994) found that the majority of illicit drug injectors were undereducated and unemployed individuals from minority groups.

With time, most young addicts who join the drug culture become increasingly withdrawn, indifferent to their friends (except those in the drug group), and apathetic about sexual activity (Tremble, Padillo, & Bell, 1994). They are likely to abandon scholastic and athletic endeavors and to show a marked reduction in competitive and achievement strivings. Most of these addicts appear to lack clear sex-role identification and to experience feelings of inadequacy when confronted with the demands of adulthood. They feel progressively isolated from the broader culture, but their feelings of group belongingness are bolstered by continued association with the addict milieu. At the same time, they come to view drugs both as a means of revolt against authority and conventional values and as a device for alleviating personal anxieties and tensions.

TREATMENTS AND OUTCOMES Treatment for narcotics addiction is initially similar to that for alcoholism in that it involves building up an addict both physically and psychologically and providing help through the withdrawal period. Addicts often dread the discomfort of withdrawal, but in a hospital setting it is less abrupt and usually involves the administration of medication that eases the distress.

After physical withdrawal has been completed, treatment focuses on helping a former addict make an adequate adjustment to his or her community and abstain from the further use of narcotics. Traditionally, however, the prognosis has been unfavorable, with many clients dropping out of treatment (Katz, Brown, et al., 2004). Withdrawal from heroin does not remove the craving for the drug. A key target in treatment of heroin addiction must be the alleviation of this craving. One approach to dealing with the physiological craving for heroin was pioneered by a research team at Rockefeller University in New York. It involved the use of the drug **methadone** in conjunction with a rehabilitation program (counseling, group therapy, and other procedures) directed toward the "total resocialization" of addicts. Methadone hydrochloride is a synthetic narcotic that is related to heroin and is equally addictive physiologically. Its usefulness in treatment lies in the fact that it satisfies an addict's craving for heroin without producing serious psychological impairment, if only because it is administered as a "treatment" in a formal clinical context (see the Unresolved Issues at the end of this chapter).

Other medications, such as buprenorphine, have been used to treat heroin addiction. It promises to be as effective a substitute for heroin as methadone but has fewer side effects (Kamien, Mikulich, & Amass, 1999). Buprenorphine operates as a partial antagonist to heroin (Lewis & Walter, 1992) and produces the "feelings of contentment" associated with heroin use (Mendelson & Mello, 1992). Yet the drug does not produce the physical dependence that is characteristic of heroin (Grant & Sonti, 1994) and can be discontinued without severe withdrawal symptoms. Like methadone, buprenorphine appears to work best at maintaining abstinence if it is provided along with behavior therapy (Bickel, Amass, et al., 1997).

Cocaine and Amphetamines (Stimulants)

In contrast to narcotics, which depress (slow down) the action of the central nervous system, cocaine and amphetamines stimulate it (speed it up).

COCAINE Like opium, **cocaine** is a plant product discovered in ancient times and used ever since. It was widely used in the pre-Columbian world of Mexico and Peru (Guerra, 1971). Because for many years it was typically very costly in the United States, cocaine was considered as the "high" for the affluent. However, with more widespread availability and lowering of prices, the drug's use increased significantly in the United States during the 1980s and 1990s—to the point where its use was considered epidemic, especially among middle- and upper-income groups. "Crack" is the street name that is applied to cocaine that has been processed from cocaine hydrochloride to a free base for smoking. The name refers to the crackling sound emitted when the mixture is heated.

In 2003, there were an estimated 2.3 million people using cocaine and over 600,000 people reported using crack cocaine during that time (Substance Abuse and Mental Health Services Administration, 2004). Cocaine-related emergency room visits increased substantially between 1978 and 2000. In 2000, there were 71 cocaine-related emergency room visits per 100,000 drug-related admissions, or about 29 percent (DAWN Report, 2001).

Like the opiates, cocaine may be ingested by sniffing, swallowing, or injecting. Also like the opiates, it precipitates a euphoric state of 4 to 6 hours' duration, during which a user experiences feelings of confidence and contentment. However, this blissful state may be preceded by headache, dizziness, and restlessness. When cocaine is chronically abused, acute toxic psychotic symptoms may occur including frightening visual, auditory, and tactual hallucinations similar to those in acute schizophrenia.

Unlike the opiates, cocaine stimulates the cortex of the brain, inducing sleeplessness and excitement as well as stimulating and accentuating sexual feelings. Dependence on cocaine also differs somewhat from dependence on opiates. It was formerly believed that tolerance was not increased appreciably with cocaine use. However, acute tolerance has now been demonstrated, and some chronic tolerance, a more persistent habituation, may occur as well (Jones, 1984). Moreover, cognitive impairment associated with cocaine abuse is likely to be an important consideration in long-term effects of the drug (Abi-Saab, Beauvais, et al., 2005; Mann, 2004). The previous view that cocaine abusers did not develop physiological dependence on the drug also has changed. Gawin and Kleber (1986) demonstrated that chronic abusers who become abstinent develop uniform, depression-like symptoms, but the symptoms are transient. Our broadened knowledge about cocaine abuse, particularly with respect to the many health and social problems resulting from dependence on the drug, has resulted in considerable modification of professional views of cocaine over the past 20 years. For example, the modifications in the DSM-IV-TR diagnostic classification reflect a significant increase in our knowledge of cocaine's addictive properties. A new disorder is described—cocaine withdrawal—that involves symptoms of depression, fatigue, disturbed sleep, and increased dreaming (Foltin & Fischman, 1997). The psychological and life problems experienced by cocaine users are often great. Employment, family, psychological, and legal problems are all more likely to occur among

Yasmine Bleeth, model and actress best known for her role on Baywatch, *"never expected to get into drugs." But over the course of several years cocaine became a serious addiction and all she could think about. At one point, cocaine use had eaten a hole the size of a dime in her nose. Her dress size dropped from size 6 to size 2. After a car accident and subsequent arrest in September 2001, Yasmine stopped all cocaine use, gained 20 pounds, and married a man she met while in rehab.*

cocaine and crack users than among nonusers. Many life problems experienced by cocaine abusers result in part from the considerable amounts of money that are required to support their habits. Increased sexual activity, often trading sex for drugs, has been associated with crack cocaine use (Weatherby et al., 1992), as has engaging in sexual activity with anonymous partners (Balshem et al., 1992). Problems in sexual functioning have been reported to be associated with crack cocaine use. Kim and colleagues (1992) reported that most users lose interest in sex and develop sexual dysfunction with prolonged usage.

Women who use cocaine when they are pregnant place their babies at risk for both health and psychological problems. Although recent research has suggested that there is no "fetal crack syndrome" similar to what has been shown with alcohol-abusing mothers (Azar, 1997), children of crack-using mothers are at risk of being maltreated as infants as well as of losing their mothers during infancy. Wasserman and Leventhal (1993) studied a group of cocaine-exposed children and a control sample of nonexposed children for a 24-month period following their birth. They found that children who were regularly exposed to cocaine *in utero* were more likely to be mistreated (23 percent compared with only 4 percent of controls). The courts today are beginning to take a stern stance with respect to mothers who use cocaine during pregnancy to the detriment of their fetus. In one case, a woman who lost her fetus as a result of crack use faced a murder charge for killing her unborn child (Associated Press, 1997). She pleaded guilty to involuntary manslaughter and received a 3-year suspended sentence.

TREATMENT AND OUTCOMES Treatment for dependence on cocaine does not differ appreciably from that for other drugs that involve physiological dependence. Kosten (1989) reported that effective cocaine-abuse treatment includes the medications such as desipramine and naltrexone (Kosten et al., 1992) to reduce cravings and psychological therapy to ensure treatment compliance, and disulfiram has been used to reduce alcohol use (Carroll, Fenton, et al., 2004). The feelings of tension and depression that accompany absence of the drug have to be dealt with during the immediate withdrawal period.

Some success in the treatment of cocaine abusers has been reported. Siqueland, Crits-Cristoph, and colleagues (2002) found that patients who remained in drug treatment longer used drugs less often after treatment than those who dropped out; and Stewart, Gossop, and Marsden (2002) found that patients who completed therapy had lower rates of drug overdose than those who failed to complete treatment. Carroll, Powers, et al. (1993) have shown that many cocaine abusers did well in maintaining treatment goals, and one-third were abstinent at a 12-month follow-up. They found several factors associated with poorer outcomes: severity of abuse, poorer psychiatric functioning, and presence of concurrent alcoholism. Higgins, Badger, and Budney (2000) found that people who were not able to sustain abstinence during the treatment had poorer outcomes following therapy.

One of the problems clinicians face in working with cocaine abusers is "dropping out": Only 42 percent of those in one study remained in treatment for six or more sessions (Kleinman et al., 1992). Another problem encountered in drug treatment is that many of the cocaine-dependent patients have severe antisocial personality disorder—a situation resulting in treatment resistance (Conway, Kane, et al., 2003; Leal, Ziedonis, & Kosten, 1994)—or are "psychosis-prone" personalities (Kwapil, 1996). Arndt and colleagues (1994) found that cocaine-dependent patients with antisocial personality characteristics made few therapeutic gains, whereas those without antisocial features made significant progress.

Is treatment always necessary for cocaine abusers to recover? An interesting study suggested that some abusers can improve without therapy. Toneatto, Sobell, et al. (1999) described a study of natural (nontreated) recovery among cocaine abusers. They reported that abusers who resolved their dependence on cocaine were similar to those who did not resolve their cocaine problems in terms of demographic characteristics, substance abuse, and psychiatric history. The successful abstainers considered their "improved self-concept" crucial to their success.

AMPHETAMINES The earliest **amphetamine** to be introduced—Benzedrine, or amphetamine sulfate—was first synthesized in 1927 and became available in drugstores in the early 1930s as an inhalant to relieve stuffy noses. However, the manufacturers soon learned that some customers were chewing the wicks in the inhalers for "kicks." Thus the stimulating effects of amphetamine sulfate were discovered by the public before the drug was formally prescribed as a stimulant by physicians. In the late 1930s, two newer amphetamines were introduced—Dexedrine (dextroamphetamine) and Methedrine (methamphetamine hydrochloride, also known as "speed"). The latter preparation is a far more potent stimulant of the central nervous system than either Benzedrine or Dexedrine and hence is considered more dangerous. In fact, its abuse can be lethal.

Initially these preparations were considered to be "wonder pills" that helped people stay alert and awake and function temporarily at a level beyond normal. During World War II, military interest was aroused in the stimulating effects of these drugs, and they were used by both Allied and German soldiers to ward off fatigue (Jarvik, 1967). Similarly, among civilians, amphetamines came to be widely used by night workers, long-distance truck drivers, students cramming for exams, and athletes striving to improve their performances. It was also discovered that amphetamines tended to suppress appetite, and they became popular with people trying to lose weight. In addition, they were often used to counteract the effects of barbiturates or other sleeping pills that had been taken the night before. As a result of their many uses, amphetamines were widely prescribed by doctors.

Today amphetamines are occasionally used medically for curbing the appetite when weight reduction is desirable; for treating individuals suffering from narcolepsy, a disorder in which people cannot prevent themselves from continually falling asleep during the day; and for treating hyperactive children. Curiously enough, amphetamines have a calming rather than a stimulating effect on many of these youngsters (see Chapter 16). Amphetamines are also sometimes prescribed for alleviating mild feelings of depression, relieving fatigue, and maintaining alertness for sustained periods of time. By far, however, the most frequent use of amphetamines is for recreational purposes, the most typical user being a young person interested in the high that the drug induces (Klee, 1998).

Since the passage of the Controlled Substance Act of 1970 (Drug Enforcement Administration, 1979), amphetamines have been classified as Schedule II controlled substances—that is, drugs with high abuse potential that require a prescription for each purchase. As a result, medical use of amphetamines has declined in the United States in recent years, and they are more difficult to obtain legally. However, it is often easy to find illegal sources of amphetamines, which thus remain among the most widely abused drugs. Amphetamines are among the most widely used illicit drugs in other countries as well—for example, in Australia (Lintzeris, Holgate, & Dunlop, 1996). In 2000, 2.4 percent of drug-related emergency room visits involved amphetamine or methamphetamine (DAWN Survey, 2000; see The World Around Us 12.4 on p. 440).

EFFECTS OF AMPHETAMINE ABUSE Despite their legitimate medical uses, amphetamines are not a magical source of extra mental or physical energy. Instead, they push users toward greater expenditures of their own resources—often to the point of hazardous fatigue. Amphetamines are psychologically and physically addictive, and the body rapidly builds up tolerance to them (Wise, 1996). Thus habituated abusers may use the drugs in amounts that would be lethal to nonusers. In some instances, users inject the drug to get faster and more intense results.

For a person who exceeds prescribed dosages, amphetamine consumption results in heightened blood pressure, enlarged pupils, unclear or rapid speech, profuse sweating, tremors, excitability, loss of appetite, confusion, and sleeplessness. Injected in large quantities, Methedrine can raise blood pressure enough to cause immediate death. In addition, chronic abuse of amphetamines can result in brain damage and a wide range of psychopathology, including a disorder known as "amphetamine psychosis," which appears similar to paranoid schizophrenia. Suicide, homicide, assault, and various other acts of violence are associated with amphetamine abuse.

TREATMENTS AND OUTCOMES Research on the effectiveness of various treatments for withdrawing patients from amphetamine is scarce (Baker & Lee, 2003). Although withdrawal from amphetamines is usually safe, some evidence suggests that physiological dependence upon the drug is an important factor to consider in treatment (Wise & Munn, 1995). In some instances, abrupt withdrawal from the chronic, excessive use of amphetamines can result in cramping, nausea, diarrhea, and even convulsions. Moreover, abrupt abstinence commonly results in feelings of weariness and depression. The depression usually peaks in 48 to 72 hours, often remains intense for a day or two, and then tends to lessen gradually over a period of several days. Mild feelings of depression and lassitude may persist for weeks or even months. If brain damage has occurred, the residual effects may include impaired ability to concentrate, learn, and remember, with resulting social, economic, and personality deterioration.

Barbiturates (Sedatives)

In the 1930s, powerful sedatives called **barbiturates** were developed. Although barbiturates have legitimate medical uses, they are extremely dangerous drugs commonly associated with both physiological and psychological dependence and lethal overdoses.

EFFECTS OF BARBITURATES Barbiturates were once widely used by physicians to calm patients and induce sleep. They act as depressants—somewhat like alcohol—to slow down the action of the central nervous system (Nemeroff, 2003) and significantly reduce performance on cognitive tasks (Pickworth et al., 1997). Shortly after taking a barbiturate, an individual experiences a feeling of relaxation in which tensions seem to disappear, followed by a physical and intellectual lassitude and a tendency toward drowsiness and sleep—the intensity of such feelings depends on the type and amount of the barbiturate taken. Strong doses produce sleep almost immediately; excessive doses are lethal because they result in paralysis of the brain's respiratory centers. Pentobarbital, a common barbiturate, appears to have even more sedating characteristics than alcohol (Mintzer, Guarino, et al., 1997). Impaired decision making and problem solving, sluggishness, slow speech, and sudden mood shifts are also common effects of barbiturates.

Excessive use of barbiturates leads to increased tolerance as well as to physiological and psychological dependence. It can also lead to brain damage and personality deterioration. Unlike tolerance for opiates, tolerance for barbiturates does not increase the amount needed to cause death. This means that users can easily ingest fatal overdoses, either intentionally or accidentally.

CAUSAL FACTORS IN BARBITURATE ABUSE AND DEPENDENCE Although many young people experiment with barbiturates, or "downers," most do not become dependent. In fact, the people who do become dependent on barbiturates tend to be middle-aged and older people who often rely on them as "sleeping pills" and who do not commonly use other classes of drugs (except possibly alcohol and minor tranquilizers). These people have been

12.4 The World Around Us

Methamphetamine—Is "Ice" Really Cool?

Methamphetamine, referred to on the streets as "crystal" or "ice" because of its appearance, is a highly addictive stimulant drug that can provide a quick and long-lasting "high." However, it is one of the most dangerous illegal drugs because of its treacherous properties and its unwelcome results. Methamphetamine is a form of amphetamine that can be "cooked" up in large quantities in makeshift laboratories in out-of-the-way places that defy and frustrate detection. This drug is relatively cheap to manufacture and is often referred to as "poor people's cocaine." It can be manufactured, for example, in a portable cooler with ingredients that can be legally obtained from any drugstore. The drug can be ingested in a variety of ways, through smoking, snorting, swallowing, or injecting. The drug's effects can be almost instantaneous if it is smoked or injected.

Methamphetamine operates by increasing the level of dopamine in the brain, and prolonged use of the drug produces structural changes in the brain (Maxwell, 2005; Wang, Volkow, et al., 2004). The severity of psychiatric symptoms associated with the drug is significantly related to the duration of use (Yoshimoto et al., 2002). Moreover, discontinuing the drug after the person has become habituated can result in problems with learning, memory, and cognitive dysfunction (Cretzmeyer, Sarrazin, et al., 2003; Rothman et al., 2000) and severe mental health problems such as paranoid thinking and hallucinations (Brecht, O'Brien, et al., 2004; Srisurapanont, Ali, et al., 2003). This drug is metabolized more slowly than other drugs such as cocaine and produces a high for a longer period of time. When the drug wears off or when users "come down from the high," they are likely to feel extremely weak, lethargic, sleepy, and depressed. Egan (2002) provided the following descriptions of two meth users from the State of Washington:

> Lacy B., 26, drives around in the rain, her skin twitching, her mind racing, her nails bitten to a pulp. She has been trying to shed her addiction and is awaiting counseling. But she also carries a grocery list under the seat of her car, with all the ingredients for cooking meth.
>
> "Solvents from the paint store, lithium from batteries, Sudafed—I know a lot of this stuff could kill me," Ms. B. said in an interview. "But I also know that it gets me through. There are times when I don't feel normal without meth."
>
> Another Snohomish County woman, a Bertina P., 33, has been drug-free for two years, but she still shudders at her low point. "I took a pocket knife and tried to lance an abscess in my mouth." She said, "I was doing my own dentistry. Lucky I didn't kill myself." (33)

Use of the drug has increased substantially over the past 10 years. Over 4.9 million people in the United States (2.3 percent of the population) had tried methamphetamine by 1998 (NIDA, 2002). In a recent survey of almost 630,000 high school students, Oetting et al. (2000) reported that methamphetamine use more than doubled between 1989 and 1996. In 1996, 1.8 percent of ninth-grade, 1.9 percent of tenth-grade, 2.5 percent of eleventh-grade, and 2.1 percent of twelfth-grade boys reported having used methamphetamine in the past 30 days. Although use among girls was less, the trend over the 7-year time span paralleled the boys' increasing use. The increasing use among women might result from one of the side effects of the drug. Wermuth (2000) pointed out that "an additional attraction is the appetite suppressant effects, especially attractive to women trying to stay thin." Interestingly, the use of methamphetamine in the United States has been somewhat of a regional phenomenon; most use has occurred in the Southwest, on the West Coast, and in Hawaii and very little use in the North, South, and Midwest (DAWN, 2001). This situation results from the fact that meth labs have been concentrated in Mexico, California, and Hawaii.

There is some evidence that people become more quickly addicted to methamphetamine and require treatment sooner than those using cocaine (Castro et al., 2000). Addicted methamphetamine users are highly resistant to treatment, and post-treatment relapse is common. In one California study of 98 methamphetamine abusers, the investigators reported that over half of the participants had returned to methamphetamine use by the time they were interviewed 2 to 3 years following therapy; 36 percent reported that they had returned to methamphetamine use within 6 months of therapy (Brecht et al., 2000).

referred to as "silent abusers" because they take the drugs in the privacy of their homes and ordinarily do not become public nuisances.

Barbiturates are commonly used with alcohol. Some users claim they can achieve an intense high by combining barbiturates, amphetamines, and alcohol. However, one possible effect of combining barbiturates and alcohol is death, because each drug potentiates (increases the action of) the other. See The World Around Us 12.5 for a discussion of pain medications abuse.

TREATMENTS AND OUTCOMES As with many other drugs, it is often essential in treatment to distinguish between barbiturate intoxication, which results from the

12.5 The World Around Us

Pain Killers: Consequences and Pain of Medications Abuse

Many people become addicted to pain medication in the course of treatment for chronic pain (Isaacson, 2004). There has been a significant increase in lifetime nonmedical use of pain relievers, with between 29 and 31 million persons age 12 or older using such drugs (Substance Abuse and Mental Health Services Administration, 2004). Pain killers such as OxyContin contain an opiate that is similar to morphine and codeine. When these substances attach to receptors in the spinal cord and brain, they block transmission of pain (FDA, 2003). Opiate medications have a high potential for abuse because they are widely available in tablet form through medical prescription for pain and are becoming more accessible through a growing illegal market. Pain killers such as OxyContin, Vicodin, and Darvon, often referred to as "hillbilly heroin," "coties," "demmies," or "dillies" on the street, are becoming a major drug problem today (FDA, 2003). These drugs are highly dangerous and can seriously affect one's lifestyle as well as producing serious health consequences, even death (Pinsky, 2004).

Talk show host, Rush Limbaugh, became addicted to pain killer OxyContin and was investigated for allegedly buying thousands of addictive pain-killers from a black-market drug ring in 2003.

The media frenzy over iconic talk show host Rush Limbaugh's alleged illegal use of pain killers (OxyContin, Lorcet, and hydrocodone) in 2003 has prompted broader attention to addiction to opoids that are widely prescribed for pain.

Rush Limbaugh was reported to authorities by his former housekeeper, who was supplying him with large quantities of OxyContin for several years. She obtained these drugs through illegal prescriptions to her and her husband. Limbaugh's excessive use of pain killers allegedly resulted in his going through detoxification on two occasions (Connor, 2003).

toxic effects of overdose, and the symptoms associated with drug withdrawal, because different procedures are required. With barbiturates, withdrawal symptoms are more dangerous, severe, and long-lasting than in opiate withdrawal. A patient going through barbiturate withdrawal becomes anxious and apprehensive and manifests coarse tremors of the hands and face; additional symptoms commonly include insomnia, weakness, nausea, vomiting, abdominal cramps, rapid heart rate, elevated blood pressure, and loss of weight. An acute delirious psychosis may develop.

For persons used to taking large dosages, withdrawal symptoms may last for as long as a month, but usually they tend to abate by the end of the first week. Fortunately, the withdrawal symptoms in barbiturate addiction can be minimized by administering increasingly small doses of the barbiturate itself or another drug that produces similar effects. The withdrawal program is still a dangerous one, however, especially if barbiturate addiction is complicated by alcoholism or dependence on other drugs.

LSD and Related Drugs (Hallucinogens)

The **hallucinogens** are drugs that are thought to induce hallucinations. However, these preparations usually do not in fact "create" sensory images but distort them, so that an individual sees or hears things in different and unusual ways. These drugs are often referred to as "psychedelics." The major drugs in this category are LSD (lysergic acid diethylamide), mescaline, and psilocybin.

LSD The most potent of the hallucinogens, the odorless, colorless, and tasteless drug **LSD** can produce intoxication with an amount smaller than a grain of salt. It is a chemically synthesized substance first discovered by the Swiss chemist Albert Hoffman in 1938. Hoffman was not aware of the potent hallucinatory qualities of LSD until he swallowed a small amount. This is his report of the experience:

> Last Friday, April 16, 1943, I was forced to stop my work in the laboratory in the middle of the afternoon and to

go home, as I was seized by a peculiar restlessness associated with a sensation of mild dizziness. On arriving home, I lay down and sank into a kind of drunkenness which was not unpleasant and which was characterized by extreme activity of imagination. As I lay in a dazed condition with my eyes closed (I experienced daylight as disagreeably bright) there surged upon me an uninterrupted stream of fantastic images of extraordinary plasticity and vividness and accompanied by an intense kaleidoscope-like play of colors. This condition gradually passed off after about two hours. (Hoffman, 1971, p. 23)

Hoffman followed up this experience with a series of planned self-observations with LSD, some of which he described as "harrowing." Researchers thought LSD might be useful for the induction and study of hallucinogenic states or "model psychoses," which were thought to be related to schizophrenia. About 1950, LSD was introduced into the United States for purposes of such research and to ascertain whether it might have medical or therapeutic uses. Despite considerable research, however, LSD did not prove to be therapeutically useful.

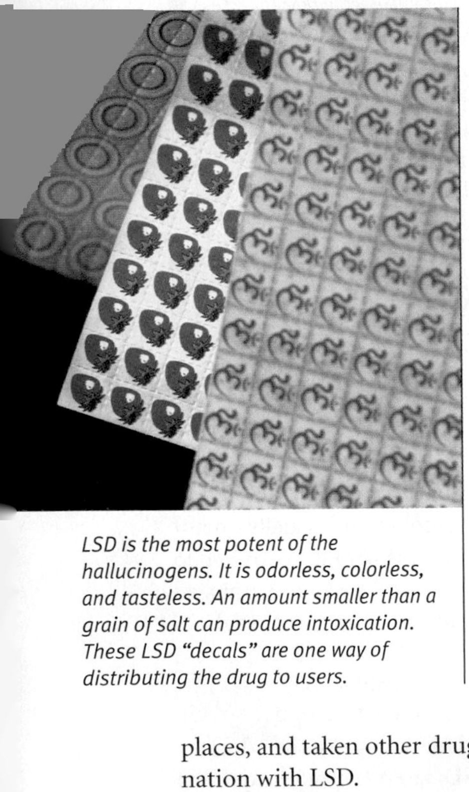

LSD is the most potent of the hallucinogens. It is odorless, colorless, and tasteless. An amount smaller than a grain of salt can produce intoxication. These LSD "decals" are one way of distributing the drug to users.

After taking LSD, a person typically goes through about 8 hours of changes in sensory perception, mood swings, and feelings of depersonalization and detachment. The LSD experience is not always pleasant. It can be extremely traumatic, and the distorted objects and sounds, the illusory colors, and the new thoughts can be menacing and terrifying. For example, while under the influence of LSD, a British law student tried to continue time by using a dental drill to bore a hole in his head (Rorvik, 1970). In other instances, people undergoing bad trips have set themselves aflame, jumped from high places, and taken other drugs that proved lethal in combination with LSD.

An interesting and unusual phenomenon that may occur some time following the use of LSD is the **flashback,** an involuntary recurrence of perceptual distortions or hallucinations weeks or even months after the individual has taken the drug. Flashbacks appear to be relatively rare among people who have taken LSD only once—although they do sometimes occur. Even if no flashbacks occur, one study found that continued effects on visual function were apparent at least 2 years after LSD use. In this study, Abraham and Wolf (1988) reported that individuals who had used LSD for a week had reduced visual sensitivity to light during dark adaptation and showed other visual problems compared with controls.

MESCALINE AND PSILOCYBIN Two other hallucinogens are **mescaline,** which is derived from the small, disclike growths (mescal buttons) at the top of the peyote cactus, and **psilocybin,** which is obtained from a variety of "sacred" Mexican mushrooms known as *Psilocybe mexicana.* These drugs have been used for centuries in the ceremonial rites of Native peoples living in Mexico, the American Southwest, and Central and South America. In fact, they were used by the Aztecs for such purposes long before the Spanish invasion. Both drugs have mind-altering and hallucinogenic properties, but their principal effect appears to be enabling an individual to see, hear, and otherwise experience events in unaccustomed ways—transporting him or her into a realm of "nonordinary reality." As with LSD, no definite evidence shows that mescaline and psilocybin actually "expand consciousness" or create new ideas; rather, they mainly alter or distort experience.

Ecstasy

The drug **Ecstasy,** or MDMA (3,4-methylenedioxymethamphetamine), is both a hallucinogen and a stimulant that is popular as a party drug among young adults. The drug was originally patented in 1913 by the pharmaceutical company Merck, supposedly to be sold as a diet pill, but the company decided against marketing the drug because of the side effects. The drug was further evaluated and tested during the 1970s and 1980s as a potential medication for use in psychological treatment for a wide range of conditions such as post-traumatic stress, phobias, psychosomatic disorders, depression, suicidality, drug addiction, and relationship difficulties (Grob, 2000). However, its value in this capacity was not supported. At present, this drug is considered a "dangerous" drug and is listed in the most restricted category by the Drug Enforcement Administration (Murray, 2001). It is currently available in the United States only through illicit means.

Ecstasy is chemically similar to methamphetamine and to the hallucinogen mescaline and produces effects similar to those of other stimulants, although some research has suggested that the drug's hallucinogenic properties exceed those of mescaline (Kovar, 1998; Parrott & Stuart, 1997). Usually about 20 minutes after ingesting Ecstasy (typically in pill form), the person experiences a "rush" sensation followed by a feeling of calmness, energy, and well-being. The effects of Ecstasy can last for several hours. People who take the drug often report an intense experience of color and sound and mild hallucinations (Fox, Parrott, & Turner, 2001; Lieb, Schuetz, et al., 2002; Soar, Turner, & Parrott, 2001) in addition to the high levels of energy and excitement that are produced. The drug

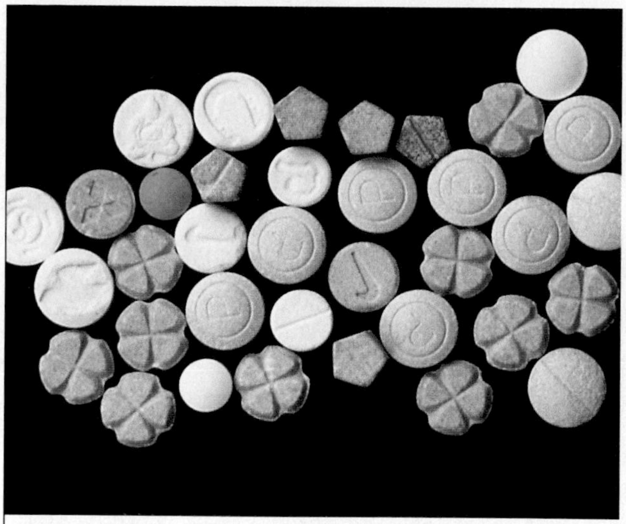

The Ecstasy drug (MDMA—3,4-Methylenedioxy-N-Methylamphetamine) is taken in pill form and is often used at "raves" or night clubs to enhance mood. Ecstasy is an illegal substance and manufacturers do not follow regulation and quality control. The popular "rave drug" is often modified to contain a mix of MDMA/MDEA and other ingredients or are made up entirely of other psychoactive substances such as amphetamine (speed) or LSD (acid).

MDMA is an addictive substance, but it is not thought to be as addictive as cocaine. Use of the drug is accompanied by a number of adverse consequences such as nausea, sweating, clenching of teeth, muscle cramps, blurred vision, and hallucinations (Parrott, 2001).

Ecstasy has been used increasingly among college students and young adults as a party enhancement or "rave" drug at dances (Boys, Lenton, & Norcross, 1997). In a survey of 14,000 college students, Strote, Lee, and Wechsler (2002) found that between 1997 and 1999, Ecstasy use increased 69 percent, from 2.8 percent to 4.7 percent. Ecstasy reportedly grew in use among eighth, tenth, and twelfth graders, as noted by the Monitoring the Future study, in which nearly 5 percent of tenth and twelfth graders and about 2 percent of eighth graders reportedly had used MDMA in the past year. However, the rate of increase slowed in the most recent survey (Substance Abuse and Mental Health Services Administration, 2004), and its frequency of use is considerably less than other drugs of abuse (Yacoubian, 2003).

As with many other illicit drugs, the recreational use of Ecstasy has been associated with personality characteristics of impulsivity and poor judgment (Morgan, 1998). Ecstasy users have been found to be more likely to use marijuana, engage in binge drinking, smoke cigarettes, and have multiple sexual partners (Strote, Lee, & Wechsler, 2002). However, Ecstasy use is also found among naïve partygoers who are provided the drug as a means of staying awake while socializing (Boys, Marsden, & Strang, 2001).

The negative psychological and health consequences (including death) of using Ecstasy have been widely reported in the literature. One recent study reported on the case of a 21-year-old man who developed panic disorder after taking Ecstasy (Windhaber, Maierhofer, & Dantendorfer, 1998); in another case study, an 18-year-old woman reportedly developed a prolonged psychosis after a single recreational use of Ecstasy (Van Kampen & Katz, 2001). The use of Ecstasy has been found to be associated with memory impairment. Parrott, Lees, and colleagues (1998) found that users of MDMA showed significantly less recall than controls participating in a memory experiment. More severe organic brain problems have also been reported. Granato, Weill, and Revillon (1997) described a case in which a 20-year-old male suffered from cerebrovascular injury after taking Ecstasy. The youth went into a coma about a minute or so after taking the drug. Upon awakening, he was found to have dissociation, delirium, visual hallucinations, and poor memory for past events. Subsequent examination showed damage to his frontal lobes and his right temporal lobe.

Marijuana

Although **marijuana** may be classified as a mild hallucinogen, there are significant differences between the nature, intensity, and duration of its effects and those induced by LSD, mescaline, and other major hallucinogens. Marijuana comes from the leaves and flowering tops of the hemp plant, *Cannabis sativa.* This plant grows in mild climates throughout the world including parts of India, Africa, Mexico, South America, and the United States. In its prepared state, marijuana consists chiefly of the dried green leaves—hence the colloquial name *grass.* It is ordinarily smoked in the form of cigarettes (variously referred to as "reefers," "joints," "stash," "weed," etc.) or in pipes. In some cultures the leaves are steeped in hot water and the liquid is drunk, much as one might drink tea. Marijuana is related to a stronger drug, **hashish,** which is derived from the resin exuded by the cannabis plant and made into a gummy powder. Hashish, like marijuana, is usually smoked.

Both marijuana use and hashish use can be traced far back into history. Cannabis was apparently known in ancient China (Blum, 1969; Culliton, 1970) and was listed in the herbal compendiums of the Chinese Emperor Shen Nung, written about 2737 B.C. Until the late 1960s, marijuana use in the United States was confined largely to members of lower-socioeconomic and minority groups and to people in entertainment and related fields, but marijuana use is commonplace today. In 2003, over 3.1 million people over 12 years of age reportedly used marijuana daily (National Survey on Drug Use and Health, 2004). The U.S. Department of Justice Statistics for 2004 (Bureau of Justice Statistics, 2004) reported that 34.9 percent of high school seniors had used marijuana within the past 12 months.

Although teen drug use declined somewhat over the past 8 years (NIDA, 2003), it has been estimated that about 7,000 Americans tried marijuana for the first time in

2003; about two-thirds of these were under age 18. In a recent national survey (Substance Abuse and Mental Health Services Administration, 2004), there were 2.6 million new marijuana users in 2002. Minority group members and Caucasians have been shown to have comparable rates of use (Brown, Flory, et al., 2004). In a separate survey of drug-related visits to the emergency room (DAWN Report, 2001), 16 percent were for marijuana abuse. Many of these emergency room visits, as one might suspect, involved the use of other substances along with marijuana.

These demonstrators are marching to City Hall in New York City to call for the legalization of marijuana.

EFFECTS OF MARIJUANA The specific effects of marijuana vary greatly, depending on the quality and dosage of the drug, the personality and mood of the user, the user's past experiences with the drug, the social setting, and the user's expectations. However, considerable consensus exists among regular users that when marijuana is smoked and inhaled, a state of slight intoxication results. This state is one of mild euphoria distinguished by increased feelings of well-being, heightened perceptual acuity, and pleasant relaxation, often accompanied by a sensation of drifting or floating away. Sensory inputs are intensified. Marijuana has the effect on the brain of altering one's internal clock (O'Leary, Block, et al., 2003). Often a person's sense of time is stretched or distorted, so that an event that lasts only a few seconds may seem to cover a much longer span. Short-term memory may also be affected, as when one notices that a bite has been taken out of a sandwich but does not remember having taken it. For most users, pleasurable experiences, including sexual intercourse, are reportedly enhanced. When smoked, marijuana is rapidly absorbed and its effects appear within seconds to minutes but seldom last more than 2 to 3 hours.

Marijuana can produce extreme euphoria, hilarity, and hypertalkativeness, but it can also produce intense anxiety and depression as well as delusions, hallucinations, and other psychotic-like behavior.

Marijuana may lead to unpleasant as well as pleasant experiences. For example, if a person uses the drug while in an unhappy, angry, suspicious, or frightened mood, these feelings may be magnified. With higher dosages and with certain unstable or susceptible individuals, marijuana can produce extreme euphoria, hilarity, and overtalkativeness, but it can also produce intense anxiety and depression as well as delusions, hallucinations, and other psychotic-like experiences. Evidence suggests a strong relationship between daily marijuana use and the occurrence of psychotic symptoms (Raphael et al., 2005).

Marijuana's short-range physiological effects include a moderate increase in heart rate, a slowing of reaction time, a slight contraction of pupil size, bloodshot and itchy eyes, a dry mouth, and increased appetite. Furthermore, marijuana induces memory dysfunction and a slowing of information processing (Pope, Gruber, et al., 2001). Continued use of high dosages over time tends to produce lethargy and passivity along with reduced life success (Lane, Cherek, et al., 2005). In such cases marijuana appears to have a depressant and a hallucinogenic effect. The effects of long-term and habitual marijuana use are still under investigation, although a number of possible adverse side effects have been related to the prolonged, heavy use of marijuana (Earleywine, 2002). For example, marijuana use tends to diminish self-control. One study exploring past substance-use history in incarcerated murderers reported that among men who committed murder, marijuana was the most commonly used drug. One-third indicated that they used the drug before the homicide, and two-thirds were experiencing some effects of the drug at the time of the murder (Spunt et al., 1994).

Some research has reported that many marijuana use abstainers reported having uncomfortable withdrawal-like symptoms such as nervousness, tension, sleep problems, and appetite change (Budney, Moore, et al., 2003; Zickler, 2002). One study of substance abusers reported that marijuana users were more ambivalent and less confident about stopping use than were cocaine abusers (Budney, Radonovich, et al., 1998).

Psychological treatment methods have been shown to be effective in reducing marijuana use in adults who are dependent on the drug (Marijuana Treatment Project Research Group, 2004) although some data suggest that many patients do not show a positive treatment response (McRae, Budney, & Brady, 2003). As with other addictive drugs, there may be among the users many individuals with serious antisocial or "psychosis-prone" personalities (Kwapil, 1996). Treatment of marijuana use is hampered by the fact that there might be an underlying personality disorder. One study compared the effectiveness of two treatments, Relapse Prevention (RP) and Support Group (SSP), with marijuana-dependent adults (Stephens, Roffman, & Simpson, 1994). Both treatment conditions resulted in substantial reduction in marijuana use in the 12 months following treatment. Relapse prevention and support discussion sessions were equally effective in bringing about changes in marijuana use.

Not all addictive disorders involve the use of substances with chemical properties that induce dependence. As discussed in The World Around Us 12.6, people can develop "addictions" to certain activities that can be just as

12.6 The World Around Us

Pathological Gambling

Although pathological gambling does not involve a chemically addictive substance, it can be considered an addictive disorder because of the personality factors that tend to characterize compulsive gamblers, the difficulties attributable to compulsive gambling, and the treatment problems involved (Grant, Kushner, & Kim, 2002). Like other addictions, pathological gambling involves behavior maintained by short-term gains despite long-term disruption of an individual's life. Judging from written history and the studies of anthropologists, gambling occurs in nearly all cultures and among all social strata. **Pathological gambling,** also known as "compulsive gambling," is a progressive disorder characterized by continuous or periodic loss of control over gambling, a preoccupation with gambling and with obtaining money for gambling, irrational behavior, and continuation of the gambling behavior in spite of adverse consequences. Estimates place the number of pathological gamblers in the United States at between 1.2 and 2.3 percent of the adult population (Volberg, 1990). Both men and women appear to be vulnerable to pathological gambling (Hing & Breen, 2001). One recent study of elderly African-Americans from two senior citizen centers documented the extent of gambling problems in this population; 17 percent were found to be heavy pathological gamblers (Bazargan, Bazargan, & Akanda 2001).

Gambling in our society takes many forms including casino gambling, betting on horse races (legally or otherwise), numbers games, lotteries, dice, bingo, and cards. Whatever an individual gambler's situation, compulsive gambling significantly affects the social, psychological, and economic well-being of the gambler's family (Lorenz & Shuttlesworth, 1983). In fact, one study found that a high proportion of pathological gamblers commit crimes that are related to gambling (Blaszczynski, McConaghy, & Frankova, 1989).

Pathological gambling seems to be a learned pattern that is highly resistant to extinction. Some research suggests that control over gambling is related to duration and frequency of playing (Scannell, Quirk, et al., 2000). However, many people who become pathological gamblers won a substantial sum of money the first time they gambled; chance alone would dictate that a certain percentage of people would have such "beginner's luck." The reinforcement a person receives during this introductory phase may be a significant factor in later pathological gambling. Because everyone is likely to win from time to time, the principles of intermittent reinforcement—the most potent reinforcement schedule for operant conditioning (see Chapter 3)—could explain an addict's continued gambling despite excessive losses.

Despite their awareness that the odds are against them, and despite the fact that they rarely or never repeat their early success, compulsive gamblers continue to gamble avidly. To "stake" their gambling, they often dissipate their savings, neglect their families, default on bills, and borrow money from friends and loan companies. Some resort to embezzlement, writing bad checks, or other illegal means of obtaining money. In a pioneering study of former pathological gamblers, Rosten (1961) found that as a group, they tended to be rebellious, unconventional individuals who did not seem to understand fully the ethical norms of society. Half of the group described themselves as "hating regulations." Often they had the unshakable feeling that "tonight is my night." Typically, they had also followed the so-called "Monte Carlo fallacy"—that after so many losses, their turn was coming up and they would hit it big. Many of the men discussed the extent to which they had "fooled themselves" by elaborate rationalizations. For example, one gambler described his previous rationalizations as covering all contingencies: "When I was ahead, I could gamble because I was playing with others' money. When I was

(continued)

behind, I had to get even. When I was even, I hadn't lost any money" (Rosten, 1961, p. 67). It is of interest to note that within a few months after the study, 13 of Rosten's 30 subjects had returned to heavy gambling, had started to drink excessively, or had not been heard from and were presumed to be gambling again.

Later studies strongly support Rosten's findings. They describe pathological gamblers as typically immature, rebellious, thrill-seeking, superstitious, basically antisocial, and compulsive (Hollander, Buchalter, et al., 2000). Research has shown that pathological gambling frequently co-occurs with other disorders particularly substance abuse such as alcohol and cocaine dependence (Kausch, 2003; Welte, Barnes, et al., 2004) and impulse disorders (Grant & Kim, 2003). Those with co-occurring substance-abuse disorders typically have the most severe gambling problems (Ladd & Petry, 2003).

The causes of impulse-driven behavior such as we see in pathological gambling are complex. Although learning undoubtedly plays an important part in the development of personality factors underlying the "compulsive" gambler, recent research in brain mechanisms that are involved in motivation, reward, and decision making could influence the underlying impulsivity in personality (Chambers & Potenza, 2003). These investigators have suggested that important neurodevelopmental events during adolescence occur in brain regions associated with motivation and impulsive behavior. Cultural factors also appear to be important in the development of gambling problems. Research with Southeast Asian refugee populations highlights the role of cultural influences in gambling. Pathological gambling is a particular problem among Southeast Asian refugees, especially those from Laos. Surveys of mental health problems have reported almost epidemic compulsive gambling among such groups (Aronoff, 1987; Ganju & Quan, 1987). Gambling is reportedly common within Southeast Asian cultures, but these refugees' gambling problems have apparently become more serious and more widespread in the United States.

Treatment of pathological gamblers has tended to parallel that of other addictive disorders. The most extensive treatment approach used with pathological gamblers is cognitive-behavioral therapy (Breen, Kruedelbach, & Walker, 2001). For example, Sylvain, Ladouceur, and Boisvert (1997) provided cognitive-behavioral therapy for 58 pathological gamblers recruited through the media. Although 18 participants dropped out at the start and 11 quit during therapy, those who remained in treatment showed significant improvement. Of those who completed therapy, 86 percent were considered "no longer" pathological gamblers at a 1-year follow-up. However, one recent study (Hodgins & el-Guebaly, 2004) reported very high relapse rates among pathological gamblers—only 8 percent were free of gambling 12 months after treatment.

Some pathological gamblers who want to change find help through membership in Gamblers Anonymous. This organization, modeled after Alcoholics Anonymous, was founded in 1957 in Los Angeles by two pathological gamblers who found that they could help each other control their gambling by talking about their experiences. Since then, groups have been formed in most major American cities.

Pathological gambling is on the increase in the United States (Potenza, 2002; Stinchfield, 2002), particularly with the widely available gambling opportunities on the Internet (Griffiths, 2003). Liberalized gambling legislation has permitted state-operated lotteries, horse racing, and gambling casinos in an effort to increase state tax revenues. In the context of this apparent environmental support and "official" sanction for gambling, it is likely that pathological gambling will increase substantially as more and more people "try their luck." Given that pathological gamblers are resistant to treatment, our future efforts to develop more effective preventive and treatment approaches will need to be increased as this problem continues to grow.

life-threatening as severe alcoholism and just as damaging, psychologically and socially, as drug abuse. One such addiction, pathological gambling, is in many ways similar to substance abuse. The maladaptive behaviors involved and the treatment approaches shown to be effective suggest that these addictive disorders are quite similar to the various drug-use and drug-induced disorders.

In Review

- What are the major physical and psychological effects of morphine and heroin use?
- What are three major causal factors in the development of opiate dependence?
- Describe the psychosocial and biological treatments for opiate dependence.
- What are the physical risks of taking Ecstasy?
- What is methamphetamine? What are the major health factors related to methamphetamine use?

Unresolved Issues

Exchanging Addictions: Is This an Effective Approach?

Withdrawal from heroin can be extremely difficult because of the intense craving that develops for the drug. Wouldn't it be great if we had a magic bullet—a medication—that would allow people who are addicted to heroin to withdraw from it painlessly? One approach that has been used for several decades involves the administration of methadone (methadone hydrochloride, a synthetic narcotic that is as addictive as heroin), often in conjunction with a psychological or social rehabilitation program that is aimed at resocialization of the abuser. The value of this treatment comes from the fact that methadone satisfies an addict's craving for heroin without producing serious psychological impairment.

Many researchers have concluded that in addition to facilitating psychological or social rehabilitation, this drug is effective at reducing the dependence on heroin (Byrne, 2000; Silverman, Higgins, Brooner, & Montoya, 1996). Thus it enables many people to experience reduced craving, allowing them to alter somewhat the often desperate life circumstances they find themselves in through trying to support their expensive and all-consuming habit.

The idea that addicts may need to be maintained for life on methadone, itself a powerful and addicting drug, has been questioned both on moral and practical grounds. Methadone advocates, however, point out that addicts on methadone can function normally and hold jobs, which is not possible for most heroin addicts. In addition, methadone is available legally, and its quality is controlled by government standards. Advocates for methadone programs point out that it is not necessary to increase the dosage over time as it is with heroin use. In fact, some patients can eventually stop taking methadone without danger of relapse to heroin addiction.

However, negative consequences are sometimes associated with the use of methadone (Miller & Lyon, 2003). Methadone patients are at increased risk for health problems such as hepatitis (McCarthy & Flynn, 2001) and cognitive impairment (Scheurich, 2005; Verdejo, Toribio, et al., 2005). In addition, many social problems, such as trading sex for drugs, persist (El-Bassel, Simoni, et al., 2001); some addicts get involved with other drugs such as cocaine (Avants, Margolin, et al., 1998; Silverman et al., 1996); suicide attempts are common (Darke & Ross, 2001); and violent deaths and drug overdoses are common among methadone patients (Sunjic & Zabor, 1999).

A great deal of research has shown that administering psychotherapy along with methadone increases the effectiveness of treatment (Woody et al., 1987). However, a persistent problem of methadone maintenance programs has been the relatively high dropout rate. Several variations in methadone maintenance programs have aimed at keeping addicts in therapy. These variations include the use of such additional drugs as clonidine (an antihypertensive drug used to treat essential hypertension and prevent headache), which aid in the detoxification process and reduce the discomfort of withdrawal symptoms. In one study, the joint use of tranquilizers such as diazepam was shown to decrease the amount of methadone consumed (Spiga et al., 2001). Another approach involves the use of behavioral shaping through contingent reinforcers (monetary vouchers) to reward abstinent patients (Preston, Umbricht, et al., 2001).

A new approach to treating opioid dependence is one that promotes drug abstinence for addicts rather than permanent maintenance on methadone (Kosten, 2003; Reilly et al., 1995). This program, referred to as "methadone transition treatment" (MTT), involves several elements over the 180-day course of treatment. During the first 100 days, the addict is provided a stable dose of methadone to begin the withdrawal from heroin. During this period the addict also receives a psychosocial intervention that includes weekly psychoeducational classes, biweekly group therapy, and 6 months of individual therapy that continues after drug maintenance has terminated. The program ends with 80 days of phaseout in which the addict is "weaned" from methadone through systematically decreasing the doses (Piotrowski, Tusel, et al., 1999).

Summary

- Addictive disorders such as alcohol or drug abuse are among the most widespread and intransigent mental health problems facing us today.
- Many problems of alcohol or drug use involve difficulties that stem solely from the intoxicating effects of the substances.
- Dependence occurs when an individual develops a tolerance for the substance or exhibits withdrawal symptoms when the substance is not available.
- Several psychoses related to alcoholism have been identified: idiosyncratic intoxication, withdrawal delirium, chronic alcoholic hallucinosis, and dementia associated with alcoholism.

- Drug abuse disorders may involve physiological dependence on substances, such as opiates—particularly heroin—or barbiturates; however, psychological dependence may also occur with any of the drugs that are commonly used today—for example, marijuana.
- A number of factors are considered important in the etiology of substance-abuse disorders. Some substances, such as alcohol and opium, stimulate brain centers that produce euphoria—which then becomes a desired goal.
- It is widely believed that genetic factors play some role in causing susceptibility through such biological avenues as metabolic rates and sensitivity to alcohol.
- Psychological factors—such as psychological vulnerability, stress, and the desire for tension reduction—and disturbed marital relationships are also seen as important etiologic elements in substance-use disorders.
- Although the existence of an "alcoholic personality type" has been disavowed by most theorists, a variety of personality factors apparently play an important role in the development and expression of addictive disorders.
- Sociocultural factors such as attitudes toward alcohol may predispose individuals to alcoholism.
- Possible causal factors in drug abuse include the influence of peer groups, the existence of a so-called "drug culture," and the availability of drugs as tension reducers or pain relievers.
- Some recent research has explored a possible physiological basis for drug abuse. The discovery of endorphins, morphine-like substances produced by the body, has led to speculation that a biochemical basis of drug addiction may exist.
- The so-called "pleasure pathway"—the mesocorticolimbic dopamine pathway (MCLP)—has come under a great deal of study in recent years as the possible potential anatomic site underlying the addictions.
- The treatment of individuals who abuse alcohol or drugs is generally difficult and often fails. The abuse may reflect a long history of psychological difficulties; interpersonal and marital distress may be involved; and financial and legal problems may be present.
- In addition, all such problems must be dealt with by an individual who may deny that the problems exist and who may not be motivated to work on them.
- Several approaches to the treatment of chronic alcohol or drug abuse have been developed—for example, medication to deal with withdrawal symptoms and withdrawal delirium, and dietary evaluation and treatment for malnutrition.
- Psychological therapies such as group therapy and behavioral interventions may be effective with some alcohol- or drug-abusing individuals. Another source of help for alcohol abusers is Alcoholics Anonymous; however, the extent of successful outcomes with this program has not been sufficiently studied.
- Most treatment programs require abstinence; however, over the past 20 years, research has suggested that some alcohol abusers can learn to control their drinking while continuing to drink socially. The controversy surrounding controlled drinking continues.

Key Terms

addictive behavior (p. 412)
alcoholism (p. 413)
amphetamine (p. 438)
barbiturates (p. 439)
caffeine (p. 431)
cocaine (p. 437)
Ecstasy (p. 442)
endorphins (p. 436)
flashback (p. 442)
hallucinogens (p. 441)
hashish (p. 443)
heroin (p. 433)
LSD (p. 441)
marijuana (p. 443)
mescaline (p. 442)
mesocorticolimbic dopamine pathway (MCLP) (p. 419)
methadone (p. 436)
morphine (p. 433)
nicotine (p. 431)
opium (p. 433)
pathological gambling (p. 445)
psilocybin (p. 442)
psychoactive drugs (p. 412)
substance abuse (p. 412)
substance dependence (p. 412)
tolerance (p. 412)
toxicity (p. 412)
withdrawal symptoms (p. 412)

CHAPTER 13

Sexual Variants, Abuse, and Dysfunctions

Loving, sexually satisfying relationships contribute a great deal to our happiness, and if we are not in such relationships, we are apt to spend a great deal of time, effort, and emotional energy looking for them. Sexuality is a central concern of our lives, influencing with whom we fall in love and mate, and how happy we are with them and with ourselves.

In this chapter we shall first look at the psychological problems that make sexual fulfillment especially difficult for some people—the vast majority of them men—who develop unusual sexual interests that are difficult to satisfy in a socially acceptable manner. For example, exhibitionists are sexually aroused by showing their genitals to strangers, who are likely to be disgusted, frightened, and potentially traumatized. Other *sexual or gender variants* may be problematic primarily to the individual: Transsexualism, for example, is a disorder involving discomfort with one's biological sex and a strong desire to be of the opposite sex. Still other variants such as fetishism, in which sexual interest centers on some inanimate object or body part, involve behaviors that, although bizarre and unusual, do not clearly harm anyone. Perhaps no other area covered in this book exposes the difficulties in defining boundaries between normality and psychopathology as clearly as variant sexuality does.

The second issue we shall consider is *sexual abuse,* a pattern of pressured, forced, or inappropriate sexual contact. During the last few decades, there has been a tremendous increase in attention to the problem of sexual abuse of both children and adults. A great deal of research has addressed its causes and consequences. As we shall see, some related issues, such as the reality of recovered memories of sexual abuse, are extremely controversial.

The third category of sexual difficulties examined in this chapter is *sexual dysfunctions,* which include problems that impede satisfactory performance of sexual acts. People who have sexual dysfunctions (or their partners) typically view them as problems. Premature ejaculation, for example, causes men to reach orgasm much earlier than they and their partners find satisfying. And women with orgasmic disorder get sexually aroused and enjoy sexual activity but have a persistent delay, or absence of, orgasm following a normal sexual excitement phase.

Much less is known about sexual deviations, abuse, and dysfunctions than is known about many of the other disorders we have considered thus far in this book. There are also many fewer sex researchers than researchers for many other disorders, so relatively few articles related to sexual deviations and dysfunctions are published. One major reason is the sex taboo. Although sex is an important concern for most people, many have difficulty talking about it openly—especially when the relevant behaviors may be socially stigmatized, as in homosexuality. This makes it hard to obtain knowledge about even the most basic facts, such as the frequency of various sexual practices, feelings, and attitudes.

Loving, sexually satisfying relationships contribute a great deal to our happiness, but our understanding of them has advanced slowly, largely because they are so difficult for people to talk about openly and because funding for research is often hard to come by.

A second reason why sex research has progressed less rapidly is that many issues related to sexuality—including homosexuality, teenage sexuality, abortion, and childhood sexual abuse—are among our most divisive and controversial. In fact, sex research is itself controversial and not well funded. Two large-scale sex surveys were halted because of political opposition even after being officially approved and deemed scientifically meritorious (Udry, 1993). Senator Jesse Helms and others had argued that sex researchers tended to approve of premarital sex and homosexuality and that this would be likely to bias the results of the surveys. Fortunately, one of these surveys was funded privately, though on a much smaller scale, and it is now considered the definitive study for the 1990s (Laumann et al., 1994; see also Laumann et al., 1999). Several smaller studies have also been published since 2000 (e.g., Bancroft et al., 2003).

Despite these significant barriers, some progress has been made in the past half-century in understanding some important things about sexual and gender variants and dysfunctions. The contemporary era of sex research was first launched by Alfred Kinsey in the early 1950s (Kinsey, Pomeroy, & Martin, 1948; Kinsey, Pomeroy, Martin, & Gebhard, 1953). Kinsey and his pioneering work are portrayed in a fascinating way in the 2004 award-winning movie *Kinsey.* However, before we discuss this progress, we first examine sociocultural influences on sexual behavior and attitudes in general. Doing so will provide some perspective about cross-cultural variability in standards of sexual conduct and remind us that we must exercise special caution in classifying sexual practices as "abnormal" or "deviant."

Sociocultural Influences on Sexual Practices and Standards

Although some aspects of sexuality and mating such as men's greater emphasis on their partner's attractiveness are cross-culturally universal (Buss, 1989, 1999), others are quite variable. For example, all known cultures have taboos against sex between close relatives, but attitudes toward premarital sex have varied considerably across history and around the world. Ideas about acceptable sexual behavior also change over time. Less than 100 years ago, for example, sexual modesty in Western cultures was such that women's arms and legs were always hidden in public. Although this is by no means the case in Western cultures today, it remains true in many Muslim countries.

Despite the substantial variability in sexual attitudes and behavior in different times and places, people typically behave as though the sexual standards of their time and place are obviously correct, and they tend to be intolerant of sexual nonconformity. Sexual nonconformists are often considered evil or sick. We do not mean to suggest that such judgments are always arbitrary. There has probably never existed a society in which Jeffrey Dahmer, who was sexually aroused by killing men, having sex with them, storing their corpses, and sometimes eating them, would be considered psychologically normal. Nevertheless, it is useful to be aware of historical and cultural influences on sexuality. When the expression or the acceptance of a certain behavior varies considerably across eras and cultures, we should at least pause to consider the possibility that our own stance is not the only appropriate one.

Because the influences of time and place are so important in shaping sexual behavior and attitudes, we begin by exploring three cases that illustrate how opinions about "acceptable" and "normal" sexual behavior may change dramatically over time and may differ dramatically from one culture to another. In the first case, America during the mid-1800s, "degeneracy theory," a set of beliefs about sexuality, led to highly conservative sexual practices and dire warnings about most kinds of sexual "indulgence." In the second case, we look briefly at the Sambia tribe in New Guinea, in which a set of beliefs about sexuality prescribe that all normal adolescent males go through a stage of homosexuality before switching rather abruptly to heterosexuality in adulthood. Finally, in the third case, we consider changes across time in the status of homosexuality in Western culture.

Case 1: Degeneracy and Abstinence Theory

During the 1750s, Swiss physician Simon Tissot developed *degeneracy theory,* the central belief of which was that semen is necessary for physical and sexual vigor in men and for masculine characteristics such as beard growth (Money, 1985, 1986). He based this theory on observations about human eunuchs and castrated animals. Of course, we now know that loss of the male hormone testosterone, and not of semen, is responsible for the relevant characteristics of eunuchs and castrated animals. On the basis of his theory, however, Tissot asserted that two practices were especially harmful: masturbation and patronizing prostitutes. Both of these practices wasted the vital fluid, semen, as well as (in his view) overstimulating and exhausting the nervous system. Tissot also recommended that married people engage solely in procreative sex to avoid the waste of semen.

A descendant of degeneracy theory, *abstinence theory,* was advocated in America during the 1830s by the Reverend Sylvester Graham (Money, 1985, 1986). The three cornerstones of his crusade for public health were healthy food (graham crackers were named for him), physical fitness, and sexual abstinence. In the 1870s Graham's most famous successor, Dr. John Harvey Kellogg, published a paper in which he ardently disapproved of masturbation and urged parents to be wary of signs that their children were indulging in it. He wrote about the 39 signs of "the secret vice," which included weakness, dullness of the eyes, sleeplessness, untrustworthiness, bashfulness, love of solitude, unnatural boldness, mock piety, and round shoulders.

As a physician, Kellogg was professionally admired and publicly influential, and he earned a fortune publishing books discouraging masturbation. His recommended treatments for "the secret vice" were quite extreme. For example, he advocated that persistent masturbation in boys be treated by sewing the foreskin with silver wire or, as a last resort, by circumcision without anesthesia. Female masturbation was to be treated by burning the clitoris with carbolic acid. Kellogg, like Graham, was also very concerned with dietary health—especially with the idea that consumption of meat increased sexual desire. Thus, he urged people to eat more cereals and nuts and invented Kellogg's cornflakes "almost literally, as anti-masturbation food" (Money, 1986, p. 186).

Given the influence of physicians like Kellogg, it should come as no surprise that many people believed that masturbation caused insanity (Hare, 1962). This hypothesis had started with the anonymous publication in the early eighteenth century in London of a book entitled *Onania, or the Heinous Sin of Self-Pollution.* It asserted that masturbation was a common cause of insanity. This idea probably arose from observations that many patients in mental asylums masturbated openly (unlike sane people, who are more likely to do it in private) and that the age at which masturbation tends to begin (at puberty in adolescence) precedes by several years the age when the first signs of insanity often appear (in late adolescence and young adulthood; Abramson & Seligman, 1977). The idea that masturbation may cause insanity appeared in some psychiatry textbooks as late as the 1940s.

Although abstinence theory and associated attitudes seem highly puritanical by today's standards, they have had a long-lasting influence on attitudes toward sex in American and other Western cultures. It was not until 1972 that the American Medical Association declared, "Masturbation is a normal part of adolescent sexual development and requires no medical management" (American Medical Association Committee on Human Sexuality, 1972, p. 40). Around the same time, the *Boy Scout Manual* dropped its antimasturbation warnings. Nonetheless, in 1994 Jocelyn Elders was fired as U.S. Surgeon General for suggesting publicly that sex education courses should include discussion of masturbation. Moreover, the Roman Catholic Church still holds that masturbation is sinful.

Case 2: Ritualized Homosexuality in Melanesia

Melanesia is a group of islands in the South Pacific that has been intensively studied by anthropologists, who have uncovered cultural influences on sexuality unlike any known in the West. Between 10 and 20 percent of Melanesian societies practice a form of homosexuality within the context of male initiation rituals that all male members of society must experience.

The best-studied society has been the Sambia of Papua New Guinea (Herdt, 1999; Herdt & Stoller, 1990). Two beliefs reflected in Sambian sexual practices are *semen conservation* and *female pollution.* Like Tissot, the Sambians believe that semen is important for many things including physical growth, strength, and spirituality. Furthermore, they believe that it takes many inseminations (and much semen) to impregnate a woman. Finally, they believe that semen cannot easily be replenished by the body and so must be conserved or obtained elsewhere. The female pollution doctrine is the belief that the female body is unhealthy to males, primarily because of menstrual fluids. At menarche, Sambian women are secretly initiated in the menstrual hut forbidden to all males.

In order to obtain or maintain adequate amounts of semen, young Sambian males practice semen exchange with each other. Beginning as boys, they learn to practice fellatio (oral sex) in order to ingest sperm, but after puberty they can also take the penetrative role, inseminating younger boys. Ritualized homosexuality among the Sambian men is seen as an exchange of sexual pleasure for vital semen. (It is ironic that although both the Sambians and the Victorian-era Americans believed in semen conservation, their solutions to the problem were radically different.) When Sambian males are well past puberty, they begin the transition to heterosexuality. At this time the female body is thought to be less dangerous, because the males have ingested protective semen over the previous years. For a time, they may begin having sex with women and still participate in fellatio with younger boys, but homosexual behavior stops after the birth of a man's first child. Most of the Sambian men make the transition to exclusive adult heterosexuality without problems and those who do not are viewed as misfits.

Ritualized homosexuality among the Melanesians is a striking example of the influence of culture on sexual attitudes and behavior. A Melanesian adolescent who refused to practice homosexuality would be viewed as abnormal, and such adolescents are apparently absent or rare. Homosexuality among the Sambia is not the same as homosexuality in contemporary America, with the possible exception of those Sambian men who have difficulty making the transition to heterosexuality.

Case 3: Homosexuality and American Psychiatry

During the past half-century, the status of homosexuality has changed enormously both within psychiatry and psychology, and for many Western societies in general. In the not-too-distant past, homosexuality was a taboo topic. Now, movies, talk shows, and television sitcoms and dramas address the topic explicitly by including gay men and lesbians in leading roles. As we shall see, developments in psychiatry and psychology have played an important part in these changes. Homosexuality was officially removed from the DSM (where it had previously been classified as a sexual deviation) in 1973 and today is no longer regarded as a mental disorder. A brief survey of attitudes toward homosexuality within the mental health profession itself again illustrates how attitudes toward various expressions of human sexuality may change over time.

HOMOSEXUALITY AS SICKNESS Reading the medical and psychological literature on homosexuality written before 1970 can be a jarring experience, especially if one subscribes to views prevalent today. Relevant articles included "Effeminate homosexuality: A disease of childhood" and "On the cure of homosexuality." It is only fair to note, however, that the view that homosexual people are mentally ill was relatively tolerant compared with some earlier views—for example, the idea that homosexual people were criminals in need of incarceration (Bayer, 1981). British and American cultures had long taken punitive approaches to homosexual behavior. In the sixteenth century, King Henry VIII of England declared "the detestable and abominable vice of buggery [anal sex]" a felony punishable by death, and it was not until 1861 that the maximum penalty was reduced to 10 years' imprisonment. Similarly, laws in the United States were very repressive until recently, with homosexual behavior continuing to be a criminal offense in some states (Posner & Silbaugh, 1996) until the 2003 Supreme Court ruling that struck down a Texas state law banning sexual behavior between two people of the same sex (*Lawrence & Garner* v. *Texas*). For the first time, this ruling established a broad constitutional right to sexual privacy in the United States.

During the late nineteenth and early twentieth centuries, several prominent sexologists such as Havelock Ellis and Magnus Hirschfeld suggested that homosexuality is natural and consistent with psychological normality. Freud's own attitude toward homosexual people was also remarkably progressive for his time and is well expressed in his touching "Letter to an American Mother" (1935).

> Dear Mrs. . . .
>
> I gather from your letter that your son is a homosexual. I am most impressed by the fact that you do not mention this term yourself in your information about him. May I question you, why you avoid it? Homosexuality is assuredly no advantage, but it is nothing to be ashamed of, no vice, no degradation, it cannot be classified as an illness. . . . Many highly respectable individuals of ancient and modern times have been homosexuals, several of the greatest men among them (Plato, Michelangelo, Leonardo da Vinci, etc.). It is a great injustice to persecute homosexuality as a crime, and cruelty too. . . .
>
> By asking me if I can help, you mean, I suppose, if I can abolish homosexuality and make normal heterosexuality take its place. The answer is, in a general way, we cannot promise to achieve it. . . .
>
> Sincerely yours with kind wishes,
>
> Freud

Beginning in the 1940s, however, other psychoanalysts, led by Sandor Rado, began to take a more pessimistic view of the mental health of homosexual people—and a more optimistic view of the possible success of therapy to induce heterosexuality. Rado (1962) believed that homosexuality develops in people whose heterosexual desires were too psychologically threatening; thus homosexuality was an escape from heterosexuality and therefore incompatible with mental health (see also Bieber et al., 1962). In the case of male homosexuality, one argument was that domineering, emotionally smothering mothers and detached, hostile fathers played a causal role. Unfortunately, these psychoanalysts based their opinions primarily on their experiences seeing gay men in therapy, who are obviously more likely than other gay men to be psychologically troubled.

HOMOSEXUALITY AS NONPATHOLOGICAL VARIATION Around 1950, the view of homosexuality as sickness began to be challenged by both scientists and homosexual people themselves. Scientific blows to the pathology position included Alfred Kinsey's finding that homosexual behavior was more common than had been previously believed (Kinsey et al., 1948; Kinsey et al., 1953). Influential studies also demonstrated that trained psychologists could not distinguish the psychological test results of homosexual subjects from those of heterosexual subjects (e.g., Hooker, 1957).

Gay men and lesbians also began to challenge the psychiatric orthodoxy that homosexuality is a mental disorder. The 1960s saw the birth of the radical gay liberation movement, which took the more uncompromising stance that "gay is good." The decade closed with the famous Stonewall riot in New York City, sparked by police mistreatment of gay men, which sent a clear signal that homosexual people would no longer tolerate being treated as second-class citizens. By the 1970s, openly gay psychiatrists and psychologists were working from within the mental health profession to have homosexuality removed from DSM-II (1968).

In the not-too-distant past, homosexuality was a taboo topic. Today, gay men and lesbian women and their everyday lives are topics prevalent in all aspects of popular culture. Also, it is more and more common for homosexual couples to raise children together.

After acrimonious debate in 1973 and 1974, the American Psychiatric Association (APA) voted in 1974 by a vote of 5,854 to 3,810 to remove homosexuality from DSM-II. This episode was both a milestone for gay rights and an embarrassment for psychiatry. The spectacle of the psychiatric nomenclature being modified on the basis of a vote rather than through the scientific consensus of experts appeared to confirm what the harshest critics of psychodiagnosis, such as Thomas Szasz (1974), had been saying—that the label "mental illness" merely reflects the values of mental health professionals.

We believe the APA made a correct decision here, because the vast majority of evidence shows that homosexuality is compatible with psychological normality. Furthermore, resolving this issue by vote is not especially problematic. The classification of any behavior as psychopathology necessitates a value judgment that the behavior is undesirable (see Chapter 1). Challenges by gay and lesbian people forced mental health professionals to confront the values question explicitly, and they made the correct determination that homosexuality is not a psychological disorder. (See Developments in Thinking 13.1.)

In Review

- What does each of the three examples of sociocultural influences on sexual practices and standards reveal about cultural differences and historical changes in what is considered acceptable and normal sexual behavior?
- How has the psychiatric view of homosexuality changed over time? Identify a few key historical events that propelled this change.

13.1 Developments in Thinking

Homosexuality as a Normal Sexual Variant

Although its current status as a nonpsychopathological sexual variant rather than a disorder might suggest that no further mention of homosexuality is warranted in an abnormal psychology textbook, we have provided a more extensive discussion, for two reasons. First, American attitudes toward homosexuality remain highly ambivalent, and at least part of this ambivalence reflects uncertainty about the causes and correlates of sexual orientation. Thus one goal is to review what is known about homosexuality to clarify why we believe it is not pathological. Second, although homosexuality is not pathological, it is sometimes related to a condition that remains in DSM-IV-TR: Gender Identity Disorder (see Chapter 11). Thus some findings about homosexuality may apply to gender identity disorder as well.

How Common Is Homosexuality?

Large, carefully selected samples from the United States (Laumann & Michael, 2000), France (ACSF Investigators, 1992), and England (Wellings et al., 1994) suggest that the rate of adult homosexual behavior is between 2 and 6 percent, with the rate of exclusive male homosexuality estimated at about 2.4 percent (LeVay & Valente, 2006). The analogous rates of exclusive female homosexuality is, however, less than 1 percent. The fact that homosexuality is relatively rare has no implications for its status as a nonpathological sexual variant because, for example, genius too is rare but not pathological. Moreover, approximately 20 percent of men and women may report having had at least one instance of sexual attraction to a member of their own sex after the age of 15 (Sell, Wypij, & Wells, 1995). Some people are also bisexual, although this may be even less common in men than exclusive homosexuality, especially since the onset of the AIDS epidemic in the mid-1980s (Masters, Johnson, & Kolodny, 1992). One intensive study of bisexuals found that for many, their homosexuality came after they had established a heterosexual orientation (Weinberg, Williams, & Pryor, 1994).

What Causes Some People to Be Homosexual and Others Heterosexual?

An important study by the Kinsey Institute for Sex Research examined the psychoanalytic hypothesis that homosexuality is associated with dysfunctional parent-child relationships and found only very limited support for it (Bell, Weinberg, & Hammersmith, 1981). For example, gay men did recall relatively distant relationships with their fathers, but the differences observed were so small that they could not account for development of sexual orientation. The most striking finding concerned childhood behavior. On average, homosexual adults recalled substantially more sex-atypical behavior than heterosexual adults. For example, gay men were more likely than heterosexual men to recall playing with girls, cross-dressing, shunning sports, and wishing they were girls. Lesbians were more likely than heterosexual women to recall enjoying sports and wishing they were boys. (See Table 13.1 on p. 456.) Similar differences have been found in many other studies (Bailey & Zucker, 1995; LeVay & Valente, 2006). Nevertheless it should also be emphasized that many gay men and lesbians appear to have been sex-typical as children.

Observations that homosexual people have sexual orientations and often other behaviors more typical of the opposite sex are consistent with the most influential current etiological model of sexual orientation: Homosexual people have been subjected to early, possibly prenatal, hormonal influences more typical of the opposite sex. Perhaps the best evidence for this hypothesis comes from the rare cases in which normal male infants have been reassigned as females shortly after birth, and reared as females, because of traumatic injury to the penis (Bradley, Oliver, et al., 1998; Diamond & Sigmundson, 1997). As adults, these individuals are primarily attracted to females, which is consistent with their prenatal biology rather than their postnatal rearing. In addition, a well-known study by Simon LeVay (1991) found gay men to be different from heterosexual men and similar to heterosexual women in the size of one region of the hypothalamus that affects sexual behavior. A later study partially replicated this finding (Byne, Tobet, et al., 2001).

Genetic factors have also been implicated in both male (Bailey & Pillard, 1991; Hamer et al., 1993) and female (Bailey et al., 1993) sexual orientation. Concordance rates have varied widely across studies, with recent, more careful studies yielding smaller figures (Bailey, Dunne, & Martin, 2000; Kendler, Thornton, Gilman, & Kessler, 2000). Nevertheless, even the most recent evidence is consistent with a moderate role for heredity. However, because at least half of the monozygotic twin pairs in the better genetic studies were discordant for sexual orientation, environmental factors are clearly also important (Bailey et al., 2000). The nature of the environmental influences is uncertain; these could include either biological (e.g., prenatal stress) or social (e.g., parental child-rearing philosophy) factors. One erroneous environmental hypothesis is that homosexual adults seduce and "recruit" younger individuals to homosexuality. There is no scientific evidence for this belief and much against it. For example, the large majority of gay men and lesbians had homosexual feelings at least a year before their first homosexual experience (Bell et al., 1981).

Is Homosexuality a Sign of Mental Disturbance?

Historically, the belief that homosexuality reflects mental disturbance has been linked to discomfort with the sexual behavior of homosexual people. For example, some have pointed to the high number of sexual partners reported by gay men (especially before the AIDS epidemic) as evidence that these men are abnormally impulsive and promiscuous. However, a more parsimonious explanation of this finding is that all men have an elevated desire for casual sex but that homosexual men have more casual sex opportunities because they interact sexually with other men (Symons, 1979). One study supporting this idea found that gay men and heterosexual men reported similar levels of interest in casual sex (Bailey, Gaulin, Agyei, & Gladue, 1994).

Several large and careful surveys have examined rates of mental problems in people with and without homosexual feelings or behavior (Fergusson et al., 1999; Herrell, Goldberg, et al., 1999; Sandfort, de Graaf, et al., 2001). Homosexual people do appear to have elevated risk for some mental problems. For example, compared with heterosexual men, gay men have higher rates of anxiety disorders and depression, and they are more likely to contemplate suicide. Lesbians also have a higher rate of substance abuse (Sandfort, de Graaf, et al., 2001). Although it remains unclear why homosexual people have higher rates of certain problems (Bailey, 1999), one plausible explanation is that such problems result from societal stigmatizing of homosexuality. Regardless, homosexuality is compatible with psychological health—most gay men and lesbians do not have mental disorders.

TABLE 13.1 Sex-Typical and Sex-Atypical Behavior in Childhood

1. As a child, did you enjoy boys' activities like baseball or football (at least somewhat)?	
Gay men	32%
Heterosexual men	89%
Lesbians	85%
Heterosexual women	57%
2. Did you enjoy girls' activities like hopscotch, playing house, or jacks?	
Gay men	46%
Heterosexual men	12%
Lesbians	33%
Heterosexual women	82%
3. Did you dress in opposite-sex clothes and pretend to be a child of the opposite sex (other than for Halloween or school plays)?	
Gay men	32%
Heterosexual men	10%
Lesbians	49%
Heterosexual women	7%

Source: From *Sexual Preference: Its Development in Men and Women,* a study by the Kinsey Institute, by Alan P. Bell, Martin S. Weinberg, and Sue Kiefer Hammersmith (1981). Reprinted by permission of Martin S. Weinberg.

SEXUAL AND GENDER VARIANTS

We now turn to the problematic sexual variants included in DSM-IV-TR. There are two general categories: paraphilias and gender identity disorders.

The Paraphilias

People with **paraphilias** have recurrent, intense sexually arousing fantasies, sexual urges, or behaviors that generally involve (1) nonhuman objects, (2) the suffering or humiliation of oneself or one's partner, or (3) children or other nonconsenting persons. To meet DSM-IV-TR criteria, these patterns must last at least 6 months. According to DSM-IV-TR (APA, 2000), five of these conditions can be diagnosed simply if the person has acted on his fantasies or urges, even if the person does not experience significant distress or impairment—which is otherwise a criterion for nearly all mental disorders (see also Maletzky, 2002). This change recognizes that certain paraphilias like exhibitionism should be diagnosed even if the individual is not bothered by them. Although mild forms of these conditions probably occur in the lives of many normal people, a paraphilic person is distinguished by the insistence and relative exclusivity with which his sexuality focuses on the acts or objects in question—without which orgasm is often impossible. Paraphilias also frequently have a compulsive quality, and some individuals with paraphilias require orgasmic release as often as four to ten times per day (Money, 1986; Weiner & Rosen, 1999). Individuals with paraphilias may or may not have persistent desires to change their sexual preferences. Because nearly all such persons are male (a fact whose etiological implications we consider later), we use masculine pronouns to refer to them.

Paraphilias are thought to be quite rare although there are no good prevalence data, in part because people are often reluctant to disclose such deviant behavior (Maletzky, 2002). The DSM-IV recognizes eight specific paraphilias: (1) fetishism, (2) transvestic fetishism, (3) voyeurism, (4) exhibitionism, (5) sexual sadism, (6) sexual masochism, (7) pedophilia, and (8) frotteurism (rubbing against a nonconsenting person). An additional category, Paraphilias Not Otherwise Specified, includes several rarer disorders such as telephone scatologia (obscene phone calls), necrophilia (sexual desire for corpses), zoophilia (sexual interest in animals; Williams & Weinberg, 2003), apotemnophilia (sexual excitement and desire about having a limb amputated), and coprophilia (sexual arousal to feces). Although the different paraphilias very often co-occur, we will discuss each of the paraphilias separately, except for frotteurism, a category that is relatively new and has not yet been satisfactorily researched. Our discussion of pedophilia is postponed, however, until a later section concerning sexual abuse.

FETISHISM In **fetishism,** the individual has recurrent, intense sexually arousing fantasies, urges, and behaviors involving the use of some inanimate object to obtain sexual gratification (see DSM-IV-TR Criteria for Several Different Paraphilias). (DSM-IV-TR states that a fetish is diagnosed only when the object is inanimate, but most sex researchers have not traditionally made this distinction.) As is generally true for the paraphilias, reported cases of female fetishists are extremely rare (Mason, 1997). The range of fetishistic objects includes hair, ears, hands, underclothing, shoes, perfume, and similar objects associated with the opposite sex. Rarely more unusual fetishes develop, as, for example, in men who are sexually fixated on people who have an amputated limb (LeVay & Valente,

DSM-IV-TR

Criteria for Several Different Paraphilias

A. FETISHISM

(1) For at least 6 months, recurrent, intense sexually arousing fantasies, urges, or behaviors involving the use of nonliving objects (e.g., female undergarments, though not if used for cross-dressing).

(2) The fantasies, urges, or behaviors cause distress or impairment in functioning.

B. TRANSVESTIC FETISHISM

(1) For at least 6 months, in a heterosexual male, recurrent, intense sexually arousing fantasies, urges, or behaviors involving cross-dressing.

(2) The fantasies, urges, or behaviors cause distress or impairment in functioning.

C. VOYEURISM

(1) For at least 6 months, recurrent, intense sexually arousing fantasies, urges, or behaviors involving the act of observing an unsuspecting person who is naked, in the process of disrobing, or engaging in sexual activity.

(2) The person has acted on these sexual urges, *or,* the sexual urges or fantasies cause marked distress or impairment.

D. EXHIBITIONISM

(1) Over a period of at least 6 months, recurrent, intense sexually arousing fantasies, urges, or behaviors involving the exposure of one's genitals to an unsuspecting stranger.

(2) The person has acted on these sexual urges, *or,* the sexual urges or fantasies cause marked distress or impairment.

E. SEXUAL SADISM

(1) Over a period of at least 6 months, recurrent, intense sexually arousing fantasies, urges, or behaviors involving real acts in which the psychological or physical suffering of the victim is sexually exciting to the person.

(2) The person has acted on these sexual urges, *or,* the sexual urges or fantasies cause marked distress or impairment.

F. SEXUAL MASOCHISM

(1) Over a period of at least 6 months, recurrent, intense sexually arousing fantasies, urges, or behaviors involving the real act of being humiliated, beaten, bound, or otherwise made to suffer.

(2) The fantasies, urges, or behaviors cause distress or impairment in functioning.

G. PEDOPHILIA

(1) Over a period of at least 6 months, recurrent, intense sexually arousing fantasies, urges, or behaviors involving sexual activity with a prepubescent child or children (generally age 13 or younger).

(2) The person has acted on these sexual urges, *or,* the sexual urges or fantasies cause marked distress or impairment.

(3) The person is at least age 16 and at least 5 years older than the child.

2006). The mode of using these objects to achieve sexual excitation and gratification varies considerably, but it commonly involves masturbating while kissing, fondling, tasting, or smelling the objects. Fetishism does not normally interfere with the rights of others, except in an incidental way such as asking the partner to wear the object during sexual encounters. Many men have a strong sexual fascination for paraphernalia such as bras, garter belts, hose, and high heels, but most do not typically meet diagnostic criteria for fetishism because the paraphernalia are not necessary or strongly preferred for sexual arousal. Nevertheless, they do illustrate the relatively high frequency of fetish-like preferences among men.

To obtain the required object, a person with a fetish may commit burglary, theft, or even assault. Probably the articles most commonly stolen by such individuals are women's undergarments. In such cases, the excitement and suspense of the criminal act itself typically reinforce the sexual stimulation and sometimes actually constitute the fetish, the stolen article itself being of little importance. One example of this pattern of fetishism is provided in the case of a man whose fetish was women's panties:

case STUDY — Panties

A single, 32-year-old male freelance photographer... related that although he was somewhat sexually attracted by women, he was far more attracted by "their panties."...[His] sexual excitement began about age 7, when he came upon a pornographic magazine and felt stimulated by pictures of partially nude women wearing "panties." His first ejaculation occurred at 13 via masturbation to fantasies of women wearing panties. He masturbated into his older sister's panties, which he had stolen without her knowledge. Subsequently he stole panties from her friends and from other women he met socially....The pattern of masturbating into women's underwear had been his preferred method of achieving sexual excitement and orgasm from adolescence until the present consultation. (Adapted from Spitzer et al., 2002, p. 247.)

Source: Adapted with permission from the *DSM-TR-Casebook: A Learning Companion to the Diagnostic and Statistical Manual of Mental Disorders,* Fourth Edition, Text Revision (Copyright 2002). American Psychiatric Publishing, Inc.

Many theories of the etiology of fetishism emphasize the importance of classical conditioning and social learning (e.g., Maletzky, 2002; Mason, 1997). For example, it is not difficult to imagine how women's underwear might become eroticized via its close association with sex and the female body. But only a small number of men develop fetishes, so there must be individual differences in conditionability of sexual responses (just as there are in the conditionability of fear and anxiety responses). Men high in sexual conditionability would be prone to developing one or more fetishes. We will later return to the role of conditioning in the development of paraphilias more generally.

TRANSVESTIC FETISHISM According to DSM-IV-TR, heterosexual men who experience recurrent, intense sexually arousing fantasies, urges, or behaviors that involve cross-dressing as a female may be diagnosed with **transvestic fetishism** (see DSM-IV-TR Criteria on p. 457). Typically, the onset of transvestism is during adolescence and involves masturbation while wearing female clothing or undergarments. R. Blanchard (1989, 1992) has termed the psychological motivation of transvestites *autogynephilia:* paraphilic sexual arousal by the thought or fantasy of being a woman (Blanchard, 1991, 1993; Zucker & Blanchard, 1997). The great sexologist Magnus Hirschfeld first identified a class of cross-dressing men who are sexually aroused by the image of themselves as women: "They feel attracted not by the women outside them, but by the woman inside them" (Hirschfeld, 1948, p. 167). Although some gay men dress "in drag" on occasion, they do not typically do this for sexual pleasure and hence are not transvestic fetishists.

In 1997 over 1,000 cross-dressing men were surveyed. The vast majority (87 percent) were heterosexual, 83 percent had married, and 60 percent were married at the time of the survey (Docter & Prince, 1997). Many managed to keep their cross-dressing a secret, at least for a while. However, wives often found out, and had a wide range of reactions, from accepting to being extremely disturbed. The following case illustrates both the typical early onset of transvestic fetishism and the difficulties the condition may raise in a marriage.

case STUDY — A Transvestite's Dilemma

Mr. A., a 65-year-old security guard, formerly a fishing-boat captain, is distressed about his wife's objections to his wearing a nightgown at home in the evening, now that his youngest child has left home. His appearance and demeanor, except when he is dressing in women's clothes, are always appropriately masculine, and he is exclusively heterosexual. Occasionally, over the past 5 years, he has worn an inconspicuous item of female clothing even when dressed as a man, sometimes a pair of panties....He always carries a photograph of himself dressed as a woman.

His first recollection of an interest in female clothing was putting on his sister's bloomers at age 12, an act accompanied by sexual excitement. He continued periodically to put on women's underpants—an activity that invariably resulted in an erection, sometimes a spontaneous emission, sometimes masturbation....He was competitive and aggressive with other boys and always acted "masculine." During his single years he was always attracted to girls....

His involvement with female clothes was of the same intensity even after his marriage. Beginning at age 45, after a chance exposure to a magazine called *Transvestia,* he began to increase his cross-dressing activity. He learned there were other men like himself, and he became more and more preoccupied with female clothing in fantasy and progressed to periodically dressing completely as a woman. More recently he has become involved in a transvestite network...occasionally attending transvestite parties.

Although still committed to his marriage, sex with his wife has dwindled over the past 20 years as his waking thoughts and activities have become increasingly centered on cross-dressing....He always has an increased urge to dress as a woman when under stress; it has a tranquilizing effect. If particular circumstances prevent him from cross-dressing, he feels extremely frustrated....

Because of disruptions in his early life, the patient has always treasured the steadfastness of his wife and the order of his home. He told his wife about his cross-dressing practice when they were married, and she was accepting so long as he kept it to himself. Nevertheless, he felt guilty . . . and periodically he attempted to renounce the practice, throwing out all his female clothes and makeup. His children served as a barrier to his giving free rein to his impulses. Following his retirement from fishing, and in the absence of his children, he finds himself more drawn to cross-dressing, more in conflict with his wife, and more depressed. (Adapted from Spitzer et al., 2002, pp. 257–59.)

Source: Reprinted with permission from the *DSM-TR-Casebook: A Learning Companion to the Diagnostic and Statistical Manual of Mental Disorders,* Fourth Edition, Text Revision (Copyright 2002). American Psychiatric Publishing, Inc.

Like other kinds of fetishism, however, transvestic fetishism causes overt harm to others only when accompanied by such an illegal act as theft or destruction of property. This is not always the case with the other paraphilias, many of which do contain a definite element of injury or significant risk of injury—physical or psychological—to one or more of the parties involved in a sexual encounter. Some of these practices have strong legal sanctions against them.

Studies have shown that transvestic men often feel sexual arousal while cross-dressing, as well as less anxiety and shyness when in their female roles. Although a transvestic man may therefore enjoy excursions into the social roles of the other sex, he may also be markedly distressed by urges to do so, and, if married, his transvestic fetishism may also cause difficulties for his wife.

VOYEURISM A person is diagnosed with **voyeurism** according to DSM-IV-TR if he has recurrent, intense sexually arousing fantasies, urges, or behaviors involving the observation of unsuspecting females who are undressing or of couples engaging in sexual activity (see DSM-IV-TR Criteria on p. 457). Frequently, such individuals masturbate during their peeping activity. Peeping Toms, as they are commonly called, commit these offenses primarily as young men.

How do some young men develop this pattern? First, viewing the body of an attractive female is sexually stimulating for many, if not most, heterosexual men. In addition, the privacy and mystery that have traditionally surrounded sexual activities tend to increase curiosity about them. Second, if a young man with such curiosity feels shy and inadequate in his relations with the opposite sex, he may accept the substitute of voyeurism, which satisfies his curiosity and to some extent meets his sexual needs without the trauma of actually approaching a female. He thus avoids the rejection and lowered self-status that such an approach might bring. In fact, voyeuristic activities often provide important compensatory feelings of power and secret domination over an unsuspecting victim, which may contribute to the maintenance of this pattern. If a voyeur manages to find a wife in spite of his interpersonal difficulties, as many do, he is rarely well adjusted sexually in his relationship with his wife, as the following case illustrates.

case STUDY — A Peeping Tom

A young married college student had an attic apartment that was extremely hot during the summer months. To enable him to attend school, his wife worked; she came home at night tired and irritable and not in the mood for sexual relations. In addition, "the damned springs in the bed squeaked." In order "to obtain some sexual gratification," the youth would peer through his binoculars at the room next door and occasionally saw the young couple there engaged in erotic activities. This stimulated him greatly, and he decided to extend his peeping to a sorority house. During his second venture, however, he was reported and was apprehended by the police. This offender was quite immature for his age, rather puritanical in his attitude toward masturbation, and prone to indulge in rich but immature sexual fantasies.

More permissive laws concerning "adult" movies, videos, and magazines in recent years have probably removed much of the secrecy from sexual behavior and also have provided an alternative source of gratification for would-be voyeurs. However, their actual effect on voyeurism is a matter of speculation because there never have been good epidemiological data on its prevalence (Kaplan & Krueger, 1997; Maletzky, 2002), although it is thought to be one of the most common paraphilias. For many voyeurs, these movies and magazines probably do not provide an adequate substitute for secretly watching the sexual behavior of an unsuspecting couple or the "real-life" nudity of a woman who mistakenly believes she enjoys privacy.

Although a voyeur may become reckless in his behavior and thus may be detected or even apprehended by the police, voyeurism does not ordinarily have any other serious criminal or antisocial behaviors associated with it. In fact, many people probably have some voyeuristic inclinations, which are checked by practical considerations such as the possibility of being caught, and by ethical attitudes concerning the right to privacy.

EXHIBITIONISM **Exhibitionism** (*indecent exposure* in legal terms) is diagnosed in a person with recurrent, intense urges, fantasies, or behaviors that involve exposing his genitals to others (usually strangers) in inappropriate circumstances and without their consent (see DSM-IV-TR Criteria on p. 457). The exposure may take place in some secluded location such as a park or in a more public place such as a department store, church, theater, or bus. In cities, an exhibitionist (also known as a flasher) often drives by schools or bus stops, exhibits himself while in the car, and then drives rapidly away. In many instances the exposure is repeated under fairly constant conditions, such as only in churches or buses, or in the same general vicinity and at the same time of day. In one case, a youth exhibited himself only at the top of an escalator in a large department store. For a male offender, the typical victim is ordinarily a young or middle-aged female who is not known to the offender, although children and adolescents may also be targeted (Murphy, 1997). Exhibitionism, which usually begins in adolescence or young adulthood, is the most common sexual offense reported to the police in the United States, Canada, and Europe, accounting for about one-third of all sexual offenses (McAnulty et al., 2001; Murphy, 1997). According to some estimates, as many as 20 percent of women have been the target of either exhibitionism or voyeurism (Kaplan & Krueger, 1997; Meyer, 1995).

In some instances, exposure of the genitals is accompanied by suggestive gestures or masturbation, but more often there is only exposure. A significant minority of exhibitionists commit aggressive acts, sometimes including coercive sex crimes against adults or children, and a subset of exhibitionists may best be considered as having antisocial personality disorder, as described in Chapter 11 (Kaplan & Krueger, 1997).

Despite the rarity of aggressive or assaultive behavior in these cases, an exhibitionistic act nevertheless takes place without the viewer's consent and may be emotionally upsetting, as is indeed the perpetrator's intent. This intrusive quality of the act, together with its explicit violation of propriety norms about "private parts," ensures condemnation. Thus society considers exhibitionism a criminal offense.

Men who engage in exhibitionism often cause emotional distress in the viewers because of the intrusive quality of the act, along with its explicit violation of propriety norms.

SADISM The term **sadism** is derived from the name of the Marquis de Sade (1740–1814), who for sexual purposes inflicted such cruelty on his victims that he was eventually committed as insane. In DSM-IV-TR, for a diagnosis of sadism, a person must have recurrent, intense sexually arousing fantasies, urges, or behaviors that involve inflicting psychological or physical pain on another individual (see DSM-IV-TR Criteria on p. 457). A closely related, but less severe, pattern is the practice of "bondage and discipline" (B & D), which may include tying a person up, hitting or spanking, and so on, to enhance sexual excitement.

In some cases, sadistic activities lead up to or terminate in actual sexual relations; in others, full sexual gratification is obtained from the sadistic practice alone. A sadist, for example, may slash a woman with a razor or stick her with a needle, experiencing an orgasm in the process. The pain inflicted by sadists may come from whipping, biting, cutting, or burning; the act may vary in intensity, from fantasy to severe mutilation and even murder. Mild degrees of sadism (and masochism, discussed below) are involved in the sexual foreplay customs of many cultures, and some couples in our own society—both heterosexual and homosexual—regularly engage in such practices, which are often quite ritualized. It is important to distinguish transient or occasional interest in sadomasochistic practices from sadism as a paraphilia. Surveys have found that perhaps 5 to 15 percent of men and women enjoy sadistic and/or masochistic activities voluntarily on occasion (Baumeister & Butler, 1997; Hucker, 1997). Paraphilic sadism and masochism, in which sadomasochistic activities are the preferred or exclusive means to sexual gratification, are much rarer; not uncommonly they co-occur in the same individual (LeVay & Valente, 2006). The situation can range from full consent of the victim to complete lack of consent, although changes to DSM-IV-TR in 2000 require that the diagnosis of sadism be reserved for cases in which the victim is nonconsenting (LeVay & Valente, 2006).

Extreme sexual sadists may mentally replay their torture scenes later while masturbating. Serial killers, who tend to be sexual sadists, sometimes record or videotape their sadistic acts. One study characterized 20 sexually sadistic serial killers who were responsible for 149 murders throughout the United States and Canada (Warren, Dietz, & Hazelwood, 1996). Most were white males in their late-twenties or early thirties. Their murders were remarkably consistent over time, reflecting sexual arousal to the pain, fear, and panic of their victims. Choreographed assaults allowed them to carefully control their victims' deaths. Some of the men reported that the God-like sense of being in control of the life and death of another human being was especially exhilarating. Eighty-five percent of the sample reported consistent violent sexual fantasies, and 75 percent collected materials with a violent theme including audiotapes, videotapes, pictures, or sketches of their sadistic acts or sexually sadistic pornography.

After a decades-long search for a psychopathic serial killer who was also a sexual sadist, Wichita, Kansas, police captured Dennis Rader (the BTK killer) in February 2005. By June 27, 2005, Rader had confessed to murdering 10 people over the previous three decades. Many of his victims were found partially unclothed and Rader reportedly obtained sexual gratification while torturing them and watching them die. Rader also sometimes practiced bondage on himself while watching pictures and videos of young attractive women.

Notorious serial killers include Ted Bundy, who was executed in 1989. Bundy confessed to the murder of over 30 young women, nearly all of whom fit a targeted type: women with long hair parted in the middle. Bundy admitted that he used his victims to re-create the covers of detective magazines or scenes from "slasher movies." Jeffrey Dahmer was convicted in 1992 of having mutilated and murdered 15 boys and young men, generally having sex with them after death. (He was subsequently murdered in prison.) Although many sadists have had chaotic childhoods, both Bundy and Dahmer came from middle-class families and had loving parents. Unfortunately, we do not have a good understanding of the causal factors involved in these extreme cases of sadism.

MASOCHISM The term **masochism** is derived from the name of the Austrian novelist Leopold V. Sacher-Masoch (1836–1895), whose fictional characters dwelt lovingly on the sexual pleasure of pain. In sexual masochism, a person experiences sexual stimulation and gratification from the experience of pain and degradation in relating to a lover. According to DSM-IV-TR (see DSM-IV-TR Criteria on p. 457), the person must have experienced recurrent, intense sexually arousing fantasies, urges, or behaviors involving the act of being humiliated, beaten, or bound, often in a ritualistic pattern of behavior (Sandnabba et al., 2002). Interpersonal masochistic activities require the participation of at least two people—one superior "disciplinarian" and one obedient "slave." In a significant minority of cases, the women who fall into such a pattern with their partners were sexually or physically abused as children (Warren & Hazelwood, 2002).

Such arrangements in mild form are not uncommon in either heterosexual or homosexual relationships. Masochists do not usually want, or cooperate with, true sexual sadists, but with individuals willing to hurt or humiliate them within limits they set. Masochism appears to be much more common than sadism and occurs in both men and women (Baumeister & Butler, 1997; Sandnabba et al., 2002). Sadomasochistic activities, including bondage and discipline, are often performed communally, within "dungeons" popular in major cities. Such activities might involve men being bound and whipped by women called "dominatrixes," who wear tight leather or rubber outfits and are paid to inflict pain and humiliation in a sexually charged sense.

One particularly dangerous form of masochism, called *autoerotic asphyxia,* involves self-strangulation to

Sadomasochistic activities, including bondage and discipline, are often performed communally, within "dungeons" popular in major cities.

the point of oxygen deprivation, which appears in these individuals to increase the intensity of orgasm by constriction of blood flow to the brain during masturbation (LeVay & Valente, 2006). Coroners in most major U.S. cities are familiar with cases in which the deceased is found hanged next to masochistic pornographic literature or other sexual paraphernalia. Accidental deaths attributable to this practice have been estimated to range between 500 and 1,000 per year in the United States (LeVay & Valente, 2006). The following is a case of autoerotic asphyxia with a tragic ending.

case STUDY **"I got tangled in the rope"**

A woman heard a man shouting for help and went to his apartment door. . . .

The woman with her two sons . . . broke into the apartment. They found the man lying on the floor, his hands tied behind him, his legs bent back, and his ankles secured to his hands. A mop handle had been placed behind his knees. He was visibly distraught, sweating, and short of breath, and his hands were turning blue. He had defecated and urinated in his trousers. In his kitchen the woman found a knife and freed him.

When police officers arrived and questioned the man, he stated that he had returned home that afternoon, fallen asleep on his couch, and awakened an hour later only to find himself hopelessly bound. The officers noted that the apartment door had been locked when the neighbors broke in . . . [and] when the officers filed their report, they noted that "this could possibly be a sexual deviation act." Interviewed the next day, the man confessed to binding himself in the position in which he was found.

A month later, the police were called back to the same man's apartment. A building manager had discovered him face down on the floor in his apartment. A paper bag covered his head like a hood. When the police arrived, the man was breathing rapidly with a satin cloth stuffed in his mouth. Rope was stretched around his head and mouth and wrapped his chest and waist. Several lengths ran from his back to his crotch, and ropes at his ankles had left deep marks. A broom handle locked his elbows behind his back. Once freed, the man explained, "While doing isometric exercises, I got tangled up in the rope." . . .

Two years passed and the man moved on to another job. He failed to appear for work one Monday morning. A fellow employee found him dead in his apartment. During their investigation, police were able to reconstruct the man's final minutes. On the preceding Friday, he had bound himself in the following manner: sitting on his bed and crossing his ankles, left over right, he had bound them together with twine. Fastening a tie around his neck, he then secured the tie to an 86-inch pole behind his back. . . . [By a complicated set of maneuvers he applied] pressure to the pole, still secured to the tie around his neck, [and] strangled himself. (From Spitzer et al., 2002, pp. 86–88.)

Source: Reprinted with permission from the *DSM-TR-Casebook: A Learning Companion to the Diagnostic and Statistical Manual of Mental Disorders,* Fourth Edition, Text Revision (Copyright 2002). American Psychiatric Publishing, Inc.

Causal Factors and Treatments for Paraphilias

Many individuals with paraphilias have explanations for their unusual sexual preferences. For example, one amputee paraphilic (whose preference is a partner with a missing limb) recalled that his fascination with female amputees originated during adolescence. He was neglected emotionally by his cold family but heard a family member express sympathetic feelings for an amputee. He developed the wish that he would become an amputee and thus earn their sympathy (see First, 2005, for a discussion of this paraphilia, known as *apotemnophilia*). This story raises many questions. Emotionally cold families are not uncom-

Men's vulnerability to paraphilias such as fetishism may be a result of their greater dependence on visual stimuli. This in turn makes them more likely to form sexual associations to nonsexual stimuli, such as women's legs or high-heeled shoes, quite possibly through a process of classical conditioning.

mon, and sympathy for amputees is nearly universal. Certainly not every male in a cold family who detects sympathy for amputees develops an amputee paraphilia. Such stories do not necessarily have any validity because we are often unaware of the forces that shape us (Nisbett & Wilson, 1977).

Several facts about paraphilia are likely to be important in their development. First, as we have already noted, nearly all persons with paraphilias are male; females with paraphilias are so rare that they are found in the literature only as case reports (e.g., Fedoroff, Fishell, & Fedoroff, 1999). Second, paraphilias usually begin around the time of puberty or early adolescence. Third, people with paraphilias often have more than one (e.g., LeVay & Valente, 2006; Maletzky, 1998). For example, the corpses of men who died accidentally in the course of autoerotic asphyxia were partially or fully cross-dressed in 25 to 33 percent of cases (Blanchard & Hucker, 1991). There is no obvious reason for the association between sexual masochism and transvestism. Why should it be so?

Money (1986) and others have suggested that male vulnerability to paraphilias is closely linked to their greater dependence on visual sexual imagery. Perhaps sexual arousal in men depends on physical stimulus features to a greater degree than in women, whose arousal may depend more on emotional context such as being in love with a partner. If so, men may be more vulnerable to forming sexual associations to nonsexual stimuli, which may be most likely to occur after puberty when the sexual drive is high. Many believe that these associations arise as a result of classical and instrumental conditioning and/or social learning that occurs through observation and modeling. When observing paraphilic stimuli (e.g., photographs of models in their underwear), or when fantasies about paraphilic stimuli occur, boys may masturbate, and the reinforcement by orgasm-release may serve to condition an intense attraction to paraphilic stimuli (e.g., Kaplan & Krueger, 1997; LeVay & Valente, 2006).

TREATMENTS FOR PARAPHILIAS The vast majority of studies concerning the treatment of paraphilias have been conducted with sex offenders. The literature concerning treatment of men with paraphilias who have not committed any offense, or who have victimless paraphilias (e.g., masochism), consists primarily of case reports because most people with paraphilias do not seek treatment for these conditions. Thus we defer discussion of the treatment of paraphilias until we discuss the treatment of sex offenders, many of whom have paraphilias.

Gender Identity Disorders

Gender identity refers to one's sense of maleness or femaleness and may be distinguished from *gender role,* which refers to the masculinity and femininity of one's overt behavior (Money, 1988). Of all behavioral traits, gender identity may have the strongest correlation with biological sex, but the correlation is not perfect. Some rare individuals feel extreme discomfort and unhappiness with their biological sex and strongly desire to change to the opposite sex. Indeed, some adults with gender identity disorders, often called transsexuals, opt for expensive and complicated surgery to accomplish just that. In DSM-IV-TR, **gender identity disorder** is characterized by two components: (1) a strong and persistent **cross-gender identification**—that is, the desire to be, or the insistence that one is, of the opposite sex—and (2) **gender dysphoria**—persistent discomfort about one's biological sex or the sense that the gender role of that sex is inappropriate. The disorder may occur in children or adults and in males or females.

GENDER IDENTITY DISORDER OF CHILDHOOD Boys with gender identity disorder show a marked preoccupation with traditionally feminine activities (Zucker, 2005; Zucker & Bradley, 1995). They may prefer to dress in female clothing. They enjoy stereotypical girls' activities such as playing dolls and playing house. They usually avoid rough-and-tumble play and often express the desire to be a girl. Boys with gender identity disorder are often ostracized as "sissies" by their peers.

DSM-IV-TR

Criteria for Gender Identity Disorder

A. A strong and persistent cross-gender identification. In children four of the following must also be present:

(1) Repeatedly stated desire to be, or insistence one is, the other sex.

(2) In boys, preference for cross-dressing in female attire; in girls, insistence on wearing stereotypical masculine clothing.

(3) Strong and persistent preferences for cross-sex roles in make-believe play or persistent fantasies of being the other sex.

(4) Intense desire to participate in the stereotypical games and pastimes of the other sex.

(5) Strong preference for playmates of the other sex.

In adolescents and adults, the disturbance is manifested by symptoms such as stated desire to be the other sex, frequent passing as the other sex, and/or desire to live or be treated as the other sex.

B. Persistent discomfort with his or her sex or sense of inappropriateness in the gender role of that sex. In boys, this could be in the form of assertion that his penis or testes are disgusting or that it would be better not to have a penis, or rejection of stereotypical male toys, games, and activities. In girls: Rejection of urinating in a sitting position, assertion that she will grow a penis, or assertion that she does not want to grow breasts or menstruate. In adolescents and adults: preoccupation with getting rid of primary and secondary sex characteristics, or other procedures to physically alter sexual characteristics to simulate the other sex.

Girls with gender identity disorder typically balk at parents' attempts to dress them in traditional feminine clothes such as dresses, preferring boys' clothing and short hair. Fantasy heroes typically include powerful male figures like Batman and Superman. They show little interest in dolls, and increased interest in sports. Although mere tomboys frequently have many or most of these traits, girls with gender identity disorder are distinguished by their desire to be a boy or to grow up as a man. Young girls with gender identity disorder are treated better by their peers than are boys with gender identity disorder, because cross-gender behavior in girls is better tolerated (Cohen-Kettenis et al., 2003; Zucker, Sanikhani, & Bradley, 1997). In clinic-referred gender identity disorder, boys outnumber girls 5 to 1 (Cohen-Kettenis et al., 2003). An appreciable percentage of that imbalance may reflect greater parental concern about femininity in boys than about masculinity in girls.

The most common adult outcome of boys with gender identity disorder appears to be homosexuality rather than transsexualism (Bradley & Zucker, 1997; Zucker, 2005). In Richard Green's (1987) prospective study of 44 very feminine boys from the community, only one sought sex change surgery by age 18. About three-quarters became gay or bisexual men who were evidently satisfied with their biological sex. However, several later studies of clinic-referred children have found that 10 to 20 percent of boys with gender identity disorder later were diagnosed as transsexual by age 16 or 18, and about 40 to 60 percent identified themselves as homosexual or bisexual, a percentage that may have increased by the time they were older (Zucker, 2005). There are several smaller prospective studies of girls with gender identity disorder that have shown that 35 to 45 percent may show persistent gender identity disorder (leading to a desire for sex reassignment surgery in many), and approximately half had a homosexual orientation.

Given that many such children typically adjust well in adulthood, should they be considered to have a mental

Boys with gender identity disorder enjoy dressing up in female clothing and make-up, and enjoy stereotypical girls' activities. As a consequence, they are often ostracized as "sissies" by their peers.

disorder as children? Some have argued that such children should not be considered "disordered" because the primary obstacle to their happiness may be a society that is intolerant of cross-gender behavior. However, most researchers who work with these children maintain that the distress and unhappiness these children and adolescents have about the discrepancy between their biological sex and their psychological gender is consistent with this being called a mental disorder (e.g., Zucker, 2005; Zucker & Spitzer, 2005). Moreover, these children are frequently mistreated by their peers and have strained relations with their parents, even though their cross-gender behavior harms no one.

Treatment Children with gender identity disorder are often brought in by their parents for psychotherapy. Specialists attempt both to treat the child's unhappiness with his or her biological sex and to ease strained relations with parents and peers. Children with gender identity disorders often have other general behavioral problems such as anxiety and mood disorders that also need therapeutic attention (Zucker, Owen, et al., 2002). Therapists try to improve peer and parental relations by teaching such children how to reduce their cross-gender behavior, especially in situations where it might cause interpersonal problems. Gender dysphoria is typically treated psychodynamically—that is, by examining inner conflicts. Controlled studies evaluating such treatment remain to be conducted (Zucker & Bradley, 2003).

TRANSSEXUALISM Transsexuals are adults with gender identity disorder who desire to change their sex, and surgical advances have made this goal partially feasible, although expensive. (Adults who have gender identity disorder and do not desire to change their sex are usually referred to as *transgendered.*) **Transsexualism** is apparently a very rare disorder. European studies suggest that approximately 1 per 30,000 adult males and 1 per 100,000 adult females seek sex reassignment surgery. Until fairly recently, most researchers assumed that transsexualism was the adult version of childhood gender identity disorder, and indeed this is often the case. That is, many transsexuals had gender identity disorder as children (despite the fact that most children with gender identity disorder do not become transsexual), and their adult behavior is analogous. This appears to be the case for all female-to-male transsexuals (individuals born female who become male). Virtually all such individuals recall being extremely tomboyish, with masculinity persisting unabated into adulthood. Most, but not all, female-to-male transsexuals are sexually attracted to women. One female-to-male transsexual had these recollections:

> [I have felt different] as far as I can remember. Three years old. I remember wanting to be a boy. Wearing boys' clothes and wanting to do all the things boys do. I remember my mother... saying, "Are you ever going to be a lady? Are you ever going to wear women's clothing?"... I can remember as I got a little older always looking at women, always wanting a woman.... I feel like a man, and I feel like my loving a woman is perfectly normal. (Green, 1992, p. 102)

In contrast to female-to-male transsexuals, there are two kinds of male-to-female transsexuals, with very different causes and developmental courses: *homosexual* and *autogynephilic transsexuals* (Blanchard, 1989; LeVay & Valente, 2006). Homosexual transsexual men are generally very feminine and have the same sexual orientation as gay men: They are sexually attracted to biological males (their preoperative biological sex). However, because these transsexual men experience their gender identity as female, they often define their sexual orientation as heterosexual and resent being labelled gay. Thus what is referred to in the research literature as a homosexual male-to-female transsexual is a genetic male seeking a sex change operation who describes himself as a woman trapped in a man's body and who is sexually attracted to heterosexual male partners (Bailey, 2003). In contrast, autogynephilic transsexuals appear to have **autogynephilia**—a paraphilia in which their attraction is to thoughts, images, or fantasies of themselves as a woman (Blanchard, 1991, 1993). This diagnostic distinction has not been made in the DSM-IV, although it is briefly mentioned. Although it may not be relevant for treatment purposes (both types of transsexuals are appropriate candidates for sex reassignment surgery), it is fundamental to understanding the diverse psychology of male-to-female transsexualism.

One important finding is that homosexual transsexuals generally have had gender identity disorder since childhood, paralleling what is found in female-to-male transsexuals as discussed above. However, because most children with gender identity disorder do not become transsexual adults (but instead become gay or bisexual men), there must be other important determinants of transsexualism. One hypothesis is that there are some prenatal hormonal influences affecting which children develop gender identity disorder and later become transsexuals. For example, primate research clearly shows that a female fetus exposed to high levels of androgens in utero usually develops masculine types of rough-and-tumble play (Goy et al., 1988; Whalen, 1996).

Autogynephilic (sometimes called heterosexual) *transsexualism* almost always occurs in genetic males who usually report a history of transvestic fetishism. However, unlike other transvestites, autogynephilic transsexuals fantasize that they have female genitalia, which can lead to acute gender dysphoria, motivating their desire for sex reassignment surgery. Autogynephilic transsexuals may report sexual attraction to women, to both men and women, or to neither. Research has shown that these subtypes of autogynephilic transsexuals (varying in sexual

Mianne Bager (a Danish-born Australian resident) is a male-to-female transsexual who has golfed professionally in women's tournaments since 2003. She is the first known female professional golfer who was born male. Before she could play women's tournaments, rule changes had to be implemented in Europe, Australia, and other countries so that it was no longer required that a competitor be female at birth.

orientation) are very similar to each other and differ from homosexual transsexuals in other important respects (Bailey, 2003; Blanchard, 1985, 1989, 1991). Unlike homosexual transsexuals, autogynephilic transsexuals do not appear to have been especially feminine in childhood or adulthood, and they typically seek sex reassignment surgery much later in life than do homosexual transsexuals (R. Blanchard, 1994). The causes of autogynephilic transsexualism probably overlap etiologically with the causes of other paraphilias but are not yet well understood.

Treatment Psychotherapy is usually not effective in helping adolescents or adults resolve their gender dysphoria (Cohen-Kettenis, Dillen, et al., 2000; Zucker & Bradley, 1995). The only treatment that has been shown to be effective is surgical sex reassignment. Initially, transsexuals awaiting surgery are given hormone treatment. Biological men are given estrogens to facilitate breast growth, skin softening, and shrinking of muscles. Biological women are given testosterone, which suppresses menstruation, increases facial and body hair, and deepens the voice. Before they are eligible for surgery, transsexuals typically must live for many months with hormonal therapy, and they generally must live for at least a year as the gender they wish to become. If they successfully complete the trial period, they undergo surgery and continue to take hormones indefinitely. In male-to-female transsexuals, this entails removal of the penis and testes and the creation of an artificial vagina. Moreover, such transsexuals must undergo extensive electrolysis to remove their beards and body hair. They also have to learn to raise the pitch of their voice. Female-to-male transsexuals typically are given mastectomies and hysterectomies and often have other plastic surgery to alter various facial features (such as the Adam's apple).

Only a subset of female-to-male transsexuals seek an artificial penis because relevant surgical techniques are still somewhat primitive and very expensive. Moreover, the artificial penis is not capable of normal erection, so those who have this surgery must rely on artificial supports to have intercourse anyway. The rest function sexually without a penis. As surgical techniques advance, this is very likely to change. A 1990 review of the outcome literature found that 87 percent of 220 male-to-female transsexuals had satisfactory outcomes (meaning that they did not regret their decisions) and that 97 percent of 130 female-to-male transsexuals had successful outcomes (Green & Fleming, 1990). More recent studies have reported similar findings. Thus the majority of transsexuals are satisfied with the outcome of sex reassignment surgery, although there is variability in the degree of satisfaction (Cohen-Kettenis & Gooren, 1999; LeVay & Valente, 2006). In spite of the reasonably good success record for transsexual patients who are carefully chosen, such surgery remains controversial because some professionals continue to maintain that it is inappropriate to treat psychological disorders through drastic anatomical changes.

In Review

- Define paraphilia, and cite eight paraphilias recognized in the DSM, along with their associated features.
- What two components characterize gender identity disorder?
- Identify the two types of male-to-female transsexuals, and describe their developmental course as well as that of female-to-male transsexuals.
- What are the most effective treatments for childhood gender identity disorder and adult transsexualism?

Sexual Abuse

Sexual abuse is sexual contact that involves physical or psychological coercion, or at least one individual who cannot reasonably consent to the contact (e.g., a child). Such abuse includes pedophilia, rape, and incest, and it concerns society more than any other sexual problem. It is somewhat ironic, then, that of these three forms of abuse, only pedophilia is included in DSM-IV-TR. This partly reflects the seriousness with which society views these offenses and its preference for treating coercive sex offenders as criminals rather than as having a mental disorder (although obviously many criminals also have mental disorders).

Childhood Sexual Abuse

The past few decades have seen intense concern about childhood sexual abuse, with an accompanying increase in relevant research. There are at least three reasons for this. First, much evidence suggests that, broadly defined, childhood sexual abuse is more common than once was assumed. Second, there are possible links between childhood sexual abuse and some mental disorders, so such abuse may be important in the etiology of some disorders (see especially Chapters 3, 5, 8, and 11). Third, some dramatic and well-publicized cases involving allegations of childhood sexual abuse have raised very controversial issues such as the validity of children's testimony and the accuracy of recovered memories of sexual abuse. We shall consider all three of these issues in turn.

PREVALENCE OF CHILDHOOD SEXUAL ABUSE The prevalence of childhood sexual abuse depends on its definition, which has varied substantially across studies. For example, different studies use different definitions of "childhood," with the upper age limit ranging from 12 to as high as 19 years. Some studies have counted any kind of sexual interaction, even that which does not include physical contact (e.g., exhibitionism); others have counted only physical contact; others have counted only genital contact; and still others have counted consensual sexual contact with a minor. Depending on which definition is used, prevalence figures have ranged from less than 5 percent to more than 30 percent. Even the lowest plausible figures justify concern.

CONSEQUENCES OF CHILDHOOD SEXUAL ABUSE Childhood sexual abuse may have both short-term and long-term consequences. The most common short-term consequences are fears, post-traumatic stress disorder, sexual inappropriateness (e.g., touching others' genitals or talking about sexual acts), and poor self-esteem (e.g., Kendall-Tackett, Williams, & Finkelhor, 1993; McConaghy, 1998). Approximately one-third of sexually abused children show no symptoms. Thus there is no single "sexual abuse" syndrome.

A number of studies have found associations between reports of childhood sexual abuse and adult psychopathology, including borderline personality disorder (Battle, Shea, et al., 2004; Fossati, Madeddu, & Maffei, 1999), somatization disorder with dissociative symptoms (Sar et al., 2004), dissociative symptoms (Chu & Dill, 1990), and dissociative identity disorder (Maldonado et al., 2002; Ross, 1999). A wide variety of sexual symptoms have also been alleged to result from early sexual abuse (e.g., Leonard & Follette, 2002; Loeb et al., 2002), ranging, for example, from sexual aversion to sexual promiscuity. However, as discussed in Chapters 8 and 11, knowledge about these hypothesized associations is very limited because of difficulties in establishing causal links between early experiences and adult behavior (see also Unresolved Issues at the end of this chapter).

CONTROVERSIES CONCERNING CHILDHOOD SEXUAL ABUSE Several types of high-profile criminal trials have highlighted the limitations of our knowledge concerning questions of great scientific and practical importance. In one type of case, children have accused adults working in day-care settings of extensive, often bizarre sexual abuse, and controversial issues have been raised about the degree to which children's accusations can be trusted. In a second type of case, adults claim to have repressed and completely forgotten memories of early sexual abuse and then to have "recovered" the memories during adulthood, typically while seeing a therapist who believes that repressed memories of childhood sexual abuse are a very common cause of adult psychopathology. Many controversial issues have been raised about the validity of these "recovered" memories.

Children's Testimony Several cases of alleged sexual abuse in day-care settings shocked the country starting in the 1980s. The most notorious was the McMartin Preschool case in California (Eberle & Eberle, 1993). In 1983 Judy Johnson complained to police that her son had been molested by Raymond Buckey, who helped run the McMartin Preschool, which her son attended. Johnson's complaints grew increasingly bizarre. For example, she accused Buckey of sodomizing her son while he stuck the boy's head in a toilet and of making him ride naked on a horse. Johnson was diagnosed with acute paranoid schizophrenia, and she died of alcohol-related liver disease in 1986. By the time she died, prosecutors no longer needed her. Children at the preschool who were interviewed began to tell fantastically lurid stories—for example, that children were forced to dig up dead bodies at cemeteries, jump out of airplanes, and kill animals with bats. Nevertheless, prosecutors and many McMartin parents believed the children. Buckey and his mother (who owned the day-care

13.2 Developments in Research

The Reliability of Children's Reports of Past Events

Abuse of children is distressingly common, and children's reports of such abuse must always be taken seriously. However, as more and more children have been brought forward to testify in court about alleged physical and sexual abuse by parents or other adults, researchers have become increasingly concerned about determining how reliable the testimony of children, especially that of *young* children, can be expected to be—especially when they have been subjected to repeated interviews over many months with highly leading questions, sometimes in a coercive atmosphere. Unfortunately, this continues to be the way in which such children are sometimes treated before the trials in which they testify.

Stephen Ceci and Maggie Bruck, leading developmental psychologists studying this problem, have conducted a series of experiments that cast grave doubt on young children's testimony if they have been exposed repeatedly to suggestive interviews with leading questions over long intervals of time (Bruck, Ceci, & Hembrooke, 2002; Ceci, Bruck, & Battin, 2000; London et al., 2005). For example, Ceci and colleagues summarized evidence that preschoolers have greater difficulty than older children or adults in distinguishing between real and imagined acts (such as whether they really touched their nose or only imagined touching it; Ceci et al., 2000; Foley et al., 1989). In one well-known study, Ceci and colleagues had an adult interview preschoolers weekly for 10 weeks about whether certain actual events (such as getting in an accident that required stitches) and certain fictitious events (such as getting their hand caught in a mousetrap and having to go to the hospital to get it removed) had occurred. Each week, the children were asked to think hard about whether the event had happened and were prompted to visualize the scene. Later, each child had a videotaped interview with a new adult and was asked to recall what happened, with the adult using probing questions. The results were striking. Over half claimed that at least one of the fictitious events had actually happened to them, and one-quarter claimed that nearly all of the fictitious events had happened to them. Their narratives describing these fictitious events were often elaborate, embellished, coherent, and emotional, and many children firmly believed that these events had happened to them, and could not be talked out of their false reports (Ceci, 1995). When psychologists who specialize in interviewing children were shown these videotapes, their accuracy at detecting real events from fictitious events was no better than chance. Similar results have been obtained for judges, social workers, and psychiatrists. Ceci's conclusion was: "Repeatedly thinking about a fictitious event can lead some preschool children to produce vivid, detailed reports that professionals are unable to discern from their reports of actual events" (1995, p. 103).

Other research by Ceci and Bruck has shown that those who interview young children about possible abuse are actually more likely to obtain accurate information if they ask open-ended questions than if they ask many specific questions (London et al., 2005). And contrary to the widely held opinion that most children will not disclose abuse they have experienced, recent studies have shown that most children with substantiated abuse do disclose the abuse within one or two sessions when questioned in formal settings. These findings are contrary to the opinion of many professionals that when children disclose abuse readily, their reports should be considered suspect. For example, consider the following interchange cited by London et al. (2005, p. 196) between a prosecutor and an expert witness in a 2001 case (*People* v. *Carroll*, p. 70):

> Q: Doctor, you mentioned earlier that with respect to child victims, it is not unusual that they would fully describe all of the events in your first interview.
> A: No.
> Q: And if they do, is it suspicious to you?
> A. To me, yes.

On the other hand, many expert witnesses are also not inclined to believe children when they deny abuse has happened:

> Indeed Dr. Snow herself admitted that she used interrogation procedures that were not intended to sift truth from error. She forthrightly admitted she was not a neutral interviewer; rather she was "an ally for the child," "biased," and not a fact collector like the police. . . . since she starts an interrogation with the assumption

facility) were tried in a trial that took $2\frac{1}{2}$ years and cost $15 million. The jury acquitted Ms. Buckey on all counts and failed to convict Raymond Buckey on any; however, he was freed only after retrial, after having spent 5 years in jail. The jurors' principal reason for not finding the defendants guilty was their concern that interviewers had coaxed the children into telling stories of abuse that were not true by using the sorts of leading or coercive methods of questioning described in Developments in Research 13.2. Moreover, subsequent research on children with reported satanic abuse found no evidence (including physical evidence) that such abuse had occurred, and so any such

that abuse occurred, she then proceeds to prove that point. . . . "I didn't believe any of those kids when they told me it didn't happen." (*State* v. *Bullock*, 1989, p. 175; cited in London et al., 2005, p. 215.)

In several other important studies, Ceci and colleagues looked at young children who had been exposed to a staged event and examined the effect of the kinds of questions the children received from an interviewer. For example, in the Sam Stone Study, Leichtman and Ceci (1995) interviewed preschool children four times over 10 weeks for details about a previously staged 2-minute visit to their day-care center by a stranger named Sam Stone. Some of the children were given no prior information about Sam Stone before his visit and were never asked suggestive questions during the four interviews; other children were given a stereotype about Sam Stone (such as that he was clumsy) before his visit and were also given leading questions suggesting that Sam Stone had done certain things consistent with the stereotype. One month later (about 14 weeks after Sam Stone's visit), all the children were interviewed by a new interviewer, who asked about two events that had not happened during Sam Stone's visit. For the children who had been given no prior stereotype about Sam Stone and no leading questions during the initial four interviews, only 10 percent of the youngest preschoolers claimed that Sam Stone had done either of these two nonevents. (Older preschoolers seldom committed such errors.) By contrast, for the younger preschoolers who were given a prior stereotype that Sam Stone was clumsy and who had been asked leading questions during the four interviews, a startling 72 percent of the youngest children claimed that Sam Stone had done either one or both of the nonevents. When gently challenged, 44 percent continued to claim that they had seen him do these things.

Videotapes of some of these forensic interviews were later shown to over 1,000 researchers and clinicians who work with children, and they were then asked to rate the children for the accuracy of their testimony. The majority of the professionals were highly inaccurate. Indeed, the videotape of the child who was least accurate was rated as most credible, and the videotape of the child who was most accurate was rated as least credible. Leichtman and Ceci (1995) concluded "the accuracy of children's reports is extremely difficult to discern when children have been subjected to repeated erroneous suggestions over long retention intervals, especially when coupled with the induction of stereotypes" (p. 20). In a later study, two groups of children who watched a memorable staged event (an archaeological dig) were later questioned about that event. One group had seen two target events during the archaeological dig that the second group did not see, and the children from the two groups were allowed to discuss it with each other before being interviewed. Results showed that having personal conversations with peers can also lead to false reports of nonexperienced events, even in the absence of misleading questions (Principe & Ceci, 2002).

Finally, Ceci's and Bruck's work also challenges the use of anatomically correct dolls (dolls with bodies showing the sex organs) to symbolically represent actions, at least for very young children. Bruck and colleagues (1995) studied 70 three-year-old boys and girls who were visiting their pediatrician, 35 of whom were given a genital exam (which involved touching the genital area but no genital insertions) and 35 of whom were not given a genital exam. Mothers were present during these exams. Five minutes later, with the mothers still present, the children were asked to describe where the doctor had touched them. They were then presented anatomical dolls and asked to point on the dolls where the doctor had touched them. When interviewed verbally, most of the children who had not received a genital exam correctly refrained from stating that their genitals had been touched. However, when given the anatomical doll, nearly 60 percent of those who had not received a genital exam claimed that the doctor had made genital and/or anal insertions and done other acts to be concerned about. On the other hand, just over half of the children who had been given a genital exam claimed that their genitals had not been touched, even though they had. Thus it seemed that the use of anatomical dolls failed to improve the accuracy of the 3-year-olds' reports of what did or did not happen. Bruck et al. (1998) reported very similar results with 4-year-olds. Although older children may make fewer errors, no one has yet shown that the use of anatomical dolls improves reporting (Bruck et al., 1995; Ceci et al., 2000).

In summary, although young children are capable of correct recall of what has happened to them, they are also susceptible to a greater variety of sources of post-event distortion than older children and adults. To a lesser degree, even adults are susceptible to a variety of sources of post-event distortion (Ornstein, Ceci, & Loftus, 1998; see also the Unresolved Issues in Chapter 8). Thus the differences should be seen as a matter of degree rather than of kind (Ceci et al., 2000).

reports of satanic abuse are scientifically very doubtful (London, Bruck, et al., 2005).

Recovered Memories of Sexual Abuse In 1990, a young woman named Eileen Franklin testified in court that she had seen her father rape and murder an 8-year-old playmate 20 years earlier. Remarkably, despite her claim to have witnessed the murder, she had no memory of the event until she "recovered" the memory by accident in adulthood (MacLean, 1992). Franklin's father was convicted and given a life sentence, although in 1995 the conviction was overturned because of two serious constitutional errors made

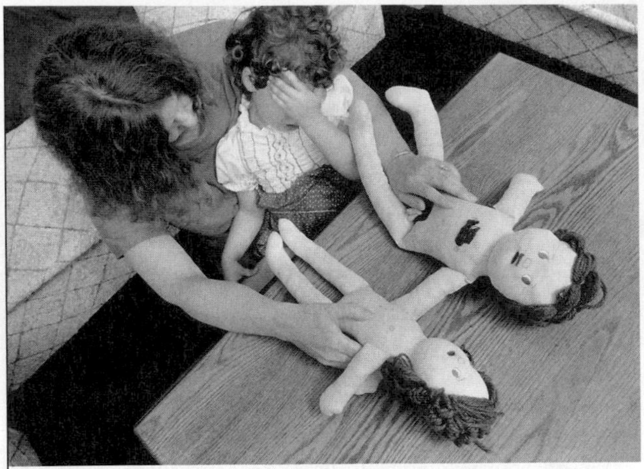

Recent evidence has suggested that the use of anatomically correct dolls to question young children about where they may have been touched in alleged incidents of sexual abuse does not improve the accuracy of their testimony relative to verbal interviews alone.

during the original trial that might have affected the jury's verdict. In another case, Patricia Burgus sued her two psychiatrists in Chicago for false-memory implantation, claiming the doctors had persuaded her through hypnosis and other therapeutic techniques "to believe that she was a member of a satanic cult, that she was sexually abused by multiple men, and that she engaged in cannibalism and abused her own children" (Brown, Goldstein, & Bjorklund, 2000, p. 3). In 1997 she was awarded $10.6 million (as far as we know, the largest judgment yet in a false-memory lawsuit).

As discussed in some detail in Chapter 8, whether traumatic experiences can be utterly forgotten and then somehow recovered intact years later has been heatedly debated during the past several decades. Some have argued that repressed memories are common (e.g., Herman, 1993) and are responsible for a great deal of psychopathology. In the controversial but very popular book *The Courage to Heal,* journalists Ellen Bass and Laura Davis asserted, "If you are unable to remember any specific instances [of sexual abuse]... but still have the feeling that something abusive happened to you, it probably did" (1988, p. 21). Yet as researchers have pointed out, there is absolutely no evidence that this statement is true. Some therapists still routinely give this book to their clients, and those clients often do report "recovering" such memories. Those skeptical about recovery of repressed memories point out that even normal, unrepressed memories can be highly inaccurate and that false memories can be induced experimentally (Loftus et al., 1995; Thomas & Loftus, 2002). For example, adolescents and adults who have been told to imagine several times having engaged in bizarre and unusual acts have sometimes come to believe that they actually performed those acts (see Chapter 8).

The debate about the validity of memories of childhood sexual abuse that arise during therapy remains extremely heated. Some researchers (the nonbelievers) maintain that the concept of repressed memory is wholly or largely invalid. In their view, virtually all "recovered memories" are false (Crews, 1995; Loftus & Ketchum, 1994; Thomas & Loftus, 2002). Others (the believers) maintain that false memories rarely occur and that recovered memories are typically valid, and they often cite cases in which the accused perpetrator confesses to the sexual abuse he is accused of (e.g., Pope, 1996). Psychologists equally familiar with the evidence have argued bitterly about this issue, and, as discussed in more detail in Chapter 8, a task force assembled by the American Psychological Association to study the issue in the mid-1990s failed to reach a consensus. This lack of consensus continues today. Indeed, this debate concerning recovered memories of sexual abuse is one of the most important and interesting contemporary controversies in the domains of psychopathology and mental health as discussed in the Unresolved Issues section in Chapter 8.

Pedophilia

According to DSM-IV-TR, **pedophilia** is diagnosed when an adult has recurrent, intense sexual urges or fantasies about sexual activity with a prepubertal child, although acting on these desires is not necessary for the diagnosis (see DSM-IV-TR Criteria on p. 457). Pedophilia frequently involves fondling or manipulation of the child's genitals, and occasionally penetration. Although penetration and associated force are often injurious to the child, injuries are usually a by-product rather than the goal they would be with a sadist (although a minority of men diagnosed with pedophilia are sexual sadists or have antisocial personality disorder or psychopathy; Cohen & Galynker, 2002). It is important to emphasize that pedophilia is defined by body maturity, not the age, of the preferred partner. Thus studies of childhood sexual abuse, which typically define childhood in terms of an age range that may extend well into adolescence, do not necessarily concern pedophilia (McAnulty et al., 2001).

Nearly all pedophiles are male, and about two-thirds of their victims are girls, typically between the ages of 8 and 11 (Cohen & Galynker, 2002). Some pedophiles (especially those who abuse prepubescent children) are relatively indifferent to the sex of their victim, but most are heterosexual or homosexual with about 1 in 2 or 3 being homosexual. Homosexual pedophiles tend to have more victims than heterosexual pedophiles (Blanchard, 2000; Cohen & Galynker, 2002).

Studies investigating the sexual responses of pedophiles have revealed several patterns of results (Barbaree & Seto, 1997; LeVay & Valente, 2006). Such studies tend to use a *penile plethysmograph* to measure erectile responses to sexual stimuli directly rather than relying on self-report. (A plethysmograph consists of an expandable band placed around the penis that is connected to a recording device.) Some men who have molested nonfamilial female children show greater sexual arousal than matched nonoffenders in response to pictures of nude or partially clad girls—and greater arousal to such pictures than to pictures of adult women. But other pedophiles respond to children as well as to adolescents and/or adults (Seto et al., 1999).

Child molesters are more likely than nonoffenders to believe that children will benefit from sexual contacts with adults and that children often initiate such contact (Cohen & Galynker, 2002; Segal & Stermac, 1990). Motivationally, many pedophiles appear to be shy and introverted, yet still desire mastery or dominance over another individual; some also idealize aspects of childhood such as innocence, unconditional love, or simplicity (Cohen & Galynker, 2002).

Pedophilia usually begins in adolescence and persists over a person's life. Many engage in work with children or youth so that they have extensive access to children; a subset never take advantage but many others do. Several studies show that men with pedophilia were much more likely to have been sexually abused as children than were rapists (Lee et al., 2002).

For several decades we have seen an increasing number of cases of pedophilia among a group long considered to be highly trustworthy: the Catholic clergy. Although the majority of priests are innocent of sexual wrongdoing, the Catholic Church has been forced to admit that a significant minority have committed sexual abuse, including pedophilia. At least 400 priests were charged with sexual abuse during the 1980s, and $400 million was paid in damages between 1985 and the early 1990s (Samborn, 1994). One very serious scandal involved James R. Porter, a 57-year-old father of four who is alleged to have sexually abused as many as 100 children when he was a priest in Massachusetts during the 1960s. Porter later admitted to his offenses and was convicted of molesting his children's baby-sitter in 1987. The Church settled a multimillion-dollar suit with 25 men whom Porter had abused while a priest.

This scandal erupted anew in 2002, with heightened publicity regarding revelations that a substantial number of priests in many cities had been sexually involved with children and adolescents—and that a significant number had been protected by their superiors. Indeed, this scandal led, after a prolonged public outcry, to the resignation of Cardinal Bernard Law of the Archdiocese of Boston. Over many years, Law had protected numerous priests who were guilty of sexual misconduct, allowing them to move from one parish to another after their sexual misconduct was discovered. Thus he allowed their sexual molestation to continue with more and more girls and boys. The Conference of Bishops subsequently adopted a policy of mandatory removal of any priest from his ministerial duties if he is known to have had sexual contact with a minor. This new policy seems to be working at least to some extent. In September 2005, for example, Cardinal Francis George of the Archdiocese of Chicago permanently removed 11 priests from public ministerial duties for reasons of sexual misconduct (*Chicago Tribune,* September 27, 2005). Similar problems of priests engaging in abuse have also occurred in Ireland (LeVay & Valente, 2006).

Former priest John Geoghan was found guilty of sexually molesting two boys, and accused of sexually molesting dozens more in several parishes in the Boston area. In January 2002, the Boston Globe *published a special report on the archdiocese's failure to stop Geoghan's cycle of abuse. This report became a catalyst for hundreds of people to come forward and expose the widespread scandal of sexual abuse and cover-up in the Catholic church. Geoghan was killed in prison in 2003.*

Incest

Culturally prohibited sexual relations (up to and including coitus) between family members such as a brother and sister or a parent and child are known as **incest.** Although a few societies have sanctioned certain incestuous relationships—at one time it was the established practice for Egyptian pharaohs to marry their sisters to prevent the royal blood from being "contaminated"—the incest taboo is virtually universal among human societies. Incest often produces children with mental and physical problems because close genetic relatives are much more likely than nonrelatives to share the same recessive genes (which often have negative biological effects) and hence to have children with two sets of recessive genes. Presumably for this reason, many nonhuman animal species, and all known primates, have an evolved tendency to avoid matings between close relatives. The mechanism for human incest avoidance appears to be lack of sexual interest in people to whom one is continuously exposed from an early age. For example, biologically unrelated children who are raised together in Israeli kibbutzim rarely marry or have affairs with others from their rearing group when they become adults (Kenrick & Luce, 2004). Evolutionarily, this makes sense. In most cultures, children reared together are biologically related.

In our own society, the actual incidence of incest is difficult to estimate because it usually comes to light only when reported to law enforcement or other agencies. It is almost certainly more common than is generally believed, in part because many victims are reluctant to report the incest or do not consider themselves victimized. Brother-sister incest is the most common form of incest, even though it is rarely reported (LeVay & Valente, 2006). The second most common pattern is father-daughter incest. It seems that girls living with stepfathers are at especially high risk for incest, perhaps because there is less of an incest taboo among nonblood relatives (Finkelhor, 1984; Masters et al., 1992). Mother-son incest is thought to be relatively rare. Frequently, incest offenders do not stop with one child in a family (Wilson, 2004), and some incestuous fathers involve all of their daughters serially as they become pubescent.

Incestuous child molesters tend to have some pedophilic arousal patterns (Barsetti, Earls, et al., 1998; Seto, Lalumiere, & Kuban, 1999), suggesting that they are at least partly motivated by sexual attraction to children, although they also show arousal to adult women. However, they differ from extrafamilial child molesters in at least two respects (Quinsey, Lalumiere, et al., 1995). First, the large majority of incest offenses are against girls, whereas extrafamilial offenses show a more equal distribution between boys and girls. Second, incest offenders are more likely to offend with only one or a few children in the family, whereas pedophilic child molesters are likely to have more victims (LeVay & Valente, 2006).

Rape

The term **rape** describes sexual activity that occurs under actual or threatened forcible coercion of one person by another (see Figure 13.1). In most states, legal definitions restrict forcible rape to forced intercourse or penetration of a bodily orifice by a penis or other object. Statutory rape is sexual activity with a person who is legally defined (by statute or law) to be under the age of consent (18 in most states), even if the underage person consents. In the vast majority of cases, rape is a crime of men against women, although in prison settings it is often committed by men against men.

It is important to note that forced sex is not unique to humans but rather occurs in many species in the animal kingdom, where it has often evolved as a reproductive strategy by males to produce more offspring. It has also existed in most human societies (including preliterate ones) at some time in history (Lalumiere et al., 2005). Across history, rape is traditionally most frequent during and following wars, when it sometimes reaches epidemic proportions. This may be because during war, men perceive few costs for the offense and it is perceived as a good way to express antagonism and contempt toward the enemy (Lalumiere et al., 2005).

PREVALENCE It might seem to be fairly straightforward to estimate the prevalence of rape, but the results of different studies have varied widely. Figures may vary in both the precise definition of rape and the way information is gathered (direct or indirect questions, for example), and when the estimates are made. For example, the U.S. Department of Justice figures from 1998 estimated that 1 in 3 women would experience rape or attempted rape at some point in their lives, with many of these being attempted but not completed rapes. But between 1993 and 2003 the number of rapes declined dramatically according to U.S. Department of Justice figures; thus rape figures for 2003 were only about one-fifth of what they had been in 1991 (LeVay & Valente, 2006).

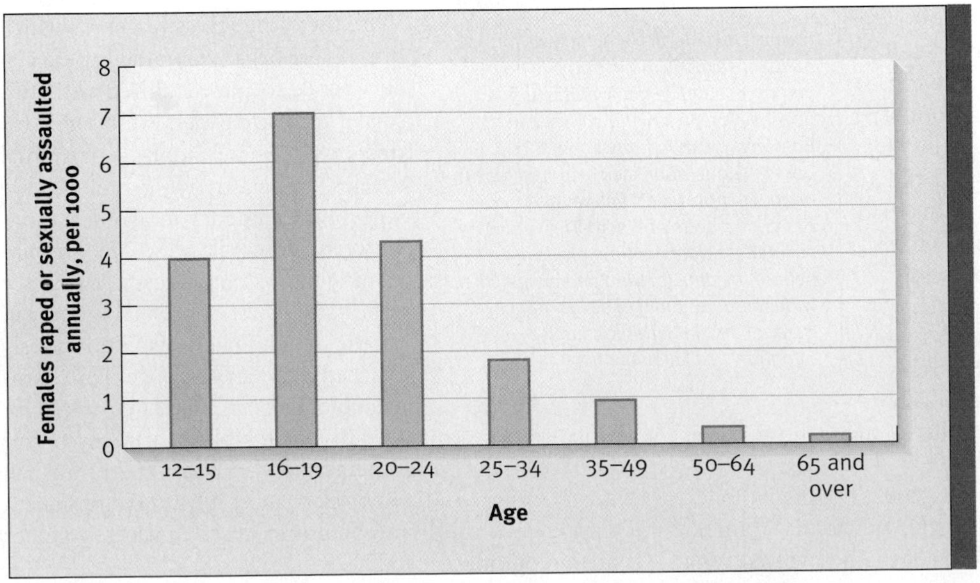

FIGURE 13.1

Age of Rape and Sexual Assault Victims

Young women are most at risk. (Data from U.S. Department of Justice, 2000a.)

IS RAPE MOTIVATED BY SEX OR AGGRESSION? Traditionally, rape has been classified as a sex crime, and society has assumed that the rapist was motivated by lust. However, in the 1970s some feminist scholars began to challenge this view, arguing that rape is motivated by the need to dominate, to assert power, and to humiliate a victim rather than by sexual desire for her (e.g., Brownmiller, 1975). Certainly from the perspective of the victim, rape—which is among women's greatest fears—is always an act of violence and is certainly not a sexually pleasurable experience, whatever the rapist's motivation.

In spite of the fact that feminist writers have argued that rape is primarily a violent act, there are many compelling reasons why sexual motivation is often, if not always, a very important factor (e.g., Ellis, 1989; Thornhill & Palmer, 2000). For example, although rape victims include females of all ages and degrees of physical attractiveness, the age distribution of rape victims is not at all random but includes a very high proportion of women in their teens and early twenties (see Figure 13.1), supporting the interpretation that rapists prefer younger (and hence usually considered more attractive) victims. This age distribution is quite different from the distribution of other violent crimes, in which the elderly are overrepresented because of their vulnerability. Furthermore, rapists usually cite sexual motivation as a very important cause of their actions. Finally, as we shall see, at least some rapists exhibit features associated with paraphilias and have multiple paraphilias (Abel & Rouleau, 1990; LeVay & Valente, 2006). Men with paraphilias are typically highly sexually motivated. Thus, there is a great deal of evidence showing that sexual desire is a factor in motivating many rapists, although not the exclusive motivational factor for all.

In the past few decades, several prominent researchers studying sex offenders have shown that all rapists actually have both aggressive and sexual motives, but to varying degrees. For example, Knight and Prentky (1990) identified four subtypes of rapists with two subtypes motivated primarily by aggression, and two subtypes motivated primarily by distorted sexual motives (see also Knight, Prentky, & Cerce, 1994). More recently, McCabe and Wauchope (2005) provided empirical support for a somewhat different classification system that also has four subtypes of rapists with differing amounts of sexual and aggressive motives. One type is largely motivated by undifferentiated anger and gratuitous aggression rather than sexual motivation; the second and third types are each motivated by displaying hostility and power over women through rape because of their own inadequacies (including sexual; the third type has a more sensitive, apologetic, and complimentary demeanor with his victim than the second); and a fourth type is motivated by sexually sadistic fantasies. At present it is not clear which scheme of classification is best, and some rapists cannot readily be characterized (LeVay & Valente, 2006).

RAPE AND ITS AFTERMATH Rape tends to be a repetitive activity rather than an isolated act, and most rapes are planned events. About 80 percent of rapists commit the act in the neighborhoods in which they reside; most rapes occur in an urban setting at night, in places ranging from dark, lonely streets to elevators and hallways, and apartments or homes. About a third or more of all rapes involve more than one offender, and often they are accompanied by beatings. The remainder are single-offender rapes in which the victim and the offender are acquainted with each other (in about two-thirds of rapes); this includes wives (Bennice & Resick, 2003).

In addition to the physical trauma inflicted on a victim, the psychological trauma may be severe, leading in a substantial number of female victims to what used to be called *rape trauma syndrome* (Burgess & Holmstrom, 1974). Since 1980 this has been recognized as posttraumatic stress disorder (see Chapter 5), which, when caused by rape, is often also associated with severe sexual problems. Other especially unfortunate factors in rape are the possibility of pregnancy or of contracting a sexually transmitted disease. A rape may also have a negative impact on a victim's marriage or other intimate relationships. Although there has been little systematic study of men who have been raped, one recent study of 40 male rape victims revealed that nearly all experienced some long-term psychological distress following rape including anxiety, depression, increased feelings of anger, and loss of self-image (Walker, Archer, & Davies, 2005).

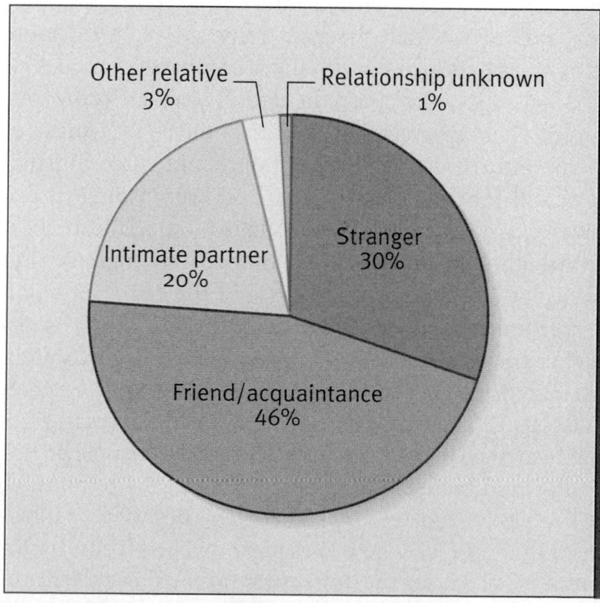

FIGURE 13.2

Most Rapes Are Not Committed by Strangers

The graph shows the relationships of perpetrators of rape and sexual assault to their victims. (Data from U.S. Department of Justice, 2000b.)

Which scenario do you think is more likely to lead to rape? It is difficult to guess because date rape is increasingly common, and rapes by casual acquaintances usually occur in dark, lonely places.

Rape, even at its least violent, is a bullying, intrusive violation of another person's integrity, selfhood, and personal boundaries that deserves to be viewed with more gravity—and its victims with more compassion and sensitivity—than has often been the case. Nevertheless, the concept of "victim-precipitated" rape, once a favorite of defense attorneys and of some police and court jurisdictions, still remains in certain circles, even though it is a myth. According to this view, a victim (especially a repeat victim), though often bruised both psychologically and physically, is regarded as the cause of the crime, often on such grounds as the alleged provocativeness of her clothing, her past sexual behavior, or her presence in a location considered risky (LeVay & Valente, 2006; Stermac, Segal, & Gillis, 1990). The attacker, on the other hand, is regarded as unable to quell his lust in the face of such irresistible provocation—and therefore is not treated as legally responsible for the act. Fortunately, *rape shield laws* began to be introduced in the 1970s. These laws protect rape victims by, for example, preventing the prosecutor from using evidence of a victim's prior sex history; however, many problems in these laws still remain (LeVay & Valente, 2006).

RAPISTS AND CAUSAL CONSIDERATIONS Information gathered by the FBI about arrested and convicted rapists suggests that rape is usually a young man's crime. According to FBI Uniform Crime Reports, about 60 percent of all rapists arrested are under 25 years old, with the greatest concentration in the 18-to-24 age group. Of the rapists who get into police records, about 30 to 50 percent are married and living with their wives at the time of the crime. As a group, they come from the low end of the socioeconomic ladder and commonly have a prior criminal record (Ward et al., 1997). They are also quite likely to have experienced sexual abuse, a violent home environment, and inconsistent caregiving in childhood (Hudson & Ward, 1997).

One subset of rapists, date rapists (a date rapist is an acquaintance who rapes a woman in the context of a date or other social interaction), have a somewhat different demographic profile in that they are often middle- to upper-class young men who rarely have criminal records. However, these men, like incarcerated rapists, are also characterized by promiscuity, hostile masculinity, and an emotionally detached, predatory personality (e.g., Knight, 1997; LeVay & Valente, 2003). Their victims are often highly intoxicated (Mohler-Keuo et al., 2004; Testa et al., 2003). What distinguishes them, primarily, is that incarcerated rapists show much higher levels of impulsive, antisocial behavior than the date rapists.

As suggested earlier, there is evidence that some rapists are afflicted by a paraphilia (Abel & Rouleau, 1990;

Freund & Seto, 1998). For example, rapists often report having recurrent, repetitive, and compulsive urges to rape. They typically try to control these urges, but the urges eventually become so strong that they act on them. Many rapists also have other paraphilias. In one study of 126 rapists, for example, 28 percent had an interest in exhibitionism and 18 percent in voyeurism (Abel & Rouleau, 1990). Most important, rapists have a characteristic pattern of sexual arousal (Abel & Rouleau, 1990; Lohr, Adams, & Davis, 1997). Most rapists are similar to normal nonoffending men in being sexually aroused by depictions of mutually satisfying, consensual intercourse. However, in contrast to normal men and other nonsexual offenders, many rapists are also sexually aroused by depictions of sexual assaults involving an unwilling victim (Lalumiere et al., 2005b). A small minority of rapists are sexual sadists, characterized by very violent assaults and aroused more by assault than by sexual stimuli.

In terms of personality, rapists are very often characterized by impulsivity, quick loss of temper, lack of personally intimate relationships, and insensitivity to social cues or pressures (Giotakos et al., 2004). Many rapists also show some deficits in social and communication skills (Emmers-Sommer et al., 2004), as well as in their cognitive appraisals of women's feelings and intentions (Ward et al., 1997). For example, they are particularly deficient in skills involved in successful conversation, which is necessary for developing consenting relationships with women. In addition, they have difficulty decoding women's negative cues during social interactions and often interpret friendly behavior as flirtatious or sexually provocative (Emmers-Sommer et al., 2004). This can lead to inappropriate behaviors that women would experience as sexually intrusive.

Estimates are that only 20 to 28 percent of rapes are ever reported, compared to 60 percent of robberies, but the number of rapes being reported has increased over the past several decades (Magid et al., 2004). Among men who are arrested, only about half are convicted; of these, only about two-thirds serve a jail term (LeVay & Valente, 2006). Convictions often bring light sentences, and a jail term does not dissuade a substantial number of offenders from repeating their crimes. The upshot of all this is that the large majority of rapists are not in prison but out among us.

Treatment and Recidivism of Sex Offenders

There is growing intolerance for sex offenders who repeat their crimes. Soon after his release from prison, convicted sex offender Earl Shriner forced a 7-year-old boy off his bike in the woods near Tacoma, Washington, and then raped and stabbed him before cutting off the boy's penis. Just before his release from prison, Shriner had confided to a cellmate that he still had fantasies of molesting and murdering children (Popkin, 1994). In a similar case, 7-year-old Megan Kanka was sexually molested and murdered by a convicted pedophile living in her neighborhood. Cases such as these have inspired a number of measures to protect society from sexual predators (see The World Around Us 13.3 on p. 476).

But are such stories representative? Are sex offenders typically incurable? Should they receive life sentences on the presumption that they are bound to offend again? Or have they been unfairly singled out by media sensationalism when they really are responsive to treatment (Berlin & Malin, 1991)? The efficacy of treatment for sex offenders is controversial, and this is the topic to which we now turn (e.g., Hanson, Gordon, et al., 2002; Maletzky, 2002).

Recidivism rates for some types of offenders are higher than they are for others (Berner et al., 2003; Rabinowitz et al., 2004). Specifically, sex offenders with deviant sexual preferences (e.g., exhibitionists, severe sadists, and those who are most attracted to children) have particularly high rates of sexual recidivism (Dickey et al., 2002; Langevin et al., 2004). One recent follow-up study of more than 300 sex offenders over 25 years found that over half were charged with at least one additional sexual offense (Langevin et al., 2004). The recidivism rate for rapists steadily decreases with age, but that for child molesters does not decline much until after age 50 (Dickey et al., 2002; Hanson, 2002).

PSYCHOTHERAPIES AND THEIR EFFECTIVENESS

Therapies for sex offenders typically have at least one of the following four goals: to modify patterns of sexual arousal, to modify cognitions and social skills to allow more appropriate sexual interactions with adult partners, to change habits or behavior that increases the chance of reoffending, or to reduce sexual drive. Attempts to modify sexual arousal patterns usually involve *aversion therapy,* in which a paraphilic stimulus such as a slide of a nude prepubescent girl for a pedophile is paired with an aversive event such as forced inhalation of noxious odors or a shock to the arm. An alternative to electric aversion therapy is *covert sensitization,* in which the patient imagines a highly aversive event while viewing or imagining a paraphilic stimulus, or *assisted covert sensitization,* in which a foul odor is introduced to induce nausea at the point of peak arousal (Maletzky, 2002).

Deviant arousal patterns also need to be replaced by arousal to acceptable stimuli (Maletzky, 2002; Quinsey & Earls, 1990). Most often, investigators have attempted to pair the pleasurable stimuli of orgasm with sexual fantasies involving sex between consenting adults. For example, patients are asked to masturbate while thinking of deviant fantasies. At the moment of ejaculatory inevitability, the patient switches his fantasy to a more appropriate theme. Although aversion therapy has been shown to be somewhat effective in the laboratory (Maletzky, 1998; Quinsey & Earls, 1990), how well this therapeutic change generalizes to the patient's outside world is uncertain if his motivation wanes. Although aversion therapy is still widely

13.3 The World Around Us

Megan's Law

On July 29, 1994, seven-year-old Megan Kanka, from Hamilton Township, New Jersey, was walking home from her friend's house when a neighbor invited her to his house to see his new puppy. The neighbor, Jesse Timmendequas, 33, was a landscaper who had lived across the street for about a year. Unknown to Megan, to Megan's parents, or to anyone else in the neighborhood, he was also a twice-convicted child molester (who lived with two other convicted sex offenders). When Megan followed him inside, he led her to an upstairs bedroom, strangled her unconscious with his belt, raped her, and asphyxiated her with a plastic bag. Timmendequas then placed Megan's body in a toolbox, drove to a soccer field, and dumped it near a portable toilet. Timmendequas was subsequently apprehended, convicted, and sentenced to death.

Megan's murder sparked outrage at the fact that dangerous sex offenders could move into a neighborhood without notifying the community of their presence. In response, the New Jersey state legislature passed Megan's Law, which mandated that upon release, convicted sex offenders register with police and that authorities notify neighbors that convicted sex offenders have moved in by distributing flyers, alerting local organizations, and canvassing door-to-door. Similar laws have been passed in many other states, and it is now possible in several states to visit a Web site containing pictures and addresses of convicted sex offenders subject to that state's Megan's Law. Some states require convictions of sex offenses to be indicated on drivers' licenses.

Although Megan's Laws have been enormously popular with state legislators and citizens, they have not been uncontroversial. Civil libertarians have objected to community notification requirements, which, they argue, endanger released offenders (who have arguably paid their debts to society) and also prevent them from integrating successfully back into society. Although the various Megan's Laws are intended to protect potential victims rather than to encourage harassment of sex offenders, the latter has occurred. For example, in July 1993, the home of convicted child rapist Joseph Gallardo was burned to the ground after citizens in Snohomish County, Washington, learned that he was about to be paroled. John Becerra, a convicted sex offender, moved into a two-story home in the New York City area in December 1995, hoping to begin a new life with his wife and their 9-year-old son. But he and his family found themselves the target of a persistent campaign of protests by their neighbors. Signs around the neighborhood warned, "Beware of Sex Offender," their car was vandalized, and rallies were held outside their home. In addition, the limited amount of relevant data has brought the effectiveness of Megan's Laws into question. A 1995 Washington State study found that in the period before that state's Megan's Law was passed, 22 percent of sex offenders who had been arrested committed another sex crime; after the law went into effect, the rate was quite similar, 19 percent (Schenk, 1998).

Recognition that some sex offenses have high recidivism rates—and uncertainty whether treatment helps—has led some states to pass laws that require involuntary commitment of dangerous offenders to psychiatric facilities even after their sentences have been served. Leroy Hendricks was convicted five times of molesting children and admitted that only his death could guarantee that he would commit no further offenses. Kansas prosecutors invoked state law to prevent his release after he served 10 years in prison, but this action was challenged as unconstitutional. The primary objection was that holding Hendricks after his sentence had been served amounted to giving him a second punishment for the same offense. In 1997 the U.S. Supreme Court ruled narrowly (5 to 4) that people such as Hendricks can be held if they are considered mentally abnormal and are likely to commit new crimes. Early signs are that once committed, few sex offenders will be released.

In order to ensure that released sex offenders will not reoffend, some states have passed legislation requiring chemical or surgical castration for certain types of sex offenders. For example, California now requires that repeat child molesters undergo chemical castration as a condition of parole. Michigan has passed a similar law applying to repeat rapists. Civil libertarians, exemplified by the ACLU, have argued that because of potentially severe side effects, such requirements violate the Constitution's ban on cruel and unusual punishment.

used for sex offenders, it is not used anymore as a sole form of treatment (Marshall, 1998).

The remaining psychological treatments are aimed at reducing the chances of sexual reoffending. *Cognitive restructuring* attempts to eliminate sex offenders' cognitive distortions, because these may play a role in sexual abuse (Maletzky, 2002). For example, an incest offender who maintained that "If my ten-year-old daughter had said no I would have stopped" might be challenged about a number of implied distortions: that a child has the capacity to consent to have sex with an adult, that if a child does not say no she has consented, and that it is the child's responsibility to stop sexual contact. In addition, *social-skills training* aims to help sex offenders (especially rapists) learn to process social information from women more effectively and to interact with them more appropriately (Maletzky, 2002; McFall, 1990). For example, some men read positive sexual connotations into women's neutral or negative messages, or believe that women's refusals of sexual advances reflect "playing hard to get." Training typically involves interaction of patients and female partners, who can give the patients feedback on their response to their interactions.

Although some studies in the treatment literature have reached positive conclusions (see Maletzsky, 2002, for a review), other studies have found essentially no differences between treated and untreated offenders (Emmelkamp, 1994; Quinsey et al., 1991; Rice et al., 1991). A recent meta-analysis of 43 studies containing nearly 10,000 sex offenders did find that treated offenders were less likely to reoffend than untreated offenders (Hanson, Gordon, et al., 2002), but the effect was modest: 12.3 percent of treated offenders were convicted of another sex offense, compared with 16.8 percent of untreated offenders. Current cognitive-behavioral techniques appeared to be much more effective than older techniques such as aversion therapy. There are also indications in the literature that certain paraphilias respond better to treatment than others (Laws & O'Donohue, 1997). For example, one very long-term follow-up (5 to 15 years) of over 2,000 sex offenders who had entered a cognitive-behavior treatment program found that child molesters and exhibitionists achieved better overall success rates than pedophiles and rapists (Maletzky & Steinhauser, 2002).

BIOLOGICAL AND SURGICAL TREATMENTS In recent years antidepressants from the SSRI category have been found to be useful in treating a variety of paraphilias by reducing paraphilic desire and behavior; they are not, however, useful in treatment of sexual offenders. The most controversial treatment for sex offenders involves castration—either surgical removal of the testes or the hormonal treatment sometimes called "chemical castration" (e.g., Berlin, 2003; Bradford & Greenberg, 1996). Both surgical and chemical castration lower the testosterone level, which in turn lowers the sex drive, allowing the offender to resist any inappropriate impulses. Chemical castration has most often involved the administration of antiandrogen steroid hormones such as Depo-Provera and Lupron, which can both have serious side effects. One uncontrolled study of the drug Lupron yielded dramatic results: Thirty men with paraphilias reported an average of 48 deviant fantasies per week prior to therapy, and no such fantasies during treatment (Rosler & Witztum, 1998; see also Maletzky & Field, 2003). However, relapse rates upon discontinuation of the drug are very high (Maletzky, 2002). Studies of surgical castration of repeat sex offenders with violent tendencies conducted in Europe and more recently in the United States had similar results (but without high rates of relapse); (Weinberger et al., 2005). These studies have typically included diverse categories of offenders, from pedophiles to rapists of adult women. Follow-up has sometimes exceeded 10 years. Recidivism rates for castrated offenders are typically less than 3 percent, compared with greater than 50 percent for uncastrated offenders (e.g., Berlin, 1994; Green, 1992; Prentky, 1997). Many feel that the treatment is brutal, unethical, and dehumanizing (Farkas & Strichman, 2002; Gunn, 1993), although this assumption has been challenged (Bailey & Greenberg, 1998). Interestingly, some recent cases have involved a request by the sex offender himself to be castrated in exchange for a lighter sentence (LeVay & Valente, 2006), and in some states a repeat offender's eligibility for probation or parole is linked to acceptance of mandated hormonal therapy (Scott & Holmberg, 2003).

COMBINING PSYCHOLOGICAL AND BIOLOGICAL TREATMENTS Not surprisingly, many treatment programs now use a combination of hormone therapy and cognitive-behavioral treatments, the hope being that the hormone treatment can be tapered off after the offender has learned techniques for impulse control (Maletzky, 2002). However, the single most important defect of nearly all available studies is the lack of randomly assigned controls who were equally motivated for treatment. Some have argued that denying treatment to sex offenders is unethical (e.g., Marshall et al., 1991). However, this could be true only if the treatment were effective, and it is not clear at this point whether it is. Research in this area is further complicated by the fact that the outcome variable in most studies is whether the man is convicted for another sex offense during the follow-up period. Because most sex offenses go unpunished (the offender is often never even caught, let alone convicted), this will exaggerate the apparent effectiveness of treatment and underestimate the dangerousness of sex offenders. Given the social importance of determining whether sex offenders can be helped and how likely they are to reoffend, it is crucial that society devote the resources necessary to answering these questions.

SUMMARY It is possible both to acknowledge that sex offenders cause immense human suffering and to feel sympathy for the plight of many offenders who have been burdened with a deviant sexual arousal pattern that has caused them great personal and legal trouble. Consider the case of Scott Murphy, a convicted pedophile:

> He lives alone with a friend, works odd hours, and doesn't go out of his way to meet neighbors. Ironically, Murphy has never been prouder of his behavior. He admits he'll never be cured and will always be attracted to young boys. But he says he is now making every attempt to steer clear of them: "I went from constantly living my whole life to molest kids to now living my whole life to not molest kids." It's a 24-hour-a-day job.

On the highway, Murphy keeps at a distance to guarantee he makes no eye contact with the young passengers in school buses. When the Sunday paper arrives at home, he immediately throws out the coupon section because the glossy ads often depict attractive boy models. He refuses to leave the office when kids might be walking to or from school and got rid of his television so the sit-com images of young boys wouldn't distract him. (Popkin, 1994, p. 67)

Society cannot allow Murphy to act on his sexual preference, nor can his past crimes be forgotten. Nevertheless, in deciding how to treat people like Scott Murphy, it is important and humane to remember that many of them have a tormented inner life.

In Review

- What are the short-term consequences of childhood sexual abuse, and why are we less certain about its long-term consequences?
- What are the major issues surrounding children's testimony about sexual abuse and adults' recovered memories of sexual abuse?
- Define pedophilia, incest, and rape, and summarize the major clinical features of the perpetrators of these crimes.
- Identify the main goals of treatment of sex offenders, and describe the different treatment approaches.

SEXUAL DYSFUNCTIONS

The term **sexual dysfunction** refers to impairment either in the desire for sexual gratification or in the ability to achieve it. The impairment varies markedly in degree, but regardless of which partner is alleged to be dysfunctional, the enjoyment of sex by both parties in a relationship is typically adversely affected. Sexual dysfunctions occur in both heterosexual and homosexual couples. In some cases, sexual dysfunctions are caused primarily by psychological or interpersonal factors. In others, physical factors are most important. In recent years, both explanations and treatments of sexual dysfunction have become more biological, although some psychological treatments have been ***empirically validated*** and psychosocial factors clearly play a causal role as well (Heiman, 2002; Heiman & Meston, 1997; Segraves & Althof, 2002).

> **research close-up**
>
> ***empirically validated***
>
> *Empirically validated treatments are treatments that have been determined to be helpful based on well-designed, scientific research by more than just one group of researchers.*

Today researchers and clinicians typically identify four different phases of the human sexual response as originally proposed by Masters and Johnson (1966, 1970, 1975). According to DSM-IV-TR, disorders can occur in any of the first three phases:

- The first phase is the **desire phase,** which consists of fantasies about sexual activity or a sense of desire to have sexual activity.
- The second phase is the **excitement phase,** characterized by both a subjective sense of sexual pleasure and physiological changes that accompany this subjective pleasure, including penile erection in the male and vaginal lubrication and clitoral enlargement in the female.
- The third phase is **orgasm,** during which there is a release of sexual tension and a peaking of sexual pleasure.
- The final phase is **resolution,** during which the person has a sense of relaxation and well-being.

Although these four phases are described as if they were distinct, it is important to remember that they are experienced by an individual as a continuous set of feelings, and biological and behavioral reactions. There are other conceivable ways to discuss and organize the sequence that occurs, but we will follow this scheme because it is the one that DSM has used to categorize dysfunctions. We will first describe the most common dysfunctions that can occur in the first three phases and then discuss causation and treatment.

How common are sexual dysfunctions? It is obviously difficult to do large-scale research on such a sensitive topic. Nevertheless, the National Health and Social Life Survey (Laumann, Paik, & Rosen, 1999) assessed sexual problems during the previous year in 3,159 randomly selected Americans by asking them if they had experienced the symptoms of any of the different sexual dysfunctions in the past 12 months. Sexual problems were very common, with 43 percent of women and 31 percent of men reporting having experienced at least one of these problems in the previous 12 months. For women, the reported rate of sexual problems decreased with age; for men it increased. Married men and women, and those with higher educational attainment, had lower rates of problems. For women, most common complaints were lack of sexual desire (22 percent) and sexual arousal problems (14 percent). For men, climaxing too early (21 percent), erectile dysfunction (5 percent), and lack of sexual interest (5 percent) were reported most frequently.

This study has been criticized by Bancroft and others (2003), however, who believe that these numbers overestimate how many people have true sexual dysfunctions. Although the Laumann et al. results are often referred to as being about sexual *dysfunction,* in fact the investigators never asked people about whether the problems caused them distress or impairment in any way; yet these are necessary criteria for making a diagnosis in DSM-IV-TR. When Bancroft and colleagues (2003) did a related survey (although just in women), they found very similar percentages to those found by Laumann et al. However, Bancroft et al. (2003) found that only about half as many reported that the problem caused them "severe distress." Nevertheless, this is still a relatively high percentage of people experiencing sexual dysfunction at some point in their lives. The DSM-IV-TR Criteria box on page 480 summarizes each of the dysfunctions covered here.

Dysfunctions of Sexual Desire

Researchers have delineated two types of sexual desire disorders. The first is **hypoactive sexual desire disorder.** It is a dysfunction in which either a man or a woman shows little or no sexual drive or interest (see DSM-IV-TR Criteria on p. 480). Research on the degree to which the diminished sex drive has a biological basis remains controversial, but in many (and perhaps most) cases (and especially in women), psychological factors appear to be more important than biological factors (Weiner & Rosen, 1999). These people usually come to the attention of clinicians only at the request of their partners, who typically complain of insufficient sexual interaction. This fact exposes one problem with the diagnosis, because it is known that preferences for frequency of sexual contact vary widely among otherwise normal individuals. Who is to decide what is "not enough"? DSM-IV-TR explicitly indicates that this judgment is left to the clinician, taking into account the person's age and the context of his or her life. In extreme cases, sex actually becomes psychologically aversive and warrants a diagnosis of **sexual aversion disorder,** the second type of sexual desire disorder. With this disorder, the person shows extreme aversion to, and avoidance of, all genital sexual contact with a partner.

Prior or current depression may contribute to many cases of sexual desire disorders (Weiner & Rosen, 1999). Although sexual desire disorders typically occur in the absence of obvious physical pathology, there is evidence that physical factors may sometimes play a role. Sexual interest, in both men and women, depends in part on testosterone (Alexander & Sherwin, 1993; LeVay & Valente, 2006). That sexual desire problems increase with age may be in part attributable to declining levels of testosterone, but testosterone replacement therapy is usually not beneficial, except possibly in women whose ovaries have been removed (Segraves & Althof, 2002). Although there has been interest since antiquity in the possibility that a drug to increase sexual desire might be found, no effective aphrodisiacs yet exist. However, one recent study has found that sustained use of bupropion (an atypical antidepressant), relative to placebo, improved sexual arousability and orgasm frequency in women who were in a committed relationship and had hypoactive sexual desire disorder (Segraves et al., 2004).

Hypoactive sexual desire disorder appears to be the most common female sexual dysfunction (Laumann et al., 1994, 1999). Despite this fact, it has inspired far less research into its origins and treatment than male dysfunctions, especially erectile disorder and premature ejaculation. One main reason for this disparity is doubtless the great importance that many men place on their ability to perform sexually. Until recently, there has also been a more general neglect of female sexuality and an implicit (though largely mistaken) societal attitude that women simply do not care much about sex.

Fortunately, this has been changing gradually in recent years (e.g., Althof et al., 2005; Basson, 2005). One emerging finding is that it is uncommon for women to

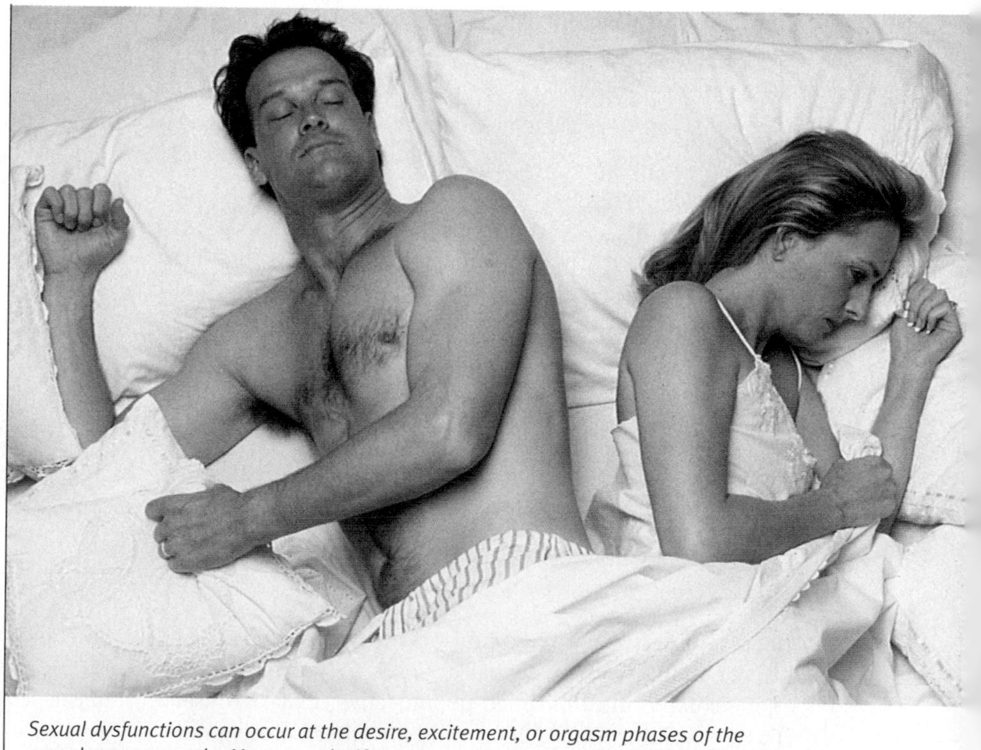

Sexual dysfunctions can occur at the desire, excitement, or orgasm phases of the sexual response cycle. Many people, if not most, will experience some sexual dysfunction sometime during their lives. If it becomes chronic or disturbing to one or both partners, it warrants treatment.

DSM-IV-TR

Criteria for Different Sexual Dysfunctions

General Criteria for All Dysfunctions

1. The disturbance causes marked distress or interpersonal difficulty.
2. The sexual dysfunction is not better accounted for by another Axis I disorder and is not due to direct effects of a substance or a general medical condition.
3. Specifiers include: Lifelong vs Acquired Types, and Generalized vs Situational Types.

Specific Criteria for Different Dysfunctions

A. *Sexual Desire Disorders:*

(1) **Hypoactive Sexual Desire Disorder:**

Persistently or recurrently deficient or absent sexual fantasies and desire for sexual activity. This judgment of deficiency or absence is made by the clinician taking into account such factors as age and context of a person's life.

(2) **Sexual Aversion Disorder:**

Persistent or recurrent extreme aversion to, and avoidance of, all (or almost all) genital sexual contact with a sexual partner.

B. *Sexual Arousal Disorders:*

(1) **Female Sexual Arousal Disorder**

Persistent or recurrent inability to attain, or to maintain until completion of the sexual activity, an adequate lubrication-swelling response of sexual excitement.

(2) **Male Erectile Disorder**

Persistent or recurrent inability to attain, or to maintain until completion of the sexual activity, an adequate erection.

C. *Orgasmic Disorders:*

(1) **Female Orgasmic Disorder**

Persistent or recurrent delay in, or absence of, orgasm following a normal sexual excitement phase. Diagnosis is made based on clinician's judgment that the woman's orgasmic capacity is less than would be reasonable for her age, sexual experience, and the adequacy of sexual stimulation she receives.

(2) **Male Orgasmic Disorder**

Persistent or recurrent delay in, or absence of, orgasm following a normal sexual excitement phase during sexual activity that the clinician, taking into account the person's age, judges to be adequate in focus, intensity, and duration.

(3) **Premature Ejaculation**

Persistent or recurrent ejaculation with minimal sexual stimulation before, on, or shortly after penetration and before the person wishes it. The clinician must take into account factors such as age, novelty of the sexual partner, or situation and recent frequency of sexual activity.

D. *Sexual Pain Disorders:*

(1) **Dyspareunia**

Recurrent or persistent genital pain associated with sexual intercourse in either a male or a female.

(2) **Vaginismus**

Recurrent or persistent involuntary spasm of the musculature of the outer third of the vagina that interferes with sexual intercourse.

cite sexual desire as a reason or incentive for sexual activity. For many women, sexual desire is only experienced after sexual stimuli have led to subjective sexual arousal (Basson, Leiblum, et al., 2003), and for others, motivation for sexual activity may involve a desire for increasing emotional intimacy, or increasing one's sense of well-being and one's self-image as an attractive female (Basson, 2003, 2005). Thus, some research suggests that the supposedly linear sequence of desire leading to arousal, leading to orgasm originally posited for women as well as men by Masters and Johnson (1970) and DSM is not very accurate for women (e.g., Basson, 2005).

Dysfunctions of Sexual Arousal

MALE ERECTILE DISORDER Inability to achieve or maintain an erection sufficient for successful sexual intercourse was formerly called *impotence.* It is now known as **male erectile disorder** or *erectile insufficiency* (see DSM-IV-TR Criteria p. 480). In lifelong erectile disorder, a man has never been able to sustain an erection long enough to accomplish a satisfactory duration of penetration. In acquired or situational erectile disorder, a man has had at least one successful experience of sexual activity requiring erection but is presently unable to produce or maintain the required level of penile rigidity. Lifelong insufficiency is a relatively rare disorder, but it has been estimated that half or more of the male population has had some experience of erectile insufficiency on at least a temporary basis.

Masters and Johnson (1975; Masters et al., 1992) and Kaplan (1975, 1987) hypothesized that erectile dysfunction is primarily a function of anxiety about sexual performance. In other reviews of the accumulated evidence, however, Barlow and colleagues (Beck & Barlow, 1984; Sbrocco & Barlow, 1996) have played down the role of anxiety per se—which under some circumstances can actually enhance sexual performance in normally functioning men and women (Barlow, Sakheim, & Beck, 1983; Palace & Gorzalka, 1990; see Sbrocco & Barlow, 1996, for a review). In one study, for example, sexually functional male subjects in a laboratory experiment were made anxious by being told that there was a 60 percent chance of their receiving an electric shock while watching an erotic film unless they had an average-sized erection. These men actually showed more sexual arousal to the film than did men who were not threatened with shock (Barlow et al., 1983).

Barlow (2002a) emphasizes that it is the cognitive distractions frequently associated with anxiety in dysfunctional people that seem to interfere with their sexual arousal. For example, one study found that nondysfunctional men who were distracted by material they were listening to on earphones while watching an erotic film showed less sexual arousal than men who were not distracted (Abrahamson et al., 1985). Barlow and colleagues hypothesize that sexually dysfunctional men and women get distracted by negative thoughts about their performance during a sexual encounter ("I'll never get aroused" or "She'll think I'm inadequate"). Their research suggests that this preoccupation with negative thoughts, rather than anxiety per se, is responsible for inhibiting sexual arousal (see also Weiner & Rosen, 1999). Moreover, such self-defeating thoughts not only decrease pleasure but also can increase anxiety if the erection does not happen (Malatesta & Adams, 1993), and this in turn can fuel further negative, self-defeating thoughts (Sbrocco & Barlow, 1996). A related finding is that men with erectile dysfunction make more internal and stable causal attributions for hypothetical negative sexual events that do men without sexual dysfunction, much as depressed people do for more general hypothetical negative events (Scepkowski et al., 2004). Combined with Bancroft et al.'s (2005) findings that fear of performance failure is a strong predictor of erectile dysfunction in both gay and heterosexual men, one can see how a vicious cycle develops in which fears of failure are sometimes followed by erectile dysfunction, which is then attributed to internal and stable causes, thereby perpetuating the problem.

Erectile problems occur in as many as 90 percent of men on certain antidepressant medications (especially the SSRIs), and are one of the primary reasons men cite for discontinuing these medications (Rosen & Marin, 2003). These problems are also a common consequence of aging. Perhaps two-thirds of men over the age of 50 have some degree of erectile dysfunction (Carbone & Seftel, 2002). However, complete and permanent erectile disorder before the age of 60 is relatively rare. Moreover, studies have indicated that men and women in their eighties and nineties are often quite capable of enjoying intercourse (Malatesta & Adams, 1993; Masters et al., 1992). For example, in one study of 202 healthy men and women between the ages of 80 and 102, it was found that nearly two-thirds of the men and one-third of the women were still having sexual intercourse, although this was not generally their most common form of sexual activity (Bretschneider & McCoy, 1988).

The most frequent cause of erectile disorder in older men is vascular disease, resulting in decreased blood flow to the penis or in diminished ability of the penis to hold blood to maintain an erection. Thus hardening of the arteries, high blood pressure, and other diseases such as diabetes that cause vascular problems often account for erectile disorder. Smoking, obesity, and alcohol abuse are associated lifestyle factors (Weiner & Rosen, 1999). Diseases that affect the nervous system such as multiple sclerosis can also cause erectile problems. For young men, one cause of erectile problems is having had *priapism*—that is, an erection that will not diminish even after a couple of hours, typically unaccompanied by sexual excitement. Priapism can occur as a result of prolonged sexual activity, as a consequence of disease, or as a side effect of certain medications. Untreated cases of priapism result in erectile dysfunction approximately 50 percent of the time (Starck, Branna, & Tallen, 1994) and thus should be regarded as a medical emergency (LeVay & Valente, 2006).

Treatment A variety of treatments—primarily medical—have been employed in recent years, often when cognitive-behavioral treatments have failed. These include: (1) medications such as yohimbine, (2) injections of smooth-muscle-relaxing drugs into the penile erection chambers (corpora cavernosa), (3) even a vacuum pump (LeVay & Rosen, 2006; Rosen, 1996). In extreme cases, penile implants may be used. These devices can be inflated to provide erection on demand. They are made of silicone rubber or polyurethane rubber. Such treatments have generally shown success in clinical trials, although they are rather extreme interventions that often evoke bothersome side effects (Rosen & Leiblum, 1995; Segraves & Althof, 2002).

In 1999 the revolutionary new drug Viagra (sildenalfil) was introduced on the U.S. market and was received with a great deal of attention. Viagra works by making nitric oxide, the primary neurotransmitter involved in penile erection, more available. Viagra is taken orally, at least an hour before sexual activity. Unlike some other biological treatments for erectile dysfunction, Viagra promotes erection only if some sexual excitation is present. Thus, contrary to some myths, Viagra does not improve libido or promote spontaneous erections (Segraves & Althof, 2002).

Clinical trials of Viagra have been impressive. In a double-blind study, over 70 percent of men receiving at least 50 mg of Viagra reported that their erections had improved, compared with fewer than 30 percent of men receiving a placebo (Carlson, 1997; see also Goldstein et al., 1998). Side effects were relatively uncommon and not serious (e.g., the most common side effect, headache, was reported by 11 percent of patients), provided that the person had no serious preexisting heart problems (Cheitlin, Hutter, et al., 1999). When heart problems do exist, Viagra should be prescribed with caution, because it can interact in dangerous ways with heart medications. Viagra has been highly successful commercially although as many as 40 percent of men who fill one prescription never refill it according to the drug company's own statistics. This is an indication of both the high prevalence of sexual dysfunction in men and the importance that people attach to sexual performance. Two other related medications introduced in 2003 to treat erectile dysfunction were Cialis (tadalafil; Padma-Nathan, McMurray, et al., 2001) and Levitra (vardenafil; Stark, Sachse, et al., 2001). There is also one study showing that the usefulness of these medications may be further enhanced in couples who also use a cognitive-behavioral treatment manual along with a weekly phone call with a therapist (Bach et al., 2004).

The once taboo topic of erectile dysfunction now gets plenty of attention through the popularity of the drug Viagra, the most popular treatment for the disorder. Viagra works by making nitric oxide, the primary neurotransmitter involved in penile erection, more available. It is taken orally, about an hour before sexual activity. Unlike some other biological treatments for erectile dysfunction, Viagra only works if sexual desire is present.

FEMALE SEXUAL AROUSAL DISORDER Formerly and somewhat pejoratively referred to as *frigidity*, **female sexual arousal disorder**—the absence of feelings of sexual arousal and an unresponsiveness to most or all forms of erotic stimulation—is in many ways the female counterpart of erectile disorder (see DSM-IV-TR Criteria on p. 480). Its chief physical manifestation is a failure to produce the characteristic swelling and lubrication of the vulva and vaginal tissues during sexual stimulation—a condition that may make intercourse quite uncomfortable.

Although the causes of this disorder are not well understood, possible reasons for this inhibition of sexual feelings range from early sexual traumatization; to excessive and distorted socialization about the "evils" of sex; to dislike of, or disgust with, a current partner's sexuality. One interesting recent study also found that women with sexual arousal disorder show lower tactile sensitivity than is seen in other women, and the lower the level of tactile sensitivity, the more severe the arousal dysfunction (Frolich & Meston, 2005). Whether this lower tactile sensitivity plays a causal role or is merely a symptom of sexual arousal disorder is not yet clear.

One reason why progress toward understanding this disorder is slow is that female sexuality may in some ways be more complicated than male sexuality. For example, it appears that the correlation between subjective sexual arousal and physiological sexual arousal (genital response) is lower for women than for men (Heiman, 1980; Laan & Everaerd, 1995). That is, it is not uncommon for women to feel unaroused sexually at a subjective level, but to have some genital response; the reverse can also occur, although less frequently. This has led to a suggestion that female sexual arousal disorder be separated into two subtypes: genital and subjective (Basson, Leiblum, et al., 2003).

Treatment Few controlled treatment studies of female arousal disorder have been conducted (Heiman, 2002), although clinical experience suggests that psychotherapy and sex therapy may play important roles. The widespread use of vaginal lubricants may effectively mask and treat the disorder in many women. In addition, because female genital response depends in part on the same neurotransmitter systems as male genital response, there has been great interest in the possibility that Viagra, Levitra, and/or Cialis would have positive effects for women analogous to its positive effects for men (Kolata, 1998). Unfortunately, enough research has now been performed to make it clear that those drugs are not as useful for women as men (Basson et al., 2002; LeVay & Valente, 2006). They do, however, seem useful for a subset of women with sexual arousal disorder, specifically those for whom the disorder is caused by sustained use of antidepressants (LeVay & Valente, 2006).

Orgasmic Disorders

PREMATURE EJACULATION **Premature ejaculation** is the persistent and recurrent onset of orgasm and ejaculation with minimal sexual stimulation. It may occur before, on, or shortly after penetration and before the man wants it to (see DSM-IV-TR Criteria on p. 480). The consequences often include failure of the partner to achieve satisfaction and, often, acute embarrassment for the prematurely ejaculating man, with disruptive anxiety about recurrence on future occasions. Men who have had this problem from their first sexual encounter often try to diminish sexual excitement by avoiding stimulation, by self-distracting, and by "spectatoring," or psychologically taking the role of an observer rather than a participant (Metz, Pryor, et al., 1997).

An exact definition of prematurity is necessarily somewhat arbitrary. For example, the age of a client must be considered—the alleged "quick trigger" of the younger man being more than a mere myth (McCarthy, 1989). Indeed, perhaps half of young men complain of early ejaculation. Not surprisingly, premature ejaculation is most likely after a lengthy abstinence (Malatesta & Adams, 1993). DSM-IV-TR acknowledges these many factors that may affect time to ejaculation by noting that the diagnosis is made only if ejaculation occurs before, on, or shortly after penetration and before the man wants it to. Premature ejaculation is the most common male sexual dysfunction at least up to age 59 (LeVay & Valente, 2006; Segraves & Althof, 2002).

In sexually normal men, the ejaculatory reflex is, to a considerable extent, under voluntary control. They monitor their sensations during sexual stimulation and are somehow able, perhaps by judicious use of distraction, to forestall the point of ejaculatory inevitability until they decide to "let go" (Kaplan, 1987). Premature ejaculators are for some reason unable to use this technique effectively. Explanations have ranged from psychological factors such as increased anxiety (Kaplan, 1987) to physiological factors such as increased penile sensitivity (Gospodinoff, 1989) and inflammation of the prostate gland (LeVay & Valente, 2006). Presently, however, no explanation has received much empirical support (LeVay & Valente, 2006).

Treatment For many years, most sex therapists considered premature ejaculation to be psychogenically caused and highly treatable via behavioral therapy such as the pause-and-squeeze technique developed by Masters and Johnson (1970). This technique requires the man to monitor his sexual arousal during sexual activity. When arousal is intense enough that the man feels that ejaculation might occur soon, he pauses, and he or his partner squeezes the head of the penis for a few moments, until the feeling of pending ejaculation passes. Initial reports suggested that this technique was approximately 60 to 90 percent effective; however, more recent studies have reported a much lower overall success rate (Rosen & Leiblum, 1995; Segraves & Althof, 2002). In recent years, with men for whom behavioral treatments have not worked, there has been increasing interest in possible use of pharmacological interventions. Antidepressants such as paroxetine (Paxil) and sertraline (Zoloft) that block serotonin reuptake have been found to prolong significantly ejaculatory latency in men with premature ejaculation (LeVay & Valente, 2006; Rowland & Slob, 1997); some antidepressants can be taken about 6 hours before anticipated intercourse, and others must be taken every day. Evidence suggests that the medications work only as long as they are being taken (Segraves & Althof, 2002).

MALE ORGASMIC DISORDER Sometimes called *retarded ejaculation* or *inhibited male orgasm,* **male orgasmic disorder** refers to the persistent inability to ejaculate during intercourse (see DSM-IV-TR Criteria on p. 480). Men who are completely unable to ejaculate are rare. About 85 percent of men who have difficulty ejaculating during intercourse can nevertheless achieve orgasm by other means of stimulation, notably through solitary masturbation (Masters et al., 1992). In milder cases a man can ejaculate in the presence of a partner, but only by means of manual or oral stimulation. Psychological treatments emphasize the reduction of performance anxiety in addition to increasing genital stimulation (Rosen & Leiblum, 1995; Segraves & Althof, 2002).

In other cases, retarded ejaculation can be related to specific physical problems such as multiple sclerosis or to the use of certain medications. For example, we noted that antidepressants that block serotonin reuptake appear to be an effective treatment for premature ejaculation. However, in other men, these same medications—especially the SSRIs—sometimes delay or prevent orgasm to an unpleasant extent (Ashton, Hamer, & Rosen, 1997; LeVay & Valente, 2006). These side effects are common but can often be treated pharmacologically with medications like Viagra (Ashton et al., 1997; LeVay & Valente, 2006).

FEMALE ORGASMIC DISORDER The diagnosis of orgasmic dysfunction in women is complicated by the fact that the subjective quality of orgasm varies widely among women, within the same woman from time to time, and depending on mode of stimulation. Nevertheless, according to DSM-IV-TR, **female orgasmic disorder** (formerly *inhibited female orgasm*) can be diagnosed in women who are readily sexually excitable and who otherwise enjoy sexual activity but who show persistent or recurrent delay in or absence of orgasm following a normal sexual excitement phase (see DSM-IV-TR Criteria on p. 480). Of these women, many do not routinely experience orgasm during sexual intercourse without direct supplemental stimulation of the clitoris; indeed this pattern is so common that it is not generally considered dysfunctional. A small percentage of women are able to achieve orgasm only through direct mechanical stimulation of the clitoris, as in vigorous digital manipulation, oral stimulation, or the use of an electric vibrator. Even fewer are unable to have the experience under any known conditions of stimulation; this condition, which is called lifelong orgasmic dysfunction, is analogous to lifelong erectile insufficiency in males. One study estimated that 10 to 15 percent of women in the United States have never experienced an orgasm (Althof & Schreiner-Engel, 2000).

What causes female orgasmic disorder is not well understood, but a multitude of contributory factors have been hypothesized. For example, some women feel fearful and inadequate in sexual relations. A woman may be uncertain whether her partner finds her sexually attractive, and this may lead to anxiety and tension that interfere with her sexual enjoyment. Or she may feel inadequate because she is unable to have an orgasm or does so infrequently. Sometimes a nonorgasmic woman will pretend to have orgasms to make her sexual partner feel fully adequate. The longer a woman maintains such a pretense, however, the more likely she is to become confused and frustrated; in addition, she is likely to resent her partner for being insensitive to her real feelings and needs. This in turn only adds to her sexual difficulties.

Treatment One important issue regarding treatment is whether women should seek it or not. Most clinicians agree that a woman with lifelong orgasmic disorder needs treatment if she is to become orgasmic. However, in the middle range of orgasmic responsiveness, our own view is that this question is best left to a woman herself to answer. If she is dissatisfied about her responsiveness, then she should seek treatment.

For those who do seek treatment, it is important to distinguish between lifelong and situational female orgasmic dysfunction. Treatment of the former, which typically begins with instruction and guided practice in masturbating to orgasm, has a high likelihood of success (Andersen, 1983; Segraves & Althof, 2002). "Situational" anorgasmia (where a woman may experience orgasm in some situations, with certain kinds of stimulation, or with certain partners, but not under the precise conditions she desires) often proves more difficult to treat, perhaps in part because it is often associated with relationship problems that may also be hard to treat (Althof & Schreiner-Engel, 2000; LeVay & Valente, 2006).

Dysfunctions Involving Sexual Pain

VAGINISMUS According to DSM-IV-TR, **vaginismus** involves an involuntary spasm of the muscles at the entrance to, and outer third of, the vagina (not due to a physical disorder) that prevents penetration and sexual intercourse (see DSM-IV-TR Criteria on p. 480). However, researchers have recently raised important questions about this diagnostic criterion. They have noted that most diagnosticians do not require a physical exam to make the diagnosis in order to confirm the presence of involuntary muscle spasm. Moreover, there are serious doubts about the reliability of involuntary spasm as the primary diagnostic criterion for vaginismus. For example, Reissing, Binik, et al. (2004) found that only about a quarter of women with diagnosed vaginismus reported experiencing spasm with attempted intercourse, and less than a third experienced spasm during a gynecological exam. However, muscle *tension* (not spasm) in the vaginal and pelvic muscles was common. Moreover, they did find that women diagnosed with vaginismus frequently experienced pain upon examination, and the researchers suggested that pain upon penetration (as well as fear and avoidance of penetration) is perhaps a more reliable diagnostic criterion than involuntary spasm.

In some cases, women who suffer from vaginismus also have sexual arousal disorder, possibly as a result of conditioned fears associated with earlier traumatic sexual experiences (e.g., Reissing, Binik, et al., 2003). In many cases, however, they show normal sexual arousal but are still afflicted with this disorder (Masters et al., 1992). This form of sexual dysfunction is relatively rare, but when it occurs, it is likely to be extremely distressing for both an affected woman and her partner and may sometimes lead to erectile or ejaculatory dysfunction in the partner (Segraves & Althof, 2002). Treatment of vaginismus typically involves a combination of banning intercourse, training of the vaginal muscles, and graduated self-insertion of vaginal dilators of increasing size. This treatment generally appears to be effective (Rosen & Leiblum, 1995; Segraves & Althof, 2002).

DYSPAREUNIA Painful coitus, or **dyspareunia,** involves persistent or recurrent genital pain associated with sexual intercourse (see DSM-IV-TR Criteria on p. 480). It can occur in men but is far more common in women—especially young women (LeVay & Valente, 2006). This is the form of sexual dysfunction most likely to have an obvious physical basis. Some examples of physical causes include: acute or chronic infections or inflammations of the vagina or internal reproductive organs, vaginal atrophy that occurs with aging, scars from vaginal tearing, or insufficiency of sexual arousal. Understandably, dyspareunia is often associated with vaginismus. Treatment of this problem usually requires addressing the specific physical problems that contribute to it, but often there may also be a conditioned psychological response that needs psychological intervention as well (Segraves & Althof, 2002).

Recently, some prominent researchers have argued against classifying dyspareunia as a "sexual disorder" rather than as a "pain disorder" (e.g., Binik, 2005). For example, Binik and colleagues argue that the pain in "sexual pain disorders" is qualitatively similar to the pain in other, nonsexual areas of the body and that the causes of "sexual pain disorder" are more similar to the causes of other pain disorders (e.g., low back pain) than to those of other sexual dysfunctions. They have recommended that dyspareunia be reclassified as a "pelvic pain disorder." It is also interesting to note in this regard that the pain of dyspareunia sometimes precedes any sexual experiences—as for example, in some adolescent girls trying to use a tampon.

In Review

- Compare and contrast the symptoms of the dysfunctions of sexual desire, arousal, and orgasm in men and women.
- Why have common female sexual dysfunctions been studied less than male sexual dysfunctions?
- What are the most effective treatments for male erectile disorder and premature ejaculation and for female orgasmic disorder?

Unresolved Issues

How Harmful Is Childhood Sexual Abuse?

Most contemporary Americans believe that childhood sexual abuse (CSA) is very harmful. This is reflected both in their concern for the victims of CSA and in their outrage at its perpetrators. The assumption of harmfulness is so deeply ingrained that many people find it shocking even to consider the alternative possibility that, at least sometimes, CSA is not very harmful. Surely, though, the issue of harm is answerable by empirical means. What do the results show?

In 1998 psychologist Bruce Rind of Temple University and two colleagues published, in the prestigious journal *Psychological Bulletin,* an article reviewing 49 previous studies that had asked college students about their sexual experiences during childhood (Rind, Tromovitch, & Bauserman, 1998). Furthermore, the studies assessed the students' current adjustment, enabling Rind and colleagues to examine the association between early sexual experiences and mental health in young adulthood. Here are some conclusions of this study:

- Correlations between childhood sexual abuse and later problems were of surprisingly small magnitude, suggesting that such experiences are not typically very harmful.
- After general family problems had been statistically controlled for, the small association between CSA and adult problems was reduced to essentially zero, suggesting that the negative family environment in which child sexual abuse often occurs might explain much of the link between CSA and later problems, rather than the sexual abuse per se.
- Incest (sex with relatives) and forced sex were both associated with more problems than sex between nominally consenting nonrelated individuals.
- Age at which CSA was experienced was unrelated to adult outcome.

At first, the study's provocative conclusions attracted little attention. However, after the conservative radio personality Dr. Laura Schlessinger learned of the study, she incited a firestorm of controversy. Both Dr. Laura and other critics accused Rind and his co-authors of giving comfort to child molesters and being insensitive to victims of CSA. The controversy culminated in 1999 with a resolution by the U.S. House of Representatives that condemned the study (Lilienfeld, 2002; Rind, Bauserman, & Tromovitch, 2000).

Rind's study was attacked on two general grounds: First, some argued that it is socially dangerous to make the kinds of claims that the authors made in their article (Ondersma, Chaffin, et al., 2001). Second, some argued the study was not strong enough, scientifically, to justify such risky conclusions. Let us examine both criticisms.

Clearly, it would be wrong to understate the harm of CSA. Victims of CSA would suffer from having their pain

(continued)

unappreciated, and we may well invest too little in solving problems related to CSA. But overstating the harm of CSA may also entail significant costs. For example, people who are led to believe that they have been gravely and permanently harmed by CSA may suffer unnecessarily if CSA does not invariably have grave and permanent consequences. If CSA is often not very harmful, we need to know that.

Assessing the validity of Rind's study is a scientific matter. *Psychological Bulletin* published a lengthy scientific critique of Rind's study (Dallam, Gleaves, et al., 2001) along with a reply by Rind and his co-authors (2001). One criticism of the original study was that it relied on college students, who may be unrepresentative. Perhaps they were able to attend college despite CSA because they were especially resilient. However, in another study, Rind analyzed data from community samples (samples not selected on the basis of educational attainment) and got virtually identical results (Rind & Tromovitch, 1997). Some of Rind's statistical decisions and analyses have also been criticized, but he has shown that his results do not change much when he analyzes the data the way his critics would. Although the question "How harmful is CSA?" has not been definitively answered by Rind's study, future research must contend with his findings.

Recently Rind (2003, 2004) has extended his discussion to the issue of how harmful *adult-adolescent* sexual relationships are (see also LeVay & Valente, 2006). The current American view, which has spread throughout the Western world, is that such relations are by definition also "childhood sexual abuse" even though marriages involving young teenagers were common in previous centuries. He reviews evidence showing that current views on this topic are driven by ideology and moral panic rather than by any empirical research showing these experiences to be harmful—especially those between adolescent boys and adult females, where considerable evidence suggests that many teenage boys see perceived benefits from such relationships regarding their sexual confidence and self-acceptance (see also LeVay & Valente, 2006). These are obviously controversial issues that deserve more careful research in the future.

summary

- Defining boundaries between normality and psychopathology in the area of variant sexuality is very difficult, in part because sociocultural influences on what have been viewed as normal or aberrant sexual practices abound.
  - Degeneracy theory and abstinence theory were very influential for long periods of time in the United States and many other Western cultures and led to very conservative views on heterosexual sexuality.
  - In contrast to Western cultures, in the Sambia tribe in Melanesia, homosexuality is practiced by all adolescent males in the context of male sexual initiation rites; these males transition to heterosexuality in young adulthood.
  - Until rather recently, in many Western cultures homosexuality was viewed either as criminal behavior or as a form of mental illness. However, since 1974 homosexuality has been considered by mental health professionals to be a normal sexual variant.
- Sexual deviations in the form of paraphilias involve persistent and recurrent patterns of sexual behavior and arousal, lasting at least 6 months, in which unusual objects, rituals, or situations are required for full sexual satisfaction. Their occurrence is nearly always in males. The paraphilias include fetishes, transvestic fetishism, voyeurism, exhibitionism, sadism, masochism, pedophilia, and frotteurism.
- Gender identity disorders occur in children and adults. Childhood gender identity disorder occurs in children who have cross-gender identification and gender dysphoria. Most boys who have this disorder grow up to have a homosexual orientation; a few become transsexuals. Prospective studies of girls who have this disorder have not yet been reported.
  - Transsexualism is a very rare disorder in which the person believes that he or she is trapped in the body of the wrong sex. It is now recognized that there are two distinct types of transsexuals: homosexual transsexuals and autogynephilic transsexuals, each with different characteristics and developmental antecedents.
  - The only known effective treatment for transsexuals is a sex change operation. Although its use remains highly controversial, it does appear to have fairly high success rates when the people are carefully diagnosed as being true transsexuals.
- There are three overlapping categories of sexual abuse: pedophilia, incest, and rape. All three kinds of abuse occur at alarming rates today.
  - Active debate persists about several issues related to sexual abuse and identification of its perpetrators. These include controversies about

- the accuracy of children's testimony and the accuracy of recovered memories of sexual abuse that often occur in psychotherapy.
  - All sexual abuse can sometimes have serious short-term and long-term consequences for its victims. What leads people to engage in sexual abuse is poorly understood at this time.
  - Treatment of sex offenders has not as yet proved highly effective in most cases, although promising research in this area is being conducted.
- Sexual dysfunction involves impairment either in the desire for sexual gratification or in the ability to achieve it. Dysfunction can occur in the first three of the four phases of the human sexual response: the desire phase, the excitement phase, and orgasm.
  - Both men and women can experience hypoactive sexual desire disorder, in which they have little or no interest in sex. In more extreme cases, they may develop sexual aversion disorder, which involves a strong disinclination to sexual activity.
  - Dysfunctions of the arousal phase include male erectile disorder and female arousal disorder.
  - Dysfunctions of orgasm for men include premature ejaculation and male orgasmic disorder (retarded ejaculation), and for women include female orgasmic disorder.
  - There are also two sexual pain disorders: vaginismus, which occurs in women, and dyspareunia (painful coitus), which can occur in women and occasionally in men.
  - In the past 35 years, remarkable progress has been made in the treatment of sexual dysfunctions.

Key Terms

autogynephilia (P. 465)
cross-gender identification (P. 463)
desire phase (P. 478)
dyspareunia (P. 484)
excitement phase (P. 478)
exhibitionism (P. 460)
female orgasmic disorder (P. 483)
female sexual arousal disorder (P. 482)
fetishism (P. 456)
gender dysphoria (P. 463)
gender identity disorder (P. 463)
hypoactive sexual desire disorder (P. 479)
incest (P. 471)
male erectile disorder (P. 481)
male orgasmic disorder (P. 483)
masochism (P. 461)
orgasm (P. 478)
paraphilias (P. 456)
pedophilia (P. 470)
premature ejaculation (P. 483)
rape (P. 472)
resolution (P. 478)
sadism (P. 460)
sexual abuse (P. 467)
sexual aversion disorder (P. 479)
sexual dysfunction (P. 478)
transsexualism (P. 465)
transvestic fetishism (P. 458)
vaginismus (P. 484)
voyeurism (P. 459)

CHAPTER 14

Schizophrenia and Other Psychotic Disorders

SCHIZOPHRENIA

When we think of severe mental illness, in all probability we think of schizophrenia. Schizophrenia occurs in people from all cultures and from all walks of life, and its characteristic symptoms have long been recognized. The disorder is characterized by an array of diverse symptoms, including extreme oddities in perception, thinking, action, sense of self and manner of relating to others. However, the hallmark of schizophrenia is a significant loss of contact with reality, referred to as psychosis. Although the clinical presentation of schizophrenia differs from one patient to another, the case of Emilio is quite typical.

case STUDY Emilio: "Eating Wires and Lighting Fires"

Emilio is a 40-year-old man who looks 10 years younger. He is brought to the hospital, his twelfth hospitalization, by his mother because she is afraid of him. He is dressed in a ragged overcoat, bedroom slippers, and a baseball cap, and he wears several medals around his neck. His affect ranges from anger at his mother ("She feeds me shit . . . what comes out of other people's rectums") to a giggling, obsequious seductiveness toward the interviewer. His speech and manner have a childlike quality, and he walks with a mincing step and exaggerated hip movements. His mother reports that he stopped taking his medication about a month ago and has since begun to hear voices and to look and act more bizarrely. When asked what he has been doing, he says "eating wires and lighting fires." His spontaneous speech is often incoherent and marked by frequent rhyming and clang associations (speech in which sounds, rather than meaningful relationships, govern word choice).

Emilio's first hospitalization occurred after he dropped out of school at age 16, and since that time he has never been able to attend school or hold a job. He has been treated with neuroleptics (medications used to treat schizophrenia) during his hospitalizations, but he doesn't continue to take his medications when he leaves, so he quickly becomes disorganized again. He lives with his elderly mother, but he sometimes disappears for several months at a time and is eventually picked up by the police as he wanders the streets. There is no known history of drug or alcohol abuse. (Modified from Spitzer et al., 2002, pp. 189–90.)

Source: Adapted with permission from the *DSM-TR-Casebook: A Learning Companion to the Diagnostic and Statistical Manual of Mental Disorders*, Fourth Edition, Text Revision (Copyright 2002). American Psychiatric Publishing, Inc.

This chapter describes the pieces of the schizophrenia puzzle as we now know them. It is important that you bear in mind from the outset that not all of the pieces or their presumed interconnections have been found, so our puzzle is far from being solved. You will recognize just how challenging and complex this disorder is—not only for patients who suffer from it and for their families who try to care for them, but also for the clinicians who attempt to treat it and the researchers who are determined to understand it.

The Epidemiology of Schizophrenia

Many people are surprised to learn that schizophrenia is about as prevalent as epilepsy. The lifetime morbid risk for developing schizophrenia is widely accepted to be around 1.0 percent (Gottesman, 1991). What this means is that 1 out of every 100 people born today who survive until at least age 55 will develop the disorder. Of course, a statistic like this does not mean that everyone has exactly the same risk. This is an average lifetime risk estimate. As we shall see later, some people (e.g., those who have a parent with

The internal suffering of the person with schizophrenia is often readily apparent, as are bizarre behavior and unusual appearance.

Children whose fathers are older at the time of their birth have 2 to 3 times the normal risk of developing schizophrenia.

schizophrenia) have a statistically higher risk of developing the disorder than do others (e.g., people who come from families where there has never been a case of schizophrenia). There are also other groups of people who seem to have an especially high risk of developing schizophrenia. For example, people whose fathers were older (aged 45–50 years or more) at the time of their birth have two to three times the normal risk of developing schizophrenia when they grow up (Byrne et al., 2003; Malaspina et al., 2001). Moreover, people of Afro-Caribbean origin living in the United Kingdom seem to have higher-than-expected rates of schizophrenia (Harrison et al., 1997). Rates of schizophrenia also seem to be unexpectedly high in western Ireland and Croatia and especially low in Papua New Guinea (Gottesman, 1991). The Hutterites, a Christian sect that migrated to the United States from Europe in the late 1800s, also show a low prevalence of schizophrenia (Nimgaonkar et al., 2000). At present, we have little idea about why this should be, although such differences are of great interest to researchers.

The vast majority of cases of schizophrenia begin in late adolescence and early adulthood. Although schizophrenia is sometimes found in children, such cases are rare (Green et al., 1992; McKenna et al., 1994). Schizophrenia can also have its initial onset in middle age or later, but again, this is not typical. Interestingly, schizophrenia tends to begin earlier in men than in women. In men, there is a peak in new cases of schizophrenia between ages 20 and 24. The incidence of schizophrenia in women peaks during the same age period, but the peak is less marked than it is for men. After about age 35, the number of men developing schizophrenia falls markedly, whereas the number of women developing schizophrenia does not. Instead, there is a second rise in new cases that begins around age 40. This is shown in Figure 14.1. Overall, the average age of onset of schizophrenia is around 25 years for men and around 29 years for women (Jablensky & Cole, 1997).

In addition to having an earlier age of onset of schizophrenia, many investigators believe that males develop a more severe form of the disorder (Leung & Chue, 2000). That belief is consistent with a brain-imaging study by Nopoulos, Flaum, and Andreasen (1997) showing that schizophrenia-related anomalies of brain structure (discussed later) are more severe in male than in female patients. Gender-related differences in illness severity may explain why some researchers have found that schizophrenia is becoming more common in males than in females (Iacono & Beiser, 1992). If women have a less severe form of schizophrenia, and if they also have more symptoms of depression (see Leung & Chue, 2000), they may either not be diagnosed at all or be diagnosed with other disorders.

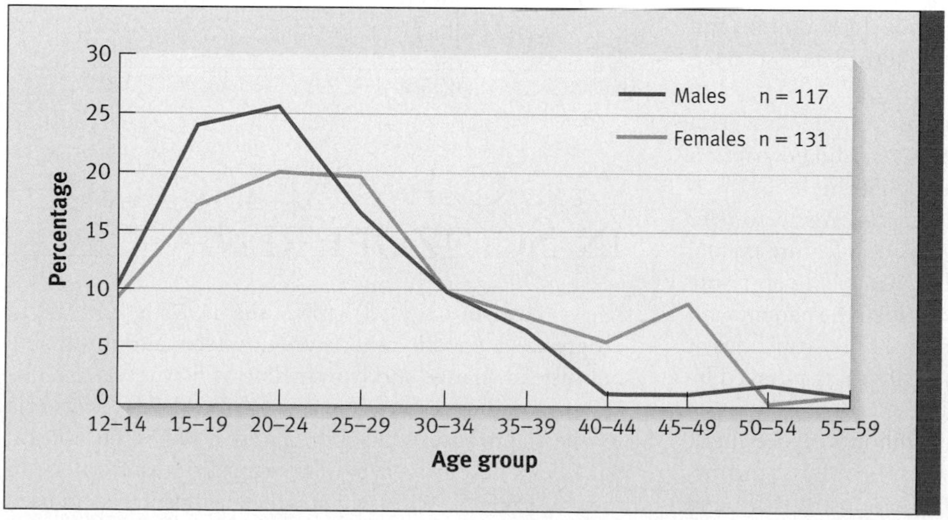

FIGURE 14.1

Age distribution of onset of schizophrenia (first sign of mental disorder) for men and women.

Source: *Haffner et al. (1998).*

What might explain the better clinical outcome of women with schizophrenia? One possibility is that female sex hormones play some protective role. When estrogen levels are low (as is true premenstrually) or are falling, psychotic symptoms in women with schizophrenia often get worse (Lindamer et al., 1997). The protective effect of estrogen may therefore help explain the delayed onset of schizophrenia in women. Declining levels of estrogen around menopause might also explain why late-onset schizophrenia is much more likely to strike women than men. And there is some evidence that this late-onset pattern in women is associated with a more severe clinical presentation (Haffner et al., 1998).

Origins of the Schizophrenia Construct

The first detailed clinical description of what we now recognize to be schizophrenia was offered in 1810 by John Haslam, the apothecary at the Bethlem Hospital in London, England. Haslam described the case of James Tilly Matthews, a married tea merchant with two children. Matthews was admitted to Bethlem in 1797, and he appears to have suffered from a variety of symptoms that are typical of schizophrenia. He was delusional, and Haslam noted that Matthews believed that "in some apartment near London Wall, there is a gang of villains profoundly skilled in Pneumatic Chemistry who assail him by means of an Air Loom" (as cited in Carpenter, 1989). Fifty years later, the Belgian psychiatrist Benedict Morel described the case of a 13-year-old boy who had formerly been the most brilliant pupil in his school but who gradually lost interest in his studies; became increasingly withdrawn, lethargic, seclusive, and quiet; and appeared to have forgotten everything he had learned. He talked frequently of killing his father. Morel thought the boy's intellectual, moral, and physical functions had deteriorated as a result of brain degeneration of hereditary origin and hence were irrecoverable. He used the term *demence precoce* (mental deterioration at an early age) to describe the condition and to distinguish it from the dementing disorders associated with old age.

It is the German psychiatrist Emil Kraepelin (1856–1926) who is best known for his careful description of what we now regard as schizophrenia. In 1896, Kraepelin (like Morel) used the term *dementia praecox* to refer to a group of conditions that all seemed to feature mental deterioration beginning early in life. Kraepelin, an astute observer of clinical phenomena, described the patient with dementia praecox as someone who "becomes suspicious of those around him, sees poison in his food, is pursued by the police, feels his body is being influenced, or thinks that he is going to be shot or that the neighbours are jeering at him" (Kraepelin, 1896). Kraepelin also noted that the disorder was characterized by hallucinations, apathy and indifference, withdrawn behavior, and an incapacity for regular work.

The term that has survived into today's diagnostic nomenclature was introduced in 1911 by a Swiss psychiatrist named Eugen Bleuler (1857–1939). Bleuler used *schizophrenia* (from the German *schizien,* meaning "to split," and *phren,* from the Greek root meaning "mind") because he believed the condition was characterized primarily by disorganization of thought processes, a lack of coherence between thought and emotion, and an inward orientation away (split off) from reality. Although the term is often thought to reflect a "Jekyll and Hyde" split personality, this is a major misconception. The splitting does not refer to multiple personalities (an entirely different form of disorder now called "dissociative identity disorder" and discussed in Chapter 8). Instead, in schizophrenia there is a split within the intellect, between the intellect and emotion, and between the intellect and external reality. Interestingly, the subtitle of Bleuler's monograph (Bleuler, 1911/1950) was "The Group of Schizophrenias," indicating that he believed this disorder was not a single diagnostic entity.

In Review

- What is the prevalence of schizophrenia? What groups of people show lower or higher rates of schizophrenia than expected?
- When does the initial onset of schizophrenia usually occur? How does this vary by gender?
- How does gender influence the severity of schizophrenia? Why might this be?
- What did Kraepelin mean by the term *dementia praecox*? How accurate is this description?
- What was Bleuler's use of the term *schizophrenia* meant to convey?
- Is schizophrenia the same thing as split personality?

The Clinical Picture in Schizophrenia

As we have mentioned earlier, the DSM is a work in progress. Diagnostic criteria are not fixed and immutable but instead change subtly over time as new research findings become available. The current DSM-IV-TR criteria for the diagnosis of schizophrenia are listed in the table on page 493. These are very similar to the diagnostic criteria in the ICD (WHO, 1992), which is the diagnostic system used in Europe and other parts of the world. In isolation, however, lists of symptoms convey little about the clinical essence of schizophrenia. In the sections that follow, we elaborate on the hallmark symptoms of this major form of psychotic disorder.

Delusions

A **delusion** is essentially an erroneous belief that is fixed and firmly held despite clear contradictory evidence. The word *delusion* comes from the Latin verb *ludere,* which means "to play." In essence, tricks are played on the mind. People with delusions believe things that others who share their social, religious, and cultural backgrounds do not believe. A delusion therefore involves a disturbance in the *content* of thought. Not all people who have delusions suffer from schizophrenia. However, delusions are common in schizophrenia, occurring in more than 90 percent of patients at some time in their illness (Cutting, 1995). In schizophrenia, certain types of delusions or false beliefs are quite characteristic. Prominent among these are beliefs that one's thoughts, feelings, or actions are being controlled by external agents (made feelings or impulses), that one's private thoughts are being broadcast indiscriminately to others (thought broadcasting), that thoughts are being inserted into one's brain by some external agency (thought insertion), or that some external agency has robbed one of one's thoughts (thought withdrawal). Also common are delusions of reference, where some neutral environmental event (such as a television program or a song played on the radio) is believed to have special and personal meaning intended only for the patient. Other strange propositions, including delusions of bodily changes (e.g., bowels do not work) or removal of organs, are also not uncommon.

Hallucinations

A **hallucination** is a sensory experience that occurs in the absence of any external perceptual stimulus. This is quite different from an illusion, which is a misperception of a stimulus that actually exists. Hallucinations can occur in any sensory modality (auditory, visual, olfactory, tactile, or gustatory). However, auditory hallucinations (e.g., hearing voices) are by far the most common, being present in up to 75 percent of patients with schizophrenia (Wing et al., 1974). In contrast, visual hallucinations occur less frequently (15 percent of patients), and tactile hallucinations are even more rare (Cutting, 1995). Hallucinations often have relevance for the patient at some affective, conceptual, or behavioral level. Patients can become emotionally involved in their hallucinations, often incorporating them into their delusions. In some cases, patients may even act on their hallucinations and do what the voices tell them to do (Stern & Silbersweig, 1998).

DSM-IV-TR

Criteria for the Diagnosis of Schizophrenia

- Two or more of the following symptoms, present for a significant portion of time during a 1-month period (less if successfully treated):
  (1) Delusions.
  (2) Hallucinations.
  (3) Disorganized speech.
  (4) Grossly disorganized or catatonic behavior.
  (5) Negative symptoms.
  (Only one symptom is required if the delusions are bizarre or if the hallucinations consist of a voice keeping up a running commentary on the person's behavior or thoughts, or two or more voices conversing with each other.)
- Dysfunction in work, interpersonal relations, or self-care.
- Signs of disturbance for at least 6 months, with at least 1 month of symptoms listed above.

Source: *Adapted with permission from the* Diagnostic and Statistical Manual of Mental Disorders, Fourth Edition, Text Revision *(Copyright 2000). American Psychiatric Association.*

In an interesting study of the phenomenology of auditory hallucinations, Nayani and David (1996) interviewed 100 hallucinating patients and asked them a series of questions about their hallucinatory voices. The majority of patients (73 percent) reported that their voices usually spoke at a normal conversational volume. Hallucinated voices were often those of people known to the patient in

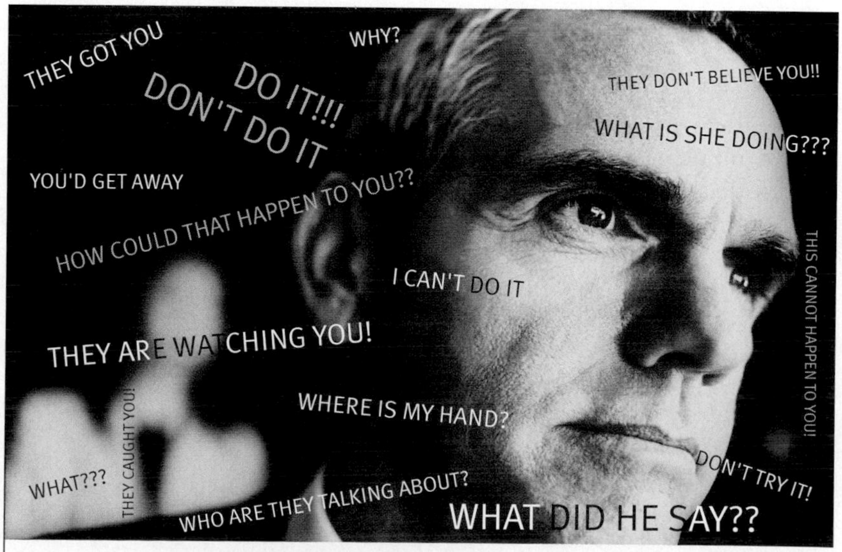

The inner world of people with schizophrenia is often confused, punctuated by alien voices, paranoia, and illogical thoughts.

real life, although sometimes unfamiliar voices or the voices of God or the Devil were also heard. Most patients reported that they heard more than one voice and that their hallucinations were worse when they were alone. Most commonly, the hallucinated voices uttered rude and vulgar expletives or else were critical ("You are stupid"), bossy ("Get the milk"), or abusive ("Ugly bitch"), although some voices were pleasant and supportive ("My darling").

Are patients who are hallucinating really hearing voices? Neuroimaging studies of hallucinating patients are beginning to provide some answers to this interesting question. Several research groups have used PET and fMRI to look at activity in the brains of patients when they are actually experiencing auditory hallucinations (Cleghorn et al., 1992; McGuire et al., 1996). Although it might be expected that patients hearing voices would show an increase of activity in areas of the brain involved in speech comprehension (e.g., Wernicke's area in the temporal lobe), imaging studies show that hallucinating patients show increased activity in Broca's area—an area of the temporal lobe that is involved in speech production. In some cases, the pattern of brain activation that occurs when patients experience auditory hallucinations is very similar to that seen when healthy volunteers are asked to imagine that there is another person talking to them (Shergill et al., 2000). Overall, the research findings suggest that auditory hallucinations occur when patients misinterpret their own self-generated and verbally mediated thoughts (inner speech or self-talk) as coming from another source. Indeed, if transcranial magnetic stimulation (where a magnetic field passing through the skull temporarily disrupts activity in underlying brain areas) is used to reduce activity in speech production areas, hallucinating patients actually show a reduction in their auditory hallucinations (Hoffman et al., 2005)! Modern technology is thus supporting a very old idea: Auditory hallucinations are really a form of misperceived subvocal speech (Gould, 1949).

Disorganized Speech

Delusions reflect a disorder of thought *content.* Disorganized speech, on the other hand, is the external manifestation of a disorder in thought *form.* Basically, an affected person fails to make sense, despite seeming to conform to the semantic and syntactic rules governing verbal communication. The failure is not attributable to low intelligence, poor education, or cultural deprivation. Years ago, Meehl (1962) aptly referred to the process as one of "cognitive slippage"; others have referred to it as "derailment" or "loosening" of associations or, in its most extreme form, as "incoherence."

In disorganized speech, the words and word combinations sound communicative, but the listener is left with little or no understanding of the point the speaker is trying to make. In some cases, completely new made-up words known as "neologisms" (literally, "new words") appear in the patient's speech. An example might be the word *detone,* which looks and sounds like a meaningful word but is a neologism. Formal thought disorder is well illustrated in the following example, which is taken from a letter written by a man with schizophrenia and addressed to Queen Beatrix of the Netherlands.

case study **Disorganized Speech: A Letter to Queen Beatrix**

I have also "killed" my ex-wife, [name], in a 2.5 to 3.0 hours sex bout in Devon Pennsylvania in 1976, while two Pitcairns were residing in my next room closet, hearing the event. Enclosed, please find my urology report, indicating that my male genitals, specifically my penis, are within normal size and that I'm capable of normal intercourse with any woman, signed by Dr. [name], a urologist and surgeon who performed a circumcision on me in 1982. Conclusion: I cannot be a nincompoop in a physical sense (unless Society would feed me chemicals for my picture in the nincompoop book).

Disorganized and Catatonic Behavior

Goal-directed activity is almost universally disrupted in schizophrenia. The impairment occurs in areas of routine daily functioning, such as work, social relations, and self-care, such that observers note that the person is not himself or herself anymore. The picture is thus one of deterioration from a previously mastered standard of performance in everyday affairs. For example, the person may no longer maintain minimal standards of personal hygiene or may exhibit a profound disregard of personal safety and health. In other cases, grossly disorganized behavior appears as silliness or unusual dress (e.g., wearing an overcoat, scarf, and gloves on a hot summer day). Many researchers attribute these disruptions of "executive" behavior to some sort of impairment in the functioning of the prefrontal region of the cerebral cortex (Lenzenweger & Dworkin, 1998).

Catatonia is an even more striking behavioral disturbance. The patient with catatonia may show a virtual absence of all movement and speech and be in what is called a *catatonic stupor.* At other times, the patient may hold an unusual posture for an extended period of time without any seeming discomfort.

Negative Symptoms

Since the days of Bleuler, two general symptom patterns or syndromes of schizophrenia have been differentiated. These are referred to as positive- and negative-syndrome schizophrenia (e.g., Andreasen, 1985; Andreasen et al., 1995). Statistical procedures have further indicated that some symptoms like disordered speech and disorganized behavior that were previously thought to reflect positive symptoms might be better separated from "true" positive symptoms like hallucinations and delusions. A disorganized symptom pattern is now also recognized (Lenzenweger et al., 1991). These symptom types are illustrated in Table 14.1.

Positive symptoms are those that reflect an excess or distortion in a normal repertoire of behavior and experience such as delusions and hallucinations. **Negative symptoms,** by contrast, reflect an absence or deficit of behaviors that are normally present. Important negative symptoms in schizophrenia include flat or blunted emotional expressiveness, alogia (very little speech), and avolition (no ability to initiate or persist in goal-directed activities). Instead, the patient may sit for long periods of time staring into space or watching TV with little interest in any outside work or social activities.

Although most patients exhibit both positive and negative signs during the course of their disorders (Breier et al., 1994; Guelfi et al., 1989), a preponderance of negative symptoms in the clinical picture is not a good sign for the patient's future outcome (e.g., Fenton & McGlashan, 1994; McGlashan & Fenton, 1993; Milev et al., 2005).

Not all negative symptoms are exactly what they seem, however. Kring and Neale (1996) studied unmedicated male patients with schizophrenia while they were watching film clips. Three different types of film clips were used, the scenes in them being either very positive, negative, or neutral in terms of the emotions they were designed to elicit in the viewers. Videotapes of how the patients looked when they were watching the films were then coded by trained raters. As might be expected, the patients with schizophrenia showed less facial expressiveness than a group of healthy controls.

What *was* surprising was that when the patients were asked about their emotional experiences during the films, they reported as much emotional feelings as the controls—and sometimes slightly more. Measures of autonomic arousal also showed that when they were watching the films, the patients exhibited more physiological reactivity than the controls did. What these findings suggest, therefore, is that even though patients with schizophrenia may sometimes not look very emotionally expressive, they are nonetheless experiencing plenty of emotion.

Positive and negative symptoms can co-occur in the same patient. This woman appears to exhibit marked social withdrawal (a negative symptom) in addition to showing bizarre behavior (a positive symptom).

In Review

- Explain the difference between positive and negative symptoms.
- What are the major symptoms of schizophrenia?
- How is a hallucination different from a delusion?

TABLE 14.1 Positive, Negative, and Disorganized Symptoms of Schizophrenia

Positive Symptoms	Negative Symptoms	Disorganized Symptoms
Hallucinations	Emotional flattening	Bizarre behavior
Delusions	Poverty of speech	Disorganized speech
	Asociality	
	Apathy	
	Anhedonia	

SUBTYPES OF SCHIZOPHRENIA

What we call "schizophrenia" in all probability encompasses a variety of disordered processes of varied etiology, developmental pattern, and outcome—perhaps more so than in the case of any other psychiatric diagnosis. This leads to much heterogeneity at the clinical, observational level. Sociocultural factors also shape the clinical presentation of the disorder. For example, compared to Mexican-American patients, Anglo-American patients with schizophrenia report fewer somatic symptoms, have more blunted affect, and exhibit more self-neglect. They also have more persecutory delusions and delusions that have a basis in science fiction or the supernatural (Weisman et al., 2000). Current classification systems have long attempted to recognize the heterogeneity in the presentation of schizophrenia by describing clinical subtypes of the disorder.

The DSM-IV recognizes several subtypes of schizophrenia. However, questions have been raised about the overall usefulness of subtyping patients. For example, there is no strong evidence that such information is helpful when it comes to planning treatment. Despite this, researchers and clinicians remain interested in exploring and refining possible subtypes of schizophrenia, perhaps because they hope such an approach will eventually yield insights into the etiology of the disorder.

Paranoid Type

The patient with **paranoid schizophrenia** shows a history of increasing suspiciousness and of severe difficulties in interpersonal relationships. The eventual clinical picture is dominated by absurd and illogical ideas and beliefs that are often highly elaborated and organized into a coherent, though delusional, framework. Persecutory delusions are the most frequent and may involve a wide range of bizarre ideas and plots. An individual may become highly suspicious of relatives or associates and may complain of being watched, followed, poisoned, talked about, or influenced by various tormenting devices rigged up by "enemies." Delusions of grandeur are also common in paranoid schizophrenia. Persons with such delusions may, for example, claim to be the world's greatest economist or philosopher, to have invented some impossible device, or to be a prominent person from the past. In some cases, this provides the justification (in the mind of delusional persons) for their being persecuted, followed, or spied upon, and it may provide a sense of identity and importance not otherwise attainable. Patients with the paranoid subtype of schizophrenia tend to function at a higher level overall and also to have more intact cognitive skills than patients with other subtypes, although the differences are not large and are not consistent across all cognitive domains (Zalewski et al., 1998). The prognosis for these patients is generally better than for patients with other types of schizophrenia (Fenton & McGlashan, 1991; Kendler, McGuire, et al., 1994).

The next clinical example will give you some sense of what a complex and highly elaborated delusional system is like. It was printed on a flier and handed to one of the authors by a man who appeared to be in his thirties. Any errors of grammar are errors in the original flier.

DSM-IV-TR

Criteria for Paranoid Schizophrenia

- Preoccupation with delusions or frequent auditory hallucinations.
- No evidence of marked disorganized speech, disorganized or catatonic behavior, flat or inappropriate affect.

case STUDY — Are You Being Mind Controlled?

Are you being or were you mind controlled to do something very stupid? Twenty-five percent of our population have what is called electronic hearing. This twenty-five percent can hear a silent radio and do not hear it. You might be one. In hearing pitch the average person hears from zero to sixteen thousand cycles. Twenty-five percent can hear up to thirty thousand cycles. The silent radio can be heard by these high hearing frequency persons. The silent radio sounds the same as thoughts in their minds.

This silent radio tricks these persons into every crime imaginable. It tricks them into bad decisions, to quit jobs, to divorce, to run away, to be sheriff saled and any stupidity possible. The broadcasters over this silent radio are government, medical, psychiatrists, religious and educational. This is an enormous budget used to destroy the innocent and helpless. The media is scared to cover this up.

This minority, which can be in any ethnic or race, has lost all rights under law because the Russians do it everywhere. It is shocking to discover very large corporation and all college have mind control departments. If you and your family constantly make bad decisions and have ruinous problems, you probably are mind controlled. Every year these mind controlled people are going down the economic ladder as they cannot be trusted. No company knows when one will be selected as a guinea pig. Who could risk a sizeable work force of persons with electronic hearing for your competitor could easily wipe you out?

Disorganized Type

Compared with the other subtypes of schizophrenia, **disorganized schizophrenia** usually occurs at an earlier age and has a gradual, insidious onset. As you can see from the table for criteria for disorganized schizophrenia, it is characterized by disorganized speech, disorganized behavior, and flat or inappropriate affect. In the past (and currently in the ICD) this subtype was called "hebephrenic schizophrenia." The case study of Emilio that you read earlier is an example of this subtype. Very gradually, the person becomes more reclusive and preoccupied with fantasies. As the disorder progresses, the clinical picture is one of emotional indifference and infantile behavior. A silly smile and inappropriate, shallow laughter after little or no provocation are common symptoms. Speech becomes difficult to understand and may include considerable baby talk, childish giggling, and a repetitious use of similar-sounding words. Hallucinations and delusions may be present, but in contrast to paranoid schizophrenia, these are not coherent or organized into a "story." Patients with disorganized schizophrenia may have severe disruptions in their abilities to take care of themselves and be unable to perform routine tasks. They sometimes also show peculiar mannerisms and other bizarre forms of behavior. These behaviors may take the form of odd facial grimaces, talking and gesturing to themselves, or sudden, inexplicable laughter and weeping. The prognosis is generally poor for individuals who develop disorganized schizophrenia. At this stage of deterioration, no form of treatment intervention yet discovered has a high likelihood of effecting more than modest gains.

People with the disorganized type of schizophrenia become emotionally indifferent and infantile and may display odd facial grimaces, talk and gesture to themselves, and break into sudden, inexplicable laughter and weeping.

Catatonic Type

The central feature of **catatonic schizophrenia** (see the table for criteria for catatonic schizophrenia) is pronounced motor signs, either of an excited or a stuporous type. Some of these patients are highly suggestible and will automatically obey commands or imitate the actions of others (echopraxia) or mimic their phrases (echolalia). Even if a patient's arm is raised to an awkward and uncomfortable position, he or she may keep it there for minutes or even hours. Ordinarily, patients in a catatonic stupor stubbornly resist any effort to change their position, may become mute, resist all attempts at feeding, and refuse to comply with even the slightest request. Catatonic patients may pass suddenly from extreme stupor to a state of great excitement, during which they seem to be under great "pressure of activity" and may become violent, being in these respects indistinguishable from some bipolar manic patients. They may talk or shout excitedly and incoherently, pace rapidly back and forth, openly indulge in sexual activities, attempt self-mutilation or even suicide, or impulsively attack and try to kill others. The suddenness and extreme frenzy of these attacks make such patients dangerous to both themselves and others. Though at one time common in Europe and North America, catatonic reactions have become less prevalent in recent years, although they are still found in less industrialized regions of the world (Cutting, 1995).

The matter is far from settled, but some clinicians interpret a catatonic patient's immobility as a way of coping with his or her reduced filtering ability and increased vulnerability to stimulation: It seems to provide a feeling of some control over external sources of stimulation, though not necessarily over inner ones. Freeman (1960) has cited

DSM-IV-TR

Criteria for Disorganized Schizophrenia

- Disorganized speech.
- Disorganized behavior.
- Flat or inappropriate affect.
- No evidence of catatonic schizophrenia.

DSM-IV-TR

Criteria for Catatonic Schizophrenia

In catatonic schizophrenia, the clinical picture is dominated by at least two of the following:

- Immobile body or stupor.
- Excessive motor activity that is purposeless and unrelated to outside stimuli.
- Extreme negativism (resistance to being moved, or to follow instructions) or mutism.
- Assumption of bizarre postures, or stereotyped movements or mannerisms.
- Echolalia or echopraxia.

the explanation advanced by one patient: "I did not want to move, because if I did everything changed around me and upset me horribly so I remained still to hold on to a sense of permanence" (p. 932).

case STUDY Anna, the Student with Catatonic Schizophrenia

Anna is a 22-year-old unmarried student of mathematics in Finland. She was brought to the psychiatric hospital by the police after she attacked a child. She had walked up to a 9-year-old girl at a bus stop and tried to strangle her. Some passersby fortunately intervened, restraining Anna, and called the police. At first she fought violently and tried to get at the child, but then suddenly she became motionless and rigid as a statue, with one arm stretched out toward the child and a wild stare on her face. When the police arrived, it was very difficult to get her into the car, because she would not move and resisted attempts to move her.

At the police station she said nothing, kept standing in an awkward position, and stared straight ahead. A physician decided that an immediate admission to the psychiatric hospital was appropriate. Anna was put on a locked ward because she was under arrest for attempted murder. When she was brought to the ward, she remained standing just inside the entrance and resisted invitations to go farther. She refused to have anything to eat and would not go into the examination room. She remained standing rigid, with her right arm stretched out in front of her, staring at her hand. She did not answer questions or respond in any way to the ward assistants. After several hours she finally had to be taken to her room and put in bed with the use of mild force. She lay in bed in the position where she had been placed, staring at the ceiling. She seemed tense, with an apprehensive and worried look on her face. She was given an injection of 10 mg of haloperidol and did not resist. Afterward she fell asleep.

During a clinical interview the next day, Anna appeared to be fully oriented. She knew she was in the hospital but would not or could not explain what had happened. At times she suddenly stiffened and stared for half a minute or so. At other times she just mechanically repeated the questions that were asked of her.

Anna's sister arrived. She said that the family had been concerned about Anna for some time. For the last 2 or 3 months she had seemed reclusive and odd, with recurrent episodes of muteness that lasted for several minutes. Several times she made peculiar statements such as, "Children are trying to destroy mathematics" and "Rational figures have a hard time." She stopped going to the university and stayed in her room, leaving it only for a walk in the evening. She seemed to be preoccupied with writing numbers on pieces of paper. (Adapted from Üstün et al., 1996.)

Undifferentiated Type

As the term implies, the diagnosis of **undifferentiated schizophrenia** is something of a wastebasket category. A person with undifferentiated schizophrenia (see the table on criteria for undifferentiated schizophrenia) meets the usual criteria for schizophrenia—including (in varying combinations) delusions, hallucinations, disordered thoughts, and bizarre behaviors—but does not clearly fit into one of the other types because of a mixed-symptom picture. People in the acute, early phases of a schizophrenic breakdown frequently exhibit undifferentiated symptoms, as do those whose clinical picture may change enough over time to warrant a change in diagnosis from a specific subtype to the undifferentiated subtype.

Residual Type

A final subtype of schizophrenia contained in DSM-IV deserves brief mention. **Residual schizophrenia** is a category used for people who have suffered at least one episode of schizophrenia but do not now show any prominent positive symptoms such as hallucinations, delusions, or disorganized speech or behavior. Instead, the clinical picture contains mostly negative symptoms (e.g., flat affect), although some positive symptoms (e.g., odd beliefs, eccen-

DSM-IV-TR

Criteria for Undifferentiated Schizophrenia

- Symptoms of schizophrenia that do not meet criteria for the Paranoid, Disorganized, or Catatonic types.

DSM-IV-TR

Criteria for the Residual Type of Schizophrenia

- Absence of prominent delusions, hallucinations, disorganized speech, and grossly disorganized or catatonic behavior.
- Continued evidence of schizophrenia (e.g., negative symptoms), or mild psychotic symptoms (e.g., odd beliefs, unusual perceptual experiences).

tric behavior) may also be present in a mild form (see the table for criteria for residual type schizophrenia).

Other Psychotic Disorders

SCHIZOAFFECTIVE DISORDER The DSM-IV recognizes a diagnostic category called **schizoaffective disorder** (see the table for criteria for schizoaffective disorder). This diagnosis is conceptually something of a hybrid in that it is used to describe people who have features of schizophrenia and severe mood disorder. In other words, the person has psychotic symptoms that meet criteria for schizophrenia but also has marked changes in mood for a substantial amount of time. Because mood disorders can be unipolar or bipolar in type, there also are two subtypes of schizoaffective disorder (bipolar and unipolar subtype).

It is still not entirely clear whether schizoaffective disorder is best regarded as a variant of schizophrenia or as a form of mood disorder. Reflecting this controversy, DSM-IV-TR lists schizoaffective disorder in the same section of the manual as schizophrenia but does not classify it as a formal subtype of schizophrenia. Instead, it is treated as a separate disorder. In general, the prognosis for these patients is somewhere between that of patients with schizophrenia and that of patients with mood disorders (Walker et al., 2004). Research suggests that the long-term (10-year) outcome is much better for patients with schizoaffective disorder than it is for patients with schizophrenia (Harrow et al., 2000).

SCHIZOPHRENIFORM DISORDER **Schizophreniform disorder** is a category reserved for schizophrenia-like psychoses that last at least a month but do not last for 6 months and so do not warrant a diagnosis of schizophrenia (see the table for criteria for schizophreniform disorder). It may include any of the symptoms described in the preceding sections but is probably most often seen in an undifferentiated form. Brief psychotic states of this sort may or may not be related to subsequent psychiatric disorder (Strakowski, 1994). At present, however, all recent-onset cases of true schizophrenia presumably must first receive a diagnosis of schizophreniform disorder. Because of the possibility of an early and lasting remission in a first episode of schizophrenic breakdown, the prognosis for schizophreniform disorder (where it is a manifestation of recent-onset schizophrenic symptoms) is better than that for established forms of schizophrenia.

DELUSIONAL DISORDER Patients with **delusional disorder,** like many people with schizophrenia, give voice to, and sometimes take actions on the basis of, beliefs that are considered completely false and absurd by those around them. Unlike individuals with schizophrenia, however, people given the diagnosis of delusional disorder may otherwise behave quite normally. Their behavior does not show the gross disorganization and performance deficiencies characteristic of schizophrenia, and general behavioral deterioration is rarely observed in this disorder, even when it proves chronic (see the table for criteria for delusional disorder). One interesting subtype of delusional disorder is erotomania. Here, the theme of the delusion involves great love for a person, usually of higher status. One study suggests that a significant proportion of women who stalk are diagnosed with erotomania (Purcell et al, 2001).

DSM-IV-TR

Criteria for Schizoaffective Disorder

- An illness during which, at some time, there is either a Major Depressive Episode, a Manic Episode, or a Mixed Episode that co-occurs with symptoms of Schizophrenia (delusions, hallucinations, disorganized speech, disorganized behavior, or negative symptoms).
- During the illness, there must be a period of at least 2 weeks where delusions and hallucinations have been present *without* mood symptoms.
- The mood symptoms are present for a substantial proportion of the total illness time.

DSM-IV-TR

Criteria for Schizophreniform Disorder

- Symptoms of schizophrenia.
- An episode of the disorder (including the prodromal, active, and residual phases) that lasts at least 1 month but less than 6 months.

DSM-IV-TR

Criteria for Delusional Disorder

- Nonbizarre delusions (i.e., involving situations that could occur in real life such as being followed or being poisoned) that last for at least 1 month.
- No evidence of full-blown schizophrenia.
- Apart from the delusion, the person's functioning is not markedly impaired; neither is behavior obviously odd or bizarre.

BRIEF PSYCHOTIC DISORDER **Brief psychotic disorder** is exactly what its name suggests. It involves the sudden onset of psychotic symptoms or grossly disorganized or catatonic behavior. Even though there is often great emotional turmoil, the episode is usually quite brief, often lasting only a matter of days (too short to warrant a diagnosis of schizophreniform disorder). After this, the person returns to his or her former level of functioning and may never have another episode again (see the table for criteria for brief psychotic disorder). Cases of brief psychotic disorder are infrequently seen in clinical settings, perhaps because they remit so quickly. Brief psychotic disorder is often triggered by stress, as illustrated in the following case.

case STUDY Four Days of Symptoms and Rapid Recovery

A 32-year-old lawyer, who has successfully practiced law for 6 years, who is married with two young sons and many close friends, and who is a popular Cub Scout leader, returns home from work to find his wife in bed with his best friend. Initially, he expresses much depression and anger, but within 2 days begins to speak of fusing with God, of dispensing peace on Earth, and of needing to fight the "giant conspiracy." He hears voices calling his name and saying, "Love, love, love." His affect becomes flat and he speaks slowly and distinctly. His sleep is not disturbed. He is admitted to a hospital, where he is treated with medication. Within 4 days he begins marital therapy with his wife. He improves rapidly. He returns to work within 5 days of the onset of his initial symptoms. (Adapted from Janowsky et al., 1987, p. 1.)

DSM-IV-TR

Criteria for Brief Psychotic Disorder

- Presence of one or more of the following: delusions, hallucinations, disorganized speech or grossly disorganized or catatonic behavior.
- The episode lasts for at least 1 day but less than 1 month, with an eventual full return to normal functioning.
- A diagnosis of Mood Disorder with Psychotic Features; Schizoaffective Disorder or Schizophrenia is ruled out.

SHARED PSYCHOTIC DISORDER Finally, many people know **shared psychotic disorder** by its French name, **folie à deux.** As the name suggests, it is a delusion that develops in someone who has a very close relationship with another person who is delusional (see the table for criteria for shared psychotic disorder). Over time, this second individual comes to believe in the delusions of the other person. In some cases, the contagion of thought may spread even further and whole families may adopt the same delusional beliefs.

DSM-IV-TR

Criteria for Shared Psychotic Disorder

- A delusion develops in the context of a close relationship with another person who already has an established delusion.
- The delusion is similar in content to that of the person who already has the established delusion.
- Other Psychotic Disorders are ruled out.

In Review

- What are the five major subtypes of schizophrenia recognized by the DSM?
- What are the major differences between schizophrenia and (a) schizoaffective disorder and (b) schizophreniform disorder?

WHAT CAUSES SCHIZOPHRENIA?

Despite an enormous research effort going back many years and continuing to the present day, this question still defies a simple answer. In the sections that follow, we discuss what is currently known about the etiology of schizophrenia. In all probability, however, no one factor can fully explain why schizophrenia develops. The old dichotomy of nature versus nurture is as misleading as it is simplistic. Psychiatric disorders are not the result of a single genetic switch being flipped. Rather, a complex interplay between genetic and environmental factors is usually responsible.

Genetic Aspects

It has long been known that disorders of the schizophrenic type are "familial" and tend to "run in families." The evidence for higher-than-expected rates of schizophrenia among biological relatives of "index" cases (that is, the diagnosed group of people who provide the starting point for inquiry, also called "probands") is overwhelming. Figure 14.2 shows the percentage of the risk of developing schizophrenia given a specific genetic relationship with someone who has the disorder. As you can see, there is a strong association between the closeness of the blood relationship (i.e., level of gene sharing or consanguinity) and the risk for developing the disorder. For example, the prevalence of schizophrenia in the first-degree relatives (parents, siblings, and offspring) of a proband with schizophrenia is about 10 percent. For second-degree relatives who share only 25 percent of their genes with the proband (e.g., half-siblings, aunts, uncles, nieces, nephews, and grandchildren), the lifetime prevalence of schizophrenia is closer to 3 percent.

Of course, that something runs in families does not automatically implicate genetic factors. The terms *familial* and *genetic* are not synonymous, and a disorder can run in a family for nongenetic reasons (if I am obese and my dog is also obese, the reasons for this are clearly not genetic!). As we have repeatedly emphasized, the interpretation of familial concordance patterns is never completely straightforward, in part because of the strong relationship between the sharing of genes and the sharing of the environments in which those genes express themselves. Although they are indispensable in providing a starting point for researchers, family studies cannot, by themselves, tell us why a disorder runs in families. To disentangle the contributions of genes and environment, we need twin and adoption studies.

TWIN STUDIES We discussed twin studies in general in Chapter 3 and more specifically in relation to anxiety and mood disorders in Chapters 6 and 7. As with the mood disorders, schizophrenia concordance rates for identical twins are routinely, and over very many studies, found to be significantly higher than those for fraternal twins or ordinary siblings. The most famous case of concordance for schizophrenia is the Genain quadruplets, summarized in The World Around Us 14.1 on page 502.

Although being a twin does not increase one's risk for developing schizophrenia (the incidence of schizophrenia among twins is no greater than that for the general population), study after study has shown a higher concordance for schizophrenia among identical, or monozygotic (MZ), twins over people related in any other way, including fraternal, or dizygotic (DZ), twins.

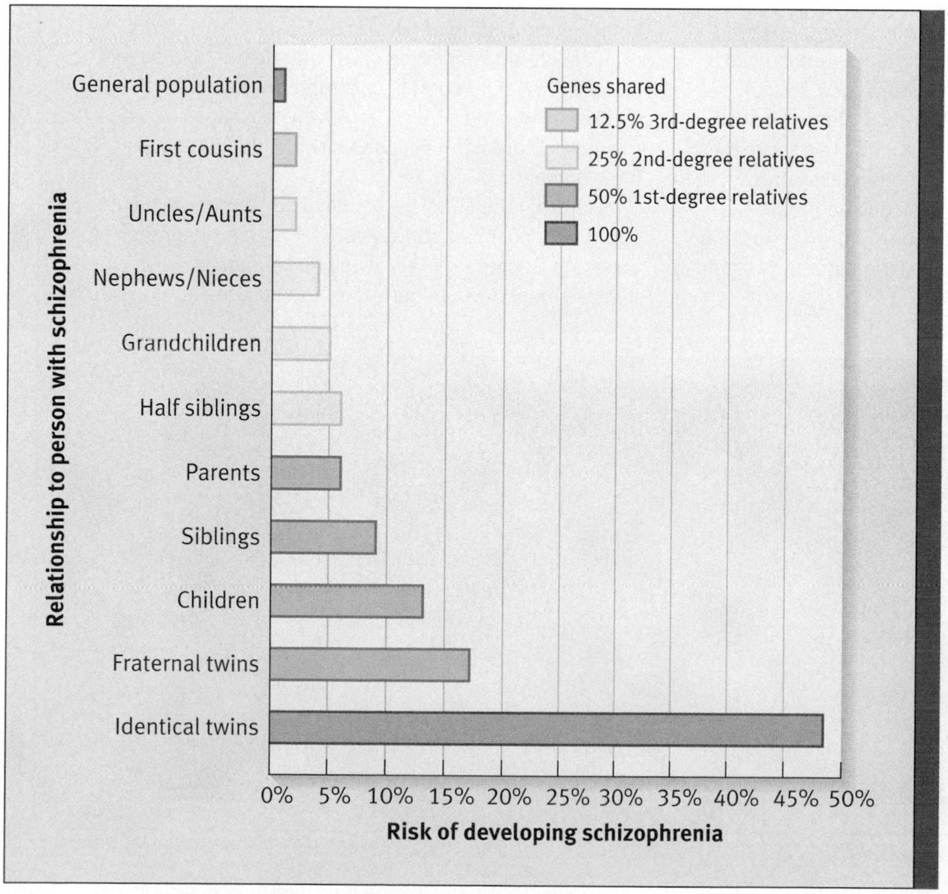

FIGURE 14.2

Lifetime age-adjusted, averaged risks for the development of schizophrenia-related psychoses in classes of relatives differing in their degree of genetic relatedness.

Source: *Compiled from family and twin studies in European populations between 1920 and 1987. From* Schizophrenia Genesis: The Origins of Madness *(p. 96), by I. I. Gottesman. Copyright © 1991 by Irving I. Gottesman. Used with permission of W.H. Freeman and Company/Worth Publishers.*

14.1 THE WORLD AROUND US

The Genain Quadruplets

The Genain quadruplets were born sometime in the early 1930s. They immediately became famous in their hometown because they were rare MZ quadruplets. What makes the Genains especially interesting, however, is that each of these genetically identical girls was to develop schizophrenia, an outcome that would be expected to occur by chance only once in approximately 1.5 billion births.

The quadruplets were hospitalized at the National Institute of Mental Health in the mid-1950s and became a focus of intensive study. David Rosenthal, the lead researcher, selected the pseudonym surname *Genain* for the girls. The word was derived from the Greek for "dreadful gene." Rosenthal also selected first names for the girls in order of their birth, using the initials of the institution, NIMH. Accordingly, the women are known to us as Nora (the firstborn), Iris, Myra, and Hester. They are all concordant for schizophrenia. However, they are discordant with regard to the severity of their illnesses.

The most severely ill Genain is Hester, who was born last and had the lowest birth weight. Hester was always the slowest to develop, and she was removed from school after eleventh grade. She has never held a job outside the home and has suffered from chronic and unremitting severe symptoms since age 18. Neurocognitive testing at NIMH revealed that, along with Nora, Hester showed a great deal of evidence of brain disturbance.

Nora, the firstborn, was always considered by the family to be the best of the four girls. She had the highest IQ and was the first to get a job. Nonetheless, after she was hospitalized at the age of 22 with hallucinations, delusions, and withdrawal, she had a long history of hospitalizations and was never able to live independently or hold a job for an extended period of time.

In contrast, Myra, who was born third, though she had some problems in her twenties (when she was questionably diagnosed as having schizophrenia), does not appear to have experienced delusions and paranoia until her mid-forties. The only one of the Genains to marry and have children, she has a clinical picture that suggests schizoaffective disorder (a blend of psychotic symptoms and mood symptoms). Although she was not psychiatrically well by any means, she was able to go off medications. She eventually went into remission and was diagnosed as having residual schizophrenia.

Finally, there is Iris. Like Nora, Iris had her first psychiatric hospitalization at age 22. She spent 12 years in a state hospital and suffered from hallucinations, delusions, and motor abnormalities. Although neurocognitive testing did not reveal any obvious brain disturbance, it is clear that she has suffered from a severe form of schizophrenia.

Why do these identical quadruplets not have identical illnesses? We simply do not know. Did Nora and Hester, being born first and last, experience more traumatic birth complications? Did Iris do less well than might have been expected from her neurocognitive test results because her parents insisted on treating the quads as though they were two sets of twins—a superior and talented set consisting of Nora and Myra, and an inferior, problematic set consisting of Iris and Hester? Did being paired with Hester somehow compromise Iris's development? Did Myra do so well (relatively) because she was the most favored and because she did not sustain any brain damage?

Why did the quadruplets develop schizophrenia at all? In all probability, there was a family history of the disorder. Mr. Genain's mother (the girls' grandmother) had a nervous breakdown in her teens and appears to have had

some symptoms of paranoid schizophrenia. It is also clear that the family environment was far from healthy and may have provided the stress that acted on the quadruplets' genetic predispositions to induce full-blown illness. Mr. Genain was very disturbed. He spent most of his time drinking and expressing his various fears and obsessions to his family. Prominent among these were fears that break-ins would occur at the home unless he patrolled the premises constantly with a loaded gun, and, especially as the girls developed into adolescence, that they would get into sexual trouble or be raped unless he watched over them with total dedication. He imposed extreme restrictions and surveillance on the girls until the time of their breakdowns. He was himself sexually promiscuous and was reported to have sexually molested at least two of his daughters. Mrs. Genain, although she apparently managed to see sexuality and sexual threats in the most innocuous circumstances, seems to have ignored the real sexual exploitation occurring in the home. In short, nothing about the family environment can be considered to have been normal.

It is a tribute to the scientific diligence of the NIMH staff and to David Rosenthal, who maintained both a human and a scientific interest in this unfortunate family, that we know so much about them (see Rosenthal, 1963; see also Mirsky & Quinn, 1988). In the Genain quadruplets we have four genetically identical women, all of whom have experienced schizophrenia in one form or another. Their disorders, however, have been different in severity, chronicity, and eventual outcome. Although this case highlights the likely role of environmental factors in the puzzle of schizophrenia, just how the combination of genes and environment shaped the destinies of Nora, Iris, Myra, and Hester remains a mystery.

E. Fuller Torrey is a noted schizophrenia researcher who has a sister with the disorder. He and his colleagues (1994) have published a review of the major literature worldwide on twin studies of schizophrenia. Their findings are summarized in Figure 14.3. The overall pairwise concordance rate is 28 percent in MZ twins and 6 percent in DZ twins. This suggests that a reduction in shared genes from 100 percent to 50 percent reduces the risk of schizophrenia by nearly 80 percent. Also note that sharing 50 percent of one's genes with a co-twin with schizophrenia is associated with a lifetime risk for schizophrenia of 6 percent. Although this is low in absolute terms, it is markedly higher than the baseline risk of 1 percent found in the general population.

If schizophrenia were exclusively a genetic disorder, the concordance rate for identical twins would, of course, be 100 percent. Although MZ concordance rates vary from one twin study to another, and some researchers report

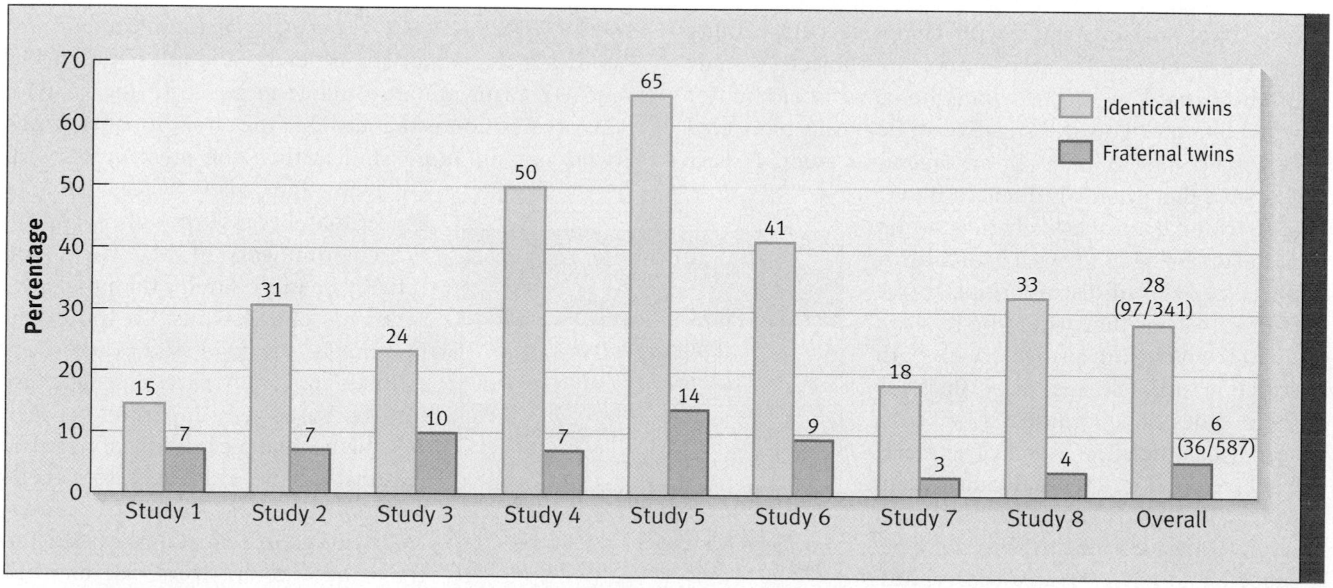

FIGURE 14.3

Pairwise twin concordance rates for schizophrenia found in eight methodologically adequate studies.

Source: *From* Schizophrenia and Manic Depressive Disorder *by E. Fuller Torrey, Ann Bowler, Edward Taylor, and Irving I. Gottesman. Copyright © 1994 by Basic Books. Reprinted by permission of Basic Books, a member of Perseus Books, L. L. C.*

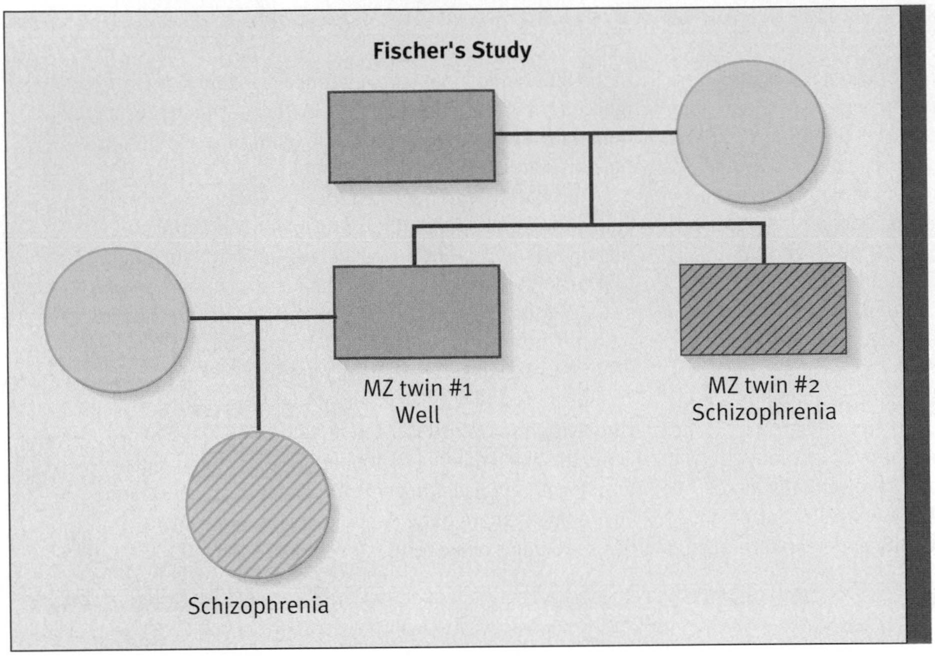

FIGURE 14.4

Because MZ twins have identical genes, the children of even the well twin have an elevated risk of schizophrenia, even if their parent did not actually suffer from the disorder.

higher rates than Torrey's 28 percent, they are never even close to 100 percent. Two conclusions can therefore be drawn: First, genes undoubtedly play a role in causing schizophrenia. Second, genes themselves are not the whole story. Twin studies provide some of the most solid evidence that the environment plays an important role in the development of schizophrenia. But why one MZ twin should develop schizophrenia when his or her co-twin does not remains a mystery.

A great deal of research attention is now being directed at studying people with a known genetic liability for schizophrenia. The most important subjects to study in this regard are MZ twins who are discordant for schizophrenia. This investigative strategy was pioneered by Fischer (1971, 1973) in an ingenious study. Fischer reasoned that genetic influences, if present, would be just as likely to show up in the offspring of the well (nonschizophrenic) twins of discordant pairs (see Figure 14.4) as they would be to show up in the offspring of the ill twins with schizophrenia (because they share all their genes in common). And, in a search of official records in Denmark, Fischer found exactly that. Subsequent to this, in a follow-up of Fischer's subjects, Gottesman and Bertelson (1989) reported an ***age-corrected*** schizophrenia ***incidence rate*** of 17.4 percent for the offspring of the nonschizophrenic (i.e., well) MZ twins. This rate, which far exceeds normal expectancy, was not significantly different from that for offspring of the schizophrenic members of discordant pairs, or from that for offspring of DZ twins with schizophrenia. Assuming that exposure to an aunt or uncle with schizophrenia (i.e, the "ill twin") would have, at most, limited etiologic significance, these results lend impressive support to the genetic hypothesis. They also, as the authors note, indicate that a predisposition to schizophrenia may remain "unexpressed" (as in the nonschizophrenic twins of discordant pairs) unless "released" by unknown environmental factors.

> **research close•up**
>
> ***age-corrected incidence rate***
>
> *Incidence is the number of new cases that develop. An age-corrected incidence rate takes into account predicted breakdowns for subjects who are not yet beyond the age of risk for succumbing to the disorder.*

ADOPTION STUDIES One major assumption that twin studies make is that any differences found between MZ and DZ twins are attributable to genes. At the heart of this assumption is the idea that the environments of MZ twins are no more similar than the environments of DZ twins. But it is very reasonable to expect that, because they are identical, the environments of MZ twins will actually be more similar than the environments of DZ twins. To the extent that this is true, twin studies will overestimate the importance of genetic factors (because some similarities between MZ twins that occur for nongenetic reasons will be attributed to genetic factors). In some cases, of course, MZ twins go to a great deal of effort to try to be different from one another. The bottom line, however, is that the assumption that MZ and DZ twins have equally similar environments can create some problems when we try to interpret the findings of twin studies.

Several studies have attempted to overcome the shortcomings of the twin method in achieving a true separation of hereditary from environmental influences by using what is called the "adoption strategy." Here concordance rates for schizophrenia are compared for the biological and the adoptive relatives of persons who have been adopted out of their biological families at an early age (preferably at birth) and have subsequently developed schizophrenia. If concordance is greater among the patients' biological than adoptive relatives, a hereditary influence is strongly suggested; the reverse pattern would argue for environmental causation.

The first study of this kind was conducted by Heston in 1966. Heston followed up 47 children who had been born to mothers who were in a state mental hospital suffering from schizophrenia. The children had been placed with relatives or into foster homes within 72 hours of their birth. In his follow-up study, Heston found that 16.6 percent of these children were later diagnosed with schizophrenia. In contrast, none of the 50 control children (selected from among residents of the same foster homes whose biological mothers did not have schizophrenia) developed schizophrenia. In addition to the greater probability of being diagnosed with schizophrenia, the offspring whose mothers had schizophrenia were also more likely to be diagnosed as mentally retarded, neurotic, and psychopathic (that is, antisocial). They also had been involved more frequently in criminal activities and had spent more time in penal institutions (Heston, 1966). These findings are often taken to suggest that any genetic liability conveyed by the mothers is not specific to schizophrenia but also includes a liability for other forms of psychopathology, but we must be careful about drawing such a conclusion. Heston's study provided no information about psychopathology in the fathers of the children. We therefore cannot know to what extent some of the problems that the children had were due to genetic liability conveyed by their fathers.

Heston's study began by identifying mothers with schizophrenia and then tracing what had happened to their adopted-away offspring. An alternative approach involves locating adult patients with schizophrenia who were adopted early in life and then looking at rates of schizophrenia in their biological and adoptive relatives. A large-scale and multifaceted adoption study of this type was undertaken in Denmark with Danish and American investigators working in collaboration (Kendler & Gruenberg, 1984; Kendler et al., 1994; Kety, 1987; Kety et al., 1968, 1978, 1994; Rosenthal et al., 1968; Wender et al., 1974). As would be expected on the basis of a genetic model, the data showed a preponderance of schizophrenia and "schizophrenia-spectrum" problems (e.g., schizotypal and paranoid personality disorder) in the biological relatives of adoptees with schizophrenia. More specifically, 13.3 percent of the 105 biological relatives had schizophrenia or schizophrenia-spectrum disorders themselves. In contrast, only 1.3 percent of the 224 adoptive parents showed such problems.

THE QUALITY OF THE ADOPTIVE FAMILY The Danish adoption studies did not include independent assessments of the child-rearing adequacy of the adoptive families into which the index children (those who developed schizophrenia) and the control children (those who did not) had been placed. It remained for Tienari and his colleagues (Tienari et al., 1987, 2000, 2004) to add this feature to their research design. The Finnish Adoptive Family Study of Schizophrenia, as it is known, has followed up the adopted-away children of all women in Finland who were hospitalized for schizophrenia between 1960 and 1979. As they grew to adulthood, the functioning of these index children was compared with the functioning of a control sample of adoptees whose biological mothers were psychiatrically healthy. Over the course of a 21-year follow-up, the index adoptees developed more schizophrenia and schizophrenia-related disorders than did the controls (Tienari et al., 2000; 2003). What sets this study apart, however, is what it tells us about the interaction between genes and environment.

One measure of the family environment that the researchers looked at was communication deviance (Wahlberg et al., 1997). Communication deviance is a measure of how understandable and "easy to follow" the speech of a family member is. Vague, confusing, and unclear communication reflects high communication deviance. What Wahlberg and colleagues found was that it was the combination of genetic risk and high communication deviance in the adopted families that was problematic. Children who were at genetic risk and who lived in families where there was high communication deviance showed high levels of thought disorder at the time of the follow-up. In contrast, the control adoptees who had no genetic risk for schizophrenia showed no thought disorder, regardless of whether they were raised in a high- or a low-communication-deviance family. Perhaps what was most remarkable, though, was the outcome for the high-risk children who were raised by adopted families low in communication deviance. These children were healthier at follow-up than any of the other three groups! In other words, if they are raised in a benign environment, even children who are at genetic risk for schizophrenia appear to do very well.

Tienari and his colleague have recently provided further evidence of a gene-environment interaction in schizophrenia (Tienari et al., 2004). Using interviews, the researchers first looked at the quality of the family environment in which the adopted children were raised. They then looked at what happened to the children who were raised in healthy versus dysfunctional families. The degree of adversity in the family environment predicted later problems in the adopted children. However, only those children who were raised in dysfunctional families *and* had high genetic risk for schizophrenia went on to develop

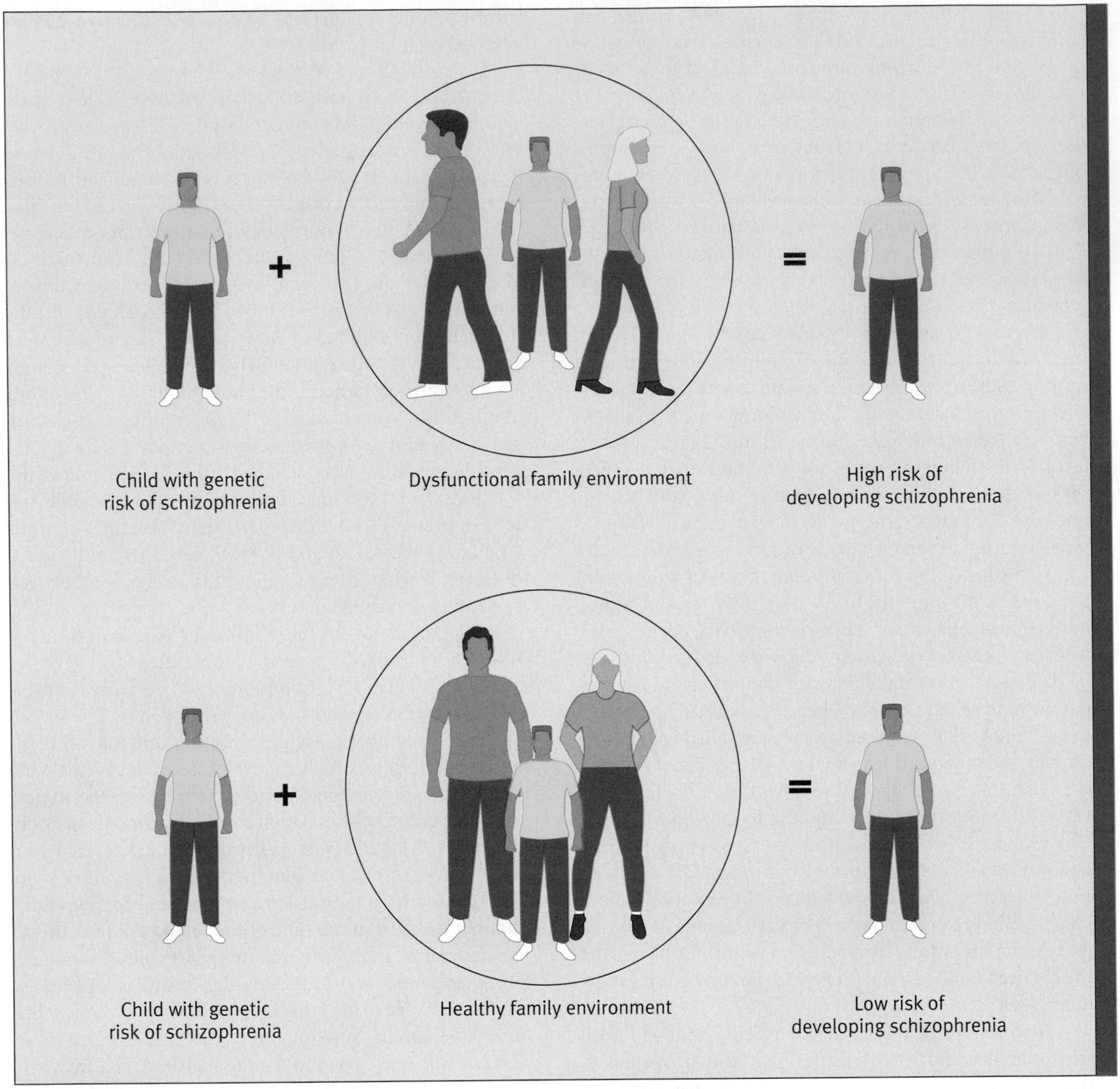

FIGURE 14.5

Children at genetic risk for schizophrenia are more likely to develop the disorder if they are raised in dysfunctional family environments. Children who do not have a genetic risk have a low risk of developing schizophrenia, even if their family environment is not healthy.

schizophrenia-related disorders themselves. Children at high genetic risk who were raised in healthy family environments did not develop problems any more frequently than children at low genetic risk (see Figure 14.5).

These findings are important because they suggest that our genetic makeup may control how sensitive we are to certain aspects of our environments. If we have no genetic risk, certain kinds of environmental influences may not affect us very much. But if we have high genetic risk, we may be much more vulnerable to certain types of environmental "risks" such as high communication deviance or adverse family environments. Findings such as these also raise the exciting possibility that certain kinds of environments may protect people with a genetic susceptibility to schizophrenia from ever developing the illness.

In summary, these findings indicate a strong interaction between genetic vulnerability and an unfavorable family environment in the causal pathway leading to schizophrenia. Of course, it could be argued that the children who went on to develop problems caused the disorganization of their adoptive families. However, there is little support for this alternative interpretation (see Tienari et al., 2004; Wahlberg et al., 1997). Some independent work reported by Kinney and colleagues (1997) also fails to show diminished mental health in adoptive parents raising children who later developed schizophrenia. Everything considered, the Finnish Adoptive Family Study has provided strong confirmation of the diathesis-stress model as it applies to the origins of schizophrenia.

MOLECULAR GENETICS Family, twin, and adoption studies have been immensely valuable in the study of schizophrenia. Family studies tell us that schizophrenia runs in families, and twin and adoption studies help us explore the relative contributions of genes and environment. These approaches also tell us about the genetic heterogeneity of schizophrenia. For example, in addition to higher rates of schizophrenia, higher rates of schizotypal personality disorder are also found in the relatives of patients with schizophrenia (Kendler et al., 1993). This supports the idea of the schizophrenia spectrum and suggests that a genetic liability to schizophrenia can sometimes manifest itself in a form of pathology that is "schizophrenia-like" but not exactly schizophrenia itself (see Fowles, 2003, for more discussion).

Traditional genetic approaches have indeed taken us a long way. But a paradigm shift is now taking place. Genetic researchers are moving away from family, twin, and adoption studies toward studies of molecular genetics. Although a detailed discussion of such approaches is technical and beyond the scope of this textbook, efforts are now under way to answer two key questions: "What is the mode of genetic transmission?" and "Where are the genes located?" Using a complex mathematical modeling technique called "segregation analysis," researchers are trying to determine whether there is a single major genetic locus for schizophrenia. Progress in this area has been frustratingly slow, not least because schizophrenia appears to be very complex genetically and because researchers are still not sure exactly what phenotype they should be looking for (remember the idea of "the schizophrenias"?). Because segregation analysis requires that we know who is "affected" and who is not, this is clearly a big problem.

It is extremely unlikely that schizophrenia will, like Huntington's disease (see Chapter 15), be explained by one mutated gene on one specific chromosome. Rather, schizophrenia probably involves several, or perhaps many, genes working together to confer susceptibility to the illness (Faraone et al., 1999; Gottesman, 1991). The individual's "dose" of schizophrenia genes may explain why one person develops schizophrenia and another develops a milder variant within the schizophrenia spectrum such as schizotypal personality disorder.

Currently, researchers are paying a lot of attention to specific regions on chromosomes 22, 6, 8, and 1, among others (Brzustowicz et al., 2000; Harrison & Owen, 2003; Kendler, 1999a; Plomin & McGuffin, 2003). They are also using known DNA markers to try to learn where aberrant genes might lie. As Faraone and colleagues (1999) aptly state, DNA markers are the "milemarkers" on our chromosomal highways. Molecular geneticists capitalize on the fact that we know the location of a few important genes that are associated with observable traits (such as genes for color blindness, for blood group, and for the human leukocyte antigen). Because genes that are close together on the same chromosome tend to stay together when genetic information is shuffled (as happens during reproduction), researchers can see whether a disorder like schizophrenia tends to co-occur with any known DNA marker traits. This is the rationale behind **linkage analysis.** Linkage analysis has been very successful in helping locate the genes associated with diseases that have well-defined models of inheritance. In schizophrenia research up to now, however, failures to replicate this success have been more the rule than the exception.

Now the focus is on looking more closely for **candidate genes** (Berry et al., 2003; Harrison & Owen, 2003). These genes are known to be involved in some of the processes that are thought to be aberrant in schizophrenia (e.g., genes implicated in dopamine metabolism). Although there are no definitive findings as yet, this approach holds a lot of potential.

Prenatal Exposures

Genes are clearly involved in the development of schizophrenia, but we also know that they are not the whole story. In recent years, researchers have begun to explore other factors that might either cause the disorder or trigger it in a genetically vulnerable person. These factors include prenatal viral infection, rhesus incompatibility, early nutritional deficiency, and perinatal birth complications.

The idea that schizophrenia might result from some kind of virus is not new. Kraepelin (1919) suggested that "infections in the years of development might have a causal significance" for schizophrenia. We also know that in the Northern Hemisphere, more people with schizophrenia are born between January and March than would be expected by chance (Waddington et al., 1999). Could some seasonal factor, such as a virus, be implicated in causing schizophrenia?

In 1957 there was a major epidemic of influenza in Finland. Studying the residents of Helsinki, Mednick and colleagues found elevated rates of schizophrenia in children born to mothers who had been in their second trimester of pregnancy at the time of the influenza epidemic (1988). The link between maternal influenza and subsequent schizophrenia in the grown offspring has now been well replicated using influenza epidemic information from other countries (see Wright et al., 1999). Risk of schizophrenia seems to be greatest when the mother gets the flu in the fourth to seventh month of gestation.

Although the size of the effect is small and influenza clearly does not account for very many cases of schizophrenia, the fact that this association exists is very provocative. How can maternal influenza set the stage for schizophrenia in the child two or three decades later? One possibility is that the mother's antibodies to the virus cross the placenta and somehow disrupt the neurodevelopment of the fetus (Waddington et al., 1999).

The idea that the mother's immune system might somehow damage the developing brain of the fetus is not as far-fetched as it might sound. Rhesus (Rh) incompatibility occurs when an Rh-negative mother carries an Rh-positive fetus (Rhesus-positive or -negative is a way of typing a person's blood). Incompatibility between the mother and the fetus is a major cause of hemolytic (blood) disease in newborns. Interestingly, Rh incompatibility also seems to be associated with increased risk for schizophrenia. Hollister, Laing, and Mednick (1996) have shown that the rate of schizophrenia is about 2.1 percent in males who are Rh-incompatible with their mothers. For males who have no such incompatibility with their mothers, the rate of schizophrenia is 0.8 percent—very close to the expected base rate found in the general population. Hollister is another example of a schizophrenia researcher who has a family member with the disorder, in this case a sister who was Rh-incompatible with her mother.

How might Rh incompatibility increase the risk for schizophrenia? One possibility is that the mechanism might involve oxygen deprivation, or hypoxia. This suggestion is supported by studies that have linked the risk for schizophrenia to birth complications. Research tells us that patients with schizophrenia are much more likely to have been born following a pregnancy or delivery that was complicated in some way (Cannon et al., 2002). Although the type of obstetric complication varies, many delivery problems (for example, breech delivery, prolonged labor, or the umbilical cord around the baby's neck) affect the oxygen supply of the newborn. Although we still have a lot to learn, the research again points toward damage to the fetal brain at a critical time of development.

The last piece of evidence that supports the idea that schizophrenia might be caused or triggered by environmental events that interfere with normal brain development comes from a tragedy that occurred in the Netherlands toward the end of World War II. In October 1944, a Nazi blockade resulted in a severe famine that affected people living in Amsterdam and other cities in the west of the country. The Dutch Hunger Winter (as it was known) continued until the Netherlands was liberated in May 1945. The population was severely malnourished during this time, and many died of starvation. Not surprisingly, fertility levels fell and the birthrate dropped precipitously. However, some children were born during this time. It now appears that those who were conceived at the height of the famine had a twofold increase in their risk of later developing schizophrenia (Susser et al., 1996). Early prenatal nutritional deficiency appears to have been the cause. Whether the problem was general malnutrition or the lack of a specific nutrient such as folate is not clear. But again, something seems to have compromised the development of the fetus during a critical stage.

Genes and Environment in Schizophrenia: A Synthesis

Without question, schizophrenia has a strong genetic component. But it is a genetically influenced, not a genetically determined, disorder (Gottesman, 2001). Schizophrenia is almost certainly polygenic and involves more than one or two genes. Current expert thinking emphasizes the notion of a multiplicity of genes that must somehow operate in concert (Gottesman, 1991; Kendler & Diehl, 1993; Moldin & Gottesman, 1997). Moreover, in the case of a person who develops schizophrenia, the predisposing genetic factors must have combined in additive and interactive ways with environmental factors, some known and some still unknown, that operate prenatally, perinatally, and also postnatally (see Gottesman, 2001).

It is also possible that the focus on MZ concordance rates has caused us to overestimate the heritability of schizophrenia. This is because some MZ and all DZ twins do not have equally similar prenatal environments. Around two-thirds of MZ embryos are *monochorionic,* which means that they share a placenta and their blood supply. The remaining MZ twins and all DZ twins are *dichorionic;* they have separate placentas and separate fetal circulations. This is shown in Figure 14.6. The higher concordance rate for schizophrenia in MZ than in DZ twins might therefore be a consequence, at least in part, of the greater potential for monochorionic MZ twins to share infections. Davis, Phelps, and Bracha (1995) have found that MZ twins who are monochorionic are much more likely to be concordant for schizophrenia (around 60 percent concordance) than MZ twins who are dichorionic (around 11 percent concordance). The concordance figure for dichorionic MZ twins is very similar to that generally reported for DZ twins. Monochorionic twins may therefore have inflated concordance rates in schizophrenia and may have caused us to overattribute to genetics what might more accurately be attributed to environmental influences.

Finally, we need to keep in mind that genes get "turned on" and "turned off" in response to environmental changes. Perhaps some environmental "hits" turn on the genes for schizophrenia. Perhaps some environments can keep the genes for schizophrenia from ever being turned on at all. And perhaps being at genetic risk makes people more susceptible to environmental insults. In a study looking at the consequences of birth complications, Cannon and colleagues (1993) found that only the people who had a parent with schizophrenia and who had birth complica-

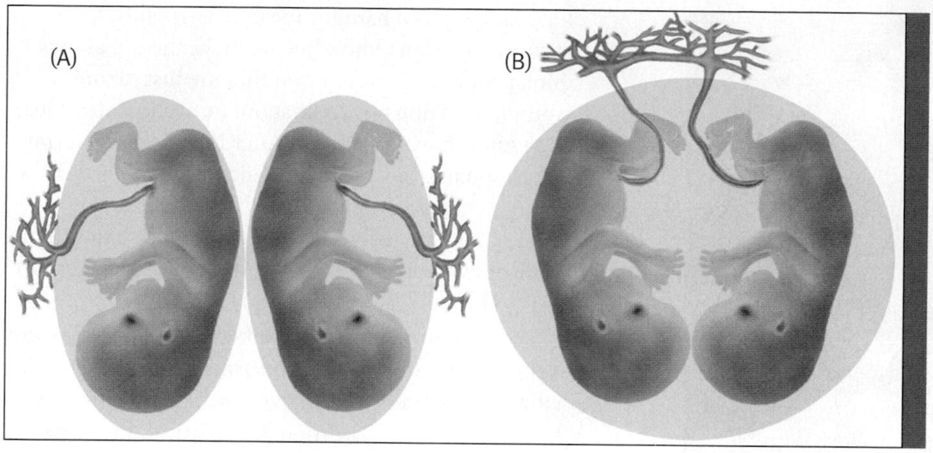

FIGURE 14.6

Chorionic Arrangements in Twins

(A) Dichorionic twins, who can be either dizygotic or monozygotic, have separate placentas and separate fetal circulation.
(B) Monochorionic twins, who are always monozygotic, have a single placenta and shared circulation.

Source: *Davis, Phelps, and Bracha (1995).*

tions were the ones who later had brain abnormalities in adulthood such as enlarged ventricles (fluid-filled spaces in the brain). Moreover, for people who had two parents with schizophrenia, the problems were even worse. In contrast, people with no family history of schizophrenia did not show enlarged ventricles, regardless of whether they experienced delivery complications when they were born. The message seems to be clear: A genetic liability to schizophrenia may predispose an individual to suffer more damage from environmental insults than would be the case in the absence of the genetic predisposition.

A Neurodevelopmental Perspective

Earlier in this chapter you learned that schizophrenia typically strikes people in late adolescence or early adulthood. Yet in the sections above, we saw that some of the factors thought to cause schizophrenia occur very early in life—in some cases before birth. How can this be? A majority of researchers now accept that schizophrenia is a neurodevelopmental disorder. The idea here is that vulnerability to schizophrenia stems from a brain lesion that occurs very early in development, perhaps even before birth. This lesion then lies dormant until normal maturation of the brain shows up the problems that result from the lesion. This may not occur until the brain is fully mature, typically late in the second decade of life (Conklin & Iacono, 2002; Weinberger, 1987).

What goes wrong? We cannot yet be certain. Brain development is a complex process that involves a programmed, orderly, and progressive sequence of events (Nowakowski, 1999). One possibility, however, is that there is a disruption in cell migration, with some cells failing to reach their target destinations. If this were to happen, the "internal connectivity" of the brain could be greatly affected. Neuronal migration is known to occur during the second trimester—exactly the period in development during which the consequences of maternal influenza seem to be most devastating.

DEVELOPMENTAL PRECURSORS OF SCHIZOPHRENIA

If the seeds of schizophrenia are sown very early in life, can we see early indications of vulnerability to the disorder before the illness itself strikes?

An ingenious series of studies reported by Elaine Walker and her colleagues nicely illustrates the association between early developmental deviation and schizophrenia risk. These investigators gathered family home movies made during the childhoods of 32 persons who eventually developed schizophrenia. Trained observers made "blind" ratings (i.e., the observers were uninformed of outcomes) of certain dimensions of the emotional (Grimes & Walker, 1994) and facial expressions (Walker et al., 1993), motor skills, and neuromotor abnormalities (Walker et al., 1994) of these children and of their healthy-outcome siblings from the same movie clips. The facial and emotional expressions and the motor competence of the preschizophrenic and the healthy-outcome children were found by the raters to differ significantly. The preschizophrenic children showed more motor abnormalities including unusual hand movements than their healthy siblings; they also showed less positive facial emotion and more negative facial emotion. In some instances these differences were apparent by age 2. Of course, we need to keep in mind that these early problems do not characterize all preschizophrenic children. But they do tell us that subtle abnormalities can be found in children who are vulnerable to schizophrenia. We should also note that a major advantage of Walker's research design was that it avoided the problem of retrospective bias. Rather than asking parents or siblings what patients were like when they were growing up, the study used home movies to provide an objective behavioral record.

Another way to explore childhood indicators without the problem of retrospective bias is to use a prospective research design. Jones et al. (1994) and Isohanni et al. (2001) studied whole cohorts of children born in particular years and followed them up over time. Both groups of researchers found evidence of delayed speech and delayed

Ratings of clips of old home movies have revealed that children who went on to develop schizophrenia showed more unusual hand movements than their healthy siblings, even when they were just two years old.
Source: *E. E. Walker (1994). Developmentally moderated expressions of the neuropathology underlying schizophrenia.* Schisophrenia Bulletin, 20, *453–480.*

motor development at age 2 in children who later went on to develop schizophrenia.

Yet another approach is to follow children who are known to be at high risk for schizophrenia by virtue of their having been born to a parent with the disorder. This strategy, pioneered by Mednick and Schulsinger (1968), has led to several other studies of high-risk children (for reviews, see Cornblatt et al., 1992; Erlenmeyer-Kimling & Cornblatt, 1992; Garmezy, 1978a, 1978b; Neale & Oltmanns, 1980; Rieder, 1979; Watt et al., 1984). Obviously, research of this kind is both costly and time-consuming. It also requires a great deal of patience on the part of researchers, because children at risk have to be identified early in their lives and then followed into adulthood. Moreover, because the majority of people with schizophrenia do not have a parent with the disorder [in fact, 89 percent of patients have no first- or second-degree relatives with schizophrenia (Gottesman, 2001)], high-risk samples are not particularly representative. Nonetheless, they have provided us with some valuable information about what people at risk look like prior to developing the full illness.

One of the most consistent findings from high-risk research is that children with a genetic risk for schizophrenia are more deviant than control children on research tasks that measure attention (Erlenmeyer-Kimling & Cornblatt, 1992). Adolescents at risk for schizophrenia are also rated lower in social competence than adolescents at risk for affective illness (Dworkin et al., 1990, 1991, 1994). Some of the social problems that these high-risk children have may result from underlying attentional problems (Cornblatt et al., 1992). This is consistent with the following comments, which come from a patient who developed schizophrenia as a child:

> It has always been hard for me to have friends. I want friends, but I don't know how to make them. I always think people are serious when they are just joking around, but I don't figure that out until a lot later. I just don't know how to adapt.... After I got back from [my first hospitalization], I really couldn't get along with anyone. That was when kids first began calling me "retard." I am not a retard, but I get confused and I can't figure out what is going on. (Anonymous, 1994, p. 587)

Echoing the findings from Walker's home movie study is evidence that early motor abnormalities might be an especially strong predictor of later schizophrenia. Using data from the New York High-Risk Study, Erlenmeyer-Kimling and colleagues (1998) reported that, of an initial group of 51 high-risk children, 10 developed schizophrenia or schizophrenia-like psychosis as adults. Of these, 80 percent showed unusual motor behavior when they were between 7 and 12 years of age. Although we might have suspected that the schizophrenia would first begin to show itself via hallucinations or delusions, it may be that the first signs of the illness can instead be found in the way that children move.

The original high-risk studies have given us many insights into the problems that characterize people at risk for schizophrenia. But researchers are now changing their strategies. A new generation of high-risk studies is focusing on the young unaffected siblings of patients with schizophrenia, rather than following children who have a parent with the disorder (Cornblatt et al., 1998). Other research groups are studying currently well young people who are at exceptionally high risk because they have two close relatives with the disorder (Miller et al., 2002). Time will tell just how informative these research designs will prove to be.

Finally, it is important to remember that studying people with a family history of schizophrenia is not the only way to study people at risk for schizophrenia. An alternative approach is to study **endophenotypes** (e.g., Miller, 1995). These are discrete, measurable traits that are thought to be linked to specific genes that might be important in schizophrenia. Accordingly, researchers are interested in people who score high on certain tests or measures that are thought to reflect a predisposition to schizophrenia. One example is subjects who score high on a self-report measure of schizotypic traits involving perceptual aberrations and magical ideation (the Per-Mag Scale; see Chapman, Chapman, & Miller, 1982; Chapman et al., 1994). An example of perceptual aberration is responding "True" to the statement "Sometimes people whom I know well begin to look like strangers." An example of magical ideation is endorsing the item "Things seem to be in different places when I get home, even though no one has been there" (see Green, 1997). Other endophenotypic risk markers for schizophrenia include abnormal performance on measures of cognitive functioning such as tests of working memory (see Barch, 2005).

Biological Aspects

Research on the structural properties of the brain in living subjects was largely unproductive until the development of modern computer-dependent technologies such as computerized axial tomography (CAT), positron emission tomography (PET), and magnetic resonance imaging (MRI). The use of these techniques in the study of the brains of people with schizophrenia has accelerated in recent years, with important results.

BRAIN VOLUME One of the most well-replicated findings concerns the brain ventricles, fluid-filled spaces that lie deep within the brain. A large number of studies have shown that, compared with controls, patients with schizophrenia have enlarged brain ventricles, with males possibly being more affected than females (see Lawrie & Abukmeil, 1998). Figure 14.7 illustrates enlarged ventricles in identical twins, one of whom suffers from schizophrenia. However, we must also point out that enlarged brain ventricles are apparent only in a significant minority of patients. Enlarged brain ventricles also are not specific to schizophrenia and can be seen in patients with Alzheimer's disease, in those with Huntington's disease, and in chronic alcoholics.

Enlarged brain ventricles are important because they are an indicator of a deficit in the amount of brain tissue. The brain normally occupies fully the rigid enclosure of the skull. Enlarged ventricles therefore imply that the brain areas that border the ventricles have somehow shrunk or decreased in volume, the ventricular space becoming larger as a result. In fact, MRI studies of patients with schizophrenia show about a 3 percent reduction in whole brain volume relative to controls (Lawrie & Abukmeil, 1998). This decrease in brain volume seems to be present very early in the illness. Even patients with a recent onset of schizophrenia have lower overall brain volumes than controls (Fannon et al., 2000; Matsumoto et al., 2001) or else show evidence of enlarged ventricles (Cahn et al., 2002). These findings suggest that some brain abnormalities may predate the illness rather than develop as a result of untreated psychosis or as a consequence of taking neuroleptic medications (Bogerts, 1993; Hoff et al., 2000). Studies of neuropsychological test performance (Heaton et al., 1994; Hoff et al., 1992) lead us to essentially the same conclusion. Patients who have only recently become ill perform about the same on neuropsychological tests as patients who have been ill for many years (and both groups obviously perform worse than controls). This suggests that many of the problems that characterize patients are present early in the illness. In other words, the neuropsychological data and the neuroanatomical data support schizophrenia being a neurodevelopmental disorder rather than a neurodegenerative or progressively deteriorating disorder (see Cannon, 1998a, 1998b; Heaton et al., 2001).

The idea that brain abnormalities in patients with schizophrenia progressively get worse with time should not be dismissed too readily, however. An MRI study of a small sample of children with schizophrenia who received brain scans on two separate occasions 2 years apart showed that their brain volumes were smaller at the second assessment (Jacobsen et al., 1998). A similar decrease in brain volume was not found in the healthy control participants. Other researchers have also reported that adult patients with schizophrenia show more rapid declines in total brain volume than healthy controls (Mathalon et al., 2001). Moreover, evidence suggests that these brain changes occur early in the illness. Cahn and colleagues (2002) measured changes in the overall volume of gray matter (which is made up of nerve cells) in patients who were experiencing their first episode of schizophrenia. Thirty-four patients and 36 matched healthy comparison subjects received MRI brain scans at the start of the study and then again 1 year later. The results showed that the volume of gray matter declined significantly over time in the patients but not in the controls. More specifically,

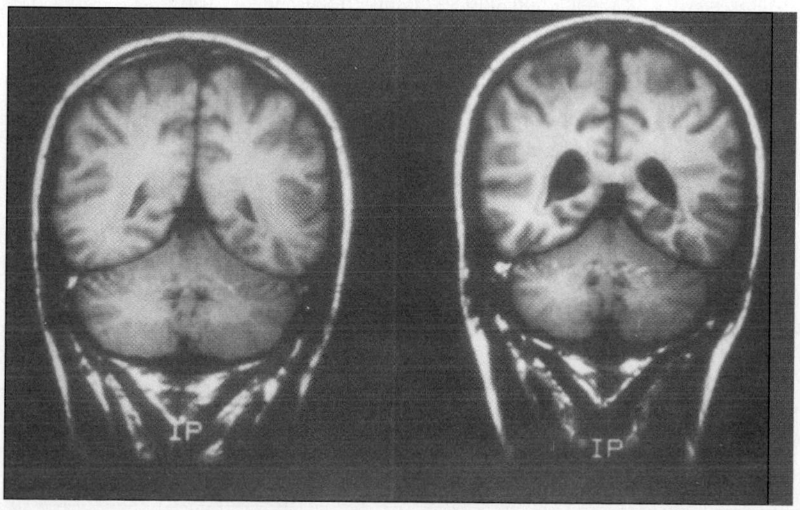

FIGURE 14.7

MRI scans of 28-year-old male identical twins, showing the enlarged brain ventricles in the twin with schizophrenia (right) compared with his well brother (left).

Source: *E. Fuller Torrey, M.D., The Treatment Advocacy Center.*

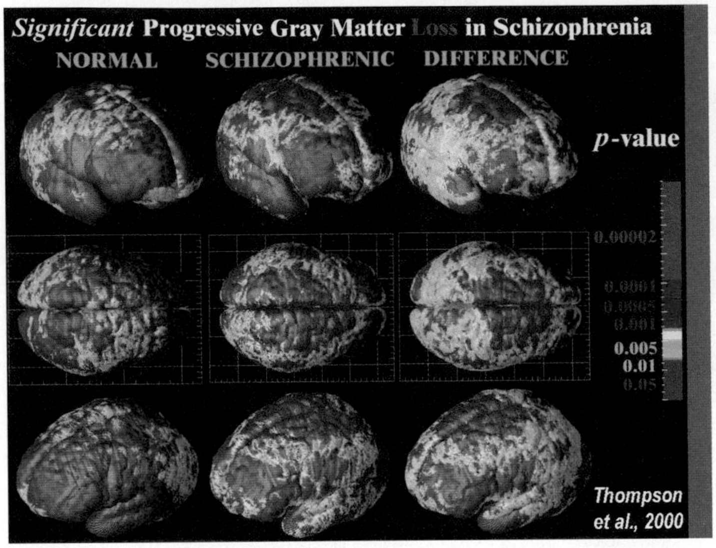

FIGURE 14.8

Compared with normal adolescents, young people with early-onset schizophrenia show a progressive loss of gray matter in their brains over time. MRI scans repeated over a 5-year period show a much greater loss of brain tissue in patients with schizophrenia than in healthy controls. Gray matter loss occurs in many brain areas, beginning in parietal cortex and spreading to temporal cortex and frontal cortex.

Source: *Thompson et al., 2000.*

there was almost a 3 percent decrease in the volume of gray matter in the patients in the 1-year period between the first and the second scans. Although progressive brain changes are not invariably found (e.g., Lieberman et al., 2001), results like these suggest that, in addition to being a neurodevelopmental disorder, schizophrenia may also be characterized by progressive brain changes. Kraepelin's use of the term *dementia praecox* may have been highly appropriate after all.

SPECIFIC BRAIN AREAS In recent years much research has focused on the question of what particular brain structures are especially involved in schizophrenia. Although much remains to be learned, there is evidence of problems

14.2 Developments in Research: Pain Insensitivity and Schizophrenia

Pain is a very familiar sensation for most of us. Yet for some patients with schizophrenia, this may not be true (Dworkin, 1994). A century ago, Kraepelin (1919/1989) observed that "the patients often become less sensitive to bodily discomfort; they endure uncomfortable positions, pricks of a needle, injuries, without thinking much about it" (p. 34); and Bleuler (1924/1988) similarly noted "an analgesia, which occurs not too rarely and which is sometimes quite complete" (p. 400).

These observations of pain insensitivity in schizophrenia are supported by anecdotal accounts and case reports in the medical and surgical literatures. One case described a male patient with schizophrenia who had a perforated bowel and who reported only occasional mild discomfort and showed surprisingly little abdominal tenderness during a physical examination (Rosenthal et al., 1990). Other reports described patients with such medical problems as a perforated and gangrenous gallbladder (Bickerstaff et al., 1988), a perforated ulcer, a broken ankle (Fishbain, 1982), and a ruptured appendix (Geschwind, 1977), who nonetheless seemed to experience little pain. In some cases the atypical presentations of some schizophrenia patients with respect to physical pain put them at risk of being misdiagnosed or of potentially serious medical problems being overlooked (Bickerstaff et al., 1988).

Pain insensitivity in schizophrenia is not a ubiquitous phenomenon, and some patients do report pain (Delaplaine et al., 1978; Torrey, 1989). What is especially interesting, however, is that a significant minority of the relatives of patients with schizophrenia also appear to have much higher pain tolerance than do controls with no family history of mental illness (Hooley & Chung, 2003; Hooley & Delgado, 2001). We have no idea as yet why this should be. However, several areas of the brain that are involved in pain perception are brain regions that have been implicated in schizophrenia. Included here are the thalamus and the anterior cingulate (Benes & Bird, 1987). The neurotransmitter glutamate is also involved in the transmission of noxious stimuli. Although pain insensitivity is a rather neglected topic in schizophrenia research (see Dworkin, 1994), it may provide us with some more clues that will help us get closer to solving the puzzle of schizophrenia.

in the frontal lobes and in the temporal lobes and such neighboring (medial temporal) areas as the amygdala, hippocampus, and the thalamus (Ettinger et al., 2001; Gur & Pearlson, 1993; Lawrie & Abukmeil, 1998; Tamminga et al., 2002; Weinberger, 1997). Again, however, we must emphasize that most patients have brains that look essentially normal and that many of the differences reported are not specific to schizophrenia. As you know from other chapters in this book, some of these brain areas are implicated in other conditions (e.g., severe mood disorders) as well. Brain areas such as the thalamus are also involved in sensitivity to pain, which, interestingly, is greatly diminished in many patients with schizophrenia, as well as in some of their relatives (see Developments in Research 14.2).

The importance of the frontal lobes is reflected in their large size relative to the rest of the brain. Many studies have demonstrated that patients with schizophrenia show abnormally low frontal lobe activation (known as "hypofrontality") when they engage in mentally challenging tasks such as the Wisconsin Card Sorting Test (WCST) or in other tests generally thought to require substantial frontal lobe involvement. Essentially, this brain area does not seem to be able to kick into action when patients perform complex tasks (see Figure 14.9). Again, however, this problem characterizes only a minority (albeit a substantial minority) of patients with schizophrenia (e.g., Buchsbaum et al., 1992; Heinrichs, 2001). Nonetheless, frontal lobe dysfunction is believed to account for some of the negative symptoms of schizophrenia and perhaps to be involved in some attentional-cognitive deficits (Cannon et al., 1998; Goldman-Rakic & Selemon, 1997).

There is also evidence that the temporal lobes (which have many connections to and from the frontal lobes) and other medial temporal areas such as the hippocampus (which is involved in memory) and the amygdala (which is involved in emotion) are compromised in schizophrenia (C; Bogerts, 1997; Haber & Fudge, 1997; Nelson et al., 1998). Here again, there are still many unresolved or unreconciled findings, and large numbers of patients have temporal lobe volumes within normal limits (Crow, 1997; Heinrichs, 2001; Weinberger, 1997). But the consensus appears to be that these regions, perhaps especially on the left side, are somehow implicated and that they may be linked to positive symptoms (Bogerts, 1997; Cannon et al.,

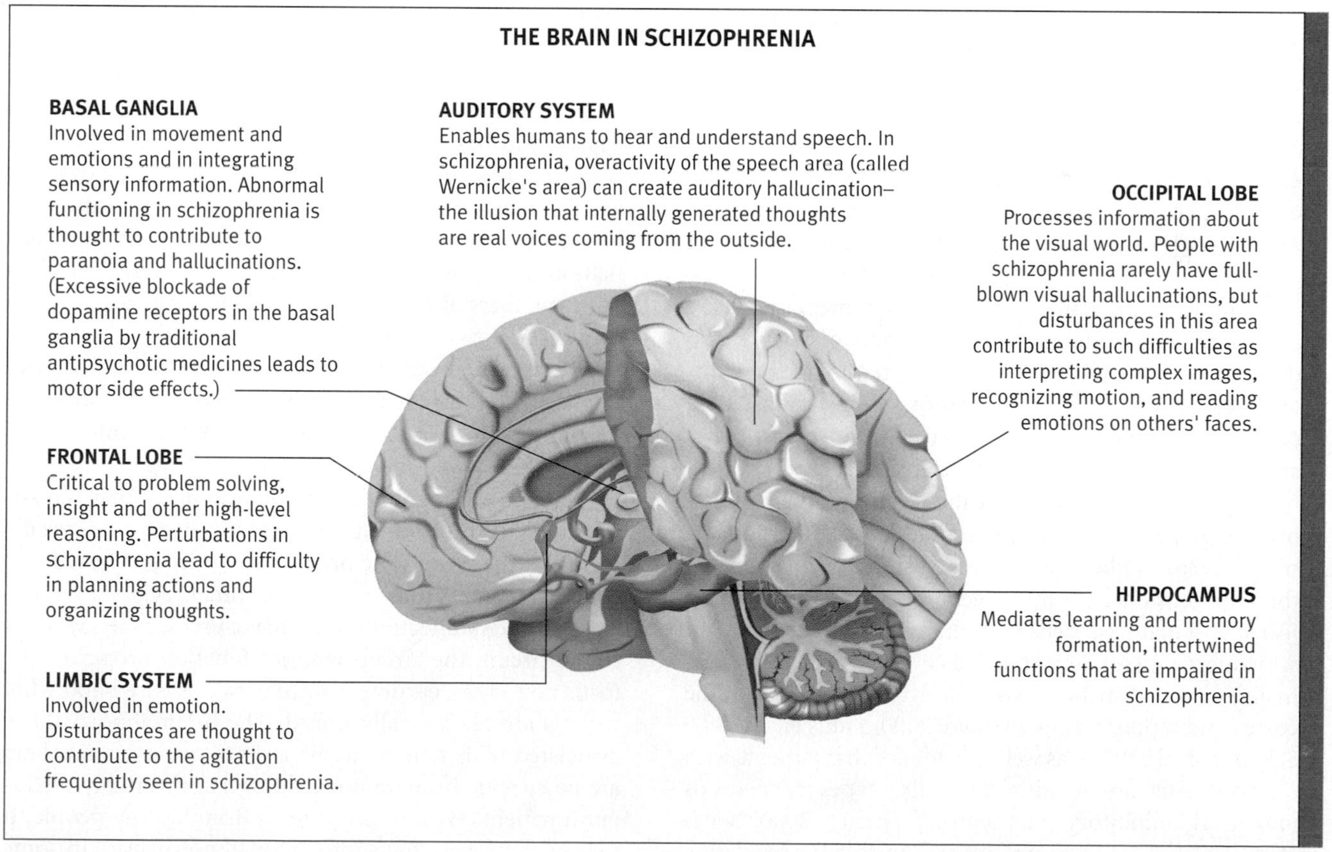

FIGURE 14.9

The Brain in Schizophrenia

Many brain regions and systems operate abnormally in schizophrenia, including those highlighted below. Imbalances in the neurotransmitter dopamine were once thought to be the prime cause of schizophrenia. But new findings suggest that impoverished signaling by the more pervasive neurotransmitter glutamate–or, more specifically, by one of glutamate's key targets on neurons (the NMDA receptor)—better explains the wide range of symptoms in this disorder.

1998; Woodruff et al., 1997). It is also interesting to note that the left temporal lobe is thought to be the last brain region to complete neuronal migration. Because of this, it may be especially vulnerable to injury and insult (Satz & Green, 1999).

Finally, evidence is emerging that the volume of the thalamus is reduced in patients with schizophrenia relative to controls (Andreasen et al., 1994; Ettinger et al., 2001). The thalamus receives virtually all incoming sensory input. This relay center of the brain connects with many different areas. It is tempting to speculate that a thalamus reduced in volume may be less able to do its job and to successfully filter out, or "gate," irrelevant information. The result may be that patients become flooded with sensory information.

CYTOARCHITECTURE As we have seen, one hypothesis about schizophrenia is that genetic vulnerabilities, perhaps combined with prenatal insults, can lead to disruption of the migration of neurons in the brain. If this is true, some cells will fail to arrive at their final destinations, and the overall organization of cells in the brain (the brain's cytoarchitecture) will be compromised. There are also other ways in which the organization of cells in the brain could be disrupted. For example, we all have an excess of synapses well into our late teens. This "neuronal redundancy" is eventually diminished by synaptic pruning, whereby unnecessary neuronal connections are essentially deleted. Programmed cell death (which involves the eradication of surplus cells) is also a natural developmental event (see Weickert & Weinberger, 1998, for a useful overview). If any or all of these processes are disrupted, the density and positioning of the cells in the brain will be in disarray.

Although the brains of people with schizophrenia are almost certainly different from the brains of people who do not have schizophrenia, the precise nature of these differences is still under investigation. Using painstaking counting techniques on postmortem brain slices, Benes and her colleagues have demonstrated that patients with schizophrenia have lower densities of neurons in certain brain regions such as the prefrontal cortex than do controls (1986). Other researchers, using more complex, three-dimensional counting techniques have reported an *increase* in neuronal density in the brains of patients with schizophrenia (see Selemon, 2004). There are also abnormalities in the distribution of cells in different layers of the cortex and hippocampus (Arnold, 2000; Kalus et al., 1997; Selemon et al., 1995), as well as evidence that patients with schizophrenia are missing particular types of neurons known as "inhibitory interneurons" (Benes, 2000; Benes et al., 1991). These neurons are responsible for regulating the excitability of other neurons. Their absence may mean that bursts of activity by excitatory neurons in the brain go unchecked. Again, research suggests that the brains of patients with schizophrenia may be less able to regulate or dampen down overactivity in certain key circuits (see Daskalakis et al., 2002). As we will see shortly, patients with schizophrenia have difficulty handling even normal levels of stress. Given what we have just learned, this makes a great deal of sense.

SYNTHESIS The brain is clearly compromised in schizophrenia, although the compromise is often very subtle. Some of the brain abnormalities that are found are likely to be genetic in origin. Others may reflect environmental insults. For example, Baaré and colleagues used MRI to study the brains of MZ and DZ twins who were discordant for schizophrenia and then compared the results for these groups to results from a group of healthy twins. What these researchers found was that the patients with schizophrenia had smaller brain volumes than their well co-twins. What was interesting, however, was that these well co-twins also had smaller brains than the healthy control twins. Baaré and his colleagues (2001) propose that genetic risk for schizophrenia may be associated with reduced brain development early in life. This is why the healthy twins who had a co-twin with schizophrenia had smaller brain volumes than the healthy controls. Baaré and his colleagues (2001) also hypothesize that patients who develop schizophrenia suffer additional brain abnormalities that are not genetic in origin. This explains why they had smaller brain volumes than their discordant co-twins. In people at genetic risk for schizophrenia (but not in those without genetic risk), a history of fetal oxygen deprivation has been shown to be associated with brain abnormalities in later life (Cannon et al., 2002). In other words, what we may have here is an excellent example of how genes can create an enhanced susceptibility to potentially aversive environmental events. Moreover, even when both members of a twin pair have identical genes (as is the case for MZ twins), if only one of them experiences the environmental insult (for example, a birth cord around the neck, creating hypoxia), this would explain why one twin might be pushed across the threshold into illness while the co-twin remained healthy.

Finally, we emphasize that it is unlikely that schizophrenia is the result of any one problem in any one specific region of the brain. The brain is comprised of functional circuits—regions that are linked to other regions by a network of interconnections. If there is a problem at any point in the circuit, the circuit will not function properly. The focus now is on learning how the brain is wired and what regions are functionally linked. The brain abnormalities associated with schizophrenia are not massive, and there are no specific brain abnormalities that invariably distinguish patients with schizophrenia from healthy people. It may be, however, that subtle brain abnormalities in some key functional circuits may wreak havoc with normal functioning (see Mendrek et al., 2004). As we gain more knowledge about how the brain does its job, perhaps we will understand more about how the brain is compromised in schizophrenia.

NEUROCHEMISTRY The idea that serious mental disorders are due to "chemical imbalances" in the brain is now commonplace. This phrase is often used to provide a general explanation of why someone has a disorder like schizophrenia. But the notion of "chemical imbalance" is vague and imprecise. All it really conveys is the widely accepted notion that alterations in brain chemistry may be associated with abnormal mental states. This idea became very clear to researchers shortly after LSD was first synthesized in 1947. The profound mental changes associated with LSD prompted those interested in schizophrenia to consider the possible biochemical basis of the disorder.

The most important neurotransmitter implicated in schizophrenia is **dopamine.** The "dopamine hypothesis" (as it is called) dates back to the 1960s and was derived from three important observations. The first is the pharmacological action of the drug chlorpromazine (Thorazine). Chlorpromazine was first used in the treatment of schizophrenia in 1952. It rapidly became clear that this drug was helpful to patients. Eventually, it was learned that the therapeutic benefits of chlorpromazine were linked to its ability to block dopamine receptors.

The second piece of evidence implicating dopamine in schizophrenia came from an entirely different direction. Amphetamines are drugs that produce a functional excess of dopamine (i.e, the brain acts as if there is too much dopamine in the system). In the late 1950s and early 1960s, it began to be seen that abuse of amphetamines led, in some cases, to a form of psychosis that involved paranoia and auditory hallucinations (Connell, 1958; Kalant, 1966; Tatetsu, 1964). There was thus clinical evidence that a drug that gave rise to a functional excess of dopamine also gave rise to a psychotic state that looked a lot like schizophrenia.

The third piece of indirect evidence linking dopamine to schizophrenia came from clinical studies that actually treated patients by giving them drugs that increase the availability of dopamine in the brain. An example here is Parkinson's disease (see Chapter 15), which is caused by low levels of dopamine in a specific brain area (the basal ganglia) and is treated with a drug called L-DOPA. Psychotic symptoms are a significant complication of treatment with L-DOPA. Again, then, the circumstantial evidence pointed to the role of dopamine in inducing psychosis.

How could dopamine induce psychosis? Activity in the dopamine system may play a role in determining how much salience we give to internal and external stimuli. Dysregulated dopamine transmission may actually make us pay more attention to and give more significance to stimuli that are not especially relevant or important. This is called "aberrant salience" (see Kapur, 2003). If this is the case, it is quite easy to see why patients might develop delusions or experience hallucinations and why psychotic experiences might be so shaped by the patient's culture and history. In the early stages of their illnesses, patients often report heightened sensory awareness ("My senses were sharpened. I became fascinated by the little insignificant things around me.") or increased meaning in events ("I felt that there was some overwhelming significance in this"). If dopamine creates aberrant salience, the person will struggle to make sense of everyday experiences that were previously in the background but that now have become inappropriately important and worthy of attention. In this way, the hum of a refrigerator could become a voice talking; or the arrival of a package could signal a threat, which then prompts the patient to look carefully at the subtle behaviors of others to see who could be a source of harm and persecution.

But how might a functional excess of dopamine in the system come about? One way is through too much dopamine available in the synapse (the gap between nerve cells that has to be "bridged" by a neurotransmitter for a nerve impulse to be carried from one neuron to another). This could be accomplished by increasing the synthesis or production of dopamine, by releasing more of it into the synapse, by slowing down the rate at which dopamine is metabolized or broken down once it is in the synapse, or by blocking neuronal reuptake (the "recycling" of dopamine back into the neuron). Any or all of these could increase the overall availability of dopamine. There is also another way in which a functional excess of dopamine could be produced or, more accurately, mimicked. If the receptors that dopamine acts on (i.e., those on the postsynaptic membrane) are especially dense and prolific or if they are especially sensitive, the effects of a normal amount of dopamine being released into the synapse would be multiplied. In other words, the system acts as though there were more dopamine available even though there really isn't. This is what we call "receptor supersensitivity."

Researchers have been acutely interested in learning about dopamine in the brains of people with schizophrenia, but research is hampered by the fact that brain dopamine can be measured only in the postmortem brain and then only with some technical difficulties. Because of this, researchers have largely had to be content to study dopamine indirectly by measuring its major metabolite (what most of it is converted into). The major metabolite of dopamine is homovanillic acid, or HVA. However, HVA is best collected in cerebrospinal fluid (CSF). This requires that the patient agree to a lumbar puncture, which involves a large needle being inserted into the spine to draw off fluid. Not only is this potentially dangerous, it also leaves the patient with a violent headache.

Studies that have examined concentrations of HVA in the CSF of patients with schizophrenia and in controls have yielded generally negative results (see Heinrichs, 2001; Owen & Simpson, 1995). The same is true of postmortem studies. In general, there seems to be no strong evidence to support the idea that patients with schizophrenia are producing more dopamine than controls are. In light of this, it is hardly surprising that more recent research efforts have moved toward exploring the idea that the problem lies not in overall dopamine levels (dopamine turnover) but in receptor sensitivity.

Most of the research has concerned a type of dopamine receptor called a D2 receptor although we know that there are at least five dopamine receptor subtypes (D1–D5) and that more may be discovered. In general, postmortem studies show that there are more D2 receptors in the brains of patients with schizophrenia than in controls—in fact, some 60 to 110 percent more (McKenna, 1997). Although this would seem to support the dopamine hypothesis of schizophrenia, there is a major problem: The drugs used to treat schizophrenia (known as "neuroleptics") are also known to cause postsynaptic receptor supersensitivity. Because virtually all patients with schizophrenia receive neuroleptics, it is impossible to know whether the increased density of D2 receptors is associated with the schizophrenia or with the neuroleptic medications the patients have received during their lives. Ironically, then, the drugs that played such a major role in the development of the dopamine hypothesis may have made it almost impossible for us to determine whether that hypothesis is correct!

But modern technology has given us a way around the problem. PET scans enable us to study the working brain and to look at the density of dopamine receptors in living patients. Even more important, PET studies can be done before patients receive any medications for their schizophrenia (so-called drug-naïve patients). Several studies have now been done. One group (Wong et al., 1986) found evidence for a more-than-twofold increase in D2 receptors in patients with schizophrenia, compared with controls, and later replicated these results (Gjedde & Wong, 1987). Another group (Farde et al., 1987, 1990) found no significant differences between the patients and the controls. So far, the decisive test of the dopamine hypothesis has not yielded decisive results. Different methodological approaches used by the different research teams may be one reason why.

What is the current status of the dopamine hypothesis? Certainly, there is support for the idea that schizophrenia involves abnormal dopaminergic function. Although much of the evidence is still circumstantial, the proliferation of dopamine receptors in the postmortem brains of schizophrenia patients clearly suggests a biologically based abnormality. Although some increase in receptor density may be the result of neuroleptic treatment, some PET studies with drug-naïve patients support the idea of receptor supersensitivity in schizophrenia. Thus researchers do not yet have good reason to abandon the dopamine hypothesis. Current thinking, however, is that schizophrenia also involves problems in other neurotransmitter systems. Before leaving our discussion of the neurochemistry of schizophrenia we take a quick look at another key neurotransmitter that is attracting a lot of attention.

Glutamate is an excitatory neurotransmitter that is widespread in the brain. As was the case for dopamine, there are a number of reasons why researchers have begun to suspect that a dysfunction in glutamate transmission might be involved in schizophrenia. First, PCP, or angel dust, is known to block glutamate receptors. PCP also induces symptoms (both positive and negative) that are very similar to those of schizophrenia. Moreover, when people with schizophrenia take PCP, it exacerbates their symptoms.

Second, physicians had to stop using ketamine, which is an anesthetic, because when it is given intravenously to normal subjects, it produces schizophrenia-like positive and negative symptoms (see Krystal et al., 2005). When given to patients whose schizophrenia is stable and well controlled, ketamine exacerbates hallucinations, delusions, and thought disorder. But what is all the more remarkable about ketamine is that it does not cause any of these problems when it is administered to children, for whom it continues to be used as an anesthetic. This suggests that age (and brain maturity) determines whether ketamine causes psychosis.

Like PCP, ketamine blocks glutamate receptors. Researchers are now exploring concentrations of glutamate in postmortem brains of patients with schizophrenia and finding lower levels of glutamate in both the prefrontal cortex and the hippocampus, compared with control subjects (Goff & Coyle, 2001). Olney and Farber (1995) have proposed that diminished activity at certain types of glutamate receptors (known as "NMDA" receptors) may not only trigger schizophrenia-like symptoms but also cause the degeneration of neurons in key brain areas. In other words, if the NMDA receptors are not normally active (perhaps because glutamate levels are low), subtle brain damage may result.

The glutamate hypothesis of schizophrenia is now attracting a lot of research attention. It is also prompting the development of new experimental drugs such as glycine that are designed to activate glutamate receptors. This research is still in its early stages but holds much promise (Goff & Coyle, 2001).

Finally, does the importance of glutamate challenge the importance of dopamine in the neurochemistry of schizophrenia? No. One action of dopamine receptors is to inhibit the release of glutamate. Simply stated, an overactive dopaminergic system could result in excessive suppression of glutamate, leading to the underactivity of the NMDA receptors. The dopamine hypothesis of schizophrenia is actually made all the more credible by discoveries about glutamate.

Neurocognition

Given all that you have learned about the brain abnormalities associated with schizophrenia, it should come as no surprise that schizophrenia patients experience problems in many aspects of their neurocognitive functioning (see Cornblatt et al., 1999, or Green, 1997, for reviews). In fact, the range of deficits is so broad that it is fair to say that schizophrenia manifests itself more in defective cognition than in defective biology (Heinrichs, 2001). For example, in reaction time studies that require subjects to respond to a stimulus as quickly and appropriately as possible, schizophrenia patients do poorly compared with controls (see Nuechterlein, 1977). They also show deficits on the Continuous Performance Task (CPT; e.g., Cornblatt et al., 1989). This task requires the subject to attend to a series of letters or numbers and then to detect an intermittently presented target stimulus that appears on the screen along with other letters or numbers (e.g., "Press when you see the number 7"). There are also problems with working memory (Barch, 2005; Park et al., 1995), which can be thought of as our "mental blackboard." Paralleling the findings for the Wisconsin Card Sort Test that we described earlier, patients with schizophrenia show less prefrontal brain activity than healthy controls when they engage in tests of working memory (Cannon et al., 2005).

Somewhere between 54 and 86 percent of people with schizophrenia also show eye-tracking dysfunction and are deficient in their ability to track a moving target such as a pendulum (Cornblatt et al., 1999). This is a skill referred to as smooth-pursuit eye movement (Holzman et al., 1988, 1998; Levy et al., 1983, 1993; Lieberman et al., 1993). In contrast, only about 6 to 8 percent of the general population show problems with eye-tracking. Especially interesting is that around 50 percent of the first-degree relatives of schizophrenia patients also show eye-tracking problems even though they do not have schizophrenia themselves (e.g., Clementz et al., 1992; Iacono et al., 1992; Levy et al., 1993 Sporn et al., 2005). This suggests that disturbances in eye-tracking have a genetic basis. Moreover, when healthy volunteers are given ketamine (the NMDA receptor antagonist, or blocker, that we described earlier), they develop eye-tracking problems similar to those found in schizophrenia patients (Avila et al., 2002). This provides us with another clue that problems with NMDA receptors (which detect the neurotransmitter glutamate) are somehow involved in the pathophysiology of schizophrenia.

Perhaps the strongest finding in the area of neurocognition and schizophrenia, however, concerns a psychophysiological measure called "P50" (see Heinrichs, 2001). When two clicks are heard in close succession, the brain (receiving the auditory signal) produces a positive electrical response to each click. This response is called P50 because it occurs 50 milliseconds after the click. In normal subjects, the response to the second click is less marked than the response to the first click because the normal brain dampens, or "gates," responses to repeated sensory events. If this didn't happen, habituation to a stimulus would never occur. Many patients with schizophrenia, in contrast, respond almost as strongly to the second click as to the first. This is referred to as "poor P50 suppression." First-degree family members of patients with schizophrenia are also more likely than controls to have problems with P50 suppression (Clementz et al., 1998). It has been suggested that poor P50 suppression is the result of problems with specific receptors in the hippocampus of the medial temporal lobe (Adler et al., 1998). As you may recall, the hippocampus is one brain region that appears to be compromised in schizophrenia. Cells in the hippocampus are also especially susceptible to damage from hypoxia during brain development.

Taken together, the weight of the evidence suggests that patients with schizophrenia have problems with the active, functional allocation of attentional resources. What this means is that they are unable to attend well on demand. Although many of the findings may not be highly specific to schizophrenia (some of the neurocognitive deficits can be found in patients with mood disorders, for example), attentional dysfunctions may be indicators of a biological susceptibility to at least some forms of schizophrenia (Cornblatt et al., 1992).

INTEGRATION Biological factors undoubtedly play a role in the etiology of schizophrenia. But genetic predispositions can be shaped by environmental factors such as prenatal exposures. We have also seen that when children at genetic risk for schizophrenia are adopted into families that show maladaptive rearing styles or deviant communication patterns, they are at increased risk of problems later on. In contrast, children at genetic risk who are adopted into healthy family environments do very well (Tienari et al., 2004; Wahlberg et al., 1997). The diathesis-stress model, whose origins largely derive from schizophrenia research, predicts exactly these sorts of scenarios (e.g., Walker & Diforio, 1997; Zubin & Spring, 1977).

Psychosocial and Cultural Aspects

DO BAD FAMILIES CAUSE SCHIZOPHRENIA? Years ago, parents were routinely assumed to have caused their children's disorders through hostility, deliberate rejection, or gross parental ineptitude. Many professionals blamed parents, and their feedback to them was often angry and insensitive. Mothers were particularly singled out for criticism. The idea of the "schizophrenogenic mother" whose cold and aloof behavior was the root cause of schizophrenia was very influential in many clinical circles (Fromm-Reichman, 1948). Not surprisingly, this was a bad thing for families. Not only were they faced with the difficulties of coping with a son or daughter who had a devastating illness (see The World Around Us 14.3 on p. 518 for a description of what it is like to live with schizophrenia in the family), but they suffered all the more because of the blame that was directed toward them by mental health professionals.

Today, things are very different. Theories that were popular 40 years ago have foundered for lack of empirical support—for example, the idea that schizophrenia was caused by destructive parental interactions (Lidz et al., 1965). Another idea that has not stood the test of time is

14.3 THE WORLD AROUND US

Mad House

Schizophrenia is a disorder that easily captures attention. Because of this, the difficulties faced by family members who must cope with the illness in a loved one can sometimes be overlooked. Schizophrenia can wreak havoc in the most healthy of families. It is hard to be the parent of a son or daughter with the disorder, and growing up with a mother or father who suffers from schizophrenia is fraught with its own set of problems.

In her book *Mad House,* Clea Simon (a Boston author; 1997) describes what it was like for her to grow up with two older siblings who developed schizophrenia. Clea was only 8 years old when her sister, Katherine, succumbed to schizophrenia at age 16. Shortly after this, her older brother, Daniel, whom she adored, also dissolved into madness. He began to hear voices while he was a freshman at Harvard, dropped out of school, and was diagnosed with schizophrenia. In her book Clea describes a happy childhood abruptly terminated by late-night phone calls from the police and from hospitals. She describes Katherine's screaming panics and how, powerless to prevent it, she watched Katherine kill her beloved hamster in a fit of rage. She also speaks of her sadness at losing the brother who doted on her and gave her piggyback rides.

Author Clea Simon grew up with two older siblings who both developed schizophrenia in their teens.

Like her parents, Clea tried to cope as best she could. She sensed her parents needed to see that she was happy, and so she acted happy. Yet she felt alone and stranded. As she approached adolescence, she also felt afraid. None of her siblings had made it through adolescence without going crazy. Following in her father's footsteps and going to Harvard, she was also acutely aware that she was retracing her brother Daniel's steps too. She made it through, but not without her own personal struggles. As the "well sibling," it has taken her many years to come to terms with what happened to her brother and sister.

the *double-bind hypothesis* (Bateson, 1959, 1960). A double bind occurs when the parent presents the child with ideas, feelings, and demands that are mutually incompatible (for example, a mother may complain about her son's lack of affection but freeze up or punish him when he approaches her affectionately). According to Bateson's etiologic hypothesis, such a son is continually placed in situations where he cannot win, and he becomes increasingly anxious. Presumably, over time, such disorganized and contradictory communications in the family come to be reflected in his own thinking. However, no solid confirmation of the pathogenicity of double-bind communications has ever been reported.

Instead, research has taught us that disturbances and conflict in families that include an individual with schizophrenia (e.g., Hirsch & Leff, 1975) may well be caused by having a severely ill and psychotic person in the family. In other words, rather than causing the schizophrenia, family communication problems could be the result of trying to communicate with someone who is severely ill and disorganized (Liem, 1974; Mishler & Waxler, 1968). Of course, some families do show unusual communication patterns that we now refer to as "communication deviance" (Singer et al., 1978; Wynne et al., 1979). Current thinking is that these amorphous and fragmented communications may actually reflect genetic susceptibility to schizophrenia on the part of the relative (Hooley & Hiller, 2001; Miklowitz & Stackman, 1992). However, as we know from the Finnish Adoption Study, adverse family environments and communication deviance probably have little pathological consequence if the child who is exposed has no genetic risk for schizophrenia (Tienari et al., 2004; Wahlberg et al., 1997).

FAMILIES AND RELAPSE Although schizophrenia is often a chronic disorder, its symptoms may be especially severe at some times (i.e., when there is a relapse) and less severe at other times (for example, during a period of remission). In 1958, George Brown and his colleagues (Brown et al., 1958) observed that how patients with schizophrenia fared clinically after they left the hospital depended a lot on what kind of living arrangement they returned to. Surprisingly, patients who returned home to live with parents or with a spouse were at higher risk of relapse than patients who left the hospital to live alone or with siblings. Brown reasoned that highly emotional family environments might be stressful to patients. Unlike researchers on the other side of the Atlantic, however, he suspected that what might be important was not the presence of markedly disturbed or pathological patient-family relationships (although those certainly existed in some families) but something much more ordinary and commonplace. Brown's hunch was that researchers should focus on "the range of feelings and emotions to be found in ordinary families" (Brown, 1985, p. 22). This was an unusual insight at the time. As Brown himself remembers, "In 1956 there was little hint in the literature of British psychiatry that the core symptoms of schizophrenia might be importantly influenced by social experience" (1985, p. 10). Viewing his insight today in the context of the diathesis-stress model, we see just how prescient Brown was.

In a series of studies, Brown and his colleagues went on to develop and refine the construct of **expressed emotion,** or **EE.** Expressed emotion is a measure of the family environment that is based on how a family member speaks about the patient during a private interview with a researcher. It has three main elements: criticism, hostility, and emotional overinvolvement (EOI). The most important of these is criticism, which reflects dislike or disapproval of the patient. Hostility is a more extreme form of criticism that indicates a dislike or rejection of the patient as a person. Finally, EOI reflects dramatic or overconcerned attitude on the part of the family member toward the patient's illness.

EE is important because it has been repeatedly shown to predict relapse in patients with schizophrenia. In a meta-analysis of 26 studies, Butzlaff and Hooley (1998) demonstrated that living in a high-EE home environment more than doubled the baseline level of relapse risk for schizophrenia patients in the 9 to 12 months after hospitalization. Moreover, even though EE predicts relapse regardless of whether the patients studied have been ill for a short, medium, or long time, EE seems to be an especially strong predictor of relapse for patients who are chronically ill.

Of course, it could be that families simply tend to be more critical of patients who are more severely ill and that this is why EE and relapse are correlated. However, a review of the literature provides no strong support for this assumption (see Hooley et al., 1995). Also, EE predicts relapse even when potentially important patient variables are controlled statistically (Nuechterlein et al., 1992). Finally, research shows that when EE levels in families are lowered (usually by clinical interventions), patients' relapse rates also decrease (Falloon et al., 1985; Hogarty et al., 1986; Lam, 1991; Leff et al., 1982; Jesus-Mari & Streiner, 1994; McFarlane et al., 1995). This suggests that EE may play a causal role in the relapse process.

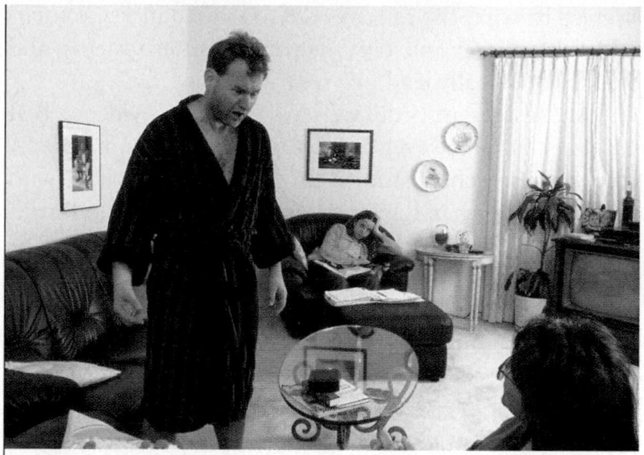

Patients with schizophrenia who live in families where there is a high level of emotional tension have more than twice the risk of relapse.

But how might EE trigger relapse? There is a great deal of evidence that patients with schizophrenia are highly stress-sensitive. Consistent with the diathesis-stress model, environmental stress is thought to interact with preexisting biological vulnerabilities to increase the probability of relapse (Nuechterlein et al., 1992). We know, for example, that independent stressful life events occur more frequently just prior to psychotic relapse than at other times (Ventura et al., 1989, 1992) and may exert their effects over longer periods of time too. Furthermore, in a thoughtful review, Walker and Diforio (1997) note that one of the primary manifestations of the stress response in humans is the release of cortisol (a glucocorticoid) from the adrenal cortex. Animal and human studies show that cortisol release triggers dopamine activity (McMurray et al., 1991; Rothschild et al., 1985). Glucocorticoid secretion also affects glutamate release (Horger & Roth, 1995; Walker & Diforio, 1997). In other words, two of the major neurotransmitters implicated in schizophrenia (dopamine and glutamate) are affected by cortisol, which is released when we are stressed.

Along these lines, Hooley and Gotlib (2000) have suggested that, to the extent that high-EE behaviors exhibited by family members are perceived as stressful by patients, these behaviors are likely to trigger the release of cortisol. In support of this idea, high-EE relatives have been found to be more behaviorally controlling of patients than low-EE relatives are (Hooley & Campbell, 2002). When they try to help, they seem to do so in rather intrusive ways (e.g., "She wouldn't go to sleep so I held her head down onto the pillow"). Furthermore, controlling behaviors such as these predict relapse in patients with schizophrenia. Quite possibly, relatives' well-meaning attempts to get patients to function better simply backfire. If patients are stressed by what the relatives do, this could increase cortisol levels, affect important neurotransmitter systems, and perhaps eventually lead to a return of symptoms.

At the present time, we have no direct evidence that this happens. However, one study is worthy of note. A group of researchers studied the behavior of patients with schizophrenia when they were involved in interactions with high-EE and low-EE relatives (Rosenfarb et al., 1995). The researchers observed that when patients said something strange (e.g., "If that kid bites you, you'll get rabies"), high-EE relatives tended to respond by being critical of the patient. What was interesting was that when this happened, it tended to be followed by another unusual remark from the patient. In other words, an increase in patients' unusual thinking occurred immediately after the patient was criticized by a family member. Although other interpretations of the findings are possible, the results of this study are consistent with the idea that negative (stress-inducing) behaviors by relatives can trigger increases in unusual thinking in patients with schizophrenia. Although we have no way of knowing what was happening to the cortisol levels of these patients, it is intriguing to speculate that increased cortisol release might somehow be involved.

URBAN LIVING Being raised in an urban environment seems to increase a person's risk of developing schizophrenia. Pederson and Mortensen (2001) studied a large sample of 1.9 million people in Denmark, a country where information about where people live is recorded in a national register and where people have to notify authorities when they change addresses in order to retain eligibility for benefits. The researchers found that children who spent the first 15 years of their lives living in an urban environment were 2.75 times more likely to develop schizophrenia in adulthood than were children who spent their childhoods in more rural settings. Other methodologically sound studies also confirm this association (Sundqusist et al., 2004). Although the reasons for the link between urban living and the later development of schizophrenia are not clear, studies of this kind raise the possibility that some cases of schizophrenia may have environmental causes (van Os, 2004). What is so problematic about urban living is still unknown, however.

Research suggests that growing up in an urban environment increases a person's risk of developing schizophrenia in adulthood.

IMMIGRATION The findings showing that urban living raises a person's risk for developing schizophrenia suggest that stress or social adversity might be important factors to consider with respect to this disorder. Supporting this idea, research is also showing that recent immigrants have much higher risks of developing schizophrenia than do people who are native to the country of immigration. Looking at the results of 40 different studies involving immigrant groups from many different parts of the world, Cantor-Grace and Selten (2005) found that first-generation immigrants (i.e., those born in another country) had 2.7 times the risk of developing schizophrenia; for second-generation immigrants (i.e., those with one or both parents having been born abroad) the relative risk was even higher at 4.5. In other words, there is something about moving to another country that appears to be a risk factor for developing schizophrenia. The following case study illustrates this.

case STUDY Schizophrenia in an Immigrant from China

A young Chinese woman was sent by her parents to live in Ireland after she lost her job in China and was unable to find another. She enrolled in language school and subsequently began to study for a master's degree in business administration. Initially she lived in a boarding house, moving later to live in a house with eight other young Chinese. Those who knew her described her as a private person who did not have many friends. She spent her time alone reading or playing solitary games.

After she learned of the unnatural deaths of two young Chinese nationals in Dublin, the young Chinese woman became extremely alarmed. She left the language school and moved back with her old landlady from the boarding house. She developed a belief that a "presence" was living in her abdomen. She also reported that multiple voices were coming from the "presence." The voices spoke Chinese and English, and they included the voices of her family, her landlady, and teachers in her language school. She also reported that the picture on a banknote that she had recently received from her family in China spoke to her, stating, "You are no longer welcome here." In addition, she developed the belief that the family with whom she had grown up was not her real family. She immediately cut off contact with them and expressed a wish to contact her "real" mother. She also stated that the CIA was looking for her but could provide no explanation of why this should be the case. (Adapted from Feeney et al., 2002.)

Why should immigration be associated with an elevated risk of developing schizophrenia? One possibility is that immigrants are more likely to receive this diagnosis because of cultural misunderstandings (Sashidharan, 1993). However, there is no convincing evidence that this is the case (Harrison et al., 1999; Takei et al., 1998). Another hypothesis is that people who are genetically predisposed to develop schizophrenia are more likely to move to live in another country. However, some of the impairments associated with the early stages of schizophrenia seem incompatible with this because negative symptoms and frontal lobe dysfunctions may make it harder to be organized enough to emigrate (see Cantor-Grace & Selten, 2005).

Perhaps the strongest clue comes from the finding that immigrants with darker skin have a much higher risk of developing schizophrenia than do immigrants with lighter skin (Cantor-Grace & Selten, 2005). This raises the possibility that experiences of being discriminated against could lead some immigrants to develop a paranoid and suspicious outlook on the world, which could set the stage for the development of schizophrenia. In support of this idea, the results of a prospective study showed that healthy people who felt discriminated against were more likely to develop psychotic symptoms over time than healthy people who did not perceive any discrimination (Janssen et al., 2003). Another possibility suggested by animal studies is that the stress that results from social disadvantage and social defeat may have an effect on dopamine release or dopamine activity in key neural circuits (Tidey & Miczek, 1996). Moreover, some of these biological changes could make people more sensitive to the effects of using illicit substances (Miczek et al., 2004). This is especially interesting in light of new evidence linking cannabis abuse to the development of schizophrenia (see Developments in Research 14.4). Although there are no definitive answers yet, environmental triggers of schizophrenia are now receiving a renewed focus of attention.

14.4 Developments in Research

Cannabis Abuse and Schizophrenia

The finding that people with schizophrenia are twice as likely as people in the general population to smoke cannabis (van Os et al., 2002) has prompted researchers to ask whether there is a causal link between cannabis abuse and the development of psychosis. A methodologically rigorous study of conscripts to the Swedish army suggests that this may indeed be the case. Compared to those who had never used cannabis, young men who were heavy cannabis users by the time they were 18 were more than 6 times more likely to have developed schizophrenia 27 years later (Zammit et al., 2002). This association also remained even after people who had used other kinds of drugs were removed from the statistical analysis.

Other studies have replicated this link (Arsenault et al., 2002; Fergusson et al., 2003; van Os, 2002) and highlighted early cannabis use as being particularly problematic. For example, Arsenault et al. (2002) reported that 10.3 percent of those who used cannabis by age 15 were diagnosed with signs of schizophrenia by age 26, compared with only 3 percent of the controls who did not use cannabis. Taken together, the research findings suggest that using cannabis more than doubles a person's risk of developing schizophrenia at a later stage of life.

A major methodological concern in studies of this kind is whether people who are in the early stages of developing psychosis are more likely to use cannabis. If this were the case, cannabis use would simply be a correlate of schizophrenia and not a cause. However, even after childhood psychotic symptoms are considered and accounted for statistically, cannabis use has still been found to be a predictor of later schizophrenia (Fergusson et al., 2003).

Of course, the majority of people who use cannabis do not develop schizophrenia. An important factor here is obviously how vulnerable a person is to developing psychosis in the first place. Those who already have some preexisting psychotic symptoms or who have a family member with schizophrenia may be particularly at risk if they use cannabis, especially if they begin early. It has been suggested that removing cannabis abuse in 15-year-olds would reduce the later development of schizophrenia in the population by 8 percent (see Arsenault et al., 2004). At the very least, parents, teachers, and health practitioners need to alert teenagers to the risks associated with cannabis use and discourage them from using it.

Immigration has been found to be a risk factor for developing schizophrenia. People who leave their native land to live in another country have almost 3 times the risk of developing schizophrenia compared to people who remain living in their home country. The stresses and social challenges that accompany immigration may be important factors.

In Review

- What evidence supports a genetic contribution to schizophrenia?
- What is the dopamine hypothesis? Describe the current status of this explanation for schizophrenia.
- What neuroanatomical abnormalities differentiate people with schizophrenia from people who do not suffer from this disorder?
- What role does the family play in the development of schizophrenia?

Treatment and Clinical Outcome

Before the 1950s the prognosis for schizophrenia was rather bleak. Treatment options were very limited and most patients were sent away to remote, forbidding, and overcrowded public hospitals. Some were put in straitjackets or treated with electroconvulsive "shock" therapy. Other were simply left to adjust to institutions that they were never expected to leave (Deutsch, 1948).

Dramatic improvement came in the mid-1950s when a class of drugs known as "antipsychotics" were introduced. Pharmacotherapy (treatment by drugs) with these medications rapidly transformed the environment of mental hospitals by calming patients and virtually eliminating wild, dangerous, and out-of-control patient behaviors. A new and more hopeful era had arrived.

CLINICAL OUTCOME The most recent studies of clinical outcome show that 15 to 25 years after developing schizophrenia, around 38 percent of patients have a generally favorable outcome and can be thought of as being recovered (Harrison et al., 2001). This does not mean that patients return to how they were before they became ill, however. Rather, it means that, with the help of therapy and medications, the patients function quite well. Unfortunately, only around 16 percent of patients recover to the extent that they no longer need any treatment. Moreover, for a minority of patients (around 12 percent), long-term institutionalization is necessary. Finally, around a third of patients show continued signs of illness, usually with prominent negative symptoms. In other words, although things now are a great deal better than they were 50 or 60 years ago, a "cure" for schizophrenia has not materialized.

Sometimes, patients who have been very severely impaired by schizophrenia show considerable improvement late in the course of their illness. As illustrated in the case below, these spontaneous improvements can occur even when there is no change in the medications that patients are taking.

Case Study: From Impairment to Improvement

The patient is a 46-year-old man who first became ill when he was 17 years old. At the time his illness began, he was hearing voices and he had grandiose delusions. He also had delusions of being persecuted.

By the time he was 30, he was living in the hospital. He experienced continuous symptoms including delusions, hallucinations, and incoherent speech. His self-care was also very poor. His symptoms showed only minimal improvement after he was treated with clozapine.

Spontaneous clinical improvement was noted when the patient was in his forties. He became less isolated and he began to spend more time doing activities. Although he had previously been incoherent when he spoke, he began to speak rationally, although there was still some poverty in the content of his speech. His self-care also improved. However, hospital staff still needed to prompt him to bathe and change his clothes. (Adapted from Murray et al., 2004.)

Can we predict which patients will do better over time? Milev and colleagues (2005) gave a comprehensive battery of clinical assessments and cognitive tests to a sample of 99 patients who were experiencing their first episode of schizophrenia. They then followed up the sample for 7 years. Although the outcome of any individual case is obviously difficult to forecast, the best predictor of overall psychosocial functioning over time was the severity of the patients' negative symptoms.

Finally, patients who live in less industrialized countries do better than patients who live in more industrialized nations (Jablensky et al., 1992). This may be because levels of expressed emotion are much lower in countries such as India than in the United States and Europe. For example, in highly industrialized cultures, more than 50 percent of families are high in expressed emotion. In contrast, studies with Mexican-American and Hindi-speaking Indian samples show that only 24 percent and 41 percent of families, respectively, are high in EE (see Karno et al., 1987; Leff et al., 1987). These differences may help explain why the clinical outcome of patients is different in different parts of the world.

Pharmacological Approaches

FIRST-GENERATION ANTIPSYCHOTICS First-generation **antipsychotics** are medications like chlorpromazine (Thorazine) and haloperidol (Haldol) that were among the first to be used to treat psychotic disorders. Sometimes referred to as **neuroleptics** (literally, "seizing the neuron"), these medications revolutionized the treatment of schizophrenia more than 50 years ago and can be regarded as one of the major medical advances of the twentieth century (Bradford et al., 2002). They are called "first-generation antipsychotics" (or "typical antipsychotics") to distinguish them from a new class of antipsychotics that have been developed much more recently. These are referred to as "second-generation" (or "atypical") "antipsychotics."

There is overwhelming evidence that antipsychotic medications help patients. Large numbers of clinical trials have demonstrated the efficacy and effectiveness of these drugs (Bradford et al., 2002). Also, the earlier patients receive these medications, the better they tend to do over the longer term (Marshall et al., 2005; Perkins et al., 2004). As we discussed earlier, first-generation antipsychotics are thought to work because they are dopamine antagonists. This means that they block the action of dopamine, primarily by blocking the D2 dopamine receptors. Although it is generally taught that antipsychotic medications take 1 to 3 weeks to work, with most clinical gains being apparent 6 to 8 weeks after the start of treatment (Bezchlibnyk-Butler & Jeffries, 2003), new data suggest that clinical changes can be seen within the first 24 hours of treatment (Kapur et al., 2005). This supports the idea that these medications work by interfering with dopamine transmission at the D2 receptors because dopamine blockade begins within hours after the patient is given antipsychotic medication.

First-generation antipsychotics work best for the positive symptoms of schizophrenia. In quieting the voices and diminishing delusional beliefs, these medications provide patients with significant clinical improvement (Jibson & Tandon, 1998). This comes at a cost, however. Common side effects of these medications include drowsiness, dry mouth, and weight gain. Many patients on these antipsychotics also experience what are known as *extrapyramidal side effects (EPS)*. These are involuntary movement abnormalities (muscle spasms, rigidity, shaking) that resemble Parkinson's disease.

African-Americans and other ethnic minorities appear to be at increased risk of extrapyramidal side effects (Lindamer et al., 1999). Such side effects are usually controlled by taking other medications. Some patients who have been treated with neuroleptics for long periods of time may also develop *tardive dyskinesia*. This involves marked involuntary movements of the lips and tongue (and sometimes the hands and neck). Rates of tardive dyskinesia are about 56 percent when patients have taken neuroleptics for 10 years or more, with females being especially susceptible (Bezchlibnyk-Butler & Jeffries, 2003). Finally, in very rare cases there is a toxic reaction to the medication that is called *neuroleptic malignant syndrome* (Viejo et al., 2003). This condition is characterized by high fever and extreme muscle rigidity and if left untreated, it can be fatal.

SECOND-GENERATION ANTIPSYCHOTICS In the 1980s a new class of antipsychotic medications began to appear. The first of these to be used clinically was clozapine (Clozaril). This drug was introduced in the United States in 1989, although clinicians in Europe had been using it prior to this. Although initially reserved for use with treatment-refractory patients (those who were not helped by other medications), clozapine is now used much more widely.

Other examples of second-generation antipsychotic medications are risperidone (Risperdal), olanzapine (Zyprexa), quetiapine (Seroquel), and ziprasidone (Geodon). The most recent addition is aripiprazole (Abilify). The reason why these medications are called "second-generation antipsychotics" is that they cause far fewer extrapyramidal symptoms than the earlier antipsychotic medications such as Thorazine and Haldol (Jibson & Tandon, 1998; Stahl, 2002). They are also remarkably effective in alleviating both the positive and the negative symptoms of schizophrenia. Current thinking is that second-generation antipsychotics work by blocking a much broader range of receptors than first-generation antipsychotics. These include the D4 dopamine receptor (which is from the same "family" as the D2 receptor) and possibly receptors for other neurotransmitters as well (Bezchlibnyk-Butler & Jeffries, 2003).

The introduction of second-generation neuroleptics has been tremendously beneficial to many patients with schizophrenia. As we have just seen, they reduce symptoms and have few motor side effects. Patients taking these newer antipsychotics are also less likely to be rehospitalized than patients taking conventional first-generation antipsychotics (Rabinowitz et al., 2001). However, these medications are not without other side effects. Drowsiness and weight gain are very common. Diabetes is also a concern (Sernyak et al., 2002). In rare cases, clozapine also causes a life-threatening drop in white blood cells known as *agranulocytosis.* For this reason, patients taking this medication must have regular blood tests.

THE PATIENT'S PERSPECTIVE Not all patients will benefit from these medications. And many who do show clinical improvement will still have problems functioning without a great deal of additional help. We must also not lose sight of what it is like for patients with schizophrenia to have to take medications every day, often for years or for a lifetime. Side effects that can sound trivial to someone on the outside can be so bad for patients that they refuse to take their medications, even when those medications give them relief from their hallucinations and delusions. The following comes from the mother of a daughter who suffers from schizophrenia:

> As a parent I also know that medication is not perfect and that the side effects can be distressing. When my daughter goes back on her medication, I feel bad seeing her shuffling or experiencing involuntary arm and mouth movements. These symptoms usually subside over time; but she also gains weight, and she hates being heavy. I think she hates taking medication most of all because she is, in a sense, admitting she is mentally ill, something she very much wants to deny. (From Slater, 1986.)

Psychosocial Approaches

Mental health professionals have been slow to realize the limitations of an exclusively pharmacological approach to the treatment of schizophrenia. In fact, so dominant was this approach that some extremely promising alternative approaches that originated in the decades prior to the 1990s were simply ignored by the majority of mental health professionals (e.g., Fairweather, 1980; Fairweather et al., 1969; Karon & Vandenbos, 1981; Paul & Lenz, 1977).

But we are now beginning to learn from our mistakes. Perhaps the most notable indication of a changing perspective on the treatment of schizophrenia comes from the American Psychiatric Association's (2004) *Practice Guideline for the Treatment of Patients with Schizophrenia.* This document makes recommendations for using medications to manage patients in various phases and at differing severities of disorder. However, it highlights the importance of psychosocial interventions as well. Some of these approaches, which are normally used in conjunction with medication, are briefly described below.

FAMILY THERAPY The literature that links relapse in patients with schizophrenia to high family levels of expressed emotion (EE) inspired several investigators to develop family intervention programs. The idea was to reduce relapse in schizophrenia by changing those aspects of the patient-relative relationship that were regarded as central to the EE construct. At a practical level, this generally involves working with patients and their families to educate them about schizophrenia, to help them improve their coping and problem-solving skills, and to enhance communication skills, especially the clarity of family communication.

In general, the results of research studies in this area have shown that patients do better clinically and relapse rates are lower when families receive family treatment (see Pitschel-Walz et al., 2001). Studies done in China indicate that these treatment approaches can also be used in other cultures (Xiong et al., 1994). Despite this, family treatment is still not a routine element in the accepted standard of care for patients with schizophrenia (Lehman et al., 1998). Given its clear benefits to patients and its considerable cost-effectiveness [Tarrier et al. (1991) calculated that family treatment results in an average cost savings of 27 percent per patient], this seems very unfortunate.

CASE MANAGEMENT Case managers are people who help patients find the services they need in order to function in the community. Essentially, the case manager acts as a broker, referring the patient to the people who will provide the needed service (e.g., help with housing, treatment, employment, and the like). Assertive community treatment programs are a specialized form of case management. Typically, they involve multidisciplinary teams with limited caseloads to ensure that discharged patients don't get overlooked and "lost in the system." The multidisciplinary team delivers all the services the patient needs (see Stein & Test, 1980; Mueser, 1998).

Assertive community treatment programs reduce the time that patients spend in the hospital. They also enhance the stability of patients' housing arrangements. These approaches seem to be especially beneficial for patients who are already high utilizers of psychiatric and community services (see Bustillo et al., 2001).

SOCIAL-SKILLS TRAINING Patients with schizophrenia often have very poor interpersonal skills (for a review, see Hooley & Candela, 1999). Their social functioning is also hampered by deficits in their abilities to recognize basic facial emotions such as happiness and anger and by deficits in making social judgments from faces compared to control subjects (Hall et al., 2004). Social-skills training is designed to help patients acquire the skills they need to function better on a day-to-day basis. These skills include employment skills, relationship skills, self-care skills, and skills in managing medication or symptoms. Social routines are broken down into smaller, more manageable components. For conversational skills, these elements might include learning to make eye contact, speaking at a normal and moderate volume, taking one's turn in a conversation, and so on. Patients learn these skills, get corrective feedback, practice their new skills using role-playing, and then use what they have learned in natural settings (Bellack & Mueser, 1993). As Green (2001, p. 139) has correctly noted, engaging in social-skills training is a bit like taking dance lessons. It does not resemble traditional "talk therapy" in any obvious manner.

The results of social-skills treatments are mixed (see Pilling et al., 2002). In some cases, treatment approaches such as this have been found to improve the specific skills that patients have and help them function better (see Kopelowicz et al., 2002). Other research studies have failed to find any significant improvements in patients' social functioning, even when very intensive social-skills training has been provided (Hogarty et al., 1991). One problem is that competent social functioning requires a broad range of skills. Social-skills training tends to target specific areas (e.g., conversational skills, managing finances, cooking a meal) that are domain-specific and do not always lead patients to be more generally competent in the world at large. Another problem is that many of the new skills that patients learn do not seem to generalize to everyday settings. Because of this, researchers are now trying to teach patients skills that transfer better to real-life situations.

Instead of teaching specific skills, the new emphasis is on helping patients deal with their neurocognitive deficits through **cognitive remediation** training. New research efforts are now trying to help patients improve some of their neurocognitive deficits (e.g., verbal memory, vigilance, and performance on card-sorting tasks) in the hope that these improvements will translate into better overall functioning (e.g., conversational skills, self-care, job skills, and so on). Unfortunately, although some of the early results looked promising (Spaulding, 1999; Wykes et al., 1999), a recent meta-analysis suggests that cognitive remediation efforts may not be particularly beneficial to patients (Pilling et al., 2002).

COGNITIVE-BEHAVIORAL THERAPY As you have already learned, cognitive-behavioral therapy (CBT) approaches are widely used in the treatment of mood and anxiety disorders as well as many other conditions (Beck, 2005). Until fairly recently, however, researchers did not consider using them for patients with schizophrenia, no doubt because patients with schizophrenia were considered too impaired. Pioneered by researchers and clinicians in the United Kingdom, cognitive-behavioral approaches are now gaining momentum in the treatment of schizophrenia. The goal of these treatments is to decrease the intensity of positive symptoms, reduce relapse, and decrease social disability. Working together, therapist and patient explore the subjective nature of the patient's delusions and hallucinations, examine evidence for and against their veracity or veridicality, and subject delusional beliefs to reality testing.

In general, the results are promising. Tarrier and his colleagues (1998, 1999) found that patients who received CBT showed decreases in their hallucinations and delusions, compared to patients who received either supportive counseling or routine care. These treatment gains were maintained a year later. Another study by Sensky and colleagues also showed that patients who received CBT had a decrease in their levels of psychosis, compared to a routine-care control group, both after 9 months of treatment and also after a 9-month follow-up (2000). But both of these studies also revealed something quite surprising. In the study by Sensky and colleagues, patients who were treated with a "befriending" intervention also did unexpectedly well. And in the other study, by the time of the 2-year follow-up, the patients who were doing the best were those who had received supporting counseling (Tarrier et al., 2000). Both of these "treatments" had initially been designed to be placebo conditions. The fact that patients who received them did so well raises some important questions. Far from being placebo treatments, individual meetings with patients that develop rapport, contain unconditional positive regard, provide social interaction, and give patients an opportunity to discuss their problems may actually produce real clinical benefits of their own.

INDIVIDUAL TREATMENT Before 1960 the optimal treatment for patients with schizophrenia was psychoanalytically oriented therapy based on a Freudian type of approach. This is what Nobel Prize–winning mathematician John Nash received when he was a patient at McLean Hospital in Massachusetts in 1958 (Nash's story is told in The World Around Us 14.5 on p. 526). By 1980, however, things had changed. Research began to suggest that in some cases, psychodynamic treatments made patients worse (see Mueser & Berenbaum, 1990). This form of individual treatment thus fell out of favor.

Individual treatment for schizophrenia now takes a different form. Hogarty and colleagues (1997a, 1997b) report on a controlled 3-year trial of what they call "personal therapy." Personal therapy is a nonpsychodynamic approach that equips patients with a broad range of coping techniques and skills. The therapy is staged, which means that it comprises different components that are administered at different points in the patient's recovery. For example, in the early stages, patients examine the relationship

14.5 THE WORLD AROUND US

A Beautiful Mind

The film *A Beautiful Mind* (based on the book of the same name by Sylvia Nasar, 1998) vividly depicts the descent of Princeton mathematician John Nash into schizophrenia, his subsequent recovery, and his winning of the Nobel Prize in economics. By any measure the film is engaging, disturbing, and wonderfully uplifting. But how accurate is it? What is the real story of John Nash?

Princeton mathematician John Nash won the 1994 Nobel Prize for his mathematical contributions to game theory. Nash's struggle with schizophrenia is depicted in the movie A Beautiful Mind.

John Forbes Nash was born in West Virginia. Even in grade school he stood out, and then he won a scholarship in high school and later attended the Carnegie Institute of Technology in 1945. He then went on to complete a Ph.D. in mathematics at Princeton, the most elite mathematics department in the world. At Princeton Nash rarely went to classes, and he alienated some people with his odd behavior, his arrogance, and his eccentricities. Although we might now regard these as early warning signs of schizophrenia, he did not develop schizophrenia at this time. Rather, he impressed his peers and colleagues by inventing a new board game and developing his ideas about the equilibrium point (the Nash equilibrium), for which he would later win the Nobel Prize.

After graduating from Princeton, Nash took a job at M.I.T., where he was regarded as shamelessly elitist, brash, boastful, and egocentric. His brilliant mind, however, meant that people tolerated his abrasive interpersonal style. Although there is no mention of this in the movie, he dated a nurse, Eleanor Stier, and fathered a son named John David. The affair was kept secret, and after the baby was born, Nash abandoned Eleanor and John David, with the result that his young son had to be placed in foster care.

Shortly after his son's birth in 1953, Nash met Alicia Larde, a talented physics major who was a student in one of his classes. They married in 1957 and all seemed to be well. However, a year later, when Alicia was pregnant, Nash went rapidly downhill. He told colleagues that he was getting coded messages from the *New York Times,* that he had delusions about men in red ties at M.I.T., and that he turned down a job at the University of Chicago because he was scheduled to become Emperor of Antarctica. He painted black spots on his bedroom wall, and in February 1958, he was hospitalized at McLean Hospital in Belmont, Massachusetts, just a few miles from M.I.T. At McLean he was diagnosed with paranoid schizophrenia, given Thorazine, and called "Professor" by the staff. Contrary to the account in the movie, Nash did not experience visual hallucinations. And even when people do experience visual hallucinations, the hallucinations rarely seem like real people. More typically, they are fleeting visual "fragments." No doubt the hallucinated roommate and his niece in the movie were a creative device to sidestep the fact that delusions (i.e., beliefs) do not play well in a visual medium.

After 50 days in McLean, Nash was released with assistance from his lawyer. He resigned from M.I.T., withdrew all the money from his pension fund, and left for Europe. Fearing for his welfare, Alicia went with him, leaving their baby, Johnny, with Alicia's mother. Nash disappeared while they were in Paris and then spent the next 9 months wandering Europe trying to renounce his U.S. citizenship. He was eventually deported.

When Nash returned to the United States, he and Alicia moved back to Princeton, and Alicia worked to support the family. Nash was offered a job at Princeton but was so delusional that he refused to sign the necessary tax forms and so could not be hired. Within 2 years of leaving McLean he was hospitalized again, this time at Trenton State Hospital in New Jersey. Trenton State was a very different environment from the country club setting of McLean. It was crowded and full of poorly treated patients. As is accurately depicted in the movie, Nash was treated with insulin coma therapy. This treatment (which had already been phased out in most other hospitals) involved an injection of insulin that led to a rapid decrease in blood sugar, coma, and convulsions. Nash received this therapy 5 days a week for 6 weeks. He was discharged 6 months later with some improvement in his symptoms.

The following year, when he was 34, Nash disappeared to Europe again. He regularly sent friends and family members postcards that were both bizarre and frightening. Later that same year, Alicia filed for divorce.

For the next several years Nash wandered around, sometimes living in Boston, spending time with his older son and Eleanor Stier, and then abruptly leaving. He began to take antipsychotics and showed some improvement. Then, like many patients, he would abruptly stop taking the medications and his symptoms would come back again. Around this time, Nash also began to hear voices.

By 1970 Nash was essentially indigent. Alicia took pity on him and took him in. She promised not to rehospitalize him and provided him with a supportive home environment. Nash became a regular visitor to Princeton, roaming the campus for a decade and leaving mathematical scribblings on blackboards and windows. He was trying to prove the existence of God through mathematics. The Princeton community was extremely tolerant of him, and slowly, perhaps because he was able to remain in a low-stress environment, Nash began to get better. He later said he willed himself to get better, rejecting what the voices said and deciding not to listen to them. At age 66, remarried to Alicia, he walked in front of the King of Sweden and received the Nobel Prize, to the delight of his jubilant colleagues. His recovery was long in coming, as was the formal recognition of his genius. Sadly, however, the Nash family is not finished dealing with schizophrenia. Nash's son with Alicia, also a mathematician, suffers from the same illness as his father.

between their symptoms and their stress levels. They also learn relaxation and some cognitive techniques. Later, the focus is on social and vocational skills. Overall, this treatment appears to be very effective in enhancing the social adjustment and social role performance of discharged patients.

In light of the unexpected findings from some of the CBT studies described above, it is likely that researchers will have a renewed interest in the elements of individual treatment for patients with schizophrenia. Although rigorous psychoanalytic approaches may be too demanding and stressful for patients, supportive forms of therapy that offer an opportunity to learn skills and yet are low key and responsive to patients' individual concerns might well be very beneficial for patients. Individual reports from patients and therapists attest to the value of such approaches (Kendler, 1999b; A Recovering Patient, 1986). Just as progress in research on schizophrenia requires a partnership between molecular biology and the social sciences, progress in the treatment of schizophrenia requires balancing pharmacology with consideration of the specific needs of the patient. For patients who are at high risk of relapse and who live with families, family-based interventions will be required. If patients have continuing and disturbing hallucinations and delusions, CBT may be appropriate. When patients are clinically stable, social-skills training and rehabilitation efforts may be helpful. But in all of this, we must not lose sight of the need of patients (and their families) for support, validation, and respectful care. The treatment of patients with schizophrenia is certainly not easy, and there is no "quick fix." Even with all of the treatment advances that have occurred, there is still a need for more high-quality, informed, and clinically sensitive care.

In Review

- What kinds of clinical outcomes are associated with schizophrenia? Is full recovery possible or typical?
- In what ways are conventional and atypical neuroleptic medications similar and in what ways are they different? How effective are these treatments for patients with schizophrenia?
- Describe the major psychological approaches used in treating schizophrenia.

unresolved issues

Can Schizophrenia Be Prevented?

Schizophrenia is a devastating and costly illness. Successful efforts to prevent it would yield enormous humanitarian and financial benefits. But is this really feasible?

The aim of *primary prevention* is to prevent new cases of a disorder or condition from ever developing. Primary intervention in schizophrenia would involve improving obstetric care for women with schizophrenia and first-degree relatives of schizophrenia patients (see Warner, 2001). Good prenatal care is known to result in fewer birth complications and fewer low-weight babies. Although such a program would not result in a major decline in the incidence of schizophrenia, it has no potential for harm. And if it prevented just a handful of new cases of schizophrenia, the savings in human suffering and money would be far from trivial.

Another possibility is to try to intervene early with people who are most at risk of developing schizophrenia. This is known as *secondary prevention*. McGorry and his colleagues in Australia have pioneered this approach, and it is widely regarded as an important public health priority (see McGorry & Jackson, 1999). One major problem, though, is how to identify people who are at risk. The screening tests that are currently being used, although acceptable in clinical settings (see Klosterkötter et al., 2001; Warner, 2001; Yung & McGorry, 1997), are too flawed to be of use in community settings. This is because they generate far too many "false positives." These are people who the test says are at risk of developing the disorder but who will not, in fact, develop schizophrenia.

Even if we could identify all of those who are truly at risk, what interventions would be appropriate? McGorry and Jackson (1999) suggest that low-dose antipsychotic medications could be used. But is it really appropriate and ethical to prescribe antipsychotic medications to someone who has no psychotic symptoms? And how harmful might it be to tell someone that he or she might develop schizophrenia? A promising (and less controversial development) is the use of cognitive therapy to prevent psychosis in people at very high risk (Morrison et al., 2004).

Perhaps the most viable form of intervention is *tertiary prevention*—early treatment for those who already have the full illness. Many researchers are now expanding their efforts in this direction. Although we do not yet have direct and compelling evidence that intense and early intervention is beneficial over the long term, there may be few serious risks associated with providing short-term inpatient care, medication, vocational rehabilitation, family support, and cognitive therapy for these patients (McGorry et al., 1996). Some patients may certainly be "overtreated." However, compared to undertreatment, this may be the more desirable choice.

summary

- Schizophrenia is the most severe form of mental illness. It is characterized by impairments in many domains and affects just under 1 percent of the population.
- Characteristic symptoms of schizophrenia include hallucinations, delusions, disorganized speech, disorganized and catatonic behavior, and negative symptoms.
- Most cases of schizophrenia begin in late adolescence or early adulthood. The disorder begins earlier in men than in women. Overall, the clinical symptoms of schizophrenia tend to be more severe in men than in women. Women also have a better long-term outcome.
- Genetic factors are clearly implicated in schizophrenia. Having a relative with the disorder significantly raises a person's risk of developing schizophrenia.
- Other factors that have been implicated in the development of schizophrenia include prenatal exposure to the influenza virus, early nutritional deficiencies, and perinatal birth complications.
- Current thinking about schizophrenia emphasizes the interplay between genetic and environmental factors.
- Even though schizophrenia begins in early adulthood, researchers believe that it is a neurodevelopmental disorder. A "silent lesion" in the brain is thought to lie dormant until normal developmental changes occur and expose the problems that result from this brain abnormality.
- Many brain areas are abnormal in schizophrenia, although abnormalities are not found in all patients. The brain abnormalities that have been found include decreased brain volume, enlarged ventricles, frontal lobe dysfunction, reduced volume of the thalamus,

and abnormalities in temporal lobe areas such as the hippocampus and amygdala.

- The most important neurotransmitters implicated in schizophrenia are dopamine and glutamate.
- Patients with schizophrenia have problems in many aspects of neurocognitive functioning. They show a variety of attentional deficits (e.g., poor P50 suppression and deficits on the Continuous Performance Test). They also show eye-tracking dysfunctions.
- Patients with schizophrenia are more likely to relapse if their relatives are high in expressed emotion (EE). High-EE environments may be stressful to patients and may trigger biological changes that cause dysregulations in the dopamine system. This could lead to a return of symptoms.
- For many patients, schizophrenia is a chronic disorder requiring long-term treatment or institutionalization. However, with therapy and medications, around 38 percent of patients can show a reasonable recovery. Only about 16 percent of patients recover to the extent that they no longer need treatment.
- Patients with schizophrenia are usually treated with first- or second-generation antipsychotic (neuroleptic) medications. Second-generation antipsychotics cause fewer extrapyramidal (motor abnormality) side effects. Antipsychotic drugs work by blocking dopamine receptors. Overall, patients taking second-generation antipsychotics do better than patients taking first-generation antipsychotic drugs.
- Psychological treatments for patients with schizophrenia include cognitive-behavioral therapy, social-skills training, and other forms of individual treatment, as well as case management. Family therapy provides families with communication skills and other skills that are helpful in managing the illness. Family therapy also reduces high levels of expressed emotion.

Key Terms

CHAPTER 15

Cognitive Disorders

The brain is an astonishing organ. Weighing around 3 pounds, it is the most complex structure in the known universe (Thompson, 2000). It is also the only organ capable of studying and reading about itself. It is involved in every aspect of our lives from eating and sleeping to falling in love. The brain makes decisions, and it contains all the memories that make us who we are. Whether we are physically ill or mentally disturbed, the brain is involved.

Because it is so important, the brain is protected in an enclosed space and covered by a thick outer membrane called the "dura mater" (literally, "hard mother" in Latin). For further protection, the brain is encased by the skull. The skull is so strong that, if it were placed on the ground and weight were applied very slowly, it could support as much as 3 tons (Rolak, 2001, p. 403)! These anatomical facts alone indicate just how precious the brain is.

But the brain cannot be protected entirely. Sometimes there is internal damage that occurs early. When structural defects in the brain are present before birth or occur at an early age, mental retardation may result (see Chapter 16). In other cases, what was a normally developed brain can suffer from internal changes that can lead to destruction of brain tissue. Depending on the nature and site of the damage, this can result in a movement disorder such as Parkinson's disease or in cognitive confusion, referred to as dementia. This dementia could be caused by Alzheimer's disease or by a stroke (so named in 1599 because this cerebrovascular event occurs so suddenly that it was likened to "a stroke of God's hand").

The brain can also be damaged by external influences. A wide variety of injuries and toxic substances may result in the death of neurons or their connections. The brain can be damaged by trauma from traffic accidents or from the repeated blows to the head that can occur in boxing or football. In short, even though it is highly protected, the brain is vulnerable to damage from many sources.

When the brain is damaged or brain functioning is in some way compromised, cognitive changes result. Although there may be other signs and symptoms (such as mood or personality changes), changes in cognitive functioning are the most obvious signs of a damaged brain. In this chapter we will discuss three major types of cognitive disorders that are recognized in DSM-IV-TR: delirium, dementia, and amnestic syndrome.

Why are cognitive disorders discussed at all in a textbook on abnormal psychology? There are several reasons. First, as their inclusion in the DSM indicates, these disorders are regarded as psychopathological conditions. Second, as you will see from the ***case study*** that follows, some brain disorders cause symptoms that look remarkably like other abnormal psychology disorders. For example, the American composer George Gershwin died at age 39 because doctors failed to recognize that what they were diagnosing as "hysteria" was really the result of a brain tumor (Jablonski, 1987). Third, brain damage can cause changes in behavior, mood, and personality. You will recognize this more clearly later when we describe the case of Phineas Gage (who survived a metal bar being blown through his head). Understanding what brain areas are involved when behavior, mood, and personality change after brain damage may help researchers better understand the biological underpinnings of many problems in abnormal psychology. Fourth, many people who suffer from brain disorders (for example, people who are diagnosed as having Alzheimer's disease) react to the news of their diagnosis with depression or anxiety. Prospective studies also suggest that depressive symptoms may herald the onset of disorders such as Alzheimer's disease (AD) by several years (Devanand et al., 1996; Wilson et al., 2002) and that episodes of depression double the risk for AD even 20 years later (Speck et al., 1995). Finally, cognitive disorders of the type we describe in this chapter take a heavy toll on family members who, for many patients, must shoulder the burden of care. Again, depression and anxiety in relatives of the patients themselves are not uncommon.

research close•up

case study

Case studies are descriptions of one specific case. Case studies can be a useful source of information and can help researchers generate hypotheses. Because of their highly selective nature, however, they cannot be used to draw any scientific conclusions.

case STUDY **A Simple Case of Mania?**

A highly successful businessman, age 45, with no previous history of psychiatric disorder began to act differently from his usual self. He seemed driven at work. His working hours gradually increased, until finally he was sleeping only 2 to 3 hours a night; the rest of the time he worked. He became irritable and began to engage in uncharacteristic sprees of spending beyond his means.

Although he felt extremely productive and claimed he was doing the work of five men, the man's boss felt otherwise. He was worried about the quality of that work, having observed several recent examples of poor business decisions. Finally, when the man complained of headaches, his boss insisted that he seek help. (Adapted from Jamieson & Wells, 1979.)

Clinicians always need to be alert to the possibility that brain impairment itself may be directly responsible for the clinical phenomena observed. Failure to do so could result in serious diagnostic errors, as when a clinician falsely attributes a mood change to psychological causes and fails to consider a neuropsychological origin such as a brain tumor (Purisch & Sbordone, 1997; Weinberger, 1984). The case you have just read concerns a man who, on first glance, looks as if he might be having an episode of mania. In fact, however, he is suffering from four tumorous masses in his brain. Clues that the patient has a brain disorder rather than a mood disorder come from the fact that he is experiencing headaches at the same time as a major change in behavior. The fact that he has no prior history of psychopathology is also another clue (see Taylor, 2000).

Brain Impairment in Adults

Prior to the revision of DSM-IV in 1994, most of the disorders to be considered in this section were called **organic mental disorders.** This term was designed to convey that there was some kind of identifiable pathology that was causing the problem (e.g., a brain tumor, stroke, drug intoxication, or the like). Recognizing this, such disorders were typically treated by neurologists. In contrast, **functional mental disorders** were brain disorders that were considered not to have an organic basis. Such disorders were treated by psychiatrists. By the time DSM-IV was published, however, it was apparent that it was wrong to assume that psychiatric disorders had no organic (or biological) component. Consider, for example, how important problems in brain neuroanatomy and neurochemistry are to our understanding of schizophrenia (see Chapter 14). The terms *functional* and *organic* were therefore dropped. What was the organic mental disorders section of the DSM has been renamed. It is now called "Delirium, Dementia, and Amnestic and other Cognitive Disorders" (see APA, 2000).

Diagnostic Issues

The DSM-IV-TR presents the diagnostic coding of various neuropsychological disorders in different and somewhat inconsistent ways. Much depends on what is causing the cognitive problem. For cognitive disorders that have an underlying medical problem as their cause, both the cognitive problem and the medical cause are listed on Axis I. Sometimes the qualifying phrase "Due to [a specified general medical condition]" is used. Then, in addition, the medical condition that is causing the cognitive problem is listed again on Axis III. Many of the common neuropsychological disorders are handled in this manner. For example, cognitive impairment associated with HIV disease might have the following DSM-IV-TR diagnostic code:

Axis I: Dementia due to HIV disease

Axis III: HIV disease

The diagnosis for dementia caused by Alzheimer's disease is managed in a similar way, with Alzheimer's disease being designated on Axis III.

Axis I: Dementia of the Alzheimer's type

Axis III: Alzheimer's disease

On the other hand, pathological brain changes that are related to the toxic effects of abusing certain substances, such as long-term, excessive alcohol consumption (see Chapter 12), are handled a little differently. In these cases, a specific etiologic notation is included in the Axis I diagnosis, as in "Substance-Induced Persisting Amnestic Disorder" (a circumscribed and characteristic type of memory impairment). No diagnosis is given on Axis III.

Axis I: Alcohol-induced persisting amnestic disorder

Axis III: None

Clinical Signs of Brain Damage

With possible minor exceptions, cell bodies and neural pathways in the brain do not appear to have the power of regeneration, which means that their destruction is permanent. When brain injury occurs in an older child or adult, there is a loss in established functioning. This loss—this deprivation of already acquired and customary skills—can be painfully obvious to the victim, adding an often pronounced psychological burden to the physical burden of having the lesion. In other cases the impairment may extend to the capacity for realistic self-appraisal (a condition called "anosognosia"), leaving these patients

15.1 Developments in Practice

Screening for Cognitive Impairment

All of us misplace our keys from time to time, drive past our intended destinations, or forget something we had planned to remember. Are these signs of cognitive impairment? Or are we just too busy and preoccupied to pay enough attention to what we are doing?

Clinicians often use a short screening test called the Mini-Mental State Examination to examine patients for cognitive impairment (see Folstein et al., 1975). Although this test is far from new, it is still the most widely used in routine clinical practice. The test has a maximum score of 30 points. A score of less than 25 suggests impairment, and a score of 20 or less is indicative of definite impairment.

During the MMSE the clinician will ask the patient questions that concern *orientation* (score 1 point if correct):

What is the year, season, month, date, day of the week?

Where are we now (country, state, city or town, building, floor of building)?

There will also be questions that assess *registration*. Here the clinician names three objects (e.g., cat, window, orange) and asks the patient to repeat them. The patient receives a score of 1 point for each object correctly repeated.

Next, the clinician will assess *attention* and *concentration*. The patient is asked to start at 100 and count backward, subtracting 7 each time until he or she gets to 65. An alternative here is to ask the patient to spell a common five-letter word such as *world* backward. This part of the test has a maximum score of 5 points.

Then the clinician will test for *recall* by asking, "Do you recall the three objects named before?" One point is given for each object correctly recalled.

This is followed by *language tests*.

The clinician will point to two objects such as a watch and a pen and ask the patient to name them (2 points).

The clinician will ask the patient to repeat a phrase such as "No ifs, ands, or buts" (1 point).

Comprehension will be assessed by asking the patient to comply with a command: "Pick up the paper in your right hand, fold it in half, and set it on the floor" (3 points).

The patient will also be asked to read a command (such as "Close your eyes") off a piece of paper and perform it (1 point).

The last part of this section requires the patient to write a simple sentence (e.g., subject, verb, object; 1 point).

Finally *construction* ability is tested by asking the patient to copy a very simple design (1 point).

relatively unaware of their losses and hence poorly motivated for rehabilitation.

Damage or destruction of brain tissue may involve only limited behavioral deficits or a wide range of psychological impairments, depending on: (1) the nature, location, and extent of neural damage, (2) the premorbid (predisorder) competence and personality of the individual, (3) the individual's life situation, and (4) the amount of time since the first appearance of the condition. Although the degree of mental impairment is usually directly related to the extent of damage, this is not invariably so. In some cases involving relatively severe brain damage, mental change is astonishingly slight. In other cases of apparently mild and limited damage, there may be profoundly altered functioning. Developments in Practice 15.1 describes a short screening test that is widely used to assess patients for possible cognitive impairment. A patient with a low score on the test would be referred for a more extensive evaluation.

Diffuse versus Focal Damage

The fundamental disorders discussed in this section are always in the strictest sense neuropsychological ones, although psychopathological problems (psychosis, mood change, etc.) may be associated with them. Some of these disorders are relatively well understood, with symptoms that have relatively constant features in people whose brain injuries are comparable in location and extent. For example, attention is often impaired by mild to moderate diffuse (i.e., widespread) damage, such as might occur with moderate oxygen deprivation or the ingestion of toxic substances such as mercury. Such a person may complain of memory problems due to an inability to sustain focused retrieval efforts, while his or her ability to store new information remains intact. As Developments in Research 15.2 shows, mild cognitive impairments can also be detected in people who have had only low-level exposure to organic solvents and other neurotoxins.

In contrast to diffuse damage, focal brain lesions involve circumscribed areas of abnormal change in brain structure. This is the kind of damage that might occur with a sharply defined traumatic injury or an interruption of blood supply (a stroke) to a specific part of the brain (see Figure 15.1). The location and extent of the damage determine what problems the patient will have. As you are aware, the brain is highly specialized (see Figure 15.2). For instance, the two hemispheres, while interacting intimately at many levels, are involved in

15.2 Developments in Research

Cognitive Impairments in Nail Salon Technicians

As you will learn in this chapter, the brain can be damaged by exposure to metals such as lead and mercury. This places many industrial workers at risk. However, the nervous system can also be damaged by exposure to organic solvents that are neurotoxic. Some of these are found in a place that most of us would not immediately think of.

Nail studios routinely use (meth)acrylates and a variety of organic solvents such as toluene, acetone, and formaldehyde that are known to be potentially damaging to the central nervous system. In a recent study, LoSasso et al. (2001) compared the neuropsychological functioning of 150 nail salon technicians with that of 148 demographically similar controls. All of the participants completed a self-report measure that assessed neuropsychological impairments in the areas of memory, verbal learning, and general cognitive efficiency.

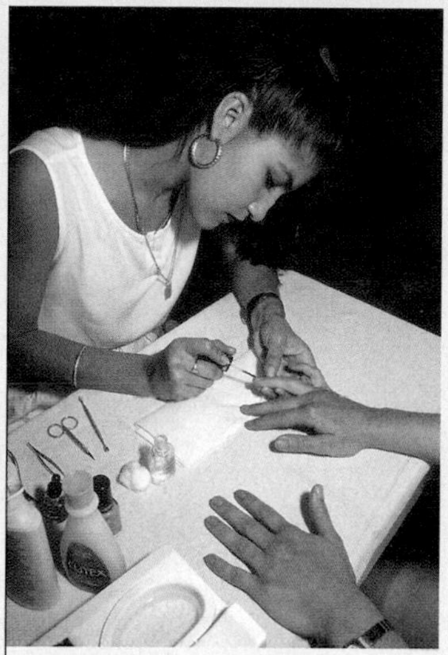

The brain can be damaged by exposure to solvents. Nail studios frequently use a variety of organic solvents that are known to be potentially damaging to the central nervous system.

What the researchers found was both interesting and disturbing. The results showed that compared to the controls, the nail salon technicians reported significantly more cognitive and neurological impairments. Many of the impairments were mild. However, the severity of the symptoms that the nail salon technicians reported was correlated with how long they had worked in the industry, as well as with such workplace factors as the size of the salon and the adequacy of ventilation. In a similar study that used psychological, neuropsychological, and sensory tests (rather than a mail-in questionnaire), LoSasso and colleagues (2002) found that nail salon technicians performed more poorly than the controls on tests of attention and information processing. The nail salon technicians also scored worse than the controls on tests of olfaction (ability to detect smells). Taken together, these findings highlight the consequences of even low-level exposure to neurotoxic substances that can be found in places where many people work and where many others routinely visit.

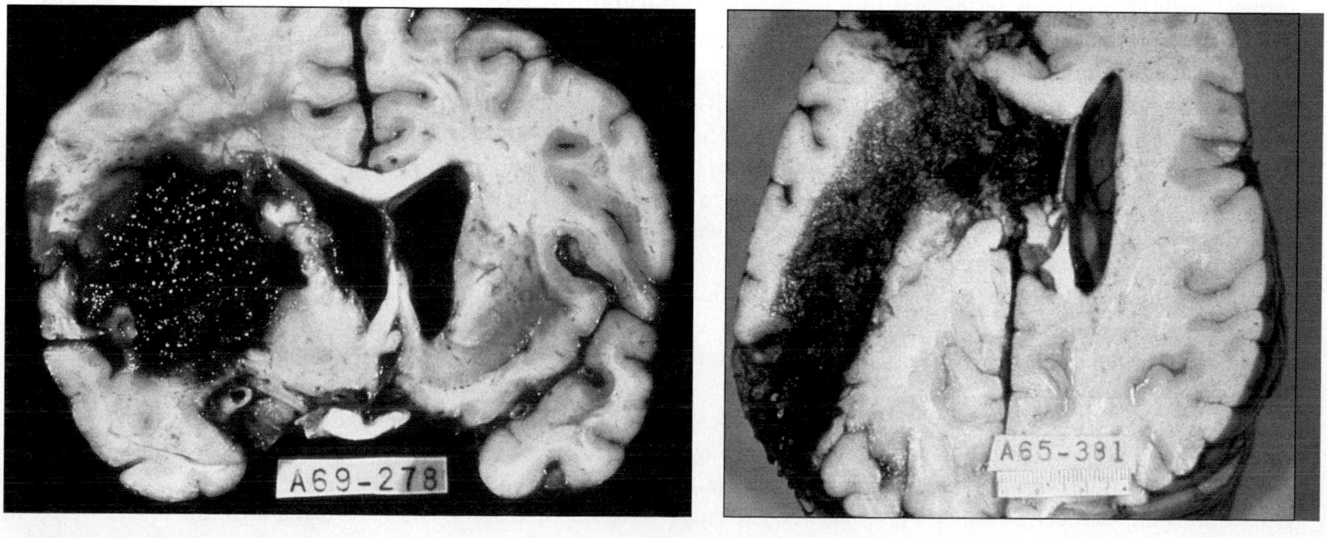

FIGURE 15.1

Cross sections of damaged brains: cerebrovascular accident of stroke (left) and bullet injury (right).

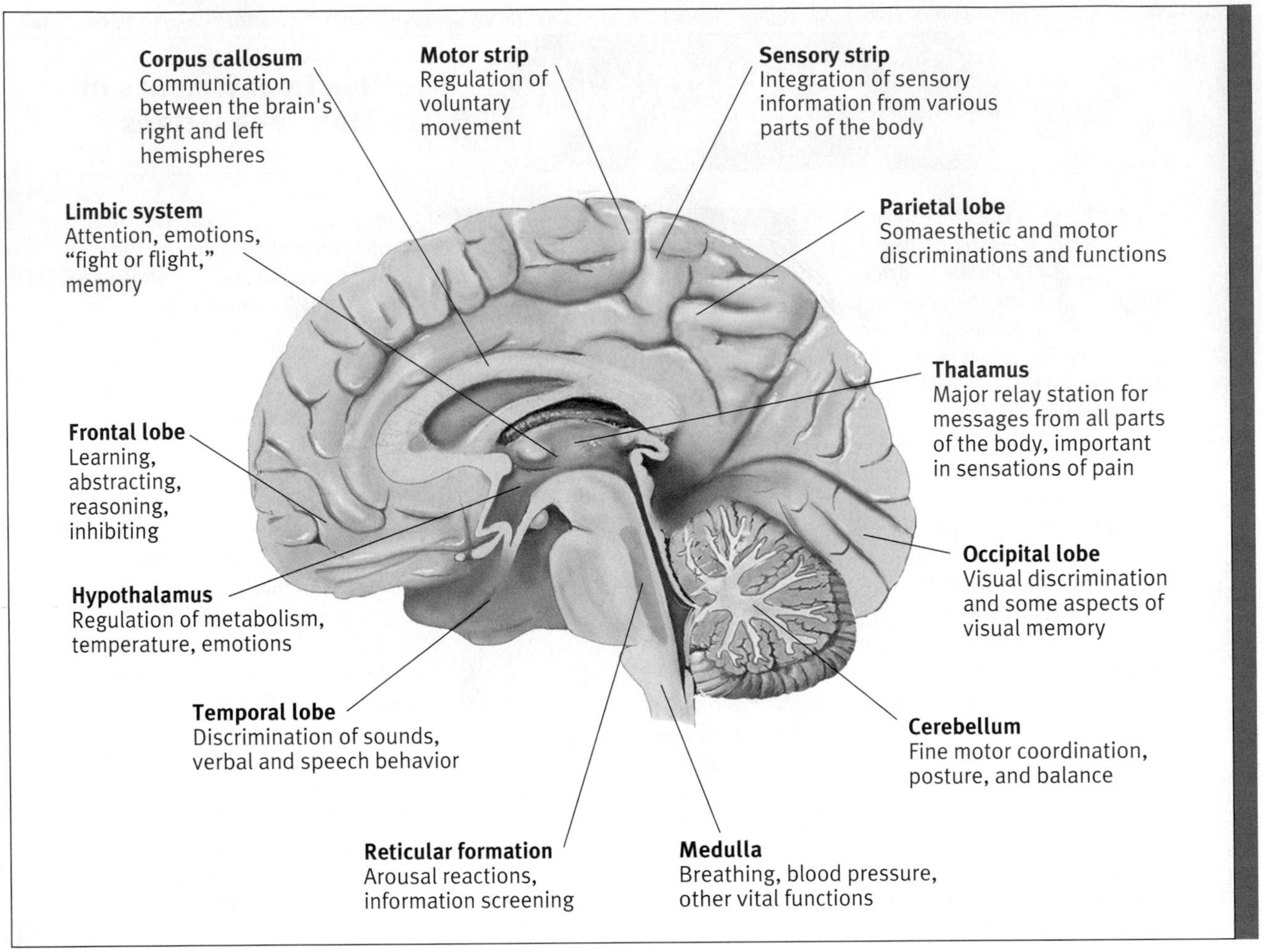

FIGURE 15.2
Brain Structures and Associated Behaviors

somewhat different types of mental processing. At the risk of oversimplifying, it is generally accepted that functions that are dependent on serial processing of familiar information, such as language and solving mathematical equations, take place mostly in the left hemisphere for nearly everyone. Conversely, the right hemisphere appears to be generally specialized for grasping overall meanings in novel situations, reasoning on a nonverbal, intuitive level, and appreciation of spatial relations. Even within hemispheres, the various lobes and regions within them mediate specialized functions.

Although none of these relationships between brain location and behavior can be considered universally true, it is possible to make broad generalizations about the likely effects of damage to particular parts of the brain. Damage to the frontal areas, for example, is associated with either of two contrasting clinical pictures: (1) behavioral inertia, passivity, apathy, and perseverative thought, or (2) impulsiveness and distractibility. Damage to specific areas of the right parietal lobe may produce impairment of visual-motor coordination, and damage to the left parietal area may impair certain aspects of language function, including reading and writing, as well as arithmetical abilities. Damage to certain structures within the temporal lobes disrupts an early stage of memory storage. Extensive bilateral temporal damage can produce a syndrome in which remote memory remains relatively intact but nothing new can be stored for later retrieval. Damage to other structures within the temporal lobes is associated with disturbances of eating, sexuality, and the emotions. Occipital damage produces a variety of visual impairments and visual association deficits, the nature of the deficit depending on the particular site of the lesion. For example, a person may be unable to recognize familiar faces. Unfortunately, many types of brain disease are general and therefore diffuse in their destructive effects, causing multiple and widespread interruptions of the brain's circuitry. Some consequences of brain disorders that have mainly focal origins but com-

TABLE 15.1 Impairments Associated with Brain Disorders

The following types of difficulties are often the consequences of brain disease, disorder, or damage.

1. *Impairment of memory.* The individual has notable trouble remembering recent events and less trouble remembering events of the remote past, with a tendency in some patients to confabulate—that is, to invent memories to fill in gaps. In severe instances, no new experience can be retained for more than a few minutes.
2. *Impairment of orientation.* The individual is unable to locate himself or herself accurately, especially in time but also in space or in relation to the personal identities of self or others.
3. *Impairment of learning, comprehension, and judgment.* The individual's thinking becomes clouded, sluggish, and/or inaccurate. The person may lose the ability to plan with foresight or to understand abstract concepts and hence to process complex information (described as "thought impoverishment").
4. *Impairment of emotional control or modulation.* The individual manifests emotional overreactivity such as easy arousal to laughter, tears, or rage.
5. *Apathy or emotional blunting.* The individual manifests emotional underreactivity, especially in cases of advanced deterioration.
6. *Impairment in the initiation of behavior.* The individual lacks self-starting capability and may have to be reminded repeatedly about what to do next, even when the behavior involved remains well within the person's range of competence. This is sometimes referred to as "loss of executive function."
7. *Impairment of controls over matters of propriety and ethical conduct.* The individual may manifest a marked lowering of personal standards in areas such as appearance, personal hygiene, sexuality, or language.
8. *Impairment of receptive and expressive communication.* The individual may be unable to comprehend written or spoken language or may be unable to express his or her own thoughts orally or in writing.
9. *Impaired visuospatial ability.* The individual has difficulty coordinating motor activity with the characteristics of the visual environment, a deficit that affects graphomotor (handwriting and drawing) and constructional (e.g., assembling things) performance.

monly appear in the context of progressively diffuse damage are shown in Table 15.1.

The Neuropsychology/ Psychopathology Interaction

Most people who have a neuropsychological disorder do not develop psychopathological symptoms such as panic attacks, dissociative episodes, or delusions. However, many show at least mild deficits in cognitive processing and self-regulation. Similarly, some people who suffer from psychopathological disorders also have cognitive deficits. For example, patients with bipolar disorder have persistent cognitive deficits that can be detected even during periods of illness remission (Cavanagh et al., 2002; Clark et al., 2002; Ferrier & Thompson, 2002). This highlights the close link between psychopathological and neuropsychological conditions.

The psychopathological symptoms that do sometimes accompany brain impairment are not always predictable and can reflect individual nuances consistent with the patient's age (see Tateno et al., 2002), her or his prior personality, and the total psychological situation confronting the patient. It is erroneous to assume that a psychological disorder—for example, a serious depression that follows a brain injury—is necessarily and completely explained by the patient's brain damage. Certainly that could be the case. However, it is also possible that the depression might be better explained by the patient's awareness of dramatically lessened competence and the loss of previous skills. After a traumatic brain injury caused by an accident or a fall, for example, around 18 percent of patients make a suicide attempt (Simpson & Tate, 2002).

People with more favorable life situations tend to fare better after brain injury than people whose lives are more disorganized or disadvantaged (Yeates et al., 1997). Intelligent, well-educated, mentally active people have enhanced resistance to mental and behavioral deterioration following significant brain injury (e.g., see Mori et al., 1997a; Schmand et al., 1997). Because the brain is the organ responsible for the integration of behavior, however, there are limits to the amount of brain damage that anyone can tolerate or compensate for without exhibiting behavior that is decidedly abnormal.

In Review

- Describe some of the major ways in which the brain can become damaged.
- What kinds of clinical symptoms are often associated with damage to the frontal, parietal, temporal, and occipital lobes of the brain?
- List nine symptoms that are typical of focal and diffuse brain damage.

Delirium

Clinical Presentation

Delirium (see the table on criteria for delirium) is a commonly occurring syndrome. It is an acute confusional state that lies between normal wakefulness and stupor or coma (see Figure 15.3). It has a sudden onset and involves a fluctuating state of reduced awareness. Essentially, delirium reflects a major change in the way the brain is working. In addition to a disturbance in level of consciousness, delirium also involves cognitive changes. Information-processing capacities are impaired, affecting such basic functions as attention, perception, memory, and thinking. Hallucinations and delusions are quite common (see Trzepacz et al., 2002). In addition, the syndrome often includes abnormal psychomotor activity such as wild thrashing about and disturbance of the sleep cycle. A delirious person is essentially unable to carry out purposeful mental activity of any kind. The intensity of the symptoms also fluctuates over the course of a 24-hour period, as described in the following case study.

DSM-IV-TR

Criteria for Delirium

- Disturbance of consciousness (i.e., reduced awareness of the environment).
- A change in cognition (e.g., memory deficit, disorientation) that is not related to dementia.
- The disturbance develops over a short period of time (usually hours to days) and tends to fluctuate over the course of the day.

Source: *Adapted with permission from the* Diagnostic and Statistical Manual of Mental Disorders, *Fourth Edition, Text Revision (Copyright 2000). American Psychiatric Association.*

Case Study — Delirium Following a Routine Operation

Mrs. Petersen is a 75-year-old widow. She was admitted to the hospital after breaking her leg. She had a routine operation, and after this, she began to show signs of confusion. Her consciousness became clouded, with reduced attention and awareness. She could not remember what had happened to her or why she was in the hospital. During the day, she showed mild and aimless hyperactive behavior. She was unable to read or watch television and could not always recognize relatives who visited her. She was seen having conversations with imaginary persons and staring at a point on the ceiling. She was irritable and would burst out in anger. She knocked her meals onto the floor and refused to take any medications. Between outbursts Mrs. Petersen calmed down and was able to sleep for up to half an hour, but at night she seemed unable to sleep at all, and the hyperactivity increased. As other patients fell asleep for the night, Mrs. Petersen started wandering about the ward waking them up again. She went into other people's rooms and tried to climb into their beds. Several times she tried to leave the hospital in her nightdress but was stopped and brought back to her room. (Adapted from Üstün et al., 1996.)

Delirium can occur in a person of any age. However, the elderly are at particularly high risk, perhaps because of brain changes caused by normal aging that lead to "reduced brain reserve." As described in the case of Mrs. Petersen, delirium is very common in the elderly after they have had surgery, patients over 80 being particularly at risk (Trzepacz et al., 2002). At the other end of the age spectrum, children are also at high risk of delirium, perhaps because their brains are not yet fully developed. Estimates of the prevalence of delirium vary widely with the age of the population studied but are somewhere in the region of 5 to 40 percent of hospitalized patients (Fann, 2000).

Delirium may result from several conditions including head injury and infection. However, the most common cause of delirium is drug intoxication or withdrawal. Toxicity from medications also causes many cases of delirium. This may explain why delirium is so common in the elderly after they have had surgery.

Treatment and Outcome

Delirium is a true medical emergency, and its underlying cause must be identified and managed. Most cases of delirium are reversible, except when the delirium is caused by a terminal illness or by severe brain trauma. Treatment involves medication, environmental manipulations, and family support (American Psychiatric Association, 1999).

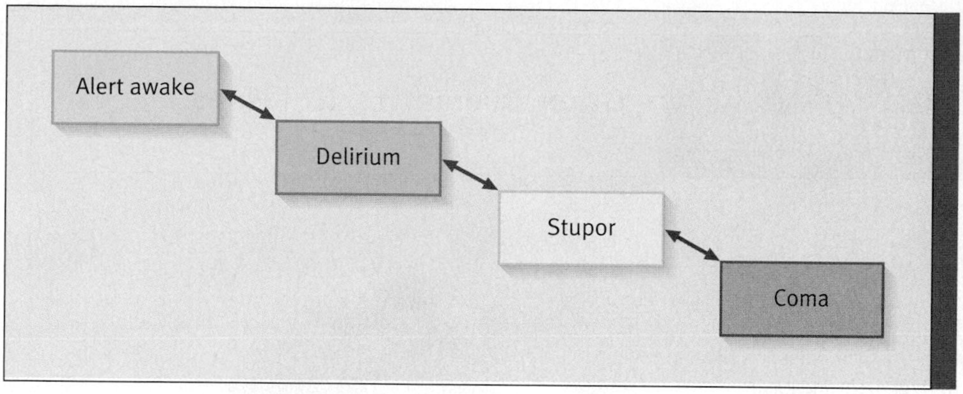

FIGURE 15.3
Continuum of Level of Consciousness

Source: *From* The American Psychiatric Publishing Textbook of Neuropsychiatry and Clinical Neurosciences, *4th ed., p. 526. Reprinted by permission of American Psychiatric Publishing, Inc.,* www.appi.org.

The medications that are used for most cases are neuroleptics (Lee et al., 2004). These are the same drugs that are used to treat schizophrenia. For delirium caused by alcohol or drug withdrawal, benzodiazepines (such as those used in the treatment of anxiety disorders) are used (Trzepacz et al., 2002). In addition, orienting techniques (such as calendars and staff prompting) and environmental modifications (e.g., nightlights) can be helpful. Some patients, however, especially elderly ones, may still have orientation problems, sleep problems, and other difficulties even months after an episode of delirium.

In Review

- What clinical features characterize the syndrome of delirium?
- Describe some common causes of delirium. Who is most at risk of developing this clinical condition?
- How is delirium treated?

Dementia

Unlike delirium, dementia is not a rapidly fluctuating condition. **Dementia** implies loss, and it is characterized by a decline from a previously attained level of functioning (see the table on criteria for dementia). The onset of dementia is typically quite gradual. Early on, the individual is alert and fairly well attuned to events in the environment. Even in the early stages, however, memory is invariably affected, especially memory for recent events. As time goes on, patients with dementia show increasingly marked deficits in abstract thinking, the acquisition of new knowledge or skills, visuospatial comprehension, motor control, problem solving, and judgment. Dementia is often accompanied by an impairment in emotional control and in moral and ethical sensibilities; for example, the person may engage in crude solicitations for sex. Dementia may be progressive (getting worse over time) or static but is more often the former. Occasionally dementia is reversible if it has an underlying cause that can be removed or treated (such as vitamin deficiency).

At least 50 different disorders are known to cause dementia (Bondi & Lange, 2001). They include degenerative diseases such as Huntington's disease and Parkinson's disease (which are described in The World Around Us 15.3). Other causes are strokes (see Ivan et al., 2004); certain infectious diseases such as syphilis, meningitis, and AIDS; intracranial tumors and abscesses; certain dietary deficiencies (especially of the B vitamins); severe or

DSM-IV-TR

Criteria for Dementia

- The development of multiple cognitive deficits manifested by both
  (1) Memory impairment.
  (2) One or more of the following cognitive disturbances:
    (a) Aphasia (language disturbance).
    (b) Apraxia (impaired ability to carry out motor tasks despite having the motor ability to do so).
    (c) Agnosia (failure to recognize or identify objects despite intact sensory function).
    (d) Disturbance in executive functioning (i.e., planning, organizing, sequencing, abstracting).
- The cognitive deficits cause significant impairment in functioning and represent a significant decline from a previous level of functioning.
- The onset of the disorder is gradual and there is continuing cognitive decline.

Source: *Adapted with permission from the* Diagnostic and Statistical Manual of Mental Disorders, *Fourth Edition, Text Revision (Copyright 2000). American Psychiatric Association.*

15.3 THE WORLD AROUND US — Other Dementing Illnesses

Parkinson's Disease

First described in 1817, Parkinson's disease is a form of "shaking palsy." It is the second most common neurodegenerative disorder (after Alzheimer's disease), with a prevalence of 1 per 1,000. The causes of Parkinson's disease are not clear, although both genetic and environmental factors are suspected.

Parkinson's disease is more common in men than in women. In general, it develops in people aged 50 to 70 years. However, the actor Michael J. Fox developed Parkinson's disease when he was only 30 years old. His book *Lucky Man* (2002) offers a moving personal account of his struggle with the illness and well describes some of its major symptoms.

> I need to explain the "on-off" phenomenon. This Jekyll-and-Hyde melodrama is a constant vexation for the P.D. patient, especially one as determined as I was to remain closeted. "On" refers to the time when the medication is telling my brain everything it wants to hear. I'm relatively loose and fluid, my mind clear and movements under control. Only a trained observer could detect my Parkinson's. During one of my "off" periods, even the most myopic layperson, while perhaps not able to diagnose P.D. specifically, can recognize that I am in serious trouble.
>
> When I'm "off," the disease has complete authority over my physical being. I'm utterly in its possession. Sometimes there are flashes of function, and I can be effective at performing basic physical tasks, certainly feeding and dressing myself (though I'll lean toward loafers and pullover sweaters), as well as any chore calling for more brute force than manual dexterity. In my very worst "off" times I experience the full panoply of classic Parkinsonian symptoms: rigidity, shuffling, tremors, lack of balance, diminished small motor control, and the insidious cluster of symptoms that makes communication—written as well as spoken—difficult and sometimes impossible.

Actor Michael J. Fox developed Parkinson's disease when he was only 30 years old. After the diagnosis, he started a foundation to fund research into a cure for the disorder.

Huntington's Disease

Huntington's disease is a rare degenerative disorder of the central nervous system that afflicts about 1 in every 10,000 people. It was first described in 1872 by the American neurologist George Huntington. The illness begins in midlife (the mean age of onset is around 40 years) and it affects men and women in equal numbers. Huntington's disease is characterized by a chronic, progressive chorea (involuntary and irregular movements that flow randomly from one area of the body to another). Patients eventually develop dementia, and death usually occurs within 10 to 20 years of first developing the illness. Huntington's disease is caused by an autosomal dominant gene on chromosome 4. This means that a person who has a parent with the disease has a 50 percent chance of developing the disease himself or herself. A genetic test can be given to at-risk individuals to determine whether they will eventually develop the disorder. However, because there is no cure for Huntington's disease, many at-risk people choose not to know what their genetic destiny is.

repeated head injury; anoxia (oxygen deprivation); and the ingestion or inhalation of toxic substances such as lead or mercury. As Figure 15.4 illustrates, the most common cause of dementia is degenerative brain disease, particularly Alzheimer's disease. In this chapter we will focus primarily on this greatly feared disorder. We will also briefly discuss dementia caused by HIV infection and vascular dementia.

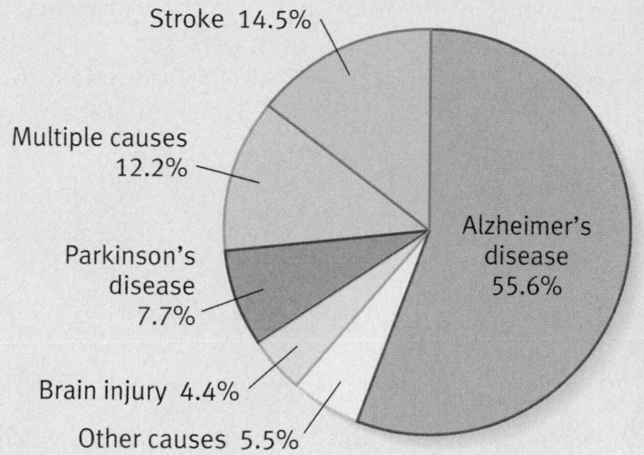

Some Treatable Causes of Dementia

- Medications
- Emotional depression
- Vitamin B_{12} deficiency
- Chronic alcoholism
- Certain tumors or infections of the brain
- Blood clots pressing on the brain
- Metabolic imbalances (including thyroid, kidney, or liver disorders)

FIGURE 15.4

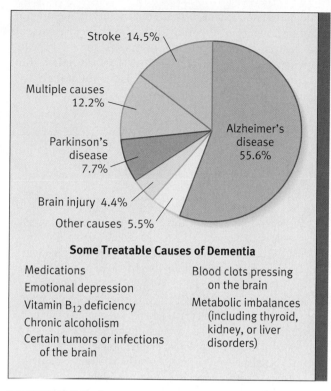

Distribution of Dementia by Probable Cause*

*Numbers do not add up to 100 percent because of rounding off.

Source: *Dennis J. Selkoe. (1993). Aging brain, aging mind. In* Mind and Brain: Readings from Scientific American *(p. 111). New York: Freeman; and Johnny Johnson, Some treatable causes of dementia,* Scientific American *(September 2003). Copyright © 2003 by Scientific American, Inc. All rights reserved. Reprinted by permission.*

Alzheimer's Disease

Alzheimer's disease (AD) takes its name from Alois Alzheimer (1864–1915), the German neuropathologist who first described it in 1907. It is the most common cause of dementia (Askin-Edgar et al., 2002). In the DSM-IV-TR it is referred to (on Axis 1) as "dementia of the Alzheimer's type." Alzheimer's disease is associated with a characteristic dementia syndrome that has an imperceptible onset and a usually slow but progressively deteriorating course, terminating in delirium and death. Public awareness of the disorder has been high since late president Ronald Reagan announced in November 1994 that he was suffering from the disease.

case STUDY — The Forgetful Mail Carrier

Hans is a 66-year-old man who has become so forgetful that his wife is now afraid to leave him alone, even in the house. At the age of 60, Hans took early retirement from his job in a government office, because for the previous 5 years he had not been able to carry out his duties properly. He constantly made mistakes when delivering the mail to different sections of the building. At the same time, he had gradually given up his hobbies and had become more and more quiet. At first, his growing forgetfulness had not been very noticeable in his home environment. Then one day, at the age of 62, when leading a hike in an area he knew well, he could not find the way home. Since then, his memory failures became ever more pronounced. He mislaid things, forgot appointments, and could no longer find his way around the area where he had lived for more than 40 years. He failed to recognize even good friends and lost interest in newspapers and television. (Adapted from Üstün et al., 1996.)

Former president Ronald Reagan raised the public's awareness of Alzheimer's disease after he announced in 1994 that he had been diagnosed with the illness. He died in 2004.

THE CLINICAL PICTURE IN AD The diagnosis of AD is made on the basis of a thorough clinical assessment of the patient but cannot be absolutely confirmed until after the patient's death. This is because an autopsy must be performed in order to see the **amyloid plaques** and **neurofibrillary tangles** that are such distinctive signs of Alzheimer neuropathology. In the living patient, the diagnosis is normally given only after all other potential causes of dementia are ruled out by case and family history,

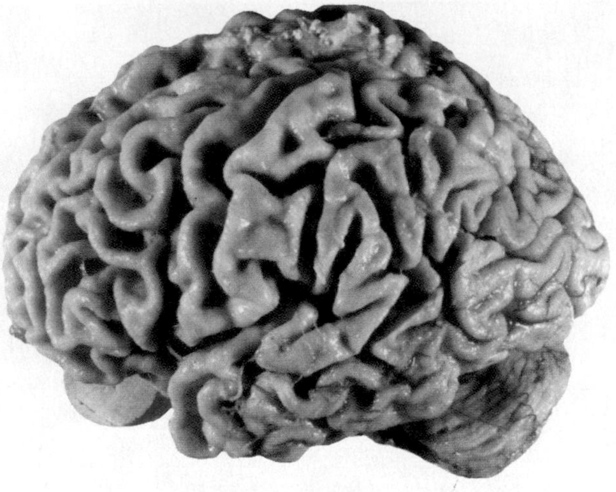

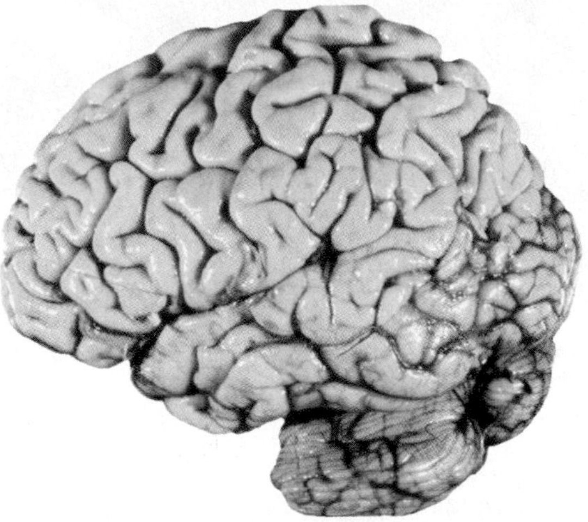

Some brain diseases, Alzheimer's among them, can be diagnosed with certainty only at autopsy. Amyloid plaques, neurofibrillary tangles, and overall brain atrophy (top) are physical evidence of Alzheimer's disease. Compare this to a healthy brain (bottom).

physical examination, and laboratory tests. Neuroimaging techniques are now being explored as a way to facilitate early diagnostic assessment of patients suspected to have AD (e.g., Devanand et al., 2000; D.H.S. Silverman et al., 2001). Although such approaches can aid in the positive diagnosis of AD, the ability of magnetic resonance imaging (MRI) to discriminate AD from other dementias is uncertain (Skoog, 2002).

Alzheimer's disease usually begins after about age 45 (Malaspina et al., 2002). Contrary to what many people believe, it is characterized by multiple cognitive deficits, not just problems with memory. There is a gradual declining course that involves slow mental deterioration. In some cases a physical ailment or some other stressful event is a milestone, but most AD victims pass into a demented state almost imperceptibly, so that it is impossible to date the onset of the disorder precisely. The clinical picture may differ markedly from one person to another, depending on the nature and extent of brain degeneration, the premorbid personality of the individual, the particular stressors present, and the degree of environmental support. The following case, which involves a man who had retired some 7 years prior to his hospitalization, is typical of the deterioration resulting from AD.

case STUDY — Restless and Wandering

During the past 5 years, the patient had shown a progressive loss of interest in his surroundings and during the last year had become increasingly "childish." His wife and eldest son had brought him to the hospital because they felt they could no longer care for him in their home, particularly because of the grandchildren. They stated that he had become careless in his eating and other personal habits and was restless and prone to wandering about at night. He could not seem to remember anything that had happened during the day but was garrulous concerning events of his childhood and middle years.

After admission to the hospital, the patient seemed to deteriorate rapidly. He could rarely remember what had happened a few minutes before, although his memory for remote events of his childhood remained good. When visited by his wife and children, he mistook them for old friends, and he could not recall anything about the visit a few minutes after they had departed. The following brief conversation with the patient, which took place after he had been in the hospital for 9 months (and about 3 months before his death), shows his disorientation for time and person.

DOCTOR: How are you today, Mr. _____?

PATIENT: Oh... hello [looks at doctor in rather puzzled way as if trying to make out who he is].

DOCTOR: Do you know where you are now?

PATIENT: Why yes... I am at home. I must paint the house this summer. It has needed painting for a long time but it seems like I just keep putting it off.

DOCTOR: Can you tell me the day today?

PATIENT: Isn't today Sunday... why, yes, the children are coming over for dinner today. We always have dinner for the whole family on Sunday. My wife was here just a minute ago but I guess she has gone back into the kitchen.

As is illustrated in this case, AD often begins with the person's gradual withdrawal from active engagement with life. There is a narrowing of social activities and interests, a lessening of mental alertness and adaptability, and a lowering of tolerance to new ideas and changes in routine. Often thoughts and activities become self-centered and childlike,

15.4 Developments in Research

The Early Detection of Alzheimer's Disease

Is it possible to detect Alzheimer's disease in its early stages? Many researchers are now actively exploring this issue. To do this, they are using a range of techniques including PET, MRI, and fMRI to study the brain both at rest and at work. In addition, they are studying not only people who have Alzheimer's disease, but also those at high risk for developing the disorder.

One high-risk group is people who are experiencing mild cognitive impairment or MCI. MCI is thought to be on a continuum between healthy aging and the earliest signs of dementia (Petersen et al., 2001). People with MCI report memory problems and perform less well on tests of memory. However, they are generally functioning at a normal level. Roughly half of people who currently have MCI will be diagnosed with AD within the next 3 to 5 years (Petersen et al., 2001). Another high-risk group is people who do not have any cognitive problems but who are considered to be at high risk for developing AD. This could be either because they have a relative with the disorder or because they have the APOE-E4 allele.

The research findings are complex and there are no definitive answers yet. However, a central part of the story involves the hippocampus, a brain area that is involved in memory. Patients with Alzheimer's disease show atrophy of the hippocamus (Chételat et al., 2003; Kubota et al., 2005). This brain area is also less active when AD patients (as compared to controls) are engaged in memory tasks (Kato et al., 2001; Sperling et al., 2003, 2005).

Interestingly, brain scans of people with MCI also show atrophy in a number of brain areas including the hippocampus (Chételat et al., 2002; Du et al., 2001; Jack et al., 1999; Van Der Flier et al., 2002; Visser et al., 1999). Moreover, when functional imaging techniques are used to watch the brain at work, people with MCI (like those with Alzheimer's disease) also show less activation in the hippocampus (Chételat et al., 2003; De Santi et al., 2001). These findings are in contrast to those found in people who are cognitively normal but who are at high risk because they carry the APOE-E4 allele. These people do not show a lack of activation in the hippocampus when they are involved in memory tasks. Instead, brain-imaging studies reveal the opposite. Rather than underactivity, people who are at genetic high risk show increased activity in various parts of the brain, including the hippocampus, when they engage in memory tasks (Bookheimer et al., 2000; Smith et al., 2002).

How can we explain these rather contradictory findings? Current thinking is that the greater degree of brain activation in people who are cognitively normal but at high risk for developing AD reflects the greater effort they need to make to manage the task. Simply put, carriers of the APOE-E4 allele may have to work harder. Because their brain tissue is still healthy (unlike AD patients and people with MCI), we see an *increase* in brain activation in response to a cognitive challenge rather than the decrease in activation that is more typical of AD patients or those with mild cognitive impairment.

Does brain-imaging research allow us to identify people who are going to develop dementia? At present the answer is no. None of the changes are specific enough yet to be able to be used to make an early diagnosis. This, however, is the goal for the future.

including a preoccupation with the bodily functions of eating, digestion, and excretion. As these changes become more severe, additional symptoms—such as impaired memory for recent events, "empty" speech (in which grammar and syntax remain intact but vague and seemingly pointless expressions replace meaningful conversational exchange, for example, "It's a nice day, but it might rain"), messiness, impaired judgment, agitation, and periods of confusion—make their appearance. The clinical picture is by no means uniform until the terminal stages, when the patient is reduced to a vegetative level.

Approximately half of all AD patients display a course of simple deterioration. That is, they gradually lose various mental capacities, typically beginning with memory for recent events and progressing to disorientation, poor judgment, neglect of personal hygiene, and loss of contact with reality to an extent that precludes independent functioning as adults. Perhaps because Alzheimer's disease damages the temporal lobes of the brain, delusions are also found in some patients (Lyketsos et al., 2000). Although delusions of persecution are predominant, delusional jealousy is sometimes seen. Here the person persistently accuses his or her partner or spouse—who is often of advanced age and physically debilitated—of being sexually unfaithful. Family members may be accused of poisoning the patient's food or of plotting to steal the patient's funds. Fortunately, punitive retribution in the form of physical attacks on the "evil-doers" is not especially common, but a combative pattern does occasionally occur, complicating the patient's management. In a study of physically aggressive AD patients, Gilley and associates (1997) found that 80 percent of them were delusional.

With appropriate treatment, which may include medication and the maintenance of a calm, reassuring, and unprovocative social environment, many people with Alzheimer's disease show some alleviation of symptoms. In general, however, deterioration continues its downward course over a period of months or years. Eventually, patients become oblivious to their surroundings, bedridden, and reduced to a vegetative state. Resistance to disease is lowered, and death usually results from pneumonia or some other respiratory or cardiac problem. It is typically taught that patients with AD live about 7 to 10 years after they are diagnosed (Bondi & Lange, 2001). However, data from a large Canadian study suggest that the average duration of life after the individual first contacts a doctor for memory problems may be as little as 3.3 years (Wolfson et al., 2001).

PREVALENCE OF AD Alzheimer's dementia is fast becoming a major public health problem, straining societal and family resources. AD accounts for a large proportion of all cases of dementia (Lyketsos et al., 2000). Although AD is not an inevitable consequence of aging (George Bernard Shaw, for example, wrote plays well into his nineties), age is clearly a major risk factor. For all of us, the brain starts to decrease in size after about age 18. By the time we reach the age of 80, our brain has lost about 15 percent of its original weight (Perl, 1999).

It has been estimated that the rate of AD doubles about every 5 years after a person reaches the age of 40 (Hendrie, 1998). Conservatively, about 1 to 2 percent of the population in the age range of 65 to 74 have AD, and about 25 percent of people older than 85 have the disease (Hendrie, 1998). It is also estimated that approximately 360,000 new cases (incidence) will occur each year and that this number will increase as the population ages (Brookmeyer et al., 1998). Currently, about 4 million people in this country have AD. In the next 50 years, this figure is expected to more than triple (Askin-Edgar et al., 2002). The future prospects regarding the prevalence of AD are therefore somewhat alarming. If we have not solved the problem of preventing AD (or arresting it in its early stages) by around that time, society will be faced with the overwhelming problem of caring for millions of demented senior citizens. The adverse family, social, and economic consequences, already considerable, could become devastating (Fisher & Carstensen, 1990).

For reasons that are not yet clear, women seem to have a slightly higher risk of developing AD than men (Askin-Edgar et al., 2002). Indeed, Alois Alzheimer's original case was a 51-year-old woman. Women tend to live longer than men, but the increased prevalence of women with AD may not be entirely explained by this. The prevalence of Alzheimer's disease is lower in non-Western developed countries such as Japan, as well as in less industrialized countries like Nigeria and India (Malaspina et al., 2002). Such observations have led researchers to suspect that environmental factors such as a high-fat, high-cholesterol diet is implicated in the development of Alzheimer's disease (Sjogren & Blennow, 2005). Also implicating diet, researchers have found that high levels of an amino acid called "homocysteine" (which is a risk factor for heart disease) seem to increase a person's risk of developing Alzheimer's disease later in life (Ravaglia et al., 2005). Levels of homocysteine in the blood can be reduced by taking folic acid and certain B vitamins. Taking statin drugs to lower cholesterol also seems to offer some protection against AD (Sparks et al., 2005).

GENETIC AND ENVIRONMENTAL ASPECTS OF AD When we picture a typical Alzheimer patient, we imagine a person of very advanced age. Sometimes, however, AD begins much earlier and affects people in their forties or fifties. In such cases, the progress of the disease and its associated dementia is often rapid (Heyman et al., 1987). Considerable evidence suggests an especially substantial genetic contribution in early-onset Alzheimer's disease (see Holmes, 2002; Malaspina et al., 2002, for reviews), although different genes may be involved in different families (Breitner et al., 1993). Genes also play a role in late-onset AD.

Cases of **early-onset Alzheimer's disease** appear to be caused by rare genetic mutations. So far three such mutations have been identified. One involves the *APP gene*, which is located on chromosome 21. The fact that a mutation of a gene on chromosome 21 has been found to be important in AD is interesting, because it has long been known that people with Down syndrome (which is caused by a tripling, or trisomy, of chromosome 21; see Chapter 16) who survive beyond about age 40 develop an Alzheimer's-like dementia (Bauer & Shea, 1986; Janicki & Dalton, 1993). They also show similar neuropathological changes (Schapiro & Rapoport, 1987). In addition, cases of Down syndrome tend to occur more frequently in the families of patients with Alzheimer's disease (Heyman et al., 1984; Schupf et al., 1994). One study has found that mothers who gave birth to a child with Down syndrome before age 35 had a 4.8 times greater risk of developing Alzheimer's disease when they were older, compared to mothers of children with other types of mental retardation (Schupf et al., 2001). Mutations of the APP gene are associated with an onset of AD somewhere between 55 and 60 years of age (Cruts et al., 1998).

Other cases of even earlier onset appear to be associated with mutations of a gene on chromosome 14 called *presenilin 1* (PS1) and with a mutation of the *presenilin 2* (PS2) gene on chromosome 1. These genes are associated with an onset of AD somewhere between 30 and 50 years of age (Cruts et al., 1998). One carrier of the PS1 mutation is even known to have developed the disorder at age 24 (Wisniewski et al., 1998). Remember, however, that these mutant genes, which are autosomal dominant genes and so nearly always cause AD in anyone who carries them, are extremely rare. The APP, PS1, and PS2 genetic mutations probably account, together, for no more than about 5 percent of cases of AD.

A gene that may play a greater role in cases of **late-onset Alzheimer's disease** is the APOE (apolipoprotein) gene on chromosome 19. This gene codes for a blood protein that helps carry cholesterol through the bloodstream. It has been discovered that differing forms (genetic alleles) of APOE differentially predict risk for late-onset AD. Three such alleles have been identified, and everyone inherits two of them, one from each parent. One of these alleles, the **APOE-E4 allele,** significantly enhances risk for late-onset AD. Thus a person may inherit zero, one, or two of the APOE-E4 forms, and his or her risk for AD increases correspondingly. Another such allele, APOE-E2, seems to convey protection against late-onset AD. The remaining and most common allele form, APOE-E3, is of "neutral" significance in predicting AD (e.g., Katzman et al., 1997; Lopez et al., 1997; Martin et al., 1997; Plassman & Breitner, 1997). APOE-E4 has been shown to be a significant predictor of memory deterioration in older individuals with or without clinical dementia (Hofer et al., 2002). The APOE-E4 allele is relatively uncommon in Chinese people compared to its frequency in people from Europe or North America. In contrast, people of African descent are especially likely to have this allele (Waters & Nicoll, 2005).

The APOE-E4 allele (which can be detected by a blood test) is overrepresented in all types of AD, including the early-onset and late-onset forms. Approximately 65 percent of patients with AD have at least one copy of the APOE-E4 allele (see Malaspina et al., 2002). Exciting as they are, however, these discoveries still do not account for all cases of AD, not even all cases of late-onset AD (e.g., Bergem et al., 1997). Many people who inherit the most risky APOE pattern (two APOE-E4 alleles) do not succumb to AD. One study found that only 55 percent of people who had two APOE-E4 alleles had developed AD by age 80 (Myers et al., 1996). And others *with* AD have no such APOE-E4 risk factor. In addition, substantial numbers of monozygotic twins are discordant for the disease (Bergem et al., 1997; Breitner et al., 1993).

Why should this be? Current thinking is that our genetic susceptibility interacts with other genetic factors and with environmental factors to determine whether we will succumb to any particular disorder. Clearly, other genes involved in the development of AD still remain to be found. However, environmental factors may also play a key role. As we have noted, the different prevalences of AD across different parts of the world suggest that diet may be an important mediating environmental variable. Other environmental factors under consideration include exposure to metals such as *aluminum,* and experiencing *head trauma.* One prospective study has found that traumatic brain injury is associated, for up to 5 years after the injury, with a fourfold increase in risk of developing Alzheimer's disease (see Malaspina et al., 2002). On the other hand, exposure to *nonsteroidal anti-inflammatory drugs* such as ibuprofen may be protective and lead to a lower risk of AD (Breitner et al., 1994; in't Veld et al., 2001; Weggen et al., 2001). This view leaves open the possibility of reducing or delaying the occurrence of AD by deliberately limiting exposure to risks and taking other preventive measures.

The German neuropathologist Alois Alzheimer was the first to recognize and describe the disease that is now named after him.

NEUROPATHOLOGY When Alois Alzheimer performed the first autopsy on his patient (she was known as Auguste D.), he identified a number of brain abnormalities that are now known to be characteristic of the disease. These are (1) senile plaques, (2) neurofibrillary tangles, and (3) the abnormal appearance of small holes in neuronal tissue, called "granulovacuoles," which derive from cell degeneration. Although plaques and tangles are also found in normal brains, they are present in much greater numbers in patients with AD.

But what goes wrong first? *Senile plaques* are made of deformed nerve cell terminals. An important observation concerning the plaques is that at their core, they contain a sticky protein substance called *beta amyloid.* This substance

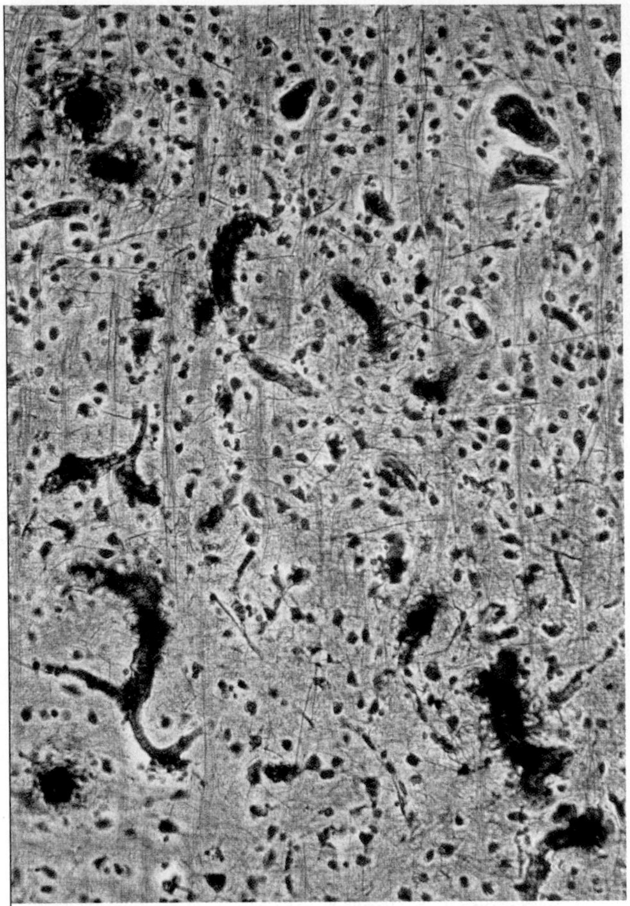

This photomicrograph of a brain tissue specimen from an Alzheimer's patient shows the characteristic plaques (dark patches) and neurofibrillary tangles (irregular pattern of strand-like fibers).

(and a chemical precursor to it) also occurs in abnormal abundance in other parts of AD patients' brains (Hardy, 2004). It is believed that accumulation of beta amyloid is what causes plaques. Having the APOE-E4 form of the APOE gene may also facilitate the aggregation of amyloid in the brain (Askin-Edgar et al., 2002). Moreover, beta amyloid has been shown to be neurotoxic. In other words, it causes cell death (Seppa, 1998). Current thinking is that the accumulation of beta amyloid plays a primary role in the development of AD.

Neurofibrillary tangles are webs of abnormal filaments within a nerve cell. These filaments are made up of another protein called *tau*. Researchers now suspect that abnormal tau protein in the neurofibrillary tangles may be caused by an increasing burden of amyloid in the brain. In other words, the presence of tau is secondary to the presence of amyloid and is a sign that the disease is progressing (Hardy, 2004). Animal studies of mice that have been genetically modified to be highly susceptible to developing AD (so-called "transgenic mice") support this idea (Götz et al., 2001; Lewis et al., 2001). If this idea proves correct, it suggests that the most promising drug treatments for Alzheimer's disease may be those that can target and prevent amyloid build-up.

Another notable alteration in AD concerns the neurotransmitter *acetylcholine* (ACh). This neurotransmitter is known to be important in the mediation of memory. Although there is widespread destruction of neurons in AD, particularly in the area of the hippocampus (Adler, 1994; Mori et al., 1997b), evidence suggests that among the earliest and most severely affected structures are a cluster of cell bodies located in the basal forebrain and involved in the release of ACh (Whitehouse et al., 1982). The reduction in brain ACh activity in patients with AD is correlated with the extent of neuronal damage (i.e., plaques, tangles) that they have sustained (Debettignles et al., 1997).

The loss of cells that produce ACh makes a bad situation much worse. Because ACh is so important in memory, its depletion contributes greatly to the cognitive and behavioral deficits that are characteristic of AD. For this reason, drugs (called "cholinesterase inhibitors") that inhibit the breakdown of ACh (and so increase the availability of this neurotransmitter) can be clinically beneficial for patients (Whitehouse, 1993; Winblad et al., 2001).

TREATMENTS AND OUTCOMES IN AD We currently have no treatment for AD that will restore functions once they have been destroyed or lost. Until something that can do this is discovered, we have only palliative measures that diminish patient and caregiver distress and relieve as far as possible those complications of the disorder such as combativeness that increase the difficulties of management.

Some common problematic behaviors associated with AD (and with other dementias as well) are wandering off, incontinence, inappropriate sexual behavior, and inadequate self-care skills. These can be somewhat controlled via behavioral approaches (see Chapter 17). Because behavioral treatments need not be dependent on complex cognitive and communication abilities (which tend to be lacking in AD patients), they may be particularly well suited for therapeutic intervention with this group. In general, reports of results are moderately encouraging in terms of reducing unnecessary frustration and embarrassment for the patient and difficulty for the caregiver (Fisher & Carstensen, 1990; Mintzer et al., 1997; Teri et al., 1997).

Active treatment research has also focused on the consistent findings of acetylcholine depletion in AD. The reasoning here is that it might be possible to improve functioning by administering drugs that enhance the availability of brain ACh. Currently, the most effective way of doing so is by inhibiting the production of acetylcholinesterase, the principal enzyme involved in the metabolic breakdown of acetylcholine. This is the rationale for administering drugs such as tacrine (Cognex) and donepezil (Aricept). Winblad and colleagues (2001) studied 286 patients who were randomly assigned to receive either medication (donepezil) or placebo for a 1-year

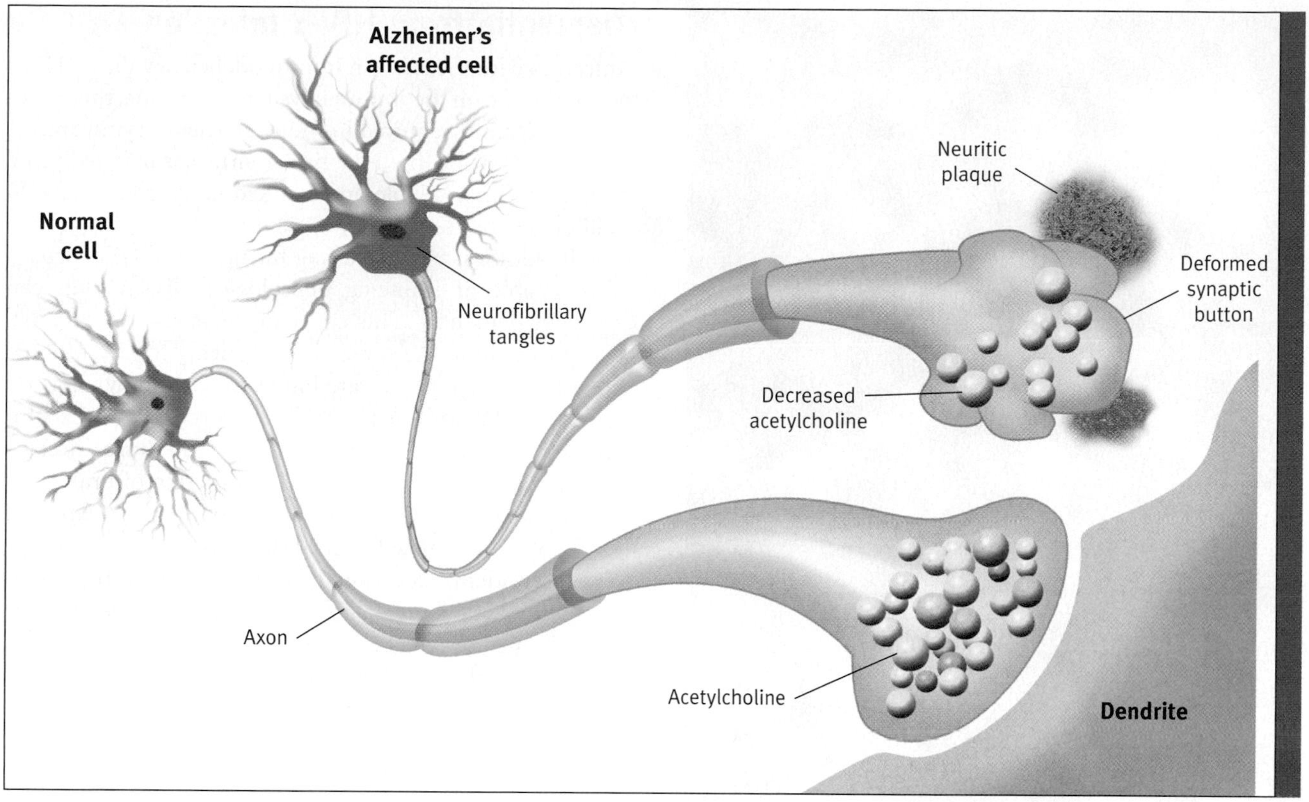

FIGURE 15.5

Depletion of Acetylcholine in Alzheimer's Patients

Alzheimer's Disease is characterized by nerve cell abnormalities that include the presence of neurofibrillary tangles, neuritic plaques of beta amyloid, and decreased levels of the neurotransmitter acetylcholine.

period. Patients' cognitive functioning and ability to perform daily activities were measured at the start of the study and again at regular intervals over the study period. Patients who received the medication did better overall than patients who received the placebo. However, all patients declined in their functioning over the course of the study. Furthermore, although donepezil does help patients a little, these gains do not mean that patients taking the drug are any less likely to avoid institutionalization than those who are not taking the medication (AD2000 Collaborative Group, 2004).

The newest medication that has been approved to treat AD is memantine, which is marketed as Namenda. Unlike other approved medications, memantine is not a cholinesterase inhibitor. Instead, it appears to regulate the activity of the neurotransmitter glutamate, perhaps by protecting cells against excess glutamate by partially blocking NMDA receptors. Memantine, which can be used alone or in combination with donepezil, appears to provide patients with some cognitive benefits (Forchetti, 2005; Reisberg et al., 2003).

Yet another line of treatment research is focused on developing vaccines that might help clear away any accumulated amyloid plaques. Although initial findings from animal research looked promising (e.g., McLaurin et al., 2002), human clinical trials of a vaccine were stopped abruptly in 2002 because of dangerous side effects. Nonetheless, researchers are continuing to explore novel treatment approaches (Gestwicki et al., 2004; Hardy, 2004; Hutter-Paier et al., 2004). Many drug companies are now working on this problem.

Unfortunately, neuronal cells that have died with the advance of Alzheimer's neuropathology are permanently lost. This means that even if some new treatment could halt a patient's progressive loss of brain tissue, he or she would still be left seriously impaired. The real key to effective intervention must therefore be seen as preventive, or at least as deployable at the first sign of Alzheimer's (see Schultz, 2000). For this reason, researchers are now exploring ways to detect AD in its very early stages (see Developments in Research 15.4 on p. 543).

TREATING CAREGIVERS It is estimated that about 30 to 40 percent of nursing home residents are AD patients. Some patients with AD also reside in mental hospitals or other types of institutional settings. Most, however, live in the community, typically with family members. This arrangement is often extremely stressful for caregivers (Fisher & Carstensen, 1990; Intrieri & Rapp, 1994; Shaw et al., 1997).

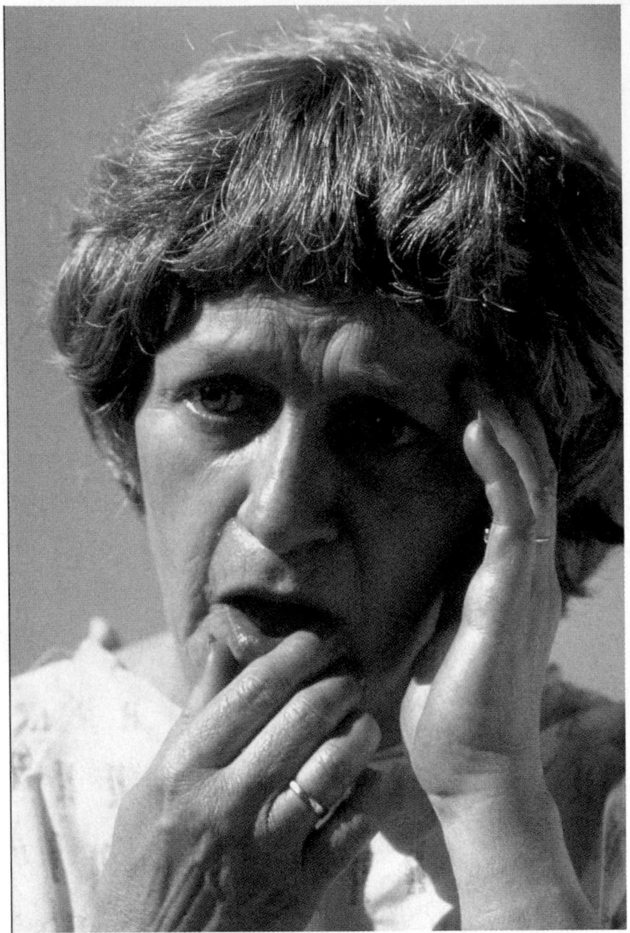

Patients with Alzheimer's disease slowly lose their mental capacities, beginning with memory and progressing to disorientation, poor judgment, and neglect of personal hygiene.

Any comprehensive approach to therapeutic intervention must consider the situation of caregivers. As the disease advances, they are confronted not only with many challenging management problems but also with the "social death" of the patient as a person and their own "anticipatory grief" (Gilhooly et al., 1994). As a group, caregivers are at extraordinarily high risk for developing depression (Cohen & Eisdorfer, 1988), especially if they are husbands caring for impaired wives (Robinson-Whelen & Kiecolt-Glaser, 1997; Tower et al., 1997). For example, one study showed that in those caregivers who were not clinically depressed, cortisol levels were essentially similar to those in patients with major depression (Da Roza, Davis & Cowen, 2001). Caregivers of patients with AD tend to consume high quantities of psychotropic medication themselves and to report many stress symptoms (Hinrichsen & Niederehe, 1994). Providing caregivers with counseling and supportive therapy is very beneficial and produces measurable reductions in their levels of depression (Mittelman et al., 2004).

Dementia from HIV-1 Infection

Infection with the Human Immunodeficiency Virus (HIV) wreaks havoc on the immune system. Over time, this infection can lead to acquired immune deficiency syndrome or AIDS. Worldwide, the HIV type 1 virus has infected more than 36 million people and resulted in approximately 20 million deaths (Kaul et al., 2005).

In addition to devastating the body, the HIV virus is also capable of inducing neurological disease that can result in dementia. This can happen in two ways. First, because the immune system is weakened, people with HIV are more susceptible to rare infections caused by parasites and fungi (Woodward, 2001). However, the virus also appears capable of damaging the brain more directly, resulting in neuronal injury and destruction of brain cells (see Snider et al., 1983; Kaul et al., 2005). Several different forms of HIV-induced central nervous system pathology have been identified, some of which appear to be associated with the emergence of psychotic (e.g., delusional) phenomena (Sewell et al., 1994).

The neuropathology of **HIV-associated dementia** involves various changes in the brain, among them generalized atrophy, edema (swelling), inflammation, and patches of demyelination (Adams & Ferraro, 1997; Gabuzda & Hirsch, 1987; Gray et al., 1988; Price et al., 1988; Sewell et al., 1994). No brain area may be entirely spared, but the damage appears to be concentrated in subcortical regions, notably the central white matter, the tissue surrounding the ventricles, and deeper gray matter structures such as the basal ganglia and thalamus. Ninety percent of AIDS patients show evidence of such changes on autopsy (Adams & Ferraro, 1997).

The neuropsychological features of AIDS, which tend to appear as a late phase of HIV infection (though often before the full development of AIDS itself), usually begin with mild memory difficulties, psychomotor slowing, and diminished attention and concentration (see Fernandez et al., 2002, for a review). Progression is typically rapid after this point, with clear-cut dementia appearing in many cases within 1 year, although considerably longer periods have been reported. In general, and consistent with autopsy findings, the neuropsychological evidence points primarily to a disruption of brain function at the subcortical level; the most reliably reported finding is that of notably delayed reaction time (Law & Mapou, 1997). The later phases of AIDS dementia include behavioral regression, confusion, psychotic thinking, apathy, and marked withdrawal.

Estimates from the early 1990s suggested HIV-related dementia was present in 20-30% of people with advanced HIV disease. Fortunately, the arrival of highly active antiretroviral therapy has not only resulted in infected people living longer but it has also reduced the prevalence of HIV-related dementia to around 10.5% (Kaul et al., 2005). However, although rates of frank dementia have decreased, around 30% of people who are infected with the HIV virus show some signs of mild cognitive impairment (McArthur, 2004). Moreover, for reasons that are not yet clear, women may be at especially high risk of HIV-related cognitive impairment (McArthur, 2004).

Treatment with antiretroviral therapy does not fully prevent the HIV virus from damaging the brain (Kaul et al., 2005). This may be because HIV penetrates into the nervous system soon after a person becomes infected. What this means is that, even though the new therapies have made HIV/AIDS a chronic but manageable condition (at least for those who have access to the necessary medications) prevention of infection remains the only certain strategy for avoiding the cognitive impairments associated with this disease.

Vascular Dementia

Vascular dementia (VAD), formerly called "multi-infarct dementia," is frequently confused with AD because of its similar clinical picture of progressive dementia and its increasing incidence and prevalence rates with advancing age. It is actually an entirely different disease in terms of its underlying neuropathology. In this disorder, a series of circumscribed cerebral infarcts—interruptions of the blood supply to minute areas of the brain because of arterial disease, commonly known as "small strokes"—cumulatively destroy neurons over expanding brain regions. The affected regions become soft and may degenerate over time, leaving only cavities. Although this disorder tends to have a more varied early clinical picture than AD (Wallin & Blennow, 1993), the progressive loss of cells leads to brain atrophy and behavioral impairments that ultimately mimic those of AD (Bowler et al., 1997).

VAD tends to occur after the age of 50 and affects more men than women (Askin-Edgar et al., 2002). Abnormalities of gait (e.g., being unsteady on one's feet) may be an early predictor of this condition (Verghese et al., 2002). Vascular dementia is less common than AD, accounting for only some 19 percent of dementia cases in a community sample aged 65 years or older (Lyketsos et al., 2000). One reason for this is that VAD has a much shorter average course because of a patient's vulnerability to sudden death from stroke or cardiovascular disease (Askin-Edgar et al., 2002). Accompanying mood disorders are also more common in vascular dementia than in Alzheimer's disease, perhaps because subcortical areas of the brain are more affected (Lyketsos et al., 2000). Occasionally, an unfortunate patient will be discovered to have both AD and VAD, a condition commonly referred to as "mixed" dementia (Cohen et al., 1997).

The medical treatment of VAD, though complicated, offers slightly more hope than that of Alzheimer's disease. Unlike AD, the basic problem of cerebral arteriosclerosis (decreased elasticity of brain arteries) can be medically managed to some extent, perhaps decreasing the likelihood of further strokes. The daunting problems that caregivers face, however, are much the same in the two conditions, indicating the appropriateness of support groups, stress reduction techniques, and the like.

In Review

- What is dementia? How is it different from delirium?
- List five diseases or clinical disorders that can cause dementia.
- Describe some of the major risk factors for Alzheimer's disease.
- What kinds of neuropathological abnormalities are typical of the Alzheimer's brain?

Amnestic Syndrome

Amnestic is just another way of saying "amnesia," and the characteristic feature of **amnestic syndrome** is strikingly disturbed memory. Immediate recall (that is, the ability to repeat what has just been heard) is not usually affected. Memory for remote past events is also usually relatively preserved. However, short-term memory is typically so impaired that the person is unable to recall events that took place only a few minutes previously. To compensate, patients sometimes confabulate, apparently making up events to fill in the void that they have in their memories.

In contrast to the dementia syndrome, overall cognitive functioning in the amnestic syndrome may remain relatively intact. The affected person may thus be able to execute a complex task if it provides its own distinctive cues for each stage of the task. This is well illustrated in the film *Memento,* where the main character, Leonard, has an amnestic disorder caused by a traumatic head injury. Although he has severe *anterograde amnesia* and is unable to hold anything in his short-term memory for more than a minute or so, he uses polaroid photographs, notes, and tattoos on his body to retain the information he needs to search for his wife's killer.

Brain damage is the root cause of amnestic disorders. Most commonly, amnestic syndrome is caused by chronic alcohol use and associated deficiency in vitamin B1 (thiamine). This was the cause of the memory loss of the patient whose case is described below. Another common cause is head trauma. Stroke, surgery in the temporal lobe area of the brain, hypoxia (oxygen deprivation), and some forms of brain infections (such as encephalitis) can also

DSM-IV-TR

Criteria for Amnestic Disorder

- The development of memory impairment (i.e., inability to learn new information or to recall previously learned information).
- The memory disturbance causes significant impairment in functioning and represents a decline from a previous level of functioning.
- The memory disturbance does not occur exclusively during the course of a delirium or a dementia.

Source: *Adapted with permission from the* Diagnostic and Statistical Manual of Mental Disorders, *Fourth Edition, Text Revision (Copyright 2000). American Psychiatric Association.*

lead to amnestic disorder. In these cases, depending on the nature and extent of damage to the affected neural structures and on the treatment undertaken, the syndrome may in time abate wholly or partially. A wide range of techniques has been developed to assist the good-prognosis amnestic patient in remembering recent events (e.g., Gouvier et al., 1997).

Moreover, because procedural memory (i.e., the ability to learn routines, skills, and actions) is often preserved in patients with amnesia, even patients without memory for specific personal experiences can still can be taught to perform tasks that might help them reenter the workforce (Cavaco et al., 2004).

case STUDY He Forgot the Name of His Daughter

A powerfully built six-footer, Charles Jackson still showed traces of a military bearing. Before he left the army a year before, he had been demoted to buck private; this was the culmination of a string of disciplinary actions for drunkenness.

For over a year he had had monthly consultations with the current interviewer. On this occasion, the interviewer asked when they had last met. Charles replied, "Well, I just don't know. What do you think?" To the follow-up question, he said he guessed he had seen the interviewer before. "Maybe it was last week."

Asking him to remain seated, the interviewer went into the waiting room to ask Mrs. Jackson how she thought her husband was doing. She said, "Oh, he's about the same as before. He sketches some. But mostly he just sits around the house and watches TV. I come home and ask him what he's watching, but he can't even tell me."

At any rate, Charles was no longer drinking, not since they had moved to the country. It was at least 2 miles to the nearest convenience store, and he didn't walk very well anymore. "But he still talks about drinking. Sometimes he seems to think he's still in the army. He orders me to go buy him a quart of gin."

Charles remembered quite a few things, if they happened long enough ago—the gin, for example, and getting drunk with his father when he was a boy. But he couldn't remember the name of his daughter, who was two and a half. Most of the time, he just called her "the girl."

The interviewer walked back into the inner office. Charles looked up and smiled.

"Have I seen you before?" asked the interviewer.

"Well, I'm pretty sure."

"When was it?"

"It might have been last week."

(Adapted from Morrison, 1995, pp. 50–51.)

In Review

- What are the most striking clinical features of amnestic syndrome?
- What are some of the major causes of amnestic syndrome?

Disorders Involving Head Injury

Traumatic brain injury (TBI) occurs frequently, affecting more than 2 million people each year in the United States. The most common cause of TBI is motor vehicle accidents. Other causes include falls, violent assaults, and sports injuries (although it is likely that the vast majority of these are never even reported). Men aged 15 to 24 are at the highest risk for brain injury. Stated simply, disorders that result from traumatic injuries to the brain are more common than any other forms of neurological disease except headache (see Silver et al., 2002, for a review). In DSM-IV-TR, brain injuries that have notable, long-standing effects on adaptive functioning are coded on Axis I using the appropriate syndromal descriptive phrase, with the qualifier "due to head trauma." (Examples include "dementia due to head trauma," "amnestic disorder due to head trauma," and the like.)

The Clinical Picture

Clinicians distinguish three general types of TBI because the clinical pictures and residual problems vary somewhat among them: (1) closed-head injury, in which the cranium remains intact; (2) penetrating head injury, in which the cranium, as well as the underlying brain, are penetrated by some object such as a bullet; and (3) skull fracture, with or without compression of the brain by fragmented bone concavity. Post-trauma epilepsy, for example, is unusual in closed-head injury but a rather common outcome of the other two forms of head injury. In closed-head injury, the damage to the brain is indirect because it is produced either by inertial forces that cause the brain to come into violent contact with the interior skull wall or by rotational forces that twist the brain mass relative to the brain stem. Not uncommonly, closed-head injury also causes diffuse neuron damage because of the inertial force. In other words, the rapid movement of the rigid cranium is stopped on contact with an unyielding object. However, the softer brain tissue within keeps moving, and this has a shearing effect on nerve fibers and their synaptic interconnections. As The World Around Us 15.5 indicates, riding roller coasters that generate high g-forces may also cause brain injury.

15.5 The World Around Us

Can Thrill Rides Cause Brain Damage?

In 1999 a 24-year-old Japanese woman developed a headache after spending the day at the Fujikyu Highland Park in Japan. During that time, she had ridden twice on each of three different roller coasters, including the Fujiyama. At 259 feet, this is the fifth tallest roller coaster in the world. It reaches speeds of over 81 miles per hour and it has a 229-foot drop. The young woman's headache lasted 4 days and was initially diagnosed as a tension headache. It was only 4 months later, after she had received an MRI scan, that it became clear that this young woman had something much more serious: She had subdural hematomas (areas of bleeding) on both sides of her brain (see Fukutake et al., 2000).

The thrill-ride-seeking public is always hungry for new and more extreme rides, and the amusement park industry has responded accordingly. In 2001, the fastest roller coaster rides were the Tower of Terror in Queensland, Australia, and Superman, The Escape at Six Flags Magic Mountain in Los Angeles, California. Both rides also have the greatest drops in the world (328 feet). Moreover, technological advances are now allowing more and more extreme rides to be developed. Some people worry, however, that such rides expose the body to dangerously high g-forces.

G-force is a measure of the acceleration of an object divided by the acceleration caused by gravity. In the United States, there are now at least 18 roller coasters that produce g-forces above 4.0 Gs. Taz's Tornado at Six Flags AstroWorld in Houston, Texas, is the most extreme at 6.5 Gs. Many others, including the Rock 'n' Roll Coaster at Disney MGM Studios in Orlando, Florida, register 5.0 Gs.

The U.S. military has studied g-forces and found that sustained (i.e., 4.2 seconds or longer) exposure to high g-forces leads to a loss of consciousness. Because people do not routinely black out when they ride roller coasters, we can assume that most of the applied g-forces that impact riders occur for less time than this. Nonetheless, the g-forces created by extreme rides may cause more than just thrills. A review of the literature (see Braksiek & Roberts, 2002) suggests that a tiny minority of riders may experience neurological injury as a consequence of riding roller coasters. Although the individual risk is slight, the rotational and positional changes that the body experiences may create small tears in delicate blood vessels. To date, there are 58 known cases of brain injuries from roller coasters, nearly all of which have occurred since 1990 (Markey, 2002). Although this risk may not be enough to dissuade you from heading to a theme park the next time you want to have some fun, it is already prompting calls for greater oversight of the industry and demands for enforceable g-force standards.

Exposure to high g-forces, such as those experienced on some theme park rides, can cause neurological injury in some individuals by creating small tears in delicate blood vessels in the brain.

Neuropsychologically significant head injuries usually give rise to immediate acute reactions such as unconsciousness and disruption of circulatory, metabolic, and neurotransmitter regulation. Normally, if a head injury is severe enough to result in unconsciousness, the person experiences **retrograde amnesia,** or inability to recall events immediately *preceding* the injury. Apparently, such trauma interferes with the brain's capacity to consolidate into long-term storage the events that were still being processed at the time of the trauma. As you learned earlier, **anterograde amnesia** (also called "post-traumatic amnesia") is the inability to store effectively in memory events that happen during variable periods of time *after* the trauma. It is also frequently observed and is regarded by many as a negative prognostic sign.

A person rendered unconscious by a head injury usually passes through stages of stupor and confusion on the way to recovering clear consciousness. This recovery of consciousness may be complete in the course of minutes, or it may take hours or days. Following a severe injury and loss of consciousness, a person's pulse, temperature, blood pressure, and important aspects of brain metabolism are all affected, and survival may be uncertain. In rare cases an individual may live for extended periods of time without regaining consciousness in a condition known as *coma.* The duration of the coma is generally related to the severity of the injury. If the patient survives, coma may be followed by delirium, marked by acute excitement and disorientation and hallucinations. Gradually the confusion may clear up and the individual may regain contact with reality. Individual courses of recovery are highly variable (Crepeau & Scherzer, 1993; Powell & Wilson, 1994).

Even when a TBI seems relatively mild and there is a good recovery, careful neuropsychological assessment may reveal subtle residual impairment. This is well illustrated in the following case.

case STUDY — Hit on the Head with a Rake

A 17-year-old girl was referred by her father for neuropsychiatric evaluation because of the many changes that had been observed in her personality during the past 2 years. She had been an A student and had been involved in many extracurricular activities during her sophomore year in high school. But now, as a senior, she was barely able to maintain a C average, was "hanging around with the bad kids," and was frequently using marijuana and alcohol. A careful history revealed that 2 years before, her older brother had hit her in the forehead with a rake, which stunned her but did not cause her to lose consciousness. Although she had a headache after the accident, no psychiatric or neurological follow-up was pursued.

Neuropsychological testing at the time of evaluation revealed a significant decline in intellectual functioning from her "preinjury" state. Testing revealed poor concentration, attention, memory, and reasoning abilities. Academically, she was unable to "keep up" with the friends she had had before her injury. She began to socialize with a group of students who had little interest in academics, and she began to see herself as a rebel. When the neuropsychological test results were explained to the patient and her family as a consequence of the brain injury, she and her family were able to understand the "defensive" reaction to her changed social behavior. (Adapted from Silver et al., 2002.)

Large numbers of relatively mild closed-head brain concussions and contusions (bruises) occur every year as a result of auto collisions, athletic injuries, falls, and other mishaps. Temporary loss of consciousness and postimpact confusion are the most common and salient immediate symptoms. Although there is controversy about whether these mild brain injuries produce significant long-standing symptoms or impairments (Dikmen & Levin, 1993; Zasler, 1993), a recent study has shown that older individuals and individuals who have TBI share several changes in information-processing speed (Bashore & Ridderinkhof, 2002).

We are also learning something about the factors that may increase a person's susceptibility to having problems after a brain injury. One important risk factor appears to be the presence of the APOE-E4 allele that we discussed earlier (Waters & Nicoll, 2005). In one study of boxers, the presence of the APOE-E4 genetic risk factor was associated with more chronic neurological deficits (Jordan et al., 1997). A study of patients being treated in a neurosurgical unit found that APOE-E4 predicted patients doing more poorly at 6-month follow-up. This was true even after controlling for such factors as severity of the initial injury (Teasdale et al., 1997).

Perhaps the most famous historical example of traumatic brain injury is the case of Phineas Gage, reported by Dr. J. M. Harlow in 1868 (here reprinted from *History of Psychiatry*, 1993, Vol. 4, pp. 271–281). Because it is of both historical and descriptive significance, it merits our attention. Incidentally, Gage's skull and the tamping iron that damaged it are on display at Harvard Medical School.

case STUDY — The Story of Phineas Gage

The accident occurred in Cavendish, Vermont, on the line of the Rutland and Burlington Railroad, at that time being built, on the 13th of September, 1848, and was occasioned by the premature explosion of a blast, when this iron, known to blasters as a tamping iron, and which I now show you, was shot through the face and head.

The subject of it was Phineas P. Gage, a perfectly healthy, strong, and active young man, twenty-five years of age. . . . Gage was foreman of a gang of men employed in excavating rock, for the road way. . . .

The missile entered by its pointed end, the left side of the face, immediately anterior to the angle of the lower jaw, and passing obliquely upwards, and obliquely backwards, emerged in the median line, at the back part of the frontal bone, near the coronal suture. . . .

The iron which thus traversed the head, is round and rendered comparatively smooth by use, and is three feet seven inches in length, one and one fourth inches in its largest diameter, and weighs thirteen and one fourth pounds. . . .

The patient was thrown upon his back by the explosion, and gave a few convulsive motions of the extremities, but spoke in a few minutes. His men (with whom he was a great favorite) took him in their arms and carried him to the road, only a few rods distant, and put him into an ox cart, in which he rode, supported in a sitting posture, fully three quarters of a mile to his hotel. He got out of the cart himself, with a little assistance from his men, and an hour afterwards (with what I could aid him by taking hold of his left arm) walked up a long flight of stairs, and got upon the bed in the room where he was dressed. He seemed perfectly conscious, but was becoming exhausted from the hemorrhage, which by this time was quite profuse, the blood pouring from the lacerated sinus in the top of his head, and also finding its way into the stomach, which ejected it as often as every fifteen or twenty minutes. He bore his sufferings with firmness, and directed my attention to the hole in his cheek, saying, "the iron entered there and passed through my head."

Some time later Dr. Harlow made the following report:

> His physical health is good, and I am inclined to say that he has recovered. Has no pain in head, but says it has a queer feeling which he is not able to describe. Applied for his situation as foreman, but is undecided whether to work or travel. His contractors, who regarded him as the most efficient and capable foreman in their employ previous to his injury, considered the change in his mind so marked that they could not give him his place again. The equilibrium or balance, so to speak, between his intellectual faculties and animal propensities, seems to have been destroyed. He is fitful, irreverent, indulging at times in the grossest profanity (which was not previously his custom), manifesting but little deference for his fellows, impatient of restraint or advice when it conflicts with his desires, at times pertinaciously obstinate, yet capricious and vacillating, devising many plans of future operations, which are no sooner arranged than they are abandoned in turn for others . . . his mind is radically changed, so decidedly that his friends and acquaintances said he was "no longer Gage."

As Stuss and colleagues (1992) have noted, Gage's persistent post-trauma difficulties are fairly characteristic for severe frontal lobe damage; emotional dyscontrol and personality alterations, including impairment of self-reflective awareness, are often prominent features of behavior change due to this type of injury. In general, however, personality disturbances secondary to traumatic brain injury are somewhat unpredictable owing to the varied structural pathology that is usually involved in such injuries (Prigatano, 1992).

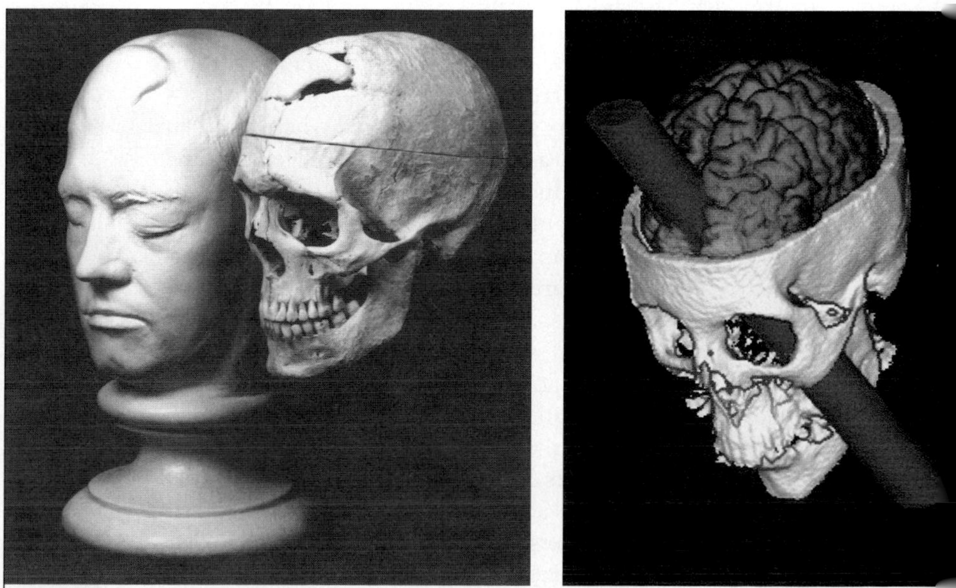

Though Phineas Gage survived when a tamping iron entered his face and shot through his head, his personality was altered such that his friends found that he was "no longer Gage."

Treatments and Outcomes

Prompt treatment of brain injury may prevent further damage, for example, when pooled blood under pressure is removed from the skull. In many instances, including some that may initially be considered mild, immediate medical treatment may have to be supplemented by a long-range program of reeducation and rehabilitation.

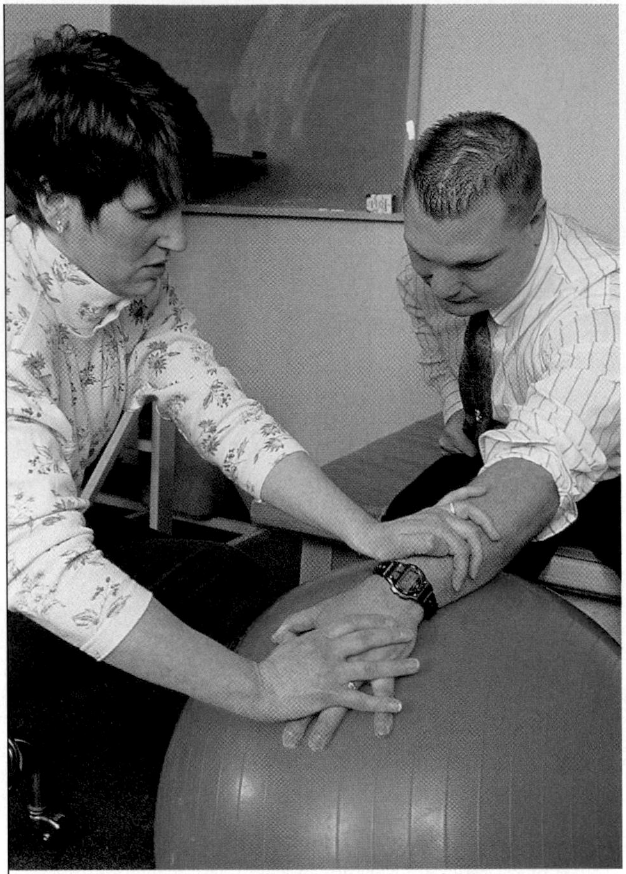
This police officer received a gunshot head wound in the line of duty and is participating in physical therapy to improve muscle tone and function in his left arm.

Although many TBI patients show few residual effects from their injury, particularly if they have experienced only a brief loss of consciousness, other patients sustain definite and long-lasting impairment. Common aftereffects of moderate brain injury include chronic headaches, anxiety, irritability, dizziness, easy fatigability, and impaired memory and concentration. Where the brain damage is extensive, a patient's general intellectual level may be markedly reduced, especially if he or she has suffered severe temporal lobe or parietal lobe lesions. Most victims have significant delays in returning to their occupations, and many are unable to return at all (Bennett et al., 1997; Dikmen et al., 1994; Goran et al., 1997). Other losses of adult social role functioning are also common (Hallett et al., 1994). Some 24 percent of TBI cases, overall, develop post-traumatic epilepsy, presumably because of the growth of scar tissue in the brain. Seizures usually develop within 2 years of the head injury. For decades after a head injury, there is also an elevated risk of depression as well as other disorders such as substance abuse, anxiety disorders, and personality disorders (Holsinger et al., 2002; Koponen et al., 2002).

In a minority of brain injury cases, dramatic personality changes occur such as those described in the case of Phineas Gage. Other kinds of personality changes include passivity, loss of drive and spontaneity, agitation, anxiety, depression, and paranoid suspiciousness. Like cognitive changes, the kinds of personality changes that emerge in severely damaged people depend, in large measure, on the site and extent of their injury (Prigatano, 1992). However, even though more than half the people who sustain TBI develop psychological symptoms, and even though alleviation of such symptoms can improve rehabilitation outcome, there are currently few studies of risk factors, pathogenesis, and treatment of these disturbances (Rao & Lyketsos, 2002).

Children who undergo significant traumatic brain injury are more likely to be adversely affected the younger they are at the time of injury and the less language, fine-motor, and other competencies they have. This is because brain damage makes it harder to learn new skills and because young children have fewer developed skills to begin with. The severity of their injury and the degree to which their environment is accommodating also affect children's recovery (Anderson et al., 1997; Taylor & Alden, 1997; Yeates et al., 1997). When the injury is mild, most children emerge without lasting negative effects (Satz et al., 1997).

Treatment of traumatic brain injury beyond the purely medical phase is often long, difficult, and expensive. It requires careful and continuing assessment of neuropsychological functioning and the design of interventions intended to overcome the deficits that remain. Not surprisingly, people from many disciplines may become involved

TABLE 15.2 Predictors of Clinical Outcome after Traumatic Brain Injury

Outcome is more favorable when there is:

- only a short period of unconsciousness or post-traumatic anterograde amnesia,
- minimal cognitive impairment,
- a well-functioning preinjury personality,
- higher educational attainment,
- a stable preinjury work history,
- motivation to recover or make the most of residual capacities,
- a favorable life situation to which to return,
- early intervention,
- an appropriate program of rehabilitation and retraining.

Sources: Bennett et al., 1997; Dikmen et al., 1994; Diller & Gordon, 1981; Mackay, 1994; MacMillan et al., 2002.

including neurologists; psychologists and neuropsychologists; occupational, physical, and speech/language therapists; cognitive rehabilitation specialists; and vocational and recreational therapists. Often, a treatment goal is to provide patients with new techniques to compensate for losses that may be permanent (Bennett et al., 1997). However, research is now showing that patients with TBI may also benefit from treatment with donepezil, an acetylcholinesterase inhibitor widely used in the treatment of Alzheimer's disease (Zhang et al., 2004). Table 15.2 shows some of the variables that are associated with patients having a more favorable outcome after a traumatic brain injury.

In Review

- What is the link between the APOE-E4 allele and problems after head injury?
- What kinds of clinical problems are associated with head injury in the short and longer term?
- What factors are associated with the degree of disability after head injury?

Unresolved Issues

Can Dietary Supplements Enhance Brain Functioning?

It is an unfortunate fact that our memories get worse as we get older. In an effort to slow this decline (which may begin as young as age 30), many people are turning to dietary supplements and herbal preparations. Herbs such as *Ginkgo biloba* (which is derived from the leaves of the ginkgo tree) are widely used and have been part of traditional Chinese medicine for centuries. Ginkgo is now approved as a treatment for dementia in Germany. But is there any scientific validity to the claims that are made?

Using meta-analysis to examine the results of over 50 studies, Oken and colleagues (1998) concluded that patients with Alzheimer's disease who received ginkgo performed better cognitively than patients who took placebo. In fact, the magnitude of the differences was comparable to that found when patients take donepezil, a drug that is widely used to treat Alzheimer's disease. However, a more recent study that was both large and methodologically sound found that patients with mild to moderate dementia did not derive any clinically meaningful benefits from taking ginkgo (van Dongen et al., 2000).

The most recent statement on this issue is a thorough review of the literature by Gold and his colleagues (2002). They note that patients who have mild to moderate cognitive impairment and who take ginkgo tend to show modest but significant improvement in cognitive functioning when compared to patients who take placebo. They also caution, however, that very few animal studies have been conducted and that the effects of ginkgo in younger people are still little explored. They conclude that ginkgo warrants further attention from researchers but that it is not yet possible to say conclusively whether ginkgo is helpful or not.

What about other supposed cognitive enhancers? Phosphatatidylserine (PS) is getting a great deal of attention in Italy as a treatment for dementia and age-related memory decline. One popular book even recommends it as a cure for poor memory (Crook & Adderly, 1998). Reviewing the evidence, however, McDaniel et al. (2002) conclude that such enthusiasm may be a little premature. Overall, the findings are inconsistent, and the increases in cognitive functioning (to the extent that they exist) may be so slight that they might not even be noticeable to the people taking the supplement. The same caution is extended to claims made for the benefits of choline, which is found in foods containing lethicin and is important for the production of the neurotransmitter acetylcholine. Although they call for more rigorous research on the issue of these and other "brain-specific nutrients," McDaniel and colleagues (2002) are not willing to conclude categorically that such supplements have no clinical value. As with Ginkgo biloba, the positive findings that exist in the literature are suggestive enough to encourage researchers to keep exploring this issue.

summary

- The DSM-IV-TR recognizes various cognitive disorders including delirium, dementia, and amnestic disorder. Typically these disorders result from transient or permanent damage to the brain. Chronic neuropsychological disorders involve the permanent loss of neural cells.
- There is no simple relationship between extent of brain damage and degree of impaired functioning. Some people who have severe damage develop no severe symptoms, whereas some with slight damage have extreme reactions.
- Although such inconsistencies are not completely understood, it appears that an individual's premorbid personality and life situation are important in determining his or her reactions to brain damage. The APOE-E4 genetic allele is also important.
- Delirium is a fluctuating condition common among the elderly. It involves a state of awareness between wakefulness and stupor or coma. It is treated with neuroleptic medications and also with benzodiazepines.
- Dementia involves a loss of function and of previously acquired skills. It has a slow onset and a deteriorating course. The most common cause of dementia is Alzheimer's disease.
- Age is a major risk factor for Alzheimer's disease as well as for other forms of dementia such as vascular dementia.
- Genes play a major role in susceptibility to and risk for Alzheimer's disease. Genetic mutations of the APP, presenilin 1, and presenilin 2 genes are implicated in early-onset AD. The APOE-E4 allele of the APOE gene is also a risk factor for AD.
- The characteristic neuropathology of Alzheimer's disease involves cell loss, plaques, and neurofibrillary tangles. Plaques contain a sticky protein called "beta amyloid." Neurofibrillary tangles contain abnormal tau protein.
- Alzheimer's disease causes the destruction of cells that make acetylcholine, a neurotransmitter important for memory. Drug treatments for AD include cholinesterase inhibitors such as donepezil (Aricept). These drugs help stop ACh from being broken down and so make more of it available to the brain.
- Amnestic disorders involve severe memory loss. The most common cause of amnestic disorders is chronic alcohol abuse.
- Head injuries can cause amnesia as well as other cognitive impairments. Retrograde amnesia is inability to recall events that preceded the trauma. Anterograde amnesia is inability to remember things that follow it.
- Any comprehensive treatment approach for cognitive disorders should also involve caregivers, who are often under a great deal of stress and have difficulty coping. They may benefit from medications as well as from support groups.

Key Terms

amnestic syndrome (P. 549)
amyloid plaques (P. 541)
anterograde amnesia (P. 552)
APOE-E4 allele (P. 545)
delirium (P. 538)
dementia (P. 539)
early-onset Alzheimer's disease (P. 544)
functional mental disorders (P. 533)
HIV-associated dementia (P. 548)
late-onset Alzheimer's disease (P. 545)
neurofibrillary tangles (P. 541)
organic mental disorders (P. 533)
retrograde amnesia (P. 552)
traumatic brain injury (TBI) (P. 550)
vascular dementia (VAD) (P. 549)

CHAPTER 16

Disorders of Childhood and Adolescence

Until the twentieth century, little account was taken of the special characteristics of psychopathology in children; maladaptive patterns considered relatively specific to childhood, such as autism, received virtually no attention at all. Only since the advent of the mental health movement and the availability of child guidance facilities at the beginning of the twentieth century have marked strides been made in assessing, treating, and understanding the maladaptive behavior patterns of children and adolescents. Still, progress in child psychopathology has lagged behind that in adult psychopathology.

In fact, the problems of childhood were initially seen simply as downward extensions of adult-oriented diagnoses. The prevailing view was one of children as "miniature adults." But this view failed to recognize special problems, such as those associated with the developmental changes that normally take place in a child or adolescent. Only recently have clinicians come to realize that they cannot fully understand childhood disorders without taking these developmental processes into account. Today, even though great progress has been made in providing treatment for disturbed children, facilities are still woefully inadequate to the task, and most children with problems do not receive psychological attention.

The numbers of children affected by psychological problems are considerable. Multisite studies in several countries have provided estimates of childhood disorder. Verhulst (1995) conducted an evaluation of the overall prevalence based on 49 studies involving over 240,000 children across many countries and found the average rate to be 12.3 percent. In most studies, maladjustment is found more commonly among boys than among girls. In one survey of psychological disorder in children, Anderson and colleagues (1987) found that 17.6 percent of 11-year-old children studied had one or more disorders, with boys and girls diagnosed at a ratio of 1.7 boys to 1 girl. The most prevalent disorders were *attention-deficit/hyperactivity disorder* and *separation anxiety disorders.* Zill and Schoenborn (1990) reported that rates of childhood disorders varied by gender, with boys having higher rates of emotional problems over the childhood and adolescent years. However, for some diagnostic problems such as eating disorders, rates are higher for girls than for boys.

Maladaptive Behavior in Different Life Periods

Several behaviors that characterize maladjustment or emotional disturbance are relatively common in childhood. Because of the manner in which personality develops, the various steps in growth and development, and the differing stressors people face in childhood, adolescence, and adulthood, we would expect to find some differences in maladaptive behavior in these periods. The fields of developmental science (Hetherington, 1998) and, more specifically, **developmental psychopathology** (Cicchetti & Rogosch, 1999) are devoted to studying the origins and course of individual maladaptation in the context of normal growth processes.

It is important to view a child's behavior in reference to normal childhood development (Silk, Nath, et al., 2000). We cannot consider a child's behavior abnormal without determining whether the behavior in question is appropriate for the child's age. For example, temper tantrums and eating inedible objects might be viewed as abnormal behavior at age 10 but not at age 2. Despite the somewhat distinctive characteristics of childhood disturbances at different ages, there is no sharp line of demarcation between the maladaptive behavior patterns of childhood and those of adolescence, or between those of adolescence and those of adulthood. Thus, although our focus in this chapter will be on the behavior disorders of children and adolescents, we will find some inevitable overlap with those of later life periods.

Varying Clinical Pictures

The clinical picture in childhood disorders tends to be distinct from disorders of other life periods. Some of the emotional disturbances of childhood may be relatively short-lived and less specific than those occurring in adulthood (Mash & Dozois, 1996). However, some childhood disorders severely affect future development. One study found that individuals who had been hospitalized as child psychiatric patients (between the ages of 5 and 17) showed excess mortality due to unnatural causes (about twice the rate of the general population) when followed up from 4 to 15 years later (Kuperman, Black, & Burns, 1988). Suicide accounted for most of these deaths, and the suicide rate was significantly greater than in the general population.

Special Vulnerabilities of Young Children

Young children are especially vulnerable to psychological problems (Ingram & Price, 2001). In evaluating the presence or extent of mental health problems in children and adolescents, one needs to consider the following:

- They do not have as complex and realistic a view of themselves and their world as they will have later, they have less self-understanding, and they have not yet developed a stable sense of identity or a clear understanding of what is expected of them and what resources they might have to deal with problems.
- Immediately perceived threats are tempered less by considerations of the past or future and thus tend to be seen as disproportionately important. As a result, children often have more difficulty than adults in coping with stressful events (Compas & Epping, 1993). For example, children are at risk for post-traumatic stress disorder after a disaster, especially if the family atmosphere is troubled—a circumstance that adds additional stress to the problems resulting from the natural disaster (La Greca, 2001).
- Children's limited perspectives, as might be expected, lead them to use unrealistic concepts to explain events. For example, a child who commits suicide may be trying to rejoin a dead parent, sibling, or pet. For young children, suicide or violence against another person may be undertaken without any real understanding of the finality of death.
- Children also are more dependent on other people than are adults. Although in some ways this dependency serves as a buffer against other dangers, because the adults around might "protect" a child against stressors in the environment, it also makes the child highly vulnerable to experiences of rejection, disappointment, and failure if these adults, because of their own problems, ignore the child.
- Children's lack of experience in dealing with adversity can make manageable problems seem insurmountable. On the other hand, although their inexperience and lack of self-sufficiency make them easily upset by problems that seem minor to the average adult, children typically recover more rapidly from their hurts.

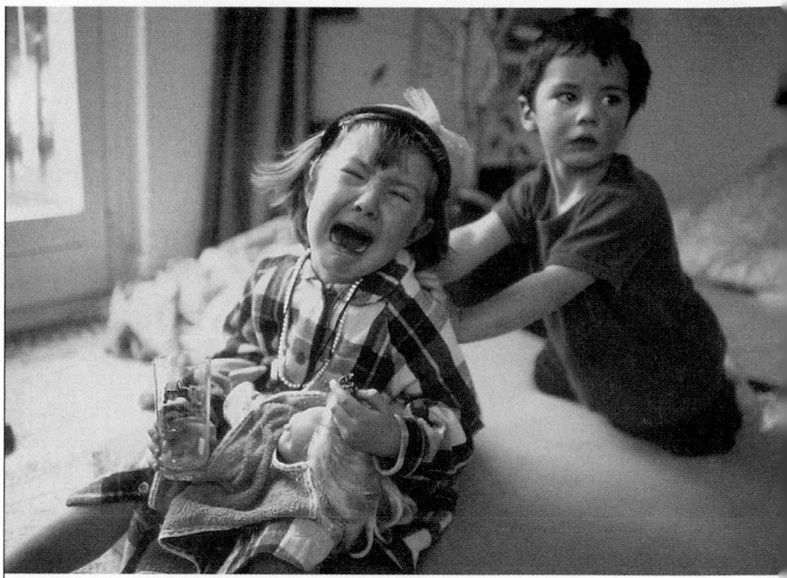

We cannot understand or consider a child's behavior as abnormal without considering the child's age and stage of development. Developmental psychopathology is devoted to studying the origins and course of maladaptation in the context of normal growth processes.

The Classification of Childhood and Adolescent Disorders

Until the 1950s no formal, specific system was available for classifying the emotional or behavioral problems of children and adolescents. Kraepelin's (1883) classic textbook on the classification of mental disorders did not include childhood disorders. In 1952, the first formal psychiatric nomenclature (DSM-I) was published and childhood disorders included. This system was quite limited and included only two childhood emotional disorders: childhood schizophrenia and adjustment reaction of childhood. In 1966, the Group for the Advancement of Psychiatry provided a classification system for children that was detailed and comprehensive. In the 1968 revision of the DSM (DSM-II), several additional categories were added. A growing concern remained, however, both among clinicians attempting to diagnose and treat childhood problems and among researchers attempting to broaden our understanding of childhood psychopathology, that the then-current ways of viewing psychological disorders in children and adolescents were inappropriate and inaccurate for several reasons. The greatest problem resulted from the fact that the same classification system that had been developed for adults was used for childhood problems, even though many childhood disorders (such as autism, learning disabilities, and school phobias) have no counterpart in adult psychopathology. The early systems also ignored the fact that in childhood disorders, environmental factors play an important part in the expression of symptoms—that is, symptoms are highly influenced by a family's acceptance or rejection of the behavior. In addition, symptoms were not considered with respect to a child's developmental level. Some of the problem behaviors might be considered age-appropriate, and troubling behaviors might simply be behaviors that the child will eventually outgrow.

In Review

- Define developmental psychopathology.
- What are several of the special psychological vulnerabilities of children?

Common Disorders of Childhood

At present the DSM-IV-TR provides diagnoses on a large number of childhood and adolescent disorders diagnosed on Axis I. In addition, several disorders involving mental retardation are diagnosed on Axis II. Space limitations do not allow us to explore fully the mental disorders of childhood and adolescence, so we have selected several disorders to illustrate the broad spectrum of problems that can occur in childhood and adolescence. Some of these disorders are more transient than many of the abnormal behavior patterns of adulthood discussed in earlier chapters—and also perhaps more amenable to treatment. Learning disorders and mental retardation, covered toward the end of the chapter, are coded on Axis II.

Attention-Deficit/Hyperactivity Disorder

Attention-deficit/hyperactivity disorder (ADHD), often referred to as "hyperactivity," is characterized by difficulties that interfere with effective task-oriented behavior in children—particularly impulsivity, excessive or exaggerated motor activity such as aimless or haphazard running or fidgeting, and difficulties in sustaining attention (Brodeur & Pond, 2001). Hyperactive children are highly distractible and often fail to follow instructions or respond to demands placed on them (Wender, 2000). Perhaps as a result of their behavioral problems, hyperactive children are often lower in intelligence, usually about 7 to 15 IQ points below average (Barkley, 1997). Hyperactive children also tend to talk incessantly and to be socially intrusive and immature. Recent research has shown that many ADHD children show deficits on neuropsychological testing that were related to poor academic functioning (Biederman, Monteaux, et al., 2004).

Children with ADHD generally have many social problems because of their impulsivity and overactivity. Hyperactive children usually have great difficulty in getting along with their parents because they do not obey rules. Their behavior problems also result in their being viewed negatively by their peers (Hoza, Mrug, et al., 2005). In general, however, hyperactive children are not anxious, although their overactivity, restlessness, and distractibility are frequently interpreted as indications of anxiety. They usually do poorly in school and often show specific learning disabilities such as difficulties in reading or in learning other basic school subjects. Hyperactive children also pose behavior problems in the elementary grades. The following case reveals a typical clinical picture.

Case Study: Gina, a Student with Hyperactivity

Gina was referred to a community clinic because of overactive, inattentive, and disruptive behavior. Her hyperactivity and uninhibited behavior caused problems for her teacher and for other students. She would impulsively hit other children, knock things off their desks, erase material on the blackboard, and damage books and other school property. She seemed to be in perpetual motion, talking, moving about, and darting from one area of the classroom to another. She demanded an inordinate amount of attention from her parents and her teacher, and she was intensely jealous of other children, including her own brother and sister. Despite her hyperactive behavior, inferior school performance, and other problems, she was considerably above average in intelligence. Nevertheless, she felt stupid and had a seriously devaluated self-image. Neurological tests revealed no significant organic brain disorder.

The symptoms of ADHD are relatively common among children seen at mental health facilities. In fact, hyperactive children are the most frequent psychological referrals to mental health and pediatric facilities, and the disorder is thought to occur in about 3 to 5 percent of school-age children (Goldman et al., 1998). However, one study reported a much higher prevalence rate of 16.1 percent for ADHD (Wolrich, Hannah, et al., 1998). The disorder occurs most frequently among preadolescent boys—it is six to nine times more prevalent among boys than among girls. ADHD occurs with the greatest frequency before age 8 and tends to become less frequent and to

Children with ADHD are described as overactive, impulsive, and having a low tolerance for frustration and an inability to delay gratification. Incessant talkers, they tend not to obey rules and often run the risk of a multitude of problems with schoolwork, teachers, and other students.

involve briefer episodes thereafter. ADHD has also been found to be comorbid with other disorders such as oppositional defiant disorder (Drabick, Gadow, et al., 2004), which we discuss later. Some residual effects, such as attention difficulties, may persist into adolescence or adulthood (Odell, Warren, et al., 1997) although, as we will see, some authorities doubt the authenticity of this syndrome in adults (Bhandary, 1997). ADHD exists in other cultures—for example, among Chinese schoolboys (Leung, Luk, et al., 1996), who show a pattern similar to that of hyperactive youngsters in the United States.

CAUSAL FACTORS IN ATTENTION-DEFICIT/HYPERACTIVITY DISORDER The cause or causes of ADHD in children have been much debated (Breggin & Breggin, 1995). It still remains unclear to what extent the disorder results from environmental or biological factors, and recent research points to both genetic (Nadder, Silberg, et al., 1998) and social environmental precursors (Hechtman, 1996). Many researchers believe that biological factors such as genetic inheritance will turn out to be important precursors to the development of ADHD (Durston, 2003). But firm conclusions about any biological basis for ADHD must await further research.

The search for psychological causes of hyperactivity has yielded similarly inconclusive results, although temperament and learning appear likely to be factors. One study suggested that family pathology, particularly parental personality problems, leads to hyperactivity in children. Morrison (1980) found that many parents of hyperactive children had psychological problems; for example, a large number were found to have clinical diagnoses of personality disorder or hysteria. Currently, ADHD

DSM-IV-TR

Criteria for Attention-Deficit/Hyperactivity Disorder

Either of the following criteria would enable a diagnosis of ADHD:

1. If six (or more) of the following symptoms of **inattention** have persisted for at least 6 months and are maladaptive for the child's developmental level:

   Inattention

   (a) often fails to give close attention to details or makes careless mistakes in schoolwork, work, or other activities
   (b) often has difficulty attending in tasks or play activities
   (c) often does not seem to listen when spoken to directly
   (d) often does not follow through on instructions and fails to finish schoolwork, chores, or duties in the workplace (not due to oppositional behavior or failure to understand instructions)
   (e) often has difficulty organizing tasks and activities
   (f) often avoids, dislikes, or is reluctant to engage in tasks that require sustained mental effort (such as schoolwork or homework)
   (g) is often easily distracted by extraneous stimuli
   (h) is often forgetful in daily activities

2. If six (or more) of the following symptoms of **hyperactivity-impulsivity** have persisted for at least 6 months to a degree that is maladaptive:

   Hyperactivity

   (a) often fidgets with hands or feet or squirms in seat
   (b) often leaves seat in classroom or in other situations in which remaining seated is expected
   (c) often runs about or climbs excessively in situations in which it is inappropriate (in adolescents or adults, may be limited to subjective feelings of restlessness)
   (d) often has difficulty playing or engaging in leisure activities quietly
   (e) is often "on the go" or often acts as if "driven by a motor"
   (f) often talks excessively

   Impulsivity

   (g) often blurts out answers before questions have been completed
   (h) often has difficulty awaiting turn
   (i) often interrupts or intrudes on others (e.g., butts into conversations or games)

Source: *Adapted with permission from the* Diagnostic and Statistical Manual of Mental Disorders, *Fourth Edition, Text Revision (Copyright 2000). American Psychiatric Association.*

is considered to have multiple causes and effects (Hinshaw, Zupan, et al., 1997). Whatever cause or causes are ultimately determined to be influential in ADHD, the mechanisms underlying the disorder need to be more clearly understood and explored. There is general agreement that there are processes operating in the brain that disinhibit the child's behavior (Nigg, 2001), and some recent research has found different EEG patterns occurring in children with ADHD (Barry, Clarke, & Johnstone, 2003). At this time, however, theorists do not agree what those central nervous system processes are.

TREATMENTS AND OUTCOMES Although the hyperactive syndrome was first described more than 100 years ago, disagreement over the most effective methods of treatment continues, especially regarding the use of drugs to calm a hyperactive child. Yet this approach to treating hyperactive children has great appeal in the medical community; one survey (Runnheim, Frankenberger, & Hazelkorn, 1996) found that 40 percent of junior high school children and 15 percent of high school children with emotional and behavioral problems and ADHD were prescribed medication, mostly **Ritalin** (methylphenidate), an amphetamine. In fact, school nurses administer more daily medication for ADHD than for any other chronic health problem (E.M. O'Connor, 2001).

Interestingly, research has shown that amphetamines have a quieting effect on children—just the opposite of what we would expect from their effects on adults (Pelham et al., 1992). For hyperactive children, such medication decreases overactivity and distractibility and, at the same time, increases their alertness (Konrad, Gunther, et al., 2004). As a result, they are often able to function much better at school (Pelham, Hoza, et al., 2002; Wender, 2000).

Fava (1997) concluded that Ritalin can often lower the amount of aggressiveness in hyperactive children. In fact, many hyperactive children whose behavior has not been acceptable in regular classes can function and progress in a relatively normal manner when they use such a drug. In a 5-year follow-up study, Charach, Ickowicz, and Schachar (2004) reported that ADHD children on medication showed greater improvement in teacher-reported symptoms than nontreated children. The possible side effects of Ritalin, however, are numerous: decreased blood flow to the brain, which can result in impaired thinking ability and memory loss; disruption of growth hormone, leading to suppression of growth in the body and brain of the child; insomnia; psychotic symptoms; and others. Although amphetamines do not cure hyperactivity, they have reduced the behavioral symptoms in about one-half to two-thirds of the cases in which medication appears warranted.

Ritalin has been shown to be effective in the short-term treatment of ADHD (Baldwin, Chelonis, et al., 2004; Spencer, 2004a). There are newer variants of the drug, referred to as "extended-release methylphenidate" (Concerta), that have similar benefits but with available doses that may better suit an adolescent's lifestyle (Mott & Leach, 2004; Spencer, 2004b).

Two other medications for treating ADHD have received recent attention in recent years. **Pemoline** is chemically very different from Ritalin (Faigel & Heiligenstein, 1996); it exerts beneficial effects on classroom behavior by enhancing cognitive processing but has less adverse side effects (Bostic, Biederman, et al., 2000). **Strattera** (atomoxetine), a noncontrolled treatment option that is more readily obtainable, is a nonstimulant medication that has recently received FDA approval (FDA, 2002). This medication, a norepinephrine reuptake inhibitor, reduces the symptoms of ADHD (Friemoth, 2005), but its mode of operation is not well understood. The side effects for the drug are decreased appetite, nausea, vomiting, and fatigue. The development of jaundice has been reported, and the FDA (2004) has warned of the possibility of liver damage that may result from use of Strattera. Although Strattera has been shown to reduce some symptoms of ADHD, further research is needed to evaluate its effectiveness and potential side effects (Barton, Mooney, & Prasad, 2005).

Although the short-term pharmacological effect of stimulants on the symptoms of hyperactive children is well established, their long-term effects are not well known (Safer, 1997a). Carlson and Bunner (1993) reported that studies of achievement over long periods of time failed to show that the medication has beneficial effects. Some concern has been expressed about some effects of the drugs such as psychotic symptoms, particularly when stimulants are used in heavy dosages over time (Breggin, 2001). The pharmacological similarity of Ritalin and cocaine, for example, has caused some investigators to be concerned over its use in the treatment of ADHD (Volkow et al., 1995). There have been some reported recreational uses of Ritalin, particularly among college students. Kapner (2003) described several surveys in which Ritalin was reportedly abused on college campuses. For example, in one survey, 16 percent of students at one university reported using Ritalin; and in another study 1.5 percent of the population surveyed reported using Ritalin for recreational purposes within the past 30 days. In many situations, college students "share" the prescription medications of friends as a means of obtaining a "high" (Kapner, 2003).

Some authorities prefer using psychological interventions in conjunction with medications (Stein, 1999). The behavioral intervention techniques that have been developed for ADHD include selective reinforcement in the classroom (DuPaul & Stoner, et al. 1998) and family therapy (Everett & Everett, 2001). Another effective approach to treating hyperactive children involves the use of behavior therapy techniques featuring positive reinforcement and the structuring of learning materials and tasks in a way that minimizes error and maximizes immediate feedback and success (Frazier & Merrill, 1998; Goldstein & Goldstein, 1998). An example is providing a hyperactive boy with immediate praise for stopping to think through a task he has been assigned before he starts to do it. The use of behavioral treatment methods for hyperactivity has reportedly been quite successful, at least for short-term gains.

The use of behavior therapy with medication in a total treatment program has reportedly shown good success. Pelham and colleagues (1993) found that both behavior modification and medication therapy significantly reduced ADHD. Medication, however, appeared to be the more effective element in the treatment.

The use of behavior modification alone in the treatment of ADHD has shown positive results. Van Lier, Muthen, et al. (2004) conducted a school-based behavioral intervention program aimed at preventing disruptive behavior in elementary school children using positive reinforcement. They found this program to be effective with ADHD children with different levels of disorder but most effective with children at lower or intermediate levels.

ADHD BEYOND ADOLESCENCE Some researchers have reported that many hyperactive children retain ADHD into early adulthood (Nigg, Butler, et al., 2002; Wender, 2000) or go on to have other psychological problems such as overly aggressive behavior or substance abuse in their late teens and early adulthood (Barkley, Fischer, et al., 2004). For example, Carroll and Rounsaville (1993) found that 34.6 percent of treatment-seeking cocaine abusers in their study met the criteria for ADHD when they were children. In a 16-year follow-up study of ADHD children, about 25 percent never completed high school, compared with 2 percent for controls (Mannuzza, et al., 1993).

More ***longitudinal research*** is clearly needed before we can conclude that children with ADHD go on to develop similar or other problems in adulthood. Mannuzza, Klein, and Moulton (2003) reported that estimates of the numbers of children with ADHD who will experience later symptoms of ADHD in adulthood are likely to vary considerably. However, some of the research cited suggests that a significant percentage of adolescents continue to have problems in later life.

> **research close•up**
>
> ***longitudinal research***
>
> *Longitudinal research involves studying and collecting baseline information on a specific group of interest (patients with a given disorder, high-risk children, etc.) and then following them up at a future date (e.g., 1, 5, or even 20 years later) to determine the changes that have occurred over the intervening period.*

Oppositional Defiant Disorder and Conduct Disorder

The next group of disorders involves a child's or an adolescent's relationship to social norms and rules of conduct. In both oppositional defiant disorder and conduct disorder, aggressive or antisocial behavior is the focus. As we will see, oppositional defiant disorder is usually apparent by about age 8, and conduct disorder tends to be seen by age 9. These disorders are closely linked (Stahl & Clarizio, 1999). However, it is important to distinguish between persistent antisocial acts—such as setting fires, where the rights of others are violated—and the less serious pranks often carried out by normal children and adolescents. Also, oppositional defiant disorder and conduct disorder involve misdeeds that may or may not be against the law; **juvenile delinquency** is the legal term used to refer to violations of the law committed by minors. (See the "Unresolved Issues" section at the end of this chapter.)

THE CLINICAL PICTURE IN OPPOSITIONAL DEFIANT DISORDER An important precursor of the antisocial behavior seen in children who develop conduct disorder is often what is now called **oppositional defiant disorder** (Webster-Stratton, 2000). The essential feature is a recurrent pattern of negativistic, defiant, disobedient, and hostile behavior toward authority figures that persists for at least 6 months (American Psychiatric Association, *DSM-IV-TR,* 2000, p. 102). This disorder usually begins by the age of 8, whereas full-blown conduct disorders typically begin from middle childhood through adolescence. Prospective studies have found a developmental sequence from oppositional defiant disorder to conduct disorder, with common risk factors for both conditions (Hinshaw, 1994). That is, virtually all cases of conduct disorder were preceded developmentally by oppositional defiant disorder, but not all children with oppositional defiant disorder go on to develop conduct disorder within a 3-year period (Lahey, McBurnett, & Loeber, 2000). The risk factors for both include family discord, socioeconomic disadvantage, and antisocial behavior in the parents (Hinshaw, 1994).

THE CLINICAL PICTURE IN CONDUCT DISORDER The essential symptomatic behavior in **conduct disorder** involves a persistent, repetitive violation of rules and a disregard for the rights of others. Conduct-disordered children show a deficit in social behavior (Happe & Frith, 1996). In general, they manifest such characteristics as overt or covert hostility, disobedience, physical and verbal aggressiveness, quarrelsomeness, vengefulness, and destructiveness. Lying, solitary stealing, and temper tantrums are common. Such children tend to be sexually uninhibited and inclined toward sexual aggressiveness. Some may engage in cruelty to animals (Becker, Stuewig, et al, 2004), bullying (Coolidge, DenBoer, & Segal, 2004), firesetting (Becker, Stuewig, et al, 2004; Slavkin & Fineman, 2000; Stickle & Blechman, 2002), vandalism, robbery, and even homicidal acts. Conduct-disordered children and adolescents are also frequently comorbid for substance-abuse disorder (Grilo, Becker, et al., 1996)

DSM-IV-TR

Criteria for Conduct Disorder

A. This disorder is a repetitive and persistent pattern of behavior in which the basic rights of others or major age-appropriate societal norms or rules are violated, as manifested by the presence of *three* (or more) of the following criteria in the past 6 months:

Aggression to People and Animals

(1) often bullies, threatens, or intimidates others

(2) often initiates physical fights

(3) has used a weapon that can cause serious physical harm to others (e.g., a bat, brick, broken bottle, knife, gun)

(4) has been physically cruel to people

(5) has been physically cruel to animals

(6) has stolen while confronting a victim (e.g., mugging, purse snatching, extortion, armed robbery)

(7) has forced someone into sexual activity

Destruction of Property

(8) has deliberately engaged in firesetting with the intention of causing serious damage

(9) has deliberately destroyed others' property (other than by firesetting)

Deceitfulness or Theft

(10) has broken into someone else's house, building, or car

(11) often lies to obtain goods or favors or to avoid obligations (i.e., "cons" others)

(12) has stolen items of nontrivial value without confronting a victim (e.g., shoplifting, but without breaking and entering; forgery)

Serious Violations of Rules

(13) often stays out at night despite parental prohibitions, beginning before age 13 years

(14) has run away from home overnight at least twice while living in parental or parental surrogate home (or once without returning for a lengthy period)

(15) is often truant from school, beginning before age 13 years

B. The disturbance in behavior causes clinically significant impairment in social, academic, or occupational functioning.

C. If the individual is age 18 years or older, criteria are not met for Antisocial Personality Disorder.

The severity of the disorder should be specified as follows:

Mild: few if any conduct problems in excess of those required to make the diagnosis **and** conduct problems cause only minor harm to others

Moderate: number of conduct problems and effect on others intermediate between "mild" and "severe"

Severe: many conduct problems in excess of those required to make the diagnosis **or** conduct problems cause considerable harm to others

Source: *Adapted with permission from the* Diagnostic and Statistical Manual of Mental Disorders, *Fourth Edition, Text Revision (Copyright 2000). American Psychiatric Association.*

Hostility and aggressive behavior have been found to play a role in the development of conduct disorder. Children who develop this disorder early in childhood are at special risk for problems later in life.

or depressive symptoms (O'Connor et al., 1998). Zoccolillo, Meyers, and Assiter (1997) found that conduct disorder was a risk factor for unwed pregnancy and substance abuse in teenage girls.

CAUSAL FACTORS IN OPPOSITIONAL DISORDER AND CONDUCT DISORDER Understanding of the factors associated with the development of conduct problems in childhood has increased tremendously in the past 20 years. Several factors will be covered in the sections that follow.

A Self-Perpetuating Cycle Evidence has accumulated that a genetic predisposition (Pliszka, 1999; Simonoff, 2001) leading to low verbal intelligence, mild neuropsychological problems, and difficult temperament can set the stage for early onset conduct disorder through a set of self-perpetuating mechanisms (Moffitt & Lynam, 1994; Slutsky, Heath, et al., 1997). The child's difficult temperament may lead to an insecure attachment because parents find it hard to engage in the good parenting that would promote a secure attachment. In addition, the low verbal intelligence and/or mild neuropsychological deficits that have been documented in many of these children—some of which may involve deficiencies in self-control functions such as sustaining attention, planning, self-monitoring, and inhibiting unsuccessful or impulsive behaviors—may help set the stage for a lifelong course of difficulties. In attempting to explain why the relatively mild neuropsychological deficits typically seen can have such pervasive effects, Moffitt and Lynam (1994) provide the following scenario: A preschooler has problems understanding language and tends to resist his mother's efforts to read to him. This deficit then delays the child's readiness for school. When he does enter school, the typically busy curriculum does not allow teachers to focus their attention on students at his low readiness level. Over time, and after a few years of school failure, the child will be chronologically older than his classmates, setting the stage for social rejection. At some point, the child might be placed into remedial programs that contain other pupils who have similar behavioral disorders as well as learning disabilities. This involvement with conduct-disordered peers exposes him to delinquent behaviors that he adopts in order to gain acceptance.

Age of Onset and Links to Antisocial Personality Disorder Children who develop conduct disorder at an earlier age are much more likely to develop psychopathy or antisocial personality disorder as adults than are adolescents who develop conduct disorder suddenly in adolescence (Hinshaw, 1994; Moffitt, 1993b). The link between conduct disorder and antisocial personality is stronger among lower-socioeconomic-class children (Lahey, Loeber, et al., 2005). It is the pervasiveness of the problems first associated with oppositional defiant disorder and then with conduct disorder that forms the pattern associated with an adult diagnosis of psychopathy or antisocial personality. Although only about 25 to 40 percent of cases of early onset conduct disorder go on to develop adult antisocial personality disorder, over 80 percent of boys with early onset conduct disorder do continue to have multiple problems of social dysfunction (in friendships, intimate relationships, and vocational activities) even if they do not meet all the criteria for antisocial personality disorder (Hinshaw, 1994; Zoccolillo et al., 1992). By contrast, most individuals who develop conduct disorder in adolescence do not go on to become adult psychopaths or antisocial personalities but instead have problems limited to the adolescent years. These adolescent-onset cases also do not share the same set of risk factors that the child-onset cases have, including low verbal intelligence, neuropsychological deficits, and impulsivity and attentional problems (Hinshaw, 1994; Moffitt & Lynam, 1994).

Environmental Factors In addition to the genetic or constitutional liabilities that may predispose a person to conduct disorder and to adult psychopathy and antisocial personality, Kazdin (1995) underscored the importance of family and social context factors as causal variables. For example, having a confused "idea" or relationship with the primary caregiver can result in disorganized early attachment and can signal later aggression in the child (Lyons-Ruth, 1996). Children who are aggressive and socially unskilled are often rejected by their peers, and such rejection can lead to a spiraling sequence of social interactions with peers that exacerbates the tendency toward antisocial behavior (Coie & Lenox, 1994). Severe conduct problems can lead to other mental health problems as well. Mason, Kosterman, et al. (2004) found that children who reported higher levels of conduct problems were nearly four times more likely to experience a depressive episode in early adulthood.

This socially rejected subgroup of aggressive children is also at the highest risk for adolescent delinquency and probably for adult antisocial personality. In addition, parents and teachers may react to aggressive children with strong negative affect such as anger (Capaldi & Patterson, 1994), and they may in turn reject these aggressive children. The combination of rejection by parents, peers, and teachers leads these children to become isolated and alienated. Not surprisingly, they often turn to deviant peer groups for companionship (Coie & Lenox, 1994), at which point a good deal of imitation of the antisocial behavior of their deviant peer models may occur.

Investigators generally seem to agree that the family setting of a conduct-disordered child is typically characterized by ineffective parenting, rejection, harsh and inconsistent discipline, and often parental neglect (Frick, 1998; Patterson, 1996). Frequently, the parents have an unstable marital relationship (Osborn, 1992), are emotionally disturbed or sociopathic, and do not provide the child with consistent guidance, acceptance, or affection. Even if the family is intact, a child in a conflict-charged home feels overtly rejected. For example, Rutter and Quinton (1984b) concluded that family discord and hostility were the primary factors defining the relationship between disturbed parents and disturbed children; this is particularly true with respect to the development of conduct disorders in children and adolescents. Such discord and hostility contribute to poor and ineffective parenting skills, especially ineffective discipline and supervision. These children are "trained" in antisocial behavior by the family—directly via coercive interchanges and indirectly via lack of monitoring and consistent discipline (Capaldi & Patterson, 1994). This all too often leads to association with deviant peers and the opportunity for further learning of antisocial behavior.

Ineffective parenting, harsh and inconsistent discipline, parental neglect, and marital discord can all contribute to oppositional defiant disorder (ODD) and conduct disorders. So can poverty and parental stress and depression.

In addition to these familial factors, a number of broader psychosocial and sociocultural variables increase the probability that a child will develop conduct disorder and, later, adult psychopathy or antisocial personality disorder. Low socioeconomic status, poor neighborhoods, parental stress, and depression all appear to increase the likelihood that a child will become enmeshed in this cycle (Capaldi & Patterson, 1994).

TREATMENTS AND OUTCOMES By and large, our society tends to take a punitive, rather than a rehabilitative, attitude toward an antisocial, aggressive youth. Thus the emphasis is on punishment and on "teaching the child a lesson." Such treatment, however, seems to intensify rather than correct the behavior.

Treatment for oppositional defiant disorder and conduct disorder tends to focus on dysfunctional family patterns described above and on finding ways to alter the child's aggressive or otherwise maladaptive behaviors (Behan & Carr, 2000; Milne, Edwards, et al., 2001).

The Cohesive Family Model Therapy for a child with conduct disorder is likely to be ineffective unless some way can be found to modify the child's environment. One interesting and often effective treatment strategy with conduct disorder is the cohesive family model (Patterson, Reid, & Dishion, 1998; Webster-Stratton, 1991). In this family-group-oriented approach, parents of children with conduct disorder are viewed as lacking in parenting skills and as behaving in inconsistent ways, thereby reinforcing inappropriate behavior and failing to socialize the children. Children learn to escape or avoid parental criticism by escalating their negative behavior. This tactic, in turn, increases their parents' aversive interactions and criticism. The child observes the increased anger in his or her parents and models this aggressive pattern. The parental attention to the child's negative, aggressive behavior actually serves to reinforce that behavior instead of suppressing it. Viewing conduct problems as emerging from such interactions places the treatment focus squarely on the interaction between the child and the parents (Patterson, Capaldi, & Bank, 1991).

Obtaining treatment cooperation from parents who are themselves in conflict with each other is difficult. Often, an overburdened parent who is separated or divorced and working simply does not have the resources, the time, or the inclination to learn and practice a more adequate parental role (Clarke-Stewart, Vandell, et al., 2000). In more extreme cases, the circumstances may call for a child to be removed from the home and placed in a foster home or institution, with the expectation of a later return to the home if intervening therapy with the parent or parents appears to justify it.

Unfortunately, children who are removed to new environments often interpret this removal as further rejection, not only by their parents but by society as well. Unless the changed environment offers a warm, kindly, and accepting yet consistent and firm setting, such children are likely to make little progress. Even then, treatment may have only a temporary effect. Faretra (1981) followed up 66 aggressive and disturbed adolescents who had been admitted to an inpatient unit. She found that antisocial and criminal behavior persisted into adulthood, though with a lessening of psychiatric involvement. Many children with conduct disorder go on to have personality disorders as adults (Rutter, 1988; Zeitlin, 1986).

Behavioral Techniques The advent of behavior therapy techniques has made the outlook brighter for children who manifest conduct disorder (Kazdin & Weisz, 2003; Nock, 2003). Teaching control techniques to the parents of such children is particularly important, so that they can function as therapists in reinforcing desirable behavior and modifying the environmental conditions that have been reinforcing maladaptive behavior. The changes brought about when parents consistently accept and reward their child's positive behavior and stop focusing on the negative behavior may finally change their perception of and feelings toward the child, leading to the basic acceptance that the child has so badly needed.

Although effective techniques for behavioral management can be taught to parents, they often have difficulty carrying out treatment plans. If this is the case, other techniques, such as family therapy or parental counseling, are used to ensure that the parent or person responsible for the child's discipline is sufficiently assertive to follow through on the program.

Anxiety Disorders of Childhood and Adolescence

In modern society, no one is totally insulated from anxiety-producing events or situations, and the experience of traumatic events can predispose children to develop anxiety disorders (Bandelow, Spaeth, et al., 2002). Most children are vulnerable to fears and uncertainties as a normal part of growing up, and children can get generalized panic disorder just as adults do. Children with anxiety disorders, however, are more extreme in their behavior than those experiencing "normal" anxiety. These children appear to share many of the following characteristics: oversensitivity, unrealistic fears, shyness and timidity, pervasive feelings of inadequacy, sleep disturbances, and fear of school (Goodyer, 2000). Children diagnosed as suffering from an anxiety disorder typically attempt to cope with their fears by becoming overly dependent on others for support and help. In the DSM, anxiety disorders of childhood and adolescence are classified similarly to anxiety disorders in adults (Albano, Chorpita, & Barlow, 1996). Research has shown that anxiety disorders are often comorbid with depressive disorders (Manassis & Monga, 2001) or may be influential in later depression (Silberg, Rutter, & Eaves, 2001); children who have these comorbid conditions often have significantly more symptoms than children who have anxiety disorders without depression (Masi, Favilla, et al., 2000).

Anxiety disorders are common among children. In fact, 9.7 percent of one community-based school sample clearly met diagnostic criteria for an anxiety-based disorder (Dadds, Spence, et al., 1997). There is a greater preponderance of anxiety-based disorder in girls than in boys (Lewinsohn et al., 1998). Among adolescents, Goodwin and Gotlib (2004) reported that panic attacks occurred in 3.3 percent in a large community-based epidemiological study.

SEPARATION ANXIETY DISORDER **Separation anxiety disorder** is the most common of the childhood anxiety disorders, reportedly occurring in 2 to 4 percent of children in a population health study and accounting for 50 percent of children seen at mental health clinics for anxiety disorders (Goodyer, 2000). Children with separation anxiety disorder exhibit unrealistic fears, oversensitivity, self-consciousness, nightmares, and chronic anxiety. They lack self-confidence, are apprehensive in new situations, and tend to be immature for their age. Such children are described by their parents as shy, sensitive, nervous, submissive, easily discouraged, worried, and frequently moved to tears. Typically, they are overly dependent, particularly on their parents. The essential feature in the clinical picture of this disorder is excessive anxiety about separation from major attachment figures, such as mother, and from familiar home surroundings. In many cases, a clear psychosocial stressor can be identified, such as the death of a relative or a pet. The following case illustrates the clinical picture in this disorder.

Case Study: Johnny's Severe Separation Anxiety

Johnny was a highly sensitive 6-year-old who suffered from numerous fears, nightmares, and chronic anxiety. He was terrified of being separated from his mother, even for a brief period. When his mother tried to enroll him in kindergarten, he became so upset when she left the room that the principal arranged for her to remain in the classroom. After 2 weeks, however, this arrangement had to be discontinued, and Johnny had to be withdrawn from kindergarten because his mother could not leave him even for a few minutes. Later, when his mother attempted to enroll him in the first grade, Johnny manifested the same intense anxiety and unwillingness to be separated from her. At the suggestion of the school counselor, Johnny's mother brought him to a community clinic for assistance with the problem. The therapist, who initially saw Johnny and his mother, was wearing a white clinic jacket, which led to a severe panic reaction on Johnny's part. His mother had to hold him to keep him from running away, and he did not settle down until the therapist removed his jacket. Johnny's mother explained that he was terrified of doctors and that it was almost impossible to get him to a physician even when he was sick.

DSM-IV-TR

Criteria for Separation Anxiety Disorder

A. Developmentally inappropriate and excessive anxiety concerning separation from home or from those to whom the individual is attached, as evidenced by three (or more) of the following:

(1) recurrent excessive distress when separation from home or major attachment figures occurs or is anticipated

(2) persistent and excessive worry about losing, or about possible harm befalling, major attachment figures

(3) persistent and excessive worry that an untoward event will lead to separation from a major attachment figure (e.g., getting lost or being kidnapped)

(4) persistent reluctance or refusal to go to school or elsewhere because of fear of separation

(5) persistently and excessively fearful or reluctant to be alone or without major attachment figures at home or without significant adults in other settings

(6) persistent reluctance or refusal to go to sleep without being near a major attachment figure or to sleep away from home

(7) repeated nightmares involving the theme of separation

(8) repeated complaints of physical symptoms (such as headaches, stomachaches, nausea, or vomiting) when separation from major attachment figures occurs or is anticipated

B. The duration of the disturbance is a least 4 weeks.

C. The onset is before age 18 years.

D. The disturbance causes clinically significant distress or impairment in social, academic, occupational, or other important areas of functioning.

Source: *Adapted with permission from the* Diagnostic and Statistical Manual of Mental Disorders, *Fourth Edition, Text Revision (Copyright 2000). American Psychiatric Association.*

When children with separation anxiety disorder are actually separated from their attachment figures, they typically become preoccupied with morbid fears, such as the worry that their parents are going to become ill or die. They cling helplessly to adults, have difficulty sleeping, and become intensely demanding. Separation anxiety is more common in girls (Majcher & Pollack, 1996), and the disorder is not very stable over time (Poulton, Milne, et al., 2001). One study, for example, reported that 44 percent of youngsters showed recovery at a 4-year follow-up (Cantwell & Baker, 1989). However, some children go on to exhibit school refusal problems (a fear of leaving home and parents to attend school) and continue to have subsequent adjustment difficulties. A disproportionate number of children with separation anxiety disorder also experience a high number of other anxiety-based disorders such as phobia and obsessive-compulsive disorder (Egger, Costello, & Angold, 2003; Kearney, Sims, et al., 2003).

When children with separation anxiety disorder are actually separated from their attachment figures, they typically become preoccupied with morbid fears, such as the worry that their parents are going to become ill or die.

SELECTIVE MUTISM Another anxiety-based disorder sometimes found in children is **selective mutism,** a condition that involves the persistent failure to speak in specific social situations—for example, in school or in social groups—that is considered to interfere with educational or social adjustment. In many cases, children with selective mutism also have a diagnosis of developmental disorder/delay (Standart & Le Couteur, 2003). Selective mutism should be diagnosed only if the child actually has the ability to speak and knows the language. Moreover, in order for this disorder to be diagnosed, the condition must have lasted for a month and must not be limited to the first month of school, when many children are shy or inhibited.

Selective (formerly referred to as "elective") mutism is apparently quite rare in clinical populations and is most typically seen at preschool age. The disorder occurs in all social strata, and in about one-third of the cases studied, the child showed early signs of the problem such as shyness and internalizing behavior (Steinhausen & Juzi, 1996).

Both biological and learning factors have been cited as possible causal factors underlying the disorder. Bar-Haim, Henkin, et al. (2004) reported that specific deficiencies in auditory nerve activity was found among children with selective mutism, and Steinhausen and Adamek (1997) reported some evidence that genetic factors play a part in selective mutism in that cases tend to occur more frequently in families in which taciturn behavior is prominent. Evidence for cultural or learning factors has also been presented. Elizur and Perednik (2003) found that both stress and family environmental factors were involved in cases of selective mutism.

Selective mutism is treated much like other anxiety-based disorders. One study reported that the symptoms were reduced substantially with fluoxetine (Motavalli, 1995), and another successful report involved a drug called "moclobemide," an MAO inhibitor (Maskey, 2001). However, family-based psychological treatment is the most commonly used therapeutic approach (Tatem & DelCampo, 1995).

CAUSAL FACTORS IN ANXIETY DISORDERS A number of causal factors have been emphasized in explanations of the childhood anxiety disorders. Parental behavior has been particularly noted as a potential influential factor in the origin of anxiety disorders in children; however, broader cultural factors are also important considerations.

Anxious children often manifest an unusual constitutional sensitivity that makes them easily conditionable by aversive stimuli. For example, they may be readily upset by even small disappointments—a lost toy or an encounter with an overeager dog. They then have a harder time calming down, a fact that can result in a buildup and generalization of surplus fear reactions.

The child can become anxious because of early illnesses, accidents, or losses that involved pain and discomfort. The traumatic effect of experiences such as hospitalizations makes such children feel insecure and inadequate. The traumatic nature of certain life changes such as moving away from friends and into a new situation can also have an intensely negative effect on a child's adjustment. Kashani and colleagues (1981) found that the most common recent life event for children receiving psychiatric care was moving to a new school district.

Overanxious children often have the modeling effect of an overanxious and protective parent who sensitizes a child to the dangers and threats of the outside world. Often, the parent's overprotectiveness communicates a lack of confidence in the child's ability to cope, thus reinforcing the child's feelings of inadequacy (Dadds, Heard, & Rapee, 1991; Woodruff-Borden et al., 2002).

Indifferent or detached parents (Chartier, Walker, & Stein, 2001) or rejecting parents (Hudson & Rapee, 2001) also foster anxiety in their children. The child may not feel adequately supported in mastering essential competencies and in gaining a positive self-concept. Repeated experiences of failure, stemming from poor learning skills, may lead to subsequent patterns of anxiety or withdrawal in the face of "threatening" situations. Other children may perform adequately but may be overcritical of themselves and feel intensely anxious and devalued when they perceive themselves as failing to do well enough to earn their parents' love and respect.

The role that social-environmental factors might play in the development of anxiety-based disorders, though important, is not clearly understood. A cross-cultural study of fears (Ollendick et al., 1996) found significant differences among American, Australian, Nigerian, and Chinese children and adolescents. These authors suggested that cultures that favor inhibition, compliance, and obedience appear to increase the levels of fear reported. In another study in the United States, Last and Perrin (1993) reported that there were some differences between African-American and white children with respect to types of anxiety disorders. White children were more likely to present with school refusal than were African-American children, who showed more PTSD symptoms. This difference might result from differing patterns of referral for African-American and white families, or it might reflect differing environmental stressors placed on the children. Several studies have found a strong association between exposure to violence and a reduced sense of security and psychological well-being (Cooley-Quille, Boyd, et al., 2001; Kliewer et al., 1998). The child's vulnerability to anxiety and depression may be induced by his or her early experiences of feeling a lack of "control" over reinforcing environmental events (Chorpita & Barlow, 1998). Children who experience a sense of diminished control over negative environmental factors may become more vulnerable to the development of anxiety than those children who achieve a sense of efficacy in managing stressful circumstances.

TREATMENTS AND OUTCOMES The anxiety disorders of childhood may continue into adolescence and young adulthood, leading first to maladaptive avoidance behavior and later to increasingly idiosyncratic thinking and behavior or an inability to "fit in" with a peer group. Typically, however, this is not the case. As affected children grow and have wider interactions in school and in activities with peers, they often benefit from experiences such as making friends and succeeding at given tasks. Teachers who are aware of the needs of both overanxious and shy, withdrawn children are often able to ensure that they will have successful experiences that help alleviate anxiety.

Biologically Based Treatments Psychopharmacological treatment of anxiety disorders in children and adolescents is becoming more common today. Birmaher, Axelson, et al. (2003) evaluated the efficacy of using fluoxetine in the treatment of a variety of anxiety-based disorders and found the medication useful. However, the cautious use of medications with anxiety-based disorders involves obtaining diagnostic clarity since these conditions often coexist with other disorders.

Psychological Treatment Behavior therapy procedures, sometimes used in school settings, often help anxious children (Kashdan & Herbert, 2001). Such procedures include assertiveness training to provide help with mastering essential competencies, and desensitization to reduce anxious behavior. Kendall and his colleagues have reported the successful use of manual-based cognitive-behavioral treatment (well-defined procedures using positive reinforcement to enhance coping strategies to deal with fears) for children with anxiety disorders (Chu & Kendall, 2004). Behavioral treatment approaches such as desensitization must be explicitly tailored to a child's particular problem, and *in vivo* methods (using real-life situations graded in terms of the anxiety they arouse) tend to be more effective than having the child "imagine" situations. Svensson, Larsson, and Oest (2002) reported successful treatment of phobic children using brief exposure.

An interesting and effective cognitive-behavioral anxiety prevention and treatment study was implemented in Australia. In an effort to identify and reduce anxiousness in young adolescents, Dadds, Spence, and colleagues (1997) identified 314 children who met the criteria for an anxiety disorder, out of a sample of 1,786 children 7 to 14 years old in a school system in Brisbane, Australia. They contacted the parents of these anxious children to engage them in the treatment intervention, and parents of 128 of the children agreed to participate. The treatment intervention involved holding group sessions with the children, in which they were taught to recognize their anxious feelings and deal with them more effectively than they otherwise would have. In addition, the parents were taught behavioral management procedures to deal more effectively with the child's behavior. Six months after therapy was completed, significant anxiety reduction was shown for the treatment group, compared with an untreated control sample.

Childhood Depression

Childhood depression includes behaviors such as withdrawal, crying, avoidance of eye contact, physical complaints, poor appetite, and even aggressive behavior and in some cases suicide (Pfeffer, 1996a, 1996b). One epidemiological study (Cohen et al., 1998) reported an association between somatic illness and childhood depressive illness, suggesting that there may be some common etiologic factors.

Currently, childhood depression is classified according to essentially the same DSM diagnostic criteria as are used for adults (American Psychiatric Association, *DSM-IV-TR*, 2000). However, recent research on the neurobiological correlates and treatment responses of children, adolescents, and adults has shown clear differences in hormonal levels and in the response to treatment (Kaufman, Martin, et al., 2001). Future neuroimaging studies are needed to explore these differences further. One modification used for diagnosing depression in children is that irritability is often found as a major symptom and can be substituted for depressed mood, as seen in the following case.

case STUDY — The Unhappy Child

Joey is a 10-year-old boy whose mother and teacher have shared their concerns about his irritability and temper tantrums displayed both at home and at school. With little provocation, he bursts into tears and yells and throws objects. In class he seems to have difficulty concentrating and seems easily distracted. Increasingly shunned by his peers, he plays by himself at recess, and at home he spends most of his time in his room watching TV. His mother notes that he has been sleeping poorly and has gained 10 pounds over the past couple of months from constant snacking. A consultation with the school psychologist has ruled out learning disabilities and attention-deficit disorder; instead, she says, he is a deeply unhappy child who expresses feelings of worthlessness and hopelessness—and even a wish that he would die. These experiences probably began about 6 months ago when his father, divorced from Joey's mother for several years, remarried and moved to another town, with the result that he spends far less time with Joey. (Adapted from Hammen & Rudolph, 1996, pp. 153–54.)

Childhood depression includes behaviors such as withdrawal, crying, avoiding eye contact, physical complaints, poor appetite, and in some extreme cases, aggressive behavior and suicide.

Depression in children and adolescents occurs with high frequency. The point prevalence (the rate at the time of the assessment) of major depressive disorder has been estimated to be between 0.4 and 2.5 percent for children and between 4.0 and 8.3 percent for adolescents (Birmaher, Ryan, et al., 1996). The lifetime prevalence for major depressive disorders in adolescents is between 15 and 20 percent (Harrington et al., 1996). One review of the epidemiology of depression in children and adolescents concluded that major depression is relatively rare in young children but more common in adolescents, with up to 25 percent lifetime prevalence (Kessler, Avenevoli, & Merikangas, 2001). A survey of 1,710 high school students found that point prevalence was 2.9 percent, that lifetime prevalence was 20.4 percent, and that suicidal ideation at some time in life was high—19 percent—in this sample (Lewinsohn et al., 1996). Before adolescence, rates of depression are somewhat higher in boys, but depression occurs at about twice the rate for adolescent girls as for adolescent boys (Hankin et al., 1998). Lewinsohn and colleagues (1993) also reported that 7.1 percent of the adolescents surveyed reported having attempted suicide in the past, and in another epidemiological study, Lewinsohn, Rohde, and Seeley (1994) pointed out that 1.7 percent of adolescents between 14 and 18 had made a suicide attempt.

CAUSAL FACTORS IN CHILDHOOD DEPRESSION The causal factors implicated in the childhood anxiety disorders are pertinent to the depressive disorders as well.

Biological Factors There appears to be an association between parental depression and behavioral and mood problems in children (Hammen, Shih, & Brennan, 2004). Children of parents with major depression were more impaired, received more psychological treatment, and had more psychological diagnoses than children of parents with no psychological disorders (Kramer, Warner, et al., 1998). This is particularly the case when the parent's depression affected the child through less-than-optimal interactions (Carter, Garrity-Rokous, et al., 2001). A controlled study of family history and onset of depression found that children from mood-disordered families had significantly higher rates of depression than those from nondisordered families (Kovacs, Devlin, et al., 1997). The suicide attempt rate has also been shown to be higher for children of depressed parents (7.8 percent) than for the offspring of control parents (Weissman et al., 1992). All these correlations suggest a potential genetic component to childhood depression, but in each case, learning could also be the causal factor.

Other biological factors might also make children vulnerable to psychological problems like depression. These factors include biological changes in the neonate as a result of alcohol intake by the mother during pregnancy. One recent study reported that prenatal exposure to alcohol is related to depression in children. M. J. O'Connor's (2001) study of children exposed to alcohol *in utero* revealed a continuity between alcohol use by the mother and infant negative affect and early childhood depression symptoms. (See Developments in Research 12.1 on p. 417 for a discussion of fetal alcohol syndrome.)

Learning Factors Learning of maladaptive behaviors appears to be important in childhood depressive disorders. There are likely to be learning or cultural factors in the expression of depression. A recent article by Stewart, Kennard, et al. (2004) reported that depression symptoms and hopelessness were higher in Hong Kong than in the United

States. In addition, a number of studies have indicated that children's exposure to early traumatic events can increase their risk for the development of depression. Children who have experienced past stressful events are susceptible to states of depression that make them vulnerable to suicidal thinking under stress (Silberg, Pickles, et al., 1999). Intense or persistent sensitization of the central nervous system in response to severe stress might induce hyperreactivity and alteration of the neurotransmitter system, leaving these children vulnerable to later depression (Heim & Nemeroff, 2001). Children who are exposed to negative parental behavior or negative emotional states may develop depressed affect themselves (Herman-Stahl & Peterson, 1999). For example, childhood depression has been found to be more common in divorced families (Palosaari & Laippala, 1996).

One important area of research is focusing on the role of the mother-child interaction in the transmission of depressed affect. Specifically, investigators have been evaluating the possibility that mothers who are depressed transfer their low mood to their infants through their interactions with them (Jackson & Huang, 2000). Depression among mothers is not uncommon and can result from several sources. Some women become depressed during pregnancy or following the delivery of their child, in part because of exhaustion and hormonal changes that can affect mood. Several investigators have reported that marital distress, delivery complications, and difficulties with the infant are also associated with depression in mothers (Campbell et al., 1990).

Depressed mothers do not respond effectively to their children (Goldsmith & Rogoff, 1997). Depressed mothers tend to be less sensitively attuned to, and more negative toward, their infants than nondepressed mothers (Murray, Fiori-Cowley, et al., 1996). Other research has shown that negative (depressed) affect and constricted mood on the part of a mother, which shows up as unresponsive facial expressions and irritable behavior, can produce similar responses in her infant (Cohn & Tronick, 1983; Tronick & Cohn, 1989). Interestingly, the negative impact of depressed mothers' interaction style has also been studied at the physiological level. Infants have been reported to exhibit greater frontal brain electrical activity during the expression of negative emotionality by their mothers (Dawson, Panagiotides, et al., 1997). Although most of these studies have implicated the mother-child relationship in development of the disorder, depression in fathers has also been related to depression in children (Jacob & Johnson, 2001).

Another important line of research in childhood depression involves the cognitive-behavioral perspective. Considerable evidence has accumulated that depressive symptoms are positively correlated with the tendency to attribute positive events to external, specific, and unstable causes and negative events to internal, global, and stable causes (Hinshaw, 1992); with fatalistic thinking (Roberts, Roberts, & Chen, 2000); and with feelings of helplessness (Kistner, Ziegert, et al., 2001). For example, the child may respond to peer rejection or teasing by concluding that he or she has some internal flaw. Hinshaw (1994) considers the tendency to develop distorted mental representations an important cause of disorders such as depression and conduct disorder. In addition, children who show symptoms of depression tend to underestimate their self-competence over time (Cole et al., 1998).

Mothers who are depressed may transmit their depression to their children by their lack of responsiveness to the child as a result of their own depression. Unfortunately, depression among mothers is all too common. Exhaustion, marital distress as a result of the arrival of children in a couple's lives, delivery complications, and the difficulties of particular babies may all play a part.

TREATMENTS AND OUTCOMES The view that childhood and adolescent depression is like adult depression has prompted researchers to treat children displaying mood disorders—particularly adolescents who are viewed as suicidal (Greenhill & Waslick, 1997)—with medications that have worked with adults. Research on the effectiveness of antidepressant medications with children is both limited (Emslie & Mayes, 2001) and contradictory at best, and some studies have found them to be only moderately helpful (Wagner & Ambrosini, 2001). Some recent studies using fluoxetine (Prozac) with depressed adolescents have shown the drug to be more effective than a placebo (DeVane & Sallee, 1996; Emslie, Rush, et al., 1997), and recent studies have shown fluoxetine to be effective in the treatment of depression along with cognitive-behavioral therapy (Treatment for Adolescents with Depression Study (TADS) Team, US, 2004) although complete remission of symptoms was seldom obtained. Antidepressant medications may have some undesirable side effects (nausea, headaches, nervousness, insomnia, and even seizures) in children and adolescents. Four accidental deaths with a drug called "desipramine" have been reported (Campbell & Cueva, 1995). However, the use of antidepressant medication for depressed adolescents has increased from three- to fivefold over the past 10 years (Zito & Safer, 2001).

Depressed mood has come to be viewed as an important risk factor in suicide among children and adolescents (Fisher, 1999; Houston, Hawton, & Sheppard, 2001). About 7 to 10 percent of adolescents report having made at least one suicide attempt (Safer, 1997b). Children who attempt suicide are at greater risk for subsequent suicidal episodes than are nonattempters, particularly within the first 2 years after their initial attempt (Pfeffer et al., 1994). Among the childhood disorders, depression especially merits aggressive treatment. Recent attention is being paid to the increased potential of suicidal ideation and behavior in children and adolescents who are taking SSRIs for their depression (Whittington, Kendall, et al., 2004). Some risk of suicide for those taking the medication has been noted (Couzin, 2004). The extent to which these medications represent an additional threat of suicide is being investigated.

An important facet of psychological therapy with children, whether for depression or anxiety or other disorders, is providing a supportive emotional environment in which they can learn more adaptive coping strategies and effective emotional expression. Older children and adolescents can often benefit from a positive therapeutic relationship in which they can discuss their feelings openly (Stark, Laurent, et al., 1999). Younger children and those with less developed verbal skills may benefit from play therapy. Controlled studies of psychological treatment with depressed adolescents have shown significantly reduced symptoms with cognitive-behavioral therapy (Brent, Holder, et al., 1997) derived from Beck's cognitive-behavioral approach (Ackerson et al., 1998), which is discussed in Chapter 7. Rawson and Tabb (1993) showed that short-term residential treatment was effective with depressed children aged 8 to 14. The predominant approach for treating depression in children and adolescents over the past few years has been the combined use of medication and psychotherapy (Skaer, Robison, et al., 2000).

Symptom Disorders: Enuresis, Encopresis, Sleepwalking, and Tics

The childhood disorders we will deal with in this section—"elimination disorders" (enuresis and encopresis), sleepwalking, and tics—typically involve a single outstanding symptom rather than a pervasive maladaptive pattern.

FUNCTIONAL ENURESIS The term **enuresis** refers to the habitual involuntary discharge of urine, usually at night, after the age of expected continence (age 5). In DSM-IV-TR, functional enuresis is described as bed-wetting that is not organically caused. Children who have primary functional enuresis have never been continent; children who have secondary functional enuresis have been continent for at least a year but have regressed.

Enuresis may vary in frequency, from nightly occurrence to occasional instances when a child is under considerable stress or is unduly tired. It has been estimated that some 4 to 5 million children and adolescents in the United States suffer from the inconvenience and embarrassment of this disorder. Estimates of the prevalence of enuresis reported in DSM-IV-TR are 5 to 10 percent among 5-year-olds, 3 to 5 percent among 10-year-olds, and 1.1 percent of children age 15 or older. An epidemiological study in China reported a 4.3 percent prevalence, with a significantly higher percentage of boys than of girls (Liu, Sun, et al., 2000). Research has shown that there are clear sex differences in enuresis, as well as age differences. In one extensive epidemiological study of enuresis in Holland, Verhulst and colleagues (1985) determined that between the ages of 5 and 8, enuresis is about two to three times more common among boys than among girls. The percentages for boys also diminish more slowly; the decline for girls between ages 4 and 6 is about 71 percent, whereas the decline for boys is only 16 percent. The researchers recommended that the upper age limit for diagnosing enuresis in boys be extended to age 8, because it is at about age 9 that approximately the same percentage of boys and girls reach "dryness"—that is, wetting the bed less than once a month.

Enuresis may result from a variety of organic conditions, such as disturbed cerebral control of the bladder (Goin, 1998), neurological dysfunction (Lunsing et al., 1991), or other medical factors such as medication side effects (Took & Buck, 1996) or having a small functional bladder capacity and a weak urethral sphincter (Dahl, 1992). One group of researchers reported that 11 percent of their enuretic patients had disorders of the urinary tract (Watanabe et al., 1994). However, most investigators have pointed to a number of other possible causal factors: (1) faulty learning, resulting in the failure to acquire inhibition of reflexive bladder emptying; (2) personal immaturity, associated with or stemming from emotional problems; (3) disturbed family interactions, particularly those that lead to sustained anxiety, hostility, or both; and (4) stressful events (Haug Schnabel, 1992). For example, a child may regress to bed-wetting when a new baby enters the family and becomes the center of attention.

Medical treatment of enuresis typically centers on using medications such as imipramine. The mechanism underlying the action of the drug is unclear, but it may simply decrease the deepest stages of sleep to light sleep, enabling the child to recognize bodily needs more effectively (Dahl, 1992). An intranasal desmopressin (DDAVP) has also been used to help children manage urine more effectively. This medication, a hormone replacement, apparently increases urine concentration, decreases urine volume, and therefore reduces the need to urinate (Dahl, 1992). The use of this medication to treat enuretic children is no panacea. Disadvantages of its use include its high cost and the fact that it is effective only with a small subset of enuretic children, and then only temporarily. Bath, Morton, Uing, and Williams (1996) reported that treatment with desmopressin was disappointing but concluded that this treatment had some utility as a way to enable children to stay dry for brief periods of time—for example, at a camp or on a holiday. Moffatt (1997) suggested that DDAVP had an important place in treating nocturnal enuresis in youngsters who have not responded well to behavioral treatment methods. It is well to remember that medications by themselves do not cure enuresis and that there is frequent relapse when the drug is discontinued or the child habituates to the medication (Dahl, 1992).

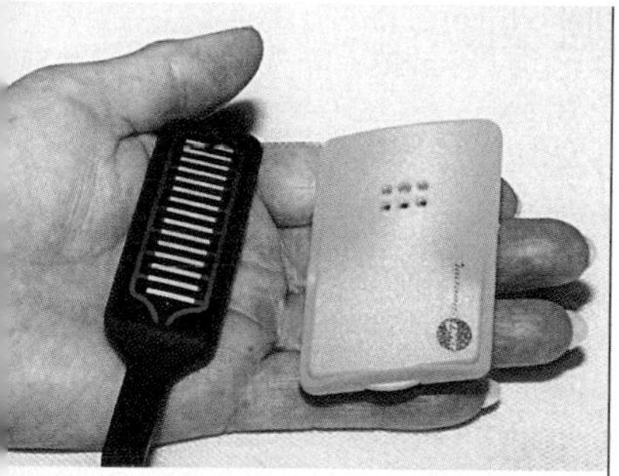

When combined with medication such as desmopressin, a urine alarm (shown here) can be very effective in treating enuresis. The child sleeps with a wetness detector, which is wired to a battery-operated alarm in his or her undergarment. Through conditioning, the child comes to associate bladder tension with awakening.

Conditioning procedures have proved to be the most effective treatment for enuresis (Friman & Warzak, 1990). Mowrer and Mowrer (1938) introduced a procedure in which a child sleeps on a pad that is wired to a battery-operated bell. At the first few drops of urine, the bell is set off, thus awakening the child. Through conditioning, the child comes to associate bladder tension with awakening. Recent evidence suggests that a "biobehavioral approach"—that is, using the urine alarm along with desmopressin—is most effective (Mellon & McGrath, 2000).

With or without treatment, the incidence of enuresis tends to decrease significantly with age, but many experts still believe that enuresis should be treated in childhood because there is presently no way to identify which children will remain enuretic into adulthood (Goin, 1998). In an evaluation of research on the treatment of bed-wetting, Houts, Berman, and Abramson (1994) concluded that treated children were more improved at follow-up than nontreated children. They also found that learning-based procedures were more effective than medications.

FUNCTIONAL ENCOPRESIS The term **encopresis** describes a symptom disorder of children who have not learned appropriate toileting for bowel movements after age 4. This condition is less common than enuresis; however, DSM-IV-TR estimated that about 1 percent of 5-year-olds have encopresis. A study of 102 cases of encopretic children yielded the following list of characteristics: The average age of children with encopresis was 7, with a range of ages 4 to 13. About one-third of encopretic children were also enuretic, and a large sex difference was found, with about six times more boys than girls in the sample. Many of the children soiled their clothing when they were under stress. A common time was in the late afternoon after school; few children actually had this problem at school. Most of the children reported that they did not know when they needed to have a bowel movement or were too shy to use the bathrooms at school.

Many encopretic children suffer from constipation, so an important element in the diagnosis is a physical examination to determine whether physiological factors are contributing to the disorder. The treatment of encopresis usually involves both medical and psychological aspects (Dawson et al., 1990). Several studies of the use of conditioning procedures with encopretic children have reported moderate treatment success; that is, no additional incidents occurred within 6 months following treatment (Huntley & Smith, 1999; Smith et al., 2000).

SLEEPWALKING (SOMNAMBULISM) Although the onset of **sleepwalking disorder** is usually between the ages of 6 and 12, the disorder is classified broadly under sleep disorders in DSM-IV-TR rather than under disorders of infancy, childhood, and adolescence (American Psychiatric Association, *DSM-IV-TR*, 2000). The symptoms of sleepwalking disorder involve repeated episodes in which a person leaves his or her bed and walks around without being conscious of the experience or remembering it later.

Statistics are meager, but the incidence of sleepwalking reported for children in DSM is high for one episode—between 10 and 30 percent. However, the incidence for repeated episodes is low—from 1 to 5 percent. Children subject to this problem usually go to sleep in a normal manner but arise during the second or third hour of sleep. They may walk to another room of the house or even outside, and they may engage in complex activities. Finally, they return to bed and in the morning remember nothing that has taken place. While moving about, sleepwalkers' eyes are partially or fully open; they avoid obstacles, listen when spoken to, and ordinarily respond to commands, such as to return to bed. Shaking them will usually awaken sleepwalkers, and they will be surprised and perplexed at finding themselves in an unexpected place. Sleepwalking episodes usually last only a few minutes (Graham, Turk, & Verhulst, 1999). The causes of sleepwalking are not fully understood. Sleepwalking takes place during NREM (non–rapid eye movement) sleep. It appears to be related to some anxiety-arousing situation that has just occurred or is expected to occur in the near future (Klackenberg, 1987).

Little attention has been devoted to the treatment of sleepwalking. Clement (1970), however, reported on the treatment of a 7-year-old boy through behavior therapy. During treatment, the therapist learned that just before each sleepwalking episode, the boy usually had a nightmare about being chased by "a big black bug." After his nightmare began, he perspired freely, moaned and talked in his sleep, tossed and turned, and finally got up and walked through the house. He did not remember the sleepwalking episode when he awoke the next morning. Assessment data revealed no neurological or other medical problems and indicated that he was of normal intelligence. He was, however, found to be a very anxious, guilt-ridden little boy who avoided performing assertive and aggressive behaviors appropriate to his age and sex (p. 23). The therapist focused treatment on having his mother awaken the boy each time he showed signs of an impending episode. After washing his face with cold water and making sure he was fully awake, the mother would return him to bed, where he was to hit and tear up a picture of the big black bug. (At the start of the treatment program, he had made up several of these drawings.)

Eventually, the nightmare was associated with awakening, and he learned to wake up on most occasions when he was having a bad dream. Thus the basic behavior therapy followed in this case was the same as that used in the conditioning treatment for enuresis, where a waking response is elicited by an intense stimulus just as urination is beginning and becomes associated with, and eventually prevents, nocturnal bed-wetting.

TICS A **tic** is a persistent, intermittent muscle twitch or spasm, usually limited to a localized muscle group. The term is used broadly to include blinking the eye, twitching the mouth, licking the lips, shrugging the shoulders, twisting the neck, clearing the throat, blowing the nose, and grimacing, among other actions. Tics occur most frequently between the ages of 2 and 14 (Evans et al., 1996). In some instances, as in clearing the throat, an individual may be aware of the tic when it occurs, but usually he or she performs the act habitually and does not notice it. In fact, many individuals do not even realize they have a tic unless someone brings it to their attention. A cross-cultural examination of tics found a similar pattern in research and clinical case reports from other countries (Staley et al., 1997). Moreover, the age of onset (average 7 to 8 years) and predominant gender (male) of cases were reported to be similar across cultures (Turan & Senol, 2000). The psychological impact that tics can have on an adolescent is illustrated in the following case.

case study — The Adolescent Who Wanted to Be a Teacher

An adolescent who had wanted very much to be a teacher told the school counselor that he was thinking of giving up his plans. When asked why, he explained that several friends had told him that he had a persistent twitching of the mouth muscles when he answered questions in class. He had been unaware of this muscle twitch and, even after being told about it, could not tell when it took place. However, he became acutely self-conscious and was reluctant to answer questions or enter into class discussions. As a result, his general level of tension increased, and so did the frequency of the tic, which now became apparent even when he was talking to his friends. Thus a vicious circle had been established. Fortunately, the tic proved amenable to treatment by conditioning and assertiveness training.

Tourette's syndrome is an extreme tic disorder involving multiple motor and vocal patterns. This disorder typically involves uncontrollable head movements with accompanying sounds such as grunts, clicks, yelps, sniffs, or words. Some, possibly most, tics are preceded by an urge or sensation that seems to be relieved by execution of the tic. Tics are thus often difficult to differentiate from compulsions, and they are sometimes referred to as "compulsive tics" (Jankovic, 1997). One recent epidemiological study in Sweden reported the prevalence of Tourette's syndrome in children and adolescents to be about 0.56 percent (Khalifa & von Knorring, 2004). About one-third of individuals with Tourette's syndrome manifest coprolalia, which is a complex vocal tic that involves the uttering of obscenities. Some people with Tourette's syndrome also experience explosive outbursts (Budman, Braun, et al., 2000). The average age of onset for Tourette's syndrome is 7, and most cases have an onset before age 14. The disorder frequently persists into adulthood. It is about three times more frequent among males than among females. Although the exact cause of Tourette's syndrome is undetermined, evidence suggests an organic basis. Because children with Tourette's syndrome can have substantial family adjustment (Wilkinson, Newman, et al., 2001) and/or school adjustment problems (Nolan & Gadow, 1997), interventions should be designed to aid their adjustment and to modify the reactions of peers to them. School psychologists can play an effective part in the social adjustment of the child with Tourette's syndrome (Walter & Carter, 1997) by applying behavioral intervention strategies that help arrange the child's environment to be more accepting of such unusual behaviors.

There are many types of tics, and many of them appear to be associated with the presence of other psychological disorders (Cardona et al., 1997), particularly obsessive-compulsive disorder (OCD). Most tics, however, do not have an organic basis but stem from psychological causes such as self-consciousness or tension in social situations, and they are usually associated with severe behavioral problems (Rosenberg, Brown, & Singer, 1995). As in the case of the adolescent boy previously described, an individual's awareness of the tic often increases tension and the occurrence of the tic.

Among medications, neuroleptics are the most predictably effective tic-suppressing drugs (Kurlan, 1997). Clonazepam, clonidine, and tiapride have all shown effectiveness in reducing motor tics; however, tiapride has shown the greatest decrease in the intensity and frequency of tics (Drtikova et al., 1996). Campbell and Cueva (1995) reported that both haloperidol and pimozide reduced the severity of tics by about 65 percent but that haloperidol seemed the more effective of the two medications. Recently, Gilbert, Batterson, Sethuraman, & Sallee (2004) reported that risperidone outperformed pimozide in tic suppression.

Behavioral intervention techniques have also been used successfully in treating tics (Woods & Miltenberger, 2001). One successful program involved several sequential elements, beginning with awareness training, relaxation training, and the development of incompatible responses and then progressing to cognitive therapy and modification of the individual's overall style of action. Finally, perfectionist expectations about self-image (which are often found in children and adolescents with tics) are addressed through cognitive restructuring (O'Connor et al., 1998).

Pervasive Developmental Disorders

The **pervasive developmental disorders (PDDs)** are a group of severely disabling conditions that are among the most difficult to understand and treat. They make up about 3.2 percent of cases seen in inpatient settings (Sverd, Sheth, Fuss, & Levine, 1995). They are considered to be the result of some structural differences in the brain that are usually evident at birth or become apparent as the child begins to develop (Siegel, 1996). There is fairly good diagnostic agreement in the determination of pervasive developmental disorders in children whether one follows the DSM-IV-TR or ICD-10 (the International Classification of Disease, published by the World Health Organization), which have slightly different criteria for some disorders (Sponheim, 1996). Several pervasive developmental disorders are covered in DSM-IV-TR—for example, **Asperger's disorder,** which is a severe and persistent impairment in social interaction that involves marked stereotypic (repetitive) behavior and inflexible adherence to routines (Mesibov, Shea, & Adams, 2001). This pattern of behavior usually appears later than other pervasive developmental disorders such as autism, but it nevertheless involves substantial long-term psychological disability. Asperger's disorder shares many features of social impairment disorder, restricted interests, and repetitive behaviors with autistic disorder although it may become manifest somewhat later than autism and in most cases is not associated with the severe delay in language development and social interactions that autism does (Khouzam, El-Gabalawi, et al., 2004). We will illustrate the developmental disorders by addressing in some detail the disorder referred to as "autism."

Autism

One of the most common and most puzzling and disabling of the pervasive developmental disorders is autistic disorder, which is often referred to as **autism** or "childhood autism" (Schopler, Yirmiya, et al., 2001). It is a developmental disorder that involves a wide range of problematic behaviors including deficits in language, and perceptual and motor development; defective reality testing; and an inability to function in social situations. The following case illustrates some of the behaviors that may be seen in an autistic child.

case STUDY **The Need for Routine**

Mathew is 5 years old. When spoken to, he turns his head away. Sometimes he mumbles unintelligibly. He is neither toilet trained nor able to feed himself. He actively resists being touched. He dislikes sounds and is uncommunicative. He cannot relate to others and avoids looking anyone in the eye. He often engages in routine manipulative activities such as dropping an object, picking it up, and dropping it again. He shows a pathological need for sameness. While seated, he often rocks back and forth in a rhythmic motion for hours. Any change in routine is highly upsetting to him.

Autism in infancy and childhood was first described by Kanner (1943). It afflicts tens of thousands of American children from all socioeconomic levels and is apparently on the increase—estimates range between 30 and 60 people in 10,000 (Fombonne, 2003; Merrick, Kandel, & Morad, 2004). The reported increase in autism in recent years is likely due to methodological differences between studies, and changes in diagnostic practice and public and professional awareness in recent years rather than an increase in prevalence (Williams, Mellis, & Peat 2005). Autism is usually identified before a child is 30 months of age and may be suspected in the early weeks of life. One study found that autistic behavior such as lack of empathy, inattention to others, and inability to imitate is shown as early as 20 months (Charman, Swettenham, et al., 1997).

THE CLINICAL PICTURE IN AUTISM DISORDER

Autistic children show varying degrees of impairments and capabilities. In this section, we will discuss some of the behaviors that may be evident in autism. A cardinal and typical sign is that a child seems apart or aloof from others, even in the earliest stages of life (Adrien et al., 1992). Mothers often remember such babies as never being cuddly, never reaching out when being picked up, never smiling or looking at them while being fed, and never appearing to notice the comings and goings of other people.

A Social Deficit Typically, autistic children do not show any need for affection or contact with anyone, and they usually do not even seem to know or care who their parents are. Several studies, however, have questioned the traditional view that autistic children are emotionally flat. These studies (Capps et al., 1993) have shown that autistic children do express emotions and should not be considered as lacking emotional reactions (Jones et al., 2001). Instead, Sigman (1996) has characterized the seeming inability of autistic children to respond to others as a lack of social understanding—a deficit in the ability to attend to social cues from others. The autistic child is thought to have a "mind blindness," an inability to take the attitude of others or to "see" things as others do. For example, an autistic child appears limited in the ability to understand where another person is pointing. Additionally, autistic children show deficits in attention and in locating and orienting to sounds in their environment (Townsend et al., 1996).

The lack of social interaction among autistic children has been well described. A behavioral observation study by Lord and Magill-Evans (1995) noted that autistic youngsters engaged in fewer social interactions than other children; however, this study also made the important observation that autistic children did not play—particularly did not show spontaneous play. In fact, much of the time, nothing was going on.

Encopresis is common (Siegel, 2003). Radford and Anderson (2003) pointed out that relatively little of the clinical descriptive literature on autistic children addresses the problem of toilet training. They noted that failing to cooperate in toilet training is a common problem and one that creates added difficulty for parents of autistic children and provided practical advice and training guidelines for dealing with this problem behavior. In addition, a high prevalence of sleep problems has been reported for autistic children (Williams, Sears, & Allard, 2004).

An Absence of Speech Autistic children have been considered to have an imitative deficit and do not effectively learn by imitation (Smith & Bryson, 1994). This dysfunction might explain their characteristic absence or severely limited use of speech. If speech is present, it is almost never used to communicate except in the most rudimentary fashion, such as by saying "yes" in answer to a question or by the use of **echolalia**—the parrot-like repetition of a few words. Whereas the echoing of parents' verbal behavior is found to a small degree in normal children as they experiment with their ability to produce articulate speech, persistent echolalia is found in about 75 percent of autistic children (Prizant, 1983).

Self-Stimulation Self-stimulation is often characteristic of autistic children. It usually takes the form of such repetitive movements as head banging, spinning, and rocking, which may continue by the hour. Other bizarre repetitive behaviors are typical. Such behavior is well described by Schreibman and Charlop-Christie (1998) and illustrated in the case of a young autistic boy.

case STUDY — Two of Everything

A. was described as a screaming, severely disturbed child who ran around in circles making high-pitched sounds for hours. He also liked to sit in boxes, under mats, and [under] blankets. He habitually piled up all furniture and bedding in the center of the room. At times, he was thought [to be] deaf, though he also showed extreme fear of loud noises. He refused all food except in a bottle, refused to wear clothes, chewed stones and paper, whirled himself, and spun objects. He played repetitively with the same toys for months, lining things in rows, collected objects such as bottle tops, and insisted on having two of everything, one in each hand. He became extremely upset if interrupted and if the order or arrangement of things [was] altered. (From Gajzago & Prior, 1974, p. 264.)

Autistic children seem to actively arrange the environment on their own terms in an effort to exclude or limit variety and intervention from other people, preferring instead a limited and solitary routine. Autistic children often show an active aversion to auditory stimuli, crying even at the sound of a parent's voice. The pattern is not always consistent, however; autistic children may at one moment be severely agitated or panicked by a very soft sound and at another time be totally oblivious to loud noise.

Intellectual Ability Much has been learned in the last few years about the cognitive abilities of autistic children (Bennetto, Pennington, et al., 1996). Compared with the

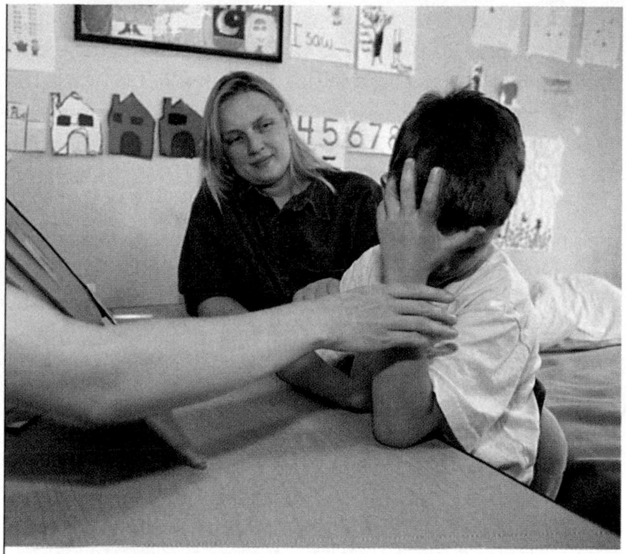

Autistic children seem to actively exclude or limit intervention from other people.

performance of other groups of children on cognitive or intellectual tasks, autistic children often show marked impairment. For example, autistic children are significantly impaired on memory tasks when compared with both normal and retarded children. Autistic children show a particular deficit in representing mental states—that is, they appear to have deficits in social reasoning but can manipulate objects (Scott & Baron-Cohen, 1996). Carpentieri and Morgan (1996) found that the cognitive impairment in autistic children is reflected in greater impairment in adaptive behaviors than is seen in mentally retarded children without autism.

Some autistic children are quite skilled at fitting objects together; thus their performance on puzzles or form boards may be average or above. Even in the manipulation of objects, however, difficulty with meaning is apparent. For example, when pictures are to be arranged in an order that tells a story, autistic children show a marked deficiency in performance. Moreover, autistic adolescents, even those who are functioning well, have difficulty with symbolic tasks such as pantomime, in which they are asked to recall motor actions to imitate tasks (e.g., ironing) with imagined objects, in spite of the fact that they might perform the task well with real objects (Rogers, Bennetto, et al., 1996).

Maintaining Sameness Many autistic children become preoccupied with and form strong attachments to unusual objects such as rocks, light switches, film negatives, or keys. In some instances, the object is so large or bizarre that merely carrying it around interferes with other activities. When their preoccupation with the object is disturbed—for example, by its removal or by attempts to substitute something in its place—or when anything familiar in the

DSM-IV-TR

Criteria for Autistic Disorder

A. Six (or more) of the following criteria from (1), (2), and (3), with at least two from (1), and one each from (2) and (3):

(1) qualitative impairment in social interaction, as manifested by at least two of the following:

(a) marked impairment in the use of multiple nonverbal behaviors such as eye-to-eye gaze, facial expression, body postures, and gestures to regulate social interaction

(b) failure to develop peer relationships appropriate to developmental level

(c) a lack of spontaneous seeking to share enjoyment, interests, or achievements with other people (e.g., by a lack of showing, bringing, or pointing-out objects of interest)

(d) lack of social or emotional reciprocity

(2) qualitative impairments in communication as manifested by at least one of the following:

(a) delay in, or total lack of, the development of spoken language (not accompanied by an attempt to compensate through alternative modes of communication such as gesture or mime)

(b) in individuals with adequate speech, marked impairment in the ability to initiate or sustain a conversation with others

(c) stereotyped and repetitive use of language or idiosyncratic language

(d) lack of varied, spontaneous make-believe play or social imitative play appropriate to developmental level

(3) restricted repetitive impairments and stereotyped patterns of behavior, interests, and activities, as manifested by at least one of the following:

(a) encompassing preoccupation with one or more stereotyped and restricted patterns of interest that is abnormal either in intensity or focus

(b) apparently inflexible adherence to specific, nonfunctional routines or rituals

(c) stereotyped and repetitive motor mannerisms (e.g., hand or finger flapping or twisting, or complex whole-body movements)

(d) persistent preoccupation with parts of objects

B. Delays or abnormal functioning in at least one of the following areas, with onset prior to age 3 years: (1) social interaction, (2) language as used in social communication, or (3) symbolic or imaginative play

Source: *Adapted with permission from the* Diagnostic and Statistical Manual of Mental Disorders, *Fourth Edition, Text Revision (Copyright 2000). American Psychiatric Association.*

environment is altered even slightly, these children may have a violent temper tantrum or a crying spell that continues until the familiar situation is restored. Thus autistic children are often said to be "obsessed with the maintenance of sameness."

CAUSAL FACTORS IN AUTISM The precise cause or causes of autism are unknown although most investigators agree that a fundamental disturbance of the central nervous system is involved (Volkmar & Klein, 2000). Many investigators believe that autism begins with some type of inborn defect that impairs an infant's perceptual-cognitive functioning—the ability to process incoming stimuli and to relate to the world. Recently, Fein (2001) presented the view that the psychological deficits in children with autism stem from a primary impairment in the domains of social attachment and communication failures. She postulated that the problem arises from deficits in the functioning of the amygdala, the almond-shaped neural structure that is believed to coordinate the actions of the autonomic nervous system and the endocrine systems. Recent MRI research has suggested that abnormalities in the brain anatomy may contribute to the brain metabolic differences and behavioral phenotype in autism (McAlonan, Cheung, et al., 2005). Whatever the physiological mechanisms or brain structures involved, evidence has accumulated that defective genes or damage from radiation or other conditions during prenatal development may play a significant role in the etiologic picture (Nicolson & Szatmari, 2003; Rutter, 2000; Waterhouse & Fein, 1997). Evidence for a genetic contribution to autism comes from examining the risk for autism in the siblings of autistic children (Micali, Chakrabarti, & Fombonne, 2004). The best estimates are that in families with one autistic child, there is a 3 to 5 percent risk of a sibling being autistic as well. Although this figure may seem low in an absolute sense, it is in fact extremely high, given the frequency of autism in the population.

Twin studies have also consistently shown higher concordance rates among monozygotic than dizygotic twins (Bailey, Le Couteur, & Gottesman, 1995). The conclusion from family and twin studies is that 80 to 90 percent of the variance in risk for autism is based on genetic factors; thus it is probably the most heritable form of psychopathology discussed in this text (Le Couteur et al., 1996). Nevertheless, the exact mode of genetic transmission is not yet understood, and it seems likely that relatives may also show an increased risk for other cognitive and social deficits that are milder in form than true autism (Smalley, 1991). In other words, just as in schizophrenia, there may be a spectrum of disorders related to autism (Gottesman & Hanson, 2005).

Some investigators have pointed to the existence of a possible genetic defect known as "fragile X," a constriction or breaking off of the end portion of the long arm of the X sex chromosome that appears to be determined by a specific gene defect (Eliez, Blasey, et al., 2001; Mazzocco, 2000; Tsai & Ghaziuddin, 1992). The fragile X syndrome occurs in about 8 percent of autistic males (Smalley, 1991). In addition, 15 to 20 percent of males with the fragile X syndrome are also diagnosed with autism, further suggesting a link between the two syndromes.

TREATMENTS AND OUTCOMES OF AUTISM The treatment prognosis for autistic disorder is poor, and because of the severity of their problems, those diagnosed with autism are often insufficiently treated (Wherry, 1996). Moreover, because of the typically poor response to treatment, autistic children are often subjected to a range of fads and "novel" approaches, which turn out to be equally ineffective.

Medical Treatment In the past, the use of medications to treat autistic children has not proved effective (Rutter, 1985). The drug most often used in the treatment of autism is haloperidol (Haldol), an antipsychotic medication (Campbell, 1987), but the data on its effectiveness do not support its use unless a child's behavior is unmanageable by other means (Sloman, 1991). More recently, clonidine, an antihypertensive medication, has been used with reportedly moderate effects in reducing the severity of the symptoms (Fankhauser et al., 1992). If irritability and aggressiveness are present, the medical management of a case might involve use of medications to lower the level of aggression (Fava, 1997; Leventhal, Cook, & Lord, 1998). Although there are no surefire medications approved for this purpose, the drug clomipramine has had some beneficial effect. However, no currently available medication reduces the symptoms of autism enough to encourage general use. We will thus direct our attention to a variety of psychological procedures that have been more successful in treating autistic children.

Behavioral Treatment Behavior therapy in an institutional setting has been used successfully in the elimination of self-injurious behavior, the mastery of the fundamentals of social behavior, and the development of some language skills (Charlop-Christie et al., 1998). Ivar Lovaas (1987), a pioneer in behavioral treatment of autistic children, reported highly positive results from a long-term experimental treatment program. The intervention developed by Lovaas and colleagues is very intensive and is usually conducted in the children's homes rather than in a clinical setting. The children are usually immersed in a one-to-one teaching situation for most of their waking hours over several years. The intervention is based on both discrimination training strategies (reinforcement) and contingent aversive techniques (punishment). The treatment plan typically enlists parents in the process and emphasizes teaching children to learn from and interact with "normal" peers in real-world situations. Of the treated children, 47 percent achieved normal intellectual functioning, and another 40 percent attained the mildly retarded level. In comparison, only 2 percent of the untreated control children achieved normal functioning, and 45 percent attained mildly retarded functioning. These remarkable results did, however, require a considerable staffing effort, with well-qualified therapists working with each child at least 40 hours per week for 2 years.

Some of the other impressive results with autistic children have also been obtained in projects that involve parents, with treatment in the home (Siegel, 2003). Treatment contracts with parents specify the desired behavior changes in their child and spell out the explicit techniques for bringing about these changes. Such "contracting" acknowledges the value of the parents as potential agents of change (Huynen, Lutzker, et al., 1996).

The Effectiveness of Treatment It is too early to evaluate the long-term effectiveness of the newer treatment methods or the degree of improvement they actually bring about. The prognosis for autistic children, particularly for children showing symptoms before the age of 2, is poor. Commonly, the long-term results of autism treatments have been unfavorable. A great deal of attention has been given to high-functioning autistic children (children who meet the criteria for autism yet develop functional speech). Ritvo and colleagues (1988) studied 11 parents who they believed met diagnostic criteria for autism (they were identified through having had children who were autistic). These individuals had been able to make modest adjustments to life, hold down jobs, and get married. But the outcome in autism, particularly in more severe cases, is usually not as positive.

One important factor limiting treatment success is the difficulty that autistic children have in generalizing behavior outside the treatment context (Handleman, Gill, & Alessandri, 1988). Children with severe developmental disabilities do not transfer skills across situations very well. Consequently, learning behavior in one situation does not appear to help them meet challenges in others.

In spite of a few remarkable cases of dramatic success, the overall prognosis for autistic children remains guarded. Less than one-fourth of the autistic children who receive treatment attain even marginal adjustment in later life. Even with intensive long-term care in a clinical facility, where gratifying improvements in specific behaviors may be brought about, autistic children are a long way from becoming normal. Some make substantial improvement during childhood, only to deteriorate, showing symptom aggravation, at the onset of puberty (Gillberg & Schaumann, 1981).

Providing parental care to autistic children is more trying and stressful than providing it to normal or mentally retarded children (Dunn, Burbine, et al., 2001). Parents of autistic children often find themselves in the extremely frustrating situation of trying to understand their autistic child, providing day-to-day care, and searching for possible educational resources for their child in the present health and educational environment. An unusually informative book on the topic of autism is *The World of the Autistic Child* (Siegel, 1996). Siegel discusses the impact that having an autistic child can have on the family—both parents and siblings—and describes ways of dealing with the problems that can arise, including the possible need of psychological treatment for other family members. The book is a particularly valuable guide to accessing the resources available for educating and treating autistic children and negotiating the confusing educational environment. Whether to seek residential placement, clearly a necessity in some situations and families, is also an important decision that parents of many autistic children must address. Efforts are being made to promote the development and growth of autistic people over their life span, in what has been referred to as the "Eden Model" (Holmes, 1998). In this approach, professionals and families recognize that autistic individuals may need to have different therapeutic regimes at different periods of their lives and that the available resources need to be structured to provide for their changing needs.

Some studies show that intensive behavioral treatment of autistic children, requiring a significant investment of time and energy on the part of therapist and parents, can bring improvement, particularly if this treatment continues at home rather than in an institution.

In Review

- Distinguish among conduct disorder, oppositional defiant disorder, and juvenile delinquency.
- Describe two common anxiety disorders found in children and adolescents.
- How do the symptoms of childhood depression compare to those seen in adult depression?
- Identify four common symptom disorders that can arise in childhood.
- What is known about the causes and treatments of autistic disorder?

Learning Disabilities and Mental Retardation

In the next two sections, we address two general conditions that can occur in children and can persist over their life span, greatly limiting their future development and psychological growth: learning disorders and mental retardation.

Learning Disabilities

The inadequate development found in **learning disabilities,** a term that refers to retardation, disorder, or delayed development, may be manifested in language, speech, mathematical, or motor skills, and it is not due to any reliably demonstrable physical or neurological defect. Of these types of problems, the best known and most widely researched are a variety of reading/writing difficulties known collectively as dyslexia. In **dyslexia,** the individual manifests problems in word recognition and reading comprehension; often he or she is markedly deficient in spelling as well. On assessments of reading skill, these persons routinely omit, add, and distort words, and their reading is typically painfully slow and halting.

The diagnosis of learning disability or disorder is restricted to those cases in which there is clear impairment in school performance or (if the person is not a student) in daily living activities—impairment not due to mental retardation or to a pervasive developmental disorder such as autism. Skill deficits due to attention-deficit/hyperactivity disorder are coded under that diagnosis. This coding presents another diagnostic dilemma, because some investigators hold that an attentional deficit is basic to many learning disorders; evidence for the latter view is equivocal (see Faraone et al., 1993). Children (and adults) with these disorders are more generally said to be "learning disabled" (LD). Significantly more boys than girls are diagnosed as learning disabled, but estimates of the extent of this gender discrepancy have varied widely from study to study.

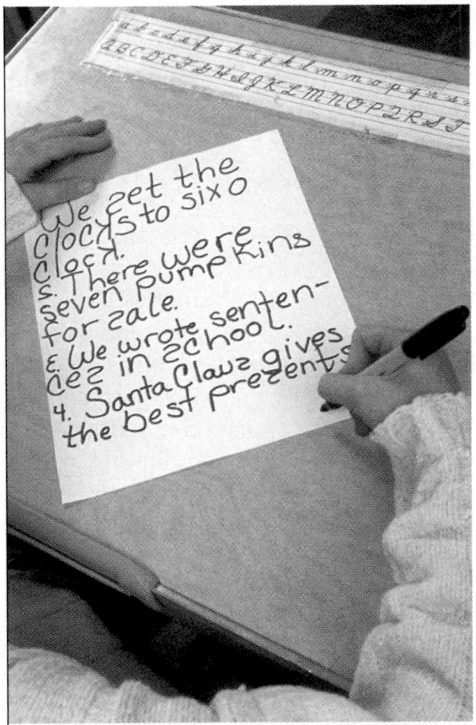

A person with dyslexia has problems with word recognition, spelling, and reading comprehension. Dyslexic people routinely omit, add, and distort written words, and their reading is typically painfully slow and halting.

Children with learning disabilities are initially identified as such because of an apparent disparity between their expected academic achievement level and their actual academic performance in one or more school subjects such as math, spelling, writing, or reading. Typically, these children have overall IQs, family backgrounds, and exposure to cultural norms and symbols that are consistent with at least average achievement in school. They do not have obvious crippling emotional problems, nor do they seem to be lacking in motivation, cooperativeness, or eagerness to please their teachers and parents—at least not at the outset of their formal education. Nevertheless, they fail, often abysmally and usually with a stubborn, puzzling persistence.

It is unfortunately the case that LD, despite its having been recognized as a distinct and rather common type of disorder for more than 40 years, and despite its having generated a voluminous research literature, still fails to be accorded the status it deserves in many school jurisdictions. Instead, many classroom teachers and school administrators resort to blaming the victim and attributing the affected child's problems to various character deficiencies (see Bearn & Smith, 1998; Fischer, 1993; Moats & Lyon, 1993). Where lockstep uniformity is the rule, as it is in most public and many alternative educational systems, a youngster who learns academic skills slowly or in a different way is treated as a troublemaker.

The consequences of these encounters between LD children and rigidly doctrinaire or regimented school systems can be disastrous to a child's self-esteem and general psychological well-being, and research indicates that these effects do not necessarily dissipate after secondary schooling ends (Aspis, 1997; Cooper, 1997; Ferri, Gregg, & Heggoy, 1997). Thus even where LD difficulties are no longer a significant impediment, an individual may bear, into maturity and beyond, the scars of many painful school-related episodes of failure.

But there is also a brighter side to this picture. High levels of general talent and of motivation to overcome the obstacle of a learning disorder sometime produce a life of extraordinary achievement. Sir Winston Churchill, British statesman, author, and inspiring World War II leader, is said to have been dyslexic as a child. The same attribution is made to Woodrow Wilson, former university professor and president of the United States, and to Nelson Rockefeller, former governor of New York and vice president of the United States. Such examples remind us that the "bad luck" and personal adversity of having a learning disorder need not be uniformly limiting; quite the contrary.

Causal Factors in Learning Disabilities

Probably the most widely held view of the causes of specific learning disabilities is that they are the products of subtle central nervous system impairments. In particular, these disabilities are thought to result from some sort of immaturity, deficiency, or dysregulation limited to those brain functions that supposedly mediate, for normal children, the cognitive skills that LD children cannot efficiently acquire. For example, many researchers believe that language-related LDs such as dyslexia are associated with a failure of the brain to develop in a normally asymmetrical manner with respect to the right and left hemispheres. Specifically, portions of the left hemisphere, where language function is normally mediated, for unknown reasons appear to remain relatively underdeveloped in many dyslexic individuals (Beaton, 1997). Recent work with functional magnetic resonance imaging (see Chapter 4) has suggested that dyslexic individuals may have a deficiency of physiological activation in a brain center believed to be involved with rapid visual processing (Travis, 1996).

Some investigators believe that the various forms of LD, or vulnerability to develop them, may be genetically transmitted. This issue seems not to have been studied with the same intensity or methodological rigor as in other disorders. Identification of a gene region for dyslexia on chromosome 6 has been reported (Schulte-Koerne, 2001). Although it would be somewhat surprising if a single gene were identified as the causal factor in all cases of reading disorder, the hypothesis of a genetic contribution to at least the dyslexic form of LD seems promising. One twin study of mathematics disability has also turned up evidence of some genetic contribution to this form of LD (Alarcon et al., 1997).

Children with learning disorders can experience deep emotional tension under normal learning circumstances.

Despite the seeming multitude of factors involved in LD, there may be some common elements. This is the position of Worden (1986), who argues that we should study the approaches taken by good learners in order to identify the areas where LD children are weak. Specialized training could then be employed to remedy the specific deficiencies. Even precise information on the manner in which LD children's learning approaches differ from those of normal children would leave unanswered questions about the sources of these differences. Nevertheless, pursuit of this idea might produce a set of rational, fine-tuned strategies for intervening to correct LD children's inefficient modes of learning.

Treatments and Outcomes

Because we do not yet have a confident grasp of what is "wrong" with the average LD child, we have had limited success in treating these children. Many informal and single-case reports claim success with various treatment approaches, but direct instruction strategies often do not succeed in transforming these children's abilities (Gettinger & Koscik, 2001), and there are few well-designed and well-executed outcome studies on specific treatments for LD.

Ellis (1993) has offered a comprehensive intervention model to facilitate learning in LD. This Integrative Strategy Instruction (ISI) has generated considerable interest among professionals in the field (see Houck, 1993; Hutchinson, 1993). Organized according to particular content areas, it envisions a variety of teacher-directed instructional strategies directed at key aspects of the learning process: orienting, framing, applying, and extending. Although the model appears not to have been rigorously tested for efficacy, its knowledge-based and systematic character is a welcome addition to analysis of the problems that LD children face. However, its application would demand high levels of administrative flexibility, teacher skill, and teacher motivation, none of which can be taken for granted in the average school environment (see Bearn & Smith, 1998; Male & May, 1997).

We have only limited data on the long-term, adult adjustments of people who grew up with the personal, academic, and social problems that LD generally entails. Two studies of college students with LD (Gregg & Hoy, 1989; Saracoglu et al., 1989) suggested that as a group they continue to have problems—academic, personal, and social—into the postsecondary education years. In a community survey of LD adults, Khan, Cowan, and Roy (1997) found that some 50 percent of them had personality abnormalities. Cato and Rice (1982) extracted from the available literature a lengthy list of problems experienced by the typical LD adult. These include—in addition to expected difficulties with self-confidence—continuing problems with deficits in the ordinary skills such as math that these people had trouble with as children. The authors did note, however, that there are considerable individual differences in these outcomes and that some adults with LD are able to manage very well.

Mental Retardation

The American Psychiatric Association (2000) in DSM-IV-TR defined **mental retardation** as "significantly subaverage general intellectual functioning . . . that is accompanied by significant limitations in adaptive functioning" (p. 41) in certain skill areas such as self-care, work, health, and safety. For the diagnosis to apply, these problems must have begun before the age of 18. Mental retardation is thus defined in terms of level of performance as well as intelligence. The definition says nothing about causal factors, which may be primarily biological, psychosocial, sociocultural, or a combination of these. By definition, any functional equivalent of mental retardation that has its onset after age 17 must be considered a dementia rather than mental retardation. The distinction is an important one, because the psychological situation of a person who acquires a pronounced impairment of intellectual functioning after attaining maturity is vastly different from that of a person whose intellectual resources were subnormal throughout all or most of his or her development.

Mental retardation occurs among children throughout the world (Fryers, 2000). In its most severe forms, it is a source of great hardship to parents as well as an economic and social burden on a community. The point prevalence rate of diagnosed mental retardation in the United States is estimated to be about 1 percent, which would indicate a population estimate of some 2.6 million people. In fact, however, prevalence is extremely difficult to pin down, because definitions of mental retardation vary considerably (Roeleveld, Zielhuis, & Gabreels, 1997). Most states have laws providing that persons with IQs below 70 who show socially incompetent or persistently problematic behavior can be classified as "mentally retarded" and, if judged otherwise unmanageable, may be placed in an institution. Informally, IQ scores between about 70 and 90 are often referred to as "borderline" or (in the upper part of the range) as "dull-normal."

Initial diagnoses of mental retardation occur very frequently at ages 5 to 6 (around the time that schooling begins for most children), peak at age 15, and drop off sharply after that. For the most part, these patterns in age of first diagnosis reflect changes in life demands. During early childhood, individuals with only a mild degree of intellectual impairment, who constitute the vast majority of the mentally retarded, often appear to be normal. Their subaverage intellectual functioning becomes apparent only when difficulties with schoolwork lead to a diagnostic evaluation. When adequate facilities are available for their education, children in this group can usually master essential school skills and achieve a satisfactory level of socially adaptive behavior. Following the school years, they usually make a more or less acceptable adjustment in the community and thus lose the identity of being mentally retarded.

TABLE 16.1 Retardation Severity and IQ Ranges

Diagnosed Level of Mental Retardation	Corresponding IQ Range
Mild retardation	50–55 to approximately 70
Moderate retardation	35–40 to 50–55
Severe retardation	20–25 to 35–40
Profound retardation	below 20–25

The various levels of mental retardation, as defined in DSM-IV-TR, are listed in Table 16.1 and described in greater detail in the following sections.

MILD MENTAL RETARDATION Mildly retarded individuals constitute by far the largest number of those diagnosed as mentally retarded. Within the educational context, people in this group are considered "educable," and their intellectual levels as adults are comparable to those of average 8- to 11-year-old children. Statements

Mildly retarded individuals constitute the largest number of those labeled mentally retarded. With help, a great majority of these individuals can adjust socially, master simple academic and occupational skills, and become self-supporting citizens.

such as the latter, however, should not be taken too literally. A mildly retarded adult with a mental age of, say, 10 (that is, intelligence test performance is at the level of the average 10-year-old) may not in fact be comparable to the normal 10-year-old in information-processing ability or speed (Weiss, Weisz, & Bromfield, 1986). On the other hand, he or she will normally have had far more experience in living, which would tend to raise the IQ score.

The social adjustment of mildly retarded people often approximates that of adolescents, although they tend to lack normal adolescents' imagination, inventiveness, and judgment. Ordinarily, they do not show signs of brain pathology or other physical anomalies, but often they require some measure of supervision because of their limited abilities to foresee the consequences of their actions. With early diagnosis, parental assistance, and special educational programs, the great majority of borderline and mildly retarded individuals can adjust socially, master simple academic and occupational skills, and become self-supporting citizens (Maclean, 1997).

MODERATE MENTAL RETARDATION Moderately retarded individuals are likely to fall in the educational category of "trainable," which means that they are presumed able to master certain routine skills such as cooking or minor janitorial work if provided specialized instruction in these activities. In adult life, individuals classified as moderately retarded attain intellectual levels similar to those of average 4- to 7-year-old children. Although some can be taught to read and write a little and may manage to achieve a fair command of spoken language, their rate of learning is slow, and their level of conceptualizing is extremely limited. They usually appear clumsy and ungainly, and they suffer from bodily deformities and poor motor coordination. Some of these moderately retarded people are hostile and aggressive; more typically, they are affable and nonthreatening. In general, with early diagnosis, parental help, and adequate opportunities for training, most moderately retarded individuals can achieve partial independence in daily self-care, acceptable behavior, and economic sustenance in a family or other sheltered environment.

SEVERE MENTAL RETARDATION Severely retarded individuals are sometimes referred to as "dependent retarded." In these individuals, motor and speech development are severely retarded, and sensory defects and motor handicaps are common. They can develop limited levels of personal hygiene and self-help skills, which somewhat lessen their dependency, but they are always dependent on others for care. However, many profit to some extent from training and can perform simple occupational tasks under supervision.

PROFOUND MENTAL RETARDATION The term "life-support retarded" is sometimes used to refer to profoundly retarded individuals. Most of these people are severely deficient in adaptive behavior and unable to master any but the simplest tasks. Useful speech, if it develops at all, is rudimentary. Severe physical deformities, central nervous system pathology, and retarded growth are typical; convulsive seizures, mutism, deafness, and other physical anomalies are also common. These individuals must remain in custodial care all their lives. They tend, however, to have poor health and low resistance to disease and thus a short life expectancy. Severe and profound cases of mental retardation can usually be readily diagnosed in infancy because of the presence of obvious physical malformations, grossly delayed development (e.g., in taking solid food), and other obvious symptoms of abnormality. These individuals show a marked impairment of overall intellectual functioning.

Brain Defects in Mental Retardation

Some cases of mental retardation occur in association with known organic brain pathology (Kaski, 2000). In these cases, retardation is virtually always at least moderate, and it is often severe. Profound retardation, which fortunately is rare, always includes obvious organic impairment. Organically caused retardation is, in essential respects, similar to dementia, except for a different history of prior functioning. In this section, we will consider five biological conditions that may lead to mental retardation, noting some of the possible interrelationships among them. Then we will review some of the major clinical types of mental retardation associated with these organic causes.

GENETIC-CHROMOSOMAL FACTORS Mental retardation, especially mild retardation, tends to run in families. Poverty and sociocultural deprivation, however, also tend to run in families, and with early and continued exposure to such conditions, even the inheritance of average intellectual potential may not prevent subaverage intellectual functioning.

Genetic-chromosomal factors play a much clearer role in the etiology of relatively infrequent but more severe types of mental retardation such as Down syndrome (discussed below) and a heritable condition known as fragile X. The gene responsible for the fragile X syndrome (FMR-1) was identified in 1991 (Verkerk, Pieretti, et al., 1991). In such conditions, genetic aberrations are responsible for metabolic alterations that adversely affect the brain's development. Genetic defects leading to metabolic alterations may, of course, involve many other developmental anomalies besides mental retardation—for example, autism (Wassink, Piven, & Patil, 2001). In general, mental retardation associated with known genetic-chromosomal defects is moderate to severe.

INFECTIONS AND TOXIC AGENTS Mental retardation may be associated with a wide range of conditions due to infection such as viral encephalitis or genital herpes

(Kaski, 2000). If a pregnant woman is infected with syphilis or HIV-1 or if she gets German measles, her child may suffer brain damage.

A number of toxic agents such as carbon monoxide and lead may cause brain damage during fetal development or after birth (Kaski, 2000). In rare instances, immunological agents such as antitetanus serum or typhoid vaccine may lead to brain damage. Similarly, if taken by a pregnant woman, certain drugs, including an excess of alcohol (West, Perotta, & Erickson, 1998; see Chapter 12), may lead to congenital malformations. And an overdose of drugs administered to an infant may result in toxicity and cause brain damage. In rare cases, brain damage results from incompatibility in blood types between mother and fetus. Fortunately, early diagnosis and blood transfusions can minimize the effects of such incompatibility.

TRAUMA (PHYSICAL INJURY) Physical injury at birth can result in retardation (Kaski, 2000). Although the fetus is normally well protected by its fluid-filled bag during gestation, and although its skull appears designed to resist delivery stressors, accidents do happen during delivery and after birth. Difficulties in labor due to malposition of the fetus or other complications may irreparably damage the infant's brain. Bleeding within the brain is probably the most common result of such birth trauma. Hypoxia—lack of sufficient oxygen to the brain stemming from delayed breathing or other causes—is another type of birth trauma that may damage the brain.

IONIZING RADIATION In recent decades, a good deal of scientific attention has been focused on the damaging effects of ionizing radiation on sex cells and other bodily cells and tissues. Radiation may act directly on the fertilized ovum or may produce gene mutations in the sex cells of either or both parents, which may lead to defective offspring. Sources of harmful radiation were once limited primarily to high-energy X rays used in medicine for diagnosis and therapy, but the list has grown to include nuclear weapons testing and leakages at nuclear power plants, among others.

MALNUTRITION AND OTHER BIOLOGICAL FACTORS It was long thought that dietary deficiencies in protein and other essential nutrients during early development of the fetus could do irreversible physical and mental damage. However, it is currently believed that this assumption of a direct causal link may have been oversimplified. In a review of the problem, Ricciuti (1993) cited growing evidence that malnutrition may affect mental development more indirectly, by altering a child's responsiveness, curiosity, and motivation to learn. According to this hypothesis, these losses would then lead to a relative retardation of intellectual facility. The implication here is that at least some malnutrition-associated intellectual deficit is a special case of psychosocial deprivation, which is also involved in retardation outcomes, as described below.

A limited number of cases of mental retardation are clearly associated with organic brain pathology. In some instances—particularly of the severe and profound types—the specific causes are uncertain or unknown, although extensive brain pathology is evident.

Organic Retardation Syndromes

Mental retardation stemming primarily from biological causes can be classified into several recognizable clinical types (Murphy, Boyle, et al., 1998), of which Down syndrome, phenylketonuria, and cranial anomalies will be discussed here. Table 16.2 presents information on several other well-known forms.

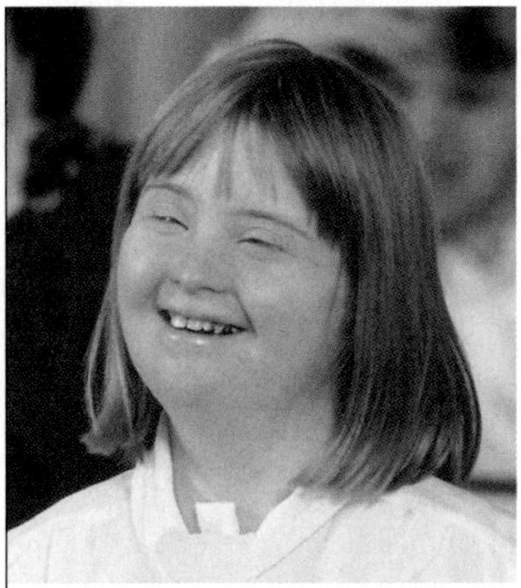

Physical features found among children with Down syndrome include almond-shaped eyes, abnormally thick skin on the eyelids, and a face and nose that are often flat and broad. The tongue may seem too big for the mouth and may show deep fissures. The iris of the eye is frequently speckled. The neck is often short and broad, as are the hands. The fingers are stubby, and the little finger is often more noticeably curved than the other fingers.

DOWN SYNDROME First described by Langdon Down in 1866, Down syndrome is the best known of the clinical conditions associated with moderate and severe mental retardation. About 1 in every 1,000 babies is diagnosed as having **Down syndrome,** a condition that creates irreversible limitations on survivability, intellectual achievement, and competence in managing life tasks. In fact, among adults with this disorder, adaptive abilities seem to decrease with increasing age, especially after 40 (Collacott & Cooper, 1997). The availability of amniocentesis and of chorionic villus sampling has made it possible to detect *in utero* the extra genetic material involved in Down syndrome, which is most often the trisomy of chromosome 21, yielding 47 rather than the normal 46 chromosomes (see Figure 16.1).

The Clinical Picture in Down Syndrome A number of physical features are often found among children with Down syndrome, but few of these children have all of the characteristics commonly thought to typify this group. The eyes appear almond-shaped, and the skin of the eyelids tends to be abnormally thick. The face and nose are often flat and broad, as is the back of the head. The tongue,

TABLE 16.2 Other Disorders Sometimes Associated with Mental Retardation

Clinical Type	Symptoms	Causes
No. 18 trisomy syndrome	Peculiar pattern of multiple congenital anomalies, the most common being low-set malformed ears, flexion of fingers, small jaw, and heart defects	Autosomal anomaly of chromosome 18
Tay-Sachs disease	Hypertonicity, listlessness, blindness, progressive spastic paralysis, and convulsions (death by the third year)	Disorder of lipoid metabolism, carried by a single recessive gene
Turner's syndrome	In females only; webbing of neck, increased carrying angle of forearm, and sexual infantilism	Sex chromosome anomaly (XO); mental retardation may occur but is infrequent
Klinefelter's syndrome	In males only; features vary from case to case, the only constant finding being the presence of small testes after puberty	Sex chromosome anomaly (XXY)
Niemann-Pick's disease	Onset usually in infancy, with loss of weight, dehydration, and progressive paralysis	Disorder of lipoid metabolism
Bilirubin encephalopathy	Abnormal levels of bilirubin (a toxic substance released by red cell destruction) in the blood; motor incoordination frequent	Often, Rh (ABO) blood group incompatibility between mother and fetus
Rubella, congenital	Visual difficulties most common, with cataracts and retinal problems often occurring together and with deafness and anomalies in the valves and septa of the heart	The mother's contraction of rubella (German measles) during the first few months of her pregnancy

Source: Based on American Psychiatric Association (1968, 1972); Clarke, Clarke, & Berg (1985); Holvey & Talbott (1972); Robinson & Robinson (1976).

which seems too large for the mouth, may show deep fissures. The iris of the eye is frequently speckled. The neck is often short and broad, as are the hands. The fingers are stubby, and the little finger is often more noticeably curved than the other fingers. Although facial surgery is sometimes tried to correct the more stigmatizing features, its success is often limited (Dodd & Leahy, 1989; Katz & Kravetz, 1989). Also, parents' acceptance of the Down syndrome child is inversely related to their support of such surgery (Katz, Kravetz, & Marks, 1997).

There are special medical problems with Down syndrome children that require careful medical attention and examinations (Merrick, Kandel, & Vardi, 2004). Death rates for children with Down syndrome have, however, decreased dramatically in the past century. In 1919 the life expectancy at birth for such children was about

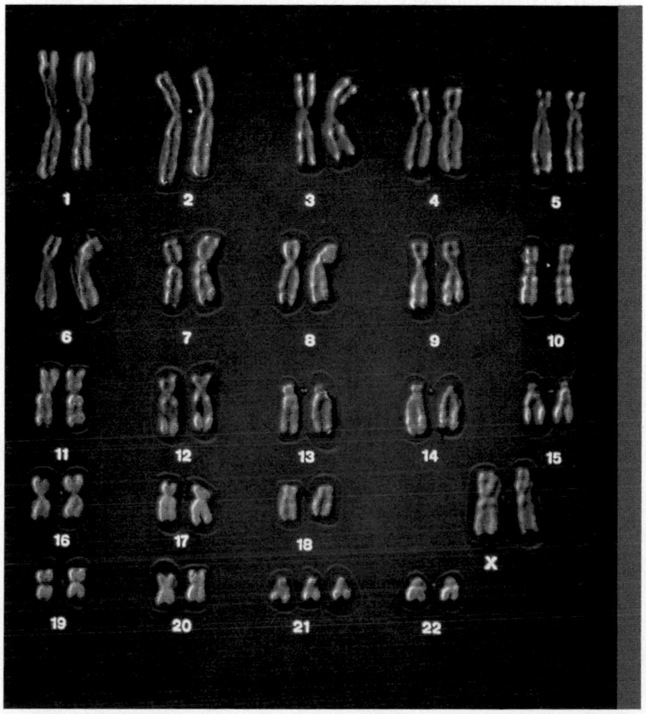

FIGURE 16.1

Trisomy of Chromosome 21 in Down Syndrome

This is a reproduction (karyotype) of the chromosomes of a female patient with Down syndrome. Note the triple (rather than the normal paired) representation at chromosome 21.

Source: *Reproduced with permission by Custom Medical Stock Photo, Inc.*

9 years; most of the deaths were due to gross physical problems, and a large proportion occurred in the first year. Thanks to antibiotics, surgical correction of lethal anatomical defects such as holes in the walls separating the heart's chambers, and better general medical care, many more of these children now live to adulthood (Hijji et al., 1997; Jancar & Jancar, 1996). Nevertheless, they appear as a group to experience an accelerated aging process (Hasegawa et al., 1997) and a decline in cognitive abilities (Thompson, 2003).

Despite their problems, children with Down syndrome are usually able to learn self-help skills, acceptable social behavior, and routine manual skills that enable them to be of assistance in a family or institutional setting (Brown, Taylor, & Matthews, 2001). The traditional view has been that Down syndrome youngsters are unusually placid and affectionate. Research has called into question the validity of this generalization (Pary, 2004). These children may indeed be very docile, but probably in no greater proportion than normal youngsters; they may also be equally (or more) difficult in various areas (Bridges & Cicchetti, 1982). In general, the quality of a child's social relationships depends on both IQ level and a supportive home environment (Alderson, 2001). Down syndrome adults may manifest less maladaptive behavior than comparable persons with other types of learning disability (Collacott et al., 1998).

Research has also suggested that the intellectual defect in Down syndrome may not be consistent across various abilities. Children with Down syndrome tend to remain relatively unimpaired in their appreciation of spatial relationships and in visual-motor coordination, although some evidence disputes this conclusion (Uecker et al., 1993). Research data are quite consistent in showing that their greatest deficits are in verbal and language-related skills (Azari et al., 1994; Mahoney, Glover, & Finger, 1981; Silverstein et al., 1982). Because spatial functions are known to be partially localized in the right cerebral hemisphere, and language-related functions in the left cerebral hemisphere, some investigators speculate that the syndrome is especially crippling to the left hemisphere.

Chromosomal abnormalities other than the trisomy of chromosome 21 may occasionally be involved in the etiology of Down syndrome. However, the extra version of chromosome 21 is present in at least 94 percent of cases. As we noted earlier, it may be significant that this is the same chromosome that has been implicated in research on Alzheimer's disease, especially given that persons with Down syndrome are at extremely high risk for Alzheimer's as they get into and beyond their late thirties (Cole et al., 1994; Janicki & Dalton, 2000; Nelson, Orme, et al., 2001; Prasher & Kirshnan, 1993). Interestingly, the APOE risk factor that is prominent in research on Alzheimer's appears not to be a significant element in the dementia experienced by Down syndrome adults (Prasher et al., 1997).

The reason for the trisomy of chromosome 21 is not clear, but the defect seems definitely related to parental age at conception. It has been known for many years that the incidence of Down syndrome increases on an accelerating slope (from the twenties on) with increasing age of the mother. A woman in her twenties has about 1 chance in 2,000 of conceiving a Down syndrome baby, whereas the risk for a woman in her forties is 1 in 50 (Holvey & Talbott, 1972). As in the case of all birth defects, the risk of having a Down syndrome baby is also high for very young mothers, whose reproductive systems have not yet fully matured. Research has also indicated that the father's age at conception is implicated in Down syndrome, particularly at higher ages (Hook, 1980; Stene et al., 1981). In one study involving 1,279 cases of Down syndrome in Japan, Matsunaga and associates (1978) demonstrated an overall increase in incidence with advancing paternal age when maternal age was controlled. The risk for fathers aged 55 years and over was more than twice that for fathers in their early twenties.

Thus it seems that advancing age in either parent increases the risk of the trisomy 21 anomaly, although the effect of maternal age is greater. It is not yet clear how aging produces this effect. A reasonable guess is that aging is related to cumulative exposure to varied environmental hazards such as radiation that might have adverse effects on the processes involved in zygote formation or development.

PHENYLKETONURIA In **phenylketonuria (PKU),** a baby appears normal at birth but lacks a liver enzyme needed to break down phenylalanine, an amino acid found in many foods. The genetic error results in retardation only when significant quantities of phenylalanine are ingested, which is virtually certain to occur if the child's condition

Today many more Down syndrome children are living to adulthood than in the past and are able to learn self-help, social, and manual skills. It is not unusual for Down syndrome children to be mainstreamed to some extent with unimpaired children, such as this boy (center, with glasses). Down syndrome children tend to remain relatively unimpaired in their appreciation of spatial relationships and visual–motor coordination; they show their greatest deficits in verbal and language-related skills.

remains undiagnosed (Grodin & Laurie, 2000). This disorder occurs in about 1 in 12,000 births (Deb & Ahmed, 2000). If the condition is not detected, the amount of phenylalanine in the blood increases and eventually produces brain damage.

The disorder usually becomes apparent between 6 and 12 months after birth, although such symptoms as vomiting, a peculiar odor, infantile eczema, and seizures may occur during the early weeks of life. Often, the first symptoms noticed are signs of mental retardation, which may be moderate to severe, depending on the degree to which the disease has progressed. Lack of motor coordination and other neurological problems caused by the brain damage are also common, and often the eyes, skin, and hair of untreated PKU patients are very pale (Dyer, 1999).

The early detection of PKU by examining urine for the presence of phenylpyruvic acid is routine in developed countries, and dietary treatment (such as the elimination of phenylalanine-containing foods such as diet soda or turkey) and related procedures can be used to prevent the disorder (Sullivan & Chang, 1999). With early detection and treatment—preferably before an infant is 6 months old—the deterioration process can usually be arrested so that levels of intellectual functioning may range from borderline to normal. A few children suffer mental retardation despite restricted phenylalanine intake and other preventive efforts, however. Dietary restriction in late-diagnosed PKU may improve the clinical picture somewhat, but there is no real substitute for early detection and prompt intervention (Pavone et al., 1993).

It appears that for a baby to inherit PKU, both parents must carry the recessive gene. Thus, when one child in a family is discovered to have PKU, it is especially critical that other children in the family be screened as well. Also, a pregnant PKU mother whose risk status has been successfully addressed by early dietary intervention may damage her at-risk fetus unless she maintains rigorous control of phenylalanine intake.

Patients with PKU are typically advised to follow a restricted diet over their life span in order to prevent cognitive impairment. Even with long-term treatment some investigators have reported mild deficits in cognitive functioning (White, Nortz, et al., 2002). However, some research has found little support for the hypothesis that deficits will occur even with dietary restrictions (Channon, German, et al., 2004).

CRANIAL ANOMALIES Mental retardation is associated with a number of conditions that involve alterations in head size and shape and for which the causal factors have not been definitely established (Maclean, 1997; Robinson & Robinson, 1976). In the rare condition known as **macrocephaly** (large-headedness), for example, there is an increase in the size and weight of the brain, an enlargement of the skull, visual impairment, convulsions, and other neurological symptoms resulting from the abnormal growth of glial cells that form the supporting structure for brain tissue.

Microcephaly The term **microcephaly** means "small-headedness." It is associated with a type of mental retardation resulting from impaired development of the brain and a consequent failure of the cranium to attain normal size.

The most obvious characteristic of microcephaly is the small head, the circumference of which rarely exceeds 17 inches, compared with the normal size of approximately 22 inches. Penrose (1963) also described microcephalic children as being invariably short in stature but having relatively normal musculature and sex organs. Beyond these characteristics, they differ considerably from one another in appearance, although there is a tendency for the skull to be cone-shaped, with a receding chin and forehead. Microcephalic children fall within the moderate, severe, and profound categories of mental retardation, but most show little language development and are extremely limited in mental capacity.

Microcephaly may result from a wide range of factors that impair brain development including intrauterine infections and pelvic irradiation during the mother's early months of pregnancy. Miller (1970) noted a number of cases of microcephaly in Hiroshima and Nagasaki that apparently resulted from the atomic bomb explosions during World War II. The role of genetic factors is not clear, although there is speculation that a single recessive gene is involved in a primary, inherited form of the disorder (Robinson & Robinson, 1976). Treatment is ineffective once faulty development has occurred; at present, preventive measures focus on the avoidance of infection and radiation during pregnancy.

Hydrocephaly **Hydrocephaly** is a relatively rare condition in which the accumulation of an abnormal amount of cerebrospinal fluid within the cranium causes damage to the brain tissues and enlargement of the skull (Materro, Junque, et al., 2001). In congenital cases, the head either is already enlarged at birth or begins to enlarge soon thereafter, presumably as a result of a disturbance in the formation, absorption, or circulation of the cerebrospinal fluid. The disorder can also arise in infancy or early childhood, following the development of a brain tumor, subdural hematoma, meningitis, or other conditions. In these cases, the condition appears to result from a blockage of the cerebrospinal pathways and an accumulation of fluid in certain brain areas.

The clinical picture in hydrocephaly depends on the extent of neural damage, which, in turn, depends on the age at onset and the duration and severity of the disorder. In chronic cases, the chief symptom is the gradual enlargement of the upper part of the head out of proportion to the face and the rest of the body. While the expansion of the skull helps minimize destructive pressure on the brain, serious brain damage occurs nonetheless. This damage leads to intellectual impairment and to such other effects as convulsions and impairment or loss of sight and hearing. The degree of intellectual impairment varies, being severe or profound in advanced cases.

Hydrocephaly can be treated by a procedure in which shunting devices are inserted to drain cerebrospinal fluid. With early diagnosis and treatment, this condition can usually be arrested before severe brain damage has occurred (Duinkerke, Williams, Rigamonti, & Hillis, 2004). Even with significant brain damage, carefully planned and early interventions that take into account both strengths and weaknesses in intellectual functioning may minimize disability (Baron & Goldberger, 1993).

Treatments, Outcomes, and Prevention

A number of programs have demonstrated that significant changes in the adaptive capacity of mentally retarded children are possible through special education and other rehabilitative measures (Berney, 2000). The degree of change that can be expected is related, of course, to the individual's particular situation and level of mental retardation.

TREATMENT FACILITIES AND METHODS One decision that the parents of a mentally retarded child must make is whether to place the child in an institution (Gath, 2000). Most authorities agree that this should be considered as a last resort, in light of the unfavorable outcomes normally experienced—particularly in regard to the erosion of self-care skills (Lynch, Kellow, & Willson, 1997). In general, children who are institutionalized fall into two groups: (1) those who, in infancy and childhood, manifest severe mental retardation and associated physical impairment and who enter an institution at an early age; and (2) those who have no physical impairments but show relatively mild mental retardation and a failure to adjust socially in adolescence, eventually being institutionalized chiefly because of delinquency or other problem behavior (see Stattin & Klackenberg-Larsson, 1993). In these cases, social incompetence is the main factor in the decision. The families of patients in the first group come from all socioeconomic levels, whereas a significantly higher percentage of the families of those in the second group come from lower educational and occupational strata.

The effect of being institutionalized in adolescence depends heavily on the institution's facilities as well as on individual factors. For the many teenagers with retardation whose families are not in a position to help them achieve a satisfactory adjustment, community-oriented residential care seems a particularly effective alternative (Alexander, Huganir, & Zigler, 1985), although great care must be taken in assessing the residents' needs and in the recruitment of staff personnel (Petronko, Harris, & Kormann, 1994). Unfortunately, many neighborhoods resist the location of such facilities within their confines and reject integration of residents into the local society (Short & Johnston, 1997).

For individuals with mental retardation who do not require institutionalization, educational and training facilities have historically been woefully inadequate. It still appears that a very substantial proportion of mentally retarded people in the United States never get access to services appropriate to their specific needs (Luckasson et al., 1992).

This neglect is especially tragic in view of the ways that exist to help these people. For example, classes for the mildly retarded, which usually emphasize reading and other basic school subjects, budgeting and money matters, and the development of occupational skills, have succeeded in helping many people become independent, productive community members. Classes for the moderately and severely retarded usually have more limited objectives, but they emphasize the development of self-care and other skills—e.g., toilet habits (Wilder et al., 1997)—that enable individuals to function adequately and to be of assistance in either a family (e.g., Heller, Miller, & Factor, 1997) or an institutional setting. Just mastering toilet training and learning to eat and dress properly may mean the difference between remaining at home or in a community residence and being institutionalized.

Today, there are probably fewer than 80,000 individuals in institutions for the retarded, less than half the number that were residents 40 years ago. Even many of these more seriously affected persons are being helped to be partly self-supporting in community-based programs (Bouras & Holt, 2000; Maclean, 1997; McDonnell et al., 1993). These developments reflect both the new optimism that has come to prevail and, in many instances, new laws and judicial decisions upholding the rights of retarded people and their families. A notable example is Public Law 94-142, passed by Congress in 1975 and since modified several times (see Hayden, 1998, for an update). This statute, termed the "Education for All Handicapped Children Act," asserts the right of mentally retarded people to be educated at public expense in the least restrictive environment possible.

During the 1970s, there was a rapid increase in alternative forms of care for the mentally retarded (Tyor & Bell, 1984). These included the use of decentralized regional facilities for short-term evaluation and training; small private hospitals specializing in rehabilitative techniques; group homes or halfway houses integrated into the local community; nursing homes for the elderly retarded; the placement of severely retarded children in more enriched foster-home environments; varied forms of support to the family for own-home care; and employment (Conley, 2003). The past 20 years have seen a marked enhancement in alternative modes of life for retarded citizens, rendering obsolete (and often leading to the closing of) many public institutions formerly devoted exclusively to this type of care.

EDUCATION AND INCLUSION PROGRAMMING Typically, educational and training procedures involve mapping out target areas of improvement such as personal grooming, social behavior, basic academic skills, and (for retarded adults) simple occupational skills (see Forness & Kavale, 1993). Within each area, specific skills are divided into simple components that can be learned and reinforced before more complex behaviors are required. Training that builds on step-by-step progression can bring retarded individuals repeated experiences of success and lead to substantial progress even by those previously regarded as uneducable (see McDonnell et al., 1993).

For mildly retarded youngsters, the question of what schooling is best is likely to challenge both parents and school officials. Many such children fare better when they attend regular classes for much of the day. Of course, this type of approach—often called **mainstreaming** or "inclusion programming"—requires careful planning, a high level of teacher skill, and facilitative teacher attitudes (Kozleski & Jackson, 1993; Stafford & Green, 1993; Wehman, 2003).

In Review

- In what ways do learning disorders differ from mental retardation?
- Compare and contrast mild, moderate, severe, and profound mental retardation.
- Describe five biological conditions that may lead to mental retardation.
- Describe some of the physical characteristics of children born with Down syndrome. What is its cause?
- What is the cause of and the preventive treatment for phenylketonuria (PKU)?

Planning Better Programs to Help Children and Adolescents

In our earlier discussion of several disorders of childhood and adolescence, we noted the wide range of treatment procedures available, as well as the marked differences in outcomes. In concluding this chapter, we will discuss certain special factors associated with the treatment of children and adolescents that can affect the success of an intervention.

Special Factors Associated with Treatment for Children and Adolescents

Mental health treatment, psychotherapy, and behavior therapy have been found to be as effective with children and adolescents as with adults (Kazdin & Weisz, 2003; Steiner, 1996), but treatments conducted in laboratory-controlled studies are more effective than "real-world" treatment situations (Weisz, Donenberg, et al., 1995; see Developments in Practice 16.1 and 16.2 on pp. 590 and 591). There are a number of special factors to consider in relation to treatment for children and adolescents, as follows:

THE CHILD'S INABILITY TO SEEK ASSISTANCE Most emotionally disturbed children who need assistance are not in a position to ask for help themselves or to transport themselves to and from child treatment clinics. Thus, unlike an adult, who can usually seek help, a child is dependent, primarily on his or her parents. Adults should realize when a child needs professional help and take the initiative in obtaining it. Sometimes, however, adults neglect this responsibility.

The law identifies four areas in which treatment without parental consent is permitted: (1) in the case of mature minors (those considered capable of making decisions about themselves); (2) in the case of emancipated minors (those living independently away from their parents); (3) in emergency situations; and (4) in situations in which a court orders treatment. Many children, of course, come to the attention of treatment agencies as a consequence of school referrals, delinquent acts, or parental abuse.

VULNERABILITIES THAT PLACE CHILDREN AT RISK FOR DEVELOPING EMOTIONAL PROBLEMS Children and youth who experience or are exposed to violence are at increased risk for developing psychological disorders (Seifert, 2003). In addition, many families provide an undesirable environment for their growing children (Ammerman et al., 1998). Studies have shown that up to a fourth of American children may be living in inadequate homes and that 7.6 percent of American youth have reported spending at least one night in a shelter, public place, or abandoned building (Ringwalt, Greene, et al., 1998). Disruptive childhood experiences have been found to be a risk factor for adult problems. For example, Reingold, Smith, et al. (2004) reported that a high risk of mental health problems in children and adolescents has been associated with the death of a parent or friend. Another epidemiological study (Susser, Moore, & Link, 1993) revealed that 23 percent of newly homeless men in New York City reported a history of out-of-home care as children. Parental substance abuse has also been found to be associated with vulnerability for children to develop psychological disorders (El-Sheikh & Buckhalt, 2003).

16.1 Developments in Practice

Family Therapy as a Means of Helping Children

To address a child's problems, it is often necessary to alter pathological family interaction patterns that produce or serve to maintain the child's behavior problems (Cooklin, 2000). Several family therapy approaches have been developed (Minuchin, 1974; Patterson, Capaldi, & Bank, 1991). These differ in some important ways—for example, in terms of how the family is defined (whether to include extended family members); what the treatment process will focus on (whether communications between the family members or the aberrant behavior of the problem family members is the focus); and what procedures are used in treatment (analyzing and interpreting hidden messages in the family communications or altering the reward and punishment contingencies through behavioral assessment and reinforcement). But whatever their differences, all family therapies view a child's problems, at least in part, as an outgrowth of pathological interaction patterns within the family, and they attempt to bring about positive change in family members through analysis and modification of the deviant family patterns (Everett & Everett, 2001).

Treatment outcome research strongly supports the effectiveness of family therapy in improving disruptive family relationships and promoting a more positive atmosphere for children (Hazelrigg, Cooper, & Borduin, 1987; Shadish et al., 1993).

High-risk behaviors or difficult life conditions need to be recognized and taken into consideration (Harrington & Clark, 1998). For example, there are a number of behaviors such as engaging in sexual acts or delinquency and using alcohol or drugs that might place young people at great risk for developing later emotional problems. Moreover, physical or sexual abuse, parental divorce, family turbulence, and homelessness (Cauce, Paradise, et al., 2000; Spataro, Mullen, et al., 2004) can place young people at great risk for emotional distress and subsequent maladaptive behavior (see The World Around Us 8.1 on p. 291 on factitious disorder by proxy and The World Around Us 16.3 on p. 592). Dodge, Lochman, and colleagues (1997) found that children from homes with harsh discipline and physical abuse, for example, were more likely to be aggressive and conduct-disordered than those from homes with less harsh discipline and those from nonabusing families.

NEED FOR TREATING PARENTS AS WELL AS CHILDREN Because many of the behavior disorders specific to childhood appear to grow out of pathogenic family interactions and result from having parents with psychiatric problems themselves (Johnson, Cohen, et al., 2000), it is often essential for the parents, as well as their child, to receive treatment. In some instances, in fact, the treatment program may focus on the parents entirely, as in the case of child abuse.

Increasingly, then, the treatment of children has come to mean family therapy, in which one or both parents, along with the child and siblings, may participate in all phases of the program. This is particularly important in situations in which the family situation has been identified as involving violence (Chaffin, Silvosky, et al., 2004). Many therapists have discovered that fathers are particularly difficult to engage in the treatment process. For working parents and for parents who basically reject the affected child, such treatment may be hard to arrange (Gaudin, 1993), especially in the case of poorer families who lack transportation and money. Thus both parental and economic factors help determine which emotionally disturbed children will receive assistance.

POSSIBILITY OF USING PARENTS AS CHANGE AGENTS In essence, parents can be used as change agents by training them in techniques that enable them to help their child. Typically, such training focuses on helping the parents understand the child's behavior disorder and teaching them to reinforce adaptive behavior while withholding reinforcement for undesirable behavior. Encouraging results have been obtained with parents who care about their children and want to help (Forehand, 1993; Webster-Stratton, 1991). Kazdin, Holland, and Crowley (1997) described a number of barriers to parental involvement in treatment that resulted in dropout from therapy. For example, coming from a disadvantaged background, having parents who were antisocial, or having parents who were under great stress tended to result in premature termination of treatment.

PROBLEM OF PLACING A CHILD OUTSIDE THE FAMILY Most communities have juvenile facilities that, day or night, will provide protective care and custody for young victims of unfit homes, abandonment, abuse, neglect, and related conditions. Depending on the home situation and the special needs of the child, he or she will later be either

16.2 Developments in Practice: Using Play Therapy to Resolve Children's Psychological Problems

Even if a child's problems are viewed as primary and in need of specific therapeutic intervention, he or she may not be motivated for therapy or be sufficiently verbal to benefit from psychotherapeutic methods that work with adults. Consequently, effective psychological treatment with children may involve using more indirect methods of therapy or providing individual psychological therapy for children in a less intrusive and more familiar way through play therapy (Hollins, 2001; Johnson, 2001).

As a treatment technique, play therapy emerged out of efforts to apply psychodynamic therapy to children. Because children are not able to talk about their problems in the way adults are, having not yet developed the self-awareness necessary, the applicability of traditional psychodynamic therapy methods to children is limited. Children tend to be oriented to the present and to lack the capability for insight and self-scrutiny that therapy requires. Their perceptions of their therapist differ from those of adult patients, and they may have the unrealistic view that the therapist can magically change their environment.

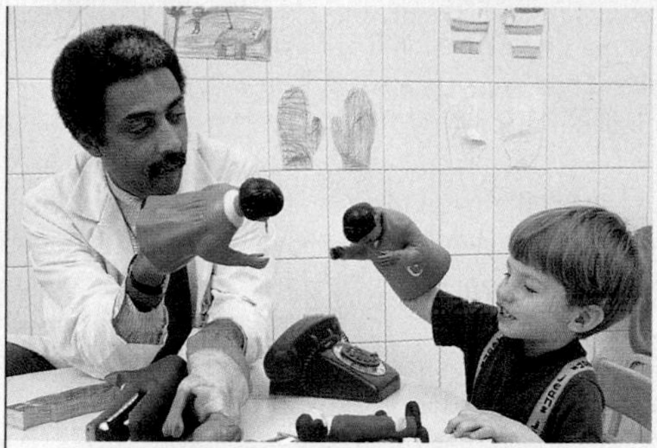

Children can often express their feelings more directly through play than in words, as shown in this play therapy session.

Through their play, children often express their feelings, fears, and emotions in a direct and uncensored fashion, providing a clinician with a clearer picture of problems and feelings (Perry & Landreth, 2001). The activity of play has become a valuable source of information about children, particularly when the sessions are consistent with their developmental level (Lewis, 1997).

In a play therapy session, the therapist usually needs to provide some structure or to guide play activities so that the child can express pertinent feelings. This might mean that the therapist asks direct questions of the child during the play session, such as "Is the doll happy now?" or "What makes the doll cry?" In addition to being a means of understanding a troubled child's problems, play activity also offers a medium for bringing about change in the child's behavior. A central process in play therapy is that the therapist, through interpretation, emotional support, and clarification of feelings (often by labeling them for the child), provides the child with a corrective emotional experience. That is, the therapist supplies the child with an accepting and trusting relationship that promotes healthier personality and relationship development. The play therapy situation enables the child to reexperience conflict or problems in the safety of the therapy setting, thereby gaining a chance to conquer fears, to acclimate to necessary life changes, or to gain a feeling of security to replace anxiety and uncertainty.

How effective is play therapy in reducing children's problems and promoting better adjustment? When compared with adult treatment studies, play therapy compares quite favorably. Casey and Berman (1985) conducted a careful study of treatment research with children and concluded that such treatment "appears to match the efficacy of psychotherapy with adults" (p. 395). Play therapy was found to be as effective as other types of treatment such as behavior therapy. In another study, in which play therapy was integrated into an 8-week intervention program to treat children with conduct disorder, the subjects showed significant gains at a 2-year follow-up (McDonald, Bellingham, et al., 1997).

returned to his or her parents or placed elsewhere. In the latter instance, four types of facilities are commonly relied on: (1) foster homes, (2) private institutions for the care of children, such as group homes, (3) county or state institutions, and (4) the homes of relatives. At any one time, more than half a million children are living in foster-care facilities.

The quality of a child's new home is, of course, a crucial determinant of whether the child's problems will be alleviated or made worse, and there is evidence to suggest that foster-home placement has more positive effects than group-home placement (Buckley & Zimmermann, 2003; Groza, Maschmeier, Jamison, & Piccola, 2003). Efforts are usually made to screen the placement facilities and maintain contact with the situation through follow-up visits, but even so, there have been cases of mistreatment in the new home (Dubner & Motta, 1999; Wilson, Sinclair, & Gibbs, 2000). In cases of child abuse, child

16.3 THE WORLD AROUND US

The Impact of Child Abuse on Psychological Adjustment

Children who are physically or sexually abused show problems in social adjustment (Beardslee & Gladstone, 2001) and are particularly likely to feel that the outcomes of events are determined by external factors beyond their own control (Kinzl & Biebl, 1992; Toth, Manly, & Cicchetti, 1992). They are also more likely to experience depressive symptoms (Bushnell, Wells, & Oakley-Browne, 1992; Emery & Laumann-Billings, 1998). As a result, abused children are dramatically less likely to assume personal responsibility for themselves, and they generally demonstrate less interpersonal sensitivity than control children. Child abuse and neglect may initiate a chain of violence. Child abuse is also associated with delinquent and criminal behavior when the victim grows up. Maxfield and Widom (1996), in a follow-up study of 908 people who were abused as children, found that their arrest rate for nontraffic offenses was significantly higher than that of a control sample of people who had not been abused as children.

Child abuse is an increasing concern in the United States (Crosson-Tower, 2002). A survey of reported incidents of child abuse in the United States found that such reports increased 1.7 percent in 1995, the total number of incidents exceeding 3.1 million. An estimated 1,215 children were killed in 1995 in child abuse incidents (National Committee to Prevent Child Abuse, 1996). The excessive use of alcohol or drugs in a family appears to increase the risk of violent death in the home (Rivera, Muellar, et al., 1997). Some evidence suggests that boys are more often physically abused than girls. It is clear that many children brought to the attention of legal agencies for abuse have been abused before. Moreover, the significantly higher rates among psychiatric inpatients of having been abused as children suggest that such maltreatment plays a causal role in the development of severe psychopathology (Read, 1997).

When the abuse involves a sexual component such as incest or rape, the long-range consequences can be profound (Paolucci, Genuis, & Violato, 2001). Adults who were sexually abused as children often show serious psychological symptoms such as a tendency to use dissociative defense mechanisms to excess, excessive preoccupation with bodily functions, lowered self-esteem (Nash et al., 1993), or a tendency to disengage as a means of handling stress (Coffey, Leitenberg, et al., 1996).

The role of sexual abuse in causing psychological problems has been the subject of several longitudinal studies. A large percentage of sexually abused children experience intense psychological symptoms following the incident (for example, the 74 percent reported by Bentovim, Boston, & Van Elburg, 1987). At follow-up, however, the improvement often seems dramatic (Bentovim et al., 1987; Conte, Berliner, & Schuerman, 1986). Several investigators have conceptualized the residual symptoms of sexual abuse as a type of post-traumatic stress disorder (PTSD) because the symptoms experienced are similar—for example, nightmares, flashbacks, sleep problems, and feelings of estrangement (Donaldson & Gardner, 1985; Koltek, Wilkes, & Atkinson, 1998).

Child abuse all too frequently produces maladaptive social behavior in its victims (Winton & Mara, 2001). The treatment of abused children needs to address their problems of inadequate social adjustment, depression, and poor interpersonal skills.

abandonment, or a serious childhood behavior problem that parents cannot control, it has often been assumed that the only feasible action was to take the child out of the home and find a temporary substitute. With such a child's own home so obviously inadequate, the hope has been that a more stable outside placement will be better for the child. But when children are taken from their homes and placed in an institution (which promptly tries to change them) or in a series of foster homes (where they obviously do not really belong), they are likely to feel rejected by their own parents, unwanted by their new caretakers, rootless, constantly insecure, lonely, and bitter.

Accordingly, the trend today is toward permanent planning. First, every effort is made to hold a family together and to give the parents the support and guidance they need for adequate childrearing. If this is impossible, then efforts are made to free the child legally for adoption and to find an adoptive home as soon as possible. This, of course, means that the public agencies need specially trained staffs with reasonable caseloads and access to resources that they and their clients may need. Children and adolescents in foster homes tend to require more mental health services than other children (dos Reis, Zito, et al., 2001).

VALUE OF INTERVENING BEFORE PROBLEMS BECOME ACUTE Over the last 25 years, a primary concern of many researchers and clinicians has been to identify and provide early help for children who are at special risk (Athey, O'Malley, et al., 1997). Rather than waiting until these children develop acute psychological problems that may require therapy or major changes in living arrangements, psychologists are attempting to identify conditions in the children's lives that seem likely to bring about or maintain behavior problems and, where such conditions exist, to intervene before development has been seriously distorted (Schroeder & Gordon, 2002). An example of this approach is provided in the work of Steele and Forehand (1997). These investigators found that children of parents who had a chronic medical condition (the fathers were diagnosed as having hemophilia, and many were HIV positive) were vulnerable to developing internalizing problems and avoidant behavior, particularly when the parent-child relationship was weak. These symptoms in the child were associated with depression in the parent. The investigators concluded that clinicians may be able to reduce the impact of parental chronic illness by strengthening the parent-child relationship and decreasing the child's use of avoidant strategies.

As described in Chapter 5, another type of early intervention has been developed in response to the special vulnerability children experience in the wake of a disaster or trauma such as a hurricane, accident, hostage-taking, or shooting (Shaw, 2003). Children and adolescents often require considerable support and attention to deal with such traumatic events, all too frequent in today's world. Individual and small-group psychological therapy might be implemented for victims of trauma (Gillis, 1993), support programs might operate through school-based interventions (Klingman, 1993), or community-based programs might be implemented to reduce the post-traumatic symptoms.

Early intervention has the double goal of reducing the stressors in a child's life and strengthening the child's coping mechanisms. It can often reduce the incidence and intensity of later maladjustment, thus averting problems for both the individuals concerned and the broader society. It is apparent that children's needs can be met only if adequate preventive and treatment facilities exist and are available to the children who need assistance.

Child Advocacy Programs

Today there are over 70 million people under age 18 in the United States (Bureau of the Census, 2001). Unfortunately, both treatment and preventive programs for our society's children remain inadequate to dealing with the extent of psychological problems among children and adolescents. In 1989 the United Nations General Assembly adopted the "U.N. Convention on the Rights of the Child," which provides a detailed definition of the rights of children in political, economic, social, and cultural areas. This international recognition of the rights of children can potentially have a great impact in promoting the humane treatment of children (Wilcox & Naimark, 1991). However, implementing those high ideals on a practical level is difficult at best.

In the United States, one approach that has evolved in recent years is mental health child advocacy. Advocacy programs attempt to help children or others receive services that they need but often are unable to obtain for themselves. In some cases, advocacy seeks to better conditions for underserved populations by changing the system (Pianta, 2001). Federal programs offering services for children are fragmented in that different agencies serve different needs; no government agency is charged with considering the whole child and planning comprehensively for children who need help. Consequently, child advocacy is often frustrating and difficult to implement (Zigler & Hall, 2000).

Outside the federal government, advocacy efforts for children have until recently been supported largely by legal and special-interest citizen's groups such as the Children's Defense Fund, a public-interest organization based in Washington, D.C. Mental health professionals have typically not been involved. Today, however, there is greater interdisciplinary involvement in attempts to provide effective advocacy programs for children (Carlson, 2001; Singer & Singer, 2000).

Although such programs have made important local gains toward bettering conditions for mentally disabled children, a great deal of confusion, inconsistency, and uncertainty still persist in the advocacy movement as a whole (Beeman & Edleson, 2000), and there is still a need to improve the accountability of mental health services for children (Carlson, 2001). In addition, the tendency at both federal and state levels has for some time been to cut back on funds for social services. Even so, some important steps have been taken toward child advocacy, and new efforts to identify and help high-risk children have been made (National Advisory Mental Health Council, 1990). If the direction and momentum of these efforts can be maintained and if sufficient financial support for them can be procured, the psychological environment for children could substantially improve.

In Review

- What special factors must be considered in providing treatment for children and adolescents?
- Why is therapeutic intervention a more complicated process with children than with adults?

UNRESOLVED ISSUES

Can Society Deal with Delinquent Behavior?

One of the most troublesome and widespread problems in childhood and adolescence is delinquent behavior. This behavior includes such acts as destruction of property, violence against other people, and various behaviors contrary to the needs and rights of others and in violation of society's laws. The term juvenile delinquency is a legal one; it refers to illegal acts committed by individuals between the ages of 8 and 18 (depending on state law). It is not recognized in DSM-IV-TR as a disorder. The actual incidence of juvenile delinquency is difficult to determine because many delinquent acts are not reported. However, some data are available:

- Of the more than 2 million young people who go through the juvenile courts each year in the United States, about a million and a half are there for delinquent acts and the remainder for status offenses such as running away that are not considered crimes for adults.
- In 2002, there were over 2.3 million juveniles arrested in the United States, which accounts for about 17 percent of all arrests; and 1,700 juveniles were involved in 1,400 murders (Federal Bureau of Investigation, 2003).
- Although most juvenile crime is committed by males, the rate has also risen for females. Female delinquents are commonly apprehended for drug use, sex offenses, running away from home, and incorrigibility, but crimes against property such as stealing have also markedly increased among this group.
- Both the incidence and the severity of delinquent behavior are disproportionately high for lower-class adolescents (Federal Bureau of Investigation, 2003).

More than two million children a year go through the juvenile justice system for committing delinquent acts.

Causal Factors

As noted in the text, only a small group of "continuous" delinquents actually evolve from oppositional defiant behavior to conduct disorder and then to adult antisocial personality; most people who engage in delinquent acts as adolescents do not follow this path (Moffitt, 1993a). The individuals who show adolescence-limited delinquency are thought to do so as a result of social mimicry. As they mature, they lose their motivation for delinquency and gain rewards for more socially acceptable behavior. Several key variables seem to play a part in the genesis of delinquency. They fall into the general categories of personal pathology, pathogenic family patterns, and undesirable peer relationships.

PERSONAL PATHOLOGY

Genetic Determinants Although the research on genetic determinants of antisocial behavior is far from conclusive, some evidence suggests possible hereditary contributions to criminality. Bailey (2000) pointed out that genetic factors in individual differences might operate through "an effect on hyperactivity and inattention, impulsivity, and physiological reactivity rather than through aggression." (p. 1861).

Brain Damage and Learning Disability In a distinct minority of delinquency cases (an estimated 1 percent or less), brain pathology results in lowered inhibitory controls and a tendency toward episodes of violent behavior. Such adolescents are often hyperactive, impulsive, emotionally unstable, and unable to inhibit themselves when strongly stimulated. The actual role that intellectual factors play in juvenile delinquency is still being debated (Lynam, Moffitt, & Stouthamer-Loeber, 1993).

Psychological Disorders Some delinquent acts appear to be directly associated with behavior disorders such as hyperactivity (Lyons, Griffin, et al., 2003) or pervasive developmental disorders (Palermo, 2004). One recent study reported that over half of delinquents showed evidence of mental disorders and 14 percent were judged to have mental disorder with substantial impairment that required a highly restrictive environment (Shelton, 2001).

Antisocial Traits Many habitual delinquents appear to share the traits typical of antisocial personalities (Bailey, 2000). They are impulsive, defiant, resentful, devoid of feelings of remorse or guilt, incapable of establishing and maintaining close interpersonal ties, and seemingly unable to profit from experience. In essence, these individuals are unsocialized.

Drug Abuse Many delinquent acts—particularly theft, prostitution, and assault—are directly associated with alcohol or drug use (Leukefeld et al., 1998). Most adolescents who abuse hard drugs such as heroin are forced to steal to maintain their habit, which can be very expensive. In the case of female addicts, theft may be combined with or replaced by prostitution as a means of obtaining money.

Pathogenic Family Patterns Of the various family patterns that have been implicated in contributing to juvenile delinquency, the following appear to be the most important.

Parental Absence or Family Conflict Delinquency appears to be much more common among youths from homes in which parents have separated or divorced than among those from homes in which a parent has died, suggesting that parental conflict may be a key element in causing delinquency. The effects of parental absence vary—for example, parental separation or divorce may be less troubling for children than parental conflict and dissension. It is parental disharmony and conflict in lieu of a stable home life that appears to be an important causal variable.

Parental Rejection and Faulty Discipline In many cases, one or both parents reject a child. When the father is the rejecting parent, it is difficult for a boy to identify with him and use him as a model for his own development. The detrimental effects of parental rejection and inconsistent discipline are by no means attributable only to fathers. Adolescents who experience alienation from their parents have been found to be more prone to delinquent behavior (Leas & Mellor, 2000).

Undesirable Peer Relationships Delinquency tends to be an experience often shared by cultural group (O'Donnell, 2004). In a classic study, Haney and Gold (1973) found that about two-thirds of delinquent acts were committed in association with one or two other people, and most of the remainder involved three or four others. Usually the offender and the companion or companions were of the same sex. Interestingly, girls were more likely than boys to have a constant friend or companion in delinquency.

Broad social conditions may also tend to produce or support delinquency (Ward & Laughlin, 2003). Interrelated factors that appear to be of key importance include alienation and rebellion, social rejection, and the psychological support afforded by membership in a delinquent gang. A recent report by the Office of Juvenile Justice and Delinquency Prevention estimated that there are 23,388 youth gangs with 664,906 members in the United States. Every state and every large city has a gang problem, and gangs are cropping up in small rural towns across the United States as well. The gang experience is male-oriented; only about 3 percent of gang members are female. In 1995 there were 46,359 gang-related crimes and 1,072 gang-related murders reported (Office of Juvenile Justice and Delinquency Prevention, 1995). The problem of gang membership is most prevalent in lower-SES areas and more common among ethnic minority adolescents (48 percent are African-Americans; 43 percent are Hispanic Americans) than among Caucasians. Although young people join gangs for many reasons, most members appear to feel inadequate in and rejected by the larger society. One recent study (Yoder, Whitlock, & Hoyt, 2003) found that a significant number of homeless youth (32 percent of the sample) become gang members. Gang membership gives them a sense of belonging and a means of gaining some measure of status and approval.

Dealing with Delinquency

If juvenile institutions have adequate facilities and personnel, they can be of great help to youth who need to be removed from aversive environments. These institutions can give adolescents a chance to learn about themselves and their world, to further their education and develop needed skills, and to find purpose and meaning in their lives. In such settings, young people may have the opportunity to receive psychological counseling and group therapy. The use of "boot camps" (juvenile facilities designed along the lines of army-style basic training) has received some support as a means of intervening in the delinquency process. One recent study reported that youth in boot camps viewed their environment as more positive and therapeutic than did those enrolled in traditional programs and that they showed less antisocial behavior at the end of the training (MacKenzie, Wilson, et al., 2001). However, the harsh, punitive programs favored by many "law and order" politicians (as noted by the Washington State Institute for Public Policy, 1995, 1998) often fail because they do not bring about the necessary behavior changes by reinforcing alternative behaviors (Huey & Henggeler, 2001).

Behavior therapy techniques based on the assumption that delinquent behavior is learned, maintained, and changed according to the same principles as other learned behavior have shown promise in the rehabilitation of juvenile offenders who require institutionalization (Ammerman & Hersen, 1997). Counseling with parents and related environmental changes are generally of vital importance in a total rehabilitation program (Perkins-Dock, 2001), but it is often difficult to get parents involved with incarcerated delinquents.

Probation is widely used with juvenile offenders and may be granted either in lieu of or after a period of institutionalization. Many delinquents can be guided into constructive behavior without being removed from their family or community. It is essential that peer group pressures be channeled in the direction of resocialization, rather than toward repetitive delinquent behavior (Carr & Vandiver, 2001). The recidivism rate for delinquents, the most commonly used measure for assessing rehabilitation programs, depends heavily on the type of offender and on the facility or procedures used. Other variables including the type of offense, family problems, having delinquent peers, ineffective use of leisure time, and conduct problems have also been related to reoffending (Cottle, Lee, & Heilbrun, 2001). The overall recidivism rate for delinquents sent to training schools has been estimated to be high (Federal Bureau of Investigation, 1998). Because juveniles who have recently been released from custody commit many crimes, it is important to intervene to provide a more positive peer culture (Springelmeyer & Chamberlain, 2001).

summary

- Children used to be viewed as "miniature adults." It was not until the second half of the twentieth century that a diagnostic classification system focused clearly on the special problems of children.
- In this chapter, the DSM-IV-TR classification system is followed in order to provide clinical descriptions of a wide range of childhood behavior problems.
- Attention-deficit/hyperactivity disorder is one of the more common behavior problems of childhood. In this disorder, the child shows impulsive, overactive behavior that interferes with his or her ability to accomplish tasks.
- The major approaches to treating hyperactive children have been medication and behavior therapy. Using medications such as amphetamines with children is somewhat controversial. Behavior therapy, particularly cognitive-behavioral methods, has shown a great deal of promise in modifying the behavior of hyperactive children.
- In conduct disorder, a child engages in persistent aggressive or antisocial acts. The possible causes of conduct disorder or delinquent behavior include biological factors, personal pathology, family patterns, and peer relationships.
- Children who suffer from anxiety or depressive disorders typically do not cause trouble for others through their aggressive conduct. Rather, they are fearful, shy, withdrawn, and insecure and have difficulty adapting to outside demands.
- The anxiety disorders may be characterized by extreme anxiety, withdrawal, or avoidance behavior. A likely cause is early family relationships that generate anxiety and prevent the child from developing more adaptive coping skills.
- Several other disorders of childhood involve behavior problems characterized by a single outstanding symptom rather than pervasive maladaptive patterns. The symptoms may involve enuresis, encopresis, sleepwalking, or tics.
- In autistic children, extreme maladaptive behavior occurs during the early years and prevents affected children from developing psychologically.
- It has not been possible to normalize the behavior of autistic children through treatment, but newer instructional and behavior modification techniques have been helpful in improving the ability of less severely impaired autistic children to function.
- When serious organic brain impairment occurs before the age of 18, the cognitive and behavioral deficits experienced are referred to as "mental retardation." Relatively common forms of such mental retardation, which in these cases is normally at least moderate in severity, include Down syndrome, phenylketonuria (PKU), and certain cranial anomalies.
- This organic type of mental deficit accounts for only some 25 percent of all cases of mental retardation. Mental retardation diagnoses, regardless of the underlying origins of the deficit, are coded on Axis II of DSM-IV-TR.
- Specific learning disorders are those in which failure of mastery is limited to circumscribed areas, chiefly involving academic skills such as reading. General cognitive ability may be normal or superior.
- Affected children are commonly described as "learning disabled" (LD). Some localized defect in brain development is often considered the primary cause of the disorder. Learning disorders create great turmoil and frustration in victims, their families, schools, and professional helpers.
- We reviewed a number of potential causes for the disorders of childhood and adolescence. Although genetic predisposition appears to be important in several disorders, parental psychopathology, family disruption, and stressful circumstances (such as parental death or desertion and child abuse) can also contribute.
- Recent research has underscored the importance of multiple risk factors in the development of psychopathology.
- There are special problems, and special opportunities, involved in treating childhood disorders. The need for preventive and treatment programs for children is always growing, and in recent years child advocacy has become effective in some states. Unfortunately, the financing and resources necessary for such services are not always readily available, and the future of programs for improving psychological environments for children remains uncertain.

Key Terms

Asperger's disorder (p. 575)
attention-deficit/hyperactivity disorder (ADHD) (p. 560)
autism (p. 575)
conduct disorder (p. 563)
developmental psychopathology (p. 558)
Down syndrome (p. 584)
dyslexia (p. 580)
echolalia (p. 576)
encopresis (p. 573)
enuresis (p. 572)
hydrocephaly (p. 587)
juvenile delinquency (p. 563)
learning disabilities (p. 580)
macrocephaly (p. 587)
mainstreaming (p. 589)
mental retardation (p. 582)
microcephaly (p. 587)
oppositional defiant disorder (p. 563)
Pemoline (p. 562)
pervasive developmental disorders (PDDs) (p. 575)
phenylketonuria (PKU) (p. 586)
Ritalin (p. 562)
selective mutism (p. 568)
separation anxiety disorder (p. 567)
sleepwalking disorder (p. 573)
Strattera (p. 562)
tic (p. 574)
Tourette's syndrome (p. 574)

CHAPTER 17

Therapy

Most of us have experienced a time or situation when we were dramatically helped by talking things over with a relative or friend. Most therapists, like all good listeners, rely on receptiveness, warmth, and empathy and take a nonjudgmental approach to the problems their clients present.

But there is more to therapy than just giving someone an opportunity to talk. Therapists also introduce into the relationship psychological interventions that are designed to promote new understandings, behaviors, or both, on the client's part. The fact that these interventions are deliberately planned and systematically guided by certain theoretical preconceptions is what distinguishes professional therapy from more informal helping relationships.

An Overview of Treatment

The belief that people with psychological problems can change—can learn more adaptive ways of perceiving, evaluating, and behaving—is the conviction underlying all **psychotherapy.** Achieving these changes is by no means easy. Sometimes a person's view of the world and her or his self-concept are distorted from pathological early relationships reinforced by years of negative life experiences. In other instances, environmental factors such as an unsatisfying job, an unhappy marriage, or financial stresses must be a focus of attention in addition to psychotherapy. Because change can be hard, people sometimes find it easier to bear their present problems than to challenge themselves to chart a different life course. Therapy also takes time. Even a highly skilled and experienced therapist cannot undo a person's entire past history and prepare him or her to cope adequately with difficult life situations within a short time. Therapy offers no magical transformations. Nevertheless, it holds promise even for the most severe mental disorders. Moreover, contrary to common opinion, psychotherapy can be less expensive in the long run than alternative modes of intervention (Gabbard et al., 1997).

It has been estimated that several hundred therapeutic approaches exist, ranging from psychoanalysis to Zen meditation. However, the era of managed care has prompted new and increasingly stringent demands that the efficacy of treatments be empirically demonstrated. This chapter will explore some of the most widely accepted pharmacological and psychological treatment approaches in use today. Although we recognize that different groups of mental health professionals often have their own preferences with respect to the use of the terms *client* and *patient*, in this chapter we use the terms interchangeably.

Why Do People Seek Therapy?

STRESSFUL CURRENT LIFE CIRCUMSTANCES People who seek therapy vary widely in their problems and in their motivations to solve them. Perhaps the most obvious candidates for psychological treatment are people experiencing sudden and highly stressful situations such as a divorce or unemployment—people who feel so overwhelmed by a crisis that they cannot manage on their own. These people often feel quite vulnerable and tend to be open to psychological treatment because they are motivated to alter their present intolerable mental states. In such situations, clients may gain considerably, in a brief time, from the perspective provided by their therapist.

PEOPLE WITH LONG-STANDING PROBLEMS Other people entering therapy have experienced long-term psychological distress and have lengthy histories of maladjustment. They may have had interpersonal problems such as an inability to be comfortable with intimacy, or they may have felt susceptible to low moods that are difficult for them to shake. Chronic unhappiness and the inability to feel confident and secure may finally prompt them to seek outside help. These people seek psychological assistance out of dissatisfaction and despair. They may enter treatment with a high degree of motivation, but as therapy proceeds, their persistent patterns of maladaptive behavior may generate resistance with which a therapist must contend. For example, a narcissistic client who expects to be praised by his or her therapist may become disenchanted and hostile when such "strokes" are not forthcoming.

RELUCTANT CLIENTS Some people enter therapy by a more indirect route. Perhaps they had consulted a physician for their headaches or stomach pains, only to be told that nothing was physically wrong with them. After they are referred to a therapist, they may at first resist the idea that their physical symptoms are emotionally based. Motivation to enter treatment differs widely among psychotherapy clients. Reluctant clients may come from many sources—for example, an alcoholic whose spouse threatens "either therapy or divorce," or a suspected felon whose attorney advises that things will go better at trial if it can be announced that the suspect has "entered therapy." In general, males are more reluctant to enter therapy than

17.1 The World Around Us

Why Are Men So Reluctant to Enter Therapy?

Compared to women, men are much more likely to resist seeking treatment from health professionals when they are experiencing difficulties. For example, they visit their primary physicians less frequently; they also visit mental health specialists less often, and they are less likely to enter psychotherapy or counseling than women are. In the case of depression, far more men than women say that they would never consider seeing a therapist; when men are depressed they are even reluctant to seek informal help from their friends. Moreover, when men do seek professional help, they tend to ask fewer questions than women do (see Addis & Mahalik, 2003).

Why is the average man, regardless of age, social background, and ethnicity, so much more reluctant than the average woman to utilize health services? One answer is that men are less able than women to recognize and label feelings of distress and to identify these feelings as emotional problems. In addition, men who subscribe to masculine stereotypes emphasizing self-reliance and lack of emotionality also tend to experience more gender-role conflict when they consider traditional counseling, with its focus on emotions and emotional disclosure. For a man who prides himself on being emotionally stoic, seeking help for a problem like depression may present a major threat to his self-esteem. Seeking help also requires giving up some control, and may run counter to the ideology that " a real man helps himself."

How can men be encouraged to seek help when they have difficulties? One basic problem is that the kinds of services that are available may not be the kinds of services that men who endorse traditional masculine roles can readily accept. In other words, for some men, there may be a mismatch between what is available and what they can psychologically tolerate. Part of the solution may be to develop treatment approaches that are based on theories of how men are socialized and that provide a better fit for men who are constrained by gender-role expectations. Another strategy is to use more creative approaches to encourage men to seek help and support. For example, television commercials for erectile dysfunction use professional basketball players and football coaches to encourage men with similar problems to "step up to the plate" and talk to their doctors. Making men more aware of other "masculine men" who have been "man enough" to go for help when they needed it may be an important step toward educating those whose adherence to masculine gender roles makes it difficult for them to acknowledge and seek help for their problems.

females are (see The World Around Us 17.1). A substantial number of angry parents bring their children to therapists with demands that their child's "uncontrollable behavior," which they view as independent of the family context, be "fixed." These parents may be surprised and reluctant to recognize their own role in shaping their child's behavior patterns.

PEOPLE WHO SEEK PERSONAL GROWTH A final group of people who enter therapy have problems that would be considered relatively normal. That is, they appear to have achieved success, have financial stability, have generally accepting and loving families, and have accomplished many of their life goals. They enter therapy not out of personal despair or impossible interpersonal involvements, but out of a sense that they have not lived up to their own expectations and realized their own potential. These people, partly because their problems are more manageable than the problems of others, may make substantial gains in personal growth.

Psychotherapy, however, is not just for people who have clearly defined problems, high levels of motivation, and an ability to gain ready insight into their behavior. Psychotherapeutic interventions have been applied to a wide variety of chronic problems. Even a severely disturbed, psychotic client may profit from a therapeutic relationship that takes into account his or her level of functioning and maintains therapeutic subgoals that are within the client's present capabilities (e.g., see Hogarty et al., 1997a, 1997b; Kendler, 1999b).

It should be clear from these brief descriptions that there is no "typical" client. Neither is there a "model" therapy. No currently used form of therapy is applicable to all types of clients, and all of the standard therapies can document some successes. Most authorities agree that client variables such as motivation to change and the severity of symptoms are exceedingly important to the outcome of therapy (Clarkin & Levy, 2004). As we will see, the various therapies have relatively greater success when a therapist takes the characteristics of a particular client into account in determining treatment approaches.

Who Provides Psychotherapeutic Services?

Members of many different professions have traditionally provided advice and counsel to individuals in emotional distress. Physicians, in addition to caring for their patients'

Many clients with psychological problems can be helped by talking with a skilled, empathetic, and nonjudgmental therapist.

physical problems, often become trusted advisers in emotional matters as well. Many physicians are trained to recognize psychological problems that are beyond their expertise and to refer patients to psychological specialists or to psychiatrists.

Another professional group who deals extensively with emotional problems is the clergy. A minister, priest, or rabbi is frequently the first professional to encounter a person experiencing an emotional crisis. Although some clergy are trained mental health counselors, most limit their counseling to religious matters and spiritual support and do not attempt to provide psychotherapy. Rather, like general-practice physicians, they are trained to recognize problems that require professional management and to refer seriously disturbed people to mental health specialists.

The three types of mental health professionals who most often administer psychological treatment in mental health settings are clinical psychologists, psychiatrists, and psychiatric social workers. These professions were briefly described in Chapter 1 (see The World Around Us 1.3). In addition to their providing psychotherapy, the medical training and licensure qualifications of psychiatrists enable them to prescribe psychoactive medications and also to administer other forms of medical treatment such as electroconvulsive therapy. In some states, appropriately supervised psychologists and other clinical specialists may now prescribe medications if they have received additional training. Although every mental health professional differs to some degree in his or her training and approach to treatment, generally, psychiatrists differ from psychologists in their predilection for treating mental disorders with a biological approach (i.e., medications), whereas psychologists generally treat patients' psychopathology by examining and in some cases changing their patients' behaviors and thought patterns.

In a clinic or hospital (as opposed to an individual practice), a wide range of treatment approaches may be used. These range from the use of drugs, to individual or group psychotherapy, to home, school, or job visits aimed at modifying adverse conditions in a client's life—for example, helping a teacher become more understanding and supportive of a child-client's needs. Often the latter is as important as treatment directed toward modifying the client's personality, behavior, or both.

This willingness to use a variety of procedures is reflected in the frequent use of a team approach to assessment and treatment, particularly in group practice and institutional settings. This approach ideally involves the coordinated efforts of medical, psychological, social work, and other mental health personnel working together as the needs of each case warrant. Also of key importance is the current practice of providing treatment facilities in the community. Instead of considering maladjustment to be an individual's private misery, which in the past often required confinement in a distant mental hospital, this approach integrates family and community resources in the total treatment approach.

The Therapeutic Relationship

The therapeutic relationship evolves out of what both client and therapist bring to the therapeutic situation. The outcome of psychotherapy normally depends on whether the client and therapist are successful in achieving a productive working alliance. The client's major contribution is his or her motivation. Clients who are pessimistic about their chances of recovery or who are ambivalent about dealing with their problems and symptoms respond less well to treatment (e.g., Mussell et al., 2000).

THE THERAPEUTIC ALLIANCE The establishment of an effective "working alliance" between client and therapist is seen by most investigators and practitioners as essential to psychotherapeutic gain. Our experiences as therapists affirm this basic observation, as does the research literature. In a very real sense, the relationship with the therapist is therapeutic in its own right.

There is much evidence that therapists' personal characteristics help determine therapeutic outcome (e.g., see Beutler et al., 2004; Blatt et al., 1996; Moyers et al., 2005). How well clients do in treatment is related to the strength of the alliance they have with their therapists (Barber et al., 2000; Kazdin et al., 2005; Martin et al., 2000). However, people who have a lot of problems often have very troubled interpersonal relationships. An important skill for any therapist therefore is the ability to foster good relationships with clients who may present some challenges in this regard.

Other factors such as the level of expertise and experience of the therapist also appear to be important, although there is considerable variability across studies (e.g., Beutler et al., 2004; Huppert et al., 2001; Lambert & Ogles, 2004) and more research is warranted. Expert therapists have been shown to be better than either experienced or novice therapists in such skills as the ability to provide a clear, coherent, and succinct account of a patient's problems (that is, to make a case formulation) and to develop an appropriate treatment plan (Eells et al., 2005).

Although definitions of the therapeutic alliance vary, its key elements are (1) a sense of working collaboratively on the problem, (2) agreement between patient and therapist about the goals and tasks of therapy, and (3) an affective bond between patient and therapist (see Constantino et al., 2001; Martin et al., 2000). Clear communication is also important. This is no doubt facilitated by the degree of shared experience in the backgrounds of client and therapist.

OTHER QUALITIES THAT ENHANCE THERAPY As already noted, the client's motivation to change is a crucial element in determining the quality of the therapeutic alliance and hence the level of success likely to be achieved in the therapeutic effort. A wise therapist is appropriately cautious about accepting an unmotivated client. Not all prospective clients, regardless of their need for treatment, are ready for the temporary discomfort that effective therapy may entail. As already described, many men, in particular, have trouble accepting the conditions that therapy may impose such as the need to report their innermost feelings. Even the motivation of self-referred clients may dissipate in the face of the painful confrontations with self and past experiences that good therapy may require.

Almost as important as motivation is a client's expectation of receiving help. This expectancy is often sufficient in itself to bring about substantial improvement (Fisher & Greenberg, 1997; Lambert et al., 1986); this may be because patients who expect therapy to be effective engage more in the process (Meyer et al., 2002). Just as a placebo often lessens pain for someone who believes it will do so, a person who expects to be helped by therapy is likely to be helped, almost regardless of the particular methods used by a therapist. The downside of this fact is that if a therapy or therapist fails for whatever reason to inspire client confidence, the effectiveness of treatment is likely to be compromised.

To the art of therapy, a therapist brings a variety of professional skills and methods intended to help people see themselves and their situations more objectively—that is, to gain a different perspective. Besides helping provide a new perspective, most therapy situations also offer a client a safe setting in which he or she is encouraged to practice new ways of feeling and acting, gradually developing both the courage and the ability to take responsibility for acting in more effective and satisfying ways.

To bring about such changes, an effective psychotherapist must help the client give up old and dysfunctional behavior patterns and replace them with new, functional ones. Because clients will present varying challenges in this regard, the therapist must be flexible enough to use a variety of interactive styles. Effective therapy depends, at least to some extent, on a good match between client and therapist. For this reason, a therapist's own personality is an important factor in determining therapeutic outcomes, quite aside from his or her background and training or the particular formal treatment plan adopted (Beutler et al., 2004; Blatt et al., 1996; Lambert, 1989). For example, a therapist who inadvertently but unfailingly takes charge in finding solutions for clients' problems will have considerable difficulty helping people who are experiencing inhibited autonomy, as in dependent personality disorder.

In Review

- What kinds of professionals provide help to people in psychological distress? In what kinds of settings does treatment occur?
- What factors are important in determining how well patients do in therapy?

Measuring Success in Psychotherapy

Evaluating treatment success is not always as easy as it might seem (Hill & Lambert, 2004). Attempts at estimating clients' gains in therapy generally depend on one or more of the following sources of information: (1) a therapist's impression of changes that have occurred, (2) a client's reports of change, (3) reports from the client's family or friends, (4) comparison of pretreatment and post-treatment scores on personality tests or on other instruments designed to measure relevant facets of psychological functioning, and (5) measures of change in selected overt behaviors. Unfortunately, each of these sources has its own limitations.

A therapist may not be the best judge of a client's progress, because any therapist is likely to be biased in favor of seeing himself or herself as competent and successful (after all, therapists are only human). In addition, the therapist typically has only a limited observational sample (the client's in-session behavior) from which to make judgments of overall change. Furthermore, therapists can inflate improvement averages by deliberately or subtly encouraging difficult clients to discontinue therapy. The problem of how to deal with early dropouts from treatment further complicates many studies of therapy outcomes. Should these patients be excluded from analyses of outcome? (After all, they have received little or none of the therapy being evaluated.) Or should they be included and counted as treatment failures? These issues have been at the heart of much debate and discussion.

Also, a client is not necessarily a reliable source of information on therapeutic outcomes. Not only may clients want to believe for various personal reasons that they are getting better, but in an attempt to please the therapist, they may report that they are being helped. In addition, because therapy often requires a considerable investment of time, money, and sometimes emotional distress, the idea that it has been useless is a dissonant one. Relatives of the client may also be inclined to "see" the improvement they had hoped for, although they often seem to be more realistic than either the therapist or the client in their evaluations of outcome.

Clinical ratings by an outside, independent observer are sometimes used in research on psychotherapy outcomes to evaluate the progress of a client; these ratings may be more objective than ratings by those directly involved in the therapy. Another widely used objective measure of client change is performance on various psychological tests. A client evaluated in this way takes a battery of tests before and after therapy, and the differences in scores are assumed to reflect progress, or lack of progress, or occasionally even deterioration. However, some of the changes that such tests show may be artifactual, as with ***regression to the mean*** (Speer, 1992), wherein very high (or very low) scores tend on repeated measurement to drift toward the average of their own distributions, yielding a false impression that some real change has been documented. Also, the particular tests selected are likely to focus on the theoretical predictions of the therapist or researcher. They are not necessarily valid predictors of the changes, if any, that the therapy actually induces, or of how the client will behave in real life. And without follow-up assessment, they provide little information on how enduring any change is likely to be.

> **research close-up**
>
> ***regression to the mean***
>
> *This reflects the statistical tendency for extreme scores (e.g., very high or very low scores) on a given measure to look less extreme at a second assessment (as occurs in a repeated-measures design). Because of this statistical artifact, people whose scores are furthest away from the group mean to begin with (e.g., people who have the highest anxiety scores or the lowest scores on self-esteem) will tend to score closer to the group mean at the second assessment, even if no real clinical change has occurred.*

Objectifying and Quantifying Change

Generalized terms such as *recovery, marked improvement,* and *moderate improvement,* which were often used in outcome research in the past, are open to considerable differences in interpretation. Today the emphasis is on using more quantitative methods of measuring change. For example, the Beck Depression Inventory (a self-report measure of depression severity) and the Hamilton Rating Scale for Depression (a set of rating scales used by clinicians to measure the same thing) both yield summary scores and have become almost standard in the pre- and post-therapy assessment of depression. Changes in preselected and specifically denoted behaviors that are systematically monitored, such as how many times a client with obsessions about contamination washes his hands, are often highly valid measures of outcome. Such techniques, including client self-monitoring, have been widely and effectively used, mainly by behavior and cognitive-behavioral therapists. In research settings, one new development is using functional magnetic resonance imaging (fMRI) to examine brain activity before and after treatment (see Developments in Research 17.2).

Would Change Occur Anyway?

What happens to disturbed people who do not obtain formal treatment? In view of the many ways in which people can help each other, it is not surprising that improvement often occurs without professional intervention. Relevant here is the observation that treatment offered by therapists has not always been clearly demonstrated to be superior in outcome to nonprofessionally administered therapies (Christensen & Jacobson, 1994). Moreover, some forms of psychopathology such as depressive episodes or brief psychotic disorder sometimes run a fairly short course with or without treatment. In other instances, disturbed people improve over time for reasons that are not apparent.

Even if many emotionally disturbed persons tend to improve over time without psychotherapy, psychotherapy can often accelerate improvement or bring about desired behavior change that might not otherwise occur. Most researchers today would agree that psychotherapy is more effective than no treatment (see Shadish et al., 2000), and

17.2 Developments in Research

Using Brain Activation to Measure Therapeutic Change

Functional magnetic resonance imaging (fMRI) is an exciting technique that can be used to measure changes in activation in the human brain. When certain areas of the brain are active and in use, it is believed that they require more oxygen. By measuring the amount of blood flow and oxygen in a given region of the brain, scientists can begin to learn what is happening in the human mind.

Research using neuroimaging to explore the changes that occur in psychotherapy is still in its infancy. However, clinical scientists are using fMRI to measure clinical change in patient populations. Nakao and colleagues (2005) studied ten outpatients with obsessive-compulsive disorder (OCD). At the start of the study, all the patients received a brain scan while they were engaged in a task that required them to think about words (e.g., *sweat, urine, feces*) that triggered their obsessions and compulsions. Patients were then treated for 12 weeks either with the SSRI fluvoxamine (Luvox) or with behavior therapy. At the end of this treatment period, the brain scanning was repeated.

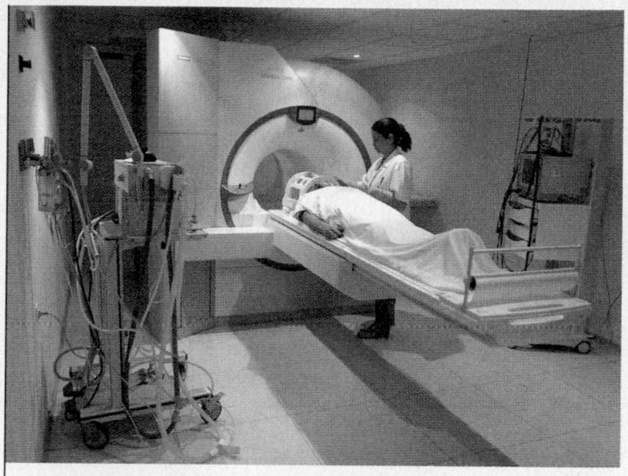

Researchers are now using functional magnetic resonance imaging (fMRI) to look at brain activity before and after treatment.

The results showed that, before treatment, certain areas of the brain thought to be involved in OCD (for example, a brain region in the frontal lobe called the "orbitofrontal cortex") were activated during the symptom-provocation task. However, after therapy, these same regions showed much less activation when the patients were challenged to think about the provocative trigger words. Several methodological problems limit the conclusions that can be drawn from this study (e.g., small number of subjects). However, research studies of this type highlight the potential of neuroimaging in treatment research and suggest that physiological changes may accompany the clinical gains that occur in psychotherapy.

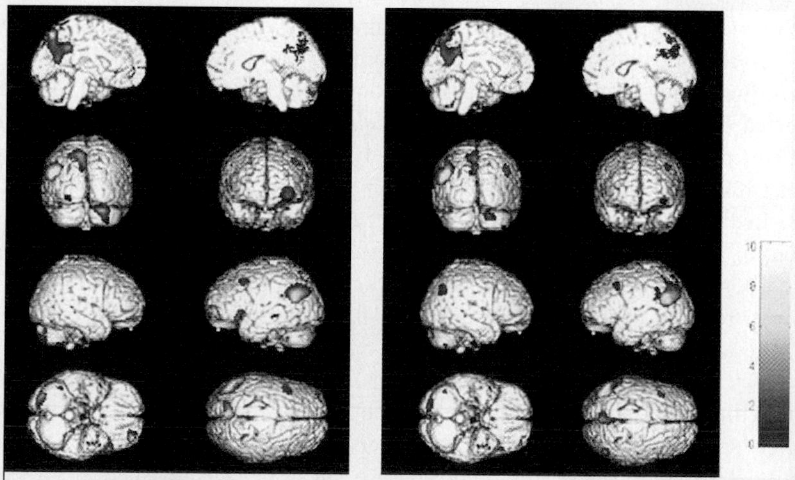

Before After

Treatment changes the patterns of brain activation of OCD patients during an experimental task. After receiving treatment, patients' brain activation patterns look similar to those of normal controls when they perform the same task. This suggests that OCD symptoms might suppress activity in key brain areas involved in cognitive performance and that treatment may help to correct this.

Source: *Nakao et al., 2005.*

indeed the pertinent evidence, widely cited throughout this entire text, confirms this strongly. The chances of an average client benefiting significantly from psychological treatment are, overall, impressive (Lambert & Ogles, 2004). Research suggests that about 50 percent of patients show clinically significant change after 21 therapy sessions. After 40 sessions, about 75 percent of patients have improved (Lambert et al., 2001).

Progress in therapy is not always smooth and linear, however. Tang and his colleagues have shown that "sudden gains" can occur between one therapy session and another (Tang & DeRubeis, 1999; Tang et al., 2002). These clinical leaps appear to be triggered by cognitive changes or by psychodynamic insights that patients experience in certain critical sessions.

Can Therapy Be Harmful?

The outcomes of psychotherapy are not invariably either neutral (no effect) or positive. Some clients are actually harmed by their encounters with psychotherapists (Lambert & Ogles, 2004; Mays & Franks, 1985; Strupp et al., 1977). According to one estimate, somewhere between 5 and 10 percent of clients deteriorate during treatment (Lambert & Ogles, 2004). Patients suffering from borderline personality disorder and from obsessive-compulsive disorder typically have higher rates of negative treatment outcomes than patients with other problems (Mohr, 1995).

Obvious ruptures of the therapeutic alliance—what Binder and Strupp (1997) refer to as "negative process" (p. 121) in which client and therapist become embroiled in a mutually antagonistic and downwardly spiraling course—account for only a portion of the failures. In other instances an idiosyncratic array of factors operate together (for example, the mismatch of therapist and client personality characteristics) to produce deteriorating outcomes. Our impression, supported by some evidence (see Beutler et al., 2004), is that certain therapists, probably for reasons of personality, just do not do well with certain types of client problems. In light of these intangible factors, it is ethically required of all therapists (1) to monitor their work with various types of clients to discover any such deficiencies, and (2) to refer to other therapists those clients with whom they may be ill-equipped to work (APA, 2002).

A special case of therapeutic harm is the problem of sex between therapist and client, typically seduction of a client (or former client) by a therapist. This is highly unethical conduct. Given the frequently intense and intimate quality of therapeutic relationships, it is not surprising that sexual attraction arises. What is distressing is the apparent frequency with which it is manifested in exploitive and unprofessional behavior on the part of therapists—all the more so in light of the fact that virtually all authorities agree that such liaisons are nearly always destructive of good client functioning in the long run (Pope et al., 1993). A prospective client seeking therapy needs to be sufficiently wary to determine that the therapist chosen is one of the large majority who are committed to high ethical and professional standards.

In Review

- What approaches can be used to evaluate treatment success? What are the advantages and limitations of these approaches?
- Do people who receive psychological treatment always show a clinical benefit?

What Therapeutic Approaches Should Be Used?

Evidence-Based Treatments

When a pharmaceutical company develops a new drug, it must obtain approval of the drug from the federal Food and Drug Administration (FDA) before that drug can be marketed. This involves, among other things, demonstrating through research on human subjects that the drug has **efficacy**—that is, that it does what it is supposed to do in curing or relieving some target condition. These tests, using voluntary and informed patients as subjects, are called **randomized clinical trials (RCTs)** or, more simply, *efficacy trials.* Although these trials may become quite elaborate, the basic design is one of randomly assigning (e.g., by the flip of a coin) half the patients to the supposedly "active" drug and the other half to a visually identical but physiologically inactive **placebo.** Usually, neither the patient nor the prescriber is informed which is to be administered; that information is recorded in code by a third party. This **double-blind** procedure is an effort to ensure that expectations on the part of the patient and prescriber play no role in the study. After a predetermined treatment interval, the code is broken and the active or placebo status of all subjects is revealed. If subjects on the active drug have improved in health significantly more than subjects on the placebo, the investigator has evidence of the drug's efficacy. Obviously, the same design could be modified to compare the efficacy of two or more active drugs, with the option of adding a placebo condition. Thousands of such studies are in progress daily across the country. They usually take place in academic medical settings and many are financially supported by the pharmaceutical industry.

Investigators of psychotherapy outcomes have attempted to apply this research design to their own field of inquiry, with necessary modifications (see Chambless & Ollendick, 2001). A source of persistent frustration has been the difficulty of concocting a credible placebo condition. Most such research has thus adopted the strategy of either competitively comparing two or more purportedly "active" therapies or using a no-treatment ("wait list") control of the same duration as the active treatment. Another problem is that therapists, even those with the same theoretical orientations, often differ markedly in the manner in which they deliver therapy. (In contrast, pills of the same chemical compound and dosage do not vary.) To test a given therapy, it therefore becomes necessary to develop a treatment manual to specify just how the therapy under examination will be delivered. Therapists in the research trial are then trained (and monitored) to make sure that their therapy sessions do not deviate significantly from the procedures outlined in the manual (e.g., see Sanderson & Woody, 1995).

Efforts to "manualize" therapy represent one way that researchers have tried to minimize the variability in patients' clinical outcomes that might result from characteristics of the therapist themselves (such as "personal charisma"). Although **manualized therapies** originated principally to standardize psychosocial treatments to fit the randomized clinical trial (RCT) paradigm, some therapists recommend extending these manualized therapies' use to routine clinical practice after efficacy for particular disorders has been established (e.g., see Wilson, 1998). Practicing clinicians, however, vary in their attitudes toward treatment manuals (Addis & Krasnow, 2000).

Efficacy or RCT studies of psychosocial treatments are increasingly common. These time-limited studies typically focus on patients who have a single DSM-IV-TR diagnosis (patients with comorbid diagnoses are sometimes excluded) and involve two or more treatment or control (e.g., wait list) conditions where at least one of the treatment conditions is a psychosocial one (another could be some biological therapy, such as a particular drug). Client-subjects are randomly assigned to these conditions, whose effects, if any, are evaluated systematically with a common battery of assessment instruments, usually administered both before and after treatment.

Efficacy studies of the outcomes of specific psychosocial treatment procedures are considered the most rigorous type of evaluation we have for establishing that a given therapy "works" for clients with a given DSM-IV-TR diagnosis. Treatments that meet this standard are often described as "empirically validated" or "empirically supported," and various lists of such treatments are now routinely published and updated (e.g., Chambless et al., 1998; Nathan & Gorman, 1998; Roth & Fonagy, 1996).

Medication or Psychotherapy?

Modern **psychopharmacology** has helped many individuals who would otherwise require hospitalization to function in their family and community settings. It has also led to the earlier discharge of those who do require hospitalization and made restraints and locked wards largely obsolete. In short, medication has led to a much more favorable hospital climate for patients and staff alike.

Nevertheless, certain issues arise in the use of psychotropic drugs. Aside from possible unwanted side effects, there is the complexity of matching drug and drug dosage to the needs of the specific patient. It is also sometimes necessary for patients to change medication in the course of treatment. In addition, the use of medications in isolation from other treatment methods may not be ideal for some disorders, because drugs themselves do not generally cure disorders. As many investigators have pointed out, drugs tend to alleviate symptoms by inducing biochemical changes, not by helping the individual understand and change the personal or situational factors that may be creating or reinforcing maladaptive behaviors. Moreover, when drugs are discontinued, patients may be at risk of relapsing. For many disorders, a variety of evidence-based forms of psychotherapy may produce more long-lasting benefits than medications alone unless the medications are continued indefinitely.

On the other hand, for some disorders for which there are known effective medications, the failure to incorporate medication into a psychotherapeutic treatment program can also lead to very serious problems. The World Around Us 17. 3 on page 608 well illustrates this point.

Combined Treatments

In the past, it was believed that medication and psychotherapy were incompatible approaches and so should not be administered together (see Gabbard & Kay, 2001). However, for many disorders the integration of medication and psychotherapy is now common in clinical practice (Thase & Jindal, 2004). One survey suggests that 55 percent of patients receive both medications and psychotherapy for their problems (Pincus et al., 1999). This integrative approach is a good example of the biopsychosocial perspective that best describes current thinking about mental disorders and that is reflected throughout this book.

Medications can be combined with a broad range of psychological approaches. In some cases, they can help patients benefit more fully from psychotherapy and can serve to reduce noncompliant behavior in therapy. In other cases, psychotherapy may be directed at the family of the patient, as, for example, in psychosocial interventions, which are designed to reduce high levels of expressed emotion and thus decrease patients' relapse rates, with the families of patients who have schizophrenia (see Chapter 14).

17.3 The World Around Us

Osherhoff v. Chestnut Lodge

Osherhoff, a physician, was severely depressed and functioning so ineffectively that his family hospitalized him at Chestnut Lodge, which at the time was a largely psychoanalytically oriented treatment facility. Osherhoff received intensive psychoanalytic treatment four times a week. He did not receive any medications.

After several months, Osherhoff's family became concerned over his lack of progress. He had lost 40 pounds, he was experiencing severe sleep disturbance, and he had such marked psychomotor agitation that his feet had become swollen and blistered from pacing. The family sought a reevaluation of his case. The staff, in a case conference, decided to continue the treatment program that had been initiated. When Dr. Osherhoff's condition worsened further, his family had him discharged and admitted to another facility, where he was treated with a combination of phenothiazines and tricyclic antidepressants. He improved markedly and was discharged in 3 months. Later he filed a suit claiming that Chestnut Lodge had not administered the proper treatment, drug therapy—an error that had caused him to lose a year of employment in his medical practice.

Preliminary court arbitration indicated an initial award of damages to Dr. Osherhoff, but the case was settled out of court before a final judgment was rendered. A number of complicated issues were involved in this case, which is described in Klerman (1990). However, it serves as an important reminder that therapists may be liable for failing to provide medication to patients with certain disorders for which medications known to be effective are available.

Overall, there is some cause to be optimistic about the combined use of drugs and psychosocial approaches, especially in the more severe disorders such as schizophrenia and bipolar disorder, although in these cases the psychotherapy often cannot start until a psychotic episode has at least begun to subside. Such integrated approaches are also appreciated and regarded as essential by the patients themselves. Here is the description of one patient with bipolar disorder, who also happens to be a prominent clinical scientist, highlighting her need for both medication and psychotherapy:

Case Study: Medications and Psychotherapy

At this point in my existence, I cannot imagine leading a normal life without both taking lithium and having had the benefits of psychotherapy. Lithium prevents my seductive but disastrous highs, diminishes my depressions, clears out the wool and webbing from my disordered thinking, slows me down, gentles me out, keeps me from ruining my career and relationships, keeps me out of a hospital, alive, and makes psychotherapy possible. But ineffably, psychotherapy heals. It makes some sense of the confusion, reins in the terrifying thoughts and feelings, returns some control and hope and possibility of learning from it all. Pills cannot, do not, ease one back into reality; they only bring one back headlong, careening, and faster than can be endured at times. Psychotherapy is a sanctuary; it is a battleground; it is a place I have been psychotic, neurotic, elated, confused, and despairing beyond belief. But, always, it is where I have believed—or learned to believe—that I might someday be able to contend with all of this.

No pill can help me deal with the problem of not wanting to take pills; likewise, no amount of psychotherapy alone can prevent my manias and depressions. I need both. It is an odd thing, owing life to pills, one's own quirks and tenacities, and this unique, strange, and ultimately profound relationship called psychotherapy. (From the autobiography of Kay Jamison, *An Unquiet Mind,* 1995, pp. 88–89.)

In addition to combined treatments being well received by patients, research suggests that there are clinical benefits to this approach, especially for patients with severe disorders (see Gabbard & Kay, 2001). For example, Keller and colleagues (2000) compared the outcomes of 519 depressed patients who were treated with an antidepressant (nefazodone), with psychotherapy (cognitive-behavioral), or with a combination of both of these treatments. In the medication-alone condition, 55 percent of patients did well. In the psychotherapy-alone condition, 52 percent of patients responded to treatment. However, patients for whom the two treatments were combined did even better, with an overall positive response rate of 85 percent. These findings echo the results of Thase et al. (1997), who conducted a large-scale analysis of single and combined treatments for patients with depression and found that the combination of medication and psychotherapy was particularly beneficial for patients with more severe and recurrent depressions. Similar clinical advantages for combining cognitive-behavioral therapy (CBT) and medications have also been reported in the treatment of panic disorder (Barlow et al., 2000), although in this study the long-term benefits of CBT were somewhat reduced for patients in the combined-treatment condition. Quite possibly, combined treatment is effective because medications and psychotherapy may target different symptoms and work at different rates. As Hollon and Fawcett (1995) note after reviewing this literature, "Pharmacotherapy appears to provide rapid, reliable relief from acute distress, and psychotherapy appears to provide broad and enduring change, with combined treatment retaining the specific benefits of each" (p. 1232).

In Review

- What are the advantages and drawbacks of using a "manualized" therapy?
- What is the difference between an effectiveness study and an efficacy study?
- What does it mean to describe a treatment as "evidence-based"?
- Why is the integration of medication and psychotherapy becoming increasingly common in clinical practice?

Pharmacological Approaches to Treatment

The field of psychopharmacology is characterized by rapid and exciting progress. Clinical breakthroughs are occurring on a regular basis, and there is now real hope for patients previously considered to be beyond help. In the following sections we discuss some of the major classes of medications that are now routinely used to help patients with a variety of mental disorders, as well as some additional treatment approaches (such as electroconvulsive therapy) that are less widely used but highly effective, especially for patients who fail to show a good clinical response to other treatments.

These drugs are sometimes referred to as "psychoactive" (literally, "mind-altering") medications, indicating that their major effects are on the brain. As we examine these medications, it is important to remember that people differ in how rapidly they metabolize drugs—that is, in how quickly their bodies break down the drugs once ingested. For example, many African-Americans metabolize antidepressant and antipsychotic medications more slowly than whites. What this means is that African-Americans sometimes show a more rapid and greater response to these medications but also experience more side effects (see U.S. Department of Health and Human Services, 2001, p. 67). Determining the correct dosage is critical, because too little of a drug can be ineffective; on the other hand, too much medication can cause toxicity that may be life-threatening, depending on the individual and the medication concerned.

Antipsychotic Drugs

As their name suggests, **antipsychotic drugs** are used to treat psychotic disorders such as schizophrenia and psychotic mood disorders. You have already read about these medications in Chapter 14. The key therapeutic benefit of antipsychotics derives from their ability to alleviate or reduce the intensity of delusions and hallucinations. They do this by blocking dopamine receptors.

Table 17.1 on page 610 lists some of the more commonly used neuroleptic drugs as well as information about typical dose ranges and the **half-life** of each drug. The half-life is the time it takes for the level of active drug in the body to be reduced by 50 percent (due to the drug being metabolized and excreted). Advantages of a long half-life include the need for less frequent dosing, less variation in the concentration of the drug in the plasma, and less severe withdrawal. Disadvantages include the risk of the drug accumulating in the body, as well as increased sedation and psychomotor impairment during the day.

Studies have found that approximately 60 percent of patients with schizophrenia who are treated with traditional antipsychotic medication have a resolution of their positive symptoms within 6 weeks, compared to only about 20 percent of those treated with placebo (see Bradford et al., 2002). These drugs are also useful in treating other disorders with psychotic symptoms such as mania, psychotic depression, and schizoaffective disorder, and they are occasionally used to treat transient psychotic symptoms when these occur in people with borderline personality disorder and schizotypal personality disorder (Koenigsberg et al., 2002). Finally, they are useful in treating Tourette's syndrome and delirium (see Chapter 15) and are sometimes used in the treatment of the delusions, hallucinations, paranoia, and agitation that can occur with Alzheimer's disease (Gitlin, 1996).

Antipsychotic medications are usually administered daily by mouth. However, some patients, particularly those

TABLE 17.1 Commonly Prescribed Antipsychotic Drugs

Drug Class	Generic Name	Trade Name	Dose Range (mg)	Half-Life (hrs)
Second Generation (Atypical)	clozapine	Clozaril	300–900	5–16
	risperidone	Risperdal	1–8	20–24
	olanzapine	Zyprexa	5–20	21–54
	quetiapine	Seroquel	100–750	6–7
	ziprasidone	Geodon	80–160	6.6
	aripiprazole	Abilify	15–30	75
First Generation (Conventional)	chlorpromazine	Thorazine	75–900	16–30
	perphenazine	Trilafon	12–64	9–21
	molindone	Moban	50–200	6.5
	thiothixene	Navane	15–60	34
	trifluroperazine	Stelazine	6–40	13
	haloperidol	Haldol	2–100	12–36
	fluphenazine	Prolixin	2–20	13–58

Sources: Bezchlibnyk-Butler & Jeffries (2003); Buckley & Waddington (2001); and Sadock & Sadock (2003).

with chronic schizophrenia, are often not able to remember to take their medications each day. In such cases, depot neuroleptics can be very helpful. These are neuroleptics that can be administered in a long-acting, injectable form. The clinical benefits of one injection can last for up to 4 weeks, which makes depot neuroleptics very valuable for patients, like the one in the following case, who need medication but are unwilling or unable to take drugs every day.

case STUDY He Forgets to Take His Medications

A 45-year-old male patient with chronic schizophrenia has a history of recurrent delusions of persecution and ideas of reference as well as auditory persecutory hallucinations. He has a history of 19 inpatient psychiatric admissions. He will generally keep outpatient appointments, but he forgets to take his antipsychotic medications and usually relapses within 2 weeks of discontinuing them. While in the hospital, he has an alleviation of his psychotic symptoms when he is given 20 mg per day of fluphenazine hydrochloride (Prolixin) orally. Because he responds well to medication but is not compliant, his psychiatrist decides to treat him with a biweekly injection of a depot neuroleptic. (Adapted from Janowsky et al., 1987.)

One very problematic side effect that can result from treatment with conventional antipsychotic medications such as chlorpromazine is **tardive dyskinesia** (see Chapter 14). Tardive (from *tardy*) dyskinesia is a movement abnormality that is a delayed result of taking antipsychotic medications. The problem of tardive dyskinesia is well illustrated in the following case. Because movement-related side effects are much less common with atypical antipsychotic medications such as clozapine (Clozaril) and olanzapine (Zyprexa), these medications are now generally preferred in the clinical management of schizophrenia. Clozapine also seems to be especially beneficial for psychotic patients at high risk of suicide (Meltzer et al., 2003).

case STUDY Suffering from Tardive Dyskinesia

A 62-year-old woman with chronic schizophrenia who has been a 20-year inpatient in a state mental hospital is noted to manifest bizarre repetitive movements of her mouth, tongue, hands, and feet. Her mouth involuntarily grimaces, and her tongue intermittently protrudes. Her fingers repetitively flex and she is often noted to rock back and forth. Her hand and feet movements appear choreiform (pronounced chor-ray-if-form; means "jerky and flowing"). The patient has a history of paranoid delusions and hallucinations, beginning 25 years previously. She has not manifested these symptoms of schizophrenia for 6 years. She has been treated with a progression of antipsychotic drugs in moderate doses for the past 18 years. (Adapted from Janowsky et al., 1987.)

In addition to having a lower risk of producing movement-related side effects, atypical antipsychotics such as clozapine (Clozaril), risperidone (Risperdal), olanzapine (Zyprexa), quetiapine (Seroquel), ziprasidone

(Geodon), and the more recently introduced aripiprazole (Abilify) have other treatment advantages. Specifically, there is evidence that atypical antipsychotics may effectively treat both the positive and the negative symptoms of schizophrenia, whereas the older, traditional neuroleptics worked mainly on the positive symptoms. This represents a major treatment advance. However, even the atypical neuroleptics have side effects, weight gain being very common and diabetes also being a clinical concern (Sernyak et al., 2002). You may recall that a more serious side effect of clozapine is a potentially life-threatening drop in white blood cells called "agranulocytosis," which occurs in 0.5 to 2 percent of patients (Stahl, 2002). Accordingly, patients must have their blood tested every week for the first 6 months of treatment and then every 2 weeks thereafter for as long as they are on the medication. Because of this, clozapine is best regarded as a medication to consider after other medications (e.g., some of the other atypical antipsychotic medications) have proved ineffective. Current thinking is that the atypical antipsychotics described above (with the exception of clozapine) are the first-choice treatments for psychosis and that clozapine and conventional antipsychotics (e.g., Haldol) are best considered as second-line therapies.

Antidepressant Drugs

SELECTIVE SEROTONIN RE-UPTAKE INHIBITORS (SSRIS) As is the case for antipsychotic medications, the drugs that were discovered first (so-called "classical antidepressants" such as monoamine oxidase inhibitors and tricyclic antidepressants) have now been replaced in routine clinical practice by "second-generation" treatments such as the SSRIs. In 1988 fluoxetine (Prozac) became the first SSRI to be released in the United States. It is now the most widely prescribed antidepressant in the world (Sadock & Sadock, 2003). Its pharmacological cousins include sertraline (Zoloft) and paroxetine (Paxil). Recent additions to the SSRI family are fluvoxamine (Luvox), which is used in the treatment of obsessive-compulsive disorder; citalopram (Celexa), which was introduced to the U.S. market in 1998; and escitalopram (Lexapro), which became available in 2002. Table 17.2 lists some of the most widely used antidepressant medications.

TABLE 17.2 Commonly Prescribed Antidepressant Drugs

Drug Class	Generic Name	Trade Name	Dose Range (mg)	Half-Life (hrs)
SSRI	fluoxetine	Prozac	10–80	4–6 days
	sertraline	Zoloft	50–200	26
	paroxetine	Paxil	10–60	21
	fluvoxamine	Luvox	50–300	15
	citalopram	Celexa	10–60	33
	escitalopram	Lexapro	10–20	27–32
SNRI	venlafaxine	Effexor	75–375	3–13
	reboxetine	Vestra	8–20	13
Tricyclic	amitriptyline	Elavil	75–300	10–46
	clomipramine	Anafranil	75–300	17–37
	desipramine	Norpramin	75–300	12–76
	doxepin	Sinequan	75–300	8–36
	imipramine	Tofranil	75–300	4–34
	nortriptyline	Aventyl	40–200	13–88
	trimipramine	Surmontil	75–300	7–30
MAOI	phenelzine	Nardil	45–90	1.5–4
	tranylcypromine	Parnate	20–60	2.4
	isocarboxazid	Marplan	30–50	N/A
Atypical	nefazodone	Serzone	100–600	2–5
	trazodone	Desyrel	150–600	4–9
	mirtazapine	Remeron	15–60	20–40
	bupropion	Wellbutrin	225–450	10–14

Sources: Bezchlibnyk-Butler & Jeffries (2003); Buckley & Waddington (2001); and Sadock & Sadock (2003).

SSRIs are chemically unrelated to the older tricyclic antidepressants and to the monoamine oxidase inhibitors (see Chapter 7). However, most antidepressants work by increasing the availability of serotonin, norepinephrine, or both. As their name implies, the SSRIs serve to inhibit the reuptake of the neurotransmitter serotonin following its release into the synapse. Unlike the tricyclics (which inhibit the reuptake of both serotonin and norepinephrine), the SSRIs selectively inhibit the reuptake of serotonin. They have become the preferred **antidepressant drugs** because they are thought to be relatively "safe": They are easier to use, have fewer side effects, and are generally not found to be fatal in overdose as the tricyclics can be. However, it should be noted that they are generally not considered more effective than the classic tricyclic antidepressants—they are simply more acceptable and better tolerated by many patients. In many cases, they are now being used by people who are not clinically depressed but just want a "pharmacological lift" (see The World Around Us 17.4).

The actress Brooke Shields is one of many public figures who have been open with the public about their experiences with depression.

Another widely used antidepressant in this drug family is venlafaxine (Effexor). This medication blocks reuptake of both norepinephrine and serotonin and is part of a new category of medications called "SNRIs" (serotonin and norepinephrine reuptake inhibitors; see Stahl, 2000). Its side effect profile resembles that of the SSRIs, and it is relatively safe in overdose. This drug seems to help a significant number of patients who have not responded well to other antidepressants, and it appears more effective than the SSRIs in the treatment of severe major depression (Thase, Entsuah, & Rudolph, 2001). Other SNRI drugs are currently in development and are expected to become clinically available in the near future.

Clinical trials with the SSRIs indicate that patients tend to improve after about 3 to 5 weeks of treatment. Patients who show at least a 50 percent improvement in their symptoms are considered to have had a positive response to treatment (see Figure 17.1). However, although considerably better, such patients are not fully well. When treatment removes all of a patient's symptoms, patients are considered to be in a period of remission (see Figure 17.2). If this remission is sustained for 6 to 12

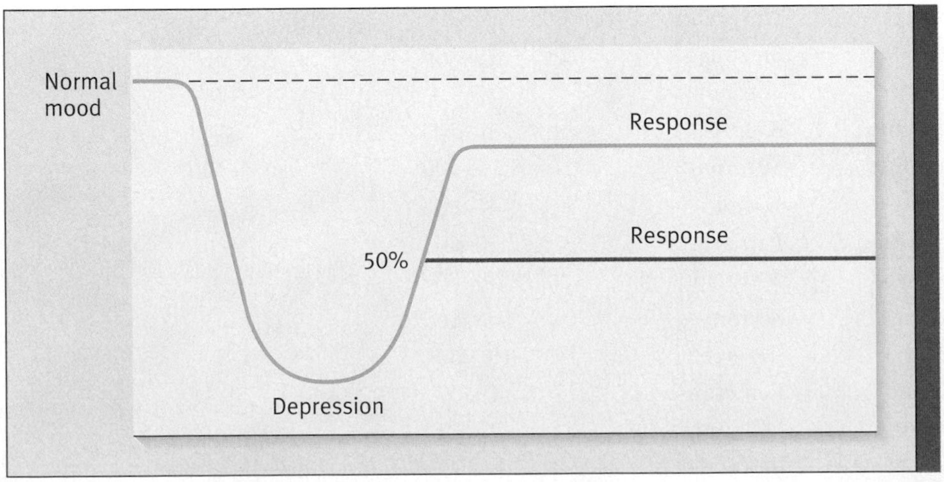

FIGURE 17.1

When treatment of depression results in at least 50 percent improvement in symptoms, it is called a response. Such patients are better, but not well.

Source: *From* Essential Psychopharmacology: Neuroscientific Basis and Practical Applications, 2E, *p. 143, by Stephen M. Stahl, copyright © Cambridge University Press, 2000. Reprinted with the permission of Cambridge University Press.*

17.4 The World Around Us

Better Living through Chemistry?

The drug Prozac and others that are pharmacologically similar to it (such as Paxil and Zoloft) are now among the drugs most prescribed by physicians. Originally recommended for the treatment of relatively severe mood disorders, they are now widely prescribed by many physicians, even those who are not psychiatrists, to ease patients' complaints of just feeling unhappy. In this respect they have come to occupy a role not unlike that of the benzodiazepines (antianxiety agents such as Valium) during the 1970s and 1980s. The pharmacological message appears to be that many people feel "better" when they have more serotonin available in the neuronal synapses of their brains.

What is the nature of this "feeling better"? Psychiatrist Peter Kramer (1993), in his popular book *Listening to Prozac,* argues that Prozac does more than ameliorate depressive states; in many instances it transforms personality, usually in a very positive, self-esteem-enhancing way. Kramer describes cases in which people claim to be functioning far better than they were before becoming depressed—literally "better than well"—or to have discovered, while on the drug, a "true" self different from and more satisfying than their previous self. In light of these effects on subjective well-being, patients are often understandably reluctant to stop taking the drug. That aspect, too, is reminiscent of the serious problems the overuse of benzodiazepines eventually caused.

Kramer suggests that the person taking Prozac experiences a diminished sensitivity to disapproval, criticism, and rejection by others. Obviously, such effects would be of considerable benefit to many people, not only people who suffer from major depression. Kramer addresses forthrightly the disturbing questions raised by the availability of a prescription drug that seems not only to ameliorate disorder but also, for many individuals, to alter their personalities, mostly in ways they find pleasing. Moreover, Kramer is undoubtedly correct when he says that Prozac is only among the first of a large number of "legitimate" drugs with comparable personality-altering properties that will eventually become available. Will these drugs be given only to people who really need them? Or are we on the verge of entering an era of "cosmetic psychopharmacology," where people may even get to choose major aspects of their personalities, just as some now choose the shapes of their noses?

months or more, the patient is considered to have recovered. In other words, he or she is fully well again.

Side effects of the SSRIs include nausea, diarrhea, nervousness, insomnia, and sexual problems such as diminished sexual interest and difficulty with orgasm (Gitlin, 1996; Nemeroff & Schatzberg, 2002). Although SSRIs help many people, as the following case study illustrates, some people have side effects that are so extreme that they are unable to continue to take their medication as prescribed. Contrary to earlier reports (e.g., Cole & Bodkin, 1990; Papp & Gorman, 1990), Prozac is no more associated with suicide than other antidepressants are (Gitlin, 1996;

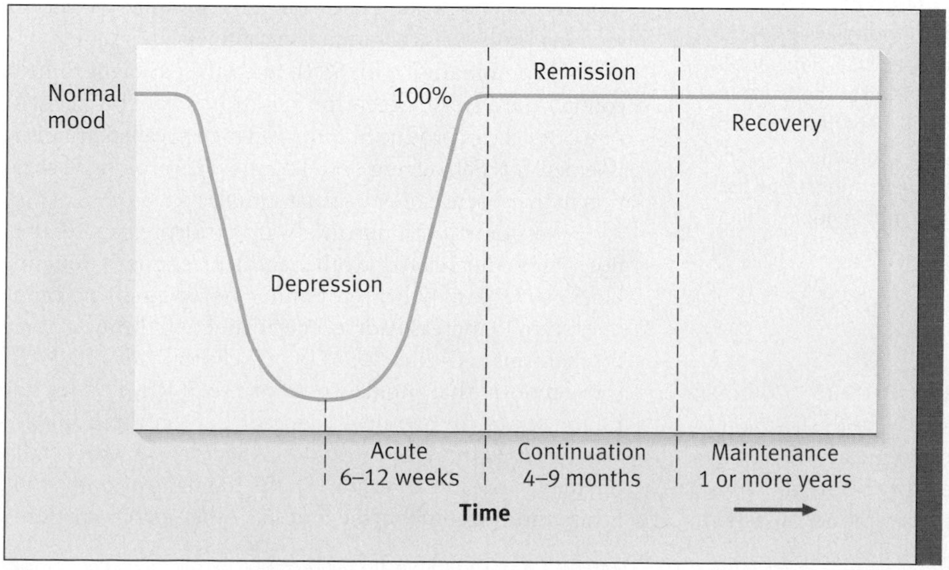

FIGURE 17.2

When treatment of depression results in removal of essentially all symptoms, it is called remission for the first several months, and then recovery if it is sustained for longer than 6 to 12 months. Such patients are not just better — they are well.

Source: *From* Essential Psychopharmacology: Neuroscientific Basis and Practical Applications, 2E, *p. 143, by Stephen M. Stahl, copyright © Cambridge University Press, 2000. Reprinted with the permission of Cambridge University Press.*

Jick et al., 2004). Because they have fewer side effects and are safer and easier to use, prescriptions for antidepressants have increased substantially in recent years.

case STUDY A Psychiatrist Gets a Taste of Her Own Medicine

Dr. G. had been a psychiatrist for many years when, during a consultation with a patient, she broke into a sweat, started to shake, and felt as if she were disintegrating. A close friend was dying of cancer and she felt weighed down and depressed. Her partner, also a psychiatrist, recommended that she take buproprion (Wellbutrin). This was an antidepressant that Dr. G. had often prescribed to her own patients, with favorable results. She began to take it herself.

Within 10 days she developed insomnia, agitation, and tremors. She lost the ability to distinguish between sadness and the side effects of the drug. She began to develop panic attacks and could barely function at work. Even so, she was terrified that she might feel worse if she stopped taking the buproprion or started taking a new drug. Determined to keep taking the medication despite her deteriorating physical and mental health, she tried to follow the advice she had given to hundreds of her own patients to stick things out. She forced herself to eat but lost 10 pounds. Sometimes she felt paranoid and wondered if she was delusional. When she wasn't working, she curled up in a fetal position and wondered if she should hospitalize herself.

After 4 weeks she had had enough. She began to taper the medication, although her symptoms, insomnia, lack of appetite, agitation, and panic attacks continued for 3 weeks after she had taken the last tablet. For a month she felt weak, as if she had just recovered from the flu.

After her experiences with buproprion, Dr. G. now describes potential side effects to her patients in much greater detail than she did before. Although she continues to prescribe the medication, she is vigilant about signs of distress in her patients. Whereas in the past she would have encouraged patients with side effects to stick it out, anticipating that these would eventually pass, she now switches her patients to a new medication at the first sign of problems. A taste of her own medicine has made her a more attentive and aware physician. (Adapted from Gartrell, 2004.)

MONOAMINE OXIDASE (MAO) INHIBITORS Although they are used infrequently now, these were the first antidepressant medications to be developed in the 1950s. These drugs were being studied for the treatment of tuberculosis when they were found to elevate the mood of patients (Gitlin, 1996). They were later shown to be effective in treating depression. Monoamine oxidase (MAO) inhibitors include isocarboxazid (Marplan), phenelzine (Nardil), tranylcypromine (Parnate), and selegiline (Eldepryl; see Chapter 7). They inhibit the activity of monoamine oxidase, an enzyme present in the synaptic cleft that helps break down the monoamine neurotransmitters (such as serotonin and norepinephrine) that have been released into the cleft. Patients taking MAO inhibitors must avoid foods rich in the amino acid tyramine (such as salami and Stilton cheese). This limits the drugs' clinical usefulness. Nevertheless, they are used in certain cases of atypical depression that are characterized by hypersomnia and overeating and do not respond well to other classes of antidepressant medication (Nemeroff & Schatzberg, 2002).

TRICYCLIC ANTIDEPRESSANTS The tricyclic antidepressants (TCAs) operate to inhibit the reuptake of norepinephrine and (to a lesser extent) serotonin once these have been released into the synapse. Their discovery was also serendipitous in that the first TCA—imipramine—was being studied as a possible treatment for schizophrenia when it was found to elevate mood. As discussed in Chapter 7, the theory that these drugs work by increasing norepinephrine activity is now known to be oversimplified. It is also known that when the tricyclics are taken for several weeks, they alter a number of other aspects of cellular functioning including how receptors function and how cells respond to the activation of receptors and the synthesis of neurotransmitters. Because these alterations in cellular functioning parallel the time course for these drugs to exert their antidepressant effects, one or more of these changes are likely to be involved in mediating their antidepressant effects (see Figure 17.3).

OTHER ANTIDEPRESSANTS Trazodone (Desyrel) was the first antidepressant to be introduced in the United States that was not lethal when taken in overdose. It specifically inhibits the reuptake of serotonin. Trazodone has heavy sedating properties that limit its usefulness. It is sometimes used in combination with SSRIs and taken at night to help counter the adverse effects the SSRIs often have on sleep. In rare cases, it can produce a condition in men called priapism (Nemeroff & Schatzberg, 2002). Priapism is prolonged erection in the absence of any sexual stimulation.

Bupropion (Wellbutrin) is an antidepressant that is not structurally related to other antidepressants. It does not block reuptake of either serotonin or norepinephrine, but it does seem to increase noradrenegic function through other mechanisms (Gitlin, 1996). One clinical advantage of bupropion is that, unlike some of the SSRIs, it does not inhibit sexual functioning (Nemeroff & Schatzberg, 2002).

Released in 1995, nefazodone (Serzone) is structurally related to trazodone. It inhibits the reuptake of both serotonin and norepinephrine and has other effects on sero-

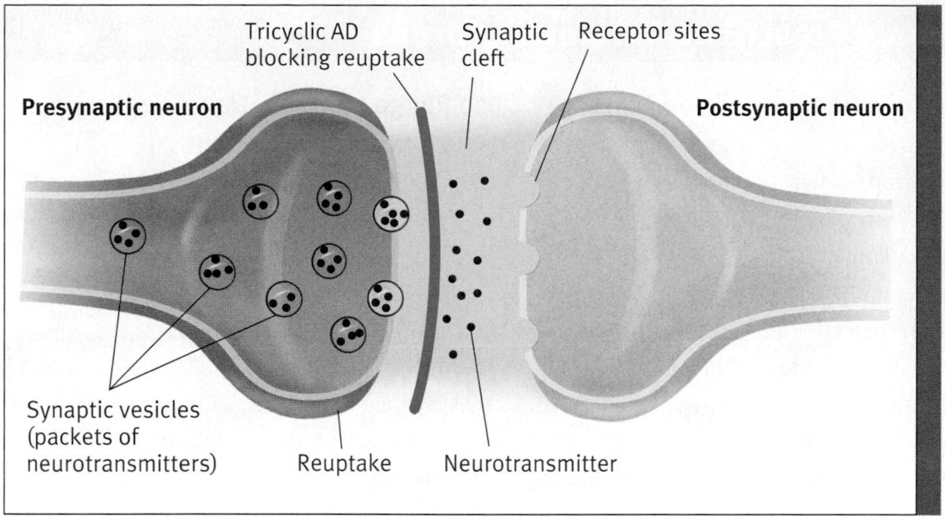

FIGURE 17.3

Tricyclic Antidepressants as Reuptake Blockers

Adapted from Gitlin, 1996, p. 287.

tonin as well. One of the major advantages of nefazodone is that (compared to the SSRIs) it does not reduce sexual responsiveness and does not produce insomnia. However, patients taking this medication need regular monitoring to ensure that the drug is not causing any liver damage.

Other drugs that facilitate serotonin and norepinephrine neurotransmission are mirtazapine (Remeron) and the newly introduced duloxetine hydrochloride, which is marketed as Cymbalta. A major side effect of Remeron is weight gain; Cymbalta, on the other hand, has been associated with decreased appetite and weight loss. As new medications are developed, they further increase the therapeutic options available to patients suffering from depression.

USING ANTIDEPRESSANTS TO TREAT ANXIETY DISORDERS, BULIMIA, AND PERSONALITY DISORDERS In addition to their usefulness in treating depression, the antidepressant drugs are also widely used in the treatment of various other disorders. As discussed in Chapter 6, SSRIs are widely used in the treatment of panic disorder, social phobia, and generalized anxiety disorder, as well as obsessive-compulsive disorder (Dougherty et al., 2002; Gitlin, 1996; Wolfe & Maser, 1994; Roy-Byrne & Cowley, 2002). However, some people with panic disorder are greatly bothered by the side effects of these drugs (which create some of the symptoms to which panic patients are hypersensitive), so they quickly discontinue the medication. SSRIs and tricyclic antidepressants are also used in the treatment of bulimia (see Chapter 9). Many, but not all, studies have shown that these antidepressants are useful in reducing binge eating and purging (Gitlin, 1996; Wilson & Fairburn, 2002). Patients with Cluster B personality disorders such as borderline personality disorder may show a decrease in certain symptoms, most notably mood lability, if they take SSRIs (Rinne et al., 2002).

Antianxiety Drugs

BENZODIAZEPINES The most important and widely used class of antianxiety (or anxiolytic) drugs are the benzodiazepines. (Another class of drugs, the barbiturates [e.g., phenobarbitol], are seldom used today except to control seizures or as anesthetics during electroconvulsive therapy.) The first benzodiazepines were released in the early 1960s. They are now the drugs of choice for the treatment of acute anxiety and agitation. They are rapidly absorbed from the digestive tract and start to work very quickly. At low doses they help quell anxiety; at higher doses they act as sleep-inducing agents and can be used to treat insomnia. For this reason, people taking these medications are cautioned about driving or operating machinery.

One problem with benzodiazepines is that patients can become psychologically and physiologically dependent on them (Gitlin, 1996; Roy-Byrne & Cowley, 2002). Patients taking these medications must be "weaned" from them gradually because of the risk of withdrawal symptoms, which include seizures in some cases. Moreover, relapse rates following discontinuation of these drugs are extremely high (Roy-Byrne & Cowley, 2002). For example, as many as 60 to 80 percent of panic patients relapse following discontinuation of Xanax (McNally, 1994). Benzodiazepine drugs include diazepam (Valium), oxazepam (Serax), clonazepam (Klonopin), alprazolam (Xanax), and lorazepam (Ativan). Table 17.3 on page 616 provides a more comprehensive list of antianxiety medications.

Benzodiazepines and related anxiolytic medications are believed to work by enhancing the activity of GABA receptors (Gitlin, 1996; Roy-Byrne & Cowley, 2002). GABA (gamma aminobutyric acid) is an inhibitory neurotransmitter that plays an important role in the way our brain inhibits anxiety in stressful situations. The benzodiazepines appear to enhance GABA activity in certain parts

TABLE 17.3 Commonly Prescribed Antianxiety Drugs

Drug Class	Generic Name	Trade Name	Dose Range (mg)	Half-Life (hrs)
Benzodiazepines	alprazolam	Xanax	0.5–10	9–20
	clonazepam	Klonopin	1–6	19–60
	diazepam	Valium	4–40	30–200
	lorazepam	Ativan	1–6	8–24
	oxazepam	Serax	30–120	3–25
	clorazepate	Tranxene	15–60	120
	chlordiazepoxide	Librium	10–150	28–100
Other	buspirone	Buspar	5–30	1–11

Sources: Bezchlibnyk-Butler & Jeffries (2003); Buckley & Waddington (2001); and Sadock & Sadock (2003).

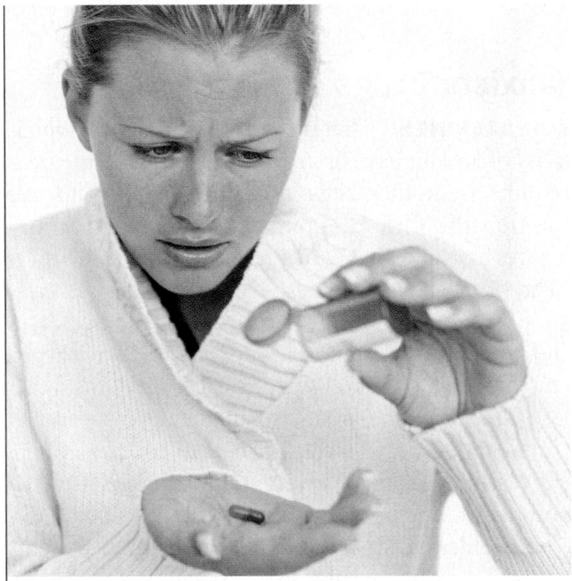

Anti-anxiety medications are widely prescribed. However, patients can become psychologically and physiologically dependent on them.

of the brain known to be implicated in anxiety such as the limbic system.

The range of applications of **antianxiety drugs** is quite broad. They are used in all manner of conditions in which tension and anxiety may be significant components, including anxiety-based and psychophysiological disorders. They are also used as supplementary treatment in certain neurological disorders to control such symptoms as convulsive seizures, but they have little place in the treatment of psychosis. They are among the most widely prescribed drugs, a fact that has caused concern among some leaders in the medical and psychiatric fields because of these drugs' addictive potential and sedating effects.

OTHER ANTI-ANXIETY MEDICATIONS The only new class of antianxiety medication that has been released since the early 1960s is buspirone (Buspar), which is completely unrelated to the benzodiazepines and is thought to act in complex ways on serotonergic functioning rather than on GABA. It has been shown to be as effective as the benzodiazepines in treating generalized anxiety disorder (Gitlin, 1996; Roy-Byrne & Cowley, 2002), although patients who have previously taken benzodiazepines tend not to respond as well as patients who have never taken them. Buspar has a low potential for abuse, probably because it has no sedative or muscle-relaxing properties and so is less pleasurable for patients. It also does not cause any withdrawal effects. The primary drawback to the use of buspirone is that it takes 2 to 4 weeks to exert any anxiolytic effects. It is therefore not useful in acute situations. Because it is nonsedating, it cannot be used to treat insomnia.

Lithium and Other Mood-Stabilizing Drugs

In the late 1940s John Cade in Australia discovered that lithium salts such as lithium carbonate were effective in treating manic disorders. One of Cade's (1949) own cases serves well as an illustration of the effects of lithium treatment.

case STUDY — Lithium Helps a Difficult Patient

Mr. W. B. was a 51-year-old man who had been in a state of chronic manic excitement for 5 years. So obnoxious and destructive was his behavior that he had long been regarded as the most difficult patient on his ward in the hospital.

He was started on treatment with a lithium compound, and within 3 weeks his behavior had improved so much that transfer to the convalescent ward was deemed appropriate. He remained in the hospital for another 2 months, during which time his behavior continued to be essentially normal. Prior to discharge, he was switched to another form of lithium salts because the one he had been taking had caused stomach upset.

He was soon back at his job and living a happy and productive life. In fact, he felt so good that, contrary to instructions, he stopped taking his lithium. Thereafter he steadily became more irritable and erratic; some 6 months following his discharge, he had to cease work. In another 5 weeks he was back at the hospital in an acute manic state.

Lithium therapy was immediately reestablished, with prompt positive results. In another month Mr. W. B. was pronounced ready to return to home and work, provided that he not fail to continue taking a prescribed dosage of lithium.

It was about 20 years before lithium treatment was introduced, around 1970, in the United States. There were at least two reasons for this delay. First, lithium had been used as a salt substitute for patients with hypertension in the 1940s and 1950s when its toxic side effects were unknown. Some tragic deaths resulted, making the medical community very wary of using it for any reason. Second, because it is a naturally occurring compound, it is unpatentable. This meant that drug companies did not find it profitable to investigate its effects. Nevertheless, by the mid-1970s it was regarded as a wonder drug in psychiatry (Gitlin, 1996). It is still widely used for the treatment of bipolar disorder and is marketed as Eskalith.

The biochemical basis of lithium's therapeutic effect is unknown. One hypothesis is that lithium, being a mineral salt, may affect electrolyte balances that may alter the activities of many neurotransmitter systems in the brain, which is consistent with its diverse clinical effects (Gitlin, 1996). So far, however, this connection remains largely speculative. Clearly, the riddle of exactly what occurs will be solved only by more and better research.

Even though we still do not know exactly how it works, there is no doubt about the effectiveness of lithium. As many as 70 to 80 percent of patients in a clear manic state show marked improvement after 2 to 3 weeks of taking lithium (Keck & McElroy, 2002b; Sadock & Sadock, 2003). In addition, as we saw in Chapter 7, lithium sometimes relieves depression, although probably mainly in patients with bipolar depression. Nevertheless, there may be a subclass of unipolar depressive patients who benefit from lithium treatment (Abou-Saleh, 1992; Gitlin, 1996).

There is increasing evidence that lithium maintenance treatment may be less reliable at preventing future episodes of mania than was once thought. For example, several studies of bipolar patients maintained on lithium for 5 years or more found that only just over one-third remained in remission. Nevertheless, discontinuation of lithium is also very risky. The probability of relapse is estimated to be 28 times higher after withdrawal than when the patient is on lithium, with about 50 percent relapsing within 6 months (Keck & McElroy, 2002b).

Side effects of lithium include increased thirst, gastrointestinal difficulties, weight gain, tremor, and fatigue. In addition, lithium can be toxic if the recommended dose is exceeded or if the kidneys fail to excrete it from the body at a normal rate. Lithium toxicity is a serious medical condition. If not treated swiftly and appropriately, it can cause neuronal damage or even death.

Despite the clinical benefits of lithium, not all patients with bipolar disorder take it exactly as prescribed. Many seem to miss the "highs" and the abundance of energy associated with their hypomanic episodes, so when faced with unpleasant side effects and the loss of these highs, they may stop taking the drug.

case study — I'd Rather Not Take It

Even though I was a clinician and a scientist, and even though I could read the research literature and see the inevitable, bleak consequences of not taking lithium, for many years after my initial diagnosis I was reluctant to take my medications as prescribed. Why was I so unwilling? Why did I have to go through more episodes of mania, followed by long suicidal depressions, before I would take lithium in a medically sensible way?

Some of my reluctance, no doubt, stemmed from a fundamental denial that what I had was a real disease. This is a common reaction that follows, rather counterintuitively, in the wake of early episodes of manic-depressive illness. Moods are such an essential part of the substance of life, of one's notion of oneself, that even psychotic extremes in mood and behavior somehow can be seen as temporary, even understandable reactions to what life has dealt.... It was difficult to give up the high flights of mind and mood, even though the depressions that inevitably followed nearly cost me my life.

My family and friends expected that I would welcome being "normal," be appreciative of lithium, and take in stride having normal energy and sleep. But if you have had stars at your feet and rings of planets through your hands, are used to sleeping only 4 or 5 hours a night and now sleep 8, are used to staying up all night for days and weeks in a row and now cannot, it is a very real adjustment to blend into a three-piece-suit schedule, which, though comfortable to many, is new, restrictive, seemingly less productive, and maddeningly less intoxicating. People

(continued)

say, when I complain of being less lively, less energetic, less high-spirited, "Well, now you're just like the rest of us," intending, among other things, to be reassuring. But I compare myself with my former self, not with others. Not only that, I tend to compare my current self with the best I have been, which is when I have been mildly manic. (Adapted from Jamison, 1995, pp. 91–93, 167.)

Source: From AN UNQUIET MIND by Kay Redfield Jamison, copyright © 1995 by Kay Redfield Jamison. Used by permission of Alfred A. Knopf, a division of Random House, Inc.

OTHER MOOD-STABILIZING DRUGS Although lithium is still widely used, other drugs are also considered first-line treatments for bipolar disorder (see Table 17.4). These include divalproic acid (Depakote) and carbamazepine (Tegretol). Other drugs that are currently being researched and used clinically as treatments for rapid cycling bipolar disorders are gabapentin (Neurontin), lamotrigine (Lamictal), and topiramate (Topamax). Many of these drugs are used in the treatment of epilepsy and are anticonvulsant agents (Keck & McElroy, 2002a, 2002b). Carbamazepine has been associated with significant side effects including blood problems, hepatitis, and serious skin conditions (Sadock & Sadock, 2003). As with lithium, careful blood monitoring of patients is required. Valproate probably has the fewest and mildest side effects, which can include nausea, diarrhea, sedation, tremor, and weight gain. Abilify, an antipsychotic medication, is also now being marketed as a treatment for bipolar disorder.

Electroconvulsive Therapy

Using convulsions to treat mental disorders dates back to the Swiss physician/alchemist Paracelsus (1493–1591), who induced a patient with "lunacy" to drink camphor until he experienced convulsions (Abrams, 2002; Mowbray, 1959). However, Ladislas von Meduna, a Hungarian physician, is generally regarded as the modern originator of this treatment approach. Von Meduna noted—erroneously, as it turned out—that schizophrenia rarely occurred in people with epilepsy. This observation caused him to infer that schizophrenia and epilepsy were somehow incompatible and to speculate that one might be able to cure schizophrenia by inducing convulsions. In an early treatment effort, von Meduna used camphor to induce convulsions in a patient with schizophrenia, who relatively quickly regained lucidity after the convulsive therapy. Later, von Meduna began to use a drug called Metrazol to induce convulsions because it operated more rapidly.

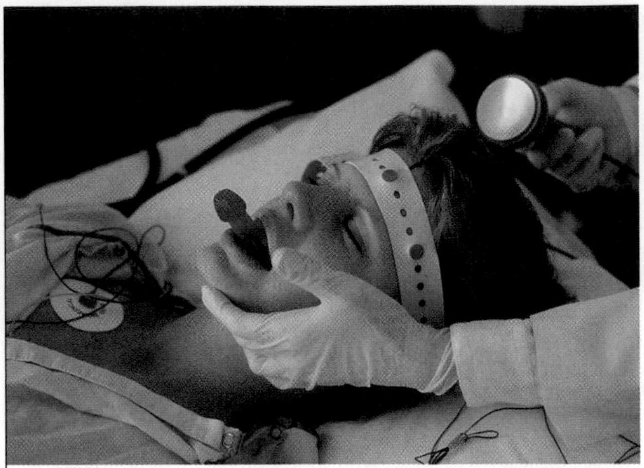

A patient who receives electroconvulsive therapy (ECT) today is given sedative and muscle-relaxant medication prior to the procedure to prevent violent contractions. In the days before such medication was available, the initial seizure was sometimes so violent as to fracture vertebrae.

Another early approach, adopted by Sakel in the 1930s, was to cause convulsions by injecting patients with insulin (see Fink, 2003). However, these chemical methods gave physicians no control over the induction and timing of the seizures. Then, in 1938, the Italian physicians Ugo Cerletti and Lucio Bini tried the simplest method of all—passing an electric current through a patient's head. This method, which became known as **electroconvulsive therapy (ECT),** is still used today. In the United States, about 100,000 patients are treated with ECT each year (Sadock & Sadock, 2003).

The general public often views ECT as a horrific and primitive form of treatment. Indeed, a number of mal-

TABLE 17.4 **Commonly Prescribed Mood-Stabilizing Medications**

Drug Class	Generic Name	Trade Name	Dose Range (mg)	Half-Life (hrs)
Lithium	lithium	Eskalith	400–1200	24
Anticonvulsants	carbamazepine	Tegretol	300–1600	16–24
	divalproex	Depakote	750–3000	6–16
	lamotrigine	Lamictal	100–500	25
	gabapentin	Neurontin	900–3600	5–9
	topiramate	Topamax	50–1300	21

Sources: Bezchlibnyk-Butler & Jeffries (2003); Buckley & Waddington (2001); and Sadock & Sadock (2003).

practice lawsuits have been brought against psychiatrists who use ECT, primarily over the failure to obtain appropriate patient consent, which can be very difficult when patients may not be legally competent to give such consent due to their illness (Abrams, 2002; Leong & Eth, 1991). However, despite the distaste with which some people regard ECT, it is a safe, effective, and important form of treatment. In fact, it is the only way of dealing with some severely depressed and suicidal patients—patients who may have failed to respond to other forms of treatment. In addition, it is often the treatment of choice for severely depressed women who are pregnant, for whom taking antidepressants may be problematic, as well as for the elderly, who may have medical conditions that make taking antidepressant drugs dangerous (Gitlin, 1996). Properly administered, ECT does not do any structural damage to the brain (Devanand et al., 1994; Gitlin, 1996). Moreover, numerous reviews evaluating the research on ECT over the past 50 years have concluded that ECT is also an effective treatment for patients with manic disorders who have not responded to pharmacotherapy (it is 80 percent effective overall with difficult-to-treat patients; e.g., Abrams, 2002; Mukherjee et al., 1994). For example, Husain and colleagues (1993) reported on the use of a long-term (2-year) treatment of an elderly woman with recurring mania. The authors pointed out that the ECT (81 sessions in all) was the only effective means of controlling her manic episodes and proved to be both safe and cost-effective.

Virtually every neurotransmitter system is affected by ECT. ECT is known to downregulate the receptors for norepinephrine, increasing the functional availability of this neurotransmitter. However, exactly how ECT works is still not fully clear (Abrams, 2002; Gitlin, 1996).

ECT can be administered in one of two ways. In *bilateral* ECT, electrodes are placed on either side of the patient's head (see Figure 17.4), and constant-current brief electrical pulses of either high or low intensity are passed from one side of the head to the other for up to about 1.5 seconds. In contrast, *unilateral* ECT (see Figure 17.4) involves limiting current flow to one side of the brain, typically the nondominant side (right side, for most people). Anesthetics allow the patient to sleep through the procedure, and muscle relaxants are used to prevent the violent contractions that, in the early days of ECT, could be so severe as to cause the patient to fracture bones. Today, if you were to observe someone receiving ECT, all you might see would be a small twitch of the hand, perhaps, as the convulsions occurred.

After the ECT is over, the patient has amnesia for the period immediately preceding the therapy and is usually somewhat confused for the next hour or so. Normally, a treatment series consists of fewer than a dozen sessions, although occasionally more are needed (Gitlin, 1996). With repeated treatments, usually administered three times weekly, the patient gradually becomes disoriented, a state that usually clears after termination of the treatments.

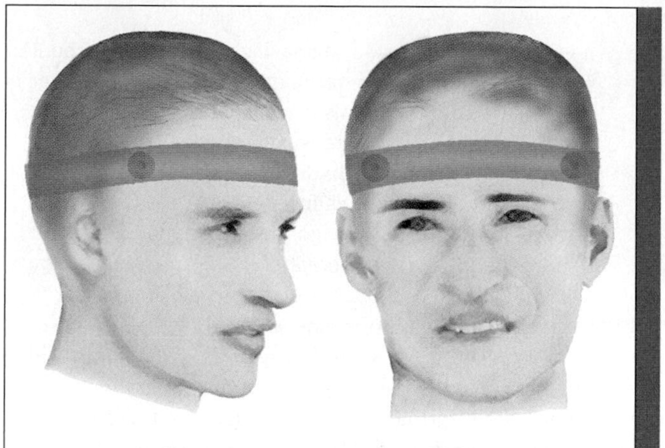

FIGURE 17.4

Unilateral and bilateral electrode placement for ECT.
Adapted from Sadock & Sadock, 2003, p. 1142.

Empirical evidence suggests that bilateral ECT is more effective than unilateral ECT (Sackheim et al., 1993). Unfortunately, bilateral ECT is also associated with more severe cognitive side effects and memory problems. Patients often have difficulty forming new memories (anterograde amnesia) for about 3 months after ECT ends. Physicians must therefore weigh the greater clinical benefits of bilateral ECT against its tendency to cause greater cognitive side effects. Some clinicians recommend starting with unilateral ECT and switching to bilateral after five or six treatments if no improvement is seen (Abrams, 2002; Gitlin, 1996).

A dramatic early example of successful ECT treatments is provided in the autobiographical account of Lenore McCall (1947/1961), who suffered a severe depressive disorder in her middle years.

case study **Using ECT to Treat Severe Depression**

Ms. McCall, a well-educated woman of affluent circumstances and the mother of three children, noticed a feeling of persistent fatigue as the first sign of her impending descent into depression. Too fearful to seek help, she at first attempted to fight off her increasingly profound apathy by engaging in excessive activity, a defensive strategy that accomplished little but the depletion of her remaining strength and emotional reserves.

In due course, she noticed that her mental processes seemed to be deteriorating—her memory appeared impaired and she could concentrate only with great difficulty. Emotionally, she felt an enormous loneliness, bleak-

(continued)

ness of experience, and increasingly intense fear about what was happening to her mind. She came to view her past small errors of commission and omission as the most heinous of crimes and increasingly withdrew from contact with her husband and children. Eventually, at her husband's and her physician's insistence, she was hospitalized despite her own vigorous resistance. She felt betrayed and shortly thereafter attempted suicide by shattering a drinking glass and ingesting its fragments. To her great disappointment, she survived.

Ms. McCall then spent nearly 4 years continuously in two separate mental hospitals, during which time she deteriorated further. She was silent and withdrawn, behaved in a mechanical fashion, lost an alarming amount of weight, and underwent a seemingly premature aging process. She felt that she emitted an offensive odor. At this time, ECT was introduced into the therapeutic procedures in use at her hospital.

A series of ECT treatments was given to Ms. McCall over about a 3-month period. Then one day, she woke up in the morning with a totally changed outlook: "I sat up suddenly, my heart pounding. I looked around the room and a sweep of wonder surged over me. God in heaven, I'm well. I'm myself. . . ." After a brief period of convalescence, she went home to her husband and children.

Neurosurgery

Although **neurosurgery** was used occasionally in the nineteenth century to treat mental disorders by relieving pressure in the brain (Berrios, 1990), it was not considered a treatment for psychological problems until this century. In 1935 in Portugal, Antonio Moniz introduced a neurosurgical procedure in which the frontal lobes of the brain were severed from the deeper centers underlying them. This technique eventually evolved into an operation known as "prefrontal lobotomy," which stands as a dubious tribute to the extremes to which professionals have sometimes been driven in their search for effective treatments for the psychoses. In retrospect, it is ironic that this procedure—which results in permanent structural changes in the brain of the patient and has been highly criticized by many within the profession—won Moniz the 1949 Nobel Prize in medicine (although he was later shot by a former patient who was, presumedly, less than grateful).

From 1935 to 1955 (when antipsychotic drugs became available), tens of thousands of mental patients in this country and abroad were subjected to prefrontal lobotomies and related neurosurgical procedures. In some settings, as many as 50 patients were treated in a single day (Freeman, 1959). Initial reports of results tended to be enthusiastic, downplaying complications (which included a 1 to 4 percent death rate) and undesirable side effects. It was eventually recognized, however, that the "side effects" of psychosurgery could be very undesirable indeed. In some instances they included a permanent inability to inhibit impulses, in others an unnatural "tranquility" with undesirable shallowness or absence of feeling. The World Around Us 17.5 describes the tragic results of the lobotomy performed on Rosemary Kennedy, sister of former president John F. Kennedy.

The introduction of the major antipsychotic drugs caused an immediate decrease in the widespread use of psychosurgery, especially prefrontal lobotomy. Such operations are rare today and are used only as a last resort for patients who have not responded to all other forms of treatment for a period of 5 years and who are experiencing extreme and disabling symptoms. Modern surgical techniques involve the selective destruction of minute areas of the brain. Psychosurgery is sometimes used for patients with debilitating obsessive-compulsive disorders (see Rauch & Jenike, 1998; Sachdev et al., 2001) or treatment-resistant severe self-mutilation (Price et al., 2001). Morgan and Crisp (2000) have also reported long-term follow-up data on four patients with intractable anorexia nervosa who were treated with leukotomy.

17.5 The World Around Us — The Tragedy of Rosemary Kennedy

One of the victims of the zeal to perform prefrontal lobotomies to alleviate behavior problems was Rosemary Kennedy, the sister of former president John F. Kennedy and senators Robert and Edward Kennedy. Rosemary was the third child of Joseph and Rose Kennedy. Born during the height of the influenza epidemic of 1918, she was a beautiful baby, with a sweet temperament. Over time, however, her mother became increasingly concerned about Rosemary's slow development compared to her brothers and sisters. When the family finally concluded that Rosemary was retarded, the best experts in the country at the time could offer no guidance and told the family that nothing could be done except to place Rosemary in an institution.

Rose Kennedy and the family rebelled against this suggestion. Instead of being institutionalized, Rosemary was kept at home. She had a special governess and many private tutors. She participated fully in the Kennedy family's activities, and she made considerable progress. By the age of 18, Rosemary was performing at a fifth-grade level in English and at a fourth-grade level in math.

Because of the considerable stigma associated with mental retardation at the time, Rosemary's parents kept her condition hidden from those outside the family, a major task because of the scrutiny the family was subjected to by the press. Although her parents and siblings were always nearby to protect her, Rosemary developed the social skills needed to be presented successfully as a debutante and later to the king and queen of England at Buckingham Palace.

The tragic failure of Rosemary Kennedy's prefrontal lobotomy is a reminder that brain surgery can permanently alter personality. Rosemary is shown here in foreground, with her sister Kathleen (left) and mother Rose (center),before the surgery.

Unfortunately, Rosemary's behavior deteriorated when, around the beginning of World War II, the family returned to the United States from England, where Joseph Kennedy had been ambassador. Some of her deterioration may have been caused by her increasing frustration at not being able to do all the things her siblings were able to do, as well as having to leave the school in England where she had felt successful. The 21-year-old Rosemary became quite violent and frequently ran away from home or her convent school, and there was considerable concern for her safety. Her father turned to the medical experts of the time, searching for a solution.

These experts convinced Joseph Kennedy that the miracle treatment he sought lay in prefrontal lobotomy. Rosemary Kennedy became one of the thousands submitted to that "desperate" cure. In Rosemary's case, the surgery was a tragic failure—all her previous accomplishments were wiped out, leaving little of her former personality and adaptive ability intact: "They knew right away that it wasn't successful. You could see by looking at her that something was wrong, for her head was tilted and her capacity to speak was almost entirely gone. There was no question now that she could no longer take care of herself and that the only answer was an institution." (Ann Gargan King, a cousin, as reported by Goodwin, 1988, p. 744.)

Although not enough controlled studies of these new psychosurgery techniques have been published to warrant firm conclusions, research has been encouraging for at least one disorder. Mindus and colleagues (1993, 1994) described an overall satisfactory result of psychosurgery in 253 severely obsessive-compulsive patients. About half of these patients were found to show at least a 35 percent reduction in intensity of symptoms after surgery. This experimental procedure is associated with relatively few negative side effects (although occasionally patients experience seizures or transient headaches). However, effects on cognition or personality are rare (Dougherty et al., 2002).

Deep brain stimulation is a new treatment approach that involves surgery but does not result in a permanent lesion being made in the brain. As Developments in Research 17.6 on page 622 illustrates, this innovative form of therapy is now being used to help patients get some relief from their unrelenting symptoms of depression.

In Review

- What kinds of disorders can be treated with antipsychotic drugs? How do these drugs help patients? What are their drawbacks?
- Why have the SSRIs largely replaced tricyclic antidepressants in routine clinical practice? What kinds of conditions can be treated with antidepressants?
- What kinds of medications can be used to treat acute anxiety and agitation? How are these medications believed to work?
- Do the clinical advantages of ECT outweigh its disadvantages?

17.6 Developments in Research

Treating Depressed Patients with Deep Brain Stimulation

A new development in the treatment of patients with severe and chronic mental health problems is deep brain stimulation. This involves stimulating patients' brains electrically over a period of several months. In one study, surgeons drilled holes into the brains of six severely depressed patients and implanted small electrodes (see Mayberg et al., 2005). Because this procedure was done under local anesthetic, the patients were able to talk to the doctors about what was happening to them and tell the doctors about the changes they experienced when the voltage through the electrodes was gradually increased. Although the patients had no cues to tell them when current was being passed through the electrodes or when the current was off, all of them reported a response to the electrical stimulation. When current was flowing into an area of the brain that is thought to be metabolically overactive in depression (the cingulate region), patients reported feelings of "sudden calmness or lightness," "connectedness", or "disappearance of the void" (p. 652). Patients also reported feeling better during these periods of stimulation.

In the days after the operation, the researchers gave patients short sessions of deep brain stimulation in which current was passed through the implanted electrodes. Using the reports of the patients as a guide, the researchers then selected the settings that would be used after the patients left the hospital to provide stimulation through an implanted pulse device.

Over the next few months, four of the six patients who received treatment with deep brain stimulation showed clinical improvement, and two patients were actually depression-free after 6 months.

Of course, from a research perspective, there are many limitations to this study. The treatment technique is also invasive. However, this innovative approach may be able to provide relief to depressed patients who have failed to show improvement with other forms of therapy without permanent lesions being made in their brains.

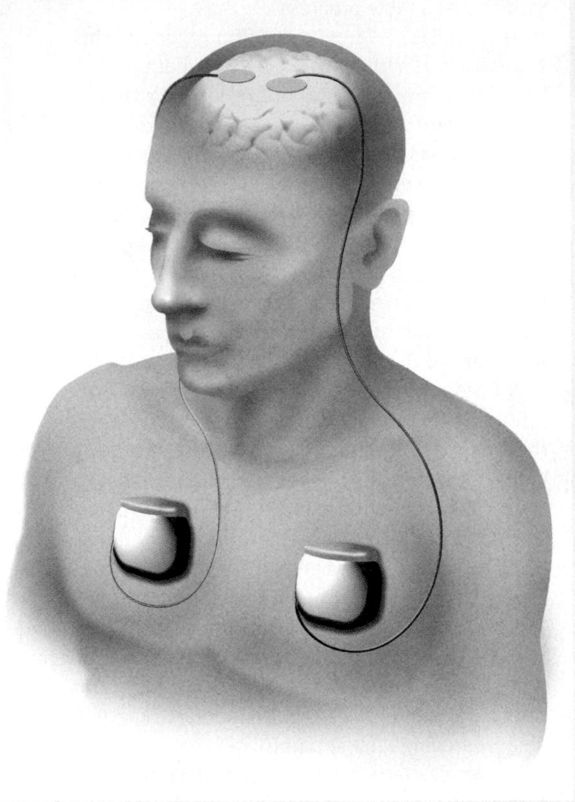

In deep brain stimulation, electrodes are implanted into the brain. These are stimulated by pulse generators implanted into the chest region.
Source: *http://www.clevelandclinic.org/neuroscience/treat/movement/images/medtronicman.gif*

Psychological Approaches to Treatment

Behavior Therapy

Behavior therapy is a direct and active treatment that recognizes the primacy of behavior, acknowledges the role of learning, and includes thorough assessment and evaluation (see Kazdin, 1984). Instead of exploring past traumatic events or inner conflicts, behavior therapists focus on the presenting problem—the problem or symptom that is causing the patient great distress. A major assumption of behavior therapy is that abnormal behavior is acquired in the same way as normal behavior—that is, by learning. A variety of behavioral techniques have therefore been developed to help patients "unlearn" maladaptive behaviors by one means or another.

EXPOSURE THERAPY A behavior therapy technique that is widely used in the treatment of anxiety disorders is exposure (see Chapter 6). If anxiety is learned, then, from the behavior therapy perspective, it can be unlearned. This is accomplished through guided exposure to anxiety-provoking stimuli. During exposure therapy, the patient or client is confronted with the fear-producing stimulus in a therapeutic manner. This can be accomplished in a very controlled, slow, and gradual way, as in **systematic desensitization,** or in a more extreme manner, as in flooding, where the patient directly confronts the feared stimulus at full strength. (An example is a housebound patient with agoraphobia being accompanied outdoors by the therapist). Moreover, the form of the exposure can be real (also known as ***in vivo* exposure**) or imaginary (**imaginal exposure**).

The rationale behind systematic desensitization is quite simple: Find a behavior that is incompatible with being anxious (such as being relaxed or experiencing something pleasant) and repeatedly pair this with the stimulus that provokes anxiety in the patient. Because it is difficult if not impossible to feel both pleasant and anxious at the same time, systematic desensitization is aimed at teaching a person, while in the presence (real or imagined) of the anxiety-producing stimulus, to relax or behave in some other way that is inconsistent with anxiety. It may therefore be considered a type of counter-conditioning procedure. The term *systematic* refers to the carefully graduated manner in which the person is exposed to the feared stimulus.

The prototype of systematic desensitization is the classic experiment of Mary Cover Jones (1924), in which she successfully eliminated a small boy's fears of a white rabbit and other furry animals. She began by bringing the rabbit just inside the door at the far end of the room while the boy, Peter, was eating. On successive days, the rabbit was gradually brought closer until Peter could pat it with one hand while eating with the other.

Joseph Wolpe (1958; Rachman & Hodgson, 1980) elaborated on the procedure developed by Jones and coined the phrase *systematic desensitization* to refer to it. On the assumption that most anxiety-based patterns are, fundamentally, conditioned responses, Wolpe worked out a way to train a client to remain calm and relaxed in situations that formerly produced anxiety. Wolpe's approach is elegant in its simplicity, and his method is equally straightforward.

A client is first taught to enter a state of relaxation, typically by progressive concentration on relaxing various muscle groups. Meanwhile, patient and therapist collaborate in constructing an anxiety hierarchy that consists of imagined scenes graded as to their capacity to elicit anxiety. For example, for a dog-phobic patient, a low-anxiety step might be imagining a small dog in the distance being walked on a leash by its owner. In contrast, a high-anxiety step might be imagining a large and exuberant dog running toward oneself. Therapy sessions consist of the patient's repeatedly imagining, under conditions of deep relaxation, the scenes in the hierarchy, beginning with low-anxiety images and gradually working toward those in the more extreme ranges. Treatment continues until all items in the hierarchy can be imagined without notable discomfort, at which point the client's real-life difficulties typically have shown substantial improvement.

Imaginal procedures have some limitations, an obvious one being that not everybody is capable of vividly imagining the required scenes. In an early study of clients with agoraphobia, Emmelkamp and Wessels (1975) concluded that prolonged exposure *in vivo* was superior to imaginal exposure. Since then, therapists have sought to use *in vivo* exposure whenever this is practical, encouraging clients to confront anxiety-provoking situations directly (Barlow, 1988, 1993). Obviously, however, this cannot be accomplished for all stimuli. In addition, an occasional client is so fearful that he or she cannot be induced to confront the anxiety-arousing situation directly (Emmelkamp & Wessels, 1975). Imaginal procedures are therefore a vital part of the therapeutic exposure repertoire. A recent development in behavior therapy is the use of virtual reality to help patients overcome their fears and phobias (e.g., Emmelkamp, 2004; Rothbaum, Hodges, et al., 2000). Such approaches are obviously helpful when the source of the patient's anxiety is something that is not easily reproduced in real life.

When a therapist has a choice, *in vivo* procedures seem to have an edge in efficiency, and possibly in ultimate efficacy, over those employing imagery as the mode of confrontation (Emmelkamp, 1994). Overall, the outcome record for exposure treatments is impressive (Barlow et al., 2002; Emmelkamp, 2004; Roth & Fonagy, 1996).

AVERSION THERAPY Aversion therapy involves modifying undesirable behavior by the old-fashioned method of punishment. Probably the most commonly used aversive stimuli today are drugs that have noxious effects, such as Antabuse, which induces nausea and vomiting when a person who has taken it ingests alcohol (see Chapter 12). In another variant, the client is instructed to wear a substantial elastic band on the wrist and to "snap" it when temptation arises, thus administering self-punishment.

In the past, painful electric shock was commonly employed in programs that paired it with the occurrence of the undesirable behavior, a practice that certainly contributed to aversion therapy's "negative image" among some segments of the public. Although aversive conditioning has been used to treat a wide range of maladaptive behaviors including smoking, drinking, overeating, drug dependence, gambling, sexual deviance, and bizarre psychotic behavior, interest in this approach is now on the decline (see Emmelkamp, 2004).

MODELING As the name implies, in **modeling** the client learns new skills by imitating another person, such as a parent or therapist, who performs the behavior to be acquired. A younger client may be exposed to behaviors or roles in peers who act as assistants to the therapist and then be encouraged to imitate and practice the desired new responses. For example, modeling may be used to promote the learning of simple skills such as self-feeding for a profoundly mentally retarded child, or more complex skills such as being more effective in social situations for a shy, withdrawn adolescent. In work with children especially, effective decision making and problem solving may be modeled when the therapist "thinks out loud" about everyday choices that present themselves in the course of therapy (Kendall, 1990; Kendall & Braswell, 1985).

Modeling and imitation are adjunctive aspects of various forms of behavior therapy as well as other types of therapy. For example, in an early classic work, Bandura (1964) found that live modeling of fearlessness, combined with instruction and guided exposure, was the most effective treatment for snake phobia, resulting in the elimination of phobic reactions in over 90 percent of the cases treated. The photographs taken during the treatment of spider phobia on page 189 of this text provide a graphic example of a similar combined approach.

SYSTEMATIC USE OF REINFORCEMENT Often referred to as "contingency management," systematic programs that manage through reinforcement to suppress (extinguish) unwanted behavior or to elicit and maintain effective behavior have achieved notable success, particularly but by no means exclusively in institutional settings.

Suppressing problematic behavior may be as simple as removing the reinforcements that support it, provided, of course, that they can be identified. Sometimes identification is relatively easy, as in the following case. In other instances, it may require extremely careful and detailed observation and analysis for the therapist to learn what is maintaining the maladaptive behavior.

case STUDY — Showing Off in Class

Billy, a 6-year-old first grader, was brought to a psychological clinic by his parents because he hated school and because his teacher had told them that his showing off was disrupting the class and making him unpopular. It became apparent, in observing Billy and his parents during the initial interview, that both his mother and his father were noncritical and approving of everything Billy did. After further assessment, a three-phase program of therapy was undertaken: (1) The parents were helped to discriminate between showing-off behavior and appropriate behavior on Billy's part. (2) The parents were instructed to show a loss of interest and attention when Billy engaged in showing-off behavior, while continuing to show their approval of appropriate behavior. (3) Billy's teacher was instructed to ignore Billy, insofar as it was feasible, when he engaged in showing-off behavior and to devote her attention at those times to children who were behaving more appropriately.

Although Billy's showing off in class increased during the first few days of this behavior therapy program, it diminished markedly after his parents and teacher no longer reinforced it. As his maladaptive behavior diminished, he was better accepted by his classmates, which, in turn, helped reinforce more appropriate behavior patterns and changed his negative attitude toward school.

Billy's was a case in which unwanted behavior was eliminated by eliminating its reinforcers. On other occasions, therapy is administered to establish desired behaviors that are missing. Examples of such approaches are *response shaping* and use of *token economies.* In **response shaping,** positive reinforcement is often used to establish, by gradual approximation, a response that is actively resisted or is not initially in an individual's behavioral repertoire. This technique has been used extensively in working with children's behavior problems.

TOKEN ECONOMIES Years ago, when behavior therapy was in its infancy, token economies based on the principles of operant conditioning were developed for use with chronic psychiatric inpatients. When they behaved appropriately on the hospital ward, patients earned tokens that they could later use to receive rewards or privileges (Paul, 1982; Paul & Lentz, 1977).

Token economies have been used to establish adaptive behaviors ranging from elementary responses such as eating and making one's bed, to the daily performance of responsible hospital jobs. In the latter instance, the **token economy** resembles the outside world, where an individual is paid for his or her work in tokens (money) that can later be exchanged for desired objects and activities. Although sometimes the subject of criticism and controversy, token economies remain a relevant treatment approach for the seriously mentally ill and those with developmental disabilities (see Corrigan, 1995; Higgins et al., 2001; Le Blanc et al., 2000; Morisse et al., 1996).

Similar reinforcement-based methods are now being used to treat substance abuse. In one study, people being treated for cocaine dependence were rewarded with vouchers worth 25 cents if their urine test came back negative (see Higgins, Wong, et al., 2000). Patients could then ask a staff member to purchase for them items from the community with the vouchers they had accumulated. Patients who received the incentive vouchers based on their abstinence from cocaine had better clinical outcomes than a comparison group of patients who also received vouchers but whose vouchers were not contingent on their abstinent behavior.

EVALUATING BEHAVIOR THERAPY Compared with some other forms of therapy, behavior therapy has some distinct advantages. Behavior therapy usually achieves results in a short period of time because it is generally directed to specific symptoms, leading to faster relief of a client's distress and to lower costs. The methods to be used are also clearly delineated, and the results can be readily evaluated (Marks, 1982). Overall, the outcomes achieved with behavior therapy compare very favorably with those of other approaches (Emmelkamp, 2004; Nathan & Gorman, 2002; Roth & Fonagy, 1996).

As with other approaches, behavior therapy works better with certain kinds of problems than with others. Generally, the more pervasive and vaguely defined the client's problem, the less likely behavior therapy is to be useful. For example, it appears to be only rarely employed to treat complex personality disorders, although dialectical behavior therapy for patients with borderline personality disorder (see Chapter 11) is an exception. On the other hand, behavioral techniques are the backbone of modern approaches to treating sexual dysfunctions, as discussed in Chapter 13. Moreover, quantitative reviews of therapeutic outcomes confirm the expectation that behavior therapy is especially effective in the treatment of anxiety disorders, where the powerful exposure techniques can be brought to bear (Andrews & Harvey, 1981; Chambless et al., 1998; Clum et al., 1993; Nathan & Gorman, 2002). Behavior therapy can even be used with psychotic patients. Although behavior therapy is far from a cure-all, it has a highly respected place among the available psychosocial treatment approaches.

Cognitive and Cognitive-Behavioral Therapy

Early behavior therapists focused on observable behavior and regarded the inner thoughts of their clients as unimportant. Because of this, these therapists were often viewed as mechanistic technicians who simply manipulated their clients without considering them as people. Starting in the 1970s, a number of behavior therapists began to reappraise the importance of "private events"—thoughts, perceptions, evaluations, and self-statements—and started to see them as processes that mediate the effects of objective stimulus conditions and thus help determine behavior and emotions (Borkovec, 1985; Mahoney & Arnkoff, 1978).

Cognitive and **cognitive-behavioral therapy** (terms for the most part used interchangeably) stem from both cognitive psychology (with its emphasis on the effects of thoughts on behavior) and behaviorism (with its rigorous methodology and performance-oriented focus). At the present time, no single set of techniques defines cognitively oriented treatment approaches. Two main themes are important, however: (1) the conviction that cognitive processes influence emotion, motivation, and behavior, and (2) the use of cognitive and behavior-change techniques in a pragmatic (hypothesis-testing) manner. In our discussion we briefly describe the rational emotive behavior therapy of Albert Ellis and then focus in more detail on the cognitive therapy approach of Aaron Beck.

RATIONAL EMOTIVE BEHAVIOR THERAPY One of the earliest developed of the behaviorally oriented cognitive therapies is the rational emotive therapy (now called **rational emotive behavior therapy—REBT**) of Albert Ellis (see Ellis & Dryden, 1997). REBT attempts to change a client's maladaptive thought processes, on which maladaptive emotional responses, and thus behavior, are presumed to depend.

Ellis posited that a well-functioning individual behaves rationally and in tune with empirical reality. Unfortunately, however, many of us have learned unrealistic beliefs and perfectionistic values that cause us to expect too much of ourselves, leading us to behave irrationally and then to feel that we are worthless failures. For example, a person may continually think, "I should be able to win everyone's love and approval" or "I should be thoroughly adequate and competent in everything I do." Such unrealistic assumptions and self-demands inevitably spell problems.

The task of REBT is to restructure an individual's belief system and self-evaluation, especially with respect to the irrational "shoulds," "oughts," and "musts" that are preventing the individual from having a more positive sense of self-worth and an emotionally satisfying, fulfilling life. Several methods are used. One method is to dispute a person's false beliefs through rational confrontation ("Why should your failure to get the promotion you wanted mean that you are worthless?").

REBT therapists also use behaviorally oriented techniques. For example, homework assignments might be given to encourage clients to have new experiences and to break negative chains of behavior. Although the techniques differ dramatically, the philosophy underlying REBT has something in common with that underlying humanistic therapy (discussed later) because both take a clear stand on personal worth and human values. Rational emotive behavior therapy aims at increasing an individual's feelings of self-worth and clearing the way for self-actualization by removing the false beliefs that have been stumbling blocks to personal growth.

BECK'S COGNITIVE THERAPIES Beck's cognitive therapy approach was originally developed for the treatment of depression (see Chapter 7) and was later extended to anxiety disorders, eating disorders and obesity, conduct disorder in children, personality disorders, and substance abuse (Beck, 2005; Beck & Emery, 1985; Beck et al., 1990, 1993; Hollon & Beck, 2004). The cognitive model is basically an information-processing model of psychopathology. A basic assumption of the cognitive model is that problems result from biased processing of external events or internal stimuli. These biases distort the way that a person makes sense of the experiences that she or he has in the world, leading to cognitive errors.

But why do people make cognitive errors at all? According to Beck (2005), underlying these biases is a relatively stable set of cognitive structures or schemas that contain dysfunctional beliefs. When these schemas become activated (by external or internal triggers), they bias how people process information. In the case of depression, people become inclined to make negatively biased interpretations of themselves, their world, and their future.

In the initial phase of cognitive therapy, clients are made aware of the connection between their patterns of thinking and their emotional responses. They are first taught simply to identify their own automatic thoughts (such as, "This event is a total disaster") and to keep records of their thought content and their emotional reactions (e.g., see Clark, 1997). With the therapist's help, they then identify the logical errors in their thinking and learn to challenge the validity of these automatic thoughts. The errors in the logic behind their thinking lead them (1) to perceive the world selectively as harmful while ignoring evidence to the contrary; (2) to overgeneralize on the basis of limited examples—for example, seeing themselves as totally worthless because they were laid off from work; (3) to magnify the significance of undesirable events—for example, seeing the job loss as the end of the world for them; and (4) to engage in absolutistic thinking—for example, exaggerating the importance of someone's mildly critical comment and perceiving it as proof of their instant descent from goodness to worthlessness. In the following case study, the therapist describes some of these errors in thinking to a depressed patient.

case STUDY Cognitive Therapy

THERAPIST: You have described many instances today where your interpretations led to particular feelings. You remember when you were crying a little while ago and I asked you what was going through your mind? You told me that you thought that I considered you pathetic and that I wouldn't want to see you for therapy. I said you were reading my mind and putting negative thoughts in my mind that were not, in fact, correct. You were making an arbitrary inference, or jumping to conclusions without evidence. This is what often happens when one is depressed. One tends to put the most negative interpretations on things, even sometimes when the evidence is contrary, and this makes one even more depressed. Do you recognize what I mean?

PATIENT: You mean even my thoughts are wrong?

THERAPIST: No, not your thoughts in general, and I am not talking about right and wrong. As I was explaining before, interpretations are not facts. They can be more or less accurate, but they cannot be right or wrong. What I mean is that some of your interpretations, in particular those relating to yourself, are biased negatively. The thoughts you attributed to me could have been accurate. But there were also many other conclusions you could have reached that might have been less depressing for you, in that they would reflect less badly on you. For example, you could have thought that since I was spending time with you, that meant I was interested and that I wanted to try and help. If this had been your conclusion, how do you think that you would have felt? Do you think that you would have felt like crying?

PATIENT: Well, I guess I might have felt less depressed, more hopeful.

THERAPIST: Good. That's the point I was trying to make. We feel what we think. Unfortunately, these biased interpretations tend to occur automatically. They just pop into one's head and one believes them. What you and I will do in therapy is to try and catch these thoughts and examine them. Together we will look at the evidence and correct the biases to make the thoughts more realistic. Does this sound all right with you?

PATIENT: Yes.

(Adapted from Blackburn & Davidson, 1990, pp. 106–7.)

Source: From *Cognitive Therapy for Depression and Anxiety: A Practitioner's Guide* by Ivy-Marie Blackburn and Kate M. Davidson, copyright © 1995. Blackwell Science.

Much of the content of the therapy sessions and homework assignments is analogous to experiments in which a therapist and a client apply learning principles to alter the client's biased and dysfunctional cognitions, and continuously evaluate the effects that these changes have on subsequent thoughts, feelings, and overt behavior. It is important to note, however, that in Beck's cognitive therapy, clients do not change their beliefs by debate and persuasion as is common in REBT. Rather, they are encouraged to gather information about themselves. For example, a young man who believes that his interest will be rebuffed by any woman he approaches would be led into a searching analysis of the reasons why he holds this belief. The client might then be assigned the task of "testing" this dysfunctional "hypothesis" by actually approaching seemingly appropriate women whom he admires. The results of the "test" would then be

According to the cognitive model, how we think about situations is closely linked to our emotional responses to them. If this young man is having automatic thoughts such as, "I'll never get to play. I'm such a loser," he is likely to be more emotionally distressed about waiting on the sideline than if he has a thought such as, "There's a lot I can learn from watching how this game is going."

thoroughly analyzed with the cognitive therapist, and any cognitive "errors" that may have interfered with a skillful performance would be discussed and corrected.

In addition, the client is encouraged to discover the faulty assumptions or dysfunctional schemas that may be leading to problem behaviors and self-defeating tendencies. These generally become evident over the course of therapy as the client and the therapist examine the themes of the client's automatic thoughts. Because these dysfunctional schemas are seen as making the person vulnerable (e.g., to depression), this phase of treatment is considered essential in ensuring resistance to relapse when the client faces stressful life events in the future. That is, if the underlying cognitive vulnerability factors are not changed, the client may show short-term improvement but will still be subject to recurrent depression.

For disorders other than depression, the general approach is quite similar. However, the nature of the patient's automatic thoughts and underlying beliefs is obviously quite different across disorders. In panic disorder, for example, the focus is on identifying the automatic thoughts about feared bodily sensations and on teaching the client to "decatastrophize" the experience of panic (Clark, 1986; Clark, Salkovskis, et al., 1994). In bulimia, the cognitive approach centers on the person's overvalued ideas about body weight and shape, which are often fueled by low self-esteem and fears of being unattractive. In addition, faulty cognitions about which foods are "safe" and which "dangerous" are explored (Agras, 1993; Fairburn, Marcus, et al., 1993; Wilson, 2005).

EVALUATING COGNITIVE-BEHAVIORAL THERAPIES

In spite of the widespread attention that Ellis's REBT has enjoyed, little research attests to its efficacy, especially for carefully diagnosed clinical populations. It appears to be inferior to exposure-based therapies in the treatment of anxiety disorders such as agoraphobia, social phobia (Haaga & Davison, 1989, 1992), and probably obsessive-compulsive disorder (Franklin & Foa, 1998). In general, it may be most useful in helping basically healthy people to cope better with everyday stress and perhaps in preventing them from developing full-blown anxiety or depressive disorders (Haaga & Davison, 1989, 1992).

In contrast, the efficacy of Beck's cognitive treatment methods has been well documented. Research suggests that these approaches are extremely beneficial in alleviating many different types of disorders (see Hollon & Beck, 2004). For depression, cognitive-behavioral therapy is at least comparable to drug treatment for all but the most severe cases (e.g., psychotic depression). It also offers long-term advantages, especially with regard to the prevention of relapse (Craighead et al., 2002). Cognitive therapy produces dramatic results in the treatment of panic disorder and generalized anxiety disorder (Hollon & Beck, 2004), and cognitive-behavioral therapy is now the treatment of choice for bulimia (Wilson & Fairburn, 2002; Wilson, 2005). Finally, cognitive approaches have promise in the treatment of conduct disorder in children (Hollon & Beck, 2004), substance abuse (Beck et al., 1993), and certain personality disorders (Beck et al., 1990; Linehan, 1993).

The combined use of cognitive and behavior therapy approaches is now quite routine. Some disagreement remains about whether the effects of cognitive treatments are actually the result of cognitive changes, as the cognitive theorists propose (Hollon & Beck, 2004; Jacobson et al., 1996). At least for depression and panic disorder, it does appear that cognitive change is the best predictor of long-term outcome, just as cognitive theory maintains (Hollon et al., 1990). Exactly what the active ingredients of cognitive treatments really are, however, is now a focus of debate and research (e.g., Teasdale et al., 2001; see also the Fall 1997 issue of *Behavior Therapy* [vol. 28, no. 4]).

Humanistic-Experiential Therapies

The humanistic-experiential therapies emerged as significant treatment approaches after World War II. In a society dominated by self-interest, mechanization, computerization, mass deception, and mindless bureaucracy, proponents of the humanistic-experiential therapies see psychopathology as stemming in many cases from problems of alienation, depersonalization, loneliness, and a failure to find meaning and genuine fulfillment. Problems of this sort, it is held, are not likely to be solved either by delving into forgotten memories or by correcting specific maladaptive behaviors.

The humanistic-experiential therapies are based on the assumption that we have both the freedom and the responsibility to control our own behavior—that we can

17.7 Developments in Practice — Motivational Interviewing

As anyone who has considered therapy knows, people tend to be ambivalent about making changes in their lives. They want to change, but they also don't want to change. Motivational Interviewing (MI; see Hettema et al., 2005) is a brief form of therapy that can be delivered in one or two sessions. It was developed as a way to help people resolve their ambivalence about change and make a commitment to treatment (Miller, 1983). At its center is a supportive and empathic style of relating to the client that has its origins in the work of Carl Rogers. However, MI differs from client-centered counseling because it also employs a more direct approach that explores the client's own reasons for wanting to change. The therapist encourages this "change talk" by asking the client to discuss his or her desire, ability, reasons, and need for change. These are reflected back by the therapist, thus exposing the client to periodic summaries of his or her own motivational statements and thoughts about change. The result is that clients can develop and strengthen their commitment to change in an active, accepting, and supportive atmosphere.

Motivational Interviewing is most often used in the areas of substance abuse and addiction. When added to the beginning of a treatment program, it appears to benefit patients, perhaps because it facilitates patients' staying in treatment and following the treatment plan. Hettema and colleagues' (2005) meta-analysis of the MI literature has also shown that MI has a large effect when it is used with ethnic minorities. In one alcoholism-treatment trial, Native American participants did better if they received four sessions of MI than if they received 12 sessions of cognitive-behavior therapy or else participated in a 12-step program (Villanueva et al., 2003). Quite possibly, the supportive and nonconfrontational style of MI may be more congruent with the typical and culturally sanctioned communication style of Native Americans and thus represent a culturally appropriate intervention. As research continues, we will learn more about the efficacy of this increasingly popular therapeutic technique and gain knowledge about the kinds of clients for whom it is most appropriate.

reflect on our problems, make choices, and take positive action. Humanistic-experiential therapists feel that a client must take most of the responsibility for the direction and success of therapy, with the therapist serving merely as counselor, guide, and facilitator. Although humanistic-experiential therapies differ in their details, their central focus is always expanding a client's "awareness."

CLIENT-CENTERED THERAPY The **client-centered** (person-centered) **therapy** of Carl Rogers (1902–1987) focuses on the natural power of the organism to heal itself (Rogers, 1951, 1961). Rogers saw therapy as a process of removing the constraints and restrictions that grow out of unrealistic demands that people tend to place on themselves when they believe, as a condition of self-worth, that they should not have certain kinds of feelings such as hostility. By denying that they do in fact have such feelings, they become unaware of their actual "gut" reactions. As they lose touch with their own genuine experience, the result is lowered integration, impaired personal relationships, and various forms of maladjustment.

The primary objective of Rogerian therapy is to resolve this incongruence—to help clients become able to accept and be themselves. To this end, client-centered therapists establish a psychological climate in which clients can feel unconditionally accepted, understood, and valued as people. Within this context, the therapist employs nondirective techniques such as empathic reflecting, or restatement of the client's descriptions of life difficulties. If all goes well, clients begin to feel free, for perhaps the first time, to explore their real feelings and thoughts and to accept hates and angers and ugly feelings as parts of themselves. As their self-concept becomes more congruent with their actual experience, they become more self-accepting and more open to new experiences and new perspectives; in short, they become better-integrated people.

In contrast to most other forms of therapy, the client-centered therapist does not give answers, interpret what a client says, probe for unconscious conflicts, or even steer the client toward certain topics. Rather, he or she simply listens attentively and acceptingly to what the client wants to talk about, interrupting only to restate in different words what the client is saying. Such restatements, devoid of any judgment or interpretation by the therapist, help the client to clarify further the feelings and ideas that he or she is exploring—really to look at them and acknowledge them.

Pure client-centered psychotherapy, as originally practiced, is rarely used today in North America, although it is still relatively popular in Europe. Motivational Interviewing is a new form of therapy that is based on this empathic style (see Developments in Practice 17.7). The following excerpt from a therapist's second interview with a young woman will serve to illustrate these techniques of reflection and clarification.

case STUDY Client-Centered Therapy

ALICE: I was thinking about this business of standards. I somehow developed a sort of a knack, I guess, of—well—habit—of trying to make people feel at ease around me, or to make things go along smoothly. . . .

COUNSELOR: In other words, what you did was always in the direction of trying to keep things smooth and to make other people feel better and to smooth the situation.

ALICE: Yes. I think that's what it was. Now the reason why I did it probably was—I mean, not that I was a good little Samaritan going around making other people happy, but that was probably the role that felt easiest for me to play. I'd been doing it around home so much. I just didn't stand up for my own convictions, until I don't know whether I have any convictions to stand up for.

COUNSELOR: You feel that for a long time you've been playing the role of kind of smoothing out the frictions or differences or what not.

ALICE: M-hm.

COUNSELOR: Rather than having any opinion or reaction of your own in the situation. Is that it?

ALICE: That's it. Or that I haven't been really honestly being myself, or actually knowing what my real self is, and that I've been just playing a sort of a false role. Whatever role no one else was playing, and that needed to be played at the time, I'd try to fill it in.

(From Rogers, 1951, pp. 152–53.)

GESTALT THERAPY In German, the term *gestalt* means "whole," and gestalt therapy emphasizes the unity of mind and body—placing strong emphasis on the need to integrate thought, feeling, and action. Gestalt therapy was developed by Frederick (Fritz) Perls (1969) as a means of teaching clients to recognize the bodily processes and emotions they had been blocking off from awareness. As with the client-centered and humanistic approaches, the main goal of gestalt therapy is to increase the individual's self-awareness and self-acceptance.

Although gestalt therapy is commonly used in a group setting, the emphasis is on one person at a time, with whom a therapist works intensively, trying to help identify aspects of the individual's self or world that are not being acknowledged in awareness. The individual may be asked to act out fantasies concerning feelings and conflicts or to represent one side of a conflict while sitting in one chair and then switch chairs to take the part of the adversary. Often the therapist or other group members will ask such questions as, "What are you aware of in your body now?" and "What does it feel like in your gut when you think of that?"

In Perls' approach to therapy, a good deal of attention is also paid to dreams, but with an emphasis very different from that of classical psychoanalysis. In gestalt theory, all elements of a dream, including seemingly inconsequential, impersonal objects, are considered to be representations of unacknowledged aspects of the dreamer's self. The therapist urges the client to suspend normal critical judgment, to "be" the object in the dream, and then to report on the experience. This is illustrated in the following case study.

case STUDY Gestalt Therapy

A college professor and therapist was preoccupied with his academic promotion and tenure and found himself unable to experience any joy. He sought the assistance of a friend who was a gestalt therapist. She asked him to conjure up a daydream, rather than a dream. The daydream that emerged spontaneously was one of skiing. The therapist asked him to be the mountain, and he began to experience how warm he was when he was at his base. As he got closer to the top, what looked so beautiful was also very cold and frozen. The therapist asked the professor to be the snow, and he experienced how hard and icy he could be near the top. But near the bottom, people ran over him easily and wore him out. When the session was finished, the professor did not feel like crying or shouting; he felt like skiing. So he went, leaving articles and books behind. In the sparkle of the snow and sun, he realized that joy in living emerges through deeds and not through words. In his rush to succeed, he had committed one of the cardinal sins against himself—the sin of not being active. (Adapted from Prochaska & Norcross, 2003, p. 183.)

PROCESS-EXPERIENTIAL THERAPY Process-experiential (PE) therapy is a relatively new treatment approach that combines client-centered therapy and gestalt therapy. Developed by Greenberg and his colleagues, (see Greenberg, 2004) this treatment emphasizes the *experiencing* of emotions during therapy. Clients are also asked to reflect on their emotions and are encouraged to create meaning from them (see Elliot et al., 2004). The therapist plays a more active role than in pure client-centered therapy and may work to guide the patient to experience emotions more vividly through a variety of different techniques. Like other humanistic-experiential therapies, the relationship with the therapist is regarded as extremely important and the vehicle through which progress in treatment is made.

EVALUATING HUMANISTIC-EXPERIENTIAL THERAPIES Many of the humanistic-experiential concepts—the uniqueness of each individual, the importance of therapist genuineness, the satisfaction that comes from realizing one's potential, the importance of the search for meaning and fulfillment, and the human capacity for choice and self-direction—have had a major impact on our contemporary views of both human nature and the nature of good psychotherapy.

However, humanistic-experiential therapies have been criticized for their lack of agreed-upon therapeutic procedures, and their vagueness about what is supposed to happen between client and therapist. In response, proponents of such approaches argue against reducing people to abstractions, which can diminish their perceived worth and deny their uniqueness. Because people are so different, they argue, we should expect different techniques to be appropriate for different cases.

Controlled research on the outcomes achieved by many forms of humanistic-existential therapy was lacking in the past. However, research in this area is now on the increase. As the number of controlled-outcome studies grows, there is evidence to suggest that these treatment approaches are helpful for patients with a variety of problems including depression, anxiety, trauma, and marital difficulties (Elliot et al., 2004).

Psychodynamic Therapies

Psychodynamic therapy is a treatment approach that focuses on individual personality dynamics, usually from a psychoanalytic or some psychoanalytically derived perspective (see Chapter 3). Psychoanalytic therapy is the oldest form of psychological therapy and began with Sigmund Freud. The therapy is mainly practiced in two basic forms: classical psychoanalysis and psychoanalytically oriented psychotherapy. As developed by Freud and his immediate followers, classical psychoanalysis is an intensive (at least three sessions per week), long-term procedure for uncovering repressed memories, thoughts, fears, and conflicts presumably stemming from problems in early psychosexual development—and helping individuals come to terms with them in light of the realities of adult life. For example, excessive orderliness and a grim and humorless focus on rigorous self-control would probably be viewed as deriving from difficulties in early toilet training.

In psychoanalytically oriented psychotherapy, the treatment and the ideas guiding it may depart substantially from the principles and procedures laid out by orthodox Freudian theory, yet the therapy is still loosely based on psychoanalytic concepts. For example, many psychoanalytically oriented therapists schedule less frequent sessions (e.g., once per week) and sit face-to-face with the client instead of having the latter recline on a couch with the analyst out of sight behind him or her. Likewise, the relatively passive stance of the analyst (primarily listening to the client's "free associations" and rarely offering "interpretations") is replaced with an active conversational style in which the therapist attempts to clarify distortions and gaps in the client's construction of the origins and consequences of his or her problems, thus challenging client "defenses" as they present themselves. It is widely believed that this more direct approach significantly shortens total treatment time. We will first examine Freud's original treatment methods, in part because of their historical significance and enormous influence; we will then look briefly at some of the contemporary modifications of psychodynamic therapy, which for the most part focus on interpersonal processes. Before we do so, however, let's consider the case of Karen.

case study — Psychodynamic Therapy

Karen was about to be terminated from her nursing program if her problems were not resolved. She had always been a competent student who seemed to get along well with peers and patients. Now, since the beginning of her rotation on 3 South, a surgical ward, she was plagued by headaches and dizzy spells. Of more serious consequence were the two medical errors she had made when dispensing medications to patients. She realized that these errors could have proved fatal, and she was as concerned as her nursing faculty about why such problems had begun in this final year of her education. Karen knew she had many negative feelings toward the head nurse on 3 South, but she did not believe these feelings could account for her current dilemma. She entered psychotherapy.

After a few weeks of psychotherapy, the therapist realized that one of Karen's important conflicts revolved around the death of her father when she was 12 years old. Karen had just gone to live with her father after being with her mother for 7 years. She remembered how upset she was when her father had a heart attack and had to be rushed to the hospital. For a while it looked as though her father was going to pull through, and Karen began enjoying her daily visits to see him. During one of these visits, her father clutched his chest in obvious pain and told Karen to get a nurse. She remembered how helpless she felt when she could not find a nurse, although she did not recall why this was so difficult. Her search seemed endless, and by the time she finally found a nurse, her father was dead.

The therapist asked Karen the name of the ward on which her father had died. She paused and thought, and then she blurted out, "3 South." She cried at length as she told how confused she was and how angry she felt toward the nurses on the ward for not being more readily available, although she thought they might have been involved with another emergency. After weeping and shaking and expressing her resentment, Karen felt calm and relaxed for the first time in months. Her symptoms disappeared, and her problems in the nursing program were relieved. (Adapted from Prochaska & Norcross, 2003, p. 28.)

FREUDIAN PSYCHOANALYSIS Psychoanalysis is a system of therapy that evolved over a period of years during Freud's long career. Psychoanalysis is not easy to describe, and the problem is complicated by the fact that many people have inaccurate conceptions of it based on cartoons and other forms of caricature. The best way to begin our discussion is to describe the four basic techniques of this form of therapy: (1) free association, (2) analysis of dreams, (3) analysis of resistance, and (4) analysis of transference. Then we will note some of the most important changes that have taken place in psychodynamic therapy since Freud's time.

Free Association The basic rule of **free association** is that an individual must say whatever comes into his or her mind, regardless of how personal, painful, or seemingly irrelevant it may be. Usually a client lies in a relaxed position on a couch and gives a running account of all the thoughts, feelings, and desires that come to mind as one idea leads to another. The therapist normally takes a position behind the client so as not to disrupt the free flow of associations in any way.

Although such a running account of whatever comes into one's mind may seem random, Freud did not view it as such; rather, he believed that associations are determined just like other events. The purpose of free association is to explore thoroughly the contents of the preconscious—that part of the mind considered subject to conscious attention but largely ignored. Analytic interpretation involves a therapist's tying together a client's often disconnected ideas, beliefs, and actions into a meaningful explanation to help the client gain insight into the relationship between his or her maladaptive behavior and the repressed (unconscious) events and fantasies that drive it.

Analysis of Dreams Another important, related procedure for uncovering unconscious material is the analysis of dreams. When a person is asleep, repressive defenses are said to be lowered, and forbidden desires and feelings may find an outlet in dreams. For this reason, dreams have been referred to as the "royal road to the unconscious." Some motives, however, are so unacceptable to an individual that even in dreams they are not revealed openly but are expressed in disguised or symbolic form. Thus a dream has two kinds of content: (1) **manifest content,** which is the dream as it appears to the dreamer, and (2) **latent content,** which consists of the actual motives that are seeking expression but that are so painful or unacceptable that they are disguised.

It is a therapist's task, in conjunction with the associations of the patient, to uncover these disguised meanings by studying the images that appear in the manifest content of a client's dream and in the client's associations to them. For example, a client's dream of being engulfed in a tidal wave may be interpreted by a therapist as indicating that the client feels in danger of being overwhelmed by inadequately repressed fears and/or hostilities.

Analysis of Resistance During the process of free association or of associating to dreams, an individual may evidence **resistance**—an unwillingness or inability to talk about certain thoughts, motives, or experiences (Strean, 1985). For example, a client may be talking about an important childhood experience and then suddenly switch topics, perhaps stating, "It really isn't that important" or "It is too absurd to discuss." Resistance may also be evidenced by the client's giving a too-glib interpretation of some association, or coming late to an appointment, or even "forgetting" an appointment altogether. Because resistance prevents painful and threatening material from entering awareness, its sources must be sought if an individual is to face the problem and learn to deal with it in a realistic manner.

Analysis of Transference As client and therapist interact, the relationship between them may become complex and emotionally involved. Often people carry over, and unconsciously apply to their therapist, attitudes and feelings that they had in their relations with a parent or other person close to them in the past, a process known as **transference.** Thus clients may react to their analyst as they did to that earlier person and feel the same love, hostility, or rejection that they felt long ago. If the analyst is operating according to the prescribed role of maintaining an impersonal stance of detached attention, the often affect-laden reactions of the client can be interpreted, it is held, as a type of projection—inappropriate to the present situation, yet highly revealing of central issues in the client's life. For example, should the client vehemently (but inaccurately) condemn the therapist for a lack of caring and attention to the client's needs, this would be seen as a "transference" to the therapist of attitudes acquired (possibly on valid grounds) in childhood interactions with parents or other key individuals.

In helping the client to understand and acknowledge the transference relationship, a therapist may provide the client with insight into the meaning of his or her reactions to others. In doing so, the therapist may also introduce a corrective emotional experience by refusing to engage the person on the basis of his or her unwarranted assumptions about the nature of the therapeutic relationship. If the client expects rejection and criticism, for example, the therapist is careful to maintain a neutral manner. Or contrarily, the therapist may express positive emotions at a point where the client feels particularly vulnerable, thereby encouraging the client to reframe and rethink her or his view of the situation. In this way it may be possible for the individual to recognize these assumptions and to "work through" the conflict in feelings about the real parent or perhaps to overcome feelings of hostility and self-devaluation that stemmed from the earlier parental rejection. In essence, the negative effects of an undesirable early relationship are counteracted by working through a similar emotional conflict with the therapist in a therapeutic setting. A person's reliving of a pathogenic past relationship in a sense re-creates the neurosis in real life, and therefore this experience is often referred to as a *transference neurosis.*

It is not possible here to consider at length the complexities of transference relationships, but a client's attitudes toward his or her therapist usually do not follow such simple patterns as our examples suggest. Often the client is ambivalent—distrusting the therapist and feeling hostile toward him or her as a symbol of authority, but at the same time seeking acceptance and love. In addition, the problems of transference are not confined to the client, for the therapist may also have a mixture of feelings toward the client. This **counter-transference,** wherein the therapist reacts in accord with the client's transferred attributions rather than objectively, must be recognized and handled properly by the therapist. For this reason, it is considered important that therapists have a thorough understanding of their own motives, conflicts, and "weak spots"; in fact, all psychoanalysts undergo psychoanalysis themselves before they begin independent practice.

The resolution of the transference neurosis is said to be the key element in effecting a psychoanalytic "cure." Such resolution can occur only if an analyst successfully avoids the pitfalls of counter-transference. That is, the analyst needs to keep track of his or her own transference or reaction to a client's behavior. Failure to do so risks merely repeating, in the therapy relationship, the typical relationship difficulties characterizing the client's adult life. Analysis of transference and the phenomenon of counter-transference are also part of most psychodynamic derivatives of classical psychoanalysis, to which we now turn.

Psychodynamic Therapy since Freud The original version of psychoanalysis is practiced only rarely today. Arduous and costly in time, money, and emotional commitment, it may take several years before all major issues in the client's life have been satisfactorily resolved. In light of these heavy demands, psychoanalytic/psychodynamic therapists have worked out modifications in procedure designed to shorten the time and expense required. A good review of some of these approaches can be found in Prochaska and Norcross (2003).

INTERPERSONAL THERAPY (IPT) Contemporary psychodynamic approaches to therapy tend to have a strongly interpersonal focus. They emphasize, in other words, what traditional Freudians would consider transferential and counter-transferential phenomena, extending these concepts to virtually all of a disturbed person's relationships, rather than considering them only in the treatment situation. Interpersonal therapy was first articulated in this country by Harry Stack Sullivan (see Chapter 3). Its central idea is that all of us, at all times, involuntarily invoke schemas acquired from our earliest interactions with others, such as our parents, in interpreting what is going on in our current relationships. Where those earlier relationships have had problematic features such as rejection or abuse, the "introjected" characteristics of those earlier interaction partners may distort in various ways the individual's ability to process accurately and objectively the information contained in current interpersonal transactions. Thus the formerly abused or rejected person may come to operate under the implicit (unconscious) assumption that the world is generally rejecting and/or abusive. The mistrust stemming from this belief is bound to affect current relationships negatively. In the worst instances it may even lead (because of the reactions of others to the client's wariness, reticence, or counteraggression) to a further confirmation that the world is a nasty if not a dangerous place—an instance of self-fulfilling prophecy (e.g., see Carson, 1982; Wachtel, 1993).

OBJECT RELATIONS, SELF-PSYCHOLOGY, AND OTHER INTERPERSONAL VARIATIONS The most extensive revisions of classical psychoanalytic theory undertaken within recent decades have been related to the object-relations perspective (in psychoanalytic jargon, "objects" are other people) and, to a lesser extent, the attachment and self-psychology perspectives (see Chapter 3; also see Prochaska & Norcross, 2003). Whether or not psychotherapy investigators and clinicians use the term *object relations* (or *attachment* or *self-psychology*) to denote their approach, increasing numbers of them describe procedures that focus on interpersonal relationship issues, particularly as they play themselves out in the client-therapist relationship (e.g., Benjamin, 1996; Frank & Spanier, 1995; Kiesler, 1996; Klerman et al., 1984; Strupp & Binder, 1984).

The greatest contribution of the interpersonal approach may be its role in the developing movement toward "integration" of the various forms of therapy. Numerous contemporary investigators and clinicians (e.g., Beutler, 1992; Blatt et al., 1996; Lazarus, 1997a, 1997b; Linehan, 1993; Safran, 1990a, 1990b; Wachtel, 1997) have pointed to the many ways in which interpersonal issues play a central role in psychodynamic, behavioral, cognitive, and even psychopharmacological therapies.

Interpersonally oriented psychodynamic therapists vary considerably in their time focus: whether they concentrate on remote events of the past, on current interpersonal situations and impasses (including those of the therapy itself), or on some balance of the two. Most seek to expose, bring to awareness, and modify the effects of the remote developmental sources of the difficulties the client is currently experiencing. These therapies generally retain, then, the classical psychoanalytic goal of understanding the present in terms of the past. What they ignore are the psychoanalytic notions of staged libidinal energy transformations and of entirely internal (and impersonal) drives that are channeled into psychopathological symptom formation.

EVALUATING PSYCHODYNAMIC THERAPY Classical psychoanalysis is routinely criticized by outsiders for being relatively time-consuming and expensive; for being based on a questionable, stultified, and sometimes cult-like approach to human nature; for neglecting a client's immediate problems in the search for unconscious conflicts in the remote past; and for there being no adequate proof of its general effectiveness. Concerning this, we note that there have been no rigorous, controlled outcome studies of classical psychoanalysis. This is understandable, given the intensive and long-term nature of the treatment and the methodological difficulties inherent in testing such an approach. Nonetheless, there are some promising but preliminary hints that this treatment approach has some value (Gabbard et al., 2002). Psychoanalysts also argue that manualized treatments unduly limit treatment for a disorder. They note that simply because a treatment cannot be standardized does not mean that it is invalid or unhelpful. Whether the clinical benefits justify the time and expense of psychoanalysis, however, remains uncertain.

In contrast, there is much more research on some of the newer psychodynamically oriented approaches, although research showing that this form of therapy works for specific diagnoses is still generally lacking. Anderson and Lambert (1995) have published a useful summary, involving quantitative analysis, of 26 efficacy studies of brief psychodynamic psychotherapy. In general, the demonstrated results of this type of therapy are quite impressive. We would single out in particular the interpersonal therapy model developed by Klerman and associates (1984), originally targeted for the problem of depression, where it has demonstrable value (de Mello et al., 2005). It has also been shown to be a promising treatment for bulimia nervosa (Fairburn, Jones, et al., 1993).

Marital and Family Therapy

Many problems brought to practitioners are explicitly relationship problems. A common example is couples or marital distress. The maladaptive behavior in these instances is shared between the members of the relationship. Extending the focus even further, a family systems approach reflects the assumption that the within-family behavior of any particular family member is subject to the influence of the behaviors and communication patterns of other family members. It is, in other words, the product of a "system" that may be amenable to both understanding and change. Addressing problems deriving from the in-place system thus requires therapeutic techniques that focus on relationships as much as, or more than, on individuals.

MARITAL THERAPY The large numbers of couples seeking help with relationship problems have made couples counseling a growing field of therapy. Typically the couple is seen together, and improving communication skills and developing more adaptive problem-solving styles are both a major focus of clinical attention. Although it is quite routine at the start of couples therapy for each partner secretly to harbor the idea that only the other will have to do the changing (e.g., Cordova & Jacobson, 1993), it is nearly always necessary for both partners to alter their reactions to the other.

For many years the gold standard of **marital therapy** has been **traditional behavioral couple therapy** (TBCT; see Christensen & Heavey, 1999). TBCT is based on a social-learning model and views marital satisfaction and marital distress in terms of reinforcement. The treatment is usually short-term (10 to 26 sessions) and is guided by a manual. The goal of TBCT is to increase caring behaviors in the relationship and to teach partners to resolve their conflicts in a more constructive way through training in communication skills and adaptive problem solving.

Research has established TBCT as an empirically supported treatment for marital distress (for a review of numerous outcome studies, see Christensen & Heavey, 1999). Approximately two-thirds of couples do well and show improvement in relationship satisfaction (Jacobson et al., 1987). However, this form of treatment does not work for all couples (Jacobson & Addis, 1993). Moreover, even among couples who show an improvement in relationship

Marital therapists try to help couples improve their communication skills and develop more adaptive ways of solving their problems.

satisfaction, the improvement may not be maintained over time (Jacobson et al., 1987).

The limitations of TBCT have led researchers to conclude that a change-focused treatment approach is not appropriate for all couples. This, in turn, has led to the development of **integrative behavioral couple therapy** (IBCT; see Jacobson et al., 2000; Wheeler et al., 2001). Instead of emphasizing change (which sometimes has the paradoxical effect of making people not want to change), IBCT focuses on acceptance and includes strategies that help each member of the couple come to terms with and accept some of the limitations of his or her partner. Of course, change is not forbidden. Rather, within IBCT, acceptance strategies are integrated with change strategies to provide a form of therapy that is more tailored to individual characteristics and the needs of the couple.

Although this is a new development in the marital therapy field, the preliminary findings are quite promising. In one study, improvement rates were 80 percent in the couples treated with IBCT versus 64 percent in couples receiving TBCT (Jacobson et al., 2000).

FAMILY THERAPY Therapy for a family obviously overlaps with couples and marital therapy but has somewhat different roots. Whereas marital therapy developed in response to the large number of clients who came for assistance with couples problems, **family therapy** began with the finding that many people who had shown marked improvement in individual therapy—often in institutional settings—had a relapse when they returned home. As you have already learned from Chapters 7 and 14, family-based treatment approaches designed to reduce high levels of criticism and family tension have been successful in reducing relapse rates in patients with schizophrenia and mood disorders (Miklowitz, 2002; Pilling et al., 2002).

Another approach to resolving family disturbances is called **structural family therapy** (Minuchin, 1974). This approach, which is based on systems theory, holds that if the family context can be changed, then the individual members will have altered experiences in the family and will behave differently in accordance with the changed requirements of the new family context. Thus an important goal of structural family therapy is changing the organization of the family in such a way that the family members will behave more supportively and less pathogenically toward each other.

Structural family therapy is focused on present interactions and requires an active but not directive approach on the part of a therapist. Initially, the therapist gathers information about the family—a structural map of the typical family interaction patterns—by acting like one of the family members and participating in the family interactions as an insider. In this way, the therapist discovers whether the family system has rigid or flexible boundaries, who dominates the power structure, who gets blamed when things go wrong, and so on. Armed with this understanding, the therapist then operates as an agent for altering the interaction among the members, which often has transactional characteristics of enmeshment (overinvolvement), overprotectiveness, rigidity, and poor conflict resolution skills. The "identified client" is often found to play an important role in the family's mode of conflict avoidance. As discussed in Chapter 9, structural family therapy has quite a good record of success in the treatment of anorexia nervosa (see Lock et al., 2001).

Eclecticism and Integration

The various "schools" of psychotherapy that we have just described used to stand more in opposition to one another than they do now. Today, clinical practice is characterized by a relaxation of boundaries and a willingness on the part of therapists to explore differing ways of approaching clinical problems (see Castonguay et al., 2003, for a discussion), a process sometimes called *multimodal therapy* (Lazarus, 1981, 1985, 1997a). When asked what their orientation is, most psychotherapists today reply "eclectic," which usually means that they try to borrow and combine concepts and techniques from various schools, depending on what seems best for the individual case. This inclusiveness even extends to efforts to combine individual and family therapies (e.g., Feldman, 1992; E. Wachtel, 1994) and to combine biological and psychosocial approaches (e.g., Feldman & Feldman, 1997; Klerman et al., 1994; Pinsof, 1995).

In Review

- Describe the different techniques that can be used to provide anxious patients with exposure to the stimuli they fear.
- In what ways are REBT and cognitive therapy similar? In what ways are they different?
- Explain the concepts of transference and counter-transference.
- What special difficulties do clinicians face when they work with couples? How have techniques of marital therapy evolved over recent years?

Psychotherapy and Society

The criticism has been raised—from both inside and outside the mental health professions—that psychotherapy can be viewed as an attempt to get people adjusted to a "sick" society rather than to encourage them to work toward its improvement. As a consequence, psychotherapy has often been considered the guardian of the status quo. This issue is perhaps easier for us to place in perspective by looking at other cultures. For example, there had been frequent allegations that psychiatry was used as a means of political control in the former Soviet Union, an abuse that was eventually officially acknowledged (see *Schizophrenia Bulletin,* 1990, vol. 16, no. 4). Although few would claim that psychiatry in most industrialized societies is used to gain control over social critics, there is nevertheless the possibility that therapists in some ways play the role of "gatekeepers" of social values. Such charges, of course, bring us back to the question we raised in Chapter 1: What do we mean by "abnormal"? That question can be answered only in the light of our values.

Social Values and Psychotherapy

In a broader perspective, there is the complex and controversial issue of the role of values in science. Psychotherapy is not, or at least should not be, a system of ethics; it is a set of tools to be used at the discretion of a therapist in pursuit of a client's welfare. Thus mental health professionals are confronted with the same kinds of questions that confront scientists in general: Should a physical scientist who helps develop weapons of mass destruction be morally concerned about how they are used? Similarly, should a psychologist or behavioral scientist who develops powerful techniques to influence or control how people behave be concerned about how those techniques are used?

Many psychologists and other scientists try to sidestep this issue by insisting that science is value-free—that it is concerned only with gathering facts, not with how they are applied. Each time therapists decide that one behavior should be eliminated or substituted for another, however, they are making a value judgment. For example, is a therapist to assume that the depression of a young mother who is abused by an alcoholic husband is an internally based disorder requiring "treatment," as once would have been the routine interpretation? Or does the therapist have a larger responsibility to look beyond individual pathology and confront the abnormality of the marital relationship? Therapy takes place in a context that involves the values of the therapist, the client, and the society in which they live. There are strong pressures on a therapist—from parents, schools, courts, and other social institutions—to help people adjust to the world as it is. At the same time, there are many counterpressures, particularly from young people who are seeking support in their (sometimes overdone) attempts to become authentic people rather than blind conformists.

The dilemma in which contemporary therapists may find themselves is illustrated by the following case study.

case STUDY — Who Needs Therapy?

A 15-year-old high school sophomore is sent to a therapist because her parents have discovered that she has been having sexual intercourse with her boyfriend. The girl tells the therapist that she thoroughly enjoys such relations and feels no guilt or remorse over her behavior, even though her parents strongly disapprove. In addition, she reports that she is quite aware of the danger of becoming pregnant and is careful to take contraceptive measures.

What is the role of the therapist in such a case? Should the girl be encouraged to conform to her parents' expectations and postpone sexual activity until she is older and more mature? Or should the parents be helped to adjust to the pattern of sexual behavior their daughter has chosen? What should be the therapist's goal? As we noted earlier, it is not unusual for individuals to be referred for psychological treatment because their behavior, though not particularly destructive or disturbing, has caused concern among family members, who want the therapist to "fix" them.

Psychotherapy and Cultural Diversity

As we have seen, the establishment and maintenance of an effective psychotherapeutic "working alliance" between client and therapist is generally regarded as a crucial and indispensable element in determining the success of the outcome. What does this mean for a client whose background is considerably different from that of the therapist?

As yet, there is little or no solid evidence that psychotherapeutic outcomes are diminished when client and therapist differ in race or ethnicity (Beutler et al., 2004; Sue et al., 1994). However, members of minority groups are seriously underrepresented in treatment research studies, and this makes it difficult to fully assess their needs and outcomes (Miranda et al., 2005; Nagayama Hall, 2001). Moreover, racial and ethnic minorities are clearly underserved by the mental health system (Snowden & Yamada, 2005; U.S. Department of Health and Human Services, 2001). However, the factors that are behind these disparities are complex and not well understood.

Many minorities are economically disadvantaged and simply do not have the health insurance they need to seek treatment. It is also difficult for patients to find the kind of therapists they want. In general, minority patients tend to prefer ethnically similar therapists over European-American therapists (Coleman, et al., 1995). Mexican-Americans state a strong preference for therapists who share their ethnic background and express the view that such therapists are more "credible" than Anglo therapists would be (Lopez et al., 1991; Ponce & Atkinson, 1989). However, finding an ethnically matched therapist may present difficulties. In one survey, for example, only 2 percent of psychiatrists, 2 percent of psychologists, and 4 percent of social workers said they were African-Americans (Holzer et al., 1998). The number of mental health professionals who are representative of other minority groups is no better (U.S. Department of Health and Human Services, 2001). The lack of trained therapists familiar with the issues important to different ethnic groups is a serious drawback, given the unique problems often associated with certain groups. This is illustrated in the following case, which concerns a Southeast Asian refugee woman in her mid-forties who was relocated to the United States.

case study — A Khmer Woman

"I lost my husband, I lost my country, I lost every property/fortune we owned. And coming over here, I can't learn to speak English and the way of life here is different; my mother and oldest son are very sick: I feel crippled, I can do nothing. I can't control what's going on. I don't know what I'm going to do once my public assistance expires. I may feel safe in a way—there is no war here, no Communist to kill or torture you—but deep down inside me, I still don't feel safe or secure. I get scared. I get scared so easily." (From Rumbaut, 1985, p. 475.)

When specialized, ethnically focused mental health programs are made available in community settings, minority clients are less likely to drop out of treatment and often do well (Snowden & Yamada, 2005). However, such programs are still lacking in many communities. Also lacking are research investigations designed to understand how culture and ethnicity affect a person's ability to access and receive psychiatric and psychological treatments. Although special funding initiatives do exist, this is still an area of research in need of much more attention and activity.

In Review

- Can psychotherapy ever be value-free? Why or why not?
- What special issues do racial and ethnic minorities face when they seek therapy?

UNRESOLVED ISSUES

Is There Bias in the Reporting of Drug Trials?

Many researchers, especially those who conduct clinical trials of drugs, receive money, directly from the pharmaceutical industry, to conduct their studies. Some academic researchers in medical schools and universities receive grants from drug companies. Other clinical investigators are actually employed by the drug companies themselves. Clinical investigators often also have other links to the pharmaceutical industry. For example, they may own stock in the company whose drug they are studying. They may also serve as consultants for drug companies or receive speaking fees from them.

Do such financial conflicts of interest have any implications for the results of the clinical trials that these researchers conduct? Interest in this issue escalated after Jesse Gelsinger, a teenager, died after he participated in a University of Pennsylvania study that was led by a researcher with a financial interest in the company that was sponsoring the research (see Bodeneheimer, 2000). Although some argue that researchers with financial ties to drug companies remain independent and objective collectors of data, others believe that such ties may subtly influence scientific judgment, leading to bias in the findings that are reported (Angell, 2000; Stossel, 2005).

In an examination of this issue, Perlis and colleagues (2005) looked at all the clinical drug trials that were reported in four of the most prestigious psychiatry journals between January 2001 and December 2003. They noted who funded the study and also determined whether authors reported financial conflicts of interest such as being employed by the drug company or owning stock in it. They then looked at the results of the clinical trials that were published.

It is noteworthy that the majority (60 percent) of the clinical trials were funded by the pharmaceutical industry. Financial conflicts of interest were also quite common (47 percent of studies). The central question, however, is whether either of these factors was associated with the likelihood that the authors reported a positive finding (i.e., drug better than placebo) for their study.

Perlis and colleagues' findings (2005) showed that the chances of a positive finding were not associated with who funded the clinical trial. In other words, receiving financial support from a drug company to do the study did not make it more likely that the drug would be reported as performing better than the placebo. However, there was an association between author conflict of interest and positive results. Specifically, when at least one author had a financial interest in the company, the odds of positive findings being reported were 4.9 times greater than when there was no conflict of interest.

How can the link between author conflict of interest and the outcome of the clinical trial be explained? One possibility is that the most senior and experienced investigators were also those who served as consultants for the drug companies, and perhaps these senior investigators also designed better clinical trials that yielded positive findings. But then again, perhaps authors with an interest in the company might have been more inclined to use research designs that could have favored the drug produced by their sponsors. Authors with financial conflicts of interest might also have been less inclined to publish negative findings that did not show the drug of their sponsors to be superior to placebo.

What are the implications here? At the very least, these findings validate the current practice of journals' requiring authors to disclose any financial links they have with industry. The findings also support calls for all clinical trials to be registered so that the results have to be reported regardless of whether they are positive or negative (Meier, 2004). Finally, these results raise the possibility that there may be subtle factors operating to undermine the objectivity of scientific researchers, perhaps even without them being fully aware of this.

SUMMARY

- Psychological treatment is aimed at reducing abnormal behavior in individuals through psychological means. The goals of psychotherapy include changing maladaptive behavior, minimizing or eliminating stressful environmental conditions, reducing negative affect, improving interpersonal competencies, resolving personal conflicts, modifying people's inaccurate assumptions about themselves, and fostering a more positive self-image.
- Although these goals are by no means easy to achieve, psychological treatment methods have been shown to be generally effective in promoting adaptive psychological functioning in many troubled people.
- Medications are also important in the treatment of many disorders. It is now common clinical practice to combine medication and psychological treatments.

- Some of the earlier antidepressant medications (e.g., tricyclics and monoamine oxidase inhibitors) have now been replaced by SSRIs and SNRIs. In general, antidepressants work through their influence on the serotonin and norepinephrine neurotransmitter systems.
- The most commonly used antipsychotic medications are the atypical neuroleptics. These improve both positive and negative symptoms and have fewer extrapyramidal symptoms (unwanted side effects involving movement) than conventional (first generation) antipsychotics.
- Although not frequently used, ECT is a safe and effective treatment for depression and other disorders. It causes some short-term cognitive side effects, especially when administered bilaterally.
- Anxiolytic medications work via their effect on the GABA system to decrease anxiety. They are widely prescribed.
- Lithium is an important medication in the treatment of mania. However, some of the newer mood-stabilizing drugs (which are also used to treat epilepsy) are now more frequently prescribed.
- Many approaches to psychological treatment have been developed to treat individuals with psychological disorders. One of the oldest approaches to psychological treatment, classical psychoanalysis, was originated a century ago by Sigmund Freud. It is rarely practiced today, and there is little empirical support for its efficacy.
- Several variants of therapy have developed out of the psychoanalytic tradition. These diverge from classical psychoanalysis on matters such as the duration of therapy and the role of primitive psychosexual drives in personality dynamics. Many of the newer psychodynamic forms of treatment emphasize the way interpersonal processes are affected by early interactions with parents and other family members.
- Behavior therapy is extensively used to treat many clinical problems. Behavior therapy approaches include exposure, aversion therapy, modeling, and reinforcement approaches.
- Cognitive or cognitive-behavioral therapy attempts to modify a person's self-statements and construal of events in order to change his or her behavior. Cognitive-behavioral methods have been used for a wide variety of clinical problems—from depression to anger control—and with a range of clinical populations. Much research attests to the efficacy of cognitive and cognitive-behavioral approaches.
- Other psychological treatment approaches include humanistic-experiential therapies and gestalt therapy.
- In addition to their use in treating individuals, some psychological treatment methods are applied to problematic relationships through marital or family therapy. These approaches typically assume that a person's problems lie partly in his or her interactions with others. Consequently, the focus of treatment is on changing the ways in which members of the social or family unit interact.
- A key element in all therapies is the development of an effective "working alliance." A principal social issue in psychotherapy is ensuring the development of a good therapeutic working alliance between client and therapist, even when they differ widely in cultural, ethnic, and/or socioeconomic backgrounds.
- Evaluation of the success of psychotherapy in producing desired changes in clients is difficult. Two criteria for doing so have evolved: efficacy and effectiveness. Research on psychotherapy, however, has shown that most treatment approaches are more effective than no treatment at all.

Key Terms

antianxiety drugs (P. 616)
antidepressant drugs (P. 612)
antipsychotic drugs (P. 609)
behavior therapy (P. 622)
client-centered therapy (P. 628)
cognitive/cognitive-behavioral therapy (P. 625)
counter-transference (P. 632)
double-blind (P. 606)
efficacy (P. 606)
electroconvulsive therapy (ECT) (P. 618)
family therapy (P. 634)
free association (P. 631)
half-life (P. 609)
imaginal exposure (P. 623)
integrative behavioral couple therapy (P. 634)
***in vivo* exposure** (P. 623)
latent content (P. 631)
manifest content (P. 631)
manualized therapy (P. 607)
marital therapy (P. 633)
modeling (P. 623)
neurosurgery (P. 620)
placebo (P. 606)
psychodynamic therapy (P. 630)
psychopharmacology (P. 607)
psychotherapy (P. 600)
randomized clinical trials (RCTs) (P. 606)
rational emotive behavior therapy (REBT) (P. 625)
resistance (P. 631)
response shaping (P. 624)
structural family therapy (P. 634)
systematic desensitization (P. 623)
tardive dyskinesia (P. 610)
token economy (P. 624)
traditional behavioral couple therapy (P. 633)
transference (P. 631)

CHAPTER 18

Contemporary and Legal Issues in Abnormal Psychology

PERSPECTIVES ON PREVENTION
Universal Interventions
Selective Interventions
Indicated Interventions
The Mental Hospital as a Therapeutic Community
Deinstitutionalization

CONTROVERSIAL LEGAL ISSUES AND THE MENTALLY DISORDERED
The Commitment Process
Assessment of "Dangerousness"
The Insanity Defense

ORGANIZED EFFORTS FOR MENTAL HEALTH
U.S. Efforts for Mental Health
International Efforts for Mental Health

CHALLENGES FOR THE FUTURE
The Need for Planning
The Individual's Contribution

UNRESOLVED ISSUES:
The HMOs and Mental Health Care

We have covered a great many topics and issues pertinent to a modern understanding of abnormal behavior on these pages. The final chapter of this book has traditionally been somewhat of a forum for several important topics in abnormal psychology that have been noted only briefly in earlier chapters. These issues are very important to understanding the field of abnormal psychology and will give the reader a broader perspective on ways our society deals with, or in some cases fails to deal with, abnormal behavior. We begin with the topic of prevention of mental disorders. Over the years, most mental health efforts have been largely restorative, geared toward helping people after they have already developed serious problems. Albee (1999) cogently makes the case that if the goal is the reduction or elimination of emotional problems in our country or the world, then a major revolution in thinking is required—the expansion of efforts at prevention.

Next, we will describe inpatient mental health treatment and the state of mental hospitals in contemporary society. We will discuss changes that have taken place and some of the forces that have affected inpatient psychiatric care today. Following this, several legal issues pertinent to psychiatric care and the hospitalization of people with severe psychological problems will be addressed. We will then briefly survey the scope of organized efforts for mental health both in the United States and throughout the world. Finally, we will consider what each of us can do to foster mental health.

Perspectives on Prevention

In the past the concepts of *primary, secondary,* and *tertiary* prevention were widely used in public health efforts to describe general strategies of disease prevention. The terminology was derived from public health strategies employed for understanding and controlling infectious physical diseases, and was thought to provide a useful perspective in the mental health field as well. However, for years there was relatively little progress in prevention. Heller (1996), for example, noted that "Until the last decade anything approaching a true prevention science did not exist" (p. 1124). In the early 1990s, the U.S. Congress directed the National Institute of Mental Health (NIMH) to work with the Institute of Medicine (IOM) to develop a report detailing a long-term prevention research program. Among other things, the IOM report focused attention on the distinction between prevention and treatment efforts (Dozois, 2004; Dozois & Dobson, 2004; Munoz, 2001; Munoz, Mrazek, & Haggerty, 1996). Prevention efforts are now classified into three subcategories:

1. **Universal interventions:** Efforts that are aimed at influencing the general population.
2. **Selective interventions:** Efforts that are aimed at a specific subgroup of the population considered at risk for developing mental health problems—for example, adolescents or ethnic minorities (Coie, Miller-Johnson, & Bagwell, 2000).
3. **Indicated interventions:** Efforts that are directed to high-risk individuals who are identified as having minimal but detectable symptoms of mental disorder but who do not meet criteria for clinical diagnosis—for example, individuals forced from their homes by a flood or some other disaster.

As shown in Figure 18.1, preventive efforts are clearly differentiated from treatment and maintenance interventions.

Universal Interventions

Universal interventions perform two key tasks: (1) altering conditions that can cause or contribute to mental disorders (risk factors) and (2) establishing conditions that foster positive mental health (protective factors). Epidemiological studies (see Chapter 1) help investigators obtain information about the incidence and distribution of various maladaptive behaviors (Dozois & Dobson, 2004) such as anxiety-based disorders (Feldner, Zvolensky, & Schmidt, 2004). These findings can then be used to suggest what preventive efforts might be most appropriate. For example, various epidemiological studies and reviews have shown that certain groups are at high risk for mental disorders: recently divorced people (Theun, 2000), the physically disabled (Mitchell & House, 2000), elderly people (King & Markus, 2000), physically abused children (Hamerman &

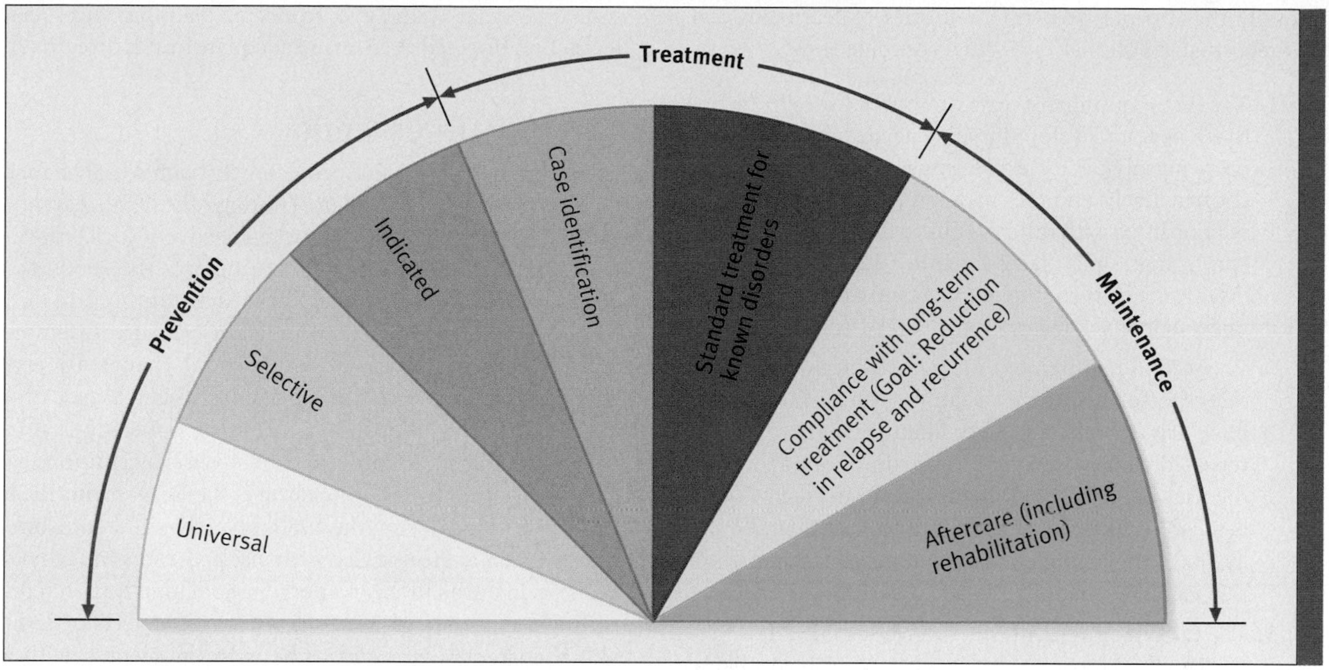

FIGURE 18.1

Classification of Prevention Strategies, Treatment, and Maintenance

The traditional terminology for describing general strategies of disease prevention in the field of public health has been revised to provide a more useful perspective on prevention efforts. The new classification system for prevention (universal, selective, and indicated strategies) is shown in this context as distinct from treatment interventions and maintenance approaches to mental health problems.

Source: *From* Reducing Risks for Mental Disorders: Frontiers for Preventive Research, *edited by P. J. Mrazek and R. J. Haggerty. Copyright © 1994 by the National Academy of Sciences. Courtesy of the National Academy Press, Washington, DC.*

Ludwig, 2000), people who have been uprooted from their homes (Caracci & Mezzich, 2001), and victims of severe trauma (Jaranson, Butcher, et al., 2004). Although findings such as these may be the basis for immediate selective or indicated prevention, they may also aid in universal prevention by telling us what to look for and where to look—in essence, by focusing our efforts in the right direction. Universal prevention is very broad and includes biological, psychosocial, and sociocultural efforts. Virtually any effort that is aimed at improving the human condition would be considered a part of universal prevention of mental disorder.

BIOLOGICAL STRATEGIES Biologically based universal strategies for prevention begin with promoting adaptive lifestyles. Many of the goals of health psychology (see Chapter 10) can be viewed as universal prevention strategies. Efforts geared toward improving diet, establishing a routine of physical exercise, and developing overall good health habits can do much to improve physical well-being. Physical illness always produces some sort of psychological stress that can result in such problems as depression, so with respect to good mental health, maintaining good physical health is prevention.

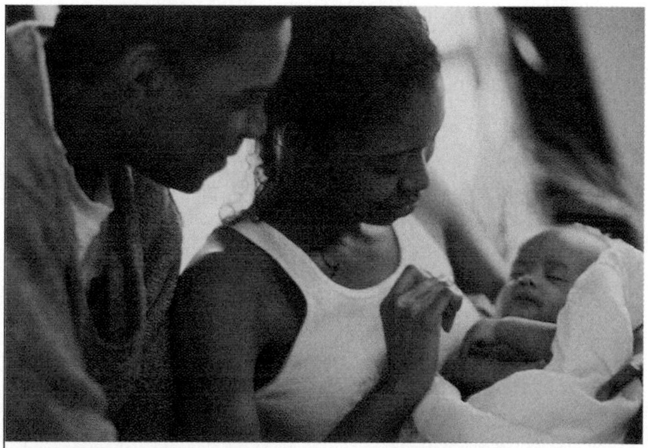

Preventing mental disorders and maintaining psychosocial health require that a person be prepared for the types of problems likely to be encountered during given life stages. For example, young people who want to marry and have children must be prepared for the tasks of building a mutually satisfying relationship and helping children develop their abilities.

PSYCHOSOCIAL STRATEGIES In viewing normality as optimal development and viewing high functioning (rather than the mere absence of pathology) as the goal, we imply that people need opportunities to learn physical, intellectual, emotional, and social competencies.

1. The first requirement for psychosocial "health" is that a person develop the skills needed for effective problem solving, for expressing emotions constructively, and for engaging in satisfying relationships with others. Failure to develop these "protective" skills places the individual at a serious disadvantage in coping with stresses and the unavoidable risk factors for mental disorder.
2. The second requirement for psychosocial health is that a person acquire an accurate frame of reference on which to build his or her identity. We have seen repeatedly that when people's assumptions about themselves or their world are inaccurate, their behavior is likely to be maladaptive. Consider, for example, the young woman who believes that being thin can bring happiness and so becomes anorexic.
3. The third requirement for psychosocial health is that a person be prepared for the types of problems likely to be encountered during given life stages. For example, young people who want to marry and have children must be prepared for the tasks of building a mutually satisfying relationship and helping children develop their abilities. Similarly, a middle-aged adult needs to be prepared for problems that are likely to arise during retirement and old age.

In recent years, psychosocial measures aimed at prevention have received a great deal of attention. The field of behavioral medicine has had substantial influence here. As we saw in Chapter 10, efforts are being made to change the psychological factors underlying unhealthful habits such as smoking, excessive drinking, and poor eating habits.

SOCIOCULTURAL STRATEGIES As has been demonstrated many times throughout this book, without a supportive community, individual development is stifled. At the same time, without responsible, psychologically healthy individuals, the community will not thrive and, in turn, cannot be supportive. The psychosocially impaired victims of disorganized communities lack the wherewithal to create better communities to protect and sustain the psychological health of those who come after them, and a persistently unprotective environment results. Sociocultural efforts toward universal prevention are focused on making the community as safe and attractive as possible for the individuals within it.

With our growing recognition of the role that pathological social conditions play in producing maladaptive behavior (in socially impoverished communities), increased attention must be devoted to creating social conditions that will foster healthy development and functioning in individuals. Efforts to create these conditions include a broad spectrum of measures—ranging from public education and Social Security to economic planning and social legislation directed at ensuring adequate health care for all.

Selective Interventions

Preventing mental health problems through social change in the community is difficult. Although the whole psychological climate can ultimately be changed by a social movement such as the civil rights movement of the 1960s, the payoff of such efforts is generally far in the future and may be difficult or impossible to predict or measure. Attempts to effect psychologically desirable social change are also likely to involve ideological and political issues that may inspire powerful opposition, including opposition from government itself. According to an analysis by Humphreys and Rappaport (1993), for example, the Reagan and Bush administrations during the 1980s severely undercut Community Mental Health Center social programs in favor of agencies involved in the "war on drugs." This effort, in redirecting attention and funds to purported defects of individual character, was said to be more in keeping with a conservative political philosophy that viewed the basic problem as one of personal moral weakness, not social disorganization. ("How should kids deal with a drug-saturated environment? Just say no.") Although drug abuse is a matter of individual behavior, it does not follow that all countermeasures must or should be directed at the individual. Some examples of more selective and effective programs will be discussed in what follows.

AN ILLUSTRATION OF SELECTIVE PREVENTION STRATEGIES Though difficult to formulate and even more difficult to mobilize and carry out, selective intervention can bring about major improvements. In this section, we will look at the mobilization of prevention resources aimed at curtailing or reducing the problem of teenage alcohol and drug abuse. Prominent social forces such as attractive television advertising, the influence of peer groups, negative parental role models, and the ready availability of many drugs are instrumental in promoting the early use of alcohol in young people. In some Central American countries, increasingly greater numbers of adolescents are succumbing to drug habits as a result of drug traffickers using youth, whom they consider forms of cheap labor, and who can more easily escape prosecution. The extent of drug use among adolescents is increasing substantially in Guatemala, El Salvador, Honduras, and Nicaragua (Boddiger, 2004).

Recent years have witnessed a decrease in the rate of alcohol and marijuana use (National Institute of Drug Abuse, 2004) in the United States. However, teenage alcohol and drug use remains one of the most significant psychological community problems (Ellickson, D'Amico, et al., 2005), and adolescent use of pain killers has increased. For example, Vicodin was used by 9.3 percent of twelfth graders, 6.2 percent of tenth graders, and 2.5 percent of eighth graders in the past year, and OxyContin was used in the past year by 5 percent of twelfth graders, 3.5 percent of tenth graders, and 1.7 percent of eighth graders. The problem of teenage drinking, particularly binge drinking, is significant among adolescents from minority groups such as American Indians, who are at especially high risk for substance-related problems given that their current alcohol use rate is extremely high. One recent survey of Bureau of Indian Affairs schools showed that 48.8 percent of the sample currently reported alcohol use, with 80 percent of the sample indicating lifetime use; three-quarters of the sample reported a lifetime use of marijuana (Centers for Disease Control, 2003). In another study, Ramirez, Crano, et al. (2004) found that Hispanic Americans showed higher usage of marijuana and inhalants than Anglo-Americans.

Heavy alcohol use among young people can lead to tragic consequences such as impaired driving (Lewis, Thombs, & Olds, 2005). Because the factors that entice adolescents to begin using alcohol and drugs are seemingly under social control, it is tempting to think that if these forces could be counterbalanced with equally powerful alternative influences, the rate of substance abuse might radically decline. But this is easier said than done. Our government has approached the drug-abuse problem with three broad strategies, all of which have proved insufficient:

1. **Interdicting and reducing the supply of drugs available.** The reduction of supply by policing our borders has had little impact on the availability of drugs. Drug interdiction programs do little to affect the supply of the two drugs most abused by adolescents—alcohol and tobacco—which are, of course, available in corner stores and even in the adolescent's home. Reducing the supply of these drugs to adolescents seems virtually impossible.
2. **Providing treatment services for those who develop drug problems.** Although much money is spent each year on treatment, treating substance abuse is perhaps the least effective way to reduce the problem. Addictive disorders are very difficult to overcome, and treatment failure-relapse is the rule rather than the exception. Therapeutic programs for those addicted to drugs or alcohol, though necessary, are not the answer to eliminating or even significantly reducing the problems in our society.
3. **Encouraging prevention.** By far the most desirable—and potentially the most effective—means of reducing the drug problem in our country is through prevention methods aimed at alerting citizens to the problems that surround drugs and teaching young people ways to avoid using them (Hawkins, Cummins, & Marlatt, 2004; Sussman, Earleywine, et al., 2004). Although past efforts have had some limited success in discouraging adolescent drug use, many initially promising prevention efforts have failed to bring about the desired reduction in substance use. There are a number of reasons for this: The intervention typically has not been conducted for long enough to show the desired effect; the intervention efforts have not been powerful enough to make a sufficient impact on the participants; or the strategy may not have been well implemented.

Efforts to teach schoolchildren about the dangers of drugs before they reach the age of maximum risk are based on the premise that if children are made aware of the dangers of drugs and alcohol, they will choose not to use them.

It is clear that traditional health or psychological intervention models aimed at individual remediation only after a youngster has become addicted to narcotics or alcohol have not significantly reduced the problem of drug and alcohol abuse among teenagers. Moreover, these treatment approaches are typically implemented only after the child has seriously compromised his or her life opportunities through drug or alcohol use. Recent epidemiological research has confirmed that early alcohol use is a strong predictor of lifetime alcohol abuse and dependence (Grant & Dawson, 1997). In recent years, therefore, prevention specialists have taken a more proactive position. They have attempted to establish programs that prevent the development of abuse disorders before young people become so involved with drugs or alcohol that future adjustment becomes difficult, if not impossible. These recent prevention strategies have taken some diverse and promising directions. We will examine several such efforts and then discuss the limitations of these prevention approaches.

Education Programs Many drug and alcohol education programs are school based and are predicated on the idea that if children are made aware of the dangers of drugs and alcohol, they will choose not to begin using them. Englander-Golden and colleagues (1986), for example, provided "Say it straight" training, in which they taught sixth through eighth graders both the dangers of drug and alcohol abuse and how to be assertive enough to resist drugs and alcohol in spite of peer pressure. In a follow-up evaluation, these investigators reported that youngsters who were trained in the program had a lower rate of drug- and alcohol-related suspensions from school than children who received no training. Another school-based prevention program developed by the organization Mothers Against Drunk Driving (MADD) involves the use of a safety curriculum for third, fourth, and fifth graders, taught by high school peer leaders, to make young children aware of the risks of underage consumption of alcoholic beverages and vehicle-related risks, especially when they are passengers in vehicles in which the driver is not alcohol-free. The curriculum benefits students by influencing their attitudes toward advertisements and increasing their intentions not to ride in a car with a driver who has been drinking (Bohman, Barker, et al., 2004).

research close•up

intervention programs for high-risk populations

This research strategy involves identifying high-risk individuals and providing special approaches to circumvent their problems; for example, identifying adolescents at risk for abusing alcohol and implementing a program to prevent the problem behavior.

Intervention Programs for High-Risk Teens Intervention programs identify high-risk teenagers and take special measures to circumvent their further use of alcohol or potentially dangerous drugs (Hawkins, Cummins, & Marlatt, 2004). Programs such as these are often school-based efforts and are not strictly prevention programs. One such program involved the early identification of young people who were having difficulties in school because of drug and alcohol use. Teachers and administrators were trained to identify and counter problems with alcohol and drug use through a fair and consistently enforced drug and alcohol policy in the schools (Newman et al., 1988–89).

Parent Education and Family-Based Intervention Programs Through their own drinking or through positive verbalizations about alcohol, parents may encourage or sanction alcohol use among teens. Some research has shown that parental involvement and monitoring reduces substance use among adolescents (Ramirez, Crano, et al., 2004). Thus, some prevention programs focus upon family interventions (Spoth, Redmond, et al., 2004) with good success. Sieving, Maruyama, et al. (2000) found that alcohol-related cognitions among teenagers were directly related to parental norms. Moreover, parents typically underestimate their own children's drug and alcohol use (Silverman & Silverman, 1987). Because of these factors, several programs have been aimed at increasing parents' awareness of the extent of the problem and at teaching them ways to deal with drug and alcohol use in the family context (Kumpfer, 2000). One such program worked with parents whose children were about to become teenagers (Grady, Gersick, & Boratynski, 1985). It first assessed parents' skills in dealing with drug-related issues and then trained parents to understand and respond empathically to youngsters who might be exposed to drugs during their adolescent years. Parents were next taught how to respond effectively to their children's questions and concerns and to help them consider alternative, more adaptive behavior.

Peer Group Influence Programs Peers exert a powerful influence on teenagers in every aspect of their lives including drug and alcohol abuse. Programs designed to help youngsters overcome negative pressures from peers focus on teaching social skills and assertiveness. Of course, peer pressure can influence a teen not to use drugs or alcohol (Orman, Veseley, et al., 2004). Peer influence seems much more powerful than the influence of adults, including teachers and parents, particularly when parents and schools fail to supervise students adequately (Voelki & Frone, 2000).

Programs to Increase Self-Esteem Programs designed to increase a sense of self-worth attempt to ensure that young people will be able to fend for themselves with more confidence and not fall into dependent, negative relationships with stronger and more dominant peers. One such program provided teenagers with social-skills training and the modeling of appropriate behaviors to reduce drug use and related negative behaviors such as truancy (Pentz, 1983). In another program, Botvin (1983) relied on cognitive-behavioral intervention techniques (for example, self-talk) to enhance teenagers' feelings of competency in basic life skills and to improve their problem-solving skills. This approach has been thought to be effective in reducing the impact of tobacco, alcohol, and marijuana use (Botvin et al., 1990).

Mass Media and Modeling Programs Recognizing the huge "market" potential of teenagers, advertisers have become adept at exploiting the tremendous value that the

Peer programs, like those offered at the Boys and Girls Clubs, focus on the positive aspects of peer pressure. Peers can exert much more influence over teen behavior than can adults in all aspects of life, including avoiding drug and alcohol abuse.

appearance of sophistication has for this age group. Most youngsters are bombarded with drug- or alcohol-related stimuli in movies and in TV commercials that are aired at those times when children are most likely to view them. Some legal prohibitions of such exploitation are now in place. And several efforts have been aimed at deglamorizing or counteracting these messages by showing commercials that graphically depict the negative aspects of alcohol and drug use (Schilling & McAlister, 1990).

Combined Prevention Programs The various prevention strategies discussed here are by no means mutually exclusive, and some approaches do not rely on a single intervention strategy but incorporate two or more (Wagenaar, Murray, et al., 2000). Project Northland—an exemplary program of research geared toward the prevention of alcohol abuse—targets junior high school students in northeastern Minnesota but also involves a much broader, community-wide intervention effort (Komro, Perry, et al., 2004; Perry, Williams, Komro, & Veblen-Mortenson, 2000). This program is discussed in Developments in Practice 18.1.

These projects have clearly shown an effective path toward reducing the extent of substance abuse in young people. Armed with appropriate information and having had some practice at resisting others around them, adolescents can stick to the decision not to use alcohol or drugs. The visible success of these programs has come to

18.1 Developments in Practice

Preventing Alcohol Abuse

Teenage drinking is a major social problem in the United States. Johnson, O'Malley, and Bachman (2000) reported that 80.3 percent of twelfth graders, 71.4 percent of tenth graders, and 51.7 percent of eighth graders have had more than "a few sips" of alcohol. Project Northland is a research study designed to prevent or reduce alcohol use among adolescents via a multilevel community-based approach (Komro, Perry, et al., 2004; Perry, Williams, Komro, Veblen-Mortenson, et al., 2000; Perry & Williams, et al., 2001). The investigators conducted their program in 24 school districts in northern Minnesota, an area that was notorious for high rates of substance abuse. Assessments were made annually to measure the use of alcohol among the identified target population and the control samples. The program employs a number of forms of intervention: a social-behavioral curriculum in the schools to make students aware of the issues, parent education programs, peer leadership, and community-wide activities to alter the messages that young people typically receive about alcohol. In this program, students complete four activity booklets as homework assignments with their parents over a period of 4 weeks. Each booklet includes activities that contain explicit behavioral objectives (for example, how to establish family rules about drinking). Elected peer leaders give students activity tasks each week, with the assistance of their teachers. These sessions are conducted in small groups.

Before the intervention program begins, teachers receive a 4-hour training session. Elected peer group leaders attend a 2-hour training session. During the intervention phase of the program, each child is asked to display score cards (signed by parents to record participation) on a prominent scoreboard. Students receive prizes (e.g., a pen) for completion of the first two booklets and a T-shirt at the end of the program. The program ends with an event at each school that brings fifth graders and their parents together for an evening program. During the week before the evening event, students work in pairs on posters with alcohol-related messages that are presented to parents during the evening event.

Project Northland staff have been able to maintain broad participation in the program for over 3 years and have shown that multilevel, targeted prevention programs for young adolescents are effective in reducing alcohol use among adolescents. Adolescents in the experimental condition show clearly lower levels of alcohol use than adolescents in the control schools. Alcohol use, cigarette smoking, and marijuana use by adolescents was reduced 21 percent more in the intervention schools than in the control schools.

Another study of an extensive and comprehensive substance-abuse prevention program was completed by Botvin and his colleagues (Botvin et al., 1995). This program involved 3,597 adolescents in 56 public schools, who were followed for 5 years beginning in the seventh grade. The initial intervention consisted of 15 classes, 10 booster sessions in the eighth grade, and 5 booster sessions in the ninth grade. The adolescents were taught specific drug resistance skills and general life skills in a classroom-based program. Like the Northland Project, this study found that drug-abuse prevention programs conducted during junior high school can produce significant and durable reductions in tobacco, alcohol, and marijuana use if they teach social resistance skills and if booster sessions are provided. There were 44 percent fewer drug users and 66 percent fewer polydrug users (tobacco, marijuana, and alcohol) in the prevention group than in the control schools.

Recognizing the huge "market" potential of teenagers, advertisers exploit the tremendous value that the appearance of sophistication has for this age group. Some efforts have been aimed at deglamorizing these messages by showing ads that graphically depict the negative aspects of alcohol and drug use, like the antismoking ad on the right.

the attention of educators in other school districts, and a number of efforts are under way to "export" these laboratory programs for broader use in America's schools. Recently, the Northland approach has been adapted for prevention projects in Croatia, Russia, and Poland as a means of fighting alcohol abuse—one of the most serious health problems in those countries (Abatemarco, West, et al., 2004; Okulicz-Kozaryn, Bobrowski, et al., 2000; Ostaszewski, Bobrowski, et al., 2000; Williams, Grechanaia, et al., 2001).

The jury is still out on the relative success of the various substance-abuse prevention programs at reducing alcohol and drug problems in adolescents. It will take time and further research efforts to determine which of the strategies, if any, are superior to the others in reducing alcohol and drug problems in adolescents. Some programs have been evaluated more extensively than others; for example, the D.A.R.E. program recently underwent an extensive number of evaluative studies that have generally concluded that the program has limited success. West and O'Neal (2004) conducted a meta-analysis by examining the results of several studies of the effectiveness of Project D.A.R.E. in preventing alcohol, tobacco, and illicit drug use among school-age youths. They concluded that the effects of the program were extremely small, indicating that D.A.R.E. is ineffective at influencing adolescents to stay away from alcohol and drug use.

Indicated Interventions

Indicated intervention emphasizes the early detection and prompt treatment of maladaptive behavior in a person's family and community setting. In some cases—for example, in a crisis or after a disaster (Garakina, Hirschowitz, & Katz 2004) (see the discussion on crisis intervention in Chapter 5)—indicated prevention involves immediate and relatively brief intervention to prevent any long-term behavioral consequences (Raphael & Wooding, 2004).

The Mental Hospital as a Therapeutic Community

In cases where individuals might be considered dangerous to themselves or others (Richards, Smith, et al., 1997) or where their symptoms are so severe that they are unable to care for themselves in the community, psychiatric hospitalization may be required. Most of the traditional forms of therapy that we discussed in Chapter 17 may, of course, be used in a hospital setting. In addition, in many mental hospitals, these techniques are being supplemented by efforts to make the hospital environment itself a "therapeutic community" (Kennard, 2004; Whiteley, 1991). That is, all the ongoing activities of the hospital are brought into the total treatment program, and the environment, or milieu, is a crucial aspect of the therapy. This approach is thus often referred to as **"milieu therapy"** (Kennard, 2000; Zimmerman, 2004). Three general therapeutic principles guide this approach to treatment:

1. Staff expectations are clearly communicated to patients. Both positive and negative feedback are used to encourage appropriate verbalizations and actions by patients.
2. Patients are encouraged to become involved in all decisions made, and in all actions taken, concerning them. A self-care, do-it-yourself attitude prevails.
3. All patients belong to social groups on the ward. The group cohesiveness that results gives the patients support and encouragement, and the related process of group pressure helps shape their behavior in positive ways.

In a therapeutic community, as few restraints as possible are placed on patients' freedom, and patients are encouraged to take responsibility for their behavior and participate actively in their treatment programs. Open wards permit patients to use the grounds and premises.

Self-government programs give patients responsibility for managing their own affairs and those of the ward. All hospital personnel are expected to treat the patients as human beings who merit consideration and courtesy. The interaction among patients—whether in group therapy sessions, social events, or other activities—is planned in such a way as to be of therapeutic benefit. In fact, it is becoming apparent that often the most beneficial aspect of a therapeutic community is the interaction among the patients themselves. Differences in social roles and backgrounds may make empathy between staff and patients difficult, but fellow patients have been there—they have had similar problems and breakdowns and have experienced the anxiety and humiliation of being labeled "mentally ill" and being hospitalized. Constructive relationships frequently develop among patients in a supportive, encouraging milieu.

Another successful method for helping patients take increased responsibility for their own behavior is the use of **social-learning programs.** Such programs normally make use of learning principles and techniques such as token economies (see Chapter 17) to shape more socially acceptable behavior (Corrigan, 1995, 1997; Mariotto, Paul, & Licht, 2002; Paul, Stuve, & Cross, 1997).

A persistent concern about hospitalization is that the mental hospital may become a permanent refuge from the world. Over the past three decades, considerable effort has been devoted to reducing the population of inpatients by closing hospitals and treating patients who have mental disorders as outpatients. This effort, which is often referred to as *deinstitutionalization,* was initiated to prevent the negative effects, for many psychiatric patients, of being confined to a mental hospital for long periods of time as well as to lower health care costs. To keep the focus on returning patients to the community and on preventing their return to the institution, contemporary hospital staffs try to establish close ties with patients' families and communities and to provide them with positive expectations about the patient's recovery.

The rise of the biological therapies described in Chapter 17 has meant that between 70 and 90 percent of patients labeled as "psychotic" and admitted to mental hospitals can now be discharged within a few weeks, or at most a few months. Recent estimates suggest that there are some 2 to 3 million chronically mentally ill individuals in America, of whom about half reside in mental hospitals and the other half in nursing homes or in the community (Regier et al., 1993).

Even where disorders have become chronic, effective treatment methods have been developed. In one of the most extensive and well-controlled studies of chronic hospitalized patients, Paul and Lentz (1977) compared the relative effectiveness of three treatment approaches:

1. Milieu therapy, focused on structuring a patient's environment to provide clear communication of expectations and to get the patient involved in the treatment and participating in the therapeutic community through the group process.
2. A social-learning treatment program, organized around learning principles and using a rigorously programmed token economy system, with ward staff as reinforcing agents. Undesirable behavior was not reinforced, whereas the accumulation of many tokens through effective functioning made a patient eligible for attractive amenities not normally available in public mental hospitals.
3. Traditional mental hospital treatments including pharmacotherapy, occupational therapy, recreational therapy, activity therapy, and individual or group therapy. No systematic application of milieu therapy or the social-learning program was given to this group.

The treatment project covered a period of 6 years: an initial phase of staff training, patient assessment, and baseline recording; a treatment phase; an aftercare phase; and a long (year and a half) follow-up. The changes targeted included resocialization, learning new roles, and reducing or eliminating bizarre behavior. There were 28 chronic schizophrenic patients in each treatment group, matched for age, sex, socioeconomic level, symptoms, and duration of hospitalization. The results of the study were impressive. Both milieu therapy and the social-learning program produced significant improvement in overall functioning and resulted in more successful hospital releases than the traditional hospital care. The behaviorally based social-learning program, however, was clearly superior to the more diffuse program of milieu therapy, as evidenced by the fact that over 90 percent of the released patients from the social-learning program remained continuously in the community, compared with 70 percent of the released patients who had had milieu therapy. The figure for the traditional treatment program was less than 50 percent.

Despite the promise of the token economy approach, emulating as it does certain "real-world" principles of exchange that the patient will face outside the institution, it has not enjoyed wide public acceptance (Paul & Lentz, 1977). Many feel that it is cruel and inhumane to expect mental patients to govern their behavior in accordance with a prescribed schedule of reinforcements. One might ask, however, whether it is more humane to consign the patient to the status of a passive and helpless recipient of whatever the environment has to offer, which in many institutional settings is not very much. Is that truly the message we want to convey about the patient's relationship to his or her environment? Probably not, especially in light of the considerable evidence that most chronic mental patients are surprisingly adept at making successful adaptations that are within their range of control.

AFTERCARE PROGRAMS Even where hospitalization has successfully modified maladaptive behavior and a patient has learned needed occupational and interpersonal skills, readjustment in the community following release may still be difficult (Seidman, 2003; Thornicraft & Tansella, 2000). Many studies have shown that in the past, up to 45 percent of schizophrenic patients have been readmitted within the first year after their discharge. Community-based treatment programs, now referred to as "aftercare programs," are live-in facilities that serve as a home base for former patients as they make the transition back to adequate functioning in the community. Typically, community-based facilities are run not by professional mental health personnel but by the residents themselves. Aftercare programs can help smooth the transition from institutional to community life and reduce the number of relapses. However, some individuals do not function well in aftercare programs. Owen, Rutherford, Jones, and colleagues (1997) found that clients who were likely to hold unskilled employment, to be nonpsychotic, to have committed a crime, or to be more transient tended to be noncompliant in aftercare programs. The investigators concluded that many of the discharged patients did not "fit" the services typically offered to released psychiatric inpatients. Those with less severe symptoms may fail because they appear to aftercare staff as not needing much help; most services are geared to those patients who exhibit more extreme symptoms.

Sometimes aftercare includes a "halfway" period in which a released patient makes a gradual return to the outside world in what were formerly termed "halfway houses."

Aftercare facilities do not always provide the safe refuge promised. Homeless people often live in large cities under austere conditions, noted in this photograph, that resemble those seen in back wards of mental institutions several decades ago.

Aftercare programs do not always live up to their name, however. Levy and Kershaw (2001) disclosed a number of problems in which relevant treatment was not made available and staff did not provide a secure environment.

Although some patients continue to have mental health problems including suicide attempts (Fenton, McGlashan, et al., 1997), and many have trouble gaining the acceptance and support of the community (Fairweather, 1994; Seidman, 2003), efforts to treat severely disturbed patients in the community are often very successful. However, as Dennes (1974) pointed out in the early years of the growth of community-based treatment, its success depends on educational and other social measures directed toward increasing community understanding, acceptance, and tolerance of troubled people who may differ somewhat from community norms.

Deinstitutionalization

The population of psychiatric patients in the United States has shrunk considerably over the past 35 years. Between 1970 and 1992, the number of state mental hospitals dropped from 310 to 273, and the patient population was reduced by 73 percent (Witkin, Atay, & Manderscheid, 1998). The deinstitutionalization movement has not been limited to the United States. On the contrary, there has been a worldwide trend to shift the care of mental patients from inpatient hospitals to community-based programs (D'Avanzo, Barbato, et al., 2003; Emerson, 2004; Honkonen, Karlsson, et al., 2003; Pijl, Kluiter, & Wiersma, 2001).

Deinstitutionalization—the movement to close down mental hospitals and to treat persons with severe mental disorders in the community—has been a source of considerable controversy. Some authorities consider the emptying of the mental hospitals a positive expression of society's desire to free previously confined persons and maintain that deinstitutionalized patients show significant improvement compared with those who remain hospitalized (Newton, Rosen, et al., 2000; Reinharz, Lesage, & Contandriopoulos, 2000), but others speak of the "abandonment" of chronic patients to a cruel and harsh existence, which for many includes homelessness, violent victimization (Walsh, Moran, et al., 2003), or suicide (Goldney, 2003). Many citizens, too, complain of being harassed, intimidated, and frightened by obviously disturbed persons wandering the streets of their neighborhoods.

Some of the reduction in mental health services over the past 25 years has come about because of changes in the health care system. (See the Unresolved Issues section at the end of this chapter.) The planned community efforts to fill the gaps in service never really materialized at effective levels (Lamb, 1998).

The number of patients residing in state and county mental hospitals sank from over half a million in 1950 (Lerman, 1981) to about 100,000 in the 1990s (Narrow et al., 1993); these figures are even more staggering when we consider that at the same time, the U.S. population grew by nearly 100 million. A number of factors have interacted to alter the pattern of mental hospital admissions and discharges over the past 40 years. Antipsychotic drugs have made it possible for many patients who would otherwise have required confinement to live in the community, but not all mental health problems can be managed with medication. In addition, changing treatment philosophy and the desire to eliminate mental institutions were bolstered by the assumption that society wanted and could afford to provide better community-based care for chronic patients outside of large mental hospitals.

In theory, closing the public mental hospitals seemed workable. The plan was to open many community-based mental health centers that would provide continuing care to the residents of hospitals after discharge. Residents would be given welfare funds (supposedly at less cost to the government than maintaining large mental hospitals) and would be administered medication to keep them stabilized until they could obtain continuing care. Many patients would be discharged to home and family; others would be placed in smaller, home-like board-and-care facilities or nursing homes.

Unforeseen problems arose, however, and in many cases, homeless shelters in metropolitan communities have become a "makeshift alternative" to inpatient mental health care (Haugland, Sigel, et al., 1997). Many residents of mental institutions had no families or homes to go to; board-and-care facilities were often substandard; and the community mental health centers were ill prepared and insufficiently funded to provide needed services for chronic patients, particularly as national funding priorities shifted during the 1980s (Humphreys & Rappaport, 1993). Many patients had not been carefully selected for discharge and were not ready for community living, and many of those who were discharged were not followed up sufficiently or often enough to ensure their successful adaptation outside the hospital.

One recent court case (*Albright* v. *Abington Memorial Hospital,* 1997) involved charges that the hospital failed to provide sufficient care for a seriously disturbed woman who later killed herself. Countless patients have been discharged to fates harsher than the conditions in any of the hospitals (Westermeyer, 1987). The following case illustrates the situation.

case STUDY — Institution to Homelessness

Dave B., 49 years old, had been hospitalized for 25 years in a state mental hospital. When the hospital was scheduled for phaseout, many of the patients, particularly those who were regressed or aggressive, were transferred to another state hospital. Dave was a borderline mentally retarded man who had periodic episodes of psychosis. At the time of hospital closing, however, he was not hallucinating and was "reasonably intact." Dave was considered to be one of the "less disturbed" residents because his psychotic behavior was less pronounced and he presented no dangerous problems. He was discharged to a board-and-care facility (actually an old hotel where most of the residents were former inpatients). At first, Dave seemed to fit in well at the facility; mostly he sat in his room or in the outside hallway, and he caused no trouble for the caretakers. Two weeks after he arrived, he wandered off the hotel grounds and was missing for several days. The police eventually found him living in the city dump. He had apparently stopped taking his medication, and when he was discovered he was regressed and catatonic. He was readmitted to a state hospital.

Recent research on the effects of deinstitutionalization has been mixed. Some reports have noted positive benefits of briefer hospitalization (Honkonen, et al., 2003; Rauktis, 2001), and some data suggest that deinstitutionalization appears not to be associated with an increased risk of homicide by people who are mentally ill (Simpson, McKenna, et al., 2004). However, others have reported problems with discharged patients and point to failures in programs to deinstitutionalize mental patients (Chan, Ungvari, & Leung, 2001; Leff, 2001).

There has been recent indication that inpatient psychiatric hospitalization may be increasing because of the failures to provide adequate mental health care for patients in need of mental health services in the community (Marcotty, 2004). A similar increase in the number of people being hospitalized has been reported in the United Kingdom (Priebe & Turner, 2003).

HOMELESSNESS By the early 1980s, cases like Dave's had become commonplace in large cities throughout the nation. Vagrants and "bag ladies" appeared in abundance on city streets and in transport terminals, and the virtually always overwhelmed shelters for homeless persons hastily expanded in futile efforts to contain the tide of recently discharged patients. Street crime soared, as did the death rate among these hapless persons, who lacked survival resources for the harsh urban environment.

The full extent of problems created by deinstitutionalization is not precisely known, partly because there has been little rigorous follow-up on patients discharged from mental hospitals. Such research investigations are difficult to conduct because the patients are transient and hard to keep track of over time. Certainly, not all homeless people are former mental patients, but deinstitutionalization has contributed substantially to the number of

18.2 THE WORLD AROUND US

Jails and Prisons: Serving as Mental Hospitals Again

The number of people with mental disorders in prison populations is alarming (Lamb & Weinberger, 1998). According to recent Justice Department statistics, over 16 percent of the people in prison in the United States (275,000) have a diagnosed mental disorder. Mentally ill persons who are evaluated in jails or prisons are twice as likely to have been homeless before their arrest. Moreover, mentally ill inmates tend to have more incarcerations than other prisoners, and more than three-quarters of them have been sentenced to jail or prison in the past. The modern trend of using prisons and jails as facilities to house mentally ill persons is, of course, not a new concept (Torrey, 1997). About 150 years ago, the great social reformer Dorothea Dix became concerned over the large number of mentally ill people confined to prisons and jails and launched a movement to develop mental hospitals to provide more humane treatment for them. Gilligen (2001) recently noted that public mental hospitals were created because many mentally ill people were being held in prisons or jails. Over time, support for those hospitals has diminished, and by the time they had degenerated into problem facilities a consensus was reached to close them down. However, they have not been replaced with adequate community mental health resources to treat severely disturbed patients. As the hospitals have emptied, the prisons and jails have begun to fill, partly with the mentally ill.

As a result of deinstitutionalization over the past 20 years and the subsequent closing of so many psychiatric facilities, there are fewer places where mentally ill patients can receive inpatient treatment. Moreover, there has been insufficient development of community-based services to provide outpatient care for people who need it. Consequently, many people become homeless because they cannot take care of themselves or because they commit crimes as a result of their uncontrolled behavior.

The high rates of psychiatrically disturbed persons in prisons and jails are a problem not only in the United States but in other countries as well (Bluglass, 2000). A recent study of prison inmates in 13 European countries reported similar high rates of mental disorder in the inmate population and indicated that countries differ widely in how they deal with the mentally disordered inmate (Blaauw, Roesch, & Kerkhof, 2000; see also Birmingham, Gray, Mason, & Grubin, 2000). Comparably high rates of mental disorder in prisons have recently been reported in New Zealand as well (Brinded et al., 1999).

Do mentally ill men and women who are incarcerated actually receive mental health treatment? A recent survey by the U.S. Department of Justice reported that 1,394 of the nation's public and private adult correctional facilities

homeless people (Lamb, 1998) and to the number of mentally ill people in prison (Butterfield, 1998; Powell et al., 1997), as described in The World Around Us 18.2.

In Review

- What are some strategies for biological, psychosocial, and sociocultural universal interventions?
- Define the term *selective intervention*. What selective intervention programs have shown promise in helping prevent teenage alcohol and drug abuse?
- What is indicated intervention?
- What problems have resulted from deinstitutionalization?

Controversial Legal Issues and the Mentally Disordered

A number of important issues are related to the legal status of mentally ill people—the subject matter of **forensic psychology** or **forensic psychiatry**—and they center on the rights of patients and the rights of members of society to be protected from disturbed individuals. For a survey of some of the legal rights that mentally ill people have gained over the years, see The World Around Us 18.3 on page 654.

The Commitment Process

Persons with psychological problems or behaviors that are so extreme and severe as to pose a threat to themselves or others may require protective confinement. Those who commit crimes, whether or not they have a psychological disorder, are dealt with primarily through the judicial sys-

provide mental health services to inmates. Almost 70 percent of the facilities that reported screen inmates when they are incarcerated, and 65 percent conduct some type of psychiatric examination. In addition, 51 percent of these facilities provide around-the-clock mental health services, but only 2 percent of the prison population live in a 24-hour treatment unit. The survey showed that 71 percent of the facilities provide counseling and 73 percent distribute medications to inmates (Beck & Maruschak, 2001). However, many authorities have reported that mental health services are typically not provided for the majority of inmates who require them (Gilligen, 2001). Teplin, Abram, and McClelland (1997) reported that only 23.5 percent of the women who needed mental health services received them while they were in jail, despite the fact that 80 percent of the sample met criteria for a lifetime mental disorder.

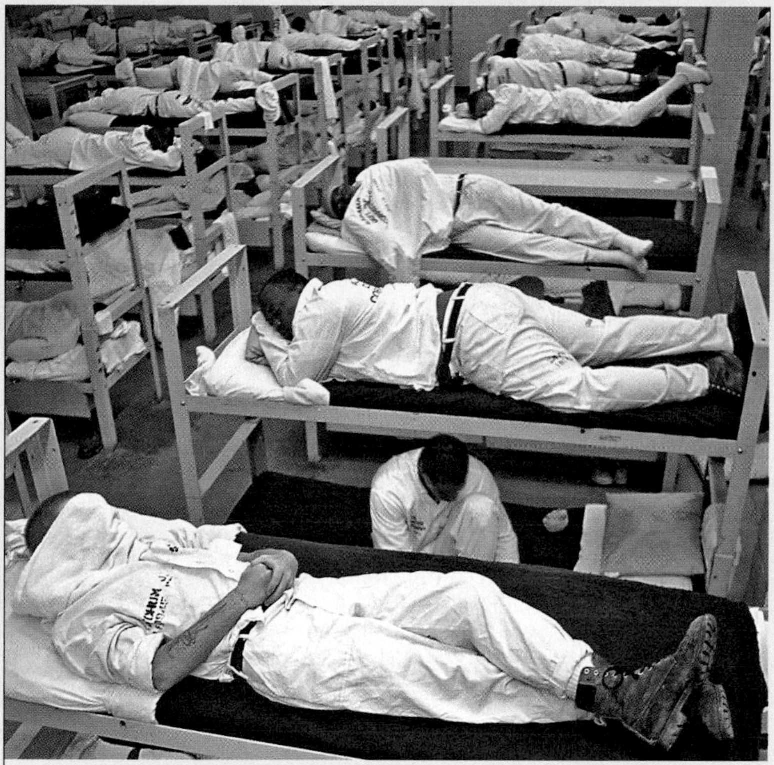

In the United States and Canada jails and prisons are extremely overcrowded and unable to implement rehabilitation efforts for those imprisoned. Inmates are typically at great risk of developing further problems such as aggression, illness, mental health problems, higher suicide rates, and increased likelihood of recidivism.

tem—arrest, court trial, and, if convicted, possible confinement in a penal institution. People who are judged to be potentially dangerous because of their psychological state may, after civil commitment procedures, be confined in a mental institution. The steps in the commitment process vary slightly depending on state law, the locally available community mental health resources, and the nature of the problem. For example, commitment procedures for a mentally retarded person are different from those for a person whose problem is alcohol abuse.

There is a distinction between voluntary hospitalization and involuntary commitment. In most cases, people accept voluntary commitment or hospitalization. In these cases, they can, with sufficient notice, leave the hospital if they wish. But in cases where a person may be considered dangerous or is unable to provide for his or her own care, the need for involuntary commitment may arise (Zerman & Schwartz, 1998).

A person's being mentally ill is not sufficient grounds for placing that person in a mental institution against his or her will. Although procedures vary somewhat from state to state, several conditions beyond mental illness usually must be met before formal involuntary commitment can occur (Simon & Aaronson, 1988). In brief, such individuals must be judged to be

- Dangerous to themselves or to others *and/or*
- Incapable of providing for their basic physical needs *and/or*
- Unable to make responsible decisions about hospitalization *and*
- In need of treatment or care in a hospital

Typically, filing a petition for a commitment hearing is the first step in the process of committing a person involuntarily. This petition is usually filed by a concerned individual such as a relative, physician, or mental health professional. When such a petition is filed, a judge appoints two examiners to evaluate the "proposed patient." In Minnesota, for example, one examiner must be a physician (not necessarily a psychiatrist); the other can be a psychiatrist or a psychologist. The patient is asked to appear voluntarily

18.3 THE WORLD AROUND US — Important Court Decisions for Patient Rights

Several important court decisions have helped establish certain basic rights for individuals suffering from mental disorders. But they have also curtailed these rights, amid continuing controversy.

- **Right to treatment.** In 1972 a U.S. district court in Alabama rendered a landmark decision in the case of *Wyatt* v. *Stickney.* It ruled that a mentally ill or mentally retarded person had a right to receive treatment. Since the decision, the state of Alabama has increased its budget for the treatment of mental illness and mental retardation by 300 percent (see Winick, 1997).
- **Freedom from custodial confinement.** In 1975 the U.S. Supreme Court upheld the principle that patients have a right to freedom from custodial confinement if they are not dangerous to themselves or others and if they can safely survive outside of custody. In *Donaldson* v. *O'Connor,* the defendants were required to pay Donaldson $10,000 for having kept him in custody without providing treatment.
- **Right to compensation for work.** In 1973 a U.S. District Court ruled in the case of *Souder* v. *Brennan* (the secretary of labor) that a patient in a nonfederal mental institution who performed work must be paid according to the Fair Labor Standards Act. Although a 1978 Supreme Court ruling nullified the part of the lower court's decision dealing with state hospitals, the ruling still applied to mentally ill and mentally retarded patients in private facilities.
- **Right to live in a community.** In 1974 a U.S. district court decided, in the case of *Staff* v. *Miller,* that released state mental hospital patients had a right to live in "adult homes" in the community.
- **Right to less restrictive treatment.** In 1975 a U.S. district court issued a landmark decision in the case of *Dixon* v. *Weinberger.* The ruling established the right of individuals to receive treatment in less restrictive facilities than mental institutions.
- **Right to legal counsel at commitment hearings.** The state Supreme Court of Wisconsin decided in 1976, in the case of *Memmel* v. *Mundy,* that an individual had the right to legal counsel during the commitment process.
- **Right to refuse treatment.** Several court decisions have provided rulings, and some states have enacted legislation, permitting patients to refuse certain treatments such as electroconvulsive therapy and psychosurgery.
- **The need for confinement must be shown by clear, convincing evidence.** In 1979 the U.S. Supreme Court ruled, in the case of *Addington* v. *Texas,* that a person's need to be kept in an institution must be based on demonstrable evidence.
- **Limitation on patients' rights to refuse psychotropic medication.** In 1990 the U.S. Supreme Court ruled, in *Washington* v. *Harper,* that a Washington State prison could override a disturbed prisoner's refusal of psychotropic medications. This decision was based on a finding that the prison's review process adequately protected the patient's rights. We see in this instance that changes in the national political climate can reverse prior trends that favored patients' rights.

Source: Grounds (2000), Hermann (1990), Mental Health Law Project (1987), Saks (2004), and Swartz et al. (2004).

for psychiatric examination before the commitment hearing. The hearing must be held within 14 days, which can be extended for 30 more days if good cause for the extension can be shown. The law requires that the court-appointed examiners interview the patient before the hearing.

When a person is committed to a mental hospital for treatment, the hospital must report to the court within 60 days on whether the person needs to be confined even longer. If the hospital gives no report, the patient must be released. If the hospital indicates that the person needs further treatment, then the commitment period becomes indeterminate, subject to periodic reevaluations.

Because the decision to commit a person is based on the conclusions of others about the person's capabilities and his or her potential for dangerous behavior, the civil commitment process leaves open the possibility of the unwarranted violation of a person's civil rights. As a consequence, most states have stringent safeguards to ensure that any person who is the subject of a petition for commitment is granted due process, including rights to formal hearings with representation by legal counsel. If there is not time to get a court order for commitment or if there is imminent danger, however, the law allows emergency hospitalization without a formal commitment hearing. In such cases, a physician must sign a statement saying that an imminent danger exists. The patient can then be picked up (usually by the police) and detained under a "hold order," usually not to exceed 72 hours, unless a petition for commitment is filed within that period.

Involuntary commitment in a psychiatric facility is largely contingent on a determination that a person is dangerous and requires confinement out of a need to protect himself or herself or society. Once committed, a patient may refuse treatment—a situation that not infrequently confronts mental health professionals working in psychiatric facilities (Grisso & Appelbaum, 1998). We will now turn to the important question of evaluating patients in terms of potential dangerousness.

Assessment of "Dangerousness"

As we have seen, although most psychiatric patients are not considered dangerous, some are violent and require close supervision—perhaps confinement until they are no longer dangerous. Few psychiatric patients are assaultive at or prior to their admission to psychiatric facilities. Rates of assaultiveness vary from setting to setting, but in all reported studies, the overall number of assaultive patients is relatively low. A history of violent behavior (Bonta et al., 1998) and some classes of mental disorder appear to be associated with violence, as an increasing number of clinical researchers in recent years have discovered (Pinard & Pagani, 2001). Although most disordered people show no tendency toward violence (Lamberg, 1998), an increased risk of violence appears more likely among some who are experiencing psychotic symptoms (Hodgins & Lalonde, 1999; Tardiff, 1998). The disorders that have an increased risk for violent behavior include schizophrenia, mania, personality disorder, substance abuse, and the more rare conditions of organic brain injury and Huntington's disease. One study from Finland (Eronen, Hakola, & Tiihonen, 1996) reported that homicidal behavior among former patients was considerably more frequent among schizophrenics and even more common among patients with antisocial personality or alcoholism. Psychiatric patients who abuse alcohol (Steadman, Mulvey, et al., 1998) were found to be notably violent.

Practitioners are often called upon to evaluate the possibility that a patient might be dangerous, and there is some evidence that mental health professionals can contribute to such an assessment (Monahan, Steadman, et al., 2001; Steadman, 2000; Szmukler, 2001), at least on a short-term basis (Binder, 1999). The determination that a patient is potentially dangerous can be difficult to make (Bauer, Rosca, et al., 2003; Heilbrun, 1997; Rogers, 2000), yet this is one of the most important responsibilities of professionals working in the field of law and psychology. A clinician has a clear responsibility to try to protect the public from potential violence or other uncontrolled behavior of dangerous patients. A dramatic incident of a failure to assess the extent of a patient's dangerousness was reported by Gorin (1980, 1982) on the television news program *60 Minutes:*

Case of violent domestic abuse. In December, 1979, Mrs. Eva B. was brutally stabbed to death by her former husband while a police dispatcher listened to her terrified screams over the telephone. Only hours before the stabbing incident occurred, Mr. B., who had attacked Mrs. B. eight times in the past, had been judged by two staff psychiatrists not to be dangerous. He had then been released, as part of his treatment, on a temporary pass from the Pilgrim State Hospital in New York. The hospital staff had released Mr. B. from confinement at this time despite the fact that both the judge and the prosecuting attorney who had been involved in his trial (for attempting to kill his wife) had independently written the New York State Department of Mental Health recommending that Mr. B. be held in the strictest confinement because of his persistent threats against Mrs. B. (Indeed, on two previous occasions, Mr. B. had escaped from the hospital and attempted to kill her.) The judge and attorney had also recommended that Mrs. B. should be warned if Mr. B. was released. Ironically, six hours after she had been murdered, a telegram from the hospital was delivered to Mrs. B.'s home warning her that her husband had not returned from his pass.

Looking beyond what appears to be some failure to follow through on the court's recommendations, this case illustrates a number of difficult yet critical dilemmas involved in trying to identify or predict dangerousness in psychiatric patients. First, it emphasizes the fact that some people are capable of uncontrolled violent behavior and hence are potentially dangerous if left unsupervised in the community. It also reflects the dilemma faced by mental health professionals, who, attempting to rehabilitate disturbed patients by gradually easing them back into society, must place some degree of trust in these individuals. Finally, and critically, it illustrates that it is very difficult—for professionals and laypersons alike—to accurately appraise "dangerousness" in some individuals.

Predicting who will become violent is very difficult. Mental health professionals typically err on the conservative side, considering some patients as more violence prone than they actually are. At the same time, they have an obligation to integrate disordered individuals back into society, a move that has occasionally met with tragic results.

ATTEMPTS TO PREDICT DANGEROUSNESS The complex problem of risk assessment or prediction of dangerousness can be likened to predicting the weather. "Ultimately, the goal of a warning system in mental health law is the same as the goal of a warning system in meteorology: to maximize the number of people who take appropriate and timely actions for the safety of life and property" (Monahan & Steadman, 1997, p. 937).

It is usually easy to determine, after the fact, that a person has demonstrated dangerous behavior but how well do mental health professionals do in predicting the occurrence of dangerous acts? Not as well as we would like (Edens, Buffington-Vollum, et al., 2005). Violent acts are particularly difficult to predict because they are apparently determined as much by situational circumstances (for example, whether a person is under the influence of alcohol) as by an individual's personality traits or violent predispositions. One obvious and significantly predictive risk factor is a past history of violence (Megargee, 2002), but clinicians are not always able to unearth this type of background information.

As already noted, some types of patients, particularly actively schizophrenic and manic individuals (Hodgins & Lalonde, 1999) and patients with well-entrenched delusions (de Pauw & Szulecka, 1988), are far more likely than others to commit violent acts. Martell and Dietz (1992) reported a study of persons convicted of pushing or attempting to push unsuspecting victims in front of New York City subway trains and found that most were both psychotic and homeless at the time of the act. Norko & Baranoski (2005) noted that although many studies point to a modest increased risk of violence associated with mental illness, particularly psychosis, other studies have not confirmed these findings.

Mental health professionals typically overpredict violence. They consider some individuals more dangerous than they actually are and usually predict a greater percentage of clients to be dangerous than actually become involved in violent acts (Megargee, 2002). Such a tendency is of course understandable from the perspective of the practitioner, considering the potentially serious consequences of releasing a violent individual. It is likely, however, that many innocent patients thereby experience a violation of their civil rights. Given a certain irreducible level of uncertainty in the prediction of violence, it is not obvious how this dilemma can be completely resolved.

THE DUTY TO PROTECT: IMPLICATIONS OF THE TARASOFF DECISION What should a therapist do upon learning that a patient is planning to harm another person? Can the therapist violate the legally sanctioned confidence of the therapy contract and take action to prevent the patient from committing the act? Today, in most states, the therapist not only can violate confidentiality with impunity but may be required by law to take action to protect people from the threat of imminent violence against them. In its original form, this requirement was conceived as a duty to warn the prospective victim.

The duty-to-warn legal doctrine was given great impetus in a California court ruling in 1976 in the case of *Tarasoff* v. *Regents of the University of California et al.* (Mills, Sullivan, & Eth, 1987). In this case, Prosenjit Poddar was being seen in outpatient psychotherapy by a psychologist at the university mental health facility. During his treatment, Mr. Poddar indicated that he intended to kill his former girlfriend, Tatiana Tarasoff, when she returned from vacation. Concerned about the threat, the psychologist discussed the case with his supervisors, and they agreed that Poddar was dangerous and should be committed for further observation and treatment. They informed the campus police, who picked up Poddar for questioning, subsequently judged him to be rational, and released him after he promised to leave Ms. Tarasoff alone. Poddar then terminated treatment with the psychologist. About 2 months thereafter, he stabbed Ms. Tarasoff to death. Her parents later sued the University of California and staff members involved in the case for their failure to hospitalize Poddar and their failure to warn Tarasoff about the threat to her life. In due course, the California Supreme Court in 1974 ruled that the defendants were not liable for failing to hospitalize Poddar; it did, however, find them liable for failing to warn the victim. Ironically, Prosenjit Poddar, the criminal, was released on a trial technicality and returned home to India. In a later analysis of the case, Knapp (1980) said that the court ruled that difficulty in determining dangerousness does not exempt a psychotherapist from attempting to protect others when a determination of dangerousness exists. The court acknowledged that confidentiality was important to the psychotherapeutic relationship but stated that the protection privilege ends where public peril begins.

The duty-to-warn ruling—which has come to be known as the **Tarasoff decision**—spelled out a therapist's responsibility in situations where there has been an explicit threat on a specific person's life, but it left other areas of application unclear. For example, does this ruling apply in cases where a patient threatens to commit suicide, and how might the therapist's responsibility be met in such a case? What, if anything, should a therapist do when the target of violence is not clearly named—for example, when global threats are made? Would the duty-to-warn ruling hold up in other states? Or might deleterious effects on patient–therapist relationships outweigh any public benefit to be derived from the duty to warn? Responding to mounting pressures for clarification, chiefly from mental health professional organizations, the California Supreme Court in 1976 issued a revised opinion called the "duty to warn doctrine." In this decision the Court ruled that the duty was to protect, rather than specifically to warn, the prospective victim, but it left vague the question of how this duty might be discharged—presumably in order to give practitioners latitude in dealing with danger to third parties. Meanwhile, however, numerous other lawsuits in other jurisdictions have been filed and adjudicated in inconsistent and confusing ways (Mills et al., 1987).

The many perplexing issues for practitioners left in the wake of Tarasoff were partly resolved, at least in California, by the legislature's adoption in 1985 of a new state law essentially establishing that the duty to protect is discharged if the therapist makes "reasonable efforts" to inform potential victims and an appropriate law enforcement agency of the pending threat. In other jurisdictions, however, the inconsistent judicial fallout from Tarasoff has continued and has been a source of much anxiety and confusion among mental health professionals, many of whom continue to believe, on ethical and clinical grounds, that strict confidentiality is an absolute and inviolable trust. A small minority of states—for example, Maryland and Pennsylvania—have explicitly affirmed that position, abandoning Tarasoff altogether (Mills et al., 1987) while 23 states impose a duty to warn but the criteria for this typically varies (Herbert, 2002). Some states have tended to limit the applicability of the duty to warn (Walcott, Cerundolo, & Beck, 2001), while one recent court decision (*Ewing* v. *Goldstein,* 2004) actually extended the ruling to include a need to warn when the therapist did not hear the threat from the patient but from a family member who communicated to the therapist that the patient had made a threat.

Official professional ethics codes, such as that of the American Psychological Association (2002), normally compel compliance with relevant laws regardless of one's personal predilections. Where the law is itself vague or equivocal, however, as it often is in this area, there is much room for individual interpretation (Kachigian & Felthous, 2004).

The Insanity Defense

Some people who are being tried for murder use the **insanity defense**—also known as the **NGRI plea** ("not guilty by reason of insanity")—in an attempt to escape the legally prescribed consequences of their crimes. These defendants claim that they were not legally responsible for their criminal acts. In technical legal terms, they invoke the ancient doctrine that their acts, while guilty ones (*actus rea*), lacked moral blameworthiness because they were not intentional since the defendants did not possess their full mental faculties at the time of the crime and did not "know what they were doing" (*mens rea*)—the underlying assumption being that "insanity" somehow precludes or absolves the harboring of a guilty intent. (See The World Around Us 18.4. on p. 658.) One of the most notorious uses of the Not Guilty by Reason of Insanity plea in American history was in the case of Jeffrey Dahmer, on trial for the murder, dismemberment, and cannibalization of 15 men in Milwaukee. In the Dahmer case, the planned insanity defense proved unsuccessful, which is the usual outcome (Steadman et al., 1993).

Jeffrey Dahmer was torturing and drowning cats and dogs by age 7. He never heard voices or broke with reality. He tricked his victims into being handcuffed (they thought it was part of a sexual game) and then dripped acid into their flesh and skulls, rendering them zombies. Then, he would engage them sexually, and would occasionally cannibalize them. Dahmer was charged with and later convicted of murder after body parts of several young men were found in his apartment. While serving his time in prison, he was bludgeoned to death by a psychotic killer in 1994.

By contrast, attorneys for John Hinckley, who shot President Reagan and his press secretary, James Brady, successfully pleaded NGRI. (See the Case Study on p. 658.) The outcome of the Hinckley case was different in a number of important respects, because the jury in this instance considered the defendant to be acting "outside of reason" and found him "not guilty by reason of insanity." At trial in June 1982, Hinckley was acquitted on those grounds. This verdict immediately unleashed a storm of public protest and generated widespread, often hasty attempts to reform the law and make the NGRI defense a less attractive option to defendants and their attorneys. Hinckley himself was committed to the care of a federally operated, high-security mental hospital, to be involuntarily detained there until such time as his disorder remits sufficiently that his release would not constitute a danger to himself or others. He remains incarcerated; however, under a 1999 federal appeals court ruling, Hinckley has been able to take supervised day trips off hospital grounds, and most recently he has requested that he be allowed to travel unescorted to his parents' home in Williamsburg, Virginia, some 3 hours away. However, his "recovery" has been questioned. Recent psychiatric testimony (Associated Press, 2003) has indicated that Hinckley still suffers from the same narcissistic personality disorder that drove him to shoot Reagan and three others in 1981.

Releasing Hinckley from custody would almost certainly bring forth another public outcry demanding abolition or limitation of the insanity defense. This unfortunate public outrage at *all* insanity defense pleas results from a persistent failure of legal scholars to examine critically and rigorously the guilt-absolving insanity construct and the *mens rea* doctrine from which it derives.

case STUDY Hinckley's Successful Insanity Plea

On March 30, 1981, in an apparent scheme to attract the attention of actress Jodie Foster, with whom he was obsessed, John Hinckley, Jr., shot six bullets at President Ronald Reagan in an assassination attempt. President Reagan was seriously injured, as was Press Secretary James Brady. At the end of his trial in 1982, Hinckley was found not guilty by reason of insanity. Since his trial, Hinckley has been confined to St. Elizabeth's Hospital in Washington, DC. After what seemed to be significant improvement in his mental health, Hinckley was allowed unsupervised visits in April 2000, but these visits were revoked when guards discovered a smuggled book on Jodie Foster in his room.

In recent years the use of the NGRI defense in trials where the defendant's life is at stake has been surrounded by controversy, largely owing to the uproar created by the outcome of the Hinckley trial (Steadman et al., 1993). Some have contended that the objection to the insanity defense in capital crimes might reflect negative social attitudes toward the insane (Perlin, 1996). There has been some concern, especially in cases of high visibility, that guilty defendants may feign mental disorder and hence avoid criminal responsibility. Good defense attorneys are of course aware of this public cynicism, which is likely to be shared by juries. They attempt to counteract it in various ways, often by portraying their purportedly "insane at the time of the act" clients as having been themselves victims of heinous and traumatic acts at an earlier time in their lives. Some of them undoubtedly were victimized, but the strategy of creating sympathy while offering a plausible explanation for the "insane" act would have a compelling attraction in any case. On the other hand, the insanity defense is often not employed where it is appropriate, as it would have been, for example, in two high-visibility cases: those of John Salvi (the abortion clinic assassin) and Theodore Kaczynski (the Unabomber). Apparently neither defendant wanted his mental state to be a part of the proceedings. Severe delusional disorder (see Chapter 14) is likely to have played a significant role in both of their crimes.

Despite some features that make it an appealing option to consider, especially where the undisputed facts are strongly aligned against the defendant, the NGRI

18.4 THE WORLD AROUND US — Controversial Not Guilty Pleas: Can Altered Mind States or Personality Disorder Limit Responsibility for a Criminal Act?

If a person commits a capital offense when his or her consciousness (and reason) is impaired, as in an altered state, should he or she be held responsible for the crime? Can using psychotropic medicine such as Prozac or Zoloft "poison" a person's mind to such an extreme degree that she or he commits murder? If a murder is committed while someone is heavily "sedated"—for example, with Xanax or Halcion—should that person be released from criminal responsibility because he or she was involuntarily intoxicated with medications prescribed by a health professional? If a person experiences "multiple personalities" and a crime is committed by one personality, should all of the personalities suffer the consequences? These defense strategies can be interesting and controversial challenges to today's legal system.

Altered States of Consciousness

In a civil trial, the jury failed to find the manufacturer of Prozac (Eli Lilly) liable in court action that resulted from a 1989 mass murder allegedly committed "under the influence" of Prozac. The murderer (Joseph Wesbecker), in a rage against his employer, killed 8 people and wounded 12 others before killing himself. Survivors and family members of several people who were killed in the incident filed a suit against Eli Lilly because the company had produced the drug Prozac, which the killer was taking at the time of the murders and which was alleged to be responsible for "intoxicating" the assassin and lowering his inhibitions. After a long trial, the jury found in favor of the manufacturer (*Fentress et al.* v. *Shea Communications et al.*, 1990).

Courts have generally not considered altered states of consciousness such as being intoxicated on drugs or alcohol sufficient grounds for an insanity defense because of the issue of volition—that is, the perpetrator of the crime consciously chose to become intoxicated in the first place. However, the question of intoxication by drugs that were taken for the purpose of medication has added a new dimension to the defense. This issue has not been fully resolved in the court system.

Altered Personality States

Possibly the most fascinating of controversial insanity pleas are those raised by the phenomenon of multiple personality disorder, now called "dissociative identity disorder" (DID), which has become a more common diagnosis in recent years. Although some professionals dispute even the existence of such a condition, others find it a plausible argument for a plea of not guilty by reason of insanity (NGRI).

The general nature of the problem can be stated quite succinctly: Within a legal system strongly oriented to the precise identification of individual responsibility for acts, what if any are the limits of the assignment of responsibility and sanctions for infractions of the law where the same physical space and body are occupied at different times by more than one distinct and legally recognizable person? Consider the following legal dilemmas:

- Who, among various co-personalities, is empowered to sign for withdrawals from a bank account?
- Are the provisions and obligations of a contract entered into by one constituent personality binding on all others, regardless of their particular desires in the matter?
- Does the swearing of an oath, as in court, apply to the entire collection of personalities, or must each be sworn individually if he or she is to testify?
- In the case of a guilty verdict for the criminal act of a given personality, where other personalities did not acquiesce in the crime, how should punishment be fairly meted out?
- If no constituent personality meets a test of insanity, is it reasonable and lawful to declare DID itself an instance of insanity?
- Has rape occurred if the co-personalities of a 26-year-old woman who had acquiesced to intercourse included one or more personalities who vehemently objected to it? (Such a case was prosecuted in Wisconsin in 1990.)
- And, of course, the most common real-life legal dilemma: Should an individual, as the primary personality, be held legally accountable for, say, a capital crime that evidence suggests may have actually been committed surreptitiously, so to speak, by an alter personality?

The scenario just mentioned has rather often been the contention underlying a plea of not guilty by reason of insanity. Usually, as in the case of the "Hillside Strangler" Kenneth Bianchi (convicted of 12 rapes and murders in California and Washington State) and in the case of a woman who kidnapped a newborn from a hospital and later claimed that an alter personality actually committed the crime (Appelbaum & Greer, 1994), the plea has failed. On a very few occasions, however, the NGRI plea has worked, as in the well-publicized 1978 case of Ohio resident Billy Milligan, who claimed to be host to ten personalities and was accused of raping four women (*New York Times,* 1994). The legal maneuvers inspired by the DID construct admittedly have a quality of whimsy about them. It is consequently difficult to convince most juries that the defendant was so taken over by an alter personality who perpetrated the crime that he or she should be absolved of guilt and responsibility.

defense has actually been employed quite rarely—in less than 2 percent of capital cases in the United States over time (Lymburner & Roesch, 1999; Steadman et al., 1993). Studies have confirmed, however, that in some jurisdictions, persons acquitted of crimes by reason of insanity spend less time, on the whole, in a psychiatric hospital than persons who are convicted of crimes spend in prison (Lymburner & Roesch, 1999). In addition, states differ widely in the amount of time that persons found not guilty by reason of insanity are actually confined. For example, one study by Callahan and Silver (1998) reported that in the states of Ohio and Maryland, nearly all persons acquitted as NGRI have been released within 5 years, whereas in Connecticut and New York, conditional release has been much more difficult to obtain. The re-arrest rates for freed NGRI claimants vary, with some studies reporting rates as high as 50 percent (Callahan & Silver, 1998; Wiederanders, Bromley, & Choate, 1997). Monson, Gunnin, and colleagues (2001) conducted a follow-up of 125 NGRI acquittees and found a similarly high re-arrest rate. These investigators reported that persons discharged to live with their family of origin or to alone/semi-independent living were more likely to maintain their conditional release and not reoffend. These investigators reported that such factors as minority status, comorbid substance abuse, and prior criminal history were associated with return to custody after release. One recent study in which an active community treatment program was implemented reported low re-arrest rates (1.4 percent) and moderate rehospitalization rates (14 percent; Parker, 2004).

case STUDY Detected Faking of the Insanity Defense

Michael McDermott testified that Michael the Archangel had sent him on a mission to prevent the Holocaust when he gunned down seven co-workers on December 26, 2000. McDermott also stated that he believed he was soulless, and that by killing he would earn a soul. McDermott claimed to have been raped by a neighbor when he was a young boy and had a history of paranoia and suicide attempts. Despite this claim of insanity, a jury found McDermott guilty in the shooting deaths of his seven co-workers. The prosecution argued that McDermott was motivated to kill because his employer was about to deduct back taxes owed to the IRS from his wages. Evidence seized from his computer showed that McDermott had researched how to fake being mentally ill. McDermott is currently serving seven consecutive life sentences for his crimes.

Up to this point in the discussion, we have used the term *insanity defense* loosely. We must now become more attentive to the many precise legal nuances involved. Established precedents that define the insanity defense are as follows:

1. **The M'Naghten Rule (1843).** Under this ruling, which is often referred to as the "knowing right from wrong" rule, people are assumed to be sane unless it can be proved that at the time of committing the act, they were laboring under such a defect of reason (from a disease of the mind) that they did not know the nature and quality of the act they were doing—or, if they did know they were committing the act, they did not know that what they were doing was wrong.
2. **The Irresistible Impulse Rule (1887).** A second precedent in the insanity defense is the doctrine of the "irresistible impulse." This view holds that accused persons might not be responsible for their acts, even if they knew that what they were doing was wrong (according to the M'Naghten Rule), if they had lost the power to choose between right and wrong. That is, they could not avoid doing the act in question because they were compelled beyond their will to commit the act (Fersch, 1980).
3. **The Durham Rule.** In 1954, Judge David Bazelon, in a decision of the U.S. Court of Appeals, broadened the insanity defense further. Bazelon did not believe that the previous precedents allowed for a sufficient application of established scientific knowledge of mental illness and proposed a test that would be based on this knowledge. Under this rule, which is often referred to as the product test, the accused is not criminally responsible if his or her unlawful act was the product of mental disease or mental defect.
4. **The American Law Institute (ALI) Standard (1962).** Often referred to as the "substantial capacity test" for insanity, this test combines the cognitive aspect of M'Naghten with the volitional focus of irresistible impulse in holding that the perpetrator is not legally responsible if at the time of the act he or she, owing to mental disease or defect, lacked "substantial capacity" either to appreciate its criminal character or to conform his or her behavior to the law's requirements.
5. **The Federal Insanity Defense Reform Act (IDRA).** Adopted by Congress in 1984 as the standard for the insanity defense to be applied in all federal jurisdictions, this act abolished the volitional element of the ALI standard and modified the cognitive one to read "unable to appreciate," thus bringing the definition quite close to M'Naghten. IDRA also specified that the mental disorder involved must be a severe one and shifted the burden of proof from the prosecution to the defense. That is, the defense must clearly and convincingly establish the defendant's insanity, in contrast to the prior requirement that the prosecution clearly and convincingly demonstrate the defendant to have been sane when the prohibited act was committed.

This shifting of the burden of proof for the insanity defense, by the way, had been instituted by many states in the wake of the Hinckley acquittal. The intent of this reform was to discourage use of the insanity defense, and it proved quite effective in altering litigation practices in the intended direction (Steadman et al., 1993).

At the present time, most states and the District of Columbia subscribe to a version of either the ALI or the more restrictive M'Naghten standard. New York is a special case. It uses a version of M'Naghten to define insanity, with the burden of proof on the defense, but an elaborate procedural code has been enacted to promote fairness in outcomes while ensuring lengthy and restrictive hospital commitment for defendants judged to be dangerous; this approach appears to have worked well (Steadman et al., 1993). In some jurisdictions, when an insanity plea is filed, the case is submitted for pretrial screening, which includes a psychiatric evaluation, review of records, and appraisal of criminal responsibility. In one study of 190 defendants who entered a plea of not criminally responsible, the following outcomes were obtained: 105 were judged to be criminally responsible, charges against 34 were dropped, and 8 defendants were agreed by both the prosecution and the defense to be insane and not responsible. A total of 134 withdrew their insanity pleas (Janofsky, Dunn, et al., 1996). The insanity defense was noted in this study to be somewhat of a "rich man's defense" in that such cases involved private attorneys rather than public defenders.

Silver (1995) found that the successful use of the NGRI defense varied widely among states. In addition, Silver reported that the length of confinement was related more to the judged seriousness of the crime than to whether the person was employing the NGRI defense. One study (Cirincione, Steadman, & McGreevy, 1995) found that an NGRI plea was most likely to be successful if one or more of the following factors were present:

- A diagnosed mental disorder, particularly a major mental disorder
- A female defendant
- The violent crime was other than murder
- There had been prior mental hospitalizations

Three states—Idaho, Montana, and Utah—have entirely abolished the attribution of insanity as an acceptable defense for wrongdoing—a somewhat draconian solution that compensates in clarity for what some feel it lacks in compassion. As expected, with the disappearance of the insanity acquittals in Montana there was a corresponding rise in the use of "incompetent to stand trial," in which the charges were actually dismissed, largely negating the desired result (more effective prosecution) of doing away with the insanity defense (Callahan, Robbins, et al., 1995).

How, then, is guilt or innocence determined? Many authorities believe that the insanity defense sets the courts an impossible task—to determine guilt or innocence by reason of insanity on the basis of psychiatric testimony. In a number of cases, conflicting testimony has resulted because both the prosecution and the defense have "their" panel of expert psychiatric witnesses, who are in complete disagreement (Marvit, 1981).

Finally, states have adopted the optional plea/verdict of **guilty but mentally ill (GBMI).** In these cases, a defendant may be sentenced but placed in a treatment facility rather than in a prison. This two-part judgment serves to prevent the type of situation in which a person commits a murder, is found not guilty by reason of insanity, is turned over to a mental health facility, is found to be rational and in no further need of treatment by the hospital staff, and is unconditionally released to the community after only a minimal period of confinement. Under the two-part decision, such a person would remain in the custody of the correctional department until the full sentence had been served. Marvit (1981) has suggested that this approach might "realistically balance the interest of the mentally ill offender's rights and the community's need to control criminal behavior" (p. 23). However, others have argued that the GBMI defense is confusing to jurors and should be eliminated (Melville & Naimark, 2002). Interestingly, in Georgia, one of the states adopting this option, GBMI defendants received longer sentences and longer periods of confinement than those who pleaded NGRI and lost. Overall, outcomes from use of the GBMI standard, which is often employed in a plea-bargaining strategy, have been disappointing (Steadman et al., 1993).

In Review

- What conditions must be met before an individual can be involuntarily committed to a mental institution? Describe the legal process that follows.
- What is the insanity (NGRI) defense in criminal cases?
- What are the implications of the Tarasoff decision for practicing clinicians?

Organized Efforts for Mental Health

Public awareness of the magnitude of contemporary mental health problems and the interest of government, professional, and lay organizations have stimulated the development of programs directed at better understanding, more effective treatment, and long-range prevention. Efforts to improve mental health are apparent not only in our society but also in many other countries, and they involve international as well as national and local organizations and approaches.

U.S. Efforts for Mental Health

In the United States in the eighteenth and nineteenth centuries, dealing with mental disorders was the primary responsibility of state and local agencies. During World War II, however, the extent of mental disorders in the United States was brought to public attention when a large number of young men—two out of every seven recruits—were rejected for military service for psychiatric reasons. This discovery led to a variety of organized measures for taking care of people with mental illness.

THE FEDERAL GOVERNMENT AND MENTAL HEALTH

In 1946, aware of the need for more research, training, and services in the field of mental health, Congress passed its first comprehensive mental health bill, the National Mental Health Act. In that same year, the National Institute of Mental Health (NIMH) was formed in Washington, DC. The agency was to serve as a central research and training center and as headquarters for the administration of a grant-in-aid program designed to foster research and training elsewhere in the nation and to help state and local communities expand and improve their own mental health services. Congress authorized the institute to provide "mental health project grants" for experimental studies, pilot projects, surveys, and general research. Today the NIMH is a separate institute under the National Institutes of Health, within the Department of Health and Human Services (NIMH, 2001).

The NIMH (1) conducts and supports research on the biological, psychosocial, and sociocultural aspects of mental disorders; (2) supports the training of professional and paraprofessional personnel in the mental health field; (3) helps communities plan, establish, and maintain more effective mental health programs; and (4) provides information on mental health to the public and to the scientific community. Two companion institutes—the National Institute on Alcohol Abuse and Alcoholism (NIAAA) and the National Institute on Drug Abuse (NIDA)—perform comparable functions in these more specialized fields.

Although the federal government provides leadership and financial aid, the states and local organizations actually plan and run most NIMH programs. Most state and local governments, however, have not been able to fund programs and facilities because of cuts in federal support. As a result, many programs devoted to mental health training, research, and service have been greatly reduced or abandoned, even as the need for them has increased. There is considerable uncertainty about the extent to which mental health problems will be included in forthcoming revisions of national health care policy and about what forms any such inclusion might take.

PROFESSIONAL ORGANIZATIONS AND MENTAL HEALTH A number of national professional organizations exist in the mental health field. These include the American Psychological Association (APA), the American Psychological Society (APS), the American Psychiatric Association (APA), the American Medical Association (AMA), the Association for the Advancement of Behavior Therapy (AABT), the American Association for Correctional and Forensic Psychology (AACFP), and the American Association for Social Work.

A key function of professional organizations is the application of insights and methods to contemporary social problems—for example, in lobbying national and local government agencies to provide more services for homeless people. Professional mental health organizations are in a unique position to serve as consultants on mental health problems and programs.

Another important function of these organizations is to set and maintain high professional and ethical standards within their special areas. This function may include (1) establishing and reviewing training qualifications for professional and paraprofessional personnel; (2) setting standards and procedures for the accreditation of undergraduate and graduate training programs; (3) setting standards for the accreditation of clinics, hospitals, or other service operations and carrying out inspections to see that the standards are followed; and (4) investigating reported cases of unethical or unprofessional conduct and taking disciplinary action when necessary.

THE ROLE OF VOLUNTEER ORGANIZATIONS AND AGENCIES Although professional mental health personnel and organizations can give expert technical advice with regard to mental health needs and programs, informed citizens are essential in planning and implementing these programs. In fact, it is primarily concerned nonprofessionals who have blazed the trails in the mental health field.

Prominent among the many volunteer mental health agencies is the National Mental Health Association (NMHA). This organization was founded in 1909 by Clifford Beers as the National Association for Mental Health and expanded by the merger of the National Committee for Mental Hygiene, the National Mental Health Foundation, and the Psychiatric Foundation; it was further expanded in 1962 by merging with the National Organization for Mentally Ill Children. The NMHA works for the improvement of services in community clinics and mental hospitals; it helps recruit, train, and place volunteers for service in treatment and aftercare programs; and it works for enlightened mental health legislation and for the provision of needed facilities and personnel. It also carries on special educational programs aimed at fostering positive mental health and helping people understand mental disorders. In addition, the National Mental Health Association has been actively involved in many court decisions affecting patient rights (1997). In several cases, the organization has sponsored litigation or served as *amicus curiae* (friend of the court) in efforts to establish the rights of mental patients to treatment, to freedom from custodial confinement, to freedom to live in the community, and to protection of their confidentiality.

The National Association for Retarded Citizens (NARC) works to reduce the incidence of mental retardation, to seek community and residential treatment centers and services for the retarded, and to carry on a program of education aimed at better public understanding of retarded individuals and greater support for legislation on their behalf. The NARC also fosters scientific research into mental retardation, the recruitment and training of volunteer workers, and programs of community action.

These and other volunteer health organizations such as Alcoholics Anonymous and the National Alliance for the Mentally Ill (NAMI) need the backing of a wide constituency of knowledgeable and involved citizens in order to succeed.

MENTAL HEALTH RESOURCES IN PRIVATE INDUSTRY Personal problems—such as marital distress or other family problems, alcohol or drug abuse, financial difficulties, and job-related stress—can adversely affect employee morale and performance. Psychological difficulties among employees may result in numerous problems such as absenteeism, accident proneness, poor productivity, and high job turnover. The National Institute for Occupational Safety and Health (NIOSH) recognizes psychological disorders as one of the ten leading work-related health problems (Millar, 1990), and work-related mental health risk factors may be increasing with changes in the economy, in technology, and in demographic factors in the workforce (Sauter, Murphy, & Hurrell, 1990). Since passage of the Americans with Disabilities Act, people with psychiatric problems cannot be discriminated against in the workplace. Employers are encouraged to alter the workplace, as needed, to accommodate the needs of persons with mental illness. Although employers often object that it is too costly to hire psychiatrically impaired persons, great benefits for society can result from integrating into productive jobs people who have disabilities but also have appropriate skills (Kramer, 1998).

A great deal more research is needed to identify specific mental health risk factors in work situations. We already know (e.g., Sauter et al., 1990) that serious unrecognized problems may exist in the following areas of job design and conditions of work.

1. **Work load and pace.** The critical factor here appears to be the degree of control the worker has over the pace of work, rather than output demand. Machine-paced assembly work may be particularly hazardous to mental health.
2. **Work schedule.** Rotating shifts and night work have been associated with elevated risk for psychological difficulties.
3. **Role stressors.** Role ambiguity (such as uncertainty about who has responsibility for what), said to be common in many work situations, has a negative impact on mental and physical health, as does role conflict (incompatible role demands).
4. **Career security factors.** Feelings of insecurity related to issues such as job future or obsolescence, career development, and encouragement of early retirement adversely affect mental and physical health.
5. **Interpersonal relations.** Poor or unsupportive relationships among work colleagues significantly increase the risk of untoward psychological reactions.
6. **Job content.** Poor mental health has been associated with work assignments involving fragmented, narrow, unvarying tasks that allow for little creativity and give the worker little sense of having contributed to the ultimate product.

Many corporations have long recognized the importance of worker mental health and of enhancing mental-health-promoting factors in the workplace, yet only recently have many of them acted on this knowledge. Today many companies have expanded their "obligations" to employees to include numerous psychological services. Employee assistance programs (EAPs) are means through which larger corporations can actively provide mental health services to employees and their family members. In general, employers have been slower to deal with issues of job design and work environment as additional means of maximizing worker mental health.

International Efforts for Mental Health

Mental health is a major issue not only in the United States but also in the rest of the world. Indeed, many of the problems in this country with regard to the treatment of mental disorders are greatly magnified in poorer countries and countries with repressive governments. The severity of the world mental health problem is reflected in the World Health Organization's estimate that mental disorders affect more than 200 million people worldwide, partly because of the significant world refugee crisis (de Jong, 2002; Watters & Ingleby, 2004). Recognition of this great problem served to bring about the formation of several international organizations at the end of World War II. Here we will briefly discuss the World Health Organization and the World Federation for Mental Health.

THE WORLD HEALTH ORGANIZATION The World Health Organization (2001) has always been keenly aware of the close interrelationships among physical, psychosocial, and sociocultural factors. Examples include the influence of rapid change and social disruption on both physical and mental health; the impossibility of major progress toward mental health in societies where a large proportion of the population suffers from malnutrition, parasites, and disease; and the frequent psychological and cultural barriers to successful programs in family planning and public health (Rutz, 2001).

Formed after World War II as part of the United Nations system, WHO's earliest focus was on physical diseases; it has helped make dramatic progress toward the conquest of such ancient scourges as smallpox and malaria. Over the years, mental health, too, became an increasing concern among the member countries. WHO's present program integrates mental health concerns with the broad problems of overall health and socioeconomic development that many member countries face (World Health Organization, 1997).

Another important contribution of WHO has been its International Classification of Diseases (ICD), which enables clinicians and researchers in different countries to use a uniform set of diagnostic categories. As we saw in Chapter 4, the American Psychiatric Association's DSM-IV classification has been coordinated with the WHO's ICD-10 classification (Sartorius et al., 1993).

THE WORLD FEDERATION FOR MENTAL HEALTH The World Federation for Mental Health was established in 1948 as an international congress of nongovernmental organizations and individuals concerned with mental health. Its purpose is to promote international cooperation among governmental and nongovernmental mental health agencies, and its membership now extends to more than 50 countries. The federation has been granted consultative status by WHO, and it assists the UN agencies by collecting information on mental health conditions all over the world (World Health Organization, 1997).

The last century witnessed an amazing openness and a lowering of previously impassable barriers between nations. Along with this increased interchange of ideas and cooperation, we expect to see a broader mental health collaboration. It is vital that greater international cooperation in the sciences and in health planning continue, along with more sharing of information and views on mental health.

In Review

- What is the role of the National Institute of Mental Health in providing care for the mentally ill?
- What is the NMHA and how does it contribute to improvement in mental health services?
- What is the WHO?

Challenges for the Future

Even though international cooperation in efforts to understand and enhance mental health is encouraging, the media confront us daily with the stark truth that we have a long way to go before our dreams of a better world are realized. Many people question whether the United States or any other technologically advanced nation can achieve mental health for the majority of its citizens in our time. Racism, poverty, youth violence, terrorism, the uprooting of developing world populations, and other social problems that contribute to mental disorder sometimes seem insurmountable.

Other events in the rest of the world affect us also, both directly and indirectly. Worldwide economic instability and shortages and the possibility of the destruction of our planet's life ecology breeds widespread anxiety about the future. The vast resources we have spent on military programs over the past half-century to protect against perceived threats have absorbed funds and energy that otherwise might have been devoted to meeting human and social needs here and elsewhere in the world. The limited resources we are now willing to allocate to mental health problems prevent our solving major problems resulting from drug and alcohol abuse, homelessness, broken families, and squalid living conditions.

The Need for Planning

If mental health problems are going to be reduced or eliminated, it seems imperative that more effective planning be done at community, national, and international levels. Many challenges must be met if we are to create a better world for ourselves and future generations. Without slackening our efforts to meet needs at home, we will probably find it essential to participate more broadly in international measures aimed at reducing group tensions and promoting mental health and a better world for people everywhere. At the same time, we can expect that measures we undertake to reduce international conflict and improve the general condition of humankind will make a significant contribution to our own nation's social progress and mental health. Both kinds of measures will require understanding and moral commitment from concerned citizens.

Within our own country and the rest of the industrialized world, progress in prolonging life has brought with it burgeoning problems in the prevalence of disorders associated with advanced age, particularly in the area of conditions such as Alzheimer's disease. Judging by the numbers of people already affected, it is not certain at this time that we will find the means of eradicating or arresting this threat before it has overwhelmed us. Planning and preparation would seem our only rational hope of forestalling a potential disaster of unprecedented magnitude; we need to make a beginning.

The Individual's Contribution

History provides clear examples of individuals whose efforts were instrumental in changing the way we think about mental health problems. Recall that Pinel took off the chains, Dorothea Dix initiated a movement to improve the conditions of asylums, and Clifford Beers inspired the modern mental health movement with his autobiographical account of his own experience with mental illness. Who will lead the next revolution in mental health is anyone's guess. What is clear is that a great deal can be accomplished by individual effort.

When students become aware of the tremendous scope of the mental health problem both nationally and internationally and of the woefully inadequate facilities for coping with it, they often ask, "What can I do?" Thus it seems appropriate to suggest a few of the lines of action that interested students can take.

Many opportunities in mental health work are open to trained personnel, both professional and paraprofessional. Social work, clinical psychology, psychiatry, and other mental health occupations are personally fulfilling. In addition, many occupations, ranging from law enforcement to teaching and the ministry, can and do play key roles in the mental health and well-being of many people. Training in all these fields usually offers individuals opportunities to work in community clinics and related facilities, to gain experience in understanding the needs and problems of people in distress, and to become familiar with community resources.

Citizens can find many ways to be of direct service if they are familiar with national and international resources and programs and if they invest the effort necessary to learn about their community's special needs and problems. Whatever their roles in life—student, teacher, police officer, lawyer, homemaker, business executive, or trade unionist—their interests are directly at stake, for although the mental health of a nation may be manifested in many ways—in its purposes, courage, moral responsibility, scientific and cultural achievements, and quality of daily life—its health and resources derive ultimately from the individuals within it. In a participatory democracy, it is they who plan and implement the nation's goals.

Besides accepting some measure of responsibility for the mental health of others through the quality of one's own interpersonal relationships, there are several other constructive courses of action open to each citizen. These include (1) serving as a volunteer in a mental hospital, community mental health center, or service organization; (2) supporting realistic measures for ensuring comprehensive health services for all age groups; and (3) working toward improved public education, responsible government, the alleviation of prejudice, and the establishment of a more sane and harmonious world.

All of us are concerned with mental health for personal as well as altruistic reasons, for we want to overcome the nagging problems of contemporary living and find our share of happiness in a meaningful and fulfilling life. To do so, we may sometimes need the courage to admit that our problems are too much for us. When existence seems futile or the going becomes too difficult, it may help to remind ourselves of the following basic facts, which have been emphasized throughout this text: From time to time, each of us has serious difficulties in coping with the problems of living. During such crises, we may need psychological and related assistance. Such difficulties are not a disgrace; they can happen to anyone if the stress is severe enough. The early detection and treatment of maladaptive behavior are of great importance in preventing the development of more severe or chronic conditions. Preventive measures—universal, selected, and indicated—are the most effective long-range approach to the solution of both individual and group mental health problems.

Statistics show that nearly all of us will at some time in our lives have to deal with severely maladaptive behavior or mental disorder either in ourselves or in someone close to us. Our interdependence and the loss to us all, individually and collectively, when any one of us fails to achieve his or her potential are eloquently expressed in the famous lines of John Donne (1624):

> No man is an island, entire of itself; every man is a piece of the continent, a part of the main. If a clod be washed away by the sea, Europe is the less, as well as if a promontory were, as well as if a manor of thy friends or of thine own were: any man's death diminishes me, because I am involved in mankind, and therefore never send to know for whom the bell tolls; it tolls for thee.

In Review

- After reading the Unresolved Issues feature, discuss the controversy over the effects of managed health care on the treatment and prevention of mental illness.
- Describe several ways in which individuals can contribute to the advancement of mental health.

unresolved issues

The HMOs and Mental Health Care

As noted in Chapter 1, in any 12-month period the lives of more than 37 million adults in this country are affected by mental illness of some kind (Kessler, Chiu, et al., 2005). Only about one in five with a disorder receives mental health treatment (Castro, 1993). It has been estimated that psychiatric treatment accounts for about one-quarter of all hospital stays in America (Kiesler & Sibulkin, 1987). Health care costs in general are reportedly rising more rapidly than any other aspect of the American economy (Resnick & DeLeon, 1995). Some businesses have spent as much on health care for employees as they have earned (O'Connor, 1996). In the 1990s health care costs skyrocketed as the number of people receiving services increased over 30 percent per year (Giles, 1993). The "gatekeeping" function of HMOs has clearly affected access to mental health care in the United States in that business decisions often take precedence over treatment need. Treatment, when it is allowed by the HMO, tends to be limited in both duration and quality. As we have seen in this chapter, mental health treatment is valuable for preventing as well as easing mental disorders. Yet the current crisis in health care has meant that mental health treatment is less readily available and that its cost is less often reimbursed.

In response to these needs, health care administrators have created a diverse array of programs in an attempt to provide services at a cost that society can afford. In **managed health care,** a system of corporations secures services from hospitals, physicians, and other providers/workers for a designated population (Frank, McDaniel, et al., 2004). Managed health care providers attempt to offer medical care at lower costs by limiting traditional services, employing stringent review procedures, and using lower-cost, brief treatment options. These systems operate by marketing health care plans to employers or individuals. For a fixed prepaid fee, employers and individuals subscribe to a health service company or a **health maintenance organization (HMO),** which entitles them to the services provided by that health plan. These programs establish a treatment staff through systems of professionals, referred to as "panels," who are considered to have efficacy and efficiency in providing a wide range of services. Some HMOs—referred to as "open-panel systems"—allow patients some choice of health providers and allow any qualified professional in the community to participate. However, most are closed-panel systems, which limit the selection of available providers. The benefits vary from plan to plan and usually include limits on the problems covered or on the maximum amount of care provided or services available. To keep costs low, some HMOs operate according to a system of "capitation," a method of payment in which a health care provider contracts to deliver all the health care services required by a population for a fixed cost or flat fee per enrolled member or employee (Sanchez & Turner, 2003). The HMO thus assumes some risk, but capitation allows for great profit if the subscriber's fees can be set higher than the cost of health services.

Mental Health Treatment—Who Decides What Kind and How Long?

In one common approach to reducing health care costs, the managed care agency negotiates a reduced price directly with the health service provider. The provider then bills the health service organization for the time spent, and the HMO can obtain "low-bid" services from the health professional (Richardson & Austad, 1994). This approach poses little financial risk to the provider. As might be apparent to the casual observer of managed care systems, the procedures for determining the amount of money paid to providers have frequently been a problem for mental health professionals—psychologists and psychiatrists (Resnick et al., 1994). The HMO representative or "gatekeeper" to reimbursement, often a medical generalist untrained in either psychiatric disorders or psychosocial interventions, controls access to therapy and sometimes the type of treatment to be provided (Resnick et al., 1994). In some systems of managed care, the gatekeeper might be a business professional who, in the view of the health service provider, is blocking adequate treatment by demanding that the clinician periodically justify treatment decisions to someone who has little or no background in mental health. Conflicts frequently develop in such situations, and patients may be deprived of appropriate and necessary care (Resnick et al., 1994).

Managed care programs differ widely in the modes and quality of mental health services provided. Although their stated intention is to provide the most effective treatments available, decisions about what treatments to provide are often based more on business factors than on treatment considerations. HMOs that are overly cost-conscious have come to be viewed by many in the mental health field as simply tending to business and neglecting the patients' needs (Karon, 1995).

Time-Limited Therapy

The mental health services typically covered by HMOs tend to favor less expensive and less labor-intensive approaches. As might be expected, pharmacotherapy is the most frequent mental health treatment provided by HMOs. About 10 percent of the population in the United States receives some prescribed psychoactive medication each year (Klerman et al., 1994), a situation that some research suggests actually reduces health care costs. Some research has also shown that cost-containment measures that are intended to reduce drug costs by restricting access to medications can—and often do—wind up increasing total health care costs (Horn, 2003). Some managed health care systems have advocated the expanded use of somatic therapies in an attempt to contain costs. Psychosocial interventions such as individual psychotherapy are discouraged or limited to relatively few sessions. Long-term psychotherapy has been virtually eliminated for all but a small number of wealthy private clients (Lazarus, 1996). On the other hand, group psychotherapy is often promoted and encouraged because it is often thought of as cost-effective.

Most managed care corporations have adopted the model of providing focused, brief, intermittent mental health treatment (Cummings, 1995) for most problems. Patients who require longer treatments or need inpatient hospitalization are typically not well served in managed care organizations. In fact, long-term mental health treatment is usually discouraged by managed health care organizations. For example, most managed care groups approve only short inpatient stays (less than 10 days) and four to six sessions of outpatient mental health treatment at a time. Few if any of the decisions regarding the amount and type of services provided are directly guided by empirical criteria. Decisions whether to cover 8 or 20 sessions of psychotherapy, for example, are arbitrary and often seem capricious to both practitioner and patient (Harwood et al., 1997).

A clear divide has developed between health service providers and managers. Available services are often governed more by financial concerns than by a mental health professional's judgment. Practitioners, as a result, are expressing disagreement over the situation. Critics of managed care argue that there is no convincing evidence that current efforts are actually controlling costs (Gabbard, 1994; Harwood et al., 1997) and that there is no scientific support for the limited-benefit options being exercised. Some data suggest that some measures that are designed to reduce drug costs by restricting access to medications can actually wind up increasing total health care costs (Horn, 2003). Some researchers have pointed out that the administrative costs for managed care centers (including high salaries for HMO executives) are exorbitant. Gabbard (1994), for example, estimated that about one-fourth of the health care expenditures in the United States go for managed care administration.

The revolution in health care has clearly created controversy in the field of psychotherapy. The mental health field is being drastically altered by economic considerations. Recently, Sanchez and Turner (2003) provided an overview of the impact of managed care on psychological practice and the provision of mental health services to clients in need. They pointed out that the economics of the current health care system have greatly impacted the practice of behavioral health care by limiting treatment to time-limited, symptom-focused services. They note that this environment has resulted in dramatic changes in the way psychological services are delivered to people in need. The most frequently cited changes include the remarkable shift of treatment decision-making power from the behavioral health care provider to policymakers. In addition, practitioners have experienced a reduction in income, which has likely impacted quality of care since less-well-trained (non-doctoral-level) therapists have taken on more responsibility and offer short-term therapeutic approaches instead of needed long-term therapy. These growing pains are likely to continue as our society attempts to come to terms with the cost of health care and the need to ensure that it is available. One thing is certain: The nature of the mental health professions is changing, and there is a growing discontent with health maintenance organizations in society today (Mechanic, 2004).

summary

- Many mental health professionals are trying not only to cure mental health problems but also to prevent them, or at least to reduce their effects.
- Prevention can be viewed as focusing on three levels: (1) universal interventions, which attempt to reduce the long-term consequences of having had a disorder; (2) selective interventions, which are aimed at reducing the possibility of disorder and fostering positive mental health efforts in subpopulations that are considered at special risk; and (3) indicated interventions, which attempt to reduce the impact or duration of a problem that has already occurred.
- Over the past 40 years, with the advent of many new psychotropic medications and changing treatment philosophies, there has been a major effort to discharge psychiatric patients into the community.
- There has been a great deal of controversy over deinstitutionalization and the failure to provide adequate follow-up of these patients in the community.
- Recent work in the area of aftercare for former mental patients has provided clearer guidelines for discharge and therapeutic follow-up.
- Being "mentally ill" is not considered sufficient grounds for involuntary commitment. There must be, in addition, evidence that the individual either is dangerous to himself or herself or represents a danger to society.
- It is not an easy matter, even for trained professionals, to determine in advance whether a person is dangerous and likely to harm others. Nevertheless, professionals must sometimes make such judgments.

- Recent court rulings have found professionals liable when patients they were treating caused harm to others. The Tarasoff decision held that a therapist has a duty to protect potential victims if his or her patient has threatened to kill them.
- The insanity plea for capital crimes is an important issue in forensic psychology. Many mental health and legal professionals, journalists, and laypersons have questioned the present use of the "not guilty by reason of insanity" (NGRI) defense.
- The original legal precedent, the M'Naghten Rule, held that at the time of committing the act, the accused must have been laboring under such a defect of reason as not to know the nature and quality of the act or not to know that what he or she was doing was wrong.
- More recent broadenings of the insanity plea, as in the American Law Institute standard, leave open the possibility of valid NGRI pleas by persons who are not diagnosed to be psychotic.
- The successful use of the NGRI defense by John Hinckley, attempted assassin of President Reagan, set off a storm of protest. One effective and widely adopted reform was to shift the burden of proof (of insanity) to the defense.
- Federal agencies such as the National Institute of Mental Health (NIMH), the National Institute on Drug Abuse (NIDA), and the National Institute on Alcohol Abuse and Alcoholism (NIAAA) are devoted to promoting research, training, and service in the mental health community.
- Several professional and mental health organizations, many corporations, and a number of volunteer associations are also active in programs to promote mental health.
- International organizations such as the World Health Organization (WHO) and the World Federation for Mental Health have contributed to mental health programs worldwide.

Key Terms

deinstitutionalization (P. 650)
forensic psychology (forensic psychiatry) (P. 652)
guilty but mentally ill (GBMI) (P. 661)
health maintenance organization (HMO) (P. 666)
indicated interventions (P. 642)
insanity defense (P. 657)
managed health care (P. 666)
milieu therapy (P. 648)
NGRI plea (P. 657)
selective interventions (P. 642)
social-learning programs (P. 649)
Tarasoff decision (P. 656)
universal interventions (P. 642)

Glossary

Many of the key terms listed in the glossary appear in boldface when first introduced in the text discussion. A number of other terms commonly encountered in this or other psychology texts are also included; you are encouraged to make use of this glossary both as a general reference tool and as a study aid for the course in abnormal psychology.

ABAB design. An experimental design, often involving a single subject, wherein a baseline period (A) is followed by a treatment (B). To confirm that the treatment resulted in a change in behavior, the treatment is then withdrawn (A) and reinstated (B).

Abnormal behavior. Maladaptive behavior detrimental to an individual and/or a group.

Abnormal psychology. Field of psychology concerned with the study, assessment, treatment, and prevention of abnormal behavior.

Abstinence. Refraining altogether from the use of a particular addictive substance or from a particular behavior.

Accommodation. Cognitive process of changing existing cognitive frameworks to make possible the incorporation of discrepant information.

Acting out. Ego-defense mechanism of engaging in antisocial or excessive behavior without regard to negative consequences as a way of dealing with emotional stress.

Activation (arousal). Energy mobilization required for an organism to pursue its goals and meet its needs.

Actuarial approach. Application of probability statistics to human behavior.

Actuarial procedures. Methods whereby data about subjects are analyzed by objective procedures or formulas rather than by human judgments.

Acute. Term used to describe a disorder of sudden onset, usually with intense symptoms.

Acute stress disorder. Disorder that occurs within 4 weeks after a traumatic event and lasts for a minimum of 2 days and a maximum of 4 weeks.

Addictive behavior. Behavior based on the pathological need for a substance or activity; it may involve the abuse of substances, such as nicotine, alcohol, or cocaine, or gambling.

Adjustment. Outcome of a person's efforts to deal with stress and meet his or her needs.

Adjustment disorder. A disorder in which a person's response to a common stressor is maladaptive and occurs within 3 months of the stressor.

Adjustment disorder with depressed mood. Moderately severe mood disorder that is similar to dysthymic disorder but has an identifiable, though not severe, psychosocial stressor occurring within 3 months before the onset of depression, and does not exceed 6 months in duration.

Adoption method. Comparison of biological and adoptive relatives with and without a given disorder to assess genetic versus environmental influences.

Adrenal cortex. Outer layer of the adrenal glands; secretes the adrenal steroids and other hormones.

Adrenal glands. Endocrine glands located at the upper end of the kidneys; consist of inner adrenal medulla and outer adrenal cortex.

Adrenaline. Hormone secreted by the adrenal medulla during strong emotion; causes such bodily changes as an increase in blood sugar and a rise in blood pressure. Also called *epinephrine.*

Advocacy. Approach to meeting mental health needs in which advocates, often an interested group of volunteers, attempt to help children or others receive services that they need but often are unable to obtain for themselves.

Advocacy programs. Programs aimed at helping people in underserved populations to obtain aid with which to improve their situations.

Affect. Emotion or feeling.

Aftercare. Follow-up therapy after release from a hospital.

Aggression. Behavior aimed at hurting or destroying someone or something.

Agitation. Marked restlessness and psychomotor excitement.

Agoraphobia. Fear of being in places or situations where a panic attack may occur, and from which escape would be physically difficult or psychologically embarrassing, or in which immediate help would be unavailable in the event that some mishap occurred.

AIDS-dementia complex (ADC). Generalized loss of cognitive functioning that eventually affects a substantial proportion of AIDS patients.

AIDS-related complex (ARC). Pre-AIDS manifestation of HIV infection involving minor infections, various nonspecific symptoms (such as unexplained fever), blood cell count abnormalities, and sometimes cognitive difficulties.

AIDS-related dementia. A progressive brain deterioration that is caused by infection from the HIV virus.

Alarm and mobilization. Selye's first stage of responding to trauma, alerting and mobilizing a person's resources for coping with the trauma.

Alcoholism. Dependence on alcohol that seriously interferes with life adjustment.

Alexithymia. Term used to denote a personality pattern in which an individual is unable to communicate distress in other than somatic language.

Alienation. Lack or loss of relationships with others.

Allostatic load. The biological cost of adapting to stress. Under conditions of high stress our allostatic load is high. When we are calm, our allostatic load is low and our bodies are not experiencing any of the physiological consequences of stress (e.g., racing heart, high levels of cortisol, etc.).

Alter identities. In a person with dissociative identity disorder, personalities other than the host personality.

Alzheimer's disease. See **Dementia of the Alzheimer's type.**

Amnesia. Total or partial loss of memory.

Amnestic syndrome. Striking deficit in the ability to recall ongoing events more than a few minutes after they have taken place, or the inability to recall the recent past.

Amniocentesis. Technique that involves drawing fluid from the amniotic sac of a pregnant woman so that sloughed-off fetal cells can be examined for chromosomal irregularities, including that of Down syndrome.

Amphetamine. Drug that produces a psychologically stimulating and energizing effect.

Amygdala. A collection of nuclei that are almond-shaped which lie in front of the hippocampus in the limbic system of the brain. It is involved in regulation of emotion and is critically involved in the emotion of fear.

Amyloid plaques. Found in the brains of people with Alzheimer's disease, these deposits of aluminum silicate and abnormal protein (beta amyloid) are believed to cause loss of neurons.

Analogue studies. Studies in which a researcher attempts to emulate the conditions hypothesized as leading to abnormality.

Anal stage. In psychoanalytic theory, stage of psychosexual development in which behavior is presumably focused on anal pleasure and activities.

Androgen. Hormone associated with the development and maintenance of male characteristics.

Anesthesia. Loss or impairment of sensitivity (usually to touch but often applied to sensitivity to pain and other senses as well).

Anhedonia. Inability to experience pleasure or joy.

Anorexia nervosa. Intense fear of gaining weight or becoming "fat," coupled with refusal to maintain adequate nutrition and with severe loss of body weight.

Anoxia. Lack of sufficient oxygen.

Antabuse. Drug used in the treatment of alcoholism.

Anterograde amnesia. Loss of memory for events that occur *following* trauma or shock.

Antianxiety drugs. Drugs that are used primarily for alleviating anxiety.

Antibody. Circulating blood substance coded for detection of and binding to a particular antigen.

Antidepressant drugs. Drugs that are used primarily to elevate mood and relieve depression. Often also used in the treatment of certain anxiety disorders, bulimia, and certain personality disorders.

Antigen. A foreign body (e.g., a virus or bacteria) or an internal threat (e.g., a tumor) that can trigger an immune response.

Antipsychotic drugs (neuroleptics). Medications that alleviate or diminish the intensity of psychotic symptoms such as hallucinations or delusions.

Antipsychotic medication. Drugs used to treat psychotic disorders (like schizophrenia); also called antipsychotics or neuroleptics.

Antisocial personality disorder (ASPD). Disorder characterized by continual violation of and disregard for the rights of others through deceitful, aggressive or antisocial behavior, typically without remorse or loyalty to anyone.

Anxiety. A general feeling of apprehension about possible danger.

Anxiety disorder. An unrealistic, irrational fear or anxiety of disabling intensity. DSM-IV-TR recognizes seven types of anxiety disorders: phobic disorders (specific or social), panic disorder (with or without agoraphobia), generalized anxiety disorder, obsessive-compulsive disorder, and post-traumatic stress disorder.

Anxiety sensitivity. A personality trait involving a high level of belief that certain bodily symptoms may have harmful consequences.

Aphasia. Loss or impairment of ability to communicate and understand language symbols—involving loss of power of expression by speech, writing, or signs, or loss of ability to comprehend written or spoken language—resulting from brain injury or disease.

APOE-4 allele. Variant of a gene on chromosome 19 that significantly enhances risk for late-onset Alzheimer's disease.

Apraxia. Loss of ability to perform purposeful movements.

Arousal. See **Activation.**

Arteriosclerosis. Degenerative thickening and hardening of the walls of the arteries, occurring usually in old age.

Asberger's disorder. Severe and sustained childhood impairment in social relationships and peculiar behaviors, but without the language delays seen in autism.

Assertive community treatment (ACT). Persistent and vigorous follow-up with and aid to patients in managing life problems.

Assertiveness therapy. Behavior therapy technique for helping people become more self-assertive in interpersonal relationships.

Assimilation. Cognitive process whereby new experiences tend to be worked into existing cognitive frameworks even if the new information has to be reinterpreted or distorted to make it fit.

Association studies. Genetic research strategy comparing frequency of certain genetic markers known to be located on particular chromosomes in people with and without a particular disorder.

Asylums. Historically, these were institutions meant solely for the care of the mentally ill.

At risk. Condition of being considered vulnerable to the development of certain abnormal behaviors.

Atrophy. Wasting away or shrinking of a bodily organ, particularly muscle tissue.

Attachment theory. Contemporary psychodynamic theory emphasizing the importance of early experience with attachment relationships in laying the foundation for later functioning throughout life.

Attention-deficit/hyperactivity disorder (ADHD). Disorder of childhood characterized by difficulties that interfere with task-oriented behavior, such as impulsivity, excessive motor activity, and difficulties in sustaining attention. Also known as hyperactivity.

Attribution. Process of assigning causes to things that happen.

Autism. Pervasive developmental disorder beginning in infancy and involving a wide range of problematic behaviors, including deficits in language, perception, and motor development; defective reality testing; and social withdrawal.

Autogynephilia. Paraphilia characterized by sexual arousal in men at the thought or fantasy of being a woman.

Autonomic nervous system. Section of the nervous system that regulates the internal organs; consists primarily of ganglia connected with the brain stem and spinal cord; may be subdivided into the sympathetic and parasympathetic systems.

Autonomic reactivity. Individual's characteristic degree of emotional reactivity to stress.

Autonomy. Self-reliance; the sense of being an independent person.

Autosome. Any chromosome other than those determining sex.

Aversion therapy. Form of behavior therapy in which punishment or aversive stimulation is used to eliminate undesired responses.

Aversive stimulus. Stimulus that elicits psychic or physical pain.

Avoidance conditioning. Form of conditioning in which a subject learns to behave in a certain way in order to avoid an unpleasant stimulus.

Avoidant personality disorder. Extreme social inhibition and introversion, hypersensitivity to criticism and rejection, limited social relationships, and low self-esteem.

Axes (of DSM). Evaluation of an individual according to five foci, the first three assessing the person's present clinical status or condition and the other two assessing broader aspects of the person's situation.

Barbiturates. Synthetic drugs that act as depressants to calm the individual and induce sleep.

Baseline. The initial level of responses emitted by an organism.

B-cell. A type of white blood cell, produced in the bone marrow, that is (along with T-cells) very important in the immune system. B-cells produce specific antibodies in response to specific antigens.

Behavioral contracting. Positive reinforcement technique using a contract, often between family members, to identify the behaviors to be changed and to specify privileges and responsibilities.

Behavioral medicine. Broad interdisciplinary approach to the treatment of physical disorders thought to have psychological factors as major aspects in their causation and/or maintenance.

Behavioral perspective. A theoretical viewpoint organized around the theme that learning is central in determining human behavior.

Behavioral sciences. Various interrelated disciplines, including psychology, sociology, and anthropology, that focus on human behavior.

Behavior genetics. Field that studies the heritability of mental disorders and other aspects of psychological functioning such as personality and intelligence.

Behaviorism. School of psychology that formerly restricted itself primarily to the study of overt behavior.

Behavior modification. Change of specific behaviors by learning techniques.

Behavior therapy. Use of therapeutic procedures based primarily on principles of classical and operant conditioning.

Benign. Of a mild, self-limiting nature; not malignant.

Binge-eating disorder (BED). Distinct from nonpurging bulimia nervosa, whereby binging is not accompanied by inappropriate compensatory behavior to limit weight gain.

Biofeedback. Treatment technique in which a person is taught to influence his or her own physiological processes that were formerly thought to be involuntary.

Biogenic amines. Chemicals that serve as neurotransmitters or modulators.

Biological clocks. Regular biological cycles of sleep, activity, hormone activity, and metabolism characteristic of each species.

Biological viewpoint. Approach to mental disorders emphasizing biological causation.

Biopsychosocial viewpoint. A viewpoint that acknowledges the interacting roles of biological, psychosocial, and sociocultural factors in the origins of psychopathology.

Bipolar I disorder. A form of bipolar disorder in which the person experiences both manic (or mixed) episodes and major depressive episodes.

Bipolar II disorder. A form of bipolar disorder in which the person experiences both hypomanic episodes and major depressive episodes.

Bipolar disorders. Mood disorders in which a person experiences both manic and depressive episodes.

Bipolar disorder with a seasonal pattern. Bipolar disorder with recurrences in particular seasons of the year.

Bisexuality. Sexual attraction to both females and males.

Blocking. Involuntary inhibition of recall, ideation, or communication (including sudden stoppage of speech).

Blood–injection–injury phobia. Persistent and disproportionate fear of the sight of blood or injury, or the possibility of having an injection. Afflicted persons are likely to experience a drop in blood pressure and sometimes faint.

Body dysmorphic disorder (BDD). Obsession with some perceived flaw or flaws in one's appearance.

Body mass index. An estimation of total body fat calculated as body weight in kilograms divided by height (in meters) squared.

Borderline personality disorder (BPD). Impulsivity and instability in interpersonal relationships, self-image, and moods.

Brain pathology. Diseased or disordered condition of the brain.

Brain waves. Minute oscillations of electrical potential given off by neurons in the cerebral cortex and measured by the electroencephalograph (EEG).

Brief Psychiatric Rating Scale (BPRS). Objective method of rating clinical symptoms that provides scores on 18 variables (e.g., somatic concern, anxiety, withdrawal, hostility, and bizarre thinking).

Brief psychotherapy. Short-term therapy, usually eight to ten sessions, focused on restoring an individual's functioning and offering emotional support.

Brief psychotic disorder. Brief episodes (lasting a month or less) of otherwise uncomplicated delusional thinking.

Bulimia nervosa. Frequent occurrence of binge-eating episodes, accompanied by a sense of loss of control of overeating and recurrent inappropriate behavior such as purging or excessive exercise to prevent weight gain.

Caffeine. A drug of dependence found in many commonly available drinks and foods.

Candidate genes. Genes that are of specific interest to researchers because they are thought to be involved in processes that are known to be aberrant in that disorder (e.g., serotonin transporter genes in depression, or dopamine receptor genes in schizophrenia).

Cardiovascular. Pertaining to the heart and blood vessels.

Case study. An in-depth examination of an individual or family that draws from a number of data sources, including interviews and psychological testing.

Castrating. Refers to any source of injury to the genitals, or, more broadly, to a threat to the masculinity of an individual.

Castration anxiety. As postulated by Freud, the anxiety a young boy experiences when he desires his mother while at the same time fearing that his father may harm him by cutting off his penis; this anxiety forces the boy to repress his sexual desire for his mother and his hostility toward his father.

Catalepsy. Condition seen in some schizophrenic psychoses, and some psychotic mood disorders, in which body postures are waxy and semirigid, with the limbs maintaining for prolonged periods any position in which they are placed.

Catatonic schizophrenia. See **Schizophrenia, catatonic type.**

Catecholamines. Class of monoamine compounds sharing a similar chemical structure. Known to be neurotransmitters—norepinephrine and dopamine.

Categorical approach. Approach to classifying abnormal behavior that assumes that (1) all human behavior can be sharply divided into the categories normal and abnormal, and (2) there exist discrete, nonoverlapping classes or types of abnormal behavior, often referred to as mental illnesses or diseases.

Catharsis. Discharge of emotional tension associated with something, such as by talking about past traumas.

CAT scan. See **Computerized axial tomography**.

Causal pattern. In a cause-and-effect relationship, a situation in which more than one causal factor is involved.

Causation. Relationship in which the preceding variable causes the other(s).

Central nervous system (CNS). The brain and spinal cord.

Cerebral arteriosclerosis. Hardening of the arteries in the brain.

Cerebral cortex. Surface layers of the cerebrum.

Cerebral hemorrhage. Bleeding into brain tissue from a ruptured blood vessel.

Cerebral laceration. Tearing of brain tissue associated with severe head injury.

Cerebral syphilis. Syphilitic infection of the brain.

Cerebral thrombosis. Formation of a clot or thrombus in the vascular system of the brain.

Cerebrovascular accident (CVA). Blockage or rupture of a large blood vessel in the brain leading to both focal and generalized impairment of brain function. Also called *stroke.*

Cerebrum. Main part of the brain; divided into left and right hemispheres.

Chemotherapy. Use of drugs to treat disorders.

Child abuse. Infliction of physical or psychological damage on a child by parents or other adults.

Child advocacy. Movement concerned with protecting rights and ensuring well-being of children.

Chorea. Pathological condition characterized by jerky, irregular, involuntary movements. See also **Huntington's disease.**

Chromosomal anomalies. Inherited defects or vulnerabilities caused by irregularities in chromosomes.

Chromosomes. Chain-like structures within cell nucleus that contain genes.

Chronic. Term used to describe a long-standing or frequently recurring disorder, often with progressing seriousness.

Chronic fatigue syndrome. A debilitating illness characterized by disabling fatigue that lasts 6 months or more and occurs with other symptoms.

Chronic major depressive disorder. A disorder in which a major depressive episode does not remit over a two year period.

Chronic schizophrenic. A schizophrenic patient whose condition has deteriorated and/or remained stable over a long period of time (years).

Circadian rhythms. The 24-hour rhythmic fluctuations in animals' sleep activity and in the metabolic processes of plants and animals. See also **Biological clocks.**

Civil commitment. Procedure whereby a person certified as mentally disordered can be hospitalized, either voluntarily or against his or her will.

Classical conditioning. A basic form of learning in which a neutral stimulus is paired repeatedly with an unconditioned stimulus (US) that naturally elicits an unconditioned response (UR). After repeated pairings, the neutral stimulus becomes a conditioned stimulus (CS) that elicits a conditioned response (CR).

Claustrophobia. Irrational fear of small enclosed places.

Client-centered (person-centered) therapy. Nondirective approach to psychotherapy, developed chiefly by Carl Rogers, that focuses on the natural power of the organism to heal itself; a key goal is to help clients accept and be themselves.

Clinical picture. Diagnostic picture formed by observation of patient's behavior or by all available assessment data.

Clinical problem checklist. Computer-administered psychological assessment procedure for surveying the range of psychological problems a patient is experiencing.

Clinical psychologist. Mental health professional with Ph.D. degree or Psy.D. degree in clinical psychology and clinical experience in assessment and psychotherapy.

Clinical psychology. Field of psychology concerned with the understanding, assessment, treatment, and prevention of maladaptive behavior.

Cocaine. Stimulating and pain-reducing psychoactive drug.

Cognition. Act, process, or product of knowing or perceiving.

Cognitive-behavioral perspective. A theory of abnormal behavior that focuses on how thoughts and information processing can become distorted and lead to maladaptive emotions and behavior.

Cognitive/cognitive-behavioral therapy. Therapy based on altering dysfunctional thoughts and cognitive distortions.

Cognitive dissonance. Condition of tension existing when several of one's beliefs and attitudes are inconsistent with each other.

Cognitive map. Network of assumptions that form a person's "frame of reference" for interpreting and coping with his or her world.

Cognitive processes (cognition). Mental processes, including perception, memory, and reasoning, by which one acquires knowledge, solves problems, and makes plans.

Cognitive remediation. Training efforts designed to help patients improve their neurocognitive (e.g., memory, vigilance) skills. The hope is that this will also help improve patients' overall levels of functioning.

Cognitive restructuring. Cognitive-behavioral therapy techniques that aim to change a person's negative or unrealistic thoughts and attributions.

Collective unconscious. Term used by Carl Jung to refer to that portion of the unconscious that he considered common to all humanity, based on wisdom acquired by our predecessors.

Coma. Profound stupor with unconsciousness.

Community mental health. Application of psychosocial and sociocultural principles to the improvement of given environments.

Community psychology. Use of community resources in dealing with maladaptive behavior; tends to be more concerned with community intervention than with personal or individual change.

Comorbidity. Occurrence of two or more identified disorders in the same psychologically disordered individual.

Compulsions. Overt repetitive behaviors (such as hand washing or checking) or more covert mental acts (such as counting, praying, saying certain words silently, or ordering) that a person feels driven to perform in response to an obsession.

Compulsive gambling. See **Pathological gambling.**

Computer assessment. Use of computers to obtain or interpret assessment data.

Computerized axial tomography (CAT scan). Radiological technique used to locate and assess the extent of organic damage to the brain without surgery.

Concordance rate. The percentage of twins sharing a disorder or trait.

Conduct disorders. Childhood and adolescent disorders that can appear by age 9 and are marked by persistent acts of aggressive or antisocial behavior that may or may not be against the law.

Confabulation. Filling in of memory gaps with false and often irrelevant details.

Confidentiality. Commitment on part of a professional person to keep information he or she obtains from a client confidential.

Conflict. Simultaneous arousal of opposing impulses, desires, or motives.

Congenital. Existing at birth or before birth, but not necessarily hereditary.

Congenital defect. Genetic defect or environmental condition occurring before birth and causing a child to develop a physical or psychological anomaly.

Conjoint family therapy. Direct involvement of the family in improving communication, interaction, and relationships among family members and fostering a family system that better meets the needs of each member.

Consciousness. Awareness of inner and/or outer environment.

Constitution. Relatively constant biological makeup of an individual, resulting from the interaction of heredity and environment.

Consultation. Community intervention approach that aims at helping individuals at risk for disorder by working indirectly through caretaker institutions (e.g., police and teachers).

Contingency. Relationship, usually causal, between two events in which one is usually followed by the other.

Continuous reinforcement. Reward or reinforcement given regularly after each correct response.

Contributory cause. A condition that increases the probability of developing a disorder but that is neither necessary nor sufficient for it to occur.

Control (comparison) group. Group of subjects who do not exhibit the disorder being studied but who are comparable in all other respects to the criterion group. Also, a comparison group of subjects who do not receive a condition or treatment the effects of which are being studied.

Conversion disorder. Pattern in which symptoms of some physical malfunction or loss of control appear without any underlying organic pathology; originally called *hysteria.*

Convulsion. Pathological, involuntary muscle contractions.

Coping strategies. Efforts to deal with stress.

Coprolalia. Verbal tic in which an individual utters obscenities aloud.

Coronary heart disease (CHD). Potentially lethal blockage of the arteries supplying blood to the heart muscle, or myocardium.

Corpus callosum. Nerve fibers that connect the two hemispheres of the brain.

Correlation. The tendency of two variables to covary. With positive correlation, as one variable goes up, so does the other; with negative correlation, one variable goes up as the other goes down.

Corticovisceral control mechanisms. Brain mechanisms that regulate autonomic and other bodily functions.

Cortisol. Human stress hormone released by the cortex of the adrenal glands.

Counseling psychology. Field of psychology that focuses on helping people with problems pertaining to education, marriage, or occupation.

Counter-transference. Psychodynamic concept that the therapist brings personal issues, based on his or her own vulnerabilities and conflicts, to the therapeutic relationship.

Couples counseling. Treatment for disordered interpersonal relationships involving sessions with both members of the relationship present and emphasizing mutual need gratification, social role expectations, communication patterns, and similar interpersonal factors.

Covert. Concealed, disguised, not directly observable.

Covert sensitization. Behavioral treatment method for extinguishing undesirable behavior by associating noxious mental images with that behavior.

Criminal responsibility. Legal question of whether a person should be permitted to use insanity as a defense after having committed a crime.

Crisis. Stressful situation that approaches or exceeds the adaptive capacities of an individual or group.

Crisis intervention. Provision of psychological help to an individual or group in times of severe and special stress.

Criterion group. Group of subjects who exhibit the disorder under study.

Cross-gender identification. The desire to be, or the insistence that one is, of the opposite sex.

Cultural-familial retardation. Mental retardation as a result of an inferior quality of interaction with the cultural environment and other people, with no evidence of brain pathology.

Cultural relativism. Position that one cannot apply universal standards of normality or abnormality to all societies.

Cyclothymic disorder. Mild mood disorder characterized by cyclical periods of hypomanic and depressive symptoms.

Cytokines. Small protein molecules that enable the brain and the immune system to communicate with each other. Cytokines can augment or enhance an immune system response or cause immunosuppression, depending on the specific cytokine that is released.

Day hospital. Community-based mental hospital where patients are treated during the day, returning to their homes at night.

Debriefing sessions. Psychological debriefing is a brief, directive treatment method that is used in helping people who have undergone a traumatic situation. This approach is often a good first step for helping people process their reaction to traumatic events. Debriefing sessions are usually conducted with small groups of trauma victims shortly after the incident for the purpose of helping them dealing with the emotional residuals of the event.

Defense mechanism. See **Ego-defense mechanism.**

Defense-oriented response. Behavior directed primarily at protecting the self from hurt and disorganization rather than at resolving the situation.

Deinstitutionalization. Movement to close mental hospitals and treat people with severe mental disorder in the community.

Delinquency. Antisocial or illegal behavior by a minor.

Delirium. State of mental confusion characterized by relatively rapid onset of widespread disorganization of the higher mental processes, caused by a generalized disturbance in brain metabolism. May include impaired perception, memory, and thinking and abnormal psychomotor activity.

Delirium tremens. Acute delirium associated with withdrawal from alcohol after prolonged heavy consumption; characterized by intense anxiety, tremors, fever and sweating, and hallucinations.

Delusions. False beliefs about reality maintained in spite of strong evidence to the contrary.

Delusional disorder. Nuturing, giving voice to, and sometimes taking action on beliefs that are considered completely false by others; formerly called *paranoia.*

Delusional system. Internally coherent, systematized pattern of delusions.

Delusion of grandeur. False belief that one is a noted or famous person, such as Napoleon or the Virgin Mary.

Delusion of persecution. False belief that one is being mistreated or interfered with by one's enemies.

Dementia. Progressive deterioration of brain functioning occurring after the completion of brain maturation in adolescence. Characterized by deficits in memory, abstract thinking, acquisition of new knowledge or skills, visuospatial comprehension, motor control, problem solving, and judgment.

Dementia of the Alzheimer's type (DAT). Disorder associated with a progressive dementia syndrome ultimately terminating in death. Onset may be in middle or old age, and symptoms include memory loss, withdrawal, confusion, and impaired judgment.

Dementia praecox. Older term for schizophrenia.

Demonology. Viewpoint emphasizing supernatural causation of mental disorder, especially "possession" by evil spirits or forces.

Denial of reality. Ego-defense mechanism that protects the self from an unpleasant reality by refusing to perceive or face it.

Dependence. Tendency to rely overly on others.

Dependent personality disorder. Extreme dependence on others, particularly the need to be taken care of, leading to clinging and submissive behavior.

Dependent variable. In an experiment, the factor that is observed to change with changes in the manipulated (independent) variables.

Depersonalization. Loss of sense of personal identity, often with a feeling of being something or someone else.

Depersonalization disorder. Dissociative disorder in which there is a loss of the sense of self.

Depression. Emotional state characterized by extraordinary sadness and dejection.

Depressive personality disorder. Provisional category of personality disorder in DSM-IV-TR that involves a pattern of depressive cognitions and behaviors that begins by early adulthood and is pervasive in nature.

Depressogenic schemas. Dysfunctional beliefs that are rigid, extreme, and counterproductive and that are thought to leave one susceptible to depression when experiencing stress.

Derealization. Experience in which the external world is perceived as distorted and lacking a stable and palpable existence.

Desensitization. Therapeutic process by means of which reactions to traumatic experiences are reduced in intensity by repeatedly exposing a person to them in mild form, either in reality or in fantasy.

Desire phase. First phase of the human sexual response, consisting of fantasies about sexual activity or a sense of desire to have sexual activity.

Deterrence. Premise that punishment for criminal offenses will deter that criminal and others from future criminal acts.

Detox center. Center or facility for receiving and detoxifying alcohol- or drug-intoxicated individuals.

Detoxification. Treatment directed toward ridding the body of alcohol or other drugs.

Developmental disorder. Problem that is rooted in deviations in the development process itself, thus disrupting the acquisition of skills and adaptive behavior and often interfering with the transition to well-functioning adulthood.

Developmental psychopathology. Field of psychology that focuses on determining what is abnormal at any point in the developmental process by comparing and contrasting it with normal and expected changes that occur.

Developmental systems approach. Acknowledgment that genetic activity influences neural activity, which in turn influences behavior, which in turn influences the environment, and that these influences are bidirectional.

Deviant behavior. Behavior that deviates markedly from the average or norm.

Diagnosis. Determination of the nature and extent of a specific disorder.

Diathesis. Predisposition or vulnerability to developing a given disorder.

Diathesis–stress model. View of abnormal behavior as the result of stress operating on an individual who has a biological, psychosocial, or sociocultural predisposition to developing a specific disorder.

Dimensional approach. Approach to classifying abnormal behavior that assumes that a person's typical behavior is the product of differing strengths or intensities of behavior along several definable dimensions, such as mood, emotional stability, aggressiveness, gender, identity, anxiousness, interpersonal trust, clarity of thinking and communication, social introversion, and so on.

Direct observation. Method of collecting research data that involves directly observing behavior in a given situation.

Directive therapy. Type of therapeutic approach in which a therapist supplies direct answers to problems and takes much of the responsibility for the progress of therapy.

Disaster syndrome. Reactions of many victims of major catastrophes during the traumatic experience and the initial and long-lasting reactions after it.

Discordant marriage. Family in which one or both of the parents are not gaining satisfaction from the relationship and one spouse may express frustration and disillusionment in hostile ways, such as nagging, belittling, and purposely doing things to annoy the other.

Discrimination. Ability to interpret and respond differently to two or more similar stimuli.

Disintegration. Loss of organization or integration in any organized system.

Disorganization. Severely impaired integration.

Disorganized schizophrenia. See **Schizophrenia, disorganized type.**

Disorientation. Mental confusion with respect to time, place, or person.

Displacement. Ego-defense mechanism that discharges pent-up feelings, often of hostility, on objects less dangerous than those arousing the feelings.

Disrupted family. Family that is incomplete as a result of death, divorce, separation, or some other circumstance.

Dissociation. The human mind's capacity to mediate complex mental activity in channels split off from or independent of conscious awareness.

Dissociative amnesia. Psychogenically caused memory failure.

Dissociative disorders. Conditions involving a disruption in an individual's sense of personal identity.

Dissociative fugue. A dissociative amnesic state in which the person is not only amnesic for some or all aspects of his or her past but also departs from home surroundings.

Dissociative identity disorder. Condition in which a person manifests at least two or more distinct identities or personality states that alternate in some way in taking control of behavior. Formerly called *multiple personality disorder.*

Distress. Negative stress, associated with pain, anxiety, or sorrow.

Disturbed family. Family in which one or both parents behave in grossly eccentric or abnormal ways and may keep the home in constant emotional turmoil.

Dizygotic (fraternal) twins. Twins that develop from two separate eggs.

DNA. Deoxyribonucleic acid, principal component of genes.

Dominant gene. A gene whose hereditary characteristics prevail, in offspring, over any recessive gene that affects the same trait.

Dopamine. Neurotransmitter from the catecholamine family that is initially synthesized from tyrosine, an amino acid common in the diet. Dopamine is produced from l-dopa by the enzyme dopamine decarboxylase.

Dopamine hypothesis. Hypothesis that schizophrenia is the result of an excess of dopamine activity at certain synaptic sites.

Double bind. Situation in which a person will be disapproved for performing a given act and equally disapproved if he or she does not perform it.

Double-bind communication. Type of faulty communication in which one person (e.g., a parent) presents to another (e.g., a child) ideas, feelings, and demands that are mutually incompatible.

Double blind study. Often used in studies examining drug treatment effects, a condition where neither the subject nor the experimenter has knowledge about what specific experimental condition (or drug) the subject is receiving.

Double depression. This condition is diagnosed when a person with dysthymia has a superimposed major depressive episode.

Down syndrome. Form of moderate to severe mental retardation associated with chromosomal abnormality and typically accompanied by characteristic physical features.

Dream analysis. Method involving the recording, description, and interpretation of a patient's dreams.

Drive. Internal conditions directing an organism toward a specific goal, often involving biological rather than psychological motives.

Drug abuse. Use of a drug to the extent that it interferes with health and/or occupational or social adjustment.

Drug addiction (dependence). Physiological and/or psychological dependence on a drug.

Drug therapy. See **Chemotherapy** and **Pharmacotherapy.**

DSM-IV-TR. Current diagnostic manual of the American Psychiatric Association.

Dwarfism. Condition of arrested growth and very short stature.

Dyad. Two-person group.

Dynamic formulation. Integrated evaluation of an individual's personality traits, behavior patterns, environmental demands, and the like to describe the person's current situation and to hypothesize about what is driving the person to behave in maladaptive ways.

Dysfunction. Impairment or disturbance in the functioning of an organ or in behavior.

Dysfunctional beliefs. Negative beliefs that are rigid, extreme, and counterproductive.

Dyslexia. Impairment of the ability to read.

Dyspareunia. Painful coitus in a male or a female.

Dysrhythmia. Abnormal brain wave pattern.

Dysthymic disorder. Moderately severe mood disorder characterized by a persistently depressed mood most of the day for more days than not for at least 2 years. Additional symptoms may include poor appetite, sleep disturbance, lack of energy, low self-esteem, difficulty concentrating, and feelings of hopelessness.

Early-onset Alzheimer's disease. Form of Alzheimer's disease that appears in people who are younger than approximately 60 years of age. Thought to be caused by rare genetic mutations.

Eating Disorder NOS. A diagnostic category reserved for disorders of eating that do not meet criteria for any other specific eating disorder.

Eating disorders. Disorders of food ingestion, regurgitation, or attitude that affect health and well-being, such as anorexia, bulimia, or binge-eating.

Echolalia. Parrot-like repetition of a few words or phrases.

Ecstasy. A human manufactured drug that is taken orally and acts as both a stimulant and a hallucinogen. The drug effects include feelings of mental stimulation, emotional warmth, enhanced sensory perception, and increased physical energy. The adverse health effects of the drug can be extreme and include symptoms of nausea, chills, sweating, teeth clenching, muscle cramping, and blurred vision.

Edema. Swelling of tissues.

EEG. See **Electroencephalogram.**

Efficacy. In a situation where treatment is tested under ideal conditions (usually in a controlled clinical trial) efficacy is how well a given treatment improves clinical outcome compared to a control or comparison condition.

Ego. In psychoanalytic theory, the rational part of the personality that mediates between the demands of the id, constraints of the superego, and the realities of the external world.

Egocentric. Preoccupied with one's own concerns and relatively insensitive to the concerns of others.

Ego-defense mechanisms. Psychic mechanisms that discharge or soothe anxiety rather than coping directly with an anxiety-provoking situation; usually unconscious and reality-distorting. Also called *defense mechanisms.*

Ego psychology. Psychodynamic theory emphasizing the importance of the ego—the "executive branch of the personality"—in organizing normal personality development.

Electra complex. Excessive emotional attachment (love) of a daughter for her father; the female counterpart of the Oedipus complex.

Electroconvulsive therapy (ECT). Use of electricity to produce convulsions and unconsciousness; a treatment used primarily to alleviate depressive and manic episodes. Also known as *electroshock therapy.*

Electroencephalogram (EEG). Graphical record of the brain's electrical activity, obtained by placing electrodes on the scalp and measuring the brain wave impulses from various brain areas.

Embolism. Lodgment of a blood clot in a blood vessel too small to permit its passage.

Emotion. Strong feeling accompanied by physiological changes.

Emotional disturbance. Psychological disorder.

Empathy. Ability to understand, and to some extent share, the state of mind of another person.

Encephalitis. Inflammation of the brain.

Encopresis. Disorder in children who have not learned appropriate toileting for bowel movements after age 4.

Encounter group. Small group designed to provide an intensive interpersonal experience focusing on feelings and group interactions; used in therapy or to promote personal growth.

Endocrine glands. Ductless glands that secrete hormones directly into the lymph or bloodstream.

Endogenous factors. Factors originating within an organism that affect behavior.

Endophenotypes. Discrete, measurable traits that are thought to be linked to specific genes that might be important in schizophrenia.

Endorphins. Opiates produced in the brain and throughout the body that function like neurotransmitters to dampen pain sensations. They also play a role in the body's building up tolerance to certain drugs.

Enuresis. Bed wetting; involuntary discharge of urine after the age of expected continence (age 5).

Environmental psychology. Field of psychology focusing on the effects of an environmental setting on an individual's feelings and behavior.

Epidemiological studies. Attempts to establish the pattern of occurrence of certain (mental) disorders in different times, places, and groups of people.

Epidemiology. Study of the distribution of diseases, disorders, or health-related behaviors in a given population. Mental health epidemiology is the study of the distribution of mental disorders.

Epilepsy. Group of disorders varying from momentary lapses of consciousness to generalized convulsions.

Epinephrine. Hormone secreted by the adrenal medulla; also called *adrenaline.*

Episodic. Term used to describe a disorder that tends to abate and recur.

Equilibrium. Steady state; balance.

Erotic. Pertaining to sexual stimulation and gratification.

Escape learning. Instrumental response in which a subject learns to terminate or escape an aversive stimulus.

Essential hypertension. High blood pressure with no specific known physical cause.

Estrogens. Female hormones produced by the ovaries.

Ethnic group. Group of people who are treated as distinctive in terms of culture and group patterns.

Etiology. Causal pattern of abnormal behavior.

Euphoria. Exaggerated feeling of well-being and contentment.

Eustress. Positive stress.

Exacerbate. Intensify.

Excitement phase. Second phase of the human sexual response, in which there is generally a subjective sense of sexual pleasure and physiological changes, including penile erection in the male and vaginal lubrication and enlargement in the female.

Exhaustion. Selye's third and final stage of responding to continued excessive trauma, in which a person's adaptive resources are depleted and the coping patterns developed during the resistance stage fail.

Exhibitionism. Intentional exposure of one's genitals to others under inappropriate circumstances and without their consent.

Existential anxiety. Anxiety concerning one's ability to find a satisfying and fulfilling way of life.

Existentialism. View of human beings that emphasizes an individual's responsibility for becoming the kind of person he or she should be.

Existential neurosis. Disorder characterized by feelings of alienation, meaninglessness, and apathy.

Existential psychotherapy. Type of therapy that is based on existential thought and focuses on individual uniqueness and authenticity on the part of both client and therapist.

Exogenous. Originating from or due to external causes.

Exorcism. Religiously inspired treatment procedure designed to drive out evil spirits or forces from a "possessed" person.

Experimental group. Group of subjects used to assess the effects of independent variables.

Experimental method. Rigorous scientific procedure by which hypotheses are tested.

Experimental research. Research that involves the manipulation of a given factor or variable with everything else held constant.

Expressed emotion (EE). Type of negative communication involving excessive criticism and emotional overinvolvement directed at a patient by family members.

Extinction. Gradual disappearance of a conditioned response when it is no longer reinforced.

Extraversion. Direction of interest toward the outer world of people and things rather than toward concepts and intellectual concerns.

Factitious disorder. Feigning of symptoms to maintain the personal benefits that a sick role may provide, including the attention and concern of medical personnel and/or family members.

Factitious disorder by proxy. A variant of factitious disorder in which a person induces medical or psychological symptoms in another person who is under his or her care (usually a child).

Factor analysis. Statistical technique used for reducing a large array of intercorrelated measures to the minimum number of factors necessary to account for the observed overlap or associations among them.

Fading. Technique whereby a stimulus causing some reaction is gradually replaced by a previously neutral stimulus, such that the latter acquires the property of producing the reaction in question.

False memories. "Memories" of events that did not actually happen, often produced by highly leading and suggestive techniques.

Familial. Pertaining to characteristics that tend to run in families and have a higher incidence in certain families than in the general population.

Family aggregation. The clustering of certain traits, behaviors, or disorders within a given family. Family aggregation may arise because of genetic or environmental similarities.

Family history (or pedigree) method. Behavior genetic research strategy that examines the incidence of disorder in relatives of an index case to determine whether incidence increases in proportion to the degree of the hereditary relationship.

Family systems approach. Form of interpersonal therapy focusing on the within-family behavior of a particular family member and the assumption that it is largely influenced by the behaviors and communication patterns of other family members.

Family therapy. A treatment approach that includes all family members, not just the identified patient.

Fantasy. Daydream; also, an ego-defense mechanism by means of which a person escapes from the world of reality and gratifies his or her desires in fantasy achievements.

Fear. A basic emotion that involves the activation of the "fight-or-flight" response of the sympathetic nervous system.

Feedback. Explicit information pertaining to internal physiological processes or to the social consequences of one's overt behavior.

Female orgasmic disorder. Persistent or recurrent delay in, or absence of, orgasm after a normal sexual excitement phase.

Female sexual arousal disorder. Sexual dysfunction involving an absence of sexual arousal and unresponsiveness to most or all forms of erotic stimulation.

Fetal alcohol syndrome. Observed pattern in infants of alcoholic mothers, in which there is a characteristic facial or limb irregularity, low body weight, and behavioral abnormality.

Fetishism. Sexual variant in which sexual interest centers on some inanimate object or nonsexual part of the body.

Fetus. Embryo after the sixth week following conception.

Fixation. Ego-defense mechanism involving an unreasonable or exaggerated attachment to some person or arresting of emotional development on a childhood or adolescent level.

Fixed-interval schedule. Schedule of reinforcement based on a fixed period of time after the previous reinforced response.

Fixed-ratio schedule. Schedule of reinforcement based on reinforcement after a fixed number of nonreinforced responses.

Flashback. Involuntary recurrence of perceptual distortions or hallucinations weeks or months after taking a drug; in post-traumatic stress disorder, a dissociative state in which the person briefly relives the traumatic experience.

Flooding. Anxiety-eliciting therapeutic technique involving having a client repeatedly experience the actual internal or external stimuli that had been identifed as producing anxiety reactions.

Folie à deux. See **Shared psychotic disorder.**

Follow-up study. Research procedure in which people are studied over a period of time or are recontacted at a later time after an initial study.

Forensic psychology and psychiatry. Branches of psychology and psychiatry dealing with legal problems related to mental disorders and the legal rights and protection of mental patients and members of society at large.

Fraternal twins. Dizygotic twins; fertilized by separate germ cells, thus not having the same genetic inheritance. May be of the same or of opposite sexes.

Free association. Method for probing the unconscious by having patients talk freely about themselves, their feelings, and their motives.

Free-floating anxiety. Anxiety not referable to any specific situation or cause.

Frontal lobe. Portion of the brain active in reasoning and other higher thought processes.

Frustration. Thwarting of a need or desire.

Frustration tolerance. Ability to withstand frustration without becoming impaired psychologically.

Fugue. Dissociative disorder that entails loss of memory for personal information accompanied by actual physical flight from one's present life situation to a new environment or a less threatening former one.

Functional mental disorders. Outdated term used to refer to disorders that were not considered to have an organic basis.

Functional MRI (fMRI). Internal scanning technique that measures changes in local oxygenation (blood flow) to specific areas of brain tissue that in turn depend on neuronal activity in those specific regions, allowing the mapping of psychological activity such as sensations, images, and thoughts.

Functional psychoses. Severe mental disorders for which a specific organic pathology has not been demonstrated.

Gambling. Wagering on games or events in which chance largely determines the outcome.

Gender dysphoria. Persistent discomfort about one's biological sex or the sense that the gender role of that sex is inappropriate.

Gender identity. Individual's identification as being male or female.

Gender identity disorder. Identification with members of the opposite sex, persistent discomfort with one's biological sexual identity, and strong desire to change to the opposite sex.

General adaptation syndrome. A model that helps explain the course of a person's biological deterioration under excessive stress; consists of three stages (alarm reaction, the stage of resistance, and exhaustion).

Generalization. Tendency of a response that has been conditioned to one stimulus to be elicited by other, similar stimuli.

Generalized anxiety disorder (GAD). Chronic excessive worry about a number of events or activities, with no specific threat present, accompanied by at least three of the following symptoms: restlessness, fatigue, difficulty concentrating, irritability, muscle tension, sleep disturbance.

General paresis. Mental disorder associated with syphilis of the brain.

Genes. Long molecules of DNA that are present at various locations on chromosomes and that are responsible for the transmission of hereditary traits.

Genetic code. Means by which DNA controls the sequence and structure of proteins manufactured within each cell and also makes exact duplicates of itself.

Genetic counseling. Counseling prospective parents concerning the probability of their having impaired offspring as a result of genetic defects.

Genetic inheritance. Potential for development and behavior determined at conception by egg and sperm cells.

Genetics. Science of the inheritance of traits and the mechanisms of this inheritance.

Genitalia. Organs of reproduction, especially the external organs.

Genital stage. In psychoanalytic theory, the final stage of psychosexual development, involving a shift from autoeroticism to heterosexual interest.

Genotype. A person's total genetic endowment.

Genotype-environment correlation. Genotypic vulnerability that can shape a child's environmental experiences.

Genotype-environment interaction. Differential sensitivity or susceptibility to their environments by people who have different genotypes.

Geriatrics. Science of the diseases and treatment of the aged.

Germ cells. Reproductive cells (female ovum and male sperm) that unite to produce a new individual.

Gerontology. Science dealing with the study of old age.

Gestalt psychology. School of psychology that emphasizes patterns rather than elements or connections, taking the view that the whole is more than the sum of its parts.

Gestalt therapy. Type of psychotherapy emphasizing wholeness of the person and integration of thought, feeling, and action.

Glucocorticoids. Adrenocortical hormones involved in sugar metabolism but also having widespread effects on injury-repair mechanisms and resistance to disease; they include cortisol.

Glutamate. An excitatory neurotransmitter that is widespread throughout the brain.

Gonads. Sex glands.

Good premorbid schizophrenia. See **Reactive schizophrenia.**

Grehlin. Grehlin is a hormone that is produced by the stomach. It stimulates appetite.

Group therapy. Psychotherapy administered to several people at the same time.

Guilt. Feelings of culpability arising from behavior or desires contrary to one's ethical principles. Involves both self-devaluation and apprehension growing out of fears of punishment.

Guilty but mentally ill (GBMI). Plea and possible verdict that would provide an alternative to pleading not guilty by reason of insanity (NGRI) and would allow for placing a defendant in a treatment facility rather than in a prison.

Habituation. Automatic process whereby a person's response to the same stimulus lessens with repeated presentations.

Half-life. Time taken for the level of an active drug or medication in the body to be reduced to 50% of the original level.

Halfway house. Facility that provides aftercare following institutionalization, seeking to ease a person's adjustment to the community.

Hallucinations. False perceptions such as things seen or heard that are not real or present.

Hallucinogens. Drugs known to induce hallucinations; often referred to as psychedelics.

Hallucinosis. Persistent hallucinations in the presence of known or suspected organic brain pathology.

Hashish. Strongest drug derived from the hemp plant; a relative of marijuana that is usually smoked.

Health maintenance organization (HMO). Health plan that provides services to employers and individuals for a fixed prepaid fee.

Health psychology. Subspecialty within behavioral medicine that deals with psychology's contributions to diagnosis, treatment, and prevention of psychological components of physical dysfunction.

Hebephrenic schizophrenia. See **Schizophrenia, disorganized type.**

Hemiplegia. Paralysis of one lateral half of the body.

Heredity. Genetic transmission of characteristics from parents to their children.

Hermaphroditism. Anatomical sexual abnormality in which a person has some sex organs of both sexes.

Heroin. Powerful psychoactive drug, chemically derived from morphine, that relieves pain but is even more intense and addictive than morphine.

Heterosexuality. Sexual interest in a member of the opposite sex.

Hierarchy of needs. Concept, articulated by Maslow, that needs arrange themselves in a hierarchy in terms of importance, from the most basic biological needs to those psychological needs concerned with self-actualization.

High-risk. Term applied to persons showing great vulnerability to physical or mental disorders.

Histrionic personality disorder. Excessive attention seeking and emotional instability, and self-dramatization.

Homeostasis. Tendency of organisms to maintain conditions that make possible a constant level of physiological functioning.

Homosexuality. Sexual preference for a member of one's own sex.

Hormones. Chemical messengers secreted by endocrine glands that regulate development of and activity in various parts of the body.

Host identity (personality). The identity in dissociative identity disorder which is most frequently encountered and carries the person's real name. This is not usually the original identity and it may or may not be the best adjusted identity.

Hostility. Emotional reaction or drive toward the destruction or damage of an object interpreted as a source of frustration or threat.

HPA axis. The hypothalamic–pituitary–adrenal (HPA) axis is a hormonal feedback system that becomes activated by stress and results in the production of cortisol.

Humanistic-experiential therapies. Psychotherapies emphasizing personal growth and self-direction.

Humanistic perspective. Approach to understanding abnormal behavior that views basic human nature as "good" and emphasizes people's inherent capacity for growth and self-actualization.

Huntington's disease. Incurable disease of hereditary origin, which is manifested in jerking, twitching movements and mental deterioration. Formerly called *Huntington's chorea.*

Hydrocephalus. Relatively rare condition in which the accumulation of an abnormal amount of cerebrospinal fluid within the cranium causes damage to the brain tissues and enlargement of the skull.

Hydrotherapy. Use of hot or cold baths, ice packs, etc., in treatment.

Hyper-. Prefix meaning "increased" or "excessive."

Hyperactivity. See **Attention-deficit/hyperactivity disorder.**

Hyperobesity. Extreme overweight; 100 pounds or more above ideal body weight.

Hypertension. High blood pressure, defined as a persisting systolic blood pressure of 140 or more and a diastolic blood pressure of 90 or greater.

Hyperthymic temperament. Personality type involving lifelong hypomanic adjustment.

Hyperventilation. Rapid breathing associated with intense anxiety.

Hypesthesia. Partial loss of sensitivity.

Hypnosis. Trance-like mental state induced in a cooperative subject by suggestion.

Hypnotherapy. Use of hypnosis in psychotherapy.

Hypo-. Prefix meaning "decreased" or "insufficient."

Hypoactive sexual desire disorder. Sexual dysfunction in which either a man or a woman shows little or no sexual drive or interest.

Hypochondriacal delusions. Delusions concerning various horrible disease conditions, such as the belief that one's brain is turning to dust.

Hypochondriasis. Preoccupation, based on misinterpretations of bodily symptoms, with the fear that one has a serious disease.

Hypomania. Mild form of mania.

Hypomanic episode. A condition lasting at least 4 days in which a person experiences abnormally elevated, expansive or irritable mood. At least 3 out of 7 other designated symptoms similar to those in a manic episode must also be present but to a lesser degree than in mania.

Hypothalamic-pituitary-adrenal-cortical axis (HPA axis). Brain-endocrine system involved in responding to stress in which the hypothalamus and pituitary send messages to the adrenal gland which releases a stress hormone that feeds back on the hypothalamus.

Hypothalamus. Key structure at the base of the brain; important in emotion and motivation.

Hypothesis. Statement or proposition, usually based on observation, that is tested in an experiment; may be refuted or supported by experimental results but can never be conclusively proved.

Hypoxia. Insufficient delivery of oxygen to an organ, especially the brain.

Hysteria. Older term used for conversion disorders; involves the appearance of symptoms of organic illness in the absence of any related organic pathology.

Id. In psychoanalytic theory, the reservoir of instinctual drives and the first structure to appear in infancy.

Identical twins. Monozygotic twins; developed from a single fertilized egg.

Identification. Ego-defense mechanism in which a person identifies himself or herself with some person or institution, usually of an illustrious nature.

Ideology. System of beliefs.

Illusion. Misinterpretation of sensory data; false perception.

Imaginal exposure. Form of exposure therapy that does not involve a real stimulus. Instead, the patient is asked to imagine the feared stimulus or situation.

Immaturity. Pattern of childhood maladaptive behaviors suggesting lack of adaptive skills.

Immune reaction. Complex defensive reaction initiated on detection of an antigen invading the body.

Immune system. The body's principal means of defending itself against the intrusion of foreign substances.

Immunosuppression. A down-regulation or dampening of the immune system. This can be short or long term and can be triggered by injury, stress, illness, and other factors.

Implicit memory. Memory that occurs below the conscious level.

Implicit perception. Perception that occurs below the conscious level.

Incentive. External inducement to behave in a certain way.

Incest. Culturally prohibited sexual relations between family members, such as a brother and sister or a parent and child.

Incidence. Occurrence (onset) rate of a given disorder in a given population.

Independent variable. Factor whose effects are being examined and which is manipulated in some way while other variables are held constant.

Index case. In a genetic study, an individual who evidences the trait in which the investigator is interested. Same as *proband.*

Indicated intervention. Early detection and prompt treatment of maladaptive behavior in a person's family and community setting.

Infantile autism. See **Autism.**

Inhibition. Restraint of impulse or desire.

Innate. Inborn.

Inpatient. Hospitalized patient.

Insanity. Legal term for mental disorder, implying lack of responsibility for one's acts and inability to manage one's affairs.

Insanity defense (NGRI). The "not guilty by reason of insanity" plea used as a legal defense in criminal trials.

Insight. Clinically, a person's understanding of his or her illness or of the motivations underlying a behavior pattern; in general psychology, the sudden grasp or understanding of meaningful relationships in a situation.

Insight therapy. Type of psychotherapy that focuses on helping a client achieve greater self-understanding with respect to his or her motives, values, coping patterns, and so on.

Insomnia. Difficulty in sleeping.

Instinct. Inborn tendency to perform particular behavior patterns under certain conditions in the absence of learning.

Instrumental (operant) conditioning. Reinforcement of a subject for making a correct response that leads either to receipt of something rewarding or to escape from something unpleasant.

Insulin coma therapy. Physiological treatment for schizophrenia that is rarely used today; it involved administration of increasing amounts of insulin until the patient went into shock.

Integrative behavioral couple therapy. Modification of traditional behavioral couple therapy that has a focus on acceptance of the partner rather than being solely change-oriented.

Intellectualization. Ego-defense mechanism by which a person achieves some measure of insulation from emotional hurt by cutting off or distorting the emotional charge that normally accompanies hurtful situations.

Intelligence. The ability to learn, reason, and adapt.

Intelligence quotient (IQ). Measurement of "intelligence" expressed as a number or position on a scale.

Intelligence test. Test used in establishing a subject's level of intellectual capability.

Intensive care management (ICM). Use of multidisciplinary teams with limited caseloads to ensure that discharged patients don't get overlooked and "lost" in the system.

Interdisciplinary (multidisciplinary) approach. Integration of various scientific disciplines in understanding, assessing, treating, and preventing mental disorders.

Intermittent reinforcement. Reinforcement given intermittently rather than after every response.

International Classification of Diseases (ICD-10). System of classification of disorders published by the World Health Organization.

Interoceptive fears. Fear of various internal bodily sensations.

Interpersonal accommodation. Process through which two people develop patterns of communication and interaction that enable them to attain common goals, meet mutual needs, and build a satisfying relationship.

Interpersonal perspective. Approach to understanding abnormal behavior that views much of psychopathology as rooted in the unfortunate tendencies we develop while dealing with our interpersonal environments; it thus focuses on our relationships, past and present, with other people.

Intrapsychic conflict. Inner mental struggles resulting from the interplay of the id, ego, and superego when the three subsystems are striving for different goals.

Introjection. Internal process by which a child incorporates symbolically, through images and memories, important people in his or her life.

Intromission. Insertion of the penis into the vagina or anus.

Introspection. Observing (and often reporting on) one's inner experiences.

Introversion. Direction of interest toward one's inner world of experience and toward concepts rather than external events and objects or people.

***In vivo* exposure.** Exposure that takes place in a real-life situation as opposed to the therapeutic or laboratory setting.

Ionizing radiation. Form of radiation; major cause of gene mutations.

Isolation. Ego-defense mechanism by means of which contradictory attitudes or feelings that normally accompany particular attitudes are kept apart, thus preventing conflict or hurt.

Juvenile delinquency. Legal term used to refer to illegal acts committed by minors.

Juvenile paresis. General paresis in children, usually of congenital origin.

Klinefelter's syndrome. Type of mental retardation associated with sex chromosome anomaly.

La belle indifférence. The unconcern about serious illness or disability that is sometimes characteristic of conversion disorder.

Labeling. Assigning a person to a particular diagnostic category, such as schizophrenia.

Lability. Instability, particularly with regard to affect.

Late-onset Alzheimer's disease. The occurrence of Alzheimer's disease in the more elderly. One gene thought to be involved in this form of Alzheimer's disease is the APOE gene.

Latency stage. In psychoanalytic theory, a stage of psychosexual development during which sexual motivations recede in importance and a child is preoccupied with developing skills and other activities.

Latent. Inactive or dormant.

Latent content. In psychoanalytic theory, repressed actual motives of a dream that are seeking expression but are so painful or unacceptable that they are disguised by the manifest content of the dream.

Law of effect. Principle that responses that have rewarding consequences are strengthened and those that have aversive consequences are weakened or eliminated.

Learned helplessness theory. A theory that animals and people exposed to uncontrollable aversive events learn that they have no control over these events and this causes them to behave in a passive and helpless manner when later exposed to potentially controllable events. Later extended to become a theory of depression.

Learning. Modification of behavior as a consequence of experience.

Learning disabled (LD). Term used to describe children who exhibit deficits in academic skills.

Leptin. Leptin is a hormone produced by fat cells that acts to reduce food intake.

Lesbian. Female homosexual person.

Lesion. Anatomically localized area of tissue pathology in an organ or a part of the brain.

Lethality scale. Criteria used to assess the likelihood of a person's committing suicide.

Libido. In psychoanalytic theory, a term used to describe the instinctual drives of the id; the basic constructive energy of life, primarily sexual in nature.

Life crisis. Stress situation that approaches or exceeds a person's capacity to adjust.

Life history method. Technique of psychological observation in which the development of particular forms of behavior is traced by means of records of a subject's past or present behavior.

Lifestyle. General pattern of assumptions, motives, cognitive styles, and coping techniques that characterize a person's behavior and give it consistency.

Lifetime prevalence. The proportion of living persons in a population who have ever had a disorder up to the time of the epidemiological assessment.

Linkage analysis. Genetic research strategy in which occurrence of a disorder in an extended family is compared with that of a genetic marker for a physical characteristic or biological process that is known to be located on a particular chromosome.

Lobotomy. See **Prefrontal lobotomy.**

Locomotor ataxia. Muscular incoordination usually resulting from syphilitic damage to the spinal cord pathways.

LSD (lysergic acid diethylamide). The most potent of the hallucinogens. It is odorless, colorless, and tasteless, and an amount smaller than a grain of salt can produce intoxication.

Lunacy. Old term roughly synonymous with *insanity.*

Lycanthropy. Delusion of being a wolf.

Lymphocyte. Generalized term for white blood cells involved in immune protection.

Macrocephaly. Rare type of mental retardation characterized by an increase in the size and weight of the brain, enlargement of the skull, visual impairment, convulsions, and other neurological symptoms resulting from abnormal growth of glial cells that form the supporting structure for brain tissue.

Macrophage. Literally, "big eater." A white blood cell that destroys antigens by engulfment.

Madness. Nontechnical term for severe mental disorder.

Magnetic resonance imaging (MRI). Internal scanning technique involving measurement of variations in magnetic fields that allows visualization of the anatomical features of internal organs, including the central nervous system and particularly the brain.

Mainstreaming. Placement of mentally retarded children in regular school classrooms for all or part of the day.

Major depressive disorder. Moderate to severe mood disorder in which a person experiences only major depressive episodes, but no hypomanic, manic or mixed episodes. *Single episode* if only one; *recurrent episode* if more than one.

Major depressive episode. A mental condition in which a person must be markedly depressed for most of every day for most days for at least 2 weeks. In addition, a total of at least 5 out of 9 designated symptoms must also be present during the same time period.

Major depressive episode with atypical features. A type of major depressive episode which includes a pattern of symptoms characterized by marked mood reactivity, as well as at least 2 out of 4 other designated symptoms.

Major depressive episode with melancholic features. A type of major depressive episode which includes marked symptoms of loss of interest or pleasure in almost all activities, plus at least 3 of 6 other designated symptoms.

Major tranquilizers. Antipsychotic drugs, such as the phenothiazines.

Maladaptive (abnormal) behavior. Behavior that is detrimental to the well-being of an individual and/or group.

Maladjustment. More or less enduring failure of adjustment; lack of harmony with self or environment.

Male erectile disorder. Sexual dysfunction in which a male is unable to achieve or maintain an erection sufficient for successful sexual gratification; formerly known as impotence.

Male orgasmic disorder. Retarded ejaculation or the inability to ejaculate following a normal sexual excitement phase.

Malingering. Consciously faking illness or symptoms of disability to achieve some specific nonmedical objective.

Managed health care. System of corporations that secures services from hospitals, physicians, and other providers for treating a designated population, with the goal of holding down health care cost.

Mania. Emotional state characterized by intense and unrealistic feelings of excitement and euphoria.

Manic-depressive psychoses. Older term denoting a group of psychotic disorders characterized by prolonged periods of excitement and overactivity (mania) or by periods of depression and underactivity (depression) or by alternation of the two. Now known as *bipolar disorders.*

Manic episode. A condition in which a person shows markedly elevated, euphoric, or expansive mood, often interrupted by occasional outbursts of intense irritability or even violence that lasts for at least 1 week. In addition at least 3 out of 7 other designated symptoms must also occur.

Manualized therapy. Standardization of psychosocial treatments (as in development of a manual) to fit the randomized clinical paradigm.

Manifest content. In psychoanalytic theory, the apparent (or obvious) meaning of a dream; masks the latent (or hidden) content.

Marijuana. Mild hallucinogenic drug derived from the hemp plant, often smoked in cigarettes called reefers or joints.

Marital therapy. See **Couples counseling.**

Masked disorder. "Masking" of underlying depression or other emotional disturbance by delinquent behavior or other patterns seemingly unrelated to the basic disturbance.

Masochism. Sexual stimulation and gratification from experiencing pain or degradation in relating to a lover.

Mass madness. Historically, widespread occurrence of group behavior disorders that were apparently cases of hysteria.

Masturbation. Self-stimulation of genitals for sexual gratification.

Maternal deprivation. Lack of adequate care and stimulation by the mother or mother surrogate.

Maturation. Process of development and body change resulting from heredity rather than learning.

Medical model. View of disordered behavior as a symptom of a disease process, rather than as a pattern representing faulty learning or cognition.

Melancholic type. Subtype of major depression that involves loss of interest or pleasure in nearly all activities, and other symptoms, including early morning awakenings, worse depression in the morning, psychomotor agitation or retardation, loss of appetite or weight, excessive guilt, and sadness qualitatively different from that usually experienced after a loss.

Meninges. Membranes that envelop the brain and spinal cord.

Mental age (MA). Scale unit indicating level of intelligence in relation to chronological age.

Mental disorder. Entire range of abnormal behavior patterns.

Mental hygiene movement. Movement that advocated a method of treatment focused almost exclusively on the physical well-being of hospitalized mental patients.

Mental illness. Serious mental disorder.

Mental retardation. Significantly subaverage general intellectual functioning that is accompanied by significant limitations in adaptive functioning and is obvious during the developmental period.

Mescaline. Hallucinogenic drug derived from the peyote cactus.

Mesmerism. Theories of "animal magnetism" (hypnosis) formulated by Anton Mesmer.

Mesocorticolimbic dopamine pathway (MCLP). Center of psychoactive drug activation in the brain. This area is involved in the release of dopamine and in mediating the rewarding properties of drugs.

Meta-analysis. A statistical method used to combine the results of a number of similar research studies. The data from each study are transformed into a common metric called the *effect size*. This allows the data from the various studies to be combined and then analyzed. You can think of a meta-analysis as being like research that you are already familiar with, except that the "participants" are individual research studies, not individual people.

Methadone. Synthetic narcotic related to heroin; used in treatment of heroin addiction because it satisfies the craving for heroin without producing serious psychological impairment.

Microcephaly. Type of mental retardation resulting from impaired development of the brain and a consequent failure of the cranium to attain normal size.

Migraine. Intensely painful, recurrent headache that typically involves only one side of the head and may be accompanied by nausea and other disturbances.

Mild (disorder). Disorder low in severity.

Milieu. Immediate environment, physical or social or both.

Milieu therapy. General approach to treatment for hospitalized patients that focuses on making the hospital environment itself a therapeutic community.

Minnesota Multiphasic Personality Inventory (MMPI/MMPI-2). Widely used and empirically validated personality scales.

Minor tranquilizers. Antianxiety drugs, such as the benzodiazepines.

Mixed episode. A condition in which a person is characterized by symptoms of both full-blown manic and major depressive episodes for at least 1 week, whether the symptoms are intermixed or alternate rapidly every few days.

Model. Analogy that helps a scientist order findings and see important relationships among them.

Modeling. Learning of skills by imitating another person who performs the behavior to be acquired.

Moderate (disorder). Disorder intermediate in severity.

Monozygotic twins. Identical twins, developed from one fertilized egg.

Mood-congruent disorders. Delusions or hallucinations that are consistent with a person's mood.

Mood disorders. Disturbances of mood that are intense and persistent enough to be clearly maladaptive.

Mood-incongruent. Delusional thinking that is inconsistent with a person's predominant mood.

Moral management. Wide-ranging method of treatment that focuses on a patient's social, individual, and occupational needs.

Moral therapy. Therapy based on provision of kindness, understanding, and favorable environment; prevalent during early part of the nineteenth century.

Morbid. Unhealthful, pathological.

Morphine. Addictive drug derived from opium that can serve as a powerful sedative and pain reliver.

Motivation. Often used as a synonym for *drive* or *activation;* implies that an organism's actions are partly determined in direction and strength by its own inner nature.

Motive. Internal condition that directs action toward some goal; the term is generally used to include both the drive and the goal to which it is directed.

Multi-infarct dementia. See **Vascular dementia.**

Multiple personality disorder. See **Dissociative identity disorder.**

Mutant gene. Gene that has undergone some change in structure.

Mutation. Change in the composition of a gene, usually causing harmful or abnormal characteristics to appear in the offspring.

Mutism. Refusal or inability to speak.

Nancy School, The. Group of physicians in nineteenth-century Europe who accepted the view that hysteria was a sort of self-hypnosis.

Narcissism. Self-love.

Narcissistic personality disorder. Exaggerated sense of self-importance, preoccupation with being admired, and lack of empathy for the feelings of others.

Narcolepsy. Disorder characterized by transient, compulsive states of sleepiness.

Narcotic drugs. Drugs, such as morphine, that lead to physiological dependence and increased tolerance.

Natural killer cell. White blood cell that destroys antigens by chemical dissolution.

Necessary cause. A condition that must exist for a disorder to occur.

Need. Biological or psychological condition whose gratification is necessary for the maintenance of homeostasis or for self-actualization.

Negative affect. The experience of an emotional state characterized by negative emotions. Such negative emotions might include anger, anxiety, irritability, and sadness.

Negative automatic thoughts. Thoughts that are just below the surface of awareness and that involve unpleasant pessimistic predictions.

Negative cognitive triad. Negative thoughts about the self, the world, and the future.

Negative correlation. A relationship between two variables such that a high score on one variable is associated with a low score on another variable.

Negative symptoms. Symptoms that reflect an absence or deficit in normal functions (e.g., blunted affect, social withdrawal).

Negative-symptom schizophrenia. Schizophrenia characterized by an absence or deficit of normal behaviors, such as emotional expressiveness, communicative speech, and reactivity to environmental events.

Negativism. Form of aggressive withdrawal that involves refusing to cooperate or obey commands, or doing the exact opposite of what has been requested.

Neologisms. New words; a feature of language disturbance in schizophrenia.

Neonate. Newborn infant.

Neoplasm. Tumor.

Nervous breakdown. General term used to refer broadly to lowered integration and inability to deal adequately with one's life situation.

Neurofibrillary tangles. Twisted and weblike nerve filaments that characterize the brains of patients with Alzheimer's disease.

Neurological examination. Examination to determine the presence and extent of organic damage to the nervous system.

Neurology. Field concerned with the study of the brain and nervous system and disorders thereof.

Neuron. Individual nerve cell.

Neurophysiology. Branch of biology concerned with the functioning of nervous tissue and the nervous system.

Neuropsychological assessment. Use of psychological tests that measure a person's cognitive, perceptual, and motor performance to obtain clues to the extent and locus of brain damage.

Neuropsychological disorders. Disorders that occur when there has been significant organic impairment or damage to a normal adolescent or adult brain.

Neuropsychological mood syndromes. Serious mood disturbances apparently caused by disruptions in the normal physiology of cerebral function.

Neuropsychological personality syndromes. Changes in an individual's general personality style or traits following brain injury of one or another type.

Neurosis. Term historically used to characterize maladaptive behavior resulting from intrapsychic conflict and marked by prominent use of defense mechanisms.

Neurosurgery. Surgery of the nervous system, especially the brain.

Neurosyphilis. Syphilis affecting the central nervous system.

Neurotic behavior. Anxiety-driven, exaggerated use of avoidance behaviors and defense mechanisms.

Neuroticism. Personality pattern including the tendency to experience anxiety, anger, hostility, depression, self-consciousness, impulsiveness, and vulnerability.

Neurotransmitters. Chemical substances that are released into a synapse by the presynaptic neuron and which transmit nerve impulses from one neuron to another.

NGRI plea. The Not Guilty by Reason of Insanity Plea, or NGRI, is a legal defense a defendant might use to claim that he or she was not guilty of a crime because of insanity.

Nicotine. Addictive akaloid that is the chief active ingredient in tobacco and a drug of dependence.

Night hospital. Mental hospital in which an individual may receive treatment during all or part of the night while carrying on his or her usual occupation in the daytime.

Nihilistic delusion. Fixed belief that everything is unreal.

Nomenclature. A formalized naming system.

Nondirective therapy. Approach to psychotherapy in which a therapist refrains from giving advice or directing the therapy. See also **Client-centered psychotherapy.**

Norepinephrine. Catecholamine neurotransmitter substance.

Norm. Standard based on the measurement of a large group of people; used for comparing the scores of an individual with those of others in a defined group.

Normal. Conforming to the usual or norm; healthy.

Normal distribution. Tendency for most members of a population to cluster around a central point or average with respect to a given trait, with the rest spreading out to the two extremes in decreasing frequency.

NREM sleep. Stages of sleep not characterized by the rapid eye movements that accompany dreaming.

Obesity. The condition of having elevated fat masses in the body. Obesity is defined as having a body mass index (BMI) of 30 or higher.

Objective tests. Structured tests, such as questionnaires, self-inventories, or rating scales, used in psychological assessment.

Object–relations theory. In psychoanalytic theory, this viewpoint focuses on an infant or young child's interactions with "objects" (that is, real or imagined people), as well as how they make symbolic representations of important people in their lives.

Observational learning. Learning through observation alone without directly experiencing an unconditioned stimulus (for classical conditioning) or a reinforcement (for instrumental conditioning).

Observational method. Systematic technique by which observers are trained to watch and record behavior without bias.

Observational research. In contrast to experimental research (which involves manipulating variables in some way and seeing what happens), in observational research the researcher simply observes or assesses the characteristics of different groups, learning about them without manipulating the conditions to which they are exposed. Sometimes called *correlational research,* although the former is the preferred term.

Obsessions. Persistent and recurrent intrusive thoughts, images, or impulses that a person experiences as disturbing and inappropriate but has difficulty suppressing.

Obsessive-compulsive disorder (OCD). Anxiety disorder characterized by the persistent intrusion of unwanted and intrusive thoughts or distressing images; these are usually accompanied by compulsive behaviors designed to neutralize the obsessive thoughts or images or to prevent some dreaded event or situation.

Obsessive-compulsive personality disorder (OCPD). Perfectionism and excessive concern with maintaining order, control, and adherence to rules.

Occipital lobe. Portion of cerebrum concerned chiefly with visual function.

Oedipus complex. Desire for sexual relations with a parent of opposite sex; specifically, the desire of a boy for his mother, with his father a hated rival.

Olfactory hallucinations. Hallucinations involving the sense of smell.

One-year prevalence. The number of cases of a specific condition or disorder that are documented in a population within a one-year period.

Operant (or instrumental) conditioning. Form of learning in which if a particular response is reinforced, it becomes more likely to be repeated on similar occasions.

Operational definition. Definition of a concept on the basis of a set of operations that can be observed and measured.

Opium. Narcotic drug that leads to physiological dependence and the development of tolerance; derivatives are morphine, heroin, and codeine.

Oppositional defiant disorder. Childhood disorder that appears by age 6 and is characterized by persistent acts of aggressive or antisocial behavior that may or may not be against the law.

Oral stage. First stage of psychosexual development in Freudian theory, in which mouth or oral activities are the primary source of pleasure.

Organic mental disorders. Outdated term used to refer to disorders that resulted from some identifiable brain pathology.

Organic viewpoint. Concept that all mental disorders have an organic basis. See also **Biological viewpoint.**

Orgasm. Third phase of the human sexual response, during which there is a release of sexual tension and a peaking of sexual pleasure.

Outcome research. Studies of effectiveness of treatment.

Outpatient. Ambulatory client who visits a hospital or clinic for examination and treatment, as distinct from a hospitalized client.

Ovaries. Female gonads.

Overanxious disorder. Disorder of childhood characterized by excessive worry and persistent fears unrelated to any specific event; often includes somatic and sleeping problems.

Overcompensation. Type of ego-defense mechanism in which an undesirable trait is covered up by exaggerating a desirable trait.

Overloading. Subjecting an organism to excessive stress, e.g., forcing the organism to handle or "process" an excessive amount of information.

Overprotection. Shielding a child to the extent that he or she becomes too dependent on the parent.

Overt behavior. Activities that can be observed by an outsider.

Ovum. Female gamete or germ cell.

Pain disorder. Experience of pain of sufficient duration and severity to cause significant life disruption in the absence of medical pathology that would explain it.

Panic. A basic emotion that involves activation of the "fight-or-flight" response of the sympathetic nervous system and that is often characterized by an overwhelming sense of fear or terror.

Panic disorder. Occurrence of repeated unexpected panic attacks, often accompanied by intense anxiety about having another one.

Panic provocation agent. A variety of biological challenge procedures that provoke panic attacks at higher rates in people with panic disorder than in people without panic disorder.

Paradigm. Model or pattern; in research, a basic design specifying concepts considered legitimate and procedures to be used in the collection and interpretation of data.

Paranoia. Symptoms of delusions and impaired contact with reality without the bizarreness, fragmentation, and severe personality disorganization characteristic of schizophrenia.

Paranoid personality disorder. Pervasive suspiciousness and distrust of others.

Paranoid schizophrenia. See **Schizophrenia, paranoid type.**

Paraphilias. Persistent sexual behavior patterns in which unusual objects, rituals, or situations are required for full sexual satisfaction.

Paraprofessional. Person who has been trained in mental health services, but not at the professional level.

Parasympathetic nervous system. Division of the autonomic nervous system that controls most of the basic metabolic functions essential for life.

Paresis. See **General paresis.**

Paresthesia. Exceptional sensations, such as tingling.

Parkinson's disease. Progressive disease characterized by a mask-like, expressionless face and various neurological symptoms, such as tremors.

Passive-aggressive personality disorder. Provisional category of personality disorder in DSM-IV-TR characterized by a pattern of passive resistance to demands in social or work situations, which may take such forms as simple resistance to performing routine tasks, being sullen or argumentative, or alternating between defiance and submission.

Pathogenic. Pertaining to conditions that lead to pathology.

Pathological gambling. Progressive disorder characterized by loss of control over gambling, preoccupation with gambling and obtaining money for gambling, and irrational gambling behavior in spite of adverse consequences.

Pathology. Abnormal physical or mental condition.

PCP. Phencyclidine; developed as a tranquilizer but not marketed because of its unpredictability. Known on the street as "angel dust," this drug produces stupor and, at times, prolonged coma or psychosis.

Pedigree (family history) method. Observation of samples of relatives of each subject or each carrier of the trait or disorder in question.

Pedophilia. Paraphilia in which an adult's preferred or exclusive sexual partner is a prepubertal child.

Perception. Interpretation of sensory input.

Perceptual filtering. Processes involved in selective attention to aspects of the great mass of incoming stimuli that continually impinge on an organism.

Perfectionism. The need to get things exactly right. A personality trait that may increase risk for the development of eating disorders, perhaps because perfectionistic people may be more likely to idealize thinness.

Performance test. Test in which perceptual-motor rather than verbal content is emphasized.

Peripheral nervous system. Nerve fibers passing between the central nervous system and the sense organs, muscles, and glands.

Perseveration. Persistent continuation of a line of thought or activity once it is under way. Clinically inappropriate repetition.

Personality. Unique pattern of traits that characterizes an individual.

Personality disorders. Gradual development of inflexible and distorted personality and behavioral patterns that result in persistently maladaptive ways of perceiving, thinking about, and relating to the world.

Personality or psychological decompensation. Inability to adapt to sustained or severe stressors.

Personality profile. Graphical summary that is derived from several tests or subtests of the same test battery or scale and that shows the personality configuration of an individual or group of individuals.

Person-centered therapy. See **Client-centered therapy.**

Pervasive developmental disorders (PDDs). Severely disabling conditions marked by deficits in language, perceptual, and motor development; defective reality testing; and inability to function in social situations.

Pessimistic attributional style. Cognitive style involving a tendency to make internal, stable, and global attributions for negative life events.

PET scan. See **Positron emission tomography.**

Phagocyte. Circulating white blood cell that binds to antigens and partially destroys them by engulfment.

Phallic stage. In psychoanalytic theory, the stage of psychosexual development during which genital exploration and manipulation occur.

Pharmacology. The science of drugs.

Pharmacotherapy. Treatment by means of drugs.

Phenomenological. Pertaining to the immediate perceiving and experiencing of an individual.

Phenotype. The observed structural and functional characteristics of a person that result from interaction between the genotype and the environment.

Phenylketonuria (PKU). Type of mental retardation resulting from a baby's lack of a liver enzyme needed to break down phenylalanine, an amino acid found in many foods.

Phobia. Persistent and disproportionate fear of some specific object or situation that presents little or no actual danger.

Physiological dependence. Type of drug dependence involving withdrawal symptoms when drug is discontinued.

Pick's disease. Form of presenile dementia.

Pineal gland. Small gland at the base of the brain that helps regulate the body's biological clock and may also establish pace of sexual development.

Pituitary gland. Endocrine gland associated with many regulatory functions.

Placebo. An inert pill or otherwise neutral intervention that produces desirable therapeutic effects because of the subject's expectations that it will be beneficial.

Placebo effect. Positive effect experienced after an inactive treatment is administered in such a way that a person thinks he or she is receiving an active treatment.

Plaques. Abnormal accumulations of protein found in the brains of patients with Alzheimer's disease.

Play therapy. Use of play activities in psychotherapy with children.

Pleasure principle. Demand that an instinctual need be immediately gratified, regardless of reality or moral considerations.

Point prevalence. The number of cases of a specific condition or disorder that can be found in a population at one given point in time.

Polygenic. Caused by the action of many genes together in an additive or interactive fashion.

Poor premorbid schizophrenia. See **Process schizophrenia.**

Positive correlation. A relationship between two variables such that a high score on one variable is associated with a high score on another variable.

Positive psychology. A new field that focuses on human traits (e.g., optimism) and resources that are potentially important for health and well-being.

Positive reinforcer. Reinforcer that increases the probability of recurrence of a given response.

Positive symptoms. Symptoms that are characterized by something being added to normal behavior or experience. Includes delusions, hallucinations, motor agitation, and marked emotional turmoil.

Positive-symptom schizophrenia. Schizophrenia characterized by something added to normal behavior and experience, such as marked emotional turmoil, motor agitation, delusions, and hallucinations.

Positron emission tomography (PET scan). Scanning technique that measures metabolic processes to appraise how well an organ is functioning.

Posthypnotic amnesia. Subject's lack of memory for the period during which he or she was hypnotized.

Posthypnotic suggestion. Suggestion given during hypnosis to be carried out by a subject after he or she is brought out of hypnosis.

Postpartum depression. Depression occurring after childbirth. Most commonly it is mild and transient (postpartum blues) but can become a major depressive episode.

Post-traumatic stress disorder (PTSD). Disorder that occurs following an extreme traumatic event, in which a person reexperiences the event, avoids reminders of the trauma, and exhibits persistent increased arousal.

Predisposition. Tendency to develop certain symptoms under given stress conditions.

Prefrontal lobotomy. Surgical procedure used before the advent of antipsychotic drugs, in which the frontal lobes of the brain were severed from the deeper centers underlying them, resulting in permanent structural changes in the brain.

Prejudice. Emotionally toned conception favorable or unfavorable to some person, group, or idea—typically in the absence of sound evidence.

Premature ejaculation. Persistent and recurrent onset of orgasm and ejaculation with minimal sexual stimulation.

Prematurity. Birth of an infant before the end of a normal period of pregnancy.

Premorbid. Existing before the onset of mental disorder.

Prenatal. Before birth.

Presenile dementia. Mental disorders resulting from brain degeneration before old age.

Prevalence. In a population, the proportion of active cases of a disorder that can be identified at a given point in, or during a given period of, time.

Primary gain. In psychodynamic theory it is the goal achieved by symptoms of conversion disorder by keeping internal intrapsychic conflicts out of awareness. In contemporary terms it is the goal achieved by symptoms of conversion disorder by allowing the person to escape or avoid stressful situations.

Primary prevention. Older term for preventive efforts aimed at reducing the incidence of a disease or disorder and fostering positive health. (See **Universal prevention.**)

Primary process thinking. Gratification of id demands by means of imagery or fantasy without the ability to undertake the realistic actions needed to meet those instinctual demands.

Proband. In a genetic study, the original individual who evidences the trait in which the investigator is interested. Same as index case.

Problem checklist. Inventory used in behavioral assessment to determine an individual's fears, moods, and other problems.

Problem drinker. Behavioral term referring to one who has serious problems associated with drinking.

Process schizophrenia. Schizophrenic pattern—marked by seclusiveness, gradual waning of interest in the surrounding world, diminished emotional responsivity, and mildly inappropriate responses—that develops gradually and tends to be long-lasting; alternatively known as *poor premorbid schizophrenia* and *chronic schizophrenia.*

Prognosis. Prediction of the probable course and outcome of a disorder.

Projection. Ego-defense mechanism of attributing one's own unacceptable motives or characteristics to others.

Projective tests. Techniques that use various ambiguous stimuli that a subject is encouraged to interpret and from which the subject's personality characteristics can be analyzed.

Prospective research strategy. Method that often focuses on individuals who have a higher-than-average likelihood of becoming psychologically disordered before abnormal behavior is observed.

Protective factors. Influences that modify a person's response to an environmental stressor, making it less likely that the person will experience the adverse effects of the stressor.

Prototypal approach. Approach to classifying abnormal behavior that assumes the existence of prototypes of behavior disorders that, rather than being mutually exclusive, may blend into others with which they share many characteristics.

Psilocybin. Hallucinogenic drug derived from a variety of mushrooms.

Psychedelic drugs. Drugs such as LSD that often produce hallucinations.

Psychiatric nursing. Field of nursing primarily concerned with mental disorders.

Psychiatric social worker. Professional who has had graduate training in social work with psychiatric specialization, typically leading to a master's degree.

Psychiatrist. Medical doctor who specializes in the diagnosis and treatment of mental disorders.

Psychiatry. Field of medicine concerned with understanding, assessing, treating, and preventing mental disorders.

Psychic trauma. Any aversive experience that inflicts serious psychological damage on a person.

Psychoactive drugs. Drugs that affect mental functioning.

Psychoactive substance abuse. Pathological use of a substance, resulting in potentially hazardous behavior or in continued use despite a persistent social, psychological, occupational, or health problem.

Psychoactive substance dependence. Use of a psychoactive substance to the point where one has a marked physiological need for increasing amounts of the substance to achieve the desired effects.

Psychoanalysis. Methods Freud used to study and treat patients.

Psychoanalytic perspective. Theory of psychopathology, initially developed by Freud, that emphasized the inner dynamics of unconscious motives.

Psychodrama. Psychotherapeutic technique in which the acting of various roles is an essential part.

Psychodynamic perspectives. Theories of psychopathology based on modification and revision of Freud's theories.

Psychodynamic therapy. Psychological treatment that focuses on individual personality dynamics, usually from a psychodynamic or psychodynamically derived perspective.

Psychogenic. Of psychological origin: originating in the psychological functioning of an individual.

Psychogenic amnesia. Amnesia of psychological origin, common in initial reactions to traumatic experiences.

Psychogenic illness. Psychologically induced or maintained disease.

Psychohistory. A field of study analyzing history according to psychoanalytic principles.

Psychological autopsy. Analytical procedure used to determine whether or not death was self-inflicted and if so, why.

Psychological need. Need emerging out of environmental interactions, e.g., the need for social approval.

Psychological screening. Use of psychological procedures or tests to detect psychological problems among applicants in pre-employment evaluations.

Psychological test. Standardized procedure designed to measure a subject's performance on a specified task.

Psychomotor. Involving both psychological and physical activity.

Psychomotor retardation. Slowing down of psychological and motor functions.

Psychoneuroimmunology. Study of the interactions between the immune system and the nervous system and the influence of these factors on behavior.

Psychopathology. Abnormal behavior.

Psychopathy. A condition involving the features of antisocial personality disorder and such traits as lack of empathy, inflated and arrogant self-appraisal, and glib and superficial charm.

Psychopharmacology. Science of determining which drugs alleviate which disorders and why they do so.

Psychophysiological (psychosomatic) disorders. Physical disorders in which psychological factors are believed to play a major causative role.

Psychophysiological variables. Measures of biological functioning including heart rate, blood pressure, EEG, and so on.

Psychosexual development. Freudian view of development as involving a succession of stages, each characterized by a dominant mode of achieving libidinal pleasure.

Psychosexual stages of development. According to Freudian theory, there are five stages of psychosexual development, each characterized by a dominant mode of achieving sexual pleasure: the oral stage, the anal stage, the phallic stage, the latency stage, and the genital stage.

Psychosis. Severe impairment in reality testing.

Psychosocial deprivation. Lack of needed stimulation and interaction during early life.

Psychosocial viewpoints. Approaches to understanding mental disorders that emphasize the importance of early experience and an awareness of social influences and psychological processes within an individual.

Psychosurgery. Brain surgery used in the past with excessive frequency in the treatment of functional mental disorders.

Psychotherapy. Treatment of mental disorders by psychological methods.

Psychotropic drugs. Drugs whose main effects are mental or behavioral in nature.

Purge. Purging refers to the removal of food from the body by such means as self-induced vomiting or misuse of laxatives, diuretics, and enemas.

Q-sort. Personality inventory in which a subject, or a clinician, sorts a number of statements into piles according to their applicability to the subject.

Racism. Prejudice and discrimination directed toward individuals or groups because of their racial background.

Randomized controlled trials. A randomized controlled trial involves a specific treatment group (the group the researchers are most interested in) as well as a control treatment group (against which the treatment group will be compared). Participants have an equal chance of being placed in either group because placement is determined randomly.

Random sample. Sample drawn in such a way that each member of a population has an equal chance of being selected; it is hoped that such a sample will be fully representative of the population from which it is drawn.

Rape. Sexual activity that occurs under actual or threatened forcible coercion of one person by another.

Rapid cycling. A pattern of bipolar disorder involving at least four manic or depressive episodes per year.

Rapport. Interpersonal relationship characterized by a spirit of cooperation, confidence, and harmony.

Rating scales. Formal structure for organizing information obtained from clinical observation and self-reports to encourage reliability and objectivity.

Rational-emotive behavior therapy (REBT). Form of psychotherapy focusing on changing a client's maladaptive thought processes, on which maladaptive emotional responses and thus behavior are presumed to depend.

Rationalization. Ego-defense mechanism that involves the use of contrived "explanations" to conceal or disguise unworthy motives for a person's behavior.

Reaction formation. Ego-defense mechanism that prevents the awareness or expression of unacceptable desires via the exaggerated adoption of seemingly opposite behavior.

Reactive schizophrenia. Schizophrenia pattern—marked by confusion and intense emotional turmoil—that normally develops suddenly and has identifiable precipitating stressors; alternatively known as *good premorbid schizophrenia, Type I schizophrenia,* and *acute schizophrenia.*

Reality principle. Awareness of the demands of the environment and adjustment of behavior to meet these demands.

Reality testing. Behavior aimed at testing or exploring the nature of a person's social and physical environment; often used more specifically to refer to testing the limits of the permissiveness of the social environment.

Recessive gene. Gene that is effective only when paired with an identical gene.

Recidivism. Shift back to one's original behavior (often delinquent or criminal) after a period of treatment or rehabilitation.

Recompensation. Increase in integration or inner organization. Opposite of *decompensation.*

Recurrence. A new occurrence of a disorder after a remission of symptom.

Recurrent. Term used to describe a disorder pattern that tends to come and go.

Referral. Sending or recommending an individual and/or family for psychological assessment and/or treatment.

Regression. Ego-defense mechanism of retreat to an earlier developmental level involving less mature behavior and responsibility.

Rehabilitation. Use of reeducation rather than punishment to overcome behavioral deficits.

Reinforcement. The process of rewarding desired responses.

Relapse. Return of the symptoms of a disorder after a fairly short period of time.

Reliability. Degree to which a measuring device produces the same result each time it is used to measure the same thing, or when two or more different raters use it.

Remission. Marked improvement or recovery appearing in the course of a mental illness; may or may not be permanent.

REM sleep. Stage of sleep involving rapid eye movements (REM); associated with dreaming.

Representative sample. Small group selected in such a way as to be representative of the larger group from which it is drawn.

Repression. Ego-defense mechanism that prevents painful or dangerous thoughts from entering consciousness.

Residual schizophrenia. See **Schizophrenia, residual type.**

Resilience. The ability to adapt successfully to even very difficult circumstances.

Resistance. Selye's second stage of responding to continuing trauma, involving finding some means to deal with the trauma and adjust to it. In psychodynamic treatment, the person's unwillingness or inability to talk about certain thoughts, motives, or experiences.

Resistance to extinction. Tendency of a conditioned response to persist despite lack of reinforcement.

Resolution. Final phase of the human sexual response, during which a person has a sense of relaxation and well-being.

Response shaping. Positive reinforcement technique used in therapy to establish, by gradual approximation, a response not initially in a person's behavioral repertoire.

Reticular activating system (RAS). Fibers going from the reticular formation to higher brain centers and presumably functioning as a general arousal system.

Reticular formation. Neural nuclei and fibers in the brain stem that apparently play an important role in arousing and alerting an organism and in controlling attention.

Retrograde amnesia. Loss of memory for events that occurred during a circumscribed period prior to brain injury or damage.

Retrospective strategy. Method of trying to uncover the probable causes of abnormal behavior by looking backward from the present.

Retrospective study. Research approach that attempts to retrace earlier events in the life of a subject.

Rigidity. Tendency to follow established coping patterns, with failure to see alternatives or extreme difficulty in changing one's established patterns.

Ritalin. Central nervous system stimulant often used to treat ADHD.

Role playing. Form of assessment in which a person is instructed to play a part, enabling a clinician to observe a client's behavior directly.

Rorschach test. Use of ten inkblot pictures to which a subject responds with associations that come to mind. Analysis of these responses enables a clinician to infer personality characteristics.

Sadism. Achievement of sexual gratification by inflicting physical or psychic pain or humiliation on a sexual partner.

Saint Vitus's dance. Name given to the dancing mania (and mass hysteria) that spread from Italy to Germany and the rest of Europe in the Middle Ages.

Sample. Group on which measurements are taken; should normally be representative of the population about which an inference is to be made.

Sampling. The process of selecting a representative subgroup from a defined population of interest.

Scapegoating. Displacement of aggression onto some object, person, or group other than the source of frustration.

Schedule of reinforcement. Program of rewards for requisite behavior.

Schema. An underlying representation of knowledge that guides current processing of information and often leads to distortions in attention, memory, and comprehension.

Schizoaffective disorder. Form of psychotic disorder in which the symptoms of schizophrenia co-occur with symptoms of a mood disorder.

Schizoid personality disorder. Inability to form social relationships or express feelings and lack of interest in doing so.

Schizophrenia. Disorder characterized by hallucinations, delusions, disorganized speech and behavior, as well as problems in self care and general functioning.

Schizophrenia, catatonic type. Type of schizophrenia in which the central feature is pronounced motor symptoms, of either an excited or a stuporous type, which sometimes make for difficulty in differentiating this condition from a psychotic mood disorder.

Schizophrenia, disorganized type. Type of schizophrenia that usually begins at an earlier age and represents a more severe disintegration of the personality than in the other types of schizophrenia.

Schizophrenia, paranoid type. Type of schizophrenia in which a person is increasingly suspicious, has severe difficulties in interpersonal relationships, and experiences absurd, illogical, and often changing delusions.

Schizophrenia, residual type. Diagnostic category used for people who have experienced a schizophrenic episode from which they have recovered enough to not show prominent symptoms but are still manifesting some mild signs of their past disorder.

Schizophrenia, undifferentiated type. Type of schizophrenia in which a person meets the usual criteria for being schizophrenic—including (in varying combinations) delusions, hallucinations, thought disorder, and bizarre behavior—but does not clearly fit into one of the other types because of a mixed symptom picture.

Schizophreniform disorder. Category of schizophrenic-like psychosis less than 6 months in duration.

Schizophrenogenic. Schizophrenia-causing.

Schizotypal personality disorder. Excessive introversion, pervasive social interpersonal deficits, cognitive and perceptual distortions, and eccentricities in communication and behavior.

Seasonal affective disorder. Mood disorder involving at least two episodes of depression in the past two years occurring at the same time of year (most commonly fall or winter), with remission also occurring at the same time of year (most commonly spring).

Secondary gain. External circumstances that tend to reinforce the maintenance of disability.

Secondary prevention. Older term for prevention techniques that typically involve emergency or crisis intervention, with efforts focused on reducing the impact, duration, or spread of a problem. (See **Selective intervention.**)

Secondary process thinking. Reality-oriented rational processes of the ego for dealing with the external world and the exercise of control over id demands.

Secondary reinforcer. Reinforcement provided by a stimulus that has gained reward value by being associated with a primary reinforcing stimulus.

Sedative. Drug used to reduce tension and induce relaxation and sleep.

Selective intervention. Mobilization of prevention resources to eliminate or reduce a particular type of problem (such as teenage pregnancy or alcohol or drug abuse).

Selective mutism. Condition that involves the persistent failure to speak in specific social situations and interferes with educational or social adjustment.

Self (ego). Integrating core of a personality that mediates between needs and reality.

Self-acceptance. Being satisfied with one's attributes and qualities while remaining aware of one's limitations.

Self-actualizing. Achieving one's full potentialities as a human being.

Self-concept. A person's sense of his or her own identity, worth, capabilities, and limitations.

Self-esteem. Feeling of personal worth.

Self-evaluation. Way in which an individual views the self, in terms of worth, adequacy, etc.

Self-ideal (ego-ideal). Person or "self" a person thinks he or she could and should be.

Self-identity. Individual's delineation and awareness of his or her continuing identity as a person.

Self-instructional training. Cognitive-behavioral method aimed at teaching a person to alter his or her covert behavior.

Self-monitoring. Observing and recording one's own behavior, thoughts, and feelings as they occur in various natural settings.

Self-reinforcement. Reward of self for desired or appropriate behavior.

Self-report data. Data collected directly from participants, typically by means of interviews or questionnaires.

Self-report inventory. Procedure in which a subject is asked to respond to statements in terms of their applicability to him or her.

Self-schemas. Our views of what we are, what we might become, and what is important to us.

Self-statements. A person's implicit verbalizations of what he or she is experiencing.

Senile. Pertaining to old age.

Senile dementia. Mental disorders that sometimes accompany brain degeneration in old age.

Sensate focus learning. Learning to derive pleasure from touching one's partner and being touched by him or her; this training is used in sexual therapy to enhance sexual feelings and help overcome sexual dysfunction.

Sensory deprivation. Restriction of sensory stimulation below the level required for normal functioning of the central nervous system.

Sentence-completion test. Projective technique utilizing incomplete sentences that a person is to complete, analysis of which enables a clinician to infer personality dynamics.

Separation anxiety disorder. Childhood disorder characterized by unrealistic fears, oversensitivity, self-consciousness, nightmares, and chronic anxiety.

Separation-individuation. According to Mahler, a developmental phase in which a child gains an internal representation of the self as distinct from representations of other objects.

Sequelae. Symptoms remaining as the aftermath of a disorder.

Serotonin. A neurotransmitter from the indolamine class that is synthesized from the amino acid tryptophan. Also referred to as 5-HT (5-hydroxytryptamine), this neurotransmitter is thought to be involved in a wide range of psychopathological conditions.

Severe (disorder). Disorder of a high degree of seriousness.

Severe major depressive episode with psychotic features. Major depression involving loss of contact with reality, often in the form of delusions or hallucinations.

Sex chromosomes. Pair of chromosomes inherited by an individual that determine sex and certain other characteristics.

Sexual abuse. Sexual contact that involves physical or psychological coercion or occurs when at least one individual cannot reasonably consent to the contact.

Sexual aversion disorder. Sexual dysfunction in which a person shows extreme aversion to, and avoidance of, all genital sexual contact with a partner.

Sexual dysfunction. Impairment either in the desire for sexual gratification or in the ability to achieve it.

Shaping. Form of instrumental conditioning; at first, all responses resembling the desired one are reinforced, then only the closest approximations, until finally the desired response is attained.

Shared psychotic disorder. Psychosis in which two or more people develop persistent, interlocking delusional ideas. Also known as *folie à deux.*

Sheltered workshops. Workshops where mentally retarded or otherwise handicapped persons can engage in constructive work in the community.

Short-term crisis therapy. Brief treatment that focuses on the immediate problem an individual or family is experiencing.

Siblings. Offspring of the same parents.

Sick role. Protected role provided by society via the medical model for a person suffering from severe physical or mental disorder.

Signs. Objective observations that suggest to a diagnostician a patient's physical or mental disorder.

Significant others. In interpersonal theory of psychological development, parents or others on whom an infant is dependent for meeting all physical and psychological needs.

Simple phobia. See **Specific phobia.**

Simple tension headaches. Common headaches in which stress leads to contraction of the muscles surrounding the skull; these contractions result in vascular constrictions that cause headache pain.

Single case research design. An experimental research design (e.g., an ABAB design) that involves only one subject.

Situational test. Test that measures performance in a simulated life situation.

Sleepwalking disorder. Disorder of childhood that involves repeated episodes of leaving the bed and walking around without being conscious of the experience or remembering it later. Also known as *somnambulism.*

Social exchange view. Model of interpersonal relationships based on the premise that such relationships are formed for mutual gratification of needs.

Social introversion. Trait characterized by shy, withdrawn, and inhibited behavior.

Socialization. Process by which a child acquires the values and impulse controls deemed appropriate by his or her culture.

Social-learning programs. Behavioral programs using learning techniques, especially token economies, to help patients assume more responsibility for their own behavior.

Social norms. Group standards concerning which behaviors are viewed as acceptable and which as unacceptable.

Social pathology. Abnormal patterns of social organization, attitudes, or behavior; undesirable social conditions that tend to produce individual pathology.

Social phobia. Fear of situations in which a person might be exposed to the scrutiny of others and fear of acting in a humiliating or embarrassing way.

Social recovery. Ability to manage independently as an economically effective and interpersonally connected member of society.

Social role. Behavior expected of a person occupying a given position in a group.

"Social" self. Façade a person displays to others, as contrasted with the private self.

Social work. Applied offshoot of sociology concerned with analyzing social environments and providing services that enhance the adjustment of a client in both family and community settings.

Social worker. Person in a mental health field with a master's degree in social work (MSW) plus supervised training in clinical or social service agencies.

Sociocultural viewpoint. Perspective that focuses on broad social conditions that influence the development and/or behavior of individuals and groups.

Socioeconomic status. Position on social and economic scale in community; determined largely by income and occupational level.

Sociogenic. Having its roots in sociocultural conditions.

Sociopathic personality. See **Antisocial personality disorder.**

Sodium pentothal. Barbiturate drug sometimes used in psychotherapy to produce a state of relaxation and suggestibility.

Soma. Greek word for body. *Somatoform* disorders involve complaints of bodily symptoms or defects suggesting the presence of medical problems but for which no organic basis can be found that satisfactorily explains the symptoms.

Somatic. Pertaining to the body.

Somatic weakness. Special vulnerability of given organ systems to stress.

Somatization disorder. Multiple complaints, over a long period beginning before age 30, of physical ailments that are inadequately explained by independent findings of physical illness or injury and that lead to medical treatment or to significant life impairment.

Somatoform disorders. Conditions involving physical complaints or disabilities that occur without any evidence of physical pathology to account for them.

Somnambulism. See **Sleepwalking disorder.**

Spasm. Intense, involuntary, usually painful contraction of a muscle or group of muscles.

Spasticity. Marked hypertonicity or continual overcontraction of muscles, causing stiffness, awkwardness, and motor incoordination.

Specific learning disorders. Developmental disorders involving deficits in language, speech, mathematical, or motor skills.

Specific phobia. Persistent or disproportionate fears of various objects, places, or situations, such as fears of situations (airplanes or elevators), other species (snakes, spiders), or aspects of the environment (high places, water).

Specifiers in mood disorders. Different patterns of symptoms that sometimes characterize major depressive episodes which may help predict the course and preferred treatments for the condition.

Sperm. Male gamete or germ cell.

Split-brain research. Research associated with split-brain surgery, which cuts off the transmission of information from one cerebral hemisphere to the other by severing the corpus callosum.

Spontaneous recovery. The return of a learned response at some time after extinction has occurred.

Stage of exhaustion. Selye's third and final stage in the general adaptation syndrome, in which an organism is no longer able to resist continuing stress; may result in death.

Stage of resistance. Second stage of the general adaptation syndrome.

Standardization. Procedure for establishing the expected performance range on a test.

Stanford-Binet. Standardized intelligence test for children.

Startle reaction. Sudden involuntary motor reaction to intense unexpected stimuli; may result from mild stimuli if a person is hypersensitive.

Statutory rape. Sexual intercourse with a minor.

Steady states (homeostasis). Tendency of an organism to maintain conditions that make possible a constant level of physiological functioning.

Stereotyping. The tendency to jump to conclusions (often negative) about what a person is like based on beliefs about that group that exist (often incorrectly) in the culture (e.g., French people are rude, homosexuals have good taste in clothes, mental patients are dangerous, etc.).

Stereotypy. Persistent and inappropriate repetition of phrases, gestures, or acts.

Stigma. Negative labeling.

Stimulants. Drugs that tend to increase feelings of alertness, reduce feelings of fatigue, and enable a person to stay awake over sustained periods of time.

Stimulus generalization. Spread of a conditioned response to some stimulus similar to, but not identical with, the conditioned stimulus.

Stress. Effects created within an organism by the application of a stressor.

Stress-inoculation therapy. Type of self-instructional training focused on altering self-statements that a person routinely makes in stress-producing situations.

Stress-inoculation training. Preventive strategy that prepares people to tolerate an anticipated threat by changing the things they say to themselves before the crisis.

Stressors. Adjustive demands that require coping behavior on the part of an individual or group.

Stress tolerance. A person's ability to withstand stress without becoming seriously impaired.

Stroke. See **Cerebrovascular accident.**

Structural family therapy. Treatment of an entire family by analysis of interaction among family members.

Stupor. Condition of lethargy and unresponsiveness, with partial or complete unconsciousness.

Sublimation. Ego-defense mechanism that channels frustrated expression of sexual energy into substitutive activities.

Substance abuse. Maladaptive pattern of substance use manifested by recurrent and significant adverse consequences related to the use of the substance.

Substance dependence. Severe form of substance use disorder involving physiological dependence on the substance, tolerance, withdrawal, and compulsive drug taking.

Substance-related disorders. Patterns of maladaptive behavior centered on the regular use of a substance, such as a drug or alcohol.

Substitution. Acceptance of substitute goals or satisfactions in place of those originally sought or desired.

Successive approximation. See **Shaping.**

Sufficent cause. A condition that guarantees the occurrence of a disorder.

Suicide. Taking one's own life.

Suicidology. Study of the causes and prevention of suicide.

Superego. Conscience; ethical or moral dimensions (attitudes) of personality.

Suppression. Conscious forcing of desires or thoughts out of consciousness; conscious inhibition of desires or impulses.

Surrogate. Substitute for another person, such as a parent or mate.

Symbol. Image, word, object, or activity that is used to represent something else.

Symbolism. Representation of one idea or object by another.

Sympathetic division. Division of the autonomic nervous system that is active in emergency conditions of extreme cold, violent effort, and emotions.

Symptoms. Patient's subjective description of a physical or mental disorder.

Synapse. Site of communication from the axon of one neuron to the dendrites or cell body of another neuron—a tiny filled space between neurons.

Syndrome. Group or pattern of symptoms that occur together in a disorder and represent the typical picture of the disorder.

System. Assemblage of interdependent parts, living or nonliving.

Systematic desensitization. Behavior therapy technique for extinguishing maladaptive anxiety responses by teaching a person to relax or behave, while in the presence of the anxiety-producing stimulus, in some other way that is inconsistent with anxiety.

Tachycardia. Rapid heartbeat.

Tactual hallucinations. Hallucinations involving the sense of touch.

Tarantism. Dancing mania that occurred in Italy in the thirteenth century.

Tarasoff decision. Ruling by a California court (1974) that a therapist has a duty to warn a prospective victim of an explicit threat expressed by a client in therapy.

Tardive dyskinesia. Neurological disorder resulting from excessive use of antipsychotic drugs. Side effects can occur months to years after treatment has been initiated or has stopped. The symptoms involve involuntary movements of the tongue, lips, jaw, and extremities.

Task-oriented response. Making changes in one's self, one's surroundings, or both, depending on the situation.

Tay-Sachs disease. Genetic disorder of lipid metabolism usually resulting in death by age 3.

T-cell. A type of white blood cell that, when activated, can recognize specific antigens. T-cells play an important role in the immune system.

Telepathy. Communication from one person to another without use of any known sense organs.

Temperament. Pattern of emotional and arousal responses and characteristic ways of self-regulation that are considered to be primarily hereditary or constitutional.

Temporal lobe. Portion of the cerebrum located in front of the occipital lobe and separated from the frontal and parietal lobes by the fissure of Sylvius.

Tension. Condition arising from the mobilization of psychobiological resources to meet a threat; physically, involves an increase in muscle tone and other emergency changes; psychologically, is characterized by feelings of strain, uneasiness, and anxiety.

Tertiary prevention. Older term for preventive techniques focused on reducing long-term consequences of disorders or serious problems. (See **Indicated prevention.**)

Testes. Male reproductive glands or gonads.

Testosterone. Male sex hormone.

Test-retest reliability. Consistency with which a test measures a given trait on repeated administrations of the test to given subjects.

Test validity. Degree to which a test actually measures what it was designed to measure.

Thematic Apperception Test (TAT). Use of a series of simple pictures about which a subject is instructed to make up stories. Analysis of the stories gives a clinician clues about the person's conflicts, traits, personality dynamics, and the like.

Therapeutic. Pertaining to treatment or healing.

Therapeutic community. Hospital environment used for therapeutic purposes.

Therapy. Treatment; application of various treatment techniques.

Thyroid. Endocrine gland located in the neck that influences body metabolism, rate of physical growth, and development of intelligence.

Thyroxin. Hormone secreted by the thyroid glands.

Tic. Persistent, intermittent muscle twitch or spasm, usually limited to a localized muscle group, often of the facial muscles.

Token economies. Reinforcement techniques often used in hospital or institutional settings in which patients are rewarded for socially constructive behaviors with tokens that can then be exchanged for desired objects or activities.

Tolerance. Need for increased amounts of a substance to achieve the desired effects.

Tourette's syndrome. Extreme tic disorder involving uncontrollable multiple motor and vocal patterns.

Toxic. Poisonous.

Toxicity. Poisonous nature of a substance.

Traditional behavioral couple therapy. Widely used form of therapy that uses behavioral approaches to bring about changes in the marital relationship.

Trait. Characteristic of a person that can be observed or measured.

Trance. Sleep-like state in which the range of consciousness is limited and voluntary activities are suspended; a deep hypnotic state.

Tranquilizers. Drugs used for reduction of psychotic symptoms (major tranquilizers), or reduction of anxiety and tension (minor tranquilizers).

Transference. In psychodynamic therapy, a process whereby clients project onto the therapist attitudes and feelings that they have had for a parent or others close to them.

Transsexualism. Individuals who identify with members of the opposite sex (as opposed to acceptance of their own biological sex) and who strongly desire to (and often do) change their sex. In most cases this is gender identity disorder in adults.

Transvestic fetishism. Achievement of sexual arousal and satisfaction by dressing as a member of the opposite sex.

Trauma. Severe psychological or physiological stressor.

Traumatic. Pertaining to a wound or injury or to psychic shock.

Traumatic brain injuries (TBI). Brain damage resulting from motor vehicle crashes, bullets or other objects entering the brain, and other severe impacts to the head.

Traumatic childhood abuse. Mistreatment in childhood severe enough to cause psychological damage.

Treatment contract. Explicit arrangement between a therapist and a client designed to bring about specific behavioral changes.

Tremor. Repeated fine spastic movement.

Twin method. The use of identical and nonidentical twins to study genetic influences on abnormal behavior.

Type A behavior pattern. Excessive competitive drive even when it is unnecessary, impatience or time urgency, and hostility.

Type D personality. Type D (for distressed) personality is characterized by high levels of negative emotions and social anxiety. Research suggests that Type D personality is linked to heart attacks.

Type I schizophrenia. Psychotic behavior of the positive syndrome variety thought to involve chiefly temporolimbic brain structures.

Type II schizophrenia. Psychotic behavior of the negative syndrome variety thought to involve chiefly frontal brain structures.

Unconscious, The. In psychoanalytic theory, a major portion of the mind, which consists of a hidden mass of instincts, impulses, and memories and is not easily available to conscious awareness yet plays an important role in behavior.

Underarousal. Inadequate physiological response to a given stimulus.

Undifferentiated schizophrenia. See **Schizophrenia, undifferentiated type.**

Undoing. Ego-defense mechanism of atoning for or magically trying to dispel unacceptable desires or acts.

Unipolar disorders. Mood disorders in which a person experiences only depressive episodes, as opposed to bipolar disorder, in which both manic and depressive episodes occur.

Universal intervention. The tasks of altering conditions that cause or contribute to mental disorders (risk factors) and establishing conditions that foster positive mental health (protective factors).

Vaginismus. Involuntary spasm of the muscles at the entrance to the vagina that prevents penetration and sexual intercourse.

Validity. Extent to which a measuring instrument actually measures what it purports to measure.

Variable. Characteristic or property that may assume any one of a set of different qualities or quantities.

Vascular dementia (VAD). A brain disorder in which a series of small strokes destroy neurons, leading to brain atrophy and behavioral impairments that are similar to Alzheimer's disease.

Vasomotor. Pertaining to the walls of the blood vessels.

Vegetative. Withdrawn or deteriorated to the point of leading a passive, vegetable-like existence.

Verbal test. Test in which a subject's ability to understand and use words and concepts is important in making the required responses.

Vertigo. Dizziness.

Virilism. Accentuation of masculine secondary sex characteristsics, especially in a woman or young boy, caused by hormonal imbalance.

Viscera. Internal organs.

Voyeurism. Achievement of sexual pleasure through clandestine "peeping," usually watching other people disrobe and/or engage in sexual activities.

Vulnerabilities. Factors that render a person susceptible to behaving abnormally.

Wechsler Intelligence Scale for Children (WISC). Standardized Intelligence Test for Children.

Withdrawal. Intellectual, emotional, or physical retreat.

Withdrawal symptoms. Physical symptoms such as sweating, tremors, and tension that accompany abstinence from some drugs.

Word salad. Jumbled or incoherent use of words by psychotic or disoriented individuals.

X chromosome. Sex-determining chromosome; all female gametes contain X chromosomes, and if the fertilized ovum has also received an X chromosome from its father, it will be female.

XYY syndrome. Chromosomal anomaly in males (presence of an extra Y chromosome) possibly related to impulsive behavior.

Y chromosome. Sex-determining chromosome found in half of the total number of male gametes; its uniting with an X chromosome provided by a female produces a male offspring.

Zygote. Fertilized egg cell formed by the union of male and female gametes.

References

JOURNAL ABBREVIATIONS

Acta Neurol. Scandin.—*Acta Neurologica Scandinavica*
Acta Psychiatr. Scandin.—*Acta Psychiatrica Scandinavica*
Add. Behav.—*Addictive Behaviors*
Addict. Dis. Treat.—*Addictive Disorders and Their Treatment*
Addict. Res. Theory—*Addiction Research & Theory*
Aggr. Behav.—*Aggressive Behavior*
Al. Res. Hlth.—*Alcohol Research & Health*
Al. Treat. Quart.—*Alcoholism Treatment Quarterly*
Alcoholism: Clin. Exper. Res.—*Alcoholism: Clinical and Experimental Research*
Am. J. Community Psychol.—*American Journal of Community Psychology*
Amer. J. Cardio.—*American Journal of Cardiology*
Amer. J. Clin. Nutri.—*American Journal of Clinical Nutrition*
Amer. J. Drug Alcoh. Abuse—*American Journal of Drug and Alcohol Abuse*
Amer. J. Epidemiol.—*American Journal of Epidemiology*
Amer. J. Foren. Psychol.—*American Journal of Forensic Psychology*
Amer. J. Geriatr. Psychiat.—*American Journal of Geriatric Psychiatry*
Amer. J. Hum. Gene.—*American Journal of Human Genetics*
Amer. J. Med. Genet.—*American Journal of Medical Genetics*
Amer. J. Med. Sci.—*American Journal of the Medical Sciences*
Amer. J. Ment. Def.—*American Journal of Mental Deficiency*
Amer. J. Ment. Retard.—*American Journal of Mental Retardation*
Amer. J. Nurs.—*American Journal of Nursing*
Amer. J. Occup. Ther.—*American Journal of Occupational Therapy*
Amer. J. Orthopsychiat.—*American Journal of Orthopsychiatry*
Amer. J. Psychiat.—*American Journal of Psychiatry*
Amer. J. Psychoanal.—*American Journal of Psychoanalysis*
Amer. J. Psychother.—*American Journal of Psychotherapy*
Amer. J. Pub. Hlth.—*American Journal of Public Health*
Amer. Psychol.—*American Psychologist*
Ann. Behav. Med.—*Annals of Behavioral Medicine*
Ann. Clin. Psychiat.—*Annals of Clinical Psychiatry*
Ann. Int. Med.—*Annals of Internal Medicine*
Ann. Neurol.—*Annals of Neurology*
Ann. NY Acad. Sci.—*Annals of the New York Academy of Science*
Ann. Sex Res.—*Annals of Sex Research*
Annu. Rev. Clin. Psychol.—*Annual Review of Clinical Psychology*
Annu. Rev. Med.—*Annual Review of Medicine*
Annu. Rev. Neurosci.—*Annual Review of Neuroscience*
Annu. Rev. Psychol.—*Annual Review of Psychology*
Annu. Rev. Sex Res.—*Annual Review of Sex Research*
Annu. Rev. Soc.—*Annual Review of Sociology*
App. Prev. Psychol.—*Applied and Preventive Psychology*
Arch. Clin. Neuropsychol.—*Archives of Clinical Neuropsychology*
Arch. Gen. Psychiat.—*Archives of General Psychiatry*
Arch. Gerontol. Geriatr.—*Archives of Gerontology and Geriatrics*
Arch. Int. Med.—*Archives of Internal Medicine*
Arch. Neurol.—*Archives of Neurology*
Arch. Sex. Behav.—*Archives of Sexual Behavior*
Austral. N.Z. J. Psychiat.—*Australian and New Zealand Journal of Psychiatry*
Behav. Chng.—*Behaviour Change*
Behav. Cog. Psychother.—*Behavioural & Cognitive Psychotherapy*
Behav. Gen.—*Behavior Genetics*
Behav. Mod.—*Behavior Modification*
Behav. Res. Ther.—*Behavior Research and Therapy*
Behav. Ther.—*Behavior Therapy*
Behav. Today—*Behavior Today*
Biol. Psych.—*Biological Psychology*
Biol. Psychiat.—*Biological Psychiatry*
BMJ—*British Medical Journal*
Brain—*Brain: A Journal of Neurology*
Brit. J. Addict.—*British Journal of Addiction*
Brit. J. Clin. Psychol.—*British Journal of Clinical Psychology*
Brit. J. Dev. Psychol.—*British Journal of Developmental Psychology*
Brit. J. Learn. Dis.—*British Journal of Learning Disabilities*
Brit. J. Psychiat.—*British Journal of Psychiatry*
Brit. Med. J.—*British Medical Journal*
Bull. Amer. Acad. Psychiat. Law—*Bulletin of the American Academy of Psychiatry and Law*
Canad. J. Behav. Sci.—*Canadian Journal of Behavioral Science*
Canad. J. Psychiat.—*Canadian Journal of Psychiatry*
Child Ab. Negl.—*Child Abuse and Neglect*
Child Adoles. Psychiat.—*Child and Adolescent Psychiatry*
Child Adoles. Psychiatr. Clin. N. Amer.—*Child and Adolescent Psychiatric Clinics of North America*
Child Develop.—*Child Development*
Child Psychiat. Human Devel.—*Child Psychiatry and Human Development*
Clin. Child Fam. Psych. Rev.—*Clinical Child & Family Psychology Review*
Clin. Chld. Fam. Psychol.—*Clinical Child & Family Psychology*
Clin. Exp. Res.—*Clinical and Experimental Research*
Clin. Geron.—*Clinical Gerontologis*
Clin. Neuropharmac.—*Clinical Neuropharmacology*
Clin. Neuropsych.—*The Clinical Neuropsychologist*
Clin. Pediat.—*Clinical Pediatrics*
Clin. Pharm.—*Clinical Pharmacy*
Clin. Psychol. Rev.—*Clinical Psychology Review*
Clin. Psychol. Sci. Prac.—*Clinical Psychology: Science and Practice*
Clin. Psychol.—*The Clinical Psychologist*
Cog. & Emo.—*Cognition and Emotion*
Cog. Behav. Neuro.—*Cognitive and Behavioral Neurology*
Cog. Behav. Ther.—*Cognitive Behaviour Therapy*
Cog. Ther. Res.—*Cognitive Therapy and Research*
Coll. Stud. J.—*College Student Journal*
Comm. Ment. Hlth. J.—*Community Mental Health Journal*
Compr. Psychiat.—*Comprehensive Psychiatry*
Contemp. Psychol.—*Contemporary Psychology*
Counsel. Psychol.—*Counseling Psychologist*
Crim. Just. Behav.—*Criminal Justice and Behavior*
Cult. Med. Psychiatr.—*Culture, Medicine, and Psychiatry*
Cultur. Psychiatr.—*Cultural Psychiatry*
Cur. Opin. Psychiat.—*Current Opinion in Psychiatry*
Curr. Dis. Psychol. Sci.—*Current Directions in Psychological Science*
Dev. Behav.—*Deviant Behavior*
Develop. Med. Child Neurol.—*Developmental Medicine & Child Neurology*
Develop. Psychol.—*Developmental Psychology*
Develop. Psychopath.—*Development and Psychopathology*
Dis. Nerv. Sys.—*Diseases of the Nervous System*
Drug Al. Dep.—*Drug & Alcohol Dependency*
Drug. Al. Rev.—*Drug & Alcohol Review*
Eat. Dis.—*Eating Disorders*
Eur. Arch. Psychiat. Clin. Neurosci.—*European Archives of Psychiatry and Clinical Neuroscience*
Europ. J. Neurosci.—*European Journal of Neuroscience*
Europ. J. Psychol. Assess.—*European Journal of Psychology Assessment*
Europ. Psychol.—*European Psychologist*
Except.—*Exceptionality*
Exp. Clin. Psychopharm.—*Experimental and Clinical Psychopharmacology*
Exper. Neurol.—*Experimental Neurology*
Fam. Hlth.—*Family Health*
Fam. Plann. Perspect.—*Family Planning Perspectives*
Fam. Process—*Family Process*
Fed. Proc.—*Federal Proceedings*
Gen. Hosp. Psychiat.—*General Hospital Psychiatry*
Harv. Rev. Psychiat.—*Harvard Review of Psychiatry*
Hlth. Psychol.—*Health Psychology*
Hong Kong J. Psychiatry—*Hong Kong Journal of Psychiatry*
Hosp. Comm. Psychiat.—*Hospital and Community Psychiatry*
Human Behav.—*Human Behavior*
Human Develop.—*Human Development*
Human Genet.—*Human Genetics*
Inf. Behav. Develop.—*Infant Behavior and Development*
Int. Clin. Psychopharm.—*International Clinical Psychopharmocology*
Int. J. Adol. Med. Hlth.—*International Journal of Adolescent Medicine and Health*
Int. J. Aging Hum. Dev.—*International Journal of Aging & Human Development*
Int. J. Clin. Exp. Hypn.—*International Journal of Clinical and Experimental Hypnosis*
Int. J. Eat. Dis.—*International Journal of Eating Disorders*
Int. J. Emerg. Mntl. Hlth.—*International Journal of Emergency Mental Health*
Int. J. Epidemiol.—*International Journal of Epidemiology*
Int. J. Neuropsychopharm.—*International Journal of Neuropsychopharmacology*

Int. J. Off. Ther. Comp. Crim.—*International Journal of Offender Therapy & Comparative Criminology*
Int. Rev. Psychiat.—*International Review of Psychiatry*
Integr. Psychiat.—*Integrative Psychiatry*
Inter. J. Addict.—*International Journal of Addictions*
Inter. J. Ment. Hlth.—*International Journal of Mental Health*
Inter. J. Psychiat.—*International Journal of Psychiatry*
Inter. J. Psychoanal.—*International Journal of Psychoanalysis*
Inter. J. Soc. Psychiat.—*International Journal of Social Psychiatry*
Intl. J. Clin. Hlth.—*International Journal of Clinical and Health Psychology*
J. Abn. Psychol.—*Journal of Abnormal Psychology*
J. Abnorm. Child Psychol.—*Journal of Abnormal Child Psychology*
J. Abnorm. Soc. Psychol.—*Journal of Abnormal and Social Psychology*
J. Addict. Dis.—*Journal of Addictive Diseases*
J. Adol. Hlth.—*Journal of Adolescent Health*
J. Affect. Dis.—*Journal of Affective Disorders*
J. Amer. Acad. Adoles. Psychiat.—*Journal of the American Academy of Adolescent Psychiatry*
J. Amer. Acad. Child Adoles. Psychiat.—*Journal of the American Academy of Child and Adolescent Psychiatry*
J. Amer. Acad. Child Psychiat.—*Journal of the American Academy of Child Psychiatry*
J. Amer. Acad. Psychiat. Law—*Journal of the American Academy of Psychiatry and Law*
J. Amer. Coll. Hlth.—*Journal of American College Health*
J. Amer. Geriat. Soc.—*Journal of the American Geriatrics Society*
J. Anxiety Dis.—*Journal of Anxiety Disorders*
J. Appl. Beh. Anal.—*Journal of Applied Behavior Analysis*
J. Appl. Psychol.—*Journal of Applied Psychology*
J. Atten. Dis.—*Journal of Attention Disorders*
J. Autism Devel. Dis.—*Journal of Autism and Developmental Disorders*
J. Behav. Assess.—*Journal of Behavioral Assessment*
J. Behav. Med.—*Journal of Behavioral Medicine*
J. Behav. Ther. Exper. Psychiat.—*Journal of Behavior Therapy and Experimental Psychiatry*
J. Chem. Depen. Treat.—*Journal of Chemical Dependency Treatment*
J. Child Fam. Stud.—*Journal of Child and Family Studies*
J. Child Psychol. Psychiat.—*Journal of Child Psychology and Psychiatry*
J. Child. Adol. Men. Hlth.—*Journal of Child and Adolescent Mental Health*
J. Child. Adol. Psychopharm.—*Journal of Child & Adolescent Psychopharmacology*
J. Clin. Child Psychol.—*Journal of Clinical Child Psychology*
J. Clin. Child. Adol. Psych.—*Journal of Clinical Child & Adolescent Psychology*
J. Clin. Exp. Neuropsych.—*Journal of Clinical and Experimental Neuropsychology*
J. Clin. Geropsychol.—*Journal of Clinical Geropsychology*
J. Clin. Psychiat.—*Journal of Clinical Psychiatry*
J. Clin. Psychol. Med. Set.—*Journal of Clinical Psychology in Medical Settings*
J. Clin. Psychol.—*Journal of Clinical Psychology*
J. Clin. Psychopharm.—*Journal of Clinical Psychopharmacology*
J. Cog. Neurosci.—*Journal of Cognitive Neuroscience*
J. Cog. Psychother.—*Journal of Cognitive Psychotherapy*
J. Cog. Rehab.—*Journal of Cognitive Rehabilitation*
J. Coll. Stud. Psychother.—*Journal of College Student Psychotherapy*
J. Comm. Psychol.—*Journal of Community Psychology*
J. Compar. Fam. Stud.—*Journal of Comparative Family Studies*
J. Cons. Clin. Psychol.—*Journal of Consulting and Clinical Psychology*
J. Couns. Psychol.—*Journal of Counseling Psychology*
J. Crisis Int. Suicide Prev.—*Journal of Crisis Intervention and Suicide Prevention*
J. Dev. Behav. Ped.—*Journal of Developmental & Behavioral Pediatrics*
J. Drug Al. Ed.—*Journal of Drug and Alcohol Education*
J. Drug Ed.—*Journal of Drug Education*
J. Drug Iss.—*Journal of Drug Issues*
J. Edu. Psychol.—*Journal of Educational Psychology*
J. Environ. Pschol.—*Journal of Environmental Psychology*
J. Exper. Psychol.—*Journal of Experimental Psychology*
J. Fam. Pract.—*Journal of Family Practice*
J. Fam. Psychol.—*Journal of Family Psychology*
J. Foren. Psychol. Pract.—*Journal of Forensic Psychology Practice*
J. Gen. Psychol.—*Journal of General Psychology*
J. Gerontol.—*Journal of Gerontology*
J. Head Trauma Rehab.—*Journal of Head Trauma Rehabilitation*
J. His. Behav. Sci.—*Journal of the History of the Behavioral Sciences*
J. Hlth. Soc. Behav.—*Journal of Health and Social Behavior*
J. Hlth. Soc. Behav.—*Journal of Health and Social Behavior*
J. Int. Neuropsycholog. Soc.—*Journal of the International Neuropsychological Society*
J. Intell. Develop. Dis.—*Journal of Intellectual Developmental Disability*
J. Intell. Dis. Res.—*Journal of Intellectual Disability Research*
J. Interpers. Violen.—*Journal of Interpersonal Violence*
J. Learn. Dis.—*Journal of Learning Disabilities*
J. Loss Trauma—*Journal of Loss & Trauma*
J. Marit. Fam. Ther.—*Journal of Marital and Family Therapy*
J. Marr. Fam.—*Journal of Marriage and the Family*
J. Ment. Deficien. Res.—*Journal of Mental Deficiency Research*
J. Ment. Hlth. Couns.—*Journal of Mental Health Counseling*
J. Ment. Sci.—*Journal of Mental Science*
J. Meth. Psychiat. Res.—*Journal of Methods in Psychiatric Research*
J. Nerv. Ment. Dis.—*Journal of Nervous and Mental Diseases*
J. Neurol. Neurosurg. Psychiat.—*Journal of Neurology, Neurosurgery, & Psychiatry*
J. Neuropsychiat. Clin. Neurosci.—*Journal of Neuropsychiatry and Clinical Neurosciences*
J. Neurosci.—*Journal of Neuroscience*
J. Occup. Hlth. Psych.—*Journal of Occupational Health Psychology*
J. Off. Rehab.—*Journal of Offender Rehabilitation*
J. Pediat. Psychol.—*Journal of Pediatric Psychology*
J. Pers. Assess.—*Journal of Personality Assessment*
J. Pers. Dis.—*Journal of Personality Disorders*
J. Pers. Soc. Psychol.—*Journal of Personality and Social Psychology*
J. Personal.—*Journal of Personality*
J. Psychiat. Neurosci.—*Journal of Psychiatry and Neuroscience*
J. Psychiat. Pract.—*Journal of Psychiatric Practice*
J. Psychiat. Res.—*Journal of Psychiatric Research*
J. Psychiat.—*Journal of Psychiatry*
J. Psychoact. Drugs—*Journal of Psychoactive Drugs*
J. Psychohist.—*Journal of Psychohistory*
J. Psychol.—*Journal of Psychology*
J. Psychopath. Behav. Assess.—*Journal of Psychopathology and Behavioral Assessment*
J. Psychopharm.—*Journal of Psychopharmacology*
J. Psychosom. Obst. Gyn.—*Journal of Psychosomatic Obstetrics & Gynecology*
J. Psychosom. Res.—*Journal of Psychosomatic Research*
J. Res. Person.—*Journals of Research in Personality*
J. Sex Marit. Ther.—*Journal of Sex and Marital Therapy*
J. Sex Res.—*Journal of Sex Research*
J. Speech Hear. Dis.—*Journal of Speech and Hearing Disorders*
J. Stud. Alcoh.—*Journal of Studies on Alcohol*
J. Sub. Abuse treat.—*Journal of Substance Abuse Treatment*
J. Subst. Abuse—*Journal of Substance Abuse*
J. Trauma. Stress.—*Journal of Traumatic Stress*
JAMA—*Journal of the American Medical Association*
Med. Clin. N. Amer.—*Medical Clinics of North America*
Men. Hlth. Asp. Dev. Dis.—*Mental Health Aspects of Developmental Disabilities*
Ment. Retard. Dev. Dis. Res. Rev.—*Mental Retardation & Developmental Disabilities Research Reviews*
Ment. Retard. Devel. Res. Rev—*Mental Retardation & Developmental Research Review*
Monogr. Soc. Res. Child Develop.—*Monographs of the Society for Research in Child Development*
N. Engl. J. Med.—*New England Journal of Medicine*
Neurobiol. Aging—*Neurobiology of Aging*
Neurosci. Lett.—*Neuroscience Letters*
Nord. J. Psychiat.—*Nordic Journal of Psychiatry*
Personal. Indiv. Diff.—*Personality and Individual Differences*
Personal. Soc. Psychol. Bull.—*Personality and Social Psychology Bulletin*
Personal. Soc. Psychol. Rev.—*Personality and Social Psychology Review*
Prim. Psychiat.—*Primary Psychiatry*
Prof. Psychol. Res. Pract.—*Professional Psychology: Research and Practice*
Prof. Psychol.—*Professional Psychology*
Prog. Neuropsychopharmacol. Biol. Psychiatry—*Progress in Neuropsychopharmacology & Biological Psychiatry*
Psych. Addict. Behav.—*Psychology of Addictive Behaviors*
Psych. Res. Neuroimag.—*Psychiatry Research: Neuroimaging*
Psych. Today—*Psychology Today*
Psychiat. Ann.—*Psychiatric Annals*
Psychiat. Clin. N. Amer.—*Psychiatric Clinics of North America*
Psychiat. News—*Psychiatric News*
Psychiat. Res.—*Psychiatric Research*
Psychiatr. Q.—*Psychiatric Quarterly*
Psychiatr. Serv.—*Psychiatric Services*
Psychol. Aging—*Psychology and Aging*
Psychol. Assess.—*Psychological Assessment*
Psychol. Bull.—*Psychological Bulletin*
Psychol. Inq.—*Psychological Inquiry*
Psychol. Med.—*Psychological Medicine*
Psychol. Meth.—*Psychological Methods*
Psychol. Rec.—*Psychological Record*
Psychol. Rep.—*Psychological Reports*
Psychol. Rev.—*Psychological Review*
Psychol. Sci. in the Pub. Int.—*Psychological Science in the Public Interest*
Psychol. Sci.—*Psychological Science*
Psychol. Women Quart.—*Psychology of Women Quarterly*
Psychopath.—*Psychopathology*
Psychopharm. Bull.—*Psychopharmacology Bulletin*
Psychosom. Med.—*Psychosomatic Medicine*
Psychother. Psychosom.—*Psychotherapy and Psychosomatics*
Q. J. Exp. Psych. [A]—*Quarterly Journal of Experimental Psychology: [A] Human Experimental Psychology*
Rev. Gen. Pscyhol.—*Review of General Psychology*
Roche Med. Imag. Comm.—*Roche Medical Image and Commentary*
Schiz. Res.—*Schizophrenia Research*
Schizo. Bull.—*Schizophrenia Bulletin*
School Psychol. Rev.—*School Psychology Review*
Sci. News—*Science News*
Scientif. Amer.—*Scientific American*
Soc. Develop.—*Social Development*
Soc. Psychiat. Psychiatr. Epidemiol.—*Social Psychiatry and Psychiatric Epidemiology*
Soc. Psychiat.—*Social Psychiatry*
Soc. Sci. Med.—*Social Science and Medicine*
Stress—*Stress: The International Journal on the Biology of Stress*
Trans. Cult. Psych. Res. Rev.—*Transcultural Psychiatric Research Review*
Transcult. Psychiat.—*Transcultural Psychiatry*

A recovering patient. (1986). "Can we talk?": The schizophrenic patient in psychotherapy. *Amer. J. Psychiat., 143*(1), 68–70.

Abatemarco, D. J., West, B., Zec, V., Russo, A., Sosiak, P., & Mardesic, V. (2004). Project Northland in Croatia: A community-based adolescent alcohol prevention intervention. *J. Drug Edu. 34*, 167–78.

Abbey, A., Zawacki, T., Buck, P. O., Clinton, A. M., & McAuslan, P. (2001). Alcohol and sexual assault. *Alcohol Research & Health, 25*(1), 43–51.

Abel, E. L. (1988). Fetal alcohol syndrome in families. *Neurotoxicology and Teratology, 10,* 1–2.

Abel, G. G., & Rouleau, J. L. (1990). The nature and extent of sexual assault. In W. L. Marshall, D. R. Laws, & H. E. Barbaree (Eds.), *Handbook of sexual assault: Issues, theories, and treatment of the offender* (pp. 9–22). New York: Plenum.

Abi-Saab, D., Beauvais, J., Mehm, J., Brody, M., Gottschalk, C., & Kosten, T. R. (2005). The effect of alcohol on the neuropsychological functioning of recently abstinent cocaine-dependent subjects. *American Journal on Addictions, 14*(2), 166–78.

Abou-Saleh, M. T. (1992). Lithium. In E. S. Paykel (Ed.), *Handbook of affective disorders* (2nd ed.). New York: Guilford.

Abraham, H. D., & Wolf, E. (1988). Visual function in past users of LSD: Psychophysical findings. *J. Abn. Psychol., 97,* 443–47.

Abrahamson, D. J., Barlow, D. H., Sakheim, D. K., Beck, J. G., & Athanasiou, R. (1985). Effects of distraction on sexual responding in functional and dysfunctional men. *Behav. Ther., 16,* 503–15.

Abramowitz, J. S., Tolin, D. F., & Street, G. P. (2001). Paradoxical effects of thought suppression: A meta-analysis of controlled studies. *Clin. Psychol. Rev., 21*(5), 683–703.

Abrams, R. (2002) *Electroconvulsive Therapy* (4th Edition). New York: Oxford University Press.

Abramson, L. Y., & Alloy, L. B. (In Press). Cognitive vulnerability to depression: Current status and developmental origins. In T. E. Joiner, J. Brown, & J. Kistner (Eds.), *The interpersonal, cognitive, and social nature of depression.* Mahwah, N. J.: Erlbaum.

Abramson, L. Y., & Seligman, M. E. P. (1977). Modeling psychopathology in the laboratory: History and rationale. In M. Maser & M. E. P. Seligman (Eds.), *Psychopathology: Experimental models.* San Francisco: Freeman.

Abramson, L. Y., Alloy, L. B., Hankin, B. L., Haeffel, G. J., MacCoon, D. G., & Gibb, B. E. (2002). Cognitive vulnerability-stress models of depression in a self-regulatory and psychobiological context. In I. H. Gotlib & C. L. Hammen (Eds.), *Handbook of depression*(pp. 268–94). New York: Guilford.

Abramson, L. Y., Metalsky, G. I., & Alloy, L. B. (1989). Hopelessness depression: A theory-based subtype of depression. *Psychol. Rev., 96,* 358–72.

Abramson, L. Y., Seligman, M. E. P., & Teasdale, J. D. (1978). Learned helplessness in humans: Critique and reformulation. *J. Abn. Psychol., 87,* 49–74.

Abramson, L., Alloy, L., & Metalsky, G. (1995). Hopelessness depression. In G. Buchanan & M. Seligman (Eds.), *Explanatory style* (pp. 113–34). Hillsdale, NJ: Erlbaum.

Ackard, D. M., Croll, J. K., & Kearney-Cooke, A. (2002). Dieting frequency among college females: Association with disordered eating, body image, and related psychological problems. *J. Psychosom. Res., 52,* 129–36.

Ackerson, J., Scogin, F., McKendree-Smith, N., & Lyman, R. (1998). Cognitive bibliotherapy for mild and moderate adolescent depressive symptomatology. *J. Cons. Clin. Psychol., 66*(4), 685–90.

ACSF Investigators. (1992). AIDS and sexual behaviour in France. Nature, 360, 407–9.

AD2000 Collaborative Group. (2004, Jun. 26). Long-term donepezil treatment in 565 patients with Alzheimer's disease (AD2000): Randomised double blind trial. *Lancet, 363,* 2105–15.

Adair, M. J. (1997). Plato's lost theory of hysteria. *Psychoanalytic Quarterly, 66,* 98–106.

Adams, H. E., Bernat, J. A., & Luscher, K. A. (2001). Borderline personality disorder: An overview. In H. E. Adams & P. B. Sutker (Eds.), *Comprehensive handbook of psychopathology* (pp. 491–508). New York: Kluwer Academic.

Adams, M. A., & Ferraro, F. R. (1997). Acquired immunodeficiency syndrome dementia complex. *J. Clin. Psychol., 53*(7), 767–78.

Addis, M. E., & Krasnow, A. D. (2000). A national survey of practicing psychologists' attitudes toward psychotherapy treatment manuals. *J. Cons. Clin. Psychol., 68,* 331–39.

Addis, M. E., & Mahalik, J. R. (2003). Men, masculinity, and the contexts of help seeking. *Amer. Psychol., 58,* 1, 5–14.

Adler, L. E., Olincy, A., Waldo, M., Harris, J. G., Griffith, J., Stevens, K., Flach, K., Nagamoto, H., Bickford, P., Leonard, S., & Freedman, R. (1998). Schizophrenia, sensory gating, and nicotinic receptors. *Schizo. Bull., 24*(2), 189–202.

Adler, T. (1994). Alzheimer's causes unique cell death. *Sci. News, 146*(13), 198.

Adrien, J. L., Perrot, A., Sauvage, D., & Leddet, I. (1992). Early symptoms in autism from family home movies: Evaluation and comparison between 1st and 2nd year of life using I.B.S.E. scale. *Acta Paedopsychiatrica International Journal of Child and Adolescent Psychiatry, 55,* 71–75.

Affleck, G., Tennen, H., Urrows, S., & Higgins, P. (1994). Person and contextual features of daily stress reactivity: Individual differences in relations of undesirable daily events with mood disturbance and chronic pain intensity. *J. of Pers. Soc. Psychol., 66*(2), 329–40.

Agras, W. S. (1982). Behavioral medicine in the 1980's: Nonrandom connections. *J. Cons. Clin. Psychol., 50*(6), 820–40.

Agras, W. S. (1993). Short term psychological treatments for binge eating. In C. Fairburn & G. T. Wilson (Eds.), *Binge eating: Nature, assessment, and treatment.* New York: Guilford.

Agras, S. W., Telch, C. F., Arnow, B., Eldredge, K., et al. (1997). One-year follow-up of cognitive-behavioral therapy for obese individuals with binge eating disorder. *J. Cons. Clin. Psychol., 65*(2), 343–47.

Agras, W. S., et al. (1992). Pharmacologic and cognitive-behavioral treatment for bulimia nervosa: A controlled comparison. *Amer. J. Psychiat., 149,* 82–87.

Agras, W. S., Walsh, T., Fairburn, C. G., Wilson, T., & Kraemer, H. C. (2000). A multicenter comparison of cognitive-behavioral therapy and interpersonal therapy for bulimia nervosa. *Arch. Gen. Psychiat., 57*(5), 459–66.

Aiken, L. R. (1996). *Rating scales and checklists.* New York: Wiley.

Akins, S., Mosher, C., Rotolo, T., & Griffin, R. (2003). Patterns and correlates of substance use among American Indians in Washington State. *J. Drug Iss., 33*(1), 45–72.

Akiskal, H. S. (1997). Overview of chronic depressions and their clinical management. In H. S Akiskal & G. B. Cassano (Eds.), *Dysthymia and the spectrum of chronic depressions* (pp. 1–34). New York: Guilford.

Akiskal, H. S. (2005). Searching for behavioral indicators of bipolar II in patients presenting with major depressive episodes: The "red sign," the "rule of three," and other biographic signs of temperamental extravagance, activation, and hypomania. *J. Affect. Dis., 84*(2–3), 279–290.

Akiskal, H. S., & Benazzi, F. (2005). Atypical depression: A variant of bipolar II or a bridge between unipolar and bipolar II. *J. Affect. Dis., 84,* 209–217.

Akiskal, H. S., & Pinto, O. (1999). The evolving bipolar spectrum: Prototypes I, II, III and IV. *Psychiat. Clin. N. Amer., 22*(3), 517–34.

Akiskal, H. S., Maser, J. D., Zeller, P. J., Endicott, J., Coryell, W., Keller, M., Warshaw, M., Clayton, P., & Goodwin, F. (1995). Switching from 'unipolar' to bipolar II. *Arch. Gen. Psychiat., 52,* 114–23.

Alarcon, M., et al. (1997). A twin study of mathematics disability. *J. Learn. Dis., 30*(6), 617–23.

Albano, A. M., Chorpita, B. F., & Barlow, D. H. (1996). Childhood anxiety disorders. In E. J. Mash & R. A. Barkley (Eds.), *Child psychopathology* (pp. 196–241). New York: Guilford.

Albee, G. W. (1999). Prevention, not treatment, is the only hope. *Counseling Psychology Quarterly, 12*(2), 133–46.

Albright v. Abington Memorial Hospital, 696 A.2d 1159 (Pa 1997).

Alcoholics Anonymous. (2002). Membership in AA. Alcoholics Anonymous Website.

Alderson, P. (2001). Down's syndrome: Cost, quality and value of life. *Soc. Sci. Med., 53,* 627–38.

Alexander, F. (1948). *Fundamentals of psychoanalysis.* New York: Norton.

Alexander, F. (1950). *Psychosomatic medicine.* New York: Norton.

Alexander, G. M., & Sherwin, B. B. (1993). Sex steroids, sexual behavior, and selective attention for erotic stimuli in women using oral contraceptives. *Psychoneuroendocrinology, 18,* 91–102.

Alexander, K., Huganir, L. S., & Zigler, E. (1985). Effects of different living settings on the performance of mentally retarded individuals. *Amer. J. Ment. Def., 90,* 9–17.

Alexopoulos, G. S., Borson, S., Cuthbert, B. N., Devanand, D. P., Mulsant, B. H., Olin, J. T., et al. (2002). Assessment of late life depression. *Biol. Psychiat., 52*(3), 164–174.

Alison, N. G. (1994). Fetal alcohol syndrome: Implications for psychologists. *Clin. Psychol. Rev., 14,* 91–111.

Allden, K., Poole, C., Chantavanich, S., Ohmar, K., Aung, N., & Mollica, R. (1996). Burmese political dissidents in Thailand: Trauma and survival among young adults in exile. *Amer. J. Pub. Hlth., 86*(11), 1561–169.

Allen, A., & Hollander, E. (2004). Similarities and differences between body dysmorphic disorder and other disorders. *Psychiat. Ann., 34*(12), 927–33.

Allerton, W. S. (1979). Psychiatric casualties in Vietnam. *Roche Med. Imag. Comm., 12*(8), 27.

Allodi, F. A. (1994). Posttraumatic stress disorder in hostages and victims of torture. *Psychiat. Clin. of N. Amer., 17,* 279–88.

Alloy, L. B., Abramson, L. Y., Gibb, B. E., Crossfield, A. G., Pieracci, A. M., Spasojevic, J., et al. (2004). Developmental antecedents of cognitive vulnerability to depression: Review of findings from the cognitive vulnerability to depression project. *J. Cog. Psychother. 18*(2), 115–133.

Alloy, L. B., Abramson, L. Y., Whitehouse, W. G., Hogan, M. E., Panzarella, C., & Rose, D. T. (In Press). Prospective incidence of first onsets and recurrences of depression in individuals at high and low cognitive risk for depression. *J. Abn. Psychol.*

Almeida, D. M. (2005). Resilience and vulnerability to daily stressors assessed via diary methods. *Curr. Dirs. Psychol. Sci., 14,* 2, 64–68.

Alpert, J. E., Uebelacker, L. A., McLean, N. E., Nierenberg, A. A., Pava, J. A., Worthington III, J. J., Tedlow, J. R., Rosenbaum, J. F., & Fava, M. (1997). Social phobia, avoidant personality disorder and atypical depression: Co-occurrence and clinical implications. *Psychol. Med., 27,* 627–633.

Alpert, J. L., Brown, L. S., Ceci, S. J., Courtois, C. A., Loftus, E. F., & Ornstein, P. A. (1996). *Working group on investigation of memories of childhood abuse: Final report.* Washington, DC: American Psychological Association.

Alterman, A. I. (1988). Patterns of familial alcoholism, alcoholism severity, and psychopathology. *J. Nerv. Ment. Dis., 176,* 167–75.

Alterman, A. I., McDermott, P. A., Cacciola, J. S., Rutherford, M. J., Boardman, C. R., McKay, J. R., & Cook, T. G. (1998). A typology of antisociality in methadone patients. *J. Abn. Psychol., 107*(2), 412–22.

Alterman, A. I., Searles, J. S., & Hall, J. G. (1989). Failure to find differences in drinking behavior as a function of familial risk for alcoholism: A replication. *J. Cons. Clin. Psychol., 98,* 50–53.

Altshuler, L. L., Bauer, M., Frye, M. A., Gitlin, M. J., Mintz, J., Szuba, M. P., Leight K. L., & Whybrow, P. C. (2001). Does thyroid supplementation accelerate tricyclic antidepressant response? A review and meta-analysis of the literature. *Amer. J. Psychiat., 158,* 1617–22.

Amato, P. R. (2000). The consequences of divorce for adults and children. *J. Marr. Fam., 62,* 1269–87.

Amato, P. R. (2001). Children of divorce in the 1990s: An update of the Amato and Keith (1991) meta-analysis. *J. Fam. Psychol., 15,* 355–70.

Amato, P. R. & Cheadle, J. (2005). The long reach of divorce: Divorce and child well-being across three generations. *J. Marr. Fam., 67*(1), 191–206.

Amato, P. R., & Booth, A. (2001). The legacy of parents' marital discord: Consequences for children's marital quality. *J. Pers. Soc. Psychol., 81,* 627–38.

Amato, P. R., & DeBoer, D. D. (2001). The transmission of marital instability across generations: Relationships skills or commitment to marriage? *J. Marr. Fam., 63,* 1038–51.

Amato, P. R., & Keith, B. (1991a). Parental divorce and adult well-being: A meta-analysis. *J. Marr. Fam., 53,* 43–58.

Amato, P. R., & Keith, B. (1991b). Parental divorce and the well-being of children: A meta-analysis. *Psychol. Bull., 110,* 26–46.

Ambrogne, J. A. (2002). Reduced-risk drinking as a treatment goal: What clinicians need to know. *Journal of Substance Abuse Treatment, 22*(1), 45–53.

American Heart Association. (2001). *2001 Heart and stroke statistical update.* Dallas, TX: Author.

American Heart Association. (2002). *2002 Heart and stroke statistical update.* Dallas, TX: Author.

American Medical Association Committee on Human Sexuality. (1972). *Human Sexuality.* (p. 40). Chicago: American Medical Association.

American Psychiatric Association. (1968). *Diagnostic and statistical manual of mental disorders* (2nd ed.). Washington, DC: Author.

American Psychiatric Association. (1994). *Diagnostic and statistical manual of mental disorders (DSM-IV)* (4th ed.). Washington, DC: Author.

American Psychiatric Association. (1999). Practice guidelines for the treatment of patients with delirium. *Amer. J. Psychiat., 156*(suppl.), 1–20.

American Psychiatric Association. (2000). *Diagnostic and statistical manual of mental disorders* (4th ed.). Washington, DC: Author.

American Psychiatric Association. (2000). *Diagnostic and statistical manual of mental disorders: DSM-IV-TR.* Washington, DC: Author.

American Psychiatric Association. (2001). Practice guideline for the treatment of patients with borderline personality disorder. *Amer. J. Psychiat., 158,* 1–52.

American Psychiatric Association. (2004). Practice guideline for the treatment of patients with schizophrenia. (2nd ed.). *Amer. J. Psychiat., 161,* (Suppl. 2), 1–56.

American Psychological Association (2002). Ethical principles of psychologists. *Amer. Psychol., 57, 12,* 1060–73.

Ammerman, R. T., & Hersen, M. (1997). *Handbook of prevention and treatment with children and adolescents.* New York: Wiley.

Ammerman, R. T., Kane, V. R., Slomka, G. T., Reigel, D. H., Franzen, M. D., & Gadow, K. D. (1998). Psychiatric symptomatology and family functioning in children and adolescents with spina bifida. *J. Clin. Psychol. Med. Set., 5*(4), 449–65.

Anand, K. J. S., & Arnold, J. H. (1994). Opioid tolerance and dependence in infants and children. *Critical Care Medicine, 22,* 334–42.

Anda, R., Williamson, D., Jones, D., Macera, C., Eaker, E., Glasman, A., & Marks, J. (1993). Depressed affect, hopelessness, and the risk of ischemic heart disease in a cohort of U.S. adults. *Epidemiology, 4,* 285–94.

Anderluh, M. B., Tchanturia, K., Rabe-Hesketh, S., & Treasure, J. (2003). Childhood obsessive-compulsive personality traits in adult women with eating disorders: Defining a broader eating disorder phenotype. *Amer. J. Psychiat., 160,* 242–47.

Andersen, A. E. (1999). The diagnosis and treatment of eating disorders in primary care medicine. In P. S. Mehler & A. E. Andersen (Eds.), *Eating disorders: A guide to medical care and complications.* Baltimore: Johns Hopkins University Press.

Andersen, A. E. (2002). Eating disorders in males. In C. G. Fairburn & K. D. Brownell (Eds.), *Eating disorders and obesity* (pp. 188–92). New York: Guilford.

Andersen, A. E., Bowers, W., & Evans, K. (1997). Inpatient treatment of anorexia nervosa. In D. M. Garner & P. E. Garfinkel (Eds.), *Handbook of treatment for eating disorders* (pp. 327–53). New York: Guilford.

Andersen, B. L. (1983). Primary orgasmic dysfunction: Diagnostic considerations and review of treatment. *Psychol. Bull., 93,* 105–36.

Anderson, C., Krull, D., & Weiner, B. (1996). Explanations: Processes and consequences. In E. T. Higgins & A. Kruglanski (Eds.), *Social Psychology: Handbook of Basic Principles* (pp. 271–96). New York: Guilford.

Anderson, E. M., & Lambert, M. J. (1995). Short-term dynamically oriented psychotherapy: A review and meta-analysis. *Clin. Psychol. Rev., 15*(6), 503–14.

Anderson, J. C., Williams, S., McGee, R., & Silva, P. A. (1987). DSM III disorders in preadolescent children. *Arch. Gen. Psychiat., 44,* 69–80.

Anderson, K. E., & Savage, C. R. (2004). Cognitive and neurobiological findings in obsessive-compulsive disorder. *Psychiat. Clin. N. Amer., 27*(1), 37–47.

Anderson, K., & Lehto, J. (1995). *Young people and alcohol, drugs and tobacco: European action plan.* Geneva: World Health Organization.

Anderson, N. B., & McNeilly, M. (1993). Autonomic reactivity and hypertension in blacks: Toward a contextual model. In J. C. S. Fray & J. G. Douglas (Eds.), *Pathophysiology of hypertension in blacks* (pp. 107–39). New York: Oxford.

Anderson, V. A., et al. (1997). Predicting recovery from head injury in young children: A prospective analysis. *J. Int. Neuropsychologic. Soc., 3*(6), 568–80.

Andrade, L., Caraveo-Anduaga, J. J., Berglund, P., Bijl, R. V., DeGraaf, R., Vollerbergh, W., et al. (2004). The epidemiology of major depressive episodes: Results from the International Consortium of Psychiatric Epidemiology (ICPE) surveys. *Int. J. Meth. Psychiat. Res., 12*(1), 3–21.

Andreasen, N. C., Arndt, S., Swayze, V., Cizadlo, T., Flaum, M., O'Leary, D., Ernhardt, J. C., & Yuh, W. T. C. (1994). Thalamic abnormalities in schizophrenia visualized through magnetic resonance image averaging. *Science, 266,* 294–98.

Andreasen, N. C., et al. (1995). Symptoms of schizophrenia: Methods, meanings, and mechanisms. *Arch. Gen. Psychiat., 52*(5), 341–51.

Andreasen, N. C. (1984). *The broken brain: The biological revolution in psychiatry.* New York: Harper & Row.

Andreasen, N. C. (1985). Positive vs. negative schizophrenia: A critical evaluation. *Schizo. Bull., 11,* 380–89.

Andreasson, S., & Brandt, L. (1997). Mortality and morbidity related to alcohol. *Alcohol and Alcoholism, 32*(2), 173–78.

Andrews, G., & Harvey, R. (1981). Does psychotherapy benefit neurotic patients? A reanalysis of the Smith, Glass, and Miller data. *Arch. Gen. Psychiat., 38,* 1203–8.

Angell, M. (2000). Is academic medicine for sale? *N. Engl. J. Med., 342,* 1516–1518.

Angst, J., & Sellaro, R. (2000). Historical perspectives and natural history of bipolar disorder. *Biol. Psychiat., 48,* 445–457.

Anisman, H., & Merali, Z. (1999). Understanding stress: Characteristics and caveats. *Alcohol Research & Health, 23,* 241–49.

Anonymous. (1994). First person account: Schizophrenia with childhood onset. *Schizo. Bull., 20,* 587–90.

Antony, M. M., & Barlow, D. H. (2002). Specific phobias. In D. H. Barlow (Ed.), *Anxiety and its disorders* (2nd ed., pp. 380–417). New York: Guilford.

Antony, M. M., Brown, T. A., & Barlow, D. H. (1997). Heterogeneity among specific phobia types in DSM-IV. *Behav. Res. Ther., 35,* 1089–1100.

Antony, M., Downie, F. , & Swinson, R. (1998). Diagnostic issues and epidemiology in obsessive-compulsive disorder. In R. Swinson, M. Antony, S. Rachman, & M. Richter (Eds.), *Obsessive-compulsive disorder: Theory, research, and treatments* (pp. 3–32). New York: Guilford.

Appelbaum, P. S., & Greer, A. (1994). Who's on trial? Multiple personalities and the insanity defense. *Hosp. Comm. Psychiat., 45*(10), Spec. Issue 965–66.

Appels, A., & Mulder, P. (1988). Excess fatigue as a precursor of myocardial infarction. *European Heart Journal, 9,* 758–64.

Arbisi, P. A., & Butcher, J. N. (2004). Relationship between personality and health symptoms: Use of the MMPI-2 in medical assessments. *Intl. J. Clin. Hlth., 4,* 571–595.

Arbisi, P. A., Ben-Porath, Y., & McNulty, J. (2002). A comparison of MMPI-2 validity in African American and Caucasian psychiatric inpatients. *Psychol. Assess., 14*(1), 3–15.

Arehart-Treichler, J. (2004). PTSD treatment focus of newest APA practice guideline. *Psychiat. News, 39,* 24–25.

Arlow, J. A. (2000). Psychoanalysis. In R. J. Corsini & D. Wedding (Eds.), *Current psychotherapies* (pp. 16–53). Itasca, IL: Peacock.

Arndt, I. O., McLellan, A. T., Dorozynsky, L., Woody, G. E., & O'Brien, C. P. (1994). Desipramine treatment for cocaine dependence: Role of antisocial personality disorder. *J. Ner. Ment. Dis., 182,* 151–56.

Arnett, P. A., Howland, E. W., Smith, S. S., & Newman, J. P. (1993). Autonomic responsivity during passive avoidance in incarcerated psychopaths. *Personal. and Indiv. Diff., 14*(1), 173–84.

Arnold, M. B. (1962). *Story sequence analysis: A new method of measuring motivation and predicting achievement.* New York: Columbia University Press.

Arnold, S. E. (2000). Hippocampal pathology. In P. J. Harrison & G. W. Roberts (Eds.), *The neuropathology of schizophrenia* (pp. 57–80). Oxford, UK: Oxford University Press.

Arnott, R., Finger, S., & Smith, C. U. (Eds.). (2003). *Trepanation: History, discovery, theory.* Lisse, the Netherlands: Swets & Zeitlinger.

Aronoff, B. (1987). *Needs assessments: What have we learned? Experiences from Refugee Assistance Programs in Hawaii.* Paper given at the Refugee Assistance Program: Mental Health Workgroup Meeting, UCLA, February 12–13.

Arrindell, W. A. (2003). Cultural abnormal psychology. *Beh. Res. Ther., 41,* 749–753.

Arsenault, L., Cannon, M., Poulton, R., Murray, R., Caspi, A., & Moffitt, T. E. (2002). Cannabis use in adolescence and risk for adult psychosis: A longitudinal prospective study. *BMJ, 325,* 1212–13.

Arsenault, L., Cannon, M., Witton, J., & Murray, R. M. (2004). Causal association between cannabis and psychosis: Examination of the evidence. *Brit. J. Psychiat., 184,* 110–17.

Ashton, A. K., Hamer, R., & Rosen, R. C. (1997). Serotonin reuptake inhibitor-induced sexual dysfunction and its treatment: A large-scale retrospective study of 596 psychiatric outpatients. *J. Sex and Marit. Ther., 23,* 165–75.

Askin-Edgar, S., White, K. E., & Cummings, J. L. (2002). Neuropsychiatric aspects of Alzheimer's disease and other dementing illnesses. In S. C. Yudofsky & R. E. Hales, *The American Psychiatric Publishing textbook of neuropsychiatry and clinical neurosciences* (pp. 953–88). Washington, DC: American Psychiatric Publishing.

Aspis, S. (1997). Self-advocacy for people with learning difficulties: Does it have a future? *Disability & Society, 12*(4), 647–54.

Associated Press. (1997, Dec. 3). Crack-using woman admits guilt in the death of her fetus.

Associated Press. (2001, Aug. 7). Fire in asylum in southern India kills 25 mentally ill patients, many chained to beds. *Daily Star International News, 3.*

Associated Press. (2003). Psychiatrist disputes Hinckley's recovery. Tuesday, Nov. 18, 2003. Posted: 8:40 PM EST (0140 GMT).

Athey, J. L., O'Malley, P., Henderson, D. P., & Ball, J. W. (1997). Emergency medical services for children:

Beyond lights and sirens. *Profess. Psychol., 28*(5), 464–70.

Atkinson, J. W. (1992). Motivational determinants of thematic apperception. In C. P. Smith, J. W. Atkinson, & J. Veroff (Eds.), *Motivation and personality: Handbook of thematic content analysis* (pp. 21–48). New York: Cambridge University Press.

Atlis, M. M., Hahn, J. & Butcher, J. N. (2005). Computer-based assessment with the MMPI-2. In J. N. Butcher (Ed.). *MMPI-2: The practioner's handbook.* (pp. 445–476). Washington, DC: American Psychological Association.

Avants, S. K., Margolin, A., Kosten, T. R., Rounsaville, B. J., & Schottenfeld, R. S. (1998). When is less treatment better? The role of social anxiety in matching methadone patients to psychosocial treatments. *J. Cons. Clin. Psychol., 66,* 924–31.

Avila, M. T., Weiler, M. A., Lahti, A. C., Tamminga, C. A., & Thaker, G. K. (2002). Effects of ketamine on leading saccades during smooth-pursuit eye movements may implicate cerebellar dysfunction in schizophrenia. *Amer. J. Psychiat., 159*(9), 1490–96.

Azar, B. (1997). Researchers debunk myth of crack baby. *Monitor, 29*(12), 14–15.

Azari, N. P., Horwitz, B., Pettigrew, K. D., & Grady, C. L. (1994). Abnormal pattern of glucose metabolic rates involving language areas in young adults with Down syndrome. *Brain & Language, 46*(1), 1–20.

Azim, H. F. (2001). Partial hospitalization programs. In W. J. Livesley (Ed.), *Handbook of personality disorders* (pp. 527–40). New York: Guilford.

Baaré, F. C., van Oel, C. J., Hulshoff Pol, H. E., Schnack, H. G., Durston, S., Sitkoorn, M. M., & Kahn, R. S. (2001). Volumes of brain structures in twins discordant for schizophrenia. *Arch. Gen. Psychiat., 58,* 33–40.

Babcock, J. C., Jacobson, N. S., Gottman, J. M., & Yerington, T. P. (2000). Attachment, emotional regulation, and the function of marital violence: Differences between secure, preoccupied, and dismissing violent and nonviolent husbands. *J. Fam. Viol., 15*(4), 391–409.

Babor, T. F. (1996). The classification of alcoholics: Typology theories from the nineteenth century to the present. *Alcohol, Health, & Research World, 20*(1), 6–14.

Bailer, U. F., Frank, G. K., Henry, S. E., Price, J. C., Meltzer, C. C., Weissfeld, L., Mathis, C. A., Drevets, W. C., Wagner, A., Hoge, J., Ziolko, S. K., McConaha, C. W., & Kaye, W. H. (2005). Altered brain serotonin 5-HT_{1A} receptor binding after recovery from anorexia nervosa measured by positron emission tomography and [Carbonyl ^{11}C] WAY-100635. *Arch. Gen. Psychiat., [62]* 1032–41.

Bailey, A., Le Couteur, A., & Gottesman, I. (1995). Autism as a strongly genetic disorder: Evidence from a British twin study. *Psychol. Med., 25*(1), 63–77.

Bailey, J. M. (1999). Homosexuality and mental illness. *Arch. Gen. Psychiat., 56,* 883–84.

Bailey, J. M. (2003) *The man who would be queen.* Washington , DC. Joseph Henry Press.

Bailey, J. M., & Greenberg, A. S. (1998). The science and ethics of castration: Lessons from the Morse case. *Northwestern Law Review, 92,* 1225–45.

Bailey, J. M., & Pillard, R. C. (1991). A genetic study of male sexual orientation. *Arch. Gen. Psychiat., 48,* 1089–96.

Bailey, J. M., & Zucker, K. J. (1995). Childhood sex-typed behavior and sexual orientation: A conceptual analysis and quantitative review. *Develop. Psychol., 31,* 43–55.

Bailey, J. M., Dunne, M. P., & Martin, N. (2000). Genetic and environmental influences on sexual orientation and its correlates in an Australian twin sample. *J. Pers. Soc. Psychol., 78,* 524–36.

Bailey, J. M., Gaulin, S., Agyei, Y., & Gladue, B. A. (1994). Effects of gender and sexual orientation on evolutionarily relevant aspects of human mating psychology. *J. Pers. Soc. Psychol. 66,* 1081–93.

Bailey, J. M., Pillard, R. C., Neale, M. C., & Agyei, Y. (1993). Heritable factors influence female sexual orientation. *Arch. Gen. Psychiat., 50,* 217–23.

Bailey, S. (2000). Juvenile delinquency and serious antisocial behavior. In M. G. Gelder, J. J. Lopez-Ibor, Jr., & N. C. Andreasen (Eds.), *New Oxford textbook of psychiatry* (pp. 1859–73). Oxford: Oxford University Press.

Baker, A., & Lee, N. K. (2003). A review of psychosocial interventions for amphetamine use. *Drug Al. Rev., 22*(3), 323–35.

Baker, D., Hunter, E., Lawrence, E., Medford, N., Patel, M., Senior, C., et al. (2003). Depersonalization disorder: Clinical features of 204 cases. *Brit. J. Psychiat., 182,* 428–33.

Baldessarini, R. J., & Hennen, J. (2004). Genetics of suicide. *Harv. Rev. Psychiat., 12*(1), 1–13.

Baldwin, A. L., Baldwin, C., & Cole, R. E. (1990). Stress-resistant families and stress-resistant children. In J. Rolf, A. S. Masten, D. Cicchetti, K. H. Nuechterlein, & S. Weintraub (Eds.), *Risk and protective factors in the development of psychopathology.* New York: Cambridge University Press.

Baldwin, R. I., Chelonis, J. J., Flake, R. A., Edwards, M. C., Field, C. R., Meaux, J. B., & Paule, M. G. (2004). Effect of methylphenidate on time perception in children with attention-deficit hyperactivity disorder. *Exp. Clin. Psychopharm., 12,* 57–64.

Ballenger, J. C. (1996). An update on pharmacological treatment of panic disorder. In H. G. Westenberg, J. A. Den Boer, & D. L. Murphy (Eds.), *Advances in the neurobiology of anxiety disorders* (pp. 229–46). Chichester, England: Wiley.

Balshem, M., Oxman, G., Van Rooyen, D., & Girod, K. (1992). Syphilis, sex and crack cocaine: Images of risk and morality. *Soc. Sci. and Med., 35,* 147–60.

Bandelow, B., Spaeth, C., Alvarez Tichauer, G., Broocks, A., Hajak, G., & Ruether, E. (2002). Early traumatic life events, parental attitudes, family history, and birth risk factors in patients with panic disorder. *Compr. Psychia., 43,* 269–78.

Bandura, A. (1964). *Principles of behavior modification.* New York: Holt, Rinehart and Winston.

Bandura, A. (1969). *Principles of behavior modification.* New York: Holt, Rinehart & Winston.

Bandura, A. (1974). Behavior theory and the models of man. *Amer. Psychol., 29*(12), 859–69.

Bandura, A. (1977a). Self-efficacy: Toward a unifying theory of behavioral change. *Psychol. Rev., 84*(2), 191–215.

Bandura, A. (1977b). *Social learning theory.* Englewood Cliffs, NJ: Prentice-Hall.

Bandura, A. (1986). *Social foundations of thought and action: A social cognitive theory.* Englewood Cliffs, NJ: Prentice-Hall.

Bandura, A. (1997). *Self-efficacy: The exercise of control.* New York: W. H. Freeman/Times Books/Henry Holt & Co.

Barbaree, H. E., & Seto, M. C. (1997). Pedophilia: Assessment and treatment. In D. R. Laws & W. O'Donohue (Eds.), *Sexual deviance: Theory, assessment, and treatment* (pp. 175–93). New York: Guilford.

Barber, J. P., Connolly, M. B., Crits-Christoph, P., Gladis, L., & Siqueland, L. (2000). Alliance predicts patients' outcome beyond in-treatment change in symptoms. *J. Cons. Clin. Psychol., 68,* 1027–32.

Barbour, K. A., Davison, G. C. (2004). Clinical interviewing. *Comprehensive handbook of psychological assessment* (Vol. 3, pp. 181–93). New York: John Wiley & Sons.

Barch, D. M. (2005). The cognitive neuroscience of schizophrenia. *Annual Review of Clinical Psychology, 1,* 12.1–12.33.

Bar-Haim, Y., Henkin, Y., Ari-Even-Roth, D., Tetin-Schneider, S., Hildesheimer, M., & Muchnik, C. (2004). Reduced auditory efferent activity in childhood selective mutism. *Biol. Psychiat., 55*(11), 1061–68.

Barkley, R. A., Fischer, M., Smallish, L., & Fletcher, K. (2004). Young adult follow-up of hyperactive children: Antisocial activities and drug use. *J. Child Psychol. Psychiat., 45*(2), 195–211.

Barkley, R. A. (1997). Behavioral inhibition, sustained attention, and executive function: Constructing a unified theory of ADHD. *Psychol. Bull., 121,* 65–94.

Barlow, D. H. (1988). *Anxiety and its disorders: The nature and treatment of anxiety and panic.* New York: Guilford.

Barlow, D. H. (2001) (Ed), *Clinical Handbook of Psychological Disorders, 3rd Edition.* Guilford: New York.

Barlow, D. H. (2004). Psychological Treatments. *Amer. Psychol., 59*(9), 869–878.

Barlow, D. H. (Ed.). (1993). *Clinical handbook of psychological disorders* (2nd ed.). New York: Guilford.

Barlow, D. H. (Ed.). (2002a). *Anxiety and its disorders: The nature and treatment of anxiety and panic* (2nd ed.). New York: Guilford.

Barlow, D. H. (Ed.). (2002b). *Handbook of assessment and treatment planning for psychological disorders* (pp. 453–80). New York: Guilford.

Barlow, D. H., & Craske, M. G. (2000). *Mastery of your anxiety and panic (MAP-3): Client workbook for anxiety and panic* (3rd ed.). San Antonio, TX: Graywind/Psychological Corporation.

Barlow, D. H., Chorpita, B., & Turovsky, J. (1996). Fear, panic, anxiety, and disorders of emotion. In D. Hope (Ed.), *Perspectives on anxiety, panic, and fear.* 43rd Annual Nebraska Symposium on Motivation (pp. 251–328). Lincoln: University of Nebraska Press.

Barlow, D. H., Gorman, J. M., Shear, M. K., & Woods, S. W. (2000). Cognitive-behavioral therapy, imipramine, or their combination for panic disorder: A randomized controlled trial. *JAMA, 283,* 2529–36.

Barlow, D. H., Raffa, S. D., & Cohen, E. M. (2002). Psychosocial treatments for panic disorders, phobias and generalized anxiety disorders. In P. E. Nathan & J. M. Gorman (Eds.), *A guide to treatments that work* (2nd ed., pp. 301–36). New York: Oxford University Press.

Barlow, D. H., Sakheim, D. K., & Beck, J. G. (1983). Anxiety increases sexual arousal. *J. Abn. Psychol., 92,* 49–54.

Barnett, D., Ganiban, J., & Cicchetti, D. (1999). Maltreatment, negative expressivity, and the development of Type D attachments from 12 to 24 months of age. *Monogr. Soc. Res. Child Develop., 64,* 97–118.

Baron, I. S., & Goldberger, E. (1993). Neuropsychological disturbances of hydrocephalic children with implications for special education and rehabilitation. *Neuropsychological Rehabilitation, 3*(4), 389–410.

Barrett, D. H., Resnick, H., Foy, D. W., & Dansky, B. S. (1996). Combat exposure and adult psychosocial adjustment among U.S. Army veterans serving in Vietnam, 1965–1971. *J. Abn. Psychol. 105*(4), 575–81.

Barringer, T. A., & Weaver, E. M. (2002). Does long-term bupropion (Zyban) use prevent smoking relapse after initial success at quitting smoking? *J. Fam. Pract., 51,* 172.

Barry, H., III. (1982). Cultural variations in alcohol abuse. In I. Al-Issa (Ed.), *Culture and psychopathology.* Baltimore: University Park Press.

Barry, R. J., Clarke, A. R., & Johnstone, S. J. (2003). A review of electrophysiology in attention-deficit/hyperactivity disorder: II. Event-related potentials. *Clinical Neurophysiology, 114*(2) 184–98.

Barsetti, I., Earls, C. M., Lalumiere, M. L., & Belanger, N. (1998). The differentiation of intrafamilial and extrafamilial heterosexual child molesters. *J. Interpers. Violen., 13*(2), 275–86.

Barsky, A. J., & Ahern, D. K. (2004). Cognitive behavior therapy for hypochondriasis: A randomized controlled trial. *JAMA, 291*(12), 1464–70.

Barsky, A. J., et al. (1998). A prospective 4- to 5-year study of DSM-III-R Hypochondriasis. *Arch. Gen. Psychiat., 55*(8), 737–44.

Barsky, A. J., Wool, C., Barnett, M. C., & Cleary, P. D. (1994). Histories of childhood trauma in adult hypochondriacal patients. *Amer. J. Psychiat., 151*(3), 397–401.

Bartholomew, K., Kwong, M. J., & Hart, S. D. (2001). Attachment. In W. J. Livesley (Ed.), *Handbook of personality disorders* (pp. 196–230). New York: Guilford.

Bartholomew, R. (1997). The medicalization of the exotic: Latah as a colonialism-bound "syndrome." *Dev. Behav., 18,* 47–75.

Bartholow, B. D., Sher, K. J., & Krull, J. L. (2003). Changes in heavy drinking over the third decade of life as a function of collegiate fraternity and sorority involvement: A prospective, multilevel analysis. *Hlth. Psychol., 22,* 618–26.

Barton, J., Mooney, P., & Prasad, S. (2005). Atomoxetine hydrochloride and executive function in children with attention-deficit/hyperactivity disorder. *J. Child Adol. Psychopharm., 15*(2), 147–49.

Bartzokis, G., Lu, P. H., Turner, J., Mintz, J., & Saunders, C. S. (2005). Adjunctive risperidone in the treatment of chronic combat-related posttraumatic stress disorder. *Biol. Psychiat., 57*(5), 474–79.

Bashore, T., & Ridderinkhof, K. R. (2002). Older age, traumatic brain injury, and cognitive slowing: Some convergent and divergent findings. *Psychol. Bull., 128*(1), 151–98.

Başoğlu, M., & Mineka, S. (1992). The role of uncontrollable and unpredictable stress in post-traumatic stress responses in torture survivors. In M. Başoğlu (Ed.), *Torture and its consequences: Current treatment approaches* (pp. 182–225). Cambridge: Cambridge University Press.

Başoğlu, M., Kiliç, C., Salcioglu, E., & Livanou, M. (2004). Prevalence of posttraumatic stress disorder and comorbid depression in earthquake survivors in Turkey: An epidemiological study. *J. Trauma. Stress., 17*(2), 133–41.

Başoğlu, M., Mineka, S., Paker, M., Aker, T., Livanou, M., & Gok, S. (1997). Psychological preparedness for trauma as a protective factor in survivors of torture. *Psychol. Med., 27,* 1421–33.

Başoğlu, M., Paker, M., Paker, O., Ozmen, E., Marks, I., Sahin, D., & Sarimurat, N. (1994). Psychological effects of torture: A comparison of tortured with nontortured political activists in Turkey. *Amer. J. Psychiat., 151,* 76–81.

Bass, E., & Davis, L. (1988). *The courage to heal.* New York: Harper & Row.

Bassett, D. R., Jr., Fitzhugh, E. C., Crespo, C. J., King, G. A., & McLaughlin, J. E. (2002). Physical activity and ethnic differences in hypertension in the United States. *Preventive Medicine, 34*(2), 179–86.

Bastiani, A. M., Rao, R., Weltzin, T., & Kaye, W. H. (1995). Perfectionism in anorexia nervosa. *Int. J. Eat. Dis., 17*(2), 147–52.

Bateson, G. (1959). Cultural problems posed by a study of schizophrenic process. In A. Auerback (Ed.), *Schizophrenia: An integrated approach.* New York: Ronald Press.

Bateson, G. (1960). Minimal requirements for a theory of schizophrenia. *Arch. Gen. Psychiat., 2,* 477–91.

Bath, R., Morton, R., Uing, A., & Williams, C. (1996). Nocturnal enuresis and the use of desmopressin: Is it helpful? *Child: Care, Health & Development, 22*(22), 73–84.

Bauer, A. M., & Shea, T. M. (1986). Alzheimer's disease and Down syndrome: A review and implications for adult services. *Education and Training of the Mentally Retarded, 21,* 144–50.

Bauer, A., Rosca, P., Khawalled, R., Gruzniewski, A., & Grinshpoon, A. (2003). Dangerousness and risk assessment: The state of the art. *Israel Journal of Psychiatry & Related Sciences, 40*(3), 182–90.

Baumeister, R. F., & Butler, J. L. (1997). Sexual masochism: Deviance without pathology. In D. R. Laws & W. O'Donohue (Eds.), *Sexual deviance: Theory, assessment, and treatment.* New York: Guilford.

Baumrind, D. (1967). Child care practices anteceding three patterns of preschool behavior. *Genetic Psychology Monographs, 75,* 43–88.

Baumrind, D. (1971). Current patterns of parental authority. *Develop. Psychol., 4*(1), 1–103.

Baumrind, D. (1975). *Early socialization and the discipline controversy.* Morristown, NJ: General Learning Press.

Baumrind, D. (1991). Effective parenting during the early adolescent transition. In P. A. Cowan & E. M. Hetherington (Eds.), *Family transitions* (pp. 111–64). Hillsdale, NJ: Erlbaum.

Baumrind, D. (1993). The average expectable environment is not good enough: A response to Scarr. *Child Develop., 64,* 1299–1317.

Baxter, L. R., Jr., Ackermann, R. F., Swerdlow, N. R., Brody, A., Saxena, S., Schwartz, J. M., Gregortich, J. M., Stoessel, P., & Phelps, M. E. (2000). Specific brain system mediation of obsessive-compulsive disorder responsive to either medication or behavior therapy. In W. K. Goodman, M. V. Rudorfer, et al. (Eds.), *Obsessive-compulsive disorder: Contemporary issues in treatment. Personality and clinical psychology series* (pp. 573–609). Mahwah, NJ: Erlbaum.

Baxter, L. R., Jr., Schwartz, J. M., & Guze, B. H. (1991). Brain imaging: Toward a neuroanatomy of OCD. In J. Zohar, T. Insel, & S. Rasmussen (Eds.), *The psychobiology of obsessive-compulsive disorder.* New York: Springer.

Baxter, L. R., Jr., Schwartz, J. M., Bergman, K. S., Szuba, M. P., Guze, B. H., Mazziota, J. C., Alazraki, A., Selin, C., Ferng, H. K., Munford, P., & Phelps, M. (1992). Caudate glucose metabolic rate changes with both drug and behavior therapy for obsessive-compulsive disorder. *Arch. Gen. Psychiat., 49,* 681–89.

Bayer, R. (1981). *Homosexuality and American psychiatry.* New York: Basic Books.

Bazargan, M., Bazargan, S., & Akanda, M. (2001). Gambling habits among aged African Americans. *Clin. Geron., 22*(3–4), 51–62.

Beach, S. R. H., & Jones, D. J. (2002). Marital and family therapy for depression in adults. In I. H. Gotlib & C. L. Hammen (Eds.), *Handbook of depression* (pp. 422–40). New York: Guilford.

Beal, A. L. (1995). Post-traumatic stress disorder in prisoners of war and combat veterans of the Dieppe raid: A 50 year follow-up. *Canad. J. Psychiat., 40*(4), 177–84.

Beardslee, W. R., & Gladstone, T. R. G. (2001). Prevention of childhood depression: Recent findings and future prospects. *Biol. Psychiat., 49*(12), 1101–10.

Bearn, A., & Smith, C. (1998). How learning support is perceived by mainstream colleagues. *Support for Learning, 13*(1), 14–20.

Beason-Hazen, S., Nasrallah, H. A., & Bornstein, R. A. (1994). Self-report of symptoms and neuropsychological performance in asymptomatic HIV-positive individuals. *J. Neuropsychiat. Clin. Neurosci., 6*(1), 43–49.

Beaton, A. A. (1997). The relation of planum temporale asymmetry and morphology of the corpus callosum to handedness, gender, and dyslexia: A review of the evidence. *Brain and Language, 60*(2), 255–322.

Beauvais, F. (1998). American Indians and alcohol. *Alcohol Health & Research World, 22,* 253–59.

Beck, A. J., & Maruschak, L. M. (2001). Mental health treatment in state prisons, 2000. *Bureau of Justice Special Report* (NCJ 188215), July. Washington, DC: Department of Justice.

Beck, A. T., & Emery, G., (with) Greenberg, R. L. (1985). *Anxiety disorders and phobias: A cognitive perspective.* New York: Basic Books.

Beck, A. T., & Weishaar, M. (2000). Cognitive therapy. In R. J. Corsini & D. Wedding (Eds.), *Current psychotherapies* (6th ed., pp. 241–72). Itasca, IL: Peacock.

Beck, A. T., Freeman, A., & Associates. (1990). *Cognitive therapy of personality disorders.* New York: Guilford.

Beck, A. T., Freeman, A., & Davis, D. D. (2004). *Cognitive therapy of personality disorders.* (2nd ed). New York: Guilford Press.

Beck, A. T., Rush, A. J., Shaw, B., & Emery, G. (1979). *Cognitive therapy of depression: A treatment manual.* New York: Guilford.

Beck, A. T., Wright, F., Newman, C., & Liese, B. (1993). *Cognitive therapy of substance abuse.* New York: Guilford.

Beck, A. T. (1967). *Depression: Causes and treatment.* Philadelphia: University of Pennsylvania Press.

Beck, A. T. (1983). Cognitive therapy of depression: New perspectives. In P. J. Clayton & J. E. Barrett (Eds.), *Treatment of depression: Old controversies and new approaches* (pp. 265–90). New York: Raven Press.

Beck, A. T. (2005). The current state of cognitive therapy: A 40-year retrospective. *Arch. Gen. Psychiat., 62,* 953–59.

Beck, A. T. (2005). The current state of cognitive therapy: A 40-year retrospective. *Arch. Gen. Psychiat., 62,* 953–959.

Beck, J. G., & Barlow, D. H. (1984). Unraveling the nature of sex roles. In E. A. Blechman (Ed.), *Behavior modification with women* (pp. 34–59). New York: Guilford.

Becker, A., Burwell, R. A., Gilman, S., Herzog, D. B., & Hamburg, P. (2002). Eating behaviors and attitudes following prolonged exposure to television among ethnic Fijian adolescent girls. *Brit. J. Psychiat., 180,* 509–14.

Becker, K. D., Stuewig, J., Herrera, V. M., & McCloskey, L. A. (2004). A study of firesetting and animal cruelty in children: Family influences and adolescent outcomes. *J. Amer. Acad. Child Adoles. Psychiat., 43,* 905–12.

Beckett, C., Bredenkamp, D., Castle, J., Groothues, C., O'Connor, T. G., & Rutter, M. (2002). Behavior patterns associated with institutional deprivation: A study of children adopted from Romania. *J. Dev. Behav. Ped., 23*(5), 297–303.

Beekman, A. T. F., Deeg, D. J. H., Smit, J. H., Comijs, H. C., Braam, A. W., de Beurs, E., et al. (2004). Dysthymia in later life: A study in the community. *J. Affect. Dis., 81*(3), 191–199.

Beeman, S. K., & Edleson, J. L. (2000). Collaborating on family safety: Challenges for children's and women's advocates. *Journal of Aggression, Maltreatment & Trauma, 3,* 345–58.

Beers, C. (1970). *A mind that found itself* (Rev. ed.). New York: Doubleday.

Beevers, C. G., & Miller, I. W. (2004). Depression-related negative cognition: Mood-state and trait dependent properties. *Cog. Ther. Res., 28*(3), 293–307.

Behan, J., & Carr, A. (2000). Oppositional defiant disorder. In A. Carr (Ed.), *What works with children and adolescents? A critical review of psychological interventions with children, adolescents and their families* (pp. 102–30). Florence, KY: Taylor & Francis/Routledge.

Bekker, M. H. (1996). Agoraphobia and gender: A review. *Clin. Psychol. Rev., 16*(2), 129–46.

Belanoff, J. K., Gross, K., Yager, A., & Schatzberg, A. F. (2001). Corticosteroids and cognition. *J. Psychiat. Res., 35*(3), 127–45.

Belar, C. D. (1997). Clinical health psychology: A specialty for the 21st century. *Hlth. Psychol., 16*(5), 411–16.

Bell, A. P., Weinberg, M. S., & Hammersmith, S. K. (1981). *Sexual preference: Its development in men and women.* Bloomington, IN: Indiana University Press.

Bell, E., Jr. (1958). The basis of effective military psychiatry. *Dis. Nerv. Sys., 19,* 283–88.

Bellack, A. S., & Mueser, K. T. (1993). Psychosocial treatment for schizophrenia. *Schizo. Bull., 19,* 317–36.

Bemporad, J. R. (1995). Long-term analytic treatment of depression. In E. E. Beckham & W. R. Leber (Eds.), *Handbook of depression* (2nd ed., pp. 404–24). New York: Guilford.

Ben Hamida, S., Mineka, S., & Bailey, J. M. (1998). Sex differences in perceived controllability of mate value: An evolutionary perspective. *J. Pers. Soc. Psychol., 75,* 953–66.

Benes, F. M., & Bird, E. D. (1987). An analysis of the arrangement of neurons in the cingulate cortex of schizophrenic patients. *Arch. Gen. Psychiat., 44,* 608–16.

Benes, F. M., Davidson, J., & Bird, E. D. (1986). Quantitative cytoarchitectural analyses of the cerebral cortex of schizophrenic patients. *Arch. Gen. Psychiat., 43,* 31–35.

Benes, F. M., McSparren, J., Bird, E. D., SanGiovanni, J. P., & Vincent, S. L. (1991). Deficits in small interneurons in prefrontal and cingulated cortices of schizophrenic and schizoaffective patients. *Arch. Gen. Psychiat., 48,* 996–1001.

Benes, F. M. (2000). Cortical pathology: A new generation of quantitative microscopic studies. In P. J. Harrison & G. W. Roberts (Eds.), *The neuropathology of schizophrenia: Progress and interpretation.* New York: Oxford University Press.

Benjamin, L. S., & Pugh, C. (2001). Using interpersonal theory to select effective treatment interventions. In J. W. Livesley (Ed.), *Handbook of personality disorders: Theory, research, and treatment* (pp. 414–36). New York: Guilford.

Benjamin, L. S. (1993). *Interpersonal diagnosis and treatment of personality disorders.* New York: Guilford.

Benjamin, L. S. (1996). A clinician-friendly version of the interpersonal circumplex: structural analysis of social behavior. *J. Pers. Assess., 66,* 248–266.

Benjamin, L. S. (2004). An interpersonal family-oriented approach to personality disorder. In M. M. MacFarlane (Ed.), *Family treatment of personality disorders: Advances in clinical practice.* (pp. 41–69). Binghampton, NY: Haworth Clinical Practice Press.

Benjamin, L. S. (2005). Interpersonal theory of personality disorders: The structural analysis of social behavior and interpersonal reconstructive therapy. In M. F. Lezenweger & J. F. Clarkin (Eds.), *Major theories of personality disorder.* (2nd ed.: pp. 157–230). New York: Guilford Press.

Benjamin, L. T., Jr. (2005). A history of clinical psychology as a profession in America (and a glimpse at its future). *Annu. Rev. Clin. Psychol, 1*(1), 1–30.

Bennett, D., Sharpe, M., Freeman, C., & Carson, A. (2004). Anorexia nervosa among female secondary students in Ghana. *Brit. J. Psychiat., 185,* 312–17.

Bennett, J. B., & Lehman, W. E. K. (1996). Alcohol, antagonism, and witnessing violence in the workplace: Drinking climates and social alienation-integration. In G. R. Vandenbos & E. Q. Bulatao (Eds.), *Violence in the workplace* (pp. 105–52). Washington: American Psychological Association.

Bennett, T. L., Dittmar, C., & Ho, M. R. (1997). The neuropsychology of traumatic brain injury. In A. M. Horton, D. Wedding, & J. Webster (Eds.), *The neuropsychology handbook* (Vol. 2, pp. 123–72). New York: Springer.

Bennetto, L., Pennington, B. F., & Rogers, S. J. (1996). Intact and impaired memory functions in autism. *Child Develop., 67*(4), 1816–35.

Benotti, P. N., & Forse, R. A. (1995). The role of gastric surgery in the multidisciplinary management of severe obesity. *American Journal of Surgery, 169,* 361–67.

Bentovim, A., Boston, P., & Van Elburg, A. (1987). Child sexual abuse—children and families referred to a treatment project and the effects of intervention. *Brit. Med. J., 295,* 1453–57.

Berenbaum, H., & Connelly, J. (1993). The effects of stress on hedonic capacity. *J. Abn. Psychol., 102*(3), 474–81.

Bergem, A. L. M., Engedal, K., & Kringlen, E. (1997). The role of heredity in late-onset Alzheimer disease and vascular dementia. *Arch. Gen. Psychiat., 54*(3), 264–70.

Berk, L. S., Tan, S. A., Nehlsen-Cannarella, S., Napier, B. J., Lewis, J. E., Lee, J. W., & Eby, W. C. (1988). Humor associated laughter decreases cortisol and increases spontaneous lymphocyte blastogenesis. *Clin. Res., 36,* 435A.

Berkman, L. F., Blumenthal, J., Burg, M., Carney, R. M., Catellier, D., Cowan, M. J., Czajkowski, S. M., DeBuk, R., Hosking, J., Jaffe, A., Kaufmann, P. G., Mitchell, P., Norman, J., Powell, L. H., Raczynski, J. M., & Schneidermann, N. (2003). Effects of treating depression and low perceived social support on clinical events after myocardial infarction: The Enhancing Recovery in Coronary Heart Diseases Patients (ENRICHD) randomized trial. *JAMA, 289,* 3106–16.

Berkman, L. F., Leo-Summers, L., & Horwitz, R. I. (1992). Emotional support and survival after myocardial infarction: A prospective population-based study of the elderly. *Ann. Int. Med., 117,* 1003–9.

Berlant, J. L. (2001). Topiramate in posttraumatic stress disorder: Preliminary clinical observations. *J. Clin. Psychiat., 62,* 60–63.

Berlin, F. S., & Malin, H. M. (1991). Media distortion of the public's perception of recidivism and psychiatric rehabilitation. *Amer. J. Psychiat., 148,* 1572–76.

Berlin, F. S. (1994, May). The case for castration, part 2. *Washington Monthly, 26,* 28–29.

Berney, T. P. (2000). Methods of treatment. In M. G. Gelder, J. J. Lopez-Ibor, Jr., & N. C. Andreason (Eds.), *New Oxford textbook of psychiatry.* Volume 2 (pp. 1989–94). Oxford: Oxford University Press.

Berns, S. B., Jacobson, N. S., & Gottman, J. M. (1999). Demand-withdraw interaction in couples with a violent husband. *J. Cons. Clin. Psychol., 67*(5), 666–74.

Bernstein, D. P., & Travaglini, L. (1999). Schizoid and avoidant personality disorders. In T. Millon, P. H. Blaney, & R. D. Davis (Eds.), *Oxford textbook of psychopathology* (pp. 523–34). New York: Oxford University Press.

Bernstein, D. P., Useda, D., Siever, L. J. (1995). Paranoid personality disorder. In W. J Livesley (Ed), *The DSM-IV personality disorders. Diagnosis and treatment of mental disorders.* (pp. 45–57). New York: Guilford.

Berrios, G. (1990). A British contribution to the history of functional brain surgery. Special Issue: History of psychopharmacology. *J. Psychopharm., 4,* 140–44.

Berry, N., Jobanputra, V., & Pal, H. (2003). Molecular genetics of schizophrenia: A critical review. *J. Psychiat. Neurosci., 28*(6), 415–29.

Beumont, P. J. V. (2002). Clinical presentation of anorexia nervosa and bulimia nervosa. In C. G. Fairburn & Kelly D. Brownell (Eds). *Eating disorders and obesity* (2nd edition). New York: Guilford Press. pp. 162–170.

Beutler, L. E., & Malik, M. I. (Eds.). (2002). *Rethinking the DSM: A psychological perspective.* Washington, DC: American Psychological Association.

Beutler, L. E., Clarkin, J. F., & Bongar, B. (2000). *Guidelines for the systemic treatment of the depressed patient.* New York: Oxford University Press.

Beutler, L. E., Malik, M., Alimohamed, S., Harwood, T. M., Talebi, H., Noble, S., & Wong, E. (2004). In M. J. Lambert (2004). *Bergin and Garfield's handbook of Psychotherapy and behavior change.* New York: John Wiley and Sons, pp. 227–306.

Beutler, L. E. (1992). Systematic treatment selection. In J. C. Norcross & M. R. Goldfried (Eds.), *Psychotherapy integration.* New York: Basic Books.

Beutler, L., & Harwood, T. M. (2002). How to assess clients in pretreatment planning. In J. N. Butcher (Ed.), *Clinical personality assessment* (2nd ed., pp. 76–95). New York: Oxford University Press.

Beveridge, A. (1997). Voices of the mad: Patients' letters from the Royal Edinburgh Asylum, 1873–1908. *Psychol. Med., 27,* 899–908.

Bezchlibnyk-Butler, K. Z., & Jeffries, J. J. (2003). *Clinical handbook of psychotropic drugs.* Seattle: Hogrefe & Huber.

Bhandary, A. N. (1997). The chronic attention deficit syndrome. *Psychiat. Ann., 27*(8), 543–44.

Bibring, E. (1953). The mechanism of depression. In P. Greenacre (Ed.), *Affective disorders* (pp. 13–48). New York: International University Press.

Bickel, W. K., Amass, L., Higgins, S. T., Badger, G. J., & Esch, R. A. (1997). Effects of adding behavioral treatment to opioid detoxification with buprenorphine. *J. Cons. Clin. Psychol., 65*(5), 803–10.

Bickerstaff, L. K., Harris, S. C., Leggett, R. S., & Cheah, K. C. (1988). Pain insensitivity in schizophrenic patients: A surgical dilemma. *Archives of Surgery, 123,* 49–51.

Bieber, I., Dain, H. J., Dince, P. R., Drellich, M. G., Grand, H. G., Gundlach, R. H., Kremer, M. W., Rifkin, A. H., Wilbur, C. B. & Bieber, T. B. (1962). *Homosexuality: A psychoanalytic study of male homosexuals.* New York: Basic Books.

Biederman, J., Monteaux, M. C., Doyle, A. E., Seidman, L. J., Wilens, T. E., Ferraro, F., Morgan, C. L., & Farone, S. V. (2004). Impact of executive function deficits and attention deficit/hyperactivity disorder (ADHD) on academic outcomes in children. *J. Cons. Clin. Psychol., 72,* 757–76.

Biederman, J., Rosenbaum, J. F., Hirschfeld, D. R., Faraone, S., Bolduc, E., Gersten, M., Meminger, S., Kagan, J., Snidman, N., & Reznick, J. S. (1990). Psychiatric correlates of behavioral inhibition in young children of parents with and without psychiatric disorders. *Arch. Gen. Psychiat., 47,* 21–26.

Bifulco, A. T., Brown, G. W., & Harris, T. O. (1987). Childhood loss of parent, lack of adequate parental care and adult depression: A replication. *J. Affect. Dis., 12,* 115–28.

Billett, E., Richter, J., & Kennedy, J. (1998). Genetics of obsessive-compulsive disorder. In R. Swinson, M. Antony, S. Rachman, & M. Richter (Eds.), *Obsessive-compulsive disorder: Theory, research, and treatment* (pp. 181–206). New York: Guilford.

Binder, R. L. (1999). Are the mentally ill dangerous? *J. Amer. Acad. Psychiat. & Law, 27*(2), 189–201.

Birmaher, B., Axelson, D. A., Monk, K., Kalas, C., Clark, D. B., Ehmann, M., Bridge, J., Heo, J., & Brent, D. A. (2003). Fluoxetine for the treatment of childhood anxiety disorders. *J. Amer. Acad. Child Adoles. Psychiat., 42*(4), 415–23.

Birmaher, B., Ryan, S. W., Williamson, D., Brent, D., Kaufman, J., Dahl, R., Perel, J., & Nelson, B. (1996). Childhood and adolescent depression: A review of the past 10 years. Part I. *J. Amer. Acad. Child Adoles. Psychiat., 35,* 1427–39.

Birmingham, L., Gray, J., Mason, D., & Grubin, D. (2000). Mental illness at reception into prison. *Criminal Behaviour and Mental Health, 10,* 77–87.

Bjorklund, D. F. (2000). *False-memory creation in children and adults: Theory, research and implications.* Mahway, NJ: Erlbaum.

Blaauw, E., Roesch, R., & Kerkhof, A. (2000). Mental disorders in European prison systems: Arrangements for mentally disordered prisoners in the prison system of 13 European countries. *International Journal of Law and Psychiatry, 23,* 649–57.

Blackburn, I. M., & Davidson, K. (1990). *Cognitive therapy for depression and anxiety.* Oxford: Blackwell Scientific.

Blair, R. J. R., Jones, L., Clark, F., & Smith, M. (1997). The psychopathic individual: A lack of responsiveness to distress cues? *Psychophysiology, 34,* 192–198.

Blanchard, E. B., & Scharff, L. (2002). Psychosocial aspects of assessment and treatment of irritable bowel syndrome in adults and recurrent abdominal pain in children. *J. Cons. Clin. Psychol., 70*(3), 725–38.

Blanchard, E. B., Appelbaum, K. A., Radnitz, C. L., Michultka, D., Morrill, B., Kirsch, C., Hillhouse, J., Evans, D. D., Guarnieri, P., Attanasio, V., Andrasik, F., Jaccard J., & Dentinger, M. P. (1990a). Placebo-controlled evaluation of abbreviated progressive muscle relaxation and of relaxation combined with cognitive therapy in the treatment of tension headache. *J. Cons. Clin. Psychol., 58,* 210–15.

Blanchard, E. B., Appelbaum, K. A., Radnitz, C. L., Morrill, B., Michultka, D., Kirsch, C., Gaurinieri, P., Hillhouse, J., Evans, D. D., Jaccard, J., & Barron, K. D. (1990b). A controlled evaluation of thermal biofeedback and thermal biofeedback combined with cognitive therapy in the treatment of vascular headache. *J. Cons. Clin. Psychol., 58,* 216–24.

Blanchard, E. B., Hickling, E. J., Barton, K., & Taylor, A. E. (1996). One-year prospective follow-up of motor vehicle accident victims. *Behav. Res. Ther., 34*(10), 775–86.

Blanchard, E. B., Hickling, E. J., Taylor, A. E., & Loos, W. (1995). Psychiatric morbidity associated with motor vehicle accidents. *J. Nerv. Ment. Dis., 183*(8), 495–504.

Blanchard, R., & Hucker, S. J. (1991). Age, transvestitism, bondage, and concurrent paraphilic activities in 117 fatal cases of autoerotic asphyxia. *Brit. J. Psychiat., 159,* 371–77.

Blanchard, R. (1985). Typology of male-to-female transsexualism. *Arch. Sex. Behav., 14,* 247–61.

Blanchard, R. (1989). The classification and labeling of nonhomosexual gender dysphorias. *Arch. Sex. Behav., 18,* 315–34.

Blanchard, R. (1991). Clinical observations and systematic study of autogynephilia. *J. Sex Marit. Ther., 17,* 235–51.

Blanchard, R. (1992). Nonmonotonic relation of autogynephilia and heterosexual attraction. *J. Abnorm. Psych., 101,* 271–76.

Blanchard, R. (1993). Varieties of autogynephilia and their relationship to gender dysphoria. *Arch. Sex. Behav., 22,* 241–51.

Blanchard, R. (1994). A structural equation model for age at clinical presentation in nonhomosexual male gender dysphorics. *Arch. Sex. Behav., 23,* 311–32.

Blanco, C., Anita, S. X., & Liebowitz, R. (2002). Pharmacotherapy of social anxiety disorder. *Biol. Psychiat., 51,* 109–20.

Blashfield, R. K., & Livesley, W. J. (1999). Classification. In T. Millon, P. H. Blaney, & R. D. Davis (Eds.), *Oxford textbook of psychopathology* (pp. 3–28). New York: Oxford University Press.

Blaszczynski, A., McConaghy, N., & Frankova, A. (1989). Crime, antisocial personality and pathological gambling. *Journal of Gambling Behavior, 5,* 137–52.

Blatt, S. J., Zuroff, D. C., Quinlan, D. M., & Pilkonis, P. A. (1996). Interpersonal factors in brief treatment of depression: Further analyses of the NIMH Treatment of Depression Collaborative Research Program. *J. Cons. Clin. Psychol., 64*(1), 162–71.

Bleuler, E. (1924). *Textbook of psychiatry.* Translated by A. A. Brill. New York: Macmillan. Reprinted by the Classics of Psychiatry and Behavioral Sciences Library, New York, 1988.

Bleuler, E. (1950). *Dementia praecox or the group of schizophrenias.* New York: International Universities Press. (Originally published in 1911)

Bloch, H. S. (1969). Army clinical psychiatry in the combat zone—1967–1968. *Amer. J. Psychiat., 126,* 289.

Block, J. H., Block, J., & Gjerde, P. F. (1986). The personality of children prior to divorce: A prospective study. *Child Develop., 57,* 827–40.

Bluglass, R. (2000). Organization of services. In M. G. Gelder, J. J. Lopez-Ibor, Jr., & N. C. Andreason (Eds.), *New Oxford textbook of psychiatry* (pp. 2123–31). Oxford: Oxford University Press.

Blum, R. (1969). *Society and drugs* (Vol. 1). San Francisco: Jossey-Bass.

Blume, E. S. (1990). *Secret survivors: uncovering incest and its aftermath in women.* New York: Wiley.

Blumenthal, J. A., Sherwood, A., Gullette, E. C. D., Georgiades, A., & Tweedy, D. (2002). Biobehavioral approaches to the treatment of essential hypertension. *J. Cons. Clin. Psychol., 70,* 569–89.

Bockhoven, J. S. (1972). *Moral treatment in community mental health.* New York: Springer.

Boddiger, D. (2004). Battling addiction. *Lancet, 364*(9438), 923–24.

Bodenheimer, T. (2000). Uneasy alliance—clinical investigators and the pharmaceutical industry. *N. Engl. J. Med., 342,* 1539–1544.

Boehm, G. (1968). At last—a nonaddicting substitute for morphine? *Today's Health, 46*(4), 69–72.

Bogerts, B. (1993). Recent advances in the neuropathology of schizophrenia. *Schizo. Bull., 19*(2), 431–45.

Bogerts, B. (1997). The temporolimbic system theory of positive schizophrenic symptoms. *Schizo. Bull., 23*(3), 423–36.

Bohman, T. M., Barker, E. D., Bell, M. L., Lewis, C. M., Holleran, L., & Pomeroy, E. (2004). Early intervention for alcohol use prevention and vehicle safety skills: Evaluating the Protecting You/Protecting Me curriculum. *Journal of Child & Adolescent Substance Abuse, 14*(1) 17–40.

Bohn, M. J. (1993). Alcoholism. *Psychiat. Clin. N. Amer., 16,* 679–92.

Boland, R. J., & Keller, M. B. (2002). Course and outcome of depression. In I. H. Gotlib & C. L. Hammen (Eds.), *Handbook of depression* (pp. 43–57). New York: Guilford.

Bolger, N. (1990). Coping as a personality process: A prospective study. *J. Pers. Soc. Psychol., 59,* 525–37.

Boll, T. J. (1980). The Halstead-Reitan neuropsychological battery. In S. B. Filskov & T. J. Boll (Eds.), *Handbook of neurophysiology.* New York: Wiley Interscience.

Bolles, R. C., & Fanselow, M. S. (1982). Endorphins and behavior. *Annu. Rev. Psychol., 33,* 87–101.

Bonanno, G. A. (2004). Loss, trauma, and human resilience: Have we underestimated the human capacity to thrive after extremely aversive events? *Amer. Psychol., 59,* 20–28.

Bonanno, G. A., & Kaltman, S. (1999). Toward an integrative perspective on bereavement. *Psychol. Bull., 125*(6), 760–76.

Bonanno, G. A., Moskowitz, J. T., Papa, A., & Folkman, S. (2005). Resilience to loss in bereaved spouses, bereaved parents, and bereaved gay men. *J. Pers. Soc. Psychol., 88*(5), 827–843.

Bonanno, G. A., Wortman, C. B., & Nesse, R. M. (2004). Prospective patterns of resilience and maladjustment during widowhood. *Psychol. Aging, 19*(2), 260–271.

Bondi, M. W., & Lange, K. L. (2001). Alzheimer's disease. In H. S. Friedman (Ed.), *The disorders: Specialty articles from the encyclopedia of mental health.* San Diego: Academic Press.

Bonta, J., Law, M., & Hanson, K. (1998). The prediction of criminal and violent recidivism among mentally disordered offenders: A meta-analysis. *Psychol. Bull., 123*(2), 123–42.

Bookheimer, S. Y., Strojwas, M. H., Cohen, M. S., Saunders, A. M., Pericak-Vance, M. A., Mazziotta, J. C., & Small, G. W. (2000). Patterns of brain activation in people at risk for Alzheimer's disease. *N. Engl. J. Med., 343,* 450–56.

Booth, B. M., Russell, D. W., Soucek, S., & Laughlin, P. R. (1992). Social support and outcome of alcoholism treatment: An exploratory analysis. *Amer. J. Drug Alcoh. Abuse, 18,* 87–101.

Booth, B. M., Russell, D. W., Yates, W. R., & Laughlin, P. R. (1992). Social support and depression in men during alcoholism treatment. *J. Subst. Abuse, 4,* 57–67.

Borkovec, T. D. (1985). The role of cognitive and somatic cues in anxiety and anxiety disorders. In A. Tuma and J. D. Maser (Eds). *Anxiety and the Anxiety Disorders* (pp. 463–478). Hillsdale, N.J: Lawrence Erlbaum Associates Inc.

Borkovec, T. D. (1994). The nature, functions, and origins of worry. In G. L. C. Davey & F. Tallis (Eds.), *Worrying, perspectives on theory, assessment, and treatment* (pp. 5–34). Sussex, England: Wiley.

Borkovec, T. D., & Ruscio, A. M. (2001). Psychotherapy for generalized anxiety disorder. *J. Clin. Psychiat., 62,* 37–42.

Borkovec, T. D., Abel, J. L., & Newman, H. (1995). Effects of psychotherapy on comorbid conditions in generalized anxiety disorder. *J. Cons. Clin. Psychol., 63*(3), 479–83.

Borkovec, T. D., Alcaine, O., Behar, E. (2004). Avoidance theory of worry and generalized anxiety disorder. In R. G. Heimberg, C. L. Turk, & D. S. Mennin (Eds.), *Generalized anxiety disorder: Advances in research and practice* (pp. 77–108). New York: Guilford Press.

Borkovec, T. D., Newman, M. G., Pincus, A. L., Lytle, R. (2002). A component analysis of cognitive-behavioral therapy for generalized anxiety disorder and the role of interpersonal problems. *J. Cons. Clin. Psychol., 70*(2), 288–298.

Bornstein, R. F. (1999). Dependent and histrionic personality disorders. In T. Millon, P. H. Blaney, & R. D. Davis (Eds.), *Oxford textbook of psychopathology* (pp. 535–54). New York: Oxford University Press.

Borthwick, A., Holman, C., Kennard, D., McFetridge, M., Messruther, K., & Wilkes, J. (2001). The relevance of moral treatment to contemporary mental health care. *J. Ment. Hlth., 10,* 427–39.

Boskind-White, M., & White, W. C. (1983). *Bulimarexia: The binge-purge cycle.* New York: Norton.

Bostic, J. Q., Biederman, J., Spencer, T. J., Wilens, T. E., Prince, J. B., Monuteaux, M. C., Sienna, M., Polisner, D. A., & Hatch, M. (2000). Pemoline treatment of adolescents with attention deficit hyperactivity disorder: A short-term controlled trial. *Journal of Child & Adolescent Psychopharmacology, 10*(3), 205–16.

Botvin, G. J. (1983). Prevention of adolescent substance abuse through the development of personal and social competence. *National Institute on Drug Abuse Research Monograph Series, 47,* 115–40.

Botvin, G. J., Baker, E., Dusenbury, L., Botvin, E. M., & Diaz, T. (1995). Long-term follow-up results of a randomized drug abuse prevention trial in a white middle-class population. *J. Cons. Clin. Psychol., 58,* 1106–12.

Botvin, G. J., Baker, E., Dusenbury, L., Tortu, S., & Botvin, E. M. (1990). Preventing adolescent drug abuse through a multimodal cognitive-behavioral approach: Results of a 3 year study. *J. Cons. Clin. Psychol., 58,* 437–57.

Bouchard, T. J., & Propping, P. (Eds.). (1993). *Twins as a tool of behavioral genetics.* New York: Wiley.

Bouchard, T. J., Jr., & Loehlin, J. C. (2001). Genes, evolution, and personality. *Behav. Gen., 31*(3), 243–73.

Bouman, T. K., Eifert, G. H., & Lejuex, C. W. (1999). Somatoform disorders. In T. Millon & P. Blaney (Eds.), *Oxford textbook of psychopathology* (pp. 444–65). New York: Oxford University Press.

Bouras, N., & Holt, G. (2000). The planning and provision of psychiatric services for people with mental retardation. In M. G. Gelder, J. J. Lopez-Ibor, Jr., & N. C. Andreason (Eds.), *New Oxford textbook of psychiatry.* Volume 2 (pp. 1007–2012). Oxford: Oxford University Press.

Bourne, P. G. (1970). Military psychiatry and the Vietnam experience. *Amer. J. Psychiat., 127*(4), 481–88.

Bouton, M. E., Mineka, S., & Barlow, D. H. (2001). A modern learning theory perspective on the etiology of panic disorder. *Psychol. Rev., 108,* 4–32.

Bouton, M. E. (1994). Conditioning, remembering, and forgetting. *J. Exper. Psychol.: Animal Behavior Processes, 20,* 219–31.

Bouton, M. E. (2002). Context, ambiguity, and unlearning: Sources of relapse after behavioral extinction. *Biol. Psychiat., 52*(10), 976–86.

Bovet, P., Perret, F., Cornuz, J., Quilindo, J., & Paccaud, F. (2002). Improved smoking cessation in smokers given ultrasound photographs of their own atherosclerotic plaques. *Preventive Medicine: An International Journal Devoted to Practice & Theory, 34*(2), 215–20.

Bowlby, J. (1960). Separation anxiety. *Inter. J. Psychoanal., 41,* 89–93.

Bowlby, J. (1969). *Attachment and loss* (Vol. 1). New York: Basic Books.

Bowlby, J. (1973). Separation: Anxiety and anger. *Psychology of attachment and loss series* (Vol. 3). New York: Basic Books.

Bowlby, J. (1980). *Attachment and loss, III: Loss, sadness, and depression.* New York: Basic Books.

Bowler, J. V., et al. (1997). Comparative evolution of Alzheimer disease, vascular dementia, and mixed dementia. *Arch. Neurol., 54*(6), 697–703.

Bowman, E. S., & Markand, O. N. (2005). Diagnosis and treatment of pseudoseizures. *Psychiat. Ann., 35*(4), 306–16.

Boys, A., Lenton, S., & Norcross, K. (1997). Polydrug use at raves by a western Australian sample. *Drug & Alcohol Review, 16*(3), 227–34.

Boys, A., Marsden, J., & Strang, J. (2001). Understanding reasons for drug use amongst young people: A functional perspective. *Hlth Ed. Res., 16*(4), 457–69.

Bradford, D., Stroup, S., & Liberman, J. (2002). Pharmacological treatments for schizophrenia. In P. E. Nathan & J. M. Gorman (Eds.), *A guide to treatments that work* (2nd ed., pp. 169–200). New York: Oxford University Press.

Bradford, J. M. W., & Greenberg, D. M. (1996). Pharmacological treatment of deviant sexual behaviour. *Annu. Rev. Sex Res., 7,* 283–306.

Bradley, S. J., & Zucker, K. J. (1997). Gender identity disorder: A review of the past 10 years. *J. Amer. Acad. Child Adoles. Psychiat., 36,* 872–80.

Bradley, S. J., Oliver, G. D., Chernick, A. B., & Zucker, K. J. (1998). Experiment of nurture: Ablatio penis at 2 months, sex reassignment at 7 months, and a psychosexual follow-up in young adulthood. *Pediatrics, 102*(1), e9.

Brake, W. G., Zhang, T. Y., Diorio, J., Meaney, M. J., & Gratton, A. (2004). Influence of early postnatal rearing conditions on mesocortical dopamine and behavioural responses to psychostimulants and stressors in adult rats. *Europ. J. Neurosci., 19,* 1863–74.

Braksiek, R. J., & Roberts, D. J. (2002). Amusement park injuries and deaths. *Annals of Emergency Medicine, 39*(1), 65–72.

Brand, M., Fujiwara, E., Kalbe, E., Steingrass, H. P., Kessler, J., & Markowitsch, H. J. (2003). Cognitive estimation and affective judgments in alcoholic Korsakoff patients. *J. Clini. Exper. Neuropsych., 25*(3), 324–34.

Brandsma, J. M., Maultsby, M. C., & Welsh, R. J. (1980). *Outpatient treatment of alcoholism: A review and comparative study.* Baltimore: University Park Press.

Branson, R., Potoczna, N., Kral, J. G., Lentes, K.-U., Hoehe, M. R., & Horber, F. F. (2003). Binge eating as a major phenotype of melanocortin 4 receptor gene mutation. *N. Engl. J. Med., 348,* 1096–103.

Braun, S. (1996). *Buzz.* (1) New York: Oxford University Press.

Braus, D., Ende, G., Weber-Fahr, W., Sartorius, A., Krier, A., Hubrich-Ungureanu, P., Ruf, M., Stuck, S., & Henn, F. A. (1999). Antipsychotic drug effects on motor activation measured by functional magnetic resonance imaging in schizophrenic patients. *Schiz. Res., 39*(1), 19–29.

Brecht, M. L., O'Brien, A., Mayrhauser, C., & Anglin, M. D. (2004). Methamphetamine use behaviors and gender differences. *Add. Behav., 29*(1), 89–106.

Breen, R. B., Kruedelbach, N. G., & Walker, H. I. (2001). Cognitive changes in pathological gamblers following a 28-day inpatient program. *Psychology of Addictive Behaviors, 15*(3), 246–48.

Breggin, P. R., & Breggin, G. R. (1995). The hazards of treating "attention deficit/hyperactivity disorder" with methylphenidate (Ritalin). *J. Coll. Stud. Psychother., 10*(2), 55–72.

Breggin, P. R. (2001). *Talking back to Ritalin.* Braintree, MA: Perseus Publishing.

Breier, A., Buchanan, R. W., Kirkpatrick, B., Davis, O. R., Irish, D., Summerfelt, A., & Carpenter, W. T. (1994). Effects of clozapine on positive and negative symptoms in outpatients with schizophrenia. *Amer. J. Psychiat., 151*(1), 20–26.

Breitner, J. C. S., Gatz, M., Bergem, A. L. M., Christian, J. C., Mortimer, J. A., McClearn, G. E., Heston, L. L., Welsh, K. A., Anthony, J. C., Folstein, M. F., & Radebaugh, T. S. (1993). Use of twin cohorts for research in Alzheimer's disease. *Neurology, 43,* 261–67.

Breitner, J. C., Gau, B. A., Welsh, K. A., et al. (1994). Inverse association of anti-inflammatory treatments and Alzheimer's disease: Initial results of a co-twin control study. *Neurology, 44,* 227–32.

Brems, C. (1995). Women and depression: A comprehensive analysis. In E. E. Beckham & W. R. Leber (Eds.), *Handbook of depression* (2nd ed., pp. 539–66). New York: Guilford.

Brems, C., & Johnson, M. E. (1997). Clinical implications of the co-occurrence of substance use and other psychiatric conditions. *Prof. Psychol., 28*(5), 437–47.

Brener, N. D., McMahon, P. M., Warren, C. W., & Douglas, K. A. (1999). Forced sexual intercourse and associated health-risk behaviors among female college students in the United States. *J. Cons. Clin. Psychol., 67*(2), 252–59.

Brennan, P. A., Le Brocque, R., & Hammen, C. (2003). Maternal depression, parent-child relationships, and resilient outcomes in adolescence. *J. Amer. Acad. Child Adol. Psychiat., 42*(12), 1469–1477.

Brennan, P. A., Raine, A., Schulsinger, F., Kirkegaard-Sorensen, L., et al. (1997). Psychosociological protective factors for male subjects at high risk for criminal behavior. *Amer. J. Psychiat., 154*(6), 853–55.

Brent, D. A., Holder, D., Kolko, D., Birmaher, B., Baugher, M., Roth, C., Iyengar, S., & Johnson, B. A. (1997). A clinical psychotherapy trial for adolescent depression comparing cognitive, family, and supportive. *Arch. Gen. Psychiat., 54,* 877–85.

Breslau, N., Kessler, R. C., Chilcoat, H. D., Schultz, L. R., Davis, G. C., & Andreski, P. (1998). Trauma and posttraumatic stress disorder in the community. *Arch. Gen. Psychiat., 55,* 626–32.

Breslau, N. (2001). The epidemiology of posttraumatic stress disorder: What is the extent of the problem? *J. Clin. Psychiat., 62,* 16–22.

Breslow, R. A., Faden, V. B., & Smothers, B. (2003). Alcohol consumption by elderly Americans. *J. Stud. Alcoh., 64,* 884–92.

Bretschneider, J. G., & McCoy, N. L. (1988). Sexual interest and behavior in healthy 80- to 102-year-olds. *Arch. Sex. Behav., 17,* 109–29.

Brewer, R. D., Morris, P. D., Cole, T. B., Watkins, S., Patetta, M. J., & Popkin, C. (1994). The risk of dying in alcohol-related automobile crashes among habitual drunk drivers. *New Engl. J. Med., 331*(8), 523–17.

Brewerton, T. D., Lydiard, R. B., Herzog, D. B., Brotman, A. W., O'Neil, P. M., & Ballenger, J. C. (1995). Comorbidity of Axis I psychiatric disorders in bulimia nervosa. *J. Clin. Psychiat., 56,* 77–80.

Brewin, C., & Holmes, E. A. (2003). Psychological theories of posttraumatic stress disorder. *Clin. Psychol. Rev., 23*(3), 339–76.

Bridges, F. A., & Cicchetti, D. (1982). Mothers' ratings of the temperament characteristics of Down's syndrome infants. *Develop. Psychol., 18,* 238–44.

Brinded, M. J., Stevens, I., Myulder, R. T., Fairley, N., Malcolm, F., & Wells, J. E. (1999). The Christchurch Prisons psychiatric epidemiology study: Methodology and prevalence rates for psychiatric disorders. *Criminal Behaviour and Mental Health, 9,* 131–43.

Brock, A. J. (1979). Galen. On the natural faculties. (English translation). Loeb Classical Library. Cambridge, MA.: Harvard University Press.

Brodeur, D. A., & Pond, M. (2001). The development of selective attention in children with attention deficit hyperactivity disorder. *J. Abn. Child Psychol., 29,* 229–39.

Brody, A. L., Saxena, S., Mandelkern, M. A., Fairbanks, L. A., Ho, M. L., & Baxter, L. R., Jr. (2001). Brain metabolic changes associated with symptom factor improvement in major depressive disorder. *Biol. Psychiat., 50,* 171–78.

Brokate, B., Hildebrandt, H., Eling, P., Fichtner, H., Runge, K., & Timm, C. (2003). Frontal lobe dysfunctions in Korsakoff's syndrome and chronic alcoholism: Continuity or discontinuity? *Neuropsychology, 17*(3), 420–28.

Brom, D., Kleber, R. J., & Defares, P. B. (1989). Brief psychotherapy for posttraumatic stress disorders. *J. Cons. Clin. Psychol., 57,* 607–12.

Brookmeyer, R., Gray, S., & Kawas, C. (1998). Projections of Alzheimer's disease in the United States and the public health impact of delaying disease onset. *Amer. J. Pub. Hlth., 88*(9), 1337–42.

Brown, A. S., Schaefer, C. A., Wyatt, R. J., Begg, M. D., Goetz, R., Bresnahan, M. A., Harvaky-Friedman, J., Gorman, J. M., Malaspina, J. M., & Susser, E. S. (2002). Paternal age and risk of schizophrenia in adult offspring. *Amer. J. Psychiat., 159*(9), 1528–33.

Brown, G. K., Have, T. T., Henriques, G. R., Xie, S. X., Hollander, J. E., & Beck, A. T. (2005). Cognitive therapy for the prevention of suicide attempts: A randomized controlled trial. *JAMA, 294*(5), 563–570.

Brown, G. W. (1985). The discovery of expressed emotion: Induction or deduction? In J. Leff & C. Vaughn, *Expressed emotion in families* (pp. 7–25). New York: Guilford.

Brown, G. W., & Harris, T. O. (1978). *Social origins of depression.* London: Tavistock.

Brown, G. W., & Harris, T. O. (1989). *Life events and illness.* New York: Guilford.

Brown, G. W., & Moran, P. M. (1997). Single mothers, poverty and depression. *Psychol. Med. 27*(1), 21–33.

Brown, G. W., Carstairs, G. M., & Topping, G. (1958). Post hospital adjustment of chronic mental patients. *Lancet, 2,* 685–89.

Brown, G. W., Harris, T. O., & Bifulco, P. M. (1985). Long-term effects of early loss of parent. In M. Rutter, C. E. Izard, & P. B. Read (Eds.), *Depression in young people: Clinical and developmental perspectives* (pp. 251–96). New York: Guilford.

Brown, J. F., & Menninger, K. A. (1940). *Psychodynamics of abnormal behavior.* New York: McGraw-Hill.

Brown, L. M., Shiang, J., & Bongar, B. (2003). Crisis intervention. In G. Stricker & T. Widiger (Eds.), *Handbook of psychology: Clinical psychology* (Vol. 8, pp. 431–51). New York: John Wiley & Sons, Inc.

Brown, P. J., Stout, R. L., & Mueller, T. (1999). Substance use disorder and posttraumtic stress disorder: Comorbidity, addiction, and psychiatric treatment rates. *Psychology of Addictive Behaviors, 13,* 115–22.

Brown, P. (1994). Toward a psychobiological model of dissociation and posttraumatic stress disorder. In S. J. Lynn & J. W. Rhue (Eds.), *Dissociation: Clinical and theoretical perspectives* (pp. 94–122). New York: Guilford.

Brown, R. D., Goldstein, E., & Bjorklund, D. F. (2000). The history and Zeitgeist of the repressed-false-memory debate: Scientific and sociological perspectives on suggestibility and childhood memory. In D. F. Bjorklund (Ed.), *False-memory creation in children and adults: Theory, research, and implications* (pp. 1–30). Mahwah, NJ: Erlbaum.

Brown, R., & Lo, R. (2000). The physical and psychosocial consequences of opioid addiction: An overview of changes in opioid treatment. *Australian & New Zealand Journal of Mental Health Nursing,* 9, 65–74.

Brown, R., Taylor, J., & Matthews, B. (2001). Quality of life: Aging and Down syndrome. *Down Syndrome: Research & Practice, 6,* 111–16.

Brown, S. A., Tate, S. R., Vik, P. W., Haas, A. L., & Aarons, G. A. (1999). Modeling of alcohol use mediates the effect of family history of alcoholism on adolescent alcohol expectancies. *Experimental and Clinical Psychopharmacology, 7*(1), 20–27.

Brown, T. A. (1996). Validity of the DSM-III-R and DSM-IV classification systems for anxiety disorders. In R. M. Rapee (Ed.), *Current controversies in the anxiety disorders* (pp. 21–45). New York: Guilford.

Brown, T. A., & Barlow, D. H. (2001). *Casebook in abnormal psychology* (2nd ed.). Belmont, CA: Wadsworth/Thomson Learning.

Brown, T. A., Campbell, L. A., Lehman, C. L., Grisham, J. R., & Mancill, R. B. (2001). Current and lifetime comorbidity of the DSM-IV anxiety and mood disorders in a large clinical sample. *J. Abn. Psychol., 110*(4), 585–99.

Brown, T. A., Chorpita, B. F., & Barlow, D. H. (1998). Structural relationships among dimensions of the DSM-IV anxiety and mood disorders and dimensions of negative affect, positive affect, and autonomic arousal. *J. Abn. Psychol., 107*(2), 179–92.

Brown, T. L., Flory, K., Lynam, D. R., Leukefeld, C., & Clayton, R. R. (2004). Comparing the developmental trajectories of marijuana use of African American and Caucasian adolescent patterns, antecedents and consequences. *Exp. Clin. Psychopharm., 12,* 47–56.

Browne, A., & Finkelhor, D. (1986). Impact of child sexual abuse: A review of the research. *Psychol. Bull. 99,* 66–77.

Browne, E. G. (1921). *Arabian Medicine.* New York: Macmillan.

Brownell, K. D., & Wadden, T. A. (1992). Etiology and treatment of obesity: Understanding a serious, prevalent, and refractory disorder. *J. Cons. Clin. Psychol., 60,* 505–17.

Brownell, K. D. (2002). Public policy and the prevention of obesity. In C. G. Fairburn & K. D. Brownell (Eds.), *Eating disorders and obesity: A comprehensive handbook* (2nd ed., pp. 619–23). New York: Guilford.

Brownell, K. (2003). *Food fight: The inside story of the food industry.* New York: McGraw-Hill.

Brownmiller, S. (1975). *Against our will: Men, women, and rape.* New York: Simon & Schuster.

Bruce, L. C., & Peebles, A. M. S. (1904). Quantitative and qualitative leukocyte counts in various forms of mental illness. *J. Ment. Sci., 50,* 409–17.

Bruch, H. (1973). *Eating disorders: Obesity, anorexia nervosa and the person within.* New York: Basic Books.

Bruck, M., Ceci, S., & Hembrooke, H. (1998). Reliability and credibility of young children's reports: From research to policy and practice. *Amer. Psychol., 53,* 136–51.

Bruck, M., Ceci., S. J., Francouer, E., & Renick, A. (1995). Anatomically detailed dolls do not facilitate preschoolers' reports of a pediatric examination involving genital touch. *J. Exper. Psychol. Applied, 1,* 95–109.

Brugha, T. S., Nienhuis, F., Bagchi, D., Smith, J., & Meltzer, H. (1999). The survey form of SCAN: The feasibility of using experienced lay survey interviewers to administer a semi-structured systematic clinical assessment of psychotic and non-psychotic disorders. *Psychol. Med., 29,* 703–11.

Bry, B. H., McKeon, P., & Pandina, R. J. (1982). The extent of drug use as a function of number of risk factors. *J. Abn. Psychol., 91*(4), 273–79.

Bryant-Waugh, R., & Lask, B. (2002). Childhood-onset eating disorders. In C. G. Fairburn & K. D. Brownell (Eds.), *Eating disorders and obesity: A comprehensive handbook* (2nd ed., pp. 210–14). New York: Guilford.

Brzustowicz, L. M., Hodkinson, K. A., Chow, E. W. C., Honer, W. G., & Bassett, A. S. (2000). Location of a major susceptibility locus for familial schizophrenia on chromosome 1q21–q22. *Science, 288,* 687–82.

Buchanan, G. M., & Seligman, M. E. P. (1995). Afterword: The future of the field. In G. M. Buchanan & M. E. P. Seligman (Eds.), *Explanatory Style* (pp. 247–52). Hillsdale, NJ: Erlbaum.

Buchsbaum, M. S., Haier, R. J., Potkin, S. G., Nuechterlein, K., Bracha, H. S., Katz, M., Lohr, J., Wu, J., Lottenberg, S., Jerabek, P. A., Trenary, M., Tafalla, R., Reynolds, C., & Bunney, W. E., Jr. (1992). Frontostriatal disorder of cerebral metabolism in never-medicated schizophrenics. *Arch. Gen. Psychiat., 49*(12), 935–41.

Buckley, M. A., & Zimmermann, S. H. (2003). *Mentoring children and adolescents: A guide to the issues.* Westport, CT: Praeger Publishers.

Buckley, P. F., & Waddington, J. L. (2001). *Schizophrenia and mood disorders: The new drug therapies in clinical practice.* London: Arnold.

Budman, C. L., Braun, R. D., Park, K. S., Lesser, M., & Olson, M. (2000). Explosive outbursts in children with Tourette's disorder. *J. Amer. Acad. Child Adoles. Psychiat., 39*(10), 1270–76.

Budney, A. J., Moore, B. A., Vandrey, R. G., & Hughes, J. R. (2003). The time course and significance of cannabis withdrawal. *J. Abn. Psychol., 112,* 393–402.

Budney, A. J., Radonovich, K. J., Higgins, S. T., & Wong, C. J. (1998). Adults seeking treatment for marijuana dependence: A comparison with cocaine-dependent treatment seekers. *Experimental and Clinical Psychopharmacology, 6*(4), 419–26.

Bühler, K. E., & Pagels, S. (2003). The influence of biography, life events and chronic difficulties on depressivity during the process of inpatient treatment of depressives. *Schweizer Archiv für Neurologie und Psychiatrie, 154*(6), 284–91.

Buhlmann, U., & Wilhelm, S. (2004). Cognitive factors in body dysmorphic disorder. *Psychiat. Ann., 34*(12), 922–26.

Bulik, C. M., & Allison, D. B. (2002). Constitutional thinness and resistance to obesity. In C. G. Fairburn & K. D. Brownell (Eds.), *Eating disorders and obesity: A comprehensive handbook* (2nd ed., pp. 22–25). New York: Guilford.

Bulik, C. M., & Kendler, K. S. (2000). "I am what I (don't) eat": Establishing an identity independent of an eating disorder. *Amer. J. Psychiat., 157*(11), 1755–60.

Bulik, C. M., & Tozzi, F. (2004). Genetics in eating disorders: State of the science. *CNS Spectrums, 9*(7), 511–15.

Bulik, C. M., Devlin, B., Bacanu, S.-A., Thornton, L., Klump, K. L., Fichter, M., Halmi, K. A., Kaplan, A. S., Strober, M., Woodside, D. B., Bergen, A. W., Ganjei, J. K., Crow, S., Mitchell, J., Rotondo, A., Mauri, M., Cassano, G., Keel, P., Berrettini, W. H., & Kaye, W. H. (2003). Significant linkage on chromosome 10p in families with bulimia nervosa. *Amer. J. Hum. Gene., 72,* 200–207.

Bulik, C. M., Sullivan, P. F., & Kendler, K. S. (2003). Genetic and environmental contributions to obesity and binge eating. *Int. J. Eat. Dis., 33,* 293–98.

Bulik, C. M. (2002). Commentary on Löwe et al., 2001. *Evidence-Based Mental Health, 5*(2), 59.

Bullman, T. A., & Kang, H. K. (1997). Posttraumatic stress disorder and the risk of traumatic deaths among Vietnam veterans. In C. S. Fullerton & R. J. Ursano (Eds.), *Posttraumatic stress disorders* (pp. 175–89). Washington, DC: American Psychiatric Press.

Bureau of Justice Statistics. (2004). *Monitoring the Future national results in use: Overview of key findings, 2003.* University of Michigan.

Bureau of the Census. (2001). *Population estimates of the United States by age and sex.* Washington, DC: U.S. Census Bureau.

Burgess, A. W., & Holmstrom, L. (1974). Rape trauma syndrome. *Amer. J. Psychiat., 131,* 981–86.

Burgess, A. W., & Holmstrom, L. (1976). Coping behavior of the rape victim. *Amer. J. Psychiat., 133,* 413–18.

Burks, V. S., Dodge, K. A., & Price, J. M. (1995). Models of internalizing outcomes of early rejection. *Develop. Psychopath., 7,* 683–95.

Burks, V. S., Laird, R. D., Dodge, K. A., Pettit, G. S., & Bates, J. E. (1999). Knowledge structures, social information processing, and children's aggressive behavior. *Soc. Develop., 8,* 220–36.

Burman, B., & Margolin, G. G. (1992). Analysis of the association between marital relationships and health problems: An interactional perspective. *Psychol. Bull., 112,* 39–63.

Burnett, A., & Peel, M. (2001). Asylum seekers and refugees in Britain: The health of survivors of torture and organized violence. *Brit. Med. J., I322,* 606–9.

Burstein, A. (1985). How common is delayed posttraumatic stress disorder? *Amer. J. Psychiat., 142*(7), 887.

Burt, K. B., Van Dulmen, M. H. M., Carlivati, J., Egeland, B., Sroufe, L. A., Forman, D. R., et al., (2005). Mediating links between maternal depression and offspring psychopathology: The importance of independent data. *J. Child Psychol. Psychiat., 46*(5), 490–499.

Burt, V. L., Whelton, P., Roccella, E. J., Brown, C., Cutler, J. A., Higgins, M., Horan, M. J., & Labarthe, D. (1995). Prevalence of hypertension in the U.S. adult population. Results from the Third National Health and Nutrition Examination Survey, 1988–1991. *Hypertension, 25,* 305–13.

Burton, G. (2001). The tenacity of historical misinformation: Titchner did not invent the Titchner illusion. *History of Psychology, 4,* 228–44.

Burton, R. (1624). *Anatomy of melancholia.* London: *Oxford.*

Busch, K. A., Fawcett, J., & Jacobs, D. G. (2003). Clinical correlates of inpatient suicide. *J. Clin. Psychiat., 64*(1), 14–19.

Bush, D. E., Ziegelstein, R. C., Tayback, M., Richter, D., Stevens, S., Zahalsky, H., & Fauerbach, J. A. (2001). Even minimal symptoms of depression increase mortality risk after acute myocardial infarction. *Amer. J. Cardio., 88,* 337–41.

Bushnell, J. A., Wells, J. E., & Oakley-Browne, M. A. (1992). Long-term effects of intrafamilial sexual abuse in childhood. *Acta Psychiatr. Scandin., 85,* 136–42.

Buss, D. M. (1989). Sex differences in human mate preferences: Evolutionary hypotheses tested in 37 cultures. *Behavioral and Brain Sciences, 12,* 1–49.

Buss, D. M. (1999). *Evolutionary psychology.* Boston: Allyn and Bacon.

Bustillo, J. R., Lauriello, J., Horan, W. P., & Keith, S. J. (2001). The psychosocial treatment of schizophrenia: An update. *Amer. J. Psychiat., 158,* 163–75.

Butcher, J. N. (Ed.). (1996). *International applications of the MMPI-2: A handbook of research and clinical applications.* Minneapolis, MN: University of Minnesota Press.

Butcher, J. N., & Dunn, L. (1989). Human responses and treatment needs in airline disasters. In R. Gist & B. Lubin (Eds.), *Psychosocial aspects of disaster.* New York: Wiley.

Butcher, J. N., & Hatcher, C. (1988). The neglected entity in air disaster planning: Psychological services. *Amer. Psychol., 43,* 724–29.

Butcher, J. N., Atlis, M., & Hahn, J. (2003). Assessment with the MMPI-2: Research base and future developments. In D. Segal (Ed.), *Comprehensive handbook of psychological assessment* (pp. 30–38). New York: John Wiley.

Butcher, J. N., Cheung, F. M., & Kim, J. (2003). Use of the MMPI-2 with Asian populations. *Psychol. Assess., 15*(3), 248–256.

Butcher, J. N., Graham, J. R., Ben-Porath, Y. S., Tellegen, A., Dahlstrom, W. G., & Kaemmer, B. (2001). *Minnesota Multiphasic Personality Inventory-2 (MMPI-2): Manual for administration and scoring* (2nd ed.). Minneapolis: University of Minnesota Press.

Butcher, J. N., Perry, J. N., & Atlis, M. (2000). Validity and utility of computer-based test interpretation. *Psychol. Assess., 12,* 6–18.

Butcher, J. N., Perry, J., & Hahn, J. (2004). Computers in clinical assessment: Historical developments, present status, and future challenges. *J. Clin. Psychol., 60,* 331–46.

Butcher, J. N., Rouse, S. V., & Perry, J. N. (2000). Empirical description of psychopathology in therapy clients: Correlates of MMPI-2 scales. Chapter in J. N. Butcher (Ed.), *Basic sources of MMPI-2* (pp. 487–500). Minneapolis: University of Minnesota Press.

Butcher, J. N., Williams, C. L., Graham, J. R., Archer, R., Tellegen, A., Ben-Porath, Y. S., & Kaemmer, B. (1992). *MMPI-A: Manual for administration, scoring, and interpretation.* Minneapolis: University of Minnesota Press.

Butcher, J. N. (1993). *User's guide for the MMPI-2 Minnesota Report: Adult Clinical System.* Minneapolis: National Computer Systems.

Butcher, J. N. (1996). Understanding abnormal behavior across cultures: The use of objective personality assessment methods. In J. N. Butcher (Ed.), *International adaptations of the MMPI-2s* (pp. 3–25). Minneapolis: University of Minnesota Press.

Butcher, J. N. (2004). Personality assessment without borders: Adaptation of the MMPI-2 across cultures. *J. Pers. Assess., 83*(2), 90–104.

Butcher, J., Derksen, J., Sloore, H., & Sirigatti, S. (2003). Objective personality assessment of people in diverse cultures: European adaptations of the MMPI-2. *Behav. Res. Ther., 41*(7), 819–840.

Butler, L. D., Duran, R. E., Jasiukaitis, P., Koopman, C., & Spiegel, D. (1996). Hypnotizability and traumatic experience: A diathesis–stress model of dissociative symptomatology. *Amer. J. Psychiat., 153,* 42–63.

Butow, P., Beumont, P., & Touyz, S. (1993). Cognitive processes in dieting disorders. *Int. J. Eat Dis., 14,* 319–30.

Butterfield, F. (1998). Prisons replace hospitals for the nation's mentally ill. *New York Times,* pp. 1–17.

Butzlaff, R. L., & Hooley, J. M. (1998). Expressed emotion and psychiatric relapse: A meta-analysis. *Arch. Gen. Psychiat., 55*(6), 547–52.

Byne, W., Tobet, S., Mattiace, L. A., Lasco, M. S., Kemether, E., Edgar, M. A., et al. (2001). The interstitial nuclei of the human anterior hypothalamus: An investigation of variation with sex, sexual orientation, and HIV status. *Hormones and Behavior, 40,* 86–92.

Byrne, A. (2000). Nine year follow up of 86 consecutive patients treated with methadone in general practice, Sydney, Australia. *Drug & Alcohol Review, 19,* 153–58.

Byrne, M., Agerbo, E., Ewald, H., Eaton, W., & Mortensen, P. B. (2003). Parental age and risk of schizophrenia. *Arch. Gen. Psychiat., 60,* 673–678.

Cachelin, F. M., & Maher, B. A. (1998). Is amenorrhea a critical criterion for anorexia nervosa? *J. Psychosom. Res., 44,* 435–40.

Cachelin, F. M., Veisel, C., Barzegarnazari, E., & Striegel-Moore, R. H. (2000). Disordered eating, acculturation, and treatment seeking in a community of Hispanic, Asian, Black, and White women. *Psychol. Women Quart., 24,* 244–53.

Cacioppo, J. T., et al. (1998). Cellular immune responses to acute stress in female caregivers of dementia patients and matched controls. *Hlth. Psychol., 17,* 182–89.

Cade, J. F. J. (1949). Lithium salts in the treatment of psychotic excitement. *Medical Journal of Australia, 36* (part II): 349–52.

Cadenhead, K. S., Light, G. A., Geyer, M. A., & Braff, D. L. (2000a). Sensory gating deficits assessed by the P50 event-related potential in subjects with schizotypal personality disorder. *Amer. J. Psychiat., 157*(1), 55–59.

Cadenhead, K. S., Swerdlow, N. R., Shafer, K. M., Diaz, M., & Braff, D. L. (2000b). Modulation of the startle response and startle laterality in relatives of schizophrenic patients and in subjects with schizotypal personality disorder: Evidence of inhibitory deficits. *Amer. J. Psychiat., 157*(10), 1660–67.

Cadoret, R. J., Yates, W. R., Troughton, E., Woodworth, G., & Stewart, M. A. (1995). Genetic-environmental interaction in the genesis of aggressivity and conduct disorders. *Arch. Gen. Psychiat., 52,* 916–24.

Caetano, R. Clark, C. L., Tam, T. (1998). Alcohol consumption among racial/ethnic minorities, *Alcohol World: Health and Research, 22*(4), 233–42.

Cahn, W., Hulsoff Pol, H. E., Lems, E. B. T. E., van Haren, N. E. M., Schnack, H. G., van der Linden, J. A., Schothorst, P. F., van Engeland, H., Kahn, R. S. (2002). Brain volume changes in first-episode schizophrenia: A 1-year follow-up study. *Arch. Gen. Psychiat., 59,* 1002–10.

Cale, E. M., & Lilienfeld, S. O. (2002). Histrionic personality disorder and antisocial personality disorder: Sex-differentiated manifestations of psychopathy. *J. Pers. Dis., 16*(1), 52–72.

Cale, E. M., & Lilienfeld, S. O. (2002). Sex differences in psychopathy and antisocial personality disorder: A review and integration. *Clin. Psychol. Rev., 22,* 1179–1207.

Callahan, L. A., & Silver, E. (1998). Factors associated with the conditional release of persons acquitted by reason of insanity: A decision tree approach. *Law and Human Behavior, 22,* 147–63.

Callahan, L. A., Robbins, P. C., Steadman, H., & Morrissey, J. P. (1995). The hidden effects of Montana's "abolition" of the insanity defense. *Psychiat. Q., 66*(2), 103–17.

Campbell, D. (1926). *Arabian medicine and its influence on the Middle Ages.* New York: Dutton.

Campbell, M. (1987). Drug treatment of infantile autism: The past decade. In H. Meltzer (Ed.), *Psychopharmacology: The third generation of progress* (pp. 1225–31). New York: Raven Press.

Campbell, M., & Cueva, J. E. (1995). Psychopharmacology in child and adolescent psychiatry: A review of the past seven years. Part 1. *J. Amer. Acad. Child Adoles. Psychiat., 34*(9), 1124–32.

Campbell, P. (1926). *Arabian medicine and its influence on the middle ages.* New York: Dutton, 1926.

Campbell, S. B., Cohn, J. F., Ross, S., Elmore, M., & Popper, S. (1990, Apr.). *Postpartum adaptation and postpartum depression in primiparous women.* International Conference of Infant Studies, Montreal.

Canetti, L., Bachar, E., & Berry, E. M. (2002). Food and emotion. *Behavioural Processes, 60,* 157–64.

Canetti, L., Bachar, E., Bonne, O., Agid, O., Lerer, B., de-Nour, A. K., & Shalev, A. Y. (2000). The impact of parental death versus separation from parents on the mental health of Israeli adolescents. *Compr. Psychiat., 41,* 360–68.

Canetto, S. S. (1997). Gender and suicidal behavior: Theories and evidence. In R. W. Maris, M. M. Silverman, & S. S. Canetton (Eds.), *Review of Suicidology, 1997* (pp. 138–67). New York: Guilford.

Cannon, M., Jones, P. B., & Murray, R. M. (2002). Obstetric complications and schizophrenia: Historical and meta-analytic review. *Amer. J. Psychiat., 159*(7), 1080–92.

Cannon, M., Jones, P. B., & Murray, R. M. (2002). Obstetric complications and schizophrenia: Historical and meta-analytic review. *Amer. J. Psychiat., 159,* 1080–1092.

Cannon, T. D. (1998a). Genetic and perinatal influences in the etiology of schizophrenia: A neurodevelopmental model. In M. F. Lenzenweger & R. H. Dworkin (Eds.), *Origins and development of schizophrenia.* Washington, DC: American Psychological Association.

Cannon, T. D. (1998b). Neurodevelopmental influences in the genesis and epigenesis of schizophrenia: An overview. *App. Prev. Psychol., 7*(1), 47–62.

Cannon, T. D., et al. (1998). The genetic epidemiology of schizophrenia in a Finnish twin cohort. *Arch. Gen. Psychiat., 55*(1), 67–74.

Cannon, T. D., Glahn, D. C., Kim, J., Van Erp, T. G. M., Karlsgodt, K., Cohen, M. S., Neuchterlein, K. H., Bava, S., & Shirinyan, D. (2005). Dorsolateral prefrontal cortex activity during maintenance and manipulation of information in working memory in patients with schizophrenia. *Arch. Gen. Psychiat., 62(10):* 1071–1080.

Cannon, W. B. (1915). *Bodily changes in pain, hunger, fear and rage.* New York: Appleton.

Cantor Grace, E., & Selten, J.-P. (2005). Schizophrenia and migration: A meta-analysis and review. *Amer. J. Psychiat., 162,* 12–24.

Cantwell, D. P., & Baker, L. (1989). Stability and natural history of DSM III childhood diagnoses. *J. Amer. Acad. Child Adoles. Psychiat., 28,* 691–700.

Capaldi, D. M., & Patterson, G. R. (1994). Interrelated influences of contextual factors on antisocial behavior in childhood and adolescence for males. In D. C. Fowles, P. Sutker, & S. H. Goodman (Eds.), *Progress in experimental personality and psychopathology research.* New York: Springer.

Capaldi, D., DeGarmo, D., Patterson, G. R., & Forgatch, M. (2002). Contextual risk across the early life span and association with antisocial behavior. In J. B. Reid, G. R. Patterson, et al. (Eds.), *Antisocial behavior in children and adolescents: A developmental analysis and model for intervention* (pp. 123–45). Washington, DC: American Psychological Association.

Capps, L., Kasari, C., Yirmiya, N., & Sigman, M. (1993). Parental perception of emotional expressiveness in children with autism. *J. Cons. Clin. Psychol., 61,* 475–84.

Capraro, R. L. (2000). Why college men drink: Alcohol, adventure, and the paradox of masculinity. *J. Amer. Coll. Hlth. 48,* 307–15.

Capron, C., & Duyme, M. (1989). Assessment of effects of socio-economic status on IQ in a full cross-fostering study. *Nature, 340,* 552–54.

Caracci, G. (2003). Violence against women. *Inter. J. Ment. Hlth., 32*(1), 36–53.

Caracci, G., & Mezzich, J. E. (2001). Culture and urban mental health. *Psychiat. Clin. N. Amer., 24*(3), 581–93.

Carbone, D. J., Jr., & Seftel, A. D. (2002). Erectile dysfunction. Diagnosis and treatment in older men. *Geriatrics, 57,* 18–24.

Cardeña, E., Butler, L., & Spiegel, D. (2003). Stress disorders. In G. Stricker & T. A. Widiger (Eds.), *Handbook of psychology: Clinical psychology* (Vol. 8, pp. 229–49). New York: John Wiley & Sons, Inc.

Cardona, F., Camillo, E., Casini, M. P., Luchetti, A., & Muscetta, A. (1997). Tic disorders in childhood: A retrospective study. *Giornale di Neuropsichiatria dell'Eta Evolutiva, 17*(2), 120–26.

Carey, G. (2003). *Human genetics for the social sciences.* London: Sage.

Carey, G., & DiLalla, D. L. (1994). Personality and psychopathology: Genetic perspectives. *J. Abn. Psychol., 103,* 32–43.

Carey, G., & Goldman, D. (1997). The genetics of antisocial behavior. In D. M. Stoff, J. Breiling, & J. D. Maser (Eds.), *Handbook of antisocial behavior* (pp. 243–54). New York: Wiley.

Carlat, D. J., Carmargo, C. A., & Herzog, D. B. (1997). Eating disorders in males: A report on 135 patients. *Amer. J. Psychiat., 154,* 1127–32.

Carlier, I. V., Lamberts, R. D., & Gersons, B. (1997). Risk factors for post-traumatic stress symptomatology in police officers: A prospective analysis. *J. Nerv. Ment. Dis. 185*(8), 498–506.

Carlson R. (1997, Apr.). *Sildenafil: An effective oral drug for impotence. Inpharma, 1085: 11-12.* Annual Meeting of the American Urological Association, New Orleans.

Carlson, C. L., & Bunner, M. R. (1993). Effects of methylphenidate on the academic performance of children with Attention Deficit Hyperactivity Disorder and learning disabilities. *School Psychol. Rev., 22,* 184–98.

Carlson, C. R., & Hoyle, R. H. (1993). Efficacy of abbreviated progressive muscle relaxation training: A quantitative review of behavioral medicine research. *J. Cons. Clin. Psychol., 61*(6), 1059–67.

Carlson, E. A., & Sroufe, L. A. (1995). Contribution of attachment theory to developmental psychopathology. In D. Cicchetti & D. J. Cohen (Eds.), *Developmental Psychopathology: Vol. 1 Theory and Methods* (pp. 581–617). New York: Wiley.

Carlson, E. A., Sampson, M. C., & Sroufe, L. A. (2003). Implications of attachment theory and research for developmental-behavioral pediatrics. *J. Dev. Behav. Ped., 24*(5), 364–379.

Carlson, E. B., & Rosser-Hogan, R. (1993). Mental health status of Cambodian refugees ten years after leaving their homes. *Amer. J. Orthopsychiat., 63,* 223–31.

Carlson, M. (2001). Child rights and mental health. *Child Adoles. Psychiatr. Clin. N. Amer., 10,* 825–39.

Carlsson, K., Petersson, K. M., Lundqvist, D., Karlsson, A., Ingvar, M., & Ohman, A. (2004). Fear and the amygdale: manipulation of awareness generates differential cerebral responses to phobic and fear-relevant (but nonfeared) stimuli. *Emotion, 4*(4), 340–353.

Carney, R. M., Freedland, K. E., Eisen, S. A., Rich, M. W., & Jaffe, A. S. (1995). Major depression and medication adherence in elderly patients with coronary artery disease. *Hlth. Psychol., 14,* 88–90.

Carney, R. M., Saunders, R. D., Freedland, K. E., Stein, P., Rich, M. W., & Jaffe, A. S. (1995). Association of depression with reduced heart rate variability in coronary artery disease. *Amer. J. Cardio., 76,* 562–64.

Carpenter, P. K. (1989). Descriptions of schizophrenia in the psychiatry of Georgian Britain: John Haslam and James Tilly Matthews. *Compr. Psychiat., 30,* 332–38.

Carpentieri, S., & Morgan, S. B. (1996). Adaptive and intellectual functioning in autistic and nonautistic retarded children. *J. Autism and Devel. Dis., 26*(6), 611–20.

Carr, M. B., & Vandiver, T. A. (2001). Risk and protective factors among youth offenders. *Adolescence, 36*(143), 409–26.

Carroll, K. M., & Rounsaville, B. J. (1993). History and significance and childhood attention deficit disorder in treatment-seeking cocaine abusers. *Compr. Psychiat., 34,* 75–82.

Carroll, K. M., Fenton, L. R., Ball, S. A., Nich, C., Frankforter, T. L., Shi, J., & Rounsaville, B. J. (2004). Efficacy of disulfiram and cognitive behavior therapy in cocaine-dependent outpatients. *Arch. Gen. Psychiat., 61*(3), 264–72.

Carroll, K. M., Power, M. D., Bryant, K. J.& Rounsaville, B. J. (1993). One-year follow-up status of treatment-seeking cocaine abusers: Psychopathology and dependence severity as predictors of outcome. *J. Nerv. Mant. Dis. 181*(2), 71–79.

Carroll, K. M., Powers, M. D., Bryant, K. J., & Rounsaville, B. J. (1993). One-year follow up status of treatment seeking cocaine abusers: Psychopathology and dependence severity as predictors of outcome. *J. Nerv. Ment. Dis., 181*(2), 71–79.

Carruthers, M., (1980). Hazardous occupations and the heart. In C. L. Cooper & R. Payne (Eds.), *Current concerns in occupational stress.* New York: Wiley.

Carson, R. C. (1982). Self-fulfilling prophecy, maladaptive behavior, and psychotherapy. In J. C. Anchin & D. J. Kiesler (Eds.), *Handbook of interpersonal psychotherapy* (pp. 64–77). New York: Pergamon.

Carstairs, G. M., & Kapur, R. L. (1976). *The great universe of Kota: Stress, change and mental disorder in an Indian village.* Berkeley, CA: University of California Press.

Carter, A. S., Garrity-Rokous, F. E., Chazan-Cohen, R., Little, C., & Briggs-Gowan, M. J. (2001). Maternal depression and comorbidity: Predicting early parenting, attachment security, and toddler social-emotional problems and competencies. *J. Amer. Acad. Child Adoles. Psychiat., 40*(1), 18–26.

Carter, J. C., & Fairburn, C. G. (1998). Cognitive behavioral self help for binge eating disorder: A controlled effectiveness study. *J. Cons. Clin. Psychol., 66*(4), 616–23.

Carter, M. M., Hollon, S. D., Carson, R., & Shelton, R. C. (1995). Effects of a safe person on induced distress following a biological challenge in panic disorder with agoraphobia. *J. Abn. Psychol., 104,* 156–63.

Carter, W. P., Hudson, J. I., Lalonde, J. K., Pindyck, L., McElroy, S. L., & Pope, H. G. (2003). Pharmacologic treatment of binge eating disorder. *Int. J. Eat. Dis., 34,* S74–S88.

Cascardi, M., O'Leary, K. D., & Schlee, K. A. (1999). Co-occurrence and correlates of posttraumatic stress disorder and major depression in physically abused women. *J. Fam. Viol., 14*(3), 227–49.

Case, R. B., Heller, S. S., & Moss, A. J. (1985). The multicenter post infarction research group: Type A behavior and survival after acute myocardial infarction. *N. Engl. J. Med., 312,* 737–41.

Casey, R. J., & Berman, J. S. (1985). The outcome of psychotherapy with children. *Psychol. Bull., 98,* 388–400.

Caspi, A., Sugden, K., Moffitt, T. E., Taylor, A., Craig, I. W., Harrington, H., McClay, J., Mill, J., Martin, J., Braithwaite, A., & Poulton, R. (2003, Jul. 18). Influence of life stress on depression: Moderation by a polymorphism in the 5HTT gene. *Science, 301,* 386–89.

Cassady, J. D., Kirschke, D. L., Jones, T. F., Craig, A. S., Bermudez, O. B., & Schaffner W. (2005). Case series: Outbreak of conversion disorder among Amish adolescent girls. *J. Amer. Acad. Child Adoles. Psychiat., 44*(3), 291–97.

Cassell, E. J. (2002). Compassion. In C. R. Snyder & S. J. Lopez (Eds.), *Handbook of positive psychology* (pp. 434–45). New York: Oxford University Press.

Cassidy, C., O'Connor, R. C., Howe, C., & Warden, D. (2004). Perceived discrimination and psychological distress: The role of personal and ethnic self-esteem. *J. Couns. Psychol., 51*(3), 329–339.

Cassidy, F., Forest, K., Murry, E., & Carroll, B. J. (1998). A factor analysis of the signs and symptoms of mania. *Arch. Gen. Psychiat., 55*(1), 27–32.

Castiglioni, A. (1924). *Adventures of the mind.* New York: Dutton.

Castonguay, L. G., Reid, J. J., & Halperin, G. S. (in press). Reconciliation and integration in psychotherapy: A strategy to address the complexity of human change. In G. Stricker & T. A. Widiger (Eds.), *Comprehensive handbook of psychology, Vol. 8. Clinical Psychology.* New York: Wiley.

Castonguay, L. G., Reid, J. J., & Halperin, G. S., & Goldfried, M. R. (2003). Psychotherapy integration. In Stricker, G., Widiger, T. A., & Weiner, I. B. (Eds.), *Handbook of Psychology: Clinical Psychology, Vol. 8.* Hoboken: John Wiley and Sons, pp. 327–366.

Castro, J. (1993, May 31). What price mental health? *Time,* pp. 59–60.

Cato, C., & Rice, B. D. (1982). *Report from the study group on rehabilitation of clients with specific learning disabilities.* St. Louis: National Institute of Handicapped Research.

Cauce, A. M., Paradise, M., Ginzler, J. A., Embry, L., Morgan, C. J., Lohr, Y., & Theofelis, J. (2000). The characteristics and mental health of homeless adolescents: Age and gender differences. *Journal of Emotional & Behavioral Disorders, 8,* 230–39.

Cavaco, S., Anserson, S. W., Allen, J. S., Castro-Caldas, A., & Damasio, H. (2004). The scope of preserved procedural memory in amnesia. *Brain, 127,* 1853–67.

Cavanagh, J. T., Van Beck, M., Muir, W., & Blackwood, D. H. R. (2002). Case control study of neurocognitive function in euthymic patients with bipolar disorder: An association with mania. *Brit. J. Psychiat., 180,* 320–26.

CBS News. (2003, Aug. 5). Autistic boy dies during exorcism. New York: Columbia Broadcasting System.

Ceci, S. J., Bruck, M., & Battin, D. B. (2000). The suggestibility of children's testimony. In D. F. Bjorklund (Ed.), *False-memory creation in children and adults: Theory, research, and implications* (pp. 169–202). Mahwah, NJ: Erlbaum.

Ceci, S. J. (1995). False beliefs: Some developmental and clinical considerations. In D. Schacter, (Ed.), *Memory distortions: How minds, brains and societies reconstruct the past.* (pp. 91–125). New York: Harvard University Press.

Centers for Disease Control. (2003). Tobacco, alcohol, and other drug use among high school students in the Bureau of Indian Affairs funded schools—United States, 2001. Washington, DC: U.S. Department of Health and Human Services.

Chaffin, M., Silvosky, J. F., Funderburk, B., Valle, L. A., Brestan, E. V., Balachova, T., Jackson, S., Lensgraf, J., & Bonner, B. L. (2004). Parent-child interaction therapy with physically abusive parents: Efficacy for reducing future abuse reports. *J. Cons. Clin. Psychol., 72,* 500–10.

Chambers, R. A., & Potenza, M. N. (2003). Neurodevelopment, impulsivity, and adolescent gambling. *Journal of Gambling Studies, 19*(1), 53–84.

Chambers, R. E. (1952). Discussion of "Survival factors . . ." *Amer. J. Psychiat., 109,* 247–48.

Chambless, D. L., & Mason, J. (1986). Sex, sex role stereotyping, and agoraphobia. *Behav. Res. Ther., 24,* 231–35.

Chambless, D. L., & Ollendick, T. H. (2001). Empritically supported psychological interventions: Controversies and Evidence. *Annu. Rev. Psychol., 52,* 685–716.

Chambless, D. L., et al. (1998). Update on empirically validated therapies, II. *Clin. Psychol., 51*(1), 3–16.

Chan, G. W. L., Ungvari, G. S., & Leung, J. P. (2001). Residential services for psychiatric patients in Hong Kong. *Hong Kong J. Psychiatry, 11*(3), 13–17.

Chan, G. W. L. (2001). Residential services for psychiatric patients in Hong Kong. *Hong Kong J. of Psychiatry, 11*(3), 13–17.

Channon, S., German, E., Cassina, C., & Lee, P. (2004). Executive functioning, memory, and learning in phenylketonuria. *Neuropsychology, 18,* 613–20.

Chapman, L. J., Chapman, J. P., & Miller, E. N. (1982). Reliabilities and intercorrelations of eight measures of proneness to psychosis. *J. Cons.Clin. Psychol., 50,* 187–95.

Chapman, L. J., Chapman, J. P., Kwapil, T. R., Eckblad, M., & Zinzer, M. (1994). Putatively psychosis-prone subjects ten years later. *J. Abn. Psychol., 103,* 171–83.

Chappel, J. N. (1993). Long-term recovery from alcoholism. *Psychiat. Clin. N. Amer., 16,* 177–87.

Charach, A., Ickowicz, A., & Schachar, R. (2004). Stimulant treatment over five years: Adherence, effectiveness, and adverse effects. *J. Amer. Acad. Child Adoles. Psychiat., 43,* 559–67.

Charlop-Christie, M. H., Schreibman, L., Pierce, K., & Kurtz, P. F. (1998). Childhood autism. In R. J. Morris, T. R. Kratochwill, et al. (Eds.), *The practice of child therapy* (pp. 271–302). Boston: Allyn and Bacon.

Charman, T., Swettenham, J., Baron-Cohen, S., Cox, A., Baird, G., & Drew, A. (1997). Infants with autism: An investigation of empathy, pretend play, joint attention, and imitation. *Develop. Psychol., 33*(5), 781–89.

Charney, D., Grillon, C., & Bremner, J. D. (1998). The neurobiological basis of anxiety and fear: Circuits, mechanisms, and neurochemical interactions (Part I). *The Neuroscientist, 4,* 35–44.

Chartier, M. J., Walker, J. R., & Stein, M. B. (2001). Social phobia and potential childhood risk factors in a community sample. *Psychol. Med., 31,* 307–15.

Chase-Lansdale, P. L., Cherlin, A. J., & Kieran, K. E. (1995). The long-term effects of parental divorce on the mental health of young adults: A developmental perspective. *Child Develop., 66,* 1614–34.

Chassin, L., Curran, P. J., Hussong, A. M., & Colder, C. R. (1996). The relation of parent alcoholism to adolescent substance use: A longitudinal follow-up. *J. Abn. Psychol., 105*(1), 70–80.

Chassin, L., Pillow, D. R., Curran, P. J., Molina, B. S., & Barrera, M. (1993). Relation of parental alcoholism in early adolescent substance use: A test of three mediating mechanisms. *J. Abn. Psychol., 102,* 3–19.

Chassin, L., Rogosch, F., & Barrera, M. (1991). Substance use and symptomatology among adolescent children of alcoholics. *J. Abn. Psychol., 100,* 449–63.

Checkley, S. (1992). Neuroendocrinology. In E. S. Paykel (Ed.), *Handbook of affective disorders* (2nd ed.). New York: Guilford.

Cheitlin, M. D., Hutter, A. M., Brindis, R. G., Ganz, P., Kaul, S., Russell, R. O., et al. (1999). Use of sildenafil (Viagra) in patients with cardiovascular disease. Technology and Practice Executive Committee. *Circulation, 99,* 168–77.

Chemtob, C. M., Hamada, R. S., Roitblat, H. L., & Muraoka, M. Y. (1994). Anger, impulsivity, and anger control in combat-related post-traumatic stress disorder. *J. Cons. Clin. Psychol., 62,* 827–32.

Chemtob, C. M., Novaco, R. W., Hamada, R. S., & Gross, D. M. (1997). Cognitive-behavioral treatment for severe anger in posttraumatic stress disorder. *J. Cons. Clin. Psychol., 65*(1), 184–89.

Chemtob, C. M., Tomas, S., Law, W., & Cremniter, D. (1997). Postdisaster psychosocial intervention: A field study of the impact of debriefing on psychological distress. *Amer. J. Psychiat., 154*(3), 415–17.

Chen, C. C., & Yeh, E. K. (1997). Population differences in ALDH levels and flushing response. In G. Y. San (Ed.), *Molecular mechanisms of alcohol.* New York: Humana.

Cheng, A. T. A., Tien, A. Y., Chang, C. J., Brugha, T. S., Cooper, J. E., Lee, C. S., Compton, W., Liu, C. Y., Yu, W. Y. , & Chen, H. M. (2001). Cross-cultural implementation of a Chinese version of the Schedules for Clinical Assessment in Neuropsychiatry (SCAN) in Taiwan. *Brit. J. Psychia., 178,* 567–72.

Cherpitel, C. J. (1997). Alcohol and injuries resulting from violence: A comparison of emergency room samples from two regions of the U.S. *Journal of Addictive Diseases, 16*(1), 25–40.

Chesney, M. (1996). New behavioral risk factors for coronary heart disease: Implications for intervention. In K. Orth-Gomer & N. Schneiderman (Eds.), *Behavioral medicine approaches to cardiovascular disease prevention* (pp. 169–82). Mahwah, NJ: Erlbaum.

Chételat, G., Desgranges, B., Sayette, V., Viader, F., Eustache, F., & Baron, J. C. (2002). Mapping gray matter loss with voxel-based morphometry in mild cognitive impairment, *NeuroReport, 13,* 1939–43.

Chételat, G., Desgranges, B., Sayette, V., Viader, F., Berkouk, K., Landeau, B., Lalevée, C., Le, D. F., Dupuy, B., Hannequin, D., Baron, J. C., & Eustache, F. (2003). Dissociating atrophy and hypometabolism impact on episodic memory in mild cognitive impairment. *Brain, 126,* 1955–67.

Chorpita, B. F., & Barlow, D. H. (1998). The development of anxiety: The role of control in the early environment. *Psychol. Bull., 124*(1), 3–21.

Chorpita, B. F. (2001). Control and the development of negative emotion. In M. W. Vasey & M. R. Dadds (Eds.), *The developmental psychopathology of anxiety* (pp. 112–42). New York: Oxford University Press.

Chowdhury, A. (1996) The definition and classification of Koro. *Cult. Med. Psychiat.,* 20, 41–65.

Christensen, A., & Heavey, C. L. (1999). Interventions for couples. In J. T. Spence, J. M. Darley, & D. J. Foss (Eds.), *Annual Review of Psychology* (pp. 165–90). Palo Alt., CA: Annual Review.

Christensen, A., & Jacobson, N. S. (1994). Who (or what) can do psychotherapy: The status and challenge of nonprofessional therapies. *Psychol. Sci., 5,* 1, 8–14.

Christiansen, B. A., Smith, G. T., Roehling, P. V., & Goldman, M. S. (1989). Using alcohol expectancies to predict adolescent drinking behavior after one year. *J. Cons. Clin. Psychol., 57,* 93–99.

Christopher, M. (2004). A broader view of trauma: A biopsychosocial-evolutionary view of the role of traumatic stress response in the emergence of pathology and or growth. *Clin. Psychol. Rev., 24,* 75–98.

Chu B. C., & Kendall, P. C. (2004). Positive association of child involovement and treatment outcome within a manual-based cognitive-behavioral treatment for children with anxiety. *J. Cons. Clin. Psychol., 72,* 821–29.

Chu, J. A., & Dill, D. L. (1990). Dissociative symptoms in relation to childhood physical and sexual abuse. *Amer. J. Psychiat., 147,* 887–92.

Cicchetti, D. & Toth, S. L. (2005). Child maltreatment. *Annu. Rev. Clin. Psychol., 1(1),* 409–438.

Cicchetti, D., & Lynch, M. (1995). Failures in the expectable environment and their impact on individual development: The case of child maltreatment. In D. Cicchetti & D. J. Cohen (Eds.), *Developmental Psychopathology: Vol. 2. Risk, disorder, and adaptation* (pp. 32–72). New York: Wiley.

Cicchetti, D., & Rogosch, F. (1999). Conceptual and methodological issues in developmental psychopathological research. In P. C. Kendall, J. N. Butcher, & G. Holmbeck (Eds.), *Research methods in clinical psychology* (2nd ed., pp. 433–65). New York: Wiley.

Cicchetti, D., & Toth, S. L. (1995a). Developmental psychopathology and disorders of affect. In D. Cicchetti & D. J. Cohen (Eds.), *Developmental Psychopathology Vol. 2: Risk, disorder, and adaptation* (pp. 369–420). New York: Wiley.

Cicchetti, D., & Toth, S. L. (1995b). A developmental psychopathology perspective on child abuse and neglect. *J. Amer. Acad. Child Adoles. Psychiat., 34*(5), 541–65.

Cicchetti, D., & Toth, S. L. (1998). The development of depression in children and adolescents. *Amer. Psychol., 53*(2), 221–41.

Cicchetti, D. (2004). An odyssey of discovery: Lessons learned through three decades of research on child maltreatment. *Amer. Psychol.,* 731–741.

Cigrang, J. A., Pace, J. V., & Yasuhara, T. T. (1995). Critical incident stress intervention following fatal aircraft mishaps. *Aviation, Space, and Environmental Medicine, 66*(9), 880–82.

Ciociola, A. A., McSorley, D. J., Turner, K., Sykes, D., & Palmer, J. B. (1999). *Heicobacter pylori* infection rates in duodenal ulcer patients in the United States may be lower than previously estimated. *American Journal of Gastroenterology, 94*(7), 1834–40.

Cirinclone, C., Steadman, H., & McGreevy, M. A. (1995). Rates of insanity acquittals and the factors associated with successful insanity pleas. *Bull. Amer. Acad. Psychiat. Law, 23*(3), 399–409.

Clark, D. A., Beck, A. T., & Alford, B. A. (1999). *Scientific foundations of cognitive theory and therapy of depression.* New York: Wiley.

Clark, D. A., Steer, R. A., & Beck, A. T. (1994). Common and specific dimensions of self-reported anxiety and depression: Implications for the cognitive and tripartite models. *Amer. J. Psychiat., 103,* 645–54.

Clark, D. A. (1997). Twenty years of cognitive assessment: Current status and future directions. *J. Cons. Clin. Psychol., 65*(6), 996–1000.

Clark, D. C. (1995). Epidemiology, assessment, and management of suicide in depressed patients. In E. E. Beckham & W. R. Leber (Eds.), *Handbook of depression* (2nd ed., pp. 526–38). New York: Guilford.

Clark, D. E., Salkovskis, P. M., Öst, L. G., Breitholtz, E., Koehler, K. A., Westling, B. E., Jeavons, A., & Gelder, M. (1997). Misinterpretations of body sensations in panic disorder. *J. Cons. Clin. Psychol., 65*(2), 203–13.

Clark, D. M., & McManus, F. (2002). Information processing in social phobia. *Biol. Psychiat., 51,* 92–100.

Clark, D. M., & Wells, A. (1995). A cognitive model of social phobia. In R. G. Heimberg, M. R. Liebowitz, D. A. Hope, & F. R. Schneier (Eds.), *Social phobia: Diagnosis, assessment, and treatment* (pp. 69–93). New York: Guilford.

Clark, D. M., Ehlers, A., McManus, F., Hackmann, A., Fennell, M., Campbell, H. et al. (2003). Cognitive therapy versus fluoxetine in generalized social phobia: A randomized placebo-controlled trial. *J. Cons. Clin. Psychol., 71*(6), 1058–1067.

Clark, D. M., Salkovskis, P. M., Hackmann, A., Middleton, H., Anastasiades, P., & Gelder, M. (1994). A comparison of cognitive therapy, applied relaxation, and imipramine in the treatment of panic disorder. *Brit. J. Psychiat., 164,* 759–69.

Clark, D. M., Salkovskis, P. M., Hackmann, A., Wells, A., Ludgate, J., & Gelder, M. (1999). Brief cognitive therapy for panic disorder: A randomized controlled trial. *J. Cons. Clin. Psychol., 67,* 583–89.

Clark, D. M. (1986). A cognitive approach to panic. *Behav. Res. Ther., 24,* 461–70.

Clark, D. M. (1996). Panic disorder: From theory to therapy. In R. M. Rapee (Ed.), *Current controversies in the anxiety disorders* (pp. 318–44). New York: Guilford.

Clark, L. A., & Harrison, J. A. (2001). Assessment instruments. In W. J. Livesley (Ed.), *Handbook of personality disorders* (pp. 277–306). New York: Guilford.

Clark, L. A., & Watson, D. (1991a). "Theoretical and empirical issues in differentiating depression from anxiety." In J. Becker & A. Kleinman (Eds.), *Psychosocial aspects of depression.* Hillsdale, NJ: Erlbaum.

Clark, L. A., & Watson, D. (1991b). Tripartite model of anxiety and depression: Psychometric evidence and taxonomic implications. *J. Abn. Psychol., 100,* 316–36.

Clark, L. A., Watson, D., & Mineka, S. (1994). Temperament, personality, and the mood and anxiety disorders. *J. Abn. Psychol., 103,* 103–16.

Clark, L. A., Watson, D., & Reynolds, S. (1995). Diagnosis and classification of psychopathology: Challenges to the current system and future directions. *Annu. Rev. Psychol., 46,* 121–53.

Clark, L. A. (1992). Resolving taxonomic issues in personality disorders: The value of large-scale analyses of symptom data. *J. Pers. Dis., 6,* 360–76.

Clark, L. A. (1999). Introduction to the special section on the concept of disorder. *J. Abn. Psychol., 108*(3), 371–73.

Clark, L. T. (2005). Issues in minority health: atherosclerosis and coronary heart disease in African Americans. *Med. Clin. N. Amer., 89*(5), 977–1001.

Clark, L., Iversen, S. D., & Goodwin, G. M. (2002). Sustained attention deficit in bipolar disorder. *Brit. J. Psychiat., 180,* 313–19.

Clarke, A. M., Clarke, A. D. B., & Berg, J. M. (Eds.). (1985). *Mental deficiency: The changing outlook* (4th ed.). London: Methuen.

Clarke-Stewart, K. A., Vandell, D. L., McCartney, K., Owen, M. T., & Booth, C. (2000). Effects of parental separation and divorce on very young children. *J. Fam. Psychol., 14*(2), 304–26.

Clarkin, J. F., & Levy, J. N. (2004). The influence of client variables on psychotherapy. In M. J. Lambert (2004). *Bergin and Garfield's handbook of Psychotherapy and behavior change.* New York: John Wiley and Sons, pp. 194–226.

Cleckley, H. M. (1941). *The mask of sanity* (1st ed.). St. Louis, MO: Mosby.

Cleckley, H. M. (1982). *The mask of sanity* (Rev. ed.). New York: Plume.

Cleghorn, J. M., Franco, S., Szechtman, B., Kaplan, R. D., Szechtman, H., Brown, G. M., Nahmias, C., & Garnett, E. S. (1992). Toward a brain map of auditory hallucinations. *Amer. J. Psychiat., 149*(8), 1062–69.

Clement, P. (1970). Elimination of sleepwalking in a seven-year-old boy. *J. Cons. Clin. Psychol., 34*(1), 22–26.

Clementz, B. A., Geyer, M. A., & Braff, D. L. (1998). Poor P50 suppression among schizophrenia patients and their first-degree biological relatives. *Amer. J. Psychiat., 155,* 1691–1702.

Clementz, B. A., Grove, W. M., Iacono, W. G., & Sweeney, J. A. (1992). Smooth-pursuit eye movement dysfunction and liability for schizophrenia: Implications for genetic modeling. *J. Abn. Psychol., 101*(1), 117–29.

Cloitre, M. (2004). Trauma and PTSD. *CNS Spectrums, 9*(9), 4–5.

Cloninger, C. R., Bayon, C., & Pszybeck, T. R. (1997). Epidemiology and Axis I comorbidity of antisocial personality. In D. M. Stoff, J. Breiling, & J. D. Maser (Eds.), *Handbook of antisocial behavior* (pp. 12–21). New York: Wiley.

Cloninger, C. R., Reich, T., Sigvardsson, S., von Knorring, A. L., & Bohman, M. (1986). The effects of changes in alcohol use between generations on the inheritance of alcohol abuse. In *Alcoholism: A medical disorder.* Proceedings of the 76th Annual Meeting of the American Psychopathological Association.

Cloninger, C. R. (1987). A systematic method for clinical description and classification of personality invariants. *Arch. Gen. Psychiat., 44,* 161–67.

Clum, G. A., Clum, G. A., & Surls, R. (1993). A meta-analysis of treatments for panic disorder. *J. Con. Clin. Psychol., 61*(2), 317–26.

Coccaro, E. F. (2001). Biological and treatment correlates. In W. J. Livesley (Ed.), *Handbook of personality disorders* (pp. 124–35). New York: Guilford.

Cockayne, T. O. (1864–1866). Leechdoms, wort cunning, and star craft of early England. London: Longman, Green, Longman, Roberts & Green.

Coffey, P., Leitenberg, H., Henning, K., Turner, T., & Bennett, R. T. (1996). The relation between methods of coping during adulthood with a history of childhood sexual abuse and current psychological adjustment. *J. Cons. Clin. Psychol., 64*(5), 1090–93.

Cohen, A. N., Hammen, C., Henry, R. M., & Daley, S. E. (2004). Effects of stress and social support on recurrence in biporal disorder. *J. Affect. Dis., 82*(1), 143–147.

Cohen, C. I., et al. (1997). "Mixed dementia": Adequate or antiquated? A critical review. *Amer. J. Geriatr. Psychiat., 5*(4), 279–83.

Cohen, D., & Eisdorfer, C. (1988). Depression in family members caring for a relative with Alzheimer's disease. *J. Amer. Geriat. Soc., 36,* 885–89.

Cohen, P., Pine, D. S., Must, A., Kasen, S., & Brook, J. (1998). Prospective associations between somatic illness and mental illness from childhood to adulthood. *Amer. J. Epidemiol., 147*(3), 232–39.

Cohen, S., Doyle, W. J., Skoner, D. P., Rabin, B. S., & Gwaltney, J. M. (1997). Social ties and susceptibility to the common cold. *JAMA, 277,* 1940–44.

Cohen, S., Tyrrell, D. A. J., & Smith, A. P. (1993). Negative life events, perceived stress, negative affect, and susceptibility to the common cold. *J. Pers. Soc. Psychol., 64*(1), 131–40.

Cohen-Kettenis, P. T., & Gooren, L. J. G. (1999). Transsexualism: A review of etiology, diagnosis, and treatment. *J. Psychosom. Res., 46,* 315–33.

Cohen-Kettenis, P. T., Dillen, C. M., & Gooren, L. J. G. (2000). [Treatment of young transsexuals in the Netherlands]. *Nederlands Tijdschrift voor Geneeskunde, 144,* 698–702.

Cohler, B. J., Stott, F. M., & Musick, J. S. (1995). Adversity, vulnerability, and resilience: Cultural and developmental perspectives. In D. Cicchetti & D. J. Cohen (Eds.), *Developmental Psychopathology: Vol. 2. Risk, disorder, and adaptations* (pp. 753–800). New York: Wiley.

Cohn, J. F., & Tronick, E. Z. (1983). Three months infant's reaction to simulated maternal depression. *Child Develop., 54,* 185–93.

Cohn, L. D., & Adler, N. E. (1992). Female and male perceptions of ideal body shapes: Distorted views among Caucasian college students. *Psychology of Women Quarterly, 16,* 69–79.

Coie, J. D., & Lenox, K. F. (1994). The development of antisocial individuals. In D. C. Fowles, P. Sutker, & S. H. Goodman (Eds.), *Progress in experimental personality and psychopathology research.* New York: Springer.

Coie, J. D., Dodge, K. A., Terry, R., & Wright, V. (1991). The role of aggression in peer relations: An analysis of aggression episodes in boys' play groups. *Child Develop., 62,* 812–26.

Coie, J. D., Lochman, J. E., Terry, R., & Hyman, C. (1992). Predicting adolescent disorder from childhood aggression and peer rejection. *J. Cons. Clin. Psychol., 60*(5), 783–92.

Coie, J. D., Miller-Johnson, S., & Bagwell, C. (2000). Prevention science. In A. J. Sameroff & M. Lewis, et al. (Eds.), *Handbook of developmental psychopathology* (2nd ed., pp. 93–112). New York: Kluwer/Plenum.

Coie, J. D. (1990). Toward a theory of peer rejection. In S. R. Asher & J. D. Coie (Eds.), *Peer rejection in childhood* (pp. 365–402). New York: Cambridge University Press.

Coie, J. D. (1996). Effectiveness trials: An initial evaluation of the FAST track program. Paper presented at the Fifth National Institute of Mental Health Conference on Prevention Research, Washington.

Coie, J. D. (2004). The impact of negative social experiences on the development of antisocial behavior. In J. B. Kupersmidt & K. A Dodge (Eds). *Children's peer relations: From development to intervention* (pp. 243–267). Washington DC: American Psychological Association.

Cole, D. A., Martin, J. M., Peeke, L. G., Seroczynski, A., & Hoffman, K. (1998). Are cognitive errors of underestimation predictive or reflective of depressive symptoms in children: A longitudinal study. *J. Abn. Psychol. 107*(3), 481–96.

Cole, G., Neal, J. W., Fraser, W. I., & Cowie, V. A. (1994). Autopsy findings in patients with mental handicap. *J. Intell. Dis. Res., 38*(1), 9–26.

Cole, J. O., & Bodkin, J. A. (1990). Antidepressant drug side effects. *J. Clin. Psychiat., 51,* 21–26.

Coleman, H. L. K., Wampold, B. E., & Casali, S. L., (1995). Ethnic minorities' ratings of ethnically similar and European American counselors: A meta-analysis. *J. Couns. Psychol., 42,* 55–64.

Collacott, R. A., & Cooper, S.-A. (1997). The five-year follow-up study of adaptive behavior in adults with Down syndrome. *J. Intell. Develop. Dis., 22*(3), 187–97.

Collacott, R. A., et al. (1998). Behavior phenotype for Down's syndrome. *Brit. J. Psychiat., 172,* 85–89.

Collaer, M. L., & Hines, M. (1995). Human behavioral sex differences: A role for gonadal hormones during early development? *Psychol. Bull., 118,* 55–107.

Collins, N. L., Dunkel-Schetter, C., Lobel, M., & Scrimshaw, S. C. M. (2004). Social support in pregnancy: Psychosocial correlates of birth outcomes and postpartum depression. In H. T. Reis, & C. E. Rusbult (Eds.) *Close Relationships: Key Readings* (pp. 35–55). Philadelphia: Taylor & Francis.

Comer, A. M., & Figgitt, D. (2000). Sertraline: A review of its therapeutic use in post-traumatic stress disorder. *CNS Drugs, 14,* 391–407.

Compas, B. E., & Epping, J. E. (1993). Stress and coping in children and families: Implications for children coping with disaster. In C. F. Saylor (Ed.), *Children and disasters* (pp. 11–28). New York: Plenum.

Conklin, H. M., & Iacono, W. G. (2002). Schizophrenia: A neurodevelopmental perspective. *Curr. Dis. Psychol. Sci., 11*(1), 33–37.

Conley, R. W. (2003). Supported employment in Maryland: Successes and issues. *Mental Retardation, 41*(4), 237–49.

Conlon, L., & Fahy, T. J. (2001). Psychological debriefing for acute trauma—a welcome demise? *International Journal of Psychological Medicine, 18*(2), 43–44.

Connell, P. (1958). *Amphetamine psychosis,* Maudsley Monographs, No. 5. London: Oxford University Press.

Connor, T. (2003, Oct. 2). Rush Limbaugh in pill probe *New York Daily News,* p. 4.

Connors, G. J., & Walitzer, K. S. (2001). Reducing alcohol consumption among heavily drinking women: Evaluating the contributions of life-skills training and booster sessions. *J. Cons. Clin. Psychol., 69*(3), 447–56.

Connors, G. J., Carroll, K. M., DiClemente, C. C., Longabaugh, R., & Donovan, D. M. (1997). The therapeutic alliance and its relationship to alcoholism treatment participation and outcome. *J. Cons. Clin. Psychol., 65,* 588–98.

Connors, G. J., Tonigan, J. S., & Miller, W. R. (2001). A longitudinal model of intake symptomatology, AA participation and outcome: Retrospective study of the project MATCH outpatient and aftercare samples. *J. Stud. Alcoh., 62*(6), 817–25.

Conrod, P. J., Pihl, R. O., & Vassileva, J. (1998). Differential sensitivity to alcohol reinforcement in groups of men at risk for distinct alcoholism subtypes. *Alcoholism: Clin. Exper. Res., 22*(3), 585–97.

Constantino, M. J., Castonguay, L. G., & Schut, A. J. (2001). The working alliance. In G. S. Tryon (Ed.), *Counseling based on process research: Applying what we know.* Boston: Allyn and Bacon.

Conte, J., Berliner, L., & Schuerman, J. (1986). *The impact of sexual abuse on children* (Final Report No. MH 37133). Rockville, MD: National Institute of Mental Health.

Conway, K. P., Kane, R. J., Ball, S. A., Poling, J., & Rounsaville, B. (2003). Personality, substance of choice and polysubstance involvement among substance dependent patients. *Drug Al. Dep., 71,* 65–75.

Conwell, Y., Duberstein, P. R., & Caine, E. D. (2002). Risk factors for suicide in later life. *Biol. Psychiat., 52*(3), 193–204.

Cook, M., & Mineka, S. (1989). Observational conditioning of fear to fear-relevant versus fear-irrelevant stimuli in rhesus monkeys. *J. Abn. Psychol., 98,* 448–59.

Cook, M., & Mineka, S. (1990). Selective associations in the observational conditioning of fear in monkeys. *J. Exper. Psychol.: Animal Behavior Processes, 16,* 372–89.

Cooke, D. J., & Michie, C. (1999). Psychopathy across cultures: North America and Scotland compared. *J. Abn. Psychol., 108*(1), 58–68.

Cooke, D. J. (1996). Psychopathic personality in different cultures: What do we know? What do we need to find out? *J. Person. Dis., 10*(1), 23–40.

Cooklin, A. (2000). Therapy, the family and others. In H. Maxwell (Ed.), *Imperial College of Science, Technology, & Medicine. Clinical psychotherapy for health professionals* (pp. 57–82). London: Whurr Publishers.

Cooley-Quille, M., Boyd, R., Frantz, E., & Walsh, J. (2001). Emotional and behavioral impact of exposure to community violence in inner-city adolescents. *J. Clin. Child Psychol., 30,* 199–206.

Coolidge, F. L., DenBoer, J. W., & Segal, D. L. (2004). Personality and neuropsychological correlates of bullying behavior. *Personal. Indiv. Diff., 36,* 1559–69.

Coons, P. M., & Bowman, E. S. (2001). Ten-year follow-up study of patients with dissociative identity disorder. *Journal of Trauma & Dissociation, 2,* 73–89.

Coons, P. M., Bowman, E. S., & Millstein, V. (1988). Multiple personality disorder: A clinical investigation of 50 cases. *J. Nerv. Ment. Dis., 176,* 519–27.

Cooper, G. L., & Dewe, P. (2004). *Stress: A brief history.* Oxford, England: Blackwell.

Cooper, M. L. (1994). Motivations for alcohol use among adolescents: Development and validation of a four-factor model. *Psychol. Assess., 6,* 117–28.

Cooper, M., Todd, G., & Wells, A. (2000). Bulimia nervosa: A cognitive therapy programme for clients. London: Jessica Kingsley Publishers.

Cooper, S.-A. (1997). Deficient health and social services for elderly people with learning disabilities. *J. Intell. Dis. Res., 41*(4), 331–38.

Cordova, J. V., & Jacobson, N. S. (1993). Couple distress. In D. H. Barlow (Ed.), *Clinical handbook of psychological disorders* (2nd ed., pp. 481–512). New York: Guilford.

Cornblatt, B. A., Green, M. F., & Walker, E. F. (1999). Schizophrenia: Etiology and neurocognition. In T. Millon, P. H. Blaney, & R. D. Davis (Eds.), *Oxford textbook of psychopathology.* New York: Oxford University Press.

Cornblatt, B. A., Lenzenweger, M. F., & Erlenmeyer-Kimling, L. (1989). The continuous performance test, identical pairs version: II. Contrasting attentional profiles in schizophrenic and depressed patients. *Psychiatry Research, 29,* 65–85.

Cornblatt, B. A., Lenzenweger, M. F., Dworkin, R. H., & Erlenmeyer-Kimling, L. (1992). Childhood attentional dysfunctions predict social deficits in unaffected adults at risk for schizophrenia. *Brit. J. Psychiat., 16* (Suppl. 18), 59–64.

Cornblatt, B. A., Obuchowski, M., Andreasen, A., & Smith, C. (1998). High-risk research in schizophrenia: New strategies, new designs. In M. F. Lenzenweger & R. H. Dworkin (Eds.), *Origins and development of schizophrenia.* Washington, DC: American Psychological Association.

Cororve, M. B., & Gleaves, D. H. (2001). Body dysmorphic disorder: A review of conceptualizations, assessment, and treatment strategies. *Clin. Psychol. Rev., 21,* 949–70.

Correa, H., Campi-Azevedo, A. C., De Marco, L., Boson, W., Viana, M. M., Guimarães, M. M., et al. (2004). Familial suicide behaviour: Association with probands sucide attempt characteristics and 5-HTTLPR polymorphism. *Acta Psychiatr. Scandin., 110,* 459–464.

Corrigan, P. W. (1995). Use of token economy with seriously mentally ill patients: Criticisms and misconceptions. *Psychiatr. Serv., 46*(12), 1258–63.

Corrigan, P. W. (1997). Behavior therapy empowers persons with severe mental illness. *Behav. Mod., 21*(1), 45–61.

Coryell, W. (1997). Do psychotic, minor, and intermittent depressive disorders exist on a continuum? *J. Affect. Dis., 45,* 75–83.

Coryell, W., Endicott, J., Keller, M., Andreasen, N., Grove, W., Hirschfeld, R. M. A., & Scheftner, W. (1989). Bipolar affective disorder and high achievement: A familial association. *Amer. J. Psychiat., 146,* 983–88.

Coryell, W., Endicott, J., Maser, J. D., Mueller, T., Lavori, P., & Keller, M. (1995). The likelihood of recurrence in bipolar affective disorder: The importance of episode recency. *J. Affect. Dis., 33,* 201–6.

Coryell, W., Solomon, D., Turvey, C., Keller, M., Leon, A. C., Endicott, J., et al. (2003). The long-term course of rapid-cycling bipolar disorder. *Arch. Gen. Psychiat., 60*(9), 914–920.

Coryell, W., & Winokur, G. (1992). Course and outcome. In E. S. Paykel (Ed.), *Handbook of affective disorders* (2nd ed.). New York: Guilford.

Coryell, W., & Young, E. A. (2005). Clinical predictors of suicide in primary major depressive disorder. *J. Clin. Psychiat., 66*(4), 412–417.

Cote, G., O'Leary, T., Barlow, D. H., Strain, J. J., Salkovskis, P. M., Warwick, H. M. C., et al. (1996). Hypochondriasis. In T. A. Widiger, A. J. Frances, H. A. Pincus, R. Ross, M. B. First, & W. W. Davis (Eds.), *DSM-IV Sourcebook, vol. 2* (pp. 933–47). Washington, DC: American Psychiatric Association.

Cottle, C. C., Lee, R. J., & Heilbrun, K. (2001). The prediction of criminal recidivism in juveniles: A meta-analysis. *Crim. Just. Behav., 28*(3), 367–94.

Cotton, N. S. (1979). The familial incidence of alcoholism. *J. Stud. Alcoh., 40,* 89–116.

Cottraux, J., & Blackburn, I. M. (2001). Cognitive therapy. In W. J. Livesley (Ed.), *Handbook of personality disorders* (pp. 377–99). New York: Guilford.

Couturier, J. L. (2005). Efficacy of rapid-rate repetitive transcranial magnetic stimulation in the treatment of depression: A systematic review and meta-analysis. *J. Psychiat. Neurosci., 30*(2), 83–90.

Couzin, J. (2004). Volatile chemistry: Children and antidepressants. *Science, 305*(5683), 468–70.

Cox, B. J. (1996). The nature and assessment of catastrophic thoughts in panic disorder. *Behav. Res. Ther., 34*(4), 363–74.

Cox, W. M., & Klinger, E. (1988). A motivational model of alcohol use. *J. Abn. Psychol., 97,* 168–80.

Coyne, J. C. (1976). Depression and the response of others. *J. Abn. Psychol., 55*(2), 186–93.

Coyne, J. C., Rohrbaugh, M. J., Shoham, V., Sonnega, J. S., Nicklas, J. M., & Cranford, J. A. (2001). Prognostic importance of marital quality for survival of congestive heart failure. *Amer. J. Cardio., 88,* 526–29.

Craig, R. J. (2004). Assessing personality and psychopathology with interviews. *Handbook of psychology* (Vol. 10, pp. 487–508). New York: John Wiley & Sons.

Craighead, W. E., Miklowitz, D. J., Frank, E., & Vajk, F. C. (2002). Psychosocial treatments for bipolar disorder. In P. E. Nathan & J. M. Gorman (Eds.), *A guide to treatments that work* (pp. 263–75). New York: Oxford University Press.

Craighead, W.E., Hart, A. B., Craighead, L. W., & Ilardi, S. S. (2002). Psychosocial treatments for major depressive disorder. In Nathan, P. E. & Gorman, J. M. (Eds.) *Treatments that work.* Pp. 245–261, New York: Oxford University Press.

Cramer, P. (2003). Defense mechanisms and physiological reactivity to stress. *J. Personal., 71,* 221–24.

Craske, M. G. (1999). *Anxiety disorders: Psychological approaches to theory and treatment.* Boulder, CO: Westview.

Craske, M. G., Barlow, D. H., & Meadows, E. (2000). *Mastery of your anxiety and panic: Therapist guide for anxiety, panic, and agoraphobia (MAP-3).* San Antonio, TX: Graywind/Psychological Corporation.

Craske, M. G., DeCola, J. P., Sachs, A. D., & Pontillo, D. C. (2003). Panic control treatment for agoraphobia. *Journal of Anxiety Disorders, 17*(3), 321–333.

Craske, M. G., Lang, A. J., Mystowski, J. L., Zucker, B. G., Bystritsky, A., & Yan-go, F. (2002). Does nocturnal panic represent a more severe form of panic disorder? *J. Nerv. & Ment. Dis., 190*(9), 611–618.

Craske, M. G., & Rowe, M. K. (1997). A comparison of behavioral and cognitive treatments of phobias. In G. C. L. Davey (Ed.), *Phobias: A handbook of theory, research and treatment* (pp. 247–80). Chichester, England: Wiley.

Craske, M. G., & Waters, A. M. (2005). Panic disorders, phobias, and generalized anxiety disorder. *Annu. Rev. Clin. Psychol., 1,* 197–225.

Creed, F., & Barsky, A. (2004). A systematic review of the epidemiology of somatisation disorder and hypochondriasis. *J. Psychosom. Res., 56,* 391–408.

Crepeau, F., & Scherzer, P. (1993). Predictors and indicators of work status after traumatic brain injury: A meta-analysis. *Neuropsychological Rehabilitation, 3*(1), 5–35.

Crerand, C. E., Sarwer, D. B., Magee, L., Gibbons, L. M., Lowe, M. R., Bartlett, S. P., et al. (2004). Rate of body dysmorphic disorder among patients seeking facial plastic surgery. *Psychiat. Ann., 34*(12), 958–65.

Cretzmeyer, M., Sarrazin, M. V., Huber, D. L., Block, R. I., & Hall, J. A. (2003). Treatment of methamphetamine abuse: Research findings and clinical directions. *J. Sub. Abuse Treat., 24*(3), 267–77.

Crews, F. (1995). *The memory wards: Freud's legacy in dispute.* New York: Granta.

Crick, N. R., & Dodge, K. A. (1994). A review and reformulation of social information-processing mechanisms in children's social adjustment. *Psychol. Bull., 115*(1), 74–101.

Crisp, A. H., Douglas, J. W. B., Ross, J. M., & Stonehill, E. (1970). Some developmental aspects of disorders of weight. *J. Psychosom. Res., 14,* 313–20.

Crits-Christoph, P., & Barber, J. P. (2000). Long-term psychotherapy. In C. R. Snyder & R. E. Ingram (Eds.), *Handbook of psychological change* (pp. 455–73). New York: Wiley.

Crits-Christoph, P., & Barber, J. (2002). Psychosocial treatments for personality disorders. In P. E. Nathan & J. M. Gorman (Eds.), *A guide to treatments that work* (pp. 544–53). New York: Oxford University Press.

Crits-Christoph, P., Gibbons, M. C., Crits-Christoph, K. (2004). Supportive-expressive psychodynamic therapy. In R. G. Heimberg, C. L. Turk, & D. S. Mennin (Eds.), *Generalized anxiety disorder: Advances in research and practice.* (pp. 293–319). New York: Guilford Press.

Crittenden, P. M., & Ainsworth, M. D. S. (1989). Child maltreatment and attachment theory. In D. Cicchetti & V. Carlson (Eds.), *Child maltreatment: Theory and research on the causes and consequences of child abuse and neglect* (pp. 432–63). Cambridge: Cambridge University Press.

Crook, T. H., III, & Adderly, B. (1998). *The memory cure.* New York: Simon & Schuster.

Crosson-Tower, C. (2002). *Understanding child abuse and neglect* (5th ed.). New York: Longman.

Crouter, A. C., & Booth, A. (2003). *Children's influence on family dynamics: The neglected side of family relationships.* Mahwah, NJ: Lawrence Erlbaum Associates.

Crow, T. J. (1997). Temporolimbic or transcallosal connections: Where is the primary lesion in schizophrenia and what is its nature? *Schizo. Bull., 23*(3), 521–24.

Crowther, J. H., Kichler, J. C., Sherwood, N., & Kuhnert, M. E. (2002). The role of family factors in bulimia nervosa. *Eat. Dis., 10,* 141–51.

Cruts, M., van Duijn, C. M., Backhovens, H., van den Broeck, M., Serneels, S., Sherrington, R., Hutton, M., Hardy, J., St. George-Hyslop, P. H., & Van Broeckhoven, C. (1998). Estimations of the genetic contribution of presenilin-1 and presenilin-2 mutations in a population-based study of presenile Alzheimer disease. *Human Molecular Genetics, 7,* 43–51.

Culbertson, F. M. (1997). Depression and gender: An international review. *Amer. Psychol., 52*(1), 25–31.

Culliton, B. J. (1970, Jan. 24). Pot facing stringent scientific examination. *Sci. News, 97*(4), 102–5.

Cummings, E. M., Goeke-Morey, M. C., & Papp, L. M. (2004). Everyday marital conflict and child aggression. *J. Abn. Psychol., 32*(2), 191–202.

Cummings, N. (1995). Impact of managed care on employment and training: A primer for survival. *Professional Psychology: Research and Practice, 26,* 10–15.

Curry, S. J. (1993). Self-help interventions for smoking cessation. *J. Cons. Clin. Psychol., 61,* 790–803.

Curtis, G. C., Magee, W. J., Eaton, W. W., Wittchen, H.-U, & Kessler, R. (1998). Specific fears and phobias: Epidemiology and classification. *Brit. J. Psychiat., 173,* 212–17.

Cutting, J., & Murphy, D. (1990). Impaired ability of schizophrenics, relative to manics or depressives, to appreciate social knowledge about their culture. *Brit. J. Psychiat., 157,* 355–58.

Cutting, J. (1995). Descriptive psychopathology. In S. R. Hirsch & D. R. Weinberger, (Eds.), *Schizophrenia* (pp. 15–27). Cambridge: Cambridge University Press.

D'Avanzo, B., Barbato, A., Barbui, C., Battino, R. N., Civenti, G., & Frattura, L. (2003). Discharges of patients from public psychiatric hospitals in Italy between 1994 and 2000. *Inter. J. Soc. Psychiat., 49*(1), 27–34.

Dadds, M. R., Heard, P. M., & Rapee, R. M. (1991). Anxiety disorders in children. *Int. Rev. Psychiat., 3,* 231–41.

Dadds, M. R., Spence, S. H., Holland, D. E., Barren, P. M., & Laurens, K. R. (1997). Prevention and early intervention for anxiety disorders: A controlled study. *J. Cons. Clin. Psychol., 65*(4), 627–35.

Dadds, M., Davey, G. C., Graham, C., & Field, A. P. (2001). Developmental aspects of conditioning processes in anxiety disorders. In M. W. Vasey and M. R. Dadds (Eds.) *The developmental psychopathology of anxiety.* (pp. 205–230). London: Oxford University Press.

Dahl, R. E. (1992). The pharmacologic treatment of sleep disorders. *Psychiat. Clin. N. Amer., 15,* 161–78.

Dain, N. (1964). *Concepts of insanity in the United States: 1789–1865.* New Brunswick, NJ: Rutgers University Press.

Dallam, S. J., Gleaves, D. H., Cepeda-Benito, A., Silberg, J. L., Kraemer, H. C., & Spiegel, D. (2001). The effects of child sexual abuse: Comment on Rind, Tromovitch, and Bauserman (1998). *Psychol. Bull.,* 127, 715–33.

Dallman, M. F., Pecorano, N., Akana, S. F., la Fleur, S. E., Gomez, F., Houshyar, H., Bell, M. E., Bhatnagar, S., Laugero, K. D., & Manalo, S. (2003, Sep. 30). Chronic stress and obesity: A new view of "comfort food." *Proceedings of the National Academy of Sciences, 100*(20), 11696–701.

Daly, M., & Wilson, M. I. (1996). Violence against stepchildren. *Curr. Dir. Psychol. Sci., 5*(3), 77–81.

Daly, M., & Wilson, M. (1988). *Homicide.* New York: Aldine de Gruyter.

Dar, R., Rish, S., Hermesh, H., Taub, M., & Fux, M. (2000). Realsim of confidence in obsessive-compulsive checkers. *J. Abn. Psychol., 109*(4), 673–678.

Dare, C., & Eisler, I. (2002). Family therapy and eating disorders. In C. G. Fairburn & K. D. Brownell (Eds.), *Eating disorders and obesity: A comprehensive handbook* (2nd ed., pp. 314–19). New York: Guilford.

Darke, S., & Ross, J. (2001). The relationship between suicide and heroin overdose among methadone maintenance patients in Sydney, Australia. *Addiction, 96,* 1443–53.

Daskalakis, Z. J., Christensen, B. K., Chen, R., Fitzgerald, P. B., Zipursky, R. B., & Kapus, S. (2002). Evidence for impaired cortical inhibition in schizophrenia using transcranial magnetic stimulation. *Arch. Gen. Psychiat., 59,* 347–54.

David, D., De Faria, L., Lapeyra, O., & Mellman, T. A. (2004). Adjunctive risperidone treatment in combat veterans with chronic PTSD. *J. Clin. Psychopharm., 24*(5), 556–58.

Davidson, A. D. (1979a, Spring). Coping with stress reactions in rescue workers: A program that worked. *Police Stress.*

Davidson, A. D. (1979b). Personal communication.

Davidson, J. R. T., Payne, V. M., Connor, K. M., Foa, E. B., Rothbaum, B. O., Hertzberg, M. A., & Weisler, R. H. (2005). Trauma, resilience and saliostasis: Effects of treatment in post-traumatic stress disorder. *Int. Clin. Psychpharm., 20*(1), 43–48.

Davidson, K., & Prkachin, K. (1997). Optimism and unrealistic optimism have an interacting impact on health-promoting behavior and knowledge changes. *Personal. Soc. Psychol. Bull., 23*(6), 617–25.

Davidson, K., MacGregor, M. W., Stuhr, J., Dixon, K., & MacLean, D. (2000). Constructive anger verbal behavior predicts blood pressure in a population-based sample. *Hlth. Psychol., 19*(1), 55–64.

Davidson, L. M., & Baum, A. (1986). Chronic stress and posttraumatic stress disorders. *J. Cons. Clin. Psychol., 54,* 303–8.

Davidson, L., Shahar, G., Stayner, et al. (2004). Supported socialization for people with psychiatric disabilities: Lessons from a randomized controlled trial. *J. Comm. Psychol., 32,* 453–77.

Davidson, M. C., Thomas, K. M., & Casey, B. J. (2003). Imaging the developing brain with fMRI. *Men. Retard. Devel. Res. Rev., 9,* 161–67.

Davidson, R. J. (2000). Affective style, psychopathology, and resilience: Brain mechanisms and plasticity. *Amer. Psychol., 55,* 1196–1214.

Davidson, R. J., Pizzagalli, D., & Nitschke, J. B. (2002). The representation and regulation of emotion in depression: Perspectives from affective neuroscience. In I. H. Gotlib & C. L. Hammen (Eds.), *Handbook of depression* (pp. 219–44). New York: Guilford.

Davidson, R. J., Pizzagalli, D., Nitschke, J. B., Putnam, K. (2002). Depression: Perspectives from affective neuroscience. *Ann. Rev. Psychol., 53,* 545–74. Annual Reviews, US.

Davis, C., Shuster, B., Blackmore, E., & Fox, J. (2004). Looking good—family focus on appearance and the risk for eating disorders. *Int. J. Eat. Dis., 35,* 136–44.

Davis, J. A., & Stewart, L. (1999). The PSA 182 airflight disaster twenty years later: What have we learned about disaster response and recovery? *Human Performance in Extreme Environments, 4*(1), 30–34.

Davis, J. O., Phelps, J. A., & Bracha, H. S. (1995). Prenatal development of monozygotic twins and concordance for schizophrenia. *Schizo. Bull., 21*(3), 357–66.

Davis, L. L., et al. (2000). Nefazodone treatment for chronic posttraumatic stress disorder: An open trial. *J. Clin. Psychopharm., 20,* 159–64.

Davis, Michael (2002). Role of NMDA receptors and MAP kinase in the amygdala in extinction of fear: Clinical implications for exposure therapy. *Europ. J. Neurosci., 16*(3), 395–398.

Dawkins, M. P. (1997). Drug use and violent crime among adolescents. *Adolescence, 32,* 395–405.

DAWN Report. (2001). *Major drugs of abuse in ED visits in 2000.* Drug Abuse Warning Network. Office of Applied Studies, Substance Abuse and Mental Health Services Administration, Washington, DC.

DAWN Survey. (2000). *Annual trends in drug related episodes. NIDA Research Report: Monitoring the Future Study.* Washington, DC: Author.

DAWN. (2002). *Mortality data from the Drug Abuse Warning Network, 2002.* Rockville, MD: U. S. Department of Health and Human Services.

Dawson, G., Panagiotides, H., Klinger, L. G., & Spieker, S. (1997). Infants of depressed and nondepressed mothers exhibit differences in frontal brain electrical activity during the expression of negative emotions. *Develop. Psychol., 33*(5), 650–56.

Dawson, P. M., Griffith, K., & Boeke, K. M. (1990). Combined medical and psychological treatment of hospitalized children with encopresis. *Child Psychiat. Human Devel., 20,* 181–290.

Deahl, M. (2000). Psychological debriefing: Controversy and challenge. *Austral. NZ J. Psychiat., 34,* 929–39.

Deale, A., Chalder, T., Marks, I., & Wessely, S. (1997). Cognitive behavior therapy for chronic fatigue syndrome. *Amer. J. Psychiat., 154*(3), 408–14.

Deb, S., & Ahmed, Z. (2000). Specific conditions leading to mental retardation. In M. G. Gelder, J. J. Lopez-Ibor, Jr., & N. Andreason (Eds.), *New Oxford textbook of psychiatry* (pp. 1954–63). New York: Oxford University Press.

Debettignles, B. H., Swihart, A. A., Green, L. A., & Pirozzolo, F. J. (1997). The neuropsychology of normal aging and dementia: An introduction. In J. A. M. Horton, D. Wedding, & J. Webster (Eds.), *The neuropsychology handbook* (Vol. 2., pp. 173–210). New York: Springer.

de Jong, J. (Ed.). (2002). *Trauma, war, and violence: Public health in socio-cultural context.* New York: Kluwer Academic/Plenum, 2002.

de Jongh, A., Muris, P., Ter Horst, T., & Duyx, M. P. M. A. (1995). Acquisition and maintenance of dental anxiety: The role of conditioning experiences and cognitive factors. *Behav. Res. Ther., 33*(2), 205–10.

Del Boca, F. K., Darkes, J., Greenbaum, P. E., & Goldman, M. S. (2004). Up close and personal: Temporal variability in the drinking of individual college students during their first year. *J. Cons. Clin. Psychol., 72,* 155–64.

Delaplaine, R., Ifabumuyi, O. I., Merskey, H., & Zarfas, J. (1978). Significance of pain in psychiatric hospital patients. *Pain, 4,* 361–66.

de Mello, F., de Jesus-Mari. J., Bacaltchuk, J., Verdeli, H., & Neugebauer, R. (2005). A systematic review of research findings on the efficacy of interpersonal therapy for depressive disorders. *Eur. Arch. Psychiat. Clini. Neurosci., 255,* 75–82.

de Mello, M. F., de Jesus, M. J., Bacaltchuk, J., Verdeli, H., & Neugebauer, R. (2005). A systematic review of research findings on the efficacy of interpersonal therapy for depressive disorders. *Europ. Arch. Pyschiat. Clin. Neurosci., 255*(2), 75–82.

Deming, M. P., Chase, N. D., & Karesh, D. (1996). Parental alcoholism and perceived levels of family health among college freshmen. *Alcoholism Treatment Quarterly, 14*(1), 47–56.

Dennes, B. (1974). Returning madness to an accepting community. *Comm. Ment. Hlth. J., 10*(2), 163–72.

Dennis, C. (2004). Asia's tigers get the blues. *Nature, 429,* 696–698.

Denollet, J., Vaes, J., & Brutsaert, D. L. (2000). Inadequate response to treatment in coronary heart disease: Adverse effects of Type D personality and younger age on 5-year prognosis and quality of life. *Circulation, 102,* 630–35.

Dent, G. W., Smith, M. A., & Levine, S. (2001). Stress induced alterations in locus coeruleus gene expression during ontogeny. *Brain Research. Devel. Brain Res., 127,* 23–30.

Department of Labor. (1999, Feb.). *Employment and earnings.* Bureau of Labor Statistics. Washington, DC: U.S. Government Printing Office.

de Pauw, K. W., & Szulecka, T. K. (1988). Dangerous delusions: Violence and misidentification syndromes. *Brit. J. Psychiat., 152,* 91–96.

Depue, R. A., & Lenzenweger, M. F. (2001). A neurobehavioral dimensional model. In W. J. Livesley (Ed.), *Handbook of personality disorders* (pp. 136–76). New York: Guilford.

Depue, R. A., & Monroe, S. M. (1986). Conceptualization and measurement of human disorder in life stress research: The problem of chronic disturbance. *Psychol. Bull., 99*(1), 36–51.

Derr, R. F., & Gutmann, H. R. (1994). Alcoholic liver disease may be prevented with adequate nutrients. *Medical Hypotheses, 42,* 1–4.

DeRubeis, R. J., Gelfand, L. A., Tang, T. Z., & Simons, A. D. (1999). Medications versus cognitive behavior therapy for severely depressed outpatients: Mega-analysis of four randomized comparisons. *Amer. J. Psychiat., 156*(7), 1007–13.

DeRubeis, R. J., Hollon, S. D., Amsterdam, J. D., Shelton, R. C., Young, P. R., Salomon, R. M., et al. (2005). Cognitive therapy vs medications in the treatment of moderate to severe depression. *Arch. Gen. Psychiat., 62,* 409–416.

DeRubeis, R. (1997, May). *Cognitive therapy IS as effective as medication for severe depression: A mega-analysis.* Paper presented at the meeting of the American Psychological Society, Washington.

DeSanti, S., de Leon, M. J., Rusinek, H., Convit, A., Tarshish, C. Y., Roche, A., Tsui, W. H., Kandil, E., Boppana, M., Daisley, K., Wang, G. J., Schlyer, D., & Fowler, J. (2001). Hippocampal formation, glucose metabolism and volume losses in MCI and AD. *Neurobiol. Aging, 22,* 529–39.

De Silva, P., Rachman, S. J., & Seligman, M. E. P. (1977). Prepared phobias and obsessions: Therapeutic outcomes. *Behav. Res. Ther., 15,* 65–78.

Deutsch, A. (1944). Military psychiatry: The Civil War 1860–1865. In J. K. Hall (Ed.), *One hundred years of American psychiatry.* New York: Columbia University Press.

Deutsch, A. (1948). *The shame of the states.* New York: Harcourt, Brace.

Devanand, D. P., et al. (1994). Does ECT alter brain structure? *Amer. J. Psychiat., 151,* 957–70.

Devanand, D. P., Michaels-Marston, K. S., Liu, X., Pelton, G. H., Padilla, M., Marder, K., Bell, K., Stern, Y., & Mayeux, R. (2000). Olfactory deficits in patients with mild cognitive impairment predict Alzheimer's disease at follow-up. *Amer. J. Psychiat., 157*(9), 1399–1405.

Devanand, D. P., Sano, M., Tang, M.-X., Taylor, S., Gurland, B. J., Wilder, D., Stern, Y., & Mayeux, R. (1996). Depressed mood and the incidence of Alzheimer's disease in the elderly living in the community. *Arch. Gen. Psychiat., 53,* 175–82.

DeVane, C. L., & Sallee, F. R. (1996). Serotonin selective reuptake inhibitors in child and adolescent psychopharmacology: A review of published experience. *J. Clin. Psychiat., 57*(2), 55–66.

DeVries, T. J., & Shippenberg, T. S. (2002). Neural systems underlying opiate addiction. *Journal of Neuroscience, 22*(9), 3321–25.

de Vries, B., & Suedfeld, P. (2005). Vancouver, The life stories of Holocaust survivors. *Int. J. Aging & Hum. Dev., 60*(3), 183–87.

Dew, M. A., Bromet, E. J., & Schulberg, H. C. (1987). A comparative analysis of two community stressors' long-term mental health effects. *Am. J. Community Psychol., 15,* 167–84.

Dew, M. A., Penkower, L., & Bromet, E. J. (1991). Effects of unemployment on mental health in the contemporary family. *Behav. Mod., 15,* 501–44.

De Zwaan, M., & Mitchell, J. E. (1999). Medical evaluation of the patient with an eating disorder: An overview. In P. S. Mehler & A. E. Andersen (Eds.), *Eating disorders: A guide to medical care and complications* (pp. 44–62). Baltimore: Johns Hopkins University Press.

Diamond, M., & Sigmundson, K. (1997). Sex reassignment at birth: Long-term review and clinical implications. *Archives of Pediatric and Adolescent Medicine, 151,* 298–304.

DiClemente, C. C. (1993). Changing addictive behaviors: A process perspective. *Curr. Dis. Psychol. Sci., 2,* 101–6.

Dikmen, S. S., & Levin, H. S. (1993). Methodological issues in the study of mild head injury. *J. Head Trauma Rehab., 8*(3), 30–37.

Dikmen, S. S., Temkin, N. R., Machamer, J. E., & Holubkov, A. L. (1994). Employment following traumatic head injuries. *Arch. Neurol., 51*(2), 177–86.

Diller, L., & Gordon, W. A. (1981). Interventions for cognitive deficits in brain-injured adults. *J. Cons. Clin. Psychol., 49,* 822–34.

Dimberg, U., & Öhman, A. (1996). Behold the wrath: Psychophysiological responses to facial stimuli. *Motivation & Emotion, 20,* 149–82.

Dimidjian, S., Hollon, S., Dobson, K. S., Schmaling, K. B., Kohlenberg, R. J., Addis, M. E., et al. (2003). Behavioral activation, cognitive therapy, and antidepressant medication. *J. Cons. Clin. Psychol.,* Manuscript submitted for publication.

Din-Dzietham, R., Nembhard, W. N., Collins, R., & Davis, S. K. (2004). Perceived stress following race-based discrimination at work is associated with hypertension in African-Americans. The metro Atlanta heart disease study 1999–2001. *Soc. Sci. Med., 58,* 449–61.

DiPietro, L., Mossberg, H.-O., & Stunkard, A. J. (1994). A 40-year history of overweight children in Stockholm: Lifetime overweight, morbidity, and mortality. *International Journal of Obesity, 18,* 585–90.

Dirkzwager, A. J. E., Bramsen, I., Adèr, H., & van der Ploeg, H. M. (2005). Secondary traumatization in partners and parents of Dutch peacekeeping soldiers. *J. Fam. Psychol., 19*(2), 217–26.

Dishion, T. P, & Patterson, G. R. (1997). The timing and severity of antisocial behavior: Three hypotheses within an ecological framework. In D. M. Stoff,

J. Breiling, & J. D. Maser (Eds.), *Handbook of antisocial behavior.* (pp. 205–217). New York: Wiley.

Dodd, B., & Leahy, J. (1989). Facial prejudice. *Amer. J. Ment. Retard., 94,* 111.

Dodge, K. A., Bates, J. E., & Pettit, G. S. (1990). Mechanisms in the cycle of violence. *Science, 250,* 1678–83.

Dodge, K. A., Laird, R., Lochman, J., & Zelli, A. (2002). Multidimensional latent-construct analysis of children's social information processing patterns: Correlations with aggressive behavior problems. *Psychol. Assess., 14,* 60–73.

Dodge, K. A., Lochman, J. E., Harnish, J. D., Bates, J. E., & Pettit, G. S. (1997). Reactive and proactive aggression in school children and psychiatrically impaired chronically assaultive youth. *J. Abn. Psychol., 106*(1), 37–51.

Dodge, K. A., Pettit, G. S., & Bates, J. E. (1994). Socialization mediators of the relation between socioeconomic status and child conduct problems. *Child Develop., 65,* 649–65.

Dodge, K. A., Pettit, G. S., Bates, J. E., & Valente, E. (1995). Social information-processing patterns partially mediate the effect of early physical abuse on later conduct problems. *J. Abn. Psychol., 104*(4), 632–43.

Dohrenwend, B. P. (2000). The role of adversity and stress in psychopathology: Some evidence and its implications for theory and research. *J. Health & Social Behavr., 41*(1), 1–19.

Dohrenwend, B. P., Neria, Y., Turner, J. B., Turse, N., Marshall, R., Lewis-Fernandez, R., & Koenen, K. C. (2004). Positive tertiary appraisals and posttraumatic stress disorder in U.S. male veterans of the war in Vietnam: The roles of positive affirmation, positive reformulation, and defensive denial. *J. Cons. Clin. Psychol., 72*(3), 417–33.

Dohrenwend, B. P., Shrout, P. E., Link, B. G., Skodol, A. E., & Stueve, A. (1995). A case-control study of life events and other possible psychosocial risk factors for episodes of schizophrenia and major depression. In C. M. Mazure (Ed.), *Does stress cause psychiatric illness?* Washington, DC: American Psychiatric Press.

Dolan-Sewell, R. T., Krueger, R. F., & Shea, M. T. (2001). Co-occurrence with syndrome disorders. In W. J. Livesley (Ed.), *Handbook of personality disorders* (pp. 84–104). New York: Guilford.

Dollard, J., & Miller, N. E. (1950). *Personality and psychotherapy.* New York: McGraw-Hill.

Domjan, M. (2002). Stepping outside the box in considering the C/T ratio. *Behavioral Processes, 62*(1–3), 103–114.

Domjan, M. (2005). Pavlonian conditioning: A functional perspective. *Annu. Rev. Psychol., 56,* 179–206.

Donaldson, M. A., & Gardner, R., Jr. (1985). Diagnosis and treatment of traumatic stress among women after childhood incest. In C. R. Filley (Ed.), *Trauma and its wake: The study and treatment of posttraumatic stress disorder* (pp. 356–77). Newbury Park, CA: Sage.

Dooley, D., & Catalano, R. (1980). Economic change as a cause of behavioral disorder. *Psychol. Bull., 87,* 450–68.

Dooley, D., Prause, J., & Ham-Rowbottom, K. A. (2000) Underemployment and depression: Longitudinal relationships. *J. Hlth. Soc. Behav., 41*(4), 421–436.

Dorahy, M. J. (2001). Dissociative identity disorder and memory dysfunction: The current state of experimental research and its future directions. *Clin. Psychol. Rev., 21,* 771–95.

Dorahy, M. J., Middleton, W., & Irwin, H. J. (2005). The effect of emotional context on cognitive inhibition and attentional processing in dissociative identity disorder. *Behav. Res. Ther., 43,* 555–68

dos Reis, S., Zito, J. M., Safer, D. J., & Soeken, K. L. (2001). Mental health services for youths in foster care and disabled youths. *Amer. J. Pub. Hlth., 91,* 1094–99.

Dougherty, D. D., Baer, L., Cosgrove, G. R., Cassem, E. H., Price, B.H., Nierenberg, A. A., et al. (2002). Prospective long-term follow-up of 44 patients who received cingulotomy for treatment-refractory obsessive-compulsive disorder. *Amer. J. Psychiat., 159*(2), 269–275.

Dougherty, D. D., Rauch, S. L., & Jenike, M. A. (2002). Pharmacological treatments for obsessive compulsive disorder. In P. E. Nathan & J. M. Gorman (Eds.), *A guide to treatments that work* (2nd ed., pp. 387–410). New York: Oxford University Press.

Dougherty, D. D., Rauch, S. L., & Jenike, M. A. (2002). Pharmacological treatments for obsessive compulsive disorder. In P. E. Nathan and J. M. Gorman (Eds). *A guide to treatments that work,* (second Edition, pp. 387–410). New York: Oxford University Press.

Dougherty, L. R., Klein, D. N., & Davila, J. (2004). A growth curve analysis of the course of dysthymic disorder: The effects of chronic stress and moderation by adverse parent-child relationships and family history. *J. Cons. Clin. Psychol., 72*(6), 1012–1021.

Downey, G., & Feldman, S. I. (1996). Implications of rejection sensitivity for intimate relationships. *J. Pers. Soc. Psychol., 70,* 1327–43.

Dozois, D. J. A. (2004). Prevention of anxiety psychopathology: Conceptual, methodological, and practical issues. *Clin. Psychol. Sci. Prac., 11*(4) 425–29.

Dozois, D. J. A., & Dobson, K. S. (Eds.). (2004). *The prevention of anxiety and depression: Theory, research, and practice.* Washington, DC: American Psychological Association.

Drabick, D. A., Gadow, K. D., Carlson, G. A., & Bromet, E. J. (2004). ODD and ADHD symptoms in Ukranian children: External validators and comorbidity. *J. Amer. Acad. Child Adoles. Psychiat., 43,* 73–82.

Draguns, J. G. (2001). Toward a truly international psychology: Beyond English only. *Amer. Psychol., 56,* 1019–30.

Draguns, J. G., & Tanaka-Matsumi, J. (2003). Assessment of psychopathology across and within cultures: Issues and findings. *Behav. Res. Ther., 41,* 755–76.

Drevets, W. C. (2000). Neuroimaging studies of mood disorders. *Biol. Psychiat., 48*(8), 813–29.

Drtikova, I., Balastikova, B., Lemanova, H., & Zak, J. (1996). Clonazepam, clonidine and tiapride in children with tic disorder. *Homeostasis in Health & Disease, 37*(5), 216.

Drug Enforcement Administration, Department of Justice. (1979). *Controlled Substance Inventory List.* Washington, DC.

Du Rocher Schudlin, T. D., Shamir, H. & Cummings, E. M. (2004). Marital conflict, children's representations of family relationships, and children's dispositions towards peer conflict strategies. *Soc. Develop., 13*(2), 171–192.

Du, A. T., Schuff, N., Amend, D., Laakso, M. P., Hsu, Y. Y., Jagust, W. J., Yaffe, K., Kramer, J. H., Reed, B., Norman, D., Chui, H. C., & Weiner, M. W. (2001). Magnetic resonance imaging of the entorhinal cortex and hippocampus in mild cognitive impairment and Alzheimer's disease. *J. Neurol. Neurosurg. Psychiat., 71,* 441–47.

Dubbert, P. M. (2002). Physical activity and exercise: Recent advances and current challenges. *J. Cons. Clin. Psychol., 70*(3), 526–36.

Dubner, A. E., & Motta, R. W. (1999). Sexually and physically abused foster care children and posttraumatic stress disorder. *J. Cons. Clin. Psychol., 67,* 367–73.

Dugas, M. J., Buhr, K., & Ladouceur, R. (2004). The role of intolerance of uncertainty in etiology and maintenance. In R. G. Heimberg, C. L Turk, & D. S. Mennin. (Eds.) *Generalized anxiety disorder: Advances in research and practice.* (pp. 143–163). New York: Guilford Press.

Duinkerke, A., Williams, M. A., Rigamonti, D., & Hillis, A. E. (2004). Cognitive recovery in idiopathic normal pressure hydrocephalus after shunt. *Cog. Behav. Neurol., 17*(3), 179–84.

Dunbar, F. (1943). *Psychosomatic diagnosis.* New York: Harper & Row.

Duncan, G. J., Brooks-Gunn, J., & Klebanov, P. K. (1994). Economic deprivation and early childhood development. *Child Develop., 65,* 296–318.

Dunn, M. E., Burbine, T., Bowers, C. A., & Tantleff-Dunn, S. (2001). Moderators of stress in parents of children with autism. *Comm. Ment. Hlth. J., 37,* 39–52.

Dunne, E. J. (1992). Following a suicide: Postvention. In B. Bongar (Ed.), *Suicide: Guidelines for assessment, management and treatment.* New York: Oxford University Press.

DuPaul, G. J., Stoner, G., et al. (1998). *Classroom interventions for ADHD.* New York: Guilford.

Durkheim, E. (1951). *Suicide: A study in sociology* (J. A. Spaulding & G. Simpson, Trans., G. Simpson, Ed). New York: Free Press. (Originally published in 1897).

Durston, S. (2003). A review of the biological bases of ADHD: What have we learned from imaging studies? *Ment. Retard. Dev. Dis. Res. Rev., 9,* 184–85.

Dworkin, R. H. (1994). Pain insensitivity in schizophrenia: A neglected phenomenon and some implications. *Schizo. Bull., 20,* 235–48.

Dworkin, R. H., Bernstein, G., Kaplansky, L. M., Lipsitz, J. D., Rinaldi, A., Slater, S. L., Cornblatt, B. A., & Erlenmeyer-Kimling, L. (1991). Social competence and positive and negative symptoms: A longitudinal study of children and adolescents at risk for schizophrenia and affective disorder. *Amer. J. Psychiat., 148,* 1182–88.

Dworkin, R. H., Green, S. R., Small, N. E. M., Warner, M. L., Cornblatt, B. A., & Erlenmeyer-Kimling, L. (1990). Positive and negative symptoms and social competence in adolescents at risk for schizophrenia and affective disorder. *Amer. J. Psychiat., 147*(9), 1234–36.

Dworkin, R. H., Lewis, J. A., Cornblatt, B. A., & Erlenmeyer-Kimling, L. (1994). Social competence deficits in adolescents at risk for schizophrenia. *J. Nerv. Ment. Dis., 182*(2), 103–8.

Dwyer, J. (2001, Oct. 9). Fighting for life 50 floors up, with one tool and ingenuity. *New York Times,* B1.

Dyer, C. A. (1999). Pathophysiology of phenylketonuria. *Mental Retardation & Developmental Disabilities Research Reviews, 5,* 104–12.

Eagly, A. H., & Karau, S. J. (2002). Role congruity theory of prejudice toward female leaders. *Psychol. Rev., 109,* 573–98.

Eagly, A.H. (2004). Prejudice: Toward a more inclusive understanding. In Department of Psychology and Institute for Policy Research (Eds.) *The Social psychology of group identity and social conflict: Theory, application, and practice* (pp. 45–64). Washington, DC: American Psychological Association.

Earleywine, M. (2002). *Understanding marijuana.* New York: Oxford University Press.

Earlywine, M., & Finn, P. R. (1990, Mar.). *Personality, drinking habits, and responses to cues for alcohol.* Paper presented at the 5th Congress of the International Society for Biomedical Research on Alcoholism and the Research Society on Alcoholism, Toronto, Canada.

Eaton, W. W., & Muntaner, C. (1999). Socioeconomic stratification and mental disorder. In A. V. Horwitz & T. L. Scheid (Eds.), *A handbook for the study of mental health: Social contexts, theories, and systems* (pp. 259–83). New York: Cambridge University Press.

Eaton, W. W., Kessler, R. C., Wittchen, H. U., & Magee, W. J. (1994). Panic and panic disorder in the United States. *Amer. J. Psychiat., 151*(3), 413–20.

Eberle, P., & Eberle, S. (1993). The abuse of innocence: The McMartin preschool trial. Amherst, NY: Prometheus Books.

Ebigbo, P. O. (1982). Development of a culture specific (Nigeria) screening scale of somatic complaints indicating psychiatric disturbance. *Cult. Med. Psychiatr., 6,* 29–43.

Edens, J. F., Buffington-Vollum, J. K., Keilen, A., Roskamp, P., & Anthony, C. (2005). Predictions of future dangerousness in capital murder trials: Is it time to "disinvent the wheel"? *Law & Human Behavior, 29*(1), 55–86.

Eells, T., T. D., Lombart, K. G., Kendjelic, E. M., Turner, L. C., Lucas, C. P. (2005). The quality of psychotherapy case formulations: A comparison of expert, experienced, and novice cognitive-behavioral and psychodynamic therapists. *J. Cons. Clin. Psychol., 73,* 579–589.

Egan, T. (2002, Feb. 6). Meth building its Hell's Kitchen in rural America. *New York Times,* A14.

Egeland, B., & Sroufe, L. A. (1981). Attachment and early maltreatment. *Child Develop., 52,* 44–52.

Egeland, J. A., Gerhard, D. S., Pauls, D. L., Sussex, J. N., Kidd, K. K., Allen, C. R., Hostetter, A. M., & Housman, D. E. (1987). Bipolar affective disorders linked to DNA markers on chromosome 11. *Nature, 325,* 783–87.

Egendorf, A. (1986). *Healing from the war.* Boston: Houghton Mifflin.

Egger, H. L., Costello, E. J., & Angold, A. (2003). School refusal and psychiatric disorders: A community study. *J. Amer. Acad. Child Adoles. Psychiat., 42*(7), 797–807.

Ehlers, A. (2000). Post-traumatic stress disorder. In M.G. Gelder, J. J. Lopez-Ibor, & N. Andreason (Eds.), *New Oxford textbook of psychiatry* (pp. 758–71). New York: Oxford University Press.

Eich, E., Macaulay, D., Loewenstein, R. J., & Dihle, P. H. (1997). Implicit memory, interpersonality amnesia, and dissociative identity disorder. Comparing patients with simulators. In D. J. Read & S. D. Lindsay (Eds.), *Recollections of trauma: Scientific evidence and clinical practice* (pp. 469–74). New York: Plenum.

Eisen, J. L., Phillips, K. A., Coles, M. E., & Rasmussen, S. A. (2003). Insight in obsessive compulsive disorder and body dysmorphic disorder. *Compr. Psychiat., 45*(1), 10–15.

Eisenberg, D. M., Davis, R. B., Ettner, S. L., Appel, S., Wilkey, S., Van Rompay, M., & Kessler, R. C. (1998). Trends in alternative medicine use in the United Sates, 1990–1997: Results of a follow-up national survey. *JAMA, 280,* 1569–75.

Eisenberger, N. J., Lieberman, M. D., & Williams, K. D. (2003). Does rejection hurt? An fMRI study of social exclusion. *Science, 302,* 290–92.

Ekselius, L., Tillfors, M., Furmark, T., & Fredrikson, M. (2001). Personality disorders in the general population: *DSM-IV* and *ICD-10* defined prevalence as related to sociodemographic profile. *Personal. Indiv. Diff., 30*(2), 311–20.

El-Bassel, N., Simoni, J. M., Cooper, D. K., Gilbert, L., & Schilling, R. F. (2001). Sex trading and psychological distress among women on methadone. *Psychology of Addictive Behaviors, 15,* 177–84.

Elder, R. W., Shults, R., Swahn, M. H., Strife, B. J., & Ryan, G. W. (2004). Alcohol-related emergency department visits among people ages 13 to 25 years. *J. Stud. Alcoh., 65*(3), 297–300.

Eliez, S., Blasey, C. M., Freund, L. S., Hastie, T., & Reiss, A. L. (2001). Brain anatomy, gender, and IQ in children and adolescents with fragile X syndrome. *Brain, 124,* 1610–18.

Elizur, Y., & Perednik, R. (2003). Prevalence and description of selective mutism in immigrant and native families: A controlled study. *J. Amer. Acad. Child Adoles. Psychiat., 42*(12), 1451–59.

Ellason, J. W., & Ross, C. A. (1997). Two-year follow-up of inpatients with dissociative disorder. *Amer. J. Psychiat., 154,* 832–39.

Ellickson, P. L., D'Amico, E. J., Collins, R. L., & Klein, D. J. (2005). Marijuana use and later problems: When frequency of recent use explains age of initiation effects (and when it does not). *Substance Use & Misuse, 40*(3), 343–59.

Ellicott, A., Hammen, C., Gitlin, M., Brown, G., & Jamison, K. (1990). Life events and the course of bipolar disorder. *Amer. J. Psychiat., 147,* 1194–98.

Elliot, R., Greenberg, L. S., & Lietaer, G. (2004). Research on experiential psychotherapies. In M. J. Lambert (2004). *Bergin and Garfield's handbook of Psychotherapy and behavior change.* New York: John Wiley and Sons, pp. 493–539.

Ellis, A., & Dryden, W. (1997). *The practice of rational emotive behavior therapy* (2nd ed.). New York: Springer.

Ellis, A. (1962). *Reason and emotion in psychotherapy.* New York: Lyle Stuart.

Ellis, A. (1989). The history of cognition in psychotherapy. In A. Freeman, K. M. Simon, L. E. Beutler, & H. Arkowitz (Eds.), *Comprehensive handbook of cognitive therapy.* (pp. 5–19). New York: Plenum.

Ellis, B. H., Fisher, P. A., & Zaharie, S. (2004). Predictors of disruptive behavior, developmental delays, anxiety, and affective symptomology among institutionally reared romanian children. *J. Amer. Acad. Child Adol. Psychiat., 43*(10), 1283–1292.

Ellis, E. S. (1993). Integrative strategy instruction: A potential model for teaching content area subjects to adolescents with learning disabilities. *J. Learn. Dis., 26*(6), 358–83.

El-Sheikh, M., & Buckhalt, J. A. (2003). Parental problem drinking and children's adjustment attachment and family functioning in moderators and mediators of risk. *J. Fam. Psychol., 17,* 510–20.

El-Sheikh, M., & Harger, J. (2001). Appraisals of marital conflict and children's adjustment, health, and physiological reactivity. *Develop. Psychol., 37,* 875–85.

Elzinga, B. M., Phaf, R. H., Ardon, A. M., & van Dyck, R. (2003). Directed forgetting between, but not within, dissociative personality states. *J. Abn. Psychol., 112*(2), 237–43.

Emerson, E. (2004). Deinstitutionalisation in England. *J. Intell. Develop. Dis., 29*(1), 79–84.

Emery, R. E., & Kitzmann, K. M. (1995). The child in the family: Disruptions in family functions. In D. Cicchetti & D. J. Cohen (Eds.), *Developmental Psychopathology: Vol. 2. Risk, disorder, and adaptation* (pp. 3–31). New York: Wiley.

Emery, R. E., & Laumann-Billings, L. (1998). An overview of the nature, causes, and consequences of abusive relationships: Toward differentiating maltreatment and violence. *Amer. Psychol., 53*(2), 121–35.

Emery, R. E. (1999). Postdivorce family life for children: An overview of research and some implications for policy. In R. A. Thompson & P. R. Amato (Eds.), *The postdivorce family: Children, parenting, and society* (pp. 3–27). Thousand Oaks, CA: Sage.

Emmelkamp, P. M. G., & Wessels, H. (1975). Flooding in imagination vs. flooding in vivo: A comparison with agoraphobics. *Behav. Res. Ther., 13*(1), 7–15.

Emmelkamp, P. M. G. (1994). Behavior therapy with adults. In A. E. Bergin & S. L. Garfield (Eds.), *Handbook of psychotherapy and behavior change* (4th ed., pp. 379–427). New York: Wiley.

EmmelkampP, M. G. (2004). Behavior therapy with adults. In M. J. Lambert (2004). *Bergin and Garfield's handbook of Psychotherapy and behavior change.* New York: John Wiley and Sons, pp. 393–446.

Emmons, R. A., & Shelton, C. M. (2002). Gratitude and the science of positive psychology. In C. R. Snyder & S. J. Lopez (Eds.), *Handbook of positive psychology* (pp. 459–71). New York: Oxford University Press.

Emslie, G. J., & Mayes, L. (2001). Mood disorders in children and adolescents: Psychopharmacological treatment. *Biol. Psychiat., 49*(12), 1082–90.

Emslie, G. J., Rush, A. J., Weinberg, W. A., Kowatch, R. A., Hughes, C. W., Carmody, T., & Rintelmann, J. (1997). A double-blind, randomized, placebo-controlled trial of fluoxetine in children and adolescents with depression. *Arch. Gen. Psychiat., 54,* 1031–37.

Engdahl, B. E., Harkness, A. R., Eberly, R. E., & Bielinski, J. (1993). Structural models of captivity trauma, resilience, and trauma response among former prisoners of war 20 and 40 years after release. *Soc. Psychiat. Psychiatr. Epidemiol., 28,* 109–15.

Englander-Golden, P., Elconin, J., Miller, K. J., & Schwarzkopf, A. B. (1986). Brief SAY IT STRAIGHT training and follow-up in adolescent substance abuse prevention. *J. Prim. Preven., 6*(4), 219–30.

Enright, S. J., & Beech, A. R. (1993a). Further evidence of reduced cognitive inhibition in obsessive-compulsive disorder. *Personal. Indiv. Diff., 14,* 387–95.

Enright, S. J., & Beech, A. R. (1993b). Reduced cognitive inhibition in obsessive-compulsive disorder. *Brit. J. Clin. Psychol., 32,* 67–74.

Epstein, E. E. (2001). Classification of alcohol-related problems and dependence. In N. Heather & T. Peters, et al. (Eds.), *International handbook of alcohol dependence and problems* (pp. 47–70). New York: John Wiley & Sons Ltd.

Epstein, J., & Klinkenberg, W. D. (2001). From Eliza to Internet: A brief history of computerized assessment. *Computers in Human Behavior, 17,* 295–314.

Epstein, R. S., Fullerton, C. S., & Ursano, R. J. (1998). Posttraumatic stress disorder following an air disaster: A prospective study. *Amer. J. Psychiat., 155*(7), 934–38.

Erblich, J., Earleywine, M., & Erblich, B. (2001). Positive and negative associations with alcohol and familial risk for alcoholism. *Psychology of Addictive Behaviors, 15*(3), 204–9.

Erdelyi, M. (1992). Psychodynamics and the unconscious. *Amer. Psychol., 47*(6), 784–787.

Erickson, S. J., Feldman, S., Shirley, S., & Steiner, H. (1996). Defense mechanisms and adjustment in normal adolescents. *Amer. J. Psychiat., 153*(6), 826–28.

Eriksen, W. (1994). The role of social support in the pathogenesis of coronary heart disease. A literature review. *Fam. Pract., 11,* 201–9.

Erlenmeyer-Kimling, L., & Cornblatt, B. A. (1992). A summary of attentional findings in the New York high-risk project. *J. Psychiat. Res., 26,* 405–26.

Erlenmeyer-Kimling, L., Roberts, S. A., Rock, D., Adamo, U. H., Shapiro, B. M., & Pape, S. (1998). Prediction from longitudinal assessments of high-risk children. In M. F. Lenzenweger & R. H. Dworkin (Eds.), *Origins and development of schizophrenia.* Washington, DC: American Psychological Association.

Ernst, N. D., & Harlan, W. R. (1991). Obesity and cardiovascular disease in minority populations: Executive summary. Conference highlights, conclusions, and recommendations. *Amer. J. Clin. Nutri., 53,* 1507S–11S.

Eron, L. D., Huesmann, L. R., Lefkowitz, M. M., & Walder, L. O. (1974). How learning conditions in early childhood—including mass media—relate to aggression in late adolescence. *Amer. J. Orthopsychiat., 44*(3), 412–23.

Eronen, M., Hakola, P., & Tiihonen, J. (1996). Mental disorders and homicidal behavior in Finland. *Arch. Gen. Psychiat., 53*(6), 497–501.

ESPAD. (2000). *The 1999 ESPAD Report: Alcohol and other drug use among students in 30 European countries.* European School Survey Project on Alcohol and Other Drugs, Stockholm, Sweden.

Estruch, R., Bono, G., Laine, P., Antunez, E., Petrucci, A., Morocutti, C., & Hillbom, M. (1998). Brain imaging in alcoholism. *European Journal of Neurology, 5*(2), 119–35.

Ettinger, U., et al. (2001). Magnetic-resonance imaging of the thalamus in first-episode psychosis. *Amer. J. Psychiat., 158,* 116–18.

Evans, D. W., King, R. A., & Leckman, J. F. (1996). Tic disorders. In E. J. Mash & R. A. Barkley (Eds.), *Child psychopathology* (pp. 436–56). New York: Guilford.

Evans, D. W., Lewis, M. D., & Iobst, E. (2004). The role of the orbitofrontal cortex in normally developing compulsive-like behaviors and obsessive compulsive disorder. *Brain & Cognition, 55*(1), 220–234.

Evans, E., Hawton, K., & Rodham, K. (2004). Factors associated with suicidal phenomena in adolescents: A systematic review of population-based studies. *Clin. Psychol. Rev., 24,* 957–979.

Evans, G., & Stecker, R. (2004). Motivational consequences of environmental stress. *J. Environ. Psych., 24*(2), 143–65.

Everett, C. A., & Everett, S. V. (2001). *Family therapy for ADHD.* New York: Guilford.

Everly, G. S., Jr., Boyle, S. H., & Lating, J. M. (1999). The effectiveness of psychological debriefing with vicarious trauma: A meta-analysis. *Stress Medicine, 15,* 229–33.

Everson, S. A., et al. (1997). Hopelessness and 4-year progression of carotid atherosclerosis: The Kuopio ischemic heart disease risk factor study. *Arteriosclerosis, Thrombosis, and Vascular Biology, 17,* 1490–95.

Ewing v. Goldstein. (2004). Cal. App.4th (No. B163112. Second Dist., Div. Eight. July 16, 2004).

Exner, J. E. (1987). Computer assistance in Rorschach interpretation. In J. N. Butcher (Ed.), *Computerized psychological assessment: A practitioner's guide.* New York: Basic Books.

Exner, J. E. (1993). *The Rorschach: A comprehensive system. Vol. 1: Basic Foundations.* New York: Wiley.

Exner, J. E. (1995). Why use personality tests? A brief historical view. In J. N. Butcher (Ed.), *Clinical personality assessment: Practical considerations* (10th ed., pp. 10–18). New York: Oxford University Press.

Exner, J. E., Jr., & Erdberg, P. (2002). Why use personality tests? A brief history and some comments. In J. N. Butcher (Ed.), *Clinical personality assessment: Practical approaches* (2nd ed., pp. 7–12). London: Oxford University Press.

Eysenck, M. W., Mogg, K., May, J., Richards, A., & Mathews, A. (1991). Bias in interpretation of ambiguous sentences related to threat in anxiety. *J. Abn. Psychol., 100,* 144–50.

Fabrega, H., Jr. (2001). Culture and history in psychiatric diagnosis and practice. *Cultural Psychiatry: International Perspectives, 24,* 391–405.

Faigel, H., & Heiligenstein, E. (1996). Medication for attention deficit hyperactivity disorder: Commentary and response. *J. Amer. Coll. Hlth., 45,* 40–42.

Fairburn, C. G., & Carter, J. C. (1997). Self-help and guided self-help for binge-eating problems. In D. M. Garner & P. E. Garfinkel (Eds.), *Handbook of treatment for eating disorders* (pp. 494–99). New York: Guilford.

Fairburn, C. G., & Harrison, P. J. (2003, Feb.). Eating disorders. *Lancet, 361,* 407–16.

Fairburn, C. G., Cooper, Z., Doll, H. A., & Welch, S. L. (1999). Risk factors for anorexia nervosa: Three integrated case-control comparisons. *Arch. Gen. Psychiat., 56,* 468–76.

Fairburn, C. G., Doll, H. A., Welch, S. L., Hay, P. J., Davies, B. A., & O'Conner, M. E. (1998). Risk factors for binge eating disorder: A community-based case control study. *Arch. Gen. Psychiat., 55*(5), 425–32.

Fairburn, C. G., Jones, R., Peveler, R. C., Hope, R. A., & O'Connor, M. (1993). Psychotherapy and bulimia nervosa: Long-term effects of interpersonal psychotherapy, behavior therapy, and cognitive behavior therapy. *Arch. Gen. Psychiat., 50*(6), 419–28.

Fairburn, C. G., Marcus, M. D., & Wilson, G. T. (1993). Cognitive-behavioral treatment for binge eating and bulimia nervosa. In C. G. Fairburn & G. T. Wilson (Eds.), *Binge eating: Nature, assessment, and treatment* (pp. 361–404). New York: Guilford.

Fairburn, C. G., Welch, S. L., Doll, H. A., Davies, B. A., & O'Connor, M. E. (1997). Risk factors for bulimia nervosa: A community-based case-control study. *Arch. Gen. Psychiat., 54*(6), 509–17.

Fairweather, G. W. (1994). *Keeping the balance: A psychologist's story.* Austin, TX: Fairweather Publishing.

Fairweather, G. W. (Ed.). (1980). *The Fairweather Lodge: A twenty-five year retrospective.* San Francisco: Jossey Bass.

Fairweather, G. W., Sanders, D. H., Maynard, H., & Cressler, D. L. (1969). *Community life for the mentally ill: An alternative to institutional care.* Chicago: Aldine.

Fallon, A. E., & Rozin, P. (1985). Sex differences in perceptions of desirable body shape. *J. Abn. Psychol., 94,* 102–5.

Fallon, B. A. (2004). Pharmacotherapy of somatoform disorders. *J. Psychosom. Res., 56,* 455–60.

Fallon, P., & Wonderlich, S. A. (1997). Sexual abuse and other forms of trauma. In D. M. Garner & P. E. Gatfinkel (Eds.), *Handbook of treatment for eating disorders* (pp. 394–423). New York: Guilford.

Falloon, I. R. H., Boyd, J. L., McGill, C. W., Williamson, M., & Razani, J. (1985). Family management in the prevention of morbidity of schizophrenia: Clinical outcome of a two-year longitudinal study. *Arch. Gen. Psychiat., 42,* 887–96.

Falsetti, S. A., Kilpatrick, D. G., Dansky, B. S., Lydiard, R. B., & Resnick, H. S. (1995). Relationship of stress to panic disorder: Cause or effect? In C. M. Mazure (Ed.), *Does stress cause psychiatric illness?* (pp. 111–47). Washington, DC: American Psychiatric Association.

Famy, C., Streissguth, A. P., & Unis, A. S. (1998). Mental illness in adults with fetal alcohol syndrome or fetal alcohol effects. *Amer. J. Psychiat., 155*(4), 552–54.

Fankhauser, M. P., Karumanchi, V. C., German, M. L., & Yates, A. (1992). A double-blind, placebo-controlled study of the efficacy of transdermal clonidine in autism. *J. Clin. Psychiat., 53,* 77–82.

Fann, J. R. (2000). The epidemiology of delirium: A review of studies and methodological issues. *Seminars in Clinical Neuropsychiatry, 5,* 86–92.

Fannon, D., Chitnis, X., Doku, V., Tennakoon, L., Ó'Ceallaigh, S., Soni, W., Sumich, A., Lowe, J., Satnamaria, M., & Sharma, T. (2000). Features of structural brain abnormality detected in first-episode psychosis. *Amer. J. Psychiat., 157,* 1829–34.

Faraone, S. V., Biederman, J., Lehman, B. F., Spencer, T., Norman, T., Seidman, L. J., Kraus, I., Perrin, J., Chen, W. J., & Tsuang, M. T. (1993). Intellectual performance and school failure in children with Attention Deficit Hyperactivity Disorder and in their siblings. *J. Abn. Psychol., 102,* 616–23.

Faraone, S. V., Tsuang, M. T., & Tsuang, D. W. (1999). *Genetics of mental disorder.* New York: Guilford.

Farde, L., Wiesel, F. A., Hall, H., Halldin, C., Stone-Elander, S., & Sedvall, G. (1987). No D2 receptor increase in PET study of schizophrenia. *Arch. Gen. Psychiat., 44,* 671–72.

Farde, L., Wiesel, F. A., Stone-Elander, S., Halldin, C., Norstrom, A. L., Hall, H., & Sedvall, G. (1990). D2 dopamine receptors in neuroleptic-naïve schizophrenic patients: A positron emission tomography study with [11C] raclopride. *Arch. Gen. Psychiat., 47,* 213–19.

Faretra, G. (1981). A profile of aggression from adolescence to adulthood: An 18-year follow-up of psychiatrically disturbed and violent adolescents. *Amer. J. Orthopsychiat., 51,* 439–53.

Farmer, A., Eley, T. C., & McGuffin, P. (2005). Current strategies for investigating the genetic and environmental risk factors for affective disorders. *Brit. J. Psychiat., 186*(3), 179–181.

Farmer, C. M., O'Donnell, B. F., Niznikiewicz, M. A., Voglmaier, M. M., McCarley, R. W., & Shenton, M. E. (2000). Visual perception and working memory in schizotypal personality disorder. *Amer. J. Psychiat., 157*(5), 781–86.

Farooqi, I. S., Matarese, G., Lord, G. M., Keogh, J. M., Lawrrence, E., Agwu, C., Sanna, V., Jebb, S. A., Perna, F., Fontana, S., Lechler, R. I., DePaoli, A. M., & O'Rahilly, S. (2002). Beneficial effects of leptin on obesity, T cell hyporesponsiveness, and neuroendocrine/metabolic dysfunction of human congenital leptin deficiency. *Journal of Clinical Investigation, 110,* 1093–103.

Fava, M., & Rosenbaum, J. F. (1995). Pharmacotherapy and somatic therapies. In E. E. Beckham & W. R. Leber (Eds.), *Handbook of depression* (2nd ed., pp. 280–301). New York: Guilford.

Fava, M. (1997). Psychopharmacologic treatment of pathologic anger. *Psychiat. Clin. N. Amer., 20,* 427–52.

Fawcett, J., Scheftner, W. A., Fogg, L., Clark, D. C., et al. (1990). Time-related predictors of suicide in major affective disorder. *Amer. J. Psychiat., 147*(9), 1189–94.

Fawcett, J. (2004). Is BDD culturally induced? *Psychiat. Ann., 34*(12), 900.

FDA. (2002). *The FDA approved Strattera.* Washington, DC: Department of Health and Human Services.

FDA. (2003). *FDA strengthens warnings for OxyContin* (TO1-30). Washington, DC: Author.

FDA. (2004). *FDA Talk paper: Warning about Strattera.* Washington, DC: Department of Health and Human Services.

Federal Bureau of Investigation. (1998). *Crime in the United States.* U.S. Government Printing Office.

Federal Bureau of Investigation. (2003). *Juvenile crime statistics.* Washington, DC: U.S. Department of Justice.

Fedoroff, J. P., Fishell, A., & Federoff, B. (1999). A case series of women evaluated for paraphilic sexual disorders. *Canadian Journal of Human Sexuality, 8,* 127–40.

Feeney, L., Kelly, B. D., Whitty, P., & O'Callaghan, E. (2002). Mental illness in migrants: Diagnostic and therapeutic challenges. *Irish Journal of Psychiatric Medicine, 19*(1), 29–31.

Fein, D. (2001). The primacy of social and language deficits in autism. *Japanese Journal of Special Education, 38,* 1–16.

Feldman, L. B., & Feldman, S. L. (1997). Conclusion: Principles for integrating psychotherapy and pharmacotherapy. *In Session: Psychotherapy in Practice, 3*(2), 99–102.

Feldman, L. (1992). *Integrating individual and family therapy.* New York: Brunner/Mazel.

Felsman, J. K., & Valliant, G. E. (1987). Resilient children as adults: A 40-year study. In E. J. Anthony & B. J. Cohler (Eds.), *The invulnerable child* (pp. 289–314). New York: Guilford.

Fenna, D., et al. (1971). Ethanol metabolism in various racial groups. *Canadian Medical Association Journal, 105,* 472–75.

Fennell, M. J. V. (1989). Depression. In K. Hawton, P. M. Salkovskis, J. Kirk, & D. M. Clark (Eds.), *Cognitive behaviour therapy for psychiatric problems: A practical guide.* Oxford, UK: Oxford University Press.

Fenton, W. S., & McGlashan, T. H. (1991). Natural history of the schizophrenia subtypes. I. Longitudinal study of paranoid, hebephrenic, and undifferentiated schizophrenia. *Arch. Gen. Psychiat., 48*(11), 969–77.

Fenton, W. S., & McGlashan, T. H. (1994). Antecedents, symptom progression, and long-term outcome of the deficit syndrome in schizophrenia. *Amer. J. Psychiat., 151*(3), 351–56.

Fenton, W. S., McGlashan, T. H., Victor, B. J., & Blyler, C. R. (1997). Symptoms, subtype, and suicidality in patients with schizophrenia spectrum disorders. *Amer. J. Psychiat., 154*(2), 199–204.

Fentress, et al. v. Shea Communications et al. (1990). Jefferson Circuit Court, No 90-CI-06033.

Ferguson, C. P., & Pigott, T. A. (2000). Anorexia and bulimia nervosa: Neurobiology and pharmacotherapy. *Behav. Ther.,* 31, 237–63.

Fergusson, D. M., Horwood, L. J., & Beautrais, A. L. (1999). Is sexual orientation related to mental health problems and suicidality in young people? *Arch. Gen. Psychiat., 56,* 876–80.

Fergusson, D. M., Horwood, L. J., & Swain-Campbell, N. R. (2003). Cannabis dependence and psychotic symptoms in young people. *Psychol. Med., 33,* 15–22.

Ferketich, A. K., Schwartzbaum, J. A., Frid, D. J., & Moeschberger, M. L. (2000). Depression as an antecedent to heart disease among women and men in the NHANES 1 Study. *Arch. Int. Med., 160*(9), 1261–68.

Fernandez, F., Ringholz, G. M., & Levy, J. K. (2002). Neuropsychiatric aspects of human immunodeficiency virus infection of the central nervous system. In S. Yudofsky & R. E. Hales (Eds.), *The American Psychiatric Association Publishing textbook of neuropsychiatry and clinical sciences* (4th ed., pp. 783–812). Washington, DC: American Psychiatric Publishing.

Ferri, B. A., Gregg, N., & Heggoy, S. J. (1997). Profiles of college students demonstrating learning disabilities with and without giftedness. *J. Learn. Dis., 30*(5), 552–59.

Ferrier, I. N., & Thompson, J. M. (2002). Cognitive impairment in bipolar affective disorder: Implications for the bipolar diathesis. *Brit. J. Psychiat., 180,* 293–95.

Ferrucci, L., Harris, T., Guralnik, J., Tracy, R., Corti, M., Cohen, H., Pennix, B., Pahor, M., Wallace, R., & Havlik, R. J. (1999). Serum IL-6 level and the development of disability in older persons. *J. Amer. Geriat. Soc, 47,* 639–46.

Fersch, E. A., Jr. (1980). *Psychology and psychiatry in courts and corrections.* New York: Wiley.

Ferster, C. B. (1974). Behavioral approaches to depression. In R. J. Friedman & M. M. Katz (Eds.), *The psychology of depression: Contemporary theory and research.* Washington, DC: Hemisphere.

Feuer, C. A., Nishith, P., & Resick, P. (2005). Prediction of numbing and effortful avoidance in female rape survivors with chronic PTSD. *J. Trauma. Stres., 18,* 165–70.

Fichter, M. M., et al. (1991). Fluoxetine versus placebo: A double-blind study with bulimic inpatients undergoing intensive psychotherapy. *Pharmacopsychiatry, 24,* 1–7.

Fields, J. Z., Turk, A., Durkin, M., Ravi, N. V., & Keshavarzian, A. (1994). Increased gastrointestinal symptoms in chronic alcoholics. *American Journal of Gastroenterology, 89,* 382–86.

Fierman, E. J., Hung, M. F., Pratt, L. A., Warshaw, M. G., Yonkers, K. A., Peterson, L. G., Epstein-Kaye, T. M., & Norton, H. S. (1993). Trauma and post-traumatic stress disorder in subjects with anxiety disorders. *Amer. J. Psychiat., 150,* 1872–74.

Figueroa, E., & Silk, K. (1997). Biological implications of childhood sexual abuse in borderline personality disorder. *J. Person. Dis., 11* (1), 71–92.

Fink, M. (2003). *A Beautiful Mind* and insulin coma: Social constraints on psychiatric diagnosis and treatment. *Harv. Rev. Psychiat., 11,* 284–290.

Fink, P., Ornbol, E., Toft, T., Sparle, K. C., Frostholm, L., & Olesen, F. (2004). A new empirically established hypochondriasis diagnosis. *Amer. J. Psychiat., 161*(9), 1680–91.

Finkelhor, D. (1984). *Child sexual abuse.* New York: Free Press.

Finkenbine, R., & Miele, V. J. (2004). Globus hystericus: A brief review. *Gen. Hosp. Psychiat., 26,* 78–82.

Finn, P. R., Sharkansky, E. J., Viken, R., West, T. L., Sandy, J., & Bufferd, S. (1997). Heterogeneity in the families of sons of alcoholics: The impact of familial vulnerability type on offspring characteristics. *J. Abn. Psychol., 106*(1), 26–36.

Finn, S. E., & Kamphuis, J. H. (2006). Therapeutic assessment with the MMPI-2. In J. N. Butcher (Ed.), *MMPI-2: The practioner's handbook.* (pp. 165–91). Washington, DC: American Psychological Association.

Finn, S. E., & Tonsager, M. E. (1997). Information-gathering and therapeutic models of assessment: Complementary paradigms. *Psychol. Assess., 9*(4), 374–85.

Fischer, J. L., Pidcock, B. W., Munsch, J., & Forthun, L. (2005). Parental abusive drinking and sibling role differences. *Al. Treat. Quart., 23*(1), 79–97.

Fischer, J. M. (1993). People with learning disabilities: Moral and ethical rights to equal opportunities. *Journal of Applied Rehabilitation Counseling, 24*(1), 3–7.

Fischer, M. (1971). Psychoses in the offspring of schizophrenic monozygotic twins and their normal co-twins. *Brit. J. Psychiat., 118,* 43–52.

Fischer, M. (1973). Genetic and environmental factors in schizophrenia: A study of schizophrenic twins and their families. *Acta Psychiatr. Scandin.,* Suppl. No. 238.

Fish, E. W., Shahrokh, D., Bagot, R., Caldji, C., Bredy, T., Szyf, M., & Meaney, M. J. (2004). Epigenetic programming of stress responses through variations in maternal care. *Ann. NY Acad. Sci., 1036,* 167–80.

Fishbain, D. A. (1982). Pain insensitivity in psychosis. *Annals of Emergency Medicine, 11,* 630–32.

Fisher, A. J. (1999). Mood disorder in suicidal children and adolescents: Recent developments. *Journal of Child Psychology & Psychiatry & Allied Disciplines, 40*(3), 315–24.

Fisher, J. D., & Fisher, W. A. (1992). Changing AIDS-risk behavior. *Psychol. Bull., 111*(3), 455–74.

Fisher, J. E., & Carstensen, L. L. (1990). Behavior management for the dementias. *Clin. Psychol. Rev., 10,* 611–30.

Fisher, S., & Greenberg, R. P. (1997). The curse of the placebo: Fanciful pursuit of a pure biological therapy. In S. Fisher & R. P. Greenberg (Eds.), *From placebo to panacea: Putting psychiatric drugs to the test.* (pp. 3–56). New York: Wiley.

Fiske, S., & Taylor, S. (1991). *Social cognition* (2nd ed.). New York: McGraw Hill.

Fitzgerald, P. B., Brown, T. L., & Daskalakis, Z. J. (2002). The application of transcranial magnetic stimulation in psychiatry and neurosciences research. *Acta Psychiatri. Scandi., 105*(5), 324–40.

Flannery, R. B. (2004). Managing stress in today's age: A concise guide for emergency services personnel. *Int. J. Emerg. Ment. Hlth., 6*(4), 205–9.

Fleming, S. K., Blasey, C., & Schatzberg, A. F. (2004). Neuropsychological correlates of psychotic features in major depressive disorders: A review and meta-analysis. *J. Psychiat. Res., 38,* 27–35.

Fletcher, P. C. (2004). Functional neuroimaging of psychiatric disorders: Exploring hidden behavior. *Psychol. Med., 34,* 577–81.

Flier, J. S., Underhill, L. H., & Lieber, C. S. (1995). Medical disorders of alcoholism. *N. Engl. J. Med., 333*(6), 1058–65.

Flor, H., & Birbaumer, N. (1993). Comparison of the efficacy of electromyographic biofeedback, cognitive-behavior therapy, and conservative medical interventions in the treatment of chronic musculoskeletal pain. *J. Cons. Clin. Psychol., 61*(4), 653–58.

Flor, H., Birbaumer, N., & Turk, D. C. (1990). The psychobiology of chronic pain. *Advances in Behaviour Research & Therapy, 12,* 47–84.

Flor, H., Birbaumer, N., Hermann, C., Ziegler, S., & Patrick, C. J. (2002). Aversive Pavlovian conditioning in psychopaths: Peripheral and central correlates. *Psychophysiology, 39*(4), 505–18.

Foa, E. B., & Kozak, M. J. (1995). DSM-IV field trial: Obsessive-compulsive disorder. *Amer. J. Psychiat., 152,* 90–96.

Foa, E. B., & Rauch, S. A. M. (2004). Cognitive changes during prolonged exposure versus prolonged exposure plus cognitive restructuring in female assault survivors with posttraumatic stress disorder. *J. Cons. Clin. Psychol., 72,* 879–84.

Foa, E. B., Zinbarg, R., & Rothbaum, B. O. (1992). Uncontrollability and unpredictability in post-traumatic stress disorder: An animal model. *Psychol. Bull., 112*(2), 218–38.

Foa, E. B., Zoellner, L. A., Feeny, N. C., Hembree, E. A., & Alvarez-Conrad, J. (2002). Does imaginal exposure exacerbate PTSD symptoms? *J. Cons. Clin. Psychol., 70,* 1022–28.

Foa, E., & Franklin, M. (2001). Obsessive-compulsive disorder. In D. H. Barlow (Ed.), *Clinical handbook of psychological disorders* (3rd ed., pp. 209–63). New York: Guilford.

Foley, M. A., Santini, C., & Sopasakis, M. (1989). Discriminating between memories: Evidence for children's spontaneous elaboration. *Journal of Experimental Child Psychology, 48,* 146–69.

Folkman, S. & Moskovitz, J. T. (2004). Coping: Pitfalls and promise. *Annu. Rev. Psychol., 55,* 745–774.

Folstein, M. F., Folstein, S., & McHugh, P. R. (1975). Mini-mental state: A practical method for grading the cognitive state of patients for the clinician. *J. Psychiat. Res., 12,* 189.

Foltin, R. W., & Fischman, M. W. (1997). A laboratory model of cocaine withdrawal in humans: Intravenous cocaine. *Experimental and Clinical Pharmacology, 5*(4), 404–11.

Fombonne, E. (2003). Epidemiological surveys of autism and other pervasive developmental disorders: An update. *J. Autism Devel. Dis., 33*(4), 365–82.

Fontenelle, L. F., Mendlowicz, M. V., Soares, I. D., & Versiani, M. (2004). Patients with obsessive-compulsive disorder and hoarding symptoms: A distinctive clinical subtype. *Compr. Psychiat., 45*(5), 375–383.

Forchetti, C. M. (2005). Treating patients with moderate to severe Alzheimer's disease: Implications of recent pharmacologic studies. *Primary Care Companion Journal of Clinical Psychiatry, 7,* 155–61.

Ford, D. E., Mead, L. A., Chang, P. P., Cooper-Patrick, L., Wang, N. Y., & Klag, M. J. (1998). Depression is a risk factor for coronary artery disease in men: The Precursors Study. *Arch. Int. Med., 158,* 1422–26.

Ford, J. D. (1999). Disorders of extreme stress following war-zone military trauma: Associated features of posttraumatic stress disorder or comorbid but distinct syndromes? *J. Cons. Clin. Psychol., 67*(1), 3–12.

Forehand, R. (1993). Twenty years of research on parenting: Does it have practical implications for clinicians working with parents and children? *Clin. Psychol., 46,* 169–76.

Forness, S. R., & Kavale, K. A. (1993). Strategies to improve basic learning and memory deficits in mental retardation: A meta-analysis of experimental studies. *Education and Training in Mental Retardation, 28*(2), 99–110.

Forsyth, J. P., Daleiden, E. L., & Chorpita, B. F. (2000). Response primacy in fear conditioning: Disentangling the contributions of UCS vs. UCR intensity. *Psychol. Rec., 50*(1), 17–34.

Forsyth, J., Eifert, G. H. (1998). Response intensity in content-specific fear conditioning comparing 20% versus 13% CO-sub-2-enriched air as unconditioned stimuli. *J. Abn. Psychol., 107*(2), 291–304.

Fossati, A., Madeddu, F., & Maffei, C. (1999). Borderline personality disorder and childhood sexual abuse: A meta-analytic study. *J. Pers. Dis., 13,* 268–80.

Fowles, D. C. (1993). Electrodermal activity and antisocial behavior: Empirical findings and theoretical issues. In J.-C. Roy, W. Boucsein, D. Fowles, & J. Gruzelier (Eds.), *Progress in electrodermal research.* London: Plenum.

Fowles, D. C. (2001). Biological variables in psychopathology: A psychobiological perspective. In P. D. Sutker & H. E. Adams (Eds.), *Comprehensive handbook of psychopathology* (3rd ed., pp. 85–104). New York: Kluwer Academic.

Fowles, D. C. (2003). Schizophrenia spectrum disorders. In I. Weiner (Series Ed.) & T. A. Widiger & G. Stricker (Vol Eds.) *Handbook of Psychology:* Vol 8. *Clinical Psychology* (pp. 65–92). New York: John Wiley and Sons.

Fowles, D. C., & Kochanska, G. (2000). Temperament as a moderator of pathways to conscience in children: The contribution of electrodermal activity. *Psychophysiology, 37*(6), 788–95.

Fox, H. C., Parrott, A. C., & Turner, J. J. D. (2001). Ecstasy use: Cognitive deficits related to dosage rather than self-reported problematic use of the drug. *J. Psychopharm., 15,* 273–81.

Fox, M. J. (2002). *Lucky man.* New York: Hyperion Press.

Fox, N. A., Henderson, H. A., Marshall, P. J., Nichols, K. E., & Ghera, M. M. (2005). Behavioral inhibition: Linking biology and behavior within a developmental framework. *Annu. Rev. Psychol., 56,* 235–262.

Frances, A., & Ross, R. (1996). *DSM-IV Case studies: A clinical guide to differential diagnosis.* Washington, DC: American Psychiatric Press.

Frank, E., & Spanier, C. (1995). Interpersonal psychotherapy for depression: Overview, clinical efficacy, and future directions. *Clin. Psychol. Sci. Pract., 2,* 349–69.

Frank, E., Kupfer, D. J., Perel, J. M., Cornes, C., Jarett, D. B., Mallinger, A. G., Thase, M. E., McEachran, A. B., & Grochocinski, V. J. (1990). Three-year outcomes for maintenance therapies in recurrent depression. *Arch. Gen. Psychiat., 47,* 1093–99.

Frank, E., Prien, R. F., Jarrett, R. B., Keller, M. B., Kupfer, D. J., Lavori, P. W., Rush, A. J., & Weissman, M. M. (1991). Conceptualization and rationale for consensus definitions of terms in major depressive disorder: Remission, recovery, relapse, and recurrence. *Arch. Gen. Psychiat., 48,* 851–55.

Frank, R. G., McDaniel, S. H., Bray, J. H., & Heldring, M. (Eds.). (2004). *Primary care psychology.* Washington, DC: American Psychological Association.

Frankenburg, F. R. (1994). History of the development of antipsychotic medications. *Psychiat. Clin. N. Amer., 17*(3), 531–41.

Franklin, M. E., & Foa, E. B. (1998). Cognitive-behavioral treatments for obsessive-compulsive disorder. In P. E. Nathan & J. M. Gorman (Eds.), *A guide to treatments that work.* (pp. 339–57). New York: Oxford University Press.

Franklin, M. E., & Foa, E. B. (2002). Cognitive behavioral treatments for obsessive compulsive disorder. In P. E. Nathan & J. M. Gorman (Eds.), *A guide to treatments that work* (2nd ed., pp. 367–86). London: Oxford University Press.

Franko, D. L., Keel, P. K., Dorer, D. J., Blais, M. A., Delinsky, S. S., Eddy, K. T., Charat, V., Renn, R., & Herzog, D. B. (2004). What predicts suicide attempts in women with eating disorders? *Psychol. Med., 34,* 843–53.

Franzen, M. D. (2001). *Reliability and validity in neuropsychological assessment.* New York: Kluwer.

Frasure-Smith, N., Lesperance, F., & Talajic, M. (1993). Depression following myocardial infarction: Impact on 6-month survival. *JAMA, 270,* 1819–25.

Frazier, M., & Merrill, K. W. (1998). Issues in behavioral treatment of attention-deficit/hyperactivity disorder. *Education & Treatment of Children, 20*(4), 441–61.

Frazier, P., & Burnett, J. (1994). Immediate coping strategies among rape victims. *J. Couns. Devel., 72,* 633–39.

Frazier, P., & Schauben, L. (1994). Causal attributions and recovery from rape and other stressful life events. *J. Soc. Clin. Psychol., 14,* 1–14.

Frazier, P., Conlon, A., & Glaser, T. (2001). Positive and negative life changes following sexual assault. *J. Cons. Clin. Psychol., 69,* 1048–55.

Freeman, T. (1960). On the psychopathology of schizophrenia. *J. Ment. Sci., 106,* 925–37.

Freeman, W. (1959). Psychosurgery. In S. Arieti (Ed.). *American handbook of psychiatry* (vol 2, pp. 1521–1540). New York: Basic Books

Freud, A. (1946). *Ego and the mechanisms of defense.* New York: International Universities Press.

Freud, S. & Breuer, J. In J. Strachey (Ed. and Trans.), *The standard edition of the complete psychological works of Sigmund Freud: Vol. 2. On the Psychical Mechanisms of Hysterical Phenomena,* (pp. 11–20). London: Hogarth Press. (originally published in 1893).

Freud, S. (1909). Analysis of a phobia in a five-year-old boy. In *Standard edition, vol 10.* London: Hogarth Press (1955). First German edition 1909.

Freud, S. (1917). Mourning and melancholia. In W. Gaylin (Ed.), *The meaning of despair: Psychoanalytic contributions to the understanding of depression.* New York: Science House.

Freud, S. (1935). Letter to an American mother. Reprinted in Paul Friedman (1959), Sexual deviations, in S. Arieti (Ed.), *American Handbook of Psychiatry* (Vol. 1). pp. 606–7. New York: Basic Books.

Freund, K., & Seto, M. C. (1998). Preferential rape in the theory of courtship disorder. *Arch. Sex. Behav., 27,* 433–43.

Frick, P. J., Cornell, A. H., Barry, C. T., Bodin, S. D., & Dane, H. E. (2003). Callous-unemotional traits and conduct problems in the prediction of conduct problem severity, aggression, and self-report of delinquency. *J. Abnorm. Child Psychol., 31*(4), 457–470.

Frick, P. J. (1998). *Conduct disorders and severe antisocial behavior.* New York: Plenum.

Friedman, H. S., Hawley, P. H., & Tucker, J. S. (1994). Personality, health, and longevity. *Curr. Dis. Psychol. Sci., 3*(2), 37–41.

Friedman, J. M. (2003). A war on obesity, not the obese. (2003). *Science, vol 299,* no. 5608, 856–858.

Friedman, M. J., & Yehuda, R. (1995). Post-traumatic stress disorder and comorbidity: Psychobiological approaches to differential diagnosis. In M. J. Friedman & D. S. Charney, et al. (Eds.), *Neurobiological and clinical consequences of stress: From normal adaptation to post-traumatic stress disorder* (pp. 429–45). Philadelphia: Lippincott Williams & Wilkins.

Friedman, M., & Rosenman, R. H. (1959). Association of specific overt behavior pattern with blood and cardiovascular findings. *JAMA, 169,* 1286.

Friemoth, J. (2005). What is the most effective treatment for ADHD in children? *J. Fam. Pract., 54*(2), 166–68.

Fries, J. (2001, Nov. 14). Mother drowned daughter, 4, in exorcism rite. *New York Times.*

Friman, P. C., & Warzak, W. J. (1990). Nocturnal enuresis: A prevalent, persistent, yet curable parasomnia. *Pediatrician, 17,* 38–45.

Fromm-Reichmann, F. (1948). Notes on the development of treatment of schizophrenics by psychoanalytic psychotherapy. Reprinted in D. M. Bullard (Ed.), *Psychoanalysis and psychotherapy: Selected papers of Freida Fromm-Reichmann.* Chicago: University of Chicago Press, 1959.

Frone, M. R. (2003). Predictors of overall and on-the-job substance use among young workers. *J. Occup. Hlth. Psych., 8,* 39–54.

Frost, R. O., Steketee, G., Williams, L. F., & Warren, R. (2000). Mood, personality disorder symptoms, and disability in obsessive compulsive hoarders: A comparison with clinical and nonclinical controls. *Behaviour Research & Therapy, 38*(11), 1071–1081.

Fruzzetti, A. E. (1996). Causes and consequences: Individual distress in the context of couple interactions. *J. Cons. Clin. Psychol., 64,* 1192–201.

Fryers, T. (2000). Epidemiology of mental retardation. In M. G. Gelder, J. J. Lopez-Ibor, Jr., & N. Andreason (Eds.), *New Oxford textbook of psychiatry* (pp. 1941–45). New York: Oxford University Press.

Fukutake, T., Mine, S., Yamakami, I., Yamaura, A., & Hattori, T. (2000). Rollercoaster headache and subdural hematoma. *Neurology, 54,* 264.

Fullerton, C. S., & Ursano, R. J. (1997). The other side of chaos: Understanding the patterns of posttraumatic stress disorder. In C. S. Fullerton & R. J. Ursano (Eds.), *Posttraumatic stress disorder* (pp. 3–20). Washington, DC: American Psychiatric Association Press.

Fulmer, R. H., & Lapidus, L. B. (1980). A study of professed reasons for beginning and continuing heroin use. *Inter. J. Addicti., 15,* 631–45.

Futterman, A., Thompson, L., Gallagher-Thompson, D., & Ferris, R. (1995). Depression in later life: Epidemiology, assessment, etiology, and treatment. In E. E. Beckham & W. R. Leber (Eds.), *Handbook of depression* (2nd ed., pp. 494–525). New York: Guilford.

Gabbard, G. O. (1994). Inpatient services: The clinician's view. In R. K. Schreter, S. S. Sharfstein, & C. A. Schreter (Eds.), *Allies and adversaries* (pp. 22–30). Washington, DC: American Psychiatric Press.

Gabbard, G. O., Gunderson, J. G., & Fonagy, P. (2002). The place of psychoanalytic treatments within psychiatry. *Arch. Gen. Psychiat., 59,* 505–10.

Gabbard, G. O., & Kay, J. K. (2001). The fate of integrated treatment: Whatever happened to the biopsychosocial psychiatrist? *Amer. J. Psychiat., 158,* 1956–63.

Gabbard, G. O., Lazar, S. G., Hornberger, J., & Spiegel, D. (1997). The economic impact of psychotherapy: A review. *Amer. J. Psychiat., 154*(2), 147–55.

Gabriel, R. A. (1987). *No more heroes. Madness and psychiatry in war.* New York: Hill and Wang.

Gabuzda, D. H., & Hirsch, M. S. (1987). Neurologic manifestations of infection with human immunodeficiency virus: Clinical features and pathogenesis. *Ann. Int. Med., 107,* 383–91.

Gajzago, C., & Prior, M. (1974). Two cases of "recovery" in Kanner syndrome. *Arch. Gen. Psychiat., 31*(2), 264–68.

Galaif, E. R., Newcomb, M. D., & Carmona, J. V. (2001). Prospective relationships between drug problems and work adjustment in a community sample of adults. *J. Appl. Psychol., 86*(2), 337–50.

Ganju, V., & Quan, H. (1987). *Mental health service needs of refugees in Texas.* Paper given at the Refugee Assistance Program: Mental Health Workgroup Meeting, UCLA, February 12–13.

Ganzini, L., Nelson, H. D., Lee, M. A., Kraemer, D. F., Schmidt, T. A., & Delorit, M. A. (2001). Oregon physicians' attitudes about and experiences with end-of-life care since passage of the Oregon death with dignity act. *JAMA, 285*(18), 2362–69.

Garakani, A., Hirschowitz, J., & Katz, C. I. (2004). General disaster psychiatry. *Psychiat. Clin. N. Amer., 27,* 391–406.

Garb, H. (1995). Using computers to make judgments: Correlation among predictors and the comparison of configural rules. *Computers in Human Behavior, 11*(2), 313–24.

Garb, H. N., Florio, C. M., & Grove, W. M. (1998). The validity of the Rorschach and the Minnesota Multiphasic Personality Inventory: Results from meta-analyses. *Psychol. Sci., 9*(5), 402–4.

Garber, J., & Horowitz, J. L. (2002). Depression in children. In I. H. Gotlib & C. L. Hammen (Eds.), *Handbook of depression* (pp. 510–40). New York: Guilford.

Gardner, J. (2000). Living with a child with fetal alcohol syndrome. *American Journal of Maternal/Child Nursing, 25*(5), 252–57.

Garfinkel, P. E. (2002). Classification and diagnosis of eating disorders. In C. G. Fairburn & K. D. Brownell (Eds.), *Eating disorders and obesity: A comprehensive handbook* (2nd ed., pp. 155–61). New York: Guilford.

Garmezy, N. (1978a). Current status of other high-risk research programs. In L. C. Wynne, R. L. Cromwell, & S. Matthysse (Eds.), *The nature of schizophrenia: New approaches to research and treatment.* New York: Wiley.

Garmezy, N. (1978b). Observations of high-risk research and premorbid development in schizophrenia. In L. C. Wynne, R. L. Cromwell, & S. Matthysse (Eds.), *The nature of schizophrenia: New approaches to research and treatment.* New York: Wiley.

Garmezy, N. (1993). Vulnerability and resilience. In D. C. Funder, R. D. Parke, et al. (Eds.) *Studying lives through time: Personality and development.* (pp. 377–398). Washington DC: American Psychological Association.

Garner, D. M. (1997). Psychoeducational principles in treatment. In D. M. Garner & P. E. Garfinkel (Eds.), *Handbook of treatment for eating disorders* (pp. 145–77). New York: Guilford.

Garner, D. M., & Garfinkel, P. E. (Eds.). (1997) *Handbook of treatment for eating disorders* (2nd ed.). New York: Guilford.

Garner, D. M., Garfinkel, P. E., Schwartz, D., & Thompson, M. (1980). Cultural expectations of thinness. *Psychol. Rep., 47,* 483–91.

Garner, D. M., Vitousek, K. M., & Pike, K. M. (1997). Cognitive-behavioral therapy for anorexia nervosa. In D. M. Garner &. P. E. Garfinkel (Eds.), *Handbook of treatment for eating disorders* (pp. 94–144). New York: Guilford.

Gartrell, N. (2004). A doctor's toxic shock. *Boston Globe Magazine,* January 4th 2004. page 58.

Gath, A. (2000). Families with a mentally retarded member and their needs. In M. G. Gelder, J. J. Lopez-Ibor, Jr., & N. C. Andreason (Eds.), *New Oxford textbook of psychiatry, Volume 2* (pp. 2002–5). Oxford: Oxford University Press.

Gaudin, J. M., Jr. (1993). Effective intervention with neglectful families. *Crim. Just. Behav., 20,* 66–89.

Gawande, A. (2001, Jul. 9). The man who couldn't stop eating. *New Yorker,* 66–75.

Gawin, F. H., & Kleber, H. D. (1986). Abstinence symptomatology and psychiatric diagnosis in cocaine abusers. *Arch. Gen. Psychiat., 43,* 107–13.

Gazdzinski, S., Durazzo, T., & Meyerhoff, D. J. (2005). Temporal dynamics and determinants of whole brain tissue volume changes during recovery from alcohol dependence. *Drug Al. Dep., 78*(3), 263–73.

Gelehrter, T. D., Collins, F. S., & Ginsburg, D. (1998). *Principles of Medical Genetics.* Baltimore: Williams and Wilkins.

Gelfand, D. M., & Teti, D. M. (1990). The effects of maternal depression on children. *Clin. Psychol. Rev., 10,* 329–53.

Gentry, W. D. (1984). Behavioral medicine: A new research paradigm. In W. D. Gentry (Ed.), *Handbook of behavioral medicine* (pp. 1–12). New York: Guilford.

Germain, A., Nofzinger, E. A., Kupfer, D. J., & Buysse, D. J. (2004). Neurobiology of non-REM sleep in depression: Further evidence of hypofrontality and thalamic dysregulation. *Amer. J. Psychiat., 161,* 1856–1863.

Gershuny, B. S., & Sher, K. J. (1998). The relation between personality and anxiety: Findings from a 3-year prospective study. *J. Abn. Psychol., 107*(2), 252–62.

Geschwind, N. (1977). Insensitivity to pain in psychotic patients. [letter]. *N. Engl. J. Med., 296,* 1480.

Gestwicki, J. E., Crabtree, G. R., & Graef, I. A. (2004). Harnessing chaperones to generate small molecule inhibitors of amyloid β aggregation. *Science, 306,* 865–69.

Gettinger, M., & Koscik, R. (2001). Psychological services for children with learning disabilities. In J. N. Huges, A. W. La Greca, & J. C. Conoley (Eds.), *Handbook of psychological services for children and adolescents* (pp. 421–35). Oxford: Oxford University Press.

Ghaemi, S. N., Hsu, D. J., Ko, J. Y., Baldassano, C. F., Kontos, N. J., & Goodwin, F. K. (2004). Bipolar spectrum disorder: A pilot study. *Psychopath., 37*(5), 222–226.

Gibbs, N. A. (1996). Nonclinical populations in research on obsessive-compulsive disorder: A critical review. *Clin. Psychol. Rev., 16*(8), 729–73.

Gilbert, D. L., Batterson, J. R., Sethuraman, G., & Sallee, F. R. (2004). Tic reduction with risperidone versus pimozide in a randomized, double-blind, crossover trial. *J. Amer. Acad. Child Adoles. Psychiat., 43*(2) 206–14.

Gilbert, J. G., & Lombardi, D. N. (1967). Personality characteristics of young male narcotic addicts. *J. Couns. Psychol., 31,* 536–38.

Giles, T. R. (1993). *Managed mental health care: A guide to practitioners, employees, and hospital administrators.* Boston: Allyn and Bacon.

Gilhooly, M. L. M., Sweeting, H. N., Whittick, J. E., & McKee, K. (1994). Family care of the dementing elderly. *Inter. Rev. Psychiat., 6*(1), 29–40.

Gill, K., Eagle Elk, M., Liu, Y., & Deitrich, R. A. (1999). An examination of ALDH2 genotypes, alcohol metabolism and the flushing response in Native Americans. *J. Stud. Alcoh., 60*(2), 149–58.

Gillberg, C., & Schaumann, H. (1981). Infantile autism and puberty. *J. Autism Develop. Dis., 11*(4), 365–71.

Gilley, D. W., et al. (1997). Psychotic symptoms and physically aggressive behavior in Alzheimer's disease. *J. Amer. Geriat. Soc., 45*(9), 1074–79.

Gillies, L. A. (2001). Interpersonal psychotherapy for depression and other disorders. In D. H. Barlow (Ed.), *Clinical handbook of psychological disorders: A step-by-step treatment manual* (pp. 309–31). New York: Guilford.

Gilligan, J. (2001). The last mental hospital. *Psychiatric Quarterly. 72*(1), 45–61.

Gilligen, J. (2001). The last mental hospital. *Psychiatric Q., 72,* 45–61.

Gillis, H. M. (1993). Individual and small-group psychotherapy for children involved in trauma and disaster. In C. F. Saylor (Ed.), *Children and disasters* (pp. 165–86). New York: Plenum.

Gilovich, T. (1991). *How do we know what isn't so: The fallibility of human reason in everyday life.* New York: Free Press.

Gitlin, M. J. (1996). *The psychotherapist's guide to psychopharmacology* (2nd ed.). New York: Free Press.

Gitlin, M. J. (2002). Pharmacological treatment of depression. In I. H. Gotlib & C. L. Hammen (Eds.), *Handbook of depression* (pp. 360–82). New York: Guilford.

Gjedde, A., & Wong, D. F. (1987). Positron tomographic quantification of neuroreceptors in human brain *in vivo,* with special reference to the D2 dopamine receptors in caudate nucleus. *Neurosurgical Review, 10,* 9–18.

Glaser, R., Kiecolt-Glaser, J. K., Speicher, C. E., & Holliday, J. E. (1985). Stress, loneliness, and changes in herpes virus latency. *J. Behav. Med., 8,* 249–60.

Glaser, R., Rice, J., Sheridan, J., Fertel, R., Stout, J., Speicher, C., Pinsky, R., Kotur, M., Post, A., Beck, M., & Kiecolt-Glaser, J. (1987). Stress-related immune suppression: Health implications. *Brain, Behavior, and Immunity, 1,* 7–20.

Glassman, A. H. (2005). Commentary: Does treating post-myocardial infarction depression reduce medical mortality? *Arch. Gen. Psychiat., 62*(7), 711–712.

Glassman, A. H. (2005). Does treating post-myocardial infarction depression reduce medical mortality? *Arch. Gen. Psychiat., 62,* 711–12.

Glassman, A. H., & Shapiro, P. A. (1998). Depression and the course of coronary artery disease. *Amer. J. Psychiat., 155*(1), 4–11.

Glatt, M. M. (1995). Controlled drinking after a third of a century. *Addiction, 90*(9), 1157–60.

Gleaves, D. H. (1996). The sociocognitive model of dissociative identity disorder: A reexamination of the evidence. *Psychol. Bull., 120,* 42–59.

Gleaves, D. H., May, M. C., & Cardena, E. (2001). Examination of the diagnostic validity of dissociative identity disorder. *Clin. Psychol. Rev., 21,* 577–608.

Gleaves, D. H., Smith, S. M., Butler, L. D., & Spiegel, D. (2004). False and recovered memories in the laboratory and clinic: A review of experimental and clinical evidence. *Clin. Psychol. Sci. Prac., 11*(1), 3–28.

Glisky, E. L., Ryan, L., Reminger, S., Hardt, O., Hayes, S. M., & Hupbach, A. (2004). A case of psychogenic fugue: I understand, aber ich verstehe nichts. *Neuropsychologia, 42,* 1132–47.

Glitz, D. A., & Balon, R. (1996). Serotonin-selective drugs in generalized anxiety disorder: Achievements and prospects. In H. G. Westenberg, J. A. Den Boer, & D. L. Murphy (Eds.), *Advances in the neurobiology of anxiety disorders* (pp. 335–58). Chichester, England: Wiley.

Glover, M. R. (1984). *The York Retreat: An early Quaker experiment in the treatment of mental illness.* York, England: William Sessions Ltd.

Goddard, A. W., Mason , G. F., Almai, A., Rothman, D. L., Behar, K. L., Petroff, O. et al. (2001). Reductions in occipital cortex GABA levels in panic disorder detected with superscript 1H-magnetic resonance spectroscopy. *Arch. Gen. Psychiat., 58*(6), 556–561.

Goddard, A. W., Mason, G. F., Rothman, D. L., Behar, K. L., Petroff, O., & Krystal, J. H. (2004). Family psychopathology and magnitude of reductions in occipital cortex GABA levels in panic disorder. *Neuropsychopharmacology, 29*(3), 639–640.

Goddard, A. W., Narayan, M., Woods, S. W., Germine, M., Gerald, L., Kramer, L. L. et al. (1996). Plasma levels of gamma-aminobutyric acid and panic disorder. *Psych. Res., 63*(2-3), 223–225.

Goff, D. C., & Coyle, J. T. (2001). The emerging role of glutamate in the pathophysiology and treatment of schizophrenia. *Amer. J. Psychiat., 158,* 1367–77.

Goffman, E. (1961). *Asylums.* New York: Doubleday.

Goin, R. P. (1998). Nocturnal enuresis in children. *Child: Care, Health, and Development, 24,* 277–88.

Gold, E. R. (1986). Long-term effects of sexual victimization in childhood: An attributional approach. *J. Cons. Clin. Psychol., 54,* 471–75.

Gold, P. E., Cahill, L., & Wenk, G. L. (2002). *Ginkgo biloba:* A cognitive enhancer? *Psychological Science in the Public Interest, 3*(1), 2–11.

Goldapple, K., Segal, Z., Garson, C., Lau, M., Bieling, P., Kennedy, S.,et al. (2004). Modulation of cortical-limbic pathways in major depression. *Arch. Gen. Psychiat., 61*(1), 34–41.

Golden, R. N., Gaynes, B. N., Ekstrom, R. D., Hamer, R. M., Jacobsen, F. M., Suppes, T., et al., (2005). The efficacy of light therapy in the treatment of mood disorders: A review and meta-analysis of the evidence. *Amer. J. Psychiat., 162*(4), 656–662.

Goldfein, J. A., Devlin, M. J., & Spitzer, R. L. (2000). Cognitive behavioral therapy for the treatment of binge eating disorder: What constitutes success? *Amer. J. Psychiat., 157*(7), 1051–56.

Golding, J. M., Cooper, M. L., & George, L. K. (1997). Sexual assault history and health perceptions: Seven general population studies. *Hlth. Psychol., 16*(5), 417–25.

Goldman, L. S., Genel, M., Bezman, R. J., & Slanetz, P. J. (1998). Diagnosis and treatment of attention-deficit/hyperactivity disorder in children and adolescents. *JAMA, 279*(14), 1100–07.

Goldman-Rakic, P. S., & Selemon, L. D. (1997). Functional and anatomical aspects of prefrontal pathology in schizophrenia. *Schizo. Bull., 23,* 437–58.

Goldney, R. D. (2003). Deinstitutionalization and suicide. *J. Crisis Int. Suicide Prev., 24,* 39–40.

Goldney, R. D. (2003). Deinstitutionalization and suicide. *J. Crisis. Int. Suicide Prev., 24,* 39–40.

Goldsmith, D. F., & Rogoff, B. (1997). Mother's and toddler's coordinated joint focus of attention: Variations with maternal dysphoric symptoms. *Develop. Psychol., 33,* 113–19.

Goldsmith, S. J., Anger, Friedfeld, K., Beren, S., & Rudolph, D. (1992). Psychiatric illness in patients presenting for obesity treatment. *Int. J. Eat. Dis., 12,* 63–71.

Goldsmith, W., & Cretekos, C. (1969). Unhappy odysseys: Psychiatric hospitalization among Vietnam returnees. *Amer. J. Psychiat., 20,* 78–83.

Goldstein, A. J., & Chambless, D. (1978). A reanalysis of agoraphobia. *Behav. Ther.,* 9, 47–59.

Goldstein, A., et al. (1974, Mar. 4). Researchers isolate opiate receptor. *Behav. Today, 5*(9), 1.

Goldstein, I., Lue, T. F., Padma-Nathan, H., Rosen, R. C., Steers, W. D., & Wicker, P. A. (1998). Oral sildenafil in the treatment of erectile dysfunction. *N. Engl. J. of Med., 338,* 20, 1397–1404.

Goldstein, S., & Goldstein, M. (1998). *Managing attention-deficit hyperactivity disorder in children: A guide for practitioners* (2nd ed.). New York: Wiley.

Golomb, M., Fava, M., Abraham, M., Rosenbaum, J. F. (1995). Gender differences in personality disorders. *Amer. J. Psychiat., 152*(4), 579–82.

Good, B. J., & Kleinman, A. M. (1985). Culture and anxiety: Cross-cultural evidence for the patterning of anxiety disorders. In A. H. Tuma & J. D. Master (Eds.), *Anxiety and the anxiety disorders.* Hillsdale, NJ: Erlbaum.

Goodlett, C. R., & Horn, K. H. (2001). Mechanisms of alcohol-induced damage to the developing nervous system. *Alcohol Research & Health, 25,* 175–84.

Goodman, S. H., & Gotlib, I. H. (1999). Risk for psychopathology in the children of depressed mothers: A developmental model for understanding mechanisms of transmission. *Psychol. Rev., 106,* 458–90.

Goodman, S. H., & Gotlib, I. H. (2002). *Children of depressed parents: Mechanisms of risk and implications for treatment.* Washington, DC: American Psychological Association.

Goodman, S. H. (2002). Depression and early adverse experiences. In I. H. Gotlib & C. L. Hammen (Eds.), *Handbook of depression* (pp. 245–67). New York: Guilford.

Goodman, W. K. (2004). Selecting pharmacotherapy for generalized anxiety disorder. *J. Clin. Psychiat., 65*(113), 8–13.

Goodwin, D. K. (1988). *The Fitzgeralds and the Kennedys: An American saga.* New York: St. Martin's Press.

Goodwin, D. W., Schulsinger, F., Hermansen, L., Guze, S. B., & Winokur, G. (1973). Alcohol problems in adoptees raised apart from alcoholic biological parents. *Arch. Gen. Psychiat., 28*(2), 238–43.

Goodwin, D. W., Schulsinger, F., Moller, N., Hermansen, L., Winokur, G., & Guze, S. B. (1974). Drinking problems in adopted and nonadopted sons of alcoholics. *Arch. Gen. Psychiat., 31*(2), 164–69.

Goodwin, F. K., & Jamison, K. R. (1990). *Manic-depressive illness.* New York: Oxford University Press.

Goodwin, F. K., Fireman, B., Simon, G. E., Hunkeler, E. M., Lee, J., & Revicki, D. (2003). Suicide risk in bipolar disorder during treatment with lithium and divalproex. *JAMA, 290*(11), 1467–1473.

Goodwin, F. K. (2003). Preventing inpatient suicide. *J. Clin. Psychiat., 64*(1), 12–13.

Goodwin, L. (1992). Alcohol and drug use in fraternities and sororities. *Journal of Alcohol and Drug Education, 37*(2), 52–63.

Goodwin, R. D., & Gotlib, I. H. (2004). Gender differences in depression: The role of personality factors. *Psychiat. Res., 126,* 135–142.

Goodwin, R. D., & Gotlib, I. H. (2004). Panic attacks and psychopathology among youth. *Acta Psychiatr. Scandin., 109*(3), 216–21.

Goodyer, I. (2000). Emotional disorders with their onset in childhood. In M. G. Gleder, J. J. Lopez-Ibor, Jr., & N. Andreason (Eds.), *New Oxford textbook of psychiatry* (pp. 1762–71). Oxford: Oxford University Press.

Goran, D. A., Fabiano, R. J., & Crewe, N. (1997). Employment following severe traumatic brain injury: The utility of the Individual Ability Profile System (IAP). *Arch. Clin. Neuropsychol., 12*(7), 691–98.

Gordis, E. (1997). Patient-treatment matching. *Alcohol Alert, 36,* 1–4.

Gordis, E. (2000). Contributions of behavioral science to alcohol research: Understanding who is at risk and why. *Experimental and Clinical Psychopharmacology, 8*(3), 264–70.

Gordis, E. (2001). Cognitive impairment and recovery from alcoholism. *Alcohol Alert.* National Institute on Alcohol Abuse and Alcoholism, No. 53, U.S. Department of Health and Human Services.

Gordis, E., Dufour, M. C., Warren, K. R., Jackson, R. J., Floyd, R. L., & Hungerford, D. W. (1995). Should physicians counsel patients to drink alcohol? *JAMA, 273,* 1–12.

Gordon, R. A. (2000). Eating disorders: Anatomy of a social epidemic (2nd ed.). London: Blackwell.

Gorenstein, E. E. (1992). *The science of mental illness.* San Diego: Academic Press.

Gorin, N. (1980). Looking out for Mrs. Berwid. *Sixty Minutes.* (Narrated by Morley Safer.) New York: CBS Television News.

Gorin, N. (1982). It didn't have to happen. *Sixty Minutes.* (Narrated by Morley Safer.) New York: CBS Television News.

Gorlick, D. A. (1993). Overview of pharmacologic treatment approaches for alcohol and other drug addictions. *Psychiat. Clin. N. Amer., 16,* 141–56.

Gorman, C. (2002). The death of an all-star. *Time,* July 8.

Gorman, J. M., & Coplan, J. D. (1996). Comorbidity of depression and panic disorder. *J. Clin. Psychiat., 57*(10), 34–41.

Gorman, J. M., Battista, D., Goetz, R. R., Dillon, D. J., Liebowitz, M. R., Fyer, A. J., Kahn, J. P., Sandberg, D., & Klein, D. F. (1989). A comparison of sodium bicarbonate and sodium lactate infusion in the induction of panic attacks. *Arch. Gen. Psychiat., 46,* 145–50.

Gorman, J. M., Kent, J. M., Sullivan, G. M., & Coplan, J. D. (2000). Neuroanatomical hypothesis of panic disorder, revised. *Amer. J. Psychiat., 157,* 493–505.

Gortner, E. T., Gollan, J. K., & Jacobson, N. S. (1997). Psychological aspects of perpetrators of domestic violence and their relationships with the victims. *Psychiat. Clin. N. Amer., 20*(2), 327–52.

Gospodinoff, M. L. (1989). Premature ejaculation: Clinical subgroups and etiology. *J. Sex Marit. Ther., 15,* 130–34.

Gossop, M., Harris, J., Best, D., Man, L., Manning, V., Marshall, J., & Strang, J. (2003). Is attendance at Alcoholics Anonymous meetings after inpatient treatment related to improved outcomes? A 6-month follow-up study. *Alcohol & Alcoholism, 38*(5), 421–26.

Gotlib, I. H., & Abramson, L. Y. (1999). Attributional theories of emotion. In T. Dalgleish & M. J. Power (Eds.), *Handbook of cognition and emotion* (pp. 613–36). Chichester, England: Wiley.

Gotlib, I. H., & Hammen, C. L. (1992). *Psychological aspects of depression: Toward a cognitive-interpersonal integration.* Chichester, UK: Wiley.

Gottesman, I. I., & Bertelson, A. (1989). Confirming unexpressed genotypes for schizophrenia: Risks in the offspring of Fischer's Danish identical and fraternal discordant twins. *Arch. Gen. Psychiat., 46,* 867–72.

Gottesman, I. I., & Hanson, D. R. (2005). Human development: Biological and genetic processes. *Annu. Rev. Psychol.,* 10–24.

Gottesman, I. I. (1991). *Schizophrenia genesis: The origins of madness.* New York: Freeman.

Gottesman, I. I. (2001). Psychopathology through a life span–genetic prism. *Amer. Psychol., 56,* 867–78.

Gottlieb, G. (1992). *Individual development and evolution: The genesis of novel behavior.* New York: Oxford University Press.

Götz, J., Chen, F., van Dorpe, J., & Nitsch, R. M. (2001). Formation of neurofibrillary tangles in P301L tau transgenic mice induced by A(42 fibrils. *Science, 293,* 1491–95.

Gould, L. N. (1949). Auditory hallucinations and subvocal speech. *J. Nerv. Ment. Dis., 109,* 418–27.

Gouvier, W. D., et al. (1997). Cognitive retraining with brain-damaged patients. In A. M. Horton, D. Wedding, & J. Webster (Eds.), *The neuropsychology handbook* (Vol. 2., pp. 3–46). New York: Springer.

Grady, K., Gersick, K. E., & Boratynski, M. (1985). Preparing parents for teenagers: A step in the prevention of adolescent substance abuse. *Family Relations Journal of Applied Family and Child Studies, 34*(4), 541–49.

Graham, J. E., Jones, L. M., & Kiecolt-Glaser, J. K. (in press). Marriage, health, and immune function: A review of key findings and the role of depression. In S. Beach (Ed.), *Relational processes and DSM-V.* Washington, DC: APPI Press.

Graham, J. R., Ben-Porath, Y. S., & McNulty, J. (1999). *Using the MMPI-2 in outpatient mental health settings.* Minneapolis: University of Minnesota Press.

Graham, P., Turk, J., & Verhulst, F. (1999). *Child psychiatry: A developmental approach.* London: Oxford University Press.

Granato, P., Weill, S., & Revillon, J. J. (1997). Ecstasy and dementia in a young subject. *European Psychiatry, 12*(7), 369–71.

Granfield, R. (2005). Alcohol use in college: Limitations on the transformation of social norms. *Addiction Research & Theory, 13*(3), 281–92.

Grant, B. F., & Dawson, D. A. (1997). Age at onset of alcohol use and its association with DSM–IV alcohol abuse and dependency: Results from the National Longitudinal Alcohol Epidemiologic Survey. *J. Subst. Abuse, 9,* 103–10.

Grant, B. F., Stinson, F. S., Dawson, D. A., Chou, P., Dufour, M., Compton, W., Pickering, R. P., & Kaplan, K. (2004). Prevalence and co-occurrence of substance use disorders and independent mood and anxiety disorders: Results from the national epidemiologic survey on alcohol and related conditions. *Arch. Gen. Psychiat., 61*(8), 807–16.

Grant, J. E., & Kim, S. W. (2003). Comorbidity of impulse control disorders in pathological gamblers. *Acta Psychiatr. Scandin., 108*(3), 203–7.

Grant, J. E., Kushner, M. G., & Kim, S. W. (2002). Pathological gambling and alcohol use disorder. *Alcohol Research & Health, 26,* 143–50.

Grant, S. J., & Sonti, G. (1994). Buprenorphine and morphine produce equivalent increases in extracellular single unit activity of dopamine neurons in the ventral tegmental area *in vivo. Synapse, 16,* 181–87.

Gray, F., Gherardi, R., & Scaravilli, F. (1988). The neuropathology of the acquired immune deficiency syndrome (AIDS). *Brain, 111,* 245–66.

Gray, J. A. (1987). *The psychology of fear and stress* (2nd ed.). New York: Cambridge University Press.

Gray, J. A., & McNaughton, N. (1996). The neuropsychology of anxiety: Reprise. In D. A. Hope (Ed.), *Nebraska Symposium on Motivation, 1995: Perspectives on anxiety, panic, and fear. Current theory and research in motivation* (Vol. 43., pp. 61–134). Lincoln: University of Nebraska Press.

Gray, M. J., Bolen, E., & Litz, B. T. (2004). A longitudincal analysis of PTSD symptome course: Delayed-onset in Somalia peacekeepers. *J. Cons. Clin. Psychol., 72,* 909–13.

Gray, M. J., Litz, B. T., Hsu, J. L., & Lombardo, T. W. (2004). Psychometric properties of the life events checklist. *Assessment, 11*(4), 330–41.

Gray-Little, B. (2002). The assessment of psychopathology in racial and ethnic minorities. In J. N. Butcher (Ed.), *Clinical personality assessment* (2nd ed., pp. 171–89). New York: Oxford University Press.

Green, B. L., Lindy, J. D., Grace, M. C., & Leonard, A. C. (1992). Chronic posttraumatic stress disorder and diagnostic comorbidity in a disaster sample. *J. Nerv. Ment. Dis., 180,* 760–66.

Green, M. F. (1997). *Schizophrenia from a neurocognitive perspective.* Needham Heights, MA: Allyn and Bacon.

Green, M. F. (2001). *Schizophrenia revealed: From neurons to social interactions.* New York: Norton.

Green, R. (1987). *The "sissy boy syndrome" and the development of homosexuality.* New Haven: Yale University Press.

Green, R. (1992). *Sexual science and the law.* Cambridge: Harvard University Press.

Green, R., & Fleming, D. (1990). Transsexual surgery followup: Status in the 1990's. In J. Bancroft, C. Davis, & H. Ruppel (Eds.), *Annual review of sex research.* Mt. Vernon, IA: Society for the Scientific Study of Sex.

Green, R. M. (1951). *Galen's hygiene.* Springfield, IL: Charles C. Thomas.

Greenberg, J. R., & Mitchell, S. (1983). *Object relations in psychoanalytic theory.* Cambridge, MA: Harvard University Press.

Greenberg, L. S. (2004). Emotion-focused therapy. *Clinical Psychology and Psychotherapy, 11,* 3–16.

Greenberg, P. E., Kessler, R. C., Birnbaum, H. G., Leong, S. A., Lowe, S. W., Berglund, P. A., et al. (2003). The economic burden of depression in the United States: How did it change between 1990 and 2000. *J. Clin. Psychiat., 64*(12), 1465–1469.

Greenberg, P. E., Sisitsky, T., Kessler, R. C., Finkelstein, S. N., Berndt, E. R., Davidson, J. R. T., Ballenger, J. C., & Fyer, A. J. (1999). The economic burden of anxiety disorders in the 1990s. *J. Clin. Psychiat., 60,* 427–35.

Greene, R. L., Robin, R. W., Albaugh, B., Caldwell, A., & Goldman, D. (2003). Use of the MMPI-2 in American Indians: II. Empirical correlates. *Psychol. Assess., 15*(3), 360–69.

Greenhill, L. L., & Waslick, B. (1997). Management of suicidal behavior in children and adolescents. *Psychiat. Clin. N. Amer., 20*(3), 641–66.

Greenough, W. T., & Black, J. E. (1992). Induction of brain structure by experience: Substrates for cognitive development. In M. R. Gunnar & C. A. Nelson (Eds.), *Minnesota Symposia on Child Psychology: Developmental Neuroscience* (Vol. 24., pp. 155–200). Hillsdale, NJ: Erlbaum.

Gregg, C., & Hoy, C. (1989). Coherence: The comprehension and production abilities of college writers who are normally achieving, learning disabled, and underprepared. *J. Learn. Dis., 22,* 370–72.

Grekin, E. R., Brennan, P. A., & Hammen, C. (2005). Parental alcohol use disorders and child delinquency: The mediating effects of executive functioning and chronic family stress. *J. Stud. Alcoh., 66*(1), 14–22.

Greve, W., & Strobl, R. (2004). Social and individual coping with threats: Outlines of an interdisciplinary approach. *Rev. Gen. Psychol., 8,* 194–207.

Grice, D. E., Halmi, K. A., Fichter, M. M., Strober, M., Woodside, D. B., Treasure, J. T., Kaplan, A. S., Magistretti, P. J., Goldman, D., Bulik, C. M., Jaye, W. H., & Berrettini, W. H. (2002). Evidence for a susceptibility gene for anorexia nervosa on chromosome 1. *American Journal of Human Genetics, 70*(3), 787–92.

Griesinger, W. (1845). *The Pathology and Therapy of Psychic Disorders,* Stuttgart: Krabbe.

Griffiths, M. (2003). Internet gambling: Issues, concerns, and recommendations. *Cyber Psychology & Behavior, 6*(6), 557–68.

Grilo, C. M. (2002). Binge eating disorder. In C. G. Fairburn & K. D. Brownell (Eds.), *Eating disorders and obesity: A comprehensive handbook* (2nd ed., pp. 178–82). New York: Guilford.

Grilo, C. M., Becker, D. F., Fehon, D. C., Edell, W. S., & McGlashan, T. H. (1996). Conduct disorder, substance use disorders, and coexisting conduct and substance use disorders in adolescent inpatients. *Amer. J. Psychiat., 153*(7), 914–20.

Grimes, K., & Walker, E. F. (1994). Childhood emotional expressions, educational attainment, and age at onset of illness in schizophrenia. *J. Abn. Psychol., 103*(4), 784–90.

Grisso, T., & Tomkins, A. J. (1996). Communicating violence risk assessments. *Amer. Psychol., 51*(9), 928–30.

Grob, C. S. (2000). Deconstructing ecstasy: The politics of MDMA research. *Addiction Research, 8*(6), 549–88.

Grob, G. N. (1994). Mad, homeless, and unwanted: A history of the care of the chronically mentally ill in America. *Psychiat. Clin. N. Amer., 17*(3), 541–58.

Grodin, M., & Laurie, G. T. (2000). Susceptibility genes and neurological disorders: Learning the right lessons from the Human Genome Project. *Arch. Neurol., 57,* 1569–74.

Gross, R., Sasson, Y., Chopra, M., & Zohar, J. (1998). Biological models of obsessive-compulsive disorder: The serotonin hypothesis. In R. P. Swinson, M. M. Antony, et al. (Eds.) *Obsessive-compulsive disorder: Theory, research, and treatment.* (pp. 141–153). New York: Guilford Press.

Grounds, A. (2000). The psychiatrist in court. In M. G. Gelder, J. J. Lopez-Ibor, Jr., & N. C. Andreason (Eds.), *New Oxford textbook of psychiatry* (pp. 2089–96). Oxford: Oxford University Press.

Grove, W. M., Zald, D. H., Lebow, B., Snitz, E., & Nelson, C. (2000). Clinical versus mechanical prediction: A meta-analysis. *Psychol. Assess., 12,* 19–30.

Groza, V., Maschmeier, C., Jamison, C., & Piccola, T. (2003). Siblings and out-of-home placement: Best practices. *Families in Society, 84*(4), 480–90.

Grundy, S. M., D'Agostino, R. B., Mosca, L., Burke, G. L., Wilson, P. W. F., Daniel, D. R., Cleeman, J. I., Roccella, E. J., Cutler, J. A., Friedmahn, L. M. (2001). Cardiovascular risk assessment based on US cohort studies. Findings from a National Heart, Lung and Blood Institute workshop. *Circulation, 104,* 491–496.

Grzywacz, J.G. & Dooley, D. (2003). "Good jobs" to "bad jobs": replicated evidence of an employment continuum from two large surveys. *Soc. Sci. Med., 56,* 1749–1760.

Guelfi, G. P., Faustman, W. O., & Csernansky, J. G. (1989). Independence of positive and negative symptoms in a population of schizophrenic patients. *J. Nerv. Ment. Dis., 177,* 285–90.

Guerje, O., Simon, G. E., Ustun, T. B., & Goldberg, D. B. (1997). Somatization in cross-cultural perspective: A World Health Organization study in primary care. *Amer. J. Psychiat., 154,* 989–95.

Guerra, F. (1971). *The pre-Columbian mind.* New York: Seminar Press.

Gull, W. (1888). Anorexia nervosa. *Lancet, i,* 516–17.

Gunderson, J. G., Zanarini, M. C., Kisiel, C. L. (1995). Borderline personality disorder. In W. J. Livesley (Ed.), *The DSM-IV personality disorders.* (pp. 141–157). New York: Guilford.

Gunn, J. (1993). Castration is not the answer. *Brit. Med. J., 307,* 790–91.

Gunnar, M. R., Broderson, L., Kreuger, K., & Rigatuso, J. (1996). Dampening of adrenocortical responses during infancy: Normative changes and individual differences. *Child Develop., 67,* 877–89.

Gunnar, M. R., Morison, S. J., Chisholm, K., & Schuder, M. (2001). Salivary cortisol levels in children adopted from Romanian orphanages. *Develop. Psychopath., 13,* 611–28.

Gupta, J. C., Deb, A. K., & Kahali, B. S. (1943). Preliminary observations on the use of Rauwolfia perpentina berth in the treatment of mental disorder. *Indian Medical Gazette, 78,* 547–49.

Gur, R. E., & Pearlson, G. D. (1993). Neuroimaging in schizophrenia research. *Schizo. Bull., 19*(2), 337–53.

Guze, S. B., Cloninger, C. R., Martin, R. L., & Clayton, P. J. (1986). A follow-up and family study of Briquet's Syndrome. *Brit. J. Psychiat., 149,* 17–23.

Haaga, D. A. F., Dyck, M. J., & Ernst, D. (1991). Empirical status of cognitive theory of depression. *Psychol. Bull., 110*(2), 215–36.

Haaga, D. A., & Davison, G. C. (1989). Outcome studies of rational-emotive therapy. In M. Bernard & R. DeGiuseppe (Eds.), *Inside rationale-motive therapy.* New York: Academic Press.

Haaga, D. A., & Davison, G. C. (1992). Disappearing differences do not always reflect healthy integration: An analysis of cognitive therapy and rational-emotive therapy. *Journal of Psychotherapy Integration, 1,* 287–303.

Haas, G. (1997). Suicidal behavior in schizophrenia. In R. W. Maris, M. M. Silverman, & S. S. Canetton (Eds.), *Review of Suicidology, 1997* (pp. 202–35). New York: Guilford.

Haber, S. N., & Fudge, J. L. (1997). The interface between dopamine neurons and the amygdala: Implications for schizophrenia. *Schizo. Bull., 23*(3), 471–82.

Hackmann, A., Clark, D. M., McManus, F. (2000). Recurrent images and early memories in social phobia. *Behav. Res. Ther.,* 38, 601–10.

Hafen, B. Q., Karren, K. J., Frandsen, K. J., & Smith, N. L. (1996). *Mind/body health: The effects of attitudes, emotions, and relationships.* Needham Heights, MA: Allyn and Bacon.

Haffner, H., et al. (1998). Causes and consequences of the gender difference in age at onset of schizophrenia. *Schizo. Bull., 24*(1), 99–114.

Halcón, L., Robertson, C. L., Savik, K., Johnson, D. R., Spring, M. A., Butcher, J. N., Westermeyer, J. J., & Jaranson, J. M. (2004). Trauma and coping in Somali and Oromo refugee youth. *J. Adol. Hlth., 35,* 17–25.

Haldane, M., & Frangou, S. (2004). New insights help define the pathophysiology of bipolar affective disorder: Neuroimaging and neuropathology findings. *Prog. Neuropsychopharmacol. Biol. Psychiatry, 28,* 943–960.

Hall, D. E., Eubanks, L., Meyyazhagan, S., Kenney, R. D., & Johnson, S. C. (2000). Evaluation of covert video surveillance in the diagnosis of Munchausen syndrome by proxy: Lessons from 41 cases. *Pediatrics, 105*(6), 1305–11.

Hall, G. (1994). Pavlovian conditioning: Laws of association. In N. J. Mackintosh (Ed.), *Animal learning and cognition* (pp. 15–43). San Diego, CA: Academic Press.

Hall, G. C., Bansal, A., & Lopez, I. R. (1999). Ethnicity and psychopathology: A meta-analytic review of 31 years of comparative MMPI/MMPI-2 research. *Psychological Assess., 11,* 186–97.

Hall, J., Harris, J. M., Sprengelmeyer, R., Sprengelmeyer, A., Young, A. W., Santos, I. M., Johnstone, E. C., & Lawrie, S. M. (2004). Social cognition and face processing in schizophrenia. *Brit. J. Psychiat., 185,* 169–170.

Hallett, J. D., Zasler, N. D., Maurer, P., & Cash, S. (1994). Role change after traumatic brain injury in adults. *Amer. J. Occup. Ther., 48*(3), 241–46.

Halmi, K. A., et al. (1991). Comorbidity of psychiatric diagnoses in anorexia nervosa. *Arch. Gen. Psychiat., 48,* 712–18.

Halmi, K. A., Sunday, S., R., Strober, M., Kaplan, A., Woodside, D. B., Fichter, M., Treasure, J., Berrettini, W. H., & Kaye, W. H. (2000). Perfectionism in anorexia nervosa: Variation by clinical subtype, obsessionality, and pathological eating behavior. *Amer. J. Psychiat., 157*(11), 1799–805.

Hamer, D. H., Hu, S., Magnuson, V. L., Hu, N., & Pattatucci, A. M. L. (1993). A linkage between DNA markers on the X chromosome and male sexual orientation. *Science, 261,* 321–27.

Hamerman, S., & Ludwig, S. (2000). Emotional abuse and neglect. In R. M. Reece (Ed.), *Treatment of child abuse: Common ground for mental health* (pp. 201–10). Baltimore: Johns Hopkins University Press.

Hammen, C. L. (1991). Generation of stress in the course of unipolar depression. *J. Abn. Psychol., 100,* 555–61.

Hammen, C. L. (1995). Stress and the course of unipolar disorders. In C. M. Mazure (Ed.), *Does stress cause psychiatric illness?* Washington, DC: American Psychiatric Press.

Hammen, C., & Gitlin, M. (1997). Stress reactivity in bipolar patients and its relation to prior history of disorder. *Amer. J. Psychiat., 154*(6), 856–57.

Hammen, C., & Rudolph, K. D. (1996). Childhood depression. In E. J. Mash & R. A. Barkley (Eds.), *Childhood psychopathology* (pp. 153–94). New York: Guilford.

Hammen, C., Shih, J. H., & Brennan, P. A. (2004). Intergenerational transmission of depression: Test of an interpersonal stress model in a community sample. *J. Cons. Clin. Psychol., 72,* 511–22.

Hammen, C. (2002). Context of stress in families of children with depressed parents. In S. H. Goodman & I. H. Gotlib (Eds.), *Children of depressed parents: Mechanisms of risk and implications for treatment* (pp. 175–99). Washington, DC: American Psychological Association.

Hammen, C. (2005). Stress and Depression. In *Annual Review of Clinical Psychology, Volume 1.* (P's 293–319). Annual Reviews: Palo Alto, CA.

Hammer, M. B., Robert, S., & Frueh, B. C. (2004). Treatment-resistant posttraumatic stress disorder: Strategies for intervention. *CNS Spectrums, 9*(10), 740–52.

Hamrick, N., Cohen, S., & Rodriguez, M. S. (2002). Being popular can be healthy or unhealthy: Stress, social network diversity, and the incidence of upper respiratory infection. *Hlth. Psychol., 21*(3), 294–98.

Hance, M., Carney, R., Freedland, K., & Skala, J. (1996). Depression in patients with coronary heart disease: A 12 month follow-up. *Gen. Hosp. Psychiat., 18,* 61–65.

Handleman, J. S., Gill, M. J., & Alessandri, M. (1988). Generalization by severely developmentally disabled children: Issues, advances, and future directions. *The Behavior Therapist, 11,* 221–23.

Haney, B., & Gold, M. (1973). The juvenile delinquent nobody knows. *Psych. Today, 7*(4), 48–52, 55.

Hankin, B. L., & Abramson, L. Y. (2001). Development of gender differences in depression: An elaborated cognitive vulnerability-transactional stress theory. *Psychol. Bull., 127,* 773–96.

Hankin, B. L., Abramson, L. Y., Miller, N., & Haeffel, G. J. (2004). Cognitive vulnerability-stress theories of depression: Examining affective specificity in the prediction of depression versus anxiety in threeprospective stuides. *Cog. Ther. & Res., 28*(3), 309–345.

Hankin, B. L., Abramson, L. Y., Moffitt, T. E., Silva, P. A., McGee, R., & Angell, K. E. (1998). Development of depression from preadolescence to young adulthood: Emerging gender differences in a 10-year longitudinal study. *J. Abn. Psychol., 107*(1), 128–40.

Hanna, G. L. (2000). Clinical and family-genetic studies of childhood obsessive-compulsive disorder. In W. K. Goodman, M. V. Rudorfer, et al. (Eds.), *Obsessive-compulsive disorder: Contemporary issues in treatment. Personality and clinical psychology series* (pp. 87–103). Mahwah, NJ: Erlbaum.

Hannigan, J. H. (1996). What research with animals is telling us about alcohol-related neurodevelopmental disorder. *Pharmacology, Biochemistry & Behavior, 55*(4), 489–500.

Hanson, R. K., Gordon, A., Harris, A. J., Marques, J. K., Murphy, W., Quinsey, V. L., et al. (2002). First report of the collaborative outcome data project on the effectiveness of psychological treatment for sex offenders. *Sexual Abuse: Journal of Research & Treatment, 14,* 169–94.

Hanson, R. (2002). Recidivism and age: Follow-up data from 4,673 sexual offenders. *J. Interpers. Violen., 17,* 1046–62.

Happe, F., & Frith, U. (1996). Theory of mind and social impairment in children with conduct disorder. *Brit. J. Develop. Psychol., 14,* 385–98.

Hardy, J. (2004). Toward Alzheimer therapies based on genetic knowledge. *Annu. Rev. Med., 55,* 15–25.

Hare, E. H. (1962). Masturbatory insanity: The history of an idea. *J. Ment. Sci., 108,* 1–25.

Hare, R. D., Cooke, D. J., & Hart, S. D. (1999). Psychopathy and sadistic personality disorder. In T. Millon, P. H. Blaney, & R. D. Davis (Eds.), *Oxford textbook of psychopathology* (pp. 555–84). New York: Oxford University Press.

Hare, R. D., McPherson, L. M., & Forth, A. E. (1988). Male psychopaths and their criminal careers. *J. Cons. Clin. Psychology, 56,* 710–14.

Hare, R. D. (1970). *Psychopathy: theory and research.* New York: Wiley.

Hare, R. D. (1980). A research scale for the assessment of psychopathy in criminal populations. *Personal. Indiv. Diff., 1,* 111–19.

Hare, R. D. (1991). *The Hare psychopathy checklist—Revised.* Toronto: Multi-Health systems.

Hare, R. D. (1998b). Psychopathy, affect and behavior. In D. J. Cooke, A. E. Forth, & R. D. Hare (Eds.), *Psychopathy: Theory, research, and implications for society.* (pp. 105–37). Dordrecht, Netherlands: Kluwer Academic Publishers.

Harlow, J. M. (1868). Recovery from the passage of an iron bar through the head. *Publication of the Massachusetts Medical Society, 2,* 327.

Harper, C., Dixon, G., Sheedy, D., & Garrick, T. (2003). Neuropathological alterations in alcoholic brains. Studies arising from the New South Wales Tissue Resource Centre. *Prog. Neuropsychopharmacol. Biol. Psychiatry, 27,* 951–61.

Harpur, T. J., Hart, S. D., & Hare, R. D. (1993). The personality of the psychopath. In P. T. Costa & T. A. Widiger (Eds.), *Personality disorders and the five-factor model of personality* (pp. 149–73). Washington, DC: American Psychological Association.

Harrington, R., & Clark, A. (1998). Prevention and early intervention for depression in adolescence and early adult life. *Eur. Arch. Psychiat. Clin. Neurosci., 248*(1), 32–45.

Harrington, R., Rutter, M., & Fombonne, E. (1996). Developmental pathways in depression: Multiple meanings, antecedents, and end points. *Develop. Psychopath., 8,* 601–16.

Harris, B. (1979). Whatever happened to Little Albert? *American Psychologist, 34,* 151–60.

Harris, T., Brown, G. W., & Bifulco, A. (1986). Loss of parent in childhood and adult psychiatric disorder: The role of lack of adequate parental care. *Psychol. Med., 16,* 641–59.

Harrison, G., Amin, S., Singh, S. P., Croudace, T., & Jones, P. (1999). Outcome of psychosis in people of Afro-Caribbean family origin. *Brit. J. Psychiat., 175,* 43–49.

Harrison, G., Glazebrook, C., Brewin, J., & Cantwell, R. (1997). Increased incidence of psychotic disorders in migrants from the Caribbean to the United Kingdom. *Psychol. Med., 27*(4), 799–806.

Harrison, G., Hopper, K., Craig, T., Laska, E., Siegel, C., Wanderling, J., Dube, K. C., Ganev, K., Giel, R., An Der Heiden, W., Holmberg, S. K., Janca, A., Lee, P. W. H., León, C. A., Malhotra, S., Marsella, A. J., Nakane, Y., Sartorius, N., Shen, Y., Skoda, C., Thara, R., Tsirkin, S. J., Varma, V. K., Walsh, D., & Wiersma, D. (2001). Recovery from psychotic illness: A 15- and 25-year international follow-up study. *Brit. J. Psychiat., 178,* 506–17.

Harrison, P. J., & Owen, M. J. (2003, Feb. 1). Genes for schizophrenia? Recent findings and their neuropathological implications. *Lancet, 361,* 417–19.

Harrow, M., Grossman, L. S., Herbener, E. S., & Davies, E. W. (2000). Ten-year outcome: patients with schizoaffective disorders, schizophrenia, affective disorders and mood-incongruent psychotic symptoms. *Brit. J. Psychiat., 177,* 421–26.

Hartmann, D. P., Barrios, B. A., & Wood, D. D. (2004). Principles of behavioral observation. *Comprehensive handbook of psychological assessment* (Vol. 3, pp. 108–27). New York: John Wiley & Sons.

Harvey, A. G., Schmidt, D. A., Scarna, A., Semler, C. N., & Goodwin, G. M. (2005). Sleep-related functioning in euthymic patients with bipolar disorder, patients with insomnia, and subjects without sleep problems. *Amer. J. Psychiat., 162,* 50–57.

Harwood, T. M., Beutler, L. E., Fisher, D., Sandowicz, M., Albanese, A. L., & Baker, M. (1997). Clinical decision making in managed health care. In J. N. Butcher (Ed.), *Personality assessment in managed health care: Using the MMPI-2 in treatment planning* (pp. 15–41). New York: Oxford University Press.

Hasegawa, S., et al. (1997). Physical aging in persons with Down syndrome: Bases on external appearance and diseases. *Japanese Journal of Special Education, 35*(2), 43–49.

Hasler, G., Drevets, W. C., Manji, H. K., & Charney, D. S. (2004). Discovering endophenotypes for major depression. *Neuropsychopharmacology, 29*(10), 1765–1781.

Hatta, S. M. (1996). A Malay cross cultural worldview and forensic review of amok. *Austral. NZ J. Psychiat., 30,* 505–10.

Hauff, E., & Vaglum, P. (1994). Chronic posttraumatic stress disorder in Vietnamese refugees. *J. Nerv. Ment. Dis., 182,* 85–90.

Haug Schnabel, G. (1992). Daytime and nighttime enuresis: A functional disorder and its ethological decoding. *Behaviour, 120,* 232–61.

Haugland, G., Sigel, G., Hopper, K., & Alexander, M. J. (1997). Mental illness among homeless individuals in a suburban county. *Psychiat. Serv., 48*(4), 504–9.

Hawkins, E. H., Cummins, L. H., & Marlatt, G. A. (2004). Preventing substance abuse in American Indian and Alaska Native youth: Promising strategies for healthier communities. *Psychol. Bull., 130,* 304–23.

Hawton, K., & Williams, K. (2002). Influences of the media on suicide. *Brit. Med. J., 325,* 1374–1375.

Hayden, M. F. (1998). Civil rights litigation for institutionalized persons with mental retardation: A summary. *Mental Retardation, 36*(1), 75–83.

Hayes, S. C. (1998). Single case experimental design and empirical clinical practice. In A. E. Kazdin (Ed.), *Methodological issues and strategies in clinical research* (pp. 419–49). Washington, DC: American Psychological Association.

Haynes, S. N. (2001). Clinical applications of analogue behavioral observation dimensions of psychometric evaluation. *Psychol. Assess., 13*(1), 73–85.

Hays, J. T., Hurt, R. D., Rigotti, N. A., Niaura, R., Gonzales, D., Durcan, M. J., Sachs, D. P. L., Wolter, R. D., Buist, A. S., Johnston, J. A., & White, J. D. (2001). Sustained-release bupropion for pharmacologic relapse prevention after smoking cessation. *Ann. Int. Med., 135*(6), 423–33.

Hayward, C., Killen, J. D., Kraemer, H. C., & Taylor, C. B. (1998). Linking self-reported childhood behavioral inhibition to adolescent social phobia. *J. Amer. Acad. Child Adoles. Psychiat., 37,* 1308–16.

Hayward, C., Killen, J. D., Kraemer, H. C., & Taylor, C. B. (2000). Predictors of panic attacks in adolescents. *J. Amer. Acad. Child Adoles. Psychiat., 39*(2), 207–14.

Hayward, C. (2003). Methodological concerns in puberty-related research. In C. Hayward (Ed.), *Gender differences at puberty* (pp. 1–14). New York: Cambridge University Press.

Hayward, P., & Wardle, J. (1997). The use of medication in the treatment of phobias. In G. C. L. Davey, (Ed.), *Phobias. A handbook of theory, research and treatment* (pp. 281–98). Chichester, England: Wiley.

Hazelrigg, M., Cooper, H., & Borduin, C. (1987). Evaluating the effectiveness of family therapies: An integrative review and analysis. *Psychol. Bull., 101,* 428–42.

Heather, J. (1995). The great controlled drinking consensus. Is it premature? *Addiction, 90*(9), 1160–63.

Heatherton, T. F., Mahamedi, F., Striepe, M., Field, A. E., & Keel, P. (1997). A 10-year longitudinal study of body weight, dieting, and eating disorder symptoms. *J. Abn. Psychol., 106*(1), 117–25.

Heaton, R. K., Gladsjo, J. A., Palmer, B. W., Kuck, J., Marcotte, T. D., & Jeste, D. V. (2001). Stability and course of neuropsychological deficits in schizophrenia. *Arch. Gen. Psychiat., 58,* 24–32.

Heaton, R., Paulsen, J. S., McAdams, L. A., Kuck, J., Zisook, S., Braff, D., Harris, M. J., & Jesta, D. V. (1994). Neuropsychological deficits in schizophrenics: Relationship to age, chronicity, and dementia. *Arch. Gen. Psychiat., 51*(6), 469–76.

Hechtman, L. (1996). Attention-deficit hyperactivity disorder. In L. Hechtman (Ed.), *Do they grow out of it?* (pp. 17–38). Washington, DC: American Psychiatric Press.

Heck, A. M., Yankovski, J. A., & Calis, K. A. (2000). Orlistat, a new lipase inhibitor for the management of obesity. *Phamacotherapy, 20,* 270–79.

Hefez, A. (1985). The role of the press and the medical community in the epidemic of "mysterious gas poisoning" in the Jordan West Bank. *Amer. J. Psychiat., 142,* 833–37.

Heilbrun, K. (1997). Prediction versus management models relevant to risk assessment: The importance of legal decision-making context. *Law and Human Behavior, 21*(4), 347–59.

Heim, C., & Nemeroff, C. B. (2001). The role of childhood trauma in the neurobiology of mood and anxiety disorders: Preclinical and clinical studies. *Biol. Psychiat., 49*(12), 1023–39.

Heim, C., Newport, J., Heit, S., Graham, Y., Wilcox, M., Bonsall, R., Miller, A., & Nemeroff, C. (2000). Pituitary-adrenal and autonomic responses to stress in women after sexual and physical abuse in childhood. *JAMA,* 284, 592–96.

Heiman, J. R. (1980). Female sexual response patterns. Interactions of physiological, affective, and contextual cues. *Arch. Gen. Psychiat., 37,* 1311–16.

Heiman, J. R., & Meston, C. M. (1997). Empirically validated treatment for sexual dysfunction. *Annu. Rev. Sex Res., 8,* 148–94.

Heimberg, R. G. (2002). Cognitive-behavioral therapy for social anxiety disorder: Current status and future directions. *Biol. Psychiat., 51,* 101–8.

Heinrichs, R. W. (2001). *In search of madness: Schizophrenia and neuroscience.* New York: Oxford University Press.

Helgeson, V. C. (2002). *The psychology of gender.* NJ: Pearson.

Heller, K. (1996). Coming of age of prevention science: Comments on the 1994 National Institute of Mental Health–Institute of Medicine Prevention Reports. *Amer. Psychol., 51*(11), 1123–27.

Heller, T., Miller, A. B., & Factor, A. (1997). Adults with mental retardation as supports to their parents: Effects on parental caregiving appraisal. *Mental Retardation, 35*(5), 338–46.

Helsing, K., Szklo, M., & Comstock, G. (1981). Factors associated with mortality after widowhood. *Amer. J. Pub. Hlth., 71,* 802–09.

Helzer, J. E., Canino, G. J., Yeh, E. K., Bland, R., et al. (1990). Alcoholism—North America and Asia: A comparison of population surveys with the Diagnostic Interview Schedule. *Arch. Gen. Psychiat., 47*(4), 313–19.

Hemphill, J. F., Templeman, T., Wong, S., & Hare, R. D. (1998). Psychopathy and crime: Recidivism and criminal careers. In D. J. Cooke, A. E. Forth, & R. D. Hare (Eds.), *Psychopathy: Theory, research, and implications for society* (pp. 375–99). Dordrecht, Netherlands: Kluwer Academic Publishers.

Hendricks, P. S., & Thompson, J. K. (2005). An integration of cognitive-behavioral therapy and interpersonal therapy for bulimia nervosa: A case study using the case formulation method. *Int. J. Eat. Dis., 37,* 171–74.

Hendrie, H. C. (1998). Epidemiology of dementia and Alzheimer's disease. *Amer. J. Geriat. Psychiat., 6,* 3–18.

Henriques, J. B., & Davidson, R. J. (1990). Regional brain electrical asymmetries discriminate between previously depressed and healthy control subjects. *J. Abn. Psychol., 99,* 22–31.

Henry, W. P., Strupp, H. H., Schacht, T. E., & Gaston, L. (1994). Psychodynamic approaches. In A. E. Bergin & S. L. Garfield (Eds.), *Handbook of psychotherapy and behavior change* (4th ed., pp. 467–508). New York: Wiley.

Henshaw, C., Foreman, D., & Cox, J. (2004). Postnatal blues: A risk factor for postnatal depression. *J. Psychosom. Obst. Gyn., 25*(3–4), 267–272.

Herbert, P. B. (2002). The duty to warn: A reconsideration and critique. *J. Amer. Acad. Psychiat. Law, 30*(3), 417–24.

Herbert, T. B., & Cohen, S. (1993). Depression and immunity: A meta-analytic review. *Psychol. Bull., 113*(3), 472–86.

Herbst-Damm, K. L., & Kulik, J. A. (2005). Volunteer support, marital status, and the survival times of terminally ill patients. *Hlth. Psychol., 24,* 2, 225–28.

Herdt, G., & Stoller, R. G. (1990). *Intimate communications: Erotics and the study of a culture.* New York: Columbia University Press.

Herman, J. L. (1993, March/April). The abuses of memory. *Mother Jones, 18,* 3–4.

Hermann, D. H. J. (1990). Autonomy, self determination, the right of involuntarily committed persons to refuse treatment, and the use of substituted judgment in medication decisions involving incompetent persons. *International Journal of Law and Psychiatry, 13,* 361–85.

Herman-Stahl, M., & Peterson, A. C. (1999). Depressive symptoms during adolescence: Direct and stress-buffering effects of coping, control beliefs, and family relationships. *Journal of Applied Developmental Psychology, 120,* 45–62.

Hermens, D. F., Williams, L. M., Lazzaro, I., Whitmont, S., Melkonian, D., & Gordon, E. (2004). Sex differences in adult ADHD: A double dissociation in brain activity and autonomic arousal. *Biological Psychology, 66*(3), 221–33.

Herrell, R., Goldberg, J., True, W. R., Ramakrishnan, V., Lyons, M., Eisen, S., et al. (1999). Sexual orientation and suicidality: A co-twin control study in adult men. *Arch. Gen. Psychiat., 56,* 867–74.

Herrmann-Lingen, C., Klemme, H., & Meyer, T. (2001). Depressed mood, physicianrated prognosis, and comorbidity as independent predictors of 1-year mortality in consecutive medical inpatients. *J. Psychosom. Res., 50,* 295–301.

Herzog, D. B., Greenwood, D. N., Dorer, D. J., Flores, A. T., Ekeblad, E. R., Richards, A., Blais, M. A., & Keller, M. B. (2000). Mortality in eating disorders: A descriptive study. *Int. J. Eat. Dis., 28,* 20–26.

Heshka, S., Greenway, F., Anderson, J. W., Atkinson, R. L., Hill, J. O., Phinney, S. D., Miller-Kovach, K., & Pi-Sunyer, F. X. (2000). Self-help weight loss versus a structured commercial program after 26 weeks: A randomized controlled study. *American Journal of Medicine, 109,* 282–87.

Hesketh, T., Ding, Q. J., & Jenkins, R. (2002). Suicide ideation in Chinese adolescents. *Soc. Psychiat. & Psychiatr. Epidemiol., 37*(5), 230–235.

Hesselbrock, M. N., Easton, C., Bucholz, K. K., Schuckit, M., & Hesselbrock, V. (1999). A validity study of the SSAGA-a comparison with the SCAN. *Addiction, 49,* 1361–70.

Hester, R. K., & Delaney, H. D. (1997). Behavioral self-control program for Windows: Results of a controlled clinical trial. *J. Cons. Clin. Psychol., 65*(4), 686–93.

Heston, L. (1966). Psychiatric disorders in foster home reared children of schizophrenic mothers. *Brit. J. Psychiat., 112,* 819–25.

Hetherington, E. M., & Parke, R. D. (1993). *Child psychology: A contemporary viewpoint* (4th ed.). New York: McGraw Hill.

Hetherington, E. M., Bridges, M., & Insabella, G. (1998) What matters? What does not? Five perspectives on the association between marital transitions and children's adjustment. *Amer. Psychol., 53,* 167–84.

Hetherington, E. M., Stanley-Hagan, M., & Anderson, E. R. (1989). Marital transitions: A child's perspective. *Amer. Psychol., 44,* 303–12.

Hetherington, E. M. (1991). The role of individual differences and family relationships in children's coping with divorce and remarriage. In P. S. Cowan & E. M. Hetherington (Eds.), *Family transitions* (pp. 165–94). Hillsdale, NJ: Erlbaum.

Hetherington, E. M. (1998). Relevant issues in developmental science: Introduction to the special series. *Amer. Psychol., 53*(2), 93–5.

Hetherington, E. M. (1999). *Coping with divorce, single patenting, and remarriage: A risk and resilience perspective.* Mahwah, NJ: Lawrence Erlbaum Associates.

Hetherington, E. M. (2003). Intimate pathways: Changing patterns in close personal relationships across time. *Family Relations: Interdisciplinary Journal of Applied Family Studies, 52*(4), 318–331.

Hetherington, E. M. (2003). Social support and the adjustment of children in divorced and remarried families. *Childhood: A Global Journal of Child Research, 10*(2), 217–236.

Hettema, J. M., Neale, M. C., & Kendler, K. S. (1995). Physical similarity and the equal-environment assumption in twin studies of psychiatric disorders. *Behav. Gen., 25*(4), 327–35.

Hettema, J. M., Neale, M. C., & Kendler, K. S. (2001). A review and meta-analysis of the genetic epidemiology of anxiety disorders. *Amer. J. Psych., 158*(10), 1568–1578.

Hettema, J. M., Prescott, C. A., & Kendler, K. S. (2001). A population-based twin study of generalized anxiety disorder in men and women. *J. Nerv. Ment. Dis., 189,* 413–20.

Hettema, J. M., Prescott, C. A., & Kendler, K. S. (2004). Genetic and environmental sources of covariation between generalized anxiety disorder and neuroticism. *Amer. J. Psych., 161*(9), 1581–1587.

Hettema, J., Steele, J., & Miller, W. R. (2005). Motivational Interviewing. *Annu. Rev. Clin. Psychol., 1,* 91–111.

HEW. (1978). *The third report on alcohol and health.* United States Department of Public Health. Washington, DC: U.S. Government Printing Office.

Heyman, A., Wilkinson, W. E., Hurwitz, B. J., Helms, M. J., et al. (1987). Early-onset Alzheimer's disease: Clinical predictors of institutionalization and death. *Neurology, 37,* 980–84.

Heyman, A., Wilkinson, W. E., Stafford, J. A., Helms, M. J., Sigmon, A. H., & Weinberg, T. (1984). Alzheimer's disease: A study of epidemiological aspects. *Ann. Neurol., 15,* 335–41.

Heymsfield, S. B., Allison, D. B., Heshka, S., & Pierson, R. N. (1995). Assessment of human body composition. In D. B. Allison et al. (Eds.), *Handbook of assessment methods for eating behaviors and weight-related problems: Measures, theory, research* (pp. 515–60). Thousand Oaks, CA: Sage.

Hibbard, S. (2003). A critique of Lilienfeld et al.'s "The scientific status of projective techniques." *J. Pers. Assess., 80,* 260–71.

Hibell, B., Anderson, B., Ahlstrom, S., Balakireva, O., Bjaranson, T., Kokkevi, A., & Morgan, M. (2000). *The 1999 ESPAD Report: Alcohol and other drugs among students in 30 European countries.* Stockholm: Swedish Council for Information on Alcohol and Drug Abuse.

Higgins, J. W., Williams, R. L., & McLaughlin, T. F. (2001). The effects of a token economy employing instructional consequences for a third-grade student with learning disabilities: A data-based case study. *Education and Treatment of Children, 24,* 99–106.

Higgins, S. T., Badger, G. J., & Budney, A. J. (2000). Initial abstinence and success in achieving longer term cocaine abstinence. *Experimental and Clinical Psychopharmacology, 8*(3), 377–86.

Higgins, S. T., Wong, C. J., Badger, G. J., Haug Ogden, D. E. H., & Dantona, R. L. (2000). Contingent reinforcement increases cocaine abstinence during outpatient treatment and 1 year of follow-up. *J. Cons. Clin. Psychol., 68*(1), 64–72.

Higuci, S. S., Matsushita, H., Imazeki, T., Kinoshita, T., Takagi, S., & Kono, H. (1994). Aldehyde de hydrogenase genotypes in Japanese alcoholics. *Lancet, 343,* 741–42.

Hijii, T., et al. (1997). Life expectancy and social adaptation in individuals with Down syndrome with and without surgery for congenital heart disease. *Clin. Pediat., 36*(6), 327–32.

Hill, A. J. (2002). Prevalence and demographics of dieting. In C. G. Fairburn & K. D. Brownell (Eds.), *Eating disorders and obesity: A comprehensive handbook* (2nd ed., pp. 80–83).

Hill, C. E., & Lambert, M. J. (2004). Methodological issues in studying psychotherapy process and outcomes. In M. J. Lambert (2004). *Bergin and Garfield's handbook of Psychotherapy and behavior change.* New York: John Wiley and Sons, pp. 84–135.

Hill, J. O., Wyatt, H. R., Reed, G. W., & Peters, J. C. (2003, Feb. 7). Obesity and the environment: Where do we go from here? *Science, 299,* 853–55.

Hiller, W., Kroymann, R., Leibbrand, R., Cebulla, M., Korn, H. J., Rief, W., et al. (2004). Effects and cost-effectiveness analysis of inpatient treatment for somatoform disorders. *Fortschritte der Neurologie, Psychiatrie, 72*(3), 136–46.

Hilsman, R., & Garber, J. (1995). A test of the cognitive diathesis stress model of depression in children: Academic stressors, attributional style, perceived competence, and control. *J. Person. Soc. Psychol., 69*(2), 370–80.

Hing, N., & Breen, H. (2001). Profiling lady luck: An empirical study of gambling and problem gambling amongst female club members. *Journal of Gambling Studies, 17*(1), 47–69.

Hinrichsen, G. A., & Niederehe, G. (1994). Dementia management strategies and adjustment of family members of older patients. *Gerontologist, 34*(1), 95–102.

Hinshaw, S. F., Zupan, B. A., Simmel, C., & Nigg, J. T. (1997). Peer status in boys with and without attention-deficit hyperactivity disorder: Predictions from overt and covert antisocial behavior, social isolation, and authoritative parents. *Child Develop., 68*(5), 880–96.

Hinshaw, S. P. (1992). Externalizing behavior problems and academic underachievement in childhood and adolescence: Causal relationships and underlying mechanisms. *Psychol. Bull., 111,* 127–55.

Hinshaw, S. P. (1994). Conduct disorder in childhood: Conceptualization, diagnosis, comorbidity, and risk status for antisocial functioning in adulthood. In D. C. Fowles, P. Sutker, & S. H. Goodman (Eds.), *Progress in experimental personality and psychopathology research.* New York: Springer.

Hinton, W. L., Tiet, Q., Giaouyen, C., & Chesney, M. (1997). Predictors of depression among refugees from Vietnam: A longitudinal study of new arrivals. *J. Nerv. Ment. Dis., 185*(1), 39–45.

Hiroto, D. S., & Seligman, M. E. P. (1975). Generality of learned helplessness in man. *J. Pers. Soc. Psychol., 31*(2), 311–27.

Hirsch, C. R., Meynen, T., & Clark, D. M. (2004). Negative self-imagery in social anxiety contaminates social interactions. *Memory, 12*(4), 496–506.

Hirsch, C., Clark, D. M., Mathews, A., & Williams, R. (2003). Self-images play a causal role in social phobia. *Behav. Res. Ther., 41*(8), 909–921.

Hirsch, S. R., & Leff, J. P. (1975). *Abnormalities in parents of schizophrenics.* London: Oxford University Press.

Hirschfeld, M. (1948). *Sexual anomalies* (p. 167). New York: Emerson.

Hirschfeld, R. M. A. (1996). Panic disorder: Diagnosis, epidemiology, and clinical course. *J. Clin. Psychiat., 57*(10), 3–8.

Hobfoll, S., Ritter, C., Lavin, J., Hulsizer, M., et al. (1995). Depression prevalence and incidence among inner-city pregnant and postpartum women. *J. Cons. Clin. Psychol., 3,* 445–53.

Hodgins, D. C., & el-Guebaly, N. (2004). Retrospective and prospective reports of precipitants to relapse in pathological gambling. *J. Cons. Clin. Psychol., 72,* 72–80.

Hodgins, S., & Lalonde, N. (1999). Major mental disorders and crime: Changes over time? In P. Cohen, C. Slomkowski, et al. (Eds.), *Historical and geographical influences on psychopathology* (pp. 57–83). Mahwah, NJ: Erlbaum.

Hoek, H. W., & van Hoecken, D. (2003). Review of the prevalence and incidence of eating disorders. *Int. J. Eat. Dis., 34,* 383–96.

Hoek, H. W. (2002). Distribution of eating disorders. In C. G. Fairburn & K. D. Brownell (Eds.), *Eating disorders and obesity: A comprehensive handbook* (2nd ed., pp. 233–37). New York: Guilford.

Hofer, S. M., Christensen, H., Mackinnon, A., Korten, A. E., Jorm, A. F., Henderson, A. F., & Easteal, S. (2002). Change in cognitive functioning associated with ApoE genotype in a community sample of older adults. *Psychol. Aging, 17*(2), 194–208.

Hoff, A. L., Riordan, H., O'Donnell, D. W., Morris, L., & DeLisi, L. E. (1992). Neuropsychological functioning of first-episode schizophreniform patients. *Amer. J. Psychiat., 149,* 898–903.

Hoff, A. L., Sakamura, M., Razi, K., Heyderbrand, G., Csernansky, J. G., & DeLisi, L. E. (2000). Lack of association between duration of untreated illness and severity of cognitive and structural brain deficits at the first episode of schizophrenia. *Amer. J. Psychiat., 157,* 1824–28.

Hoffman, A. (1971). LSD discoverer disputes "chance" factor in finding. *Psychiat. News, 6*(8), 23–26.

Hoffman, R. E., Gueorguieva, R., Hawkins, K. A., Varanko, M., Boutros, N. N., Wu, Y-T, Carroll, K., & Krystal, J. H. (2005). Temporoparietal transcranial magnetic stimulation for auditory hallucinations: Safety, efficacy and moderators in a fifty patient sample. *Biol. Psychiat., 58,* 97–104.

Hofmann, S. G., & Barlow, D. H. (2002). Social phobia. In D. H. Barlow (Ed.), *Anxiety and its disorders* (2nd ed., pp. 454–76). New York: Guilford.

Hogarty, G. E., Anderson, C. M., Reiss, D. J., Kornblith, S. J., Greenwald, D. P., Javna, C. D., & Madonia, M. J. (1986). Family psychoeducation, social skills training, and maintenance chemotherapy in the aftercare treatment of schizophrenia. *Arch. Gen. Psychiat., 43,* 633–42.

Hogarty, G. E., Anderson, C. M., Reiss, D. J., Kornblith, S. J., Greenwald, D. P., Ulrich, R. F., & Carter, M. (1991). Family psychoeducation, social skills training, and maintenance chemotherapy in the aftercare treatment of schizophrenia. 2. Two-year effects of a controlled study in relapse and adjustment. *Arch. Gen. Psychiat., 48,* 340–47.

Hogarty, G. E., et al. (1997a). Three-year trials of personal therapy among schizophrenic patients living with or independent of family: I. Description of study and effects on relapse rate. *Amer. J. Psychiat., 154*(11), 1504–13.

Hogarty, G. E., et al. (1997b). Three-year trials of personal therapy among schizophrenic patients living with or independent of family, II: Effects on adjustment of patients. *Amer. J. Psychiat., 154*(11), 1514–24.

Hoge, C. W., Castro, C. A., Messer, S. C., McGurk, D., Cotting, D. I., & Koffman, R. L. (2004). Combat duty in Iraq and Afghanistan, mental health problems, and barriers to care. *N. Engl. J. Med., 351,* 13–32.

Holder, H. D., Longabaugh, R., Miller, W. R., & Rubonis, A. V. (1991). The cost effectiveness of treatment for alcohol problems: A first approximation. *J. Stud. Alcoh., 52,* 517–40.

Hollander, E., Buchalter, A. J., & DeCaria, C. M. (2000). Pathological gambling. *Psychiat. Clin. N. Amer., 23*(3), 626–42.

Hollander, E., DeCaria, C. M., Nitescu, A., Gully, R., Suckow, R. F., et al. (1992). Serotonergic function in obsessive-compulsive disorder: Behavioral and neuroendocrine responses to oral m-chlorophenylpiperazine and fenfluramine in patients and healthy volunteers. *Arch. Gen. Psychiat., 49,* 21–28.

Holliday, J., Wall, E., Treasure, J., & Weinman, J. (2005). Perceptions of illness in individuals with anorexia nervosa: A comparison with lay men and women. *Int. J. Eat. Dis., 37,* 50–56.

Hollins, S. (2001). Psychotherapeutic methods. In A. Dosen & K. Day (Eds.), *Treating mental illness and behavior disorders in children and adults with mental retardation* (pp. 27–44). Washington, DC: American Psychiatric Press.

Hollister, J. M., Laing, P., & Mednick, S. A. (1996). Rhesus incompatibility as a risk factor for schizophrenia in male adults. *Arch. Gen. Psychiat., 53,* 19–24.

Hollon, S. D., & Beck, A. T. (1994). Cognitive and cognitive-behavioral therapies. In A. E. Bergin & S. L. Garfield (Eds.), *Handbook of psychotherapy and behavior change* (4th ed., pp. 428–66). New York: Wiley.

Hollon, S. D. & Beck, A. T. (2004). Cognitive and Cognitive Behavioral Therapies. In M. J. Lambert (2004). *Bergin and Garfield's handbook of Psychotherapy and behavior change.* New York: John Wiley and Sons, pp. 447–492.

Hollon, S. D., & Fawcett, J. (1995). Combined medication and psychotherapy. In G. O. Gabbard (Ed.), *Treatments of psychiatric disorders* (Vol. 1., 2nd ed., pp. 1221–36). Washington, DC: American Psychiatric Press.

Hollon, S. D., DeRubeis, R. J., & Evans, M. D. (1987). Causal mediation of change in treatment for depression: Discriminating between nonspecificity and noncausality. *Psychol. Bull., 102,* 139–49.

Hollon, S. D., DeRubeis, R. J., Shelton, R. C., Amsterdam, J. D., Salomon, R. M., O'Reardon, J. P., et al. (2005a). Prevention of relapse following cognitive therapy vs medications in moderate to severe depression. *Arch. Gen. Psychiat., 62,* 417–422.

Hollon, S. D., Evans, M., & DeRubeis, R. (1990). Cognitive mediation of relapse prevention following treatment for depression: Implications of differential risk. In R. Ingram (Ed.), *Psychological aspects of depression.* New York: Plenum.

Hollon, S. D., Haman, K. L., & Brown, L. L. (2002). Cognitive-behavioral treatment of depression. In I. H. Gotlib & C. L. Hammen (Eds.), *Handbook of depression* (pp. 383–403). New York: Guilford.

Hollon, S. D., Stewart, M. O., & Strunk, D. (In Press). Cognitive behaviour therapy has enduring effects in the treatment of depression and anxiety. *Annu. Rev. Psychol.*

Hollon, S. D., Thase, M. E., & Markowitz, J. C. (2002). Treatment and prevention of depression. *Psychological Science in the Public Interest, 3*(2, suppl.), 39–77.

Holmes, C. (2002). Genotype and phenotype in Alzheimer's disease. *Brit. J. Psychiat., 180*(2), 131–34.

Holmes, D. L. (1998). *Autism through the lifespan: The Eden Model.* Bethesda, MD: Woodbine House.

Holmes, T. H., & Rahe, R. H. (1967). The social readjustment rating scale. *J. Psychosom. Res., 11*(2), 213–18.

Holroyd, K. A. (2002). Assessment and psychological management of recurrent headache disorders. *J. Cons. Clin. Psychol., 70*(3), 656–77.

Holsboer, F. (1992). The hypothalamic-pituitary-adrenocortical system. In E. S. Paykel (Ed.), *Handbook of affective disorders* (2nd ed.). New York: Guilford.

Holsinger, T., Steffens, D. C., Helms, P. C., Havlik, R. J., Bretiner, J. C., Guralnik, J. M., & Plassman, B. L. (2002). Head injury in early adulthood and the lifetime risk of depression. *Arch. Gen. Psychiat., 59*(1), 17–22.

Holtzworth-Munroe, A., & Meehan, J. C. (2004). Typologies of men who are maritally violent: Scientific and clinical implications. *J. Interpers. Viole., 19*(12), 1369–1389.

Holvey, D. N., & Talbott, J. H. (Eds.). (1972). *The Merck manual of diagnosis and therapy* (12th ed.). Rahway, NJ: Merck, Sharp, & Dohme Research Laboratories.

Holzbeck, E. (1996). Thiamine absorption in alcoholic delirium patients. *J. Stud. Alcoh., 57*(6), 581–84.

Holzer, C. E., Goldsmith, H. F., & Ciarlo, J. A. (1998). Effects of rural-urban county type on the availability of health and mental health care providers. In R. W. Manderscheid & M. J. Henderson (Eds.), *Mental health, United States.* Rockville, MD: Center for Mental Health Services.

Holzman, P. S., et al. (1998). How are deficits in motion perception related to eye-tracking dysfunction in schizophrenia? In M. F. Lenzenweger & R. H. Dworkin (Eds.), *Origins and development of schizophrenia* (pp. 161–84). Washington, DC: American Psychological Association.

Holzman, P. S., Kringlen, E., Matthysse, S., Flanagan, S. D., Lipton, R. B., Cramer, G., Levin, S., Lange, K., & Levy, D. L. (1988). A single dominant gene can account for eye tracking dysfunctions and schizophrenia in offspring of discordant twins. *Arch. Gen. Psychiat., 45,* 641–47.

Honkonen, T., Karlsson, H., Koivisto, A. M., Stengård, E., & Salokangas, R. K. R. (2003). Schizophrenic patients in different treatment settings during the era of deinstitutionalization: Three-year follow-up of three discharge cohorts in Finland. *Austral. N.Z. J. Psychiat., 37*(2), 160–68.

Hook, E. B. (1980). Genetic counseling dilemmas: Down's syndrome, paternal age, and recurrence risk after remarriage. *Amer. J. Med. Genet., 5,* 145–51.

Hooker, E. (1957). The adjustment of the male overt homosexual. *Journal of Projective Techniques, 21,* 18–30.

Hooley, J. M., & Campbell, C. (2002). Control and controllability: Beliefs and behavior in high and low expressed emotion relatives. *Psychol. Med., 32*(6), 1091–99.

Hooley, J. M., & Candela, S. F. (1999). Interpersonal functioning in schizophrenia. In T. Millon, P. H. Blaney, & R. D. Davis (Eds.), *Oxford textbook of psychopathology.* New York: Oxford University Press.

Hooley, J. M., & Chung, R. J. (2003). Pain insensitivity in relatives of patients with schizophrenia and bipolar disorder. In M. F. Lenzenweger & J. M. Hooley (Eds.), *Principles of experimental psychopathology: Essays in honor of Brendan Maher* (pp. 157–71). Washington, DC: American Psychological Association.

Hooley, J. M., & Delgado, M. L. (2001). Pain insensitivity in the relatives of schizophrenia patients. *Schizophrenia Research, 47,* 265–73.

Hooley, J. M., & Gotlib, I. H. (2000). A diathesis-stress conceptualization of expressed emotion and clinical outcome. *App. Prev. Psychol., 9,* 135–51.

Hooley, J. M., & Hiller, J. B. (2001). Family relationships and major mental disorder: Risk factors and preventive strategies. In B. R. Sarason & S. Duck (Eds.), *Personal relationships: Implications for clinical and community psychology* (pp. 61–87). New York: Wiley.

Hooley, J. M., & Teasdale, J. D. (1989). Predictors of relapse in unipolar depressives: Expressed emotion, marital distress, and perceived criticism. *J. Abn. Psychol., 98,* 229–35.

Hooley, J. M., Rosen, L. R., & Richters, J. E. (1995). Expressed emotion: Toward clarification of a critical construct. In G. Miller (Ed.), *The behavioral high-risk paradigm in psychopathology* (pp. 88–120). New York: Springer.

Horger, B. A., & Roth, R. H. (1995). Stress and central amino acid systems. In M. J. Friedman, D. S. Charney, & A. Y. Deutch (Eds.), *Neurobiological and clinical consequences of stress: From normal adaptation to PTSD.* Philadelphia: Lippincott.

Horn, S. D. (2003). Limiting access to psychiatric services can increase total health care costs. *Drug Benefit Trends, 15*(Suppl. I), 12–18.

Horowitz, M. J., & Solomon, G. F. (1978). Delayed stress response syndromes in Vietnam veterans. In C. R. Figley (Ed.), *Stress disorders among Vietnam veterans: Theory, research, and treatment.* New York: Brunner/Mazel.

Horowitz, M. J., Merluzzi, R. V., Ewert, M., Ghannam, J. H., Harley, D., & Stinson, C. H. (1991). Role-relationship models of configuration (RRMC). In M. Horowitz (Ed.), *Person schemas and maladaptive interpersonal patterns* (pp. 115–54). Chicago: University of Chicago Press.

Horowitz, M. J., Wilner, N., & Alvarez, W. (1979). Impact of Events Scale: A measure of subjective stress. *Psychosom. Med., 41,* 209–18.

Houck, C. K. (1993). Ellis's "potential" Integrative Strategy Instruction model: An appealing extension of previous efforts. *J. Learn. Dis., 26*(6), 399–403.

Houston, K., Hawton, K., & Sheppard, R. (2001). Suicide in young people aged 15–24: A psychological autopsy study. *J. Affect. Dis., 63*(1–3), 159–70.

Houts, A. C., Berman, J. S., & Abramson, H. (1994). Effectiveness of psychological and pharmacological treatments for nocturnal enuresis. *J. Cons. Clin. Psychol., 62,* 737–45.

Howland, R. H., & Thase, M. E. (1999). Affective disorders: Biological aspects. In T. Millon, P. H. Blaney, et al. (Eds.), *Oxford textbook of psychopathology. Oxford textbooks in clinical psychology* (Vol. 4., pp. 166–202). New York: Oxford University Press.

Hoza, B., Mrug, S., Gerdes, A. C., Hinshaw, S. P., Bukowski, W. M., Gold, J. A., Kraemer, H. C., Pelham, W. E., Wigal, T., & Arnold, L. E. (2005). What aspects of peer relationships are impaired in children with Attention Deficit/Hyperactivity Disorder? *J. Cons. Clin. Psychol., 73,* 411–23.

Hsu, L. K., Benotti, P. N., Dwyer, J., Roberts, S. B., Saltzman, E., Shikora, S., Rolls, B. J., & Rand, W. (1998). Nonsurgical factors that influence the outcome of bariatric surgery: A review. *Psychosom. Med., 60,* 338–46.

Hucker, S. J. (1997). Sexual sadism: Psychopathology and theory. In D. R. Laws & W. O'Donohue (Eds.), *Sexual deviance: Theory, assessment, and treatment* (pp. 210–24). New York: Guilford.

Hudson, J. L., & Rapee, R. M. (2001). Parent-child interactions and anxiety disorders: An observational study. *Behav. Res. Ther., 39*(12), 1411–27.

Huey, S. J., & Henggeler, S. W. (2001). Effective community based interventions for antisocial and delinquent adolescents. In J. H. Hughes, A. M. La Greca, & J. C. Conoley (Eds.), *Handbook of psychological services for children and adolescents* (pp. 301–22). Oxford: Oxford University Press.

Hufford, M. R. (2001). Alcohol and suicidal behavior. *Clin. Psychol. Rev., 21*(5), 797–811.

Hughes, A. L. (1992). The prevalence of illicit drug use in six metropolitan areas in the United States: Results from the 1991 National Household Survey on Drug Abuse. *Brit. J. Addict., 87,* 1481–85.

Hughes, J. R., Higgins, S. T., & Hatsukami, D. K. (1990). Effects of abstinence from tobacco: A critical review. In L. T. Kozlowski, H. Annis, & H. D. Cappell, et al. (Eds.), *Recent advances in alcohol and drug problems* (Vol. 10, pp. 317–97).

Humphreys, K., & Rappaport, J. (1993). From community mental health movement to the war on drugs: A study of the definition of social problems. *Amer. Psychol., 48*(8), 892–901.

Humphry, D., & Wickett, A. (1986). *The right to die: Understanding euthanasia.* New York: Harper & Row.

Hunsley, J., & Bailey, J. M. (1999). The clinical utility of the Rorschach: Unfulfilled promises and an uncertain future. *Psychol. Assess., 11*(3), 266–77.

Hunt, W. A. (1993). Are binge drinkers more at risk of developing brain damage? *Alcohol, 10,* 559–61.

Hunter, E. C. M., Phillips, M. L., Chalder, T., Sierra, M., & David, A. S. (2003). Depersonalization disorder: A cognitive-behavioural conceptualisation. *Behav. Res. Ther., 41,* 1451–67.

Hunter, E. J. (1978). The Vietnam POW veteran: Immediate and long-term effects. In C. R. Figley (Ed.), *Stress disorders among Vietnam veterans.* New York: Brunner/Mazel.

Huntjens, R. J. C., Peters, M. L., Postma, A., Woertman, L., Effting, M., & van der Hart, O. (2005). Transfer of newly acquired stimulus valence between identities in dissociative identity disorder (DID). *Behav. Res. Ther., 43,* 243–55.

Huntjens, R. J. C., Postma, A., Peters, M. L., Woertma, L., & van der Hart, O. (2003). Interidentity amnesia for neutral, episodic information in dissociative identity disorder. *J. Abn. Psychol., 112*(2), 290–97.

Huntley, E., & Smith, L. (1999). Long-term follow-up of behavioral treatment for primary encopresis in people with intellectual disability in the community. *J. Intell. Dis. Res., 43*(6), 484–88.

Hurley, D. (2005, April 19). Divorce rate: It's not as high as you think. *The New York Times.*

Husain, M. M., Meyer, D. E., Muttakin, M. H., & Weiner, M. F. (1993). Maintenance ECT for treatment of recurrent mania. *Amer. J. Psychiat., 150,* 985.

Hussong, A. M., Hicks, R. E., Levy, S. A., & Curran, P. J. (2001). Specifying the relations between affect and heavy alcohol use among young adults. *J. Abn. Psychol., 110*(3), 449–61.

Hutchins, R. M. (Ed). (1952). *The dialogues of Plato.* Translated by B. Jowett. Chicago: William Benton/Encyclopaedia Britannica.

Hutchinson, N. L. (1993). Integrative Strategy Instruction: An elusive ideal for teaching adolescents with learning disabilities. *J. Learn. Dis., 26*(7), 428–32.

Hutter-Paier, B., Huttenen, H. J., Puglielli, L., Eckman, C. B., Kim, D. Y., Hofmeister, A., Moir, R. D., Domnitz, S. B., Frosch, M. P., Windisch, M., & Kovacs, D. M. (2004). The ACAT inhibitor CP-113,818 markedly reduces amyloid pathology in a mouse model of Alzheimer's disease. *Neuron, 44,* 227–38.

Huynen, K. B., Lutzker, J. R., Bigelow, K. B., Touchette, R. E., & Campbell, R. V. (1996). Planned activities for mothers of children with developmental disorders. *Behav. Mod., 20*(4), 406–27.

Iacono, W. G., & Beiser, M. (1992). Are males more likely than females to develop schizophrenia? *Amer. J. Psychiat., 149*(5), 1070–74.

Iacono, W. G., Moreau, M., Beiser, M., Fleming, J. A., & Lin, T. (1992). Smooth-pursuit eye tracking in first-episode psychotic patients and their relatives. *J. Abn. Psychol., 101(1),* 104–116.

Iancu, I., Dannon, P. N., Lustig, M., Sasson, Y., & Zohar, J. (2000). Preferential efficacy of serotonergic medication in obsessive-compulsive disorder: From practice to theory. In W. K. Goodman & M. V. Rudorfer, et al. (Eds.), *Obsessive-compulsive disorder: Contemporary issues in treatment. Personality and clinical psychology series* (pp. 303–13). Mahwah, NJ: Erlbaum.

Iezzi, T., Duckworth, M. P., & Adams, H. E. (2001). Somatoform and factitious disorders. In P. Sutker & H. Adams (Eds.), *Comprehensive handbook of psychopathology* (pp. 211–58). New York: Kluwer Academic/Plenum.

Ikemi, Y., Ago, Y., Nakagawa, S., Mori, S., Takahashi, N., Suematsu, H., Sugita, M., & Matsubara, H. (1974). Psychosomatic mechanism under social changes in Japan. *J. Psychosom. Res., 18*(1), 15–24.

Ilechukwu, S. T. (1992). Magical penis loss in Nigeria: Report of a recent epidemic of a koro-like syndrome. *Trans. Cult. Psych. Res. Rev., 29*(2), 91–108.

in't Veld, B. A., Ruitenberg, A., Hofman, A., Launer, L. J., van Duijn, C. M., Stijnen, T., Breteler, M. M. B., & Stricker, B. H. C. (2001). Nonsteroidal anti-inflammatory drugs and the risk of Alzheimer's disease. *N. Engl. J. Med., 345,* 1515–21.

Ingram, R. E., & Price, J. M. (Eds.). (2001). *Vulnerability to psychopathology: Risk across the lifespan.* New York: Guilford.

Ingram, R. E., Scott, W., & Siegle, G. (1999). Depression: Social and cognitive aspects. In T. Millon, P. H. Blaney, et al. (Eds.), *Oxford textbook of psychopathology* (pp. 203–26). New York: Oxford University Press.

Intrieri, R. C., & Rapp, S. R. (1994). Self-control skillfulness and caregiver burden among help-seeking elders. *J. Gerontol., 49*(1), P19–P23.

Iribarren, C., Sidney, S., Bild, D. E., Liu, K., Markovitz, J. H., Roseman, J. M., & Matthews, K. (2000). Association of hostility with coronary artery calcification in young adults: The CARDIA study. Coronary Artery Risk Development in Young Adults. *JAMA, 283*(19), 2546–51.

Irwin, M., Daniels, M., Smith, T. L., Bloom, E., & Weiner, H. (1987). Impaired natural killer cell activity during bereavement. *Brain, Behavior, and Immunity, 1,* 98–104.

Isaac, M., Janca, A., Burke, K. C., Costa e Silva, J. A., et al. (1995). Medically unexplained somatic symptoms in different cultures: A preliminary report from Phase I of the World Health Organization International Study of Somatoform Disorders. *Psychother. Psychosom., 64,* 88–93.

Isaacson, J. H. (2004). Early detection and treatment of prescription drug abuse in primary care. In N. A. Cummings, M. P. Duckworth, W. T. O'Donohue, & K. E. Ferguson (Eds.), *Early detection and treatment of substance abuse within integrated primary care.* Reno, NV: Context Press.

Ishiwaka, S. S., Raine, A., Lencz, T., Bihrle, S., & LaCasse, L. (2001). Autonomic stress reactivity and executive functions in successful and unsuccessful criminal psychopaths from the community. *J. Abn. Psychol., 110*(3), 423–32.

Isohanni, M., Jones, P., Moilanen, K., Veijola, J., Oja, H., Koiranen, M., Jokelainen, J., Croudace, T., & Järvelin, M.-R. (2001). Early developmental milestones in adult schizophrenia and other psychoses. A 31-year follow-up of the North Finland 1966 birth cohort. *Schizophrenia Research, 52,* 1–19.

Ivan, C. S., Seshadri, S., Beiser, A., Au, R., Kase, C., Kelly-Hayes, M., & Wolf, P. A. (2004). Dementia after stroke: The Framingham study. *Stroke, 35,* 1264–68.

Jablensky, A., & Cole, S. (1997). Is the earlier age of onset of schizophrenia in males a confounded finding? Results from a cross-cultural investigation. *Brit. J. Psychiat., 170,* 234–40.

Jablensky, A., et al. (1992). Schizophrenia: Manifestations, incidence, and course in different cultures. A World Health Organization ten-country study. *Psychological Medicine Monograph Supplement, 20,* 1–97.

Jablonski, E. (1987). *Gershwin.* New York: Doubleday.

Jack, C. R., Jr., Petersen, R. C., Xu, Y. C., O'Brien, P. C., Smith, G. E., Ivnik, R. J., Boeve, B. F., Waring, S. C., Tangalos E. G., & Kokmen, E. (1999). Prediction of AD with MRI-based hippocampal volume in mild cognitive impairment. *Neurology, 52,* 1397–1403.

Jackson, A. P., & Huang, C. C. (2000). Parenting stress and behavior among single mothers of preschoolers: The mediating role of self efficacy. *Journal of Social Service Research, 26,* 29–42.

Jacob, T., & Johnson, S. L. (2001). Sequential interactions in the parent–child communications of depressed fathers and depressed mothers. *J. Fam. Psychol., 15*(1), 38–52.

Jacobsen, L. K., Giedd, J. N., Castellanos, F. X., Vaituzis, A. C., Hamburger, S. D., Kumra, S., Lenane, M. C., & Rapoport, J. L. (1998). Progressive reduction in temporal lobe structures in childhood-onset schizophrenia. *Amer. J. Psychiat., 155,* 678–85.

Jacobson, E. (1971). *Depression: Comparative studies of normal, neurotic, and psychotic conditions.* New York: International Universities Press.

Jacobson, N. S., & Addis, M. E. (1993). Research on couples and couple therapy: What do we know? Where are we going? *J. Cons. Clin. Psychol., 61,* 85–93.

Jacobson, N. S., Christensen, A., Prince, S. E., Cordova, J., & Eldridge, K. (2000). Integrative behavioral couple therapy: An acceptance-based, promising new treatment for couple discord. *J. Cons. Clin. Psychol., 68,* 351–55.

Jacobson, N. S., Dobson, K. S., Truax, P. A., Addis, M. E., Koerner, K., Gollan, J. K., Gortner, E., & Prince, S. E. (1996). A component analysis of cognitive behavioral treatment for depression. *J. Cons. Clin. Psychol., 64,* 295–304.

Jacobson, N. S., Gottman, J. M., Waltz, J., Rushe, R., Babcock, J., & Holtzworth-Munroe, A. (1994). Affect, verbal content, and psychophysiology in the arguments of couples with a violent husband. *J. Cons. Clin. Psychol., 62,* 982–88.

Jacobson, N. S., Martell, C. R., & Dimidjian, S. (2001). Behavioral activation treatment for depression: Returning to contextual roots. *Clin. Psychol. Sci. Prac., 8*(3), 255–70.

Jacobson, N. S., Schmaling, K. B., & Holtzworth-Monroe, A. (1987). A component analysis of behavioral marital therapy: Two-year follow-up and prediction of relapse. *J. Marit. Fam. Ther., 13,* 187–95.

Jamieson, R., & Wells, C. (1979). Manic psychosis in a patient with multiple metastatic brain tumors. *J. Clin. Psychiat., 40,* 280–83.

Jamison, K. R. (1993). *Touched with fire.* New York: Free Press.
Jamison, K. R. (1995). *An Unquiet Mind.* New York: A. A. Knopf.
Jamison, K. R. (1999). *Night falls fast: Understanding suicide.* New York: Vintage Books.
Janca, A., Isaac, M., Bennett, L. A., & Tacchini, G. (1995). Somatoform disorders in different cultures: A mail questionnaire survey. *Soc. Psychiat. Psychiatr. Epidemiol., 30,* 44–48.
Jancar, J., & Jancar, P. J. (1996). Longevity in Down syndrome: A twelve year survey (1984–1995). *Italian Journal of Intellectual Impairment,* 9(1), 27–30.
Janet, P. (1901). *The mental state of hystericals: A study of mental stigmata and mental accidents.* New York: Putnam.
Janet, P. (1907). *The major symptoms of hysteria.* New York: Macmillan.
Jang, K. L. (2005). *The behavioral genetics of psychopathology: A clinical guide.* Mahwah, NJ: Lawrence Erlbaum Associates.
Janicak, P. G., Dowd, S. M., Strong, M. J., Alam, D., & Beedle, D. (2005). The potential role of repetitive transcranial magnetic stimulation in treating severe depression. *Psychiatr. Ann., 35*(2), 138–145.
Janicki, M. P., & Dalton, A. J. (1993). Alzheimer disease in a select population of older adults with mental retardation. *Irish Journal of Psychology: Special Issue, Psychological aspects of aging 14*(1), 38–47.
Janicki, M. P., & Dalton, A. (2000). Prevalence of dementia and impact on intellectual disability services. *Mental Retardation, 38,* 276–88.
Jankovic, J. (1997). Phenomenology and classification of tics. *Neurologic Clinics, 15*(2), 267–75.
Janofsky, J. S., Dunn, M. H., Roskes, E. J., Briskin, J. K., & Rudolph, M. S. (1996). Insanity defense pleas in Baltimore city: An analysis of outcome. *Amer. J. Psychiat., 153*(11), 1464–68.
Janowsky, D. S., Addario, D., & Risch, S. C. (1987). *Pharmacology case studies.* New York: Guilford.
Janssen, I., Hanssen, M., Bak, M., Bijl, R. V., De Graaf, R., Vollebergh, W., McKenzie, K., & van Os, J. (2003). Discrimination and delusional ideation. *Brit. J. Psychiat., 182,* 71–76.
Jaranson, J. M., & Popkin, M. K. (1998). *Caring for victims of torture.* Washington, DC: American Psychiatric Press.
Jaranson, J. M., Kinzie, J. D., Friedman, M., Ortiz, S. D., Friedman, M. J., Southwick, S., Kastrup, M., & Mollica, R. (2001). Assessment, diagnosis, and intervention. In E. Gerrity, T. M. Keane, & F. Tuma (Eds.), *The mental health consequences of torture* (pp. 249–75). New York: Kluwer/Plenum.
Jaranson, J., Butcher, J. N., Halcón, L., Johnson, D. R., Robertson, C., Savik, K., Spring, M., & Westermeyer, J. (2004). Somali and Oromo refugees: Correlates of torture and trauma. *Amer. J. Pub. Hlth., 94,* 591–97.
Jaranson, J., Butcher, J. N., Halcón, L., Johnson, D. R., Robertson, C., Savik, K., Spring, M., & Westermeyer, J. (2004). Somali and Oromo refugees: Correlates of torture and trauma. *Amer. J. Pub. Hlth., 94,* 591–97.
Jarvik, M. E. (1967). The psychopharmacological revolution. *Psych. Today, 1*(1), 51–58.
Jason, L. A., Richman, J. A., Friedberg, F., Wagner, L., Taylor, R., & Jordan, K. M. (1997). Politics, science, and the emergence of a new disease: The case of chronic fatigue syndrome. *Amer. Psychol., 52*(9), 973–83.
Jeffrey, R. W., Adlis, S. A., & Forster, J. L. (1991). Prevalence of dieting among working men and women: The healthy worker project. *Hlth. Psychol., 10,* 274–81.
Jenike, M. A. (2000). Neurosurgical treatment of obsessive-compulsive disorder. In W. K. Goodman, M. V. Rudorfer, et al. (Eds.), *Obsessive-compulsive disorder: Contemporary issues in treatment. Personality and clinical psychology series* (pp. 457–82). Mahwah, NJ: Erlbaum.
Jibson, M. D., & Tandon, R. (1998). New atypical antipsychotic medications. *J. Psychiat. Res., 32,* 215–28.
Jick, H., Kaye, J. A., Jick, S. S. (2004). Antidepressants and the risk of suicidal behaviors. *JAMA,* Jul 21, 292(3): 338–343.
Jindal, R. D., Thase, M. E., Fasiczka, A. L., Friedman, E. S., Buysse, D. J., Frank, E., et al. (2002). Electroencephalographic sleep profiles in single-episode and recurrent unipolar forms of major depression: II. Comparision during remission. *Biol. Psychiat., 51,* 230–236.
Joffe, R. T., & Offord, D. R. (1990). Epidemiology. In G. MacLean (Ed.), *Suicide in children and adolescents.* Toronto: Hogrefe & Huber.
Johnson, C. L., Stuckey, M. K., Lewis, L. D., & Schwartz, D. M. (1982). Bulimia: A descriptive survey of 316 cases. *Int. J. Eat. Dis., 2,* 3–16.
Johnson, D. E. (2000). Medical and developmental sequelae of early childhood institutionalization in Eastern European adoptees. In C. A. Nelson (Ed.), *The Minnesota symposia on child psychology: The effects of early adversity on neurobehavioral development. Minnesota symposia on child psychology* (Vol. 31, pp. 113–62). Mahwah, NJ: Erlbaum.
Johnson, F., & Wardle, J. (2005). Dietary restraint, body dissatisfaction, and psychological distress: A prospective analysis. *J. Abn. Psychol., 114,* 119–25.
Johnson, J. D., O'Connor, K. A., Deak, T., Spencer, R. L., Watkins, L. R., & Maier, S. F. (2002). Prior stressor exposure primes the HPA axis. *Psychoneuroimmunology, 27,* 353–65.
Johnson, J. G., Cohen, P., Kasen, S., & Brook, J. S. (2002a). Childhood adversities associated with risk for eating disorders or weight problems during adolescence or early adulthood. *Amer. J. Psychiat. 159*(3), 394–400.
Johnson, J. G., Cohen, P., Kotler, L., Kasen, S., & Brook, J. S. (2002b). Psychiatric disorders associated with risk for the development of eating disorders during adolescence and early adulthood. *J. Cons. Clin. Psychol., 70,* 5, 1119–28.
Johnson, J. G., Cohen, P., Smailes, E., Kasen, S., Oldham, J. M., & Skodol, A. E. (2000). Adolescent personality disorders associated with violence and criminal behavior during adolescence and early childhood. *Amer. J. Psychiat., 157,* 1406–12.
Johnson, L., O'Malley, P., & Bachman, J. (2000). *Monitoring the future: Overview of key findings.* Ann Arbor: University of Michigan News and Information Services.
Johnson, L., O'Malley, P., & Bachman, J. (2000). Monitoring the future: Overview of key findings. Ann Arbor: University of Michigan News and Information Services.
Johnson, N. J., Backlund, E., Sorlie, P. D. et al. (2000). Marital status and mortality: The National Longitudinal Mortality Study. *Annals of Epidemiology, 10,* 224–238.
Johnson, S. L., & Miller, I. (1997). Negative life events and time to recovery from episodes of bipolar disorder. *J. Abn. Psychol., 106*(3), 449–57.
Johnson, S. L., & Roberts, J. E. (1995). Life events and bipolar disorder: Implications from biological theories. *Psychol. Bull., 117,* 434–49.
Johnson, S. P. (2001). Short-term play therapy. In G. L. Landreth (Ed.), *Innovations in play therapy: Issues, process, and special populations* (pp. 217–35). Philadelphia: Brunner-Routledge.
Joiner, T. E. (1997). Shyness and low social support as interactive diatheses, with loneliness as mediator: Testing an interpersonal-personality view of vulnerability to depressive symptoms. *J. Abn. Psychol., 106*(3), 386–94.
Joiner, T. E. (2002). Depression in its interpersonal context. In I. H. Gotlib & C. L. Hammen (Eds.), *Handbook of depression* (pp. 295–313). New York: Guilford.
Joiner, T. E., & Metalsky, G. I. (1995). A prospective test of an integrative interpersonal theory of depression: A naturalistic study of college roommates. *J. Pers. Soc. Psychol., 69*(4), 778–88.
Joint National Committee on Detection, Evaluation, and Treatment of High Blood Pressure. (1997). The sixth report of the Joint National Committee on Detection, Evaluation, and Treatment of High Blood Pressure (JNC VI). *Arch. Int. Med., 157,* 2413–45.
Jones, E., & Wessely, S. (2002). Psychiatric battle casualties: An intra- and interwar comparison. *Brit. J. Psychiat., 178,* 242–47.
Jones, L. (1992). Specifying the temporal relationship between job loss and consequences: Implication for service delivery. *The Journal of Applied Social Sciences, 16,* 37–62.
Jones, M. C. (1924). A laboratory study of fear: The case of Peter. *Pedagogical Seminary, 31,* 308–315.
Jones, P. B., Rodgers, B., Murray, R., & Marmot, M. (1994). Child developmental risk factors for adult schizophrenia in the British 1946 birth cohort. *Lancet, 344,* 1398–1402.
Jones, R. (1984). The pharmacology of cocaine. *National Institute on Drug Abuse Research Monograph Series 50.* Washington, DC: National Institute on Drug Abuse.
Jones, R. S. P., Zahl, A., & Huws, J. C. (2001). First hand accounts of emotional experiences in autism: A qualitative analysis. *Disability & Society, 16,* 393–401.
Jones, S. H., Hare, D. J., & Evershed, K. (2005). Actigraphic assessment of circadian activity and sleep patterns in bipolar disorder. *Bipolar Disorders, 7*(2), 176–186.
Jordan, B. D., Relkin, N. R., Ravdin, L. D., Jacobs, A. R., Bennett, A., & Gandy, S. (1997). Apolipoprotein E (4 associated with chronic traumatic brain injury in boxing. *JAMA, 278,* 136–40.
Judd, L. L., Akiskal, H. S., Maser, J. D., Zeller, P. J., Endicott, J., Coryell, W., Paulus, M., et al. (1998). A prospective 12-year study of subsyndromal and syndromal depressive symptoms in unipolar major depressive disorders. *Arch. Gen. Psychiat., 55,* 694–700.
Judd, L. L., Akiskal, H. S., Schetteler, P. J., Endicott, J., Maser, J., Solomon, D. A., et al. (2002). The long-term natural history of the weekly symptomatic status of bipolar I disorder. *Arch. Gen. Psychiat., 59*(6), 530–37.
Judd, L. L., Akiskal, H. S., Schettler, P. J., Coryell, W., Maser, J., Rice, J. A., et al. (2003). The comparative clinical phenotype and long term longitudinal episode course of bipolar I and II: A clinical spectrum or distinct disorders? *J. Affect. Dis., 73*(1–2), 19–32.
Judd, L. L., Paulus, M. P., Zeller, P., Fava, G. A., Rafanelli, C., Grandi, S., et al. (1999). The role of residual subthreshold depressive symptoms in early episode relapse in unipolar major depressive disorder. *Arch. Gen. Psychiat., 56*(8), 764–65.
Judd, L. L., Schettler, P. J., Akiskal, H. S., Maser, J., Coryell, W., Solomon, D., et al. (2003). Long-term symptomatic status of bipolar I vs. bipolar II disorders. *Int. J. Neuropsychopharm., 6*(2), 127–137.
Judd, L. L. (1997). The clinical course of unipolar major depressive disorders. *Arch. Gen. Psychiat., 54*(11), 989–91.
Kachigian, C., & Felthous, A. R. (2004). Court responses to Tarasoff statutes. *J. Amer. Acad. Psychiat. Law, 32*(3), 263–73.
Kaelber, C. T., Moul, D. E., & Farmer, M. E. (1995). Epidemiology of depression. In E. E. Beckham & W. R. Leber (Eds.), *Handbook of depression* (2nd ed., pp. 3–35). New York: Guilford.
Kagan, J. (1997). Temperament and the reactions to unfamiliarity. *Child Develop., 68*(1), 139–43.
Kagan, J. (2003). Biology, context and developmental inquiry. *Annu. Rev. Psychol., 54,* 1–23.
Kagan, J., Snidman, N., McManis, M., & Woodward, S. (2001). Temperamental contributions to the affect family of anxiety. *Psychiat. Clin. N. Amer., 2,* 677–88.
Kahler, C. W. (1995). Current challenges and an old debate. *Addiction, 90*(9), 1169–71.
Kalant, O. J. (1966). *The amphetamines: Toxicity and addiction.* Brookside Monographs, No. 5. Toronto: University of Toronto Press.
Kalarchian, M. A., Wilson, G. T., Brolin, R. E., & Bradley, L. (1998). Binge eating in bariatric surgery patients. *Int. J. Eat. Dis., 23*(1), 89–92.

Kalat, J. W. (1998). Biological Psychology. 5th Edition, Belmont, CA: Wadsworth Publishing Company.

Kalat, J. W. (2001). *Biological psychology* (7th ed.) Belmont, CA: Wadsworth.

Kalichman, S. C., Hunter, T. L., & Kelly, J. A. (1993). Perceptions of AIDS susceptibility among minority and nonminority women at risk for HIV infection. *J. Cons. Clin. Psychol., 60*(5), 725–32.

Kalus, O., Bernstein, D. P., & Siever, L. J. (1995). Schizoid personality disorder. In W. J. Livesley (Ed.), *The DSM-IV personality disorders.* (pp.58–70). New York: Guilford.

Kalus, P., Senitz, D., & Beckmann, H. (1997). Cortical layer I changes in schizophrenia: A marker for impaired brain development? *Journal of Neural Transmission, 104,* 549–59.

Kamien, J. B., Mikulolcho, S. K., & Amass, L. (1999). Efficacy of buprenorphine: Naloxone tablet for daily vs. alternate day opioid dependency. *Drug Dependency Inc.* National Institute on Drug Abuse Monograph # 179. Washington, DC: U.S. Government Printing Office.

Kamphaus, R. W., & Kroncke, A. P. (2004). "Back to the Future" of the Stanford-Binet Intelligence Scales. *Comprehensive handbook of psychological assessment* (pp. 77–86). New York: John Wiley & Sons.

Kang, H. K., Natelson, B. H., Mahan, C. M., Lee, K. Y., & Murphy, F. (2003). Post-traumatic stress disorder and chronic fatigue syndrome-like illness among Gulf War veterans: A population-based survey of 30,000 veterans. *Amer. J. Epidemiol., 157,* 141–48.

Kannell, W. B., Wolf, P. A., Garrison, R. J., Cupples, L. A., & D Agostino, R. B. (1987). *The Framingham study: an epidemiological investigation of cardiovascular disease.* Bethesda, MD: National Heart, Lung and Blood Institute.

Kanner, L. (1943). Autistic disturbances of effective content. *Nervous Child, 2,* 217–40.

Kaplan, H. S. (1974). *The new sex therapy.* New York: Brunner/Mazel.

Kaplan, H. S. (1987). *The illustrated manual of sex therapy* (2nd ed.). New York: Brunner/Mazel.

Kaplan, M. S., & Krueger, R. B. (1997). Voyeurism: Psychopathology and theory. In D. R. Laws & W. O'Donohue (Eds.), *Sexual deviance: Theory, assessment, and treatment* (pp. 297–310). New York: Guilford.

Kapner, D. A. (2003). Recreational use of Ritalin on college campuses. *Info Fact Resources.* Washington, DC: US. Department of Justice.

Kapur, N. (1999). Syndromes of retrograde amnesia: A conceptual and empirical synthesis. *Psychol. Bull., 125,* 800–25.

Kapur, S. (2003). Psychosis as a state of aberrant salience: A framework linking biology, phenomenology, and pharmacology in schizophrenia. *Amer. J. Psychiat., 160,* 13–23.

Kapur, S., Arenovich, T., Agid, O., Zipursky, R., Lindborg, S., & Jones, B. (2005). Evidence for the onset of antipsychotic effects within the first 24 hours of treatment. *Amer. J. Psychiat., 162,* 939–46.

Karavasilis, L., Doyle, A. B., & Markiewicz, D. (2003). Associations between parenting style and attachment to mothe in middle childhood and adolescence. *International Journal of Behavioral Development, 27*(2), 153–164.

Kario, K., & Ohashi, T. (1997). Increased coronary heart disease mortality after the Hanshin-Awaji earthquake among the older community on Awaji Island. Tsuna Medical Association. *J. Amer. Geriat. Soc., 45,* 610–13.

Karnesh, L. J. (with collaboration of Zucker, E. M.). (1945). *Handbook of psychiatry.* St. Louis: Mosby.

Karno, M., Golding, J. M., Sorenson, S. B., & Burnam, M. A. (1988). The epidemiology of obsessive-compulsive disorder in five U.S. communities. *Arch. Gen. Psychiat., 45,* 1094–99.

Karno, M., Jenkins, J. H., de la Selva, A., Santana, F., Telles, C., Lopez, S., & Mintz, J. (1987). Expressed emotion and schizophrenic outcome among Mexican-American families. *J. Nerv. Ment. Dis., 175*(3), 143–51.

Karon, B. P. (1995). Provision of psychotherapy under managed health care: A growing crisis and national nightmare. *Professional Psychology: Research & Practice, 26*(1), 5–9.

Karon, B. P., & Vandenbos, G. R. (1981). *Psychotherapy of schizophrenia: Treatment of choice.* New York: Jason Aronson.

Kashani, J. H., Hodges, K. K., Simonds, J. F., & Hilderbrand, E. (1981). Life events and hospitalization in children: A comparison with a general population. *Brit. J. Psychiat., 139,* 221–25.

Kashdan, T. B., & Herbert, J. D. (2001). Social anxiety disorder in childhood and adolescence: Current status and future directions. *Clinical Child & Family Psychology Review, 4,* 37–61.

Kaski, M. (2000). Aetiology of mental retardation: General issues and prevention. In M. G. Gelder, J. J. Lopez-Ibor, Jr., & N. Andreason (Eds.), *New Oxford textbook of psychiatry* (pp. 1947–52). New York: Oxford University Press.

Kato, T., Knopman, D., & Liu, H. Y. (2001). Dissociation of regional activation in mild AD during visual encoding—a functional MRI study. *Neurology, 57,* 812–16.

Katz, E. C., Brown, B. S., Schwartz, R. P., Weintraub, E., Barksdale, W., & Robinson, R. (2004). Role induction: A method for enhancing early retention in outpatient drug-free treatment. *J. Cons. Clin. Psychol., 72,* 227–34.

Katz, L. F., & Gottman, J. M. (1997). Buffering children from marital conflict and dissolution. *J. Clin. Child Psychol., 26*(2), 157–71.

Katz, R., & McGuffin, P. (1993). The genetics of affective disorders. In L. J. Chapman, J. P. Chapman, & D. C. Fowles (Eds.), *Progress in experimental personality and psychopathology research* (Vol. 16). New York: Springer.

Katz, S., & Kravetz, S. (1989). Facial plastic surgery for persons with Down syndrome: Research findings and their professional and social implications. *Amer. J. Ment. Retard., 94,* 101–10.

Katz, S., Kravetz, S., & Marks, Y. (1997). Parents' and doctors' attitudes toward plastic facial surgery for persons with Down syndrome. *J. Intell. Develop. Dis., 22*(4), 265–73.

Katzman, R., et al. (1997). Effects of apolipoprotein E on dementia and aging in the Shanghai Survey of Dementia. *Neurology, 49*(3), 779–85.

Katzmarzyk, P. T., & Davis, C. (2001). Thinness and body shape of *Playboy* centerfolds from 1978 to 1998. *International Journal of Obesity and Related Metabolic Disorders, 25*(4), 590–92.

Kaufman, J., & Zigler, E. (1989). The intergenerational transmission of child abuse. In D. Cicchetti & V. Carlson (Eds.), *Child maltreatment: Theory and research on the causes and consequences of child abuse and neglect* (pp. 129–50). Cambridge: Cambridge University Press.

Kaufman, J., Martin, A., King, R. A., & Charney, D. (2001). Are child-, adolescent-, and adult-onset depression one and the same disorder? *Biol. Psychiat., 49*(12), 980–1001.

Kausch, O. (2003). Patterns of substance abuse among treatment-seeking pathological gamblers. *J. Sub. Abuse Treat., 25*(4), 263–70.

Kawachi, I., Colditz, G., Ascherio, A., et al. (1994). Prospective study of phobic anxiety and risk of coronary heart disease in men. *Circulation, 89,* 1992.

Kawachi, I., Sparrow, D., Vokonas, P., et al. (1994). Symptoms of anxiety and risk of coronary heart disease: The normative aging study. *Circulation, 90,* 2225.

Kawachi, I., Sparrow, D., Vokonas, P., et al. (1995). Decreased heart rate variability in men with phobic anxiety (data from the normative aging study.) *Amer. J. Cardiol., 75,* 882.

Kaye, W. H. (2002). Central nervous system neurotransmitter activity in anorexia nervosa and bulimia nervosa. In C. G. Fairburn & K. D. Brownell (Eds.), *Eating disorders and obesity: A comprehensive handbook* (2nd ed., pp. 272–77). New York: Guilford.

Kaye, W. H., Bulik, C. M., Thornton, L., Barbarich, N., Masters, K. Price Foundation Collaborative Group. (2004). Comorbidity of anxiety disorders with anorexia and bulimia nervosa. *Amer. J. Psychiat., 161,* 2215–21.

Kaye, W. H., Frank, G. K., Meltzer, C. C., Price, J. C., McConaha, C. W., Crossan, P. J., Klump, K. L., & Rhodes, L. (2001). Altered serotonin 2A receptor activity in women who have recovered from bulimia nervosa. *Amer. J. Psychiat., 158*(7), 1152–55.

Kaye, W. H., Greeno, C. G., Moss, H., Fernstrom, J., Fernstrom, M., Lilenfeld, L. R., Weltzin, T. E., & Mann, J. J. (1998). Alterations in serotonin activity and psychiatric symptoms after recovery from bulimia nervosa. *Arch. Gen. Psychiat.,* 55, 927–35.

Kaye, W. H., Gwirtsman, H. E., George, D. T., & Ebert, M. H. (1991). Altered serotonin activity in anorexia nervosa after long-term weight restoration. *Arch. Gen. Psychiat.,* 48, 556–62.

Kazdin, A. E. (1984). Integration of psychodynamic and behavioral psychotherapies: Conceptual versus empirical synthesis. In H. Arkowitz & S. B. Messer (Eds.), *Psychoanalytic therapy and behavior therapy: Is integration possible?* (pp. 139–70). New York: Plenum.

Kazdin, A. E. (1995). Conduct disorder. In F. C. Verhulst & H. M. Koot (Eds.), *The epidemiology of child and adolescent psychopathology* (pp. 258–90). New York: Oxford University Press.

Kazdin, A. E. (1998). *Research Design in Clinical Psychology.* (3rd Edn.) Boston, MA: Allyn and Bacon.

Kazdin, A. E. (1998a). Conduct disorder. In R. J. Morris, T. R. Kratochwill, et al. (Eds.), *The practice of child therapy* (3rd ed., pp. 199–230). Boston: Allyn and Bacon.

Kazdin, A. E. (1998b). Drawing valid inferences from case studies. In A. E. Kazdin (Ed.), *Methodological issues and strategies in clinical research* (pp. 403–17). Washington, DC: American Psychological Association.

Kazdin, A. E. (1998c). *Research design in clinical psychology.* Needham, MA: Allyn and Bacon.

Kazdin, A. E., & Nock, M. K. (2003). Delineating mechanisms of change in child and adolescent therapy: Methodological issues and research recommendations. *J. Child Psychol. Psychiat., 44*(8), 1116–1129.

Kazdin, A. E., & Weisz, J. R. (2003). *Evidence-based psychotherapies for children and adolescents.* New York: Guilford Press.

Kazdin, A. E., Holland, L., & Crowley, M. (1997). Family experience of barriers to treatment and premature termination from child therapy. *J. Cons. Clin. Psychol., 65*(3), 453–63.

Kazdin, A. E., Marciano, P. L., & Whitley, M. K. (2005). The therapeutic alliance in cognitive-behavioral treatment of children referred for oppositional, aggressive, and antisocial behavior. *J. Cons. Clin. Psychol., 73,* 726–730.

Kearney, C. A., Sims, K. E., Pursell, C. R., & Tillotson, C. A. (2003). Separation anxiety disorder in young children: A longitudinal and family analysis. *J. Clin. Child & Adol. Psych., 32*(4), 593–98.

Keck, P. E., & McElroy, S. L. (2002a). Carbamazepine and valproate in the maintenance treatment of bipolar disorder. *J. Clin. Psychiat., 63*(110), 13–17.

Keck, P. E., & McElroy, S. L. (2002b). Pharmacological treatments for bipolar disorder. In P. E. Nathan & J. M. Gorman (Eds.), *A guide to treatments that work* (2nd ed., pp. 277–300). New York: Oxford University Press.

Keefe, F. J., Dunsmore, J., & Burnett, R. (1992). Behavioral and cognitive-behavioral approaches to chronic pain: Recent advances and future directions. *J. Cons. Clin. Psychol., 60*(4), 528–36.

Keefe, F. J., Smith, S. J., Buffington, A. L. H., Gibson, J., Studts, J. L., & Caldwell, D. S. (2002). Recent advances and future directions in the biopsychosocial assessment and treatment of arthritis. *J. Cons. Clin. Psychol., 70*(3), 640–55.

Keel, P. K., & Klump, K. L. (2003). Are eating disorders culture-bound syndromes? Implications for conceptualizing their etiology. *Psychol. Bull., 129*(5), 747–69.

Keel, P. K., & Mitchell, J. E. (1997). Outcome in bulimia nervosa. *Amer. J. Psychiat., 154*(3), 313–21.

Keel, P. K., Dorer, D. J., Eddy, K. T., Franko, D., Charatan, D. L., & Herzog, D. B. (2003). Predictors of mortality in eating disorders. *Arch. Gen. Psychiat., 60,* 179–83.

Keel, P. K., Mitchell, J. E., Miller, K. B., Davis, T. L., & Crow, S. J. (1999). Long-term outcome of bulimia nervosa. *Arch. Gen. Psychiat., 56*(1), 63–69.

Keller, M. B., & Boland, R. J. (1998). Implications of failing to achieve successful long-term maintenance treatment of recurrent unipolar major depression. *Biol. Psychiat., 44*(5), 348–60.

Keller, M. B., Hirschfeld, R. M. A., & Hanks, D. (1997). Double depression: A distinctive subtype of unipolar depression. *J. Affect. Dis., 45*(1–2), 65–73.

Keller, M. B., McCullough, J. P., Klein, D. N., Arnow, B., Dunner, D. L., Gelenberg, A. J., Markowitz, J. C., Nemeroff, C. B., Russell, J. M., Thase, M. E., Trivedi, M. H., & Zajecka, J. (2000). A comparison of nefazodone, the cognitive behavioral-analysis system of psychotherapy, and their combination for the treatment of chronic depression. *N. Engl. J. Med., 342,* 1462–70.

Keller, M. B., Yonkers, K. A., Warshaw, M. G., Pratt, L. A., Golan, J., Mathews, A. O., et al. (1994). Remission and relapse in subjects with panic disorder and agoraphobia: A prospective short interval naturalistic follow-up. *J. Nerv. Ment. Dis., 182,* 290–96.

Keller, M. C., & Nesse, R. M. (2005). Is low mood an adaptation? Evidence for subtypes with symptoms that match precipitants. *J. Affect. Dis., 86,* 27–35.

Kelley, J. E., Lumley, M. A., & Leisen, J. C. C. (1997). Health effects of emotional disclosure in rheumatoid arthritis patients. *Hlth. Psychol., 16*(4), 331–40.

Kellner, R. (1985). Functional somatic symptoms and hypochondriasis: A survey of empirical studies. *Arch. Gen. Psychiat., 42,* 821–33.

Kelsoe, J. R. (1997). The genetics of bipolar disorder. *Moskovskogo Nauchno-Issledovatel'Skogo Instituta Psikhiatrii, 27*(4), 285–92.

Kenardy, J., Arnow, B., & Agras, S. W. (1996). The aversiveness of specific emotional states associated with binge eating in obese patients. *Austral. NZ J. Psychiat., 30*(6), 839–44.

Kenchaiah, S., Evans, J. C., Levy, D., Wilson, P. W. F., Benjamin, E. J., Larson, M. G., Kannel, W. B., & Vasan, R. S. (2002). Obesity and the risk of heart failure. *N. Engl. J. Med., 347,* 305–13.

Kendall, P. C., & Braswell, L. (1985). *Cognitive-behavioral therapy for impulsive children.* New York: Guilford.

Kendall, P. C., Holmbeck, G., & Verduin, T. (2004). Methodology, design, and evaluation in psychotherapy research. In M. J. Lambert (Ed.). *Bergin and Garfield's Handbook of Psychotherapy and Behavior Change.* (5th edn.). New York: John Wiley and Sons. pp. 16–43.

Kendall, P. C. (1990). Cognitive processes and procedures in behavior therapy. In C. M. Franks, G. T. Wilson, P. C. Kendall, & J. P. Foreyt (Eds.), *Review of behavior therapy: Theory and practice* (pp. 103–37). New York: Guilford.

Kendall-Tackett, K. A., Williams, L. M., & Finkelhor, D. (1993). Impact of sexual abuse on children: A review and synthesis of recent empirical studies. *Psychol. Bull., 113,* 164–80.

Kendler, K. S. (1996). Major depression and generalised anxiety disorder: Same genes, (partly) different environments—revisited. *Brit. J. Psychiat, 168*(30), 68–75.

Kendler, K. S. (1997). The diagnostic validity of melancholic major depression in a population-based sample of female twins. *Arch. Gen. Psychiat., 54,* 299–304.

Kendler, K. S. (1999a). Molecular genetics of schizophrenia. In D. S. Charney, E. J. Nestler, & B. S. Bunney (Eds.), *The neurobiology of mental illness* (pp. 203–13). New York: Oxford University Press.

Kendler, K. S. (1999b). Long-term care of an individual with schizophrenia: Pharmacological, psychological, and social factors. *Amer. J. Psychiat., 156,* 124–28.

Kendler, K. S., & Diehl, S. R. (1993). The genetics of schizophrenia: A current, genetic-epidemiologic perspective. *Schizo. Bull., 19* (2), 261–85.

Kendler, K. S., & Gardner, C. O. (1998). Boundaries of major depression: An evaluation of DSM-IV criteria. *Amer. J. Psychiat., 155*(2), 172–77.

Kendler, K. S., & Gardner, C. O. (1997). The risk for psychiatric disorders in relatives of schizophrenic and control probands: A comparison of three independent studies. *Psychol. Med., 27,* 411–419.

Kendler, K. S., & Gruenberg, A. M. (1984). An independent analysis of the Danish adoption study of schizophrenia: VI. The relationship between psychiatric disorders as defined by DSM-III in the relatives and adoptees. *Arch. Gen. Psychiat., 41,* 555–64.

Kendler, K. S., & Karkowski-Shuman, L. (1997). Stressful life events and genetic liability to major depression: Genetic control of exposure to the environment? *Psychol. Med., 27,* 539–47.

Kendler, K. S., Bulik, C. M., Silberg, J., Hettema, J. M., Myers, J., & Prescott, C. A. (2000). Childhood sexual abuse and adult psychiatric and substance use disorders in women. *Arch. Gen. Psychiat., 57*(10), 1–14.

Kendler, K.S., Gardner, C. O., & Prescott, C. A. (2001). Panic syndromes in a population-based sample of male and female twins. *Psychol. Med., 31,* 989–1000.

Kendler, K. S., Gardner, C. O., & Prescott, C. A. (2002). Toward a comprehensive developmental model for major depression in women. *Amer. J. Psychiat., 159*(7), 1133–1145.

Kendler, K. S., Gardner, C. O., & Prescott, C. A. (2003). Personality and the experience of environmental adversity. *Psychol. Med., 33,* 1193–1202.

Kendler, K. S., Gruenberg, A. M., & Kinney, D. K. (1994). Independent diagnoses of adoptees and relatives as defined by DSM-III in the provincial and national samples of the Danish adoption study of schizophrenia. *Arch. Gen. Psychiat., 51*(6), 456–68.

Kendler, K. S., Hettema, J. M., Butera, F., Gardner, C. O., & Prescott, C. A. (2003). Life event dimensions of loss, humiliation, entrapment, and danger in the prediction of onsets of major depression and generalized anxiety. *Arch. Gen. Psychiat., 60,* 789–796.

Kendler, K. S., Karkowski, L. M., & Prescott, C. A. (1999a). Causal relationship between stressful life events and the onset of major depression. *Amer. J. Psychiat., 156*(6), 837–41.

Kendler, K. S., Karkowski, L. M., & Prescott, C. A. (1999b). Fears and phobias: Reliability and heritability. *Psychol. Med., 29,* 539–53.

Kendler, K. S., Karkowski, L. M., & Prescott, C. A. (1998) Stressful life events and major depression: Risk period, long-term contextual threat and diagnostic specificity. *J. Nerv. Ment. Dis., 186,* 661–669.

Kendler, K. S., Karkowski, L. M., Neale, M. C., & Prescott, C. A. (2000). Illicit psychoactive substance use, heavy use, abuse, and dependence in a U.S. population-based sample of male twins.*Arch. Gen. Psychiat., 57*(3), 1–18.

Kendler, K. S., Kessler, R. D., Walters, E. E., MacLean, C., et al. (1995). Stressful life events, genetic liability, and onset of an episode of major depression in women. *Amer. J. Psychiat., 152(2),* 833–42.

Kendler, K. S., Kuhn, J., & Prescott, C. A. (2004). The interrelationship of neuroticism, sex, and stressful life events in the prediction of episodes of major depression. *Amer. J. Psychiat., 161*(4), 631–636.

Kendler, K. S., McGuire, M., Gruenberg, A. M., O'Hare, A., Spellman, M., & Walsh, D. (1993). The Roscommon family study: Schizophrenia-related personality disorders in relatives. *Arch. Gen. Psychiat., 50,* 781–88.

Kendler, K. S., Myers, J., Prescott, C. A., & Neale, M. C. (2001). The genetic epidemiology of irrational fears and phobias in men. *Arch. Gen. Psychiat., 58,* 257–265.

Kendler, K. S., Neale, M. C., Kessler, R. C., Heath, A. C., & Eaves, L. J. (1992a). Generalized anxiety disorder in women: A population-based twin study. *Arch. Gen. Psychiat., 49,* 267–72.

Kendler, K. S., Neale, M. C., Kessler, R. C., Heath, A. C., & Eaves, L. J. (1992b). The genetic epidemiology of phobias in women: The interrelationship of agoraphobia, social phobia, situational phobia, and simple phobia. *Arch. Gen. Psychiat., 49,* 273–81.

Kendler, K. S., Neale, M. C., Kessler, R. C., Heath, A. C., & Eaves, L. J. (1992d). Panic disorder in women: A population-based twin study. *Psychol. Med., 23,* 397–406.

Kendler, K. S., Thornton, L. M., & Gardner, C. O. (2000). Stressful life events and previous episodes in the etiology of major depression in women: An evaluation of the "Kindling" hypothesis. *Amer. J. Psychiat., 157,* 1243–51.

Kendler, K. S., Thornton, L. M., Gilman, S. E., & Kessler, R. C. (2000). Sexual orientation in a U.S. national sample of twin and nontwin sibling pairs. *Amer. J. Psychiat., 157,* 1843–46.

Kendler. K. S., Walters, E. E., & Kessler, R. C. (1997). The prediction of length of major depressive episodes: Results from an epidemiological sample of female twins. *Psychol. Med., 27,* 107–17.

Kendler, K. S., Walters, E. E., Neale, M. C., Kessler, R. C., Heath, A. C., & Eaves, L. J. (1995). The structure of the genetic and environmental risk factors for six major psychiatric disorders in women: Phobia, generalized anxiety disorder, panic disorder, bulimia, major depression, and alcoholism. *Arch. Gen. Psychiat., 52,* 374–83.

Kenis, G., & Maes, M. (2002). Effects of antidepressants on the production of cytokines. *The International Journal of Neuropharmacology, 5,* 401–12.

Kennard, D. (2000). Therapeutic communities. In M. G. Gelder, J. J. Lopez-Ibor, Jr., & N. C. Andreason (Eds.), *New Oxford textbook of psychiatry* (pp. 1483–90). Oxford: Oxford University Press.

Kennard, D. (2004). The therapeutic community as an adaptable treatment modality across different settings. *Psychiatr. Q., 75*(3), 295–307.

Kennedy, B. L., Lynch, G. V., & Schwab, J. J. (1998). Assessment of locus of control in patients with anxiety and depressive disorders. *J. Clin. Psychol., 54*(4). 509–515.

Kent, G. (1997). Dental phobias. In G. C. L. Davey (Ed.), *Phobias. A handbook of theory, research and treatment* (pp. 107–27). Chichester, England: Wiley.

Kernberg, O. F. (1985). *Borderline conditions and pathological narcissism.* Northvale, NJ: Jason Aronson.

Kernberg, O. F. (1996). A psychoanalytic theory of personality disorders. In J. F. Clarkin & M. F. Lenzenweger (Eds.), *Major theories of personality disorder* (pp. 106–40). New York: Guilford.

Kernberg, O. F. (1996). A psychoanalytic theory of personality disorders. In J. F. Clarkin & M. F. Lenzenweger (Eds.), *Major theories of personality disorder.* (pp. 106–140). New York: Guilford.

Kernberg, O. F. (1998). Pathological narcissism and narcissistic personality disorder: Theoretical background and diagnostic classification. In E. F. Ronningstam (Ed.), *Disorders of narcissism: Diagnostic, clinical, and empirical implications* (pp. 29–51). Washington, DC: American Psychiatric Press.

Kershner, J. G., Cohen, N. J., & Coyne, J. C. (1998). Expressed emotion in families of clinically referred and nonreferred children: Toward a further understanding of the expressed emotion index. *J. Fam. Psychol., 10*(1), 97–106.

Kessler, R. C. (2003). Epidemiology of women and depression. *J. Affect. Dis., 74*(1), 5–13.

Kessler, R. C., & Merikangas, K. R. (2004). The National Comorbidity Survey Replication (NCS-R). *Int. J. Method. Psych., 13*(2), 60–68.

Kessler, R. C., & Zhao, S. (1999). Overview of descriptive epidemiology of mental disorders. In C. S. Aneshensel & J. C. Phelan (Eds.), *Handbook of sociology of mental health. Handbook of sociology and social research* (pp. 127–50). New York: Kluwer/Plenum.

Kessler, R. C., Avenevoli, S., & Merikangas, K. R. (2001). Mood disorders in children and adolescents: An epidemiologic perspective. *Biol. Psychiat., 49*(12), 1002–14.

Kessler, R. C., Berglund, P., Borges, G., Nock, M., & Wang, P. S. (2005). Trends in suicide ideation, plans, gestures, and attempts in the United States. *JAMA, 293*(20), 2487–2495.

Kessler, R. C., Berglund, P., Chiu, W. T., Demler, O., Heeringa, S., Hiripi, E., Jin, R., Pennell, B.-P., Walters, E. E., Zaslavsky, A., & Zheng, H. (2004). The US National Comorbidity Survey Replication (NCS-R): Design and field procedures. *Int. J. Method. Psych. Res., 13*(2), 69–92.

Kessler, R. C., Berglund, P., Demler, O., Jin, R., & Walters, E. E. (2005b). Lifetime prevalence and age-of-onset distributions of DSM-IV disorders in the National Comorbidity Survey Replication. *Arch. Gen. Psychiat., 62,* 593–602.

Kessler, R. C., Berglund, P., Demler, O., Jin, R., Koretz, D., Merikangas, K. R., et al. (2003). The epidemiology of major depressive disorder: Results from the National Comorbidity Survey Replication. *JAMA, 289*(23), 3095–3105.

Kessler, R. C., Berglund, P., Demler, O., Jin, R., Merikangas, K. R., & Walters, E. E. (2005a). Lifetime prevalence and age-of-onset distributions of *DSM-IV* disorders in the National Comorbidity Survey Replication. *Arch. Gen. Psychiat., 62,* 593–602.

Kessler, R. C., Chiu, W. T., Demler, O., & Walters, E. E. (2005b). Prevalence, severity, and comorbidity of 12-month *DSM-IV* disorders in the National Comorbidity Survey Replication. *Arch. Gen. Psychiat., 62,* 617–627.

Kessler, R. C., McGonagle, K. A., Zhao, S., Nelson, C. B., Hughes, M., Eshleman, S., Wittchen, H.-U., & Kendler, K. S. (1994). Lifetime and 12-month prevalence of DSM-III-R psychiatric disorders in the United States: Results from the national comorbidity survey. *Arch. Gen. Psychiat., 51,* 8–19.

Kessler, R. C., Nelson, C. B., McGonagle, K. A., Liu, J., Swartz, M., & Blazer, D. G. (1996). Comorbidity of DSM-III-R major depressive disorder in the general population: Results from the U.S. national comorbidity survey. *Brit. J. Psychiat, 168*(suppl. 30), 17–30.

Kessler, R. C., Sonnega, A., Bromet, E., Hughes, M., & Nelsom, C. B. (1995). Post-traumatic stress disorder in the National Comorbidity Study. *Arch. Gen. Psychiat., 52,* 1048–60.

Kety, S. S. (1974). From rationalization to reason. *Amer. J. Psychiat., 131,* 957–63.

Kety, S. S. (1987). The significance of genetic factors in the etiology of schizophrenia. *J. Psychiat. Res., 21,* 423–29.

Kety, S. S., Rosenthal, D., Wender, P. H., & Schulsinger, F. (1968). The types and prevalence of mental illness in the biological and adoptive families of adopted schizophrenics. In D. Rosenthal & S. S. Kety (Eds.), *The transmission of schizophrenia.* Elmsford, NY: Pergamon.

Kety, S. S., Rosenthal, D., Wender, P. H., Schulsinger, F., & Jacobsen, B. (1978). The biologic and adoptive families of adopted individuals who became schizophrenic: Prevalence of mental illness and other characteristics. In L. C. Wynne, R. L. Cromwell, & S. Matthyse (Eds.), *The nature of schizophrenia: New approaches to research and treatment* (pp. 25–37). New York: Wiley.

Kety, S. S., Wender, P. H., Jacobsen, B., Ingraham, L. J., Jansson, L., Faber, B., & Kinney, D. K. (1994). Mental illness in the biological and adoptive relatives of schizophrenic adoptees: Replication of the Copenhagen study in the rest of Denmark. *Arch. Gen. Psychiat., 51*(6), 442–55.

Keys, A., Brozek, J., Henschel, A., Mickelson, O., & Taylor, H. L. (1950). *The biology of human starvation.* Minneapolis: University of Minnesota Press.

Khalifa, N., & von Knorring, A. L. (2004). Prevalence of tic disorders and Tourette syndrome in a Swedish school population. *J. Amer. Acad. Child Adoles. Psychiat., 43*(2) 206–14.

Khan, A., Cowan, C., & Roy, A. (1997). Personality disorders in people with learning disabilities: A community survey. *J. Intell. Dis. Res., 41*(4), 324–30.

Khazaal, Y., Zimmerman, G., & Zullino, D. F. (2005). Depersonalization—current data. *Canad. J. Psychiat., 50*(2), 101–7.

Khouzam, H. R., El-Gabalawi, F., Pirwani, N., & Priest, F. (2004). Asperger's disorder: A review of its diagnosis and treatment. *Compr. Psychiat., 45*(3), 184–91.

Kici, G., & Westhoff, K. (2004). Evaluation of requirements for the assessment and construction of interview guides in psychological assessment. *Europ. J. Psychol. Assess., 20,* 83–98.

Kidson, M., & Jones, I. (1968). Psychiatric disorders among aborigines of the Australian Western Desert. *Arch. Gen. Psychiat., 19,* 413–22.

Kiecolt-Glaser, J. K., McGuire, L., Robles, T. F., & Glaser, R. (2002a). Emotion, morbidity, and mortality: New perspectives from psychoneuroimmunology. *Ann. Rev. Psychol., 53,* 83–107.

Kiecolt-Glaser, J. K., McGuire, L., Robles, T. F., & Glaser, R. (2002b). Psychoneuroimmunology: Psychological influences on immune function and health. *J. Cons. Clin. Psychol., 70*(3), 537–47.

Kiecolt-Glaser, J. K., Page, G. G., Marucha, P. T., MacCallum, R. C., & Glaser, R. (1998). Psychological influences on surgical recovery: Perspectives from psychoneuroimmunology. *Amer. Psychol., 53*(11), 1209–18.

Kiecolt-Glaser, J., & Glaser, R. (1988). Psychological influences in immunity: Implications for AIDS. *Amer. Psychol., 43,* 892–98.

Kiehl, K. A., Smith, A. M., Hare, R. D., Mendrek, A., Forster, B. B., Brink, J., & Liddle, P. F. (2001). Limbic abnormalities in affective processing by criminal psychopaths as revealed by functional magnetic resonance imaging. *Biol. Psychiat., 50,* 677–84.

Kiesler, C. A., & Sibulkin, A. E. (1987). *Mental hospitalization: Myths and facts about a national crisis.* Newbury Park, CA: Sage.

Kiesler, C. A., & Simpkins, C. G. (1993). *The unnoticed majority in inpatient psychiatric care.* New York: Plenum.

Kiesler, D. J. (1996). *Contemporary interpersonal theory and research.* New York: Wiley.

Kiev, A. (1972). *Transcultural psychiatry.* New York: Free Press.

Kihlstrom, J. F. (1994). One hundred years of hysteria. In S. J. Lynn & J. W. Rhue (Eds.), *Dissociation: Clinical and theoretical perspectives* (pp. 365–94). New York: Guilford.

Kihlstrom, J. F. (2001). Dissociative disorders. In P. B. Sutker & H. E. Adams (Eds.), *Comprehensive handbook of psychopathology* (3rd ed., pp. 259–76). New York: Kluwer Academic/Plenum.

Kihlstrom, J. F. (2002). To honor Kraepelin ...: From symptoms to pathology in the diagnosis of mental illness. In L. E. Beutler & M. L. Malik (Eds.), *Rethinking the DSM: A psychological perspective* (pp. 279–303). Washington, DC: American Psychological Association.

Kihlstrom, J. F., & Schacter, D. L. (2000). Functional amnesia. In F. Boller & J. Grafman (Eds.), *Handbook of neuropsychology* (2nd ed., *Vol 2: Memory and its disorders,* ed. L. S. Cermak; pp. 409–27). Amsterdam: Elsevier Science.

Kihlstrom, J. F., Glisky, M. L., & Angiulo, M. J. (1994). Dissociative tendencies and dissociative disorders. *J. Abn. Psychol., 103*(1), 117–24.

Kihlstrom, J. F., Tataryn, D. J., & Hoyt, I. P. (1993). Dissociative disorders. In P. B. Sutker & H. E. Adams (Eds.), *Comprehensive handbook of psychopathology* (pp. 203–34). New York: Plenum.

Killen, J. D., Fortmann, S. P., Davis, L., & Varady, A. (1997). Nicotine patch and self-help video for cigarette smoking cessation. *J. Cons. Clin. Psychol., 65*(4), 663–72.

Kilzieh, N., Akiskal, H. S. (1999). Rapid-cycling bipolar disorder: An overview of research and clinical experience. *Psychiat. Clin. N. Amer., 22,* 585–607.

Kim, A., Galanter, M., Castaneda, R., & Lifshutz, H. (1992). Crack cocaine use and sexual behavior among psychiatric inpatients. *Amer. J. Drug Alcoh. Abuse, 18,* 235–46.

Kim, K., & Jacobs, S. (1995). Stress bereavement and consequent psychiatric illness. In C. M. Mazure (Ed.), *Does stress cause psychiatric illness?* Washington, DC: American Psychiatric Association.

King, C. A. (1997). Suicidal behavior in adolescence. In R. W. Maris, M. M. Silverman, & S. S. Canetton (Eds.), *Review of Suicidology, 1997* (pp. 61–95). New York: Guilford.

King, D. A., & Markus, H. F. (2000). Mood disorders in older adults. In S. K. Whitbourne (Ed.), *Psychopathology in later adulthood* (pp. 141–72). New York: Wiley.

King, L. J. (1999). A brief history of psychiatry: Millennia past and present—Part II. *Ann. Clin. Psychiat., 2,* 47–54.

Kinney, D. K., Holzman, P. S., Jacobsen, B., Jansson, L., Faber, B., Hildebrand, W., Kasell, E., & Zimbalist, M. E. (1997). Thought disorder in schizophrenic and control adoptees and their relatives. *Arch. Gen. Psychiat., 54*(5), 475–79.

Kinsey, A. C., Pomeroy, W. B., & Martin, C. E. (1948). *Sexual behavior in the human male.* Philadelphia: Sanders.

Kinsey, A. C., Pomeroy, W. B., Martin, C. E., & Gebhard, P. H. (1953). *Sexual behavior in the human female.* Philadelphia: Saunders.

Kinzl, J., & Biebl, W. (1992). Long-term effects of incest: Life events triggering mental disorders in female patients with sexual abuse in childhood. *Child Ab. Negl., 16,* 567–73.

Kirk, S. A., & Kutchins, H. (1992). *The selling of DSM: The rhetoric of science in psychiatry.* Hawthorne, NY: Aldine de Gruyter.

Kirkland, G. (1986). *Dancing on My Grave.* New York: Doubleday.

Kirmayer, L. J., & Groleau, D. (2001). Affective disorders in cultural context. *Cultural Psychiatry: International Perspectives, 24,* 465–78.

Kirmayer, L. J., Young, A., Hayton, B. C. (1995). The cultural context of anxiety disorders. *Cultur. Psychiat., 18*(3), 503–21.

Kirmayer, L. J. (1991). The place of culture in psychiatric nosology: Taijin Kyofusho and DSM III-R. *J. Nerv. Ment. Dis., 179,* 19–28.

Kirsch, I., Lynn, S. J., & Rhue, J. W. (1993). Introduction to clinical hypnosis. In J. W. Rhue, S. J. Lynn, & I. Kirsch (Eds.), *Handbook of clinical hypnosis* (pp. 3–22). Washington, DC: American Psychological Association.

Kistner, J. A., Ziegert, D. I., Castro, R., & Robertson, B. (2001). Helplessness in early childhood: Prediction of symptoms associated with depression and negative self-worth. *Merrill-Palmer Quarterly, 47*(3), 336–54.

Klackenberg, G. (1987). Incidence of parasomnias in children in a general population. In C. Guilleminault (Ed.), *Sleep and its disorders in children* (pp. 99–113). New York: Raven Press.

Klee, H. (1998). The love of speed: An analysis of the enduring attraction of amphetamine sulphate for British youth. *Journal of Drug Issues, 28*(1), 33–56.

Klein, D. F. (1981). Anxiety reconceptualized. In D. F. Klein & J. Rabkin (Eds.), *Anxiety: New research and changing concepts.* New York: Raven Press.

Klein, D. N., & Shih, J. H. (1998). Depressive personality: Association with DSM-III-R mood and personality disorders and negative and positive affectivity, 30-month stability, and prediciton of course of axis I depressive disorders. *J. Abn. Psychol., 107*(2), 319–327.

Klein, D. N., & Vocisano, C. (1999). Depressive and self-defeating (masochistic) personality disorders. In T. Millon, P. H. Blaney, & R. D. Davis (Eds.), *Oxford textbook of psychopathology* (pp. 653–73). New York: Oxford University Press.

Klein, D. N., Durbin, C. E., Shankman, S. A., & Santiago, N. J. (2002). Depression and personality. In I. H. Gotlib & C. L. Hammen (Eds.), *Handbook of depression* (pp. 115–40). New York: Guilford.

Klein, D. N., Schwartz, J. E., Rose, S., & Leader, J. B. (2000). Five-year course and outcome of dysthymic disorder: A prospective, naturalistic follow-up study. *Amer. J. Psychiat., 157*(6), 931–39.

Klein, D. N. (1999). Commentary on Ryder and Bagby's "Diagnostic viability of depressive personality disorder: Theoretical and conceptual issues." *J. Pers. Dis., 13*(2), 118–27.

Klein, M. (1934). A contribution to the psychogenesis of manic-depressive states. In *Contributions to psychoanalysis, 1921–1945* (pp. 282–310). London: Hogarth Press.

Kleinknecht, R. A., Dinnel, D. L., & Kleinknecht, E. E. (1997). Cultural factors in social anxiety: A comparison of social phobia symptoms and Taijin Kyofusho. *J. Anxiety Dis., 11*(2), 157–77.

Kleinman, A. (1988). *Rethinking psychiatry: From cultural category to personal experience.* New York: Free Press.

Kleinman, A. (2004). Culture and depression. *N. Engl. J. Med., 351*(10), 951–953.

Kleinman, A. M., & Good, B. J. (1985). *Culture and depression.* Berkeley, CA: University of California Press.

Kleinman, A. M. (1986). *Social origins of distress and disease: Depression, neurasthenia and pain in modern China.* New Haven, CT: Yale University Press.

Kleinman, P. H., Kang, S., Lipton, D. S., & Woody, G. E. (1992). Retention of cocaine abusers in outpatient psychotherapy. *Amer. J. Drug Alcoh. Abuse, 18,* 29 43.

Klem, M. L., Wing, R. R., McGuire, M. T., Seagle, H. M., & Hill, J. O. (1997). A descriptive study of individuals successful at long-term maintenance of substantial weight loss. *Amer. J. Clin. Nutri., 66,* 239–46.

Klerman, G. L., Weissman, M. M., Markowitz, J. C., Glick, I., Wilner, P. J., Mason, B., & Shear, M. K. (1994). Medication and psychotherapy. In A. E. Bergin & S. L. Garfield (Eds.), *Handbook of psychotherapy and behavior change* (4th ed., pp. 734–82). New York: Wiley.

Klerman, G. L., Weissman, M. M., Rounsaville, B. J., & Chevron, E. S. (1984). *Interpersonal psychotherapy of depression.* New York: Basic Books.

Klerman, G. L. (1990). The psychiatric patient's right to effective treatment: Implications of *Osherhoff* v. *Chestnut Lodge. Amer. J. Psychiat., 147,* 409–18.

Kliewer, W., Lepore, S. J., Oskin, D., & Johnson, P. D. (1998). The role of social and cognitive processes in children's adjustment to community violence. *J. Cons. Clin. Psychol., 66*(1), 199–209.

Klinger, E., & Kroll-Mensing, D. (1995). Idiothetic assessment. In J. N. Butcher (Ed.), *Clinical personality assessment: Practical considerations* (pp. 267–77). New York: Oxford University Press.

Klinger, E. (1979). Modes of normal conscious flow. In K. S. Pope & J. L. Singer (Eds.), *The stream of consciousness: Scientific investigations into the flow of human experience.* New York: Plenum.

Klingman, A. (1993). School-based intervention following a disaster. In C. F. Saylor (Ed.), *Children and disasters* (pp. 187–210). New York: Plenum.

Kloner, R. A., Leor, J., Poole, W. K., & Perritt, R. (1997). Population-based analysis of the effect of the Northridge earthquake on cardiac death in Los Angeles County, California. *Journal of the American College of Cardiology, 30,* 1174–80.

Klosterkötter, J., Hellmich, M., Steinmeyer, E. M., & Schultze-Luttter, F. (2001). Diagnosing schizophrenia in the initial prodromal phase. *Arch. Gen. Psychiat., 58,* 158–64.

Kluft, R. P. (1993). Basic principles in conducting the treatment of multiple personality disorder. In R. P. Kluft & C. G. Fine (Eds.), *Clinical perspectives on multiple personality disorder* (pp. 53–73). Washington, DC: American Psychiatric Press.

Kluft, R. P. (1999). Dissociative identity disorder. In N. Miller & K. Magruder (Eds.), *Cost-effectiveness of psychotherapy: A guide for practitioners, researchers, and policymakers* (pp. 306–13). New York: Oxford University Press.

Klump, K. L., Strober, M., Bulik, C. M., Thornton, L., Johnson, C., Devlin, B., Fichter, M., Halmi, K. A., Kaplan, A. S., Woodside, D. B., Crow, S., Mitchell, J., Rotondo, A., Keel, P., Berrettini, W. H., Plotnicov, K., Pollice, C., Lilenfeld, L. R., & Kaye, W. H. (2004). Personality characteristics of women before and after recovery from an eating disorder. *Psychol. Med., 34,* 1407–18.

Knapp, S. (1980). A primer on malpractice for psychologists. *Profess. Psychol., 11*(4), 606–12.

Knight, R. A. (1997). *A unified model of sexual aggression: Consistencies and differences across noncriminal and criminal samples.* Paper presented at meeting of the Association for the Treatment of Sexual Abusers, Arlington, VA.

Knight, R., & Prentky, R. (1990). Classifying sexual offenders: The development and corroboration of taxonomic models. In W. L. Marshall, D. R. Laws, & H. E. Barbaree (Eds.), *Handbook of sexual assault: Issues, theories, and treatment of the offender* (pp. 23–52). New York: Plenum.

Knight, R., Prentky, R., & Cerce, D. (1994). The development, reliability, and validity of an inventory for the multidimensional assessment of sex and aggression. *Crim. Just. Behav., 21,* 72–94.

Kocsis, J. H., Zisook, S., Davidson, J., Shelton, R., Yonkers, K., Hellerstein, D. J., Rosenbaum, J., & Halbreich, U. (1997). Double-blind comparisons of sertraline, imipramine, and placebo in the treatment of dysthymia: Psychosocial outcomes. *Amer. J. Psychiat., 154*(3), 390–95.

Kodituwakku, P. W., Kalberg, W., & May, P. A. (2001). The effects of prenatal alcohol exposure on executive functioning. *Alcohol Research & Health, 25,* 198.

Koenigsberg, H. W., Kernberg, O. F., Stone, M. H., Appelbaum, A. H., Yeomans, F. E., & Diamond, D. (2000). *Borderline patients: Extending the limits of treatability.* New York: Basic Books.

Koenigsberg, H. W., Woo-Ming, A. M., & Siever, L. J. (2002). Pharmacological treatments for personality disorders. In P. E. Nathan & J. M. Gorman (Eds.), *A guide to treatments that work* (2nd ed., pp. 625–54). New York: Oxford University Press.

Kohut, H., & Wolff, E. (1978). The disorders of the self and their treatment: An outline. *Inter. J. Psychoanal., 59,* 413–26.

Kolata, G. (1998, Apr. 4). New drug for impotence raises hope for its use by women, too. *New York Times.*

Kolata, G. B. (1981). Fetal alcohol advisory debated. *Science, 214,* 642–46.

Koltek, M., Wilkes, T. C. R., & Atkinson, M. (1998). The prevalence of posttraumatic stress disorder in an adolescent inpatient unit. *Canad. J. Psychiat., 43*(1), 64–68.

Komaroff, A. L., & Buchwald, D. S. (1998). Chronic fatigue syndrome: An update. *Ann. Rev. Med., 49,* 1–13.

Komro, K. A., Perry, C. L., Veblen-Mortenson, S., Bosma, L. M., Dudovitz, B. S., Williams, C., Jones-Webb, R., & Toomey, T. L. (2004). Brief report: The adaptation of Project Northland for urban youth. *J. Pediat. Psychol., 29*(6), 457–66.

Konrad, K., Gunther, T., Hanisch, C., & Herpertz-Dahlmann, B. (2004). Differential effects of methylphenidate on attentional functions in children with attention-deficit/hyperactivity disorder. *J. Amer. Acad. Child Adoles. Psychia., 43*(2) 191–98.

Koob, G. F., Mason, B. J., De Witte, P., Littleton, J., & Siggins, G. R. (2002). Potential neuroprotective effects of acamprosate. *Alcoholism: Clinical & Experimental Research, 26*(4), 586–92.

Kopelowicz, A., Liberman, R. P., & Zarate, R. (2002). Psychosocial treatments for schizophrenia. In P. E. Nathan & J. M. Gorman (Eds.), *A guide to treatments that work* (2nd ed., pp. 201–28). New York: Oxford University Press.

Koponen, S., Taiminem, T., Portin, R., Himanen, L., Isoniemi, H., Heinonen, H., Hinkka, S., & Tenuvuo, O. (2002). Axis I and Axis II psychiatric disorders after traumatic brain injury: A 30-year follow up study. *Amer. J. Psychiat., 159,* 1315–21.

Korkeila, J., Lehtinen, V., Tuori, T., & Helenius, H. (1998). Patterns of psychiatric hospital service use in Finland: A national register study of hospital discharges in the early 1990's. *Soc. Psychiat. Psychiatr. Epidemiol., 33,* 218–23.

Koss, M. P. (1983). The scope of rape: Implications for the clinical treatment of victims. *Clin. Psychol., 36,* 88–91.

Koss, M. P., & Figueredo, A. J. (2004). Cognitive mediation of rape's mental health impact: Constructive replication of a cross-sectional model in longitudinal data. *Psychol. Women Quart., 28*(4), 273–86.

Kosslyn, S. M., Cacioppo, J. T., Davidson, R. J., Hugdahl, K., Lovallo, W. R., Spiegel, D., & Rose, R. (2002). Bridging psychology and biology: The analysis of individuals in groups. *Amer. Psychol., 57*(5), 341–51.

Kosten, T. R. (1989). Pharmacotherapeutic interventions for cocaine abuse: Matching patients to treatments. *J. Nerv. Ment. Dis., 177,* 379–89.

Kosten, T. R. (1997). Substance abuse and schizophrenia. *Schizo. Bull., 23,* 181–86.

Kosten, T. R. (2003). Buprenorphine for opioid detoxification: A brief review. *Addict. Dis. Treat., 2*(4), 107–12.

Kosten, T. R., & Rounsaville, B. J. (1986). Psychopathology in opioid addicts. *Psychiat. Clin. N. Amer., 9,* 515–32.

Kosten, T. R., Silverman, D. G., Fleming, J., & Kosten, T. A. (1992). Intraveneous cocaine challenges during naltrexone maintenance: A preliminary study. *Biol. Psychiat., 32,* 543–48.

Kovacs, M., Devlin, B., Pollack, M., Richards, C., & Mukerji, P. (1997). A controlled family history study of childhood-onset depressive disorder. *Arch. Gen. Psychiat., 54,* 613–23.

Kovar, K. A. (1998). Chemistry and pharmacology of hallucinogens, entactogens and stimulants. *Pharmacopsychiatry, 31*(Suppl. 2), 69–72.

Kozak, M. J., Liebowitz, M. R., & Foa, E. B. (2000). Cognitive behavior therapy and pharmacotherapy for obsessive-compulsive disorder: The NIMH-sponsored collaborative study. In W. K. Goodman & M. V. Rudorfer, et al. (Eds.), *Obsessive-compulsive disorder: Contemporary issues in treatment. Personality and clinical psychology series* (pp. 501–30). Mahwah, NJ: Erlbaum.

Kozleski, E. B., & Jackson, L. (1993). Taylor's story: Full inclusion in her neighborhood elementary school. *Except., 4*(3), 153–75.

Kraepelin, E. (1883). *Compendium der psychiatrie.* Leipzig: Abel.

Kraepelin, E. (1896). Dementia praecox. In J. Cutting & M. Shepherd (1987), *The clinical roots of the schizophrenia concept: Translation of seminal European contributions on schizophrenia* (pp. 13–24). Cambridge: Cambridge University Press.

Kraepelin, E. (1899). *Psychiatrie. Ein lehrbuch fur studierende und aerzte* (6th ed.). Leipzig: Barth.

Kraines, E. (1989). *Dementia preacox and paraphrenia.* (R. M. Barclay, Trans.) Edinburgh, Scotland: E & S Livingstone. (Original work published 1919)

Kraines, S. H. (1948). *The therapy of the neuroses and psychoses* (3rd ed.). Philadelphia: Lea & Febiger.

Kramer, P. D. (1993). *Listening to Prozac: A psychiatrist explores antidepressant drugs and the remaking of the self.* New York: Viking Penguin.

Kramer, R. A., Warner, V., Olfson, M., Ebanks, C. M., Chaput, F., & Weissman, M. M. (1998). General medical problems among the offspring of depressed parents: A 10-year follow-up. *J. Amer. Acad. Child Adoles. Psychiat., 37*(6), 602–11.

Kramer, R. M. (1998). Paranoid cognition in social systems: Thinking and acting in the shadow of doubt. *Personal. Soc. Psychol. Rev., 2*(4), 251–75.

Krantz, D. S., & McCeney, M. K. (2002). Effects of psychological and social factors on organic disease: A critical assessment of research on coronary heart disease. *Ann. Rev. Psychol., 53,* 341–69.

Kranzler, H. R., Armeli, S., Feinn, R., & Tennen, H. (2004). Targeted Naltrexone treatment moderates the relations between mood and drinking behavior among problem drinkers. *J. Cons. Clin. Psychol., 72,* 317–27

Kranzler, H. R., Del Boca, F. K., & Rounsaville, B. (1997). Comorbid psychiatric diagnosis predicts three-year outcomes in alcoholics: A posttreatment natural history study. *J. Stud. Alcoh., 57*(6), 619–26.

Kring, A. M., & Neale, J. M. (1996). Do schizophrenic patients show a disjunctive relationship among expressive, experiential, and psychophysiological correlates of emotion? *J. Abn. Psychol., 105,* 249–57.

Krippner, S. (1994). Cross-cultural treatment perspectives on dissociative disorders. In S. J. Lynn & J. W. Rhue (Eds.), *Dissociation: Clinical and theoretical perspectives* (pp. 338–64). New York: Guilford.

Kroll, J., & Bachrach, B. (1984). Sin and mental illness in the Middle Ages. *Psychol. Med., 14,* 507–14.

Kronfol, Z., & Remick, D. G. (2000). Cytokines and the brain: Implications for clinical psychiatry. *Amer. J. Psychiat., 157*(5), 683–94.

Krueger, R. F., Hicks, B. M., Patrick, C. J., Carlson, S. R., Iacono, W. G., & McGue, M. (2002). Etiologic connections among substance dependence, antisocial behavior, and personality: Modeling the externalizing spectrum. *J. Abn. Psychol., 111*(3), 411–24.

Krystal, J. H., Cramer, J. A., Krol, W. F., Kirk, G. F., & Rosenheck, R. A. (2001). Naltrexone in the treatment of alcohol dependence. *N. Engl. J. Med., 345*(24), 1734–39.

Krystal, J. H., Deutsch, D. N., & Charney, D. S. (1996). The biological basis of panic disorder. *J. Clin. Psychiat., 57*(10), 23–31.

Krystal, J. H., Perry, E. B., Gueorguieva, R., Belger, A., Madonick, S. H., Abi-Dargham, A., Cooper, T. B., MacDougall, L., Abi-Saab W., & D'Souza, C. (2005). Comparative and interactive psychopharmacologic effects of ketamine and amphetamine. *Arch. Gen. Psychiat., 62,* 985–95.

Kubota, T., Ushijima, Y., Yamada, K., Okuyama, C., Kizu, O., & Nishimura, T. (2005). Diagnosis of Alzheimer's disease using brain perfusion SPECT and MRI imaging: Which modality achieves better diagnostic accuracy? *European Journal of Nuclear Medicine and Molecular Imaging, 32,* 414–21.

Kuch, K. (1997). Accident phobia. In G. C. L. Davey (Ed.), *Phobias. A handbook of theory, research and treatment* (pp. 153–62). Chichester, England: Wiley.

Kulhara, P., & Chakrabarti, S. (2001). Culture and schizophrenia and other psychotic disorders. *Cultural Psychiatry: International Perspectives, 24,* 449–64.

Kumar, A., Li, Y., Patil, S., & Jain, S. (2005). A haplotype of the angiotensin gene is associated with hypertension in African Americans. *Clinical and Experimental Pharmacoloy and Physiology, 32*(5–6), 495–502.

Kumpfer, K. L. (2000). Strengthening family involvement in school substance abuse prevention programs. In W. B. Hansen, S. M. Giles, & M. D. Fearnow-Kenney (Eds.), *Improving prevention effectiveness* (pp. 127–37). Greensboro, NC: Tanglewood Research.

Kunda, Z. (1999). *Social cognition: Making sense of people.* Cambridge, MA: M.I.T. Press.

Kuperman, S., Black, D. W., & Burns, T. L. (1988). Excess mortality among formerly hospitalized child psychiatric patients. *Arch. Gen. Psychiat., 45,* 277–82.

Kupersmidt, J. B., Coie, J. D., & Dodge, K. A. (1990). The role of poor peer relationships in the development of disorder. In S. R. Asher & J. D. Coie (Eds.), *Peer rejection in childhood* (pp. 274–308). New York: Cambridge University Press.

Kupersmidt, J. B., Coie, J. D., & Howell, J. C. (2004). Resillience in children exposed to negative peer influences. In K. I. Maton, C.J. Schellenbach, B. J. Leadbeater, & A. L. Solarz (Eds.) *Investing in children, youth, families, and communities: Strenths-based research and policy* (pp. 251–268). Washington DC: American Psychological Association.

Kupfer, D. J. (2005). The increasing medical burden in bipolar disorder. *JAMA, 293*(20), 2528–2530.

Kurlan, R. (1997). Treatment of tics. *Neurologic Clinics, 15*(2), 403–9.

Kushner, M. G., Thuras, P., Kaminski, J., Anderson, N., Neumeyer, B., & Mackenzie, T. (2000). Expectancies for alcohol to effect tension and anxiety as a function of time. *Addictive Behaviors, 25*(1), 93–98.

Kwapil, T. R. (1996). A longitudinal study of drug and alcohol use by psychosis-prone and impulsive-nonconforming individuals. *J. Abn. Psychol., 105*(1), 114–23.

La Greca, A. M., Silverman, W. K., Vernberg, E. M., & Prinstein, M. J. (1996). Symptoms of posttraumatic stress disorder in children after Hurricane Andrew: A prospective study. *J. Cons. Clin. Psychol., 64*(4), 712–23.

La Greca, A. (2001). Children experiencing disasters. In J. H. Hughes, A. M. La Greca, & J. C. Conoley (Eds.), *Handbook of psychological services for children and adolescents* (pp. 195–222). London: Oxford University Press.

La Rue, A., & Swanda, R. (1997). Neuropsychological assessment. In P. D. Nussbaum (Ed.), *Handbook of neuropsychology and aging* (pp. 360–84). New York: Plenum.

Laan, E., & Everaerd, W. (1995). Determinants of female sexual arousal: Psychophysiological theory and data. *Annu. Rev. Sex Res., 6,* 32–76.

Lacerda, A. L. T., Keshavan, M. S., Hardan, A. Y., Yorbik, O., Brambilla, P., Sassi, R. B., et al. (2004). Anatomic evaluation of the orbitofrontal cortex in major depressive disorder. *Biol. Psychiat., 55,* 353–358.

Lachar, D., Bailley, S. E., Rhoades, H. M., Espadas, A., Aponte, M., Cowan, K. A., Gummatira, P., Kopecky, C. R., & Wassef, A. (2001). New subscales for an anchored version of the Brief Psychiatric Rating Scale: Construction, reliability, and validity in acute psychiatric admissions. *Psychol. Assess., 13,* 384–95.

Ladd, C. O., Huot, R. L., Thrivikraman, K. V., Nemeroff, C. B., Meaney, M. J., & Plotsky, P. M. (2000). Long-term behavioral and neuroendocrine adaptations to adverse early experience. In E. A. Meyer & C. B. Saper (Eds.), *Progress in brain research: Vol 122. The biological basis for mind-body interactions.* Amsterdam: Elsevier.

Ladd, G. T., & Petry, N. M. (2003). A comparison of pathological gamblers with and without substance abuse treatment histories. *Exper. Clin. Psychopharm., 11,* 202–9.

Lahey, B. B., Loeber, R., Burke, J. D., & Applegate, B. (2005). Predicting future antisocial personality disorder in males from a clinical assessment in childhood. *J. Cons. Clin. Psychol., 73,* 389–99.

Lahey, B. B., McBurnett, K., & Loeber, R. (2000). Are attention-deficit/hyperactivity disorder and oppositional defiant disorder developmental precursors to conduct disorder? In A. J. Sameroff, M. Lewis, et al. (Eds.), *Handbook of developmental psychopathology* (2nd ed., pp. 431–46). New York: Kluwer.

Laird, R. D., Jordan, K. Y., Dodge, K. A., Pettit, G. S., & Bates, J. E. (2001). Peer rejection in childhood, involvement with antisocial peers in early adolescence, and the development of externalizing behavior problems. *Develop. Psychopath., 13,* 337–54.

Lally, S. J. (2003). What tests are acceptable for use in forensic evaluations? A survey of experts. *Prof. Psychol: Res. Pract., 34,* 434–47.

Lam, A. G., & Sue, S. (2001). Client diversity. *Psychother., 38,* 479–86.

Lam, D. H. (1991). Psychosocial family intervention in schizophrenia: A review of empirical studies. *Psychol. Med., 21,* 423–41.

Lamb, H. R., & Weinberger, L. E. (1998). Persons with severe mental illness in jails and prisons: A review. *Psychiatr. Serv., 49*(4), 483–92.

Lamb, H. R. (1998). Deinstitutionalization at the beginning of the new millennium. *Harvard Review of Psychiatry, 6,* 1–10.

Lambe, E. K., Katzman, D. K., Mikulis, D. J., Kennedy, S. H., & Zipursky, R. B. (1997). Cerebral gray matter volume deficits after weight recovery from anorexia nervosa. *Arch. Gen. Psychiat., 54*(6), 537–42.

Lamberg, L. (1998). Mental illness and violent acts: protecting the patient and the public. *JAMA, 280,* 407–8.

Lambert, M. J. & Ogles, B. M. (2004). The efficacy and effectiveness of psychotherapy. In M. J. Lambert (2004). *Bergin and Garfield's handbook of Psychotherapy and behavior change.* New York: John Wiley and Sons, pp. 139–193.

Lambert, M. J., Hansen, N. B., & Finch, A. E. (2001). Patient-focused research: Using patient outcome data to enhance treatment. *J. Cons. Clin. Psychol., 69*(2), 159–72.

Lambert, M. J., Shapiro, D. A., & Bergin, A. E. (1986). The effectiveness of psychotherapy. In S. L. Garfield & A. E. Bergin (Eds.), *Handbook of psychotherapy and behavior change.* New York: Wiley.

Lambert, M. J. (1989). The individual therapist's contribution to psychotherapy process and outcome. *Clin. Psychol. Rev., 9,* 469–85.

Lambert, M. J. (2004). *Bergin and Garfield's handbook of Psychotherapy and behavior change.* New York: John Wiley and Sons.

Lane, S. D., Cherek, D. R., Pietras, C. J. & Steinberg, J. L. (2005). Performance of heavy marijuana-smoking adolescents on a laboratory measure of motivation. *Add. Behav., 30*(2), 815–28.

Lang, P. J., Davis, M., & Öhman, A. (2000). Fear and anxiety: Animal modes and human cognitive psychophysiology. *J. Affec. Dis., 61,* 137–59.

Lang, P. J. (1968). Fear reduction and fear behavior: Problems in treating a construct. In J. M. Shlien (Ed.), *Research in psychotherapy* (Vol. 3). Washington, DC: American Psychological Association.

Lang, P. J. (1971). Application of psychophysiological methods to the study of psychotherapy and behavior modification. In A. E. Bergin & S. L. Garfield (Eds.), *Handbook of psychotherapy and behavior change.* New York: Wiley.

Lang, P. J. (1985). The cognitive psychophysiology of emotion: Fear and anxiety. In A. H. Tuma & J. D. Maser (Eds.), *Anxiety and the anxiety disorders.* Hillsdale, NJ: Erlbaum.

Lang, P. (1970). Autonomic control. *Psych. Today, 4*(5), 37–41.

Lange, W. R., Cabanilla, B. R., Moler, G., Bernacki, E. J., & Frankenfield, D. (1994). Preemployment drug screening at the Johns Hopkins Hospital, 1989 and 1991. *Amer. J. Drug Alcoh. Abuse, 20,* 35–46.

Lapham, S. C., Smith, E., Baca, J. C., Chang, L., Skipper, B. J., Baum, G., & Hunt, W. C. (2001). Prevalence of psychiatric disorders among persons convicted of driving while impaired. *Arch. Gen. Psychiat., 58,* 943–49.

Lasser, K., Boyd, J. W., Woolhandler, S., Himmelstien, D. U., McCormick, D., & Bor, D. H. (2000). Smoking and mental illness: A population-based prevalence study. *JAMA, 284,* 2606–10.

Last, C. G., & Perrin, S. (1993). Anxiety disorders in African-American and white children. *J. Abnorm. Child Psychol., 21,* 153–64.

Latner, J. D., & Stunkard, A. (2003). Getting worse: The stigmatization of obese children. *Obesity Research, 11*(3), 452–56.

Laufer, R. S., Brett, E., & Gallops, M. S. (1985). Dimensions of posttraumatic stress disorder among Vietnam veterans. *J. Nerv. Ment. Dis., 173*(9), 538–45.

Laumann, E. O., Gagnon, J. H., Michael, R. T., & Michaels, S. (1994). *The social organization of sexuality: Sexual practices in the United States.* Chicago: The University of Chicago Press.

Laumann, E. O., Paik, A., & Rosen, R. C. (1999). Sexual dysfunction in the United States: Prevalence and predictors. *JAMA, 281,* 537–44.

Law, W. A., & Mapou, R. L. (1997). Neuropsychological findings in HIV-1 disease and AIDS. In A. M. Horton, D. Wedding, & J. Webster (Eds.), *The neuropsychology handbook* (Vol. 2, pp. 267–308). New York: Springer.

Lawrie, S. M., & Abukmeil, S. S. (1998). Brain abnormality in schizophrenia. *Brit. J. Psychiat., 172,* 110–20.

Lazarus, A. A. (Ed.). (1985). *Casebook of multimodal therapy.* New York: Guilford.

Lazarus, A. A. (1981). *The practice of multimodal therapy.* New York: McGraw-Hill.

Lazarus, A. A. (1997a). *Brief but comprehensive psychotherapy: The multimodal way.* New York: Springer.

Lazarus, A. A. (1997b). Through a different lens: Commentary on "Behavior Therapy: Distinct but Acculturated." *Behav. Ther., 28*(4), 573–75.

Lazarus, A. A. (Ed.). (1996). *Controversies in managed mental health care.* Washington, DC: American Psychiatric Press.

Leal, J., Ziedonis, D., & Kosten, T. (1994). Antisocial personality disorder as a prognostic factor for pharmacotherapy of cocaine dependence. *Drug and Alcohol Dependence, 35,* 31–35.

Leas, L., & Mellor, D. (2000). Prediction of delinquency: The role of depression, risk-taking, and parental attachment. *Behavior Change, 17*(3), 155–66.

Le Blanc, L. A., Hagopian, L. P., & Maglieri, K. A. (2000). Use of a token economy to eliminate excessive inappropriate social behavior in an adult with developmental disabilities. *Behavioral Interventions, 15,* 135–43.

LeBlond, R. F., DeGowin, R. L., & Brown, D. D. (2004). *DeGowin's diagnostic examination.* New York: McGraw-Hill.

Le Couteur, A., Bailey, A., Goode, S., Pickles, A., Robertson, S., Gottesman, I., & Rutter, M. (1996). A broader phenotype of autism: The clinical spectrum in twins. *J. Child Clin. Psychiat., 37*(7), 785–801.

Lebra, W. (Ed.). (1976). Culture-bound syndromes, ethnopsychiatry and alternate therapies. In *Mental health research in Asia and the Pacific* (Vol. 4). Honolulu: University Press of Hawaii.

LeDoux, J. E. (2000). Emotion circuits in the brain. *Annu. Rev. Neurosci., 23,* 155–184.

Lee, P. E., Gill, S. S., Freedman, M., Bronskill, S. E., Hillmer, M. P., & Rochon, P. A. (2004). Atypical antipsychotic drugs in the treatment of behavioral and psychological symptoms of dementia. *BMJ, 329,* 75–78.

Lee, S., & Katzman, M. A. (2002). Cross-cultural perspectives on eating disorders. In C. G. Fairburn & K. D. Brownell (Eds.), *Eating disorders and obesity: A comprehensive handbook* (2nd ed., pp. 260–64). New York: Guilford.

Lee, S., Ho, T. P., & Hsu, L. K. (1993). Fat-phobic and non-fat-phobic anorexia nervosa: A comparative study of 70 Chinese patients in Hong Kong. *Psychol. Med., 23*(4), 999–1017.

Lees-Roitman, S. E., Cornblatt, B. A., Bergman, A., Obuchowski, M., Mitropoulou, V., Keefe, R. S. E., Silverman, J. M., & Siever, L. J. (1997). Attentional functioning in schizotypal personality disorder. *Amer. J. Psychiat., 154*(5), 655–660.

Lefcourt, H. M. (2002). Humor. In C. R. Snyder & S. J. Lopez (Eds.), *Handbook of positive psychology* (pp. 619–31). New York: Oxford University Press.

Leff, J. (2001). Can we manage without the mental hospital? *Austral. N.Z. J. Psychiat., 35*(4), 421–27.

Leff, J., Kuipers, L., Berkowitz, R., Eberlein-Fries, R., & Sturgeon, D. (1982). A controlled trial of social intervention in the families of schizophrenic patients. *Brit. J. Psychiat., 141,* 121–34.

Leff, J., Wig, N. N., Ghosh, A., Bedi, H., Menon, D. K., Kuipers, L., Korten, A., Ernberg, G., Day, R., Sartorius, N., & Jablensky, A. (1987). Influence of relatives' expressed emotion in the course of schizophrenia in Chandigarh. *Brit. J. Psychiat., 151,* 166–73.

Le Grange, D., & Lock, J. (2005). The dearth of psychological treatment studies for anorexia nervosa. *Int. J. Eat. Dis., 37,* 79–91.

Le Grange, D., Telch, C. F., & Tibbs, J. (1998). Eating attitudes and behaviors in 1,435 South African Caucasian and non-Caucasian college students. *Amer. J. Psychiat., 155*(2), 250–54.

Lehman, A. F., Steinwachs, D. M., Dixon, L. B., Postrado, L., Scott, J. E., Fahey, M., Fischer, P., Hoch, J., Kasper, J. A., Lyles, A., Shore, A., & Skinner, E. A. (1998). Patterns of usual care for schizophrenia: Initial results from the Schizophrenia Patient Outcomes Research Team (PORT) Client Survey. *Schizo. Bull., 24*(1), 11–20.

Lehto, J. (1995). *Approaches to alcohol control policy: European alcohol action plan.* Geneva: World Health Organization.

Leichtman, M. D., & Ceci, S. J. (1995). The effects of stereotypes and suggestions on preschoolers' reports. *Develop. Psychol., 31,* 568–78.

Leichtman, M. (2002). Behavioral observations. In J. N. Butcher (Ed.), *Clinical personality assessment* (2nd ed., pp. 303–18). New York: Oxford University Press.

Leit, R. A., Pope, H. G., & Gray, J. J. (2001). Cultural expectations of muscularity in men: The evolution of *Playgirl* centerfolds. *Int. J. Eat. Dis., 29*(1), 90–93.

Leitenberg, H., et al. (1994). Comparison of cognitive-behaviour therapy and desipramine in the treatment of bulimia nervosa. *Behav. Res. Ther., 32,* 37–46.

Lencz, T., Raine, A., Scerbo, A., Redmon, M., Brodish, S., Holt, L., & Bird, L. (1993). Impaired eye tracking in undergraduates with schizotypal personality disorder. *Amer. J. Psychiat., 150,* 152–54.

Lengweiler, M. (2003). Psychiatry beyond the asylum: The origins of German military psychiatry before World War I. *History of Psychiatry, 14,* 14–62.

Lenz, G., & Demal, U. (2000). Quality of life in depression and anxiety disorders: An explanatory follow-up study after intensive cognitive behaviour therapy. *Psychopath., 33,* 297–302.

Lenzenweger, M. F., & Dworkin, R. H. (Ed.). (1998). *Origins and development of schizophrenia: Advances in experimental psychopathology.* Washington, DC: American Psychological Association.

Lenzenweger, M. F., Dworkin, R. H., & Wethington, E. (1991). Examining the underlying structure of schizophrenic phenomenology: Evidence for a 3-process model. *Schizo. Bull., 17,* 515–24.

Leon, G. R., Keel, P. K., Klump, K. L., & Fulkerson, J. A. (1997). The future of risk factor research in understanding the etiology of eating disorders. *Psychopharm. Bull., 33*(3), 405–11.

Leonard, K. E., & Senchak, M. (1996). Prospective prediction of husband marital aggression within newlywed couples. *J. Abn. Psychol., 105,* 369–80.

Leong, G. B., & Eth, S. (1991). Legal and ethical issues in electroconvulsive therapy. *Psychiat. Clin. N. Amer., 14,* 1007–16.

Leproult, R., Copinschi, G., Buxton, O., & Cauter, E. V. (1997). Sleep loss results in an elevation of cortisol the next evening. *Sleep, 20,* 865–70.

Lerman, P. (1981). *Deinstitutionalization: A cross-problem analysis.* Rockville, MD: U.S. Department of Health and Human Services.

Leserman, J., Pettito, J. M., Golden, R. N., Gaynes, B. N., Gu, H., Perkins, D. O. (2000). The impact of stressful life events, depression, social support, coping and cortisol on progression to AIDS. *Amer. J. Psychiat., 157,* 1221–28.

Lesperance, F., Frasure-Smith, N., Theroux, P., & Irwin, M. (2004). The association between major depression and levels of soluble intercellular adhesion molecule 1, interleukin-6, and C-reactive protein in patients with recent acute coronary syndromes. *Amer. J. Psychiat., 161,* 271–77.

Leukefeld, C. G., Logan, P. R., Clayton, C., Martin, R., Zimmerman, A., Milch, R., & Lynam, D. (1998). Adolescent drug use, delinquency, and other behaviors. In T. P. Gullotta, G. R. Adams, & R. Montemayor (Eds.), *Advances in adolescent development: An annual book series.* (Vol. 9, pp. 98–128). Thousand Oaks, CA: Sage.

Leung, A., & Chue, P. (2000). Sex differences in schizophrenia, a review of the literature. *Acta Psychiatr. Scandin., 101,* 3–38.

Leung, P. W., Luk, S. L., Ho, T. P., Taylor, E., Mak, F. L., & Bacon-Shone, J. (1996). The diagnosis and prevalence of hyperactivity in Chinese boys. *Brit. J. Psychiat., 168,* 486–96.

Levav, I., Kohn, R., Golding, J. M., & Weisman, M. M. (1997). Vulnerability of Jews to affective disorders. *Amer. J. Psychiat., 154*(7), 941–47.

LeVay, S. (1991). A difference in hypothalamic structure between heterosexual and homosexual men. *Science, 253,* 1034–37.

Levenstein, S. (2002). Psychosocial factors in peptic ulcer and inflammatory bowel disease. *J. Cons. Clin. Psychol., 70*(3), 739–50.

Levenston, G. K., Patrick, C. J., Bradley, M. M., & Lang, P. J. (2000). The psychopath as observer: Emotion and attention in picture processing. *J. Abn. Psychol., 109*(3), 373–85.

Leventhal, B. L., Cook, E. H., & Lord, C. (1998). The irony of autism. *Arch. Gen. Psychiat., 55,* 643–44.

Leventhal, H., Patrick-Muller, L., & Leventhal, E. A. (1998). It's long-term stressors that take a toll: Comment on Cohen et al. (1988). *Hlth. Psychol., 17*(3), 211–13.

Levin, F. R., & Hennessey, G. (2004). Bipolar disorder and substance abuse. *Biol. Psychiat., 56,* 738–748.

Levine, R. E., & Gaw, A. C. (1995). Culture-bound syndromes. *Psychiat. Clin. N. Amer.: Cultural Psychiatry, 18*(3), 523–36.

Levor, R. M., Cohen, M. J., Naliboff, B. D., & McArthur, D. (1986). Psychosocial precursors and correlates of migraine headache. *J. Cons. Clin. Psychol., 54,* 347–53.

Levy & Kershaw. (2001, Apr. 18). *New York Times,* p. A20.

Levy, D. L., Holzman, P. S., Matthysse, S., & Mendell, N. R. (1993). Eye tracking dysfunction and schizophrenia: A critical perspective. *Schizo. Bull., 19*(3), 461–536.

Levy, D. L., Yasillo, N. J., Dorcus, E., Shaughnessy, R., Gibbons, R. D., Peterson, J., Janicak, P. G., Gaviria, M., & Davis, J. M. (1983). Relatives of unipolar and bipolar patients have normal pursuit. *Psychiat. Res., 10,* 285–93.

Lewinsohn, P. M. (1974). A behavioral approach to depression. In R. J. Friedman & M. M. Katz (Eds.), *The psychology of depression: Contemporary theory and research.* New York: Halstead Press.

Lewinsohn, P. M., & Essau, C. A. (2002). Depression in adolescents. In I. H. Gotlib & C. L. Hammen (Eds.), *Handbook of depression* (pp. 541–59). New York: Guilford.

Lewinsohn, P. M., & Gotlib, I. H. (1995). Behavioral theory and treatment of depression. In E. E. Beckham & W. R. Leber (Eds.), *Handbook of depression* (2nd ed., pp. 352–75). New York: Guilford.

Lewinsohn, P. M., Gotlib, I. H., Lewinson, M., Seeley, J. R., & Allen, N. B. (1998). Gender differences in anxiety disorders and anxiety symptoms in adolescents. *J. Abn. Psychol. 107*(1), 109–17.

Lewinsohn, P. M., Hoberman, H. M., Teri, L., & Hautzinger, M. (1985). An integrative theory of depression. In S. Reiss & R. Bootzin (Eds.), *Theoretical issues in behavior therapy* (pp. 331–59). San Diego: Academic Press.

Lewinsohn, P. M., Hops, H., Roberts, R. E., Seeley, J. R., & Andrews, J. A. (1993). Adolescent psychopathology: I. Prevalence and incidence of depression and other DSM-III-R disorders in high school students. *J. Abn. Psychol., 102,* 133–44.

Lewinsohn, P. M., Joiner, T. E., & Rohde, P. (2001). Evaluation of cognitive diathesis-stress models in predicting major depressive disorder in adolescents. *J. Abn. Psychol., 110*(2), 203–15.

Lewinsohn, P. M., Rohde, P., & Seeley, J. R. (1994). Psychosocial risk factors for future adolescent suicide attempts. *J. Cons. Clin. Psychol., 62,* 297–305.

Lewinsohn, P. M., Rohde, P., & Seeley, J. R. (1996). Epidemiology of adolescent suicide. *Clin. Psychol. Sci. Prac., 3,* 25–46.

Lewinsohn, P. M., Rohde, P., Seely, J. R., Klein, D. N., & Gotlib, I. H. (2003). Psychosocial functioning of young adults who have experienced and recovered from major depressive disorder during adolescence. *J. Abn. Psychol., 112*(3), 353–363.

Lewis, C. F., & Ednie, K. (1997). Koro and homicidal behavior. *Amer. J. Psychiat., 154,* 1169.

Lewis, D. O., Yeager, C. A., Swica, Y., Pincus, J. H., & Lewis, M. (1997). Objective documentation of child abuse and dissociation in 12 murderers with Dissociative Identity Disorder. *Amer. J. Psychiat., 154*(12), 1703–10.

Lewis, J. W., & Walter, D. (1992). Buprenorphine: Background to its development as a treatment for opiate dependence. In J. D. Blaine (Ed.), *Buprenorphine: An alternative treatment for opioid dependence* (pp. 5–11). Washington, DC: U.S. Department of Health and Human Services.

Lewis, J., Dickson, D. W., Lin, W.-L., Chisholm, L., Corral, A., Jones, G., Yen, S.-H., Sahara, N., Skipper, L., Yager, D., Eckman, C., Hardy, J., Hutton, M., & McGowan, E. (2001). Enhanced neurofibrillary degeneration in transgenic mice expressing mutant tau and APP. *Science, 293,* 1487–91.

Lewis, O. (1997). Integrated psychodynamic psychotherapy with children. *Child Adoles. Psychiat. Clin. N. Amer., 6*(1), 53–68.

Lewis, S. (1992). Sex and schizophrenia: Vive la différence. *Brit. J. Psychiat., 161,* 445–50.

Lewis, T. F., Thombs, D. L., & Olds, R. S. (2005). Profiles of alcohol- and marijuana-impaired adolescent drivers. *Addict. Res. Theory, 13*(2), 145–54.

Lezak, M. D. (1995). *Neuropsychological assessment* (3rd ed.). New York: Oxford University Press.

Lidz, T., Fleck, S., & Cornelison, A. R. (1965). *Schizophrenia and the family.* New York: International Universities Press.

Lieb, R., Schuetz, C. G., Pfister, H., von Sydow, K., & Wittchen, H. (2002). Mental disorders in ecstasy users: A prospective-longitudinal investigation. *Drug & Alcohol Dependence, 68,* 195–207

Lieb, R., Wittchen, H.-U., Hofler, M., Fuetsch, M., Stein, M., & Merikangas, K. R. (2000). Parental psychopathology, parenting styles, and the risk of social phobia in offspring: A prospective-longitudinal community study. *JAMA, 57,* 859–66.

Lieberman, J. A., Jody, D., Alvir, J. M. J., Ashtari, M., Levy, D. L., Bogerts, B., Degreef, G., Mayerhoff, D. I., & Cooper, T. (1993). Brain morphology, dopamine, and eyetracking abnormalities in first-episode schizophrenia: Prevalence and clinical correlates. *Arch. Gen. Psychiat., 50*(5), 357–68.

Lieberman, J., Chakos, M., Wu, H., Alvir, J., Hoffman, E., Robinson, D., & Bilder, R. (2001). Longitudinal study of brain morphology in first episode schizophrenia. *Biol. Psychiat., 49,* 487–99.

Liebman, J. M., & Cooper, S. J. (1989). *The neuropharmacological basis of reward.* New York: Clarendon Press.

Liebowitz, M. R., Salman, E., Jusino, C. M., Garfinkel, R., et al. (1994). Ataque de nervios and panic disorder. *Amer. J. Psychiat., 151*(6), 871–875.

Liem, J. H. (1974). Effects of verbal communications of parents and children: A comparison of normal and schizophrenic families. *J. Cons. Clin. Psychol., 42,* 438–50.

Lifton, R. J. (2005). Americans as survivors. *N. Engl. J. Med., 352*(22), 2263–65.

Lilenfield, L. R., Kaye, W. H., Greeno, C. G., Merikangas, K. R., Plotnicov, K., Pollice, C., Rao, R., Strober, M., Bulik, C. M., & Nagy, L. (1998.) A controlled family study of anorexia nervosa and bulimia nervosa. *Arch. Gen. Psychiat., 55,* 603–10.

Lilienfeld, S. O. (1992). The association between antisocial personality and somatization disorders: A review and integration of theoretical models. *Clin. Psychol. Rev., 12,* 641–62.

Lilienfeld, S. O. (2002). When worlds collide: Social science, politics, and the Rind et al. (1998) child sexual abuse meta-analysis. *Amer. Psychol., 57,* 176–88.

Lilienfeld, S. O., & Loftus, E. F. (1998). Repressed memories and World War II: Some cautionary notes. *Profess. Psychol.: Res. Prac., 29,* 471–75.

Lilienfeld, S. O., & Loftus, E. F. (1999). A step backwards in the recovered memory debate. *Profess. Psychol.: Res. Prac., 30,* 623.

Lilienfeld, S. O., & Lynn, S. J. (2003). Dissociative identity disorder: Multiple personalities, multiple controversies. In S. O. Lilienfeld & S. J. Lynn (Eds.), *Science and pseudoscience in clinical psychology* (pp. 109–42). New York: Guilford Press.

Lilienfeld, S. O., & Marino, L. (1999). Essentialism revisited: Evolutionary theory and the concept of mental disorder. *J. Abn. Psychol., 108*(3), 400–11.

Lilienfeld, S. O., Lynn, S. J., Kirsch, I., Chaves, J. F., Sarbin, T. R., Ganaway, G. K., & Puwell, R. A. (1999). Dissociative identity disorder and the sociocognitive model: Recalling lessons of the past. *Psychol. Bull., 125,* 507–23.

Lindamer, L. A., Lohr, J. B., Harris, M. J., & Jeste, D. V. (1997). Gender, estrogen, and schizophrenia. *Psychopharm. Bull., 33*(2), 221–28.

Lindamer, L., Lacro, J. P., & Jeste, D. V. (1999). Relationship of ethnicity to the effects of antipsychotic medications. In J. M. Herra & W. B. Lawson (Eds.), *Cross cultural psychiatry* (pp. 193–203).

Linden, W., Stossel, C., & Maurice, J. (1996). Psychosocial interventions for patients with coronary artery disease. *Arch. Int. Med., 157,* 745–52.

Lindman, R. E., & Lang, A. R. (1994). The alcohol-aggression stereotype: A cross-cultural comparison of beliefs. *Inter. J. Addict., 29,* 1–13.

Linehan, M. M. (1993). *Cognitive-behavioral treatment of borderline personality disorder: The dialectics of effective treatment.* New York: Guilford.

Linehan, M. M., Armstrong, H. E., Suarez, A., Allmon, D., & Heard, H. L. (1991). Cognitive-behavioral treatment of chronically parasuicidal borderline patients. *Arch. Gen. Psychiat., 48,* 1060–64.

Linehan, M. M., Heard, H. L., & Armstrong, H. E. (1993) Naturalistic follow-up of a behavioral treatment for chronically parasuicidal borderline patients. *Arch. Gen. Psychiat., 50,* 971–74.

Linehan, M. M., Tutek, D. A., Heard, H. L., & Armstrong, H. E. (1994). Interpersonal outcome of cognitive behavioral treatment for chronically suicidal borderline patients. *Amer. J. Psychiat., 151*(12), 1771–76.

Link, B. G. (2001). Stigma: Many mechanisms require multifaceted responses. *Epidemiologia e Psichiatria Sociale, 10,* 8–11.

Lintzeris, N., Holgate, F., & Dunlop, A. (1996). Addressing dependent amphetamine use: A place for prescription. *Drug and Alcohol Review, 15*(2), 189–95.

Lishman, W. A. (1990). Alcohol and the brain. *Brit. J. Psychiat., 156,* 635–44.

Lissau, I., & Sorensen, T. I. A. (1994). Parental neglect during childhood and increased risk of obesity in young adulthood. *Lancet, 343,* 324–27.

Littrell, J. (2001). What neurobiology has to say about why people abuse alcohol and other drugs. *Journal of Social Work Practice in the Addictions, 1*(3), 23–40.

Liu, X., Sun, Z., Uchiyama, M., Li, Y., & Okawa, M. (2000). Attaining nocturnal urinary control, nocturnal enuresis, and behavioral problems in Chinese children aged 6 through 16 years. *J. Amer. Acad. Child Adol. Psychiat., 39,* 1557–64.

Livesley, J. W. (2001). Conceptual and taxonomic issues. In W. J. Livesley (Ed.), *Handbook of personality disorders* (pp. 3–38). New York: Guilford.

Livesley, W. J. (1995). Past achievements and future directions. In W. J. Livesley (Ed.), *The DSM-IV personality disorders.* (pp. 497–506). New York: Guilford.

Livesley, W. J., Jang, K. L., & Vernon, P. A. (1998). Phenotypic and genetic structure of traits delineating personality disorder. *Arch. Gen. Psychiat., 55*(10), 941–48.

Lochner, C., & Stein, D. J. (2003). Heterogeneity of obsessive-compulsive disorder: A literature review. *Har. Rev. Psychiat., 11*(3), 113–132.

Lock, J., le Grange, D., Agras, W. S., & Dare, C. (2001). *Treatment manual for anorexia nervosa: A family-based approach.* New York: Guilford.

Loewenthal, K. M., MacLeod, A. K., Cook, S., Lee, M., & Goldblatt, V. (2003). Beliefs about alcohol among UK Jews and Protestants: Do they fit the alcohol depression hypothesis? *Soc. Psychiat. Psychiatr. Epidemiol., 38,* 122–27.

Loewenthal, K., Goldblatt, V., Gorton, T., Lubitsch, G., Bicknell, H., Fellowes, D., & Sowden, A. (1995). Gender and depression in Anglo-Jewry. *Psychol. Med., 25,* 1051–63.

Loftus, E. F., & Bernstein, D. M. (2005). Rich false memories: The royal road to success. In A. F. Healy (Ed.), *Experimental cognitive psychology and its applications: Decade of behavior* (pp. 101–13). Washington, DC: American Psychological Association.

Loftus, E. F., & Ketchum, K. (1994). *The myth of repressed memory: False memories and allegations of sexual abuse.* New York: St Martin's.

Loftus, E. F., Feldman, J., & Dashiell, R. (1995). The reality of illusory memories. In D. Schacter, J. Coyle, L. Sullivan, M. Mesulam, & G. Fischbach (Eds.), *Memory distortions: Interdisciplinary perspectives.* Cambridge: Harvard University Press.

Lohr, B. A., Adams, H. E., & Davis, J. M. (1997). Sexual arousal to erotic and aggressive stimuli in sexually coercive and noncoercive men. *J. Abn. Psychol., 106,* 230–42.

Long, J. V. F., & Valliant, G. E. (1984). Natural history of male psychological health, XI: Escape from the underclass. *Amer. J. Psychiat., 141,* 341–46.

Looper, K. J., & Kirmayer, L. J. (2002). Behavioral medicine approaches to somatoform disorders. *J. Cons. Clin. Psychol., 70,* 810–27.

Lopez, O. L., et al. (1997). The apoliproprotein E e4 allele is not associated with psychiatric symptoms or extra-pyramidal signs in probable Alzheimer's disease. *Neurology, 49*(3), 794–97.

Lopez, S. R., & Guarnaccia, P. J. (2005). Cultural dimensions of psychopathology: The social world's impact on mental illness. In J. E. Maddux & B. A. Winstead (Eds.), *Psychopathology: Foundations for a contemporary understanding.* Mahwah, NJ: Lawrence Erlbaum Associates.

Lopez, S. R., Lopez, A. A., & Fong, K. T. (1991). Mexican Americans' initial preferences for counselors: The role of ethnic factors. *J. Couns. Psychol., 38,* 487–96.

Lord, C., & Magill-Evans, J. (1995). Peer interactions of autistic children and adolescents. *Develop. Psychopath., 7,* 611–26.

Lorenz, A. R., & Newman, J. P. (2002). Deficient response modulation and emotion processing in low-anxious Caucasian psychopathic offenders: Results from a lexical decision task. *Emotion, 2*(2), 91–104.

Lorenz, V. C., & Shuttlesworth, D. E. (1983). The impact of pathological gambling on the spouse of the gambler. *J. Comm. Psychol., 11,* 67–76.

LoSasso, G. L., Rapport, L. J., & Axelrod, B. N. (2001). Neuropsychological symptoms associated with low-level exposure to solvents and (meth)acrylates among nail technicians. *Neuropsychiatry, Neuropsychology, & Behavioral Neurology, 14*(3), 183–89.

LoSasso, G. L., Rapport, L. J., Axelrod, B. N., & Whitman, R. D. (2002). Neurocognitive sequelae of exposure to organic solvents and (meth)acrylates among nail-studio technicians. *Neuropsychiatry, Neuropsychology & Behavioral Neurology, 15*(1), 44–55.

Losel, F. (1998). Treatment and management of psychopaths. In D. J. Cooke, A. E. Forth, & R. D. Hare (Eds.), *Psychopathy: Theory, research, and implications for society.* (pp. 303–354). Dordrecht, Netherland: Kluwer Academic Publishers.

Lovaas, O. I. (1987). Behavioral treatment of normal educational and intellectual functioning in young autistic children. *J. Cons. Clin. Psychol., 44,* 3–9.

Loving, T. J., Heffner, K. L., Kiecolt-Glaser, J. K., Glaser, R., & Malarkey, W. B. (2004). Stress hormone changes and marital conflict: Spouses' relative power makes a difference. *J. Marr. Fam., 66*(3), 595–612.

Löwe, B., Zipfel, S., Buchholz, C., Dupont, Y., Reas, D. L., & Herzog, W. (2001). Long-term outcome of anorexia nervosa in a prospective 21-year follow-up study. *Psychol. Med.,* 31, 881–90.

Lozano, B. E., & Johnson, S. L. (2001). Can personality traits predict increases in manic and depressive symptoms? *J. Affect. Dis., 63*(1-3), 103–11.

Luchins, A. S. (1989). Moral treatment in asylums and general hospitals in 19th-century America. *J. Psychol.: Interdisciplinary & Applied, 123*(6), 585–607.

Luckasson, R., Coulter, D. L., Polloway, E. A., Reiss, S., Schalock, R. L., Snell, M. E., Spitalnik, D. M., & Stark, J. A. (1992). *Mental retardation: Definition, classification, and systems of supports* (9th ed.). Washington, DC: American Association on Mental Retardation.

Ludwig, A. M., Brandsma, J. M., Wilbur, C. B., Bendfelt, F., & Jameson, D. H. (1972). The objective study of a multiple personality: Or, are four heads better than one? *Arch. Gen. Psychiat., 26,* 298–310.

Luecken, L. J., & Lemery, K. S. (2004). Early caregiving and physiological stress responses. *Clin. Psychol. Rev., 24,* 171–91.

Lukas, C., & Seiden, H. M. (1990). *Silent grief: Living in the wake of suicide.* New York: Bantam Books.

Lundgren, J. D., Danoff-Burg, S., & Anderson, D. A. (2004). Cognitive-behavior therapy for bulimia nervosa: An empirical analysis of clinical significance. *Int. J. Eat. Dis., 35,* 262–274.

Lunsing, R. J., Hadders Algra, M., Touwen, B. C., & Huisjes, H. J. (1991). Nocturnal enuresis and minor neurological dysfunction at 12 years: A follow-up study. *Develop. Med. Child Neurol., 33,* 439–45.

Luntz, B. K., & Widom, C. S. (1994). Antisocial personality disorder in abused and neglected children grown-up. *Amer. J. Psychiat., 151,* 670–74.

Luten, A., Ralph, J., & Mineka, S. (1997). Depressive attributional style: Is it specific to depression vs. anxiety vs. negative affect? *Behav. Res. Ther., 35,* 703–19.

Lutgendorf, S. K., Russell, D., Ullrich, P., Harris, T., & Wallace, R. (2004). Religious participation, Interleukin-6, and mortality in older adults. *Hlth. Psychol., 23,* 5, 465–75.

Lutgendorf, S., Garand, L., Buckwalter, K. C., Reimer, T. T., Hong, S., & Lubaroff, D. (1999). Life stress, mood disturbance, and elevated interleukin-6 in healthy older women. *Journals of Gerontology. Series A, Biological Sciences and Medical Sciences,* 54A M434–M439.

Luthar, S.S. (2003). *Resilience and vulnerability: Adaption in the context of childhood adversities.* New York: Cambridge University Press.

Lyketsos, C. G., Steinberg, M., Tschanz, J. T., Norton, M. C., Steffens, D. C., & Breitner, J. C. S. (2000). Mental and behavioral disturbances in dementia: Findings from the Cache County study on memory and aging. *Amer. J. Psychiat., 157*(5), 708–14.

Lykken, D. T. (1957). A study of anxiety in the sociopathic personality. *J. Abn. Soc. Psychol., 55*(1), 6–10.

Lykken, D. T. (1995). *The Antisocial Personalities.* Hillsdale, NJ: Erlbaum.

Lymburner, J. A., & Roesch, R. (1999). The insanity defense: Five years of research (1993–1997). *International Journal of Law & Psychiatry, 22*(3–4), 213–20.

Lynam, D. R. (2002). Fledgling psychopathy. *Law & Human Behavior, 26*(2), 255–59.

Lynam, D., Moffitt, T. E., & Stouthamer-Loeber, M. (1993). Explaining the relation between IQ and delinquency: Class, race, test motivation, school failure, or self-control. *J. Abn. Psychol., 102,* 187–96.

Lynch, P. S., Kellow, J. T., & Willson, V. L. (1997). The impact of deinstitutionalization on the adaptive behavior of adults with mental retardation. *Education & Training in Mental Retardation & Developmental Disabilities, 32*(3), 255–61.

Lynn, S. J., Knox, J. A., Fassler, O., Lilienfeld, S. O., & Loftus, E. F. (2004). Memory, trauma, and dissociation. In G. M. Rosen (Ed.), *Posttraumatic stress disorder: Issues and controversies* (pp. 163–86). New York: John Wiley & Sons Ltd.

Lyon, H. M., Startup, M., & Bentall, R. P. (1999). Social cognition and the manic defense: Attributions, selective attention, and self-schema in bipolar affective disorder. *J. Abn. Psychol., 108*(2), 273–82.

Lyons, J. S., Griffin, G., Quintenz, S., Jenuwine, M., & Shasha, M. (2003). Clinical and forensic outcomes from the Illinois Mental Health Juvenile Justice Initiative. *Psychiatr. Serv., 54*(12), 1629–34.

Lyons-Ruth, K. (1996). Attachment relationships among children with aggressive behavior problems: The role of disorganized early attachment patterns. *J. Cons. Clin. Psychol., 64*(1), 64–73.

Lytton, H. (1980). *Parent-child interaction: The socialization process observed in twin and singleton families.* New York: Plenum.

Lyubomirsky, S., Caldwell, N. D., & Nolen-Hoeksema, S. (1998). Effects of ruminative and distracting responses to depressed mood on retrieval of autobiographical memories. *J. Pers. Soc. Psychol., 75,* 166–77.

Lyvers, M. (2000). "Loss of control" in alcoholism and drug addiction: A neuroscientific interpretation. *Experimental and Clinical Psychopharmacology, 8*(2), 225–45.

Ma, S. H., & Teasdale, J. D. (2004). Mindfulness-based cognitive therapy for depression: Replication and esploration of differential relapse prevention effects. *Journal of Cons. Clin. Psychol., 72*(1), 31–40.

Maccoby, E. E., & Martin, J. A. (1983). Socialization in the context of the family: Parent-child interaction. In E. M. Hetherington (Ed.), *Socialization, personality, and social development: Vol. 4. Handbook of child psychology.* New York: Wiley.

MacDonald, A. W., III, & Carter, C. S. (2002). Cognitive experimental approaches to investigating impaired cognition in schizophrenia: A paradigm shift. *J. Clin. Exp. Neuropsych., 7,* 873–82.

MacDonald, M. R., & Kuiper, N. A. (1983). Cognitive-behavioral preparations for surgery: Some theoretical and methodological concerns. *Clin. Psychol. Rev., 3,* 27–39.

Mackay, L. E. (1994). Benefits of a formalized traumatic brain injury program within a trauma center. *J. Head Trauma Rehab., 9*(1), 11–19.

MacKenzie, D. L., Wilson, D. B., Armstrong, G. S., & Glover, A. R. (2001). The impact of boot camps and traditional institutions on juvenile residents: Perceptions, adjustment, and change. *Journal of Research in Crime & Delinquency, 38*(3), 279–313.

Mackinnon, A., & Foley, D. (1996). The genetics of anxiety disorders. In H. G. Westenberg, J. A. Den Boer, & D. L. Murphy (Eds.), *Advances in the neurobiology of anxiety disorders* (pp. 39–59). Chichester, England: Wiley.

MacLean, H. N. (1992). *Once upon a time.* New York: HarperCollins.

Maclean, W. E., Jr. (Ed.). (1997). *Ellis' handbook of mental deficiency: Psychological theory and research.* Mahwah, NJ: Erlbaum.

MacLeod, A. K. (1999). Prospective cognitions. In T. Dalgleish & M. J. Power (Eds.), *Handbook of cognition and emotion* (pp. 267–80). Chichester, England: Wiley.

MacLeod, C., Campbell, L., Rutherford, E., & Wilson, E. (2004). The causal status of anxiety-linked attentional and interpretive bias. In J. Yiend (Ed.) Cognition, emotion and psychopathology: *Theoretical, empirical and clinical directions.* (pp. 172–189). New York: Cambridge University Press.

MacMillan, P. J., Hart, R., Martelli, M., & Zasler, N. (2002). Pre-injury status and adaptation following traumatic brain injury. *Brain Injury, 16*(1), 41–49.

Maddi, S. R., Bartone, P. T., & Puccetti, M. C. (1987). Stressful events are indeed a factor in physical illness: Reply to Schroeder and Costa. *J. Pers. Soc. Psychol., 52,* 833–43.

Maddock, R. J., Buonocore, M. H., Kile, S. J., & Garrett, A. S. (2003). Brain regions showing increased activation by threat-related words in panic disorder. *Neuroreport: For rapid communication of neuroscience research, 14*(3), 325–328.

Maddux, J. E., Gosselin, J. T., & Winstead, B. A. (2005). Conceptions of psychopathology: A social constructionist perspective. In J. E. Maddux & B. A. Winstead (Eds.), *Psychopathology: Foundations for a contemporary understanding.* Mahwah, NJ: Lawrence Erlbaum Associates.

Maddux, J. F., Vogtsberger, K. N., Prihoda, T. J., Desmond, D. F., Watson, D. D., & Williams, M. L. (1994). Illicit drug injectors in three Texas cities. *Inter. J. Addict., 29,* 179–94.

Magee, W. J., Eaton, W. W., Wittchen, H., McGonagle, K. A., & Kessler, R. C. (1996). Agoraphobia, simple phobia, and social phobia in the National Comorbidity Survey. *Arch. Gen. Psychiat., 53,* 159–68.

Maher, B. A., & Maher, W. R. (1985). Psychopathology: 1. From ancient times to the eighteenth century. In G. A. Kimble & K. Schlesinger (Eds.), *Topics in the history of psychology* (pp. 251–94). Hillsdale, NJ: Erlbaum.

Maher, B. A., & Maher, W. R. (1994). Personality and psychopathology: A historical perspective. *J. Abn. Psychol., 103,* 72–77.

Mahoney, G., Glover, A., & Finger, I. (1981). Relationship between language and sensorimotor development of Down's syndrome and nonretarded children. *Amer. J. Ment. Def., 86,* 21–27.

Mahoney, M., & Arnkoff, D. (1978). Cognitive and self-control therapies. In S. Garfield & A. Bergin (Eds.), *Handbook of psychotherapy and behavior change: An empirical analysis.* New York: Wiley.

Mai, F. (2004). Somatization disorder: A practical review. *Canad. J. Psychiat., 49*(10), 652–62.

Maier, S., Seligman, M., & Solomon, R. (1969). Pavlovian fear conditioning and learned helplessness. In B. A. Campbell & R. M. Church (Eds.), *Punishment and aversive behavior.* New York: Appleton-Century-Crofts.

Maier, S. E., & West, J. R. (2001). Drinking patterns and alcohol related birth defects. *Alcohol Research & Health, 25,* 168–74.

Maier, S. F. (2001). Exposure to the stressor environment prevents the temporal dissipation of behavioral depression/learned helplessness. *Biol. Psychiat., 49*(9), 763–73.

Maier, S. F., & Watkins, L. R. (1998). Cytokines for psychologists: Implications of bidirectional immune-to-brain communication for understanding behavior, mood, and cognition. *Psychol. Rev., 105*(1), 83–107.

Maier, S. F., Watkins, L. R., & Fleshner, M. (1994). Psychoneuroimmunology: The interface between behavior, brain, and immunity. *Amer. Psychol., 49*(12), 1004–17.

Maiuro, R. D., Cahn, T. S., Vitaliano, P. P., Wagner, B. C., & Zegree, J. B. (1988). Anger, hostility, and depression in domestically violent versus generally assaultive men and nonviolent control subjects. *J. Cons. Clin. Psychol., 56,* 17–23.

Majcher, D., & Pollack, M. (1996). Childhood anxiety disorders. In L. Hechtman (Ed.), *Do they grow out of it?* (pp. 139–70). Washington, DC: American Psychiatric Press.

Malaspina, D., Corcoran, C., & Hamilton, S. P. (2002). Epidemiologic and genetic aspects of neuropsychiatric disorders. In S. C. Yudofsky & R. E. Hales, *The American Psychiatric Publishing textbook of neuropsychiatry and clinical neurosciences* (pp. 323–415). Washington, DC: American Psychiatric Publishing.

Malaspina, D., Harlap, S., Fennig, S., Heiman, D., Nahon, D., Feldman, D., & Susser, E. (2001). Advancing paternal age and the risk of schizophrenia. *Arch. Gen. Psychiat., 58,* 361–67.

Malatesta, V. J., & Adams, H. (1993). The sexual dysfunctions. In P. Sutker & H. Adams (Eds.), *Comprehensive textbook of psychopathology.* New York: Plenum.

Malcolm, R. (2003). Pharmacologic treatments manage alcohol withdrawal, relapse prevention. *Psychiat. Ann., 33*(9), 593–601.

Maldonado, J. R., & Spiegel, D. (2001). Somatoform and factitious disorders. *Review of psychiatry series, 20,* 95–128.

Maldonado, J. R., Butler, L. D., & Spiegel, D. (2002). Treatments for dissociative disorders. In P. E. Nathan & J. M. Gorman (Eds.), *A guide to treatments that work* (2nd ed., pp. 463–96). New York: Oxford University Press.

Male, D. B., & May, D. S. (1997). Burnout and workload in teachers of children with severe learning difficulties. *Brit. J. Learn. Dis., 25*(3), 117–21.

Maletzky, B. M. (1998). The paraphilias: Research and treatment. In P. E. Nathan & J. M. Gorman (Eds.), *A guide to treatments that work* (pp. 472–500). New York: Oxford University Press.

Maletzky, B. M. (2002). The paraphilias: Research and treatment. In P. E. Nathan & J. M. Gorman (Eds.), *A guide to treatments that work* (pp. 525–58). New York: Oxford University Press.

Malhi, G. S., Ivanovski, B., Szekeres, V., & Olley, A. (2004a). Bipolar disorder: It's all in your mind: The neuropsychological profile of a biological disorder. *Can. J. Psychiat., 49*(12), 813–819.

Malhi, G. S., Lagopoulos, J., Owen, A. M., & Yatham, L. N. (2004). Bipolaroids: Functional imaging in bipolar disorder. *Acta Psychiatr. Scandin., 110,* 46–54.

Malin, D. H. (2001). Nicotine dependence: Studies with a laboratory model. *Pharmacology, Biochemistry, & Behavior, 70*(4), 551–59.

Malkoff-Schwartz, S., Frank, E., Anderson, B., Sherrill, J. T., Siegel, L., Patterson, D., & Kupfer, D. J. (1998). Stressful life events and social rhythm disruption in the onset of manic and depressive bipolar episodes: A preliminary investigation. *Arch. Gen. Psychiat., 55*(8), 702–7.

Manassis, K., & Monga, S. (2001). A therapeutic approach to children and adolescents with anxiety disorders and associated comorbid conditions. *J. Amer. Acad. Child Adoles. Psychiat., 40*(1), 115–17.

Mangweth, B., Hudson, J. I., Pope, H. G., Hausman, A., De Col, C., Laird, N. M., Beibl, W., & Tsuang, M. T. (2003). Family study of the aggregation of eating disorders and mood disorders. *Psychol. Med., 33,* 1319–23.

Manji, H. K., & Lenox, R. H. (2000). The nature of bipolar disorder. *J. Clin. Psychiat., 61,* 42–57.

Mann, A. (2004). *Cocaine abusers' cognitive deficits compromise treatment.* Washington, DC: NIDA.

Mann, J. J., Brent, D. A., & Arango, V. (2001). The neurobiology and genetics of suicide and attempted suicide: A focus on the serotonergic system. *Neuropsychopharmacology, 24*(5), 467–77.

Mannuzza, S., Klein, R. G., & Moulton, J. L., III. (2003). Persistence of attention-deficit/hyperactivity disorder into adulthood: What have we learned from the prospective follow-up studies? *J. Atten. Dis., 7*(2) 93–100.

Mannuzza, S., Klein, R., Bessler, A., Malloy, P., & LaPadula, M. (1993). Adult outcome of hyperactive boys: Educational achievement, occupational rank, and psychiatric status. *Arch. Gen. Psychiat., 50,* 565–76.

Manson, S. M. (1995). Culture and major depression: Current challenges in the diagnosis of mood disorders. *Psychiat. Clin. N. Amer.: Cultural Psychiatry, 18*(3), 487–501.

Manuck, S. B., et al. (1991). Individual differences in cellular immune response to stress. *Psychol. Sci., 2*(2), 111–15.

Marangell, L. B., Ketter, T. A., George, M. S., Pazzaglia, P. J., Callahan, A. M., Parekh, P., Andreason, P. J., Horwitz, B., Herscovitch, P., & Post, R. (1997). Inverse relationship of peripheral thyrotropin-stimulating hormone levels to brain activity in mood disorder. *Amer. J. Psychiat., 145*(2), 224–30.

March, J., & Leonard, H. (1998). Obsessive-compulsive disorder in children and adolescents. In R. Swinson, M. Antony, S. Rachman, & M. Richter (Eds.), *Obsessive-compulsive disorder: Theory, research, and treatment* (pp. 367–94). New York: Guilford.

Marcotty, J. (2004). Outpatient psychiatric care is scarce: One result has been an increase in psychiatric admissions in Minnesota. *Minneapolis Star and Tribune,* Section B, pp. 1–2.

Marcus, M. D. (1997). Adapting treatment for patients with binge-eating disorder. In D. M. Garner & P. E. Garfinkel (Eds.), *Handbook of treatment for eating disorders* (pp. 484–93). New York: Guilford.

Margolis, R. D., & Zweben, J. E. (1998). *Treating patients with alcohol and other drug problems: An integrated approach.* Washington, DC: American Psychological Association.

Margraf, J., Ehlers, A., & Roth, W. T. (1986a). Sodium lactate infusions and panic attacks: A review and critique. *Psychosom. Med., 48,* 23–51.

Margraf, J., Ehlers, A., & Roth, W. (1986b). Biological models of panic disorder and agoraphobia—A review. *Behav. Res. Ther., 24,* 553–67.

Mari, J. D. J., & Streiner, D. L. (1994). An overview of family interventions and relapse on schizophrenia: Meta-analysis of research findings. *Psychol. Med., 24,* 565–78.

Marijuana Treatment Project Research Group. (2004). Brief treatments for cannabis dependence: Findings from a randomized multi-site trial. *J. Cons. Clin. Psychol., 72,* 455–66.

Mariotto, M. J., Paul, G. L., & Licht, M. H. (2002). Assessment in inpatient and residential settings. In J. N. Butcher (Ed.), *Clinical personality assessment* (2nd ed., pp. 466–90). New York: Oxford University Press.

Maris, R. W. (1997). Social forces in suicide: A life review, 1965–1995. In R. W. Maris, M. M. Silverman, & S. S. Canetton (Eds.), *Review of Suicidology, 1997* (pp. 42–60). New York: Guilford.

Maris, R. W., Berman, A. L., & Silverman, M. M. (2000). *Comprehensive textbook of suicidology.* New York: Guilford.

Markey, E. (2002). *List of documented brain injuries on thrill rides triples.* Press release from the office of Ed Markey, United States Congress, Massachusetts Seventh District, May 7, 2002.

Markham, D. (2003). Attitudes towards patients with a diagnosis of "borderline personality disorder": Social rejection of dangerousness. *J. Ment. Hlth., 12,* 595–612.

Markovitz, J. H., Shuster, J. L., Chitwood, W. S., May, R. S., & Tolbert, L. C. (2000). Platelet activation in depression and the effects of sertraline treatment: An open label study. *Amer. J. Psychiat., 157,* 1006–08.

Markovitz, P. (2001). Pharmacotherapy. In W. J. Livesley (Ed.), *Handbook of personality disorders* (pp. 475–93). New York: Guilford.

Markowitsch, H. J. (1999). Functional neuroimaging correlates of functional amnesia. *Memory, 7*(5–6), 561–83.

Marks, I., & Nesse, R. M. (1991). Fear and fitness: An evolutionary analysis of anxiety disorders. Paper presented at the Eleventh National Conference on Anxiety Disorders. Chicago, IL.

Marks, I., Swinson, R. P., Başoğlu, M., & Kunch, K. (1993). Alprazolam and exposure alone and combined in panic disorder with agoraphobia: A controlled study in London and Toronto. *Brit. J. Psychiat., 162,* 776–87.

Marks, M., Yule, W., & De Silva, P. (1999). Post-traumatic stress disorder in airplane cabin crew attendants. *Human Performance in Extreme Environments, 4*(1), 128–32.

Marlatt, G. A., & Vandenbos, G. R. (Eds.). (1997). *Addictive behaviors: Readings on etiology, prevention, and treatment.* Washington, DC: American Psychological Association.

Marlatt, G. A., Baer, J. S., Kivahan, D. R., Dimeoff, L. A., Larimer, M. E., Quigley, L. A., Somers, J. M., & Williams, E. (1998). Screening and brief intervention for high-risk college student drinkers: Results from a 2-year follow up assessment. *J. Cons. Clin. Psychol., 66*(4), 604–15.

Marlatt, G. A. (1985). Cognitive assessment and intervention procedures for relapse prevention. In G. A. Marlatt & J. R. Gordon (Eds.), *Relapse prevention.* New York: Guilford.

Marsella, A. J. (1980). Depressive experience and disorder across cultures. In H. C. Triandis & J. Draguns (Eds.), *Handbook of cross-cultural psychology* (Vol. 6). Boston: Allyn and Bacon.

Marshall M., Lewis, S., Lockwood, A., Drake, R., Jones, P., & Croudace, T. (2005). Association between duration of untreated psychosis and outcome in cohorts of first-episode patients. *Arch. Gen. Psychiat., 62,* 975–83.

Marshall, R. D., & Klein, D. F. (1995). Pharmacotherapy in the treatment of posttraumatic stress disorder. *Psychiat. Ann., 23*(10), 588–89.

Marshall, W. L., Jones, R., Ward, T., Johnston, P., & Barbaree, H. E. (1991). Treatment outcome with sex offenders. *Clin. Psychol. Rev., 11,* 465–85.

Martell, D. A., & Dietz, P. E. (1992). Mentally disordered offenders who push or attempt to push victims onto subway tracks in New York City. *Arch. Gen. Psychiat., 49*(6), 472–75.

Martin, D. J., Garske, J. P., & Davis, M. K. (2000). Relation of the therapeutic alliance with outcome and other variables: A meta-analytic review. *J. Cons. Clin. Psychol., 68,* 438–50.

Martin, E. S., et al. (1997). Studies in a large family with late-onset Alzheimer disease (LOAD). *Alzheimer Disease and Associated Disorders, 11*(3), 163–70.

Martin, P. R., Singleton, C. K., & Hiller-Sturmhöfel, S. (2003). The role of thiamine deficiency in alcoholic brain disease. *Al. Res. Hlth., 27,* 134–42.

Marvit, R. C. (1981). Guilty but mentally ill—an old approach to an old problem. *Clin. Psychol., 34*(4), 22–23.

Mash, E. J., & Dozois, D. J. A. (1996). Child psychopathology: A developmental perspective. In E. J. Mash & R. A. Barkley (Eds.), *Child psychopathology* (pp. 3–60). New York: Guilford.

Masi, G., Favilla, L., Mucci, M., & Millepiedi, S. (2000). Depressive comorbidity in children and adolescents with generalized anxiety disorder. *Child Psychiat. Human Devel., 30*(3), 205–15.

Maskey, S. (2001). Selective mutism, social phobia and moclobemide: A case report. *Clinical Child Psychology & Psychiatry, 6,* 363–69.

Mason, F. L. (1997). Fetishism: Psychopathology and theory. In D. R. Laws & W. O'Donohue (Eds.) *Sexual deviance: Theory, assessment, and treatment.* (pp. 75–91). New York: Guilford.

Mason, W. A., Kosterman, R., Hawkins, J. D., Herrenkohl, T. I., Lengua, L. J., & McCauley, E. (2004). Predicting depression, social phobia, and violence in early adulthood from childhood behavior problems. *J. Amer. Acad. Child Adoles. Psychiat., 43*(3), 307–15.

Masten, A. S., & Coatsworth, J. D. (1995). Competence, resilience, and psychopathology. In D. Cicchetti & D. J. Cohen (Eds.), *Psychopathology: Vol. 2. Risk, disorder, and adaptation* (pp. 715–52). New York: Wiley.

Masten, A. S., & Coatsworth, J. D. (1998). The development of competence in favorable and unfavorable environments: Lessons from research on successful children. *Amer. Psychol., 53,* 205–20.

Masten, A. S., Best, K., & Garmezy, N. (1990). Resilience and development: Contributions from the study of children who overcome adversity. *Develop. Psychopath., 2,* 425–44.

Masten, A. S., Burt, K. B., Roisman, G. I., Obradovic, J., Long, J. D., Tellegen, A. (2004). Resources and resilience in the transition to adulthood: Continuity and change. *Develop. Psychopath., 16,* 1071–1094.

Masten, A. S. (2001). Ordinary magic: Resilience processes in development. *Amer. Psychol., 56,* 227–38.

Masters, W. H., & Johnson, V. E. (1966). *Human sexual response.* Boston: Little, Brown.

Masters, W. H., & Johnson, V. E. (1970). *Human sexual inadequacy.* Boston: Little, Brown.

Masters, W. H., & Johnson, V. E. (1975). *The pleasure bond: A new look at sexuality and commitment.* Boston: Little, Brown.

Masters, W. H., Johnson, V. E., & Kolodny, R. C. (1992). *Human sexuality.* New York: HarperCollins.

Mataix-Cols, D., Rauch, S. L., Baer, L., Eisen, J. L., Shera, D. M., Goodman, W. K., et al. (2002). Symptom stability in adult obsessive-compulsive disorder: Data from a naturalistic two-year follow-up study. *Amer. J. Psychiat., 159*(2), 263–268.

Mataix-Cols, D., Wooderson, S., Lawrence, N., Brammer, M. J., Speckens, A., Phillips, M. L. (2004). Distinct neural correlates of washing, checking, and hoarding symptom dimensions in obsessive-compulsive disorder. *Arch. Gen. Psychiat., 61*(6), 564–576.

Matarazzo, J. D. (1986). Computerized clinical psychological test interpretations: Unvalidated plus all mean and no sigma. *Amer. Psychol., 41,* 14–24.

Materro, M., Junque, C., Poca, M. A., & Sahuquillo, J. (2001). Neuropsychological findings in congenital and acquired childhood hydrocephalus. *Neuropsychology, 11*, 169–78.

Mathalondolf, D. H., Sullivan, E. V., Lim, K. O., & Pfefferbaum, A. (2001). Progressive brain volume changes and the clinical course of schizophrenia in men: A longitudinal magnetic resonance imaging study. *Arch. Gen. Psychiat., 58*, 48–157.

Mathew, S. J., Coplan, J. D., & Gorman, J. M. (2001). Neurobiological mechanisms of social anxiety disorder. *Amer. J. Psychiat., 158*, 1558–67.

Mathews, A. & MacLeod, C. (2005). Cognitive vulnerability to emotional disorders. *Annu. Rev. Clin. Psychol., 1*(1), 167–195.

Mathews, A. & MacLeod, C. (2005). Cognitive vulnerability to emotional disorders. *Annu. Rev. Clin. Psychol., 1*(1), 167–195.

Mathews, A. M., & MacLeod, C. (1994). Cognitive approaches to emotion and emotional disorders. *Ann. Rev. Psychol., 45*, 25–50.

Mathews, A., & MacLeod, C. (2002). Induced processing biases have causal effects on anxiety. *Cog. & Emo., 16*(3), 331–354.

Mathews, S. J., Shungu, D. C., Mao, X., Smith, E. L. P., Perera, G. M., Kegeles, L. S., et al. (2003). A magnetic resonance spectroscopic imaging study of adult nonhuman primates exposed to early-life stressors. *Biol. Psychiat., 54*(7), 727–735.

Matsumoto, H., Simmons, A., Williams, S., Hadjulis, M., Pipe, R., Murray, R., & Frangou, S. (2001). Superior temporal gyrus abnormalities in early-onset schizophrenia: Similarities and differences with adult-onset schizophrenia. *Amer. J. Psychiat., 158*(8), 1299–304.

Matsunaga, E., Tonomura, A., Hidetsune, O., & Yasumoto, K. (1978). Reexamination of paternal age effect in Down's syndrome. *Human Genet., 40*, 259–68.

Matthews, K. A., & Gump, B. B. (2002). Chronic work stress and marital dissolution increase risk of posttrial mortality in men from the Multiple Risk Factor Intervention Trial. *Arch. Int. Med., 162*, 309–15.

Mattia, J. I., & Zimmerman, M. (2001). Epidemiology. In W. J. Livesley (Ed.), *Handbook of personality disorders* (pp. 107–23). New York: Guilford.

Mattson, M. E., & Riley, E. P. (1998). A review of the neurobehavioral deficits in children with fetal alcohol syndrome or prenatal exposure to alcohol. *Alcoholism: Clin. Exper. Res., 22*(2), 279–94.

Mattson, M. E., Allen, J. P., Longabaugh, R., Nickless, C. J., et al. (1994). A chronological review of empirical studies matching alcoholic clients to treatment. *J. Stud. Alcoh. 12*, 16–29.

Matza, L. S., Revicki, D. A., Davidson, J. R., & Stewart, J. W. (2003). Depression with atypical features in the national comorbidity survey. *Arch. Gen. Psychiat., 60*, 817–826.

Maxfield, M. G., & Widom, C. S. (1996). The cycle of violence: Revisited six years later. *Archives of Pediatric and Adolescent Medicine, 150*, 390–95.

Maxwell, J. C. (2005). Emerging research on methamphetamine. *Cur. Opin. Psychiat., 18*(3), 235–42.

May, P. A., & Gossage, J. P. (2001). Estimating the prevalence of fetal alcohol syndrome. *Alcohol Research & Health, 25*, 159–67.

Mayberg, H. S., Lozano, A. M., Voon, V., McNeely, H. E., Seminowicz, D., Hamani, C., Schwalb, J. M., & Kennedy, S. H. (2005). Deep brain stimulation for treatment-resistant depression. *Neuron, 45*, 651–660 March 3.

Mayou, R. A., Ehlers, A., & Hobbs, M. (2000). Psychological debriefing for road traffic accident victims: Three-year follow-up of a randomised controlled trial. *Brit. J. Psychiat., 176*, 589–93.

Mays, D. T., & Franks, C. M. (Eds.). (1985). *Negative outcome in psychotherapy and what to do about it.* New York: Springer.

Mazziotta, J. (1996). Mapping mental illness: A new era. *Arch. Gen. Psychiat., 53*(7), 574–76.

Mazzocco, M. M. (2000). Advances in research on the fragile X syndrome. *Mental Retardation & Developmental Disabilities Research Reviews, 6*, 96–106.

McAlonan, G. M., Cheung, V., Cheung, C., Suckling, J., Lam, G. Y., Tai, K. S., Yip, L., Murphy, D. G. M., & Chua, S. E. (2005). Mapping the brain in autism. A voxel-based MRI study of volumetric differences and intercorrelations in autism. *Brain: 128*(2), 268–76.

McAnulty, R. D., Adams, H. E., & Dillon, J. (2001). Sexual disorders: The paraphilias. In P. B. Sutker & H. E. Adams (Eds.), *Comprehensive handbook of psychopathology* (pp. 749–73). New York: Kluwer/Plenum.

McCabe, R. E., Antony, M. M., Summerfield, L. J., Liss, & Swinson, R. P. (2003). Preliminary examination of the relationship between anxiety disorders in adults and self-reported history of teasing or bullying experiences. *Cog. Behav. Ther., 32*(4), 187–193.

McCall, L. (1961). Between us and the dark. Originally published in 1947. Summary in W. C. Alvarez, (1961) *Minds That Came Back.* Philadelphia: J. B. Lippincott.

McCann, I. L., Sakheim, D. K., & Abrahamson, D. J. (1988). Trauma and victimization: A model of psychological adaptation. *Counsel. Psychol., 16*, 531–94.

McCann, J. T. (1999). Obsessive-compulsive and negativistic personality disorders. In T. Millon, P. H. Blaney, & R. D. Davis (Eds.), *Oxford textbook of psychopathology* (pp. 585–604). New York: Oxford University Press.

McCarroll, J. E., Ursano, R. J., & Fullerton, C. S. (1995). Symptoms of PTSD following recovery of war dead: 13–15-month follow-up. *Amer. J. Psychiat., 152*(6), 939–41.

McCarthy, B. W. (1989). Cognitive-behavioral strategies and techniques in the treatment of early ejaculation. In S. R. Leiblum & R. C. Rosen (Eds.), *Principles and practice of sex therapy* (2nd ed., pp. 141–67). New York: Guilford.

McCarthy, J. J., & Flynn, N. (2001). Hepatitis C in methadone maintenance patients. Prevalence and public policy implications. *Journal of Addictive Diseases, 20*, 19–31.

McCarthy, M. (1990). The thin ideal, depression, and eating disorders in women. *Behav. Res. Ther., 28*, 205–18.

McCaslin, S., Jacobs, G. A., Meyer, D. L., Johnson-Jimenez, E., Metzler, T. J., & Marmar, C. R. (2005). How does negative life change following disaster response impact distress among Red Cross responders? *Prof. Psychol.: Research and Practice, 36*, 246–53.

McClelland, G. M., & Teplin, L. (2001). Alcohol intoxication and violent crime: Implications for public health policy. *American Journal on Addictions, 10*(suppl.), 70.

McClelland, L., & Crisp, A. (2001). Anorexia nervosa and social class. *Int. J. Eat. Dis., 29*, 150–56.

McCloud, A., Barnaby, B., Omu, N., Drummond, C., & Aboud, A. (2004). Relationship between alcohol use disorders and suicidality in a psychiatric population: In-patient prevalence study. *Brit. J. Psychiat., 184*, 439–45.

McCrady, B. S., Epstein, E. S., & Kahler, C. W. (2004). Alcoholics Anonymous and relapse prevention as maintenance strategies after conjoining behavioral alcohol treatment for men: 18 month outcomes. *J. Cons. Clin. Psychol., 72*, 870–78.

McCullough, J. P., Klein, D. N., Borian, F. E., Howland, R. H., Riso, L. P., Keller, M. B., et al. (2003). Group comparisons of *DSM-IV* subtypes of chronic depression: Validity of the distinctions, part 2. *J. Abn. Psychol., 112*(4), 614–622.

McDaniel, M. A., Maier, S. F., & Einstien, G. O. (2002). "Brain-specific" nutrients: A memory cure? *Psychological Science in the Public Interest, 3*(1), 12–38.

McDonald, L., Bellingham, S., Conrad, T., Morgan, A., et al. (1997). Families and schools together (FAST): Integrating community development with clinical strategies. *Families in Society, 78*(2), 140–55.

McDonnell, J., Hardman, M. L., Hightower, J., & Keifer-O'Donnel, R. (1993). Impact of community-based instruction on the development of adaptive behavior of secondary-level students with mental retardation. *Amer. J. Ment. Retard., 97*(5), 575–84.

McEwen, A., Preston, A., & West, R. (2002). Effect of a GP desktop resource on smoking cessation activities of general practitioners. *Addiction, 97*(5), 595–97.

McEwan, B. S. (1998). Protective and damaging effects of stress-mediators. *N. Engl. J. Med., 338*, 171–79.

McEwen, B. S., & Stellar, E. (1993). Stress and the individual. *Arch. Int. Med., 153*, 2093–101.

McFall, M. E., Murburg, M. M., Ko, G. N., & Veith, R. C. (1990). Autonomic responses to stress in Vietnam combat veterans with posttraumatic stress disorder. *Biol. Psychiat., 27*(1), 1165–75.

McFall, R. M. (1990). The enhancement of social skills: An information-processing analysis. In W. L. Marshall, D. R. Laws, & H. E. Barbaree (Eds.), *Handbook of sexual assault: Issues, theories, and treatment of the offender* (pp. 311–30). New York: Plenum.

McFarlane, W. R., Lukens, E., Link, B., Dushay, R., Deakins, S. A., Newmark, M., Dunne, E. J., Horen, B., & Toran, J. (1995). Multiple-family groups and psychoeducation in the treatment of schizophrenia. *Arch. Gen. Psychiat., 52*, 679–87.

McGlashan, T. H., & Fenton, W. S. (1993). Subtype progression and pathophysiologic deterioration in early schizophrenia. *Schizo. Bull., 19*(1), 71–84.

McGorry, P. D., & Jackson, H. J. (1999). *The recognition and management of early psychosis.* Cambridge: Cambridge University Press.

McGorry, P. D., Edwards, J., Mihalopoulos, C., Harrigan, S. M., & Jackson, H. J. (1996). EPPIC: An evolving system of early detection and optimal management. *Schizo. Bull., 22*(2), 305–26.

McGue, M. (1998). Behavioral genetic models of alcoholism and drinking. In K. E. Leonard & H. T. Blane (Eds.), *Psychological theories of drinking and alcoholism.* New York: Guilford.

McGuffin, P., Rijsdijk, F., Andrew, M., Sham, P., Katz, R., & Cardno, A. (2003). The heritability of bipolar affective disorder and the genetic relationship to unipolar depression. *Arch. Gen. Psychiat., 60*, 497–502.

McGuire, P. K., Silbersweig, D. A., Wright, I., & Murray, R. M. (1996). The neural correlates of inner speech and auditory verbal imagery in schizophrenia: Relationship to auditory verbal hallucinations. *Brit. J. Psychiat., 169*(2), 148–59.

McGuire, W. J. (1994). Uses of historical data in psychology: Comments on Munsterberg (1899). *Psychol. Rev., 101*, 243–47.

McIvor, R. J., & Turner, S. W. (1995). Assessment and treatment approaches for survivors of torture. *Brit. J. Psychiat., 166*, 705–11.

McKenna, K., Gordon, C. T., & Rapoport, J. L. (1994). Childhood-onset schizophrenia: Timely neurobiological research. *J. Amer. Acad. Child Adoles. Psychiat., 33*(6), 771–81.

McKenna, P. J. (1997). Pathogenesis: The dopamine hypothesis. In *Schizophrenia and related syndromes* (pp. 135–63). Hove, East Sussex, UK: Psychology Press.

McKnight Investigators. (2003). Risk factors for the onset of eating disorders in adolescent girls: Results of the McKnight Longitudinal Risk Factor Study. *Amer. J. Psychiat., 160*, 248–54.

McLaurin, J., Cecal, R., Kierstead, M. E., Tian, X., Phinney, A. L., Manea, M., French, J. E., Lambermon, M. H. L., Darabie, A. A., Bown, M. E., Janus, C., Chishti, M. A., Horne, P., Westaway, D., Fraser, P. E., Mount, H. T. J., Przybylski, M., & St. George-Hyslop, P. (2002). Therapuetically effective antibodies against amyloid-β peptide target amyloid-β residues 4–10 and inhibit cytotoxicity and fibrillogenesis. *Nature Medicine, 8*(11), 1263–69.

McLoyd, V. C. (1998). Socioeconomic disadvantage and child development. *Amer. Psychol., 53*, 185–204.

McLoyd, V. C. (1998). Socioeconomic disadvantage and child development. *Amer. Psychol., 53*(2), 185–204.

McMahon, T. J. & Giannini, F. D. (2003). Substance-abusing fathers in family court: Moving from popular stereotypes to therapeutic jurisprudence. *Family Court Review, 41*(3), 337–353.

McMillan, J. C., Smith, E. M., & Fisher, R. H. (1997). Perceived benefit and mental health after three types of disaster. *J. Cons. Clin. Psychol., 65*(5), 733–39.

McMinn, M. R., Buchanan, T., Ellens, B. M., & Ryan, M. K. (1999). Technology, professional practice, and ethics: Survey findings and implications. *Profess. Psychol.: Res. and Prac., 30*(2), 165–72.

McMurran, M., & Hollin, C. R. (1993). *Young offenders and alcohol related crime.* New York: Wiley.

McMurray, R. G., Newbould, E., Bouloux, G. M., Besser, G. M., & Grossman, A. (1991). High-dose nalolone modifies cardiovascular and neuroendocrine function in ambulant subjects. *Psychoneuroendocrinology, 16,* 447–55.

McNally, R. J., Bryant, R. A., & Ehlers, A. (2003). Does early intervention promote recovery from posttraumatic stress? *Psychol. Sci. in the Pub. Int., 4,* 45–79.

McNally, R. J., Clancy, S. A., Barret, H. M., & Parker, H. A. (2005). Reality monitoring in adults reporting repressed, recovered, or continuous memories of childhood sexual abuse. *J. Abn. Psychol. 114*(1), 147–152.

McNally, R. J. (1994). *Panic disorder: A critical analysis.* New York: Guilford.

McNally, R. J. (2000). Information-processing abnormalities in obsessive-compulsive disorder. In W. K. Goodman, M. V. Rudorfer, et al. (Eds.), *Obsessive-compulsive disorder: Contemporary issues in treatment. Personality and clinical psychology series* (pp. 106–16). Mahwah, NJ: Erlbaum.

McNally, R. J. (2002). Anxiety sensitivity and panic disorder. *Biol. Psychiat., 51,* 938–46.

McNally, R. J. (2004a). Is traumatic amnesia nothing but psychiatric folklore? *Cog. Behav. Ther., 33*(2), 97–101.

McNally, R. J. (2004b). The science and folklore of traumatic amnesia. *Clin. Psychol. Sci. Prac., 11*(1), 29–33.

McNicholas, F., Slonims, V., & Cass, H. (2000). Exaggeration of symptoms or psychiatric Munchausen's syndrome by proxy? *Child Psychology & Psychiatry Review, 5,* 69–75.

McNulty, J. P. (2004). Commentary: Mental illness, society, stigma, and research. *Schizo. Bull., 30*(3), 573–75.

McRae, A. L., Budney, A. J., & Brady, K. F. (2003). Treatment of marijuana dependence: A review of the literature. *J. Sub. Abuse Treat., 24,* 369–76.

McReynolds, P. (1996). Lightner Witmer: Little-known founder of clinical psychology. *Amer. Psychol., 51,* 237–40.

McReynolds, P. (1997). Lightner Witmer: The first clinical psychologist. In W. G. Bringmann, H. E. Luck, R. Miller, & C. E. Early (Eds.), *A pictorial history of psychology* (pp. 465–70). Chicago: Quintessence Books.

Mechanic, D. (2004).The rise and fall of managed care. *J. Hlth. Soc. Behav., 45*(Suppl.), 76–86.

Medical Council on Alcoholism. (1997). *Alcohol-related liver disease.* London: Author.

Mednick, S. A., & Schulsinger, F. (1968). Some premorbid characteristics related to breakdown in children with schizophrenic mothers. In D. Rosenthal & S. S. Kety (Eds.), *The transmission of schizophrenia* (pp. 267–91). Oxford: Pergamon.

Mednick, S. A., Machon, R. A., Huttunen, M. O., & Bonnet, D. (1988). Adult schizophrenia following prenatal exposure to an influenza epidemic. *Arch. Gen. Psychiat., 45,* 189–92.

Meehl, P. E. (1962). Schizotaxia, schizotypy, schizophrenia. *Amer. Psychol., 17,* 827–38.

Meehl, P. E. (1990a). Toward an integrated theory of schizotaxia, schizotypy, and schizophrenia. *J. Personal. Dis., 4,* 1–99.

Megargee, E. I. (2002). Assessing the risk of aggression and violence. In J. N. Butcher (Ed.), *Clinical personality assessment* (2nd ed., pp. 435–50). New York: Oxford University Press.

Meier, B. (2004, Sept. 9). Major medical journals will require registration of trials. *New York Times,* p. C11.

Mellon, M. W., & McGrath, M. L. (2000). Empirically supported treatments in pediatric psychology: Nocturnal enuresis. *J. Pediat. Psychol., 25,* 193–214.

Meltzer, H. Y., Alphs, L., Green, A. I., Altamura, A. C., Anand, R., Bertoldi, A., Bourgeois, M., Chouinard, G., Islam, Z., Kane, J., Krishnan, R., Lindenmayer, J.-P., & Potkin, S., for the InterSePT Study Group. (2003). Clozapine treatment for suicidality in schizophrenia. *Arch. Gen. Psychiat., 60,* 82–91.

Melville, J. D., & Naimark, D. (2002). Punishing the insane: The verdict of guilty but mentally ill. *J. Amer. Acad. Psychiat. Law, 30,* 553–55.

Mendelson, J. H., & Mello, N. (1992). Human laboratory studies of buprenorphine. In J. D. Blaine (Ed.), *Buprenorphine: An alternative treatment for opiate dependence* (pp. 38–60). Washington, DC: U.S. Department of Health and Human Services.

Mendrek, A., Laurens, K. R., Kiehl, K. A., Ngan, E. T. C., Stip, E., & Liddle, P. F. (2004). Changes in distributed neural circuitry function in patients with first-episode schizophrenia. *Brit. J. Psychiat., 185,* 205–14.

Meneses, A. (1999). 5-HT system and cognition. *Neuroscience & Biobehavioral Reviews, 23,* 1111–25.

Meneses, A. (2001). Could the 5-Ht-sub (1B) receptor inverse agonism affect learning consolidation? *Neuroscience & Biobehavioral Reviews, 25,* 193–201.

Mental Health Law Project. (1987, Oct.). Court decisions concerning mentally disabled people confined in institutions. *MHLP Newsletter.* Washington, DC.

Merbaum, M., & Hefez, A. (1976). Some personality characteristics of soldiers exposed to extreme war stress. *J. Cons. Clin. Psychol., 44*(1), 1–6.

Merbaum, M. (1977). Some personality characteristics of soldiers exposed to extreme war stress: A follow-up study of post-hospital adjustment. *J. Clin. Psychol.,* 33, 558–62.

Merikangus, K. R., & Swendsen, J. D. (1997). Genetic epidemiology of psychiatric disorders. *Epidemiological Reviews, 19*(1), 144–55.

Merikangus, K. R., Zhang, H., Avenevoli, S., Acharya, S., Neuenschwander, M., & Angst, J. (2003). Longitudinal trajectories of depression and anxiety in a prospective community study. *Arch. Gen. Psychiat., 60*(10), 993–1000.

Mermelstein, H. T., & Basu, R. (2001). Can you ever be too old to be too thin? Anorexia nervosa in a 92-year-old woman. *Int. J. Eat. Dis., 30*(1), 123–26.

Merrick, J., Kandel, I. & Vardi, G. (2004). Adolescents with Down syndrome. *Int. J. Adol. Med. Hlth., 16*(1), 13–19.

Merrick, J., Kandel, I., & Morad, M. (2004). Trends in autism. *Int. J. Adol. Med. Hlth., 16*(1), 75–78.

Mersky, H., & Potter, P. (1989). The womb lay still in ancient Egypt. *Brit. J. Psychiat., 154,* 751–53.

Mersky, H. (1995). *The analysis of hysteria: Understanding conversion and dissociation.* Gaskell, England: Royal College of Psychiatrists.

Mesibov, G. B., Adams, L. W., & Klinger, L. G. (1997). *Autism: Understanding the disorder.* New York: Plenum.

Mesibov, G. B., Shea, V., & Adams, L. W. (Eds.). (2001). *Understanding asperger syndrome and high-functioning autism.* Boston: Kluwer.

Metz, M. E., Pryor, J. L., Nesvacil, L. J., Abuzzahab, F., & Koznar, J. (1997). Premature ejaculation: A psychophysiological review. *J. Sex Marit. Ther., 23,* 3–23.

Meyer, B., Pilkonis, P. A., Krupnick, J. L., Egan, M. K., Simmens, S. J., & Sotsky, S. M. (2002). Treatment expectancies, patient alliance, and outcome: Further analyses from the National Institute of Mental Health Treatment of Depression Collaborative Research Program. *J. Cons. Clin. Psychol., 70,* 1051–55.

Meyer, C. B., & Taylor, S. E. (1986). Adjustment to rape. *J. Pers. Soc. Psychol., 50,* 1226–34.

Meyer, G. J., Mihura, J. L., & Smith, B. L. (2005). The interclinician reliability of Rorschach interpretation in four data sets. *J. Pers. Assess., 84,* 296–314.

Meyer, G., Finn, S. E., Eyde, L. D., Kay, G. G., Moreland, K. L., Dies, R. R., Eisman, E. J., Kubiszyn, T. W., & Reed, G. M. (2001). Psychological testing and psychological assessment: A review of evidence and issues. *Amer. Psychol., 56,* 128–65.

Meyer, J. K. (1995). Paraphilias. In H. I. Kaplan & J. B. Sadock (Eds.), *Comprehensive textbook of psychiatry.* (6th ed., pp. 1334–47). Baltimore: Williams and Wilkins.

Meyer, R. E., & Mirin, S. M. (1979). *The heroin stimulus: Implications for a theory of addiction.* New York: Plenum.

Meyer, R. G. (2003). *Case studies in abnormal behavior* (6th ed.). Boston: Allyn & Bacon.

Mezulis, A. H., Abramson, L. Y., Hyde, J. S., & Hankin, B. L. (2004). Is there a universal positivity bias in attributions? A meta-analytic review of individual, developmental, and cultural differences in the self-serving attributional bias. *Psychol. Bull., 130*(5), 711–747.

Mezulis, A. H., Abramson, L. Y., Hyde, J. S., & Hankin, B. L. (2004). Is there a universal positivity bias in attributions? A meta-analytic review of individual, developmental, and cultural differences in the self-serving attributional bias. *Psychol. Bull., 130*(5), 711–747.

Mezzich, J. E., Kirmayer, L. J., Kleinman, A., Fabrega, H., Jr., Parron, D. L., Good, B. J., Lin, K. M., & Manson, S. M. (1999). The place of culture in DSM-IV. *J. Nerv. Ment. Dis., 187,* 457–64.

Micale, M. S. (1995). *Approaching hysteria: Disease and its interpretation.* Princeton, NJ: Princeton University Press.

Micali, N., Chakrabarti, S., & Fombonne, E. (2004). The broad autism phenotype. *Autism, 8,* 21–37.

Michelson, D., Stratakis, C., Hill, L., Reynolds, J., Galliven, E., Chrousos, G., & Gold, P. (1996). Bone mineral density in women with depression. *N. Engl. J. Med., 335,* 1176–81.

Miczek, K. A., Covington, H. E., Nikulna, E. M., & Hammer, R. P. (2004). Aggression and defeat: Persistent effects on cocaine self-administration and gene expression in peptidergic and aminergic mesocorticolimbic circuits. *Neuroscience and Biobehavioral Reviews, 27,* 787–802.

Middeldorp, C. M., Cath, D. C., & Boomsma, D. I. (2005). The comorbidity of anxiety and depressionin the perspective of genetic epidemiology: A review of twin and family studies. *Psychol. Med., 35*(5), 611–624.

Miklowitz, D. J., & Stackman, D. (1992). Communication deviance in families of schizophrenic and other psychiatric patients: Current state of the construct. In E. F. Walker, R. H. Dworkin, & B. A. Cornblatt (Eds.), *Progress in Experimental Personality and Psychopathology Research,* Vol. 15. New York: Springer.

Miklowitz, D. J. (2002). Family focused treatment for bipolar disorder. In S. G. Hofmann & M. C. Tompson (Eds.), *Treating chronic and severe mental disorders: A handbook of empirically supported interventions* (pp. 159–74). New York: Guilford.

Milani, R., Lavie, C., & Cassidy, M. (1996). Effects of cardiac rehabilitation and exercise training programs on depression in patients after major coronary events. *Amer. Heart J., 132,* 726–32.

Milev, P., Ho, B.-C., Arndt, S., & Andreasen, N. C. (2005). Predictive values of neurocognition and negative symptoms on functional outcome in schizophrenia: A longitudinal first-episode study with 7-year follow-up. *Amer. J. Psychiat., 162,* 495–506.

Millar, A., Espie, C. A., & Scott, J. (2004). The sleep of remitted bipolar outpatients: A controlled naturalistic study using actigraphy. *J. Affect. Dis., 80,* 145–153.

Millar, J. D. (1990). Mental health and the workplace: An interchangeable partnership. *Amer. Psychol., 45*(10), 1165–66.

Miller, G. E., Stetler, C. A., Carney, R. M., Freedland, K. E., & Banks, W. A. (2002). Clinical depression and inflammatory risk markers for coronary heart disease. *Amer. Jour. Cardio., 90,* 1279–83.

Miller, G. (1995). *The behavioral high-risk paradigm in psychopathology.* New York: Springer-Verlag.

Miller, J. D., Reynolds, S. K., & Pilkonis, P. A. (2004). The validity of the five-factor model prototypes for personality disorders in two clinical samples. *Psychol. Assess., 16,* 310–33.

Miller, K., & Rasco, L. (Eds.). (2004). *The mental health of refugees: Ecological approaches to healing and adaptation.* Mahwah, NJ: Lawrence Erlbaum Publishers, Inc.

Miller, L. J. (2002). Postpartum depression. *JAMA, 287*(6), 762–65.

Miller, M. B., Useda, J. D., Trull, T. J., Burr, R. M., & Minks-Brown, C. (2001). Paranoid, schizoid, and schizotypal personality disorders. In H. E. Adams & P. B. Sutker (Eds.), *Comprehensive handbook of psychopathology* (pp. 535–58). New York: Kluwer Academic.

Miller, N., & Lyon, D. (2003). Biology of opiates affects prevalence of addiction, options for treatment. *Psychiat. Ann., 33,* 559–64.

Miller, P. M., Byrne, M., Hodges, A., Lawrie, S. M., & Johnstone, E. C. (2002). Childhood behavior, psychotic symptoms and psychosis onset in young people at high risk of schizophrenia: Early findings from the Edinburgh High Risk Study. *Psychol. Med., 32,* 173–79.

Miller, R. (1970). Does Down's syndrome predispose children to leukemia? *Roche Report, 7*(16), 5.

Miller, T. Q., Smith, T. W., Turner, C. W., Guijarro, M. L., & Haller, A. J. (1996). A meta-analytic review of research on hostility and physical health. *Psychol. Bull., 119,* 322–48.

Miller, W. R. (1983). Motivational Interviewing with problem drinkers. *Behav. Psychotherapy, 11,* 147–172.

Miller, W. R., & Rollnick, S. (2003). [Book review of Motivational interviewing: Peparing people for change]. *J. Stud. Alcoh., 63*(6), 776–77.

Miller, W. R., & Wilbourne, P. L. (2002). Mesa Grande: A methodological analysis of clinical trials of treatment for alcohol use disorders. *Addiction, 97*(3), 265–77.

Miller, W. R., Benefield, R. G., & Tonigan, J. S. (1993). Enhancing motivation for change in problem drinking: A controlled comparison of two therapist styles. *J. Cons. Clin. Psychol., 61*(3), 455–61.

Miller, W. R., Brown, J. M., Simpson, T. L., Handmaker, N. S., Bien, T. H., Luckie, L. F., Montgomery, H. A., Hester, R. K., & Tonigan, J. S. (1995). What works? A methodological analysis of the alcohol treatment outcome literature. In R. K. Hester & W. R. Miller (Eds.), *Handbook of alcoholism treatment approaches: Effective alternatives* (pp. 12–44). Needham, MA: Allyn and Bacon.

Miller, W. R., Leckman, A. L., Tinkcom, M., & Rubenstein, J. (1986). *Longterm follow-up of controlled drinking therapies.* Paper given at the Ninety-fourth Annual Meeting of the American Psychological Association, Washington, DC.

Miller, W. R., Walters, S. T., & Bennett, M. E. (2001). How effective is alcoholism treatment in the United States? *J. Stud. Alcoh., 62*(2), 211–20.

Millon, T. (1981). *Disorders of personality: DSM-III, Axis II.* New York: Wiley.

Millon, T. & Martinez, A. (1995). Avoidant personality disorder. In W. J. Livesley (Ed.), *The DSM-IV personality disorders.* (pp. 218–233). New York: Guilford.

Millon, T., & Davis, R. D. (1995). The development of personality disorders. In D. Cicchetti & D. J. Cohen (Eds.), *Developmental psychopathology: Vol. 2. Risk, disorder, and adaptation* (pp. 633–76). New York: Wiley.

Millon, T., & Davis, R. D. (1999). Developmental pathogenesis. In T. Millon, P. H. Blaney, & R. D. Davis (Eds.), *Oxford textbook of psychopathology* (pp. 29–48). New York: Oxford University Press.

Millon, T., & Radovanov, J. (1995). Passive-aggressive (negativistic) personality disorder. In W. J. Livesley (Ed.), *The DSM-IV personality disorders.* (pp. 312–325). New York: Guilford.

Mills, M. J., Sullivan, G., & Eth, S. (1987). Protecting third parties: A decade after Tarasoff. *Amer. J. Psychiat., 144*(1), 68–74.

Milne, J. M., Edwards, J. K., & Murchie, J. C. (2001). Family treatment of oppositional defiant disorder: Changing views and strength-based approaches. *Family Journal—Counseling & Therapy for Couples & Families, 9*(1), 17–28.

Milns, R. D. (1986). Squibb academic lecture: Attitudes towards mental illness in antiquity. *Austral. NZ J. Psychiat., 20,* 454–62.

Milos, G., Spindler, A., Ruggiero, G., Klaghofer, R., & Schnyder, U. (2002). Comorbidity of obsessive compulsive disorders and duration of eating disorders. *Int. J. Eat. Dis., 31,* 284–89.

Mindus, P., Nyman, H., Lindquist, C., & Meyerson, B. A. (1993). *Neurosurgery for intractable obsessive-compulsive disorder, an update.* Paper presented at the International Workshop on Obsessive Disorder, Vail, CO.

Mindus, P., Rasmussen, S. A., & Lindquist, C. (1994). Neurosurgical treatment for refractory obsessive-compulsive disorder: Implications for understanding frontal lobe function. *J. Neuropsychiat. Clin. Neurosci., 6,* 467–77.

Mineka, S., & Ben Hamida, S. (1998). Observational and nonconscious learning. In W. T. O'Donohue (Ed.), *Learning and behavior therapy* (pp. 421–39). Needham Heights, MA: Allyn and Bacon.

Mineka, S., & Cook, M. (1986). Immunization against the observational conditioning of snake fear in monkeys. *J. Abn. Psychol., 95,* 307–18.

Mineka, S., & Cook, M. (1993). Mechanisms underlying observational conditioning of fear in monkeys. *J. Exper. Psychol.: General, 122,* 23–38.

Mineka, S., & Kelly, K. A. (1989). The relationship between anxiety, lack of control and loss of control. In A. Steptoe & A. Appels (Eds.), *Stress, personal control and health.* Brussels-Luxembourg: J. Wiley.

Mineka, S., & Zinbarg, R. (1995). Conditioning and ethological models of social phobia. In R. Heimberg, M. Liebowitz, D. Hope, & F. Schneier (Eds.), *Social phobia: Diagnosis, assessment, and treatment.* New York: Guilford.

Mineka, S., & Zinbarg, R. (1996). Conditioning and ethological models of anxiety disorders: Stress-in-Dynamic Context Anxiety Models. In D. Hope (Ed.), *Perspectives on Anxiety, Panic, and Fear: Nebraska Symposium on Motivation.* Lincoln: University of Nebraska Press.

Mineka, S., Cook, M., & Miller, S. (1984). Fear conditioned with escapable and inescapable shock: Effects of a feedback stimulus. *J. Exper. Psychol., 10,* 307–23.

Mineka, S., Gunnar, M., & Champoux, M. (1986). Control and early socioemotional development: Infant rhesus monkeys reared in controllable versus uncontrollable environments. *Child Develop. 57,* 1241–56.

Mineka, S., Rafaeli, E., & Yovel, I. (2003). Cognitive biases in emotional disorders: Social-cognitive and information processing perspectives. In R. Davidson, H. Goldsmith, & K. Scherer (Eds.), *Handbook of affective science.* Amsterdam: Elsevier.

Mineka, S., Watson, D., & Clark, L. A. (1998). Comorbidity of anxiety and unipolar mood disorders. In J. T. Spence, J. M. Darley, & D. J. Foss (Eds.), *Annu. Rev. Psychol., 49,* 377–412.

Mineka, S., Yovel, I., & Pineles, S. (2002). Toward a psychological model of the etiology of generalized anxiety disorder. In D. J. Nutt, K. Rickels, & D. J. Stein (Eds.), *Generalized anxiety disorder: Symptomatology, pathogenesis and management.* London: Martin Dunitz.

Mineka, S. (1985a). Animal models of anxiety-based disorders: Their usefulness and limitations. In A. H. Tuma & J. D. Maser (Eds.), *Anxiety and the anxiety disorders.* Hillsdale, NJ: Erlbaum.

Mineka, S. (1985b). The frightful complexities of the origins of fears. In F. R. Brush & J. B. Overmier (Eds.), *Affect, conditioning, and cognition: Essays on the determinants of behavior.* Hillsdale, NJ: Erlbaum.

Ming, E. E., Adler, G. K., Kessler, R. C., Fogg, L. F., Matthews, K. A., Herd, J. A., & Rose, R. M. (2004). Cardiovascular reactivity to work stress predicts subsequent onset of hypertension: The air traffic controller health change study. *Psychosom. Med., 66*(4), 459–65.

Mintzer, J. E., et al. (1997). Effectiveness of a continuum of care using brief and partial hospitalization for agitated dementia patients. *Psychiatr. Serv., 48*(11), 1435–39.

Mintzer, M. Z., Guarino, J., Kirk, T., Roache, J. D., & Griffiths, R. R. (1997). Ethanol and Pentobarbital: Comparison of behavioral and subjective effects in sedative drug abusers. *Experimental and Clinical Psychopharmacology, 5*(3), 203–15.

Minuchin, S. (1974). *Families and family therapy.* Cambridge, MA: Harvard University Press.

Miranda, J., Bernal, G., Lau, A., Kohn, L., Hwang, W-C, & LaFramboise, T. (2005). State of the science on psychosocial interventions for ethnic minorities. *Annu. Rev. Clin. Psychol., 1*(1), 113–142.

Miranda, J., Bernal, G., Lau, A., Kohn, L., Hwang, W-C., & La Framboise, T. (2005). State of the science on psychosocial interventions for ethnic minorities. *Annu. Rev. Clin. Psychol.,* 1, 113–142.

Mirsky, A. F., & Quinn, O. W. (1988). The Genain quadruplets. *Schizo. Bull., 14,* 595–612.

Mishler, E. G., & Waxler, N. E. (1968). *Interaction in families: An experimental study of family processes and schizophrenia.* New York: Wiley.

Mitchell, A., & House, A. (2000). Medical and surgical conditions and treatments associated with psychiatric disorder. In Gelder et al. (Eds.), *New Oxford textbook of psychiatry* (pp. 1138–53). Oxford: Oxford University Press.

Mitchell, J. E., Pomeroy, C., & Adson, D. E. (1997). Managing medical complications. In D. M. Garner & P. E. Garfinkel (Eds.), *Handbook of treatment for eating disorders* (pp. 383–93). New York: Guilford.

Mitchell, P., Wilhelm, K., Parker, G., Austin, M. P., Rutgers, P., & Malhi, G. S. (2001). The clinical features of bipolar depression: A comparison with matched major depressive disorder patients. *J. Clin. Psychiat., 62,* 212–16.

Mittelman, M. S., Roth, D. L., Coon, D. W., & Haley, W. E. (2004). Sustained benefit of supportive intervention for depressive symptoms in the caregivers of patients with Alzheimer's disease. *Amer. J. Psychiat., 161,* 850–56.

Moats, L. C., & Lyon, G. R. (1993). Learning disabilities in the United States: Advocacy, science, and the future of the field. *J. Learn. Dis., 26*(5), 282–94.

Moeller, F. G., & Dougherty, D. M. (2001). Antisocial personality disorder, alcohol and aggression. *Alcohol Research & Health, 25*(1), 5–11.

Moene, F. C., Spinhoven, P., Hoogduin, K., & Dyck, R. V. (2003). A randomized controlled clinical trial of a hypnosis-based treatment for patients with conversion disorder, motor type. *Int. J. Clin. Exp. Hypn., 51*(1), 29–50.

Moffatt, M. E. (1997). Nocturnal enuresis: A review of the efficacy of treatments and practical advice for clinicians. *Developmental and Behavioral Pediatrics, 18*(1), 49–56.

Moffitt, T. (1993a). Adolescence-limited and life-course-persistent antisocial behavior: A developmental taxonomy. *Psychol. Rev., 100,* 674–701.

Moffitt, T., Caspi, A., & Rutter, M. (2005). Strategy for investigating interactions between measured genes and measured environments. *Arch. Gen. Psychiat. 62*(5), 473–481.

Moffitt, T. E. (1993b). The neuropsychology of conduct disorder. *Develop. Psychopath., 5,* 135–51.

Moffitt, T. E., & Caspi, A. (2001). Childhood predictors differentiate life-course-persistent and adolescence-limited antisocial pathways among males and females. *Develop. Psychopath., 13*(2), 355–75.

Moffitt, T. E., Caspi, A., Harrington, H., & Milne, B. J. (2002). Males on the life-course-persistent and adolescence-limited antisocial pathways: Follow-up at age 26 years. *Develop. Psychopath., 14,* 179–207.

Moffitt, T. E., & Lynam, D. (1994). The neuropsychology of conduct disorder and delinquency: Implications for understanding antisocial behavior. In D. C. Fowles, P. Sutker, & S. H. Goodman (Eds.), *Progress in experimental personality and psychopathology research.* New York: Springer.

Mohr, D. C. (1995). Negative outcome in psychotherapy: A critical review. *Clin. Psychol. Sci. Prac., 2,* 1–27.

Moldin, S. O., & Gottesman, I. I. (1997). Genes, experience, and chance in schizophrenia—Positioning for the 21st century. *Schizo. Bull., 23*(4), 547–61.

Möller, J., Theorell, T., de Faire, U., Ahlbom, A., & Hallqvist, J. (2005). Work related stressful life events and the risk of myocardial infarctions: Case-control and case-crossover analyses with the Stockholm Heart Epidemiology Programme (SHEEP). *Journal of Epidemiology and Community Health, 59,* 1, 23–30.

Molnar, B. E., Berkman, L. F., & Buka, S. L. (2001). Psychopathology, childhood sexual abuse and other childhood adversities: Relative links to subsequent suicidal behaviour in the US. *Psychol. Med., 31,* 965–977.

Monahan, J., & Steadman, H. J. (1997). Violent storms and violent people: How meteorology can inform risk communication in mental health law. *Amer. Psychol., 51*(9), 931–38.

Monahan, J., Steadman, H. J., Silver, E., Appelbaum, P. S., Robbins, P. C., Mulvey, E. P., Roth, L. H., Grisso, T., & Banks, S. (2001). *Rethinking risk assessment: The MacArthur study of mental disorder and violence.* Oxford: Oxford University Press.

Money, J. (1985). *The destroying angel.* (pp. 17–31, 51–52, 61–68, 83–90, 107–20, 137–48) Buffalo, NY: Prometheus Books.

Money, J. (1986). *Lovemaps: Clinical concepts of sexual/erotic health and pathology, paraphilia, and gender transposition.* New York: Irvington.

Money, J. (1988). *Gay, straight, and in-between.* (p. 77). New York: Oxford University Press.

Money, J., & Ehrhardt, A. A. (1972). *Man & woman, boy & girl: Differentiation and dimorphism of gender identity from conception to maturity.* Baltimore: Johns Hopkins University Press.

Monroe, S. M., & Hadjiyannakis, K. (2002). The social environment and depression: Focusing on severe life stress. In I. H. Gotlib & C. L. Hammen (Eds.), *Handbook of depression* (pp. 314–40). New York: Guilford.

Monroe, S. M., & Harkness, K. L. (2005). Life stress, the "kindling" hypothesis, and the recurrence of depression: Considerations from a life stress perspective. *Psychol. Rev., 112*(2), 417–445.

Monroe, S. M., & Simons, A. D. (1991). Diathesis-stress theories in the context of life stress research: Implications for the depressive disorders. *Psychol. Bull., 110,* 406–25.

Monroe, S. M., Roberts, J. E., Kupfer, D. J., & Frank, E. (1996). Life stress and treatment course of recurrent depression: II. Postrecovery associations with attrition, symptom course, and recurrence over 3 years. *J. Abn. Psychol., 105*(3), 313–28.

Monson, C. M., Gunnin, D. D., Fogel, M. H., & Kyle, L. L. (2001). Stopping (or slowing) the revolving door: Factors related to NGRI acquittees' maintenance of a conditional release. *Law and Human Behavior, 25*(3), 257–66.

Montague, C. T., Farooqi, I. S., Whitehead, J. P., Soos, M. A., Rau, H., Wareham, N. J., Sewter, C. P., Digby, J. E., Mohammed, S. N., Hurst, J. A., Cheetham, C. H., Earley, A. R., Barnett, A. H., Prins, J. B., & O'Rahilly, S. (1997, Jun. 26). Congenital leptin deficiency is associated with severe early-onset obesity in humans. *Nature, 387,* 903–8.

Monterosso, J. R., Flannery, B. A., Pettinati, H. M., et al. (2001). Predicting treatment response to naltrexone: The influence of craving and family history. *American Journal of Addictions, 10*(3), 258–68.

Mora, G. (1967). Paracelsus' psychiatry. *Amer. J. Psychiat., 124,* 803–14.

Morey, L. C., Skinner, H. A., & Blashfield, R. K. (1984). A typology of alcohol abusers: Correlates and implications. *J. Abn. Psychol., 93,* 408–17.

Morey, L. C. (1988). Personality disorders in DSM-III and DSM-III-R: Convergence, coverage, and internal consistency. *Amer. J. Psychiat., 145,* 573–77.

Morgan, J. F., & Crisp, A. H. (2000). Use of leucotomy for intractable anorexia nervosa: A long-term follow-up study. *Int. Jo. Ea. Diso., 27,* 249–58.

Morgan, M. J. (1998). Recreational use of "ecstasy" (MDMA) is associated with elevated impulsivity. *Neuropsychopharmacology, 19*(4), 252–64.

Morgan, W. G. (2002). Origin and history of the earliest Thematic Apperception Test pictures. *J. Pers. Assess., 79*(3), 422–45.

Morganstern, J., Labouvie, E., McCrady, B. S., Kahler, C. W., & Frey, R. M. (1997). Affiliation with Alcoholics Anonymous after treatment: A study of its therapeutic effects and mechanisms of action. *J. Cons. Clin. Psychol., 65*(5), 768–77.

Morganstern, J., Langenbucher, J., Labouvie, E., & Miller, K. J. (1997). The comorbidity of alcoholism and personality disorders in a clinical population. *J. Abn. Psychol., 106*(1), 74–84.

Mori, E., et al. (1997a). Medial temporal structures relate to memory impairment in Alzheimer's disease: An MRI volumetric study. *J. Neurol. Neurosurg. Psychiat., 63*(2), 214–21.

Mori, E., et al. (1997b). Premorbid brain size as a determinant of reserve capacity against intellectual decline in Alzheimer's disease. *Amer. J. Psychiat., 154*(1), 18–24.

Moriarty, K. M., Alagna, S. W., & Lake, C. R. (1984). Psychopharmacology: An historical perspective. *Psychiat. Clin. N. Amer., 7*(3), 411–33.

Morihisa, J. M. (Ed). (2001). Advances in brain imaging. *Review of Psychiatry, 20,* 123–70.

Morisse, D., Batra, L., Hess, L., Silverman, R., & Corrigan, P. (1996). A demonstration of a token economy for the real world. *App. Prev. Psychol., 5,* 41–46.

Morris, T. L. (2001). Social phobia. In M. W. Vasey & M. R. Dadds (Eds.), *The developmental psychopathology of anxiety* (pp. 435–58). New York: Oxford University Press.

Morrison, A. P., French, P., Walford, L., Lewis, S., Kilcommons, A., Green, J., Parker, S., & Bentall, R. P. (2004). Cognitive therapy for the prevention of psychosis in people at ultra-high risk: Randomised controlled trial. *Brit. J. Psychiat., 185,* 291–97.

Morrison, J. (1980). Adult psychiatric disorders in parents of hyperactive children. *Amer. J. Psychiat., 137*(7), 825–27.

Morrison, J. (1995). *DSM-IV made easy: The clinicians guide to diagnosis.* New York: Guilford.

Mosak, H. H. (2000). Adlerian psychotherapy. In R. J. Corsini & D. Wedding (Eds.), *Current psychotherapies* (pp. 54–98). Itasca, IL: Peacock.

Moscato, B. S., Russell, M., Zielezny, M., Bromet, E., Egri, G., Mudar, P., & Marshall, J. R. (1997). Gender differences in the relation between depressive symptoms and alcohol problems: A longitudinal perspective. *Amer. J. Epidemiol., 146*(11), 966–74.

Moser, P. W. (1989, Jan.). Double vision: Why do we never match up to our mind's ideal? *Self,* pp. 51–52.

Moss-Morris, R., & Petrie, K. J. (2001). Discriminating between chronic fatigue syndrome and depression: A cognitive analysis. *Psychol. Med., 31,* 469–79.

Motavalli, N. (1995). Fluoxetine for (s)elective mutism. *J. Amer. Acad. Child Adoles. Psychiat., 34*(6), 701–2.

Mott, F. W. (1919). *War neuroses and shell shock.* Oxford: Oxford Medical Publications.

Mott, F. W. (1919). *War neuroses and shell shock.* Oxford: Oxford Medical Publications.

Mott, T. F., & Leach, L. (2004). Is methylphenidate useful for treating adolescents with ADHD? *J. Fam. Pract., 53*(8), 659–61.

Mowbray, R. M. (1959). Historical aspects of electric convulsant therapy. *Scott Medical Journal, 4,* 373–78.

Mowrer, O. H., & Mowrer, W. M. (1938). Enuresis—a method for its study and treatment. *Amer. J. Orthopsychiat., 8,* 436–59.

Mowrer, O. H. (1947). On the dual nature of learning: A reinterpretation of "conditioning" and "problem solving." *Harvard Educational Review, 17,* 102–48.

Moyers, T. B., Miller, W. R., & Henrdickson, M. L. (2005). How does motivational interviewing work? Therapist interpersonal skill predicts client involvement within motivational interviewing sessions. *J. Cons. Clin. Psychol., 73,* 590–598.

Mrazek, P. J., & Haggerty, R. J. (1994). *Reducing risks for mental disorders: Frontiers for prevention intervention research.* Washington, DC: National Academy Press.

Mueser, K. T., & Berenbaum, H. (1990). Psychodynamic treatment of schizophrenia. Is there a future? *Psychol. Med., 20,* 253–62.

Mueser, K. T., et al. (1998). Models of community care for severe mental illness: A review of research on case management. *Schizo. Bull., 24*(1), 37–74.

Mukherjee, S., Sackeim, H. A., & Schnur, D. B. (1994). Electroconvulsive therapy of acute manic episodes: A review of 50 years' experience. *Amer. J. Psychiat., 151,* 169–76.

Munoz, R. F., Mrazek, P. J., & Haggerty, R. J. (1996). Institute of Medicine report on prevention of mental disorders: Summary and commentary. *Amer. Psychol., 51*(11), 1116–22.

Munoz, R. F. (2001). How shall we ensure that the prevention of onset of mental disorders becomes a national priority? *Prevention & Treatment, 4,* np.

Murphy, C. C., Boyle, C., Schendel, D., Decoufle, P., & Yeargin-Allsopp, M. (1998). Epidemiology of mental retardation in children. *Mental Retardation & Developmental Disabilities Research Review, 4,* 6–13.

Murphy, C. M., Meyer, S. L., & O'Leary, K. D. (1994). Dependency characteristics of partner assaultive men. *J. Abn. Psychol., 103,* 729–35.

Murphy, D. L., Greenburg, B., Altemus, M., Benjamin, J., Grady, T., & Pigott, T. (1996). The neuropharmacology and neurobiology of obsessive-compulsive disorder: An update on the serotonin hypothesis. In H. G. Westenberg, J. A. Den Boer, & D. L. Murphy (Eds.), *Advances in the neurobiology of anxiety disorders* (pp. 279–97). Chichester, England: Wiley.

Murphy, G. C., & Athanasou, J. A. (1999). The effect of unemployment on mental health. *J. Occup. Org. Psychol., 72,* 83–99.

Murphy, J. M. (1976). Psychiatric labeling in cross-cultural perspective. *Science, 191,* 1019–28.

Murphy, W. D. (1997). Exhibitionism: Psychopathology and theory. In D. R. Laws & W. O'Donohue (Eds.), *Sexual deviance: Theory, assessment, and treatment* (pp. 22–39). New York: Guilford.

Murray, G. K., Leeson, V., & McKenna, P. J. (2004). Spontaneous improvement in severe, chronic schizophrenia and its neurological correlates. *Brit. J. Psychiat., 184,* 357–58.

Murray, J. B. (2001). Ecstasy is a dangerous drug. *Psychol. Rep., 88*(3), 895–902.

Murray, L. & Cooper, P. (1997). Postpartum depression and child development. *Psychol. Med., 27,* 253–60.

Murray, L., Fiori-Cowley, A., Hooper, R., & Cooper, P. (1996). The impact of postnatal depression and associated adversity on early mother-infant interactions and later infant outcomes. *Child Develop., 67*(5), 2512–26.

Musante, G. J., Costanzo, P. R., & Friedman, K. E. (1998). The comorbidity of depression and eating dysregulation processes in a diet-seeking obese population: A matter of gender specificity. *Int. J. Eat. Dis., 23*(1), 65–75.

Mussell, M. P., Mitchell, J. E., Crosby, R. D., Fulkerson, J. A., Hoberman, H. M., & Romano, J. L. (2000). Commitment to treatment goals in prediction of group cognitive-behavioral therapy treatment outcome for women with bulimia nervosa. *J. Cons. Clin. Psychol., 68,* 432–37.

Musselman, D. L., Lawson, D., Gumnick, J. F., Manatunga, A., Penna, S., Goodkin, R. S., Nemeroff, C. B., & Miller, A. H. (2001). Paroxetine for the prevention of depression induced by high dose interferon-alpha. *N. Engl. J. Med., 344,* 961–66.

Musselman, D. L., Marzec, U. M., Manatunga, A., Penna, S., Reemsnyder, A., Knight, B. T., Naron, A., Hanson, S. R., & Nemeroff, C. B. (2000). Platelet reactivity in depressed patients treated with paroxetine: Preliminary findings. *Arch. Gen. Psychiat., 57,* 875–82.

Mustanski, B. S., Viken, R. J., Kaprio, J., & Rose, R. J. (2003). Genetic influences on the association between personality risk factors and alcohol use and abuse. *J. Abn. Psychol., 112,* 282–89.

Myers, J. K., Weissman, M. M., Tischler, G. L., Holzer, C. E., Leaf, P. J., & Stoltzman, R. (1984). Six-month prevalence of psychiatric disorders in three communities: 1980 to 1982. *Arch. Gen. Psychiat., 41,* 959–67.

Myers, R. H., Schaefer, E. J., Wilson, P. W., D'Agostino, R., Ordovas, J. M., Espino, A., Au, R., White, R. F., Knoefel, J. E., Cobb, J. L., McNulty, K. A., Beiser, A., & Wolf, P. A. (1996). Apolipoprotein E (4 association with dementia in a population-based study: The Framingham study. *Neurology, 46,* 673–77.

Nadder, T. S., Silberg, J. L., Eaves, L. J., Maes, H. H., & Meyer, J. M. (1998). Genetic effects on ADHD symptomatology in 7- to 13-year-old twins: Results from a telephone survey. *Behav. Gen., 28*(2), 83–99.

Nagayama Hall, G. C. (2001). Psychotherapy research with ethnic minorities: Empirical, ethical, and conceptual issues. *J. Cons. Clin. Psychol., 69*(3), 502–10.

Nakao, T., Nakagawa, A., Yoshiura, T., Nakatani, E., Nabeyama, M., Yoshizato, C., Kudoh, A., Tada, K., Yoshioka, K., Kawamoto, M., Togao, O., & Kanba, S. (2005). Brain activation of patients with obsessive-compulsive disorder during neuropsychological and symptom provocation tasks before and after symptom improvement: A functional magnetic resonance imaging study. *Biol. Psychiat., 57,* 901–910.

Narby, J. (1982). The evolution of attitudes towards mental illness in preindustrial England. *Orthomolecular Psychiatry, 11,* 103–10.

Narrow, W. E., Regier, D. A., Rae, D. S., Manderscheld, R. W., & Locke, B. Z. (1993). Use of services by persons with mental and addictive disorders: Findings from the National Institute of Mental Health Epidemiologic Catchment Area Program. *Arch. Gen. Psychiat., 50,* 95–107.

Nasar, S. (1998). *A Beautiful Mind.* New York: Simon and Schuster.

Nash, M. R., Hulsey, T. L., Sexton, M. C., Harralson, T. L., & Lambert, W. (1993). Long-term sequelae of childhood sexual abuse: Perceived family environment, psychopathology, and dissociation. *J. Cons. Clin. Psychol., 61*(2), 276–83.

Nathan, P. E. & Gorman, J. M. (2002). *Treatments that work.* New York: Oxford University Press.

Nathan, P. E., & Gorman, J. M. (Eds.). (1998). *A guide to treatments that work.* New York: Oxford University Press.

National Advisory Mental Health Council. (1990). *National plan for research on child and adolescent mental disorders.* Washington, DC: National Institute of Mental Health.

National Center for Injury Prevention and Control. (2004). *Suicide: Fact sheet.* Retrieved August 3, 2005, from http://www. cdc. gov/ncipc/factsheets/ suifacts. htm.

National Committee to Prevent Child Abuse. (1996). *Study of the national incidence and prevalence of child abuse and neglect.* Washington, DC: Author.

National Institute for Drug Abuse. (1998). *Director's report:* 1997. Washington, DC: Author.

National Institute of Drug Abuse. (2004). *Results from the annual Monitoring the Future (MTF) survey.* Washington, DC: U.S. Department of Health and Human Services.

National Institutes of Health. (2001). *Alcohol: Research and Health,,* 25, 241–306.

National Mental Health Association. (1997). *Working for America's mental health.* Alexandria, VA: Author.

National Survey on Drug Use and Health. (2004). *The NSDUH Report.* Rockville, MD: US. Department of Health and Human Services.

National Youth Violence Prevention Resource Center. (2003). *Youth suicide facts.* Retrieved August 3, 2005, from http://www. safeyouth. org/scripts/faq/ suicidefacts. asp.

Nayani, T. H., & David, A. S. (1996). The auditory hallucination: A phenomenological survey. *Psychol. Med., 26*(1), 177–89.

Neale, J. M. (1988). Defensive functions of manic episodes. In T. F. Oltmanns & B. A. Maher (Eds.), *Delusional beliefs* (pp. 138–56). New York: Wiley.

Neale, J. M., & Oltmanns, T. F. (1980). *Schizophrenia.* New York: Wiley.

Neighbors, C., Larimer, M. E., & Lewis, M. A. (2004). Targeting misperceptions of descriptive drinking norms: Efficacy of a computer-delivered personalized normative feedback intervention. *J. Cons. Clin. Psychol., 72,* 202–17.

Neisser, U. (Ed.). (1982). *Memory observed: Remembering in natural contexts.* San Francisco: Freeman.

Neisser, U. (1967). *Cognitive psychology.* New York: Appleton Century Crofts.

Nelson, C. A. & Bloom, F. E. (1997). Child development and neuroscience. *Child Develop., 68*(5), 970–987.

Nelson, C. A., Bloom, F. E., Cameron, J. L., Amaral, D., Dahl, R. E., & Pine, D. (2002). An integrative, multidisciplinary approach to the study of brain-behavior relations in the context of typical and atypical development. *Develop. Psychopath., 14*(3), 499–520.

Nelson, L., Orme, D., Osann, K., & Lott, I. T. (2001). Neurological changes and emotional functioning in adults with Down syndrome. *J. Intell. Dis. Res., 45,* 450–56.

Nemeroff, C. B., & Schatzberg, A. F. (1998). Pharmacological treatment of unipolar depression. In P. E. Nathan & J. M. Gorman (Eds.), *A guide to treatments that work* (pp. 212–25). Oxford, England: Oxford University Press.

Nemeroff, C. B., & Schatzberg, A. F. (2002). Pharmacological treatments for unipolar depression. In P. E. Nathan & J. M. Gorman (Eds.), *A guide to treatments that work* (pp. 229–43). New York: Oxford University Press.

Nemeroff, C. B. (2003). Anxiolytics: Past, present, and future agents. *J. Clin. Psychiat., 64* (Suppl. 3), 3–6.

Nemeroff, C. B. (2004). Neurobiological consequences of childhood trauma. *J. Clin. Psychiat., 65*(1), 18–28.

Nesdale, D., Rooney, R., & Smith, L. (1997). Migrant ethnic identity and psychological distress. *Journal of Cross-Cultural Psychology, 28*(5), 569–88.

Nesse, R. M. (2000). Is depression an adaptation? *Arch. Gen. Psychiat., 57*(1), 14–20.

New York Times. (1994, May 9). Multiple personality cases perplex legal system, pp. 143.

Newcomb, M. D., Galaif, E. R., & Locke, T. F. (2001). Substance use diagnoses within a community sample of adults: Distinction, comorbidity, and progression over time. *Profess. Psychol.: Res. Prac., 32*(3), 239–47.

Newman, L., Henry, P. B., DiRenzo, P., & Stecher, T. (1988–89). Intervention and student assistance: The Pennsylvania model. Special Issue: Practical approaches in treating adolescent chemical dependency: A guide to clinical assessment and intervention. *J. Chem. Depen. Treat., 2*(1), 145–62.

Newton, L., Rosen, A., Tennant, C., Hobbs, C., Lapsley, H. M., & Tribe, K. (2000). Deinstitutionalisation for long-term mental illness: An ethnographic study. *Austral. NZ J. Psychiat., 34,* 484–90.

Neziroglu, F., Roberts, M., & Yaryura-Tobias, J. (2004). A behavioural model for body dysmorphic disorder. *Psychiat. Ann., 34*(12), 915–20.

Ng, B.-Y., & Chan Y.-H. (2004). Psychosocial stressors that precipitate dissociative trance disorder in Singapore. *Austral. N. Z. J. Psychol., 38*(6), 426–32.

Ng, B.-Y. (1999). Hysteria: A cross-cultural comparison of its origins and history. *History of Psychiatry, 10,* 287–301.

Ng, D. M., & Jeffery, R. W. (2003). Relationships between perceived stress and health behaviors in a sample of working adults. *Hlth. Psychol. 22*(6), 638–42.

NIAAA. (2001). Monitoring the Future. National Institutes of Mental Health. Washington, DC: Author.

NIAAA. (2002, Apr.). A call to action: Changing the culture of drinking at U.S. colleges. NIH publication no. 02-5010.

NIAAA. (2004). *Alcohol alert* (No. 61). Rockville, MD: U.S. Department of Health and Human Services.

Niaura, R., & Abrams, D. B. (2002). Smoking cessation: Progess, priorities, and prospectus. *J. Cons. Clin. Psychol., 70*(3), 494–509.

Nichter, M., & Nichter, M. (1991). Hype and weight. *Medical Anthropology, 13*(3), 249–84.

Nicolson, R., & Szatmari, P. (2003). Genetic and neurodevelopmental influences in autistic disorder. *Canad. J. Psychiat., 48*(8), 526–37.

NIDA Survey. (2003). *Trends in drug related episodes. NIDA Research Report: Monitoring the Future Study.* Washington, DC: Author.

Niederehe, G., & Schneider. (1998). Treatments for depression and anxiety in the aged. In P. E. Nathan & J. M. Gorman (Eds.), *A guide to treatments that work* (pp. 270–87). New York: Oxford University Press.

Niederhofer, H., & Staffen, W. (2003). Comparison of disulfiram and placebo in treatment of alcohol dependence of adolescents. *Drug. Al. Rev., 22*(3), 295–97.

Nigg, J. T. (2001). Is ADHD a disinhibitory disorder? *Psychol. Bull., 127*(5), 571–98.

Nigg, J. T., Butler, K. M., Huang-Pollock, C. L., & Henderson, J. M. (2002). Inhibitory processes in adults with persistent childhood onset ADHD. *J. Cons. Clin. Psychol., 70*(1), 153–57.

Nimgaonkar, V. L., Fujiwara, T. M., Dutta, M., Wood, J., Gentry, K., Maendel, S., Morgan, K., & Eaton, J. (2000). Low prevalence of psychoses among the Hutterites, an isolated religious community. *Amer. J. Psychiat., 157*(7), 1065–70.

NIMH. (2001). *Facts about the National Institute of Mental Health.* Washington, DC: U.S. Government Printing Office 00-47-43.

Nisbett, R. E., & Wilson, T. D. (1977). Telling more than we can know: Verbal reports on mental processes. *Psychol. Rev., 84,* 231–59.

Nissen, M. J., Ross, J. L., Willingham, D. B., MacKenzie, T. B., & Schacter, D. L. (1988). Memory and awareness in a patient with multiple personality disorder. *Brain and Cognition, 8,* 117–34.

Nixon, R. D., & Bryant, R. A. (2005). Are negative cognitions associated with severe acute trauma responses? *Behav. Chng., 22*(1), 22–28.

Nobakht, M., & Dezhkam, M. (2000). An epidemiological study of eating disorders in Iran. *Int. J. Eat. Dis., 28,* 265–71.

Noble, E. P. (Ed.). (1979). *Alcohol and health: Technical support document.* Third special report to the U.S. Congress (DHEW Publication No. ADM79–832). Washington, DC: U.S. Government Printing Office.

Nock, M. K. (2003). Progress review of the psychosocial treatment of child conduct problems. *Clin. Psychol. Sci. Prac., 10,* 1–28.

Nolan, E. E., & Gadow, K. D. (1997). Children with ADHD and tic disorder and their classmates: Behavioral normalization with methylphenidate. *J. Amer. Acad. Child Adoles. Psychiat., 36*(5), 597–604.

Nolen-Hoeksema, S. (1990). *Sex differences in depression.* Stanford, CA: Stanford University Press.

Nolen-Hoeksema, S. (2002). Gender differences in depression. In I. H. Gotlib & C. L. Hammen (Eds.), *Handbook of depression* (pp. 492–509). New York: Guilford.

Nolen-Hoeksema, S., & Corte, C. (2004). Gender and self-regulation. In R. F. Baumeister & K. D. Vohs (Eds.) *Handbook of self-regulation: Research, theory, and applications.* (pp. 411–421). New York: Guilford Press.

Nolen-Hoeksema, S., & Girgus, J. S. (1994). The emergence of gender differences in depression during adolescence. *Psychol. Bull., 115*(3), 424–43.

Nolen-Hoeksema, S., Larson, J., & Grayson, C. (1999). Explaining the gender difference in depressive symptoms. *J. Person. Soc. Psychol., 77*(5), 1061–72.

Nolen-Hoeksema, S., Morrow, J., & Fredrickson, B. L. (1993). Response styles and the duration of episodes of depressed mood. *J. Abn. Psychol., 102*(1), 20–28.

Nopoulos, P., Flaum, M., & Andreasen, N. C. (1997). Sex differences in brain morphology in schizophrenia. *Amer. J. Psychiat., 154*(12), 1648–54.

Norko, M., & Baranoski, M. V. (2005). The state of contemporary risk assessment research. *Canad. J. Psychiat., 50*(1), 18–26.

Norris, F. H., & Kaniasty, K. (1994). Psychological distress following criminal victimization in the general population: Cross-sectional, longitudinal, and prospective analyses. *J. Cons. Clin. Psychol., 62,* 111–23.

Novy, D. M., Blumentritt, T. L., Nelson, D. V., & Gaa, A. (1997). The Washington University Sentence Completion Test: Are the two halves alternate forms? Are the female and male forms comparable? *J. Pers. Assess., 68*(3), 616–27.

Nowakowski, R. S. (1999). Prenatal development of the brain. In E. Z. Susser, A. S. Brown, & J. M. Gorman (Eds.), *Prenatal exposures in schizophrenia* (pp. 61–85). Washington, DC: American Psychiatric Press.

Nuechterlein, K. H. (1977). Reaction time and attention in schizophrenia: A critical evaluation of the data and theories. *Schizo. Bull., 3,* 373–428.

Nuechterlein, K. H., Snyder, K. S., & Mintz, J. M. (1992). Paths to relapse: Possible transactional processes connecting patient illness onset, expressed emotion, and psychotic relapse. *Brit. J. Psychiat., 161*(suppl. 18), 88–96.

O'Brien, D. (1979, Mar.). Mental anguish: An occupational hazard. *Emergency,* 61–64.

O'Brien, K. M., & Vincent, N. K. (2003). Psychiatric comorbidity in anorexia and bulimia nervosa: Nature, prevalence, and causal relationships. *Clin. Psychol. Rev., 23,* 57–74.

O'Carroll, R. E., Smith, K. B., Grubb, N. R., Fox, K. A. A., & Masterton, G. (2001). Psychological factors associated with delay in attending hospital following a myocardial infarction. *J. Psychosom. Res., 51*(4), 611–14.

O'Conner, T. G., Marvin, R. S., Rutter, M., Olrick, J. T., & Britner, P. A. (2003). Child-parent attachment following early institutional deprivation. *Develop. Psychopath., 15*(1), 19–38.

O'Connor, B. P., McGuire, S., Reiss, D., Hetherington, E. M., & Plomin, R. (1998). Co-occurrence of depressive symptoms and antisocial behavior in adolescence: A common genetic liability. *J. Abn. Psychol., 107*(1), 27–37.

O'Connor, E. M. (2001, Dec.). Medicating ADHD: Too much? Too soon? *Monitor on Psychology,* 50–51.

O'Connor, M. J. (2001). Prenatal alcohol exposure and infant negative affect as precursors of depressive features in children. *Infant Mental Health Journal, 22*(3), 291 99.

O'Connor, S. J. (1996). Who will manage the managers? In A. Lazarus (Ed.), *Controversies in managed mental health care* (pp. 383–401). Washington, DC: American Psychiatric Press, Inc.

O'Donnell, C. R. (Ed.). (2004). *Culture, peers and delinquency.* Binghamton, NY: Haworth Press.

O'Donnell, I., & Farmer, R. (1995). The limitations of official suicide statistics. *Brit. J. Psychiat., 166,* 458–61.

O'Donnell, R., Rome, D., Godin, M., & Fulton, P. (2000). Changes in inpatient utilization and quality of care performance measures in a capitated HMO population, 1989–1999. *Psychiat. Clin. N. Amer., 23*(2), 319–33.

O'Donoghue, E. G. (1914). *The story of Bethlehem Hospital from its foundation in 1247.* London: Adelphi Terrace.

O'Farrell, T. J., Murphy, C. M., Stephan, S. H., Fals-Stewart, W., & Murphy, M. (2004). Partner violence before and after couples-based alcoholism treatment for male alcoholic patients: The role of treatment involvement and abstinence. *J. Cons. Clin. Psychol., 72,* 202–17.

O'Hara, M., & Gorman, L. L. (2004). Can postpartum depression be predicted. *Prim. Psychiat., 11*(3), 42–47.

O'Hara, M., Schlecte, J., Lewis, D., & Varner, M. (1991). Controlled prospective study of postpartum mood disorders: Psychological, environmental, and hormonal variables. *J. Abn. Psychol., 100,* 63–73.

O'Hara, M., Zekoski, E., Philipps, L., & Wright, E. (1990). Controlled prospective study of postpartum mood disorders: Comparison of childbearing and nonchildbearing women. *J. Abn. Psychol., 99,* 3–15.

O'Leary, K. D. (2000). Are women really more aggressive than men in intimate relationships? Comment on. *Psychol. Bull., 126*(5), 685–89.

O'Leary, K. D., & Schumacher, J. A. (2003). The association between alcohol use and intimate partner violence: Linear effect, threshold effect, or both? *Add. Behav., 28,* 1575–85.

O'Malley, S. S., Jaffe, A. J., Rode, S., & Rounsaville, B. (1996). Experience of a "slip" among alcoholics treated with naltrexone or placebo. *Amer. J. Psychiat., 153*(2), 281–83.

O'Malley, S. S., Krishnan-Sarin, S., Farren, C., Sinha, R., & Kreek, M. J. (2002). Naltrexone decreases craving and alcohol self-administration in alcohol-dependent subjects and activates the hypothalamo-pituitary-adrenocortical axis. *Psychopharmacology, 160*(1), 19–29.

O'Shea, B. (2001). Post-traumatic stress disorder: A review for the general psychiatrist. *International Journal of Psychiatry in Clinical Practice, 5,* 11–18.

Odell, J. D., Warren, R. P., Warren, W., Burger, R. A., & Maciulis, A. (1997). Association of genes within the major histocompatibility complex with attention-deficit hyperactivity disorder. *Neuropsychobiology, 35*(4), 181–86.

Office of Juvenile Justice and Delinquency Prevention. (1995). *1995 Youth Gang survey.* Washington, DC: U.S. Government Printing Office.

Office of Technology Assessment. (1993). *Biological components of substance abuse and addiction.* Washington, DC: United States Congress, Office of Technology Assessment.

Ohayon, M. M., & Shatzberg, A. F. (2002). Prevalence of depressive episodes with psychotic features in the general population. *Amer. J. Psychiat., 159*(11), 1855–1861.

Öhman, A. (1996). Perferential preattentive processing of threat in anxiety: Preparedness and attentional biases. In R. M. Rapee (Ed.), *Current controversies in the anxiety disorders* (pp. 253–90). New York: Guilford.

Öhman, A., & Mineka, S. (2001). Fears, phobias, and preparedness: Toward an evolved module of fear and fear learning. *Psychol. Rev., 108,* 483–522.

Öhman, A., & Soares, J. (1993). On the automatic nature of phobic fear: Conditioned electrodermal responses to masked fear-relevant stimuli. *J. Abn. Psychol., 102,* 121–32.

Öhman, A., Dimberg, U., & Öst, L. G. (1985). Animal and social phobias: Biological constraints on learned fear responses. In S. Reiss & R. Bootzin (Eds.), *Theoretical issues in behavior therapy* (pp. 123–75). New York: Academic Press.

Okasha, A., & Okasha, T. (2000). Notes on mental disorders in Pharaonic Egypt. *History of Psychiatry, 11,* 413–24.

Oken, B. S., Storzbach, D. M., & Kaye, J. A. (1998). The efficacy of *Ginkgo biloba* on cognitive function in Alzheimer disease. *Arch. Neurol., 55,* 1409–15.

Okulicz-Kozaryn, K., Bobrowski, K., Borucka, A., Ostaszewski, K., & Pisarska, A. (2000). Poprawnosc realizacji programu domowych detektywow a jego skutecnosc. *Alkoholizm I Narkomania Tom, 13*(2), 235–54.

Ollendick, T. H., Yang, B., King, N. J., Dong, Q., et al. (1996). Fears in American, Australian, Chinese, and Nigerian children and adolescents: A cross-cultural study. *Journal of Child Psychology & Psychiatry & Allied Sciences, 37*(2), 213–20.

Olney, J. W., & Farber, N. B. (1995). Glutamate receptor dysfunction and schizophrenia. *Arch. Gen. Psychiat., 52,* 998–1007.

Olson, K. R. (2001). Computerized psychological test usage in APA accredited training programs. *J. Clin. Psychol., 57,* 727–36.

Ondersma, S. J., Chaffin, M., Berliner, L., Cordon, I., & Goodman, G. S. (2001). Sex with children is abuse: Comment on Rind, Tromovitch, and Bauserman (1998). *Psychol. Bull., 127,* 707–14.

Oquendo, M. A., & Mann, J. J. (2000). The biology of impulsivity and suicidality. *Borderline Personality Disorder, 23*(1), 11–25.

Oren, D. A., & Rosenthal, N. E. (1992). Seasonal affective disorders. In E. S. Paykel (Ed.), *Handbook of affective disorders* (2nd ed., pp. 551–67). New York: Guilford.

Orman, R. F., Veseley, S., Aspey, C. B., McLeroy, K. R., Rodine, S., & Marshall, L. (2004). The potential protective effect of youth assets on adolescent alcohol and drug use. *Amer. J. Pub. Hlth., 94,* 1425–30.

Orne, M. T., Dinges, D. F., & Orne, E. C. (1984). On the differential diagnosis of multiple personality in the forensic context. *Int. J. Clin. Exp. Hypn., 32,* 118–69.

Ornstein, P. A., Ceci, S. J., & Loftus, E. F. (1998). Adult recollections of childhood abuse: Cognitive and developmental perspectives. *Psychology, Public Policy, and Law, 4,* 1025–51.

Osborn, A. F. (1992). Social influences on conduct disorder in mid-childhood. *Studia Psychologica, 34,* 29–43.

Oscar-Berman, M., Shagrin, B., Evert, D. L., & Epstein, C. (1997). Impairments of brain and behavior. *Alcohol Health and Research World, 21*(1), 65–75.

Öst, L. G., & Hugdahl, K. (1981). Acquisition of phobias and anxiety response patterns in clinical patients. *Behav. Res. Ther., 19,* 439–47.

Öst, L. G., & Hugdahl, K. (1985). Acquisition of blood and dental phobia and anxiety response patterns in clinical patients. *Behav. Res. Ther., 23*(1), 27–34.

Öst, L. G. (1987). Age of onset of different phobias. *J. Abn. Psychol., 96,* 223–29.

Öst, L-G., & Hellström, K. (1997). Blood-injury-injection phobia. In G. C. L. Davey (Ed.), *Phobias. A handbook of theory, research and treatment.* (pp. 63–80). Chichester, England: Wiley.

Ost, L-G., Alm, T., Brandberg, M., & Breitholtz, E. (2001). One vs. five sessions of exposure and five sessions of cognitive therapy in the treatment of claustrophobia. *Behav. Res. & Ther., 39*(2), 167–183.

Öst, L-G. (1997). Rapid treatment of specific phobias. In G. C. L. Davey (Ed.), *Phobias. A handbook of theory, research and treatment* (2nd ed., pp. 227–46). Chichester, England: Wiley.

Ostaszewski, K., Bobrowski, K., Borucka, A., Okulicz-Kozaryn, K., & Pisarska, A. (2000). Evaluating innovative drug-prevention programmes: Lessons learned. In R. Neaman, M. Nilson, & U. Solberg (Eds.), *Evaluation: A key tool for improving drug prevention* (pp. 75–85). Luxembourg: European Monitoring Centre for Drugs and Drug Addiction.

Ostberg, V. (2002). Children in classrooms: peer status, status distribution and mental well-being. *Soc. Sci. Med., 56*(1), 17–29.

Ouimette, P., & Brown, P. J. (Eds.). (2004). *Trauma and substance abuse: Causes, consequences and treat-*

ment of comorbid disorders. Washington, DC: American Psychological Association.

Overall, J. E., & Hollister, L. E. (1982). Decision rules for phenomenological classification of psychiatric patients. *J. Cons. Clin. Psychol., 50*(4), 535–45.

Overmier, J. B., & Seligman, M. E. P. (1967). Effects of inescapable shock upon subsequent escape and avoidance learning. *Journal of Comparative and Physiological Psychology, 63,* 23–33.

Owen, C., Rutherford, M. J., Jones, M., Tennant, C., & Smallman, A. (1997). Noncompliance in psychiatric aftercare. *Comm. Ment. Hlth. J., 33,* 25–34.

Owen, F., & Simpson, M. D. C. (1995). The neurochemistry of schizophrenia. In S. R. Hirsch & D. R. Weinberger (Eds.), *Schizophrenia* (pp. 253–74). Cambridge: Cambridge University Press.

Owens, K., Asmundson, G., Hadjistavropoulos, T., & Owens, T. J. (2004). Attentional bias toward illness threat in individuals with elevated health anxiety. *Cog. Ther. Res., 28*(1), 57–66.

Ozer, E. J., & Weiss, D. S. (2004). Who develops posttraumatic stress disorder? *Curr. Dirs. Psychol. Sci., 13,* 169–72.

Ozer, E. J., Best, S. R., Lipsey, T. L., & Weiss, D. S. (2004). Predictors of posttraumatic stress disorder and symptoms in adults: A meta analysis. *Psychol. Bull., 129,* 52–73.

Pachter, H. M. (1951). *Magic into science: The story of Paracelsus.* New York: Schumen.

Padma-Nathan, H., McMurray, J. G., Pullman, W. E., Whitaker, J. S., Saoud, J. B., Ferguson, K. M., et al. (2001). On-demand IC351 (Cialis) enhances erectile function in patients with erectile dysfunction. *International Journal of Impotence Research, 13,* 2–9.

Page, W. F., Engdahl, B. E., & Eberly, R. E. (1997). Persistence of PTSD in former prisoners of war. In C. S. Fullerton & R. J. Ursano (Eds.), *Posttraumatic stress disorder* (pp. 147–58). Washington, DC: American Psychiatric Press.

Palace, E. M., & Gorzalka, B. B. (1990). The enhancing effects of anxiety on arousal in sexually dysfunctional and functional women. *J. Abn. Psychol., 99,* 403–11.

Palermo, M. T. (2004). Pervasive developmental disorders, psychiatric comorbidities, and the law. *Int. J. Off. Ther. Comp. Crim., 48*(1), 40–48.

Palmstierno, T. (2001). A model for predicting alcohol withdrawal delirium. *Psychiatr. Serv., 52*(6), 820–23.

Palosaari, U., & Laippala, P. (1996). Parental divorce and depression in young adulthood: Adolescents' closeness to parents and self-esteem as mediating factor. *Acta Psychiat. Scandin., 93*(1), 20–36.

Pan, H. S., Neidig, P. H., & O'Leary, K. D. (1994). Predicting mild and severe husband-to-wife physical aggression. *J. Cons. Clin. Psychol., 62,* 975–81.

Paolucci, E. O., Genuis, M. L., & Violato, C. (2001). A meta-analysis of the published research on the effects of child sexual abuse. *J. Psychol., 135*(1), 17–36.

Papanicolaou, D. A., Wilder, R. I., Manolagas, S. C., & Chrousos, G. P. (1998). The pathophysiologic roles of interleukin-6 in human disease. *Ann. Int. Med., 128,* 127–37.

Papp, L., & Gorman, J. M. (1990). Suicidal preoccupation during fluoxetine treatment. *Amer. J. Psychiat., 147,* 1380.

Pargament, K. I., & Mahoney, A. (2002). Spirituality. In C. R. Snyder & S. J. Lopez (Eds.), *Handbook of positive psychology* (pp. 646–59). Oxford University Press.

Paris, J. (1999). Borderline personality disorder. In T. Millon, P. H. Blaney, & R. D. Davis (Eds.), *Oxford textbook of psychopathology* (pp. 628–52). New York: Oxford University Press.

Paris, J. (2001). Psychosocial adversity. In W. J. Livesley (Ed.), *Handbook of personality disorders* (pp. 231–41). New York: Guilford.

Park, S., Holzman, P. S., & Goldman-Rakic, P. S. (1995). Spatial working memory deficits in the relatives of schizophrenic patients. *Arch. Gen. Psychiat., 52,* 821–28.

Parker, G. F. (2004). Outcomes of assertive community treatment in an NGRI conditional release program. *J. Amer. Acad. Psychiat. Law, 32*(3), 291–303.

Parker, G., Gladstone, G., & Chee, K. T. (2001). Depression in the planet's largest ethnic group: The Chinese. *Amer. J. Psychiat., 158*(6), 857–64.

Parker, I. (2004, Aug. 2). The gift. *The New Yorker,* p. 54–63.

Parker, J. G., Rubin, K. H., Price, J. M., & DeRossier, M. E. (1995). Peer relationships, child development, and adjustment: A developmental psychopathology perspective. In D. Cicchetti & D. J. Cohen (Eds.), *Developmental psychopathology: Vol. 2. Risk, disorder, and adaptation* (pp. 96–161). New York: Wiley.

Parra, C., Esteves, F., Flykt, A., & Ohman, A. (1997). Pavlonian conditioning to social stimuli: Backward masking and the dissociation of implicit and explicit cognitive processes. *Europ. Psychol., 2*(2), 106–117.

Parra, C., Esteves, F., Flykt, A., & Öhman, A. (1997). Pavlovian conditioning to social stimuli: Backward masking and the dissociation of implicit and explicit cognitive processes. *European Psychologist, 2,* 106–17.

Parrott, A. C., & Stuart, M. (1997). Ecstasy (MDMA), amphetamine, and LSD: Comparative mood profiles in recreational polydrug users. *Human Psychopharmacology, 12*(5), 501–04.

Parrott, A. C., Lees, A., Garnham, N. J., Jones, M., & Wesnes, K. (1998). Cognitive performance in recreational users of MDMA or "ecstasy": Evidence for memory deficits. *J. Psychopharmacol., 12*(1), 79–83.

Parrott, A. C. (2001). Human psychopharmacology of Ecstasy (MDMA): A review of 15 years of empirical research. *Human Psychopharmacology Clinical & Experimental, 16*(8), 557–77.

Pary, R. J. (2004). Behavioral and psychiatric disorders in children and adolescents with Down Syndrome. *Ment. Hlth. Asp. Dev. Dis., 7,* 69–76.

Patel, V., & Sumathipala, A. (2001). International representation in psychiatric literature: Survey of six leading journals. *Brit. J. Psychiat., 178,* 406–9.

Patrick, C. J., & Lang, A. R. (1999). Psychopathic traits and intoxicated states: Affective concomitants and conceptual links. In M. E. Dawson, A. M. Schell, & A. H. Bohmelt (Eds.), *Startle modification: Implications for neuroscience, cognitive science, and clinical science.* Cambridge, UK: Cambridge University Press.

Patrick, C. J., Bradley, M. M., & Lang, P. J. (1993). Emotion in the criminal psychopath: Startle reflex modulation. *J. Abn. Psychol., 102*(1), 82–92.

Patrick, C. J., Cuthbert, B. N., & Lang, P. J. (1994). Emotion in the criminal psychopath: Fear image processing. *J. Abn. Psychol., 103,* 523–34.

Patrick, C. J. (1994). Emotion and psychopathy: Startling new insights. *Psychophysiology, 31*(4), 319–30.

Patterson, G. R. (1979). Treatment for children with conduct problems: A review of outcome studies. In S. Feshbach & A. Fraczek (Eds.), *Aggression and behavior change: Biological and social processes.* New York: Praeger.

Patterson, G. R. (1996). Characteristics of developmental theory for early onset delinquency. In M. F. Lenzenweger & J. L. Haugaard (Eds.), *Frontiers of developmental psychopathology* (pp. 81–124). New York: Oxford University Press.

Patterson, G. R., & Yoerger, K. (2002). A developmental model for early- and late-onset delinquency. In J. B. Reid, G. R. Patterson, et al. (Eds.), *Antisocial behavior in children and adolescents: A developmental analysis and model for intervention* (pp. 147–72). Washington, DC: American Psychological Association.

Patterson, G. R., Capaldi, D., & Bank, L. (1991). An early starter model for predicting delinquency. In D. Pepler & K. H. Rubin (Eds.), *The development and treatment of childhood aggression* (pp. 139–68). Hillsdale, NJ: Erlbaum.

Patterson, G. R., DeGarmo, D. S., & Knutson, N. (2000). Hyperactivity and antisocial behaviors: Comorbid or two points in the same process? *Develop. Psychopath., 12*(1), 91–106.

Patterson, G. R., Reid, J. B., & Dishion, T. J. (1998). Antisocial boys. In J. M. Jenkins & K. Oatley (Eds.), *Human emotions: A reader* (pp. 330–36). Malden, MA: Blackwell.

Patton, G. C., Johnson-Sabine, E., Wood, K., Mann, A. H., & Wakeling, A. (1990). Abnormal eating attitudes in London schoolgirls—a prospective epidemiological study: outcome at twelve month follow-up. *Psychol. Med., 20*(2), 383–394.

Paul, G. L. (1982). *The development of a "transportable" system of behavioral assessment for chronic patients.* Invited address. University of Minnesota, Minneapolis.

Paul, G. L., & Lentz, R. J. (1977). *Psychosocial treatment of chronic mental patients: Milieu versus social-learning programs.* Cambridge, MA: Harvard University Press.

Paul, G. L., Stuve, P., & Cross, J. V. (1997). Real-world inpatient programs: Shedding some light—A critique. *App. Prev. Psychol., 6*(4), 193–204.

Paul, L. K., Schieffer, B., & Brown, W. S. (2004). Social processing deficits in agenesis of the corpus callosum: Narratives from the Thematic Apperception Test. *Arch. Clin. Neuropsychol., 19*(2), 215–25.

Paul, T., Schroeter, K., Dahme, B., & Nutzinger, D. O. (2002). Self-injurious behavior in women with eating disorders. *Amer. J. Psychiat., 159*(3), 408–11.

Pauli, P., & Alpers, G. W. (2002). Memory bias in patients with hypochondriases and somatoform pain disorder. *J. Psychom. Res., 52,* 42–53.

Pauls, D. L., Alsobrooke, J. P., Goodman, W., Rasmussen, S., & Leckman, J. F. (1995). A family study of obsessive-compulsive disorder. *Amer. J. Psychiat., 152*(1), 76–84.

Pauls, D. L., Raymond, C. L., & Robertson, M. (1991). The genetics of obsessive-compulsive disorder: A review. In J. Zohar, T. Insel, & S. Rasmussen (Eds.), *The psychobiology of obsessive-compulsive disorder.* New York: Springer.

Pauls, D. L., Towbin, K. E., Leckman, J. F., Zahner, G. E., & Cohen, D. J. (1986). Gilles de la Tourette's Syndrome and obsessive-compulsive disorder. *Arch. Gen. Psychiat., 43,* 1180–2.

Pavlov, I. P. (1927). *Conditioned reflexes.* London: Oxford University Press.

Pavone, L., Meli, C., Nigro, F., & Lisi, R. (1993). Late diagnosed phenylketonuria patients: Clinical presentation and results of treatment. *Developmental Brain Dysfunction, 6*(1–3), 184–87.

Pearlstein, T. (2000). Antidepressant treatment of posttraumatic stress disorder. *J. Clin. Psychiat., 61,* 40–43.

Pederson, C. B., & Mortensen, P. B. (2001). Evidence of a dose-response relationship between urbanicity during upbringing and schizophrenia risk. *Arch. Gen. Psychiat., 58,* 1039–46.

Pediatric OCD Treatment Study. (2004). Cognitive-behavior therapy, sertraline, and their combination for children and adolescents with obsessive-compulsive disorder: The pediatric OCD treatment study (POTS) randomized controlled trial. *JAMA, 292*(16). 1969–1976.

Peek, R. M., Jr., & Blaser, M. J. (1997). Pathophysiology of *Helicobacter pylori*-induced gastritis and peptic ulcer disease. *Amer. J. Med., 102,* 200–07.

Peeke, P. M., & Chrousos, G. P. (1995). Hypercortisolism and obesity. In G. P. Chrousos, R. McCarty, et al. (Eds.), *Stress: Basic mechanisms and clinical implications* (pp. 515–60). New York: New York Academy of Sciences.

Pelham, W. E., Carlson, C., Sams, S. E., Vallano, G., Dixon, M. J., & Hoza, B. (1993). Separate and combined effects of methylphenidate and behavior modification on boys with attention-deficit hyperactivity disorder in the classroom. *J. Cons. Clin. Psychol., 61,* 506–15.

Pelham, W. E., Jr., Hoza, B., Pillow, D. R., Gnagy, E., Kipp, H. L., Greiner, D. R., Waschbusch, D. A., Trane, S., T., Greenhouse, J., Wolfson, L., & Fitzpatrick, E. (2002). Effects of methylphenidate and expectancy on children with ADHD behavior, academic performance, and attributions in a summer treatment program and regular classroom setting. *J. Cons. Clin. Psychol., 70,* 320–25.

Pelham, W. E., Murphy, D. A., Vannatta, K., Milich, R., Licht, B. G., Gnagy, E. M., Greenslade, K. E., Greiner, A. R., & Vodde-Hamilton, M. (1992). Methylphenidate and attributions in boys with attention-deficit hyperactivity disorder. *J. Cons. Clin. Psychol., 60,* 282–92.

Penk, W. E., Rierdan, J., Losardo, M., & Robinowitz, R. (in press). The MMPI-2 and assessment of posttraumatic stress disorder (PTSD). In J. N. Butcher (Ed.), *MMPI-2: The practitioner's guide.* Washington, DC: American Psychological Association.

Penk, W., Drebing, C., & Schutt, R. (2002). PTSD in the workplace. In J. C. Thomas & Michel Hersen (Eds.), *Handbook of mental health in the workplace* (pp. 215–48). Thousand Oaks, CA: Sage.

Pennebaker, J. W. (1997). *Opening up: The healing power of expressing emotions.* New York: Guilford.

Penrose, L. S. (1963). *Biology of mental defect* (3rd ed.). New York: Grune & Stratton.

Pentz, M. A. (1983). Prevention of adolescent substance abuse through social skill development. *National Institute on Drug Abuse Research Monograph Series, 47,* 195–232.

Perkins, D. O., Lieberman, J. A., Gu, H., Tohen, M., McEvoy, J., Green, A. I., Zipursky, R. B., Strakowski, S. M., Sharma, T., Kahn, R. S., Gur, R., & Tollefson, G. (2004). Predictors of antipsychotoic treatment response in patients with first-episode schizophrenia, schizoaffective disorder and schizophreniform disorders. *Brit. J. Psychiat., 185,* 18–24.

Perkins-Dock, R. E. (2001). Family interventions with incarcerated youth: A review of the literature. *International Journal of Offender Therapy & Comparative Criminology, 45*(5), 606–25.

Perl, D. P. (1999). Abnormalities in brain structure on postmortem analysis of dementias. In D. S. Charney, E. J. Nestler, & B. S. Bunney (Eds.), *Neurobiology of mental illness.* New York: Oxford University Press.

Perlin, M. L. (1996). Myths, realities, and the political world; the anthropology of insanity defense attitudes. *Bull. Amer. Acad. Psychiat. Law, 24*(1), 5–25.

Perlis, R. P., Perlis, C. S., Wu, Y., Hwang, C., Jospeh, M., & Nierenberg, A. A. (2005). Industry sponsorship and financial conflict of interest in the reporting of clinical trials in psychiatry. *Amer. J. Psychiat., 162,* 1957–1960.

Perls, F. S. (1969). *Gestalt therapy verbatim.* Lafayette, California: Real People Press.

Perreira, K. M., & Sloan, F. A. (2001). Life events and alcohol consumption among mature adults: A longitudinal analysis. *J. Stud. Alcoh., 62*(4), 501–8.

Perris, C. (1992). Bipolar-unipolar distinction. In E. S. Paykel (Ed.), *Handbook of affective disorders* (2nd ed.). New York: Guilford.

Perry, C. L., Williams, C. L., Komro, K. A., & Veblen-Mortenson, S. (2000). Project Northland: A community-wide approach to prevent young adolescent alcohol use. In W. B. Hansen, S. M. Giles, & M. D. Fearnow-Kenney (Eds.), *Improving prevention effectiveness* (pp. 225–423). Greensboro, NC: Tanglewood Research.

Perry, C. L., Williams, C. L., Komro, K. A., Veblen-Mortenson, S., Forster, J. L., Lachter, R. B., Pratt, L. K., Dudovitz, B., Munson, K. A., Farbakhsh, K., Finnegan, J., & McGovern, P. (2000). Project Northland high school interventions: Community action to reduce adolescent alcohol use. *Health Education and Behavior, 27*(1), 29–49.

Perry, C. L., Williams, C. L., Komro, K. A., Veblen-Mortenson, S., Stigler, M. H., Munson, K. A., Farbakhsh, K., Jones, R. M., & Forster, J. L. (2001). Project Northland: Long-term outcomes of community action to reduce adolescent alcohol use. *Health Education Research: Theory & Practice, 16*(5), 101–15.

Perry, J., Miller, K., & Klump, K. (2006). Treatment planning with the MMPI-2. In J. N. Butcher (Ed.), *MMPI-2: The practioner's handbook* (pp. 143–63). Washington, DC: American Psychological Association.

Perry, L. H., & Landreth, G. L. (2001). Diagnostic assessment of children's play therapy behavior. In G. L. Landreth (Ed.), *Innovations in play therapy: Issues, process, and special population* (pp. 155–78). Philadelphia: Bruner-Routledge.

Pert, C. B., & Snyder, S. H. (1973, Mar. 9). Opiate receptor: Demonstration in nervous tissue. *Science, 179*(4077), 1011–14.

Peter, R., & Siegrist, J. (2000). Psychosocial work environment and the risk of coronary heart disease. *International Archives of Occupational and Environmental Health, 73,* S41–S45.

Petersen, R. C., Doody, R., Kurz, A., Mohs, R. C., Morris, J. C., Rabins, P. V., Ritchie, K., Rossor, M., Thal, L., & Winblad, B. (2001). Current concepts in mild cognitive impairment. *Arch. Neurol., 58,* 1985–92.

Peterson, C., & Seligman, M. E. P. (1987). Explanatory style and illness. *J. Personal., 55,* 237–65.

Peterson, C., et al. (1998). Catastrophizing and untimely death. *Psychol. Sci., 9*(2), 127–30.

Peterson, C., Maier, S. F., & Seligman, M. E .P. (1993). *Learned helplessness: A theory for the age of personal control.* New York: Oxford University Press.

Petrak, J., & Hedge, B. (Eds.). (2002). *The trauma of sexual assault: Treatment, prevention and practice.* Chichester, UK: Wiley.

Petrakis, I. L., Gonzalez, G., et al. (2002). Comorbidity of alcoholism and psychiatric disorders. *Alcohol Research & Health, 26,* 81–89.

Petronko, M. R., Harris, S. L., & Kormann, R. J. (1994). Community-based behavioral training approaches for people with mental retardation and mental illness. *J. Cons. Clin. Psychol., 62*(1), 49–54.

Petrovic, V. (2004). Level of psychopathology in children with war related trauma. *Psychiatry Today, 36*(1), 17–28.

Pfeffer, C. R., Hurt, S. W., Kakuma, T., Peskin, J., Siefker, C. A., & Nagbhairava, S. (1994). Suicidal children grow up: Suicidal episodes and effects of treatment during follow-up. *J. Amer. Acad. Child Adoles. Psychiat., 33,* 225–30.

Pfeffer, C. R. (1996a). Suicidal behavior in response to stress. In C. R. Pfeffer (Ed.), *Severe stress and mental disturbance in children* (pp. 327–46). Washington, DC: American Psychiatric Association.

Pfeffer, C. R. (1996b). Suicidal behavior. In L. Hechtman (Ed.), *Do they grow out of it?* (pp. 121–38). Washington, DC: American Psychiatric Press.

Pfefferbaum, B., Call, J. A., & Sconzo, G. M. (1999). Mental health services for children in the first two years after the 1995 Oklahoma City terrorist bombing. *Psychiatr. Serv., 50*(7), 956–58.

Phares, V., Duhig, A. M., & Watkins, M. M. (2002). Family context: Fathers and other supporters. In S. H. Goodman & I. H. Gotlib (Eds.), *Children of depressed parents: Mechanisms of risk and implications for treatment* (pp. 203–25). Washington DC: American Psychological Association.

Phillips, K. A., & Diaz, S. F. (1997). Gender differences in body dysmorphic disorder. *J. Nerv. Ment. Dis., 185,* 570–77.

Phillips, K. A., Grant, J., Siniscalchi, J., & Albertini, R. S. (2001). Surgical and nonpsychiatric medical treatment of patients with body dysmorphic disorder. *Psychosomatics, 42,* 504–10.

Phillips, K. A. (2000). Body dysmorphic disorder: Diagnostic controversies and treatment challenges. *Bulletin of the Menninger Clinic, 64,* 18–35.

Phillips, K. A. (2004). Treating body dysmorphic disorder using medication. *Psychiat. Ann., 34*(12), 945–53.

Phillips, K. (1996). *The broken mirror: Understanding and treating body dysmorphic disorder.* New York: Oxford University Press.

Phillips, K. (2001). Body dysmorphic disorder. In K. Phillips (Ed.), *Somatoform and factitious disorders* (pp. 67–94). Washington, DC: American Psychiatric Association.

Phillips, M. L., & Sierra, M. (2003). Depersonalization disorder: A functional neuroanatomical perspective. *Stress, 6*(3), 157–65.

Phillips, M. L., Drevets, W. C., Rauch, S. L., & Lane, R. (2003). Neurobiology of emotion perception II: Implications for major psychiatric disorders. *Biol. Psychiat., 54,* 515–528.

Phillips, S. (2002). Free to speak: Clarifying the legacy of witchhunts. *Journal of Psychology and Christianity, 21,* 25–37.

Pianta, R. C. (2001). Implications of a developmental systems model for preventing and treating behavioral disturbances in children and adolescents. In J. N. Hughes, A. M. La Greca, et al. (Eds.), *Handbook of psychological services for children and adolescents* (pp. 23–41). London: Oxford University Press.

Pickering, T. G. (2001). Mental stress as a causal factor in the development of hypertension and cardiovascular disease. *Current Hypertension Reports, 3,* 249–54.

Pickworth, W. B., Rohrer, M. S., & Fant, R. V. (1997). Effects of abused drugs on psychomotor performance. *Experimental and Clinical Psychopharmacology, 5*(3), 235–41.

Pigott, T. A., & Seay, S. (2000). Pharmacotherapy of obsessive-compulsive disorder: Overview and treatment-refractory strategies. In W. K. Goodman, M. V. Rudorfer, et al. (Eds.), *Obsessive-compulsive disorder: Contemporary issues in treatment. Personality and clinical psychology series* (pp. 277–302). Mahwah, NJ: Erlbaum.

Pijl, Y., & Pijl, Y. J. (2001). Deinstitutionalization in the Netherlands. *Eur. Arch. Psychiat. Clin. Neurosci., 251*(3), 124–29.

Pijl, Y., Kluiter, H., & Wiersma, D. (2001). Deinstitutionalisation in the Netherlands. *Eur. Arch. Psychiat. Clin. Neurosci., 25,* 124–29.

Pike, K. M., & Mizushima, H. (2005). The clinical presentation of Japanese women with anorexia nervosa and bulimia nervosa: A study of the Eating Disorders Inventory-2. *Int. J. Eat. Dis., 37,* 26–31.

Pike, K. M., Dohm, F., Striegel-Moore, R. H., Wilfley, D. E., & Fairburn, C. G. (2001). A comparison of black and white women with binge eating disorder. *Amer. J. Psychiat., 158*(9), 1455–60.

Pike, K. M., Walsh, B. T., Vitousek, K., Wilson, G. T., & Bauer, J. (2003). Cognitive behavioral therapy in the posthospitalization treatment of anorexia nervosa. *Amer. J. Psychiat., 160*(11): 2046–2049.

Pilkonis, P. A. (2001). Treatment of personality disorders in association with symptom disorders. In W. J. Livesley (Ed.), *Handbook of personality disorders* (pp. 541–54). New York: Guilford.

Pilling, S., Bebbington, P., Kuipers, E., Garety, P., Geddes, J., Martindale, B., Orbach, G., & Morgan. C. (2002). Psychological treatments in schizophrenia: II. Meta-analysis of randomized controlled trials of social skills training and cognitive remediation. *Psychol. Med., 32,* 783–91.

Pinard, G. F., & Pagani, L. (Eds.). (2001). *Clinical assessment of dangerousness: Empirical contributions.* New York: Cambridge University Press.

Pincus, H. A., Zarin, D. A., Tanielian, T. L., Johnson, J. L., West, J. C., Pettit, A. R., Marcus, S. C., Kessler, S. C., & McIntyre, J. (1999). Psychiatric patients and treatments in 1997: Findings from the American Psychiatric Association Practice Research Network. *Arch. Gen. Psychiat., 56,* 441–49.

Pineles, S.L., & Mineka, S. (2005). Attentional biases to internal and external sources of potential threat in social anxiety. *J. Abn. Psychol., 114*(2), 314–318.

Pines, M., & Schlapobersky, J. (2000). Group methods in adult psychiatry. In Gelder et al. (Eds.), *New Oxford textbook of psychiatry* (pp. 1442–62). Oxford: Oxford University Press.

Pinsof, W. M. (1995). *Integrative problem-centered therapy: A synthesis of family, individual, and biological therapies.* New York: Basic Books.

Piotrowski, C., & Keller, J. W. (1992). Psychological testing in applied settings: A literature review from 1982–1992. *Journal of Training and Practice in Professional Psychology, 6,* 74–82.

Piotrowski, C., & Zalewski, C. (1993). Training in psychodiagnostic testing in APA approved PsyD and PhD clinical psychology programs. *J. Pers. Assess., 61,* 394–405.

Piotrowski, C., Belter, R. W., & Keller, J. M. (1998). The impact of "managed care" on the practice of psychological testing: Preliminary findings. *J. Pers. Assess., 70,* 441–47.

Piotrowski, N. A., Tusel, D. J., Sees, K. L., Reilly, P. M., Banys, P., Meek, P., & Hall, S. M. (1999). Contingency contracting with monetary reinforcers for abstinence from multiple drugs in a methadone program. *Experimental and Clinical Psychopharmacology, 7*(4), 399–411.

Piper, A., & Merskey, H. (2004a). The persistence of folly: A critical examination of dissociative identity disorder. Part I. The excesses of an improbable concept. *Canad. J. Psychiat., 49*(9), 592–600.

Piper, A., & Merskey, H. (2004b). The persistence of folly: A critical examination of dissociative identity disorder. Part II. The defence and decline of multiple personality or dissociative identity disorder. *Canad. J. Psychiat., 49*(10), 678–83.

Piper, A. (1998). Repressed memories from World War II: Nothing to forget. Examining Karon and Widener's (1997) claim to have discovered evidence for repression. *Profess. Psychol.: Res. Prac., 29,* 476–78.

Piper, W. E., & Joyce, A. S. (2001). Psychosocial treatment outcome. In W. J. Livesley (Ed.), *Handbook of personality disorders* (pp. 323–43). New York: Guilford.

Pi-Sunyer, X. (2003, Feb. 7). A clinical view of the obesity problem. *Science, 299,* 859–60.

Pitschel-Walz, G., Leucht, S., Bäuml, J., Kissling, W., & Engel, R. R. (2001). The effects of family interventions on relapse and rehospitalization in schizophrenia—A meta-analysis. *Schizo. Bull., 27*(1), 73–92.

Pizzagalli, D. A., Nitschke, J. B., Oakes, T. R., Hendrick, A. M., Horras, K. A., Larson, C. L., et al. (2002). Brain electrical tomography in depression: The importance of symptom severity, anxiety, and melancholic features. *Biol. Psychiat., 52,* 73–85.

Plassman, B. L., & Breitner, J. C. (1997). The genetics of dementia in late life. *Psychiat. Clin. N. Amer., 20*(1), 59–76.

Plato. (no date). *The laws, Vol. 5* G. Burges (Tr) London: George Bell & Sons.

Platte, P., Zelten, J. F., & Stunkard, A. J. (2000). Body image in the Old Order Amish: A people separate from "The World." *Int. J. Eat. Dis., 28,* 408–14.

Pliszka, S. R. (1999). The psychobiology of oppositional defiant disorder and conduct disorder. In H. C. Quay & A. E. Hogan (Eds.), *Handbook of disruptive behavior disorders* (pp. 507–24). New York: Kluwer.

Plomin, R. (1986). *Development, genetics and psychology.* Hillsdale, NJ: Erlbaum.

Plomin, R. (1990). The role of inheritance in behavior. *Science, 248,* 183–88.

Plomin, R. & McGuffin, P. (2003). Psychopathology in the postgenomic era. *Annu. Rev. Psychol., 54,* 205–228.

Plomin, R., & Daniels, D. (1987). Why are children in the same family so different from one another? *Behavioral and Brain Sciences, 10,* 1–15.

Plomin, R., & DeFries, J. C. (Eds.). (2003). *Behavioral genetics in the postgenomic era.* Washington, DC: American Psychological Association.

Plomin, R., & McGuffin, P. (2003). Psychopathology in the postgenomic era. *Ann. Rev. Psychol., 54,* 205–228.

Plomin, R., DeFries, J. C., McClearn, G. E., & McGuffin, P. (2001). *Behavioral genetics* (4th ed.). New York: Worth.

Pogarell, O., Hamann, C., Popperl, G., Juckel, G., Chouker, M., Zaudig, M., et al. (2003). Elevated brain serotonin transporter availability in patients with obsessive-compulsive disorder. *Biol. Psychiat., 54*(12), 1406–1413.

Polich, J. M., Armor, D. J., & Braiker, H. B. (1981). *The course of alcoholism: Four years after treatment.* New York: Wiley Interscience.

Polivy, J., & Herman, C. P. (1985). Dieting and binging: A causal analysis. *Amer. Psychol., 40*(2), 193–210.

Polivy, J., Herman, C. P., & Boivin, M. (2005). Eating disorders. In J. E. Maddux & B. A. Winstead (Eds.), *Psychopathology: Foundations for a contemporary understanding.* Mahwah, NJ: Lawrence Erlbaum Associates.

Polo, C. (1997). *Del Padre Jofre al jofrismo. La Locura y sus instuciones.* Valencia: Disputacion de Valencia, 125–40.

Polvan, N. (1969). Historical aspects of mental ills in Middle East discussed. *Roche Reports, 6*(12), 3.

Pomeroy, C., & Mitchell, J. E. (2002). Medical complications of anorexia nervosa and bulimia nervosa. In C. G. Fairburn & K. D. Brownell (Eds.), *Eating disorders and obesity: A comprehensive handbook* (2nd ed., pp. 278–85). New York: Guilford.

Pompili, M., Mancinelli, I., Giradi, P., Ruberto, A., & Tatarelli, R. (2004). Suicide in anorexia nervosa: A meta-analysis. *Int. J. Eat. Dis., 36,* 99–103.

Ponce, F. Q., & Atkinson, D. R. (1989). Mexican-American acculturation, counselor ethnicity, counseling style, and perceived counselor credibility. *J. Couns. Psychol., 36,* 203–8.

Pope Innocent VIII The papal Bull/The Malleus Maleficarum. First published in 1486.

Pope, H. G., Gruber, A., Choi, P., Olivardia, R., & Philips, K. (1997). Muscledysmorphia. An underrecognized form of body dysmorphic disorder. *Psychosomatics, 38,* 548–57.

Pope, H. G., Hudson, J. I., Bodkin, J. A., & Oliva, P. (1998). Questionable validity of "dissociative amnesia" in trauma victims: Evidence from prospective studies. *Brit. J. Psychiat., 172,* 210–15.

Pope, H. G., Jr., Gruber, A. J., Hudson, J. I., Huestis, M. A., & Yurgelun-Todd, D. (2001). Neuropsychological performance in long-term cannabis users. *Arch. Gen. Psychiat., 58,* 909–15.

Pope, K. S. (1996). Memory, abuse, and science: Questioning claims about the false memory syndrome epidemic. *Amer. Psychol., 51,* 957–74.

Pope, K. S., Sonne, J. L., & Holroyd, J. (1993). *Sexual feelings in psychotherapy: Explorations for therapists and therapists-in-training.* Washington, DC: American Psychological Association.

Pope, K. W., & McNally, R. J. (2002). Nonspecific placebo effects explain the therapeutic benefits of magnets. *Scientific Review of Alternative Medicine, 6,* 10–14.

Popkin, J. (1994, Sept. 19). Sexual predators. *U.S. News and World Report,* 65–73.

Pories, W. J., & MacDonald, K. G. (1993). The surgical treatment of morbid obesity. *Current Opinion in General Surgery,* XX, 195–205.

Posner, R. A., & Silbaugh, K. B. (1996). *A guide to America's sex laws.* Chicago: University of Chicago Press.

Post, R. M. (1992). Transduction of psychosocial stress into the neurobiology of recurrent affective disorder. *Amer. J. Psychiat., 149*(8), 999–1010.

Post, R. M., Weiss, S. R. B., & Smith, M. A. (1995). Sensitization and kindling: Implications for the evolving neural substrates of post-traumatic stress disorder. In M. J. Friedman, D. S. Charney, et al. (Eds.), *Neurobiological and clinical consequences of stress: From normal adaptation to post-traumatic stress disorder* (pp. 203–24). Philadelphia: Lippincott-Raven.

Potash, J. B., DePaulo, J. R. (2000). Searching high and low: A review of the genetics of bipolar disorder. *Bipolar Disorders, 2,* 8–26.

Potenza, M. N. (2002). A perspective on future directions in the prevention, treatment, and research of pathological gambling. *Psychiat. Ann., 32*(3), 203–07.

Poulton, R., Milne, B. J., Craske, M. G., & Menzies, R. G. (2001). A longitudinal study of the etiology of separation anxiety. *Behav. Res. Ther., 39*(12), 1395–410.

Powell, G. E., & Wilson, S. L. (1994). Recovery curves for patients who have suffered very severe brain injury. *Clinical Rehabilitation, 8*(1), 54–69.

Powell, T. A., Holt, J. C., & Fondacaro, K. M. (1997). The prevalence of mental illness among inmates in a rural state. *Law & Human Behavior, 21*(4), 427–38.

Prasher, V. P., & Kirshnan, V. H. (1993). Age of onset and duration of dementia in people with Down syndrome: Integration of 98 reported cases in the literature. *International Journal of Geriatric Psychiatry, 8*(11), 915–22.

Prasher, V. P., et al. (1997). ApoE genotype and Alzheimer's disease in adults with Down syndrome: Meta-analysis. *Amer. J. Ment. Retard., 102*(2), 103–10.

Pratt, L., Ford, D., Crum, R., Armenian, H., Galb, J., & Eaton, W. (1996). Depression, psychotropic medication, and risk of myocardial infarction. *Circulation, 94,* 3123–29.

Presnell, K., & Stice, E. (2003). An experimental test of the effect of weight-loss dieting on bulimic pathology: Tipping the scales in a different direction. *J. Abn. Psychol., 112,* 166–70.

Pressman, S. D., Cohen, S., Miller, G. E., Barkin, A., Rabin, B. S., & Treanor, J. J. (2005). Loneliness, social network size, and immune response to influenza vaccination in college freshmen. *Hlth. Psychol., 24,* 3, 297–306.

Preston, K. L., Umbricht, A., Wong, C. J., & Epstein, D. H. (2001). Shaping cocaine abstinence by successive approximation. *J. Cons. Clin. Psychol., 69*(4), 643–54.

Pretzer, J. L., & Beck, A. T. (1996). A cognitive theory of personality disorders. In J. F. Clarkin & M. F. Lenzenweger (Eds.), *Major theories of personality disorder.* (pp. 36–105). New York: Guilford.

Price, B. H., Baral, I., Cosgrove, G. R., Rauch, S. L., Nierenberg, A. A., Jenike, M. A., & Cassem, E. H. (2001). Improvement in severe self-mutilation following limbic leucotomy: A series of 5 consecutive cases. *J. Clin. Psychiat., 62,* 925–32.

Price, R. W., Brew, B., Sidtis, J., Rosenblum, M., Scheck, A. C., & Cleary, P. (1988). The brain in AIDS: Central nervous system HIV-1 infection and the AIDS dementia complex. *Science, 239,* 586–92.

Prichard, J. C. (1835). *A treatise on insanity.* London: Sherwood, Gilbert, & Piper.

Priebe, S., & Turner, T. (2003). Reinstitutionalisation in mental health care: This largely unnoticed process requires debate and evaluation. *Brit. Med. J., 326*(7382), 175–76.

Prigatano, G. P. (1992). Personality disturbances associated with traumatic brain injury. *J. Cons. Clin. Psychol., 60*(3), 360–68.

Prigerson, H., Bierhals, A. J., Kasl, S. V., Reynolds, C. F., et al. (1997). Traumatic grief as a risk factor for mental and physical morbidity. *Amer. J. Psychiat., 154*(5), 616–23.

Prigerson, H. G., Maciejewski, P. K., & Rosenheck, R. A. (2002). Population attributable fractions of psychiatric disorders and behavioral outcomes associated with combat exposures among US men. *Amer. J. Pub. Hlth., 9,* 59–63.

Prince, M. (1910). *The dissociation of a personality.* New York: Longmans, Green.

Prizant, B. M. (1983). Language acquisition and communicative behavior in autism: Toward an understanding of the "whole" of it. *J. Speech Hear. Dis., 46,* 241–49.

Prochaska, J. O., & Norcross, J. C. (2003). *Systems of psychotherapy* (5th ed.). Pacific Grove, CA: Brooks/Cole.

Project MATCH Group. (1997). Project MATCH: Rationale and methods for a multisite clinical trial matching patients to alcoholism treatment. *Alcoholism: Clin. Exper. Res., 17*(6), 1130–45.

Psychological Corporation. (1997). *Wechsler Memory Scale III manual.* San Antonio, TX: Author.

Purcell, R., Pathé, M., & Mullen, P. E. (2001). A study of women who stalk. *Amer. J. Psychiat., 158*(12), 2056–60.

Purdon, C. (2004). Empirical investigations of thought suppression in OCD. *J. Behav. Ther. Exper. Psychiat., 35*(2), 121–136/

Purisch, A. D., & Sbordone, R. J. (1997). Forensic neuropsychology: Clinical issues and practice. In A. M. Horton, D. Wedding, & J. Webster (Eds.), *The neu-*

ropsychology handbook (Vol. 2., pp. 309–56). New York: Springer.
Putnam, F. W., Guroff, J. J., Silberman, E. K., Barban, L., & Post, R. M. (1986). The clinical phenomenology of multiple personality disorder: Review of 100 recent cases. *J. Clin. Psychiat., 47,* 285–93.
Putnam, F. W. (1984). The psychophysiologic investigation of multiple personality disorder: A review. *Psychiat. Clin. N. Amer., 7,* 31–39.
Putnam, F. W. (1997). *Dissociation in children and adolescents: A developmental perspective.* New York: Guilford.
Putnam, S. P., Sanson, A. V., & Rothbart, M. K. (2002). Child temperament and parenting. In M. H. Bornstein (Ed.), *Handbook of parenting: Vol: Chidren and parenting* (2nd ed.: pp. 255–277). Mahwah, NJ: Lawrence Erlbaum Associates.
Pynoos, R. S., Frederick, C., Nader, K., Arroyo, W., Steinberg, A., Eth, S., Nunez, F., & Fairbanks, L. (1987). Life threat and posttraumatic stress in school-age children. *Arch. Gen. Psychiat., 44,* 1057–63.
Quinsey, V. L., & Earls, C. M. (1990). The modification of sexual preferences. In W. L. Marshall, D. R. Laws, & H. E. Barbaree (Eds.), *Handbook of sexual assault: Issues, theories, and treatment of the offender* (pp. 279–95). New York: Plenum.
Quinsey, V. L., Lalumiere, M. L., Rice, M. E., & Harris, G. T. (1995). Predicting sexual-offenses. In J. C. Campbell (Ed.), *Assessing dangerousness: Violence by sexual offenders, batterers, and child abusers* (pp. 114–37). Thousand Oaks, CA: Sage.
Quinton, D., & Rutter, M. (1988). *Parenting breakdown: The making and breaking of intergenerational links.* Aldershot, Hants: Avebury.
Rabinowitz, J., Lichtenberg, P., Kaplan, Z., Mark, M., Nahon, D., & Davidson, M. (2001). Rehospitalization rates of chronically ill schizophrenic patients discharged on a regimen of risperidone, olanzapine, or conventional antipsychotics. *Amer. J. Psychiat., 158*(2), 266–69.
Rabow, J., & Duncan-Schill, M. (1995). Drinking among college students. *Journal of Alcohol & Drug Education, 40*(3), 52–64.
Rachman, J. G., & Hodgson, R. (1980). *Obsessions and compulsions.* Englewood Cliffs, NJ: Prentice-Hall.
Rachman, S. J. (1990). *Fear and courage.* New York: Freeman.
Rachman, S. J. (1997). Claustrophobia. In G. C. L. Davey (Ed.), *Phobias: A handbook of theory, research and treatment* (pp. 163–81). Chichester, England: Wiley.
Rachman, S., & Shafran, R. (1998). Cognitive and behavioral features of obsessive-compulsive disorder. In R. Swinson, M. Antony, S. Rachman, & M. Richter (Eds.), *Obsessive-compulsive disorder: Theory, research, and treatment* (pp. 51–78). New York: Guilford.
Radden, J. (Ed.). (2000). *The nature of melancholy: From Aristotle to Kristeva.* New York: Oxford University Press.
Radford, J., & Anderson, M. (2003). Encopresis in children on the autistic spectrum. *Early Child Development & Care, 173*(4), 375–82.
Rado, S. (1962). *Psychoanalysis of behavior II,* (p. 96). New York: Grune & Stratton.
Ramey, C. H., & Weisberg, R. W. (2004). The "poetical activity" of Emily Dickinson: A further test of the hypothesis that affective disorders foster creativity. *Creativity Research Journal, 16*(2–3), 173–185.
Ramirez, J. R., Crano, W. D., Quist, R., Burgoon, M., Alvaro, E. M., & Grandpre, J. (2004). Acculturation, familism, parental monitoring, and knowledge as predictors of marijuana and inhalant use in adolescents. *Psych. Addict. Behav., 18,* 3–11.
Ramirez, J. R., Crano, W. D., Quist, R., Burgoon, M., Alvaro, E. M., & Grandpre, J. (2004). Acculturation, familism, parental monitoring, and knowledge as predictors of marijuana and inhalant use in adolescents. *Psych. Addict. Behav., 18,* 3–11.
Ramstedt, M. (2003). Alcohol consumption and liver cirrhosis mortality with and without mention of alcohol—the case of Canada. *Addiction, 98*(9), 1267–76.
Rantanen, T., Penninx, B. W., Masaki, K., Lintunen, T., Foley, D., & Guralnik, J. M. (2000). Depressed mood and body mass index as predictors of muscle strength decline in old men. *J. Amer. Geriat. Soc., 48,* 613–17.
Rao, V., & Lyketsos, C. (2002). Psychiatric aspects of traumatic brain injury. *Psychiat. Clin. N. Amer., 25*(1), 43–69.
Rapee, R. M. (1996). Information-processing views of panic disorder. In R. M. Rapee (Ed.), *Current controversies in the anxiety disorders* (pp. 77–93). New York: Guilford.
Rapee, R. M. (2001). The development of generalized anxiety. In M. W. Vasey & M. R. Dadds (Eds.), *The developmental psychopathology of anxiety* (pp. 481–503). New York: Oxford University Press.
Rapee, R. (2002). The development and modification of temperamental risk for anxiety disorders: Prevention of a lifetime of anxiety? *Biol. Psychiat., 52*(10), 947–957.
Raphael, B., & Wooding, S. (2004). Debriefing: Its evolution and current status. *Psychiat. Clin. N. Amer., 27,* 407–23.
Raphael, B., Wooding, S., Stevens, G., & Connor, J. (2005). Comorbidity: Cannabis and complexity. *J. Psychiat. Pract., 11*(3), 161–76.
Rapoport, J. (1989). *The boy who couldn't stop washing: The experience and treatment of obsessive-compulsive disorder.* New York: Penguin.
Rapp, J. T., Miltenberger, R. G., Galensky, T. L., Ellingson, S. A., Stricker, J., Garlinghouse, M., & Long, E. S. (2000). Treatment of hair pulling and hair manipulation maintained by digital-tactile stimulation. *Behav. Ther., 31,* 381–93.
Raskin, V. D. (1993). Psychiatric aspects of substance use disorders in childbearing populations. *Psychiatr. Clin. N. Amer., 16,* 157–65.
Rasmussen, S., & Eisen, J. L. (1991). Phenomenology of OCD: Clinical subtypes, heterogeneity and coexistence. In J. Zohar, T. Insel, & S. Rasmussen (Eds.), *The psychobiology of obsessive-compulsive disorder.* New York: Springer.
Rauch, S. L., & Savage, C. R. (2000). Investigating cortico-striatal pathophysiology in obsessive-compulsive disorders: Procedural learning and imaging probes. In W. K. Goodman, M. V. Rudorfer, et al. (Eds.), *Obsessive-compulsive disorder: Contemporary issues in treatment. Personality and clinical psychology series* (pp. 133–54). Mahwah, NJ: Erlbaum.
Rauch, S. L., Phillips, K. A., Segal, E., Makris, N., Shin, L. M., Whalen, P. J., et al. (2003). A preliminary morphometric resonance imaging study of regional brain volumes in body dysmorphic disorder. *Psych. Res. Neuroimag., 122,* 13–19.
Rauktis, M. (2001). The impact of deinstitutionalization on the seriously and persistently mentally ill elderly: A one-year follow-up. *Journal of Mental Health & Aging, 7*(3), 335–48.
Raulin, M L., & Lilienfeld, S. O. (1999). Research strategies for studying psychopathology. In T. Millon, P. H. Blaney, & R. D. Davis (Eds.), *Oxford textbook of psychopathology.* New York: Oxford University Press.
Ravaglia, G., Forti, P., Maioli, F., Martelli, M., Servadei, L., Brunetti, N., Porcellini, E., & Licastro, F. (2005). Homocysteine and folate as risk factors for dementia and Alzheimer disease. *Amer. J. Clin. Nutri., 82,* 636–43.
Rawson, H. E., & Tabb, C. L. (1993). Effects of therapeutic intervention on childhood depression. *Child and Adolescent Social Work Journal, 10,* 39–52.
Rawson, R. A., Huber, A., McCann, M., Shoptaw, S., Farabee, D., Reiber, C., & Ling, W. (2002). A comparison of contingency management and cognitive-behavioral approaches during methadone maintenance treatment for cocaine dependence. *Arch. Gen. Psychiat., 59*(9), 817–24.
Read, J. (1997). Child abuse and psychosis: A literature review and implications for professional psychology. *Profess. Psychol., 28*(5), 448–56.
Read, J. P., Wood, M. D., Kahler, C. W., Maddock, J. E., & Palfai, T. P. (2003). Examining the role of drinking motives in college student alcohol use and problems. *Psych. of Addict. Beh., 17,* 13–23.
Reardon, M. L., Lang, A. R., & Patrick, C. J. (2002). An evaluation of relations among antisocial behavior, psychopathic traits, and alcohol problems in incarcerated men. *Alcoholism, 26*(8), 1188–97.
Redmond, D. E., Jr. (1985). Neurochemical basis for anxiety and anxiety disorders: Evidence from drugs which decrease human fear of anxiety. In A. H. Tuma & J. D. Maser (Eds.), *Anxiety and the anxiety disorders.* Hillsdale, NJ: Erlbaum.
Reed, S. D., Katkin, E. S., & Goldband, S. (1986). Biofeedback and behavioral medicine. In F. H. Kanfer & A. P. Goldstein (Eds.), *Helping people change: A textbook of methods* (3rd ed.). Elmsford, NY: Pergamon.
Regehr, C., & Hill, J. (2000). Evaluating the efficacy of crisis debriefing groups. *Social Work with Groups, 23,* 69–79.
Regier, D. A., Boyd, J. H., Burke, J. D., Rae, D. S., Myers, J. K., Kramer, M., Robins, L. N., George, L. K., Karno, M., & Locke, B. Z. (1988). One-month prevalence of mental disorders in the United States. *Arch. Gen. Psychiat., 45,* 877–986.
Regier, D. A., Narrow, W. E., Rae, D. S., Manderscheid, R. W., Locke, B. Z., & Goodwin, F. K. (1993). The de facto US mental and addictive disorders service system: Epidemiologic Catchment Area prospective 1-year prevalence rates of disorders and services. *Arch. Gen. Psychiat., 50,* 85–94.
Rehm, L. P., & Tyndall, C. I. (1993). Mood disorders: Unipolar and bipolar. In P. B. Sutker & H. E. Adams (Eds.), *Comprehensive handbook of psychopathology* (2nd ed.). New York: Plenum.
Reich, R. (2001). *The future of success.* New York: Knopf.
Reichenberg, A., Yirmiya, R., Schuld, A., Kraus, T., Haak, M., Morag, A., & Pollmacher, T. (2001). Cytokine-associated emotional and cognitive disturbances in humans. *Arch. Gen. Psychiat., 58,* 455–52.
Reid, J. B., Patterson, G. R., & Snyder, J. (Eds.). (2002). *Antisocial behavior in children and adolescents: A developmental analysis model for intervention.* Washington, DC: American Psychological Association.
Reilly, P. M., Banys, P., Tusel, D. J., Sees, K. L., Krumenaker, C. L., & Shopshire, M. S. (1995). Methadone transition treatment: A treatment model for 180-day methadone detoxification. *Int. J. Addict., 30,* 387–402.
Reilly-Harrington, N. A., Alloy, L. B., Fresco, D. M., & Whitehouse, W. G. (1999). Cognitive styles and life events interact to predict bipolar and unipolar symptomatology. *J. Abn. Psychol., 108*(4), 567–78.
Reingold, A. A., Smith, D. W., Ruggiero, K. J., Saunders, B. E., Kilpatrick, D. G., & Resnick, H. (2004). Loss, trauma exposure and mental health in a representative sample of 12–17 year old youth: Data from the National Survey of Adolescents. *J. Loss Trauma, 9,* 1–19.
Reinharz, D., Lesage, A. D., & Contandriopoulos, A.-P. (2000). II. Cost-effectiveness analysis of psychiatric deinstitutionalization. *Canad. J. Psychiat., 45,* 533–38.
Reisberg, B., Doody, R., Stöffler, A., Schmitt, F., Ferris, S., & Möbius, H. J. (2003). Memantine in moderate-to-severe Alzheimer's disease. *N. Engl. J. Med., 348*(14), 1333–41.
Reisman, J. M. (1991). *A history of clinical psychology.* New York: Hemisphere Press.
Reitan, R. M., & Wolfson, D. (1985). *The Halstead-Reitan Neuropsychological Test Battery: Theory and clinical interpretation.* Tuscon, AZ: Neuropsychology Press.
Reitan, R. M., & Wolfson, D. (2000). The neuropsychological similarities of mild and more severe head injury. *Arch. Clin. Neuropsychol., 15,* 433–42.
Rescorla, R. A. (1974). Effect of inflation of the unconditioned stimulus value following conditioning.

Journal of Comparative and Physiological Psychology, 86, 101–6
Rescorla, R. A. (1988). Pavlovian conditioning: It's not what you think it is. *Amer. Psychol., 43,* 151–60.
Resick, P. A. (2001). *Stress and trauma.* London: Psychology Press.
Resnick, R. J., & DeLeon, P. (1995). The future of health care reform: Implications of 1994 elections. *Profess. Psychol.: Res. & Prac., 26*(1), 3–4.
Resnick, R. J., Bottinelli, R., Puder-York, M., Harris, H. B., & O'Keffe, B. E. (1994). Basic issues in managed mental health services. In R. L. Lowman & R. J. Resnick (Eds.), *The mental health professional's guide to managed care.* Washington, DC: American Psychological Association.
Reynaud, M., Leleu, X., Bernoux, A., Meyer, L., Lery, J. F., & Ruch, C. (1997). Alcohol use disorders in French hospital patients. *Alcohol and Alcoholism, 32*(6), 749–55.
Rholes, W. S. & Simpson, J. A. (2004). Ambivalent attachment and depressive symptoms: The role of romantic and parent-child relationships. *J. Cog. Psychother., 18*(1), 67–78.
Ricciuti, H. N. (1993). Nutrition and mental development. *Curr. Dir. Psychol. Sci., 2*(2), 43–46.
Rice, M. E., & Harris, G. T. (1997). The treatment for adult offenders. In D. M. Stoff, J. Breiling, & J. D. Maser (Eds.), *Handbook of antisocial behavior.* (pp. 425–435). New York: Wiley.
Rice, M. E., Quinsey, V. L., & Harris, G. T. (1991). Sexual recidivism among child molesters released from a maximum security psychiatric institution. *J. Cons. Clin. Psychol., 59,* 381–86.
Richards, J., Smith, D. J., Harvey, C. A., & Pantelis, C. (1997). Characteristics of the new long-stay population in an inner Melbourne acute psychiatric hospital. *Austral. NZ J. Psychiat., 31*(4), 488–95.
Richardson, L. M., & Austad, C. S. (1994). Realities of mental health practice in managed-care settings. In R. L. Lowman & R. J. Resnick, et al. (Eds.), *The mental health professional's guide to managed care* (pp. 151–67).Washington, DC: American Psychological Association.
Rieder, R. O. (1979). Children at risk. In L. Bellak (Ed.), *The schizophrenic syndrome.* New York: Basic Books.
Rief, W., Hiller, W., & Margraf, J. (1998). Cognitive aspects of hypochondriasis and the somatization syndrome. *J. Abn. Psychol., 107,* 587–95.
Rief, W., Shaw, R., & Fichter, M. M. (1998). Elevated levels of psychophysiological arousal and cortisol in patients with somatization syndrome. *Psychosom. Med., 60,* 198–203.
Rijnders, C. A., van den Berg, J. F. M., Hodiamont, P. P. G., Nienhuis, F. J., Furer, J. W., Mulder, J., & Giel, R. (2000). Psychometric properties of the schedules for clinical assessment in neuropsychiatry (SCAN-2.1). *Soc. Psychiat. Psychiat. Epidemiol., 35,* 348–52.
Rind, B., & Tromovitch, P. (1997). A meta-analytic review of findings from national samples on psychological correlates of child sexual abuse. *J. Sex Res., 34,* 237–55.
Rind, B., Bauserman, R., & Tromovitch, P. (2000). Science versus orthodoxy: Anatomy of the congressional condemnation of a scientific article and reflections on remedies for future ideological attacks. *App. Prev. Psychol., 9,* 211–26.
Rind, B., Tromovitch, P., & Bauserman, R. (1998). A meta-analytic examination of assumed properties of child sexual abuse using college samples. *Psychol. Bull., 124,* 22–53.
Rind, B., Tromovitch, P., & Bauserman, R. (2001). The validity and appropriateness of methods, analyses, and conclusions in Rind et al. (1998): A rebuttal of victimological critique from Ondersma et al. (2001) and Dallam et al. (2001). *Psychol. Bull., 127,* 734–58.
Ringwalt, C. L., Greene, J. M., Robertson, M., & McPheeters, M. (1998). The prevalence of homelessness among adolescents in the United States. *Amer. J. Pub. Hlth., 88*(9), 1325–29.
Rinne, T., van der Brink, W., Wouters, L., & van Dyck, R. (2002). SSRI treatment of borderline personality disorder: A randomized, placebo-controlled clinical trial for female patients with borderline personality disorder. *Amer. J. Psychiat., 159,* 2048–54.
Ritchie, E. C., & Owens, M. (2004). Military issues. *Psychiat. Clin. N. Amer., 27,* 459–71.
Rittson, B. (1995). *Community and municipal action on alcohol: European alcohol action plan.* Geneva: World Health Organization.
Ritvo, E., Brothers, A. M., Freeman, B. J., & Pingree, J. C. (1988). Eleven possibly autistic parents. *J. Autism Devel. Dis., 18,* 139–43.
Rivera, F. P., Muellar, B. A., Somes, G., Mendoza, C. T., Rushforth, N. B., & Kellerman, A. L. (1997). Alcohol and illicit drug abuse and the risk of violent death in the home. *JAMA, 278*(7), 569–75.
Rivera, R. P., & Borda, T. (2001). The etiology of body dysmorphic disorder. *Psychiat. Ann., 31,* 559–63.
Ro, O., Martinsen, E. W., Hoffart, A., & Rosenvinge, J. (2005). Two-year prospective study of personality disorders in adults with longstanding eating disorders. *Int. J. Eat. Dis., 37,* 112–18.
Roberts, N. A., & Levinson, R. W. (2001). The remains of the workday: Impact of job stress and exhaustion on marital interaction in police couples. *J. Marr. Fam., 63*(4), 1052–67.
Roberts, R. E., Roberts, C. R., & Chen, I. G. (2000). Fatalism and risk of adolescent depression. *Psychiatry: Interpersonal & Biological Processes, 63*(3), 239–52.
Robins, C. J., Ivanoff, A. M., & Linehan, M. M. (2001). Dialectical behavior therapy. In W. J. Livesley (Ed.), *Handbook of personality disorders* (pp. 437–59). New York: Guilford.
Robins, L. N. (1978). Aetiological implications in studies of childhood histories relating to antisocial personality. In R.D. Hare & D. Schalling (Eds.), *Psychopathic behavior: Approaches to research.* (pp. 255–71). Chichester, UK: Wiley.
Robins, L. N. (1991). Conduct disorder. *J. Child Psychol. Psychiat., 32,* 193–212.
Robins, L. N., & Regier, D. A. (Eds.). (1991). *Psychiatric disorders in America.* New York: Free Press.
Robinson, N. M., & Robinson, H. B. (1976). *The mentally retarded child* (2nd ed.). New York: McGraw-Hill.
Robinson, R. G., & Downhill, J. E. (1995). Lateralization of psychopathology in response to focal brain injury. In R. J. Davidson & K. Hugdahl (Eds.), *Brain asymmetry* (pp. 693–711). Cambridge, MA: MIT Press.
Robinson-Whelen, S., & Kiecolt-Glaser, J. (1997). Spousal caregiving: Does it matter if you have a choice? *J. Clin. Geropsychol., 3*(4), 283–89.
Robles, T. F., Glaser, R., & Kiecolt-Glaser, J. K. (2005). Out of balance: A new look at chronic stress, depression, and immunity. *Curr. Dirs. Psychol. Sci., 14,* 2, 111–15.
Roca-Bennasar, M., Gili-Planas, M., Ferer-Perez, V., & Bernardo-Arroyo, M. (2001). Mental disorders and medical conditions: A community study in a small island in Spain. *J. Psychosom. Res., 50,* 39–44.
Rodin, J. (1993). *Body traps.* New York: Norton.
Roeleveld, N., Zielhuis, G. A., & Gabreels, F. (1997). The prevalence of mental retardation: A critical review of recent literature. *Develop. Med. Child Neurol., 39*(2), 125–32.
Roemer, L., Molina, S., & Borkovec, T. D. (1997). An investigation of worry content among generally anxious individuals. *J. Nerv. Ment. Dis., 185*(5), 314–19.
Roemer, L., Orsillo, S. M., & Barlow, D. H. (2002). Generalized anxiety disorder. In D. H. Barlow (Ed.), *Anxiety and its disorders* (2nd ed., pp. 477–515). New York: Guilford.
Rogers, C. R. (1951). *Client-centered therapy.* Boston: Houghton Mifflin.
Rogers, C. R. (1959). A theory of therapy, personality, and interpersonal relationships as developed in the client-centered framework. In S. Koch (Ed.), *Psychology: A study of a science* (Vol. 3., pp. 184–256). New York: McGraw-Hill.
Rogers, C. R. (1961). The process equation of psychotherapy. *Amer. J. Psychother., 15,* 27–45.
Rogers, R. (2000). The uncritical acceptance of risk assessment in forensic practice. *Law and Human Behavior, 24*(5), 595–605.
Rogers, R. (2004). Dianostic, explanatory, and detection models of Munchausen by proxy: Extrapolations from malingering and deception. *Child Ab. Negl., 28,* 225–39.
Rogers, S. J., Bennetto, L., McEvoy, R., & Pennington, B. F. (1996). Imitation and pantomine in high-functioning adolescents with autism spectrum disorders. *Child Develop., 67*(5), 2060–73.
Rogosch, F. A., Cicchetti, D., & Toth, S. L. (2004). Expressed emotion in multiple subsystems of the families of toddlers with depressed mothers. *Develop. Psychopath., 16*(3), 689–706.
Rohling, M. L., Meyers, J. E., & Millis, S. R. (2003). Neuropsychological impairment following traumatic brain injury: A dose response analysis. *Clin. Neuropsych., 17,* 289–302.
Rolak, L. A. (2001). *Neurology secrets* (3rd ed.). Philadelphia: Hanley and Belfus.
Romach, M. K., & Sellers, E. M. (1998). Alcohol dependency: Women, biology, and pharmacotherapy. In E. F. McCance-Katz & T. R. Kosten (Eds.), *New treatments for chemical addictions.* Washington, DC: American Psychiatric Press.
Ronningstan, E. (1999). Narcissistic personality disorder. In T. Millon, P. H. Blaney, & R. D. Davis (Eds.), *Oxford textbook of psychopathology* (pp. 674–93). New York: Oxford University Press.
Rorvik, D. M. (1970, Apr. 7). Do drugs lead to violence? *Look,* 58–61.
Rosen, R. C., & Leiblum, S. J. (1995). Treatment of sexual disorders in the 1990s: An integrated approach. *J. Cons. Clin. Psychol., 63,* 877–90.
Rosen, R. C. (1996). Erectile dysfunction: The medicalization of male sexuality. *Clin. Psychol. Rev., 16,* 497–519.
Rosenberg, L. A., Brown, J., & Singer, H. S. (1995). Behavioral problems and severity of tics. *J. Clin. Psychol., 51*(6), 760–67.
Rosenfarb, I. S., Goldstein, M. J., Mintz, J., & Nuechterlein, K. H. (1995). Expressed emotion and subclinical psychopathology observable within the transactions between schizophrenic patients and their family members. *J. Abn. Psychol., 104,* 259–67.
Rosenman, R. H., Brand, R. J., Jenkins, C. D., Friedman, M., & Straus, R. (1975). Coronary heart disease in the Western Collaborative Group Study: Final follow-up experience of 8 1/2 years. *JAMA, 233,* 872–77.
Rosenthal, D. (Ed.). (1963). *The Genain quadruplets.* New York: Basic Books.
Rosenthal, D., Wender, P. H., Kety, S. S., Schulsinger, F., Welner, J., & Ostergaard, L. (1968). Schizophrenics' offspring reared in adoptive homes. In D. Rosenthal & S. S. Kety (Eds.), *The transmission of schizophrenia* (pp. 377–92). New York: Pergamon.
Rosenthal, S. H., Porter, K. A., & Coffey, B. (1990). Pain insensitivity and schizophrenia: Case report and review of the literature. *General Hospital Psychiatry, 12,* 319–22.
Rosenzweig, M. R., Breedlove, S. M., & Leiman, A. L. (2002). *Biological psychology: An introduction to behavioral, cognitive, and clinical neuroscience* (3rd ed.). Sunderland, MA: Sinauer.
Rosler, A., & Witztum, E. (1998). Treatment of men with paraphilia with a long-acting analogue of gonadotropin-releasing hormone. *New Engl. J. Med., 338,* 416–22.
Ross, C. A. (1997). *Dissociative identity disorder: Diagnosis, clinical features, and treatment of Multiple Personality* (2nd ed.). New York: Wiley.
Ross, C. A. (1999). Dissociative disorders. In T. Millon & P. Blaney (Eds.), *Oxford textbook of psychopathology* (pp. 466–81). New York: Oxford University Press.

Ross, C. A., et al. (1990). Structured interview data on 102 cases of multiple personality disorder from four centers. *Amer. J. Psychiat., 147,* 596–601.

Ross, C. A., et al. (1991). Abuse histories in 102 cases of multiple personality disorder. *Canad. J. Psychiat., 36,* 97–101.

Rossini, E. D., & Moretti, R. J. (1997). Thematic Apperception Test (TAT) interpretation: Practice recommendations from a survey of clinical psychology doctoral programs accredited by the American Psychological Association. *Profess. Psychol.: Res. Prac., 28*(4), 393–98.

Rost, K., Kashner, T. M., & Smith, G. R. (1994). Effectiveness of psychiatric intervention with somatization disorder patients: Improved outcomes at reduced costs. *General Hospital Psychiatry, 16,* 381–87.

Rosten, R. A. (1961). *Some personality characteristics of compulsive gamblers.* Unpublished dissertation, UCLA.

Roth, A., & Fonagy, P. (1996). *What works for whom? A critical view of psychotherapy research.* New York: Guilford.

Roth, M., & Mountjoy, C. Q. (1997). The need for the concept of neurotic depression. In H. S Akiskal & G. B. Cassano (Eds.), *Dysthymia and the spectrum of chronic depressions* (pp. 96–129). New York: Guilford.

Roth, S., & Lebowitz, L. (1988). The experience of sexual trauma. *J. Trauma. Stress, 1,* 79–107.

Rothbart, M. K., & Ahadi, S. A. (1994). Temperament and the development of personality. *J. Abn. Psychol., 103,* 55–66.

Rothbart, M. K., Ahadi, S. A., & Evans, D. E. (2000). Temperament and personality: Origins and outcomes. *J. Pers. Soc. Psychol., 78,* 122–35.

Rothbart, M. K., Derryberry, D., & Hershey, K. (2000). Stability of temperament in childhood: Laboratory infant assessment to parent report at seven years. In V. J. Molfese & D. L. Molfese (Eds.), *Temperament and personality development across the life span* (pp. 85–119). Mahwah, NJ: Erlbaum.

Rothbaum, B. O., Hodges, L., Smith, S., Lee, J. H., & Price, L. (2000). A controlled study of virtual reality exposure therapy for the fear of flying. *J. Cons. Clin. Psychol., 68,* 1020–26.

Rothbaum, B.O., Hodges, L., Anderson, P.L., Prices, L., & Smith, S. (2002). Twelve-month follow-up of virtual reality and standard exposure therapies for the fear of flying. *J. Cons. Clin. Psychol., 70*(2), 428–432.

Rothbaum, F., Weisz, J., Pott, M., Miyake, K., & Morelli, G. (2000). Attachment and culture security in the United States and Japan. *Amer. Psychol., 55,* 1093–104.

Rothbaum, F., Weisz, J., Pott, M., Miyake, K., & Morelli, G. (2001). Deeper into attachment and culture. *Amer. Psychol., 56,* 827–29.

Rothman, R. B., Paratilla, J. S., Dersch, C. M., Carroll, F. I., Rice, K. C., & Baumann, M. H. (2000). Methamphetamine dependence: Medication development efforts based on the dual deficit model of stimulant addiction. *Ann. NY Acad. Sci., 914,* 71–81.

Rothschild, A. J., Langlais, P. J., Schatzberg, A. F., Walsh, F. X., Cole, J. O., & Bird, E. D. (1985). The effects of a single dose of dexamethasone on monoamine and metabolite levels in rat brains. *Life Sciences, 36,* 2491.

Rothschild, A. J., Williamson, D. J., Tohen, M. F., Schatzberg, A., Andersen, S. W., Van Campen, L. E., et al. (2004). A double-blind, randomized study of olanzapine and olanzapine/fluoxetine combination for major depression with psychotic feaures. *J. Clin. Psychopharm., 24*(4), 365–373.

Rousseau, C., Drapeau, A., & Corin, E. (1996). School performance and emotional problems in refugee children. *Amer. J. Orthopsychiat., 66*(2), 239–51.

Rowland, D. L., & Slob, A. K. (1997). Premature ejaculation: Psychophysiological considerations in theory, research, and treatment. *Annu. Rev. Sex Res., 8,* 224–53.

Roy, A., Nielsen, D., Rylander, G., Sarchipone, M., & Segal, N. (1999). Genetics of suicide in depression. *J. Clin. Psychiat., 60,* 12–17.

Roy-Byrne, P. P., & Cowley, D. S. (2002). Pharmacological treatments for panic disorder, generalized anxiety disorder, specific phobia, and social anxiety disorder. In P. E. Nathan & J. M. Gorman (Eds.), *A guide to treatments that work* (2nd ed., pp. 337–66). New York: Oxford University Press.

Rozanski, A., Blumenthal, J. A., & Kaplan, J. (1999). Impact of psychological factors on the pathogenesis of cardiovascular disease and implications for therapy. *Circulation, 99,* 2192–217.

Rozensky, R. H., Sweet, J. J., & Tovian, S. M. (1997). *Psychological assessment in medical settings.* New York: Plenum.

Rozin, P., Kabnick, K., Pete, E., Fischler, C., & Shields, C. (2003). The ecology of eating: Smaller portion sizes in France than in the United States help explain the French paradox. *Psychol. Sci., 14*(5), 450–54.

Rubonis, A. V., & Bickman, L. (1991). Psychological impairment in the wake of disaster: The disaster's psychopathology relationship. *Psychol. Bull., 109*(3), 384–99.

Ruhmland, M., & Margraf, J. (2001). Efficacy of psychological treatments for panic and agoraphobia [German]. *Verhaltenstherapie, 11,* 41–53.

Rumbaut, R. (1985). Mental health and the refugee experience: A comparative study of Southeast Asian refugees. In T. C. Owan (Ed.), *Southeast Asian mental health: Treatment, prevention, services, training, and research* (pp. 443–86). Washington, DC: National Institute of Mental Health.

Runnheim, V. A., Frankenberger, W. R., & Hazelkorn, M. N. (1996). Medicating students with emotional and behavioral disorders and ADHD: A state survey. *Behavioral Disorders, 21*(4), 306–14.

Rurup, M. L., Muller, M. T., Onwuteaka-Philipsen, B. D., Van Der Heide, A., Van Der Wal, G., & Van Der Maas, P. J. (2005). Requests for euthanasia or physician-assisted suicide from older persons who do not have a severe disease: An interview study. *Psychol. Med., 35*(5), 665–671.

Ruscio, J., & Ruscio, A. M. (2000). Informing the continuity controversy: A taxometric analysis of depression. *J. Abn. Psychol., 109*(3), 473–87.

Rush, B. (1812). *Medical inquiries and observations upon diseases of the mind.* Philadelphia: Grigg and Elliot.

Russell, G. F. M. (1997). The history of bulimia nervosa. In D. M. Garner & P. E Garfinkel (Eds.), *Handbook of treatment for eating disorders* (2nd ed., pp. 11–24). New York: Guilford.

Russo, J., Vitaliano, P. P., Brewer, D. D., Katon, W., & Becker, J. (1995). Psychiatric disorders in spouse caregivers of care recipients with Alzheimer's disease and matched controls: A diathesis-stress model of psychopathology. *J. Abn. Psychol., 104,* 197–204.

Rutledge, P. C., & Sher, K. J. (2001). Heavy drinking from the freshman year into early young adulthood: The roles of stress, tension-reduction drinking motives, gender and personality. *J. Stud. Alcoh., 62*(4), 457–66.

Rutter, M. (1979). Maternal deprivations. 1972–1978: New findings, new concepts, new approaches. *Child Develop., 50,* 283–305.

Rutter, M. (1985). The treatment of autistic children. *Journal of Child Psychiatry, 26*(2), 193–214.

Rutter, M. (1987). Psychosocial resilience and protective mechanisms. *Amer. J. Orthopsychiat., 51,* 316–31.

Rutter, M. (1988). Epidemiological approaches to developmental psychopathology. *Arch. Gen. Psychiat., 45,* 486–500.

Rutter, M. (1990). Psychosocial resilience and protective mechanisms. In J. Rolf, A. S. Masten, D. Cicchetti, K. H. Nuechterlein, & S. Weintraub (Eds.), *Risk and protective factors in the development of psychopathology.* New York: Cambridge University Press.

Rutter, M. (1991). Nature, nurture, and psychopathology: A new look at an old topic. *Develop. Psychopath., 3,* 125–36.

Rutter, M. (2000). Genetic studies of autism: From the 1970s into the millennium. *J. Abnorm. Child Psychol., 28,* 3–14.

Rutter, M. (2001). Resilience reconsidered: Conceptual considerations, empirical findings, and policy implications. In J. P. Shonkoff & S. J. Meisels (Eds.), *Handbook of early childhood intervention* (2nd ed., pp. 651–82). New York: Cambridge University Press.

Rutter, M. L., Kreppner, J. M., & O'Connor, T. G. (2001). Specificity and heterogeneity in children's responses to profound institutional privation. *Brit. J. Psychiat., 179,* 97–103.

Rutter, M., & Maughan, B. (1997). Psychosocial adversities in childhood and adult psychopathology. *J. Personal. Dis., 11,* 4–18.

Rutter, M., & Quinton, D. (1984a). Long term follow-up of women institutionalized in childhood: Factors promoting good functioning in adult life. *Brit. J. Dev. Psychol., 18,* 255–34.

Rutter, M., & Quinton, D. (1984b). Parental psychiatric disorder: Effects on children. *Psychol. Med., 14,* 853–80.

Rutter, M., Andersen-Wood, L., Beckett, C., Bredenkamp, D., Castle, J., Dunn, J., Ehrich, K., Groothues, C., Harborne, A., Hay, D., Jewett, J., Keaveney, L., Kreppner, J., Messer, J., O'Connor, T., Quinton, D., & White, A. (1999). Developmental catch-up, and deficit, following adoption after severe global early privation. In S. J. Ceci & W. M. Williams (Eds.), *The nature-nurture debate: The essential readings* (pp. 107–33). Malden, MA: Blackwell.

Rutter, M., Silberg, J., & Simonoff, E. (1993). Whither behavioral genetics?—A developmental psychopathological perspective. In R. Plomin & G. McClearn (Eds.), *Nature, nurture, and psychology* (pp. 433–56). Washington, DC: American Psychological Association.

Rutz, W. (2001). Mental health in Europe—the World Health Organization's perspective: Diversities, possibilities, shortcomings and challenges. *Primary Care Psychiatry, 7*(3), 117–19.

Ryder, A. G., & Bagby, R. M. (1999). Diagnostic viability of depressive personality disorder: Theoretical and conceptual issues. *J. Pers. Dis., 13*(2), 99–117.

Ryff, C. D., Keyes, C. L. M., & Hughes, D. L. (2003). Status inequalities, perceived discrimination, and eudiamonic well-being: do the challenges of minority life hone purpose and growth. *J. Hlth. Soc. Beha., 44(3), 275–291.*

Sachdev, P., Troller, J., Walker, A., Wen, W., Fulham, M., Smith, J. S., & Matheson, J. (2001). Bilateral orbitomedial leucotomy for obsessive compulsive disorder: A single-case study using positron emission tomography. *Austral. NZ J. Psychiat., 35,* 648–90.

Sackeim, H. A., Haskett, R. F., Mulsant, B. H., Thase, M. E., Mann, J. J., & Pettinati, H. M., et al. (2001). Continuation pharmacotherapy in the prevention of relapse following electroconvulsive therapy: A randomized controlled trial. *JAMA, 285*(10), 1299–307.

Sackheim, H. A., Prudic, J., Devanand, D. P. Kiersky, J. E. Fitzsimons, L., Moody, B. J., McElhiney, M. C., Coleman, E. A., & Settembrino, J. M. (1993). Effects of stimulus intensity and electrode placement on the efficacy and cognitive effects of electroconvulsive therapy. *N. Engl. J. Med., 328,* 839–846.

Sadock, B. J., & Sadock, V. A. (2003). *Kaplan and Sadock's synopsis of psychiatry.* Philadelphia: Lippincott, Williams, & Wilkins.

Safer, D. J. (1997a). Central stimulant treatment of childhood attention-deficit hyperactivity disorder: Issues and recommendations from a U.S. perspective. *CNS Drugs, 7*(4), 264–72.

Safer, D. J. (1997b). Self-reported suicide attempts by adolescents. *Annals of Clinical Psychiatry, 9*(4), 263–69.

Safran, J. D. (1990a). Towards a refinement of cognitive therapy in light of interpersonal theory: I. Theory. *Clin. Psychol. Rev., 10,* 87–105.

Safran, J. D. (1990b). Towards a refinement of cognitive therapy in light of interpersonal theory: II. Practice. *Clin. Psychol. Rev., 10,* 107–21.

Saks, E. R. (2004). Refusing care: Forced treatment and the use of psychiatric advance directives. *J. Foren. Psychol. Pract., 4*(4), 35–50.

Salkovskis, P. M. (1989). Cognitive-behavioural factors and the persistence of intrusive thoughts in obsessional problems. *Behav. Res. Ther., 27,* 677–82.

Salkovskis, P. M., & Bass, C. (1997). Hypochondriasis. In D. M. Clark & C. G. Fairburn (Eds.), *Science and practice of cognitive behaviour therapy* (pp. 313–39). Oxford: Oxford University Press.

Salkovskis, P. M., & Kirk, J. (1997). Obsessive-compulsive disorder. In D. M. Clark & C. G. Fairburn (Eds.), *Science and practice of cognitive behaviour therapy* (pp. 179–208). New York: Oxford University Press.

Salkovskis, P. M., & Warwick, M. C. (2001). Meaning, misinterpretations, and medicine: A cognitive-behavioral approach to understanding health anxiety and hypochondriasis. In V. Starcevic & D. Lipsitt (Eds.), *Hypochondriasis: Modern perspectives on an ancient malady* (pp. 202–22). New York: Oxford University Press.

Salkovskis, P. M., Clark, D. M., & Gelder, M. G. (1996). Cognition-behavior links in the persistence of panic. *Behav. Res. Ther., 34*(5/6), 453–58.

Salkovskis, P. M., Wroe, A. L., Gledhill, A., Morrison, N., Forrester, E., Richards, C., Reynolds, M., & Thorpe, S. (2000). Responsibility attitudes and interpretations are characteristic of obsessive compulsive disorder. *Behav. Res. Ther., 38,* 347–72.

Salmivalli, C., & Nieminen, E. (2002). Proactive and reactive aggression among school bullies, victims, and bully-victims. *Aggr. Behav., 28,* 30–44.

Salmivalli, C., & Voeten, M. (2004). Connections between attitudes, group norms, and behavior in bullying situations. *International Journal of Behavioral Adjustment, 28*(3), 246–258.

Salter, A. (1949). *Conditioned reflex therapy.* New York: Creative Age Press.

Samborn, R. (1994, Jul. 4). Priests playing hardball to battle abuse charges. *National Law Journal, 16,* A1.

Samelson, F. (1980). J. B. Watson's Little Albert, Cyril Burt's twins, and the need for a critical science. *American Psychologist, 35,* 619–25.

Samet, S., Liu, X., & Hasin, D. (2004, Jul.). *Primary and substance induced depression and relapse in substance abusers.* Paper presented at the Annual Convention of the American Psychological Association, Honolulu, HI.

Sampson, R. J., Morenoff, J. D., & Gannon-Rowley, T. (2002). Assessing "neighborhood effects": social processes and new directions in research. *Ann. Rev. Soc., 28,* 443–478.

Sanchez, L., & Turner, S. M. (2003, Feb.). Practicing psychology in the era of managed care: Implications for practice and training. *Amer. Psychol., 58*(2), 116–29.

Sanchez, M. M., Ladd, C. O., & Plotsky, P. M. (2001). Early adverse experience as a developmental risk factor for later psychopathology: Evidence from rodent to primate models. *Develop. Psychopath., 13,* 419–49.

Sanders, M. R., Shepherd, R. W., Cleghorn, G., & Woolford, H. (1994). The treatment of recurrent abdominal pain in children: A controlled comparison of cognitive-behavioral family intervention and standard pediatric care. *J. Cons. Clin. Psychol., 62*(2), 306–14.

Sanderson, W. C., & Woody, S. (1995). Manuals for empirically validated treatments. *Clin. Psychol., 48*(4), 7–11.

Sanderson, W. C., Rapee, R. M., & Barlow, D. H. (1989). The influence of an illusion of control on panic attacks induced via inhalation of 5.5%-carbon-dioxide-enriched air. *Arch. Gen. Psychiat., 46,* 157–62.

Sandfort, T. G. M., de Graaf, R., Bijl, R. V., & Schnabel, P. (2001). Same-sex sexual behavior and psychiatric disorders: Findings from the Netherlands mental health survey and incidence study (NEMESIS). *Arch. Gen. Psychiat., 58,* 85–91.

Santor, D. A., & Coyne, J. C. (2001). Examining symptom expression as a function of symptom severity item performance on the Hamilton Rating Scale for Depression. *Psychol. Assess., 13*(1), 127–39.

Santry, H. P., Gillen, D. L., & Lauderdale, D. S. (2005). Trends in bariatric surgical procedures. *JAMA, 294,* 15, 1909–1917.

Sapolsky, R. M. (1994). *Why zebras don't get ulcers.* New York: W. H. Freeman.

Sapolsky, R. M. (2000). Glucocorticoids and hippocampal atrophy in neuropsychiatric disorders. *Arch. Gen. Psychiat., 57,* 925–35.

Sar, V., Akyüz, G., Kundakçi, T., Kiziltan, E., & Dogan, O. (2004). Childhood trauma, dissociation, and psychiatric comorbidity in patients with conversion disorder. *Amer. J. Psychiat., 161*(12), 2271–76

Saracoglu, B., Minden, H., & Wilchesky, M. (1989). The adjustment of students with learning disabilities to university and its relationship to self-esteem and self-efficacy. *J. Learn. Dis., 22,* 590–92.

Sarbin, T. R. (1997). On the futility of psychiatric diagnostic manuals (DSMs) and the return of personal agency. *App. Prev. Psychol., 6*(4), 233–43.

Sartorius, N., Kaelber, C. T., Cooper, J. E., Roper, M. T., Rae, D. S., Gulbinat, W., Ustun, T. B., & Regier, D. A. (1993). Progress toward achieving a common language in psychiatry: Results from the field trial of the clinical guidelines accompanying the WHO classification of mental and behavioral disorders in ICD-10. *Arch. Gen. Psychiat., 50,* 115–24.

Satz, P., & Green, M. F. (1999). Atypical handedness in schizophrenia: Some methodological and theoretical issues. *Schizo. Bull., 25,* 63–78.

Satz, P., et al. (1997). Mild head injury in children and adolescents: A review of studies (1970–1995). *Psychol. Bull., 122*(2), 107–31.

Sauter, S. L., Murphy, L. R., & Hurrell, J. J., Jr. (1990). Prevention of work-related psychological disorders: A national strategy proposed by the National Institute for Occupational Safety and Health (NIOSH). *Amer. Psychol., 45*(10), 1146–58.

Saxena, S., Brody, A.L., Ho, M.L., Alborzian, S., Maidment, K.M., Zohrabi, N., et al. (2002). Differential cerebral metabolic changes with paroxetine treatment of obsessive-compulsive disorder vs major depression. *Arch. Gen. Psychiat., 59,* 250–261.

Saxena, S., Brody, A.L., Maidment, K.M., Smith, E.C., Zohrabi, N., Katz, E., et al. (2004). Cerebral glucose metabolism in obsessive-compulsive hoarding. *Amer. J. Psychiat., 161*(6), 1038–1048.

Sbrocco, T., & Barlow, D. H. (1996). Conceptualizing the cognitive component of sexual arousal: Implications for sexuality research and treatment. In Salkovskis, P. M. (Ed.), *Frontiers of cognitive therapy* (pp. 419–49). New York: Guilford.

Scannell, E. D., Quirk, M. M., Smith, K., Maddern, R., & Dickerson, M. (2000). Females' coping styles and control over poker machine gambling. *Journal of Gambling Studies, 16*(4), 417–32.

Schacter, D. L., Norman, K. A., & Koutstaal, W. (2000). The cognitive neuroscience of constructive memory. In D. F. Bjorklund (Ed.), *False-memory creation in children and adults* (pp. 129–68). Mahwah, NJ: Erlbaum.

Schapiro, M. B., & Rapoport, S. I. (1987). "Pathological similarities between Alzheimer's disease and Down's syndrome: Is there a genetic link?": Commentary. *Integr. Psychiat., 5,* 167–69.

Schatzberg, A. F., Rush, A. J., Arnow, B. A., Banks, P. L. C., Blalock, J. A., Borian, F. E., et al. (2005). Chronic depression: Medication (Nefazodone) or psychotherapy (CBASP) is effective when the other is not. *Arch. Gen. Psychiat., 62,* 513–520.

Scheff, T. J. (1984). *Being mentally ill: A sociological theory* (2nd ed.). New York: Aldine.

Scheier, M. F., & Carver, C. S. (1987). Dispositional optimism and physical well-being: The influence of generalized outcome expectancies on health. *J. Personal., 55,* 169–210.

Scheier, M. F., & Carver, C. S. (1992). Effects of optimism on psychological and physical well-being: Theoretical overview and empirical update. *Cog. Ther. Res., 16*(2), 201–28.

Schenk, J. W. (1998, Mar. 9). Do "Megan's Laws" make a difference? Pariah status may not deter sex offenders. *U.S. News and World Report,* p. 27.

Scheurich, A. (2005). Neuropsychological functioning and alcohol dependence. *Current Opinion in Psychiatry, 18*(3), 319–23.

Schieffelin, E. L. (1985). Cultural analysis of depressive affect: An example from New Guinea. In A. Kleinman & B. Good (Eds.), *Culture and depression: Studies in the anthropology and cross-cultural psychiatry of affect and disorder* (pp. 102–33). Berkeley and Los Angeles: University of California Press.

Schildkraut, J. J. (1965). The catecholamine hypothesis of affective disorders: A review of supporting evidence. *Amer. J. Psychiat., 122,* 509–22.

Schilling, R. F., & McAlister, A. L. (1990). Preventing drug use in adolescents through media interventions. *J. Cons. Clin. Psychol., 58,* 416–24.

Schleifer, S. J., Keller, S. E., & Stein, M. (1985). Central nervous system mechanisms and immunity: Implications for tumor responses. In S. M. Levy (Ed.), *Behavior and cancer* (pp. 120–33). San Francisco: Jossey-Bass.

Schleifer, S. J., Keller, S. E., Bond, R. M., Cohen, J., & Stein, M. (1989). Major depressive disorder and immunity: Role of age, sex, severity, and hospitalization. *Arch. Gen. Psychiat., 46,* 81–87.

Schmand, B., et al. (1997). The effects of intelligence and education on the development of dementia: A test of the brain reserve hypothesis. *Psychol. Med., 27*(6), 1337–44.

Schmidt, N. B., Lerew, D. R., & Jackson, R. J. (1997). The role of anxiety sensitivity in the pathogenesis of panic: Prospective evaluation of spontaneous panic attacks during acute stress. *J. Abn. Psychol., 106,* 355–65.

Schmidt, N.B., & Lerew, D.R. (2002). Prospective evaluation of perceived control, predictability, and anxiety sensitivity in the pathogenesis of panic. *J. Psychopath. Behav. Assess., 24*(4), 207–214.

Schneider, M. L. (1992). The effects of mild stress during pregnancy on birthweight and neuromotor maturation in Rhesus monkey infants *(Macaca mulatta). Inf. Behav. Develop., 15,* 389–403.

Schneider, R. H., Alexander, C. N., Staggers, F., Orme-Johnson, D. W., Rainforth, M., Salerno, J. W., Shappard, W., Castillo-Richmond, A., Barnes, V. A., & Nidich, S. I. (2005). A randomized controlled trial of stress reduction in African-Americans treated for hypertension for over one year. *American Journal of Hypertension, 18,* 88–98.

Schneiderman, N., Ironson, G., & Siegel, S. D. (2005). Stress and health: Psychological, behavioral, and biological determinants. *Annu. Rev. Clin. Psychol., 1,* 1–22.

Schnyder, U. (2005). Why new psychotherapies for posttraumatic stress disorder? *Psychother. Psychosom., 74*(4), 199–201.

Schoeneman, T. J. (1984). The mentally ill witch in textbooks of abnormal psychology: Current status and implications of a fallacy. *Profess. Psychol., 15*(3), 299–314.

Schopler, E., Yirmiya, N., Shulman, C., & Marcus, L. M. (Eds.). (2001). *The research basis for autism intervention.* Boston: Kluwer.

Schreiber, F. R. (1973). *Sybil.* New York: Warner Paperback.

Schreibman, L., & Charlop-Christie, M. H. (1998). Autistic disorder. In T. H. Ollendick, M. Hersen, et al. (Eds.), *Handbook of child psychopathology* (3rd ed., pp. 157–79). New York: Plenum.

Schroeder, C. S., & Gordon, B. N. (2002). *Assessment and treatment of childhood problems: A clinician's guide (2nd ed.).* New York: Cambridge University Press.

Schuckit, M. A., Tipp, J. E., Smith, T. L., & Bucholtz, K. K. (1997). Periods of abstinence following the onset of alcohol dependence in 1853 men and women. *J. Stud. Alcoh., 58,* 581–89.

Schudson, M. (1995). Collective memory and modes of distortion. In D. Schachter, J. Coyle, L. Sullivan, M. Mesulam, & G. Fishbach (Eds.), *Memory distortion: Interdisciplinary perspectives.* Cambridge: Harvard University Press.

Schulsinger, F., Knop, J., Goodwin, D. W., Teasdale, T. W., & Mikkelsen, U. (1986). A prospective study of young men at high risk for alcoholism. *Arch. Gen. Psychiat., 43,* 755–60.

Schulsinger, F. (1972). Psychopathy: Heredity and environment. *Inter. J. Ment. Hlth., 1,* 190–206.

Schulte-Koerne, G. (2001). Genetics of reading and spelling disorder. *Journal of Child Psychology & Psychiatry & Allied Disciplines, 42*(8), 985–97.

Schultz, R. K., Braun, B. G., & Kluft, R. P. (1989). Multiple personality disorder: Phenomenology of selected variables in comparison to major depression. *Dissociation, 2,* 45–51.

Schultz, S. K. (2000). Dementia in the twenty-first century. *Amer. J. Psychiat., 157*(5), 666–68.

Schulz, R., Drayer, R. A., & Rollman, B. L. (2002). Depression as a risk factor for the non-suicide mortality in the elderly. *Biol. Psychiat., 52*(3), 205–225.

Schulze-Rauschenbach, S. C., Harms, U., Schlaepfer, T. E., Maier, W., Falkai, P., & Wagner, M. (2005). Distinctive neurocognitive effects of repetitive transcranial magnetic stimulation and electroconvulsive therapy in major depression. *Brit. J. Psychiat., 186,* 410–416.

Schupf, N., Kapell, D., Lee, J. H., Ottman, R., & Mayeux, R. (1994). Increased risk of Alzheimer's disease in mothers of adults with Down's syndrome. *Lancet, 344*(8919), 353–56.

Schupf, N., Kapell, D., Nightingale, B., Lee, J. H., Mohlenhoff, J., Bewley, S., Ottman, R., & Mayeux, R. (2001). Specificity of the fivefold increase in AD in mothers with Down syndrome. *Neurology, 57*(6), 979–84.

Schupp, H.T., Ohman, A., Junghofer, M., Weike, A.I., Stockburger, J., & Hamm, A.O. (2004). The facilitated processing of threatening faces: An ERP analysis. *Emotion, 4*(2), 189–200.

Schwartz, C. E., Snidman, N., & Kagan, J. (1996). Early childhood temperament as a determinant of externalizing behavior in adolescence. *Develop. Psychopath., 8*(3), 527–37.

Schwartz, C. E., Snidman, N., & Kagan, J. (1999). Adolescent social anxiety as an outcome of inhibited temperament in childhood. *J. Amer. Acad. Child Adoles. Psychiat., 38,* 1008–15.

Schwartz, D., Dodge, K. A., & Coie, J. D. (1993). The emergence of chronic peer victimization in boys' play groups. *Child Develop., 64,* 1755–72.

Schwartz, J. M., Stoessel, P. W., Baxter, L. R., Martin, K. M., & Phelps, M. E. (1996). Systematic changes in cerebral glucose metabolic rate after successful behavior modification treatment of obsessive-compulsive disorder. *Arch. Gen. Psychiat., 53,* 109–13.

Schwarzwald, J., Weisenberg, M., Waysman, M., Solomon, Z., & Klingman, A. (1993). Stress reaction of school-age children to bombardment by SCUD missiles. *J. Abn. Psychol., 102,* 404–10.

Scott, F. J., & Baron-Cohen, S. (1996). Logical, analogical, and psychological reasoning in autism: A test of the Cosmides theory. *Develop. Psychopath., 8,* 235–45.

Searles, J. S. (1991). The genetics of alcoholism: Impact on family and sociological models of addiction. *Family Dynamics of Addiction Quarterly, 1,* 8–21.

Sears, S. R., & Stanton, A. L. (2001). Physician-assisted dying: Review of issues and roles for health psychologists. *Hlth. Psychol., 20*(4), 302–10.

Seeley, M. F. (1997). The role of hotlines in the prevention of suicide. In R. W. Maris, M. M. Silverman, & S. S. Canetton (Eds.), *Review of Suicidology, 1997* (pp. 251–70). New York: Guilford.

Segal, Z. V., & Stermac, L. E. (1990). The role of cognition in sexual assault. In W. L. Marshall, D. R. Laws, & H. E. Barbaree (Eds.), *Handbook of sexual assault* (pp. 161–75). New York: Plenum.

Segerstrom, S. C., & Miller, G. E. (2004). Psychological stress and the human immune system: A meta-analytic study of 30 years of inquiry. *Psychol. Bull., 130,* 610–30.

Segraves, T., & Althof, S. (2002). Psychotherapy and pharmacotherapy for sexual dysfunctions. In P. E. Nathan & J. M. Gorman (Eds.), *A guide to treatments that work* (pp. 497–524). New York: Oxford University Press.

Seidman, E. (2003). Fairweather and ESID: Contemporary impact and a legacy for the twenty-first century. *Am. J. Community Psychol., 32*(3–4), 371–75.

Seifert, K. (2003). Childhood trauma: Its relationship to behavioral and psychiatric disorders. *Forensic Examiner, 12,* 27–33.

Selemon, L. D. (2004). Increased cortical neuronal density in schizophrenia. *Amer. J. Psychiat., 161,* 9.

Selemon, L. D., Rajkowska, G., & Goldman-Rakic, P. S. (1995). Abnormally high neuronal density in the schizophrenic cortex. *Arch. Gen. Psychiat., 52,* 805–18.

Seligman, M. E. P. (1971). Phobias and preparedness. *Behav. Ther., 2,* 307–20.

Seligman, M. E. P. (1974). Depression and learned helplessness. In R. J. Friedman & M. M. Katz (Eds.), *The psychology of depression: Contemporary theory and research.* Washington, DC: Hemisphere.

Seligman, M. E. P. (1975). *Helplessness: On depression, development, and death.* San Francisco: Freeman.

Seligman, M. E. P. (1990). Why is there so much depression today? The waxing of the individual and the waning of the commons. In R. E. Ingram (Ed.), *Contemporary psychological approaches to depression.* New York: Plenum.

Seligman, M. E. P. (1998). Afterword—A plea. In P. E. Nathan & J. M. Gorman (Eds.), *A guide to treatments that work* (pp. 568–71). New York: Oxford University Press.

Seligman, M. E. P., & Binik, Y. (1977). The safety signal hypothesis. In H. Davis & H. M. B. Hurwitz (Eds.), *Operant-Pavlovian interactions* (pp. 165–88). Hillsdale, NJ: Erlbaum.

Seligman, M. E. P., Walker, E. F., & Rosenhan, D. L. (2001). *Abnormal psychology.* New York: Norton.

Sell, R. L., Wypij, D., & Wells, J. A. (1995). The prevalence of homosexual behavior and attraction in the United States, the United Kingdom, and France: Results of national population-based samples. *Arch. Sex. Behav., 24,* 235–48.

Selling, L. S. (1943). *Men against madness.* New York: Garden City Books.

Selye, H. (1956). *The stress of life.* New York: McGraw-Hill.

Selye, H. (1976a). *Stress in health and disease.* Woburn, MA: Butterworth.

Selye, H. (1976b). *The stress of life* (2nd ed.). New York: McGraw-Hill.

Senft, R. A., Polen, M. R., Freeborn, D. K., & Hollis, J. F. (1997). Brief intervention in a primary care setting for hazardous drinkers. *American Journal of Preventive Medicine, 13*(6), 464–70.

Sensky, T., Turkington, D., Kingdon, D., et al. (2000). A randomized controlled trial of cognitive behavioral therapy for persistent symptoms in schizophrenia resistant to medication. *Arch. Gen. Psychiat., 57,* 165–72.

Seppa, N. (1998, Jul. 4). Amyloid can trigger brain damage. *Sci. News, 154,* 4.

Sernyak, D. L., Leslei, D. L., Alarcon, R. D., Losonczy, M. F., & Rosenheck, R. (2002). Association of diabetes mellitus with use of atypical neuroleptics in the treatment of schizophrenia. *Amer. J. Psychiat., 159,* 561–66.

Serper, M. R., Goldberg, B. R., & Salzinger, K. (2004). Behavorial assessment of psychiatric patients in restrictive settings. *Comprehensive handbook of psychological assessment* (Vol. 3, pp. 320–45). New York: John Wiley & Sons.

Seto, M. C., & Barbaree, H. E. (1995). The role of alcohol in sexual aggression. *Clin. Psychol. Rev., 15*(6), 545–66.

Seto, M. C., Lalumiere, M. L., & Kuban, M. (1999). The sexual preferences of incest offenders. *J. Abn. Psychol., 108,* 267–72.

Sewell, D. W., Jeste, D. V., Atkinson, J. H., Heaton, R. K., Hesselink, J. R., Wiley, C., Thal, L., Chandler, J. L., & Grant, I. (1994). HIV-associated psychosis: A study of 20 cases. *Amer. J. Psychiat., 151*(2), 237–42.

Shadish, W. R., Matt, G. E., Navarro, A. M., & Phillips, G. (2000). The effects of psychological therapies under clinically-representative conditions: A meta-analysis. *Psychol. Bull., 126,* 512–529.

Shadish, W. R., Montgomery, L. M., Wilson, P., Wilson, M. R., Bright, I., & Okwumabua, T. (1993). Effects of family and marital psychotherapies: A meta-analysis. *J. Cons. Clin. Psychol., 61*(6), 992–1002.

Shaffer, T. W., Erdberg, P., & Haroian, J. (1999). Current nonpatient data for the Rorschach, WAIS-R and MMPI-2. *J. Pers. Assess., 73,* 305–16.

Shafran, R., & Rachman, S. (2004). Thought-action fusion. *J. Beh. Ther. & Exper. Psychiat., 35*(2), 87–107.

Shalev, A. Y. (2000). Biological responses to disasters. *Psychiat. Q., 71*(3), 277–88.

Shalev, A. Y. (2001). What is posttraumatic stress disorder? *J. Clin. Psychiat., 62,* 4–10.

Shalev, A. Y., Bonne, O., & Eth, S. (1996). Treatment of posttraumatic stress disorder: A review. *Psychosom. Med., 58,* 165–82.

Shapiro, A. K., & Morris, L. A. (1978). The placebo effect in medical and psychological therapies. In S. L. Garfield & A. E. Bergin (Eds.), *Handbook of psychotherapy and behavior change* (2nd ed., pp. 369–410). New York: Wiley.

Shapiro, F. (1996). Eye movement desensitization and reprocessing (EMDR): Evaluation of controlled PTSD research. *J. Behav. Ther. Exper. Psychiat., 27,* 209–18.

Sharkey, J. (1997, Sept. 28). You're not bad, you're sick. It's in the book. *New York Times,* pp. 1, 5.

Shaw, J. A. (2003). Children exposed to war/terrorism. *Clin. Child Fam. Psych. Rev., 6*(4), 237–46.

Shaw, W. S., et al. (1997). Longitudinal analysis of multiple indicators of health decline among spousal caregivers. *Ann. Behav. Med., 19*(2), 101–9.

Shea, M. T. (1995). Interrelationships among categories of personality disorders. In W. J. Livesley (Ed.), *The DSM-IV personality disorders* (pp. 397–406). New York: Guilford.

Sheehan, D. Z. (1982). Panic attacks and phobias. *N. Engl. J. Med., 307,* 156–58.

Sheehan, D. Z. (1983). *The anxiety disease.* New York: Bantam Books.

Shekelle, R. B., Hulley, S. B., Neaton, J. D., Billings, J. D., Borhani, N. O., Gerace, T. A., Jacobs, D. R., Lasser, N. L., Mittlemark, M. B., & Stamler, J. (1985). The MRFIT behavior pattern study, II: Type A behavior and incidence of coronary heart disease. *Amer. J. Epidemiol., 122,* 559–70.

Sheline, Y. I., Sanghavi, M., Mintun, M. A., & Gado, M. H. (1999). Depression duration but not age predicts hippocampal volume loss in medically healthy women with recurrent major depression. *J. Neurosci., 19*(12), 5034–5043.

Shelton, D. (2001). Emotional disorders in young offenders. *Journal of Nursing Scholarship, 33*(3), 259–63.

Shepherd, J., & Brickley, M. (1996). The relationship between alcohol intoxication, stressors, and injury in urban violence. *British Journal of Criminology, 36*(4), 546–66.

Sheps, D. S., McMahon, R. P., Becker, L., Camey, R. M., Freeland, K. E., Cohen, J. D., Sheffield, D., Goldberg, A. D., Ketterer, M. W., Pepine, C. J., Raczynski, J. M., Light, K., Krantz, D. S., Stone, P. H., Knatterud, G. L., & Kaufmann, P. G. (2002). Mental stress-induced ischemia and all-cause mortality in patients with coronary artery disease. *Circulation, 105,* 1700–84.

Sher, K. J., Bartholow, B. D., & Nanda, S. (2001). Short and long term effects of fraternity and sorority membership on heavy drinking: A social norms perspective. *Psychol. Addict. Behav., 15,* 42–51.

Sher, K. J., Wood, M. D., Wood, P. D., & Raskin, G. (1996). Alcohol outcome expectancies and alcohol use: A latent variable cross-lagged panel study. *J. Abn. Psychol., 105*(4), 561–74.

Sher, K., Grekin, E. R., & Williams, N. A. (2005). The development of alcohol use disorders. *Ann. Rev. Clin. Psychol., 1*(1), 493–523.

Shergill, S. S., Brammer, M. J., Williams, S. C. R., Murray, R. M., & McGuire, P. K. (2000). Mapping auditory hallucinations in schizophrenia using functional magnetic resonance imaging. *Arch. Gen. Psychiat., 57,* 1033–38.

Sheung-Tak, C. (1996). A critical review of Chinese koro. *Cult., Med. Psychiat., 20,* 67–82.

Shevlin, M., Hunt, N., & Robbins, I. (2000). A confirmatory factor analysis of the Impact of Event Scale using a sample of World War II and Korean War veterans. *Psychol. Assess., 12*(4), 414–17.

Shields, A., Ryan, R. M., & Cicchetti, D. (2001). Narrative representations of caregivers and emotion dysregulation as predictors of maltreated children's rejection by peers. *Develop. Psychol., 37,* 321–37.

Shigenobu, K. (2001). Psychoimmunology: A dialogue between the brain and the immune system. *Journal of the International Society of Life Information Science, 19,* 141–43.

Shively, C. A., Clarkson, T. B., & Kaplan, J. R. (1989). Social deprivation and coronary artery atherosclerosis in female cynomolgus monkeys. *Atherosclerosis, 77,* 69–76.

Shneidman, E. S. (1997). The suicidal mind. In R. W. Maris, M. M. Silverman, & S. S. Canetton (Eds.), *Review of Suicidology, 1997* (pp. 22–41). New York: Guilford.

Shonk, S. M., & Cicchetti, D. (2001). Maltreatment, competency deficits, and risk for academic and behavioral maladjustment. *Develop. Psychol., 37,* 3–17.

Short, K. H., & Johnston, C. (1997). Stress, maternal distress, and children's adjustment following immigration: The buffering role of social support. *J. Cons. Clin. Psychol., 65*(3), 494–503.

Shrestha, N. M., Sharma, B., Van Ommeren, M., et al. (1998). Impact of torture on refugees displaced within the developing world: Symptomatology among Bhutanese refugees in Nepal. *JAMA, 280,* 443–48.

Siegel, B. (1996). *The world of the autistic child.* New York: Oxford University Press.

Siegel, B. (2003). *Helping children with autism learn.* New York: Oxford University Press.

Siegel, J. M., & Kuykendall, D. H. (1990). Loss, widowhood, and psychological distress among the elderly. *J. Cons. Clin. Psychol., 58,* 519–24.

Siever, L. J., Bernstein, D. P., & Silverman, J. M. (1995). Schizotypal personality disorder. In W. J. Livesley (Ed.), *The DSM-IV personality disorders.* (pp. 71–90). New York: Guilford.

Sieving, R. E., Maruyama, G., Williams, C. L., & Perry, C. L. (2000). Pathways to adolescent alcohol use: Potential mechanisms of parent influence. *Journal of Research on Adolescence, 10*(4), 489–514.

Sigal, J. J., Rossignol, M., & Perry, J. C. (1999). Some psychological and physical consequences in middle-aged adults of underfunded institutional care. *J. Nerv. Ment. Dis., 187,* 57–59.

Sigal, J. J., Silver, D., Rakoff, V., & Ellin, B. (1973, Apr.). Some second-generation effects of survival of the Nazi persecution. *Amer. J. Orthopsychiat., 43*(3), 320–27.

Sigman, M. (1996). Behavioral research in childhood autism. In M. F. Lenzenweger & J. L. Haugaard (Eds.), *Frontiers of developmental psychopathology* (pp. 190–208). New York: Oxford University Press.

Silberg, J. L., Pickles, A., Rutter, M., Hewitt, J., Simonoff, E., Maes, H., Carbonneau, R., Murrelle, L., Foley, D., & Eaves, L. (1999). The influence of genetic factors and life stress on depression among adolescent girls. *Arch. Gen. Psychiat., 56,* 225–32.

Silberg, J. L., Rutter, M., & Eaves, L. (2001). Genetic and environmental influences on the temporal association between earlier anxiety and later depression in girls. *Biol. Psychiat., 49,* 1040–49.

Silberg, J., Rutter, M., Neale, M., & Eaves, L. (2001). Genetic moderation of environmental risk for depression and anxiety in adolescent girls. *Brit. J. Psychiat., 179,* 116–21.

Silk, J. S., Nath, S. R., Siegel, L. R., & Kendall, P. C. (2000). Conceptualizing mental disorders in children: Where have we been and where are we going? *Develop. Psychopathol., 12,* 713–35.

Silove, D., Steel, Z., McGorry, P., Miles, V., & Drobny, J. (2002). The impact of torture on post-traumatic stress symptoms in war-affected Tamil refugees and immigrants. *Compr. Psychiat., 43,* 49–55.

Silver, E. (1995). Punishment or treatment? Comparing the lengths of confinement of successful and unsuccessful insanity defendants. *Law and Human Behavior, 19*(4), 375–88.

Silver, J. M., Hales, R. E., & Yudofsky, S. C. (2002). Neuropsychiatric aspects of traumatic brain injury. In S. Yudofsky & R. E. Hales (Eds.), *The American Psychiatric Association Publishing textbook of neuropsychiatry and clinical sciences* (4th ed., pp. 625–72). Washington, DC: American Psychiatric Publishing.

Silverman, D. H. S., Small, G. W., Chang, C. Y., Lu, C. S., Kung de Alburto, M. A., Chen, W., Czernin, J., Rapoport, S. I., Pietrini, P., Alexander, G. E., Schapiro, M. B., Jagust, W. J., Hoffman, J. M., Welsh-Bohmer, K. A., Alavi, A., Clark, C. M., Salmon, E., de Leon, M. J., Mielke, R., Cummings, J. L., Kowell, A. P., Gambhir, S. S., Hoh, C. K., & Phelps, M. E. (2001). Positron emission tomography in evaluation of dementia: Regional brain metabolism and long-term outcome. *JAMA, 286,* 2120–27.

Silverman, J. A. (1997). Anorexia nervosa: Historical perspective on treatment. In D. M. Garner & P. E Garfinkel (Eds.), *Handbook of treatment for eating disorders* (2nd ed., pp. 3–10). New York: Guilford.

Silverman, K., Higgins, S. T., Brooner, R. K., & Montoya, I. D. (1996). Sustained cocaine abstinence in methadone maintenance patients through voucher-based reinforcement therapy. *Arch. Gen. Psychiat., 53*(3), 409–15.

Silverman, M. M. (1997). Current controversies in suicidology. In R. W. Maris, M. M. Silverman, & S. S. Canetton (Eds.), *Review of Suicidology, 1997* (pp. 1–21). New York: Guilford.

Silverman, W. H., & Silverman, M. M. (1987). Comparison of key informants, parents, and teenagers for planning adolescent substance abuse prevention programs. *Psychology of Addictive Behaviors, 1*(1), 30–37.

Silverstein, A. B., Legutki, G., Friedman, S. L., & Takayama, D. L. (1982). Performance of Down's syndrome individuals on the Stanford-Binet Intelligence Scale. *Amer. J. Ment. Def., 86,* 548–85.

Simeon, D., Gross, S., Guralnik, O., & Stein, D. J. (1997). Feeling unreal: 30 cases of DSM-III-R depersonalization disorder. *Amer. J. Psychiat., 154,* 1107–13.

Simeon, D., Guralnik, O., Schmeidler, J., & Knutelska, M. (2004). Fluoxetine therapy in depersonalization disorder: Randomised controlled trial. *Brit. J. Psychiat., 185*(1), 31–36.

Simeon, D., Guralnik, O., Schmeidler, J., Sirof, B., & Knutelska, M. (2001). The role of childhood interpersonal trauma in depersonalization disorder. *Amer. J. Psychiat., 158,* 1027–33.

Simeon, D., Hollander, E., Stein, D. J., & Cohen, L. (1995). Body dysmorphic disorder in the DSM-IV field trial for obsessive-compulsive disorder. *Amer. J. Psychiat., 152,* 1207–9.

Simon, C. (1997). *Mad house.* New York: Doubleday.

Simon, G. E. (2002). Management of somatoform and factitious disorders. In P. E. Nathan & J. M. Gorman (Eds.), *A guide to treatments that work* (2nd ed., pp. 447–61). New York: Oxford University Press.

Simon, N. M., Otto, M. W., Wisniewski, S. R., Fossey, M., Sagduyo, K., Frank, E., et al. (2004). Anxiety disorder comorbidity in bipolar disorder patients: Data from the first 500 participants in the systematic treatment enhancement program for bipolar disorder. *Amer. J. Psychiat., 161*(12), 2222–2229.

Simon, R. J., & Aaronson, D. E. (1988). *The insanity defense.* New York: Praeger.

Simonoff, E. (2001). Gene-environment interplay in oppositional defiant and conduct disorder. *Child Adoles. Psychiatr. Clin. N. Amer., 10*(2), 351–74.

Simons, A. D., Angell, K. L., Monroe, S. M., & Thase, M. E. (1993). Cognition and life stress in depression: Cognitive factors and the definition, rating, and generation of negative life events. *J. Abn. Psychol., 102,* 584–91.

Simons, R. C., & Hughes, C. C. (Eds.). (1985). *The culture bound syndromes.* Boston: Reidel.

Simpson, A. I. F., McKenna, B., Moskowitz, A., Skipworth, J., & Barry-Walsh, J. (2004). Homicide and mental illness in New Zealand, 1970–2000. *Brit. J. Psychiat., 185*(5), 394–98.

Simpson, G., & Tate, R. (2002). Suicidality after traumatic brain injury: Demographic, injury and clinical correlates. *Psychol. Med., 32,* 687–97.

Singer, D. G., & Singer, J. L. (Eds.). (2000). *Handbook of children and the media.* Thousand Oaks, CA: Sage.

Singer, M. T., Wynne, L. C., & Toohey, M. L. (1978). Communication disorders and the families of schizophrenics. In L. C. Wynne, R. L. Cromwell, & S. Matthysse (Eds.), *The nature of schizophrenia: New approaches to research and treatment* (pp. 499–511). New York: Wiley.

Sink, M. (2004 Nov. 8). Drinking deaths draw attention to okd campus problem. *The New York Times,* p. A14.

Siqueland, L., Crits-Christoph, P., Gallop, R., Barber, J. P., Griffin, M. L., Thase, M. E., Daley, D., Frank, A., Gastfriend, D. R., Blaine, J., Connolly, M. B., & Gladis, M. (2002). Retention in psychosocial treatment of cocaine dependence: Predictors and impact on outcome. *American Journal on Addictions, 11*(1), 24–40.

Sjogren, M., & Blennow, K. (2005). The link between cholesterol and Alzheimer's disease. *World Journal of Biological Psychiatry, 6*(2), 85–97.

Skaer, T. L., Robinson, L. M., Sclar, D. A., & Galin, R. S. (2000). Treatment of depressive illness among children and adolescents in the United States. *Current Therapeutic Research, 61,* 692–705.

Skinner, B. F. (1951). How to teach animals. *Scientif. Amer., 185,* 26–29.

Skinner, B. F. (1990). Can psychology be a science of mind? *Amer. Psychol., 45,* 1206–10.

Skodol, A. E., et al. (1993). Comorbidity of DSM-III-R eating disorders and personality disorders. *Int. J. Eat. Dis., 14,* 403–416.

Skodol, A. E., Oldham, J. M., Hyler, S. E., & Stein, D. J. (1995). Patterns of anxiety and personality disorder comorbidity. *J. Psychiat. Res., 29*(5), 361–74.

Skodol, A. E., Rosnick, L., Kellman, H. D., Oldham, J. M., & Hyler, S. E. (1991). Development of a procedure for validating structured assessments of Axis II. In J. Oldham (Ed.), *Personality disorders: New perspectives on diagnostic validity.* Washington, DC: American Psychiatric Press.

Skogg, I. (2002). Magnetic-resonance imaging to assess Alzheimer's disease. *Lancet, 359*(9317), 1538–39.

Slater, E. (1986). First person account: A parent's view on enforcing medication. *Schizo. Bull., 12,* 291–92.

Slavkin, M. L., & Fineman, K. (2000). What every professional who works with adolescents needs to know about firesetters. *Adolescence, 35*(140), 759–73.

Slicker, E. K., & Thornberry, I. (2002). Older adolescent well-being and authoritative parenting. *Adolescent & Family Health, 3*(1), 9–19.

Sloman, L. (1991). Use of medication in pervasive developmental disorders. *Psychiat. Clin. N. Amer., 14,* 165–82.

Slovenko, R. (2001). The stigma of psychiatric discourse. *Journal of Psychiatry & Law, 29,* 5–29.

Slutske, W. S., Heath, A. C., Dinwiddie, S. H., Madden, P. A., & Bucholz, K. K. (1998). Common genetic risk factors for conduct disorder and alcohol dependence. *J. Abn. Psychol., 107*(3), 363–74.

Slutske, W., Heath, A. C., Dunne, M. P., Statham, D. J., Dinwiddie, S. H., Madden, P. A. F., Martin, N. G., & Bucholz, K. K. (1997). Modeling genetic and environmental influences in the etiology of conduct disorder: A study of 2,682 adult twin pairs. *J. Abn. Psychol., 100*(2), 266–79.

Smalley, S. L. (1991). Genetic influences in autism. *Psychiat. Clin. N. Amer., 14,* 125–39.

Smith, C. D., Andersen, A. H., Kryscio, R. J., Schmitt, F. A., Kindy, M. S., Blonder, L. X., & Avison, M. J. (2002). Women at risk for AD show increased parietal activation during a fluency task. *Neurology, 58,* 1197–1202.

Smith, G. T., Goldman, M. S., Greenbaum, P. E., & Christiansen, B. A. (1995). Expectancy for social facilitation from drinking: The divergent paths of high-expectancy and low-expectancy adolescents. *J. Abn. Psychol., 104,* 32–40.

Smith, I. M., & Bryson, S. (1994). Imitation and action in autism: A critical review. *Psychol. Bull., 116*(2), 259–73.

Smith, L., Smith, P., & Lee, S. K. Y. (2000). Behavioral treatment of urinary incontinence and encopresis in children with learning disabilities: Transfer of stimulus control. *Develop. Med. Child Neurol.,* 42, 276–79.

Smith, P. M., Reilly, K. R., Miller, N. H., DeBusk, R. F., & Taylor, C. B. (2002). Application of a nurse-managed inpatient smoking cessation program. *Nicotine & Tobacco Research, 4*(2), 211–22.

Smith, R. G., Monson, R. A., & Ray, D. C. (1986). Psychiatric consultation in somatization disorder: A randomized controlled study. *N. Engl. J. Med., 314,* 1407–13.

Smith, R. S., & Maes, M. (1995). The macrophage-T lymphocyte theory of schizophrenia: Additional evidence. *Medical Hypotheses, 45,* 135–41.

Smith, T. W., & Ruiz, J. M. (2002). Psychosocial influences on the development and course of coronary heart disease: Current status and implications for research and practice. *J. Cons. Clin. Psychol., 70*(3), 548–68.

Smith, T. W., Orleans, C. T., & Jenkins, C. D. (2005). Prevention and health promotion: Decades of progress, new challenges, and an emerging agenda. *Hlth. Psychol., 23,* 2, 126–31.

Smith, W. (1989). *A profile of health and disease in America.* New York: Facts on File.

Smolak, L., & Murnen, S. K. (2002). A meta-analytic examination of the relationship between child sexual abuse and eating disorders. *Int. J. Eat. Dis., 31*(2), 136–50.

Smyth, J. M. (1998). Written emotional expression: Effect sizes, outcome types, and moderating variables. *J. Cons. Clin. Psychol., 66*(1), 174–84.

Snider, W. D., Simpson, D. M., Nielsen, S., Gold, J. W., Metroka, C. E., & Posner, J. B. (1983). Neurological complications of acquired immune deficiency syndrome: Analysis of 50 patients. *Ann. Neurol., 14*(4), 403–18.

Snitz, B. E., Hellinger, A., & Daum, I. (2002). Impaired processing of affective prosody in Korsakoff's syndrome, *Cortex, 38*(5), 797–803.

Snowden, L. R., & Yamada, A-M. (2005). Cultural differences in access to care. *Annu. Rev. Clin. Psychol., 1,* 143–166.

Snyder, C. R., & Lopez, S. J. (2002). *Handbook of positive psychology.* New York: Oxford University Press.

Snyder, P. J., & Nussbaum, P. D. (1998). *Clinical neuropsychology: A pocket handbook for assessment.* Washington, DC: American Psychological Association.

Soar, K., Turner, J. J. D., & Parrott, A. C. (2001). Psychiatric disorders in Ecstasy (MDMA) users: A literature review focusing on personal predisposition and drug history. *Human Psychopharmacology Clinical & Experimental, 16,* 641–45.

Sobell, M. B., & Sobell, L. C. (1995). Controlled drinking after 25 years: How important was the great debate? *Addiction, 90*(9), 1149–53.

Sokol, M. S., & Pfeffer, C. R. (1992). Suicidal behavior of children. In B. Bongar (Ed.), *Suicide: Guidelines for assessment, management and treatment.* New York: Oxford University Press.

Solomon, D. A., Leon, A. C., Endicott, J., Coryell, W. H., Mueller, T. I., Posternak, M. A., et al. (2003). Unipolar mania over the course of a 20-year follow-up study. *Amer. J. Psychiat., 160*(11), 2049–2051.

Solomon, D. A., Leon, A. C., Endicott, J., Mueller, T. I., Coryell, W., Shea, M. T., et al. (2004). Psychosocial impairment and recurrence of major depression. *Compr. Psychiat., 45*(6), 423–430.

Solomon, D. A., Leon, A. C., Mueller, T. I., Coryell, W., Teres, J. J., Posternak, M. A., et al. (2005). Tachyphylaxes in unipolar major depressive disorder. *J. Clin. Psychiat., 66*(3), 283–290.

Sonnenberg, S. M. (1988). Victims of violence and post-traumatic stress disorder. *Psychiat. Clin. N. Amer., 11,* 581–90.

Southwick, S. M., Yehuda, R., & Morgan, C. A. (1995). Clinical studies of neurotransmitter alterations in post-traumatic stress disorder. In M. Friedman & D. S. Charney, et al. (Eds.), *Neurobiological and clinical consequences of stress: From normal adaptation to post-traumatic stress disorder* (pp. 335–49). Philadelphia: Lippincott-Raven.

Spanos, N. P. (1994). Multiple identity enactments and multiple personality disorder: A sociocognitive perspective. *Psychol. Bull., 116,* 143–65.

Spanos, N. P. (1996). *Multiple identities and false memories: A sociocognitive perspective.* Washington, DC: American Psychological Association.

Spanos, N. P., Weekes, J. R., & Bertrand, L. D. (1985). Multiple personality: A social psychological perspective. *J. Abn. Psychol., 94,* 362–76.

Sparks, D. L., Sabbagh, M. N., Connor, D. J., Lopez, J., Launer, L. J., Browne, P., Wassar, D., Johnson-Traver, S., Lochhead, J., & Ziolkowski, C. (2005). Atorvastatin for the treatment of mild to moderate Alzheimer disease: Preliminary results. *Arch. Neurol., 62*(5), 753–57.

Spataro, J., Mullen, P. M., Burgess, P. M., Wells, D. L., & Moss, S. A. (2004). Impact of child sexual abuse on mental health: Prospective study in males and females. *Brit. J. Psychiat., 184,* 416–21.

Spaulding, W. D., Fleming, S. K., Reed, D., & Sullivan, M. (1999). Cognitive functioning in schizophrenia: Implications for psychiatric rehabilitation. *Schizo. Bull, 25,* 275–89.

Speck, C. E., Kukull, W. A., Brenner, D. E., Bowen, J. D., McCormick, W. C., Teri, L., Pfanschmidt, M. L., Thompson, J. D., & Larson, E. B. (1995). History of depression as a risk factor for Alzheimer's disease. *Epidemiology, 6,* 366–69.

Speed, J. (1996). Behavioral management of conversion disorder: Retrospective study. *Archives of Physical Medicine and Rehabilitation, 77,* 435–54.

Speer, D. C. (1992). Clinically significant change: Jacobson and Truax (1991) revisited. *J. Cons. Clin. Psychol., 60*(3), 402–8.

Speier, P. L., Sherak, D. L., Hirsch, S., & Cantwell, D. P. (1995). Depression in children and adolescents. In E. E. Beckham & W. R. Leber (Eds.), *Handbook of depression* (2nd ed., pp. 467–93). New York: Guilford.

Spencer, T. J. (2004a). ADHD treatment across the life cycle. *J. Clin. Psychiat., 65*(Suppl. 3), 22–26.

Spencer, T. J. (2004b). Non stimulant treatment of adult attention deficit hyperactivity disorder. *Psychiat. Clin. N. Amer., 27,* 373–83.

Sperling, R. A., Bates, J. F., Chua, E. F., Cocchiarella, A. J., Rentz, D. M., Rosen, B. R., Schacter, D. L., & Albert, M. S. (2003). FMRI studies of associative encoding in young and elderly controls and mild Alzheimer's disease. *J. Neurol. Neurosurg. Psychiat., 74,* 44–50.

Spiga, R., Huang, D. B., Meisch, R. A., & Grabowski, J. (2001). Human methadone self-administration: Effects of diazepam pretreatment. *Experimental & Clinical Psychopharmacology, 9,* 40–46.

Spitzer, R. L. (1999). Harmful dysfunction and the DSM definition of mental disorder. *J. Abn. Psychol., 108*(3), 430–32.

Spitzer, R. L., Skodol, A. E., Gibbon, M., & Williams, J. B. W. (1981). *DSM-III casebook.* Washington, DC: American Psychiatric Association.

Spitzer, R. L., Gibbon, M., Skodol, A. E., Williams, J. B. W., & First, M. B. (1989). *DSM-III-R casebook.* Washington, DC: American Psychiatric Press.

Spitzer, R. L., Gibbon, M., Skodol, A. E., Williams, J. B. W., & First, M. B. (Eds.). (1994). *DSM-IV casebook* (4th ed.). Washington, DC: American Psychiatric Press.

Spitzer, R. L., Gibbon, M., Skodol, A. E., Williams, J. B. W., & First, M. B. (Eds.). (2002). *DSM-IV-TR casebook: A learning companion to the Diagnostic and Statistical Manual of Mental Disorders, Fourth Edition, Text Revision.* Washington, DC: American Psyciatric Press.

Sponheim, B. (1996). Changing criteria for autistic disorders: A comparison of the ICD-10 research criteria and DSM-IV with DSM-IIIR, CARS, and ABC. *J. Autism Devel. Dis., 26*(5), 513–25.

Sporn, A., Greenstein, Gogtay, Sailer, F., Hommer, D. W., Rawlings, R., Nicholson, R., Egan, M. F., Lenane, M., Gochman, P., Weinberger, D. R., & Rapoport, J. L. (2005). Childhood-onset schizophrenia: smooth pursuit eye-tracking dysfunction in family members. *Schiz. Res., 73,* 243–252.

Spoth, R., Redmond, C., Shin, C., & Azevedo, K. (2004). Brief family intervention effects on adolescent substance initiation school-level growth curve analyses 6 years following baseline. *J. Cons. Clin. Psychol., 72,* 535–42.

Springelmeyer, P. G., & Chamberlain, P. (2001). Treating antisocial and delinquent youth in out-of-home settings. In J. H. Hughes, A. M. La Greca, & J. C. Conoley (Eds.), *Handbook of psychological services for children and adolescents* (pp. 285–99). Oxford: Oxford University Press.

Spunt, B., Goldstein, P., Brownstein, H., & Fendrich, M. (1994). The role of marijuana in homicide. *Inter. J. Addict., 29,* 195–213.

Squires-Wheeler, E., Friedman, D., Amminger, G. P., Skodol, A., Looser-Ott, S., Roberts, S., Pape, S., & Erlenmeyer-Kimling, L. (1997). Negative and positive dimensions of schizotypal personality disorder. *J. Personal. Dis., 11*(3), 285–300.

Srinivasagam, N. M., Kaye, W. H., Plotnicov, K. H., Greeno, C., Weltzin, T. E., & Rao, R. (1995). Persistent perfectionism, symmetry, and exactness after long-term recovery from anorexia nervosa. *Amer. J. Psychiat., 152*(11), 1630–34.

Srisurapanont, M., Ali, R., Marsden, J., Sunga, A., Wada, K., & Monteiro, M. (2003). Psychotic symptoms in methamphetamine psychotic in-patients. *Int. J. Neuropsychopharm. 6*(4), 347–52.

Sroufe, L. A., Duggal, S., Weinfeld, N., & Carlson, E. (2000). Relationships, development, and psychopathology. In A. J. Sameroff & M. Lewis (Eds.), *Handbook of developmental psychopathology* (2nd ed., pp. 75–91). New York: Kluwer/Plenum.

Stafford, S. H., & Green, V. P. (1993). Facilitating preschool mainstreaming: Classroom strategies and teacher attitude. *Early Child Development & Care, 91,* 93–98.

Stahl, N. D., & Clarizio, H. F. (1999). Conduct disorder and comorbidity. *Psychology in the Schools, 36*(1), 41–50.

Stahl, S. M. (2002). *Essential psychopharmacology of antipsychotics and mood stabilizers.* Cambridge: Cambridge University Press.

Stahl, S. M. (2000). *Essential psychopharmacology: Neuroscientific basis and practical applications* (2nd ed.). Cambridge, UK: Cambridge University Press.

Staley, D., Wand, R., & Shady, G. (1997). Tourette Disorder: A cross-cultural review. *Compr. Psychiat., 38*(1), 6–16.

Standart, S., & Le Couteur, A. (2003). The quiet child: A literature review of selective mutism. *Child & Adolescent Mental Health, 8*(4), 154–60.

Starck, L. C., Branna, S. K., & Tallen, B. J. (1994). Mesoridazine use and priapism. *Amer. J. Psychiat., 151,* 946.

Stark, K. D., Laurent, J., Livingston, R., Boswell, J., & Swearer, S. (1999). Implications of research for the treatment of depressive disorders during childhood. *App. Prev. Psychol., 8*(2), 79–102.

Stark, S., Sachse, R., Liedl, T., Hensen, J., Rohde, G., Wensing, G., et al. (2001). Vardenafil increases penile rigidity and tumescence in men with erectile dysfunction after a single oral dose. *European Urology, 40,* 181–88.

Stattin, H., & Klackenberg-Larsson, I. (1993). Early language and intelligence development and their relationship to future criminal behavior. *J. Abn. Psychol., 102*(3), 369–78.

Steadman, H. J. (2000). From dangerousness to risk assessment of community violence: Taking stock at the turn of the century. *Journal of the American Academy of Psychiatry & Law, 28*(3), 265–71.

Steadman, H. J., McGreevy, M. A., Morrissey, J. P., Callahan, L. A., Robbins, P. C., & Cirincione, C. (1993). *Before and after Hinckley: Evaluating insanity defense reform.* New York: Guilford.

Steadman, H. J., Mulvey, E. P., Monahan, J., Robbins, P. C., Appelbaum, P. S., Grisso, T., Roth, L. H., & Silver, E. (1998). Violence by people discharged from acute psychiatric inpatient facilities and by others in the same neighborhoods. *Arch. Gen. Psychiat., 55,* 393–401.

Steele, R. G., & Forehand, R. (1997). The role of family processes and coping strategies in the relationship between parental chronic illness and childhood internalizing problems. *J. Abnorm. Child Psychol., 25,* 83–94.

Steer, R. A., Clark, D., Beck, A. T., & Ranieri, W. F. (1995). Common and specific dimensions of self-reported anxiety and depression: A replication. *J. Abn. Psychol., 104*(3), 542–45.

Steiger, H., & Seguin, J. (1999). Eating disorders: Anorexia nervosa and bulimia nervosa. In T. Millon, P. H. Blaney, & R. D. Davis (Eds.), *Oxford textbook of psychopathology* (pp. 365–89). New York: Oxford University Press.

Stein, D. B. (1999). *Ritalin is not the answer.* San Francisco: Jossey-Bass.

Stein, J. (1970). *Neurosis in contemporary society: Process and treatment.* Belmont, CA: Brooks/Cole.

Stein, L. I., & Test, M. A. (1980). Alternative to mental hospital treatment: I. Conceptual model, treatment program, and clinical evaluation. *Arch. Gen. Psychiat., 37,* 392–97.

Stein, M.B. (2004). Public health perspectives on generalized anxiety disorder. *J. Clin. Psychiat., 65*(113), 3–7.

Stein, M.B., Heimberg, R.G., & Stein, M.B. (2004). Well-being and life satisfaction in generalized anxiety disorder: Comparison to major depressive disorder in a community sample. *J. Affect. Dis., 79*(1–3), 161–166.

Stein, M.B., Jang, K.L., & Livesley, W.J. (2002). Heritability of social anxiety-related concerns and personality characteristics: A twin study. *J. Nerv. Ment. Dis., 190*(4), 219–224.

Steiner, H. (1996). *Treating adolescents.* San Francisco: Jossey-Bass.

Steinhausen, H. C. (2002). The outcome of anorexia nervosa in the 20th century. *Amer. J. Psychiat., 159,* 1284–93.

Steinhausen, H. C., & Adamek, R. (1997). The family history of children with elective mutism: A research report. *Eur. Child Adoles. Psychiat., 6*(2), 107–11.

Steinhausen, H. C., & Juzi, C. (1996). Elective mutism: An analysis of 100 cases. *J. Amer. Acad. Child Adoles. Psychiat., 35*(5), 606–14.

Steketee, G. S. (1993). *Treatment of obsessive-compulsive disorder.* New York: Guilford.

Steketee, G., & Barlow, D. H. (2002). Obsessive-compulsive disorder. In D. H. Barlow (Ed.), *Anxiety and its disorders* (2nd ed., pp. 516–50). New York: Guilford.

Steketee, G., & Foa, E. B. (1985). Obsessive-compulsive disorder. In D. H. Barlow (Ed.), *Clinical handbook of psychological disorders.* (pp. 69–144). New York: Guilford.

Steketee, G., & Frost, R. (2004). Compulsive hoarding: Current status of research. *Clin. Psychol. Rev., 23,* 905–927.

Stene, J., Stene, E., Stengel-Rutkowski, S., & Murken, J. D. (1981). Paternal age and Down's syndrome, data from prenatal diagnoses (DFG). *Human Genet., 59,* 119–24.

Stephens, R. S., Roffman, R. A., & Simpson, E. E. (1994). Treating adult marijuana dependence: A test of the relapse prevention model. *J. Cons. Clin. Psychol., 62,* 92–99.

Stermac, L. E., Segal, Z. V., & Gillis, R. (1990). Social and cultural factors in sexual assault. In W. L. Marshall, D. R. Laws, & H. E. Barbaree (Eds.), *Handbook of sexual assault* (pp. 143–60). New York: Plenum.

Stern, E., & Silbersweig, D. A. (1998). Neural mechanisms underlying hallucinations in schizophrenia: The role of abnormal front-temporal interactions. In M. F. Lenzenweger & R. H. Dworkin (Eds.), *Origins and development of schizophrenia* (pp. 235–46). Washington, DC: American Psychological Association.

Stewart, D., Gossop, M., & Marsden, J. (2002). Reductions in non-fatal overdose after drug misuse treatment: Results from the National Treatment Outcome Research Study (NTORS). *Journal of Substance Abuse Treatment, 22*(1), 1–9.

Stewart, S. H., Finn, P. R., & Pihl, R. O. (1990, Mar.). *The effects of alcohol on the cardiovascular stress response in men at high risk for alcoholism: A dose response study.* Paper presented at the annual meeting of the Canadian Psychological Association, Ottawa.

Stewart, S. M., Kennan, B. D., Hughes, C. W., Mayes, T. L., Emslie, G. J., Lee, P. W. H. et al. (2004). A cross-cultural investigation of cognitions and depressive symptoms in adolescents. *J. Abn. Psych., 113*(2), 248–257.

Stewart, S. M., Kennard, B. D., Lee, P. W. H., Hughes, C. W., Mayes, T., Emslie, G. J., & Lewinsohn, P. M. (2004). A cross-cultural investigation of cognitions and depressive symptoms in adolescents. *J. Abn. Psychol., 113*(2), 248–57.

Stewart, S.E., Geller, D.A., Jenike, M., Pauls, D., Shaw, D. Mullin, B., et al. (2004). Long-term outcome of pediatric obsessive-compulsive disorder: A meta-analysis and qualitative review of the literature. *Acta Psychiatr. Scandin., 110*(1), 4–13.

Stice, E. (2001). A prospective test of the dual-pathway model of bulimic pathology: Mediating effects of dieting and negative affect. *J. Abn. Psychol., 110*(1), 124–35.

Stice, E. (2002). Risk and maintenance factors for eating pathology: A meta-analytic review. *Psychol. Bull., 128*(5), 825–48.

Stice, E., Presnell, K., & Spangler, D. (2002). Risk factors for binge eating onset in adolescent girls. A 2-year prospective study. *Hlth. Psychol., 21*(2), 131–38.

Stickle, T. R., & Blechman, E. A. (2002). Aggression and fire: Antisocial behavior in firesetting and nonfiresetting juvenile offenders. *J. Psychopath. Behav. Assess, 24,* 177–93

Stinchfield, R. (2002). Youth gambling: How big a problem? *Psychiat. Ann., 32*(3), 197–202.

Stith, S. M., Smith, D. B., Penn, C. E., Ward, D. B., & Tritt, D. (2004). Intimate partner physical abuse penetration and victimization risk factors: A meta-analytic review. *Aggression & Violent Behavior, 10*(1), 65–98.

Stolberg, R. A., Clark, D. C., & Bongar, B. (2002). Epidemiology, assessment, and management of suicide in depressed patients. In I. H. Gotlib & C. L. Hammen (Eds.), *Handbook of depression* (pp. 581–601). New York: Guilford.

Stolberg, R., & Bongar, B. (2002). Assessment of suicide risk. In J. N. Butcher (Ed.), *Clinical personality assessment* (2nd ed., pp. 376–407). New York: Oxford University Press.

Stone, G. C., Weiss, S. M., Matarazzo, J. D., Miller, N. E., Rodin, J., Belar, C. D., Follick, M. J., & Singer, J. E. (Eds.). (1987). *Health psychology: A discipline and a profession.* Chicago: University of Chicago Press.

Stone, J., Zeidler, M., & Sharpe, M. (2003). Misdiagnosis of conversion disorder. *Amer. J. Psychiat., 160*(2), 391.

Stone, S. (1937). Psychiatry through the ages. *J. Abnorm. Soc. Psychol., 32,* 131–60.

Stossel, T. P. (2005). Regulating academic-industrial research relationships—solving problems or stifling progress? *N. Engl. J. Med., 353,* 1060–1065.

Strakowski, S. M. (1994). Diagnostic validity of schizophreniform disorder. *Amer. J. Psychiat., 151*(6), 815–24.

Strange, R. E., & Brown, D. E., Jr. (1970). Home from the wars. *Amer. J. Psychiat., 127*(4), 488–92.

Strauman, T. J., Lemieux, A. M., & Coe, C. L. (1993). Self-discrepancy and natural killer cell activity: Immunological consequences of negative self-evaluation. *J. Pers. Soc. Psychol., 64*(6), 1042–52.

Strauss, R. S., & Pollack, H. A. (2003). Social marginalization of overweight children. *Archives of Pediatric and Adolescent Medicine, 157*(8), 746–53.

Strean, H. S. (1985). *Resolving resistances in psychotherapy.* New York: Wiley Interscience.

Street, A. E., King, L. A., King, D. W., & Riggs, D. S. (2003). The associations among male-perpetrated partner violence, wives' psychological distress and children's behavior problems: A structural equation modeling analysis. *J. Compar. Fam. Stud., 34*(1), 23–40.

Street, W. (1994). *A chronology of noteworthy events in American psychology.* Washington, DC: American Psychological Association.

Striegel-Moore, R. H., Dohm, F. A., Kraemer, H. C., Taylor, C. B., Daniels, S., Crawford, P. B., & Schreiber, G. B. (2003). Eating disorders in white and black women. *Amer. J. Psychiat., 160,* 1326–31.

Strober, M. (1997). Consultation and therapeutic engagement in severe anorexia nervosa. In D. M. Garner & P. E. Garfinkel (Eds.), *Handbook of treatment for eating disorders* (2nd ed., pp. 229–47). New York: Guilford.

Strober, M. (2004). Managing the chronic, treatment-resistant patient with anorexia nervosa. *Int. J. Eat. Dis., 36,* 245–55.

Strober, M., Freeman, R., Lampert, C., Diamond, J., & Kaye, W. (2000). Controlled family study of anorexia nervosa and bulimia nervosa: Evidence of shared liability and transmission of partial syndromes. *Amer. J. Psychiat., 157*(3), 393–401.

Stroebe, M. S., & Stroebe, W. (1983). Who suffers more? Sex differences in health risks of the widowed. *Psychol. Bull., 93*(2), 279–301.

Strote, J., Lee, J. E., & Wechsler, H. (2002). Increasing MDMA use among college students: Results of a national survey. *Journal of Adolescent Health, 30*(1), 64–725.

Strupp, H. H., & Binder, J. L. (1984). *Psychotherapy in a new key: A guide to time-limited dynamic psychotherapy.* New York: Basic Books.

Strupp, H. H., Hadley, S. W., & Gomes-Schwartz, B. (1977). *Psychotherapy for better or worse: An analysis of the problem of negative effects.* New York: Jason Aronson.

Stueve, A., Dohrenwend, B. P., & Skodol, A. E. (1998). Relationships between stressful life events and episodes of major depression and nonaffective psychotic disorders: Selected results from a New York risk factor study. In B. P. Dohrenwend (Ed.), *Adversity, stress, and psychopathology* (pp. 341–57). New York: Oxford University Press.

Stuss, D. T., Gow, C. A., & Hetherington, C. R. (1992). "No longer Gage": Frontal lobe dysfunction and emotional changes. *J. Cons. Clin. Psychol., 60*(3), 349–59.

Substance Abuse and Mental Health Services Administration. Office of Applied Studies. (2004). *Results from the 2003 National Survey on Drug Use and Health: National findings* (NSDUH Series H-25, DHHS Publication No. SMA 04-3964). Rockville, MD: Author.

Sue, S. (1998). In search of cultural competence in psychotherapy and counseling. *Amer. Psychol., 53,* 440–48.

Sue, S. (1999). Science, ethnicity, and bias: Where have we gone wrong? *Amer. Psychol., 54,* 1070–77.

Sue, S. & Chang, J. (2003). The state of psychological assessment in Asia. *Psychol. Assess., 15*(3), 306–310.

Sue, S., Zane, N., & Young, K. (1994). Research on psychotherapy with culturally diverse populations. In A. E. Bergin & S. L. Garfield (Eds.), *Handbook of psychotherapy and behavior change* (pp. 783–820). New York: Wiley.

Sugerman, H. J., Fairman, R. P., Sood, R. K., Engle, K., Wolfe, L., & Kellum, J. M. (1992). Long-term effects of gastric surgery for treating respiratory insufficiency of obesity. *Amer. J. Clin. Nutri., 55*(2, suppl.), 597S–601S.

Sullivan, E. V., Deshmukh, A., Desmond, J. E., Lim, K. O., & Pfefferbaum, A. (2000). Cerebellar volume decline in normal aging, alcoholism, and Korsakoff's Syndrome relation to Ataxia. *Neuropsychology, 14*(3), 341–52.

Sullivan, J., & Chang, P. (1999). Review: Emotional and behavioral functioning in phenylketonuria. *J. Pediat. Psychol., 24,* 281–99.

Sullivan, P. F. (2002). Course and outcome of anorexia nervosa and bulimia nervosa. In C. G. Fairburn & K. D. Brownell (Eds.), *Eating disorders and obesity: A comprehensive handbook* (2nd ed., pp. 226–30). New York: Guilford.

Sullivan, P. F., Neale, M. C., & Kendler, K. S. (2000). Genetic epidemiology of major depression: Review and meta-analysis. *Amer. J. Psychiat., 157*(10), 1552–62.

Sundquist, K., Frank, G., & Sundquist, J. (2004). Urbanisation and incidence of psychosis and depression. Follow-up study of 4.4 million women and men in Sweden. *Brit. J. Psychiat., 184,* 293–98.

Sunjic, S., & Zabor, D. (1999). Methadone syrup-related deaths in New South Wales, Australia, 1990–95. *Drug & Alcohol Review, 18,* 409–15.

Susser, E., Moore, R., & Link, B. (1993). Risk factors for homelessness. *Amer. J. Epidemiol., 15,* 546–66.

Susser, E., Neugebauer, R., Hoek, H. W., Brown, A. S., Lin, S., Labovitz, D., & Gorman, J. (1996). Schizophrenia after prenatal famine. *Arch. Gen. Psychiat., 53,* 25–31.

Sussman, S., Earleywine, M., Wills, T., Cody, C., Biglan, T., Dent, C. W., & Newcomb, M. D. (2004). The motivation, skills, and decision-making model of "drug abuse" prevention. *Substance Use & Misuse, 39,* 1971–2016.

Sutker, P. B., & Allain, A. N. (1995). Psychological assessment of aviators captured in World War II. *Psychol. Assess., 7,* 66–68.

Sutker, P. B., & Allain, A. N. (2001). Antisocial personality disorder. In H. E. Adams & P. B. Sutker (Eds.), *Comprehensive handbook of psychopathology* (pp. 445–90). New York: Kluwer Academic.

Sutker, P. B., Allain, A. N., Johnson, J. J., & Butters, N. M. (1992). Memory and learning performances in POW survivors with history of malnutrition and combat veteran controls. *Arch. Clin. Neuropsychol., 7,* 431–44.

Sutton, J., Smith, P. K., & Swettenham, J. (1999). Bullying and "theory of mind": A critique of the "social skills deficit" view of antisocial behaviour. *Soc. Develop., 8,* 117–27.

Sutton, S. K., Vitale, J. E., & Newman, J. P. (2002). Emotion among women with psychopathy during picture perception. *J. Abn. Psychol., 111*(4), 610–19.

Suzuki, M., Zhou, S. Y., Hagino, H., Takahashi, T., Kawasaki, Y., Nohara, S., Yamashita, I., Matsui, M., Seto, H., & Kurachi, M. (2004). Volume reduction of the right anterior limb of the internal capsule in patients with schizotypal disorder. *Psychiatry Research: Neuroimaging, 130*(3), 213–25.

Svensson, L., Larsson, A., & Oest, L.-G. (2002). How children experience brief-exposure treatment of specific phobias. *J. Comm. Psychol., 31*(1), 80–89.

Sverd, J., Sheth, R., Fuss, J., & Levine, J. (1995). Prevalence of pervasive developmental disorder in a sample of psychiatrically hospitalized children and adolescents. *Child Psychiat. Human Devel., 25*(4), 221–40.

Swartz, M., Swanson, J. W., & Elbogen, E. B. (2004). Psychiatric advance directives: Practical, legal, and ethical issues. *J. Foren. Psychol. Pract., 4*(4), 97–107.

Swendsen, J., Hammen, C., Heller, T., & Gitlin, M. (1995). Correlates of stress reactivity in patients with bipolar disorder. *Amer. J. Psychiat., 152*(5), 795–97.

Sylvain, C., Ladouceur, R., & Boisvert, J. M. (1997). Cognitive and behavioral treatment of pathological gambling: A controlled study. *J. Cons. Clin. Psychol., 65*(5), 727–32.

Symes, L. (2000). Arriving at readiness to recover emotionally after sexual assault. *Archives of Psychiatric Nursing, 14,* 30–38.

Symonds, M. (1976). The rape victim. Psychological patterns of response. *Amer. J. Psychoanal., 36*(1), 27–34.

Symons, D. (1979). *The evolution of human sexuality.* New York: Oxford University Press.

Sypeck, M. F., Gray, J. J., & Ahrens, A. H. (2004). No longer just a pretty face: Fashion magazines' depictions of ideal female beauty from 1959–1999. *Int. J. Eat. Dis., 36,* 342–47.

Szasz, T. (1974). *The myth of mental illness* (Rev. ed., pp. 17–80). New York: Harper & Row.

Szasz, T. S. (1999). *Fatal freedom: The ethics and politics of suicide.* Westport, CT: Praeger.

Szmukler, G. (2001). Violence risk prediction in practice. *Brit. J. Psychiat., 178,* 84–85.

Takahashi, K., Miura, S., Mori-Abe, A., Kawagoe, J., Takata, K., Ohmichi, M., & Kurachi, H. (2005). Impact of menopause on augmentation of arterial stiffness with aging. *Gynecologic and Obstetric Investigation, 60,* 162–66.

Takei, N., Persaud, R., Woodruff, P., Brockington, I., & Murray, R. M. (1998). First episodes of psychosis in Afro-Caribbean and white people: An 18-year follow-up population-based study. *Brit. J. Psychiat., 172,* 147–54.

Takeshita, T. K., Morimoto, X., Mao, Q., Hashimoto, T., & Furyuama, J. (1993). Phenotypic differences in low Km Aldehyde de hydrogenase in Japanese workers. *Lancet, 341,* 837–38.

Tamminga, C. A., Thaker, G. K., & Medoff, D. R. (2002). Neuropsychiatric aspects of schizophrenia. In S. Yudofsky & R. E. Hales (Eds.), *The American Psychiatric Association Publishing textbook of neuropsychiatry and clinical sciences* (4th ed., pp. 989–1048). Washington, DC: American Psychiatric Publishing.

Tang, T. Z., & DeRubeis, R. J. (1999). Sudden gains and critical sessions in cognitive-behavioral therapy for depression. *J. Cons. Clin. Psychol., 67,* 894–904.

Tang, T. Z., Luborsky, L., & Andrusyna, T. (2002). Sudden gains in recovering from depression: Are they also found in psychotherapies other than cognitive-behavioral therapy? *J. Cons. Clin. Psychol., 70,* 444–47.

Tardiff, K. (1998). Unusual diagnoses among violent patients. *Psychiat. Clin. N. Amer., 21*(3), 567–76.

Tareen, A., Hodes, M., & Rangel, L. (2005). Non-fat phobic anorexia nervosa in British South Asian adolescents. *Int. J. Eat. Dis., 37,* 161–65.

Tarrier, N., Kinney, C., McCarthy, E., Humphreys, L., Wittkowski, A., & Morris, J. (2000). Two-year follow-up of cognitive-behavioral therapy and supportive counseling in the treatment of persistent symptoms in chronic schizophrenia. *J. Cons. Clin. Psychol., 68* (5), 917–22.

Tarrier, N., Lowson, K., & Barrowclough, C. (1991). Some aspects of family interventions in schizophrenia, II: Financial considerations. *Brit. J. Psychiat., 159,* 481–84.

Tarrier, N., Wittkowski, A., Kinney, C., McCarthy, E., Morris, J., & Humphreys, L. (1999). Durability of the effects of cognitive-behavioral therapy in the treatment of chronic schizophrenia: 12-month follow-up. *Brit. J. Psychiat., 174,* 500–04.

Tarrier, N., Yusupoff, L., Kinney, C., McCarthy, E., Gledhill, A., Haddock, G., & Morris, J. (1998). Randomised controlled trial of intensive cognitive behaviour therapy for patients with chronic schizophrenia. *Brit. Med. J., 317*(7154), 303–7.

Tatem, D. W., & DelCampo, R. L. (1995). Selective mutism in children: A structural family therapy approach to treatment. *Contemporary Family Therapy: An International Journal, 17*(2), 177–94.

Tateno, A., Murata, Y., & Robinson, R. G. (2002). Comparison of cognitive impairment associated with major depression following stroke versus traumatic brain injury. *Psychosomatics, 43*(4), 295–301.

Tatetsu, S. (1964). Methamphetamine psychosis. *Folia Psychiatrica et Neurologica Japonica* (suppl. 7), 377–80.

Tavel, M. E. (1962). A new look at an old syndrome: Delirium tremens. *Arch. Int. Med., 109,* 129–34.

Taylor, C., & Meux, C. (1997). Individual cases: The risk, the challenge. *Int. Rev. Psychiat., 9*(2), 285–302.

Taylor, C. B., Youngblood, M. E., Catellier, D., Veith, R. C., Carney, R. M., Burg, M. M., Kaufmann, P. G., Shuster, J., Mellman, T., Blumenthal, J. A., Krishnan, R., Jaffe, A. S. (2005). Effects of antidepressant medication on morbidity and mortality in depressed patients after myocardial infarction. *Arch. Gen. Psychiat., 62,* 792–98.

Taylor, H. G., & Alden, J. (1997). Age-related differences in outcomes following childhood brain insults: An introduction and overview. *J. Int. Neuropsychologic. Soc., 3*(6), 555–67.

Taylor, R. L. (2000). *Distinguishing psychological from organic disorders: Screening for psychological masquerade* (2nd ed.). New York: Springer.

Taylor, S. (2003). Anxiety sensitivity and its implications for understanding and treating PTSD. *J. Cog. Psychother., 17*(2), 179–86.

Taylor, S., & Asmundson, G. J. G. (2004). *Treating health anxiety: A cognitive-behavioural approach.* New York: Guilford Press.

Taylor, W. S., & Martin, M. F. (1944). Multiple personality. *J. Abnorm. Soc. Psychol., 39,* 281–300.

Teasdale, G. M., Nicoll, J. A. R., Murray, G., et al. (1997). Association of apolipoprotein E polymorphism with outcome after head injury. *Lancet, 350,* 1069–71.

Teasdale, J. (1988). Cognitive vulnerability to persistent depression. *Cognition and Emotion, 2,* 247–74.

Teasdale, J. D. (1996). Clinically relevant therapy: Integrating clinical insight with cognitive science. In P. M. Salkovskis (Ed.), *Frontiers of cognitive therapy* (pp. 26–47). New York: Guilford.

Teasdale, J. D., Scott, J., Moore, R. G., Hayhurst, H., Pope, M., & Paykel, E. S. (2001). How does cognitive therapy prevent relapse in residual depression? Evidence from a controlled trial. *J. Cons. Clin. Psychol., 69*(3), 347–57.

Tein, J. Y., Sandler, I., & Zautra, A. (2000). Stressful life events, psychological distress, coping and parenting of divorced mothers: A longitudinal study. *J. Fam. Psychol., 14,* 27–41.

Telch, C. F., & Stice, E. (1998). Psychiatric comorbidity in women with binge eating disorder: Prevalence rates from a non-treatment-seeking sample. *J. Cons. Clin. Psychol., 66*(5), 768–76.

Telch, M. J., Schmidt, N. B., LaNae Jaimez, T., Jacquin, K. M., & Harrington, P. J. (1995). Impact of cognitive-behavioral treatment on quality of life in panic disorder patients. *J. Cons. Clin. Psychol., 63*(5), 823–30.

Telcher, M. H., Glod, C. A., Magnus, E., Harper, D., Benson, G., Krueger, K., & McGreenery, C. E. (1997). Circadian rest-activity disturbances in seasonal affective disorder. *Arch. Gen. Psychiat., 54,* 124–30.

Tennant, C. (2001). Work-related stress and depressive disorders. *J. Psychosom. Res., 51*(5), 697–704.

Tennen, H., & Affleck, G. (1987). The costs and benefits of optimistic explanations and dispositional optimism. *J. Personal, 55,* 377–93.

Teplin, L. A., Abram, K. M., & McClelland, G. M. (1997). Mentally disordered women in jail: Who receives services? *Amer. J. Pub. Hlth., 87*(4), 604–9.

Terasahjo, T. & Salmvivalli, C. (2003). "She is not actually bullied." The discourse of harassment in student groups. *Aggr. Behav., 29*(2), 134–154.

Teri, L., et al. (1997). Behavioral treatment of depression in dementia patients: A controlled clinical trial. *J. Gerontol.,* Series B, 52B, P159–P166.

Thapar, A., Holmes, J., Poulten, K., & Harrington, R. (1999). Genetic bias of attention deficit and hyperactivity. *Brit. J. Psychiat., 174,* 105–111.

Thase, M. E., & Howland, R. H. (1995). Biological processes in depression: An updated review and integration. In E. E. Beckham & W. H. R. Leber (Eds.), *Handbook of depression* (2nd ed., pp. 213–79). New York: Guilford.

Thase, M. E., & Jindal, R. D. (2004). Combining psychotherapy and pharmacotherapy for the treatment of mental disorders. In M. J. Lambert (2004). *Bergin and Garfield's handbook of Psychotherapy and behavior change.* New York: John Wiley and Sons, pp. 743–766.

Thase, M. E., Entsuah, A. R., & Rudolph, R. L. (2001). Remission rates during treatment with venlafaxine or selective serotonin reuptake inhibitors. *Brit. J. Psychiat., 178,* 234–41.

Thase, M. E., Greenhouse, J. B., Frank, E., Reynolds, C. F., III, Pilkonis, P. A., Hurley, K., Grochocinski, V., & Kupfer, D. J. (1997). Treatment of major depression with psychotherapy or psychotherapy–pharmacotherapy combinations. *Arch. Gen. Psychiat., 54,* 1009–15.

Thase, M. E., Jindal, R., & Howland, R. H. (2002). Biological aspects of depression. In I. H. Gotlib & C. L. Hammen (Eds.), *Handbook of depression* (pp. 192–218). New York: Guilford.

Thase, M. E., Salloum, I. M., & Cornelius, J. D. (2001). Comorbid alcoholism and depression: Treatment issues. *J. Clin. Psychiat., 62,* 32–41.

Theodorou, S., & Haber, P. S. (2005). The medical complications of heroin use. *Cur. Opin. in Psychiat., 18*(3), 257–63.

Theorell, T., Emdad, R., Arnetz, B., & Weingarten, A. (2001). Employee effects of an educational program for managers at an insurance company. *Psychosom. Med., 63,* 724–33.

Theun, F. (2000). Psychiatric symptoms and perceived need for psychiatric care after divorce. *Journal of Divorce & Remarriage, 34,* 61–76.

Thomas, A. K., & Loftus, E. F. (2002). Creating bizarre false memories through imagination. *Memory and Cognition, 30,* 423–31.

Thomas, J. D., & Riley, E. P. (1998). Fetal alcohol syndrome: Does alcohol withdrawal play a role?, *Alcohol World: Health and Research, 22*(1), 47–53.

Thompson, P. M., Vidal, C., Giedd, J. N., Gochman, P., Blumenthal, J., Nicolson, R., Toga, A. W., & Rapoport, J. L.. (2001). Mapping adolescent brain changes reveals dynamic wave of accelerated gray matter loss in very early-onset schizophrenia. *Proceedings of the National Academy of Sciences, 98, 20,* 11650–5.

Thompson, R. A., & Nelson, C. A. (2001). Developmental science and the media: Early brain development. *Amer. Psychol., 56,* 5–15.

Thompson, R. F. (2000). *The brain: A neuroscience primer* (3rd ed.). New York: Worth.

Thompson, S. B. N. (2003). Rate of decline in social and cognitive abilities in dementing individuals with Down's syndrome and other learning disabilities. *Clin. Geron., 26*(3–4), 145–53.

Thornicroft, G., & Tansella, M. (2000). Planning and providing mental health services for a community. In M. G. Gelder, J. J. Lopez-Ibor, Jr., & N. C. Andreason (Eds.), *New Oxford textbook of psychiatry* (pp. 1547–58). Oxford: Oxford University Press.

Tidey, J. W., & Miczek, K. A. (1996). Social defeat stress selectively alters mesocorticolimbic dopamine release: An in vivo micro-dialysis study. *Brain Research, 721,* 140–49.

Tien, A. Y., & Eaton, W. W. (1992). Psychopathologic precursors and sociodemographic risk factors for the schizophrenia syndrome. *Arch. Gen. Psychiat., 49*(1), 37–46.

Tienari, P., Lahti, I., Sorri, A., Naarala, M., Moring, J., Wahlberg, K.-E., & Wynne, L. C. (1987). The Finnish adoptive family study of schizophrenia. *J. Psychiat. Res., 21,* 437–45.

Tienari, P., Wynne, L. C., Läksy, K., Moring, J., Nieminen, P., Sorri, A., Lahti, I., & Wahlberg, K.-E. (2003). Genetic boundaries of the schizophrenia spectrum: Evidence from the Finnish adoptive family study. *Amer. J. Psychiat., 160,* 1587–94.

Tienari, P., Wynne, L. C., Moring, J., Läksy, K., Nieminen, P., Sorri, A., Lahti, I., Wahlberg, K.-E., Naarala, M., Kurki-Suonio, K., Saarento, O., Koistinen, P., Tarvainen, T., Hakko, H., & Miettunen, J. (2000). Finnish adoptive family study: Sample selection and adoptee DSM-III-R diagnoses. *Acta Psychiatr. Scandin., 101,* 433–43.

Tienari, P., Wynne, L. C., Sorri, A., Lahti, I., Läksy, K., Moring, J., Naarala, M., Nieminen, P., & Wahlberg, K.-E. (2004). Geneotype-environment interaction in schizophrenia-spectrum disorder. *Brit. J. Psychiat., 184,* 216–22.

Tillfors, M. (2004). Why do some individuals develop social phobia? A review with emphasis on the neurobiological influences. *Nord. J. Psychiat., 58*(4), 267–276.

Time. January 15, 1973, p. 53.

Tims, F. M., Leukefeld, C. G., & Platt, J. J. (2001). *Relapse and recovery in addictions.* New Haven: Yale University Press.

Tinker, J. E., & Tucker, J. A. (1997). Motivations for weight loss and behavior change strategies associated with natural recovery from obesity. *Psychology of Addictive Behaviors, 11,* 98–106.

Tizard, J. (1975). Race and IQ: The limits of probability. *New Behaviour, 1,* 6–9.

Tomarken, A. J., Mineka, S., & Cook, M. (1989). Fear-relevant selective associations and covariation bias. *J. Abn. Psychol., 98,* 381–94.

Tomarken, A. J., Simien, C., & Garber, J. (1994). Resting frontal brain asymmetry discriminates adolescent children of depressed mothers from low-risk controls. *Psychophysiology, 31,* 97–98.

Toneatto, T., Sobell, L. C., Sobell, M. B., & Rubel, E. (1999). Natural recovery from cocaine dependence. *Psychology of Addictive Behaviors, 13*(4), 259–68.

Tong, J., Miao, S. J., Wang, J., Zhang, J. J., Wu, H. M., Li, T., & Hsu, L. K. G. (2005). Five cases of male eating disorders in Central China. *Int. J. Eat. Dis., 37,* 72–75.

Tonigan, J. S., Toscova, R., & Miller, W. R. (1995). Meta-analysis of the literature on Alcoholics Anonymous. *J. Stud. Alcoh., 57*(1), 65–72.

Took, K. J., & Buck, B. L. (1996). Enuresis with combined risperidone and SSRI use. *J. Amer. Acad. Child Adoles. Psychiat., 35*(7), 840–41.

Torgersen, S., Kringlen, E., & Cramer, V. (2001). The prevalence of personality disorders in a community sample. *Arch. Gen. Psychiat., 58*(6), 590–96.

Torgersen, S., Lygren, S., Oien, P. A., Skre, I., Onstad, S., Edvardsen, J., Tambs, K., & Kringlen, E. (2000). A twin study of personality disorders. *Compr. Psychiat., 41*(6), 416–25.

Torgersen, S. (1993). Genetics. In A. S. Bellack & M. Hersen (Eds.), *Psychopathology in adulthood.* Needham Heights, MA: Allyn and Bacon.

Torrey, E. F., Bower, A. E., Taylor, E. H., & Gottesman, I. I. (1994). *Schizophrenia and manic-depressive disorder: The biological roots of mental illness as revealed by the landmark study of identical twins.* New York: Basic Books.

Torrey, E. F. (1989). Headache in schizophrenia and seasonality of births. *Biolog. Psychiat.,* 852–53.

Torrey, E. F. (1997). *Out of the shadows: Confronting America's mental illness crisis.* New York: Wiley.

Toth, S. L., Manly, J. T., & Cicchetti, D. (1992). Child maltreatment and vulnerability to depression. *Develop. Psychopath., 4,* 97–112.

Tower, R. B., Kasl, S. V., & Moritz, D. J. (1997). The influence of spouse cognitive impairment on respondents' depressive symptoms: The moderating role of marital closeness. *J. Gerontol.,* Series B, 52B(5), S270–S278.

Townsend, J., Harris, N. S., & Courchesne, E. (1996). Visual attention abnormalities in autism: Delayed orienting to location. *J. Int. Neuropsycholog. Assoc., 2,* 541–50.

Townsley, R., Turner, S., Beidel, D., & Calhoun, K. (1995). Social phobia: An analysis of possible developmental factors. *J. Abn. Psychol., 104,* 526–31.

Tozzi, F., Sullivan, P. F., Fear, J. L., McKenzie, J., & Bulik, C. M. (2003). Causes and recovery in anorexia nervosa: The patient's perspective. *Int. J. Eat. Dis., 33,* 143–54.

Trasler, G. (1978). Relations between psychopathy and persistent criminality-methodological and theoretical issues. In R. D. Hare & D. Schalling (Eds.), *Psychopathic behavior: Approaches to research.* New York: Wiley.

Travis, J. (1996). Visualizing vision in dyslexic brains. *Sci. News, 149,* 105.

Treatment for Adolescents with Depression Study (TADS) Team, US. (2004). Fluoxetine, cognitive-behavioral therapy, and their combination for adolescents with depression: Treatment for Adolescents with Depression Study (TADS) randomized controlled trial. *JAMA,* August 18, 807–820.

Tremble, J., Padillo, A., & Bell, C. (1994). *Drug abuse among ethnic minorities, 1987.* Washington, DC: U.S. Department of Health and Human Services.

Trim, R. S., & Chassin, L. (2004). Drinking restraint, alcohol consumption and alcohol dependence among children of alcoholics. *J. Stud. Alcoh., 65*(1), 122–25.

Tronick, E. Z., & Cohn, J. F. (1989). Infant-mother face-to-face interaction: Age and gender differences in coordination and miscoordination. *Child Develop., 59,* 85–92.

Trope, H. (1997). *Locura y sociedad en la valencia de los siglos XV al XVII: Los locos del Hospital de los Inocentes sus instituciones La Locura y sus instuciones.* Valencia: Disputacion de Valencia, 141–54.

Trzepacz, P. T., Meagher, D. J., & Wise, M. G. (2002). Neuropsychiatric aspects of delirium. In S. C. Yudofsky & R. E. Hales (Eds.), *The American Psychiatric Publishing textbook of neuropsychiatry and clinical neurosciences* (pp. 525–64). Washington, DC: American Psychiatric Publishing.

Tsai, A. G., & Wadden, T. A. (2005). Systematic review: An evaluation of major commercial weight loss programs in the United States. *Ann. Int. Med.,* 142(1), 56–66.

Tsai, A., Loftus, E., & Polage, D. (2000). Current directions in false-memory research. In D. Bjourkund (Ed.), *False-memory creation in children and adults: Theory, research, and implications* (pp. 31–44). Mahwah, NJ: Erlbaum.

Tsai, G. E., Condie, D., Wu, M., & Chang, I. (1999). Functional magnetic resonance imaging of personality switches in a woman with dissociative identity disorder. *Harvard Review of Psychiatry, 7,* 119–22.

Tsai, J. L., & Chentsova-Dutton, Y. (2002). Understanding depression across cultures. In I. H. Gotlib & C. L. Hammen (Eds.), *Handbook of depression* (pp. 467–91). New York: Guilford.

Tsai, J. L., Butcher, J. N., Munoz, R. F., & Vitousek, K. (2001). Culture, ethnicity, and psychopathology. In P. B. Sutker & H. E. Adams (Eds.), *Comprehensive handbook of psychopathology* (3rd ed., pp. 105–27). New York: Kluwer/Plenum.

Tsai, L. Y., & Ghaziuddin, M. (1992). Biomedical research in autism. In D. M. Berkell (Ed.), *Autism* (pp. 53–76). Hillsdale: Erlbaum.

Tseng, W. S. (1973). The development of psychiatric concepts in traditional Chinese medicine. *Arch. Gen. Psychiat., 29*(4), 569–75.

Tseng, W., Asai, M., Kitanishi, K., McLaughlin, D. G., & Kyomen, H. (1992). Diagnostic patterns of social phobia: Comparison in Tokyo and Hawaii. *J. Nerv. Ment. Dis., 180,* 380–85.

Tseng, W. (2001). *Handbook of cultural psychiatry.* San Diego: Academic Press.

Tsuang, M. T., Taylor, L., & Faraone, S. V. (2004). An overview of the genetics of psychotic mood disorders. *J. Psychiat. Res., 38,* 3–15.

Tucker, G. J. (1998). Editorial: Putting DSM-IV in perspective. *Amer. J. Psychiat., 155*(2), 159–61.

Tuke, D. H. (1882). *History of the insane in the British Isles.* London: Kegan, Paul, Trench.

Tuomisto, M. T. (1997). Intra-arterial blood pressure and heart rate reactivity to behavioral stress in normotensive, borderline, and mild hypertensive men. *Hlth. Psychol., 16*(6), 554–65.

Turan, M., & Senol, S. (2000). Tic disorders in children and adolescents. *Psikiyatri Psikoloji Psikofarmakoloji Dergisis, 8,* 215–20.

Turner, J. R. (1994). *Cardiovascular reactivity and stress: Patterns of physiological response.* New York: Plenum.

Turrisi, R., Wiersma, K. A., & Hughes, K. K. (2000). Binge-drinking-related consequences in college students: Role of drinking beliefs and mother–teen communications. *Psychology of Addictive Behaviors, 14*(4), 342–55.

Turrisi, R. (1999). Cognitive and attitudinal factors in the analysis of alternatives to binge drinking. *Journal of Applied Social Psychology, 29,* 1510–33.

Twenge, J. M. & Campbell, W. K. (2002). Self-esteem and socioeconomic status: A meta-analytic review. *Personal. Soc. Psychol. Rev., 6*(1), 59–71.

Twenge, J. M., & Nolen-Hoeksema, S. (2002). Age, gender, race, socioeconomic status, and birth cohort difference on the children's depression inventory: A meta-analysis. *J. Abn. Psychol., 111*(4), 578–588.

Tyor, P. L., & Bell, L. V. (1984). *Caring for the retarded in America: A history.* Westport, CT: Greenwood Press.

Tyrka, A. R., Cannon, T. D., Haslam, N., Mednick, S. A., Schulsinger, F., Schulsinger, H., & Parnas, J. (1995). The latent structure of schizotypy: I. Premorbid indicators of a taxon of individuals at risk for schizophrenia-spectrum disorders. *J. Abn. Psychol., 104*(1), 173–183.

U.S. Committee for Refugees. (2001). *World refugee survey.* Washington, DC: Immigration and Refugee Services of America.

U.S. Department of Health and Human Services. Public Health Service. (1997). *Survey of heroin use in the United States.* Rockville, MD: Author.

U.S. Department of Health and Human Services. (2001). *Mental health: Culture, race, and ethnicity—A supplement to mental health: A report of the Surgeon General.* Rockville, MD: U.S. Department of Health and Human Services, Public Health Service, Office of the Surgeon General.

Uchino, B. N., Cacioppo, J. T., & Kiecolt-Glaser, K. G. (1996). The relationships between social support and physiological processes: A review with emphasis on underlying mechanisms and implications for health. *Psychol. Bull., 119,* 488–531.

Udry, J. R. (1993). The politics of sex research. *J. Sex Res., 30,* 103–10.

Uecker, A., Mangan, P. A., Obrzut, J. E., & Nadel, L. (1993). Down syndrome in neurobiological perspective: An emphasis on spatial cognition. *J. Clin. Child Psychol., 22*(2), 266–76.

Uhde, T. W. (1990). Caffeine provocation of panic: A focus on biological mechanisms. In J. C. Ballenger (Ed.), *Neurobiology of panic disorder* (pp. 219–42). New York: Wiley-Liss.

Ullman, S. E., & Filipas, H. H. (2001). Predictors of PTSD symptom severity and social reactions in sexual assault victims. *J. Trauma. Stress., 14*(2), 369–89.

USDHHS. (1994). Preventing tobacco use among young people: A report of the Surgeon General. U.S. Department of Health and Human Services.

Üstün, T. B., Ayuso-Mateos, S., Chatterji, S., Mathers, C., & Murray, C. J. L. (2004). Global burden of depressive disorders in the year 2000. *Brit. J. Psychiat., 184,* 386–392.

Üstün, T. B., Bertelsen, A., Dilling, H., van Drimmelen, J., Pull, C., Okasha, A., Sartorius, N., and other ICD-10 Reference and Training Directors. (1996). *ICD-10 casebook. The many faces of mental disorders: Adult case histories according to ICD-10.* Washington, DC: American Psychiatric Press.

Vaillant, G. E., Gale, L., & Milofsky, E. S. (1982). Natural history of male alcoholism: II. The relationship between different diagnostic dimensions. *J. Stud. Alcoh., 43*(3), 216–32.

Valdez, R., & Williamson, D. F. (2002). Prevalence and demographics of obesity. In C. G. Fairburn & K. D. Brownell (Eds.), *Eating disorders and obesity: A comprehensive handbook* (2nd ed., pp. 417–21). New York: Guilford.

Valentiner, D. B., Foa, E. B., Riggs, D. S., & Gershuny, B. S. (1996). Coping strategies and posttraumatic stress disorder in female victims of sexual and nonsexual assault. *J. Abn. Psychol., 105*(3), 455–58.

Van Der Flier, W. M., Van Den Heuvel, D. M., Weverling-Rijnsburger, A. W., Bollen, E. L., Westendorp, R. G., Van Buchem M. A., & Middelkoop, H. A. (2002). Magnetization transfer imaging in normal aging, mild cognitive impairment, and Alzheimer's disease. *Ann. Neurol., 52,* 62–67.

van der Kolk, B. A., & Saporta, J. (1993). Biological responses to psychic trauma. In J. P. Wilson, B. Raphael, et al. (Eds.), *International handbook of traumatic stress syndromes* (pp. 25–33). New York: Plenum.

van Dongen, M. J., van Rossum, E., Kessels, A., Sielhorst, H., & Knipschild, P. (2000). The efficacy of Ginkgo for elderly people with dementia and age-associated memory impairment: New results of a randomized clinical trial. *J. Amer. Geriat. Soc., 48,* 1183–94.

Van Doren, C. V. (1938). *Benjamin Franklin.* New York: Penguin.

Van Kampen, J., & Katz, M. (2001). Persistent psychosis after a single ingestion of "ecstasy." *Psychosomatics: Journal of Consultation Liaison Psychiatry, 42*(6), 525–27.

Van Lier, P. A. C., Muthen, B. O., van der Sar, R. M., & Crijnen, A. A. M. (2004). Preventing disruptive behavior in elementary schoolchildren: Impact of a universal classroom-based intervention. *J. Cons. Clin. Psychol., 72,* 467–78.

van Ommeren, M., de Jong, J. T. V. M., Sharma, B., Komproe, I., Thapa, S. B., & Cardena, E. (2001). Psychiatric disorders among tortured Bhutanese refugees in Nepal. *Arch. Gen. Psychiat., 58,* 475–82.

van Os, J., Bak, M., Hanssen, M., Bijl, R. V., de Graaf, R., & Verdoux, H. (2002). Cannabis use and psychosis: A longitudinal population-based study. *Amer. J. Epidemiol., 156,* 319–27.

van Os, J. (2004). Does the urban environment cause psychosis? *Brit. J. Psychiat., 184,* 287–88.

Van Ree, J. M. (1996). Endorphins and experimental addiction. *Alcohol, 13*(1), 25–30.

VandenBos, G. R. (1986). Psychotherapy research: A special issue. *Amer. Psychol., 41,* 111–12.

Vandereycken, W. (2002). History of anorexia nervosa and bulimia nervosa. In C. G. Fairburn & Kelly D. Brownell (Eds). *Eating disorders and obesity* (2nd edition). New York: Guilford Press. pp. 151–154.

Vargas, M. A., & Davidson, J. (1993). Posttraumatic stress disorder. *Psychiat. Clin. N. Amer., 16,* 737–48.

Vasiljeva, O. A., Kornetov, N. A., Zhankov, A. I., & Reshetnikov, V. I. (1989). Immune function in psychogenic depression. *Amer. J. Psychiat., 146,* 284–85.

Vastag, B. (2003, Apr. 9). Experimental drugs take aim at obesity. *JAMA, 289*(14), 1763–64.

Veale, D., & Riley, S. (2001). Mirror, mirror on the wall, who is the ugliest of them all? The psychopathology of mirror gazing in body dysmorphic disorder. *Behav. Res. Ther., 39,* 1381–93.

Vega, W. A., Zimmerman, R. S., Warheit, G. J., Apospori, E., & Gil, A. G. (1993). Risk factors for early adolescent drug use in four ethnic and racial groups. *Amer. J. Pub. Hlth., 83,* 185–89.

Velasquez, M. M., Maurer, G. G., Crouch, C., & DiClemente, C. C. (2001). *Group treatment of substance abuse.* New York: Guilford.

Velting, D. M., & Gould, M. S. (1997). Suicide contagion. In R. W. Maris, M. M. Silverman, & S. S. Canetton (Eds.), *Review of Suicidology, 1997* (pp. 96–137). New York: Guilford.

Ventura, J., Nuechterlein, K. H., Hardesty, J. P., & Gitlin, M. (1992). Life events and schizophrenic relapse after withdrawal of medication. *Brit. J. Psychiat., 161,* 615–20.

Ventura, J., Nuechterlein, K. H., Lukoff, D., & Hardesty, J. P. (1989). A prospective study of stressful life events and schizophrenic relapse. *J. Abn. Psychol., 98,* 407–11.

Verdejo, A., Toribio, I., Orozco, C., Puente, K. L., & Pérez-García, M. (2005). Neuropsychological functioning in methadone maintenance patients versus abstinent heroin abusers. *Drug Al. Dep., 78*(3), 283–88.

Verghese, J., Lipton, R. B., Hall, C. B., Kuslansky, G., Katz, M. J., & Buschke, H. (2002). Abnormality of gait as a predictor of non-Alzheimer's dementia. *N. Engl. J. Med., 347,* 1761–68.

Verhulst, F. C., & Achenbach, T. M. (1995). Empirically based assessment and taxonomy of psychopathology: Cross cultural applications. A review. *Eur. Child Adoles. Psychiat., 4,* 61–76.

Verhulst, F. (1995). A review of community studies. In F. Verhulst & H. Koot (Eds.), *The epidemiology of child and adolescent psychiatry* (pp. 146–77). Oxford: Oxford University Press.

Verhulst, J. H., Van Der Lee, J. H., Akkerhuis, G. W., Sanders-Woudstra, J. A. R., Timmer, F. C., & Donkhorst, I. D. (1985). The prevalence of nocturnal enuresis: Do DSM-III criteria need to be changed: A brief research report. *J. Child Psychol. Psychiat., 26*(6), 983–93.

Verkerk, A. J. M. H., Pieretti, M., et al. (1991). Identification of a gene (FMR-1) containing a CGG repeat coincident with a breakpoint cluster region exhibiting length variation in fragile X syndrome. *Cell, 65,* 905–14.

Verona, E., Patrick, C. J., & Joiner, T. E. (2001). Psychopathy, antisocial personality, and suicide risk. *J. Abn. Psychol., 110*(3), 462–70.

Vickers, K., & McNally, R.J. (2004). Panic disorder and suicide attempt in the National Comorbidity Survey. *J. Abn. Psychol., 113*(4), 582–591.

Videbech, P., Ravnkilde, B., Kristensen, S., Egander, A., Clemmensen, K., Rasmussen, N., & Gjedde, A. (2003). The Danish/PET depression project: Poor verbal fluency performance despite normal prefrontal activation in patients with major depression. *Psychiatry Research: Neuroimaging, 123*(1), 49–63.

Viejo, L. F., Morales, V., Puñal P., Pérez, R. L., & Sancho, R. A. (2003). Risk factors in neuroleptic malignant syndrome. *Acta Psychiat. Scandin., 107,* 45–49.

Villanueva, M., Tonigan, J. S., & Miller, W. R. (2003). A retrospective study of client-treatment matching: differential treatment response of Native American alcoholics in project MATCH. Alcohol. *Clin. Exp. Res., 26* (Suppl.) A 83.

Villasante, O. (2003). The unfulfilled project of the model mental hospital in Spain: Fifty years of the Santa Isabel Madhouse, Leganis (1851–1900). In T. Dening (Ed.), *Hist. Psychiat., 14*(53, Pt. 1), 3–23.

Viney, W. (1996). Dorthea Dix: An intellectual conscience for psychology. In G. A. Kimble, C. A. Boneau, & M. Wertheimer (Eds.), *Portraits of pioneers in psychology* (pp. 15–33). Washington, DC: American Psychological Association.

Viney, W., & Bartsch, K. (1984). Dorthea Lynde Dix: Positive or negative influence on the development of treatment for the mentally ill? *Social Science Journal, 21,* 71–82.

Vinokur, A. D., Price, R. H. & Caplan, R. D. (1996). Hard times and hurtful partners: How financial strain affects depression and relationship satisfaction of unemployed persons and their spouses. *J. Pers. Soc. Psychol., 71,* 166–79.

Visser, P. J., Scheltens, P., Verhey, F. R., Schmand, B., Launer, L. J., Jolles, J., & Jonker, C. (1999). Medial temporal lobe atrophy and memory dysfunction as predictors for dementia in subjects with mild cognitive impairment. *J. Neurol, 246,* 477–85.

Vitousek, K. B. (2002). Cognitive-behavioral therapy for anorexia nervosa. In C. G. Fairburn & K. D. Brownell (Eds.), *Eating disorders and obesity: A comprehensive handbook* (2nd ed., pp. 308–13). New York: Guilford.

Voelki, K. E., & Frone, M. R. (2000). Predictors of substance use at school among high school students. *J. Edu. Psychol., 92*(3), 583–92.

Vogeltanz, N. D., & Hecker, J. E. (1999). The roles of neuroticism and controllability/predictability in physiological response to aversive stimuli. *Personal. Indiv. Diff., 27,* 599–612.

Vogeltanz-Holm, N. D., Wonderlich, S. A., Lewis, B. A., Wilsnack, S. C., Harris, T. R., Wilsnack, R. W., & Kristjanson, A. F. (2000). Longitudinal predictors of binge eating, intense dieting, and weight concerns in a national sample of women. *Behav. Ther., 31,* 221–35.

Volberg, R. A. (1990, Aug.). *Estimating the prevalence of pathological gambling in the United States.* Paper presented at the Eighth International Conference on Risk and Gambling.

Volkmar, F. R., & Klein, A. (2000). Autism and the pervasive developmental disorders. In M. G. Gelder, J. J. Lopez-Ibor, Jr., & N. C. Andreason (Eds.), *New Oxford textbook of psychiatry* (pp. 1723–34). Oxford, England: Oxford University Press.

Volkow, N. D., Ding, Y. S., Fowler, J. S., Ashby, C., Liebermann, J., Hitzemann, R., & Wolf, A. P. (1995). Is methylphenidate like cocaine? Studies on their pharmacokinetics and distribution in the human brain. *Arch. Gen. Psychiat., 52,* 456–63.

Volpicelli, J. R. (2001). Alcohol abuse and alcoholism: An overview. *J. Clin. Psychiat., 62,* 4–10.

Volz, H.-P., Nenadic, I., Gaser, C., Rammsayer, T., Haeger, F., & Sauer, H. (2001). Time estimation in schizophrenia: An fMRI study at adjusted levels of difficulty. *Neuroreport: For Rapid Communication of Neuroscience Research, 12,* 313–16.

Von Haller, A. (1782) *Elementa Physiologiae Corporis Humani.* Lausanne, Julium Henricum Pott,

Wachtel, E. (1994). *Treating troubled children and their families.* New York: Guilford Press.

Wachtel, P. L. (1993). *Therapeutic communication: Principles and effective practice.* New York: Guilford.

Wachtel, P. L. (1997). *Psychoanalysis, behavior therapy, and the relational world.* Washington, DC: American Psychological Association.

Wadden, T. A., Brownell, K. D., & Foster, G. D. (2002). Obesity: Responding to the global epidemic. *J. Cons. Clin. Psychol., 70*(3), 510–25.

Wadden, T. A., Foster, G. D., & Letizia, K. A. (1994). One-year behavioral treatment of obesity: Comparison of the moderate and severe caloric restriction and the effects of weight maintenance procedures. *J. Cons. Clin. Psychol., 62,* 165–71.

Waddington, J. L., O'Callaghan, E., Youssef, H. A., Buckley, P., Lane, A., Cotter, D., & Larkin, C. (1999). Schizophrenia: Evidence for a "cascade" process with neurodevelopmental origins. In E. Z. Susser, A. S. Brown, & J. M. Gorman (Eds.), *Prenatal exposures in schizophrenia* (pp. 3–34). Washington, DC: American Psychiatric Press.

Waelde, L. C., Koopman, C., Rierdan, J., & Speigel, D. (2001). Symptoms of acute stress disorder and posttraumatic stress disorder following exposure to disastrous flooding. *Journal of Trauma & Dissociation, 2*(2), 37–52.

Wagenaar, A. C., Murray, D. M., Gehan, J. P., Wolfson, M., Forster, J. L., Toomery, T. L., Perry, C. L., & Jones-Webb, R. (2000). Communities mobilizing for change on alcohol: Outcomes from a randomized community trial. *J. Stud. Alcoh., 61*(1), 85–94.

Wagner, K. D., & Ambrosini, P. J. (2001). Childhood depression: Pharmacological therapy/treatment (pharmacotherapy of childhood depression). *J. Clin. Child Psychol., 30*(1), 88–97.

Wahlberg, K.-E., Wynne, L. C., et al. (1997). Gene-environment interaction in vulnerability to schizophrenia: Findings from the Finnish adoptive family study of schizophrenia. *Amer. J. Psychiat., 154*(3), 355–62.

Wakefield, J. C. (1992a). The concept of mental disorder: On the boundary between biological facts and social values. *Amer. Psychol., 47*(3), 373–88.

Wakefield, J. C. (1992b). Disorder as harmful dysfunction: A conceptual critique of DSM-III-R's definition of mental disorder. *Psychol. Rev., 99*(2), 232–47.

Wakefield, J. C. (1997). Normal inability versus pathological disability: Why Ossorio's definition of mental disorder is not sufficient. *Clin. Psychol. Sci. Prac., 4*(3), 249–58.

Walcott, D. M., Cerundolo, P., & Beck, J. C. (2001). Current analysis of the Tarasoff duty: An evolution towards the limitation of the duty to protect. *Behavioral Sciences & the Law, 19*(3), 325–43.

Waldman, I. D., & Slutske, W. S. (2000). Antisocial behavior and alcoholism: A behavioral genetic perspective on comorbidity. *Clin. Psychol. Rev., 20*(2), 255–87.

Walker, D.L., Ressler, K.J., Lu, K-T., & Davis, M. (2002). Facilitation of conditioned fear extinction by systemic administration or intra-amygdala infusions of D-cycloserine as assessed with fear-potentiated startle in rats. *J. Neuroci., 22*(6), 2343–2351.

Walker, E. F., & Diforio, D. (1997). Schizophrenia: A neural diathesis–stress model. *Psychol. Rev., 104,* 667–85.

Walker, E. F., Grimes, K. E., Davis, D. M., & Smith, A. J. (1993). Childhood precursors of schizophrenia: Facial expressions of emotion. *Amer. J. Psychiat., 150*(11), 1654–60.

Walker, E. F., Savoie, T., & Davis, D. (1994). Neuromotor precursors of schizophrenia. *Schizo. Bull., 20*(3), 441–51.

Walker, E., Kestler, L., Bollini, A., & Hochman, K. M. (2004). Schizophrenia: Etiology and course. *Ann. Rev. Psychol., 55,* 401–30.

Wall, T. L., Shea, S. H., Chan, K. K., & Carr, L. G. (2001). A genetic association with the development of alcohol and other substance use behavior in Asian Americans. *J. Abn. Psychol., 110*(1), 173–78.

Wallace, J., Schneider, T., & McGuffin, P. (2002). Genetics of depression. In I. H. Gotlib & C. L. Hammen (Eds.), *Handbook of depression* (pp. 169–91). New York: Guilford.

Waller, N. G., & Ross, C. A. (1997). The prevalence and biometric structure of pathological dissociation in the general population: Taxometric and behavior genetic findings. *J. Abn. Psychol., 106,* 499–510.

Waller, N., Putnam, F. W., & Carlson, E. B. (1996). Types of dissociation and dissociative types: A taxometric analysis of dissociative experiences. *Psychol. Meth., 1,* 300–21.

Wallin, A., & Blennow, K. (1993). Heterogeneity of vascular dementia: Mechanisms and subgroups. *Journal of Geriatric Psychiatry and Neurology, 6*(3), 177–88.

Walsh, B. T. (2002). Pharmacological treatment of anorexia nervosa and bulimia nervosa. In C. G. Fairburn & K. D. Brownell (Eds.), *Eating disorders and obesity: A comprehensive handbook* (2nd ed., pp. 325–29). New York: Guilford.

Walsh, B. T., & Garner, D. M. (1997). Diagnostic issues. In D. M. Garner &. P. E. Garfinkel (Eds.), *Handbook of treatment for eating disorders* (pp. 25–33). New York: Guilford.

Walsh, B. T., Wilson, G. T., Loeb, K. L., Devlin, M. J., Pike, K. M., Roose, S. P., Fleiss, J., & Waternaux, C. (1997). Medication and psychotherapy in the treatment of bulimia nervosa. *Amer. J. Psychiat., 154*(4): 523–531.

Walsh, E., Moran, P., Scott, C., McKenzie, K., Burns, T., Creed, F., Tyler, P., Murray, R. M., & Fahy, T. (2003). Prevalence of violent victimization in severe mental illness. *Brit. J. Psychiat., 183,* 233–38.

Walter, A. L., & Carter, A. S. (1997). Gilles de la Tourette's syndrome in childhood: A guide for school professionals. *School Psychol. Rev., 26*(1), 28–46.

Wang, G. J., Volkow, N. D., Chang, L., Miller, E., Sedler, M., Hitzemann, R., Zhu, W., Logan, J., Ma, Y., & Fowler, J. S. (2004). Partial recovery of brain metabolism in methamphetamine abusers after protracted abstinence. *Amer. J. Psychiat., 161*(2), 242–48

Wang, J. (2005). Work stress as a risk factor for major depressive episodes. *Psychol. Med., 35,* 865–871.

Wang, P. S., Berglund, P., Olfson, M., Pincus, H. A., Wells, K. B., & Kessler, R. C. (2005). Failure and delay in initial treatment contact after the first onset of mental disorders in the National Comorbidity Survey Replication. *Arch. Gen. Psychiat., 62,* 603–13.

Wang, P. S., Lane, M., Olfson, M., Pincus, H. A., Wells, K. B., & Kessler, R. C. (2005). Twelve-month use of mental health services in the United States. *Arch. Gen. Psychiat., 62,* 629–40.

Ward, C. I., & Laughlin, J. E. (2003). Social contexts, age, and juvenile delinquency: A community perspective. *J. Child Adol. Men. Hlth., 15,* 13–25.

Ward, M. J. (1946). *The snake pit.* New York: Random House.

Ward, T., McCormack, J., Hudson, S. M., & Polaschek, D. (1997). Rape: Assessment and treatment. In D. R. Laws & W. O'Donohue (Eds.), *Sexual deviance: Theory, assessment, and treatment* (pp. 356–93). New York: Guilford.

Warner, M. D., Dorn, M. R., & Peabody, C. (2001). Survey on the usefulness of trazodone in patients with PTSD with insomnia or nightmares. *Pharmacopsychiatry, 34,* 128–31.

Warner, R. (2001). The prevention of schizophrenia: What interventions are safe and effective? *Schizo. Bull., 27,* 551–62.

Warnes, H. (1973). The traumatic syndrome. *Ment. Hlth. Dig., 5*(3), 33–34.

Warren, J. I., Dietz, P. E., & Hazelwood, R. R. (1996). The sexually sadistic serial killer. *Journal of Forensic Sciences, 41,* 970–74.

Wasco, S. M., Campbell, R., Howard, A., Mason, G. E., Staggs, S. L., Schewe, P., & Riger, S. (2004). A statewide evaluation of services provided to rape survivors. *J. Interpers. Violen., 19*(2), 252–63.

Washington State Institute for Public Policy. (1995). *Boot camps: A Washington state update and overview of national findings* (#95-06-1201). Olympia, WA: Author.

Washington State Institute for Public Policy. (1998). Trends in at-risk behaviors of youth in Washington, 1998 update. (Seminar 3162). Olympia, WA: Author.

Wasserman, D. R., & Leventhal, J. M. (1993). Maltreatment of children born to cocaine-dependent mothers. *Archives of Pediatrics and Adolescent Medicine, 147,* 1324–28.

Wasserman, J. D. (2003). Assessment of intellectual functioning. *Handbook of psychology* (Vol. 10, pp. 417–42). New York: John Wiley & Sons.

Wasserstein, S. B., & La Greca, A. M. (1996). Can peer support buffer against behavioral consequences of parental discord? *J. Clin. Child. Psychol., 25*(2), 177–82.

Wassink, T. H., Piven, J., & Patil, S. R. (2001). Chromosomal abnormalities in a clinic sample of individuals with autistic disorder. *Psychiatric Genetics, 11*(2), 57–63.

Watanabe, H., Kawauchi, A., Kitamori, T., & Azuma, Y. (1994). Treatment system for nocturnal enuresis according to an original classification system. *European Urology, 25,* 43–50.

Waterhouse, L., & Fein, D. (1997). Genes tPA, Fyn, and FAK in autism? *J. Autism Devel. Dis., 27*(3), 220–23.

Waters, R. J., & Nicoll, J. A. R. (2005). Genetic influences on outcome following acute neurological insults. *Current Opinion in Critical Care, 11,* 105–10.

Watkins, S. S., Koob, G. F., & Markou, A. (2000). Neural mechanisms underlying nicotine addiction: Acute positive reinforcement and withdrawal. *Nicotine & Tobacco Research, 2,* 19–37.

Watson, A. C., Otely, E., Westbrook, A. L., Gardner, A. L., Lamb, T. A., Corrigan, P. W., & Fenton, W. S. (2004). Changing middle schoolers' attitudes about mental illness through education. *Schizo. Bull., 30*(3), 563–72.

Watson, D., Clark, L. A., & Harkness, A. R. (1994). Structures of personality and their relevance to psychopathology. *J. Abn. Psychol., 103,* 18–31.

Watson, D., Clark, L. A., Weber, K., Assenheimer, J. S., Strauss, M. E., & McCormick, R. A. (1995a). Testing a tripartite model: I. Evaluating the convergent and discriminant validity of anxiety and depression symptom scales. *J. Abn. Psychol., 104,* 3–14.

Watson, D., Clark, L. A., Weber, K., Assenheimer, J. S., Strauss, M. E., & McCormick, R. A. (1995b). Testing a tripartite model: II. Exploring the symptom structure of anxiety and depression in student, adult, and patient samples. *J. Abn. Psychol., 104,* 15–25.

Watson, D., Gamez, W., & Simms, L. J. (2005). Basic dimensions of temperament and their relation to anxiety and depression: A symptom-based perspective. *Journal of Res. Person., 39*(1), 46–66.

Watson, D. (2002). Positive affectivity: The disposition to experience pleasurable emotional states. In C. R. Snyder & S. J. Lopez (Eds.), *Handbook of positive psychology* (pp. 106–19). New York: Oxford University Press.

Watson, J., & Raynor, R. (1920). Conditioned emotional reactions. *Journal of Genetic Psychology, 37,* 394–419.

Watson, J. (1924). *Behaviorism.* New York: The People's Institute Publishing Co., Inc.

Watson, S., Gallagher, P., Ritchie, J. C., Ferrier, I. N., & Young, A. H. (2004). Hypothalamic-pituitary-adrenal axis function in patients with bipolar disorder. *Brit. J. Psychiat., 184,* 496–502.

Watson, T. L., Bowers, W. A., & Andersen, A. E. (2000). Involuntary treatment of eating disorders. *Amer. J. Psychiat., 157*(11), 1806–10.

Watt, N. F., Anthony, E. J., Wynne, L. C., & Rolf, J. E. (Eds.). (1984). *Children at risk for schizophrenia: A longitudinal perspective.* Cambridge: Cambridge University Press.

Wattar, U., Sorensen, P., Buemann, I., Birket-Smith, M., Salkovskis, P. M., Albertsen, M., et al. (2005). Outcome of cognitive-behavioural treatment for health anxiety (hypochondriasis) in a routine clinical setting. *Behavioural and Cognitive Psychotherapy, 33*(2), 165–75.

Watters, C., & Ingleby, D. (2004). Locations of care: Meeting the mental health and social care needs of refugees in europe. *International Journal of Law & Psychiatry, 27*(6), 549–70.

Weatherby, N. L., Shultz, J. M., Chitwood, D. D., & McCoy, H. V. (1992). Crack cocaine use and sexual activity in Miami, Florida. *J. Psychoact. Drugs, 24,* 373–80.

Webster-Stratton, C. (1991). Annotation: Strategies for helping families with conduct disordered children. *J. Child Psychol. Psychiat., 32,* 1047–62.

Webster-Stratton, C. (2000). Oppositional-defiant and conduct-disordered children. In M. Hersen & R. T. Ammerman (Eds.), *Advanced abnormal child psychology* (2nd ed.; pp. 387–412). Mahwah, NJ: Erlbaum.

Wechsler, H., Davenport, A., Dowdall, G., Moeykens, M. S., & Castillo, S. (1994, Dec.). Health and behavioral consequences of binge drinking in college. *JAMA,* 1672–77.

Wechsler, H., Dowdall, G. W., Maenner, G., Gledhill-Hoyt, J., & Lee, H. (1998). Changes in binge drinking and related problems among American college students between 1993 and 1997. *J. Amer. Coll. Hlth., 47*(2), 57–68.

Weggen, S., Eriksen, J. L., Das, P., Sagi, S. A., Wang, R., Pietrzik, C. U., Findlay, K. A., Smith, T. E., Murphy, M. P., Bulter, T., Kang, D. E., Marquez-Sterling, N., Golde, T. E., & Koo, E. H. (2001). A subset of NSAIDs lower amyloidogenic A(42 independently of cyclooxygenase activity. *Nature, 414,* 212–16.

Wegner, D. M. (1994). Ironic processes of mental control. *Psychol. Rev., 101*(1), 34–52.

Wehman, P. (2003). Workplace inclusion: Persons with disabilities and coworkers working together. *Journal of Vocational Rehabilitation, 18*(2), 131–41.

Wehr, T. A., & Goodwin, F. K. (1987). Can antidepressants cause mania and worsen the course of affective illness? *Amer. J. Psychiat., 144,* 1403–11.

Weickert, C. S., & Weinberger, D. R. (1998). A candidate molecule approach to defining developmental pathology in schizophrenia. *Schizo. Bull., 24*(2), 303–16.

Weinberg, M. S., Williams, C. J., & Pryor, D. W. (1994). *Dual Attraction.* New York: Oxford University Press.

Weinberger, D. R. (1984). Brain disease and psychiatric illness: When should a psychiatrist order a CAT scan? *Amer. J. Psychiat., 141,* 1521–27.

Weinberger, D. R. (1987). Implications of normal brain development for the pathogenesis of schizophrenia. *Arch. Gen. Psychiat., 44,* 660–69.

Weinberger, D. (1997). On localizing schizophrenic neuropathology. *Schizo. Bull., 23(3)* 537–540.

Weiner, D. B. (1979). The apprenticeship of Philippe Pinel: A new document, "Observations of Citizen Pussin on the insane." *Amer. J. Psychiat., 136*(9), 1128–34.

Weiner, D. N., & Rosen, R. C. (1999). Sexual dysfunctions and disorders. In T. Millon, P. H. Blaney, & R. D. Davis (Eds.), *Oxford textbook of psychopathology* (pp. 410–43). New York: Oxford University Press.

Weiner, I. (1998). *Principles of Rorschach interpretation.* Hillsdale, NJ: Erlbaum.

Weisman, A. G., López, S. R., Ventura, J., Nuechterlein, J. H., Goldstein, M. J., & Hwang, S. (2000). A comparison of psychiatric symptoms between Anglo-Americans and Mexican-Americans with schizophrenia. *Schizo. Bull., 26,* 817–24.

Weiss, B., Weisz, J. R., & Bromfield, R. (1986). Performance of retarded and nonretarded persons on information-processing tasks: Further tests of the similar structure hypothesis. *Psychol. Bull., 100,* 157–75.

Weisse, C. S. (1992). Depression and immunocompetence: A review of the literature. *Psychol. Bull., 111*(3), 475–89.

Weissman, M. M., & Markowitz, J. C. (2002). Interpersonal psychotherapy for depression. In I. H. Gotlib & C. L. Hammen (Eds.), *Handbook of depression* (pp. 404–21). New York: Guilford.

Weissman, M. M., Fendrich, M., Warner, V., & Wickramaratne, P. (1992). Incidence of psychiatric disorder in offspring at high and low risk for depression. *J. Amer. Acad. Child Adoles. Psychiat., 31,* 640–48.

Weisz, J. R., & Weiss, B. (1991). Studying the referability of child clinical problems. *J. Cons. Clin. Psychol., 59,* 266–73.

Weisz, J. R., Donenberg, G. R., Han, S. S., & Weiss, B. (1995). Bridging the gap between laboratory and clinic in child and adolescent psychotherapy. *J. Cons. Clin. Psychol., 63*(5), 688–701.

Weisz, J. R., McCarty, C. A., Eastman, K. L., Chaiyasit, W., & Suwanlert, S. (1997). Developmental psychopathology and culture: Ten lessons from Thailand. In S. Luthar, J. Burack, D. Cicchetti, & J. Weisz (Eds.), *Developmental psychopathology: Perspectives an adjustment, risk, and disorder* (pp. 568–92). Cambridge, England: Cambridge University Press.

Weisz, J. R., Suwanlert, S., Chaiyasit, W., & Walter, B. R. (1987). Over and undercontrolled clinic-referral problems among Thai and American children and adolescents: The wat and wai of cultural differences. *J. Cons. Clin. Psychol., 55,* 719–26.

Weisz, J. R., Suwanlert, S., Chaiyasit, W., Weiss, B., Achenbach, T. M., & Eastman, K. L. (1993). Behavior and emotional problems among Thai and American adolescents: Parent reports for ages 12–16. *J. Abn. Psychol., 102,* 395–403.

Weisz, J. R., Weiss, B., Suwanlert, S., & Chaiyasit, W. (2003). Syndromal structure of psychopathology in children of Thailand and the United States. *J. Cons. Clin. Psychol., 71*(2), 375–385.

Weizman, R., Laor, N., Barber, Y., Selman, A., Schujovizky, A., Wolmer, L., Laron, Z., & Gil-Ad, I. (1994). Impact of the Gulf war on the anxiety, cortisol, and growth hormone levels of Israeli civilians. *Amer. J. Psychiat., 151,* 71–75.

Welin, C., Lappas, G., Wilhelmsen, L. (2000). Independent importance of psychological factors for prognosis after myocardial infarction. *Journal of Internal Medicine, 247,* 629–39.

Wells, A. (1999). A cognitive model of generalized anxiety disorder. *Behav. Mod., 23,* 526–55.

Wells, A., & Butler, G. (1997). Generalized anxiety disorder. In D. M. Clark & C. G. Fairburn (Eds.), *Science and practice of cognitive behaviour therapy* (pp. 155–78). New York: Oxford University Press.

Wells, A., & Clark, D. M. (1997). Social phobia: A cognitive perspective. In G. C. L. Davey (Ed.), *Phobias: A handbook of description, treatment, and theory.* Chichester, England: Wiley.

Wells, A., & Papageorgiou, C. (1995). Worry and the incubation of intrusive images following stress. *Behav. Res. Ther., 33,* 579–83.

Welte, J. W., Barnes, G. M., Wieczorek, W. F., Tidwell, M. C., & Parker, J. C. (2004). Risk factors for pathological gambling. *Add. Behav., 29*(2), 323–35.

Wender, P. H., Kety, S. S., Rosenthal, D., Schulsinger, F., Ortmann, J., & Lunde, I. (1986). Psychiatric disorders in the biological and adoptive families of adopted individuals with affective disorders. *Arch. Gen. Psychiat., 43,* 923–29.

Wender, P. H., Rosenthal, D., Kety, S. S., Schulsinger, F., & Weiner, J. (1974). Cross-fostering: A research strategy for clarifying the role of genetic and experimental factors in the etiology of schizophrenia. *Arch. Gen. Psychiat., 30*(1), 121–28.

Wender, P. H. (2000). *ADHD: Attention deficit hyperactivity disorder in children and adults.* Oxford: Oxford University Press.

Wenzlaff, R. M., Wegner, D. M., & Klein, S. B. (1991). The role of thought suppression in the bonding of thought and mood. *J. Pers. Soc. Psychol., 60*(4), 500–08.

West, J. R., Perotta, D. M., & Erickson, C. K. (1998). Fetal alcohol syndrome: A review for Texas physicians. *Medical Journal of Texas, 94,* 61–67.

West, S. L., & O'Neal, K. K. (2004). Project D.A.R.E. outcome effectiveness revisited. *Amer. J. Pub. Hlth., 94*(6), 1027–29.

Westen, D. (1998). The scientific legacy of Sigmund Freud: Toward a psychodynamically informed psychological science. *Psychol. Bull., 124*(3), 333–371.

Westermeyer, J. (1987). Public health and chronic mental illness. *Amer. J. Pub. Hlth., 77*(6), 667–68.

Westermeyer, J. (1989). Paranoid symptoms and disorders among 100 Hmong refugees: A longitudinal study. *Acta Psychiatr. Scandin., 80*(1), 47–59.

Westermeyer, J. (2001). Personal communication to J. N. Butcher.

Westermeyer, J., & Janca, A. (1997). Language, culture and psychopathology: Conceptual and methodological issues. *Transcult. Psychiatry, 34,* 291–311.

Westermeyer, J., & Kroll, J. (1978). Violence and mental illness in a peasant society: Characteristics of violent behaviors and 'folk' use of restraints. *Brit. J. Psychiat., 133,* 529–41.

Westermeyer, J., Neider, J., & Callies, A. (1989). Psychosocial adjustment of Hmong refugees during their first decade in the United States. A longitudinal study. *J. Nerv. Ment. Dis., 177,* 132–39.

Westermeyer, J., Williams, C. L., & Nguyen, N. (Eds.). (1991). *Mental health and social adjustment: A guide to clinical and prevention services.* Washington, DC: U.S. Government Printing Office.

Weyer, J. (1583). *On the Deceits of the Demons* (the translation is from the second edition in 1583) Ttrans. John Shea, Binghamton, New York: Medieval and Renaissance Texts and Studies, 1991.

Whalley, H. C., Simonotto, E., Flett, S., et al. (2004). fMRI correlates of state and trait effects in subjects at genetically enhanced risk of schizophrenia. *Brain, 127,* 478–91.

Wheeler, J. G., Christensen, A., & Jacobson, N. S. (2001). Couple distress. In D. H. Barlow (Ed.), *Clinical handbook for psychological disorders* (3rd ed., pp. 609–30). New York: Guilford.

Wherry, J. S. (1996). Pervasive developmental, psychotic, and allied disorders. In L. Hechtman (Ed.), *Do they grow out of it?* (pp. 195–223). Washington, DC: American Psychiatric Press.

Whiffen, V. L., & Clark, S. E. (1997). Does victimization account for sex differences in depressive symptoms? *Brit. J. Clin. Psychol., 36,* 185–93.

White, D. A., Nortz, M. J., Mandernach, T., Huntington, K., & Steiner, R. (2002). Age-related working memory impairments in children with prefrontal dysfunction associated with phenylketonuria. *J. Int. Neuropsycholog. Soc., 8,* 1–11.

White, I., Altmann, D. R., & Nanchahal, K. (2002). Alcohol consumption and mortality: Modelling risks for men and women at different ages. *Brit. Med. J., 325*(7357), 1032–41.

White, K., & Davey, G. (1989). Sensory preconditioning and UCS inflation in human "fear" conditioning. *Behav. Res. & Ther., 2,* 161–66.

White, K. S., & Barlow, D. H. (2002). Panic disorder and agoraphobia. In D. H. Barlow (Ed.), *Anxiety and its disorders* (2nd ed., pp. 328–79). New York: Guilford.

Whitehouse, P. J., et al. (1982). Alzheimer's disease and senile dementia: Loss of neurons in the basal forebrain. *Science, 215,* 1237–39.

Whitehouse, P. J. (1993). Cholinergic therapy in dementia. *Acta Neurol. Scandin., 88*(Suppl. 149), 42–45.

Whiteley, J. S. (1991). Developments in the therapeutic community. *Psychiatriki, 2*(1), 34–41.

Whitfield, K. E., Weidner, G., Clark, R., & Anderson, N. B. (2002). Sociodemographic diversity and behavioral medicine. *J. Cons. Clin. Psychol., 70*(3), 463–81.

Whiting, P., Bagnall, A. M., Snowden, A. J., Cornell, J. E., Mulrow, C. D., & Ramirez, G. (2001). Interventions for the treatment and management of chronic fatigue syndrome: A systematic review. *JAMA, 286,* 1360–68.

Whittington C. J., Kendall, T., Fonagy, P., Cottrell, D., Cotgrove, A., & Boddington, E. (2004). Selective serotonin reuptake inhibitors in childhood depression: Systematic review of published versus unpublished data. *Lancet, 363,* 1341–45.

Whittington, C. J., Kendall, T., & Pilling, S. (2005). Are the SSRIs and atypical antidepressants safe and effective for children and adolescents? *Current Opinion in Psychiatry, 18,* 21–25.

Whybrow, P. C. (1997). *A mood apart.* New York: Basic Books.

Widiger, T. A., & Bornstein, R. F. (2001). Histrionic, dependent, and narcissistic personality disorders. In H. E. Adams & P. B. Sutker (Eds.), *Comprehensive handbook of psychopathology* (pp. 509–34). New York: Kluwer Academic.

Widiger, T. A., & Clark, L. A. (2000). Toward DSM-V and the classification of psychopathology. *Psychol. Bull., 126*(6), 946–63.

Widiger, T. A., & Corbitt, E. M. (1995). Antisocial personality disorder. In W. J. Livesley (Ed.), *The DSM-IV personality disorders* (pp. 103–126). New York: Guilford.

Widiger, T. A., & Frances, A. (1985). Axis II personality disorders: Diagnostic and treatment issues. *Hosp. Comm. Psychiat., 36,* 619–27.

Widiger, T. A., & Sanderson, C. J. (1995). Toward a dimensional model of personality disorders. In W. J. Livesley (Ed.), *The DSM-IV personality disorders* (pp. 433–58). New York: Guilford.

Widiger, T. A., Frances, A. J., Pincus, H. A., Davis, W. W., & First, M. B. (1991). Toward an empirical classification for the DSM-IV. *J. Abn. Psychol., 100*(3), 280–88.

Widiger, T. A., Trull, T. J., Clarkin, J. F., Sanderson, C. J., & Costa, P. T. (2002). A description of the DSM-IV personality disorders with the five-factor model of personality. In P. T. Costa, Jr., & T. A. Widiger (Eds.), *Personality disorders and the five-factor model of personality* (pp. 89–102). Washington, DC: American Psychological Association.

Widiger, T. A. (2001). Official classification systems. In W. J. Livesley (Ed.), *Handbook of personality disorders: Theory, research, and treatment* (pp. 60–83). New York: Guilford.

Widiger, T., & Rogers, J. (1989). Prevalence and comorbidity of personality disorders. *Psychiat. Ann., 19,* 132–36.

Widiger, T., & Trull, T. J. (1993) Borderline and narcissistic personality disorders. In P. B. Sutker & H. E. Adams (Eds.), *Comprehensive handbook of psychopathology* (2nd ed.). New York: Plenum.

Widom, C. S. (1977). A methodology for studying noninstitutionalized psychopaths. *J. Cons. Clin. Psychol., 45,* 674–83.

Widom, C. S. (1978). An empirical classification of female offenders. *Crim. Just. Behav. 5*(1), 35–52.

Wiederanders, M. R., Bromley, D. L., & Choate, P. A. (1997). Forensic conditional release programs and outcomes in three states. *International Journal of Law and Psychiatry, 20,* 249–57.

Wilbur, R. S. (1973, Jun. 2). In S. Auerbach (Ed.), POWs found to be much sicker than they looked upon release. *Los Angeles Times,* Part I, p. 4.

Wilcox, B. L., & Naimark, H. (1991). The rights of the child: Progress toward human dignity. *Amer. Psychol., 46,* 49–52.

Wilder, D. A., et al. (1997). A simplified method of toilet training adults in residential settings. *J. Behav. Ther. Exper. Psychiat., 28*(3), 241–46.

Wildes, J. E., Emery, R. E., & Simons, A. D. (2001). The roles of ethnicity and culture in the development of eating disturbance and body dissatisfaction: A meta-analytic review. *Clin. Psychol. Rev., 21*(4), 521–51.

Wilfley, D. E., Friedman, M. A., Dounchis, J. Z., Stein, R. I., Welch, R. R., & Ball, S. A. (2000). Comorbid psychopathology in binge eating disorder: Relation to eating disorder severity at baseline and following treatment. *J. Cons. Clin. Psychol., 68*(4), 641–49.

Wilfley, D. E., Schwartz, M. B., Spurrell, E. B., & Fairburn, C. G. (2000). Using the Eating Disorder Examination to identify the specific psychopathology of binge eating disorder. *Int. J. Eat. Dis., 27*(3), 259–69.

Wilfley, D. E., Welch, R. R., Stein, R. I., Spurrell, E. B., Cohen, L. R., Saelens, B. E., Dounchis, J. Z., Frank, M. A., Wiseman, C. V., & Matt, G. E. (2002). A randomized comparison of group cognitive-behavioral therapy and group interpersonal psychotherapy for the treatment of overweight individuals with binge-eating disorder. *Arch. Gen. Psychiat., 59,* 713–21.

Wilkinson, B. J., Newman, M. G., Shytle, R. D., Silver, A. A., Sandberg, P. R., & Sheehan, D. (2001). Family impact of Tourette's syndrome. *J. Child Fam. Stud., 10,* 477–83.

Williams, C. L., Grechanaia, T., Romanova, O., Komro, K. A., Perry, C. L., & Farbakhsh, K. (2001). Russian–American partners for prevention: Adaptation of a school-based parent–child programme for alcohol use prevention. *European Journal of Public Health, 11,* 314–21.

Williams, J. M., Watts, F. N., MacLeod, C., & Mathews, A. (1997). *Cognitive psychology and emotional disorders.* Chichester, England: Wiley.

Williams, K. E., Chambless, D. L., & Ahrens, A. (1997). Are emotions frightening? An extension of the fear of fear construct. *Behav. Res. Ther., 35*(3), 239–48.

Williams, K., Mellis, C., & Peat, J. K. (2005). Incidence and prevalence of autism. *Advances in Speech Language Pathology, 7*(1), 31–40.

Williams, P. G., Sears, L. L., & Allard, A. (2004). Sleep problems in children with autism. *Journal of Sleep Research, 13*(3), 265–68.

Williams, R. B., Barefoot, J. C., Blumenthal, J. A., Helms, M. J., et al. (1997). Psychosocial correlates of job strain in a sample of working women. *Arch. Gen. Psychiat., 54*(6), 543–48.

Williams, R. B., Jr., Barefoot, J. C., Califf, R. M., Haney, T. L., Saunders, W. B., Pryor, D. B., Hlatky, M. A., Siegler, I. C., & Marks, D. B. (1992). Prognostic importance of social and economic resources among medically treated patients with angiographically documented coronary artery disease. *JAMA, 267,* 520–24.

Williamson, D. A., Womble, L. G., Smeets, M. A. M., Netemeyer, R. G., Thaw, J. M., Kutlesic, V., & Gleaves, D. H. (2002). Latent structure of eating disorder symptoms: A factor analytic and taxometric investigation. *Amer. J. Psychiat., 159*(3), 412–18.

Williamson, S., Harpur, T. J., & Hare, R. D. (1991). Abnormal processing of affective words by psychopathic individuals. *Psychophysiology, 28,* 260–73.

Wilson, D. K., Kliewer, W., & Sica, D. A. (2004). The relationship between exposure to violence and blood pressure mechanisms. *Current Hypertension Reports, 6*(4), 321–26.

Wilson, G. T. (1998). Manual-based treatment and clinical practice. *Clin. Psychol. Sci. Prac., 5,* 363–75.

Wilson, G. T. (2002). The controversy over dieting. In C. G. Fairburn & K. D. Brownell (Eds.), *Eating disorders and obesity: A comprehensive handbook* (2nd ed., pp. 93–97). New York: Guilford.

Wilson, G. T. (2005). Psychological treatment of eating disorders. *Annu. Rev. Clin. Psychol., 1,* 439–465.

Wilson, G. T., & Fairburn, C. G. (1993). Cognitive treatments for eating disorders. *J. Cons. Clin. Psychol., 61*(2), 261–69.

Wilson, G. T., & Fairburn, C. G. (1998). Treatments for eating disorders. In P. E. Nathan & J. M. Gorman (Eds.), *A guide to treatments that work* (pp. 501–30). New York: Oxford University Press.

Wilson, G. T., & Fairburn, C. G. (2002). Treatments for eating disorders. In P. E. Nathan & J. M. Gorman (Eds.), *A guide to treatments that work* (2nd ed., pp. 559–92). New York: Oxford University Press.

Wilson, K., Gibson, N., Willan, A., & Cook, D. (2000). Effect of smoking cessation on mortality after myocardial infarction. *Arch. Int. Med., 160,* 939–44.

Wilson, K., Sinclair, I., & Gibbs, I. (2000). The trouble with foster care: The impact of stressful events on foster care. *British Journal of Social Work, 30,* 193–209.

Wilson, M. (1993). DSM-III and the transformation of American psychiatry: A history. *Amer. J. Psychiat., 150,* 399–410.

Wilson, M. I., & Daly, M. (1996). Male sexual proprietariness and violence against wives. *Curr. Dis. Psychol. Sci., 5,* 2–7.

Wilson, R. S., Barnes, L. L., Mendes de Leon, C. F., Aggarwal, N. T., Schneider, J. S., Bach, J., Pilat, J., Beckett, L. A., Arnold, S. E., Evans, D. A., & Bennett, D. A. (2002). Depressive symptoms, cognitive decline, and the risk of AD in older persons. *Neurology, 59,* 364–70.

Winblad, B., Engedal, K., Sioininen, H., Verhey, F., Waldeman, G., Wimo, A., Wetterholm, A.-L., Zhang, R., Haglund, A., Subbiah, P., & the Donepezil Nordic Study Group. (2001). A 1-year, randomized, placebo-controlled study of donepezil in patients with mild to moderate AD. *Neurology, 57*(3), 489–95.

Windhaber, J., Maierhofer, D., & Dantendorfer, K. (1998). Panic disorder induced by large doses of 3,4-methylenedioxymethamphetamine resolved by paroxetine. *J. Clin. Psychopharmacol., 18*(1), 95–96.

Wing, J. K., Cooper, J. E., & Sartorius, N. (1974). *Measurement and classification of psychiatric symptoms.* Cambridge: Cambridge University Press.

Winick, B. J. (1997). *The right to refuse mental health treatment.* Washington, DC: American Psychological Association.

Winokur, G., & Tsuang, M. T. (1996). *The natural history of mania, depression, and schizophrenia.* Washington, DC: American Psychiatric Press.

Winslow, J. T., & Insel, T. R. (1991). Neuroethological models of obsessive-compulsive disorder. In J. Zohar, T. Insel, & S. Rasmussen (Eds.), *The psy-*

chobiology of obsessive-compulsive disorder. New York: Springer.

Winston, A. P., Jamieson, C. P., Madira, W., Gatward, N. M., & Palmer, R. L. (2000). Prevalence of thiamin deficiency in anorexia nervosa. *Int. J. Eat. Dis., 28,* 451–54.

Winston, A., Laikin, M., Pollack, J., Samstag, L.W., McCullough, L., & Muran, C. (1994). Short-term psychotherapy of personality disorders. *Amer. J. Psychiat., 151,* 190–94.

Winters, K. C., & Neale, J. M. (1985). Mania and low self-esteem. *J. Abn. Psychol., 94,* 282–90.

Winton, M. A., & Mara, B. A. (2001). *Child abuse and neglect: Multidisciplinary approaches.* Boston: Allyn and Bacon.

Wise, R. A., & Munn, E. (1995). Withdrawal from chronic amphetamine elevates baseline intracranial self-stimulation thresholds. *Psychopharmacology, 117*(2), 130–36.

Wise, R. A. (1996). Addictive drugs and brain stimulation reward. *Annual Review of Neuroscience, 19,* 319–40.

Wiseman, C. V., Gray, J. J., Mosimann, J. E., & Ahrens, A. (1992). Cultural expectations of thinness in women: An update. *Int. J. Eat. Dis.., 11,* 85–89.

Wisniewski, T., Dowjat, W. K., Buxbaum, J. D., Khorkova, O., Efthimiopoulos, S., Kulczycki, J., Lojkowska, W., Wegiel, J., Wisniewski, H. M., & Frangione, B. (1998). A novel Polish presenilin-2 mutation (P117L0 is associated with familial Alzheimer's disease and leads to death as early as the age of 28 years). *Neuroreport, 9,* 217–21.

Witkiewitz, K., & Marlatt, G. A. (2004). Relapse prevention for alcohol and drug problems: That was Zen, this is Tao. *Amer. Psychol., 59*(4), 224–35.

Witkin, M. J., Atay, J., & Manderscheid, R. W. (1998). Trends in state and county mental hospitals in the U.S. from 1970 to 1992. *Psychiat. Serv., 47*(10), 1079–81.

Witvliet, C. V., Ludwig, T. E., & Vander Laan, K. L. (2001). Granting forgiveness or harboring grudges: Implications for emotion, physiology, and health. *Psychol. Sci., 12*(2), 117–23.

Woelwer, W., Burtscheidt, W., Redner, C., Schwarz, R., & Gaebel, W. (2001). Out-patient behaviour therapy in alcoholism: Impact of personality disorders and cognitive impairments. *Acta Psychiatrica Scandinavica, 103,* 30–37.

Woike, B. A., Osier, T. J., & Candela, K. (1996). Attachment styles and violent imagery in thematic stories about relationships. *Personal. Soc. Psychol. Bull., 22,* 1030–34.

Wolfe, B. E., & Maser, J. D. (1994). Treatment of panic disorder: Consensus statement. In B. E. Wolfe & J. D. Maser (Eds.), *Treatment of panic disorder. A consensus development conference* (pp. 237–55). Washington, DC: American Psychiatric Press.

Wolff, H. G. (1960). Stressors as a cause of disease in man. In J. M. Tanner (Ed.), *Stress and psychiatric disorder.* London: Oxford University Press.

Wolff, P. H. (1972). Ethnic differences in alcohol sensitivity. *Science, 175,* 449–50.

Wolfson, C., Wolfson, D. B., Asgharian, M., M'Lan, C. M., Ostbye, T., Rockwood, K., & Hogan, D. B. (2001). A reevaluation of the duration of survival after the onset of dementia. *N. Engl. J. Med., 344,* 1111–16.

Wolpe, J., & Rachman, S. J. (1960). Psychoanalytic evidence: A critique based on Freud's case of Little Hans. *J. Nerv. Ment. Dis., 131,* 135–45.

Wolpe, J. (1958). *Psychotherapy by reciprocal inhibition.* Stanford, CA: Stanford University Press.

Wolpe, J. (1988). *Life without fear. Anxiety and its cure.* Oakland, CA: New Harbinger Publications, Inc.

Wolpe, J. (1993). Commentary: The cognitivist oversell and comments on symposium contributions. *J. Behav. Ther. Exper. Psychiat., 24*(2), 141–47.

Wolrich, M. L., Hannah, J. N., Baumgaertel, A., & Feurer, I. D. (1998). Examination of DSM-IV criteria for attention deficit disorder in a county-wide sample. *Journal of Developmental & Behavioral Pediatrics, 19*(3), 162–68.

Wong, D. F., Wagner, H. N., Jr., Tune, L. E., Dannals, R. F., Pearlson, G. D., Links, J. M., Tamminga, C. A., Broussolle, E. P., Ravert, H. T., & Wilson, A. A. (1986). Positron emission tomography reveals elevated D2 dopamine receptors in drug-naïve schizophrenics. *Science, 234,* 1558–63.

Wood, J. M., Nezworski, M. T., Garb, H. N., & Lilienfeld, S. O. (2001). Problems with the norms of the Comprehensive System for the Rorschach: Methodological and conceptual considerations. *Clin. Psychol. Sci. Prac., 8,* 397–402.

Woodruff, P. W. R., et al. (1997). Auditory hallucinations and the temporal cortical response to speech in schizophrenia: A functional magnetic resonance imaging study. *Amer. J. Psychiat., 154*(12), 1676–82.

Woodruff-Borden, J., Morrow, C., Bourland, S., & Cambron, S. (2002). The behavior of anxious parents: Examining mechanisms of transmission of anxiety from parent to child. *Journal of Clinical Child & Adolescent Psychology, 31*(3), 364–74.

Woods, D. W., & Miltenberger, R. G. (2001). *Tic disorder, trichotillomania, and other repetitive disorders.* New York: Kluwer.

Woods, S. W., Charney, D. S., Goodman, W. K., & Heninger, G. R. (1987). Carbon dioxide-induced anxiety: Behavioral, physiologic, and biochemical effects of 5% CO2 in panic disorder patients and 5 and 7.5% CO2 in healthy subjects. *Arch. Gen. Psychiat., 44,* 365–75.

Woodside, D. B., Bulik, C. M., Halmi, K. A., Fichter, M. M., Kaplan, A., Berrettini, W. H., Strober, M., Treasure, J., Lilenfeld, L., Klump, K. K., & Kaye, W. H. (2002). Personality, perfectionism, and attitudes toward eating in parents of individuals with eating disorders. *Int. J. Eat. Dis., 31*(3), 290–99.

Woodside, D. B., Bulik, C. M., Thornton, L., Klump, K. L., Tozzi, F., Fichter, M., Halmi, K. A., Kaplan, A. S., Strober, M., Devlin, B., Bacanu, S.-A., Ganjei, K., Crow, S., Mitchell, J., Rotondo, A., Mauri, M., Cassano, G., Keel, P., Berrettini, W. H., & Kaye, W. H. (2004). Personality in men with eating disorders. *J. Psychosom. Res., 57,* 273–78.

Woodside, D. B., Carter, J. C., & Blackmore, E. (2004). Predictors of premature termination of inpatient treatment for anorexia nervosa. *Amer. J. Psychiat., 161,* 2277–81.

Woody, G. E., McLellan, A. T., Luborsky, L., & O'Brien, C. P. (1987). Twelve month follow-up of psychotherapy for opiate dependence. *Amer. J. Psychiat., 144,* 590–96.

Woody, S. R., & Teachman, B. A. (2000). Intersection of disgust and fear: Normative and pathological views. *Clin. Psychol. Sci. Prac., 7,* 291–311.

Worden, P. E. (1986). Prose comprehension and recall in disabled learners. In S. J. Ceci (Ed.), *Handbook of cognitive, social and neuropsychological aspects of learning disabilities* (Vol. 1, pp. 241–62). Hillsdale, NJ: Erlbaum.

Workman, E. A., & La Via, M. F. (1987). T-lymphocyte polyclonal proliferation: Effects of stress and stress response style on medical students taking national board examinations. *Clinical Immunology and Immunopathology, 43,* 308–13.

World Health Organization. (1992). *ICD-10 classification of mental and behavioral disorders: Clinical descriptions and diagnostic guidelines.* Geneva: Author.

World Health Organization. (1994). *Schedules for clinical assessment in neuropsychiatry.* Geneva: Author.

World Health Organization. (1997). *World Health Organization Report, 1997: Conquering suffering, furthering humanity.* Geneva: Author.

World Health Organization. (1999). *World Health Report.* Available: www.who.int/en/

World Health Organization. (2001). *The World Health Report 2001. Mental Health: New Understanding, New Hope.* Geneva: Author.

World Health Organization. (2005). *International suicide statistics resource page.* Retrieved August 3, 2005, from http://www. befrienders. org/suicide/ statistics. htm.

Worthington, E. R. (1978). Demographic and preservice variables as predictors of post-military adjustment. In C. R. Figley (Ed.), *Stress disorders among Vietnam veterans.* New York: Brunner/Mazel.

Wright, P., Takei, N., Murray, R. M., & Sham, P. C. (1999). Seasonality, prenatal influenza exposure, and schizophrenia. In E. Z. Susser, A. S. Brown, & J. M. Gorman (Eds.), *Prenatal exposures in schizophrenia* (pp. 89–112).Washington, DC: American Psychiatric Press.

Wykes, T., Reeder, C., Corner, J, Williams, C., & Everitt, B. (1999). The effects of neurocognitive remediation on executive processing in patients with schizophrenia. *Schizo. Bull., 25,* 291–306.

Wynne, L. C., Toohey, M. L., & Doane, J. (1979). Family studies. In L. Bellak (Ed.), *The schizophrenic syndrome.* New York: Basic Books.

Xiong, W., Phillips, R., Hu, X., Wang, R., Dai, Q., Kleinman, J., & Kleinman, A. (1994). Family-based intervention for schizophrenic patients in China. *Brit. J. Psychiat., 165,* 239–47.

Yacoubian, G. S., Jr. (2003). Tracking Ecstasy: Trends in the United States with data from three national drug surveys. *J. Drug Ed., 33,* 245–58.

Yager, J., Grant, I., & Bolus, R. (1984). Interaction of life events and symptoms in psychiatric patient and nonpatient married couples. *J. Nerv. Ment. Dis., 171*(1), 21–25.

Yan, L. J., Hammen, C., Cohen, A. N., Daley, S. E., & Henry, R. M. (2004). Expressed emotion versus relationship quality variables in the prediction of recurrence in bipolar patients. *J. Affect. Dis., 83,* 199–206.

Yang, B., & Clum, G. A. (1996). Effects of early negative life experience on cognitive functioning and risk for suicide: A review. *Clin. Psychol. Rev., 16*(3), 177–95.

Yanovski, S. Z., & Yanovski, J. A. (2002). Obesity. *N. Engl. J. Med., 346,* 591–602.

Yapko, M. D. (1994). *Suggestions of abuse: True and false memories of childhood sexual trauma.* New York: Simon & Schuster.

Yeates, K. O., et al. (1997). Preinjury family environment as a determinant of recovery from traumatic brain injuries in school-age children. *J. Int. Neuropsycholog. Soc., 3*(6), 617–30.

Yehuda, R. (Ed.). (2002). *Treating trauma survivors with PTSD.* Washington, DC: American Psychiatric Association.

Yehuda, R., Southwick, S. M., Giller, E. L., et al. (1992). Urinary catecholamine excretion and severity of PTSD symptoms in Vietnam combat veterans. *J. Nerv. Ment. Dis., 180,* 321–25.

Yeung, A. C., Vekshtein, V. I., Krantz, D. S., Vita, J. A., Ryan, T. J., Ganz, P., & Selwyn, A. P. (1991). The effects of atherosclerosis on the vasomotor response of coronary arteries to mental stress. *N. Engl. J. Med., 325,* 1551–56.

Yoder, K. A.,Whitlock, L. B., & Hoyt, D. R. (2003). Gang involvement and membership among homeless and runaway youth. *Youth and Society, 34,* 441–67.

Yoshimoto, S., Iyo, M., Ouchi, Y., Matsunaga, T., Tsukada, H., Okada, H., Etsuji, F., Fatatsibashi, M., Takei, N., & Morim, N. (2001). *Amer. J. Psychiat., 158,* 1206–14.

Yoshimoto, S., Minabe, Y., Kawai, M., Suzuki, K., Iyo, M., Isoda, H., Sakahara, H., Ashby, C. R. Jr., , Takei, N. & Mori, N. (2002). Metabolite alterations in basal ganglia associated with methamphetamine-related psychiatric symptoms: A proton MRS study. *Neuropsychopharmacology, 27*(3), 453–461.

Yung, A. R., & McGorry, P. D. (1997). Is pre-psychotic intervention realistic in schizophrenia and related disorders? *Austral. NZ J. Psychiat., 31,* 799–805.

Zahl, D. L., & Hawton, K. (2004a). Media influences on suicidal behaviour: An interview study of young people. *Behav. Cog. Psychother., 32*(2), 189–198.

Zahl, D. L., & Hawton, K. (2004b). Repetition of deliberate self-harm and subsequent suicide risk: Long-term follow-up study of 11,583 patients. *Brit. J. Psychiat., 185,* 70–75.

Zakowski, S. G., Hall, M. H., Cousino Klein, L., & Baum, A. (2001). Appraised control, coping, and stress in a community sample: A test of the goodness-of-fit hypothesis. *Ann. Behav. Med., 23*,158–65.

Zakowski, S., Hall, M. H., & Baum, A. (1992). Stress, stress management, and the immune system. *App. Prev. Psychol., 1,* 1–13.

Zalewski, C., et al. (1998). A review of neuropsychological differences between paranoid and nonparanoid schizophrenia patients. *Schizo. Bull., 24*(1), 127–46.

Zametkin, A., & Liotta, W. (1997). The future of brain imaging in child psychiatry. *Child Adoles. Psychiat. Clin. N. Amer., 6*(2), 447–60.

Zammit, S., Allebeck, P., Andréasson, S., Lundberg, I., & Lewis, G. (2002). Self-reported cannabis use as a risk factor for schizophrenia: Further analysis of the 1969 Swedish conscript cohort. *BMJ, 325,* 1199–1201.

Zanarini, M. C., Williams, A. A., Lewis, R. E., Reich, R. B., Vera, S. C., Marino, M. F., Levin, A., Yong, L., & Frankenburg, F. R. (1997). Reported pathological childhood experiences associated with the development of borderline personality disorder. *Amer. J. Psychiat., 154*(8), 1101–06.

Zasler, N. D. (1993). Mild traumatic brain injury: Medical assessment and intervention. *J. Head Trauma Rehab., 8*(3), 13–29.

Zeev, K., Iancu, I., & Bodner, E. (2001). A review of psychological debriefing after extreme stress. *Psychiatr. Serv., 52*(6), 824–27.

Zeidner, M. (1993). Coping with disaster: The case of Israeli adolescents under threat of missile attack. *Journal of Youth and Adolescence, 22,* 89–108.

Zeitlin, H. (1986). *The natural history of psychiatric disorder in childhood.* New York: Oxford University Press.

Zellner, D. A., Harner, D. E., & Adler, R. L. (1989). Effects of eating abnormalities and gender on perceptions of desirable body shape. *J. Abn. Psychol., 98,* 93–96.

Zerman, P. M., & Schwartz, H. I. (1998). Hospitalization: voluntary and involuntary. In R. Rosner (Ed.), *Principles and practice of forensic psychiatry* (pp. 111–17). London: Oxford University Press.

Zettergren, P. (2003). School adjustment in adolescence for previously rejected, average and popular children. *British Journal of Educational Psychology, 73*(2), 207–221.

Zhang, L., Plotkin, R. C., Wang, G., Sandel, E., Lee, S. (2004). Cholinergic augmentation with donepezil enhances recovery in short-term memory and sustained attention after traumatic brain injury. *Archives of Physical and Medical Rehabilitation, 85,* 1050–55.

Zheng, Y. P., & Lin, K. M. (1994). A nationwide study of stressful life events in Mainland China. *Psychosom. Med., 56,* 296–305.

Zhu, J., Weiss, L. G., Prifitera, A., & Coalson, D. (2004). The Wechsler Intelligence and Achievement Tests. *Comprehensive handbook of psychological assessment* (Vol. 1, pp. 51–75). New York: John Wiley & Sons.

Zickler, P. (2002). *Study demonstrates that marijuana smokers experience significant withdrawal.* Washington, DC: NIDA.

Zigler, E. F., & Hall, N. W. (2000). *Child development and social policy: Theory and applications.* New York: McGraw-Hill.

Zilberman, M., Tavares, H., & el-Guebaly, N. (2003). Gender similarities and differences: The prevalence and course of alcohol- and other substance-related disorders. *J. Addict. Dis., 22,* 61–74.

Zilboorg, G., & Henry, G. W. (1941). *A history of medical psychology.* New York: Norton.

Zill, N., & Schoenborn, G. A. (1990). Developmental, learning, and emotional problems: Health of our nation's children. *Advance data: National Center for Health Statistics* (Number 190).

Zimmerman, D. P. (2004). Psychotherapy in residential treatment: Historical development and critical issues. *Child Adoles. Psychiat. Clin. N. Amer., 13*(2), 347–61.

Zimmerman, M., & Coryell, W. (1990). Diagnosing personality disorders in the community. A comparison of self report and interview measures. *Arch. Gen. Psychiat., 47,* 527–31.

Zinbarg, R., & Mohlman, J. (1998). Individual differences in the acquisition of affectively valenced associations. *J. Pers. Soc. Psychol., 74,* 1024–40.

Ziolko, H. U. (1996). Bulimia: A historical outline. *Int. J. Eat. Dis., 20,* 345–58.

Zito, J., & Safer, D. J. (2001). Services and prevention: Pharmacoepidemiology of antidepressant use. *Biol. Psychiat., 49,* 1121–27.

Zoccolillo, M., Meyers, J., & Assiter, S. (1997). Conduct disorder, substance dependence, and adolescent motherhood. *Amer. J. Orthopsychiat., 67*(1), 152–57.

Zoccolillo, M., Pickles, A., Quinton, D., & Rutter, M. (1992). The outcome of conduct disorder: Implications for defining adult personality disorder and conduct disorder. *Psychol. Med., 22,* 971–86.

Zorillo, E. P., Luborsky, L., McKay, J. R., Rosenthal, R., Houldin, A., Tax, A., McCorkle, R., Seligman, D. A., & Schmidt, K. (2001). The relationship of depression and stressors to immunological assays: A meta-analytic review. *Brain, Behavior, and Immunity, 15,* 199–226.

Zubin, J., & Spring, B. J. (1977). Vulnerability: A new view of schizophrenia. *J. Abn. Psychol., 86,* 103–26.

Zucker, K. J., & Blanchard, R. (1997). Transvesticfetishism: Psychopathology and theory. In D. R. Laws & W. O'Donohue (Eds.), *Sexual deviance: Theory, assessment, and treatment.* (pp. 253–79). New York: Guilford.

Zucker, K. J., & Bradley, S. J. (1995). *Gender identity disorder and psychosexual problems in children and adolescents.* New York: Guilford.

Zucker, K. J., Owen, A., Bradley, S. J., & Ameeriar, L. (2002). Gender-dysphoric children and adolescents: A comparative analysis of demographic characteristics and behavioral problems. *Clinical Child Psychology and Psychiatry, 7,* 398–411.

Zucker, K. J., Sanikhani, M., & Bradley, S. J. (1997). Sex differences in referral rates of children with gender identity disorder: Some hypotheses. *J. Abnorm. Child Psychol., 25,* 217–27.

Zvolensky, M. J., Effert, G. H., Lejuex, C. W., & McNeil, D. W. (1999). The effects of offset control over 20% carbon-dioxide-enriched air on anxious response. *J. Abn. Psychol., 108,* 624–32.

Zvolensky, M. J., Lejuez, C. W., & Eifert, G. H. (1998). The role of offset control in anxious responding: An experimental test using repeated administrations of 20%-carbon-dioxide-enriched air. *Behav. Ther., 29,* 193–209.

Zvolensky, M.J., Eifert, G.H., & Lejuez, C.W. (2001). Offset control during recurrent 20% carbon dioxide-enriched air induction: Relation to individual difference variables. *Emotion, 1*(2), 148–165.

Zweben, A. (2001). Integrating pharmacotherapy and psychosocial interventions in the treatment of individuals with alcohol problems. *Journal of Social Work Practice in the Addictions, 1*(3), 65–80.

Zwelling, S. S. (1985). *Quest for a cure.* Williamsburg, VA: The Colonial Williamsburg Foundation.

credits

Chapter 1: p. 1: © Dennis D. Potokar/Photo Researchers, Inc.; p. 3: © Rudi Von Briel/PhotoEdit; p. 6T: © Paul Cookney/Professional Sports/Topham/The Image Works; p. 6B: © Ethel Wolvowitz/The Image Works; p. 7: © TIM SHAFFER/Reuters/Landov; p. 11L: © Carol Beckwith & Angela Fisher/HAGA/The Image Works; p. 11R: © Dan Budnik/Woodfin Camp & Associates; p. 12: © Andy Rain/Liaison/Getty Images; p. 14: © Esbin-Anderson/The Image Works; p. 16: © Richard Lord/PhotoEdit; p. 18: © David Turnley/CORBIS; p. 23: © Volker Steger/Photo Researchers, Inc.; **Chapter 2:** p. 27: © Royalty-Free/CORBIS; p. 29: © The Granger Collection, New York; p. 31: © 2006 Museum of Fine Arts. Boston. William Francis Warden Fund, 57.356. Copyright © 2006 The Munch Museum/The Munch-Ellingsen Group/Artists Rights Society (ARS), New York.; p. 32T: © The Granger Collection, New York; p. 32B: © The Granger Collection, New York; p. 35: © Stapleton Collection/CORBIS; p. 36: © Tate Gallery, London/Art Resource, NY; p. 37: © Réunion des Musées Nationaux/Art Resource, NY; p. 38T: Mary Evans Picture Library; p. 38B: Courtesy of the author; p. 40: © Stock Montage, Inc.; p. 41: © Jerry Cooke/CORBIS; p. 42: Dr. Joe Westermeyer; p. 44: © Mario Tama/Getty Images; p. 46: © National Library of Medicine/Photo Researchers, Inc.; p. 47: The Wellcome Trust; p. 48: © Bettmann/CORBIS; p. 50T: © Bettmann/CORBIS; p. 50B: © Bettmann/CORBIS; p. 51T: © The Granger Collection, New York; p. 51M: © The Granger Collection, New York; p. 51B: Mary Evans Picture Library; p. 52T: © The Granger Collection, New York; p. 52ML: © Stock Montage, Inc.; p. 52MR: © Stock Montage, Inc.; p. 52B: © Underwood & Underwood/CORBIS; **Chapter 3:** p. 57: © Stockbyte; p. 59: © AFP Photo/Tom Mihalek/Getty Images; p. 61: © Will Hart; p. 64: © Joe Raedle/Getty Images; p. 67: © SPL/Photo Researchers, Inc.; p. 69: AP/Wide World Photos; p. 72: © Peter Dazeley/zefa/CORBIS; p. 76: © Royalty-Free/CORBIS; p. 77: © Laura Dwight Photography/Peter Arnold Inc.; p. 78L: © Bettmann/CORBIS; p. 78R: Margaret S. Mahler Psychiatric Research Foundation; p. 79L: The William Alanson White Institute; p. 79R: The Association for the Advancement of Psychoanalysis; p. 82: © James Marshall/CORBIS; p. 84T: Linda A. Cicero/Stanford News Service; p. 84B: © Chuck Savage/ImageState/International Stock Photography Ltd.; p. 85: University of Pennsylvania; p. 86: © Christopher Bissel/Getty Images/Stone; p. 90L: AP/Wide World Photos; p. 90R: AP/Wide World Photos; p. 91: © Rachel Epstein/The Image Works; p. 92: © David Young-Wolff/PhotoEdit; p. 93: © Nancy Ney/Getty Images/DK Stock; p. 96: © J. Greenberg/The Image Works; p. 98: © Lindsay Hebberd/CORBIS; p. 100: © James Marshall/CORBIS; p. 103: © A. Ramey/PhotoEdit; **Chapter 4:** p. 107: © Keith Brofsky/Getty Images/Photodisc Green; p. 109: © Getty Images/PhotoDisc Blue; p. 111: © Lester Lefkowitz/CORBIS; p. 112: © James D. Wilson/Woodfin Camp & Associates; p. 113: Eisenberger, N. J., Lieberman, M. D., & Williams, K. D. (2003). Does rejection hurt? An fMRI study of social exclusion. *Science*, 302, 290–292; p. 116: © Andrea Morini/Getty Images/Digital Vision; p. 117: © Mary Kate Denny/PhotoEdit; p. 119: National Library of Medicine; p. 120L: © Peter Vandermark/Stock Boston, LLC.; p. 120R: Rorschach Museum; p. 122: University of Minnesota; p. 123: Courtesy of the author; p. 131: © Spencer Grant/PhotoEdit; p. 132: © Charles Gupton/CORBIS; p. 138: AP/Wide World Photos; **Chapter 5:** p. 143: © David Leeson/Dallas Morning News; p. 144L: © John Berry/The Image Works; p. 144R: © Tony Freeman/PhotoEdit; p. 146: © Thomas Friedman/Photo Researchers, Inc.; p. 147: AP/Wide World Photos; p. 149L: © Jeff Greenberg/PhotoEdit; p. 149R: © Dion Ogust/The Image Works; p. 150: © G. & M. David de Lossy/Getty Images/Image Bank; p. 155: AP/Wide World Photos; p. 156T: © Judy Sloan Reich/South-Florida Sun-Sentinel; p. 156B: © 2005, The Washington Post. Photo by David Finkel. Reprinted with Permission.; p. 160: © Pallava Bagla/CORBIS; p. 164 : United States Coast Guard; p. 170: AP/Wide World Photos; p. 172: © Mario Tama/Getty Images; p. 174: AP/Wide World Photos; p. 175: AP/Wide World Photos; **Chapter 6:** p. 179: © PIERRE PERRIN/CORBIS SYGMA; p. 181: © Peter Weimann/Animals, Animals/Earth Scenes; p. 183: © mediacolor's/Alamy; p. 185T: © SW Productions/Getty Images/Photodisc Green; p. 185B: © Spencer Grant/PhotoEdit; p. 186: Susan Mineka; p. 187: © Michael Newman/PhotoEdit; p. 189: no credit needed; p. 190L: © Bob Mahoney/The Image Works; p. 190R: Delft University of Technology; p. 191: © David Young-Wolff/PhotoEdit; p. 192: © Bob Daemmrich/Stock Boston, LLC.; p. 193: © Antonio Mo/Getty Images/Taxi; p. 197: © David Gifford/Photo Researchers, Inc.; p. 203: © Willie Hall Jr./The Image Works; p. 206: © Kevin Horan/Stock Boston, LLC; p. 208: © Christopher Bissell/Getty Images/Stone; p. 212: © David Young-Wolff/PhotoEdit; p. 213: Pearson Education U.S. ELT/Scott Foresman; p. 215: © Nancy Kaszerman/ZUMA Press; **Chapter 7:** p. 225: © Jake Wyman/Getty Images/Photonica; p. 229R: © BananaStock/Alamy; p. 229L: © Mike Schroeder/argus/Peter Arnold Inc.; p. 231: © Alex James Photographic/Getty Images/Photonica; p. 234: © David Pollack/CORBIS; p. 238: Richard Davidson; p. 241: © Alison Wright/CORBIS; p. 242: © Lawrence Migdale/Getty Images/Stone; p. 245: © Robert Mora/Getty Images; p. 248: © Steven Rubin/The Image Works; p. 251: © Lee Snider/The Image Works; p. 256L: © Bettmann/CORBIS; p. 256R: © Time & Life Pictures/Mansell/Getty Images; p. 260: © Royalty-Free/CORBIS; p. 269: © Frank Micelotta/Getty Images; p. 271L: © Bettmann/CORBIS; p. 271R: © CORBIS Sygma; p. 275: © Mary Kate Denny/PhotoEdit; **Chapter 8:** p. 279: © Laurent/Yakou/Photo Researchers, Inc.; p. 282: © Royalty-Free/CORBIS; p. 285: © Stock4B/CORBIS; p. 286: © Bruce Ayers/Getty Images/Stone; p. 288: © Topham/The Image Works; p. 289: © Francoise Sauze/Science Photo Library/Photo Researchers, Inc.; p. 291: AP/Wide World Photos; p. 292L: © Andy Schwartz/PhotoFest; p. 292R: © Andy Schwartz/PhotoFest; p. 295: © Mike Okoniewsky/The Image Works; p. 296: © SUMMIT ENTERTAINMENT/THE KOBAL COLLECTION/ROTHENBERG, DANNY; p. 301: AP/Wide World Photos; p. 303: © Bettmann/CORBIS; **Chapter 9:** p. 311: © Max Oppenheim/Getty Images/Photographer's Choice; p. 312L: © Ezra Shaw/Getty Images; p. 312R: © Tim Graham/CORBIS; p. 313L: © NMSB/Custom Medical Stock Photos; p. 315: © Jack Kurtz/The Image Works; p. 318: © Firefly Productions/CORBIS; p. 324L: © Valentino Maria Chandoha/

CORBIS; p. 324R: AP/Wide World Photos; p. 325: © David Young-Wolff/PhotoEdit; p. 329: © Archivo Iconografico, S.A./CORBIS; p. 336T: © Dennis MacDonald/PhotoEdit; p. 336B: © Tony Freeman/PhotoEdit; p. 337: © V.C.L./Getty Images/Taxi; p. 338L: © Steve Azzara/CORBIS SYGMA; p. 338R: © Najlah Feanny/CORBIS; p. 339: © FogStock LLC/Index Stock; **Chapter 10:** p. 343: © Henry Sims/Getty Images/The Image Bank; p. 344: © Bob Daemmrich/Stock Boston, LLC.; p. 348T: © Dynamic Graphics Group/Creatas/Alamy; p. 348B: © Thomas Hoeffgen/Getty Images/Stone; p. 352TL: AP/Wide World Photos; p. 352TR: © Robin Nelson/Photo Edit; p. 352B: © David Young-Wolff/PhotoEdit; p. 359: © Suzie Packard/Alamy; p. 361: © GOODSHOOT/Alamy; p. 363: © Bill Losh/Getty Images/Taxi; p. 366: © Tony Savino/The Image Works; **Chapter 11:** p. 371: © Ann Cutting/Getty Images/Workbook Stock; p. 374: © Frank Siteman/Stock Boston, LLC.; p. 375: © Geri Engberg/The Image Works; p. 379: © M. Antman/The Image Works; p. 383: © Philip Lee Harvey/Getty Images/Stone; p. 385L: Otto Kernberg; p. 385R: Norton Professional Books; p. 386: © Dr. P. Marazzi/Science Photo Library/Photo Researchers, Inc.; p. 387: © Patrick Olear/PhotoEdit; p. 389: © David Young-Wolff/PhotoEdit; p. 391: © Erik Dreyer/Getty Images/Stone; p. 400: © Bettmann/CORBIS; p. 403: © Jasper White/Getty Images/Photonica; **Chapter 12:** p. 411: © Stockbyte Royalty Free Photos/PictureQuest; p. 414: © Paul Conklin/PhotoEdit; p. 416: © Patrick Ward/CORBIS; p. 417B: Mattson, S. N., Jernigan, T. L., & Riley, E. P., (1994). MRI and prenatal alcohol exposure. *Alcohol Health & Research World*, 18 (1), 49–52; p. 417T: © George Steinmetz; p. 422: © Spencer Grant/PhotoEdit; p. 425: © David Turnley/CORBIS; p. 429: © Spencer Grant/PhotoEdit; p. 430: © Bill Aron/PhotoEdit; p. 432: © BAUMGARTNER OLIVIA/CORBIS SYGMA; p. 433: © Dennis McDonald/PhotoEdit; p. 435: © Topham/The Image Works; p. 437L: © Mitchell Gerber/CORBIS; p. 437R: AP/Wide World Photos; p. 441: AP/Wide World Photos; p. 442: © TEK Image/Science Photo Library/Photo Researchers, Inc.; p. 443: © Scott Houston/CORBIS; p. 444L: © Bill Aron/PhotoEdit; p. 444R: AP/Wide World Photos; **Chapter 13:** p. 449: © Jack Slomovits/Getty Images/Digital Vision; p. 450: © Ken Chernus/Getty Images/Taxi; p. 454: © Rachel Epstein/The Image Works; p. 459: © Network Photographers/Alamy; p. 460: © Jutta Klee/CORBIS; p. 461: © Bo Rader/The Wichita Eagle/Pool/Reuters/CORBIS; p. 462: © Howard Kingsnorth/Getty Images/Stone; p. 463: © Thomas Hoeffgen/Getty Images/Stone; p. 464: © Chris Warren/Alamy; p. 466: © WILL BURGESS/Reuters/CORBIS; p. 470: © Mary Ellen Mark; p. 471: AP/Wide World Photos; p. 474L: © Rob Lewine/CORBIS; p. 474R: © David Young-Wolff/PhotoEdit; p. 479: © Bill Bachmann/Stock Boston, LLC.; p. 482: © Robert Laberge/Getty Images; **Chapter 14:** p. 489: © Betsie Van Der Meer/Getty Images/Photonica; p. 490: © Barbara J. Feigles/Stock Boston, LLC.; p. 491: © Phil Borden/PhotoEdit; p. 493: not needed; p. 495: © Grunnitus Studios/Photo Researchers, Inc.; p. 497: © Mary Ellen Mark; p. 502: NIMH/Courtesy of Edna A. Morlok; p. 510: Courtesy of Dr. E.E. Walker; p. 511: E. Fuller Torrey, M.D., (The Treatment Advocacy Center, www.psychlaws.org) and Daniel Weinberger; p. 512: Dr. Paul Thompson, Laboratory of Neuro Imaging at UCLA; p. 518: Susan Wilson/Clea Simon; p. 519: © Michael Newman/Photo Edit; p. 520: © Tony Savino/The Image Works; p. 522: © A. Ramey/Stock Boston, LLC; p. 526: © BOB STRONG/AFP/Getty Images; **Chapter 15:** p. 531: © Wolfgang Schmidt/Das Fotoarchiv/Peter Arnold Inc.; p. 535T: © Robert Fried/Stock Boston, LLC.; p. 535B: Pearson Education/PH College; p. 540: © Seth Wenig/Reuters/CORBIS; p. 541: © Reuters/CORBIS; p. 542: Robert D. Terry, MD.; p. 545: © CORBIS; p. 546: © CNRI/Photo Researchers, Inc.; p. 548: © SIU/Peter Arnold Inc.; p. 551: © Getty Images/Stone; p. 553L: The Francis A. Countway Library of Medicine; p. 553R: Damasio H, Grabowski T, Frank R, Galaburda AM, Damasio AR: The return of Phineas Gage: Clues about the brain from a famous patient. *Science*, 264:1102–1105, 1994. Department of Neurology and Image Analysis Facility, University of Iowa.; p. 554: © Hank Morgan/Photo Researchers, Inc.; **Chapter 16:** p. 557: © Jeff Greenberg/Omni-Photo Communications, Inc.; p. 559: © Ursula Markus/Photo Researchers, Inc.; p. 561: © David Young-Wolff/PhotoEdit; p. 564: © Michael Newman/PhotoEdit; p. 565: © Stockbyte; p. 568: © David Young-Wolff/PhotoEdit; p. 570: © Nancy Richmond/The Image Works; p. 571: © Laura Dwight/PhotoEdit; p. 573: Courtesy of Alpha Consultants LTD; p. 577: © Jan Sonnenmair/Aurora & Quanta Productions Inc; p. 579: AP/Wide World Photos; p. 580: © Will Hart/PhotoEdit; p. 581: © Stephanie Maze/CORBIS; p. 582: © Chris Ware/The Image Works; p. 584: © Mike Greenlar/The Image Works; p. 585: © Science Photo/Custom Medical Stock; p. 586: © Richard Hutchings/PhotoEdit; p. 591: © Michael Heron/Michael Heron Photography; p. 594: AP/Wide World Photos; **Chapter 17:** p. 599: © JP Fankhauser/Getty Images/Photonica; p. 602: © David Buffington/Getty Images/Photodisc Green; p. 605B: Reprinted from *Biological Psychiatry*, V 57: 901–910, Nakaoa et al., "Brain activation of patients with obsessive-compulsive disorder during neuropsychological and symptom provocation tasks before and after symptom improvement: A functional magnetic resonance imaging study", © 2005, with permission from Society of Biological Psychiatry.; p. 605T: © FETHI BELAID/AFP/Getty Images; p. 612: AP/Wide World Photos; p. 616: © Stockbyte Platinum/Alamy; p. 618: © Will & Deni McIntyre/Photo Researchers, Inc.; p. 621: © Keystone/Hulton Archive/Getty Images; p. 627: © J. Gerard Smith/Photo Researchers, Inc.; p. 633: © Zigy Kaluzny/Getty Images/Stone; **Chapter 18:** p. 641: © Stockdisc/SuperStock; p. 643: © Steve Prezant/CORBIS; p. 645: © Michael Newman/PhotoEdit; p. 646: © Robert Harbison; p. 648L: © Susan Van Etten/PhotoEdit; p. 648R: © Bill Aron/PhotoEdit; p. 650: © Lee Snider/The Image Works; p. 653: © Fritz Hoffmann/The Image Works; p. 655: © Jose Luis Pelaez, Inc./CORBIS; p. 657: © Reuters/CORBIS; p. 658: © Bettmann/CORBIS; p. 660: AP/Wide World Photos

Name Index

The letters t and f following page numbers stand for table and figure.

SUBJECT INDEX

The letters t and f following page numbers stand for table and figure.